MACMILLAN
COMPENDIUM

Cultures of the World

MACMILLAN
COMPENDIUM

Cultures of the World

**SELECTIONS FROM THE
TEN-VOLUME**

Encyclopedia of World Cultures

Edited by

Melvin Ember
Carol R. Ember

REFERENCE

MACMILLAN LIBRARY REFERENCE USA

New York

Copyright © 1999 Macmillan Library Reference; © 1996 (Appendix); © 1991-1996
Human Relations Area Files, Inc

Interior Design by Kevin Hanek
Cover Design by Judy Kahn

Macmillan Library Reference USA
1633 Broadway, 7th Floor
New York, NY 10019

Manufactured in the United States of America

Printing number
1 2 3 4 5 6 7 8 9 10

ISBN: 0-02-865367-X
LC #: 99-25220

Library of Congress Cataloging-in-Publication Data

Encyclopedia of world cultures.   Selections.
    Cultures of the world : selections from the ten-volume
encyclopedia of world cultures / edited by Melvin Ember, Carol R.
Ember.
        p.   cm.—(Macmillan compendium)
    Includes bibliographical references.
    ISBN 0-02-865367-X (hardcover : alk. paper)
    1. Ethnology Encyclopedias.   I. Ember, Melvin.   II. Ember, Carol
R.   III. Title.   IV. Series.
    GN307.E532   1999
    305.8′003—dc21   99-25220
                                                                        CIP

Cover photos (clockwise from left): Peruvian woman © Ric Ergenbright/Corbis;
Hawaiian woman © Douglas Peebles/Corbis; Himba woman of Namibia, Africa ©
Sharna Balfour, ABPL/Corbis; Native American family © Pete Saloutos/The Stock
Market; men in Scottish dress © Dewitt Jones/Corbis; Japanese children © David
Ball/The Stock Market. Flag montage © Reza Estakhrian/Tony Stone Images.

This paper meets the requirements of ANSI/NISO Z39.48-1992 (Permanence of
Paper).

Table of Contents

v

Table of Contents

Preface

This volume is an abridged version of the award-winning ten-volume *Encyclopedia of World Cultures*, which was organized and prepared by the Human Relations Area Files (HRAF) at Yale University, and published by G.K. Hall/Macmillan Library Reference between 1991 and 1996.

In preparing the original encyclopedia, HRAF was guided by a distinguished editorial board who provided advice on which cultures to include and on which scholars to ask to write the summaries. One of the unique features of this encyclopedia is that the nearly 1,000 contributors who wrote the entries were usually anthropologists and other social scientists who had firsthand research experience living or working with the people whose cultures they summarized.

Three criteria guided the editors in selecting entries for this compendium. The first was population size. We tried to include most of the largest cultures. But relying on population size alone would skew the volume towards a few world regions, so we also tried to include the larger cultures within each world region. Our third criterion was that the culture is discussed often in the anthropological and other literatures.

The cultures described in this compendium are listed alphabetically within every region of the world. The cultural summaries range up to five or six pages in length. They provide a mix of information—demographic, historical, social, economic, political, and religious. But the emphasis is on the culture, on the ways of life of the people, past and present. This is an anthropological compendium, designed for comparing the ways of life of cultures around the world. Hence the authors followed a standardized outline; each summary usually provides information on a core list of topics, including the following:

CULTURE NAME: The name used most often in the anthropological and social science literatures to refer to the culture, or the name the group uses for itself.

ETHNONYMS: Alternative names for the culture, including alternative spellings.

ORIENTATION
- **Identification.** Location of the culture and the derivation of its name and ethnonyms.
- **Location.** Where the culture is located and a description of the physical environment.
- **Demography.** Population history and recent reliable population figures or estimates.
- **Linguistic Affiliation.** The name of the language spoken and/or written by the culture, the language family it belongs to, and variation in how the language is used.

HISTORY AND CULTURAL RELATIONS: The origins and history of the culture, and the past and current nature of relationships with other groups.

SETTLEMENTS: The location of settlements, types of settlements, types of structures, housing design, and materials.

ECONOMY
- **Subsistence and Commercial Activities.** The primary methods of obtaining, consuming, and distributing food, money, and other necessities.
- **Industrial Arts.** Implements and objects produced by the culture either for its own use or for sale or trade.
- **Trade.** Patterns of trade with other groups.
- **Division of Labor.** How basic economic tasks are assigned by age, gender, ability, occupational specialization, and status.
- **Land Tenure.** Rules and practices concerning the allocation of land and land-use rights to members of the culture and to outsiders.

KINSHIP
- **Kin Groups and Descent.** Rules and practices concerning kin groups such as lineages and clans, and the basis of membership.
- **Kinship Terminology.** The system of kin terms used, and information about unique features of the system.

MARRIAGE AND FAMILY
- **Marriage.** Rules and practices concerning reasons for marriage, types of marriage, economic aspects of marriage, where couples live after they get married, divorce, and remarriage.
- **Domestic Unit.** Description of the basic household unit, its type, size, and composition.
- **Inheritance.** Rules and practices concerning the inheritance of property.
- **Socialization.** Rules and practices concerning child rearing including caretakers, values inculcated, child-rearing methods, initiation rites, and education.

SOCIOPOLITICAL ORGANIZATION
- **Social Organization.** Rules and practices concerning social status, primary and secondary groups, and social stratification.
- **Political Organization.** Rules and practices concerning leadership, politics, governmental organizations, and decision making.
- **Social Control.** The sources of conflict within the culture and informal and formal social control mechanisms.
- **Conflict.** The sources of conflict with other groups and informal and formal means of resolving conflicts.

RELIGION AND EXPRESSIVE CULTURE
- **Religious Beliefs.** The nature of religious beliefs including beliefs in supernatural entities, traditional beliefs, and the effects of major religions.
- **Religious Practitioners.** The types, sources of power, and activities of religious specialists such as shamans and priests.
- **Ceremonies.** The nature, types, and frequencies of religious and other ceremonies and rites.
- **Arts.** The nature, types, and characteristics of artistic activities including literature, music, dance, carving, and so on.
- **Medicine.** The nature of traditional medical beliefs and practices and the influence of scientific medicine.
- **Death and Afterlife.** The nature of beliefs and practices concerning death, the deceased, funerals, and the afterlife.

BIBLIOGRAPHY: A selected list of publications about the culture. The list usually includes publications that describe both the traditional and the contemporary culture.

AUTHOR'S NAME: The name of the author of the summary.

FEATURES

To add visual appeal and enhance the usefulness of the volume, the page format was designed to include the following helpful features.

- **Call-out Quotations:** These relevant, often provocative quotations are highlighted in the margin to promote exploration and add visual appeal to the page.

- **Cross-references:** Appearing at the base of many margins, "See also" cross-references also cite related articles to encourage further research.
- **Notable Quotations:** Found throughout the text in the margin, these thought-provoking quotations will complement the topic under discussion.
- **Definitions:** Brief definitions of important terms in the main text can also be found in the margin.
- **Sidebars:** Appearing in a gray box, these provocative asides relate to the text and amplify topics.
- **Index:** A thorough index provides thousands of additional points of entry into the work.
- **Country Listing:** A list of cultures by country.

ACKNOWLEDGMENTS

Cultures of the World contains over one hundred illustrations. Acknowledgments of sources for illustrations can be found within the illustration captions.

We are grateful to all of these scholars and experts for their contributions to this important reference work. We would also like to thank the in-house staff whose hard work and creativity made this book possible.

Melvin Ember
President of HRAF
Carol R. Ember
Executive Director of HRAF

AKAN

Ethonyms: none

Orientation

The Akan comprise a cluster of peoples living in southern and central Ghana and in southeastern Ivory Coast. They form a series of distinct kingdoms and share a common language, known as Twi, which has many dialects. Twi is a tonal language and, since missionary work during the eighteenth and nineteenth centuries, has been written in Roman script.

The total Akan population numbers some five or six million. The main constituent kingdoms include Akyem, Akwamu, Akuapem, and Kwahu; the Anyi cluster of some fifteen kingdoms; Asante (with Ahanta and Wasa); the Attie cluster of four kingdoms; the Baule cluster of some seven kingdoms; Brong; and the several Fante states.

History

The long, complex history of the Akan peoples is one of internecine conflicts and, since the eighteenth century, of opposition to the encroachment of various colonial powers: the Dutch, Portuguese, Danish, French, and English. In addition, there have been continual threats from the Islamic peoples of the southern Saharan fringe. Essentially all these conflicts have been over monopolies in trade, first across the Sahara with northern Africa and, in later centuries, across the Atlantic with the countries of Europe and the Americas.

It appears certain that there were early cultural and commercial links with the empires of the southern Sahara, the latter consisting mainly of the exchange of gold from the Akan region for salt and other commodities from the Sahara. Many of the cultural traits of the Akan indicate that their kingdoms may, in many cases, be considered successor-states to ancient Ghana and Mali. Also evident are many cultural similarities with forest peoples to their east, such as the Fon, Yoruba, and Edo, although these must have developed many centuries ago.

Economy and Settlement

The Akan are almost all forest dwellers; the exceptions are a few outlying groups northward in the savanna and eastward in the hills and valley of the Volta River.

The basic crops are forest root plants (including yams, cocoyams, sweet potatoes, plantains) and trees (including oilpalm, many other palms, and cocoa). In many areas, minerals—especially gold and bauxite—have been and remain important. Some Akan kingdoms have lacked gold sources, their political weakness reflecting the lack of this valuable trade commodity. Livestock have never been of great importance, but in some areas hunting has been so until the late twentieth century. For most of the Akan kingdoms, trade—mainly in gold—has been a crucial resource. Weaving in cotton and silk is of a technically and aesthetically high order, and much commerce is built around it. Wood carvings have also become a valuable commodity, especially with the rise of the tourist trade in the late twentieth century.

The basic Akan pattern of settlement is extremely variable but, in the main, is one of towns each centered on the palace of its chief. Attached to these towns, but away from them in less densely inhabited land, are villages and farms, some large and long-lasting and others little more than clusters of the houses of single small families. The houses in the larger towns, constructed of materials that can last for several years before they crumble, are set along permanent roads. The dwellings in the villages are made of less durable materials and are typically arranged with no plan and no clearly marked center, being merely clusters of the houses of kin.

Men and women share in labor, but both may own farms and houses and both may provide the labor for them. In former times, until the end of the nineteenth century, much or most farm labor was supplied by various forms of servile persons: slaves, pawns, and many categories of "servant." Today different types of sharecropping and labor hired for cash are the most prevalent, although domestic peonage is still common.

Kinship, Family, and Marriage

All Akan groups recognize matrilineal descent. The basic group is the clan, of which there are eight; they are dispersed among the many kingdoms. Members of a subclan tend to occupy a single town or village. The clan is an exogamous group. It is comprised of constituent groups that may be referred to as lineages, but these do not form any kind of segmentary lineage system, lineages being attached to others by propinquity and the power and wealth of the host lineage. Although there has been much confusion in accounts of the Akan peoples between matriliny and matriarchy, authority within clans and lineages is held firmly by men, succession being from a man to his brother or to his closest sister's son.

♦ **matrilineal descent**
The practice of tracing kinship affiliation only through the female line.

Marriage is expected to be exogamous, and is extremely simple. There is no bride-wealth, the union being effected by the transfer of rum or other drink and some money from the groom to the bride's immediate family. Divorce is extremely easy and may be initiated by either men or women. The most usual causes are adultery and the barrenness of wives.

Legitimacy is important both for inheritance and to define a person as having, or not having, slave ancestry. It demands not only a proper marriage, however short-lasting, but also a recognized pater: he gives the child his own spiritual identity and his or her name; he admits his responsibility for the child's education, and he has the expectation that the child will carry out the father's funerary rites.

A child inherits his or her blood from the mother, and character or temperament from the father. Maternal blood ensures the child's membership in the *abusua* (clan or lineage); paternity bestows membership in one of nine other groups or categories. Although some accounts claim the Akan descent system is one of double descent, this view appears to be based on a misreading of the actual roles of the two lines of descent.

Despite being jurally matrilineal, inheritance is to some extent divided between sister's children and a man's own children. The basic principle is that lineage-inherited property goes to sisters' children, and property acquired with the help of a man's wife and children is distributed among the latter at his death.

The Akan practiced slavery, obtaining slaves from northern slave dealers, usually Muslims. War captives, criminals, persons who opposed local chiefs, and many local ritual leaders were also enslaved. Slaves were used for domestic and field labor, for sale to traders across the Sahara and across the Atlantic, and as sacrifices to royal and other ancestors. In the middle of the nineteenth century, slaves amounted to half of the population in many towns.

Political Organization

The several Akan peoples each consist of a single kingdom ruled by a king, *omanhene* (lit., "state-chief"). The king comes from whatever clan provides the royal line in a particular kingdom, and is chosen in rotation from one of this clan's kingly lineages (there are often other, nonkingly, lineages within a royal clan). He is elected by various officials, of which the most important is the *ohemmaa* (or similar terms; lit. "woman-chief" and usually translated in the literature as "queen-mother") although she is typically not the actual mother but a senior woman of the clan, who "knows" genealogy and may have her own court and be assisted by

AKAN WARRIOR

An Akan man wearing a feather headdress in Akrokerri. Warfare is used as a means of extending territory and controlling external trade. Ghana, Africa. (© Werner Forman/Corbis)

various officials. Criteria for the selection of a king include assumed competence, general personality, and the fact that kingly lines usually rotate in providing the king. Once selected, the king is "enstooled"—that is, seated upon the stool of kingship. His former status is annulled symbolically, his debts and lawsuits are settled, his clothing and personal possessions stored; he is then symbolically reborn and given the identity of one of his forebears. He assumes the royal name and title borne by that previous ruler.

A king has his palace, in which work members of his court. Details vary considerably, but, in general, the royal officials comprise several categories: those from the royal clan itself; those representing the remainder of the people; and ritual officials, drummers, and others who were considered the "children" of the king, being recruited from many sources, including royal slaves, and often observing patrilineal descent.

The king is a sacred person. He may not be observed eating or drinking and may not be heard to speak nor be spoken to publicly (speaking only through a spokesman or "linguist," *okyeame*). He is covered from the sky by a royal umbrella, avoids contact with the earth by wearing royal sandals, and wears insignia of gold and elaborate and beautiful cloth of royal design. In the past, an Akan king held power over the life and death of his subjects and slaves. These powers were eroded during colonial rule, but today an Akan king remains extremely powerful, representing his people both politically and ritually and acting as a focus for the identity of his kingdom. By far the most powerful is the king of Asante, who has the largest of all the Akan kingdoms, the Asantehene at Kumasi.

Warfare has historically been a central institution, a means of extending of territory and controlling external trade. An Akan state is typically divided into five or six military formations or "wings," each under the authority of a wing chief. Beneath the wing chiefs, who are chosen by the king, are the chiefs of the main towns of a kingdom. The latter are from the town's ruling line.

Religion

Indigenous Akan religion is based upon the worship of a High God, various spirits or deities, and ancestors. The High God—known as Onyame, Onyankopon, and by other names—is the Creator, now otiose; he is accompanied by Asase Yaa, the goddess of the earth. The ancestors live in the land of the dead and may demand offerings, in the past including those of slaves. The royal ancestors

are at the heart of the ritual protection of a kingdom. They are "fed" at shrines in the form of blackened stools of wood and kept in the "stool rooms" in palaces and houses. Traditionally, the stools were anointed with human blood, gunpowder, and spider webs, and given alcoholic drink; human sacrifices are no longer made. Spirits or deities are many, and the living can communicate with them through prayer, sacrifice, and possession. Each has its own *osofo*, or priest; an *okomfo* is a living spirit medium who interprets the words of a spirit who is consulted to remove sickness and human disasters. Each kingdom and town has, or had in past years, an annual purification ritual, known as *odwira*, in which the king, the office of kingship, the kingdom, and the town are purified of the pollution of the preceding year; this is often known in the literature as a "yam festival."

The Akan have largely been Christian since the nineteenth century, except for most kings, who have had to retain their indigenous religious status and practices. European Christian missions were highly successful, bringing not only Christianity but also education, and most Akan have been literate for a long time. Islam has a long history among the Akan, having been introduced by early traders from the north. Royalty made use of Muslim scribes for court duties. The Akan have a long history of "prophets" of many kinds—Christian, Muslim, and "heathen"—and of separatist Christian movements. All these various forms of religious belief and activity exist side by side, and most people have recourse to all of them, according to their particular needs and wishes.

Bibliography

Busia, K. A. (1951). *The Position of the Chief in the Modern Political System of Ashanti*. London: Oxford University Press, for the International African Institute.

McCaskie, T. C. (1995). *State and Society in Pre-Colonial Asante*. Cambridge and New York: Cambridge University Press.

McLeod, M. D. (1981). *Asante*. London: British Museum Publications, for the Trustees of the British Museum.

Rattray, R. S. (1923). *Ashanti*. Oxford: Clarendon Press.

Rattray, R. S. (1927). *Religion and Art in Ashanti*. Oxford: Clarendon Press.

Rattray, R. S. (1929). *Ashanti Law and Constitution*. Oxford: Clarendon Press.

Wilks, Ivor (1975). *Assante in the Nineteenth Century*. London and New York: Cambridge University Press.

—MICHELLE GILBERT

The Akan king is a sacred person. He may not be observed eating or drinking and may not be heard to speak nor be spoken to publicly.

AMHARA

Ethonym: Amara

Orientation

IDENTIFICATION. The term "Amhara" is derived from *amari*, meaning "one who is pleasing, agreeable, beautiful, and gracious." Amhara culture is often identified with Abyssinian culture, which is regarded as the heir to the cultural blending of ancient Semitic and Cushitic (African) patterns; other heirs are the Tigre-speaking people of Eritrea, and the Tegreñña speakers of northern Ethiopia. The name "Ethiopia" is derived from an ancient Greek term meaning "people with sunburned faces" and has been revived to designate the present-day state, which also includes non-Abyssinians. The Amhara themselves often use the term "Amhara" synonymously with "Ethiopian Orthodox (Monophysite) Christian," although their own, more precise expression for this religion is "Towahedo" (Orthodox). In the past, books on Ethiopia have often referred to this religion as "Coptic," derived from the Greek term for Egyptian. Until Haile Selassie was crowned emperor in 1930, the Coptic metropolitan of Alexandria, Egypt, had also been the head of this Ethiopian church and had appointed Ethiopian archbishops.

LOCATION. Ethiopia is located in the northeastern part of Africa, roughly between 5° and 16° N and 33° and 43° E. It is mountainous, separated from the Red Sea by hot lowland deserts; a steep escarpment in the west borders the hot lowland in Sudan. The mountain-fortress type of landscape has frequently enabled the plateau people to retain their independence against would-be invaders. Begemder, Gojam, and Welo are Amharic speaking, as are parts of Shewa since Amhara expansion under emperor Menilek II in the 1880s.

DEMOGRAPHY. According to the 1984 census, the population of Ethiopia was estimated as 42 million. Of these, 28 percent referred to themselves as "Amhara," and 32 percent stated that they spoke Amharic at home. Hence, about 14 million could be identified as Amhara, subject to qualification by the effects of Amharization during the rule of Emperor Haile Selassie (1930–1974) and the political strife against Amhara domination since then. Ethiopia is essentially a rural country. Apart from the capital, Addis Ababa, few towns have a permanent population in excess of 10,000: Gonder, the old caravan town on the way from the highlands to the Sudan; Harer, the coffee city; and Dire Dawa, the railroad junction to the coast. The many small towns are essentially marketplaces, serving the farming hinterland.

LINGUISTIC AFFILIATION. There are three major linguistic families in Ethiopia: Cushitic, Semitic, and Nilo-Saharan. Cushitic and Semitic are two families of the Afro-Asian Phylum. Nilo-Sarahan languages of the Sudanic Phylum predominate along the northern and western escarpment. Cushitic includes Oromo (formerly called Galla), Sidamo, Somali, and Agau. Semitic languages, spoken mainly in the northern half of the country, are related to the Ge'ez language, which was spoken there from about the first half of the first millennium B.C. and had a writing system from which the present Amharic writing is derived. Ge'ez ceased to be spoken before the fourteenth century A.D., but it survives in the Orthodox liturgy to this day. It has been the language of religious and historical documents almost until the present, and linguists have referred to it as "Ethiopic." Amharic is related to Ge'ez but contains strong influences from Cushitic. It has been important since the fourteenth century A.D., when the earliest Amharic document, "Songs of the Kings," was written. Amharic, which is the predominant language on the plateau of northwest-central Ethiopia, is now the official national language of Ethiopia.

History and Cultural Relations

There is a paucity of reliable data about the prehistory of Ethiopia because archaeological excavation was long prohibited. Three procedures can be followed, however: interpretation of surface archaeological sites, tracing ancient trade routes, and linguistic analysis. Rock paintings resemble those of Libya; others depict cattle without humps, suggesting an early population of cattle breeders prior to the entry from Yemen of breeders of humped cattle (which are predominant today), via the Bab al-Mandab. The elaborate obelisks at Aksum, 27 to 30 meters tall, with false doors and windows (which have counterparts in ancient Yemen), appear to fall into the Semitic period of about 500 B.C. to A.D. 300.

Certain basic trade routes—for instance, the iron route—have scarcely changed in thousands of years. Salt must still be brought in from the coast of the Red Sea. Ivory, gold, and slaves were brought from the south to pay for imports. Wild coffee was brought from the south of Ethiopia to Yemen, perhaps to pay for humped *sebu* cattle. *Mashella* (guinea corn) may have originated on the western Ethiopian plateau and spread westward from there. Foreign trade was given great impetus when the camel was introduced to those Ethiopian regions too dry for donkeys, about A.D. 100. There is a record of hunting expeditions by the Ptolemean rulers of Egypt in Ethiopia. Ptolemy III (245–222 B.C.) placed at the port of Adulis (near present-day Mesewa) a Greek inscription recording that he captured elephants, and an inscribed block of stones with magical hieroglyphs. At the same port about A.D. 60, a Greek merchant named Periplus recorded the importation of iron and the production of spears for hunting elephants, and in A.D. 350 Aeizana, king of Aksum, defeated the Nubians and carried off iron and bronze from Meroë.

The Abyssinian tradition of the Solomonic dynasty, as told in the Ge'ez-language book *Kebra Nagast* (Honor of the Kings) refers to the rule of Menilek I, about 975–950 B.C. It relates that he was the son of Makeda, conceived from King Solomon during her visit to Jerusalem. Interrupted in A.D. 927 by sovereigns of a Zagwe line, the Solomonic line was restored in 1260 and claimed continuity until Emperor Haile Selassie was deposed in 1974. Abyssinian churches are still built on the principle of Solomon's temple of Jerusalem, with a Holy of Holies section in the interior. Christianity came to Aksum in the fourth century A.D., when Greek-speaking Syrians converted the royal family. This strain of Christianity retained a number of Old Testament rules, some of which are observed to this day: the consumption of pork is forbidden; circumcision of boys takes place about a week after birth; upper-level priests consider Saturday a day of rest, second only to Sunday; weddings preferably take place on Sunday, so that the presumed deflowering, after nightfall, is considered to have taken place on the eve of Monday. Ecclesiastic rule over Abyssinia was administered early on by the archbishop of Alexandria, detached only after World War II. At the Council of Chalcedon in A.D. 451, the theological Monophysites of Alexandria, including the Abyssinians, had broken away from the European church; hence the designation "Coptic."

The spread of Islam to regions surrounding it produced relative isolation in Ethiopia from the seventh to the sixteenth centuries. During this period, the Solomonic dynasty was restored in 1260 in the province of Shewa by King Yekuno Amlak, who extended his realm from Abyssinia to some Cuchitic-speaking lands south and east. Amharic developed out of this linguistic blend. From time to time, Europeans heard rumors of a Prester John, a Christian king on the other side of the Muslim world. Using a vast number of serfs on feudal church territories, Abuna (archbishop) Tekle Haymanot built churches and monasteries, often on easily defensible hilltops, such as Debra Libanos monastery in Shewa, which is still the most important in Ethiopia.

With the Muslim conquest of Somali land in 1430, the ring around Abyssinia was complete, and recently Islamicized Oromo (Galla) seminomadic tribes from the south invaded through the Rift Valley, burning churches and monasteries. Some manuscripts and church paintings had to be hidden on islands on Lake Tana. When a second wave of invaders came, equipped with Turkish firearms, the Shewan king Lebna Dengel sent a young Armenian to Portugal to solicit aid. Before it could arrive, the Oromo leader Mohammed Grañ ("the left-handed") attacked with the aid of Arabs from Yemen, Somalis, and Danakils and proceeded as far north as Aksum, which he razed, killing the king in battle in 1540. His children and the clergy took refuge on and north of Lake Tana. One year later, Som Christofo Da Gama landed at Mesewa with 450 Portuguese musketeers; the slain king's son, Galaudeos (Claudius), fought on until he died in battle. The tide turned, however, and in 1543 Mohammed Grañ fell in battle.

Shewa nevertheless remained settled by Oromo, who learned the agriculture of the region. The royal family had only a tent city in what became the town of Gonder. There the Portuguese built bridges and castles, and Jesuits began to convert the royal family to Roman Christianity. King Za Dengel was the first royal convert, but the Monophysite clergy organized a rebellion that led to his removal. His successor, King Susneos, had also been converted but was careful not to urge his people to convert; shortly before his death in 1632, he proclaimed religious liberty for all his subjects.

The new king, Fasilidas (1632–1667), expelled the Portuguese and restored the privileges of the Monophysite clergy. He—and later his son and grandson—employed workmen trained by the Portuguese to build the castles that stand to this day. Special walled paths shielded the royal family from common sight, but the king, while sitting under a fig tree, judged cases brought before him. A stone-lined water pool was constructed under his balcony, and a mausoleum entombed his favorite horse. All these structures still exist. But the skills of stonemasonry later fell into disuse; warfare required mobility, which necessitated the formation of military tent cities. Portuguese viticulture was also lost (though the name of the middle

♦ **Mohammed**
The Arab prophet of Islam, who received the Quran from the Angel Gabriel. Although most venerated, he is not considered a deity, for in Islam there is no god but Allah. He lived from about A.D. 570 to 632.

elevation remains "Woyna Dega"), and the clergy had to import raisins to produce sacramental wine.

Gonder had been abandoned by the Solomonic line when a usurping commoner chieftain, Kassa, chose it as the location to have himself crowned King Theodore in 1855. He defeated the king of Shewa and held the dynastic heir, the boy Menilek II, hostage at his court. Theodore realized the urgency of uniting the many ethnic groups of the country into a nation, to prevent Ethiopia from losing its independence to European colonial powers. Thinking that all Europeans knew how to manufacture cannons, Theodore invited foreign technicians and, at first, even welcomed foreign missionaries. But when the latter proved unable to cast cannons for him and even criticized his often violent behavior, he jailed and chained British missionaries. This led to the Lord Napier expedition, which was welcomed and assisted by the population of Tigray Province. When the fort of Magdalla fell, Theodore committed suicide. A conservative Tigray chief, Yohannes, was crowned at Aksum.

In 1889 the Muslim mahdi took advantage of the disarray in Ethiopia; he razed Gonder and devastated the subprovince of Dembeya, causing a severe and prolonged famine. Meanwhile, the Shewan dynastic heir, Menilek II, had grown to manhood and realized that Ethiopia could no longer isolate itself if it were to retain independence. He proceeded, with patient persistence, to unify the country. As an Amhara from Shewa, he understood his Oromo neighbors and won their loyalty with land grants and military alliances. He negotiated a settlement with the Tigray. He equipped his forces with firearms from whatever source, some even from the Italians (in exchange for granting them territory in Eritrea).

His policies were so successful that he managed to defeat the Italian invasion at Adwa, in 1896, an event that placed Ethiopia on the international map diplomatically. Empress Taitu liked the hot mineral springs of a district in Shewa, even though it was in an Oromo region, and the emperor therefore agreed to build his capital there, naming it "Addis Ababa" (new flower). When expanding Addis Ababa threatened to exhaust the local fuel supply, Menilek ordered the importation of eucalyptus trees from Australia, which grew rapidly during each three-month rainy season.

Menilek II died in 1913, and his daughter Zauditu became nominal head; a second cousin, Ras Tafari Makonnen, became regent and was crowned King of Kings Haile Selassie I in 1930. He made it possible for Ethiopia to join the League of Nations in 1923, by outlawing the slave trade. One of his first acts as emperor was to grant his subjects a written constitution. He allied himself by marriage to the Oromo king of Welo Province. When Mussolini invaded Ethiopia in 1935, Emperor Haile Selassie appeared in Geneva to plead his case before the League, warning that his country would not be the last victim of aggression. The Italian occupation ended in 1941 with surrender to the British and return of the emperor. During succeeding decades, the emperor promoted an educated elite and sought assistance from the United States, rather than the British, in various fields. Beginning in about 1960, a young, educated generation of Ethiopians grew increasingly impatient with the slowness of development, especially in the political sphere. At the same time, the aging emperor, who was suffering memory loss, was losing his ability to maintain control. In 1974 he was deposed, and he died a year later. The revolutionary committees, claiming to follow a Marxist ideology, formed military dictatorships that deported villagers under conditions of great suffering and executed students and each other without legal trials. Dictator Mengistu Haile Mariam fled Ethiopia in May 1991 as Eritrean and Tigrayan rebel armies approached from the north. The country remains largely rural; traditional culture patterns and means of survival are the norm.

Economy

Much Amhara ingenuity has long been invested in the direct exploitation of natural resources. An Amhara would rather spend as much time as necessary searching for suitably shaped hard or soft saplings for a walking cane than perform carpentry, which is traditionally largely limited to constructing the master bed (*alga*), wooden saddles, and simple musical instruments. Soap is obtained by crushing the fruit of the *endod* (*Pircunia abyssinica*) bush. Tannin for depilation of hides and curing is obtained from the yellow fruit of the *embway* bush. Butter is preserved and perfumed by boiling it with the leaves of the *ades* (myrtle) bush. In times of crop failure, edible oil is obtained by gathering and crushing wild-growing sunflower seeds (*Carthamus tinctorus*). If necessary, leaves of the *lola* bush can be split by women to bake the festive bread *dabbo*. The honey of a

See also

Akan

small, tiny-stingered bee (*Apis dorsata*) is gathered to produce alcoholic mead, *ṭej*, whereas the honey of the wild bee *ṭazemma* (*Apis Africans miaia*) is gathered to treat colds and heart ailments. Fishing is mostly limited to the three-month rainy season, when rivers are full and the water is muddy from runoff so that the fish cannot see the fishers. Hunting elephants used to be a sport of young feudal nobles, but hunting for ivory took place largely in non-Amhara regions. Since rifles became available in Amhara farming regions, Ethiopian duikers and guinea fowl have nearly disappeared.

Subsistence farming provides the main economy for most rural Amhara. The traditional method required much land to lie fallow because no fertilization was applied. Cattle manure is formed into flat cakes, sun dried, and used as fuel for cooking. New land, if available, is cleared by the slash-and-burn method. A wooden scratch plow with a pointed iron tip, pulled by oxen, is the main farming tool. Insecurity of land tenure has long been a major factor in discouraging Amhara farmers from producing more than the amount required for subsistence. The sharecropping peasant (*gabbar*) was little more than a serf who feared the (often absentee) feudal landlord or military quartering that would absorb any surplus. The revolutionary government (1975–1991) added additional fears by its villagization program, moving peasants at command to facilitate state control and deporting peasants to the south of Ethiopia, where many perished owing to poor government planning and support.

The preferred crop of the Amhara is *tyeff* (*Eragrostis abyssinica*; *Poa abyssinica*), the small seeds of which are rich in iron. At lower or drier elevations, several sorghums (durras) are grown: *mashella* (*Andropogon sorghum*), often mixed with the costlier tyeff flower to bake the flapjack bread *injera*; *zengada* (*Eleusina multiforma*), grown as crop insurance; and *dagussa* (*Eleusine coracana*, or *tocusso*), used as an ingredient in beer together with barley. Wheat (*Triticum* spp.), *sendē*, is grown in higher elevations and is considered a luxury. Barley (*Hordeum* spp.), *gebs*, is a year-round crop, used primarily for brewing *talla*, a mild beer, or to pop a parched grain, *gebs qolo*, a ready snack kept available for guests. Maize, *baher mashella*, is recognized as a foreign-introduced crop.

The most important vegetable oil derives from *nug* (*Guizotia abyssinica*), the black Niger seed, and from *talba* (*Linum usitatissimum*), flax seed. Cabbage (*gomen*) is regarded as a poor food.

Chick-peas are appreciated as a staple that is not expected to fail even in war and famine; they are consumed during the Lenten season, as are peas. Onions and garlic are grown as ingredients for *woṭ*, the spicy stew that also contains beans, may include chicken, and always features spicy red peppers—unless ill heath prevents their consumption. Lentils substitute for meat during fasting periods. The raising of livestock is traditionally not directly related to available pasture, but to agriculture and the desire for prestige. Oxen are needed to pull the plow, but traditionally there was no breeding to obtain good milkers. Coffee may grow wild, but the beans are usually bought at a market and crushed and boiled in front of guests; salt—but not sugar—may be added.

DIVISION OF LABOR. Although much needed, the castelike skilled occupations like blacksmithing, pottery making, and tanning are held in low esteem and, in rural regions, are usually associated with a socially excluded ethnic grouping. Moreover, ethnic workmanship is suspected of having been acquired by dealings with evil spirits that enable the artisans to turn themselves into hyenas at night to consume corpses, cause diseases by staring, and turn humans into donkeys to utilize their labor. Such false accusations can be very serious. On the other hand, the magic power accredited to these workers is believed to make their products strong, whereas those manufactured by an outsider who might have learned the trade would soon break. The trade of weaving is not afflicted by such suspicions, although it is sometimes associated with Muslims or migrants from the south.

LAND TENURE. Land tenure among traditional rural Amhara resembled that of medieval Europe more than that found elsewhere in Africa. Feudal institutions required the gabbar to perform labor (*hudad*) for his lord and allocated land use in exchange for military service, *gult*. In a system resembling the European entail, inheritable land, *rest*, was subject to taxation (which could be passed on to the sharecroppers) and to expropriation in case of rebellion against the king. Over the centuries, endowed land was added to fief-holding church land, and *debber ager*. Royal household lands were classified as *mādbet*, and *melkenya* land was granted to tax collectors. Emperor Haile Selassie attempted to change the feudal system early in his administration. He defeated feudal armies, but was stymied in abrogating feudalistic land tenure, especially in the Amhara region, by feudal lords such as Ras Kassa. The parliament that he

♦ **serf**
In medieval Europe, a tenant farmer who subsisted by farming land owned by a lord or landowner. Serfs were generally bound to the land they farmed and their rights to move from the land were greatly restricted.

Amhara social organization is linked to land tenure of kinfolk, feudalistic traditions and the church, ethnic division of labor, gender, and age status.

had called into existence had no real power. All remaining feudal land tenure was abrogated during the revolutionary dictatorship (1975–1991), but feudalistic attitudes practiced by rural officials, such as *shum shir* (frequently moving lower officials to other positions to maintain control), appear to have persisted.

Kinship

The extended patrilocal, patrilineal, patriarchal family is particularly strong among holders of rest land tenure, but is found, in principle, even on the hamlet level of sharecroppers. There are several levels of kin, *zemed*, which also include those by affinity, *amachenet*. In view of the emphasis on seeking security in kinship relations, there are also several formal methods of establishing fictive kinship, *zemed hone*, provided the person to be adopted is *attentam* ("of good bones," i.e., not of Shanqalla slave ancestry). Full adoption provides a breast father (*yetut abbat*) or a breast mother (*yetut ennat*). The traditional public ceremony included coating the nipples with honey and simulating breast-feeding, even if the child was already in adolescence.

Marriage and Family

MARRIAGE. There are three predominant types of marriage in Amhara tradition. Only a minority—the priesthood, some older persons, and nobility—engage in eucharistic church marriage (*qurban*). No divorce is possible. Widows and widowers may remarry, except for priests, who are instead expected to become monks.

Kin-negotiated civil marriage (*semanya*; lit., "eighty") is most common. (Violation of the oath of marriage used to be penalized by a fine of 80 Maria Theresa thalers.) No church ceremony is involved, but a priest may be present at the wedding to bless the couple. Divorce, which involves the division of property and determination of custody of children, can be negotiated. Temporary marriage (*damoz*) obliges the husband to pay housekeeper's wages for a period stated in advance. This was felt to be an essential arrangement in an economy where restaurant and hotel services were not available. The term is a contraction of *demewez*, "blood and sweat" (compensation). The contract, although oral, was before witnesses and was therefore enforceable by court order. The wife had no right of inheritance, but if children were conceived during the contract period, they could make a claim for part of the fa-

ther's property, should he die. Damoz rights were even recognized in modern law during the rule of Emperor Haile Selassie.

Socialization in the domestic unit begins with the naming of the baby (giving him or her the "world name"), a privilege that usually belongs to the mother. She may base it on her predominant emotion at the time (e.g., Desta [joy] or Almaz [diamond]), on a significant event occurring at the time, or on a special wish she may have for the personality or future of her baby (Seyum, "to be appointed to dignity").

SOCIALIZATION. Breast-feeding may last two years, during which the nursling is never out of touch with the body of the mother or another woman. Until they are weaned, at about age 7, children are treated with permissiveness, in contrast to the authoritarian training that is to follow. The state of reason and incipient discipline begins gradually at about age 5 for girls and 7 for boys. The former assist their mothers in watching babies and fetching wood; boys take sheep and cows to pasture and, with slingshots, guard crops against birds and baboons. Both can be questioned in court to express preferences concerning guardianship in case of their parents' divorce. Neglect of duty is punished by immediate scolding and beating.

Formal education in the traditional rural church school rarely began before age 11 for boys. Hazing patterns to test courage are common among boys as they grow up, both physically and verbally. Girls are enculturated to appear shy, but may play house with boys prior to adolescence. Adolescence is the beginning of stricter obedience for both sexes, compensated by pride in being assigned greater responsibilities. Young men are addressed as *ashker* and do most of the plowing; by age 18 they may be addressed as *gobez*, signifying (strong, handsome) young warrior. On the Temqet (baptism of Jesus) festival, the young men encounter each other in teams to compete in the game of *guks*, a tournament fought on horseback with blunt, wooden lances, in which injuries are avoided by ducking or protecting oneself with leather shields. At Christmas, a hockeylike game called *genna* is played and celebrated by boasting (*fukkara*). Female adolescents are addressed as *qonjo* (beautiful), no longer as *leja-gered* (servant maid), unless criticized. Singing loudly in groups while gathering firewood attracts groups of young men, away from parental supervision. Young men and women also meet following the guks and genna games, wearing new clothes and traditional makeup and hairstyles. Outdoor flirting reaches a peak on Easter (Fassika), at the end of the dry season.

DOMESTIC UNIT. The traditional age of a girl at first marriage may be as young as 14, to protect her virginity, and to enable the groom to tame her more easily. A groom three to five years older than the bride is preferred. To protect the bride against excessive violence, she is assigned two best men, who wait behind a curtain as the marriage is consummated; later, she may call on them in case of batter.

The term *shemagelyē* signifies an elder and connotes seriousness, wisdom, and command of human relations within the residential kin group or beyond. He may be 40 years of age and already a grandfather. There is no automatic equivalency for elder women, but they can take the *qob* of a nun and continue to live at home while working in the churchyard, baking bread and brewing beer for the priests. Only women past menopause, usually widows, are accepted as nuns by the Monophysite Aybssinian church. Younger women are not considered sufficiently serious to be able to deny their sex drives.

INHERITANCE. When death is approaching, elder kin of the dying person bring the confessor, and the last will concerning inheritance is pronounced. Fields are given to patrilineal descendants, cattle to all offspring. Personal belongings, such as oxhide mats and a *shamma* (toga), may be given to the confessor, who administers last rites and assigns a burial place in the churchyard. Endowments to the church are handled by the *qes gobez*.

Sociopolitical Organization

Social organization is linked to land tenure of kinfolk, feudalistic traditions and the church, ethnic division of labor, gender, and age status. The peasant class is divided between landowning farmers, who, even though they have no formal political power, can thwart distant government power by their rural remoteness, poor roads, and weight of numbers, and the sharecroppers, who have no such power against local landlords. Fear of a person who engages in a skilled occupation, *ṭebib* (lit., "the knowing one," to whom supernatural secrets are revealed), enters into class stratification, especially for blacksmiths, pottery makers, and tanners. They are despised as members of a lower caste, but their products are needed, and therefore they are tolerated. Below them on the social scale are the descendants of slaves who used to be imported from the negroid Shanqalla of the Sudanese border, or the Nilotic Barya, so that both terms became synonymous with "slave."

Social control is traditionally maintained, and conflict situations are resolved, in accordance with the power hierarchy. Judges interpret laws subjectively and make no sharp distinction between civil

♦ **caste**
An endogamous hereditary group, usually with a distinct hereditary occupation, who have a virtually immutable position in a hierarchy. Although the caste system is most elaborated throughout South Asia, castes have also been reported in Tibet, Japan, Korea, Burundi, and the American South.

SETTLEMENTS

The typical rural settlement is the hamlet, *tis*, called *mender* if several are linked on one large hill. The hamlet may consist of two to a dozen huts. Thus, the hamlet is often little more than an isolated or semi-isolated farmstead, and another hamlet may be close by if their plowed fields are near. Four factors appear to determine where a hamlet is likely to be situated: ecological considerations, such as water within a woman's walking distance, or available pasturage for the flock; kinship considerations—persons within a hamlet are nearly always related and form a family economic community; administrative considerations, such as inherited family ownership of land, tenancy of land belonging to a feudal lord of former times, or continuing agreement with the nearby church that had held

the land as a fief up to 1975 and continues to receive part of the crop in exchange for its services; and ethnic considerations. A hamlet may be entirely inhabited by Falasha blacksmiths and pottery makers or Faqi tanners. Most of the Falasha have now left Ethiopia.

To avoid being flooded during the rainy season, settlements are typically built on or near hilltops. There is usually a valley in between, where brooks or irrigation canals form the border for planted fields. The hillsides, if not terrace farmed, serve as pasturage for all hamlets on the hill. Not only sheep and goats, but also cows, climb over fairly steep, bushy hillsides to feed. Carrying water and branches for fuel is still considered a woman's job, and she may have to

climb for several hours from the nearest year-round water supply. The hamlet is usually patrilocal and patrilineal. When marriage occurs, usually early in life, a son may receive use of part of his father's rented (or owned) field and build his hut nearby. If no land is available owing to fragmentation, the son may reluctantly be compelled to establish himself at the bride's hamlet. When warfare has killed off the adult males in a hamlet, in-laws may also be able to move in. Some hamlets are fenced in by thorn bushes against night-roving hyenas and to corral cattle. Calves and the family mule may be taken into the living hut at night. There is usually at least one fierce reddish-brown dog in each hamlet.

Amhara

Verbal arts are highly esteemed in Amhara culture, but there is a pronounced class distinction between the speech of the rustic peasant and upper-class speech.

and criminal procedures. In addition to written Abyssinian and church laws, there are unwritten codes, such as the payment of blood money to the kin of a murder victim. An aggrieved person could appeal to a higher authority by lying prostrate in his path and shouting "*abyet*" (hear me). Contracts did not have to be written, provided there were reliable witnesses. To obtain a loan or a job, a personal guarantor (*wās*) is necessary, and the wās can also act as bondsman to keep an accused out of jail. The drama of litigation, to talk well in court, is much appreciated. Even children enact it with the proper body language of pointing a toga at the judge to emphasize the speech.

Religion and Expressive Culture

The religious belief of most Amhara is Monophysite—that is, Tewahedo (Orthodox) Christianity, to such an extent that the term "Amhara" is used synonymously with "Abyssinian Christian." Christian Amhara wear a blue neck cord (*meteb*), to distinguish themselves from Muslims. In rural regions, the rules of the church have the de facto force of law, and many people are consecrated to church functions: priests, boy deacons and church students, chorister-scribes, monks, and nuns. Besides the ecclesiastical function of the *qes* (parish priest), the chorister-scribe—who is not ordained—fulfills many services. He translates the liturgy from Ge'ez to Amharic, chants and sometimes composes devotional poetry (*qēnē*), and writes amulets. The latter may be unofficial and discouraged by the priests, but ailing persons believe strongly in them and may use them to prevent disease. Prior to examinations, church students often chew and swallow a *Datura* weed called *astenager* (lit., "to stimulate talk") to enhance memory of biblical quotations and other details learned by rote and to aid correct pronunciation of the liturgy.

CEREMONIES Ceremonies often mark the annual cycle for the public, despite the sacredotal emphasis of the religion. The calendar of Abyssinia is Julian, but the year begins on 11 September, following ancient Egyptian usage, and is called *amete mehrāt* (year of grace). Thus, the Abyssinian year 1948 A.M. corresponds roughly with the Gregorian (Western) A.D. 1956. The new year begins with the month of Meskerem, which follows the rainy season and is named after the first religious holy day of the year, Mesqel-abeba, celebrating the Feast of the Cross. On the seventeenth day, huge poles are stacked up for the bonfire in the evening, with much public parading, dancing, and feasting. By contrast, Christmas (Ledet) has little social significance except for the genna game of the young men. Far more important is Epiphany (Ṭemqet), on the eleventh day of Ṭer. Ceremonial parades escort the priests who carry the *tabot*, symbolic of the holy ark, on their heads, to a water pool. There are all-night services, public feasting, and prayers for plentiful rains.

This is the end of the genna season and the beginning of the guks tournaments fought on horseback by the young men. The long Lenten season is approaching, and clergy as well as the public look forward to the feasting at Easter (Fassika), on the seventeenth day of Miyazya. Children receive new clothes and collect gifts, chanting house to house. Even the voluntary fraternal association *mehabber* is said to have originated from the practice of private communion. Members take turns as hosts at monthly meetings, drinking barley beer together with the confessor-priest, who intones prayers. Members are expected to act as a mutual aid society, raising regular contributions, extending loans, even paying for the *tazkar* (formal memorial service) forty days after a member's death, if his family cannot afford it.

ARTS. Verbal arts—such as *bedanya fit* (speaking well before a judge)—are highly esteemed in general Amhara culture, but there is a pronounced class distinction between the speech of the rustic peasant, *balager* (hence *belegē*, unpolished, sometimes even vulgar), and *chowa lij*, upper-class speech. A further differentiation within the latter is the speech of those whose traditional education has included *sewassow* (Ge'ez: grammar; lit., "ladder," "uplifting"), which is fully mastered mainly by church scholars; the speeches of former emperor Haile Selassie, who had also mastered sewassow, impressed the average layperson as esoteric and hard to understand, and therefore all the more to be respected. In the arts of politeness, veiled mockery, puns with double meanings, such as *semmena-worq* (wax and gold), even partial knowledge of grammar is an advantage. The draping of the toga (shamma) is used at court and other occasions to emphasize spoken words, or to communicate even without speech. It is draped differently to express social status in deference to a person of high status, on different occasions, and even to express moods ranging from outgoing and expansive to calm sobriety, to sadness, reserve, pride, social distance, desperate pleading, religious devotion, and so on. Artistic expression in the fine arts had long been linked to the church, as in paintings, and sponsorship by feudal lords who could afford it, especially when giving feasts celebrated with a variety of musical instruments.

MEDICINE. The basic concepts and practices of Amhara medicine can be traced to ancient Egypt and the ancient Near East and can also be attributed to regional ecological links within Ethiopia. Often no sharp distinctions are made between bodily and spiritual ailments, but there are special occupations: the *woggesha* (surgeon-herbologist) is a pragmatist in practice; the *debtera* (scribe) invokes the spirit world. The latter is officially or unofficially linked to the church, but the *zar* cult is apart and may even be female dominated. Its spirit healing has a complex cosmology; it involves the social status of the patient and includes group therapy. The chief zar doctor is often a matriarch who entered the profession when she herself was possessed by a spirit; she has managed to control some powerful spirits that she can then employ in her battles to overcome the spirits that possess her patients. No cure is expected, only control through negotiation and appeasement of the offended spirit, in the hope of turning it into a *weqabi* (protective spirit).

Many men consider the zar cult effeminate and consult its doctors by stealth only, at night. Husbands may resent the financial outlays if their wives are patients, but fear the wives' relapse into hysterical or catatonic states. Women, whose participation in the Abyssinian church is severely limited, find expression in the zar cult. The zar doctors at Gonder hold their annual convention on the twenty-third night of the month of Yekatit, just before the beginning of the Monophysite Christian Lent (Kudade; lit., "suffering"). There is much chanting, dancing, drumming, and consumption of various drinks at the love feasts of the zars. Poor patients who are unable to pay with money or commodities can work off their debts in labor service to the cult—waitressing, weaving baskets, fetching water and fuel, brewing barley beer, and so forth. They are generally analyzed by the zar doctor as being possessed by a low-status zar spirit.

By contrast, possession by an evil spirit (*buda*) is considered more serious and less manageable than possession by a zar, and there is no cult. An effort is made to prevent it by wearing amulets and avoiding ṭebib persons, who are skilled in trades like blacksmithing and pottery making. Since these spirits are believed to strike beautiful or successful persons, such individuals—especially if they are children—must not be praised out loud. If a person sickens and wastes away, an exorcism by the church may be attempted, or a *tanqway* (diviner-sorcerer) may be consulted; however, the latter recourse is considered risky and shameful.

DEATH AND AFTERLIFE. When an elder is near death, other elders from his kin group bring the confessor and say to him, "Confess yourself." Then they ask him for his last will—what to leave to his children and what for his soul (the church). The confessor gives last rites and, after death, assigns a burial place in the churchyard. The corpse is washed, wrapped in a shamma, carried to church for the mass, and buried, traditionally without a marker except for a circle of rocks. Women express grief with loud keening and wailing. This is repeated when kinfolk arrive to console. A memorial feast (tazkar) is held forty days after the death of a man or a woman, when the soul has the earliest opportunity to be freed from purgatory. Preparations for this feast begin at the time of the funeral: money is provided for the priest to recite the *fetet*, the prayer for absolution, and materials, food, and drink are accumulated. It is often the greatest single economic expenditure of an individual's lifetime and, hence, a major social event. For the feasting, a large, rectangular shelter (*dass*) is erected, and even distant kin are expected to participate and consume as much talla and woṭ as available.

Bibliography

Hoben, Alan (1973). *Land Tenure among the Amhara of Ethiopia: The Dynamics of Cognatic Descent.* Chicago: University of Chicago Press.

Levine, Donald M. (1965). *Wax and Gold: Tradition and Innovation in Ethiopian Culture.* Chicago: University of Chicago Press.

Messing, Simon D. (1985). *Highland Plateau Amhara of Ethiopia.* Edited by Lionel M. Bender. 3 vols. New Haven: HRAFlex Books, Human Relations Area Files.

Molvar, R. K. (1980). *Tradition and Change in Ethiopia: Social and Cultural Life as Reflected in Amharic Fictional Literature ca. 1930–1974.* Leiden: E. J. Brill.

Young, Alan L. (1975). "Magic as a Quasi-Profession: The Organization of Magic and Magical Healing among Amhara." *Ethnology* 14:245–265.

—SIMON D. MESSING

BEMBA

Ethonyms: Babemba, Chibemba, Chiwemba, Ichibemba, Wemba

The Bemba are the largest ethnic group in the Northern Province of Zambia, where they occupy the high plateau land between 9° and 12° S and between 29° and 32° E, covering the whole dis-

◆ **cult**
The beliefs, ideas, and activities associated with the worship of a supernatural force or its representations, such as an ancestor cult or a bear cult.

trict of Kasama and much of Mpika, Chinsali, Luwingu, and Mporokoso districts. The 1986 Zambian census placed the Bemba population at approximately 1,700,000 in Zambia, with another 150,000 in neighboring countries.

Some seventeen or eighteen ethnic groups in this general area of Zambia comprise the Bemba-speaking peoples, and they form with the Bemba a closely related culture cluster. All of these peoples are predominantly agricultural and have a matrilineal-matrilocal emphasis. They practice shifting cultivation, growing finger millet (*Eleusine corocana*), which is the staple crop in the eastern part of the area, including among the Bemba, and manioc among the western groups. There is a general absence of cattle because this area is within the tsetse belt, but the Bemba do have a few sheep and goats. The Bemba-speaking peoples, together with several other ethnic clusters, are generally considered to comprise a broader cultural-linguistic category known as the Central Bantu.

The Bemba recognize the following distinctive marks of societal membership: a common name, Babemba; a common language, Cibemba, which in their eyes forms a distinct dialect; distinctive scarification, a vertical cut on each temple behind the eyes, almost one inch long; common historical traditions; and allegiance to a common paramount chief, the *citimukulu*, whose rule of the Bemba territory is unquestioned.

Descent, sib affiliation, and succession to office follow the matrilineal line, and marital residence is matrilocal. Each individual belongs to a matrilineal lineage, which determines his succession to different offices and his status in the community. He also belongs to an exogamous, matrilineal sib (*mukoa*), which is important for certain hereditary offices. There are about thirty sibs among the Bemba, and they are ranked according to status based on their relations with the royal crocodile sib. Inheritance is relatively unimportant, since there are few forms of inheritable wealth.

Despite this matrilineal orientation, the Bemba kinship system in some ways is bilateral in nature. The kin group to which a person constantly refers in everyday affairs is the *lupwa*, a bilateral group of near relatives on both sides of his family (i.e., a kindred), who join in religious ceremonies, matrimonial transactions, mortuary ritual, and inheritance. This group may be more important to a Bemba than his matrilineal sib. In addition, a patrilineal emphasis has been increasing in the late twentieth century, including a broadening of the father's authority within the family.

Superimposed upon this kinship base is a highly centralized, hierarchical, and authoritarian political system consisting of three main levels of organization: the state, the district, and the village. As previously noted, the state is ruled by a paramount chief (citimukulu), whose office is hereditary within a royal sib. His authority is nearly absolute, and he is believed to have supernatural powers. The citimukulu is assisted by a council consisting of thirty to forty hereditary officials (the *bakabilo*), many of royal descent, and each responsible for some special ritual duty kept secret from the ordinary members of the society.

The Bemba state is divided into political districts (*ifyalo*; sing. *icalo*), usually five or more in number. Each icalo is a geographical unit with a more or less fixed boundary and name, and it is also a ritual unit. A hereditary, territorial chief (*mfumu*) rules over each icalo. These chieftainships are arranged in order of precedence, according to their nearness to the center of the country and the antiquity of their offices. To the most important of these chiefdoms the citimukulu appoints his nearest relatives. In 1933 there were three major districts: the citimukulu's personal district (called Lubemba—the center of the country), comprised of 160 villages; the Ituna district, with 69 villages; and Icinga district, with 76 villages. Each territorial chief also has his own councillors.

Each territorial chief has under him a number of subchiefs, who might rule over very small tracts of country, or rather, over a few villages. A district or territorial chief is also chief of his own village (*musumba*), and there is a significant difference in size between a chief's village and a village with a commoner as headman. The average Bemba village is rather small in size, with 30 to 50 huts and a population range of about 60 to 160. In contrast, chief's villages are very much larger in size. In the old days, a chief's village might have had thousands of inhabitants; in 1934, the villages of important chiefs had 400 to 600 huts. They were divided into quarters, ruled over by loyal supporters of the chief. The nucleus of a commoner Bemba village consists of the headman's matrilocal extended family. In older villages, such as Kasaka, there may be three or four related matrilocal family groups. The heads of these family groups are the most influential members of the community; they are known as the "great ones of the village" (*bakalamba*). It can be seen that rank is a marked feature of Bemba society. It is based ultimately on kinship—real or fictive—with the paramount chief and, derivatively, with the territorial chiefs.

♦ **shifting cultivation**
A form of horticulture in which plots of land are cleared and planted for a few years and then left to fallow for a number of years while other plots are used. Also called swidden, extensive, or slash-and-burn cultivation.

The religious beliefs and practices of the Bemba are related to their social organization, particularly the matrilineal basis of the society. Traditionally the Bemba-speaking people adhered to a house religion, in which the married woman was in charge of all the domestic ritual and had access to the divine through the intercession of her forebears. She was the one who led the veneration of the recently dead at the small house shrine. She also led the public remembrance services to the ancient guardians of the land. Furthermore, the knowledge of the community's religious heritage and the guidelines for worshiping the transcendent were passed on by the women during the ceremonies of initiation.

The original house religion of the Bemba was radically altered during the centralization of chiefly authority and the imposition of Bemba paramountcy, which occurred around 1700. The chiefs manipulated Bemba religion to enhance their own power. The worship of the spirits (*imipashi*) of dead chiefs—both paramount and territorial chiefs—has since become an essential element of Bemba religion. The focus shifted from the traditional house shrine, attended by the housewife, to the court cult, where the royal relics were venerated along with other magical objects. This cult had slowly acquired more power and authority than the ritual of the house shrine, in spite of the insistence on service to the immediate family spirits and to the guardians of the land by women.

The first Christian missionaries arrived toward the end of the nineteenth century, when chiefly power was being used in particularly cruel ways. The common people regarded these missionaries as liberators, who by their medical and social work seemed to have preferential regard for the poor and for those who suffered. Women accepted them as allies in their struggle to restore the house cult, the family spirits, and the guardians of the land. The Western missionaries were seen as the messengers of God pointing the way to a better future, and as such their teaching was incorporated into the already existing worldview of the people.

From the 1920s to the 1950s, women experienced increasing difficulties with the further demands of what was called the "new way." By then, their sacred position had come under severe attack. At that time a Western style of education, with its emphasis on modernity, was strongly emphasized within Bemba society. The Protestants and the Catholics competed for the allegiance of boys and young men. Both groups saw the religious role of women as reactionary and dangerous. Their teaching was considered pagan and was discouraged as much as possible.

Women found redress only by turning to prophets who pushed for a return to older customs and traditions. For example, Emilio Mulolani, a fervent lay preacher, was in favor of the restoration of the house cult, and taught that men and women were equal, especially in the act of procreation, which was sacred. Many women were influenced by these ideas and expressed the need to have the Christian message expressed in the religious concepts of the domestic cult.

By 1964, however, with Zambian independence, it was still apparent that women were not equal partners in religious matters. Widespread spirit possession within Bemba society, which has become incorporated into Bemba Christianity, may be a cultural response to the reduction of the woman's role in the religious sphere.

Bibliography

Hinfelaar, Hugo F. (1994). *Bemba-Speaking Women of Zambia in a Century of Religious Change (1892–1992)*. Leiden: E. J. Brill.

Labrecque, Éd. (1931). "Le marriage chez les babemba." *Africa* 4:209–221.

Richards, Audrey I. (1940). "The Political System of the Bemba Tribe—North-Eastern Rhodesia." In *African Political Systems*, edited by Meyer Fortes and E. E. Evans-Pritchard, 83–120. London: International African Institute.

Richards, Audrey I. (1956). *Chisungu: A Girl's Initiation Ceremony among the Bemba of Northern Rhodesia*. London: Faber & Faber.

Slaski, J. (1950). "Peoples of the Lower Luapula Valley." In *Bemba and Related Peoples of Northern Rhodesia*, by Wilfred Whitely, 77–100. Ethnographic Survey of Africa: East Central Africa: Part 2. London: International African Institute.

Whiteley, Wilfred (1950). *Bemba and Related Peoples of Northern Rhodesia*, 1–32, 70–76. Ethnographic Survey of Africa: East Central Africa, Part 2. London: International African Institute.

BERBERS OF MOROCCO

Ethnyms: "Imazighen" (sing. Amazigh) since 1980 has come to refer to all North African Berbers, whereas distinct names refer to regional subgroups, almost all territorially discontinuous from each other: Irifiyen (sing. Arifi) refers to the

The Bemba recognize a common name, Babemba; a common language, Cibemba; distinctive scarification; common historical traditions; and allegiance to a common paramount chief.

Almost every Berber family in the Rif region has a cow, a few goats and chickens, and a mule or donkey, as well as the ubiquitous guard dog.

Rifians of northeastern Morocco; Imazighen, again and in its original meaning, to the Berbers of central and southeast-central Morocco; Ishilhayen (sing. Ashilhay), to the Shluh or Swasa (sing. Susi) of southwestern Morocco; Iqbaʾiliyen (sing. Aqbaʾili), to the Kabyles of the Algerian Jurjura; Ishawiyen (sing. Ashawi), to the Shawiya of the Algerian Aurès; Imzabiyen (sing. Amzabi), to the oasis dwellers of the Algerian Mzab; and Imajeghen (sing. Amajegh), to the Ahaggar Tuareg of the southern Algerian Sahara, with similar names for other Tuareg groups in Mali and Niger. In this article, only the three Moroccan regional subgroups will be discussed.

Orientation

IDENTIFICATION. "Berber" refers to any native speaker of a dialect of the Berber language, although many—if not most—Arabic speakers in North Africa are also Berber by descent, even if they have lost the language. Especially in Morocco, "Imazighen" is today the preferred vernacular name for the three main regional subgroups of Berbers themselves, and its feminine form, "Tamazight," refers to their language. In the northern Moroccan Rif, encompassing the provinces of El Hoceima and Nador and part of Taza, major tribal groups include the Aith Waryaghar, Ibuqquyen, Aith ʿAmmarth, Igzinnayen, Thimsaman, Axt Tuzin, Aith Saʿid, Aith Wurishik, and Iqarʿayen. In the larger and properly Imazighen region embracing the Middle Atlas and Central High Atlas chains, the Saghro (pronounced "Saghru") massif, and the Presaharan oasis regions and encompassing parts of Kenitra, Meknes, Fès, and Taza provinces and all of Khenifra, Azilal, Ouarzazate, and Rachidia provinces, major tribal groups include the Zimmur, Ait Ndhir, Ait Yusi, Ait Warayin, Iziyyan, Ait Imyill, Ait Mhand, Ait Massad, Ait Sukhman, Ihansalen, Ait Siddrat, AitʿAtta, Ait Murghad, Ait Hadiddu, Ait Izdig, AitʿAyyash, and Ait Saghrushshn. In the Ishilhayen region embracing the Western High Atlas, the Sus Valley, and the Anti-Atlas and parts of the Essaouira, Marrakech, and Ouarzazate provinces and all of Agadir, Taroudant, and Tiznit provinces, important tribal groups include the Ihahan, Imtuggan, Iseksawen, Idemsiren, Igundafen, Igedmiwen, Imsfiwen, Iglawn, Ait Wawzgit, Id aw-Zaddagh, Ind aw-Zal, Id aw Zkri, Id aw Zkri, Isaffen, Id aw-Kansus, Isuktan, Id aw-Tanan, Ashtuken, Illalen, Id aw-Ltit, Ammeln, AitʿAli, Mjjat, l-Akhsas, Ait Ba ʿAmran, and Ait n-Nuss.

LOCATION. Of the three major Moroccan Berber-speaking areas, the northern Rif runs from roughly 34°30′ to 35°20′ N and from 2°30′to 4°30′ W; the central region from roughly 29°30′ to 34°00′ N and from 3°30′ to 6°30′ W; and the southwestern region from roughly from 29°30′ to 31°30′ N and from 7°00′ to 10°30′ W. In Morocco, too, all three Berber-speaking areas are essentially mountainous. The highest peak in the Rif chain (actually just west of the Rif proper) is Adrar n-Tidighin, at 2,458 meters. The two highest in the Central and Eastern Atlas are Adrar Mgun and Adrar n-l-ʿAyyashi, at 4,071 meters and 3,737 meters, respectively. The highest peak in the Western Atlas and highest in the country is Adrar n-Tubkal, at 4,165 meters. The Atlas chain forms the backbone of Moroccan geography and orography. The higher mountains are always snow-covered in winter and during the rainy season. Precipitation is irregular, however, and only the higher areas receive more than 100 days' rainfall per year, generally much less. Morocco and Algeria are semiarid countries, and, even in the mountains, summers are hot, with temperatures often reaching more than 30° C. The western part of the Rif chain, inhabited by Arabic-speaking Jbala and not by Rifians, is one of the few parts of the country to receive more than 200 centimeters of rainfall per year. The eastern part—the Rif proper—is much drier and badly deforested. Overpopulation and the infertility of the soil have brought about a long-standing Rifian labor migration. The same is largely true of the Anti-Atlas, another area of strong Berber labor migration. Only the Middle Atlas has considerable agricultural and stock-raising potential. Since Moroccan independence from France in 1956, many Berbers have become urban dwellers as well. Tangier, Tétouan, and Fès have long been urban centers for Rifians, and since 1936 Casablanca has become a major center for the Ishilhayen or Swasa.

DEMOGRAPHY. Morocco has never had a census taken along ethnolinguistic lines—and neither has Algeria. At the beginning of the colonial period in 1912, when France annexed Morocco and leased its northern tier, the Rif chain, and the Ifni enclave on the southwest coast to Spain, the population was an estimated 4.5 million, of which an estimated 40 percent was Berber speaking. The remainder speak Arabic, the official language in both countries. As of 1960, Morocco's population was 11.2 million, and by 1972, 15.7 million. By 1993, it had risen to 27 million, as had that of Algeria. Berber was only given nominal recognition as a second language by the authorities in both countries in 1994 and censuses of Berber speakers have pointedly not been taken. In-depth figures can be provided only for the 1960 Moroccan census, which, entirely by interpolation, yielded roughly 903,000 Rifians, 1,573,000 Imazighen, and 1,724,000 Ishilhayen/Swasa, amounting to a total of 4.2 million—or 37.5 percent.

LINGUISTIC AFFILIATION. "Berber" is primarily a linguistic term and designation; the Berber or Tamazight language belongs to the Hamitic or African Branch of the Hamito-Semitic or Afro-Asiatic Family. Dialects of Berber are spoken here and there all over North Africa, from Morocco to the Siwa oasis in western Egypt and from the Algerian Jurjura to Mali and Niger, but in no case is Berber the national language of any country in which it is spoken. The various dialects (Tharifith or Rifian, Tamazight "Proper" or Central Atlas Highland, and Tashilhit or Southwestern Atlas Highland in Morocco; Taqba'ilit, Tashawit, and Tamahaq or Ahaggar Tuareg in Algeria; other Tuareg dialects in Burkina Faso, Mali, and Niger; and various oasis dialects from Algeria to western Egypt) are all closely related from grammatical and syntactical standpoints but in no case to the point of total mutual comprehensibility. Many contemporary Berber speakers also know colloquial Arabic, and some even know literary Arabic, French, and Spanish.

History and Cultural Relations

The Berbers are the autochthonous inhabitants of North Africa. The sedentary agricultural tribes are largely old and long established, and certain important tribal names in the Rif may go back almost to the beginnings of Islam in Morocco in the late eighth century. Berber identification with Islam thus goes back itself to the initial Arab conquests in the late seventh century, barring initial resistance and certain resultant heresies. The sedentary Ishilhayen tribes of the Western Atlas are probably also long established, although there is little Arabic documentation on them prior to the early fifteenth century. The transhumant Imazighen tribes of Central Morocco are more recent, although the great northwest passage of Imazighen from the Saghro massif across the Atlas in search of grass for their sheep began about 1550 and was still unfinished when the Franco-Spanish protectorate was established in 1912. Primary resistance to colonial penetration was heaviest in the Berber-speaking areas. In the Rif,

it was led by Muhammad bin 'Abd al-Krim al-Khattabi of the Aith Waryaghar in a major two-front war—first against Spain in 1921, then against both Spain and France in 1925–1926. In the Atlas, although the French won over to their side the three major *quyad* (sing. *qa'id*), the tribal leaders of the Imtuggan, the Igundafen, and the Iglawn, resistance nonetheless began in 1913 and continued piecemeal, on a tribe-by-tribe basis for the most part, until the Ait 'Atta of the Saghro and the Ait Murghad and Ait Hadiddu of the eastern Central Atlas were "pacified" in 1933, and the Anti-Atlas was fully occupied the following year.

During this period, the French made the mistake of promulgating the "Berber Dahir," or decree of 1930, which placed all Berber tribes in their zone (although not those of the Spanish-held Rif) under the jural aegis of customary-law tribunals. In effect, this subtracted them from the jurisdiction of the Sharia, of Muslim law as enjoined by the Quran. At Moroccan independence in 1956, the Berber Dahir was rescinded, and normal Muslim law courts under *qudat* (sing. *qadi*) were installed in the Berber-speaking areas. Since about 1986, customary law appears to be coming back in small and low-key ways, but not to the extent of resuscitating collective oaths.

♦ **Sharia**
Quaranic law.

A Berber bride-to-be dons her robe at a mass engagement festival in Imilchil. Birth, marriage, and death are the three most important individual ceremonies. Imilchil, Morocco. (Nik Wheeler/Corbis)

Settlements

Precolonial settlements varied according to region. In the Rif, local communities (*dshur*; sing. *dshar*) consisted of highly dispersed individual homesteads, one-floored, flat-roofed structures of mud and stone, with rooms formed around a central courtyard. Each was at least 300 meters from the next and housed either a large nuclear family or an extended one of father and married sons or of brothers and their wives and children. Since the 1970s, however, owing to unprecedented labor migration to Western Europe, the Rif has become "urbanized," with apartment-type buildings now studding the countryside. In the Central Atlas, local communities (*timizar*; sing. *tamazirt*) consisted of three or four fortlike structures called *qsur* (Arabic; sing. *qsar*) or *igharman* (Tamazight; sing. *igharm*). Made of adobe and stone, these structures stood three or four stories high. Each had a central courtyard and internal staircases leading to individual rooms of the various nuclear families (*tashat*; pl. *tashatin*) comprising the several patrilineages (*ighsan*; sing. *ighs*; lit., "bone") that constituted the tribal section (*taqbilt*; pl. *tiqbilin*). The igharman were generally named after one of the sections, and these names were usually replicated in other localities. Imazighen who take their sheep on transhumance up into the Atlas in spring live in black goat-hair tents while pasturing them during the summer in special reserves called *igudlan* (sing. *agudal*), which have rigid opening and closing dates and which are usually owned exclusively by the group in question. The Imazighen return to their permanent igharman in the fall for agricultural operations. The villages (*l-mwada*ʿ sing. *l-muda*ʿ) of the Ishilhayen show features combining the Central Atlas igharman with Rifian-type homesteads in the lower areas and compact Kabyle-type villages in the higher ones. Collective storehouses (*agadir*; pl. *igudar*, but also igharm), still to be found in the Central Atlas, also existed in this area but were abandoned during the colonial period.

Economy

SUBSISTENCE AND COMMERCIAL ACTIVITIES. Except for the transhumant Imazighen tribes of central Morocco, Berber groups traditionally consisted of sedentary subsistence agriculturalists, although a limited transhumance has been reported for parts of the Western Atlas. In the Rif, a wide variety of crops was grown, albeit on a much lesser scale: in particular, barley and wheat, plus maize and broad beans, supplemented by fig, olive, almond, and walnut trees. *Kif* (*Cannabis sativa*) became a semilegal cash crop on the western fringe of the area only after independence. Almost every family has a cow, a few goats and chickens, and a mule or donkey, as well as the ubiquitous guard dog. Being transhumants, all the Imazighen tribes have sheep, and the southern ones also have camels for transport. For plowing, two cows or a cow and a mule or donkey may be yoked together; lending of individual animals by one farmer to another for plowing or threshing is the norm. Crops grown by the Imazighen and Ishilhayen differ somewhat, but wheat and barley are still staples. Turnips are common in the higher mountains, and, in some areas, apples and potatoes have, since the mid-1980s, become cash crops, which are trucked to Marrakech and elsewhere. Since 1970, however, traditional agriculture, in the Rif in particular, has been disappearing as Moroccans and Algerians have continued to swell the ranks of industrial workers in Europe.

INDUSTRIAL ARTS. In the Rif, important traditional crafts were blacksmithing, pottery, basketry, and utilitarian wood-work such as plow handles and yokes. Blacksmithing was done by members of a totally endogamous, low-status occupational group from one tribe, the Axt Tuzin, which also provided lowstatus musicians who doubled as mule and donkey breeders. Women made pottery by hand in the Rif, but low-status, endogamous Black men used the pottery wheel in the Atlas (the same group that provided the blacksmiths of southern Morocco). There is strikingly little economic specialization in the region at large, however, and local men do craft work as needed. Only blacksmithing and, in the Imazighen and Ishilhayen areas, pottery making carry occupational stigmata. Silversmithing and pack-saddle making, occupations formerly practiced by rural Jews, did as well, but all the latter migrated to Israel shortly after independence.

TRADE. All trade in rural North Africa is carried out in the *suq* (market), found in almost every tribal territory of sufficient size and named both for the day of the week on which it is held and for the tribe in whose land it is located. Large tribes, like the Aith Waryaghar of the Rif (who are unique in North Africa for having special women's markets, without economic value, which are forbidden to men), may have several markets held on different days and in different tribal sections, whereas in the Imazighen region markets are often located not in the centers of tribal terri-

◆ **transhumance**
Seasonal movements of a society or community. It may involve seasonal shifts in food production between hunting and gathering and horticulture or the movement of herds to more favorable locations.

tories but on their fringes, as among the Ait 'Atta. Local and European goods could be bought or sold at most markets during the colonial period, when markets also became effective centers of tribal control by the colonial power. Since the postindependence upsurge of labor migration to Europe, however, many Rifian markets have now become full-fledged urban centers where, even in the 1960s, such items as transistor radios were readily available, since replaced by color televisions.

DIVISION OF LABOR. In precolonial times, feuding and warfare were everywhere male occupations, as is true today of agriculture, driving animals, and, very occasionally, hunting. Women do all the housework (except for making tea for guests, a male occupation) and perform two agricultural tasks: helping the men with the harvest and taking newly cut grain in baskets to the threshing floor. Men build the houses but women whitewash the walls and blacken and smooth the floors, bring in manure to the collective manure pile, milk the animals, and fetch water and firewood. Poultry and rabbits are also exclusively female concerns. Marketing was traditionally a man's job, but, even in colonial times, poorer and older women could be seen vending at market stalls, and today women are as numerous in the markets as are men. Smaller boys and girls both herded goats on the slopes, and girls tended younger children. At home the sex division of labor has remained much as it was traditionally, but both sexes have become exposed to more varied occupational opportunities. Greater emphasis on schooling has made small boys especially less available for household chores.

LAND TENURE. Agricultural land is traditionally inherited patrilaterally throughout Morocco, but whether or not it is divided up among sons on their father's death or remains in indivision is a question that, in most cases, must be resolved on the spot. As land in the Rif is a scarce resource, Rifians tend always to divide it; conflicts and feuds over landownership were inherent in their social structure, whereas transhumant Imazighen were more inclined to remain in indivision. Land closest to settlements is, in all areas, generally used for agricultural purposes, with or without irrigation; land farther away is used for grazing and tends to be held by the community in indivision. In addition, a very few communities in the Rif, and probably in the Anti-Atlas, have some *habus* land, donated by individuals to the local mosque or pious foundation for religious or charitable purposes, although this last is much more an urban than a rural phenomenon.

Kinship

KIN GROUPS AND DESCENT. Everywhere in North Africa except among some of the Tuareg groups of the Central Sahara, descent is patrilineal, and residence is patrilocal. The fundamental unit of Berber social organization is the patrilineage (*dharfiqth* [pl. *dharfiqin*]; in the Rif, ighs among the Imazighen and *afus* [lit. "hand"; pl. *ifassen*] among the Ishilhayen), which is seldom more than four to six generations in depth in the Rif and only four in the Atlas, where, however, it is corporate in character, unlike the Rifian lineage. Exogamy or endogamy is a matter of choice and circumstance: Rifians favor the former and Imazighen the latter, where possible.

KINSHIP TERMINOLOGY. Both Arabic and most Berber kinship terminologies (those of the Tuareg apart) are, as they stand, "Sudanese," in Murdock's terminology; however, Rifians, Ishilhayen, and Algerian Kabyles all have the classificatory term *ayyaw* (fem. *dhayyawxth*), meaning variously "father's sister's child," "sister's child," "daughter's child," and, asymmetrically, "son's child," and its existence thus turns these kinship systems from "Normal Sudanese" into "Modified Omaha." As for terms of address, all close kin, whether patrilateral or matrilateral, are addressed either by the appropriate kin term or by name, or, especially if in an ascending generation, by the kin term plus the name. The same holds generally true for known elders of any sort in terms of their kinship distance from the speaker.

Marriage and Family

MARRIAGE. In the Rif, unlike the practice in certain other Berber-speaking areas, parallel-cousin marriage with the father's brother's daughter was permitted, although not highly regarded. These marriages accounted for 12 percent of a total of 1,625 marriages recorded between 1953 and 1955 among the Aith Waryaghar (3 percent true father's brother's daughter marriages and 9 percent classificatory—that is, not with true father's brother's daughter, but within the lineage). By far the most common form was local-lineage exogamy—marriages between lineages within the same tribal section—at 54 percent, whereas marriages between spouses of different sections accounted for 22 percent, and marriages with spouses of other tribes (both male and female) amounted again to 12 percent. Polygynous mar-

♦ **endogamy**
Marriage within a specific group or social category of which the person is a member, such as one's caste or community.

♦ **exogamy**
Marriage outside a specific group or social category of which the person is a member, such as one's clan or community.

riages accounted for 11 percent of the total (with each co-wife having her separate dwelling or household), secondary or successive marriages for 5 percent, and 3 percent of marriages terminated in divorce. There was a high rate of widow inheritance (as opposed to levirate) at 5 percent, but sororate, although permitted, accounted for only 0.8 percent. Marriage by exchange of sisters accounted for 2.5 percent, as did two brothers marrying two sisters; 20 percent of all marriages—whether endogamous or exogamous—were between individuals of different generations, even though they may have been of nearly equivalent ages (Hart 1976, 217–229).

Among the Imazighen of south-central Morocco, parallel-cousin marriage with the father's brother's daughter is strongly favored, but among the Ait ʿAtta of Usikis on the south-central slope of the Atlas, it accounted for only 17 percent of 313 marriages recorded between 1961 and 1962 (of which only 3 percent were with true father's brother's daughter and 14 percent were with the classificatory father's brother's daughter, within the lineage). Lineage exogamy within the section accounted for 42 percent, intersectional marriages within the community of Usikis for 39 percent, and extracommunity or extratribal marriages for only 2 percent. Plural marriages accounted for 9 percent of the total, secondary or successive ones for 4 percent. Three percent of marriages ended in divorce; the rate of widow inheritance was 3 percent and that of the sororate only 1 percent. Of all marriages, endogamous or exogamous, 10 percent were cross-generational (Hart 1981, 148–151, 251–253).

Bride-wealth or bride-price is heavy in the Rif but minimal in the Imazighen region. Normally only a husband can initiate divorce (except in cases of impotency). Bride-wealth is generally returned in such cases, but children remain with their fathers. Childlessness is a normal cause for divorce.

DOMESTIC UNIT. The nuclear family (Rifian: *nubth* [lit., "turn"; pl. *nubath*]; Tharifith: *tashat* [lit., "hearth"]) of father, mother, and unmarried children constitutes the domestic unit, all of whose members eat together when guests are not present, but—owing to the prevalence of male labor migration to Europe—women are now often de facto heads of rural households.

INHERITANCE. Land is inherited patrilaterally. Although the Sharia stipulates that, for purposes of inheritance, one son equals two daughters, with one-eighth subtracted at a man's death for his widow, in areas like the Imazighen region,

where customary law prevailed until independence, daughters generally got nothing and tended rather to be inherited by their fathers' brothers, in order to be married off to the latters' sons.

SOCIALIZATION. Under maternal and grandparental supervision, all Berber communities are characterized by a high degree of sibling caretaking, with elder siblings taking care of younger ones while their mothers do household work. Grandparents and grandchildren are close, but sex segregation begins when boys and girls reach 6 or 7 years of age and start to herd goats. By the time they reach puberty, which traditionally is not long before the age to marry, it is fully ingrained.

Sociopolitical Organization

SOCIAL ORGANIZATION. The agnatic lineage or patrilineage (Rifian: dharfiqth; Imazighen: ighs; Ishilhayen: afus) was, until after Moroccan independence from France and Spain in 1956, the basic social unit, with a depth of four to six generations in the Rif and of only four among the Imazighen. Among the latter, however, it was corporate in character, which was not, or not always, the case in the Rif. In the latter half of the twentieth century and particularly since the 1970s as a result of labor migration, the patrilineage has been overshadowed in importance by the nuclear family. Above the patrilineage is the local community, and above this the tribal section (Rifian: *rba*ʿ or *khums*, Imazighen/Ishilhayen: taqbilt), and finally the tribe itself. Within certain Moroccan tribes in precolonial times, sections were grouped together to form five primary units or "fifths" (*khamsa khmas*)—as among the Aith Waryaghar of the Rif and the Ait ʿAtta of the Saghro and Central Atlas—which might differ widely from each other in terms of function; however, except in southern Morocco and the Presaharan oases, there is no formal hierarchy, and indeed among Berber lay tribesmen everywhere there has always been a fierce egalitarianism. In the south, holy lineages descended from the Prophet Mohammed (very numerous in Morocco, even among Berbers) form a top stratum. The mass of lay and illiterate White Berber tribespeople form the middle stratum, and the many residential clusters (or qsur) of *haratin*—sedentary Black date-palm cultivators, some of whom stand traditionally in a clientage relationship to specific Berber tribal sections—form the bottom one. This precolonial social stratification, however, is today turning into a class system based mainly on wealth and economic considerations.

POLITICAL ORGANIZATION. In the precolonial Rif, the highest unit of political integration was the tribe (*dhaqbitsh*, which like "taqbilt" is derived from Arabic *qabila*), although as a unit it was invoked far less often than the section (rba᾽ or khums). A three-tiered system of representative councils (aitharbi᾽in, *agraw*), for the community, the section, and the tribe, respectively, was convoked as needed and generally met in the suq in any case. The councillors (Rifian: *imgharen*; sing.

amghar) were always tribal notables. As of the late nineteenth century, the choice of top tribal quyad, although generally ratified by sultanic decree, tended to confirm local strongmen in their positions. Among the Imazighen tribes, annual elections for chiefs at the tribal, sectional, and community levels were held in spring through rotation and complementarity of participant sections. Each year, it was the turn of one of the sections to provide the chief; its members sat apart, and

RELIGION AND EXPRESSIVE CULTURE

Religious Beliefs

All Moroccans, whether Berbers or Arabs, are Sunni (i.e., orthodox and mainstream) Muslims of the Maliki rite, which predominates in North Africa. Their beliefs are exactly the same as those of Sunni Muslims elsewhere. It should be noted, however, that Islam in rural North Africa has traditionally placed a strong emphasis on *baraka* (lit., "blessing"), the charisma and miracle-working abilities of *shurfa᾽* (sing. *sharif*), descendants of the Prophet, whose shrines dot the countryside and whose living representatives have traditionally been mediators of conflicts between lineages or sections of lay Berber tribesmen.

Religious Practitioners

In Islam, there is, in theory, no intermediary between man and God, but every Moroccan rural community, whether Berber or Arab, has its *fqih* or schoolmaster, who teaches the boys to recite the Quran. The fqih, who is contracted by the community on an annual basis, leads the prayers in the mosque and gives the Friday sermon. He also writes charms (from Quranic verses) with a view to curing diseases, although any elements of witchcraft and sorcery that do not involve the use of (Arabic) writing are generally the preserve of women.

Ceremonies

The major ceremonies in the individual life cycle are birth, marriage, and death, with the first haircut and circumcision as additional rites for small boys. Circumcision, although not specifically mentioned in the Quran, is nonetheless practiced by all Muslims. Rifians perform it when boys reach 2 years of age, whereas the Imazighen tend to wait until boys are 5 or 6—they are told by their elders to bear it bravely. There is no female circumcision. The marriage ceremony is the most important, lengthy, and elaborate ritual for both sexes. In addition, everyone observes the normal Muslim religious festivals of the lunar year. During the first ten days of the first month, the ʿAshura is celebrated; in Morocco, children are invariably given toys and other presents at this time of year. The month-long fast of Ramadan, in the ninth month, is followed immediately by the ʿAyd al-Saghir or Small Feast to break the fast. The ʿAyd al-Kabir or Great Feast, when every householder must sacrifice a sheep, occurs in the last month of the year and coincides with the hajj, the pilgrimage to Mecca.

Arts

The only specialized arts among Berbers are performed by women and consist, among Rifians, of pottery decoration and, among Imazighen in the Middle Atlas, of rug weaving.

Medicine

Traditional healers continue to flourish, but today hospitals and clinics are also much in use.

Death and Afterlife

Death may be attributed either to natural or supernatural causes, and every community has its cemetery. If the deceased is a man, his body is washed and enshrouded by the fqih, and if a woman, by another woman. Anyone who dies in the morning is buried the same afternoon and anyone who dies at night is buried the following morning, in a hole that must be only a spread handspan plus an extra half-thumb length in width. Of overriding importance in the orientation of an Islamic grave is the *qibla,* the direction of Mecca. In Morocco, the body is therefore placed in the grave more or less on its right side, with its face turned toward Mecca, while the fqih intones an appropriate chapter of the Quran. Only men attend funerals, and among the Imazighen the kinsmen of the deceased give a feast seven days after the death for those who mourned at the burial. In the Rif, a widow gives a feast forty days after her husband's death, which theoretically marks the end of the mourning period. Ideally, it should also correspond to the obligatory *ʿidda,* or three-month period between widowhood, or divorce, and remarriage, in order to determine paternity in case of pregnancy. Anyone who dies during Ramadan will go to paradise immediately, far faster than at any other time of year. The Quran is quite specific on the subject both of paradise, *ajinna,* and of hell, *jahannama;* it also teaches that two invisible recording angels sit on everyone's shoulders, one recording good deeds, the other bad ones.

Berbers of Morocco

SOCIOPOLITICAL ORGANIZATION

Under maternal and grandparental supervision, all Berber communities are characterized by a high degree of sibling caretaking.

members of the other sections selected the chief from among them. The chief's badge of office was a blade of grass that the electors placed in his turban. Among the Ait 'Atta, this procedure took place, until final "pacification" by the French in 1933, at the tribal capital and supreme court seat of Igharm Amazdar, in the Saghro. Given the egalitarian ideology, the top chief, or *amghar n-ufilla*, like the lesser chiefs, had little power and could be removed from office before his year was up if he were deemed unfit in any way, or if the year in question had been a bad or calamitous one. Conversely, if he were an able leader during war and if under his term of office the harvest had been good and the sheep had grown fat, he was likely to stay on for another year, or even longer. Today tribes have been nominally eradicated administratively, and the tribal sections have given way to the rural commune, but the communal councils are still elected and representative bodies that meet every week in the markets to deliberate on local issues.

SOCIAL CONTROL. In the Rif and elsewhere, the sectional council was competent to handle most misdemeanors, such as theft or land disputes, but woundings and murders generally fell under the competence of the tribal council (*aitharbi' in n-tqbitsh*). Prohibitively heavy fines (*haqq*; lit., "truth, right") were imposed by the council members on anyone who committed a murder in the market or on any path leading to or from it on market day, the day before it, and the day after it. In all Berber areas, especially among the Imazighen, the most effective and drastic form of sociopolitical control was the collective oath (Tamazight: *tagallit*), in which a man accused of any crime had to attest his innocence backed up by his agnates. One did this in front of a saint's shrine, with the number of agnates, as his cojurors, varying with the gravity of the offense. Supernatural sanctions of death or blindness in the event of perjury acted as a powerful incentive against swearing falsely. Although bin 'Abd al-Krim decollectivized Rifian oaths in 1922, they persisted in the Atlas until the end of the colonial period, with the rescinding of the Berber Dahir. By colonial times (after the Rifians were defeated in 1926), vengeance killings became far less common than they had been prior to 1921; these cases were handled by the courts of the protecting power. The qa'id's tribunal heard lesser cases and the qudat were concerned with torts. Since about 1986, customary law, now under the aegis of local specialists, has been reintroduced in embryonic form in most Moroccan Berber tribal areas, and this development is evidently looked upon with favor by the tribes in question.

CONFLICT. In the precolonial Rif in particular, both blood feuds (between lineage groups) and vendettas (within lineages, and generally between brothers and their sons) were endemic. Among the Aith Waryaghar, the latter outnumbered the former by about two to one: of the 193 conflicts recorded by Hart (1994) for the period from approximately 1880 to 1921, 122 were vendettas as opposed to only 71 feuds, indicating the lack of a corporate base in the Rifian lineage. Alliance networks, called *lfuf* (sing. *liff*), conceived as equal in size but usually not so in fact, either embraced whole tribal sections or cleaved them in two, but essentially they did not extend beyond individual tribal borders. However, given the emphasis on corporate lineages in the Imazighen, and possibly the Ishilhayen regions as well, the emphasis here was on feud. Feuding was partially responsible for a degree of dispersal of individuals, given the fact that it was customary for a murderer, with or without his coresponsible agnatic kinsmen, to flee from home and seek exile in another tribe. In all regions, however, the resolution of conflicts between groups was the work of *imrabdhen* (sing. *amrabit*) or *igurramen* (sing. *agurram*), members of holy and generally charismatic lineages descended from the Prophet; conflict mediation between lay tribesmen was part of their stock-in-trade.

Bibliography

Bourdieu, Pierre (1962). *The Algerians*. Translated by Alan C. M. Ross. Boston: Beacon Press.

Bousquet, Georges-Henri (1961). *Les berbères*. Que Sais-Je? no. 718. Paris: Presses Universitaires de France. Originally published in 1957.

Chiapuris, John (1979). *The Ait Ayash of the High Moulouya Plain: Rural Social Organization in Morocco*. University of Michigan Museum of Anthropology, Anthropological Papers, no. 69. Ann Arbor: University of Michigan Press.

Gellner, Ernest (1969). *Saints of the Atlas*. London: Weidenfeld & Nicholson.

Gellner, Ernest, and Charles Micaud, eds. (1973). *Arabs and Berbers: From Tribe to Nation in North Africa*. London: Duck-worth.

Hart, David M. (1976). *The Aith Waryaghar of the Moroccan Rif: An Ethnography and History*. Viking Fund Publications in Anthropology, no. 55. Tucson: University of Arizona Press.

Hart, David M. (1981). *Dadda ʿAtta and His Forty Grandsons: The Socio-Political Organisation of the Ait ʿAtta of Southern Morocco.* Wisbech, Cambridgeshire: MENAS Press.

Hart, David M. (1984a). *The Ait ʿAtta of Southern Morocco: Daily Life and Recent History.* Wisbech, Cambridgeshire: MENAS Press.

Hart, David M. (1984b). "Segmentary Systems and the Role of `Five Fifths' in Tribal Morocco." In *Islam in Tribal Societies: From the Atlas to the Indus,* edited by Akbar S. Ahmed and David M. Hart, 66–105. London: Routledge & Kegan Paul. Originally published in 1967.

Hart, David M. (1989). "Rejoinder to Henry Munson, Jr.: 'On the Irrelevance of the Segmentary Model in the Moroccan Rif.'" *American Anthropologist* 91: 765–769.

Hart, David M. (1992). "Tradicion, continuidad y modernidad en el derecho consuetudinario islamico: Ejemplos del marruecos bereber y de las agencias tribales pujtunes de Pakistan." In *Amazigh-Tamazight: Debate Abierto,* edited by Vicente Moga Romero, 133–150. Aldaba, no. 19. Melilla: Universidad Nacional de Educacion a Distancia (UNED).

Hart, David M. (1993). "Four Centuries of History on the Hoof: The Northwest Passage of Berber Sheep Transhumants across the Moroccan Atlas, 1550–1912." *Morocco: Journal of the Society for Moroccan Studies* 3:21–55.

Hart, David M. (1994). "Conflits extérieurs et vendettas dans le Djurdjura algérien et le Rif marocain." *Awal: Cahiers d'Études Berbères* 11:95–122.

Hart, David M. (1995). *Traditional Society and the Feud in the Moroccan Rif.* Wisbech, Cambridgeshire: MENAS Press; Rabat: Faculté des Lettres et des Sciences Humaines, Université Mohammed V. In press.

Hart, David M., ed. and trans. (1975). *Emilio Blanco Izaga: Colonel in the Rif.* 2 vols. Ethnography Series, HRAFlex Books, MX3–001. New Haven: Human Relations Area Files.

Kraus, Wolfgang (1991). *Die Ayt Hdiddu: Wirtschaft und Gesellschaft im zentralen Hohen Atlas.* Oesterreichische Akademie der Wissenschaften, Philosophisch-Historische Klasse, Sitzungsberichte, 574. Band, Veroeffentlichungen der ethnologischen Kommission, Bd. 7. Vienna: Verlag der oesterreichischen Akademie der Wissenschaften.

Montagne, Robert (1930). *Les berbères et le Makhzen dans le sud du Maroc: Essai sur la transformation politique des Berbères sedentaires (groupe Chleuh).* Paris: Félix Alcan.

Montagne, Robert (1973). *The Berbers: Their Social and Political Organisation.* Translated by David Seddon. London: Frank Cass. Originally published in French in 1931.

Murdock, George Peter (1960). *Social Structure.* New York: Macmillan. Originally published in 1949.

Neumann, Wolfgang (1987). *Die Berber: Vielfalt und Einheit einer alten nordafrikanischen Kultur.* Cologne: DuMont Verlag. Originally published in 1983.

Raha Ahmed, Rachid, ed. (1994). *Imazighen del Magreb entre Occidente y Oriente: Introduccion a los bereberes.* Granada: Copisteria La Gioconda.

Royaume du Maroc, Ministère de l'Économie Nationale, Division de la Coordination Économique et du Plan (1962). *Population rurale du Maroc: Recensement démographique (juin 1960).* Rabat: Service Central des Statistiques.

Vinogradov, Amal Rassam (1974). *The Ait Ndhir of Morocco: A Study of the Social Transformation of a Berber Tribe.* University of Michigan Museum of Anthropology, Anthropological Papers, no. 55. Ann Arbor: University of Michigan Press.

Waterbury, John (1972). *North for the Trade: The Life and Times of a Berber Merchant.* Berkeley, Los Angeles, and London: University of California Press.

—DAVID M. HART

EWE AND FON

Ethonym: Fon: Dahomeans

Orientation

IDENTIFICATION. "Ewe" is the umbrella name for a number of groups that speak dialects of the same language and have separate local names, such as Anlo, Abutia, Be, Kpelle, and Ho. (These are not subnations but populations of towns or small regions.) Closely related groups with slightly different mutually comprehensible languages and cultures may be grouped with Ewe, notably Adja, Oatchi, and Peda. Fon and Ewe people are often considered to belong to the same, larger grouping, although their related languages are mutually incomprehensible. All these peoples are said to have originated in the general area of Tado, a town in present-day Togo, at about the same latitude as Abomey, Benin. Mina and Guin are the descendants of Fanti and Ga people who left the Gold Coast in the seventeenth and eighteenth centuries, settling in the Aneho and Glidji areas, where they intermarried with Ewe, Oatchi, Peda, and Adja. The Guin-Mina and Ewe languages are mutually comprehensible, although there are significant structural and lexical differences.

Ewe and Fon

The Atlantic commerce in slaves was a significant aspect of Ewe and Fon life for two centuries.

LOCATION. Most Ewe (including Oatchi, Peda, and Adja) live between the Volta River in Ghana and the Mono River (to the east) in Togo, from the coast (southern boundary) northward just past Ho in Ghana and Danyi on the western Togolese border, and Tado on the eastern border. Fon live primarily in Benin, from the coast to Savalou, and from the Togolese border almost to Porto-Novo in the south. Other Fon-and Ewe-related groups live in Benin. Borders between Ghana and Togo, as well as between Togo and Benin, are permeable to innumerable Ewe and Fon lineages with family on both sides of the border.

Pazzi (1976, 6) describes locations of the different groups with historical references, including the migrations out of Tado, principally to Notse, in present-day Togo, and to Allada, in present-day Benin. Ewe who left Notse spread from the lower basin of the Amugan to the valley of the Mono. Two groups left Allada: Fon occupied the plateau of Abomey and the entire plain that spreads from the Kufo and Weme rivers to the coast, and Gun settled between Lake Nokwe and the Yawa River. Adja remained in the hills surrounding Tado and in the plain between the Mono and Kufo rivers. Mina are the Fante-Ane from Elmina who founded Aneho, and Guin are the Ga immigrants from Accra who occupied the plain between Lake Gbaga and the Mono River. They encountered there the Xwla or Peda people (whom the Portuguese of the fifteenth century named "Popo"), whose language also overlaps with the Ewe language.

The coastal areas of Benin, Togo, and southeastern Ghana are flat, with numerous palm groves. Just north of the beach areas is a string of lagoons, navigable in some areas. An undulating plain lies behind the lagoons, with a soil of red laterite and sand. The southern parts of the Akwapim ridge in Ghana, about 120 kilometers from the coast, are forested and reach an elevation of about 750 meters. The dry season usually lasts from November through March, including the period of dry and dusty harmattan winds in December, which lasts longer farther north. The rainy season often peaks in April-May and September-October. Temperatures along the coast vary from the twenties to the thirties (centigrade), but may be both hotter and cooler farther inland.

DEMOGRAPHY. According to estimates made in 1994, there are more than 1.5 million Ewe (including Adja, Mina, Oatchi, Peda, and Fon) living in Togo. Two million Fon and almost a half-million Ewe live in Benin. While the government of Ghana does not keep a census of ethnic groups (so as to reduce ethnic conflict), Ewe in Ghana are estimated at 2 million, including a certain number of Ga-Adangme who were more or less assimilated to Ewe groups linguistically and politically, although they have maintained much of their pre-Ewe culture.

LINGUISTIC AFFILIATION. Pazzi's (1976) comparative dictionary of Ewe, Adja, Guin, and Fon languages demonstrates that they are very closely related, all originating centuries ago with the people of the royal city of Tado. They belong to the Kwa Language Group. Numerous dialects exist inside the family of Ewe proper, such as Anlo, Kpelle, Danyi, and Be. Adja dialects include Tado, Hweno, and Dogbo. Fon, the language of the Kingdom of Dahomey, includes the Abomey, Xweda, and Wemenu dialects as well as numerous others. Kossi (1990, 5, 6) insists that the overarching name for this extended family of languages and peoples should be Adja rather than Ewe/Fon, given their common origin in Tado, where the Adja language, mother of the other tongues, is still spoken.

History and Cultural Relations

The Adja Kingdom of Tado, in an area constantly populated since prehistory and known for metal-working and other crafts, was situated near the east bank of the Mono River, at about the same latitude as Abomey. It was probably built by immigrants from the Oyo Kingdom or from Ketu, to the east (Nigeria). Most Adja people today still live in and around Tado. Fon and Ewe peoples are the descendants of emigrants from Tado who intermarried with other groups they encountered en route to their present-day locations.

Ewe populations today are the result of various migrations moving west and toward the coast, eventually dominated by emigrants of the Adja Kingdom of Tado, who first settled in the new vassal kingdom of Notse. Early in the seventeenth century they left Notse in several groups and settled farther south and west. Their descendants eventually became the Anlo, Abutia, Be, and Kpelle, as well as the Oatchi, further south and east, in the Vogan area.

Anlo Ewe, who settled in the Volta region, in what is now the southeastern corner of the Republic of Ghana, were located in one of the strategic areas of the Atlantic slave trade. In 1683 Keta was already an important slave market. By 1727 Dutch and English slave traders were posted in

Aflao, and in 1784 the Danes built a fort in Keta; Anlo territory thus became a center for the Atlantic trade. Anlo Ewe participated in the capture and sale of slaves to Europeans, and many were themselves sold into slavery and taken to the New World.

In close contact with their militarily superior and more politically centralized Asante neighbors, Anlo nevertheless were a separate polity and have maintained an Ewe identity until the present. Dominated by Akwamu during the first third of the eighteenth century, they joined with them and the army of Ouidah to war against Allada. Numerous other local wars with—and against—Akan armies involved Anlo Ewe during the seventeenth through nineteenth centuries.

Trading with Europeans was an aspect of Anlo Ewe life almost from the beginning of their settlement in the area. Bremen missionaries and other Christian emissaries set anchor in Eweland both in the Volta region and inland on the (now) Togolese side during the nineteenth century. Various Ewe populations were under close colonial supervision during the British regime on the Gold Coast and during German control of Togoland. After World War I, approximately a third of Togoland, including much of Eweland, became a part of the Gold Coast; the remainder of the country taken from the Germans became a French protectorate called Togo. Thus Eweland was split in two, and remains so today. Ewe, who were mostly "southerners," were among the first in the two countries to receive an education in British and French colonial schools.

Fon are among those who left Tado to found the Kingdom of Allada; some of them subsequently left Allada, around 1610, and migrated toward Abomey, where they succeeded in dominating the native Dahomey population some 70 years later. Fon created the royal city of Abomey (where the famous "Amazons" had their headquarters), and other Fon founded the city of Ouidah. The two cities were linked, both high places of slave commerce during the Atlantic Trade. The Brazilian Francisco de Souza, a key figure on the Slave Coast of the late eighteenth and early nineteenth centuries, established slave trading posts and built forts both in Aneho among the Mina (now in Togo) and in Ouidah among the Fon (now in Benin).

The Fon Kingdom of Dahomey, which lasted from 1625 until its defeat by the French in 1893, is legendary, thanks to numerous visitors and their accounts, from those of Bosman (seventeenth century), Norris (eighteenth century), and Burton (nineteenth century), to those of twentieth-century ethnographers, including Le Herissé (1911) and Herskovits (1938). Focal to the Atlantic trade on the Slave Coast, the kingdom was expansionist but highly centralized only in and around its main cities—Abomey, Allada, and (much later) Ouidah—high places of art, courtly ceremony, and commerce with Europeans. The kingdom was said to include a territory much larger than it could effectively control, from the Volta River in the west to Badagary in the east, and northward to the 8th parallel. Its coastline, however, extended only 16 kilometers on either side of Ouidah. Although it was thus about 39,000 square kilometers in area, the king had authority only within some 10,400 square kilometers of that territory. Numerous wars and intrigues, including captures and contests of nerves with European envoys, mark the history of the Kingdom of Dahomey. Its more cruel kings were renowned for human sacrifice (always a royal prerogative), the stunning extent of which is described in perhaps exaggerated terms by some writers (e.g., Herskovits 1938, 2:52–56).

Although many Ewe and Fon are Christian (perhaps the highest percentage among the Ghana Ewe), the majority continue to practice Vodu or Tro worship, which has remained the religion of the Adja-Tado peoples for centuries.

Settlements

Ewe and Fon live mostly in villages and towns, although there are some more isolated farming compounds. Rectangular mud brick houses and concrete brick dwellings with gabled or corrugated-iron roofs are predominant except along the ocean, where there are numerous palm-frond huts with straw- or palm-thatch gabled roofs. Small huts or buildings are often clustered in a single compound with an open court, all surrounded by a mud wall. In ocean-front fishing villages, fragile palm-frond fences give some privacy to clusters of small huts. People living in the same compound are usually members of the same patrilineage (*to-fome*), although kinship is extremely open to outside recruitment; fictive kin may even predominate in certain cases. Large villages may have central market-places. Today there are a number of cities and large towns in which Ewe and Fon constitute the largest portion of the population. Ewe are a majority in Tema and Aflao (Ghana) and in Lome, Kpalime, and Tsévié (Togo). Adja dominate in Tado, and Mina-Guin in the Glidji-

Aneho area (Togo). Abomey, Allada, Ouidah, Grand Popo, Cotonou, and other towns in Benin are largely populated by Fon and related groups.

Economy

SUBSISTENCE AND COMMERCIAL ACTIVITIES. Ewe and Fon are farmers, fishermen, and market women. Nowadays they occupy all the positions and jobs to be found in government, civil service, business, and production. Staple crops are yams, maize, and manioc. (Millet was once important). Beans, peas, peanuts, sorghum, sweet potatoes, onions, okra, peppers, gourds, papayas, bananas, plantains, mangoes, pineapples, oil palms, and some rice and cocoa are also grown. Animals raised include pigs, sheep, goats, dogs, chickens, guinea fowl, ducks, and pigeons. Fishing is of primary importance along the coast and in the Volta region. Cash crops include palm kernels, peanuts, copra, castor beans, kapok, and, by far the most important, coffee and cocoa.

Along the coast, from Accra to Porto-Novo, hundreds of thousands of Ewe and Fon women work in the ports and markets. From Lome to Cotonou, Ewe and Fon market women—both wholesalers and retailers—have a near monopoly on the internal economy. Even in small villages, many women are traders and retailers, selling anything from homemade fermented corn porridge to Coca Cola, often specializing in a single item such as fresh or home-smoked fish, imported Dutch wax cloth, fresh fruits and vegetables, or trade beads.

INDUSTRIAL ARTS. Ewe and Fon engage in pottery making, wood sculpting (mostly for religious use), and basketwork; in the past, every village had a blacksmith.

TRADE. Ewe have traded with Asante and Fante, and Fon have traded with Yoruba and Hausa for as long as they have had their present identity. The slave trade and the salt trade brought other traders from the north of present Ewe and Fon regions, including as far north as Burkina Faso (formerly Upper Volta) and perhaps Mali and Niger. Portuguese traders reached the coast in the fifteenth century, even before the Ewe and Fon had migrated that far. By the seventeenth century, when the Volta region had become home to an Ewe polity and the Kingdom of Dahomey had regular relations with Ouidah, European commercial envoys were no longer a novelty on what was then called the Slave Coast. The Atlantic commerce in slaves was a significant aspect of Ewe and Fon life for two centuries.

Market activities are central in all Ewe and Fon regions. Women almost always have something to sell on market days, including foodstuffs they make themselves. They often buy their husband's or brothers' catch of fish fresh from the sea or river and take it straight to various markets. Or they smoke the fish and take them to markets farther inland. Today European, U.S., and Chinese goods are available even in small Ewe and Fon village markets more than 150 kilometers from the coast, often taken there by local women who buy the goods in coastal cities. In Togo, Ewe and Mina are said to be trading peoples willing to travel far to engage in commerce, thereby distinguishing themselves from more northern and more strictly agricultural groups who stay closer to the land.

DIVISION OF LABOR. Apart from the special status of kings in the Kingdom of Dahomey and occasionally chiefs in Ewe regions, who did not perform manual labor, the main division of labor is along gender lines. Men do heavy agricultural labor such as clearing the land and staking yam vines; they fish, hunt, and build houses. Women participate in the above activities also, such as preparing the palm-frond walling or fencing necessary to hut building, taking charge of butchered animals and fish, and carrying out almost all agricultural tasks except the very heaviest. Women also carry headloads as heavy as any load men can carry. Although it is often said that only women headload, this is patently untrue. Women are in charge of most market activities, although they may hire men to help them. One of the few items usually sold by men in the market is beef, often brought by Hausa or other Muslim traders. Most other kinds of work, including cooking, may be done by women and men, and even the above-mentioned divisions of labor are not absolute. Women and children may join with men in pulling in the enormous and heavy fishing nets from the surf after a catch. Gender-specific cash savings and work collectives abound, enabling members to have their own banking as well as support in house building, clearing land, harvesting, fishing, marketing, and all other labors. Especially notable are the Fon *dokpwe*, or cooperative, and the Ewe *esodjodjo*, or *tontine* (French). Both women and men engage in child care, although women are considered to have greater responsibility in this regard. Groups of men and groups of women may take care of any and all village children in their vicinity at any given time.

LAND TENURE. Anyone from a particular region can farm on land that is not occupied by

♦ **copra**
The dried flesh of the coconut used as the basis of oils, soaps, cosmetics, and dried coconut. Beginning in the 1860s copra became the chief commercial export in most Pacific islands.

anyone else. Inside a settlement, a person wishing to employ land must ask permission of the village chief or the elders of the lineage owning the land. Formerly, rights have extended only to use of land; there was no absolute right to the land itself. In the Kingdom of Dahomey, land was by definition the property of the king. In most Ewe regions, land is inherited and administered by elders of each patriline; any lineage member may build or farm on lineage land as long as she or he respects the rights of others nearby who are already established on the land. Widows of patriline members or other persons not members of the lineage may stay on the land and farm it, but it cannot pass definitively into another lineage. Only in the last few generations has land come to be alienable from lineage tenure by being mortgaged or sold. It is possible for palm groves and other wealth on the land to be passed on matrilineally, especially in Anlo and Glidji, where Akan matrilineal practices have influenced Ewe groups. Land not already belonging to a lineage (of which there is scarcely any now) may be acquired personally through simply clearing the land, or buying it from non-Ewe or non-Fon owners; the owner may dispose of such land without consulting lineage elders. Both women and men have rights to lineage land, often now called "inheritance of land," but, in areas where land is scarce, women have difficulty claiming such rights. Where lineage land is now alienable, plot by plot (e.g., southern Togo), women may, with difficulty, have a share in the proceeds of sales.

Marriage and Family

MARRIAGE. Most Ewe and Fon marriages are patrilocal, although neolocal residence has become popular in the late twentieth century. Polygyny is the rule if a man has means to marry more than one wife. It is often said that an abuse of polygyny leads wives to leave their husbands for other men, often younger and as yet unmarried, so that women also tend to have more than one husband in their lifetimes. Fon marriages are of two general types, one more prestigious than the other. Prestigious marriage includes payments by the groom to the bride's father or premarital farm labor performed by a man for his future father-in-law. Such bride-wealth or work gives a man control over his children. When this is not performed, the mother and her family have all rights over the children; thus, this sort of marriage is less desirable or prestigious for a husband. Herskovits (1938) outlines thirteen different variations of these two major marriage categories. A man must

never refuse a wife offered him, and divorce may be initiated only by the wife's family. In many Ewe groups, marriage is less marked by bride-wealth or bride-service, and even if a man offers only the required drinks and cloths to his bride and her family, he may claim the children as members of his own patriline. In case of separation, a father may keep his children with him, although in many cases wives are allowed to raise the children, and rotation of children between divorced parents is perhaps as common among Ewe as it is in the United States. Among Anlo families, it is often the father's sister who arranges the marriage when a young man wishes a certain young woman to be his wife. The simple giving of gifts to the young woman and her family and the sharing of drinks and libations, often a modest affair, is, even so, a marriage ceremony and a binding ritual that links two lineages and sets in motion serious obligations. Pregnancy makes a marriage complete. In the Kingdom of Dahomey, virginity was demanded of brides in prestigious marriages. In Anlo, too, the marriage-payment might be less if the bride was found not to be a virgin; today many couples become intimate before arranging a marriage. Christian Ewe and Fon proceed according to the arrangements prescribed in their churches.

DOMESTIC UNIT. Patrilineal three- or four-generational extended family compounds, as well as agnatic extended family compounds, are common. Another model is a nuclear-family household (often with children from previous marriages) that eventually is joined by other relatives, such as the couple's younger siblings, cousins, nieces, nephews, and foster children. If the husband has not vowed monogamy, in time, other wives and their children may come to expand the compound (each wife with her own hut or little house). In many cases, other wives and their children form separate households. Adolescent boys may have collective sleeping quarters separate from their mothers and sisters.

INHERITANCE. Most Fon property, including land, is inherited patrilineally, although some lineage land remains. Among Ewe groups, lineage land and whatever is on it—palm groves, houses, fields, and shrines—ideally remains within the lineage, although much lineage land is being broken up and sold nowadays. Rights to lineage land are primarily patrilineal. Cloth wealth and jewelry sometimes become lineage property too, along with ancestral stools. Individual property, which may include rights to land and fields, may be inherited patrilineally or matrilineally, depending on the Ewe subgroup. (In Anlo and Glidji, for ex-

♦ **neolocal residence**
The practice of a newly married couple living apart from the immediate kin of either party.

ample, much private property, including oil-palm trees, is inherited matrilineally.) In some areas the eldest son inherits land rights, but livestock and other individual property go to a man's sister's son. In Lome inheritance is mixed.

SOCIALIZATION. Virtually everyone, but especially older siblings, takes care of the children. Grandparents, both female and male, also spend considerable time with children. Fishermen in from the sea often sit around in groups during the afternoon, playing boardgames and watching over young children at the same time. Toddlers are passed from person to person, including adolescent boys, who appear to enjoy taking their turns. Mothers and all female relatives carry babies on their backs for much of the day; sometimes doting fathers or other male relatives also wrap babies and toddlers on their backs. Ewe adolescents experiment with sexuality early in their teen years, and nowadays pregnancy at a young age, even if the mother is unmarried, is not especially discouraged in many communities. Thus virginity is not as highly valued as it once was. Young girls help their mothers, often caring for smaller children or carrying loads to market, boys as young as 10 may go to sea with the men and go over the side of the pirogue to drive a school of fish into the nets. In-

land, young boys and girls help perform agricultural tasks and care for animals. Children are present at all important social and religious events and may, at a very early age, become "spouses" of important spirits or gods, thus inheriting sizable responsibilities and the special, often prestigious, identity, that goes with them. Children as young as 10 may go into trance during Vodu (Fon and Guin-Mina) or Tro (Anlo Ewe) possession ceremonies. They also enjoy such events as recreation and take advantage of opportunities for drumming, singing, and dancing performances; teenagers and young adults may court during and after such religious rituals.

Sociopolitical Organization

SOCIAL ORGANIZATION. There is virtually no formal hierarchy in many Ewe groups, except for the difference between slaves and their owners in times past. Even this crucial difference is now subject to ritual, during which some Ewe worship the spirits of their ancestors' slaves, thereby turning the tables on their past position of superiority. In Anlo there is some prestige in "royal" lineages, but there is no real class system other than that brought into existence by the capitalist economy,

KINSHIP

Kin Groups and Descent

Descent is primarily patrilineal, although among Ewe groups there are sometimes elements of double descent or of influence from Akan matriliny, such as rights of mother's brother in sister's children (including rights to pawn them). Fon have exogamous patrisibs composed of lineages, but in the Kingdom of Dahomey the royal sib had exceptional rules. Princesses married commoners and their children belonged to the royal sib, as did the offspring of royal princes. Cross-cousin marriage is preferred among most Ewe and Fon groups, particularly with mother's brother's daughter. Anlo Ewe established a clan (hlo) system soon after their arrival in Anlo. Long-term Anlo residents are still divided into some thirteen clans, including the Blu clan, which was

specifically created for resident strangers, made "Ewe" by virtue of their clan belonging. During certain periods, there has been a preference for clan endogamy.

Kinship Terminology

Brothers, sisters, and all first cousins are referred to as *novi;* father is referred to as *to,* and mother is referred to as *no.* Classificatory mothers and fathers, siblings, and cousins are also referred to by these terms. Other terms may differ between Ewe groups and between Ewe and Fon. An Iroquois system for parents' generation is general among Ewe, except that in some regions father's brothers are *ata* rather than versions of to or *eto* (Anlo), reserved for father; and mother's sisters are *na* rather than no or *eno,* which is reserved for mother. The most sig-

nificant variations are terms for father's sisters—*ete* (Anlo) or *tasi* (Guin-Mina)—and mother's brothers—*nyrui* (Anlo) or *nyine* (Guin-Mina). The Iroquois aspects are clearer in terms of address, which lump together parents, parents' same-sex siblings, and Ego's older siblings and cousins: *efo* (father or father's brothers), *fofo* or *fofovi* (younger uncle; cousin or brother older than Ego), *fogan* (older uncle or eldest brothers and cousins); *da* or *dada* (mother, mother's sisters), *davi* or *dadavi* (younger aunt, cousin or sister older than Ego), and *dagan* (older aunts and eldest cousins and sisters). Mother's brother and father's sister, however, do not have specific terms of direct address, but are addressed more formally as nyrui and ete. Fon employ descriptive terms for avuncular and nepotic kinsmen; cousin terminology is also descriptive.

which now touches all Ewe and Fon to some extent, and especially those who live in towns and cities. In the Kingdom of Dahomey, the royal lineages were effectively an elite who did not labor. Both Ewe and Fon had domestic slaves, who often married nonslaves and had children with them. The children in some communities were a sort of in-between class; in other localities, they were free. In any case, after two or three generations, they were no longer tied to a slave class.

POLITICAL ORGANIZATION. Although the Anlo polity was called a "state" at various periods, Green (1981, 1995) maintains it was not a true state but rather an attempt at centralization. The organizing principles were religious and clan-based rather than political or military in the strict sense. The Anlo did not have expansionist ambitions to compare with those of their Asante neighbors, who often ruled over them, or those of their Fon neighbors to the east, who maintained a royal city and a standing army. As early as the seventeenth century in the Volta region, elders were at the head of lineages, wards (lineage residential units), and villages. The *awoamefia* (political and spiritual leader, or chief priest) resided in Anloga. At the turn of the twentieth century, Ewe polities were divided into about 120 independent divisions. Each division had a number of villages, with a subchief in each one, and its own capital, with a paramount chief and military commander-inchief. Succession was patrilineal. Today political organization in villages may be quite egalitarian, although chiefs and elders (both male and female) do have more decision-making authority than younger adults. Fon villages had village autonomy before they were consolidated into a kingdom in the seventeenth century, and thus each village chief was a "king" (*toxosu*) to whom the heads of each compound answered. The Kingdom of Dahomey forced these chiefs to swear loyalty to the ruler or be sacrificed (some were sold into slavery). Sibs in Fon villages have considerable political influence, as do clans in Anlo and lineages and religious societies in other Ewe regions; the chief is hardly all-powerful.

SOCIAL CONTROL. Although during the colonial period chiefs had considerable control (and still do as far as administrative decisions are concerned), authority is widely distributed in villages and regions. Whereas all Ewe and Fon are nominally under the jurisdiction of British- and French-inspired legal systems, the laws of the ancestors and the moral frameworks of Vodu worship tend to have just as much, if not more, authority than official law in many communities.

Even in colonial and precolonial periods, the office of chief and the ranks of the elders were usually filled with men (and some women) who were linked to religious orders.

Individual behavior for many is constantly interpreted and adjusted through the lenses of Afa (or Fa) divination, which includes the "laws of destiny," or the "law-deity who brought me here" (*esesidomeda*). Thus, supernatural sanctions are more powerful than state legal systems for numerous Ewe and Fon. In the Kingdom of Dahomey, kings were tyrannical according to numerous sources; village chiefs, in keeping with earlier practices, were not. Decisions of village chiefs had to be reported to the king, however, so that final control was in his hands. The king's tribunal of chiefs was expected to judge harshly so that the king himself could demonstrate clemency by lightening the sentence. During the colonial period, there was great tension between certain Ewe Vodu orders and colonial administrators who claimed the Vodu "courts" were presuming to take the place of official courts. Numerous shrines were thus destroyed by German and British authorities. Vodu worshipers often did not consider the powers of the colonial governments to be legitimate.

CONFLICT. Conflict in villages is typically brought to a group of "judges," including the chief, Vodu priests, and both male and female elders. The entire village has the right to attend, and whoever wishes to speak may do so. Often divorce cases, theft, assault, and instances of injury through witchcraft do not go before official courts of law. Even cases that do go before official courts of law, including murder, may be rejudged by Vodu priests and communities because the conflict at the source of the crime is not thought to be merely personal. All conflict is a reflection of the social body in its relationship to the rest of the cosmos.

Religion and Expressive Culture

RELIGIOUS BELIEFS. Various Vodu (Fon) and Tro (Ewe) orders are at the foundation of Fon and Ewe religion. A High God exists, according to numerous informants. Ewe may say that Mawu is the creator, similar to the Christian god, or, for some, more like the diffuse life force of the universe. For yet others, Mawu is the "mother/father" of all the Trowo (powerful spirits or deities). Among Fon, Mawu and Lisa are a couple, twins, or a female (Mawu) and male (Lisa) hermaphrodite divinity. Fon may say the world was created

Ewe and Fon

RELIGION AND EXPRESSIVE CULTURE

Conflict in Ewe and Fon villages is typically brought to a group of "judges," including the chief, Vodu priests, and both male and female elders.

by Nana-Buluku, who gave birth to Mawu and Lisa. For others, Nana-Buluku, Mawu, and Lisa are all Vodus, and there is no all-powerful separate creator. Among Anlo Ewe, Nyigbla, the deity of the Sacred Forest is very important, as well as the entire pantheon of Yehve spirits, including Heviesso, god of thunder and lightning, and Avle, a goddess who sometimes impersonates men. Gu or Egu, the warrior and hunter god of iron, is central among all Ewe and Fon groups. There are a number of other Tro and Vodu orders, including Gorovodu, which is popular across Ewe and Fon populations in Ghana, Togo, and Benin. Mama Tchamba, a related order, involves the worship of the spirits of slaves from the north that Ewe once owned and married. The selfhood of each individual is involved with these major deities and spirit personalities. They are also protectors, healers, judges, and consummate performers. All Vodu and Tro orders work hand in hand with Afa (or Fa) divination, a complex interpretive framework within which each person has a life sign (*kpoli*), of which there are a total of 256. Each sign is connected to a set of plants and animals, stories and songs, dietary taboos, Vodus, and dangers and strengths, all associated with each other, as though clan-related. Events, projects, activities, and relationships also have their own Afa signs. Everything in the universe is related to Afa texts and themes, as though nature itself were divided into exogamous clans.

Many Ewe and Fon have become Christians; given their proximity to the coast, these ethnic groups were among the first to accept Christianity in the eighteenth and nineteenth centuries. Certain Christian groups originating in West Africa, such as Aladura and Celeste, have a considerable following on the coast.

RELIGIOUS PRACTITIONERS. Vodu and Tro priests are usually men, but postmenopausal women may become priestesses. The great majority of spirit hosts or "wives" of the Vodus are women. Priests, priestesses, and "wives" of the Yehve deities (Sosi, Avlesi, Dasi, etc.) do not usually practice trance. Afa diviners are almost always men, although it is said that a woman can become a diviner if she wishes.

CEREMONIES. Vodu and Tro ceremonies are compelling performances for both insiders and outsiders. Worshipers who begin dancing to the drum music may go into trance. Spirits who possess their "wives" may have messages for the community, may take part in judging certain cases of conflict, and may heal the sick. Above all, they are dancing gods, and there are aesthetic conven-

tions that have long traditions. In Vodu orders where possession is not usual, ceremonies are all the more dazzling because of the perfection of their collective execution. Rows of dancers, all clothed in ceremonial attire, move across a ritual space as one person, performing specific movements. Drums always provide a sort of text or context for movement, including narrative associations and instruction. Ceremonies are events during which symbolic associations are reinforced, individual and collective identity is stated, certain aspects of identity and power are recalled and redistributed, healing and admonishment take place, and, above all, collective exhilaration, ecstasy, and awe are produced. Ceremonies are always gifts to the gods.

Afa divination involves numerous complicated rituals based on a binary system of questions and responses, and permutations of the 256 life signs associated with collections of oral texts.

ARTS. Some Ewe men specialize in weaving prized *kente* cloth (similar to that of Asante), worn during all important occasions. The weaving is done on small looms that produce narrow strips of brightly colored cloth that must be sewn together to make a kente 76 to 152 centimeters wide and as long as 4.5 meters. There are numerous combinations of colors and patterns that bear great significance for the wearers. Now batik art, brought from Indonesia, is practiced in Togo and is popular among tourists. Fon artists are widely known for their appliqué hangings with legendary motifs from the Kingdom of Dahomey and Vodu culture. Elaborate engraving or carving of calabashes is another Fon art. Brass casting (using the *cireperdue*, or lost-wax method) has been practiced by the Fon since early times. Brass workers belonged to special guilds in the Kingdom of Dahomey; they created some of the more striking objects constituting the king's wealth. Silverwork was also mastered. Both Ewe and Fon still carve wooden *bocio* figures for spiritual practices, as well as Legba statues (guardian deities) and other Vodu god-objects. Earthen Legbas are also common. Some god-objects, entirely abstract in form, are confected as a collage-sculpture, with numerous ingredients including cowry shells, goat horns, cows' tails, birds' claws, iron bells, and tree roots, all united with red clay and glazed with the blood of sacrificial animals. Drums of many different kinds are produced for specific ceremonies. Vodu costumes for spirit possession may be richly adorned with cowries sewn on in patterns. All of the objects necessary for Afa (Ewe) or Fa (Fon) divination are also created with great care and elaboration; thus they are sometimes bought by Europeans as objects of art. Stools are important to Ewe and Fon lineages. They are often carved with narrative detail so that their symbolic significance is inscribed for future generations to see.

MEDICINE. Today many Fon and Ewe seek medical assistance in modern clinics and hospitals and go to Western-trained doctors. They may also frequent local healers and Vodu priests who employ plants and carbonized ingredients, as well as rituals to address illness and conflicts playing themselves out in a person's body and soul. Vodu medicine is not hostile to modern biomedicine. Upon asking Afa, though divination, what to do about illness, a sufferer may be told by Afa to go to a doctor in town. Vodu medicine is particularly effective in cases of madness. Ingestion of roots and plants, as well as "speaking pain and desire" to the Vodus make it possible for the alienated to mourn losses and go on with life once again.

DEATH AND AFTERLIFE. Upon death, certain aspects of the person are lost forever in their individuated form, whereas other aspects, for example, the *djoto*, or reincarnation soul, will come back in the next child born to the lineage. The *luvo*, or death soul, may linger for some time after death, looking just like the person in life and frightening loved ones with demands for attention and its cravings to be still with the living. According to some informants, the person as constituted in life does not survive death, but parts of the personality may indeed continue and even join with Vodus, as part of the conglomerate energy and personality of a deity. Others say that the spirit realm mirrors human life in every aspect, so that after death individuals go on in much the same way as before. Funerals are the single most important event in a person's history, more lavish and expensive than any other celebration or feast. Groups of drummers are hired, and mourners may dance throughout the night for several nights in succession. Attending funerals and contributing to them financially and with food and drink are among the most binding obligations for lineage members, neighbors, friends, chiefs, and Vodu worshipers (above all, for those who belong to the same order as the deceased).

Bibliography

Argyle, W. J. (1966). *The Fon of Dahomey*. Oxford: Clarendon Press.

Blier, Suzanne-Preston (1995). *African Vodun: Art, Psychology, and Power*. Chicago and London: University of Chicago Press.

Green, Sandra E. (1981). "The Anlo Ewe: Their Economy, Society, and External Relations in the Eighteenth Century." Ph.D. dissertation, Northwestern University.

Green, Sandra E. (1983). "Conflict and Crisis: A Note on the Workings of the Political Economy and Ideology of the Anlo-Ewe in the Precolonial Period." *Rural Africana* 17:83–96.

Green, Sandra E. (1985). "The Past and Present of an Anlo-Ewe Oral Tradition." *History in Africa* 12: 73–87.

Green, Sandra E. (1988). "Social Change in Eighteenth-Century Anlo: The Role of Technology, Markets, and Military Conflict." *Africa* 58(1): 70–86.

Green, Sandra E. (Forthcoming 1995). *Gender, Ethnicity, and Social Change on the Upper Slave Coast: A History of the Anlo-Ewe*.

Herskovits, Melville J. ([1938] 1967). *Dahomey: An Ancient West African Kingdom*. (Vols. 1, 2). Evanston, Ill.: Northwestern University Press.

Kossi, Komi E. (1990). *La structure socio-politique et son articulation avec la pensée religieuse chez les aja-tado du sud-est Togo*. Stuttgart: Franz Steiner Verlag.

Le Herissé, A. (1911). *L'ancien royaume du Dahomey*. Paris.

Manoukian, Madeline (1952). *The Ewe-Speaking People of Togoland and the Gold Coast*. London: International African Institute.

Mignot, Alain (1985). *La terre et le pouvoir chez les guin du sudest du Togo*. Paris: Publications de la Sorbonne.

Pazzi, Roberto (1976). *L'homme evé, aja, gen, fon et son univers*. Lome: reneotyped.

Riviere, Claude (1981). *Anthropologie religieuse des evé du Togo*. Lome: Les Nouvelles Éditions Africaines.

Rosenthal, Judy (Forthcoming 1995). *Foreign Tongues and Domestic Bodies: Personhood, Possession, and the Law in Ewe Gorovodu*.

Surgy, Albert de (1988). *Le système religieux des evhe*. Paris: L'Harmattan.

Université Nationale du Bénin; Faculté des Letters, Arts, et Sciences Humaines; Départment d'Histoire et d'Archéologie (1977). *Actes du Colloque international sur les civilisations aja-ewé*. Cotonou: Université Nationale du Bénin.

Verger, Pierre (1957). *Notes sur le culte des orisa et vodun à Bahía, la baie de tous les saints, au Brésil et à l'ancienne Côte des Esclaves en Afrique*. Dakar: Mémoires de l'Institut Français d'Afrique Noire, no. 51.

—JUDY ROSENTHAL

FULANI

Ethonyms: Bororo'en, Fellaata, Fellah, Filani, Fula, Fulata, Fulbe, Hilani, Peul, Toroobe

Fulani

A major problem in reckoning the Fulani population is that Fulani are found in twenty nations in a wide swath of Africa.

Orientation

IDENTIFICATION. "Fulbe" is the preferred self-name of the group the Hausa term the "Fulani" or "Hilani." In French countries, they tend to be termed "Peul" or "Fulata." Because of their spread over a wide area and their assumption of cultural traits from surrounding groups, there is great confusion regarding the nature of Fulani ethnicity. This confusion is reflected in the confounding and conflating of names for particular segments or local groups of Fulbe, such as Toroobe and Bororo'en, with the entire ethnic group.

LOCATION. The Fulani live in an area that stretches from Ouadaï, a city east of Lake Chad, to Senegal's Atlantic shore. There are groups of Fulani as far east as the border of Ethiopia.

DEMOGRAPHY. Estimates of the number of Fulani vary. A major problem in reckoning the population is that Fulani are found in twenty nations in a wide swath of Africa—from Mauritania and Senegal to Sudan, Ethiopia, and Kenya. Only Liberia may not have any Fulani settlements. It seems reasonable to accept an estimate of 7 to 8 million nomadic Fulani and 16 million settled Fulani.

LINGUISTIC AFFILIATION. The language is variously known as "Fulfulde," "Pulaar," "Fula," or "Peul," among other names. It belongs to the West African Subfamily of the Niger-Congo Group, along with Wolof, Serer, and Temne. There are many variations and dialects of Fulfulde. The influence of surrounding peoples is clearly seen in its local variations. Fulfulde is generally written in Roman script, although in the past it was written in Arabic.

History and Cultural Relations

A search for the origin of the Fulani is not only futile, it betrays a position toward ethnic identity that strikes many anthropologists as profoundly wrong. Ethnic groups are political-action groups that exist, among other reasons, to attain benefits for their members. Therefore, by definition, their social organization, as well as cultural content, will change over time. Moreover, ethnic groups, such as the Fulani, are always coming into—and going out of—existence.

Rather than searching for the legendary eastern origin of the Fulani, a more productive approach might be to focus on the meaning of Fulani identity within concrete historical situations and analyze the factors that shaped Fulani ethnicity and the manner in which people used it to attain particular goals.

People whom historians identify as Fulani entered present-day Senegal from the north and east. It is certain that they were a mixture of peoples from northern and sub-Saharan Africa. These pastoral peoples tended to move in an eastern direction and spread over much of West Africa after the tenth century.

Their adoption of Islam increased the Fulanis' feeling of cultural and religious superiority to surrounding peoples, and that adoption became a major ethnic boundary marker. The Toroobe, a branch of the Fulani, settled in towns and mixed with the ethnic groups there. They quickly became noted as outstanding Islamic clerics, joining the highest ranks of the exponents of Islam, along with Berbers and Arabs. The Town Fulani (Fulbe Sirre) never lost touch with their Cattle Fulani relatives, however, often investing in large herds themselves. Cattle remain a significant symbolic repository of Fulani values.

The Fulani movement in West Africa tended to follow a set pattern. Their first movement into an area tended to be peaceful. Local officials gave them land grants. Their dairy products, including fertilizer, were highly prized. The number of converts to Islam increased over time. With that increase, Fulani resentment at being ruled by pagans, or imperfect Muslims, increased.

That resentment was fueled by the larger migration that occurred during the seventeenth century, in which the Fulani migrants were predominantly Muslim. These groups were not so easily integrated into society as earlier immigrants had been. By the beginning of the eighteenth century, revolts had broken out against local rulers. Although these revolts began as holy wars (jihads), after their success they followed the basic principle of Fulani ethnic dominance.

The situation in Nigeria was somewhat different from that elsewhere in West Africa in that the Fulani entered an area more settled and developed than that in other West African areas. At the time of their arrival, in the early fifteenth century, many Fulani settled as clerics in Hausa citystates such as Kano, Katsina, and Zaria. Others settled among the local peoples during the sixteenth and seventeenth centuries. By the seventeenth century, the Hausa states had begun to gain their independence from various foreign rulers, with Gobir becoming the predominant Hausa state.

The urban culture of the Hausa was attractive to many Fulani. These Town or Settled Fulani became clerics, teachers, settlers, and judges—and in many other ways filled elite positions within the Hausa states. Soon they adopted the Hausa language, many forgetting their own Fulfulde language. Although Hausa customs exerted an influence on the Town Fulani, they did not lose touch with the Cattle or Bush Fulani.

These ties proved useful when their strict adherence to Islamic learning and practice led them to join the jihads raging across West Africa. They tied their grievances to those of their pastoral relatives. The Cattle Fulani resented what they considered to be an unfair cattle tax, one levied by imperfect Muslims. Under the leadership of the outstanding Fulani Islamic cleric, Shehu Usman dan Fodio, the Fulani launched a jihad in 1804. By 1810, almost all the Hausa states had been defeated.

Although many Hausa—such as Yakubu in Bauchi—joined dan Fodio after victory was achieved, the Fulani in Hausaland turned their religious conquest into an ethnic triumph. Those in Adamawa, for instance, were inspired by dan Fodio's example to revolt against the kingdom of Mandara. The leader was Modibo Adamu, after whom the area is now named. His capital is the city of Yola. After their victories, the Fulani generally eased their Hausa collaborators from positions of power and forged alliances with fellow Fulani.

Settlements

For the fully nomadic Fulani, the practice of transhumance, the seasonal movement in search of water, strongly influences settlement patterns. The basic settlement, consisting of a man and his dependents, is called a *wuru*. It is social but ephemeral, given that many such settlements have no women and serve simply as shelters for the nomads who tend the herds.

There are, in fact, a number of settlement patterns among Fulani. In the late twentieth century there has been an increasing trend toward livestock production and sedentary settlement, but Fulani settlement types still range from traditional nomadism to variations on sedentarism. As the modern nation-state restricts the range of nomadism, the Fulani have adapted ever increasingly complex ways to move herds among their related families: the families may reside in stable communities, but the herds move according to the availability of water. Over the last few centuries, the majority of Fulani have become sedentary.

Those Fulani who remain nomadic or seminomadic have two major types of settlements: dry-season and wet-season camps. The dry season lasts from about November to March, the wet season from about March to the end of October. Households are patrilocal and range in size from one nuclear family to more than one hundred people. The administrative structure, however, crosscuts patrilinies and is territorial. Families tend to remain in wet-season camp while sending younger males—or, increasingly, hiring non-Fulani herders—to accompany the cattle to dry-season camps.

Town Fulani live in much the same manner as the urban people among whom they live, maintaining their Fulani identity because of the prestige and other advantages to which it entitles its members. In towns, Fulani pursue the various occupations available to them: ruler, adviser to the ruler, religious specialist, landlord, business, trade, and so forth.

Economy

SUBSISTENCE AND COMMERCIAL ACTIVITIES. The Fulani form the largest pastoral nomadic group in the world. The Bororo'en are noted for the size of their cattle herds. In addition to fully nomadic groups, however, there are also semisedentary Fulani—Fulbe Laddi—who also

FULANI GIRL

A Fulani girl carries a large pot on her head. In Fulani society, women have two essential roles, that of sister and daughter. Jalingo, Nigeria. (Kerstin Geier; ABPL/Corbis)

Young Fulani children are treated with great gentleness and are rarely disciplined. Adults seek to avoid giving them any emotional shocks.

farm, although they argue that they do so out of necessity, not choice. A small group, the Fulbe Mbalu or Sheep Fulani, rely on sheep for their livelihood.

The Toroobe are outstanding clerics in the Sunni branch of Islam. They have generally intermarried with Hausa and no longer speak Fulfulde. They are found practicing other urban trades: teaching, serving in government positions, engaging in legal activities, renting property, financing trade, and so forth.

Many of the other Town Fulani were actually slaves of the Fulani who now identify with the group because of their high prestige. These urban dwellers engage in all the trades one finds in Hausa towns from crafts to long-range trade throughout Africa and the world.

INDUSTRIAL ARTS. The Fulani are not particularly noted for industrial arts, except for those associated with cattle. They do engage in leatherworking and some craft production. Many of their former slaves who have assumed Fulani ethnicity follow the basic crafts of other West Africans: silver- and goldsmithing, ironworking, basket making, and similar crafts.

TRADE. The Fulani are engaged in long-distance trade, generally involving cattle, with their Hausa colleagues. Often the Hausa are also butchers who control West African cattle markets by controlling access to Fulani cattle.

DIVISION OF LABOR. Herding cattle is a male activity. Tending and milking cattle, however, are women's work. Women may also sell dairy products; their graceful movement with containers of milk or cheese is a common sight in West African towns. Adolescent males traditionally have been in charge of moving the herds, whereas their elders deal with the political decisions and negotiate with sedentary people for the safe movement of the herds through farmlands.

LAND TENURE. Land is held by—and inherited through—the patrilineage. As the Fulani have become increasingly sedentary—generally as a result of the pressure of the modern nation state and its centralized control—rights in land have become increasingly important.

Kinship

KIN GROUPS AND DESCENT. The Fulani are patrilineal and patrilocal. Kinship and seniority are vital to their way of life. The basic elements of kinship are sex, age, and generation. Full siblings tend to unite against half-siblings, although halfsiblings with the same mother do share a special bond.

The Fulani have a principle of generational seniority that is embodied in the general organization of lineages. There are four general lineages, all traced to descent from a common ancestor and his sons; however, everyday groups cut across these *yettore* lines. Such groups developed to meet historical needs. Over time, patrilineages—much shallower than the four general lineages—emerged. These patrilineages, in turn, are intersected by territorial groups under men called "guides."

Patrilineages are named and consist of three ascending generations. They are coresidential, and members cooperate in pastoral pursuits. The patrilineage controls marriage and is endogamous. A clan is a cluster of lineages, and the clan members generally share a wet-season camp.

KINSHIP TERMINOLOGY. There is a good deal of ambiguity in the Fulani use of kinship terms. Thus, any of these terms can be used to refer to a specific person or a range of people. Part of this ambiguity results from the Fulani preference for close marriage so that any person might, in fact, be addressed or referred to by any of several terms.

Goggo is used for father's sister or paternal aunt. *Bappanngo* is father's brother, whereas *kaawu* refers to mother's brother; *dendiraado* designates a cross cousin, and *sakike* is a sibling. *Baaba* is father, and *yaaye* is mother; *biddo* or *bu* is a child. These terms are often combined, however. Thus, *sakiraabe* refers to both siblings and cousins of all sexes. A true sibling if elder is termed *mawniyo*; if younger, *minyiyo*. *Maama* refers both to grandparents, of either sex, and their *sakiraabe* and their grandchildren. When it is necessary to distinguish male from female, a term may be added: *biddi* for male, and *dibbo* for female.

Marriage and Family

MARRIAGE. Ideally, the Fulani do not practice birth control because the perfect or model Fulani marriage will produce many children. Toward that goal, the Fulani marry young. No special value is placed on virginity, and women are not shy about boasting about their various experiences. In fact, the Fulani expect young women to bring sexual experience to marriage. There are even special dances in which women select mates, with the proviso that the mate selected not be her fiancé or a particular category of relative—one to whom she could be affianced, for example.

At the same time, a woman is expected to display appropriate modesty whenever the subject of marriage arises, for marriage confers on her a special status. There has been some confusion regarding what constitutes the marriage ceremony among the Fulani. Because neither bride nor groom may be present at the ceremony, owing to shame-avoidance taboos, the significance of the cattle ceremony (*koowgal*) has often been overlooked. In that ceremony, the bride's father transfers one of his herd to the groom, legalizing the marriage. There may also follow a more typical Islamic ceremony, termed *kabbal*. Again, neither bride nor groom may actually be present at the ceremony.

An important public acknowledgment of the marriage is the movement of the bride to her husband's village, termed *bangal*. The women of that village come to greet her, and the welcome is a rite of passage for the bride. The bride's status increases with each child she has, especially with the birth of males.

The Fulani prefer endogamy. Their first choice of a marriage partner is a patrilateral parallel cousin. If that is not possible, their other choices are for the partners to share a great-grandfather, a great-great grandfather, or a patrilateral cross cousin.

DOMESTIC UNIT. A man is allowed four wives. Each wife brings cattle with her to the marriage. It is a major obligation for a woman to milk the cattle and prepare the dairy products. A woman receives respect from her sons and daughters-in-law.

INHERITANCE. Lineage members inherit cattle and widows. Among Town Fulani, inheritance generally follows Islamic prescriptions, with the exception that generally women do not contest their inheritance with their full brothers.

SOCIALIZATION. At 2 years of age, children are weaned. A child's father remains distant throughout its life. Women provide for children's needs. Thus, a mother and her daughters tend to the needs of her sons. A young girl first plays at carrying dolls on her back and then moves on to carrying her baby brother.

Among the Pastoral Fulani, baby girls are given amulets for fertility and boys for virility. Mothers take care to preserve and shape their children's conformity to the Fulani ideal notions of beauty. Mothers attempt to lengthen their children's noses by pressing them between their fingers, stretching, and squeezing hard. They also attempt to shape their children's heads into the ideal round shape.

Acquiring a culture is perceived as acquiring something that is found. The Fulani term is *tawaangal*. There is a sense that no one invented

nor can change these traditions, for they define what it is to be Fulani.

Young children are treated with great gentleness and are rarely disciplined. Adults seek to avoid giving them any emotional shocks. Most training is given by a child's mother and the other women of the compound. They are believed to be more capable of patience and reciprocity. Young girls are initiated into their adult work through games. The young girl carries her doll. At 2 or 3 years old her ears are pierced, six holes in her right ear and six in her left. Almost as soon as she can walk well, she is placed into the middle of a circle of dancing women who begin to teach her to dance and praise her efforts lavishly.

Indeed, the transition to adulthood proceeds in smooth steps. At about 5 years of age, girls are taught the rules of the moral code -*mbo*. There are to be no sexual relations of any kind with brothers. A woman may not look at her fiancé in the face. She must demonstrate respect for elders and must never mention her future parents-in-law. Women have two essential roles in Fulani society, that of sister and daughter. Either at her naming ceremony or just before she leaves her father's home for her husband's, a woman's father presents her with a heifer. There is shame for a man on entering his daughter's home; however, the strong affection he demonstrates for his grandchildren is meant to show his affection for his daughter as well.

Young boys play at taking care of the cattle and performing men's work. Mothers come to rely more on sons than on daughters because daughters will leave the compound upon marriage.

Sociopolitical Organization

SOCIAL ORGANIZATION. The Fulani are many different people. Among those who term themselves "Fulani" are former slaves and members of castes or guilds, such as blacksmiths or bards. It is important to note that the Fulani hold that belonging to society itself is dependent on the will of the individual.

POLITICAL ORGANIZATION. Fulani tend to be the ruling caste among Islamic communities in the northern areas of West Africa. They control the various northern emirates in what was Northern Nigeria, for example. They also play a major role in the modern governments of many West African states.

Among the Cattle Fulani, a leader (*ardo*) of a territorial group has a major role. Patrilineages play an important part in regulating day-to-day

♦ cousin, parallel
Children of one's parent's siblings of the same sex— one's father's brothers' and mother's sisters' children.

matters and in controlling cattle. They also govern marriages and widow inheritance.

CONFLICT. Kinship and regional groups regulate conflict within and between groups. The Fulani often come into conflict with settled populations among which they pass. Alliances with Town Fulani help resolve a number of disputes between Fulani and their neighbors. The Fulani are quick to resort to combat in the defense of their interest but also have a reputation for waiting for the opportune moment to seek revenge if the situation demands patience.

Religion and Expressive Culture

RELIGIOUS BELIEFS. Over 90 percent of the Town Fulani are Muslims. It is, in fact, rather difficult to discover any Fulani—Town or Cattle—who admits to not being Muslim, no matter how lax his or her practice may be. The Fulani share many beliefs with other West African Muslims. They use Islam both as a means to distinguish themselves from others, through the reputation of Fulani clerics, and as a link to members of other African groups.

At the same time, there is belief in the steady-state nature of culture that preceded Islam. Culture is seen to be unchanging and constant from generation to generation. The only improvement a Cattle Fulani sees possible is to have more children than his or her parents. Otherwise, the appropriate thing to do is to live according to the code of the ancestors.

That code stresses the symbolic importance of cattle in defining Fulani ethnicity. There is also a requirement to respect one's seniors and to love one's mother. The ethos of the Fulani is best summed up in the concept of *palaaku*. It portrays the ideal Fulani as one who has stoic sobriety, reserve, and strong emotional ties to cattle. At the same time, the model Fulani is gentle in demeanor. His carriage conveys a proud reserve, almost a disdain toward non-Fulani. It is said that no one knows what a Fulani is thinking. The true Fulani is physically as well as psychologically distant from other people, especially non-Fulani. Moreover, he is enjoined from displays of strong emotions. His demeanor is taciturn, loathing the boisterousness of others. Wealth is not to be vulgarly displayed but carefully and quietly tended.

The Fulani have a number of taboos. They may not pronounce the name of a spouse, a first son, a first daughter, a father or mother, or a parent-in-law or the names of the parents of any beautiful girl or young woman. In addition to observing the usual Islamic dietary laws, they may not eat goat meat, lest they become lepers.

RELIGIOUS PRACTITIONERS. As Muslims, the Fulani share with other Muslims reliance on traditional Islamic religious practitioners and are themselves prominent members of the Islamic clerical class. In common with other West Africans, however, Fulani will frequent local religious practitioners who have established reputations for their curative powers and supernatural abilities.

CEREMONIES. Varios life-cycle events—naming, acceptance of young girls into the group, marriage, first child, and so on—are marked by ceremonies. The Shar'o ceremony demonstrates to the community that a young man has come of age. In it, adolescent friends take turns beating each other across the chest with their walking sticks. No sign of pain or discomfort can be shown. Although adolescents have died in this ceremony, young men are eager to participate and display their scars with pride throughout their lives.

ARTS. The Fulani are noted for their oral literature, which celebrates the concept of palaaku and serves to define Fulani identity. Fulani oral literature has been influenced both by surrounding peoples and by Islam. The major categories of Fulani literature are poetry, history, story, legend, proverb, magic formula, and riddle. Many of these genres are sung, either by amateurs or by professionals.

MEDICINE. The Fulani participate in a number of medical systems. One is an Islamic system, basically derived from the Arabs and through them from Greco-Roman sources. They share many traditions with the groups among whom they live. Since the onset of British colonization—around the turn of the twentieth century—they have been exposed to Western medical practices. In common with other West Africans, they have incorporated elements from these various systems in a rather syncretistic and pragmatic fashion.

DEATH AND AFTERLIFE. If one lives up to the palaaku code and obeys Allah's laws, there will be rewards in the afterlife. The Fulani, in common with other Muslims, believe in an afterlife of material rewards for the followers of Allah.

Bibliography

Azarya, Victor (1978). *Aristocrats Facing Change.* Chicago: University of Chicago Press.

Ba, Amadou Hampata (1990). "Out of the Land of Shadows." *UNESCO Courier*, May, 22–25.

Dupire, Marguerite (1973). "Women in a Pastoral Society." In *Peoples and Cultures of Africa*, edited by Elliott P. Skinner, 297–303. Garden City, N.Y.: Doubleday.

Eguchi, Paul K. (1993). "Fulbe-ness' in Fulbe Oral Literature of Cameroon." In *Unity and Diversity of a People: The Search for Fulbe Identity*, edited by Paul K. Eguchi and Victor Azarya, 181–200. Senri Ethnological Studies, no. 35. Osaka: National Museum of Ethnology.

Eguchi, Paul K., and Victor Azarya, eds. (1993). *Unity and Diversity of a People: The Search for Fulbe Identity*. Senri Ethnological Studies, no. 35. Osaka: National Museum of Ethnology.

Frantz, Charles (1981). "Settlement and Migration among Pastoral Fulbe in Nigeria and Cameroun." In *Contemporary Nomadic and Pastoral Peoples*, edited by Philip Carl Salzman, 57–94. Studies in Third World Society, Publication no. 17. Williamsburg, Va.: College of William and Mary, Department of Anthropology.

Hopen, C. Edward (1984). "Fulani." In *Muslim Peoples: A World Ethnographic Survey*. 2nd ed., rev. and expanded, edited by Richard V. Weekes, 257–261. Westport, Conn.: Greenwood Press.

Riesman, Paul (1977). *Freedom in Fulani Social Life: An Introspective Ethnography*. Translated by Martha Fuller. Chicago: University of Chicago Press.

Salamone, Frank A. (1985). "Colonialism and the Emergence of Fulani Ethnicity." *Journal of Asian and African Studies* 20:170–201.

Schultz, Emily A. (1981). *Image and Reality in African Interethnic Relations: The Fulbe and Their Neighbors*. Studies in Third World Society, Publication no. 11. Williamsburg, Va.: College of William and Mary, Department of Anthropology.

Stenning, Derrick J. (1959). *Savannah Nomads: A Study of the Wodaabe Pastoral Fulani of Western Bornu Province, Northern Region, Nigeria*. London: International African Institute; Oxford University Press.

Wilson, Wendy (1990). "Women Pastoralists and Project Participation." *Sage* 7:18–23.

Wilson-Haffenden, James Rhodes (1967). *The Red Men of Nigeria: An Account of a Lengthy Residence among the Fulani or "Red Man," and other Pagan Tribes of Central Nigeria*. London: Cass.

Wyatt-Brown, Bertram (1988). "The Mask of Obedience: Male Slave Psychology in the Old South." *American Historical Review* 93:1228–1252.

—FRANK A. SALAMONE

GANDA

Ethnyms: Buganda, Luganda

The Ganda are a group of people who live in the province of Buganda in Uganda. The Ganda refer to themselves as "Baganda" (sing. Muganda), and they refer to their language as "Luganda." Luganda is a Bantu language. Linguistically, Luganda can be placed within the Interlacustrine Group of the Northern Zone of Bantu languages or within the Central Branch of the Niger-Congo Language Family.

Buganda is one of four provinces within the country of Uganda. It is located on the northern and western shores of Lake Victoria, from 2° N to 1° S. It stretches for about 320 kilometers along the shore and extends inland about 130 kilometers. The land area of Buganda is about 45,000 square kilometers, and the elevation averages about 1,200 meters above sea level. The Ganda occupy the northwestern shore of Lake Victoria, a region characterized by flat-topped hills separated from each other by swampland.

Although the number of Africans living in Buganda, according to the 1950 census, was 1,834,128, only 1,006,101 of these people were ethnically Ganda. The overall density was 42 persons per square kilometer. At about the time of European contact (c. 1862), there were 3,000,000 Ganda. Civil wars, famine, and disease had reduced their number to about 2,000,000 by 1911. In 1986 their population was estimated at 2,352,000 (Grimes 1988).

Along with Bunyoro, Toro, Ankole, and Kiziba, Buganda is one of the Lacustrian kingdoms. The Ganda are people of mixed origins, whose ancestors migrated to their present location over the past 600 years. Historically, they were known as a warlike people who conquered many of their neighbors. At the time of White contact, the Ganda kingdom was at the height of its power.

The first contact with Westerners occurred in 1862, and missionaries arrived in Buganda soon thereafter. In the Buganda Agreement of 1900, Buganda was designated a province of Uganda. In 1962 the status of Uganda changed from that of a British protectorate to an independent nation and a member of the Commonwealth of Nations. In the Uganda Agreement, the position of the king (*kabaka*) was confirmed, and the native system of administration was preserved. The central government of Buganda Province consists of the kabaka, three ministers, and a legislative assembly (*lukiiko*). For administrative purposes, the province is divided into counties, subcounties, and parishes.

The Ganda are primarily an agricultural society; their staple crops are bananas and yams. Cotton was introduced as a market crop early in the twentieth century. In addition, sweet potatoes, taro, manioc, maize, millet, peanuts, beans, squashes, gourds, sesame, tomatoes, and sugarcane are grown. Ownership of cattle is a sign of wealth,

Traditionally, Ganda villages consisted of a number of households, each one surrounded by its banana gardens, spread out over the top of a hill.

and goats, chickens, and a few sheep are also kept. The banana has been of great importance in Ganda life. Typically, each household had a banana grove, which supplied the major food needs of the family. A grove could produce for as long as seventy years and required only a little weeding and mulching, work that was commonly done by women. According to the Ganda, one woman working in a banana grove provided food for ten men. Because of the banana, the Ganda have not needed to follow a pattern of shifting agriculture, and the land has been able to support a fairly dense population.

Traditionally, villages consisted of a number of households, each one surrounded by its banana gardens, spread out over the top of a hill. Villages were made up of between 60 and 100 adult males, together with their families, in a hierarchical system. All land was considered to be owned by the kabaka, who appointed local chiefs to administer specific territories. The chiefs, in turn, had subchiefs under them. At the bottom of this hierarchy was the village headman.

Land was controlled by patrilineal clans, each of which was protected by a major and a minor totem. Clan estates were administered by the heads of the clans, who were confirmed by the kabaka. Tribute—in the form of goods and services—flowed from the clans, to the chiefs, to the kabaka. For the kabaka, clan affiliation was different. There was a royal family, rather than a royal clan, and the children of the kabaka were affiliated with their mothers' clans. The succession to the kingship was in the male line: sons, grandsons, and brothers were eligible to inherit the title. In addition to his role as monarch, the kabaka was the head of all the clans in the kingdom. Through this latter role, the position of the king was reinforced, insofar as he was directly related to every family in the kingdom. Because of the kabaka's dual function, the Ganda consider it inconceivable for their society to exist without a king. Nevertheless, the chieftainship has declined in importance, and villages have become more dispersed and now lack the central focus of a chief's house. The residents of a village no longer get together except for marriage feasts and funerals.

The traditional religion of the Ganda was based on beliefs in the spirits of the dead. Prophets and mediums were able to consult with these spirits, which had influence over the affairs of the living. Although all of the Ganda are now considered to be Christian or Muslim (a small minority), vestiges of the traditional religion can still be observed. For example, sorcery, traditional medicine, spirit possession, and ancestor worship are some of the elements of the traditional religion that are sometimes practiced today.

Bibliography

Apte, David E. (1967). *The Political Kingdom of Uganda: A Study in Bureaucratic Nationalism.* 2d ed. Princeton, N.J.: Princeton University Press.

Fallers, Margaret Chave (1960). *The Eastern Lacustrine Bantu (Ganda and Soga).* London: International African Institute.

Grimes, Barbara F. (1988). *Ethnologue: Languages of the World.* Dallas: Summer Institute of Linguistics.

Mair, Lucy Philip (1934). *An African People in the Twentieth Century.* London: G. Routledge & Sons.

Mair, Lucy Philip (1940). *Native Marriage in Buganda.* London: Oxford University Press for the International Institute of African Languages and Cultures.

Ray, Benjamin C. (1991). *Myth, Ritual, and Kingship in Buganda.* New York: Oxford University Press.

Richards, Audrey Isabel (1960). "The Ganda." In *East African Chiefs: A Study of Political Development in Some Uganda and Tanganyika Tribes*, edited by Audrey I. Richards, 41–77. London: Faber & Faber for the East African Institute of Social Research.

Richards, Audrey Isabel (1966). *The Changing Structure of a Ganda Village: Kisozi 1892–1952.* Nairobi: East African Publishing House.

Richards, Audrey Isabel, ed. (1954). *Economic Development and Tribal Change: A Study of Immigrant Labour in Buganda.* Cambridge: W. Heffer and Sons for the East African Institute of Social Research.

Roscoe, John (1911). *The Baganda: An Account of Their Native Customs and Beliefs.* London: Macmillan.

Southwold, Margin (1965). "The Ganda of Uganda." In *Peoples of Africa*, edited by James L. Gibbs, Jr., 81–118. New York: Holt, Rinehart & Winston.

HAUSA

Ethnonyms: Afnu (the Kanuri term) or Afunu; Arna or Azna, Bunjawa, Maguzawa (non-Muslims) Aussa; Haoussa, al Hausin

Orientation

IDENTIFICATION. The Hausa constitute the largest ethnic group in West Africa. The term "Hausa" actually refers to the language and, by extension, to its native speakers, of whom there are about 25 million.

LOCATION. The Hausa are scattered across the savanna of northern Nigeria, the adjacent area of Niger, and, as a result of extensive migration, in enclaves in various African cities as far south as the Atlantic coast. The focal homeland covers an area about 640 kilometers wide, from Lake Chad to the east to the Niger River in the west. It extends from 11° to 14° N and from about 2° to 14° E. The annual rainfall ranges from about 50 centimeters in the north to 100 centimeters in the south.

DEMOGRAPHY. There are approximately 22.5 million Hausa in West Africa. According to the last census, carried out in 1963, 80 percent of the Hausa are rural, 20 percent urban. Even with the tremendous urbanization of the 1970s and 1980s, economic problems have led to return migrations to the countryside. Thus, the 80:20 ratio may still stand. Among the Hausa, there is high infant mortality. If a child survives his or her first two years, he or she will probably live to age 50. Risk decreases until one reaches middle age, but many Hausa survive into their 70s and 80s.

LINGUISTIC AFFILIATION. A Chadic language, Hausa is related to Arabic, Hebrew, Berber, and other Afroasiatic Family members. Proper tone and stress are imperative. Hausa, which was originally written in Arabic script, has a centuries-old literary tradition, but it is also the language of trade and, next to Swahili, is the most widely spoken African language.

Settlements

The Hausa classify their settlements as cities, towns, or hamlets. The cities have wards for foreigners, including Tuareg, Arabs, Nupe, Kanuri, and others. The capital cities are walled, and residents live in walled compounds with interior courtyards. Those of the well-to-do are whitewashed and decorated with plaster arabesques. The women's quarters are separate. Urban compounds may house sixty to a hundred persons. Although the Hausa accord urban living the most prestige, they are primarily rural. Each village contains a capital, as well as several hamlets; the capital is divided into wards, housing families of the same occupational group. Traditional village compounds are walled or fenced; materials range from baked clay to mud or cornstalks. Compounds characteristically contain an entrance hut, an open shared cooking and work area, a hut for the compound head, and separate huts for each of his wives. Newer housing is rectangular and concrete. The number of people living in a rural compound ranges from one to thirty, the average being ten.

Economy

SUBSISTENCE AND COMMERCIAL ACTIVITIES. Agriculture is the main economic activity. Grain is the staple diet, including Guinea corn, millet, maize, and rice. The Hausa also grow and eat root crops and a variety of vegetables. Cotton and peanuts are processed and used locally, but part of the harvest is exported. The Hausa practice intercropping and double-cropping; their

HISTORY AND CULTURAL RELATIONS

Hausa history is one of immigration and conquest. The Hausa nation has evolved from the incorporation over hundreds of years of many different peoples who joined the original stock. They are united by a common language and adherence to a common religion, Islam. According to tradition, the Hausa people derive from the Hausa *bakwai*, the "true" seven states, of which Daura (named after its female founder) is considered the most senior. In the myth of origin, Bayajidda, the son of the king of Baghdad, arrived in Daura via Bornu. He killed the snake that occupied the well, impeding the townspeople's access to the water. As a reward, Bayajidda married the queen. Their son Bawo was the progenitor of six sons, thereby founding six

states—Daura, Katsina, Zazzau (Zaria), Gobir, Kano, and Rano. Bayajidda's son by his first wife, Magira (a Kanuri woman), founded Biram, the seventh state.

In fact, it is not known when the movement of peoples actually occurred; neither has the migrants' place of origin been pinpointed. The seven Habe kingdoms were formed by a coalescence of strangers with local folk. The emergence of states in Hausaland was apparently associated with the establishment of capital cities as centers of power. They were different from earlier settlements in that they were cosmopolitan, fortified, and each the seat of a king who was recognized as the superior power throughout the surrounding area.

Before 1804, Habe kings ruled over Hausaland; following 1804, the Fulani took over, and by mid-century the Hausa were stratified into three tiers: the hereditary ruling Fulani, the appointive ruling class dominated by Fulani, and the Habe commoners.

Hausa relations with others are considerable, because of their extensive involvement with trade and Islam. There is considerable exchange with the Kanuri to the east, the nomadic Tuareg, and southern Nigerians (Igbo, Yoruba); in their diaspora settlements, other ethnic groups that share their cultural orientation, such as the Wangara, the Zabarama, the Adar, the Nupe, are often lumped together with them as "Hausa."

main implement is the hoe. The Cattle Fulani provide the Hausa with meat, yogurt, and butter.

Most men also practice a second occupation; ascriptive and ranked, these include aristocratic officeholder, scholar, Islamic cleric (imam), artisan, trader, musician, and butcher. As good Muslims, the urban women are in seclusion (rural women much less so), and therefore dependent upon their husbands for their maintenance; they are economically active from behind the compound walls, however, primarily in order to finance their daughters' dowries. Their work, which includes sewing and selling prepared food and jewelry, is an offshoot of their domestic persona.

INDUSTRIAL ARTS. There are full-time specialists only where there is an assured market for craft products. Men's crafts include tanning, leatherworking, saddling, weaving, dying, woodworking, and smithing. Iron has been mined, smelted, and worked as far back as there are Hausa traditions. Blacksmiths have a guildlike organization, and many are hereditary.

TRADE. Trade is complicated and varied. Some traders deal in a particular market, as distinguished from those who trade in many markets over a long distance. This dual trade strategy, augmented by the contributions of the Cattle Fulani, enabled the Hausa to meet all of their requirements, even during the nineteenth century. The markets are traditional to Hausa society and carry social as well as economic significance; male friends and relatives meet there, and well-dressed marriageable young women pass through, to see and be seen. The Hausa differentiate rural from urban settlements in terms of the size and frequency of the markets.

There is also customary exchange that takes place outside of the market. Gift exchanges are practiced at life-cycle celebrations such as childbirth, naming, marriage, and death; other exchanges are framed by religion (alms, tithes, fixed festivals) and politics (expressing relations of patronage/clientage).

DIVISION OF LABOR. Hausa society traditionally observes several divisions of labor: in public administration, it is primarily men who may be appointed, although some women hold appointed positions in the palace. Class determines what sort of work one might do, and gender determines work roles. When women engage in income-producing activities, they may keep what they earn. Because of purdah, many women who trade are dependent upon children to act as their runners.

LAND TENURE. The rural householder farms with his sons' help; from the old farm, he allocates to them small plots, which he enlarges as they mature. New family fields are cleared from the bush.

Kinship

KIN GROUPS AND DESCENT. Although the domestic group is based on agnatic ties, and even as Hausa society is patriarchal, descent is basically bilateral; only the political aristocracy and urban intelligentsia observe strict patrilineality, everyone else practicing bilaterality.

KINSHIP TERMINOLOGY. Hausa kinship terminology cannot be classified according to standard anthropological categories because of the number of alternative usages. For example, a man's siblings and his parallel or cross cousins are called *'yanuwa* (children of my mother); cross cousins, however, are also referred to and addressed as *abokan wasa* (joking relations), and special terms distinguishing elder and younger brother and sister may also be applied to both parallel and cross cousins.

Marriage and Family

MARRIAGE. Adult Hausa society is essentially totally married. Ideal marriage is virilocal/patrilocal, and it is polygynous: a man is allowed up to four wives at a time. The term in Hausa for co-wife is *kishiya*, from the word for "jealousy," often but not always descriptive of co-wife relations. Once men begin to marry, they are rarely single despite divorce because most are polygynous; nearly 50 percent of the women are divorced at some point, but there is such pressure to be married and have children that they tend not to stay unmarried long. Important social distinctions identify women in terms of their marital status. By custom, girls marry at the age of 12 to 14. There is some disagreement in the literature regarding the respectful nature of singlehood. Divorce is a regular occurrence, not surprisingly, given the brittle and formal relationship between spouses. Both men and women have a right to divorce, but for men it is easier. After divorce, most weaned children are claimed by their father.

Marriage is marked by bride-price, given by the groom's family to the bride, and a dowry for the bride provided by her family. Marriage is classified according to the degree of wife seclusion and according to whether it is a kin or nonkin union. Bilateral cross-cousin marriage is preferred.

♦ **purdah**
Seclusion of women; mainly a Muslim custom in South Asia and Middle East.

♦ **bride-price**
The practice of a groom or his kin giving substantial property or wealth to the bride's kin before, at the time of, or after marriage.

DOMESTIC UNIT. The ideal household is the agnatically based *gandu* (family farm), formed by a man with his sons and their wives and children. After the senior male's death, the brothers may stay on together for a time. More frequently, each brother's household becomes a separate economic unit.

INHERITANCE. Consistent with Islamic practice, a woman can own and inherit in her own right, but her inheritance rights are subordinate to those of men. All of the wives married to a man at the time of his death are entitled, together with their children, to share one-quarter of his total estate if there are no agnatic descendants, or one-eighth of his estate if there are agnatic descendants. Women own property such as houses and land together with consanguines, even after marriage, and they inherit only half as much as their brothers.

Succession to leadership of the agnatic group and leadership of the compound is collateral. Farmland is inherited in the male line, the gandu being collectively owned by brothers.

SOCIALIZATION. Women observe a postpartum taboo on sexual intercourse for a year and a half to two years, during which time the child is breast-fed. Toddlers are weaned onto soft foods and then to the standard diet. An older sister carries the infant on her back when the mother is busy, which extends into a special attachment between an adult man and his elder sister.

From infancy, boys and girls are treated differently. Boys are preferred; as they age, they learn that they are superior to girls and consequently to distance themselves from them and identify with things masculine. It is imperative for boys to separate from their mothers. Girls are trained to self-identify in terms of their sex role: domestic (female) skills are taught to young women as they mature. They are admonished to be submissive and subordinate to males. As children, boys and girls are rigidly sex-stereotyped into appropriate behavior.

Sociopolitical Organization

SOCIAL ORGANIZATION. One of the most salient principles in Hausa society is the segregation of adults according to gender. Throughout Hausaland, seclusion of married women is normative, and the extradomestic impact of sexual segregation and stratification is that women are legal, political, and religious minors and the economic wards of men. Although women are central to kinship matters, they are excluded from extradomestic discussion and decision making. Both within the household and in the public domain, patriarchal authority is dominant and reinforced by spatial separation of the sexes.

The senior wife of the compound head, the *mai gida*, is the *uwar gida*. She may settle minor disputes among residents and give advice and aid to the younger women. Domestic authority rests with the male head of compound/household.

From childhood, males and females develop bond friendships with members of the same sex, a practice continued into adulthood and marked by reciprocal exchanges. Given their seclusion, women tend to formalize their bond ties more than men do. Formal relationships that emphasize differences in status (patron/client) are also established by women, as they are by men.

POLITICAL ORGANIZATION Organizational structure is hierarchic; the centralized kingdoms, known as emirates, are the primary groupings; districts are secondary and village areas tertiary.

The institutions of kinship, clientship, and office (and, in the past, slavery) in the emirates, have provided the fundamentals of Hausa government from the sixteenth century until the middle part of the twentieth century. Rank regulates relations between commoners and rulers.

"Traditional and modern government proceeds through a system of titled offices . . . , each of which is in theory a unique indissoluble legal corporation having definite rights, powers and duties, special relations to the throne and to certain other offices, special lands, farms, compounds, horses, praise songs, clients, and, formerly, slaves" (Smith 1965, 132). In most states, major offices are traditionally distributed among descent groups, so that rank and lineage intertwine. The traditional offices differed in rewards, power, and function, and were territorially based with attendant obligations and duties. Within communities, the various occupational groups distribute titles, which duplicate the ranks of the central political system.

Clientship links men of unequal status, position, and wealth. It is a relationship of mutual benefit, whereby the client gains advice in his affairs at the minimum and protection, food, and shelter at the maximum. The patron can call upon the client to serve as his retainer.

In applying his notion of government to Kano, the Fulani religious and political leader Usman dan Fodio, when he launched his successful jihad against the king of Gobir in 1804, he followed the basic premise of a theocracy within a legalistic

One of the most salient principles in Hausa society is the segregation of adults according to gender. Throughout Hausaland, seclusion of married women is normative.

framework; government, and its chief agent, the emir, were perceived as an instrument of Allah.

SOCIAL CONTROL. Legal affairs fall under the jurisdiction of the emir, and he is guided by Islamic law. The Quran, the word of Allah, and its *hadith*, the traditions of the Prophet Mohammed, along with the dictates of secular reasoning provide answers to legal questions. The Sharia, the canon law of Islam, is fundamentally a code of obligations, a guide to ethics. Sanctions of shame and ostracism compel conformity to Hausa and Islamic custom.

CONFLICT. When disputes arise, the Hausa may opt to go to court, submit to mediation, or leave it to Allah. The basic process involves deference to mediation by elders.

Religion and Expressive Culture

RELIGIOUS BELIEFS. About 90 percent of the Hausa are Muslims. "The traditional Hausa way of life and Islamic social values have been intermixed for such a long time that many of the basic tenets of Hausa society are Islamic" (Adamu 1978, 9). Islam has been carried throughout West Africa by Hausa traders.

Adherents are expected to observe the five pillars of Islam—profession of the faith, five daily prayers, alms giving, fasting at Ramadan, and at least one pilgrimage to Mecca (the hajj). Within Hausa society, there are sects (brotherhoods) of adherents; of these, the Tijaniya, Qadriya, and Ahmadiyya have been important. Wife seclusion is basic to the Hausa version of Islam, although it is believed that the institution is more a sign of status than of religious piety.

Even among some Muslims, as among the Maguzawa pagans, spirit cults persist. One, the Bori, has more female than male adepts; cultists are believed to be possessed by particular spirits within the Bori pantheon.

RELIGIOUS PRACTITIONERS. Although such personnel as imams and teachers (*mallamai*; sing. *mallam*) have no churchly functions or spiritual authority, they do tend to assume or accept some measure of spiritual authority in certain contexts.

CEREMONIES. Men are enjoined to attend Friday prayers at the mosque. Men and women celebrate the three main annual festivals of Ramadan, Id il Fitr, and Sallah. Life-cycle events—birth, puberty, marriage, death—are also marked.

ARTS. The arts are limited to those forms allowed by Islam; the Hausa use Islamic design in their architecture, pottery, cloth, leather, and weaving. Music is an integral part of Hausa life

and can be classified in terms of function and audience: for royalty, for dancing pleasure, and for professional guilds. Each category has its own instruments, which include drums as well as string and wind instruments. Poetry exists in an oral tradition, as practiced by the praise singers and the oral historians, and also in the written tradition of the learned.

MEDICINE. There is a tricultural system that consists of strong traditional roots set in the framework of a predominantly Islamic mode, now augmented by Western medicine. The Bori spirit-possession cult is relied upon for various kinds of curing, and this involves diagnosing the particular spirit giving the sick person trouble.

DEATH AND AFTERLIFE. Burial is in the Islamic manner. Upon death, the individual passes on into the realm of heaven (paradise) or hell, consistent with Islamic teaching.

Bibliography

Adamu, Mahdi (1978). *The Hausa Factor in West African History*. London: Oxford University Press.

Coles, Catherine, and Beverly Mack, eds. (1991). *Women in Twentieth Century Hausa Society*. Madison: University of Wisconsin Press.

Hill, Polly (1972). *Rural Hausa: A Village and a Setting*. Cambridge: Cambridge University Press.

Paden, John (1974). *Religion and Political Culture in Kano*. Berkeley and Los Angeles: University of California Press.

Smith, Mary F. (1981). *Baba of Karo*. New Haven: Yale University Press. Originally published in 1954.

Smith, M. G. (1965). "The Hausa of Northern Nigeria." In *Peoples of Africa*, edited by James L. Gibbs, Jr., 119–155. New York: Holt, Rinehart & Winston.

—DEBORAH PELLOW

IGBO

Ethonyms: Ala Igbo, Ani Igbo, Ibo, Ndi Igbo

Orientation

IDENTIFICATION. Igbo is the language spoken in Ala Igbo or Ani Igbo (Igboland) by the people who are collectively referred to as "Ndi Igbo"; their community is known as "Olu no Igbo" ("those in the lowlands and uplands"). Before European colonialism, the Igbo-speaking peoples, who shared similarities in culture, lived in localized communities and were not unified under a single cultural identity or political framework, although unifying processes were present via expansion, ritual subordination, intermarriage, trade, cultural exchange, migration, war, and conquest. Villages and village groups were generally identified by distinct names of their ancestral founders or by specific names such as Umuleri, Nri, Ogidi, Nnobi, Orlu, Ngwa, Ezza, and Ohaffia.

There are several theories concerning the etymology of the word "Igbo" (wrongly spelled "Ibo" by British colonialists). Eighteenth-century texts had the word as "Heebo" or "Eboe," which was thought to be a corruption of "Hebrew." "Igbo" is commonly presumed to mean "the people." The root -bo is judged to be of Sudanic origin; some scholars think that the word is derived from the verb gboo and therefore has connotations of "to protect," "to shelter," or "to prevent"—hence the notion of a protected people or a community of peace. According to other theorists, it may also be traced to the Igala, among whom onigbo is the word for "slave," oni meaning "people."

Igbo-speaking peoples can be divided into five geographically based subcultures: northern Igbo, southern Igbo, western Igbo, eastern Igbo, and northeastern Igbo. Each of these five can be further divided into subgroups based on specific locations and names. The northern or Onitsha Igbo are divided into the Nri-Awka of Onitsha and Awka; the Enugu of Nsukka, Udi, Awgu, and Okigwe; and those of the Onitsha town. The southern or Owerri Igbo are divided into the Isu-Ama of Okigwe, Orlu, and Owerri; the Oratta-Ikwerri of Owerri and Ahoada; the Ohuhu-Ngwa of Aba and Bende; and the Isu-Item of Bende and Okigwe. The western Igbo (Ndi Anioma, as they like to call themselves) are divided into the northern Ika of Ogwashi Uku and Agbor; the southern Ika or Kwale of Kwale; and the Riverrain of Ogwashi Uku, Onitsha, Owerri, and Ahoada. The eastern or Cross River Igbo are divided into the Ada (or Edda) of Afikpo, the Abam-Ohaffia of Bende and Okigwe, and the Aro of Aro. The northeastern Igbo include the Ogu Uku of Abakaliki and Afikpo.

LOCATION. Today Igbo-speaking individuals live all over Nigeria and in diverse countries of the world. As a people, however, the Igbo are located on both sides of the River Niger and occupy most of southeastern Nigeria. The area, measuring over 41,000 square kilometers, includes the old provinces of Onitsha, Owerri, East Rivers, Southeast Benin, West Ogoja, and Northeast Warri. In contemporary Nigerian history, the Igbo have claimed all these areas as the protec-

torate of the "Niger Districts." Thus began the process of wider unification and incorporation into wider political and administrative units. Presently, they constitute the entire Enugu State, Anambra State, Abia State, Imo State, and the Ahoada area of Rivers State; Igbo-speaking people west of the Niger are inhabitants of the Asaba, Ika, and Agbo areas of Delta State.

DEMOGRAPHY. In 1963 the Igbo numbered about 8.5 million and by 1993 had grown to more than 15 million (some even claim 30 million, although there has been no widely accepted census since 1963). They have one of the highest population densities in West Africa, ranging from 120 to more than 400 persons per square kilometer. Igbo subcultures are distributed in six ecological zones: the northern Igbo in the Scarplands, the northeastern Igbo in the Lower Niger, the eastern Igbo in the Midwest Lowlands, the western Igbo in the Niger Delta, the southeastern Igbo in the Palm Belt, and the southern Igbo in the Cross River Basin.

LINGUISTIC AFFILIATION. Igbo is classified in the Kwa Subgroup of the Niger-Congo Language Family, which is spoken in West Africa. It is though that between five and six thousand years ago, Igbo began to diverge from its linguistic related neighbors such as the Igala, Idoma, Edo, and Yoruba languages. There are many dialects, two of which have been widely recognized and are used in standard texts: Owerri Igbo and Onitsha Igbo. Of the two, Owerri Igbo appears to be the more extensively spoken.

History and Cultural Relations

Contemporary views in Igbo scholarship dismiss completely earlier claims of Jewish or Egyptian origin—that is, "the Hamitic hypothesis"—as "the oriental mirage." Instead, there are two current opinions as a result of evidence derived from several sources that take into account oral history, archaeology, linguistics, and art history. One suggests the Awka-Orlu uplands as the center of Igbo origin, from which dispersal took place. The second and more recent opinion suggests the region of the Niger-Benue confluence as the area of descent some five thousand years ago, and the plateau region, that is, the Nsukka-Okigwe Cuesta, as the area of Igbo settlement. This first area of settlement would include Nsukka-Okigwe and Awka-Orlu uplands. The southern Igbo would constitute areas of later southward migration.

Until about 1500, major economic, social, and political transformations led to continuous outward migrations from overpopulated and less fer-

Traditional Igbo social life is based on membership in kinship groups and parallel but complementary dual-sex associations, which are of great importance to the integration of society.

tile Igbo core areas to more fertile lands, particularly east of the lower Niger River. The Igbo had cultural relations with their various neighbors, the Igala, Ijaw (Ijo), Urhobo, Edo, and Yoruba. From 1434 to 1807, the Niger coast was a contact point between European and African traders. This was also the period of trade in slaves; this activity resulted in the development of many centralized states owing to greater economic accumulation and the development of more destructive weapons of war. The Portuguese came to Nigerian coastal towns between the fifteenth and sixteenth centuries; they were the first Europeans to make contact with the Igbo. The Dutch followed in the seventeenth century, and the British came in the eighteenth century. In the late nineteenth century, mission Christianity and colonialist interest worked together for the colonization of Igboland. The Church Missionary Society and the Catholic Mission opened their missions in Onitsha in 1857 and 1885, respectively.

Economy

SUBSISTENCE AND COMMERCIAL ACTIVITIES. Subsistence farming characterizes agriculture among traditional Igbo people. The chief agricultural products include yams, cassava, and taro. Other important subsidiary crops include cocoyams, plantains, maize, melons, okra, pumpkins, peppers, gourds, and beans. Palm products are the main cash crops. The principal exports include palm oil and, to a lesser extent, palm kernels. Trading, local crafts, and wage labor are also important in the Igbo economy. High literacy rates among the Igbo have helped them obtain jobs as civil servants and business entrepreneurs since Nigeria gained independence in 1960.

INDUSTRIAL ARTS. The Igbo blacksmiths of Awka are renowned for their ironsmithing. Men's wood carving and women's pottery and patterned woven cloth are of very high quality, and Igbo carpenters can be found all over Nigeria. The stylized character of Igbo masks consists of figures with beak noses, slit eyes, and thin lips.

TRADE. The Ikwo and Ezza in the Abakaliki Division of Ogoja produce a substantial surplus of yams for trade. Women dominate rural retail-market trade. Trading is a major social and economic function of women in traditional Igbo society. Women engage in all sorts of economic activities to make money to purchase the essentials they need. They make mats and pottery and weave cloth. Women do most of the petty trade, which is very active. The manufacture and trade of pottery are almost exclusively the domain of

women. Igbo also process palm oil and palm kernels, which they market with the surplus crops from their farm stock, and generally monopolize the sale of cooked foods. They mine and sell salt.

DIVISION OF LABOR. There is a sexual division of labor in the traditional setting. Men are mainly responsible for yam cultivation, and women for other crops. Usually, the men clear and prepare the land, plant their own yams, cut stakes and train the yam vines, build the yam barns, and tie the harvest. The women plant their own varieties of yam and "women's crops," which include cassava, cocoyams, pumpkins, and peppers. They also weed and harvest the yams from the farm. With regard to palm products, the men usually cut the palm fruit and tap and then sell the palm wine. They also sell palm oil, which the women prepare. In general, women reserve and sell the kernels.

LAND TENURE. Most farmland is controlled by kinship groups. The groups cooperatively cultivate farmland and make subsequent allocations according to seniority. To this end, rights over the use of land for food cultivation or for building a house depend primarily on agnatic descent, and secondarily on local residence. It is Igbo custom that a wife must be allocated a piece of land to cultivate for feeding her household.

Kinship

KIN GROUPS AND DESCENT. Igbo society places strong emphasis on lineage kinship systems, particularly the patrilineage, although some Igbo groups, such as the Ohaffia, have a matrilineal descent system, whereas groups like the Afipko Igbo have a double descent system. In all the Igbo groups, one's mother's people remain important throughout one's life.

KINSHIP TERMINOLOGY. The *umunna*, children of one father or a localized patrilineage, is made up of specific compound families, which consist of even more basic matricentric household units of each mother and siblings. The umunna is made up of both male and female cognates of an Igbo man's father's lineage. All blood-related kinship groups are bound in the morality or ethics of *umunne*, the ritualized spirit of a common mother. *Ndi-Umune*, or *ikwunne*, is the term used to describe the mother's agnates.

Marriage and Family

MARRIAGE. Marriage is not a matter for the man and woman alone; it concerns the close kin of both. Marriage arrangements are negotiated between the families of the prospective bride and

♦ **cassava**
A plant of the genus Manihot (also known as manihot, manioc, tapioca, and yuca), cultivated by aboriginal farmers for its nutritious starch roots.

♦ **agnatic descent (patrilineal descent)**
The practice of tracing kinship affiliation only through the male line.

groom. With regard to the paternity of the wife's children, they belong to the lineage of the husband. When a woman has children out of wedlock, however, they belong to her natal lineage, and not to that of the children's father. Igbo have also institutionalized marriage options permitting "female husbands" in woman-to-woman marriages, in special circumstances. Some daughters with a male status (i.e., "male daughters") do not even have to marry to procreate.

Although females are brought up looking forward to this dual role, it would be misleading to think that the major roles of women in Igbo society are as wife and mother, since Igbo women are prominent in public life as an organized force in both economics and politics. A significant part of a young girl's or a young man's childhood training is geared toward their future roles in the family and as useful and responsible citizens. Women are fully involved in matchmaking and usually participate directly or indirectly in the actual negotiations of marital arrangements for their sons or their daughters, in cooperation with the male members of the families concerned. Women have powerful and active behind-the-scene roles in seeking out the girls they would like their sons to marry. The approval of the mother is vital because the young bride is generally expected to live with her mother-in-law and to serve her for the first few months of marriage, until the new couple can set up an independent household and farmland.

DOMESTIC UNIT. Most Igbo lived in villages made up of dispersed compounds. A compound was typically a cluster of huts belonging to individual household units. The typical Igbo village consisted of loose clusters of homesteads scattered along cleared paths that radiated from a central meeting place. The village meeting place usually contained the shrines or temples and groves of the local earth goddess and also served as the market. Large communities often had two such units. Most local communities contained anywhere between 40 and 8,000 residents. Homesteads were generally comprised of the houses of a man, his wives, his children, and sometimes his patrilineal cousins. They were often surrounded by mud walls and were nearly always separated from neighboring homesteads by undergrowth or women's gardens. Northern Igbo women normally decorated the mud walls of their houses with artwork. In the south, houses were made of mud on a stick framework; usually either circular or rectangular, the houses were thatched with either palm leaves or grass and were floored with beaten mud. Co-wives had their own rooms,

kitchens, and storerooms. Young children and daughters usually stayed with their mothers, whereas the males lived in separate houses. Population pressure and European architecture has forced significant changes in these old settlement ideals, introducing (cement) brick houses lacking aesthetic appeal.

INHERITANCE. The bulk of inheritance allotments are granted to the eldest son, who, at the time of the inheritance, becomes responsible for the welfare of his younger siblings. If the eldest son is a minor at the time of his father's death, a paternal uncle will take charge of the property and provide for the deceased brother's family. There is also marriage by inheritance, or levirate—a widow may become the wife of her brother-in-law. In some localities, widows may become the wives of the deceased father's sons by another wife.

Sociopolitical Organization

SOCIAL ORGANIZATION. Traditional Igbo social life is based on membership in kinship groups and parallel but complementary dual-sex associations, which are of great importance to the integration of society. The associations take several forms, including age grades, men's societies, women's societies, and prestige-title societies such as the Nze or Ozo for men and the Omu, Ekwe, or Lolo for women. The interlocking nature of these groups prevents the concentration of authority in any one association. Age sets are informally established during childhood. Respect and recognition among the Igbo are accorded not only on the basis of age, but also through the acquisition of traditional titles. In Igbo society, an individual may progress through at least five levels of titles. One could liken the acquisition of titles to the acquisition of academic degrees. Titles are expensive to obtain, and each additional title costs more than the preceding one; they are, therefore, considered a sure means to upward mobility.

POLITICAL ORGANIZATION. The basic political unit among the Igbo is the village. Two types of political systems have been distinguished among the Igbo on both sides of the Niger River: the democratic village republic type, found among the Igbo living to the east of the Niger River, and the constitutional monarchy type, found among Igbo in Delta State and the riverine towns of Onitsha and Ossomali. Most of the villages or towns that have the latter type of political system have two ruling monarchs—one female and one male. The *obi* (male monarch) is theoretically the father of the whole community, and the *omu* (female monarch) is theoretically the mother of the

Although many Igbo people are now Christians, traditional Igbo religious practices still abound.

whole community; the duties of the latter, however, center mainly around the female side of the community.

Women engage in village politics (i.e., manage their affairs, separately from the men). They do this by establishing their own political organizations, which come under an overall village or town Women's Council under the leadership of seasoned matriarchs. It was this organizational system that enabled Igbo women and Ibibio women to wage an anticolonial struggle against the British in 1929 known as the Women's War (Ogu Umunwayi).

Both types of political systems are characterized by the smallness in size of the political units, the wide dispersal of political authority between the sexes, kinship groups, lineages, age sets, title societies, diviners, and other professional groups. Colonialism has had a detrimental effect on the social, political, and economic status of traditional Igbo women, resulting in a gradual loss of autonomy and power.

Religion and Expressive Culture

RELIGIOUS BELIEFS. Although many Igbo people are now Christians, traditional Igbo religious practices still abound. The traditional Igbo religion includes an uncontested general reverence for Ala or Ana, the earth goddess, and beliefs and rituals related to numerous other male and female deities, spirits, and ancestors, who protect their living descendants. Revelation of the will of certain deities is sought through oracles and divination. The claim that the Igbo acknowledge a creator God or Supreme Being, Chukwu or Chineka, is, however, contested. Some see it as historical within the context of centralized political formations, borrowings from Islam and Christianity, and the invention of sky (Igwe) gods. The primordial earth goddess and other deified spirits have shrines and temples of worship and affect the living in very real and direct ways, but there are none dedicated to Chukwu. Ala encapsulates both politics and religion in Igbo society by fusing together space, custom, and ethics (*omenala*); some refer to Ala as the constitutional deity of the Igbo.

The Igbo concept of personhood and the dialectic between individual choice/freedom and destiny or fate is embodied in the notion of *chi*, variously interpreted as spirit double, guardian angel, personal deity, personality soul, or divine nature. Igbo have varied accounts of myths of origin because there are many gods and goddesses. According to one Igbo worldview, Chukwu created the visible universe, *uwa*. The universe is divided into two levels: the natural level, uwa, or human world, and the spiritual level of spirits, which include Anyanwu, the sun; Igwe, the sky; Andala (or Ana), the earth; women's water spirits/goddesses, and forest spirits. Through taboos, the Igbo forge a mediatory category of relations with nature and certain animals such as pythons, crocodiles, tigers, tortoises, and fish.

RELIGIOUS PRACTITIONERS. There are two different kinds of priests: the hereditary lineage priests and priests who are chosen by particular deities for their service. Diviners and priests—those empowered with *ofo*, the symbol of authority, truth, and justice—interpret the wishes of the spirits, who bless and favor devotees as well as punish social offenders and those who unwittingly infringe their privileges, and placate the spirits with ceremonial sacrifices.

DEATH AND AFTERLIFE. The living, the dead, and the unborn form part of a continuum. Enshrined ancestors are those who lived their lives well and died in a socially acceptable manner (i.e., were given the proper burial rites). These ancestors live in one of the worlds of the dead that mirrors the world of the living. The living pay tribute to their ancestors by honoring them through sacrifices.

IGBO MASK

An Igbo mask. The stylized character of Igbo masks consists of figures with beak noses, slit eyes, and thin lips. Nigeria. (© Werner Forman/Corbis)

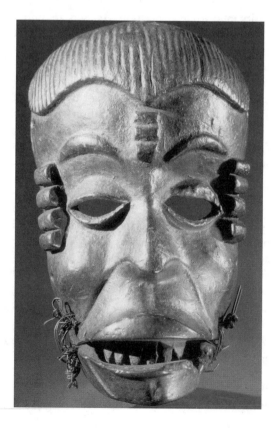

Bibliography

Achebe, Chinua (1958). *Things Fall Apart*. London: Heinemann.

Afigbo, A. E. (1971). *The Warrant Chiefs: Indirect Rule in Southern Nigeria, 1891–1928*. New York: Humanities Press.

Afigbo, A. E. (1981). *Ropes of Sand: Studies in Igbo History and Culture*. Ibadan and Oxford: Ibadan University Press and Oxford University Press.

Amadiume, Ifi (1987a). *Afrikan Matriarchal Foundations: The Igbo Case*. London: Karnak House.

Amadiume, Ifi (1987b). *Male Daughters, Female Husbands: Gender and Sex in an African Society*. London: Zed Books.

Anyanwu, U. D. and J. C. U. Aguwa, eds. (1993). *The Igbo and The Tradition of Politics*. Enugu: Fourth Dimension.

Arinze, F. A. (1970). *Sacrifice in Ibo Religion*. Ibadan: Ibadan University Press.

Basden, G. T. (1966). *Niger Ibos*. London: Frank Cass.

Cole, Herbert (1982). *Mbari: Art and Life among the Owerri Igbo*. Bloomington: Indiana University Press.

Cole, Herbert, and Chike Aniakor (1984). *Igbo Arts: Community and Cosmos*. Los Angeles: University of California, Museum of Cultural History.

Forde, D., and G. I. Jones (1962). *The Ibo and Ibibio-Speaking People of South-Eastern Nigeria: Ethnographic Survey of Africa*. London: Stone & Cox.

Green, M. M. (1947). *Ibo Village Affairs*. New York: Praeger.

Henderson, Richard N. (1972). *The King in Every Man*. New Haven: Yale University Press.

Hodder, B. W. (1969). *Markets in West Africa: Studies of Markets and Trade among the Yoruba and Ibo*. Ibadan: Ibadan University Press.

Horton, R. (1976). "Stateless Societies in the History of West Africa." In *History of West Africa*, edited by J. F. Ade Ajayi and Michael Crowder. Vol. 1, 72–113. London: Longman.

Isichei, Elizabeth (1976). *A History of the Igbo People*. New York: St. Martin's Press.

Isichei, Elizabeth (1978). *Igbo Worlds: An Anthology of Oral Histories and Historical Descriptions*. Philadelphia: Institute for the Study of Human Issues.

Leith-Ross, Sylvia (1939). *African Women: A Study of the Ibo of Nigeria*. London: Faber & Faber.

Metuh, E. I. (1981). *God and Man in African Religion: A Case Study of the Igbo of Nigeria*. London: Chapman.

Nsugbe, Philip (1974). *Ohaffia, A Matrilineal Ibo People*. Oxford: Clarendon Press.

Nzimiro, Ikenna (1972). *Studies in Ibo Political Systems*. Berkeley and Los Angeles: University of California Press.

Ohadike, D. C. (1994). *Anioma*. Athens: Ohio University Press.

Onwuejeogwu, M. A. (1981). *An Igbo Civilization: Nri Kingdom & Hegemony*. London: Ethiope Publishing.

Uchendu, V. C. (1965). *The Igbo of Southeast Nigeria*. New York: Holt, Rinehart & Winston.

—IFI AMADIUME

KANURI

Ethonyms: Beri-beri, Bornu, Yerwa

Orientation

The Kanuri are the dominant ethnic group of Borno Province in northeastern Nigeria. They number over 3 million in Nigeria, about 500,000 in Niger, 100,000 in Chad, and 60,000 in Cameroon. They are called "Beri-beri" by the Hausa, but they seldom use the term themselves. Bornu Emirate, the major division of the province and the Kanuri homeland, has a history as a political entity that stretches back at least 1,100 years. It has been a Muslim emirate since the eleventh century. Bornu Emirate is located between 11°00' and 13°00' N and 11°00' and 13°30' E. It is bordered on the north by the Republic of Niger, on the northeast by Chad, and on the east by Cameroon. Kanuri may be found in all of the major cities of northern Nigeria and in the neighboring sections of Chad and Niger. The southwestern section of the Republic of Niger is predominantly Kanuri.

The Kanuri language has the largest number of speakers of the Central Saharan Language Family, which has speakers from northern Nigeria to the Central Sudan. Kanuri is unrelated to Hausa, which is the most commonly spoken language in northern Nigeria. Most Kanuri can speak some Hausa.

The climate of the Kanuri region is typical sub-Saharan savanna. Rainfall averages 56 to 69 centimeters per year, nearly all of it falling from June to September. The harmattan, the wind off of the Sahara, blows cool from mid-December to mid-March, and then may heat up to 38° C. The temperature may remain that high for weeks at a time, until the rains start in June. Most of Borno is flat, except for the southwest, where the rugged Bauchi plateau rises steeply. The eastern part, on the shores of Lake Chad, is marshy. Because of the flatness of the terrain, the summer rains create swamps, and travel becomes impossible. The soil is sandy and is covered with scrub brush, scattered

The Kanuri diet consists of a vegetable soup poured over millet; the diet is universal, but the soup contents vary according to socioeconomic class.

thorny trees, and occasional baobabs. There are also large flat surfaces of hard green clay at the bottoms of ridges, which provide material for buildings and pottery.

History and Cultural Relations

Although there are semilegendary views about early Kanuri roots in Yemen, little is known of the earliest phases of Kanuri culture. Contemporary Kanuri are the descendants of the ruling Saifawa family of the Kanem Empire. As a result of civil war, this family left Kanem in the fourteenth century and, after nearly a century of internal strife, established a new empire southwest of Lake Chad. This empire was and is known as Bornu, although Borno is now its official name. The area to which the Saifawa moved was inhabited by various peoples about whom little is known. Now they are known collectively as the Sau—reputedly a race of giants. For a period of several centuries, the efforts of the Saifawa to consolidate their power and expand their kingdom's boundaries led to the incorporation of many distinctive groups within Kanuri society. This process has not ended. Intermarriage, commerce, politics, and other factors have combined to produce a people who are culturally heterogeneous.

The Kanuri have had a strong influence on surrounding peoples, which include the Budum of Lake Chad, the Mandara and Kotoko (or Mogori) who live southeast of the Kanuri, the Marghi of the Damboa district, the Babur in the hills south of the Kanuri, the Bolewa located southwest of the Kanuri, and the Bede of Gashua, within the Kanuri territory. All of these groups have acquired various aspects of Kanuri culture, mainly the Kanuri language and Islam. Many, including the Hausa, were at one time subjects of the Kanuri Empire.

Economy

The Kanuri are sedentary hoe agriculturists, although almost all of the men practice some other occupation as well. The economy is complex, with commerce, transportation, and construction constituting the other main elements of the private business sector. Government and public-service jobs provide another major source of employment today; manufacturing and industry are still relatively unimportant.

Millet is the staple food crop, supplemented by guinea corn (sorghum). Groundnuts (peanuts) are grown for sale. Hunting is of minor significance, but fish are an important resource to villages along the shores of Lake Chad and the Yobe

River. Horses are symbols of prestige. Most households use donkeys as draft animals. Sheep and goats are commonly kept. For beef, most Kanuri rely on the pastoral Shuwa and Fulbe (Fulani, Peul) cattle herders, with whom they exchange grain and craft work for the beef they need. In a few areas, the Kanuri keep large herds of cattle.

The Kanuri diet consists of large quantities of millet, served either as porridge or as dumplings. A vegetable soup, also containing meat, groundnut oil, salt, and other condiments—especially red peppers—is poured over the millet. The diet is universal, but the soup contents vary according to socioeconomic class. Cooked foods are sold in the markets, and a wide range of canned foods are available to city dwellers. Goats and sheep are slaughtered for religious ceremonies. Islamic food taboos are observed.

Kinship, Marriage, and Family

The basic socioeconomic unit is the virilocal extended family, each of which occupies a single walled compound. Although this type of unit is the ideal, neolocality is actually more common. In the case of traditional aristocracy and royalty, the households included slaves, concubines, and numerous retainers and adopted children in addition to the nuclear family. At this social level, the household is not strictly a kin group, although the relations are patterned on kin relations, and kin terms are used.

Social relations in Kanuri society are generally patterned upon those of the idealized family, the most common being the father-son/superior-subordinate relation. A man's prestige is based on the size of his household and the number of his patron-client relationships. His followers provide farm and household labor, support, and defense; in return, he provides food, clothing, bride-price, and possibly a bride, to each of them. Given that a man's status increases or diminishes with that of his household, regardless of his position within it, there is a premium on loyalty to the master.

For men, marriage usually occurs first at about age 20, and for women, at about age 14. The preferred marriage for a man is to a young virgin, 10 to 14 years of age. But this is a very expensive form of marriage, and most men cannot afford it as a first marriage, when they are themselves usually in their late teens to mid-twenties. The more common first marriage is to a divorcée, for whom the bride-wealth payments are much lower. The rate of divorce is extremely high, approaching 80 percent of all marriages. In case of divorce, children stay with the father. Marriage between cousins sometimes occurs, a form that also results in a reduced bride-price.

In accordance with Islamic law, polygyny is permitted. Concubinage is also practiced, although far less commonly than polygyny. Ideally, married Kanuri women are secluded. This practice is rare in rural areas, where the economic role of women is vital, but it is rather common in large cities, such as Maiduguri.

Although agnatic relations take precedence for legal matters and inheritance, kin relations are recognized through both lines. Kin terms make no distinctions for agnates above the parental generation or for cousins, who are all classed as brothers and sisters. Agnates generally live together in their own wards within a city, town, or village. Although there are no corporate lineages as such, in the eyes of the law these groups of neighboring agnates are treated as corporate units, in the sense that they are responsible for the actions of their members. People without agnates upon whom they can depend are social outcasts.

Sociopolitical Organization

The Kanuri live in settlements ranging in size from the large city of Maiduguri—which is the capital of Borno and has a population of 80,000—to tiny hamlets of three or four households. About two-thirds of the population live in villages of from 1,000 to 5,000 people. About one-quarter live in cities of more than 10,000. Hamlets are found about every 1.5 to 3 kilometers, and larger villages every 8 or 10 kilometers. Settlements are composed of walled compounds, made up of mud- or grass-mat-walled houses, with thatched conical roofs. Farms extend in a circle from the settlement, with scattered farms, pastures, and free land beyond.

Before European contact, Bornu was a feudal state, with royal lineages, a landholding aristocracy, peasants, and slaves. Today, in almost all cases, important political leaders are descendants of the aristocratic lineages, but popular elections have added commoners to their ranks. When the British took control at the beginning of the twentieth century, they abolished slavery and took over the top decision-making positions, but they left most of the social system intact. In small villages, there is little or no labor specialization, and differences in wealth are slight. In towns and cities, however, social stratification is pronounced, and differences in wealth may be great. New trading opportunities, Western education, and political power through election and financial support of others have all served to create a situation in which there are many commoners who have become as wealthy as the aristocrats.

Relationships between social unequals, in which each person has diffuse obligations to and expectations of the other, is still an integral part of Kanuri culture today. In the past, the principal contrast was between the nobility and royalty, on the one hand, and commoners, on the other. Today this contrast is being transformed to one between the modern, educated, bureaucratic elite and the traditional, illiterate peasantry. Occupations that are related to politics and religion have high status, whereas those that are associated with things thought to be dirty have low status. Quranic scholars and individuals with political positions have high status, but barbers, blacksmiths, well diggers, tanners, and butchers have very low status. In between are the great bulk of commoners who are farmers, artisans, and traders. Musicians (classed as beggars) and moneylenders (who, because they charge interest, are viewed as violators of Islamic law) hold the lowest status of all.

Another major dimension of social inequality in Borno is between men and women. In a pattern that reflects Islamic law as it is interpreted locally, women are legally and socially inferior to men, and they are considered a major source of instability. Accordingly, various civil and social rights are denied to women.

The Bornu Emirate is a political entity and is viewed as such by its inhabitants. Its present political structure is a result of the colonial era, but is still largely based on precolonial values, traditions, and ideology. The *shehu*, or king, is both the political and the religious leader of the emirate. There are twenty-one districts, each with a district head—usually a member of the aristocracy—and a district capital. The districts are composed of villages, each with its own headman (*lawan*), and of towns and cities, each of which may have more than one headman. Villages, towns, and cities are composed of wards and surrounding hamlets. Wards and hamlets are each run by a *bullama*, usually the founder or senior male.

Religion

The Kanuri have been Muslims since the eleventh century. Law, education, and social organization are the parts of their culture that have been most affected by Islam. The Malakite version of Islamic law is administered by an *alkali* (judge) who has been trained at the Kano Law School. Traditional education is in the Quran. Social organization

♦ **polygyny**
The marriage of one man to more than one woman at a time.

emphasizes the importance of the nuclear family and the supreme authority of the father.

Today Islam is the central ideological force in the daily lives of the Kanuri, affecting the thinking and behavior of the people in every way. The full ritual calendar of the Muslim year is followed, the fast is faithfully kept by all who are required to do so by traditional laws, and the other pillars of Islam are religiously followed by the great majority. Despite the strength of this orthodoxy, a few superimposed superstitious practices, such as the wearing of charms and amulets, are considered by most of the populace as acceptably Islamic. Of the various Sufi brotherhoods in Nigeria, the dominant one in Borno appears to be that of the Tijaniya.

Bibliography

Botting, Douglas (1961). *The Knights of Bornu*. London: Hodder & Stoughton.

Cohen, Ronald (1960). *The Structure of Kanuri Society*. Ann Arbor: University Microfilms.

Cohen, Ronald (1961). "The Success that Failed: An Experiment in Culture Change in Africa." *Anthropologica*, n.s. 3:21–36.

Cohen, Ronald (1967). *The Kanuri of Bornu*. New York: Holt, Rinehart & Winston.

Low, Victor N. (1972). *Three Nigerian Emirates: A Study in Oral History*. Evanston, Ill.: Northwestern University Press.

Murdock, George P. (1959). *Africa: Its People and Their Culture History*. New York: McGraw-Hill.

Peshkin, Alan (1970). "Education and Modernism in Bornu." *Comparative Education Review* 14: 283–300.

Peshkin, Alan (1972). *Kanuri Schoolchildren: Education and Social Mobilization in Nigeria*. New York: Holt, Rinehart & Winston.

Rosman, Abraham (1966). *Social Structure and Acculturation among the Kanuri of Northern Nigeria*. Ann Arbor: University Microfilms.

Tessler, Mark A., William M. O'Barr, and David H. Spain (1973). *Tradition and Identity in Changing Africa*. New York: Harper & Row.

KHOI

Ethonyms: Herders of southern Africa, Khoikhoi (Khoekhoe) Hottentots, Khoisan

Orientation

IDENTIFICATION. "Hottentot" was the collective name given to indigenous herders of southern Africa by early travelers from Europe.

As herders, they were distinguishable from both the hunter-gatherer "Bushmen" (or San) and from crop farmers (Bantu-speaking people). They had no collective name for themselves, but they identified strongly with various clan names, such as "Chochoqua," "Goringhaiqua," or "Gorachoqua." Twentieth-century scholars have tended to identify a number of ethnic divisions within the Khoi that are associated with geographically and socially distinct regions: "Cape Hottentots," "Eastern Cape Hottentots" (sometimes classified together as "Cape Khoikhoi"), "Korana" (!Kora), and "Naman" (Nama).

The term "Hottentot"—and especially its abbreviated version, "Hotnot"—have acquired derogatory connotations, and the preferred terms "Khoi" or "Khoikhoi" (meaning "the real people") are most commonly used in the literature today.

LOCATION. At the time that the first European settlers arrived in southern Africa (mid-seventeenth century), Khoi populations were located around the Cape of Good Hope and along and inland from the southwestern and western coasts—roughly south from 22° N and west from 25° E. This whole area is a winter-rainfall region, but, whereas the southwestern parts have an annual rainfall of up to 76 centimeters per year, much of the northern and inland areas are semi-desert with sparse and irregular rainfall (less than 13 centimeters per year). Archaeological evidence suggests that the Khoi had previously been more widely distributed (especially to the east), but had been displaced by the arrival of crop farmers (Bantu-speaking people) whose southward migration eventually ended around A.D. 500 on the boundary between the summer and winter rainfall regions (near present-day Port Elizabeth). European settlement at the Cape similarly resulted in the rapid displacement of Khoi populations, who were eventually forced into the most arid and remote areas. Today Khoi herders are found only in isolated reserve areas in South Africa and Namibia.

DEMOGRAPHY. Although some historians (e.g., Stow) have estimated the total Khoi population in the mid-seventeenth century at less than 50,000, it is unlikely that their number was less than 200,000. The main reason for this lack of agreement seems to be the different definitions of the population in question. For example, some estimates excluded population north of the Orange River, while others included the Einiqua (about whom very little is known). There is widespread agreement, however, that this population was decimated during the eighteenth century—by the smallpox epidemics, through intermarriage with other populations, and through incorporation into settler society. The 1805 Cape census recorded only 20,000 "Hottentots," but this figure included people of mixed descent and excluded significant populations that were not yet part of Cape Colony. Present population estimates are similarly hampered by the problem of definition: most descendants of the Khoi are wage laborers who have been incorporated into the broader category of "Coloured" and do not identify themselves as either "Khoi" or "Hottentot." If the term "Khoi" is used in the narrower sense, however, to refer only to those descendants of the indigenous herders who continue to practice a herding life-style on communal lands, the current population (in South Africa and Namibia) is well below 20,000.

LINGUISTIC AFFILIATION. The languages spoken by the Khoi and the San (Bushmen) were part of a broad family of Khoisan languages (clearly distinguishable from the Bantu languages spoken by the neighboring agricultural Nguni and Sotho). The Khoisan languages, well-known for the prevalence of a range of different clicks, can be subdivided into Khoikhoi (Hottentot) and San (Bushmen) languages. Whereas all Khoi herders spoke one of a number of mutually understandable Khoikhoi languages, some groups of San hunters also spoke Khoikhoi languages. Khoikhoi languages have largely been replaced by Afrikaans and are rapidly disappearing in South Africa today—very few young people, even in the reserve areas, retain more than a smattering of their traditional language. In Namibia, it is still the mother tongue of most of the few thousand remaining Khoi herders.

History and Cultural Relations

Khoi herders have lived in southwestern Africa for at least 2,000 years. Until recently, it was generally accepted that a distinct group of herder Khoi, originating in Central Africa, had migrated south with their herds of fat-tailed sheep, eventually displacing hunting populations in those areas where they chose to settle. Contemporary theories acknowledge that, given the close linguistic, cultural, and racial links between the Khoi and the San, the emergence of a herding life-style was more complex than this simple model would suggest.

Some San hunters were incorporated into Khoi populations, and some Khoi herders lost their stock and became hunters. It is also possible that some San populations acquired stock and thus adopted a herder life-style. Notwithstanding

such fluidity, there is much evidence that Khoi and San saw themselves as being different. In particular, the Khoi viewed people without stock as inferior and despised those hunters who stole their stock. A system of clientship developed whereby individual San (commonly referred to as "Sonqua") were adopted as servants by the pastoralists.

European settlers were initially interested in the Khoi as trading partners. To provide fresh supplies to ships rounding the Cape, Europeans obtained stock through barter. Khoi were very careful of their breeding stock and did not ordinarily kill cattle for food; tensions arose as they became increasingly reluctant to part with their animals. When settlers themselves began to farm, the resultant struggle over land increased tensions and led to open conflict. Gradually, the Khoi herders were displaced from the area around the Cape and forced to retreat to more remote and arid regions. While it is true that their numbers were decimated by smallpox epidemics, many were also incorporated into settler society as domestic and farm workers. At the same time, some settlers moved away from the Cape, intermarried with Khoi women, and adopted a life close to that of the Khoi pastoralists. Their descendants became known as "Basters" (bastards)—people of mixed descent—who learned to speak Dutch (later Afrikaans) and were educated in Christiantiy.

There was significant interaction between the remaining "pure" Khoi and the Dutch-speaking Basters; gradually, therefore, no clear division could be drawn between the two. In some instances, Khoi and Basters combined into single sociopolitical groupings.

By the turn of the twentieth century, little remained of the traditional pastoral life-style of the Khoi. In many areas, however, descendants of the Khoi had managed to retain rights to land by recognizing that missionaries could offer some protection from encroaching Dutch farmers. By 1900, numerous mission stations had been established, and these areas eventually became the reserves where seminomadic pastoralism is still practiced today.

Settlements

Unlike the San, who lived in very flexible and mobile bands generally numbering fewer than 50 persons, the basic village encampment (or *kraal*) of the precolonial Khoi was significantly larger, incorporating well over 100 persons (some vil-

The Khoisan languages are well-known for the prevalence of a range of different clicks.

♦ **pastoralism**
A type of subsistence economy based on the herding of domesticated grazing animals such as sheep or cattle.

See also

San-speaking Peoples

lages included several hundred). The basic housing structure was a round hut (*matjieshuis*) made of a frame of saplings that was covered with reed mats. Each village encampment consisted primarily of members of the same patrilineal clan.

Economy

SUBSISTENCE AND COMMERCIAL ACTIVITIES. Although subsistence activity was centered on the care of herds of sheep and cattle, hunting and the collection of wildplant foods were also important. In general, cattle were only slaughtered for ritual purposes, but their milk was an essential part of the diet. The Khoi used oxen to carry loads and to ride on. Fat-tailed sheep were slaughtered more regularly (their fat was highly prized), and their skins were used for clothing. Ewes were also milked.

A majority of the contemporary population in the reserves is still involved with herding (primarily of sheep and goats) on communal land. Today most of the produce is sold outside the reserves. Notwithstanding the significance of herding, wage labor outside the reserves is the major source of income.

INDUSTRIAL ARTS AND TRADE. The Khoi manufactured skins into clothing, bags, and blankets, and threaded reeds together to make sleeping mats and mats to cover their round houses. Mat houses provided very practical accommodation, especially in warmer climates. During warm days they offered a cool, relatively bright shelter, with the crevices between the reeds allowing air to circulate. During the rains, the reeds would swell as they absorbed water and therefore offer good protection against leaks. During the cold months, the inside of the house could be lined with skins to offer extra insulation against the elements. This structure also had the advantage that it could be dismantled and reerected every few months in response to the changing seasons or when grazing in the surrounding area became depleted.

The Khoi made pottery, some of which had distinctive pointed bases and handles, which could be tied to their oxen when moving, or to hut poles. They made spears with fire-hardened tips, but generally used iron tips, which they obtained from neighboring Bantu-speaking peoples or, more recently, from European ships and settlers.

DIVISION OF LABOR. Women milked the cows and ewes and collected plant foods; herding and hunting activities were the preserve of men. The construction of mat houses was a task shared by men and women: men cut and planted the

saplings and tied them together with leather thongs to form a frame, and women collected the reeds and manufactured the mats. With the introduction of modern dwelling structures, women have largely taken over the entire task of constructing traditional homes, and men have become responsible for the erection of modern (primarily corrugated-iron or brick) housing. Many contemporary households in the reserves have both modern and traditional structures—the latter being reserved for cooking activities (the domain of women).

LAND TENURE. In precolonial times, several clan-based villages were united into much larger units called tribes or hordes, which ranged in size from a few hundred to several thousand individuals. The most significant aspect of tribal integrity related to the various clans' unrestricted access to communal tribal land. Local clans could move around and utilize pasture, water resources, game, and wild fruit and vegetables within the tribal area (although individual clans tended to move in a regular pattern in a specific tract of tribal land). The relatively low population density prior to the arrival of Europeans meant that there was limited competition for any given piece of land, and the extent of tribal land was thus defined not so much in terms of exact boundaries as with reference to land around key water holes as well as areas with better pasture.

The communal character of land tenure has been retained in most of the contemporary reserves, and local populations have resisted government's attempts to create individual farms. Although specific plots of land are allocated to individual farmers in some of the reserves (where crop cultivation is possible), such plots are not privately owned and remain under the control of the local communities.

Kinship

KINSHIP GROUPS AND DESCENT. The exogamous patrilineal clan was the basic unit of social organization. Although tribal groupings were unstable and mobile, and were not composed exclusively of clan members, the Khoi kept detailed oral genealogies of the origins of various clans and of the relationship between them. This knowledge was very important, since precedence within tribes and clans was by primogeniture.

During most of the twentieth century, descent has been used as an important indication of status—higher status being associated with "White" blood. More recently, the opposite trend has been

♦ **primogeniture**
A rule of inheritance that gives the exclusive right of inheritance to the first-born son.

emerging: people are keen to emphasize their Khoi history.

KINSHIP TERMINOLOGY. Individuals were given both patrilineal clan names and "great names"—names inherited by a group of brothers from their mother, or of sisters from their father. In this way, men shared their name with their maternal grandfather, and women with their maternal grandmother. These names were closely associated with the pattern of institutionalized joking and avoidance relationships between kin.

Sociopolitical Organization

SOCIAL ORGANIZATION. Although precolonial village encampments generally included some members of other clans, as well as some dependents or servants (San or impoverished Khoi from other clans), patrilineal descent formed the basis of social organization.

POLITICAL ORGANIZATION. Each village recognized the authority of a headman, a hereditary position passed on to the eldest son of the founding ancestor and so forth for every generation. Headmen provided leadership regarding decision making within the village (e.g., determining when and where to move), as well as acting as mediator or judge in criminal or civil disputes. Although villages enjoyed a fair degree of autonomy, several villages were united to form a horde or tribe. As with clan-based villages, tribes had a kinship base. They were composed of a number of linked clans, with the seniority of one of the clans being recognized. (In one example, five of seven clans were descended from one of five brothers, with the remaining two being offshoots of these. The clan descended from the eldest brother was the senior clan.) The head of the senior clan was acknowledged as the chief of the tribe. The tribal chief controlled access to the tribal resources, but there was a clear recognition that neither the land, nor the resources left on it, could become the property of individuals (and this included the chief). Chiefs commanded a great deal of respect through their individual ability and effort (often accumulating very large herds), but they still remained dependent on the wishes of the tribal council, a group consisting of the headmen of all the other clans. Colonial governments succeeded in coopting many leaders (chiefs or headmen) by formally recognizing their position as "captains."

SOCIAL CONTROL. Criminal and civil disputes were handled by the chief and his council (or, in some cases, by the village headmen). More recently, however, such cases have been handled by the captain (i.e., a government appointee), by management boards in the various reserves, or by state courts.

CONFLICT. During precolonial times, relations between Khoi and San groups were often

MARRIAGE AND FAMILY

Marriage

Clans were exogamous, and men from one clan thus had to seek wives in another. Given the geographical proximity of related clans, it was possible for many men to find wives within the tribe; however, marriage between members of different tribes was also common. Marriage served as a powerful social mechanism to unite members of the tribe or to link different tribes together. This bond was reinforced by the custom that the bridegroom had to spend the first few months of marriage (often until the birth of the couple's first child) living at the village of his parents-in-law. (This practice has sometimes been referred to as bride-service). Thereafter, residence was patrilocal. Marriage usually involved the transfer of cattle from the groom's family to the bride's parents. Polygyny was permitted but not very common.

Inheritance

Individual clans or tribes controlled access to land and the resources on it, but there was a clear understanding that land could not become the property of individuals. By contrast, all stock were individually owned, and a wealthy stock owner was accorded high status. Wealthier stock owners almost invariably acquired their stock through inheritance. Customary inheritance patterns varied: in some tribes, the inheritance was shared among all the children; in others, only sons inherited; in yet others, the eldest son was the only heir.

Socialization

Parents were responsible for training their children in the basic subsistence skills, following the basic sexual division of labor. Very close relationships existed between grandparents and their daughters' children, and between children and their mother's brothers. Relationships between brothers and sisters and between a father's sister and her brother's children were respectful and formal.

Khoi

RELIGION AND EXPRESSIVE CULTURE

By the turn of the twentieth century, little remained of the traditional pastoral Khoi life-style; in many areas, however, their descendants managed to retain rights to land.

strained. Khoi accusations that San had stolen their livestock sometimes resulted in open warfare. The pressure on land associated with European settlement gave rise to warfare not only between Khoi and the Dutch farmers, but also between different Khoi tribes. It is generally assumed that Khoi political groupings were too small and weak to offer much resistance to the settlers (who had access to firearms and horses). The Khoi did offer significant resistance, however. Various tribes could and did unite against the common enemy, the most notable episode being the Khoikhoi War of Independence (1799–1803). Although ultimately unsuccessful, it showed that the Khoi were capable of mobilizing the support of many different tribal groupings (in this particular case, they also joined forces with Bantu-speaking Xhosa) and of presenting a united force.

Religion and Expressive Culture

RELIGIOUS BELIEFS. Khoi have been under missionary influence for a considerable length of time, and relatively little information regarding religious beliefs is available. A range of myths that have been recorded shed some light on pre-Christian beliefs. Special significance was attached to the moon (it has been claimed that the Khoi "worshiped" the moon) and to two central good beings, Tsụi-//goab (the deity) and Haiseb or Heitsi-eibib (the folk hero). The Khoi also believed in ghosts and witches, but not in the power of ancestors; however, there is some evidence that the spirits of the dead were involved in curing rituals.

RELIGIOUS PRACTITIONERS. Some individuals played a dominant role in healing or rainmaking rituals, but it would be incorrect to view them as specialist religious practitioners. There is some mention of magicians, but very little is known of the methods they employed.

CEREMONIES. The central theme of virtually all Khoi ritual was the idea of transformation or transition from one status to another. Most rituals marked the critical periods of change in a person's life—birth, puberty, adulthood, marriage, and death. In all of these rituals, the concept of *!nau* was central. !Nau was seen as a state of particular vulnerability and danger. The ceremonies all involved a period of seclusion associated with increased !nau. During these periods of social withdrawal, certain substances (notably water) were avoided, whereas others (such as fire or the *buchu* plant) were associated with protection. Of particular interest is the part played by livestock—not only in feasting associated with the rituals, but in the rituals themselves. In contrast with water, domestic stock seemed always to be associated with protection (e.g., feeding babies with the milk of cows or ewes, or the wearing of parts of a slaughtered animal, as in the case of female puberty rituals).

MEDICINE. Besides the healing rituals (often taking the form of trance-dancing), much use was made of the medicinal properties of various plants. All adult Khoi possessed a basic knowledge of plant usage, but certain individuals were seen to have developed higher levels of expertise. Some of this knowledge remains important today.

DEATH AND AFTERLIFE. Besides natural causation, death under exceptional circumstances was often attributed to the evil being //Gâuab, to ghosts, or to the violation of certain ritual avoidances. Burials took place as soon as possible after death. The Khoi did not have a well-developed conception of an afterlife, and funeral ceremonies were appropriately unelaborated.

Bibliography

Barnard, Allan (1992). *Hunters and Herders of Southern Africa: a Comparative Ethnography of the Khoisan Peoples.* Cambridge: Cambridge University Press.

Carstens, W. Peter (1966). *The Social Structure of a Cape Coloured Reserve.* Cape Town: Oxford University Press.

Elphick, Richard (1977). *Kraal and Castle: Khoikhoi and the Founding of White South Africa.* Johannesburg: Ravan Press.

Engelbrecht, J. A. (1936). *The Korana: An Account of Their Customs and Their History, with Texts.* Cape Town: Maskew Miller.

Hoernlé, A. Winifred (1913). *Richtersveld: The Land and its People.* Johannesburg: Council of Education, Witwatersrand.

Marais, J. S. (1968). *The Cape Coloured People: 1652–1937.* Johannesburg: Witwatersrand University Press.

Schapera, I. (1930). *The Khoisan Peoples of South Africa: Bushmen and Hottentots.* London: George Routledge & Sons.

Smith, Andrew B., ed. (1995). *Einigualand: Studies of the Orange River Frontier.* Cape Town: University of Cape Town Press.

Stow, George W. (1905). *The Native Races of South Africa: A History of the Intrusion of the Hottentots and Bantu into the Hunting Grounds of the Bushmen, the Aborigines of the Country.* London: Swan Sonnenschein.

Wilson, Monica, and Leonard Thompson, eds. (1969). *The Oxford History of South Africa*. Oxford: Clarendon Press.

—EMILE BOONZAIER

KIKUYU

Ethonyms: Gekoyo, Gigikuyu, Gikiyu

Orientation

The Kikuyu, a major ethnic group of Kenya, numbered about 4.4 million in 1987, accounting for about 20 percent of Kenya's population of 25 million. The Kikuyu refer to themselves as "Mugikuyu" (sing.) or "Agikuyu" (pl.). The Kikuyu language, which has three predominant dialects, is linguistically related to other Bantu-speaking groups in central Kenya, including the Kamba, Embu, Mbere, Tharaka, and Meru.

History and Cultural Relations

The Kikuyu share common historical roots with the Kamba, Embu, Mbere, Tharaka, and Meru. All of these groups date back to a prototype population known as the Thagicu. Migrating from the north, the Thagicu settled in the Mount Kenya region sometime between the twelfth and fourteenth centuries. As splinter groups formed, one of the groups migrated south and settled on the southwestern slopes of Kirinyaga (Mount Kenya). Archaeological evidence suggests that the people who settled there hunted game, herded sheep and goats, and worked with iron to make simple tools and weapons.

There were additional Bantu migrations from the northeast, followed by periods of settlement, intermarriage, and further splintering of the Thagicu in the fifteenth and sixteenth centuries. The Kikuyu trace their descent from one of the splinter groups that settled at the convergence of the Tana (Thagana) and Thika rivers. From the settlement at Ithanga, subgroups migrated in several directions, some north to Nyeri, others northeast to Kirinyaga, and some south to Murang'a over the next two centuries. Some migrated further south than Murang'a, toward Kiambu, in the eighteenth century, and came into contact with a hunting people they called the Aathi. They intermarried with the Aathi and acquired land from them in exchange for goats.

As different Kikuyu settled in different areas, a clan structure emerged. Each clan traced its descent back to a specific female ancestor. According to Kikuyu mythology, there were nine (or nine plus one) original clans. Two clans, the Acera and Agaciku, are thought to have formed through contact with neighboring Kamba. The largest clan is the Anjiru; its members were formerly renowned as great warriors and medicine men. The Aithaga clan was known for its ironworks, and its members were also thought to have the power to control rain. Other clans include the Ambui, Angari, Aithiegeni, Aithirandu, and Aithanga. According to Kikuyu myths, Kikuyu and Mumbi were the male and female progenitors of the nine clan ancestors.

Economy

The Kikuyu were originally hunter-gatherers, but they gradually adopted horticultural practices. The first crops grown by the Kikuyu were cocoyams, sweet potatoes, bananas, and millet. The cultivation of crops was traditionally segregated by gender. Men cultivated yams and bananas, whereas women grew sweet potatoes and millet. Women also gathered a variety of wild spinachlike greens, tubers, such as arrowroot (taro), and berries. Sugarcane was grown and honey collected from hives in the forest for the production of beer. Maize was introduced early in the nineteenth century and has become a major staple crop. When it is used for domestic consumption, it is usually grown by women, but when it is sold as a commodity, it is more often grown by men.

Many foods have been added to the traditional crops of the Kikuyu. European potatoes, cassava, and rice have been added to the cultivated crops, as well as legumes, which include dwarf beans, cowpeas, pigeon peas, kidney beans, lentils, and garden peas. Today Kikuyu also grow cabbage, tomatoes, onions, carrots, kale, and swiss chard. They season their foods with salt, chili peppers, or curry. A great variety of fruits is grown in the area. In addition to bananas, these include passion fruits, mangoes, papayas, loquats, plums, pineapples, oranges, and avocado pears. Women and children especially enjoy fruits, which they sell in local markets.

Although Kikuyu were formerly hunters, Kenyan game laws prohibit them from hunting today. Meat of wild game (antelope, impalas, bushbucks) and from herd animals (goats, sheep, and African cattle) was the prerogative of men. Pork and fish were prohibited, and game birds and other fowl were eaten only occasionally; eggs were not a part of the diet. Women rarely ate meat and then only when it was handed to them by their husbands. Today meat is served only on special occasions—to celebrate a ceremony, such as

Although Kikuyu were formerly hunters, Kenyan game laws prohibit them from hunting today.

♦ cassava
A plant of the genus Manihot *(also known as manihot, manioc, tapioca, and yuca), cultivated by aboriginal farmers for its nutritious starch roots.*

Irua (circumcision), or to welcome an important visitor. Cash crops, such as tea, coffee, and rice, were not grown until the 1940s, and, in some areas of Kenya, much later, but they have become an important part of the economy.

Kinship, Marriage, and Family

The nuclear family, which consists of a husband and wife, or wives, and children, is the basic social unit of Kikuyu society. As children grow up and form their own families, a subclan (*mbari*) is formed. Each mbari contains a hundred to a thousand families, and each member of an mbari knows from which ancestor, or which daughter of Kikuyu and Mumbi, they originate. The Kikuyu family is considered to be circular, rather than linear as in Western cultures. Each new generation replaces their grandparents, who are then free to become ancestors. The need to replace four grandparents is an important reason for having a minimum of four children, and more children gives honor to the parents' siblings.

Extended families living together form a homestead (*mucii*; pl. *micii*), and several micii together form into larger units, roughly equivalent to villages or hamlets.

Ideally, the mucii includes the paternal head of the family, his wives or wife, their unmarried children, often his married sons, and sometimes single male or female relatives. The Kikuyu are traditionally polygynous, but with the influence of Christianity and Western education, the trend has been toward monogamy. If a man chooses to marry more than one wife, theoretically he must provide *ruracio* (bride-wealth) and a separate house for each within the homestead.

Sociopolitical Organization

The concept of *mariika* (age sets; sing. *riika*) is of central importance within Kikuyu society. Mariika provide a way of keeping track of groups of people (both male and female) who were circumcised in different years. The circumcision group (generation) is given a name that identifies it with a particular event or characteristic of the group. Members of a particular riika, circumcised at the same time, were given a rank in the age groupings. The rank defined the behavior of individual members within a riika and their behavior toward members of other age groups, both younger and older. The older a riika became, the more respect it was given. Mariika function as agents of gender-segregated social control.

A strong bond of friendship forms between members of the same riika during Irua (circumcision ceremonies) and continues as a form of mutual social aid throughout their lives. Younger Kikuyu, however, are usually circumcised in hospitals today, and have a much weaker concept of mariika than earlier generations. In place of Irua, modern young Kikuyu find peer bonds in the school setting. Furthermore, the strict social segregation between the sexes seems to be breaking down as young people of both sexes come into contact with one another in primary classrooms, on the playground, and through church activities.

In the past, the transition from one life stage to another in Kikuyu society was marked by rites of passage. Each stage was given a special name for both males and females. Stages of life for the Kikuyu included newborn, infant, uncircumcised boy or girl, circumcised boy or girl, married, married with children, and old age.

Political authority in precolonial Kenya was decentralized. No kings, chiefs, or bureaucratic institutions existed. For the most part, political authority was collective at every level, and decisions were generally reached by the oldest males of kin groups or political units in council. Although the councils made some important decisions for the group as a whole, their primary role was judicial—the settlement of disputes between kin groups. The collective prestige of the elders in

council, as the representatives of tradition and the ancestors, gave their words weight and their decisions authority. Women also had a council, the function of which was to deal with domestic concerns, matters of the farms, and the discipline of female social and ritual life. Women were excluded from politics and were usually prevented from holding rights in land.

The imposition of foreign rule on the Kikuyu drastically altered their social and political structures and disrupted their traditional ways of life. European settlement policies had an even more drastic effect on the Kikuyu as land was virtually taken away from thousands of resident Kikuyu without adequate compensation.

Religion and Expressive Culture

In the traditional religion of the Kikuyu, the elders, or the older people within a clan, were considered to be the authority of God (Ngai). They used to offer to Ngai propitiatory sacrifices of animals, in chosen places that were considered sacred, usually near a fig tree or on the top of a hill or mountain. Even today there are large sacred trees where people sometimes gather for religious or political meetings or particular feasts. Mount Kenya, especially for the clans who live on its slopes, is considered the home of God.

The medicine man was a powerful person in traditional Kikuyu society. People would come to him to learn the future, to be healed, or to be freed from ill omens. The primary apparatus of the medicine man consisted of a series of gourds, the most important of which was the *mwano*, or divination gourd. It contained pebbles picked up from the river during his initiation, as well as small bones, marbles, small sticks, old coins, pieces of glass and any other object that might instill wonder in the eyes of his patients.

With European contact and the arrival of missionaries at the end of the nineteenth century, conversion of the Kikuyu to Christianity began with the establishment of missions throughout Kenya. Conversion was slow for the first thirty or forty years because of the missions' insistence that the Kikuyu give up a large part of their own cultures to become Christians. Although many Kikuyu became Christians, resistance to changing their customs and traditions to satisfy Western religious standards was very strong. Many Kikuyu took a stand over the issue of female circumcision. Missionaries insisted that the practice be stopped, and the Kikuyu were just as adamant that it was an integral part of their lives and culture. The issue eventually became tied to the fight for political independence and the establishment of Kikuyu independent schools.

The Kikuyu have no unique written language; therefore, much of the information on their traditional culture has been gleaned from their rich oral traditions. The oral literature of the Kikuyu consists, in part, of original poems, stories, fables, myths, riddles, and proverbs containing the principles of their philosophy, system of justice, and moral code. An example of Kikuyu music is the *Gicandi*, which is a very old poem of enigmas sung by pairs of minstrels in public markets, with the accompaniment of musical instruments made from gourds.

Bibliography

Clough, Marshall (1990). *Fighting Two Sides: Kenyan Chiefs and Politicians*. Niwot, Colo.: University Press of Colorado.

Davison, Jean (1989). *Voices From Mutira: Lives of Rural Gikuyu Women*. Boulder, Colo.: Lynne Rienner Publishers.

Hedlund, Hans G. B. (1992). *Coffee, Co-operatives and Culture: An Anthropological Study of a Coffee Co-operative in Kenya*. Nairobi: Oxford University Press.

Kenyatta, Jomo (1979). *Facing Mount Kenya: The Traditional Life of the Gikuyu*. London: Heinemann.

Muriuki, Godfrey (1985). *People Round Mount Kenya; Kikuyu*. 2nd ed. London: Evans Bros.

Presley, Cora Ann (1992). *Kikuyu Women, the Mau Mau Rebellion, and Social Change in Kenya*. Boulder, Colo.: Westview Press.

Prins, Adriaan Hendrik Johan (1970). *East African Age-Class Systems: An Inquiry into the Social Order of Galla, Kipsigis, and Kikuyu*. Westport, Conn.: Negro Universities Press.

KONGO

Ethonyms: Bembe, Kongo, Kunyi, Manianga, Mboma, Mpangu, Ndibu, Ntandu, (N)Sandi, Solongo, Vili, Yombe, all with or without the plural prefix "Ba." "MuKongo" or "Mwisi Kongo" refers to an individual. The people call their homeland "Kongo." The language is KiKongo (KiBembe, etc.)

Orientation

IDENTIFICATION. The BaKongo, numbering three to four million, live in west-central Africa, in a roughly triangular area extending from Pointe-Noire, Congo, in the north, to Luanda, Angola, in the south, and inland to Kinshasa, Zaire. The unitary character of the Kongo group and the identity of the various subgroups are artifacts of colonial rule and ethnography.

Kongo

Most Kongo men and many women work in urban areas for most of their working lives. The rural population consists disproportionately of children and elderly people.

LOCATION. Neither the internal nor the external boundaries of the Kongo group can be defined with any precision. The northern part of the Kongo territory is forested, whereas the southern is mainly savanna grasslands with forest galleries. The Zaire (Congo) River fights its way to the sea by a series of cataracts from Malebo Pool, between Kinshasa and Brazzaville, through the rugged Crystal Mountains, whose elevations range from 200 to 400 meters. The vegetation does not differ from that of other parts of tropical Africa; the soil is predominantly lateritic, varying in fertility from the forested bottomlands to the coarse grass and sparse orchard-bush of nearly barren hills. The long dry season lasts from mid-May to September, the short rainy season from October to mid-December, the short dry season from mid-December to February, and the long rainy season from February to mid-May. The average temperature in Brazzaville is 25° C. Because the upper waters of the Zaire extend north of the equator, the flow of the river is fairly constant; high water levels occur in mid-December, low water levels between 15 July and 15 August. Until about 1900, the fauna included lions, hippopotamuses, leopards, elephants, several species of antelope, chimpanzees, giant otters, buffalo, gorillas, and snakes of many kinds, poisonous and nonpoisonous. Animals frequently hunted included wild pigs, cane-cutter rodents, civet cats, bats, and field rats. Fish abound in the rivers. Virtually all large animals except crocodiles have now been killed off by hunters and, since 1970, as a consequence of increasingly rapid destruction of forest habitats. Natural resources include petroleum (in the Cabinda enclave, on the coast) and noncommercial amounts of gold, bauxite, and copper.

DEMOGRAPHY. In 1960 the Kongo population in Zaire (Belgian Congo) was approximately 951,000, not including the city of Kinshasa, whose population of 70,000 was about half Kongo. A similar number of BaKongo were located in Congo (formerly the French colony of Moyen Congo), with a corresponding concentration in Brazzaville. By 1970, the population of the major urban areas had tripled; it continued to grow thereafter, although, since 1990, there has been some return to rural areas, for economic and political reasons. Demographic information pertaining to the BaKongo of Angola is lacking; northern Angola was embroiled in civil war during most of the thirty years after 1960, when thousands of Kongo refugees moved temporarily to Zaire. In general, the BaKongo of Zaire are much better documented than those of either Angola or Congo.

LINGUISTIC AFFILIATION. KiKongo is a Western Bantu language whose several dialects constitute Group H of M. Guthrie's classification. A form of KiKingo, called KiLeta, functions as a lingua franca for many Kongo-related peoples further east. The younger generation of BaKongo in Congo and Zaire, especially in the cities, speak only Lingala, which is increasingly becoming the national language of Zaire.

History and Cultural Relations

The legendary origin of most of the Kongo peoples is Mbanza Kongo, the capital of the Kongo Kingdom, founded perhaps in the thirteenth century but long since reduced to a village—São Salvador—in northern Angola. In 1485 the Portuguese sailor Diego Cão brought the first Europeans to Kongo. Shortly afterward, most of the nobility converted to Christianity. During the sixteenth century, Kongo maintained diplomatic relations with Portugal and the Vatican.

The growth of the Atlantic slave trade in the seventeenth century favored the development of petty states on the coast, notably the kingdom of Loango in modern Cabinda. Increasing Portuguese intervention in Kongo politics, culminating in the defeat of the Kongo king in 1665, brought to an end the relatively centralized period of Kongo government, despite an effort in 1704, led by the prophet Beatrice Kimpa Vita, to revive the kingdom. By the eighteenth century, the typical Kongo settlement was a village of from 200 to 500 inhabitants. The BaKongo were thereafter increasingly integrated into the Atlantic commerce. Their main function was to act as porters and middlemen between the European stations on the coast and the Tio and BoBangi traders at Malebo Pool, where navigation downstream on the Zaire ceased to be possible. The population was stratified into free and slave. From the effective end of the slave trade in 1863 until the creation of the Free State in 1885, slaves were used mostly for agricultural production intended for the European settlements on the coast.

When the European powers divided Africa among themselves in 1885, the Zaire Basin, named the "Congo Free State," was allotted to Leopold II, king of the Belgians. His agents, led by Henry Morton Stanley, took over the interior, including the territory of the BaKongo, where they set up police posts, established trade routes of their own, and more or less forcibly recruited much of the male population as porters and laborers. Similarly violent processes of occupation in the neighboring French and Portuguese colonies, with associated epidemics of sleeping sickness, killed off as much as three-quarters of the population.

In 1908 international protest and fiscal mismanagement forced Leopold to hand over his colony to Belgium, as the Belgian Congo. Effective administration of all three colonial territories was in place by about 1920. Thereafter, the combined effect of state and, more especially, Catholic- and Protestant-mission education, helped to make the BaKongo one of the most Westernized and most influential groups in French Congo, Belgian Congo, and Angola, although they never formed a coherent international bloc. In 1960 Kongo politicians emerged as heads of newly independent states in both Kinshasa and Brazzaville, only to be replaced during subsequent civil strife.

Settlements

Besides the capital cities of Brazzaville (Congo) and Kinshasa (Zaire), the principal urban centers are the ports of Pointe-Noire, Matadi, and Boma. BaKongo predominate in the many towns of their home region but are also found in towns and cities throughout their respective countries. In their own rural areas, BaKongo live in scattered villages varying in population from a few dozen to a few hundred persons. Constructed of adobe, burned brick, or wattle and daub, with roofs of thatch or corrugated iron, the houses shelter single individuals or married couples. Usually, there are two rooms, the inner one reserved for sleeping and storage. A separate kitchen at the back of the house is the center of the female domain.

Kinship

KIN GROUPS AND DESCENT. In Zairean law, all traditional kinship groupings have been abolished and replaced by a modified type of European family. In practice, every MuKongo identifies himself by reference to his mother's clan and the village in which it is domiciled. Exogamous local sections of each matrilineal clan are divided into landowning houses, and these, in turn, into lineages functioning as inheritance groups.

KINSHIP TERMINOLOGY. BaKongo can trace their relationship to others through only one of several routes, depending on the situation. Two persons occupying the same status with respect to any third party are said to be "siblings," *mpangi*.

When reckoning is by clans, this principle generates a terminological pattern of the Crow type, in which mother's brother's daughter is equated with "child," *mwana*, and father's sister's daughter with "father," *se*. When reckoning is traced from individual to individual, the pattern becomes Hawaiian, meaning that all cousins are called "sibling." Most kinship terms apply to relatives of either sex.

Marriage and Family

MARRIAGE. Monogamy is required by law, but many men have long-standing, quasi-domestic relationships with more than one woman. Traditionally, marriage with a classificatory patrilateral cross cousin was preferred, but no one may marry into a closely related lineage. Couples are expected to go through traditional wedding formalities, but official recognition is extended only to legally registered marriages. A man is obliged to support his children, whether he married their mother or not, and there is no status of illegitimacy.

DOMESTIC UNIT. By tradition, a married woman and man have separate budgets, the wife being responsible for the provision of food (except meat) and the husband for clothes and other bought goods. Each disposes independently of any surplus, but in Zaire the government favors making women dependent on their husbands. Children are raised cooperatively by neighboring and relate women.

INHERITANCE. Increasingly, especially in urban areas, children inherit from their fathers.

Sociopolitical Organization

SOCIAL ORGANIZATION. Matrilineal descent groups of every level are led by a headman (*nkazi*) with at least nominal authority. Civil affairs, subject to traditional or "customary" regulation (*fu kia nsi*), are managed by committees consisting, as appropriate, of representatives of an individual's father's and mother's clans, along with patrifilial children and grandchildren. Such bilateral committees also represent the individual or his lineage at weddings, funerals, and lawsuits. In the conduct of such affairs, the skill of the orator (*nzonzi*), that is, the ability to influence the gathering by authoritative references to tradition and apt proverbs, is greatly esteemed. Official communications and conclusions are registered by exchanging symbolic gifts of food and money.

POLITICAL ORGANIZATION. Indigenous chieftainship no longer has any effective exis-

*The BaKongo have
a reputation as a
nonviolent people.*

tence, although, in Zaire, the government, for its own purposes, occasionally convenes people it regards as "customary chiefs." Local politics focuses on rights to land—that is, the rights of the "first occupant." Others who wish to use the land, acknowledging the primacy of the owning house, are supposed to be the descendants of slaves or refugees. Arguments about who is a slave and who is not depend on the recitation of tradition and pedigree, supported by the testimony of neighboring descent groups, and may drag on for generations. The basic unit of rural government in Zaire, roughly corresponding to a U.S. county, is the "collectivity," known in colonial times as the "sector" and, later, as the "commune." Its officers, elected or appointed as the policy of the day may decree, form the lowest rank of the national territorial bureaucracy, which is responsible for local taxation, road maintenance, and public order. The Kongo area in northern Angola has been ravaged by civil war for decades.

SOCIAL CONTROL. Elders are believed to exercise a kind of witchcraft on behalf of their dependents, but also to use it against them should they feel that their wishes have been ignored.

They may also be accused of misusing this power. Witchcraft capacity (*kundu*) is said to be acquired from other witches for a fee, ultimately requiring the sacrifice of a relative to be "eaten" by the witch coven.

CONFLICT. The BaKongo have a reputation as a nonviolent people. Physical violence is, in fact, rare among them, although they think of themselves as under constant attack by hostile relatives and neighbors, "witches" exercising occult powers. Appropriate committees of elders mediate disputes, and diviners may be consulted in serious cases; often the diviner is a "prophet" (*ngunza*) of a Christian denomination.

Religion and Expressive Culture

The BaKongo are Christians, mostly Catholic, but with a strong Protestant minority in all three countries, affiliated with British, U.S., and Swedish evangelical missions. Church-related schools and hospitals provide the best available education and medical care. Between 10 and 15 percent of the population belong to local Pentecostal churches, most of which trace their origin to the celebrated Kongo prophet Simon Kim-

ECONOMY

Subsistence and Commercial Activities

Most men and many women work, or seek work, in urban areas for most of their working lives. The rural population consists disproportionately of children and elderly people. In urban areas, wages are rarely sufficient to support even a single individual; therefore, people depend on innumerable petty occupations, legal and illegal, to make ends meet. In rural areas, families export as much food to town as they can, earning cash with which to pay taxes and school fees and to buy hardware, clothes, and small luxuries. Domestic animals include goats, sheep, pigs, and poultry; commercial cattle ranches supply meat to the towns. The BaKongo grow manioc, several kinds of yam, maize, peanuts, and various pulses, as well as bananas, avocados, citrus fruits, and palm nuts. A major handicap to the rural economy is the expense and unreliability of transportation. After 1985, the national

economy virtually disintegrated, leaving most BaKongo, urban and rural, in dire straits.

Industrial Arts

In rural areas, some men weave baskets and mats, and a few continue the traditional techniques of ironworking; a few women make pots.

Trade

Villages within reach of a truck route may hold a market on Saturdays. Unlicensed traders bring manufactured goods from town for sale or barter, and may make cash advances to rural producers. In town, most women supplement their incomes by buying goods in small quantities and selling still smaller amounts, but a certain number have become successful wholesalers and importers.

Division of Labor

Although both women and men work for wages when they can, men predominate in the better-paying and more prestigious occupations. In rural areas, men cultivate forest crops, including fruit trees, whereas savanna crops are appropriate to women. Men hunt; women fish and catch small rodents.

Land Tenure

In principle, in Zaire all land belongs to the state, from which commercial developers may obtain use rights. In practice, in rural areas unattractive to capitalists, traditional rules of land tenure prevail. Land is owned by matrilineal descent groups called "houses" and is available for use to the members of the house, to in-marrying women, and to the children and grandchildren of male members. Fruit trees, also inherited matrilineally, are owned separately from the land on which they stand.

bangu, who preached and healed the sick for a few months in 1921 before being imprisoned for life by the Belgian authorities. His son Joseph Diangienda (deceased) founded and led the now international Church of Jesus Christ on the Earth by the Prophet Simon Kimbangu. Kimbanguist-related movements have included Khakism in Congo in the 1930s and Tokoism in Angola in the 1950s.

ARTS. Indigenous arts, including sculpture and music, have been almost entirely suppressed by European influence. The traditional pentatonic scale can still be heard in the songs of women, especially as sung at funerals and in connection with the cult of twins. A variety of percussion instruments and idiophones (drums, silt gongs, clapperless bells, rattles) are employed at parties and religious services. In Kinshasa, the BaKongo contribute substantially to Zaire's internationally famous popular dance music.

MEDICINE. BaKongo of all walks of life commonly consult healers and magical experts (*nganga*) to deal with not only illnesses but also afflictions such as marital disputes, unemployment, traffic accidents, and theft. Such experts, concentrated in the towns, include non-BaKongo. A distinction is made between afflictions sent by God, which are "natural," and those in which an element of witchcraft is involved. Sufferers and their families commonly essay a series of treatments for the same problem, visiting both the diviner and the hospital.

DEATH AND AFTERLIFE. Funerals are important occasions of social gathering and family expenditure. Ideally, the bodies of the dead should be taken back to their natal villages if death occurs in town. Cemeteries are considered to be dangerous places, not to be visited casually. The land of the dead is thought of as situated on the other side of a body of water, sometimes identified with the Atlantic. The life of the dead continues that of the living in another place but inverts it, in such a way that to the dead, who become white, nighttime is daylight. All exceptional powers among the living are thought to be obtained from the dead, either legitimately, as in the case of chiefs and elders, or illegitimately, in the case of witches. In modern belief, benevolent powers from the land of the dead tend to be consolidated under the name "Holy Spirit," and evil powers as "Satan."

Bibliography

Bockie, Simon (1993). *Death and the Invisible Powers: The World of Kongo Belief*. Bloomington: Indiana University Press.

Dupré, Georges (1985). *Naissances d'une société: Historique et histoire chez les Beeme du Congo*. Paris: OSTROM.

Janzen, John M. (1978). *The Quest for Therapy in Lower Zaire*. Berkeley and Los Angeles: University of California Press.

MacGaffey, Wyatt (1970). *Custom and Government in the Lower Congo*. Berkeley and Los Angeles: University of California Press.

MacGaffey, Wyatt (1986). *Religion and Society in Central Africa*. Chicago: University of Chicago Press.

Thornton, John K. (1983). *The Kingdom of Kongo*. Madison: University of Wisconsin Press.

—WYATT MACGAFFEY

LOZI

Ethonyms: Barotse, Barozi, Barutse, Kololo, Marotse, Marutse, Rotse, Rozi, Rutse, Silozi, Tozui

Orientation

IDENTIFICATION. Concentrated around the Zambezi River plain lying at 14°30′ to 16°00′ S by 23°00′ E, the Lozi consist of a number of interrelated ethnic groups located along the Zambezi River in Barotse Province of western Zambia. As used here, the term "Lozi" refers both to the Lozi proper and to those groups that have become subject to and assimilated into the Lozi proper. These groups include the Kwanda, Makoma (Bamakoma), Mbowe (Mamboe), Mishulundu, Muenyi (Mwenyi), Mwanga, Ndundulu, Nygengo, Shanjo, and Simaa. In addition to being members of the Lozi-dominated Barotse Kingdom, these peoples share similar customs, speak the Lozi language (Kololo), and intermarry. The Barotse Kingdom incorporated a number of other ethnic groups, such as the Tonga, Lukolwe, and Subia, but these groups have remained somewhat distinct in language and customs.

DEMOGRAPHY. Population data for the Lozi are poor, based mainly on estimates, and do not lend themselves to an assessment of demographic trends. Figures for the whole of Barotse Province (including non-Lozi) place the population at 295,741 in 1938 and 361,905 in 1963. The 1938 estimates suggest figures of about 67,000 for the Lozi ethnic group itself and 105,000 for the Luyana group (the Lozi and related groups that consider themselves to have common origins). If assimilated peoples are included, the Lozi population in 1938 reached over 160,000. More recent

The Lozi consist of a number of interrelated ethnic groups located along the Zambezi River in Barotse Province of western Zambia.

estimates place the Lozi at 380,800 in Zambia (1986); 8,070 in Zimbabwe (1969), and 50,000 in Mozambique (1988).

LINGUISTIC AFFILIATION. Lozi (Kololo) is the common language of Barotse Province, although many inhabitants speak other Bantu languages as well. Lozi has been classified as a Bantu language of the Benue-Congo Family, within the larger Niger-Congo Group. The Lozi language derives largely from the Sotho dialect spoken by the Kololo, who conquered the Lozi, but it exhibits some modifications, especially in phonetics and vocabulary.

History and Cultural Relations

The history of the Barotse Kingdom begins with the southward movement of the Luyi people sometime around 1600. Luyi history is characterized by a series of expansionary conquests and the absorption of numerous other peoples under their rule. Luyi domination was temporarily interrupted when they were conquered by the Kololo, a group of invaders from the south, who ruled the kingdom from 1838 to 1864. In 1864 one of the Luyi (now known as Lozi) princes reestablished his group's dominance by conquering the Kololo. By then, however, British and Portuguese interests had begun to penetrate the area. The first treaties between the British and the Lozi, signed in 1890 and 1900, placed the Lozi under the authority of the British South Africa Company, but allowed them considerable autonomy in self-government. During the twentieth century, there were a series of changes in the larger political institutions to which the Lozi were subordinate. From 1924 to the 1950s, they were a part of Northern Rhodesia, under the rule of the British Colonial Office. Subsequently, they were incorporated into the Federation of Rhodesia and Nyasaland, and in 1964 Barotse Province became part of the newly proclaimed Republic of Zambia. Each of these political developments brought changes to the sociopolitical organization of the Lozi; the indigenous political organization increasingly lost power and functions, and the territorial extent of Lozi domination was constricted.

Settlements

The Lozi occupy small, compact villages, often surrounded by a fence or palisade and usually arranged with a cattle corral or open plaza in the center. Although village sites persist over time, there is a great deal of flux in village population. Flooding of the Zambezi River necessitates aban-donment of villages in the flood plains during part of the year. In some cases, all or most of a village's population will move together to their lands on higher sites. Sometimes, however, the entire village will disperse, with its members joining kin from other villages. Besides this annual flux, there is a continual flow of people from one village to another for various reasons. The prevailing house type is that of a round hut with a low cylindrical wall of rush mats or of wattle and daub and a conical thatched roof.

Economy

SUBSISTENCE AND COMMERCIAL ACTIVITIES. In a habitat characterized by great seasonal and ecological variation, it is not surprising that the Lozi subsistence economy is both mixed and complex. Lozi agriculture produces such staples as bulrush millet, cassava, sorghum, and maize, plus a number of lesser crops, including groundnuts, sweet potatoes, beans, and melons. Agricultural crops, methods, and intensity vary with the location of the plot, the type of soil, the amount of moisture, and the population's needs. Most cultivation is done with hoes, the plow being a relatively recent, and not always practical, introduction. Fallowing, manuring, crop rotation, and construction of drainage ditches are known to the Lozi and applied where deemed necessary. Most Lozi also keep domestic animals—cattle in particular, but also poultry, goats, and sheep. Hunting, collecting, and fishing are all important adjuncts to the subsistence economy, and the Lozi use a variety of technical equipment in these activities.

INDUSTRIAL ARTS. The Lozi are skilled ironworkers. Blacksmiths smelt the iron ore obtained from stream and river beds and from swamp soils to produce axe, hoe, and mattock heads, snuff spoons, crocodile hooks, knife blades, dagger blades, iron ankle-rings, hammers, and other items. A skilled and experienced blacksmith will often embellish his work with punched ornamentations or bosses. Many utilitarian pots are vase shaped and without handles; some of these are decorated around the neck with patterns of a lighter or darker color, others are highly polished to give the appearance of glaze. Large urn-shaped maize bins are made of unbaked clay and also have clay lids. On the front of these vessels, close to the bottom, is a semicircular opening protected by an interior slide, which may be lowered or raised by horizontal handles.

The average Lozi can carve a knobkerrie or a handle for an axe or a hoe; the Lozi also produce excellent dugout canoes. Many of the wooden artifacts used by the Lozi, such as stools, bowls, and dishes, are probably obtained in trade from neighboring tribes.

TRADE. Traditionally, economic exchange was carried on through barter and redistribution by the king, and trade between the Lozi and surrounding bush tribes formed a very important part of the economy. Fish and cattle, held in abundance by the Lozi, were bartered for bulrush millet; cassava meal; iron; many types of woods, bark, and grasses; and various tribal specialties of the bush people. Trade between the Lozi and the outside world began to develop in the nineteenth century, particularly with Arab and European traders. Although Loziland had few profitable exports, owing to its remoteness from the outside world, the Lozi did have ivory, beeswax, and slaves, which were exchanged for luxury items of the industrialized world. As the economic balance changed during World War II, cattle and dried fish began to be exported to centers of industry in the Rhodesias (now Zambia and Zimbabwe). Today the Lozi are part of a full-fledged cash economy with market mechanisms.

DIVISION OF LABOR. The division of labor in subsistence pursuits largely follows sex lines. Men are responsible for livestock, hunting, most of the fishing, and the more arduous agricultural tasks; women do most of the work in agriculture and collecting, a little fishing, and most of the routine domestic chores. Occupational specialization was limited in the past, but has become increasingly important. Migration for wage labor opportunities has become a major means of support for the Lozi.

LAND TENURE. In traditional Lozi society, all land and its products belonged to the king, and the king was obligated to provide his subjects with land and protection. In addition, every subject had the right to fish in public waters, hunt on public lands, and to use the natural raw materials of the land (e.g., clay, iron ore, grasses, reeds, trees). In return for the use of the land and its products, the king had the right to claim the allegiance of everyone living on his land, to demand tribute from their produce, to control the building of villages, and to pass laws affecting land tenure and use. In addition, the king retained direct control over unallocated land, had residuary rights to land for which an heir could not be found, and potentially had the right to give unused land to landless people or to use it for his own purposes or for public works. Land allotted by the king to villages was held in the name of the village headman, who, in turn, distributed parcels of land to his fellow villagers.

When an individual is given land from the king, he doesn't really own it. He has ownership of, or access to, that land only as long as he occupies his position within the village. Valued property, such as garden plots and fishing sites, were attached to particular villages and, specifically, to certain individuals or families within those villages. If a man leaves a village, he loses his rights to all land within that village. Once land has been acquired by right of blood or adoption, a family member (male) has the right to use it and to transmit it to his own heirs, and this right is protected by the courts, even against the wishes of the headman.

Kinship, Marriage, and Family

KINSHIP. The Lozi possess no unilinear kin groups. Despite a slight patrilineal bias, kinship is reckoned bilaterally, with relations traced as widely as possible through both consanguineal and affinal ties. They have eight noncorporate name groups called *mishiku* (sing. *mushiku*), and a man can claim membership in any or all of them, provided that he is a direct descendant in any line of a person who was a member.

MARRIAGE. Marriages are legitimated by the payment of a small bride-price. The practice of bride-service has fallen out of use, and postmarital residence is usually in the community of the groom. Polygyny is common, but the Lozi do not practice polyandry. Co-wives are accorded relatively equal status, although they are ranked according to order of marriage. The senior wife has a few privileges, such as first consideration in the distribution of food produced by the husband, but she has no authority over her co-wives. Neither levirate nor sororate are practiced. Divorce rates are high, and an individual Lozi may have had several partners during his or her lifetime. Marriages between close relatives, extending to third cousins, are prohibited; some cousin marriages occur despite this prohibition, but with the proviso that they may not be dissolved by divorce.

DOMESTIC UNIT. Residence patterns in marriage are loosely structured. Formerly, initial residence was matrilocal, whereas permanent residence later on was usually patrilocal. However, a man could take up residence in the village of any grandparent, and possibly even in the wife's fa-

In traditional Lozi society, all land and its products belonged to the king, who was obligated to provide his subjects with land and protection

ther's village, if there were no available locations in his father's village. Incidences of avunculocal residence have also been reported for the Lozi.

The nuclear family constitutes the basic economic unit of Lozi society. In polygynous marriages, each wife has a separate dwelling and her own gardens and animals to tend. She has the rights of disposition of her own produce and receives a share of the husband's produce. Cooperation in production and consumption between co-wives is highly variable. The traditional ideal is that each wife produces only for her husband and her own children, but it appears that there has been an increased tendency away from this ideal of separateness. In the past it was common for one wife to prepare food for the whole polygynous unit.

Sociopolitical Organization

During the days of the Lozi Kingdom, there was no higher territorially based organization than the village, except for the kingdom as a whole. Beginning with British rule, however, territorial organization was introduced, with villages organized into districts, districts organized into Barotse Province, and the province, in turn, forming a part of a larger political unit or state. In contrast, the Lozi Kingdom was hierarchically organized into a system of nonterritorial political sectors. Members of a sector owed allegiance to the sector head, a man who held a senior title in the Lozi court. These sectors were dispersed throughout the kingdom and served as judicial, military, and administrative units.

The Lozi Kingdom was highly stratified socially. At the top was the royalty (*linabi* and *bana bamulena*), composed of all those who could trace their descent from a king bilaterally within four to five generations. Husbands of princesses and commoners related to royalty were also of high status. Below them were the ordinary commoners. Slaves and serfs formed the lowest strata. (The institutions of serfdom and slavery were abolished in 1906.) The king was the ultimate authority. In earlier times, a chief princess held almost equivalent power over the southern portion of the kingdom, but British rule eroded her powers. In addition, the Lozi courts had a number of stewards, councilors, and members of royalty, all of whom participated in decision making. The most important office next to that of the king was that of *ngambela*, chief councilor, sometimes referred to as the "imperial chancellor," a commoner who represented the commoners' interests in the court.

Allocation of power within the Lozi power structure was highly complex and dichotomized. Commoner interests were balanced against royal interests from the top down.

The prerogatives and functions of the king and his courts have undergone steady erosion since the beginning of British colonial rule. As part of a larger political unit, the king was no longer the ultimate power. Power in judicial matters was first limited to minor legal cases and later placed completely within the Zambian judicial system. Similarly, the right to collect tribute was taken from the king. By 1965, most of the governance of the Lozi was through Zambian national agencies, and the right to distribute land rights was virtually the only power that the king could still exercise.

Sanctions maintaining relationships among the Lozi are general and diffuse; breaches of their rules lead to far more serious consequences than a lawsuit in court. Penalties applied to an erring kinsman may range not only from loss of rights to cattle and land, but also the loss of support from fellow kinsmen in various economic endeavors. Conscience and sentiments are major factors in inducing conformity and in making redress for wrongs. Generally, the settlement of everyday problems and the administration of justice is handled at the village level. Should the verdict not satisfy the parties involved, the case is passed along to the next level in a hierarchial court system, until satisfaction is obtained.

Historically, warfare was very common among the Lozi. Lozi kings fought not so much to enrich themselves, although they obviously increased their power and prestige through successful military operations, but to obtain land and cattle, to add to their subject population, and to extend the area of tribute-exchange in which the conquered shared. At the height of their power, the Lozi ruled over some twenty-five tribes of from 300,000 to 400,000 people spread over an area of some 200,000 square kilometers. After British rule was established in 1890, the Lozi domain was restricted to Barotse Province of Rhodesia (later, Zambia). In traditional society, rebellion against the authority of the king was common. Often contenders for power were the king's councilor or groups of councilors, who had enlisted a prince of the royal family on their behalf. When a group of councilors mutinied against a king, because of the king's policies or because he favored another group of councilors, they attacked neither the kingship itself nor the rights of the royal family to it. Each party put forward its royal candidate for the throne and fought in his name. Clearly, com-

♦ **avunculocal
residence**
*The practice of a newly
married couple residing in
the community or household
of the husband's mother's
brother.*

moners could only seek power by serving their own royal candidate for the kingship.

Religion and Expressive Culture

RELIGIOUS BELIEFS. The Lozi are primarily monotheistic, but they retain a number of beliefs about spirits and other supernatural beings. Elaborate rituals and offerings are focused on the burial sites of former kings and chief princesses. Priests mediate between the Lozi and the spirits of their former rulers. There is a different set of beliefs and practices concerning commoner ancestors, and rituals concerning these spirits takes place on an individual level. Sorcery, divination, exorcism, and the use of amulets are all elements in the Lozi religious system.

CEREMONIES. The Lozi ceremonial calendar is largely defined by the state of the flood. The two great national events of the year are the moves of the king between his home on the plain at the time of rising flood, and his eventual return after the flood waters fall. The initial move is made following the appearance of the new moon and after sacrifices are made at all the royal graves. Amid the booming of the royal drums, the king, traveling on the royal barge and accompanied by the princes and councilors of his court, proceeds to one of his capitals located on high land above the floodplain. This procession is followed by the migration of the commoners in their dugout canoes. As the flood recedes, the king is enjoined by the royal drummers to move back to the plain so that the people can return to their normal economic pursuits. At this time, the king makes his return journey along a canal dug by one of his predecessors. This trip is accompanied with far less ceremony than the original voyage entailed. Upon the return of the king to his capital, much dancing, especially of the *ngomalume* (royal dance) variety, takes place.

ARTS. Lozi artistic expression includes ironic folktales, maxims, and songs about people, objects, and places, all of which are rich in historical allusion and proverbial wisdom. There is a band of musicians within the king's court; they sing as well as play musical instruments. These musicians perform on state occasions, or otherwise at the king's command. The instruments used by this band include a wide variety of drums (kettle, friction, small tube-shaped drums, and war drums), marimbas, the *kangomhbro* or *zanza* (ten pieces of metal fixed around a plate of hardwood on an empty calabash), various stringed instruments made of the ribs of fan palms, iron bells, rattles, and pipes of ivory, wood, or reeds.

MEDICINE. Diviners usually dance to work themselves into a frenzy and into a state of spirit possession to cure their patients. According to the Lozi, almost all disease is caused by sorcery. To combat these diseases, a witch doctor (*naka*) is called in to perform rites of exorcism over the patient. The naka, who possesses real if limited medical knowledge, may be a member of the local community or may be invited from a neighboring village or from an outside tribe. The diseases treated by exorcism are psychic disorders that are usually attributed to possession by a malevolent spirit. These disorders are called *maimbwe, liyalay, macoba,* and *kayongo.* The method of curing involves exorcistic dancing combined with the inhalation of the vapor from boiling concoctions of bark, roots, and leaves. There are also a number of less common curing ceremonies, such as the one performed when a child becomes possessed by a hunter ancestor.

DEATH AND AFTERLIFE. At the point of death, the individual's eyes and mouth are kept open. When death occurs, the body is flexed so that the knees come up under the chin. The body is then removed from the hut through a special opening cut in the side of the dwelling for this purpose. As the body is taken to the cemetery for burial, spells are scattered on the road to prevent the return of the ghost to haunt the village. Men dig the grave while women stand around the grave site and check to see if the grave is deep enough. Men are buried facing east, whereas women face the west. When the grave is ready, two relatives of the deceased climb into the grave to receive the body. The personal possessions of the deceased are then placed around the corpse. Relatives kneeling around the open grave then gently push dirt into the hole, while those within place dirt around the body. The grave is then completely filled. On top of the grave are placed a broken anthill and a wooden plate or some other object that has been broken with an axe stroke (dead like its owner), in the belief that they will accompany the individual to the other world. The grave of a person of status, which is situated to the side of the commoner's cemetery, is surrounded by a circular barrier of grass and branches. After returning to the village the people mourn for several days. As a sign of grief, the kin of the deceased wear their skin cloaks inside out. The hut of the deceased is pulled down, the roof being placed near the grave, while the remaining possessions of the dead person are burned so that nothing will attract the ghost back to the village. Sons and brothers of the deceased build miniature shelters in their court-

Elaborate rituals and offerings are focused on the burial sites of former Lozi kings and chief princesses. Priests mediate between the Lozi and the rulers' spirits.

Historically, the Lunda are remarkable for their drive to maintain local autonomy while simultaneously building up wide-ranging social, economic, and political networks.

yards, bearing the name of the dead, in which the spirit may come and find protection. At times of sickness or disaster, the kin of the deceased go to these shelters to worship and seek the spirit's aid.

The funeral rites for a king are far more elaborate. Before his death, each king selects or builds a village in which he will be buried, peopling it with councilors, priests, and other personnel. At his death, the king is buried in a huge grave at this site. This is then surrounded by a fence of pointed stakes and the markings of royalty erected around the location. Trees, obtained from the bush, are planted at the royal grave so that from a distance the site stands out distinctly on the flat plain. The Lozi believe that these royal graves are infused with great supernatural power, affecting the lives not only of the royal heirs but of all the inhabitants of Loziland. Each grave has its resident priest, who makes offerings at the site. The royal ancestors are believed to act as intermediaries between Nyambe (the supreme god) and man.

At death, the spirit of the deceased goes to a "halfway house" on the way to the spirit world. Here the deceased, if a man who has the appropriate tribal marks (*matumbekela*) on his arms and holes in his ears, is received by Nyambe, or if a woman, by Nasilele (Nyambe's wife), and then placed on the road to the spirit world proper. If matumbekela and holes through the ears were lacking, the man was given flies for food and not welcomed; he was put on a road that meandered and became narrower and narrower until it ended in a desert where the man would die of hunger and thirst.

Bibliography

Gluckman, Max (1965). *The Ideas in Barotse Jurisprudence.* New Haven: Yale University Press.

Kalaluka, Likando (1979). *Kuomboka: A Living Traditional Culture among the Malozi People of Zambia.* Lusaka: Neczam.

Murdock, George Peter (1959). *Africa: Its Peoples and Their Culture History.* New York, Toronto, and London: McGraw-Hill.

Murray, Lynn Loreen (1972). *The Origins of North-Western Rhodesia.* Kingston, Ont.

—RONALD JOHNSON

LUNDA

Ethonyms: Akosa, Aluunda, Aruund, Eastern Lunda, Imbangala, Ishindi Lunda, Kanongesha Lunda, Kazembe Mutanda Lunda, Luapula Lunda, Lunda-Kazembe (Cazembe), Lunda-Ndembu, Luunda, Musokantanda Lunda, Ndembu, Northern Lunda, Ruund, Southern Lunda, Western Lunda

Orientation

IDENTIFICATION. "Lunda" is the most widely used English term to refer to literally hundreds of social groups whose oral histories link them in varying ways to a far-flung empire that controlled trade and tribute in much of Central Africa from the sixteenth through the nineteenth centuries. Local names for groups tend to reflect either geographical position, topographical features, or names of founding lineages of local ruling dynasties.

LOCATION. The Lunda are broadly distributed in eastern Angola, southern Zaire, and northern and western Zambia. Most of this territory is characterized by high plateau ranging between 1,200 and 1,500 meters above sea level. The vegetation-soil types are generally described as Northern Brachystegia woodlands on clayey plateau soils in the extreme north, Northern Brachystegia woodlands on Kalahari Contact soils in the central region, and Cryptosepalum forest and Cryptosepalum-Brachystegia woodland on upland and central sands in the south. The landscape, however, is broken up into myriad micro-ecological niches, corresponding to bands of changing soil type and variations in elevation. The most common are thick forest, forest of low stunted trees, gallery forest along rivers, grassy plains, and sparse shrub land at the edge of plains. There are three rather distinct seasons. There is a rainy season that runs from roughly September to April, during which time 15 to 28 centimeters of rain may fall. May to July is the cold, dry season, during which time the temperature regularly drops down to around 4° C, and night frost sometimes occurs in low-lying valleys. August to September is the hot dry season, with temperatures regularly soaring into the 30s (C).

DEMOGRAPHY. No reliable census figures exist for the number of individuals who consider themselves Lunda. A rough estimate is 500,000 in Angola, 750,000 in Zaire, and 200,000 in Zambia. Population densities range as low as 0.8 persons per square kilometer in some rural areas, but reach extremely high ratios in urban areas of all three countries.

LINGUISTIC AFFILIATION. The Lunda language is Western Bantu at its root, with some overlay of Eastern Bantu and with local influences from the languages of people who existed in Central Africa before the Bantu expansion. A core vocabulary is mutually intelligible over vast areas, but understanding decreases as one moves away from the central point. Some groups, such as the Luapula Lunda, have almost completely adopted the language of the people among whom they settled.

Settlements

The traditional village was a collection of small circular clay houses with straw-thatched roofs, arranged in a circle around a central meeting house. Members of alternate generations would build on opposing hemispheres of the circle. Banana, tobacco, and a few specialty crops would be planted around the periphery, with the main food gardens fanning out some distance from the village. Hectares of forest would separate individual villages. Villages would range in size from less than a dozen individuals to several hundred people in the villages of chiefs or senior headmen. More than 10,000 people were known to have occupied the court of the paramount chief at Musumba.

Today villages of square or rectangular houses tend to form straight lines along roadways and major paths, clustering at crossroads. Small towns, where life takes a more urban tempo, dot Lunda territory.

Economy

SUBSISTENCE AND COMMERCIAL ACTIVITIES. Subsistence production consists mainly of cassava—the basic staple—supplemented by maize, bananas, pumpkins, pineapples, sweet potatoes, yams, beans, groundnuts, tomatoes, cabbages, and a wide variety of other vegetable crops. Millet and sorghum, once the major food crops, are today grown primarily by women, for the production of alcoholic beverages. Goats, sheep, pigs, chickens, and a few cattle are present in most areas. Game is fairly abundant and is secured either through hunting or trapping. Honey, mushrooms, fruits, berries, and other wild foods are regularly gathered in the forest. Fishing with hook and line, nets, and traps is a popular activity.

Cassava, maize, pineapples, and sunflowers are the major commercial crops. Since the mid-

HISTORY AND CULTURAL RELATIONS

Before the sixteenth century, the basic institution of the Lunda was believed to have been the segmentary matrilineage. Each lineage segment occupied its own small territory (*mpat*), mostly along the Kalanyi River in present-day Zaire. They raised millet and sorghum as well as other crops, but fishing was the activity for which they were most noted. Each mpat was probably centered on an ideal location for fishing, with crops being planted in the fertile alluvial soils along the riverbank. By all indications, this system was extremely productive; Lunda territory was dotted with a rapidly expanding number of independent domains, each with its own headman.

Shortly after 1600, a centralized polity emerged that attracted traders from both the Atlantic and Indian Ocean coasts of Africa. The Lunda capital was located at Musumba, in present-day Zaire, but several major Lunda clusters existed with populations exceeding 10,000 people each. With four large standing armies, an array of titled court fig-

ures and a large complex bureaucracy, the Lunda became an empire capable of controlling the terms of trade and exacting tribute over a wide area.

The Lunda have a long history of spawning émigrés who, through political manipulation or outright conquest, have reformulated the social and economic landscape of Central Africa. During the 1600s, one set of émigrés left the Lunda center, traveled west, and played a seminal role in the formation of the Kasanje Kingdom in Angola. Another set of émigrés traveled south to form the Luvale ruling dynasty. During the mid-1700s, royal lineages from the Lunda center traveled south to form the polities of Kanongesha, Ishindi, Musokantanda, and Kazembe Mutanda. A fifth group traveled east and established a polity along the Luapula River in Zambia. The impetus for most of this movement was the attempt to control strategic positions in the rapidly expanding long-distance trade network. Caravans from both coasts, with up to a thousand merchants

and carriers, were crisscrossing Central Africa on a regular basis in search of marketable commodities, and in need of vast quantities of food. Some Lunda groups specialized in providing ivory, slaves, copper, wild rubber, and other goods that fueled the trade. Other groups ventured into the commercial production of food. Still others grew wealthy by levying taxes on the movement of men and materials through their territory, particularly at strategic river crossings. Most of these polities remain in direct tributary relations with the Lunda center at Musumba.

With the formal establishment of colonialism in the late 1800s, the Lunda were subjected to a tripartite division among the European powers of England, Portugal, and Belgium (later France). The long-distance caravan system was curtailed. The Lunda in each of the three colonial territories were relegated to the margins of newly emerging centers of economic activity. Little has changed in the era of independence.

1980s, fish farming has become an increasingly widespread activity.

INDUSTRIAL ARTS. Traditionally, the Lunda were well known for copper- and iron-smithing, pottery, basket making, mat weaving, and woodworking. Local craft production, however, declined precipitously under colonial rule and persists today at a very low level.

TRADE. Precolonial trade was characterized by a vast array of goods from both Europe and the Indian Ocean nations flowing into the Lunda region in exchange for copper, iron, ivory, skins, slaves, honey and wax, rubber, and food. During the colonial era, 1884–1964, external trade was forcefully curtailed. Today there is extensive inter-regional trade between Lunda in Angola, Zaire, and Zambia, exploiting the differing price structures of each country. The trade consists mainly of foodstuffs, particularly dried fish and game meat, in exchange for manufactured commodities such as sugar, salt, cooking oil, clothing, and household utensils.

DIVISION OF LABOR. Males, females and children all plant cassava extensively. Men are responsible for cutting trees and clearing the fields. Women do all the processing and cooking. Men are responsible for providing the household with protein foods, either by hunting, trapping, fishing, raising domestic stock, or through cash purchases. Men are also responsible for all village construction and for providing tools, as well as some clothing, for wives and children. Women provide most of the child care, with some assistance from husbands and older children. Women also secure and maintain the cooking and other household utensils.

LAND TENURE. Land is rather abundant throughout most of the Lunda territory and is, therefore, rarely a subject of dispute. Traditional use rights are established by requests made to local chiefs and senior headmen. Requests for land are generally denied only if a prior claim exists. Owing to the practice of shifting cultivation, fields as well as entire villages move frequently, and land is not generally considered an inheritable commodity. Access to land in or near towns is granted through local government councils, often on a ninety-nine-year lease basis. The civil war in Angola has, since 1975, made all land tenure uncertain in that country. Zambia has held national discussions on the future of land tenure in rural areas.

Kinship

KIN GROUPS AND DESCENT. Most Lunda are matrilineal, but only the lineages of chiefs or certain headmen are remembered with great genealogical depth. Most matrilineages, however, are quite extensive geographically. Attendance at weddings, funerals, and initiation ceremonies serves to keep individuals in touch with matrikin over vast areas of Angola, Zaire, and Zambia. The matrilineage rarely acts as a corporate group, but it does provide a potential network for support and hospitality should the need arise. Personal relations cultivated over time, rather than cultural prescriptions, determine the degree of closeness and frequency of social interaction.

KINSHIP TERMINOLOGY. The Lunda use an Iroquois kinship terminology system. The major features include a merging of same-sex siblings by the descending generation. Both mother and mother's sister are called by the same term, *mama*. Both father and father's brother are called *tata*. Distinctions are made for the father's sister (*tatankaji*) and mother's brother (*mandumi*). Likewise, cross cousins (children of mother's brother or father's sister) are distinguished from parallel cousins (children of mother's sister or father's brother). The latter are addressed using sibling terms. Hierarchy based on age defines relationships among the Lunda. Most kin terms reflect, or are appended by terms that reflect birth order or relative age—for example, *yaya* (older brother or sister), *mwanyika* (younger brother or sister), *-mukulumpi* (-the elder), *-kansi* (-the younger).

Marriage and Family

MARRIAGE. Traditionally among the Lunda there has been a slight preference for cross-cousin marriages. Little pressure is exerted, however, and individuals generally enjoy a great deal of latitude in the choice of marriage partners. Many marriages take place across ethnic boundaries. In the past, couples would live uxorilocally for the first few years of marriage, with the husband performing bride-service for his in-laws by assisting with agricultural tasks and village construction. Later the couple would reside patrilocally. Today a wife generally moves to her husband's village immediately upon the completion of an exchange of bride-wealth and the performance of a simple ceremony. Bride-wealth may consist of agricultural commodities, tools, household utensils, clothing, and a small amount of cash. Couples today may also choose to marry in civil ceremonies in town, or in Christian ceremonies in any of the numerous churches in Lunda territory, with or without bride-wealth. The Lunda possess one of the highest rates of divorce noted in the anthropological literature. In the 1950s it was recorded that nearly

66 percent of all marriages ended in divorce. By the 1980s, the divorce rate had dropped to around 33 percent. Polygyny is permitted, but probably less than 1 in 50 men actually has more than one wife at a time.

DOMESTIC UNIT. Ideally, each mature adult has his or her own house. Children tend to sleep with their mother when they are very young, with a grandparent in their preteen years, and in single-sex "dormitories" as young adults. Houses are grouped together into distinct villages, the core of which is usually a set of matrilineally related males, ideally uterine brothers and their wives and children. Extended and classificatory kin, as well as friends and visitors, are also present in most villages. In some respects the matricentric bond can be viewed as the basic unit of society. Because divorce and remarriage are frequent, women with their children oscillate between the villages of their matrilineal kin and those of their successive husbands. There is strict division of labor by gender; the labor of children is under the control of the mother. Productive individualism is the norm, but consumption tends to be communal. Households could be defined as those who habitually dine from the same pot.

INHERITANCE. Titles, positions of leadership, cash, and other precious articles are inherited matrilineally. Individuals are traditionally buried with their few utilitarian personal possessions, such as tools, clothing, and household utensils. Standing crops and domestic stock are consumed by the funeral party.

SOCIALIZATION. Boys remain under the authority and guidance of their mothers until they have undergone the circumcision rite. Girls remain with their mothers until they marry. Older siblings play an active role in supervising and educating younger siblings. The grandparent-grandchild relationship is extremely close. They are permitted a degree of informality and intimacy denied in other relationships. In theory, at least, a grandparent cannot deny any request made by a grandchild. Traditionally, every adult in a village was said to be responsible for educating and socializing every child in the village. Today, however, public schools and churches play an increasingly important role in shaping the ideas and ideals of the youth.

Sociopolitical Organization

SOCIAL ORGANIZATION. Lunda individuals tend to be embedded in social networks made up of numerous distinct, yet often overlapping, social units. These include the household, the village, the matrilineage, local cohorts, ritual cults, religious communities, occupational associations, civic clubs, and perhaps political parties. These

The Lunda can be described as botanists par excellence, with nearly a hundred different medicinal plants recorded as being in use.

LUNDA CHIEFTAN

Lunda chief Tshombe Kabwit. The central governments of Zaire and Zambia continue to recognize tradtional leaders as the custodians of rural lands. Zaire. (Daniel Lainé/Corbis)

social units vary in their methods of recruitment, the claims they make on the individual, and the benefits they offer in return. Individual commitment to particular social units varies over the course of a lifetime as people's ambitions, capacities, and strategies change. Lunda enjoy a great deal of flexibility in residential affiliation and choice of personal association. The social landscape is fluid and ever-changing.

Hierarchy, expressed in an idiom of age, is the dominant feature of traditional social organization. Notions of hierarchy are embedded in the language; they are expressed in routine greetings, and they set the norms of daily social interaction. The hierarchy extends from the most recently born up to the paramount chief. It cuts across lineages, villages, and national boundaries.

POLITICAL ORGANIZATION. Historically, the Lunda are remarkable for their drive to maintain local autonomy while simultaneously building up wide-ranging social, economic, and political networks. During the sixteenth through nineteenth centuries, the Lunda king at Musumba (Mwantiyanvwa) was able to exact tribute from wide areas of Central Africa. Otherwise, he made few demands and exerted little influence on daily village life. Headmen oversee the affairs of each village. The longest-standing headman in a particular area is generally recognized as the senior headman. Subchiefs preside over clearly defined territories. The power of headmen, senior headmen, and chiefs resides in their ability to mobilize a consensus on local issues. They possess little coercive force and cannot dictate the course of events. Shifting agriculture and residential mobility enable individuals to simply leave the territory of an unpopular leader.

Today the central governments of Zaire and Zambia continue to recognize traditional leaders as the custodians of rural lands. There are, however, national structures (i.e., executive, legislative, and judicial bureaucracies of government) superimposed on the traditional framework, as well as representatives of the ruling political party. In reality, the relationship between government bureaucrats, party functionaries, and traditional leaders is fluid, highly variable, and often quite volatile. Functional power tends to gravitate toward the most powerful local personality rather than toward particular positions.

Conditions brought about by the civil war in Angola have not been conducive to the formation of any stable political organization among the Lunda of that country.

SOCIAL CONTROL. Most petty crimes and misdeeds are handled by informal local gatherings presided over by headmen, senior headmen, and chiefs. The focus is primarily on restitution, through the imposition of fines paid to the aggrieved party. Individuals dissatisfied with the outcome of local negotiations may carry the case first to local constitutional courts, and then to higher courts of appeal. There is a clear preference, however, for dealing with these problems locally, as constitutional courts tend to punish offenders by imposing fines paid to the court or by incarcerating the offender, rather than requiring restitution to the aggrieved party. Serious crimes, as well as those committed in urban areas, are mandated directly to constitutional courts.

CONFLICT. Most of Lunda territory is lightly policed, and serious conflicts are rare. The local docket is dominated by cases of untethered domestic animals straying into neighbors' gardens, accusations of adultery, and the occasional drunken brawl, most of which are swiftly resolved. In Angola, however, conflict of a military nature was a constant concern during the civil war.

Religion and Expressive Culture

RELIGIOUS BELIEFS. Traditionally, it was believed that Nzambi, the supreme deity, created the universe and all its inhabitants. He endowed each type of living entity with a unique set of capacities that alone determine its fortune. Humans were uniquely blessed with the gift of intellect. Nzambi plays no role in the day-to-day interaction of his creation, nor does he favor any one of his creatures over the others. He requires no formal worship. Human appeals for supernatural intervention are directed mostly toward the ancestors. The spirits of the dead tend to remain in the area where they resided during life, and they continue to be concerned with the welfare of their living kin. Ancestral spirits particularly wish to be remembered for their contributions to the world of the living. Remembrance takes three forms: mentioning an ancestor's name in daily conversation, propitiating an ancestor during communal meals, and naming a newborn after a favored ancestor. Neglected ancestors are said to afflict their living kin with a range of diseases, primarily infertility for women and lack of hunting success for men. Ancestors may also afflict kin who are not living properly (e.g., quarreling and not sharing).

The Lunda metaphysical world is also inhabited by a variety of invisible beings with sinister intent toward humans. These beings, under the nominal control of human witches, can likewise cause debilitating illness and even death if not discovered and neutralized.

The twentieth-century influx of U.S. and European missionaries into Lunda territory has led to a proliferation of religious beliefs. Evangelical Protestant, Catholic, and independent churches now dot the landscape. The earliest missionaries adopted the local term, Nzambi, to refer to the High God, implying in some respects that they were not attempting to introduce a new God but were simply bringing new information about the old Lunda High God. All local religions thus proclaim Nzambi as the supreme deity. They differ, however, in their beliefs about Nzambi's secular and spiritual requirements, preferred forms of worship, areas of intervention, and the benefits offered.

RELIGIOUS PRACTITIONERS. Traditionally, it was the task of diviners to ascertain whether it was an ancestor or an invisible being who was responsible for a particular human affliction. A *chimbuki* (medicine man) would then be responsible for performing an elaborate ritual that would appease and neutralize the afflicting entity. The chimbuki would be assisted in the ritual by a coterie of individuals who have themselves been afflicted, yet survived the same sort of metaphysically induced illness being experienced by the patient. Herbal medicines (both ingested and applied to the patient's body), the manipulation of symbolic objects, and the adherence to strict taboos on foods and personal behavior are the dominant features of such rituals.

Today priests, pastors, deacons, and spiritual counselors of various sorts compete for prominence with traditional healers. The majority of Lunda regularly attend one of the Christian churches in their area, yet most still rely on herbal medicines and participate in traditional healing rituals.

CEREMONIES. In addition to the vast repertoire of curing rituals, the Lunda perform ceremonies to mark most important transitions in life (i.e., birth, marriage, coming of age, and death). The boys' initiation rite (*mukanda*) and the girls' initiation rite (*nkanga*) are the most elaborate. Mukanda today is a month-long ritual during which time groups of boys, mostly between the ages of 10 and 15, are isolated in forest camps where they are first circumcised, then instructed and tested in productive skills, cultural history, and social etiquette. They are also subjected to hard labor and harsh discipline. Mukanda begins and ends with a public ceremony that entails round-the-clock singing, dancing, feasting, storytelling, and perhaps the appearance of masked figures believed to be the embodiment of nature spirits. Mukanda is heavily laden with symbolism

meant to signify the cultural unity of all Lunda men, at one level, and the interrelatedness of all Lunda, male and female, at another. Upon completion of mukanda, a boy received the full complement of rights and duties bestowed on all adult Lunda males.

Nkanga differs markedly from mukanda. Girls are initiated individually in the village, rather than in groups in the forest. They are relieved of all physical labor, pampered, groomed, and sung to, for up to three months. They are not subjected to any physical operation. Like the boys, however, they are instructed in productive skills, cultural history, and social etiquette. Much of the instructional focus and symbolic expression is on augmenting reproductive capacity and on child-rearing competency. For most of nkanga, a girl remains isolated from males in a small seclusion hut, where she is regularly visited by elder women from the surrounding area. A young attendant is assigned to each girl, to be her constant companion and to attend to her every need. A girl is to remain silent throughout nkanga, speaking only in whispers to her attendant should the need arise. Nkanga, likewise, begins and ends with a well-attended public ceremony characterized by great revelry, most notably the singing of ribald songs extolling female virtues while denigrating male vices. Symbolically, nkanga possesses many levels of meaning. It expresses the unity of females in opposition to males, while simultaneously asserting the unity of all Lunda under matrilineal principles of social organization. Like mukanda, nkanga also symbolizes the death of one's former self, and rebirth as a new social persona. Gifts, primarily clothing and cash, are heaped on the new adult member of society.

ARTS. A few professional wood-carvers and basket makers continue to produce locally. Most decorative objects, music, and performances, however, are produced by dedicated amateurs, solely for local enjoyment.

MEDICINE. The Lunda can be described as botanists par excellence. Nearly a hundred different medicinal plants have been recorded as being in use, from which herbal specialists can concoct a vast array of composite remedies. Even very young children tend to be competent in the preparation of herbal remedies for such simple ailments as headaches, stomach aches, colds, influenza, and muscle aches and pains. The local population also accepts and seeks out Western pharmaceutical drugs, viewing them as being akin to traditional herbal preparations, albeit more powerful because they are believed to be more concentrated, especially injections. Nevertheless,

Most appeals for supernatural intervention are directed toward ancestors.

most individuals in rural areas still try one or more herbal preparations before resolving to visit a clinic. This is so in part because most traditional medicines can be gathered in the course of daily activities such as going to the fields and gardens, drawing water from the river, trekking to distant pastures to round up the goats and sheep, or going to the bush to hunt, trap, or fish. A visit to one of the few clinics in the area, however, tends to break up the daily routine, often forcing people to walk great distances, to wait in long lines, perhaps only to receive pills instead of the much more highly desired injections. Elaborate curing rituals are the prescribed medicine for spirit-induced ailments.

DEATH AND AFTERLIFE. Death may be attributed to either natural or supernatural causes. It is invariably accompanied by accusations of witchcraft, threats of retaliation, the questioning of long-standing relationships, and, occasionally, divination to ascertain the true cause of death. In the case of married individuals, the surviving spouse is generally required to pay a substantial sum (*mpepi*) to the lineage of the deceased, regardless of culpability. Individuals are buried in cemeteries shared by clusters of villages. A complex cleansing ritual is performed to remove the aura of death from the village and to appease the recently departed and ease his or her passage into the afterlife. Traditionally, it was believed that the spirit of a deceased individual remained in the area he or she inhabited during life, watching over living kin and reestablishing contacts with friends and relatives who had died earlier. Today the multiplicity of ideas about the afterlife spawned by various Christian denominations competes for prominence with traditional notions.

Bibliography

Bustin, Edouard (1975). *Lunda under Belgian rule: The Politics of Ethnicity*. Cambridge: Harvard University Press.

Chinyanta, Munona (1989). *Mutomboko Ceremony and the Lunda-Kazembe Dynasty*. Lusaka: Kenneth Kaunda Foundation.

Cunnison, Ian G. (1959). *The Auapula Peoples of Northern Rhodesia: Custom and History in Tribal Politics*. Manchester: Manchester University Press.

Dias de Carvalho, Henrique A. (1890). *Ethnographia e historia tradicional dos povos da Lunda*. Lisbon: Imprensa Nacional.

Hoover, J. Jeffrey (1978). "The Seduction of Ruwej: Reconstructing Ruund History (the Nuclear Lunda: Zaire, Angola, Zambia)." Ph.D. dissertation, Yale University.

McCulloch, Merran (1951). *The Southern Lunda and Related Peoples (Northern Rhodesia, Belgian Congo, Angola)*. London: International African Institute.

Poewe, Karla, O. (1981). *Matrilineal Ideology: Male-Female Dynamics in Luapula, Zambia*. New York: Academic Press.

Pritchett, James A. (1989). "Continuity and Change in an African Society: The Kanongesha Lunda of Mwinilunga Zambia." Ph.D. dissertation, Harvard University.

Schecter, Robert E. (1976). "History and Historiography on a Frontier of Lunda Expansion: The Origins and Early Development of the Kanongesha." Ph.D. dissertation, University of Wisconsin.

Turner, Victor W. (1957). *Schism and Continuity in an African Society: A Study of Ndembu Village Life*. Manchester: Manchester University Press.

Turner, Victor W. (1967). *The Forest of Symbols: Aspects of Ndembu Ritual*. Ithaca, N.Y.: Cornell University Press.

Turner, Victor W. (1968). *The Drums of Affliction: A Study of Religious Processes among the Ndembu of Zambia*. Oxford: Clarendon Press.

—JAMES ANTHONY PRITCHETT

LUYIA

Ethonyms: Abaluhya, Abaluyia, Baluyia, Bantu Kavirondo, Luhya

Orientation

IDENTIFICATION. "Abaluyia" is the preferred name for the people once called the "Bantu Kavirondo" because of their proximity to Lake Victoria's Kavirondo Gulf. "Abaluyia" refers to the nation, tribe, or ethnic group, "Omuluyia" to an individual, and "Luluyia" to the language they speak. There are seventeen Luluyia-speaking subnations in Western and Nyanza provinces of Kenya: Bakhayo (Abakhayo), Bukusu (Babukusu, Kitosh [derogatory], Vugusu), Banyala (Abanyala), Basonga (Abasonga), Banyore (Abanyore), Batsotso (Abatsotso), Idakho (Abetakho, Babetakho), Isukha (Abesukha, Babesukha), Kabras (Abakabras), Kisa (Abakisa, Bakisa), Logoli (Avalogoli, Maragoli), Marachi (Abamarachi, Bamaraki, Marach), Marama (Abamarama, Bamarama), Samia (Abasamia, Basamia), Tachoni (Abatachoni, Kitosh), Tiriki (Batiriki), and Wanga (Abawanga, Bawanga). Some Luluyia speakers are found in eastern Uganda: the Gisu (Abagisu, Bagisu, Bamasaba, Masaba), Gwe (Abagwe), Nyole (Abanyole, Abanyuli), and

Samia. The ethnic label "Abaluyia" is Kenyan, however, and is not used by Ugandan Luluyia speakers. The label has been associated with this part of Kenya since the 1930s, and elders from the region accepted the designation during the 1960s.

LOCATION. The Abaluyia region, which includes eastern Uganda, extends roughly from the equator to 1°10' N and from 34°00' to 35°15' E. It is bounded on the south by Nyanza Province and Lake Victoria (elevation 1,127 meters), on the north by Mount Elgon (elevation 4,296 meters), and on the east by the Rift Valley. The majority of the Abaluyia live in Western Province, Kenya, which consists of four districts: Bungoma, Busia, Kakamega, and Vihiga. Most of the region (90 percent) is highly suited for agriculture, but there are interspersed rocky and sandy areas. Temperatures range from about 32° C in the south to 5–10° C near Mount Elgon. There are two rainy seasons, the long rains from March to June or July and the short rains from August to October. Rainfall ranges from 76 centimeters per year in the southernmost region to 155 centimeters per year around the area of the Kakamega Forest—a 315–square-kilometer, isolated primeval rain forest teeming with many unique plant, primate, bird, and insect species. Large carnivores (e.g., leopards), large mammals (e.g., elephants), and ruminants (e.g., gazelles) were once common throughout western Kenya, but they have been gone since at least the 1950s or 1960s. Although eucalyptuses and euphorbias are common, deforestation of the entire region, including the Kakamega Forest, poses a serious threat.

DEMOGRAPHY. Wagner (1949) estimated that there were less than 350,000 Abaluyia in 1937. The Abaluyia, with a total population of 3.5 million, are now the second-largest ethnic group in Kenya. There are at least 1.5 million Luluyia speakers in Uganda, but—unlike the Kenyan Abaluyia—they do not consider themselves a single ethnic group. Population densities range from more than 2,000 persons per square kilometer in the south (Vihiga District) to less than 200 persons per square kilometer near Mount Elgon. Although there is now some evidence of fertility decline, total fertility rates, until the late 1980s, exceeded nine and ten births per woman of childbearing age.

LINGUISTIC AFFILIATION. Luluyia is a Western Bantu language. The Abaluyia subnations speak mutually understandable dialects, but subnations that border each other are more likely to understand one another's dialect. Some of the dialects (Lubukusu, Kisamia) are tonal. Many contemporary Luluyia speakers also know English, Kiswahili, Dholuo, and/or Luganda.

History and Cultural Relations

Luluyia-speaking groups have occupied the same East African region for up to 500 years; they displaced long-established foraging and herding peoples. The Abaluyia subnations, most of which probably originated from central Africa, were originally clans with diverse historical origins that grew large and then split into subclans. The eighteenth and nineteenth centuries were characterized by widespread warfare between Abaluyia subnations and neighboring ethnic groups, especially the Buganda, Luo, Nandi, Maasai, and Iteso. The Bagisu, Bakhayo, Bukusu, Banyala, Batsotso, Kabras, Nyole, Marachi, Marama, Samia, and Tachoni constructed fortressed settlements during this period. These were walled with thorns and surrounded by moats.

During the colonial period (1895–1963), the British, whose goal was to pacify the area and facilitate the completion of the Uganda Railway, made several unsuccessful attempts to unite politically the Luluyia-speaking subnations. In 1895 the Bukusu waged an unsuccessful war of resistance, the Chetambe War, against the British. The first train reached Kisumu in 1901. The Abaluyia region was split in two in 1902, when the British established the current boundary between Kenya and Uganda. As a result, the subnations in Kenya and Uganda have different colonial histories and different political economies. In 1909, in a futile attempt to unite the subnations, the British anointed Nobongo Mumia of the Wanga "kingdom" the "supreme" chief. The Abaluyia, however, never had a single paramount chief prior to British colonial rule. The Ugandan Nyole were dominated by the Baganda; various clan leaders in Kenya aligned themselves with or resisted the British. The Kenyan Abaluyia did not develop a unified ethnic identity until the 1930s, and the Ugandan Luluyia speakers have never had a single ethnic identity.

The Friends African Mission, the Mill Hill Mission, the Church of God, and the Church Missionary Society (Anglican) were all established in the region between 1902 and·1906; mission schools were established shortly thereafter. A brief gold rush (1929–1931) was followed by land confiscation and alienation. Today nearly all Abaluyia are Christians, although some Abaluyia—especially around Mumias town—practice Islam. Universal primary education has been achieved in much of western Kenya.

Prior to the colonial period, the highest level of Luyia political integration was the clan, and the clan headman was the most powerful figure.

Settlements

Precolonial Abaluyia villages were loosely organized around single localized lineages (*enyumba*; pl. *tsinyumba*). Abaluyia homesteads consisted of circular compounds surrounded by euphorbias, thorns, or clay walls. Structures within the compounds followed a prescribed layout, although there were variations. Houses were circular with thatched roofs. The first wife's house was directly opposite the gate, with the houses of junior wives organized to the left and right, according to seniority. The married sons' houses were near the gate and were arranged according to birth order. Because unmarried children who had reached puberty were not permitted to sleep under the same roof as their parents, unmarried sons slept in special houses called *chisimba* (sing. *esimba*). Girls, and sometimes younger boys, slept with classificatory grandmothers in girls' houses (*ekogono* or *eshibinze*). The compound usually had one or more elevated granaries, and animals were often kept in separate structures. Nowadays settlements are organized more like neighborhoods. Mud houses are usually square and often roofed with iron sheets. Modern block houses with tile roofs line the major roads. Compounds are often crowded and may be laid out less formally. They are surrounded by euphorbias, shrubs, rows of trees, or fences. In some places, girls' houses no longer exist: girls sleep in their mothers' kitchens, but older boys continue to sleep in separate dwellings. Granaries are still common in the Bukusu area but are rare in Maragoli and Banyore.

Economy

SUBSISTENCE AND COMMERCIAL ACTIVITIES. The Abaluyia are now primarily farmers who keep cattle, but in precolonial times men hunted, and animal husbandry was even more important. The Banyala and the Samia were known for their expertise in fishing, and quail and insects were eaten throughout the region. Finger millet, sorghum, sesame, pumpkins, sweet potatoes, yams, beans, and bananas were the most important crops in precolonial times. Nowadays the main crop is maize intercropped with beans; millet and sorghum are less common. In addition to the traditional crops, other important contemporary crops include green beans, red beans, bananas, groundnuts (peanuts), *sukuma wiki* (kale), cabbages, potatoes, and cassava. The major cash crops are tea, coffee, sugarcane, cotton, and sunflower seeds. Farms are tilled entirely with iron hoes in the hillier, more densely populated areas, whereas hoes are commonly used with ox-drawn plows and tractors in the northern and western regions. Cattle (zebu, mixed, and grade), goats, sheep, chickens, ducks, and turkeys are common.

INDUSTRIAL ARTS. Formerly, the important crafts were blacksmithing, pottery, basketry, woodworking (particularly, the manufacture of drums), and weaving. Blacksmithing had been passed down patrilineally in some clans. The Samia (especially the Abang'aale clan) were particularly well known for blacksmithing and mining of iron ore. Manufacture of pottery was more often a woman's than a man's task—although Bukusu women of childbearing age could not quarry clay. Pots, which were usually traded and owned by women, were considered utilitarian. There was not much specialization in the manufacture of everyday wood tools (e.g., hoe handles), but specialists still make drums, lyres, stools, and wood carvings.

TRADE. The subnations of the Abaluyia traded among one another during the precolonial era. Iron hoes, spear points, and ivory, for example, could be traded for grains or animals. Precolonial trade covered a distance of no more than 72 kilometers, but there were three precolonial markets where Luo, Nandi, and Abaluyia came together to trade baskets, wooden tools, quail, and various foodstuffs for cattle, fish, tobacco, and so forth. During the colonial era, various weekly regional and local market centers developed, where local and European goods could be bought or bartered. Wagner counted sixty-four recognized markets in 1937. By 1990, in addition to dozens of rural, market, and local trading centers, there were at least ten urban centers in Western Province, Kenya, where one could buy everything from Diet Coke to Michael Jackson tapes.

DIVISION OF LABOR. In precolonial times, hunting and warfare were important men's work. Horticulture was mainly women's work. Men cleared fields, but women usually prepared soil, planted, weeded, and harvested. Only men planted trees, although women cared for them. Large animals were the domain of men and unmarried boys. Traditionally, the men milked the cattle in most of the subnations, but nowadays women often do it. Women owned and cared for poultry. Both women and men were involved in marketing: the women sold pots, products grown in kitchen gardens, dried fish, fruits, and grains bought from farmers in other regions. Only men took animals to market. House building has many stages, each with a division of labor; however, women generally repaired walls and floors, whereas men prepared thatching materials. Children contributed to subsistence: girls mainly in the home and fields, boys mainly with the herds. Boys and girls helped out with other tasks, such as tending younger children, gathering wood, and fetching water. Girls helped their mothers in selling. Nowadays men's and women's roles are more varied. Although the sexual division of labor at home has not changed much, both men and women have a broader range of occupational opportunities. Schoolteacher, agricultural-extension worker, and sugar-factory worker are common occupations of rural Abaluyia. The sexual division of labor in agriculture has changed somewhat as agriculture has intensified. Modern Abaluyia children usually attend school and are less available to perform chores.

LAND TENURE. Traditionally, land was inherited patrilineally. Among the Kenyan Abaluyia, families owned land, and this land was referred to as the *omulimi gwa guga* (lands of the grandfather). A man apportioned his land to sons as they married but could not alienate the omulimi gwa guga. Women had use rights on their husbands' farms but could not inherit land. Mothers could, however, hold land in trust for sons. When his mother died, the last-born son would inherit the land she farmed. Communal lands, such as surplus lands or those used for grazing, were under the control of the clan and administered by the *luguru* (headman). Women are permitted to inherit land in contemporary Kenya but more often acquire land by purchasing it themselves. Communal grazing lands are now rare because of population pressure. Most land is registered, and buying and selling of land are individual affairs. Land disputes are handled in courts or in sublocation meetings convened by assistant chiefs.

Kinship

KIN GROUPS AND DESCENT. The exogamous patrilineal clan (*oluyia*) is the fundamental unit of Abaluyia social organization. Clans may also have several exogamous subclans. There were at least 750 Abaluyia clans by the mid-twentieth century. Each clan has an animal, plant, or bird totem, as well as an ancestor for whom the clan is usually named.

KINSHIP TERMINOLOGY. The Abaluyia use an Iroquoian system that incorporates classificatory kinship terminology. Grandparents and grandchildren are called by the same kin terms—*guga* for grandfathers, grandsons, and great-grandsons, *guku* for grandmothers, granddaugh-

ters, and great-granddaughters. Distinctions are made for the father's sister (*senje*) and mother's brother (*khotsa*), but clan relatives of the same generation (e.g., women and female in-laws) are called by the same term (in this case, *mama*). Cousins are addressed by sibling terms, but, in some places, cross cousins are distinguished in reference.

Marriage and Family

MARRIAGE. Traditional Abaluyia marriage is patrilocal. Polygyny rates vary among the subnations, and bride-wealth, consisting of animals and money, is usually exchanged. Many types of exchange occurred during the marriage process, and male elders conducted the negotiations. Wives were chosen for their good character and the ability to work hard. Men were also chosen for these qualities, as well as soberness and ability to pay bride-wealth. After marriage, co-wives usually had separate dwellings but would often cook together. New wives were not permitted to cook in their own houses until their own cooking stones were set up in a brief ceremony. This was often after the birth of one or several children. Childlessness was usually blamed on the woman. In some subnations, a woman whose husband died lived in a state of ritual impurity until she was inherited by the dead husband's brother. Divorce may or may not have involved return of bride-wealth cattle. In the case of divorce or serious witchcraft accusations, the woman could return to her natal home without her children, who remained with their fathers.

Abaluyia women in contemporary Kenya choose among a variety of marriage options, including the traditional bride-wealth system, Christian marriage with or without bride-wealth, elopement, and single parenthood. Women with more education may command a higher bride-wealth. Bride-wealth in Bungoma remains stable, but in Maragoli and some other regions, bride-wealth may be declining or disappearing.

DOMESTIC UNIT. A married man heads one or more households. A typical household consists of a husband, a wife, and their children. Other family members may join these households, including the wife's sisters, the husband's other children, and foster children. Since mature relatives of adjacent generations do not sleep in the same house, grandmothers and older children often occupy adjacent houses; however, all usually eat from the same pot. These rules have not changed much, although many rural households are now

◆ **patrilocal**
The practice of a newly married couple residing in the community of the husband's kin. Virilocal is sometimes used in a more restrictive sense to indicate residence in the household of the husband's family.

*After marriage, co-
wives usually had
separate dwellings
but would often cook
together.*

headed by women because of long-term male wage-labor migration.

INHERITANCE. Land is inherited patrilineally.

SOCIALIZATION. Abaluyia communities are characterized by a high degree of sibling involvement in caretaking, under the general supervision of the mothers and grandmothers in the homestead. Although mothers play a primary role in child rearing, small children and infants may be left with older siblings while their mothers do other work. Although fathers play a minimal role, they are often the ones who take children for medical care. Grandparents and grandchildren have close relationships. Until the mid- to late twentieth century, girls learned about marriage and sexuality from their grandmothers. In the Abaluyia subnations that circumcise, boys are admonished by male elders and taught to endure the pain of circumcision without flinching, a sign that they have the strength of character to endure other hardships they may face. Contemporary Abaluyia grandparents play an even greater role in child rearing because they are thrust more and more into foster-parent roles.

Sociopolitical Organization

SOCIAL ORGANIZATION. Although some clans were known for particular roles and strengths during the eighteenth through early-twentieth centuries, leadership has come from a variety of clans and subnations over the years. The range of social stratification among the Abaluyia extends from the landless to poor, middle-level, and rich farmers, depending upon such factors as the size of the plot owned and the number of animals kept. There is a developing class system but no formal hierarchy.

POLITICAL ORGANIZATION. Prior to the colonial period, the highest level of political integration was the clan, and the clan headman was the most powerful figure. In some of the subnations, patron-client relationships developed between powerful clan heads and landless men who would serve as warriors. These big-men later gained power through alliances with the British, but there were no precolonial chiefs among the Abaluyia. Nevertheless, some clans and individuals were viewed as having particularly good leadership abilities. In Kenya, the traditional headman system changed in 1926 with the institution of *milango* headmen (usually, they were also luguru headmen), then the *ulogongo* system in the 1950s. Currently, villages are headed by luguru, sublocations are headed by government-hired and -paid

assistant chiefs, and a paid chief leads at the location level.

SOCIAL CONTROL. Crimes, misdeeds, land disputes, and the like were originally handled by the clan. Nowadays, in Kenya, these matters proceed initially to the headmen and assistant chiefs, who deal with local disputes at a monthly *baraza* (community meeting). Unresolved cases may be taken up by the location chief, district officer, or district commissioner; final recourse may be sought in the Kenyan court system.

CONFLICT. During the eighteenth and nineteenth centuries, Abaluyia subnations and clans often raided and warred against each other and against their non-Abaluyia neighbors. This warfare accelerated toward the end of the nineteenth century with the arrival of the British and the introduction of firearms. Pax Britannica was achieved in 1906, but feuds and rivalries continued within clans and subclans even into the postcolonial era. The Marachi and Wanga eventually formed military alliances with the British, but others, such as the Bukusu, waged wars of resistance. Conflicts are now rare, although political events in Kenya in the 1990s have resulted in some interethnic fighting at the margins of the Abaluyia region.

Religion and Expressive Culture

RELIGIOUS BELIEFS. There is a sharp distinction between precolonial religious beliefs and contemporary ones. Prior to missionization, the Abaluyia believed in a High God, Were, as well as in the concept of ancestral spirits. Some said that Were lived on Mount Elgon. Ancestral spirits had power in everyday life and could cause illness and death. After 1902, the first U.S. Quaker missionaries arrived in Kaimosi and began to convert the Tiriki and Maragoli with varying success. Other missions followed, and the schooling and wage-labor opportunities available to the converted were very attractive to the ambitious. By the 1930s, at least six Christian missions were in place in western Kenya, boasting 50,000 converts. Nowadays, worshipers of ancestral spirits are rare; nearly everyone is a Christian, Muslim, or self-described "backslider." It is important to note, however, that missionary teachings have not abolished certain traditional practices; for example, beliefs in ancestral powers are still widespread.

RELIGIOUS PRACTITIONERS. Traditional practitioners included garden magicians and rain magicians. Witchcraft, sorcery, and traditional healing continue to play a role in Abaluyia communities. Both men and women can be healers or practice witchcraft. A common witchcraft accusation is that a person is a night runner—that is, he or she keeps a leopard in the house and runs naked at night rattling neighbors' doors and windows. Untimely deaths may be blamed on witchcraft and sorcery. Beliefs in poisoning or nonspecific causation of death, illness, or misfortune by witchcraft or sorcery are common. Traditional healers undergo a kind of ritual healing themselves and are indoctrinated by other healers. Healers may also have expertise with herbal medicines.

CEREMONIES. Transitions from one life stage to the next are the most celebrated events. The important transitions for women are coming of age, marriage, and giving birth, whereas initiation is the most important event for men. In some subnations (Batsotso, Banyore, Kisa, Marama, and Wanga), six lower teeth were extracted in childhood; others extracted only one (Idakho, Isukha) or two (Bukusu). The extraction of teeth varied widely and was probably borrowed from neighboring ethnic groups. Men and women were often scarified at marriage, but now only the very old have any scarification. Male circumcision is important in the Bukusu, Banyore, Batsotso, Banyala of Kakamega District, Idakho, Isukha, Kabras, Kisa, Logoli, Marama, Tachoni, Tiriki, and Wanga subnations. The Gisu also circumcise. Some subnations neighboring the Luo do not circumcise, including the Bakhayo, Basonga, Gwe, Marachi, Samia and some Banyole. Circumcision ceremonies vary between subnations, although the stages usually consist of a period of preparation, the circumcision day, and a subsequent period of seclusion. The Bukusu and Tachoni have cyclical age-set systems with names that repeat about every one hundred years. Bukusu and Tachoni circumcise every two years. Some Abaluyia subnations are similar to the Logoli, who circumcise once every ten years and whose circumcision groups are named after a current event. Traditionally, boys were usually circumcised between ages 12 and 18 but could be circumcised earlier or later. A requirement of a traditional circumcision is demonstration of bravery. Even a flinch or change of expression can result in lifelong shame and disgrace. Nowadays circumcisions are done at younger ages, and boys may be circumcised in hospitals. Female circumcision was once practiced only by the Tachoni and the Bukusu, who probably adopted it from their Kalenjin neighbors.

ARTS. There are few specialized arts in the Abaluyia region. Houses are sometimes painted on the outside, especially during the Christmas season.

MEDICINE. Contemporary Abaluyia seek medical assistance in a variety of settings, including hospitals and clinics, and from both community health workers and traditional healers.

DEATH AND AFTERLIFE. Death may be attributed to both natural and supernatural causes. The deceased are usually buried on their own compounds. Abaluyia funerals typically involve a period of wailing immediately after the death, a time when the body of the deceased can be viewed, and the funeral itself. During the period after the funeral, animals are slaughtered, widows' roles are considered, and some family members shave their heads. In some Abaluyia subnations, the announcement of the death of an important man or woman may have been accompanied by a cattle drive. Funeral celebrations can involve great expense and last for several days and nights, often accompanied by dancing and drums. Widows are ritually unclean for a period after the death of their spouses and are subject to a number of prohibitions. Traditionally, the widow sometimes wore her dead husband's clothes until she was inherited by his brother. Musambwa were believed to have an active role in the world of the living, and, in former times, people would call upon them to change their fortunes. Illness and death were attributed to angry musambwa.

Bibliography

Bradley, Candice (1993). *Bibliography of Western Province, Kenya.* African Studies, University of Wisconsin.

de Wolf, Jan Jacob (1983). "Circumcision and Initiation in Western Kenya and Eastern Uganda: Historical Reconstructions and Ethnographic Evidence." *Anthropos* 78:369–410.

Makila, F. E. (1978). *An Outline History of the Babukusu of Western Kenya.* Nairobi: Kenya Literature Bureau.

Munroe, Robert L., and Ruth H. Munroe (1989). *Logoli Time Allocation.* Cross-Cultural Studies in Time Allocation, vol. 5. New Haven: HRAF.

Osogo, John (1965). *Life in Kenya in the Olden Days: The Baluyia.* Nairobi: Oxford University Press.

Sangree, Walter H. (1965). "The Bantu Tiriki of Western Kenya." In *Peoples of Africa*, edited by J. Gibbs. New York: Holt, Rinehart & Winston.

Ssennyonga, Joseph (1978). "Population Growth and Cultural Inventory: The Maragoli Case." Doctoral thesis, University of Sussex.

Wagner, Gunter (1949–1956). *The Bantu of Western Kenya.* 2 vols. London: Oxford University Press.

A common Luyia witchcraft accusation is that a person is a night runner, keeping a leopard in the house and running naked at night, rattling neighbors' doors and windows.

Wandibba, Simiyu (1985). *History and Culture in Western Kenya: The People of Bungoma District Through Time*. Nairobi: Gideon S. Were Press.

Weisner, Thomas S. (1979). "Urban-Rural Differences in Sociable and Disruptive Behavior of Kenya Children." *Ethnology* 18:153–172.

Were, Gideon S. (1967). *A History of the Abaluyia of Western Kenya c. 1500–1930*. Nairobi: East African Publishing House.

Whyte, Michael A., and Susan Reynolds Whyte (1984–1985). "Peasants and Workers: The Legacy of Partition among the Luyia-speaking Nyole and Marachi." *Journal of the Historical Society of Nigeria* 12:139–158.

—CANDICE BRADLEY

According to oral traditions, the Maasai migrated to their present area and adopted a boy they found there, who became the ancestor of the Loonkidongi dynasty of prophets.

MAASAI

Ethonyms: Ilmaasai, Masai (also Maa, which refers to all those peoples who speak the Maasai language)

Orientation

IDENTIFICATION. The Maasai comprise a federation of tribal sections whose economy is based on nomadic pastoralism. Most prominent among them are the Purko and Kisonko, and also among the core groups are the Damat, Kaputiei, Keekonyukie, Loita, Koitokitok, Loodokilani, Matapato, Salei, and Serenket. More peripheral, and with different clans but sharing the Maasai age system, are the Dalalekutuk, Laitayok, Moitanik, Siria, and Uasinkishu, and also the agricultural Arusha. More peripheral still, with their own independent age systems, are the Parakuyu, Samburu, and Tiamus. Because each tribal section is effectively autonomous, both economically and socially, there is a considerable diversity in custom between sections.

LOCATION. The designated Maasai region covers some 100,000 square kilometers, divided between southern Kenya, where most of the Maasai live, and northern Tanzania, where the land is more arid and the population sparse. The principal rains come in the spring. The dry season typically covers the six summer months, extending occasionally to periods of eighteen months or more when the rains fail in some part of the region.

DEMOGRAPHY. There are rather more than one-quarter of a million Maasai, with a broad balance between the sexes. A high rate of polygyny is achieved by delaying the age of marriage of young men as compared with that of girls. During their extended period of bachelorhood, youths are still regarded as warriors (*moran*).

LINGUISTIC AFFILIATION. Maa (Maasai) is classed as a Paranilotic language.

History and Cultural Relations

According to oral traditions, the Maasai migrated from the north to their present area, probably before A.D. 1800, and adopted a boy they found there, who became the ancestor of the Loonkidongi dynasty of prophets. From this time on, and under the patronage of successive prophets, these oral traditions relate to the military dominance of the Maasai over their neighbors, who emulated Maasai warrior practices. This military emphasis led in the earlier period to internecine competition between the Maasai and the more peripheral Maa peoples, and then, following a disastrous cattle epidemic and famine in the 1880s, to civil war among the Maasai proper, who were seeking to recover their fortunes at each other's expense.

The civil wars were ended by colonial intervention in the areas, which were split between British and German rule—now Kenya and Tanzania, respectively. The two halves have developed separately since then, while retaining close cultural links as "one people." In Kenya, it was largely Maasai land that was alienated for European colonization through two controversial treaties. These treaties confined the Maasai to their present reserve, where they have remained largely isolated from change, even since independence in 1963. A volume on the (Kisonko) Maasai written by a German military administrator, M. Merker (1904), provides the most lucid account of the Maasai of early colonial Tanzania. Since then, the demise of the system of warrior villages in Tanzania suggests greater administrative interference into their internal affairs than was the case in Kenya. More recently, the Maasai as a nomadic people have proved an intractable problem for the Tanzanian government's policy of accommodating dispersed populations in settled villages during the 1970s ("villagization").

Settlements

The significant residential groupings are the locality, the village, and the polygynous homestead, or joint family. The locality typically corresponds to a natural water-catchment area, within which interaction is most frequent and elders meet to discuss the issues that affect the community at large and the villages within it. Villages are dispersed throughout the locality, but have little social identity of their own. They are built primarily as a protection against the dangers of the bush at night. During the day, the cattle go out to graze, and social life extends to the wider neighborhood and locality. The significant unit within the village is the cluster of huts and stock corrals that comprise the joint-family homestead, of which there are typically four or five within each village. It is the joint family that has the greatest continuity, and the family head has almost total autonomy in handling its internal affairs. Such families may migrate to another locality at any time, leaving their huts and village space to be occupied by any newcomers to the village. Huts and villages tend to be more substantial and permanent in the less nomadic, upland areas.

Contrasting with the elders' villages, both ideologically and in size, are the warrior villages (*manyat*), which are built to protect the area from marauders. Typically, there are three or four warrior villages in any tribal section, and the warriors who are associated with them claim considerable autonomy from the elders and adopt a contrasting life-style that emphasizes their dependence on one another and their lack of domesticity.

Economy

SUBSISTENCE AND COMMERCIAL ACTIVITIES. The life-style of the Maasai is oriented toward their herds of cattle, although sheep and goats play an important part in their diet, especially during the dry season, when milk is scarce. The need to graze stock necessitates dispersal over the widest area that is consistent with the availability of grazing and access to water, especially in the dry season. Traditionally, in the most severe famines, Maasai could merge temporarily with neighboring Dorobo hunters and gatherers. During the twentieth century, as the area that is suitable for hunting has contracted and as opportunities for employment have opened up, many of those whom circumstances have squeezed out of the Maasai pastoral economy have drifted toward the fringes of urban society, seeking employment—notably as security guards.

INDUSTRIAL ARTS. Blacksmiths, especially in the past, produced spears and ornaments. Associated with the dirt of their craft, they were despised and not allowed to intermarry with Maasai, who were not involved with blacksmithing.

TRADE. Traditionally, sheep and goats were traded with neighboring peoples for vegetable produce. Although the opportunity to migrate for wage labor had been available earlier, it was not until the 1960s that Maasai, who traditionally sold their stock only from absolute necessity, entered the monetary economy; they remain essentially self-sufficient.

DIVISION OF LABOR. Boys herd the stock, assisted by older males and girls as the need arises, and under the overall supervision of the family head. At night, responsibility for the herds passes to the women. Women also look after their dependent children, maintain the domestic supply of firewood and water, and milk the cattle. Warriors are expected to defend the herds.

LAND TENURE. Each tribal section claims sole grazing rights in its own territory, and indi-

YOUNG MAASAI

Three Maasai youth. Visual arts among the Maasai focus on body decoration and on beaded ornaments. Tanzania, Africa. (Stephen Frink/Corbis)

vidual elders may develop and claim wells for watering stock. In times of need, however, it is a major premise that Maasai land and water belong ultimately to all Maasai and that no one should be denied access, even across the boundaries between tribal sections. This principle conflicts with two economic trends that began in the 1960s and have been steadily gaining force, which entail a shift toward local ownership of land: the encroachment of agriculture and the government's attempts to confine Maasai to group ranches. Neither of these developments is consistent with the erratic nature of droughts.

Kinship

KIN GROUPS AND DESCENT. The Maasai are a patrilineal people, with shallow dispersed lineages that extend for only one or two generations beyond the oldest living elders. These lineages are identified with the membership of a clan. Today the bonds and restrictions of clanship are weak, and clan membership tends to acquire significance only by default, as, for example, when the members of a migrant family find themselves isolated from close friends or kin.

KINSHIP TERMINOLOGY. Although kinship terminology is broadly of the Omaha type, there is a general preference to address others by the use of teknonyms or, among close kin and affines, to establish gift terms that emphasize mutual respect.

Sociopolitical Organization

SOCIAL ORGANIZATION. The most distinctive feature of Maasai society is the age system, which stratifies adult males into age sets, spaced apart by about fifteen years. Each age set is further divided into two successive subsets, the "right-hand," followed by the "left-hand." Of primary importance in the community is the subset of warriors who have been most recently initiated. In their physical prime, they form their warrior villages during this period, until the next subset captures the limelight. It is the establishment of such successive arrays of warrior villages, every seven years or so, that symbolizes the autonomy of the warrior ideal and the temporary independence of each warrior from his father. This independence extends to those mothers of moran who are "seconded" to the warrior villages of their sons.

Each warrior village is a cultural ideal that proclaims the close fraternity among all warriors. They disown any individual claims to property and are obliged to share their time, their food, and even the girls who are their mistresses. The restrictions on their diet and behavior keep them in

MARRIAGE AND FAMILY

Marriage

Marriages are arranged by the elders, without consulting the bride or her mother. Polygyny is an ideal that is achieved by most older men. As a result of their being younger than men at the time of marriage, most women become widows, and it is understood that they should not remarry.

Domestic Unit

The father is the key figure in the patriarchal family, and, theoretically, his control is absolute—subject only to interference by close senior elders in situations of crisis. Traditionally, as long as the father was alive, no son had final control over his cattle nor over his choice in marriage; this is still the norm in pastoral areas, away from the townships. In practice, as they age, older men rely on their sons to take over the management of the family, and it is the subservience of women that is the most permanent feature of the Maasai family. After her husband's death, even a forceful widow is subordinate to her sons in the management of her herd, and she finds herself wholly unprotected if she has no sons.

Inheritance

At marriage, a bride is allocated a herd of cattle, from which all her sons will build up herds of their own, overseen by their father, who also makes gifts of cattle to his sons over the course of his life. When the parents die, the oldest son inherits the residue of his father's herd, and the youngest inherits the residue of his mother's allocated cattle. Daughters inherit nothing at all.

Socialization

The warrior village plays a key role in the socialization of men. Boys are taken away by their older warrior brothers as herders and are taught to respond to the discipline of the warrior village. Then, in due course, as warriors within their own village, they are expected to develop an unquestioning acceptance of the authority of their peers to emerge to elderhood with a strong sense of loyalty to this peer group.

A girl's childhood is dominated by a strict avoidance, even a fear, of her father and other elders. Her marriage prospects and her family's reputation hinge on her ability to develop an acute sense of respect. She is socialized to accept her subservience to her future husband—himself an elder—and to the elders at large.

each other's company, reinforcing their dependence on their peers.

The warrior villages of one subset are abandoned before the initiation of the next subset of warriors, and retirement to elderhood entails a dispersal into smaller and often more remote villages, in order to exploit fully the available grazing lands and water for livestock. As elders, the mens' prime concern is to establish their families and herds. The transition to elderhood thus entails a transformation from a young man who had been heavily dependent on his peers to a self-reliant and self-interested veteran. The independence of each stock owner within the elder's village is popularly seen as the converse of the close dependency that was nurtured within the warrior village, just as the image of the patriarch is the converse of the popular image of the selfless warrior.

POLITICAL ORGANIZATION. Authority within the age system resides in the linkage of alternating age sets (A-B-C-D-E-F . . .), whereby elders of age set A bring a new age set, C, to life in a ceremony that includes the kindling of a fire: they then become the "firestick patrons" of the members of age set C and are responsible for promoting them as warriors in stages toward elderhood. Similarly, C will eventually be patrons to age set E, creating a linkage of age sets, A-C-E- . . ., which is separate from a parallel firestick linkage among age sets B-D-F. . . . This dual system of accountability entails an ambivalent combination of rivalry between adjacent age sets (especially in the south) and of hostility between young and old (especially in the north).

SOCIAL CONTROL. Social control among the Maasai rests ultimately on the general belief in the power of elders to bless and to curse, which is linked to their moral superiority in all spheres. The power of firestick patrons over warriors, of fathers over their children, and of all senior kin resides in their power to curse.

CONFLICT. Conflict among the Maasai focuses primarily on various aspects of warriorhood. The warriors are seen as the defenders of Maasai herds even today, although cattle raiding occurs only on a minor scale as compared with what went on in the past. More pressing are the problems that are internal to the Maasai, those of accommodating the warriors. On the one hand, there is a strained relationship between warriors and elders over stock theft and adultery by the warriors, both of which stem from their prolonged bachelorhood and from the food shortages they often endure, in contrast to the lives led by the wealthy

and polygynous elders. On the other hand, there is the rivalry that exists between successive subsets of warriors. The privileges that are claimed by each subset of warriors in their prime are denied their successors until these novices are capable of assuming them in a display of force. This rivalry can lead to fierce infighting. The succession of age sets and subsets is far from smooth, therefore, and the warrior ideal continues to dominate, even after almost a century of peace.

Religion and Expressive Culture

RELIGIOUS BELIEFS. The Maasai believe in an omnipresent God (Nkai), but they have no means of knowing their God's form or intentions. Inasmuch as God has human attributes, they might be described as those of extreme age. Respect for the knowledge of the oldest living men and for their ritual power to bless and to curse is magnified in the profound respect for their all-powerful and all-knowing God.

Pronounced beliefs in sorcery are also evident, particularly at times of misfortune and at major sacrifices. The characteristics of the supposed sorcerers may be viewed as a grotesque caricature of the competitive instincts that are popularly attributed to individual elders, emphasizing their greed and envy of the good fortune of others.

RELIGIOUS PRACTITIONERS. The widespread concern with sorcery is associated with the Loonkidongi dynasty of prophets. Each tribal section has its own prophet, who is seen as helping its members to cope with the endemic sorcery, by providing them with protective medicines and advice for their ceremonies. The prophet is regarded with awe as a type of all-seeing godfather, but his power to curb sorcery is also thought to derive from his knowledge of sorcery as a Loonkidongi, and popular attitudes toward other members of this dynasty are highly ambivalent. The Loonkidongi tend to live in small colonies on the borders between Maasai tribal sections, where they are suspected of providing a breeding ground for discontent, practicing sorcery among themselves, and even secretly selling evil charms to would-be Maasai sorcerers.

CEREMONIES. The promotion of warriors to elderhood entails a series of extended ceremonies. The first of two high points of this process is the *eunoto* ceremony, when warriors are "raised" to senior-warrior status. For this occasion, they come from their separate villages and form a single village. They are led by a ritual leader (*olotuno*), who is sometimes thought to shoulder the misfortunes of his peers and is there-

The most distinctive feature of Maasai society is the age system, which stratifies adult males into age sets, spaced apart by about fifteen years.

The Mende household unit is represented by at least one man and perhaps several of his brothers, with all of their wives and children.

fore destined to an early death or an impoverished life. Shortly after the eunoto, the warriors abandon their warrior village and return with their mothers to their fathers' villages. The second high point of their career as an age set is the *olghesher* ceremony, which finally unites the "right-hand" and "left-hand" subsets, promoting them jointly to senior elderhood. They are now endowed with the power to bless and to curse and to become firestick patrons of the next new age set.

Their age-set rituals also serve to unite the Maasai federation as a people. The Keekonyukie section in the north and the Kisonko section in the south each have a central role in unifying the Maasai through synchronizing their shared age system. At the inception of each age set, all Maasai are oriented toward the north, waiting for the ritual cue from the Keekonyukie, when boys from the northern tribal sections compete to seize an ox's horn. Only after this ritual has occurred can the new age set be inaugurated in other tribal sections. About twenty-five years later, it is the Kisonko who must first perform olghesher, finally promoting the whole age set and giving it a name that is adopted by all Maasai. Meanwhile, other tribal sections must wait in turn for this lead before they too can follow suit. These two ritual cues, alternating between north and south and between firestick linkages in a fifteen-year cycle, provide a common orientation in space and in time for the Maasai, punctuating their life courses as individuals and reiterating the unity of all Maasai.

Women's ceremonies invariably stem from a widespread concern for their fertility, and, at such times, their dancing is a central feature. These dances sometimes amount to a display of anger and even violence against the elders, and they provide an arena within which women's subservience is temporarily reversed. Even elders share in the belief that these dances will restore fertility and bring the community back to harmony.

ARTS. Visual arts among the Maasai focus predominantly on body decoration and on the beaded ornaments that are displayed by warriors and complemented by the beaded ornaments of girls and young women—notably in the trousseau of a bride. These decorations are prominently displayed in their dances, which are themselves a popular art form, frequently with a competitive idiom. Elders do not perform in display dances, but their oratory has many parallels with dance, with gestures used to delineate the space around them and to structure their rhetoric, holding the attention of the audience with a display of the panache that they learned as warriors in their youthful dancing.

MEDICINE. In addition to the prophets, lesser members of the Loonkidongi dynasty serve as diviners who claim the power to diagnose illnesses and the causes of misfortune and to prescribe a range of herbal medicines and ritual cures. Their secrets are carefully withheld from other Maasai and are linked to a range of "poisons" that are associated with their powers of sorcery, if they are provoked.

DEATH AND AFTERLIFE. There are no elaborate mortuary practices among the Maasai and no beliefs in afterlife. For a parent, however, there is a sense akin to immortality in leaving behind a family whose very existence stems from a life that has been dedicated to care and attention. To leave no successors is to face oblivion in the fullest sense, and it may be taken as a sign of having been cursed.

Bibliography

Gulliver, P. H. (1962). *Social Control in an African Society: A Study of the Arusha, Agricultural Maasai of Northern Tanganyika*. London: Routledge & Kegan Paul.

Merker, M. (1904). *Die Maasai*. Berlin: Dietrich Reimer.

Spencer, Paul (1976). "Opposing Streams and the Gerontocratic Ladder: Two Models of Age Organization in East Africa." *Man* 11:153–175.

Spencer, Paul (1988). *The Maasai of Matapato: A Study of Rituals of Rebellion*. Manchester: Manchester University Press.

—PAUL SPENCER

MENDE

Ethonyms: Boumpe, Hulo, Kossa, Kosso

The Mende are a group of people who live primarily within the southern third of Sierre Leone. Historically, they are rather recent arrivals to this area, appearing no earlier than the sixteenth century as invading forces advancing from the south. Linguistically, the Mende are related to Niger-Kordofanian and Niger-Congo groupings; they have at least two major dialects—Kpa and Ko—and two less prominent dialects—Waanjama and Sewawa. In 1987 the Mende numbered about one million, of whom 75 to 80 percent were Kpa Mende and most of the remaining portion, Ko Mende. The Mende comprise about 30 percent of Sierre Leone's total population.

The small country of Sierre Leone, of which the Mende occupy the southern portion, lies very close to the equator on the western coast of Africa. The climate is distinguished by a dry season from October to May and a wet season from June to October. There is much variation in humidity, sunshine, and rainfall, depending on the terrain, the distance from the coast, and the time of year. Until the twentieth century, much of the terrain consisted of forests, which have since been greatly reduced by clearing for farming. Farmbush is the dominant vegetation type of the southern part of the country, where the Mende reside.

The Mende live primarily in villages of 70 to 250 residents, which are situated from 1.5 to 5 kilometers apart. There is little or no mechanization over the greater part of rural Mende country. Mende farmers use hoes and machetes, but few other tools. Coffee, cocoa, and ginger are grown as cash crops, whereas rice, pepper, groundnuts, beniseed, and palm oil are grown for local consumption. Rice cooperatives have been formed in some rural areas.

Work is divided by gender: men attend to the heavy work of clearing the land for planting rice while women are occupied with cleaning and pounding rice, fishing, and weeding the planted crops. This routine is followed during ten months of every year, with a couple of months left around the New Year, when they can spend more time in the village engaging in domestic pursuits like house building.

The household unit is represented by at least one man and perhaps several of his brothers, with all of their wives and children. One or more brothers and married sisters usually leave sooner or later and are incorporated into other residential units. The senior male has moral authority—the right to respect and obedience—over the family as a whole, especially with regard to the negotiation of debts, damages, and bride-wealth.

Because of their recent origins, their contact with other peoples in the area, their involvement in the slave trade, and the strong influence of Islam and later colonial powers, as well as missionary contact, it is difficult and perhaps misleading to speak of the traditional culture of the Mende. Mende culture is an eclectic blend that has resulted from all of these different influences. Mende religion, likewise, has native elements—a Supreme Being, ancestral spirits, secret societies, and witch finders—that coexist with and are sometimes interspersed with adherence to Christian or Islamic beliefs.

Bibliography

Gittins, Anthony J. (1987). *Mende Religion: Aspects of Belief and Thought in Sierra Leone*. Wort und Werk. Nettetal: Steyler Verlag.

Harris, W. T., and H. Sawyerr (1968). *The Springs of Mende Belief and Conduct*. Freetown: Sierra Leone University Press; Oxford University Press.

Jedrej, M. C. (1974). "An Analytic Note on the Land and Spirits of the Sewa Mende." *Africa* 44:38–45.

MOSSI

Ethnyms: "Moose" is the currently favored form according to the nationally adopted orthography. It is traditionally written "Mossi"; "Moshi" formerly appeared frequently in British and Ghanaian writing. "Mosi" also occurs. One conteporary scholar who employs the officially favored spelling notes for his Anglophone readers that the pronunciation is "MOH-say" (Fiske 1991, 24).

Orientation

IDENTIFICATION. The Mossi are the most prominent ethnic group in the modern nation of Burkina Faso (formerly Upper Volta). They are also well known in the anthropological literature as a society with an especially high rate of labor migration to neighboring countries. They are noted historically for their resistance to the regionally dominant Islamic states and missionaries, although their culture shows numerous Islamic influences.

LOCATION. The traditionally Mossi areas expanded at the moment of French conquest (1896–1897) from the central core, or so-called Mossi plateau, of Burkina Faso. There are also significant numbers of Mossi in Ivory Coast (where they are the second-largest ethnic group) and in Ghana. The core area, however, is approximately 11°30′ to 14°00′ N and 0°00′ to 3°00′ E. Names and boundaries of local government units have changed repeatedly in the modern era; Mossi country can be defined generally as the area of Burkina containing the cities of Ouahigouya, Kongoussi, Kaya, Koudougou, Ouagadougou, Manga, Tenkodogo, Koupela, and Boulsa.

The Mossi states were well placed for trade; they were "inland" from the great bend of the Niger River, where the empires of Ghana, Mali, and Songhay rose and fell. At the same time, they were north of Asante and the other Akan states that come to prominence as trade shifted from

Sacrifices for the sake of fertility or to call down rain are performed by the Mossi when conditions demand.

trans-Saharan toward European outposts on the coast.

Because of the proximity of Mossi country to the more prosperous (at times) economies of Ghana and Ivory Coast, the relatively dense Mossi population, and the poverty (in colonial and postcolonial economic terms) of Burkina Faso, very substantial numbers of Mossi have drawn upon their precolonial trade and frontier traditions of movement, working and even settling in neighboring countries.

DEMOGRAPHY. The Mossi make up approximately half of the population of Burkina Faso. The national censuses of 1975 and 1985 did not report national statistics for ethnicity. The 1961 sample survey reported 49 percent of the population of the then Upper Volta to be Mossi. If that figure is carried forward to the 1985 population of 7,964,705, there would then be some 3.9 million Mossi. The 49-percent figure, apart from deriving from a 10-percent sample, was often suspected of having been politically manipulated to deny the dominant ethnic group in the new country formal majority status. Therefore, a figure of 4 million or so Mossi should be considered the minimum. The 1994 *CIA World Factbook* estimates the population of Burkina Faso as 10,134,661 in July of 1994; that same source estimates the Mossi population as 2.5 million, lower than the 4.96 million that is 49 percent of the 1994 estimated population. Given that estimates of the Mossi population of Burkina Faso residing outside the country as labor migrants at any one time range as high as 20 percent, a higher figure is plausible.

LINGUISTIC AFFILIATION. The name of the Mossi language was usually written as Moré, although the 1976 national standards stipulate "Moore." It is also encountered as "Molé" or, in more recent works, "Mooré." Labeled "Mossi" in Greenberg's classification (1963), it is a member of the Voltaic of Niger-Congo; "Molé-Dagbané" is also found as a label for the grouping. In recent scholarship, "Moore" is placed in the Oti-Volta Subgroup of the Gur languages; a recent summary notes that "Gur" is common in English and German writing, whereas French scholars more often use "langues voltaïques."

History and Cultural Relations

The Mossi states have existed for at least 500 years; the exact dates and origins of the states and their ruling clans are still debated by scholars. The Mossi were in conflict with the Song-hay Empire in the period from 1328 to 1333, and again between 1477 and 1498. In general terms, the Mossi were strong enough that they were never conquered until the French arrived in 1896–1897, but they were not strong enough to do more than raid the kingdoms along the Niger. Their expansion was by annexing other, often stateless, peoples at the edges of Mossi polities, peoples whose general culture was the same and whose languages were related. Within one generation of the French conquest, French writers had already employed the term *mossification* to describe the assimilationist expansion of the Mossi states into surrounding communities.

Settlements

Rural communities are dispersed: each extended-family compound is surrounded by fields; households are therefore 75 to 100 meters apart. When millet is fully grown (with stalks up to 4 meters), each compound is invisible to others. Boundaries may be based upon natural features like streams, but the dispersed settlement pattern forces recognition that communities are social and political—not geographic—units. It is often impossible to assign a compound to one village or another on a basis of location. Households are compounds of adobe, usually circular, houses with thatched roofs and surrounded by adobe walls. Although metal roofs are hotter and noisier and hence less comfortable than thatch, their prestige value and lessened maintenance has made them common, if not yet dominant, in the countryside.

District chiefs tended to live in noticeably larger compounds, but in villages that otherwise resembled ordinary ones. Kings, however, lived in larger towns or cities—places with artisans, sizable markets, and links to long-distance trade.

In the colonial and postcolonial periods, there has been an increase in movement to towns, but also an increase in ease of communication for rural villages and in capital available to them from their migrant members.

The modern ease of communications—better roads and motor transport, railroads, and telecommunications—has greatly expanded the social field within which individuals and families live and move while still remaining participating members of their home social and ritual communities. The still-high rate of labor migration nowadays takes place within a network of relatives and neighbors already in a several-country region, who can house and sponsor, if not directly employ, the new migrant.

Economy

SUBSISTENCE AND COMMERCIAL ACTIVITIES. The basis for life throughout the region was (and is) the cultivation of millet and sorghum. Millet flour is made into porridge, eaten with a sauce of meat and/or leaves and condiments. Sorghum is made into beer. Because of the lack of substantial agricultural surpluses, together with a cultural expectation that each household head grow his own millet for subsistence, almost everyone was a farmer. Many cultivators also engaged in local market trading; indeed, sale of beer on market days was the main source of independent income for women. As is usual for West Africa, markets are on a regional rotation; for the Mossi, that cycle is seven days. When a market falls on a Friday, it is especially large and well attended. Formally non-Muslim, this is one of the several ways in which Mossi culture is affected by the Sahelwide presence of Islam.

INDUSTRIAL ARTS. In common with inhabitants of their larger region, Mossi blacksmiths and potters are distinct, castelike, descent groups living in specially named villages or neighborhoods.

TRADE. Besides the local markets, which involved much of the population, there are also, among the Mossi, long-distance traders, the Yarsé. Of Mandé origin, from what is now Mali, they settled among the Mossi. They were not unusual in their assimilation of Mossi culture and language, but are distinct from other Mossi in their retention of Islam, a necessary affiliation for Sahelian traders. Mossi exported cattle, donkeys, and cotton cloth (in large, strip-woven "wheels") and imported salt, kola nuts, and luxury goods.

DIVISION OF LABOR. Work in household fields is done by all family members. When a cooperative work group is held, women in the host household prepare beer and porridge for the participants. Women are generally responsible for food preparation, including collecting water and firewood. Spinning cotton is done by women, whereas weaving the thread into cloth and sewing the strips into panels and clothing is done by men. Precolonial iron smelting and contemporary smithing were/are the preserve of specific lineages, which in some but not all Mossi societies are endogamous; throughout West Africa, iron is associated with the earth, and smiths are held in spiritual awe and frequently segregated from the rest of society. Pottery is likewise made by specialist lineages, which also provide drummers who set the rhythm for large cultivating and threshing parties.

LAND TENURE. Land is held by virtue of membership in one's patrilineage, although, in cases where sufficient land is available, it may also be let by the lineage to affinal kin or outright strangers. As heritage from the ancestors to the living lineage members, land is not alienable, but is rather held in trust for future descendants. The lineage allocates fields to households on the basis of need, dividing at intervals both the fields within the settlement that surround the houses, and those further away.

Kinship

KIN GROUPS AND DESCENT. The formal organization of Mossi society is by patrilineal descent groups. Lineages are grouped into larger clans, which share a presumed common ancestor and a totemic animal whose avoidance as food is explained by the clan origin myth. Individual lineages within a clan may not be able to trace any genealogical links beyond their apical ancestor. In general, with the exception of chiefly lineages whose members have claims to power to maintain, genealogies are shallow and mutable. For most cultivators, all that is necessary is enough depth of genealogy (perhaps three generations) to clearly validate one's rights to a house plot and fields. Whereas formal authority in a lineage is assigned by genealogical seniority, in day-to-day life other elders, with perhaps less seniority but more wisdom, function as leaders. Indeed, a man might be represented in marriage negotiations by an elder not of his lineage, if circumstances of local knowledge and standing made that desirable.

KINSHIP TERMINOLOGY. A consequence of the relative weakness (or, in positive terms, the adaptive flexibility) of the patrilineages is that there is only one word—*buudu*—for "clan" and "lineage"; it spans all descent-based groups above the immediate household compound. Members of a clan share a surname, although the formalities and mutability of this practice are not well studied.

Marriage and Family

MARRIAGE. Marriages are arranged by lineage heads. Lineages are exogamous within the local community, with clear genealogical connections. People could and did move from village to village, making it possible for nearby members of

◆ **exogamous**
Marriage outside a specific group or social category of which the person is a member, such as one's clan or community.

*Mossi marriages are
arranged by lineage
head.*

one's clan to be genealogically distinct enough to allow intermarriage. Indeed, there is a continuum ranging from those close kin with whom marriage is forbidden, to complete strangers (even non-Mossi) as spouses. In between are clan members who are eligible marriage partners, and closer still to oneself are clan members too close genealogically to marry, but too far away genealogically to remarry widows from one's own lineage. Mossi marriage includes levirate and sororate. Polygyny was practiced, within the economic limits of a man's need for additional household labor and the prestige of multiple wives, against his ability to pay the compensating goods and services required by his wives' lineages.

In addition to marriages arranged (or accepted) by local lineages, members of chiefly lineages or prominent commoners might be granted a wife by a chief or king. Such a marriage obligated the recipient to betroth a daughter or sister to the king or chief in return. The chief might then marry that woman, but would be more likely to award her to another man, expanding the web of marriage ties and obligations centered on the chief. This practice, *pugsiure*, was not often a factor in the lives of ordinary cultivators, but it was not unknown for a man of renown to be rewarded with a wife by his political superiors.

Polygyny is not an option for Christian Mossi; some villages are predominantly Christian, but the overall Mossi population is only 10 percent Christian.

DOMESTIC UNIT. The classic Mossi household was comprised of a man, his younger brothers and any married sons, their wives, and children. This household unit, the *zaka*, in turn contained residential areas for each husband and his family. Houses were usually round adobe structures with conical thatched roofs; each adult had his or her own house, and others served as kitchens and animal pens. Adobe walls surrounded the entire compound and subdivided it into households. A cleared "patio" area, to the west of the compound, was conceptually part of the living unit; it contained granaries and sunshades under which guests were entertained; only close kin or close friends would enter the compound itself.

INHERITANCE. Goods and livestock were inherited by patrilineal descendants—in principle by sons, but in practice by children of both genders. Land, houses, and granaries were the property of the lineage, not of the individual, and were inherited within the descent group as much on the basis of need as on that of seniority.

SOCIALIZATION. Children were raised within the extended-family compound. Muslim boys (as in Yarsé communities) might receive religious instruction from the local *maalam* and, in unusual cases, travel for advanced instruction. Similarly, within the Mossi religion, an occasional individual might travel to gain education as a seer or healer.

In modern Burkina Faso, even after large increases in the number of schools relative to the period of French rule (which ended in 1961), formal education still does not reach most children, including the Mossi. The 1990 estimate for literacy of those older than age 15 nationwide was 18 percent, with men estimated at 28 percent and women 9 percent. The increase in Islam has increased the number of children, chiefly boys, receiving instruction in basic Arabic and the Quran.

Sociopolitical Organization

SOCIAL ORGANIZATION. The Mossi, in common with other Voltaic peoples, state and stateless, were organized in patrilineally defined lineages within clans. Membership in such units, however, was only rigidly constrained for those of royal and chiefly descent. Ordinary cultivators could and did incorporate new members into their lineages, whether affinal kin (sisters' sons seeking better opportunities matrilaterally) or outright strangers, even non-Mossi.

POLITICAL ORGANIZATION. Survey literature often refers to the Mossi Empire. In fact, there were three independent kingdoms and around fifteen dependencies and interstitial buffers. The three kingdoms, in order of seniority, but not power, were Tenkodogo (Tankudugo), Ouagadougou (Wogodogo), and Yatenga. An easterly fourth kingdom, Fada N'Gurma, is sometimes counted as a Mossi state. The polities, as in most of Africa, were based on control of trade, whether of sources or routes. The burden of the state on the ordinary cultivators, then, was not great. Kings and chiefs possessed *naam*, the supernatural power required to rule others, which was conferred in consequence of a ruler having been properly chosen and installed. It is this intertwining of political power and religious legitimization that accounted for the well-known Mossi resistance to Islam. An occasional king or chief might convert, as several Ouagadougou kings did in the 1700s, but the system as a whole could not separate a ruler from the religion that conferred his power.

Kings had court officials who were each responsible for a sector of the kingdom; district chiefs in turn had twenty or more village chiefs reporting to them. Proper selection and validation indicated the possession of naam, without which one could not validly rule, but the officeholders were picked from their predecessor's patrilineage. Kings, district chiefs, and village chiefs all bore the title *naba*, with a geographic qualifier (e.g., Tenkdogo Naba, Koupela Naba). Only the king of Ouagadougou, the Mogho Naba, had a title (chief of Mossi country) that was not tied to a place-name; he was by far the most powerful of the various Mossi kings and chiefs.

Since Burkina Faso became independent in 1961, traditional kings and chiefs are not formally recognized by the government and its colonially derived administrative structure. They remain locally important, however, and have served as deputies during periods when there has been an elected legislature.

SOCIAL CONTROL. Lineages, and village elders generally, exerted a good deal of influence upon people and their behavior. A society in which several crucial tasks (cultivating, weeding, harvesting, threshing, and, not least, roof replacement) depended on cooperative work groups allows effective ostracism for nonparticipation. The complex of Mossi chiefdoms and states and the expanding Mossi frontier at their edges allowed resettlement as a means of improving one's opportunities or escape from a difficult community, even before the French colonial regime intentionally stimulated massive labor migration by imposing a head tax payable in francs. Village chiefs represented the state and resolved differences brought to them.

In independent Burkina Faso, courts and police exist as well, although their impact on the countryside is variable. The avowedly revolutionary government of Thomas Sankara in the 1980s created "revolutionary defense committees" in every community, including rural villages, but their impact during that period and since the overthrow of that government in 1987 has not been reported.

CONFLICT. Military power was cavalry based. As was true across the Sahel, the absence of wheeled transport and semiarid conditions made garrisons impossible owing to the inability to feed a concentration of horses. In consequence, the power of a political center depended on its ability to mobilize local chiefs, with their horses and dependents.

The Mossi states were, however, strong enough to survive wars with the Muslim empires of the great bend of the Niger River, to their north. The Mossi are noted as the major—if not the only—Sahelian states to withstand the spread of Islam in the region. Mossi forces, like those of the other states around them, raided the stateless peoples around their perimeters for slaves. As a result of the loose nature of Mossi states and their weak military basis, there was also conflict between them. At the time of the French conquest, the oldest—but smallest and weakest—Mossi state, Tenkodogo, was engaged in a war of mutual raids with a chiefdom to its north, which in turn was a dependency of a buffer state on the edge of the largest Mossi kingdom, Ouagadougou.

Religion and Expressive Culture

RELIGIOUS BELIEFS. There are three major components to Mossi religion. One is the general African belief in an otiose "High God," who created the universe but has no role in its daily life. There are lesser, but more relevant, supernatural powers that govern the two major elements of life: soil fertility and rainfall. They are worshiped by conducting rituals at specific sites, often trees (or sites where one grew) or rock outcrops. Lastly, and most immediately, are the ancestors in one's patrilineage, who play an active role in regulating the behavior and success of their descendants. In the interests of the lineage, the ancestors link the past, present, and future.

Because of the close ties between Mossi religion and political organization, most Mossi—apart from the Yarsé long-distance traders—did not become Muslims. The French conquest in 1896–1897 undermined the traditional religion by implying that it was no longer effective in the face of superior outside forces. The French sent Catholic missionaries, and, very reluctantly, admitted U.S. Protestant missionaries in 1921, but cultural differences and the demands of Christianity have limited its impact. The first African cardinal in the Catholic church is a Mossi, however. Islam has a long-standing presence in the region, and, because its proselytizers are Africans, Mossi have been converting to Islam at an increasing rate. The lack of ethnic statistics at the national level makes numbers imprecise, and the more traditionally Muslim areas (west of the Mossi) would affect the totals, but the current estimate that Burkina is 50 percent Muslim suggests a clear trend toward conversion.

RELIGIOUS PRACTITIONERS. The Mossi are known ethnographically for a formal dichotomy between political and spiritual power: the political power of the chiefs, signified by the naam, is offset by the religious power of the *teng-*

♦ **seer**
One who foresees the future; a diviner.

Mossi

Mossi men were buried to the west of the cleared area west of their compounds; women were buried in household fields.

soba, or "earth-owner." In much of West Africa, an important distinction is drawn between wild land and animals, and domesticated animals and farmland. Ownership of land is not merely vested in an ongoing descent group, but is validated by the presumption that the family in question "domesticated" unsettled land, thereby gaining both title to it and access to the supernatural forces controlling its fertility. Since the Mossi political system is founded upon an origin myth of immigrant cavalry, the political rulers cannot claim spiritual power over the land. That power is retained by the lineage of the tengsoba, presumed to be the descendants of the autochtonous people, the original settlers who antedated the Mossi military. This dichotomy, and its ability to check royal abuse with refusal to perform vital fertility rituals, was so well known ethnographically that James G. Frazer had swept it into *The Golden Bough* by 1919, barely twenty-two years after the Mossi had been conquered. Whereas the dichotomy is fundamental to a number of Voltaic societies as well as the Mossi states of Yatenga and Ouagadougou, it is not found in the original Mossi state of Tenkodogo. There, the autochtonous people, the Bisa, were not assimilated into Mossi society, which instead relies upon sisters' sons to perform fertility rituals; the dichotomy in this case is between the lineage and its non-member relative.

Lineage rituals, propitiating ancestors rather than earth spirits, are performed by the eldest male; lineage members from even scores of kilometers away may send chickens to be sacrificed by the lineage head on the ancestral graves. Finally, funerals are performed by the household head of the deceased, who may be the heir of the latter.

CEREMONIES. Sacrifices for the sake of fertility or to call down rain are performed when conditions demand, by "earth-owners" or, in the case of Tenkodogo, a "sister's son" of the local lineage. Ancestor-oriented rituals, even at the kingdom level, are lineage or clan based; that is, even a king's harvest thanksgiving, although it is immense in scale and takes precedence over everyone else's, is, strictly speaking, offered to his ancestors for the sake of his harvest, rather than to those of the collective inhabitants of his realm. Inhabitants of a given district are not able to perform sacrifices to thank their ancestors until their district chief has performed his.

This harvest festival, which occurs after the millet has been harvested in late autumn, but before it is threshed in midwinter, is the *basega*; the chief's or king's is the *na'basega*.

ARTS. Mossi men weave cotton cloth, using the strip looms common in West Africa. Pottery, made by specialist lineages, is decorated with inscribed and painted designs. The western Mossi share the traditions of wood sculpture and masked dancing with the societies to their west, but these practices are not found in Tenkodogo. Unlike some other Voltaic peoples, the Mossi do not paint designs on their adobe walls and houses. Until banned by the modern government, facial scarification in locally distinctive patterns was practiced.

MEDICINE. Traditionally, curing was in the hands of one's family and individuals locally renowned as healers. Modern medicine is now available to the Mossi, within the limitations imposed by the fact that Burkina Faso is among the poorest nations in both Africa and the world.

DEATH AND AFTERLIFE. Men were buried to the west of the cleared area west of their compounds. Women were buried in household fields; the funeral was performed by members of their own patrilineages. As is common in Africa, elders are venerated because their accumulated knowledge and experiences form the collective information in societies without written records. They are also considered "almost ancestors"; upon death, they become part of the generalized community of ancestors who watch over their living descendants and intervene to reward or punish behavior. Because of the shallowness of commoner genealogies, the ancestors one addresses in rituals like the basega are a collectivity, not named spirits whose individual intercession might be requested.

Bibliography

Fiske, Alan Page (1991). *Structures of Social Life: The Four Elementary Forms of Human Relations.* New York: Free Press.

Greenberg, Joseph H. (1963). *The Languages of Africa.* Indiana University Research Center in Anthropology, Folklore, and Linguistics, Publication no. 25. The Hague: Mouton.

Hammond, Peter B. (1966). *Yatenga: Technology in the Culture of a West African Kingdom.* New York: Free Press.

McMillan, Della E. (1995). *Sahel Visions: Planned Settlement and River Blindness Control in Burkina Faso.* Tucson: University of Arizona Press.

Schildkrout, Enid (1978). *People of the Zongo: The Transformation of Ethnic Identities in Ghana.* Cambridge: Cambridge University Press.

Skinner, Elliott P. (1964). *The Mossi of the Upper Volta: The Political Development of a Sudanese People.* Stanford, Calif.: Stanford University Press. Reprint, with supplementary chapter. 1989. *The Mossi of Burkina Faso: Chiefs, Politicians, and Soldiers.* Prospect Heights, Ill.: Waveland Press.

Skinner, Elliott P. (1974). *African Urban Life: The Transformation of Ouagadougou.* Princeton, N.J.: Princeton University Press.

—GREGORY A. FINNEGAN

NANDI AND OTHER KALENJIN PEOPLES

Ethonyms: Chebleng'. Keiyo: Elgeyo. Kipsigis: Lumbwa, Sotek. Kony: Bong'om, Bok, Elgon Maasai, Elgonyi, Sabaot. Marakwet: Cherang'any, Maragweta, Sengwer. Nandi: Chemwal, Teng'wal. Okiek: Akiy, Dorobo, Ogiek Pokot: Pakot, Suk. Sebei: Kipsorai, Mbai, Sabaot, Saping', Sor. Terik: Nilotic Tiriki, Nyang'ori. Tugen: Cherangani, Kamasia.

Orientation

IDENTIFICATION. The Kalenjin are related East African peoples (Kipsigis, Nandi, Keiyo, Tugen, Marakwet, Endo, Sabaot, Terik, Okiek) who form one branch of the Highland Nilotes, formerly referred to as "Southern Nilo-Hamites" or sometimes "Nandi-speaking peoples." This description focuses on the Nandi; about one-third of all Kalenjin and second-largest of the Kalenjin subgroups, they are geographically the most centrally located.

LOCATION. The Kalenjin live mainly in the highland of western Kenya, although the Sebei and some Pokot are located in eastern Uganda. Physical environment and ecological adaptation vary throughout Kalenjin country. The Nandi and Kipsigis live primarily on high plateaus with good agricultural potential: average elevation of 1,800 to 2,000 meters, thick topsoil, and 150 to 200 centimeters of rain annually distributed over the entire year. Many of the Kalenjin groups (Keiyo, Tugen, Marakwet/Endo) live along escarpments in the Rift Valley system, and the Sabaot on Mount Elgon. In these cases, most cultivation occurs between 1,350 and 2,000 meters, animals are herded in low-lying plains, and some communities may be situated at elevations of over 2,700 meters. The pastoral Pokot, the northernmost Kalenjin, live in arid lowlands where little cultivation is possible. The Okiek, mountain-forest-dwelling Kalenjin speakers, historically are foragers.

DEMOGRAPHY. There are probably just over 2 million Kalenjin, at least 95 percent of whom live in Kenya. The Kipsigis were 32 percent of all the Kenya Kalenjin in the 1969 census, followed by the Nandi (27 percent), Pokot (13 percent), Tugen (8.6 percent), Keiyo (8.5 percent), Marakwet (6 percent), Sabaot (4.2 percent), and Okiek (less than 1 percent by official census figures, but perhaps undercounted). The number of Uganda Sabaot (Sebei) is close to their number in Kenya. In the 1979 census, there were 1,652,243 Kalenjin in Kenya. They were the fifth-largest ethnic group—10.8 percent of the population. The vast majority of Kalenjin are rural, and population density differs greatly throughout Kalenjin country owing to highly varied ecological conditions.

LINGUISTIC AFFILIATION. Although the Kalenjin are regarded as a unit on the basis of speaking a common language, there are numerous dialects. All of them, it seems, are mutually intelligible with practice, although not necessarily immediately. Nandi and Kipsigis are distinguished by small sound and terminology differences, similar to the difference between English as spoken in Britain and the United States. Speakers of these dialects cannot immediately understand Pokot, Sabaot, and regional variants of Marakwet. Greenberg (1963) classifies Kalenjin as a Southern Nilotic language (Eastern Section, Nilotic Branch, Eastern Sudanic Language Family). Aside from Tatoga, which is spoken by a few small peoples of northern Tanzania, the nearest language to Kalenjin is Maasai.

History and Cultural Relations

The oral traditions of all the Nilotic peoples of East Africa refer to northern origins. There is a consensus among historians and linguists that the Plains and Highland Nilotes migrated from a region near the southern border of Ethiopia and Sudan shortly before the beginning of the Christian Era and diverged into separate communities shortly thereafter. Ehret (1971) believes that pre-Kalenjin who already were cattle keepers and had age sets lived in the western Kenya highlands 2,000 years ago. Presumably, these people absorbed other populations already living in the region. From some time after A.D. 500 to about A.D. 1600, there seems to have been a series of migrations eastward and southward from near Mount Elgon. Migrations were complex, and there are competing theories about their details.

Nandi and Other Kalenjin Peoples

SETTLEMENTS

In Nandi, individual title to land replaced a system in which land was plentiful and all who lived in a community had the right to cultivate it.

The Nandi and Kipsigis, in response to Maasai expansion, borrowed from the Maasai some of the traits that distinguish them from other Kalenjin: large-scale economic dependence on herding, military organization and aggressive cattle raiding, and centralized religious-political leadership. The family that established the office of *orkoiyot* (warlord/diviner) among both the Nandi and Kipsigis were nineteenth-century Maasai immigrants. By 1800, both the Nandi and Kipsigis were expanding at the expense of the Maasai. This process was halted in 1905 by the imposition of British colonial rule.

Introduced during the colonial era were new crops/techniques and a cash economy (Kalenjin men were paid wages for their military service as early as World War I); conversions to Christianity began (Kalenjin was the first East African vernacular to have a translation of the Bible). Consciousness of a common Kalenjin identity emerged to facilitate action as a political-interest group during and after World War II—historically, the Nandi and Kipsigis raided other Kalenjin as well as the Maasai, Gusii, Luyia, and Luo. The name "Kalenjin" is said to derive from a radio broadcaster who often used the phrase (meaning "I tell you"). Similarly, "Sabaot" is a modern term used to mean those Kalenjin subgroups who use "Subai" as a greeting. Nandi and Kipsigis were early recipients of individual land titles (1954), with large holdings by African standards because of their historically low population density. Economic development schemes were promoted as independence (1964) approached, and afterward many Kalenjin from more crowded areas resettled on farms in the former White Highlands near Kitale. Today's Kalenjin are among the most prosperous of Kenya's ethnic groups. Kenya's second president, Daniel arap Moi, is a Tugen.

Settlements

The typical settlement pattern is scattered. Groups of family homesteads make up a neighborhood (Nandi: *koret*), and today (in Kenya) several neighborhoods are combined into a sublocation, the smallest unit of government administration. Neighborhood size varies, but twenty to fifty or sixty households is typical. Among the Nandi, Kipsigis, pastoral Pokot, and Sebei, local communities historically were not, or were only to a limited extent, kin-based; among some other Kalenjin, they were based on patrilineal clans. Most Kalenjin combined neighborhoods to form a *pororiet*, a unit with mutual-defense functions.

Old-style houses are round, of wattle and daub, thatched, and divided internally into two rooms; the back room traditionally sheltered sheep and goats. Modern houses (still the minority) are usually square and of permanent material, with iron-sheet roofs. A typical household consists of a small extended family, or a nuclear family with some attached nonnuclear kin, living in a compound composed of several individual houses facing each other.

Economy

SUBSISTENCE AND COMMERCIAL ACTIVITIES. The Kalenjin are essentially semipastoralists. Cattle herding is thought to be ancient among them. Although the real economic importance of herding is slight compared to that of cultivation among many Kalenjin groups, they almost all display a cultural emphasis on and an emotional commitment to pastoralism. Cattle numbers have waxed and waned; however, cattle/people ratios of 5:1 or greater (typical of peoples among whom herding is economically dominant) have been recorded only for the pastoral Pokot. In their late-nineteenth-century heyday of pastoralism, the Nandi and the Kipsigis approached this ratio; 1–3:1 is more typical of the Kalenjin, and in some communities the ratio is even lower than 1:1.

The staple crop was eleusine, but maize replaced it during the colonial era. Other subsistence crops include beans, pumpkins, cabbages, and other vegetables as well as sweet and European potatoes and small amounts of sorghum. Sheep, goats, and chickens are kept. Iron hoes were traditionally used to till; today plows pulled by oxen or rented tractors are more common. The importance of cash crops varies with land availability, soil type, and other factors; among the Nandi and the Kipsigis, it is considerable. Surplus maize, milk, and tea are the major cash crops. Kalenjin farms on the Uasin Gishu plateau also grow wheat and pyrethrum.

In most communities there are a few wage workers and full-time business persons (shopkeepers, tailors, carpenters, bicycle repairmen, tractor owners) with local clienteles. It is common for young married men to be part-time entrepreneurs. Historically, women could brew and sell beer; this became illegal in the early 1980s. Some men work outside their communities, but labor migration is less common than elsewhere in western Kenya.

INDUSTRIAL ARTS. Traditionally, there were no full-time craft specialists. Most objects were manufactured by their users. The blacksmith's art was passed down in families in particular localities, and some women specialized in pottery.

TRADE. Traditionally, women conducted a trade of small stock for grain between pastoral-emphasis and cultivation-emphasis (often non-Kalenjin) communities. Regular local markets were rare prior to the colonial era. Today large towns and district centers have regular markets, and women occasionally sell vegetables in sublocation centers.

DIVISION OF LABOR. There was little traditional division of labor except by age and sex. Men cleared land for cultivation, and there is evidence that married men and women cooperated in the rest of the cultivation process. Husbands and wives did not (except during a limited historical period)—and do not—typically cultivate separately, other than the wife's vegetable garden. Today women do more cultivation if their husbands are engaged in small-scale business activities. Children herded cattle close to the homestead, as well as sheep and goats; warriors (young initiated men) herded cattle in distant pastures. Women and girls milked, cooked, and supplied water and firewood. Today boys are the main cowherds, and girls are largely responsible for infant care. The children's role in domestic labor is extremely important, even though most children now attend school.

LAND TENURE. In Nandi, individual title to land replaced a system in which land was plentiful, all who lived in a community had the right to cultivate it, and a man could move with his family to any locality in which he had a sponsor. Land prepared for cultivation, and used regularly, was viewed as belonging to the family that used it, and inherited from mother to son. The tenure systems of other Kalenjin were mainly similar. The Kerio Valley groups cultivated on ridges and at the foot of ridges, using irrigation furrows that required collective labor to maintain. This labor was provided by clan segments, which cleared and held land collectively, although cultivation rights in developed fields were held by individual families.

Kinship

All Kalenjin have patrilineal clans, but clans do not universally have strong cooperative functions other than regulating marriage (with various rules). Specific patrilineal links are traced for only three to four generations.

Kin terminology is basically Omaha. The most common sibling terms do not differentiate gender. There are a large number of specific terms for types of affines.

Marriage and Family

MARRIAGE. Traditionally, marriage took place in two stages: *ratet*, a small ceremony after which the couple lived together, and *tunisiet*, a large public feast held only at the completion of bride-wealth payment. Among the Nandi, these stages have typically occurred in rapid succession since about the turn of the twentieth century; among some other Kalenjin, at least during certain periods, a separation of many years has been customary, probably depending on availability of cattle or other livestock. Most Kalenjin—with some exceptions, notably the Okiek—pay bride-wealth in cattle. Once payment is complete, marriage is theoretically irrevocable. Traditional divorce grounds and proceedings exist, but divorce is in fact extremely rare, even in modern times. Permanent separations occur but do not technically negate marriage.

Polygyny is prestigious and, in the 1970s, was practiced by about 25 percent of ever-married Nandi men. Christians were monogamous slightly more frequently than non-Christians. Woman-woman marriage, found among Nandi, Kipsigis, and, since about the mid-twentieth century, among Keiyo, is not customary among other Kalenjin. Both women and men are active in negotiating marriages and reconciling separated couples. Husbands are jurally dominant, with the right to beat wives for certain offenses. Wives are publicly deferential; private relations are more nearly egalitarian. Leisure is spent with same-gender companions more than with one's spouse.

DOMESTIC UNIT. Each wife has her own field, cattle, and house within the family compound. A separate farm for each wife is the ideal. Compounds may include the husband's parents or mother, and other kin, depending on circumstances. Brothers and their wives may share a compound, although this is rare.

INHERITANCE. Traditional norms of cattle inheritance have been extended to land, money, and other property. Each wife's house-property consists of cattle given to her at marriage, acquired by her on her own, or given as bride-wealth for her daughters. These may be inherited only by

*Woman-woman
marriage, found
among Nandi,
Kipsigis, and, since
the mid-twentieth
century, among
Keiyo, is not
customary among
other Kalenjin.*

Nandi and Other Kalenjin Peoples

SOCIOPOLITICAL ORGANIZATION

her own sons (or, in Nandi and Kipsigis, the sons of her wife). A man's other property is inherited in equal shares by each wife's house. Failing lineal heirs, a man's property reverts to his brothers or their sons, a woman's to her co-wives' sons.

SOCIALIZATION. Infants are treated indulgently, but strict obedience (enforced by corporal punishment) is expected from children by about the age of 6. Routine care of infants and toddlers is largely the responsibility of girls between ages 8 and 10. Children are economically important and have heavy responsibilities. It is common to spend a part of childhood fostered by a relative, helping with domestic work in exchange for board and school fees.

Adolescent initiation (circumcision for boys and clitoridectomy for girls, and instruction for both) is a key feature of Kalenjin life and ethnic identity. These are sex-segregated rituals for most, but not all, Kalenjin groups. Adolescents are allowed a period of license to indulge in courtship and sexual play—before initiation for girls and afterward for boys. Girls marry directly following initiation; boys become warriors. Today some (mostly highly educated) girls refuse initiation.

Sociopolitical Organization

SOCIAL ORGANIZATION. Rotating age sets formerly existed among all Kalenjin, with the same or nearly the same names in all groups. There were eight sets among the Tugen, Marakwet, and Sabaot and seven among the Keiyo, Nandi, and Kipsigis (with some evidence that there may have been eight formerly). The Marakwet, Tugen, and Sabaot have formalized age sets for women, and other Kalenjin probably once had them. Members of younger age sets defer to members of older age sets. Men initiated together have a very high level of solidarity: they spend much time together, form work teams, try to live in the same neighborhood and marry sisters (wife's sister's husband is an important reciprocal kin type), and may not marry each other's daughters. Aside from territorial units and clans, there were no other formal associations.

RELIGION AND EXPRESSIVE CULTURE

Religious Beliefs

The statistical majority of Kalenjin are nominally Christian, but many still follow traditional beliefs and practices. They believed in one god, with many names, identified with the sun and now believed to be identical to the Christian God. Prayers were addressed primarily to God. The *oiik* (sing. *olindet*), or spirits of dead ancestors, were also believed able to intervene in human life. They were occasionally, but not systematically, propitiated. Thunder was another named supernatural being. Inchoate evil spirits were believed to lurk on pathways, especially at night, and cause harm.

Religious Practitioners

Every neighborhood has elders who serve as ritual experts. Diviners foretell events by patterns of pebbles poured from a calabash. The Kalenjin also believe in an array of different named types of sorcerers and witches.

Ceremonies

Formerly, there was an important communitywide festival, *kipsunde,* after the harvest. The major ceremonies now are the life-cycle rituals, many (e.g., those for for newborns) restricted to the family. The most important larger ritual is initiation.

Arts

The most highly developed visual art is decorative beadwork. Expressive culture and leisure activities include storytelling, singing and dancing, beer drinking (for men), and games of strategy. A lyrelike stringed instrument traditionally accompanied singing but is now becoming rare.

Medicine

Traditionally, "doctors" (male), with primarily supernaturally based skills, could ascertain the cause of bad luck or illness and treat it.

These practitioners still treat patients, particularly for mental illness. Female herbalists' and midwives' skills are more technical than supernatural.

Death and Afterlife

Death customs varied. The Nandi buried only infants and elders. Corpses of adults were left to be consumed by hyenas. In some Kalenjin groups (e.g., Marakwet), only barren people were left for scavengers. Death was polluting, and corpse handlers (sons or other close kin) had to be ritually purified and compensated from the estate. Many stories refer to an afterlife that is an idealized version of precolonial Kalenjin life. In a family ceremony, elders decided which ancestral spirit has been reincarnated in a newborn infant.

POLITICAL ORGANIZATION. Most political action took place in the *kokwet*, or council of the locality (today, sublocation council). Theoretically, any married man could be an active participant; in fact, a small group of influential elders formed the core. Women could observe—but not speak unless invited. Local councils sent representatives to occasional meetings of pororiet councils. Such councils continue to be important under the leadership of a government-appointed sublocation chief.

Traditionally, there were no central authorities, although the Nandi and Kipsigis came close to having chiefs in the head orkoiyot. All the Kalenjin had men called orkoiyot, believed to have power to control weather and foretell events. The nineteenth-century Nandi and Kipsigis came to rely on one central authority to coordinate warfare (through representatives on pororiet councils) and predict the success of raids. The orkoiyot was rewarded with a share of the booty of successful raids, and his family became wealthy and powerful. For its short existence, this office was passed from father to son.

SOCIAL CONTROL. Internal conflicts and norm violations are brought before neighborhood elders' courts. In modern Kenya, serious offenses are automatically matters for the police and government courts; other disputes can become police matters if someone files charges, but the elders' court is still the main arena for litigation. Offending parties would normally comply with fines imposed by elders; elders could also order punishments (e.g., beating) to be administered by offenders' age sets. People convicted of witchcraft were ordered to be put to death by their own kin. Traditionally, local groups of women could sanction men deemed guilty of "crimes against women."

CONFLICT. Cattle raiding was extremely important in the social life of the pastoral Kalenjin. The warrior age grade (youngest initiated age set) was responsible for defending cattle, and acquiring their own fortunes in captured cattle. War was not specifically for territory, but the Nandi and the Kipsigis did expand territorially at the expense of the Maasai. Whereas the Nandi and the Kipsigis did not raid each other, they did at times raid other Kalenjin.

Bibliography

Ehret, Christopher (1971). *Southern Nilotic History: Linguistic Approaches to the Study of the Past.* Evanston, Ill.: Northwestern University Press.

Goldschmidt, Walter (1976). *The Culture and Behavior of the Sebei.* Berkeley and Los Angeles: University of California Press.

Greenberg, Joseph H. (1963). Indiana University Research Center in Anthropology, Folklore, and Linguistics, Publication 25. *The Languages of Africa.* The Hague: Mouton.

Huntingford, G. W. B. (1953). *The Nandi of Kenya: Tribal Control in a Pastoral Society.* London: Routledge & Kegan Paul.

Kipkorir, B. E., with F. B. Welbourn (1973). *The Marakwet of Kenya.* Nairobi: East African Literature Bureau.

Oboler, Regina Smith (1985). *Women, Power, and Economic Change: The Nandi of Kenya.* Stanford, Calif.: Stanford University Press.

Orchardson, Ian (1961). *The Kipsigis.* Nairobi: East African Literature Bureau.

Peristiany, J. G. (1939). *The Social Institutions of the Kipsigis.* London: Routledge & Kegan Paul.

—REGINA SMITH OBOLER

NYAMWEZI AND SUKUMA

Ethonyms: Banyamwezi, Basukuma

Orientation

IDENTIFICATION. The Nyamwezi and Sukuma are two closely related ethnic groups that live principally in the region to the south of Lake Victoria in west-central Tanzania. When using ethnic names, they describe themselves as "Banyamwezi" (sing. Munyamwezi) and "Basukuma" (sing. Musukuma) respectively; they refer to their home areas as "Bunyamwezi" or "Unyamwezi," and as "Busukuma." The term "Sukumaland" is sometimes used for the Sukuma area. The name "Sukuma" literally means "north," but it has become a term of ethnic identification.

LOCATION. The Nyamwezi and Sukuma region lies between 2°10' and 6°20' S and 31°00' and 35°00' E. The Nyamwezi "home" area is in Tabora Region and western Shinyanga Region, and Sukumaland lies to the north and east, covering eastern Shinyanga Region and also Mwanza Region. There has been much population movement in and beyond these areas, and members of both groups have also settled on the coast and elsewhere. Sukuma and members of other groups, such as the Tusi and the Sumbwa, are often found in Nyamwezi villages, but Sukuma villages are ethnically more homogeneous. Sukuma took over the Geita area of Mwanza Region during the colonial period, and they have expanded farther west since then. They have also moved down into Nzega and the neighboring Igunga District, and some have migrated into the southern highland areas of Tanzania, and even into Zambia. These Sukuma movements have stemmed from political factors, such as colonial cattle-culling policies, and from local overcrowding and deteriorating soil conditions. The two areas form a large and undulating tableland, most of it at elevations between 1,150 and 1,275 meters. There are several rivers in the region, but most of them do not flow during the drier months. The year can be broadly divided into a rainy season, from about November until April, and a dry season the rest of the year. Average annual rainfall is about 75 centimeters for most of the Sukuma area, and about 90 centimeters for Unyamwezi, but there is much variation from year to year and from place to place. Across the region, there is a regular sequence of soil and vegetation zones. The upper levels are dry woodland typified by trees of the Brachystegia-Isoberlinia association; these areas are often called *miombo* country, after one of these trees. Lower areas of grass and thornbush steppe are also common, and in Sukumaland there are large tracts of park steppe interspersed with baobabs.

DEMOGRAPHY. Estimates of the modern population are difficult to make because Tanzanian censuses no longer record the ethnic affiliation of enumerated local populations. According to Tanzanian newspaper reports based on official estimates, there were 1 to 1.5 million Nyamwezi and between 3 and 3.5 million Sukuma in 1989. Census figures for 1978 show a wide range of population densities, from 73.3 per square kilometer in the Mwanza Region to 10.7 per square kilometer in the Tabora Region. Since then, population growth in Tanzania generally has been about 2.8 percent per annum, but densities have also been influenced by population movement.

LINGUISTIC AFFILIATION. Although sometimes classed as two closely related languages, Nyamwezi and Sukuma are probably best considered as a single Bantu language with several mutually intelligible dialects. These features include a seven-vowel system, use of tone, true negative tenses, class prefixes to indicate size, and the restriction of double prefixes to determined situations. In addition to their own dialect, most people today also speak Swahili.

History and Cultural Relations

It is not known how long the people have inhabited the area. The first clear written references to Nyamwezi occur in the early nineteenth century. According to local traditions, most of the region was uninhabited until the seventeenth century, when chiefly families began to arrive from various directions. Some are said to have come as hunters. As the population grew, new chiefdoms were formed by expansion and division. Trading visits to the coast and other areas were common in the nineteenth century, and Indian and Arab traders visited the area from the coast. Tabora was established as an Arab settlement, probably in the 1840s. John Hanning Speke and Richard Francis Burton were the first European visitors, in 1857. During the next thirty years, foreign traders, explorers, and missionaries made frequent visits, and local traders continued to travel to the coast. Exports included ivory and slaves, and imports included cloth and, later, guns. Secular aspects of chieftainship seem to have developed strongly at this time, and Arab intervention in local politics brought them into conflict with a rising chief, Mirambo, whom Henry Morton Stanley described as the Napoleon of Central Africa. Mirambo established his influence over many other chiefdoms in the Nyamwezi and southern Sukuma areas, but this "empire" broke up shortly after his death in 1884. The colony of German East Africa was established in 1890, and the area was brought under control by 1893. The Germans ruled through local chiefs who were expected to keep order and collect taxes. Several chiefdoms that

SUKAMA CONTAINER

A container made by the Sukuma of Tanzania. The Nyamwezi and Sukuma live south of Lake Victoria in west-central Tanzania. (Paul Almasy/© Corbis)

had formerly had matrilineal succession to the chieftainship changed to patrilineal succession under German rule. The British formally took over the administration of the country in 1919, three years after the expulsion of the Germans from Tabora during World War I. British rule continued until Tanzanian independence in 1961. Several changes were made in the number and internal organization of the chiefdoms in this period, and communications were extended and improved. Many people were moved from areas where sleeping sickness was prevalent into new settlements. Cotton was developed as a cash crop in Sukumaland. Since independence, chieftainship, as a political office, has been abolished, and the development of collective forms of village organization has been encouraged, albeit without much success.

Settlements

In the nineteenth century large compact villages were common, especially among the Nyamwezi. As the country became peaceful, people moved out to build in their own fields. The dispersal of settlement continued until the first years of independence, and villages passed through phases of expansion and decline as soils became worn out and the age structure of their populations changed. In the mid-1970s new compact villages, ideally of 250 households, were established by decree throughout this and other parts of Tanzania. Each household had a 0.4−hectare plot within the village on which to build and cultivate, and families also had access to fields in surrounding land. The 0.4−hectare plots were commonly arranged in blocks of ten between new village streets. This policy has since been relaxed, and some settlements are said to be disbanding.

Economy

SUBSISTENCE AND COMMERCIAL ACTIVITIES. Agriculture and cattle keeping are the chief economic activities. Most families grow food for themselves and attempt to produce some surplus for the market. Maize, sorghum, and rice are the main food crops sold, and cotton and tobacco are produced in substantial quantities. Other crops include groundnuts, beans, cassava, and some vegetables and fruits. The main cattle owners are Sukuma. Some families own very large herds of a thousand head or more, but smaller herds are more usual. Small stock are also raised.

Most families still use hoes, but plows pulled by oxen are quite common. Some richer people own tractors that they hire out to others, in addition to using them to cultivate large areas for themselves.

INDUSTRIAL ARTS. Traditional crafts include building, ironwork, pottery, basketry, drum making, and stool carving. These crafts are usually part-time occupations, and some have declined as foreign goods have been imported. Bow and arrow making has enjoyed a resurgence with the rise of Sungusungu. Some carpenters make Western-type chairs and other furniture, and some men work as sewing-machine operators in local shops.

TRADE. Local caravans down to the coast ceased in colonial times, but people continued to go as porters and migrant laborers. Shops were largely owned by Asians and Arabs, but after independence local shopkeepers became common in the villages and towns. Private trade was discouraged by the state for many years, and cooperative shops and state trading agencies were established. The private sector has persisted, however, and there are many successful businesses, especially among the Sukuma.

DIVISION OF LABOR. There is a strong sexual division of labor. In general, men do shorter, heavy tasks, and women do more repetitive chores. Cattle are mainly men's concern, as are ironworking and machine sewing. Only men hunt. Pottery is women's work. Some urgent tasks, such as harvesting, are done by both sexes. Most diviners are men. The state has been keen to draw women into politics, but only moderate progress has been made.

LAND TENURE. Under the chiefs, land could be acquired in several ways. A villager might clear new land or obtain cleared land from a village headman. He might also inherit land with agreement from the headman. The chief was said to be "owner" of the land; this meant that those who held it were his subjects, and that the prosperity of the chiefdom depended on him and his ancestors. There was some variation in the degree of control that chiefs and headmen exercised over land. Fields could not customarily be sold, but those who had cleared land could often lend it to others and pass it on to heirs. In the 1960s, once chieftainship was abolished, land started to be sold, but this was stemmed by government. Later, land was defined as belonging to a village as the agent of the state. Villagers were allocated land for their own use, and some land was retained for communal production. Some villagers are now returning to live on their former holdings.

The main Nyamwezi and Sukuma kin groups were those vested with political office, and were mainly based on descent from former chiefs and other officeholders.

Kinship

KIN GROUPS AND DESCENT. The main kin groups in the area were those vested with political office. Since independence, their importance has diminished, although they still provide valuable personal networks for their members. The groups were mainly based on descent from former chiefs and other officeholders. Officeholders were also a focus for sets of relatives who clustered around them. Some Sukuma classify themselves into "clans" defined in terms of their members' chiefdom of origin. For most people, kinship is important mainly for interpersonal relations. A person's kin are widely dispersed, and villages are not typically kinship units. The main structural elements of the kinship system are oppositions between male and female, senior and junior, and proximal and alternate generations. One notable feature of behavior between kin is the division between those with whom one is familiar or jokes, and those whom one "respects" or avoids. This runs partly along generation lines and is at its strongest between affines. Sexual difference is also a factor. Thus, brothers-in-law joke with each other, and there is avoidance between a man and his daughter-in-law and mother-in-law. Known kin should not marry. A main determinant of people's status vis-à-vis their kin is the form of their parents' marriage.

KINSHIP TERMINOLOGY. Some features of the kinship system are reflected in the Iroquoian kinship terminology used by the Nyamwezi, which distinguishes kin from affines, mother's kin from father's kin in proximal generations, cross cousins from siblings and ortho-cousins, and proximal from alternate generations. Parental and great-grandparental generations are merged, as are those of grandparents and great-great-grandparents. Similar patterns are followed in the terms for junior generations. Some puzzling Crow features (father's sister's son = father) have been reported for the traditional Sukuma terminology.

Marriage and Family

MARRIAGE. Local forms of marriage fall into two main classes, marriage with bride-wealth and marriage without bride-wealth. In bride-wealth marriage, a husband customarily acquires full rights over the children his wife bears. He should receive bride-wealth for his daughters and provide it for his sons, and his children should inherit from him. He also has customary rights to compensation for his wife's adultery. Adultery is still an offense if no bride-wealth has been given,

but compensation is not customarily paid. Rights over children of non-bride-wealth unions are mainly vested in maternal kin, unless the father makes redemption payments for them. These payments are larger for a daughter than for a son. The verb *kukwa* is used for these payments and also for paying bride-wealth. Bride-wealth marriage is more common in prosperous areas and times. The verb *kutola* is commonly used for both forms of marriage. A man "marries," and a woman "is married." Residence at marriage varies but is increasingly neolocal. Patrivirilocal residence is most common when bride-wealth is paid, but sons often move away eventually. Bride-service with initial uxorilocal residence is reported to have existed formerly among the Sukuma. Polygyny is a common male ambition, but polygynous marriages are relatively unstable. Many men have been polygynous, but, with the main exception of chiefs in the past, older men are less polygynous than those in their forties. More generally, divorce is frequent. Women's first marriages in which bride-wealth has been paid are the most stable.

DOMESTIC UNIT. Before the 1970s, homesteads sometimes contained a dozen or more people, although most were smaller. They commonly consisted of a man and his wife or wives, their resident children, and perhaps the spouse and the children of one or more of the resident children. Other close relatives of the head of the homestead might also be present. Homesteads were the largest units in which members of one sex regularly ate together. They contained one or more households that were distinct food-producing and child-rearing units. The household was the basic economic unit and the husband-wife relation was its key element. This has been reinforced in new compact village where each 0.4–hectare plot is assigned to a *familia* (modern Swahili) based on a couple and their children. Neighboring households collaborate in a wide range of activities.

INHERITANCE. Questions of inheritance are usually resolved within the families concerned. Customarily only sons of bride-wealth marriages, or redeemed sons, inherit the main forms of wealth. Such heirs should look after the needs of daughters. Sometimes one son looks after an inheritance for all his siblings. Unredeemed children are in a weak position; they may fail to inherit either from their father or from their mother's kin, whose own children may take precedence.

SOCIALIZATION. Socialization takes place largely within the family and village. Ceremonies within a few days of birth symbolize a baby's fu-

♦ **uxorilocal residence (matrilocal residence)**
The practice of a newly married couple residing in the community of the wife's kin. Uxorilocal *is sometimes used in a more restrictive sense to indicate residence in the household of the wife's family.*

ture as a male or female member of society. Girls especially learn their gender roles quite early, through participation in household tasks. Boys help in herding and other work but have more free time than do girls during their teens. There are no formal age groups or ceremonies of initiation into adulthood. Primary schooling is now compulsory, but parents sometimes keep children from school if their labor is required. Training in citizenship is part of the school curriculum.

Sociopolitical Organization

Before independence the main forms of political organization were the chiefdoms and the villages. Neighbors, and also kin, collaborate in many activities, and there are several ritual and secular associations and societies. Since independence, as part of the Republic of Tanzania, the area inhabited by the Nyamwezi and the Sukuma has been subject to its laws and constitution. It falls administratively within Mwanza, Shinyanga, and Tabora regions, which contain several administrative districts. These districts are segmented into divisions, which, in turn, contain wards, within which there are officially constituted villages. There are governmental and party officials at each level, and a series of elected committees. Since 1973, villages have been the basic unit of organization, although, within them, ten-house groups are recognized. In the early 1980s a new grass-roots village-security organization—Sungusungu or Busalama—emerged, and it has spread to all parts of the area. All able-bodied village men belong to the local Sungusungu group, and there is sometimes a women's wing.

Conflicts have occurred between the Revolutionary party (CCM) and Sungusungu, but there has also been some cooperation between them, and the groups are now legally recognized. Each village has its own group, but there is also some intervillage collaboration. Single-party rule is due to end, and multiparty elections are planned in the mid-1990s.

SOCIAL CONTROL. There are official district-level courts, and below these there are primary courts. These administer national and some customary law. Neighbors' courts dealt with many disputes in the past, but nowadays Sungusungu groups hear cases. Their function is to maintain village security against cattle thieves and other enemies, including witches in some areas. Members are armed with bows and arrows, which have proved to be effective weapons for them, and with whistles for sounding alarms.

CONFLICT. Since World War I, the area has been relatively peaceful. The independence struggle was active but mainly nonviolent. Class conflict is not yet strongly developed, although there are substantial differences in wealth in some areas. Initial official reactions to Sungusungu were mainly negative, but the groups received qualified support from Julius Nyerere and some other leading Tanzanian figures. Government has since tried to control the groups and encourage their development elsewhere, but there are signs that enthusiasm for the system is declining among villagers themselves.

Religion and Expressive Culture

RELIGIOUS BELIEFS. With the main exceptions of the villages around Tabora and of areas around some Christian missions, neither Islam nor Christianity has flourished strongly among villagers. Religion in the area, like society itself, is accretive rather than exclusive.

Beliefs in a High God are widely held but involve no special cult. Ancestor worship is the main element in the religious complex. Chiefs' ancestors are thought to influence the lives of the inhabitants of their domains, but ordinary ancestors only affect their own descendants. Belief in witchcraft is widespread and strong.

RELIGIOUS PRACTITIONERS. In addition to the High God and the ancestors, some nonancestral spirits are believed to influence some people's lives. Spirit-possession societies, such as the Baswezi, deal with such attacks and recruit the victims into membership. As a link between belief and action, the diviner (*mfumu*) is a key figure in religious life; diviners interpret the belief system for individuals and groups. They decide which forces are active and help people to deal with them. Although it is not strictly an hereditary art, people often take up divination when a misfortune is diagnosed as having been induced by a diviner ancestor who wishes them to do so. There are often several diviners in a village, but only one or two are likely to attract a wide clientele. All diviners, like their neighbors, engage in farming and participate fully in village life.

CEREMONIES. Divination takes many forms, the most common being chicken divination, in which a young fowl is killed and readings are taken from its wings and other features. Sacrifices and libations, along with initiation into a spirit-possession or other society, may result from a divinatory séance. Divination and subsequent rituals may divide people, especially if witchcraft is diagnosed, but in many contexts the system al-

*As a link between belief and action, the diviner (*mfumu*) is a key figure in religious life; diviners interpret the belief system for individuals and groups.*

lows villagers to express their solidarity with each other without loss of individual identity. In addition to ritual focused upon individuals and attended by their kin and neighbors, there is some public ceremonial at village and wider levels. Chiefly rituals are still sometimes performed, and there are ceremonies to cleanse a village of pollution when a member dies.

ARTS. Representational art is not strongly developed; it has mainly ritual functions. Music and dancing are the main art forms, and drums are the main instruments, although the nailpiano (a box with metal prongs that twang at different pitches) and other instruments are also found. Traditional songs are sung at weddings and at dances, but new songs are also composed by dance leaders. Male dance teams are the most common, but some female and mixed teams perform. Ritual and other societies have their own dance styles. Transistor radios are now widespread. Local and visiting jazz and other bands play in the towns.

MEDICINE. Diviners and other local experts provide herbal and other forms of treatment for illness. Shops sell some Western medicines, including aspirin and liniments. Village dispensaries and state and mission hospitals also provide Western medicine. People commonly use both Western and indigenous treatments rather than trusting wholly in either.

DEATH AND AFTERLIFE. Funerals are important rituals for bereaved families and their kin and neighbors. Neighbors dig the grave and take news of the death to relatives of the deceased who live outside the village. The dead become ancestors who may continue to affect the lives of their descendants and demand appeasement. The idea that the dead live on in their descendants is expressed in terms of shared identity between alternate generations.

Bibliography

Abrahams, Ray G. (1967). *The Peoples of Greater Unyamwezi*. Ethnographic Survey of Africa. London: International African Institute.

Abrahams, Ray G. (1981). *The Nyamwezi Today*. Cambridge: Cambridge University Press.

Abrahams, Ray G. (1987). "Sungusungu: Village Vigilante Groups in Tanzania." *African Affairs*, April, 179–196.

Abrahams, Ray G., and Sufian Bukurura (1993). "Party Bureaucracy and Grass-Roots Initiatives in a Socialist State: The Case of Sungusungu Vigilantes in Tanzania." In *Socialism: Ideals, Ideologies, and Local Practices*, edited by Chris Hann, 92–101. London: Routledge.

Malcom, D. W. (1953). *Sukumaland: An African People and Their Country*. London: Oxford University Press.

—RAY G. ABRAHAMS

SAN-SPEAKING PEOPLES

Ethnonyms: G | wi, G | | ana, Hai | | om, Kxoe (Makwengo), Nharo (Naro); !Koõ (!Xoõ), !Xu; Zhu | õasi (!Kung)

Orientation

IDENTIFICATION. The term "San" has replaced "Buchman" as an ethnographic term designating both the contemporary and the precolonial southern African peoples who speak, or spoke, languages containing click consonants and who have been described as hunter-gatherers or foragers. Thus, San-speaking peoples do not constitute an ethnic group in the usual sense. The most widely known are those who call themselves "Zhu | õasi" (!Kung or Juwasi in most ethnographies), although the other peoples mentioned above have also been extensively described; about ten other groups have been well studied by linguists. In Botswana, all these peoples are called collectively "Basarwa," and this term is often seen in recent ethnographic literature.

LOCATION. The Zhu | õasi live in the semi-arid *savdveld* (savanna) of northwestern Botswana (Ngamiland) and in adjacent parts of Namibia. The !Xu, whose anglicized ethnonym is the source of the name "!Kung," live in the better-watered tropical open woodlands of southern Angola. The Axoe live along the Okavango River, in the Caprivi Strip of Namibia; the Hai | | om occupy a large part of north-central Namibia, between the Cunene River and the Etosha Pan. The Nharo live in the limestone karst zone of the Ghansi District of Botswana. The G | wi, G | | ana, and !Koõ live throughout the poorly watered central sand zone of Botswana, extending into Namibia, in conditions most closely approximating true desert. The | | Anikhoe, the so-called Swamp Bushmen, live in the Okavango Delta floodplain; the Deti live along the Botletli River. Several other peoples who are called San in the ethnographic literature speak Khoe languages and live in the hill, *mopane*-forest, and salt-pan environments of eastern Botswana. These highly diverse geophysical regions share a number of features: seasonal rains, falling mainly as localized thunderstorms during the hot months, October to May; high variation in average annual rainfall—around 45 centimeters in Ngamiland, some 50 percent higher in Angola, and 50 percent lower in central Botswana; summer temperatures that often exceed 37° C; and cool winters, with night temperatures as low as -4° C in Botswana and Namibia.

DEMOGRAPHY. In 1980 the most reliable sources estimated that about 30,000 San-speaking peoples lived in Botswana, about 12,000 in Namibia, and about 8,000 in Angola—representing about 3 percent of the population of Botswana, 1.2 percent of that of Namibia, and 0.1 percent of Angola's people. The Zhu ǀ õasi, who previously had wide birth spacing and a low birthrate, now have one of the highest recorded birthrates in the world, according to 1980 statistics, with 6.7 live births per 1,000 women of childbearing age. Zhu ǀ õasi infant mortality, at 85 per 1,000 births, is comparatively low by African standards, as is child mortality. Life expectancy at birth was 45 years for Zhu ǀ õasi in the 1960s, but improved nutrition and health care have probably lengthened life spans; survivors to age 5 have good prospects of living into their 70s. There are no comparable statistics for other San speakers, but health-ministry surveys suggest that similar demographic profiles may be found in Botswana.

LINGUISTIC AFFILIATION. San languages are usually classified as being in the Khoisan Family; there are three sets of these languages, each with its own history. Zhu ǀ õasi, !Xu, and Au ǀ ǀ ei (formerly spoken around Lake Ngami, now with few living speakers) are mutually intelligible and together constitute the Northern Khoisan Group; they are grammatically, syntactically, and lexically distinct from other Khoisan languages. G ǀ wi, G ǀ ǀ ana, Kxoe, Nharo, and ǀ ǀ Anikhoe, plus Deti, Buga, Tshukhoe, Kwa, and several others, form the Khoe Group, formerly Central Khoisan, which is closely related to the Nama that is spoken by Khoi peoples (often called Hottentots in the past); Hai ǀ ǀ om is a dialect of Nama. In general, the geographically adjacent Khoe languages (e.g., G ǀ wi and G ǀ ǀ ana) are very similar and are mutually intelligible, whereas those farther apart (e.g., Nharo and Deti) are structurally alike but become progressively less interintelligible. The principal extant Southern Khoisan languages are !Koõ and Tsassi, spoken across a long, narrow band of the southern Kalahari. All Khoisan languages are predominantly monoand bisyllabic and tonal, and they contain click consonants (which are conventionally represented by ǀ, !, and ǀ ǀ—al-though Bantu orthography, which uses *c* for ǀ and, *q* for !, and *x* for ǀ ǀ, is preferable in nonlinguistic contexts). The replacement of click by nonclick consonants is common in the Khoe languages of eastern Botswana, where some of these languages are being completely replaced by Setswana.

History and Cultural Relations

Accumulating archaeological and archival evidence provides the basis for a more comprehensive reconstruction of the later prehistory of southern Africa than was possible as recently as 1970, when it was generally thought that Bantu-speaking peoples arrived only two or three centuries ago, bringing with them grain horticulture and cattle-sheep-goat pastoralism. It is now known that cattle and sheep were widely kept, almost certainly by Khoisan-speaking peoples, beginning about 2,000 years ago; both the Khoe languages and Zhu ǀ õasi contain indigenous vocabularies for stock keeping, indicating that some of these pastoralist-foragers must have been San speakers. About 500 years later, Bantu-speaking agro-pastoralists spread into many parts of the region, introducing sorghum, millet, and probably goats, as well as metallurgy; linguistic evidence suggests that speakers of Nguni and Sotho-Tswana Bantu languages obtained cattle from Khoisan peoples. Since that time, mixed economies that combine foraging, herding, and farming in varying proportions have been predominant. Nevertheless, it has not been uncommon for local groups of both Bantu and Khoisan speakers to rely exclusively on foraging when drought, disease, raiding, or political subjugation have made herding and farming impossible; San peoples in this condition have been the subjects of most ethnographic studies. Interregional and transcontinental trade is archaeologically documented from the ninth century, when iron and copper jewelry, glass beads from Asia, and cowrie shells from the Indian Ocean were widely distributed and reached even into the Kalahari and Ngamiland. The Portuguese Atlantic-coast trade penetrated from the Congo through Angola into Namibia and Botswana in the seventeenth century and was recorded a hundred years later by the first Europeans to enter those areas; these observers noted that many different groups of San speakers engaged with Bantu and Nama speakers in such trade, which followed ancient routes of communication and exchange. European hunter-merchants accelerated this trade, beginning in the 1840s. Throughout the 1880s, until the market collapsed, San speakers were major providers of

♦ **pastoralism**
A type of subsistence economy based on the herding of domesticated grazing animals such as sheep or cattle.

San settlements are composed of one to a dozen or more homesteads, each containing a set of separate households, the heads of which are ideally related.

ivory and ostrich feathers, for which the merchants paid with European goods. Horses and donkeys were introduced by these merchants; donkeys, especially, became important economic assets. Most of the San-speaking peoples became impoverished during the period from 1850 to 1920, but some of them (the Deti and a few Zhu | õasi, for example) retained modest herds. Many, especially in southern and eastern Botswana, became serfs of Twsana patrons; a few became marginal foragers, partially dependent on their serf and client kin. Labor migration to South African gold mines, which began in the 1890s, increased dramatically for San speakers in the 1950s, when efforts to recruit them were intensified in order to augment insufficient Bantu labor. Different groups were variably affected: as many as 50 percent of Kwa men were absent from their villages at any given time, but only 10 percent of Zhu | õasi men ever went to the mines. Opportunities to work in the mines are no longer available to San speakers.

Settlements

San settlements are composed of one to a dozen or more homesteads, each containing a set of separate households, the heads of which are ideally related as parent and child or as descendants of common grandparents, that is, as siblings and first cousins. Larger settlements may contain 200 or 300 persons. Many homesteads, as well as individual households today—and probably all of them in precolonial times—also set up temporary encampments near seasonal rain pools, from which their members hunt and collect wild-plant products; livestock are usually kept there as well, and fields may be cultivated nearby. In Botswana, settlements rarely contain only persons of a single language group; in Ngamiland, for example, Zhu | õasi, ‡Au | | ei, Nharo, Nama, Mbanderu, Mbukushu, and Tswana homesteads may all be found in the same settlement. Houses within a homestead are normally built close together and usually face a common open area, but homesteads within a settlement may be 2 to 3 kilometers apart; clients and persons employed as herders tend to live adjacent to their patrons and employers. Conical grass huts are frequently used, especially at temporary encampments, but round, one-room, wattle-and-daub houses with thatched roofs are more common among most groups.

Economy

SUBSISTENCE AND COMMERCIAL ACTIVITIES. Although famed as foragers, fewer than 5 percent of San-speaking peoples have relied on foraging for the bulk of their subsistence during the twentieth century; even these few have depended on herding-farming relatives and on neighbors for dietary supplements of meat, milk, and grains, as well as for supplies of such desired goods as iron for arrow points and spears, metal containers, glass beads, tobacco, and, when obtainable, sugar, coffee, and tea. Herding-farming San speakers also forage, as do rural Bantu speakers (the poorer of whom obtain 25 percent of their livelihood from foraging). It has been reported that during the 1970s hunting provided 11 percent of the diet of the Zhu | õasi, whereas gathered plants contributed 85 percent of the calories that were consumed by those who owned no livestock and 10 percent to 68 percent of the caloric intake of stock owners. Large antelope—eland, kudu, gemsboks—and giraffes still provide the bulk of the dietary meat, but small antelope, birds, and reptiles are also important. Seasonal and annual variation is great; the proportion of the diet that is obtained by hunting may rise to 30 percent during the dry winter months (May to August) but falls to less than 1 percent during the wet summer (December to February). Those Khoe speakers who live along rivers and in the delta rely heavily upon fish, the abundance of which is also highly seasonal. The contribution of gathered plants, about 100 species, is subject to similar fluctuation. For example, in September and October *mongongo* nuts may supply as much as 90 percent of the calories of Zhu | õasi who own no livestock, but these nuts are seldom available from November to March. Mongongo groves are restricted to narrow ecological zones; most San-speaking groups rely on more widely distributed wild nuts and legumes (mainly *marula* nuts and species of *Bauhinia* beans). Goats are kept by individuals in all San-speaking groups, but fewer than one-third of households own any of these animals; cattle ownership is even more restricted, but the Deti are wealthy in these animals, as are small proportions of families in several other groups. Goats are readily slaughtered for home consumption and are sold locally for slaughter by others. Cattle are milked and are eaten when they die; when available, surplus oxen and old bulls are slaughtered for important ritual occasions and may also be sold. The few owners of large herds fatten oxen for commercial sale. Crops are grown by most homesteads and, where conditions are favorable (i.e., in Angola and eastern-southern Botswana), contribute substantially to subsistence. Mixed fields are usual; these are planted with some combination of sorghum, millet, maize, sweet-reed (a type of sugarcane), cowpeas, and melons. Women sell home-brewed beer. The cash purchase of maize meal, sugar, coffee and tea, soap, cosmetics, clothing, and utilitarian household items has increased since the late 1970s.

INDUSTRIAL ARTS. Leatherworking was important in the past, as was blacksmithing, but no longer. A few women in the riverine-delta area still weave baskets for local use and for sale.

TRADE. The majority of San speakers live in or near villages, in which one or more small shops are located. Those who live in the central Kalahari, in western Ngamiland, and on many cattle posts rely primarily on itinerant traders and on informal arrangements with periodic visitors. Fairly often they travel on foot, donkey, or horseback to the nearest shop, which may be 100 kilometers away.

DIVISION OF LABOR. Women bear the major responsibility for child care, but men play important supporting roles. Adolescents learn their adult roles mainly from older members of their respective sexes. Men hunt the larger animals, but women collect smaller species, such as tortoises, and may assist in the monitoring of snare lines. Women gather the greater quantity of plant foods, but men bring in smaller amounts as well, especially after successful hunts. Men of all groups do the heavier work of cattle management (well digging, corral building, branding, slaughtering). In some groups, women may participate in herding and be responsible for milking (as among the Zhu ǀ õasi). Elsewhere, these may be considered inappropriate activities for women (as among most Khoe speakers). Among the Zhu ǀ õasi, relative age modifies the division of labor, in that older cohorts and siblings have some directional control over their juniors. Leadership positions—which may be held by either men or women in a related set of families—do not relieve the leaders from obligations of work, but they do provide avenues for disproportionate long-term gains; the terms for "leader" in the Zhu ǀ õasi and Khoe languages are derived from words that designate "wealth." Diviners and curers, who also may be women as well as men, are generally held in high esteem.

LAND TENURE. Land tenure is vested in a set of related families whose claim to generationally inherited rights to a particular area is considered legitimate. Generally, individuals acquire two such rights bilaterally through their parents. Residence in one of these tenure areas and regular

SOCIOPOLITICAL ORGANIZATION

Social Organization

Residence is based on bilateral kinship. Nonresident associations are also important. Among the Zhu ǀ õasi, *hxaro* networks link persons who are related through common great-grandparents over distances of 200 kilometers or more; the Nharo and a few other Khoe groups have similar exchange networks. Hxaro (the Zhu ǀ õasi term) is a system of delayed reciprocity, with obligations attached to partners; important partnerships are frequently inherited from parents, and marriages are often arranged through these channels. To celebrate marriages, childbirth, and girls' puberty initiations, gifts—called *kamasi* in Zhu ǀ õasi and *kamane* in Nharo—are given in a separate series of exchanges. Zhu ǀ õasi are sets, ǀ *arakwe,* are composed of persons who are not necessarily kin; these age sets now have few functions, but they appear to have been important in the past, when they probably were central to the hxaro framework for long-distance trade. Zhu ǀ õasi name groups, which once may have functioned as clans, are now almost entirely forgotten; the Kxoe and some eastern Khoe have analogous residual forms.

Political Organization

All San-speaking groups have positions of hereditary leadership; the term ǀ ǀ *xaiha,* derived from a root designating "wealth," is usually translated as "chief." These leaders now have limited authority of a traditional kind, but among the Zhu ǀ õasi they are usually elected to state-created posts such as chairman of the village-development committee.

Social Control

Ridicule, verbal abuse, dispersal, and divination are the usual means of maintaining social order, but consensually sanctioned executions and murders were not uncommon in the past. Minor disputes are adjudicated in informal hearings in which all interested parties participate. Nowadays village headmen appointed by district councils hear minor civil cases; more serious cases are referred to local and district courts.

Conflict

For many years, all San speakers have engaged in small-scale fighting among themselves and their neighbors, but there are no special war officers, and no particular prestige follows success in battle.

Ridicule, verbal abuse, dispersal, and divination are the usual means of maintaining social order among the San-speaking peoples.

participation with relatives in the other are essential if a person wishes to retain these rights. Seasonal movement within tenures is common, as is vesting among relatives in different tenures. The current leader of a landholding group is in most cases also the nominal "owner" of the land. Nonresidents must obtain permission from this person to use the land; such permission is rarely refused to kin and rarely given to others.

Kinship

KIN GROUPS AND DESCENT. All San speakers reckon kinship bilaterally; membership in Zhu | õasi and Khoe local descent groups is determined by rights that are inherited through either father or mother or through both. The Hai | | om, who in the past lived in patrilineal local groups, reckon descent unilineally.

KINSHIP TERMINOLOGY. Zhu | õasi terminology is of the Eskimo type, with older siblings and cousins distinguished by sex; all Khoe and !Koõ terminologies are Iroquois, with bifurcate-merging avuncular terms.

Marriage and Family

MARRIAGE. The majority of marriages are monogamous, with polygyny being restricted to the wealthier men. Marriages are ideally arranged by parents, in consultation with senior members of the kinship group. The Zhu | õasi prefer bilateral-cousin marriages, excluding first cousins; Khoe speakers prescribe cross-cousin marriage, including first cousins. The !Koõ permit marriage only to more distant relatives. The Zhu | õasi prefer virilocal postmarital residence for couples who are related matrilaterally and vice versa; the other groups prefer uxorilocal residence. Bride-service was once required, but today it is often replaced by marriage payments in livestock. Divorce is common until a child is born to a couple, after which time it is rare.

DOMESTIC UNIT. Each family has its own hut; adolescent children often build small huts for themselves next to those of their parents. Each wife in a polygynous family has her own hut. Families prefer to live in homesteads that include other members of their extended family.

INHERITANCE. Land-tenure rights are inherited at birth. Personal property and partnerships devolve from parent to child during the lifetimes of both.

SOCIALIZATION. Children are instructed from infancy in proper forms of etiquette, especially toward kin. Corporal punishment is applied and ridicule is used, but threats are very rare. In the past, groups of adolescent boys were initiated in seclusion, but this is no longer done; circumcision is reported only for the Tshukhoe. Zhu | õasi, Nharo, and G | wi girls still go through a brief initiation at first menstruation. No female genital mutilation has been recorded for any group. Scarification of the face, back, chest (for men), and thighs (for women) was commonly applied to mark important life events, but is seldom done now.

Religion and Expressive Culture

RELIGIOUS BELIEFS. The Zhu | õasi and the !Koõ each divide their chief deity into a creator, who now plays little active role in earthly affairs, and an administrator, whom they hold responsible for all that happens on earth. Some Khoe speakers incorporate these roles in one being. All believe in lesser spirits, who are ancestors. Ecumenism is characteristic of southern African peoples, who share numerous mythic themes: many ideas have been transferred among the different cosmologies of the region, including the various Christian forms that were added during the nineteenth century.

RELIGIOUS PRACTITIONERS. There are no religious practitioners other than the diviners and curers.

CEREMONIES. The main ceremonies among San speakers are dance performances; these are usually attended by members of an extended family, but may include other relatives. The girls' initiation dance is restricted to relatives of the initiate—one adult-male relative plays a central ritual role. Male initiation, which was important in the past, is no longer performed.

ARTS. San-speaking peoples have long been famed for beadwork, both of ostrich-eggshell beads, which they manufacture, and of glass beads, which they purchase or obtain in trade. They are widely believed to be responsible for the fine rock paintings of southern Africa. Recently three men (two Zhu | õasi and one Nharo) have gained recognition as watercolorists; in 1980 one of them received a prize at the Botswana National Art Show.

MEDICINE. Both men and women may be curers, but most diviners are men; often both roles are combined in a single person. Divination is directed toward the analysis of problems, such as the source of misfortune, the location of stray livestock, or the cause of illness. Divination takes two forms: in one, a set of bones or disks is thrown, and the resultant patterns are interpreted; in the other, a dance is performed, during which one or more practitioners may go into a trance. Cures are almost exclusively attained through the dance performances, usually involving trance, which are directed toward physical and psychological healing as well as social well-being.

DEATH AND AFTERLIFE. Death is a passing into a spiritual realm that is distinct from the material realm. To the Zhu | õasi, human death is senseless because people are not properly earthly food; it can be explained, however, by the belief that the administrator deity feeds on the people he causes to die. Recently dead relatives are dangerous because their spirits yearn for their kin and may attempt to bring about their early deaths in order to be reunited; this danger recedes as memory of the deceased dims with time.

Bibliography

Barnard, Alan (1991). *Hunters and Herders: A Comparative Ethnography of the Khoisan Peoples.* Cambridge: Cambridge University Press.

Denbow, James (1984). "Prehistoric Herders and Foragers of the Kalahari: The Evidence for 1500 Years of Interaction." In *Past and Present in Hunter Gatherer Studies,* edited by Carmel Schrire, 175–193. Orlando, Fla.: Academic Press.

Lee, Richard (1979). *The !Kung San: Men, Women, and Work in a Foraging Society.* Cambridge: Cambridge University Press.

Silberbauer, George (1981). *Hunter and Habitat in the Central Kalahari Desert.* Cambridge: Cambridge University Press.

Vossen, Rainer, and Klaus Keuthmann, eds. (1986). *Contemporary Studies on Khoisan: In Honor of Oswin Köhler on the Occasion of his 75th Birthday.* Hamburg: Helmut Buske.

Wilmsen, Edwin (1989). *Land Filled with Flies: A Political Economy of the Kalahari.* Chicago: University of Chicago Press.

Wilmsen, Edwin, and James Denbow (1990). "Almost Outcasts: Paradigmatic History of San-Speaking Peoples and Current Attempts at Reconstruction." *Current Anthropology* 31:489–524.

—EDWIN N. WILMSEN

SHONA

Ethonyms: Karanga (historical)

Orientation

IDENTIFICATION. The Shona-speaking peoples comprise about 80 percent of the population of Zimbabwe, with significant groups in Mozambique. Most of what follows applies to the Shona in Zimbabwe, who have been extensively studied.

There are a number of linguistic subgroups of Shona: the Zezuru, who inhabit the central plateau of Zimbabwe; the Karanga, to the south; the Korekore, to the north and dropping into the Zambezi Valley; the Manyika, to the east; the Tavara, in the Zambezi Valley in Mozambique and in the extreme northeast of Zimbabwe; the Ndau, in the southeast of Zimbabwe and stretching down to the coast in Mozambique; and the Kalanga, in the southwest of Zimbabwe and overflowing into Botswana.

These linguistic classifications led to the formation of distinct ethnic classifications in colonial times. Historically, however, neither the subgroups nor the Shona as a whole comprised distinct political or ethnic units. The Kalanga and the Ndau, in particular, have been considerably influenced by neighboring Nguni peoples.

LOCATION. Central Shona country is the high plateau of Zimbabwe, with an elevation of 1,200 meters or more, a temperate climate, and an annual rainfall of 70 to 100 centimeters. The Zambezi Valley, in the north, is hotter and drier, as is the southwest. Few Shona now inhabit the eastern highlands, which are cool and wet. Generally, the colonial administration moved the majority of Shona away from the best farmland, into areas where the soils are sandy and thin and where the amount of rainfall is less favorable for agriculture.

DEMOGRAPHY. The Shona population is estimated to have been slightly more than half a million early in the twentieth century. There has been rapid population increase in Zimbabwe throughout the twentieth century: there are around 8,000,000 Shona in Zimbabwe and perhaps half a million outside. Approximately 26 percent of the population reside in urban areas. Life expectancy at birth is 57, and the population growth rate is estimated at 3 percent.

LINGUISTIC AFFILIATION. The Shona language is tonal and is one of the Bantu Group. There is relative ease of communication with neighboring peoples. A kind of pidgin Bantu, *chilapalapa*, based largely on Zulu and Afrikaans, is widely spoken in the region, especially in the towns.

History and Cultural Relations

The ancestors of the Shona settled in their region in the first millennium A.D., introducing settled agriculture, cattle, and iron mining to the area. Although the Shona have been organized, for the

The Shona-speaking peoples comprise about 80 percent of the population of Zimbabwe.

♦ **pidgin**
A second language very often made up of words and grammatical features from several languages and used as the medium of communication between speakers of different languages.

most part, into small, independent chiefdoms, from time to time during the course of their history, conglomerations of chiefdoms have been united into larger states. Control of trade in gold and ivory with Arabs and Portuguese on the coast constituted both a motive and a support for political rulers to expand their spheres of influence. From the twelfth century onward, techniques of drystone walling were developed by the Karanga in the south, who, with the formation of large states, constructed a number of large stone buildings.

In the nineteenth century, the Shona were disturbed by Nguni migrations from the south, particularly by the Ndebele who, possessing superior military techniques, settled in and dominated the southeast of what is now Zimbabwe. Colonial settlement came at the end of the century. An uprising against the settlers was defeated. Independence came after further wars in Rhodesia and Mozambique in the 1960s and 1970s.

From the nineteenth century onward, the Shona have migrated to work in the mines of South Africa. After the colonial settlement of southern Rhodesia, employment became available within the country, on farms and mines, and particularly in the growing industrial cities. Some groups were moved off their land to make way for settlers who wanted to farm it.

Widespread education was introduced by various groups of missionaries, who also established hospitals and diverse forms of technical training, including training in improved agriculture. These services were subsequently taken over and expanded by government. Plow agriculture is now prevalent.

Settlements

There were some large stockaded villages prior to colonial settlement, but in some areas people lived in scattered family hamlets. The dominant settlement pattern is one of villages with homesteads spread out in lines next to agricultural land. The traditional homestead included a number of round, pole-and-mud huts with conical thatched roofs. These huts have largely been replaced by brick houses, roofed with zinc, sometimes in the traditional style of round huts.

Economy

SUBSISTENCE AND COMMERCIAL ACTIVITIES. In precolonial times the main crops were various types of millet. Now, except in the drier areas, maize is predominant. Groundnuts and various vegetables are also grown for relish. Early in the colonial period, farmers grew surpluses for sale. Cash crops such as tobacco and cotton are also grown. Today, shortages of land are acute in many areas, and few Shona are able to make much of an income from farming. Agriculture is largely supported by salaried or wage labor in the towns. A cash income in the family allows for expenditure on implements and on quality seed and fertilizers, which increase agricultural output.

Except in the low-lying, tsetse-fly-infested areas, cattle are widely kept. Traditionally, cattle comprised the main indicator of wealth. They retain importance in this respect in the rural areas and have the added utility of providing draft power. Other domestic animals include goats, sheep, pigs, donkeys, and various types of poultry.

INDUSTRIAL ARTS. In the rural areas everyone is involved in agriculture and there are no full-time specialists. In the past there was extensive iron and gold smelting, but all the surface gold has now been mined, and superior iron is now obtained from modern plants. One still finds blacksmiths in many villages, however. Traditional crafts of basketwork and pottery are still widespread. One now finds carpenters, builders, tailors, and other semiskilled specialists in many rural areas. Women engage in sewing and knitting, now often on a cooperative basis.

TRADE. Although there is a long history of trade both between Shona groups and with outsiders, there were traditionally no markets in Shona settlements. These are now well established in cities, towns, and many rural centers of administration and trade. Even the remotest areas have access to some stores in which basic consumer goods are sold.

DIVISION OF LABOR. The division of labor in Shona society is primarily based on sex. Women make pottery, do all the domestic work, and perform many of the less strenuous agricultural tasks. Men are responsible for more strenuous (but less time-consuming) agricultural work, raising cattle, hunting, and ironwork. They are also involved in politics, which requires much sitting around and talking.

Certain men, such as a chief or a man with many daughters, can expect to have dependents do chores for them. People with good incomes from wages or salaries are now able to employ others to do some of their agricultural work.

LAND TENURE. Traditionally, every adult man was given land by his father or village headman. Land could not be bought or sold; it was returned to the community for redistribution when no longer in use. Now there is a scarcity of agricultural land in most communities, and land rights are carefully guarded and inherited. Land has acquired a commercial value. Grazing land, however, remains communal and, except in freehold commercial-farming areas, is habitually overused.

Kinship

KIN GROUPS AND DESCENT. Patrilineal groups are the basic unit of economic cooperation and, usually, of residence: extended families traditionally shared a homestead or lived in adjacent homesteads. Except in chiefly families, such a group is rarely more than three or four generations in depth, and it is easy for an individual to attach instead to matrilateral relatives. The descendants of a deceased woman may occasionally gather for ritual purposes.

KINSHIP TERMINOLOGY. Patrilineal kin are classified according to sex, generation, and seniority by age. Parallel matrilateral kin are accorded the same terms as patrilineal kin. Other matrilateral kin are classified simply by sex.

Marriage and Family

MARRIAGE. Polygyny was traditionally preferred, but the cost of living, and especially of education, has made monogamy more common. The preferred form of marriage is virilocal, with the payment of bride-price, traditionally in cattle but now in cash and kind. Bride-service was formerly an alternative; in the remoter low-lying areas where cattle are not kept, it remains a prominent part of marriage transactions. Occasionally, a young girl may be pledged to a wealthy man against help in time of extreme hardship. Divorce, although discouraged, is common and usually involves the return of a proportion of the bride-price, depending on the duration of the marriage and the number of children born.

Traditionally, the sexual activities of women were strictly controlled, and girls were inspected for virginity at marriage. Such controls have largely broken down.

DOMESTIC UNIT. In a polygynous marriage, the domestic unit was usually a wife and her children. Such a unit was usually allocated its own fields for subsistence purposes. A nuclear family is now the most common domestic unit.

INHERITANCE. A man's status, wives, and possessions may be inherited by his brother or by his adult child. The inheritor takes responsibility for the family of the deceased. Adelphic succession results in the position of chieftainship rotating between houses descended from different wives of the founder of the dynasty. Adelphic inheritance sometimes poses problems in a modern family, when the deceased husband's kin take all the family property, leaving the wife destitute. A woman's personal property is inherited by her daughters.

SOCIALIZATION. Infants are pampered and receive much personal attention until the age of 3 or 4, resulting in rapid development of motor and cognitive skills. Thereafter, they are strictly disciplined. Children receive much personal attention from peers and a number of adults in the extended family. Although importance is attached to authority structures, including authority based on age among siblings, this authority is diffused among a number of older persons. Now, with more emphasis on the elementary family, authority often rests entirely with the family head and is more open to abuse.

Sociopolitical Organization

SOCIAL ORGANIZATION. Shona societies are primarily organized around kinship. Relations between nonkin may be formalized in bond friendship, which imposes mutual obligations of hospitality, material assistance, and certain ritual services. Heavy tasks, such as thatching a house, clearing or plowing a field or reaping the harvest, may be performed by work parties, at which neighbors work and are rewarded with supplies of millet beer. Attendance at such parties imposes obligations of reciprocation.

POLITICAL ORGANIZATION. The principal Shona political unit was the chiefdom. A hereditary chief was ultimately responsible for the distribution of land, for appeasing the territorial spirit guardians, and for settling disputes. Larger chiefdoms were sometimes subdivided into wards, each with its ward headman. The details of distributing land and settling minor disputes were left to the village headmen, but in the colonial era his main function became keeping a tax register.

Although the traditional political authorities are still recognized in order to maintain Shona culture and values, they now have little power. Dispute settlement is now in the hands of elected presiding officers, and land distribution is controlled by government administrators.

SOCIAL CONTROL. Serious crimes, such as incest and homicide, used to be in the control of the guardian spirits, through their mediums. All

Relations between Shona nonkin may be formalized in bond friendship, which imposes mutual obligations of hospitality, material assistance, and certain ritual services.

*The most important
religious
practitioners among
the Shona are spirit
mediums, men or
women chosen by
particular spirits to
be their host.*

other offenses were dealt with by a hierarchy of courts from the village level to the chiefly level. Now offenses are dealt with by a hierarchy of government-controlled courts, from the community level to the High Court.

CONFLICT. Warfare between the scattered Shona chiefdoms was rare. A number of Shona groups suffered from raids by Ndebele armies during the nineteenth century. Tensions between the Shona and the Ndebele have not yet been totally resolved.

Religion and Expressive Culture

RELIGIOUS BELIEFS. The ancestor cult is the dominant feature of Shona religion. Ancestors are largely benign; they protect their descendants from malign influences, both human and spiritual. Ancestors make their wishes known through the mediums they possess and often through causing their descendants to suffer mild but persistent illness. They dislike dissension among their descendants and are therefore a force for keeping groups together. Ancestors can be extremely dangerous; when they become angry, they can cause multiple deaths.

Ancestors of chiefly lineages often have a political function. They support and control the chiefly office and are often involved in the selection of a new chief. These spirit guardians are believed to care for all who live in their territory. They are responsible for rain and fertility. In some parts of Shona country, remote hero spirits can take on these territorial and political functions.

Most Shona have a vague idea of a remote High God but no traditional cult in his honor. Among the Karanga and the Kalanga, however, there is a cult of the High God Mwari, with a complex organization, which overshadows local chiefly or territorial cults. Partly through use of the name by missionaries, knowledge of Mwari has now spread throughout Shona country.

There are a variety of lesser spirits that may provide individuals with particular skills or protection. Belief in witchcraft and sorcery is widespread and can become obsessive, particularly under the strain of survival in urban environments.

Around 25 percent of the Shona belong to a variety of Christian denominations, and many ideas from Christianity have penetrated the thought of non-Christians. Among the denominations Shona have embraced are a number of independent churches that emphasize prophecy and healing through possession by the Holy Spirit.

RELIGIOUS PRACTITIONERS. The most important practitioners are spirit mediums, men or women who have been chosen by particular spirits to be their hosts. From time to time, a medium becomes possessed by the spirit, and the spirit is believed to act and speak through the host. Hosts may have relatively unimportant spirits and have little function other than providing entertainment at possession dances. They may have healing spirits and thus be primarily concerned with divination and healing, or they may have ancestral spirits or politically important territorial spirits.

In the south, the cult of Mwari has a specialized priesthood that cares for a number of hill shrines and performs ceremonies at them. Otherwise, any adult male, and occasionally an adult female, may perform routine ceremonies in honor of deceased ancestors.

CEREMONIES. Most important ceremonies involve offerings of millet beer to the spirits concerned. Small libations are poured, and the remainder is consumed by the gathering, amid singing and dancing. Sacrifices may occasionally be offered to ancestors and territorial spirits but are regularly offered to Mwari. Spirits may also be honored with gifts of cloth or money, handed over to the medium.

ARTS. The most important musical instrument is the *mbira*, consisting of up to thirty finely tuned metal reeds, set on a wooden base and played inside a gourd resonator. The reeds are plucked with fingers and thumbs. The Shona also have a variety of drums, and in different parts of the country one finds horns, friction bows, gongs, panpipes, and xylophones.

Visual arts were relatively undeveloped in precolonial times. More recently, fine wood and stone carving have become widespread.

MEDICINE. Western medicine is widely available in Shona country and is widely accepted for most ailments. A wide range of herbs and charms are available for ordinary ailments or protection against them. When illness is persistent or when it is accompanied by tension in the community, spiritual causes are suspected and traditional healers are consulted. These divine the cause by dice or through spirit possession and prescribe both ritual and herbal remedies. Such healers may also prescribe charms for good fortune in various domains. A common result of divination is that a spirit wants the sick person to become its host; in such cases, healing may be achieved through possession trances. Traditional healing is particularly effective in dealing with psychological tensions: responsibility is transferred to spirits, and the whole community is involved in sorting out the problem.

DEATH AND AFTERLIFE. Although the ancestral cult is important, traditional Shona rarely speak about an afterlife; a person's future after death is vaguely thought to depend on having descendants who will remember the deceased and hold rituals in his or her honor. Funeral ceremonies are performed to take a dead person away from the community and to keep him or her away. For an adult with descendants, an additional ceremony a year or more later welcomes the deceased into the company of benign ancestors and back into the homestead.

Bibliography

Beach, David N. (1980). *The Shona and Zimbabwe, 900–1850*. Gweru: Mambo Press.

Bourdillon, M. F. C. (1987). *The Shona Peoples*. 3rd ed. Gweru: Mambo Press.

Ellert, Henrik (1984). *The Material Culture of Zimbabwe*. Harare: Longman.

Gelfand, Michael (1979). *Growing Up in Shona Society*. Gweru: Mambo Press.

—M. F. C. BOURDILLON

SOMALIS

Ethonyms: Samaale, Soomaali

Orientation

IDENTIFICATION. The Muslim Somalis of the Horn of Africa speak the Somali language and live in the Somali Democratic Republic (Somalia). There are also substantial numbers of Somalis in neighboring countries: the southern half of Djibouti, the eastern part of Ethiopia, and the northeastern part of Kenya. There are large stable settlements of Somalis in the north of Tanzania and in the Yemeni city of Aden. Although Somalis regard themselves as ethnically one people, there are several subgroups based on patrilineal descent. The term "Somali" is popularly held to derive from the expression *so maal*, or "come and milk," an expression used among nomads, which alludes to the pastoral subsistence and the Somali ideal of hospitality.

LOCATION. Somalia is located between 1°30′ S and 11°30′ N and 41°00′ and 51°25′ E; it extends over an area of 638,000 square kilometers. Somalia has a warm climate: daytime temperatures range from 25° C to 35° C. There is high humidity along the coastal plains. The country is traversed by two perennial rivers, the Jabba and the Shabelle. Average annual rainfall is less than 60 centimeters. There are two rainy seasons, *gu'* (April to June) and *dayr* (October to November).

DEMOGRAPHY. In 1994 the population of Somalia was officially estimated to be 6.67 million. The average population density varies between 9.4 and 13.3 persons per square kilometer; however, density is substantially higher along the riverbanks. A rapid urbanization rate has brought 20 percent of the population to urban centers, with the bulk of this population living in the capital, Mogadishu. With an average life expectancy of about 46 years (1975), more than 58 percent of Somalis are below 20 years of age.

LINGUISTIC AFFILIATION. The Somali language, Af-Soomaali, belongs to the East Cushitic Branch of Afroasiatic languages. It is closely related to languages of some of the neighboring peoples: the Oromo, the Rendille, and the Boni. These languages are sometimes referred to as the "Sam" languages. The Afar language, too, has many similarities with Somali. The Somali people also share many important cultural traits with these linguistically related groups. Somali has adopted a substantial amount of vocabulary from Arabic, but, since 1972, the Latin alphabet has been used for writing. The language has a number of different dialects, most of which are mutually intelligible. The dialects that standard Somali speakers find most difficult to comprehend are the Af-May dialects that are spoken in the south.

History and Cultural Relations

There are two major versions of how the Somali people came into possession of their current territory. Some oral-historical evidence suggests that Somalis gradually spread from the north of the country toward the west and, pushing Oromo and Bantu peoples ahead of them, appeared in the south only during the last millennium. According to another version that possibly relates to movements of a much earlier date, the "Sam"-language speakers first emerged east of Lake Turkana in Kenya. Proto-Somali speakers spread to the northeast from the Tana River and into the Somali Peninsula. Neither of the versions can draw support from archaeological finds. There is evidence that two northern port towns, Zeila and Berbera, were already flourishing in 100 B.C. During the first half of the twentieth century, the coastal settlements along the southern shore, in

The Somali people are divided into six major clusters of patrilineal clans, usually labeled clan-families, that are internally segmented.

Somalis

In the late 1980s a bloody civil war between Somali government troops and several resistance groups led to a mass exodus of at least 400,000 northern Somalis to Ethiopia.

the Benadir region, became established as important commercial centers, with trade networks extending along substantial parts of the East African coast and into the interior of the Horn. During the nineteenth century, Benadir ports came under the dominion of the Omani sultanate, and southern Somali agriculture received an influx of imported slave labor. In the late nineteenth century southern Somalia became an Italian colony; the northern part of country was colonized by the British. After the Italians were defeated during World War II, they were granted their former colony in United Nations trusteeship from 1950 until the independence and unification of the two former colonies in 1960. The frail parliamentary democracy that was installed was overthrown in a 1969 coup d'état that brought Major General Mohammed Siad Barre to power. During some two decades of military rule, the Soviet Union and the United States succeeded one another as Somalia's chief ally. In 1977–1978 Somalia sought unsuccessfully to take from Ethiopia the Ogaden region, which is inhabited primarily by ethnic Somalis. The final resolution of that conflict was not reached until the spring of 1988. In the late 1980s a bloody civil war between Somali government troops and several resistance groups led to a mass exodus of at least 400,000 northern Somalis to Ethiopia.

Settlements

There are two major types of Somali villages. One is the densely clustered nomadic encampment, with portable huts (sing. *aqal*) occupied by five to ten families that stay in the vicinity of the pastures of their herds. Another type of village is found among sedentary cultivators and agro-pastoralists. These are permanent settlements, with an average of five hundred inhabitants and about one hundred mud huts (sing. *mundul*) with thatched roofs. An increasingly common type of building is the tin-roofed mud house (*baraako*). Settlement in these villages may be more dispersed than in the nomadic encampments and may also seasonally include some of the villagers' nomadic kin. The permanent villages are surrounded by farms, and in the center of each village a mosque and a market can often be found. In the grazing areas, small groups of young herders often reside in the open.

Economy

SUBSISTENCE AND COMMERCIAL ACTIVITIES. Animal husbandry is traditionally the major subsistence activity, and the only one in large parts of northern and central Somalia. A wealthy household in the north may have several hundred camels and also considerable numbers of cattle, sheep, and goats. The commercialization of the livestock sector has made livestock and livestock products into the single most important contributor to the gross national product. The total number of camels in Somalia was estimated to be 6.4 million in 1987. Herd management continues to be carried on according to traditional methods, with transhumance between water holes and suitable pastures. In the south, nomadic pastoralism is often mixed with rain-fed agriculture, primarily of sorghum and maize. Other crops include vegetables, fruits, and sesame. With the exception of large foreign-owned banana plantations, agriculture is largely unmechanized, and most crops are planted, weeded, and harvested with hoes and knives. The consumption of fish is increasing, but the 3,300 kilometers of seashore remain little exploited. Hunting is generally seen as defiling and is left to groups that most other Somalis see as inferior.

INDUSTRIAL ARTS. Every one of the larger Somali villages has inhabitants who specialize in the manufacture of iron goods, pottery, and leatherwork. Often such artisans belong to groups that are considered inferior. Larger villages may

SOMALI MEAL

Two Somali women cook outside of a hut. Household chores are traditionally the domain of women and elder daughters in Somalia. (Liba Taylor/Corbis)

also host some tailors and, in the riverine zones, sesame-mill operators.

TRADE. Although the bulk of agricultural production is for family consumption, the sale of surplus in small-scale markets provides important income for most families. Both crops and animal produce are traded. Women have come to play increasingly important roles in commercial activities.

DIVISION OF LABOR. Polygynously formed households assume specialized functions within the larger family economy. One wife and her children may be chiefly responsible for the camels, whereas another such sibling group is assigned the agricultural work. The herding and milking of camels is the exclusive domain of men, but women and children usually tend the small stock. Both men and women engage in farm work. Child rearing and household chores are the tasks of women and their elder daughters. Somali men often express embarrassment if they stay for a long period in the home.

LAND TENURE. Pastoral territorial control of rangelands is primarily centered on the water sources that are available within an area. Thus, although there exists some association between a clan group and a certain tract of land, more definite property rights are articulated regarding wells and other water points. Pastoral territorial feuding is most marked where routes of migration conflict with the interests of cultivators. Agricultural territory belongs to the person who has cleared or inherited the land, and, theoretically, it may be sold or rented as that person sees fit. In colonial times, a form of community control was exercised; members of the same village or kin group were given the first option to buy farmland. The military regime has since introduced a system of centralized farm registration, and there have been reports that wealthy urban settlers use the system to appropriate rural estates from small-scale farmers.

Kinship

KIN GROUPS AND DESCENT. The Somali system of patrilineal descent embraces the whole nation in a genealogical grid and claims ultimate descent from the Qurayshitic lineage of the prophet Mohammed. At the level of residential groupings, a set of patrilineally related kinsmen will form the nucleus of a kin group, to which other people are joined by ties of affinity or matrilaterality. For practical purposes, the genealogical depth of a residential kin group rarely goes beyond four or five generations; however, in matters

such as feuding and payment of blood-wealth, the range of agnatically related kinsmen who are involved is greatly expanded.

KINSHIP TERMINOLOGY. Parental siblings are referred to by bifurcate-collateral terms. Cousin terms are either Sudanese or Hawaiian. Where the latter prevails, it is usually for reasons of politeness, just as any stranger of approximately the same age as Ego may be addressed as "brother/sister." Seniority is emphasized in the use of intragenerational terms. Many intergenerational terms are used self-reciprocally, so that, for instance, a man addresses his son as "father."

Sociopolitical Organization

Somalia, constitutionally a socialist republic, is divided into regions, districts, and subdistricts. At each of these administrative levels, there is an elected body of officials and a parallel assembly of members of the Socialist party. The traditional form of sociopolitical organization, based on clan membership, was formally abolished and condemned as "tribalism" in 1971, yet clans and agnatic groupings remain the focus of articulation of all important societal matters. The modern administrative system is in many parts of the country only superimposed upon the old system of segmentary lineages, and it has by no means replaced that system.

SOCIAL ORGANIZATION. The Somali people are divided into six major clusters of patrilineal clans, usually labeled clan-families, that are internally segmented. For most purposes, the largest social unit is a clan (*qabiil*) or a subclan that may vary in size between a few thousand and a hundred thousand members. Based on the reckoning of agnatic descent, clans are internally divided into lineages and sublineages, the size of which rarely exceeds a few hundred to a thousand members. In the north, there are additional small scattered groups of despised artisans and serfs that are collectively known as *sab*. In the south, there are large numbers of such small groups of people—some of whom are descendants of former slaves—who are frequently called in as farm labor. Known collectively as *boon* (inferior), they are regarded and treated as second-class citizens. Marriage with members of these groups is not permitted. In the southern regions of Somalia, it is possible to be "adopted"—given full membership—in a clan, even though one is the descendant of another clan. The sedentary villages in the south often have a leadership that is independent from that of the clan.

♦ **agnatic descent (patrilineal descent)**
The practice of tracing kinship affiliation only through the male line.

POLITICAL ORGANIZATION. Interclan and interlineage affairs are handled by committees of clan elders, supervised by the clan chief, the *suldaan* or *ugas*. In the north, there exists a system of contractual agreements between different agnatic groupings, and the fines that are to be exacted for different breaches of customary law are specified. These agreements also specify the range of solidarity within the different contracting segmentary lineages. In the south, the lineages that constitute a clan are less likely to contract such agreements on their own, but the clan as a whole will agree on blood-wealth size, grazing rights, and other arrangements with other clans. Political life in rural Somali society has always been marked by negotiation, counseling, and free debate—features that inspired Ioan M. Lewis to title his major work on the northern Somali "A Pastoral Democracy" (1961).

SOCIAL CONTROL. The traditional means of social control are closely linked with the clanship system. Lineage elders and chiefs are expected to ensure that the conduct of lineage members conforms to customary law, both in internal dealings and in affairs with other agnatic groups. Traditional cooperatives and associations, such as water-hole (war) maintenance groups, have their own sets of rules to guide their internal affairs, and they elect headmen to be responsible for doing so. Nowadays the police force is involved in most rural affairs and will often act together with local leaders. The *guulwada*, or "victory-carriers," a paramilitary militia, are frequently relied upon to implement government decisions. Another government agency, the National Security Service (NSS), has also had a high degree of presence, even in remote rural settings.

CONFLICT. Feuding and armed conflicts over grazing and water rights are not uncommon. In the past, conflicts often emerged following cattle or camel raids. In the war zones in the north of the country and along the Ethiopian border, a considerable supply of submachine guns and other light weaponry exists.

Religion and Expressive Culture

RELIGIOUS BELIEFS. Somalis are Sunni Muslims, the vast majority of whom follow the Shafi rite. Islam probably dates as far back as the thirteenth century in Somalia. In the nineteenth century Islam was revitalized, and popular versions of it developed following the proselytizing of *shuyukh* (sing. *shaykh*) belonging to different Sufi orders.

MARRIAGE AND FAMILY

Marriage

In northern Somalia, marriages were traditionally contracted between previously non-related families, explicitly to enable the establishment of new alliances. In the south, the favorite spouse is a patrilateral parallel cousin, real or classificatory. As a Muslim, each Somali man has the right to be married to four women. Although viri-patrilocal and neolocal residence are characteristic of both endogamous and exogamous marriages, several clans practice an initial period of uxorilocal residence that, lasting as it occasionally does for many years, may develop into a permanent residence. The divorce rate is high. In one southern study, half of all rural women in their fifties had been married more than once.

Domestic Unit

The principal domestic unit is the uterinesibling group (*bah*), but it is not a closely bounded unit; many such groups have more distant relatives living with them, sometimes for extended periods. The descendants of a man, divided into several uterine-sibling groups, are collectively called a *reer*. This term means "people" and is, in principle, applicable to any level of agnatic grouping.

Inheritance

Sons generally receive an equal share of the father's property, whereas the rights of the daughters are less secure. Although daughters theoretically should inherit half the share that is allotted to each of their brothers, they have in several areas traditionally been allowed to inherit neither camels nor landed property. The ambitious 1975 family-law reform, stipulating that daughters should have equal rights to inheritance, has had little impact in either rural or urban areas.

Socialization

The duties of child rearing are essentially the mother's, although the father will take part in Quranic and religious education. The mother is usually aided in her task by both her sisters and her elder daughters. The values of respect for both seniority and the integrity of others are constantly emphasized. Small children are rapidly taught their position within the age hierarchy, but it is noteworthy how often parents will treat seriously even the most inchoate statement of a younger child.

The Muslim faith forms an integral part of daily social life. The activities of Catholic and Protestant missionaries have never been successful. Somali scholars debate the extent to which Somali Muslims may have incorporated elements of a pre-Islamic religion. Some of the terms for "God" (e.g., Wag) are also found among the neighboring non-Muslim peoples. In urban areas, groups have appeared that, inspired by the Egyptian Muslim Brotherhood (Akhiwaan Muslimin), propagate a more orthodox Islam and criticize the government on moral grounds.

A variety of spiritual beings are believed to inhabit the world. The *jinny*, the only category of spirits that Islam recognizes, are generally harmless if they are left undisturbed. Other categories of spirits, such as *ayaamo*, *mingis*, and *rohaan*, are more capricious and may bring illness by possessing their victims. Groups of those who are possessed often form cults seeking to soothe the possessing spirit.

RELIGIOUS PRACTITIONERS. The Somali culture distinguishes between a religious expert (*wadaad*) and a person who is preoccupied with worldly matters. There is no formal hierarchy of clergy, but a wadaad may enjoy considerable respect and may assemble a small party of followers with whom to settle in a rural community. The five standard Muslim prayers are generally observed, but Somali women have never worn the prescribed veils. Villagers and urban settlers frequently turn to the wadaad for blessings, charms, and advice in worldly matters.

CEREMONIES. Somalis do not worship the dead, but they do perform annual commemorative services at their graves. Pilgrimages (sing. *siyaaro*) to the tombs of saints are also prominent events in ritual life. The Muslim calendar includes the celebration of `Iid al Fidr (the end of Ramadan), Araafo (the pilgrimage to Mecca), and Mawliid (the birthday of the Prophet). Among the non-Muslim ceremonies, the *dab-shiid* (the lighting of the fire), at which all household members jump across the family hearth, is most widely performed.

ARTS. Somalis enjoy a broad variety of alliterated oral poetry and songs. Famous poets may come to enjoy nationwide prestige.

MEDICINE. Illnesses are attributed both to abstract entities and emotions and to tangible causes. Somali nomads discovered the role of mosquitoes in the spread of malaria long before this connection was scientifically proven. The medical system is a plural one: patients have a free choice between herbal, religious, and Western medicines.

DEATH AND AFTERLIFE. Although graves are insignificant looking, the symbolic dimensions of funerals are considerable. The corpse is seen as harmful and must be disposed of rapidly. Within the local community, relations with the deceased must be cleared of grievances, and his or her passage from "this world" (*addunnyo*) to the "next world" (*aakhiro*) ensured. Funerals serve as a reminder to the living of the return of the Prophet and the approaching day of judgment (*qiyaame*), when the faithful will have nothing to fear, but sinners will be sent to hell.

Bibliography

Cassanelli, Lee V. (1982). *The Shaping of Somali Society: Reconstructing the History of a Pastoral People, 1600–1900*. Philadelphia: University of Pennsylvania Press.

Helander, Bernhard (1990). *The Slaughtered Camel: Coping with Fictitious Descent among the Hubeer of Southern Somalia*. Uppsala: Acta Universitatis Upsaliensis.

Lewis, Ioan M. (1961). *A Pastoral Democracy: A Study of Pastoralism and Politics among the Northern Somali of the Horn of Africa*. London: Oxford University Press.

—BERNHARD HELANDER

SONGHAY

Ethonyms: Gao borey, Kado, Kwaara borey, Songhoi, Songhrai

Orientation

The Songhay are the fourth-largest ethnic group in Niger, West Africa. There are also considerable Songhay populations in Mali and Benin. They are closely related culturally to the Zarma. The Songhay are spread over a large area of eastern Mali, western Niger, and northern Benin. The largest concentrations are in eastern Mali and western Niger. In eastern Mali, the Songhay population lives along the Niger River from east of Lake Debo to south of Ansongo. In Niger, Songhay live along the Niger River from Firgoun to Sansane-Hausa, as well as west of the Niger north of Niamey in the region of Tera. In regions far from the Niger, the geography consists of laterite plateaus broken by occasional mesas. The vegetation in Songhay country, which is by and large scrub desert, is sparse. Water is deep and in short supply,

In precolonial times, Songhay social organization consisted of nobles, other free Songhay, and captives who could be sold, but whose offspring were considered members of noble families.

except in the land along the Niger River, which is lush with wild vegetation as well as vegetable and fruit gardens. The climate of Songhay country, like that of Zarma country, consists of a single rainy season that begins in June and ends in September. Average rainfall varies from 20 centimeters in the north of Songhay country to roughly 40 centimeters in the south. The average high temperature, as in Zarma country, is 36° C, but temperatures reach the mid-40s at the peak of the hot season in mid-May. The average low temperature is 22° C.

History and Cultural Relations

The Songhay trace their origins to the coming of Aliman Za (or Dia) to the Niger River (near Koukya) in the latter part of the eighth century. With the help of iron weapons, Za conquered the indigenous populations of Gabibi (hunters and farmers) and Sorko (fishers). Aliman Za, probably a Lemta Berber from southern Libya, founded the Za dynasty of Songhay that endured from the latter part of the eighth century to 1491 and the death of Sonni Ali Ber, who was succeeded by Askia Mohammed Toure (founder of the Askiad, the second and last dynasty of Songhay). During the reigns of Sonni Ali Ber and Askia Mohammed, the Songhay Empire reached the zenith of its imperial power. The weaknesses and avarice of most of Askia Mohammed's successors—his sons—sapped Songhay of its strength. In 1591 a small Moroccan force sent to Songhay by El Mansur routed a much larger Songhay army, marking the end of the Songhay Empire. Descendants of Askia Mohammed continued to rule a unified southern state of Songhay until 1660, in what is today Niger. Rivalries among the ruling princes, however, precipitated the balkanization of the south into five principalities: Garuol, Tera, Dargol, Kokoro, and Anzuru. These principalities remained independent until the coming of the French military in 1898.

Settlements

Like Zarma villages, Songhay villages are usually nucleated settlements of round mud or thatched dwellings with straw roofs. In these villages, one also finds an increasing number of rectangular mud-brick houses with either thatch or corrugated-tin roofs. Villages far from the Niger River are surrounded by cultivated fields (mostly of millet) and by bush areas. There are substantial rice fields and garden plots around the riverine villages.

Economy

Nonriverine Songhay are dryland farmers who cultivate millet as a principal subsistence crop. Most farmers do not sell their grain after the harvest. Millet is cultivated along with cowpeas, sorrel, and groundnuts. Sorghum and manioc are also cultivated in regions with heavy soils. In riverine areas, rice is cultivated. In both riverine and nonriverine areas, dry-season gardens are also cultivated. Gardeners harvest mangoes, guavas, citrus fruits, papayas, dates, and bananas, as well as tomatoes, carrots, peppers, lettuce, cabbages, squashes, sorrel, and okra. The Songhay, like the Zarma, rely heavily upon the household for agricultural labor, but rice cultivators often hire nonkin to harvest their crops.

Like the Zarma, the Songhay are well-known migrants. During the colonial period, both Songhay and Zarma migrated in droves to the colonial Gold Coast, where they were known collectively as either "Zabrama" or "Gao." In Ghana, Nigeria, Togo, and Ivory Coast, Songhay today are cloth merchants as well as *nyama-nyama ize* ("the children of disorder"), who sell a variety of goods. In Niger, Songhay men sell surplus millet and rice and engage in transport and commerce; women sell cooked foods and condiments.

Kinship

As with the Zarma, the patrilineage and lineage segments are the most significant kinship groupings. Descent is also patrilineal. Unlike their Zarma cousins, however, the Songhay also recognize noble lineages, principally those whose apical ancestor is Askia Mohammed Toure (*maiga*), Sonni Ali Ber (*sohanci*), or Faran Maka Bote (*sorko*). The Songhay employ Iroquois cousin terminology, using bifurcate-merging terms.

Marriage and Family

Polygyny is highly valued among the Songhay, as it is among the Zarma, but the great percentage of Songhay households are monogamous—primarily for economic reasons. Among Songhay nobles, firstborn sons are pressured to marry their parallel cousins (father's brother's daughters), in order to maintain the purity of the noble lineage.

Sociopolitical Organization

The household is the fundamental unit of Songhay social organization. Beyond the household is the village quarter (*kurey*), which elects a quarter chief (*kurey koy*). The neighborhood chiefs constitute a village council, which elects the village chief (*kwaara koy*). Whereas the Zarma profess a rather egalitarian ideology, the Songhay do not. Village chiefs are accorded deference, especially if they are of noble descent, which is usually the case in major towns.

In precolonial times, Songhay social organization consisted of nobles, other free Songhay, and captives. The latter were originally prisoners taken in precolonial raids. Captives could be sold, but their offspring were considered members—albeit stigmatized—of noble families. Captives became weavers, smiths, and bards.

The most important political authorities in Songhay country are various paramount chiefs. These men are appointed in Songhay villages of historical consequence (Dargol, Tera, Kokoro, Ayoru, Yatakala). Such chiefs are always of noble descent, and they have at least symbolic authority over the village chiefs in their jurisdiction.

Religion and Expressive Culture

RELIGIOUS BELIEFS. According to Songhay religious beliefs, there are a number of paths that situate Songhay in the cosmos. These paths are magic, possession, ancestor worship, witchcraft, and Islam. Islam is superficially important, in that every town has a mosque, and larger towns have Friday mosques. Possession, magic (and sorcery), ancestor worship, and witchcraft, however, are the vital components of Songhay belief. Most Songhay towns have possession troupes and magician-healers, as well as suspected witches.

RELIGIOUS PRACTITIONERS. For Muslims, there are marabouts, Islamic clerics who either heal the sick or lead the community in prayer. Some Songhay communities have imams, who teach Islamic philosophy to lesser clerics. There are also healers as well as priests who are associated with the possession cults and are also healers in their own right.

CEREMONIES. Muslim ceremonial activities are the most frequent rituals practiced among the Songhay (daily prayers, weekly prayer, the Ramadan fast, and the Tabaski). There are also spirit-possession ceremonies, which in some Songhay towns occur at least once a week. The most important spirit-possession ceremonies are the *genji bi hori*, a festival in which Songhay make offerings to the black spirits that control pestilence, and the *yenaandi*, or rain dance. Both of these ceremonies are held in the hot season.

Bibliography

Boulnois, J., and B. Hama (1953). *Empire de Gao: Histoire, coutumes et magi des Songhai*. Paris: Maisonneuve.

Gabbal, Jean-Marie (1988). *Les génies du fleuve*. Paris: Presses de la Renaissance.

Kati, Mahmoud (1912). *Tarikh al-Fattach*. Translated by M. Delafosse. Paris: Maisonneuve.

Olivier de Sardan, J-P. (1982). *Concepts et conceptions songhay-zarma: Histoire, culture, société*. Paris: Nubia.

Olivier de Sardan, J-P. (1984). *Sociétés songhay-zarma*. Paris: Karthala.

Rouch, Jean ([1960] 1989). *La religion et la magie songhay*. Brussels: Éditions de l'Université de Bruxelles.

es-Saadi, Mohammed (1900). *Tarikh es-Soudan*. Translated by O. Houdas. Paris: Leroux.

Stoller, Paul (1989). *Fusion of the Worlds: An Ethnography of Possession among the Songhay of Niger*. Chicago: University of Chicago Press.

Stoller, Paul, and Cheryl Olkes (1987). *In Sorcery's Shadow*. Chicago: University of Chicago Press.

—PAUL STOLLER

SWAHILI

Ethonyms: none

Orientation

The people known as Swahili (sing. Mswahili, pl. Wa Swahili) live along the narrow East African coastline and the adjacent islands (Zanzibar, Pemba, and Mafia) between southern Somalia and northern Mozambique; they also live in the Aomoro Islands and northwestern Madagascar, and there are Swahili settlements in the far African interior near Lake Tanganyika. On the coast, they live in distinct settlements within approximately 2 kilometers of the seas, placed on creeks and on the leeward sides of the many small islets that are protected from the Indian Oceam. Their language, KiSwahili, with its many dialects, belongs to the Sam Family of Northeastern Bantu and has many loanwords from Arabic. It has long been used in a debased form as a lingua franca throughout eastern Africa. It was traditionally written in Arabic script but today Roman script is mostly used. The name "Swahili" comes from the Arabic *Swahili* ("coast" or "margin"). The term was first used to refer to the eighteenth-century coast dwellers by the colonial rulers of the time, the Omani of the sultanate of Zanzibar; they prefer to use the names of their local settlements,

Open conflict is unusual among the Swahili; however, finita, *intrigue and backbiting, is a well-recognized aspect of Swahili domestic and social life.*

such as Mvita (Mombasa), Unguja Zanzibar, or Amu (Lamu). "Swahili" is essentially the name others have given them. They number between 200,000 and 400,000, censuses being unreliable because self-designations have varied from one period to another.

History and Cultural Relations

Pre-Swahili settlements are reported from the first century onward, mainly in Arabic and Chinese medieval records, and later in those of the Portuguese and other Europeans. Many Swahili claim Arabic and other Asian origins, but these claims, rather than having a historical basis, reflect ambitions to deny African origins (i.e., those of their slaves). They suffered under Portuguese rule from 1498 until 1729, when they were forcibly incorporated into the sultanate of Zanzibar. In the nineteenth century they came under the rule of Britain and Germany, and in the 1960s they were incorporated into the independent states of Kenya and Tanzania, not always with their approval. As Muslims, the Swahili have felt themselves distinct from the non-Muslim majorities of these countries, which have rarely supported the social and political wishes of the Swahili, who are remembered as slave traders and owners.

Economy

The basis of Swahili economy has been the long-distance commerce between the interior of Africa and the countries of the northern Indian Ocean, in which they played the role of middlemen merchants. Their settlements, strung along the coastline, have been urban—some closely built-up places and others more like large villages—but all are known by the same Swahili term, *mji*. The commerce, now virtually extinguished, lasted for almost two thousand years. Raw and unprocessed items from Africa (e.g., ivory, slaves, gold, grain, mangrove poles) were exchanged for processed commodities from Asia (e.g., textiles, beads, weapons, porcelain). The oceangoing sailing vessels from Asia and the foot caravans from the interior met at the coast, where the Swahili merchants provided safe harbors and the many complex skills and facilities needed for mercantile exchange.

"Stone-towns"—permanent houses built with "stone" (coral block), set in narrow streets, and often surrounded by walls—provided these services. Interspersed with these are the "Country-towns," large villagelike places of impermanent housing that have provided the Stone-towns with food-

stuffs and labor but have not themselves taken direct part in the long-distance commerce. The whole has formed a single *oikumene*, never a single polity, but a congeries of towns with a single underlying structure. Country-towns grow foodstuffs in gardens and fields; Stone-towns once had large plantations worked by slave labor for the growing of export grains, their own food coming mainly from the Country-towns.

The staple foods are rice and sorghums; the most important of the many other crops and trees are the coconut, banana, tamarind, mango, and clove (the last grown mainly in large plantations formerly owned by Omani Arabs). Fishing is important everywhere, and few livestock are kept.

Labor has been provided from three sources: the family and kin group, slaves, and hired laborers. In the Country-towns, men and women are, in most respects, considered equal and their respective labor as being complementary: men have the heavier work—as contract laborers on clove plantations and in the largest towns such as Mombasa, Zanzibar City, and Dar es Salaam. In the Stone-towns, domestic and agricultural work was carried out by slaves until the beginning of the twentieth century. Since then, it has been done in most towns by hired and "squatter" labor from the Country-towns and by non-Swahili immigrants. Shortage of seasonal labor has always been a serious problem in all the Swahili settlements; this remains true today.

Kinship, Marriage, and Family

There is a wide variation in forms of descent and kin group among the Swahili settlements. Country-towns are divided into moieties, and these into wards or quarters. The wards, composed of clusters of cognatically related kin, are the corporate and landholding units. Marriage is preferred between cross and parallel cousins; it is seen largely as a way to retain rights over land within the small kin group. Authority is held by senior men and women, and all local groups are regarded as equal in rank.

Within the Stone-towns, the main social groups are in most cases patrilineal subclans and lineages. The clans are distributed among the coastal towns and even in southern Arabia, from which immigrant origin is often claimed. These towns are likewise divided into moieties and constituent wards, the former once providing indigenous forms of government; their structural opposition is expressed in fighting at certain rituals, football matches, and poetry competitions. The corporate groups are the lineages, segments of subclans, that, in the past, acted as business houses and owned the large permanent houses that are so marked a feature of these towns. The subclans are ranked, position depending largely on antiquity of claimed immigration and settlement, as well as on commercial wealth and standing. Members of these mercantile lineages are known as "patricians."

Marriages are centrally important and weddings the most elaborate rituals. In the Stone-towns, the preferred marriage forms vary. For firstborn daughters, they should be between close paternal parallel cousins. Bride-wealth and dowry are both transferred, as are residential rights (not full ownership, which is vested in the lineage) for the daughter in her lineage house, marriage thus being uxorilocal. Marriages of later-born daughters are more usually with cross cousins, often in neighboring Stone-towns so as to make and retain useful commercial ties. Stone-town weddings are traditionally elaborate and costly, the bride needing to show her virginity and so her purity, which reflects upon the honor and reputation of her husband. Country-town weddings are basically similar but less elaborate and less ritualized.

Divorce is permitted under Islamic law: it is easy for husbands but extremely difficult for wives. The marriages of firstborn patrician daughters are monogamous (although concubinage was frequent), and divorce has been rare; all other marriages have often been polygynous, and divorce has been and is extremely common, as high as 90 percent in some areas.

Today Swahili women undergo initiation (without physical operation) at puberty, in order to be permitted to marry. Boys nowadays are not initiated but are circumcised in infancy; in the past there was more elaborate male initiation. Both boys' and girls' socialization after infancy takes the form of Islamic education in the Quranic schools attached to mosques, and consists largely of moral and theological learning based on knowledge of the Quran, although instruction in poetry and music has been an important part of their training to become pious Muslims. Today most children also attend nonreligious schools in order to acquire "Western" education, but religious education retains its central place, and overtly Christian schools are totally avoided.

Sociopolitical Organization

Swahili towns have traditionally been autonomous, many at one time being ruled by kings and queens. (Lamu Town, ruled by an oligarchy, was an exception.) Country-town local government remains largely in the hands of small, indigenous government organs, known as "the Four Men" and similar titles, representing constituent wards.

The Swahili patricians kept and traded in slaves; the Country-towns did neither. Slaves, numbering between 25 percent and 50 percent of the total population, were obtained from the interior from indigenous rulers and used as trade commodities, for house- and fieldwork, and as concubines. Slavery was abolished under the British in 1897 in Zanzibar and Tanganyika and in 1907 in Kenya. Its abolition brought the traditional mercantile economy largely to an end.

Open conflict has been—and remains—unusual among the Swahili, and institutions such as the feud are not known; however, *fitina*, intrigue and backbiting, is a well-recognized aspect of Swahili domestic and social life. Nevertheless, the towns have frequently waged war against one another, as part of wider processes of colonial subordination. The Omani sultanate of Zanzibar extended its sway along the coast during the eighteenth and nineteenth centuries by attacking towns in turn, using other towns as allies; local opposition to Zanzibar hegemony was soon put down by the sultans' forces of mercenary troops from outside eastern Africa. The Swahili also revolted against German rule in Tanganyika in the early years of the twentieth century and were put down with great brutality by German-led troops. The Zanzibar Revolution of 1964 removed the Omani colonial administration, and there have since been many small clashes, often couched in religious terms, with the forces of independent Kenya.

Religion and Expressive Culture

The Swahili are Sunni Muslims; even though their former Omani rulers of the sultanate of Zanzibar were Ibadhi, the Swahili were shown religious tolerance. The first mosques on the coast date from about the mid-tenth century, the identity of Swahili as Muslims dating also from that period. The central building of every town is its mosque, typically placed in a space between the two moieties; the male population assembles there on Fridays (women are not permitted to attend). In most towns, a Muslim school is built next to the mosque. There may be many mosques in a large town, built and administered privately and entailed for charitable purposes. Swahili religion

Open conflict has been—and remains—unusual among the Swahili.

♦ **dowry**
The practice of a bride's kin giving substantial property or wealth to the groom or to his kin before or at the time of marriage.

is comprised of two aspects: orthodox Islam, or *dini*, and the set of local beliefs and practices known as *mila*, which are perhaps almost always originally pre-Islamic. It is often held that the dini is Arabian and associated with men, whereas the mila is African and associated with women. Both men and women, however, see themselves as orthodox Muslims, and in fact almost all observe the practices of the mila. An important part of the mila is spirit possession, which is largely practiced and controlled by women, even though they stress their Islamic purity. Women who are possessed typically join associations, even though these are in most case controlled by men, and most such associations have members of both free and of slave ancestry.

The Swahili recognize as crucial to the maintenance of their identity the concepts of *ustaarabu* ("civilization") and *utamaduni* ("urbanity"), both linked to Islam and contrasted to what they see as the *ushenzi* ("barbarism") of the other, non-Muslim peoples of eastern Africa. Important rites that maintain these concepts include the originally pre-Islamic "New Year," Mwaka or Nauroz, at which the towns are symbolically purified, and the regular Islamic ceremonies of Id-al-Fitr and other occasions, along with the regular public reading known as *maulidi*, that deal with the life and deeds of the Prophet.

Closely linked to religious beliefs and practice are forms of medical healing. Herbal medicines and possession by "doctors" are employed, as well as prayer and ritual purification. In the latter, the main practitioners are members of the clans known as Sharifu, composed of people who claim to be direct descendants of the Prophet and who live scattered in the coastal towns. All Swahili believe in the existence of many categories of both evil and good spirits, and also in that of witches and sorcerers, whose activities can be controlled by recourse to "doctors" who use both pre-Islamic and Islamic means.

The Swahili practice certain forms of visual art—the carving of elaborate wooden doors and furniture, the making of gold and silver jewelry—but the art most highly regarded is poetry. Swahili poetry is complex and of many kinds; like Islamic scholarship and knowledge, it is open to both women and men (and formerly, also to slaves). Poetry is used for both devotional and historical writings, the latter taking the form of the "chronicles" that relate the founding of the various towns and other key historical events. Today poetry is composed for both domestic and town occasions, such as weddings and competitions at New Year,

and also for political purposes on radio and television.

Bibliography

Cooper, Frederick (1977). *Plantation Slavery on the East Coast of Africa.* New Haven: Yale University Press.

Middleton, John (1992). *The World of the Swahili: An African Mercantile Civilization.* New Haven: Yale University Press.

Pouwels, Randall L. (1987). *Horn and Crescent: Cultural Change and Traditional Islam on the East African Coast, 800–1900.* Cambridge: Cambridge University Press.

Sheriff, A. M. H. (1987). *Slaves, Spices, and Ivory in Zanzibar.* Athens: Ohio University Press.

—JOHN MIDDLETON

SWAZI

Ethonyms: Ebantfu ba kwa Ngwane (the people of Ngwane), emaSwati, emaSwazi, Swati

Orientation

IDENTIFICATION. "Swazi" refers to the nation, tribe, or ethnic group, or an individual, "siSwati" to the language. SiSwati speakers are found in Swaziland, South Africa, and Mozambique.

LOCATION. The Swazi reside in Swaziland, a small, land-locked country of 17,363 square kilometers, which is perched on the edge of the southern African escarpment. It is bounded on three sides by South Africa and on the fourth by Mozambique, both countries in which many ethnic Swazis reside. Four distinctive topographic steps largely determine the characteristics of Swaziland's natural environment: the high veld, averaging 1,219 meters in elevation, with forests and grassy hills; the middle veld, averaging 610 meters in elevation, with hills and palatable grasses suited for livestock and rich soils good for agriculture; the low veld, averaging 274 meters in elevation, with tall grasses suited for grazing but usually not for dry-land agriculture; and the Lubombo mountain range, a narrow plateau averaging about 610 meters in elevation, with a warm, subhumid climate and basaltic soils suited for arable agriculture. Several rivers—the Mbeluzi, Ngwavuma, Great Usutu, Komati, and Lomati—cut through the high veld, middle veld, and Lubombo Mountains.

DEMOGRAPHY. Swazi identity is based on allegiance to a dual monarchy, headed by a hereditary king, titled by his people *ingwenyama* (lion), and a queen mother, *indlovukati* (Lady Elephant). Ethnic Swazis living in the Republic of South Africa and in Mozambique are not under their effective political control, however. Within Swaziland, the population (the great majority of which is Swazi) was estimated at 860,000 in 1992, with an annual growth rate of about 3.4 percent. Most Swazis live in rural homesteads, but, in the middle veld, where nearly one-half of the Swazi population resides, rural homesteads are interspersed with densely populated settlements around employment centers. The two major cities are Mbabane and Manzini.

LINGUISTIC AFFILIATION. SiSwati is a tonal Bantu language of the Nguni Group, closely related to Zulu and, more distantly, to Xhosa. It is spoken in Swaziland and in the Eastern Transvaal Province of the Republic of South Africa. Little has been published in siSwati.

History and Cultural Relations

Swazi history dates back to the late sixteenth century, when the first Swazi King, Ngwane II, settled southeast of modernday Swaziland. His grandson Sobhuza I established a permanent capital and drew within a centralized political system the resident Nguni and Sotho people. During the mid-nineteenth century, Sobhuza's heir, Mswati II, from whom the Swazis derive their name, expanded the Swazi nation to an area much larger than modern Swaziland. Mswati established contact with the British. By the late nineteenth century, Mswati's successor, Mbandzeni, granted Europeans land concessions for grazing and prospecting, thus unwittingly giving rise to serious, prolonged conflicts regarding land-usage rights. In 1894 the Boer and British powers granted the South African Boer Republic of the Transvaal control over Swaziland. After the Anglo-Boer War (1899–1902), Britain made Swaziland a protectorate. The Partitions Proclamation of 1907 confirmed the concessionaires control of two-thirds of the land, which was contested in 1922 by King Sobhuza II. Today the Swazi nation controls about two-thirds of the land area. Swaziland became independent in 1968.

Settlements

The ordinary Swazi derives rights to land access and use by virtue of his/her residence or membership in a particular homestead (*umuti*). According to Hilda Kuper and Brian Marwick, the homestead is patriarchal, with a male homestead head (*umnumzana*) assuming primary powers, but the position of the main wife is important in family life. The homestead head determines resource allocation such as land distribution, makes major decisions regarding both production (plowing and types of crops grown) and economic expenditures, and mobilizes homestead labor.

The traditional Swazi homestead was circular in shape; the dwelling huts and cooking huts were built around the circumference of a circle, forming two "horns" embracing the courtyard and partially enclosing the cattle byre. Homestead residents have access as individuals to arable land and as members of the larger community to communal pasturage. Following the arrival of Europeans in Swaziland, homesteads changed; customarily tenured land was reduced in area, fragmented, and taxed. New agricultural methods, new hybrid seeds and fertilizers, and new technologies were introduced. At the same time, men migrated within Swaziland and to South Africa in search of income, thereby reducing labor power, altering sex roles, and changing the locus of decision making within homesteads. When homestead production activities changed, the social composition and physical organization of homesteads also changed.

Economy

SUBSISTENCE AND COMMERCIAL ACTIVITIES. Swazi homesteads focus on subsistence agricultural activities—primarily the cultivation of maize, sorghum, beans, groundnuts, and sweet potatoes. Maize had been essentially unknown until the mid-nineteenth century, at which time it was introduced and gradually replaced sorghum as the staple crop. Despite the importance of agriculture to the homestead economy, cattle are the basis of wealth and status. Swazi have the "cattle complex" typical of many eastern African tribes: cattle provide for individual food and clothing needs as well as serving wider economic and ritual purposes.

INDUSTRIAL ARTS. Smithing, a hereditary occupation for men that requires long apprenticeship, is surrounded by taboos. It was, at one time, the most exacting and remunerative of the industrial arts. The iron hoes, knives, and various kinds of spears (weapons of war) produced by smiths were in great demand. The smithy was built at a distance from the homestead and put off limits to women. In the past, the Swazi also had specialists in copper and brass. Today wood carving is important but is mainly limited to functional ob-

Swazi identity is based on allegiance to a dual monarchy, headed by a hereditary king, titled ingwenyama *(lion), and a queen mother,* indlovukati *(Lady Elephant).*

jects, such as meat dishes and spoons. Wood carvers are not required to enter a restricted apprenticeship and do not receive the status accorded healers, or even smiths. Pottery making lies within the domain of women, who, using the coil technique, produce different sizes and shapes of drinking and cooking vessels. Swazi specialists do not have at their disposal markets comparable to those found in West Africa.

TRADE. Swaziland's main export crop is sugar, based on irrigated cane. Several other cash crops, including maize, rice, vegetables, cotton, tobacco, citrus fruits, and pineapples, are traded both within and outside the country. Its mineral wealth, which consists of iron ore, coal, diamonds, and asbestos, is mined for export. Meat and meat products are also exported. The industrial estate at Matsapha produces processed agricultural and forestry products, garments, textiles, and many light manufactures. The main imports are motor vehicles, heavy machinery, fuel and lubricants, foodstuffs, and clothing.

DIVISION OF LABOR. Swazi division of labor proceeds according to sex, age, and pedigree. Most men know how to construct house frames and cattle kraals, plow, tend and milk cattle, sew skins, and cut shields. Some men are (or were in the past) particularly accomplished at warfare, animal husbandry, hunting, and governing. Most women know how to hoe, tend small livestock, thatch, plait ropes, weave mats/baskets, grind grain, brew beer, cook foods, and care for children; some women specialize in pot- and mat making. Age determines who will perform tasks associated with ritual performances. Rank determines who

will summon people for work parties in district and national enterprises and who will supervise the workers. Work parties, sometimes consisting of hundreds or thousands of workers, compete in separate groups of men and women and receive customary rewards of thanks from the host according to rank, age, sex, and locality.

LAND TENURE. Land-access rights in Swazi areas (as opposed to freehold areas established by the colonial land partition of 1907) are held by the community as a whole, and the king, representing the entire Swazi nation, is responsible for its allotment to chiefs. The chiefs, in their turn, distribute land to homestead heads. Swazi citizens can pledge allegiance to a chief and rulers and thereby obtain rights to land according to four acquisition methods: *kukhonta* (direct grant by the chief), *kubekwa* (direct grant by another individual), inheritance, and *kuboleka umhlaba* (being "lent" land by another individual). Rose (1992) has maintained that land disputes commonly center around problems of use rights, boundaries, cattle trespass, inheritance, natural-resource ownership and management, or chiefly legitimacy and territorial jurisdiction. In the late twentieth century land disputes have intensified or become more frequent, as populations have expanded or migrated toward employment centers. New varieties of disputes, often in association with development projects (e.g., construction of buildings, roads, or dams) have arisen.

Marriage and Family

MARRIAGE. Clan membership is important in regulating marriage and succession. Marriage

SWAZI WARRIOR

A Swazi warrior dressed in traditional costume in a field. Swazis were engaged in tribal warfare until the imposition of European control in the late 1880s. Swaziland. (Phillip Perry; Frank Lane Picture Agency/Corbis)

with a person of one's own paternal clan is prohibited (although permissible for the king) but allowed with a woman of the maternal clan. At one time, a preferred form of marriage was the sororate, in which a man married his wife's sister, who became the subsidiary wife (*inhlanti*). A woman retains her paternal clan name upon marriage, but her children acquire at birth their father's clan name. Paternal rights are acquired by the man's family through the transfer to the woman's family of bride-wealth (*lobola*)—valuables such as cattle (and, in modern times, possibly cash). Bride-wealth varies with the rank and education of the bride. Marital residence is virilocal; the bride goes to live with her husband and in-laws. In contemporary Swaziland, several forms of marriage are found: traditional marriages—"love" matches, arranged marriages, and marriage by capture, the latter being uncommon and not always involving the exchange of bride-wealth—as well as Christian marriages. More individuals are eloping or remaining single. The marriage ceremony, particularly for high-ranking couples, involves numerous and sometimes protracted ritualized exchanges between the families of the man and the woman, including singing, dancing, wailing, gift exchange, and feasting. Divorce, which is discouraged in association with traditional marriages, although permissible in situations of adultery, witchcraft, and sterility, proceeds according to a variety of arrangements.

DOMESTIC UNIT. Within a complex homestead are households, each household (*indlu*) generally consists of one nuclear family (a man, his wife and their children) whose members share agricultural tasks and eat from one kitchen. When there are several households on the homestead, each consists of a simple polygynous family, an extended agnatic family, or a complex family grouping. Sometimes a wife has an attached co-wife (*inhlanti*), who, along with her children, forms part of the same "house." A married son and his wife and dependents occasionally form another house within the wider "house" of his mother.

INHERITANCE. Upon the death of a homestead head (*umnumzana*), the family council of agnates (including full and half-brothers of the head, his own and brothers' senior sons, etc.) meet to discuss the disposal of his estate. The council primarily considers the household divisions prevailing within the homestead group during the life of the head as well as the land allocations made by him during his life. In monogamous families, the largest land allocation and administrative responsibilities usually go to the oldest son, whereas in large polygynous families, the largest land allocation and administrative responsibilities usually go to the oldest son of the senior wife who is named the general heir (*inkosana*) and acts as guardian over the special heirs of each wife's house's estate. When a woman dies, her property (e.g., her pots, mats, and implements) goes, by tradition, to the wife of her eldest son, who resides in the same homestead or village, unlike her married daughters. In contemporary Swaziland, traditional rules of inheritance are not applicable when a Christian marriage, which disallows polygyny and which is governed by Roman-Dutch law, is contracted.

SOCIALIZATION. Preadolescent girls play and help their mothers with minor domestic chores and child care, whereas preadolescent boys play and run errands around the homestead until

---

KINSHIP

Kin Groups and Descent

At the center of each Swazi homestead is the biological family, extended through classificatory kinship to maternal and paternal groups, the largest of which is the clan. The clan, as the farthest extension of kinship, contains a number of lineages in which direct descent can be genealogically traced over three to eight generations. The exogamous patrilineal clan (*sibongo*), with members usually residing in the same locality (*sifundza*), is the fundamental unit of Swazi social organization.

Kinship Terminology

One's father is called *ubabe*, whereas father's older brother is *ubabe lomkhulu*, and father's younger brother is *ubabe lomncane*. One's father's sister is *ubabe lomsikati* (female father). One's own mother, the other wives of his/her father, and his/her mother's sisters are called *umake*. One's father's brother's wife is also umake, and one's mother's sister's husband is also ubabe. One's mother's brother and his wife are called *umalume*. Grandfathers are called *ubabemkhulu*, and grandmothers *ugogo*, but the kinship terms can be specified by the addition of explanatory words (e.g., the paternal grandfather may be called *ubabemkhulu lotala babe* to distinguish him from the maternal grandfather). All grandchildren are *umtukulu*.

*Swazis believe that
most serious
illnesses do not
simply happen; they
are created and sent
by a person of ill
will.*

they are old enough to accompany their age mates to the fields with the herds. Fathers sometimes play a small role in child rearing, particularly if they are employed at distant locations within Swaziland or in South Africa. The Swazi have not circumcised males since King Mswati's reign in the mid-nineteenth century, but both boys and girls traditionally had their ears cut (*ukusika tindlebe*). By custom, a boy who has reached puberty is tended by a traditional healer, and a girl who has had her first menstruation is isolated in a hut for several days and instructed by her mother about observances and taboos. A boy learns about manhood and service to the king when he joins his age (warrior) regiment (*libutfo*).

Sociopolitical Organization

SOCIAL ORGANIZATION. During the seventeenth and eighteenth centuries, the dominant Dlamini clan created a hierarchy of control by amalgamating and ranking through conquest, treaty, and peaceful incorporation over seventy disparate, equal clans under a hereditary monarchy. The Swazi hierarchical ranking system came to consist of several units: the polygynous patriarchal family, the hierarchy of clans and lineages, the dual monarchy, the age grades, and the groups of specialists. The stability of the ruling elite's control was achieved through a balance of power among the king, his mother, princes, and commoners, as well as between the dual monarchy and the chiefs. Moreover, Swazi hierarchy harmoniously blended authoritarian political privileges of birth with egalitarian participation in age classes and councils. With the coming of Europeans in the late nineteenth century, the traditional hierarchy was forced to compete with a new, colonial administrative hierarchy that was based upon race and oriented toward the accumulation of wealth. After Swaziland achieved independence in 1968, a complex administrative system was fused together from parts of the dual hierarchy. Currently, traditional hierarchical arrangements are most threatened by the developing class system that found root in the economic and social changes of the colonial period.

POLITICAL ORGANIZATION. Swaziland's government is a monarchy. Its political organization is characterized by dualism: the parallel political structures consist of a "traditional" and a "modern" (postcolonial) hierarchy. At the apex of the traditional hierarchy is the Swazi monarch, who as a member of the Dlamini clan, holds supreme executive, legislative, and judicial power. He governs with the assistance of his traditional

advisers. At the middle level of the traditional hierarchy are chiefs who consult with their council of elders (*bandlancane*), and at the lowest level are homestead heads who consult with their *lusendvo* (lineage council). The modern structure, through which the monarch's power is also delegated, consists of modern, statutory bodies, such as a cabinet and a parliament that passes legislation (subject to approval by the king), which is administered in four regions, and less formal governmental structures, consisting of Swazi Courts and forty subregional districts in which the traditional chiefs are grouped.

SOCIAL CONTROL. The colonial powers altered some Swazi customary legal rules and procedures and imposed Roman-Dutch law as the general law. As a result, Swaziland developed a dual system of law and courts consisting of traditional councils, in which procedures are not controlled by legislative enactments or by codified legal rules, and modern courts, which have been formalized by national legislation. Traditional councils consist of the clan/lineage council (lusendvo), the chief's council (bandlancane), and the king's council. Modern courts consist of both Swazi and European-influenced courts at lower levels, including the Swazi Courts, two Courts of Appeal, the Higher Swazi Court of Appeal, and the king on the Swazi-influenced side, and the Subordinate Courts, the High Court, and the Court of Appeal on the European-influenced side. The Swazi Courts Act of 1950 provided for the formal composition of customary courts, the type of law they may apply (customary law), the procedure to be followed, and the limits of the courts' jurisdiction over persons. Swazis may exercise some discretion, depending upon individual circumstances, in choosing which legal forum to pursue a case.

CONFLICT. Swazis were engaged in tribal warfare until the imposition of European control in the late nineteenth century. Following the arrival of European concessionaires, severe conflicts developed between Swazis and Europeans regarding alienated land. Throughout history, conflicts arose between Swazi clan and lineage members (commonly co-wives and half-brothers) in association with daily interactions and were often attributed to suspected acts of witchcraft and sorcery. In modern-day Swaziland, interpersonal conflicts are influenced by many social and economic changes, including altered sex roles, increased job competition, labor migration, and the growth of an educated elite. Some Swazis believe that the legal prohibition of "witch finding" exacerbates conflicts by protecting evildoers who promote themselves at the workplace and in personal affairs through the use of magic. New of intensified pressures upon status relationships in stratified Swazi society are also producing conflicts.

Religion and Expressive Culture

RELIGIOUS BELIEFS. Adherents of traditional religion believe(d) in an aloof Supreme Being known as Mkhulumnqande, who fashioned the earth but who demands no sacrifices and is neither worshiped nor associated with the ancestral spirits. Swazi men play important roles in Swazi traditional religious life, offering sacrifices for the ancestral spirits, who are ranked, as are humans. Despite the important role of men in religious matters, female diviners also communicate with spirits, and the queen mother acts as custodian of rain medicines. Swazi ancestral spirits take many forms, sometimes possessing people and influencing their welfare, primarily their health.

Methodists established the first mission in Swaziland. Currently, many Christian sects exist in Swaziland, ranging from the more eclectic Catholics to the more rigid Afrikaner Calvinists. A majority of Swazis are registered as "Christian." Many converts belong to nationalistic Separatist "Zionist" churches, which practice a flexible dogma and great tolerance of custom. Christianity as practiced by Swazis has been influenced by existing traditions, including beliefs in ancestral spirits, and traditional religion has been influenced by Christianity.

RELIGIOUS PRACTITIONERS. Swazi practitioners of traditional religious beliefs articulate belief systems and link the spirit and human worlds. Their primary role, as healers, is to identify and correct the imbalances between these worlds, imbalances that lead to human misfortunes and illnesses. Swazi healers are of three types: herbalist (about 50 percent), diviner-medium (about 40 percent), and Christian faith healers (about 10 percent). Diviners are usually accorded more prestige than herbalists because ancestral spirits are believed to work through them directly. They are called to their profession through spirit possession and may become novices-in-training in a ritual school run by a master diviner. Although the healer categories overlap, in general, herbalists work primarily with natural materia medica (e.g., roots, bark, leaves), whereas diviner-mediums diagnose the "mystical" causes of illness, rely on spirit possession, and perform the femba ceremony, through which agents of illness are removed. Since the late colonial period (1960s), most healers (more than 80 percent) have been officially registered and are thus subject to taxation. Many belong to healers' organizations.

CEREMONIES. The annual ritual of kingship, the Incwala, a ceremony rich in Swazi symbolism and only understandable in terms of the social organization and major values of Swazi life, has been described in numerous writings by Hilda Kuper. According to her, the central figure is the king, who alone can authorize its performance. The Incwala reflects the growth of the king, and his subjects play parts determined by their status, primarily rank and sex. Before this ceremony (which is sometimes described as a first-fruits ceremony or a ritual of rebellion) can be performed during a three-week period each year, considerable organizational and preparatory activities must be undertaken. For example, water and sacred plants are collected at distant points to strengthen and purify the king. Thereafter, the oldest warrior regiment opens the Incwala. Sacred songs that are concerned with the important events of kingship (a king's marriage to his main ritual wife, the return of ancestral cattle from the royal grave, and the burial of kings) as well as dances are performed. Themes of fertility and potency predominate. Celebrants are adorned in striking clothing, including feathers of special birds and skins of wild animals. Kuper maintains that the Incwala symbolizes the unity of the state and attempts to reinforce it; therefore, it dramatizes power struggles between the king and the princes, or between the aristocrats and commoners, with the Swazi king ultimately triumphing. Kuper, Beidelman, and other scholars have discussed other Swazi royal rituals, including the reed dance and rainmaking rites, as well as ceremonies that involve Swazis as individuals or groups, including funerals, marriages, and initiations.

ARTS. Swazi implements and utensils, such as clay pots and baskets, are unornamented, serving mainly a utilitarian purpose. Wood carvers did not traditionally produce masks or sculptured figures, although in the late twentieth century schools have encouraged woodcraft for the tourist trade. Musical instruments are crafted to accompany popular singing and dancing activities; among those instruments used either in the past or present are the *luvene* (hunting horn), *impalampala* (kudu bull horn), *ligubu* (calabash attached to a wooden bow), and *livenge* (wind instrument made from a plant). Drums and European instruments have been introduced.

The annual ritual of kingship, the Incwala, is a ceremony rich in Swazi symbolism.

MEDICINE. Swazis resort to various medical practitioners, primarily biomedical or traditional practitioners. Traditional practitioners retain their high standing among the Swazi, as indicated by their relatively high ratio within the general population: currently, about one person in 110. About half of traditional healers are female, and the vast majority are diviner-mediums. Swazis believe that most serious diseases do not simply happen: they are created and sent by a person of ill will. Furthermore, Swazis differentiate between diseases or conditions regarded as "African" or "Swazi" and those that are foreign, emphasizing that the former, such as madness caused by sorcery, is a Swazi disease best treated by traditional medicine and practitioners, and that the latter, such as cholera, is a foreign disease best treated by Western orthodox medicine and biomedical practitioners. According to Green (1987), Swazi healers claim to be most effective in healing sexually transmitted diseases, sorcery and bewitchment types of ailments, children's illnesses, and migraines. By tradition, a recognized Swazi healer-diviner would commonly receive an initial gift of a goat, spear, or other articles, an intermediary gift of meat from a beast that was slaughtered during treatment, and a cow given in thanks for effecting a successful cure. The diviner's fee did not constitute a regular stipulated payment but did depend on her or his technique and the seriousness of the situation. Nowadays a healer may demand set fees for particular medicines and services.

DEATH AND AFTERLIFE. Swazi mortuary ritual varies with both the status of the deceased and his or her relationship with different categories of mourners. The more important the deceased, the more elaborate the rites given the corpse (particularly so for the king). The closer the relationship through blood or marriage of the deceased and a mourner, the greater the stereotyped performance demanded by the spirit from the mourner. A headman is traditionally buried at the entrance of the cattle enclosure, and his widows, children, siblings, and other relatives are expected to grieve dissimilarly and for different lengths of time. Widows grieve longer than do widowers. A widow may be expected to continue her husband's lineage through the levirate (*ngena*), in which she is taken over by a brother of her deceased husband. The spirit of the deceased may manifest itself in illness and in various omens; sometimes it materializes in the form of a snake. Ancestral spirits, acting as custodians of correct behavior and moral standards, inflict suffering on their descendants only as just punishment, not out of malice. The head of the family appeals to the ancestors and directs offerings to them at specific domestic events such as births, marriages, and deaths and during hut-building activities.

Bibliography

Beidelman, T. O. (1966). "Swazi Royal Ritual." *Africa* 36(4): 373–405.

Bowen, Paul N. (1993). *A Longing for Land: Tradition and Change in a Swazi Agricultural Community*. Aldershot: Avebury, Ashgate.

Gailey, Charles R. (1968). "Changes in the Social Stratification of the Swazi, 1936–1967." Ph.D. dissertation, University of South Africa.

Gort, Enid (1987). *Changing Traditional Medicine in Rural Swaziland: A World Systems Analysis*. Ann Arbor: University Microfilms International.

Green, E. C. (1987). "The Integration of Modern and Traditional Health Sectors in Swaziland." In *Anthropological Praxis*, edited by R. Wulff and S. Fiske, 87–97. Boulder, Colo.: Westview Press.

Holleman, J. F. (1964a). "The Land Use Survey." In *Experiment in Swaziland*, edited by J. F. Holleman, 52–57. Cape Town: Oxford University Press.

Hughes, A. J. B. (1962). "Some Swazi Views on Land Tenure." *Africa* 32(3): 253–278.

Hughes, A. J. B. (1972). *Land Tenure, Land Rights, and Land Communities on Swazi Nation Land: A Discussion of Some Inter-relationships between the Traditional Tenurial System and Problems of Agrarian Development*. Monographs of the Institute for Social Research, no. 7.

Kuby, David Joseph (1980). *Elitism and Holiness in Swazi Conversion*. Ann Arbor: University Microfilms International.

Kuper, Hilda (1947a). *An African Aristocracy: Rank among the Swazi*. London: Oxford University Press for the International African Institute.

Kuper, Hilda (1947b). *The Uniform of Color in Swaziland: A Study of White-Black Relationships in Swaziland*. Johannesburg: Witwatersrand University Press.

Kuper, Hilda (1963). *The Swazi: A South African Kingdom*. New York: Holt, Rinehart & Winston.

Kuper, Hilda (1978). *Sobhuza II: Ngwenyama and King of Swaziland*. London: Gerald Duckworth & Co.

Marwick, Brian Allan (1940). *The Swazi: An Ethnographic Account of the Swaziland Protectorate*. Cambridge: Cambridge University Press.

Ngubane, Harriet (1983). "The Swazi Homestead." In *The Swazi Rural Homestead*, edited by Fion de Vletter, 95–122. Mbabane: University of Swaziland, Social Science Research Unit.

Nhlapo, Ronald Thandabantu (1992). *Marriage and Divorce in Swazi Law and Custom.* Mbabane: Websters.

Rose, Laurel L. (1991). "Swaziland: Witchcraft and Deviance." In *Deviance: Anthropological Perspectives,* edited by Morris Freilich, Douglas Raybeck, and Joel Savishinsky. New York: Bergin & Garvey.

Rose, Laurel L. (1992). *The Politics of Harmony: Land Dispute Strategies in Swaziland.* Cambridge: Cambridge University Press.

Rosen-Prinz, Beth (1976). "Urbanization and Political Change: A Study of Urban Local Government in Swaziland." Ph.D. dissertation, University of California, Los Angeles.

Russell, Margo (1983). "Boundaries and Structures in the Swaziland Homestead." Research paper no. 6. University of Swaziland, Social Science Research Unit.

Sibisi, Harriet (1980). "Sociological Observations on Some Aspects of Rural Development in Swaziland." Traditional Securities and the Response to "Modern" Economic Opportunities, Paper no. 3. Ministry of Agriculture and Cooperatives. Mbabane.

—LAUREL L. ROSE

TEMNE

Ethonym: Timmannee

Orientation

LOCATION. The Temne occupy some 29,000 square kilometers of Sierra Leone's Northern Province, specifically in the districts of Bombali, Karene, Kambia, Port Loko, and Tonkolili. They are bounded on the west by the nearly absorbed Bullom; on the north by the Susu, Limba, and Loko; on the east by the Kuranko and Kono; and on the south by the Sherbro and Mende. The area occupied predominantly by Temne thus stretches roughly west from 11°20′ E, to the Atlantic and from 8°20′ to 9°20′ N. In elevation most of the Temne area is below 150 meters, excluding only isolated hills and the extreme eastern portion. Rainfall averages between 254 and 305 centimeters annually, with higher averages of 305 to 356 centimeters along the Atlantic beaches and the extreme eastern portion. Ninety to 95 percent of the annual rainfall is received during the period from May through November, the rainy season. Much of Sierra Leone was once covered by forest, but it has been almost completely cleared; the only primary forest remaining is in the remote reserves. Most of the area is farmed using the slash-and-burn technique, whether it is secondary forest, savanna, or mixed trees on grassland. Small stock are kept, but comparatively few cattle—and these only of the dwarf Ndama strain.

DEMOGRAPHY. Of Sierra Leone's 4.5 million people, about one-third are Temne. Population density is highest in the west, in the Kambia and Port Loko districts (57 to 96 persons per square kilometer), and lower in the east (20 to 58 persons per square kilometer). Both fertility and mortality estimates are high for Temne in particular and for Sierra Leone as a whole.

LINGUISTIC AFFILIATION. The Temne language is included in Greenberg's West Atlantic category and in Dalby's MEL category (with Bullom, Gola, and Kissi in Sierra Leone and others to the north), which is a subdivision of West Atlantic. Dalby found at least five Temne dialects: Western (with variations in the Sanda area), Yoni, Bonbali, Western Kunike, and Eastern or Deep Kunike. The major cleavage is between a grouping of the first four and the Eastern or Deep Kunike, which is nearly unintelligible to speakers of the other dialects. There is no lingua franca in use, although the pidgin English of the Freetown area, known as Krio, has come close to serving as such since the early twentieth century.

History and Cultural Relations

There is no archaeological record for the present-day Temne area that covers the precontact era. Oral traditions, however, are fairly consistent in citing a Temne migration from the northeast, from the Fouta Djallon plateau area in the Republic of Guinea. Subsequent movements of small groups criss-crossed the Temne area in all directions.

There were Temne speakers along the coast when the first Portuguese ships arrived, probably in the 1460s. Temne were indicated on subsequent Portuguese maps, and references to them and brief vocabularies appear in the texts. Trade began, albeit on a small scale, in the fifteenth century with the Portuguese and expanded in the late sixteenth century with the arrival of British traders, and later traders of other nations. Slaves, gold, ivory and local foodstuffs were exchanged for European trade goods—mostly cloth, firearms, and hardware.

Temne

The chief of each Temne chiefdom is said to "own" the land comprising it, having "bought it" and the people on it during his installation ceremonies.

As Temne traders were in contact with the permanent European factories in the river mouths, so did they establish and maintain relations with the settlement at Freetown after its founding in the late eighteenth century. This settlement, inspired by philanthropic abolitionists, was regarded ambivalently by Temne traders, who had long been involved in the profitable export slave trade. In the nineteenth century, following abolition, Freetown became the primate trade entrepôt, attracting trade caravans from Temne and beyond. Creoles from Freetown moved progressively upcounty to trade in the second half of the nineteenth century, and relations with the Temne and other were not always amicable. The British colonial government at Freetown followed a policy of "stipendiary bribery" punctuated by threats to use armed force in an attempt to prevent Temne and other chiefs from hindering trade from and with areas farther inland. When diplomacy failed, British expeditions invaded the Temne area of Yoni (1889) and then at Tambi (1891).

The Protectorate of Sierra Leone was proclaimed in 1896, and, subsequently, a colonial overadministration was instituted. The traditional Temne chiefdoms became units of local government, and a house tax was levied to support the colonial administration. Armed rebellion broke out in 1898, first in Mende country and later in the western Temne area, where a Temne chief, Bai Bureh, led successful campaigns and became a folk hero. The colonial era began again after 1898, with a more effective administration and increased penetration of the hinterland. Railway construction and, later, feeder roads were pushed in an effort to increase exports. Towns developed to meet the needs of government and increased trade, and expatriate firms and Lebanese and Creole traders expanded their activities throughout Temne and adjacent areas. Schools developed slowly under Christian missions and, later, under government aegis. For the Temne, culture change accelerated.

Portuguese Christian missionary efforts began before the Protestant Reformation but had no lasting effects on the Temne. The Protestant presence accompanied the founding of Freetown in the late eighteenth century; Church Missionary Society representatives were active up the Rokel River and elsewhere in Temne country through the nineteenth century. In the 1890s the Soudna Mission was the first American mission in the Temne area; American Wesleyans and the Evangelical United Brethren subsequently joined the field.

Muslim contacts probably go back several centuries, and fifteenth-century Portuguese were cognizant of Muslim peoples. Early traders, holy men, and warriors brought Islam into the Temne area from the north (Susu) and northeast (Fula, Mandinka, and so on). Through the nineteenth century, as the volume of trade grew, Muslim influences increased; in the late twentieth century a significant proportion of Temne claim to be Muslim converts.

Settlements

Traditionally, Temne resided in villages that varied in size and plan. During the nineteenth century, the village of a chief was larger and included people from several patriclans; often it was either palisaded or had a walled fortress/redoubt built nearby, where the population could reside in times of emergency. Other villages in a chiefdom were built by those given land-use rights by the chief; subsequently, other patrikin groups settled if they were given land-use rights by the initial grantee. If a household farmed land at some distance, people would build a hamlet (*tagbom*; Krio: *fakai*) to reduce travel. Paths connecting villages were often paralleled by secret paths used only by local people. During the colonial era, public paths were cleared and secret paths fell into disuse; village palisades and mud walls were left to deteriorate. When the motor road system developed, villages cut paths to the roads, and some villages, in whole or in part, relocated along them. The compact village plan gave way to a linear pattern along the roads, where larger garden areas separated houses.

The traditional Temne house was round, of varying diameter, with walls of mud plastered over a stick frame; the roof frame, of wooden poles connected by stringers, was conical and covered with bunches of grass thatching. Rectangular houses with a gabled roof became more commonplace during the colonial era. Houses became larger—and also fewer—after the "Hut Tax" was instituted. Chiefs and some subchiefs had rectangular, open-sided structures with thatch roofs, which they used for hearing court cases and for various ceremonies. Some associations, (e.g., Poro, Wunde) had small buildings for regalia. Adobe-brick and cement-block structures were introduced during the colonial era, along with iron-pan and tile roofs.

Economy

SUBSISTENCE AND COMMERCIAL ACTIVITIES. The Temne have long been predominantly farmers of upland/dry rice, intercropped with a variety of secondary crops. Some swamp/wet rice was grown from at least the nineteenth century in inland swamps and seasonal ponds and in cleared overflow areas along the lower Scarcies River, a development pushed by the colonial administration from the 1930s. Rice surplus to household needs was exchanged. Peanuts, cassava, and other crops were planted on the previous year's rice farm, and around and behind the house were gardens. Oil palms and fruit and other trees provided additional foodstuffs. Through most of the nineteenth century, wooden farming tools (hoes, digging sticks, and knives) continued to be used, although they were progressively being replaced by iron hoes, cutlasses, and knives made by local blacksmiths and, subsequently, imported. Most village households keep chickens; some also keep ducks, sheep and/or goats, dogs, and cats. A few maintain cattle, at least part of the time. Nearly all of the cattle are bred outside the Temne area. Hunting, formerly of some significance, has decreased as the human population has increased. Fishing in the interior rivers and permanent ponds is more important, and a wide variety of techniques is used; off the coast, the western Temne engage in fairly intensive fishing activity, dry the catch, and trade much of it inland.

INDUSTRIAL ARTS.   Other than a few long-distance traders, itinerant Poro and Ragbenle society officials, traditional diviners/healers and Mori men, and mercenary warriors, almost no Temne made a living by specializing in an economic activity other than farming. Some farmers, male and female, possessed one or more specialized skills and made some supplementary income from them. For men, the main specialized skills were those related to iron smelting and working, weaving, woodworking, leatherworking, fishing, hunting and trapping, and drumming. The twentieth century brought new forms of specialized knowledge (e.g., carpentry, stonemasonry, sewing, tailoring, literacy) and imported manufactured goods that precipitated the loss of some traditional craft skills.

TRADE.   Some western Temne were involved in export trade from the late fifteenth century on, whereas many eastern Temne were little involved before the late nineteenth century. Trade, the exchange of goods and services by bartering and/or selling, operated on basically three levels in the nineteenth century: first, horizontal exchanges between households in a village or a group of neighboring villages; second, interchiefdom/regional trade; and third, long-distance trade. The latter two were usually bulking and break-bulking marketing chains. Spatially, long-distance trade patterns were usually dendritic in form. Nineteenth-century trade depended upon canoes and porters head-loading goods over footpaths. The colonial administration brought changes to facilitate a growing volume of trade goods. The construction of a narrow-gauge railway (the SLGRR) brought the establishment of towns along the route, which served as bulking and break-bulking centers and locations for marketplaces. The building of feeder roads extended the areas served by the SLGRR; the completion of an integrated, nationwide road system subsequently led to the closing of the railway. Government programs to increase agricultural productivity were begun; the rice research station at Rokupr and government-run oil-palm plantations and oil mills were the most important of these efforts. The establishment of the Sierra Leone Produce Marketing Board (SLPMB) was of pivotal importance for exports and for income possibilities for the government. Gold, most of it produced further inland than the Temne are, had been traded from Sierra Leone since the fifteenth century but had its last peak in the 1930s; iron was first exported in 1933, from the mine at Marampa, by the Sierra Leone Development Company (SLDC/DELCO); and

SORCERER

A Temne man wears the costume of the sorcerer bird in Sierra Leone, Africa. (Charles & Josette Lenars/Corbis)

Each individual's second name indicates the paternal clan with which Temne are affiliated.

diamonds were exported after the formation of the Sierra Leone Selection Trust in 1935. Although the diamond areas were outside Temne country, large numbers of Temne migrated as wage laborers in this initially illegal business.

DIVISION OF LABOR. In farming, the traditional gender division of tasks, which never held for domestic slaves, has substantially broken down in the twentieth century, although men still do most of the clearing and hoeing, and women do most of the weeding. Basically, Temne have always had—and have today—a household mode of production: most farmwork is done by members of the household on its own farmland. At times of peak labor input, cooperative work groups are utilized when possible, for hoeing (Kabotho) harvesting (Ambira), and so on. Domestic slavery in Sierra Leone ended in 1926, but, before then, wealthier Temne used slave workers as well. A household's food and income production is augmented by selling or bartering surplus products locally, in the marketplaces of provincial towns, or to builders. Remittances from household members who have migrated also help. Little wage labor is used in agriculture.

LAND TENURE. The chief of each chiefdom is said to "own" the land comprising it, given that he "bought it" and the people on it during that part of his installation ceremonies usually called "Makane." The land/chiefdom was originally secured by the chiefly kin group by occupation of vacant land or by conquest. According to tradition, chiefs "gave" portions of land to immigrants to farm, and the receivers reciprocated with a *lambe*, a return gift, to the grantor-chief as seal on the agreement. The receivers, in turn, could reallocate portions of their land to others, receiving a lambe from them. Such transfers were regarded as permanent. After 1900, as the best farmland became shorter in supply, temporary land-use rights were negotiated with a lambe to seal the deal. Land-use rights became temporary and lambe, now of real economic and not merely symbolic value, had to be given annually; lambe thus increasingly resembled "rent," in our terms. Outright, permanent sale of farmland does not occur.

Kinship

Each individual's second name indicates the patriclan (*s. abuna*) with which she or he is affiliated. There are twenty-five to thirty such patriclans. The names are mostly of Mande origin and are also found among several neighboring ethnic groups. Most patriclans have alternative names, and each is usually geographically concentrated,

resulting from isolation during migration. In general, however, Temne patriclans are dispersed and are neither ranked nor exogamous. Each patriclan has several totems—usually of animals, birds, fish, or plants—and prohibitions on seeing, touching, eating, or using that vary considerably from one area to another. Penalties for violating a prohibition are mild, and many adults do not know what the prohibitions are until a diviner diagnoses the cause of a misfortune. Early sources and some contemporary Temne indicate that a common patriclan bond was formerly of significant social importance, but that is not the case today. Each patriclan consists of smaller, localized segments or patrilineages, each of which is comprised of a number of (usually extended) families, each of which in turn usually forms the core of a household. Temne kinship terminology is the type that Murdock calls "Eskimo," in which mother's brothers and sisters are not differentiated terminologically from father's brothers and sisters. In discourse, seniority is indicated more often than laterality. A person is usually closest to and receives most assistance from his or her own (father's) patrilineage, but often ties with the mother's patrilineage are nearly as important; Temne speak of their mother's patrilineage as their "second line of help and protection."

Marriage and Family

MARRIAGE. To be married is strongly desired by adult Temne, especially in the rural agrarian context, where subsistence is very difficult for a single adult, especially if that adult has children. In the traditional Temne marriage system, bride-wealth, comprised of consumer goods and/or money, passes from the groom's kin group to the bride's and/or to guardians and is subsequently distributed more widely. The exchange of bridewealth and dowry or counterpayment seals the transfer of rights and obligations from the bride's father/guardian; this transfer marks a true marriage from other forms, which may be equally permanent but not as acceptable to the kin groups concerned. The rights transferred are those with respect to domestic service, labor and the income from that labor, children, and sexual services. All subsequent major decisions are made by the husband, who may or may not consult with his wife. Marriage ceremonies differ between Muslim and non-Muslim Temne; both differ from Christian rites.

Although the incidence of polygynous marriages has declined since the 1950s, especially in urban areas, nearly four of every ten married men still had two or more wives in 1976, and six of every ten married women were part of a polygynous family. A polygynously married man's first wife becomes the head wife/manager. Co-wife tensions can lead to discord but usually do not.

Since the 1950s, divorce rates have increased in both rural and urban areas; urban rates are higher than rural rates at any given time. There are generally accepted grounds for a husband, and also for a wife, to secure a divorce. If a wife initiates proceedings, the bride-wealth must be returned; if a husband, it is usually forfeit. Previous divorce(s) are a barrier to remarriage only in rare instances.

DOMESTIC UNIT. The male- or female-headed household is the primary residential unit. There are various types of households, but most have a family (husband, wife or wives, and their children) as the core. Some are complex (two or more married men, either father and son or two brothers), often with other, more-distant kin or even strangers in residence. The household head resolves disputes by mediation and moot proceedings and represents the household in village affairs.

INHERITANCE. Land-use rights and most portable forms of wealth are inherited patrilineally; womens' jewelry, clothing, and rare other items pass from mother to daughter. Disputes occur between the deceased's brothers, between his sons, and between his brothers and his sons.

SOCIALIZATION. A child is socialized by a comparatively large number of people including parents, older siblings and elders in the household where he or she grows up. For a variety of reasons, fosterage is common; many children are raised outside the parental household. Significant socialization formerly took place during a girl's initiation into the Bundu society and a boy's initiation into Poro. Since about the 1940s, however, initiates into both societies have been younger and have spent little time receiving training in seclusion. Both societies helped prepare adolescents for their roles in adult life. Socialization continued intermittently throughout adult life as people learned from new experiences and patterned their behavior on role models who came to be widely respected and even revered.

Sociopolitical Organization

SOCIAL ORGANIZATION. Traditionally, chiefly kin groups enjoyed superior status, as did big-men, such as wealthier farmers and traders, successful subchiefs or village headmen, society officials, Muslim "holy men," prominent warriors, and the heads of large households. There were wealth differentials between households, based on size, access to farmland, numbers of domestic slaves, and people with specialized skills; the head's prestige was largely determined by his household's relative wealth. As the colonial era progressed and the urban population grew, a social-class system developed, based on wealth as traditionally defined, on money, on nontraditional occupations, and on literary in English. Elderly males dominated traditional society, and there was a marked "upward flow of wealth" to such men. Slaves, children, junior males, and most females were largely powerless.

POLITICAL ORGANIZATION. The Temne were traditionally organized into fifty-odd chiefdoms, each under a titled chief (ɔ *bai*), whom the British would later call a "paramount chief." Some of the larger chiefdoms were sectioned, but usually each large village or group of smaller villages had its own untitled subchief (ɔ *kapr*). Each village also had an elected headman. In the chief's village there usually resided four to six titled subchiefs, who served their chief as advisors and facilitators. One of these, usually titled *kapr mə sə m*, served as interim ruler after his chief's demise. A chief selected his subchiefs, and they were installed with him. Each subchief, titled or not, selected a sister's daughter as his helper (*mankapr*), and each chief selected one or more sister's daughters to help him. These "female subchiefs" had only ritual—not administrative—duties.

In the western and northern Temne chiefdoms, the chiefs and subchiefs are installed and buried with Muslim ceremonies and bear titles such as *alkali*, *alimany*, and *santigi*. Elsewhere, the Ramena, Ragbenle, or Poro societies perform these rites; there is considerable variation. In the "society chiefdoms," the chief is divine; he has a mystical connection with the chiefdom and the line of previous chiefs. These chiefs have prohibitions—some on their own behavior, and others on the behavior of people toward them.

Chiefly succession systems are either alternating between two patriclans or two lineages within one patriclan, or rotating among three or more lineages of one chiefly patriclan. The fixed rotational patterns were often abrogated. In the nineteenth century it was not unknown for a man who didn't want the job to be selected.

The intrachiefdom power game was primarily a struggle between the chief and those big-men who supported him and those big-men who opposed him. In some instances, the chief and his supporters ruled tyrannically; in others, the chief became a manipulated figurehead. Some chiefs were well liked and had a broad base of popular support; others were disliked, distrusted, and generally opposed.

Elderly males dominated traditional Temne society, with a marked "upward flow of wealth" to such men; slaves, children, junior males, and most females were largely powerless.

With the proclamation of the Protectorate in 1896, the chiefdoms became units of local government, and the chiefs, on stipend, became low-level administrative bureaucrats. Some small chiefdoms were amalgamated to make fewer, economically more viable units. Each British district commissioner worked with and through the paramount chiefs of the chiefdoms comprising his district. As chiefly administrative responsibilities widened, nonliterate chiefs had to hire literate assistants, chiefdom clerks. After the Native Administration (N.A.) system was implemented, the chiefs' courts were more closely regulated, and, in the larger chiefdoms, N.A. messengers/police were hired. In 1951 a district council was created in each district, comprised initially of the paramount chiefs and an equal number of elected members and chaired by the district commisioner. When political parties were first formed in the 1950s, they dealt with the chiefs and depended upon them as "ward healers" to turn out their voters for elections.

SOCIAL CONTROL. Among nineteenth-century Temne, the law did not have the preeminent place in the resolution of disagreements and conflicts in the way court systems do in twentieth-century democracies. There was no separate, largely independent judiciary; sociopolitical lead-

RELIGION AND EXPRESSIVE CULTURE

Religious Beliefs

The traditional Temne creator-High God is Kurumasaba, who, in judging the Temne, is thought to be kind, generous, just, and infallible. Kurumasaba is never approached directly, only through patrilineal ancestors as intermediaries. These ancestors also judge their descendants. Sacrifices are offered to them to obtain help for the living. Various nonancestral spirits, some regarded as good and helpful, others as mischievous and even vicious, also receive sacrifices and make agreements to help or—at least not to harm—the living. Temne also believe in witches (rashir), individuals, both male and female, who can make victims fall idle, have an accident, or even die. The identity of a witch may be determined by several divinatory techniques and, once identified, can be countered by magical medicines. Especially useful are "swearing medicines," which bring illness and death to an identified witch, thief, or other target. Borrowings from Islam and Christianity have altered many traditional beliefs during the twentieth century.

Religious Practitioners

Traditional diviners used various methods and made protective charms for individuals to protect farms from thieves and to protect a house or farm from witches. These specialists paid for the necessary knowledge from established practitioners during an apprenticeship. Morimen, itinerant Muslims, provided the same range of services with different methods. Officials of the major associations (Poro, Ragbenle, Bundu, and so on) used techniques particular to their group. Confidence in particular practitioners and particular techniques varies over time.

Ceremonies

Ceremonies are held for most life-stage transitions for both sexes. For women, circumcision, coming of age, initiation into the Bundu society, marriage, and giving birth are paramount. For men, circumcision, initiation into the Poro society, marriage, and fathering children are most important. The primary public ceremonies are those that mark the end of initiation of groups into Bundu and Poro, both for ordinary initiates and the rarer initiation of officials, and those that are part of the installation or burial of a chief. The principal Christian and Muslim holidays are also marked by ceremonies (e.g., Christmas and the end of Ramadan).

Arts

Graphic and plastic arts are essentially limited to the adornment of utilitarian objects and the masks and other items used by the various societies. In the past, the Ragbenle masks, especially, were many and varied.

The verbal arts are stressed, and Temne use riddles and proverbs in instruction, engage in storytelling that verges on dramatic performance, and employ vocal music and drumming on various occasions. Jewelry is becoming more popular.

Medicine

Disease and ill health are viewed in terms of obvious surface "symptoms" (e.g., fever, rash, swelling) and the "underlying causes" of those symptoms (e.g., witchcraft, being caught by a swearing medicine). Symptoms can be relieved by traditional and/or Western medicine, but these have no effect on the underlying cause(s), which require divination and the proper supernatural response.

Death and Afterlife

Relatives assemble after a death, and the corpse is washed, oiled, and dressed in good clothing. Burial usually occurs in or near the deceased's house. Mourning periods and the number and form of sacrifices vary with the status of the deceased. Divination of the cause of death was usual in the past. Witches require special burial procedures, and society officials and chiefs are also prepared and buried in special ways. One common thread in all is the attempt to appease the spirit of the deceased and prevent disturbance of the living in the future.

ers tried certain cases as a prerogative of their positions. Rather than applying abstract ideals of justice, equity, and good conscience, these leaders made decisions in light of the particular political and social settings in each specific instance. Disagreements and conflicts between individuals and groups were adjudicated at, first, the kin-group and residence-group level; second, at the association level (especially the Poro and Bundu societies); and third, at the chiefdom and subchiefdom level (in a chief's court). The first level used primarily moot proceedings, the second usually inquisitory techniques, and the third, a kind of adversarial contest. In the colonial court system, only courts of those chiefs recognized as paramounts served as local courts. Somewhat modified, the system continues today.

CONFLICT. Raiding and warfare among Temne and between Temne and people of other groups were long-standing. In the eighteenth and nineteenth centuries raids were carried out to steal foodstuffs and people, both disposed of in domestic and foreign trade. People on and near the coast tried to prevent inland traders from having direct contacts and thus preserve middleman profits for themselves. A period of "trade wars" occurred in the second half of the nineteenth century, and a body of professional warriors developed then. These were fulltime, itinerant mercenaries, known for their cruelty and fearlessness, who inspired terror and specialized in quick, surprise raids. For defense, Temne surrounded larger villages with walls of tree trunks and mud and built separate fortresses, to which people from several smaller villages could retire in times of emergency. The establishment of the colonial overgovernment put an end to Temne raiding and warfare.

Bibliography

Biji, Esu (1913). "Temne Land Tenure." *Journal of the African Society* 12:407–420.

Dalby, David (1962). "Language Distribution in Sierra Leone." *Sierra Leone Language Review* 1:62–67.

Dalby, David (1965). "The MEL Languages: A Reclassification of Southern `West Atlantic.'" *African Language Studies* 6:2–17.

Dorjahn, Vernon R. (1959). "The Organization and Functions of the *Ragbenle* Society of the Temne." *Africa* 29:156–170.

Dorjahn, Vernon R. (1960). "The Changing Political System of the Temne." *Africa* 30:110–139.

Dorjahn, Vernon R. (1962a). "African Traders in Central Sierra Leone." In *Markets in Africa*, edited by Paul Bohannan and George Dalton, 61–98. Evanston, Ill.: Northwestern University Press.

Dorjahn, Vernon R. (1962b). "Some Aspects of Temne Divination." *Sierra Leone Bulletin of Religion* 4:1–9.

Dorjahn, Vernon R. (1975). "Migration in Central Sierra Leone: The Temne Chiefdom of Kolifa Mayoso." *Africa* 45:28–47.

Dorjahn, Vernon R. (1977). "Temne Household Size and Composition: Rural Changes Over Time and Rural-Urban Differences." *Ethnology* 16:105–127.

Dorjahn, Vernon R. (1982). "The Initiation and Training of Temne *Poro* Members." In *African Religious Groups and Beliefs*, edited by Simon Ottenberg, 35–62. Sadar: Archana Publications.

Dorjahn, Vernon R. (1988). "Changes in Temne Fertility." *Ethnology* 37:376–390.

Dorjahn, Vernon R. (1990). "The Marital Game, Divorce, and Divorce Frequency among the Temne of Sierra Leone." *Anthropological Quarterly* 63: 169–182.

Fyfe, Christopher H. (1956). "European and Creole Influence in the Hinterland of Sierra Leone before 1896." *Sierra Leone Studies*, n.s. 6:113–123.

Fyfe, Christopher H. (1962). *A History of Sierra Leone*. London: Oxford University Press.

Gamble, David P. (1963). "The Rokel River and the Development of Inland Trade in Sierra Leone." *Odu*, n.s. 3:45–70.

Greenberg, Joseph H. (1963). *The Languages of Africa*. Indiana University Research Center in Anthropology, Folklore, and Linguistics, Publication no. 25. The Hague: Mouton.

Ijagbemi, E. Ade (1973). *Gbanka of Yoni*. Freetown: Sierra Leone University Press.

Laing, Alexander G. (1825). *Travels in the Timanee, Kooranko, and Sulima Countries of Western Africa*. London: John Murray.

Littlejohn, James (1960). "The Temne *Ansasa*." *Sierra Leone Studies* 13:32–35.

Loveridge, A. J. (1957). "The Present Position of the Temne Chiefs of Sierra Leone." *Journal of African Administration* 9:115–120.

McCulloch, M. (1950). *Peoples of Sierra Leone*. International African Institute. Ethnographic Survey of Africa, Western Africa, Part 2. London: International African Institute.

Sayers, E. F. (1927). "Notes on the Clan or Family Names Common in the Area Inhabited by Temne-Speaking Peoples." *Sierra Leone Studies* 10:14–108.

Sisay, O. (1939). "Funeral Ceremonies among the Temne." *Sierra Leone Studies* 21:94–100.

Skinner, David E. (1978). "Mande Settlement and the Development of Islamic Institutions in Sierra Leone." *International Journal of African Historical Studies* 11:32–62.

Thomas, Northcote W. (1916). *Anthropological Report on Sierra Leone*. Part 1. London: Harrison & Sons.

Wylie, Kenneth C. (1977). *The Political Kingdoms of the Temne: Temne Government in Sierra Leone, 1825–1910.* New York: Africana Publishing Co.

— VERNON R. DORJAHN

TIV

Ethnonyms: Munchi, Munshi, Tivi

Orientation

IDENTIFICATION. The Tiv (sing. Or-Tiv) are a group of about a million people who live on both sides of the Benue River, 220 kilometers from its confluence with the Niger, in Nigeria. "Tiv" is the name of the common ancestor from whom all are descended. In Hausa they are called "Munshi" or "Munchi."

LOCATION. The heartland of Tivland stretches from about 6°30′ to 8°00′ N and from 8°00′ E to 10°00′ E, although Tiv settlements are also found north and east of that area. In the southeast, Tivland borders the foothills of the Cameroons, from whence the Tiv say they originally came. Some hills, especially in southern Tivland, are as high as 1,200 meters. The undulating plains of tall grasses (as much as 3 meters high), dotted with savanna trees, lose elevation until they reach the Benue, at about 100 to 120 meters. The Tiv, who are an expanding people, are well along in their occuptaion of the similar plain that extends northward from the river toward the Jos Plateau.

DEMOGRAPHY. The earliest estimate of the Tiv population, in 1933, was 600,000. In 1950 the count was about 800,000. By 1990, the figure had climbed to more than a million. The density of population in Tivland in 1950 was about 166 per square kilometer, but that figure is misleading. In the southern area, where the Tiv reside adjacently with the small groups of peoples they know collectively as the Udam, the density rises to at least 1,430 per square kilometer.

LINGUISTIC AFFILIATION. There is a single Tiv language intelligible to all, although regional dialects allow one to distinguish the area from which a person comes. The language is classified as the only example of its subdivision (on the same level as Bantu languages) of the Niger-Congo Language Family.

History and Cultural Relations

The Tiv say they emerged into their present location from the southeast. "Coming down," as they put it, they met the Fulani, with whom they still recognize a joking relationship. The earliest recorded European contact was in 1852, when Tiv were found on the banks of the Benue. In 1879 their occupation of the riverbanks was about the same as in 1950. British occupying forces entered Tivland from the east in 1906, when they were called in to protect a Hausa and Jukun enclave that Tiv had attacked. The Tiv said in 1950 that they had defeated this British force, then later invited the British in. The southern area was penetrated from the south; what southern Tiv call "the eruption" of the British there occurred in 1911.

Dutch Reformed missionaries from South Africa entered Tivland in 1911; they were joined, and then succeeded, by U.S. Protestants in the 1940s and 1950s. Catholic missions arrived in the 1920s.

The early administration, coming as it did from the east where Tiv had come under the influence (but not the hegemony) of Jukun and Hausa kingdoms, established "District Heads," who were influential men to whom the British gave authority in which other Tiv did not concur. That system was extended beyond the area of Jukun influence to other Tiv, causing disturbances. Beginning in 1934, the administration created Tiv experts—men who learned the Tiv language and stayed for far longer periods of time than most colonial officers stayed with any given people. Their reports provided a firm basis for administrative reform.

Settlements

The Tiv say—and archaeological sites confirm—that before the British "eruption" they lived in stockaded villages of perhaps 500 to 600 people. After the Pax Britannica became effective, they "went to the farm," establishing smaller compounds spread more or less evenly over the land. In 1950 these compounds contained from 12 to 120 people. Eighty-three percent of the males in each compound were members of the patrilineage associated with the area; the other 17 percent were descendants of daughters of the lineage living temporarily with their maternal patrilineages.

Reception huts, each identified by the name of a mature male member of the compound, are arranged in a circle or an oval, their entrances facing in toward the center. Behind each reception hut is a sleeping hut for each of that man's wives. A recently married son may build his wife a sleeping hut behind his mother's hut before he has a reception hut of his own. Reception huts are circular, with conical thatched roofs supported on posts. They are open on the sides and as much as

♦ **joking relationship**
A form of customary kin relation in which certain categories of kin (e.g., in-laws) engage in sexual or other forms of joking.

9 meters in diameter. Sleeping huts have solid walls and are usually no more than 4.5 meters in diameter; each contains a cooking fireplace with a storage platform built above it. Granaries of several sorts are associated with sleeping huts.

Economy

SUBSISTENCE AND COMMERCIAL ACTIVITIES. The Tiv are subsistence farmers. Their main crops—like those of peoples to their south—are yams, cassava, and sweet potatoes; they have in common with the peoples to their north grain crops, particularly sorghum, millet, and maize. Peanuts, peppers, several types of cucurbit, tomatoes, okra, and cotton are grown. Mango trees abound, although the fruit is eaten only by children; oranges were introduced by British agricultural officers. The Tiv gather greens, mushrooms, seeds, leaves, and plants to be used in sauces. They keep goats, sheep, chickens, ducks, and guinea hens; sleeping sickness prevented the keeping of cattle or horses. Tiv men set great store by hunting, but in most areas all game has been hunted out.

INDUSTRIAL ARTS. Pottery is made by women; weaving of cotton cloth is done by young men; baskets are woven by men and boys. Chairs, both indigenous chairs and deck chairs, are made by mature men, as are beds, stools, mortars, and grinding stones. The Tiv share the general West African respect for blacksmiths; they made and hafted hoes, digging sticks, and spearheads as recently as the 1950s. All specialists is such crafts are farmers.

TRADE. Although markets were indigenous, their importance and number increased vastly with the Pax Britannica. Markets meet every five days except in areas associated with mission compounds, where they are held on Fridays or Saturdays. Every area in Tivland maintains a calendar built on five-day market cycles. Goods move from smaller markets to large central markets, from which they are exported, particular in the south.

DIVISION OF LABOR. Tiv gender ideas are expressed primarily in terms of the division of labor, although the ideas penetrate every aspect of their culture. Men do the hard labor of clearing land and making mounds for planting yams; they also run the legal, political, and religious systems. Women do the rest of the farm work: weeding (which is often done by parties of women), harvesting, and carrying the crops to the granaries and storehouses in the compound. Women cook and are in charge of child rearing but traditionally had help from older children, either their own or those they "borrowed" from kin.

LAND TENURE. Tiv land tenure, closely associated with residence, is an integral part of political and social organization.

Kinship

KIN GROUPS AND DESCENT. All Tiv reckon patrilineal descent from their earliest ancestor. They see themselves—all one million of them—as a single patrilineage. Tiv had two sons, the ancestors of the major division of the group. They divide themselves at every generation, thus forming an immense lineage system. The genealogies collected in the early 1950s were from fourteen to eighteen generations from Tiv, the original ancestor, to living elders. Obviously, to get that number of people in that number of generations, there has to be a "correction factor." The eight senior, hence largest, levels of lineage form the core of the political organization; they are probably resistant to change. The most recent four or five generations are relevant to exogamy and land tenure; their genealogy is generally known. Where the political and domestic systems overlap, there is likely to be a dispute about ancestral names.

The Tiv see their large-scale patrilineal genealogy as the basis of their land-tenure system. Every Tiv male has a right to a farm beside that of his full brother; their collective farms belong beside those of their half-brothers. The sons of their common father have farms beside the farms of their father's brothers' sons. So it continues, through the generations. All geographical locations that do not accord with the genealogy are given special explanations.

A lineage is called a *nongo* ("line"). The Tiv call their own patrilineal lineage, at all levels, their *ityo*. Their mother's patrilineal lineage is their *igba*. The more distant in the genealogy their ityo and their igba, the greater number of people each contains; this factor can be important in computing political influence.

KINSHIP TERMINOLOGY. The major distinctions made by kinship terms are between lineals and collaterals. *Ter* means father, both grandfathers, and all male ascendants. If Tiv want to distinguish the generations, they say "great ter" for the older generation and "little ter" for the junior one. *Ngo* means mother, both grandmothers, and all female ascendants. *Wan* means child and all of one's descendants. The word is also used for all male members of one's agnatic lineage (ityo) younger than oneself and all female members of

Tiv marriage is brittle. Divorce is inaugurated by women, never by men (although men may behave badly enough that they know their wives will leave them).

any age. "Child of my mother" (*wanngo*) is anyone with whom I share a female ascendant. "Child of my father" (*wanter*) is anyone with whom I share a male ascendant. People who share both a father and a mother at any level are called *wangban*—as is anyone with whom a kinship relationship can be traced by two paths. There is one word for all affines—it means "outside." The words for husband and wife are the words for male and female; a co-wife is a *wuhe*.

Marriage and Family

MARRIAGE. The Tiv, at first European contact, used an involved form of exchange marriage. The ideal was that two men exchanged full sisters. The children were then double cousins. Seldom, however, could that be arranged. Therefore, one of the lineages (usually three or four generations deep) was called a "ward-sharing group." Each woman in the group was assigned to one of the men of the group—her "guardian"—who then exchanged her for a wife. Nevertheless, the Tiv usually "followed their own hearts" in matters of marriage and eloped. That meant that the exchange system was a network of long-term debts between lineages. The debts sometimes took several generations to straighten out. The British administration outlawed exchange on the stated principle that they could never administer justice under so complex a system. They and the Dutch Reformed missionaries pressed for a form of bride-wealth marriage, which the Tiv saw in terms of their own system of *kem* marriage. "Kem" means "to accumulate." By 1950, bride-wealth was paid, a little at a time, more or less over the life of the marriage.

Tiv marriage is brittle. Divorce is inaugurated by women, never by men (although men may behave badly enough that they know their wives will leave them). Children of nursing age go with the mother, of course; a boy returns to his father's compound when he is about 8 years old, a girl in time to be married from her father's compound.

DOMESTIC UNIT. Every married woman has her own hut, at least after the birth of her first child. The husband's reception hut is surrounded by the huts of his wives. Each married woman has her own store of food; she cooks and takes food to her husband every day, and he shares it with all the children present. The children also eat with their mothers. Several such polygynous families, linked by the agnatic links of the husband/fathers, live in the same compound. Their compound is next to those of his agnatically close kinsmen.

INHERITANCE. Land is not, properly speaking, inherited. It is a right of lineage membership. Ritual positions are not inherited. A man's personal property is taken over by his sons and grandsons, a woman's personal property by her daughters-in-law.

Sociopolitical Organization

SOCIAL ORGANIZATION. Tiv social organization is based on the lineage system. Market courts are secondary. Age-sets were important in some ritual situations.

POLITICAL ORGANIZATION. Tiv political organization was traditionally based solely on the lineage principle. That principle was recognized by the colonial government, which nevertheless added a hierarchy of offices, one for each lineage level recognized by the government. Market organizations were often used for political purposes.

SOCIAL CONTROL. Social control was achieved through the lineage system.

CONFLICT. Traditionally, there were struggles and wars between lineages (which were limited by the lineage system) and conflicts between the Tiv and their neighbors (in which case all Tiv were "against" all the neighbors). The usual means of settling conflict within the lineage was by a moot of elders who met, heard the cases, and made decisions. They did not have—and by and large did not need—the right to enforce their decisions.

Religion and Expressive Culture

RELIGIOUS BELIEFS. The Tiv recognize an otiose god called Aondo (Sky) who created the universe, but they do not postulate that he has any current interest in them. They acknowledge ancestral spirits and, sometimes, make offerings to them—but do not pray to them or regard them as either good or evil. Evil is to be found in the hearts of human beings—it is called *tsav*. Tsav, set in motion by evil men using forces that the Tiv call *akombo*, caused misfortune. Each akombo is a disease or symptom, as well as being a set of special symbols. The ritual task is, by sacrifice and medicines, to keep the akombo repaired.

RELIGIOUS PRACTITIONERS. The Tiv utilize diviners. Most Tiv men also come to be masters of at least some akombo, a few of many akombo. A man who has mastered an akombo carries out rites when that akombo is implicated in a curing ceremony.

CEREMONIES. Akombo ceremonies are performed in order that individual people (and, very occasionally, communities) can recover from illness already manifest or else may prosper in general.

ARTS. The Tiv decorate almost everything. They produce some sculpture, little of it of the high quality that is known in much West African art.

MEDICINE. Herbal medicines are known to most Tiv elders. The masters of specific akombo specialize in the medicines associated with that akombo. Only after the akombo ceremony is carried out can the medicine be effective.

DEATH AND AFTERLIFE. The Tiv say that they do not know whether there is an afterlife and that a funeral ceremony is like calling down the path to a person who is departing—one cannot be sure how much of the message the person heard.

Bibliography

Bohannan, Laura, and Paul Bohannan (1953). *The Tiv of Central Nigeria*. London: International African Institute.

Bohannan, Paul (1954). *Tiv Land Tenure*. London: Her Majesty's Stationery Office.

Bohannan, Paul (1957). *Justice and Judgment among the Tiv*. London: Oxford University Press for International African Institute.

Bohannan, Paul, and Laura Bohannan (1968). *Tiv Economy*. Evanston, Ill.: Northwestern University Press.

Keil, Charles (1979). *Tiv Song*. Chicago: University of Chicago Press.

—PAUL BOHANNAN

TONGA

Ethonyms: Balumbila, Batoka, Batonga, Bawe, Toka

Orientation

IDENTIFICATION. The Tonga occupy much of Southern Province in Zambia (formerly Northern Rhodesia), spilling over on the east into Zimbabwe (once Southern Rhodesia or Rhodesia). Tonga in Kalomo and Livingstone districts are known as Toka; to the north are Plateau Tonga; Gwembe Tonga live in Gwembe District and in nearby Zimbabwe. The Tonga never formed a single political unit. Today they are an ethnic group united by common language and in opposition to other Zambian ethnic groups, with whom they compete.

LOCATION. Tonga country, Butonga, lies between 16° and 18° S and 26° and 29° E, bounded on the north by the Kafue and Sanyati rivers, in Zambia and Zimbabwe, respectively. Its southern boundary follows the Zambezi and Gwai rivers. It includes the southern Zambian plateau, which rises to more than 1,000 meters, the escarpment hills facing the Middle Zambezi Valley, the Zambezi plain lying some 600 meters below the plateau, and the escarpment hills within Zimbabwe. The Middle Zambezi Valley is knows as Gwembe Valley. Average annual rainfall varies from nearly 80 centimeters at the escarpment edges to 40 centimeters in northern Gwembe Valley. Drought years are frequent. Rains are expected by mid-November and taper off through March and April, when the cold dry season begins. June and July may bring light frost. In late August the hot dry season begins abruptly. Temperatures in northern Gwembe may reach 45° C. The Zambian Railway and a highway paralleling it cross the plateau south to north, giving access to markets for agricultural produce first created when copper mines were opened in Zaire and Zambia in the 1920s. This led to European farming settlement, the building of small townships dominated by Indian shopkeepers, and cash cropping by Plateau Tonga. Since the completion of Kriba Hydroelectric Dam in 1958, much of the Zambezi plain and the lower reaches of its tributary rivers have been flooded by Kariba Lake. Over 54,000 Gwembe Tonga were displaced from the river plain to new habitats in the hills above Kariba Lake or in more arid country below Kariba Dam. They also became more accessible.

DEMOGRAPHY. In 1980 Southern Province had an estimated population of 791,296, at an average density of 7.9 per square kilometer, some of whom were non-Tonga immigrants. Many Tonga have emigrated to Central Province since the 1940s in search of agricultural land or urban jobs. In 1969 Tonga speakers comprised slightly over 10 percent of the Zambian population; in the 1980s they probably numbered over 800,000. There were approximately 40,000 Tonga settled in Zimbabwe in the 1950s. Birthrates are high; the rate of population increase is around 2.8 percent per annum.

LINGUISTIC AFFILIATION. The Tonga speak dialects of ciTonga, a Central Bantu language, along with other languages of central and north-

*Tonga society was
once strongly
egalitarian despite
differences in wealth
and the existence of
slavery; slaves were
incorporated into
the descent group of
the owner.*

ern Zambia and adjacent regions in Zaire. It was committed to writing by missionaries in the early twentieth century and today has a minute literature, but Tonga writers prefer to write in English, the official language of Zambia. The Central Plateau dialect is becoming the standard used in schools and for broadcasting.

History and Cultural Relations

Tonga oral history is local history of no great time depth. Archaeological sites on the southern plateau associated with the arrival of the Tonga from the northwest date from the twelfth century A.D. Although they were shifting cultivators who had cattle, they also relied on game and fish. Their crafts included pottery and ironwork; a few scraps of copper remain. There is little evidence of differences in status or of long-distance trade. Sites in northern Gwembe from much the same period have richer assemblages and may not have been Tonga sites. Finds from Ingombe Ilede indicate trade contacts with the Indian Ocean. Some fourteenth- and fifteenth-century graves contained trade beads and worked gold, copper, and bronze. Ingombe Ilede may have been an outpost of one of the Shona kingdoms. Shona speakers still live nearby. In the eighteenth and nineteenth centuries northern Gwembe was visited by Portuguese and Chikunda from Mozambique, who first sought ivory and slaves, and then settled. In general, the nineteenth century was a time of turmoil: Toka country was occupied for a few years by Makololo from southern Africa; in the last half of the century, Lozi raiders from the Upper Zambezi and Ndebele raiders from Zimbabwe harassed all of Tonga country, and the Lozi established hegemony among the Toka. In the 1890s the British South Africa Company had little difficulty in annexing Tonga country and administering it as part of the newly created Northern Rhodesia that, in 1923, was handed over to the British Colonial Office. Early administrators organized the country into districts and created a skeletal administration based on appointed village headmen. These headmen were grouped into chieftaincies under appointed chiefs, who were responsible to a district administrator. Much land was taken for European settlement. After 1923, native reserves were set aside and allocated to the three divisions into which Tonga were by then grouped, under councils called the Plateau Tonga, the Toka-Leya, and the Gwembe Tonga native authorities. Missions arrived at the beginning of the twentieth century. They established schools and, on the plateau, provided instruction in plow agriculture. The Plateau Tonga developed a cash-crop economy by the 1930s; the Toka, with poorer soils, and the Gwembe Tonga, cut off by the escarpment, continued to work as labor migrants, usually in Zimbabwe, until after Zambian independence in 1964. Independence removed restrictions on African access to employment and the use of lands reserved for European development.

Settlements

Plateau villages in the late nineteenth century were small clusters of round pole-and-mud huts with associated granaries and cattle pens, frequently housing a single extended family or a small number of kinsmen with their dependents, including slaves. Shifting cultivation encouraged the relocation of villages; these occasions provided the opportunity for dissidents to hive off. In the west, the placement of homesteads along long ridges to avoid floods led to larger aggregates. On the Zambezi plain, where alluvial soils permitted long-term cultivation, villages were stable and could contain up to 400 or 500 people. Early colonial administrators amalgamated small villages and required each village to have a minimum of 10 able-bodied male taxpayers, who had to build near their appointed headman. When these rules were relaxed in the 1950s, plateau villages were already somewhat stabilized by the placement of schools, by the planting of fruit trees, and by the construction of more permanent housing; nevertheless, villages rarely contained more than 300 people. Gwembe villages began to fragment after their relocation to the hills in 1958. Many Tonga now live in cities or in the small towns of the province, which are commercial and service centers for rural people.

Economy

SUBSISTENCE AND COMMERCIAL ACTIVITIES. The Tonga were hoe cultivators whose staple crops were sorghums and millets until well into the twentieth century. Maize, cucurbits, groundnuts, ground peas, sweet potatoes, tobacco, and cannabis were additional crops. Livestock included cattle (in areas where tsetse flies were absent), goats, sheep, dogs, and chickens. Hunting, fishing, and gathering wild produce were important. Plow agriculture, using oxen, is now universal. Many Plateau Tonga have substantial farms of more than a hundred hectares, as well as large herds of cattle. Some own small tractors that they hire to neighbors. Maize has been the primary plateau crop since the 1930s, but farmers have also experimented with beans, cotton, and sunflowers. They began to keep pigs in the 1930s. The shift to plowing in much of Gwembe came in the late 1950s. Gwembe farmers raise maize, sorghums, bulrush millet, and, since the 1970s, cotton, now the main cash crop, which, like maize, is sold to governments depots. Income is also derived through the sale of cattle, goats, chickens, and out-of-season vegetables. Tobacco is no longer an important crop. Pigs were recently introduced. Hunting is now important only in some sections of Gwembe and on the western plateau. Commercial fisheries exist on the Kafue River and on Kariba Lake, where most fishers are immigrants. Rural diets continue to rely upon plants collected in the bush.

INDUSTRIAL ARTS. Crafts were part-time occupations despite being practiced by specialists, among them blacksmiths, woodworkers, potters, and basket makers. Work at a craft was validated by the belief that an ancestor required a given person to carry on the skill. Other specialists were diviners, herbalists, song makers, and hunters. Old crafts, in abeyance because of a preference for factory-made imports, were revived after the 1970s when the difficulty of transportation and the high cost of foreign goods made imports difficult to obtain. Production is now for the tourist trade as well as local use. New crafts include carpentry, brick making, auto repair, tailoring, and needlework.

TRADE. Marketplaces and shops are twentieth-century phenomena; earlier, trade took the form of direct exchange based on equivalences. Marketplaces are located in townships, where women are prominent as traders. Shops exist both in townships and villages and usually have male owners. In the townships, shop owners are frequently Indians.

DIVISION OF LABOR. Building houses, clearing fields, taking care of cattle, woodworking, blacksmithing, hunting, and most fishing are the responsibilities of men. They work in their own fields and usually do the plowing. They are hawkers and shop owners and work in a wide variety of paid jobs. Women are potters and basket makers. They do much of the agricultural work, gather wild produce, fish with baskets, process food, brew beer, care for small stock, do much transport, plaster huts, and provide most care of children. Increasingly, they plow. Some also work for wages, as shop assistants or house servants, but also in professional positions. Both men and women are ritual experts and both are politically active.

LAND TENURE. Alluvial fields along the Zambezi were lineage property but were allocated to individual men and women. In general, rights in a field belonged to the person who cleared it and were transferable. Where shifting cultivation prevailed, land was not inherited. A man was expected to clear fields for himself and for each wife. Wives controlled the produce from their own fields, which they stored in their own granaries. The crop from the husband's field was his. Uncleared land is now scarce, and fields are kept in permanent cultivation. Sale of land in former reserve areas in prohibited, and land is obtained through loan, gift, or inheritance. Grazing areas are held in common. Claims to fishing and hunting grounds are now unimportant, except on Kariba Lake, where the government licenses *kapenta* (*Limnothrissa miodon*) fishing outfits and assigns them sites along the lake. Land pressure has led to emigration. The emergence of a landless rural class is imminent. Already, smallholders hire themselves to farmers who need additional labor. Cultivators are also being dispossessed as government allocates large tracts to multinational agribusinesses in hopes of spurring production.

Marriage and Family

MARRIAGE. Polygyny is common and may be increasing as farmers marry additional wives to obtain labor for expanded operations. Christians divide on whether monogamy is necessary. Childhood betrothal was abandoned by Plateau Tonga in the 1920s and by Gwembe Tonga in the 1950s. Cross cousins of both types were preferred spouses among Plateau Tonga and in the Gwembe hills, whereas Plains Tonga preferred marriage into the descent groups of their grandfathers. Most marriages linked people of the same village or neighborhood. Marriage today is usually initiated by elopement or when the woman is pregnant. Both damages and marriage payments are required, even in Christian marriages, and their value is steadily inflating. Young couples are initially attached to a relative's homestead; formerly, they did not have the right to their own cooking fire or to make beer for ancestral offerings until several years after marriage. A second wife may be attached to the household of the first wife for the probationary period; thereafter each wife is independent. Couples who begin married life in urban areas usually establish an independent household immediately. Divorce was and is common. Households headed by a single woman are increasingly common, although even early in the twentieth century some women chose to have

♦ **shifting cultivation**
A form of horticulture in which plots of land are cleared and planted for a few years and then left to fallow for a number of years while other plots are used. Also called swidden, extensive, or slash-and-burn cultivation.

Tonga

Monogamous Tonga women share their dwellings with their husbands; polygynous men move from wife to wife. Only unmarried men have their own houses.

children by lovers rather then accept a husband's domination. Couples do not hold property in common; upon divorce, each spouse retains his or her assets. Once equitable, this practice now places women at a disadvantage because the property they helped earn can be claimed by the husband. They also lose when widowed because the husband's assets are taken by his kin. Therefore, women try to build up their own assets, which they safeguard by sending to their own kin. Widows are ideally inherited by someone in the husband's descent group, but this practice is increasingly controversial, especially among Christians.

DOMESTIC UNIT. Each established wife or senior single woman is expected to cook for herself, her children, and other dependents and to send food to her husband. Women, girls, and very young boys of the homestead eat either together, sharing food, or separately, each woman eating alone with her children. Men and boys of the homestead eat together, sharing the food contributed by all the women. Each woman has her own dwelling. Monogamous women share the dwelling with their husbands; polygynous men move from wife to wife. Only unmarried men have their own houses. Co-wives have separate fields and separate granaries.

INHERITANCE. As the inheritance council held when the funeral ends, claims are canvassed. The father of the deceased, or his heir, can claim a share in stock and, today, money, but the bulk of the estate goes to matrilineal kin who appoint someone to become the guardian of the new spirit. This person is the primary heir, but stock and other possessions are distributed among a large number of claimants. The heir becomes the ritual parent of any children of the deceased and

has claims upon their services and property, including marriage payments for daughters. In the past the preferred heir was of the same or alternate generation. Sons and daughters do not have the right to inherit, but in rural areas they may be given one or more head of cattle, and courts increasingly argue that those who work to increase the wealth of their father should benefit from that labor. Widows may be permitted to retain their fields but can be driven away if they refuse to be inherited.

SOCIALIZATION. Infants and children are raised by parents and siblings, and frequently by other kin. Grandparents often care for children after divorce. Today children are exchanged between urban and rural areas to work for relatives or to attend school. Training in the past was oriented toward ensuring that children acquired skills essential to rural life; now families urge children to succeed at school so they can get good jobs and provide support to parents and siblings.

Sociopolitical Organization

SOCIAL ORGANIZATION. Tonga society was once strongly egalitarian despite differences in wealth and the existence of slavery. Slaves were incorporated into the descent group of the owner, and they or their descendants might then be chosen as spirit guardians. The colonial administration abolished slavery. Today few know whose ancestors were or were not slaves. Lineages claiming priority of settlement within a neighborhood were said to hold *katongo* in that area, which amounted to a right to provide custodians for local shrines and sometimes a right to receive a portion of game killed. In southern Gwembe, status differences were more apparent. Today status reflects

KINSHIP

Tonga belong to the clans and matrilineal descent groups of their mothers, although children also identify with their fathers and the descent groups of the latter. Residence is usually virilocal. The residential group, or homestead, usually consists of a man, his wife or wives, and their children. Sons may settle initially with their father but are likely to join other kin or establish their own homestead on the death or divorce of their parents. Descent groups disperse, but matrilineal kin assemble for funerals as long as common descent is remembered, and those living in proximity consult frequently. They inherit from each other and, in the past, formed a mutual defense and vengeance group. Residential units based on multilateral linkages, however important at any one time, are ephemeral. Continuity is created by the ties of matrilineal descent. Some fourteen clans exist. People with the same clan name are assumed to be related. Clanship provides a means of legitimating associations, which over time can be converted into kinship. The system of clan joking links clans for the provision of essential services at funerals and in some other tense situations.

Alternate generations are merged. Within-generation speakers refer to each other as senior or junior. On the plateau and in the Gwembe hills, Iroquois cousin terms are used. Plain dwellers use Crow cousin terms.

success in exploiting new economic opportunities, including education. Teachers and others with technical training, along with shop owners and wealthier farmers, form an emerging rural elite.

POLITICAL ORGANIZATION. The Republic of Zambia is a single-party state organized into provinces and districts with their own administrations. Districts are divided into wards, and these into branches and sections. Elected councillors provide the effective grassroots political organization and have replaced the chieftaincy/village hierarchy that was the backbone of the colonial administration. Chiefs and village headmen still exist, but headmen have few functions, and chiefs act primarily as land allocators and ceremonial heads. Political initiative flows from the central government. As much as possible, the Tonga maintain their independence by avoiding contact with authority except when it might work to their advantage. Prior to the colonial era, and even much later, political leadership was usually provided by "big-men," whose exercise of power did not create a permanent office. Hereditary political office was the exception. Usually the political community was the neighborhood, of perhaps a thousand people, whose name derived from a geographical feature. Political authority was shared by senior men and women who assembled to settle disputes and organize communal rituals. Neighborhood residents were expected to attend each other's funerals. They had to observe ritual restrictions associated with "the work of the neighborhood," which centered on the agricultural cycle. They came together at local shrines to appeal for rain. Neighborhoods are still important under the party organization. Branch and section councillors summon people for communal labor: repairing roads, building additions to the local school, and other community work. Gwembe neighborhoods also have drum teams that perform at local funerals and represent the neighborhood on ceremonial occasions.

SOCIAL CONTROL. Homestead members were expected to settle their own differences. Neighborhood moots dealt with quarrels between descent groups or general issues. Direct action to enforce rights or redress injury was common, but cross-cutting ties of kinship damped down the possibility for prolonged feuding. Gossip and the fear of sorcery were important mechanisms of social control. The colonial administration instituted chief's courts and delegated to headmen the right to settle village disputes. Messengers attached to the chief's court provided an embryonic police force, reinforced by district messengers un-

der the authority of the district commissioner. In 1964 elected party officers took over adjudication at the neighborhood level, and local courts are no longer under the jurisdiction of chiefs. Courts are responsible to the Ministry of Justice, which appoints their members and regulates procedures. Courts are still expected to operate within customary law unless it clashes with national legislation. Police units, party vigilantes, and other representatives of the central government are constant reminders of the centralization of authority.

CONFLICT. In years of hunger, neighborhood once raided neighborhood to obtain food, and neighbor stole from neighbor. In the Zambezi plain, lineage members quarreled over the allocation of alluvial fields, and adjacent cultivators accused each other of moving boundary marks. When cattle or other stock invaded fields, damages were demanded. There were quarrels over adultery, the flight of wives, and failure to meet marriage payments. Deaths, illnesses, and other misfortune led to accusations of sorcery. Many of these grounds for conflict still exist, and theft of livestock has increased vastly, as has armed banditry along the roads. The availability of alcohol, since beer has become commercialized, has increased the amount of physical violence.

Religion and Expressive Culture

RELIGIOUS BELIEFS. Tonga have been exposed to Christian missions of many denominations since the beginning of the twentieth century. More recently, they have been evangelized by Pentecostal and Apostolic groups originating in the towns. Churches exist in many neighborhoods. Many people consider themselves Christians, but they may also adhere to some aspects of earlier Tonga belief and practice.

The Tonga recognized the existence of a creator god, Leza, now identified with the Christian God but formerly not responsive to human appeals. *Basangu* are spirits concerned with the fate of neighborhood communities and sometimes with larger regions. *Mizimo* are the spirits of the dead, concerned with the affairs of their own kin. Adult men and women become mizimo after death. Mizimo of parents are the most important, but offerings are also made to any former member of the descent group, to siblings of the father, and to grandparents. Invading spirits, *masabe*, attack individuals, as do ghosts, *zelo*. In the twentieth century new masabe are frequently recognized; recent ones have been Angels, Negroes, and the Regiment. Many Christians say these, along with

Many consider themselves Christians, but also adhere to some aspects of early Tonga belief and practice.

the spirits of the dead and the community spirits, are demons.

The world is basically good. Evil exists through the malice of human beings who try to obtain power to maximize their own interests by use of medicines. Suffering may also occur because of failure to deal correctly with spiritual forces.

RELIGIOUS PRACTITIONERS. Adult men and women serve as officiants at offerings to their ancestors. Spirit guardians are appointed to make such offerings on behalf of the children and grandchildren of the deceased. Shrine custodians perform rituals at neighborhood shrines and first-fruit rituals at their homes. Spirit mediums and diviners discover the will of spirits. Many women and some men are subject to possession by masabe and, when treatment is completed, may treat others similarly afflicted. Since the 1970s, some Tonga have become heads of evolving cults. Witch finders, today based in the towns, provide a means of controlling sorcerers. Evangelists, pastors, and other Christian leaders are other religious figures.

CEREMONIES. Christians attend church services, and Christmas and Easter are now days of feasting. Appeals for rain and community protection are held at local shrines, but such rites are now rare among Plateau Tonga. Mediums are consulted by neighborhood delegations to learn why communal spirits are angry and how to renegotiate relationships with them. The spirits may demand an offering of beer or the sacrifice of a chicken, goat, or cow, after which those attending share a communion meal. Men and women pour an offering of beer at the doorway of a dwelling or at a special spirit shrine in the doorway. The beer should be made from grain grown in the field of the supplicant. Possession by invading spirits is treated by holding the appropriate dance and drama, through which the demands of the spirit are enacted.

ARTS. Wood carving, pottery, basketry and metalwork are utilitarian, although fine pieces are made. Beadwork was formerly elaborate, but beads are now scarce and styles have changed. Music is important: Gwembe Tonga pride themselves on their drum teams; musical instruments include several types of drums, antelope-horn flutes, rattles, hand pianos, musical bows, and crude xylophones. Guitars, homemade banjos or ukeleles, and accordions cater to new musical interests. Men compose elaborate songs describing personal adventures or embodying insulting comments toward others. Women compose lullabies, dirges, and other songs. Beer drinking is enlivened by dramatic dancing.

MEDICINE. Illness is attributed to the anger of ancestral spirits, sorcery, the misuse of medicines acquired for success, the use of a tabooed substance, or spirit invasion. Minor illnesses are considered normal. Treatment may involve driving out an invading ghost through fumigation, sucking out the intrusive object, cupping (drawing blood by suction), pacifying an indignant ancestor, or taming an invading alien spirit through a dance, as well as the use of medicines. Herbalists supplement the widespread knowledge of home remedies. Medicines are infused and drunk, rubbed into cuts, or used in fumigation. People also use Western medicine, dispensed by hospitals, local health centers, private doctors, and herbalists.

DEATH AND AFTERLIFE. Infants and small children are given abbreviated funerals, and their spirits return to their mother's womb to be reborn. Adults receive elaborate funerals in preparation for their return as ancestral spirits at the end of the funeral, when the chosen guardian is pointed out to the spirit. If possible, beer is poured in its honor, to which it summons fellow spirits, thereby becoming acceptable to them. Burial is immediate, and usually close to the dwelling of the deceased; some villages have established cemeteries. Formerly, bodies were buried in the fetal position; today they are laid at full length and, if possible, in a coffin. Christians attend and pray over the grave even if the deceased was not a Christian.

Bibliography

Colson, Elizabeth (1958). *Marriage and the Family among the Plateau Tonga.* Manchester: Manchester University Press.

Colson, Elizabeth (1960). *Social Organization of the Gwembe Tonga.* Manchester: Manchester University Press.

Colson, Elizabeth, and Thayer Scudder (1988). *For Prayer and Profit: The Ritual, Economic, and Social Importance of Beer in Gwembe District, Zambia, 1950–1982.* Stanford, Calif.: Stanford University Press.

Holy, Ladislas (1986). *Strategies and Norms in a Changing Matrilineal Society: Descent, Succession, and Inheritance among the Toka of Zambia.* Cambridge: Cambridge University Press.

Reynolds, Barry (1968). *The Material Culture of the Peoples of the Gwembe Valley.* Manchester: Manchester University Press.

Scudder, Thayer (1962). *The Ecology of the Gwembe Tonga.* Manchester: Manchester University Press.

Vickery, Kenneth (1986). *Black and White in Southern Zambia: The Tonga Plateau Economy and British Imperialism, 1890–1939.* New York: Greenwood Press.
—ELIZABETH COLSON

TROPICAL-FOREST FORAGERS

Ethonyms: Aka: Babinga, Bayaka, Biaka, Mbenzele. Asua: Aka, Bambuti. Baka: Bangombe. Bofi: Babinga. Bongo: Akoa, Bazimba. Efe: Bambuti. Kasia Twa. Kola: Bagyeli. Mbuti: Basua, Kango. Medzan: Tikar. Ntomba Twa. Rwanda and Burundi Twa.

Orientation

IDENTIFICATION. The term "tropical-forest foragers," or "pygmies," refers to ethnolinguistically diverse peoples distributed across the forested regions of Central Africa who are particularly short in stature and who traditionally have lived by specializing in hunting and gathering wild forest resources, which they consume themselves or trade to neighboring farmers in exchange for cultivated foods. There are exceptions to these generalizations: some "pygmies" are tall, independent from farmers, and live in the savanna. There is so much diversity among these groups that it is impossible to describe a "pygmy" culture. That there is no generic term other than the European word "pygmy" (derived from the Greek *pyme*, meaning a unit of measure equivalent to the distance from the elbow to a knuckle) bears testimony to the absence of any pan-"pygmy" awareness or culture. Forest foragers in most areas are unaware of the existence of "pygmies" in other regions, and there is currently no sense of solidarity among the different populations. Unfortunately, no term has been developed to replace the derogatory term "pygmy."

Multinational logging, the establishment of conservation parks and reserves in the tropical forest, gold and diamond mining, central-government programs and policies to sedentarize "pygmies," and more farmers moving into the forest because of population increases outside the forest areas are just some of the forces dramatically influencing forest foragers today. Traditional forager-farmer relations are breaking down, and most forest foragers today also farm, although it may only amount to planting a field in the middle of the forest or near a village and then abandoning it to hunt and gather until it is close to harvesttime.

Few forest foragers receive health or education services from national governments.

LOCATION, LINGUISTIC AFFILIATION, AND DEMOGRAPHY. Forest foragers are distributed discontinuously across nine different African countries (Rwanda, Burundi, Uganda, Zaire, the Central African Republic, Cameroon, Equatorial Guinea, Gabon, and Congo). Most forest foragers live in the Congo Basin and are usually found within 5° N or S of the equator and between 10° and 30° E. There is enormous diversity in the natural environments occupied by forest foragers of the Congo Basin—from upland dense tropical rain forest to lowland swamps to mixed savanna-forest environments. Ethnolinguistic diversity is also evident. The estimated 30,000 to 35,000 Aka, who live in southeastern Central African Republic, speak a Bantu language, whereas the 3,000 or so Asua of the Ituri Forest of northeastern Zaire speak a Sudanic language. About 10,000 Efe also reside in the Ituri Forest and speak a related Sudanic language. The Baka of southwestern Cameroon, who number about 30,000 to 40,000 individuals, speak a language classified as Oubanguian, as do the roughly 3,000 Bofi of the forest-savanna areas of southeastern Central African Republic. Other Bantu-language speakers among forest foragers are the estimated 2,000 Bongo of western Gabon, the 3,500 Kola of the southeastern coast of Cameroon, the 7,500 Mbuti of the Ituri Forest of northeastern Zaire, the 250 Medzan of the forest-wet savanna region of central Cameroon, the 14,000 Ntomba Twa of the Lake Tumba area of central Zaire, an unknown number of Kasai Twa inhabiting the forest-wet savanna areas of southern Zaire, and 10,000 Rwanda and Burundi Twa living in the western portions of those two nations.

Settlements

The Aka, Asua, Baka, Efe, and Mbuti are relatively mobile; they live in temporary spherical huts. The Bongo, Kola, and Twa tend to be more sedentary; they build rectangular, mud-thatch village houses. Average camp sizes of the Aka, Baka, Efe, and Mbuti are relatively small, ranging from 17.8 inhabitants among the Efe to 37.4 among the Mbuti. Baka and Efe camps tend to be closer to villages than are Aka and Mbuti camps (4 to 8 kilometers versus 5 to 40 kilometers).

Economy

In the late twentieth century most forest foragers are specialized in extracting resources from the forest (e.g., game meat, honey, caterpillars) and

In the late twentieth century most tropical-forest foragers are specialized in extracting resources from the forest (e.g., game meat, honey, caterpillars) and thus are often nomadic.

thus are often nomadic. Some of these resources are traded to farmers for such foods as manioc, maize, and plantains and for iron implements, salt, tobacco, and clothes. In many areas of Central Africa, specific clans of forest foragers have traditional relations with specific clans of farmers, and these relationships are transmitted from one generation to the next, creating a complex web of economic and social exchange that leads to high levels of cooperation and support. Today most forest foragers live in association with farmers, but the nature and extent of the association varies substantially.

Among the Aka, Bofi, Bongo, and Kola, a type of cooperative net hunting is practiced, in which men, women, and children all participate; other groups utilize some combination of bows and arrows, spears, and snares.

Kinship, Descent, and Marriage

Aka, Baka, Efe, and Mbuti utilize Hawaiian kinship terminologies and reckon descent patrilineally. The Efe and Mbuti practice sister exchange, and the Aka and Baka require bride-service. Postmarital residence is very flexible in each of these four groups, but there is a tendency toward patrilocality in all of them. Polygyny rates vary from 3 percent among the Efe to 20 percent among the Baka. Efe also have one of the highest intermar-

riage rates with farmers: 13 percent of Efe women have married a neighboring farmer.

The Aka, Efe, and Mbuti have relatively high levels of multiple care giving; Aka and Mbuti fathers are especially active care givers. Infants are indulged: they are held virtually all the time and attended immediately when they fuss or cry, and they nurse on demand. Children grow up in multiage play groups, and autonomy is greatly encouraged. Male circumcision and adolescent tooth pointing are practiced by all three groups.

Sociopolitical Organization

Patriclans are common to all forager groups, but their function tends to be less pronounced by comparison to clan organization among farmers. Forest foragers are often members of the same patriclans as those of their traditional farming trading partners. Patrilineage ideology is not strong: mother's relatives are recognized, often with specific terms. Patriclans are "shallow," in that most foragers recall two or three generations in the clan, whereas farmers frequently can cite five or six generations.

Most forest foragers are known for their relatively egalitarian social systems. They maintain this egalitarianism through prestige avoidance, rough joking, and pervasive sharing.

ITURI FOREST

Anthropologist Nadine Peacock sits among a group of Tropical Forest Foragers outside a hut in a clearing in the Ituri Forest. Zaire. (Anthro/Photo)

Religion and Expressive Culture

RELIGIOUS BELIEFS. Origin stories often make reference to a god who created the world, the forest, and the first humans, after which she or he withdrew to the sky and paid no more attention to the affairs of the world. A certain powerful forest spirit influences the "living dead" (i.e., the souls of dead forest foragers).

RELIGIOUS PRACTITIONERS. All the forager groups have traditional healers, and several of them (e.g., the Aka, Baka, and Mbuti) recognize the supernatural abilities of great hunters, who can communicate with the supernatural world, make themselves invisible, and take the forms of various animals.

CEREMONIES. Each of the forager groups has several hunting rituals; their nature, occurrence, frequency, and intensity depend on hunting success, failure, and uncertainty. Among the Aka and Baka, the most important hunting rituals are linked to elephant hunting. Honey is symbolic of life substance, and gathering of the first honey is preceded by collective ceremonies, music, and dance.

The most important ceremonies follow death. The forest spirit participates in these, either through the sound of a trumpet (among the Efe and Mbuti) or dancing under a raffia mask (among the Aka and Baka).

MUSIC. Forest-forager music is distinct from that of farmers of Central Africa. It exhibits complex vocal polyphony; yodeling is incorporated, but there is a relative lack of musical instruments. Varying by region, the latter include whistles, two-stringed bows, and drums. Unison singing is seldom realized. Collective songs have superimposed parts. The lyrics are usually not important; they may consist of meaningless vowels and syllables.

Bibliography

Bahuchet, Serge (1993). *Dans la forêt d'Afrique Centrale: Les pygmées aka et baka.* Paris: Peeters-SELAF.

Bailey, Robert C., Serge Bahuchet, and Barry S. Hewlett (1992). "Development in the Central African Rainforest: Concern for Forest Peoples." In *Conservation of West and Central African Rainforests,* edited by K. Cleaver, M. Munasinghe, M. Dyson, N. Egli, A. Peuker, and F. Wencélius, 260–269. Washington, D.C.: World Bank.

Cavalli-Sforza, L. L., ed. (1986). *African Pygmies.* Orlando, Fla.: Academic Press.

Kent, Susan, ed. (Forthcoming 1996). *Cultural Diversity among Twentieth-Century African Foragers.* Cambridge: Cambridge University Press. [Chapters on tropical-forest foragers by B. Hewlett, M. Ichikawa, and D. Joiris.]

Turnbull, Colin (1965). *The Mbuti Pygmies: An Ethnographic Survey.* Anthropological Papers of the American Museum of Natural History. New York: Museum of Natural History.

—BARRY S. HEWLETT

TSWANA

Ethonyms: Batswana, Bechuana (colonial appellation)

Orientation

IDENTIFICATION. Batswana are divided into a number of subgroups or "tribes": Bahurutshe, Bakaa, Bakgatla, Bakwena, Bamalete, Bangwaketse, Bangwato, Barolong (Seleka and Tshidi), Batawana, Batlhaping, Batlharo, and Batlokwa. There are approximately twenty-five totems (sing. *seanô* or *serêtô*), which crosscut "tribal" boundaries.

LOCATION. The Batswana region extends from approximately the Okavango River in the northwest, running southeast to the upper reaches of the Limpopo and southwest to the Kuruman area, northeast of the Orange River. In South Africa the majority of Batswana are in the north, in the region that was British Bechuanaland in colonial times, subsequently included the disconnected blocks that constituted nominally independent Bophuthatswana under the apartheid regime, and is now in the Northwest District. Although many Batswana were forced into the overcrowded homeland of Bophuthatswana after 1960, many others remained throughout South Africa, particularly in the urban areas around Johannesburg, in what is now the province of Guateng. There are also Batswana in Namibia and Zimbabwe. Batswana live in all parts of Botswana but are concentrated most heavily in the eastern part of the country, along a strip running east and west of the rail line that extends from South Africa north into Zimbabwe. This is also the region of Botswana that receives the greatest amount of rainfall and has the best agricultural potential. West of this region is the Kalahari (Kgalagadi) Desert (which is not considered a true desert but has sandy soils and is characterized by a lack of permanent surface water), where Batswana reside along with other ethnic groups, predominantly Bakgalagadi and Basarwa (Bushmen). Agriculture is practiced in the Kalahari but

*Batswana are
known for their
large, nucleated
villages, which can
comprise as many as
30,000 people.*

is extremely risky. Livestock (particularly cattle) raising has become widespread in the Kalahari since the 1960s, when numerous boreholes were drilled, and this, along with drought and over-hunting, has led to the diminution of game (most of the large mammals of Africa are found in Botswana) in the region. The Central Kalahari and Chobe Game reserves are protected from livestock grazing and are still rich in game. The climate is semiarid subtropical; average daily maximum temperature reaches 33° C in summer and 22° C in winter. Average rainfall ranges from 65 centimeters in the northeast to 25 centimeters in the southwest.

DEMOGRAPHY. The population of Botswana is approximately 1.4 million. Ethnic affiliation has not been recorded in the census since 1946; whether ethnic Batswana ("Batswana" can also refer to all citizens of Botswana, regardless of ethnic affiliation) make up the majority in the country remains a contentious issue. Most Batswana live in rural areas, but Botswana has the highest urbanization rate in Africa. There are over 2 million Batswana in South Africa. In Botswana, the population growth rate is 3.5 percent.

LINGUISTIC AFFILIATION. Setswana is a Bantu language of the western Sotho group. (The prefix "Se*f*" refers to "language/culture of," "Bo*f*" refers to "land of," and "Ba*f*" refers to "people," whereas "Mo*f*" is the singular.) There are a number of dialects within Setswana, all of which are mutually intelligible. Sekgalagadi (which is spoken by the Bakgalagadi) and the languages of many other neighboring groups are sufficiently similar to Setswana to be classified by some scholars as dialects, although this is debated by others. Setswana and English are official languages of Botswana and Setswana is one of eleven official languages in South Africa. Many Batswana also speak English, Afrikaans, or other Southern African Bantu languages; many adult men speak Fanagalo, the language of the mines.

History and Cultural Relations

New archaeological evidence continues to push the arrival of Bantu speakers into the Batswana area further back in time; it is now assumed that they arrived in southeastern Botswana around A.D. 600 or 700, displacing, absorbing, and/or living among Khoisan foragers and pastoralists. Ancestors of Sotho speakers are believed to have been in the area by about A.D. 1200, and by 1500 the major Batswana tribes/chiefdoms/nations began to form, through a process of fission and amalgamation of agnatic groupings, as they spread northward and westward from the Transvaal, in search of better watered pastureland.

A period of warfare, political disruption, and migration commonly termed the *difiqane* (Zulu: *mfecane*) characterized the first quarter of the nineteenth century. These wars have conventionally been attributed to the rise of the Zulu state and to the innovative forms of political and military organization of its leader, Shaka. The causes of the difiqane have become a subject of late twentieth-century debate; it is now argued that European trade and slaving initially precipitated the period of warfare. The difiqane engendered a period of chaos, during which Batswana polities experienced varying degrees of suffering, impoverishment, political disintegration, death, and forced movement. At the same time, however, some groups, particularly the western Batswana chiefdoms, eventually prospered and strengthened to the extent that they incorporated refugees and livestock. Batswana polities are noted for their capacity to absorb foreign peoples, to turn strangers into tribespeople, and to do so without compromising the integrity of their own institutions. Socioeconomic mechanisms such as *mafisa* (which provided for the lending of cattle) and the ward system of tribal administration facilitated the integration of foreigners. Not all peoples were welcomed into the Tswana fold; some remained foreigners, and some became subjects. The latter category includes peoples of the desert (Bakgalagadi and Bushmen) who are accorded a servile status termed "Batlhanka" or "Bolata."

European traders and missionaries (of the British nonconformist sects) began to arrive in the Batswana region in the first two decades of the nineteenth century. Trade (ivory, furs, and feathers being the most valued items) escalated after this period, and control over this trade dramatically empowered some Batswana chiefs, who were able to consolidate their control over extensive areas. By the mid-nineteenth century, Afrikaners, newly settled in the Transvaal, posed a threat to Batswana; Batswana chiefdoms acquired firearms to protect themselves, and many Batsana moved westward, into the area that is now Botswana. Christian missions were established throughout the region in the nineteenth century; today most Batswana profess to be Christian.

The discovery of diamonds and gold in the 1860s and 1870s in southern Africa led to the industrialization of South Africa and the introduction of the migrant-labor system, which continues to draw thousands of Batswana men to the mines (although recruitment from Botswana has been restricted since 1979). In 1885 the Bechuanaland Protectorate was established in the north of the region, and, in the south, British Bechuanaland was established as a Crown colony; ten years later it was annexed to the Cape. In 1966 Botswana achieved independence. In 1910 British Bechuanaland was incorporated into the Union of South Africa; in 1977, under the apartheid regime, the Tswana ethnic "homeland" of Bophutatswana was granted nominal independence by South Africa, but no other nation recognized it; in 1994, in conjunction with the first all-race elections in South Africa and the dismantling of apartheid, Bophutatswana was reincorporated into South Africa.

Settlements

Batswana are noted for their large, nucleated villages, which can comprise as many as 30,000 people. Large compact villages or towns are associated with the aridity of the areas and the necessity of settling near reliable water sources and under chiefly power. In the past, chiefs were able to control the movements of people, the allocation of land, and the timing of agricultural activity through their centrality in rituals performed to ensure agricultural fertility. Town or village residence is the norm, but Batswana disperse their economic activities and typically have temporary residences at their agricultural fields (as far as 40 kilometers from the village) and near their grazing lands. Grazing lands are less demarcated than agricultural lands and can be hundreds of kilometers from the village. This settlement pattern can be envisioned as a series of concentric circles, with the main village residence in the center, agricultural fields surrounding the inner circle, grazing lands comprising the outer circle, and the bush beyond. There is a social dimension to this model, in that (with the exception of the temporary residences) those of highest rank tend to reside in the center, whereas those of lowest rank, especially members of servile groups such as Bushmen, reside on the periphery. Most Batswana continue to maintain a rural residence, even as urbanization increases. With the decline of chiefly power, more Batswana have established their primary residence at smaller centers, often near their agricultural fields.

Villages are organized into wards, each with its own headman, who is ideally closely related to the chief—or appointed by him—and is responsible to him. Wards are based on the patrilineal model, but many have absorbed nonagnates or nonrelatives. Within wards, compounds, which tend to be close to one another, are surrounded by perimeter bush or stone fences. Internal low mud walls separate living from cooking and other spaces. Each married couple has a house (traditionally, a round mud hut with a thatch roof, although rectangular concrete block houses with tin roofs are becoming popular) in which they and some younger children may sleep; there are additional huts for sleeping and storage. Raised granaries are less common now than in the past. Kitchen areas are usually inside the perimeter fence and enclosed by a bushfence firebreak.

Economy

SUBSISTENCE AND COMMERCIAL ACTIVITIES. Batswana have been called a peasant-proletariat to reflect the fact that they have been migrating to the mines, and to a lesser extent, to the White commercial farms of South Africa, for over a century and that wages constitute their single largest source of revenue. Mine contacts were temporary, often enabling the migrant to return home for the plowing season; until the late twentieth century, migrants were prevented by South African law from establishing permanent residence at their place of employment. New forms of employment have been emerging, especially in Botswana, where diamond mining has led to dramatic economic growth. State-sponsored welfare is important in both countries.

Local economic activities center on agro-pastoralism. Batswana rely on ox-drawn iron plows (but tractors are becoming increasingly common); the principal crop is sorghum. They also grow maize, beans, sweet-cane, and some millet. Some farmers engage in commercial agriculture. Batswana husband goats, sheep, and most importantly, cattle. Cattle are valuable for local exchange, for ritual purposes, for their milk, and less so for their meat; their sale provides an important source of revenue for rural peoples. Most households also keep chickens, and, in the east, some keep pigs. Hunting is far less important than it was in the past, when game was plentiful.

INDUSTRIAL ARTS. Batswana have long been tied to the South African industrial economy and have purchased items that formerly were made locally; these include most metal goods. In the past, men worked in metal, bone, and wood; women made pots, and both sexes did basketwork. These skills were often passed from parents to children. Some men still specialize in skin preparation and sewing, usually for trade, and men still make some wooden items, such as yokes for livestock. In northern Botswana, women make

♦ **peasant**
Small-scale agriculturalists producing only subsistence crops, perhaps in combination with some fishing, animal husbandry, or hunting. They live in villages in a larger state, but participate little in the state's commerce or cultural activities. Today, many peasants rely on mechanized farming and are involved in the national economy, so they are called post-peasants *by anthropologists.*

Tswana

Many Batswana own vast amounts of property and have highly remunerative employment, but far greater numbers are welfare recipients.

baskets, many of which are exported. Women build "traditional" Tswana huts, whereas men specialize in European-style thatch and "modern"-style houses. The latter are highly specialized skills. As in much of Africa, children fashion toys out of fence wire, tin cans, old tires, and almost anything they can acquire.

TRADE. Archaeological evidence points to the great antiquity of local and long-distance trade. Marketplaces were not common in the region; most trade occurred among neighbors or with itinerant peddlers; in the early nineteenth century Griqua traders from the south traveled into the region; they were followed by Europeans. Trade increased with the arrival of missionaries during the nineteenth century, many of whom encouraged such commerce as a means of bringing "civilization" to the area. Europeans and, later, Asians established shops over the course of the colonial period. Virtually all villages now have trading stores, and many individuals—especially women—are "hawkers" who engage in trade from their compounds. Botswana is part of the South African Customs Union, and virtually every commodity is available in both countries.

DIVISION OF LABOR. In pre-European times, men tended livestock, hunted, prepared fields, engaged in warfare, and participated in the formal public political arena. Women tended fields, gathered wild foods, and were responsible for the domestic arena, including looking after domestic fowl. With the introduction of the ox-drawn plow in the nineteenth century, men assumed the task of plowing, but women continued to perform most other agricultural work. The division of labor became less strict as more men migrated for wage labor and women increasingly engaged in livestock activities, especially plowing and milking. Boys worked extensively with livestock and spent long periods away from home at cattle posts. All children helped in the fields, and girls helped their mothers, especially with looking after younger siblings. Although wage labor has been available for men for over a century, until about the 1970s, women had little opportunity for wage employment; those jobs available were largely as domestics and on White-owned farms. In the late twentieth century greater opportunity exists for both men and women, but men still have an advantage over women.

LAND TENURE. Traditionally, the right to use (but not to sell) agricultural land was inherited patrilineally by sons; women received access to agricultural lands as wives. Closely related agnatic kin tended to have fields in the same general area, which facilitated cooperation. Pastureland was in

theory communal, but often areas were associated with particular groups. Since the advent of boreholes, the land surrounding them has become increasingly associated with (but not formally owned by) the borehole owners.

In Botswana, the majority of people live in the districts (former tribal reserves), where most land is held in common. Some areas, as provided under the Tribal Grazing Land Policy established in 1975, have been demarcated as commercial ranch land, and wealthy Batswana who are willing to invest in infrastructure (fences, boreholes, etc.) may take out long-term leases. Other land has been reserved as wildlife-management areas. Permission to use land in the communal areas is obtained from land boards. The land cannot be sold. Unlike in Botswana, where very little land was given over to Europeans, in South Africa Blacks were given only 13 percent of the land after 1913.

Kinship

KIN GROUPS AND DESCENT. Agnation is emphasized in Batswana kinship: along with primogeniture, it traditionally had the greatest influence on inheritance of property and succession to office. Individuals were identified with and came under the jural authority of their agnatic group (*kgotla*, or the diminutive *kgotlana*); however, the formation of discrete agnatic units was and continues to be inhibited by the marriage system, which permits cousin marriages of all kinds. Patrilineal parallel-cousin marriages of near kin, although practiced mainly by the elite but permitted to all, serve to complicate the principle of unilineality and create ambiguous and overlapping links. Thus, there is a cognatic element to the system, which places emphasis upon kindreds (sing. *losika*) and gives greater license to individuals to "construct" their social networks than is found in many patrilineal societies.

KINSHIP TERMINOLOGY. With the exceptions of the term for cross cousin (*ntsala*) and the term for sibling of the opposite sex (*kgaitsadi*), virtually all Batswana kinship terms imply relative seniority and thus, relative authority. It is a classificatory system that distinguishes cross from parallel cousins (parallel cousin terms are the same as sibling terms), siblings of the same sex (these are distinguished by seniority) from those of the opposite sex, father's sister (*rrakgadi*) from mother's sister (*mmangwane* ["small mother"]), and mother's brother (*malome*) from father's brother (*rrangwane* ["small father"]). Parents' older siblings are referred to by grandparental terms (*rremogolo* ["great-father"], *mmemogolo* [great-mother]). There is considerable variation in the use of affinal terms.

Sociopolitical Organization

SOCIAL ORGANIZATION. The Batswana developed powerful chiefdoms in the nineteenth century; members were internally ranked into royals (*dikgosana*), commoners (*badintlha*), immigrants absorbed into the tribe (*bafaladi*), and non-Batswana clients (*bolata*). High rank brought both privilege and responsibility; for instance the chief (*kgosi*) could command stray cattle (*matimela*), labor, and first fruits from the harvest, but was also expected to display largesse to his followers. The system of rank, privilege, and responsibility has been much eroded but not eradicated. Now rank, patron-client relations, and class coexist as forms of stratification. Many Batswana own vast amounts of property and have highly remunerative employment, but far greater numbers are welfare recipients.

POLITICAL ORGANIZATION. In the precolonial period the most powerful Batswana chiefs presided over large tributary states. Subchiefs and headmen who presided over wards and villages outside the capital were responsible to the chief. Chiefly power and succession were open to challenge, resulting at times in dynastic contests and tribal secession. Chiefs controlled the timing of initiation ceremonies and, thus, the creation of new regiments; these regiments provided chiefs with a labor and military force. In Botswana, the House of Chiefs was established at independence; the House advises but cannot make law. Chiefs and headmen have been incorporated into the civil service and preside over customary courts in Botswana. Traditional leaders have also played a role in South Africa, and the postapartheid government elected in 1994 is developing a policy toward them.

SOCIAL CONTROL. Socialization, positive and negative social sanction, and fear of illness or other misfortune are powerful means of social control; however, when behavior violates custom or law, means of redress exist. Although not systematically codified, customary law (*maloa*) and legal protocol are highly developed among the Batswana. Less serious crimes can be dealt with by the families of the parties involved. If a problem cannot be resolved at that level, it is taken to the kgotla. "Kgotla" refers both to a group of people and the place where they meet. Each ward has a kgotla, over which a headman presides. Villages have a central kgotla, and the central kgotla of the tribal capital is presided over by the chief. All men, and, in the late twentieth century, women,

may speak at the kgotla and advise the chief. If a case cannot be resolved at a minor kgotla, it moves up the system and may eventually be tried at the chief's kgotla, which, in Botswana, is sanctioned by government. Certain offenses, such as murder, are addressed by the civil court system.

CONFLICT. In precolonial times Batswana groups fought among themselves and with others over territory, trade routes, and control over subject peoples. They raided for livestock and other property. British control and the demarcation of tribal boundaries in the late nineteenth century significantly diminished intergroup conflict. In the early twentieth century chiefs began to employ lawyers in their disputes with other chiefs. Ethnic tension is minimal but not absent and appears to be on the rise in the 1990s. Many Batswana were involved and some lost their lives in the antiapartheid struggle. Violence accompanied the dismantling of Bophutatswana in 1994, as some leaders were reluctant to relinquish their power.

Religion and Expressive Culture

RELIGIOUS BELIEFS. Although Batswana received Christian missionaries in the early nineteenth century and most belong to a church today, precolonial beliefs retain strength among many Batswana. Missionaries brought literacy, schools, and Western values, all of which facilitated the transition to migrant wage labor. In precolonial times Batswana believed in a Supreme Being, Modimo, a creator and director, but nonetheless distant and remote. More immediate and having a greater influence in daily affairs were the ancestors, Badimo. Ancestor worship was reflected in the respect given to the elders and their capacity to influence the young; after death, their spirits left their bodies to join others. Badimo were venerated and invoked; appeals were addressed to them, and they were placated with sacrifices, prayers, and appropriate behavior. Badimo intervened actively in daily life and they could withdraw their support, rendering their descendants vulnerable to disease and misfortune. Most Batswana today belong to African Independent churches that incorporate Christian and non-Christian practices, beliefs, and symbols.

RELIGIOUS PRACTITIONERS. Most people have some knowledge of medicinal plants; *dingaka* (doctors; sing. *ngaka*), however, are specialists in healing and magic. "Dingaka" is a collective term referring to many different types of specialties, which among others include rainmaking, compound protection, avenging sorcery, and women's reproductive health. Formerly, dingaka presided over rituals and aided the chief in protecting and controlling the village and tribe. Dingaka apprentice with others, often paying them a cow. Many divine using a set of bones: the interpretation of how they fall determines the source of a patient's problem. *Baloi* (sorcerers; sing. *moloi*)

manipulate substances for malevolent purposes. Baloi are believed to work by day or by night; in the latter case, they meet together, often transform into animals, and may cause their victims to do the same. Much illness and misfortune is attributed to their powers. Practitioners of the

MARRIAGE AND FAMILY

Marriage

Traditionally, Batswana marriage was a process marked by a number of rituals and exchanges between the two families. No single ritual or exchange was definitive in confirming the existence of a marriage. Bridewealth (*bogadi*—typically eight head of cattle) exchange was the most elaborate materially and ritually but it often occurred several years after the couple had been cohabitating, after children had been born, and occasionally after the death of the wife. Church and civil marriage have begun to replace traditional marriage, which has removed some of the ambiguity in marital status, but many people who observe "modern" marriage procedures still conduct traditional rituals and pay bride-wealth. Some tribes have prohibited bride-wealth.

Polygyny, although not absent, is no longer common; serial monogamy and "concubinage" have, in some instances, replaced polygyny. Arranged marriages have largely ceased; however, despite the fact that spouses now choose each other, family approval is usually still sought and not always granted. Decisions are based less on the identity of the new spouse than on his or her family, the assumption being that families, not just spouses, are being joined together and that the right family will produce the right spouse. Family members (and sometimes even the chief) intervene if there are marital problems. The consequences of conjugal separation vary with the type of marriage and the stage of the marriage process. Civil marriages require formal divorce if the parties wish to remarry in the same way. If a "traditional" marriage dissolves, the wife usually returns to her natal home, taking some household property if she is the ag-

grieved party. Bride-wealth is almost never returned, attesting to the fact that its primary function is to affiliate children. The affiliation of children born before marriage or after divorce or widowhood is ambiguous and a subject of negotiation.

Batswana postmarital residence is ideally patrilocal; in some areas, overcrowding prevents this ideal from being realized. In addition, neolocal residence is common in urban areas, although most urban households maintain a rural residence.

Domestic Unit

A compound (*lolwapa*) typically houses a family or multifamily unit, including foster children and, occasionally, nonkin dependents or servants. It is headed by the senior male—or female, if she is single. The eldest (sometimes the youngest) married son often resides with his wife and children in his parents' compound and eventually assumes headship of it. Younger married sons build their compounds near those of their parents, and co-wives maintain their own compounds adjacent to one another or separated by those of married sons or unmarried daughters. Grandparents may live with their children or occupy a nearby compound. If the latter is the case, they usually maintain close links with their children and "eat from the same pot." Over 40 percent of rural households in Botswana are now headed by single mothers.

Inheritance

Primogeniture and agnation are the most critical factors influencing inheritance. A man's eldest son inherits most of his cattle,

other property, and political office, although the latter can be contested. Younger sons receive fewer numbers of cattle from their fathers. Daughters are occasionally given livestock, although a daughter's cattle may remain with her brothers upon marriage or be transferred to her husband. Daughters inherit their mother's household utensils. A deceased person's personal effects are inherited by his linked maternal uncle or the uncle's survivor. Boys and, sometimes, girls inherit an ox from their maternal uncle after they have given him a specified gift—usually a bull, first animal hunted, or first paycheck.

Socialization

Both sexes nurture children, but their care and upbringing are largely the responsibility of women and other children, particularly girls. Grandmothers devote much time to child rearing. It is often believed that a young mother is not ready to entirely care for her own children, and elder female kin take on the responsibility—either keeping children with them or regularly intervening and training the young mother. As young women increasingly pursue employment or education, infants and children are sent to live with their grandmothers. The conventional two-year breast-feeding period is being reduced. In the past initiation ceremonies existed for boys (*bogwêra*) and girls (*bojale*). During the confinement away from the village, the children were subjected to hardships and tutored in adult responsibilities and knowledge. These ceremonies were made illegal by the British and are now undergoing somewhat of a revival, although their functions in terms of education have been largely replaced by formal education.

African Independent churches (e.g., a *baporafota* [prophet] or a *baruti* [minister or teacher]) also engage in healing. Their training is considered less rigorous than that of the dingaka.

CEREMONIES. There are many ceremonies to mark life-cycle events: these include birth, the end of the three-month postpartum confinement, several marriage ceremonies, bridewealth payment, and death. Increasingly, funerals have become the most elaborate life-cycle rituals. Funerals used to be conducted shortly after death but now the use of mortuaries has enabled funerals to be postponed. Thus, the expectations in terms of attendance, quality of coffin, and level of hospitality have escalated, and many more people can be notified and material resources assembled. Funerals have become one of the main venues for the expression of cultural, time, and resource commitment, both on the part of the aggrieved family and those attending, who are expected to work at the funeral and who expect to be fed. In the past initiations into adulthood were elaborate ceremonies lasting a few months, in which girls and boys were taken separately to the bush in the winter. The boys were circumcised. Other ceremonies tied to the agricultural cycle, such as those to initiate planting, to make rain, and first-fruits rituals, are no longer regularly practiced.

ARTS. There are few specialized arts. Beadwork is practiced by some, and children are often adorned (sometimes for protection from malevolent forces) with beads and other decorations. Compounds and houses are often beautifully designed and painted. Song (*pina*) and dance (*pino*) are highly developed forms of artistic expression. Choirs perform and compete with each other on official and ritual occasions. They compose lyrics that offer narratives and critiques of the past and present.

MEDICINE. Batswana have an extensive local pharmacopoeia. Medicines (*ditlhare* ["trees"] or *melemò*) are used for treating ailments in humans and animals, for fortification, protection, fertility, injury, making rain, and so on. Batswana seek medical help from a number of sources, including clinics and hospitals, traditional practitioners, and Christian healers. Western medicine is more or less universally acknowledged for its ability to treat symptoms, but other healers are frequently sought in order to address the causes of illness and misfortune.

DEATH AND AFTERLIFE. Death is usually considered to have both natural and supernatural causes. Traditionally, men were buried in their cattle kraals and women in the compounds. Small children were buried under houses. Many people are still buried in this fashion, although cemeteries are increasingly used. Funerals are highly elaborated, expensive, and can last up to a week. Livestock are slaughtered during the funeral to feed guests. Priests and, often, traditional healers preside over funerals, administering rites to the bereaved that are directed toward exorcising thoughts of the dead from the living so that they will not "go mad" from their grief. After death, elders become ancestors (Badimo). People who die with regrets are believed to become ghosts (*dipoko*); their souls remain in the grave by day but rise at night to haunt the living.

Bibliography

Alverson, Hoyt (1978). *Mind in the Heart of Darkness: Value and Self-Identity among the Tswana of Southern Africa*. New Haven: Yale University Press.

Comaroff, Jean (1985). *Body of Power, Spirit of Resistance: The Culture and History of a South African People*. Chicago: University of Chicago Press.

Comaroff, Jean, and John Comaroff (1991). *Of Revelation and Revolution: Christianity, Colonialism, and Consciousness in South Africa*. Chicago: University of Chicago Press.

Comaroff, John L. (1978). "Rules and Rulers: Political Processes in a Tswana Chiefdom." *Man* 13:1–20.

Comaroff, John L. (1980). "Bridewealth and the Control of Ambiguity in a Tswana Chiefdom." In *The Meaning of Marriage Payments*, edited by John L. Comaroff, 29–49. London and New York: Academic Press.

Comaroff, John L., and Jean Comaroff (1992). *Ethnography and the Historical Imagination*. Boulder, Colo.: Westview Press.

Comaroff, John L., and S. A. Roberts (1981). *Rules and Processes: The Cultural Logic of Dispute in an African Context*. Chicago: University of Chicago Press.

Good, Kenneth (1992). "Interpreting the Exceptionality of Botswana." *Journal of Modern African Studies* 30(1): 69–95.

Gulbrandsen, Ornulf (1986). "To Marry—or Not to Marry: Marital Strategies and Sexual Relations in a Tswana Society." *Ethnos* 51:7–28.

Gulbrandsen, Ornulf (1993). "The Rise of the North-Western Tswana Kingdoms." *Africa* 63:550–582.

Hitchcock, Robert (1980). "Tradition, Social Justice, and Land Reform in Central Botswana." *Journal of African Law* 24:1–34.

Holm, J., and P. Molutsi, eds. (1989). *Democracy in Botswana*. Gaborone: Macmillan.

Kerven, Carol, and Pamela Simmons (1981). *Bibliography on the Society, Culture, and Political Economy of*

Post-Independence Botswana. National Migration Study. Gaborone.

Kinsman, Margaret (1983). "Beasts of Burden: The Subordination of Southern Tswana Women." *Journal of Southern African Studies* 10:39–54.

Kuper, Adam (1970). *Kalahari Village Politics: An African Democracy.* London: Cambridge University Press.

Kuper, Adam (1978). "Determinants of Form in Seven Tswana Kinship Terminologies." *Ethnology* 17: 239–286.

Kuper, Adam (1982). *Wives for Cattle: Bridewealth and Marriage in Southern Africa.* London and Boston: Routledge & Kegan Paul.

Lagassick, Martin (1969). "The Sotho-Tswana Peoples before 1800." In *African Societies in Southern Africa*, edited by L. Thompson. London: Heinemann.

Lye, W. F., and C. Murray (1980). *Transformations on the Highveld: The Tswana and Southern Sotho.* Cape Town and London: David Philip.

Molutsi, P., and J. Holm (1990). "Developing Democracy When Civil Society Is Weak: The Case of Botswana." *African Affairs* 89:323–340.

Parson, J., ed. (1990). *Succession to High Office in Botswana.* Ohio University Monographs in International Studies, Africa Series, no. 54. Athens: Ohio University Press.

Parsons, N. Q. (1977). "The Economic History of Khama's Country in Botswana." In *Roots of Rural Poverty in Central and Southern Africa*, edited by R. Palmer and N. Q. Parsons, 113–142. Berkeley and Los Angeles: University of California Press.

Peters, Pauline (1983). "Gender, Developmental Cycles, and Historical Process: A Critique of Recent Research on Women in Botswana." *Journal of Southern African Studies* 10:101–122.

Peters, Pauline (1994). *Dividing the Commons: Politics, Policy, and Culture in Botswana.* Charlottesville and London: University of Virginia Press.

Roberts, Simon (1972). *Tswana Family Law.* London: Sweet & Maxwell.

Roberts, Simon (1986). "The Tswana Polity" and "Tswana Law and Custom." *Journal of Southern African Studies* 12:75–87.

Schapera, Isaac (1938). *A Handbook of Tswana Law and Custom.* London: Oxford University Press for the International African Institute.

Schapera, Isaac (1940a). *Married Life in an African Tribe.* London: Faber.

Schapera, Isaac (1940b). "The Political Organization of Ngwato in the Bechuanaland Protectorate." In *African Political Systems*, edited by M. Fortes and E. E. Evans-Pritchard, 56–82. London: Oxford University Press for the International African Institute.

Schapera, Isaac (1943a). *Native Land Tenure in the Bechuanaland Protectorate.* Alice: Lovedale Press.

Schapera, Isaac (1943b). *Tribal Legislation among the Tswana of the Bechuanaland Protectorate.* Monographs on Social Anthropology, no. 9. London: London School of Economics.

Schapera, Isaac (1947). *Migrant Labour and Tribal Life: A Study of Conditions in the Bechuanaland Protectorate.* London: Oxford University Press.

Schapera, Isaac (1950). "Kinship and Marriage among the Tswana." In *African Systems of Kinship and Marriage*, edited by A. R. Radcliffe-Brown and C. D. Forde, 140–165. London: Oxford University Press for the International African Institute.

Schapera, Isaac (1952). *The Ethnic Composition of Tswana Tribes.* Monographs on Social Anthropology, no. 11. London: London School of Economics.

Schapera, Isaac (1965). *Praise-Poems of Tswana Chiefs.* Oxford: Oxford University Press.

Schapera, Isaac (1970). *Tribal Innovators: Tswana Chiefs and Social Change.* London: Athlone Press.

Schapera, Isaac, and John Comaroff (1991). *The Tswana.* Rev. ed. London: Kegan Paul International in Association with the International African Institute.

Solway, Jacqueline (1994). "From Shame to Pride: Politicized Ethnicity in the Kalahari, Botswana." *Canadian Journal of African Studies* 24(2): 254–274.

Werbner, Richard (1971). "Local Adaptation and the Transformation of an Imperial Concession in Northeastern Botswana." *Africa* 41:32–41.

Werbner, Richard, ed. (1982). *Land Reform in the Making: Tradition, Public Policy, and Ideology in Botswana.* London: Rex Collings.

Wylie, Diana (1990). *A Little God: The Twilight of Patriarchy in a Southern African Chiefdom.* Hanover, N.H.: University Press of New England for Wesleyan University Press.

—JACQUELINE S. SOLWAY

TUAREG

Ethonyms: Kel Tagelmust, Kel Tamacheq, Tamacheq, Targui. There are also numerous names designating the different political confederations and descent groups. These latter are often preceded by "Kel," which denotes "people of."

Orientation

IDENTIFICATION. The Tuareg, a seminomadic, Islamic people who speak a Berber language, Tamacheq, live in the contemporary nation-states of Niger, Mali, Algeria, and Libya. They are believed to be descendants of the North African Berbers and to have originated in the Fezzan region of Libya but later to have expanded into areas bordering the Sahara, assimilating into their traditionally stratified society the sedentary farming peoples from regions south of the Sahara. Tuareg traded with these populations and also raided them for slaves. Thus, Tuareg display diverse physical and cultural traits ranging from Arabic influences to influences stemming from south of the Sahara. "Tuareg," the term by which they are most commonly known today, is actually a term of outside, possibly Arabic origin. It was imposed as a gloss, or cover-term, to designate the ethnicity and culture of a people who, although unified by their common language and culture, belong to diverse social strata based on descent, have different geographic origins, and practice varied subsistence patterns of stock-breeding, oasis gardening, caravanning, professional Quranic scholarship, and smithing. There are also names for numerous subdivisions of Tuareg, based upon precolonial descent groups and confederations. Many Tuareg call themselves "Kel Tamacheq" (people of the Tamacheq language), "Kel Tagelmust" (people of the veil, a reference to the distinctive practice of men's face veiling), and other more specific terms. There are names referring to the precolonial social categories based on descent, still ideologically important in rural communities: *imajeghen*, denoting nobility, refers to those Tuareg of aristocratic origin; *imghad* refers to those of the tributary social stratum; *inaden* refers to smith/artisans; and *iklan* and *ighawalen* denote, respectively, peoples of various degrees of servile and client status. Currently, there is disagreement regarding which term to use to refer to these peoples as a group. "Tuareg" still predominates in most English-language historical and ethnographic literature. "Touareg" and "Targui" are often found in French-language sources. Many contemporary local intellectuals of Niger and Mali refer to themselves as "Tuareg," but some have expressed a preference for "Kel Tamacheq." For purposes of standardization, the term "Tuareg" is used in this article.

LOCATION. The Saharan regions where Tuareg originated—southern Algeria, western Libya, eastern Mali, and northern Niger—are still the regions where they predominate today. During the late twentieth century, many Tuareg have migrated to rural and urban areas farther south—into Sahelian and coastal regions of West Africa—because of drought, famine, and political tensions with the central governments of Mali

and Niger. Since the early 1990s, some Tuareg have joined an armed insurrection against those governments (Bourgeot 1990, 129–162). A few Tuareg have emigrated to France. The Saharan and Sahelian regions of Mali and Niger, where most Tuareg still live are the principal biomes to which the culture is adapted (Baier and Lovejoy 1977; Bernus 1981). The topography includes volcanic mountains, flat desert plains, rugged savanna, and desert-edge borderlands where agriculture is possible only with daily irrigation. The major ranges are the Ahaggar Mountains in Algeria and the Aïr Mountains in Niger. Temperatures range from 4° C at night in the brief cold season, from December to March, upward to 54° C during the day in the hot season. There is a short and unreliable rainy season between June and September; annual precipitation often amounts to less than 25 centimeters. Pasturelands have been diminishing, and, consequently, livestock herds are shrinking. Many herds were decimated in the droughts of 1967–1973 and 1984–1985. During the brief cold season, there are high winds and sandstorms.

DEMOGRAPHY. Tuareg constitute about 8 percent of the population of Niger (U.S. Department of State 1987). The total population of Tamacheq speakers who identify themselves culturally as Tuareg has been estimated at about 1 million (Childs and Chelala 1994, 16).

LINGUISTIC AFFILIATION. There are numerous dialects of Tamacheq, a language of the Berber Family. French sources (Fraternité Charles de Foucauld 1968, 1) list the three major dialects as "Tamaheq" (in the Ahaggar Mountains of Algeria and in the Tassili mountain range in the Ajjer region of Mali), "Tamacheq" (in the desert-edge region along the River Niger and in the Adrar des Iforas of Mali), and "Temajeq" (in the Aïr Mountains of Niger). In many other sources (Rodd 1926; Nicolaisen 1963; Bernus 1981), the major language is called "Tamacheq," without specifying dialectal distinctions, a usage also adopted in this article. Tuareg also use a written script known as Tifinagh. Many contemporary Tamacheq speakers also speak Songhay, Hausa, or French.

History and Cultural Relations

Early origins and migrations of the various confederations of Tuareg are related in oral traditions and have been documented by Rodd (1926), Nicolaisen (1963), and Bernus (1981). Early events are also recorded in Tifinagh inscriptions on Saharan rocks and in Arabic manuscripts such as the Agadez Chronicle. Many of these written records were lost when the central Sahara was plundered by French colonial patrols after the unsuccessful 1917 Tuareg revolt against France.

The Tuareg came to prominence as stockbreeders and caravanners in the Saharan and Sahelian regions at the beginning of the fourteenth century, when trade routes to the lucrative salt, gold, ivory, and slave markets in North Africa, Europe, and the Middle East sprang up across Tuareg territory. Nicolaisen (1963, 411) suggests that the first Tuareg to come to the Aïr region were caravan traders who were attracted by the area's excellent grazing grounds. As early as the seventh century A.D., there were extensive migrations of pastoral Berbers, including the two important groups related to contemporary Tuareg: the Lemta and the Zarawa. Invasions of Beni Hilal and Beni Sulaym Arabs into Tuareg Tripolitania and Fezzan pushed Tuareg southward to Aïr (Nicolaisen 1963, 411). Among these was a group of seven clans, allegedly descended from daughters of the same mother, a matrilineal myth widespread among many Tuareg groups, with cultural vestiges today in the high social prestige and economic independence of women. These matrilin-

eally based social institutions, manifested in inheritance and descent, mythology and ritual, counterbalance more recent Islamic elements in the culture. In the late nineteenth century European exploration and military expeditions in the Sahara and along the Niger River led to incorporation of the region into French West Africa. By the early twentieth century, the French had brought the Tuareg under their colonial domination. As a result, Tuareg forfeited their rights to tariff collection and protection services for trans-Saharan camel caravans. Ocean routes had diverted most of the trade to the coast of Africa. Laws against raiding and slavery were strictly enforced.

After independence and the establishment of nationstates in the region in the early 1960s, the Tuareg continued to lose economic strength and political power. They had resisted, first, French, and later, central-state schools and taxes, suspicious of them as strategies to forcibly sedentarize them and gain control over their destiny. As a result, Tuareg tend to be underrepresented today in jobs in the new infrastructure of the towns, as well as in central governments in the region. These governments imposed restrictions on trade with neighboring countries, in order to protect na-

DUST STORM

A Tuareg camp outside Timbuktu during a dust storm. Harmattan winds are hot and dry, blowing from areas of southern Sahara, carrying huge amounts of dust. Near Timbuktu, Mali. (Wolfgang Kaehler/Corbis)

tional economic interests. Droughts and decreasing value of livestock and salt—the last remaining export commodity of the Tuareg—have weakened a once strong and diverse local economy (Childs and Chelala 1994, 17). Development programs involving the Tuareg from the 1940s to the 1970s failed miserably because they worked against the traditional pastoral production systems. During the 1984–1985 drought, some Tuareg men, calling themselves *ishumar* (a Tamacheq variant of the French verb *chomer*, denoting "to be unemployed"), left for Libya, where they received military training and weapons. In the early 1990s they returned to their homes and demanded autonomy. Since that time, there has been continuous guerrilla warfare in some regions of Mali and Niger. Some Tuareg have been forced into refugee camps in neighboring countries (e.g., Mauritania).

Settlements

Precolonial Tuareg communities were predominantly rural and nomadic, with a few urban settlers. Today most Tuareg are seminomadic and remain in rural areas. Rural communities range from clusters of six to ten nomadic tents, temporarily camped to follow herds in search of pasture, to semisedentarized hamlets with compounds of tents and adobe houses reflecting the mixed subsistence of herding and gardening, to fully sedentarized hamlets, the inhabitants of which engage primarily in irrigated gardening. In all communities, each tent or compound corresponds to the nuclear household. Each compound is named for the married woman, who owns the nomadic tent, made by elderly female relatives and provided as a dowry, from which she may eject her husband upon divorce. Within compounds in more sedentarized areas, residential structures are diverse: there may be several tents, a few conical grass buildings, and sometimes, among the more well-to-do, an adobe house, built and owned by men. There are thus significant changes taking place in the property balance between men and women as a result of sedentarization.

Economy

SUBSISTENCE AND COMMERCIAL ACTIVITIES. Traditionally, occupations corresponded to social-stratum affiliation, determined by descent. Nobles controlled the caravan trade, owned most camels, and remained more nomadic, coming into oases only to collect a proportion of the harvest from their client and servile peoples. Tributary groups raided and traded for nobles and also herded smaller livestock, such as goats, in usufruct relationships with nobles. Peoples of varying degrees of client and servile status performed domestic and herding labor for nobles. Smiths manufactured jewelry and household tools and performed praise songs for noble patron families, serving as important oral historians and political intermediaries. Owing to natural disasters and political tensions, it is now increasingly difficult to make a living solely from nomadic stockbreeding. Thus, social stratum, occupation, and socioeconomic status tend to be less coincident. Most rural Tareg today combine subsistence methods, practicing herding, oasis gardening, caravan trading, and migrant labor. Nomadic stockbreeding still confers great prestige, however, and gardening remains stigmatized as a servile occupation. Other careers being pursued in the late twentieth century include creating art for tourists, at which smiths are particularly active, as artisans in towns, and guarding houses, also in the towns. On oases, crops include millet, barley, wheat, maize, onions, tomatoes, and dates.

TRADE. The caravan trade, although today less important than formerly, persists in the region between the Aïr Mountains and Kano, Nigeria. Men from the Aïr spend five to seven months each year on camel caravans, traveling to Bilma for dates and salt, and then to Kano to trade them for millet and other foodstuffs, household tools, and luxury items such as spices, perfume, and cloth.

DIVISION OF LABOR. Most camel herding is still done by men; although women may inherit and own camels, they tend to own and herd more goats, sheep, and donkeys. Caravan trade is exclusively conducted by men. A woman may, however, indirectly participate in the caravan trade by sending her camels with a male relative, who returns with goods for her. Men plant and irrigate gardens, and women harvest the crops. Whereas women may own gardens and date palms, they leave the work of tending them to male relatives.

Kinship

KIN GROUPS AND DESCENT. The introduction of Islam in the seventh century A.D. had the long-term effect of superimposing patrilineal institutions upon traditional matriliny. Formerly, each matrilineal clan was linked to a part of an animal, over which that clan had rights (Casajus 1987; Lhote 1953; Nicolaisen 1963; Norris 1975, 30). Matrilineal clans were traditionally impor-

Droughts and decreasing value of livestock and salt have weakened a once strong and diverse Tuareg economy.

The Tuareg came to prominence as stockbreeders and caravanners in the Saharan and Sahelian regions at the beginning of the fourteenth century.

tant as corporate groups, and they still exert varying degrees of influence among the different Tuareg confederations. Most Tuareg today are bilateral in descent and inheritance systems (Murphy 1964; 1967). Descent-group allegience is through the mother, social-stratum affiliation is through the father, and political office, in most groups, passes from father to son.

KINSHIP TERMINOLOGY. Tuareg personal names are used most frequently in addressing all descendants and kin of one's own generation, although cousins frequently address one another by their respective classificatory kinship terms. Kin of the second ascending generation may be addressed using the classificatory terms *anna* (mother) and *abba* (father), as may brothers and sisters of parents, although this is variable. Most ascendants, particularly those who are considerably older and on the paternal side, are usually addressed with the respectful term *amghar* (masc.) or *tamghart* (fem.). The most frequently heard kinship term is *abobaz*, denoting "cousin," used in a classificatory sense. Tuareg enjoy more relaxed, familiar relationships with the maternal side, which is known as *tedis*, or "stomach" and associated with emotional and affective support, and more reserved, distant relations with the paternal side, which is known as *aruru*, or "back" and associated with material suport and authority over Ego. There are joking relationships with cousins; relationships with affines are characterized by extreme reserve. Youths should not pronounce the names of deceased ancestors.

Marriage and Family

MARRIAGE. Cultural ideals are social-stratum endogamy and close-cousin marriage. In the towns, both these patterns are breaking down. In rural areas, class endogamy remains strong, but many individuals marry close relatives only to please their mothers; they subsequently divorce and marry nonrelatives. Some prosperous gardeners, chiefs, and Islamic scholars practice polygyny, contrary to the nomadic Tuareg monogamous tradition and contrary to many women's wishes; intolerant of co-wives, many women initiate divorces.

DOMESTIC UNIT. Tuareg groups vary in postmarital-residence rules. Some groups practice virilocal residence, others uxorilocal residence. The latter is more common among caravanning groups in the Aïr, such as the Kel Ewey, who adhere to uxorilocal residence for the first two to three years of marriage, during which time the husband meets the bride-wealth payments, fulfills

obligations of groom-service, and offers gifts to his parents-in-law. Upon fulfillment of these obligations, the couple may choose where to live, and the young married woman may disengage her animals from her herds and build a separate kitchen, apart from her mother's.

INHERITANCE. Patrilineal inheritance, arising from Islamic influence, prevails, unless the deceased indicated otherwise, before death, in writing, in the presence of a witness: two-thirds of the property goes to the sons, one-third to the daughters. Alternative inheritance forms, stemming from ancient matriliny, include "living milk herds" (animals reserved for sisters, daughters, and nieces) and various preinheritance gifts.

SOCIALIZATION. Fathers are considered disciplinarians, yet other men, particularly maternal uncles, often play and joke with small children. Women who lack their own daughters often adopt nieces to assist in housework. Although many men are often absent (while traveling), Tuareg children are nonetheless socialized into distinct, culturally defined masculine and feminine gender roles because male authority figures—chiefs, Islamic scholars, and wealthy gardeners—remain at home rather than departing on caravans or engaging in migrant labor, and these men exert considerable influence on young boys, who attend Quranic schools and assist in male tasks such as gardening and herding. Young girls tend to remain nearer home, assisting their mothers with household chores, although women and girls also herd animals.

Sociopolitical Organization

Precolonial Tuareg society was characterized by servility in a multiethnic setting (Baier and Lovejoy 1977, 393). This pattern arose partly as an adaptation to cycles of drought in the Sahara. In the core area of Tuareg operations, the desert, outsiders were acquired as domestic servants, herders, and farmers. Formerly, persons could belong to individuals, tribal sections, or to offices. Those persons who were in areas beyond direct control, particularly the herders, were more like clients than slaves. Still further away, in the savanna, some were settled on agricultural estates administered by resident agents and occupied a position somewhat between that of tenant farmers and serfs. The former clients and slaves now simply owe hospitality to their former masters. Traditionally, Tuareg social stratification guaranteed that power to make economic decisions remained in the hands of a few. Yet political power in the pastoral nomadic society was fragmented. At the

♦ **virilocal residence (patrilocal residence)**
The practice of a newly married couple residing in the community of the husband's kin. Virilocal is sometimes used in a more restrictive sense to indicate residence in the household of the husband's family.

lowest level was the camp (*eghiwan*) of five or six families of four or five members each, with dependents (including slaves). There were half as many dependents as free Tuareg. Two to twenty camps formed a descent-group section (*tawsit*). The male noble heads of the noble clan of the descent-group section traditionally have chosen chiefs from members of their own clan, but election usually is confirmed by all components of the section. Officeholders keep their positions for life, but traditional powers have been curtailed by colonial and postcolonial governments. Tenure of office has depended on the willingness of all nobles of the section to pay a small tribute to the chief each year (Briggs 1960, 146; Jean 1909, 175–176; Baier and Lovejoy 1977, 397). These traditional chiefs, called *chefs de tribus*, now serve as government links in collecting taxes and registering children for school. A group of sections recognizing a common leader constitutes the next level, the drum group, or confederation. Together, the noble clans of the confederations elect the *amenokal*, or sultan. His precolonial function was to conduct peaceful relations with outsiders or to lead expeditions against enemies; today he acts as a liaison with the central government.

SOCIAL CONTROL. In the traditional segmentary system, no leader had power over his followers solely by virtue of a position in a political hierarchy. Wealth was traditionally enough to guarantee influence. Nobles acted as managers of large firms and controlled most resources, although they constituted less than 10 percent of the population. Even traditionally, however, there were no cut-and-dry free or slave statuses. Below the aristocracy were various dependents whose status derived from their position in the larger system (e.g., whether attached to a specific noble or noble section); they had varying degrees of freedom. Tuareg assimilated outsiders, who formed the servile strata, on a model of fictive kinship: a noble owner was expected to be "like a father" to his slave. Vestiges of former tribute and client-patron systems persist today, but also encounter some resistance. On some oases, nobles still theoretically have rights to dates from date palms within gardens of former slaves, but nowadays the former slaves refuse to fetch them, obliging nobles to climb the trees and collect the dates themselves.

CONFLICT. In principle, members of the same confederation are not supposed to raid each other's livestock, but such raids do occur (Casajus 1987). In rural areas today, many local-level disputes are arbitrated by a council of elders and Islamic scholars who apply Quranic law, but individuals have the option of taking cases to secular courts in the towns.

Religion and Expressive Culture

RELIGIOUS BELIEFS. The local belief system, with its own cosmology and ritual, interweaves and overlaps with Islam rather than standing in opposition to it. In Islamic observances, men are more consistent about saying all the prescribed prayers, and they employ more Arabic loanwords, whereas women tend to use Tamacheq terms. There is general agreement that Islam came from the West and spread into Aïr with the migration of Sufi mystics in the seventh century (Norris 1975). Tuareg initially resisted Islam and earned a reputation among North African Arabs for being lax about Islamic practices. For example, local tradition did not require female chastity before marriage. In Tuareg groups more influenced by Quranic scholars, female chastity is becoming more important, but even these groups do not seclude women, and relations between the sexes are characterized by freedom of social interaction.

RELIGIOUS PRACTITIONERS. In official religion, Quranic scholars, popularly called *ineslemen*, or marabouts, predominate in some clans, but anyone may become one through mastery of the Quran and exemplary practice of Islam. Marabouts are considered "people of God" and have obligations of generosity and hospitality. Marabouts are believed to possess special powers of benediction, *al baraka*. Quranic scholars are important in rites of passage and Islamic rituals, but smiths often act in these rituals, in roles complementary to those of the Quranic scholars. For example, at babies' namedays, held one week following a birth, the Quranic scholar pronounces the child's name as he cuts the throat of a ram, but smiths grill its meat, announce the nameday, and organize important evening festivals following it, at which they sing praise songs. With regard to weddings, a marabout marries a couple at the mosque, but smiths negotiate bride-wealth and preside over the evening festivals.

CEREMONIES. Important rituals among Tuareg are rites of passage—namedays, weddings, and memorial/funeral feasts—as well as Islamic holidays and secular state holidays. In addition, there is male circumcision and the initial men's face-veil wrapping that takes place around the age of 18 years and that is central to the male gender role and the cultural values of reserve and modesty. There are also spirit-possession exorcism rituals (Rasmussen 1995). Many rituals integrate

Tuareg

**RELIGION AND
EXPRESSIVE CULTURE**

*In Tuareg culture,
there is great
appreciation of
visual and aural
arts. There is a
large body of music,
poetry, and song.*

Islamic and pre-Islamic elements in their symbolism, which incorporates references to matrilineal ancestresses, pre-Islamic spirits, the earth, fertility, and menstruation.

ARTS. In Tuareg culture, there is great appreciation of visual and aural arts. There is a large body of music, poetry, and song that is of central importance during courtship, rites of passage, and secular festivals. Men and women of diverse social origins dance, perform vocal and instrumental music, and are admired for their musical creativity; however, different genres of music and distinct dances and instruments are associated with the various social strata. There is also the sacred liturgical music of Islam, performed on Muslim holidays by marabouts, men, and older women.

Visual arts consist primarily of metalwork (silver jewelry), some woodwork (delicately decorated spoons and ladles and carved camel saddles), and dyed and embroidered leatherwork, all of which are specialties of smiths, who formerly manufactured these products solely for their noble patrons. In rural areas, nobles still commission smiths to make these items, but in urban areas many smiths now sell jewelry and leather to tourists.

MEDICINE. Health care among Tuareg today includes traditional herbal, Quranic, and ritual therapies, as well as Western medicine. Traditional medicine is more prevalent in rural communities because of geographic barriers and political tensions. Although local residents desire Western medicines, most Western-trained personnel tend to be non-Tuareg, and many Tuareg are suspicious or shy of outside medical practioners (Rasmussen 1994). Therefore rural peoples tend to rely most upon traditional practitioners and remedies. For example, Quranic scholars cure predominantly men with verses from the Quran and some psychological counseling techniques. Female herbalists cure predominantly women and children with leaves, roots, barks, and some holisitic techniques such as verbal incantations and laying on of hands. Practitioners called *bokawa* (a Hausa term; sing. *boka*) cure with perfumes and other non-Quranic methods. In addition, spirit possession is cured by drummers.

DEATH AND AFTERLIFE. In the Tuareg worldview, the soul (*iman*) is more personalized than are spirits. It is seen as residing within the living individual, except during sleep, when it may rise and travel about. The souls of the deceased are free to roam, but usually do so in the vicinity of graves. A dead soul sometimes brings news and, in return, demands a temporary wedding with its client. It is believed that the future may be foretold by sleeping on graves. Tuareg offer libations of dates to tombs of important marabouts and saints in order to obtain the al-baraka benediction. Beliefs about the afterlife (e.g., paradise) conform closely to those of official Islam.

Bibliography

Baier, Stephen, and Paul Lovejoy (1977). "The Desert-Side Economy of the Central Sudan." In *The Politics of Natural Disaster: The Case of the Sahel Drought*, edited by M. H. Glantz, 144–175. New York: Praeger.

Bernus, Edmond (1981). *Touaregs nigeriens: Unité culturelle d'un peuple pasteur.* Paris: Éditions de l'Office de la Recherche Scientifique et Technique d'Outre-Mer (ORSTOM).

Bourgeot, André (1990). "Identité touaregue: De l'aristocracie à la révolution." *Études Rurales* 120: 129–162.

Briggs, Lloyd Cabot (1960). *Tribes of the Sahara.* Cambridge: Harvard University Press.

Casajus, Dominique (1987). *La tente dans l'essuf.* Paris and London: Cambridge University Press.

Childs, Larry, and Celina Chelala (1994). "Drought, Rebellion, and Social Change in Northern Mali: The Challenges Facing Tamacheq Herders." *Cultural Survival Quarterly*, Winter, 16–20.

Fraternité Charles de Foucauld (1968). *Initiation a la langue des touaregs de l'Aïr.* Niamey and Agadez, Niger: Petites Soeurs de Charles de Foucauld; Service Culturel de l'Ambassade de France.

Jean, C. (1909). *Les touareg de sud-est: L'Aïr.* Paris: Émile Larose Librairie-Éditeur.

Lhote, Henri (1953). *Touareg du Hoggar.* Paris: Payot.

Murphy, Robert (1964). "Social Distance and the Veil." *American Anthropologist* 66:1257–1274.

Murphy, Robert (1967). "Tuareg Kinship." *American Anthropologist* 69:163–170.

Nicolaisen, Johannes (1963). *Ecology and Culture of the Pastoral Tuareg.* Copenhagen: National Museum of Copenhagen.

Norris, H. T. (1975). *The Tuareg: Their Islamic Legacy and Its Diffusion into the Sahel.* Wilts, Eng.: Aris & Phillips.

Rasmussen, Susan J. (1994). "Female Sexuality, Sexual Reproduction, and the Politics of Medical Intervention in Niger: Kel Ewey Tuareg Perspectives." *Culture, Medicine, and Psychiatry* 18:433–464.

Rasmussen, Susan J. (1995). *Spirit Possession and Personhood among the Kel Ewey Tuareg.* Cambridge: Cambridge University Press.

Rodd, Lord Of Renell (1926). *The People of the Veil.* London: Anthropological Publications.

United States Department of State (1987). "Niger." *Background Notes*, 1–8. Washington, D.C.: Bureau of Public Affairs.

—SUSAN J. RASMUSSEN

WOLOF

Ethonyms: Chelofes, Galofes, Guiolof, Gyloffes, Ialofes, Iolof, Jalof, Jolof, Olof, Ouoloff, Valaf, Volof, Wollufs, Yaloffs, Yolof

Orientation

IDENTIFICATION. The Wolof constitute a large ethnic group inhabiting the West African country of Senegal, a former French colony, and Gambia, a former British colony. "Wolof" is the name by which the people refer to themselves, and it is also the name of their indigenous language. They manifest a highly conscious sense of ethnic identity and ethnic pride.

LOCATION. The great majority of the Wolof are concentrated in northwestern Senegambia, between the Senegal and Gambia rivers (16°10′ to 13°30′ N); the Atlantic Ocean lies to the west, and Wolof territory extends inland to about 14° 30′ W. This entire area has a tropical climate and a fairly flat landscape. Whereas the northern section has a predominantly semidesert environment called the Sahel, to the south, a grassy savanna gradually emerges with increasing numbers of shrubs and trees. This shift in vegetation coincides with an increase in the average annual rainfall, which ranges from 38 centimeters or less in the north to around 100 centimeters in the south. The rainy season lasts from June into October, and the rest of the year is distinctly dry. Because there is very little or no surface water through most of the area, villages generally depend on wells for all of their water needs except agriculture.

DEMOGRAPHY. The Wolof are the dominant ethnic group in Senegal, both politically and numerically. Rapid population increase since the early 1960s, in combination with the Wolofization of members of other ethnic groups, resulted in a 1976 census estimate of about 2,000,000 Senegalese Wolof, around 41 percent of the total population. It must be noted, however, that these figures are crude approximations.

LINGUISTIC AFFILIATION. The Wolof language has been classified within the Northern Branch of the West Atlantic Subfamily of the Niger-Congo Language Family. The most closely related languages are Serer and Fula. The Lébu, a separate ethnic group, speak a distinct Wolof dialect. Although French remains the official language of Senegal, Wolof has become the de facto national vernacular.

History and Cultural Relations

The first substantial documentary information on the Wolof dates from the travels of Ca da Mosto from 1455 to 1457. According to oral traditions, however, it was probably during the preceding century that the Wolof were unified into a loose political federation known as the Dyolof Empire, centered in northwestern Senegal. Around the middle of the sixteenth century, this empire fragmented into its component parts, giving rise to the four major Wolof kingdoms of Baol, Kayor, Dyolof proper, and Walo. The subsequent history of these kingdoms is rife with political intrigue, rebellions, exploitation, and warfare, both against one another and against the Moors. European contacts did not become of major significance, except for the slave trade, until the nineteenth century. Gradually, a few commercial centers were established along the coast, the principal ones being the key slave ports of Saint Louis and Gorée. Peanut growing was introduced into Senegal around 1840, and peanuts soon became the main export. In the 1850s, primarily to protect their economic interests, the French launched their first serious attempts to conquer the Wolof kingdoms. The Wolof put up a bitter resistance, but, by the end of the century, they were completely subjugated; French colonial rule lasted until the independence of Senegal in 1960. During this same period, the Wolof, who had a long and ambivalent (often hostile) involvement with Islam, became rapidly and thoroughly Islamicized. The French stimulated the development of urban centers, which became the major sources of Westernization during the twentieth century.

Settlements

The bulk of the Wolof, about 70 to 75 percent, are rural villagers; the remainder constitute an important element in many of the larger urban centers of Senegal and in the Gambian capital of Banjul. The average size of Wolof villages tends to be quite small, with a mean population range of about 50 to 150, but up to 1,000 or 2,000 people inhabit some political centers. Most Wolof villages have one of two types of settlement plan: a village consisting of two or three separate groups of residential compounds with no central focus, or a nucleated village with the residential compounds grouped around a central plaza, where a

Land, marital disputes, and political factionalism are the major sources of conflict in Wolof villages. Physical violence rarely occurs except in the political arena.

mosque is usually located. In either type of village, compounds generally consist of square huts (traditionally round, as is still true in Gambia) with walls made of millet stalks or *banco* (an adobelike material), and conical, thatched roofs. In addition, there are several small cooking huts, storehouses, and animal shelters, all enclosed by a millet-stalk fence. More affluent villagers may have one or more modern, multiroom, rectangular houses constructed of cement blocks with tile or corrugated tin roofs. Many Wolof villages have an attached hamlet or encampment of Fulbe who "belong" to the village and herd their cattle.

Economy

SUBSISTENCE AND COMMERCIAL ACTIVITIES. The subsistence economy is based on agriculture, which in turn depends on rainfall. Wide annual variations in rainfall may result in poor harvests, causing widespread hunger and deprivation. The basic subsistence crop and staple food is millet (mainly *Pennisetum gambicum*); the main cash crop is peanuts (*Arachis hypogaea*). The second major foodstuff is rice, but it is not grown by most villagers and must be purchased. Manioc (cassava) is often a cash crop. The main domestic animals that serve as sources of meat are chickens, goats, and sheep. Fish, another important source of protein, is usually purchased in dried or smoked form. In each village a few people own cattle, but these are considered more as a sort of wealth reserve than a food resource. Beef tends to be eaten only when cattle are killed for a ceremonial feast. There are agricultural cooperatives, centered in the larger villages, that help farmers obtain loans and agricultural machinery and coordinate the marketing of the peanut harvest to the government.

INDUSTRIAL ARTS. In addition to agriculture, many villagers engage in a wide variety of specialized crafts, among them metalworking, leatherworking, weaving, the dyeing of cloth, tailoring, pottery and basketry making, hairdressing, house building, and thatching. There are two types of smiths: blacksmiths, who mostly make agricultural tools, and jewelers, who work in gold or silver. Much less weaving is done than formerly because bolts of manufactured cloth are available for purchase. Some village men are employed outside the villages in modern industries such as phosphate mining.

TRADE. Regional and urban marketplaces are the principal centers for the sale and purchase of foodstuffs and other types of goods. Some bartering occurs, but most transactions make use of the national currency, the CFA franc.

DIVISION OF LABOR. Two major factors structure the division of labor: social status and sex. Certain occupations—smith, leatherworker, and praise singer and drummer—are the prerogatives of males in several hierarchically ranked, castelike social groups; a separate status group formerly did the weaving, but now it is done by descendants of slaves. The making of mortars, pestles, and the like is done by a specialized Fula-speaking group that wanders from village to village. Other male occupations include clearing fields, harvesting, house building, thatching, fishing, herding, and butchering. Men also fulfill most religious and political roles. Female occupations include caring for children; managing the household; planting, weeding, and harvesting crops; gathering wild plants; drawing water; collecting firewood; engaging in petty trade; and practicing midwifery. Women of the castelike groups also make pottery. Both sexes may make basketry.

LAND TENURE. Traditionally, agricultural land has been "owned" by patrilineages. Land is inherited patrilineally within a lineage and controlled by the head of the patrilineage, to whom the users pay a tithe or rent (*waref*). This system has been changing since Senegal passed its Domaine Nationale law in 1964. This law attempts to do away with the traditional form of land control, which the government viewed as exploitative, by transferring the ownership of all land to the state. The state then grants parcels to the farmers currently working them, thereby eliminating all types of land rents and tribute. The full implementation of this law could have a major effect on Wolof society.

Kinship

KIN GROUPS AND DESCENT. The basic social units in a village are the residential groups, which usually occupy a single compound. These groups generally have at their core a patrilocal extended family but may also include unrelated members. Each such corporate group has as its head the senior male of the dominant family unit. Groups of contiguous residential groups usually consist of patrilineages. The larger and more important patrilineages may have segments in several villages. Traditionally, the patrilineages have been the pivotal kin groups at the political-legal level, especially with respect to the control of land and political offices. The senior male of a patrilineage becomes its official head, the *laman*. The

Wolof also recognize the *meen*, a matrilineal descent line. There is a good deal of controversy in the literature as to whether or not the meen truly constitutes a matrilineage, and thus whether or not the Wolof have a double descent system (cf. Diop 1985 and Irvine 1973 for opposing viewpoints—pro and con, respectively—on this issue). In modern times the meen does not constitute a corporate group, nor does it have any politico-jural functions. The meen is important because it is believed to be the main source of one's moral character and because it includes those maternal relatives to whom one turns for help in times of trouble such as illness or economic problems.

KINSHIP TERMINOLOGY. The Wolof have bifurcate-merging kin terms in the first ascending (parental) generation (i.e., father's brother and mother's sister are called by the same terms as father and mother, respectively, whereas father's sister and mother's brother are called by separate terms). The cousin terminology does not fit any of the standard classifications. Parallel cousins are called by the same terms as one's siblings; cross cousins are differentiated both from parallel cousins and from one another, but they are not called by distinct terms. Rather, they are called "child of the father's sister" and "child of the mother's brother," respectively. There is a joking relationship between cross cousins: one's matrilateral cross cousins are called "master," and one's patrilateral cross cousins are called "slave."

Marriage and Family

MARRIAGE. Social status and kinship are the two factors most influential in regulating marriage. The castelike groups form two pairs of endogamous units: the smiths and leather-workers constitute one unit, the praise singers and former weavers the other. In addition, the higher-ranking "nobles" and the lower-ranking "slaves" each form endogamous groups. But a "noble" man may marry a "slave" woman under special circumstances. Bilateral cross-cousin marriage is the preferred form, with priority given to marriage between a man and his mother's brother's daughter. Parallel-cousin marriage was once forbidden, but this prohibition is no longer in force. According to Islamic law, a man may have up to four legal wives, and in fact about 45 percent of Wolof men have at least two wives. Sororate and levirate are still practiced. The basic marital residence pattern is patrilocal, although there are some cases of temporary avunculocal residence. Divorce is rather frequent.

DOMESTIC UNIT. The main residential group may or may not constitute an integrated household. It is often composed of more than one family unit. Family units that form a single cooking unit and eat together constitute a single domestic unit. Separate domestic units tend to be established within a residential group when there have been disputes between family units or when one of the family units is of a lower social rank and unrelated to the others.

INHERITANCE. Both inheritance of material goods and succession to important kinship and political roles are determined patrilineally. The Wolof divide these goods and roles into two categories, *nombo* and *alal*. The former term is associated with land, wives, and social positions such as the headship of a residential group, of a patrilineage, or of a village, each of which passes first to a man's brother, secondly to his father's brother's sister, and only when none of these are left do they pass to his son (all but the wives). The term "alal" applies to money, cattle, and houses, which are inherited directly by a man's sons. (Formerly, slaves were also "alal.") As for matrilineal inheritance, it is believed that if the mother is a witch, the children will be witches. If only the father is a witch, the children will be able to see into the witches' world but will not actually be witches.

SOCIALIZATION. Children are weaned at about 1.5 to 2 years of age, and are carried on the mother's back until that time. Boys live in their mother's hut until they are circumcised at about 8 to 12 years of age. Physical punishment of children is strongly disapproved of and rarely inflicted. Some children attend primary schools, which are available in the larger villages.

Sociopolitical Organization

SOCIAL ORGANIZATION. Wolof society is characterized by a relatively rigid, complex system of social stratification. This system consists of a series of hierarchically ranked social groups in which membership is ascribed by bilateral descent, except when one parent (usually the mother) is of a lower-ranking group, in which case the children are always ranked in the lower group. In the literature, these groups are usually called "castes" or, less frequently, "social classes." The application of these concepts to the Wolof data has created analytical problems rather than increasing understanding of the system; thus, the component groups will be referred to here as status groups. These status groups are organized into three major hierarchical levels. First, there is an upper level that in preconquest times was divided

♦ **kin terms,
bifurcate-merging**
*A system of kinship
terminology in which
members of the two descent
groups in the parental
generation are referred to by
different kin terms.*

into several status groups including royalty and nobility; the socially prominent commoners (i.e., village and regional chiefs, large landowners, and religious leaders); peasants; and slaves of the Crown, who were ranked equivalent with the prominent commoners, and from whom were drawn the king's warriors. In modern times, these groups have essentially merged into a single status group, the nobility. Second is the level of the occupationally defined status groups—smiths, leatherworkers, and *griots* (praise singers and musicians), together with the former weavers. The third level is composed of the descendants of slaves. The latter are differentiated into status groups that are named and ranked according to the status groups of their former masters (e.g.,

slave-praise singer). This stratification system is a crucial aspect of village social life and remains significant in the urban areas.

POLITICAL ORGANIZATION. Wolof politics have been characterized by authoritarianism, manipulation, exploitation, intrigue, and factionalism. The four traditional kingdoms had basically similar political systems: a complex hierarchy of political officials and territorial commands headed by a ruler whose power depended to an important extent upon his slave warriors. These political structures were destroyed by the French conquest and replaced by the system of French colonial administration. The latter, in turn, was replaced by the current Senegalese national state. Political organization at the village level has re-

RELIGION AND EXPRESSIVE CULTURE

Religious Beliefs

Nearly all Wolof are Muslims; they are mainly organized into two Sufi orders or brotherhoods, the Tijaniyya and the Muridiyya. Men become members of an order upon circumcision, whereas women become members upon marriage, joining the same order as their husbands. The main tenets of Islam are generally adhered to, but the Wolof version of Islam clearly shows an emphasis on social relations rather than on abstract theology. Along with Islam, there is continuing adherence to many traditional (i.e., pre-Islamic) magic-oreligious beliefs and practices. This traditional system emphasizes belief in malevolent spirits (jinn) and witches and the need to protect oneself from them.

Religious Practitioners

Among Muslims, the basic complementary religious roles are those of *taalibé*, a disciple, and marabout (seriñ), a religious leader. There is a hierarchy of marabouts ranging from those who have only an elementary knowledge of the Quran and little influence, up to the powerful heads of the Sufi orders. There is also the *muqaddam*, who has authority to induct new members into a order, and the imam (yélimaan). Within the traditional magico-religious system, there are a

variety of ritual specialists, including the *jabarkat*, who is a combination shaman and sorcerer; the *lugakat*, who magically cures victims of snakebite; the *ndëpukat*, usually a female, who performs the *ndëp* ceremony to cure the mentally ill; and the *botal mbar*, who is in charge of newly circumcised boys.

Ceremonies

The Wolof observe the major Muslim festivals, the most important for them being Korité, the feast at the end of Ramadan, and Tabaski, the feast of the sacrifice of sheep. The principal life-cycle ceremonies include the naming ceremony (*nggentée*), and the circumcision ceremony for boys. It is likely that circumcision was a pre-Islamic Wolof custom, given that the key ritual specialists and practices are non-Islamic.

Arts

There is a striking lack of emphasis on art. Most notably, the Wolof do not carve wooden sculptures or masks as many other West African peoples do. Dancing is performed mostly by women of the praise-singer group. Several musical instruments are played, especially drums and a type of guitar called *xalam*. Wandering actors occasionally perform in the villages at night,

singing and dancing satirical skits that become more and more lewd as the night deepens. Smiths make filigree jewelry.

Medicine

The Wolof make use of most available medication and medical practitioners—modern, Muslim, or traditional. Nearly all Wolof wear numerous amulets that are believed to have the power to protect the wearer from illness, evil spirits, witchcraft, or other harm. The most common function of marabouts at the village level is to make these amulets, which consist of passages from the Quran written on slips of paper encased in leather packets. The shaman (jabarkat) may also be hired to make amulets, in which case the leather casings contain pieces of magical roots or leaves.

Death and Afterlife

After the death of a person, the usual Muslim funeral ceremonies are followed. Burial is within a few hours unless the death occurs at night. Formerly, members of the praise-singer group were "buried" in hollow baobab trees, so as not to contaminate the earth. Suicide is rare, and it is believed that the soul of a suicide goes straight to hell.

tained many traditional features, but there is much local and regional variation. The top political officials in most villages are of noble status. The office of village chief, the *borom dekk*, is hereditary within the patrilineage of the village founder, but the village notables (who include the patrilineage heads) also have a voice in his selection, and the official appointment must be made by a government official. The chief is officially responsible for administering village affairs, collecting taxes, maintaining order in the village, and acting as an intermediary between villagers and higher-level officials. The chief is usually also a Muslim religious leader, a *seriñ* (marabout). To assist him, the chief may appoint a council selected from the most important village notables. The chief also appoints the *yélimaan* (imam) and the *saltigé*. The imam is the religious leader of the village and leads the prayers in the mosque. The saltigé, whose position is hereditary within a particular patrilineage, was traditionally the leader of the village warriors and of hunting parties. Nowadays he directs the public works in the village and acts as an intermediary between the young men of the village and the chief. The heads of the major patrilineages are politically very influential, especially the ones who are also *chefs de quartier* (i.e., heads of the sectors into which some villages are divided for particular activities or situations). Finally, there are the heads of the residential compounds.

SOCIAL CONTROL. The system of social control is characterized by hierarchy, reciprocity, suppression of overt hostility, and the use of intermediaries to settle disputes. Gossip and ridicule, or fear of them, are effective means of social control because of the importance of maintaining one's status and prestige. Formal controls are exercised by the courts and by political officials—especially the village chief and regional officials. People readily resort to the courts to settle important differences. Muslim tribunals are headed by a *qadi*, who judges cases on the basis of Malikite law or traditional customs (*ada*), depending on the matter at issue; civil courts administer a legal system derived from French law.

CONFLICT. In modern times, land, marital disputes, and political factionalism are the major sources of conflict in the villages. Physical violence rarely occurs except in the political arena.

Bibliography

Diop, Abdoulaye-Bara (1981). *La société wolof: Tradition et changement*. Paris: Éditions Karthala.

Diop, Abdoulaye-Bara (1985). *La famille wolof: Tradition et changement*. Paris: Éditions Karthala.

Gamble, David P. (1957). *The Wolof of Senegambia*. Ethnographic Survey of Africa, Western Africa, Part 14. London: International African Institute.

Irvine, Judith T. (1973). "Caste and Communication in a Wolof Village." Ph.D. dissertation, University of Pennsylvania.

Lagacé, Robert O. (1963–1964). "Ethnographic Fieldnotes." Manuscript.

—ROBERT O. LAGACÉ

YORUBA

Ethnonyms: Anago, Awori, Egba, Egbado, Ekiti, Ibadan, Ife, Ifonyin, Igbomina, Ijebu, Ijesha, Ketu, Kwara, Ondo, Owo, Oyo, Shabe

Orientation

IDENTIFICATION. The name "Yoruba" appears to have been applied by neighbors to the Kingdom of Oyo and adopted by missionaries in the mid-nineteenth century to describe a wider, language-sharing family of peoples. These peoples have gradually accepted the term to designate their language and ethnicity in relation to other major ethnic groups, but among themselves they tend to use the subgroup ethnonyms listed above.

LOCATION. The Yoruba peoples reside in West Africa between approximately 2° and 5° E and between the seacoast and 8° N. Today this area occupies most of southwestern Nigeria and spills into the People's Republic of Benin (formerly Dahomey) and Togo. Yoruba homelands, roughly the size of England, straddle a diverse terrain ranging from tropical rain forest to open savanna countryside. The climate is marked by wet and dry seasons.

LINGUISTIC AFFILIATION. Yoruba belongs to the Kwa Group of the Niger-Congo Language Family. Linguists believe it separated from neighboring languages 2,000 to 6,000 years ago. Despite its divergent dialects, efforts are being made to standardize the language for use in the media and primary schools.

DEMOGRAPHY. The Yoruba-speaking population of Nigeria was estimated to be 20 million in the early 1990s.

History

The movement of populations into present Yorubaland appears to have been a slow process that began in the northeast, where the Niger and Benue rivers meet, and spread south and south-

There is a striking lack of emphasis on art among the Wolof; they do not carve wooden sculptures or masks as many other West African peoples do.

west. Archaeological evidence indicates Stone Age inhabitants were in this area between the tenth and second centuries B.C. By the ninth century A.D., blacksmithing and agriculture had emerged at Ife, a settlement that reached an artistic and political zenith between the twelfth and fourteenth centuries and is mythologized as the cradle of Yoruba peoples. Political development also appears to have been slow and incremental. Never unified politically, the Yoruba at contact were organized in hundreds of minor polities ranging from villages to city-states to large kingdoms, of which there were about twenty. Expansion took place through the federation of small communities and, later, through aggressive conquest. The famed Kingdom of Oyo, which emerged in the fourteenth century, relied heavily on trade and conquest to make it West Africa's largest coastal empire. At its peak in the late seventeenth century, seventy war chiefs lived in the capital city.

For many Yoruba, urbanism was a way of life. Europeans learned of the city of Ijebu Ode early in the sixteenth century, when they exchanged brass bracelets for slaves and ivory. The Ijebu Yoruba were, and continue to be, known for their business acumen. Commerce with Europe expanded in the seventeenth and eighteenth centuries as the New World demand for slaves increased. This lucrative trade stimulated competition, a thirst for increased power, and a rise in internal warfare that laid waste to the countryside and depopulated vast areas. Oyo declined in the late eighteenth and early nineteenth centuries, but urban populations expanded, and two new states emerged, Ibadan and Egba, founded by wartime refugees.

Following the abolition of the slave trade, missionaries arrived in the 1840s, and Great Britain annexed a small strip of the Yoruba-dominated coastland—the Settlement of Lagos—in 1861. Gradually, British forces and traders worked their way inland; by the dawn of the twentieth century, all Yoruba were brought into the empire. Early exposure to Christian education and economic opportunities gave the Yoruba an advantage in penetrating European institutions. By the time of Nigerian independence (1960), they had taken over most high administrative positions in their region, making theirs a relatively smooth transition to a Westernized bureaucratic government.

Cultural Relations

Neighboring groups are the Bariba, Nupe, Hausa, Igala, and Idoma to the north; the Edo (Benin),

Ijo, Urhobo, and Igbo to the east; and the Fon, Ewe, and Egun to the west. Since precolonial times, there has been extensive contact among population groups and, consequently, much cultural blending in the borderlands.

Settlements

From early times, Yoruba settlements varied in size from hunting and farming camps to cities, the largest of which had 20,000 to more than 60,000 inhabitants by the 1850s. Most indigenous capitals were circular, densely settled, and protected by earthen walls. Typically, a royal compound measuring around a hectare and a market occupied the centers. Clustered around them in pie-shaped wedges were the residences of chiefly and commoner families. Agricultural lands lay outside the walls, and farmers commuted from town to farm. The usual in-town residence was a rectangular compound, the outer walls consisting of contiguous rows of rooms that surrounded an inner courtyard used for cooking, domestic work, and social life. Buildings were constructed of mud bricks and covered with thatch. Today they are of concrete blocks or concrete-washed walls roofed with tin or zinc. Compounds are being replaced by large multistoried, freestanding structures, arranged in two long rows of rooms bisected by a central corridor.

Economy

SUBSISTENCE AND COMMERCIAL ACTIVITIES. The precolonial economy was primarily based on agriculture and trade, although fishing, hunting, and crafts were significant. As recently as 1950, two-thirds of the men were farmers. Depending on the ecological zone, the main food crops included beans, yams, and, later, cassava and maize. The main cash crops have been kola and cocoa in the forest belt and cotton and, more recently, tobacco elsewhere. Intercropping and swidden methods have been practiced, with fallow periods ranging from three to ten years following a typical three-year cultivation period. Until around the mid-twentieth century, mechanization and draught animals were lacking; the main tools are still the hoe, ax, and machete. Yoruba women seldom farm, although they may assist with harvesting or transporting produce. Farmers have suffered in the late twentieth century from fluctuating world prices for cash crops, civil war, and an oil boom, all of which have driven many into urban employment in commercial, governmental, and service sectors.

♦ **swidden**
The field or garden plot resulting from slash-and-burn field preparation.

INDUSTRIAL ARTS. Men traditionally practiced metalworking, wood carving, and weaving. Since the mid-nineteenth century, they have also taken up carpentry, tailoring, and shoemaking. Artisans often belonged to guilds. Women's crafts included pottery making, spinning, dyeing, weaving, and basketry; dressmaking was added in the nineteenth century.

TRADE. An extensive system of marketing and long-distance trade is a hallmark of Yoruba history. Precontact overland commerce emphasized kola, woven cloth, and salt; coastal trade with Europeans involved slaves, cloth, ivory, and, by the nineteenth century, palm products. Both men and women conducted long-distance commerce. Women organized local trade networks and markets and, as a consequence, were given official roles in public affairs. Markets still meet daily, at night, and in periodic cycles of four or eight days. Their revenues still help to support local government.

DIVISION OF LABOR. There is a division of labor according to sex and a clear division of finances. Husbands and wives keep their work and accounts separately, each taking responsibility for some household and child-care expenses. Labor also is divided according to age: heavy work is reserved for the young; the load lightens with age. The goal is to gain sufficient wealth to control the labor of others and thereby free oneself from physical work and from being accountable to a superior.

LAND TENURE. Most land is held corporately by descent groups and allocated to members according to need. Rights to use farmland and housing are primarily patrilateral in the north (although rights can be acquired through female agnates) and cognatic in the south. Tenant farming, sharecropping, and leasing were introduced by the British. The land-tenure system was changed in 1978 when the Nigerian government took control of all unoccupied or unused land and rights to allocate it.

Kinship

KIN GROUPS AND DESCENT. Descent groups are important in marking status, providing security, and regulating inheritance. There are strong bilateral tendencies, but agnatic ties are emphasized among northern Yoruba, among whom descent groups once were largely coterminus with residence, but not among southern Yoruba, who tend to have more dispersed residences and stress cognatic ties. Descent groups have names and founding ancestors, and in some

cases they own chieftaincy titles. Women rarely succeed to the titles, although their sons can. Descent groups formerly regulated marriage, agriculture, and family ceremonies and maintained internal discipline. Elder male members still act as decision makers, adjudicators, and administrators; formerly, they served as representatives in civic affairs. Extended-family relationships are individually cultivated and are important for mobilizing various types of support.

KINSHIP TERMINOLOGY. The few basic kinship terms are applied in a classificatory manner. Except for mother/father, grandmother/grandfather, and wife/husband, there are no gender-specific terms; senior siblings are distinguished from junior siblings; no cousin distinctions are made; and all children are addressed by the same term regardless of sex or age. To indicate more precise relationships, descriptive phrases must be used.

Marriage and Family

MARRIAGE. Marriage is prohibited among people who can trace a biological relationship. There are no ideal partners. First marriages still may be arranged by elders, who assess the suitability of spouses in terms of mental and physical health, character, or propitiousness of the union. Some marriage alliances were arranged for political or economic reasons. The type of ritual and amount of bride-wealth depended on the status of the partners. Marital residence was patrilocal but in the late twentieth century has become neolocal. Men traditionally married, and some continue to marry, polygynously. Increasingly since the mid-twentieth century, marriages between educated men and women reflect personal choice. Divorce is now common, although it is said to have been rare in precolonial times.

DOMESTIC UNIT. Agnatically related men often shared the same large compound, taking separate sections for their wives and children. Each wife had a separate room but cooked for and made conjugal visits to her husband in rotation. Until the age of puberty, children slept in their mothers' rooms; youths moved to a common room, and girls soon moved to the compounds of their husbands.

INHERITANCE. Landed property is inherited corporately following descent-group lines; other property such as money or personal belongings is divided among direct heirs, with equal shares going to the set of children born to each wife. Nothing is passed to a senior relative or wife unless

Until the mid-twentieth century, mechanization and draught animals were lacking among the Yoruba; the main tools are still the hoe, ax, and machete.

*Each Yoruban is
said to be endowed
with an inner force
that determines his
or her destiny.*

there is a will. Wives and slaves were once inherited by junior siblings.

SOCIALIZATION. The closest ties are between mother and child. Mothers indulge their children, whereas fathers are more remote and strict. A child is treated permissively until about age 2, after which physical punishment and ridicule are used to regulate behavior. Pre-Western and pre-Islamic education stressed economic and psychological independence, but not social independence. Children learned occupations from parents of the same sex by participating from age 5 or 6 in their work. Imitation and games played a large part in socialization.

Sociopolitical Organization

SOCIAL ORGANIZATION. Social status was and still is determined according to sex, age, descent group, and wealth. These features determine seniority in social relationships and govern each actor's rights, obligations, and comportment vis-à-vis others. In the past, elder males ideally held most positions of civic authority, although senior women were known to do so. Emerging class distinctions are calculated according to wealth, education, and occupation. High prestige also goes to

people who are generous, hospitable, and helpful to others.

POLITICAL ORGANIZATION. The indigenous political system consisted of a ruler and an advisory council of chiefs who represented the significant sectors of a society: descent groups, the military, religious cults, age grades, markets, and secret societies. Such representatives advised, adjudicated, administered, and set rules. The ruler performed rituals, conducted external affairs, kept peace, and wielded general powers of life and death over his subjects. Palace officials acted as intermediaries between the king and chiefs of outlying towns and tributary holdings. The political structure of each village or town replicated, in smaller scale, the structure of the capital. Kingship and some chiefships were hereditary. Primogeniture was not practiced; rather, branches of a ruling house were allowed to choose, in turn, from among competitor-members. Other titles could be achieved or bestowed as an honor. Today the ancient political systems survive with new functions as arms of local government.

SOCIAL CONTROL. Depending on gravity and scale, disputes or crimes were judged by descent group leaders, chiefs, rulers, or secret societies. Order was maintained by these same authorities and their aides. Deterrents included fear of harsh punishment, supernatural retribution, curses, ostracism, and gossip.

CONFLICT. Internal struggles for power were strongest between the monarch and town or warrior chiefs. External conflict involved raiding for slaves and booty and large-scale warfare. From 1967 to 1970, a civil war pitted Yoruba and northern peoples against their eastern neighbors; the battle ravaged the nation and depleted its resources. Hostility, precipitated by the quest for power and national resources, persists along ethnic and subgroup lines.

Religion and Expressive Culture

RELIGIOUS BELIEFS. The ancient Yoruba religious system has a pantheon of deities who underpin an extensive system of cults. Rituals are focused on the explanation, prediction, and control of mystical power. Formerly, religious beliefs were diffused widely by itinerant priests whose divinations, in the form of verses, myths, and morality tales, were sufficiently standardized to constitute a kind of oral scripture. In addition to hundreds of anthropomorphic deities, the cosmos contains a host of other supernatural forces. Mystical power of a positive nature is associated with

**YORUBA
HEADRESS**

Front view of a Yoruba headdress, made with glass beads and grass cloth. West Africa. (North Carolina Museum of Art/Corbis)

ancestors, the earth, deities of place (especially hills, trees, and rivers), and medicines and charms. Power of an unpredictable, negative nature is associated with a trickster deity; with witches, sorcerers, and their medicines and charms; and with personified powers in the form of Death, Disease, Infirmity, and Loss. Individuals inherit or acquire deities, through divination or inspiration.

Christianity was introduced from the south in the midnineteenth century; Islam came from the north in the seventeenth or eighteenth century. Today Yoruba allegiances are divided between the two global faiths, yet many simultaneously uphold aspects of the ancient religious legacy. Syncretistic groups also blend Islam or Christianity with Yoruba practices.

RELIGIOUS PRACTITIONERS. Priests and priestesses exercised considerable influence in precolonial times. They were responsible for divining, curing, maintaining peace and harmony, administering war magic, and organizing extensive rites and festivals. Many duties of political and religious authorities overlapped.

CEREMONIES. Rituals are performed largely to appease or gain favor. They take place at every level, from individuals to groups, families, or whole communities. In addition to rites of passage, elaborate masquerades or civic festivals are performed for important ancestors, to celebrate harvest, or, formerly, to bring victory in war.

ARTS. The Yoruba are known for their contributions to the arts. Life-size bronze heads and terracottas, sculpted in a classical style between A.D. 1000 and 1400 and found at the ancient city of Ife, have been widely exhibited. Other art forms are poetry, myth, dance, music, body decoration, weaving, dyeing, embroidery, pottery, calabash carving, leather- and beadworking, jewelry making, and metalworking.

MEDICINE. Yoruba medicine involves a full spectrum of ritual, psychological, and herbal treatments. Rarely practiced in isolation, curing is as dependent on possession, sacrifices, or incantations as medicinal preparations. Curing is learned through an apprenticeship and revealed slowly, because treatments are closely guarded secrets.

DEATH AND AFTERLIFE. Each individual is endowed with an inner force that determines his or her destiny. It is part of one's "multiple soul," which after death either resides in the sky with other mystical powers or is reincarnated. As ancestors, the dead influence the living, and sacrifices are made to gain their favor. Funeral rites are commensurate with one's importance in life—

simple for children but elaborate for authority figures.

Bibliography

Bascom, William (1969). *The Yoruba of Southwestern Nigeria*. New York: Holt, Rinehart & Winston.

Eades, J. S. (1980). *The Yoruba Today*. Cambridge: Cambridge University Press.

Fadipe, N. A. (1970). *The Sociology of the Yoruba*. Ibadan: University of Ibadan Press.

Lloyd, P. C. (1965). "The Yoruba of Nigeria." In *Peoples of Africa*, edited by James L. Gibbs, Jr., 549–582. New York: Holt, Rinehart & Winston.

Smith, Robert S. (1988). *Kingdoms of the Yoruba*. 3rd ed. Madison: University of Wisconsin Press.

—SANDRA T. BARNES

ZANDE

Ethonyms: Much of the literature uses "Azande." Some early writers refer to the "Niam-Niam," but this term is now regarded as inaccurate. The westernmost groups call themselves "Nzakara" and are so termed in the literature.

Orientation

IDENTIFICATION. The Zande, whose homelands lie within three modern African states (Republic of the Sudan, Zaire, Central African Republic), constitute a large and complex amalgam of originally distinct ethnic groups, united by culture and, to a considerable extent, by political institutions and by language. Because they originated in kingdoms founded by conquest, however, some scattered enclaves of earlier peoples still speak their original languages.

LOCATION. The Zande homeland extends for some 800 kilometers from west to east (13° to 30° E, i.e., from the Kotto River, a tributary of the Ubangi, to the foothills of the Bahr-al-Ghazal watershed) and about 400 kilometers from north to south (from 6° to 3° N, most of their land lying north of the Uele River). Most, therefore, live in sparsely wooded savanna country—a vast plain crossed by many small, tree-fringed streams—but the Zande of the Congo Basin live on the threshold of tropical rain forest, which grows denser with proximity to the equator. The habitat, climate, rainfall, and vegetation are thus quite divergent; in general, the rains fall from April to October, but the pattern varies not only geographically but also over time.

♦ **trickster**
A character in folklore who plays tricks on his enemies.

DEMOGRAPHY AND LINGUISTIC AFFILIATION. There are said to be approximately a million Zande (about 300,000 of them Nzakara speakers). Of these, about 400,000 live in Zaire, 300,000 in Sudan, and 300,000 in the Central African Republic—where the population is said to be decreasing. In terms of Greenberg's categories (1963), the Zande language belongs to the Eastern Branch of the Adamawa-Eastern Language Family in the Niger-Congo Group; a newer classification places Zande within the Ubangi Branch of the Adamawa-Ubangi Group. Zande and Nzakara speech forms are mutually comprehensible, although these languages differ in some 30 percent of their lexicon.

Settlements

The traditional settlement pattern, later revived with some variations toward the end of the colonial period, was in scattered homesteads, often widely separated from each other by cultivations and forest. Each was home to one man, his wife or wives, his children, and other unmarried dependents. His nearest neighbors were, in precolonial times, usually his closest male relatives and their households. A chief or his deputy would settle near a stream, with kinsmen and clients nearby, connected by radial paths; a king's court was a more elaborate version of the same plan: it was connected by narrow but well-maintained roads to the homesteads of chiefs. More recent settlements range from towns with modern health and educational facilities to hamlets comprising three or four homesteads, still sited in traditional fashion near a stream. Homesteads include two main types of traditional thatched huts: an older, round type with conical roof and a newer, square, gable-roofed type. Also traditional are round clay granaries, usually with access through a movable roof or lid, which are often used as temporary shelters during periods of intensive cultivation. In towns, new houses are usually square; a corrugated-iron or sheet-metal roof is a sign of relative wealth.

Economy

SUBSISTENCE AND COMMERCIAL ACTIVITIES. In western Zande country, cassava has displaced the former main food staple, eleusine millet. Maize, rice, sorghum, sweet potatoes, peanuts, squashes, okra, legumes, greens, and bananas are grown in fields and gardens. Goats have now been added to the traditional domestic animals, dogs and chickens. The diet is supplemented by the game men hunt and the fish women catch. In the dry season, termites are eaten as a delicacy.

In colonial times, traditional patterns of shifting cultivation were disrupted by cotton growing and other economic schemes and consequent resettlement. Hunting became less important, but it is still practiced away from the main roads. A number of new activities generated cash income. Some men worked for wages on government projects; tobacco was grown as well as cotton, and some craft products were sold.

Since independence, coffee has become an important cash crop in western Zandeland, and in many areas some cotton is still grown. Roads have everywhere deteriorated, however, making it more difficult to market crops. Some villages off the main road remain virtually self-sufficient, buying "luxury items" such as manufactured soap, cloth, and kitchen utensils with money from the sale of subsistence-crop surpluses, any local cash crop, game, craft work, palm wine, or cassava spirits.

INDUSTRIAL ARTS. The Zande have long been known as expert blacksmiths, potters, and wood carvers; many of their techniques were borrowed from the Mangbetu. A few smiths still operate as nearly full-time specialists, but most of their work consists of repairing blades and tools; iron smelting has ceased. Zande still make pots, carve wooden utensils, and weave baskets and mats.

TRADE. Markets are a comparatively recent introduction but are increasingly relied upon as more Zande live in or near towns, and self-sufficiency decreases.

DIVISION OF LABOR. Subsistence cultivation was and remains the province of women, who also prepare and cook food and make palm wine and cassava spirits. Men build and maintain traditional homesteads, hunt, and practice the various crafts; they are also, where applicable, the wage earners. Commoners formerly provided labor in the extensive eleusine plantations that enabled kings to feed large numbers of retainers and visitors at court.

LAND TENURE. The homestead and its surrounding gardens and fields long remained the main landholding unit; homesteads were separated from each other by considerable stretches of bush, which made it easy for them to shift their locations and for a younger kinsman to set up his own near that of the lineage head. Modern resettlement has disrupted this pattern. Cultivable areas are, in Sudan at least, subject to artificial limitation: married sons often have to reside some distance from the paternal homestead.

Kinship

KIN GROUPS AND DESCENT. The society as a whole exhibits a strong patrilineal bias, but relationships are not traced back for more than a couple of generations; local ties have long been based on cognatic, political, and personal criteria rather than on unilineal descent. Accordingly, there is very little interest in tracing the interrelationships of the widely dispersed named patriclans, many of which undoubtedly represent remnants of Zande-conquered peoples.

KINSHIP TERMINOLOGY. Simple terms exist for mother and parallel kin (except mother's brother) of her lineage and generation, for father and parallel kin of his lineage and generation, for mother's brother and matrilateral cross cousins, for own-generation same-sex parallel elder kin, and for own-generation same-sex parallel younger kin; there are two terms (male/female Ego) for same-generation opposite-sex parallel kin and for child and parallel members of child's generation, and there is a mutual term for grandparent/grandchild. All other terms are compound.

Marriage and Family

MARRIAGE. Marriage is normally contracted by payment of bride-wealth. It is virilocal and ideally polygynous, although, in practice, not many men are able to afford more than one wife. Kings and nobles had more wives than other men, many of them of commoner origin; they would occasionally give wives "for nothing" to reward retainers and warriors. Traditional bride-wealth took the form of iron spears; Zande rulers formerly provided their pages and courtiers with spears to enable them to marry, but the Bandia dynasty of the Nzakara seems to have provided wives directly instead. In the 1920s it became easier for young men to marry; they were no longer dependent on their elders for bride-wealth spears but could buy their own with money earned in the

HISTORY AND CULTURAL RELATIONS

The Zande were formed by military conquest, beginning probably in the first half of the eighteenth century; they were led by two different dynasties that were similar in organization yet differed in origin and political strategy. The Vungara clan, starting out from near present-day Rafai, in the south of the Central African Republic, overran a large number of small preexisting peoples, whom they incorporated—politically, but also, in varying degrees, culturally and linguistically—into the main body of the Zande people. Their kingdoms—from Zemio eastward—remained both fissiparous and expansionist until the era of European colonization. Over the same period, a non-Zande dynasty, the Bandia, starting out from southwest of Bangassou in northern Zaire, expanded first east and then north; their territorial expansion seems to have ended around 1855, to be followed by in-depth consolidation. In contrast to the Vungara, the Bandia, although they remained a distinct "foreign" dynasty, adopted the Nzakara/Zande language and customs of their subjects. Both dynasties apparently owe their success to superior political and military organization; they seem to have possessed no determining technological superiority. Both still constitute a recognizable aristocracy in the areas of their former domination.

A number of important cultural features are said to have been derived from the Mangbetu, a similarly organized people living to the south of the Uele River who were never subdued by the Zande. Contact and sporadic conflict with Arabs seem to date from the second half of the eighteenth century but resulted in neither Arab domination nor any profound cultural influence—except for the acquisition of guns, which helped safeguard continued Zande autonomy and reinforced the existing political system.

The first European travelers arrived in the 1860s. Toward the end of the nineteenth century, the Zande came under three different colonial administrations—Belgian, French, and Anglo-Egyptian, the frontiers of which have been inherited by their respective successor states.

The main impact of colonial rule was, at first, the end of the wars that had up to then been both culturally and structurally endemic between the Vungara-led kingdoms. Colonial administrations also imposed changes in the settlement pattern (away from the traditional scattered homesteads along the banks of streams, toward settlement along newly built or widened roads). In addition, they introduced labor recruitment for government or concessionary-company projects, particularly road building and cotton growing. In other respects the Azande were—except near the towns—shielded by colonial officials from Arab and other outside influences. Since independence, British officials in Sudan have been replaced largely by northern, Islamic Sudanese; many Zande are said to have trickled across the border into Zaire.

Zande

The traditional Zande settlement pattern, later revived, was in scattered homesteads, often widely separated from each other by cultivations and forest.

service of the European administration. Nowadays most bride-wealth is in cash, although it may also include goats, cloth, sacks of cassava, and so forth. A young man's family usually contributes, but he often scrapes together some of the money himself, and thus has some say in the matter.

DOMESTIC UNIT. Within the traditional homestead, each wife had her own sleeping hut for herself and her young children, but the hut of a man's senior wife might be rather better built. Such homesteads are still the rule in villages off the main road. In towns and large villages, administrative and mission influence has resulted in second and subsequent wives often living alone, with only occasional visits from the husband.

INHERITANCE. The property of commoners, their wives, and any debts or vengeance obligations are inherited by their patrilineal male kin. Competition often arises between representatives of the senior and junior branches of a lineage. It is important to the Zande that organic witchcraft, *mangu*, may be transmitted by a man to some of his sons and by a woman to some of her daughters.

SOCIALIZATION. Small children share their mother's life, and girls may do so until marriage, thus learning women's occupations. In precolonial days, many boys served as pages at royal or noble courts. When these courts disappeared, ritual circumcision of pubescent boys in the forest (almost certainly borrowed from neighboring tribes) replaced such service as an initiation into manhood. This tradition has also fallen into disuse.

Sociopolitical Organization

POLITICAL ORGANIZATION. In precolonial times, the vast Zande homeland consisted of a number of tribal kingdoms, separated from each other by wide fringes of unpopulated bush. Among Zande speakers, most of these kingdoms, the number and sizes of which varied over time, were ruled by members of the Vungara dynasty, except for the westernmost kingdom, Rafai. In Rafai the ruler was, like those of the similarly organized Nzakara kingdoms, a member of the Bandia dynasty, which was recognized by the Vungara as its equal. These kingdoms, born of conquest, were sustained by more or less continual warfare.

Each kingdom was divided into provinces, which were administered mainly by the king's younger agnates, although in some eastern Vungara kingdoms Bandia governors were also at times appointed. In each kingdom, the central province was under the monarch's personal rule.

Governors, although bound to pay tribute and assist the king in war, had considerable autonomy and ruled over deputies of their own. In each kingdom and each province, the ruler's court was centrally situated, and roads radiated out from it to the courts or homesteads of subordinates.

Under colonial rule, and even where the British preference for "indirect rule" held sway, this political system inevitably decayed. Western-style education produced new leaders; in Sudan, in 1954, an educated commoner defeated the son of the ruling prince in a local election. In the Central African Republic, mayors and village chiefs are still often of Vungara or Bandia descent, but national-level officials, usually non-Zande, are appointed from the capital.

SOCIAL ORGANIZATION. The homestead remains the common unit for most day-to-day activities, although men congregate in larger numbers for activities such as hunting. In colonial times, closed associations, open to both sexes, were important for the collective performance of magical rites. These associations, probably of non-Zande origin, remain popular in present-day Zaire. They have been described as quite elaborately organized, but individual associations seem to have been short-lived. Kings and princes, as well as both colonial and postcolonial governments, have generally regarded them with disfavor.

SOCIAL CONTROL. Day-to-day behavior is largely governed by the universal belief that most misfortunes are caused by witchcraft and that a witch will only attack those against whom he has a grudge. In precolonial days, serious accusations (e.g., of adultery or of murder by witchcraft) were brought to a ruler's court and resolved by oracle consultations in the ruler's presence. For adultery with a nonroyal wife, fines were exacted; witchcraft resulting in death was generally settled by magical vengeance. The adulterous lover of a royal wife, or a persistently murderous witch, might be put to death. Nowadays serious accusations (e.g., of witchcraft in connection with deaths by drowning or other accidents) can be handled by consulting a Nagidi prophetess and may, if her verdict is confirmed by local-government courts, result in prison sentences.

CONFLICT. Within the Vungara dynasty, conflict normally resulted in war, especially over succession to a recently dead king, but also in cases of rebellion against a reigning one. Changes in the number and size of kingdoms ensued. Among commoners, conflict, when not resolved amicably, was usually carried on by magical means directed against a suspected witch by the opposing party.

Religion and Expressive Culture

RELIGIOUS BELIEFS. Zande tend to attribute a soul, *mbisimo* (under certain circumstances separable from the body), to both animate and inanimate beings; in traditional belief, the souls of people became ghosts after death. Ghosts were believed to inhabit earth caverns in the bush, as did the Supreme Being, Mbori, who partook in their ghostly nature. In Nzakara-speaking areas, where the word "Mbori" did not exist, "Zagi" referred not only to the Supreme Being, but also to the outside universe in general, and ancestor spirits had concomitantly greater importance. Mission influence has ensured that Mbori is today almost universally associated with the Christian God and that the ghosts, once regarded as potentially benevolent, propitiable ancestors, are more and more associated with evil. Catholic and Protestant congregations are well established and numerous, and have, widely if superficially, affected traditional beliefs and other cultural features. Belief in witchcraft remains important, however, and both belief in and the practice of magic seem to be on the increase.

Witchcraft, *mangu*, is seen as an organic phenomenon, hereditary in the male line for men, and in the female for women. It need not be conscious; its action is understood as psychic. A witch sends out his or her "witch soul," *mbisimo mangu*, said to be visible at night, to consume the *mbisimo pasio*, "flesh soul," of the victim's organs. Witches are also believed to cause other kinds of misfortune by less clearly defined means. Although their mode of action is mysterious, witches are not seen as in any way supernatural, but as part of the normal order of things. They are believed not to be able to operate at any great distance; commoners are usually unable to bewitch nobles or vice versa. Witchcraft is assumed to be at least a factor in all misfortune; for remedial action, it is thus important to identify the witch. Identification was formerly achieved through divination by witch doctors or by means of various oracles, especially one in which a poison, *benge*, was administered to chickens, the outcome depending on whether or not the fowl survived. The use of benge was already severely discouraged in colonial times, and such oracles are now used very rarely, and never officially. Witch doctors are largely a phenomenon of the past, as are the closed associations through which people formerly sought both offensive and defensive magic. For consultations, including the identification of witches, recourse is now often to (generally female) diviners, who are prophetesses of the "native" Zande Christian church (Nzapa Zande), which now shares the people's allegiance with the European and American missions.

RELIGIOUS PRACTITIONERS. The traditional cult of domestic ancestor shrines required no specialized priesthood. Matters of witchcraft and magic have always been determined by part-time specialists/practitioners. Witch doctors, who were trained in the use of magical medicines, operated at public séances; Nagidi are believed to derive their power directly from God and are, for day-to-day purposes, consulted in private.

CEREMONIES. The most important ceremonies were formerly witch doctors' séances. One or more witch doctors, in colorful ceremonial dress, would dance and sing to musical accompaniment before commencing their divination. The circumcision of pubescent boys also forms part of an elaborate series of ceremonies; others were associated with initiation into the (now defunct) magical-medicine associations.

ARTS. Music, both instrumental and vocal, is very important in Zande culture; traditional instruments—wooden gongs, skin drums, whistles, xylophones, and large bow harps—also accompany singing and dancing. Harps are occasionally decorated with carved human heads; otherwise, nonutilitarian carving is poorly developed.

MEDICINE. Zande apply generally known common-sense cures to minor ailments. All serious diseases are attributed to witchcraft and are accordingly combated by magical medicine. The general term *ngua*, which originally meant simply "plant" or "tree," once covered both good and bad "medicines" of every sort. Nowadays Zande distinguish between protective or curative "medicine," which is increasingly becoming known by the Arabic term *dawa*, and ngua used as vengeance "medicine." Magical "medicines" are used, not only to ward off (or avenge) misfortune, but to obtain successful harvests, human fertility, good hunting, and other benefits, including job promotions and success in examinations. Such "medicines" are bought from people believed to have the requisite knowledge; payment is held indispensable if they are to be efficacious.

DEATH AND AFTERLIFE. All deaths, except those of very small children, are attributed to witchcraft or magic and call for magical vengeance. Upon death, the soul (mbisimo) becomes

Day-to-day Zande behavior is largely governed by the universal belief that most misfortunes are caused by witchcraft.

Zulu social, political, and economic interests have been represented since 1975 by the Zulu National Cultural Liberation Movement (Inkatha Ye Sizwe, commonly known as Inkatha).

a ghost, which in some sense may be present in the homestead ghost shrine, but also dwells with other ghosts and with the Supreme Being, Mbori, in earth caves in the forest.

Bibliography

Baxter, P. T. W., and A. Butt (1953). *The Azande and Related Peoples of the Anglo-Egyptian Sudan and the Belgian Congo.* London: International African Institute.

Calonne-Beaufaict, A. de (1921). *Azande.* Brussels: Lamertin.

Dampierre, E. de (1967). *Un ancien royaume bandia du Haut-Oubangui.* Paris: Plon.

Evans-Pritchard, E. E. (1937). *Witchcraft, Oracles, and Magic among the Azande.* Oxford: Clarendon Press.

Evans-Pritchard, E. E. (1971). *The Azande.* Oxford: Clarendon Press.

Greenberg, Joseph H. (1963). *The Languages of Africa.* Indiana University Research Center in Anthropology, Folklore, and Linguistics, Publication no. 25. The Hague: Mouton.

Lagae, C. R. (1926). *Les azande ou niam-niam.* Brussels: Vromant.

—EVA GILLIES

ZULU

Ethonyms: Kaffir, KwaZulu

Orientation

The Zulu are located primarily in Zululand (28° S, 32° E), which is part of the province of Natal of the Republic of South Africa. The Zulu language is classified as a dialect of Nguni, a Zone S language of the South Eastern Area of Bantu proper. Before the days of Shaka, the early nineteenth-century king who consolidated the North Nguni tribes, the term *abakwaZulu* referred to members of the Zulu "clan," descendants of a man named Zulu. With Shaka's political conquests, the term "Zulu" came to include some hundreds of Nguni "clans," all of whom paid allegiance to the Zulu king. Many South African peoples, including the Zulu, are also called "Kaffirs," meaning "infidels," a name which was bestowed on them by early Arab traders.

Gluckman (1972) quotes a population estimate of 100,000 for the early nineteenth century, but he feels that this estimate is too low. According to the 1967 census, the Zulu population was 3,340,000. Berglund (1976) gives the population as 4,130,000. The population in 1986 was estimated at 5,960,000, distributed thus: 5,700,00 in South Africa, 37,500 in Malawi, 15,000 in Swaziland, and 228,000 in Lesotho.

History and Cultural Relations

The Zulu have a reputation as "a proud, fierce, recklessly brave though barbaric warrior race" (Ngubane 1977, viii). In 1815 Shaka, a descendant of the Zulu "clan" originator, came to power. Shaka, who is often referred to as the "Black Napoleon," organized a standing army and proceeded to conquer many of the surrounding Nguni "clans." The results of this turbulent period were widespread; tribes such as the Matabele, Shangana, and Ngoni were formed by people fleeing in Shaka's wake. During Shaka's regin, the first European trading company was established in Port Natal (later Durban). Up to that point, there had been only sporadic contact with Whites. In 1828 Shaka was assassinated by his brother Dingane. In 1835 the missionary Gardner established himself among the Zulu. Piet Retief and a number of Boer Trekkers were massacred by Dingane in 1838. After Dingane's defeat at the Battle of Blood River, his brother Mpande made an alliance with the Boers and forced Dingane into exile. In 1843 Natal became a Crown colony. Mpande was succeeded in 1872 by his son Cetshwayo, during whose reign the Zulu war of 1879-1880 took place. Britain established a magistracy in 1887, and in 1910 Natal became a part of the Union of South Africa. The end of the era of effective Zulu monarchs came with the death of Cetshwayo's son, Dinzulu, in 1913. As with the other indigenous South Africans, the Zulu were outcastes in White-controlled South Africa. Establishment of indigenous control in the 1990s brought conflict with the Xhosa and then accommodation. Zulu social, political, and economic interests have been represented since 1975 by the Zulu National Cultural Liberation Movement (Inkatha Ye Sizwe), commonly known as Inkatha or the Inkatha party.

Economy

Traditionally, the Zulu economy depended upon cattle and a considerable amount of agriculture. Villages were economically self-sufficient. Agriculture was the sphere of women, whereas cattle were tended by the men. Crops grown were mealies, Kaffir maize, pumpkins, watermelons, calabashes, native sugar reeds, and various kinds of tubers and beans. Although there was considerable ritual and magic associated with agriculture, the most impressive agricultural ceremonial was the First Fruits ceremony. This was held late in December, and in it the king partook of the new crops. The ceremony also included a magical strengthening of the king and a general military review.

A man's wealth was counted in cattle. Cattle provided the mainstays of the diet (meat and *amasi*, a form of soured milk), hides for clothing and shields, as well as the means of acquiring wives through *lobola*, or bride-price. In addition, cattle had enormous ritual value. Sacrifice of cattle was the principal means of propitiating the ancestors.

The modern Zulu are poor, with agricultural yield below subsistence level. Women still till the fields, but most men travel to the towns seeking work. Cattle are still a symbol of wealth, although the holdings are low. Cattle are seldom slaughtered for meat—usually only for ritual occasions. According to Clarke and Ngobese (1975), poverty and malnutrition were so severe that the traditional robust Zulu physique is changing and the Zulu are "becoming a puny, stunted and mentally enfeebled people."

Kinship and Sociopolitical Organization

Traditional Zulu political organization was hierarchical, with the king at the apex. Authority was delegated to chiefs of districts and from them to homestead heads. The lowest level of political and kinship organization was the *umuzi*, variously translated as "village," "kraal," or "homestead." These settlements were patrilocal extended-family or clan barriors. Polygyny was the norm and was often sororal. Each kraal was the homestead of a male, which included a separate hut for each of his wives. The huts were arranged, according to the status of the wives, around the central cattle kraal. Villages were moved every few years. The kraal head had the responsibility of keeping law and order and settling disputes. Disputes that could not be settled in the kraal or cases of a special nature were dealt with by the district head.

Zulu society was organized into patrilineal sibs. Through a process of growth, subdivision, and incorporation of aliens, the sib developed into a "tribe," which, however, was still known by the name of the ancestor of the dominant sib. The sibs were divided into lineages, which were composed of descendants of a common ancestor in the near past.

The king, the head of the Zulu "tribe" or "clan," had judicial and legislative power. The legislation, formed by consultation with old men or the council, was not of enormous significance, consisting of orders for the regiments to marry or

ZULU CHIEF

Portrait of a Zulu chief in traditonal dress. Authority is delegated from the king to chiefs of specific districts. South Africa. (Guy Stubbs; ABPL/Corbis)

announcements about campaigns. The council of the king consisted of headmen or the heads of important families who were required to live at the royal kraal for certain periods to advise the king.

Shaka made a number of military innovations, not the least of which was a reorganization of the regimental system. An *intanga* consisted of a group of men of roughly the same age who lived at the royal kraal, tended to the king's cattle, and formed the standing army. According to Reader (1966), the regimental system, although not organized for war, is still an active institution in Zulu society.

Religion

Despite some belief in spirits, there was no real worship of them. Religion was primarily concerned with ancestor worship. Divination was the means of discovering the wishes of the ancestors, and sacrifice of cattle was the means of propitiation. Sorcery and witchcraft were quite common. Missionaries have been in Zululand since 1835, and apparently have been quite successful: more than half the population is reckoned as Christian. According to Ngubane (1977) and others, Christianity does not conflict with ancestor worship or belief in witchcraft.

Bibliography

Berglund, Axel-Ivar (1976). *Zulu Thought-Patterns and Symbolism*. Uppsala: Swedish Institute of Missionary Research.

Bryant, A. T. (1970). *Zulu Medicine and Medicine-Men*. Cape Town: C. Struik.

Clarke, Liz, and Jane Ngobese (1975). *Women without Men: A Study of 150 Families in the Ngutu District of Kwazulu*. Durban: Institute for Black Research.

Gluckman, Max (1972). "Moral Crisis: Magical and Secular Solutions." In *The Allocation of Responsibility*, edited by Max Gluckman. Manchester: Manchester University Press.

Klopper, Sandra (1989). *Mobilizing Cultural Symbols in Twentieth Century Zululand*. Cape Town: Centre for African Studies.

Krige, E. J. (1968). "Girl's Puberty Songs and Their Relation to Fertility, Health, Morality, and Religion among the Zulu." *Africa* 38:173-198.

Ngubane, Harriet (1977). *Body and Mind in Zulu Medicine*. London: Academic Press.

Raum, O. F. (1967). "The Interpretation of the Nguni First Fruit Ceremony." *Paideuma* 13:148-163.

Reader, D. H. (1966). *Zulu Tribe in Transition: The Makhanya of Southern Natal*. Manchester: Manchester University Press.

Vilakazi, A. (1962). *Zulu Transformation*. Pietermaritzburg: University of Natal Press.

HAKKA

Ethonyms: Haknyin, K'e-chia, Kejia, Keren, Lairen, Ngai, Xinren

Orientation

IDENTIFICATION. "Hakka" is the Yue (Cantonese) pronunciation of the term that translates literally as "guests" or "stranger families" or, less literally, as "settlers" or "newcomers." The name "Hakka" (in Mandarin, "Kejia") is likely to have originated from the descriptive term used before the seventeenth century in population registers to distinguish recent immigrants from earlier Yue inhabitants. During the nineteenth century, in certain contexts, the term "Hakka" carried negative implications, but by the early twentieth century, following a period of ethnic mobilization, "Hakka" became more widely accepted as an ethnic label.

LOCATION. Hakka are widely scattered throughout the southeastern provinces of the People's Republic of China (PRC), but most are concentrated in northeastern Guangdong, east of the North River, in the mountainous, less fertile region of Meizhou Prefecture. Meizhou, which includes the seven predominantly Hakka counties that surround Meixian (located at approximately 24° N and 116° E), is considered the Hakka "heartland" and is claimed by many Hakka as their native place. Sizable Hakka populations are also found in southwestern Fujian, southern Jiangxi, eastern Guangxi, Hainan Island, Hong Kong, Taiwan, and, in lesser numbers, in regions of Sichuan and Hunan. By the twentieth century Hakka could be found on virtually every continent, from South and Southeast Asia and the Pacific to Europe, North and South America, Africa, and the Caribbean.

DEMOGRAPHY. Estimated at over 38 million in the People's Republic of China in 1990, the Hakka population accounts for approximately 3.7 percent of the total Chinese population. In 1992, the International Hakka Association placed the total Hakka population worldwide at approximately 75 million.

LINGUISTIC AFFILIATION. Today many Hakka throughout the world no longer speak Hakka, but traditionally the Hakka language was the single most important cultural feature that served to distinguish Hakka from other Chinese. The version of Hakka dialect spoken in Meixian is considered the standard form and can be transcribed into standard Chinese characters as well as other Chinese vernaculars. While many Hakka claim that the Hakka language is more like Mandarin than Cantonese is, linguists classify Hakka as Southern Chinese along with Yue and Min (Hokkien) languages, signifying that these dialects developed from a variety of Chinese spoken in southern China between the first and third centuries A.D. Hakka, once classified by linguists as part of the Gan-Kejia Subgroup, is now considered a separate category.

History and Cultural Relations

The Hakka have had a long history of conflict and competition with other Chinese groups over scarce land and resources. In Fujian and Taiwan they suffered from hostile relations with Min, and in Guangdong they fought with Yue speakers. Hakka-Yue conflicts were particularly violent throughout the middle of the nineteenth century, in the aftermath of the Taiping Rebellion, and during the Hakka-Bendi Wars (1854–1867). At that time, negative stereotypes and descriptions of the Hakka began to appear in both Chinese and foreign texts. The worst insult, which was recounted by Yue to foreign missionaries, was the implication that the Hakka, with their strange language and unfamiliar dress and customs, were not in fact Chinese but were more closely related to other "barbarian" or "tribal" people. Such accusations infuriated the Hakka, who proudly sought to defend their identity and set the record straight. Since then, studies of Hakka history, based largely on genealogical evidence and other historical records, as well as linguistic evidence, support and substantiate Hakka claims to northern Chinese origins. In the People's Republic of China the Hakka are officially included in the category of Han Chinese.

Today most Hakka and non-Hakka scholars agree that the ancestors of those who later became known as "Hakka" were Chinese who came from southern Shanxi, Henan, and Anhui in north-central China. From the "cradle of Chinese civilization," these proto-Hakka gradually moved southward in five successive waves of migration. Historians do not agree, however, on the exact time and sequence of the earliest migrations. Most historians place the first migration during the fourth century at the fall of the Western Jin dynasty, when Hakka ancestors reached as far south as Hubei, south Henan, and central Jiangxi. The next period is less debated. By the late ninth and early tenth centuries, with the disorder created during the late Tang dynasty, the ancestors of the present-day Hakka moved farther south into Jiangxi, Fujian, and Guangdong. The third wave,

The Hakka have had a long history of conflict and competition with other Chinese groups over scarce land and resources.

Hakka

The Hakka have long enjoyed a reputation as extremely skilled and hardworking agriculturists who can render the least desirable land productive.

which stretched from the beginning of the twelfth century to the middle of the seventeenth, was caused by the exodus of the Southern Song dynasty and their supporters in a southward flight from the Mongol invasion. This dislodged people from Jiangxi and southwestern Fujian and forced them further into the northern and eastern quarters of Guangdong. By the end of the Yuan dynasty (A.D. 1368), northern and eastern Guangdong were exclusively Hakka. The fourth wave, which lasted from the mid-seventeenth century to the mid-nineteenth century, began with the Manchu conquest, and during the Qing dynasty, migration expanded into the central and coastal areas of Guangdong, Sinchuan, Guangxi, Hunan, Taiwan, and southern Guizhou. By the time of the fifth wave, beginning at the middle of the nineteenth century, conflicts between the Hakka and the Yue increased. Triggered by population pressure, the Hakka-Bendi (Yue) Wars, and the large Hakka involvement in the Taiping Rebellion, the fifth wave of migration sent Hakka emigrants to seek better lives farther afield—to the southern part of Guangdong, to Hainan Island, and overseas to Southeast Asia (especially Malaya and Borneo). The establishment of the People's Republic of China and China's announcement of the intent to reclaim Hong Kong in 1997 have created what might be called the sixth wave of migration, which has continued the flow of Hakka overseas, especially to the United States, Australia, and Canada.

Settlements

As later arrivals in most of the Chinese areas where they settled, the Hakka were generally forced into the higher elevations to the hilly, less productive, and less desirable land. Such was the case in Guangdong, Guangxi, and the New Territories of Hong Kong, where the Yue had already settled the more fertile river valleys, and also in Taiwan where the Min speakers owned the better land. During the eighteenth and nineteenth centuries, in regions of Guangdong, Hakka residence patterns differed from those of the Yue. As opposed to the Yue, who were more likely to live in more densely populated towns or in large, single-surname villages surrounded by fields, smaller numbers of Hakka were sparsely dispersed among the hills on land that they often rented from Yue landlords. In other regions Hakka and Yue occupied separate villages in the same areas; Hakka villages were more likely to be multisurnamed. As a result of their often hostile relations with other groups, Hakka architectural style often differed from that of their Chinese and non-Chinese neighbors. In southwestern Fujian and in northern Guangdong, Hakka built circular or rectangular, multistoried, fortresslike dwellings, designed for defensive purposes. These Hakka "roundhouses" were built three or four stories high, with walls nearly a meter thick, made of adobe or tamped earth fortified with lime. The structures vary in size; the largest, resembling a walled village, measures over 50 meters in diameter. Although the Hakka maintain the reputation of living in poor, marginal, rural areas, Hakka today also reside in urban, cosmopolitan regions.

Economy

SUBSISTENCE AND COMMERCIAL ACTIVITIES. The Hakka have long enjoyed a reputation as extremely skilled and hardworking agriculturalists who can render the least desirable land productive. In the course of their history, the Hakka often farmed wasteland rejected by others or worked as tenants. Where the land permitted, they grew rice and vegetables. In poorer areas sweet potatoes were their staple. Much of the agricultural labor was performed by women, who, unlike other Chinese, did not have their feet bound. Female agricultural labor, marketing, and cutting of wood from the hillsides for fuel were especially necessary tasks in villages where Hakka men sought work overseas. As early as the Southern Song dynasty, Hakka men sought their fortunes by joining the military. The Taiping army, the Nationalist forces of Sun Yatsen, and the Communist army during the Long March were all comprised of large numbers of Hakka soldiers. Overseas, Hakka worked as railway builders, plantation hands, and miners. Today, Hakka are still known for their reputation for hard physical labor, and the women who are commonly seen working at construction sites in Hong Kong are often Hakka.

INDUSTRIAL ARTS. During the nineteenth century, Hakka peasants often had to supplement their agricultural work with other occupations. They were also silver miners, charcoal makers, itinerant weavers, dockworkers, barbers, blacksmiths, and stonecutters.

TRADE. The Hakka are best known for their agricultural, martial, and scholarly skills and for their achievement in political, academic, and professional occupations, but they are not known for their involvement in commercial enterprises. However, a number of successful entrepreneurs are Hakka or are of Hakka ancestry. For example, T. V. Soong, founder of the Bank of China, and

Aw Boon Aw, who made his fortune selling Tiger Balm, were both Hakka. In Calcutta today, the Hakka minority are successful entrepreneurs in the leather and tanning industry.

DIVISION OF LABOR. The Hakka do not follow the traditional Chinese strict sexual division of labor. Women have long had a reputation for participating in hard physical labor—in fact, they perform many traditionally male occupations such as farming and construction. Because of the Hakka women's reputation for diligence and industriousness, during the nineteenth and early twentieth centuries poor non-Hakka valued Hakka women as wives.

LAND TENURE. As latecomers in many of the regions where they settled, the Hakka were often tenants of the Yue or Min or owned only top-soil rights to land while the Yue or Min owned bottom-soil rights. Before the Communist Revolution, Hakka were more likely to be tenants than landlords and therefore many poor and landless Hakka peasants benefited from land reform in the early 1950s.

Kinship

KIN GROUPS AND DESCENT. The Hakka trace descent patrilineally, and extended patrilineal kin groups combine to create lineages. The lineage commonly consists of a group of males who trace descent from one common ancestor, who live together in one settlement, and who own some common property. At least nominally, the lineage, including the wives and daughters, is un-der the authority of the eldest male in age and generation. Whenever possible, Hakka lineages traditionally set up ancestral halls. These buildings are usually not as ornate as those of the Cantonese, and their ancestral tablets only make reference to the name of the founding ancestor. Hakka rules for inclusion of forebears in ancestor worship are broader and more egalitarian than those of the Cantonese, and they often include men and women, rich and poor.

KINSHIP TERMINOLOGY. Hakka kinship terms follow the general Han Chinese pattern, which may be referred to as "bifurcate collateral" or as "both classificatory and descriptive" (Feng 1948, 129). They typically have a very large number of kinship terms for the paternal side and less differentiation on the maternal side. Many kinship terms distinguish affinal and consanguineal kin and indicate age in relation to Ego or Ego's parents. They also commonly use such kinship terms as "father's younger brother" or "elder sister" to refer to fictive kin. Hakka kinship terms reflect the assimilation of a woman into her husband's family. Unlike Yue women in parts of Guangdong, who have separate terms of address for their husbands' parents, Hakka women use the same terms as their husbands to address his parents and other relatives.

Sociopolitical Organization

SOCIAL ORGANIZATION. Like other Chinese, the Hakka have organized communities along kinship lines and ties to a common native

---

MARRIAGE AND FAMILY

Marriage

Like other Chinese, Hakka practice surname exogamy. Marriage traditionally was arranged, often village exogamous, and also patrilocal. Hakka marriage ceremonies suggest the transfer of women from one family to another and the incorporation of women into their husband's household and lineage rather than the establishment of bonds between two families. Wives are included in ancestral worship of their husband's lineage. Many Hakka claim that polygynous marriages were rare among the Hakka, yet until recently polygynous marriages were found among poor Hakka villagers in the New Territories of Hong Kong.

Domestic Unit

The domestic unit was ideally an extended patrilineal kin group comprised of several generations. Traditionally this group would have included a husband and wife, their unmarried daughters, and their married sons with their wives and children.

Inheritance

A man's estate was traditionally divided equally among his sons. Daughters might inherit some movable property at marriage, but did not share significantly in the parents' estate.

Socialization

As reflected in Hakka songs and sayings, Hakka girls are taught that they should learn "the appropriate skills expected of the wife of an important official, as well as know how to cook, clean, and work hard." The Hakka also instruct their children in the value of education and bodily cleanliness. There is little evidence that Hakka patterns of child rearing and socialization are significantly different from those of other Chinese. Respect for parents, elders, and obligations to the family is a commonly held value.

◆ **Taoism (Daoism)**
An ancient Chinese philosophy that seeks to recognize and control the essential forces (ch'i) in nature and all living things.

◆ **Buddhism**
A world religion, founded by Siddhartha Gautama or Sakyamuni, "the enlightened one," in the sixth century B.C. The two major branches of Buddhism are Mahayana Buddhism and Hinayana (Theravada) Buddhism.

◆ **Confucianism**
A moral and philosophical religious tradition based on the teaching of Confucius (Kongzo), who lived in northern China from about 551 to 479 B.C.

place. Alliances based on shared dialect or ethnic identity are also important. Other groups sometimes view the Hakka as being exclusive or "clannish," but they view themselves as being unified and cooperative. Two international Hakka organizations, the Tsung Tsin (Congzheng) Association and the United Hakka Association (Kexi Datonghui), were organized by Hakka intellectuals and elite in the early 1920s in order to promote Hakka ethnic solidarity and foster a public understanding of Hakka culture. In 1921, over 1,000 delegates representing Hakka associations worldwide attended a conference in Canton to protest the Shanghai publication of *The Geography of the World*, which described the Hakka as non-Chinese. Today these international Hakka voluntary organizations have branches reaching from Taiwan, Hong Kong, and Singapore to the United States, Canada, and beyond.

POLITICAL ORGANIZATION. Although Hakka political organization is not easily distinguished from that of the larger society in which they are situated, the Hakka have long played an important role in Chinese politics, despite their economic disadvantages. During the Qing dynasty, the Hakka fared well in the imperial examinations and ascended into the imperial bureaucracy. Today they are disproportionately well represented in the government of the People's Republic of China (PRC). While they comprise close to 4 percent of the population of the PRC, they represent a far greater proportion of government leaders. Among the most well-known Hakka political figures are Deng Xiaoping; Zhu De, the military commander during the Long March; Marshal Ye Jiangying, leader of the Peoples Liberation Army; and former Communist Party Secretary Hu Yaobang. Outside of the PRC, Hakka leaders include Taiwan's President Lee Teng-hui; Singapore's President Lee Kwan Yew; Burma's Prime Minister Ne Win; and the governor-general of Trinidad and Tobago, Sir Solomon Hochoy. Some sources also assert that Dr. Sun Yatsen was Hakka.

SOCIAL CONTROL. Like other Chinese, Hakka have been subject to the larger forces of the Chinese government bureaucracy and state control; on the local level, senior males had the most formal authority before 1949. Social pressure, strict traditional rules of obedience, and filial piety also help to minimize conflict.

CONFLICT. Today, as in the past, village leaders in rural communities often resolve conflicts on the local level. During the nineteenth century, conflicts often grew into long-term violent feuds. Longer-lasting feuds between Hakka villages, between Hakka lineages, or between the Hakka and the Yue were often over land or property, theft, marriage agreements, or other personal conflicts. The theft of a water buffalo and a broken marriage agreement between a Yue man and a Hakka woman were contributing events that helped escalate Hakka-Yue conflicts into large-scale armed conflicts during the 1850s. Conflicts between Hakka Christian converts and non-Christian Chinese were also common during the nineteenth and early twentieth centuries.

Religion and Expressive Culture

RELIGIOUS BELIEFS. The Hakka do not have their own distinct religion, but like most other Chinese, traditionally practiced a blend of Daoism, Buddhism, Confucianism, and "folk" religion, subject to regional variation. The Hakka traditionally believed that ancestral spirits could influence the lives of the living and thus required special care, offerings, and worship. They erected homes, located graves, and built ancestral halls according to the principles of *feng shui* (geomancy). In many communities, Hakka beliefs and practices closely resemble those of the Yue; however, in other cases, anthropologists have also observed important differences. For example, during the nineteenth century the Hakka did not worship as many of the higher-level state-sanctioned gods or Buddhist deities, placed more weight on Daoist beliefs and ancestor worship, and were more likely to practice spirit possession than other Chinese in Guangdong. Some missionaries characterize the Hakka as having more "monotheistic tendencies" than other Chinese; these tendencies may have contributed to the fact that relatively larger numbers of the Hakka converted to Christianity during the nineteenth and early twentieth centuries than did other Han Chinese. In some parts of Hong Kong, the Hakka have fewer shrines and ancestral altars in their homes than the Cantonese.

RELIGIOUS PRACTITIONERS. The same religious practitioners—Buddhist and Daoist priests, spirit mediums, feng shui experts, and various types of fortune-tellers—were observed among the Hakka during the nineteenth century as among the Yue. During the late nineteenth and early twentieth centuries Hakka Christian missionaries became particularly active in parts of Guangdong and Hong Kong.

CEREMONIES. The Hakka have traditionally observed the most common Chinese life-cycle rituals and calendrical festivals, including the Lunar New Year, the Lantern Festival, Qing Ming, the Mid-Autumn Festival, the Dragon Boat Festival, Chong Yang, and Winter Solstice. The Hakka generally do not celebrate Yu Lan, the festival to appease "hungry ghosts," which is popular among other Chinese.

ARTS. The Hakka are known for their folk songs, especially the genre of mountain songs that were once commonly sung by women, sometimes in a flirtatious dialogue with men, as they worked in the fields or collected fuel along the hillsides. These songs are often love songs, but they also touch on topics such as hard work, poverty, and personal hardships. Although their clothes were traditionally plain, most Hakka women used to weave intricately patterned bands or ribbons, which they commonly wore to secure black rectangular headcloths or the flat, circular, fringed Hakka hats. These are still worn by some older Hakka women in Hong Kong and some regions of Guangdong.

MEDICINE. The Hakka traditionally depended on spirit healers, Chinese doctors, and traditional herbal remedies.

DEATH AND AFTERLIFE. Christian- or Buddhist-derived ideas of hell exist among the Hakka, as do ideas concerning the influence of the spirits of the dead and their occasional return to earth. One nineteenth-century Protestant missionary observed that the Hakka were not very familiar with the Buddhist karmic concept of one's life influencing rebirth or the Buddhist idea of hell with its tortures and purgatory. Instead, he asserted that the Hakka ascribed to the Daoist idea that "the righteous ascend to the stars and the wicked are destroyed" (Eitel 1867, 162–163).

Bibliography

Char Tin Yuk (1929). *The Hakka Chinese—Their Origin and Folk Songs.* Reprint. 1969. San Francisco: Jade Mountain Press.

Cohen, Myron L. (1968). "The Hakka or 'Guest People': Dialect as a Sociocultural Variable in Southeastern China." *Ethnohistory* 15(3):237–252.

Constable, Nicole, ed. (forthcoming, 1994). *Guest People: Studies of Hakka Chinese Identity.* Berkeley and Los Angeles: University of California Press.

Eitel, E. J. (1867). "Ethnographical Sketches of the Hakka." *Notes and Queries on China and Japan* 1(12): 161–163.

Feng, H. C. (1948). *The Chinese Kinship System.* Cambridge: Harvard University Press.

Leong, S. T. (1985). "The Hakka Chinese of Lingnan: Ethnicity and Social Change in Modern Times." In *Ideal and Reality: Social and Political Change in Modern China*, 1860–1949, edited by David Pong and Edmund S. K. Fung, 287–327. New York: University Press of America.

Moser, Leo J. (1985). "The Controversial Hakka: 'Guests' from the North." In *The Chinese Mosaic: The Peoples and Provinces of China*, by Leo J. Moser, 235–255. Boulder, Colo., and London: Westview Press.

—NICOLE CONSTABLE

HAN

Ethonyms: Chinese, Han Chinese, Hua, Zhongguo ren

Orientation

IDENTIFICATION. Han people are both numerically and politically dominant in mainland China, Taiwan, and the city-state of Singapore; they also reside in nearly every country in the world as Overseas Chinese. In mainland China, where they constituted 91 percent of the population in the 1990 census, they are officially and conventionally known as "Han," a name that originally belonged to a river in central China and was adopted by China's first long-ruling imperial dynasty, which reigned from 206 B.C.E. to 220 C.E. Designation as "Han" distinguishes them from the diverse minority peoples such as Mongols, Uigurs, Tibetans, Miao, and others. Outside mainland China, the term "Han" is less frequently used, and the people usually refer to themselves by some variant of the term "Zhongguo ren," which in Mandarin Chinese means "people of the central country" and is usually translated into English as "Chinese." (The European terms "Chinese" and "China" are of disputed origin.)

LOCATION. The majority of the Han people are concentrated in the eastern half of mainland China. Drawing a line from the Xing'an Mountains in northeastern China, across the northern bend of the Yellow River, through the foothills that separate Sichuan from Tibet, and across the northern part of Yunnan Province to the border of Myanmar (Burma), the area to the east and south of the line has sufficient rainfall for intensive grain agriculture, whereas the area to the north and west is drier and more conducive to pastoralism. Historically, the agrarian civilization built by Han people was confined to the agricultural areas. Even though the drier northern and western regions sometimes came under the rule of Han-dominated regimes, they were not intensively col-

Han people are both numerically and politically dominant in mainland China, Taiwan, and Singapore; they also reside in nearly every country in the world.

onized by Han people until the twentieth century. The only areas outside this region that are now predominantly Han are the islands of Hainan, colonized during the last thousand years; Taiwan, settled by Han during the last 400 years; and Singapore, colonized only since the nineteenth century.

Within the core area of Han settlement, there is great climatic and geographic variation. In the northern region, centered on the drainage area of the Yellow River, winters are cold, summers are hot, rainfall is marginal, and agriculture has traditionally been based on dry grains, such as wheat, millet, sorghum, and barley. In the central region, centered on the drainage of the Yangzi River, and in the southern regions, winters are mild, summers hot and humid, and rainfall heavy, permitting multiple cropping and irrigated crops, especially wet-field rice.

DEMOGRAPHY. For the past 2,000 years at least, Han people or their precursors have probably always constituted between 15 and 25 percent of the world's population. An imperial census taken in the year 2 C.E. counted over 59 million people; by the beginning of the Qing dynasty in 1644, the population of the Chinese empire was probably around 200 million, the great majority of them Han. This had grown to about 450 million

by 1850 and was more than 580 million (and over 90 percent Han) in 1953, when the People's Republic of China took its first comprehensive census. Population grew rapidly in the 1950s and 1960s (with a large setback in the famine years of 1960–1962), finally inducing the People's Republic to institute a series of increasingly strict population-control plans, culminating in the one-child-per-family policy begun in 1979. These policies, largely though not completely successful, have reduced the population growth rate in recent years, but population continues to expand, and the 1990 census showed a total population in mainland China of 1,113,682,501, of whom 1,042,482,187, or 91.8 percent, were Han.

Outside mainland China, the Republic of China government on Taiwan also encouraged population control since the late 1950s, but through much gentler means, relying (ultimately successfully) on urbanization, economic development, and a strong propaganda campaign to curb population growth. The population of the island was 19.8 million in 1988, of whom over 98 percent were Han.

Together with Overseas Chinese populations of approximately 27 million in Asia (mostly Southeast Asia), over 2 million in the Americas, and perhaps 1 million elsewhere, the total Han Chinese population worldwide in 1992 is probably slightly over 1.1 billion.

LINGUISTIC AFFILIATION. Han people (with the exception of some Overseas Chinese) are all speakers of one or another of the languages usually known as Chinese, which comprise a branch of the Sino-Tibetan Language Family. All are tonal languages and rely on word order rather than morphology to express grammatical relationships.

For essentially political reasons, both the People's Republic of China on the mainland and the Republic of China on Taiwan consider Chinese to be a single language consisting of a series of dialects (*fangyan* or "local speeches"), but nearly all linguists agree that several of these are best classified as separate languages since they are mutually unintelligible and differ greatly in phonology and vocabulary, though only slightly in syntax. The majority of Chinese speakers, including most inhabitants of the Yellow River drainage and parts of the Yangzi drainage as well as southwestern China, speak one of the dialects collectively known as Mandarin. Other important Chinese languages include Wu in eastern China, Gan in most of Jiangxi Province, Xiang in most of Hunan Province, Yue or Cantonese in the far south and

SPRING FESTIVAL

A Han Chinese boy at the Spring Festival in Quinghai Province, China. (John Slater/Corbis)

overseas, Min in Fujian and Taiwan as well as overseas, and Hakka or Kejia in a widely dispersed series of communities mainly in the south and overseas. Many of these groups are themselves highly differentiated into mutually unintelligible local dialects; the Min-speaking areas of Fujian, in particular, are known for valley-by-valley dialect differences.

This regional linguistic diversity has been countered over the course of history by the unity of the written language. Chinese writing extends back at least to the fourteenth century B.C.E., when pictographic and ideographic signs were used to represent syllables of a spoken language. The specific forms of these signs or characters have changed since then and many have been added, but the basic principles of the writing system have persisted. Each character represents both a concept and a sound, so that, for example, *ming* meaning "bright" and *ming* meaning "name," though pronounced identically in Standard Mandarin, are written with different characters. The characters themselves can be pronounced in any Chinese language, however, making written communication feasible between speakers of related but different spoken languages.

Throughout the imperial period, the standard written language was what is now known as Classical Chinese, evolved over the centuries from what was presumably a representation of the speech of around the fourth to second centuries B.C.E. By late imperial times (1368–1911), the standard written language was far different from any spoken vernacular; in fact, literacy was largely, though not entirely, confined to the ruling scholar-elite.

In the twentieth century, a fundamental transformation of the nature and purpose of literacy has led to the elimination of the classical written language and its replacement by *baihua* or "plain speech," a written approximation of the Mandarin spoken in and around the capital city of Beijing. In addition, both the Republican and People's Republic governments have made Beijing Mandarin into a standard spoken language, called *guoyu* or "national language" by the Republic and *putonghua* or "ordinary speech" by the People's Republic. All schools in both the mainland and Taiwan use written baihua and spoken Mandarin as the medium of instruction. Thus, most younger speakers in the non-Mandarin regions of the mainland, as well as nearly everyone under about age 60 in Taiwan, can use Mandarin as a second language, and literacy in baihua is over 80 percent in the mainland and nearly universal in Taiwan.

History and Cultural Relations

The probable Neolithic forebears of the Han were farming in the valleys of the Yellow River and its major tributaries as early as 6000 B.P. In the late third and early second millennia B.C.E., a series of city-states arose in the same area; the best-documented of these, historically and archaeologically, are the Xia (centered in the Fen River valley), the Shang (centered in the western part of the North China Plain), and the Zhou (centered in the Wei River valley). Traditional historiography portrays these as successive "dynasties," but they are best seen as successively dominant city-states. By the later part of the period of Shang dominance (c. 1400–1048 B.C.E.), written records afford us a portrayal of a highly stratified, kin-based state. The Zhou conquest of Shang in 1048 initially brought about little social change, but throughout the 800–year reign of Zhou kings, China was transformed fundamentally by the intensification of agriculture, the development of bureaucracy, the invention of iron technology, and the spread of commerce and urbanism. The latter part of the Zhou reign, referred to as the Spring and Autumn (771–482) and Warring States (481–221) periods, saw great demographic and economic expansion as well as the development of rival systems of political and social philosophy that formed the basis of Chinese intellectual life for the entire imperial period, which lasted from the unification of China by the Qin in 221 B.C.E. and continued until the overthrow of the Qing in 1911.

The 2,000 years of imperial Chinese history encompass great cultural change within a self-consciously continuous tradition. The first long-lasting imperial dynasty, the Han (206 B.C.E.–220 C.E.), was characterized by the development of a cultural and political orthodoxy often known as Confucianism—an attempt to create a social, political, and cosmic order on the basis of highly developed ideas of individual and social morality. The breakup of the Han was followed by a period of disunity, during which Buddhism became an important cultural force; the early part of the next unifying dynasty, the Tang (618–906 C.E.) witnessed the flourishing of a cosmopolitan culture, but its later years were marked by a partially xenophobic tendency. In the late Tang and Song (960–1280), the late imperial culture took shape; it was characterized by a bureaucratic ruling class, deriving its legitimacy from philosophical ortho-

Han

*In the People's
Republic of China,
Han culture is not
seen as intrinsically
superior, but Han
people are
considered more
advanced.*

doxy, and an economy involving an increasingly free peasantry interacting with large urban commercial, manufacturing, and administrative centers. This basic pattern was consolidated in the Ming period (1368–1644) and persisted with changes into the nineteenth century, when intensive interaction with the industrializing, expansionist Western countries led to a series of reevaluations of traditional forms and ultimately to Republican and Communist revolutions.

The overthrow of the Qing in 1911, led partly by Han ethnic nationalists, resulted in the establishment of the Republic of China. Under this banner, a series of regimes, culminating in that of the Nationalist party, or Guomindang, ruled parts of mainland China until 1949, when they retreated to the island of Taiwan, where the Nationalist party remains in power today. On the mainland of China, the Communist party, founded in 1921, gained control over the whole country in 1949, when they established the People's Republic of China and set about building a Socialist—and ultimately a Communist—society. Increasingly radical collectivist reforms culminated in the Great Leap Forward and Peoples Communes in 1958–1960, resulting in one of the largest famines in world history and in the Great Proletarian Cultural Revolution of 1966–1976. Utopian ideological and educational ideas combined with rather rigid Socialist social policy and strict Socialist economics and caused cultural stultification and economic stagnation. Beginning in 1979, the ruling Communist party initiated the Reforms, loosening the ideological grip, decollectivizing agriculture, beginning a slow transition from a planned to a market economy (by no means finished as of 1998), and expanding commercial, diplomatic, and cultural ties to foreign countries.

Both preimperial and imperial China developed in interaction with surrounding cultures. In addition to the advanced civilization in northern China, by the end of the first millennium B.C.E. there were other centers of advanced technology in southwestern China; these were linked with more distant centers in what is now Southeast Asia. The earliest historical accounts, probably written around 800 B.C.E., already refer to non-Chinese peoples inhabiting the four directions surrounding the Chinese center. Since that period, proto-Chinese and then Han culture has expanded, mainly southward and southwestward, to its present extent, through intermarriage, conquest, assimilation, and cultural interchange. It is certain that the Han people of central and southern China are partially descended from the non-

Han peoples displaced and assimilated by the Han expansion. The cultural interchange, however, has not been entirely one-way, and southern and particularly southwestern Chinese languages, customs, religion, and other cultural elements show strong signs of influence from the non-Han inhabitants either completely displaced, as in most of the Yangzi valley, or still living in contact with the Han, as in most of the southwest.

Cultural interaction on China's northern frontiers, by contrast, has involved the ecological boundary between agriculture and herding—pastoral peoples of Central Asia have not been easily displaced or assimilated into Han society and culture. Several times in Chinese history, tribal confederations to the north or northeast of China have adopted some of the bureaucratic features of the Chinese state and used these along with their considerable military skills to conquer all or part of China and establish their own imperial dynasties. The most prominent of these have been the Toba, who established the Wei dynasty (386–534 C.E.); the Khitan, who established the Liao (907–1125); the Jurchen, who established the Jin (1115–1260), the Mongols, who established the Yuan (1234–1368); and the Manchu, descendants of the Jurchen, who ruled the Qing, the last imperial dynasty, which lasted from 1644–1911. In all of these regimes, Han people played a prominent part, but in many cases the tension between an imperial ideology, which was universalistic, and a more particular ethnic ideology of Han difference contributed to the ultimate breakup of the regime.

In both the Republic and People's Republic governments, Han leaders and officials have been overwhelmingly predominant. Leaders of the Republic, although recognizing the existence of non-Han peoples within China's political borders, based much of their legitimacy on the continuing superiority of Han civilization along with the adoption of modern technology and limited modern social forms from the West. In the People's Republic, by contrast, the multiethnic nature of China is celebrated in state ritual and protected in law. Han culture is not seen as intrinsically superior, but Han people in general are considered more advanced, because they were already moving from feudalism to capitalism at the beginning of the People's Republic, whereas many non-Han minorities were still in early feudalism or even earlier stages of the historical progression of modes of production. During the Cultural Revolution (1966–1976), this meant the imposition of modern, Socialist (in reality, Han) cultural forms on non-Han peoples; since the Reforms, Han cultural hegemony has been less emphasized, but certain aspects of assimilation continue through the education system and through various schemes for economic and social development and modernization.

In Overseas Chinese communities this process is somewhat reversed; Han people who migrate undergo various degrees of cultural assimilation to the host country. In Thailand, for example, many people of Chinese origin simply become Thai after a few generations; they remember their Chinese heritage but cease to identify with Chinese as an ethnic group. In North America, where ethnic distinctions are often based on racial distinctiveness and Chinese are easily distinguishable from Euro-Americans by sight, people usually lose most of their Chinese language and culture after a few generations but retain the emotional and cognitive group ties of ethnic identity.

Settlements

In agrarian China, 80 to 90 percent of the population lived in rural areas, most of them in nucleated villages concentrated in plains and valleys. In less productive areas of northern China and in mountainous areas in the south, villages rarely exceeded a few hundred in population; in more productive rice areas in eastern and southern China, a village could contain two thousand or more people. (In much of Sichuan and a few other areas, isolated farmsteads predominated.) Before the advent of modern transport, each village was within walking distance of a standard market town, a basic-level urban center with a periodic market and one or more commercial streets with small stores and teahouses. From the standard market town, with a thousand or a few thousand people, up to the largest cities, containing several hundred thousand each, there was a hierarchy of commercial and administrative centers, each level with a larger population, more commercial activities, and more services available.

Traditional rural housing was built of tamped mud or sun-dried mud bricks in most areas, or of fired bricks for those who could afford them. House styles vary regionally; the most common general variants are houses built on two, three, or four sides of an enclosed courtyard, usually with peaked thatch, tile, or slate roofs, and multistory houses (usually of brick and often with flat roofs) built in rows along a street, with courtyards in front or in back. Both types, in higher-density arrangements, were also found in traditional cities; courtyard housing predominated in primarily residential areas and row housing, often with the store downstairs and the family quarters upstairs, in commercial areas. Wealthier families built larger and more elaborate structures on the same principles.

In recent times all these styles are still found, but in large cities most housing built since 1949 on the mainland has consisted of four-to-six story (and more recently much taller) concrete apartment blocks in which families are allocated one or more rooms. In Taiwan urban housing is also of the apartment-block type, but apartments are much larger and better appointed. Over the past 40 years or so, rural housing of mud has gradually been replaced by more substantial brick and/or concrete structures; mud houses disappeared in Taiwan in the 1970s and in some parts of the mainland in the 1980s, but in more remote and poorer parts of mainland China people are still building new mud housing.

Economy

SUBSISTENCE AND COMMERCIAL ACTIVITIES. The great commercial revolution in Chinese history occurred in the late Tang and Song periods, which saw the transformation from a basically subsistence economy to one of a peasantry firmly tied into local and long-distance trade networks. From then until the twentieth century, the great majority of the 80 to 90 percent of Han families who tilled the soil were also dependent on markets for purchase of cloth, oil, implements, furniture, condiments, alcohol (and later tobacco), and a variety of services. To obtain cash to purchase these goods and to pay taxes, they sold grain and, in some areas, commercial food and nonfood crops as well as home-produced handicrafts. By the Qing period, some areas in eastern China were given over entirely to the production of such nonfood crops as silk and cotton, and many farmers near cities grew mainly vegetables. Still, most peasants in most places continued to grow grain.

Grain agriculture was and still is predominantly onecrop, dry grains in the north and double-crop, dry grain and rice or two crops of rice in the south. Rice agriculture in particular is highly productive, and since the first green revolution in the Song period, constant improvement of varieties and intensification of effort have allowed increases in production, in surpluses, in population density, and in the commercialization of agriculture. In modern times, there has been some mechanization of agriculture as well as the expansion of irrigation to some parts of the north but in many places traditional technologies continue with little

In traditional Han rural communities people had many children; they acted affectionately toward small children although they did not lavish immense attention on them.

change other than the addition of chemical fertilizer and insecticides.

INDUSTRIAL ARTS. Chinese peasants were using the ironbladed plow in the preimperial era, and Chinese soldiers fought with iron weapons. Chinese inventors developed the three devices Francis Bacon considered to be most essential to the Age of Discovery in the West (paper, the compass, and gunpowder); during the Song dynasty Chinese engineers developed the spinning jenny and the steam engine, the invention of which is traditionally considered to have set off the Industrial Revolution in Europe. Why the Industrial Revolution did not begin in China in 1050 instead of England in 1750 is still a subject for dispute, but seems to be attributable to economic rather than technological factors.

In the late imperial period, however, Chinese invention and technology began to lag behind those of Europe and North America, and China's industrial weakness was a major factor in its humiliation by Western powers in the nineteenth and twentieth centuries. Contemporary Chinese industry is that of a developing country, derived from, and in many cases technologically and economically inferior to, the comparable industries of Japan, Western Europe, and North America. Since 1979, China has shifted from a one-sided emphasis on heavy industry to a more consumer-oriented industry and from national self-sufficiency to increased reliance on foreign trade and investment.

TRADE. Local and interregional trade were vital to the economy of late imperial China; in addition, trade and tribute formed an important part of the Ming and Qing regimes' relations with their Inner Asian and, to a lesser extent, their Southeast Asian neighbors. Because of the size of the Chinese economy, however, foreign trade has been less important overall than for many polities in both the late imperial and modern times.

Certain regions of China have subsisted heavily on trade. Coastal Guangdong and Fujian were important trading centers in the Song, Yuan, and Ming periods; much of the overseas migration of Han people was for purposes of trading; and Overseas Chinese in the nineteenth and twentieth centuries have controlled much of the commerce of Thailand, Cambodia, Malaysia, Indonesia, and the Philippines and are prominent in overseas trading from Polynesia to Japan to North and South America. Han-dominated Singapore and Hong Kong are primarily trading economies, and Taiwan, which has always had a substantial agricultural population, now derives substantial surpluses from manufactures for export.

DIVISION OF LABOR. The basic division of labor in agrarian China was set out in Confucian social philosophy: scholar-bureaucrats ranked at the top, because they provided the wisdom and knowledge to maintain the social order. Next came farmers, who produced the necessary goods; then artisans, who added value with their skills; last were merchants, who merely moved things around. By late imperial times, merchants had acquired power and influence beyond their lowly normative position, as well as the ability to convert wealth into prestige by investing in land and education. In contemporary mainland China, the basic division of labor has until very recently been that between peasants—bound to subsistence labor on the land by restrictive social policy and using traditional, human- and animal-powered technologies to grow food—and urban workers and officials, working for wages in factories or at various kinds of desk jobs. Since the 1979 Reforms this distinction has begun to break down, with much rural and increasing amounts of urban private commercial and entrepreneurial activity.

The division of labor by gender was nearly absolute in imperial China, except among the poorest classes. Women were barred from holding office and prevented by foot binding from many kinds of physical labor. They worked hard at domestic tasks, however, in all but the most elite families. These tasks included the production of textiles for home use and for sale, as well as some assistance in agricultural tasks and care of livestock. During the Republican period, women gained some forms of legal and educational equality and began to take on a limited number of professional positions, as well as being hired as low-wage industrial laborers. Foot binding basically disappeared by the 1930s, enabling women to do more kinds of work.

In Communist China, women have gained full legal equality, and the participation of women in all walks of life has been a prominent feature of propaganda, especially during the Cultural Revolution. This equality probably always existed more in theory than in practice, though, and, since the Reforms, there has been some backsliding. There is much evidence of job discrimination, but it is less overt—women are considered suitable for and do pursue just about any career in business, the professions, or the public sector, but expectations that they also manage a household and care for children have kept them from achieving equality in practice.

LAND TENURE. For the last 1,500 years, land tenure in China has involved a struggle between the tendencies of governments to allocate land administratively and the tendencies of a commerical economy to make land into a freely exchangeable commodity. In the early Tang dynasty, the equal-field system allocated land to families according to their population and their social rank; this system, which was never universal, broke down entirely by the middle of the dynasty. The early Ming emperors also advocated an in-kind rather than a cash economy and looked with disfavor on land transactions. Finally, between 1956 and 1979, the Communist party collectivized all agricultural land.

In between these government efforts at domination, land has been a marketable commodity and has tended to concentrate in the hands of landlord classes in some areas, though not in others. In the late imperial and Republican periods, most land in northern China was worked by owner-cultivators, whereas much greater proportions of the rich rice lands of the south were held by noncultivating landlords. Tenancy arrangements in these areas were of three sorts: tenants paid either a share of the crop, a fixed rent in kind, or a fixed rent in cash. In general, there does not seem to have been a strong trend toward greater or lesser concentration of land from the Ming period to the twentieth century, but the forms of tenure tended to gravitate away from more paternalistic, "feudal" forms involving personal service and patronistic protection and toward more strictly commercial forms involving cash or in-kind rents and little else.

The Communist party based much of its appeal to peasants in the 1921–1949 revolutionary struggle on a promise to eliminate the power and wealth of the exploitative landlord class. This was done in a sometimes violent program of land reform in 1949–1951 and was followed in the middle 1950s with a series of collectivization campaigns, culminating in the establishment of the large, centralized Peoples Communes in 1958. The communes were rather quickly decentralized as unworkable, however, and from 1962 to 1978 land in effect belonged to a production team—a group of twenty to forty households whose members were compensated in shares of the collective harvest by a complex system of labor points. The Reforms of 1979 involved a devolution of land rights (except for purchase and sale) and agricultural labor organization to the individual family; in effect, the prerevolutionary landlord system has been restored with the state rather than the private landlord claiming rights to part of the crop.

Marriage and Family

MARRIAGE. In late imperial China, parents or other seniors inevitably arranged their children's first marriages. Surname exogamy was absolute in most areas, and village exogamy was often, though not always, the rule.

There were four types of marriage widely practiced in late imperial times. Major marriage was a patrilocal union between a young adult woman and a young adult man; this was the normative form everywhere and the model form almost everywhere. It involved both a bride-price (some or all of which would return to the couple as an indirect dowry) and a dowry in furniture, household items, clothing, jewelry, and money, paid for partly out of the groom's family's contribution and partly out of the bride's family's own funds. In the ideal major marriage, bride and groom laid eyes on each other for the first time at their wedding ceremony; this ideal was not always observed.

Minor marriage involved the transfer of a young girl (anywhere from a few days old to 8 or 10 years old, depending on the region and the individual case) from her natal family to her prospective husband's family, where she was raised as a low-status daughter of that family and then forced into a conjugal union with her "foster brother" when she was in her late teens. This form of marriage, practiced mainly in certain parts of the south, had the advantages of avoiding costly bride-price and dowry payments and of binding the bride more closely to her husband's family. It had the disadvantages of having low prestige and often a lack of sexual attraction between the partners, especially if the bride had been brought in very young.

Uxorilocal marriage involved the transfer of a man to a woman's household and was practiced mainly in the south and in situations where a couple with no sons needed either a laborer to work their land, descendants to continue the family line, or both. In some areas, an uxorilocal son-in-law changed his surname to that of the wife's family; in others, he kept his surname, and the children were divided between the two surnames according to a prenuptial contract. In many areas of the north, uxorilocal marriage was not practiced at all; in some parts of the south and southwest, it accounted for as much as 10 to 20 percent of all unions. In the absence of uxorilocal marriage, or as a complement to it, the alternative was adoption of an agnate or, in some cases, of an unrelated boy.

Delayed-transfer marriage was practiced primarily in Guangdong, and involved a woman's re-

In late imperial China, parents or other seniors inevitably arranged their children's first marriage.

♦ **agnate**
A paternal kinsman.

maining in her natal home after her marriage, sometimes until the birth of a child and sometimes permanently. This custom was common among many non-Han peoples in the south and southwest and may have influenced Han practice in these areas. At the same time, delayed-transfer marriage was most common in areas where women had economic autonomy because of their wage-earning power in the silk industry; perhaps a combination of these factors accounts for this highly localized practice. In addition to marriage, the wealthiest Han men in the late imperial and Republican periods often took concubines, sexual partners whose status was less than that of a wife and whose children were legally children of the wife rather than of their birth mothers. Since concubines were social and sexual ornaments not expected to do domestic labor, only the richest men could consider concubinage. Multiple wives, as opposed to concubines, were not ordinarily permitted to Han men.

In late imperial times, men could remarry after the death or (rarely) divorce of a wife; widows were normatively discouraged from remarrying, but often remarried anyway because of economic straits. By law, a remarrying widow would have to leave her children with her husband's family, because they belonged to his patriline.

Reform of marriage practices has been a keystone of social reformers' programs from the late nineteenth century on. The early efforts of Republican governments were successful only among educated urban classes, but in the PRC and in contemporary Taiwan, change has been much greater. The Marriage Law of 1950 in the People's Republic prohibited underage marriage, arranged marriage, minor marriage, bride-price, and concubinage and gave women full rights to divorce. Although not all the ideals embodied in this law have become universal practice, in urban China people usually marry in their mid-twenties by mutual consent and reside virilocally, neolocally, or uxorilocally according to individual preference and availability of housing. Spartan weddings of the collectivist era have given way to lavish banquets and huge dowries, at least among those who have benefited economically from the Reforms. In rural China spouses still often depend on relatives or neighbors to introduce them, but they know each other before the wedding and can call the plans off if they do not get along. With the increased prosperity of much of the countryside, bride-price and dowry have risen dramatically since the 1970s. The prohibition against same-surname marriages seems to have disappeared.

In Taiwan, love marriage is the ideal in theory and practice, and there is little difference between urban and rural practice in that wealthy, densely networked society. Wedding banquets are lavish, and dowries include such things as cars and real estate. Marital residence, as in mainland cities, depends on individual circumstances and preferences, though there is still some pressure to reside patrilocally. Minor marriage, while not illegal, no longer exists.

DOMESTIC UNIT. The Han domestic unit was usually coterminous with the property-holding unit. Its developmental cycle was the result of the processes of virilocal marriage and family division. Sons and their wives were expected to reside with the parents until the parents' death, at which time the sons would divide their household and property. If a couple had more than one son, their household would progress from nuclear (a married couple with children, recently separated from the husband's brothers) to stem (the couple with sons, unmarried daughters, and the wife and children of one son), to joint (the couple with sons, their wives, and their children), and back to nuclear when the original couple died and their sons divided their household and property. Demographic differences, of course, meant that not every family went through all the phases of this cycle in every generation—a couple with only one son, for example, could never be the head of a joint family, and an eldest son whose own son had children while his parents were still alive would never head a nuclear family. Censuses of local communities usually show from 5 to 20 percent joint families at any one time, with the balance about equally divided between nuclear and stem families.

This familial configuration produced a constellation of alliances and rivalries. Sons, for example, often resented the absolute authority of their fathers, but cultural norms of filial devotion prevented them from expressing this resentment. Sons and their mothers, by contrast, often remained close throughout their lifetimes, making the position of the son's wife, a potential rival for her husband's affection, a very difficult one, especially in the early years of her marriage. Mother-in-law/daughter-in-law rivalry is a recurrent theme of literature and folklore. Brothers, because of their increasing loyalty to their wives, developed rivalries over the course of their adult lives, culminating in almost inevitable family division when their parents died or sometimes before.

In recent times, the developmental cycle has simplified in most cases. In urban mainland

China, the nationalization of property and housing has removed the economic hold parents once had over their adult children. The emotional ties remain, and they can be satisfied through a network of linked nuclear and stem families, who share child care, meals, and sometimes financial resources, but who do not coreside. In rural areas, collectivization of property spelled the end of joint families, but one son continues to reside with the parents after his marriage. In Taiwan many families have become geographically extended, retaining some common property rights though often scattered over a series of houses and/or flats. In addition, the rapidly declining birthrates in both areas mean that the personnel to form joint families are rarely available anymore; this trend will become even more acute in the future.

INHERITANCE. In traditional Chinese law, inheritance was equal and patrilineal. Daughters received dowry upon marriage, but at most periods this did not include land or other real property. In some areas, the eldest son received a slightly larger share than his brothers; in others, the eldest son's eldest son received a small share. In the absence of a son, a daughter inherited rather than a distant male agnate; such an heiress often married uxorilocally.

Daughters in Taiwan under the Republic now have an equal share in inheritance by law, but they usually waive this right formally when they marry. Daughters also have such a right in the People's Republic, but until very recently there has been no significant property to inherit, and little documentation is available on current practices there.

SOCIALIZATION. Little is known of socialization in earlier periods of Chinese history, but in traditional rural communities in the nineteenth and twentieth centuries people had many children; they acted affectionately toward small children although they did not lavish immense attention on them due to alternative obligations. Mothers were primary caretakers, while older sisters, grandmothers, fathers, grandfathers, and other relatives often took a secondary part. People generally indulged boys more than girls, since boys were the link to the future of the family line as well as potential sources of security in old age. Where resources were short, girls might be neglected or even killed at birth if they could not readily be adopted by a wealthier family.

When children reached the age of 7 or so, there was somewhat of a hardening of attitudes, as indulgence and care gave way to discipline, which meant learning farming or other practical skills and conventional morality for most boys, learning household skills and modesty for most girls, and learning the classical Confucian texts for boys of elite families or aspiring to be of the scholar-elite. From this age on, father-son tensions developed.

In the twentieth century, childhood has been altered in important ways by the spread of education (almost universal for a few years, at least, in mainland China in the late 1980s, and completely universal for both sexes through at least grade six or nine in Taiwan, Hong Kong, and Singapore) and by the decline in fertility. Children cannot be significant sources of labor, but they can provide hope of social mobility through educational advancement, outside of remote areas of the rural mainland. They must therefore be pushed to do well in school, but also must be afforded time to study. The decline in fertility means more attention to the individual child and also higher expectations. Mainland Chinese psychologists have recently started studies of the "little emperors and empresses" that many people think today's only children have become.

Sociopolitical Organization

POLITICAL ORGANIZATION. Throughout imperial, Republican, and Communist China, varying political philosophies have all emphasized the creation and maintenance of order by establishing benevolent authority and preserving proper relationships between superior and subordinate. At the same time, counterideologies have stressed egalitarianism, distrust of authority, and mass action. The interplay of these two themes has shaped Chinese political history for more than 2,000 years.

For the twenty-one centuries of the imperial era, the ideology of order took the form of reverence for the emperor and respect for his appointed ministers and officials. The emperor was often referred to as Tian Zi, or "Son of Heaven," indicating that he played a pivotal ritual role in ordering the relationships between the human world and the cosmos. In addition, his formal power in human society was theoretically absolute, and most emperors were active executives as well as symbolic foci.

The power and position of the emperor were both supported and circumscribed by the ideology and actions of the bureaucratic officials. Beginning in the late Tang period, the officials were primarily drawn from the gentry or literati class, a nonhereditary group whose primary economic base was landlordism and whose ideological basis of legitimacy was their knowledge of the political philosophy of the Confucian school, which emphasized government by virtuous men as the key to social order and harmony. The literati needed the emperor (otherwise they would have nowhere to serve), and the emperor needed the literati (he needed men to administer his realm), but there was always tension between them, with the literati fearing the despotic tendencies of emperors and emperors fearing the factionalism, localism, and class privilege of the literati.

The literati, or gentry, also formed a kind of hinge between the formal hierarchical structure of the bureaucracy and the kinship-, locality-, and religion-based structures of local society. Because the literati participated both as subordinates in the imperial bureaucracy and as leaders of local communities, their loyalties were divided. From the standpoint of the ordinary peasants, the literati were their neighbors and relatives and, at the same time, their landlords and often tax collectors.

In times of prosperity, this system was relatively stable, due at least partly to the system of civil-service examinations, in which almost all males were eligible to participate, and to the free market in land, which allowed economic as well as political status mobility. But when corruption, mismanagement, natural disaster, foreign invasions, or other destabilizing factors were introduced, the links between emperor and literati and between literati and peasant became strained and eventually the regime was unable to restore order, causing periods of chaos and eventually the overthrow of the dynasty and its replacement by a new and vigorous ruling house. In these periods of interdynastic turmoil, counterideologies, such as those held by Buddhist and Daoist millennarian sects, successfully challenged the imperial orthodoxy for a while but eventually retreated when a new regime was consolidated. This dynastic cycle repeated itself every few centuries over the imperial era.

In the nineteenth century, however, this political system was fundamentally altered in response to the threat posed by European and U.S. colonial and imperialist expansion. After China was forced to sign a series of unequal treaties with the Western powers, Chinese intellectuals were forced to reevaluate their political institutions and increasingly found them wanting as responses to the advance of world capitalism. Socialism, anarchism, militarism, liberal democracy, and finally Marxism all gained their advocates in the late nineteenth and early twentieth centuries.

The political ideology of the Republic was an amalgam of traditional ideas and Western concepts of socialism and democracy; neither of these, however, was realized, and the government became more conservative in the 1930s and 1940s as its rivalry with the Communist party increased, culminating in the 1949 establishment of the People's Republic. That Communist government bases its ideology on the Marxist ideas of class struggle and of the proletariat as a vanguard class; it implemented its programs through a combination of all-pervasive propaganda and a party-state political organization that penetrated every village, factory, and neighborhood in the country.

Initially, the Communist party in power followed a course of Socialist development based on the earlier Soviet experience, but Mao Zedong's impatience with the slowness of orderly Socialist development led to radical, voluntarist politics of mass movements in the Great Leap Forward and the Cultural Revolution. Especially in the latter period, the party and state organizations themselves became targets of populist propaganda and mass action, and orderly development was shunted aside in favor of voluntarist fervor. With the Reforms of 1979, however, the party retreated both from its mass-action mode of operation and from its immediate Socialist goals. China has increasingly become a conventional one-party bureaucratic state, interested more in furthering economic growth and suppressing dissent than in directing the lives of the populace in much detail.

SOCIAL CONTROL AND CONFLICT. Traditional Chinese political philosophy emphasized the avoidance of conflict and the creation of social harmony by rule of an elite of morally cultivated scholars. Law and litigation were considered backup measures applicable only in the partial breakdown of moral government and society. Disputes ought ideally to be settled locally by lineages, villages, guilds, and other unofficial organizations, and were only supposed to come before the courts when local settlement failed. Nevertheless, Chinese magistrates were often overwhelmed with litigation, and legal codes were in fact highly developed.

Both the Republican and People's Republic governments have adapted European-derived notions of law and legality, but in neither case have these entirely superseded the earlier ideas and institutions of rule by virtuous officials. Especially in the People's Republic, most disputes are mediated by semiofficial mediation committees or by local officials, and neither legal codes nor procedures are highly developed.

Many Han people are reluctant to enter disputes and will go to great lengths of politeness and accommodation to avoid conflict. When conflict does begin, it is often difficult to stop. Most people are worried about maintaining face, or the feeling that one is respected by the community, and losing a legal dispute threatens loss of face as much as it threatens loss of money, land, or other material goods. For this reason, avoidance of conflict and persistence in conflict both continue to be features of Han culture.

Religion and Expressive Culture

RELIGIOUS BELIEFS AND PRACTICES. Han religion is conveniently, though oversimplistically, divided into three elite, literate traditions—State Religion, Daoism, and Buddhism; a series of folk beliefs and practices that varies widely in regional detail but contains a common substratum; and the beliefs and practices of various syncretic sects. None of these religious traditions is completely independent of any of the others, and with the exception of the sects, adherents of one tradition rarely reject or oppose the others.

Han folk religion is centered around the efforts of individuals and communities to create and maintain harmony in relationships between the human and the cosmic order. The soul is a necessary complement to the body in forming a whole person; as the physiology of the body must harmonize internally and with the external environment, the soul must harmonize with cosmic forces of time and space. If the soul leaves the body unintentionally, listlessness, madness, and eventually death can result, but the soul can intentionally leave the body in mediumistic séance, to be replaced by a deity, or in shamanistic travel to the realms of the dead. Upon death, the soul disperses to the Earth, where it remains in the bones, to the realm of the dead, where it takes up an existence roughly similar to that on Earth, and to the

---

KINSHIP

Kin Groups and Descent

Han people have had patrilineal kin groups since the period of the earliest written history, and a hierarchical arrangement of clans was the basis of stratification in the feudal order of the Shang and Zhou periods. Nothing is known about the kin group organization of the nonruling classes before the Song period.

In the Song period, the Chinese patrilineage as we now know it began to appear. The core of this type of lineage includes all male descendants of a founding ancestor; women tend to become more attached as they grow older to their husbands' and sons' lineages and to relinquish their minor roles as sisters and daughters of their natal lineages.

Han lineages, until very recent times, have been rigorously exogamous (even a common surname was enough to prohibit marriage in the late imperial period), and with patrilocal marital residence this resulted in lineage villages or even lineage districts populated almost entirely by members of a single lineage. Particularly in the core areas of southern and eastern China, where agriculture and commerce were most developed, lineages often held large amounts of land collectively, using the income from tenant rents to fund ritual, educational, and sometimes even military activities. Such wealthy lineages often contained corporate, property-holding, sublineages within them, and a large lineage of 10,000 or more members might have ten or more genealogical levels of property-holding segments. Such lineages were highly stratified internally, often containing both scholar officials and ordinary peasants.

The importance of lineages varied greatly by region and locally, however, and probably only a minority of Han people in the late imperial period were members of a large, powerful lineage; indeed, many were not members of any lineage at all. In the overall social structure, lineages were one important kind of corporation, but they might be locally eclipsed by local, occupational, ethnic, or sectarian organizations.

The new government effectively destroyed the power bases of lineages when they confiscated all lineage-held land in the Land Reform and replaced lineage-based local governments with structures responsible to the party. But lineages remained localized during the collectivist period, and, since the 1979 Reforms, lineages have returned in some areas to the local scene in limited ways, sponsoring ritual and other activities and becoming the focus of local loyalties.

Kinship Terminology

Kinship terminology reflects the patrilineal bias of kinship relations. Agnatic cousins are partially equated with siblings and distinguished from both cross cousins and matrilateral parallel cousins, who are ordinarily not distinguished from each other. Some Chinese kin terminology systems display Omaha features, such as the equation of mother's brother with wife's brother with son's wife's brother. The most important distinction is between elder and younger relatives; elder relatives are always addressed with a kin term, whereas younger relatives are addressed by name. Rural people in some areas use kin terms to address people of a senior generation who are not relatives.

wooden or paper spirit tablet where people worship it as an ancestor.

Like society, the cosmos has an ideal order, represented by the relationships of time and space. Every person, through the soul, is part of this order, and it is prudent to maintain a position that is harmonious with the order. To do so, people harmonize important actions in time by consulting specialist horoscope readers or widely available almanacs; they harmonize their use of space by consulting geomancers, specialists in the harmonious siting of houses, public buildings, and especially graves—where the bones must be placed in a site and a direction that will preserve harmony between soul and environment and bring good fortune to descendants.

In addition to living humans, the cosmos is inhabited by purely spiritual beings, souls without bodies, which are of three kinds. Ancestors are the souls of agnatic forebears, worshiped at graves and in tablets with daily incense and food offerings on holidays. They are ordinarily benign beings and will harm their descendants only if neglected or insulted. Ghosts are the souls of people who are angry at having died an unnatural death or being without descendants; they are malicious and capricious—dangerous particularly to children. People propitiate them on regular occasions and when they have cause to expect ghostly attack. Gods are the souls of people who have lived particularly meritorious lives and have retained spiritual power that they can use to benefit worshipers. People worship them at home and in temples; specific gods are often patrons to particular neighborhoods, villages, cities, guilds, or even social clubs, and the yearly religious ritual to a community's god is one of its most important occasions.

This folk religion has, over the years, absorbed and assimilated elements from the State Religion, Daoism, and Buddhism. Folk religion is not an independent system, since specialists trained in one or another of the elite traditions are necessary to carry out many rituals on behalf of folk believers. Magistrates and officials up to the emperor performed rituals for harmony that would prevent natural and human disasters; Buddhist monks and Daoist priests performed exorcisms, funerals, soul-retrievals, and healing rituals. Yet each of the elite traditions also has its literary, specialist side, engaged in only by the specialist practitioners or literate lay adherents.

State Religion was the ritual basis of the imperial regime, the site of the emperor's and the officials' cosmic ordering functions. In postimperial times, it has largely been supplanted by the secular rituals of the Republican and Communist regimes, though adulation and worship of Mao Zedong, particularly during the Cultural Revolution, amounted to a sort of deification.

Daoism is still an active force in China. Beginning from the late Zhou period, Daoism developed both as a philosophy of living in harmony with nature and as a system of esoteric rituals designed to confer personal immortality, cure disease, and superimpose a superior, eternal order of unchanging life on the earthly order of daily and seasonal change, life and death, growth and decay. The priests of this latter tradition were important in the development of science and medicine in imperial China, though their actions seem at odds with the natural harmony practices advocated by the philosophical Daoists.

Buddhism was introduced to China from India beginning in the early centuries of the Common Era and by Tang times was firmly established as one of the primary religions of China. Chinese Buddhist monks went on to develop some of the most sophisticated Mahayanist philosophies, some of which spread to Japan and Korea as well. Mahayana Buddhism combines the original Buddhist goals of realization of the transitoriness of material existence with a posited cosmology of myriad Buddhas and bodhisattvas (Buddhas-to-be) who are potential helpers of those who believe. The Buddhist tradition in China thus afforded its adherents everything from a sophisticated system of philosophy and psychology, to the opportunity for monastic meditative practice toward the goal of relief from existence, to help from Buddhist divinities enshrined in local temples. Over the last thousand years, many Buddhist and Daoist divinities, beliefs, and practices were absorbed into the folk religion, so that bodhisattvas function as local gods, for example, and Buddhist monks are as likely as Daoist priests to perform funerals, exorcisms, and other rites for the common people.

Sectarian traditions emerged periodically in Chinese history; by late imperial times most sectarian groups held a syncretic series of beliefs taken from Daoism, folk religion, the official tradition, and particularly from the Maitreya (Buddha of the Future) tradition of Mahayana Buddhism. Exclusivist in their membership, often secret in their activities, many sects fomented millennarian uprisings, especially at times of dynastic turmoil and decline. Other sects were quietistic, striving for personal salvation rather than social revolution. Because of their exclusivist practices and their intermittent advocacy of violent social change, imperial, Republican, and Communist governments have all persecuted the sectarians, but they have reemerged after the Reforms in mainland China, and draw a large following in Taiwan, where they have entered a quietistic phase and currently pose little threat to the sociopolitical order.

Foreign religions other than Buddhism have historically had limited appeal to Han people. Islam has been present in China for over a thousand years, and there are Muslims throughout the northwest and in most cities of China. Muslims, however, are not considered Han in mainland China; they are given the separate ethnic designation of Hui. There was a Jewish community at Kaifeng in Henan for several hundred years; its members were largely assimilated by the late nineteenth century. Christian missionaries have proselytized in China intermittently since the Tang period; their most recent period of intense activity in the late nineteenth and early twentieth centuries produced perhaps 4 million converts to both Protestant and Catholic Christian churches—suppressed in the Cultural Revolution, they are reviving in the Reform period. But Christians remain a tiny minority of Han people, probably no more than 10 million converts and adherents.

During the most radical periods of the People's Republic, all Han religion was suppressed, and very little activity went on. Since the Reforms, folk religion in particular has revived in many areas, particularly in the south and southeast, with many temples rebuilt and traditional funerals and other rituals quite common. A certain number of Buddhist monasteries and Daoist temples have been allowed to reopen, but it seems unlikely that the elite practitioners of either of these traditions will soon regain their former numbers or prominence.

ARTS. Early Chinese literature consists primarily of historical and philosophical prose as well as various kinds of poetry. The earliest extant poems, probably transcriptions of folk songs, date from the eighth century B.C.E.; since then there is an unbroken tradition of poetry both as a folk form and as a gentlemanly literary endeavor. In classical poetry, lyric and narrative forms are both found, but the epitome of the tradition is the short lyric on the themes of nature, the transience of life, or male friendship.

Fiction is a rather late entrant to Chinese literature, with the earliest extant stories written in a semivernacular style in the Tang period. In the late imperial period, the multivolume episodic novel, written in vernacular style, gained great popularity; its themes range from historical romance to Buddhist fantasy to psychological family chronicle. Fiction and political essays, now written entirely in the vernacular or baihua, have been the primary genres in the postimperial period.

Painting has been preeminent among the visual arts. The earliest extant paintings reside on the walls of Buddhist temples and caves; painting on paper or silk survives from as early as the Song period. The two major traditions of classical painting were the court tradition, depicting urban or rural scenes in meticulous detail, along with portraiture, and the literati tradition of more suggestive and evocative landscapes and still lifes. In recent times, Chinese painters have pursued a mix of traditional literati styles, adaptations of Western oils and other media, and systematization of folk styles. Communist attempts to institute Stalinist-style Socialist Realism in arts and literature have been largely abandoned by serious artists in the Reform period.

Along with painting goes calligraphy, an art engaged in by almost all literati in the imperial period and still widely learned and practiced today. Not only professional artists but also political leaders and other prominent persons are asked to inscribe their characters on important public buildings and monuments, and good calligraphy is still universally admired.

Other visual arts have not been accorded the same status as painting or calligraphy, but the works, usually by anonymous artists, show every bit as much skill and style. Wood carving, jade and other stone carving, and the architecture of palaces, private homes, and gardens are all highly sophisticated.

MEDICINE. For more than 2,000 years Han people developed a complex system of medical theory based on humoral balance and imbalance, and a series of diagnostic and therapeutic modes used to maintain and restore such balances. Diagnosis is primarily by history taking and a complex system of twelve or twenty-four different pulses; therapeutic modes include the administration of humorally active medicines orally and topically as well as the stimulation of a series of surface points with needles (acupuncture) or burning moxa (moxibustion). Practitioners of this tradition included both professionals and literati-amateurs, and they developed an extensive literature of manuals and pharmacopoeias.

In twentieth-century China there have been ongoing debates over the scientific validity and

For more than 2,000 years Han people developed a complex system of medical theory based on humoral balance and imbalance, and a series of diagnostic and therapeutic modes.

practical utility of this tradition and whether it still has a place in a world dominated by Western allopathic medicine. At present, traditional Chinese medicine is still practiced in mainland China, and there are special medical schools to train Chinese doctors. There is also considerable research on the biochemistry and physiology of traditional pharmaceuticals and point-stimulating procedures. In recent years as well, acupuncture has received attention and respect in Western countries, and several states in the United States now regulate its practice and license its practitioners.

At the same time, allopathic medicine is now the dominant form of practice in both the mainland and Taiwan. More important than clinical practice, however, have been the extensive public-health measures taken by the Japanese colonial and Republican governments in Taiwan and by the People's Republic on the mainland; these have brought the morbidity and mortality patterns of both Chinese areas close to those of the industrialized nations.

Bibliography

Ebrey, Patricia Buckley (1981). *Chinese Civilization and Society: A Sourcebook*. New York: Free Press.

Huang Shu-min (1989). *The Spiral Road: Changes in a Chinese Village through the Eyes of a Communist Party Leader*. Boulder, Colo.: Westview Press.

Naquin, Susan, and Evelyn Rawski (1987). *Chinese Society in the Eighteenth Century*. New Haven: Yale University Press.

Norman, Jerry (1988). *Chinese*. Cambridge: Cambridge University Press.

Skinner, G. William (1985). "Presidential Address: The Structure of Chinese History." *Journal of Asian Studies* 44:271–292.

Spence, Jonathan D. (1990). *The Search for Modern China*. New York and London: Norton.

Wolf, Arthur P., and Chieh-shan Huang (1980). *Marriage and Adoption in China*. Stanford, Calif.: Stanford University Press.

—STEVAN HARRELL

MIAO

Ethonyms: Bai Miao (White), Cowrie Shell Miao, Hei Miao (Black), Hmong, Hua Miao (Flowery), Hung Miao (Red), Magpie Miao, Qing Miao (Blue/Green)

Orientation

IDENTIFICATION. The various Miao groups are for the most part an unstratified agricultural people found in the uplands of several provinces of China and related to the Hmong of Southeast Asia. They are distinguished by language, dress, historical traditions, and cultural practice from neighboring ethnic groups and the dominant Han Chinese. They are not culturally homogeneous and the differences between local Miao cultures are often as great as between Miao and non-Miao neighbors. The term "Miao" is Chinese, and means "weeds" or "sprouts." Chinese minority policies since the 1950s treat these diverse groups as a single nationality and associate them with the San Miao Kingdom of central China mentioned in histories of the Han dynasty (200 B.C.–A.D. 200).

LOCATION. About half of China's Miao are located in Guizhou Province. Another 34 percent are evenly divided between Yunnan Province and western Hunan Province. The remainder are mainly found in Sichuan and Guangxi, with a small number in Guangdong and Hainan. Some of the latter may have been resettled there during the Qing dynasty. The wide dispersion makes it difficult to generalize about ecological settings. Miao settlements are found anywhere from a few hundred meters above sea level to elevations of 1,400 meters or more. The largest number are uplands people, often living at elevations over 1,200 meters and located at some distance from urban centers or the lowlands and river valleys where the Han are concentrated. Often, these upland villages and hamlets are interspersed with those of other minorities such as Yao, Dong, Zhuang, Yi, Hui, and Bouyei. Most live in the fourteen autonomous prefectures and counties designated as Miao or part-Miao. Among the largest of these are the Qiandongnan Miao-Dong Autonomous Prefecture and Qiannan Bouyei-Miao Autonomous Prefecture established in Guizhou in 1956, the Wenshan Zhuang-Miao Autonomous Prefecture of Yunnan established in 1958, and the Chengbu Miao Autonomous Country in Hunan organized in 1956. In addition, there are Miao present in at least ten other autonomous units where they are a minority among the minorities. Some Miao villages are within *minzuxiang* (minority townships), in areas that have a high concentration of minority peoples but not autonomous status, as is the case in Zhaotong Prefecture in northeastern Yunnan.

DEMOGRAPHY. The 1990 census reports a population of 7,398,677 Miao. This is an increase of almost 47 percent over the 1982 census figure of 5,036,377. Some of the growth is due to natural increase (as of 1990 the Miao were not limited to one or two children) and some to the recognition of additional population as Miao and better census procedures.

LINGUISTIC AFFILIATION. According to Chinese language classification, the Miao languages belong to the Miao-Yao Branch of Sino-Tibetan. Officially, these languages are termed *fangyin* (dialects) although they are not mutually intelligible. There are at least three main languages, further divisible into distinct and separate sublanguages or dialects of varying degrees of closeness. The Miao languages are tonal. Xiangxi, spoken in western Hunan by close to one million speakers, is associated with the Red Miao. It is comprised of two sublanguages. The larger of the two has been taken as standard and given a romanization for school texts and other local publications. The Qiandong language of central and eastern Guizhou is associated with the Black Miao. It has three major subdivisions. The most widespread of the three has well over a million speakers, and is taken as the official standard. The others, with a half million speakers each, are regarded as dialects and, as of this writing, have no official recognition. The Chuanqiandian languages are spoken by White, Flowery, and Blue Miao. There are at least seven major subdivisions, each further divided into a number of local dialects. At present only Chuanqiandianci (White Miao) and Diandongbei (Hua Miao) are officially recognized. Both of these formerly used a phonetic script, introduced by missionaries at the turn of the century. The script has been supplanted by a government-introduced romanization. In addition there are some eight additional fangyin, with several thousand speakers each, which do not fit into any of the major categories. Most of the Miao in Hainan are Yao speakers, and some Miao elsewhere speak only Dong or Chinese.

History and Cultural Relations

Chinese scholarship links the present-day Miao to tribal confederations that moved southward some 2,000 years ago from the plain between the Yellow River and the Yangtze toward the Dongting Lake area. These became the San Miao mentioned in Han dynasty texts. Over the next thousand years, between the Han and the Song dynasties, these presumed ancestors of the Miao continued to migrate westward and southward, under pressure from expanding Han populations and the imperial armies. Chinese texts and Miao oral history establish that over those years the ancestors settled in western Hunan and Guizhou, with some moving south into Guangxi or west along the Wu River to southeastern Sichuan and into Yunnan. The period was marked by a number of uprisings and battles between Miao and the Han or local indigenous groups, recalled in the oral histories of local groups. Though the term "Miao" was sometimes used in Tang and Song histories, the more usual term was "Man," meaning "barbarians." Migration continued through the Yuan, Ming, and early Qing, with some groups moving into mainland Southeast Asia. The retreat from Han control brought some into territories controlled by the Yi in northeast Yunnan/northwest Guizhou. The various migrations can also be seen as "vertical" migrations into the undeveloped hillside and mountain areas that were of lesser interest to Han. Depending on the terrain, the settled farming cited in Miao historical myths gave way to shifting slash-and-burn agriculture, facilitated by the introduction of the Irish potato and maize in the sixteenth century, and the adoption of high-altitude/cool-weather crops like barley, buckwheat, and oats. Farming was supplemented by forest hunting, fishing, gathering, and pastoralism. During the Qing, uprisings and military encounters escalated. There were major disturbances in western Hunan (1795–1806) and a continuous series of rebellions in Guizhou (1854–1872). Chinese policies toward the Miao shifted among assimilation, containment in "stockaded villages," dispersal, removal, and extermination. The frequent threat of "Miao rebellion" caused considerable anxiety to the state; in actuality, many of these uprisings included Bouyei, Dong, Hui, and other ethnic groups, including Han settlers and demobilized soldiers. At issue were heavy taxation, rising landlordism, rivalries over local resources, and official corruption. One of the last Miao uprisings occurred in 1936 in western Hunan in opposition to Guomindang (Republican) continuation of the *tuntian* system, which forced the peasants to open up new lands and grow crops for the state.

From Song on, in periods of relative peace, government control was exercised through the *tusi* system of indirect rule by appointed native headmen who collected taxes, organized corvée, and kept the peace. Miao filled this role in Hunan and eastern Guizhou, but farther west the rulers were often drawn from a hereditary Yi nobility, a system that lasted into the twentieth century. In Guizhou, some tusi claimed Han ancestry, but were probably drawn from the ranks of assimilated Bouyei, Dong, and Miao. Government documents refer to the "Sheng Miao" (raw Miao), meaning those living in areas beyond government

Throughout the Republican period, the government favored a policy of assimilation for the Miao and strongly discouraged expressions of ethnicity.

control and not paying taxes or labor service to the state. In the sixteenth century, in the more pacified areas, the implementation of the policy of *gaitu guiliu* began the replacement of native rulers with regular civilian and military officials, a few of whom were drawn from assimilated minority families. Land became a commodity, creating both landlords and some freeholding peasants in the areas affected. In the Yunnan-Guizhou border area, the tusi system continued and Miao purchase of land and participation in local markets was restricted by law until the Republican period (1911–1949).

Throughout the Republican period, the government favored a policy of assimilation for the Miao and strongly discouraged expressions of ethnicity. Southwestern China came under Communist government control by 1951, and Miao participated in land reform, collectivization, and the various national political campaigns. In the autonomous areas created beginning in 1952, the Miao were encouraged to revive and elaborate their costumes, music, and dance, while shedding "superstitious" or "harmful" customs. Some new technology and scientific knowledge was introduced, along with modern medicine and schooling. The Miao suffered considerably during the Cultural Revolution years, when expressions of ethnicity were again discouraged, but since 1979 the Miao have been promoted in the media and the government has encouraged tourism to the Miao areas of eastern and central Guizhou.

Settlements

At higher elevations, as on the plateau straddling Guizhou and Yunnan, settlements are rarely larger than twenty households. An average village in central Guizhou might have 35 or 40 households, while in Qiandongnan villages of 80 to 130 families are common, and a few settlements have close to 1,000 households. Villages are compact, with some cleared space in front of the houses, and footpaths. In some areas houses are of wood, raised off the ground, and with an additional sleeping and storage loft under a thatched or tiled roof. Elsewhere they are single-story buildings made of tamped earth or stone depending on local conditions. Windows are a recent introduction. Animals are now kept in outbuildings; in the past they were sheltered under the raised house or kept inside. Many settlements are marked by a grove of trees, where religious ceremonies are held.

**MIAO
CRAFTSWOMAN**

A Miao woman embroidering. The Miao are known for the complexity and sophistication of their weaving, embroidery, and brocade and batik work, though little of it is marketed. Kaili, Guizhou, China. (Keren Su/Corbis)

Economy

SUBSISTENCE AND COMMERCIAL ACTIVITIES. Economic strategies vary. The Hua Miao were shifting-swidden agriculturalists, growing buckwheat, oats, corn, potatoes, and hemp, and using a simple wooden hand plow or hoe. Sheep and goats were fed on nearby pasture land. Additionally the Hua Miao hunted with crossbow and poisoned arrows and gathered foodstuffs in the forests. In parts of Guizhou, the Miao more closely resembled their Han neighbors in their economic strategies as well as in their technology (the bullock-drawn plow, harrowing, use of animal and human wastes as fertilizer). The Cowrie Shell Miao in central Guizhou were settled farmers growing rice in flooded fields, and also raising millet, wheat, beans, vegetables, and tobacco. Their livestock was limited to barnyard pigs and poultry, with hunting and gathering playing a very minor role. Some of the Black Miao in southeast Guizhou combine intensive irrigated terrace farming of rice with dry-field upland cropping.

INDUSTRIAL ARTS. Women continue to spin and weave cotton, hemp, ramie, and wool for home use, and to produce garments with elaborate batik and embroidered designs that vary by area and dialect and serve as subethnic markers. Complex silver necklaces, bracelets, earrings, and headdresses are a well-developed craft specialty for men and again are closely associated with ethnicity. They are not usually sold outside the local Miao community. Carpenters, basket makers and blacksmiths can be found among some Miao groups.

TRADE. No Miao communities are self-sufficient. All depend on the market for pottery, salt, processed foods, and various daily necessities. In Guizhou there is great demand for silver for making jewelry. What the Miao have to sell varies greatly by area. The Hua Miao market wool, hides, sheep and goats, wild game, firewood, and a variety of forest products. The Cowrie Shell Miao market agricultural produce, poultry and pigs, bamboo shoots, and home-crafted grass raincoats and sandals. Different areas have their specialties, such as cattle, horses, bamboo baskets, and herbal medicines. Before 1949, some Miao sold opium, but more often poppy growing and production of raw opium was the required rent for cropland and the profits went to the landlord and middlemen. Very few Miao were full-time merchants or traders.

DIVISION OF LABOR. Both sexes engage in agriculture, care of livestock, and fishing, and men contribute some labor to domestic chores like cooking, gathering firewood, and child care. Men are expected to do the heaviest work, including plowing. Women sometimes participated on short hunting trips, but trips of several days or several weeks were undertaken by groups of men; hunting trips are now illegal. Labor exchange and cooperation between households was common even before collectivization.

LAND TENURE. Prior to the 1950s land reform, some Miao were smallholders. Many, if not most, were tenants on lands owned by Han, Yi, Hui, and others. Few were true landlords, and most who rented out land were likely to work part of their holdings themselves with family labor. All land is now owned by the state, including undeveloped mountain and forest lands, thus limiting any expansion beyond lands officially assigned to an individual or village. In the process, pastoralism and forest hunting/gathering have been reduced. Before land reform, some Miao areas followed the practice of lineage or hamlet ownership of mountain and hillside lands even where some private holdings existed. People could open new lands for farming and settlement, share village pastures, or hunt away from their home area.

Kinship

Generally, Miao have been pressured to take Chinese surnames, which are transmitted patrilineally. Descent is said to be patrilineal, and in some places the Han patrilineage form has been adopted. However, matrilineal kin are important in some areas. In practice, there is strong evidence that the system is bilateral. No serious comparative study of kin terms and lineage organization is yet available, and some of the writings on the subject suggest Miao politeness in telling Han investigators what they want to hear.

Marriage and Family

MARRIAGE. Marriages generally require parental consent but are based on mutual attraction and choice. In the past, many communities had "youth houses" where unmarried young people could gather. Groups of young men traveled around to court girls in other villages. In the absence of parental consent, elopement was an alternative. Festivals and trips to periodic markets still provide an opportunity for young people to meet, engage in antiphonal singing and dancing, and establish new friendships. Since the 1950s, travel restrictions and state disapproval of premarital sexual behavior has increased the parental role in marriage arrangement. Marriages are monoga-

Miao have often been pressured to take Chinese surnames, which are transmitted patrilineally.

mous. Marriage outside the dialect or language group is rare. Divorce and remarriages are permitted. Postmarital residence is usually in the man's home village but only the youngest son lives with his parents after his marriage, and in instances where there are no sons a family may bring in a son-in-law or an aged widow or widower might join her married daughter's household. In some areas, there is delayed transfer of the bride until after the birth of her first child, or the practice of starting out with residence with the bride's family.

DOMESTIC UNIT. The two-generation nuclear family is statistically the most common. Relations between spouses, and between parents and children, are more egalitarian than among the Han. Economic, social, and ritual ties are retained with natal kin. Visiting kinsfolk are welcome guests, and may come for extended visits.

INHERITANCE. At marriage, sons and daughters receive property and assistance in building a new house. Marriage portions previously included livestock as well as household goods, tools, jewelry, and cloth. The youngest son and his descendants inherit the parental house and remaining wealth. A couple without sons will live with a daughter, who stands as heir.

SOCIALIZATION. Both parents are involved in child rearing. Verbal skills and work skills are valued. Children are expected to assist with work tasks from an early age. Some tasks, such as gathering firewood or caring for livestock, are not gender-linked, and both sexes are encouraged to take responsibility and act independantly. Mothers teach their daughters to spin and weave and to do batik and embroidery, and sons learn hunting skills from their fathers. Since the 1950s, most boys and some girls attend primary school. Relatively few continue on to middle school since this usually involves boarding schools far from their home communities.

Sociopolitical Organization

SOCIAL ORGANIZATION. Given the long period of Chinese rule, it is not possible to reconstruct precontact organization, though some areas still retain older lineage and clan names. Owing to dispersion, population decimation, and frequent migration, the multisurname settlement seems to be the most common. Villages do not seem to have been formally linked by any kind of tribal organization. There was little class differentiation in the villages, and no formal political structure. Respected knowledgeable elders, heads of family groups, and religious experts of both genders served as informal leaders. Among the more Sini-

cized, landlords and those who had some literacy in Chinese exercised power in the community. Under the present system, those who are members of the Communist party stand as the official leaders of the community.

Religion and Expressive Culture

RELIGIOUS BELIEFS. Religious beliefs and activities vary by locale and subethnic identity. The situation is further complicated by partial adoption of elements of folk Daoism and Buddhism, or by conversion to Christianity (as among segments of the White and Flowery Miao). Traditional religious beliefs concern powerful suprahuman forces associated with sacred groves, stones, caves, and other natural phenomena, as well as with bridges and wells. Other protective spirits guard the household and hamlet. The latter are sometimes thought of as dragons. It is believed that at death, the soul divides into three parts, one of which returns to protect the household as an ancestral spirit. There is also concern with evil spirits and with ghosts of those who died bad deaths and who may cause illness and misfortune. Religious beliefs are supported by a complex series of sung or chanted poetic myths, which treat the creation of the universe, the doings of divine beings and culture heroes, and early Miao history.

RELIGIOUS PRACTITIONERS. Most religious ritual is performed or guided by various part-time specialists who act as priests, diviners, or shamans for the local community or for kin groups. Most of them are males. They engage in ordinary work, and only the most important religious activities require them to don special items of dress and decoration to mark them from others. There are no written texts for learning the chants, songs, dances, and rituals: they are memorized. If called by a family, specialists receive a small payment (often in foodstuffs) for their assistance. Shamans play a key role at funerals and postburial rites. They are also involved in analysis and healing of illness: some are skilled in herbal medicine as well as ritual procedures. Shamans also provide explanations of the possible causes of misfortune and can provide protective amulets. Ceremonies on behalf of the village community or a gathering of kin from several villages are conducted by skilled male elders who function as priests, following ritual procedures, administering the necessary animal and food sacrifices, and chanting the songs and myths without going into trance or communicating directly with the supernaturals and spirits. Some ceremonies are led by the male head of household on behalf of his immediate family.

CEREMONIES. The calendrical year holds a number of set ceremonies that vary from group to group in content, purpose, and timing. For example, some groups now celebrate the lunar New Year along with their Han neighbors, whereas others celebrate the year's start in the tenth lunar month, following the harvest, and mark it with bullfights and cattle sacrifices. Others mark the New Year with cockfights or sacrifice of pigs and chickens, or intervillage assemblages enlivened by antiphonal singing, dancing, and the playing of the *lusheng*. Among the important festivals found in many (not all) Miao communities are the Dragon Boat Festival, which is synchronic with the Han festivities to a large extent, and the Mountain Flower festivals, which were an important institution for bringing together marriageable young people from different hamlets. The Drum Society festivals are held by dispersed kin groups to honor their ancestors every seven, ten, or twelve years, and are not strictly tied to the calendar. Most festivals involve the lavish offering of animal sacrifices, and for this reason the state has discouraged them.

ARTS. The Miao are well known for the complexity, sophistication, and variety of their weaving, embroidery, and brocade and batik work, though little of it is commodified. Their elaborate silver jewelry is also famous. There is a rich heritage of oral literature (myths, history, tales, and songs). The ability to play the lusheng or other instruments and to sing and improvise songs is highly prized. Generally the Miao do not have graphic arts: the absence of god figures or painting of supernatural beings is a deliberate internal marker that differentiates them from Han and some neighboring groups.

MEDICINE. Aside from the shaman's extensive knowledge, ordinary persons also have some knowledge of plants and other materials that have healing properties. The Chinese invert this by claiming that Miao women engage in magical poisoning (gu), but all evidence suggests this is a Han myth rather than Miao practice. Divination and exorcism of ghosts and evil spirits are also a part of healing.

DEATH AND AFTERLIFE. The human soul is comprised of three parts. After death, one resides at the grave; another must be led safely through the journey to the other world where it rejoins the ancestors, and the third must be led safely back home where it serves as a protective ancestral spirit to the living. Thus, burial and postmortuary rituals require the skills and knowledge of a shaman to lead the mourners in ritual and perform the necessary sequence of ceremonies.

Bibliography

Bai Ziran, ed. (1988). *A Happy People: The Miaos*. Beijing: Foreign Languages Press.

Fan Yumei, et al., eds. (1987). *Zhongguo shaoshu minzu fengqinglu* (Customs of China's national minorities). Chengdu: Sichuan Nationalities Press.

Mickey, Margaret P. (1947). *The Cowrie Shell Miao of Kweichow*. Peabody Museum Papers, vol. 32, no. 1. Cambridge, Mass.

National Minorities Commission, Guizhou Provincial Editorial Group, ed. (1986–1987). *Miaozu shehui lishi diaocha* (Research on the society and history of the Miao). 3 vols. Guiyang: Guizhou Peoples Press.

National Minorities Commission, Yunnan Provincial Editorial Group, and Li Zhaolun, eds. (1982). *Yunnan Miaozu Yaozu shehui lishi diaocha* (Research on the society and history of the Yunnan Miao and Yao). Kunming: Yunnan Nationalities Press.

Schein, Louisa (1989). "The Dynamics of Cultural Revival among the Miao in Guizhou." In *Ethnicity and Ethnic Groups in China*, edited by Chiao Chien and Nicholas Tapp. Hong Kong: Chinese University Press.

Wu Xinfu (1990). "Lun Miaozu lishishang de sici de da qianxi" (On the four great migrations in Miao history). *Minzu Yanjiu* 6:103–111.

—NORMA DIAMOND

Traditional Miao religious beliefs concern powerful suprahuman forces associated with sacred groves, stones, caves, and other natural phenomena, as well as with bridges and wells.

MONGOLS

Ethonyms: Menggu (in Chinese), Monggol (in Mongolian)

Orientation

IDENTIFICATION. Mongols live in a number of different countries. The Siberian Buriats and the Kalmuk Oirats on the Volga reside in the Russian Federation; the Barga, Khiangan, Juu Ud, Khorchin or Jirem, Chakhar, Shiliingol, Alshaa, Ordos, Tumed, Daurs, and a small community of Buriat Mongols live in the Inner Mongolian Autonomous Region (IMAR), People's Republic of China (PRC); the Oirat (or Deed) Mongols live in Qinghai Province and in the Xinjiang Autonomous Region, PRC; the Khalkha, along with a small population of Buriat and a larger one of Oirats, live in the Mongolian People's Republic (MPR).

LOCATION. The range of Mongolian culture extends from northeastern Manchuria (125° E)

The range of Mongolian culture extends from northeastern Manchuria westward to eastern Xinjiang.

westward to eastern Xinjiang (80° E). A north-south geographical projection extends in the south from the Ordos Desert, 37° N, northward to Lake Baikal in Siberia at 53° N. Mongols also live in Qinghai Province and along the lower Volga and Don rivers. There is a small remmant Mongolian community in Yunnan Province in the PRC.

The MPR, nearly four times the size of California, is wedged between Russia, to its north, and Inner Mongolia to the south. Ecologically, Mongols in Central Asia live in a landlocked, arid region. There is, nevertheless, much topographical diversity. In both the MPR and the IMAR there are high mountians; rich, wooded areas with rivers, streams, and lakes; and rolling plains of grass (steppes). The Mongolian plateau is the origin of many important Asian rivers. The Yellow River cuts through northwestern Inner Mongolia. The climate is characterized by warm summers and very cold, dry winters. The climate varies by region. At Ulaanbaatar (in Russian, Ulan Bator), capital of the MPR, the average temperature ranges from 18° C in July to below 0° C in January; whereas in Alshaa County in southwestern Inner Mongolia the temperatures can range from 37.7° C for July to below 0° C for January.

DEMOGRAPHY. Mongols constitute 90 percent of the MPR's 1,943,000 total population. In contrast, Mongols constitute only 13.5 percent (2,681,000 Mongols and 60,000 Daurs) of the IMAR's 19,850,000 total population. The population in both regions is expanding. The MPR financially rewards families with six or more children, whereas the PRC, in 1986, restricted urban and peasant Mongolian families to two children. The new policy does not apply to pastoral Mongols.

LINGUISTIC AFFILIATION. The Mongolian language is similar to other Altaic languages (Turkish, Uigur, Kitan, Jurchen, and Manchu). In the MPR the largest and most important dialect is Khalkha. In the MPR Oirat is the only other main dialect, whereas in the IMAR dialects may be divided into many regions: in the center there is the Chahar-Shiliingol dialect, which is closely related to standard Khalkha; in the northeast Barga and Buriat are spoken; in the southeast the major dialect is Khorchin; in the northwest it is Alshaa; and in the southwest it is the Ordos dialect. The Oirat or Kalmuck dialect is spoken in northwestern Xinjiang, Qinghai, and the western part of the MPR. With the exception of the Daurs, who speak a separate language in northeastern Inner Mongolia, the dialects are more or less mutually intelligible. Historically, the Mongols adopted a Uigur or vertical script under the leadership of Chinggis (Genghis) Khan (1206–1227). In 1946, the MPR formally adopted the Russian Cyrillic alphabet. The Uigur script remains the official script in the IMAR. In the MPR the official language is Mongolian, whereas in the IMAR both Mandarian and Mongolian are the official languages of government publication and documentation.

Settlements

The Mongols have always lived in a variety of dwellings: temporary grass shelters, the standard yurt (*ger*) with a wooden latticework frame covered with felt, a permanent dwelling made from adobe brick, and multistory apartment complexes. Because of the fierce north winds, dwellings face the southeast. Today, 51 percent of the MPR's Mongolian population lives in cities, whereas the majority of the IMAR Mongols are farmers. The largest city in the MPR is Ulaanbaatar (population over 500,000). A few other "large" cities with a population of more than 10,000 are Choibalsan, Darkhan, and Erdenet. In the IMAR the three largest cities are Baotou (more than 500,000), Huhhot (491,950), and Wuhai (under 40,000).

Economy

SUBSISTENCE AND COMMERCIAL ACTIVITIES. The Mongols no longer concentrate on raising horses, cattle, camels, sheep, and goats. Instead there is a preference for sheep, which have the highest market value. Mongols continue to hunt a variety of animals: wild antelope, rabbits, pheasants, ducks, foxes, wolves, and marmots. In the mountainous areas they formerly hunted bears, deer, sable, and ermine.

The Mongols have used irrigation and dry-farm methods for centuries. Mongolian peasants grow barley, wheat, oats, corn, buckwheat, millet, potatoes, sugar beets, garlic, cabbage, onions, carrots, sorghum, and fruit trees (especially apples), and raise pigs and sheep. Among herders a typical diet consists primarily of millet, milk tea, dairy products, mutton, *kumiss* (fermented mare's milk) and liquor (*khar arkhi*). Of the total land area in the MPR, about 65 percent is used for pasturage and fodder. In the MPR, most wheat is grown on state farms and fodder on collectives. With only 15 percent of its labor force employed in industry, the MPR relies on imports from the former Soviet Union for most of its industrial goods. The majority of Mongols living in the IMAR are peasants, with smaller numbers of herders and urbanites. The region is economically subsidized by the Chinese state.

INDUSTRIAL ARTS. Historically, Mongolian artisans were honored and respected. They worked in gold, silver, iron, wood, leather, and textiles. Recently the applied arts have increased in importance because of export demands and tourist preference.

TRADE. Historically, Mongols supplemented their economy by trade and raiding. They never developed a merchant class. On a regular basis the Mongols traded animals, fur, and hides for grain, tea, silk, cloth, and manufactured items with Chinese and Russian trading companies. The Mongols also traded with each other during the *naadam*, which continues to function in the IMAR as a trade-marriage-entertainment fair. Most trade in the MPR is with the former USSR and eastern Europe, whereas most trade in the IMAR is either with other Chinese provinces or with the United States and Japan.

DIVISION OF LABOR. The gender division of labor is complementary. Among herders, women and children milk, churn butter, cook, sew, and perform child-care duties, whereas the men tend the cattle, horses, and camels, collect hay, and hunt wild game and occasionally wolves. Both sexes tend and shear sheep. In agricultural settings, men construct dwellings and plant, irrigate, weed, and harvest the crops, whereas women cook, clean, sew, perform child care, and assist with the planting and harvesting. In urban settings both men and women work for a wage. Women are responsible for most of the household chores and childcare duties.

LAND TENURE. In the MPR, collectivization, after failing in the 1920s, was reintroduced in the late 1950s and has remained the predominant mode of production. In China, collectivization was first introduced in the late 1950s. In the early 1980s it was rejected in favor of the responsiblity system, which extended to both farmer and herder long-term contracts to use the land.

Kinship, Marriage, and Family

KINSHIP. The kinship system (i.e., relations governed by rules of marriage, filiation, and descent) was strongly patrilineal in the past, but its larger units, the clans and lineages, lost many of their functions to the Manchu administrative institutions. Among herders the *ail*, a group of households consisting of kin and nonkin that migrated together, formed a discrete social unit. The functions of the ail included mutual help in times

HISTORY AND CULTURAL RELATIONS

Mongols were an insignificant northern tribe until the early thirteenth century. Under the leadership of Chinggis Khan they were transformed into a large nomadic segmentary state. Khubilai (Kublai) Khan established the Yuan dynasty (1260–1368) and shifted the political center of Mongolian power from Karakorum (near Ulan Bator) to northern China (near Beijing). Mongol power declined after the Mongol dynasty in China was overthrown in 1368.

The Manchus, who conquered China in 1644, divided Mongolian territory into the geographical regions of Outer Mongolia and Inner Mongolia. They also reorganized the Mongols into a banner administration system that bound Mongols to a specific locality, thereby effectively curtailing migration. The collapse of the Manchu (or Qing) dynasty in 1911 resulted in the formation of autonomous regions in Outer Mongolia and among the Bargas. As Russia fell into a civil war, China abolished the newly formed regions, and thereby provoked the formation of the first Mongolian political parties. In Feburary 1921 White Russians entered Outer Mongolia and drove out Chinese forces; in July 1921, the Russian Red Army drove out the Whites and installed a "constitutional monarchy." The MPR was officially formed in 1924. Khorloogiin Choibalsan and Sukhbaatar (in Russian, Suke Bator) formed and led the early Revolutionary party, and Choibalsan served from 1939 to 1952 as premier. In the 1930s the Japanese formed a new government (Meng-Jiang) in central Inner Mongolia, headed by the Mongolian prince Demchigdonggrub (Dewang). The Japanese army withdrawal in 1945 enabled Soviet-Mongolian military units to enter Inner Mongolia and Manchuria. It was not until after the Soviets had rejected political unification that the majority of Inner Mongolian leaders agreed to back the Chinese Communist party. The MPR and USSR have several long-term economic and "friendship" agreements. In 1987, the MPR established diplomatic relations with the United States.

The MPR is, ethnically, relatively homogeneous. The Kazaks, who live in the west, are the MPR's largest minority group (4 percent), followed by the Russian and Chinese urbanites (2 percent each). There was considerable resentment of Soviet domination of the MPR. The Soviet Union, however, was also regarded as a useful protector against China, as is its successor, the Russian Federation. Inner Mongolia is an ethnically diverse region. Ethnic relations between Mongols and Han Chinese continue to swing between mild antagonism and overt hostility. Most Mongols in the IMAR regard themselves as citizens of the PRC.

*After the
introduction of
Lamaist Buddhism,
Mongols switched
from earthen burial
to "sky burial" —
the body was left out
on the steppes to be
eaten by wild
animals.*

of trouble, common kinship rituals (weddings, hair-cutting rites, funerals, etc.), and economic exchange (payment of marriage expenses). Within urban settings, situational use of kinship ties is preferred over other corporate forms of kinship.

MARRIAGE. Within the domestic cycle, there is more importance placed on marriage than on birth or death. Mongols typically married young: for girls it was at age 13 or 14, for boys a few years later. Today Mongolian peasants marry in their early twenties and immediately start a family. Urban Mongols, especially the college-educated, delay marriage until their late twenties and, sometimes, early thirties. Except for urbanites, there is no dating tradition and marriages continue to be arranged. Premarital sex is common among Mongolian herders in the IMAR. Post-marital residence is almost exclusively patrilocal. Birth control is discouraged in the MPR and encouraged in the IMAR. Among peasants and herders, divorce is rare.

DOMESTIC UNIT. Historically, the main kinship groups are the nuclear and extended family and the patronymic group (a group of agnatically related men with their wives and children). Within the MPR collective farm the household remains the basic domestic unit. Among the Mongols in the PRC the primary domestic units are the nuclear and stem family.

INHERITANCE. Until the seventh century and the establishment of Buddhist estates, "property" was defined only as movable property. Wives in Mongolian society had rights to inherit property. Under Communism that right continues to be guaranteed by law. The eldest son inherited part of the family wealth at the time of his marriage, and the youngest son inherited the remaining family property after both parents had died.

SOCIALIZATION. Historically, cultural transmission occurred informally between parent and child. The common means of discipline are verbal reprimand and corporal punishment. In the MPR, primary education after the age of eight is free and compulsory. Ten years of schooling are required. Ninety percent of the Mongols in the MPR are literate. In the IMAR most Mongols attend primary school. In urban areas, most attend middle school. Very few Mongols attend college.

Sociopolitical Organization

Mongols, throughout Central Asia, lived under governments that promoted a Marxist-Leninist political philosophy with a single, dominant political party. The MPR, the PRC, and the former USSR had a politburo, the chief policy-making body that follows the directives of the Central Committee. In March 1990 the MPR politburo proposed to give up its monopoly on power in favor of a more democratic constitution. In the 1992 parliamentary elections the former Communist party won by a large margin.

SOCIAL ORGANIZATION. Traditionally, Mongolian society was organized around lay and ecclesiastical social classes. Social worth in the present-day MPR and the IMAR is determined by occupation in the command economy. The introduction of market incentives in the IMAR countryside reduced the influence of minor officials but did not undermine the power of the high-ranking officials.

POLITICAL ORGANIZATION. There were six leagues under the Manchu dynasty, which the MPR reorganized into eighteen provinces (*aimags*) and thirteen municipalites. In the MPR, a new administrative unit, the *sumun*, became the county administrative unit. The banner (*khoshuun*) level, between the province and sumun, was abolished. In Inner Mongolia, the Guomindang continued the traditional banner system. In 1947, the Communists established the IMAR and continued the banner administrative organization.

SOCIAL CONTROL. Mongols did not develop a codified legal system until the thirteenth century. The Mongol legal code included categories ranging from religious to criminal law. These codes lasted until the Communist party came to power. The legal codes developed in both the MPR and the IMAR stress collective over individual rights. Everyday affairs are regulated primarily by social censure.

CONFLICT. Historically, at the heart of the Mongolian-Chinese conflict there has been the question of land use. Throughout much of the early twentieth century, the migration of Chinese peasants pushed the herders into inferior pastureland. This led to periodic conflict. Ethnic conflict is, more or less, a moot issue in the MPR, whereas in the PRC's autonomous regions it is not. The Han Chinese believe the state's affirmative-action policy provides too many benefits. The Mongols argue that state has not provided enough benefits.

Religion and Expressive Culture

RELIGIOUS BELIEFS AND PRACTICES. Historically, the primary religions of the Mongols were shamanism and animism. Mongols believed that the shaman had the capability of "soul travel" and could cure the sick. In the sixteenth century

Lamaist Buddhism incorporated into its cosmology many shamanistic symbols and rites. Under the Manchus Lamaism flourished. Monastic centers were developed. The 1921 Revolution in Outer Mongolia brought an attack on Buddhism as a superstition. During the Cultural Revolution all but two of Inner Mongolia's 2,000 temples and shrines were destroyed. In the MPR the state has restricted the performance of festivals associated with shamanism and Lamaist Buddhism. In the IMAR, however, the obooshrine ritual festival continues to be an important community event. The oboos are thought to be inhabited by spirits and deities of localities. In the southwestern Ordos region the Chinggis Khan Memorial continues to draw Mongols from throughout the IMAR. There is also a small community of Mongolian Moslems located in the Alshaa Banner in western IMAR.

ARTS. Mongolian culture is noted for its epic poetry and music. Modern Russian folk songs and dances, performed in Mongolian, are popular in both the MPR and the IMAR.

MEDICINE. Disease and sickness were regarded as the result of evil influences and wrongdoing. The most common diseases were smallpox, typhoid fever, bubonic plague, and syphilis. The Russian and Chinese doctors cured syphilis and reduced the occurrence of the other dieases. Modernization has meant increased access to Western medicinal facilities. In the MPR women now give birth in hospitals, whereas in the IMAR herders and farmers continue to give birth in their homes. Longevity has increased in both rural and urban areas, primarily due to hygienic and medical development.

DEATH AND AFTERLIFE. After the introduction of Lamaist Buddhism, Mongols switched from earthern burial to "sky burial"—the body was left on the steppes to be eaten by wild animals. Today "sky burial" continues only in the Ujemchin districts of Shiliingol and among the Oirat (or Deed) Mongols living in the Haixi Prefecture of Qinghai. In other banners and districts, rural Mongols bury the dead in community graveyards. In urban China they are cremated.

Bibliography

Humphrey, C. (1978). "Postoral Nomadism in Mongolia: The Role of Herdsmen's Cooperatives in the National Economy." In *Development and Change*, 133–160. London: Sage.

Jacchid, Sechin, and Paul Hyer (1979). *Mongolia's Culture and Society*. Boulder, Colo.: Westview Press.

Rupen, Robert (1979). *How Mongolia Is Really Ruled.* Stanford, Calif.: Hoover Institution Press.

Vainshtein, Sevyan (1979). *Nomads of South Siberia.* Edited with an introduction by Caroline Humphrey. Cambridge: Cambridge University Press.

—WILLIAM JANKOWIAK

TIBETANS

Ethonyms: Bodpa, Bhotia (Chinese terms for Tibetans)

Orientation

IDENTIFICATION. The Tibetans are a Central Asian group living primarily on the high plateau of southwestern China and throughout sections of the Himalayas. The term "Tibet," which appeared in various forms on early maps of Arabic explorers, is thought to be derived either from the Tibetan term for "upper Tibet," *stod bod*, or from the early Indian name for Tibet, *bhot*. Ethnic Tibetans often refer to themselves by the place-names of their geographic area or a tribal name, such as the Ladakhi and Zanskari people of northern India and the Golock tribal people of Amdo.

LOCATION. Prior to 1959, the majority of Tibetans lived on the Central Asian plateau bounded on the south by the Himalayas, on the west by the Karakorum, on the east by the Tangkula Mountains, and on the north by the Kunlun Mountains and the Taklamakan Desert. This is a high mountain plateau of more than 3.9 million square kilometers, which averages 12,000 feet above sea level, has extreme temperature fluctuations, and receives 46 centimeters or less of annual precipitation.

Following 1959, a substantial number of Tibetans migrated from the plateau to Bhutan, Nepal, India, and other countries. There are currently several large reserves of Tibetans in India, some with as many as 5,000 inhabitants.

DEMOGRAPHY. Estimates of the Tibetan population are subject to dispute. No internal census was taken prior to 1950; various foreign visitors estimated the total population of Tibetans at between 3 and 6 million. The fighting in the 1950s over control of the plateau caused substantial human loss. The 1990 Chinese figures for the total population of ethnic Tibetans within Chinese borders is 4.5 million, about half in the Tibet Autonomous Region, the rest in Qinghai, Gansu, Sichuan, and Yunnan provinces. The Indian government has estimated the number of ethnic Tibetans currently in India at approximately 100,000.

◆ **Himalayas**
The world's highest mountain range, stretching over 2,200 kilometers eastward from Kashmir through Nepal, Sikkim, Bhutan, and northeast India to form the boundary between South Asia and Tibet.

LINGUISTIC AFFILIATION. Tibetan belongs to the Tibetan-Burmese Branch of the Sino-Tibetan Language Family. It is also known as "Bodish." There are two Tibetan languages, Central Tibetan and Western Tibetan, with many regional dialects spoken throughout the plateau, the Himalayas, and parts of South Asia. Tibetan is monosyllabic with no consonant clusters, five vowels, twenty-six consonants, an ablaut verb system, tones and a subject-object-verb word order. The Tibetan script is a readaptation of a northern Indian script devised for the first historical king around A.D. 630.

History and Cultural Relations

Archaeological and linguistic evidence indicate that people entered the plateau from the northeast approximately 13,000 years ago. In time they migrated throughout the plateau and settled in larger numbers along the Tsangpo River, which runs parallel to the Himalayas in the southern region. In this southernly arc, Tibetan kingdoms began to develop as early as A.D. 400, according to some commentators. The oldest extant example of Tibetan writing, which dates from around A.D. 767, indicates the presence in this region of a settled kingdom. Tibetan history begins with the Tibetan Empire period (A.D. 632 to 842): armies conquered and controlled large sections of Central Asia to the northwest and northern China and Mongolia to the northeast. After the murder of the last king of the Yarlung dynasty, decentralization ensued and many smaller states were formed throughout the plateau. Buddhism, which had first been introduced during the empire period, gained popularity during this time and became a central feature of Tibetan ethnicity.

In the thirteenth century one sect of Tibetan Buddhism (the Sa skyas pa), with the help of Mongolian supporters, took control of much of central Tibet and established a theocracy that lasted for 100 years. Three secular dynasties followed between the years 1354 and 1642—the Phagmogru, the Rinpung, and the Tsangpa. In the middle of the seventeenth century the Gelugspa, or Yellow Hat sect of Tibetan Buddhism, with the help of Mongolian supporters of their charismatic leader, the Dalai Lama, took control of the central part of the plateau, which they held for 300 years. British incursion into the country from the south and Chinese incursions from the north in the twentieth century demonstrated that the Tibetans had not cultivated military strength. In late 1950 the army of the People's Republic of China marched into eastern Tibet and claimed sovereignty over the plateau but left the Dalai Lama as leader and administrator of the country. A decade of negotiation and military skirmishes ensued, which culminated in a general uprising and the flight of the Dalai Lama and thousands of his supporters to India in 1959.

The plateau and contiguous areas of Tibetan settlement are now part of the People's Republic of China (PRC) and divided between the Tibet Autonomous Region and the neighboring provinces of Qinghai, Gansu, Sichuan, and Yunnan, where several prefectures or counties are designated for Tibetans as autonomous areas. In Dharamsala, India, the Dalai Lama heads the administration of the government-in-exile of Tibet, which oversees the affairs of over 100,000 Tibetans in exile in India, Nepal, and abroad. Negotiations conducted in the 1980s did not produce any compromises nor result in the return of the Dalai Lama to Tibet.

Settlements

Tibetans are traditionally divided into groups according to geographic origin, occupation, and social status. The plateau was divided into five general regions, each with a distinctive climate: the northern plain, which is almost uninhabited; the southern belt on the Tsangpo River, which is

TIBETAN WOMAN

A Tibetan woman carries a bundle of sticks on her back along a dirt path in the Himalaya Mountains. Paths such as this are used to reach resources and to link trading centers. Nepal. (Zuiki Eshet/The Stock Market)

the heart of the agricultural settlements; western Tibet, a mountainous and arid area; the southeast, which has rich temperate and subtropical forests and more rainfall; and the northeast terrain of rolling grasslands dotted with mountains, famous for its herding. Traditionally, settlement patterns were determined by region and by the three major occupations: peasant farming, nomadic herding, and monkhood. Peasants lived in single dwellings as well as village clusters, whereas nomads lived in tents, camping both individually and in clusters as they followed their herds through seasonal migration patterns. Monks lived in monasteries of varying sizes, some reportedly with as many as 10,000 individuals. There are only three major urban centers, all located in the southern belt of the plateau. The nonnomadic society was also divided into hierarchic social groups ranging from the ruler and the noble elite to private landowners, peasants, and craftspersons.

Since the incorporation of Tibet into the PRC after 1950, many Han Chinese have migrated onto the plateau, primarily to the urban centers, where they now outnumber the ethnic Tibetans. Nomads were originally settled into camps but have recently been allowed to resume transhumance patterns.

Economy

SUBSISTENCE AND COMMERCIAL ACTIVITIES. Prior to 1950, Tibetan farmers' primary crop was high-altitude barley, with wheat, buckwheat, peas, mustard, radishes, and potatoes following in importance.

Irrigation systems were coordinated by the village, which was also the cooperative unit for corvée. Nomads raised yaks (animals particularly suited to the high altitude and severe climate of the north), sheep, a cow-yak cross-breed, and at lower altitudes, cattle and goats. At annual or biennial markets throughout Tibet, rural nomads and farmers exchanged produce and purchased other commodities. For distant nomadic communities, annual grain-trading expeditions occurred in the late fall; each encampment of tents functioned as a unit and each family contributed a member or supplies to the group traveling down to the market in the lower regions. The large urban centers, such as the capital city of Lhasa, had daily markets displaying goods from all over the world. Particular areas of Tibet were well known for the production of certain crops or the manufacture of certain items or raw products. For example, bamboo for pens and high-quality paper came from the southeast, excellent horses from

the northeast, wood products from the east, and gold, turquoise, and other gems from two or three specific areas in the south and west. Currently, most of the manufactured products in Tibet come from urban centers in the PRC, but local markets in the rural areas continue to allow for pastoralist-peasant exchange.

INDUSTRIAL ARTS. Tibetans practiced a wide range of traditional trades, including flour milling, canvas painting, paper making, rope braiding, wool and fiber processing, weaving and textile production, tanning, metalwork, carpentry, and wood carving. Individual household or small-scale production was the norm, with the exception of a few activities, such as the printing of religious manuscripts and books, which was handled at large monasteries on more of a mass-production basis.

TRADE. There is evidence of Tibetans trading extensively both on and off the plateau as early as the seventh century A.D.—exporting raw materials and importing manufactured products. Overland routes to China, India, Nepal, and Central Asia allowed the large-scale export of animals, animal products, honey, salt, borax, herbs, gemstones, and metal in exchange for silk, paper, ink, tea, and manufactured iron and steel products. The government granted lucrative yearly monopolies on products such as salt. In the nineteenth century and the first half of the twentieth, British, Russian, and Chinese missions to Tibet tried to control trade and open markets in the country. Since 1950 trade has been regulated by the PRC.

DIVISION OF LABOR. There were traditional distinctions in wealth and status among both the peasants and nomads. Hired laborers and servants freed wealthier families from most of the manual labor of daily life. Social distinctions between aristocrats and commoners or between different strata of the commoner class were reflected in dress, housing, and speech used to one's superiors, peers, and inferiors.

Although Tibetan women are in charge of child rearing, food preparation, cooking, and other domestic activities and men do the bulk of the work outside of the home, both genders are commonly capable of performing all basic household and nonhousehold tasks. In the monasteries and nunneries, same-sex occupants perform all of the household and external tasks for the community. In larger cities, butchering, metalworking, and other low-status crafts were traditionally confined to particular groups.

LAND TENURE. Prior to 1955, much of the Tibetan plateau was considered the ultimate

Historically, Tibetans have left the functions of the military, thought to be irreligious, to foreign groups such as the Mongols or Chinese.

property of the central government in Lhasa and the ruler of Tibet, the Dalai Lama. Each peasant household had a deed, in the name of the eldest male, to the property that it farmed. Many of the peasant farmers were also organized into estates, which were an intermediate form of title holding by monasteries, incarnate lamas, or aristocratic families. The laborers attached to the estate owed taxes and corvée to the lord and were not free to move elsewhere without permission. Being bound to an estate, however, did not prevent some families from hiring others to fulfill their obligations to the lord or from traveling for purposes of trade and pilgrimage. These three levels of ownership constituted the bulk of Tibetan land tenure before 1950. Land-reform policies in Tibet under the Communist government have involved a few experiments with collective farming and ownership. Most rural peasants still farm the land of their family household, but intermediate titles have generally been extinguished.

Kinship

KIN GROUPS AND DESCENT. The most important functioning kin group is the extended family constituted as a household. Family names, which are carried by the males of some families, reflect the patrilineal inheritance pattern and are also used to demarcate the noble families.

KINSHIP TERMINOLOGY. Formal kinship terminology in the southern region, among the peasant population, distinguishes between patri- and matrilaterals at the second ascending generation, is bifurcate-collateral at the first ascending generation, and shows a typical Hawaiian generational pattern at Ego's generation level. In practice, this system results in a strong bias toward distinguishing between one's matrilateral and one's patrilateral kin for the purposes of inheritance. For relatives of his or her own level, including cousins, the average Tibetan simply uses the terms "brother" and "sister." There is local and regional variation in terminology throughout the plateau.

Marriage and Family

MARRIAGE. Among the peasants of the southern arc of the Tibetan plateau, traditional marriage patterns exhibited a great deal of variety and flexibility through the individual's life cycle. The seven forms of marriage were: fraternal polyandry (a set of brothers marries one woman), father-son and unrelated male polyandry, sororal polygyny (a set of sisters marries one man), mother-daughter and unrelated female polygyny,

and monogamy. Monogamy was the most frequent form of marriage. Traditionally, Tibetans calculated the degree of relation allowed in marriage as five generations back on the mother's side and seven on the father's, although many were unable to determine genealogy this far back. Although of astrological and cosmological import, marriage was viewed as a nonreligious joining of two households and individuals. Postmarital residence was generally virilocal.

Marriages were class-endogamous. Serfs from different manors who wished to marry required permission from their lords or their lords' agents. Yellow sect lamas do not marry, but lamas of most other sects are free to do so.

DOMESTIC UNIT. The peasant household was the chief domestic unit; it was often, but not necessarily constituted of three generations of males and their wives and children. Individuals of both genders rotated in and out of the household with great flexibility.

INHERITANCE. Although the traditional inheritance pattern for peasant land was patrilineal descent and primogeniture, both males and females could inherit land or receive it as a gift. Maintenance of the household as the landholding, tax-paying unit could be accomplished by any member of the family. Personal property could also be inherited by any member of the family, although women commonly passed on to their daughters their jewelry, clothing, and other personal possessions. Monks and nuns did not inherit. Wills, oral or written, could alter the inheritance pattern.

SOCIALIZATION. Tibetans dote on their children but believe in strong discipline and religious instruction. Traditionally, the pattern in Tibet was to raise children to follow the same occupations as their parents unless they chose to become traders or take religious vows and leave the family. Only those children entering government service were given formal education.

Sociopolitical Organization

SOCIAL ORGANIZATION. The web of bilateral kin associated with households was the basis for local social organization. Villages had headmen and head irrigators who coordinated agricultural projects.

Titleholders coordinated estates into social units. Monasteries and nunneries operated as independent social units within communities. Tibetans also form associations called *skyid sdug* for a variety of purposes: to coordinate prayers, dances, singing, religious festivals, marriages, pilgrimages, funerals, commercial ventures, and other activities.

POLITICAL ORGANIZATION. Much of the Tibetan plateau has been governed, since as early as the seventh century, by a central dynasty or theocracy with a small administrative bureaucracy. This bureaucracy was supplied with officials from the elite nobility and the monasteries in exchange for intermediate title to estates of land. For 300 years prior to 1950, the government was headed by a Buddhist monk, the Dalai Lama, who, upon death, reincarnated into a small child and resumed leadership in a new body. Under his leadership, the bureaucracy was divided into an ecclesiastical branch and a secular branch that handled a redistributive economy based on taxation by household. Networks of monasteries controlled by sects of Tibetan Buddhism were also important political players. Local authority was placed in the village headman or estate steward, who coordinated tax collection and corvée and handled local disputes. Historically, Tibetans have embraced the union of religion and politics and left the functions of the military, thought to be irreligious, to foreign groups such as the Mongols or Chinese. Since 1950 Tibet has been gradually incorporated into the government of the PRC.

SOCIAL CONTROL. Tibetans have an ancient and unique set of legal procedures that were based on early law codes and commonly used throughout the plateau. There were few governmental sanctions for any crimes other than murder and treason. A variety of forums was available for the settlement of disputes, and most cases remained open until all parties had agreed. Traditional social control was based on family and village relations.

CONFLICT. Conflict occurred over land boundaries, animal ownership, commercial agreements, injuries, fights, and a wide range of other issues. In general, it was disdained as an indication of a lack of religious training.

Religion and Expressive Culture

RELIGIOUS BELIEFS. Tibetans are devoutly religious. Tibetan Buddhism, the religion of the entire population except for a tiny Muslim minority, is a syncretic mix of Indian Buddhism, Tantrism, and the local pantheistic religion. The organization of the religion, its public practice, and the observance of religious holidays are coordinated primarily by monasteries associated with temples. The priests, called lamas, were estimated to constitute from one-sixth to one-fourth of the population prior to 1950. Although the goal of Tibetan Buddhism is individual enlightenment, the social organization of the religion rests on a laity that is expected to support the religious practices of the monastic population. Thus, Tibetans contributed sons, produce, savings, and labor to the monasteries to acquire religious merit.

RELIGIOUS PRACTITIONERS. Monasteries of various sects of Tibetan Buddhism were the centers of educational training in all the basic arts, crafts, and professions, including medicine. Monk initiates were divided into groups according to social status and ability and given training for a variety of tasks. The degree of religious teacher, *dge bshe*, required more than ten years of diligent study, memorization of texts, practice in debate, and examinations. Monks conducted most public religious ceremonies (including operatic performances), which constituted the bulk of Tibetan ceremonial life and followed the traditional Buddhist calendrical cycle. Oracles, mediums, and exorcists were also commonly monks but could be local peasants in rural areas. In western Tibet and pastoral areas of Qinghai, an earlier form of Buddhism mixed with the pre-Buddhist native religion (Bon) is practiced.

ARTS. Tibetan traditional arts focused on religious worship and included scroll paintings of deities, sculpture, carved altars, religious texts, altar implements, statues of precious metal inlaid with gems, appliquéd temple hangings, operatic costumes for religious performances, religious music, and religious singing. Most of these crafts were carried out by monks in monasteries. In addition to collections of older Buddhist scriptures, Tibetan writing and literature includes works on history, philosophy, medicine, mathematics, and astronomy as well as works of fiction and poetry. Local peasants produced utilitarian household objects for their own use or purchased them at a local market. Women wore multibanded front aprons, regionally specific headdresses, and jewelry.

MEDICINE. Tibetan medicine evolved over a thousand years into a series of nonintrusive techniques including listening to blood flow through the wrist, analysis of urine and anatomical parts, listening to the heart and lungs, questioning the patient, and administering carefully prepared herbal pills. The body is considered to be composed of various elements balanced by nutrition, religious practices, mental states, and relations with deities. The training process for physicians was long and often limited to monks.

DEATH AND AFTERLIFE. Tibetans practice sky-burial, a process of returning the corporal body to the environment by pulverizing the parts

For 300 years, prior to 1950, the government of Tibet was headed by a Buddhist monk, the Dalai Lama, who, upon death, reincarnated into a small child and resumed leadership in a new body.

and leaving them exposed to the elements and the vultures. An individual's karmic seeds are thought to remain in *bar do*, a liminal zone, for forty-nine days after death, during which time they enter a new body (that of a human, a hell being, a god, or an animal) to start a new life cycle. This recurrent process of life, death, and rebirth continues until an individual achieves enlightenment.

Bibliography

Aziz, Barbara (1978). *Tibetan Frontier Families.* Durham, N.C.: Carolina Academic Press.

Dalai Lama (1962). *My Land and My People.* New York: Potala Corporation.

French, Rebecca (in press, 1993). *The Golden Yoke: The Legal System of Buddhist Tibet.* Ithaca, N.Y.: Cornell University Press.

Snellgrove, David, and Hugh Richardson (1980). *A Cultural History of Tibet.* Boulder, Colo.: Prahna Press.

—REBECCA R. FRENCH

ZHUANG

Ethnonyms: Buban, Budai, Budong, Bulong, Buman, Bumin, Buna, Bunong, Bupian, Bushuang, Butu, Buyang, Buyue, Gaolan Nongan, Tulao

Orientation

IDENTIFICATION. The Zhuang are the largest of China's minority peoples. Their autonomous region covers the entire province of Guangxi. They are a highly Sinicized agricultural people and are closely related culturally and linguistically to the Bouyei, Maonan, and Mulam, who are recognized by the state as separate ethnicities.

LOCATION. Most Zhuang live in Guangxi, where they constitute about 33 percent of the population. They are concentrated in the western two-thirds of the province and neighboring regions of Guizhou and Yunnan, with a smaller group in Lianshan in northern Guangdong. For the most part, villages are in the mountainous areas of Guangxi. Numerous streams and rivers provide irrigation, transportation, and more recently, hydroelectric power. Much of the province is subtropical, with temperatures averaging 20° C, reaching 24 to 28° C in July and lows between 8 and 12° C in January. During the rainy season, from May to November, annual rainfall averages 150 centimeters.

DEMOGRAPHY. According to the 1982 census, the Zhuang population was 13,378,000. The 1990 census reports 15,489,000. According to 1982 figures, 12.3 million Zhuang lived in the Guangxi Autonomous Region, with another 900,000 in adjacent areas of Yunnan (mainly in the Wenshan Zhuang-Miao Autonomous Prefecture), 333,000 in Guangdong, and a small number in Hunan. At least 10 precent of the Zhuang are urban. Elsewhere, population density ranges from 100 to 161 persons per square kilometer. The reported birth rate in recent years is 2.1, which is in line with China's family-planning policies.

LINGUISTIC AFFILIATION. The Zhuang language belongs to the Zhuang Dai Branch of the Tai (Zhuang-Dong) Language Family, which includes Bouyei and Dai and is closely related to the standard Thai language of Thailand and the standard Lao of Laos. The eight-tone system resembles that of the Yue (Cantonese) dialects of the Guangdong-Guangxi area. There are also many loanwords from Chinese. Zhuang consists of two closely related "dialects," which are termed "northern" and "southern": the geographical dividing line is the Xiang River in southern Guangxi. Northern Zhuang is more widely used and is the base for the standard Zhuang encouraged by the Chinese government since the 1950s. A romanized script was introduced in 1957 for newspapers, magazines, books, and other publications. Prior to that, literate Zhuang used Chinese characters and wrote in Chinese. There was also Zhuang writing that used Chinese characters for their sound value only, or in compound forms that indicated sound and meaning, or created new ideographs by adding or deleting strokes from standard ones. These were used by shamans, Daoist priests, and merchants, but were not widely known.

History and Cultural Relations

The Sinicization of the Tai-speaking peoples of the Lingnan (Guangdong and Guangxi) has been a long process. Chinese forces first penetrated the area in 211 B.C., sparking local resistance and the creation of the Nan-Yue Kingdom, which expanded its rule to what is now northern Vietnam. In 111 B.C., Nan-Yue was integrated into the Han dynasty domain but not until the Tang (c. 600 A.D.) was state control established. Military farm colonies opened the way for further Han Chinese settlement. The indigenous Tai peoples either assimilated or were pushed westward or into the uplands, whereas the newcomers settled in the lowlands and interior river valleys. The crushing of a major Zhuang uprising in Guangdong during the Song led to further assimilation or dispersement of the ancestors of the current-day Zhuang. From the incoming Han settlers, the Zhuang adopted new agricultural techniques, where applicable, such as the iron plow, application of manure fertilizer, triple-cropping of rice, and more sophisticated irrigation systems. In the western part of Guangxi, the Zhuang remained in control of much of the area suitable for wetfield rice agriculture, as well as holding sway in the uplands where the introduction of Chinese technology was less feasible. From Tang onward, successive dynasties, landlord officials, and state-appointed local landlords ruled a large part of the Zhuang area, with most of the population reduced to tenancy and owing feudal service. This system continued into the nineteenth century, despite a number of major peasant uprisings. In the 1850s Guangxi was the origin point for the Taiping Rebellion, and Zhuang played an active role in the Taiping army and leadership. In 1927, the predominantly Zhuang area near Pai-se (Bose) was one of the earliest soviets. In 1949, the Zhuang of western Guangxi, who regarded themselves as oppressed by former Chinese governments, were warmly receptive to the Liberation army and new government. In 1952, a Zhuang autonomous region was organized in western Guangxi: By 1958, all of Guangxi became a Zhuang autonomous region, shared with the Han and with other ethnicities such as Yao, Miao, Maonan, Dong, Mulam, Jing, and Hui (Chinese Muslims). Soon after, the government organized the Zhuang-Miao Autonomous Prefecture in southeastern Yunnan and the Lianshan Zhuang-Yao Autonomous County in Guangdong. In 1984, Zhuang together with other minority people accounted for about one-third of the cadres (government employees and officials) in these areas.

Settlements

Some Zhuang areas in Guangxi are relatively homogenous, while elsewhere Zhuang villages are scattered between villages of other nationalities. Zhuang villages range in size from 20 to 2,000 persons, with a few larger communities that are traditional marketing centers located along riverways or a crossroad. Often, a village or cluster of villages traces its descent from a common male ancestor. In multilineal villages, houses tend to group according to surname (patrilineage). Newcomers to the area live on the outskirts, often at a considerable distance. Typical villages are located on a mountain slope facing a river. Under Han influence, most Zhuang have adopted the one-story brick house, but some retain the wooden-pile house common to other ethnic groups in the area: a two-story structure, with living quarters upstairs, and the lower floor serving as stables and storage rooms. Both styles nowadays have tiled roofs.

Economy

SUBSISTENCE AND COMMERCIAL ACTIVITIES. Paddy rice, dry-field uplands rice, glutinous rice, yams, and maize are staples, with double- or triple-cropping in most areas. Many tropical fruits (pineapple, banana, orange, sugarcane, litchi, mango) are grown, as well as a number of vegetables. River fisheries add protein to the diet, and most households raise pigs and chickens. Oxen and water buffalo serve as draft animals but are also eaten. Hunting and trapping are a very minor part of the economy, and gathering activities focus on mushrooms, medicinal plants, and fodder for the livestock. There is additional income in some areas from tung oil, tea and tea oil, cinnamon and anise, and a variety of ginseng. During the agricultural slack seasons, there are now increased opportunities to find construction work or other kinds of temporary jobs in the towns.

INDUSTRIAL ARTS. Most villages have always had some craft specialists skilled in carpentry, masonry, house building, tailoring, and the weaving of bamboo mats. Brocades, embroidered works, and batiks made by Zhuang women are famous throughout China and were mentioned as early as the Tang dynasty. Ordinarily, the Zhuang tend to dress like their Han neighbors, but ethnic dress has reemerged and is now encouraged by the state.

TRADE. Households are heavily dependent on local markets for obtaining daily necessities and luxury goods and for selling their own products such as vegetables, fruits, fish, poultry, furniture, herbs, and spices. Participation in the market is also a social pastime. Both sexes participate in market trading. These periodic markets, held every three, five, or ten days, are now the site of township, district, and county governments. A small number of Zhuang are shopkeepers in a village or market town, and with the recent reforms some now are long-distance traders, bringing clothing from Guangdong Province for resale on the local markets.

DIVISION OF LABOR. Men are responsible for plowing and management of the draft animals, while women are primarily responsible for transplanting rice in the flooded fields, weeding, and harvesting. Young men are more likely to be educated and are encouraged to learn an artisan

According to the 1990 census, the Zhuang population was 15,489,000.

skill or seek an urban job. The development of forestry and industries in the area makes some wage labor available. With adult women engaged in agriculture, the tasks of child care, feeding of domestic animals, and some of the housework is taken on by the elderly members of the family.

LAND TENURE. From the Tang through much of the Qing dynasty, a feudal landownership system was prevalent, in which households received land-use rights for their own subsistance in return for labor on the landowner's estates and other labor services. A more commercialized landlord system developed from the eighteenth century on into the twentieth, creating a large number of poor peasants. Under the current reforms, land is allocated on contract to households, according to the number of people registered as rural residents. A village administrative committee (formerly a production brigade or team under the socialist economy) oversees the allotments of arable land, particularly irrigated fields. The contract is usually for five years. All land now belongs to the state, but use rights and redistribution rest with the village. Conflicts over land boundaries between households, villages, or even townships and counties are not uncommon. Population density is now high relative to available land.

Kinship

KIN GROUPS AND DESCENT. Beyond the three-generation household, the significant group is the localized patrilineage, which shares a common surname and traces descent from a common ancestor. There is an elder recognized as the head, and households participate together at ancestral worship ceremonies, weddings, and funerals, with the lineage branch head directing. There are no reliable data on local variations of kinship termi-

nology. The mother's brother plays an important role for his nieces and nephews, from choosing their name and participating in their marriage arrangements to playing a role in their parents' funerals.

Marriage and Family

MARRIAGE. Marriages are surname exogamous, and usually village exogamous as well. There is some preference for a boy to marry his mother's brother's daughter, whereas marriage with parallel cousins is forbidden. In the past there was also a preference for early engagements and for a girl to be five or six years older than her prospective groom. Perhaps because of the age difference, there was delayed transfer of the bride: after the marriage ceremony she remained with her parents, making frequent visits to her in-laws to assist with planting and harvest, but maintaining her social freedoms and natal residence until the birth of her first child. Only then did she move to her husband's village. Sinicized Zhuang utilize go-betweens, matching of horoscopes, sending of gifts to the girl's family, sending of a dowry, and the general patterns of Han marriage practice. However, older patterns or borrowings from neighboring ethnic groups also continue. Groups of unmarried boys visit to serenade eligible girls at their homes; there are singing parties for groups of unmarried youth (and those not yet living with their spouses); and there are other opportunities for young people to choose a spouse for themselves. In the past, there were "elopement" marriages, accepted by the family and community. Divorce is frowned upon, and if it occurs, fathers retain custody of their sons. Remarriage is permitted.

DOMESTIC UNIT. The domestic unit is monogamous and nuclear except for youngest

SOCIOPOLITICAL ORGANIZATION

Social Organization

Prior to 1949, village organization was based on the patrilineage and on villagewide religious activities focused on gods and spirits who protected the community and assured the success of the crops and livestock. Ceremonies were led by recognized village elders.

Political Organization

Since 1949, various government-designated forms of organization have appeared. At present, villages are administered by a committee; and the next-highest level is the township government, which is responsible for a number of villages and which manages agriculture, local industry, and collection of taxes and required quota sales to the state.

Within the village and township there are branches or groups of the Communist party, the Women's Federation, and the Youth League, all of which seek to ensure that party policy is carried out. While some problems are handled informally by family or community, some matters go through government courts at the township, district, or county level. About one-third of government employees in Guangxi are Zhuang.

sons, who are obliged to live with their parents. Residence is generally patrilocal: about 20 percent of marriages bring the groom to the wife's village.

INHERITANCE. The youngest son inherits a larger share of the parental property. Both sons and daughters inherit movables, and also parental debts. In the absence of surviving offspring, other lineage members inherit.

Religion and Expressive Culture

RELIGIOUS BELIEFS. Ancestral worship differs from that of the Han in that it includes "kings" and mythic or historical heroes and heroines as well as actual ancestors in the patriline. The names of the ancestors, written on strips of red paper, are displayed on home altars together with the names of other spirits to be honored and receive special offerings at Spring Festival and at the Festival of the Dead in the seventh lunar month. In addition, there are a variety of local gods drawn from precontact religion or fused with gods from the Chinese folk tradition. These include Tudigong, who protects the village boundaries from his crossroads temple; She Shen, who is the village tutelary spirit; the Mountain Spirit (some mountains are sacred and should not be opened to farming); the Dragon King (Long Wang), who also protects the villages; and a number of spirits drawn from the pantheon of natural forces. Both Daoism and Buddhism or a fusion of the two are important in community life, particularly at the time of funerals. Catholic and Protestant missionaries came to the area in the late nineteenth century, but the number of followers is small and mostly limited to the urban areas.

RELIGIOUS PRACTITIONERS. Female divination specialists treat sickness and in trance can communicate with spirits and ghosts. A second kind of local shaman, who is male, differs in that he serves at an altar and is skilled in either the Zhuang writing system or a Zhuang reading of Chinese characters. His texts, which serve as a basis for performance (songs, chants), include myths, history and geography, astronomy, and tales. He performs at funerals, local festivals, and at times of crisis. The sacrifices of oxen, chickens, and other livestock are in part used to pay him for his service. Daoist priests, who are also part-time practitioners, perform at many of the same events as the shaman. They chant in Chinese and use Han texts. Buddhism in the Zhuang areas has been strongly influenced by Daoism and earlier traditional religion. The priests can marry and are semivegetarian. They cast horoscopes, serve as ge-omancers, and exorcise ghosts, as well as chanting sutras at life-crisis times.

CEREMONIES. Honoring ancestors at home altars and in ancestral halls is of key importance. The Chinese Qingming Festival for sweeping ancestral graves (third lunar month) is often combined with an Ox Birthday Festival and ceremonies for the goddess who protects at birth and during infancy.

ARTS. There is a rich repertoire of songs, dances, local opera, oral literature, and music. Hundreds of decorated bronze drums have been found in archaeological sites in the region, and there are frescoes dating back some 2,000 years at sites along the Zuo River.

MEDICINE. Divination, shamanistic healing, and herbal medicines from an older tradition are augmented by borrowings from Chinese traditional medicine (cupping, acupuncture) and the more recent introduction of clinics and health stations using both Chinese and Western medicine.

DEATH AND AFTERLIFE. Souls of the dead enter a netherworld but can continue to assist the living. Corpses are wrapped in white cloth and buried after three days, together with some of their favorite items of daily use. Daoist priests preside over the funeral: in some areas, two special singers are called upon to sing traditional mourning songs. The corpse is disinterred after three years and the bones are cleaned and placed in a pottery urn that is deposited in a cave or grotto. Those who died violent or untimely deaths are potentially evil spirits. Their bones are burned and a Daoist priest is called to transform the ashes into proper ancestors. Families arrange "spirit marriages" to appease the souls of those who died unmarried.

Bibliography

Gu Youzhi, and Lu Julie (1985). "Zhuangzu yuanshi zongjiao de fengjianhua" (The feudal transformation of early Zhuang religion). In *Zhongguo shaoshu minzu zongjiao* (Religions of China's national minorities), edited by Song Enchang, 301–315. Kunming: Yunnan Peoples Press.

Liang Tingwang (1986). *Zhuangzu fengsu ji* (Customs of the Zhuang). Beijing: Central Minorities Institute.

Ma Yin, ed. (1989). *China's Minority Nationalities*, 371–379. Beijing: Foreign Languages Press.

Song Enchang, ed. (1980). *Yunnan shaoshu minzu shehui diaocha yanjiu* (Social researches on Yunnan's minorities). Vol. 2. Kunming: Yunnan Peoples Press.

—LIN YUEH-HWA AND NORMA DIAMOND

Souls of the Zhuang dead enter a netherworld but can continue to assist the living. Families arrange "spirit marriages" to appease the souls of those who died unmarried.

East and
Southeast Asia

AINU IN EAST ASIA

Ethonyms: Aino, Emischi, Ezo, Hokkaidō Ainu, Kurile Ainu, Sakhalin Ainu

Orientation

The Ainu are a group of people in northern Japan whose traditional life was based on a hunting, fishing, and plant-gathering economy; the word *ainu* means "man." Only about 18,000 Ainu now live on Hokkaidō, the northernmost island of Japan, but the population was much larger in the past and their homeland included at least southern Sakhalin, the Kurile Islands, northern parts of Honshū (the main island of Japan), and adjacent areas.

Not only was their hunting-gathering economy vastly different from that of the neighboring Japanese, Koreans, and Chinese, who had been agriculturalists for several millennia, but they spoke a language of their own, and certain physical characteristics distinguished them from their neighbors.

Far from being monolithic, Ainu culture has been rich in intracultural variation. This article introduces only some of the major differences and similarities among the three major Ainu groups: the Kurile, Sakhalin, and Hokkaido Ainu. The Hokkaidō Ainu and the Sakhalin Ainu reside on the island of Hokkaidō and the southern half of the island of Sakhalin, respectively. Some use the term "Kurile Ainu" to refer only to the Ainu who occupied the central and northern Kurile Islands, excluding the Ainu on the southern Kuriles, whose way of life was similar to that of the Hokkaidō Ainu. Others use the label "Kurile Ainu" to refer to the Ainu on all the Kurile Islands, which is the practice followed in this article. The island of Sakhalin south of 50° N had always been the homeland of the Sakhalin Ainu, while the territory north of 50° N belonged to the Gilyaks and other peoples.

History and Cultural Relations

The Sakhalin Ainu, with an estimated population between 1,200 and 2,400 in the first half of the twentieth century, most likely migrated from Hokkaidō, possibly as early as the first millennium A.D., but definitely by the thirteenth century. They had extensive contacts with native populations on Sakhalin and along the Amur, including the Gilyaks, Oroks, and Nanais. It is likely that Chinese influence reached the island by the first millennium A.D. and intensified during the thirteenth century when northern Sakhalin submitted to Mongol suzerainty subsequent to the Mongol conquest of China. The period between 1263 and 1320 saw the Mongol colonization and "pacification" of the Gilyaks and the Ainu. The Sakhalin Ainu fought valiantly until 1308, finally submitting to the suzerainty of the Yuan dynasty, the Mongolian dynasty that ruled China and to whom the Ainu were forced to pay tribute. The tribute system, together with trade with other peoples along the way, merged with the Japanese-Hokkaidō Ainu trade during the fifteenth century. As a result, Japanese ironware reached the Manchus while Chinese brocade and cotton made their way to Osaka in western Japan. With the weakening of Manchu control over Sakhalin, the tribute system was abandoned at the beginning of the nineteenth century. By then, the Japanese and Russians were racing to take political control of the island and exploit its rich natural resources.

The impact of the Japanese government on the Sakhalin Ainu intensified under the Meiji government established in 1868. Many Japanese were sent to southern Sakhalin to exploit its resources. The Sakhalin Ainu came under Russian control in 1875 when southern Sakhalin came under Russian control, but Japan regained the area in 1905; the territory north of 50° N remained under Russian control throughout history. Between 1912 and 1914, the Japanese government placed the Sakhalin Ainu, except those on the remote northwest coast, on reservations, drastically altering their way of life. With the conclusion of World War II, southern Sakhalin again was reclaimed by the USSR and most of the Ainu were resettled on Hokkaidō.

The history of contact with outsiders is equally important for the Hokkaidō Ainu, whose territory once extended to northeastern Honshū. As the Japanese central government expanded its control toward the northeast, the Ainu were gradually pushed north from their southernmost territory. Trade between the Ainu and the Japanese was established by the mid-fourteenth century. With the increased power of the Matsumae clan, which claimed the southwestern end of Hokkaidō and adjacent areas, the trade became a means for the Japanese to exploit the Ainu during the sixteenth century. Although there were numerous revolts by the Ainu against Japanese oppression, the revolt in the mid-seventeenth century by a famous Ainu political leader, Shakushain, was the most significant. Shakushain rose to the forefront of the Ainu resistance in the mid-1660s, but his forces were crushed when the Matsumae samurai

♦ **pacification**
The cessation of warfare by indigenous peoples enforced by colonial nations or their agents.

broke the truce, slaying Shakushain and his retinue. This event marked the last large-scale resistance by the Hokkaidō Ainu.

In 1779, the Matsumae territory on Hokkaidō came under the direct control of the Tokugawa shogunate in order to protect Japanese interests against Russian expansion southward. The administrative hands changed again in 1821 to the Matsumae and then back to the shogunate in 1854. Drastic changes took place shortly after the establishment of the Meiji government in 1868, as the new government abolished residential restrictions for the Ainu and the Japanese, allowing them to live anywhere on Hokkaidō. The Japanese were encouraged to emigrate to Hokkaidō to take advantage of the natural resources. Most significant, the new government issued the Hokkaidō Aboriginal Protection Act. The Ainu on Hokkaidō were forced to attend Japanese schools established by the government and to register in the Japanese census. Beginning in 1883, the Ainu were granted plots of land and encouraged to take up agriculture. They were removed from their settlements and resettled on land more suited to agriculture, causing drastic changes in Ainu society and culture.

The long history of Ainu contact with outsiders, especially the Japanese, has undermined the Ainu way of life. The Ainu have long been a minority population in Japanese society, suffering prejudice, discrimination, and economic impoverishment. In recent years, the Ainu have made positive efforts to improve their social and political position in Japanese society as well as to establish their own cultural identity.

In addition to ecological factors, the history of contact with outsiders is responsible to a large degree for the major differences in the way of life among these groups of Ainu. For example, because of a lack of contact with metal-using populations, the Kurile Ainu continued to use stone and bone implements and to manufacture pottery long after the Hokkaidō and Sakhalin Ainu had started to use metal goods obtained in trade with their neighbors. The Ainu on the central and northern Kuriles had long been in contact with the Aleuts and Kamchadals. From the end of the eighteenth century, Russians and Japanese, who were hunting sea otters in the area for their furs, exploited the Ainu and transmitted diseases, causing a decline in the population. In 1875 the central and northern Kuriles came under the political control of the Japanese government, which made several attempts to "protect" the Ainu, but the last survivor in this area died in 1941.

Settlements

There was considerable variation in the permanency of Ainu settlements. Until the turn of the century, the basic pattern of the Sakhalin Ainu was a seasonal alternation of settlement between a summer settlement on the shore and a winter settlement farther inland. In the winter settlement, they built semisubterranean pit-houses. Ainu settlements were usually located along the shore, with houses in a single line parallel to the shore. The Kurile Ainu migrated even more frequently. In contrast, on Hokkaidō, permanent settlements were located along the rivers, which were rich in

ECONOMY

The Ainu were basically a hunting-gathering population but fish from the sea, rivers, and lakes was an important source of food for most Ainu. Ainu men fished and hunted sea and land mammals, while women were responsible for gathering plants and storing food for the cold season. Large animals such as bear, deer (in Hokkaidō), musk deer, and reindeer (in Sakhalin) were usually caught using individual techniques of hunting, although cooperation among individuals sometimes took place, especially among the Hokkaidō Ainu. They used the bow and arrow, the set-trap bow, the spear, and various kinds of traps for hunting land mammals, often combining different methods. The hunting techniques of the Hokkaidō Ainu were on the whole technologically more developed than those of other Ainu. They used trained dogs for hunting, and, in some areas, even for fishing. In addition, they used aconite and stingray poison for hunting, which ensured that wounded animals would fall to the ground within a short distance. Large fish such as trout and salmon were important foods, obtained by means of detachable spearheads. The Ainu also used nets, various traps, weirs, and the line and fishhook.

Animal domestication was most highly developed among the Sakhalin Ainu, who engaged in selective breeding to create strong and intelligent male sled dogs and in castration of the dogs to preserve their strength for pulling the sleds, which were an important means of transportation during the harsh winters. The Hokkaidō Ainu alone engaged in small-scale plant domestication prior to the introduction of agriculture by the Japanese government.

fish from mouth to source—an unusual situation for hunter-gathers.

Most Ainu settlements, regardless of region, were small, usually consisting of fewer than five families. An exception was the Hidaka-Tokachi District on Hokkaidō, which enjoyed the most abundant natural resources and the densest population of all the Ainu lands. Here, especially along the Saru River, a few settlements housed about thirty families, and more than half the settlements in the valley exceeded five families.

Kinship, Marriage, and Family

There are some basic features of sociopolitical organization that are shared by most of the Ainu groups, although their finer workings vary from region to region. Among most Ainu groups, the nuclear family is the basic social unit, although some extended families are present. In most Ainu settlements, males related through a common male ancestor comprise the core members who collectively own a hunting ground or a river with good fish runs. Although some scholars emphasize that among the Ainu along the Saru River in Hokkaidō women related through females comprise a corporate group, the exact nature of the group is unclear. Among these Hokkaidō Ainu, an individual is prohibited from marrying a cousin on his or her mother's side. Among most Ainu groups, a few prominent males in the community practice polygyny.

Sociopolitical Organization

Nowhere among the Ainu does political organization extend beyond the settlement, although occasionally a few extremely small settlements form a larger political unit, or a small settlement belongs politically to an adjacent larger settlement. Ainu political leaders are usually not autocratic; elders in the settlement are usually involved in decision making and executing the rules.

Although the formalized ideology prohibits women from participating in the major religious activities that provide the basis of sociopolitical powers for males, there are a number of culturally constituted ways for women to exercise nonformalized power, as discussed in the section on shamanism.

Religion and Expressive Culture

Separation of religious dimensions of Ainu life from others distorts the way Ainu view their lives, since religion is the perspective that pervades their life. Thus, even the disposal of discarded items such as food remains and broken objects is guided by the spatial classification of the Ainu universe and its directions, which derive from religious and cosmological principles. What we call economic activities are religious activities to the Ainu, who regard land and sea animals as deities and fish and plants as products of deities.

RELIGIOUS BELIEFS. An important concept in the Ainu belief system is the soul, owned by most beings in the Ainu universe. According to tradition, the soul becomes perceptible when it leaves the owner's body. For example, when one dreams, one's soul frees itself from the sleeping body and travels, even to places where one has never been. Likewise, a deceased person may appear in one's dreams because the soul of the deceased can travel from the world of the dead to that of the living. During a shamanistic performance, the shaman's soul travels to the world of the dead to snatch back the soul of a dead person, thereby reviving the person nearing death.

This belief underlies the Ainu emphasis on proper treatment of the dead body of humans and all other soul owners in the universe, resulting in elaborate funeral customs ranging from the bear ceremony, discussed later, to the careful treatment of fish bones, which represent the dead body of a fish. Without proper treatment of a dead body, its soul cannot rest in peace in the world of the dead and causes illness among the living to remind the Ainu of their misconduct. Shamans must be consulted to obtain diagnosis and treatment for these illnesses.

The soul has the power to punish only when it has been mistreated. Deities (*kamuy*), in contrast, possess the power to punish or reward at will. Some scholars believe that among the Ainu nature is equated with the deities. Others claim that only certain members of the universe are deified. The Ainu consider all animal deities to be exactly like humans in appearance and to live just like humans in their own divine country—an important point in Ainu religion. Animal deities disguise themselves when visiting the Ainu world to bring meat and fur as presents to the Ainu, just as Ainu guests always bring gifts. The bear thus is not itself the supreme deity but rather the mountain deity's disguise for bringing the gift of bear meat and hide.

In most regions, the goddess of the hearth (fire) was almost as important as the bear. Referred to as "Grandmother Hearth," she resides in the hearth, which symbolizes the Ainu universe. Other important deities include foxes, owls (the deity of the settlement), seals, and a number of other sea and land animals and birds. The impor-

The Ainu have long been a minority population in Japanese society, suffering prejudice, discrimination, and economic impoverishment, but have made positive efforts to improve their position.

What we call economic activities are religious activities to the Ainu, who regard land and sea animals as deities, and fish and plants as products of deities.

tance of each varies from region to region. In addition, there are the goddess of the sun and moon (in some regions, the sun and moon represent two phases of one deity), the dragon deity in the sky, the deity of the house, the deity of the *nusa* (the altar with *inaw*, ritual wood shavings), the deity of the woods, the deity of water, and others.

Evil spirits and demons—called variously *oyasi*, *wenkamuy* (evil deity), etc.—constitute another group of beings in the universe who are more powerful than humans. They exercise their destructive power by causing misfortunes such as epidemics. The smallpox deity is an example. Some of them are intrinsic or by definition bona fide demons, whereas others become demons. For example, if a soul is mistreated after the death of its owner, it turns into a demon. The Ainu devote a great deal of attention to evil spirits and demons by observing religious rules and performing exorcism rites. Human combat with demons is a major theme in Ainu epic poems, discussed later. Characteristically, the deities never deal directly with the demons; rather, they extend aid to the Ainu if the latter behave as directed.

RELIGIOUS PRACTITIONERS. Shamanism is not an exclusively male role. Sakhalin Ainu shamanism differs considerably from Hokkaidō Ainu shamanism. Among the Sakhalin Ainu, with regard to the symbolic structure, the shamanistic ritual represents the process of cooking, a role assigned to women in Ainu society. Shamanism is highly valued among the Sakhalin Ainu, and highly regarded members of society of both sexes, including heads of settlements, may become shamans. Although shamans sometimes perform rites for divinations of various sorts and for miracles, most rites are performed to diagnose and cure illnesses. When shamans are possessed by spirits, they enter a trance and the spirit speaks through their mouths, providing the client with necessary information such as the diagnosis and cure of an illness or the location of a missing object.

Among the Hokkaidō Ainu, shamanism is not highly regarded and shamans are usually women, who collectively have lower social status than men. The Hokkaidō Ainu shaman also enters a possession trance, but she does so only if a male elder induces it in her by offering prayers to the deities. Although she too diagnoses illnesses, male elders take over the healing process. Male elders must consult a shaman before they make important decisions for the community. In other words, the politically powerful male cannot even declare a war without consulting the shaman—an in-

triguing cultural mechanism to balance formalized and nonformalized power.

CEREMONIES. Among the rich and varied Ainu religious beliefs and practices, the bear ceremony is perhaps the most important religious ceremony among both the Sakhalin and Hokkaidō Ainu, for whom the bear represents the supreme deity in disguise. From the Ainu perspective, the bear ceremony is a "funeral ritual" for the bear. Its purpose is to send the soul of the bear back to the mountains through a proper ritual so the soul will be reborn as a bear and revisit the Ainu with gifts of meat and fur.

The process of the bear ceremonial takes at least two years. Among the Sakhalin Ainu another, less elaborate, "after ceremony" follows several months after the major ceremony, thereby further extending the process. A bear cub, captured alive either while still in a den or while walking with its mother upon emerging from the den, is usually raised by the Ainu for about a year and a half. Sometimes women nurse these cubs. Although the time of the ceremony differs according to region, usually it is held at the beginning of the cold season; for the Sakhalin Ainu, it takes place just before they move inland to their winter settlement.

The bear ceremony combines deeply religious elements with the merriment of eating, drinking, singing, and dancing. All participants don their finest clothing and adornments. Prayers are offered to the goddess of the hearth and the deity of the house, but the major focus of the ceremony is on the deity of the mountains, who is believed to have sent the bear as a gift to humans. After the bear is taken out of the "bear house," situated southwest of the house, the bear is killed. The Sakhalin Ainu kill the bear with two pointed arrows, while the Hokkaidō Ainu use blunt arrows before they fatally shoot the bear with pointed arrows, and then strangle the dead or dying bear between two logs. Male elders skin and dress the bear, which is placed in front of the altar hung with treasures. (Ainu treasures consist primarily of goods such as swords and lacquerware obtained in trade with the Japanese. They are considered offerings to the deities and serve as status symbols for the owner.) After preliminary feasting outside at the altar, the Ainu bring the dissected bear into the house through the sacred window and continue the feast.

Among the Hokkaidō Ainu, the ceremony ends when the head of the bear is placed at the altar on a pole decorated with ritual wood shavings (inaw). An elder offers a farewell prayer while shooting an arrow toward the eastern sky—an act signifying the safe departure of the deity. The Sakhalin Ainu bring the bear's skull, stuffed with ritual shavings, bones, eyes, and, if a male bear, the penis, to a sacred place in the mountains. They also sacrifice two carefully chosen dogs, whom they consider to be servant-messengers of the bear deities. Although often taken as a cruel act by outsiders, the bear ceremony expresses the Ainu's utmost respect for the deity.

The bear ceremonial is at once religious, political, and economic. The host of the bear ceremony is usually the political leader of the community. It is the only intersettlement event, to which friends and relatives as well as the politically powerful from nearby and distant settlements may come to participate. Offerings of trade items, such as Japanese lacquerware or swords and Chinese brocades, are a display of wealth, which in turn signifies the political power of the leader and his settlement.

The bear ceremony expresses the formalized cosmology in which men are closer to the deities than are women. The officiants of the ceremony must be male elders and the women must leave the scene when the bear is shot and skinned.

ARTS. While Ainu religion is expressed through rituals as well as in daily routines like the disposal of fish bones, nowhere is it better articulated than in their highly developed oral tradition, which is comparable to the Greek tradition. For the Ainu, the oral tradition is both a primary source of knowledge about the deities and a guide for conduct. There are at least twenty-seven native genres of oral tradition, each having a label in Ainu, that may be classified into two types: verses (epic or lyric) to be sung or chanted, and narrative prose. While the prose in some genres is in the third person, first-person narration is used in the rest: a protagonist tells his own story through the mouth of the narrator-singer. The mythic and heroic epics are long and complex; some heroic epics have as many as 15,000 verses. While the mythic epics relate the activities of deities, the heroic epics are about the culture hero who, with the aid of the deities, fought demons to save the Ainu and became the founder of the Ainu people. Among the Hokkaidō Ainu, the culture hero descended from the world of the deities in the sky and taught the Ainu their way of life, including fishing and hunting and the rituals and rules governing human society. Some scholars contend that the battles fought by the culture hero are battles that the Ainu once fought against invading peoples.

Ainu carving, weaving, embroidery, and music are of high aesthetic quality. Traditionally, these activities were a part of their daily lives rather than separate activities. While Hokkaidō Ainu relied most extensively on garments made of plant fibers, the Sakhalin Ainu wore garments made of fish skin and animal hides. The Kurile Ainu, who knew basketry but not weaving, used land- and sea-mammal hides and bird feathers for their clothing.

Bibliography

Ainu Bunka Hozon Taisaku Kyōgikai (Committee on the Protection of Ainu Culture), ed. (1970). *Ainu minzokushi* (The Ainu people). Tokyo: Daiichi Hōki.

Batchelor, John (1927). *Ainu Life and Lore: Echoes of a Departing Race.* Tokyo: Kyobunkwan. Reprint. 1971. New York: Johnson Reprint Corp.

Chiri, Mashio (1973–1976). *Chiri Mashio chosakushū* (Collected works by Chiri Mashio). 5 vols. Tokyo: Heibonsha.

Harrison, John (1953). *Japan's Northern Frontier.* Gainesville: University of Florida Press.

Hattori, Shiro, ed. (1964). *Bunrui Ainugo hōgen jiten* (An Ainu dialect dictionary with Ainu, Japanese, and English indexes). Tokyo: Iwanami Shoten.

Hilger, Mary Inez (1968). "Mysterious 'Sky People': Japan's Dwindling Ainu." In *Vanishing Peoples of the Earth*, edited by Robert L. Breeden, 92–113. Washington, D.C.: National Geographic Society.

Higler, Mary Inez (1971). *Together with the Ainu.* Norman: University of Oklahoma Press.

Kindaichi, Kyōsuke (1925). *Ainu no kenkyū* (Study of the Ainu). Tokyo: Naigai Shōbō. Reprint. 1944. Tokyo: Yashima Shōbō.

Koganei, Yoshikio (1893–1894). "Beiträge zur physischen Anthropologie der Aino." *Mitteilungen der medizinichen Fakultät der Kaiserlichen Universitat zu Tōkyō* 2:1–249, 251–402.

Munro, Neil Gordon (1963). *Ainu Creed and Cult.* New York: Columbia University Press.

Murdock, George Peter (1934). "The Ainus of Northern Japan." In *Our Primitive Contemporaries*, 163–191. New York: Macmillan.

Nihon Minzokugaku Kyōkai, ed. (1952). *Saru Ainu kyōdō chōsa hōkoku* (Report of the joint research on the Saru Ainu). *Minzokugaku Kenkyu* 16(3–4).

Ohnuki-Tierney, Emiko (1974). *The Ainu of the Northwest Coast of Southern Sakhalin.* New York: Holt, Rinehart & Winston. Reprint. 1984. Prospect Heights, Ill.: Waveland Press.

Ohnuki-Tierney, Emiko (1981). *Illness and Healing among the Sakhalin Ainu.* Cambridge and London: Cambridge University Press.

Piłsudski, Bronislov (1912). *Materials for the Study of the Ainu Language and Folklore.* Cracow: Spółka Wydawnicza Polska.

Takakura, Shinichirō (1960). *The Ainu of Northern Japan: A Study in Conquest and Acculturation*. Transactions of the American Philosophical Society, n.s. 50, p. 4. Philadelphia.

Torii, Ryūzo (1919). "Études archéologiques et ethnologiques: Les Ainou des Îles Kouriles." *Journal of the College of Science* (Tokyo Imperial University) 42.

Watanabe, Hitoshi (1973). *The Ainu Ecosystem*. Seattle, Wash.: University of Washington Press.

Yamamoto, Toshio (1970). *Karafuto Ainū jukyo to mingu* (Houses and artifacts of the Sakahlin Ainu). Tokyo: Sagami Shōbō.

—EMIKO OHNUKI-TIERNEY

The Balinese avoid the open expression of conflict. Villagers who have protracted quarrels such as legal disputes over inheritance usually try to avoid each other.

BALINESE

Ethnyms: none

Orientation

IDENTIFICATION. The Balinese live on the island of Bali, in the archipelago nation of Indonesia. Both their language, Balinese, and religion, Balinese Hinduism, reflect a Malayo-Polynesian culture influenced by Buddhism and Hinduism.

LOCATION. Bali is located between 8° and 8°50′ S and 114°20′ and 115°40′ E. The area is 5,580 square kilometers. The climate is tropical with two seasons, rainly between October and March and dry between April and September.

DEMOGRAPHY. In 1989 the population of Bali was about 2,782,038, of which perhaps 5 percent were Chinese, Muslim, and other minorities. The annual population increase was 1.75 percent. Denpasar, the capital, had a population of 261,263.

LINGUISTIC AFFILIATION. Balinese is an Austronesian language of the Malayo-Javanic Subgroup. Despite phonological similarity with the languages of eastern Indonesia, Java has been a stronger linguistic and literary influence. Balinese was influenced by Indian languages both directly and through contact with Javanese. The earliest (eighth century A.D.) inscriptions found in Bali are in both Sanskrit and Old Balinese. Balinese has levels of speech that require speakers to adjust vocabulary to their relative caste position and reflect feelings about both the person spoken to and the subject matter spoken about. These levels are most elaborate when discussing the human body and its functions, with nine levels of vocabulary for some lexical items. Balinese script was derived from the Pallava writing systems of southern India.

History and Cultural Relations

Archaeological remains, inscriptions, and literary and oral historical accounts indicate that an indigenous population in Bali came into increasing contact with travelers from Java after the fifth century A.D. These outsiders brought Hindu and Buddhist ideas of religion, language, and political organization. It is not known whether the travelers were themselves from the subcontinent, Indianized inhabitants of Java, or both. In the eleventh century A.D., Airlangga, son of a Balinese king and a Javanese queen, became the first ruler to unite Bali with an eastern Javanese kingdom. For the following three centuries the Balinese were intermittently ruled from the east Javanese kingdom of Majapahit, which fell to Islamic forces in 1515. Court officials then fled to Balinese kingdoms where they strengthened the Indianized literary and statecraft traditions that endured in Bali, which was not influenced by Islam. For the next three centuries Bali had small kingdoms, several of which periodically dominated one or more of the others. The Dutch colonial government largely ignored Bali, which had no good harbor on the northern trade route, until the middle of the nineteenth century. In 1855 the first resident Dutch official arrived in north Bali and colonial control over the island increased thereafter until absolute direct governance was imposed by defeating the southern kingdoms militarily in 1906 and 1908. Direct Dutch colonial rule lasted until the Japanese occupied the island from 1942 to 1945. After World War II there was fighting in Bali between those who supported Indonesian independence and forces attempting to reestablish Dutch colonial rule.

Settlements

The Balinese define a village as the people who worship at a common village temple, not as a territorial unit. In fact, inhabitants almost always live in a contiguous area and both colonial and national governments have sought to redefine the village as a territorially based administrative unit. Settlements are centered on the village temple and public buildings, which are usually situated at the intersection of a major and minor road. Both the village and the house yards within it are ideally laid out, with the most sacred buildings in the area nearest Mount Agung, the abode of the gods, and the profane structures nearest the sea, the region of more ambivalent spiritual beings. Families live in house yards that are open, walled areas containing buildings, including a family temple facing the direction of Mount Agung, one or more pavilions for sleeping and sitting, a kitchen, and a refuse area where pigs are kept. Wealthy families have large yards with brick, tileroofed buildings decorated with fine carvings in stone and wood.

Poor families have smaller yards with buildings and walls being made of mud and wattle.

Economy

SUBSISTENCE AND COMMERCIAL ACTIVITIES. For centuries the Balinese have been wet-rice farmers whose irrigation system regulates planting on mountain slopes and seaside plains. Yearly double-cropping is common and the national government supports the introduction of several strains that permit three annual crops in certain areas. Small mechanized plows can be used only in level areas. More commonly, water buffalo pull plows in small family fields, often steep terraces on the mountainsides. Although the volcanic soil is naturally rich, multiple-crop schemes require chemical fertilization. The government protects the rice price and buys all excess harvest for redistribution. In the west of the island there is a profitable coffee-growing region and in the north oranges are a cash crop. The local Balinese economy is based almost entirely on agriculture and government employment in offices and schools. Although Bali has a large tourist trade, most local households do not participate in this kind of economic activity.

INDUSTRIAL ARTS. There is no heavy industry in Bali and little light manufacturing. In tourist areas, carvers and painters produce objects for sale to visitors, often on consignment from art shops.

TRADE. In towns, goldsmiths, tailors, and other merchants provide consumer goods. Each town has a market for vegetables, fruit, packaged and other foodstuffs, and animals such as pigs and chickens. Such markets are also held on a rotating basis in some villages. Villagers, often women, bring agricultural items to sell and return home with manufactured goods to peddle either door-to-door or in small shops. Alternatively, merchants may go to the village to buy agricultural goods or to sell such items as cloth, patent medicines, or soap. Men sell cattle in a central market.

DIVISION OF LABOR. In agricultural activities men plow and prepare the fields. Men and women plant and harvest manually in large groups, while weeding is done by family members. Women keep the gardens, care for the pigs, and keep small snack stalls; they often control the income they gain from these activities. Men care for the cattle that are kept in garden areas. Women care for the children, assisted by the husband or other family members. Although men and women replace each other in domestic and agricultural chores when necessary, there is a stricter distinction between men's and women's ritual work. Men are the priests and women make the elaborate offerings used in rituals.

LAND TENURE. Legally, rice and garden land are owned and registered in the name of an individual man, although his sons may be working his holdings. Villagers consider land to belong to a patrilineal descent group with the current owner inheriting the right to use, or dispose of, the land. Royal families formerly had large holdings.

MARRIAGE AND FAMILY

Marriage

Residence after marriage is patrilocal. Although men may have more than one wife, most marriages are monogamous. Ideally women should not marry men of lower caste or kinship group; a family acknowledges inferiority toward their daughter's husband's group. To avoid such an admission in areas where kin groups are strong and opposed, there is a preference for ancestor-temple group endogamy. In other areas most marriages are village-endogamous with wealth and personal attraction playing an important part in marriage choice. Divorce rules vary but generally a woman married less than three years returns to her father's home with nothing. If she has been married more than three years, and is not adulterous, she receives a percentage of what the couple has earned after the marriage, but none of her husband's inheritance. Children of a marriage remain with their father. When a woman has been chosen by her father as his heir, the divorce rules are applied in reverse.

Domestic Unit

The domestic unit consists of people who eat from the same kitchen. The household includes the husband, wife, children, patrilateral grandparents, and unmarried siblings.

Inheritance

The Balinese inherit patrilineally. A man without sons may choose a daughter to inherit or allow his brothers to divide his property. The family house yard is inherited by the oldest or the youngest son, who is then responsible for any old people or siblings still living there.

Socialization

Children are cared for by their parents, grandparents, and older siblings. They are treated with great affection. Boys are taught to be lively and capable, while girls are encouraged to be responsible and attractive.

Kinship

KIN GROUPS AND DESCENT. Balinese distinguish different types of kinship relationships. Each type, from the smallest to the most inclusive, is described as a group of men, related through a common ancestor, who worship with their families at a common ancestor temple. The group is organized around the performance of rituals twice a year at these temples. The household has a temple in the house yard. The men (and their families) who divide an inheritance have a larger local ancestor temple. These inheritance groups can be joined into larger putative kin groups, which assert, but cannot trace, descent from a common ancestor. A family may be active only in a small, local ancestor group or they may see themselves as part of a series of nested groups with alliances in other parts of the island. Larger kin groups are likely to form and be strong in factionalized areas and times. Kin-group membership is reckoned patrilaterally but matrilateral kinship is also remembered.

KINSHIP TERMINOLOGY. Kin terms are Hawaiian or generational with all men of father's generation bilaterally referred to as "father," and so on with mother, cousins, grandparents, and children. Individuals have a teknonym that indicates their gender, caste, and birth order. Children are called by this teknonym and adults are called "father of . . ." or "mother of . . ." after the birth of their first child. Old people are known as "grandfather or grandmother of. . . ."

Sociopolitical Organization

SOCIAL ORGANIZATION. Balinese individuals and kin groups identify themselves as being members of one of four hereditary caste groups. These groups are said to have in the past corresponded to occupational categories, although this is no longer the case. Ninety percent of the population is Sudra, the group said to have been farmers and considered to be of lower caste. Certain ritual activities are reserved to priests of the Brahman caste and the former rulers who were of the Ksaytria and Wesia castes, but other members of these groups are, and were, farmers and merchants. Families belonging to the three higher castes are more likely to be part of supravillage ancestor-temple groups.

POLITICAL ORGANIZATION. Bali is one of the twenty-eight provinces of the nation of Indonesia. The province is divided into seven regions (*kabupaten*), each of which is subdivided into districts (*kecamatan*). Districts are divided into villages (*desa*), which are composed of subunits (*banjar*). The units above the village level carry out regional and national policy. The village-level officials are elected by the village council, which is made up of male heads of household. These leaders execute governmental policies such as registration of land sales, births and deaths, and also organize local projects including the repair of facilities and the holding of local elections.

SOCIAL CONTROL. Above the village level there is a police force. In the village there is a system of fines for residents who do not attend meetings or group work projects. However, informal control mechanisms such as gossip and group pressure are used more frequently.

CONFLICT. The Balinese avoid the open expression of conflict. Villagers who have protracted quarrels such as legal disputes over inheritance usually try to avoid each other. Supravillage conflict formerly led to warfare.

Religion and Expressive Culture

RELIGIOUS BELIEFS. Balinese Hinduism mixes Hinduism with animistic traditions. Each temple congregation holds periodic rituals to placate and please the supernaturals and thereby protect the group's peace and prosperity. The Balinese make offerings to their ancestors, spirits connected to places, and other supernaturals, some with Indic names.

RELIGIOUS PRACTITIONERS. The larger ceremonies are conducted by Brahman priests. Lower-caste priests care for temples and perform local ceremonies.

CEREMONIES. Rituals are performed on several cycles, the most important being the six-month cycle. Every six months there are island-wide ceremonies, and each temple has an anniversary ritual every six months. There are also life-cycle rituals arranged by families, the most important being the cremation.

ARTS. Rituals, whether family or village, may include music, dance, drama, and shadow-play performances. In ritual context artistic performance has a sacred association. Stone and wood carving in home or temple indicates high prestige for the owner or congregation. Royal and wealthy people have supported artistic performances and productions, in part as a display of their prestige. Tourist art includes paintings, carvings, and shortened secular performances.

MEDICINE. Government medical care is widely available and used. Indigenous medicine holds that illness or other misfortunes can be caused by angry spirits or ancestors, witchcraft, or imbalance in the bodily humors.

DEATH AND AFTERLIFE. A person's caste, wealth, and prestige are reflected in the size and elaborateness of his or her funeral. Living descendants must perform rituals that move the deceased souls through the afterlife to rebirth in a younger member of the family. Neglect of these rituals may cause the dead ancestor to make family members ill.

Bibliography

Belo, Jane (1949). *Bali: Rangda and Barong.* Monographs of the American Ethnological Society, 16. Seattle and London: University of Washington Press.

Belo, Jane (1960). *Trance in Bali.* New York: Columbia University Press.

Geertz, Clifford (1980). *Negara: The Theatre State in Nineteenth Century Bali.* Princeton N.J.: Princeton University Press.

Geertz, Hildred, and Clifford Geertz (1975). *Kinship in Bali.* Chicago: University of Chicago Press.

Swellengrebel, J. L., et al. (1960). *Bali: Life, Thought, and Ritual.* The Hague: W. van Hoeve.

Swellengrebel, J. L., et al. (1969). *Bali: Further Studies in Life, Thought, and Ritual.* The Hague: W. van Hoeve.

—ANN P. McCAULEY

BATAK

Ethonyms: Batak subsocieties include Angkola-Sipirok, Dairi-Pakpak, Karo, Mandailing, Simelungun, and Toba

Orientation

IDENTIFICATION. The Batak subsocieties are closely related, rapidly modernizing ethnic monority groups whose rural home regions are in the rugged highlands and plains near North Sumatra's Lake Toba. The word "Batak" may have originally been an epithet used by Muslim lowlanders to refer to the mountain peoples in a derogatory way, as "primitives." Today the term is much less stigmatic and is used in some subsocieties, such as the Toba, as an everyday ethnic designation. Some of the groups along the borders of the Batak regions (e.g., Karo, Mandailing) eschew the label "Batak" in favor of their subsociety designations. Although the Batak societies share close dialects and similar social structural patterns, they never have had any significant political

unity. During Dutch colonial times they were loose tribal confederations, with some chiefdom formation in border areas. Ethnic boundaries shift often and ethnic identity is labile. Today, with large numbers of city migrants and greater political power in multiethnic competition, many Batak are reemphasizing their Batak ethnic character, and inventing "ancient Batak village traditions" through their use of the mass media and by staging lavish rituals.

LOCATION. The Batak home regions surround Lake Toba in North Sumatra, spanning the large highland region between the Acehnese and Gayo-Alas peoples to the north and the Minangkabau to the south. The home regions include heavily forested mountains, now crosscut with passable roads, and wide, fertile plains, laid out into rice paddies and grazing land. The Batak farm areas straddle the Bukit Barisan, Sumatra's main northwest-southeast mountain chain. North Sumatra has a distinct rainy season (September-December) and a pronounced hot, dry period (May-August).

DEMOGRAPHY. North Sumatra had a 1989 population of 10,330,091. Most of this population is Batak, with smaller numbers of Javanese, Indonesian-Chinese, Acehnese, and Minangkabau. There is also a large Batak diaspora population in multiethnic cities such as Jakarta, Bandung, and Surabaya. Many Bataks moved to Javanese cities in the 1920s and 1930s for employment as clerks, teachers, and newspaper writers and editors (the Bataks were one of Outer-Island Indonesia's first deeply literate peoples). This migration pattern has continued, augmented by Bataks from poorer families seeking jobs in the army and transportation.

LINGUISTIC AFFILIATION. The Batak dialects are Western Austronesian languages closely related to Malay, Javanese, and Tagalog. The Toba, Angkola, and Mandailing dialects are quite similar and mutually intelligible, while Karo, Kairi-Pakpak, and Simelungun are generally not understood outside their home areas. No Batak language is mutually intelligible with the national language, Bahasa Indonesia, although the latter is widely known throughout the Batak home regions. Batak languages have a conversational level and a more esoteric oratory level, used in *adat* (ancient custom) ceremonies. Genres of speech here include verse-form verbal duels, mythic chants, dirges, and clan genealogies. Literacy in the Latin alphabet is widespread (introduced in Dutch colonial public schools and mission schools, beginning in the 1850s in Angkola and Mandail-

♦ **Austronesian languages**
A large group of languages (formerly called "Malayo-Polynesian") including about 450 in Oceania. They are found mostly on the coasts in Melanesia and New Guinea, but otherwise throughout Polynesia and Micronesia.

Batak

HISTORY AND
CULTURAL
RELATIONS

BATAK HOUSE

Traditional Batak houses are carved and have high peaks. The "complete" village is a small model of the cosmos and a replica of the entire social order. Sumatra, Indonesia. (Charles & Josette Lenars/Corbis)

ing). There was also an old Batak script, a syllabary based on Sanskrit-derived court-writing systems from west or south Sumatra. Little used or even known today, the Batak script was once a runic code for divination and spells, for village priests.

History and Cultural Relations

Despite the relative inaccessibility of the highlands, the Batak groups have been deeply shaped by influences from neighboring cultures. Many words for Batak political leaders and religious concepts show Indian influence, as do Batak divination and astrological lore. Border areas such as Karo and Mandailing model their traditional political systems on the nearby state societies, Aceh and Minangkabau. Islam was introduced to the southern Batak lands from Minangkabau in the 1820s, on the eve of the Dutch incursion into the area. By the 1850s, they had established a civil administration in the southern Batak areas, a region they hoped to use as a buffer between Muslim Aceh and Muslim Minangkabau. The Dutch gradually extended their control northward through Toba, encountering armed resistance from the charismatic warrior chief, Sisingamangaraja XII. By 1910 all Batak areas were under Dutch control, schools had been established in Toba, Angkola,

and Mandailing, and missionary Christianity was thriving in Toba. By the 1920s, literate Batak had established a cosmopolitan city culture of newspapers and book publishing in Medan and Sibolga; writers were turning their attention to nationalist and anti-Dutch concerns. North Sumatra was occupied by the Japanese from 1942 to 1945. Since the Indonesian national revolution of 1945–1949, the region has remained an economically vital part of the Indonesian state. Owing to population pressure on over-used farmland, out-migration to cities continues.

Settlements

Village size varies greatly by subsociety: some Toba rice-farming villages have only 4 or 5 houses, while some Mandailing and Angkola villages have 100 to 200 houses. Market towns dot the highlands too, serving as hubs for large numbers of mountain villages. In Karo and Toba, some traditional villages remain, with Great Houses (carved, high-peaked, adat houses, for several families linked through clanship and marriage alliance). More common today are Malay-style houses, divided into rooms and roofed with zinc, not thatch. Throughout the Batak areas the "complete" village is both a small model of the cosmos and a replica of the entire social order, with all its requisite interlocking parts. These consist of the village founders and their close lineage mates, their traditional wife givers (who have provided the founders with brides and blessings over many generations), and their traditional wife receivers, who marry the founders' daughters and provide the village with labor services and physical protection. Cosmic as well as social order is maintained, it is thought, if all three partners mutually support each other and keep the "flow of blessings" circulating through human society and the agricultural realm. Similar patterns of thought are found throughout eastern Indonesia.

Economy

SUBSISTENCE AND COMMERCIAL ACTIVITIES. All regions are rice-cultivation areas, combining dry fields with extensive, terraced paddies. One rice crop per year is typical in some of the less fertile uplands, although wide plainlands sometimes support two crops. Government development projects are spreading green-revolution varieties of high-yield rice throughout the province. Cash crops (coffee, tobacco, cloves, cinnamon) have been grown since colonial times; market gardening also supplements rice production (peppers, cabbage, tomatoes, beans).

Government projects encourage the cultivation of peanuts and fish farming. Traditional forest products such as camphor and incense are still collected, as is forest rubber. Karo is a major fruit and vegetable exporter. Domestic animals include chickens, ducks, water buffalo, goats, and (in non-Muslim areas) pigs. Outside the agricultural sector, Batak work in the transportation industry, in cloth sales, and in Sumatra's ubiquitous markets.

INDUSTRIAL ARTS. Market towns typically have mechanics, carpenters, house builders, tailors, and road-pavement crews, while village men make fish nets and women weave ceremonial textiles and make rattan baskets. In larger towns, shops and repair businesses are owned by Indonesian-Chinese entrepreneurs.

TRADE. Since at least early colonial times, the highlands have been crosscut by trade routes for salt, salted fish, dried hot peppers, and cooking oil—the basic ingredients, with rice and greens, of the standard village meal. Since the 1950s, paved roads and crushed stone roads have been extended to many village areas, augmenting the old colonial main routes between market centers. Bus transport to Medan and Padang is dependable and frequent.

DIVISION OF LABOR. Farm families tend to share household tasks and field labor among the men, women, and children. Heavy planting and harvest tasks are often done by larger work groups, recruited by age (groups of adolescents) or clan and marriage-alliance ties to the farm family in question. Some wealthier village families hire poorer relatives to work their land, on a sharecropping basis. In pre-Dutch times southern Batak high chiefs had slaves who worked as their house servants and field laborers.

LAND TENURE. In the ideal situation, family rice land is not to be bought and sold but should pass to sons and their households, with a smaller share going to daughters. In practice, some families do sell paddy land, for school tuition or other pressing needs; in addition, the establishment of new villages east of the traditional Batak lands has opened up new farming territory. Traditional houses and lineage heirlooms pass down through the patriline. Parents often circumvent the strict patrilineal inheritance rules for land by bestowing land gifts on favored daughters at their weddings or on the birth of their first child.

Kinship

KIN GROUPS AND DESCENT. The Batak peoples have kinship systems similar to the Kachin of highland Burma. They have patrilineal clans, divided into localized lineages (often centered on ancestral houses and tombs). Lineages of different clans are linked together through asymmetrical marriage alliance—Lineage A will get its wives from Lineage B of another clan. Lineage B will thus serve as the politically and ritually superordinate alliance partner to A, showering it with fertility blessings, good luck, and supernatural protection. Lineage A in turn will give its daughters in a second direction to C, of still another clan. Lineage C will then become A's own subordinate alliance partner. Lineages of varying time-depths are the operative units in this marriage system. Today, many lineages have members in several villages as well as in migrant communities in the multiethnic cities. Clans are very large, never meet corporately, and in fact often straddle two ethnic subsocieties such as Toba and Angkola. Some Batak peoples imagine that all clans originated in a Toba ancestral home, and spread outward from there because of ancient clan wars. Much adat ceremonial activity is directed toward contacting lineage ancestors and securing their blessings.

Marriage and Family

MARRIAGE. As noted, the ideal marriage involves a young man and a young woman from two linked lineages that have a long-standing alliance relationship. In practice, many marriages forge bonds between lineages with no previous alliance; that situation is usually accepted as a means "to widen the sphere of kin-term usage" and to provide more alliance partners for support. When families are conforming to the ideal, however, a man would marry his exact mother's brother's daughter. This marriage would repeat the marriage his father made in the previous generation: both the older man and his son would have obtained brides from the same house in the same traditional wife-giver lineage. Elaborate gift exchange accompanies marriage in many subsocieties. The bride brings ritual textiles and various foods (identified with femininity) to her new house, while the bridegroom's family gives countergifts of bride-wealth payments, jewelry, and livestock. Such exchange is conceptualized as part of a complementary opposition scheme in which wife givers and wife receivers work together to produce a fertile marriage, which in turn empowers the village. Residence is ideally with or near the new husband's parents for several years, after which the new couple formally split off to set up their own household. In prenational times some areas such as Karo and Toba had large, multifam-

In the ideal Batak marriage alliance, a man would marry his exact mother's brother's daughter, thus repeating the marriage his father made in the previous generation.

♦ **adat/adet**
The customary law of the indigenous peoples of Indonesia. Also used in a more general sense to mean the overarching rules governing social behavior.

ily houses, with a full complement of wife givers and wife takers. Lower-class people never had such large and complex houses. Divorce, much discouraged in the adat oratory, is possible under Islamic law and Indonesian civil law. For wealthier families, given the fact that marriage alliance carries so many larger political implications, divorce is shameful. When Batak migrant men marry women from other, non-Batak ethnic groups, a new bride is sometimes adopted into a lineage as her groom's mother's brother's daughter.

DOMESTIC UNIT. There are several household types: (1) older married couples living with married sons and their other unmarried children; (2) new couples just separated from such parental households; (3) young married couples with children; and (4) older couples with several unmarried relatives sharing the same house. Many migrants from the cities move back to their home villages temporarily and live with relatives, so household structure is extremely fluid. Multifamily wife giver/wife receiver "complete" households have been rare in recent decades.

INHERITANCE. Sacred property such as old rice land, lineage heirlooms, and the ancestral house should pass down the patriline, whereas bride-wealth goods circulate among houses linked through marriage alliance. Daughters can obtain rice land as bridal gifts from their fathers. In some areas, the eldest son and the youngest son get the larger share of heritable goods, and the youngest son and his wife are obligated to care for his aged parents.

SOCIALIZATION. Attendance at public school or at Muslim school is compulsory and dominates children's lives today. The national schools stress Indonesian patriotism and "modern values." At home, older siblings have a large role in the care of younger brothers and sisters, frequently carrying them around in tight cloth slings. Young children are rarely scolded or even reprimanded; children are cajoled into obeying with small food or cash gifts.

Sociopolitical Organization

The Batak subsocieties are part of the multiethnic nation of Indonesia, centered in the capital of Jakarta and dominated by the Javanese. North Sumatra is a province of the nation, and all Bataks are citizens. The civil servants who administer the area are, for the most part, Batak themselves.

SOCIAL ORGANIZATION. Like other Southeast Asians, Batak tend to pay great attention to social hierarchy. In this area, this is phrased in terms of traditional social-class background (aristocrat, free commoner, or slave descendant),

closeness to the founder lineage of a person's home village, and occupation prestige (with farm labor at the bottom and salaried office work at the top). Using a system of indirect rule, the Dutch rigidified the old Batak class systems, strengthening the hand of the traditional nobles. Poorer families looked to the colonial schools as a means for their children to escape class discrimination in farm villages.

POLITICAL ORGANIZATION. Each Batak area has a dual political organization today: the bureaucracy of the national Indonesian government extends from the province of North Sumatra down to the village level (with civil officials, a police force, and a judiciary), while Batak villages have their councils of elders, their chiefs (*rajas*), and their chiefs' councils, selected according to genealogical position in each area's founder clans. Village clusters and larger chieftaincy domains are organized according to both marriage alliance and descent ties, in a pattern reminiscent of traditional social organization in eastern Indonesia. The chiefs and their councils supervise adat ceremonials and some points of inheritance law and marriage, and serve as the prestigious, morally upright "old guard" of their villages. The government officials, for their part, control the secular political sphere.

SOCIAL CONTROL. Violent crime and business law are under the control of the national government and their police force, while traditional councils exercise some moral control over everyday village social order. Adat leaders can exact fines for disallowed marriages; they also supervise the payment of bride-wealth, a major source of tension. In some areas fear of witchcraft and sorcery is common and articulates with factional disputes. Poisoners are often thought to lurk just over the next hill (a common ethnic boundary-maintenance device).

CONFLICT. Until Dutch pacification efforts in the mid-1800s, intervillage warfare and lineage-to-lineage feuding were quite common, given severe pressure for the farmland. After the colonial era, this legacy of intense intergroup rivalry took new forms: conflict within the Protestant church, conflict among lineages to see which one can put on the most lavish ancestor-commemoration ceremony, and conflict over access to modern jobs. At the village level factionalism is bitter, constant, and quick-changing, based on competition for land and, today, government favors.

Religion and Expressive Culture

RELIGIOUS BELIEFS. Virtually all Batak have converted to Islam or Protestant Christianity over the last 170 years, although in some areas beliefs that spirits can infest people and make them ill remain strong. An older Batak pantheon of creator deities and mythical clan founders has largely been eclipsed by the world religions. Batak converts often speak of an older "Age of Darkness" before their forefathers found out about "true religion." The southern Batak areas of Angkola-Sipirok and Mandailing converted to Islam starting in the 1820s; these are markedly pious, learned areas today, with many hajji and Quranic schools. Toba is a similarly serious, well-schooled Christian area, with many ministers and religious teachers. Karo is a region of much more recent conversions: pagan areas remain, and some villagers and townspeople converted to world religions in 1965, to avoid being labeled Communist sympathizers in the national unrest attending the establishment of the Suharto regime.

Each area has a varying syncretic blend of Islamic or Christian figures with indigenous spirits; the latter are a very minor part of the system of thought in long-converted areas. With increasing literacy, the old creator deities and the figures of myth have generally been demoted to the status of folklore figures.

RELIGIOUS PRACTITIONERS.   All areas have the standard religious personnel of world Islam and Christianity, as well as curer-diviners who contact supernaturals through trances and perform exorcisms.

CEREMONIES.   Most areas have split off adat, or custom, from *agama*, or true religion (that is, Islam or Christianity). This strategem allows Batak to remain pious monotheists and to maintain an elaborate round of adat ceremonies, with ritual speeches, dances, processions, and gift exchange. Adat ceremonies focus on lineage ancestors, births in the lineage, and marriage alliance (with long, contentious weddings).

ARTS.   Nineteenth-century European missionaries discouraged carving and ritual dirges and dances, fearing these were blasphemous. This eliminated much of Toba's magnificent traditional sculpture and masked dances. House architecture in the old Great-House style has become too expensive to maintain today; few "Cosmic Houses" remain. Batak textile arts still thrive, as these cloths are still a vital part of marriage and mortuary exchange.

MEDICINE.   Modern, scientific medicine is practiced by a thin network of government health workers, based in clinics, while curer-diviners practice alongside them, concentrating now on "spirit infestations" and some aspects of childbirth and poison control.

DEATH AND AFTERLIFE.   Resilient beliefs in powerful lineage ancestors exist in some areas in tandem with the afterlife theories of Christianity and Islam. Adat's ceremonial speeches can be used to invoke the blessings of long-dead lineage ancestors. Masked dancers once served as mediums for ancestors to interact with living persons, but such performances have now been redefined as quaint customs.

Bibliography

Carle, Rainer, et al. (1987). *Cultures and Societies of North Sumatra*. Berlin: D. Reimer Verlag.

Cunningham, Clark N. (1958). *The Postwar Migration of the Toba-Bataks to East Sumatra*. Yale University Southeast Asia Studies, Cultural Report no. 5. New Haven.

Kipp, Rita Smith, and Richard Kipp, eds. (1983). *Beyond Samosir: Recent Studies of the Batak Peoples of Sumatra*. Ohio University Papers in International Studies, Southeast Asia Series, no. 62. Athens.

Siagian, T. P. (1966). "A Bibliography of the Batak Peoples." *Indonesia* 2:161–185.

Singarimbun, Masri (1975). *Kinship, Descent, and Alliance among the Karo Batak*. Berkeley and Los Angeles: University of California Press.

Vergouwen, J. C. (1933). *The Customary Law of the Toba Bataks of Northern Sumatra*. The Hague: Martinus Nijhoff.

—SUSAN RODGERS

BURAKUMIN

Ethonyms: Eta, Hinin (historic, derogatory); Hisabetsumin; Outcaste; Shin-Heimin (historic, often derogatory); Tokushu Burakumin (often derogatory)

Orientation

IDENTIFICATION.   It is important to note that neither historic outcastes nor Burakumin are racially distinguishable from the majority of Japanese, despite some common beliefs and academic writings that propose non-Japanese racial origins for Burakumin. Although in the historic period the mainstream Japanese subjected outcastes to strict dress codes and often required them to wear pieces of leather on their outer garments to signify their status, in contemporary Japan there is little to isolate the Burakumin from the majority population. Except for their reported

Nineteenth-century European missionaries discouraged Batak carving and ritual dirges and dances, fearing these were blasphemous, and so eliminated much magnificent traditional sculpture and masked dances.

Burakumin

informality of dress code, language, and behavior, Burakumin do not differ from the Japanese majority in appearance, language, and most other cultural practices.

Burakumin exclusively or dominantly occupy many small communities or areas in a community; indeed, their culture name means "hamlet or community people." (In this article, "Burakumin" is used to designate the people, "buraku" to designate their communities.) The names "Eta" and "Hinin" were used through the Middle Ages to refer to outcastes of various sorts. Eta was derived from the Japanese word for leatherworker, a name that was later spelled differently in Chinese characters to mean "plenty of defilement," which suits the popular perception of their occupation. Hinin means "nonhuman." After the abolition of caste in 1871, these words were replaced by Shin-Heimin (new commoners), Hisabetsumin (discriminated people), Tokushu Burakumin (special community people), or Burakumin.

Since the Burakumin look and behave much like the majority population, others most commonly identify Burakumin by their place of origin. Although Burakumin may choose to "pass" as non-Burakumin to avoid various forms of discrimination, they risk having their identity scrutinized if others discover their place of birth and original residence. Local people know certain areas in a locality to be buraku, and they see any connection to such areas as signifying outcaste origin. Even when a person from a buraku moves to a different region in Japan, background investigation or accident may reveal his or her origin, and this discovery often results in stigmatization of the person's professional, social, personal, and emotional life.

LOCATION. Burakumin communities are more heavily distributed in western Japan, particularly in the prefectures of Hyogo, Okayama, Hiroshima, Ehime, and Fukuoka. Urban centers in western Japan, such as Kyoto and Osaka, have large numbers of buraku. In contrast, the Tokyo metropolitan area, situated in eastern Japan, has a surprisingly small number of buraku.

DEMOGRAPHY. There are some arguments about how many buraku and Burakumin exist in Japan today. The General Affairs Agency census in 1985 reported that there were then 1,163,372 Burakumin and 4,594 buraku in Japan. Independent scholars of the Burakumin issue criticize these figures as much too small and say they do not reflect the reality of the Burakumin situation. Their estimates suggest that 2 to 3 million Burakumin and approximately 6,000 buraku currently exist in Japan.

The Burakumin are heavily concentrated in the western part of Japan. According to the above-mentioned statistics, Hyōgo has the largest number of Burakumin (153,236), followed by Osaka (143,305), Fukuoka (135,956), Nara (62,175), and Okayama (56,687). In eastern Japan, Saitama, Gumma, and Tochigi prefectures have relatively high numbers of Burakumin. There are no known Burakumin in the northernmost prefecture of Hokkaidō.

Before the 1920 census no comprehensive demographic data existed; however, some regional records were available. The population survey of Kyoto in 1715 recorded 11 outcaste communities with a population of 2,064; in 1800 4,423 outcastes were reported in Osaka; the National Census of 1871 counted 261,311 Eta, 23,480 Hinin, and 79,095 other categories of outcastes. The 1920 census reported that there were 4,890 buraku and 829,675 Burakumin in Japan; by 1935, the number of buraku had increased to 5,367 and that of Burakumin to almost 1 million.

As a general tendency the Burakumin population was increasing faster than the general population of Japan in the last century. The official abolition of outcaste status and assimilation efforts seem to have had no influence over the persistence of Burakumin. Continuous recruitment of new members by marriage and high birthrates in Burakumin communities account for this tendency.

LINGUISTIC AFFILIATION. The linguistic affiliation of the Burakumin is identical to that of mainstream Japanese. Some ethnographic reports indicate that their speech tends to be more informal and colloquial than that of the mainstream Japanese. In contemporary Japan, where most Burakumin children are educated in the same formal schooling system as other Japanese children, any community or occupational jargon Burakumin may have developed historically is bound to decrease or even to disappear.

History and Cultural Relations

The history of outcastes in Japan dates back to its early historic period, beginning in the eighth century A.D. (Nara period). Under the centralized bureaucratic government with imperial leadership, clan-based groups called Uji and Kabane became associated with often exclusive occupational guilds, or *be*. These guilds included leatherworkers, caretakers of the dead and tombs, and butchers—the traditional occupations of later outcastes.

The practitioners of these occupations gradually became separated from the majority society through the ancient to early feudal periods as unclean, undesirable, lowly, and less than human, and Japanese society denied them rights granted to its mainstream members. In addition to encompassing the traditional occupational groups, the outcaste community absorbed people who dropped out of the social systems because of poverty or criminal behavior, as well as those who failed to be an integral part of the stable society, for instance, runaway peasants, flood-plain dwellers, and itinerant entertainers of all sorts.

Toward the end of the twelfth century the failing economic system based on peasantry and heavy taxation helped cause the decline of imperial power and the rise of the military class, which marked the beginning of the feudal age. The consequent political instability and poverty affected commoners most severely, and a large number of peasants lost their financial means and social affiliation and were forced out of their homes and their assigned land. Because all peasants of the time were legally bound to their land and it was illegal for them to leave it, there was no place for them in the social system, and they became a transient population. Together with all other kinds of people who were excluded from the socioeconomic system, they joined traditional outcastes, to form the medieval outcaste population.

Historic evidence indicates that the medieval outcastes' occupation and residence varied. They engaged seasonally in work ranging from street performing, street sweeping, and leatherworking to unauthorized religious practices, changing their residence to accommodate their seasonal occupation.

This fluid population of outcastes gradually evolved into more specialized occupational groups throughout the feudal age. In the period of continuous military confrontations, from the fifteenth to the sixteenth century, warlords invited outcaste leatherworkers to their territories in order to secure the supply of military gear. The increasing demand for leather goods required a large number of outcastes in the industry and accelerated the occupational differentiation of outcastes.

In the seventeenth century the Tokugawa shogunate consolidated the systematic and legal discrimination against outcastes in Japan. After conquering warlords in most of the territory known today as Japan, the Tokugawa government set out to establish a strict administrative system that ensured social and economic stability for nearly three centuries. Incorporation of the outcaste below the rigidly divided castes of warriors, farmers, artisans, and merchants was a strategy for

detracting from the dissatisfaction of lower castes: no matter how difficult their lives may have been they were still better than those of the "nonhuman" outcastes.

Eta and Hinin were two major categories of outcaste in this period. The most crucial differences between the two were the terms of their status and the areas of their occupational specialization. The Eta inherited their status and tended to engage in farming, craftwork, and community services. Hinin were usually those who had been degraded to outcaste status as a punishment and who could be reinstated to other castes; their occupations were usually unskilled or transient. Entertainers also fell into this latter category.

Although outcastes in the Tokugawa period varied in occupation and worked as leatherworkers, basket and sandal makers, temple caretakers, crematory workers, butchers, entertainers, laborers, and farmers, others commonly treated them as nonhumans and forced them into hard labor, economic difficulties, and poor living conditions. Outcastes lived in designated segregated districts or separate communities, and occupational necessity determined their access to the public areas. Government-imposed dress codes prohibited any ornaments and narrowly defined types and quality of garments allowed for outcastes.

Their services and the products of their labor belonged to the government authority, and until later in the period there was no direct compensation for their work; instead, the government allowed them the "privileges" of begging and gathering from the commoners who benefited from the outcastes' services. This practice led to the common but untrue belief that outcastes were "beggars" and not a productive part of society, and it strengthened the discriminatory perception of and behavior toward outcastes.

Toward the end of the nineteenth century, a major political change occurred. The shogunate failed in economic reforms and mismanaged the inevitable contacts with foreign countries. After negotiations among political leaders, the emperor was restored in 1868 as the sole political power of Japan, supported by low-rank warrior-class technocrats. The new government's priority was to modernize and Westernize the then "backward" nation. In 1871 the government emancipated the outcastes as a part of this modernization effort.

This emancipation brought no real change in the discrimination against outcastes. Discriminatory practices against Burakumin persisted in almost every aspect of life, and the government made little effort to enforce its declaration of

Burakumin

Subtle forms of discrimination and vague but definite prejudice against Burakumin are the most common problems of contemporary Japan.

"equality." In the municipal house registration government officials recorded former outcastes as "Shin-Heimin" (new commoners), thus clearly distinguishing them from the traditional commoners. Segregated residence also continued, although there were no more legal restrictions. The only change that occurred was a negative one: the industries that outcastes had traditionally dominated were now open to everyone, and nonoutcaste investors began to venture into leatherwork and other crafts, threatening the small-scale former outcaste manufacturers and placing a heavy economic strain on many Burakumin. In addition, rapid political and economic changes caused financial difficulties to common people, and their frustration often found outlets in "Eta-gari" (an outcaste hunt).

Many political and cultural movements characterize the struggle of former outcastes or Burakumin throughout modern history. Reconciliation and assimilation movements represent one side of their efforts, which argues that the poverty and different life-style of Burakumin caused the persisting discrimination and that the improvement of Burakumin living standards and cultural assimilation into the mainstream society are essential to eliminate the discrimination. The other side of the scale is the more aggressive political movement that defines the Burakumin situation as a class issue and the result of victimization rooted within the mainstream society. People who support this position assert the responsibility of the larger society for positive changes in Burakumin issues. These movements, aided by the democratic constitution instituted after World War II, the Law for Special Measures for Dōwa Projects (1969), and the Law for Special Measures for Regional Improvement (1982), have succeeded in improving the Burakumin situation and reducing discrimination to a certain extent.

More than a hundred years after emancipation, however, the deep root of discrimination against Burakumin is far from dead; indeed, it is finding a new soil in the complex social problems of contemporary Japan. While subtle forms of discrimination and vague but definite prejudice against Burakumin are the most common problems, some recent incidents show that hostility between the majority population and Burakumin still exists. A group of teenagers in Yokohama beat and killed homeless people in the 1980s, and day laborers from buraku participated in an outbreak of street riots in Osaka in 1991. The Law for Special Measures for Regional Improvement expired in March 1992, and the Japanese legislature concluded that

there was no more need for this antidiscrimination law and decided not to renew it. The future development of the Burakumin movement under the new legal conditions is uncertain.

The long, continuing history of outcaste/Burakumin discrimination contains certain underlying ideas that have developed and supported the structure of discrimination and segregation in Japanese society. The most well-argued aspect of this discrimination centers on religious beliefs about the protection of ritual cleanliness. Teachings of Shintoism, the native religion of Japan, place a strong emphasis on ritual cleanliness as the essential part of righteousness, which is to be strictly guarded from contamination by death and blood. The introduction of Buddhism in the sixth century, and its recognition as a state religion from the eighth century onward, added to this view of death and blood as taboo, as the imperial and shogunate governments fully embraced the Buddhist doctrine against killing in their official policies. Thus the Japanese considered occupations that dealt with death or bloodshed "unclean" and contacts with them defiling. (This view that outcastes and their descendants are "unclean" is strong even today among many Japanese.) Still, the society needed to care for the dead properly according to the religious requirements, dispose of animal carcasses, and produce leather goods; the solution to this dilemma was the segregation of people who engaged in such occupations from the general population.

Furthermore, at the heart of the outcaste existence, which has served the contradictory needs of Japanese society, is the connection between the outcastes' continuing economic importance and their lack of access to political power. For instance, Hijiri priests in ancient Japan were extremely important religious figures, as they were knowledgeable in the agricultural calendar and counseled farmers with the proper timing for seasonal activities. The Yamato clan, the politicoreligious power in the early historic period, saw them as competition and eventually made them outcastes. The Hijiri priests thereafter played the same economic role in agricultural communities but were devoid of political influence.

In the feudal age, repeated civil wars increased the demand for leather goods, and thus it was very important for feudal lords to have outcaste leatherworkers, called "Kawata" or "Eta," under their control. In the later feudal age, lords often assigned outcastes to the cultivation of marginal land, used them as virtual slaves in various enterprises to improve the local cash economy, or placed them in dangerous situations such as those of guards and low-status detectives. In spite of the crucial roles they played in the feudal society, their ascribed outsider status effectively prevented them from gaining any political power. In the later Tokugawa period some of the outcastes became quite affluent and influential. A legend from this period depicts the defensive reaction of the government: an Eta was killed in Edo (later Tokyo), and the head of the outcastes in Edo appealed to the magistrate; he ruled that an Eta was worth one-seventh of a regular person, and therefore one regular person had to murder seven Eta before he could be convicted.

In modern industrial Japan, Burakumin workers supply cheap, disposable labor to industry as part-time workers or day laborers. Burakumin also work more often than mainstream Japanese for small businesses and factories that belong to the lower stratum of the hierarchical industrial structure of modern Japan. Thus they frequently suffer from having unstable incomes and few benefits.

Some theorists also have postulated that the existence of outcastes is a reincorporating mechanism of sociocultural deviation. The outcaste population has been increasing constantly, largely because of the continuous flow of new members from mainstream society, either directed by authority or pressured by economic failure or loss of social affiliations. Japanese culture holds it as ideal to be average and to keep to one's place in society, and deviation from the norm is strongly discouraged from early childhood. This cultural emphasis has successfully incorporated most of the population most of the time, thus creating a largely homogeneous society. However, there were people throughout history who were excluded from the majority society, and students of discrimination issues have discovered the historical systematic segregation of those who failed to be normative or who lost legitimate status in society. Existence of outcastes may be the way Japanese culture coped with unwanted segments of society, keeping them usefully under control yet isolated from others.

These three factors—the perceived need for ritual cleanliness juxtaposed with the economic need for "unclean" occupations; the desire to keep those with economic power from having political power; and the need to purge mainstream society of undesirable elements—together have established, supported, legitimized, and, most important, depoliticized the discrimination issues. Many mainstream Japanese still accept arguments that postulate non-Japanese origins, inherent inferiority, and ritual uncleanliness of outcastes; thus, the differential treatment of Burakumin seems almost "natural" to them. There is no evidence, however, to support such hypotheses. It is rather, as summarized above, a political, economic, and ideological manipulation throughout Japanese history that has created discrimination against Burakumin.

Settlements

Both historic outcastes and Burakumin have lived in segregated communities of one sort or another. In the feudal age their segregation was strictly enforced and people of outcaste status were forced to live in undesirable locations, often on the outskirts of or completely outside a mainstream community. The modern Japanese officially have abolished such segregation, but it continues to exist in the form of de facto ghettos, recognized as "Tokushu Buraku" (special community), or simply buraku. The term "Dowa Chiku" (assimilation district) is often used in the same fashion.

The conditions in buraku are typically poor, characterized by inferior sanitation, insufficient space and privacy, old housing structures, poorly maintained streets, and a lack of public and recreational areas. Improvement of living conditions has been a great concern for Burakumin. The government has made efforts over the last several decades to improve the living environment and educational opportunities in buraku. Roughly half of Burakumin live in Dōwa Chiku, which are designated target areas for the assimilation projects. In these districts, government-funded programs are being executed to improve housing, sanitation, and public services so as to match the living standard of buraku to that of mainstream communities.

Yet the reality of the buraku is less than ideal. Economic hardship and discrimination deeply rooted in Japanese people, both mainstream and Burakumin, are probably two major reasons for the slow change and persistence of age-old issues regarding the buraku.

Economy

Outcastes traditionally specialized in leatherwork, basketry, sandal making, temple caretaking, street sweeping, butchering, street performance, tenant farming, and unauthorized religious practices. Until the end of the feudal age, outcastes dominated these occupations; at the time of their emancipation, nonoutcaste businesses began to operate in some of these trades, and often drove former outcastes out of business.

Today some Burakumin still are involved in the traditional crafts and trades, but many of them

When a Burakumin moves to a different region in Japan, background investigation or accident may reveal his or her origin, often resulting in stigmatization of the person's life.

The upper-class Burakumin are constantly at odds with the lower-class Burakumin, since the former do not necessarily share the strong sense of alienation common among the latter.

work as factory hands, day laborers, and all sorts of unskilled laborers. In general, their wage levels are low, and their economic struggle in the face of the overall affluence of the Japanese is striking. Many Burakumin work for small businesses, earn minimum wage with few work benefits, and suffer from insufficient and unstable incomes. The comparison of average annual income per household in 1984 reveals that the Burakumin household average was then approximately 60 percent of the national average. The percentage of fully employed Burakumin is significantly lower than that of the overall Japanese labor force. Lower educational achievement and occupational discrimination further hinder the economic advancement of Burakumin. As a consequence a significant number of Burakumin rely on government welfare to survive.

INDUSTRIAL ARTS. Outcaste leatherworkers of the feudal age made beautiful horse gear and armor, some of which still survives. Basketry and sandal making are among the most important—and rapidly forgotten—craft traditions in which historic outcastes and traditional Burakumin produced essential items for the common people.

Kinship

Burakumin kinship practice generally follows that of the mainstream Japanese.

Marriage and Family

MARRIAGE AND DOMESTIC LIFE. Burakumin marriage practice and family life are similar to those of the mainstream Japanese, except for certain minor differences reported in ethnographic literature. Marriage and sexual relationships in buraku tend to be more informal and unstable. Extramarital relationships are not uncommon, and, because of the frequency of unstable marriage alliances, they are socially accepted in many cases. An unmarried household head is very common, and many households consist of a single parent and (often illegitimate) children. Economic situations and the mobility of spouses influence postmarital residence; it may take many forms that mainstream society considers irregular. Because of discrimination and long-lasting segregation, endogamy within buraku has been dominant, but the younger generations increasingly are opting for intermarrige with non-Burakumin.

INHERITANCE. Observers have reported that Burakumin inheritance practice is more informal than that of the mainstream Japanese, presumably because of the flexible and often unstable

Burakumin family structure. Ultimogeniture, which is very rare among the mainstream Japanese, is not uncommon among Burakumin.

SOCIALIZATION. Reflecting the informality of buraku life, socialization of Burakumin children is generally less strict than that of mainstream Japanese. Economic hardship and unstable family structure force many Burakumin parents to leave their children for long hours with their relatives, with neighbors, or sometimes at home without adult supervision. Some children were raised in family craft shops beside the working parents. The educational standard is generally lower among Burakumin than among mainstream Japanese. Analysts believe that economic difficulties, discrimination, and a lack of motivation and role models are the main causes of this problem.

Sociopolitical Organization

SOCIAL ORGANIZATION AND SOCIAL CONTROL. Although Burakumin as a whole are situated in the lowest stratum of Japanese society, there is a distinct socioeconomic differentiation within Burakumin communities. The higher level of their stratification mainly consists of better-educated, financially more secure, lower-middle-class small-business owners and administrators who now often work outside buraku. The first Burakumin leadership came from this class. A typical Burakumin of the lower level, however, would be undereducated, marginally employed, and often on a government relief program because of insufficient or unstable income. Migrant workers, day laborers, and some factory hands belong to this group.

The upper-class Burakumin are constantly at odds with the lower-class Burakumin, since they do not necessarily share the strong sense of alienation common among the lower-class Burakumin. Assimilation into mainstream Japanese society is a historically popular theme among them, and some even view lower-class Burakumin as a "burden" to their effort to eliminate discrimination through self-improvement.

The *oyabun-kobun* relationship is an important factor in the internal organization of buraku. Oyabun-kobun is a traditional concept of hierarchical relationship between a superior who acts as a parent figure (oyabun) and an inferior who takes the role of a child (kobun). Ordinary people and also criminal organizations (*yakuza*) commonly have adopted this informal hierarchy. Buraku oyabun are very influential in the community, and they often act as job-placement agents or middlemen between Burakumin manufacturers and non-

Burakumin buyers. In this relationship of mutual interests and dependency, an oyabun is expected to supply a fair share of steady jobs to kobun and to negotiate with outside buyers or employers, and a kobun is obliged to accept an oyabun's offers and to complete the assignment satisfactorily. However, since the oyabun is in a dominant position, the relationship is not symmetric and so a kobun may follow an oyabun unwillingly for fear of losing jobs or being ostracized.

POLITICAL ORGANIZATION. As citizens of Japan, Burakumin today participate in the Japanese political system through voting. As a strong interest group, Burakumin regularly send their representatives to the Diet and the local legislatures.

The current situation is the achievement of a long political struggle since the 1871 emancipation. Burakumin formed their first organization, Bisaku Heimin Kai (Bisaku Common People's Association), in 1902 in Okayama Prefecture, in reaction to the harsh discrimination that continued after emancipation. A year later they founded Dai Nippon Dōhō Yūwa Kai (Greater Japan Fraternal Conciliation Society), the first nationwide organization of Burakumin. Their movement was called the Yūwa (reconciliation) movement, and their goals were to eliminate discrimination against Burakumin through self-help and through

the improvement of living conditions, educational standards, and economic conditions in buraku. In 1919, Burakumin leaders gathered for the first time with government officials, representatives from the aristocracy, and scholars at Dōjō Yūwa Taikai (Sympathetic Reconciliation Convention) to discuss the discrimination issue.

In the 1920s, many Burakumin leaders became dissatisfied with the Yūwa movement, which was not seeking positive changes in awareness among the majority Japanese. It was also a time of social radicalism in Japan, and Burakumin activists started the "leveling" movement to eliminate all inequalities and discrimination through political channels. They formed the Zenkoku Suiheisha (National Levelers' Society) in 1922. Their slogan was "tetteiteki kyūdan" (thorough denunciation): when they found a discriminatory behavior or statement, they summoned the person responsible for the incident and demanded a public apology. Although this method was successful in some cases of discrimination, both the mainstream society and the moderate sector of Burakumin movements viewed it as violent and so resisted the campaign.

At the same time, the radical branch of Suiheisha was becoming increasingly critical of the denunciation method, and it began to insist on a more radical, even anarchistic approach to the issue. By 1925 the internal differences were becom-

RELIGION AND EXPRESSIVE CULTURE

Religious Beliefs

Historically most Buddhist sects rejected outcastes, as most outcastes violated the Buddhist taboos against death and killing through their occupations. The Jōdo Shinshu or Shinshu sect, whose founding philosophy roughly translates as "restoring righteousness in evil men," and the Nichirenshu sect, which preached the salvation of common people, were the only sects that accepted outcastes, and even today they are the most common Buddhist sects to which Burakumin belong. Outcaste members were, however, subject to segregation within the religious organization, as was apparent in the Tokugawa period practices of eta-dera (temples exclusively for a outcastes) and eta-za (segregated seating for outcastes

when they attended the same temples as regular people).

In the modern period Christian missionaries took special interest in the buraku's social problems, and their belief in the equality of human beings before God attracted many Burakumin to this religion.

Religious Practitioners

In addition to training institutionalized priests like those in the mainstream Japanese society, outcaste communities produced many unauthorized practitioners of Shintoism, Buddhism, and various folk religions. Hijiri priests, diviners, and ceremonial performers are the most prominent examples. They served the religious and ceremonial needs of commoners who could not afford the ser-

vices of authorized priests or who sought alternatives to the institutional religions.

Arts

(The traditional occupational specializations of outcastes included those of performing artists, such as actors, singers, dancers, and street entertainers. Founders of two of the most important theatrical traditions in Japan were outcastes. The dancer/actress Okuni performed the earliest form of Kabuki play on the floodplain in Kyoto. Kanami and Zeami, a father and son who began the Noh play in the fourteenth century, were also of outcaste origin, and at the height of their success they performed for the shogun of the time and enjoyed considerable prosperity and political influence.

ing too large to reconcile, and in 1926 radical segments formed separate organizations. The moderate group established the Nihon Suiheisha (Japan Levelers' Society) to continue the policies of the original Suiheisha movement.

Although Burakumin movements saw a brief moment of victory in 1935 and 1936 when they succeeded in sending their own representatives to the Fukuoka Prefectural Assembly and to the House of Representatives, Japan's increasing militarism and patriotism began to interfere with their political activities. In 1940 Suiheisha was dissolved and its members decided to support Yamato Hōkōku Undo (Japan Patriotic Movement), which was founded to coordinate the patriotic efforts of Burakumin.

Burakumin movements, which were virtually nonexistent during World War II, quickly revived at the end of the war with the support of the new constitution, which guaranteed freedom of expression and equal rights to all citizens. In 1947 Burakumin formed the Buraku Kaihō Zenkoku Iinkai (National Committee for Buraku Liberation). In 1955 the organization changed its name to Buraku Kaihō Dōmei (Buraku Liberation League, or BLL). However, Communist influence began to split the organization from inside, and more radical Communists separated from BLL and formed the Buraku Liberation League Normalizing Liaison Association, which aimed to redirect the Liberation League by introducing a more Marxist-oriented position.

Throughout the postwar period Burakumin organizations have been successful in a number of legal battles and in denunciation of discriminatory publications and behavior. They also have made remarkable advances in education, including the improvement of educational opportunities for Burakumin and the introduction of antidiscrimination education programs in public schools.

CONFLICT. Both Burakumin and the historic outcastes have been scapegoats in times of social unrest and economic difficulties. Numerous reports of riots and associated Eta-gari (outcaste hunts) after the political transition in the late nineteenth century demonstrate how violence toward Burakumin became the outlet for insecurity and frustration among commoners at the time. Burakumin did not have much protection against this aggression, but the hardship accelerated their effort to form an organized movement against discrimination. Today the Buraku Liberation League's denunciation program is a popular tool for correcting discriminatory behavior and think-

ing, but some scholars and Burakumin activists question its legal basis and actual effectiveness.

Bibliography

Brameld, Theodore (1968). *Japan: Culture, Education, and Change in Two Communities.* New York: Holt, Rinehart & Winston.

Buraku Liberation Research Institute, ed. (1977). *Discrimination against Buraku, Today.* Osaka: Buraku Kaihō Kenkyūsho.

Buraku Liberation Research Institute, ed. (1985). *White Paper on Human Rights in Japan.* Osaka: Buraku Kaihō Kenkyūsho.

De Vos, George A., and Hiroshi Wagatsuma (1966). *Japan's Invisible Race: Caste in Culture and Personality.* Berkeley and Los Angeles: University of California Press.

Donoghue, John D. (1977). *Pariah Persistence in Changing Japan.* Washington, D.C.: University Press of America.

Kawamoto, Shoichi (1985). *Hisabetsu Buraku no Kōzō to Keisei.* Tokyo: Sanichi Shōbō.

Miyoshi, Shoichiro (1980). *Hisabetsu Buraku no Keisei to Tenkai.* Tokyo: Kashiwa Shōbō. Rev. ed. 1991.

Neary, Ian (1989). *Political Protest and Social Control in Prewar Japan.* Atlantic Highlands, N.J.: Humanities Press International.

Takagi, Masayuki (1991). "A Living Legacy of Discrimination." *Japan Quarterly* (July-September): 283–290.

Wolferen, Karel von (1989). *The Enigma of Japanese Power.* New York: Knopf.

Yoshino, I. Roger, and Sueo Murakoshi (1977). *The Invisible Visible Race.* Osaka: Buraku Kaihō Kenkyūsho.

—SAWA KUROTANI BECKER

BURMESE

Ethonyms: Burmans, Myanmarese

Orientation

IDENTIFICATION. The Burmans speak Burmese (a Tibeto-Burman language) and live in the central plain of Burma, in the Union of Burma, which was renamed Myanmar in 1990. "Burman" is the name of the people of this region, while "Burmese" refers to the language and culture of these people and to other citizens of Myanmar. The Burmans are over-whelmingly adherents of Theravada Buddhism.

LOCATION. Myanmar lies between India and China and also borders Thailand. The central plain formed by the Irrawaddy River and the Salween River is the home of the Burman, while the hill country around the plain is populated by Karen, Kachin, Chin, Shan, and some smaller tribal groups. The climate is dominated by the monsoon, which brings a rainy season lasting from June to October, followed by a brief cool season, and then a four- or five-month hot and dry season.

DEMOGRAPHY. In 1992 the population of Myanmar was estimated at 42.6 million. The official count, at the 1998 census estimate, was 33 million. Population growth is estimated at about 3 percent per year. Burmese speakers are about 70 percent of the national population.

LINGUISTIC AFFILIATION. Burmese is a part of the Tibeto-Burmese Family, a Subfamily of the Sino-Tibetan Family. Outside the Sino-Tibetan Family—which includes Kachin, Chin, and several tribal languages on the China border—Tai (various dialects in the Shan states), Mon-Khmer (lower Burma), and some Indian languages on the western frontier are spoken in Myanmar.

History and Cultural Relations

The Burmans apparently migrated south from Yunnan, along with several other linguistic and cultural groups, more than 3,000 years ago. The Mons, the Tai, and the Burmans, the predominant population, were all of the same physical type called southern Mongoloid. The history of Burma begins with King Anawratha in 1057, when the king conquered the Mons in southern Burma and brought back, according to legend, a complete copy of the three books of the Pali canon, the basis of Theravada Buddhism.

Anawratha proceeded to make Theravada Buddhism the official religion of his kingdom, driving out other varieties of Buddhism and attempting to suppress and regulate forms of animism. This dynasty reigned for about two and one-half centuries.

The conquest of Yunnan by Kublai Khan shook the Burmese throne along with the rest of mainland southeast Asia, and after the fall of the capital at Pagan various principalities under shifting Tai, Mon, and Burman rulers held sway in various parts of the country. A new Burmese dynasty arose in Pegu and later shifted to Ava as its capital, giving an inland central-valley orientation to this and future Burmese regimes.

European trade and frontier squabbles led to three Anglo-Burman wars; the peacock throne was toppled and the last king Thibaw and his queen were sent into exile. Under British rule Burma became a province of India. Lower Burma was turned into one of the world's largest exporters of rice, while teak, rubies, and other products continued to enter world markets. A sort of ethnic division of labor took place with Europeans at the economic and political top, and most of the Burmans locked into the lower spaces of the classic plural or export economy. This export economy was hard hit by the world depression of the 1930s, and a rising nationalism combined with hard times led to the Saya San rebellion, suppressed by the British.

In World War II the Japanese occupied Burma and granted it nominal independence. The Japanese trained the "Thirty heroes" who became the military leaders of the independence movement called the "Thakins." Burma received independence in 1948 and proceeded to attempt to rebuild a war-ravaged country.

Upon its founding, the Union of Burma was plagued by ethnic unrest from separatist movements among the Karens (KNDO was the name of the armed insurgency) and various Communist and other insurgent groups, as well as vicious political in-fighting among the Thakins and other Burmese leaders. The hero of the independence movement, Aung Sang, and members of his cabinet, were assassinated by opponents. U Nu was elected prime minister, but the troubles with separatists, insurgents, and political disunity continued, leading to a caretaker government of the army under the command of General Ne Win. U Nu won another election, but in 1962 the army again took control, and a single-party government under Ne Win runs Myanmar, despite elections that gave a majority to the opposition party.

Settlements

Villages are the predominant form of human settlement. Over 65,000 villages make Myanmar a mainly rural country. Villages are of three kinds. In Upper Burma the village surrounded by a palisade or a fence is common. Ingress and egress are through a village gate, and the fence or palisade is often manned by village guards. There are also clustered villages without a boundary fence. These villages do not have regular plans and usually lack public buildings. The only major difference between houses is that some have one story, others two. Monasteries are always placed outside the bounds of the village. Fields lie beyond the village, usually within walking distance, but houses are set among trees and fruit crops. The third settlement type is a line village strung out along a road or

There is no strong domestic division of labor among the Burmese; men cook and tend babies, and women are barred only from the monkhood.

river bank. Towns and cities are found near or on major rivers and waterways, indicating both irrigation centers and transport networks. Yangon (formerly Rangoon) is now a major Burmese city and the nation's capital; Mandalay is the home of former kings and the cultural capital.

Economy

SUBSISTENCE AND COMMERCIAL ACTIVITIES. Wet-rice cultivation dominates agricultural activity. Most of that crop is now consumed domestically because the export industry has shriveled under the centralized control of the military powers. Upland, rain-fed rice is common in Upper Burma above the 100–centimeter rain line, and in the hill country slash-and-burn agriculture (swidden agriculture rather than crop rotation) is practiced. Cotton, maize, peanuts, onions, and other crops are produced. Logging, especially of teak for export, is still an important industry. There is an active fishing industry in Burmese waters, and dried shrimp and fish are important components in the diet. Mining of rubies and the export of jade are successful industries. Drilling for and refining oil are on a small scale, hardly for export. Among Burmese handicrafts, lacquer ware is distinctive. Wood carving, stone sculpting, and brass casting are local industries. Tobacco, cheroots, and cigars

are produced. There is a small livestock industry, some jute processing, and a little tin and tungsten mining. The economy, however, remains overwhelmingly agricultural and extractive.

In the sector of industry and mining, technology is slightly obsolete but appropriate; in agriculture, on the other hand, most of the technology is geared to the small rice producer. A wooden plow with metal share yoked to a pair of bullocks, the wooden-toothed harrow, the sickle, the metal-bladed hoe, a long knife, ropes and twine of various grasses, and the forked stick comprise the long-standing farming kit. Bamboo and wood items are ubiquitous, and iron and metal nearly so. Modern technology is represented by the sewing machine, the loudspeaker and amplifier, the battery-run transistor radio, some guns, and an occasional vehicle. In the cities an assortment of machines and vehicles dating from World War II predominates.

Kinship

The kinship system counts relatives on both the mother's and father's side, and there are no kinship-based groups beyond the family. It is not the category of kinship that is important, but rather the personal relations cultivated, relative age, generation, and the sex of persons who are linked. Age, sex, and generation, in fact, are the major axes for ordering most social relations. Beyond the nuclear family, terms of address reflect relative age, seniority, and respect rather than the degree or category of kinship.

Marriage and Family

Most marriages are monogamous. Marriages are not a sacramental affair and are arranged by families, but usually on the request of one or the other of the potential marriage partners. Divorce is easy, informal, but infrequent after the arrival of children. Families tend to be nuclear and to live in their own compound, but many households (the really effective unit) are made up of extended families or compound families. This results in part from the normal cycle of family formation and dissolution rather than from a preference for larger than nuclear families. The strongest bond in the family is the mother-daughter relationship, which is lifelong. There is no strong domestic division of labor; men cook and tend babies, and women are barred only from the monkhood.

Sociopolitical Organization

Myanmar is made up of fifteen states and divisions, all centralized under a single bureaucracy run by the army and its mass organization, the Lanzin party. This was constitutionally set up in 1974. Below this formal structure are the villages, linked by various agencies in a hierarchy reaching from the village to the prime minister's office. The village has an elected headman and he is the link between the bureaucracy and the party. There are agencies of the central government in contact with the villagers, but it is chiefly the army and the mass party that impinge on the local organization, which tries to settle its disputes at the local level.

Religion and Expressive Culture

Buddhism is a pervading force in Burmese society. The hillsides dotted with pagodas, the hosts of saffron-robed monks, and innumerable monasteries all proclaim the breadth and depth of Buddhist belief and practice in Myanmar. Almost all Burmans (more than 95 percent) are Buddhist. There are also Christians, chiefly among the Karen, Kachin, and Chin, and a sprinkling of Muslims and Hindus. Buddhism is Theravada, although this distinction is only meaningful to the learned or sophisticated monk or abbot. The religion of the ordinary Burman is *boda batha*, the way of the Buddha.

Burmese Buddhism is characterized by consensual elements of knowledge, belief, and practice that are separate from the more specialized knowledge of the Pali Canon and the commentaries known to some learned monks. The ideas of *kan* (related to karma) and *kutho* (merit) underlie religious practice. Kan is the moral nucleus earned throughout many lives that goes on from life to life in the never-ending chain of rebirth, until the very remote end of nirvana, when rebirth ends. Rebirth, in form and place, is determined by the accumulated merits and demerits earned in previous existences. A person can be reborn in one of the three levels of existence: this world, the hells below, or the various heavens above. The whole worldview of Buddhism is summed up in the continually heard refrain: *aneiksa* (change, the impermanence of everything), *dokhka* (life is suffering), and *anatta* (no self, the ego is an illusion). The next most common summary of the belief system is the repetition of the triple jewel: I take refuge in the Buddha, I take refuge in the teaching, and I take refuge in the monkhood. The monkhood (*sangha*) is loosely organized into two principal sects without significant doctrinal splits. Monks (*pongyi*) are highly honored, and most Burmese boys spend some time in a monastery after an induction ceremony (*shinbyu*) mimicking the Buddha's renunciation of secular life.

Supplementary to the Buddhist worldview are belief systems involved with crisis management, prediction, and divination. *Nats* are the most important of these systems. These spirits are mainly malevolent and must be propitiated at stated times and places to avoid harm and evil. There are also ghosts, demons, spirits, and goblins in the forest, caves, and natural features capable of causing trouble to people.

Alchemy, astrology, and horoscope casting are employed in attempts to read the future disposition of forces toward the affairs of individuals. There is a system of curing and healing depending on notions of a balance of elements in the patient.

ARTS. The *pwe* (a play, or a song and dance performance), often lasting several days and nights, often accompanies the ritual calendar.

Bibliography

Nash, Manning (1973). *The Golden Road to Modernity: Village Life in Contemporary Burma*. Chicago: University of Chicago Press.

Shway Yoe {James George Scott} (1882). *The Burman, His Life and Notions*. Reprint. 1963. New York: W. W. Norton & Co.

Spiro, Melford E. (1970). *Buddhism and Society: A Great Tradition and Its Burmese Vicissitudes*. New York: Harper & Row.

Steinberg, David (1980). *Burma's Road Toward Development, Growth, and Ideology under Military Rule*. Boulder, Colo.: Westview Press.

Tinker, Hugh (1959). *The Union of Burma: A Study of the First Years of Independence*. London and New York: Oxford University Press.

—MANNING NASH

CENTRAL THAI

Ethonyms: Khon Thai, Siamese Tai, Syam, Tai, T'ai, Thai

Orientation

IDENTIFICATION. The Central Thai speak the Central Thai (Tai-Shan) dialect, live in central and southern Thailand, and are predominantly of the Buddhist faith. The Thai name for their country is "Müang Thai," meaning "the free country," and their self-name is "Khon Thai," meaning "the free people." The terms "Siam" and "Siamese" were used mainly by Westerners; "Siam" was the official name of the country from about 1825 until 1930.

Central Thai

LOCATION. Thailand is located between 6° and 21° N and 98° and 106° E. The Central Thai primarily occupy the central alluvial plain dominated by the Chao Phraya (Menam) River. This river basin covers approximately one-fifth of the total area of the country. The monsoon winds bring on a rainy season that lasts from May or June to October or November.

DEMOGRAPHY. In 1992 the population of Thailand was estimated as 57,200,000. The population density averages 111.5 persons per square kilometer and the population is growing at the rate of 3 percent per year. Tai-speaking peoples constitute approximately 80 percent of the population of Thailand. Approximately 13 million of the nation's population speak the Central Tai dialect. Speakers of other dialects of Tai are the Tai-Yuan of the north, the Tai-Lao of the northeast, and the Pak-Tai of the south. Malay-speaking Muslims constitute approximately 4 percent of the population of Thailand, and Chinese, who live primarily in the cities, constitute roughly 14 percent. Bangkok, the capital city, had an estimated population of 5,832,843 in 1989.

LINGUISTIC AFFILIATION. Scholars have not reached a consensus on the affiliation of the Tai language. Tai has traditionally been considered a branch of the Sinitic Family (which includes various Chinese languages and Tibetan), but there seems to be substantial evidence that there are relationships between Tai, Kadai, and Indonesian subgroups and that these three languages should be classified together as a branch of the Proto-Austric Family (which includes the languages of the Philippines, Melanesia, Polynesia, Micronesia, and Indonesia). Tai is also related to Laotian and Shan. It is monosyllabic and tonal. The Thai script has forty-four consonants, thirty vowels, and nine tonal signs.

History and Cultural Relations

The original home of the Thai people was in the Chinese province of Yunnan. They are believed to have migrated south in successive waves, beginning perhaps as early as about A.D. 1050. The first Thai capital in the area now known as Thailand was established in 1280 at Sukothai. The capital was moved from there to Ayuthia, to Tonburi, and finally, in 1783, to Bangkok, where it has remained. The Kingdom of Thailand has never been colonized by any Western nation, but some territory was lost to the British and French empires when Europeans entered the rice and teak markets during the nineteenth century. The opening of the commercial rice market changed the Thai economy from one of subsistence to one of cash, producing profound economic, demographic, and social changes during the twentieth century. Thailand's absolute monarchy became a constitutional monarchy after a revolution in 1932. In spite of the king's loss of political power, the monarchy has retained its prestige and symbolic value, especially among rural Thai. Political trends since the revolution include a pro-Western foreign policy coupled with very deliberate efforts toward modernization, authoritarian government (in spite of the constitutional veneer), and encouragement of nationalism embodied in the phrase "king, country, religion."

Settlements

Villages range in size from about 300 to 3,000 persons. Some villages are spatially distinct while others are administrative subdivisions in an area of continuous settlement. There are three major village types: strip, clustered, and dispersed. In the strip pattern, houses are strung along both sides of a waterway or road, with open fields stretching behind. In the cluster pattern, houses are built in a roughly circular pattern among fruit trees, coconut palms, or rice fields; the settlement is connected to the main road by a path or cart track. In the dispersed pattern, each nuclear family lives on its own land, surrounded by its rice fields or orchards. Houses are connected by waterways or paths, and much travel is by boat. Prominent in villages are the temple compound and the school, with a few shops scattered nearby. Two styles of housing are common throughout Thailand. The first, for the more affluent, is the sturdy, paneled or clapboard-walled house of teak or mahogany, raised off the ground, with planked floor, a few windows, and a roof of attap palm, tile, or corrugated iron. The second type of house is a low-pitched gabled house on a bamboo frame with a roof and perhaps a porch, thatched with palm or grass, and with sides of the same or of woven bamboo or matting, and earthen floors.

Economy

SUBSISTENCE AND COMMERCIAL ACTIVITIES. Wet-rice agriculture dominates the Thai economy, with about 80 percent of Thailand's population living in rural agricultural communities. Ordinary rice is produced both as a dietary staple and for cash sales. Agriculture is not widely mechanized in spite of development efforts, and plowing is still done mainly with a single metal-shod plow drawn by bullocks or water buffalo. The crop is harvested by hand. Thai farmers also

---

♦ **monsoon**
Regular and persistent winds that blow in the Indian Ocean, coming from the southwest between June and August and from the northeast between October and December. The southwest monsoon is the main rain-bearing one.

See also

Shan

grow maize, yams, chilies, cassava, eggplant, and beans. Commercial crops beyond rice include sugarcane, tobacco, rubber, coconut, and cotton. Each household catches fish, an important source of food, using nets, scoops, spears, baskets, and hooks. Domestic animals include pigs, chickens, ducks, cattle, and water buffalo.

INDUSTRIAL ARTS. Most villages have part-time or seasonal specialists such as sewing-machine operators, blacksmiths, and boat builders. In some areas there are brass, pottery, and charcoal manufacturers and silk- and cotton-weaving home industries. For the most part, though, industrial and commercial tasks are performed by the Chinese, while the Thai farm and govern.

TRADE. Small stores, peddlers, and markets are found throughout rural Thailand. Women bring home-grown produce to the market for sale or to supply other merchants.

DIVISION OF LABOR. The Central Thai are notable for the near absence of a division of labor by sex. Theirs is one of the few cultures in the world where women as well as men plow and harrow. Both sexes also fish. The traditional home tasks are assigned to women, but men also cook, tend babies, clean house, and wash clothes.

LAND TENURE. Since the emergence of the commercial rice market in the mid-nineteenth century, the population has grown steadily. The amount of land devoted to rice cultivation has increased, although there has been little modernization of agricultural technology. The combination of population growth and the increasing production of rice has resulted in landlessness for growing numbers of people. The nonavailability of land has produced a class of laborers who cannot expect to gain their subsistence from the land. Since traditional Thai culture is based on self-sufficient rice agriculture or individually owned land, this situation is producing major changes in Thai society, including permanent or seasonal migration of men to the large cities for wage labor.

Marriage and Family

MARRIAGE. Although polygynous marriage has long been part of Thai culture, most marriages today are monogamous. Marriages are theoretically arranged by the parents, but there is quite a bit of freedom in the choice of marriage partners. Since fellow villagers are often considered relatives, marriages are usually locally exogamous. Marriage with second cousins is allowed. The independent family household, established soon after marriage, is the ideal. More often, though, the couple resides for a short time with the wife's

family. Residence with either the wife's or the husband's family on a more permanent basis is becoming more frequent. Divorce is common and is effected by mutual agreement, common property being divided equally.

DOMESTIC UNIT. Those people who cook and eat meals around the same hearth are considered a family. This group, averaging between six and seven persons, not only lives and consumes together, but also farms cooperatively. The nuclear family is the minimal family unit, with grandparents, grandchildren, aunts, uncles, co-wives, cousins, and children of spouses added on. Membership in the household unit requires that one perform an acceptable amount of work.

INHERITANCE. Property is divided equally among surviving children, but the child who cares for the parents in their old age (often a younger daughter) ordinarily receives the homestead in addition to her share.

SOCIALIZATION. Infants and children are raised by both parents and siblings and, in recent times, by other household members. Emphasis is placed on independence, self-reliance, and respect for others. The Central Thai are notable for almost never using physical punishment in child rearing.

Sociopolitical Organization

Thailand is a constitutional monarchy with a king as head of state and a prime minister as head of the government.

SOCIAL ORGANIZATION. Thai society is hierarchically organized on the basis of age, occupation, wealth, and residence. The rural farmers stand below the artisans, merchants, and government officials of the cities. The clergy stand as a group apart from society. Social classes, in the sense of stable, ranked statuses, are absent in the presence of considerable social mobility. Many interpersonal relationships, however, are hierarchical, and patron-client relationships are common.

POLITICAL ORGANIZATION. Thailand is divided into seventy-three provinces (*changwat*). The provinces are divided into districts (*amphoe*), and these into municipal areas and communes (*tambon*). Each tambon is composed of several numbered hamlets (*muban*), which appear to be primarily administrative divisions. Tambon seem to range in size from 1,400 to 7,000 people. Each muban has a headman (*phuyaiban*) and the head man of the tambon, the *kamnan*, is chosen from among the phuyaiban. The muban, and probably the tambon as well, are groups whose functions appear to be purely administrative, since only oc-

The Central Thai is one of the few cultures in the world where women as well as men plow and harrow.

In spite of the Thai king's loss of political power, the monarchy has retained its prestige and symbolic value, especially among rural Central Thai.

casionally do the natural communities coincide with them. Thus a village may be composed of people from two different tambon and several different muban. They constitute a community in the sense that all the people of the village recognize the village temple and the government school. There does not appear to be a native Thai term for such a "natural" community and if asked the name of his or her village, the average inhabitant would probably refer to the temple that serves it. The Thai government provides a wide range of services including schools, police, courts, health services, tax collection, and the registration of vital information. District governments maintain the highways, canals, bridges, schools, and irrigation systems.

SOCIAL CONTROL.   To a large extent, social control is maintained by a Buddhist value system, which places a premium on avoiding conflict and fleeing rather than fighting. Gossip is an important informal source of social control. Because the natural community has no administrative structure, the temple committee, made up of monks and lay people, often concerns itself with village issues as well as temple affairs.

CONFLICT.   In the past, warfare generally arose from disputes over succession to the throne, misbehavior of a vassal, and conflicts with neighboring states. Since the late 1880s a national military establishment on the European model has existed. Since the 1930s military personnel have taken an increasingly active role in politics.

Religion and Expressive Culture

Buddhism is a central and unifying force in Thai society. There are over 31,000 temples and the Thai regularly give gifts to the temple, attend festivals, and have their sons ordained.

RELIGIOUS BELIEFS.   Theravada Buddhism is the official religion of Thailand (95 percent of the population); there are also Muslims (4 percent), and small numbers of Christians, Hindus, Confucians, and animists. Various supernatural beings play a role in village life. They include the guardian spirits of houses and villages, harvest beings such as the Rice Mother, possession spirits who cause illness, and helpful spirits who provide guidance.

RELIGIOUS PRACTITIONERS.   About 85 percent of Thai men are ordained priests, although only a small minority makes the priesthood its life work. The head priest at each temple maintains the basic rules of the monastic order. Priests read sermons, sing blessings, and participate in life-cycle rituals. They often also play a central role in village government. In addition to priests there are exorcists, spirit doctors, and diviners who mediate between humans and the spirit world through incantations, charms, possession, and sympathetic action.

CEREMONIES.   The religious calendar includes the New Year's Festival in April; the day of birth, enlightenment, and death of the Buddha in May; Lent from July to October; and the Festival of Lights in November. In addition, there is an annual fair and days set are aside for presenting robes and food to the priests.

ARTS.   Although now discouraged by the government, the tattooing of men is still common. Both art and architecture are characterized by subtlety of design and form, with considerable use of amulets, mystical drawings, and both public and private statuary. Traditional musical instruments such as gongs, clappers, wooden blocks, and the long drum are used alongside Western instruments such as saxophones, flutes, and horns. Dance dramas, repartee performances, and shadow plays are a common form of theatrical entertainment in rural villages.

MEDICINE.   Illness is attributed to fright, prolonged adversity, spirit possession, and an imbalance of elements in the body. Locally purchased home remedies and the services of healers are commonly used.

KINSHIP

Kin Groups and Descent

Three types of kin group have been described: (1) multihousehold compounds that share productive equipment and have cooperative work teams; (2) hamlet clusters that contain independent households of kindred joined either by work reciprocity or by the domination of one wealthy household; and (3) linked hamlets of kin who live at a distance from each other but who are joined by shared life-cycle rites, provision of help to visiting kin, and assistance in securing shelter and employment for migrating kin. Descent is bilateral.

Kinship Terminology

Hawaiian-type cousin terms are used. The social emphasis on age is reflected by the fact that most kinship terms indicate the relative ages of people.

DEATH AND AFTERLIFE. The funeral is the most important life-cycle event because it signifies the launching of the deceased into his or her next existence. Rebirth occurs after a stay in purgatory, the length of which is determined by one's sinfulness. The older and more prestigious the deceased, the more elaborate the funeral rites. The formal mourning period is seven days, after which the body is taken to the house or a morgue where it may be kept for days or even years until it is cremated.

Bibliography

Donner, Wolf (1978). *The Five Faces of Thailand: An Economic Geography.* New York: St. Martin's Press.

Phillips, Herbert P. (1966). *Thai Peasant Personality: The Patterning of Interpersonal Behavior in the Village of Bang Chan.* Berkeley and Los Angeles: University of California Press.

Sharp, R. Lauriston, and Lucien M. Hanks (1978). *Bang Chan: Social History of a Rural Community in Thailand.* Ithaca, N.Y.: Cornell University Press.

Terwiel, Berend J. (1975). *Monks and Magic: An Analysis of Religious Ceremonies in Central Thailand.* Lund: Student-litteratur; London: Curzon Press.

—M. MARLENE MARTIN AND DAVID LEVINSON

CHINESE IN SOUTHEAST ASIA

Ethonyms: Huaqiao, Huaren, Sangley (in the Philippines), Tangren (Mandarin)

Orientation

IDENTIFICATION. The Chinese in Southeast Asia once referred to themselves as "Huaqiao" (Chinese sojourners) but now describe themselves as "Huaren" (Chinese people). Another common ethnonym for Chinese, "Zhongguo ren" (people of the Central Kingdom), is avoided in Southeast Asia because it holds overtones of political allegiance to China: the Overseas Chinese live outside the political boundaries of China and are citizens or permanent residents of a variety of Southeast Asian nations. The southern Chinese, who form the core of immigrants to Southeast Asia, also refer to themselves as "Tangren" (people of Tang), alluding to the fact that their ancestors migrated to southern China at the demise of the Tang dynasty in the tenth century A.D. In the Philippines they are called "Sangley," from a Southern Min word referring to "{those who} do business."

LOCATION. Overseas Chinese are found in cities throughout Southeast Asia, and although populations may be found in rural areas, the Chinese are overwhelmingly urban. In Southeast Asian cities they are visible in their capacity as merchants, with shops sometimes clustered in distinctive "Chinatowns."

DEMOGRAPHY. Migration to Southeast Asia originated primarily in the coastal area of southeastern China, in particular Fujian, Guangdong, and Hainan, and reached its peak in the second half of the nineteenth century, spurred by new opportunities created by the opening of treaty ports after the First Opium War. The only predominantly Chinese population in Southeast Asia is that of Singapore, where an estimated 2 million Chinese form 76 percent of a population of 3 million. In Malaysia, the Chinese form a large minority, currently estimated at 34 percent of a population of 18 million. In Indonesia, where the Chinese are only 3 percent of the total population of 195 million, there are 5 to 6 million Chinese; in Thailand, the Chinese population has been recently estimated as 5 to 6 million or more in a total population of 57 million; in the Philippines there are 600,000 in a population of 62 million; in Cambodia, 300,000 in a population of 8.5 million; in Laos, 25,000 in a population of 4 million. In Vietnam in the mid-seventies there were perhaps 2 million Chinese, but many have since become refugees. Demographic statistics do not always reveal the extent of the Overseas Chinese presence, since partially assimilated Chinese may not be counted as "Chinese" in a census report even though they maintain Chinese identity.

ASSIMILATION. Chinese who settled in Southeast Asia before the mid-nineteenth century were likely to intermarry and become assimilated to local populations, or to develop new social forms syncretized from elements of Chinese and local cultures. Examples include the mestizos of the Philippines, the Peranakans of Indonesia, and the Baba of Singapore and Malaysia. In contemporary Indonesia and Malaysia, cultural assimilation is now less common: the practice of Islam is now an important expression of ethnic and national identity for "peoples of the soil," and this tends to form an obstacle to intermarriage and full assimilation. By contrast, Chinese have tended to assimilate more readily in the Buddhist countries of mainland Southeast Asia. In Thailand, for example, assimilation has been relatively easy for Chinese; at the same time a population of "Sino-Thai," who have maintained distinctively Sinitic cultural practices while adopting the Thai language and Thai names, has persisted. On the one hand, assimilation has resulted from the relative absence of barriers to intermarriage into a population that shares a common world religion in Buddhism, and on the other hand it is the result of government policy, which since 1948 has restricted Chinese-language instruction in formerly Chinese-medium educational institutions. In Vietnam, it was once axiomatic that Chinese found low barriers to assimilation, since Vietnam had been deeply influenced by Sinitic culture, adopting Chinese characters, Mahayana Buddhism, and for a time a bureaucratic structure of government in which candidates for high office were selected through an examination system modeled on that of imperial China. However, colonial rule and its political aftermath have had an impact on the position of Chinese populations in Southeast Asia. For example, in the period of French colonial rule, French regulations discouraged Vietnamese but encouraged Chinese participation in commerce, and in 1970 it was estimated that while Chinese Vietnamese were only 5.3 percent of the total population, they controlled 70–80 percent of the commerce of Vietnam. In the aftermath of the Vietnam War, the Chinese Vietnamese became a political target, and many fled or were driven out of Vietnam. The Chinese Kampucheans were labeled urban "exploiters" by Pol Pot, and it is estimated that 200,000 perished between 1975 and 1979.

LINGUISTIC AFFILIATION. Overseas Chinese speak a variety of Sinitic regional languages, drawn from three language groups that are not mutually intelligible. Major regional languages include Min (Northern and Southern), Yue, and Hakka. Within Overseas Chinese communities, Chinese also identify themselves by their topolect of origin (misleadingly termed a "dialect"). Topolects of Southern Min include Fujian (Hokkien, Fukien), Chaozhou (Chaochow, Taechew, Teochew), and Hainan. Topolects of Northern Min include Fuzhou (Foochow, Hockchew), Xinghua (Henghua), and Fuqing (Hockchia). Speakers of Yue (Cantonese, Guangfu, Yueh) and Hakka (Hokka, Ke, Kechia, Kejia, Kek, Kheh) are also widely found in Southeast Asia. A single urban community in Southeast Asia might include speakers of eight or more Sinitic topolects, and in such situations, one topolect tends to become the lingua franca for that community. For example, the Fujian topolect of Southern Min (Hokkien) is dominant in many Overseas Chinese communities in Malaysia, Singapore, Indonesia, and the Philippines, whereas another Southern Min

topolect, Chaozhou (Teochew), dominates in Thailand. There are also long-resident Chinese populations who speak Southeast Asian languages as the language of the home: an estimated 65 percent of Chinese Indonesians speak Indonesian in the home; an estimated 80 percent of Chinese Thai speak Thai. In some cases, Chinese has been creolized with Southeast Asian languages: Baba Malay, formed from Hokkien and Malay, is spoken in Singapore and Malaysia; Peranakan Indonesian, formed from Indonesian, Javanese, and Hokkien, is used in Indonesia. The Chinese regional languages share a single written language, which was once learned through diverse literary registers of the regional languages. Since the Republican Revolution of 1911, the written language has been learned through Mandarin-medium education, which was for a time a force for Chinese nationalism in Southeast Asia as well as in China. With the exception of Singapore, Southeast Asian governments have in the postcolonial era promoted national languages at the expense of Chinese-medium education, thus eroding one important base for the continuation of Sinitic culture in Overseas Chinese communities. For example, the Indonesian government promotes Bahasa Indonesia as the medium of education and public discourse, and it has restricted Chinese-medium education and the Chinese-language press. In Malaysia, mastery of the national language, Bahasa Melayu, is increasingly indispensable to public life. However, Mandarin Chinese continues to be a medium of instruction in Chinese-medium primary schools and private secondary schools, and the Chinese-language press has persisted. In the Philippines, Chinese-language instruction has been restricted since 1973, and the new generation of Chinese Filipinos is considered more Filipino than Chinese in outlook. The command of Chinese languages is useful in business, and allows Chinese to maintain ethnic ties across national boundaries; this is one important motive for the maintenance of Chinese-language ability in the context of Southeast Asia.

History and Cultural Relations

Chinese Buddhist monks paid early visits to Southeast Asia, but regular trading visits did not begin until the fourteenth century. Chinese were drawn to the rich entrepôts of Malacca, Manila, and Batavia as trade developed between Europe and Asia in the following centuries, and they were also attracted in considerable numbers to work in Ayuthia, Thailand. In 1842, Great Britain and

China signed the Treaty of Nanking, which ceded the island of Hong Kong to Britain and opened five treaty ports to British trade and residence, including Xiamen (Amoy) and Fuzhou (Foochow) in Fujian Province. Labor migration was encouraged, and a thriving "coolie trade" brought many Chinese men (and a much smaller population of Chinese women) from these ports to work in parts of the world where labor was needed, including colonial Southeast Asia. The coolies met with varied fates: some returned to China after their sojourn in Southeast Asia; some perished under arduous working conditions and ill treatment; and some stayed, the most successful prospering greatly under the protective umbrella of European colonial rule. In the colonial period, Overseas Chinese were frequently middlemen between the European colonists and Southeast Asian producers or consumers. In the Federated Malay States and the Straits Settlements, for example, Chinese bid for contracts to manage the lucrative opium farms and controlled opium distribution on behalf of the British. In Indonesia, Chinese farmers collected taxes and worked as labor contractors for the Dutch; they were also moneylenders and dominated internal trade. The legendary successes of a few who amassed great wealth reinforced the stereotype of Chinese migration as a form of economic colonialism that exploited Southeast Asian resources and the Southeast Asian "peoples of the soil."

Settlements

In urban Southeast Asia, opulently decorated temples, *kongsi* (collective ancestral halls), dialect associations, and Chinese chambers of commerce are among the most impressive expressions of Chinese cultural identity and presence. A common form of construction combines place of work and residence in shop-houses, connected and fronted by a 1.5–meter covered veranda. Businesses frequently cluster: for example, fabric sellers, jewelry dealers, and sellers of ritual paraphernalia each will have a territory within the business district. Where allowed, food is hawked on every corner; also common are Chinese restaurants, in which large groups can be entertained at wedding or festival banquets. In Singapore and elsewhere, development and modernization have created new settlement forms that stand beside the old: many Chinese now reside in high-rise apartments or suburban housing estates, and shops and restaurants cluster in malls as well as in rows of shop-houses.

BANGKOK MARKET

A Chinese businessman counts his money in the Pak Klong market, a wholesale food and flower market. Overseas Chinese have found their economic niche primarily in commerce. Bangkok, Thailand. (Kevin R. Morris/Corbis)

Chinese society in Southeast Asia tends to be stratified, with relative wealth or poverty definitive of social status.

Economy

SUBSISTENCE AND COMMERCIAL ACTIVITIES. Overseas Chinese have found their economic niche primarily in commerce, though in the context of the modern state they have diversified into a variety of occupations. The family-run business is common and describes a range of undertakings, from modest ventures involving the cooperation of husband and wife (with children sometimes providing labor) to multinational firms run by family members trained in the latest management techniques and employing nonfamily members. Increasingly, employees in Chinese-managed firms are multiethnic rather than exclusively Chinese.

TRADE. Overseas Chinese have historically been traders and middlemen in Southeast Asia. Chinese business networks are legendary for the extent of their international linkages, which often follow family or ethnic networks.

DIVISION OF LABOR. Husband and wife frequently cooperate in running family firms. Household work is primarily managed by women, and children often assist in this work. Unmarried children also frequently help out in small family businesses.

Kinship

KIN GROUPS AND DESCENT. In Chinese society, descent is patrilineal, and each child is given his or her father's surname, one of the Chinese "100 surnames." With the exception of Singapore and Malaysia, Chinese in Southeast Asia have been urged or required to adopt non-Chinese names as a step toward identification with the nations in which they live. Many surname groups have kongsi that maintain genealogical records for that surname, though the importance of this aspect of identity has waned somewhat.

KINSHIP TERMINOLOGY. The extensive and detailed Chinese kinship terminology distinguishes members of the patrilineage from matrilateral kin, as well as marking generation and birth order. Maintenance of the Chinese kinship terminology is a fundamental aspect of a claim to Chinese identity for creolized Chinese such as the long-resident Baba community of Melaka (Malacca), Malaysia.

Marriage and Family

MARRIAGE. Urban Chinese generally marry in their twenties or thirties, and residence after marriage is often with the husband's family. It is common to marry across subethnic ("dialect") group boundaries; Overseas Chinese tend toward a high degree of religious tolerance, and religious differences are in general not a barrier to intermarriage. Chinese have intermarried with members of local Southeast Asian populations; however, intermarriage with a Muslim entails conversion to Islam and so, to some extent, loss of Chinese identity—thus the rate of intermarriage has been lower in Malaysia and Indonesia than elsewhere in Southeast Asia. Divorce in traditional Chinese society was difficult: a woman who left her husband would give up her children who, as members of her husband's patrilineage, would remain with their father's family. This is no longer the case; women have a much higher likelihood of getting custody rights under modern laws than they did in the prewar period. With the increasing economic independence of women, and with residence in extended families often replaced by nuclear-family residence, divorce is no longer as strongly discountenanced as it once was.

DOMESTIC UNIT. The extended patrilineal family persists, and at the most developed phase in the cycle a family may include parents, unmarried sons and daughters, and married sons with their wives and children. The nuclear family, however, is increasingly the norm, and young couples who can afford to do so establish independent residences.

INHERITANCE. Property is passed from the husband to his wife and children upon death; however, the patrilineal custom of leaving property to sons persists. Men, while living, may give property and financial support to persons who are not legal heirs (such as "little wives" and their children), who may be helped with gifts, support in achieving educational goals, or loans to aid them in business ventures.

SOCIALIZATION. Child-rearing responsibilities fall primarily to the mother, though grandparents or other relatives sometimes tend children, freeing the mother to seek employment. Children are taught to respect their elders by using the appropriate terms of address and, ideally, to show deference to authority by not defending themselves when criticized. Education follows the standard of the country in which children reside: Chinese-medium education has been restricted throughout Southeast Asia (except in Singapore and in Malaysia, where the constraints are relatively moderate), and government-designed curriculums attempt to orient the younger generation toward identification with Southeast Asian national cultures. Chinese cultural forms are often transmitted outside the educational system by community-based cultural and recreational clubs.

Sociopolitical Organization

SOCIAL ORGANIZATION. Chinese society in Southeast Asia tends to be stratified, with relative wealth or poverty definitive of social status. At the same time, Overseas Chinese maintain crosscutting links between classes through membership in associations that link members through bonds like those of "dialect" group and shared surname. The leaders of associations such as the Chinese chamber of commerce may be called upon to represent the interests of the Chinese community and to promote community aims. With the exception of Singapore, at the national level Overseas Chinese continue to tend to exercise economic rather than political power and influence.

SOCIAL CONTROL. Overseas Chinese live in modern states, and are subject to the legal and political systems of those states. Within their communities, concern with "face" or reputation promotes acts of public-spirited generosity. Chinese culture is imbued with ethical ideas drawn from Buddhism, Taoism, and Confucianism, and celebrates heroic figures who embody these ideals; the notion of karma gives hope of superior rebirth to those who are moral in their present lives.

CONFLICT. Overseas Chinese came to Southeast Asia with a tradition of self-policing. In the nineteenth century, secret societies (*tongs*) maintained forces of fighting men, and violent confrontation between rival secret societies was common, as was fighting between members of different subethnic groups (Cantonese against Hokkien, for example). In contemporary Overseas Chinese communities, a minority of Overseas Chinese are involved in the "underground economies" of the area, and illicit business activities such as prostitution, the drug trade, and illegal gambling have their own "police force" in the form of gangs that provide protection to those involved in these activities. Conflict between Chinese and majority populations has occasionally erupted into violence in Southeast Asia. Outbreaks of anti-Chinese violence are often ascribed to resentment of the favorable economic position of the Chinese, a position that is, to some extent, the legacy of European colonial rule.

Religion and Expressive Culture

RELIGIOUS BELIEFS. Chinese religious culture is syncretic, and Chinese "popular" religion is comprised of elements of Buddhism, Taoism, and Confucianism. The practice of Chinese religious culture involves performing the rituals of ancestor worship and participation in the cycle of public festival events: both are coordinated by the rhythms of the lunar calendar. Some Chinese are also active in the support of such world religions as Mahayana Buddhism, Theravada Buddhism (Sri Lankan and Thai), and Christianity.

Chinese religious culture is polytheistic and involves worship and placation of a variety of hierarchically arranged supernatural beings. The most basic division is that between heaven and earth. At the top of the heavenly hierarchy are spiritual beings who transcend human life, like the Lord of Heaven; next are the spirits of human beings who have, through their spiritual cultivation and perfection, transcended the human cycle of death and rebirth to become Buddhas, Bodhisattvas, or Immortals; next are the venerated spirits of human heroes. Earth, by contrast, is associated on the one hand with gods of the earth, who are territorial protectors, and on the other with the "prison of earth," or hell, which is governed by an appointed bureaucracy modeled on the courts of the district magistrates of prerepublican China. Ghosts are thought to be potentially malevolent beings who may cause human suffering when provoked.

RELIGIOUS PRACTITIONERS. Buddhist monks and Taoist priests contribute to Chinese religious culture by performing funeral rituals and the rites associated with public festivals. Buddhism functions as a world religion as well as serving the needs of religious culture. Buddhist monasteries offer education and retreats for lay Buddhists. Buddhist monks and Taoist priests ideally base their authority on spiritual self-cultivation and on mastery of the traditional texts chanted in ritual performance. Spirit mediums by contrast are ordinary persons whose special abilities belong to the spirits who possess them. Spirit mediums engage in ritual performances and folk healing, and they are frequently consulted for aid when Chinese encounter medical or personal problems that do not resolve themselves and thus are thought to have a spiritual cause. Christian missionaries were active during the colonial period in establishing schools and promoting conversion to a variety of Christian religions; Christianity also has a presence among the Chinese of Southeast Asia. While women may become Buddhist nuns or spirit mediums, Chinese women do not tend to become religious practitioners, in part because they are considered ritually impure as the result of menstruation and childbirth.

CEREMONIES. Participants in Chinese religious culture perform the rites of ancestor wor-

Overseas Chinese came to Southeast Asia with a tradition of self-policing. In the nineteenth century, secret societies (tongs) maintained forces of fighting men.

ship, offering food, drink, and incense on a family altar on the first and fifteenth days of the lunar month. Offerings are also made at this time to the Lord of Heaven, a select number of gods on the family altar, and the gods of the earth. In addition, major ancestral offerings are made during the Qing Ming festival on the fifth day of the fourth lunar month, on the fourteenth or fifteenth day of the seventh lunar month, and on the twenty-second day of the twelfth lunar month. Festivals are celebrated to honor or placate a range of deities, and community members worship in the temple during the festive period and enjoy the Chinese opera or stage show performed in the deity's honor. Religious practitioners are frequently involved in the celebration of festivals; Buddhist monks or Taoist priests may be engaged to perform elaborate rituals, in particular during the Hungry Ghosts festival; spirit mediums perform dramatic rituals such as firewalking or "washing" in hot oil in the festivals that honor their patron deities.

ARTS. Chinese art forms are frequently linked with the affirmation of cultural identity in the Southeast Asian context. They include traditional music, Chinese opera and puppet theater (most commonly performed at temple festivals), Chinese dance, painting, calligraphy, and literature, including works written in Chinese and English as well as in a variety of Southeast Asian languages. Overseas Chinese also engage in a variety of crafts, including gold- and silversmithing, furniture making, and the design and manufacture of batik textiles.

MEDICINE. Modern medicine is used side by side with Chinese medicine. Overseas Chinese consult acupuncturists, bonesetters, herbalists, and Chinese traditional doctors as well as modern medical practitioners. Certain illnesses and mental disturbances (including anxiety) are ascribed to "collisions" with members of the spirit world or to the action of black magic. When such causation is suspected, the ill person is frequently taken to visit a spirit medium, who diagnoses the cause and offers a magical cure.

DEATH AND AFTERLIFE. Funeral rituals draw kin together with members of the groups in which the deceased participated to perform the ceremonies that transform the deceased into an ancestor, represented on the family altar with a spirit tablet. Funerals may express the social status of the deceased both through the scale of ritual performance and the scale of events such as the funeral cortege that transports the coffin to the grave or crematorium. Rituals of salvation may be performed by Taoist priests or Buddhist monks or nuns. The Taoist ceremonies performed forty-nine days after the death dramatically depict the soul's journey through the courts of hell, where it is given a potion of forgetfulness and sent on to a new rebirth. This ceremony offers the soul paper models of goods that the soul is thought to need in its new life (a house, money, servants, a car), and these are burned at the conclusion of the ritual.

Bibliography

Coughlin, Donald (1960). *Double Identity: The Chinese in Modern Thailand.* Hong Kong: Hong Kong University Press.

Cushman, Jennifer, and Wang Gungwu, eds. (1988). *Changing Identities of the Southeast Asian Chinese since World War II.* Hong Kong: Hong Kong University Press.

DeBernardi, Jean (1992). "Space and Time in Chinese Religious Culture." *History of Religions* 31:247–268.

Halpern, Joel Martin (1964). *Economy and Society of Laos: A Brief Survey.* Monograph Series, no. 5. New Haven: Southeast Asian Studies, Yale University.

Lim, Linda Y. C., and L. A. Peter Gosling (1983). *The Chinese in Southeast Asia.* Vol. 1, *Ethnicity and Economic Activity.* Vol. 2, *Identity, Culture, and Politics.* Singapore: Maruzen Asia.

Pan, Lynn (1990). *Sons of the Yellow Emperor: The Story of the Overseas Chinese.* London: Mandarin Paperback.

Purcell, Victor W. W. S. (1965). *The Chinese in Southeast Asia.* London: Oxford University Press.

Skinner, G. William (1957). *Chinese Society in Thailand: An Analytical History.* Ithaca, N.Y.: Cornell University Press.

Somers Heidhues, Mary F. (1974). *Southeast Asia's Chinese Minorities.* Camberwell, Australia: Longman.

Suryadinata, Leo (1989). *The Ethnic Chinese in the ASEAN States: Bibliographic Essays.* Singapore: Institute of Southeast Asian Studies.

Tan Chee Beng (1988). *The Baba of Melaka: Culture and Identity of a Chinese Peranakan Community in Malaysia.* Kuala Lumpur: Pelanduk.

Wee, Vivienne (1988). *Who Are the Chinese?* Working Paper no. 90. Singapore: National University of Singapore, Department of Sociology.

Wickberg, Edgar (1965). *The Chinese in Philippine Life, 1850–1898.* New Haven: Yale University Press.

Wilmott, Donald (1960). *The Chinese of Semarang: A Changing Minority Community in Indonesia.* Ithaca, N.Y.: Cornell University Press.

Wilmott, William E. (1967). *The Chinese in Cambodia.* Vancouver: University of British Columbia Press.

—JEAN DeBERNARDI

DUSUN

Ethonyms: Idäan, Kadazan, Kalamantan, Kiaus, Piasau Id'an, Saghais, Sipulotes, Sundayak, Tambunwhas (Tambunaus), Tuhun Ngaavi

Orientation

IDENTIFICATION. The Dusun live in northern Borneo and speak several regional dialects of a language belonging to the Austronesian family. The Dusun name for themselves, in the Penampang regional dialect, is "Tuhun Ngaavi" (the people). Dusun commonly have recognized differences among themselves through the use of geographic designations (e.g., Tambunan, Penampang, Tempassuk, etc.) and on the basis of dominant subsistence activity in rice agriculture, employing the descriptors *tuhun id ranau* (people of the wet rice fields) or *tuhun id sakid* (people of the hill rice fields) to note a distinction between subsistence based on irrigated rice and on swidden rice cultivation. The term "Dusun" has been used by Europeans, who, in the nineteenth century, adopted the colloquial Malay language usage, *orang dusun* (people of the orchards) as a standard reference term. The recent ethnological literature refers to this population as "Dusun," or has grouped the culture with a larger entity, the Kalimantan nation, which includes the Kalabit, Milanau, and Murut peoples of northern Borneo. In the years following the inclusion (on 16 September 1963) of the former British colony of North Borneo into the new nation of Malaysia as the state of Sabah, the Dusun people began to employ the term "Kadazan" to refer to themselves and to distinguish their culture and society from other indigenous populations in Sabah. Today many Dusun view the name "Dusun" as a legacy of European colonial domination and as a disparaging ethnic identification that discounts their long cultural history and knowledge as a people well-adapted to a demanding local environment.

LOCATION. The Dusun population is found in the Malaysian state of Sabah, which comprises an area of 73,710 square kilometers on the northern tip of the island of Borneo between 4° and 7° N and 115° and 119° E. Dusun communities are located along Sabah's narrow eastern and northern coastal plains and in the central mountain interior ranges and valleys, with a few communities located in the headwater areas of the Labuk and Kinabatangan rivers. Sabah's climate is marked by a high average annual temperature (27° C) and humidity, seasonal heavy rains, gusty winds, and bright sunshine. These climatic factors vary somewhat with altitude and location in Sabah. Annual rainfall in the two yearly monsoon seasons (May to October, November to April) may total between 254 and 520 centimeters, depending on local topography. There may be dry periods of two to four weeks each year when the monsoon winds change direction. Monsoon rainstorm winds sometimes blow at gale force, while heavy rainfall often brings widespread flooding, particularly in Sabah's lowlying areas. The monsoon seasons are characterized by a period of several months when days have hot, sunny, and humid mornings followed by afternoon thunderstorms.

DEMOGRAPHY. The 1960 census of North Borneo conducted by the British colonial government reported a total population of 454,421 persons with 306,498 individuals noted as members of "indigenous tribes." The Dusun were the most numerous of the twelve indigenous groups counted in that census, totaling 145,229 persons or approximately 47 percent of the indigenous population and 32 percent of the total population. A 1980 government census notes a total Sabah population of 955,712 persons. However, the census does not provide specific figures for the twenty-eight groups listed under the heading of *pribumi* or "indigenous" peoples, totaling 742,042 persons. It is possible to estimate, however, that in 1980 the Dusun population comprised at least 101,000 more persons than in 1960, based on an average annual rate of growth in Sabah of approximately 4 percent. A more accurate estimate of the 1980 Dusun population, based on a higher rate of population growth (approximately 6 percent annually) would place the total Dusun population at approximately 319,750 persons, or 43 percent of the Sabah pribumi population at that time. A reasonable estimate of the Dusun population in 1989, based on a 6 percent annual rate of population increase between 1980 and 1989, would be a total of about 492,400 persons. In 1989, the Dusun were the largest ethnic group in Sabah, followed by the Chinese.

LINGUISTIC AFFILIATION. The Dusun language is classified as part of the Northwestern Group of Austronesian languages and is related to languages spoken in Borneo, Indonesia, the Philippines, Taiwan, and Madagascar.

History and Cultural Relations

The origin of the Dusun population is uncertain at present. Existing archaeological and physical anthropological evidence, considered with the results of historical and comparative studies, suggests that the Dusun are descendants of popula-

The Dusun population is found in the Malaysian state of Sabah on the northern tip of Borneo.

Dusun

SETTLEMENTS

*British colonial rule
lasted for eighty-two
years, during which
power, authority,
and law were
usually imposed
unilaterally and
with little regard for
Dusun tradition.*

♦ **swidden cultivation**
*A form of horticulture in
which plots of land
(swiddens, jhums) are
cleared and planted for a
few years and then left to
fallow for a number of years
while other plots are used.
The system is now mostly
used in certain tribal areas
of central and northeastern
India. Also called shifting or
slash-and-burn cultivation,
or jhuming.*

tions migrating into northern Borneo in successive waves some time about 4,000 to 5,000 years ago (and possibly earlier). They brought with them a Neolithic, or food-producing, way of life, based on swidden cultivation supplemented by hunting and foraging. Change in Dusun life, derived from contacts with other cultures, has been taking place for a long period. The historical record indicates contact, particularly in coastal communities in western and northern Sabah, between Dusun and Indians, Chinese, Malays, and Europeans. Thus, beginning after the seventh century B.C., Indian traders and travelers en route by boat to and from south China stopped briefly along the western and northern Borneo coasts to replenish supplies or seek shelter from severe South China Sea weather. These Indian travelers included various types of craftsmen and Brahman and Buddhist teachers and priests. During the time of the Western Han Empire (202 B.C. to A.D. 9), Chinese traders and religious pilgrims traveling to and from India also were in contact with the coastal peoples of western and northern Borneo, seeking local products. Chinese trade with India, with stops by ships along the coasts of Borneo, expanded several times until A.D. 1430, and included the establishment of some trading settlements, such as the one founded in A.D. 1375 at the mouth of the Kinabatangan river in the eastern part of north Borneo by a Chinese trader (Wang Sen-ping). These contacts between northern Borneo native peoples and Chinese traders and travelers over many centuries introduced a wide range of Chinese cultural forms to Bornean populations, and brought them the techniques and tools of irrigated rice agriculture using the water buffalo as a principal source of power in field preparation. Between the ninth and thirteenth centuries A.D. the early Malay Buddhist kingdom of Srivijaya, centered in the area of the present-day city of Palembang, Sumatra, dominated the southern and southwestern coasts of Borneo. Representatives of this kingdom made contact with people along the coasts of western and northern Borneo. Then the powerful Hindu kingdom of Majapahit, located in Java, exercised state power in the same coastal areas of Borneo beginning in the early fourteenth century A.D. Islamic influences and cultural forms spread to the area as the state of Malacca, ruled by a Muslim prince, exerted its domination in the fifteenth century A.D. Some European cultural influences reached the western and northern Borneo coasts as traders sought local products, particularly spices, following the conquest of Malacca by a

Portuguese fleet in A.D. 1511. Regular and intensive contacts between Europeans and the coastal peoples of Borneo did not begin until after the mid-nineteenth century A.D., as the British sought to establish protectorates to maintain the safety of trade routes through the South China Sea. In northern Borneo, a private chartered company was established by British investors in 1881, which ruled the area as a sovereign entity until 15 July 1946, when British North Borneo became a British colony. British colonial rule continued for seventeen more years, until North Borneo became the state of Sabah in Malaysia in September 1963. Thus the Dusun were in regular contact with British cultural and social forms for eighty-two years, during which power, authority, and law were usually imposed unilaterally and with little regard for Dusun tradition. These contacts brought Dusun to realize they were citizens of a Malaysian state, and also brought them into regular contact with a new national language (Bahasa Melayu) and an emphasis by the national government on Muslim religious traditions, values, and social practices.

Settlements

Dusun communities traditionally number (as of 1959) about 300 to 400 persons and range from a low of about 100 persons to over 1,000 persons. Most Dusun communities are distinct, compact, or nucleated entities set in the center of, or directly adjacent to, food-producing areas. Dusun settlements employing swidden cultivation have a "longhouse" type of dwelling, or a series of nuclear-family apartments built on one level, fronted by a common veranda and covered by a common roof. Some Dusun swidden communities have several longhouses grouped closely together. Dusun communities basing their food production on irrigated rice agriculture often contain a number of separate nuclear-family dwellings grouped closely together in a type of "divided longhouse" form (e.g., family apartments no longer fronted by a common veranda or covered by a common roof) and are arranged along the length of a footpath, often on a rise or bluff overlooking nearby rice fields. Coconut palms, fruit trees, and other useful plants are grown near the houses in compact Dusun settlements using irrigated rice farming. In both types of Dusun community, family members move out at the beginning of the day to tend fields, perform various tasks connected with agriculture, or forage and hunt in nearby jungle areas. Structures in both kinds of Dusun community traditionally have hardwood support posts with split-bamboo sides and floors and either a bamboo-tile or *atap* palm-thatch roof.

Economy

SUBSISTENCE AND COMMERCIAL ACTIVITIES. Today irrigated rice agriculture is the dominant food-producing activity in Dusun communities. The rice is grown for use as a meal several times a day. The irrigated rice crop is set out initially as seedlings in nursery plots, then hand transplanted into small plots, less than a hectare in size, that are prepared by both women and men. Field preparation involves repair of the low earthen dikes used to retain the water that flows across the fields, as well as the repair of the irrigation systems employed by Dusun to bring water from nearby streams and rivers. The irrigation systems often involve transporting water across ravines through bamboo or wooden conduits and call for considerable practical knowledge of hydrodynamics, especially in leading water to fields located at a distance from a stream. Dusun wet-rice agriculture traditionally involves breaking the soil with a hoe and plowing the field with a flat-board harrow that has wooden teeth attached to the underside, pulled by a water buffalo wearing a woven rattan harness. The rice crop is harvested by hand and initially winnowed in fields on woven, split-bamboo mats. Further winnowing of the rice crop may occur near grain storehouses where any surplus is held until required for food or trade. The irrigated rice cycle is divided into eleven named phases, each associated with a specific kind of work activity and associated with ritual and ceremonial activities, including a communitywide harvest celebration. Dusun families also plant and tend small gardens near their houses, where they may grow some twenty-five types of foodstuff, including the sweet potato, greater yam, manioc, bottle gourd, various types of bean, squashes, chilies, and a wide variety of other garden crops. The borders of garden areas are used to cultivate trees and shrubs bearing coconuts, bananas, breadfruit, mango, papaya, durian, limes, and other fruits that supplement the daily rice diet. A half-dozen plants also are cultivated near Dusun houses or garden plots for use in manufacturing tools, shelter, and clothing. These plants include bamboo, kapok, betel palms, indigo, and derris. Dusun also eat the shoots of bamboo plants. A variety of domestic animals provide food, power, and raw materials for the Dusun. Chickens and ducks are common fowl, and geese are sometimes kept. Pigs and water buffalo both are used by Dusun as food; the buffalo is employed as a power source in rice agriculture. Pigs and water buffalo also play an important role in ritual activities that are a vital part of Dusun life. Dogs and cats are kept as domestic animals in most households, the dogs serving as hunting companions and the cats reducing the rat population in houses and rice-storage structures.

INDUSTRIAL ARTS. Dusun communities usually have part-time and seasonal male and female specialists expert in the making and repair of tools and implements used in agriculture and hunting and foraging activities. They also make and repair buffalo harnesses and plows and weave rattan fish traps and split-bamboo baskets of various kinds, rice-sifting trays, and other implements used in everyday storage and the carrying of foodstuffs. Metal tools, ceramic containers, and cloth traditionally have been obtained by Dusun from Chinese traders or merchants.

TRADE. The Dusun have depended for centuries upon these traders for manufactured goods. In addition, weekly markets exist in most Dusun areas of Sabah. Here Dusun women bring local produce for sale or barter. Such markets are also places for buying various manufactured goods.

DIVISION OF LABOR. Traditional household tasks are assigned to Dusun females, although males are expected to undertake household work if their wives are ill, in the late stages of pregnancy, or absent from the community for a time. Dusun men perform the heavy labor associated with house and storehouse building and getting wood and bamboo supplies for this purpose. Men and women work together in most swidden rice agricultural tasks, including field repair, planting, harvesting, and weeding. Men undertake the clearing and firing of fields in the preparation of swidden rice cultivation because these activities are considered too dangerous for women. The construction and repair of irrigation channels used in wet-rice agriculture tend to be the task of men, although women often participate. Men are expected to participate in infant and child care. Dusun women do not hunt, are not skilled in the weapons used in the hunt, and have little knowledge of hunting lore. The weaving of split-bamboo mats, field hats, and sifting trays are the exclusive domain of women; males have scant knowledge or skill in such work.

LAND TENURE. Irrigated wet-rice agriculture is based on a set of cultural beliefs concerning the use and inheritance of land. Individual ownership and the inheritance of irrigated fields by descendants of landowners form the cornerstones of this system of land tenure. A steadily increasing

Dusun have specific social groups made up of descendants of a particular founding ancestor, whose activities are told in legend and folklore on special occasions.

population has placed significant pressure on the ownership and inheritance of irrigated rice lands and has resulted recently in the growth of a group of young Dusun unable to own land. This has caused migration of many young people to the towns and cities of Sabah to seek wage-labor incomes. Thus Kota Kinabalu, the Sabah state capital, grew from 21,719 persons in 1960 to 108,725 persons in 1980.

Marriage and Family

MARRIAGE.   Marriages are typically monogamous, although polygynous marriage is permitted between older, wealthy males and younger females believed capable of producing healthy infants. Dusun commonly prohibit marriage with any first or second cousin and view marriage with third cousins as distasteful. There is some freedom in choosing marriage partners, within limits set by Dusun culture. Following an arrangement to marry between a man and a woman, often made in secret, formal discussions concerning marriage are initiated by the man's father, paternal grandfather, or a father's brother with the woman's father,

paternal grandfather, or a father's brother. Marriage involves direct and substantial payment by a groom to the father of the bride. Marriages tend to be locally exogamous. Following marriage, couples routinely establish independent family households close to both their families, although a newly married couple may reside initially with the groom's father and occasionally with the bride's father while working to accumulate enough wealth to establish an independent household. Termination of marriage, other than through death of a spouse, requires initial arbitration by a community leader, then a formal hearing if the effort at reconciliation fails. A ritual fine may be required of an individual found to be at fault in the dissolution of a marriage.

DOMESTIC UNIT.   The nuclear family is the minimal family unit occupying a household. Some relatives may be added to the nuclear family as the need arises to support them, particularly if they are aged, ill, or handicapped. These relatives are expected to assist in some way in the household unit.

INHERITANCE.   The Dusun traditionally follow the general principle that all children should receive a fair share of the estates of their parents. A child who cares for an aged parent before death may receive some special additional consideration in property inheritance. A husband has little control over the property brought to a marriage by his wife. The Dusun have developed and use a traditional system for deciding complex questions concerning the distribution of property.

SOCIALIZATION.   Parents tend to share the care of infants and young children. Older siblings often care for infants and young children when parents are away from the household at work. The process of cultural transmission traditionally provides for a long period of freedom from most tasks for maturing children, with few restrictions on their behavior. Then, at about 11 or 12 years of age, children are expected to begin to participate in daily work activities and to be responsible members of their families and community. Prior to this age children are considered by parents to be naturally inclined to noisiness and illness, somewhat temperamental, easily offended, quick to forget, and prone to wandering away from home. Dusun parents try to shape this nature through use of a wide variety of specific physical and verbal rewards and punishments. Because infants and young children are not viewed as competent humans until they reach about 11 or 12 years of age, they are not judged harshly or punished by parents when they misbehave.

KINSHIP

Kin Groups and Descent

Descent in Dusun culture is bilateral. Ego-oriented kindreds also are present and are active in celebration of important events in the life of an individual. For Dusun, a kindred is a group of relatives recognizing their relationship to a particular individual without regard to whether the relationship is traced through a male or female relative. Dusun also have specific social groups, all members of which are descendants of a particular founding ancestor, whose activities are told in legend and folktale on special occasions of ritual feasting and ceremony, and in whose name some land and moveable property are owned. These ancestor-oriented kin groups conventionally have regulated marriage between members through insistence on the practice of endogamy.

Kinship Terminology

Dusun traditionally employ Eskimo cousin terminology. They also emphasize the relative ages of unrelated persons through use of special kin terms.

Sociopolitical Organization

The Dusun jurisdictional hierarchy is traditionally organized at the level of the local community. In the past they have given no attention to larger sociopolitical entities such as parish, district, province, or a political state. Their communities are led by males selected through an informal, community-wide consensus, who hold formal office as "headmen" (*mohoingon*) with wide powers. This office is viewed by Dusun as nonhereditary in its succession.

SOCIAL ORGANIZATION. Society is traditionally organized about several territorially based divisions that serve as a focal point for the performance of certain ritual and ceremonial activities. These territorial divisions may contain one or several mutual-aid groups whose members assist each other in heavy work (for example, house building or field clearing). Dusun society is also organized on the basis of age, sex, personal and family wealth, and the region of residence. Seniority in age, for both females and males, plays an important part in social life. Women are widely respected for their specialized craft, ritual, and ceremonial knowledge.

POLITICAL ORGANIZATION. Dusun are citizens of the nation of Malaysia, a federal parliamentary democracy based on the British model. Malaysia contains thirteen states, each with an elected assembly and headed by a chief minister. In Sabah, the state assembly has forty-eight seats. The chief minister, Mr. Joseph Pairin Kitingan, a 49–year-old Dusun, is a Christian and the first Dusun to qualify as a lawyer in Malaysia. First elected to office in 1985 in an upset victory over the candidates of two Muslim-led political parties, Mr. Kitingan's political party (PBS, or Parti Bersatu Sabah—Sabah United Party) gained control of the state government by winning a majority of seats in the assembly. Following state-court challenges by members of the previous state government and their allies, Mr. Kitingan called another assembly election in 1986. During the two-month election campaign there were violent incidents that included rioting and bombings by political activists supporting the main opposition party, Bersatu Rakyat Jelata (Sabah People's Union or Berjaya). The PBS party of Mr. Kitingan increased its majority in the Sabah state assembly in the elections held in May 1986, and Mr. Kitingan continued in office as chief minister. In June 1986 the PBS party became part of the Barisan Nasional (National Front) political party, an alliance of thirteen parties that presently is the ruling party in Malaysia. Thus, the Dusun now live in a complex nation-state political setting organized significantly beyond their traditional sociopolitical concerns. A head of state with the power of constitutional oversight, a prime minister directing a national government and substantial internal security and defense forces, and a bicameral parliament—all these are distant democratic forces affecting daily Dusun life through executive and legislative decisions.

SOCIAL CONTROL. Social control in Dusun communities is maintained largely through informal sanctions, including shame, mockery, gossip, and ridicule, with some use of shunning behavior. The Dusun have also developed more formal means of dealing at the community level with individuals accused of serious violations of the norms and mores of traditional life. Dusun have several techniques for litigating complaints against individuals. Litigation occurs in the context of a body of abstract principles that are imbued with an aura of tradition, or *koubasan*, which provides a moral and ethical authority that binds all persons involved in litigation to that body of abstract principles. Litigation in Dusun communities is conducted by a village leader (the mohoingon) who functions in ways that establish facts in a case and who may administer one or several tests of truth. The leader also has the power to levy various fines and several kinds of punishment against persons found guilty of vio-

DUSUN HARVEST DANCE

Dusun children wearing baskets on their backs perform the Dusun Harvest Dance. Public ritual performances associated with the agricultural cycle are regular features of Dusun culture. Sabah, Malaysia. (Nik Wheeler/Corbis)

*Seniority in age
plays an important
part in Dusun social
life. Women are
widely respected for
their specialized
craft, ritual, and
ceremonial
knowledge.*

lating traditional behavior. Litigation is a public process.

CONFLICT. Dusun traditionally have engaged in conflict between communities, with organized raiding parties of men seeking to engage in hand-to-hand combat persons, social groups, or communities believed to have caused an imbalance of personal or community fortune (*nasip tavasi*) and luck (*ki nasip*). Such armed conflict usually arose from an effort to restore the fate or luck of individuals or a community that had been made bad (*aiso nasip, talat*) through the real or supposed acts of some individual, group, or other community. The objective of combat was to secure trophies for a display that publicly symbolized a full restoration of good fortune and luck. Among such trophies were the severed heads of individuals vanquished in close combat. Head trophies were given special care, often stored in particular places, including house eaves, and formed an integral part of special rituals and ceremonies held periodically in Dusun communities to note formally that community and individual luck and fortune remained in balance. Following 1881, the Chartered Company acted vigorously, but until near the time of World War II with limited success, to suppress head-taking combat. Such conflict has not subsequently been a feature of Dusun life.

Religion and Expressive Culture

The Dusun traditionally are animists, believing there is a direct and continuing relationship between the events of daily life and a complex world of good and evil supernatural beings and unseen forces. Dusun also believe that proper ritual and ceremonial acts can be interposed between humans and supernatural beings and forces in an attempt to modify, or even to control, events that cause humans to fall ill, be uncertain, lose their luck, feel pain, or become fearful.

RELIGIOUS BELIEFS. Dusun conceptions of the universe include a variety of malevolent supernatural beings and forces believed to be responsible for the personal crises of human life, including accidents, illness, and death. These harmful beings include entities and forces that have existed since the time of the creation of the world, as well as the souls of the dead doomed by the creator being to an eternity of wandering and cannibalism because of evil deeds performed while alive. A group of beneficial spirit beings and forces is also believed to be important in keeping order in the universe and in daily human life. The most important of these supernatural beings and forces in

everyday life is the "spirit of the rice," a female entity who serves as the guardian of the rice crop and rice storehouse and in whose name specific rituals are performed at times of rice planting and harvest. In addition, Dusun traditionally believe in the existence of a specific class of named supernaturals whose attributes and powers are known and used by ritual specialists as they seek to divine and control events leading to life crises. A creator force, personified into a being called "Asundu," who has a legendary history and is possessed of awesome powers, is said to have shaped the universe and to direct the destiny of all its inhabitants. A specific power of the creator, believed to be derived from the inexhaustible store of the power of this being, is said to provide for the curative and restorative powers of female and male ritual specialists. Objects, geographic locations, and persons are said to be imbued with considerable amounts of this power and must be treated with respect or avoided if possible. A special designation (*apagun*) and carved symbols are used by Dusun to "wall off" such locations or objects from inadvertent human contact. Today, large numbers of Dusun have become Christians and so reject many animistic beliefs and practices. Some have also become Muslims.

RELIGIOUS PRACTITIONERS. Some male and female individuals in each Dusun community are specially knowledgeable in the many ritual and ceremonial acts used to mediate between humans and the supernatural world. These rituals and ceremonies involve spirit possession, use of symbolic objects, recitation of lengthy sacred verses, and often center upon specific individuals, places, or crops afflicted with a disease or ill fortune. The effectiveness of a ritual or ceremony is said to depend upon precisely following correct procedures and the accurate recitations of verses. Female ritual specialists tend to concentrate on curing and divination regarding individual illness and bad fortune. Male ritual specialists tend to concern themselves with alleviation or prevention of a worldwide scope. The verses recited by female and male ritual specialists are often expressed in an archaic form of the Dusun language not known or widely used in a community; they are learned through long apprenticeship to senior ritual specialists.

CEREMONIES. Public performances of ritual acts, many concerned with the annual swidden and irrigated rice agricultural cycle, are a regular feature. Ceremonies marking individual life-cycle stages or transitions (for example, birth, marriage, and death) are also important.

ARTS. Art and house architecture are imbued with forms and designs common to other native Bornean peoples. Many of these art forms are believed by Dusun to express a "spiritual" (*id dasom ginavo*) intent or quality, and are said to exhibit their deep understanding, or *ginavo*, and respect for Dusun tradition, or *koubasan*. Traditional musical instruments include a bamboo mouth harp, a bamboo-and-gourd wind instrument, and gongs of various sizes obtained in the past from Chinese traders. Dusun men have traditionally practiced tattooing of their necks, forearms, and shoulders with intricate designs of deep spiritual meaning.

MEDICINE. Personal illness is believed by Dusun to derive from bad fortune, various actions taken by harmful supernatural beings and forces, and the malign intentions of human adversaries. A wide range of medicinal remedies, derived from various plant and animal products and made into different lotions and poultices, is used to help alleviate and cure illness. Special importance is attached to a variety of a swamp-plant root that is believed to have magical and curative powers and is used by female specialists when seeking to divine and cure personal illness.

DEATH AND AFTERLIFE. The Dusun believe that following death the spirit of an individual proceeds to the supernatural world. There the spirits of the dead are said to rest near the creator being in a world similar to the human world but lacking disease, bad fortune, failed crops, and combat, where all things are new and never in need of replenishment. Some spirits of the dead are believed not to reach the place of the dead since they are captured en route by harmful spirits or eaten by cannibal spirits. A period of formal mourning, which includes a number of ritual and ceremonial actions, is intended to ease the transition of the dead to their new life in the afterworld.

Bibliography

Evans, I. H. N. (1922). *Among Primitive Peoples in Borneo*. Philadelphia: Lippincott.

Evans, I. H. N. (1953). *The Religion of the Tempasuk Dusuns of North Borneo*. Cambridge: Cambridge University Press.

Hurlbut, H. M. (1985). "Social Organization and Kinship among the Labuk Kadazan People." *Philippine Journal of Linguistics*, no. 15 (December 1984)-16 (June 1985), pp. 55–70.

Rutter, O. (1922). *British North Borneo*. London: Constable & Co.

Rutter, O. (1929). *The Pagans of North Borneo*. London: Hutchinson & Co.

Williams, T. R. (1965). *The Dusun: A North Borneo Society*. New York: Holt, Rinehart & Winston.

Williams, T. R. (1969). *A Borneo Childhood: Enculturation in Dusun Society*. New York: Holt, Rinehart & Winston.

—THOMAS RHYS WILLIAMS

FILIPINO

In its broadest sense, "Filipino" (fem. "Filipina") refers to citizens of the Republic of the Philippines, a grouping that numbered an estimated 62,380,000 people in 1992. "Filipino," however, is often used in a more restricted sense to refer to Christian Filipinos, who comprise 93 percent of the population. Muslims (4 percent) and others, including animists ("pagans"), comprise the remaining 7 percent. Relations between Christian Filipinos and Muslims (who live mainly on Mindanao Island) are troubled, with the former often viewing the latter as violent, warlike, and backward. Efforts by Muslim political groups to achieve independence continue. Roman Catholicism was introduced to the Philippines by the Spanish in the 1500s and 84 percent of the population is now Roman Catholic, with another 9 percent Protestant. The major Christian ethnic groups, ranked according to their estimated population in 1962–1963, are the Cebuan (6,529,800), Tagalog (5,694,000), Ilocano (3,158,500), Panayan (2,817,300), Bikolan (2,108,800), Samaran (1,488,600), Pampangan (875,500), and the Pangasinan (666,000). Smaller groups include the Ibanag (314,000), Aklan (304,000), Hantik (268,000), Sambal (72,000), Ivantan (11,800), Itawas (11,800), and Isinai (11,500). Bisayan is a generic label that encompasses Cebuans, Panayans, and Samarans.

Many Filipinos distinguish among the different Christian Filipino groups on the basis of stereotypical perceptions of these groups. Thus, Tagalogs are seen as proud, boastful, and talkative; Pampangans as independent, self-centered, and materialistic; Ilocanos as hard-working, aggressive, and with an eye toward the future; and Bisayans as musical, passionate, fun-loving, and brave. Identification with one's group is strong and remains a marker of social identity even in overseas communities.

Christian Filipinos live mainly in coastal lowlands and valleys, primarily on Luzon, Samar, Leyte, Cebu, Bohol, Siquijor, Panay, and Negros Islands. Most Christian Filipinos on Mindanao are recent immigrants.

Relations between Christian Filipinos and Muslims are troubled, with the former (who live mainly on Mindanao Island) often viewing the latter as violent, warlike, and backward.

Philippine languages are grammatically and phonetically similar to one another and all are classified as Austronesian. Filipino (Pilipino), based on Tagalog, is the national language, with English an important second language. Despite the Spanish influence, the Spanish language was never widely spoken.

The Philippines were probably settled initially through many small migrations from mainland Southeast Asia. Chinese influence was felt early and was substantial. With the exception of Mindanao and other islands in the south, influence from the islands that now form Indonesia was minimal. Spanish contact began with Magellan's visit in 1521 and officially ended in 1898 when Spain ceded control to the United States. In addition to Roman Catholicism, which made the Philippines the only predominantly Roman Catholic nation anywhere in Asia, the Spanish brought the roman alphabet, private ownership of land, the Gregorian calendar, and various New World plants such as cassava, maize, and sweet potatoes. The American period (1898–1946) saw the introduction of national public education, the English language, and agricultural and industrial development. During World War II the country was occupied by Japan, and in 1946 it became an independent republic.

The economy continues to center on agriculture, especially rice, sugarcane, and hemp. Foresting has long been an important industry, and deforestation is now a growing problem. Industrial activity is mainly around Manila and focuses on the processing of agricultural products.

The nuclear family, one's kindred and personal alliances, and godparenthood (*compadrazgo*) are the central features of family life and social relations. Much attention has been paid to the "familial" nature of Filipino society and the emphasis placed on the family as compared to the individual.

Filipino Roman Catholicism is a synthesis of the Roman Catholicism brought by the Spanish and some animistic beliefs of the traditional cultures. Especially important among the latter are beliefs in spirits of the land and ancestors' souls who influence the lives of the living.

Bibliography

Hart, Donn V. (1975). "Christian Filipinos." In *Ethnic Groups of Insular Southeast Asia*, edited by Frank M. LeBar. Volume 2, *Philippines and Formosa*, 16–22. New Haven: HRAF Press.

Kurian, George T. (1987). "Philippines." In *Encyclopedia of the Third World*. 3rd ed., 304–307. New York: Facts on File.

Schirmer, Daniel B., and Stephen Rosskamm Shalom, eds. (1987). *The Philippines Reader: A History of Colonialism, Neocolonialism, Dictatorship, and Resistance*. Boston: South End Press.

Steinberg, David (1982). *The Philippines: A Singular and Plural Place*. Boulder, Colo.: Westview Press.

HMONG

Ethnonyms: Man, Meo, Miao, Mong

Orientation

IDENTIFICATION. The Hmong have migrated to Southeast Asia from the mountainous parts of southwestern China, where many still remain. They have settled in the mountainous regions of northern Laos, northern Vietnam, and northern Thailand, and there are small groups of Hmong in Myanmar (Burma) near the Chinese border. Since the ending of the Indochina wars large numbers of Hmong refugees from Laos have been resettled in Western countries, including the United States. There are two main cultural divisions of the Hmong in Southeast Asia, marked by differences of dialect and custom, between the White Hmong and the Green Hmong (who pronounce their name as "Mong"). Hmong religion is based on domestic ancestral worship and shamanism, and they speak dialects of the Miao Branch of the Miao-Yao Language Family.

LOCATION. Southwestern China, Myanmar, and northern Indochina form a unified geographical zone characterized by four main mountain ranges outcropping from the eastern Himalayas and the Tibetan plain, with a semitropical climate and dense tropical rain forest in some areas. At around 1,000 meters deciduous trees give way to evergreen forest. Mountain peaks range from 2,535 meters in Thailand to 7,470 meters in southern China. North-south-running mountain ranges separate fertile alluvial river valleys united in the past only by a network of caravan routes.

DEMOGRAPHY. There are some 2 million Hmong speakers in China, approximately 200,000 in Laos, 300,000 in Vietnam, and 50,000 in Thailand. More than 30,000 others are in refugee camps along the Thai border with Laos. More than 100,000 have been resettled in Western countries.

LINGUISTIC AFFILIATION. Hmong forms part of the Western Branch of the Miao languages, which also include Hmu and Kho Xyong. Miao is related at its upper levels to the Yao dialects, from which a Proto-Miao-Yao can be re-

♦ **Indochina**
That area of mainland Southeast Asia occupied by the nations of Vietnam, Laos, Cambodia, and Thailand. The region is so named to reflect the strong cultural influences from both India and China.

constructed. No relationship to other languages has been firmly established, although the whole group has been influenced strongly by Chinese. The Miao-Yao languages are usually classed as Sino-Tibetan, although some scholars disagree with this. Hmong has eight tones and a complex phonology.

History and Cultural Relations

The Miao were first recorded in Chinese annals as a rebellious people banished from the central plains around 2500 B.C. by the legendary Yellow Emperor (Huang Di) of China. Because the Hmong today retain traces in their culture of the earliest known forms of Chinese social organization, some specialists have considered them the aboriginal inhabitants of China, predating the Han. Their legends, however, have led others to speculate that they may have originated from a northern polar region. Records exist of the Miao in China from 1300 to 200 B.C.; from then until A.D. 1200 they were subsumed under the generic Chinese term for southern barbarians (Man). There are, however, good records of the Miao from 1200 to the present, and we can be fairly certain that they refer to the ancestors of the Hmong. Most focus on the many uprisings of the Miao against the Chinese state, bearing witness to a long historical displacement of the Hmong and other southern Chinese minority people from the centers of power as the Han Chinese population slowly expanded southward. Hmong began migrating into Southeast Asia around 1800. The last major Miao rebellions in China were in 1856.

In Vietnam and Laos, the Hmong fell under the authority of the French colonial government. A major Hmong rebellion against excessive levies on opium production broke out in Laos in 1919; it took the authorities several years to suppress the revolt, which assured the Hmong of a measure of self-representation. During the Indochina wars, Hmong loyalties were severely fragmented among the royalists, neutralists, and opposition in Laos, and large numbers fled to Thailand when the Pathet Lao gained control of their country in 1975. In Thailand a similar polarization occurred as a result of the 1959 ban on opium production; the ban failed to suppress opium production, giving rise to a government policy of tolerating an illegal practice. Many Hmong supported the armed rural struggle of the Communist Party of Thailand against the government in the 1960s and early 1970s, which has now largely ended. Policies of tolerance toward opium production have also ended, and this may facilitate Hmong acceptance of the many programs targeted at replacing opium-poppy cultivation with alternative cash crops.

SETTLEMENTS

Houses are usually built directly on the ground rather than on piles. They were traditionally made out of upright wooden shingles notched together or bound with hemp rope and creepers without the use of nails, and thatched with teak leaves or cogon grass. In some parts of China the Hmong live in houses made out of adobe or stone after the Chinese fashion; in Laos and Thailand some have adopted the Thai style of housing. Richer households may be able to invest in zinc or polystyrene roofing, while poorer families may have to construct their houses entirely out of pieces of split bamboo and rough matting. The traditional village numbered only about seven houses, but today, owing to reasons of security and the need for intensive cultivation of the land, villages of between seven and fifty households are more common. They are often arranged in a horseshoe pattern just beneath the crest of a mountain, and are, if possible, sheltered by a belt of forest and located close to a source of water. New villages are carefully sited according to the principles of a geomantic system aimed at ensuring a fundamental harmony between man and the forested environment. Water is often piped down the mountain to the village through a series of semitroughs formed out of lengths of split bamboo, and is collected, usually by women, in wooden or metal buckets. In some areas wells are maintained, or tap systems have been constructed. Usually tall clumps of cooling bamboo, peach, or banana are maintained near the village, while the neighboring slopes are devoted to herbal gardens. Raised wooden granaries are constructed near each house to protect against scavengers; small chicken coops or stables may also be built. Pigs traditionally are not penned but left free to clear the village of refuse. In some villages shops are maintained, often by Chinese traders.

A major Hmong rebellion against excessive levies on opium production broke out in Laos in 1919; it took authorities several years to suppress the revolt.

Economy

SUBSISTENCE AND COMMERCIAL ACTIVITIES. The Hmong economy is based on the integrated cultivation of dry rice, maize, and opium poppy as a cash crop. Rice forms the staple diet in most of Southeast Asia, where maize is primarily used as animal fodder, but in southern China and at higher elevations the cultivation of rice for subsistence is replaced by that of maize, millet, or buckwheat. Hunting and gathering play subsidiary parts in the economy, while the domestic husbandry of pigs and chickens provides the main source of protein. In certain areas the Hmong have surrendered the shifting cultivation of dry rice in favor of intensive irrigated rice cultivation on permanent terraced fields laboriously constructed on the flanks of mountains.

Maize and poppy form an integrated cycle because they can be planted successively in the same fields. Maize is usually planted in the fifth or sixth month, after the rice has been planted, and it is harvested in the eighth or ninth month, allowing opium poppy to be planted in the same fields for harvest after the New Year, at the end of the twelfth month. Forests must be burned off for the shifting cultivation of dry rice early in the year, and dried out before rice can be dibbled in the fields fertilized by the nitrogenous ashes. While rice fields can only be used for two to three years, maize fields can be continually replanted for some eight years. It has been argued that the increasing overpopulation of the hill areas of Thailand has led to increases in the length of time the same parcel of land is kept under cultivation, resulting in declining rice yields that force the Hmong to produce opium as a cash crop to buy rice from lowland traders. Opium is the best crop to grow because it adapts well to harsh soil conditions and there is a ready market for it. Many Hmong families are indebted to traders (who tend to be of Yunnanese origin) for their rice, and so must continue to produce opium in order to survive.

INDUSTRIAL ARTS. The Hmong do not produce their own pottery, but are famous for their silverwork, and in most villages there are blacksmiths specializing in the production of farming tools and weapons. Chinese silversmiths also often are employed; there are no full-time craft specialists among the Hmong. Women, however, spend a large proportion of their time spinning, weaving, and embroidering hemp and cotton in the intricate needlework of traditional Hmong clothing.

TRADE. The most significant trading activity is that of opium for cash or rice. This takes place on an individual household basis, with organized paramilitary groups whose representatives visit villages on a regular basis, through itinerant traders who travel to the villages after the opium harvest to make their purchases, or through the medium of shopkeepers settled in the villages. There are no full-scale regional markets among the Hmong communities, although individual Hmong may visit lowland markets occasionally to make important purchases and sometimes to sell forest products or vegetables.

DIVISION OF LABOR. There is no full-time occupational specialization in traditional Hmong society, all adult members of which are farmers. Individuals, however, may specialize as wedding go-betweens, blacksmiths, or funeral specialists. The most prestigious specialization is that of the shaman, whose duties are to cure illness and prevent misfortune. The main division of labor in agricultural work is between men and women. Women take most of the responsibility for housework and child care but also play a crucial part in agricultural activities. Child labor is also important in agricultural work.

LAND TENURE. As traditional shifting cultivators, the Hmong have, in general, lacked permanent titles to land and, often, citizenship rights in the countries in which they are settled. Attempts have been made by the Thai government to encourage permanent settlement by issuing land-use certificates, but these remain limited. However, in some areas where the Hmong have turned to permanent forms of rice agriculture, they have obtained land-use rights. In general, land-use rights in shifting cultivation belong to the one who first clears the land, and lapse after an indeterminate period of noncultivation.

Kinship

KIN GROUPS AND DESCENT. Hmong society is divided into a number of named exogamous patrilineal clans similar to the Chinese surname groups. The ideal number of these, when they are referred to in ritual discourse, is twelve, but there are in fact more than this, some having been founded by inmarrying Chinese males. Within the clans, the lineage is the basis of Hmong social organization, and the local segment of the lineage acts as the major corporate ritual and political body at the village level. Major lineage differences within a clan are distinguished by variations of ritual at household and funeral ceremonies.

KINSHIP TERMINOLOGY. Hmong kinship terminology is more generative than inclusive, distinguishing relatives on the basis of generation, sex, and relative age, and above all between affinal relatives and relatives by descent. As in the Chinese system, patrilateral parallel cousins (having the same surname) are distinguished from all other cousins by a special term. It has been suggested that the system was once a bilateral one that has been considerably influenced by the Chinese system.

Marriage and Family

MARRIAGE. Polygyny is permitted and two or three cowives may inhabit the same house. Owing to the high bride-wealth demanded at weddings, however, it is only the richer men who can afford to take a second wife. On marriage a woman is completely incorporated into her husband's descent group and will be worshiped by his descendants as an ancestor, retaining only her original clan name. The levirate is practiced among the wives of elder brothers. Marriages can be arranged by parents but are more often the result of the free choice of the spouses. Premarital sex is allowed, and marriages often take place at the first pregnancy. A rare form of marriage by capture also exists, usually in the case of parental disapproval of a match. On marriage a woman moves to her husband's home, except in uncommon instances where a family has only daughters or the groom cannot afford to pay the bride-wealth, in which case uxorilocal residence occurs. Divorce, which is very rare, is almost always initiated by men. The fact that the wife's natal family may be unwilling to return her bride-wealth acts as a sanction against divorce. Suicide may be the only recourse left to an unhappy wife, yet the threat of suicide can itself prove a powerful sanction.

DOMESTIC UNIT. The household is the main unit of economic cooperation and also the most fundamental unit of ritual worship. Households vary in composition from nuclear and stem to more extended types, since usually some time after marriage, or at the birth of a child, a son will move out with his family to form a new household. These may range in size from one to twenty-five members, including, for example, the children of several living or deceased siblings, and unmarried women of several generations. Such large households, however, are rare.

INHERITANCE. Shifting cultivation means that there is no land to inherit and little other her-itable property. What wealth a family possesses will usually be divided equally among its sons. The house and its belongings, however, will usually go to the youngest son, who is expected to remain in the house to care for his aged parents.

SOCIALIZATION. Literacy remains uncommon despite state efforts to educate Hmong children in Thai, Lao, Vietnamese, or Chinese. Attendance at rituals provides an important occasion for young boys to learn their traditional customs, while women are educated in the skills of embroidery and singing by their mothers or elder female siblings and friends. Fathers play a large part in teaching young children to speak, and other local languages are often acquired individually at a later stage. Participation in agricultural work by all capable members of the household leads to an early familiarization with subsistence skills.

Sociopolitical Organization

SOCIAL ORGANIZATION. Hmong social organization is based on the kinship system, divided into patrilineal clans that define affinal relations, and subdivided into local lineages formed out of individual households. The ritual head of the lineage is its oldest living member; ranking within the lineage is on the basis of age seniority, but is largely egalitarian.

POLITICAL ORGANIZATION. There is no political organization above the village level in traditional Hmong society. An assembly of male lineage elders makes local decisions and discusses problems or arbitrates disputes. At these assemblies women also take informal part. The ritual head of the lineage and its shamans enjoy the most prestige and authority in decision-making activities. In many areas local headmen of villages are appointed to deal with external affairs. These men do not necessarily enjoy full authority over their own lineages and cannot represent other lineages in the same village, but tend to be those most skilled in dealing with outsiders.

SOCIAL CONTROL. Social control is largely maintained through the importance attached to traditional customs that distinguish the Hmong from other ethnic groups and affirm the unity of the lineage. The knowledge of these customs tends to be the preserve of lineage elders and shamans. Gossip and occasionally accusations of witchcraft also act as mechanisms of social control. The authority of a father (who controls bride-wealth payments) over his sons, and of men over women, is a fundamental feature of this system.

♦ **levirate**
The practice of requiring a man to marry his brother's widow.

Hmong

*Communication
with the otherworld
is the basis of
Hmong religion,
divided into
domestic worship
and shamanism.*

CONFLICT.   Any member of the lineage has the right to summon the lineage to war, although in practice it is the views of the eldest that will be the most respected. In case of conflicts with other ethnic groups or emergencies, the Hmong send out scouting parties in pairs from each village to report on the situation. Conflicts within Hmong society generally take place between local lineages and rarely involve related clan members. The great majority of these disputes concerns marriages and bride-wealth payments, children born out of wedlock, and extramarital affairs. Conflicts over land and the adoption of Christianity also occur, but these are rare.

Religion and Expressive Culture

RELIGIOUS BELIEFS.   The Hmong otherworld is closely modeled on the Chinese otherworld, which represents an inversion of the classical Chinese bureaucracy. In former times, it is believed, humans and spirits could meet and talk with one another. Now that the material world of light and the spiritual world of darkness have become separated, particular techniques of communication with the otherworld are required. These techniques form the basis of Hmong religion, and are divided into domestic worship and shamanism.

RELIGIOUS PRACTITIONERS.   Every male head of a household practices the domestic worship of ancestral spirits and household gods represented at different sites in the architecture of the Hmong house. Particular rituals must be performed by him in honor of these spirits, most during the New Year celebrations. Whereas domestic worship is conducted for the benefit of individual households by their heads, shamanism is only practiced by a few men in each lineage, and is for the benefit of others since its primary purpose is to cure illness. Illness is often diagnosed by the shaman as the result of soul loss; his task is to recall the wandering soul and so restore health.

SUPERNATURALS.   The two malevolent Lords of the other-world are Ntxwj Nyug and Nyuj Vaj Tuam Teem. Saub is a kindly deity who periodically comes to the rescue of humanity, and Siv Yis was the first shaman, to whom Saub entrusted some of his healing powers to protect humankind from the diseases with which Ntxwj Nyug afflicted them. Household and ancestral spirits (*dab*) are distinguished from the tutelary spirits of the shaman (*neeb*). Within the household there are special altars to the spirits of wealth and sickness, of the bedroom, the front door, the loft, the house post, and the two hearths.

CEREMONIES.   The major calendrical ceremony is New Year, when the household spirits are renewed, the ancestral spirits honored, and the shamanic spirits dispatched temporarily to the otherworld. New clothes are donned, parties of villagers visit other villages, antiphonal songs are sung by courting couples, and courting games of catch are played. Each household sacrifices domestic animals and holds feasts. Weddings are also celebrated with great display.

ARTS.   Needlework, embroidery, and the chanting of love songs are particularly esteemed artistic skills. The playing of the reed pipes, the notes of which are said to express the entirety of Hmong customs, is an art that takes many years to acquire. New dances, song forms, and pictorial arts have appeared in the context of the refugee camps.

MEDICINE.   Herbal medicine is a specialty of many women who maintain special altars to the spirits of medicine. Forms of massage and magical therapy are also used. Shamanism remains the primary medical and therapeutic technique, although modern medicines are employed extensively.

DEATH AND AFTERLIFE.   The ritual specialist at death is not necessarily a shaman, whose business is to preserve life. The purpose of the funeral and mortuary rites is to ensure the safe dispatch of the reincarnating soul to the otherworld. Funerals last a minimum of three days, attended by all local male kin within the household of the deceased. The reed pipes are played each day and a special song is sung to guide the reincarnating soul on its journey. Cattle must be slaughtered. The corpse of the deceased is inhumed in a geomantically selected site. On the third day after burial the grave is renovated, and a special propitiatory ritual is performed thirteen days after death for the ancestral soul, which will protect the household. A final memorial service to release the reincarnating soul, held a year after death, is somewhat similar to the funeral; and some years after death, in the case of severe illness or misfortune, a special propitiatory ritual may be performed for the same spirit.

On the way back to the village of its ancestors, the reincarnating soul must collect its "coat," or placenta, buried beneath the floor of the house. The dangers and pitfalls of this journey are pictured in the poetic geography of the funeral song, which parallels the long historical journey of the Hmong from a country probably to the north of China. The song describes the creation of the first couple, the deluge, and the first drought, and represents a historical journey back to the origins of humanity, to which the deceased must return before being reborn.

Bibliography

Cooper, Robert G. (1984). *Resource Scarcity and the Hmong Response: Patterns of Settlement and Economy in Transition.* Singapore: Singapore University Press.

Geddes, W. R. (1976). *Migrants of the Mountains: The Cultural Ecology of the Blue Miao (Hmong Njua) of Thailand.* Oxford: Clarendon Press.

Hendricks, Glenn L., Bruce T. Downing, and Amos S. Deinard, eds. (1986). *The Hmong in Transition.* Minneapolis: University of Minnesota; Center for Migration Studies.

Lemoine, Jacques (1972). *Un village Hmong Vert du Haut Laos: Milieu, technique et organisation sociale.* Paris: Centre National de la Recherche Scientifique.

Lin Yüeh-Hwa (1940). "The Miao-Man Peoples of Kweichow." *Harvard Journal of Asiatic Studies* 5:261–345.

Ruey Yih-Fu (1960). "The Magpie Miao of Southern Szechuan." In *Social Structure in South-East Asia,* edited by George P. Murdock, 143–155. Viking Fund Publications in Anthropology, no. 29. Chicago: Quadrangle Books.

—NICHOLAS TAPP

IBAN

Ethonyms: Dayak, Dyak, Sea Dayak

Orientation

IDENTIFICATION. The name "Iban" is of uncertain origin. Early scholars regarded it as originally a Kayan term, *hivan,* meaning "wanderer." The use of the name by those Iban in closer association with Kayan gives support to this possibility. Other Iban, of Sarawak's First and Second Divisions, used the name "Dayak," and even today consider "Iban" a borrowed term. The participation of a few Iban in alliances with Malays for coastal piracy in the nineteenth century led to their being called "Sea Dayaks."

LOCATION. Iban are to be encountered in all of the political divisions of the island of Borneo, but in the largest numbers in the Malaysian state of Sarawak, on the northwest coast. They have lived predominantly in the middle-level hills of the island, and during the last 150 years, fully half have moved onto the delta plains. Within the past 25 years, 20 percent of Sarawak's Iban have moved into the state's urban centers.

DEMOGRAPHY. There were approximately 400,000 Iban in the state of Sarawak in 1989 (368,208 in 1980). Reliable figures for Kalimantan, the Indonesian part of the island, are unavailable.

LINGUISTIC AFFILIATION. The Iban language is distinct from other Bornean languages, and though it shares a limited number of words with Malay it is not a Malay dialect.

History and Cultural Relations

The Iban trace their origins to the Kapuas Lake region of Kalimantan. With a growing population creating pressures on limited amounts of productive land, the Iban fought members of other tribes aggressively, practicing headhunting and slavery. Enslavement of captives contributed to the necessity to move into new areas. By the middle of the nineteenth century, they were well established in the First and Second Divisions, and a few had pioneered the vast Rejang River valley. Reacting to the establishment of the Brooke Raj in Sarawak in 1841, thousands of Iban migrated to the middle and upper regions of the Rejang, and by the last quarter of the century had entered all remaining divisions. The most dramatic changes in the past three decades have been abandonment of longhouses and permanent settlement in Sarawak's towns and cities. Iban have lived near other ethnic groups with whom they have interacted. The most important of these societies have been the Malays, Chinese, Kayan and, during the Brooke Raj and the period of British colonialism, Europeans. The dynamic relations between Iban and these societies have produced profound changes in Iban society and culture.

Settlements

Iban settlements are still predominantly in the form of longhouses. During the time when headhunting was endemic, the longhouse provided a sound strategy of defense. It continues to be a ritual unit, and all residents share responsibility for the health of the community. A longhouse is an attenuated structure of attached family units, each unit built by a separate family. The selection of different building materials and the uneven skills of Iban men who build their own houses are apparent in the appearance of family units, some with floors of split bamboo, others with planed and highly polished hardwood floors. The average width of a family unit is 3.5 meters, but the depth, that is, the distance from front to back, varies widely. A longhouse may include as few as 4 families with 25 residents in a structure less than 15

♦ **longhouse**
A large, rectangular-shaped dwelling with a wood frame covered by planks, bark, mats, or other siding and usually housing a number of related families.

meters long, or as many as 80 families with 500 residents in a house about 300 meters long. Access to a longhouse is by a notched-log ladder or stairs. At the top of the ladder is an uncovered porch (*tanju'*) on which clothing, rice, and other produce may be dried. Inside the outer wall is a covered veranda (*ruai*), which is the thoroughfare for traffic within the house, where women and old men sit during the daytime weaving or carving, and where families gather in the evening to recount the day's events or to listen to folklore told by storytellers. Beyond the inner wall is the family apartment (*bilik*), where the family cooks and eats its meals, stores its heirlooms, and sleeps. Above the bilik and extending halfway over the ruai is a loft (*sadau*), where the family's rice is stored in a large bark bin and where unmarried girls sleep. The longhouse is constructed with its front to the water supply and preferably facing east. The core of each longhouse community is a group of siblings or their descendants. Through interethnic marriages, members of other societies may become part of Iban settlements and are assimilated as "Iban" in a generation or two. Until the past quarter-century, all Iban lived in or were related to longhouse settlements. Life in the longhouse was considered "normal," and those few people who lived in single-family dwellings apart from the longhouse were thought to be possessed by an evil spirit. Within the past 25 years, through a process of social and economic differentiation, many affluent Iban have built single-family houses. In the towns to which Iban are moving, they live scattered among Chinese and Malays in squatters' communities.

Economy

SUBSISTENCE AND COMMERCIAL ACTIVITIES. The primary activity of a majority of Iban is rice farming. In the hills, farmers practice swidden cultivation of fields averaging one hectare. Each family maintains its own seed bank of rice, and plants between one dozen and two dozen varieties in any year. At the center of its field they plant their sacred rice (*padi pun*), a gift of some spirit to an ancestor, which has been retained over generations to recall the origins of that family. Given the uncertainties of rice farming in the hills, dozens of ritual acts are performed to ensure a successful crop. At the end of April, the head of the house holds a meeting of all family heads to discuss farm sites and an approximate date for the first rites. The meeting ensures that all residents coordinate their activities and that the rice matures at about the same time. Simultaneous maturation is critical because it

IBAN RESIDENCE

An Iban woman drying pepper in front of a longhouse. Longhouses were originally designed as defensive structures against headhunters; today, a longhouse may include 4 to 80 families, depending on size. Skrang River Longhouse, Sarawak, Malaysia. (Dave G. Houser/Corbis)

helps reduce the losses of any one family to insects, birds, and wild animals, who spread themselves over several fields rather than concentrate on just one. It also permits families to coordinate their harvest rituals. Auguries are taken in June, farms are cleared in June and July, and burned over in August or September. When the rice has ripened, it is informed through ritual that it is to be harvested and transported back to the longhouse. On the last day of harvest, farmers make an offering to the final stand of rice to ensure that the soul of the rice will return to the house with them, and not remain behind in the ground. In the plains, farmers practice farming of wet rice in permanent fields. Introduction of herbicides, pesticides, and commercial fertilizers has permitted Iban to remove vegetation, control weeds and insects, and increase the yields of their farms. With much greater control over the success of their efforts, farmers rely much less on ritual. In addition to rice, farmers plant gourds, pumpkins, cucumbers, maize, and cassava. Rice is complemented with a variety of jungle vegetables and fruits collected by men and women for consumption with the evening and morning meals. Fishing has provided the principal source of protein in the Iban diet, but logging and the consequent silting of many streams and rivers have greatly reduced the numbers of fish. Techniques of fishing are sophisticated and adjusted according to the conditions of the waters. Fish traps are placed in constricted streams, and large nets are inclined over larger streams. Fish are taken with a seine or with hooks. Hunting of wild pigs and deer, using dogs, traps, and nets, varies from community to community, according to the region, forest conditions, and animal population. Almost all families keep chickens and pigs, and every longhouse has dogs. Chickens, pigs, and water buffalo are used in sacrifices, and eggs are an essential ingredient of any offering.

The most important commercial activity for the largest number of Iban men has been the institutionalized *bejalai*, or journey to work for wages. In some longhouses almost all able-bodied men are away at any given time, working for a distant logging company or in the oilfields of northern Borneo. Wage earning enabled men to buy jars, gongs, and other valuables for their families. Rubber and pepper have provided an unstable source of income, as has cocoa, a recent introduction. The attraction of salaried jobs is one of the principal reasons for Iban urban migration. Iban are employed in every major occupational category in Sarawak's cities.

INDUSTRIAL ARTS. Iban women are superb weavers using the backstrap loom. Most men are skilled in the use of the piston bellows. In addition to weaving blankets and other cloths, women weave mats and baskets.

TRADE. Iban collect bamboo and rattans for their own use or for sale. Natural rubber and the illipe (*Bassia* sp., the Indian butter tree) nut, which is available about every fourth year, are other important collectibles. Ironwood, sawed as logs or cut as poles, is becoming increasingly scarce.

DIVISION OF LABOR. Domestic chores, such as cooking and tending the bilik, are performed primarily by women. Both men and women collect wild foods for family consumption and, among Iban living near towns, for sale. Men fell trees and do the heavier farm work, fish, hunt, and take on contracts with logging and oil companies. In urban contexts, both men and women perform office jobs.

LAND TENURE. Rights to land are established by clearing and farming it, or by occupying it. Rights to the use of farmland are vested in the bilik-family, and are held in perpetuity. These rights are maintained in the living memory of the residents of each longhouse. Boundaries are indicated by land-forms or trees, or are marked by planting a row of bamboo. Except for the land overshadowed by the eaves of the long-house, there is no land to which a community holds rights. With the introduction of surveys and titles to land in the early 1900s, Iban who lived closer to government centers obtained titles to their land, under which rights of individual familes to land could be verified. As a result of increased population and the commercialization of land, some Iban have bought land for investment and speculation.

Kinship

KIN GROUPS AND DESCENT. The fundamental unit of Iban society is the bilik-family, a group of five or six persons defined by kinship and affinity. Depending upon negotiations at a couple's marriage, there is an almost even chance that their children will be born into the family of either the wife or the husband. Iban families are part of a widely ramifying kinship system that developed in response to Iban mobility. The *suku juru* and *kaban belayan* correspond to the kindred. The former connotes kin ties originating with one's grandparents and includes persons to the degree of first cousin. The latter is any group of people who share rights of reciprocity with an Iban, and may include nonkin and even non-

The most important commercial activity for the largest number of Iban men has been the institutionalized bejalai, *or journey to work for wages.*

Iban. More inclusive groups include "the brotherhood" and "food sharers," made up of distant kin who would be invited to one's festivals, or whose festivals an Iban would attend. Attachment is ambilateral and descent is ambilineal. Although some Iban are capable of reconstructing genealogies up to fifteen generations in depth, such reconstructions are selective and illustrate the Iban practice of "genealogizing" so as to establish ancestral ties with strangers.

KINSHIP TERMINOLOGY. Terms of reference are Eskimo and the terms of address are Hawaiian.

Marriage and Family

MARRIAGE. Preferred and proscribed marriages are commonly recognized. Though parents prefer to arrange their children's marriages, especially educated young people would rather choose their own mates. Marriage is preferably with a person between the degree of first and fifth cousin. Distinctions are made between parallel and cross cousins; marriages between the former are avoided. Although most Iban marriages are monogamous, isolated instances of sororal and nonsororal polygyny occur. Marriage between a man and a woman who are related as members of adjacent generations is not approved, but propitiatory rites can be performed if, for example, an aunt and nephew insist on marrying. Marriage within the kin group is preferred to protect property rights and to avoid union with a descendant of slaves or a person of ill fortune. Residence is ambilocal or neolocal. Divorce may be initiated by either partner and, with mutual consent, is relatively easy.

DOMESTIC UNIT. The bilik-family is an autonomous unit, able to join with other units of a longhouse or to detach itself. Iban become members of a family through birth, adoption, marriage, or incorporation. The family is responsible for construction of its own unit, production of its own food, and management of its own affairs. In a sample of 1,051 families, 60 percent were comprised of parents and children, 40 percent included grandparents. The family is a kin-based, corporate group that holds in trust land, sacred rice, sacred charms, ritual formulas, taboos, and heirloom gongs and jars. Traditionally, one son or daughter remained in the bilik to ensure continuity over time. With urban migration and mail service making possible postal remittances, an increasing number of parents have no adult child residing in the bilik with them.

INHERITANCE. Male and female children share equally in rights to real and other property so long as they remain members of their natal bilik. Children who move out of the bilik at marriage or for any other reason receive a small portion of the family estate, and in theory relinquish all rights to family land. In fact, however, they retain the right to request land for farming at the annual meeting commencing the agricultural year.

SOCIALIZATION. At birth an infant becomes the center of attention and the subject of numerous rituals. Weaning is casual and discipline relaxed. During the farming season, children are left in the care of older people. By age 5, children wash their own clothes and by 8, girls help with domestic chores. Traditionally adolescent males would undertake "the initiate's journey," a trip of several months or years, from which they were expected to return with trophies. Adolescent females demonstrate their maturity with diligence and in the weaving of ceremonial cloths, baskets, and mats.

Sociopolitical Organization

SOCIAL ORGANIZATION. Each longhouse, as each bilik, is an autonomous unit. Traditionally the core of each house was a group of descendants of the founders. Houses near one another on the same river or in the same region were commonly allied, marrying among themselves, raiding together beyond their territories, and resolving disputes by peaceful means. Regionalism, deriving from these alliances, in which Iban distinguished themselves from other allied groups, persists in modern state politics. Essentially egalitarian, Iban are aware of long-standing status distinctions among themselves, recognizing the *raja berani* (wealthy and brave), *mensia saribu* (commoners), and *ulun* (slaves). Prestige still accrues to descendants of the first status, disdain to descendants of the third.

POLITICAL ORGANIZATION. Prior to the arrival of the British adventurer James Brooke there were no permanent leaders, but the affairs of each house were directed by consultations of family leaders. Men of influence included renowned warriors, bards, augurs, and other specialists. Brooke, who became Rajah of Sarawak, and his nephew, Charles Johnson, created political positions—headman (*tuai rumah*), regional chief (*penghulu*), paramount chief (*temenggong*)—to restructure Iban society for administrative control, especially for purposes of taxation and the suppression of head-hunting. The creation of permanent political positions and the establishment of political parties in the early 1960s have profoundly changed the Iban.

SOCIAL CONTROL. Iban employ three strategies of social control. First, from childhood, they are taught to avoid conflict, and for a majority every effort is made to prevent it. Second, they are taught by story and drama of the existence of numerous spirits who vigilantly ensure observation of numerous taboos; some spirits are interested in preserving the peace, while others are responsible for any strife that arises. In these ways, the stresses and conflicts of ordinary life, especially life in the longhouse, in which one is in more or less constant sight and sound of others, have been displaced onto the spirits. Third, the headman hears disputes between members of the same house, the regional chief hears disputes between members of different houses, and government officers hear those disputes that headmen and regional chiefs cannot resolve.

CONFLICT. Major causes of conflict among Iban have traditionally been over land boundaries, alleged sexual improprieties, and personal affronts. Iban are a proud people and will not tolerate insult to person or property. The major cause of conflict between Iban and non-Iban, especially other tribes with whom Iban competed, was control of the most productive land. As late as the first two decades of the twentieth century, the conflict between Iban and Kayan in the upper Rejang was serious enough to require the second rajah to send a punitive expedition and expel the Iban forcefully from the Balleh River.

Religion and Expressive Culture

RELIGIOUS BELIEFS. Religious beliefs and behavior pervade every part of Iban life. In their interpretations of their world, nature, and society, they refer to remote creator gods, who brought the elements and a structured order into existence; the bird-god Sengalang Burong, who directs their lives through messages borne by his seven sons-in-law; and the popular gods, who provide models for living. Iban religion is a product of a holistic approach to life, in which attention is paid to all events in the waking and sleeping states. The religion involves an all-embracing causality, born of the Iban conviction that "nothing happens without cause." The pervasiveness of their religion has sensitized them to every part of their world and created an elaborate otherworld (Sebayan), in which everything is vested with the potential for sensate thought and action. In Iban beliefs and narratives trees talk, crotons walk, macaques become incubi, jars moan for lack of attention, and the sex of the human fetus is determined by a cricket, the metamorphized form of a god.

Though the gods live in Panggau Libau, a remote and godly realm, they are unseen, ubiquitous presences. In contrast to the exclusive categories of Judaism and Christianity, "supernaturals" and "mortals" interact in all activities of importance. In contrast to the gods who are more benevolently inclined towards mortals, Iban believe in and fear a host of malevolent spirits. These spirits are patent projections onto a cosmic screen of anxieties and stresses suffered by Iban: the menacing father figure, the vengeful mother, the freeloader, and becoming lost in the forest. Iban strive to maintain good life and health by adherence to customary laws, avoidance of taboos, and the presentation of offerings and animal sacrifices.

RELIGIOUS PRACTITIONERS. There are three religious practitioners: the bard (*lemambang*), the augur (*tuai burong*), and the shaman (*manang*). Individually or in teams, bards are invited to chant at all major rituals. They are highly respected men, capable of recalling and adapting, as appropriate, chants that go on for hours. The augur is employed for critical activities such as farming or traveling. The shaman is a psychotherapist who is consulted for unusual or persistent ailments.

CEREMONIES. Iban rituals (*gawa, gawai*) may be grouped into four major categories: (1) one dozen major and three dozen minor agricultural festivals; (2) healing rituals, performed by the shaman, commencing in the bilik and progressing to the outer veranda; (3) ceremonies for the courageous, commemorating warfare and headhunting; and (4) rituals for the dead. Iban of all divisions perform rituals of the first two categories. Ceremonies to honor warriors have assumed greater importance in the upper Rejang, and rituals for the dead have been much more elaborated in the First and Second divisions of Sarawak.

ARTS. The Iban have created one of the most extensive bodies of folklore in human history, including more than one dozen types of epic, myth, and chant. Women weave intricate fabrics and men produce a variety of wood-carvings.

MEDICINE. Though they have a limited ethnopharmacology, Iban have developed an elaborate series of psychotherapeutic rituals.

DEATH AND AFTERLIFE. Life and health are dependent upon the condition of the soul (*samengat*). Some illnesses are attributed to the wandering of one of an Iban's seven souls, and the shaman undertakes a magical flight to retrieve and return the patient's soul. Boundaries between life and death are vague, and at death the soul

In Iban beliefs trees talk, jars moan for lack of attention, and the sex of a human fetus is determined by a cricket, the metamorphized form of a god.

The wealthy Ifugao aristocrats are known as kadangyan. *The possession of a* hagabi, *a large hardwood bench, secures their status symbolically.*

must be informed by a shaman that it must move on to Sebayan. Crossing "The Bridge of Anxiety," the soul is treated to all imaginable pleasures, many of which are proscribed for the living. After an undetermined period of revelry, the soul is transformed into spirit, then into dew, in which form it reenters the realm of the living by nourishing the growing rice. As rice is ingested, the cycle of the soul is completed by its return to human form. Gawai Antu, the Festival of the Dead, may be held from a few years to 50 years after the death of a member of the community. The main part of the festival occurs over a three-day period, but takes months or even years to plan. The primary purpose of the festival is to honor all the community's dead, who are invited to join in the ritual acts. The festival dramatizes the dependence of the living and dead upon each other.

Bibliography

Freeman, Derek (1970). *Report on the Iban*. Monographs on Social Anthropology, no. 41. London: London School of Economics. {Issued in 1955}

Jensen, Erik (1974). *Iban Religion*. Oxford: Clarendon Press.

Sutlive, Vinson H. (1978). *The Iban of Sarawak*. Arlington Heights, Ill.: AHM Publishing Corp. Reprint. 1988. Prospect Heights, Ill.: Waveland Press.

—VINSON H. SUTLIVE, JR.

IFUGAO

Ethonyms: Ifugaw, Ipugao, Yfugao

Orientation

The Ifugao are a rice-growing people who live in a mountainous region of Luzon in the Philippines. The Ifugao homeland of Ifugao Province (17° N, 121° E) occupies less than 750 square miles in the center of northern Luzon. Of the 106,794 Ifugao in 1970, 25,379 lived outside the province of Ifugao. Population density may reach 400 per square mile. The Ifugao language is Austronesian and is most closely related to Bontok and Kankanai.

History and Cultural Relations

The renowned Ifugao system of terraced rice growing appears to have developed indigenously over a period of at least four centuries. Ifugao contact with the outside world was mainly with American military officers and schoolteachers early in this century. Later, transportation improved and allowed people to travel to earn wages. After World War II, the production and sale of wood carvings became important.

Settlements

Hamlets (*buble*) of eight to twelve dwellings, housing a total of thirty or more people, are built on hillocks on the sides of valleys. The houses (*bale*) are built on terraces close to rice fields. They and the granaries are made of timber and rest on four posts, with thatched roofs; the only difference in design between the two is that houses are larger and have hearths. There are also temporary buildings, such as houses for the unmarried, which are built on the ground. Houses once had a shelf for the skulls of enemies taken in battle. The typical household consists of the nuclear family; once children are old enough to take care of themselves, they go to live in boys' houses and girls' houses.

Economy

The Ifugao depend greatly on their wet-rice pond fields. The majority—84 percent—of their diet is derived from agriculture, most of it from the wet fields; 10 percent is from the fish, clams, and snails living in those wet fields. The Ifugao grow taro, cotton, beans, radishes, cabbage, and peas in those same fields, but they raise sweet potatoes and corn elsewhere in swidden fields. A man's status depends on his rice fields. Irrigation is accomplished by dikes and sluices. Pond fields range in size from just a few square meters to more than one hectare, the average size being 270 square meters.

Kinship

Kinship terminological categories are relatively few; several types of relationship are described by the same term. For example, all kin of Ego's generation are known by the same term. A second term applies to one's child, nephew, or niece, and a third to one's mother and one's parents' sisters. Bilateral kinship relationships are the most important social ties. Every individual is a member of an exogamous bilateral kindred that extends to one's great-great-grandparents and third cousins. It is responsible for the welfare of its members, and formerly the Ifugao activated it in times of feud. One's kindred becomes allied with one's spouse's kindred at marriage.

Sociopolitical Organization

Traditionally, social differentiation has been based on wealth, measured in terms of rice land, water

MARRIAGE AND FAMILY

Monogamy is the norm, but the wealthy sometimes practice polygyny. The incest prohibition extends to first cousins; more distant cousins may be married only on payment of livestock penalties. Ifugao courtship takes place in the girls' houses (*agamang*). Before a wedding, temporary trial marriages sometimes occur. Wealthy parents arrange marriages through intermediaries, and they make decisions concerning their children's use and inheritance of property. Families exchange gifts and maintain close relations following marriage. Divorce may occur by mutual consent, or with the payment of damages if contested. Grounds for divorce include bad omens, childlessness, cruelty, desertion, and change of affections. There is a vast difference in property allocation if the couple has children. Childless partners each take whatever they brought individually into the marriage through inheritance and then divide commonly acquired joint property equally; if there are children, all property goes to the children. A widow or widower may marry again only after making a payment to the deceased spouse's family; the payment is reduced if the second spouse is of that same family. Postmarital residence is typically close to the largest rice field acquired by either partner, but newlyweds may initially spend some time with the parents of either the groom or the bride. Both sexes may inherit property and debts from both parents, although the firstborn receives the greatest share. An illegitimate child has the right to receive support from his or her natural father's family but no right to inherit from his estate.

buffalo, and slaves. The wealthy aristocrats are known as *kadangyan*. The possession of a *hagabi*, a large hardwood bench, secures their status symbolically. They maintain their high status by giving feasts and by displaying their heirlooms, including hornbill headdresses, gold beads, swords, gongs, and antique Chinese jars. Kadangyan tend to class endogamy. The less wealthy are known as *natumok*; they have little land, which forces them to borrow rice from the kadangyan at high interest rates. Because of these high rates, it is nearly impossible for natumok to rise to kadangyan status. The poor, *nawatwat*, have no land; most of them work as tenant farmers and servants to the kadangyan.

The Ifugao have little by way of a formal political system; there are no chiefs or councils. There are, however, approximately 150 districts (*himputonā'an*), each comprised of several hamlets; in the center of each district is a defining ritual rice field (*putonā'an*), the owner (*tomona'*) of which makes all agricultural decisions for the district.

Bilateral kinship obligations provide most of the political control. Beyond local areas, in which people are controlled largely by kinship behavior, are areas that are more and more unfriendly the farther outward one goes; at a certain point one reaches what was formerly known as a "war zone," within which Ifugao once fought head-hunting battles.

Social control is a combination of kinship behavior and control by a *monbaga*, a legal authority whose power rests on his wealth, knowledge of customary legal rules (*adat*), and especially a large supporting group of kin who stand behind his decisions. The monbaga's main sanctions are death and fines. The degree of wealth of the offender or the degree of his or her kinship relatedness mitigate the severity of the punishment; the less wealthy or the more distantly related the offender, the more likely that death is the sanction. However, the monbaga could not control feuding between kin groups within the larger group and warfare with outsiders. Feuds were often of long duration; if they ended at all, they were most often concluded by intermarriage between the feuding groups. Warfare often took the form of raiding, with up to 100 men in a war party. Raiders not only collected heads for display on the skull shelves of expedition leaders, but also took slaves for sale to lowlanders. Blood feuds and warfare ended with the U.S. occupation of the Philippines, head-taking by mid-century.

Religion and Expressive Culture

The complexity of Ifugao religion is based in part on the complex Ifugao cosmology. The Ifugao divide the universe into the known earth, *pugao* (the people refer to themselves as "Ipugao," or "inhabitants of the known earth"); the sky world, *kabunian*; the underworld, *dalum*; the downstream area, *lagod*; and the upstream area, *daiya*. Each of these five regions has large numbers of spirits. The spirits have individual names and each belongs to one of thirty-five categories, among them hero ancestors, celestial bodies, natural phenomena, and diseases. In addition, the Ifugao have deities; these figures are immortal, are able to change form or become invisible, and are mobile.

Ifugao priests are men who take their positions voluntarily and after a period of apprenticeship. Their job is to serve the members of their kindreds by invoking the spirits of deceased ancestors and deities. Priests do not make their living from their priestly activities, although they are compensated with meat, drink, and prestige.

Rituals and ceremonies—for the purposes of augury, omenology, hunting success, agricultural abundance, prestige feasts, etc.—typically make use of as many as fifteen priests. Priests recite myths to give them power over the deities and hero ancestors named in them, by way of inviting them to possess their bodies. Invoking deities may involve chanting for more than five hours. Once in the priest, a deity is given an offering (which may be betel, chicken claw, pig, chicken, etc.) and is fed rice and wine (through the body of the priest). Finally, an exhortation is made to the deity.

Illness is caused by deities taking souls in cooperation with ancestors. Priests treat illness through divination and curing rituals, in an effort to have the deity return the soul. If the deity does not do so, the sick individual dies. A corpse is washed, its orifices are plugged, and it is placed in an honorary death chair (corpses of kadangyan people are given insignias). There the body lies in state guarded by a fire and a corpse tender, and it is "awakened" each night; the wealthier the deceased, the longer this period lasts (up to thirteen days). Burial is in a family sepulcher or in a coffin that is placed either in a mausoleum or under the house. Sometimes secondary burials take place three to five years later, especially if the deceased is unhappy and causing illness among the living. Some Ifugao groups bury males and females separately and inter children in jars.

Bibliography

Barton, Roy Franklin (1919). "Ifugao Law." *University of California Publications in American Archaeology and Ethnology* 15:1–186.

Barton, Roy Franklin (1922). "Ifugao Economics." *University of California Publications in American Archaeology and Ethnology* 15:385–446.

Barton, Roy Franklin (1930). *The Half-Way Sun: Life among the Headhunters of the Philippines.* New York: Brewer & Warren.

Barton, Roy Franklin (1946). "The Religion of the Ifugaos." *American Anthropological Association Memoir* 65:1–219.

Conklin, Harold C. (1980). *Ethnographic Atlas of Ifugao: A Study of Environment, Culture, and Society in Northern Luzon.* New Haven: Yale University Press.

Lambrecht, Francis (1932). "The Mayawyaw Ritual, 1. Rice Culture and Rice Ritual." *Publications of the Catholic Anthropological Conference* 4:1–167.

Lambrecht, Francis (1955). "The Mayawyaw Ritual, 6. Illness and Its Ritual." *Journal of East Asiatic Studies* 4:1–155.

JAPANESE

Ethonyms: Nihonjin, Nipponjin

Orientation

IDENTIFICATION. The Japanese people, the majority of whom live in the archipelago known as Japan, which lies off the eastern coast of the Asian continent, speak the Japanese language. Japan, the most technologically advanced society in the world today, officially was transformed from a feudalistic country to a nation-state in 1871. It remains a homogeneous society in that less than 1 percent of the population is classified as non-Japanese and immigration to Japan is regulated carefully. A considerable amount of emigration has taken place since the end of the last century, largely to the United States, Canada, and South America. The indigenous religious system is Shinto; Buddhism was brought to Japan from China via Korea in the sixth century. The majority of Japanese people today classify themselves as both Shinto and Buddhist, and just over 1 percent as Christian. A large proportion of the population is, however, effectively secular in orientation. The Japanese identify themselves in terms of what is taken to be a shared biological heritage, birth in Japan, and a common language and culture. Although Japan is a postindustrial society and has, particularly since World War II, been thoroughly exposed to North American and European cultures and values, the sense of a shared past and unique cultural heritage remains central in creating a modern Japanese identity.

LOCATION. Japan consists of four main islands—from north to south, Hokkaidō, Honshū, Shikoku, and Kyūshū—in addition to a number of island chains and a thousand smaller islands. It occupies less than 0.3 percent of the world's land area and is about one twenty-fifth the size of the United States. Japan lies in the temperate zone, at the northeastern end of the monsoon region, and has four distinct seasons. Rainfall is abundant. Japan is subject to numerous earthquakes and, in

♦ **archipelago**
A sea or broad expanse of water interspersed with islands or groups of islands; the term often is used for island groups themselves.

late summer, to typhoons. Rugged mountain chains, several of them containing active volcanoes, account for more than 72 percent of the total land area, and numerous swift, shallow rivers flow from the mountains to the sea. Relatively little land is available for agriculture, just over 14 percent today; dwellings and roads occupy another 7 percent, leaving most of the countryside covered by dense, cultivated forests.

DEMOGRAPHY. The population of Japan is just over 123 million people, with a density of 326 persons per square kilometer in the habitable areas, making it one of the most densely populated countries in the world. About 76 percent of the Japanese people live in cities; well over half of urban dwellers reside in one of four metropolitan areas made up of the sixteen prefectures around Tokyo, Ōsaka, Nagoya, and Kitakyūshū. The Tokyo megalopolis is comprised of about 30 million people and contains the administrative unit known as the Central Tokyo Metropolitan Area—approximately 11 million people, a population on the decline because of a small but steady exodus of families who favor suburban residence.

Life expectancy at birth is 75.91 years for men and 81.77 years for women, the longest in the world for both sexes. In 1935 the average life expectancy was 47 for men and 50 for women, and thus it has increased by about 30 years in just over half a century, an extremely rapid rate of change. The proportion of those aged 65 and over is increasing rapidly. At present the elderly comprise about 15 percent of the population, but this figure is expected to rise to more than 23 percent early in the next century. At the same time the birthrate is falling; it is estimated at present to be 1.37 live births per 1,000 population per year, insufficient to replace the current population.

In 1721 the feudal government instituted regular, nationwide census taking with surveys repeated every six years. It is estimated from these records that Japan's population remained stable at about 30 million from the early eighteenth century until the latter part of the nineteenth century. Japan ranks seventh in the world in terms of population.

LINGUISTIC AFFILIATION. Japanese is a polysyllabic, highly inflected language. It is usually assigned to the Altaic Group of languages, which includes Korean, Mongolian, and Turkish languages and is not related to Chinese. The indigenous peoples of Japan were most probably the Ainu, a very small number of whose descendants now live in the northernmost island of Hokkaidō.

It is widely accepted that the Ainu and Japanese languages are unrelated and that the Japanese of today are primarily descended from peoples who migrated long ago from the Asian mainland and displaced the Ainu, driving them northward.

It is estimated that Proto-Korean and Proto-Japanese separated from each other about 6,700 years ago, sometime after the first distinctive society, known as the Jōmon, was established in Japan. However, pottery dating back about 12,000 years, the oldest known in the world, indicates that a well-developed social organization (possibly that of the Ainu) was present before the arrival of peoples from the Asian mainland. Although Japanese is predominantly an Altaic language, it has some similarities to Austronesian, a linguistic group associated with Micronesia, Melanesia, and Southeast Asia; it is usually assumed that continuous cultural contact and possibly repeated migrations from these areas to Japan over many centuries account for these similarities.

From about 300 B.C. the Jōmon culture was gradually transformed and largely replaced by the vital Yayoi culture, whose archaeological remains give clear evidence of sustained contact with China. With the establishment of the Yayoi culture the foundations for the present-day Japanese language were clearly established.

Written Japanese is complex because it makes use of Chinese characters (*kanji*), of which approximately 2,000 must be used just to read a newspaper. The reading of Chinese characters in Japanese texts is particularly formidable because most have more than one reading, usually depending on whether they appear singly or in combinations. In addition, two separate forms of phonetic syllabic script, both derived originally from Chinese characters, are used together with the Chinese characters. One, *katakana*, is used largely to express words of foreign origin; the other, *hiragana*, is reserved principally for inflectional endings and suffixes, which are extensively employed in Japanese but which do not exist in Chinese. In addition many technical words, acronyms, and so on are expressed today in roman letters.

Both syllabic scripts were developed by the eighth century, but at first they were not integrated with the Chinese script. At that time hiragana was used for personal correspondence and classical Japanese poetry: it was known as "women's hand." Early Japanese literature was set down entirely in what was thought of as this "pure" Japanese style, while Chinese characters were used for official and religious documents.

Written Japanese is complex because it makes use of Chinese characters (kanji), of which approximately 2,000 must be used just to read a newspaper.

See also

Ainu

Burakumin

*Beginning in the
seventeenth century,
the Tokugawa
shogunate isolated
Japan from the
outside world for
more than 265
years.*

History and Cultural Relations

The most comprehensive record of early Japan that remains was written by the Chinese some time before A.D. 300. It portrays the Japanese as law-abiding people, fond of drink, concerned with divination and ritual purity, familiar with agriculture (including wet-rice cultivation), expert at fishing and weaving, and living in a society where social differences were expressed through the use of tattooing or other bodily markings. Among the early rulers of Japan some were women, the most famous of whom is Himiko of Yamatai. Current mythology reconstructs the first Japanese state as created around a "divine" emperor, a direct descendant of the sun goddess Amatarasu, in about 660 B.C., in what is now known as the Kinki region. Historical records dating to about the fifth century A.D. can be accepted as reasonably reliable. Early historical society was tribal in organization, divided into a large number of family groupings established as agricultural, craft, and ritual-specialist communities, some of which were exceedingly wealthy. In the early seventh century Chinese-style centralized bureaucratic rule was adopted; later, with the Taika reform in the mid-seventh century, many more Chinese institutions were embraced, followed by the building of the Chinese-style capital city of Nara in the eighth century. Although all authority theoretically was concentrated in the hands of the emperor, throughout Japanese history until the late nineteenth century, in contrast to China, emperors were usually dominated by a succession of court families and military rulers.

After the transfer in A.D. 794 of the capital to Heian-kyo, later to become Kyōto, a period of artistic development took place until the early twelfth century. During this period contacts with China were disrupted, allowing Japan to develop its own distinctive cultural forms. The world's first novel, *The Tale of Genji* by Murasaki Shikibu, was written at this time together with other major literary works; Buddhism not only was consolidated as a religion but also became a political force to reckon with. A succession of civil dictators, all members of the Fujiwara family, manipulated successive emperors in order to control the country. Under them taxation of peasants became oppressive, but at the same time the state entered into opulent decline, leading to an eventual loss of power over the outlying regions. Competing dominant families, notably the Minamoto and the Taira, who had been thrust temporarily into the background by the Fujiwara, returned to Kyōto to impose military control there. The Taira ruled for thirty years but eventually succumbed to Minamoto Yoritomo, who ousted them and took firm control of Japan. Yoritomo went on to establish a military government in Kamakura in eastern Honshū and persuaded the emperor to grant him the hereditary title of shogun; thus began an era of military rule that lasted for seven centuries. It was at Kamakura that the samurai code of discipline and chivalry was conceived and developed, while the imperial household remained in Kyōto, producing a succession of puppet emperors.

The groundwork for feudalism, built on the ruins of the centralized Chinese-style bureaucratic state, was laid down during the Kamakura shogunate. On the whole, the lot of the Japanese peasants was better than that of European serfs in that they often retained some rights over land and largely were protected from crippling taxes. During the fourteenth century there was a short-lived restoration of imperial rule, followed by a new military government established by the Ashikaga family in Kyōto, which lasted for two centuries. This was a time of prosperity and the full flowering of Bushidō (the way of the warrior), including the aesthetic and religious expression of this discipline. The Portuguese Jesuit Francis Xavier first arrived in Kyūshū during the sixteenth century, followed by other Christian missionaries and then traders. Toward the end of the century a plague of civil wars broke out in Japan, which continued until order finally was restored by the military leader Hideyoshi Toyotomi in 1590. The pacification and unification of the country was completed by the first of the Tokugawa shoguns, Ieyasu, who then moved the seat of the shogunate to Edo, now Tokyo. As part of the process of consolidation, the shogunate virtually isolated Japan from the outside world, a situation that lasted for more than 265 years. Ieyasu and his son persecuted foreign missionaries and Japanese who had converted to Christianity. All contact with foreigners was restricted to the island of Deshima off the coast of Nagasaki.

Japanese feudalism reached a final, centralized stage under the Tokugawas, and neo-Confucianism, with its hierarchical ordering of society, was made a central part of the ideology. Strict class divisions were enforced between samurai, peasants, merchants, and artisans. Respect and obedience were the code of the day. During this period literacy and numeracy became widespread, and the foundations for a modern society were well established. A self-conscious cultivation of indigenous Japanese traditions, including Shintō, took hold among certain samurai, who would become politically active in the eventual restoration of the emperor. At the same time Japan came increasingly under pressure to open its shores to the outside world, and the resulting internal turbulence led to the collapse of the shogunate. This was followed by the Meiji Restoration of 1868, in which the emperor once again gained full sovereignty and set up the imperial capital in the city that was known from then on as Tokyo.

During the Meiji era a modern nation-state was firmly consolidated, a constitution was promulgated, a central government was established, the Tokugawa class system was abolished, a national system of education was put in place, a modern legal code was adopted, and a formidable military and industrial machine was assembled. The entire country threw itself into the process of modernization, for which purpose European—and, to a much lesser extent, American—models were initially emulated. Japan's victories in both the Sino-Japanese War of 1894–1895 and the Russo-Japanese War of 1904–1905 and its annexation of Korea in 1910 established Japan as a world power. Its place in the modern world order was further consolidated at the end of World War I, which Japan had entered on Britain's side under the provision of the Anglo-Japan Alliance of 1902. During the 1920s the worldwide recession affected the Japanese economy, most particularly because of its great dependence on foreign trade. By 1925 most small industries had been crushed by the monopolies of the giant corporations headed by extremely wealthy and powerful families. Faltering confidence in the government was reinforced by the exposure of a number of scandals. The military, which was suspicious of both the giant corporations and politicians, seized the moment and thus helped propel Japan toward World War II, although undoubtedly the freezing of Japanese assets by the United States and the embargo placed by the Americans on oil shipments to Japan triggered an already inflammatory situation.

The Japanese finally surrendered after two atomic bombs had been dropped, one on Hiroshima and another on Nagasaki. During the American occupation, which lasted from 1945 to 1951, Shintō was abolished as a state religion; elections, in which women could vote for the first time, were held; new political parties were established; and a new constitution was formulated. Under Prime Minister Shigeru Yoshida the country made formidable strides towards democratic self-government. Japan soon entered a phase of rapid economic growth, which has since been transformed into a low-growth economy geared to "internationalization." Today the Japanese are trying to integrate economic success with what they describe as a "humanistic" and more "spiritually" oriented life-style.

Settlements

The history of housing in Japan reflects two primary influences: the indigenous influence of climate, land formation, and natural events (typhoons and earthquakes); and the external influence of foreign architectural design. Traditional Japanese architecture is made of wood with deep projecting roofs as protection against the monsoon rains. By the sixteenth century the typical Japanese house with a joined-skeleton frame of post-and-beam construction and elaborate joinery was common. The floor is raised above the ground, its posts resting on foundation stone, which allows the entire structure to bounce during an earthquake. This type of house is still dominant in rural settings and remains also in urban areas, usually squeezed among concrete buildings today.

In cities, most people live in apartments or housing corporations; land prices and taxes are exorbitant, making the buying of homes nearly impossible in the city centers. The suburbs have encroached ever deeper into the countryside, where house prices are a little cheaper, and many people commute for as many as four hours to and from work each day. The required coordination between government and the private sector makes city planning extremely difficult in Japan. Nevertheless, recent years have seen the emergence of policies systematically designed to develop larger-scale housing and industrial projects in regional areas rather than a simple restructuring of the megalopolis.

Economy

SUBSISTENCE AND COMMERCIAL ACTIVITIES. The postwar economy of Japan is based on a competitive-market, private-enterprise system. Less than 8 percent of the population remains fully occupied with agricultural production, although many families retain farming as a secondary occupation. The most usual pattern is that the wife works the farm while the husband is employed full-time in business or industry. Rice remains the principal crop, although its production is strictly controlled and there are financial incentives for diversification. Over the past forty years there has been a steady reallocation of labor from

The history of Japanese housing reflects the indigenous influence of climate, land formation, and natural events; and the external influence of foreign architectural design.

agriculture and a large number of relatively inefficient small-scale industrial and service occupations to highly productive, technologically sophisticated enterprises. The majority of the population is occupied today in manufacturing, business, financing, service, and the communication industries. Japan consistently has kept its unemployment rate at 2.5 percent or lower—by far the lowest in the industrialized nations. Most businesses are privately owned, and demand for goods and services determines what will be produced and at what prices. The role of government in the economy is indirect, largely through close cooperation with business, wide dissemination of information to shape incentives, and provision of research and development funds.

Despite the steady reallocation of labor, not all production is concentrated in giant companies. Small units of production remain very prevalent; for example, more than half the workers in manufacturing are in enterprises with fewer than 100 workers. Japan is an exceedingly wealthy country, with the second-largest gross national product (GNP) in the world. There is a reasonably good distribution of income across the population; abject poverty is virtually nonexistent.

INDUSTRIAL ARTS. Throughout Japanese history the production of ceramics, cloth, silk, paper, furniture, metal implements, and so on has been carried out by individuals in extended households, by professional artisans, and in cottage industries. Techniques were usually passed on from one generation of specialist families to another, sometimes over hundreds of years. A few such families remain in existence, although it has become increasingly difficult to find successors. Distinguished craftspeople are sometimes recognized by the government as "national treasures." Today the bulk of industrial arts is mass-produced, and workers are trained in an apprenticeship system or in technical schools, but handmade crafts continue to be highly valued and play a major role not only in the art world and the tourist industry but also in daily life.

TRADE. Most trade in Japan is organized and conducted by the nine very large, highly diversified commercial houses known as *sōgō shōsha*, which structure and facilitate the flow of goods, services, and money among client firms. These trading houses operate both within Japan and internationally. The total sales of these nine firms account for about 25 percent of Japan's GNP, and the imports and exports handled by them amount to about half of foreign trade. These companies originated in the Meiji period, and today maintain a system of domestic offices linked by the latest communication techniques to a worldwide network of overseas offices. Japan's trade is characterized by the export of finished products and the import of raw materials, of which oil is perhaps the most strategic. At present the nation has an enormous trade surplus with most of its international trading partners.

DIVISION OF LABOR. Since 1945 Japan has adopted a comprehensive legal framework dealing with labor conditions including labor relations, labor protection, and social security. Labor conditions are managed largely by the Ministry of Labor. The Labor Standards Law of 1947 contains a "bill of rights" for individual workers and guarantees minimum wages, maximum hours of work, and so on. Many white-collar workers are nevertheless required to put in long hours of overtime work. About one-third of Japanese workers are unionized; almost all Japanese unions are organized at the level of the enterprise, and they include in their membership blue- and white-collar workers and, often, low-level managerial personnel. Branch unions often form an enterprisewide federation, which in turn may participate in a national industrywide federation. Most union activity takes place, however, at the level of the enterprise.

PRODUCTION LINE

Japanese women at work on a television production line. Today, the majority of the population is employed in manufacturing, business, financing, service, and the communication industry. Near Osaka, Japan.

The school system is designed to be egalitarian and, in theory, entrance into the work force is based on educational merit. In practice, graduation from certain schools provides a greater guarantee of entry into the top universities, graduation from which facilitates entry into the professions and high-ranking civil service jobs. Employment based on personal connections is still prevalent in Japan. A provision for equal wages for equal work regardless of gender was adopted in 1947, but discrimination against women in the workplace continues to the present time. In April 1986 the Equal Employment Opportunity Law, designed to eliminate gender inequalities, was passed, followed in 1988 by the Labor Standards Law. These laws remove many of the restrictions placed on working women—in particular, the number and timing of the hours they can work each day. In practice, considerable social pressure remains for a woman to give up work during her first pregnancy. When they return to work, women are very often hired as part-time employees, although their working hours are long, and many of them work a six-day week. Employers are not required to pay benefits to such employees, who can be hired and fired easily during economic cycles of expansion and contraction.

LAND TENURE. At the end of World War II, nearly 50 percent of the population still lived in rural surroundings. At that time 36 percent of the farm families owned 90 percent or more of their land; another 20 percent owned between 50 and 90 percent; 17 percent owned 10 to 50 percent; and 27 percent owned less than 10 percent. Tenants paid rent in kind. Landholdings were, and remain, small (1 hectare on average). Land reform was carried out during the Allied occupation, including the transfer to the government of all land owned by absentee landlords. Today 90 percent of the farmland is owned and worked by individual families. Of urban land area, over 77 percent is residential, nearly 11 percent industrial, and just over 12 percent commercial. Urban residences are small and prohibitively expensive, on average more than three times the cost of housing in the United States. Many families live in apartments for years until they can afford a down payment on a house. Approximately 65 percent of the families in Japan own their home, but in the metropolitan areas this number falls below 30 percent.

Kinship

KIN GROUPS AND DESCENT. The most usual living arrangement in Japan today is the nuclear family—more than 60 percent of the households are of this type, and the number has increased steadily throughout this century. Another 16 percent are single-person households. Just over 20 percent of households are extended, most of which are in rural areas. This type of household, known traditionally as the *ie*, is thought today to have been typical of living arrangements in Japan until well into this century, although in reality there was always considerable regional and class variation in connection with household composition. The ie usually was comprised of a three-generation household of grandparents, parents, and children; it was not extended laterally under one roof. In many regions of Japan in prewar years more than one household could comprise the ie, and households existed in a hierarchical grouping known as the *dozoku*, composed of one senior household and "stem" or branch households situated nearby. The traditional ie, a corporate economic unit, was patrilineal and patrilocal, and the head of the household was held responsible for the well-being and activities of all family members. The household, rather than individual family members, was taken as the basic unit of society, a situation that still applies for many purposes today.

KINSHIP TERMINOLOGY. The kinship system is bilateral, and includes relatives connected to both husband and wife. Cognates and affines are addressed by the same terms. In this system horizontal ties are usually stressed over vertical ties, and hence the kinship system is ideally complementary to the hierarchical lineage system. Honorifics are built into the terms used to address or refer to grandparents, parents, and older siblings within the family. Terms for brothers and sisters are differentiated according to age. When referring to one's own family members beyond the confines of the family, however, the honorifics are dropped and the terms are changed.

Marriage and Family

MARRIAGE. Marriage in Japan until the Meiji period had been characterized as an institution that benefited the community; during the Meiji period it was transformed into one that perpetuated and enriched the extended household (ie); and, in postwar years, it has again been transformed—this time into an arrangement between individuals or two nuclear families. Today marriage in Japan can be either an "arranged" union or a "love" match. In theory an arranged marriage is the result of formal negotiations involving a mediator who is not a family member, culminating in a meeting between the respective families, includ-

Many Japanese men spend extended periods of time away from home on business, either elsewhere in Japan or abroad.

ing the prospective bride and groom. This is usually followed, if all goes well, by further meetings of the young couple and ends in an elaborate and expensive civic wedding ceremony. In the case of a love marriage, which is the preference of the majority today, individuals freely establish a relationship and then approach their respective families. In response to surveys about marriage customs, most Japanese state that they underwent some combination of an arranged and love marriage, in which the young couple was given a good deal of freedom but an official mediator may have been involved nevertheless. These two arrangements are understood today not as moral oppositions but simply as different strategies for obtaining a partner. Less than 3 percent of Japanese remain unmarried; however, the age of marriage is increasing for both men and women: early or mid-thirties for men and late twenties for women are not unusual today. The divorce rate is one-quarter that of the United States.

DOMESTIC UNIT. The nuclear family is the usual domestic unit, but elderly and infirm parents often live with their children or else in close proximity to them. Many Japanese men spend extended periods of time away from home on business, either elsewhere in Japan or abroad; hence the domestic unit often is reduced today to a single-parent family for months or even years at a time, during which period the father returns rather infrequently.

INHERITANCE. Freedom to dispose of one's assets at will has been a central legal principle in Japan since the implementation of the Civil Code at the end of World War II. Inheritance without a will (statutory inheritance) is overwhelmingly the case today. In addition to financial assets, when necessary, someone is named to inherit the family genealogy, the equipment used in funerals, and the family grave. The order of inheritance is first to the children and the spouse; if there are no children, then the lineal ascendants and spouse; if there are no lineal ascendants, then the siblings and the spouse; if there are no siblings, then the spouse; if there is no spouse, procedures to prove the nonexistence of an heir are initiated, in which case the property may go to a common-law wife, an adopted child, or other suitable party. An individual may disinherit heirs by means of a request to the family court.

SOCIALIZATION. The mother is recognized as the primary agent of socialization during early childhood. The correct training of a child in appropriate discipline, language use, and manners is known as *shitsuke*. It is generally assumed that in-

fants are naturally compliant, and gentle and calm behavior is positively reinforced. Small children are rarely left on their own; they also are not usually punished but instead are taught good behavior when they are in a cooperative mood. Most children today go to preschool from about the age of 3, where, in addition to learning basic skills in drawing, reading, writing, and mathematics, emphasis is on cooperative play and learning how to function effectively in groups. More than 94 percent of children complete nine years of compulsory education and continue on to high school; 38 percent of boys and 37 percent of girls receive advanced education beyond high school.

Sociopolitical Organization

SOCIAL ORGANIZATION. Japan is an extremely homogeneous society in which class differences were abolished at the end of the last century. An exception was the *burakumin*, an outcaste group, the majority of whom are descendants of ritually "unclean" people (leatherworkers, butchers, grave diggers). Although discrimination against burakumin was made illegal after the war, many continue to be severely stigmatized, and most of them live close to the poverty line.

Japan is widely recognized as a vertically structured, group-oriented society in which the rights of individuals take second place to harmonious group functioning. Traditionally, Confucian ethics encouraged a respect for authority, whether that of the state, the employer, or the family. Age and gender differences also were marked through both language and behavioral patterns. Women traditionally were expected to pay respect first to their fathers, then to their husbands, and finally, in later life, to their sons. Although this hierarchy is no longer rigidly enforced, it is still very evident in both language and interpersonal behavior.

Social groups of all kinds in Japan frequently are described as "familylike"; a strong sense of group solidarity is fostered consciously at school and work, leading to a highly developed awareness of insiders and outsiders. Competition between groups is keen, but the vertical structuring of loyalty, which overarches and encompasses the competing entities, usually ensures that consensus can be obtained at the level of whole organizations and institutions. The finely tuned ranking order that pervades Japanese organizations today is modeled on fictive kinship relationships characteristic of superiors and their subordinates in the traditional workplace. These relationships are often likened to bonding between parents and children and are present not only in the labor force but also in the worlds of the arts and entertainment, in gangster organizations, and so on. Despite the pervasiveness of hierarchy, institutional affiliation is recognized as more important than social background in contemporary Japan. This preference combined with the existence of a highly uniform educational system leads, paradoxically, to a reasonably egalitarian social system.

POLITICAL ORGANIZATION. The 1947 postwar constitution proclaimed the Diet as the highest organ of state power and the sole law-making authority of the state. The Diet is divided into two elected chambers: the lower chamber, or the House of Representatives, where a term of office lasts for four years; and the upper chamber, or the House of Councillors, whose members serve a six-year term. Of the two, the House of Representatives holds more power. Much of the business of each house is conducted in standing committees to which special committees may be added as the need arises. Executive power resides in the cabinet, at whose head is the prime minister. The cabinet is directly responsible to the Diet. The House of Representatives chooses the prime minister, who then selects the cabinet. The power of the prime minister is curbed severely by rival intraparty factions, and cabinet posts are reshuffled frequently, both of which processes influence decision making. The judiciary is, in theory, independent of the government, and the supreme court has the power to determine the constitutionality of any law, regulation, or official act. However, supreme court judges are appointed by the cabinet and in turn influence the appointment of other judges.

Throughout the postwar years the authority of the central government has been consolidated. The relatively conservative Liberal Democratic Party has been repeatedly reelected to power ever since its formation in 1955, a situation brought about in part by its close connection with wealthy interest groups, a highly effective and far-flung bureaucracy, and an electoral system imbalanced in favor of votes from rural areas. Since the 1960s a series of active citizens' movements interested in consumer and environmental issues has repeatedly challenged the ruling party, resulting in some policy changes. Japan is frequently described as a society where a preponderance of political power that takes precedence over all other social activities exists at every level of society. Furthermore, the implementation of power is designed above all to carry forward group objectives rather than individual rights or interests.

The emperor presently is described in the constitution as the "symbol of the people and the unity of the nation" but holds no formal political power. On New Year's day 1946 the then Emperor Hirohito formally announced that he was an ordinary human being, thus breaking the tradition, which had existed since prehistory, of attributing semidivine status to Japanese emperors. Nevertheless, at the enthronement of Hirohito's son in 1991, Shintō ceremonies were performed, including rituals involving divinities. The lives of the imperial family remain very secluded and carefully controlled by the Imperial Household Agency; their existence provides, among other things, a focus for nationalistic sentiment, which at times is strongly expressed.

SOCIAL CONTROL. Law enforcement is carried out by a police system organized into prefectural forces and coordinated by a National Police Agency. Public safety commissions supervise police activities at both the national and prefectural levels. Particularly at the local level, the police force enjoys wide public support and respect, although this is tinged with a certain ambivalence because the police remain strongly associated with prewar authoritarianism. Local police are required to visit every home in their jurisdiction twice a year to gather information on residents; this activity is generally regarded positively by citizens. Police are also required to participate actively in community organizations and activities, and they maintain close links with local governments. The crime rate in Japan is exceptionally low for an urban, densely populated society, in part because segments of each community cooperate actively with the police in crime-prevention activities.

CONFLICT. Serious conflict in Japan is dealt with under the rubric of the legal system, which is organized so that out-of-court resolutions are by far the most usual. Compromise and conciliation by third-party mediators are widely practiced. Japan has relatively few lawyers and judges, and cases that go to court take an exceptionally long time to reach settlement.

Religion and Expressive Culture

RELIGIOUS BELIEFS. There are more than 200,000 religious organizations in Japan, the majority of them either Shintō or Buddhist in orientation. Since neither of these religions is exclusive, a situation of religious pluralism has existed for more than ten centuries and today most of the population claims to be both Shintoist and Buddhist, with about 1 percent being Christian. Shintō is the indigenous animistic religion of Japan. Known as the "way of the *kami* (deities)," it is both a household and a local-community reli-

There are more than 200,000 religious organizations in Japan.

gion. The doctrine is largely unwritten, religious statuary is uncommon, and Shintō shrines are simple but elegant wooden structures usually situated in a sacred grove of trees, entry to which is gained through an archway known as a *tōri*. The divine origin of the imperial family is one of the basic tenets of Shintō; after the Meiji Restoration and particularly during World War II, Shintō came to be regarded as a state religion with the emperor as its head and was intimately associated with nationalism. State Shintō was abolished under the postwar constitution, but as a community religion it does still play a very important role in many aspects of Japanese ceremonial and symbolic life, in particular with childhood ceremonies and weddings.

Buddhism was introduced to Japan from India via China and Korea in the middle of the sixth century. By the eighth century it was adopted as the state religion, but practitioners still turned to China as the source of authority. From the ninth century Buddhism spread throughout the population in Japan and gradually took on a distinctive Japanese form associated particularly with the Pure Land, Nichiren, and Zen sects. From the seventeenth century, for more than 250 years, Buddhism enjoyed political patronage under the Tokugawa shogunate, but with the restoration of the emperor and the establishment of state-supported Shintō in the second half of the nineteenth century, there was a movement to disestablish Buddhism. In the postwar years, most of the population has become essentially secular, and Buddhist priests are contacted almost exclusively for funerals and memorial services. The tourist industry is now a major source of support for the better-known temples and shrines.

Neither Confucianism nor Taoism constitutes a separate religion in Japan, but these traditions have contributed deeply to Japanese life and have influenced both Shintō and Buddhism. Confucianism, largely in the form known as Neo-Confucianism, provided the foundation for ethical relationships in both government and daily life, particularly from the seventeenth century onward. Although no longer officially sanctioned, its tenets continue to influence daily life. Religious Taoism, like Confucianism, was imported from China to Japan and actively supported from the sixth century. It has had a long-lasting influence on popular religious beliefs, particularly in connection with sacred mountains, firewalking, and purification rituals of all kinds. All of these religious traditions have contributed to a greater or lesser degree to the following features that charac-

terize Japanese religious principles: a veneration for ancestors; a belief in religious continuity of the family, living and dead; a close tie between the nation and religion; pluralism in religious beliefs; a free exchange of ideas among religious systems; and religious practice centered on the use of prayer, mediation, amulets, and purification rites.

RELIGIOUS PRACTITIONERS. Any male may train for the priesthood, but in smaller temples and shrines the position of head priest is often passed on from father to son or adopted son. Celibacy is not required, and the wives of priests often receive some formal training and participate in the running of the temple. Larger temples take in acolytes who, after years of discipline, may be assigned to subsidiary temples. Buddhist priests are often very accomplished at traditional arts, in particular calligraphy. In Shintō shrines young women, often daughters of priests and supposedly virgins, assist with many shrine activities.

CEREMONIES. Religious activities at a Shintō shrine reflect the seasonal changes and are associated particularly with the planting and harvesting of rice. These celebrations are still held in many shrines, together with important purification ceremonies at the New Year and midyear to wash away both physical and spiritual pollution. The major festival days are the New Year's festival, on the first day of the first month, the girls' festival on the third day of the third month, the boys' festival on the fifth day of the fifth month, the star festival on the seventh day of the seventh month, and the chrysanthemum festival on the ninth day of the ninth month. These festivals are celebrated both in the home and at shrines. A newborn child is usually dedicated to the service of a deity at a shrine on his or her first trip out of the house, and at ages 3, 5, and 7 children are again presented at the shrine dressed in traditional clothes. Marriage is also associated with the Shinto shrine, but most people, although they often use traditional dress replete with Shintō-derived symbolism, have secular marriages. Public ceremonies at Buddhist temples are less frequent, the most important being the annual *bon* ceremony, in which the dead are believed to return for a short while to earth, after which they must be returned safely to the other world. Some temples occasionally hold healing ceremonies, conduct tea ceremonies, or participate in *setsubun*, a purification ceremony to welcome spring.

ARTS. Prehistoric artifacts, such as the *haniwa* figures found in the tombs of the Yamato rulers of early Japan, are often thought to represent a purity and simplicity of design that has remained characteristic of Japanese art until the present day. Art of the early historical period is dominated by Buddhist statuary, which reveals a mastery of both woodwork and metalwork. During the Heian period a distinctive style of literature and art associated with the court was developed, including long, horizontally rolled narrative scrolls and a stylized form of painting that made use of brilliant color and a formalized perspective. The mid-fourteenth to the mid-sixteenth centuries are considered to have been the formative period for all the major Japanese art forms that survive to the present time, including ink painting and calligraphy, the Nō drama, ceramics, landscape gardening, flower arranging, the tea ceremony, and architecture that makes extensive use of natural wood and subordinates the building to its natural surroundings. The Tokugawa period was characterized by the emergence of literature and art forms associated with the newly emerging urban classes, which flourished side by side with earlier forms of religious and ruling-class artistic expression. Extensive use was made of the woodblock print by urban residents of feudal Japan as a medium for portraying daily life at that time. Since the middle of the nineteenth century Japanese art has come under the influence of both Europe and North America. Traditional art forms still flourish and change in a society that today produces some of the most sophisticated and innovative art, photography, architecture, and design in the world.

Literature and poetry (of which the haiku and the tanka are perhaps the most famous forms) have both flourished throughout Japanese history. The Kabuki theater, for popular consumption, in which the performers are all male, first appeared in the Tokugawa period, as did Bunraku, the puppet theater. The modern Japanese novel took form in the middle of the last century and is particularly well known for its introspection and exploration of the concept of self, together with a sensitivity to minute details.

MEDICINE. Japan has a complex, pluralistic medical system that is dominated today by a technologically sophisticated biomedicine. The earliest references to healing are recorded in the chronicles of mythological and early historical times. Shamanistic practices were present from at least A.D. 400 together with the use of medicinal-plant materials. Two theories of disease causation were dominant at this time: contact with polluting agents, such as blood and corpses; and possession by spirits. The secular, literature Chinese medical tradition was first brought to Japan in the sixth century by Buddhist priests. Grounded in the philosophical concepts of yin and yang, in which a harmonious relationship between the microcosm of the human body and the macrocosm of society and the universe is central, this system, known in Japan as *kanpo*, makes use of herbal material together with acupuncture, moxibustion, and massage as therapeutic techniques. It remained dominant until shortly after the restoration of the emperor in 1867, at which time European medicine was adopted as the official medical system.

The Japanese government established a national health-insurance system in 1961, becoming the first Asian country to do so. Today, Japan has a well-supplied, reasonably efficient modern healthcare system. Nevertheless, healing practices conducted by religious practitioners, both Shintoists and Buddhists, remain prevalent, and there has been an extensive revival of kanpo. The practice of herbal medicine is limited today to qualified physicians, and acupuncturists and other traditional practitioners must be licensed; some of these practitioners work within the national insurance system. Many ordinary physicians make use of herbal medicines in addition to synthetic drugs.

DEATH AND AFTERLIFE. In Japan death is believed to take place when the spirit is separated irrevocably from the body. Between life and death is an interim stage of forty-nine days in which the spirit lingers in this world until finally it is settled peacefully in the realm of the dead. Annual memorial services must be held for the dead and it is not until the thirty-third or fiftieth year after death that the spirit loses its individual identity and is fused with the spirits of the ancestors. Most Japanese do not adhere closely to this tradition today, but they still retain some sensitivity to these ideas. Yearly Buddhist observances in August at the bon festival for the souls of the dead continue to remind people of the links between the living and the dead, and of the possibility of spirits of the dead returning to earth. There is also a widely shared Buddhist-derived belief that one can attain a form of eternity or enlightenment while still in this world through the realization of one's full potential on earth. This tradition is associated particularly with the martial arts, the tea ceremony, and other forms of traditional arts and crafts, as well as with meditation.

Bibliography

Beardsley, Richard K., John W. Hall, and Robert E. Ward (1959). *Village Japan*. Chicago and London: University of Chicago Press.

Bestor, Theodore C. (1989). *Neighborhood Tokyo*. Stanford, Calif.: Stanford University Press.

Boscaro, Adriana, Franco Gatti, and Massimo Raveri, eds. (1990). *Rethinking Japan: Social Sciences, Ideology, and Thought*. 2 vols. Folkestone, Kent: Japan Library; New York: St. Martin's Press.

Embree, John F. (1939). *Suye Mura, a Japanese Village*. Chicago: University of Chicago Press.

Gluck, Carol (1985). *Japan's Modern Myths: Ideology in the Late Meiji Period*. Princeton, N.J.: Princeton University Press.

Hardacre, Helen (1989). *Shinto and the State, 1868–1988*. Princeton, N.J.: Princeton University Press.

Jansen, Marius B. (1980). *Japan and Its World: Two Centuries of Change*. Princeton, N.J.: Princeton University Press.

Nakane, Chie (1970). *Japanese Society*. Berkeley and Los Angeles: University of California Press.

Norbeck, Edward (1976). *Changing Japan*. 2nd ed. New York: Holt, Rinehart & Winston.

Okimoto, Daniel I., and Thomas P. Rohlen (1988). *Inside the Japanese System: Readings on Contemporary Society and Political Economy*. Stanford, Calif.: Stanford University Press.

—MARGARET LOCK

JAVANESE

Ethonyms: Orang Djawa, Tijang Djawi, Wong Djawa

Orientation

IDENTIFICATION. The Javanese are Indonesia's largest ethnic group and the world's third-largest Muslim ethnic group, following Arabs and Bengalis. "Wong Djawa" or "Tijang Djawi" are the names that the Javanese use to refer to themselves. The Indonesian term for the Javanese is "Orang Djawa." The term *djawa* has been traced to the Sanskrit word *yava*, "barley, grain." The name is of great antiquity and appears in Ptolemy's *Geography*.

LOCATION. The Javanese primarily occupy the provinces of East and Central Java, although there are also some Javanese on other Indonesian islands. Java, one of the largest islands of Indonesia, is located between 6° and 9° S and 105° and 115° E. The climate is tropical, with a dry season from March to September and a wet season from September to March. Mountains and plateaus are somewhat cooler than the lowlands.

DEMOGRAPHY. The Javanese population was 2 million in 1775. In 1900 the population of the island was 29 million and in 1990 it was estimated to be over 109 million (including the small island of Madura). Jakarta, the capital city, then had a population of about 9.5 million people. Some areas of Java have close to the highest rural population density in the world: the average density is 1,500 persons per square mile and in some areas it is considerably higher. In 1969 Jay reported a population density of 6,000–8,000 persons per square kilometer in residential areas of rural Modjokuto. Population growth combined with small and fragmented land-holdings has produced severe problems of overcrowding and poverty.

LINGUISTIC AFFILIATION. The Javanese are bilingual. They speak Bahasa Indonesia, the Indonesian national language, in public and in dealings with other ethnic groups, but at home and among themselves they speak Javanese. The Javanese language belongs to the West Indonesian Branch of the Hesperonesian Subfamily of the Malayo-Polynesian Family. Javanese has a literary history dating back to the eighth century. The language has nine styles of speech, the uses of which are determined by principles of etiquette. There is a trend toward simplification of speech levels.

History and Cultural Relations

Wet-rice agriculture and state organization were present in Java before the eighth century. Indian influence between the eighth and fourteenth centuries produced a number of petty Shaivite/Buddhist kingdoms. The Madjapahit Empire flourished near the present city of Surabaja during the fourteenth and fifteenth centuries, during which time Indian Muslims and Chinese dominated international trade. When the center of power shifted to port towns during the sixteenth century, Indian and Malay Muslims dominated trade. The aristocracy adopted a form of Islam that had been influenced by south Indian religious beliefs, and Islam spread.

The Mataram Kingdom rose in the sixteenth century and flourished until the middle of the eighteenth century. First the Portugese, and later the Dutch, dominated trade during this period. The Dutch East India Company divided Mataram into several vassal states around 1750 and later these states came under the rule of the Dutch colonial government. Except for a brief period of British rule, Java remained under Dutch rule; it was opened to private Dutch enterprise after 1850. A nationalist movement arose in the early twentieth century and communism was introduced. There was an unsuccessful revolution in the late 1920s. After Japanese occupation during World War II, Indonesia declared its independence. The Dutch transferred sovereignty to Indonesia in 1949 after four years of warfare.

Settlements

High population density imparts an urban quality to all of Java, including the rural areas. The majority of the population lives in small villages and towns and approximately 25 percent lives in cities. Population is evenly distributed and villages are often separated by no more than a few hundred meters. Villages are never more than 8 kilometers from a town. Although there are a number of towns and cities in Java, the only cities with true urban and industrial characteristics are Jakarta, Surabaja, and Semarang. Landholdings are small and fragmented.

The typical village house is small and rectangular. It is built directly on the ground and has a thatched roof. The inside has earthen floors and its small compartments are divided by movable bamboo panels. House styles are defined by the shape of the roof. Village houses that reflect urban influence have brick walls and tiled roofs. Large open pavilions at the front are typical of houses of high-ranking administrative officers and members of the nobility.

Economy

SUBSISTENCE AND COMMERCIAL ACTIVITIES. Java has a dual economy with industrial and peasant sectors. The Dutch established plantations based on a Western model of business organization. This segment of the economy is now concerned with estate agriculture, mining, and industry. It is highly capitalized and it produces primarily for export. Wet-rice agriculture is the principal activity of the peasant economy; fishing is important in coastal villages. Animal husbandry is not developed for want of space. A number of dry-season crops are produced for sale, and there are also some small-scale cottage industries and a local market system.

INDUSTRIAL ARTS. Small-scale industries are not well developed because of problems in capital, distribution, and marketing. Cottage industries in Central Java Province are silver work, batik, handweaving, and the manufacture of native cigarettes.

TRADE. There are local markets, each servicing four to five villages throughout rural Java. The retailers are usually women.

DIVISION OF LABOR. Javanese are primarily farmers, local traders, and skilled artisans. Inter-

mediate trade and small industry are dominated by foreign Asians, and the large plantations and industries are owned by Europeans. In precolonial Java, the population was divided between royalty, with its court and the nobility, and the peasantry. Two more classes emerged under colonialism and with the development of administrative centers. These classes are landless laborers and government officials, or *prijaji*. The prijaji are generally urban and there are several statuses. In rural areas farming remains the predominant occupation. Some people engage in craft specializations and trade but these occupations are usually part-time. The majority of everyone's time is spent on farming. In rural areas learned professionals such as teachers, spiritual leaders, and puppeteers are usually people from affluent families. These latter occupations have considerable prestige but they are also practiced only part-time. Local and central government officials have the highest prestige.

LAND TENURE. Traditionally much of the land was held communally and communities recruited corvée (unpaid labor) for the king, the nobility, or the colonial government. Even today, communal land is reserved for schools, roads, and cemeteries and for support of the village headman and his staff. The corvée consisted of a group of villagers (*kuli*), who constituted the productive la-

SHADOW PLAY

A Javanese puppet seller. Shadow plays use puppets to dramatize stories from Java's past. Java, Indonesia. (Jan Butchofsky-Houser/Corbis)

Interpersonal conflict, anger, and aggression are repressed or avoided in Javanese society; it is difficult to express differences of opinion.

bor force of the village. Communal land was allotted for usufruct as compensation to the kuli. In some places the kuli became a hereditary status included with the inheritance of the land. In addition, many Javanese villages have tracts of communal land allotted to the population for usufruct on a rotating basis. Individual holdings are small.

Kinship

KIN GROUPS AND DESCENT. Descent is bilateral and the basic kin group is the nuclear family (*kulawarga*). Two kindredlike groups are recognized by the Javanese. One is the *golongan*, an informal bilateral group whose members usually reside in the same village and who participate together in various ceremonies and celebrations. The *alur waris*, the second kindredlike group, is a more formal unit involved in caring for the graves of ancestors.

KINSHIP TERMINOLOGY. Four principles govern Javanese kinship terminology. First, the system is bilateral; that is, the kin terms are the same whether the link is the father or the mother. The second principle is generational; that is, all the members of each generation are verbally grouped. The third principle is seniority, a principle that subdivides each generation into junior and senior categories. Finally, the fourth principle is gender. There is a slight distinction made between nuclear-family relatives and others.

Marriage and Family

MARRIAGE. Individuals usually choose their own spouses, although parents sometimes arrange marriages. Marriage is prohibited between members of the nuclear family, half siblings, and second cousins. Several types of marriage are disapproved of but people can avoid the supernatural sanctions associated with them by performing protective rituals. The idea of preferred marriages is not widely known.

Marriage formalities include a gift to the bride's parents from the groom's relatives, a meeting of the bride's relatives at her house the night before the ceremony, civil and religious ceremonies and transactions, and a ceremonial meeting of the couple. Divorce is common and is accomplished according to Muslim law.

Most marriages are monogamous. Polygyny is practiced only among the urban lower class, orthodox high-ranking prijaji, and the nobility.

There is no fixed postmarital residence rule, although the ideal is neolocal. Uxorilocal residence is common in southern Central Java Province. High-ranking prijaji and the nobility tend toward residence in either of the parents' homes. Urban prijaji are neolocal.

DOMESTIC UNIT. The Javanese term for "household" is *somah*. Peasants and the average urban prijaji live in monogamous nuclear-family households with an average population of five to six. High-ranking prijaji and the nobility have polygynous uterolocal extended families and are larger.

INHERITANCE. Dwellings and their surrounding garden land are inherited by a married daughter or granddaughter after a period of coresidence. Fruit trees, domestic animals, and cultivable land are inherited equally by all the children, while heirlooms are usually inherited by a son.

SOCIALIZATION. Children are treated indulgently until the age of two to four when inculcation and discipline begin. The most common methods of discipline are snarling, corporal punishment, comparison to siblings and others, and threat of external disapproval and sanctions. The latter type of discipline encourages children to be fearful and shy around strangers. Mothers are the primary socializing agents, as well as sources of affection and support, while fathers are more distant. Older siblings often take care of young children. First menstruation for girls is marked simply by a *slametan*, or communal meal, while for boys circumcision, occurring between the ages of 6 and 12, is an important and dramatic event.

Religion and Expressive Culture

RELIGIOUS BELIEFS. Virtually all Javanese are Muslims. In reality, the religion of the Javanese is syncretic, with Islam being laid over spiritual and mystical beliefs of Hindu-Buddhist and indigenous origins. The difference in degree of adherence to the doctrines of Islam constitutes a dichotomy that pervades Javanese culture. The *santri* are strict in their adherence to Islam while the abangan are not. This dichotomy has class and political-party implications.

The peasant abangan knows the general structure of Islam but does not follow it to the letter. The abangan religion is a blend of indigenous beliefs, Hinduism-Buddhism, and Islam. In addition to Allah, abangan believe in several Hindu deities and numerous spirits that inhabit the environment. Abangan also believe in a form of magical power that is possessed by the *dukun*, who is a specialist in magical practices, a curer, and/or a sorcerer.

The prijaji abangan religious practice is similar to that of the peasant abangan but it is somewhat more sophisticated. It has an elaborate philosophy of fate and is quite mystical. Asceticism and the practice of meditation are characteristic of prijaji abangan religion. Sects under the leadership of gurus are typical.

The santri are present among all social levels but they predominate in the commercial classes. The santri diligently comply with Islamic doctrine. They perform the required prayers five times a day, attend communal prayers at the mosque every Friday, fast during the month of Ramadan (Pasa), do not eat pork, and make every effort to perform the pilgrimage to Mecca at least once.

RELIGIOUS PRACTITIONERS. There are several types of religious practitioner in Islam. There are sects consisting of a guru or *kijaji* (teacher) and *murid* (disciple) dyads that are hierarchically organized. Individual kijaji attract students to their *pondoks* or *pesantren* (monasterylike schools) to teach Muslim doctrines and laws. In addition to the dominance of Islam, magic and sorcery are widely practiced among the Javanese. There are many varieties of dukun, each one dealing with specialized kinds of ritual such as agricultural rituals, fertility rituals, etc. Dukun also perform divination and curing.

CEREMONIES. The communal meal, the slametan, is central to abangan practice and is sometimes also performed by santri. The function of the slametan is to promote *slamet*, a state of calmness and serenity. The slametan is performed within a household and it is usually attended by one's closest neighbors. Occasions for a slametan include important life-cycle events and certain points in the Muslim ceremonial calendar; otherwise it is performed for the well-being of the village.

ARTS. Geertz (1964) describes three art "complexes," each involving different forms of

---

SOCIOPOLITICAL ORGANIZATION

Social Organization

Javanese social classes have a long history. During the time of the Mataram Kingdom, peasants were ruled by a landed nobility or gentry representing the king. The king allotted land to some people in an appanage system. Merchants lived in coastal and port towns where international trade was in the hands of Chinese, Indians, and Malays. The port towns were ruled by princes. This pattern prevailed until the colonial period. During that period, in addition to the peasantry, two new classes arose, nonpeasant laborers and the prijaji. The prijaji, descendants of the precolonial administrative gentry, were "white-collar" workers and civil servants. There was a class of nobles (*ndara*) who could trace their descent from the rulers of the Mataram Kingdom.

During the twentieth century, there has been a trend toward an egalitarian social system and a drive to make upward mobility available to all. By the middle of the twentieth century, peasants comprised the largest class and there was a growing class of landless agricultural laborers.

Political Organization

Indonesia is an independent republic and the head of state is President Suharto. The capital of Indonesia is Jakarta and the ministries of the national government are located there. The ministries have branches at various levels from which they administer services. There are three provinces (*propinsi*) in Java. In addition, the Special Region of Jogjakarta, or Daerah Istimewa Jogjakarta, has provincial status. There are five residencies (*karésidènen*) in each province. Each residency contains four or five districts (*kawédanan*) and each district has four or five subdistricts (*katjamatan*). There are ten to twenty village complexes (*kalurahan* in Javanese, *desa* in Indonesian) in each subdistrict. The smallest unit of administration is the *dukuhan* and each kalurahan contains two to ten of them. Some dukuhan contain a number of smaller villages or hamlets also called desa. The kalurahan or desa is headed by an official called a *lurah* and the dukuhan is headed by a *kamitua*.

Social Control

In rural areas the neighborhood exerts the greatest pressures toward conformity with social values. The strongest sanctions are gossip and shunning. Kin seem to have less force than the neighborhood in exerting social control.

Conflict

Interpersonal conflict, anger, and aggression are repressed or avoided in Javanese society. In Java it is difficult to express differences of opinion. Direct criticism, anger, and annoyance are rarely expressed. The major method of handling interpersonal conflict is by not speaking to one another (*satru*). This type of conflict resolution is not surprising in a society that represses anger and expression of true feelings. Concern with maintaining peaceful interactions results in not only the avoidance of conflict and repression of true feelings, but also in the prevalence of conciliatory techniques, particularly in status-bound relationships. One source of antagonism is between adherents of different religious orientations; this is related to class differences, prijaji versus abangan villagers, and has much to do with rapid social change.

music, drama, dance, and literature. The Javanese shadow play, the *wajang*, is known worldwide and is central to the *alus* (refined) art complex. The wajang uses puppets to dramatize stories from the Indian epics, the Mahabharata and the Ramayana, or from Java's precolonial past. Wajang performances are accompanied by *gamelan* (percussion orchestras), which also have achieved worldwide fame. Another art form associated with the alus complex is batik textile dyeing. The alus art complex is classical and traditional and is largely the domain of the prijaji. The other two art complexes are more popular, nationally shared, and Western-influenced.

MEDICINE. Doctors practicing scientific medicine are present and are consulted in Java, especially in urban areas, but curers and diviners continue to be important in all of Javanese culture. In addition to the dukun who perform magic rites, there are many dukun who cure illnesses. These latter dukun include curers who use magic spells, herbalists, midwives, and masseurs. It is said that even urban prijaji who regularly consult medical doctors may also consult dukun for particular illnesses and psychosomatic complaints.

DEATH AND AFTERLIFE. Funerals are held within hours of death and they are attended by neighbors and close relatives who are able to arrive in time. A coffin is built and a grave is dug quickly while a village official performs rituals. A simple ceremony is held at the home of the deceased followed by a procession to the graveyard and burial. A slametan is held with food provided by neighbors. Javanese funerals are marked with the same emotional restraint that characterizes other social interactions. Graves are visited regularly, especially at the beginning and end of the fasting month, and they are tended by relatives. The Javanese believe in continuing ties with the dead and especially ties between parents and children. Children hold a number of slametans at intervals after death with the last held 1,000 days after the death. There are varying beliefs about life after death, including the standard Islamic concepts of eternal retribution, beliefs in spirits or ghosts who continue to influence events, and belief in reincarnation, the last sternly condemned by the orthodox Muslims.

Bibliography

Dewey, Alice G. (1962). *Peasant Marketing in Java.* New York: Free Press of Glencoe.

Geertz, Clifford (1964). *The Religion of Java.* New York: Free Press of Glencoe.

Geertz, Clifford (1975). *The Social History of an Indonesian Town.* Westport, Conn.: Greenwood Press.

Geertz, Hildred (1961). *The Javanese Family: A Study of Kinship and Socialization.* New York: Free Press of Glencoe.

Jay, Robert (1969). *Javanese Villagers: Social Relations in Rural Modjokuto.* Cambridge and London: MIT Press.

Williams, Linda B. (1990). *Development, Demography, and Family Decision Making: The Status of Women in Rural Java.* Boulder, Colo.: Westview Press.

—M. MARLENE MARTIN

KACHIN

Ethnyms: Dashan, Jinghpaw, Khang, Singhpo, Theinbaw

Orientation

IDENTIFICATION. "Kachin" comes from the Jinghpaw word "GaKhyen," meaning "Red Earth," a region in the valley of the two branches of the upper Irrawaddy with the greatest concentration of powerful traditional chiefs. It refers to a congeries of Tibeto-Burman-speaking peoples who come under the Jinghpaw political system and associated religious ideology. The main people of this group are the Jinghpaw; their language is the lingua franca and the ritual language of the group. In Jinghpaw, they are called "Jinghpaw Wunpaung Amyu Ni" (Jinghpaw and related peoples). The Singhpo are their kin in the Hukawng Valley and in northeasternmost India, closely associated with the Ahom rulers of that part of Assam from the thirteenth century. "Theinbaw" is the Burmese form. "Khang" is the Shan word for Kachin, whom the Chinese used to call "Dashan." Other than Jinghpaw (Chinese spelling, Jingpo), the Kachin are comprised of Maru (own name, "Lawngwaw"), Atsi (Szi, Zaiwa—the majority Kachin population in Yunnan), Lashi, and speakers of the Rawang language of the Nung group, Achang (Burmese term, "Maingtha," meaning "people of the {Shan} state of Möng Hsa"), and some in-resident communities of Lisu speakers (Yawyin, in Burmese). Lashi and Atsi-Maru (and smaller groups akin to Maru) are called "Maru Dangbau" (the Maru branch) in Jinghpaw.

LOCATION. Kachin are located primarily in the Kachin State of Myanmar (Burma) and parts of the northern Shan State, southwestern Yunnan in China, and northeasternmost India (Assam and Arunachal Pradesh), between 23° and 28° N and 96° and 99° E. The Maru Dangbau are found mainly along the Myanmar-China border in this range. It is a region of north-south ranges, dissected by narrow valleys. In the valleys there are also Shan (Dai, in Yunnan) and Burmans, and those Kachin who are more heavily influenced by Shan culture. In the far north there are peaks as high as 5,000 meters but the Kachin settlements and swiddens normally range between 1,200 and 1,900 meters or so, while the two main towns in Myanmar's Kachin State (Myitkyina and Bhamo, originally a Burman and a Shan town respectively) are about 330 meters in elevation. Snow is always found on the highest northern peaks, and the upper elevations are subject to cold-season frosts. There are more than 50 days of frost a year at higher elevations. Rainfall occurs mainly in the monsoon season (between June and October) and is between 190 and 254 centimeters on average. Temperatures are substantially lower on the high eastern slopes over the China border and in the northern Shan State. The forest cover is mixed evergreen/deciduous broadleaf monsoon forest, with subtropical forest at lower elevations, including teak (*Tectona grandis*).

DEMOGRAPHY.   There are no reliable census reports from recent decades from Myanmar. Projections from the estimates of the 1950s (then about half a million in all) suggest a total Kachin population of perhaps a million or more, of which Yunnan contains over 100,000 and India but a few thousand. Average population density is uneven. Because of the relatively poor growing conditions of the eastern zone and the adjacent northern Shan State, there was a greater tendency for Kachins to incorporate valley areas originally belonging to the Shan, as well as to practice swiddening on grassland rather than on forested slopes. In the intermediate zone along the north-south part of the Myanmar-China border, however, the relative density was especially high, owing to profitable concentration along the Chinese caravan trade routes there; the associated high incidence of raiding caused some villages to practice high-slope terracing of wet-rice fields rather than rely exclusively on swiddening. These historical conditions restricted access to enough forested upland to permit rotation cycles that were long enough for fallow fields to revert to natural cover. Even in the more fertile zone of the west, conditions of warfare and trade sometimes led to high density and resulted in grassland rather than forest swiddening, with associated tendencies toward erosion. Overall, many villages had twenty houses or fewer, with more than five persons each, on average.

LINGUISTIC AFFILIATIONS.   All the Kachin languages are of the Tibeto-Burman Family. Jinghpaw and its dialects (chiefly Sinli, in the south, which is the Standard Jinghpaw of the schools based in the towns of Bhamo and Myitkyina; Mungun in Assam; Gauri {Hkauri} in the east; and Hkaku in the north and west {known as the Red-Earth country}) are an autonomous branch of the family, while the languages of the Maru Dangbau are in the Burmese-Lolo Branch, akin to Burmese. Nung is less certainly placed in Tibeto-Burman, while Lisu is a Loloish language in the Lolo-Burmese Branch.

History and Cultural Relations

There are Chinese mentions of Kachin in Yunnan going back to the fourteenth or fifteenth century, and there are obscure references to what must be Singhpo clients in the chronicles of the Ahom Kingdom in Assam, dating as early as the thirteenth century. There are similar mentions in the chronicles of some Khamti Shan principalities from the Upper Chindwin, while Leach argues that the prototypical Kachin chiefly (Gumchying Gumtsa) domains of the Red-Earth country may have arisen in the context of Khamti conquest of the area and displacement of Tibetan traders from the region of Putao (Hkamti Long). However, the first historical light on them comes from the end of the eighteenth and the start of the nineteenth century. Their spread was connected with the spread of the Shan (and Ahom) Tai-speaking peoples of the region's valleys, with whom Kachin have had a symbiotic relation. There are more Shan borrowings than any other in the Jinghpaw lexicon, and Shan-Buddhist ideas (and terms) are found in the ideological rhetoric associated with the Gumlao version of their political system ("Gumlao" means "rebellious aristocrats"; see below). Most of the ethnography comes from the work of American Protestant and European Catholic missionaries, who started work in the Bhamo area in the late nineteenth century, and later extended to the Kachin areas in the Shan States and northward to and beyond Myitkyina, which the railway reached in 1899. The rest of what we know, aside from professional ethnography, comes from the records and diaries of British colonial officers and associated traders. There are Chinese sources for the Yunnan Kachin, only now becoming available outside China, and these show a long-standing place for Jinghpaw in the Tusi system of imperially appointed political-cum-customs agents in this borderland of Southeast Asia, the Kachin chiefs being subordinate to

♦ **Tibeto-Burman**
A subfamily of languages found mainly in Tibet, Myanmar (Burma), Nepal, and northeastern India. The larger family is called Sino-Tibetan and also includes the Chinese languages.

Usually the youngest Kachin son inherits his father's house and office; other property may go in the father's lifetime as dowry to his daughters and marriage settlements on the older sons.

local Shan princes in this context. There was an expansion of Kachin settlement toward the east and south from late in the eighteenth century, in which the Kachin followed the growth of the Chinese overland caravan trade, especially with the rise and spread of commercial opium growing. This led to a flowering of the Gumlao political system, owing to the injection into Kachin politics of new sources of wealth from involvement in the trade and from the levying of tribute on the caravans. It also led to more confrontation of Kachin with Shan, and to instances of Kachin taking over minor Shan valley principalities. There is also indication that a much earlier period saw a similar development of centers of political power in the Red-Earth country, when the chiefs there were able to collect tribute from the annual influx of itinerant Tibetan pack traders going to Burma and even Siam and wintering in Kachin territory, where they gathered forest products for sale farther on. In the Third Anglo-Burmese War of 1885, while the British were taking Mandalay, the Kachin were also trying to take advantage of the collapse of royal Burma, and it was thought that, had the British failed to reach Mandalay when they did, the Kachin (and Shan?) might have reached it first. During the British imperium in Burma and India most of Kachinland was under the Frontier Administration, but the Triangle, north from Myitkyina, between the two branches of the Irrawaddy, was largely unadministered until just before the Japanese invasion of 1942. The Kachin State has been a constituent of the Union of Burma (now Myanmar) since that country regained independence in 1948, and the President-elect on the eve of the socialist military coup of 1962 was a Kachin chief, the Sama Duwa Sinwa Nawng. Since the coup, however, the Kachin have been a major element in the multiethnic insurgency against the Myanmar government throughout the mountains of the Myanmar-China-Thailand border region, which has led to the extension of Kachin communities into northern Thailand. In 1953 a Jingpo Autonomous Region was established in southwestern Yunnan in China; the Peoples' Republic of China has proved a magnet and refuge for some of the insurgent leaders from Myanmar. Kachins have served prominently in Burma's armed forces (as also in British times), and some hundreds served, some in Europe, during the First World War.

Settlements

Traditional Kachin villages usually had far fewer than 100 households; the larger villages existed for defense, but the requirements of swidden agriculture led to segmentation of villages. In the old days many were stockaded. Houses were built on piles. There were three sorts of houses. In regions with strong hereditary chiefs ruling multivillage tracts, the chief's house was sometimes up to 30 meters long (10 meters wide), occupied as a single dwelling by the extended household of the chief. These were generally on steep mountain terraces. This form of dwelling served to symbolize the ownership of the tract by the lineage of the chief. Since livestock were considered individual household property rather than lineage property, they were not kept under the "longhouse." In some pioneer Gumlao settlements there were real longhouses, composite structures with separately owned individual household apartments along a corridor. Again, livestock were kept separately. These longhouses symbolized the cooperative nature of the Gumlao political order.

The rest of the Kachin lived and continue to live in individual household dwellings. Water supply was a critical factor in village size and placement, but villages that were high up for defense purposes were often distant from their water supply. Most villages were entered through a sacred grove marked by posts serving to elicit prosperity from the gods, and by shrines to the spirit of the earth, where community sacrifices were held.

The other kind of building that exists today is the household granary. The house posts and beams are made of wood, floors and walls of woven split bamboo, roof thatched with grass. Domestic tasks like weaving and rice pounding are done under the overhanging front gable of the house, under which the larger animals are also kept. Inside, the house is partitioned lengthwise. The left (up-slope) side consists of sleeping apartments; the right side is left open for cooking, storage, and entertainment. At the end of the apartments is a space for the household spirit and ancestral spirits not yet sent to the land of the dead. In front of the house are altars to spirits and large X-shaped posts to which cattle are bound during sacrifices aggrandizing the household. The main external decoration is the pair of hornlike ornaments over the front roof peak on important aristocratic houses. Inside chiefs' houses there are various symbolically carved boards and posts signifying the ritual claim to spiritual sources of general prosperity in the sky world and the nether world, and a head of a buffalo sacrificed at the construction.

Economy

SUBSISTENCE AND COMMERCIAL ACTIVITIES. Traditionally, all Kachins were farmers and there was no full-time occupational specialization. Save where Kachin settlements have encroached on Shan valley principalities, there is swidden farming. The main staple crop is rice, and the burnt-over swidden is cultivated with a short, heavy-handled hoe and planted with a planting stick, the crop being reaped with a knife or sickle. Swiddens, especially in the colder, less well rainfed eastern zone, are also planted with maize, sesame, buckwheat, millet, tobacco, and various species of pumpkin. Vegetables and fruits are planted in house-yard gardens. People also raise some cotton and opium poppy. As one goes east into the Dehong of Yunnan, cultivation is a mixture of upland wet-rice terraces, monsoon swiddening, and grassland swiddening. Rice farming starts in February or March, and the cut slopes are burnt over and planted before the onset of the monsoon in June; harvesting is in October. Grain, which is threshed by being trampled by buffalo, is stored by December. Kachins do not generally use a swidden for more than three years at a time. Fallowing ideally takes at least twelve years, but field rotation does not usually require moving the settlement; villages often last half a century or more.

Fishing with traps and poison is common, but economically insignificant. Hunting with traps, snares, deadfalls, pellet bows, and guns is especially common in the agriculturally slack cold season between December and February. Cattle, buffalo, pigs, dogs, and fowl are bred for sacrifice but generally not for eating. Pigs are fed cooked mash in the evening but scavenge during the day. Some dogs are used in hunting, and some horses are kept.

Boiled rice with a vegetable stew and sometimes meat or fish are eaten three times a day. There is an aversion to eating cats, dogs, horses, monkeys, sheep, and goats. Tobacco and betel are commonly chewed. Opium smoking has been widespread in the last century or so. Rice beer is prepared, the malted mash also being taken during heavy work and on journeys, while the liquor is also distilled. These drinks are essential to hospitality and to ritual sacrifice.

INDUSTRIAL ARTS. Most metalware is obtained from Shan and Chinese, but in some northern regions there are lineages of blacksmiths who smelt ore. No pottery making is reported, though earthenware pots are common. Bamboo, cane, and grass are used to weave mats, baskets, and house walls. Woodworking and carving are not elaborate. Women weave on the belt loom, producing elaborate, largely floral-geometric designs, with some embroidery.

TRADE. Trade is mainly with Shan and Chinese (and Burmese) for salt, metalware, and the prestigious heirloom wares exhibited by aristocratic lineages. Kachins attend the markets held every five days in Shan towns, where they sell small amounts of garden and forest produce. The extent of Kachin involvement in opium growing and trading is in dispute, but the poppy was commonly cultivated in the area, though perhaps mainly by non-Jinghpaw. Trade with the Chinese caravans that came through the region carrying, among other things, opium, was a major source of wealth for the settlements of the intermediate zone; chiefs extracted considerable revenue from traders in their domains.

DIVISION OF LABOR. Men clear and burn the swiddens, hunt, go on raids, and assume most political and religious roles. Women have full responsibility for weeding, harvesting, transporting, and threshing; both men and women cook and brew from the crops, marketing any surplus. Women fetch water and firewood; they prepare raw cotton for weaving their own clothing and make their husbands' (largely Shan-style) clothes from commercial cloth.

LAND TENURE. Forest lands in a tract are village property and there is no private property in swidden land. Chiefs or the joint rulers of a Gumlao community have the sole right to allow people to live in a village and the sole right to dispose of land to those wishing to use it, but may not refuse any resident household use of swidden lands. Deciding when and where to shift swidden sites and assigning swidden plots are the prerogative of the chief and the elders. Irrigated lands can be inherited and sold to a fellow villager, but never to an outsider; this right follows the rule that a cultivator may not be dispossessed from a plot while it is in use.

Kinship

KIN GROUPS AND DESCENT. Descent is agnatic and there are eponymous clans with fixed correspondences between clan names in the different languages. The five aristocratic clans are descended from the sons of Wahkyet-wa, youngest brother among the ancestors of the Shan, Chinese, and other peoples. These brothers were descendants of Ningawn-wa, eldest brother of the Madai nat, chief of the sky spirits. The aristocratic clans are, in order of precedence, Marip,

♦ **betel**
*The leaf of the betel vine (*Piper betle*), chewed after meals with slaked lime, catechu, and* betel *or areca nut, as a savory.*

279

Lahtaw, Lahpai, N'Hkum, and Maran. The clans are divided into major lineages and these into lesser segments and local lineage groups, and it is especially to the last that exogamy strictly applies, although all the clans are exogamous in theory. In some regions a form of marriage called *hkau wang magam* is practiced, which prohibits marrying into a lineage from which a wife has been taken until the fourth generation, and requires a marriage with a mother's brother's daughter's daughter's daughter (MBDDD). In such cases the MB-DDD may turn out to be in one's own lineage, and the requirement must still be met. Some traditional lineage genealogies recited by bards are very long, though the number of generations back to the common ancestor seems to be a fixed number (i.e., genealogical telescoping). Clans are sometimes spoken of as if they were tribes because major chiefly domains have a majority of their residents in the chief's clan, which owns the village tract. In Jinghpaw proper, the wife acquires no membership in her husband's clan and lineage, but in Gauri she acquires it to some extent, and this difference corresponds to differences in the ease of divorce and in the recovery of marriage payments in such cases; in Jinghpaw proper, recovery is made from the wife's family, while in Gauri it is made mainly from her seducer, if any.

KINSHIP TERMINOLOGY. Kinship terminology is bifurcatemerging, with Omaha-type cousin terminology. The members of the lineage from which wives are taken and given, respectively, are referred to (by male speakers) with affinal terms (save that in the second descending generation the members of one's wife-taking groups are called by grandchild terms and the members of the second ascending generation of the wife-giving group are given grandparent terms). On the other hand, the wife takers of one's wife takers are all "grandchildren" and the men of one's wife givers' wife givers are all "grandfathers," regardless of generation. Furthermore, a male Ego calls the men in his own generation, whether wife giver or wife taker, by the same "brother-in-law" term (*hkau*); he calls the women in nonascending generations and men of descending generations of his wife-giving group "wife's younger sibling" (*nam*); and he calls the members of the three central generations of his wife takers, exclusive of the men of his own generation, by the term *hkri*, meaning "sister's children." Women of ascending generations of one's own lineage are "aunts by consanguinity" (*moi*) and the men of corresponding generations of wife takers are "uncle-by-marriage" (*gu*); women of the three central gener-

ations of wife givers' wife givers are *ni*, etymologically an "aunt" term, which has primary reference to the wives of classificatory mother's brothers (*tsa*, first ascending male wife giver). There are terms for actual husband and wife, and real/classificatory siblings are distinguished by age relative to the speaker.

Marriage and Family

MARRIAGE. Traditionally premarital sex was allowed; adolescents used to gather in the front apartment of a house evenings for singing, recitations of love poetry, and lovemaking. These relations need not, and some of them could not, lead to marriage. Fines are levied in favor of a girl's family for fathering a bastard. Parents try to arrange marriages to ally with other lineages, but negotiations are turned over to go-betweens. Bride-price is paid by the groom's father and the latter's lineage mates and may involve lengthy negotiations with payments extending over many years; there may also be a year or two of bride-service. The bride's family provides her with a dowry and helps defray the wedding costs. Polygyny, not common, is allowed, and often arises from the obligation to take on the widow of a real or classificatory brother. Some chiefs have several wives, some of them Shan or Burmese, and these cases arise from the need for marriages of state. Exogamy is more theoretical than strict, and it is quite possible to marry even a somewhat distant consanguine (*lawulahta*). This follows from the two principles of asymmetrical marriage alliance and lineage segmentation. The first has a single rule: one may not take wives from the same lineages to which one gives wives; the reversal of an alliance is a major offense against the whole social order. Since wife givers (*mayu* in Jinghpaw) outrank their wife takers (*dama* in Jinghpaw) ritually and in rights and duties to one another, wife givers can extort a great deal from their wife takers, from which derives the auxiliary principle of diversification of alliances. Far from its being a rule that one should normally marry a woman from a wife-giver lineage, it is often thought strategic to negotiate a new alliance. This possibility reinforces the tendency for lineages to segment (or fission) when they become too large and have to compete for limited social and economic resources. It follows that one's distant lineage mates may well have separated themselves and have their own marriage networks, in which case each has effectively become a distinct unit of marriage alliance, and hence can intermarry. In Kachin ideology, however, exogamy and marriage-alliance relations are fixed once and for all among the five aristocratic clans, with the result that this ideological model of the system has the five clans marrying in a circle (e.g., Lahtaw, Marip, Maran, N'Hkum, Lahpai, Lahtaw, each being wife giver to the next). This is consistent with the rules. Wife giver–wife taker relations, and the restrictions against reversing them, are not transitive. They extend only to certain of the wife givers of one's own immediate wife giver (and of the wife taker of one's own immediate wife taker) because a woman's lineage brothers hold a sort of lien on the children, so that her husband's lineage must pay off that lien (to the natal lineage of her actual mother) along with paying the marriage price to her lineage. In principle the rank distinction between aristocrats and commoners (*du ni* and *darat ni* respectively) is rigid, but for the same reasons that clan exogamy is only a fiction, so is this. The politics of marriage alliance combined with the tendency for local lineage segments to constitute separate entities occasionally allows a rising commoner lineage of wealth and power to get a major wife from a lineage in an aristocratic clan that may have fallen on hard times, if the alliance is suitable to the two parties and the prices paid are appropriately inflated. There are, however, some clans that figure as unequivocal commoners (not merely darat ni but *darat daroi*, "utter commoners"); an example is the clan Labya, properly called Labya *mi-wa*, indicating that it is of Chinese origin and has been included fairly recently in the Kachin system.

DOMESTIC UNIT. Ideally, residence is virilocal, but uxorilocal marriage is not notably uncommon. This is especially true in the case of a noninheriting son, whose claims on the assistance of his real or classificatory mother's brother, whose daughter is a preferential wife, may be greater than those on his own father.

INHERITANCE. Usually the youngest son (*uma*) inherits his father's house and office, if any, while much of the movable property may go, in the father's lifetime, as dowry to his daughters and as marriage settlements on the older sons. The youngest son in return is expected to support the parents in their old age and arrange their funerals. A childless man's estate reverts to his brothers or lineage mates and their heirs. The principle of ultimogeniture is modified by the fact that an eldest son is thought to succeed in some measure to the powers of the "mother's brother" or wife-giver line and in any case is next in line after the youngest in succession, so that the position of an eldest son of a youngest-son line is especially important. This

may be an idea associated with the Gumlao political order, but compare the mythical genealogy of the chiefly clans.

Sociopolitical Organization

POLITICAL ORGANIZATION. There are several versions of the system. Gumchying Gumtsa chiefs are the ritual models of chiefdom and the base for this kind of organization is the Red-Earth country. Their authority derives from their monopoly of priests and bardic reciters of genealogical myths, through which ritual specialists they control access to the spirits who make human occupancy of the land possible. They claim the right to various services and dues from their subjects, notably a hind quarter of all animals (wild and domestic) that are killed in the tract, and so are called "thigh-eating chiefs." Gumlao communities reject on principle the hereditary privileges of chiefs. In particular, they believe that all aristocrats of the community are equal, that is, all householders who can get someone to sponsor the essential Merit Feasts and sacrifices. It is a mistake to call this a "democratic" system, since its principle is wider access by aristocrats to chieflike privileges (though they reject the thigh-eating dues); a Gumlao man is called *magam*, which signifies an aristocrat though not a chief (*duwa*) by strict succession. Gumlao is based on the idea that a noninheriting son who can find wealth and a place to set himself up may try to get an important Gumchying Gumtsa chief to sponsor him in a feat that will raise him to standing as a full chief; but first he must temporarily renounce all claims to standing (*gumyu*, which literally means "to step down from privilege") while he awaits the sponsoring rites. When local and historical circumstances conspire to make wealth more generally accessible, there are aristocrats who will not bother with sponsorship at all, since sponsorship becomes expensive and has to be postponed proportionally to the demand for it. They simply assume the ritual attributes, although not the thigh-eating privileges, of chiefdom. This seems to be the root of the Gumlao movement. Not surprisingly, as conditions ease there will be *gumlao magam* who again seek sponsorship as full chiefs, at which point Gumlao tracts turn again into Gumchying Gumtsa domains. The oscillation is fueled by a perennial ideological debate about the allowable sources of ritual privilege, as well as by the combined effects of the principle of lineage segmentation and the tendencies toward disaffection brought about through primogeniture. When a Kachin chief in close contact with Shan be-

♦ **virilocal**
Residence in the household of the husband's family.

♦ **uxorilocal**
Residence in the household of the wife's family.

♦ **primogeniture**
A rule of inheritance that gives the exclusive right of inheritance to the first-born son.

*Kachin Priests
officiate at
sacrificial rites and
can act as sorcerers.*

comes more like a Shan prince (*sawbwa*, or *tsao-fa*), often because he has taken over lowland Shan territories or because he desires political recognition on the part of other sawbwas, he will try to assert even greater power over his "subjects" and may even abandon Kachin priestly services and the closely connected reliance on upland farming. Such a chief is called "Gumsa duwa," a Gumsa chief. In tending toward becoming Shan and asserting a sharp distinction between "rulers" and "subjects" incompatible with the claims and intricacies of the Kachin marriage-alliance system (a Shan prince, of course, simply takes and gives wives as tribute), and in giving up the ritual basis of his authority, he will tend to lose the allegiance of the Kachin manpower on which his real power depends. The alternative is the compromise status of Gumrawng Gumsa (pretentious chiefs), who claim exclusive right over a village and maintain enough upland swiddens to satisfy the Kachin priests who must serve them, but remain unconnected with the hierarchy of Kachin authority deriving from the rules of strict succession and sponsorship, have no authority outside the village, and are not recognized outside the village as thigh-eating chiefs. Traditional Kachin chiefs, not being absolute rulers, rarely acted apart from the wishes of the council of household elders. In Yunnan, where Kachin chiefs have long had a place within the Tusi system in the context of Shan principalities, it is not unknown for agents (*suwen*, probably a Chinese title) to usurp much of the power of the chiefs, even though these administrative agents may be commoners.

CONFLICT.   Suppressed upon the extension of British rule, Kachin warfare was mainly guerilla action, raiding, and ambush, with sporadic instances of cannibalism and head-hunting reported.

Religion and Expressive Culture

Christian missionaries have already been mentioned. At present most, if not all, Kachin communities are Christian, and the social rift between Catholic and Protestant communities sometimes is quite deep. Recent years have also seen some Government-sponsored Buddhist-missionary activity among Kachins in Myanmar.

RELIGIOUS BELIEFS.   One class in Kachin religion includes the major deities, named and common to all Kachin, remote ancestors of commoner and aristocrat alike. These Sky Nat (*mu nat*—the word "nat" means a spirit Lord) are ultimately children of the androgynous Creator (Woishun-Chyanun), whose "reincarnation" is Shadip, the chief of the earth nats (*ga nat*), the

highest class of spirit. The youngest sky nat (senior by ultimogeniture) is the Madai Nat, who can be approached only by chiefs, whose ultimate ancestor was his eldest brother and dama, Ningawn-wa, who forged the earth. A direct daughter of Madai Nat was the wife of the first Kachin aristocrat. Below all these in rank are the *masha nat*, the ancestor nats of lineages; that of the uma, or youngestson line of thigh-eating chiefs, has special importance. There is also a vague sort of "High God," Karai Kasang, who has no myths (except that he seems to have something to do with the fate of the souls of the dead) and who Leach thinks is a projection of the Christian God of the missionaries; this spirit's name makes no sense in the Kachin language. Below all these are minor spirits such as household guardians and the spirits of immediate ancestors, witch spirits (*hpyi*) who possess those accused of unconscious hereditary witchcraft, and the *maraw*, unpersonified "fates" to be placated; they can upset the best laid plans and the boons granted by higher deities. Beyond these are the uniformly hostile ghosts and spirits, whose evil works are not, as Leach claimed, man's punishment for infraction of proper obligations.

RELIGIOUS PRACTITIONERS.   There are mediums and diviners; a medium works by trance and is inexplicably chosen for his or her calling, while divination is a learned skill. These are basically private practitioners. There are also priests (*dumsa*) who officiate at sacrificial rites, and the rather scarce *jaiwa*, or bards, who preserve and recite genealogies and associated myths at great Merit Feasts (*manau*) in which chiefs and other high aristocrats proclaim and validate the ancestral sources of their authority. These are all learned offices, never hereditary, and they are essential to the ritual practices of aristocracy and chiefdom. Priests have two sorts of sacrificial assistants (ritual butchers). Of all these offices, only that of medium may be exercised by women. Priests, bards, and sacrificers are paid with a portion of the sacrifice. Priests also can work as sorcerers. The main work in treating illnesses is intercession with spirits by some or all of these officiants. The chief has the ritual duty of declaring sabbaths from all work at the time of rites held for recurrent or exceptional communal times of crisis such as plagues or junctures in the agricultural cycle (e.g., just before the first sowing the chief and his priests make offerings to the spirit of the earth, which is followed by a four-day sabbath).

DEATH AND AFTERLIFE.   One cause of death is said to be that the cord that the Creator holds, thus sustaining the soul, is eventually gnawed away by spirits. Spirits can also entice the soul from the body, and death ensues if the soul cannot be found and enticed back home. Ultimately myth has it that death came to Kachin mankind because human beings originally had to attend ceremonies of the sky-spirit people, and, as dama, had to contribute costly gifts. This cost so much that Sut Wa Madu, the ancestor who founded the *sut manau* (Feast of Merit, a major ritual connection between the two worlds), decided to hold a mock funeral, thus enticing the sky people to attend and bring gifts. The female sun spirit (Jan nat, one of the Sky Nats) felt that this compromised the asymmetrical relations between mayu and dama, and she decreed that if there were to be human funerals, then men would have to suffer death—not so much as a punishment as in order to restore the net balance of the relationship with a quitclaim payment of men's souls. This tale expresses the ultimate paradox of an asymmetrical alliance relation; for the net circulation of the system is impossible to maintain asymmetrically when there are fewer than three parties to the relationship. On the one hand, with payments going all one way, the system lacks completeness, or closure. On the other hand, payments in an asymmetrical relation cannot go both ways. Burial is a week after death; this interval is used to try to ensure the separation of the spirit of the deceased from the world of the living, a task aided by a priest, who makes offerings to the ghost and asks it to go away. The final obsequies may be postponed for as much as a year on account of the expense. Then the priest recalls the soul from its temporary limbo and tells it the route to the land of the dead. If thereafter divination shows that the spirit has not gone, it will be installed in the household altar, which had been temporarily removed from the house at the time of the death and is now reinstalled.

Bibliography

Carrapiet, W. J. S. (1929). *The Kachin Tribes of Burma*. Rangoon: Superintendent of Government Printing and Stationery.

Friedman, Jonathan (1979). *System, Structure, and Contradiction*. Copenhagen: National Museum of Denmark.

Gilhodes, Charles (1922). *The Kachins: Religion and Customs*. Calcutta: Catholic Orphan Press.

Hanson, Olaf (1913). *The Kachins: Their Customs and Traditions*. Rangoon: American Baptist Mission Press.

Leach, Edmund R. (1954). *Political Systems of Highland Burma*. Cambridge: Harvard University Press; London: G. Bell & Sons.

Leach, Edmund R. (1961). *Rethinking Anthropology* (chapters 2, 3, and 5). London: Athlone Press.

Lehman, F. K. (1977). "Kachin Social Categories and Methodological Sins." In *Language and Thought: Anthropological Issues*, edited by William McCormack and Stefan Wurm, 229–250. The Hague: Mouton.

Lehman, F. K. (1989). "Internal Inflationary Pressures in the Prestige Economies of the Feast-of-Merit Complex." In *Ritual, Power, and Economy: Upland-Lowland Contrasts in Mainland Southeast Asia*, edited by Susan D. Russell, 89–102. Occasional Paper 14. DeKalb: Northern Illinois University, Center for Southeast Asian Studies.

Lintner, Bertil (1990). *Land of Jade: A Journey through Insurgent Burma*. Bangkok: White Lotus.

Maran, LaRaw (1967). "Towards a Basis for Understanding the Minorities of Burma: The Kachin Example." In *Southeast Asian Tribes, Minorities, and Nations*. Vol. 1, edited by Peter Kunstadter, 125–146. Princeton, N.J.: Princeton University Press.

—F. K. LEHMAN

Among the Kachin one cause of death is said to be that the cord that the Creator holds, thus sustaining the soul, is eventually gnawed away by spirits.

KAREN

Ethonyms: Kareang, Kariang, Kayin, Pwo, Sgaw, Yang

Orientation

IDENTIFICATION. Historically, the written Burmese term "Karen" probably came from the word "Kayin," referring to the particular group of peoples in eastern Myanmar (Burma) and western Thailand who speak closely related but different Sino-Tibetan languages. The Central Thai or Siamese word for Karen is "Kariang," presumably borrowed from the Mon term "Kareang." The Northern Thai or Yuan word "Yang," the origins of which may be Shan or from the root word *nyang* (person) in many Karen languages, is applied to the Karen by Shans and Thais. The designation "Karen" in fact includes several different subgroups, each with its own language and name. The largest, Sgaw and Pwo, have differences of dialect within their languages. The Sgaw or Skaw refer to themselves as "Pwakenyaw." The Pwo term for themselves is "Phlong" or "Kêphlong." The Burmese identify the Sgaw as "Bama Kayin" (Burmese Karen) and the Pwo as "Talaing Kayin" (Mon Karen). Thais sometimes use "Yang" to refer to the Sgaw and "Kariang" to refer to the Pwo, who live mainly south of the Sgaw. The word "Karen" was probably brought to Thailand from Burma by Christian missionaries. The term "White Karen" has been used to identify Christian Karen of the hill Sgaw. Other important subgroups include the Kayah and Pa-O. Prior to Burmese independence the Burmese term for the Kayah was "Kayin-ni," from which the English "Karen-ni" or "Red Karen" derived; Luce identifies them as "Eastern Bwe" or "Bghai." The Burmese term for the Pa-O is "Taungthu," adapted by the Shans as "Tong-su." Karennet (Kayin-net, or Black Karen) were listed in the 1911 census. Luce's classification of minor Karen languages listed in the 1931 census includes Paku; Western Bwe, consisting of Blimaw or Bre(k), and Geba; Padaung; Gek'o or Gheko; and Yinbaw (Yimbaw, Lakü Phu, or Lesser Padaung). Additional groups listed in the 1931 census are Monnepwa, Zayein, Taleing-Kalasi, Wewaw, and Mopwa. Scott's *Gazetteer* of 1900 lists the following: "Kekawngdu," the Padaung name for themselves; "Lakü," the self-name of the Bre; "Yintale" in Burmese, "Yangtalai" in Shan, for a branch of Eastern Karenni; the Sawng-tüng Karen, also known as "Gaung-to," "Zayein," or "Zalein"; Kawn-sawng; Mepu; Pa-hlaing; Loilong; Sinsin; Salon; Karathi; Lamung; Baw-han; and the Banyang or Banyok. These early sources are often inconsistent and lack adequate references for further research or clarification.

Recently anthropologists have remarked on the limitations of identifying the Karen primarily on the basis of language or name, noting that the complex and fluid Karen group identity is a cluster of traits that includes, among other things, language, political and social organization, religion, and material culture. Populations of Karen speakers may differ in these traits. Hinton and stresses economic and political interests as more significant to Karen identity than cultural features or "ethnic" distinctions. Some contemporary writings on the question of Karen identity place more importance on the belief of the Karen in the distinctiveness of their language as a cultural marker than they do on the objective linguistic distinctiveness of Karen languages. Other writings emphasize the contemporary Thai-Burmese political-economic context in which Karen ethnic identity is forged.

LOCATION. Until the mid-eighteenth century the Karen lived mainly in the forested mountainous regions of eastern Burma, where the hills are divided by long narrow valleys running north to south from the Bilauktaung and Dawna ranges along the Salween River system to the broad high plateau of the Shan uplands. Today Karen reside in both Myanmar and Thailand, within the area between 10° and 21° N and between 94° and 101° E. Karen settlements are found in the hills along the border between the two countries along the length of Tenasserim into the Shan plateau from 10° N as far as 21° N. Most Karen inhabit Myanmar, in both lowland ricegrowing plains and hill regions, with large numbers in the central Irrawaddy Delta, in the Irrawaddy and Sittang valleys from the coast to about 19° N, and in the northern part of Tenasserim. In Thailand most of the Karen settlements are along the hilly western border and range northward and eastward to the Mekong from approximately 12°00′ N to 20°30′ N. Karen villages are located in three distinct physical environments: the lowland plains of the Irrawaddy, Sittang, and Salween deltas and the coast of Tenasserim; the Pegu Yoma, a hilly range between the Irrawaddy and the Sittang; and the Shan upland, which varies geographically from a rolling high plateau (1,000 meters in elevation on average) in the Shan State to the north-south hills and narrow valleys of the Kayah and Karen states and interior Tenasserim to the south. These hill regions are covered with tropical rain forest that contains great varieties of vegetation, ranging from towering hard-woods to dense bamboo and vines that fires burn off during the hot dry season. The tropical-monsoon climate has two seasons, the monsoon from mid-May through September and the dry season from October through April. It is cold from November to February and becomes extremely hot in March and April, before the advent of the cooling monsoon rains. The precipitation range is from less than 200 centimeters annually in the southwestern Shan State to more than 254 centimeters in the central Irrawaddy Delta and more than 500 centimeters in Tenasserim.

DEMOGRAPHY. Karen are the largest "tribal" minority in both Myanmar and Thailand. Although recent census figures for Myanmar are unavailable, their population there, projected from 1,350,000 in the 1931 census, is estimated at more than 3 million. Karen in Thailand number approximately 185,000, with about 150,000 Sgaw, 25,000 Pwo Karen, and much smaller populations of B'ghwe or Bwe (about 1,500) and Pa-O or Taungthu; together these groups comprise about 56 percent of the highland minority people of Thailand. Approximately one-third of the Karen population in Myanmar lives in the Karen State or administrative division. The Sgaw Karen, with a population of over 1 million, have settlements in the mountainous Karen State, in the Shan uplands, and to a lesser extent in the Irrawaddy and Sittang deltas. The Pwo Karen (approximately 750,000) inhabit primarily the Irrawaddy Delta. The Pa-O live mainly in southwestern Shan State. The approximately 75,000 Kayah, or Red Karen, live almost entirely in Kayah State, the smallest state in Myanmar. Political and economic circumstances have affected demographics. Since the early 1980s between 10,000 and 20,000 Karen from Burma have been living in refugee camps in Thailand. Outside Myanmar and Thailand, there is a growing community of Karen immigrants in Bakersfield, California.

LINGUISTIC AFFILIATION. Despite the linguistic and numerical importance of the Karen, surpisingly few studies of Karen languages have been conducted in recent times. There continues to be controversy concerning the linguistic affiliation of the Karen group of languages, although it is widely accepted that within the Sino-Tibetan Stock all Karen linguistic subgroups are related to each other. Pwo and Pa-O form one subgroup, with Sgaw and several related languages forming another. Lehman and Hamilton cite André Haudricourt's view that Karen falls in the Tibeto-Burman classification. Benedict and Shafer both position Karen as a distinct Sino-Tibetan Division, the Karenic. Luce and to some extent Jones, on the other hand, argue that Karen is linguistically related to Thai. The most generally accepted view is that the Karen languages are a divergent subfamily of the Tibeto-Burman Language Family. Matisoff notes the similarity in phonology and basic vocabulary of Karen dialects to Lolo-Burmese, the other major Tibeto-Burman Language Subgroup in Thailand with similar tone systems, the same paucity of final consonants, and a comparably rich set of vowels. He points out that syntactically Karen's atypical placement of the object after the verb may be the reason some linguists have set it apart genetically from the other Tibeto-Burman languages.

History and Cultural Relations

The early history of the Karen remains problematic, and there are various theories regarding their migrations. It appears that Karen peoples originated in the north, possibly in the high plains of Central Asia, and emigrated in stages through China into Southeast Asia, probably after the Mon but before the Burmese, Thai, and Shan reached what is now Myanmar and Thailand. Their slash-and-burn agricultural economy is an indication of their original adaptation to hill life.

Eighth-century A.D. inscriptions mention the Cakraw in central Burma, who have been linked with the modern Sgaw. There is a thirteenth-century inscription near Pagan bearing the word "Karyan," which may refer to Karen. Seventeenth-century Thai sources mention the Kariang, but their identity is unclear. By the eighteenth century, Karen-speaking people were living primarily in the hills of the southern Shan states and in eastern Burma. They developed a system of relations with the neighboring Buddhist civilizations of the Shan, Burmese, and Mon, all of whom subjugated the Karen. European missionaries and travelers wrote of contact with Karen in the eighteenth century. During the turmoil among the Burman, Yuan, and Siamese kingdoms in the second half of the eighteenth century, the Karen, whose villages lay along the armies' routes, emerged as a significant group. Many Karen settled in the lowlands, and their increased contact with the dominant Burman and Siamese led to a sense of oppression at the hands of these powerful rulers. Groups of Karen made numerous mostly unsuccessful attempts to gain autonomy, either through millennarian syncretic religious movements or politically. The Red Karen, or Kayah, established three chieftainships that survived from the early nineteenth century to the end of British

PROVIDER

A Karen woman prepares betel nut for chewing. Women gather foods, medicinal plants, and firewood, as well as engage in paddy fishing and in the preparation of food and alcoholic drinks. Chiang Rai, Thailand. (Earl Kowall/Corbis)

Karen

The Karen National Union (KNU) promoted Karen autonomy, but after Aung Sun's assassination in 1947 hopes for an independent Karen state were shattered.

rule. In Thailand Karen lords ruled three small semifeudal domains from the mid-nineteenth century until about 1910. British and American Christian missionaries arrived in Burma after the British annexation of lower Burma in 1826. The Karen, many of whom had converted to Christianity, had a distinctive though ambiguous relationship with the British, based on shared religious and political interests; prior to World War II they were given special representation in the Burmese Legislative Assembly. Christian missionary activity may have been the most important factor in the emergence of Karen nationalism, through the development of schools, a Karen literate tradition, and ultimately an educated Karen elite whose members rose in the ranks of the British colonial service. In 1928 the Karen leader, Dr. Sir San C. Po, argued for an autonomous Karen state within a federation. During the war, the Karen remained loyal to the British after the Japanese occupation; there was increased antipathy between the Karen and Burmans, who were backed by the Japanese. After the war, the British prepared for Burma's independence. The Karen National Union (KNU) promoted Karen autonomy, but after Aung San's assassination in 1947 hopes for an independent Karen state were shattered. Since Burmese independence in 1948, the Karen relationship with Burma has been primarily political. The old Karen-ni states formed Kayah State, and in 1952 the Burmese government established Karen State with Pa-an as its capital. During the 1964 peace negotiations, the name was changed to the traditional Kawthoolei, but under the 1974 constitution the official name reverted to Karen State. Many Karen, especially those in the lowland deltas, have assimilated into Burmese Buddhist society. In the hill regions many resist Burmese influence and some support, directly or tacitly, the insurgent KNU movement, which has been at war since 1949, in its efforts to achieve independence from Burmese rule. It is currently in a coalition with other ethnic groups and Aung San Suu Kyi's party, the National League for Democracy, which supports the formation of a union of federal states. The Kawthoolei (the name for the KNU territory) government has the difficult task of interacting with the Karen revolutionary military hierarchy and with the heterogeneous Karen population, which consists of both nonhierarchical traditional hill Karen and more educated delta Christian Karen who have joined them. Movement back and forth across the Thai-Myanmar border continues as Karen villagers cross to cut

swiddens and Karen political refugees arrive in increasing numbers in Thailand's Mae Hon Son Province. In Thailand the Karen are facing assimilation into Thai society through mass education, the economic necessity of engaging in wage labor for Thai employers, and the assimilation of highland Karen into a generalized "hill tribe" category generated by Thai and foreign tourists.

Settlements

Contemporary Karen settlement patterns vary considerably as a result of geographical diversity and cultural contact. Research in the past twenty years has focused on Thai Karen; no comparable research has been done in Burma. Traditional Karen villages, compact and stockaded, consist of houses and granaries. Population figures for Thai highland Karen indicate an average of twenty-three houses in a village (Kunstadter 1983), a figure similar to those reported in the 1920s by Marshall for Karen hill villages in Burma. In upland and lowland Pwo Karen villages matrilineal kin arrange their houses together; this practice may derive from the traditional Karen longhouse. Stern (1979) includes David Richardson's description of Karen villages on the upper Khwae Noi in 1839–1840 containing three to six longhouses, each holding several families with a separate ladder for each. Sgaw Karen village names often reflect their pattern of settlement in valleys at the headwaters of streams. The history of Karen settlement indicates the importance of the village as a community, as village sites are frequently moved but continue to retain their name and identity.

The predominant village unit is the house, usually inhabited by five to seven family members. Anderson and Marshall in the 1920s described villages in which longhouses were characteristic (and in some cases the only structure), accommodating twenty to thirty families. Both longhouses and separate houses in the hill villages are made from bamboo, sometimes in combination with wood timbers; they have thatched roofs and require reconstruction in a new location every few years. Houses in upland valleys are generally more substantial, made of wooden posts with plank floors and walls, although bamboo is often used. Today roofs of teak leaf or grass thatch, which must be rethatched annually, are being replaced by corrugated iron sheets by those who can afford them in both hill and valley villages. In the plains Karen villages of Myanmar, the housing follows lowland-Burmese style. Traditionally and still today, most Karen houses in Myanmar and Thailand are raised above the ground with the multiple purposes of protection from floods or wild animals and shelter for domestic animals.

Economy

SUBSISTENCE AND COMMERCIAL ACTIVITIES. Traditionally hill Karen were subsistence cultivators practicing swidden agriculture. Today, their economy is mainly subsistence-oriented, requiring two sectors to produce enough food for survival: an agricultural sector based on swiddening and wet-rice cultivation, and a cash or market economy. Most hill Karen have taken up wet-rice agriculture only within the past generation, and the annual ritual cycle is still associated with the longer swidden rice-growth cycle. Swidden rice fields are generally burned and planted at the beginning of the wet season (March–April); rice is harvested in October, threshed in November, and stored in granaries. Swidden cultivators may harvest tea and cultivate maize, legumes, yams, sweet potatoes, peppers, chilies, and cotton. Tobacco, betel leaves and nuts, and fruits including bananas, durians, and mangoes are grown in the valley bottomlands. Plains and valley Karen are wet-rice agriculturalists who follow the same cycle as the Burmese and Mon. Village Karen of all ages participate in hunting and gathering. Hill Karen males still hunt for subsistence, pursuing birds, squirrels, lizards, deer, and wild pigs. They use crossbows, slingshots, snares, traps, and guns. Gathering, a more important food supplement than hunting, is done also for trade; women and children may collect roots, leaves, bamboo shoots, herbs and bark for medicinal purposes, wild fruits, frogs, small lizards, insects, paddy crabs, ant larvae, honey, beeswax, mushrooms, firewood, weeds for pig food, stick lac, and snakes. Both plains and hill Karen fish for consumption or trade. Plains Karen follow Burmese techniques. Hill and valley Karen techniques include pond fishing, bamboo poles with lines and hooks, throw nets with lead weights made by male villagers, bamboo fish traps, surrounds using jute rope, and paddy fishing with baskets.

Hill Karen generally keep water buffalo, oxen, pigs, chickens, and dogs. Water buffalo are used in wet-rice production, and oxen for pulling carts. Some buffalo and oxen are raised to be sold for profit. Traditionally pigs were used in ceremonies such as weddings, funerals, and lineage rituals. Although pigs are still used for these purposes today, in the Thai hills they are more often raised for sale to the Thais. Christian Karen raise pigs for their own consumption or for trade. Chickens are also used ceremonially, and chickens and eggs are sold at market. Cattle are usually corralled, whereas pigs and chickens are allowed to forage by day and sleep at the household by night. Buddhist plains Karen keep cattle and buffalo. Karen occasionally trap elephants in the wild and are noted as elephant handlers; most mahouts in Myanmar and Thailand are Karen.

INDUSTRIAL ARTS. Weaving, almost exclusively the domain of women, is done in both plains and hill Karen households, but it is more important in the hills. Hill Karen use only the traditional belt loom, whereas plains Karen use either the belt loom or the Burmese fixed-frame loom. In the past, cotton was ginned, whipped, spun on a wheel, dyed, and woven at home. At present some hill Karen still grow and spin their own cotton thread, but much of the thread is bought in local markets. Dye, which was derived from plants or minerals, is now often purchased, bringing new variations in the traditional colors. Articles including clothing, blankets, and highly prized shoulder bags are woven in the traditional Karen symbolic and decorative patterns unique to each subgroup, for household use and for markets as far away as Chiengmai and Toungoo. Bamboo baskets and mats are made by highland women for household use or for sale. Men make most of the tools and implements for agriculture, fishing, hunting, and construction. The machete is the most common tool.

TRADE. The cash or market sectors of Karen subsistence economies are important but vary greatly. Traditionally Karen have traded cotton cloth, forest products, game, and domestic animals to Burmese and Mon in exchange for rice, pottery, salt, and fish paste. Hill Karen carry on trade in Burmese, Shan, and Thai markets, whereas lowland Karen are tied into the Burmese economy. The hill Karen studied by Hinton (1975) were engaged in raising livestock and selling them to the Northern Thai, wage labor in the city, renting out elephants to timber contractors, and sale of forest products. Hamilton, Kunstadter, and Rajah described hill Karen participation in lowland wage-labor, trade, and cash-market economies as consisting of the picking and selling of tea and the sale of livestock, forest products, household-manufactured tools, and woven goods. Tourism has become a significant source of income for Thai hill Karen.

DIVISION OF LABOR. Women gather foods, medicinal plants and herbs and firewood, and engage in paddy fishing; they raise pigs and chickens, carry water, prepare rice for cooking, prepare

The Karen are facing assimilation into Thai society through mass education and the economic necessity of engaging in wage labor for Thai employers.

alcoholic drinks, raise cotton, spin, and weave. Men hunt, tend the buffalo and oxen, plow, build houses, cut timber, and make mats and baskets. Fishing, sowing, reaping, threshing, winnowing, and some cooking are done by both men and women.

LAND TENURE. Land use and rights to swiddens vary depending on local politics, ecological stability, and population demands on resources. Usufructuary rights to swiddens and fallow swiddens are common. Traditionally each village had its accepted farming areas in which community members were free to use what they needed as long as they selected plots within swiddens designated by the village chief and elders. Today the need to remain on a site permanently in order to own the paddy fields for wet-rice cultivation has forced many hill Karen, particularly in Thailand, to give up swiddening or to overwork and thus lower the productivity of nearby swidden fields.

Marriage and Family

MARRIAGE. A Karen may marry anyone who is not closely related (i.e., anyone except siblings, first cousins, and lineage mates). Among Pwo and Sgaw Karen there are proscriptions against certain matrilineal and intergenerational marriages. Patrilateral parallel second cousins may marry, but matrilateral parallel cousins of any degree may not because the latter are of the same lineage or of the same female spirit. Marriage is monogamous. Courting takes place on social occasions such as weddings, funerals, and communal planting and harvesting. Proposals, which require parental approval, are made by the young man or woman, although a go-between is often used. Premarital sex is prohibited, and 15 to 20 percent of bridegrooms pay a fine for having broken the rule. The marriage ceremony involves rituals to the Lord of Land and Water marking the union of the new couple and the husband's incorporation into the bride's parents' household. The ritual and wedding feast in the bride's village can last three days. After marriage the bride gives up her long white dress for the black embroidered blouse and red-and-black tubular sarong of married women; men continue to wear the traditional red fringed shirt.

Residence is usually matrilocal. Up to 30 percent of Karen marriages are village-exogamous. The groom moves to the house of the bride's father and eventually may establish a new household in that village. Postmarital residence depends

KINSHIP

Kin Groups and Descent

There is much scholarly controversy regarding the Karen kinship system, which is probably best characterized as a cognatic or bilateral system with matrilineal descent. Marshall described a group of matrilineally related persons participating in certain rituals for their ancestral spirit. The leader was the oldest living female of the line. Iijima, Hamilton, and others have observed these ancestral rituals taking place among both Sgaw and Pwo Karen matrilineages.

Kinship Terminology

Hamilton notes that the Karen bilateral system of filiation does not result in a descent group, but a set of statuses for structuring relationships. Matrilineal descent, on the other hand, indicates a person's genealogical connection to his or her mother's relatives. A Karen man and woman who are directly related to each other through a pair of sisters, for example, should not marry because they are members of the same matrilineage, although if there is even one male in the descent chain they may marry. Karen kinship terminology is overall quite similar among subgroups. A person equates his or her father's brother with his or her mother's brother. For grandparents and great-grandparents, male collaterals (maternal or paternal) of the same generation are equated, as are females. There are separate terms for generations, equating all children in each generation. Ego calls siblings only by birth-order terms, and may add a suffix to denote gender. The Sgaw term *dau'pywae* (*dang phu vwi* in Pwo) refers to the sibling set. Ego equates all cousins, but may add one of two suffixes to distinguish lineage members from nonmembers. People distinguish their own children from their brothers' children and their sisters' children, whom they equate with the children of their cousins. Birth order is important, but is usually used only in the first ascending and descending generation.

as much on availability of agricultural land resources as on ideal uxorilocal pattern, binding villages in an interdependent net of relationships.

DOMESTIC UNIT. The normal domestic unit is the nuclear family, made up of husband, wife, and unmarried children. In the hills each nuclear family traditionally occupied either an apartment in a longhouse or a separate house in the village.

INHERITANCE. Property is generally divided into three shares, with equal parts going to the eldest (*a' vwi shiae* in Pwo Karen) and youngest children (*a' oe dae*) and slightly smaller shares to middle children (*a' oa 'klae*). Inheritance takes place ideally before the death of the parents, to avoid disputes and the bad luck brought by personal property containing the dead person's *k'la* (*kala*), or spirit. The youngest child, preferably a girl, cares for the parents until their deaths and controls their property. Widows retain control of their property until remarriage.

Divorce is discouraged and rarely occurs: 5 to 6 percent of marriages in the Thai hills, and about double that in lowlands and towns, end in divorce. Divorce may be initiated by either partner and is granted upon payment of compensation to the divorced party. The wife keeps the house and the children; other property is divided equally, except for any paddy land that was previously owned by one of the partners.

SOCIALIZATION. There has been little research on traditional Karen childbirth and socialization practices. Karen women fear complications in childbirth, knowing this to be a common cause of death. There are dietary restrictions and other taboos that pregnant women must observe. To ease the birth, midwives cast magical spells and conduct ceremonies to placate spirits. Traditionally a mother sits by the fire for three days after the birth of her child; during this period rituals are held and amulets are used to protect and purify both mother and child. There is a naming ceremony when the child is one month old. Children are taught to emulate the same-sex parent. Young girls and boys both carry water, collect firewood, and care for younger siblings; both transplant rice in paddy fields, although boys do so less frequently than do girls. By puberty children do only the work that is appropriate to their gender. Education for Karen in Burma was formalized in missionary schools, which devised a Karen script based on Burmese and also taught English and Burmese. The Burmese and Thai governments have promoted the establishment of government schools in tribal villages or towns, to which Karen children are sent to live. The Karen National Union runs its own school system in Kawthoolei, where they teach English and Karen.

Sociopolitical Organization

SOCIAL ORGANIZATION. Traditional Karen social organization is based on the residential units of the household, the lineage segment, the village, and the village complex. Several nuclear households are linked together through matrilineal descent and matrilocal residence to form a lineage segment. The village structure forms around one or more lineage segments linked by marriage and/or descent. The village may split, with one or more segments separating to form daughter villages, resulting in a village complex that shares kin and spirit connections. Several more or less related village complexes make up a local subgroup. Each of the four residential units, the household, the lineage segment, the village, and the village complex, performs specific ritual, social, political, or economic functions. Nonresidential matrilineages may crosscut an area. Lineage rites (*oxe chuko* in Sgaw; *oxe pgo* in Pwo) require the presence of all descendants of the matrilineal group (*dopuweh*) regardless of which village they live in; attachment is to the line, not to the locality. Karen society is generally undifferentiated and unstratified, although status is accorded to wealth and age. Wealth is counted in livestock and rice, with elephant owners enjoying the highest status. The young are expected to defer always to elders in the family and to members of the village council of elders, as well as in intervillage and lineage-segment relationships. Karen ethnic identity, despite geographic and ecological diversity, social and cultural differentiation, a large gap between the illiterate and the well-educated elite, and a variety of religions ranging from traditional animism to Buddhism, Protestantism, and Catholicism, seems to maintain itself in the context of dominant social groups.

POLITICAL ORGANIZATION. The village is the most important political unit. It is headed by a chief or headman (*dang khaw* in Pwo) and a council of elders. Chieftainship is hereditary in the male lineal or collateral line. Traditionally the chief had both secular and religious functions, and his authority rested as much on his personal influence as it did on his institutional role. As the spiritual link to the village spirits, he is vested with the power to act on behalf of the village. Kunstadter (1979) has noted the contrast in authority structure between inherently unstable Thai Karen hill villages and long-established, relatively stable valley villages. In the hills, the ambiguity of the

♦ **animism**
A type of religious belief in which the world is made to move and becomes alive because of spiritual (soul) forces in beings and things.

*The most significant
traditional
ceremony among
the Karen is the
propitiation of the
bgha by all
matrilineally
related kin, led by
the eldest and most
senior woman.*

inheritance principle by which authority can be established when there is no clear heir has led to frequent fission of villages. The subsequent rapid dispersal of the Karen population has helped them succeed in their demographic and geographic competition with other highland peoples. In contrast to the autonomy and egalitarian political structure at the traditional village level, Karen have lived for generations under the authority of other peoples: Mon, Shan, Siamese/Thai, Burmese, and British. The institution of the elected or appointed headman, separate from the traditional chief, has been imposed by British, Burmese, Thai, and now Kawthoolei authorities to deal by consensus with the bureaucracies of national or colonial governments. The Free Karen State of Kawthoolei is democratic, with an electoral system consisting of village, township, district, and national representatives.

SOCIAL CONTROL. Traditionally any disputes were solved through the village headman and council of elders. As both spiritual and political leader, the village headman might deal with behavioral problems through social sanctions and/or spirit propitiation. For example, there are strong sanctions against adultery, which is seen as an affront to the Lord of Land and Water; he must be assuaged by ritual sacrifice by the guilty parties, and possibly even their banishment, to avert a natural disaster striking the community. Today traditional village authority exists in the contexts of Thai, Burmese, and Kawthoolei authority, each with its own political and administrative structures to which villagers must respond regarding criminal complaints, taxation, the recording of marriages, births, and deaths, and so on.

CONFLICT. Historically intervillage raids and Karen slave raids into Shan territory were common prior to British intervention. Weapons included spears, swords, guns, and shields. Today the primary conflict, which affects both sides of the Thai-Myanmar border, is the ongoing war between the Burmese military and the Karen National Union.

Religion and Expressive Culture

RELIGIOUS BELIEFS. Indigenous Karen religion is animistic, rooted both in nature and in the ancestral matrilineage. It is based on belief in cosmogonic deities and several important supernatural powers, which are propitiated by specific rituals and ceremonies. This indigenous religious system includes the concepts of k'la (*kala*), or life principle, which is possessed by humans, animals, and some inanimate objects, and *pgho*, an imper-

sonal power. Many Karen in the plains of Burma and in the highlands of Thailand embraced Buddhism through contact with Burman, Mon, Shan, and Thai Buddhists. In 1828 Ko Tha Byu became the first Karen to be converted by Christian missionaries, beginning conversions on a scale unprecedented in Southeast Asia. This is often explained by the striking parallels between Karen cosmogonic myths and the Old Testament. By 1919, 335,000, or 17 percent of Karen in Burma, had become Christian. In some areas Karen religion was syncretic, incorporating Buddhism and/or Christianity into indigenous religious practices. This sometimes took the form of a millennarian cult with a powerful leader and with elements of Karen nationalism envisioning a new order on Earth in which the Karen would be powerful. The data in Thailand indicate that of Pwo Karen, 37.2 percent are animist, 61.1 percent Buddhist, and 1.7 percent Christian; of Sgaw Karen, 42.9 percent are animist, 38.4 percent Buddhist, and 18.3 percent Christian (1977). Although current figures are unavailable for Myanmar, it is estimated that most Pwo and Pa-O Karen practice Buddhism and animism, that many Sgaw Karen are now Christians, mainly Baptist, and that most Kayah are Catholic.

The Karen cosmogonic myth tells of Y'wa, a divine power who created nature, including the first man and woman, and of Mü Kaw li, the basically feminine deity, who in serpent form teaches them their culture, including rice production, the identity of the ancestral spirit (*bgha; ther myng khwae* in Pwo), rites of propitiation of various spirits, and methods for securing k'la. Y'wa gives the Karen a book, the gift of literacy, which they lose; they await its future return in the hands of younger white brothers. The American Baptist missionaries interpreted the myth as referring to the biblical Garden of Eden. They saw Y'wa as the Hebrew Yahweh and Mü Kaw li as Satan, and offered the Christian Bible as the lost book. Bgha, associated mainly with a particular matrilineal ancestor cult, is perhaps the most important supernatural power. The other significant supernatural power, called the "Lord of Land and Water" or "Spirit of the Area" (Thi Kho Chae Kang Kho Chae), protects the well-being of the people in the village with which he is associated. There are also local deities associated with elements of nature such as trees and rivers, or with agriculture (e.g., the rice goddess).

RELIGIOUS PRACTITIONERS. The two major traditional religious practitioners are the village headman, who is the ritual specialist who leads the ceremony to the Lord of Land and Water, and the eldest woman of the senior line of the matrilineage, who officiates at the sacrificial feast for the ancestral spirit, bgha. There are people endowed with pgho, the impersonal supernatural power, including prophets (*wi*) and medicine teachers (*k'thi thra*); some Karen possessing pgho became leaders in syncretic millennial religious movements. There are also witches or "false prophets" (*wi a'bla*) who put their power to evil purposes.

CEREMONIES. The most significant traditional ceremony is probably the propitiation of the bgha by all the matrilineally related kin, led by the eldest and most senior woman. A sacrificial feast is held at least annually to prevent the bgha from consuming the k'la of kin-group members. Iijima suggests this collective ritual expresses the essence of traditional Karen identity. Rites of sacrifice to the local Lord of Land and Water, held each year for territorial protection, are officiated over by the village headman. In addition, agricultural and life-cycle rituals are conducted, local spirits are supplicated with offerings or minor ceremonies, and k'la is secured by ordinary people or specialists.

ARTS. Weaving (discussed above), with embroidery and seed work embellishing many woven garments, is the most notable Karen art. Karen make jewelry from silver, copper, and brass; ornaments of wool or other materials; beads; rattan or lacquered-thread bracelets; and traditionally earplugs of ivory or silver studded with gems. In the Thai hills, males are still tattooed for adornment. Music, both vocal and instrumental, is performed with nearly all traditional religious rituals, and Karen ballads and love songs are sung on many occasions. Karen ceremonial bronze drums, crafted by Shan artisans, are treasured as ritual objects by Karen householders—as well as by art collectors in Bangkok and abroad. Karen Christians have developed music that combines traditional Karen, church, and Western popular music.

MEDICINE. The causes of illness and death are traditionally spiritual. Marlowe notes that for Sgaw Karen, illness is the system through which the spirits of places (*da muxha*) and spirits of the ancestors (*sii kho muu xha*) signal their displeasure or their desire to be fed. K'la can become detached from human bodies during vulnerable times such as sleep or contact with the k'la of a person who has died, and must be ritually secured to the body to avoid illness or even death. Divination using chicken bones, feathers, eggs, or grains of rice is often employed to find the spiritual origin of a dis-

ease. In the case of k'la or soul loss, a shaman may be summoned to perform a soul-calling ceremony. There are rites of propitiation for various nature and ancestor spirits that cause illnesses. Karen also use herbal and animal-derived medicines.

DEATH AND AFTERLIFE. Karen have two categories of death: "natural" death resulting from old age and certain diseases, and "violent" death resulting from accidents, magic, attacks by spirits, childbirth, and murder. Some non-Christian Karen believe in an afterlife in a place of the dead, which has higher and lower realms ruled over by Lord Khu See-du. The k'la leaves the body at death; eventually it will be reincarnated in a proper body but, as a ghost, it can possess the body of another person. In traditional villages family and friends gather to sing eulogies and make music (today this may take the form of amplified pop music) to send off the newly liberated spirit and ensure that it does not remain in the place of the living, thus bringing bad luck. The dead person's possessions, which emanate the owner's k'la, may be removed from the village. The dead body is washed, dressed in the finest clothing, and buried in a coffin or mat. On their return from the burial ground villagers erect obstacles to prevent the k'la of the deceased from following. Animist and Buddhist funerals may be extensive rites involving the slaughter of many animals, whereas Christian funerals are much simpler.

Bibliography

Benedict, Paul (1972). *Sino-Tibetan: A Conspectus.* Cambridge: Cambridge University Press.

Bradley, David (1983). "Identity: The Persistence of Minority Groups." In *Highlanders of Thailand*, edited by John McKinnon and Wanat Bhruksasri, 46–55. Kuala Lumpur: Oxford University Press.

Burling, Robbins (1969). "Proto-Karen: A Reanalysis." *Occasional Papers of the Wolfenden Society in Tibeto-Burman Linguistics*, no. 1:1–116. Ann Arbor, Mich.

Falla, Jonathan (1991). *True Love and Batholomew: Rebels on the Burmese Border.* Cambridge: Cambridge University Press.

Hamilton, James W. (1976). *Pwo Karen: At the Edge of Mountain and Plain.* American Ethnological Society Monographs, no. 60. St. Paul, Minn.: West Publishing.

Hinton, Peter (1979). "The Karen, Millennialism, and the Politics of Accommodation to Lowland States." In *Ethnic Adaptation and Identity: The Karen on the Thai Frontier with Burma*, edited by Charles F. Keyes, 81–98. Philadelphia: Institute for the Study of Human Issues.

♦ **ancestor spirits**
Ghosts of deceased relatives who are believed to have supernatural powers that can influence the lives of the living.

Hinton, Peter (1983). "Do the Karen Really Exist?" In *Highlanders of Thailand*, edited by John McKinnon and Wanat Bhruksasri, 155–168. Kuala Lumpur: Oxford University Press.

Iijima, Shigeru (1979). "Ethnic Identity and Sociocultural Change among Sgaw Karen in Northern Thailand." In *Ethnic Adaptation and Identity: The Karen on the Thai Frontier with Burma*, edited by Charles F. Keyes, 99–118. Philadelphia: Institute for the Study of Human Issues.

Jones, Robert B. (1961). *Karen Linguistic Studies: Description, Comparison, and Texts*. University of California Publications in Linguistics, vol. 25. Berkeley and Los Angeles.

Keyes, Charles F. (1977). *The Golden Peninsula: Culture and Adaptation in Mainland Southeast Asia*. New York: Macmillan.

Keyes, Charles F. (1979). "The Karen in Thai History and the History of the Karen in Thailand." In *Ethnic Adaptation and Identity: The Karen on the Thai Frontier with Burma*, edited by Charles F. Keyes, 25–62. Philadelphia: Institute for the Study of Human Issues.

Klein, Harold (1991). "The Karens of Burma: Their Search for Freedom and Justice." Manuscript.

Kunstadter, Peter (1979). "Ethnic Group, Category, and Identity: Karen in Northern Thailand." In *Ethnic Adaptation and Identity: The Karen on the Thai Frontier with Burma*, edited by Charles F. Keyes, 119–164. Philadelphia: Institute for the Study of Human Issues.

Kunstadter, Peter (1983). "Highland Populations in Northern Thailand." In *Highlanders of Thailand*, edited by John McKinnon and Wanat Bhruksasri, 15–45. Kuala Lumpur: Oxford University Press.

Lehman, F. K. (1979). "Who Are the Karen, and If So, Why? Karen Ethnohistory and a Formal Theory of Ethnicity." In *Ethnic Adaptation and Identity: The Karen on the Thai Frontier with Burma*, edited by Charles F. Keyes, 215–253. Philadelphia: Institute for the Study of Human Issues.

Lewis, Paul, and Elaine Lewis (1984). *Peoples of the Golden Triangle*. London: Thames & Hudson.

Luce, Gordon H. (1959). "Introduction to the Comparative Study of Karen Languages." *Journal of the Burma Research Society* 42(1): 1–18.

Luce, Gordon H. (1959). "Old Kyaukse and the Coming of the Burmans." *Journal of the Burma Research Society* 42(1): 73–109.

Marlowe, David (1979). "In the Mosaic: The Cognitive and Structural Aspects of Karen-Other Relationships." In *Ethnic Adaptation and Identity: The Karen on the Thai Frontier with Burma*, edited by Charles F. Keyes, 165–214. Philadelphia: Institute for the Study of Human Issues.

Marshall, Harry Ignatius (1922). "The Karen People of Burma: A Study in Anthropology and Ethnology." *Ohio State University Bulletin* 26(13).

Matisoff, James (1983). "Linguistic Diversity and Language Contact." In *Highlanders of Thailand*, edited by John McKinnon and Wanat Bhruksasri, 56–86. Kuala Lumpur: Oxford University Press.

Po, San C. (1928). *Burma and the Karens*. London: Elliot Stock.

Rajah, Ananda (1986). "Remaining Karen." Ph.D. dissertation, Australian National University.

Scott, J. George, and J. P. Hardiman (1900). *Gazetteer of Upper Burma and the Shan States*. Pt. 1, vols. 1–2. Rangoon: Government Printing.

Shafer, Robert (1955). "Classification of the Sino-Tibetan Languages." *Word* 11:94–111.

Stern, Theodore (1979). "A People Between: The Pwo Karen of Western Thailand." In *Ethnic Adaptation and Identity: The Karen on the Thai Frontier with Burma*, edited by Charles F. Keyes, 63–80. Philadelphia: Institute for the Study of Human Issues.

—NANCY POLLOCK KHIN

KHMER

Ethonyms: Cambodian, Kampuchean, Khmae

Orientation

IDENTIFICATION. The term "Khmer" designates the dominant ethnic population (and the language) of Cambodia. The term "Cambodian" is also used for inhabitants of the country, including some non-Khmer ethnic groups. Khmer often refer to their nation as *srok khmae*, the country of the Khmer, and to themselves as "Khmae" (Khmer). The English designation "Cambodia" (or French "Cambodge") are Westernized transliterations of Kambuja, a Sanskrit name used by some ancient kingdoms in this region. From 1975 to early 1989 the country was called Kampuchea but was subsequently renamed Cambodia.

LOCATION. Cambodia is situated between approximately 10° and 15° N and 102° and 108° E. The country's interior is largely a lowland plain, rising to low mountains in the southwest and northwest, and high plateaus in the northeast. Running roughly north to south are two major waterways: the Mekong river in the eastern part of the country, and the Tonle Sap, a huge lake and river in the west, the two rivers converging at the capital city of Phnom Penh. Many smaller rivers and streams crosscut the lowlands. The climate is mainly hot and humid, with a rainy season from about June to November.

DEMOGRAPHY. Population figures are only approximations, given the absence of any census since 1962. In 1992 Cambodia had about 8.5 million people, with estimates of population increase ranging from about 1.5 to 3.0 percent per year. The current population is much smaller than it might otherwise have been because of tremendous mortality under conditions of warfare, revolution, and famine between 1969 and 1980. The death rate was particularly high during the Democratic Kampuchean regime between 1975 and 1979, with estimates ranging from one to two million deaths from illness, starvation, or execution. At the time, men had a higher mortality rate than women, thus creating a skewed sex ratio in which females constitute 60–80 percent of the adult population in some communities. Other ethnic groups in Cambodia are Vietnamese, Chinese, the Muslim Cham (also called the Khmer Islam, although their language and religion are distinct from those of the Khmer), and various highland "tribal" groups collectively known as the Khmer Loeu ("up-land Khmer," although their languages and cultures differ from those of the lowland Khmer). All of these minorities comprised about 15 percent of the total population in the early 1970s, but many fled or died during the subsequent turmoil and they are now estimated to be about 10 percent of the total population.

LINGUISTIC AFFILIATION. Khmer belongs to the Mon-Khmer Family that some linguists place within a larger Austroasiatic Language Stock. It is related to the languages of the Mon people in Burma and to a number of other Mon-Khmer-speaking groups in various parts of mainland Southeast Asia and India. Khmer is nontonal and largely disyllabic, and has a special vocabulary to speak to and about royalty and Buddhist monks. The Khmer script is derived from an ancient south Indian writing system.

History and Cultural Relations

The prehistoric origins of the Khmer are not clear. After the first century A.D., complex polities emerged in this region. Ancient Khmer civilization reached a peak during the Angkor period (A.D. 802–1432), when the famous Angkor Wat and other monumental structures were built, and Khmer kings ruled an irrigation-based empire extending beyond the boundaries of present-day Cambodia. Khmer power subsequently declined, and the kingdom was subject to periodic encroachments by the neighboring Thai and Vietnamese. In 1864 Cambodia became a protectorate under French colonial rule, and in 1887 Cambo-

dia, Laos, and Vietnam were designated the Union of French Indochina. After World War II (during which the country was occupied by the Japanese), Cambodia was granted independence from France, in 1953. Until 1970 the country was a constitutional monarchy with a figurehead king and real political power vested in a prime minister, assembly, and ministries. The major political leader during this time was Norodom Sihanouk (who again became head of state in 1991). In 1970 a military coup by Lon Nol overthrew Sihanouk, abolished the monarchy, and established the Khmer Republic. In the early 1970s the country was in turmoil with internal problems, repercussions from the war in Vietnam that precipitated U.S. bombing of Cambodia, and civil war between the government and Communist revolutionaries commonly known as the Khmer Rouge. In 1975 the Khmer Rouge triumphed and renamed the country Democratic Kampuchea (DK). Under the leadership of Pol Pot, the communistic DK regime attempted to restructure Cambodian society and culture radically: it evacuated people from urban centers into rural areas; reorganized the population into communes and work teams with collectivized ownership, production, and distribution; suppressed Buddhism; and imposed harsh living conditions and discipline that led to many deaths from lack of food, exhausting work loads, illness, and executions. In late 1978 the Vietnamese entered Kampuchea to combat DK incursions into Vietnam, and by early 1979 they drove the Khmer Rouge out of the country. The Vietnamese installed a new government, named the People's Republic of Kampuchea (PRK), with Khmer officials and Vietnamese advisers and occupying troops. The Vietnamese advisers and soldiers gradually withdrew, and the country was renamed the State of Cambodia (SOC) in 1989, although it retained officials from the PRK. The PRK/SOC government was opposed by so-called resistance forces composed of three factions: a Sihanouk group; supporters of a former prime minister named Son Sann; and die-hard Khmer Rouge who had fled to the northwest region bordering on Thailand. In late 1991 the contending groups negotiated a political settlement that called for a temporary governing council composed of representatives from the current government and resistance groups, with United Nations peacekeeping forces and teams to supervise eventual open elections. At this time it was not yet clear what the precise nature of the new government would be, though Sihanouk was again recognized as head of state.

♦ **Mon-Khmer**
A language family, formerly called "Kolarian"; its main distribution is throughout Southeast Asia. In India the family is represented by only a number of tribal languages spoken in the east-central parts of the country, notably Santali, Munda, and Oraon.

♦ **Austroasiatic**
A language family, formerly called "Kolarian"; its main distribution is throughout Southeast Asia. In India the family is represented by only a number of tribal languages spoken in the east-central parts of the country, notably Santali, Munda, and Oraon.

Khmer

The term "khmer" designates the dominant ethnic population and language of Cambodia.

♦ **wet rice**
*Varieties of the rice plant (*Oryza sativa*) grown in irrigated fields.*

♦ **collectivization**
*A process by which peasant farms were converted into large-scale, mechanized economic units. The process began in the late 1920s and during the early 1930s resulted in a great loss of life and economic displacement (through famine and deportation). The system of state farms (*sovkhozy*) and collective farms (*kolkhozy*) began to break up in the 1990s.*

Settlements

Village size ranges from a few hundred to over a thousand people. Rural settlements are of three basic types: houses may be strung out in a linear fashion along a roadway or stream, arranged in a relatively compact cluster, or dispersed among rice fields. Among the houses are trees, shrubs, and kitchen gardens, with rice paddies around or alongside the settlement. A community may have its own Buddhist temple compound (*wat*), and possibly a school.

The traditional Khmer-style house is gable-roofed, rectangular, and raised on piles, with access by stairs or ladder. Depending on a family's means, a house may have thatch or wooden walls, a thatch or tile roof, bamboo or wooden floors, and wood or concrete pilings. During the DK period, however, most of the population had to live in small thatch houses built directly on the ground, and many people continue to have such homes because they cannot afford to build houses in the traditional style. The interior of poorer homes is basically an open space with cloth, thatch, or wooden partitions; and there are minimal furnishings apart from wooden platforms used for sitting and sleeping. More prosperous homes have several rooms and more furniture. Kitchens are often partitioned off, although some households cook beside or beneath the house. City dwellers may live in Western-style houses or apartments.

Economy

SUBSISTENCE AND COMMERCIAL ACTIVITIES. Cambodia has a predominantly agricultural economy. Most Khmer are rural peasants with smallholdings who grow wet rice for subsistence and sometimes for sale. River-bank dwellers, however, often emphasize fruit and vegetable production (*chamkar*). Mechanized agriculture is very rare, and cultivation is carried out with relatively simple implements: a metal-tipped wooden plow pulled by draft animals, a hoe, and hand-held sickles. Irrigation systems are not widespread, and most cultivation depends on rainfall. Villagers obtain additional food from trees and kitchen gardens that produce a variety of herbs, vegetables, and fruits (e.g., basil, pepper, beans, cucumbers, sweet potatoes, mangoes, bananas, coconuts, sugar palms, etc.), and from fishing with poles, scoops, or traps in flooded rice paddies or local waterways. (There are also fishing villages along large rivers and Lake Tonle Sap, though the inhabitants may be non-Khmer.) It

should also be noted that villagers are part of a larger market economy requiring money to buy various necessities. They therefore commonly engage in various side pursuits (e.g., temporary menial labor in the city, making palm sugar for sale) to earn cash. Cambodia's main exports are rubber (grown on formerly French plantations), beans, kapok, tobacco, and timber. The most common domestic animals are cattle, water buffalo, pigs, chickens, ducks, dogs, and cats.

INDUSTRIAL ARTS. Most villagers can do basic carpentry and make certain items such as thatch, baskets, and mats. There are also part- or full-time artisans who engage in home production of various goods (e.g., cotton or silk scarves and sarongs, silver objects, pottery, bronzeware, etc.). Industrial manufacturing and processing of goods are very limited.

TRADE. Except for the DK period when money and trade were abolished, there have long been peddlers, shops, and markets in both the countryside and urban centers. The PRK government initially advocated a semisocialist economy, but the SOC has openly espoused a capitalist market system. Prior to 1975 commerce was primarily in the hands of Chinese or Sino-Khmer; at present, there are still Chinese merchants but more Khmer may be moving into trade. Khmer villagers sell surplus produce or vend other items to one another, to itinerant merchants, or in local or urban markets.

DIVISION OF LABOR. While there is some gender division of labor, a number of tasks may be done by either sex. The current shortage of males in the adult population means that women must sometimes undertake activities that were customarily performed by men. Men plow fields, collect sugarpalm liquid, do carpentry, and purchase or sell cattle and chickens. Women sow and transplant rice and have primary responsibility for such domestic activities as cooking, laundry, and child care, although men can also do these if necessary. Women control household finances and handle the sale or purchase of rice, pigs, produce, and other goods.

LAND TENURE. Prior to 1975 most Khmer peasants owned small amounts of land for cultivation; landlessness and absentee landlordism were not widespread but did exist in some regions. During the DK regime, communal ownership replaced private property. In the PRK, after an initial period of partial collectivization, land was redistributed to individuals and private property was formally reinstated in 1989. Land, like other property, is owned by both males and females.

Kinship

KIN GROUPS AND DESCENT. There are no organized kin groups beyond the family, but an individual recognizes a kindred or circle of relatives (*bong p'on*) by blood and marriage on both paternal and maternal sides of the family. Ideally there should be affection and mutual aid among kin; discord between relatives is thought to be punished by ancestral spirits. There is usually considerable interaction among kin, but an individual may have close ties with certain relatives and not others. Descent is bilateral.

KINSHIP TERMINOLOGY. Formal terms of reference for cousins are Eskimo, but terms of address are Hawaiian. Kin terms denote relative age in Ego's generation and distinguish among parents' siblings according to age relative to one's parents. Kin terms are often used to address nonkin of the same or lower social status.

Marriage and Family

MARRIAGE. Marriages are predominantly monogamous. Before 1975 polygyny was legal but not common; it was forbidden by the DK regime and remains so under the present-day government. With the current shortage of males, however, there are reports that some men have multiple if informal "wives." A young man may initiate a marriage proposal by asking his parents to send a go-between to negotiate with a young woman's parents; the woman and her parents may then accept or reject the proposal. In other cases, parents themselves arrange marriages for their children. The groom's family customarily gives a monetary gift to the bride's parents to help defray wedding expenses borne by her family. There are no rules of community endogamy or exogamy, and cousin marriage is permitted. A married couple may live in its own household, with either the wife's or husband's family, or possibly with other relatives. Residence with the wife's family, especially in the early years of marriage, is common but not a strict rule. Choice of residence depends on circumstances, and a couple may shift residence over time as situations change. Divorce can be initiated by either husband or wife on various grounds. Each person takes back whatever individual property was brought to the marriage, while any common property is divided.

DOMESTIC UNIT. Households may be either a nuclear family of parents and unmarried children, or some sort of extended family. The latter is commonly a three-generational unit composed of parents, a married child and his or her spouse and children, but extended families can include various other kin. Because of the high mortality rate during the DK period, during which many families were decimated, present-day households may consist of varying combinations of relatives; there has also been an increase in the number of single-parent families (with usually a widow). Members of a household commonly share work, resources, and produce.

INHERITANCE. Inheritance is bilateral, and transmission of property occurs either at the time a child marries or when parents die. Parents ideally try to give each child some sort of equitable inheritance (whether land, money, or goods), but in practice some children may get more than others because of individual needs or parental favoritism.

SOCIALIZATION. Children have various caretakers in addition to parents: elder siblings, grandparents, and other older relatives. Child rearing is generally permissive. Children are instructed primarily by word and by example, and physical punishment was rare in pre-1975 village life. Youngsters are, however, expected to display proper behavior and learn essential skills as they grow older.

Sociopolitical Organization

In 1992 the State of Cambodia was headed by a president/head of state, a prime minister, a council of ministers, and an elected national assembly.

SOCIAL ORGANIZATION. Pre-1975 Cambodia was hierarchical, although some social mobility was possible. Several socioeconomic strata were differentiated on the basis of relative wealth and prestige: an elite of Khmer aristocrats and high-ranking officials; a middle stratum of urban people in commerce, professions, and white-collar occupations (many of whom were Chinese or Vietnamese); and a bottom layer of peasants and workers. Theravada Buddhist monks constituted a separate social category and received enormous respect. Within a village some families were more prosperous than others, but economic differences were not great. Individuals were given differential prestige and authority based on age, religiosity, or personal qualities. The DK regime attempted to level social classes and create an egalitarian society by making virtually everyone live like peasants, but a new social hierarchy emerged with the DK cadre at the top. After 1979 Cambodia experienced several years of generalized poverty, but recent economic revival is stimulating the reemergence of socioeconomic differentiation.

POLITICAL ORGANIZATION. Cambodia is comprised of eighteen provinces (*khayt*) that are

The Khmer death rate was particularly high during the Democratic Kampuchean regime, with one to two million estimated deaths due to illness, starvation, or execution.

further divided into smaller administrative units of districts (*srok*), subdistricts (*khum*), and finally towns and villages (*phum*). Each province, district, subdistrict, and village has its own administrative personnel who oversee matters concerning the territorial unit and are responsible to the next higher level of government.

SOCIAL CONTROL.   At the community level, social control is maintained through socialization from childhood into norms of proper conduct and through use of informal sanctions such as gossip or ostracism. Individuals seek to avoid the "embarrassment" or "shame" of improper behavior, as well as to earn religious merit by following the major Buddhist rules of conduct (do not lie, steal, drink alcoholic beverages, fornicate, or kill living creatures). Certain kinds of misbehavior are thought to bring punishment from supernatural beings, usually in the form of illness. Although police and law courts exist, many people avoid using them except when absolutely necessary.

CONFLICT.   Within the community, open confrontation between individuals is rare because cultural norms discourage aggressive anger and conflict. On the larger societal level, governments since the time of the ancient kingdoms have maintained military forces to deal with internal unrest and conflict with other polities. Cambodia has experienced several decades of warfare since the late 1960s: repercussions from the war in Vietnam, civil war between government troops and Khmer Rouge Communist rebels in the early 1970s, conflict between DK and Vietnam in the late 1970s, and continued fighting through the 1980s between the government and "resistance forces" consisting mainly of Khmer Rouge.

Religion and Expressive Culture

Theravada Buddhism is the dominant religion of Cambodia, but Khmer religion actually combines Buddhism, animistic beliefs and practices, and elements from Hinduism and Chinese culture into a distinctive blend.

RELIGIOUS BELIEFS.   Theravada was the official state religion from about the fifteenth century. Buddhism and other religions were crushed during the DK period. Buddhist temples were destroyed or desecrated, monks were killed or forced to leave the holy order, and Buddhist observances were forbidden. After 1979 Theravada gradually revived, and it was once again officially recognized by the state in 1989. Relatively few Khmer are Christian. The Cham (Khmer Islam) minority group is Muslim, while the Khmer Loeu or upland tribal peoples traditionally had their own distinctive religions.

KHMER NEW YEAR

A Khmer artist paints decorations for the New Year celebration. There are several annual Buddhist ceremonies, of which the New Year celebration is one of the most important. Soc Trang Province, Vietnam. (Michael Freeman/Corbis)

A variety of supernatural entities populates the universe. These include spirits in the natural environment or certain localities, guardian spirits of houses and animals, ancestral spirits, demon-like beings, ghosts, and others. Some spirits are generally benign and can be helpful if propitiated, but others can cause sickness if they are displeased by lack of respect or by improper behavior.

RELIGIOUS PRACTITIONERS. Each Buddhist temple has resident monks who follow special rules of behavior, conduct religious observances, and are accorded respect as exemplars of the virtuous life. A man can become a monk for a temporary period of time, and prior to 1975 many Khmer males did so at some point in their lives. Some men remain monks permanently. The practice continues, but there are now fewer temples and monks than before 1975. In addition to monks, the *achar* is a sort of lay priest who leads the congregation at temple ceremonies and presides over domestic life-cycle rituals. Other religious specialists deal more with the realm of spirits and magical practices: *kru*, who have special skills such as curing sickness or making protective amulets; mediums (*rup arak*), who communicate with spirits; and sorcerers (*tmop*), who can cause illness or death.

CEREMONIES. There are many annual Buddhist ceremonies, the most important of which are the New Year celebration in April, the Pchum ceremony honoring the dead in September, and Katun festivals to contribute money and goods to the temple and monks. Life-cycle ceremonies marking births, marriages, and deaths are conducted at home. Weddings are particularly festive occasions. There are also rituals connected with healing, propitiation of supernatural spirits, agriculture, and other activities, as well as national observances such as boat races at the Water Festival in Phnom Pehn.

ARTS. Music and dance are important elements of Khmer culture that occur in ordinary village life as well as in formal performances in the city. Traditional instruments include drums, xylophones, and stringed and woodwind instruments, although popular music incorporates Western instruments. There are classical, folk, and social dances, traditional and popular songs, and theater. Literature includes folktales, legends, poetry, religious texts, and dramas. Artistry is also expressed in architecture, sculpture, painting, textiles, metalware, or even the decorations on a rice sickle.

MEDICINE. Illness may be explained and treated according to Western biomedicine, and/or attributed to other causes such as emotional distress or supernatural spirits. Treatment for the latter can include folk medicines, Chinese procedures such as moxibustion, and rituals conducted by kru healers. Traditional and biomedical procedures may be combined to cure illness.

DEATH AND AFTERLIFE. Funerals are one of the two most important life-cycle ceremonies. Cremation is customary and is carried out, along with attendant rituals, as soon as possible after death. Pieces of bone that remain after cremation are put in an urn kept at home or placed in a special structure at the Buddhist temple. According to Buddhist doctrine an individual goes through successive reincarnations, and one's position in the next life will be determined by meritorious and virtuous conduct in this life. Only exceptional persons similar to Buddha might achieve *nirvana* and release from the cycle of reincarnations.

Bibliography

Chandler, David C. (1983). *A History of Cambodia.* Boulder, Colo: Westview Press.

Ebihara, May (1968). *Svay: A Khmer Village in Cambodia.* Ann Arbor, Mich.: University Microfilms.

Ebihara, May (1984). "Revolution and Reformulation in Kampuchean Village Culture." In *The Cambodian Agony*, edited by David Ablin and Marlowe Hood. Armonk, N.Y.: M. E. Sharpe.

Vickery, Michael (1986). *Kampuchea: Politics, Economics, and Society.* London: Frances Pinter; Boulder, Colo.: Lynne Rienner Publishers.

— MAY EBIHARA

KOREAN

Ethonyms: Chosŏn, Han'guk

Orientation

IDENTIFICATION. Because Korea is an ethnically homogeneous nation, there are no ethnonyms per se. There are, however, several alternative names used by outsiders as well as natives, all of which come from the names of previous states or dynasties. The name "Korea" comes from the Koryŏ dynasty (918–1392). "Han'guk" is an abbreviation of "Taehan Min'guk" (Republic of Korea), which is used exclusively by South Koreans. Its origin can be traced to "Taehan Che'guk" (Great Han Empire), the new name of the Yi dynasty (1392–1910) chosen in 1897. "Chosŏn" originated from Old Chosŏn (2333–194 B.C.), the first Korean state that possessed a bronze culture. The Yi dynasty was also named "Chosŏn"

Funerals are one of the two most important life-cycle ceremonies in the Khmer culture.

and North Korea prefixed it for the name of its regime, "Chosŏn Minjuju-ŭi Inmin Konghwa'guk" (Democratic People's Republic of Korea). From "Chosŏn," meaning "morning calm and freshness," Korea acquired the epithet by which it is known, the "land of the morning calm."

LOCATION. The Korean Peninsula and its associated islands lie between 33°06′ and 43°01′ N and between 124°11′ and 131°53′ E. Of the entire peninsula's area of 219,015 square kilometers, South Korea is 98,477 square kilometers, including islands and excluding the 1,262 square kilometers of the Demilitarized Zone (DMZ), about 45 percent of the entire peninsula. Korea is geomorphologically characterized by abundant hills and mountains, which occupy nearly 70 percent of its territory. Low hills, plains, and basins along the rivers are located in the south and the west, whereas the eastern slope is steep with high mountains and without significant rivers and plains. Winter is long, cold, and dry. January is the coldest month, and its average temperatures range from about 2° C in southeastern Korea to about -21° C in parts of the northern mountainous region. Summer is short, hot, and humid, with late monsoon rains. In the hottest month, July, temperatures average between 21° C and 27° C. Annual rainfall varies from year to year, and ranges from 50 centimeters in the northeastern inland region to 140 centimeters on the southern coast. About 70 percent of the annual rainfall occurs from June through September.

DEMOGRAPHY. The population of South Korea has grown rapidly since the birth of the republic in 1948. Accelerating between 1955 and 1966, it reached 29.2 million, with an annual average growth rate of 2.8 percent; but the growth rate declined significantly during the period of 1966 to 1985, falling to an annual average of 1.7 percent. Thereafter, the annual average growth rate was less than 1 percent. As of 1 January 1989, the population of South Korea was slightly over 42.1 million. The population of North Korea for 1989 is unavailable, but it was estimated to be over 21 million in 1987. South Korea's Economic Planning Board estimates that its population will increase to between 46 and 48 million by the end of the twentieth century, with growth rates ranging between 0.9 and 1.2 percent. Since Korea is one of the world's most homogeneous nations ethnically and racially, the population of other national origins is negligible and the legal status of such aliens is mostly temporary. However, as of 1988 nearly 4 million ethnic Koreans live outside the peninsula: 1.7 million in China; 1.2 million in the United States and Canada; 680,000 in Japan; 85,000 in Central and South America; 62,000 in the Middle East; 40,000 in western Europe; 27,000 in other Asian countries; and 25,000 in Africa.

LINGUISTIC AFFILIATION. Although the remote origins of the Korean language are disputed among linguists, it is generally believed that the prototype of the Korean language belongs to the Ural-Altaic Language Group and specifically to the Altaic Language Family, which includes Turkish, Mongolian, Japanese, Korean, and others. Modern Korean is descended from the language of the Silla Kingdom (57 B.C.–A.D. 935). The prolonged political and cultural influence of the Chinese upon Korea had a profound impact upon the written and spoken Korean language, especially from the Confucian classics. The Japanese attempted to stifle the Korean tongue completely toward the end of their colonial rule (1910–1945), but they failed to leave more than a minimum trace of their language on Korean. Prior to the invention of Han'gŭl in 1446, Korean borrowed Chinese characters, using either the sounds or the meanings of certain Chinese characters. Even today, Koreans use Chinese characters alongside their own written language, as the Japanese do. Although the Korean language displays some regional variations both in vocabulary and pronunciation, there are no mutually unintelligible dialects. Variations are recognized between North and South Korea, resulting from a prolonged separation of the two Koreas.

History and Cultural Relations

Recent archaeological evidence has revealed that Paleolithic humans began to inhabit the Korean Peninsula some 40,000 to 50,000 years ago. It is not yet known, however, whether the contemporary Korean people are the descendants of the Paleolithic inhabitants. The Korean people commonly trace their origins to the founding of the state of Old Chosŏn, which arose in the northwestern corner of the peninsula. Several kingdoms and dynasties succeeded it; by the seventh century, the peninsula was united under the Silla Kingdom. The inhabitants of the peninsula have suffered from frequent foreign intruders, and the history of Korea can be told in terms of geopolitical adversities. Because Korea is located in the middle of the Far East, it has always been vulnerable to attacks from neighboring states. In addition to invasion and domination by Chinese dynasties over the centuries, nomadic northern tribes have continually intruded on Korea. The rise and fall of Chinese dynasties has had a profound impact on the security of Korea. Two full-scale Japanese invasions into Korea in the sixteenth century devastated the Korean Yi dynasty. Taewŏn'gun (1821–1898) of the Yi dynasty adopted a policy of isolationism in direct response to Western incursion, but in the mid-nineteenth century Japan, China, Russia, some European nations, and the United States pressured Korea to open its doors to outsiders in the name of modernization. Competing foreigners clashed on Korean soil, which led to the Russo-Japanese War (1904–1905). Victory in this conflict provided Japan with a firm base for sole control of the peninsula, which it annexed in 1910 and maintained as a colony until 1945. Despite persistent foreign threats, invasions, and incursions, the peninsula has been united since the seventh century, except in rare and temporary instances, and has remained undivided, protected on its northern border by two rivers, the Yalu and Tumen.

The peninsula was, however, divided in 1945 along the 38th parallel by the United States and the Soviet Union at the start of the cold war. This division eventually led to the fratricidal Korean War (1950–1953), as a result of which the existing demarcation at the 38th parallel was broadened to form the DMZ. Since the peninsula has been divided, the two Koreas have taken distinctly different paths. Whereas South Korea is evolving into a liberal democracy after years of authoritarian and military rule, North Korea has emerged as a committed Communist society. By 1992, North Korea was one of very few Communist countries remaining in the world. Beginning in 1971, there has been a continuing series of inter-Korea talks, although these discussions have alternated between dialogue and tension. Nevertheless, despite a prolonged division, a civil war, and the differences in ways of life, all Koreans share a strong common belief that they are the same brethren (*tong'jok* and *min'jok*).

Settlements

Before recent economic growth and industrialization accelerated urbanization, most Koreans lived in the countryside. In 1910 when Japan colonized Korea, the urban population of Korea was no more than 3 percent of the total population. Traditionally Korean villages were located along the southern foothills, and many Koreans believed that an ideal site for a house or village must have a hill behind it and a stream in front.

In some villages the population consists solely of members of one lineage; other villages have many different lineages. The size of villages varies, ranging from 10 to 150 households. Most of the housing consists of one-story structures made of stone or homemade bricks. Formerly, some of the houses had thatch roofs, which have been replaced by tile or slate roofs as part of the New Village movement that began in 1970. Traditionally, rooms were heated by the *ondol* method, and hot air from burning wood outdoors warmed the stone floor. Now coal, oil, and electricity are replacing wood.

Rural settlement patterns have been altered significantly by a massive migration from rural to urban to industrialized areas beginning in the mid-1960s. In this period, at least 9 million farmers and their families, nearly a quarter of the total population, are estimated to have left their farms and moved to cities. In 1988, the urban population reached over 78 percent. In mid-1989, the population of Seoul, the capital, was more than 10.5 million, nearly one-fourth of the entire South Korean population, with a population density of 17,365 persons per square kilometer. Construction of large numbers of high-rise apartment complexes in Seoul and other cities has alleviated housing shortages to some extent and has determined the major settlement pattern of urban Korea.

Economy

SUBSISTENCE AND COMMERCIAL ACTIVITIES. Before the 1900s, Koreans lived as subsistence farmers of rice, barley, sorghum, and other crops and satisfied most of their basic needs through their own labor or through barter. Fishery products in the coastal villages were popular. The Japanese introduced some heavy industries, locating them in the north, and improved Korean infrastructure for obvious reasons. In the meantime, the south remained mainly agricultural, with some light industry. Division of the peninsula made it impossible for Koreans to exchange products between northern industries and southern farms. The Korean economy lost its balance.

A drastic transformation of the Korean subsistence economy took place after the mid-1960s as South Korea adopted a policy of economic modernization, emphasizing export-oriented industrialization and growth. A series of five-year economic plans beginning in 1962 has exceeded the goals originally set, and growth rates have been phenomenal. Real growth was 12.5 percent between 1986 and 1988, and 6.5 percent in 1989. South Korea became the world's tenth-largest steel producer by 1989 and began exporting auto-

Despite a prolonged division, a civil war and differences in ways of life, all Koreans share a strong common belief that they are the same brethren.

A drastic transformation of the Korean subsistence economy took place after the mid-1960s as South Korea adopted a policy of economic modernization.

mobiles, ships, electronic goods, textiles, shoes, clothing, and leather products. Because of South Korea's emphasis on industrialization, the relative importance of the agricultural sector has steadily declined. By January 1989, agriculture, fishing, and forestry employed approximately 13 percent of the total industrial work force and generated 10.2 percent of gross domestic product. At the same time, farmers increased their income (by 24.4 percent in 1988) by raising cash crops, thus increasingly becoming commercial farmers.

INDUSTRIAL ARTS. A variety of implements and objects of industrial arts is available. Most popular are manufacturing replicas of the Koryŏ and Yi dynasty celadons. Lacquerware and items with mother-of-pearl inlay are popular. "Knots" with silk thread for accessories are another product, manufactured using ancient arts. Most of these are sold domestically, but some limited quantities are made for export.

TRADE. Since Korea's economic modernization has become oriented toward industrialization and growth, Koreans place a great emphasis on export. Annual trade in 1988 was more than $900 billion, and South Korea became the world's tenth-largest trading nation. Main export items include textiles, clothing, electronic and electric equipment, footwear, machinery, steel, rubber tires and tubes, plywood, and fishing products. Major import items are machinery, electronic and electrical equipment, petroleum and petroleum products, steels, grain, transport equipment, chemicals, timber and pulp, raw cotton, and cereals. South Korea achieved a surplus of more than $4.6 billion in the balance of payment for trade in 1989.

DIVISION OF LABOR. During the Koryŏ and Yi dynasties, until it was outlawed in 1894, division of labor by class was pervasive: *yangban* (nobility), mainly the scholar-officials, were largely exempt from manual labor performed by commoners. Division of labor by gender was also prominent, strongly influenced by Confucian-oriented values: men were primarily responsible for outside labor as providers, whereas women performed domestic tasks. Despite the existence of male preference in many jobs and occupational ranks, the gender gap is narrowing, especially for highly educated women in the cities. Domestic work, however, has continued to be the work of women. In the case of urban working women, their burden has become doubly onerous. In the rural villages an increasing number of women participate in agricultural work, even in the rainfall (nonirrigated) field, which was not the traditional pattern.

LAND TENURE. Traditionally, the king owned all land and granted it to his subjects. Although specific parcels of land tended to remain within the same family from generation to generation (including communal land owned by clans and lineages), land occupancy, use, and ownership patterns were legally ambiguous and widely divergent. The Japanese conducted a comprehensive land survey between 1910 and 1920 as their colonization began, in order to identify landownership. Farmers whose families had farmed the same land for generations but who could not prove ownership to the colonial authorities lost their land. Those farmers either became tenants or were forced to leave the land, emigrating to the cities or overseas. At the time of liberation, almost half (48.9 percent) of farm households were landless tenants, and another 34.6 percent were part-time part-tenants, whereas only 1.4 percent were owner-cultivators. After 1945, the American occupation authorities confiscated and redistributed the land held by the Japanese colonial government, although they allowed Koreans to retain their private property. The South Korean government then carried out a land reform in 1949 whereby Koreans with large landholdings had to divest most of their land to those who actually tilled it. Land reform provided for a more equitable distribution of available land. However, by 1989, more than 30 percent of Korean farmland was cultivated by landless tenants whose numbers were estimated to be 67 percent of the total farm population.

Kinship

KIN GROUPS AND DESCENT. The rule of descent in Korea was and still is patrilineal in principle, although a bilateral trend has begun to emerge. The origin of patrilineal rule may be prehistoric, but it first gained strength through Chinese influence beginning in the first half of the first century B.C. The patrilineal rule of descent gave rise to a number of elaborate kin groups, lineages, and clans. Most lineages and clans maintain written genealogical records following the patrilineal rule. There are over 1,000 clans in Korea, each of which includes scores of lineages. Some genealogies published recently tend to list female members who were already married to members of other clans.

KINSHIP TERMINOLOGY. The influence of Chinese Confucianism has altered the original kinship terminology, especially in kinship nomenclature for reference terms among those of yangban origin. As far as the terms of address for cousins are concerned, Korean kinship can be classified as a modified Hawaiian type, although male paternal parallel cousins are favored over other cousins.

Sociopolitical Organization

SOCIAL ORGANIZATION. When Korea was still a preindustrial and agricultural society, predominant forms of social organization were family- and kinship-centered institutions such as lineages (minimum and maximum) and clans. Kin-based organizations are still present and considered to be important. However, recent industrialization, urbanization, and massive migration have resulted in movement away from lineage- and neighborhood-based social relations toward functionally based relations. Both formal and informal social organizations are formed in factories, shops, and offices. Branches of many multinational organizations are also present. Organizations based on school ties are now pivotal.

POLITICAL ORGANIZATION. Following the division of Korea, South Korea became a democratic republic, whereas North Korea remains a communist dictatorship. South Korea is in its sixth republic. The most recent constitution was approved in October 1987, effective February 1988, and mandates a strong president, elected for one five-year term, and 224 members of the 229–member National Assembly, elected by popular vote for four-year terms. Political parties appoint the remaining officials according to a proportional formula. An independent judicial branch, with the Supreme Court at its apex, administers justice. South Korea has nine provinces, which are divided into counties, cities, townships, towns, and villages, and six provincial-level cities.

MARRIAGE AND FAMILY

Marriage

Traditional marriages were thoroughly arranged, particularly among the noble class as a form of class endogamy. The ideal form of marriage was and is monogamy. Although arranged marriages are still popular in rural villages, an increasing number of educated and urban Koreans choose their own mates. Many of them use a compromise form between arranged marriage and free choice: parents, kin, and friends recommend several candidates equal in their qualifications and leave the final selection to the persons who are going to be married (mat'sŏn). Semiprofessional matchmakers are emerging in the cities; they arrange marriages between children of the newly rich and privileged class, charging high commissions for their services.

The rule of residence used to be patrilocal, but a growing number of young couples practice neolocal residence. Marital bonds have been so strong in the past that divorce was infrequent, even unthinkable. Now the number of divorces among educated, young, urban Koreans is increasing yearly. Divorce no longer carries a stigma, and remarriage does not have many guidelines.

Domestic Unit

In accordance with increasing urbanization and industrialization, the extended family is no longer a domestic unit. The predominant form of household unit, especially in the cities, is the nuclear family, although a transitional form of stem family is also common. The average number of people in households was slightly over 5 in the 1960s and 1970s, but that number had decreased to 4.1 by the mid-1980s.

Inheritance

The rule of inheritance has evolved over a long period of time. Prior to the 1600s, sons and daughters inherited equally, but since the 1800s primogeniture has been the rule, although ultimogeniture occurred in some remote mountain villages. Even after liberation in 1945 and the revision of the civil code in 1977—and despite an effort to upgrade the position of women in inheritance—the current civil code specifies the rule of primogeniture by giving 5 percent more to the eldest son than to other sons and unmarried daughters. A married daughter's share is a quarter of the allotment given to her brothers.

Socialization

In their early years children receive a great deal of affection, indulgence, and nurturing from both parents. Infants and toddlers are seldom separated from their mothers or left unattended. Parents encourage children to be dependent, obedient, and cooperative. They usually introduce prohibitive norms only as the children grow older, and they apply punishments for disobedience rather than wrongdoing. The primary agency for socialization is gradually changing from extended family to nuclear family, thus making parents more influential than grandparents, and prohibitive norms are gradually being replaced by permissive norms. Because of the influence of the Confucian heritage, Koreans have an obsession for education: they value formal education as the single most important factor for individual success and upward mobility. Currently, Korea has six years of compulsory education, and over 93 percent of the population is literate. About 35 percent of the student-age group attended colleges and universities in 1989, one of the world's highest percentages.

SOCIAL CONTROL. Traditionally, any conflict or dispute in a family, a village, or even among villages has been settled mainly by informal control, through the mediation of either heads of households or village elders. However, formal control mechanisms have replaced the informal social controls. In the past, Koreans were reluctant to take their grievances to the courts and even took offense at the idea, but nowadays they are not so averse to the legal process.

CONFLICT. The Korean Peninsula is the only remaining part of the world where a cold war remnant of ideological conflict and tension exists. Although various levels of inter-Korean talks have taken place since 1971, as of 1992 no significant progress has yet been made. Recently, in South Korea, regional conflict and resentment—especially between Chŏlla and Kyŏngsang provinces—have arisen because of the domination of South Korea's politics and business by people from Kyŏngsang Province. The three most recent presidents, all of whom were ex-generals, came from Kyŏngsang Province. The South Korean government has made a conscious effort—including the construction of a new four-lane highway between the two provincial capitals in 1984—to reduce, if not eliminate, a potentially harmful animosity between these regions.

Religion and Expressive Culture

RELIGIOUS BELIEFS. Koreans have been inclusive rather than exclusive in their religious beliefs, and the majority of them have opted for expressing no religious preference. Because of this, it is difficult for anyone to give an accurate religious census of Korea. Polytheistic shamanism and other animistic beliefs appear to be the oldest forms of religion, dating back to prehistoric time. South Korea has a great diversity of religious traditions, including Buddhism, Confucianism, Ch'ŏndogyo, Christianity, and as many as 300 new religious sects. Among the 1985 Korean religious population of 17 million (about 42.6 percent of the total population), over 480,000 (2.8 percent) claimed that they were Confucianists, over 8.07 million (46.9 percent) were Buddhists, more than 8.34 million (48.5 percent) claimed to be Christian (both Roman Catholic and Protestant), and the remaining 310,000 (1.8 percent) belonged to various other religions. Some estimate that by the early 1990s over a quarter of the entire South Korean population was Christian. South Korea has the highest percentage of Christians of any country in East Asia or Southeast Asia with the exception of the Philippines, and the growth rate is unusually high.

RELIGIOUS PRACTITIONERS. Shamanism is performed by shamans, most of whom are women, by holding shamanic ritual, *kut*, in order to gain good fortune for clients, cure illnesses by exorcising evil spirits, or propitiate local or village gods. Shamans formerly were of low social status and were victims of discrimination. Recently, with growing nationalism, the dances, songs, and incantations of kut have been revitalized. Buddhism is experiencing a modernization movement: "mountain Buddhism" is changing toward "community Buddhism," and "temple-centered Buddhism" is turning into "socially relevant Buddhism." Accordingly, the role of monks goes beyond the religious sphere, and their worldly possessions are also modernized. Some clergymen and priests in Christian churches have become outspoken advocates of human rights, critics of the government, and sympathizers with the union movement.

CEREMONIES. Despite the strength of Christianity, most families in South Korea observe the Confucian practice of honoring their dead ancestors on the anniversaries of their death days, New Year's Day, and other holidays such as *hansik* (the 105th day after the winter solstice) and *ch'usŏk* (the fifteenth day of the eighth lunar month). The people conduct rituals and ceremonies in honor of Confucius each spring and autumn at the Confucian shrines. Shamans can hold kut at their clients' request. Buddhists pray day and night on Buddha's birthday, the eighth day of April lunar month, which is often followed by a street parade in the cities; Christians celebrate Christmas Day in their churches. Both of these days are national holidays.

ARTS. Koreans have practiced the arts since prehistoric times, especially painting, sculpture, various handicrafts, and music. The walls of tombs of the Koguryŏ Kingdom (37 B.C.–A.D. 668) revealed multicolor paintings of birds, animals, and human figures. Over the centuries, Chinese art as well as Buddhism and Confucianism have influenced Korean arts: bronze images of Buddha, stone carvings, stone pagodas, and temples are influenced by Buddhism; poetry, calligraphy, and landscape paintings are influenced by Confucianism. There are many unique Korean arts, including folk paintings (*min'hwa*); Koryŏ and Yi dynasty celadons are well known. Because of their fame, many Korean potters were taken back to Japan during the Japanese invasions of Korea in the 1590s. The influence of the Western arts, especially drama, motion pictures, music, and dances, has been pronounced.

MEDICINE. Modern Occidental medicine is the dominant form of medical practice, and since 1991 virtually all South Koreans have had medical insurance. Traditional practice of medicine, however, is not uncommon. Shamanic rituals are performed and herbal remedies are used to cure various illnesses. Shops selling traditional medicines, including ginseng, are common.

DEATH AND AFTERLIFE. Christian ideas of the afterlife involve heaven and hell; reincarnation is the belief of Buddhists. Although Confucian teaching on the afterlife is uncertain and implicit, Koreans who observe ancestor worship believe that death is not a final termination but a transformation. In Korean folk belief, death means a departure from this world to the "otherworld." The otherworld is not necessarily located far away from this world but may be over the mountains. Death is thought to be a rite of passage, and the dead are generally considered to be similar to the living. Elaborate ancestor-worship rites, offering various foods as to a living person, spring out of these beliefs.

Bibliography

Brandt, Vincent S. R. (1971). *A Korean Village: Between Farm and Sea.* Cambridge: Harvard University Press.

Janelli, Roger L., and Dawnhee Yim Janelli (1982). *Ancestor Worship and Korean Society.* Stanford, Calif.: Stanford University Press.

Kendall, Laurel (1985). *Shamans, Housewives, and Other Restless Spirits: Women in Korean Ritual Life.* Honolulu: University of Hawaii Press.

Kim, Choong Soon (1988). *Faithful Endurance: An Ethnography of Korean Family Dispersal.* Tucson: University of Arizona Press.

Kim, Choong Soon (1992). *The Culture of Korean Industry: An Ethnography of Poongsan Corporation.* Tucson: University of Arizona Press.

Sorensen, Clark W. (1988). *Over the Mountains Are Mountains: Korean Peasant Households and Their Adaptations to Rapid Industrialization.* Seattle: University of Washington Press.

—CHOONG SOON KIM

LAO

Ethnyms: Lao Loum, Lao Meui, Lao Neua, Lao Phuan, Lao Yuon

Orientation

IDENTIFICATION. The Lao are a lowland people who speak the Lao language and live in Laos and parts of northeast Thailand. They are predominantly Buddhist, but also respect animist spirits. The traditional Lao name for their country is "Pathet Lao," meaning "the country of the Lao," but this name was also applied to the insurgent Communists during the Second Indochina War. The present name for the country is the Lao People's Democratic Republic.

LOCATION. Laos extends 1,400 kilometers in a northwest-southeast direction between 14° and 23° N and 100° and 108° E. The Lao live primarily in the valleys of the Mekong River and its tributaries, at elevations below 1,000 meters. Northeast Thailand on the right bank of the Mekong is also home to many more Lao than presently live in Laos; they are called Lao (or Thai) Isan after the Thai name for that region. The north and east of Laos is characterized by rugged mountains and narrow valleys, while the terrain close to the Mekong and south of the capital, Vientiane, is more level and more heavily populated. Numerous non-Lao minority groups inhabit the upland areas of Laos throughout the country. The tropical monsoonal climate has three seasons: a warm rainy season lasting from June to November, a cool dry season from December to February, and a hot dry season from March to May.

DEMOGRAPHY. The population of Laos is about 4.2 million, of which about 2 million are Lao. The population density in Laos averages 17 persons per square kilometer. Separate demographic data are not available for the Lao, but national population growth is about 2.9 percent per year, and the crude birth rate is about 47 per thousand. Life expectancy at birth in Laos is about 50 years.

LINGUISTIC AFFILIATION. Lao is included in the Tai Family of languages. Numerous dialects, for the most part mutually comprehensible, are spoken by different subgroups across the country and in northeast Thailand. Lao is a monosyllabic, tonal language, with numerous borrowings from Pali and Sanskrit. Orthography was simplified following the accession of the present government in 1975, and was made completely phonetic. The writing system uses twenty-six consonants and eighteen vowel symbols that can be combined to represent twenty-eight vowel sounds. There are two tone markers.

History and Cultural Relations

Original Lao settlers were part of the overall Tai migrations from southern China, beginning over 2,000 years ago. By the eighth century, Tai groups had settled through much of northern Southeast

The Lao are a lowland people who speak the Lao language and live in Laos and parts of northeast Thailand.

Asia, commonly in semi-independent *muang*, or principalities, each under the leadership of a local lord. Shifting alliances and the rise and fall of petty kingdoms continued until King Fa Ngum first unified a Lao state in 1353, with its capital at Luang Prabang and encompassing all of present-day Laos and northeast Thailand. This kingdom of Lan Sang (Million Elephants) lasted about 200 years, but disintegrated under the Burmese invasions of the late sixteenth century. King Soulingna Vongsa briefly revived the kingdom during the latter half of the seventeenth century, but it again foundered and remained divided variously under Thai, Burmese, and Vietnamese influence and control until the French entered in 1893. French colonial rule served to unify the Lao provinces on the left bank of the Mekong, and reestablished the royal house of Luang Prabang under a French protectorate, but otherwise had little effect on village life. Two major periods of war (the nationalist struggle against the French between 1944 and 1954 and the Second Indochina War between 1956 and 1975) disrupted Lao villages and distorted the development of Lao towns. A Communist government took control of the present area of the Lao People's Democratic Republic in late 1975, ushering in a period of revolutionary enthusiasm, reorganization, out-migration, and consolidation. The mainly subsistence economy of Lao villages continued after 1975, but was modified by government efforts to establish collective work groups and villagewide agricultural cooperatives and to bring education and administrative oversight to rural areas. By the early 1980s the hardships of war and rapid revolutionary transformation had diminished, returning village life to approximately the same level and style as in the early 1960s. In the late 1980s, Laos gradually allowed the entry of foreign businesses and tourists, and took tentative steps toward greater political openness.

Lao and Thai have long been closely aligned culturally, and prior to 1975 the Mekong was more a communication path than a frontier. The absence of good education in Laos prompted many Lao to study in Thailand, and villages in border regions regularly participated in each other's traditional celebrations and festivals. Prior to the 1970s the Lao educational system was based on a French curriculum, and a small Lao elite was educated at French schools elsewhere in Indochina or in France itself.

Settlements

Most Lao live in villages of from ten to several hundred families. Villages are usually of the cluster type, although a number established since 1975 have been laid out in rectangular or linear patterns along a central road or a strip of public land. Few Lao villages include families of other ethnic groups. Houses are made of wood or bamboo and built on stilts above the ground. The grounds under and around the house accommodate a rice granary, family livestock and poultry, vehicles, a kitchen garden, craft equipment, and perhaps a kitchen lean-to. Towns have developed as market and administrative centers, often on the site of old muang capitals. They are ethnically diverse but few have populations over 5,000, except for some provincial capitals.

Economy

SUBSISTENCE AND COMMERCIAL ACTIVITIES. The Lao economy is based on subsistence rice production, usually in paddies, but also in swiddens in hilly areas. The rice-growing season extends from about June through December; dry-season vegetable crops are planted in some areas where water can be carried. A few villages with irrigation systems grow a second rice crop during the dry season. Most rural families have livestock including water buffalo, brahmin cattle, pigs, and poultry. Buffalo are the main source of farm draft power.

INDUSTRIAL ARTS. In the past Lao women wove most of the cloth for their family's clothing, but manufactured clothing is now steadily replacing all but the traditional woman's skirt (*pha sin*). Many villages have artisans such as blacksmiths, carpenters, or boatwrights, who are dependent on farming but practice their specialty when the need arises. Some villages specialize in activities such as pottery, charcoal, or tobacco production.

TRADE. Although most Lao villages have access to market goods, trade is very limited, primarily because roads are poor or nonexistent. Traveling merchants who sold medicines and household goods, and bought farm produce and handicrafts, were strongly discouraged in the first years of the new government but are now reappearing. Rural families can also sell small agricultural surpluses and forest products at district market towns. A state marketing network buys and sells produce and dry goods on an irregular basis.

DIVISION OF LABOR. Different farming and household tasks tend to be assigned to men and women, though the division is not rigid and anyone can perform any task without social disapproval. Women and girls are primarily responsible for cooking, household maintenance, carrying water, and care of small domestic animals. They also transplant rice and weed swidden fields. Men and older boys are primarily responsible for the care of buffalo and oxen, for hunting, and for plowing the paddy or clearing the swidden fields. The oldest working man in the household directs household rice production and represents the family in temple rituals and village councils. Both men and women plant swiddens, harvest, thresh and carry rice, and work in the gardens. Most Lao petty traders have been women.

LAND TENURE. In the past, all land theoretically belonged to the king; now all land belongs to the state. In practice, use rights may be bought and sold, but there is little trade in land. Paddyland holdings are relatively equally distributed, with only a few influential families owning more than 20 hectares prior to 1975. Presently paddy holdings average around 1 hectare per family, with few families controlling more than 3 hectares. Except in urban areas, almost all families have access to some farm land. Swidden fields are used temporarily by farmers who claim no permanent rights to these fields.

Kinship

KIN GROUPS AND DESCENT. Descent is bilateral. Surnames have been adopted only over the last several decades. Wives usually take their husband's last name. Kin groups are defined partly by choice: siblings and immediate maternal and paternal relatives are recognized by everyone, but more distant relatives may be recognized only if the kin relationship has been cultivated. Kinship relationships are recognized and reinforced through sharing of goods and produce, labor reciprocity, and participation in family and religious rituals.

KINSHIP TERMINOLOGY. Kinship terms differentiate by gender, by relative age (e.g., younger brother, older sister), by generation, and by side of the family.

Marriage and Family

MARRIAGE. Marriage partners are not prescribed. Young people often marry cousins or others from their own village. Marriage partners may be proposed either by parents or by the young people, but parents of both families are generally consulted and must approve in order for traditional marriage negotiations to proceed. Bride-price varies greatly, but usually includes gold, one or more animals, and, these days, cash. The marriage ceremony itself takes place at the bride's family home and is a Brahmanic/animist ceremony. Polygyny was practiced but uncommon be-

fore 1975, but has been prohibited by the present government. Divorce is discouraged, though it may be initiated by either party. Initial residence varies, but is usually uxorilocal; patrilocal residence is also common. Most couples establish an independent residence after several years, though there is a strong tendency for the youngest daughter to continue to live with her parents to care for them in their old age.

DOMESTIC UNIT. The domestic unit is usually a nuclear family but may include grandparents and/or siblings or other relatives, often on the wife's side. The average household consists of six to eight persons. Two or more related households may farm together and store their rice in a common granary.

INHERITANCE. The custodial daughter and her in-marrying husband often inherit the house compound and much of the parental paddy land. Other children may receive an inheritance when they marry or leave home, with sons and noncustodial daughters receiving relatively equal shares. The content and the timing of each child's inheritance is determined by the parents. The passing on of house and field ownership to the custodial child and spouse signals the passing of authority to the next generation.

SOCIALIZATION. Children learn by observation and direct instruction. Infants and very young children are indulged; older children are expected to obey their elders and help with family tasks. By age five, girls help with household work; by age nine, boys pasture cattle or buffalo. By adolescence, children can carry out nearly all adult subsistence tasks, at least with supervision. Both boys and girls attend village schools, although usually only a few boys are encouraged to continue their education in the district or provincial capital.

Sociopolitical Organization

SOCIAL ORGANIZATION. Lao society lacks rigid social classes and no longer has a hereditary elite. Buddhist monks and school teachers are accorded respect, as are elders. Socioeconomic stratification is limited, particularly in rural villages where there is little or no occupational differentiation, and is based on wealth, occupation, and age. The household and extended-kin group form the basis for village social organization. Labor exchange groups for farming or other tasks are usually drawn from the entire village, or from the neighborhood, if it is a larger village.

POLITICAL ORGANIZATION. Laos is a Communist state governed by the Lao People's

Most Lao couples establish an independent residence; but the youngest daughter is likely to keep living with her parents to care for them in their old age.

Revolutionary Party through the party's Central Committee and the Council of Ministers. As of 1989 there was no constitution, although People's Assemblies had been elected at the district, province, and national level. Laos is administratively divided into 16 provinces (*khoueng*) and the municipality of Vientiane. Provinces are subdivided into districts (muang), subdistricts (*tasseng*) and villages (*baan*), although the tassengs are beginning to be abolished. Villages are "natural communities." They are governed by a locally elected headman and village council. Muang officials are appointed by the provincial or national government, and are responsible for most administrative duties such as tax collection, school supervision, and agricultural improvement; they are also the main link in communicating policies promulgated by the central government to the village. Budgetary and personnel constraints severely limit the scope of government services. Most villages have at least a one- or two-grade school, but no health services. The level and quality of education increase with proximity to district and provincial towns.

SOCIAL CONTROL. In the village, social control is based on the need to maintain a good reputation in the community. Numerous family economic and life-cycle activities require the sup-

port and cooperation of fellow villagers, which will be withheld from those seen as dishonest, lazy, or uncooperative. In extreme cases, persons have been accused of witchcraft and expelled from a village.

CONFLICT. Whenever possible, open conflict is avoided in Lao society. Intermediaries are used informally to express or resolve discontent. Intervillage conflict is uncommon among Lao villages, but ethnic prejudice has led to disputes between Lao and hill-tribe villages, often over land use and animal grazing. A civil war between leftist and royalist factions continued between 1956 and 1975, and was closely tied to the war in Vietnam.

Religion and Expressive Culture

RELIGIOUS BELIEFS. Most Lao are Theravada Buddhists, but also practice aspects of animist worship. Small numbers have been converted to Christianity. Lao believe in spirits that inhabit certain locations, such as rivers, rice fields, or groves of trees. In addition, villages may have tutelary spirits and there is a goddess of the rice crop. Many of these spirits, especially village spirits and the rice goddess, received regular offerings in the past, but the present government has strongly discouraged such rituals. Malevolent ghosts or other spirits can possess people, and/or cause illness, which must be exorcised by a spirit doctor.

RELIGIOUS PRACTITIONERS. The traditional ideal was for all men to become Buddhist monks for at least a short period. Today only a few choose to be ordained. Monks officiate at cyclical religious ceremonies and festivals, as well as at Buddhist household ceremonies and funerals. Occasionally they become active community leaders. Spirit practitioners are commonly elderly men, and there are mediums of both sexes. Practitioners are called upon to officiate at weddings, birth-related rituals, and numerous informal ceremonies, called *basi* or *sou khouan*, marking such life events as recovery from illness, departure on or return from a journey, or construction of a new home.

CEREMONIES. The Buddhist lunar calendar has a festival (*boun*) at the full moon of almost every month. The most important calendrical ceremonies are Buddha's enlightenment in the sixth month (May), the beginning and end of Lent (July and October), and New Year (15 April). Vientiane celebrates the That Luang festival in November. Families may also sponsor Buddhist ceremonies to bless the house, gain merit, or ordain a

HOLY MEN

Lao Monks leaving Wat Wisunalat, the oldest temple in Luang Prabang. Lao are predominantly Buddhist, but also respect animist spirits. Laos. (Brian Vikander/Corbis)

son. Animist *basi* ceremonies are performed by individual households.

ARTS. Classical music, dance, and literature are strongly influenced by the Hindu epics such as the Rāmāyana, and are similar to Thai and Khmer court forms. One popular form of folk music uses the *khene*, a bamboo-and-reed mouth organ accompanying one or two singers (*mo lam*) who improvise stories, banter, and courting dules. Buddhist temple architecture is characterized by steep tiled roofs, with frescoes and mosaic decorations on the walls depicting events in the Buddha's lives.

MEDICINE. Illness is traditionally ascribed to imbalance of the body's spirits, spirit possession, or simply to change in weather. Western notions of germs and disease are now common, however, and use of patent medicines and antibiotics rivals traditional herbal and spirit cures among families who can afford them.

DEATH AND AFTERLIFE. According to Buddhist belief, death is followed by rebirth in a life appropriate to one's past karma. Following death by natural causes, the body is kept at home for one to three days, during which time villagers come to pay their respects and assist the family of the deceased during a more or less continuous wake. The body is usually cremated, but in some cases may be buried.

Bibliography

Condominas, Georges (1962). *Essai sur la société rurale lao de la région de Vientiane*. Vientiane: Royaume du Laos, Ministère des Affaires Rurales; UNESCO.

Ireson, W. Randall, and Carol J. Ireson (1989). "Laos: Marxism in a Subsistence Rural Economy." *Bulletin of Concerned Asian Scholars* 21 (2–4): 59–75.

Stuart-Fox, Martin (1987). *Laos: Politics, Economy, and Society*. London: Frances Pinter.

—W. RANDALL IRESON AND CAROL IRESON

MAKASSAR

Ethonyms: Macassarese, Makassaren, Makassarese, Mangkasaren

Orientation

IDENTIFICATION. The Makassar live in the southern corner of the southwestern peninsula of Sulawesi (formerly the Celebes), Indonesia. Along with the Bugis, with whom they share many cultural features, they have been famous for centuries as seafaring traders and agents of Islam in the eastern part of the Malay Archipelago. Their name for themselves is "Tu Mangkasara'," meaning "people who behave frankly."

LOCATION. Makassar territory is roughly between 5° and 7° S, and 119°20′ and 120°30′ E, including the island of Salayar. The Makassar inhabit the volcanic mountainous area around Mount Bawakaraeng/Lompobattang, which is traversed by a number of rivers, as well as the coastal plains, where most settlements are inhabited by a mixed Bugis-Makassar population. Except for the areas east of the volcano massif, where rainfalls are more evenly distributed over the year, the rainy season lasts from October to April.

DEMOGRAPHY. The Makassar number about 1.8 million, with an average population density of some 245 persons per square kilometer (excluding the provincial capital Ujung Pandang). The rate of population increase in the rural areas is low today, which results from an increasing migration to the towns as well as from national birth-control projects. Makassar constitute some 72 percent of the population of Ujung Pandang (formerly Makassar), the remainder being composed of ethnic groups from all over Indonesia, including a large number of Chinese.

LINGUISTIC AFFILIATION. Makassar belongs to the West Indonesian Subgroup of the Austronesian Language Family, and is most closely related to Bugis, Mandar, and several Toraja languages. It is subdivided into five mutually intelligible dialects (Lakiung, Bantaeng, Turatea, Selayar, and Konjo, the latter being classified as a separate language by some linguists), of which the "Standard Makassar," the Lakiung dialect, spoken in the western regions, is most widely used (74 percent). There are two speech levels, the higher of which is more complex in regard to morphology and lexicon. Today, few people are capable of using the high variety. The Makassar have a syllabic script comprised of nineteen characters and four additional vowel signs, which was created in the sixteenth century on the basis of Sanskrit writing and is still used, mainly by older people.

History and Cultural Relations

According to written traditions, there were a number of minor Makassar principalities in the fourteenth century. A divine princess (*tumanurung*) is said to have descended from heaven around the year 1400. She is believed to have founded the kingdom of Gowa, which was based upon a confederation of the former minor principalities. Although this and many similar myths

The Makassar live in the southern corner of the southwestern peninsula of Sulawesi, Indonesia.

Makassar

The Makassar have a name for themselves, "Tu Mangkasara," meaning "people who behave frankly."

from South Sulawesi clearly reveal an Indian influence, the impact of Hinduism on Makassar culture was comparatively slight. Among several rival Makassar kingdoms, Gowa became dominant in the sixteenth and seventeenth centuries, exercising political and economic control over the eastern part of the archipelago. Gowa's political structure was strictly hierarchical, with the king presiding over councils of subordinate rulers, ministers, and various other functionaries. Political relations with neighboring kingdoms, including those of the Bugis, were extended through intermarriage among the ruling noble families. In 1669 the Dutch captured the capital of Gowa, but rebellions and piracy continued until 1906, when the colonial troops conquered the interior regions and killed the king of Gowa. Under colonial rule as well as after Indonesia gained independence (1949), nobles were incorporated into the administrative hierarchy. Today many Makassar nobles, who are still regarded by the local population as people of a higher order, occupy prominent governmental positions in the rural regions. In the course of history the Makassar have established colonies along many coasts all over Indonesia. Principal cultural changes were brought about by the spread of Islam (which arrived on the peninsula in 1605), as well as by the growth of the town of Ujung Pandang (during the last decades of our century), where a Western-oriented life-style is now becoming dominant.

Settlements

Whereas settlements in the coastal plains usually consist of several hundred houses, villages in the interior regions are much smaller, containing from 10 to 150 houses. In some cases, the houses are clustered around sacred places; in others, they are built along both sides of a path, with the front gables oriented toward the sacred peaks of Mount Bawakaraeng/Lompobattang. Traditionally, villages were located amid the rice fields and gardens, with an average distance of some 3 kilometers from one settlement to another. In the course of current resettlement projects, many highland villages are being moved to places that are accessible by asphalt roads. In these cases, traditional settlement patterns cannot be maintained. The house is raised on wooden (formerly bamboo) piles. It is rectangular in shape and provided with a gable roof. Partitions of the gable formerly indicated the social status to which the owner belonged. No part of the house is decorated by engravings or anything similar. The interior is divided into a main room, kitchen, and

(mostly only one) sleeping quarter. While formerly up to twenty people resided in a single house, nowadays most houses are inhabited by an average of five persons. Bamboo, as the traditional material for house building, has been largely replaced by wood and corrugated iron, but even in the rural locations an increasing number of houses are built of bricks. This hampers mobility, which was characteristic of the traditional local settlement pattern, since old-style houses could be moved from one place to another within a few hours.

Economy

SUBSISTENCE AND COMMERCIAL ACTIVITIES. While fishing is the basis of the economy along the coasts, the cultivation of rice, which is the staple food, dominates in the interior regions. Wet-rice agriculture is to be found both in the lowlands and in the mountainous regions. In the latter, dry rice, maize, and cassava are also staple crops. Other important crops are coconuts, coffee, bananas, cloves, and many kinds of fruit and vegetable. Agriculture is hardly mechanized, especially in the highlands. Only part of the wet-rice fields are mechanically irrigated, and both plowing and harvesting are done in a traditional fashion. In spite of governmental efforts to increase the production of rice (by introducing new varieties of rice, fertilizers, and pesticides), rice agriculture in the backcountry is predominantly self-sufficient. Coffee is the only product that is considered a cash crop by the peasants in these areas. Domestic animals include water buffalo and cattle (both used to draw the plow), goats, chickens, and dogs. Except for dogs, all domestic animals are eaten, but only on ritual occasions. The ordinary daily diet consists of rice, maize, cassava, vegetables, and dried fish, the latter being available in the markets.

INDUSTRIAL ARTS. The traditional art of weaving is no longer practiced in most regions. House building, basketry, and the production of mats are commonly considered professional activities. Blacksmiths are full-time specialists in most villages, but in general occupy very low social positions. In several places along the coast, traditional boat building has survived despite the recent emergence of motorboats.

TRADE. The Makassar have for centuries been renowned for their skill as traders; seafaring trade is still very important in coastal locations. Markets, spread all over the country, are dominated in most cases by professional traders. For the majority of the population, products such as tobacco, salt, dried fish, and clothes can only be obtained in the market.

DIVISION OF LABOR. In general, the division of labor is strict because of the rigid separation of the sexes in everyday life. According to tradition, home tasks are assigned exclusively to women, and female traders are found in every market. In agriculture, men do the hard work, such as plowing and carrying rice bundles after harvest, and in some regions harvest the rice.

LAND TENURE. Rice fields and gardens that are part of the traditional village territory are individually owned by either men or women. In addition, everyone has the theoretical opportunity to rent or purchase untilled land, which formerly belonged to the nobility, and nowadays is governmental property. Since such land is very expensive to rent or purchase, these modes of extending control over resources are rarely practiced. In some regions most of the land is controlled by rich (mostly noble) patrons, but sharecropping among relatives is practiced everywhere.

Kinship

KIN GROUPS AND DESCENT. Descent is bilateral. The inhabitants of a village or a cluster of neighboring villages consider themselves to belong to a single localized kin group, which according to tradition is endogamous. In practice, however, intermarriage between many villages is the rule, resulting in complex, widespread kin networks. Hence it is really impossible to establish any boundaries between over-lapping kin groups. The proximity or distance of kin relations is defined in terms of an individual's personal kindred (*pammanakang*), which encompasses his or her consanguineal relatives as well as the latters' spouses. Although the definition of a person's kindred is very important for marriage strategy (since marriage taboos are formulated with respect to the pammanakang), the evaluation of social rank depends largely on membership in bilateral descent groups (ramages). The members of any such ramage trace their descent to a real or fictive ancestor through either father or mother. Like the village kin groups, ramages are not localized, but rather comprise countless numbers of individuals who are dispersed all over the country. Distinct terms are only applied to those ramages in which membership entitles one to succession to traditional political offices. Since all ramages are agamous, most individuals are members of two or more descent groups, which in addition are ordered hierarchically. Though descent is traced equally through males and females, patrilateral kin ties are emphasized in regard to succession to an office. On the other hand, there is a tendency to focus on matrilateral relations for the organization of rituals relating to the founding ancestors of a ramage.

KINSHIP TERMINOLOGY. A terminology of the Eskimo type is used. Terminological differentiation of gender is confined to the terms for father, mother, husband, and wife, while in all other cases a "female" or "male" is added to the respective term of reference. Aside from the terms for "younger sibling" and "elder sibling," the age of relatives is sometimes indicated by adding a "young" or "old" to the term of reference. Teknonymy is common, though not the rule.

Marriage and Family

MARRIAGE. In the rural locations, marriage is still arranged exclusively by the parents and/or close relatives, since according to tradition communication between unmarried young people of different sexes is strictly prohibited. Normatively, social strata are endogamous, and the groom's social rank must be higher than or at least equal to the bride's. Marriage between second cousins is preferred among the commoners, while only nobles are allowed to marry a first cousin. The bride-price is divided into "spending money" (*balanja*), which is used by the bride's family to cover the costs of the wedding feast, and a "rank-price" (*sunrang*), which is given to the bride. Both the balanja and the sunrang reflect the bride's social rank. A weak economic position of the groom's family or normative obstacles to marriage often result in elopement. There is no dominant pattern of postmarital residence. Polygyny is confined to wealthy people, because a separate household must be provided for each wife. Traditionally, divorce could be initiated only by the husband, and was fairly rare. By way of contrast, divorce is now more common, and follows Islamic law.

DOMESTIC UNIT. An average household is comprised of a nuclear family as well as close relatives who do not possess a house, in many cases including spouses of adult children. A household is considered a unit consisting of people living and consuming together; the factor of kinship is of secondary importance in this respect.

INHERITANCE. Sons and daughters inherit equally. If the deceased person has no children, his or her property is given to other consanguineal relatives. In case of divorce, children receive the house and the rank-price once given to the mother.

SOCIALIZATION. Children are raised by both parents, elder siblings, and other relatives or

Makassar girls over the age of seven traditionally were forbidden to communicate with male individuals— except for their closest relatives— until they got married.

household members. All adults, elder siblings, and cousins must be respected, and are addressed by honorific terms. Girls over the age of 7 traditionally were forbidden to communicate with male individuals—except for their closest relatives—until they got married. While mobility and bravery are considered important features of male behavior, girls are supposed to occupy balancing positions within the social group. Physical punishment is common.

Sociopolitical Organization

SOCIAL ORGANIZATION. The most important aspect of social organization is the subtle differentiation of social rank. Makassar society is divided into nobility, commoners, and (formerly) slaves. Each of these strata is internally differentiated, with every individual ranked on a continuous social scale. A person's rank is primarily determined by that of his or her ascendants. Since descent is traced bilaterally, the definition of a person's rank depends on the different levels of rank that have been transmitted through either male or female individuals in the ramages of which he or she is a member. Marriage provides the main means for upward mobility, but low descent rank may also be compensated for by bravery, religious or secret knowledge, education, wealth, polite behavior, and (recently) occupation. Hence the boundaries between the main strata and between the various substrata are not as fixed as seems to be indicated by the comparatively few levels of marriage rank-price. Both ramages and village kin groups constitute social units for the worship of ancestors and sacred heirlooms. Owing to the principles of bilateral descent, the composition of these worship communities is flexible.

POLITICAL ORGANIZATION. Traditionally, a kingdom was comprised of several principalities, each of which in turn consisted of a number of vil-

RELIGION AND EXPRESSIVE CULTURE

Religious Beliefs

Islam is the dominant religion, and in the urban context various Muslim brotherhoods are very influential. On the other hand, especially in the backcountry, religious beliefs and rituals are still based largely on traditional concepts. In the traditional religion a number of deities, who are believed to dwell on the peak of the sacred mountain, occupy prominent positions. Soil, plants, and animals are considered the property of supernatural beings, which must be presented with regular offerings. In addition, the souls of the ancestors are believed to exert direct influence on the everyday life of their descendants. Owing to the increasing influence of Islam, syncretistic beliefs now prevail even in remote locations.

Religious Practitioners

In most villages, traditional priests (*sanro or pinati*) still perform various rituals, while Islamic functionaries (*imang*) play significant roles in official religious life. In rural locations, the position of imang is for the most part an honorary office. The imang is called upon to perform marriages, circumcisions, and death rituals, all of which imply elements from both traditional religion and Islam. Divorces in accordance with Islamic law are granted by imangs holding official positions in the local administration.

Ceremonies

Agricultural rituals are still performed in accordance with tradition, while all rites of passage nowadays include Islamic elements. Most significant are rituals centering on sacred heirlooms, which in many cases involve the making or redemption of personal vows. In addition, all periodic Islamic feasts are celebrated.

Arts

Arts play a minor role among the Makassar, and material culture is characterized by extreme plainness. There are a few dances, which now have acquired the status of mere folklore. Most musical instruments that are today considered traditional are of Indian or Arabic origin (boat-lutes, flutes, clarinets, *rebab*, and *gambus*). Elements of old Makassar music are now incorporated into Western-style popular music. Poetry and the recitation of ancient heroic legends are valued highly, although many stylistic peculiarities of the high variety of the Makassar language are liable to vanish soon.

Medicine

In case of illness, seers are commonly consulted. Illness is often attributed to a former vow that has not been redeemed yet, to sorcery and witchcraft, or to malevolent ancestor souls. Since the majority of the population cannot afford consulting a trained physician, traditional healers are still very important even in the urban context.

Death and Afterlife

In the course of the funerary rituals, the soul of the deceased is incorporated into the realm of the supernatural. Whether a soul will be benevolent or malevolent depends mainly on its former owner's behavior during life. Formerly, the community of ancestor souls was considered an integral part of the social group of the living; more recently, notions of hell and paradise (as found in Islam) have gained increasing significance.

lage territories. On each level the political structure was based on a myth, according to which leadership originated from a divine being (the tu-manurung) who, before ascending back to heaven, left an object on earth that was henceforth believed to contain a divine spirit. Such sacred heirlooms (kalompoang) legitimated the political authority of noble rulers (on the levels of kingdoms and principalities) as well as that of commoner village rulers. Both noble and commoner rulers were assisted by various functionaries organized in councils. Nowadays the traditional system has been adapted to the pan-Indonesian administrative structure. In most regions, Makassar nobles hold prominent offices on the administrative levels of kabupaten, kecamatan, and desa, while village rulers were either installed as, or supplanted by, formal village heads. However, kalompoang and informal traditional leaders are still held in high esteem.

SOCIAL CONTROL. The most significant means of maintaining social control is the concept of siri' (shame, honor, self-respect). Anyone seriously offending another person's siri' runs the risk of being killed, without any external authority being involved in the affair. Only in some cases, such as conflict over matters of land tenure or other kinds of property, are leaders requested to settle disputes. In precolonial times, the violation of marriage taboos was punished by drowning.

CONFLICT. Makassar claim to be looking for, rather than avoiding, conflict. Conflict arises quickly over matters of siri', which in particular relates to guarding one's own social rank and esteem, as well as that of one's female relatives. Because the local government and police now exercise control over rural communities, however, there is an increasing tendency to settle disputes peacefully.

Bibliography

Chabot, Hendrik Th. (1950). *Verwantschap, stand en sexe in Zuid-Celebes.* Groningen and Jakarta: J. B. Wolters.

Friedericy, Herman J. (1933). "De standen bij de Boegineezen en Makassaren." *Bijdragen tot de Taal-, Land- en Volkenkunde* 90:447–602.

Rössler, Martin (1987). *Die soziale Realität des Rituals: Kontinuität und Wandel bei den Makassar von Gowa (Süd-Sulawesi/Indonesien).* Berlin: D. Reimer.

Röttger-Rössler, Birgitt (1989). *Rang und Ansehen bei den Makassar von Gowa (Süd-Sulawesi/Indonesien).* Berlin: D. Reimer.

—MARTIN RÖSSLER

MALAY

Ethonyms: Malayan, Malaysian, Melayu

Orientation

Malays live chiefly in peninsular Malaysia, where they are more than half of the population. Malays also live in East Malaysia (Sabah and Sarawak), on the coasts of Sumatra and other islands of Indonesia, extending up to the Sulu Sea of the southern Philippines. The name "Malay" is sometimes used for all of these people and refers to a cultural area called Malaysia, which ranges from southern Thailand to the Sulu Sea. This cultural sense of Malaysia never had any political unity, and "Malaysia" now refers to peninsular Malaysia (West Malaysia) and Sabah and Sarawak (East Malaysia). Malay (Bahasa Melayu) belongs to the Malayo-Polynesian Family of languages, which extend from mainland Southeast Asia to Easter Island in the Pacific. Malay is similar to modern Indonesian to about the degree that British and American English are similar, except that Indonesian shows the effects (both in structure and vocabulary) of long contact with Dutch, while Malay exhibits English influences. Malay is written in a Latin alphabet (Rumi) and a derived Indian script (Jawi).

DEMOGRAPHY. There are more than eight million Malays in Malaysia, about 90 percent of them in peninsular Malaysia. On the peninsula, Malays tend to live in the river delta areas and the wet-rice (padi or sawah) growing regions. Towns and cities have large Chinese and Indian populations. The Malays are clustered on the east coast in the states of Kelantan, Terengganu, and Pahang. Sizable populations of Malays are also found along the west coast, in Johor, and in Singapore. The population density is about 125 persons per square mile, and the rate of increase is about 2.4 percent per year (2.8 percent in East Malaysia).

History and Cultural Relations

Malays were part of the migration southward from Yunnan and eastward from the paninsula to the Pacific islands where Malayo-Polynesian languages still predominate. Malays came in several, probably continuous, waves, pushing aside people who are now the Orang Asli (aboriginals) and the pre-Islamic or proto-Malay. Early Chinese and Indian visitors and voyagers from about 600 B.C. reported on village farming and metalusing settlements of Malays. The earliest historical date on

There are more than eight million Malays in Malaysia.

Malay

Recently there has been a move, especially among the Malay young and those in the university, to return to a more vigorous and purer form of Islam.

the peninsula is about A.D. 1400. The actual history begins with the Malacca Sultanate (1402–1511), although there is mention of Malaya in the maritime empire of Srivijaya that was based on Java about A.D. 700. The trading empire based on control of the Strait of Malacca was the center of the diffusion of Islam throughout Malaysia. This spread, which was led by teachers and sufis, was peaceful. Between the 1500s and the 1800s there were struggles among competing groups such as the Acehnese, the Bugis, and the Minangkabau for dominance on the peninsula, while Melaka struggled with the Dutch and other European powers who sought to straddle the commerce in the strait. The British founded Penang in 1786, then developed Singapore and took over Melaka to form the Straits Settlements; then they intervened on the mainland in the fratricidal wars of the Sultans and formed the Federated Malay States, and in 1909 they merged all of the above with the unfederated states to form Malaya. With the expansion of Western enterprise in tin mining, rubber, and palm plantations, Malaya imported Indian and Chinese populations to form a plural society in which Malays were just under half. With the outbreak of World War II the Japanese occupied Malaya and were expelled with the defeat of the Japanese empire. A twelve-year war called the "emergency" followed, and Malaya received its independence in 1957. For a brief time Singapore was part of the union, but is now independent. A brief war with Indonesia called the "confrontation" settled rival claims on Borneo. Civil unrest caused by communal tensions among the Malays and Chinese ushered in a period of centralized rule from 1969 to 1972, but since then Malaysia has had a working parliamentary system with coalitions among the major communal groups. Malaysia keeps close cultural ties with Indonesia and is taking a larger role in the world of Islam.

Settlements

Malay settlements tend to be strung out along the mouths of rivers, on stretches of beach, or in ribbons along a road or highway. The settlement is a village (*kampung*) made up of various houses, often built on stilts and set among orchard crops, with rice fields outside the bounds of the village. The kampung usually has no public building, unless it has a *surau* (chapel) or a small mosque. Towns and cities are the product of immigrant populations and commercial and administrative activities, with a few cities combining the above with transport centers. Markets are held in the

towns; produce flows in from the countryside via trishaw, boat, truck, bus, and train. In addition to the village patterns there are plantation line settlements. Urbanization and the formation of towns are rapidly increasing, and the cities are the fastest-growing type of settlement in Malaysia.

Economy

Wet-rice growing is the chief occupation of the Malay farmer, now often accomplished with modern irrigation systems that allow double cropping. This crop is consumed within Malaysia. The paddy farmers, who sell their rice in a market economy, are likely to be sharecroppers or tenants, not a rural proletariat. Fishing is the next-largest occupation of Malays, and this too is a small-scale commercial operation. Like most rural dwellers, the Malay peasant is engaged in smallholder rubber tapping, and just under half of the rubber production of Malaysia comes from smallholders rather than from the estates or plantations. Malays are only slightly engaged in tin mining, but they are increasingly involved in factory work and modern occupations, especially on the west coast. They are involved in transportation to and trading in the local *pasar* markets and, increasingly, in government, professional, and town- and urban-based salary occupations. Because paddy farming is a low-paying occupation engaged in virtually by Malays only, Malay income is below that of other ethnic groups; it is government policy to reduce the income differential between Malays on the one hand and Chinese and Indians on the other. Certain Malay arts and crafts still flourish, especially on the east coast with its dense Malay occupation. Batik cloth is woven and dyed, and silver-, brass-, and ironwork are produced and sold. Malaysia has been the fastest-growing economy of mainland Southeast Asia during the 1970s and 1980s.

Kinship

Malay kinship terminology is structured by generation, each generation having its set; by gender, male and female being differentiated within generations; and by seniority, older and younger among siblings and birth order within a family. If other status terms are available, like titles, occupations, pilgrimage or other sorts of *pangkat*, they are preferred over personal names or kin terms. There are no descent groups among the Malay, except for the matrilineages and clans among the Minangkabau of Negri Sembilan, who follow a form of customary law (*adat*) based on matrilineal descent and inheritance; this is different from the rest of the Malays, who follow bilateral norms of inheritance and descent, without formal groups. The heirs, a category called *waris*, are stipulated in Islamic usage, but equal inheritance is followed just as often.

Marriage and Family

Marriage is expected of every adult person in the society. Up to four wives are permitted under Islamic law, but the over-whelming majority of unions are monogamous. Couples are married by registering with a religious official, usually the local imam. A woman needs the consent of a male guardian to marry. Many marriages are arranged, but the consent and knowledge of the parties is sought and required. Marriage takes place after a series of gifts and counter-gifts between the families, including both bride-price and dowry. The public ceremony of marriage often takes the form of a *bersanding*, a kind of copy of a royal Hindu-style wedding. Feasting accompanies this marriage ritual. Divorce is common, simple, and frequent in an individual's life. The high rate of divorce in Kelantan and other Malay states still defies full explanation, but the ease with which a man can sever a marriage by pronouncing a verbal intention to do so must contribute to the high rate of Malay divorce. The nuclear family in neolocal residence is the preferred and most common family form; other forms of compound or extended family are but phases in a domestic cycle culminating with the nuclear family in its own compound. One common feature of Malay family life is the frequency of adoption. Childless couples may ask relatives for the opportunity to bring up one of their children, and this request is rarely refused. Adoption is partly caused by the necessity of having children to participate in the kampung-wide activities of gift exchange and feasting, from which childless couples would be barred. Children are highly valued, permissively indulged when young, but taught the proper elements of deferential behavior and speech as they grow up. A well-socialized child exhibits *budi bahasa*, the language and character of the properly raised, while ill manners are scorned as *kurang ajar*, or lacking education.

Sociopolitical Organization

Malaysia is a constitutional monarchy with a parliamentary system and a prime minister. The parliament has an upper and a lower house, and operates much like the Indian model after which it was fashioned. At the head is a king, however, chosen from the nine hereditary rulers (sultans) and serving for five years. The other two states on the peninsula are headed by governors. Below this national government with its bureaus, departments, military, constabulary, and other agencies, are the state governments with their chief ministers and departments. The day-to-day work of the government as it affects and impinges on the ordinary Malay comes through the district officer and his staff. The district officer has command of regional officers (*penggawas*), and this lowest level of the state civil service is in contact with local kampung headmen (*penghulu*), some of whom are elected, others chosen from above. With all of this formal political organization goes a system of civil courts and Islamic domestic law courts, and a flourishing political culture of competing parties and their branch organizations. Police constables and courts contain and settle disputes, and the various officers of civil government often adjudicate troubles, as does the leader of the congregation (imam). If there is a learned, pious man (*alim*), he will often be called in for advice on amelioration of conflict.

Religion and Expressive Culture

Malays are Muslims, and their Islamic faith is of the Sunni variety. This religion stresses the observance of the five pillars of Islam but also pays attention to the sincerity of belief by enjoining interior states of pious intent called *niat*. In some towns and cities Sufi brotherhoods exist. In the Malay areas of the northeast, much Islamic belief and practice is transmitted in residential boarding schools called *pondok*, under the tutelage of learned *tok guru*. Recently there has been a movement, especially among the young and in the university, to return to a more vigorous and purer form of Islam. This movement is called *dakwah*, from the Arabic word for a "call" back to religion. The compulsory beliefs of Islam include a severe monotheism, angels, judgment day, and Mohammed as the final prophet who received the Quran from God via the angel Gabriel. Malays should make their pilgrimage to Mecca if they are able, and there is always a waiting list of Malay pilgrims seeking passage to Mecca. The ritual calendar is geared to Islamic holidays, and the end of the fasting month of Ramadan sees the major holiday of *hari raya pusa* marked by feasting and visiting among relatives and friends. Underlying Islamic belief and practice are earlier beliefs and practices from Hindu and animistic sources. These *hantu-hantu* (as the spirits, goblins and ghosts of pre- or non-Islamic provenience are called) are mainly to be avoided, overcome, or

♦ **neolocal residence**
The practice of a newly-married couple living apart from the immediate kin of either party.

propitiated, and are not much different from similar power in other cultures of Southeast Asia. The major venue of these spirits and forces is the curing ceremony, where a *bomoh* or *dukun* will undertake to cure a patient by an elaborate trance and body-smoking ritual. The bomoh calls on his familiar spirit from the world of spirits to remove the source of illness from the patient. There is also a large list of Malay poisons and herbal medicines used in treatment by bomohs. Bone-setting is another common form of local medical practice, and midwives still assist in the majority of deliveries.

ARTS. The major form of entertainment is still the *wayang kulit*, the shadow play derived from the Hindu epics. The performance may cover several nights and the puppet master must be paid for his performance, either by a host or by communal contribution. Top-spinning and kite-flying contests are still part of adult entertainment. *Bersilatea*, the Malay form of the martial arts, is enjoying a revival in both the countryside and the cities.

Bibliography

Firth, Raymond (1975). *Malay Fishermen: Their Peasant Economy.* New York: W. Norton & Co.

Ginsburg, Norton, and C. F. Roberts, Jr. (1958). *Malaya.* Seattle: University of Washington Press.

Nash, Manning (1974). *Peasant Citizens: Politics, Religion, and Modernization in Kelantan, Malaysia.* Athens: Ohio University Center for Southeast Asia Studies.

Swift, M. G. (1965). *Malay Peasant Society in Jelebu.* London: Athlone Press.

Wang Gungwu, ed. (1964). *Malaysia: A Survey.* New York: Frederick Praeger.

—MANNING NASH

MINANGKABAU

Ethonym: Menangkabau

Orientation

IDENTIFICATION. The Minangkabau are similar to their neighbors, the Malays, from whom they differ most notably in reckoning descent through females. It is this feature that has attracted the greatest interest of scholars. There are references to the relationships between the two cultures in Minangkabau folklore. For example, the first two Minangkabau persons were Parapatiah (Malay *perpatih*) and Katamangguangan (Malay *temenggong*), corresponding to the terms for systems of customary law governing descent through females (Minangkabau *adaik parapatiah*) and descent through males (Malay *adat temenggong*). The most common folk etymology of "Minangkabau" depends on its resemblance to the words *manang* (victory) and *karbau* (water buffalo). In this explanation, the ethnic name refers to a "buffalo victory" won by clever villagers who selected as their champion an unweaned female calf, armed with a knife on its nose harness, which in its frantic search for nourishment castrated and thereby defeated a champion Javanese bull.

LOCATION. The traditional Minangkabau homeland, West Sumatra Province in Indonesia, is centered on the Padang Highlands (Darek, "land above water"), which are part of a chain of mountains near and parallel to the western coast of Sumatra. Several peaks are more than 3,000 meters in elevation and some are active volcanos. The highlands, in few places more than 60 kilometers from the Indian Ocean, are divided into three territories (*luhat*), each of which is associated with a *rantau* (peripheral area). Additionally the *pasisia* (coastal area) is part of the traditional homeland. Rainfall is adequate for most crops throughout the area. Mountain lakes provide irrigation for wet-rice fields in flat parts of the highlands.

DEMOGRAPHY. There are approximately eight million Minangkabau in Indonesia, about half of them in West Sumatra; 300,000 or more live in Malaysia. Minangkabau have been migrating (*marantau*) to other areas in Indonesia and Malaysia for many centuries. Most large cities thus have sizable Minangkabau communities. Populations in rural areas of the traditional homeland tend to be unbalanced in favor of females and the elderly. Those in urban and rantau areas tend to be unbalanced in favor of males and the young.

LINGUISTIC AFFILIATION. Closely related to Malay, Minangkabau belongs to the Western Group of Austronesian languages.

History and Cultural Relations

According to myth, the first Minangkabau came from the volcanic peak Marapi. In one version, the founders arrived during an immense flood, when the part of the peak above water was no larger than an egg. In another, the founders emerged directly from the crater. Their descendants spread first into the three core areas (*luhak*) in the highlands, and then into the periphery (rantau) of the homeland.

This homeland is bordered by the Batak homeland to the north, the Malay homelands of

♦ **Austronesian languages**
A large group of languages (formerly called "Malayo-Polynesian") including about 450 in Oceania. They are found mostly on the coasts in Melanesia and New Guinea, but otherwise throughout Polynesia and Micronesia.

Riau and Jambi to the east, the Kerintji homeland to the south, and the Indian Ocean to the west. From the thirteenth century onward the Acehnese, whose homeland lies north of that of the Batak, were the dominant sea traders along the west coast of Sumatra. They were a major source of Islamic influence on Minangkabau culture. Minangkabau trade also extended eastward to the Malay-dominated Strait of Malacca. A series of fifth-to-sixteenth century Malay and Javanese trading empires (Melayu, Sri vijaya, Majapahit, and Malacca) strongly influenced the development of Minangkabau society and culture. These empires provided the economic context of Minangkabau emigration, and they provided the cultural inspiration for royal institutions at Pagarruyong, the seat of the Minangkabau king.

According to myth, the first king (Maharajo Dirajo) was a son of Iskandar Zulkarnain (Alexander the Great). Traditional history indicates that a Javanese prince or aristocrat named Adityavarman became the first king, but perhaps as late as the fifteenth century.

Tome Pires of Portugal was, in the sixteenth century, among the first western European travelers to mention the Minangkabau. During the seventeenth century the Dutch traded for gold and black pepper in native ports along the Minangkabau coast. The Dutch East India Company contracted with local rulers for a trade monopoly. By 1641, with the capture of Melaka town, the Dutch dominated much of the trade on the eastern coast of Sumatra as well. Nonetheless, the economy and social structure of Minangkabau society did not change significantly until the nineteenth century, after the Dutch colonial government replaced the Dutch East India Company. The Paderi Wars, a factor spurring development of administrative complexity, began early in the nineteenth century as a local expression of the Wahabi fundamentalist movement in Islam. Initially, the conflict was a Minangkabau affair between adat traditionalists and Islamic fundamentalists; but it developed into an anti-Dutch war, which prompted the development of more comprehensive colonial administration.

Colonial government modified native political structure by defining a new, more elaborate hierarchy of administrative districts and leadership positions, and by adhering strictly to inheritance of offices and ignoring traditional ancillary concerns regarding the size and prosperity of rival kin groups. New civil-service positions and schools that provided the necessary Western education for gaining these positions were opened to the Minangkabau. This produced a new type of Minangkabau elite. Broad economic changes also occurred, beginning in 1847 with the forced delivery of crops for export associated with the development of coffee plantations in the highlands, but changing at the beginning of the twentieth century to rapid expansion of commercial agriculture.

Settlements

The basic territorial units are the traditional *nagari* (village states), about 500 of which now constitute the homeland area. Natural and man-made features of the landscape mark the boundaries between them. Each nagari is a self-sufficient community with agricultural lands, gardens, houses, prayer houses, a mosque, and a community meeting hall. Ordinarily there is a central open market and scattered coffee shops, but no business district as such. Some old long wooden houses are propped high on foundations and have roofs that bow down deeply at mid-length and rise steeply to the gabled ends. There are also other styles of house. Houses line both sides of the roads, which link all houses. Fruit trees of many sorts shade the houses, rice fields lie behind the houses, and fields for dry cultivation are beyond the rice fields.

Economy

SUBSISTENCE AND COMMERCIAL ACTIVITIES. Ecological conditions vary from place to place: well-watered valleys and gentle slopes support wet-rice cultivation; drier hills support commercial crops such as cinnamon, coffee, fruit, and rubber; mountain lakes, rivers, and sea coasts support fishing; forests support collection of wild products; and village compounds support vegetable gardening, crafts, and petty commerce. The economy of each nagari is a particular mixture of these activities. Moreover, the distant rantau communities of emigrants contribute to the economies of their respective home nagari. The coastal towns support business of every sort and scale.

INDUSTRIAL ARTS. Blacksmithing, carpentry, wood carving, weaving, tailoring, jewelry, and pottery are the common industrial arts.

TRADE. Minangkabau men are among the most widely known and active traders in Southeast Asia. Their heavy involvement in trade outside the Minangkabau homeland area is related to the fact that they cannot inherit Minangkabau rice land.

DIVISION OF LABOR. Men's work includes the harvesting of rice, commercial agriculture, fishing, metal- and woodworking, and trade. Women's work includes vegetable gardening, transplanting and weeding of rice fields, preparation of food, care of children and the household, and some crafts such as weaving and pottery.

LAND TENURE. Individual households ordinarily gain use of traditional wet-rice land and house land through matrilineal inheritance. Newly opened land belongs to those who clear it and plant it. It may be sold or inherited as part of a man's personal property; but it becomes traditional land within a few generations, and then its use is based on matrilineal inheritance.

Kinship

KIN GROUPS AND DESCENT. Matrilineal descent groups (*suku*) vary in size and segmentary organization, depending on the vicissitudes of reproductive and economic success over many generations. Some scholars cite myths and terms for groups as evidence of moiety and phratry organization, but these features are not actually present in Minangkabau society. The largest social grouping below the nagari level is the matriclan or suku (quarter), of which there are usually four or more. Matriclans are subdivided into subclans that are also referred to as suku except when distinguishing them from other segmentary levels of organization. In that case, the subclan may be called a

payuang, or "umbrella," in reference to the symbol of office of the elected leader of such a group. Members of the same subclan may not be able to trace genealogical relationships but nonetheless consider themselves close relatives. Each subclan is subdivided into genealogically isolated lineages, for which there is no special term. Lineages are subdivided into lesser units that can be distinguished as *sabuah paruik* or "of one womb." These are the primary corporate landholding units. Finally, the sabuah paruik consists of several small domestic groups called *urang sapariuak* (persons of one cooking pot). Some of these units consist of more than one household. Royal kinship was patrilineal.

KINSHIP TERMINOLOGY. Terminology is generational or Hawaiian in type. However, special terms for mother's brother (*mamak*) and for sister's child (*kamanakan*), and other expressions identifying groups of relatives with common interests in property—*dunsanak sa'iniyek* (relatives with the same remote ancestress), *dunsanak sa'uci* (relatives with the same great-grandmother), and *dunsanak sa'anduang* (relatives with the same grandmother)—clearly indicate the importance of matrilineal descent.

Marriage and Family

MARRIAGE. Members of the same matriclan are not supposed to marry. Cross-cousin marriage is preferred, especially between a woman and her father's sister's son. Residence after marriage is uxorilocal. Polygyny is allowed but is not common. Many marriages simply lapse through desertion. Divorce according to Islamic law is possible.

DOMESTIC UNIT. The core of the traditional domestic unit consists of a woman, her married and unmarried daughters, and her daughters' children. Her adult sons or grandsons who are not yet married sleep in the local prayer house (*surau*); those who are married sleep as guests in the houses of their wives. Her husband is a guest in her house, as are her daughters' husbands. Each married woman has her own room in which to receive her husband. Members and guests of the household socialize and work in a great common room that runs full length through the middle of the traditional house, with rows of bedrooms on either side. As the original family matures and expands, older women without young children move to small houses built near the great house. Such house compounds are heritable property occupied by succeeding generations of women and their families.

NEWLYWEDS

Minangkabau bride and groom. The bride wears an elaborate headdress and the groom wears a songket cloth skullcap. Minangkabau women control the house, and their husbands are considered guests. West Sumatra, Indonesia. (Lindsay Hebberd/Corbis)

Such traditional houses still exist in most nagari, but now they are often outnumbered by smaller and more modern houses occupied by nuclear or stem families in which men are less clearly guests in the houses of their wives. If a man builds a modern house for his wife using his own resources, the house is his until his wife or daughter inherits it. Households in rantau areas also tend to be nuclear or stem families.

INHERITANCE. There are two types of property in traditional law (*adaik*): *harato pancarian* (earned property) and *harato pusako* (ancestral property). Earned property generally involves goods produced for exchange: the means of production are individually owned, and can be inherited by children of either sex. Rules of distribution of such inheritance may be Islamic, in which case male heirs receive full shares and female heirs half shares. Or, traditional rules may be followed, in which case the heirs of males are males and the heirs of females females. Examples of harato include craft goods and newly acquired land.

Ancestral property involves goods produced for immediate consumption and the means of production, which are communally owned and can be inherited only by females. The best example of harato pusako is land for wet-rice production. A right to the use of such land passes from mother to daughters and is closely supervised by the matrilineal group that owns it. Usually this is at the sabuah paruik (sublineage) level, but it might be at higher or lower levels depending on the segmentary structure of the actual kinship group and the number of generations since the acquisition of the land. Also, if there are many heirs and the plot of land is not large, the right to use the land may be rotated year-by-year among the different heirs. The male leaders (mamak, or "mother's brother") of the matrilineal group are the arbiters in matters of inheritance.

Minangkabau distinguish between *harato pusako tinggi* or "high ancestral property" and *harato pusako randah* or "low ancestral property." High ancestral property has been inherited over a period of so many generations that the incident of its initial acquisition has been forgotten, whereas low ancestral property has been inherited for only a few generations, and the incident of its initial acquisition through labor or purchase is still remembered. Low ancestral property is available for use only by the heirs of the ancestress who first acquired it. High ancestral property is available for use by a wider range of members of the corporate landholding group.

The relative importance of these two modes of inheritance, one for earned property and the other for ancestral property, varies from place to place in the Minangkabau area. Nagari in the well-watered plains, in which wet-rice production is the main economic concern, are more involved with ancestral property (harato pusako) and matrilineal law (adaik parapatiah). Those located in the dry hills and in urban areas, where the production of commodities is more important than the production of rice, are more involved with earned property (harato pancarian) and patrilineal law (adat temenggong). Also, patrilineal inheritance is more important among royal and aristocratic families and in communities where fundamentalist Islamic precepts are important.

SOCIALIZATION. Mothers and fathers socialize children. Weaning may be traumatic, but toilet training is not early or harsh. A father helps his children gain an education and he takes a strong interest in helping find appropriate husbands for his daughters. Children also receive the attention of the mother's brother, who as an adult male of the same corporate group has a strong interest in their success. Older siblings are strongly involved in the socialization of their younger siblings.

Sociopolitical Organization

SOCIAL ORGANIZATION. The various lineage groups constitute the main apparatus of social organization. Social and economic class differences based on differential access to property, leadership positions, and education have always existed.

POLITICAL ORGANIZATION. Some loose alliances of the past among groups of nagari were organized into permanent districts for modern administrative purposes. Other modern districts are not based on traditional alliances. West Sumatra is now divided into eight districts (*kabupaten*), which are divided into subdistricts (*kecamatan*), and further into nagari. Also, there are six municipalities (*kota madya*) in the province. Each nagari has a mayor (*wali nagari*) elected by the village council but approved by the *bupati*, who is the government-appointed head of the district. At the village-council level and below are the chiefs (*panghulu*) of the various lineage segments who adjudicate property rights and other matters of traditional law and receive labor service (*serayo*) from other lineage members in return.

SOCIAL CONTROL AND CONFLICT. National police and courts as well as traditional (adaik) and Islamic courts operate. Conflicts in-

The core of the traditional Minangkabau domestic unit consists of a woman, her married and unmarried daughters, and her daughters' children.

volve disputes over property and leadership positions, and differences between religious beliefs and practices of traditional Shafi'i and modern fundamentalists.

Religion and Expressive Culture

RELIGIOUS BELIEFS. Minangkabau are Muslims of the Sunni sect and the Shafi'i school of jurisprudence. The requirements of Islamic faith are simple: confession of faith, five daily prayers, fasting during the month of Ramadan, giving alms, and pilgrimage to Mecca (hajj) if possible. Because Minangkabau are born Muslims, many do not follow all of these practices; nor are they aware of the technical aspects of their religious belief and practice, Sunni or Shafi'i. Most simply follow the practices of their parents. A few individuals know a great deal about Islam, having studied in local *madrasah* schools or with religious scholars who have studied in Mecca or Medina.

RELIGIOUS PRACTITIONERS. Religious officials include the imam (head of the mosque), *khatib* (the preacher), *kadi* (religious judge), and *bilal* (caller to prayer). Additionally, there are *urang siak* and *ulama* (pious persons who know about religion).

CEREMONIES. Important ceremonial occasions include the weekly Friday sermon, beginning and ending the fast each day during the month of Ramadan to honor the Holy Quran, the feast days at the end of Ramadan, the feast days before the month for going on the hajj, the birthday of the Prophet Mohammed, and *khenduri* (ritual feasts) to celebrate any sort of change in social status.

ARTS. Poetry, music, architectural decoration, and portraiture are notable art forms practiced by Minangkabau.

MEDICINE. Herbal remedies (*jamuan*) and word charms (*jampi*) are used.

DEATH AND AFTERLIFE. Death is viewed in Islamic terms and burials are carried out according to Islamic law. Deaths of married persons involve changes in relationships between lineage segments of different clans, which are reflected in the series of funeral ceremonies that occurs after a death.

Bibliography

Chadwick, R. J. (1991). "Matrilineal Inheritance and Migration in a Minangkabau Community." *Indonesia* 51:47–81.

Graves, Elizabeth E. (1981). *The Minangkabau Response to Dutch Colonial Rule in the Nineteenth Cen-*

tury. Monograph Series, Publication no. 60, Cornell Modern Indonesia Project. Ithaca, N.Y.: Cornell University, Southeast Asia Program.

Josselin de Jong, J. P. B. de (1951). *Minangkabau Social Formations: Indonesian Peasants and the World Economy.* Cambridge Studies in Social Anthropology. Cambridge: Cambridge University Press.

Kato, Tsuyoshi (1982). *Matriliny and Migration: Evolving Minangkabau Traditions in Indonesia.* Ithaca, N.Y., and London: Cornell University Press.

Thomas, Lynn L., and Franz von Benda-Beckmann, eds. (1985). *Change and Continuity in Minangkabau: Local, Regional, and Historical Perspectives on West Sumatra.* Monographs in International Studies, Southeast Asia Series, no. 71. Athens: Ohio University Center for International Studies and Center for Southeast Asian Studies.

— RONALD PROVENCHER

SHAN

Ethonyms: Burmese Shan, Chinese Shan, Dai, Hkamti Shan, Ngiaw, Ngio, Pai-I, Tai Khe, Tai Khun, Tai Long, Tai Lu, Tai Mao, Tai Nu, Thai Yai

Orientation

IDENTIFICATION. The people refer to themselves as "Tai," often with a second term identifying their particular Tai group. "Shan" is a Burmese term that Europeans use. The word "Shan," used by colonial writers, refers to any non-Siamese Tai group. Burmese refer to these people as "Shan" and many of these people also use "Shan" as a broad label to refer to themselves and other lowland Tai peoples in Myanmar (Burma), southern China, and northern Thailand. Siamese refer to Shan living in Thailand and in the northern area of the Shan State as "Thai Yai" (big Thai); the people in this area refer to themselves as "Tai Long" (great Tai). Northern Thai refer to Shan as "Ngio" or "Ngiaw," a term Shan find pejorative. Chinese refer to Shan living in southern China as "Dai" or "Pai-I." There are a number of different Tai groups living in this area, including the Tai Lu, similar to the Northern Thai; Tai Mao, similar to the Tai Long, who refer to them as "Tai Nu" (northern Tai) or "Tai Khe" (Chinese Tai). Those in Kengtung, Myanmar, refer to themselves as "Tai Khun."

LOCATION. Shan are widespread in mountain valleys in southern China, eastern Myanmar (the Shan State), and northern Thailand. As in the rest of monsoon Asia, there is a hot dry season

♦ Quran
Divinely inspired holy book of Islam, written down by the Prophet Mohammed at the dictation of the Angel Gabriel in about A.D. 610–630.

from February until June, when the rains begin. These last until October or November, followed by a colder season until February. In the higher elevations of Myanmar and southern China there are frosts.

DEMOGRAPHY. Population estimates are practically meaningless. Reports from Myanmar systematically underreport minority populations; a 1931 British census reported 1.3 million Shan in Burma. Thai census figures do not include a separate Shan figure since most are Thai citizens. The third Chinese national census, in 1982, lists the number of Dai as 839,000.

LINGUISTIC AFFILIATION. Shan speak Thai, linguistically related to Siamese and Lao. Tai Long, Tai Mao, Tai Khun, and Tai Lu all have separate scripts: Tai Long resembles Burmese; Tai Mao, an angular Tai Long; and Tai Khun and Tai Lu, Northern Thai. The scripts were primarily used for religious texts and court chronicles. Most men learned to read and write when they were ordained as novices or monks; some women also learned to read and write.

History and Cultural Relations

Shan migrated from southern China around A.D. 1000, eventually establishing numerous small states in the mountainous region of northern Burma. Shan princes have been involved in the politics of the region, paying tribute to Burma, China, and Chiang Mai at various times. After the British conquest of Burma, most Shan states paid tribute to Burma, although the more easterly states were establishing relationships with Chiang Mai and Central Thailand. At this time there were eighteen major states ruled by princes and twenty-five states ruled by lesser officials. During the British period the Shan states were administered indirectly, through their ruling princes. During this period, borders were drawn administratively separating the Shan in Thailand from those in Burma. At Burmese independence the Shan states were consolidated into the Shan State. Since the 1950s Shan in Burma (now Myanmar) have been engaged in a military struggle to regain control of their area. Their goals range from forming an independent state to being federally associated with a changed Burmese state. Shan in Thai areas are not engaged in this struggle.

Settlements

Shan villages are nucleated settlements ranging from 10 to 500 or more households.

Economy

SUBSISTENCE AND COMMERCIAL ACTIVITIES. The majority of Shan are farmers growing rice to eat and a variety of crops to sell. Ideally Shan grow rice in irrigated fields; however, in areas where there is limited irrigable land, they also slash-and-burn fields to grow hill rice. In Thailand farming is becoming mechanized as people buy small tractors to replace water buffalo and as they use threshing machines for both rice and soybeans. Farming in Myanmar is not mechanized. What cash crops people grow depend on local ecology and the village's location; near towns and larger villages people grow vegetables to sell in the market. Elsewhere, they grow soybeans, peanuts, garlic, onions, sunflowers, pumpkins, sesame, chili peppers, pineapples, bananas, coconuts, and betel nuts.

INDUSTRIAL ARTS. People use bamboo to make a variety of baskets, mats, and handles for knives and other implements. Metal parts such as knife blades are purchased. In Myanmar, Shan make traditional carrying bags, clothes, carvings, and paintings.

TRADE. In the past, Shan men participated in the oxen caravan trade moving industrial goods from India and Burma into northern Thailand. With the development of roads, this caravan trade has disappeared. Now industrial goods move through Thailand into Myanmar in exchange for gems, cattle, and traditional Shan goods. Shan act as wholesalers, moving these goods through northwestern Thailand and eastern Myanmar. In the past, Shan women engaged in more local trade in food and domestic goods. With better transportation, most of this trade has been replaced by markets where women are the retailers.

DIVISION OF LABOR. Men plow and harrow the irrigated fields and women transplant irrigated rice, although occasionally men may help transplant. Men hunt. Women do most of the domestic work such as laundry, cooking, and carrying water. These tasks are often delegated to a competent girl or occasionally to a boy.

LAND TENURE. Hill fields are held in usufruct and not sold. Traditionally irrigated fields were held in usufruct but could be used as security for loans or mortgaged. In Thailand people are now acquiring legal title to their irrigated fields, gardens, and house sites.

Kinship

KIN GROUPS AND DESCENT. Descent is bilateral. Kinship is not an organizing principle in

The Shan world is populated with beings ranked on a continuum of power, with human beings falling somewhere near the middle.

♦ **usufruct**
The right to use land or property without actually owning it.

Shan

Shan society; people recognize a wide range of others who are their kin and those who behave toward them as if they were kin.

KINSHIP TERMINOLOGY. Kin terms distinguish relative age and sex with different terms for older/younger siblings and older/younger siblings of one's mother or father. Kin terms are used primarily as terms of address because Shan do not refer to people by their name without an address term or title. Even when using titles such as "teacher" or "ex-monk," a kin term precedes it.

Marriage and Family

MARRIAGE. There are no preferred marriage partners. With the restriction that children of siblings are considered too closely related to marry, choice of marriage partner is left to the individual. Once a marriage partner is chosen and meets with parental approval, the parents negotiate the gifts from the groom's side to the bride and the contributions from the bride's side. If the match does not meet with parental approval the couple may elope, although this usually entails smaller exchanges. Postmarital residence is usually initially with the wife's household, although this arrangement is negotiable; after a period of time, the couple establishes an independent household. Divorce is easy; the couple separates and divides any common property. If there are children, older relatives may encourage the couple to settle their disputes. Children may choose to live with either parent or some other relative.

DOMESTIC UNIT. A household consists of the people who live, work, and eat together, minimally a couple and their children. Occasionally one person or a divorced or widowed spouse and his or her children will maintain an independent household. Households may also contain grandparents, married children, and distant relatives. Unlike among Northern Thai, there is no restriction on more than one married couple living in the same household.

INHERITANCE. Inheritance is bilateral; half siblings have shares in their parent's property and in property their parent helped develop.

SOCIALIZATION. Children are taken care of by their parents and other relatives. Small children are indulged and humored but are taught early to share with younger children. Once they reach age 6 or 7 they are expected to understand and do what they are told. Children are allowed to play together without adult supervision, although if there is fighting adults quickly break it up. Both boys and girls take early responsibility for washing their own clothes, but girls are likely to have more domestic chores.

Religion and Expressive Culture

RELIGIOUS BELIEFS. In some characterizations of Theravada Buddhism, Shan beliefs and practices may be considered unorthodox. Nevertheless, Shan identify themselves as Theravada Buddhists. By so doing, they classify themselves with other lowland groups and distinguish themselves from upland "tribal" peoples. Although they are Buddhist, the worldview of the Shan centers on the idea of "power protection" and its unequal distribution. Power protects people from the con-

SOCIOPOLITICAL ORGANIZATION

Social Organization

Shan social organization is inherently hierarchical, based on age, gender, and wealth.

Political Organization

Traditionally Shan were members of numerous small states ruled by princes having relationships with China, Burma, and northern Thailand. Other lower-ranking officials dealt with clusters of villages and individual villages. Government officials were viewed as one of the five natural disasters. Shan villages in Thailand are administered as is the rest of Thailand, with elected village headmen and village-cluster headmen responsible to an appointed district officer. Shan in China are administered as a minority group in an autonomous region.

Social Control

Within communities, gossip and the desire to maintain a good reputation are important means of maintaining order. If there are fights or thefts people may appeal to the police.

Conflict

In the precolonial period Shan fought with Burmese, other Shan, Chinese, Northern Thai, and other neighboring groups in succession disputes and assorted alliances. Now Shan in Myanmar are actively in conflict with the Burmese, the national Communist party, and, occasionally, other Shan groups.

sequences of their actions, allowing them to behave as they choose. Because more powerful beings exist and may behave capriciously, people need to enter into a relationship with more powerful others for their own protection. One gains power protection through the practice of restraint or relying on the protection of more powerful others. Buddhas and Buddhist monks are the most powerful beings. Powerful beings associated with Buddhism are more reliably benevolent while others, such as government officials or spirits, are less likely to be benevolent. The world is populated with beings ranked on a continuum of power, with human beings falling somewhere near the middle. Beings with more power than humans include Buddhas, cadastral spirits of the village, and spirits associated with fields, households, and the forest. Beings less powerful than humans, although still dangerous, include spirits that arose from violent deaths or from women dying in childbirth and disease spirits. People, rice, and water buffalo have spirits whose loss causes illness or death.

RELIGIOUS PRACTITIONERS. There are Buddhist monks, novices, and nuns; temple lay readers; traditional curers; and caretakers of the cadastral-spirit altar. All except the caretaker of the cadastral-spirit altar draw on the power associated with Buddhism. The traditional curer's ability to cure comes from his keeping of precepts, his practice of restraint, and his reliance on his teachers and on the Buddhas.

CEREMONIES. The Buddhist lunar calendar structures the ceremonial cycle with four holy days each month falling on the days of full, dark, and half-moons. There are temple festivals celebrating events in the Buddha's life, such as the anniversaries of his birth, his enlightenment, his first sermon, and his death; other festivals entail the construction of sand pagodas, and the firing of rockets before or after the rainy season and to honor the end of the retreat during the three months of rain. Wealthy villages and temples celebrate more of these events than do poorer ones. However, all villages at least hold a festival after the end of the rains' retreat. Once a year villages as a whole invite monks to chant to remove misfortune and to renew the village and its constituent households' barriers against misfortune. The village cadastral spirit is also feasted at least once a year. Households may sponsor a range of ceremonies including Buddhist ordinations, funerals, merit making for the dead, marriages, first bathing ceremonies for infants, and invitations for monks to chant in the house.

ARTS. Mostly these are impermanent decorations such as carved and decorated fruit offered to the Buddha image or monks and elaborately decorated coffin carriers, money trees, and pagodas celebrating the end of the rains' retreat. In Myanmar, Shan still weave traditional shoulder bags and carve small objects such as Buddha images from marble and jade. Shan in Chiang Mai were known for their silverwork.

MEDICINE. Shan accept and use Western medicine where available and when the ailment responds to such treatment. They also use the four elements—earth, water, wind, and fire—together with hot and cold to diagnose and treat illness. Buddhist verses are important in curing, either being blown over the patient or recited over water for the patient to drink.

DEATH AND AFTERLIFE. Funerals occur three to seven days after death. In Thailand everyone is cremated, although in the recent past people dying "bad deaths" were buried. Shan in Myanmar and China still bury people who die a "bad death." Buddhist monks officiate at funerals; Shan believe that only monks can transfer merit from the living to the dead. After a short period, during which the spirit may remain waiting for people to make merit for it, it is reborn.

Bibliography

Durrenberger, E. Paul (1981). "The Southeast Asian Context of Theravada Buddhism." *Anthropology* 5: 45–62.

Durrenberger, E. Paul, and Nicola Tannenbaum (1989). *Analytical Perspectives on Shan Agriculture and Village Economics.* Yale University Southeast Asian Studies Monograph Series, no. 37. New Haven.

Mangrai, Sao Saimong (1965). *The Shan States and the British Annexation.* Cornell University Southeast Asia Program, Data Paper no. 57. Ithaca, N.Y.

Tannenbaum, Nicola (1987). "Tattoos: Invulnerability and Power in Shan Cosmology." *American Ethnologist* 14:693–711.

Tannenbaum, Nicola (1989). "Power and Its Shan Transformation." In *Ritual, Power, and Economy: Upland-Lowland Contrasts in Mainland Southeast Asia*, edited by Susan D. Russell, 67–88. Occasional Paper no. 14. DeKalb: Northern Illinois University, Center for Southeast Asian Studies.

Yangwhe, Chao Tzang {Eugene Thaike} (1987). *The Shan of Burma: Memoirs of a Shan Exile, Local History and Memoirs.* Singapore: Institute of Southeast Asian Studies.

—NICOLA TANNENBAUM

The Shan identify themselves as Theravada Buddhists.

The usual derivation of the name "Tagalog" is from taga ilog, *meaning "inhabitants of the river."*

♦ **Neolithic period**
A stage in the development of human culture characterized by the use of polished or ground stone tools. It follows the Paleolithic period and precedes the Bronze Age.

See also

Filipino

TAGALOG

Ethnonym: Pilipino (also Wikang Pambansa—"national language")

Orientation

IDENTIFICATION. The Tagalog language is the basis of Pilipino, the national language of the Republic of the Philippines since 1937, and has been taught from the first grade throughout the archipelago since the early 1950s. Thus most Filipinos (60–70 million) under the age of 50 speak, read, and write Tagalog as at least a second language, while some 10 to 15 percent (perhaps 10 million) have learned it as their first language. This article deals only with the latter group. The usual derivation of the name "Tagalog" is from *taga ilog*, meaning "inhabitants of the river."

LOCATION. The Tagalog-speaking area is oriented toward Manila Bay and is concentrated mostly within 80 to 320 kilometers of the megalopolis of Manila on the island of Luzon. It lies within the Tropic of Cancer from 10° to 16° N and from 119° to 123° E. It consists of the provinces of Bataan, Bulacan, Rizal, Cavite, Batangas, Laguna, Quezon, parts of Nueva Ecija and Camarines Norte, Marinduque, Polillio, parts of Mindoro and Palawan, and many smaller islands. The topography includes mountains up to 2,000 meters and uplands with tropical rain forest cover as well as a wide range of lowland coastal and inland environments. Monsoon seasons vary from location to location, and there are dramatic differences in annual rainfall (152 to 457 centimeters) and length of wet and dry periods. Typhoons, earthquakes, volcanic eruptions, droughts, floods, and malarial vectors form ever-present threats for the people of the area.

DEMOGRAPHY. As of 1991 the population in this "heartland" of the Tagalog area (Katagalugan) was over 10.9 million in approximately 23,920 square kilometers (325 persons per square kilometer). Probably another 100,000 people whose first language is Tagalog live elsewhere in the Philippines and abroad.

LINGUISTIC AFFILIATION. Tagalog belongs to the Malayan Branch of the Austronesian Phylum. The dialect of Tagalog spoken in Manila is often called "Taglish" because of the high percentage of American English words.

History and Cultural Relations

Tagalog civilization has been a distinctive configuration for at least one thousand years, subject to the various cultural influences operative in mainland and insular Southeast Asia since the Neolithic period. Long before the Spanish began colonization in the last half of the sixteenth century, Tagalog society on Luzon was organized in loose "confederations" of local groupings sometimes called "kingdoms." In general, Tagalogs had a system of writing (a syllabary derived from Sanskrit), an advanced technology including metallurgy, a complicated social system with hierarchical classes (including a category of individuals termed "slaves" by early Spanish sources), and religious patterns that varied regionally. The Indonesian empires of Sri Vijaya and Majapahit left their imprint on language, religion, and technology—through both trade and settlement. The Chinese for centuries used ports along the western coast of Luzon as stopping points in their trade with the Spice Islands to the south and local trading centers. Islamic sultanates had been established around Manila Bay not long before the Spanish began almost 350 years of occupation in the middle of the sixteenth century. During the seventeenth and eighteenth centuries Manila was one of the major seaports of the world as the transshipment point in the famous Manila galleon trade that exchanged silver from Mexico for silks and other luxury wares of China. By the middle of the nineteenth century, strong resistance to Spanish rule had developed in the Philippines, especially in the Tagalog area, which produced the national heroes José Rizal, Andres Bonifacio, and Emiliano Aguinaldo. Before Americans came to the Philippines during the Spanish-American War in 1898 there was a full-scale insurrection in process, which continued against the American occupation until 1902. The first Republic of the Philippines was established during this time at the Barasoin Church in Malolos, Bulacan, 48 kilometers northwest of Manila, in the midst of what is considered the land of the deepest (*malalim*) and purest dialect of Tagalog. American colonial control officially lasted almost fifty years. During World War II, the battles of Bataan and Corregidor, as well as the Death March, occurred in the Tagalog area. Independence was granted in 1946 after a three-year occupation by the Japanese. Until 1952 the insurgent Hukbalahap army waged some of its most intensive battles against the new Republic of the Philippines in the Tagalog provinces. Recently the American presence and influence have lessened, with Japan, Australia, New Zealand, and European countries becoming important economically and technologically. In the early Spanish period most of the people of the Philippines were called "Moros" and later "Indios." The term "Filipino" then referred to persons of Spanish descent born there.

Settlements

In lowlands where irrigated rice was the basis of subsistence, settlements were distributed along waterways before the introduction of highways and railroads during the Spanish period. As this network of roads and railroads expanded, housing was extended along them even in upland areas where houses were usually dispersed in clusters oriented to land-holdings and water supply. In both areas larger settlements served as markets and religious centers. Coastal settlements were clusters near sources of fresh water. Nonunilineal kinship ties were, and still are, foci for neighborhood and community. With the introduction of Roman Catholicism under the Spanish, the settlements became centralized around a church, chapel, or shrine (possibly continuing pre-Spanish patterns). By the beginning of the nineteenth century the larger settlements had complex central plazas with concentrations of population. Manila and several of the provincial capitals developed into urban centers. The houses have been of two major types: movable and nonmovable. Movable houses were built on stilts of bamboo and wood with thatch or metal roofs. Until recently, masonry houses were built mostly in the towns and cities. Manila and the other urban centers of the Tagalog area are rapidly becoming truly metropolitan districts. Manila, though an integral part of Tagalog society, is also a nexus for integration of almost all segments of the nation.

Economy

SUBSISTENCE AND COMMERCIAL ACTIVITIES. There have been extensive changes in rural areas since independence, brought on by improved communication, roads, and expansion of electrical power resources. There are several distinct types of land use. North of Manila, the Tagalog provinces form the southern edge of the "rice bowl" of the Philippines. South and west of Manila the provinces of Cavite and Batangas form a predominantly upland dry-farming and fruit-producing region. The latter is noted for its peddlers, who have traditionally roved the length and breadth of Luzon. To the south and east is a mixed region of sugarcane, coconuts, and terraced rice. In many areas mechanization is replacing water buffalo, horses, and oxen. Fishing, both deep-water and riverine, is important wherever possible. There is an almost unending inventory of local enterprises, including production of salt, vinegar, hard-boiled and fertilized duck eggs (*balut*, a national delicacy), alcoholic beverages, clothing and mosquito netting, implements, and containers. Commercial activities on a large scale take place mostly in Manila, but there are regional centers for the commercial processing of copra, sugarcane, and other products. Rice is a basic commodity around which life is oriented. Many Tagalog families living in Manila or other nonagricultural areas usually have ties to one or more rural communities within commuting distance and receive a share of crops raised by their relatives or tenants.

INDUSTRIAL ARTS. For centuries even remote communities have been part of networks of trade because people depended on the markets for things they could not make for themselves. There have been, however, certain regional specialties, for example the famous *balisong*, a collapsible pocket knife made in the province of Batangas, and the wood carving of the towns of Laguna Province, just south of Manila.

TRADE. The ancient, highly developed, and fascinating market system connects local networks to Manila and its international port. A crucial commercial relationship is the institution of the *suki*, a self-reciprocal term referring to the tie between a seller and a regular customer. Overseas Chinese have been important in trade and financial institutions over the centuries.

DIVISION OF LABOR. Division of labor (*hanapbuhay*, occupation) by gender is highly variable. Both men and women hold professional positions in medicine, law, education, and politics. Traditionally, men in lowland rice areas were responsible for the care of irrigation systems, preparation of fields, and heavier work (although women could participate). Teenaged women under the supervision of an older woman planted, and everyone harvested. In some upland areas, however, planting and harvesting were not divided so specifically. New methods of rice production are bringing about changes in all of this. Sugarcane production is usually a commercial enterprise requiring seasonally determined wage labor. Copra production, intensive fishing, and fish-pond management are predominantly male occupations. In general, division of labor within the family is highly contingent; either gender can be called upon for both household duties and economic activities. Women often control family finances and enterprises.

LAND TENURE. Patterns of ownership and rights to the use of land are also variable. In pre-

For centuries even remote Tagalog communities have been part of networks of trade, because people depended on markets for things they could not make for themselves.

Tagalog kinship is extended as far as can be determined; strangers often begin interaction by comparing names of relatives to see if there are any ties.

Spanish times usufruct operated in both lowland and upland areas because both paddies and swiddens were prepared on new land. During the Spanish period, with its imposed regulations and land grants, large areas of land came under the ownership of a relatively few Tagalog and non-Tagalog families and the various religious orders. Thus most Tagalogs came to live on land that belonged to someone else and worked the land either as tenants or as paid laborers. Frequently, the tenancy rights were inherited according to local custom within interrelated extended families. Cadastral surveys over the years have established legal boundaries, often with permanent markers. Since the early twentieth century, legislation has slowly caused division of some large holdings. Further, in some regions tenants have been able to buy the land, often renting it as a tenancy to others.

Kinship

KIN GROUPS AND DESCENT. The basic unit is the sibling group, *kamagkapatid* (*kapatid* = sibling). Usually there are terms for firstborn and lastborn: *panganay* and *bunso*. In some communities and families, terms borrowed from Chinese are used for numerical order of birth. Each marriage produces a nuclear family, *kamaganakan* (*anak* = child), which is part of a bilaterally extended family with genealogical ties traced from specific ancestors (or sibling groups). Extended families are further affiliated in complex webs of obligation and rights (reckoned polylineally) through ties of marriage into a grouping sometimes called the *angkan* or *pamilia* and identified by patrilineal inheritance of surnames, which can be retained by women after marriage. The angkan may be a fairly definite unit, but more often it is similar to the U.S. pattern called the "family of the Smiths, Jones, etc." Kinship is extended as far as can be determined, so that strangers often begin interaction by comparing names of relatives to see if there are any ties. Affinity and ritual kinship are strongly embedded in the formation and recognition of wider relationships between individuals and families. Relationships, though dependent on genealogical and ritual ties, are continually instigated, maintained, and strengthened by proper behavior on the part of individuals showing acceptance of obligation and responsibility. This reciprocity is most often expressed by the term *utang na loob*, or debt (*utang*) of volition-free will (*na loob*). Some analysts have emphasized the other meaning of *loob*, "inside" (as opposed to *labas*, "outside"), which signifies a recognition that two individuals fall within the same network of inherited obligation. Utang na loob is initially produced by an unsolicited "gift," which creates or increases obligation within the receiver. The greatest obligation is to God and parents, who give life to the individual. Kinship relations are extended to nonrelatives or intensified between relatives through ritual sponsorship of individuals at baptism (*binyag*), confirmation (*kumpil*), and marriage (*kasal*).

KINSHIP TERMINOLOGY. Referential and vocative terminologies including alternatives are mixtures of Tagalog, Spanish, and Chinese and vary from area to area. Referential terminology is very close to "Yankee" or Eskimo, while vocatively it can be more Hawaiian. There is no unilateral emphasis. Great-grandparents, grandparents, and parents' siblings are differentiated by gender. Cousins are not distinguished vocatively from siblings, and parents' siblings can be equated with parents. However, cousins are differentiated referentially from siblings to the third degree by numerically distinctive terms; beyond that, they are considered *malayo* (distant). There is a basic term for sibling (kapatid) and another for cousin (*pinsan*), either of which can be modified by adding a term indicating gender. Own children, grandchildren, and great-grandchildren are differentiated from the descendants of siblings and cousins by separate basic terms with gender and generation modifiers. The prefix *mag-* attached to a term indicates a dyadic relationship: *magama*, father and child; *magina*, mother and child; *magkapatid*, two siblings; etc. Some affinal terms are not gender-specific: *asawa* (spouse); *biyenan* (parent-in-law); *manugang* (child-in-law). Some affinal terms *are* gender-specific: spouse's own siblings are *hipag* (female) and *bayaw* (male); but their spouse's siblings of either gender are *bilas*. Ritual terms are: *kumari/kumpari* (cogodmother/godfather) used between sponsors and parents of sponsored individuals; *inaanak* (godchild); and the usual kinship terms are extended to all sides of the ritual connection. Vocative terminology is primarily age- or status-based. Most frequently the personal name of the younger or junior person is used while the older or senior is addressed by a derivation of the referential term: *ina* is derived from *nanay* (mother); *ka* is from kapatid; etc. Relative status as to age or prestige of relatives and nonrelatives is often indicated by the use of *po*, *ho*, or *oh* in a descending order during conversation.

Marriage and Family

MARRIAGE. Marriage (kasal) generally follows the proscriptions of the Roman Catholic church, but cousin marriages of all degrees occur. The degree permitted or encouraged varies from area to area and from family to family; however, there is frequently pressure to marry within the third degree and if possible within the local group. Divorce (*diborsiyo*) has not been legal for centuries, but separation (*hiwalay*) occurs.

DOMESTIC UNIT. In rural areas, where dwelling space is less limited, the preferred pattern is for each nuclear family to have a separate dwelling as soon as possible. Normally one child and spouse remain in the parental home, but as population pressure increases multiple households are increasingly becoming the rule. Parents share household chores and care of children. As children are able, they take over many household duties including care of their younger siblings and cooking. Frequently, the wife begins to engage in more intense economic activities. There are usually three or more generations present in the household, but in most cases only one or two nuclear families with young children.

INHERITANCE. The root term for inheritance is *mana*. Personal property is inherited equally by siblings. Houses usually become the property of the child who has remained to care for the parents. Rights to tenancies or ownership of land can either descend in a strictly bilateral fashion leading to segmentation of holdings of sibling groups over the generations, or be maintained by naming one sibling steward, with all having a share in the land's output dependent upon input.

SOCIALIZATION. Young children are cared for by members of the household, extended family, and neighbors in general (*mga kapitbahay* or *paligid*). Probably one of the more crucial experiences a Tagalog undergoes comes upon assuming responsibility for a younger sibling, cousin, or other relative. The residential and extended family group is the nurturing environment, and provides opportunities for the building of much *utang na loob*.

Sociopolitical Organization

The head of state in the Republic of the Philippines is a president (*pangulo*). There are two legislative houses (one elected by district and the other at large) and a series of appointed courts and judges with a supreme court at the summit.

SOCIAL ORGANIZATION. Tagalog society seems to have a strongly kinship-based set of parameters, although nonkin are generally incorporated in networks of reciprocal obligation and interaction. There are horizontal class distinctions based on wealth and closeness to economic resources and political power, which are crosscut vertically by genealogical and ritual ties of kinship so that the lower and upper classes are linked at various levels into a series of pyramidal (but ill-defined) networks. Their boundaries and internal relationships are constantly being rearranged.

POLITICAL ORGANIZATION. The Tagalog-speaking area (Katagalugan), as part of the Philippines (Bayan ng Pilipinas), is divided into provinces (singular, *lalawigan*), each with an elected governor and legislative body. Provinces are divided into municipalities (singular, *bayan* or *munisipyo*). One of the municipalities is designated provincial capital. Each municipality has an elected mayor and council. There is usually a central area (also called the bayan or munisipyo) where municipal business is carried on, with an administration building, frequently a market, and religious center. The municipality is divided into segments called *baryo*, *nayon*, or *baranggay*. These basic units have had an elected head since the middle 1950s called *tiniente del baryo*, who was promoted to *kapitan del baryo* a few years later. There is also an elected baryo council representing subdivisions called *sitio* or *pook*. At each level police, education, public works, etc. are managed by presidential appointees.

SOCIAL CONTROL. Aside from the legal system and police functions, most Tagalog communities outside the urban centers operate according to local custom similar to the *adat* found elsewhere in insular Southeast Asia. Local officials exert power insofar as they are personally re-

A Tagalog boy in the back of his family's car. Tagalogs are predominantly Roman Catholic, but there are several other religious groups represented. Manila, Philippines. (Paul Sanders/Corbis)

spected and have influence with people involved in disputes. Ostracism and ridicule are often used as means for social control.

Religion and Expressive Culture

RELIGIOUS BELIEFS. Tagalogs are predominantly Roman Catholic, but there are several other formal religious groups with significant membership. Most Protestant sects are represented in the area to a minor degree. However, both the Iglesia ni Cristo (Church of Christ), a Protestant group established locally in the Philippines, and the Aglipayan Church, a group founded by a priest (Gregorio Aglipay) who broke away from Catholicism, have significant memberships. There are also many local sects and cults.

There are generally two levels to religious belief. One is the expressed set of tenets of Roman Catholicism or other formal religion. The other is interpretation and modification of these as individual and local belief systems. Education and exposure to general scientific knowledge long ago penetrated to most parts of the Tagalog area, but mysticism is still strong and individuals seek personal experience with the unknown and unseen through acts of penitence and contrition. The continuing vagaries of life in an environment prone to catastrophic storms, earthquakes, volcanic eruptions, and social upheaval reinforce the traditional fatalism expressed in the phrase *bahala na*, or "it's all up to God."

RELIGIOUS PRACTITIONERS. The religious hierarchies are centered mostly in Manila and are staffed predominantly by Tagalog priests and ministers. Most municipalities have resident Roman Catholic clergy in a church (*simbahan*) who service chapels (*bisitas* or *ermitas*) in outlying barrios. There are still individuals who have special powers for curing and making contact with spirits of the deceased. The terminology for these and their specialties is highly variable from region to region. Most communities have annual fiestas celebrating a patron saint, the Virgin Mary, or a local manifestation of Christ. These are usually sponsored and managed by a highly organized group of volunteers who are in charge of one year's activities.

CEREMONIES. The annual cycle universally includes Christmas and Easter and their phases. Among others, the day of Saint John the Baptist is widely celebrated, especially in relation to waterways. Good Friday each year produces activity from penitents of various sorts, including whipping and actual crucifixion at spots considered especially sanctified. Baptism, confirmation, marriage, and funerals are regular parts of all lives.

ARTS. Tagalogs have long been noted for excellence in all the arts. Since the introduction of printing in 1593 at Binondo, Manila, there has developed an extensive literature published in Tagalog (and other Philippine languages), Spanish, and English, including poetry, drama, novels, short stories, essays, and criticism. As early as 1606, poems were being printed in Tagalog by Fernando Bagonbanta. Among many famous writers since then have been Francisco Baltazar (Balagtas, "Prince of Tagalog Poets"), whose *Florante at Laura* is a classic and whose pseudonym is associated with the traditional *balagtasan* or contest in verse. The works of José Rizal, especially his romantic novels *Noli me tángere* and *El filibusterismo*, which eventually brought on his execution by the Spanish in 1896 and made him into a national martyr, have been published in many languages. There is a flourishing Tagalog movie and television industry and all the media use Tagalog extensively. A traditional art form that survives is the *kundiman* or love song.

MEDICINE. Modern medical treatment is available in all parts of the Tagalog area through medical schools, hospitals, clinics, and a national health service. Traditional knowledge of herbs is still important and used. Dietary regimes and bodily care reflect long-held concepts of the relationship between good health and adaptation to the environment.

DEATH AND AFTERLIFE. Although the usual Christian beliefs regarding death and afterlife are followed, there are at least two widespread conceptual frameworks present. One holds that the body returns to the four elements: earth, water, fire, and air. The other maintains that the spirit (*kaluluwa*) of the deceased spends a certain amount of time in the immediate neighborhood before departing to an afterworld. Secondary burial has frequently been practiced (i.e., placement of the body in a grave or niche, followed after a period by transfer of the bones to an ossuary). All Souls' Day (Araw ng mga Kaluluwa) is the occasion for visiting the cemetery (*libingan*).

Bibliography

Blair, Emma Helen, and James Robertson (1903–1909). *The Philippine Islands, 1493–1898.* . . . 55 Vols. Cleveland, Ohio: A. H. Clark Co.

Eggan, Fred (1955). *The Philippines.* 4 Vols. New Haven: Human Relations Area Files.

Hollnsteiner, Mary R. (1955). *The Dynamics of Power in a Philippine Municipality.* Quezon City: University of the Philippines, Community Development Research Council.

Kaut, Charles (1961). "*Utang na Loob*: A System of Contractual Obligation among Tagalogs." *Southwestern Journal of Anthropology* 17:256–272.

Kaut, Charles (1965). "The Principle of Contingency in Tagalog Society." *Asian Studies* 3:1–15.

Lynch, Frank, and Ronald S. Hymes (1984). "Cognitive Mapping in the Tagalog Area." In *Philippine Society and the Individual: Selected Essays of Frank Lynch, 1949–1976*, edited by Aram A. Yengoyan and Perla Q. Makil, 127–164. Ann Arbor: University of Michigan, Center for South and Southeast Asian Studies.

—CHARLES KAUT

VIETNAMESE

Ethonyms: Annamese, Cochinchinese, Kinh, Tonkinese

Orientation

IDENTIFICATION. The Vietnamese speak the Vietnamese language and live in the Socialist Republic of Vietnam. Significant numbers of Vietnamese, especially since 1975, are now found in most Western countries, including the United States, France, Australia, and Canada. Remnants of earlier Vietnamese migrations still exist in northeastern Thailand and New Caledonia. Many Vietnamese have also lived in Cambodia and Laos for many decades. Under French colonial rule Vietnam was divided into three separate political entities: Tonkin (north Vietnam), Annam (central Vietnam), and Cochinchina (south Vietnam). Foreigners have sometimes used these terms as designators of ethnicity (e.g., the "Tonkinese"), sometimes employing the term "Annamese" to include all Vietnamese. This usage is offensive to Vietnamese, who all refer to themselves as "Vietnamese," sometimes using "northern," "central," or "southern" as adjectives to designate region of origin. Ethnic Vietnamese also refer to themselves as *kinh*, meaning "lowlanders," as opposed to highland "tribespeople."

LOCATION. Vietnam is located between 8°30' and 23° N and between 102° and 109° E. Very narrow and elongated in the center, it is wider in the south and in the north. The country lies to the south of China and east of Laos and Cambodia, with a long coastline on the South China Sea. Although some three-quarters of Vietnamese national territory is hilly or mountainous, ethnic Vietnamese have lived mainly in the lowland plains.

DEMOGRAPHY. The population of Vietnam is about 68.5 million, over 20 percent of whom live in urban areas. Population density is over 207 per square kilometer. About 85 percent of the total population is ethnic Vietnamese. There are many highland ethnic minorities, including numerous Tai-speaking groups as well as Hmong (Meo), Nung, and Muong in the northern highlands and Austronesian-speaking groups (e.g., Rhadé and Jarai) and Mon-Khmer (Austroasiatic)-speaking groups (e.g., Bahnar, Sedang, Stieng, Mnong, and Katu) in the southern highlands. A sizable and long-established ethnic Chinese population lives mostly in urban areas of the south, although many left the country between 1975 and 1980. Many ethnic Khmer live in parts of the Mekong Delta. The Red River and Mekong deltas, containing less than a quarter of the total land area, hold almost 60 percent of the population and over 70 percent of all ethnic Vietnamese. Population density in these core areas is often very high (over 2,000 persons per square mile), but in highland areas it is often under 25 per square mile and rarely exceeds 150 per square mile. Both the southern and the northern regimes during the division of Vietnam (1955–1975), as well as more recently the Socialist Republic of Vietnam, had programs to resettle Vietnamese into the highlands, but they encountered numerous difficulties and achieved only limited results.

LINGUISTIC AFFILIATION. Vietnamese is a monosyllabic and tonal language of composite origin, basically Mon-Khmer (Austroasiatic), but with elements derived from Tai and Sinitic languages.

History and Cultural Relations

The early inhabitants of the area apparently were Negritos. Some 4,000 years ago Austronesian (Indonesian) migrants from the north were moving into the area that is now north Vietnam. Later, Austroasiatic (Mon-Khmer and Malayo-Polynesian) peoples arrived. Then, about 2,500 years ago Viet (Yueh) and Tai peoples moved down from southern China. Out of this mixture of genes, languages, and cultures arose Van Lang, considered to have been the first Vietnamese kingdom. In mid-third century B.C. Van Lang was overrun by and incorporated into another state to the north, forming the kingdom of Au Lac. Then Au Lac was incorporated into an even larger and more powerful state: Nam Viet (Nan Yueh in Chinese), centered on Canton. Local leadership and culture were little disrupted in the Red River Delta, although new cultural elements entered from the north. In 111 B.C. the region was incorporated into the expanding Han Empire in China and the Red River Delta was part of the

The traditional Vietnamese village was a highly nucleated settlement surrounded by a bamboo hedge or sometimes by an earthen wall.

Chinese empire for a thousand years. Local hereditary leadership was used by both Nam Viet and early Han rulers, but as infrastructure and more intensive production techniques developed, pressure increased for more complete Sinicization of local culture and administration. In A.D. 39 the Trung sisters led the traditional local elite in a popularly supported revolt that flourished briefly but was suppressed in A.D. 43, ending hereditary leadership. The new hybrid elite of the Red River Delta kept and developed a sense of regional identity; the local language and many non-Chinese customs were retained. Revolts came periodically until A.D. 939 when independence from Chinese rule was achieved, although China would remain a military threat and a continuing source of cultural influence. What is now central Vietnam was then the kingdom of Champa. The Cham spoke an Austronesian language, had a powerful Indian influence on their culture and political organization, and also had a strong maritime orientation. Over the next six centuries Vietnam displaced or assimilated the Cham and extended Vietnamese territory down the coast to the plains and foothills east of Saigon, which they took and occupied during the seventeenth century. The Vietnamese then expanded at the expense of Cambodia, settling the western Mekong Delta in the eighteenth century and the eastern portion in the nineteenth. But between 1859 and 1883 all of Vietnam fell under French colonial control. South Vietnam (called Cochinchina) was a French colony; central Vietnam (called Annam) and northern Vietnam (called Tonkin) became protectorates. Together with Cambodia and Laos, they constituted French Indochina. A public school system established by the French in 1908 disseminated elements of Western culture in Vietnam, influencing but not destroying Vietnamese culture. In 1945 a popular revolution erupted against French rule. As this movement came under increasingly strong Communist control, however, some Vietnamese became disaffected. In 1955 Vietnam gained independence from France but was divided into the Socialist Republic of Vietnam in the northern half and the anti-Communist Republic of Vietnam in the southern half. About 900,000 Vietnamese relocated from the north to the south, while 90,000 or so others moved from south to north. A Communist-led revolution in the south evoked heavy American support for the Republic of Vietnam, adding American influence to the already heterodox southern region, and led to the invasion of the south by northern troops. After a devastating war,

Communist forces in 1975 took over all of Vietnam, the foreign troops departed, and the Socialist Republic of Vietnam was established in 1976.

Settlements

The traditional Vietnamese village, typical of lowland northern and central Vietnam, was a highly nucleated settlement surrounded by a bamboo hedge or sometimes by an earthen wall. Each village had a communal hall (*dinh*) that served as a sanctuary for the cult of the village guardian spirit and as a public meeting hall. Mahayana Buddhist temples were also common. These villages tended to be tightly bounded and relatively closed communities (both physically and socially) with an elaborate community structure, located along roads or waterways or on knolls or hillsides. Houses were built with mud or brick walls, thatched or tile roofs, and earthen or concrete floors. In the more recently settled southern region, especially in the western Mekong Delta, settlements have been more scattered and less tightly bounded, with a less well-defined community structure. Some southern villages had no dinh. Most are strung out along roads or waterways and some households are scattered over the countryside. Houses have walls of woven bamboo, brick, or wood, earthen or concrete floors, and roofs of palm leaves, thatch, or, in recent decades, corrugated iron or metal sheets made from recycled aluminum cans.

Kinship

KIN GROUPS AND DESCENT. The structure of Vietnamese kinship involves logical opposition and functional complementarity between two models. Especially in northern and central Vietnam, patrilineage has been the dominant form, with emphasis on hierarchy and solidarity. But bilateral tendencies, with greater egalitarian emphasis, have always been present, most strongly in the south. In recent years Socialist policies have reinforced bilateral tendencies, weakened patrilineage, and strengthened the nuclear family. Descent is patrilineal, but with increasingly strong bilateral tendencies.

KINSHIP TERMINOLOGY. Vietnamese kinship terminology is of the Sudanese type, highly descriptive. There are different terms for father's siblings and mother's siblings, and father's older brother is terminologically distinguished from his younger brother.

Marriage and Family

MARRIAGE. Although free choice in marriage is now the law and is quite common, arranged marriages and the use of matchmakers persist, and parents and important elders wield much influence. In the northern and central regions, villge endogamy and patrilocal residence have been the norm and are still common. Polygynous marriage, once common, is now illegal; but it has not disappeared.

DOMESTIC UNIT.   Households average from five to seven persons, but they vary greatly in size. Most consist of a nuclear family, often supplemented with one or more other close relatives, and function as a single economic unit, sharing the work and resources.

INHERITANCE.   In general, all children inherit equally, although sons, especially eldest sons, are sometimes favored. The oldest, or sometimes the youngest, son (or even the youngest daughter) may stay at home to care for aging parents and inherit the house.

SOCIALIZATION.   The attitude toward young children is very permissive, but older children are much more strictly controlled and disciplined. Boys have somewhat more freedom than girls and, although the tendency is weakening, are likely to get more education. Family solidarity is emphasized over independence, and nurturance/dependency relationships over self-reliance.

Sociopolitical Organization

SOCIAL ORGANIZATION.   Vietnamese social organization entails complex interaction between two contradictory sets of ideas. Traditionally, individual Vietnamese have been firmly embedded in powerful corporate groups, first and foremost in a family. A family was part of a lineage and of a village. Villages were aggregated into the state through a national civil service. Within families, lineages, and villages a strict, maledominant hierarchy was common. These biases persist in Vietnamese society. Relative age, rank, titles, degrees, and other status markers remain significant determinants of attitudes and behavior in social interaction. Yet at each level a distinct set of more open and egalitarian institutions has always been present: bilateral family ties, mutual aid groups, shamanistic cults, and Buddhist practices. Situational shifting between these two logically contradictory but on the whole functionally complementary domains at every level has been and to a large extent remains the essence of Vietnamese

ECONOMY

Subsistence and Commercial Activities

Vietnam is a poor country, with an annual per capita income of less than U.S. $200. Agriculture, the dominant sector of the economy, emphasizes the cultivation of wet rice, but the production of secondary food crops (maize, yams, manioc, beans) and industrial crops (rubber, tea, coffee, pineapple, citrus fruits, sugar, tobacco, jute) has increased in recent decades. Despite efforts to mechanize agriculture, water buffalo and human beings still do most of the farm work. Pigs, chickens, ducks, cattle, and fish ponds are common. Many coastal villages specialize in fishing. Home gardens play an important role in the household economy.

Industrial Arts

Small-scale food processing, charcoal making, and handicrafts (furniture, lacquerware, pottery, silk, baskets) play an important economic role. Sewing machines are widespread. Mining and metalworking are important in the north. Some industries (cement, textiles, chemicals, steel) are well established, but efforts to build heavy industry have been impeded by war and a weak economic base.

Trade

While small shops, stalls, street peddlers, and market squares are common, and Vietnamese women are especially active in petty retail and trade, until recently ethnic Chinese dominated many wholesale activities. Government efforts to socialize the economy in 1978 closed tens of thousands of small private businesses that were replaced by a state trading network, but some private enterprise has now returned.

Division of Labor

Traditionally women have had charge of domestic affairs, including finances. Men dominated public affairs, the professions, and agricultural activity. Extended warfare and government regulations have given women greater opportunities in all areas, but much de facto division of labor by gender persists.

Land Tenure

The ratio of people to arable land is one of the most unfavorable in the world for an agricultural country. Most landholdings have been collectivized under Communist rule. Each household in a collective is permitted to have some land for its own use; private plots (about 5 percent of the land area) typically produce from 10 to 20 percent or more of the total yield.

The official Vietnamese government ideology is basically atheistic, and the state is committed by its constitution to combat "backward life styles and superstitions."

social organization. In recent decades state ideology and legal codes have weakened the strength of traditional social groupings and hierarchies; but the new Socialist men and women and the new Socialist society envisioned by state planners since 1955 in the north and 1975 in the south remain more of an ideal than an actuality as older patterns reemerge in new forms. Vietnamese social organization is changing, but the extent and precise nature of change is still unclear and unevenly distributed from region to region.

POLITICAL ORGANIZATION. The Socialist Republic of Vietnam is a Communist state divided into thirty-nine provinces and three autonomous municipalities. Provinces are divided into districts, districts into villages and townships. Each such unit has its own People's Council, the main public organ of state authority, and a People's Committee, the executive agent of the People's Council and the major administrative body. The Communist party of Vietnam plays a major role in all spheres at all levels, however, imposing parameters of discourse and action and setting social and economic goals. The Communist party is designated by the constitution to be the "sole force leading the state and society," and the executive branch of government is virtually an extension of the Central Committee of the party.

SOCIAL CONTROL. Traditionally families, lineages, and villages could be held corporately responsible for the actions of their members. Concern for the welfare and reputation of one's family has served to constrain misbehavior. Gossip and ridicule have been important weapons for social control because of a concern for "face." Now neighborhood committees and Communist party cells and organizations monitor behavior and rebuke deviance. Self-criticism and public-criticism sessions are used to check antisocial tendencies.

CONFLICT. Local disputes have often involved competition for scarce water or land; historically much conflict has arisen from Vietnam's southern expansion and from resistance to encroachment upon Vietnam's territorial integrity and independence from the north. Ideological disputes have torn the country and region apart for the past fifty years, while regional rivalry has reemerged with national independence. Within groups, conflict often involves perceived slights in regard to respect behavior and relative status. Underlying such sensitivities there are both high psychological stakes and competition over the control of resources. Vietnam, with the twelfth-largest population in the world, has maintained

the fourth-largest army and a large public-security apparatus, despite a weak economy.

Religion and Expressive Culture

The official ideology of the Socialist Republic of Vietnam is basically atheistic, and the state is committed by its constitution to combat "backward life styles and superstitions." While official policy guarantees freedom of religion, secular activities of religious groups are severely circumscribed, and activist religious leaders have been jailed.

RELIGIOUS BELIEFS. Popular Vietnamese religion is a mixture of ritual and belief derived from animist, Confucian, Taoist, and Buddhist sources. Veneration of ancestors is a very important part of this syncretic system, as are many elements of Mahayana Buddhist practice and belief. But only a minority of Vietnamese could properly be called Confucianists or Buddhists. Beliefs in astrology, geomancy, and the intervention of spirits in human life are all widespread. Traditional villages had cults to a village guardian spirit. There are perhaps over 5 million Roman Catholics in Vietnam. Many Vietnamese are nominally Buddhists, but active members of organized Buddhist churches probably number only 3 or 4 million, mostly in and around Ho Chi Minh City and Hue. The Cao Dai, numbering between 1 and 2 million and limited to the south and south-central regions, combine folk religion and Christian beliefs. The Hoa Hao, limited to one portion of the western Mekong Delta, with about 2 million adherents, are a puritanical, poor, peasant-based sect committed to a simplified and austere Buddhist doctrine. There are also a small number of Protestant Christians and other small sects built around prophets or charismatic leaders. For some Vietnamese, Marxism seems to function as a secular religion and appears to have acquired some sacred aspects. Ho Chi Minh, "the father of independence," is to some a cult figure similar to traditional heroes worshiped as powerful spirits after their death.

Village guardian spirits were once important cult figures, but now less so. Some spirits are believed to provide assistance if venerated, or illness and misfortune if ignored. People who die violent deaths are thought to linger as angry spirits and bring misfortune if not propitiated. There are many categories of malevolent or potentially malevolent spirits, among them ghosts (*ma*), and demons (*guy*). There are numerous minor deities who may intervene in human life for good or ill, and a generally benevolent category of supernatural, *tien*, a "fairy" or "genie."

RELIGIOUS PRACTITIONERS. Buddhist monks are to be found in many villages. They do not automatically enjoy high respect or exert influence in village affairs, although some may achieve these things. Catholic priests and many Cao Dai and Hoa Hao leaders are respected leaders in their communities. Shamans, fortune-tellers, and a variety of other specialists in dealing with the supernatural may build up a group of clients or followers.

CEREMONIES. The most widespread and important ceremonies involve the ancestors. Death-anniversary celebrations, New Year's festivities, and other events bring the ancestors back to visit the family, where they must be ritually greeted. The Midyear (Wandering Souls) festival is widely observed. Christians celebrate Christmas and Easter. Many households have, in addition to altars for the ancestors, small shrines to various spirits (the earth god, Shakyamuni, the goddess of mercy, the god of wealth, etc.) and present ritual offerings once or twice a month.

ARTS. Literary arts, especially poetry, are highly prized. A wide variety of musical forms and instruments is popular. Many southerners enjoy reformed opera, musical dramas with humorous elements. Some people like Western music, everything from classical to rock and roll. While guitars and pianos are popular, some people still play traditional stringed instruments with great skill. Fine arts and architecture reveal both Western and Chinese influence. Skits and impromptu musical performances or recitations of verse are popular at many kinds of gatherings.

MEDICINE. Illness is attributed to many causes: it may be organic or owing to germs, but it also may be caused by fright or hardship, heartbreak, an imbalance of elements, a curse, or spirit possession. Picking the right kind of treatment is essential. There are many specialists in the supernatural who diagnose and treat illness in a variety of ways, often sharing clients with modern medical centers and with Vietnamese or Chinese herbalists. Vitamin injections, tonics and elixirs of many kinds, and special dietary regimens are also used. Sometimes women feel called to worship a particular spirit or deity, and illness is the penalty for failure to make offerings. Protective talismans and amulets and ritual support for protector spirits are used to ward off illness.

DEATH AND AFTERLIFE. Funerals (and sometimes reburials) were elaborate and costly affairs, especially for the well-to-do, but they are now less so. Ritual support for the deceased is most crucial. Those not honored by a cult become errant spirits, unhappy and harmful. A series of rituals elevates the deceased into the ranks of the ancestors. Ancestors return to visit the family on death-anniversary celebrations and special family occasions. Major life events are reported to the ancestors.

Bibliography

Gourou, Pierre (1936). *Les paysans du delta tonkinois.* Paris: École Francaise d'Extrême-Orient. Translated as *Peasants of the Tonkin Delta.* 1955. New Haven: Human Relations Area Files.

Hickey, Gerald C. (1964). *Village in Vietnam.* Chicago: Aldine.

Hy Van Luong (1989). "Vietnamese Kinship: Structural Principles and the Socialist Transformation in Northern Vietnam." *Journal of Asian Studies* 48: 741–756.

Le Thi Que (1986). "The Vietnamese Family Yesterday and Today." *Interculture* 92:1–38.

Rambo, Arthur Terry (1973). *A Comparison of Peasant Social Systems of Northern and Southern Viet-nam: A Study of Ecological Adaptation, Social Succession, and Cultural Evolution.* Monograph Series, no. 3. Carbondale: Southern Illinois University Center for Vietnamese Studies.

Rambo, Arthur Terry (1982). "Vietnam: Searching for Integration." In *Religion and Societies: Asia and the Middle East*, edited by Carlo Caldarola, 407–444. Berlin: Mouton.

—NEIL JAMIESON

Death-anniversary celebrations, New Year's festivities, and other events bring Vietnamese ancestors back to visit the family, where they must be ritually greeted.

ALBANIANS

Ethnym: Albanois, Arbëresh, Arnauts, Arvanits, Illyrians, Shiptare

Orientation

IDENTIFICATION. The name "Albanian" derives from the ancient town of Albanopolis, mentioned by Ptolemy in the second century B.C. and located within present-day Albania. Etymologically this derives from the Latin *albus*, "white," a possible reference to the whiteness of the nearby mountains. "Arbëresh" comes from Albanian *arbër*, a term for Albanians in Italy. "Arbanit," "Arvanit"—designating Greek Albanians—changed to "Arbërit" and "Arbëreshët," which were initially names for Catholic Albanians only. "Arnaut" derives from the Ottoman designation and—like "Albanoi," the original French name—is to be found in older sources. "Illyrian" is the name for the autochthonous population that lived partly on modern Albanian territory, from the time of the Iron Age, and it is sometimes used in Albanian nationalist literature as a designation for "ancestral Albanians." "Shiptare," "sons of the eagle," originally the self-designation of the people of the northern highlands only, is in modern Albanian the correct ethnonym for all Albanian people.

LOCATION. Present-day Albania covers an area of 28,748 square kilometers located between 39°38′ and 42°39′ N and 19°16′ and 21°4′ E and is bordered by the Adriatic and Ionian seas to the west, Montenegro, Serbia, and Macedonia to the north and east, and Greece to the south. Seventy-six percent of Albania is hill and mountain, 23.4 percent plains. The climate is Mediterranean in the coastal plains and foothills. In the mountain area of inner Albania, the climate becomes more continental, with less dry summers and cooler, often snowy winters.

DEMOGRAPHY. In 1990 there were about 3.25 million Albanians in Albania, 35 percent of them urban. The population growth rate is up to 2 percent per year with an extremely high birthrate of 24 per 1,000 inhabitants (1985–1990 average). The population has the youngest average age in Europe, with 33.9 percent under 14, 51.8 percent between 15 and 49, and only 14.3 percent above 50 in 1985. Life expectancy is 69 for men and 74 for women. More than a third of all Albanians live outside Albania's political borders, which were fixed in 1913 after the Balkan Wars. More than 2 million Albanians live in Kosovo in the Republic of Serbia, Yugoslavia, with others in Montenegro and Macedonia. There is also a large Albanian community in Greece, mainly in the Tshamaria (Greek Epirus), in the Peloponnesos, in Thrace, in Greek Macedonia, and on the islands of Angistri, Euboea, Hydra, Poros, Spetsai, etc. There are another 100,000 in south Italy and Sicily, descendants of religious refugees from the Ottoman advance in the fifteenth and sixteenth centuries. Thousands of Albanians have come very recently (1990–1991) as political refugees to Greece, Italy, and other western European states. There are also Albanian enclaves in Turkey, Egypt, Russia, and the United States.

LINGUISTIC AFFILIATION. Albanian is the sole member of one branch of Indo-European languages. There are two main dialects whose names are also the names of the two main regional groups in Albania, which are also differentiated by their traditional social organization: Tosk, influenced by Turkish, roughly to the south of the Shkumbin River; and Gheg, with many Romance, Greek, and Slavonic influences, to the north. The modern official Albanian language dates from the period 1908 to 1912, when, as a result of the nation-building process, the language was standardized on the Tosk variant and the Latin alphabet was introduced.

History and Cultural Relations

Archaeological and prehistoric evidence for Illyrian settlements on Albanian territory date from the second millennium B.C. At first influenced by ancient Greek civilization, Illyria belonged to the Roman Empire after 168 B.C. From the fourth to the sixth centuries the Illyrians suffered Hun and Gothic invasions, and from the sixth century Slavs began to settle on Illyrian territory. In Kosovo the plains settlers withdrew into the mountains, thus laying the historical foundations for modern territorial disputes between Serbs and Albanians in Yugoslavia. From 750 the area was under Byzantine rule, and from 851 to 1014 it belonged to the Bulgarian Empire. Later came the Normans (1081–1185) and Neapolitans (the "Regnum Albaniae" of Charles of Anjou in coastal Albania, 1271), and the country became part of the Great Serbian Empire from 1334 to 1347 under Stefan Dušan. The Venetians then claimed the area until 1393, when the Ottoman Empire absorbed it; the area finally declared its independence in 1912.

Today Albania is relatively homogeneous ethnically. The 1976 Albanian constitution recognizes

◆ **Iron Age**
The fourth stage in the development of Western civilization, characterized by the production and use of iron tools and objects. Beginning in southeastern Europe in about 1200 B.C., the Iron Age followed the Bronze Age.

◆ **Roman Empire**
The state centered in Rome, founded as a republic in 509 B.C., established as an empire in 27 B.C., the western half of which collapsed in the fifth century A.D. The Roman Empire was the dominant force in the Mediterranean region, North Africa, and much of Europe.

Today 35.5 percent of the Albanian population is urban, 64.5 percent rural. The relatively low urbanization rate is probably a result of state restrictions on mobility.

national minorities and guarantees minority rights concerning language, folklore, and tradition, but not religion. The Greeks (5.2 percent) live mainly in the Albanian Epirus. Thousands of Albanian Greeks have gone to Greece since the end of 1990 over a border that had been virtually closed for decades. The Balkan Romanians (0.5 percent), also known as Aromuns or Vlachs, are regarded as an assimilated minority. Their earlier nomadic pastoralism came to an end through restrictions on their mobility after World War II, when political borders were closed, and through the socialist government's collectivization of agriculture. In the thirteenth century, Vlach pastoralists, artisans, and traders founded their capital, Voskopoja, in southern Albania, which in the seventeenth and eighteenth centuries became a center for international trade and cultural relations (with Venice, Vienna, and Budapest) with an educated class. More than 100,000 Vlachs were still recorded in Albania around the turn of the century. There are also groups of Macedonians (0.4 percent) and Montenegrins (0.2 percent). The Gypsies (less than 0.2 percent), both Sinti and Roma (Albanian *evgjitë*, a reference to a formerly assumed Egyptian origin, or *kurbetë*), were compelled by state programs to settle down permanently. In the cities they live in apartment blocks or single dispersed apartments, though separate residential quarters for Gypsies can still be found. Traditionally basket makers, smiths, and tinkers, today they are employed as street cleaners or in road construction, being socially marginalized. A very few Blacks (Albanian *arigi*), the descendants of Ottoman slaves, also live in Albania. Many Jews were taken from Albania to Israel in January 1991 by Operation Flying Carpet.

Settlements

Today 35.5 percent of the Albanian population is urban, 64.5 percent rural. The relatively low urbanization rate is probably a result of state restrictions on mobility. Virilocal marriage leads many Albanian women to live in urban areas. About 80 percent of the population today lives in apartment blocks built in the Socialist period. Besides the capital, Tirana, the main regional centers are Durrës (the main port), Shkodër, Elbasan, Vlorë, and Korcë. In presocialist days villages were composed of groups of houses surrounded by farmland and pastures. Stone and wood were the main materials used in house building. The Ottoman influence can clearly be seen in the widespread enclosure of houses by stone walls for religious reasons and the use of stone, originally for defensive purposes, in

the first floor, timber in the second. Also typical of Albania is the *kula*, a fortified dwelling of stone with slits for windows in the lower floor and closable windows above, adapted to the threat of brigandage, foreign (especially Ottoman) invasions, and, above all, feuds. The one-room house of stone and timber with a central fireplace is the basic unit, sometimes extended with additional buildings into larger farms. Because of the sloping terrain, many houses are built perpendicularly on several levels against the slope, thus utilizing all possible space. In areas with a more Mediterranean climate, a veranda added to the basic unit serves in summer as a place for cooking, sleeping, and living. In the south one also finds the manor houses of the former feudal rulers (patrons) in both rural and urban areas, some of which were built for defense. In the plains both these and ordinary houses often show the influence of Italian architecture.

Economy

SUBSISTENCE AND COMMERCIAL ACTIVITIES. The extended household was basically self-sufficient, with property and labor held in common. Surplus produce was sold in sometimes distant markets to provide weapons, household utensils, bride-wealth, etc. During the Socialist period farming and stock raising were carried out by cooperatives and collective farms, and many villagers commuted to jobs in industry and state services. Privatization started in the early 1980s, after expropriations had led to the slaughter of stock by protesting farmers and consequent meat shortages. As a result, the government introduced a *brigade* economy (a brigade being a cooperative workers' unit representing approximately the population of a former village), and workers sold the surplus products at state shops at prices guaranteed by the state. No research has been carried out on the secondary economy in Albania, but people evidently provided themselves with *raki* (a spirit), vegetables, herbs, and fruits on the black market. Since 1990, a transformation toward a free-market economy has been going on. Industrial production declined by about 50 percent in 1991. Strikes, especially in the mines, the worthlessness of the Albanian currency, and a 60 percent unemployment rate currently are the main features of a very unstable economic situation.

INDUSTRIAL ARTS. In the past there were urban centers and certain streets in the cities where male artisans and specialists sold various products of pottery, metal, and wood: for example, agricultural and household tools, instruments, religious icons in Eastern Orthodox areas, ironwork, silver and gold filigree, embroidery, and other needlework. Ottoman style influenced carvings in wood for interior decoration all over Albania. Shepherds carved their crooks. Farmers produced and carved wooden spoons, pipes, distaffs, spindles, and musical instruments such as flutes, the *cifteli* (a two-stringed mandolin), and the *lahuta* (a one-stringed instrument); some regions were famous for their ornamented carved wooden chairs, cradles, and bridal chests. Women worked for family needs and in many urban and rural regions for the market, specializing in textiles.

TRADE. Until the fall of Constantinople in 1453, an important trade route between Rome and Byzantium, the Via Egnatia, passed through Durrës. In the nineteenth century, Orthodox Greek and Vlach citizens in the southern parts of Albania traded with the Ottoman Empire, economic centers in the north being Shkodër and Prizren (the latter now in Kosovo). Economic relations with Yugoslavia ended two years after the proclamation of the Albanian Socialist People's Republic in 1946. From 1949 Albania was a member of the Soviet-East European Council of Mutual Economic Assistance, and the Soviet Union was the most important trading partner until 1961, when relations were broken off. Economic assistance was provided by China from 1961 until 1978, when it ended and Chinese experts withdrew. In 1968 Albania left the Warsaw Pact. Until May 1990 the constitution did not permit the raising of foreign loans, and this restricted foreign loans, and this restricted foreign investment. In recent years Albania has exported different types of ore and metals (primarily iron ore and chromite), electricity, gas, agricultural products, some finished goods (textiles, handicrafts, etc.), building materials, chemical products, plastics, and cigarettes and tobacco. Grain, luxury goods, machinery, vehicles, chemical and electromechanical products were imported. The principle of "no import without export," broadly realized until 1987, was intended to guarantee economic autarchy. The increasing deterioration of Eastern European economies—Albania's major trading partners—together with the problems of drought and an inflexible system of central planning, have led to severe shortages. Since September 1991 the Albanian population has been supported largely through European Community programs designed to avoid further movements of refugees.

DIVISION OF LABOR. In general, the men of the clan society were concerned with agriculture and stock raising. Transhumant pastoralism, lumbering, and hunting were men's seasonal tasks. In addition to housekeeping, women were responsible for small-scale production such as weaving and sewing for the household or for one's dowry, plus dairy farming and child care. Often, when a family was involved in a feud, the men went into hiding and the women took over their work too. The household head was allowed a horse in order to represent the family to the outside world, and he also decided the organization of labor among the agnates. He appointed his female counterpart, the "mistress of the house" (*zonjë*, not necessarily his wife), who was similarly responsible for the female labor of the household. In modern times, the socialist constitution declared women equal to men. In reality this principle often creates an added burden for women, because in public life they are employed equally with men in agricultural and industrial production and in civilian and military service, whereas their emancipation in private life, though official policy, is often more theory than fact.

LAND TENURE. In the clan society land was owned jointly by the clan and owned locally by the agnates of an extended household. In the plains latifundia (*çiftlics*) developed when the formerly independent villages were integrated into the patronage system in Ottoman times. With the weakening of the Ottoman Empire, regional feudal rulers (beys), Albanian converts to Islam with lucrative positions in the Ottoman administration, extended their power and kept the mostly Eastern Orthodox peasants under their control as tenants. Endogamous family aristocracies arose, the best-known from 1778 being the Bushatli family, with large properties around Shkodër in northern Albania, and the family of Ali Pasha of Tepelena (1785–1822), with extensive landholdings in present-day Greek and Albanian Epirus. In the area around the city of Tirana up to the neighboring mountainous district of Mati, the two systems met and a mixed system of land tenure developed. Family heads were already known as beys, and some estates belonged to wealthier families, but in general land still was communally held by the different clans. The Albanian beys were expropriated after the war, when socialist land reforms in 1946 divided the land among farmers formerly dependent on feudal landlords. Later, the land was nationalized and collectivized in state farms, though this action was delayed somewhat in mountain areas because of a combination of underdeveloped infrastructure and popular resistance. People were organized in

◆ **latifundia**
Large estates of the Roman Empire that were often the local or regional centers of political and economic power. Large estates based on the latifundia model existed in many regions of Europe up to the present time, for example in Italy and Spain. Typically the land was owned by a single family and passed on through inheritance, with the land actually being worked by serfs.

◆ **European Community (EC)**
A political and economic association of twelve Western European nations, formally founded in 1992 and to be established in 1993 following ratification by the parliaments of the member nations.

cooperatives, first on the level of single villages and later in groups of villages. Since the collapse of socialism, a process of privatization of land has been set in motion, accompanied and hampered by numerous conflicts.

Kinship

KIN GROUPS AND DESCENT. Gheg clan society lasted until the 1950s in northern Albania.

Those who claimed descent from a common, sometimes mythical or fictitious male ancestor were organized in an ideally exogamous patriclan or *fis* found in many villages with lineages at the village or *mehala* level. Understood as a "brotherhood" or *vellezeri*, these included a variable number of communal extended households, called *shpi* or *shtëpi* (literally, "house"), each consisting of the nuclear families of a number of brothers, with up

MARRIAGE AND FAMILY

Marriage

Residence in Albanian clan society was strictly virilocal. Marriage arrangements were always exogamous and made by the head of the household. Children were betrothed sometimes even before birth, often in respect of an existing alliance or in order to establish friendship or peace with another clan. Religious differences between the families were no obstacle. A part of the bride-price was paid after the girl was born, the balance when she was old enough to be handed over to the bridegroom's relatives, who picked her up in a marriage procession. Girls were married between the ages of 13 and 16, boys between 15 and 18. Regionally, dowry also was given to the girl by her family, and if she was widowed and sent home, she could take with her whatever remained. Levirate was also practiced. Sometimes young widows were resold, the profit being shared between her former husband's family and her own. A wife was regarded as her husband's property, as were her children; unmarried women belonged to their fathers. If a wife failed to give birth to a son, her husband was allowed to divorce her by cutting off a piece of her dress and sending her home to her family. Such a woman was considered worthless and she had almost no chance of being married again. Church influence ended the practice of taking a woman without marrying her until she proved her fertility. A woman's only possibility of escaping an unwanted marriage without causing bloodshed between the families involved was to promise perpetual virginity as a *verdzin*, which entailed the difficult task of finding a number (which varied according to region) of co-jurors from her own

clan who would agree to feud if she failed to maintain her oath. A verdzin was allowed to take over male responsibilities and duties, and in some areas she dressed like a man. In the mountains there was often a shortage of women, causing a regional explosion in the amount of bride-price, which in turn led to marriage by capture in some cases. Socialism prohibited traditional customs concerning marriage and promised the free choice of partner to both sexes.

Domestic Unit

In the anthropological literature the extended household organized by fraternal principle is known by the original Serb word *zadruga* (see "Kin Groups and Descent").

Inheritance

Leadership positions traditionally were not inherited but achieved. One exception was the public post of a *bayraktar* or standard-bearer (see "Political Organization"), though even here, merit was the basis of a holder's choice of his successor from among his sons. Another exception was the position of captain (*kapedan*), or head of the clan, which was transmitted hereditarily through the Gjomarkaj family of the large clan of Mirditë, who were the keepers of all knowledge about the "Kanun" or traditional law (see "Social Control"). The Kanun also regulated inheritance for the household and specified that land and other property never be divided up but always remain communal within the agnatic group, with the household head having control over its use. Land could not be bequeathed to the church by anyone

without permission of the clan assembly. In the event of the deaths of their husbands or fathers, women were left to the charge of their respective agnates. In the case of the minority of a sole male heir or of the total lack of male heirs, an elder sister could choose to become a verdzin as a classificatory male household head to care for the property and keep it together for subsequent generations.

Socialization

On the third day after birth (*poganík*) three fairies would predict a child's fortune, according to traditional belief. Although baptized after three to four weeks, the child was actually initiated into the community of the house through the ritual of the first haircut when the child was about one year old. A lack of sons or of children altogether was regarded as a misfortune. Ritual techniques and amulets protected children from the evil eye. Fathers often exchanged their young sons to raise them even more strictly, and children were only allowed to speak when spoken to. A man had to carry weapons (a rifle or pistol) to be taken seriously. Girls were introduced to domestic work very early. The main concerns of child care and education were developing toughness and respect for elders, especially men. Initially the socialist government faced high rates of illiteracy, which has now almost vanished. Today children normally attend a crèche from about 6 months old, before going to kindergarten and then, from the age of about 6, to school. Socialist state education stressed the symbolic "triangle of education, productive work, and physical and military training."

to ninety individuals in some cases. Genealogies, understood as a tree, were carefully remembered and handed down through the generations through epic songs and tales as origin myths.

KINSHIP TERMINOLOGY. Kin ties were defined by blood given to the children only through the patriline. A wife's or mother's kin were her parental family; her father and brothers were responsible for her until she married. Accordingly, mother's brother and mother's son had special terms, but apparently there was no specific kin terminology for their children. All matrilateral cousins, cross as well as parallel, were potential marriage partners but not any patrilateral cousins, relations with whom constituted incest. In the traditional extended household, patrilateral cousins of any degree were called brothers and sisters, patrilateral uncles of any degree fathers or uncles. When the actual father and mother became very old, the eldest brother and sister were given the terms for father and mother. Thus the terminology was at least partly classificatory, with bifurcate-merging features.

Sociopolitical Organization

SOCIAL ORGANIZATION. The agnatic descent system has already been discussed under "Kin Groups and Descent." The institutions of godparenthood, arising out of the rites of a child's first haircut and baptism, and blood brotherhood extended social ties further for the whole family.

POLITICAL ORGANIZATION. The lord of the house or *zot i shpis* represented his extended family in the assembly of village elders, no member of which had any wealth or other privileges. One or more of its most respected members (*plak* or *drye-plak*) also represented the village in the assembly of clan elders (*kuvënd*). Each clan also had one or more "standard-bearers" or bayraktars, military leaders with administrative and juridical functions in times of peace. The area in which the zot i shpis recruited his followers was known as a *bayrak*, which might or might not coincide with a clan (fis) territory. Some clans therefore had more than one standard-bearer, while in other cases one bayraktar would be responsible for more than one clan. He had the right to convene the clan assembly and preside over it for military purposes. The assembly had executive and juridical functions concerning the community (questions of territory, religion, politics, and law), whereas cases concerning single persons or lineages were decided at village assembly level. In the plains these traditional forms of political organization were replaced by the Ottoman administration, which introduced a feudal structure. Under socialism, the state and the Communist party organized politics on the local level. As part of the collapse of socialism in Eastern Europe in the early 1990s, Albania is moving rapidly toward a democratic system. In 1991 Albania became a member of the Conference on Security and Cooperation in Europe, and in March 1992 the Democratic party, which had been founded only in 1990, won the second free election in Albania with a majority of more than 70 percent.

SOCIAL CONTROL. Gheg customary law was transmitted orally. The clan and village assemblies administered and modified justice for 500 years by always referring to a territorial ruler, to Lek Dukagjin, or in certain areas to Skanderbeg, both of whom were said to have codified existing customary law. In 1913 the Franciscan scholar Shtjefen Gjecov collected the laws referring to Dukagjin in the Mirdita clan's area, where it was said to have been preserved best. In 1933, many years after Gjecov's mysterious death, this collection was published as *Kanuni i Lek Dukagjinit*, a code based on the concepts of honor and blood. A person had to guard the honor of his family and clan, which was conceptualized through the patriline as consisting of the same blood, and the honor of wives. There was also a collective liability lasting generations regarding the actions of any clan member, maintained through an internal hierarchy reflecting the closeness of kin. The doctrine of "blood for blood" found in the Kanun led to institutionalized feud, which clearly defined the responsibilities of the "debtor of the blood" and the "master of the blood" and their respective successors in vengeance.

CONFLICT. Moral death was more threatening than any intervention by the church, as this Albanian saying makes clear: "You fast for the soul and you kill for honor." The idea of feud as ultimately producing family cohesion and at the same time preventing crime and disputes must be seen in the context of a system that took no action in relation to disputes or murders within a household. Since the latter concerned blood within a family, no feud would result. Quarrels arose through disputes about marriage arrangements, territory, theft, murder, and slander, whose respective values were also defined by the Kanun. For example, a guest's security had to be extremely well maintained according to strict regulations, which ensured mobility for all in an insecure environment. Misfortune for or the mistreatment of a guest could provoke blood vengeance or bring forth sanctions (such as burning the host's house) following a

Albanian children were betrothed sometimes even before birth, often in respect of an existing alliance or in order to establish peace with another clan.

decision of the village community. Blood payments or an oath of allegiance, *besa*, were among the institutionalized ways of ending a feud, with regional variations regarding the degree to which this was consistent with one's honor.

Religion and Expressive Culture

RELIGIOUS BELIEFS. In 1967 Albania was proclaimed the first atheist state in the world, and it remained so until December 1990, when the process of democratization under the head of state and party leader, Ramiz Alia, allowed people to admit their faith freely. About 70 percent were registered in a presocialist census as being of Muslim origin, 20 percent Eastern Orthodox, especially in the south, and the rest Catholic. Today there seems to be a tendency to define oneself as Catholic, motivated by a desire to move closer to the West. The old Albanian sayings, "Where the sword is, is the faith," and "The belief of an Albanian is to be an Albanian"—the latter being current right up to and including the socialist period, when it was used for political purposes— throw some light on conversions such as those from the seventeenth to the nineteenth centuries under Ottoman rule, when observance of the Islamic religion became the key to the possession of civic rights. Under Ottoman rule, "Crypto-Christianity" and religious syncretism became very common. After the schism of 1054 north Albania became Roman Catholic, the south Greek Orthodox. Under the Ottomans Catholicism survived only in remoter areas. Four autocephalous Orthodox dioceses were maintained in Tirana, Berat, Gjirokastër, and Korcë until 1967, when atheism was proclaimed. From the fifteenth century on, the Bektashis, a Shiite pantheistic order of dervishes who did not distinguish between Muslim and non-Muslim members, attained great popularity, their monasteries or *tekkë* being spread all over Albania, with their center at the holy tomb of Saint Sari Saltik in Krujë. Typical of the pre-Christian traditional beliefs is the dichotomy of light and dark, equivalents to male and female, sun and moon, good and evil, as can be seen in symbols and figures used in legends, myths, fairy tales (e.g., *kulshedra*, "monster," versus *dragoni*), oaths, curses, tattoos, amulets, handicrafts, on gravestones, etc. There were also beliefs concerning vampires and witchcraft, the interpretation of omens, the observation of natural phenomena for predictions, etc. Taboos of an apotropaic character were also found; for example, the wolf's name was never pronounced out loud.

RELIGIOUS PRACTITIONERS. Neither Catholic priests nor bishops, nor Muslim clergymen (*hoxha* and *sheikh* among the Sunnis), nor abbots (*baba*, sing.; *baballar*, pl.) among the Bektashis, could supply every village. Some were wanderers, all were respected as God's men, and there is evidence that the nearest available were consulted by people of any faith when necessary. Clerics were not allowed to keep house dogs because their houses had to be open all night to parishioners or passing strangers, though Eastern Orthodox and Muslim priests' houses were not considered sacred, and theft from them therefore was not considered sacrilegious. Besides their more or less important role in life-cycle rites and as consultants, priests had an educational role, since the Ottoman administration allowed religious bodies (Franciscans, Jesuits) to run schools. Jesuits sometimes succeeded in ending feuds, because of the belief that they were sent by the pope and had the power to take away God's blessing for one's family for generations to come. In the years after World War II many religious leaders were sent to prison or executed.

CEREMONIES. Life-cycle rites traditionally occurred at birth, the first haircut, sometimes the first nail cutting, marriage, and death. Further rites included the swearing of an oath on a rock, a gravestone, an altar, the doorstep of a church, a meteor, a glowing coal, and on natural phenomena such as the sun, moon, fire, plains, mountains, etc., as well as the besa or renunciation of feud. Rites of the yearly cycle consisted of pre-Christian customs as well as church festivals and processions, which were often shared by people of every faith. Some days involved taboos on certain activities or certain food. Other occasions involved the lustration and blessing of water, farmland, the harvest, agricultural instruments, livestock, houses, children, plants, etc. Under socialist rule religious ceremonies were prohibited and replaced by military and nationalist public celebrations such as First May Day processions, the birthday of the former party leader Enver Hoxha, the anniversary of his death, etc. New Year's Day became the most important festivity of the year.

ARTS. Albanian epic songs were the original vehicle for tradition and local history in a culture without writing. Typical heroic epics (e.g., the epic cycle "The Brothers Muji and Halili," songs of Skanderbeg) were monophonic and sung by professional wandering artists on social occasions, or by private musicians in the family or with friends, who accompanied themselves with the one-stringed lahuta. The telling of fairy tales for adults as well as for children was popular and assured the survival of both cosmological conceptions and old legends. Norms and values were also transmitted through anecdotes, sayings, and riddles. These traditional features are still cultivated and are performed every five years at a major festival of folklore in Gjirokastër, an old city in the south. Also still performed are, for example, the women's "vessel song," polyphonic and monophonic songs with specific regional features, and likewise a variety of men's and women's dances. The best-known modern Albanian writer is Ismail Kadare, born in 1939, who in his novels brings to life traditional conditions in Albania and the individual's experiences under the Ottomans.

MEDICINE. Medicine was traditionally practiced either by local specialized folk doctors (*hekim*), by dervishes, or by "wise old women" with herbal knowledge and knowledge of necessary ritual incantations said to have been inherited from their ancestors. Doctors were highly regarded and were often also considered soothsayers. Christian and Muslim saints were appealed to for help through pilgrimages to holy places such as monasteries, saintly tombs, holy waters and springs, etc. Diseases were attributed to evil forces and malevolent ghosts (*vila*). The latter had a deadly touch, could cast the evil eye, and often symbolized the illness itself. Under socialism the replacement of these traditions through the continuous development of a network of hospitals, medical research institutions, care centers, and maternity stations was regarded as one of the government's most challenging tasks. Modern medicine emphasizes information and prevention. The state bears the expenses for medical treatment and medicine. There were about 714 inhabitants per doctor in 1983, a figure that approximates the European standard.

DEATH AND AFTERLIFE. Wailing, scratching one's face, cutting or tearing out one's hair, wearing clothes inside out, etc. are all recognized modes of mourning. Usually this is done by female dependents and neighbors, rarely also by men, and sometimes female mourners are hired. In the south some mourning takes the form of a repeated antiphonal two-verse song sung by a leading mourner followed by a female chorus. Burial follows on the same day or, if a person dies in the afternoon, on the next morning, after a procession to church. Females bid farewell with a last kiss in front of the door, men inside the church. In some areas the bodies of important males are dressed in their most typical costume, with their rifle and other things associated with them (like a cigarette in the corner of the mouth), and then seated in their own yard on a chair to say their last goodbye to those who gather there. Mourning is continued for forty days in the

IN PRAYER

A Muslim Albanian man in prayer at a mosque. Most Albanians are Muslim; others are Orthodox and Catholic. Berat Mosque, Berat, Albania. (Arne Hodalic/Corbis)

house of the deceased and repeated at certain intervals at the graveside. In Eastern Orthodox areas traditionally the remains were exhumed after three years and the bones placed in a bone house. The good are believed to have an easy death, the bad a hard one. Life is thought to leave a person through the mouth. As well as having a decorated wooden cross, the grave is surrounded by stones either as a protection from the corpse becoming a vampire (the stones hold the corpse down) or as stepping-stones leading the dead on their way to the other world. To make their voyage easier the dead also have coins placed in their mouths (in some areas also apples or other travel supplies). In the mountains, the sites associated with particular murders, especially those resulting from feuds, are indicated with mounds of stones, called *murana*.

Bibliography

Çabej, Eqrem (1966). "Albanische Volkskunde." In *Südost-Forschungen*, edited by M. Bernath, 333–387. Vol. 25. Munich: R. Oldenbourg.

Durham, Edith (1909). *High Albania*. Boston: Beacon Press.

Hahn, J. G. von (1854). *Albanesische Studien*. Vol. 3. Jena.

Hasluck, Margaret (1954). *The Unwritten Law in Albania*. London: Cambridge University Press.

Lienau, Cay, and Günter Prinzing, eds. (1986). *Albanien: Beiträge zur Geographie und Geschichte*. Berichte aus dem Arbeitsgebiet Entwicklungsforschung am Institut für Geographie Münster, vol. 12. Münster: Verlag Dr. Cay Lienau.

Shytock, Andrew J. (1988). "Autonomy, Entanglement, and the Feud: Prestige Structures and Gender Value in Highland Albania." *Anthropological Quarterly* 61: 113–118.

Whitaker, Ian (1968). "Tribal Structure and National Politics in Albania, 1910–1950." In *History and Social Anthropology*, edited by I. M. Lewis. London and New York: Tavistock.

—STEPHANIE SCHWANDNER

ASHKENAZIC JEWS

Ethonym: none

Orientation

The term "Ashkenaz" is derived from a geographic designation in the Hebrew Bible. It is an ethnonym that at one time was applied rather precisely to the German-speaking areas, especially the Rhineland. Ashkenazic Jews have lived across most of northern, central, and eastern Europe, and they have been culturally distinctive roughly since the time of the Holy Roman Empire. However, no group of Jewish communities fits neatly into the standard concept of a "cultural region." With the exception of contemporary Israel, it has been many centuries since Jews constituted a cultural majority within a given territorial region. In fact, it would be more appropriate to speak of Ashkenazim using Mikhail Bakhtin's notion of the chronotope—a field of human interaction defined synthetically along the dimensions of time and space—which would allow us to see these Jews in their interaction with cultural and historical developments among the surrounding populations.

This becomes clear when we try to define the boundaries of Ashkenazic Jewry, which are coterminous with the boundaries of the Yiddish language area. In the seventeenth and eighteenth centuries, Amsterdam and Venice were major Yiddish publishing centers. Dialects of Yiddish were spoken as far north as northern Germany. After the first partition of Poland at the end of the eighteenth century, masses of Jews were incorporated into the westernmost portions of the Russian Empire. The "center of gravity" of Ashkenazic Jewry shifted steadily eastward during the latter parts of the eighteenth and nineteenth centuries for two reasons. First, the western European Ashkenazic communities lost cultural vigor and distinctiveness with the rise of the western European Enlightenment and the possibility of legal emancipation. Second, the Jews of the Russian and Austro-Hungarian empires experienced a massive growth in population. We might employ geological imagery, therefore, and think of Ashkenazic Jewry as a continent that became largely submerged in the modern period, leaving islands in western Europe—particularly Alsace, where Yiddish was spoken until World War II—and that experienced a gradual buildup and then sudden eruption of a mountain range on its eastern borders.

Owing to assimilation, emigration, and genocide, memoir literature generally constitutes the best source of ethnographic information on Ashkenazic Jews. The only extant communities that should properly be called "Ashkenazic" are those in which Yiddish is still spoken. These fall into two categories. The first consists of groups of elderly, usually secularist eastern European Jewish émigrés, centered in Israel, France, the United States, Canada, and a few other countries. The second includes a number of flourishing Hasidic

♦ **Enlightenment**
A social and philosophical movement of the eighteenth century that emphasized the use of reason and scientific explanation, rational thinking, and the questioning of traditional authority.

See also

Jews of Israel

communities, especially in Israel and New York City. The Hasidic communities utilize Yiddish in newspapers and in schools and adult religious study, and many Hasidic families continue to speak Yiddish at home.

Like Middle Eastern Jews, Ashkenazim display four of the major criteria of a distinctive cultural entity: religion, region, language, and political-economic position.

Religion

The cultural-religious system of Ashkenazic Jewry represents a fundamental continuity of the Rabbinic Judaism encapsulated in the Mishnah and the Babylonian Talmud. These compendiums concentrate to a large degree on the problem of adapting Biblical law, intended for a free Israelite polity centered on the temple rituals, to a situation in which Jewish communities were dispersed in other lands and lacked a ritual center. Therefore, they serve Diaspora Jews as a model for cultural adaptation and reconstitution in changing circumstances, and they help explain the persistence of Jewish collective identity through the centuries. The Talmud in particular also contains a great deal of narrative, biographical, and legendary material. The great focus in traditional Ashkenazic culture on Talmud and Bible study fostered an imaginative identification with the past generations whose lives were described therein. Furthermore, the Talmudic model of textual interrogation and dialogue contributed to a close link between textual and oral culture. While in principle Talmudic learning was open to all Jewish males, social stratification and economic pressures generally kept it the province of an elite. In certain periods and places, women were encouraged especially to study the Prophets and Chronicles.

The Ashkenazic sense of time and space was conditioned to a large extent by reiterations of the belief that the Messiah might come at any time to gather all the dispersed Jews in the land of Israel. The ritual cycle remained fixed to the lunar calendar, maintaining powerful associations with the agricultural cycle of Palestine. This system ensured both a rough correspondence between the celebration of festivals and the seasons of the year and also a certain disjuncture between the Jewish calendar on the one hand and the secular and Christian solar calendars on the other. Jewish interaction with the coterritorial populations was also shaped by the significant place of Jews in the folklore and religion of Christianity.

During periods of relative peace and prosperity, it was possible for marriage patterns to conform somewhat to ideals that stressed both the means of engaging in commerce and the leisure and competence to engage in Talmudic scholarship. The ideal marriage, therefore, was one between a young scholar who had studied full-time into his teens and the daughter of a successful merchant capitalist. The bride's family was expected to provide a dowry, often including support of the couple for a few years so the husband could continue his study, after which he would either go into business or find a rabbinic position. This pattern, to the degree it ever held as a norm, failed in largely the modern period under the combined pressures of increased pauperization, communal dislocation, and the ideology of personal choice.

Between the late eighteenth and the early twentieth century, religious Ashkenazic Jews were profoundly divided between Hasidim—enthusiastic, often mystical, and in a sense "populist" followers of the eighteenth-century charismatic leader known as Baal Shem Tov (Master of the Good Name)—and Misnagdim (literally, "opponents"), who fiercely defended traditional standards of social hierarchy, learning, worship, and observance.

Beginning in the nineteenth century, various movements arose as problematic syntheses of Ashkenazic culture—especially the Yiddish language—and the Enlightened or sometimes Social Democratic ideologies of modern Europe. A particularly powerful modern Yiddish culture briefly flourished, grounded in generations of Jews who experienced traditional religious childhood and education and then sought to frame new ideals within the older idioms of Ashkenazic Judaism. Zionism, the only such movement that proved to be an effective historical experiment, synthesized the traditional motif of the messianic return to the land of Israel with modern European ideologies of nationalism and colonialism.

Religious roles in Ashkenazic society were highly segregated according to gender. Separate seating was maintained at synagogue services. To varying degrees, rules governing women's modesty (shaving the head after marriage, not singing in public) were strictly maintained. Since domestic life was governed by religious law, women nevertheless had major "religious" responsibilities, and they often possessed informal authority in various matters.

Region

Ashkenazic Jews generally inhabited all of Europe, except for Iberia and the Mediterranean

The Ashkenazic sense of time and place was largely conditioned by the belief that the Messiah might come at any time to gather all of the dispersed Jews in the land of Israel.

Ashkenazic Jews

LANGUAGE

Yiddish served to unify Jews within particular communities and provided a means of communication between Jews living across a huge territory.

♦ **middleman minority**
A term used to describe an ethnic or racial group that occupies a middle economic position between the supplier and the consumer in a national, regional, or local economy. Usually the group is segregated from the rest of society because of racial or ethnic differences.

lands. Yiddish folklore displays a high consciousness of the regional variations among Ashkenazic Jews. Some of the most prominent markers of variation are dialect and culinary style. In recent times, these regional variations have become hypostatized into a contrast between "Litvaks"—Jews from the northeastern portion of the Russian Pale of Settlement (those eastern portions of the Russian Empire to which Jewish residents were legally confined), comprising historic Lithuania—and "Galicianers"—Jews in the Austro-Hungarian province of Galicia. Other ethnically significant regional designations include White Russia, the Ukraine, Bukovina, Hungary, and central ("Congress") Poland.

Ashkenazic Jewry since the late nineteenth century has been overwhelmingly associated with eastern Europe. In the decades before World War II, Poland, with 3.3 million Jews, had a larger Jewish population than any other country in the world. Other nations with large pre-World War II Jewish populations were Hungary (825,000), Romania (609,000), Germany (566,000), and France (350,000). In 1986, Poland had only 6,000 Jews, Hungary 80,000, Romania 45,000, and Germany 38,000. The largest population remaining in pregenocide "Ashkenazic" lands is located in the nations that were previously republics of the Soviet Union, especially Russia, Belarus, and Ukraine; though the Jews there are currently emigrating in large numbers. Major populations of descendants of Ashkenazic immigrants are located in Israel, the United States, France, Canada, South Africa, Australia, and Latin America. Except in Israel and to a much lesser degree France, the ethnic designation "Ashkenazic" (insofar as it ever had significant currency) has lost ground to the more general designation "Jewish."

Language

The Yiddish language, which is the single most distinctive marker of Ashkenazim, was the most widely used of numerous Diaspora Jewish languages, each of which synthesized Hebrew and Aramaic elements with lexical and syntactic bases of the coterritorial languages or dialects. It should not be supposed that the Hebrew and Aramaic elements were mere remnants of a time when those languages were Jewish vernaculars. Rather, the fact that Bible and Talmud study were at the heart of Ashkenazic culture meant that words, phrases, and loan translations from the religious texts were constantly interacting with the vernacular and shaping the evolution of the Jewish language.

Nor is Yiddish a variant of any single Germanic dialect belonging to a single time or place. Yiddish served to unify Jews within particular communities, and it also provided a means of communication between Jews living across a huge territory, among populations speaking a wide range of different languages. The distinctiveness of Yiddish became more obvious when Jews from Germanic-speaking lands moved into Slavic territories. Yet the language was as porous as the people were separatist, and it thus contains within itself traces of the entire cultural history of the Ashkenazim. The distinctiveness of the Hebrew alphabet also helped identify distinctive Jewish language use, even (or especially) in "secular" texts whose lexical corpus is almost indistinguishable from non-Jewish German usages.

Women and "uneducated" men were the earliest intended audience of Yiddish texts. Religious books in Yiddish, such as formalized supplications to God and an interpretive translation of the Bible, were popular long before the nineteenth century, as were Yiddish versions of the post-medieval adventure-story collections. These texts served as the basis for the growth of a secularist Yiddish literature in the nineteenth and early twentieth century.

Political-Economic Situation

In the "classic" period of Ashkenazic Jewry—before the massive shocks of industrialization, Enlightenment, nationalism, and world wars—Ashkenazim fulfilled the role of a middleman minority. In western Europe, they were variously bankers, peddlers, artisans, and the like. In eastern Europe, they fulfilled all these roles as well, but they were also utilized by the nobility as agents in the development and extraction of capital from new agricultural territories. Thus, Jews had a large percentage of state liquor monopolies in the nineteenth-century Russian Empire, and they often managed the estates of absentee nobility. Jews also served as cultural intermediaries, bringing news of the world especially to isolated peasants.

During the "classic" period, the Jewish communities were marked by a high degree of self-definition and communal autonomy. Their right to settle in a given location and to engage in business was granted by various local authorities, whether bishop, noble, or king. They were sometimes protected by these authorities and sometimes harassed or expelled at the instigation of coterritorial commercial classes or religiously inspired mobs. The rights of particular Jewish families to settle or go into business in a certain spot were frequently controlled by the community itself, which was able to deploy sanctions of Jewish law such as the *khazoke* (proprietary rights to a given "concession") and the *herem hayishuv* (ban on free settlement).

The loss of the middleman-minority sociocultural "slot," the increased threats to Jewish well-being over the course of perhaps three centuries, and the erosion of Ashkenazic Jewish cultural distinctiveness are closely and causally linked. The authority of the traditional texts and the rabbinic elite were undermined by the progressivist philosophy of the Enlightenment. The corporatist status of the premodern Jewish communities was rendered obsolete by the evolution of the inclusive Western nation-state. The masses of Jews in eastern Europe lost the artisanal and petty-commercial bases of their livelihoods, and they found little alternative opportunity in the new industrialism. Today, those descendants of the Ashkenazim who value their distinctive cultural heritage are struggling to find new ways to integrate past and present.

Bibliography

Gutman, Israel, ed. (1990). *The Encyclopedia of the Holocaust*. 4 vols. New York: Macmillan.

Katz, Jacob (1971). *Tradition and Crisis*. New York: Shocken.

Kugelmass, Jack, and Jonathan Boyarin (1983). *From a Ruined Garden: The Memorial Books of Polish Jewry*. New York: Schocken.

Memoirs of Glueckel of Hameln (1932). Translated, with introduction and notes, by Marvin Lowenthal. New York: Harper Brothers.

Tillem, Ivan L., ed. (1987). *The 1987–88 Jewish Almanac*. New York: Pacific Press.

Weinreich, Max (1980). *The History of the Yiddish Language*. Chicago: University of Chicago Press.

Zborowski, Mark, and Elizabeth Herzog (1952). *Life Is with People: The Culture of the Shtetl*. New York: Shocken.

—JONATHAN BOYARIN

AUSTRIANS

Ethonym: Burgenländer, Kärntner, Niederösterreicher, Oberösterreicher, Osterreicher, Salzburger, Steierer, Tiroler, Vorarlberger, Wiener

Orientation

IDENTIFICATION. Austria is a national culture of early twentieth-century origin (1919). It was created out of the six German-speaking provinces of the Austro-Hungarian Empire and the city of Vienna. An eighth province, containing many Hungarian and Croatian speakers, Burgenland, was added in 1945. The national culture is created by a communication system that tries to generate implicit agreement on a small set of values, especially those emphasizing historic, linguistic, and cultural similarities. This system includes the centralized curriculum of the schools, the programming of the national media monopoly, the discourse surrounding national and provincial elections and similar issues reported in the popular press, and customs of various types, including those regarding clothing, food and drink, recreational tastes, and use of dialect. In spite of these linguistic and cultural similarities, the provinces retain social, political, and ideological identities that have resisted complete integration. Also, the national culture is rejected by a growing minority that seeks unification with Germany. The forging of a national identity has fallen disproportionately on the urban centers, notably Vienna.

LOCATION. Austria is bounded on the north by the Czech and Slovak Federative Republic and Germany; on the east by Hungary; on the south by Slovenia, Croatia, and Italy; and on the west by Switzerland and Liechtenstein. Its location is approximately 46° to 49° N and 9° to 17° E. The spine of the Alps runs west to east through the center of Austria. Only the extreme east and northeast edges of the area are hilly lowland plains. The mountains drain primarily north into the Danube River system. Most of the country has alpine climate with a restricted growing season. In the lowlands, the climate is continental with warm, dry summers, humid autumns, and cold, wet winters. Average high temperature in January is −1° C, while in June it is 18° C. Elevation is a stronger determinant of local climate than latitude.

DEMOGRAPHY. The total population in the 1981 census was 7,574,085. Vienna had the largest concentration of population at 1,524,510, followed by Lower Austria (1,431,400), Upper Austria (1,276,807), Steiermark (1,188,878), Tirol (591,069), Carinthia (537,137), Salzburg (446,981), Vorarlberg (307,220), and Burgenland (270,083). Through migration and changing birthrates, the western provinces and highland areas have lost population to the eastern provinces and urban areas. Twenty-three percent of the population lives in villages of 2,500 or less, 32 percent in market towns of 2,500 to 10,000, 15

Austria was created out of the six German-speaking provinces of the Austro-Hungarian Empire and the city of Vienna in 1919.

See also

Germans

After World War II, the four Allied powers each occupied a separate sector of Austria; sovereignty was returned under the condition of perpetual Austrian political neutrality.

percent in cities of 10,000 to 100,000, and 30 percent in cities of 100,000 or more. The population structure has been altered by the mortality of two highly destructive wars in this century and the differential male mortality of advanced industrial societies.

LINGUISTIC AFFILIATION. Most Austrians speak the Southern (Bavarian) dialect of German, a branch of the Indo-European Language Family. Vorarlbergers speak the Alemannic dialect of German more commonly found in northern Switzerland and Swabia. In border provinces, one can find concentrations of speakers of Italian, Slovene, Croatian, Hungarian, and Czech. In Vienna one can find established enclaves of these languages, as well as speakers of Turkish, Serbian, Greek, Russian, Polish, French, Spanish, Arabic dialects, Persian, and English.

History and Cultural Relations

Although each province has a documentary history stretching back to the Roman occupation, the events relevant to the formation of the national culture begin after the First World War. After losing the war, the Austro-Hungarian Empire disintegrated into a number of nation-states—Hungary, Czechoslovakia, and Yugoslavia—based primarily on language affiliation. The German-speaking provinces, some with sizable non-German populations, became the (First) Republic of Austria. Other provinces, some with large German populations, especially in the regional centers, were ceded to Italy (South Tirol), Poland (Galicia), and Romania (Transylvania). National integration was hampered by postwar famine, disease, the loss of provincial markets and areas of supply, and the inflationary cycle and depression of 1926–1938. Pan-German nationalist political ideologies that linked the small, vulnerable Austria to the more powerful German state to the north were popular alternatives to Austrian nationalism, and in 1938 a majority of the country welcomed "Anschluss," the annexation of Austria by the Third Reich. The struggle between German and Austrian nationalism led to cultural warfare that severely damaged—or even, in some cases, destroyed—the country's Jewish, Gypsy, Croatian, and Slovene communities during World War II. After the war, the four Allied powers each occupied a separate sector of the country and of Vienna. In 1955, sovereignty was returned to Austria under the condition of perpetual political neutrality. The war experience, the failure of Pan-Germanism, the permanent neutrality, and the legacy of the destruction of the minority communities became the basis for a new national identity in the Second Republic of Austria.

Germany remains the most significant cultural focus outside Austria. The Austrian schilling is tied to the German mark in international money markets. German corporations are heavily invested in the Austrian economy. The German press is read and German trends in government, society, and consumption are closely monitored. Austria also has important relationships with Hungary and the Czeck and Slovak Federative Republic. Although relations were strained after the dissolution of the Austro-Hungarian Empire and the erection of political barriers in the 1950s and 1960s, the three countries now maintain a cordial association. Currently, their citizens may freely cross their frontiers without visas. Ethnic conflicts have created difficult relations with three other neighbors. In northern Italy (South Tirol), German-speaking Tirolese separatists still wage guerrilla actions against Italian institutions from Austria. Although the Austrian government deplores these actions and has successfully prosecuted offenders, relations with Italy have been strained for many years. German nationalist sentiment has also antagonized Yugoslavia. Croatian minorities in Burgenland and Slovene communities in Carinthia have been subject to discrimination by local and provincial officials. Of all its neighbors, Romania has the most strained relations with Austria. A large number of Protestant Upper Austrians migrated to Transylvania after the Counter-Reformation, but they maintained links to their original communities. These new communities were under the direct threat of "Romanianization" and the destruction of their ethnic identities. After the 1989 rebellion in Romania, however, the threat was mitigated and relations between the countries improved.

Settlements

Austrian ethnographers speak of six identifiable rural settlement forms: (1) single, isolated farms with field blocks; (2) hamlets with tenant holdings; (3) nucleated villages with strip fields; (4) linear villages with strip fields extending through wooded areas; (5) villages built around a central green with rationalized fields; and (6) villages built along a street with rationalized fields. The more diffuse settlements (types 1, 2, and 4) are found in alpine zones. The more nucleated settlements (type 3, 5, and 6) are found in lowland areas. Urban settlements are primarily riverine, nucleated, and, originally, walled. These features derive from the early modern period of town formation (1350–1650) in central Europe when waterways were used as transport routes and there was a high level of political and military insecurity. The most important regional centers—Innsbruck (Tirol), Salzburg (Salzburg), Linz (Upper Austria), Villach and Klagenfurt (Carinthia), Eisenstadt (Burgenland), Graz (Steiermark), and Saint Pölten and Wiener Neustadt (Lower Austria)—are of this type. Vienna, with 20 percent of the national population, is a world-class metropolis and a center for elite entertainments and tourism. It was originally a Roman frontier fortress (Vindobona, A.D. 140) that declined in the post-Roman period only to revive with the building of Saint Stephan's Cathedral in the twelfth century. It was a center of commerce in the early modern period, when it enjoyed staple rights over traffic up and down the Danube. Economic development stagnated in the seventeenth and eighteenth centuries as the Habsburg dynasty transformed the city into a ceremonial and administrative center for the empire. The industrial transformation of the metropolis began late (1820s) and proceeded at a leisurely pace. The razing of the city's walls in 1857 and the development of the broad Ring Boulevard around the central district heralded the beginning of modern city government and planning. By the mid-1890s, all but two of the current twenty-three districts had been annexed from previously autonomous suburbs and the population had swollen to its historic high of 2 million people, two-thirds of whom had been born elsewhere and migrated to the city for industrial employment.

Economy

SUBSISTENCE AND COMMERCIAL ACTIVITIES. Eighty-five percent of Austrians subsist by selling their labor for wages. However, 10 percent of the population in 1982 maintained a self-sufficient agricultural subsistence. The remaining 5 percent represent various professions who subsist on a fee-for-service basis. Among wage earners, more than half are salaried, white-collar employees in the commercial sector or government service. The blue-collar workers, four in ten of whom are certified as skilled, earn an hourly wage based on a 35- to 40-hour work week. All workers and employees work under contract standards established by the federal government and modified to suit the requirements of specific sectors and industries. All wage earners are currently guaranteed four weeks of paid vacation per year, with additional weeks added with seniority. An extensive program of federally administered benefits (health and unemployment insurance, pensions, general relief, family assistance, housing support, retraining programs, and continuing education) is funded through a gradual and progressive income tax. These taxes tend to level the net incomes of wage earners dramatically.

INDUSTRIAL ARTS. Specialty metals, food processing, chemicals (especially petrochemicals), machine tools, and micro-electronics are currently the basis for the greatest industrial-sector growth. Major exports include winter-sports articles, dairy products, and construction materials (lumber and concrete). Real-estate transactions are important to the urban regional economies. Tourism is also an important source of regional income, especially in Vienna and the Tirol.

DIVISION OF LABOR. A person's work life begins around age 15 and lasts through the early 60s. Retirement is a respected state, made all the more palatable by high pension payments. During a person's work life, promotions to higher pay and responsibility are age-related, although one can find fast-track promotions in young industries and government. Two-fifths of working-age women are employed outside the home. Among urban households of three persons or more, more than 75 percent of adult women are wage earners. In the rural areas, women are more likely to work at home. In two-income households, women continue to perform the traditional household-maintenance and child-care roles.

LAND TENURE. In the alpine zones, land tenure is held within family corporations under the leadership of a single person, usually the senior male. As the elevation drops, land is rented for varying periods of time from a titleholder who may reside elsewhere. In lowland regions, land tends to be held by corporations, many of which are wholly owned within families, but with leadership shared among a number of persons.

Kinship, Marriage, and Family

KINSHIP. The most important kinship group is the bilateral *Familie*. The group tends to be coterminous with the household in both urban and rural zones. Relations between lineal relatives, especially parents and their married children or siblings, is recognized with the cover term *Grossfamilie*. These extended family ties are activated through frequent visiting. Families are embedded within a wider bilateral kindred, the *Verwandschaft*. This grouping is activated for life-cycle events.

MARRIAGE. Marriages are monogamous. The age of marriage in urban centers coincides

RELIGION AND EXPRESSIVE CULTURE

Beliefs

Since the Counter-Reformation, Roman Catholicism has dominated Austrian religious belief. Although Eastern Orthodox, Protestants, Jews, Muslims, and Buddhists exist in Austria, they have no power to influence the interpretation of public morality to the extent that the Roman Catholics can. Although church and state are officially separate, the Christian Democratic party represents the interests of the Roman Catholic church in political affairs. In rural zones, this Catholicism can be very conservative. Passion plays with anti-Semitic themes, Latin liturgy, and antimodern ideologies predominate. In urban zones, religious practice is generally sporadic, often limited to life-cycle events.

Arts

In painting, literature, music, architecture, and theater, Austria has produced a significant number of Europe's masters. These artists are celebrated, often deified, in specialized museums, theaters, and concert halls in all of the regional centers, but especially Vienna and Salzburg. Two themes predominate in Austrian arts: an elaborately developed and sophisticated agro-romanticism that glorifies the rural landscape, and an introspective, highly psychologized celebration of modern metropolitan life. These themes coincide with the polarities of Austrian national consciousness: provincialism and cosmopolitanism.

Medicine

In the nineteenth century, Austrian, especially Viennese, medicine was in the vanguard of the development of modern, industrial medical science. Popular beliefs about health, however, retain a much older, humoral character. Much emphasis is placed on the good and ill effects of winds (fresh air, the alpine *Förn*), on the balance of hot and cold meals, and on the natural movements of the body. Homeopathic alternatives to school medicine are so popular that these cures are included in the national health system.

Death and Afterlife

Debilitating disease is feared more than death itself. Death imagery is very important in folk songs, betraying a lighthearted fatalism. Cemeteries play an important role in community life and are visited around 1 November each year. Evergreen wreaths symbolizing resurrection to eternal life are placed on graves.

---

with the establishment of a career track (early twenties), but many delay marriage until their thirties. In alpine zones, the European late-marriage pattern can be found. The decision to marry signifies an intention to have children, since cohabitation without marriage, even within one's parents' house, is tolerated. The Roman Catholic practice of permanent marriage between sexually chaste partners remains prevalent among the rural population. According to state law, divorce can be initiated by either husband or wife, and remarriage is permitted. Marriages tie two extended families together. As soon as possible after the marriage, the couple establishes a neolocal residence within close proximity to one of the families, most frequently the wife's family. After the birth of children, the mother returns to wage earning after a maximum two years of paid leave. Close kin are employed for preschool child care.

INHERITANCE. Where land tenure is held within the family under the leadership of a single individual (alpine practice), the ideology of inheritance specifies that the entire estate should go to the firstborn male offspring. In the absence of that heir, the next oldest child inherits. In all other situations, landed or not, inheritance ideology tends to be bilateral and partible.

SOCIALIZATION. Weaning from the breast occurs within 3 to 6 months. There is strong pressure toward early toilet training, which is often completed by the end of the child's second year. Grandparents play an important role in early childhood development. Disciplinary styles differ between the parents, with the father establishing a harsher, more physical approach, and the mother a more patient and verbal one. Preschool activities begin in the child's third year and regular kindergarten/elementary school in the fifth year. All of these institutions are state-supported. Primary school occupies the years 6 through 10 and emphasizes basic social, reading, writing, and arithmetic skills. Secondary school proceeds from ages

10 through 14. At age 10, the child is tested and tracked into either a continuing elementary school, a basic high school (Hauptschule), or a college-preparatory high school (Gymnasium). Education continues through the mandatory fifteenth year in either vocational schools, teacher-training institutes, apprenticeships, or continuing college-preparatory schools. The wage market relies on the school system for credential certification. Thus, educational decisions are among the most important an Austrian will make.

Sociopolitical Organization

SOCIAL ORGANIZATION. The class structure in Austria has both formal and informal principles. There are five named classes and an all-but-invisible underclass. The named classes are "Bauern" (farmers, especially those with land tenure), "Arbeiter" (workers, especially skilled workers), "Kleinbürger" (bureaucrats, artisans, small-property holders, and shopkeepers), "Grossbürger" (wealthy property owners, industrialists, successful artists, and intellectuals), and "Adelsstand" (nobility with inherited wealth and land). This last class is in decline because public use of one's noble title is now illegal. Families belong to classes; individuals belong to families. Class affiliation is determined by the control of wealth and property or, in lieu of wealth, by educational achievement and the prestige of the position that one's credentials can command. Since real increases in wealth are all but impossible, achieving a higher educational level than one's parents is one of the few paths to social mobility. People tend to socialize, educate, and marry within classes and localities, producing closed, class-based, localized networks that are often activated to solve problems.

POLITICAL ORGANIZATION. Austria is a parliamentary democracy. Representatives are selected for its bicameral legislature from lists prepared by the political parties. The majority party in Parliament or a coalition of parties then names the government ministers. These ministers establish policy, propose laws, and govern the republic on a day-to-day basis. A largely ceremonial official, the federal president, is elected by direct popular vote. Each province has a legislature and a governorship that retain much control over the implementation of federal law. Currently there are four political parties represented in the federal and provincial legislatures: the Social Democrats (Sozialistische Partei Österreichs), the traditional party of working-class interests; the Christian Democrats (Österreichische Volkspartei), the party of clerical, commercial, and industrial interests; the German Nationalists (Freheitliche Partei Österreichs), who call themselves "liberals" but bear no relation in platform or rhetoric to contemporary European liberal parties; and the Green Party (Österreichische Grünen), which represents the environmentalist movement in Austria. A coalition of Christian and Social Democrats has frequently formed the government since the formation of the Second Republic (1955). The Social Democrats enjoyed a majority government from 1971 to 1983. A Communist party also exists and held seats in Parliament in the 1950s and 1960s but is no longer an important political movement. National Socialism is illegal, but at least one fascist underground group operates in the country.

SOCIAL CONTROL. The centralized bureaucracy established under the old empire continues to maintain the most publicly visible institutions of social control. Hardly anything of importance to Austrians can take place without a tax stamp, license, or permit. Conformity to group values is established by gossip within tightly maintained kindreds and networks of acquaintances.

CONFLICT. The Austrian legal system is Napoleonic. Courts and police have sweeping powers to investigate conflicts. The accused must prove innocence by impeaching government evidence. Violent crimes are reported, but they appear to occur less frequently than in other advanced industrial societies. However, property crimes and white-collar crime, especially embezzlement and corruption, are common. Conflicts also occur between the majority group and resident minorities. Former guest workers from Greece, Yugoslavia, and Turkey, who now reside in Vienna, are often the subject of hate graffiti, racist language, and discrimination in employment and housing. Anti-Semitic and anti-Gypsy sentiment is quite common in private discourse and the public media. Private conflicts and alienation are among the biggest social problems Austrians face. Rates of alcoholism, suicide, and absenteeism are among the highest in European societies.

Bibliography

Cole, John W., and Eric R. Wolf (1974). *The Hidden Frontier: Ecology and Ethnicity in an Alpine Valley.* New York: Academic Press.

Honigmann, John (1963). "The Dynamics of Drinking in an Austrian Village." *Ethnology* 2:157–169.

Naroll, Raoul, and Frada Naroll (1962). "Social Development of a Tyrolese Village." *Anthropological Quarterly* 35:103–120.

♦ **guest workers**
A term originally coined in Germany for immigrant workers who have been invited and/or contracted by the host country or individual agents for a specified term.

Ringel, Erwin (1984). *Die österreichische Seele: 10 Reden über Medizin, Politik, Kunst und Religion*. Vienna: Hermann Böhlaus Nachf.

Rotenberg, Robert (1992). *Time and Order in Metropolitan Vienna*. Washington, D.C.: Smithsonian Institution Press.

—ROBERT ROTENBERG

BASQUES

Ethonym: Eskualdunak, Euskaldunak, Vascos

Orientation

IDENTIFICATION. Basques inhabit the area of southwestern Europe where the western spur of the Pyrenees meets the Cantabrian seacoast. Their territory straddles the French-Spanish frontier, providing a distinction between Spanish Basques and French Basques. There are four traditional regions (Bizkaia, Gipuzkoa, Nafarroa, Araba) on the Spanish side and three (Lapurdi, Behe-Nafarroa, and Zuberoa) on the French side. Basques refer to their homeland as "Euskal-Herria" (land of the Basques) or "Euskadi" (country of the Basques). While the seven regions have not been unified for nearly a millennium, the Basques remain one of Europe's most distinctive ethnic groups.

LOCATION. The Basque country is located between 41° to 43° N and 0° to 3° W. It contains 20,747 square kilometers, of which 17,682 square kilometers are on the Spanish side of the frontier. The Basque country contains three ecological zones. The northern zone is comprised of the Cantabrian seacoast and interior foothills. It has a maritime climate and is one of the wettest regions in Europe. The ridges of the Pyrenees constitute a central zone with an alpine climate. The southern zone, or about two-thirds of the Basque country, is in the rain shadow of the Pyrenees and has a continental climate.

DEMOGRAPHY. In 1975 the population was 2,871,717, of which only 229,383 persons resided on the French side. Population density varies greatly by region. Highly urbanized Bizkaia has 533 persons per square kilometer, while rural Behe-Nafarroa has only 22. There are an estimated 828,000 Basque speakers. Basque language proficiency is distributed unevenly, being concentrated primarily in the northern and central ecological zones. It is also more pronounced in rural and fishing communities than in the urban centers. In recent years there has been a vigorous campaign by Basque nationalists to encourage Basque language acquisition. It has met with considerable (though not total) success. All Basques are fluent in either French or Spanish (some in both), depending on which side of the border they inhabit. Use of the Basque language has declined over the centuries in places where it was spoken previously, and use of French and Spanish has increased because of the influx of non-Basque speakers into the area.

LINGUISTIC AFFILIATION. Basque is an agglutinative language and employs the Roman alphabet. It is the sole representative of its own language family. Scholars have tried to demonstrate affinities between Basque and languages from disparate parts of the world, particularly languages in the Caucasus Mountains of Russia. Another possibility is that Basque is linked to Ibero, a language spoken throughout the Iberian Peninsula in pre-Roman times.

History and Cultural Relations

The uniqueness of the language underscores the mystery of the origins of the Basques. Some scholars have suggested that they may even be the direct descendants of Cro-Magnons and the Upper Paleolithic cave painters active in southwestern Europe about 15,000 years ago. Until the Middle Ages Basques were an enclaved, pastoralist people, fierce in resisting the intrusions of outsiders and regarded as barbarians by them. Romans, Goths, Franks, and Moors all controlled parts of the Basque Country without ever quite subjugating it. It was a Basque force that attacked Charlemagne's rear guard as it traversed the Pass of Roncesvalles, killing Roland and giving rise to the famous epic *The Song of Roland*. After A.D. 1000 the several Basque regions came increasingly under the influence of emerging European kingdoms and duchies. Subsequently the embryonic states of England, France, and Spain fought for control over the regions, which frequently became pawns in larger power plays. Sovereignty over the various Basque regions shifted according to the fortunes of battle or the whims of marital alliances among Europe's royalty. Basques retained, however, a considerable degree of autonomy in their own affairs, codified in written *fueros* or charters. This relative autonomy was reflected in the custom whereby the monarchs of Castille, upon ascending the throne, were required to travel to the town of Guernica to swear beneath a sacred oak to respect Basque laws. Coastal Basques were Europe's earliest whalers. Their shipbuilding and navigational skills made them Iberia's most noted seafarers. By the early fifteenth century (and pos-

---

♦ **agglutinative language**
A language in which morphemes are combined into words without substantially modifying their form or losing their meaning.

♦ **continental climate**
In the Köppen system, a climate characterized by large seasonal temperature variations, with hot summers, cold winters, and year-round precipitation.

sibly earlier) Basques were crossing the Atlantic for whaling and cod fishing off the Labrador coast. Basques crewed the ships of Columbus and Magellan. (The Basque Elcano was the first to circumnavigate the globe.) Basque mariners, mercenaries, merchants, and missionaries swelled the ranks of Spain's colonial elite, providing much of the shipping in the American trade and capital for development of the colonies and becoming major figures in both the civil and ecclesiastical administrations. The French Revolution, with its strong centralist tendencies, destroyed the political autonomy of Lapurdi, Behe-Nafarroa, and Zuberoa. Many of their residents resisted and were sent to the guillotine or to concentration camps. In the nineteenth century Basques fought on the losing side of Spain's two Carlist Wars, relinquishing much of their political autonomy in defeat. This, coupled with the late nineteenth-century influx of Spanish workers to Basque industries, which threatened to make Basques a minority in their homeland, caused concern. By 1900 a modern Basque nationalist movement had emerged to confront Madrid's policies in the Basque country. The nationalists contested elections when allowed to do so, gaining control of many municipalities and the provincial assemblies of Gipuzkoa and Bizkaia. When the Spanish Civil War erupted in 1936, those two provinces remained loyal to the republic, fielded an army, and elected an autonomous government that issued passports and coined its own currency. Within nine months the Basques were defeated by Franco, many were executed or imprisoned, thousands were exiled, and the Basque government had been removed to Paris. During the Franco years there was systematic repression of Basque culture. Consequently, in the late 1950s disaffected Basque youths founded an organization known as "ETA" (Euskadi ta Azkatasuna, or "Basque Country and Freedom") with the goal of complete independence from Spain. Its opposition to Franco escalated into violence, providing Europe with one of its most virulent terrorist movements. Franco's death in 1975 ushered in an era of democracy in Spain. Mainline Basque nationalists collaborated in the framing of a new constitution that accorded considerable autonomy to the regions.

Settlements

In the northern ecological zone there are major cities such as Bilbo (Bilbao), Donastia (San Sebastian), and Baiona (Bayonne), as well as regional manufacturing centers of considerable importance (Eibar, Mondragon, Irun). There are many coastal fishing villages with 5,000–10,000 inhabitants. The interior foothills have peasant villages ranging from 500 to 3,000 inhabitants. The village usually encompasses a river valley and the surrounding hillsides. The nucleus, with church, school, taverns, town hall, handball court or fronton (jai alai arena), general stores, and offices of a few professionals (doctor, veterinarian, pharmacist, postmaster) is located on the valley floor. The surrounding hillsides contain *baserriak*, or farmsteads (sing., *baserria*), either isolated from one another or clustered into hamlets of ten or twelve dwellings surrounded by their collective landholdings. The dwellings are massive stone structures, often three stories tall. The ground floor is for animal stables, the second floor is living space, while the third is used to store hay and other crops.

Economy

SUBSISTENCE AND COMMERCIAL ACTIVITIES. Only about 20 percent of the population is engaged in agriculture. In Bizkaia and Gipuzkoa more than 50 percent of the active labor force is employed in industry. Until recently the Basque baserria was a mixed-farming enterprise in which the emphasis was upon self-sufficiency. The farm family grew its own wheat, corn, vegetables, fruits, and nuts and raised poultry, rabbits, pigs, cows, and sheep. Land held in common by the village was an important source of animal pasturage, ferns for animal bedding, limestone for fertilizer, and wood for fuel and building materials. Over the past fifty years there has been increasing commercialization of agriculture. Cropland has been converted either to intensive vegetable growing or fodder production for dairy farming, both to supply urban markets. Agriculture is mechanized, though on a small scale because of the steep terrain. In the central ecological zone there is little permanent settlement. In the summer months shepherds ascend with their flocks and loggers cut hardwood species (oak and beech). In the southern ecological zone agriculture is of the large-estate variety with widely dispersed "agrotowns" surrounded by large holdings. The main crops are the Mediterranean trilogy of wheat, olives, and grapes. Near the Ebro River there is extensive irrigation that permits vegetable growing on a large commercial scale. Basque coastal fishing villages today send their fleets into the Cantabrian and Irish seas for hake, anchovies, and sea bream, and as far as the coasts of western Africa in search of tuna. Some of the vessels are state-of-the-art with mechanical nets,

Some scholars have suggested that the Basques might be the direct descendants of Cro-Magnons and the Upper Paleolithic cave painters active about 15,000 years ago.

refrigeration, and sonic depth finders and helicopters for finding their quarry.

INDUSTRIAL ARTS. The Basque country is one of Iberia's most industrialized regions. The city of Bilbo (Bilbao) houses many heavy industries, including steel plants and shipbuilding facilities. It is also one of western Europe's major ports for off-loading petroleum from supertankers. Smaller industrial towns specialize in modern consumer goods ranging from plastics to sewing machines. There is also an arms industry. Industrial pollution is a major problem in the Basque country, causing poor air quality in the cities, which is exacerbated by traffic congestion. Most of the rivers are notably polluted.

TRADE. While some farmers and fishermen market their products directly in nearby towns and cities, the Basque country now has an efficient network of commercial outlets including supermarkets and department stores.

DIVISION OF LABOR. There is considerable equality between the sexes. In agriculture women frequently work alongside men at the same tasks. In urban areas women are increasingly employed in industry and services. Domestic chores remain, however, largely the purview of women.

LAND TENURE. To be the owner of a farm was socially prestigious and represented economic security in a society in which arable land was at a premium. However, developments over the past fifty years have produced both a glut and a scarcity of land. On the one hand, the inability of peasant agriculture to generate sufficient income to support a twentieth-century life-style has prompted many families simply to abandon agriculture, departing for a city and either letting their baserria fall into disuse or planting it with pines for eventual sale to the paper-pulp industry. On the other hand, many urbanites are now buying or renting baserriak and converting them into chalets—weekend refuges from urban ills.

Kinship

KIN GROUPS AND DESCENT. The urban Basque family is of the nuclear variety, maintaining its own apartment. In the southern ecological zone the nuclear family also predominates in rural districts. On the baserriak the stem family is the basic social form. Kinship is reckoned bilaterally; there is an Ego-centrically defined kindred but it is important only at the marriage or death of the defining member. Neighbors, usually unrelated, play a key role in rural Basque society. One's *lenbizikoatia*, or "first of the neighborhood," is the household of first recourse in a crisis. The larger *auzoa*, or neighborhood, is the source of social intimacy and support.

KINSHIP TERMINOLOGY. Eskimo-type terms are used. Sibling terms differ according to whether the speaker is male or female.

Marriage and Family

MARRIAGE. Basques are monogamous and exercise considerable personal choice in selecting spouses. However, people regard the marriage of the designated male or female heir to the baserria as a household affair. The parents transfer ownership of the farm to the newlyweds as part of the marital arrangements. Small villages tend to be endogamous and cousin marriage is not infrequent, including some unions between first cousins.

DOMESTIC UNIT. The heir to the baserria and spouse form a stem-family household with his or her parents. Unmarried siblings of the heir may remain in residence in their natal households until death, but they are subject to the authority of the active male and female heads. The family works the baserria together, with children and the elderly contributing to the lighter tasks as well. In the urban areas the apartment-dwelling nuclear family, possibly with a live-in servant for the affluent, is the domestic unit. It may also contain a spinster aunt or aging parent.

INHERITANCE. Ownership of the baserria is transferred to a single heir in each generation. In parts of the Basque country custom dictates male primogeniture unless the candidate is blatantly unsuitable. Out-marrying siblings of the heir are provided with dowries. They also share equally in the "personal" wealth of their deceased parents (e.g., money, jewelry, etc.). In urban areas the offspring usually share equally in the estate of the deceased, although the national legal codes favor one recipient with a maximum of one-third of the total.

SOCIALIZATION. Children are raised by everyone in the household. In the case of affluent urbanites the household may also include a female domestic servant who doubles as a nanny. On the baserriak families emphasize subordination of individual interests to the well-being of the domestic unit. One child is socialized as the heir, and his or her siblings are raised with the understanding that they should leave. This system has made the rural Basque country a seedbed of emigrants.

Sociopolitical Organization

The Basque country is a part of Spain and France, both constitutional democracies.

SOCIAL ORGANIZATION. Basque society is suffused with an egalitarian ethos. The owner of a

---

♦ **primogeniture**
A rule of inheritance that gives the exclusive right of inheritance to the first-born son.

♦ **stem family**
A residential group composed of a nuclear family and one or more additional members who do not comprise a second nuclear family.

baserria is extolled as an *etxekojaun* (lord of the household) and his spouse as *etxekoandria* (lady of the household). Basque fishermen are similarly proud and independent. The Basque country was largely untouched by western European feudalism, and there is a common belief that every Basque is a noble. There is considerable social mobility, and wealth differences do not automatically determine social status. However, there is an urban Basque plutocracy of factory owners, bankers, and wealthy professionals who relate more to the Spanish and French national elites than to their fellow Basque peasants, shopkeepers, etc. There is a near castelike division between Basques and non-Basques, with the latter constituting much of the lower-class, urban proletariat. Non-Basques are the frequent targets of resentment and discrimination.

POLITICAL ORGANIZATION. At the municipal level communities are governed by an elected mayor and town council. The three regions in France form, with Bearn, the "Département des Pyrénées Atlantiques" with its seat of government in Pau. Each of the four provinces in Spain has its own popularly elected assembly or *diputación*. Nafarroa now constitutes its own autonomous region within the Spanish state. Gipuzkoa, Bizkaia, and Araba together form the Autonomous Community of Euskadi. This regional government is funded largely by the participating diputaciónes. With its capital in Vitoria (Gasteiz), it has its own popularly elected president, parliament, and ministries. It controls some mass media, the educational system, economic development, and cultural affairs. All foreign relations are handled by Madrid. Basques elect representatives to the Spanish and French parliaments as well.

SOCIAL CONTROL. Social control at the local level is largely through peer pressure. The parish priest exercises moral influence beyond the strictly religious sphere.

CONFLICT. The Basque area is heavily policed, particularly on the Spanish side. The Spanish "Guardia Civil" is an omni-present, largely despised factor in local life. Even political moderates tend to regard their homeland as "occupied," and removal of this force is one of the main demands of Basque nationalists of all persuasions. Clashes between the *guardias* and the ETA have produced more than 600 deaths over the past three decades.

Religion and Expressive Culture

RELIGIOUS BELIEFS. With very few exceptions Basques are Roman Catholic. Even the smallest village has its own church. There are several major monasteries. Basque Catholicism has strong Jansenistic overtones.

RELIGIOUS PRACTITIONERS. While possibly the last people in western Europe to convert to Christianity, the Basques have produced such titans of the Catholic church as Saint Ignatius of Loyola and Saint Francis Xavier. There is strong Marist devotion focused on icons of the Virgin Mary housed in several churches. Until recently there were so many religious vocations that Basque priests and nuns regularly staffed Catholic missions in Africa, Asia, and Latin America. Since the Second Vatican Council church attendance and religious vocations have plummeted, prompting the closure of some churches. Formerly Basques believed in witches and legendary supernatural dwellers of mountain caverns and forest fastnesses.

ARTS. Practically every village has its folkdance group. The *txistu* (flute) and drum, played simultaneously by a single performer, are the distinctive musical instruments. There are *bertsolariak*, or versifiers, capable of spontaneously composing and singing rhymes on any subject. Such performances are a part of every village festival, and regional and national championships are held periodically. In the fine arts Basques have produced several composers of note (Arriaga, Guridi, Ravel), writers (Baroja, Unamuno), painters, and sculptors (including the world-famous Eduardo Chillida).

MEDICINE. Even the most remote villages have access to modern medical care. Nevertheless, beliefs in the efficacy of certain folk treatments (usually herbal) persist. Some of the older generation still fear the evil eye.

DEATH AND AFTERLIFE. A funeral is the most important life ritual in Basque society, triggering a year-long series of ceremonies involving the deceased's household, neighborhood, kindred, and village. Failure to conduct them is felt to compromise the deceased's smooth transition to the afterlife. Otherwise standard Christian beliefs in heaven, purgatory, and hell obtain.

Bibliography

Douglass, William A. (1969). *Death in Murelaga: Funerary Ritual in a Spanish Basque Village*. Seattle: University of Washington Press.

Douglass, William A. (1975). *Echalar and Murelaga: Opportunity and Rural Exodus in Two Spanish Basque Villages*. London: C. Hurst.

Greenwood, Davydd J. (1976). *Unrewarding Wealth: The Commercialization and Collapse of Agriculture in*

Even political moderates tend to regard their homeland as "occupied." The Spanish "Guarda Civil" is an omni-present, largel despised factor in local life.

♦ **autonomous region (AR)**
An autonomous (usually, ethnically based) region of a Union republic. In the former Soviet Union there were eight autonomous regions.

a Spanish Basque Town. Cambridge: Cambridge University Press.

Ott, Sandra (1981). *The Circle of Mountains: A Basque Shepherding Community*. Oxford: Clarendon Press.

Zulaika, Joseba (1988). *Basque Violence: Metaphor and Sacrament*. Reno: University of Nevada Press.

—WILLIAM A. DOUGLASS

BOSNIAN MUSLIMS

Ethonym: Bošnjaci Muslimani

The Bosnian Muslims of the former Yugoslavia, living in the independent state of Bosnia-Hercegovina, number about 1.8 million, or roughly 8 percent of the total previous Yugoslavian population. They constitute the majority ethnoreligious group in the state (44 percent of its population with Serbs making up 31 percent and Croats 17 percent [1991 census]). Since all three groups share in the same Serbian or Croatian linguistic tradition, the distinctiveness of the Bosnian Muslims is primarily based on religious affiliation (the Serbs are Eastern Orthodox Christians and the Croats are Catholic). There is a further, demographic distinction to be made as well. Although there is strong Muslim representation in

> *Even after the establishment of the Communist government after World War II, authorities tolerated Bosnian Muslim religious observances and institutions, including Islamic schools.*

REFUGEE

A Bosnian Muslim boy reads scriptures aloud in a refugee camp. Ljubljana, Slovenia. (Bojan Brecelj/Corbis)

See also

Croats, Serbs

the countryside, their presence is markedly high in the cities. There has been some dispersal of Bosnian Muslims to territory beyond the state. This emigration has largely been in response to politicomilitary movements such as the occupation and later annexation of the territory by the Austro-Hungarian Empire, the incorporation of the region into the Kingdom of the Serbs, Croats, and Slovenes in 1918, and the installation of a Communist regime in the years following World War II. Many of these émigrés went to Turkey, although others settled in the United States, particularly in the last emigration wave.

Beginning in the mid- to late fifteenth century, when the Ottoman Empire ruled the region, Islam came to Bosnia. Mass conversions took place, although there is no evidence to support a charge that coercion was involved. However, these conversions were centered within the landowning classes and among the free peasantry, whereas the serfs of the region remained by and large Christian.

Bosnia-Hercegovina is predominantly rural and agricultural, and the Bosnian Muslim population is largely involved in agrarian pursuits. Cereal farming and livestock keeping are the centerpieces of the rural economy. Of those animals raised, sheep are the most important. In this respect, they differ little from their non-Muslim neighbors. Their traditional, patrilocal, extended farm households (*zadruga*) also are of a type common to ethnic groups throughout the Balkans. All household members contribute to their collective economic well-being, with the bulk of the heavy agricultural labor and livestock care falling to the males. In the cities, Bosnian Muslims are heavily represented in craft production and tend to dominate the professions and civil-service posts.

Kinship is reckoned patrilineally, but in daily life this emphasis has few applications. Traditionally, the tie among brothers, and perhaps first cousins as well, was more important, as from this pool of kin the cooperative group of the zadruga was formed. The establishment of fictive kin ties through sponsorship roles is also limited; the only occasion for which a sponsor is recruited is the "first haircut" rite of passage for male children. The family generally chooses the sponsor from outside of the Muslim community, so that this ritual provides the occasion for forming alliances with non-Muslim neighbors.

Ideally, marriage among Bosnian Muslims is endogamous. When a marriage does occur between a Bosnian Muslim and an "outsider," that outsider is generally a Muslim of some other ethnic group. In rural areas, marriage to a non-Muslim is extremely uncommon, although it has increased in frequency in the urban areas. Polygyny, though practiced prior to its prohibition by state law, was rare.

In religious matters, Bosnian Muslim practice is similar in most particulars to that of Turkish Muslims. Even after the establishment of the Communist government in the years after World War II, authorities tolerated Bosnian Muslim religious observance and institutions. This toleration extended to Islamic schools, which were allowed to continue to operate, but only in addition to, rather than as a replacement for, the compulsory state educational system.

Bibliography

Cole, John W., and Sam Beck (1981). *Ethnicity and Nationality in Eastern Europe.* Amsterdam: University of Amsterdam.

Lockwood, William G. (1975). *European Moslems: Economy and Ethnicity in Western Bosnia.* New York: Academic Press.

Smajlovic, Ahmed (1980). "Muslims in Yugoslavia." *Journal of the Institute of Muslim Affairs* 2:132–144.

—NANCY E. GRATTON

BRETONS

Ethonym: Breizhiz, Bretoned

Orientation

IDENTIFICATION. Brittany is the westernmost region (formerly called a province) of France comprising the four departments (large administrative units in France, roughly equivalent to U.S. states) of Côtes-du-Nord, Ille-et-Vilaine, Finistère, and Morbihan. The Breton population is predominantly of Celtic descent.

LOCATION. Brittany is effectively a large peninsula, bounded on three sides by water: the English Channel to the north and the Atlantic Ocean to the west and south. The peninsula is 160 kilometers wide at its eastern boundary and 90 kilometers wide at the west; it is 215 kilometers long and has 2,800 kilometers of coastline. Numerous islands are associated with the Breton mainland both historically and culturally: they are located on all three sides of the peninsula and contribute an additional 700 kilometers of coastline. Although transected by the 47th parallel (the same as Quebec in Canada), Brittany enjoys a rel-

atively mild climate due to the Gulf Stream that courses around the peninsula. Winter is moderate with little or no snow or ice. Summer is cool, with temperatures ranging between 4.4 and 18° C. Rain falls throughout the year (on average 104 centimeters), and land and sea breezes are nearly always present. The peninsula is in general of low elevation, its highest point reaching only 384 meters in the Monts d'Arrée in the northwest. Although low, the interior lands are not generally flat but consist of gently rolling slopes and small hills. Undulating cultivated fields enclosed by dense boundary-marking hedges (*bocages*) are typical of the landscapes offered in interior Brittany. Moorland (*landes*) is also extensive in the north-central and northwestern sectors. The coast is marked by numerous inlets and estuaries, rugged cliffs, and imposing outcroppings of rocks and crags along the northern and western sides; the south in general affords easier access to the ocean and to many fine beaches. Bretons have for generations expressed the contrast between the interior and the coast with the epithets *armor*, "the sea," and *argoat*, "the forest" (reflecting an age when the interior was heavily wooded).

DEMOGRAPHY. Historically one of the most densely populated regions of France, Brittany has, through high losses in human life suffered during the two world wars and through emigration, dwindled from 6.5 percent (1.83 million) of the French population in 1801 to 4.98 percent (2.7 million) in 1982, and the population continues gradually to decrease. Bretons constitute a unique ethnolinguistic constellation within the territorial boundaries of France, but they are linked culturally and historically to the Celts of the British Isles (the Irish, Welsh, and Scots). Originally a farming and maritime population on the whole, Brittany has in the past twenty-five years lost more than half of its farming families and many of its fishing families to cities in Brittany or elsewhere in France (especially to Paris)—or, to a lesser extent, to other countries. The toll of emigration has been only partially offset in recent years by immigrant workers originating chiefly from Mediterranean countries.

LINGUISTIC AFFILIATION. The Breton language belongs to the Brythonic Branch of the Celtic Family of languages. It is thus closely related to Cornish (now extinct) and to Welsh, and more distantly related to the Celtic languages in the Goidelic Branch—Irish Gaelic, Scots Gaelic, and Manx. It is estimated that there are 500,000–600,000 speakers of Breton in Brittany; probably all Breton speakers nowadays also know French.

♦ Celts
An Indo-European people of Iron Age and pre-Roman Europe who ranged from the British Isles to Asia Minor. Modern-day descendants of the Celts include the Irish, Highland Scots, Welsh, Cornish, and Bretons.

See also
French

Bretons

Breton soil has long been the site of armed conflict; early Bretons fought Frankish and Norse invaders and attempted to gain or maintain sovereignty and territorial integrity.

History and Cultural Relations

The presence of this originally insular Celtic population on the Continent is accounted for by their migrations from the British Isles that took place between the third and fifth centuries A.D., apparently set off by the military and territorial pressures exerted by advancing groups of Angles and Saxons. Their settlement in Brittany was permanent, and Bretons managed for a time (ninth-tenth centuries) to create an independent state, but they were subsequently besieged by both Frankish (the future French) and Norman invaders, which reduced the amount of territory under their control. In 1488 Breton forces were definitively defeated in battle by the French, and in 1532 Brittany was officially annexed to the French state. However, throughout the ancien régime, Brittany retained its own parliament and administrative autonomy. Because of these facts and the sheer physical distance of Brittany from Paris, the Breton "province" was able to retain its distinctive Celtic culture and language, particularly in nonurban areas, which meant most of the vast inland territories of the province. The majority of the Breton people did not assimilate linguistically and culturally into the French nation until the nineteenth century, with the imposition of the military draft and obligatory public education, the creation of a network of highways and railways, and the development of industry. World War I greatly accelerated the assimilation process through the patriotic rallying of the populace and through the disproportionate loss of lives to the war effort (12 percent of Bretons were killed in World War I, though they represented only 6.5 percent of the total French population at that time). The interwar years saw the development of a significant movement for Breton autonomy; for some Bretons this meant also a return to the Breton language and traditional cultural values that they felt had been seriously threatened, if not destroyed, by the French. The movement for political autonomy from France is not so strong today, but there continues to be significant agitation among the people for the development of higher levels of cultural, linguistic, and economic self-determination.

Most Bretons perceive themselves as constituting a distinct ethnic or cultural group within France, at least historically. Divisions within the Breton population are chiefly along class and political lines, though tensions at times are manifested between Bretons and non-Breton immigrant groups in urban areas. Many Bretons also identify with the wider Celtic community; cultural and intellectual exchanges between Brittany and Wales, Ireland, and Scotland have been occurring for a very long time.

Settlements

Small hamlets and dispersed farmsteads characterized the settlement pattern in rural Brittany for centuries. Larger agglomerations of population were found in the parish headquarters—the *plous* (in Latin, *plebs*, "people"), which, although based on a church, were by no means limited to religious activities, but served economic and social functions as well. The area covered by a plou could vary widely—between roughly 10 and 100 square kilometers. As the population grew, the plous were subdivided into segments (*trevioù*), which in turn would grow into new parishes. The inheritance of this settlement and naming system is still very much in evidence in modern Brittany, where place names beginning in "Plou-" and "Tre-" are abundant (especially in the northwestern regions). The traditional rural house is rectangular, constructed of granite, with a roof of thatch or slate whose gables at each end are topped by a chimney; older houses have but one or two rooms, and appended structures, such as a stable (which would share a wall with the house), add to the impression of size. The traditional style is evident in many new houses throughout Brittany, though today they may be of cement, are whitewashed, and are far more spacious. Most of the major urban agglomerations in Brittany are found strung along or with access to the coast, the most important of which are (proceeding counterclockwise from the northeast) Saint Malo, Saint Brieuc, Morlaix, Brest, Concarneau, Quimper, Lorient, and Vannes. All of these support commercial maritime activities. The only major interior city is Rennes, historically the capital of the province; nowadays it is an industrial center (for the Citroën automobile, printing, and communications industries) and home to one of the two major universities located within Brittany (the other being in the coastal city of Brest).

Economy

SUBSISTENCE AND COMMERCIAL ACTIVITIES. Subsistence polyculture was the economic basis for the majority of Bretons living in the interior regions, and fishing and algae gathering for the coastal folk, until the early decades of the twentieth century. Since the two world wars, especially World War II, agriculture has modernized greatly, which has had two important results: first, it has meant the loss of countless small farms and the migration of farming families to the cities; but second, it has also increased the efficiency of agricultural production to the point that Brittany now ranks as the leading agricultural region of France, exporting such products as chicken, pork, fresh and canned vegetables, potatoes, milk, and butter. Fish and crustaceans are also an important economic and culinary resource, as well as a major attraction to tourists. Bretons, too, who in earlier epochs partook but little of marine products, have come to appreciate their own "fruits of the sea." The traditional diet consisted of potatoes, bread, buckwheat crepes, porridge, salt pork, eggs, cider, and milk; relatively little meat or fish was consumed until after World War II. Brittany experienced rapid industrialization after 1960, coming to it later but more intensively than other regions of France. Industries associated with agriculture—canneries, dairies, animal feed producers, slaughterhouses and packing plants, agricultural machinery manufacturers—constitute the largest industrial sector; however, other types of significant industrial activity include mining (of granite, slate, and kaolin), construction (including boats and ships), telecommunications, automobiles, and public works. In spite of considerable industrial growth since over the past thirty years, not all industries have prospered continuously (e.g., naval construction has markedly declined since 1975), and unemployment rates rose as high as 11 percent in parts of Brittany in the 1980s. A boom in tourism, on the other hand, has spawned a sizable hostelry industry; recent decades have also witnessed a sharp increase in the "secondary residence" building business. Finally, certain Parisian and multinational companies engaged in light industry requiring a sizable labor force have been attracted to Brittany because of the lower salaries accepted by a largely young, nonunionized, female workforce of rural origin.

INDUSTRIAL ARTS. Woodworking is a traditional Breton craft that has much declined in the wave of machine-turned furniture, yet is still practiced by skilled artisans. Pottery making continues as an important artisanal craft of considerable commercial value.

TRADE. The 1970s brought to Brittany the first supermarket chains, which now flourish throughout the region. Another development has been that of the "commercial centers" where, in addition to food, it is possible to purchase almost any consumer good that can be carted out of the store. These are located on the outskirts of cities such as Rennes, Brest, Quimper, and Lorient, and they draw customers from urban and rural environs alike. Such giant enterprises have threatened, though not entirely eliminated, the family-run specialty shops that used to be the norm. In addition, the tradition of weekly or biweekly open-air markets has remained robust in medium-sized towns.

DIVISION OF LABOR. In its days as a rural, strongly Catholic society, male-female division of labor was much as in other premodern agricultural societies, with women having the primary responsibility for food preparation, washing, rearing children, weaving, sewing, etc., while men did the majority of the heavy farmwork and took care of the farm machinery and equipment. With the advent of farm mechanization and the "desertification" of the farm—especially by women—this pattern is no longer so straightforward. Probably a majority of adult women work in the paid labor force at some time in their lives and manage households that have been enhanced with up-to-date services and utilities. Many women have moved into professional and technical spheres of employment. Nevertheless, shopping, cooking, and child rearing are much more likely to be done by women than by men, while mechanical and heavy industrial work are still within the male province.

LAND TENURE. In the Middle Ages, the *domaine congéable* was developed in Brittany whereby land was held by one owner, while the buildings, orchards, tools, livestock, etc. were owned by the occupant. This system gradually was replaced by private (individual or family) ownership of the complete farm. The fragmentation of holdings through the partible inheritance system (also a problem elsewhere in France) has over the generations reduced many fields to such small dimensions that they are unworkable in this age of mechanized agriculture. Many families therefore have sold their parcels to larger, wealthier farmers or to agribusinesses. Yet private ownership of a house and plot of land (for a garden) remains a goal for many Bretons.

Kinship, Marriage, and Family

KINSHIP. Lineage is traced cognatically, but the naming system is patronymic. Women used to retain their patronyms after marriage, a practice that has been largely supplanted in this century by the French vironymic system. Fictive kinship in the form of godparent-godchild relations was a very important part of the social fabric for a long

♦ levirate
The practice of requiring a man to marry his brother's widow.

time; often the godparent would in fact be real kin—an unmarried aunt or uncle, for example. The extended family—consisting of three generations and often collateral kinfolk—was the basic social unit in the countryside, but this has been broken up through the emigration of rural families to the cities or to other regions of France. Nuclear families are now in general the rule.

MARRIAGE. The marriage ceremony remains an important celebration for the individual and the family, and most couples choose to have both the civil and the church ceremonies performed (only the former is strictly necessary). In traditional rural Brittany marriages were the occasion for days-long revelry, with hundreds of people invited to partake in the feasting and games. It was not unusual for multiple marriages to take place—that is, two or more sisters would marry two or more brothers. The levirate was also practiced. Postmarital residence could be either uxori- or virolocal; nowadays it is chiefly neolocal. Young couples tend to have their children early in the marriage. Through birth control practices, couples can limit the size of their families to the desired two or three children (in contrast with past generations of couples who were pressured by the church to produce as many offspring as possible). Divorce is fully legal but still stigmatized.

DOMESTIC UNIT. The basic unit is now the nuclear family, though this may expand as needed to accommodate elderly or invalid relatives.

INHERITANCE. Bilateral partible inheritance has long been customary in Brittany, though generally only one child would inherit the farm (whether it was the oldest or the youngest varied

SOCIOPOLITICAL ORGANIZATION

Brittany, formerly a province under the ancien régime, today is qualified as a "region" within the republic of France; it is sometimes grouped with other western-lying departments under the generic title of "l'Ouest" (the West). Administratively, it consists of the four departments noted earlier (a fifth department, Loire-Atlantique, was recently reassigned to another region). Each department has delegates elected to the National Assembly under a multiple-party system that represents Communist, Christian democratic, socialist, and right-wing viewpoints. Departments also have *préfets* (chief executive officers) who are appointed by the central government and are not necessarily of Breton origin.

Social Organization

The traditional social organization revolved around the extended family as the basic unit of kinship and subsistence; however, local groupings of families into hamlets and plous was another important organizational component in which people could provide material and psychological support for one another through mutual cooperative efforts (e.g., at harvest time, at birth and death). Vertical class divisions also organized people and activities, more stringently in the past than now, into peasant, bourgeois, aristocrat, religious, and secular classes.

Political Organization

Implementation of national policies at the regional level is carried out through the French system of departmental, arrondissement, and cantonal divisions (these are in decreasing order of jurisdiction). There is also a regional council with elected representatives empowered to make some decisions independent of the central government. Local matters are considered at the level of the commune, which is presided over by a mayor and municipal councillors (elected positions).

Social Control

The Catholic church historically played a key role in social control (and in reproduction); its influence has steadily diminished in the present century. On an informal level, gossip—within the neighborhood or village—remains a powerful tool of social control. At the formal level of control and conflict resolution, the French legal system—based on the Napoleonic Code—has been in effect since 1804.

Conflict

Breton soil has been the site of much armed conflict throughout its history as Bretons early on fought Frankish and Norse invaders and attempted to gain or maintain sovereignty and territorial integrity; from the eleventh century until annexation of Brittany to France in 1532, innumerable bloody confrontations—on both land and sea—took place as English and French forces vied for Breton territory. Internal conflict has also erupted intermittently, notably following the French Revolution, when Republicans and Royalists were pitted against one another. The 1930s witnessed the rise of syndicalism and the workers' assertion of their rights vis-à-vis employers and unfavorable economic policies. Brittany was occupied by the Germans during World War II; the civilian population suffered considerable losses, and internal conflict again arose here (as elsewhere in France) between collaborationists and *résistants*. Post-World War II years have witnessed protests and demonstrations against the central government's economic policies regarding French regions, against nuclear power plants in Brittany, and in favor of greater economic, cultural, and linguistic autonomy.

locally). The remaining siblings were recompensed with other property or goods. The female's equal right of inheritance has, through the centuries, been one of the distinctive features of Breton culture vis-à-vis the French (and other non-Celtic Europeans).

SOCIALIZATION. Although corporal punishment of children is not unknown, Bretons have for long relied on verbal admonishment and instruction through a rich repertoire of proverbs and aphorisms. Appeal to Christian models of behavior and, in earlier days, the inculcation of a fear of hell and the wrath of God were also regularly deployed in the socialization process.

Religion and Expressive Culture

RELIGIOUS BELIEFS AND PRACTICES. The vast majority of Bretons are of the Catholic faith, though practice of religion (regular attendance at mass, confession, etc.) has waned throughout this century, particularly among men. However, baptism, marriage, and funeral rites within the Catholic church are still pervasive. Historically Bretons have been noted for their deep religiosity, their profusion of saints (most are unique to Brittany) and chapels, their religious festivals—such as the *pardons*—and their pilgrimages. Pardons, marked by singing and dancing as well as religious observances, are still much in evidence today, though the religious underpinnings of these celebrations have been undermined by commercialism and tourism. A salient festival, known as *la grande troménie*, still takes place in western Brittany every six years, in which participants walk 12 kilometers bearing saints' icons, visiting the chapels and sacred spots believed to be inhabited by the saints within the parish.

ARTS. Brittany's visual arts consist of many elements: centuries of architectural styles applied to both secular and religious structures (the Roman and Gothic influences are manifest, in addition to the Breton refinement of the tall, pointed spire so typical of its churches); statuary that is perhaps most memorably displayed in the magnificent calvaries (which depict scenes from the gospels with stone statues) and ossuaries that are the companions to many churches; centuries-old traditions of painting and tapestry; and a rich complex of artisanal crafts. Traditional music of Brittany focuses on two wind instruments—the *biniou* (a small bagpipe) and the oboelike *bombarde*—which are typically paired together in performances. Troops of biniou players are also popular. The Celtic harp has been reintroduced in recent decades; and the accordion has also been a popular instrument in this century. Literary production in the Breton language has seen a great upward surge in diversity and quality since the 1920s following centuries of neglect, which was a result of the castigation and repression of the spoken Breton language by the French and by Breton authorities representing their policies.

MEDICINE. Traditional Breton medicine drew on homemade herbal remedies; but there was also reliance on a person called a *diskonter*, who could dispel illnesses or disorders with special incantations (handed down from generation to generation within certain families). Today Breton medicine is almost completely in the hands of highly trained medical specialists in the national health system.

DEATH AND AFTERLIFE. Bretons tend to prepare for death—ensuring well in advance that their cemetery plot or place in the family vault is secured and selecting their funerary garb. Cremation is seldom practiced. Many superstitions accompany appropriate conduct when a close relative has died: for example, the doors and windows of the deceased's house should be left open to permit the soul (thought to assume the shape of an insect) to leave easily; mirrors should be turned to face the wall. Relatives accompany the deceased to the church, where a mass is said prior to burial, after which the family returns home for a ceremonial meal. In the first year following a person's death, a number of services will be held in the deceased's name to assist the soul in its journey to the *anaon* (the world beyond); such at least was the traditional belief and practice. The legendary death figure is Ankou, represented as a skeleton with a scythe, often riding a wooden cart. Tradition has it that the sound of his cart creaking portends the death of someone in the neighborhood. In popular belief of times past, hell (*ifern*) was conceptualized as a glacial place rather than as an inferno, seen in references to *ifern yen* ("cold hell") in fifteenth- to seventeenth-century liturgical literature.

Bibliography

Badone, Ellen (1989). *The Appointed Hour: Death, Worldview, and Social Change in Brittany*. Berkeley: University of California Press.

Bonneton, Christine, ed. (1979). *Bretagne: Ecologie, économie, art, littérature, langue, histoire, traditions populaires*. Le Puy: C. Bonneton.

Delumeau, Jean, directeur (1969). *Histoire de la Bretagne*. Toulouse: Privat.

Meynier, Andre (1984). *Atlas et géographie de la Bretagne*. Rev. ed. Lausanne: Flammarion.

The vast majority of Bretons are of the Catholic faith.

Segalen, Martine (1985). *Quinze générations de Bas-Bretons: Parenté et société dans le pays bigouden Sud, 1720–1980.* Paris: Presses Universitaires de France.

—LENORA A. TIMM

BULGARIANS

Ethnonym: Bulgarini, Bulgars

Orientation

IDENTIFICATION. Bulgaria is identified variously on the basis of geographical, cultural, and political factors as part of eastern Europe, southeastern Europe, the Balkans, the Slavic countries, the South Slavic countries, and, until recently, the Communist bloc. The most likely origin of the name "Bulgarian" is from the Turkic verb meaning "to mix," reflecting the mixture of various Turkic tribes that invaded the region and established the first Bulgarian polity.

LOCATION. Bulgaria is located on the eastern part of the Balkan Peninsula, between 41°14′ and 44°13′ N and 22°21′ and 28°36′ E. It is bordered by Romania to the north, Yugoslavia to the west, Greece to the southwest and south, Turkey to the southeast, and the Black Sea to the east. The country has a varied topography consisting of mountains, foothills, and plains. The major feature is the Balkan mountain chain, which runs across the center of the country in an east-west direction, turning northward in the west. The Danubian Plain lies to the north of the Balkans; and the upper Thracian Plain, to the south. Bulgaria abuts the Rhodope, Rila, and Pirin massif, located to the south and southwest. The topography has a strong influence on the climate, dividing the country into two climatic zones. In the north the climate is eastern European continental, with hot summers and cold winters. The Balkan range shields the south from cold winter winds, producing a modified Mediterranean climate with milder winters and hot dry summers.

DEMOGRAPHY. In 1988 the population of the country was 8,973,600. Approximately 85 percent are ethnically Bulgarian. There is much concern about the low birthrate among Bulgarians, which has dropped from one of the highest in Europe in the 1870s to the current level, which barely exceeds the rate necessary to sustain existing population levels. This dynamic has led to an increase in the average age of the population. The other major demographic shift has been in the urban component of the population, which has grown from only 20 percent in 1900 to 66 percent in 1988.

LINGUISTIC AFFILIATION. Bulgarian is classified as a South Slavic language and is written with the Cyrillic alphabet. However, the contemporary grammar and vocabulary show diverse influences, especially Turkish. There are various regional dialects in the country, with the major difference being between eastern and western variants. Other languages in border regions—such as Serbian in the northwest, Macedonian in the southwest, and Romanian in the north-central area—are increasingly influential. Regional dialects are becoming less pronounced as a result of national standardization in education and the rising importance of national media, especially television.

History and Cultural Relations

The Bulgarian lands have been the domain of diverse cultures, including Thracian, Greek, Roman, and Byzantine. Contemporary Bulgarians, however, trace their origins to Slavs who came from the area north of the Carpathians between the fifth and sixth centuries and the subsequent incursion of Turkic tribes from central Asia in the seventh century. The latter are referred to as "Bulgars" or "proto-Bulgarians," and it is from this group that the Bulgarians got their name. Although the "proto-Bulgarians" quickly dominated the region politically, they adopted the customs of the Slavic settlers, which then formed the basis of Bulgarian culture.

Bulgaria's fortunes vis-à-vis numerous hostile neighbors rose and fell over the subsequent years. The most significant event was the fall to Ottoman domination in 1396. Ottoman dominion lasted nearly 500 years and had a significant impact on Bulgarian language, culture, and economic development. The sizable Turkish minority in Bulgaria and the strained relations between Bulgarians and Turks at both the individual and national levels are, in part, consequences of this period. Likewise, the stereotypical good relations between Bulgarians and Russians that epitomized the socialist era can also be traced back to the Ottoman period, since it was the Russian army that liberated Bulgaria from Ottoman control in 1877.

Besides the Turkish minority, which accounts for approximately 10 percent of the population of Bulgaria, Gypsies are the only other sizable group with which Bulgarians interact regularly. The latter are marginalized and stigmatized as a rule; traditionally they have lived separately in distinct neighborhoods, although they are becoming more

♦ **Balkans**
The easternmost of the three major peninsulas of southern Europe and the collective name for the nations located there—Bosnia and Herzegovina, Slovenia, Croatia, Yugoslavia, Romania, Albania, Bulgaria, Greece, and the European section of Turkey.

♦ **Cyrillic alphabet**
A writing system developed in the ninth century for Slavic languages. Russian, Serbian, Bulgarian, and other Slavic languages today are written with somewhat different versions of the basic Cyrillic alphabet.

integrated residentially with Bulgarians. Some large cities also have groups of guest workers and students. The largest group of foreign workers are Vietnamese who were sent to work in Bulgaria for five-year periods in exchange for Bulgarian products exported to Vietnam. The contractual arrangement between the two countries was terminated and most Vietnamese were expected to return to Vietnam in the early 1990s. Students come primarily from the Middle East and Africa. For the most part relations between these foreigners and Bulgarians take place in the formal context of work or school. Outside of these contexts, relations are minimal and sometimes strained.

Settlements

The location of original settlements in the area was determined by defensive concerns. As settlements expanded, the presence of water and gentle terrain became dominant factors as well, and larger settlements grew up along rivers and in the foothills at the edges of the fertile plains. Contemporary villages are distributed along important travel routes connecting larger towns. In most of the country villages are concentrated settlements with houses in close proximity to each other around a village square. This area of habitation is surrounded by the land that villagers cultivate. Because of migration and demographic changes, many smaller villages have lost their population base and are basically hamlets. As their current population is primarily elderly, their long-term survival is questionable. Larger villages are faring better as a result of governmental migration restrictions, economic development, and closer integration with nearby urban settlements.

Traditional village houses were constructed of wood and plastered with mud. They were small, one-story constructions with one to three rooms. A similar style of house was also constructed from mud bricks or stone and plaster. While some examples of these houses are still evident in contemporary villages, the predominant model is a two-story house with several rooms made of brick and finished with a stucco-type plaster. Urban areas have the same type of constructions, but since the 1950s the large, multistory, concrete apartment building, usually in groups forming a complex, has come to dominate the urban housing scene.

Economy

SUBSISTENCE AND COMMERCIAL ACTIVITIES. Traditional subsistence was structured around agriculture and herding. The relative importance of these two activities varied regionally: agriculture dominated the plains; sheep- and goatherding typified the mountain regions; and a more balanced combination of both characterized intermediate zones. These resources were augmented by small-scale commodity production and the sale of excess agricultural products. Commercial agricultural production characterized a few areas, such as the Rose Valley, which is famous for the production of rose oil. Elsewhere, the level of commercial production was inhibited by the small size of holdings, which were often barely sufficient for subsistence purposes and typically widely dispersed. Reciprocal labor sharing was an important element of the subsistence strategy, and some individuals from agriculturally poorer regions migrated seasonally to work in the plains. The crop base varied regionally but usually combined grain, fruit, and vegetable production.

The agricultural situation changed radically with the collectivization of land in the 1950s. Villagers then started working for the cooperative farm and raising additional crops and animals for their own use on small personal plots granted by the cooperative for subsistence purposes. Since the 1960s the development of industrial enterprises and the possibility of commuting to work in towns has turned many villagers into nonagricultural workers who continue to acquire some subsistence needs from their personal plots.

INDUSTRIAL ARTS. Bulgarians traditionally practiced many trades, often in addition to agricultural work. Wood- and metalworkers provided villagers with such necessities as building materials, furniture, horse/donkey carts, and wine barrels. Textile crafts were perhaps the most important, including spinning, weaving, knitting, and sewing. The major products were clothing and household textiles such as bed covers and rugs. Particular designs and colors of clothing distinguished different regions of the country. While all households were involved in domestic textile production, some regions developed significant woolen and braid industries during the Ottoman period. Today textile industries are again a major component of the national economy. Other major sectors of contemporary industry include machine building, metalworking, and food processing. Chemical and electronic industries are important growth sectors.

TRADE. After liberation from Ottoman control Bulgarians began exporting agricultural products—primarily foodstuffs—to Germany, Austria, Great Britain, and other western European countries. The sale of foodstuffs to Germany increased significantly in the context of World War

Ottoman domination lasted nearly 500 years and had a significant impact on Bulgarian language, culture and economic development.

II. After the war the nature of trade shifted radically. Bulgaria became part of the Council for Mutual Economic Assistance, and trade—now state-controlled—shifted to the other members of this Communist economic alliance, especially the Soviet Union. With increasing industrialization the profile of exports also shifted to include a balance of agricultural and industrial products. The major imports were fuels, raw materials, and machinery. In the 1970s trade with Western Europe began to develop again on a small scale, and since 1989 there has been a major attempt to establish economic connections with developed capitalist countries.

DIVISION OF LABOR. In the agricultural subsistence economy labor was divided on the basis of sex and age. Women took care of most domestic activities, including cooking, cleaning, spinning, and weaving. Sewing was done by both men and women, but outer garments were often made by village tailors who were men. In the fields women hoed while men plowed and sowed, but everybody helped in the harvest. Both men and women took care of the animals, with men tending to horses and butchering. Children were primarily responsible for pasturing animals and collecting water. In the socialist era both men and women moved increasingly into wage labor. This has softened the rigidity of the sexual division of labor, but many of the same divisions are operative in the personal plot production and domestic activity of villagers.

LAND TENURE. In Ottoman times land was held by the sultan, who granted rights to collect tribute or tax to Ottoman lords. After liberation most land was divided up among Bulgarian cultivators, but villages retained some areas of pasture and forest as communal property. Schools and churches also had associated lands for their support. After World War II, the controlling Communist government pursued a policy of collectivization. Villagers retained a small "personal plot" of land for their own subsistence use, but the government took control of most land amenable to an economy of scale through village cooperatives. Following collectivization, the trend was toward increasing the size of agricultural production units, first by consolidating cooperatives and subsequently by integrating several cooperatives into large administrative units called agroindustrial complexes. This trend began to wane in the mid-1980s, and with the decline of Communist party influence since 1989, there has been strong official support for reprivatization of agricultural production.

Kinship

KIN GROUPS AND DESCENT. Bulgarians trace kinship bilaterally and the major kin group is the kindred. Close relatives are always members of one's kindred, but the importance of more distant relatives is shaped significantly by such factors as geographical distance, frequency of interaction, and interdependence in informal economic activities. Affinal relations between families of married couples are valued and fictive kin relations like godparenthood are of continuing importance.

KINSHIP TERMINOLOGY. The designation of kin follows the Eskimo system with some refinements, such as additional terms for many affinal relations.

Marriage and Family

MARRIAGE. Marriage was nearly universal and usually occurred when the man and woman were in their early twenties. Village endogamy was common, though marriage of individuals from neighboring villages was also frequent. Spouses met in the context of village life, and village work bees were major occasions for courtship. Spouse selection was based on mutual attraction, and while relatives made their feelings known, they rarely forced a couple to marry against their will. Women were expected to bring a dowry, which commonly consisted of furniture, clothing, and household textiles. Some textiles were given as gifts to wedding guests, and the remainder used by the new couple. Postmarital residence was patrilocal, with the bride going to live in the house of the groom. Divorce was viewed negatively and rarely occurred. Widows and widowers could remarry but only each other. Today marriage is still nearly universal but separation, divorce, and remarriage are fairly common. Also, as there are more contexts for interaction across localities, spouses are more likely to come from more distant locations than in the past, and neolocal residence is not uncommon. The civil ceremony has replaced the religious one, but the remainder of festivities of the traditional wedding, such as the feasts and gift giving, have been retained, if not expanded.

DOMESTIC UNIT. Bulgaria is well known for the historical importance of large patrilocally extended households known as *zadrugas*, typically consisting of a couple, several married sons, and their families. This pattern was disappearing by the turn of the century, and since that time the three-generation stem family has predominated

♦ **affinal**
Related by marriage.

♦ **endogamy**
Marriage within a specific group or social category of which the person is a member, such as one's caste or community.

in rural areas. Nuclear family households are also very common, sometimes cooperating economically with related households. In urban areas the nuclear family model is the predominant domestic form, though it is not uncommon to find an elderly parent living with one of his or her children.

INHERITANCE. Partible inheritance was legally and socially prescribed. Traditionally, daughters often received less than sons and sometimes forfeited their patrimony or gave it to a favorite brother. Brothers inherited equally, but in the case of stem families the son who stayed at home to take care of his parents received more, usually in the form of the house and other buildings. This son was typically the youngest.

SOCIALIZATION. Traditionally the household and the village provided the major context for socialization of children into adults. Children learned by observation and experience. With a reduction in the number of children per couple and the increasing role of socialist education, the process has changed. Parents indulge their children and do not encourage independence, perhaps in opposition to socialist education, which until recently stressed political ideology and commitment.

Sociopolitical Organization

SOCIAL ORGANIZATION. Village social organization was built around the household and the network of connections between households based on kin relations and socioeconomic cooperation. Connections with neighbors were particularly significant in this network. In the presocialist era neighborhoods were the basis of labor-sharing groups and informal socializing. After collectivization, cooperative brigades were also organized on the basis of neighborhood. Social stratification was minimal as the vast majority of village households were smallholding proprietors. The major social divisions were between agriculturalists, the village artisans, and the intelligentsia; the last group included the mayor, the doctor, the priest, and schoolteachers. The few households with larger landholdings had higher status, but this situation was reversed after World War II when large holdings were expropriated and wealth became a target of punitive political action. Subsequently, the advantages and power associated with political positions controlled by the Communist party were the primary basis of village differentiation. Other associations important in the village in the Socialist era were the Communist Youth League and the Fatherland Front.

POLITICAL ORGANIZATION. The Ottomans allowed villages to administer much of their own affairs, usually through a council of household heads. In the years following independence, the state administered local villages by appointing mayors who maintained law and order and acted as local judges. Since World War II, the Communist party has dominated local political organization through the appointment of mayors and party secretaries who follow the directions of higher party organs. In addition to the village leaders there is a local Communist party organization of all village party members and a village council with appointed representatives from each neighborhood. There is also an Agrarian party organization in most villages, though until 1989 it followed Communist party policy. In 1988 multi-candidate elections for local administrators were held. In 1990 the constitutionally guaranteed political monopoly of the Communist party was abolished and a multiparty national parliament was democratically elected. Multiparty local elections were held in 1991.

SOCIAL CONTROL. Traditionally the mayor, the village policeman, and the priest were the main forces of social control. Gossip and the threat of ostracism, however, were more important and ensured that formal sanctions were seldom needed. Major conflicts usually involved disputes between two parties to a financial transaction or disputes between siblings over the division of the inheritance. Such disputes divided not only the families involved but other related families as well. Even after the conflict was legally resolved, the family units often remained estranged. With collectivization the inheritance of land became less important, though the division of other resources sometimes still causes conflicts. Most conflicts are resolved by the village leaders.

CONFLICT. Bulgarians do not have any major conflicts with other groups, although relations with Gypsies and Turks are sometimes strained. Gypsies are stereotyped as lazy and dishonest, so they are obvious scapegoats when there is theft in the community or problems at places where they work. Conflicts with Turks can be traced in large part to the government's attempt to assimilate them by restricting the use of the Turkish language and forcing Turks to change their names to Bulgarian names. Such conflicts are primarily restricted to those regions where Turks predominate.

Religion and Expressive Culture

RELIGIOUS BELIEFS. The majority of Bulgarians are adherents of the Eastern Orthodox church, whose beliefs they combine with non-Christian ideas about forces of evil such as the evil eye

Folklore is an important part of traditional and contemporary Bulgarian culture. Folk songs are varied and many of them are connected to the struggle against Ottoman control.

♦ **evil eye**
The belief that a certain person can perform harm to another simply by wishing him or her harm (casting the evil eye). In South Asia mothers are especially fearful for their young children and may use amulets or other devices as protection against the evil eye.

and bad fortune. There are also several thousand Protestants of various affiliations, approximately 3,500 Jews, and a group of Bulgarian Muslims called Pomaks. A large segment of Bulgarians are not religious at all. This number increased during the Communist regime as a result of state-sponsored atheism, but even before World War II many villagers were not devoutly religious.

RELIGIOUS PRACTITIONERS. Traditionally, certain older women in villages had reputations for preventing or countering evil forces, while the Eastern Orthodox priest was considered to be the major intermediary with God and the forces of good.

CEREMONIES. The most important religious ceremonies (in addition to regular church services and religious holidays) were christenings, weddings, the blessing of a new house, and funerals. The Communist government provided civil replacements for weddings, funerals, and christenings, though some Bulgarians continued to have religious rituals performed as well.

ARTS. Folklore is an important element of traditional and contemporary Bulgarian culture. Folk songs are varied and many of them are connected to the struggle against Ottoman control. After the liberation they served as the basis for subsequent compositions. Singing was an important social activity, as work groups and drinking parties would often erupt into song. Folk dancing likewise served important social functions, and regular dances in the spring and summer brought together much of the village at the village square. Such singing and dancing continues in the contemporary context, though with somewhat less frequency. The Communist government promoted folklore as a symbol of Bulgarian identity and sponsored numerous professional folklore ensembles and amateur festivals. Many villages and towns have amateur folk ensembles who perform in these festivals. Larger villages and towns also have amateur drama and choral clubs that perform for the village. Textile arts were also of traditional importance, especially the weaving of intricately patterned cloth and rugs. Contemporary Bulgarians have achieved excellence in many art forms, and some of their artists, such as opera singers, have gained worldwide recognition.

MEDICINE. Treatment for illness traditionally included a variety of possibilities: religious actions, such as drinking holy water and kissing icons; non-Christian magical incantations believed to counter or exorcise evil forces; herbal treatments using local plants and their products (such as garlic, wine, and brandy); and consulting a physician. Traditionally the last option was the last resort, but in contemporary Bulgaria it is more often the first response to sickness, though often in combination with folk treatments.

**FESTIVE
TRADITIONS**

Three Bulgarian girls carry baskets while wearing elaborate headdresses. Folklore and cultural traditions are widely promoted; many towns have folk ensembles who perform at festivals. Bulgaria. (Syvain Grandadam/Corbis)

DEATH AND AFTERLIFE. Ideas about the afterlife are extensive, though many Bulgarians deny believing them. Traditionally, bodies had to be buried within twenty-four hours. At death the soul is believed to begin a forty-day journey to the other world. Many necessities for this journey and subsequent life, such as lighted candles, food, wine, clothing, and money, are buried with the corpse or laid on the grave. These supplies are replenished by relatives of the deceased in rituals conducted at the grave site on significant anniversaries of the death, including three days, forty days, six months, and one year. In addition there are several days in the Eastern Orthodox religious calendar devoted to the dead when everyone goes to the graveyard to light candles, lay out food, and pour wine on the graves of their relatives. The Communist government promoted civil funerals to replace religious ones and developed an annual civil ceremony at graveyards for honoring the dead. Bulgarians participated in both, and even in civil ceremonies much of the religious ritual was retained.

Bibliography

Crampton, R. J. (1987). *A Short History of Modern Bulgaria.* Cambridge: Cambridge University Press.

McIntyre, Robert J. (1988). *Bulgaria: Politics, Economics, and Society.* London: Pinter.

Markov, Georgi (1984). *The Truth That Killed.* Translated by Liliana Brisby. New York: Ticknor & Fields.

Sanders, Irwin (1948). *Balkan Village.* Lexington: University of Kentucky Press.

Silverman, Carol (1983). "The Politics of Folklore in Bulgaria." *Anthropological Quarterly* 56:55–61.

Whitaker, Roger (1979). "Continuity and Change in Two Bulgarian Communities: A Sociological Profile." *Slavic Review* 38:259–271.

—GERALD W. CREED

CASTILIANS

Ethonym: none

Orientation

IDENTIFICATION. Castilians are the people of Castile, the interior lands of the Meseta, the central plateau of Spain, traditionally a region of rural smallholdings and the historic seat of what eventually became the Spanish kingdom. The name "Castile" derives from the great many frontier castles to be found in the region.

LOCATION. There are two officially recognized regional units that bear the name "Castile" (Castile-and-Leon, and Castile-La Mancha), but historically and ethnographically, "Castile" refers to the tablelands (Meseta) of interior Spain, divided by the Sierra de Guadarrama, which runs east-west across the center of the region. Annual rainfall is scanty, averaging 70 centimeters, and most of it falls in the spring and winter. In late spring and early summer, thundershowers are common, but they bear inadequate moisture and often bring hail, which damages local crops. At one time, all of Spain was heavily forested in pine. Of the much-reduced forest lands of today, most are to be found in Castile. Other than these woodlands, the Castilian terrain is either scrub-covered or under cultivation. Soils are poor to mediocre, and the principal water courses (running east-west) are the Duero and Tagus rivers.

DEMOGRAPHY. Reliable population figures specific to Castile are not readily ascertainable, but one may roughly estimate that of the 1986 total population of Spain (38,700,000), three-fourths live in the Castilian region. This number is misleading, however, for Castile is a predominantly rural smallholding region, where average population densities are low but are offset by the fact that the region also contains massive urban concentrations in cities such as Madrid, Toledo, and Valladolid. Throughout the region, the demographic trend has been toward the depopulation of the rural sector as its residents migrate toward urban centers or abroad.

LINGUISTIC AFFILIATION. Of the six recognized Spanish dialects (Andalucian, Aragonese, Asturian, Castilian, Leonese, and Valencian) Castilian is the official one. Indeed, the linguistic designation "Spanish" refers specifically to the Castilian dialect—much to the discontent of many other Spanish (but non-Castilian) speakers. More than 28,000,000 speakers of the language are estimated in Spain alone, although not all of these speakers reside in the historic region of Castile. Castilian, along with the other five Spanish dialects, is a member of the North Central Ibero-Romance Family, and it displays strong lexical similarities (greater than 80 percent) with Portuguese, Catalan, and Italian. Less closely related, but still quite similar (greater than 70 percent lexical similarity) are French, Rheto-Romance, Sardinian, and Romanian.

The linguistic designation "Spanish" refers specifically to the Castilian dialect.

See also

Galacians

*The Inquisition,
begun in 1478
under the control of
the Spanish
monarchy, was
directed from Castile
to root out heresy
and crush what
remained of Muslim
religious practice.*

History and Cultural Relations

Originally populated by Iberian and later Ibero-celtic peoples, Castile was for a time ruled by Rome and, later, the Moors. For a time it was governed by counts under the supremacy of Asturias and Leon; it was later annexed by Sancho of Navarre (1026–1035), who gave Castile to his son Ferdinand I in 1033. Leon was united to Castile in 1037, separated in 1065, and reunited under Alfonso VI in 1072, who also annexed Galicia. Afterward, Castile and Leon were separated but were finally reunited under Ferdinand III in 1230, when he conquered large parts of southern Spain from the Moors. Other noted kings were Alfonso X and Pedro the Cruel.

Isabella of Castile married Ferdinand of Aragon in 1469, and became queen of Castile in 1474. Ferdinand became king of Aragon in 1479, from which time Castile and Aragon were united. Under Ferdinand and Isabella, not only was the Spanish territory consolidated, but authority was finally centralized in the hands of a single royal government, and Castile became the regional seat of that authority. Prior to this centralization, the independence of feudal nobles meant that the territory was riven with lawlessness and disorder. By legislating property and personal rights and stripping the nobility and the great crusading orders of much of their former independence and power, Ferdinand and Isabella gained great support among the populace. The ruling pair acquired from the pope the right to nominate all the higher ecclesiastical officers in Spain, and they used that right to reform the church by filling its offices with men of unquestioned orthodoxy and unwavering loyalty to the crown. Thus the church became an extension of royal power.

The Inquisition, begun in 1478 under the control of the monarchy, was directed from Castile to root out heresy and crush what remained of Muslim religious practice, often bloodily. The Inquisition soon developed an independence and momentum of its own, and by 1492 it had far exceeded its original purpose of ensuring that Moors and Jews were expelled from the country. In 1609, Philip III ordered the expulsion of the Moriscos (descendants of Christianized Moors) as well. As a result, when Charles II took the throne in 1665, he inherited a country that had been stripped of nearly all of its tradespeople and artisans. Agriculture declined; arts and literature degenerated.

In 1700, the death of King Charles II of Spain opened the door to dispute over who should be his successor. France favored Charles II's own choice, Philip of Anjou (grandson of Louis XIV), of the Bourbons. But France's adversaries of the time were less pleased with this choice, and they formed a "Grand Alliance" in an attempt to wrest control from the French favorite. Thus began the Wars of Spanish Succession, which raged throughout Europe until 1713–1714, ending with the Peace of Utrecht and leaving Philip V on the throne.

In 1808, Napoleon's brother Joseph succeeded to the throne. His efforts to modernize Spanish institutions led to a backlash against liberalism. By this time the populace consisted of wealthy noble, ecclesiastic, and military groups on the one hand and poor agriculturalists on the other. Because crafts and trade had been largely the province of the original Jewish and Moorish peoples in Spain, when they were suppressed and later expelled from the region there was no powerful or progressive middle class to serve as a source of reformist sentiment, so that such movements became concentrated in the military and among the intellectuals. In 1822, the crown reacted against liberal pressures, and Ferdinand VII acted against the wishes of his own people to secure the assistance of other European powers in controlling his now rebellious colonies in the Americas. Ferdinand set aside established laws of succession and transmitted the throne to Isabella II in 1833, sparking the Carlist Wars (1833–1840), in which supporters of his brother Charles challenged her succession. In 1868, a revolution drove Isabella from the throne, and the period that followed was a confused succession of contenders—each briefly securing, then losing, control over the country.

In 1870, the throne was offered to Leopold of Hohenzollern-Sigmaringen. This move incited a diplomatic crisis in Europe as a whole, and for the French in particular, precipitating the outbreak of the Franco-Prussian War. Still unable to settle their problems of government within the country, the Spanish offered the throne to Prince Amadeo of Savoy, but he abdicated in frustrated discouragement three years later. Then a brief period of republican rule ensued, which lasted until 1875, when Alfonso XII assumed the crown and restored peace to the nation. When he died in 1885, he was succeeded by his posthumous son, Alfonso XIII. Until Alfonso was declared of age in 1902, however, Maria Cristina (widow of Alfonso XII) served as regent.

The last of Spain's colonial holdings in the Americas broke out into open revolt, beginning with the island of Cuba in 1895. U.S. intervention resulted in the loss by Spain of not only Cuba but also Puerto Rico, the Philippines, and Guam, which resulted in the impoverishment of the Spanish economy. A coup d'etat in 1923 established General Primo de Rivera as chief minister of the Spanish cabinet with dictatorial powers, and he managed to enforce a period of quiescence, though one could hardly call it peace, until 1931, when revolution broke out.

Alfonso XIII fled Spain in 1931, and a republican constitution provided for the confiscation of church property, the suppression of religious instruction in the schools, and the expulsion of all religious orders. The attacks on the church, intended to destroy a major source of the monarchy's power and influence, were resented by the largely pious population. This policy, as well as plans for land reform and an attempt to curb the power of the military, alienated the three most powerful traditional elements of Spanish society. The "Popular Front," composed of leftists (including Communists and Socialists), won the election in 1936. The disgruntled military reacted by revolting, initiating the Spanish Civil War in 1936, aided by arms, planes, and artillery from Germany and Italy. The Soviets aided the Republican side against the Fascist "Nationals," but the Nationalists, under General Francisco Franco, emerged victorious in 1939.

The Franco regime remained nominally neutral but actively favored the Axis powers during World War II, so in the postwar years there was no incentive for the Allied powers to provide economic development aid to Spain. Thus Spain was left out of the Marshall Plan for aid to Europe. These postwar years are known in Castile as the "years of hunger," when the economy was so devastated that even the dogs and cats disappeared from Spanish streets—they either starved to death or were eaten. Although Franco continued in power (he was made acting head of state for life), Spain was in theory still a monarchy.

By 1950, economic recovery was slow at best, and the government's efforts at social and economic reform simply meant a greater intrusion of the state into the lives of individuals, minor industrial development of the urban centers, and the introduction of foreign firms. This meant that the rural areas benefited little from development, except for Franco's public-works schemes. Agriculture remained largely unchanged, and people from predominantly rural areas, including Castile, were forced to emigrate to the major cities and foreign countries. In 1973, Franco made Adm.

CASTILIAN WOMAN

Castilian women combining thread. The division of labor is clearly marked in Castilian society, where men are visible in the public spheres and women in the private spheres. Central Spain. (Franz-Marc Frei/Corbis)

Louis Carrero Blanco prime minister in the hope that Blanco would continue his policies after the end of Franco's rule. However, Basque terrorists assassinated the admiral six months after his appointment. The admiral was replaced by Carlos Arias Navarro (Arias). Franco's death, in November 1975, returned power to the crown. King Juan Carlos selected Adolfo Suarez as prime minister, inaugurating a period of massive reform, both political and economic. A new Spanish constitution was passed in 1978 and was hailed as the most liberal constitution in Western Europe. It defined Spain as a parliamentary monarchy with no official religion and prescribed a limited role for the armed forces, the abolition of the death penalty, and an extension of suffrage. But although political reform earned the government a great deal of popular support, resentment and dissatisfaction grew among the military. When Suarez resigned the premiership in 1981, and before his successor was sworn in a month later, this dissatisfaction was vented in a rightist coup attempt which, although foiled, persuaded the government to take steps to appease the military. Since that time, the country has attempted greater economic development, particularly of its agriculture, and has moved toward greater provincial autonomy.

Settlements

Although there are a number of large urban centers in the region, Castile is essentially rural, characterized by small towns and villages that are tied closely to a mixed agricultural, vinicultural, and forestal economy. Nonurban settlements are called *pueblos*. Small or large, the pueblo is a nucleated settlement, consisting of a central plaza surrounded by shops and (in the larger towns) municipal buildings, themselves surrounded by residential structures. At one side of the plaza is the town church, with its tall belfry that (characteristically) harbors the large nest of a crane. The oldest houses in Castilian villages often combine dwelling, stable, and barn, constructed with separate entrances for the residential and livestock portions. On the residential side, the upper floor consists of bedrooms and perhaps an attic space. The traditional Castilian kitchen has as its center a *chimenea*—an open-hearthed fireplace, around which are hung great cooking pots. Many village homes lack running water, but every settlement has a public fountain. The houses of the more well-to-do are frequently constructed of stone, although stucco is a frequently encountered building material.

Economy

SUBSISTENCE AND COMMERCIAL ACTIVITIES. Although smallhold farming is the linchpin of the regional economy, it is rare for an individual or household to live off agricultural income alone. Income provided by the family farm is augmented by small-scale animal and poultry husbandry, by public-works employment, and by individual enterprises such as beekeeping, shopkeeping, and other such supplementary economic pursuits. On the farms, alternate-year dry-farming/fallow rotations are customary. Barley and wheat are the important cash crops and are harvested in the summer. Grapes are commonly grown and are harvested in October. Even in those parts of the region not important for wine production, a farm will generally have small grape arbors, from whose fruit a household will press its own wine. Sugar beets, introduced as a cash crop about fifty years ago, provide a winter harvest. Other common crops, grown for local consumption rather than for sale, are melons, pumpkins, carob beans, lentils, and chickpeas. Traditional farming methods—using a chiselpoint plow, handsowing, weeding by hand-held hoe, and harvesting by scythe—have only slowly been replaced by mechanized means. Chemical fertilizers have slowly replaced manure since the early to mid-1950s. Animals are raised both for fieldwork and for food. Oxen, once the most important draft animals, have largely been replaced by mules. Sheep husbandry was once the heart of the Castilian economy, and in the eighteenth century huge flocks, raised for their wool, were common. Today, however, the number of sheep has declined drastically, and they are mostly raised for their meat, which is an important component of the local diet. Of all animals raised for food, the pig is most important, and nearly every family raises one or two. Commercial swine herds began to be established in the 1960s, as did commercial poultry production. Large-scale cattle-raising operations exist in some parts of the region, where pasturage makes it possible. A very important nonagricultural product is pine resin, from which tar, turpentine, and other resin derivatives are made. Forestry-based industries have always been under strict state control, and they can only be carried out in compliance with the regulations of the local forest district office. Even when trees are on privately held property, there are strictly enforced rules regarding the start and end of tapping season, which trees may be cut, and whether or not new forests may be opened up for exploitation.

INDUSTRIAL ARTS. There are few industries in rural Castile. Sawmills and the production of pine-resin derivatives are two such enterprises. In the past, local artisans crafted the tools, utensils, and other consumer goods used by the villagers of Castile, but today the people are more likely to depend upon the stores of the neighboring towns or cities to provide such items.

TRADE. Items produced regionally for export to the rest of the country and beyond Spain's borders include pine-resin products, meat, dairy, and poultry products, cereals, and, in some areas, wine and sugar beets.

DIVISION OF LABOR. In Castile, the division of labor according to sex is best understood according to the distinction between the public and private spheres—to males belongs the world of paid labor, to females the domestic tasks. This division is not complete, however, for it is crosscut by considerations of class and by the demands of the household farm. Generally speaking, in poorer households, a woman may need to seek paid employment in order to supplement the otherwise inadequate cash income of her husband. In any case, the heavy work of farming and all specialized agricultural and forestal jobs are the province of men. The task of threshing wheat falls to the male youths of the farm household. While economic necessity may force a woman to take on paid domestic work or seek employment in a local shop without seriously damaging her reputation, there is no such mitigating circumstance to justify a man's assumption of "woman's work"—a man who does so is simply not considered a "real" man.

LAND TENURE. Agricultural land is privately owned, in smallholdings. The pine forests are owned by the *communidad*, a group of neighboring villages. This form of organization derives from medieval times, when clusters of villages and hamlets were under the authority of a ruling lord who maintained his seat in a nearby city. These affiliated settlements held large tracts of land, much of it forested, in common under the dominion of the lord. Although the individual settlements eventually achieved politically independent status as *municipios* in the sixteenth century, their confederation in the communidads remained in place with regard to forests and pasture lands. Today, the primary role of the communidad is to apportion the income realized from commonly held lands and to regulate the use of such lands in order to protect future income. For the pine forests, this means that the rights to harvest the trees or their resin—but not the property rights to the land itself—are periodically allocated by communidad authorities.

Kinship

Kinship is reckoned bilaterally. Fictive kinship in the form of godparenthood is of social and ritual importance, but as godparents tend to be chosen from within the bilaterally determined consanguinal kin circle (grandparents, aunts, or uncles) it does not usually result in the extension of kin-based rights and obligations beyond the preexisting family group. The single most important kin group is the nuclear family. The term *pariente* (kinsman) refers to all consanguineal relatives, but family loyalty tends largely to focus on one's siblings and parents. This loyalty, however, is frequently contradicted by disputes, particularly over inheritance.

Marriage and Family

MARRIAGE. Marriage is a milestone in the lives of individuals and for the community. Young village girls will pray to the saints to bring them husbands, and fiestas are occasions for girls to flirt with the boys they favor. For males, it is only upon marriage that full adult status is achieved. It is nearly unheard of for a male to marry prior to the completion of his national military service, and couples do not care to marry before achieving at least a minimal degree of independence, so that couples tend to postpone marriage until about the age of twenty-five. There is strong social pressure for individuals to marry within their own socioeconomic class. When exceptions occur, they usually involve a male of higher class and status marrying "beneath" his station—rarely the other way around. Marriages between first cousins can and do occur, but they require special church dispensation. Parents exercise a great deal of control in the selection of their children's prospective spouses, but they do not arrange the actual match. Rather, a young man and woman will develop an interest in one another, and should they desire marriage the young man will formally request that the woman's parents consider him as a formal suitor. Upon the acquiescence of the woman's parents, the couple may begin holding hands in public, and they are invited to social occasions together. Propriety is carefully maintained during courtship, for not only the reputation of the couple but also that of their respective families may be damaged by scandal. A young woman is expected to be modest and, above all, chaste before marriage. Upon becoming formally engaged, the bride-to-be begins to prepare her trousseau of linen and clothing, all finely embroidered by the young woman, or handed down to her by her

It remains rare for a couple to marry outside of the church in most of Castile.

♦ **fictive kinship**
A social relationship, such as blood brotherhood or godparenthood, between individuals who are neither affines nor consanguines but who are referred to or addressed with kin terms and treated as kin. See also compadrazgo

*Castilian
participation in the
arts remains vital
and ranges through
the various musical
genres, the visual
arts and
architecture, film,
theater, literature,
and bullfighting.*

mother. In much of Castile, the groom pays a small sum (traditionally not to exceed 10 percent of his fortune, now often a token sum). Until relatively recently, marriages throughout Spain were recognized only when consecrated by the church, but with the introduction of laws allowing religious choice in the 1960s, civil ceremonies became permissible. Still it remains rare for a couple to marry outside of the church in most of Castile. The ceremony is held in the parish church of the bride. During the ceremony, a white veil is held over the bride's head and the groom's shoulders, to symbolize the submissive role a proper wife should adopt toward her husband. Spiritual sponsors (godparents) stand with the bride and groom at the ceremony. These traditionally were the father of the bride and the mother of the groom, but they now may be aunts and uncles or influential friends. There are strong prohibitions against adultery and divorce.

DOMESTIC UNIT. A new domestic unit is established with marriage, and it is expected that a couple will live apart from the parents of either spouse. However, the parents of the new bride usually will provide substantial assistance in the purchase or building of the new home, so that the couple generally takes up residence in the vicinity of the bride's parents.

INHERITANCE. Inheritance is bilateral—each child can expect to inherit an equal share of each parent's property.

SOCIALIZATION. Child rearing is a mother's responsibility. The relation between father and child is distant, and it remains so between father and son throughout their lives. Concern for the good name of oneself and one's family in the face of possible gossip or censure is very high.

Sociopolitical Organization

SOCIAL ORGANIZATION. There are three broad social classes represented in the region: a small upper class consisting of families descending from the old nobility, wealthy industrialists, and high government officials; a small middle class of professionals, government functionaries, and the clergy; and a predominantly agricultural working class. The first two categories are largely urban—in the villages, most residents share similar opportunities and access to resources, at least in principle, so that an egalitarian ethic is the rule. Informal authority is conceded to a villager on the basis of age, economic success, or other personal qualities. Castilian village society is highly individualistic, with weak, limited institutional venues for cooperative action. One such institution is the

cofradia, or lay religious society, which is dedicated to the veneration of a specific saint and cooperates in the planning of Lenten ceremonies and processions.

SOCIAL CONTROL AND CONFLICT. In the villages, the strongest mechanism for social control is the fear of loss of reputation. While municipal authorities can and do enforce public law, behaviors are kept in check informally through the fear of incurring the disapprobation of one's neighbors, of inciting gossip and scandal.

Religion and Expressive Culture

RELIGIOUS BELIEFS. Within predominantly Catholic Spain, Castile has the reputation of being one of the most religiously conservative regions. Church attendance by both men and women is generally high on Sundays and holy days of obligation, although it is usually only women who attend daily services. Religious belief and practice assume a rather personalized character in Castile as elsewhere in Spain, and cofradias (Catholic lay brotherhoods and sisterhoods devoted to particular saints) are important to community and ritual life. In 1967, the passage of the Religious Liberty Law granted rights of free worship for non-Catholics throughout Spain, but the country and the region of Castile remain strongly Catholic.

RELIGIOUS PRACTITIONERS. The village priest has traditionally exercised a great deal of authority over his congregation regarding questions of the faith and secular affairs, but this control appears to be somewhat on the wane.

CEREMONIES. Within the liturgical calendar of the Catholic church, the most important ceremonial occasions are Christmas and Easter, as well as the feast day for the patron saint of the village, when nearly everyone will attend mass regardless of their usual level of church attendance during the rest of the year. But much of Castilian ceremonial life, although tied to the religious calendar, has a strong secular flavor as well. The patron saint's feast day is the occasion for a village-wide fiesta, planned by village officials and involving soccer matches, bullfights, dances, band concerts, and fireworks. A parade of *gigantes* (giants) and *cabezudos* (big heads) marches through the streets of the village, headed by a band playing spirited tunes. The gigantes are 3–meter-tall effigies of Ferdinand and Isabella made of huge papier-mâché heads over long robes that conceal the man carrying them. Cabezudos are papier-mâché heads depicting historical, ethnic, and fantasy caricatures and also are worn by men. Life-cycle events (baptism, marriage, funerals) involve churchly ritual.

ARTS. Castile possesses a long and brilliant artistic heritage—a result in part of its historic role as the seat of the Spanish court, with its provision of royal patronage. Today Castilian participation in the arts remains vital and ranges through the various musical genres (today including everything from rock to opera), the visual arts and architecture, film, theater, literature, and bullfighting. Outside of Spain, the most famous of Castile's literary figures is Cervantes. But this great productivity in the arts retains little ethnic specificity, unlike the distinctive regional flavor of works produced by Andalusians, for example, or Catalans. This universality, too, may be the result of Castile's heritage as the seat of Spanish government, and the cosmopolitanism of its courtly, and later governmental, patrons. Except locally—and for certain ceremonial practices, such as the processions of the big heads and giants—Castilian artistic production has come to draw on influences originating throughout the Spanish culture as a whole, and/or to participate in the larger, international sphere, rather than to celebrate or reaffirm regional or folk themes.

MEDICINE. Modern medical care and facilities are available and used throughout Castile, as is the case for nearly all of Spain. Folk medical practices have, as a result, largely been lost. While in the more remote, rural areas there may still be some reliance on herbal remedies, and while it is still not uncommon to find people seeking the intervention of one or another saint in the case of illness or injury, such practices and beliefs are secondary to modern medical treatment.

DEATH AND AFTERLIFE. Mortuary belief and practice are conducted within the general context of Catholicism. The priest officiates over funerals and also confers the sacrament of extreme unction. The body of the deceased is interred after an appropriate mass has been said. Friends and close relatives of the bereaved are expected to provide support, beginning with their willingness to keep vigil over the corpse until burial. The body is carried in its coffin to the church in which a burial mass is said, then to the ceremony for burial, which traditionally is attended only by men. Throughout Castile, the family of the deceased traditionally hosted a funeral banquet, but this practice has fallen into disuse. The hiring of paid mourners and the distribution of food to the poor in conjunction with burials are two other traditional customs that now are encountered less frequently. A widow is expected to assume black mourning clothing, or at least a black head scarf.

Bibliography

Aceves, Joseph (1971). *Social Change in a Spanish Village*. Cambridge, Mass.: Schenkman.

Hooper, John (1986). *The Spaniards: A Portrait of the New Spain*. New York: Viking.

Kenny, Michael (1961). *A Spanish Tapestry: Town and Country in Old Castile*. London: Cohen & West.

—NANCY E. GRATTON

CATALANS (PAÏSOS CATALANS)

Ethonym: Catalonians

Orientation

IDENTIFICATION. Catalans can be defined by participation in the historical polity of Catalonia, which occupies the northwest Mediterranean coast and and eastern Pyrenees. Some areas of the formerly independent political unit now form separate regions in contemporary Spain and France: Valencia, the Balearics, and Roselló (Pyrénées Orientales). Andorra constitutes an independent state. Together these are known as the "Països Catalans" (Catalan countries). The traditional primary language of the polity is Catalan, a Romance language, although most inhabitants are bilingual (in Spanish or French). In the contemporary Països Catalans—after two centuries of industrial development and immigration—language, residence, cultural traits (food, arts, etc.), heritage, and political affiliation are complex and ambivalent markers of ethnic, class, and national membership.

LOCATION. Catalonia is located between 40° and 42° N and 0° and 3° E. Roselló lies at about 42° N and between 1° and 4° E. Valencia falls between 38° and 40° N and 2° W and 1° E. The Balearic Islands lie between 38° and 40° N and between 1° and 4° E. The total land surface is 69,032 square kilometers; in Spain, the Països Catalans occupy 13 percent of the land surface while in France, Roselló occupies less than 1 percent of the land surface. The countryside is predominantly mountainous, dropping from the Pyrenees (above 3,000 meters) and the Iberian system to the Mediterranean coast. The most important rivers, the Ebre (Ebro) and Xùquer (Júcar), originate outside the Països Catalans, while the rest of the hydrographic network consists of small, intermittent rivers that flood periodically. The climate is Mediterranean, characterized by a season in which heat and dryness

HISTORY AND CULTURAL RELATIONS

Settlement in Catalonia antedates historical records, with Paleolithic and Neolithic remains. Successive immigrations have included Celts, Iberians, Phoenicians, Greeks, Romans (who established a capital in Tarragona in the first century B.C.E.), Jews, Visigoths, Arabs, and Gypsies. Barcelona was reconquered from the Arabs in 801 and became capital of the Frankish county of Catalonia. Catalonia became independent about 988, uniting with the Kingdom of Aragon in the twelfth century. Balears and Valencia were reconquered from Arab domination in the thirteenth century. The Catalan-Aragonese empire also extended into Sardinia, Naples, Sicily, and Greece as its mercantile society and culture flourished. At the end of the fifteenth century, its population neared 700,000. In 1469, King Ferdinand of Aragon and Catalonia wed queen Isabella of Castile and Leon, uniting the two kingdoms that became the foundation of Spain. For centuries thereafter, Catalans struggled to preserve political and cultural autonomy as the Mediterranean region lost power to Atlantic states.

Bids for independence were defeated by the central state in 1640–1659 (at which time Roselló was incorporated into France) and in the early eighteenth century. Nonetheless, the subsequent growth of trade with Spain's New World colonies and of industry, especially textiles, gave Catalonia new economic power in the nineteenth century. In the twentieth century, a rich Catalonia has attracted immigrants from the rest of Spain while seeking to redefine its relationship to the centralized state. Under the Second Spanish Republic (1931–1939), especially during the Spanish Civil War of 1936–1939, Catalans sought new forms of autonomous government; Franco's victory brought an intense repression of the polity, its culture, and its language. Under the Spanish democratic regime (1977–), the Països Catalans have regained autonomy within the reorganized state, and a revitalization of Catalan language and culture has been evident in Spain, with repercussions as well in France.

coincide from June to September, with strong rains in September/October and April/May. The eastern and southern regions are extremely arid (less than 30 centimeters precipitation per year).

DEMOGRAPHY. Regional populations of the Països Catalans are: Catalonia, 6,079,903 (1987); Valencia, 2,918,714 (1987); Balearics, 671,233 (1987); Roselló, 349,100 (1986); and Andorra, 49,976 (1986). Catalans constitute 28 percent of the population of Spain; Catalans in France, by contrast, represent less than 1 percent of the national population. Population density averages 176 persons per square kilometer, and the population is stable. Approximately 9,000,000 speak Catalan; almost all are bilingual. Immigrants account for the majority of Spanish or French monolinguals.

LINGUISTIC AFFILIATION. Catalan is a Romance language derived from Latin and written with the Roman alphabet. It has 7 vowels and 27 consonants. Dialects are associated with the historical divisions previously cited, including Valencian, Mallorquí, Menorquí, and Eivissenc.

Settlements

Catalans have been urban for millennia. Major cities include Barcelona (with a metropolitan area of 3,000,000), Valencia, Palma de Mallorca,

Tarragona, Perpinyà (Perpignan), Lleida, and Girona. All tend to be based on Roman models, although they have undergone extensive development subsequently, especially in the past century. Cities tend to be centered on civil, Catholic church, and commercial activities, which form a core network rather than occupying a single central space. The urban landscape is extremely dense, as is typical of the Mediterranean. Residences, long associated with professional quarters and workplaces, are now more often separated from work and tend to reflect class-linked variations on a shared pattern of multistory apartment buildings. The rural Països Catalans center on the *mas*, an agricultural household production unit, with dispersed populations in the north and larger villages in the south. Northern houses consist of extended-family dwellings above barns and storage areas, developed on a Roman pattern; southern houses are simpler but encompass wide variations. Since the industrial era, rural areas have been invaded from urban centers and by intensive tourism, both internal and external.

Economy

SUBSISTENCE AND COMMERCIAL ACTIVITIES. Roughly 10 percent of the active population of the Països Catalans is engaged in agriculture, with 45 percent in industry and 45 percent in service. The last is the most productive sector (60 percent of the net product), mainly because of international tourism.

Agricultural production is dominated by arboriculture: citrus, grapes, and olives, all of which are now highly industrialized in production. The need for irrigation constrains other crops, although rice is characteristic of Valencian agriculture and cuisine. The typical production unit is a *horta* (*huerta*), a small, single-family irrigated garden of less than one hectare. These gardens produce domestic foodstuffs as well as flowers and specialties for urban markets. Domestic animals may include cattle, pigs, and sheep, but milk and meat products are generally industrialized. Fishing, despite a long economic and cultural tradition, has largely disappeared.

The Països Catalans lack natural energy resources for industry; growth relied on imported fuels until the construction of nuclear reactors. Cottage industries in the eighteenth century gave way to family-controlled urban factories and rural mill towns (*colònies*) in the nineteenth. Textiles were the foundation of growth; chemicals, leather, construction materials, automobiles, and appliances have also been important, organized as government or multinational corporations. Commerce and finance were linked to industrial growth, especially in the development of a petite bourgeoisie (shopkeeper and small merchant) infrastructure.

DIVISION OF LABOR. This follows gender and class. Women of rural and working-class households participate actively in the production process; middle-class and upper-class women have been less incorporated into the labor market than in similar developed areas. Class division has been a source of conflict for centuries.

LAND TENURE. The Països Catalans are typified by small and medium landholdings; even among the bourgeoisie, money tends to be heavily invested in land, both rural and urban.

Kinship, Marriage, and Family

KIN GROUPS AND DESCENT. Traditional Catalan kinship is based on the stem family and a designated heir, generally an elder male. This pattern has been increasingly nuclearized in cities, although ties across generations remain strong. Descent is bilateral; kinship terminology is equivalent to the rest of Latin Europe with an emphasis on the nuclear family and designation of generational and affinal distance.

MARRIAGE. Catalans are monogamous, following Catholic tradition. Civil marriage has been permitted in Spain since 1968, divorce since the 1980s. Both were available earlier in France. There are no marriage rules beyond minimal Catholic exogamy, although land and economic interests have shaped marriages in rural areas as well as among urban elites. In rural traditions, the inheriting couple resides with the heir's family. Neolocal residence is more common in the city, although economic limitations on space may preclude it.

DOMESTIC UNIT. Coresidence of the productive unit has been a cultural ideal, and the unit may include grandparents, siblings and families, children and spouses; this is more common in the countryside than in cities. The past three decades have seen a dramatic rupture in domestic relations throughout the Països Catalans.

INHERITANCE. In Catalan customary law, two-thirds of the property was given to the designated heir, and the rest was divided equally among all surviving children, including the heir, constituting the dowry or a professional stake for other siblings. After 1555, three-quarters was allotted to the heir. Customary law may still be invoked, but generally equipartite division seems to dominate, at least in cities.

SOCIALIZATION. Children are raised primarily by mothers with help of other female kin or servants. Fathers have variable but limited involvement. Schooling was dominated by the Roman Catholic church until the establishment of post-Franco governments, which have greatly expanded all youth services.

Sociopolitical Organization

The Països Catalans today encompass regions in Spain and France and the independent state of Andorra.

SOCIAL ORGANIZATION. Catalan society, since the Middle Ages, has been divided into socioeconomic groups based on occupation, descent, wealth, and prestige markers (education, cultural goods). Medieval and early modern categories of nobility, clergy, merchants, and artisans have given way since the nineteenth century to modern capitalist divisions. Successive waves of modern immigrants have been incorporated as workers with marked social and cultural discrimination. Conflict has been intense and often violent.

POLITICAL ORGANIZATION. The Països Catalans now comprise three autonomous Spanish regions and eight provinces—Catalunya (four

The Països Catalans today encompass regions in Spain and France and the independent state of Andorra.

Catalans (Països Catalans)

RELIGION AND EXPRESSIVE CULTURE

Catalan culture is one of the richest in Europe, traceable to the artistic, architectural, and literary golden age in the Middle Ages and early modern period.

provinces), the Comunitat Valenciana (three), Illes Balears (one)—as well as a French department and the Principat of Andorra, administered by *sindics* representing its joint rulers, the bishop of the Seu d'Urgell and the president of France. Local administration is heavily fragmented. Municipal and autonomous governments ("Generalitats" in Catalonia and Valencia, the "Consell" in Balears) have been elected by universal suffrage in Spain since 1977. France has a longer tradition, but in Andorra voting citizens account for only 25 percent of the population. Spain and France have party systems in which class and nationalist interests are debated. Services are distributed among all levels of government. Taxes are paid to municipal governments and to the state, which redistributes part of them: the Spanish national budget is 25 percent for local administrations, 10 percent for autonomous regions, and 65 percent for national services. Països Catalan citizens also vote for European parliament members and participate in Common Market programs.

SOCIAL CONTROL. Values of authority, tradition, and the importance of appearance are inculcated through school, home, and church. Formal systems of control include police, prisons, and the army, organs of the national state against which Catalan governments have attempted to construct their own agencies. Conflict between Catalonia and the central state, as well as internal class conflicts, have been recurrent themes of Catalan history.

Religion and Expressive Culture

RELIGIOUS BELIEFS AND PRACTICES. For centuries, the Roman Catholic church has provided the dominant belief system, while also being an important actor in Catalan society. This identification of the Catholic church and Catalan culture has been weakened by industrialization, secularism, and cultural contact. Most Catalans are Catholic by baptism and observe other Catholic life-cycle rites, but many do not practice regularly. Only one-third of those in Spanish Catalonia identified themselves as Catholic in 1988. Jews lived in the area until their expulsion in the early modern period; synagogues and mosques are now found in Barcelona and other metropolitan centers as a result of recent immigration. There are also active Protestant and evangelical communities, the latter including many Gypsies. Religious leaders are generally specialized males, but Catalonia also has many men and women in religious orders in schools and charity work as well as monasteries and convents.

CEREMONIES. The religiously based calendar, now secularized and politicized, includes: New Year's Day (January 1); Reis (Epiphany and distribution of gifts, January 6); Carnestoltes (Carnivals); Pasqua Florida (Easter); Pasqua Granada (Pentecost); Sant Jordi (feast of Saint George, the patron saint, April 23); a group of primarily summer festivals of fire and fireworks—Sant Josep (feast of Saint Joseph, or "Falles" in Valencia, March 19), Sant Antoni (feast of Saint Anthony, June 13, in Balears), Sant Joan (feast of Saint John, June 24) and Sant Pere (feast of Saint Peter, June 29); Dia dels Difunts (Day of the Dead, November 2); and Nadal (Christmas, December 25). Sunday is the general weekly holiday. Saints and apparitions of the Virgin Mary figure in regional and local cycles as well as folklore, legend, toponyms, and personal names.

ARTS. Catalan culture is one of the richest in Europe, traceable to the artistic, architectural, and literary golden age in the Middle Ages and early modern period. Urban, elite, and educated culture has coexisted with folk traditions to the present. Urban culture declined in the seventeenth and eighteenth centuries, but it revived in the nineteenth century with the growth of industrial wealth. Catalan expression, however, was limited by Francoist repression. Well-known figures from the Països Catalans, important in development of local and international culture, include: Ramon Llull, Ausiàs Marc, and Ramon Muntaner in early writings; Salvador Espriu, Vincente Blasco Ibáñez, and Llorenç Villalonga in contemporary literature; Salvador Dalí, Joan Miró, and Pablo Picasso (formative period) in painting; Antoni Gaudí, Aristides Maillol, and Josep Lluís Sert in architecture and plastic arts; and Pablo Casals and Montserrat Caballé in music. Folk traditions of note include music and dancing, especially the *sardana*, a Mediterranean circle dance that has become a national symbol; gastronomy and wine; ceramics; and various forms of textile design.

Bibliography

Elliott, J. H. (1963). *The Revolt of the Catalans: A Study in the Decline of Spain (1598–1640)*. Cambridge: Cambridge University Press.

Gran enciclopedia catalana (1968–1980). 15 vols. Barcelona: Editorial Gran, Enciclopedia Catalana. 2nd ed. forthcoming.

Hansen, Edward (1977). *Rural Catalonia under the Franco Regime: The Fate of Rural Culture since the Spanish Civil War*. Cambridge: Cambridge University Press.

McDonough, Gary (1986). *Good Families of Barcelona: A Social History of Power in the Industrial Era.* Princeton: Princeton University Press.

Vilar, Pierre (1962). *La Catalogne dans l'Espagne moderne.* Paris: S.E.V.P.E.N.

Woolard, Kathryn A. (1989). *Double Talk: Bilingualism and the Politics of Ethnicity in Catalonia.* Stanford: Stanford University Press.

—CARLES CARRERAS AND GARY W. MCDONOGH

CROATS

Ethonym: Croatians, Hrvati

Orientation

IDENTIFICATION. Croatians are a Slavic people. They began to form as a distinct group in the seventh century as part of a process completed during the modern national integration in the nineteenth and twentieth centuries. At various times, the Croatian name has been used not only for the contemporary Croats but also for two other Slavic tribes (in the vicinity of Krakow, Poland, and in northeast Bohemia). It was used for the first time as a personal name (Horóathos, Horúathos) in the second to third centuries in Tanais on the river Don and on some historic monuments (Trpimir, dux Chroatorum; Branimir, dux Cruatorum) from the ninth century. Science has not yet solved the question of the origin and meaning of the name "Croat(ian)."

LOCATION. Croatia encompasses 56,538 square kilometers and is located between 42° 23′ and 46° 32′ N and 13° 30′ and 19° 26′ E. The north plain—the biggest, most populated, and economically most active part of the country—is separated from the coastal part in the south (east coast of the Adriatic Sea) by the central mountainous region. Considering its location, Croatia is a Pannonian and Adriatic region, at the juncture of the central Danubian Plain and the Mediterranean. The climate in the north is continental, in the central region mountainous, and in the south Mediterranean.

DEMOGRAPHY. The majority of Croats (3.5 million) lives in Croatia itself; an additional million live in Bosnia and Herzegovina, Serbia, and Slovenia. It is estimated that Croatian emigrants in western Europe, the Americas, Australia, and New Zealand number more than 3 million. Although the number of live births exceeded by 3 percent the number of deceased persons between the censuses of 1971 and 1981, there were 100,000 fewer Croatians because they identified themselves as Yugoslavs.

LINGUISTIC AFFILIATION. The Croatian language is a South Slavic language and encompasses three major dialects (Štokavian, Čakavian, and Kajkavian). Literary Croatian, developed since the twelfth century on a South Štokavian base (with some influence of other dialects) was accepted in the first half of the nineteenth century as the national language. Since then it has been standardized and has become the uniform means of communication in professional, scientific, and artistic expression. The alphabet is Latin (twenty-five consonants and five vowels). In the past, Slavic alphabets were employed, including *glagoljica*, which was used in some areas around the Adriatic until the nineteenth century.

Settlements

The percentage of rural population by residence has always been very high, with significant differences between geographic regions, ranging in the 1980s from a high of about 70 percent in the central region to a low of 40 percent in southern Croatia. Traditionally, there were wide differences among different settlements in the house style and interior design. Today, however, there is a tendency toward uniformity. Settlements are either clustered (mainly in the north and south) or dispersed (mainly in the hinterland of the south and central regions). Clustered settlements are either compact and centered on a square or stripped into perpendicular streets. In the south, houses are made of stone, with roofs of reed (the oldest tradition), stone slabs, or convex tiles (the newest tradition). They are usually two-story buildings along the coast and one-story buildings in the coastal hinterland. Elsewhere, the material is wood (oak logs or trimmed wooden planks), clay mixed with chaff, or more recently brick (at first adobe) and concrete. The roofs are covered either with shingles, thatch, or flat tiles (the most recent tradition). Houses were one-story buildings.

History and Cultural Relations

After settling into today's homeland in the seventh century, Croatians organized a state. From the beginning of the twelfth century, after the demise of the national royal dynasty, the Croatian state unified with Hungary (linked by the same ruler); after 1527, the Austrian royal family of Habsburg ruled Croatia. With the consolidation of the Republic of Venice on a large section of Croatian coast (only the Republic of Dubrovnik kept its independence) and with the Turkish con-

See also

Bosnian Muslims, Serbs

*Croatian history has
been marked by a
struggle for national
and cultural
survival, for
maintenance of state
independence, and
for territorial
integrity.*

quests since the fifteenth century, Croatian lands were divided and to a certain extent the ethnic structure was changed (emigration of Croatians and immigration of Balkan and central European peoples). Subsequently, Croatian history has been marked by a struggle for national and cultural survival, for maintenance of state independence, and for territorial integrity. Following the disintegration of the Austro-Hungarian monarchy in World War I the Croatians removed themselves from it, proclaimed independence, and joined the new South Slav state (the Kingdom of Serbs, Croatians, and Slovenes, renamed the Kingdom of Yugoslavia in 1929). After the liberation struggle in World War II and socialist revolution, Croatia became a federal state (Socialist Republic of Croatia) in the Socialist Federal Republic of Yugoslavia. In 1991, following the fall of Communist rule and a bloody civil war, Croatia became an independent state, the Republic of Croatia.

In the course of developments since the mid-nineteenth century, Croatia has lived through political, social, and economic change. Since the time of Christianization in the early centuries after settling the region, Croatians have belonged to the Western-European cultural milieu. The organizational foundation of the contemporary scientific and artistic life is a branchlike system consisting of institutions of higher education (e.g., University of Zagreb since 1669; universities in Split, Osijek, and Rijeka); scientific institutions (e.g., the Yugoslav Academy of Sciences and Arts since 1867, renamed the Croatian Academy of Sciences and Arts in 1991; the Archive of Croatia and the National University Library in Zagreb); museums, galleries, and theaters (e.g., the central Croatian National Theater in Zagreb); and academies of arts. The cultural life is expressed also in literary and fine arts, films, and radio and television programs.

ECONOMY

Subsistence and Commercial Activities

Somewhat less than half of the population of Croatia is economically active (working outside the home). About 45 percent of the active population is employed in the service sector, 35 percent in industry and 20 percent in agriculture. Eighty-five percent of the agricultural activity is on small peasant farms and 15 percent on state farms. Until 1990, peasant farms were limited by law to 15 hectares (of cultivable surface) and therefore, although it is widely mechanized, agricultural production is not very profitable. The predominant agricultural products are maize, wheat, milk, and meat. The production of wine and fruits is also important, while production of industrial plants (flax, hemp, sunflowers, etc.) is less significant. Almost all agricultural products are used by the domestic population; only a small part of the produce (meat, maize, tobacco, and wine) is exported.

Industrial Arts

The dominant industries are shipbuilding, textiles, and food processing. Less important are the chemical and timber industries. The industrial sector of the Croatian economy creates 50 percent of the gross national product (GNP) while employing one-third of the working population. In the 1960s and 1970s big industrial enterprises were developed in Croatia, while in the 1980s smaller ones, especially in electronics, metalworking, and plastics, also emerged there. The problems faced by industry are insufficient energy (most oil is imported), and the need to import chemical products, raw materials, and industrial machinery.

Trade

About 10 percent of the Croatian working population employed in trade creates about 17 percent of the Croatian GNP. Large state enterprises (stores, supermarkets, specialized shops) dominate this sector. Recently, small specialized private shops (fruit and vegetable stores, stores for other food products and textiles) have been emerging.

Division of Labor

Traditionally, women were assigned domestic tasks (cleaning, cooking, tending babies, etc.) but also shared some agricultural tasks, which otherwise were dominated by men. Today, women are still occupied by household and family work, but women also comprise one-third of the work force. They are most frequently employed in education and medicine, where they outnumber men, and also in tourism and trade.

Kinship, Marriage, and Family

KINSHIP.   Descent is traced patrilineally and the social emphasis on father's lineage is reflected in more elaborated terminology for father's relatives. Kin groups were based traditionally on patrilocal residence and patrimony, which was jointly owned and managed by a father and his married sons (*zadruga*). Matrilineal kin was less important in social practice and lived at a distance. Further patrilineal kin often inhabited the same hamlet or nearby villages. The zadruga system disappeared by the early twentieth century, and because of migrations and intensive urbanization, patrilineal kin groups are presently more dispersed, with their interaction mostly limited to yearly or life-cycle rituals, while in everyday practice one's mother's and father's relatives have equally important roles. Post-World War II family law gave a married woman the opportunity to keep her maiden name or hyphenate it with her husband's surname. This practice indicates a shift toward bilaterality. Children, however, rarely receive other than their father's surname. Inheritance of parental property also has become largely bilateral.

MARRIAGE.   Marriages are monogamous. In the past, they were arranged by corporate kin groups and parents. Marriage partners were sought from neighboring hamlets and villages (regional endogamy). Residence was traditionally patrilocal. As a consequence of rural-urban migrations as well as education and employment of women, ambilocal residence has become predominant, while neolocality is the ideal for young couples. The divorce rate is constantly rising (177 per 1,000 marriages in 1988), peaking in the city of Zagreb, where every third marriage ends in divorce. Divorces are "no-fault," by agreement, with laws mainly oriented toward the protection of the rights of children.

DOMESTIC UNIT.   The domestic unit is that group of people who sleep and eat "under one roof" and who jointly manage family (*obitelj*) resources. The structure of this group has changed from the zadruga type to three-generational stem family (parents with children and one or two grandparents), nuclear family (parents with children), and even smaller "fragmented" types of domestic unit. While the three-generational family is still common in rural areas, the average number of persons in domestic units in Croatia is hardly above three. Less than half of the domestic units have a nuclear family structure, whereas others include single persons (16 percent), childless couples (24.6 percent), mothers with children (8.4 percent) and fathers with children (1.5 percent). The reasons of such fragmentation, besides divorce, are labor migration, a drop in the fertility rate, and a decrease in contracted marriages.

INHERITANCE.   Traditionally, sons inherited equal shares of patrimony, while daughters married out with dowries in land, cattle, or money. Presently property is divided equally among all children, often allotted to them gradually during the parents' life, in order to help the children establish their own households. Remaining property is divided equally upon the parents' death. However, cases of daughters who fight for their share in court against their brothers are not infrequent.

SOCIALIZATION.   Children are raised by parents or grandparents. Great emphasis is placed on achievement through education as it is the main means of climbing the social ladder. For this reason children are often excused from assuming early responsibilities in domestic and productive spheres. Socioeconomic opportunities are limited, and parents sacrifice their labor and money to support their children for a long time, frequently into adulthood.

Sociopolitical Organization

SOCIAL ORGANIZATION.   Since the socialist revolution of 1945, no social classes have been officially recognized, but there are distinguishable social strata. The class of large land-owners and industrialists was discredited after World War II, making wealth only a minor marker of social class. Instead, occupations associated with education and with access to power (as in the case of the bureaucratic elite) have become a major basis of social stratification. Differences in the standard of living and in subjective evaluations of status exist between the agricultural and industrial population, that is, between the rural and urban populations. Since the 1970s the difference has been diminishing because of secondary urbanization of rural settlements, on the one hand, and deteriorating quality of life in the cities, on the other. A trend toward stratification on the basis of wealth has developed, since the sector of private artisans, entrepreneurs, merchants, services, and professions is gaining strength again. Considerable social mobility is secured through the educational system, which is open to everyone. Yet, many social routes are also open through informal personal networks and loyalties, such as those based on familism and localism.

POLITICAL ORGANIZATION.   From 1945 to 1991, Croatia was one of six federal republics that

*The new government
declared the
independence of
Croatia in October
1991, amid civil
war and aggression
from Serbia.*

made up the Socialist Federal Republic of Yugoslavia. After the death of Marshall Tito in 1980, it elected a delegate to the board of the "Presidency"—the collective head of the Yugoslavian state—and a number of delegates to the Federal Assembly, the supreme body of government. As a federal state within Yugoslavia, Croatia had its own government, of which the parliament (Sabor) and the president of its executive council were the supreme bodies. A multiparty political system was reestablished in 1990. The nationalist Croatian Democratic Union (HDZ) won the parliamentary elections that year, taking the majority of seats in the Sabor and having its leader indirectly elected president of Croatia. The new government declared the independence of Croatia in October 1991, amid civil war and aggression from Serbia. Croatia is still divided into 115 communes (opčina), each comprising a number of villages and hamlets. Their population varies in size and density. Communes are clustered into 10 municipalities, each with a major urban center. The division reflects historical, cultural, economic, and administrative divisions so that regional identity and loyalty remains strong. A significant portion of rural-urban migration takes place within municipalities, oriented toward regional urban centers. Each opčina has an assembly and its executive council and president. There are also boards which take care of schools, health services, public roads, and the local economy; offices for tax collection, vital statistics, and urban planning; and courts and police. An opčina center also has secondary schools and religious establishments.

SOCIAL CONTROL. Under the former system, a strong mechanism of social control, both institutionalized and ideological, was the League of Communists, which, although formally separate from the state, exerted influence at all levels of social organization. Preceding the elections of 1990, there was a proliferation of alternative movements (ecological movements, initiatives for democratic reform, new women's movements, agitation for human rights, etc.), creating considerable social impact and causing a concomitant weakening of the ideological grip of the league. In 1990, the league was renamed the Socialist party and became oppositional after the elections. A number of other movements were transformed into political parties at the same time. Informally, gossip and personal alliances on the basis of kinship and common local origin remain strong means of social control.

CONFLICT. Dominant values regarding conflict and warfare are ambivalent, because of the complex history of Croatia: historical border areas (the mountainous zone) emphasize fighting for freedom and undefeatable frontierspeople, while areas of historical feudal states with a tightly controlled population place more value on passive resistance, mediation, clever avoidance of imposed duties, and outwitting opponents in inconspicuous ways. Under the Yugoslav system, courts were formally independent from the legislative and executive branches of government, but politics had influenced them greatly nevertheless. Courts were organized on five levels: communal, regional, state, federal, and supreme courts. In addition to regular courts, there were mediating agencies of different kinds, for business conflicts (e.g., "Social Defense of Self-Management") or for private matters (e.g., obligatory counseling with a social worker before divorce). Reform of the judicial system is pending.

Religion and Expressive Culture

RELIGIOUS BELIEFS AND PRACTICES. Croatians are mainly Roman Catholic, with small percentages of Uniates (Eastern Orthodox Christians, recognizing the pope), Protestants, and Muslims. Some pre-Christian elements have been integrated into Christian beliefs and practices. Other influences on Croatian religious beliefs and practices have come from European and Near Eastern cultures, from rural and urban traditions alike, resulting in an amalgam of different heritages. Sacred and religious aspects of traditional culture were neglected during the Socialist period because religion was relegated solely to the private sphere of life. The first post-Communist government is reintroducing the Catholic church into public life in many conspicuous ways.

In traditional culture, there had been many beliefs connected with the dead, as well as many beliefs in fairies, vampires (who disturb their relatives by sucking their blood), witches (demonic women), mythic female beings who determine the fate of children, or others who choke people during sleep. There is still a widespread belief in the evil eye, in the power of casting spells over people or over their property, and in various protective magical acts. Traditionally, people paid special respect to animals to which they attributed supernatural properties (e.g., snake as a house protector). Such beliefs have disappeared or are slowly fading away, but they have been transmitted through and persist in myths, legends, tales, and poems.

CEREMONIES. Ceremonies and rituals can be divided into several types—annual celebrations associated with church holy days, life-cycle events, and work rituals (the last group is connected with harvest, building of a house, etc.). The most prominent among calendrical rituals are those of Christmas Eve—*badnjak*, the burning of the yule log, an older tradition; the decoration of a Christmas tree, a newer tradition; and all sorts of practices linked to the cult of the deceased—and *koleda*, men's processions during the period between Christmas and New Year's. Mardi Gras carnival celebrations featuring processions and burning of a straw effigy have been revived recently thanks to the mass media and tourist agencies. In spring, in addition to Easter celebrations (including coloring of eggs), there used to be various village processions (on St. George's Day, First of May, Ascension Day, Whitsuntide, etc.) and bonfires (especially on St. John's Day in June). Those processions and bonfires were apotropaic rituals meant for the protection of people, fields, and cattle and for promoting fertility. There were also new rituals created in the Socialist period, such as celebrations of Workers' Day on 1 May and of International Women's Day on 8 March. Both were canceled in 1991. Among life-cycle rituals, most important are those centering on birth, marriage, and death. Today some new ones have emerged (e.g., the day of graduation, especially in cities), while the old ones have an impoverished repertoire. A wedding traditionally has been the most important family and community event. It once consisted of a complex of ritual events such as solemn carrying over of the bride's trousseau, humorous negotiations over false brides when the wedding party arrived at the bride's house, and symbolic acts by the bride upon arrival at bridegroom's home (holding a male child in her lap, sweeping the floor, starting the fire on the hearth, etc). Death gave rise to numerous beliefs, most important being the belief in life after death, marked by feasting ceremonies and loud laments for the deceased (*naricanje*).

ARTS. A wide variety of folk music is found among Croatians. Specific features are exhibited in tonal relationships of tunes and instrumental melodies. The musical styles range from a rather old, narrow-intervals style (in which the intervals in the tonal ranges are sometimes narrower than the intervals between the twelve equal semitones in an octave), in central and south Croatia, to a widespread contemporary style called "in bass" singing,

in eastern Croatia. Folk music is interwoven with all kinds of everyday and festive activities (especially working songs, weddings, and spring processions). Today, its main function is entertainment. The main instruments used to accompany the singing are cordophones and aerophones. Dances differ as much as do tunes and instruments. Today they are almost restored to their pre-World War II forms, thanks to their revival on stage; forms include the couple dance, a closed circle dance (*drmeš*), and circles and lines. Artistic expression can be found on decorative clothes, wood carving, pottery, pictures painted on glass, metalwork, and even egg painting. Oral literature is dominated by epic poetry. Among lyric poetry, the Dalmatian ballads are noteworthy (Adriatic coast). The earliest records of oral literature are from the sixteenth century and point to a wide variety of genres. Croatian art also includes church architecture, frescoes, reliefs, and decorated facades and balconies.

In the twentieth century, painting, sculpture, and music have exploded in various styles. Architecture suffered under the planned socialist economy.

MEDICINE. Folk medicine was imbued with magic, but it was also rational, especially in the identification, preparation, and use of medicinal herbs. The pharmaceutical industry has incorporated some of this folk knowledge in the production of herbal drugs.

Bibliography

Erlich, Vera Stein (1966). *Family in Transition*. Princeton: Princeton University Press.

Gavazzi, Milovan (1939). *Godina dana hrvatskih narodnih običaja* (Yearly cycle of Croatian folk customs). Zagreb: Matica Hrvatska.

Historical Maps of Croatia from the Penguin Atlas of World History (1992). Zagreb: Croatian Information Centre.

"Hrvati" (Croats) (1988). In *Enciklopedija Jugoslavije*, edited by Jakov Sirotković. Vol. 5, 1–151. Zagreb: Jugoslavenski Leksikografski Zavod.

Grupković, D., ed. (1989). *Statistički kalendar Jugoslavije* (The statistical calendar of Yugoslavia). Vol. 35. Belgrade: Savezni Zavod za Statistiku.

Grupković, D., ed. (1990). *Statistički godisnjak Jugoslavije* (The statistical yearbook of Yugoslavia). Vol. 37. Belgrade: Savezni Zavod za Statistiku.

Šeparovic, Zvonimir (1992). *Documenta Croatica*. Zagreb: Croatian Society of Victimology.

—JASNA CAPO, JAKOV GELO, TRPIMIR MACAN, AND OLGA SUPEK

There is still a widespread Croatian belief in the evil eye, in the power of casting spells over people or over their property, and in various protective magical acts.

CZECHS

Ethonym: Češi or Cechové (plural), Čech (singular), referring to people whose native language is Czech and, more specifically, to those native to or residing in Bohemia (Čechy), Moravané (plural), Moravan (singular), referring to the Czech-speaking population native to or residing in Moravia (Morava)

Orientation

IDENTIFICATION. Czechs constitute 94.2 percent (1986) of the population of the Czech Republic (*Česká republica*, hereafter CR), which is federated with the Slovak Republic (SR) in the Czech and Slovak Federative Republic (*Česká a Slovenská Federativní Republika*, or CSFR).

LOCATION. CR is bounded by Poland on the north, Germany on the north and west, Austria on the south, and the Slovak Republic on the east. The geographic location of CR is between 12°05′ and 18°51′ E and 51°03′ and 48°33′ N; the area is 78,864 square kilometers. Historically, CR consists of Bohemia, the largest province, in the west; Moravia, to the east of it; and the part of Silesia just below the northern Moravian border with Poland. Bohemia is ringed by low mountain ranges, with the highest peak (Sněžka) reaching an altitude of 1,602 meters. The southern half of Bohemia's interior is an elevated plateau; in the northern half, the distinguishing feature is the plain along the Labe (Elbe) River. The dominant feature of Moravia is the basin of the Morava River separating the Bohemian massif from the westernmost extension of the Carpathian Mountains in SR. The climate of CR is predominantly continental, with some influence of oceanic weather systems. Summers are warm, winters cold. The average temperature in Prague, the capital, varies from a high of 19.9° C in July to a low of −0.8° C in January, with an annual average of 9.7° C. The average precipitation is around 70 centimeters per year, with the summer months being the wettest. The higher elevations along the border receive more moisture than the interior. The main Bohemian river, the Labe, is joined by the Vltava (Moldau) about 32 kilometers north of Prague and empties into the North Sea north of Hamburg. The Morava, which flows from the north, marks the boundary in southern Moravia between CR and SR, and some 50 kilometers farther south it empties into the Danube.

DEMOGRAPHY. Historically, CR has been a land of small towns (10,000 to 30,000 inhabitants), their distribution reflecting the pattern of medieval settlement and growth. The relatively early industrialization of the area has increased the concentration of population in cities at the expense of rural areas. While the rural exodus continues to the present day, the inhabitants of metropolitan areas, especially Prague, tend to buy or build summer cottages in the country and to spend much of their free time away from the city, especially during the summer. The years immediately following World War II were marked by high population mobility. The border regions, inhabited from the thirteenth century on by a high proportion of German-speaking people, were resettled by Czechs after World War II when more than 2.5 million Bohemian and Moravian Germans were transferred from the country or chose to leave. The population of CR is 10,365,000 (1989 estimate), with a population density of 131 per square kilometer (1988 estimate). Of this total, 94.2 percent are Czechs and 3.9 percent Slovaks, with the remainder divided among several ethnic minorities (0.7 percent Polish, 0.5 percent German, with several other groups represented). Prague is the largest city and capital, as well as the federal capital, with a population of 1,206,098 (as of the end of 1987). Brno, the second-largest city and unofficial capital of Moravia, has a population of about 400,000.

LINGUISTIC AFFILIATION. As a West Slavic language, Czech is a member of the Indo-European Language Family. It is most closely related to Slovak, with which it is mutually intelligible. Spoken Czech is differentiated into regional dialects still to be heard in Moravia and several marginal areas of Bohemia, but interdialects—especially Common Czech—have been replacing local and regional dialects at an increasing rate. Literary Czech is the form of the language used in writing and formal communication. Czech makes use of the Latin (Roman) alphabet supplemented by several diacritical marks.

History and Cultural Relations

After the fall of the Great Moravian Empire at the beginning of the tenth century, much of today's Slovak Republic was incorporated into the Hungarian state, while Prague developed as the center of what was to become the Bohemian Kingdom. The crowning of the first Bohemian king took place in 1085 and the title became hereditary in 1198. The peak of medieval civilization was attained during the second half of the fourteenth century; the first university in central Europe was established in Prague in 1348. The

♦ **Carpathian Mountains**
A mountain range in east-central Europe in the Czech and Slovak Federative Republic, Poland, Hungary, Romania, and nations that were formerly part of the Soviet Union.

See also

Slovaks

beginning of the fifteenth century was marked by the teachings of Jan Hus, a Czech religious reformer, and, after his death at the stake in Constance in 1415, by wars against the propapal King Sigismund. When the Bohemian throne became vacant in 1526, a member of the Habsburg dynasty was elected Bohemian king. Less than a century later, in 1620, when the Czech estates were defeated in the battle of White Mountain (Bílá Hora) near Prague, the Bohemian Kingdom lost its independence and its provinces were declared the hereditary property of the Habsburg family. Wholesale emigration—resulting from forcible re-Catholicization, the effects of the Thirty Years' War (1618–1648), and epidemics of plague and other diseases—reduced the population of Bohemia by about one-half and that of Moravia by about one-fourth. A period referred to as "the darkness" (*temno*) ensued, and it was not until the end of the eighteenth century that the Czech national revival began. Independence for the Czechs arrived in 1918 with the breakup of the Austro-Hungarian Empire. The Czechoslovak Republic, which resulted from the political reorganization of Europe in the aftermath of World War I, included not only the historic Bohemian Kingdom (Bohemia, Moravia, and a part of Silesia) but also Slovakia and Carpathian Ruthenia in the extreme east. The new republic lasted a mere twenty years. Following the infamous Munich Agreement of 1938, Bohemia and Moravia lost over a third of their combined area to Germany. On 15 March 1939 Germany annexed the remainder and declared it a protectorate, thus effectively ending the independent existence of the Czechoslovak Republic. (Slovakia became a nominally independent state under the protection of the Third Reich.) Czechoslovakia was reestablished in 1945, though without Carpathian Ruthenia, which was ceded to the USSR. The majority of the population wished to continue the democratic tradition of the interwar period and hoped to establish the country as a bridge between West and East. However, in February 1948 the Communists took over the government, and Czechoslovakia became part of the cultural, economic, and political orbit of the Soviet Union. On 1 January 1969, four months after the Warsaw Pact armies put a stop to attempts to create "socialism with a human face," the federalization of the Czechoslovak Socialist Republic into the Czech Socialist Republic and the Slovak Socialist Republic took place. The transformation of Czechoslovakia from a rigid Communist country into a democracy began in November 1989 and

was accomplished bloodlessly with remarkable speed. One of Czechoslovakia's best-known dissidents, the playwright Václav Havel, became president on 29 December 1989.

The Czechs have always considered themselves as belonging culturally to western Europe, and no more so than after they were incorporated into the sphere of Soviet influence in the late 1940s. Because they constitute the westernmost Slavic outpost, surrounded as they are by speakers of German, and because of the memory of official Germanization during much of the eighteenth century as well as forcible Germanization during World War II, the potential for ethnic tension between Czechs and Germans has always existed. In prewar Czechoslovakia (1918–1939), the attitude of the Czechs toward the much less urbanized Slovaks was patronizing. After World War II, the relationship between the two peoples continued to be asymmetrical until 1969, when the federalization of the country helped to bring about a measure of dynamic balance between them. Ethnic tensions resurfaced in 1990 as a result of Slovak expectations of a greater degree of autonomy.

Economy

SUBSISTENCE AND COMMERCIAL ACTIVITIES. Before World War II, agriculture, commerce, and industry were for the most part in private hands. After the Communist takeover in 1948, commerce and industry were completely nationalized, and virtually all agricultural production came to be based on unified agricultural cooperatives (1,025 in 1987) and state farms (166 in 1987). The cooperatives employed about four times as many workers as the state farms. Because of a fairly high level of mechanization, the total number of persons engaged in agriculture is about one-fourth of those employed in industry.

INDUSTRIAL ARTS. During the nineteenth century, Bohemia became the industrial heart of the Austro-Hungarian Empire. It was known not only for its heavy industry but also for a long and distinguished tradition of ceramic, glass, and textile manufacture.

TRADE. Until the introduction of socialism after World War II, the economy was to a considerable extent capitalistic. After 1948, all commerce was managed and controlled by the state. The inefficiency of central planning was compensated for by a "second economy"—obtaining goods or services in short supply by barter or by paying someone willing to perform a service on a private basis. Relying on acquaintances to get

One of Czechoslovakia's best-known dissident, the playwright Václav Havel, became president on 29 December, 1989.

things done (networking) was widespread. Privatization of business and industry began in 1990, but it is likely to proceed slowly. A vigorous economy may take years to reestablish.

DIVISION OF LABOR. Women have made significant strides since World War II in terms of education, employment opportunities, and participation in public life, and they have benefited from social legislation. However, some of the discriminatory practices and behaviors found in many parts of the world exist in CR as well—in particular, the disproportionately large number of women in the lower half of the pay scale and the excessive demands on employed women to do far more than their share of child-rearing and household tasks.

LAND TENURE. Since the late 1940s, the vast majority of land has been publicly owned. The few exceptions include small gardens, adjacent to family dwellings or on the outskirts of large towns, and small plots (on the order of half a hectare) that members of unified agricultural cooperatives are allowed to hold for family use.

Kinship, Marriage, and Family

KINSHIP. For the Czechs, the effective kin group is limited to the closest relatives. Most people consider collateral relatives beyond uncles, aunts, and first cousins to be rather distant and are likely to see them only at weddings or funerals. Descent is bilateral, with family names patronymic. Kinship terminology is of the Eskimo type, emphasizing both lineal descent and generation membership.

MARRIAGE. For much of this century the selection of a spouse and the decision to marry has rested with the young couple. Before World War II, education and economic standing of the prospective bride and groom were of considerable importance. Men did not usually marry until they completed their education and were launched in their careers, typically in their late twenties or early thirties; women at marriage were for the most part in their early or mid-twenties. In 1986, the average age of individuals marrying for the first time was much lower: 35.7 percent of women were below 20 years of age, 51.9 percent of women and 58.4 percent of men between 20 and 24, and 23.8 percent of men between 25 and 29. Wedding celebrations rarely exceed one day. The most desired postmarital residence is neolocal; however, housing shortages in big cities since World War II have made that goal difficult to attain. Divorce, relatively rare at the beginning of the century, is now quite common: there were 2.2 divorces per 100 marriages in 1919, but 37 per 100 in 1987. The two-child family is the ideal, although childless families among careeroriented spouses are not uncommon. The number of legally approved abortions per 100 births amounted to 62.4 in 1986.

DOMESTIC UNIT. The nuclear family has long been the typical domestic group, especially in the cities.

INHERITANCE. Inheritances in former times helped perpetuate differences between the rich and poor. Under socialism, the importance of inheritance diminished. Nevertheless, most parents make every effort to help their children become comfortable.

SOCIALIZATION. Until World War II, middleclass women as a rule did not hold a job but stayed home to manage the household and take care of children. At present, with women accounting for 46.3 percent (1987) of those employed in the national economy, small children not cared for by mothers on generous maternity leave are enrolled in nurseries or are in the care of relatives, especially grandmothers. Mothers tend to exercise more authority over children than do fathers. Parents tend more to criticize than to praise their children. Czechs place a high value on education and on academic titles. In terms of values, chil-

MODERN PRAGUE

Czechs walk through the public square in Prague. Since industrialization, there has been a rural exodus to the larger cities, to find work. Prague, Czech Republic. (Dave Bartruff/Corbis)

dren are brought up to be egalitarian, individualistic, personally orderly, pragmatic, rational, hardworking (for one's own benefit), peaceful, present-oriented, and materialistic.

Sociopolitical Organization

SOCIAL ORGANIZATION. The traditional tripartite social structure—a sizable working class including the peasants, the middle class, and a relatively small upper class—gave way during Communism to a "classless" society with two distinct classes: privileged members of the higher echelons of the Communist party and the rest of the population. Material benefits also accrued to successful artists and to those who performed valuable services or distributed goods in short supply.

POLITICAL ORGANIZATION. Between 1918 and 1939, political life was characterized by a large number of rival political parties. Between 1948 and 1990, there were only three, all part of the National Front, but the Communist party had a monopoly on power. The free national election in June of 1990 was again characterized by the rivalry of a large number of political parties. The republic as a whole (CSFR) has two legislative houses—the Chamber of Nations and the Chamber of the People. The highest administrative organs of CR are the Czech National Council, the government of CR, the supreme court, the office of the prosecutor genreal, and the defense council. Administration on the level of the region (*kraj*), district (*okres*), and community (*obec*) continues to be in the hands of the respective national councils, but some administrative changes are under consideration.

SOCIAL CONTROL. Conformity with the law is maintained by a police force and a strict and efficient court system. Since the end of 1989, political dissent is again tolerated. A tradition of strong bureaucracy, inherited from Austro-Hungarian times, continues unabated.

CONFLICT. The Czechs view their history as a series of conflicts with the surrounding German-speaking population. The most recent expressions of this conflict were the German occupation of the area from 1939 to 1945 and the removal of the great majority of Germans after World War II.

Religion and Expressive Culture

RELIGIOUS BELIEFS AND PRACTICES. Christianity was introduced to the area during the ninth century by both German and Byzantine missions. By the time the bishopric of Prague was established in 973, Latin had replaced Old Church Slavic as the liturgical language. A serious breach with Rome occurred during the early part of the fifteenth century as a result of the reformational movement inspired by Jan Hus. His "Protestant" legacy became an important aspect of Czech national heritage, having been further reinforced by the efforts at forcible re-Catholicization of the population during the Counter-Reformation and the association of Catholicism with the Habsburg rule. The history of Bohemia accounts in large measure for the nature of post-World War I religious sentiments: the generally lukewarm Catholicism among the Czechs (but less so in Moravia); the fairly devout Protestantism represented by several sects; the establishment of the Czechoslovak Church (a splinter from Roman Catholicism) in 1920; and the rise of agnosticism and atheism. Many urban Czech Catholics went to church only to be baptized and married, and eventually they received their last rites and were buried by a priest. The attitude toward religion was rational rather than emotional. Relations among the members of various religious organizations were marked by tolerance. After 1948 the Communist government became hostile to organized religion and discouraged religious beliefs and observances by a variety of means, including intimidation and persecution. While the relations between the state and the Roman Catholic church were adversarial between 1948 and 1989, there was some resurgence of religious commitment in recent years, especially among young people. Nominally, at least, the country is predominantly Roman Catholic, but reliable figures concerning religious preference have not been available since the end of the last war. Christmas is the only religious holiday officially recognized, even though observances have in part been secularized. While Jan Hus is regarded as a national hero who laid down his life in defense of the truth, St. Wenceslaus (Václav), murdered around 930, is considered the country's patron saint.

ARTS. The Czechs have a long and rich tradition in the arts, both folk and elite. Music is the most popular of the arts. There is a great deal of truth in the saying "*Co Čech, to muzikant*" (Every Czech is a musician). In literature, lyric poetry has surpassed in quality both prose and dramatic writing.

MEDICINE. Use of medicinal plants, based on empirical evidence gained over centuries, for the most part was replaced by use of synthetic drugs during the course of the first half of this century. In general, Czech medicine has followed the course of Western medicine and at present is keeping up with modern advances. Health care,

The Czechs have always considered themselves as belonging culturally to western Europe, and no more so than after they were incorporated into the sphere of Soviet influence in the late 1940s.

The Danes live in the country of Denmark and Danish is their national language.

including hospitalization and drugs, is available free or at nominal cost. Health spas are numerous and popular.

Bibliography

Nyrop, Richard F., ed. (1982). *Czechoslovakia: A Country Study.* 2nd ed. Washington, D.C.: United States Government.

Paul, David W. (1981). *Czechoslovakia: Profile of a Socialist Republic at the Crossroads of Europe.* Boulder, Colo.: Westview Press.

Salzmann, Zdenek, and Vladimír Scheufler (1986). *Komárov: A Czech Farming Village.* Enl. ed. Prospect Heights, Ill.: Waveland Press.

Statistická ročenka Československé Socialistické Republiky (Statistical yearbook of the Czechoslovak Socialist Republic). Prague and Bratislava: SNTL and ALFA. [Appears annually, now with an adjusted title.]

—ZDENEK SALZMANN

DANES

Ethonym: Scandinavians (includes Faroese, Finns, Icelanders, Norwegians, and Swedes)

Orientation

IDENTIFICATION. The Danes live in the country of Denmark and Danish is their national language. The state-affiliated church is Protestant, historically a branch of the Lutheran church. Danes outside of Denmark, particularly in the United States, tend to become highly assimilated, with almost on development of ethnic neighborhoods or enclaves. The term "Dane" (Danish "Dansker"), as the name of people living in what is now Denmark, can be traced to the early Middle Ages when the Old Nordic term "Danir" was in use. Between the ninth and eleventh centuries, Old English chronicles referred loosely to all Scandinavians who invaded England as Danes (Dena).

To comprehend Danish national character in our time it is necessary to look back to Denmark of the eighteenth century. At that time, Danish cultural distinctiveness was not really evident on manorial estates or in towns. Aristocrats and burghers each lived in terms of Europe-wide cultural norms that tended to blur and diminish their uniqueness as Danes. A national identity was to be found, however, in the way of life of the majority of the population who lived on farms and in villages. The roots of a Danish identity reach deeply into peasant culture.

LOCATION. Geographically, Denmark is the most northerly extension of the West European Plain, which projects into Scandinavia as the peninsula of Jutland. Jutland points northward toward Norway and Sweden. Denmark also includes several hundred islands. On the largest island, Zealand, the capital city of Copenhagen lies within view of Malmö on the southern shore of Sweden. Copenhagen is located on "The Sound" (Øresund), which narrowly separates Denmark from Sweden and which provides valuable, strategic shipping links between the North Atlantic and the Baltic Sea.

DEMOGRAPHY. Denmark has a population of 5.1 million. Probably because they number so few and live in propinquity with other nations, many Danes speak a second language. German was the most popular before World War II, but now it is English.

LINGUISTIC AFFILIATION. Like most Europeans, the Danes speak an Indo-European language. The three most widely distributed branches of this family are the Romance languages, the Slavic languages, and the Germanic languages. Danish is a Germanic language, and thus it is less distantly related to German and Dutch than it is to other European languages such as French or Russian. However, it has its closest ties to neighboring Scandinavian languages. The oldest known example of a Scandinavian language is a Gothic translation of parts of the Bible surviving from the fourth century. The modern Scandinavian languages in addition to Danish are Norwegian, which many Danes can understand, as well as Swedish, Icelandic, and Faroese. Although Finns share in Scandinavian culture and a minority of Finns speak Swedish as their family tongue, the Finnish language as such is non-Indo-European.

History and Cultural Relations

Denmark was formerly a large nation. To the south, its territory included Holstein and Schleswig, which were conquered by Germany in 1864. (Part of Schleswig was returned to Denmark through a referendum held after World War I.) To the northeast, it included the provinces of Scania, Halland, and Blekinge, which became the southernmost provinces of Sweden in 1660. Until 1814 Norway and Denmark were united under the Danish crown. Westward to the Atlantic Ocean, the Kingdom of Denmark includes the Faroe Islands and Greenland. Iceland acquired independent nation status after World War I, subject only to a personal union under the Danish crown. It became completely independent of Denmark in 1944.

Denmark is an industrialized, urbanized nation with virtually universal literacy. Danes are full participants in the international culture of the modern world. Denmark is a member of the European Community (Common Market). A century ago, most were peasants in what was then an impoverished developing nation. They were similar in culture to peasant villagers in neighboring Germany to the south and in Sweden and Norway to the north. Like the rest of Europe, however, the lives of some Danes of the nineteenth century, as well as of earlier times, were not shaped by peasant culture. Those who belonged to the ruling class lived on large estates, followed customs shared by aristocrats throughout Europe, and spoke either French or German in addition to Danish. They looked to the royal court of the king of Denmark for cultural leadership. Townspeople were also different in many aspects of culture, since they lived from crafts, merchandising, and service occupations rather than agriculture. In the seventeenth and eighteenth centuries, German was widely spoken in Danish towns, but by the nineteenth century most spoke Danish as their family language. Culturally, they were influenced by town life in other parts of western Europe, particularly in Germany, since many artisans spent a year or more working abroad before returning to Denmark as journeymen. No comparable custom united Danish townswomen with women in other parts of Europe.

Economy

SUBSISTENCE AND COMMERCIAL ACTIVITIES.
Denmark today relies upon a diversified economy based primarily on service industries, trade, and manufacturing. Less than 10 percent of the population engages in agriculture, fishing, and forestry. Danish agriculture is known for its cooperatives, particularly in the production of butter, cheese, eggs, bacon, and ham. Danish beer and *snaps* (aquavit) have acquired an international market. The fishing industry supplies markets in Europe beyond Denmark. In American stores one is most likely to encounter Danish marinated herring. From industrial enterprises products of modern design are shipped throughout the world, particularly Danish furniture, ceramics, and plastics. The Danes pioneered in producing furniture that was functional as well as handsome. They have designed chairs in response to studies of spinal biomechanics and have created tables to serve multiple purposes, such as those that con-

vert to desks or collapse for storage against a wall in small apartments. For purposes of international trade, the Danes also have designed furniture to be shipped in disassembled, compact forms that make handling easy and save some shipping costs. The Danish merchant marine, growing out of their own interisland maritime needs, includes large shipping companies, such as the Maersk Lines, that constitute an important source of revenue for the nation. In collaboration with Sweden and Norway, Denmark also operates the Scandinavian Airline System (SAS) for international travel. Taxes are heavy in order to provide citizens with a wide range of welfare benefits that include excellent child care and school opportunities, extensive health benefits, and exceptional housing and care for the aged. Workers live very well by international standards. Although housing is in short supply, most Danes can afford small houses or apartments, dress well, and drive their own automobiles.

LAND TENURE AND DIVISION OF LABOR.
In historic Denmark, peasants lived in a form of village settlement, known as the open field system, in which communalism was central. The village territory was divided into two or three large fields, in each of which every landholder possessed scattered plots. The unit of work was not the individual plot, however, but the large field. Because fields were worked as units, it was essential that villagers agree on the nature and timing of many of their activities. Meeting in a dwelling or at a central place in the village, they followed old customs for village decision making that were common throughout Denmark. Schedules were agreed upon and implemented. Although cattle were individually owned, they were brought together daily to form single village herds, which grazed on the village common or on stubble left after fields were harvested. It was the custom for villagers to help individuals who fell sick. As a community, they supervised the use of communal facilities such as the meadow, commons, square, pond, hay field, and church. They cooperated in much of what they did, and a communal spirit was the product. By the nineteenth century, major agricultural reforms had changed the old peasant community. The chief reform was to abolish the common system by parceling out the village land. They also consolidated scattered holdings so that each villager ended up owning fields located more or less in one place. Individual management replaced communalism. Gradually, some landowners moved their farmsteads away from the village, resulting in a scattered settlement pattern of vil-

Nonviolence is the essence of the Danish polity. At all levels, governmental and nongovernmental, disputes are resolved through the highly developed art of compromise.

lages with interspersed farmsteads. Less fertile soils in western Jutland were settled by farmers who established isolated farmsteads rather than villages. During the nineteenth century, many other changes took place in association with these basic changes in land tenure and the division of labor. Yet, a sense of communalism persisted. Villages continued to manage their affairs by convening meetings of landowners. "Folk high schools," introduced by N. F. S. Grundtvig (1783–1872) and now found throughout Scandinavia, raised the level of education and prepared ordinary people for participation in democratic government. Toward the end of the nineteenth century and during the first decades of the twentieth, communalism reasserted itself as Danish farmers distinguished themselves by their ability to submit individual wishes to group decisions and to form voluntary common-interest associations. The successful creation of farming cooperatives across the nation became one of the foundations of the modernization of Danish agriculture. Meanwhile, the government of the nation shifted to that of a democratic, constitutional monarchy.

Kinship, Marriage, and Family

KINSHIP. Danish kinship nomenclature was and is bifurcate-collateral in type, differing from English primarily in that uncles, aunts, and grandparents are terminologically distinguished as father's side or mother's side, and blood relatives are always distinguished from relatives by marriage. For example, Danes distinguish father's brother from mother's brother and mother's mother from father's mother. They trace descent bilaterally, but a patrilineal emphasis was visible in the inheritance of property primarily through the male line until recent times, when gender became less determinative. Aristocrats also demonstrate their patrilineal emphasis in the inheritance of family names through the male line. Peasants did not get family names until late in the nineteenth century. Until then, one simply got the name of one's father. Thus Peter Rasmussen was the son of Rasmus Andersen, who in turn was the son of Anders Jensen, and so on. Daughters took the last names of their fathers or husbands.

MARRIAGE. Women married into the circumstances of their grooms, whether landed or landless. Property owners tended to arrange marriages for their sons and daughters so that the young couple could have a farm of their own. Marriage was neolocal insofar as newlyweds usually set up housekeeping on their own. A patrilocal quality was imparted, however, by the ten-

dency to settle in the community of the groom's family or even to take over the farm of the groom's parents. Divorce was difficult to obtain legally and was strongly censured by village opinion and church morality. Adultery in the village was regarded as highly reprehensible. Unmarried mothers were ostracized. A woman encountered no difficulty, however, if a pregnancy occurred before marriage but in betrothal, especially when a gold ring had been given to the young woman. Many couples hitherto only casually joined saved the situation when a pregnancy occurred by announcing that they were engaged. Premarital sexual activity was, in fact, common, and young men in many villages were permitted to sleep over in the bed of a young woman in the custom called night courting. Village customs thus set the stage for the sexual freedom and independence of both women and men that is characteristic of Denmark today.

FAMILY. Traditionally, the Danes practiced monogamy. They lived in nuclear families that became stem families when old parents were cared for by an inheriting son. Today, many children are born to parents united in consensual unions. Single-parent families are common. One-fourth of all marriages terminate in divorce. The stem family has become obsolete as retired parents are provided with good care by the welfare system.

INHERITANCE. Primogeniture was formerly the rule. Younger sons acquired farms by purchase or partial inheritance, worked as landless laborers residing in small cottages, or migrated to town to find work or enter a trade. Beginning in the nineteenth century, many of these younger sons and daughters migrated to the United States, particularly to Michigan and Wisconsin. Inheritance today no longer discriminates consistently on the basis of birth order and gender.

SOCIALIZATION. The Danes characteristically welcomed the birth of both boys and girls. In traditional village life, children's play was permitted, but it was unsupervised and unsupported. Children created their own toys. Even in the nineteenth century, most boys and girls went to school enough to become literate. From earliest childhood, however, they were expected to contribute to the work of the family by tending livestock such as flocks of fowl, carrying water, and helping adults at their work. Consistent with an ethic of village communalism—though the principle is long extinct in its historical form—children today still are taught to control and suppress aggression. The censorship of movies in recent decades did not permit the showing of violence but made no objection to films showing sexually

RELIGION AND EXPRESSIVE CULTURE

Religious Beliefs and Practices

The village church with its state salaried priest united each community for the Sunday church service. The confirmation ritual was a high point in the life of each boy and girl, serving as a rite of passage into adult status. In the twentieth century the Danes became increasingly secularized. Although confirmation is still important, state-supported churches today are usually almost empty for Sunday services.

Arts

The fine arts and classical music receive state support and are highly appreciated in educated circles. The Danes are best known for their success in modern design. At the same time, they preserve an affection for folk songs and folk culture in a society that values its peasant heritage. The nation maintains an unusually fine system of folk museums, including parks containing authentic, renovated buildings salvaged from premodern times.

Medicine

In the old days, villagers tended to circumvent medical doctors by going directly to apothecaries for diagnosis and treatment. They also had recourse to village healers (known as clever or wise men and women or as sorcerers). Much that healers did was based upon standard medical practice of the time, including herbs, cupping, and bleeding, but they also utilized amulets and other magical practices. Bone-setters and midwives were also part of the historic health-care scene. Only midwives survive at present in a country that supports state-of-the-art medical facilities and personnel.

Death and Afterlife

Traditional Danish beliefs paralleled those of other north European Protestant peoples. They feared hell and strived to be worthy of heaven—some with anguish, but many with little obvious concern.

explicit scenes as long as nobody was maimed or killed. The Danish child is encouraged to be dependent on his or her mother more than is true for an American child. The principal form of discipline is guilt. The mother lets the child know how hurt she is and how bad she feels because of his or her behavior. Adult Danes thus show a psychiatric vulnerability to any loss of dependency through death, separation, or divorce. They also tend to be obedient citizens.

Sociopolitical Organization

SOCIAL ORGANIZATION. Class divisions are muted now in a country with a strong egalitarian ethic. Ethnic minorities have changed the character of the nation somewhat in recent decades. Early in the century, Polish migrant workers settled in some areas of the nation, and since World War II foreign workers from as far away as southern Europe and the Middle East have become permanent residents. Contemporary families tend to isolate themselves from one another. Attitudes surviving from an older communalism and from socialization practices result, however, in acquiescence to democratic forms of governing at every level. They also persist in the widespread activities of voluntary associations, which stem from the mutual-assistance societies and the cooperative movement of the late nineteenth century. The societies were forerunners of social insurance.

POLITICAL ORGANIZATION. Denmark became a constitutional monarchy in 1848. Universal suffrage is practiced. Now ruled by a unicameral legislature, the government is headed by a prime minister. Recently a bourgeois coalition has formed the government. Previously, leadership was most often in the hands of the Social Democrats.

SOCIAL CONTROL. The Danes have some continental (Napoleonic) aspects in their legal system—for example, judges who are career civil servants and the use of lay judges. They also include some common-law (English) aspects, such as criminal jury trials. On the whole, they are closer to common law, because they mainly follow an accusatorial rather than an inquisitorial system. The courts are strong and untainted, backed by a humane penal system and police who do not carry guns.

CONFLICT. Nonviolence is the essence of the Danish polity, reflecting continuities with a history of communalism. At all levels, governmental and nongovernmental, disputes are resolved through the highly developed art of compromise. The Danes pioneered in the global expansion of the Swedish institution of the ombudsman. Appointed by parliament, the ombudsman is empowered to investigate governmental activity but may not compel the implementation of his recommendations other than through reasoned persuasion or publicity.

Bibliography

Anderson, Barbara G. (1990). *First Fieldwork: The Misadventures of an Anthropologist*. Prospect Heights, Ill.: Waveland Press.

Anderson, Robert T. (1975). *Denmark: Success of a Developing Nation*. Cambridge, Mass.: Schenkman.

Anderson, Robert T., and Barbara G. Anderson (1964). *The Vanishing Village: A Danish Maritime Community*. Seattle: University of Washington Press.

Anderson, Stanley V. (1967). *The Nordic Council: A Study of Scandinavian Regionalism*. Seattle: University of Washington Press.

Hansen, Judith Friedman (1980). *We Are a Little Land: Cultural Assumptions in Danish Everyday Life*. New York: Arno Press.

—ROBERT ANDERSON AND STANLEY ANDERSON

DUTCH

Ethonym: Dutchmen, Dutchwomen; Hollanders (in a narrow definition for the people of the provinces of North and South Holland, in colloquial language for all Dutch); further differentiated according to provincial affiliation: Brabander, Drentenaar, Fries, Groninger, Limburger, Zeeuw

Orientation

IDENTIFICATION. The origin of the name "Dutch" is supposed to be a corruption of the word "Duits" referring to the Germanic origin of the Dutch. The word "Netherlands" probably stems from the Rhineland. Since the twelfth century the lower Rhine basin north of Cologne has been referred to as "netherland" (lowland) in contrast to the "overland" (highland) south of Cologne.

LOCATION. The Netherlands is situated between 50° and 54° N and 3° and 7° E. The Netherlands is bordered by the North Sea to the north and the west, Germany to the east, and Belgium to the south. The West Frisian Islands—Texel, Vlieland, Terschelling, Ameland, Schiermonnikoog, and Rottumeroog—are situated north of the Frisian coast. The climate is maritime: wet, with mild winters and cool summers. The Netherlands consists of low-lying land, part of which (in the west and north) is below sea level. This makes water management a crucial strategy. The fight against the water has resulted in programs of land reclamation, dike construction, and drainage of marshlands, generating such amazing infrastructural achievements as the Zuider Zee Works, the Delta-works, and the canalization of the big rivers. The Netherlands is comprised of three geographic regions: the zones of large-scale agriculture in the north, the regions of mixed agricultural-recreational use in the east and south, and the highly urbanized areas in the west. The Netherlands still possesses overseas territories, which consist of a number of islands in the Caribbean, collectively called "the Dutch Antilles": the Leeward Islands of Aruba, Curacao, and Bonaire north of the Venezuelan coast; and the Windward Islands of Saba, Saint Eustacius, and Sint Maarten 900 kilometers farther north. The total population of the Dutch Antilles amounts to 250,000 people of multiethnic origin.

DEMOGRAPHY. In 1991 the Dutch population was 15 million and the population density was about 440 persons per square kilometer, which makes the Netherlands one of the most densely populated countries in the world. Up to 1970 there was rapid population growth (more than 1 percent per year), declining to less than 0.6 percent in 1990. The declining growth rate was caused by an unexpectedly rapid decrease of the marital fertility rate since the 1960s, when modern contraceptive devices became available. Coupled with a low death rate, the decreasing birthrate results in an aging population. While the natural growth is decreasing, immigration is increasing and 4.3 percent of the population is of non-Dutch origin, especially with an Antillian, Surinamese, South Moluccan, and Mediterranean background.

LINGUISTIC AFFILIATION. Dutch is a member of the Germanic Language Group (Western Continental) and is related to Afrikaans, German, Yiddish, Frisian, English, and Luxembourgeois. It is spoken in Europe by about 16–17 million people spread over the kingdom of the Netherlands and the northern half of Belgium. Outside the continent of Europe it is spoken in Indonesia by the Dutch who live there and in the Dutch Antilles. Cape Dutch (Afrikaans), spoken in the Union of South Africa, has developed into an independent language. In the course of the state-building process, High Dutch, originally the language of the province of Holland, gradually was adopted as the language of daily intercourse by all the provinces. A peculiar position is occupied by Frisian in the province of Friesland, which is separated from the Dutch dialects by a sharp linguistic boundary line.

History and Cultural Relations

Julius Caesar found the country peopled by tribes of Germanic stock. By the end of the third century the Franks swarmed over the Rhine and took possession of the whole of the southern and central Netherlands. In A.D. 843 the Verdun treaty assigned the central part of the Frankonian Empire (comprising the whole of the later Netherlands) to what was to become Germany. Up to the fourteenth century the history of the Netherlands was the history of the various feudal states into which the Frankonian Empire was gradually divided. Cities played an important part in the development of the Netherlands. The eleventh to the thirteenth centuries were rich in municipal charters granting the citizens considerable rights, counteracting the privileges of the feudal lords. The most powerful and flourishing were the cities of Flanders. They formed the central market and exchange of the world's commerce. In the north a number of "free cities" were established—Dordrecht, Leyden, Haarlem, Delft, Vlaardingen, Rotterdam, Amsterdam—to equal the Flemish cities in power.

In the fifteenth century the Netherlands fell under the dominion of the house of Burgundy. When the sole heiress of the Burgundian possessions, Mary, married Maximilian of Austria in 1477, the long domination of the Roman Catholic house of Habsburg began, bringing the Netherlands into the huge and incongruous collection of states that the wars and marriages of the Habsburgs had brought together. The Netherlands, prosperous under the Burgundy rule, had to make large financial sacrifices to pay for the many wars of the emperor. Opposition emerged in the cities. As a result, the burghers of the cities, the lower gentry, and the nobility united under the leadership of the Prince of Orange (William the Silent) to fight Habsburg domination. This uprising resulted in the separation of the seven northern provinces of the Netherlands from the south (which was to become Belgium). Each developed into distinct political, religious, social, and economic units. Enacted in the Protestant Union of Utrecht in 1579, the northern provinces formed a republic under the legislation of the State-General (the board of representatives of the provinces) and the reign of the stadt-holder,

William of Orange, who became the symbol of political unity. In 1673 the seven provinces voted to make the stadtholderate hereditary in the house of Orange. William—born the third William in the house of Orange—attempted to centralize and consolidate his government, put down the feudal liberties in the provinces, and free himself from constitutional checks. He was unable, however, to establish absolute monarchy, and the United Provinces remained a decentralized patrician republic until 1795. Married in 1677 to Mary, the king of England's niece, William became king of England in 1689. In the aftermath of the French Revolution liberalism made its entry. Rebellious citizens, aided by French troops, overthrew the stadtholder. From 1795 to 1814 the Netherlands was under French rule. Liberalism, however, turned out to be a disappointment for the Dutch citizens. In 1814, freed from the French, they returned the house of Orange. The Netherlands became a monarchy, though a constitutional one. It was not until the nineteenth century that modernization started—later and more gradually than elsewhere in western Europe. Also in the nineteenth century, the cultural differences between the various ideological and political groups were institutionalized, generating separate organizations for each group in almost every area of life. This development of parallel organizations ("pillars") is called "pillarization." The pluralistic society that developed after 1917 had its origin in this "pillarized" structure.

During World War I the Netherlands kept its neutrality, nonetheless suffering from the economic crises caused by the war. World War II brought German occupation from 1940 to 1945. The postwar reconstruction of the Netherlands generated the modern Dutch industrial welfare state. Processes of European integration led to increasing cooperation with other European states: the Netherlands joined the European Economic Community (EEC)—the Common Market—in 1957. After World War II the Dutch had to cope with their colonies' struggle for independence. Decolonization did not take a peaceful course. The proclamation of the Republic of Indonesia, which was the former Dutch East Indies, provoked military intervention by the colonial authorities. Under international pressure, however, the Dutch government agreed to transfer sovereignty to the young Indonesian republic. In 1962 the Netherlands had to cede New Guinea to Indonesia; and in 1975 Suriname gained independence.

♦ **Franks**
A Germanic people who occupied Gaul and formed a kingdom that replaced the fallen Roman government in the fifth and sixth centuries A.D. The Frankish kingdom is considered to be the beginning of modern France.

Settlements

The Dutch population is irregularly spread over
the territory. The three provinces in the west
(North and South Holland and Utrecht, collectively known as "Randstad Holland") are highly
urbanized and most densely populated: almost
half of the population lives there. The north (the
provinces of Groningen, Friesland, Drente, Over-
ijssel, and South Flevoland) has a rural and relatively small population. The provinces in the east
(Gelderland) and south (Limburg, North Brabant, and Zeeland) show a mixed pattern of
urban-rural settlements.

Economy

**SUBSISTENCE AND COMMERCIAL ACTIVI-
TIES.** Dutch agriculture is highly commercialized and specialized. The cities have been a market for the country's agrarian products from the
twelfth century onward. After the Agrarian Crisis
of 1880 the Dutch farmers specialized in labor-
intensive horticulture and dairy farming. Intensive fertilization, agrarian training and research,
reorganization of small farms, land consolidation,
and Common Market agreements increased productivity.

INDUSTRIAL ARTS. Throughout its history,
Dutch industry has depended heavily on the importation of raw materials to supply its major industries: the production of foodstuffs and stimu-
lants, which developed when raw material was
imported from the colonies; the nineteenth-
century clothing- and footwear-manufacturing
and metal industries; and the primary twentieth-
century industry, the production of petrochemicals. There is today an increasing number of
mergers between both national and multinational
enterprises. After the emergence of modern industry in the mid-nineteenth century, the significance of agriculture for the national product diminished steadily, while the significance of the
secondary sector increased until it fell behind the
growing services sector after 1960.

TRADE. The small size and the spacial position of the Netherlands (especially the location at
waterways strategic for maritime and inland shipping) are of enduring significance for the international economic relations of the country. Where
the waterways meet, the big seaports have risen;
in fact, Amsterdam and Rotterdam's Europort is
the world's largest harbor. Traditionally the
Dutch have been traders and merchants. Since
the fifteenth century the Netherlands has been a
seagoing nation, owing their affluence to the exploitation of overseas provinces and to a prospering trade. The seventeenth and eighteenth
centuries were characterized by commercial capi-

talism: as the trade center of the world the Netherlands maintained and even increased its wealth by trade and the trade-related industries. This era has become known as the "Golden Age."

DIVISION OF LABOR. The Dutch labor force consists of 7 million people, with only 38.8 percent being female. Despite the growth of the female work force since the 1960s, labor participation of married women has remained considerably lower in the Netherlands than in other European countries. During the 1960s the Dutch population could not meet the growing demands for labor because the work force was overskilled. Consequently, the Dutch labor market in the 1990s is characterized by a large number of jobless people and at the same time a large number of foreign workers who are employed in the lower-paid and lower-skill jobs.

LAND TENURE. In about 1500 the east and south (the sandy soil regions) were characterized by traditional village communities structured according to the peasant model. Peasants formed the majority of the agrarian population until the mid-nineteenth century, dwelling on very small and unspecialized family farms. Alternative work outside agriculture was lacking. Specialization in cash crops and cattle breeding was impossible because of capital shortage. The peasant family was almost self-sufficient and productivity was low. In the west and north (the clay soil regions) agriculture developed according to the farmer model. In these areas feudalism never gained a foothold. In Holland the polders (land reclaimed from the sea) provided the people with land acquired in ownership or in leasehold on businesslike conditions. Village communities were of no significance in these areas; the farmers lived dispersed over the land on their own farmsteads. They produced for a market, and their enterprises were capital-intensive. After the agrarian crises, modernization led to production increase.

Kinship

KIN GROUPS AND DESCENT. Dutch kinship is bilateral with a patrilateral kinship preference. Until recently, this descent pattern was reflected in the custom of adopting the husband's name after marriage. This practice is changing with women's emancipation.

KINSHIP TERMINOLOGY. Kin terms follow the Eskimo system.

Marriage and Family

MARRIAGE. In preindustrial society, marriage was possible only after acquiring economic independence. The rural population and urban craftsmen used to marry at a later age. The choice of a marriage partner followed endogamous preference. People married within the same occupational sector or social group, the same religious or political pillar, or at least the same village or age group. Maintaining and increasing wealth were crucial motives in arranging marriages among the aristocracy and freeholding farmers. Among urban craftsmen there was more opportunity for individual choice than among the propertied classes. Romantic love was the basis of marriage more often among the urban population than among the rural.

DOMESTIC UNIT. The nuclear family is a typical Dutch phenomenon. The Dutch even have a special word for it: *gezin*. The stem family has never been of any significance in the Netherlands, not even in the rural areas. Since the nineteenth century the concept of the nuclear family has been invested with strong moral feelings. State policy was aimed at fostering and protecting the nuclear family; extramarital relations were condemned as deviant and antisocial. After World War II, several factors—including the emancipation of women, a decline in the number of household members, and an increase in the number of single-member households—resulted in more people living together without marriage, more children being born outside marriage, and more marriages ending in divorce.

INHERITANCE. In Dutch rural society it was common that one of the children, usually the oldest son, inherited the patrimony. Impartible inheritance was both customary and legally mandated. Among the urban bourgeoisie—where money, not land, was involved—the children were more equally treated when it came to inheritance. The bourgeois pattern has become the prevailing standard in modern society.

SOCIALIZATION. As early as the seventeenth century, the urban middle classes began to treat children not as small adults but as members of a different age group, with their own wants and needs. This attitude became standard in the nineteenth century, partly because of the increasing use of contraceptive measures, which resulted in a decreasing birthrate within the nuclear family and a consequent increase in the time and attention that could be spent on individual children. A number of factors contributed to this concern with keeping the family size small. One powerful incentive was the high cost of raising the next generation. A good education and dowry had come to be considered necessary expenses. More-

◆ **stem family**
A residential group composed of a nuclear family and one or more additional members who do not comprise a second nuclear family.

*The Dutch burden of
taxation is heavy,
making considerable
collective
expenditures possible
and resulting in an
excellent set of
social services.*

over, providing loving care for a child required an enormous effort that could not be bestowed on an unlimited number of offspring. This attitude first emerged among the urban middle classes, who increasingly did not require married women to work outside the home. Thus, middle-class women were able to give much attention to their domestic and maternal tasks. The life cycle of children changed: the interval between puberty and marriage was recognized as a special stage in life.

Sociopolitical Organization

SOCIAL ORGANIZATION. Although the standard of living is high, it is lower than in some neighboring countries. The burden of taxation is heavy, making considerable collective expenditures possible and resulting in an excellent set of social services. The media, labor unions, public organizations, associations, and club life are defined by the typical Dutch phenomenon of pillarization. Dutch society is characterized by complex social stratification, based on partly converging and partly conflicting criteria. As far as political and economic power relations are concerned, tokens of nineteenth-century class society can still be found in modern Dutch society. However, regional, religious, ethnic affiliation, and life-style factors modify social and economic class differences. The Netherlands is famous for tolerance toward ethnic minorities. Since World War II, Dutch society has developed into a multiethnic society. The persistent flood of allochthonous people, coupled with a growing unemployment rate, however, causes more and more tension and conflict.

POLITICAL ORGANIZATION. In the nineteenth century parliamentary democracy emerged. The monarch, subject to the constitution, is head of state. The Dutch Lower Chamber is constituted by direct elections by all enfranchised Dutch citizens, while the Dutch Upper Chamber is elected by the provincial states. A political breakthrough happened in 1918 when general elections were established; from that time on the seats in the Lower Chamber were held by representatives of political parties. Dutch political life is characterized by a large number of small political parties competing for votes. Since 1900, when party politics emerged, an average of eleven parties have been represented in parliament each term. The most important movements in Dutch political life have been liberalism, denominationalism, and socialism.

SOCIAL CONTROL. During the Dutch republic (sixteenth to nineteenth centuries) Dutch village life was relatively unrestricted by the central government. Within the village community, however, mechanisms of social control operated. Social mobility was low and social stratification kept people in their places. Consolidation of property formed an important consideration in marriage arrangements. There were almost no illegitimate children. When a girl got pregnant, strong social pressure was exerted on her to marry, especially in Protestant areas. The authority of the older generation was respected. The moral demands of diligence and austerity were internalized and determined the attitude toward life of both young and old. Calvinism, especially north of the big rivers, intensified this propensity as well as the rejection of amusement and diversion. Although city life was less restrained, Dutch mentality, characterized by a strong sense of values, put a check on urban allure. Thus, the image of the Dutch people as tidy, diligent, and hard-working citizens does have historical roots. Since the 1960s, however, the image of the Dutch has changed. The Netherlands has made headlines as the country of the Provo movement (the organized provocative behavior of young people against the authorities, which manifested itself especially in Amsterdam in 1965–1967), insubordinate bishops, long-haired soldiers with their own trade union, and permissiveness in drug use and pornography. The country is famous for its high rate of petty crime, blurred standards, squatting, and civil disobedience—phenomena that the international press has labeled "the Dutch disease."

CONFLICT. At home the Netherlands has witnessed a peaceful development through the ages. In political and social life, physical violence was the exception. The pillarized society was characterized by a pacific policy at home. Violence was applied in the process of colonization and in colonial wars abroad. In the twentieth century the situation has reversed: the Netherlands has tried to take a strictly neutral position in external armed conflict (World War I and World War II); at home pacification relations have given way to occasionally violent conflicts between social and ethnic groups, between generations, and between pressure groups.

Religion and Expressive Culture

RELIGIOUS BELIEFS. The conflict between Roman Catholicism and Calvinism since the Reformation has fundamentally influenced the nature of Dutch society, creating its unique pillarized character. The basic organizational principle in many spheres, at the local as well as national level, is religious, not economic, affiliation. Although this pillarization has begun to erode, it is still quite evident, especially in rural communities where it colors all social relations. Although the Netherlands is characterized by secularization, other more informal ways of expressing religious feelings have emerged.

RELIGIOUS PRACTITIONERS. Parish priests and parsons have always had an important impact on Dutch mentality, political conviction, and voting behavior. Even people's private lives were ruled by standards of behavior set by the clergy. Ecclesiastical directives influenced the development of taboos on sexual activities and social contact between persons of different social classes. For Catholics the rules were dictated by the pope but translated and mediated by the clergy, with adaptations to local culture. The Protestants did not rely on religious mediators as heavily as did the Catholics, as their religious experience did not lie in the community but in the heart of the individual. Compared to their Catholic counterparts, the parsons were weak and their power limited.

CEREMONIES. Since the fifteenth century Dutch popular culture has increasingly been put under pressure by the bourgeois elite. The tales, riddles, rhymes, feasts, and rituals were suppressed to give way to high culture. Popular culture provided not only diversion and amusement but also an outlet for social tensions and instability, complaints of social abuses, and expression of religious feelings. The Catholic church tried to absorb these elements of popular culture into official religion; Protestantism, however, went on the offensive against popular culture.

ARTS. Art blossomed in the seventeenth century (i.e., the Golden Age). Many Dutch painters from that period have become famous: for example, Rembrandt van Rijn, Jan Vermeer, Frans Hals, Pieter de Hooch, and Jacob van Ruisdael. Because rich burghers and merchants, not the church and court, were the most important patrons of the artists, the art of painting became specialized. Some painters painted only landscapes, others painted exclusively portraits or still lifes. As far as music is concerned, the composer and organist Jan Pieterszoon Sweelinck became well known for his organ playing. Since the seventeenth century, Dutch art has aroused relatively modest international attention, aside from a small number of celebrities such as the painters van Gogh, Mondrian, and Appel. Cultural life is traditionally focused on the big cities, where large orchestras, theater companies, and museums of regional significance have been established in the twentieth century.

MEDICINE. In the Netherlands a modern pharmaceutical industry of international significance has developed. Big concerns have concentrated their research activities in the Netherlands. This has led to a widespread penetration of medical standards and medical consumption, resulting in a "medicalization" of everyday life that has come to be such a public-health problem that alternative medicine has recently taken root.

DEATH AND AFTERLIFE. In the twentieth century compulsory institutionalized mourning has lost much of its force, while the personal side of mourning has been accentuated and privatized. Funerals characterized by public display have given way to cremations in private. As religious beliefs have declined, the dominant standard of bereavement behavior has become more informal and individualized, making higher demands on self-regulation and self-restraint. As far as dying is concerned, the ritual and rigid regime of silence has relaxed, and more informal and varied codes of behavior- and emotion-management have spread.

Bibliography

Boissevain, J., and J. Verrips, eds. (1989). *Dutch Dilemmas: Anthropologists Look at the Netherlands.* Assen and Maastricht: Van Gorcum.

Diederiks, H. A., et al. (1987). *Van agrarische samenleving naar verzorgingsstaat: De modernisering van West-Europa sinds de 15de eeuw.* Groningen: Wolters-Noordhoff.

Goudsblom, J. (1967). *Dutch Society.* New York: Random House.

Schama, S. (1987). *The Embarassment of Riches: An Interpretation of Dutch Culture in the Golden Age.* New York: Knopf.

Sinner, L. (1973). *De wortels van de Nederlandse politiek: De 42 politieke partijen sinds 1848.* Amsterdam: Wetenschappelijke Uitgeverij.

Wouters, C. (1990). *Van minnen en sterven: Informalisering van de omgangsvormen rond sex en dood.* Amsterdam: Bert Bakker.

—HEIDI DAHLES

ENGLISH

Ethonym: Engl

Orientation

IDENTIFICATION. England, unlike Scotland, Wales, or Northern Ireland, does not constitutionally exist, and thus it has no separate rights, administration, or official statistics. The Church

Many Dutch painters from the seventeenth century have become famous: for example, Rembrandt van Rijn, Jan Vermeer, Frans Hal, Pieter de Hooch, and Jacob van Ruisdael.

See also
Irish, Highland Scots, Lowland Scots, Welsh

English

of England is its main distinctive institution. The English maintain their separate identity in sports (soccer, cricket, and rugby) and heritage; this is manifest in the monarchy, aristocracy, and associated pageantry, parliament, pride in their country, and love for their local community (with the local pub being an integrating institution). English poetry, literature, and art is also distinctive. With the decrease of specialized industry, an increase in mass marketing, and greater population mobility, English distinctiveness is threatened. However, measures such as restoration and protection of city centers, the countryside, and historic buildings—along with the movement for greater control and participation in local affairs—help counter the trend toward homogeneity.

LOCATION. England constitutes the largest land area and highest population density of any of the four units of the United Kingdom. It is also the most intensely industrialized region. Located off the northwest coast of continental Europe, it is bounded on the north by Scotland and on the west by Wales. It is located approximately between 49°56′ and 55°49′ N and 1°50′ E and 5°46′ W (not including the Channel Islands). Geographically, England constitutes 130,863 square kilometers or 53 percent of the land area of the United Kingdom and is divided into the uplands and lowlands. Following a line joining the mouths of the Tees and Exe rivers, the uplands in the northwest are characterized by rocky and mountainous areas while the lowlands of the southeast contain gentle rolling country with some hills. For the United Kingdom as a whole, the terrain is 30 percent arable, 50 percent meadow and pasture, 12 percent waste or urban, 7 percent forest, and 1 percent inland water. The climate is variable and mild for its latitudes. Rainfall for the south is 90 centimeters, with the southwest receiving 105 to 158 centimeters per year, while the extreme east gets 63 centimeters. The mean temperature for England in July is 16° C; in January and February it is 5° C. However, the north is slightly colder than the south; winter in the north averages 70 days of frost while the south averages 13.

DEMOGRAPHY. The English number 46,168,120 (1989 estimate), 81.5 percent of the population of the United Kingdom. They have maintained their relative proportion of the United Kingdom population, but the proportion of younger and older people has increased because the birthrate declined between 1921 and 1942 and then increased after World War II. The population is primarily urban and suburban. In 1921, more than 40 percent of the people lived in the six great conurbations that center on London. After World War II, there was movement from the inner cities to the suburban fringes and beyond, with the inner cities showing a marked decrease. However, English population density is among the highest in the world, averaging 840 persons per square mile in 1981 for England and Wales and rising to 12,600 for the greater London area.

LINGUISTIC AFFILIATION. The English language is of the Indo-European Family. Its parent tongue is the West Germanic Group of Proto-Indo-European. The closest related languages are German, Netherlandic, and Frisian. There is considerable dialectical variation, the most distinctive being in Lancashire, Cornwall, and parts of East London. Radio, television, and transportation are causing these differences to diminish, with the style of the southeast becoming the standard. However, there is no difference in literary style between the various regions.

History and Cultural Relations

Early English history is marked by immigration. Although not the first, the Celts began arriving around 2,500 to 3,000 years ago. England became part of the Roman Empire in A.D. 43. After the Roman withdrawal in A.D. 410, waves of Jutes, Angles, and Saxons arrived and established control, in spite of Danish incursions from the eighth through the eleventh centuries. By the fifth century A.D., the term "English"—"Angelcynn," meaning "angel kin"—was applied to the Teutonic inhabitants collectively. By the eleventh century, the term included the Celtic and Scandinavian elements and all natives of England, except for the Normans, who remained separate for several generations after their conquest in 1066. The signing of the Magna Carta in 1215 guaranteed the rights of rule by law, a point of pride for the English. In 1301, Edward of Caernarvon, son of King Edward I of England, was created Prince of Wales. The Hundred Years' War (1338–1453) resulted in the claim to large parts of France being lost, and the War of the Roses (1455–1485) led to the Tudor monarchy, which in turn led to a distinctively flourishing English civilization. In 1534, religious independence from the pope was established. Under Queen Elizabeth I, England became a major naval power and its colonies and trade expanded. In 1603, James VI of Scotland succeeded to the throne of England as King James I, and the island of Britain was united under one royal family. After a civil war (1642–1649), a republic under Oliver Cromwell was established, but the monarchy was restored in 1688, confirming the sover-

◆ **United Kingdom**
Also known as Britain or Great Britain, the term refers to England, Scotland, Wales, and Northern Ireland.

eignty of the English Parliament and the English Bill of Rights. By increasing colonial holdings and industrial power in the eighteenth century, the United Kingdom became a world power. Although victorious in both world wars, the country lost its position of world leadership, but it continued its industrial growth. During the postwar period, the Labor party governments passed some socialist legislation nationalizing some industries and expanding social security; but the Thatcher government reversed that trend and increased the role of private enterprise.

Since the Norman Conquest in 1066, a relatively homogeneous population has been maintained. However, England has been a haven for refugees ranging from the Huguenots in the seventeenth century to persecuted Jews in the twentieth. Starting in the 1950s, population homogeneity has been challenged by the immigration of West Indians and South Asians. They comprise about 4 percent of England's population (2 percent of the United Kingdom's population). Laws curbing immigration and prohibiting racial discrimination have been enacted, but racial tensions are present, especially in the inner urban centers of London and West Midlands where 60 percent of the immigrants reside.

Settlements

About 90 percent of England's population is urban or suburban, and less than 3 percent of its people are engaged in agriculture. Thus, there is a structure of towns, villages, and cities where one sees scattered groups of high-density residence patterns. In spite of the large urban sprawl, England has extensive tracts of farms with smaller villages engulfed by trees, copses, hedgerows, and fields. Settlement patterns are classed into seven categories: conurbations, cities, boroughs, towns, villages, hamlets, and farms. Conurbations refer to the large complexes of densely populated urban areas with a complex of suburbs and towns surrounding or within a large city. A city is a large important borough. A borough is a town possessing a municipal corporation with special privileges conferred by royal charter (a city can have boroughs within it). A town can be incorporated or not incorporated within a conurbation, but either way it is a small cluster of buildings, which has an independent government with greater powers of rating (taxation), paving, and sanitation than those of a village. The village is smaller than a town and has less independence, and a hamlet is smaller still, often without a church. An examination of settlement patterns of towns, villages, and hamlets reveals a great variety of planned or unplanned settlements, with buildings at regular or random intervals. They can be clustered around a center, with its own structure of roads or lanes, or linear, along the sides of a road or field. Farmsteads generally comprise the farming family.

Economy

SUBSISTENCE AND COMMERCIAL ACTIVITIES. For planning purposes, England is divided into eight regions, but it can be grouped into four divisions comprising the north, Midlands, southeast, and southwest. The north contains about one-third of the total land area and one-third of the population. Although there is some dairy and grazing livestock production, the division is highly industrial, comprising 35 percent of England's manufacturing labor force (43 percent of England's total work force in manufacturing). Most cities are near coal fields. Old, stable industries have declined, leading to unemployment. Emigration from the region has been high, although the region continues to have a slight population increase. The Midlands has about half of its workers employed in manufacturing industries, making automobiles, metal goods, and related products. About 3 percent of them work in coal and iron ore fields and 1.5 percent in mixed farming. It is common to find villages that specialize (locks and keys in Willenhall, needles and hooks in Ridditch, and so on). In the southeast, more than 60 percent of the labor force is in service industries such as construction and public administration, 32 percent in manufacturing, and less than 2 percent in agriculture. Electrical equipment, machinery, paper, printing, and publishing are the leading industries. The southwest has a lower population. Dairy farming is prominent and manufacturing employs 32 percent of the labor force. Many people retire there and tourism is important. However, unemployment is also high. In essence, England has been going through a long process of change. In the nineteenth century, the north, which was previously underdeveloped and backward, became the powerhouse or "workshop of the world." As the United Kingdom lost its prominence in the world economy, the north also lost its importance and power shifted to the southeast.

INDUSTRIAL ARTS. Service industries employ about half of England's work force, while a third of the workers are in manufacturing and engineering. The remainder are in agriculture, construction, mining, and energy.

TRADE. Three types of trade take place in English communities. The traditional institution

England is a constitutional monarchy. There is no written constitution, and so statutes, common law, and practice guide governance.

In English society, the aristocracy, "new society," middle class, and working class are the primary units. The landed aristocracy is the only aristocracy.

is the central market, which is often covered but open. It has stalls that sell everything from fish to clothes. Within neighborhoods there are clusters of specialty shops which usually comprise a grocer, butcher, newsstand, appliance store, and sweet shop. Since 1970, chain enterprises in fast food and groceries have developed and expanded.

DIVISION OF LABOR. There is a hierarchy and division of labor with limited mobility. In manufacturing, jobs are specialized according to skill and hierarchy of class is maintained where bosses have authority over subordinates. Division of labor according to gender is diminishing in the workplace as well as the domestic sphere. Class consciousness is decreasing, with the upwardly mobile young urban professional (Yuppie) becoming a dominant role model.

LAND TENURE. Land in England is privately owned.

Kinship, Marriage, and Family

KINSHIP. The most important kin group is the extended family, which generally includes all known relatives. Although descent is not strictly lineal, the family name is traced patrilineally. However, relationship through the female line is acknowledged informally. If he has no male heir, a son may incorporate the name of his mother's family as his family name in a hyphenated form. Kin relationships are strongly influenced by distance, stage of life, and closeness of relationship. In practice, the mother-daughter relationship dominates and it is around the wife's mother that much family activity is determined. Other members of the kin group are included if they live nearby. However, neighbors are very important in providing companionship and social support, and these friendships are often maintained after a person has moved away.

MARRIAGE. The emphasis on marital status has decreased in the last decade. Self-esteem and status are now determined by a career, whereas previously they centered on having a spouse and children. Today people often delay marriage and children until their career aspirations stabilize. Generally marriages are by the choice of the male and female. Abortion is legal and divorce is acceptable; both have increased in the postwar era.

DOMESTIC UNIT. The nuclear family is the most prevalent domestic unit. It consists of the mother, father, and juvenile children. During times when housing was scarce, it was common

SOCIOPOLITICAL ORGANIZATION

England is a constitutional monarchy. There is no written constitution, and so statutes, common law, and practice guide governance. The monarch is the chief of state and controls the executive branch. The prime minister is the head of the government and has a cabinet. The legislative section is a bicameral Parliament composed of a House of Commons and a House of Lords; primary power lies with the House of Commons. There is also a court system, with the House of Lords being the highest level.

Social Organization

In English society, the aristocracy, "new society," middle class, and working class are the primary units. The landed aristocracy is the only aristocracy. Alongside the aristocracy is the new society, the self-made rich. In the nineteenth century, wealth did not buy power, because it was concentrated in the aristocracy. However, the aristocracy has lost its monopoly on power. At present, most Britons see themselves as belonging either to the middle or working class. What makes a person claim membership to one of these two classes varies; economic affluence and occupation are not consistent indicators. Also, the middle class is fragmenting with each group defining itself in opposition to other groups.

Political Organization

Under the central government, the country is divided into municipalities, counties, and parliamentary constituencies. In 1974, the conurbations were detached from existing counties and designated as metropolitan counties.

Social Control

The court system, sense of tradition, public opinion, and mass media all work together to promote conformity and resolve conflicts in English society.

Conflict

Since England has not suffered from invasions since the Norman Conquest, there is no focused animosity against any particular group, although some resentment toward the Germans exists as a result of the two world wars. Internal conflicts have been primarily with Northern Ireland. They started in 1968 with demonstrations by Catholics who charged that they were discriminated against in voting rights, housing, and employment. Violence and terrorism has intensified between the Irish Republican Army (which is outlawed), Protestant groups, police, and British troops. Racial tensions between the white English community and the West Indies and South Asians have developed recently, but they have not resulted in ongoing terrorism and violence.

for a newly married couple to live with the wife's family. Among the landed gentry residence for the eldest son was patrilocal while other offspring resided elsewhere.

INHERITANCE. Traditionally, inheritance was through the male line. The aristocracy maintained its wealth by a system of primogeniture, where the estate went to the eldest son. Other sons had to serve in the army, the church, or business, or vanish into obscurity or poverty. Now, inheritance is according to the wishes of the owner of the resources. He or she dictates the inheritance by a will or testament. If there is no will, it is probated in a court.

SOCIALIZATION. Parents, peers, and media are three primary influences for socialization. Parents discipline, but corporal punishment is not acceptable. Evaluation by one's peers is important for English children. Television, videos, rock music, advertising, and other forms of popular media culture exert a strong influence on children.

Religion and Expressive Culture

RELIGIOUS BELIEFS AND PRACTICES. Although England is a secular country, about one-half of the population is baptized in the Anglican church; however, only 10 million are communicant members. Roman Catholics number 6 million, and the rest belong to nonconformist free churches such as Methodist or Baptist. Except for some areas of Irish settlements in the northwest, religious tolerance persists.

The Church of England traces its history back to the arrival of Christians in Britain during the second century. It has preserved much of the tradition of medieval Catholicism while holding on to the fundamentals of the Reformation. It broke with the Roman papacy during the reign of Henry VIII (1509–1547). The church has gone through persecution and was also influenced by the Puritans. Nevertheless, it has maintained an episcopal form of government, with the monarchy acting as the secular head of the English church and the Archbishop of Canterbury having spiritual prominence.

ARTS. England has a strong and distinctive tradition in literature, theater, and architecture. In literature, writers tend to focus on their particular region, while in plays they are more likely to deal with England as a whole. In architecture, the English have borrowed from other cultures, but they have transformed the concepts into a characteristically English style. England has also become a leader in popular culture with musical groups that have captured international promi-

nence. London is the theater center for the English-speaking world.

MEDICINE. England's national health service provides quality care. However, the system has declined somewhat under the Thatcher government and private practice has increased.

DEATH AND AFTERLIFE. In the Anglican church, exactly what happens at death is a mystery. However, Anglicans believe that the individual "is received by God into his arms," which is taken to mean the person passes into a timeless and spaceless relationship with God, unlike that which is experienced in this life. Funerals are conducted by a priest or minister a day or two after death.

Bibliography

Bonfield, Lloyd, Richard M. Smith, and Keith Wrightson, eds. (1986). *The World We Have Gained*. Oxford: Basil Blackwell.

Helweg, Arthur W. (1986). *Sikhs in England*. 2nd ed. Delhi: Oxford University Press.

Newby, Howard (1979). *Social Change in Rural England*. Madison: University of Wisconsin Press.

Noble, Trevor (1981). *Structure and Change in Modern Britain*. London: Batsford Academic and Educational.

Priestley, J. B. (1934). *English Journey*. New York and London: Harper Brothers.

Sampson, Anthony (1983). *The Changing Anatomy of Britain*. New York: Random House.

United Kingdom, Government of. Central Office of Information (1989). *Britain 1989: An Official Handbook*. London: Her Majesty's Stationery Office.

Young, Michael, and Peter Willmott (1957). *Family and Kinship in East London*. Baltimore: Penguin.

—ARTHUR W. HELWEG

FINNS

Ethonym: Karelians or Karjalaiset, Suomalaiset, Tavastians or Hämäläiset

Orientation

IDENTIFICATION. Finns constitute the majority of the citizens of the Republic of Finland, which has a Swedish-speaking minority as well as Saami (Lapp) and Gypsy minorities.

LOCATION. Finland is located approximately between 60° and 70° N and 20° and 32° E and is bordered on the east by Russia, on the south by the Gulf of Finland and Estonia, on the west by the Gulf of Bothnia and Sweden, and on the north

♦ Gypsy
A generic term for a diverse group of people who live or formerly lived a nomadic life-style.

See also

Peripatetics, Saami, Swedes

397

and northwest by Norway. Four physiographic-biotic regions divide the country. An archipelagic belt embraces the southwestern coastal waters and the Aland Islands. A narrow coastal plain of low relief and clay soils, historically the area of densest rural settlement and mixed farming production, extends between the Russian and Swedish borders. A large interior plateau contains dense forests, thousands of lakes and peat bogs, and rocky infertile soils associated with a glacially modified landscape containing numerous drumlins and eskers. This interior lake and forest district lies north and east of the coastal plain toward the Russian border. Beyond the Arctic Circle, forests give way to barren fells, extensive bogs, some rugged mountains approaching 1,300 meters, and the large rivers of Lapland. Continental weather systems produce harsh cold winters lasting up to seven months in the interior eastern and northern districts. Annual fluctuation in daylight is great, and long summer days permit farming far to the north. The climate in southern and western Finland is moderated by the warm waters of the Gulf Stream and the North Atlantic Drift Current, where more than half of the 60–70 centimeters of annual precipitation falls as rain. Maximum summer temperatures may be as high as 35° C with a mean July reading of 13–17° C. Minimum winter temperatures fall below −30° C with mean February readings of −3° to −14° C.

DEMOGRAPHY. In 1987 the population of Finland was about 4,937,000,95 percent of whom were ethnically and linguistically Finnish. High mortality from wars and famine dampened Finland's population growth between the sixteenth and late nineteenth centuries. Over the past century falling birthrates and heavy emigration have perpetuated a very low population growth. Dramatic internal migration accompanied Finland's economic transformation between the 1950s and mid-1970s, when agriculture and the forestry industry were rapidly mechanized. At that time many young people left the rural areas of eastern and northeastern Finland to work in the urban industrialized south. While 75 percent of the Finnish population lived in rural areas just prior to World War II, by the early 1980s 60 percent of Finns were urban dwellers. Other substantial Finnish populations live in Russia, the United States, Canada, and Sweden, and smaller numbers have settled in Australia, South Africa, and Latin America.

LINGUISTIC AFFILIATION. Finnish belongs to the family of farflung Finno-Ugric languages in northeastern Europe, Russia, and western Siberia, including Saami (Lapp) and Hungarian.

KEEPING WARM

A Finnish father and son in warm fur hats. Children are taught independence and respect from an early age in Finland. (Yann Arthus-Bertrand/ Corbis)

The languages most closely related to Finnish are Estonian, Votish, Livonian, Vepsian, and the closely allied Karelian dialects of the Balto-Finnic Branch. Although Finnish was established as a written language as early as the sixteenth century, its official status in Finland did not become equivalent to Swedish until after the Language Ordinance of 1863. Finnish is a euphonious language with a wealth of vowels and diphthongs, and its vocabulary has many Germanic and Slavic loanwords.

History and Cultural Relations

Human habitation in Finland dates to the early postglacial period in the late eighth century B.C., long before Finno-Ugric migrations into the area from the east. Earlier evidence indicated that the ancestors of the Finns migrated into southwestern Finland from Estonia as recently as the first century A.D. during the early Roman Iron Age. Recent research, including paleoecological evidence of agricultural grain pollens dating to the second millennium B.C., suggests a much earlier proto-Finnish presence. By the beginning of the Bronze Age, around 1200 B.C., these proto-Finnish or Finnic tribes were geographically divided. Those in southwestern Finland were heavily influenced by Scandinavian cultures, while those in the interior and eastern districts had ties with peoples of the Volga region. A series of crusades by the expanding Swedish Kingdom between the 1150s and 1293 was the vehicle for spreading the Roman Catholic church into Finland. By the time of the Lutheran Reformation in the early sixteenth century, the Swedish crown had strong control of colonial Finland, and a modified estate system forced Finnish peasants to participate in the wars of their Swedish lords. The destruction of Finnish settlements and crops, as well as large population losses, resulted from conflicts between the Swedish and Russian empires. By the mid-eighteenth century strong Finnish separatist movements were growing. Russia finally conquered Finland during the Napoleonic Wars of 1808–1809, annexing it as an autonomous grand duchy. The nineteenth century was a period of coalescence of Finnish national consciousness in scientific thought, politics, art, and literature, as exemplified by Elias Lönnrot's 1835 compilation of Finnish and Karelian rune songs in the famous Finnish epic poem, the *Kalevala*. This movement served as a counterpoint to a growing Russification of Finnish institutions, and Finland declared its independence immediately after the Russian Revolution of 1917. However, like Russia the new Finnish state was immediately embroiled in a civil war, the result of growing class tension between property owners (the counter-revolutionary "White" forces) and landless farm, forest, and factory workers (the "Red" forces) who wanted a socialist state. The scars from that strife had not entirely healed when Finland was united by its conflicts with the Soviet Union during World War II. Finland surrendered several eastern territories amounting to 10 percent of its area, and 420,000 Karelian Finns in those ceded areas chose to migrate across the newly formed national boundaries to Finland, requiring a massive resettlement and rural land-reform program. After World War II the Finnish parliamentary state actively pursued an official policy of neutrality combined with expanded trade and cultural contacts with the Soviet Union, a political adaptation known as the Paasikivi-Kekkonen Line.

Swedish is the second official language of Finland and is spoken by about 6 percent of the population. Living primarily in the southwestern part of the country, Swedish colonists and Swedish-speaking Finns had for centuries been the source of a ruling elite. Swedish was the language of commerce, the courts, and education, and Finnish was regarded as a peasant language until the nationalist movement of the nineteenth century advanced Finnish as an official, written, and cultural language of the majority. Political tensions arising from this ethnolinguistic division have largely faded as the Swedish-speaking minority declines in size and assimilates through frequent marriage with Finnish speakers. By contrast, Finland's 4,400 Saami or Lapps have largely avoided assimilation into the cultural mainstream, having been displaced from the southern part of the country by northward colonizing Finns over the past 2,000 years. Separateness is now reinforced as much by the economic marginality and limited educational opportunities in Finnish Lapland as by cultural-linguistic enclavement. Gypsies have lived in Finland since the sixteenth century and, perhaps, have endured the greatest prejudice of any minority. They number between 5,000 and 6,000, and in recent decades government measures have attempted to improve their economic situation and mitigate overt discrimination.

Settlements

With the rise of permanent agricultural settlements in the fertile plains of western and southern Finland in the Middle Ages, communal ownership and management practices were employed so that an entire hamlet, including fifteen to twenty

The nineteenth century was a period of coalescence of Finnish national consciousness—a counterpoint to a growing Russification of Finnish institutions.

closely spaced farms, assumed joint ownership of fields, forests, and pastures. Land reforms in the eighteenth and nineteenth centuries broke down the communal villages, but the newly created individual farmsteads retained a modified courtyard arrangement with dwelling units, sauna or bathhouse, grain and food storage buildings, livestock barns, and hay sheds enclosing an inner yard. Wooden domestic architecture displayed a high level of woodworking skill and embellishment, with two-storied houses marking prosperous farms. However, in the eastern and interior areas of Finland agricultural settlement occurred at a later date, and it was characterized by a more flexible system of landownership and farmstead organization. The persistence of "burn-beating" cultivation (*poltta kaskea, kaskiviljelys*), a form of pioneer extensive farming of the conifer forests, involved mobile populations and a dispersed pattern of settlement. Remote individual farms or extended dual-family holdings were won from the forest, often along favored glacial esker ridges or "home hills" (*harju, vaara*). While these historical patterns of settlement affect the present rural landscape, six of every ten Finns now live in urban areas. The largest cities are greater Helsinki, with 950,000 people in the 1980s, and Tampere and Turku, each with a population of 250,000. The majority of Finnish residential dwellings of all types have been constructed since World War II, many of them consisting of apartment-house complexes in the large cities. Social and emotional adjustment to this urban landscape has been problematic for many recently uprooted migrants from the countryside.

Economy

SUBSISTENCE AND COMMERCIAL ACTIVITIES. Livestock raising was a major element in the Finnish peasant economy, but always in combination with activities such as fishing, hunting, tar production, and peddling. Wood as a commercial product did not become part of the farming economy until liberalized marketing policies, improved sawmilling techniques, and foreign demand for wood products converged in the late nineteenth century. The precariousness of crop cultivation in Finland, coupled with the emergence of new international markets for butter during the Russian colonial period (1808–1917), intensified production based on dairy cattle. Gradually, cultivated grasses replaced grains and wild hay as a source of cattle pasturage and fodder, and after the turn of the century farmers began establishing cooperative dairies (*osuusmeijerit*). The

general shift toward commercial agriculture coincided with the decline of the old burn-beating system. Nonetheless, many farm families in northern and eastern Finland maintained an essentially subsistence orientation into the 1950s. Increased mechanization and specialization in farm production (dairy cattle, hogs, or grains) since the 1960s has occurred as the Finnish labor force has moved into manufacturing and service industries. Less than 11 percent of the labor force is now involved in agriculture and forestry. However, the rural economy is still based on modestsized family-owned farms where marketing of timber from privately owned forest tracts is an important means of financing agricultural operations. Milk is prominent in the diet as a beverage and as the basic ingredient in a variety of curdled, soured, or cultured milk products; in broths used for soups, stews, and puddings; and in regional specialty dishes such as "cheese bread" (*juustoleipa*). There are notable differences between western and eastern Finland in bread making and in the manner of souring milk.

INDUSTRIAL ARTS. Handicraft and artisan traditions were well developed, and some have survived the conversion to industrial manufacturing. Men specialized in making furniture, harnesses, and wooden vessels or "bushels" (*vakka*) and in various kinds of metalwork. The sheath knife (*puukko*) was a versatile men's tool, and it continues to symbolize maleness in recreational hunting and fishing contexts. Women specialized in textiles and lace making. The woven woolen wall rug (*ryijy*) has become a particularly popular art form in Finnish homes, emblematic of a family's patrimony.

TRADE. By the Middle Ages local markets and fairs were important in the Finnish economy, the latter often held in the vicinity of churches and associated with saints' days or other aspects of the religious calendar. Furs and naval stores comprised a large share of the export trade at that time, much of it destined for the cities of the Hanseatic League. German and Swedish merchants were prominent in Finland's early Baltic port cities. After the mid-nineteenth century Finland's foreign trade shifted toward Saint Petersburg and Russian markets with lumber, paper, and agricultural products becoming the chief exports. Since World War II, forest products have remained crucial to Finland's export economy, but these are now complemented by sophisticated metal, electronics, engineering, and chemical products. In recent years Finland's trade with countries in the European Community has expanded and is reinforced by its membership in the European Free Trade Association.

DIVISION OF LABOR. The rural economy positions women as the primary cattle tenders and men as field and forest workers. On the one hand, being a good *emäntä* (or farm wife) involves a deft balance of cow care, child care, food processing, meal preparations, arduous cleaning chores in both cowshed and house, and ritual displays of hospitality for visiting neighbors, friends, and relatives. Men, on the other hand, are symbolically and practically associated with the outdoor domain, preparing and maintaining pastures and hayfields, cutting wood, coordinating labor with other farms, and operating and maintaining machinery. However, a decline in availability of work crews of kin and friends and a concomitant increase in mechanization have contributed to some convergence in male and female work roles. A complicating factor is that young Finnish women have left the countryside in greater numbers than men in recent years. Existing farms have aging personnel and few assisting family members, and some farmers are forced into bachelorhood.

LAND TENURE. Historically in western Finland it was customary for a farm to be passed on to the eldest son, or possibly to the eldest daughter's husband. In eastern Finland a pattern of dividing land among all adult male family members prevailed. Such regional patterns have largely faded, and intergenerational transfers of land have become highly variable throughout Finland. Despite a bias toward patrilineal transmission, farms can be inherited by sons or daughters, oldest or youngest offspring, or they can be divided or jointly held by multiple heirs. However, at the beginning of the twentieth century a landless proletariat comprised half of Finland's rural population. A major agrarian reform was the Crofters' Law of 1918, serving to create holdings for landless rural poor and unfavorably situated tenant farmers. The latter reform also served to redistribute land to ex-servicemen and Karelian refugees in the wake of World War II.

Kinship

KIN GROUPS AND DESCENT. Finnish kinship is basically bilateral, thus creating overlapping personal kindreds (*sukulaiset*) derived from one's father's and mother's relatives.

KINSHIP TERMINOLOGY. Kin terms conform to the Eskimo system in Ego's generation. In the first ascending generation, terminology is

MARRIAGE AND FAMILY

Marriage

Endogamous tendencies characterized marriage in Finnish rural society, with mates frequently chosen from the same village, parish, or rural commune. This tendency was most pronounced in the eastern districts among large Karelian joint families and those of the same background and status. Night courting and bundling rituals achieved a high degree of elaboration among the youth of southwestern Finland. Originally, bilocal marriages began with engagement and leave-taking (*läksiäiset*) ceremonies at the bride's home and ended with wedding rites (*häät*) held at the groom's home. Under church influence these were replaced by unilocal weddings staged at the bride's home. In recent years community and regional endogamy has declined. In the strict sense marriage rates have also declined, as cohabitation has become more common in urban areas. However, the latter pattern preserves some of the "trial marriage" aspects of earlier times when weddings were performed to finalize a marriage after a woman had conceived a child.

Domestic Unit

Historically, joint families were common in the eastern Karelian area where a founding couple, their adult male children, and the latter's in-marrying wives formed multiple-family farm households that were among the largest (20–50 persons) in Scandinavia. Elsewhere in Finland it has been common for only one child to remain on the parents' farmstead, and smaller stem and nuclear families have prevailed. Overall, family size has become smaller under the impact of urbanization, dropping from an average of 3.6 persons in 1950 to 2.7 by 1975.

Inheritance

A common historical pattern was for a son to take over a farm and care for his parents in their old age. As suggested previously (see under "Land Tenure"), the custom of patrilineal transmission is changing, perhaps as differential migration to cities alters the sex ratios of rural areas. In many cases, relinquishing coheirs (usually siblings who move away) must be compensated for their shares in a farm by the remaining heir, and often this is done with timber income from a farm's forest tracts.

Socialization

Gritty perseverance (*sisu*), personal autonomy and independence, and respect for the autonomy of others are central themes in Finnish child training and the Finnish personality.

*Young Finnish
women have left the
countryside in
greater numbers
than men in recent
years. Existing
farms have aging
personnel and few
assisting family
members.*

lineal for females and bifurcate-collateral for males.

Sociopolitical Organization

SOCIAL ORGANIZATION. Prior to the nineteenth century Finnish society was divided into peasants (*talonpojat*), burghers, clergy, and nobility. Subsequent economic change fostered the wane of the clergy and nobility and an expansion of entrepreneurial and working classes. In recent decades considerable social mobility and an egalitarian ethos have emerged with increasing economic prosperity, progressive social welfare, an open educational system, and consensus politics. While Finns themselves may not always recognize clear economic class divisions, they are likely to be conscious of status attached to educational and honorific titles and to political-party affiliations. From an external view, the currently unfolding class system includes: farmers; working class (nonrural manual laborers); petite bourgeoisie (shopowners, small entrepreneurs); lower middle class (lower-income service sector); upper middle class (higher-income white-collar professionals); and upper class (corporate owners and managers).

POLITICAL ORGANIZATION. The administrative district or commune (*maalaiskunta*) is a locale embodying a sense of community and self-identification for its residents. It often coincides with the historically deeper church parish, and it is a local unit of self-government that generally collects taxes, regulates economic affairs, and maintains public order. Every four years a communal council is elected to manage local affairs. Much of a council's work is implemented by a communal board comprised of members appointed to reflect the council's political-party composition. With as many as a dozen political parties in Finland, *kunta* government is sometimes represented by opposing coalitions of socialist and nonsocialist party interests.

SOCIAL CONTROL. The institution of a village-governing alderman was part of the authoritarian moral environment in the dense rural settlements of southern and western Finland. Village fight groups and fights (*kylätappelut*) were ritualized conflicts, sometimes associated with weddings, which integrated communities via rivalry relationships. In the sparsely settled eastern interior, social life was more individualistic and social control less formal. In contemporary Finnish society, independent courts and centrally organized police forces maintain public order.

CONFLICT. Finland's historical position as a frontier of colonization, military incursion, and subordination to external contesting empires is part of the Finnish collective conscience. Strategic victories by Finnish troops against invading Soviet forces during the "Winter War" of 1939–1940 are symbolically integral to the lore and identity of many Finns. By contrast, the "reign of terror" following Finland's civil war of 1917–1918 profoundly polarized the Finnish middle classes and working classes, with the latter remaining especially alienated and embittered.

Religion and Expressive Culture

RELIGIOUS BELIEFS. Traditional Finnish conceptions of the supernatural had much in common with those of other Balto-Finnic peoples. The creation of the world was associated with the culture hero Väinämöinen, and the cosmos was layered into an underworld of the dead, a middle world of the living, and a sky-heaven supported by a giant pillar. Supernatural beings or deities included a god of the sky (Ilmarinen), a raingiving god (Ukko), who was converted to a supreme or universal god under Christian influence, and other spirits of nature such as Tapio, a forest guardian of game. Many old features of Finnish-Karelian religion were preserved within the Russian Orthodox faith, which currently includes about 56,000 members in Finland. However, Lutheranism, which contributed to an erosion of native Finnish religion, embraces 90 percent of the population. Revivalist movements, like Laestadianism, have flourished within the context of the Lutheran church.

RELIGIOUS PRACTITIONERS. Prior to Christian and medieval Scandinavian influence, Finnish religion was embedded in shamanism with practitioners mediating between the present world and the altered consciousness of the upper and nether realms of the universe. Traces of this tradition, perhaps, survive in the divinatory practices of the seer or *tietäjä*. Evangelical Lutheran clergy, elected by local parish members, are the prominent religious specialists in contemporary society.

CEREMONIES. Bear ceremonialism was part of the Finns' ancient hunting traditions. Ritual slaying, feasting, and returning the skull and bones of a bear to the earth were fundamental to sending the animal's soul back to its original home and, thereby, facilitating its reincarnation. Ceremonies to promote farming and livestock became associated with holidays and the cult of the saints in the Christian calendar. Lutheran church life-cycle rites surrounding baptism, confirmation, marriage, and death remain significant for most Finns.

ARTS. Finnish culture is known for its rune song (folk poetry) traditions, which were synthesized in the epic *Kalevala*, a powerful symbol of national identity and source of artistic inspiration. In recent decades, innovative functionalist movements have distinguished Finnish architecture and the design of furniture, ceramics, glass, and textiles.

MEDICINE. As a symbol of cleansing and purity, the sauna was a focus of therapeutic and curing activity as well as ritualized social bathing. It was common to give birth in saunas prior to the availability of hospitals in this century, and cupping and bloodletting were performed there. Generally, the sauna is still seen as a remedy for pain and sickness.

DEATH AND AFTERLIFE. Living and dead kin formed a close unity in traditional Finnish and Karelian belief, and death was viewed largely as transfer to a new residence. The complex rituals accompanying death were orchestrated by women who arranged the wake, washed and shrouded the body, and sometimes sang laments to send the deceased, along with food and implements, to the place of the family ancestors. Memorial feasts were held six weeks and one year after death. Those who passed on to the realm of the dead (a place known as Manala or Tuonela) remained a profound moral force among living descendants. Days set aside for commemorating the dead were eventually adapted to a Christian calendar under Roman Catholic and Russian Orthodox influence.

Bibliography

Engman, Max, and David Kirby, eds. (1989). *Finland: People, Nation, State*. London: Hurst & Co.

Jarvenpa, Robert (1988). "Agrarian Ecology, Sexual Organization of Labor, and Decision Making in Northeastern Finland." In *The Social Implications of Agrarian Change in Northern and Eastern Finland*, edited by Tim Ingold, 76–90. Helsinki: Finnish Anthropological Society.

Lander, Patricia Slade (1976). *In the Shadow of the Factory: Social Change in a Finnish Community*. Cambridge, Mass.: Schenkman.

Pentikäinen, Juha Y. (1989). *Kalevala Mythology*. Bloomington: Indiana University Press.

Sarmela, Matti (1969). *Reciprocity Systems of the Rural Society in the Finnish-Karelian Culture Area*. FF Communications, no. 207. Helsinki: Suomalainen Tiedeakatemia.

Siikala, Anna-Leens (1987). "Finnic Religions." In *The Encyclopedia of Religion*, edited by Mircea Eliade. Vol. 5, 323–330. New York: Macmillan.

Solsten, Eric, and Sandra W. Meditz, eds. (1990). *Finland: A Country Study*. Washington, D.C.: Federal Research Division, Library of Congress.

Talve, Ilmar (1980). *Suomen Kansankulttuuri* (Finnish folk culture). Helsinki: Suomalaisen Kirjallisuuden Seura.

Vuorela, Toivo (1964). *The Finno-Ugric Peoples*. Indiana University Uralic and Altaic Series, no. 39. Bloomington: Indiana University Publications.

—ROBERT JARVENPA

FLEMISH

Ethonym: Flamencos (Spanish), Flandres (French), Flemings, French-Flemish, Northern Belgians, Southern Dutch, Vlaamingen (Dutch), Vlamisch (German)

Orientation

IDENTIFICATION. The Flemish are an admixture of the original Celtic inhabitants of the region, Roman invaders and settlers in this remote outpost of the empire, and Salian Franks, who invaded the Roman empire in the fifth century. The name "Vlaanderen," Flanders, derives from a Carolingian district, Pagus Flandrensis, of the eighth century. Today, the Flemish are the ethnic majority in the kingdom of Belgium and an ethnic minority in France.

LOCATION. For the most part, the Flemish people are culturally integrated into the nation of Belgium, playing an equal role in national politics and social life. Belgium, located at 51° N and 4° E, southwest of the Netherlands, northeast of France, and northwest of Germany and Luxembourg, is comprised of Flanders and Wallonia, the French-speaking area of the country, separated by a linguistic border that runs east-west. Flanders is the northern region, composed of low-lying and coastal areas bordering the North Sea and reaching inland to the hills of Brabant. Some Flemish live in the north-east regions of France, in an area known as French-Flanders. Others have migrated to Africa and the New World. Political and religious divisions have through the centuries divided a people previously united by a common language and cultural traditions into distinct national ethnicities: the Dutch, the French-Flemish, and the Belgian Flemish.

DEMOGRAPHY. The population of Belgium in 1990 was roughly 9,868,000 divided into 58 percent Flemish, 32 percent Walloon, with the remaining 10 percent a mixture of German speakers,

The Flemish are the ethnic majority in the kingdom of Belgium and an ethnic minority in France.

See also

French

Jews, Muslims, and others. The number of Flemish in France and elsewhere is unknown.

LINGUISTIC AFFILIATION. The Flemish speak numerous dialects of Flemish Dutch, called Vlaams, which is distinct from the Dutch spoken in the Netherlands (Nederlands). Regional dialect differences are characterized by vowel and consonant changes, distinct word differences, and unique expressions that refer metaphorically to regional history. An identification of language use with culture is not possible; however, French-speaking Flemish in both France and Belgium retain traits specific to Flemish culture. In France, where the use of regional dialects has been actively discouraged and proscribed in the schools, the Flemish have developed an ethnic political movement that emphasizes the use of the Flemish language at home, practice of Flemish art forms, and training in traditional industrial skills and work patterns.

History and Cultural Relations

The original Celtic tribes of the North Sea coastal regions became part of the Roman Empire when they were conquered in 57 B.C. by the armies of Julius Caesar. (The name "Belgium" derives from the original inhabitants of the region, labeled the Gallia Belgica by the Romans.) During this time, the inhabitants of southern Belgium were heavily influenced by Latin culture, giving rise to Latinate cultural traditions and the use of a Latin language. In the north, the cultural influence of Rome was weaker. The invasion of Salian Franks in the fifth century abruptly interrupted the period of Latin influence and established a Germanic Frankish kingdom, which included the use of a Germanic language. The linguistic border that crosses Belgium is believed to mark the extent of Frankish influence. In the ninth century, Charlemagne united independent Frankish regions into a vast kingdom, of which Flanders was a central part. In the division of Charlemagne's kingdom upon his death, Flanders came under the control of his son, Lothair, comprising Lotharingia. Weak governments under Lothair and his successors resulted in a process of fragmentation that gave rise to the feudal period, extending from the ninth to the twelfth centuries (A.D. 862–1128), during which distinct principalities, counties, and duchies were established. The county of Flanders, the duchy of Brabant, and the bishopric of Liege were three of the most politically dominant. In spite of political, organizational, and language divisions, similar cultural traditions and a prosperous textile industry led to a degree of political cooperation between districts. From 1128 to 1278, the authority of nobles was challenged by the growing political power of city-dwelling burghers who gained political and military control of transportation and trade. During the Burgundian period, 1384–1482, a series of noble marriages and alliances unified the smaller principalities while preserving and extending citizen authority and the relative economic autonomy of cities. During the fifteenth and sixteenth centuries, under a balance of power between nobles and free citizens, Flemish cities established a trade association in London and became central to trans-European trade, as members of the German Hanse. This period, considered the golden age of Flemish culture, produced great works of art and music. However, the process of consolidation into yet larger political bodies was not favorable for the Flemish. When Flanders became part of the kingdom governed by the Spanish Habsburgs (1506–1700), the people became subject to authoritarian structures foreign to developing cultural traditions. The rule of the Spanish proved disastrous for the Flemish people; during the years of the Spanish Inquisition, many were tortured or killed for religious and political dissent. In an attempt to end Spanish rule, the region went to war against Spain, resulting in the separation of the northern from the southern Flemish, the creation of the independent nation of Holland comprised of liberated northern provinces, and the continued subjugation of the "Spanish Netherlands." The Flemish and the French-speaking Walloons continued to live under the Spanish until the War of Spanish Succession, 1700–1713, when the territories passed to the Austrian Habsburgs. During this period, French became the dominant language for social and political life; the Flemish became marginalized as a national identity grew. In 1794, Napoleon conquered and annexed the Flemish and Walloon territories for France. After his defeat in 1815, the Treaty of Vienna assigned these areas to the new kingdom of the Netherlands, under the rule of King William I. However, the years of economic and political separation between the Dutch and the Flemish, the years of a common fate with Wallonia, and the quite different economic and political positions of the Dutch and the Belgians in a world economy proved to be stronger political factors than a common heritage in a more distant past. Belgians—both Walloons and Flemish—revolted against the Dutch in 1830, proclaiming Belgium as an independent nation. In 1831, they elected Prince Leopold of Saxe-

Coburg-Gotha as king, defined their government as a constitutional monarchy, and instituted a bicameral parliament with democratic representation. Although Flemish leaders were an integral part of Belgian independence efforts, the Flemish played a minority role in national politics until the early 1900s, because of the predominance of French language and culture during the period of French and Austrian control. In 1914, Germany invaded Belgium. Many of the battles of World War I were fought in Flanders, which sustained enormous damage in both urban and rural areas and suffered great loss of life. Again, in 1940, Germany invaded. In an attempt to avoid the devastation it had suffered in World War I, the king quickly surrendered to the Germans. The strategy was ineffective and deadly. Belgian Jews and Gypsies were exported and killed by the Nazis. Many Flemish and Walloons were conscripted and sent to work in German factories and labor camps. The nation was occupied and became one of the most embattled fronts of the war, in both Wallonia and Flanders. In 1944, Belgium was liberated by Canadian, Australian, and American forces. The postwar period was a time of rebuilding, but it was also internally divisive and disruptive for the Belgian people. German collaborators were punished, and the king was forced to give up his rule to his son. Partly because of the favoritism shown by the Germans for the Flemish during the war, ethnic tensions between Flemish and Walloon increased. Also, Belgian colonial holdings in Africa were lost either through civil unrest or the granting of independence to restive former colonies. During the 1960s and 1970s, ethnic divisiveness in Belgium was largely resolved with the creation of independent Flemish and Walloon assemblies, which each have authority over cultural, social, political, and regional administrative affairs of their respective groups. At this time Flemish was recognized as an official state language. The Flemish regions also gained in relative economic importance, while Wallonia experienced a decline in the heavy industries—notably in steel and coal. Flanders's importance rose as well in international trade, high-tech manufacturing, industrial agriculture, tourism, and fishing. Today, the Flemish enjoy full political and social equality with the Walloons.

Settlements

Early settlement sites were located along natural waterways and on protected coastal bays. Larger settlements grew up at trading points, located on natural overland and water transportation routes.

The human hand has greatly altered the Flemish landscape, by building canals, by dredging and straightening natural rivers, and by creating dikes and stabilizing sand dunes to create dry land out of marsh and to reclaim coastal floodplains. Walled cities are the hallmark of Flemish settlements, but villages, manorial estates, religious complexes, and farms are also significant. Dwellings and public buildings are made of local brick and cut limestone. Few buildings are constructed of wood, because of its scarcity, but early structures include half-wood upper stories, half-timbered buildings with brick infilling, and wooden roofs. Flemish "art cities," including Bruges, Ghent, and Antwerp, are noted for their skillfully carved stone and brick buildings. Stone and brick masonry, slatework, lead-pipe forming, and other building trades were highly developed industrial arts from the twelfth to the eighteenth centuries, as is evident today in the finely constructed bridges, churches, city and guild halls, stockmarkets, and municipal markets. Residences dating from the seventeenth and eighteenth centuries were often built in a distinctly Flemish "stepped-gable" style, the echoes of which are reflected in more recent architecture. To this day, residences are "human-scale," building up rather than out. Residents often make space available on the ground floor for business activities: hence, the ubiquitous *winkelshuis*, "shop house," or *handelshuis*, "business residence."

Economy

SUBSISTENCE AND COMMERCIAL ACTIVITIES. Today, Flanders has primarily an industrial and postindustrial economy, depending on the service and tourist industries. In recent years, economic activity in Flanders has expanded in final-step manufacturing, electronics, computer technology, and industrial agriculture. The economy has contracted in heavy industry, such as steel manufacture and boat building. The North Sea cities are commercial fishing centers, supporting largescale fish processing. Several coastal cities are important ports for industrial production, raw materials, and agricultural produce. The fertile, flat land remains an agro-industrial center. Farmers grow vegetables, fruit, animal feed, forage, and grains, which in turn support large commercial baking, meat-processing, vegetable-oil extraction, commercial fiber-processing, and vegetable- and fruit-canning enterprises.

INDUSTRIAL ARTS. The Flemish are noted for small-scale artisanal production of foods and luxury goods. Chocolate, lace, tapestry, glass, and

Many of the battles of World War I were fought in Flanders, which sustained enormous damage in both urban and rural areas and suffered great loss of life.

Residences dating from the seventeenth and eighteenth centuries were often built in a distinctly Flemish "stepped-gable" style.

pottery are notable. Early Flemish dominance was based on the production and finishing of cotton, linen, and woolen cloth.

TRADE. Flemish social values and cultural institutions are rooted in protoindustrial and industrial production for trade. The rise of early trade networks established Flemish municipal independence from an overarching feudal system and helped to install a system of government by a council of citizen representatives. Flemish cities established and joined trade associations that supported and facilitated trading relationships throughout Europe. Today, the Flemish character and culture are heavily influenced by traditions of trade, both on a large and small scale. The existence and persistence of the *zelfstandigen*, or independent self-employed business families, serves to define the Flemish people as independent economic actors.

DIVISION OF LABOR. In Belgium, occupational specialization is based on knowledge, training, and ability, but access to education and job training is limited by social class, ethnicity, gender, and economic status. Access to some occupations is facilitated only through family connections or kinship ties. In bicultural Brussels, some occupations are thought to be restricted ethnically, with the Flemish dominating many of the working-class occupations. Work is divided along gender and age lines in business, in the family, and in the household, as well, although not so strictly in practice as in widely held gender ideologies. For women, work in small firms and commercial enterprises is overlain so completely on domestic gender roles that household and business-related tasks are often difficult to distinguish: for example, wives of business owners receive visitors in the home as wives, and they also "help" their husbands as unpaid receptionists, office assistants, and business administrators in household-based firms.

LAND TENURE. Land is owned legally by individuals or by corporate groups, such as business investors or religious orders. Ownership is enforced by the legal system, based on written records of ownership through purchase or inheritance. Rights to use and allocate the use of land and other property are held solely by the legal owner(s). Businesses and business profits are owned solely by the individuals or legal entities that have invested either property or money—but not labor, energy, or time—into those concerns.

Kinship

KIN GROUPS AND DESCENT. Kinship is recognized bilaterally by family naming practices, but with an emphasis on the patriline. Upon marriage, the family names from both husband and wife are combined into a "household" name by which the nuclear family it creates is known; thus Geert DeJonge (the groom) and Kristin Vandeputte (the bride) create the family DeJonge-Vandeputte, but only the wife (and the business they operate, if any) adopts the combined last name. The children from this couple are given the family name DeJonge, unless the wife's family name is of high social rank.

KINSHIP TERMINOLOGY. Most kin terms are based on descent/ascent and collateral relationships, and they are distinguished by gender: *moeder, vader, grootmoeder, grootvader* (mother, father, grandmother, grandfather); *dochter, zoon* (daughter, son); *zuster, broer* (sister, brother); *tante, oom* (aunt, uncle); *neef, nicht* (nephew, niece). Other kin terms are ascriptive, denoting a social, fictive kinship that echoes genealogical kinship but indicates specific social responsibilities and duties, such as *meter, peter* (godmother, godfather).

Marriage and Family

MARRIAGE. Marriage unites an adult male and female into an economic unit ideally distinct from the natal families of each. Marriages are arranged by the bride and groom themselves, but with family influence. The economic aspects of marriage are not often explicitly expressed (people prefer to say they marry because they love one another or they wish to raise children together), but marriage is clearly an economic partnership between spouses and between their natal families. Notably, *zelfstandige* (self-employed) couples and farmers work together in income-producing enterprises. Compatibility in work, the willingness to divide labor, and a shared work ethic are important reasons to marry a particular spouse when anticipating this work in adulthood. Men and women typically marry for the first time in their teens or early twenties, and they begin childbearing soon thereafter. Families of two to four children are the norm. Second and subsequent marriages are common following the death of, or separation from, one's first spouse. Legal divorce is increasingly common, but it is considered a misfortune particularly for children and wives who depend economically on husbands. Coworking couples will find it expedient not to divorce when marital difficulties arise because divorce can have a detrimental effect on business. In such cases, couples will remain married but live apart, creating social-sexual alliances with others. There are few institutions that cater to the single adult.

Subtle social sanctions are brought to bear on adults who remain single past the middle thirties without a legitimate reason, such as entry into the priesthood. Extramarital alliances, both purely sexual as well as those that result in children, are common for both men and women, but they are not often maintained openly. Wealthy Flemish men and women may maintain semipermanent liaisons for years. A secondary common-law spouse is not uncommon.

DOMESTIC UNIT. The nuclear family, composed of husband, wife, and their children, is the ideal family form. Coresident extended families are not common. Unmarried adults will commonly live with aged parents until marriage. Married couples establish new households when they wed, or shortly thereafter. Often in "business families," whose members work in the same trade, several nuclear families of kin will live in adjacent housing, next to or above the workspace. Old people who can no longer care for themselves are often cared for in old-age homes run by religious orders, sociopolitical unions, or insurance organizations. There are similar institutions for the mentally and physically disabled and the mentally ill. In recent years, young unmarried adults have begun to live apart from parents in shared housing. Alternative households and unmarried cohabitation are still uncommon.

INHERITANCE. Inheritance is strictly partible and is governed by state laws. A property owner's estate is to be divided equally between legitimate heirs. If a spouse survives, he or she is entitled to use rights to the home the couple previously shared. Business property is handled as the personal property of the owner and willed separately in ways that often result in the disinheritance of individuals who invest years of labor in the business.

SOCIALIZATION. Children are allowed carefree childhoods, without major work responsibilities. Creative, imaginative play is encouraged. Children are much loved and spoiled. Older relatives and neighbors and older children are charged with care of little ones, teaching them a rich children's culture of play songs and rhymes as well as good behavior, which is defined as showing respect for elders, keeping quiet, following instructions well, and being resourceful. Willful and stubborn behavior on the part of children is tolerated and even admired as the first sign of a strong and independent character. Few children work, but the children of business owners often work part-time as "helpers" at as early as 8 years old. This experience is viewed as good preparation for following in a family trade. Flemish children are formally educated in schools, with the majority enrolled in private Catholic schools. After elementary grades, children are then either expressly guided to or given a choice between a trade-oriented education, a liberal education, professional training, or business training. An apprenticeship system survives in the half-time work-study programs of some vocational schools, but students still reside at their parents' home.

Sociopolitical Organization

SOCIAL ORGANIZATION. The Flemish are socially divided into distinct social groupings defined by family pedigree and history, nobility, family business history, language use, personal occupation, and visible wealth. Both men and women try to "marry up" or marry within their social level. Gender is an important social divider; women typically do not receive as much from their natal families in terms of business training or education as men do. Women are expected to join their husband's family, fate, and fortune upon marriage. Because a woman's social status as a wife is therefore more significant to her social position in adulthood than her status as a daughter, courtship and marriage constitutes an important socialranking process for women.

POLITICAL ORGANIZATION. Both small communities and large cities are directed politically by *raden*, elected bodies of representatives from distinct districts. As mandated by law, all adults must vote. Representatives from Flemish districts are elected to the Flemish regional assemblies and to the parliament. These representatives make law and defend the interests of the Flemish in formulating national policy. Belgium is a constitutional monarchy, with a king at its head. The king has primarily symbolic power as the most important unifying force in the nation. Kingship is inherited through the male line and devolves only to males. The Flemish in France are not recognized officially as a political or ethnic body within the nation of France. Their participation in French political life is viewed as regional, rather than ethnic, participation.

SOCIAL CONTROL. Conflicts inherent in Flemish culture are those that center on control over private property and conflicting interpretations of private versus public interest. State social control is accomplished by means of a judicial system that interprets the laws enacted by legislators and enforced by state and local police. Cultural mechanisms of social control consist of social sanctions, public and private censure of nonconforming behavior, and effective socialization

The Flemish in Belgium played a minority role in national politics until the early 1900s, because of the predominance of the French language and culture during French and Austrian control.

The Flemish are overwhelmingly Roman Catholic. Membership in the Catholic church is the norm, regardless of personal religious belief.

of children and young adults. Violence against the person is not tolerated, with one exception. Stiff legal penalties are levied for crimes against unrelated persons, but the state allows intrafamily violence to continue by a policy of nonintervention in nuclear-family affairs. Spouse and child abuse, as well as mistreatment of the elderly, are problems in all social classes.

CONFLICT. In recent years, social conflicts have arisen and divided the Flemish over social policy issues such as abortion, which has divided the nation of Belgium in ways that crosscut social-class, ethnic, and religious differences. The Flemish people do not present a unified view on the basic question of whether abortion should be a legally protected right or a crime, nor on how it should be defined by law or handled in the courts. Such policy issues have been addressed in the past by face-to-face meetings among legislators, religious leaders, the king, and cabinet advisers, in which compromise positions have been reached and made law. National-level conflict exists between the Walloons and the Flemish centering on the dynamics of economic change in the nation of Belgium. In France, conflict over issues of ethnic and regional autonomy continue to simmer and, on occasion, boil over.

Religion and Expressive Culture

RELIGIOUS BELIEFS. The Flemish are overwhelmingly Roman Catholic. Membership in the Catholic church is the norm, regardless of personal religious belief. Although nearly everyone is baptized and learns Catholic doctrine in catechism classes or Catholic school, many Flemish people are not practicing Catholics or are active nonbelievers. Leaving the church in an official act of excommunication, however, creates myriad social difficulties, because many social services are linked with the parish or other church institutions. Flanders has a small Protestant community composed of Flemish converts to Jehovah's Witnesses, the Mormon church, and other Christian sects. In addition, there is an active, large, and dynamic Jewish community, particularly in Brussels, Antwerp, and the coastal area; an ephemeral surviving Gypsy community; and a growing community of Muslims in Brussels. "Flemish" Jews and Muslims have not adopted the culture of their neighbors, and they continue to practice their faiths in separate ethnic communities. However, Belgian religious minorities often speak the language of the region in which they live and participate in Belgian social and political life.

RELIGIOUS PRACTITIONERS. Priests and nuns organize most religious functions. Lay religious leaders are active in parish associations and participate in the organization of religious ceremonies and church services. The Freemasons also comprise an important quasireligious group in Flemish culture, establishing ties of brotherhood that crosscut social, religious, and ethnic differences. Freemasons have been influential in liberal party politics and in the process of defining a middle-class Flemish political interest.

CEREMONIES. Baptism, first communion, and confirmation mark the child's entry into the Catholic family and community. There are no official rituals marking entry into adulthood—except perhaps graduation from school, military service (for men), and marriage. The Flemish celebrate many days in the Catholic religious calendar that mark events in Christ's life. Also, there are a series of folk processions, rooted in historic events and legend, often using masks and papier-mâché "giants" (e.g., the Kattestoet in Ghent). Other ceremonies mark religious miracles, such as the Procession of the Holy Blood in Bruges, or are more purely commercial, on the order of street theater, combining spectacle with romantic reformulations of history.

ARTS. Flemish literature, painting, sculpture, music, and dance are highly developed arts, comprising Flemish regional and ethnic styles, as well as participating in widespread European art movements. Early Flemish literature, written in local dialect, is linked with the growth in political importance of the Flemish population, depicting folk heroes that personify the political and social character of the Flemish. More recent literature is often nihilistic or surreal, influenced by the damage inflicted by both world wars on the Flemish psyche. Many of the great early works of Flemish musical composition are liturgical pieces for voice and organ, for example Orlando de Lassus's Gregorian compositions. The exceptional works of the Flemish primitives—including Memling, Bosch, and the Van Eycks—and the numerous Flemish masters, such as Rubens, were commissioned by noble patrons throughout Europe. More recent Flemish painting and sculpture often highlight the pleasures and pains of rural life, but others, such as works by Ensor, depict urban decadence and cultural decay. Folk arts, notably street singing, folk opera, and marionette and hand puppetry, have revived in recent years as part of the folk movement. Antwerp has a tradition of puppet theater that often crosses into the realm of political and social critique. In the plastic arts, tapestry and lace manufacture have evolved from early products of cottage industry into domestic crafts. Today, lace is simultaneously a fine art, a hobby craft, and a tourist art; and many varieties of lace are available for sale, collection, and display.

MEDICINE. Modern medical care is provided in state-run hospitals and clinics and is also available through private doctors and health practitioners. The scientific model of medicine is widely accepted, but health maintenance often involves folk beliefs regarding the use of herbs, mineral and saltwater baths, and the use of certain foods as preventative cures. Many Flemish also believe in the curative value of Oriental medical treatments, such as acupuncture. Devout Catholics often pray for divine assistance with health problems, posting placards of thanks to the Virgin Mary in churches. Many Flemish people avoid dental care, with a resulting loss of teeth from decay.

DEATH AND AFTERLIFE. Beliefs about death and an afterlife are shaped by Catholic doctrine. Funerals are sad and frequently private events, shared only by the deceased's family, close friends, and neighbors. The death of a child is a particularly sad and private event. Public displays of grief are not common. Graves, located on church grounds or nearby, are cared for by the survivors of the deceased. National graveyards of the fallen of World Wars I and II, located in northern Flanders, are maintained by the nations whose dead are buried there. For the Flemish, these vast graveyards are monuments to sacrifice and freedom, symbolic of a national and Flemish resolve to work for international peace and political compromise.

Bibliography

De Meeus, A. (1962). *History of the Belgians*. Translated by G. Gordon. New York: Praeger.

Goris, Jan Albert (1945). *Belgium*. Berkeley: University of California Press.

Huggett, F. E. (1969). *Modern Belgium*. New York: Praeger.

Lijphart, Arend, ed. (1981). *Conflict and Coexistence in Belgium: The Dynamics of a Culturally Divided Society*. Berkeley: University of California Press, Institute of International Studies.

Pirenne, Henri (1915). *Early Democracies in the Low Countries: Urban Society and Political Conflict in the Middle Ages and the Renaissance*. Translated by J. V. Saunders. New York: Harper & Row.

Riley, R. C. (1989). *Belgium*. World Bibliographic Series, edited by R. G. Neville, vol. 104. Oxford: Clio Press.

Van Houtte, J. A. (1977). *An Economic History of the Low Countries, 800–1800*. New York: St. Martin's Press.
—MERIELLE K. FLOOD

FRENCH

Ethonym: none

The French are citizens of France (the French republic). Including the island of Corsica, France occupies 549,183 square kilometers and in 1990 had an estimated population of 56,184,000. About 10 percent of the population is composed of immigrants and workers from Italy, Spain, Portugal, and other European nations and refugees from former French colonies in Southeast Asia and Africa. French is the language of France and about 90 percent of the people are Roman Catholics, with a large Muslim population made up mainly of immigrants from northern Africa, especially Algeria. A strong Parisian-centered government and centralized authority began to emerge in the tenth century, and in the twentieth century mass communication has strengthened French nationalism at the expense of the regional cultures. Still, though, there are viable regional cultures and marked linguistic variations. Among the major regional cultures are the Alsatians in the east; the Corsicans on the Mediterranean island of Corsica; the Bretons in the northwest; the Burgundians, Auvergnats, and Aveyronnais in central France; and Aquitaine, Occitans, Provencal, and the Basques in the south.

Bibliography

Kurian, George T. (1990). *Encyclopedia of the First World*. 2 vols. New York: Facts on File.

Worldmark Encyclopedia of the Nations (1988). 7th ed. New York: Worldmark Press.

GAELS (IRISH)

Ethonym: Celts, Gaedhils, Irish countrymen and countrywomen, Kelts

Orientation

IDENTIFICATION. The Gaelic language (Gaedhilge) is a primary cultural marker of Gaels living on the Atlantic fringe of Ireland, distinguishing them from the English-speaking Irish of Ulster and the Irish republic in general.

About ten percent of the French population is composed of immigrants and workers from European nations, and refugees from former French colonies in Southeast Asia and Africa.

LOCATION. Apart from Iceland, the Gaelic enclaves represent the westernmost culture of the Old World. They are found along the south and west coasts of the republic, and these pockets, called "Gaeltachts," have had a special protected status since 1956. They are located in seven discontinuous areas: western Donegal, western Mayo, western Galway, the Aran Islands, western Kerry, western Cork, and south-western Waterford. Only in these areas is Gaelic still widely spoken, though English is learned in school and also used. They are completely rural areas, and their economic development is tightly regulated; indeed, the frequency of Atlantic gales and the poor soil make farm improvement especially difficult. The number of primarily Gaelic speakers has steadily declined since the great potato famine of 1845–1848, and since then the boundary of their habitat has correspondingly been retreating westward. Although a century ago they covered the western half of the island of Ireland, today Gaelic enclaves are found discontinuously between 51°40′ and 55°20′ N and 7°30′ and 10°30′ W.

DEMOGRAPHY. In 1981 1,018,413 Gaelic speakers were claimed for the Republic of Ireland (including 72,774 in the Gaeltachts), perhaps 20,000 in Northern Ireland, and a few thousand more who had settled in England, Australia, or North America. The number of Gaelic speakers (1,018,413)—which is 31.6 percent of the total population of the republic—does not come close to expressing the reality, since most of the self-identified "Irish speakers" are English speakers who learned some Irish in school. The number of speakers has really been declining for some centuries. Thus for example in the entire island in 1851 there were 319,602 speakers of Gaelic only, plus 1,204,684 bilingual in Gaelic and English. By 1901 these figures had dropped to 20,953 monoglots and 620,189 bilinguals. This trend has continued until recent times. However, the decline in numbers of Gaelic speakers cannot be explained simply by general population decline in the country. The closely related phenomena of population decline, high rates of underemployment, overseas emigration, the rural incidence of anomie, and the creation of the "Congested Districts Board" in 1891 must be considered together, as they apply in particular to what later became categorized as the Gaeltachts. In these areas the government has since 1891 made modest attempts to improve living conditions in what were recognized to be the poorest, least arable, and least developed parts of the country; but despite the board's activities and the creation of Roinn na Gaeltachta in 1956 to promote welfare in the Gaeltachts, the introduction of better housing, cooperative dairies, and certain welfare facilities has done nothing to hold the population in these areas. Typically today they contain an "old" population of widows, widowers, and other elderly people who have never married. While there are, of course, some young people too, many have moved to the Dublin area on the other side of the country or gone overseas. With national unemployment throughout Ireland (and Ulster) at 18 percent in 1989—and higher in the Gaeltachts—no reversal of this demographic trend is in sight.

LINGUISTIC AFFILIATION. Gaelic, Irish, or Erse is an ancient language of the Indo-European Family. It is not closely related to the neighboring English but instead is one of the languages forming the small subfamily of modern Celtic, a relic of the ancient Celtic that reached in pre-Roman times from Britain and Iberia as far as Asia Minor. The modern Celtic languages, in addition to Irish, are Scottish Gaelic (also called Erse), Welsh, Breton or Armoric, Cornish (extinct in 1777), and Manx (virtually extinct by 1990). Most of them have an ancient literature. Two other important languages that had disappeared by about the fifth century A.D. were Gaulish and British. All Celtic languages have certain non-Indo-European features, such as positioning of the verb at the beginning of the sentence, which are otherwise known to us from Berber and Ancient Egyptian. Gaelic currently has the status of "first official language" in the Republic of Ireland, and because of urban migration the largest pocket of Gaelic speakers today is in Dublin County.

History and Cultural Relations

The long history of Gaelic speakers in Ireland has been marked by the production of noble epic poetry but also by the depredations of Viking marauders and later by the suppression of the language by English soldiers and settlers in the country. Parallel with this military suppression of the Irish peasantry was the outlawing of the Gaelic tongue, which inevitably led to the "hedge schools" of the seventeenth and eighteenth centuries, so called because they had to meet in secret behind hedges. Irish literature and classical learning were both imparted in Gaelic. By the nineteenth century, village schools teaching in English were becoming widespread. The founding of the nationalistic Gaelic League in 1893 put the Gaelic language into a new light: from then on it was promoted (by urbanized, English-speaking Irish) as the language of what would one day be-

See also

Irish

come the Irish Free State (formed in 1922); and the literary revival of Gaelic that the league initiated has marked the twentieth century. But those in the Gaeltachts found little comfort in being patronized by city intellectuals, and otherwise they saw no real extension for the utility of Gaelic.

Economy

SUBSISTENCE AND COMMERCIAL ACTIVITIES. A mixed subsistence economy prevails throughout the Gaeltachts, with some farm surplus being produced for sale to neighbors or in local markets. Since these areas are near the coasts, ocean fishing used to be a prominent activity. Its importance has diminished considerably, partly because of the risks to older men that would come from going out in frail boats, but partly too because recent commercial trawling by both Irish and European Community boats has largely destroyed the breeding grounds on the sea bottom. The remaining boatmen today are more likely to put to sea to take a group of tourists for an outing. Other aspects of the traditional mixed economy are still observable, however. Cows and poultry are kept for domestic needs; goats or pigs are sometimes found. Horses and donkeys are used in all Gaeltachts to pull the carts and implements used in farmwork and dairying. Oats and potatoes are important crops, along with hay for winter feed, and some wheat, rye, and barley are also grown for bread. Timber is extremely scarce, requiring the reuse of old rafters and even the collection of driftwood. The common heating and cooking fuel is peat cut from the local bogs and dried for a month or more before being brought home. Cooking stoves using canned gas are now common. Sundry farm products are sold, privately or through cooperatives. There are also two major sources bringing money in from beyond the Gaeltacht: tourism, and numerous government subsidies. Since many villagers claim to be unemployed they can obtain unemployment benefits ("the dole"); others receive old-age pensions from age 66 on. There are small financial incentives given for speaking Gaelic in the home or for supporting an incapacitated family member. In addition to these sources, many families receive cash remissions from relatives overseas, especially in Massachusetts, Chicago, and New York. Of these various sources, the provision of meals and accommodation ("country teas" and "farm holidays") to tourists (high-school students, urban Irish, and English and Americans) are among the most remunerative today.

INDUSTRIAL ARTS. There are very few towns in the Gaeltachts and virtually no industri-

IRISH FISHERMAN

Two Gaelic fishermen on a grounded fishing boat. Ocean fishing used to be an important activity, before large-scale commercial fishing damaged the breeding grounds. Tory Island, Republic of Ireland. (Peter Turnley/ Corbis)

SETTLEMENTS

Villages are small, usually with 100–200 inhabitants, and consist of dispersed farmsteads, each surrounded by a few acres of farmland (or "townland"). There are four important centers of interaction in a Gaelic village: the pub or pubs; the post office or store (if there is one); the space outside the church; and the crossroads, which was the traditional place for dancing, gossip, and interaction among the young people on a summer's evening. The main farmhouse is usually next to another building that houses cattle, horses, donkeys, and farm implements. This latter building may be a relatively new structure, or else the ancestral home of the family that they have recently relinquished to their animals. Prehistoric and medieval stone buildings (*clocháin*) have sometimes been preserved in this manner. The traditional Gaelic home is a long one-storied cottage divided into three rooms, its long axis roughly oriented east-west. The west room has a special position in Irish folklore, for it is where the aging parent or parents traditionally live out their last years amid family mementos before "going west." The middle room, the largest, is the general living and dining room, and also serves as the kitchen. It has two external doors, on the north and the south sides of the house. The small eastern room is a bedroom, but in the more northerly Gaeltachts it is common for the living room to have a protrusion or "outshot," which also can contain a bed. The cottages are sturdily built of cut stone, with wooden rafters supporting a thatched roof. The kitchen fire provides the only heat, and so peat (the usual fuel) is burning there fairly constantly. An adjustable iron pot hanger (*croch*) hangs over it to support a pot or kettle; the smoke escapes up a chimney.

alization. Boats, carts, and houses used to be made by Gaelic villagers. Now few have the skills or the need, as cars slowly replace carts and contractors build modern houses for the people. In earlier times coastal villages had large fishing vessels, but by the present century most fishermen only had small four-man canoes (called *curragh* in the north, *naomhóg* farther south). There were no shipbuilding yards for these vessels, which were built by the boatmen themselves and are still repaired by them. Small seaports no doubt used once to have a thriving shipbuilding and repairing industry for larger vessels.

TRADE. A large village may often serve as a shopping center for a Gaeltacht, and a small town always exists somewhere nearby, perhaps an hour's bus ride away. Here a handful of shops, nearly as many pubs, a government office or two, and perhaps a weekly market supply the basic needs of the rural community.

DIVISION OF LABOR. With little perceptible class differentiations among the Gaelic peasantry, division of labor along lines of gender and age is normal. Men do the fishing, dairying, and farmwork, and they cut and cart the peat, until at 60 or 70 they become too old for all this and have to rely on their sons. Women do the housework and may also handle the dairying and the feeding of domestic animals. They are largely responsible for bringing up the children. The entire family has to go into the fields in July or August to turn the hay repeatedly and then stack it. Children are normally at school, but they are given chores to perform around the house or farm and may work hard during the summer vacation.

LAND TENURE. About 6 percent of Ireland is allocated to the Gaeltachts, and they are home to about 10,000 small farmers. These areas, however, contain some of the worst farmland in the country. It has been estimated that about 80 percent of the Gaeltacht land is mountainside, bog, or marshland, good only for grazing sheep or digging out peat: the good arable land is in the central and eastern parts of the country. Land tenure is intimately linked with the arranging of marriages and with migration. In the present century marriages are still often arranged, but the small farmer can reasonably give his land to just one son: any other sons have to go elsewhere for work, emigrate overseas, or join the priesthood. But the one son who stays on the farm of his ancestors inherits everything at his marriage. Generally, a formal contract is drawn up by a solicitor in which the old farmer agrees to transfer ownership of land, home, and livestock to his son upon the latter's marriage. This contract then becomes a key part of the young man's marriage arrangements and also takes the place of a will. The money may be used to help support the old farmer and his wife in their retirement in the west room, or it may become the dowry with which one of their daughters is married off. All too often nowadays, though, no suitable girl willing to marry a young farmer is available, and so he goes through life remaining unmarried while he toils on the land and supports his aging parents. As long as the father does not legally hand the property over to his son, the latter will remain there in a web of obligations and delayed expectations.

Kinship

KIN GROUPS AND DESCENT. In Gaelic culture, *clann* has a different meaning than the Scottish clan and the common anthropological term. The Irish clann traces descent through both males and females; thus, a clann is the entirety of all persons descended from the clann progenitor (regardless of whom those persons may have married). This means that an individual will belong to several clanns simultaneously: his or her father's one or more clanns, plus his or her mother's. The clann is not necessarily exogamous. There are other categories of kin that overlap with the clann. A person has a body of known relatives recognized as his or her kindred ("my people," *mo mhuintir*). A smaller kinship group is made up of those people considered relatives "by blood" (*gaolta*). Membership in these groupings corresponds to a very different system of naming than the Christian-name-plus-surname pattern of Anglo-Saxon lands. A person's descent is actually named, going back to one, two, or three patrilineal ancestors. There are also surnames, but the well-known O' of so many Irish names occurs less often in Gaelic: O' means "son of." Women instead carry the term *Ní*, "daughter of." Neither of these terms is used in a surname except on very formal occasions.

KINSHIP TERMINOLOGY. The Gaelic kinship system uses bifurcate-collateral terminology, which is very different from the English system so widespread in Ireland.

Marriage and Family

MARRIAGE. A woman's marriage traditionally centered on finding a young man who stood to inherit a farm and then paying a dowry to his parents. Even today, arranged marriages along these lines still occur. It has also long been thought desirable, however, for a farmer's daughter to marry someone with a shop in a nearby town; in this way the woman can hope for a somewhat easier life than if she marries into another farm. At the same time her family can expect little favors from the shop that she helps to run, while her in-laws can expect some fresh farm produce whenever her relatives come to town. This tendency of girls to move to the towns in marriage—or even to migrate to Dublin, Liverpool, or London to work as chambermaids or in other service occupations—has contributed to the steady depopulation of the Gaeltachts during the past century. Since World War II, the tendency for both male and female youths to migrate has been enhanced by the ease of air travel and the knowledge that they can find well-paid jobs in Massachusetts or Chicago. Nowadays everyone seems to have at least one relative in the United States.

DOMESTIC UNIT. Six types of household can be found in the Gaeltachts: (1) single-person households; (2) joint-sibling households, with unmarried or widowed brothers or sisters living together; (3) widow/widower households, including married or unmarried children; (4) *nepotal households*, defined by Fox as "households consisting of an uncle/aunt with his/her married/unmarried nephew/niece"; (5) extended households, consisting of father and mother with their unmarried children, one married child with spouse, and perhaps grandchildren; (6) nuclear households, made up of parents with their dependent children. In each case the household is viewed as a family and is a labor unit.

INHERITANCE. A young man whose father owns land and livestock can hope to inherit these at the time of his marriage, rather than at his father's death. A marriage contract thus often replaces a will. If there are more sons, only one will have hopes of getting the small farm, since the land cannot usually be divided among several sons.

SOCIALIZATION. All children get an informal education in daily activities by helping their parents around the home or on the farm. Gaeltacht children nowadays are usually educated at village schools provided by local government authorities. The average school-leaving age is 16, and after that boys tend to work on the farm, at least for a while. Girls are likely to emigrate sooner than their brothers. A few of these young people attend universities or theological colleges, in preparation for careers that will almost certainly keep them away from their home villages.

Sociopolitical Organization

SOCIAL ORGANIZATION. Gaelic villages are usually acephalous entities with a tendency toward exogamy.

POLITICAL ORGANIZATION. Ireland is a sovereign, independent, democratic republic. At the national level is an elected president (An

The long history of Gaelic speakers in Ireland has been marked by the production of epic poetry, plus suppression of the language by English soldiers and settlers.

*In Gaelic religious
belief the Trinity is
less often the
orthodox triad of
Father, Son, and
Holy Ghost than the
distinctly Irish one
of Jesus, Mary, and
Joseph.*

Uachtarán), a partially elected senate (Seanad Eireann), and the Assembly (the Dáil Éireann) in Dublin, which has 166 representatives (*teachta dala*) elected by universal adult suffrage and proportional representation; in the Assembly the Gaeltachts are represented through their several parliamentary constituencies. Of the two major parties, Fianna Fail draws most support in the Gaeltachts because of its pro-Gaelic policies, and it forms the current government. At the local level are twenty-seven county councils in the republic, made up of elected members.

SOCIAL CONTROL.   The formal authorities in Irish villages are police constables (*gardai*). Gaeltacht villages do not have elected mayors, and the moral leader of a community is likely to be the parish priest. His threat of supernatural sanctions for wrongdoing is taken very seriously. Gossip and public opprobrium are also strong forces of social control. Not long ago, another powerful deterrent was the fear of what the fairies might do to one at night. Even now, one of the worst things one can ever say about a neighbor is to hint that he or she is in league with the Devil and thus is an agent of evil powers.

CONFLICT.   Incidence of crime in the Gaeltachts is generally very low, rarely involving more than occasional petty theft or drunk and disorderly behavior. The people of the Gaeltachts are not directly involved with the current strife in Northern Ireland.

Religion and Expressive Culture

RELIGIOUS BELIEFS.   The religion in the Gaeltachts is generally Roman Catholicism, and in most of them Protestant churches account for less than 5 percent of believers. Vestiges of ancient pre-Christian practice and belief are nonetheless still to be observed (for example, in some annual festivals).

With Roman Catholicism so widespread, the usual Christian beliefs in the Trinity are universal. But in Gaelic belief the Trinity that people acknowledge is less often the orthodox triad of Father, Son, and Holy Ghost than the distinctly Irish one of Jesus, Mary, and Joseph—with Mary being the dominant figure in the Holy Family. A lively cult of saints is also found everywhere, many of them distinctively Irish ones. Saint Patrick (Pádraig) was the semimythical bearer of Christian civilization to the pagan Irish. Rich legend surrounds all of the Irish saints and dozens of other Christian saints. Clearly many minor gods, goddesses, and other spirits of pagan times were incorporated into Christian faith during the

Middle Ages, to such an extent that much of the idiosyncrasy of Irish Catholicism can be traced by a folklorist back to pagan custom and belief. Some of the ancient cults have been kept alive in innocent-looking folk customs and a huge corpus of epic poetry. On the borderline of Christian belief is the Devil ("Black Nick" or "Old Nick," as he is usually called), a powerful presence still active in the world. He takes the form of a black dog, a cat, or an anthropomorphic figure with tail and cloven feet. The Devil, like a more powerful form of the fairies, is potentially harmful, causing some disease, crop failure, or other disasters. He even possesses selected humans, thereby making them into his agents. People hope they have a guardian angel who will protect them from the advances of the Devil; otherwise they must rely on rosaries and Christian prayer. People also commonly have a personal saint, chosen not so much on the basis of his or her history as on whether the saint is known to be a powerful intercessor with God. Other beings of the supernatural world are the fairies or elves, the cobbler (*leipreachán*), and the vindictive female ghost or banshee (*bean sídhe*, "the white woman"). In addition many people believe in ghosts, the wandering souls of the dead (*taidhbhsí*).

RELIGIOUS PRACTITIONERS.   Pagan practitioners of healing and witchcraft are no longer to be found, and the parish priest is now the ubiquitous spiritual shepherd of his flock. While a few of these men are from the Gaeltachts themselves, most of them are from other parts of Ireland: they were trained at Maynooth College and learned Gaelic for the ministry. Mass is now commonly said in Gaelic in the Gaeltacht communities.

CEREMONIES.   Christenings, weddings, and funerals are religious rites celebrated by the parish priest at his church. But beyond these life-cycle ceremonies are others marking the annual cycle, many of them grounded in pre-Christian antiquity. The Gaelic annual cycle includes: Saint Brighid's Day, 1 February; Shrove Tuesday (just before Lent); Chalk Sunday (the first Sunday of Lent); Lent; Saint Patrick's Day; Easter; May Day, 1 May; Midsummer, 23 June; Michaelmas, 29 September; Samhain (Halloween or All Souls' Day), 31 October–1 November; Christmas; Saint Stephen's Day, 26 December. As elsewhere throughout modern Europe, many of these calendrical observances are becoming past memories.

ARTS.   The traditional arts of the Gaeltacht are music, storytelling, and poetry, all still very much alive. The pride of many communities today is the local teller of folktales (*seanchaí*) or the singer of mythical epics (*scéalaí*). Their skills are usually heard in the pubs, shebeens (*scíbíní*), and nighttime dance parties (*ceilidh*), essential scenes for community interaction. The tourist trade has brought forth several other arts, among them pottery and knitting, which might seem traditional to the culture but in fact are not.

MEDICINE. Ireland is divided into a large number of "Dispensary Districts," each with at least one doctor and some nurses on duty. Thus the government makes modern health care available in the Gaeltachts, as elsewhere, and for those of low income it is free. There are also some "herb doctors," unlicensed and untrained folk healers who practice their craft in Gaelic villages, making use of various herbs as well as talismans and charms. Theirs is of course a traditional lore in these areas, specific to the flora of the Atlantic fringe.

DEATH AND AFTERLIFE. Christian burial is universally practiced in hallowed ground in the Gaeltachts, but it is preceded by the distinctive Irish institution of a wake. The principal realms of the other world in Christian thought are heaven, purgatory, and hell. People see heaven as a calm and peaceful place where the dead are reunited with friends and relatives; thus, people look forward to this afterlife, and the thought of it makes present troubles easier to bear. Despite much skepticism about the existence of hell, many Gaels do see it as a place of fire and punishment that will engulf evildoers. Purgatory is often seen in the folk eschatology as a part of this world, not the afterlife.

Bibliography

Arensberg, Conrad M., and Solon T. Kimball (1968). *Family and Community in Ireland*. 2nd ed. Cambridge, Mass.: Harvard University Press.

Brody, Hugh (1973). *Inishkillane: Change and Decline in the West of Ireland*. London: Allen Lane, Penguin Press.

Cresswell, Robert (1969). *Une communauté rurale de l'Irlande*. Paris: Institut de l'Ethnologie, Musée de l'Homme.

Danaher, Kevin (1972). *The Year in Ireland*. Cork: Mercier Press.

Evans, E. Estyn (1957). *Irish Folk Ways*. London: Routledge & Kegan Paul.

Fox, Robin (1978). *The Tory Islanders: A People of the Celtic Fringe*. Cambridge: Cambridge University Press.

Freeman, T. W. (1960). *Ireland: A General and Regional Geography*. 2nd ed. London: Methuen & Co.

Gregory, Augusta (1970). *Visions and Beliefs in the West of Ireland Collected and Arranged by Lady Gregory: With Two Essays and Notes by W. B. Yeats*. London: Colin Smythe. [Several other editions.]

Mac Gobhan, Micí (1962). *The Hard Road to Klondike*. Translated by Valentin Iremonger. London: Routledge & Kegan Paul.

Messenger, John (1969). *Inis Beag, Isle of Ireland*. New York: Holt, Rinehart & Winston.

Ó Crohan, Tomás (1934). *The Islandman*. Translated by Robin Flower. New York: Charles Scribner's Sons. [Several later editions.]

O'Sullivan, Maurice (1933). *Twenty Years A-growing*. Translated by Moya Llewelyn Davies and George Thomson. New York: Viking Press. [Several later editions.]

Sayers, Peig (1973). *Peig: The Autobiography of Peig Sayers of the Great Blasket Island*. Translated by Bryan MacMahon. Dublin: Talbot Press. [Several later editions.]

Scheper-Hughes, Nancy (1979). *Saints, Scholars, and Schizophrenics—Mental Illness in Rural Ireland*. Berkeley: University of California Press.

—PAUL HOCKINGS

The people of Galicia in Spain inhabit the northwestern corner of the Iberian Peninsula, directly north of Portugal.

GALICIANS

Ethonym: Galego, Gallego

Orientation

IDENTIFICATION. The people of Galicia in Spain (*o pobo galego* in Galician) inhabit the northwestern corner of the Iberian Peninsula, directly north of Portugal. They speak Castilian Spanish and Galician, the latter a Romance language that is parent to modern Portuguese. They are predominantly Roman Catholic. The name "Galicia" is derived from the name for the people in the region when the Romans arrived in the second century B.C.E., the *gallatae*, but there is disagreement about the ethnic source of the people, with many celebrating a Celtic origin.

LOCATION. Galicia lies between 42° and 44° N and 7° and 9° W. The 29,434 square kilometers in the region take the form of a rough square bounded by the Bay of Biscay (Sea of Cantabria) to the north, the Atlantic Ocean to the west, the River Miño separating Galicia from Portugal to the south, and the mountain ranges of León and Asturias to the east. The coasts of Galicia are indented with drowned estuaries (*rías*). About 80 percent of the region lies above 300 meters, with the highest ranges (some with peaks over 1,800

See also

Castilian

Nearly everyone owns land in Galicia, but it is precious little; "Galicians never use handkerchiefs; they till them" is a frequent assertion.

meters) forming an effective eastern barrier between Galicia and the rest of Spain.

Galicia has a mild climate, averaging between 7.2° and 18.9° C through the year. Frequent rain, drizzle (*calabobos*), and heavy mists (*brétemas*) contribute to the 76 to 203 centimeters of rain that falls over an average of 150 days per year.

Galicia's isolation has led to the region's being one of the few in Europe where the original postglacial mammalian fauna remain virtually intact. Of the 500–600 wolves left in Iberia today, for example, most are in Galicia.

DEMOGRAPHY. In 1980 the population of Galicia was estimated at approximately 3 million inhabitants (about 424 per square kilometer), with a growth rate of less than 1 percent per year. The urban areas account for about 30 percent of the total population. Galicia is the sixth most populated of the fourteen regions of Spain, with about 7.5 percent of the country's inhabitants.

LINGUISTIC AFFILIATION. Nearly every Galician uses Castilian Spanish, but about 80 percent of the population also speaks Galician (*galego*), which, along with Castilian, is taught in the grade schools and studied in the university. The use of Galician has rapidly expanded since the region became autonomous. Historically, Galician was one of the principal and mutually comprehensible Hispano-Romance dialects spoken in the northern third of the Iberian Peninsula. When the Christian reconquest of Spain began (by the tenth century), speakers of each of these dialects gradually moved south. The central Castilian-dominated swath gradually grew broader, cutting off the southward expansion of the dialects of Leonese, Navarro-Aragonese, and Catalan, with a substantial strip in the west populated by speakers of Galician. In the twelfth and thirteenth century, Portugal began to take shape and finally was separated from Galicia at the River Miño, leaving the two languages to develop independently.

History and Cultural Relations

The Iberians migrated to Spain in the third millennium B.C.E., probably from the eastern Mediterranean, likely encountering the Basques in the peninsula. They lived in small tribal groups, isolated from one another by geography, and each with a distinct regional and political identity. When the Celts crossed the Pyrenees into Spain (sixth century B.C.E.), their cultural influence, which included gender equality, ultimately triumphed. Augustus romanized the Iberians in 19 B.C.E., cutting up the peninsula into a series of

provinces. Galicia as a kingdom was founded by the Germanic Suevi in 409 after the Visigoths drove them into the peninsula. The Visigoths defeated the Suevi in 585. Early in the eighth century armies from North Africa began their invasion of Spain, initiating the Moorish epoch, which lasted until 1492 when Ferdinand and Isabella triumphed over Boabdil at Granada. Early in this period, the shrine of Saint James was established at Santiago de Compostela (813), with Saint James subsequently becoming the symbolic commander and Spain's patron saint in the reconquest struggle after the battle of Clavijo (844). Pilgrims flocked to the shrine from throughout Europe, bringing the region into contact with the Christendom of France and Italy for the first time. In the fifteenth century Ferdinand and Isabella unified Spain, and Galicia began to be considered an underprivileged, conservative province, remote from the Castilian center to the south; even the fact that Francisco Franco was born in Galicia and returned for frequent visits did notably little to change this attitude. A strong sense of autonomy now pervades the region, however, and Galicia is developing considerable self-esteem through its language, industry, and rising tourist business.

Settlements

Outside the major cities, most of Galicia's population is spread in some 29,000 hamlets and tiny settlements called *aldeas* with an average population of 80 people. The cultural focus of each village is the church, which draws upon perhaps a dozen family groups that work together and are often related. In the mountain villages, a small oval house with a thatched roof (*choza* or *palloza gallega*) can still be seen occasionally. In the aldeas, the houses are generally single-family dwellings made up of slabs of gray granite hewn from Galician bedrock. The animals frequently live on the ground floor or in an adjoining enclosure. Almost all village houses have their own *hórreo*, a rodent-proof granary (built on stilts) for storing maize and potatoes. In the cities, the older buildings are constructed of granite, while the new multistoried apartment houses are typically constructed of poured concrete or bricks faced with stone or concrete.

Economy

SUBSISTENCE AND COMMERCIAL ACTIVITIES. Old shipbuilding, tanning, and sawmill industries have declined, leaving fishing and agricultural crops to dominate the Galician economy.

The small farms (*minifundios*) produce maize, potatoes, turnips, cabbages, small green peppers, apples, pears, and grapes. Although tractors are common, plowing on some farms is still done with a single blade or pointed prod pulled by oxen; heavy wooden-wheeled carts (*carros chiriones*, "screeching carts") are still seen. Harvesting is frequently by hand. A textile industry has produced income in the region, as have petrochemical and automobile factories. Tungsten, tin, zinc, and antimony are mined. Tourism is also growing, with the beaches of the various estuaries on the Atlantic coast (the Rías Atlas and Rías Bajas) being particularly attractive.

Emigration is the traditional way of alleviating land pressure and keeping the region's problems within manageable proportions; these days, however, greater prosperity is causing fewer than an estimated 10,000 per year to leave for Latin America and Europe, compared with the 230,000 who emigrated to Latin America between 1911 and 1915. In Buenos Aires, so many Galicians have immigrated that all people who have immigrated from Spain in the last century are called *gallegos*. There are Galician communities in all the big towns of Spain, France, Germany, and Switzerland. The Galicians' capacity for hard work is matched only by their ability to save. The strategy is to save as quickly as possible for a rapid return to Galicia. Some of the savings brought back by migrants go into land, but much more is invested in houses and in food and drink businesses.

TRADE. Small stores, café-bars, street vendors, and open-air markets are found throughout Galicia. Homegrown produce or other homemade products are brought (usually by women and not infrequently on their heads) to the markets to sell or to supply other merchants.

DIVISION OF LABOR. In 1980, 46 percent of the region's labor force (1,175,400 persons) was engaged in agriculture, 16.3 percent in industry, 8 percent in construction, and 27.1 percent in services; 2.6 percent of the available labor force was unemployed.

In Galicia, more than 75 percent of the women work for pay, generally sharing the same jobs as the men. Both women and men work the farms, tend the animals, sell fish, run café-bars and markets, and serve as heads of households. The traditional home tasks are also assigned to women, but men will tend babies and do housework.

LAND TENURE. Nearly everyone owns land in Galicia, but it is precious little; most plots are from 1 to 2.5 hectares. There are few examples of

Galicians

GALICIAN HORREO

A Galician granary, or horreo. Small farms produce crops such as maize, potatoes, turnips, and apples. Harvesting is often done by hand. Galicia, Spain. (Nik Wheeler/Corbis)

large landholding such as in the south. "Galicians never use handkerchiefs; they till them" is a frequent assertion, reflecting the scarcity and dimensions of the landholdings.

Kinship, Marriage, and Family

KIN GROUPS AND DESCENT. Galician descent is generally patrilineal, with children taking their father's family name and appending their mother's. The wife, however, does not add her husband's name to her own, retaining her own name throughout her life. She may choose to use her husband's name after his death so that she is known as "[her name], widow of [husband's name]."

KINSHIP TERMINOLOGY. The Galician kinship system is much like that found in the United States. Cousins are distinguished from brothers and sisters, but all cousins are placed in the same category. Aunts and uncles are distinguished from parents and labeled separately according to gender. No other relatives are referred to by the same terms used for members of the nuclear family.

MARRIAGE AND FAMILY. Galician marriages are monogamous, and there is considerable freedom in the choice of marriage partners, although social pressures function to keep the economic classes fairly rigid. The nuclear family is usual. Only 10 percent of households could be termed extended or joint. As long as both elderly parents are alive, they tend to stay in their homes. After a spouse dies, the widower may move to the home of a married child, but widows who are accustomed to the daily tasks of running a household generally try to reside alone rather than rely on their children. Also, among adults in Galicia with older children, it is rare to find a couple without most of their children residing either permanently or temporarily away from the village.

INHERITANCE.   The surviving spouse is the automatic heir to the deceased spouse's property, and all children regardless of gender, age, or place of residence divide the property of both parents equally. Because longevity is a feature of Galician society, late inheritance of property forces most children, even those with wealthy parents, to be on their own for long periods. Young women may remain at home to care for their aged parents in return for some advantage when the property is divided.

Sociopolitical Organization

After forty years under the dictatorship of Francisco Franco (1936–1975), Spain is now a parliamentary monarchy with a king as the head of state and a president as head of the government.

POLITICAL ORGANIZATION.   Galicia is an autonomous region of Spain and is governed by the Xunta de Galicia (the Galician Assembly). The region is divided into four provinces (La Coruña, Lugo, Orense, and Pontevedra), each with its own governing body. There are further administrative divisions for the municipalities and the hamlets. In 1992, Spain will be admitted to full partnership in the European Community (EC).

Religion and Expressive Culture

RELIGIOUS BELIEFS AND PRACTICES.   Roman Catholicism is overwhelmingly the central religious force in Galician society, although men tend to be less obviously religious than women. Catholic churches, cathedrals, monasteries, and various types of shrines, including distinctive high stone crosses (*cruceiros*), dot the landscape. Mormons and Jehovah's Witnesses are actively proselytizing in the region, but they are gaining only a smattering of converts.

The beliefs of most Galicians are infused with a vigorous strain of supernaturalism. Ceremonies connected with these beliefs are frequently celebrated simultaneously with traditional Catholic ceremonies. Fig-symbol amulets, scapulars, and objects to ward off the evil eye, for example, are often sold close to the church where a religious rite is being celebrated. Various types of people are commonly believed to have supernatural powers: *meigas* (who provide love and curing potions), *barajeras* (who cast out evil and foretell the future), and *brujas* (who are believed to cause harm). A common saying is *Eu non creo nas bruxas, ¡pero habel-as hainas!*, or "I don't believe in brujas, but they exist!"

A considerable number of sites in Galicia have profound religious significance. For example, the Galicians, other Spaniards, and a vast number of Europeans consider Santiago de Compostela, in the La Coruña Province, to be one of the great spiritual centers of the world, ranking equally with Jerusalem and Rome. Early in the Christian reconquest, the bones of Saint James were believed to be uncovered in the area (in 813). Saint James (Santiago) subsequently was ensconced as the rallying figure in the ultimately successful wars against the Moors. A vast number of faith-promoting Saint James stories permeate the beliefs of Galicia, and the symbols of Saint James (cockle shells and the distinctive cross of Saint James) are ubiquitous.

CEREMONIES.   Saint's day celebrations, popular religious excursions (*romerías*), night festivals on the eve of a religious festival (*verbenas*), and the whole traditional calendar of Catholic observances provide rhythm to the lives of Galicians. A considerable number of nonreligious observances are threaded through the calendar of observances—for example, the "Disembarking of the Vikings" at Catoira, which vigorously reenacts the attack of a marauding Viking fleet in the tenth century.

Throughout Galicia a great number of varying charms, incantations, rites, and sympathetic actions are performed at each step in the life cycle.

MEDICINE.   In case of illness, the usual Galician pattern is to consult a medical doctor first. If the illness does not subside, then the person doubts that the illness is medical and may consult a healer (*curandero* or *curandera*) who can cure with herbs or other nonmedical remedies.

ARTS AND CRAFTS.   Galicia is famous for its folk dance groups, which are accompanied by the skirl of Galician bagpipes (*gaitas*). Various vocal and instrumental groups (some even cranking medieval hurdy-gurdies) sing and play popular Galician music. Thriving groups of artisans produce works in silver and gold, ceramics, fine porcelain, jet (*azabache*), lace, wood, and stone.

Galician literature today maintains characteristics developed during the Middle Ages; it is largely a literature of lyrical poetry. Notable Galician writers include Rosalía de Castro, who expressed the deep nostalgia (*morriña*) of nineteenth-century emigrants; Manuel Curros Enríquez, whose poems exalt the regionalist spirit of Galicia; and Valle-Inclán, noted for his elegant poetic prose.

REGIONAL FOODS. Galician restaurateurs command considerable respect in Spain. The estuaries produce shellfish of all kinds, from the famous cockleshells of Saint James to lobsters, mussels, shrimps, oysters, clams, and crabs. *Caldo gallego* is a broth of turnips, cabbage or greens, and white beans. At most bars and at all sorts of outdoor celebrations, there are roast sardines, octopus, squid, little green peppers (the famous *pimientos de Padrón*), and *churros* (doughnutlike tubes of fried pastry). Many of the cheeses are traditionally in the shape of breasts (called *tetillas*). A strong liquor called *aguardiente* or *orujo* is served burned (*queimada*) with lemon peel and sugar.

Bibliography

Buechler, Hans, and J.-M. Buechler (1981). *Carmen: The Autobiography of a Spanish Galician Woman*. Cambridge, Mass.: Schenkman.

Fraguas, Antonio (1988). *Romarías e Santuarios*. Vigo: Galaxia.

Lisón Tolosana, Carmelo (1971). *Antropología cultural de Galicia*. Madrid: Akal/Universitaria.

Mariño Ferro, Xosé Ramón (1985). *Cultura popular*. Santiago de Compostela: Museo do Pobo Galego.

—EUGENE VALENTINE AND KRISTIN B. VALENTINE

GERMANS

Ethonym: Alemanes (Spanish), Allemands (French), Deutschen (German)

Orientation

IDENTIFICATION. The Germans are a cultural group united by a common language and a common political heritage. In the past, the term "German" could rightly be applied to many of those now regarded as Dutch, Swiss, or Austrian. These peoples developed separate identities as their lands split politically from a broader German area. Other regional identities—for example, Bavarian, Prussian, Saxon, and Swabian—were largely subordinated to a common German identity in the course of a nationalist movement that began during the Napoleonic Wars and led to the founding of the German Reich in 1871. Today's Germans include especially the citizens of the newly reunited Federal Republic of Germany, though enclaves of ethnic Germans persist in parts of eastern Europe, Ukraine, and Russia.

LOCATION. Germany fits roughly between 47° and 55° N and 6° and 15° E. Prior to World War II, however, Germany included other surrounding territories and extended eastward into what is now Poland and the western regions of the former Soviet Union. The German terrain rises from the northern coastal plain to the Bavarian Alps in the south. The Rhine, Weser, Elbe, and Oder rivers run toward the north or northwest, emptying into the North and Baltic seas and draining northern, central, and southwestern Germany. The Danube has its source in the Black Forest and then runs eastward, draining southern Germany and emptying eventually into the Black Sea. Germany has a temperate seasonal climate with moderate to heavy rainfall.

DEMOGRAPHY. Following normal modern European patterns, Germany's population rose from about 25 million in 1815 to 67 million in 1914, despite the loss of more than 3 million emigrants. The population continued to rise in the first half of this century, though this trend was hindered by heavy losses in the two world wars. When World War II ended, approximately 7 million ethnic Germans left Eastern Europe and resettled in Germany. An additional 3 million East Germans fled to West Germany before the construction of the Berlin Wall in 1961. The current population of Germany is estimated to be about 78,000,000, with 61,500,000 residing in the western Länder, or federal states, and 16,500,000 in the new states of former East Germany. In 1986 West Germany's growth rate was slightly negative and East Germany's nearly zero. The population is, however, augmented by more than 4.5 million foreign workers and a new wave of immigrants from eastern Europe. Since antiquity, Germany's largest settlements have been located along the river valleys and the northern coast. Today, three-quarters of the population occupies urban settlements in these areas. Nevertheless, less than half of about 100 independently administered cities in Germany have a population of more than 200,000, and only three cities—Berlin, Hamburg, and Munich—have more than a million inhabitants.

LINGUISTIC AFFILIATION. German belongs to the Germanic Branch of the Indo-European Family of languages. The major German dialect groups are High and Low German, the languages of the southern highlands and the northern lowlands, respectively. Low German dialects, in many

The Germans are a cultural group united by a common language and a common political heritage.

See also

Austrians; Swiss, German

*Postwar themes in
German literature
and cinema include
especially the Nazi
past, the Westernized
or Socialist present,
and resulting
problems of German
identity.*

ways similar to Dutch, were spoken around the mouth of the Rhine and on the northern coast but are now less widespread. High German dialects may be divided into Middle and Upper categories, which, again, correspond to geographic regions. The modern standard is descended largely from East Middle High German and was shaped in part by the Lutheran Bible and by the language of officialdom in the emerging bureaucracies of the early modern period. The standard was firmly established with political unification in the late nineteenth century, and twentieth-century migrations have further contributed to dialect leveling. Nevertheless, local and regional dialects have survived and in some places have reasserted themselves.

History and Cultural Relations

German-speaking peoples first entered the historical record when tribal groups migrating southward reached the Roman frontiers along the Rhine and the Danube. Some crossed over and merged with southern or western European populations; others stayed behind to farm or to build on the outposts abandoned by Rome. In the Middle Ages, the area now known as Germany presented a variegated sociogeographic landscape, characterized by both peasant agriculture and riverine and coastal commerce. Rival royal and noble houses sought to establish administrative bases through expanding their domains, controlling clerical appointments, or, by the thirteenth century, colonizing the eastern marches. As the struggles among emperors, popes, and nobles continued, many cities enjoyed political autonomy and prosperity. Urban manufacture and commerce suffered during the religious wars, when the German princes tried to co-opt the church administration and consolidate their territories. Conflicts beginning with the Protestant Reformation culminated in the Thirty Years' War, which devastated central Europe economically and fragmented it politically. By 1648 Germany was divided into more than 300 small principalities. France's revolutionary army struck the first blow for centralization by bringing western Germany under direct French rule and organizing the rest of Germany into a handful of tributary states. On the eve of Napoleon's defeat, Germany spawned a nationalist movement that in many ways anticipated similar movements in eastern Europe and the third world. Because of its famous army and the industrial strength of its newly acquired Rhine Province, Prussia prevailed over Austria in the struggle for intra-German hege-

mony. Germany was united in 1871 under a partially liberalized but still largely autocratic Prussian regime. Germany's bid for global hegemony failed in World War I and again under Hitler in World War II. In 1949 the zones occupied by the French, British, and Americans combined to form the Federal Republic of Germany (West Germany), and later that same year the Soviet zone became the German Democratic Republic (East Germany). The two German states persisted as Western and Soviet client states until 1989, when reform in the Soviet Union contributed to the fall of the East German regime. The new German currency union was formed on 1 July 1990, and political unification followed on 3 October.

Economy

INDUSTRY AND TRADE. The tradition of urban handicrafts and riverine commerce, large and readily available coal deposits, and economic and political union all contributed to the dramatically successful industrialization of the Rhine-Ruhr region and the Elbe River valley in the latter half of the nineteenth century. Following World War II, West Germany again emerged as one of the strongest economies of the West European industrial core. East Germany's socialist economy was successful by Eastern bloc standards, but it crumbled when it was incorporated into the West German market. In the last decade of the twentieth century, the new federal states of the east face wholesale rebuilding. Germans describe their economy as a "social market," where the welfare state ameliorates the extreme effects of competitive private enterprise. Automobiles, aircraft, chemicals, machine tools, and optical and electronic equipment are among the most important products of Germany's export-oriented economy. German industry is distinguished by long-range planning; cooperation between private enterprise, government, banks, and unions; and a highly skilled work force. In the postwar period, West Germany has traded primarily with European Community partners and NATO allies, but the reunited Germany is renewing traditional trade relationships with eastern Europe and the peoples of the former Soviet Union.

AGRICULTURE AND LAND TENURE. In Germany, the reform of feudal land tenure was not completed until the late nineteenth century. East of the Elbe, where Prussian nobles had managed large estates, reform resulted in the creation of a landless rural proletariat. Peasants of the highly subdivided southwest were often forced to migrate either to the cities or overseas, though some became owners of small farms. The free northern peasantry was most successful in making the transition from feudal obligations to private ownership, though here too expropriation and consolidation were common. The Nazis espoused an agrarian ideology, but the trend toward industrialization and rural depopulation continued. The southwestern and northern zones now lie in former West Germany, where 5 percent of the work force is employed on privately owned farms averaging just 16 hectares. Under the now defunct East German regime, the Prussian estates were transformed into large-scale, state-run agricultural enterprises, which employed 11 percent of the work force. In both regions, further reduction in agricultural production may be anticipated, since the state subsidies that sustained it have been withdrawn or are under attack.

DIVISION OF LABOR. Germany's work force includes laborers, entrepreneurs, clerical workers and other employees, managers and administrators, and professionals. Class membership is determined partly through education and individual ability and partly through family background. German labor is represented by well-organized and aggressive unions, which, however, often cooperate with capital and the state in long-range economic planning. German women are accorded equality in the workplace de jure, though equal pay, child care, maternity benefits, and abortion are still subjects of debate and shifting legislation.

Kinship, Marriage, and Family

KINSHIP. The Germans trace descent bilaterally and employ an Eskimo kinship terminology. Many of the standard kin terms are recognizable as English cognates, though there is some variation by dialect.

MARRIAGE AND DOMESTIC UNIT. Today's marriages are individualistic "love matches" but similarities in class, ethnicity, and religious affiliation are often considerations in these matches. The household is based on the nuclear family, which joins occasionally with members of a wider kindred in the course of the annual festive cycle. Divorce is a legally codified dissolution of marriage; Germans resort to divorce in about three out of ten cases. Since recent legislation protects the rights of unwed mothers and their offspring, many Germans are forgoing or postponing marriage: in 1987 an estimated 40 percent of West German couples under 35 were unwed.

INHERITANCE. Rights to private property and legal inheritance, guaranteed by the Basic Law of the Federal Republic of Germany, are typically exercised within the nuclear family or the wider kindred. Now that East Germany is subject to West German law, the courts will be busy resolving the conflicting claims to property resulting from a half-century of expropriation under the Nazi and Socialist party regimes.

SOCIALIZATION. Germany's school system differs from state to state, but in most cases students are split between vocational and university preparatory tracks. The vocational track includes nine years of school and further part-time vocational training, with a paid apprenticeship. The university preparatory track requires attendance at the humanistic *Gymnasium* and successful completion of the *Abitur*, a university entrance examination. Germany has a highly differentiated system of higher education, including sixty-two universities and technical colleges in former West Germany and fifty-four in former East Germany.

Sociopolitical Organization

SOCIAL ORGANIZATION. Modern German voluntary associations, or *Vereine*, first appeared among the bourgeoisie during the Enlightenment but spread throughout the population as laws governing free assembly in the various German states were liberalized in the course of the nineteenth century. Prior to 1848, voluntary associations were typically both nationalist and republican in orientation. After the founding of the Reich, they split into politically opposed bourgeois, Catholic, and working-class blocs. Under the Third Reich, Germany's dense network of voluntary associations was co-opted by the Nazi party. East Germany's Socialist Unity party pursued a similar strategy but, again, with less success. The Basic Law of the Federal Republic of Germany guarantees German citizens the right to free assembly, and voluntary associations are correspondingly numerous. Today, club life helps shape the local festive calendar and is an important constituent of local identities and status relations. Many local associations belong to umbrella organizations and thus help integrate members into social networks beyond the community.

POLITICAL ORGANIZATION. The Federal Republic of Germany has succeeded in realizing many of the liberal reforms first proposed at the Frankfurt Parliament of 1848 and first attempted during the Weimar Republic (1919–1933). Germany is now a parliamentary democracy, where public authority is divided among federal, state, and local governments. In federal elections held every four years, all citizens who are 18 or older are entitled to cast votes for candidates and parties, which form the *Bundestag*, or parliament, on the basis of vote distribution. The majority party or coalition then elects the head of the government. Similarly, states and local communities elect parliaments or councils and executives to govern in their constitutionally guaranteed spheres. Each state government also appoints three to five representatives to serve on the *Bundesrat*, or federal council, an upper house that must approve all legislation affecting the states. Germany's most important political parties are: the Christian Democratic Union and its corresponding Bavarian party, the Christian Social Union; the Social Democratic party; the Free Democratic party; the Greens; and the Party of Democratic Socialism, the successor to the East German Socialist Unity party. In the latter 1980s, the right-wing Republican party gained some seats in local and regional councils, but after the fall of the East German regime their constituency dwindled. The first free all-German national election since 1932 was held on 2 December 1990 and resulted in the confirmation of the ruling Christian Democratic/Free Democratic coalition.

Germany's free press produces hundreds of daily newspapers with a total circulation of 25 to 30 million. Post, telephone, and telegraph facilities are federally owned and managed. Radio and television stations are "corporations under public law," which are run by autonomous bodies and monitored by political parties in proportion to their representation in state and federal parliaments. These measures are intended to prevent the media from being manipulated for propaganda purposes, as they were by the Nazis and, with somewhat less success, by the former East German government. As of 1973, East Germans had legal access to West German television broadcasts, which contributed in no small measure to undermining the legitimacy of the Socialist regime.

SOCIAL CONTROL. It has often been noted that German society still retains a small-town ethos, which arose in the early modern period under conditions of political and economic particularism. Indeed, many Germans adhere to standards of *Bürgerlichkeit*, or civic morality, that lend a certain neatness and formality to behavior in everyday life. Public standards are further en-

RELIGION AND EXPRESSIVE CULTURE

Religious Beliefs and practices

The Germans have been predominantly Christian since the early Middle Ages. A large German-Jewish minority was driven out or destroyed by the Nazi regime between 1933 and 1945; it is represented today by a returning community of perhaps 100,000. Approximately 56 percent of all Germans are Protestant and 37 percent Roman Catholic. Protestant populations are concentrated in the northern, central, and eastern regions, and Catholics predominate in the south and in the Rhineland. Since the eighteenth century many Germans have opted for secular alternatives to religion, including rationalism, romanticism, nationalism, socialism, and, most recently, consumerism or environmentalism.

Ceremonies

Germany's festive calendar includes a cycle of Christian holidays, which are observed especially but not exclusively by Catholics. In October, many towns celebrate harvest festivals that combine regional traditions with modern tourist attractions. Carnival, or *Fastnacht*, is celebrated throughout Germany but especially in the Rhineland and the south. The carnival season begins on 11 November and ends on Mardi Gras with parades and "fools' assemblies" organized by local voluntary associations.

Arts

Germans have made major contributions to all of the typically Western fine arts, especially music. The folk traditions of Germany's various provinces declined with industrialization and urbanization, but some are still maintained as expressions of local patriotism or in connection with the promotion of tourism. A distinctively German cinema had its origins in the Weimar Republic and was revived in West Germany after the war. Postwar themes in German literature and cinema include especially the Nazi past, the Westernized or Socialist present, and resulting problems of German identity.

Medicine

Germans were among the leaders in the development of both Western biomedicine and national health insurance. Biomedical health care in Germany is extensive and high-quality. Alongside biomedicine there is a strong German tradition of naturopathic medicine, including especially water cures at spas of various kinds. Water cures have been opposed by some members of the West German biomedical establishment but are regularly subsidized by statutory West German health insurance agencies.

forced by a strong emphasis on the rule of law. This is, perhaps, in part a legacy of Germany's bureaucratic tradition and in part a response to the criminal activities of the Hitler regime. Today, Germany is regulated by a larger body of legislation than exists in either Britain or France.

Bibliography

Applegate, Celia (1990). *A Nation of Provincials: The German Idea of Heimat.* Berkeley: University of California Press.

Ardagh, John (1987). *Germany and the Germans: An Anatomy of Society Today.* New York: Harper & Row.

Craig, Gordon (1982). *The Germans.* New York: Meridian.

Lowie, Robert H. (1954). *Toward Understanding Germany.* Chicago: University of Chicago Press.

Peukert, Detlev (1987). *Inside Nazi Germany: Conformity, Opposition, and Racism in Everyday Life.* London: B. T. Batsford.

Spindler, George (1973). *Burgbach: Urbanization and Identity in a German Village.* New York: Holt, Rinehart & Winston.

Walker, Mack (1971). *German Home Towns.* Ithaca, N.Y.: Cornell University Press.

—JOHN R. EIDSON

GREEKS

Ethonym: Ellines, Hellenes

Orientation

IDENTIFICATION. Greeks constitute an ethnic group of great longevity, tracing their origins to the first appearance of complex society in southeastern Europe. A common sense of culture, language, and religion signified by the term "Greek" (Hellene) developed in antiquity and has endured, with changes, to the present. Greek identity today emphasizes early Greek civilization, the Christian traditions of the Byzantine Empire, and the concerns of the modern Greek nation established in 1831. Throughout Greek history, members of other groups were periodically assimilated as Greeks, while Greeks themselves migrated in a worldwide diaspora. The ethnic Greeks now residing outside the Hellenic republic equal those within. This article, however, is restricted to the latter.

LOCATION. The southernmost extremity of the Balkan Peninsula, Greece is located between 34° and 41° N and 19° and 29° E. It contains 15,000 kilometers of coastline and over 2,000 is-

lands fanning into the Mediterranean Sea. The total land surface is 131,947 square kilometers, of which 80 percent is hilly or mountainous with only scattered valleys and plains. Nine geographical regions are generally recognized. Macedonia, Epirus, and Thrace form Greece's northern border with Albania, Macedonia (that section of what was Yugoslavia that is now seeking recognition as a separate nation), Bulgaria, and Turkey. The southern mainland includes Thessaly, central Greece, and the Peloponnesos. The Ionian Islands to the west of the mainland, the Aegean Islands (including the Cyclades and Dodecanese) to the east, and Crete to the south constitute the major island regions. The climate varies from Mediterranean to central European with generally hot, dry summers and cool, wet winters.

DEMOGRAPHY. The 1991 Greek census recorded 10,042,956 citizens, of whom 96 percent were ethnic Greeks. There were also small numbers of Jews, Turks, Slavo-Macedonians, Gypsies, Albanians, Pomaks, Armenians, Lebanese, Filipinos, Pakistanis, North Africans, recent refugees from eastern Europe, and transhumant shepherd groups, including Koutsovlachs, Aromani, and Sarakatsani. The national population has increased greatly from its 1831 level of 750,000, because of territorial accretion, the immigration of

GREEK DELICACIES

Greek Easter pastries lie on trays in a kitchen. Easter and Holy Week are the most important of twelve annual Great Feasts. Greek Islands, Greece. (Adam Woolfitt/Corbis)

*Struggle and
competition among
different families is
a major theme of
Greek life. Familial
conflicts emerge over
land, flocks,
political office, and
a variety of local
affairs.*

Greeks from outside Greece, and a rate of natural increase annually averaging 1.5 percent prior to 1900 and 1 percent thereafter. This growth was countered, however, by massive emigration to North America, northern Europe, Australia, and other locations throughout the nineteenth and twentieth centuries. The once sizable Turkish, Bulgarian, and Serbian populations living within current Greek boundaries also fell to minimal levels after several treaties and population exchanges around the time of World War I.

LINGUISTIC AFFILIATION. The primary language of Greece is Greek, an Indo-European language first attested around 1400 B.C. Modern Greek has two major forms: *katharevousa*, a formal, archaizing style devised by Greek nationalist Adamantis Korais in the early nineteenth century; and *dimotiki*, the language of ordinary conversation, which has regional variations. Many Greeks mix these forms according to demands of context and meaning, and the choice of one or the other for schooling and public discourse has been a political issue. Hellenic Orthodox church services are conducted in yet another Greek variant, *koine*, the language of the New Testament. While 97 percent of Greek citizens speak Greek as their primary language, there are small groups who also speak Turkish, Slavo-Macedonian, Albanian, Vlach (a Romanian dialect), Pomak (a Bulgarian dialect), and Romany.

History and Cultural Relations

The ancient origins of the Greek people remain obscure and controversial, particularly as regards the relative importance of conquering invasions, external influence, and indigenous development. Most now agree that by 2000 B.C. Greek speakers inhabited the southern mainland, at the same time that non-Greek Cretans developed Minoan civilization. Mycenaean society, arising in the Peloponnesos around 1600 B.C., spread Greek language and culture to the Aegean Islands, Crete, Cyprus, and the Anatolian coast through both conquest and colonization. By the rise of the classical city-states in the seventh to eighth centuries B.C., Greek identity was firmly in place throughout these regions as well as Greek colonies near the Black Sea, southern Italy, Sicily, and North Africa. The Macedonian kings, Philip II and his son, Alexander the Great, spoke Greek and embraced Greek culture. They conquered and united Greek lands and built an empire stretching to India and Egypt during the fourth century B.C. These Hellenistic kingdoms quickly crumbled, and Greek dominions gradually fell to the Roman

Empire during the first and second centuries B.C. Greeks lived as a conquered but valued cultural group under the Romans. After this empire split in A.D. 330, the eastern half, centered in Constantinople and unified by the new religion of Christianity, quickly evolved into the Byzantine Empire, in which Greeks controlled much of the eastern Mediterranean world for over one thousand years. The Venetian-led Fourth Crusade seized Constantinople in 1204, reducing the Byzantine Empire to a much smaller territory, established Frankish feudal principalities in much of what is now Greece. Both Byzantine and Frankish holdings eventually fell to the advancing Ottoman Empire, which conquered Constantinople in 1453. The Ottoman Turks treated Greeks as a distinct ethnic group, forcing them to pay taxes and often work on Turkish estates but allowing them to keep both identity and religion. Inspired by nationalistic ideals, and supported by England, France, and Russia, the Greek War of Independence (1821–1829) against the Turks produced the modern nation of Greece in 1831. The original nation contained only the southern mainland and some Aegean islands, but it gradually expanded through successive wars and treaties with the Turks and other neighbors. Nevertheless, attempts to gain the predominantly Greek areas of Constantinople, the western coast of Anatolia, and Cyprus were not successful. Compulsory population exchanges after World War I removed most Greeks from the first two areas, as well as most Turks and other non-Greeks from Greece.

Settlements

Greeks have been very mobile throughout their history. Areas of population concentration have shifted, and villages have come and gone with transitions from one period to another. Since establishment of the Greek nation, there has been much movement from upland, interior villages to lowland and coastal ones. Hundreds of new villages have been founded in the process. There has also been increasing migration from all villages to a few large cities. Greece became over 50 percent urbanized in the late 1960s. Metropolitan Athens now houses nearly one-third of the national population. Villages, which now average 500 inhabitants, can be compact clusters around a central square, linear strings along a road, or even sometimes scattered housing dispersed over a region. Market towns, ranging between 1,000 and 10,000 residents, are intermediaries between various regions and such major cities as greater Athens, Thessaloniki, Patras, Iraklion, and Volos.

Economy

SUBSISTENCE AND COMMERCIAL ACTIVITIES. Under the Ottomans, most Greeks were peasants or craftsmen. At the end of this period, however, a few shippers and merchants rose to power and wealth by mediating between the expanding capitalist economies of western Europe and the Ottomans. After independence, Greece entered a fully "marketized" economy from a largely dependent position. Feudal estates were replaced by small family-farming operations. While an elite class continued, their wealth did not foster national economic development. Greece remains at the bottom of European Community economic indicators. Subsistence agriculture of grain, olives, and vines has given way to cash cropping of these and other produce such as cotton, tobacco, and fresh fruits. The difficulties inherent in farming on mountainous terrain have led many to seek urban or foreign employment. By 1990,

less than one-third of the Greek population were farmers.

INDUSTRIAL ARTS. Greece is one of the least industrialized European nations. While carpentry, metalworking, and similar shops exist in all Greek towns, other industry is heavily concentrated in Athens, Thessaloniki, and a few other cities. Work is often organized along family lines, and in 1990, 85 percent of Greek manufacturing units had less than ten employees. The most important industries are food, beverage, and tobacco processing, with textile, clothing, metallurgical, chemical, and shipbuilding operations following.

TRADE. At independence, Greeks exported currants and other produce to northern Europe, importing metal goods, coffee, sugar, grain, and dried fish in return. While trade has since increased greatly, it remains heavily weighted against Greece and toward its current trading partners—Germany, Italy, France, the United States, Japan, and Saudi Arabia. Greece now exports textiles,

SOCIOPOLITICAL ORGANIZATION

Social Organization

Kinship, ritual kinship, local connections, and patronage shape Greek social relations. People operate through networks of known and trusted others, extending their relationships outward through these. Status accrues from a combination of honorable behavior, material wealth, and education. Social stratification varies between city and countryside. In rural areas, large landowners, professionals, and merchants are at the top; farmers, small shopkeepers, and skilled workers in the middle; and landless farm workers at the bottom. In cities, bankers, merchants, shipowners, industrialists, wealthy professionals, and bureaucrats compose the upper stratum; executives, civil servants, shopkeepers, office workers, and skilled workers the middle; and unskilled workers the bottom. In both cases, the middle class is the majority, and there is considerable opportunity for upward social mobility.

Political Organization

The modern Greek state, initially established as a monarchy guided by northern European

nations, has emerged as a republic with a unicameral legislature headed by a prime minister as head of government and a president as ceremonial head of state. Public officials are elected by universal adult suffrage. For the last two decades, two main political parties have alternated control of the government: the conservative Nea Dimokratia party, and the Socialist PASOK party. The political system is highly centralized, with considerable power residing in national ministries and offices. The nation contains approximately 50 *nomoi* (districts), each divided into eparchies (provinces), *demoi* (municipalities), and *koinotites* (communities). Local officials, elected on the basis of patronage and personality as well as political party, oversee regional affairs.

Social Control

Struggle and competition among different families is a major theme of Greek life. Familial conflicts emerge over land, flocks, political office, and a variety of local affairs. Insults, ridicule, feuds, and even theft sometimes result. The formal legal system is based on codified Roman civil law, with a

network of civil, criminal, and administrative courts. Towns have a corps of city police, while rural regions have a gendarmerie modeled on the French system.

Conflict

Greece has a standing army and universal male conscription. Turkey is perceived as the greatest threat to national security, and the Turkish occupation of Cyprus since 1974 has caused considerable regional tension. Greece's relations with its northern neighbors, stable for some time, have recently become more tenuous as the Eastern bloc dissolves into separate ethnically based nationalities and the boundaries established after World War I are called into question. On a broader level, Greece's strategic location involves it in various international struggles. A member of NATO since 1952, Greece generally has been aligned with the West.

tobacco, produce, ores, cement, and chemicals while importing food, oil, cars, electronic items, and other consumer goods. Partially offsetting this unfavorable balance are receipts from shipping and tourism and remittances from Greeks abroad. Greece initiated membership in the European Community in 1962, becoming a full member in 1981.

DIVISION OF LABOR. Despite the importance of women's productive work in farming, household maintenance, and familial businesses, wage labor outside the family has been male-dominated until recently. At present, many Greek women work for wages only until they marry, and only 30 percent of wage earners are women. Of the total labor force in 1990, less than 29 percent were in agriculture, about 30 percent in manufacturing, and the rest in the service sector. Emigration to find work abroad has generally kept Greek unemployment rates under 5 percent.

LAND TENURE. At independence, prime agricultural lands were controlled by Turkish (and a few Greek) overlords and by Hellenic Orthodox monasteries. The new government established a series of land reforms, whereby large estates were distributed to poor and landless peasants during the nineteenth century. The practice of bilateral partible inheritance has since led to considerable farm fragmentation, whereby familial holdings average 3 hectares scattered in several different plots.

Kinship

KIN GROUPS AND DESCENT. The relatives who share a household are a basic unit of economic cooperation and collective identity. Extending outward from the household, loose networks of both consanguineal and affinal kin provide social support. This bilateral kindred is often referred to as a *soi*, although this term has an agnatic bias in certain regions. Marriage connects family lines, as does ritual kinship. Those chosen as wedding sponsors or godparents stand in a special relationship to the entire kindred.

KINSHIP TERMINOLOGY. Greek terminology follows a cognatic (or Eskimo) pattern. The gender of cousins is denoted by different endings, and in some regions more distant cousins are distinguished from first cousins. There also exist special terms for men married to two sisters and women married to two brothers. The terms for bride and groom broadly refer to people married by various members of one's family.

Marriage and Family

MARRIAGE. Greeks exhibit higher marriage and lower divorce rates than northern Europeans.

Marriage is monogamous, and it is forbidden between first cousins by the Hellenic Orthodox Church. Civil marriage outside the church has only recently been allowed. Divorce is permitted by both law and religion, and, since 1982, it can be granted through common consent. Marriages were commonly arranged by parents until the last few decades. Both families take an active interest in the groom's potential inheritance and the bride's dowry. Men and women generally marry in their mid- to late twenties. Postmarital residence is normally neolocal with respect to the actual house or apartment, although some couples reside temporarily with either the bride's or groom's parents. With respect to the village or neighborhood where a new rural couple resides, however, postmarital residence tends toward virilocality on the mainland and uxorilocality in the islands. The urban pattern is more complex, although much uxorilocality occurs in Athens.

DOMESTIC UNIT. The nuclear family household is statistically the most common, although stem families and other combinations of close kin also form households, as a result of economic need, recent migration, and variations during the life cycle. Elderly parents often reside with an adult child toward the end of their lives. House or apartment ownership is a major familial goal, and considerable resources are directed toward this. Greece ranks at the top of the European Community in per capita construction of dwellings.

INHERITANCE. By both custom and law, all children inherit equally from their parents. Daughters generally receive their share as dowry when they marry, and sons receive theirs when the parents retire or die. Dowries consist of land, houses, livestock, money, a trousseau, furnishings, and, more recently, apartments, household appliances, education, and a car. Significant dowry inflation has occurred during the last few decades, a circumstance favoring female inheritance over male. A 1983 law correspondingly limited the use of the dowry. Whether called a wedding gift or dowry, however, the practice of providing daughters with much of their inheritance at marriage continues.

SOCIALIZATION. Parents assume primary responsibility for raising children, assisted by many members of the kindred. Godparents also look after a child's material and spiritual welfare. Most children are minimally disciplined during early childhood; later they are actively trained into their proper roles through example, admonition, teasing, and comforting designed to teach such traits as wariness, cleverness, family loyalty, verbal proficiency, and honorable behavior. Nine years of formal education are both free and compulsory. A full 82 percent of Greek children complete twelve years of secondary education, and another 17 percent attend university.

Religion and Expressive Culture

RELIGIOUS BELIEFS. Over 97 percent of Greece's population belongs to the Hellenic Orthodox church, a branch of Eastern Orthodoxy. Since the Byzantine Empire, and particularly after the schism between eastern and western Christianity in 1054, Eastern Orthodoxy has been part of Greek ethnic identity. Proselytization by other religions is legally forbidden. There are only small numbers of Muslims, Roman Catholics, other Christians, and Jews. The formal theology of Eastern Orthodoxy is often mixed with informal beliefs in fate, the devil, and other supernatural forces.

RELIGIOUS PRACTITIONERS. During the last few centuries, various nationally based Eastern Orthodox churches separated from the patriarch of Constantinople, among them the Hellenic Orthodox church, established in 1833. Each of these fifteen autocephalous churches runs its own affairs, while recognizing the historical and spiritual importance of the patriarch. Except for a few regions, the Hellenic Orthodox church is governed by the Holy Synod convened by the bishop of Athens. The church hierarchy includes bishops of the approximately 90 dioceses, as well as monks and nuns. While these clergy are celibate, priests may marry. Most priests have families, and many continue to practice a trade or farm in addition to performing their religious duties. Members of the local community voluntarily maintain the church building and assist with weekly services.

CEREMONIES. The Sunday liturgy is the most significant weekly ritual of the Hellenic Orthodox church. There are also twelve annual Great Feasts, of which Easter and the Holy Week preceding it are the most important. Other rituals mark various points in the life cycle, particularly birth, marriage, and death. Baptism and confirmation of infants are performed simultaneously, and infants can then receive communion.

ARTS. Displays of ancient and Byzantine art in museums, public archaeological sites, and reproductions permeate the Greek landscape, attracting tourists and symbolizing Greek identity. Contemporary artistic expression draws from folk, religious, and international traditions in varying ways. Weaving, knitting, embroidery, carving, metalworking, and pottery remain active crafts in most regions. Dancing demonstrates individual and group identity and is an integral part of most celebrations. Contemporary composers work with the instruments and motifs of folk music, particularly the more urban bouzouki, as well as the clarinet, *santouri* (dulcimer), violin, lute, and drums. Contemporary literature, film, and theater echo pan-European styles, and Greece counts two Nobel laureates among its modern authors, George Seferis and Odysseus Elytis. Television and cinema, both foreign and domestic, are prevalent and very popular.

MEDICINE. Scientific medicine is well developed and accepted. Hospitals and clinics exist in most towns, and the National Health Service sends doctors to more remote areas. Hospital births have largely replaced the use of midwives. Abortions performed by both doctors and lay practitioners are a major means of birth control and may equal live births in number. The belief that illness stems from emotional, moral, and social causes coexists with the formal medical system. Folk healers, generally women, are sometimes called to use divination, spells, and herbal remedies against both sickness and such forces as the evil eye.

DEATH AND AFTERLIFE.

Death practices follow Hellenic Orthodox ritual modified by other beliefs, regional traditions, and contemporary circumstances. Upon death, a person's soul is thought to leave the body: at first it remains near the house, but gradually it moves farther away, until finally, after a year's time, it reaches God, who pronounces judgment and consigns the soul to paradise or hell. The body is buried within twenty-four hours of death with ceremonies at both house and local church led by the priest and female mourners who sing ritual laments. Important rituals are performed at the grave both forty days and one year after the death. After several years, the bones generally are exhumed from the ground and placed in a community ossuary.

Bibliography

Campbell, John (1964). *Honour, Family, and Patronage: A Study of Institutions and Moral Values of a Greek Mountain Community*. Oxford: Clarendon Press.

Danforth, Loring M. (1989). *Firewalking and Religious Healing: The Anastenaria of Greece and the American Firewalking Movement*. Princeton: Princeton University Press.

Dimen, Muriel, and Ernestine Friedl, eds. (1976). *Regional Variation in Modern Greece and Cyprus: Toward*

Over 97 percent of Greece's population belongs to the Hellenic Orthodox church, a branch of Eastern Orthodoxy.

a Perspective on the Ethnography of Greece. New York: Annals of the New York Academy of Science.

Friedl, Ernestine (1962). *Vasilika: A Village in Modern Greece*. New York: Holt, Rinehart & Winston.

Herzfeld, Michael (1985). *The Poetics of Manhood: Contest and Identity in a Cretan Mountain Village*. Princeton: Princeton University Press.

Hirschon, Renee (1989). *Heirs of the Greek Catastrophe: The Social Life of Asia Minor Refugees in Piraeus*. Oxford: Clarendon Press.

—SUSAN BUCK SUTTON

HIGHLAND SCOTS

Ethonym: Celts, Celtic, Highlander, Scots, Scottish, and sometimes Scotch, West coast islanders sometimes refer to themselves and others by island names, such as a Lewis man, a Barra woman.

Middle English "Scottes," Old English "Scottas," Late Latin "Scotus" are references to Gaelic people from northern Ireland who settled in Scotland about A.D. 500.

Orientation

IDENTIFICATION AND LOCATION. The Highlands of Scotland include the lands north of a line from the town of Inverness on the northeast running south and west to a point 56° N and 5° W in Scotland, encompassing the shires of Caithness, Sutherland, Ross and Cromarty, Inverness, and Argyll, as well as the islands making up the Inner and Outer Hebrides. Geographically, this area is characterized by rolling rock-faced hills and scattered lakes and rivers, interspersed with land covered by a thin layer of peaty soil. Temperatures along the coasts are fairly consistent (4.4° to 13° C) with colder temperatures inland. In mid-June, daylight may extend to midnight; in mid-December, there is daylight for only a few hours.

DEMOGRAPHY. The 1981 census reported a population of 200,000, an increase of 14.3 percent over the previous decade. There was also a slight increase in population from 1951 to 1971. These figures indicate a change in what had been a steady decline in population beginning in the mid-1700s. These increases are the result of gains in the number of people in the urban and burgh populations, which have offset losses in rural areas.

LINGUISTIC AFFILIATION. Historically, the early settlers spoke Gaelic. English has been the official language since 1754, but there remain some local dialect variations of Gaelic spoken in a few areas of the west coast, Argyll, Sutherland, Skye, and the Western Isles. Recent attempts to renew interest in written and spoken Gaelic have been undertaken, including Gaelic programming on BBC-Scotland.

History and Cultural Relations

The division of Scotland into two cultural areas, the Highlands and the Lowlands, can be traced to the works of early writers who romanticized rural life in northern Scotland. Anthropological research, which began in the 1950s, accepted this distinction, and most of the ethnographic data have been collected in small rural communities.

The history of the Highlands has been characterized by a number of events that have led to the present-day conditions. There has been a steady deforestation of the Highlands since 1700. The clan system was broken up following the 1715 and 1745 conflicts with England. An increase in population, coupled with declining resources, placed great hardships on the people throughout the eighteenth century. The nineteenth century proved even more calamitous. In the Hebrides, for example, the cheviot was introduced in 1810; the kelp industry diminished after 1821; the potato blight occurred in 1828; and the herring disappeared in 1830. The cheviot, a species of sheep able to withstand severe winter conditions, replaced people who were cleared from the land beginning in 1828. The years 1846 and 1847 witnessed the potato famine throughout the Highlands. The policy of the government was that the laird was responsible for the welfare of the people living on estates. In 1883 the Napier Commission redefined the responsibility of government, an action which eventually led to the government's becoming the largest landholder in the Highlands and thus having greater responsibility for the social and economic needs of the residents. The 1886 Crofter Act gave lands to individuals and established the crofting system.

Settlements

Inverness is the largest city, with a population of 57,000 in 1981. On the east coast, the town of Wick is the largest remaining sea-fishing port. On the west coast, Kyle of Lochalsh, Ullapool, Mallaig, and Stornaway have active fish sales and harbor facilities. The settlement pattern in these communities focuses on the harbor. Houses are close together and there are few streets. Another settlement pattern is associated with crofting. Crofting was established with the 1886 Crofting Act. The croft is a 0.4- to 2-hectare parcel of land, on which the crofter has the right to build a

♦ **clan**
A unilineal descent group in which people claim descent from a common ancestor but cannot demonstrate this descent.

See also

English, Gaels, Lowland Scots, Welsh

house. In addition, the crofter enjoys common rights to grazing land and access to peat as a source of fuel. Crofting has largely disappeared, and crofts today are often holiday homes used only during the summer months, with the grazing rights given or rented to others. The majority of crofting townships are located along the coast at an elevation lower than 75 meters. This pattern reflects the dual adaptation of crofting-fishing. Croft houses are usually one-story dwellings arranged in a scattered or lineal pattern with wide separation between dwellings. The crofting community might contain a post office and a small shop. The most recent housing and settlement pattern is attached flats built by the Forestry Commission to house employees engaged in re-forestation efforts.

Economy

WORK CYCLES IN CROFTING. While the Highland Scots have a somewhat mixed economy, most of the literature focuses on crofting and fishing. The intensity of participation in these activities is partially determined by seasonal changes. In crofting communities agricultural work requires interhousehold cooperation for tilling, planting, and peat cutting from March to April. Potatoes and oats are the main agricultural products. Harvesting of oats is in August; potatoes in October. Intense and extended cooperation is required in April or May when lambing takes place.

WORK CYCLES IN FISHING. Fishing has had a differential impact on local economies, either as a food source or wage labor. In the Outer Hebrides, agriculture has never provided enough for self-sufficiency, and incomes have been supplemented by exporting cattle or by fishing. During the summer months, herring is available fresh; for the winter, salt herring is purchased. In the nineteenth and the early twentieth century, crofters worked on foreign-owned boats engaged in commercial herring fishing. The crofter-fishermen, and sometimes women, would follow the migrating herring north to Shetland and then down the east coast to East Anglia in England. In other locations (e.g., Skye) there was very little fishing by crofters. Since World War II some Highland Scots have obtained grants and loans, along with training, to become commercial fishermen. They are found at the major ports on both the east and west coasts. Smaller boats are sometimes used by the crofter-fishermen to catch lobsters, which can provide a cash income. There has been some attempt to develop small fish-processing factories that employ local labor. In general,

since the turn of the twentieth century there has been a decline in the numbers of crofter-fishermen. But in those areas that have specialized in fishing the population has either remained constant or has increased.

TOURISM. Another contribution to local economies is tourism. The clearances of the eighteenth and nineteenth centuries were not only responsible for the depopulation of the Highlands; they also introduced tourism. Deer and salmon, once a source of food, attracted and continue to attract outsiders who are willing to pay for the rights to hunt and fish these animals. The pheasant was even introduced in the middle of the nineteenth century as a sport bird. Hunting and fishing do provide employment for gamekeepers and gillies, along with temporary work for beaters who drive the game to waiting hunters. Poaching of deer, salmon, and sea trout may provide some illegal income for Highlanders. But the major source of tourist income comes during the summer months. These temporary visitors require housing, camping sites, food, and other services that employ local labor and younger workers from other parts of Great Britain. When the migrant labor and the tourists leave at the end of the summer, public entertainments, such as galas and dances, disappear.

INDUSTRIAL ARTS. Knitting, weaving, and craft work for export provide income for some Highlanders. This is largely a home industry.

DIVISION OF LABOR. In crofting communities, male/female distinctions in labor vary by activity and historical time period. In the Hebrides, during the herring days, the most significant group of wage earners were the "herring girls," women who followed the herring fleet, gutting and packing the fish. On Lewis, when the men were away fishing, the croft and home were operated by women. In traditional activities such as peat gathering, men cut the peat blocks while women lifted them into creels and took them to where they were stacked. In Glen Fhraoich, the household was democratic in principle, but two major activity domains existed. The women's domain included the interior of the house, the "green" and the "byre." The area between the house and the byre, which contained the peat pile, henhouse, and clothes-line were also included in her domain. The men's domain encompassed the wider croft area, the fields, peat bogs, and common grazing area. In addition, men were the only wage laborers. This same pattern was observed on Lewis, except that the men's domain included the fishing boat as well. Decisions

Where there are inheritance considerations, Highland Scot marriages are often postponed until the person is over the age of 30 or until after the death of parents.

◆ **United Kingdom**
Also known as Britain or Great Britain, the term refers to England, Scotland, Wales, and Northern Ireland.

involving major purchases were joint unless one partner relinquished his/her authority. In crofting, the household is the economic unit, and regardless of the number of people in the household, there is only one male and one female in charge. Armstrong found that women in Kilmory worked in the fish factory, shops, or in activities associated with tourism. With the decline of the male-dominated fishing industry, the role of women has become increasingly important. On Barra, Valee found decreasing differences in the sexual division of labor. In the study of Kinlochleven, an industrial community, there were fewer and lower-paying jobs for females than for males.

Outside the household, the division of labor is rooted in occupational differences. On Harris, this distinction is sometimes marked by language. Crofters or fishermen speak Gaelic; professionals speak English. In Kintyre there is casual labor including road work, forestry, and seasonal services to tourists. On Islay the major occupations are working in the distillery, limestone quarrying, and farm and estate work. The historical trend has been away from employment in agriculture. For the Highlands, including Orkney and Shetland, between 1871 and 1971 the proportion of agricultural workers declined from 40.5 percent of the work force to 9.9 percent.

DEVELOPMENT. In 1965, the Highlands were designated a development area, and the Highlands and Islands Development Board was established to increase industrial production, alleviate unemployment, and stem out-migration. Grants have been given to maintain crofting and develop local industries. Another development scheme has been the reforestation of certain areas of the Highlands. Although forestry accounts for just over 2 percent of the total employment, it is four times more important to the Highlands than to the United Kingdom as a whole. The oil industry has contributed to some local commercial, service, and construction industries. A major theoretical dispute related to the role of development has emerged in the recent literature on the Highlands. One observation is that the Highlands are simply underdeveloped and have had a history of boom-and-bust cycles since 1700. Others suggest that the Highlands are part of a larger capitalistic economy, and "traditionalism" is an adaptive response to that economy, not some form of vestigial survival from a past state of peasantry. Condry observes that characteristics associated with "traditional" Highlands culture were "modern" practices of the past, and he suggests that

such "modern" practices of the present will become absorbed into future "traditionalism."

Kinship, Marriage, and Family

KIN GROUPS AND DESCENT. While descent is bilateral, there is an emphasis upon patrilateral kin in actual practice. The household is the organizational unit of descent and consists of an unbroken line of males.

KINSHIP TERMINOLOGY. Kinship terminology differs depending on whether English or Gaelic is used. Gaelic has fewer terms than English (e.g., English "uncle" is "mother's brother" in Gaelic). Naming of children usually follows the tradition of "turn and turn about": one spouse chooses a name for one child; the other spouse selects the name of the next child.

MARRIAGE. The selection of spouses depends upon demographic possibilities and economic conditions. Where there are inheritance considerations, marriages are often postponed until the person is over the age of 30 or until after the death of parents. Marriages are sometimes postponed if there is a shortage of housing. If women have migrated from an area, the remaining men may face a shortage of eligible women that necessitates their going outside the community for wives. The overall pattern seems to be a shift from community endogamy to exogamy. There are few reports on nuptial rituals. However, one study reported that wedding gifts tend to be lavish and are publicly displayed. Weddings are usually held in hotels, and guests are transported to the wedding and the postnuptial celebration by bus.

DOMESTIC UNIT. The household is the organizational unit of kinship, and much of crofting life can be understood in reference to problems related to the formation of households. Spinsters, for example, are explained as those reluctant to give away inherited property and the power associated with that property when they marry. Property is a consideration prior to marriage, especially among crofters where extended families may occupy the croft. Under these conditions, the person who moves into the croft of their spouse is subservient to the spouse's parents until they die. In noncroft settings the pattern is neolocality. Regardless of the economic base, the function of marriage is to produce children, and the household is established for this purpose.

FAMILY. The boundaries of "family" are determined by propinquity. Kin living nearby are included as family; those who have moved away, even if they are closer kin, are not. The household

WORKING PEAT

Men in the Highlands of Scotland turn peat to dry, then cut it in March and April. Crofting and fishing are economically important for Highland Scots. Loch Assynt, Scotland. (Macduff Everton/Corbis)

is the smallest unit with which one identifies and through which one is identified. The attributes of the male head of the household characterize all members of that household. Thus, if the male is viewed as clever, all members of the household are viewed as clever. The household consists of the male head, his wife, their children, and, if only daughters, the eldest's husband. Adult siblings have equal rights to remain in the household, but each is expected to contribute to the household. Outside the household, emotions are rarely publicly expressed. However, members of the household engage in intimate joking relationships. The structure of the household can produce conflict. In disputes between wife and mother, husband is expected to support his wife. In households where there is a wife and sister-in-law and the wife is the female head of house by virtue of her marriage, the sister-in-law may feel proprietary rights because she was a member of the household first. Beyond the household are more inclusive identifiers. From less to more inclusive are the household, the croft, the township, the glen (demarcated by a steep hill dividing townships), and the parish.

INHERITANCE. In croft systems, propinquity and sex are determinates of inheritance. The eldest and remaining son usually inherits the croft. When there is only a daughter, her husband becomes the head of the household after his father-in-law dies, and his sons will inherit.

Sociopolitical Organization

SOCIAL ORGANIZATION. The clan was a historical political group with a hereditary chief who controlled lands in common. Consanguine links between members was either demonstrated or stipulated. The clan system was abolished in 1746 after the battle of Culloden. Today the term "clan" is used to designate all the descendants of a particular person, usually cognates.

In general, few distinctions in social status are found. Where a laird is present in a community, he is recognized as a leader. A laird is the traditional landowner. The factor, the man who manages land for the laird, is usually respected because of his role in mediating relationships between laird and crofters. High status or prestige may vary by institutional arrangement. Religious prestige is highest for ministers, missionaries, and lay elders. Cultural prestige is awarded to bards, musicians, and "Gaelic scholars." Political-communal prestige is associated with "good" works such as participation in local committees. In Gaelic-speaking communities this category is usually occupied by "outsiders" whose work is done in English—for example, the schoolteacher(s), the local doctor, and the nurse(s). Prestige distinctions are

Among the Highland Scots, one is expected to carry out business relationships with people one knows and on a personal basis, not with outsiders.

governed by Calvinistic virtues, which, if pursued, will result in high standing in the bank and the community. Display of wealth is considered immoral and there is a marked absence of distinctions in housing, food, and clothing. Vocatively, social distinctions are often reflected in terms of address. Professionals (most often outsiders) are addressed by formal title (e.g., Mr., Mrs., Dr.). Persons from the community are addressed by first name.

POLITICAL ORGANIZATION. The principal units of local government are either the town or the county councils, which are made up of elected and appointed officials.

SOCIAL CONTROL. Leveling seems to be a powerful force in maintaining social similarities. Locals who return to the community with a formal education are often disliked because they showed evidence of a desire to "get ahead." Persons whose peat stacks are not neat will lose prestige. One is expected to carry out business relationships with people one knowns and on a personal basis. Outsiders, and agencies outside the community, are viewed as too far away for meaningful interaction.

Alcoholism rates are high for Scotland in general and the Highlands in particular. The islands of Lewis and Harris have an alcoholism rate six times higher than Scotland. They also have the highest admission rates for involutional melancholia in the United Kingdom. The ethic that one does not publicly criticize others takes precedence over drunken behavior, which often leads to a general disregard for the problem at the local level. Very low rates are reported for delinquency.

CONFLICT. Personal disputes do occur. Darling reports that petty bickering often occurs about precise boundary lines between properties. In households where no will has been left, intense intrafamily conflict may occur.

Religion and Expressive Culture

RELIGIOUS BELIEFS AND PRACTICES. Both Catholicism and Protestantism are practiced in the Highlands. Evangelical Protestantism came in the early nineteenth century. It is associated with the breakup of the clan and opposition to the system of laird-appointed ministers of the Church of Scotland. The Free Church broke from the Established Church (Presbyterian) in 1843 over the issue of land reform. It has become the church of the people and has the largest number of adherents. The Church of Scotland has a smaller number of parishioners and tends to be the church of those with official power. On Lewis, the three

principal churches are the Free Church of Scotland, the Established Church of Scotland, and the Free Presbyterian Church. The Free Church is the largest, but the Free Presbyterian is perhaps the most influential regarding community sentiment. It espouses the Calvinistic doctrine of self-denial, otherworldly orientation, and the notion of the elect. The elect are those chosen by God. The church offers the greatest single social outlet for women, who otherwise lead a life largely restricted to the household. Women are also a majority in both the Free Church and the Church of Scotland.

Catholic and Protestant communities vary in their involvement in social issues. The Protestants are most active. In Protestant communities the rates of alcoholism and mental disorders are highest.

MEDICINE. Medical care is provided by local physicians under the National Health system. For those illnesses or accidents outside the capability of local health-care units, patients are transported to regional or national hospitals. The aging of the population has led to greater demand for Home Help Services and a large percentage of social-service funding is allocated for this government program. Home Help provides services for the aged and infirm who are unable to take care of themselves, and it provides employment for women who might otherwise be ineligible for other support.

DEATH AND AFTERLIFE. In Catholic Barra, when death is imminent, the priest is called to deliver the last rites, after which the close relatives maintain a constant vigil. After death, the responsibilities for the funeral are assumed by the oldest able-bodied male relative. Women usually volunteer to wash and clothe the body. Some social activities may be curtailed for the period between death and the funeral. Usually this includes the neighborhood of the deceased as well as close family members. Pallbearers are male. The eldest responsible male walks in front of the casket; the eldest responsible female follows the casket. Catholics and Protestants are buried in the same cemetery.

Bibliography

Condry, Edward (1983). *Scottish Ethnography*. Association for Scottish Ethnography, Monograph no. 1. Social Science Research Council. New York.

Ennew, J. (1977). "The Impact of Oil-Related Industry on the Outer Hebrides, with Particular Reference to Stornoway, Isle of Lewis." Ph.D. dissertation, University of Cambridge.

Parman, Susan M. (1972). "Sociocultural Change in a Scottish Crofting Township." Ph.D. dissertation, Rice University, Houston, Tex.

Vallee, F. G. (1954). "Social Structure and Organization in a Hebridean Community: A Study of Social Change." Ph.D. dissertation, London School of Economics.

—ED KNIPE

HUGARIANS

HUNGARIANS

Ethnonym: Magyarok, Magyars

Orientation

IDENTIFICATION. Hungarians are the most populous group in the Finno-Ugric Subfamily of the Ural-Altaic people. They are considered to be the descendants of the Magyar tribes that migrated from the Ural mountain region and that settled in the Carpathian Basin during the ninth century. Hungary (Magyarország) was declared a republic (Magyar Köztársaság) in October 1989.

LOCATION. A landlocked country since 1920, Hungary is bounded on the north by the Czech and Slovak Federative Republic, on the east by Ukraine and Romania, on the west by Austria, and on the south-southwest by Slovenia, Croatia, and Yugoslavia. The country occupies 93,030 square kilometers or 1 percent of the total land area of Europe. It is located between 45°48′ and 48°35′ N, and 16°05′ and 22°58′ E. To the east of the Danube River lies the Great Hungarian Plain (Alföld) with some of the finest agricultural land in the country. To the west of the river is Transdanubia (Dunántúl). With the exception of low mountains in the north and rolling hills and low mountains in Transdanubia, most of Hungary is flat: 8 percent of its land area lies less than 200 meters above sea level. The country is located in a transitional zone between maritime and continental climates. Most winters are cold, and the summers are hot. The average annual temperature is 8° C in the north and 12° C in the south.

DEMOGRAPHY. In January of 1989 Hungary's population was estimated at 10,590,000 with an ethnic composition of 97.7 percent Magyar, 0.5 percent German, 0.3 percent Slovak, 0.8 percent Gypsy, 0.3 percent Croatian, and 0.4 percent other. The population density averages 114 persons per square kilometer. More than one-fourth of the population is over the age of retirement, which is 55 for women and 60 for men. With a very low birthrate, one of the highest mortality rates in Europe for mature and middle-aged men, and the highest suicide rate in the world, Hungary's population has been decreasing since 1981. Also, in part because of high outmigration from villages, the rural population has declined since World War II. Now 42 percent of the country's population is concentrated in rural settlements, but many Hungarians commute and work in cities. Urban dwellers make up about 58 percent of the population; 20 percent of the total population resides in Budapest, Hungary's capital city.

LINGUISTIC AFFILIATION. All the neighboring cultures belong to the Indo-European Family of languages, but Hungarian is a member of the eastern division, the Ugric Group of the Finno-Ugric Language Family. Hungarian is an agglutinative language, without prepositions and auxiliary words; it is characterized by an extensive use of suffixes. It is written in Latin script with additional letters and diacritical marks. This language is spoken by about 10 million people within Hungary and an additional 5 million distributed around the world. From the 5 million about 3.5 million live in the surrounding countries (Romania, the Czech and Slovak Federative Republic, Yugoslavia, Austria, and Ukraine), while the remaining 1.5 million settled in Canada, the United States, and elsewhere. Hungarian is distantly related to Estonian and Finnish.

History and Cultural Relations

The tribal Magyars, Uralo-Altaic nomadic people by origin, entered the Carpathian Basin in 896, led by Árpád, their chieftain. After several military campaigns into western Europe and the Balkans, the Hungarian state was established in 1000 under King Stephen I, who accepted Christianity for the country. This conversion was confirmed by Pope Sylvester II, who symbolized with a gift of a crown Hungary's entry into the European feudal community. The Latin alphabet was introduced, but the original runic script (rovásírás) was used for centuries. In the early twelfth century King Coloman "the Scholar" abolished witch hunts and updated all previous laws governing the country's affairs. King Béla III in 1180 ordered record keeping for all official business. A century later, in 1222 King Andreas II issued "the Golden Bull" (Aranybulla), a code that specified both the nation's rights and the king's obligation to uphold the country's laws. A more representative parliamentary system was introduced in 1384. In the thirteenth century Hungary was invaded by Tartars, reducing the population to one-tenth of its

Hungarians have a very low birthrate, one of the highest mortality rates in Europe for mature and middle-aged men, and the highest suicide rate in the world.

SOCIOPOLITICAL ORGANIZATION

Political Organizations

In October 1989, Hungary was declared a republic. There are nineteen counties within the country. Hungary is presently undergoing very rapid and radical changes with the development of parliamentary democracy. Potential changes in political, administrative, and state structures are envisioned.

Social Control

The county and national court systems attempt to resolve conflicts and maintain conformity. At the same time, public opinion, gossip, and tradition are still strong forces in many rural settlements, where often village customs continue to function as a largely self-contained "legal system," independent of the state.

Conflict

The history and cultural relations of the Magyars were laden with internal and external conflicts. Some of these continue into the present. Most explicitly on the domestic scene there is discord between the Magyar and the Gypsy populations, and in the international arena there is considerable friction between Hungary and the governments of Romania and the Czech and Slovak Federative Republic.

former size. After Turks invaded the Balkans, János Hunyadi and Fr. Capistrano won a decisive victory in 1456 at Nándorfehérvár (now Belgrade, Yugoslavia). Christian church bells tolling daily at noon still commemorate this victory. During his reign between 1458 and 1490 Matthias Corvinus, the son of János Hunyadi, built up both the economy and a powerful nation-state, while he introduced the culture of the Renaissance. At that time, the population of Hungary equaled that of England and France (4 million people). After Matthias's death, however, there came a period of feudal anarchy and, for the serfs, destitution and oppression. A peasant revolt in 1514 was crushed by the Magyar nobility. After the peasant war still heavier burdens were imposed on the serfs. Ottoman Turks defeated the weakened country in 1526 at Mohács and occupied the central plains of Hungary for 156 years. Hungary's western and northern regions were ruled by the Austrian Habsburgs. The eastern zone and Transylvania became a semi-independent principality. Thousands of Serbs, Romanians, and others fled from the Turkish-occupied Balkans to this principality. In 1557 the Diet of Torda, Transylvania, enacted a law proclaiming freedom of religion. Finally, in the late 1600s Habsburg forces drove the Turks out of Hungary. Then the Habsburgs took control, reunited the country, and settled thousands of Germans in depopulated areas. Led by Ferenc Rákóczi, Hungarians rose in 1703 against Habsburg colonization but were defeated, with Russian intervention, in 1711. Reform movements culminated in another attempt to obtain freedom in the revolt of 1848–1849, led by Lajos Kossuth, which was ultimately crushed by the Habsburgs with the aid of the Russian czar. War-weakened Austria compromised in 1867. The dual monarchy of Austria-Hungary was established with internally independent Hungary sharing common external services and military. Defeated with the other central powers during World War I, Hungary was forced to sign the Treaty of Trianon at Versailles in 1920. This treaty compelled Hungary to cede 68 percent of its land and 58 percent of its population: Transylvania and Bánát to Romania, Slovakia and Carpatho-Ruthenia to Czechoslovakia, Croatia and Bácska to Yugoslavia, Port Fiume to Italy, and the western part of the country to equally defeated Austria. After the dissolution of the Austro-Hungarian dual monarchy, Hungary first became a republic in 1918. Then for 131 days in 1919 it had a Communist government, and in 1920 it became and remained for the entire interwar period a constitutional monarchy with Admiral Nicholas Horthy as regent. After regaining some lost territories between 1937 and 1941 with the help of Italy and Germany, Hungary joined the Axis powers in World War II. Soviet troops entered and occupied Hungary and the 1945 Armistice returned the country to its 1937 borders. A year later the country was declared a republic, and free elections were held in 1947. Even though the Smallholders' party won, it was forced out by Communists who were trained in and supported by Moscow. In 1956 there was a popular revolution against repressive Communist rule, which had included punitive measures against private peasants and a forced policy of heavy industrialization. Soviet forces crushed the revolution and made János Kádár the new leader of what was then called the People's Republic of Hungary. Imre Nagy and other leaders of the revolution were executed; tens of thousands died or were deported, and 200,000 people fled the country to the West. In 1963 there was a sweeping amnesty for political prisoners. The New Economic Mechanism, launched in 1968, introduced, among other things, elements of a market economy, and it helped to improve living standards. In the spirit of Soviet glasnost (openness) and perestroika (restructuring), Hungarians started strong movements for democratization in 1987. They removed János Kádár from power and rehabilitated the names of Imre Nagy and others. The ruling Communist party renamed itself, opposition parties were legalized, and freedom of press was extended. Free elections were held in 1990 and more radical political and economic changes are occurring.

Settlements

Geographical conditions influenced the development of regionally varied settlement patterns, along with many historical events, like the long Turkish occupation and Habsburg political and economic domination. In addition to the populous peasant towns, in rural Hungary there is still evidence of *tanyas*, or single isolated farmsteads, regular villages with geometrically designed streets, and irregular streetless villages that were settled by *hads* (agnatic kin groups) and *nagycsaládok* (extended families) in clustered and random style. Until a relatively recent attempt to integrate all buildings and farmyards into one section, in the northern and central parts of the Great Hungarian Plain most villages and boroughs had *kertes*, or *kétbeltelkes* settlements, meaning that the dwellings and farmyards were separated from one another.

Economy

SUBSISTENCE AND COMMERCIAL ACTIVITIES. Depending on the region, the rural economy was and is currently based on agriculture (including grains, tobacco, flax, peppers, melons, fruits), viniculture, animal husbandry (with a focus on raising cattle, pigs, horses), and forestry. Today, however, men and some women regularly commute between villages and urban industrial and mining centers. Also, light industrial plants were established in rural settlements, where village women work. Most village households, therefore, have wage income both from agriculture and industry. Traditional patterns of groups work projects and mutual help (*kaláka*) continue to be visible in such activities as house building and harvesting, as well as weddings, funerals, and other important rites of passage.

INDUSTRIAL ARTS. Depending on the area, larger settlements had potters, glazed earthenware makers, furrier-embroiderers, fancy honey-cake makers, wood-carvers, and other specialists. In addition to rural craft production, larger cities boasted sophisticated traditions of crafts.

TRADE. Throughout the countryside national fairs are frequently held, and there are weekly markets where villagers sell their produce and livestock. In addition, there are general and specialty stores, and in larger towns there are Western-style supermarkets. In 1973 Hungary joined the General Agreement on Tariffs and Trade. A decade later it was admitted to the International Monetary Fund. The country exports many of its products throughout the world.

DIVISION OF LABOR. Traditionally there was a marked sexual and age-group division of labor. In rural Hungary the eldest male was the head of household. Men's special jobs included plowing, reaping, building, and woodwork. Cooking, baking, cleaning, child rearing, weaving, and embroidering were considered the women's domain. Currently, because of out-migration and regular commuting of young and middle-aged men, there is increasing feminization and aging of village populations. Despite the major changes within the structure of agriculture, industry, and services, much of the traditional sexual division of labor remains.

LAND TENURE. Prior to 1945, land was privately owned either in small (often unviably small) plots by peasants or in large estates by aristocrats and wealthy families. In the land reform of 1945, large estates were redistributed among poor families across the country. After 1948 the Communist party and the government attempted to collectivize all agricultural properties and finally succeeded in 1961. As of the 1980s, 93 percent of arable land is cultivated in cooperative or state farms. With changes in property rights imminent, the possibility of increasing amounts of acreage becoming privatized is very likely.

Kinship, Marriage, and Family

KINSHIP. In traditional Hungarian society an individual was identified principally by his or her place in a kinship organization. In Hungarian address and reference terms, one does not distinguish between paternal and maternal relatives (or

*Both urban and
rural Hungarians
consult seers who act
as mediators and
through whom they
communicate with
their dead.*

between parallel and cross cousins). Rather, kin from both the father's and mother's side are included in a common class. Kinship is bilaterally reckoned. Traditionally, however, more emphasis was placed on the paternal kin than on the maternal because of the "male-centric" worldview in Hungarian rural society and the economically more beneficial inheritance system to males along the patriline. There is no uniform reckoning or terminology of kinship. Rather, an urban and a rural system coexist in Hungary. The urban system reflects nuclear family organization, and the rural system and its many regional variants depict the traditional extended family organization. Generally, Hungarian kinship terminology is descriptive and sharply distinguishes between affinal kin, consanguineous kin, and fictive kin. In Hungarian, like in other Finno-Ugric languages, there is a systematic differentiation between elder and younger brothers (*báty, öcs*), and between elder and younger sisters (*növér, hug*). The fictive kinship of godparenthood (*keresztkomaság*) is a highly significant, lifelong alliance.

MARRIAGE. Even though only the birth of a child transforms a couple into a family, marriage is the emblem of maturity and conveys a status of adulthood, particularly in rural communities. Weddings are very elaborate, opulent affairs. Being unmarried after the age of 20–22 for women and 25–27 for men is negatively sanctioned. Traditional patterns of wife beating continue. Divorces are increasingly common, particularly in urban areas. According to 1987 data, there were 2.8 divorces per 1,000 inhabitants in the country.

DOMESTIC UNIT. Depending upon socioeconomic circumstances, both the nuclear family and various forms of the joint or extended family organization were present even within the same rural settlement in traditional times. Extended families were maintained the longest among some Hungarian subethnic groups, for example among the Palóc, Matyó, and Seklers. While there are still a number of multigenerational families who live under the same roof and share "the same bread" today the most frequent form is the independently residing nuclear family.

INHERITANCE. According to an 1840 law, property was to be divided equally among all surviving children regardless of gender. Most often, however, land was either divided equally among sons or the entire land property and the family dwelling were given to the eldest or most capable son. Other sons were given their share in money. Daughters, who of course married out of the paternal household, either gave up their rights to inherit real property or were paid a small sum. Of-

ten it was the responsibility of mothers to provide their daughters with proper dowries.

SOCIALIZATION. In the past, with a pattern of patrilocal postmarital residence, the mother, older siblings, and the female kin in the paternal household were responsible for the upbringing of children. Independence at an early age, respect for elders, and conformity to local and familial values were stressed. Currently, with the increasingly frequent pattern of neolocal postmarital residence, most rural children are raised by their mothers, maternal natal kin, and the village nursery and elementary schools. Even though today there is strong orientation toward child-centeredness, corporal punishment is still frequent.

Religion and Expressive Culture

RELIGIOUS BELIEFS. Approximately 62 percent of the population is Roman Catholic, 25 percent Protestant, 3 percent Eastern Orthodox, 1 percent Jewish. Some of the practices combine elements of Christian and ancient pagan folk beliefs and customs.

CEREMONIES. Some of the most important celebrations of the church calendrical year include namedays (*névnapok*), New Year's Day, Carnival (*Farsang*), the village patron saint's day (*búcsu*), Easter, Whitsuntide, All Saints' Day, and Christmas. In addition, rituals tied to the agricultural calendar include new bread, harvest, and grape-harvest festivals. National holidays commemorate significant historical events.

ARTS. There is considerable regional differentiation in Hungarian folk art. Still, most designs are floral, and often even the geometric motifs are turned into monumental and colorful flowers. On furniture, wood carvings, paintings, and pottery patriotic symbols such as heroes of liberty, the national shield of Hungary, and the red, white, and green of the national flag appear. Pentatonic music, *csárdás* dances, and traditional rural architecture are also noteworthy representations of Hungarian art. Of course, urban forms of literature and the plastic arts have consistently represented all significant artistic expressions known throughout Europe.

MEDICINE. Since the early 1950s, Hungarian medical care has been socialized. Women give birth in hospitals rather than at home, and regional doctors and medical clinics take care of the ill. Among other things, drafts are assumed to cause some infirmities. There are home remedies, such as herbal teas and compresses, that are believed to help various health problems.

DEATH AND AFTERLIFE. A number of ancient beliefs and customs still surround the dying and the dead, as well as the mortuary practices and funerals. It is believed that before leaving for the life hereafter, the deceased's spirit lingers on for a while in or near the body. Elaborate rituals both during the preparation of the body for the coffin and during the funeral procession ensure that the spirit will not cause harm to the living but that it can find its way to the netherworld. Both urban and rural people sometimes consult seers (*halottlátók*), who act as mediators and through whom they communicate with their dead.

Bibliography

Andrew, János (1982). *The Politics of Backwardness in Hungary, 1925–1945.* Princeton: Princeton University Press.

Balassa, Iván, and Gy. Ortutay (1984). *Hungarian Ethnography and Folklore.* Budapest: Corvina.

Bell, Peter (1984). *Peasants in Socialist Transition: Life in a Collectivized Hungarian Village.* Berkeley: University of California.

Dégh, Linda (1989). *Folktales and Society: Storytelling in a Hungarian Peasant Community.* Bloomington: Indiana University.

Fél, Edit, and Tamás Hofer (1969). *Proper Peasants: Traditional Life in a Hungarian Village.* Viking Fund Publications in Anthropology. Chicago: Aldine; Budapest: Corvina.

Ferge, Zsuzsa (1979). *A Society in the Making: Hungarian Social and Societal Policy.* New York: M. E. Sharpe.

Illyés, Gyula (1936). *People of the Puszta.* Budapest: Corvina. Reprint. 1967.

Lukács, John (1988). *Budapest 1900: A Historical Portrait of a City and Its Culture.* New York: Weidenfeld & Nicolson.

Macartney, C. A. (1962). *Hungary: A Short History.* Chicago: Aldine.

Ortutay, Gyula, et al. *Magyar néprajzi lexikon* (The encyclopedia of Hungarian ethnography). 5 vols. Budapest: Akadémiai Kiadó.

Sozan, Michael (1979). *The History of Hungarian Ethnography.* Washington, D.C.: University Press of America.

—ÉVA V. HUSEBY-DARVAS

ICELANDERS

Ethnym: none

Orientation

IDENTIFICATION. Icelanders speak Icelandic and trace their origins to settlers who came from Norway in the ninth century. According to the Icelandic literary-historic tradition, it was an early settler who gave the island its foreboding name when he was forced to return to Norway because he fished and hunted all summer and failed to lay up hay for his livestock. Today Icelanders enjoy a long life expectancy and one of the highest standards of living in the world.

LOCATION. Iceland is an island in the North Atlantic Ocean, located between Greenland and Norway, just south of the Arctic Circle. It covers 103,000 square kilometers, of which about 1,000 are cultivated, 20,000 pasture, 12,000 covered by glaciers, and 67,000 covered by lava, sands, and other wastelands. Volcanic activity continues. The Gulf Stream moderates the climate. The average annual temperature in Reykjavik, the capital, is 5° C. January averages −0.4° C and July 11.2° C. Average annual precipitation in Reykjavik is 80.5 centimeters.

DEMOGRAPHY. The total 1983 population was 237,894, about 2.3 persons per square kilometer. There were 128,221 people living in the area of the capital, and 87,106 in Reykjavik itself. There were 211,716 living in towns and villages of more than 200 people, and 26,178 in rural areas.

LINGUISTIC AFFILIATION. Icelandic is a Germanic language akin to Norwegian. Some call medieval Icelandic, the language of the Icelandic historic-literary tradition, Old Norse. Icelandic retains the full case structure, and some claim it is virtually unaltered since medieval times, though many modern Icelanders disagree. There are no family names. Everyone has one or two names and is referred to as son or daughter after his or her father. Directories are organized alphabetically by first name.

History and Cultural Relations

A number of medieval Icelandic manuscripts have been preserved. They include a compilation of stories collected just within the living memory of some of the earliest settlers about the settlement itself (the "Book of Settlements"); a grammatical treatise; the family sagas, composed during the thirteenth century about events of earlier periods; the Sturlunga sagas about contemporary thirteenth-century events; lawbooks; biographies of churchmen; other religious writings; and compilations of and commentaries on poetry and mythology. This is a unique record of a stratified society without a state, provided by the people of the society themselves. Romanticized nationalistic treatments of this tradition are common and are related to the ideology of the nineteenth-century Icelandic independence movement. This

Iceland has a strongly egalitarian ideology and the distribution of income is more equal than in most other societies; there has never been any Icelandic royalty.

influence remains in some Scandinavian and other treatments of Icelandic culture and history. While scholars continue to debate the reliability of the documents of the Icelandic literary-historic tradition, most agree about the following history. Iceland was settled by people from Norway beginning in the ninth century. Each nonchieftain belonged to the assembly group of a chieftain. The society was stratified, but there was no state system. In A.D. 930 a General Assembly based on the model of Norwegian assemblies was established. One "law speaker" was elected every three years to memorize the customs and laws and recite one-third of them at each annual meeting of the assembly. He had no executive authority, but he could be consulted on points of law. The chieftains in assembly changed laws and heard cases. The assembly was not a parliamentary structure nor in any way did it resemble a democracy. Under pressure from the king of Norway in 1000, Christianity was adopted as the general religion of the island by arbitration at the meeting of the General Assembly. With Christianity came bishops and, in 1096, a tithe law. Early in the twelfth century the laws were written. A period of strife among chieftains resulted in the concentration of power into the hands of a few families in the thirteenth century, and in 1242 the remaining chieftains surrendered to the king of Norway. In 1380 Norway came under Danish rule, bringing Iceland with it. During the Reformation, in 1550, Catholicism was replaced by Lutheranism. From 1602 until 1787 there was a trade monopoly to prevent Icelanders from trading with British, German, and other fishermen and traders. In 1918 home rule was granted. During World War II, the Germans occupied Denmark and the British occupied Iceland. At the invitation of the British and occupied Iceland, the United States established military bases to free the British for other war tasks. Iceland became an independent republic in 1944. The American bases remain as NATO bases. Their presence is hotly debated in Iceland. Some argue they are Iceland's contribution to NATO while others argue they contradict Iceland's independence. Language, geography, and history place Iceland in the sphere of Scandinavian culture.

Economy

SUBSISTENCE AND COMMERCIAL ACTIVITIES. Iceland has always depended on trade. The growing season is too short for any crop but grass, cultivated as feed for cattle and sheep. Fishing and hunting have always supplemented livestock production. The relative place of each component in the economic system has changed over the centuries. Initially, livestock production was important both for domestic consumption and for production of woolen goods for trade with Europe for metal and wood products. Fishing provided additional food, and cod may have been traded commercially since medieval times. During the period of Danish colonial rule, livestock production predominated. As Danish rule weakened toward the end of the nineteenth century, and local capital accumulation became possible, fishing communities grew along the coast and merchants developed foreign markets for fisheries products. Modern Iceland has an industrial economy based on fishing, fish processing, and fish exporting. Icelanders enjoy a high standard of living with 508 cars, 525 telephones, 266 television sets, and 2 physicians per 1,000 inhabitants in 1983.

INDUSTRIAL ARTS. Iceland's fishing and fish processing industries are among the most innovative and modern in the world. From their trawlers to their line boats and freezing plants, they take advantage of the most modern technology and innovations in all fields from computer science to plastics. Hydroelectric plants provide electricity for an aluminum processing factory.

TRADE. The nation exports fish and fish products and imports most of its consumer goods.

DIVISION OF LABOR. Most Icelandic adults work, including most married women. As in other industrialized countries, the question is not so much one of division of labor as division of rewards such as wages and prestige. Icelandic women are generally paid less than their male counterparts. Women are usually assigned less desirable and less remunerative work in fish processing plants, for example. They are underrepresented on the faculty of the University of Iceland. This overall inequity may be in the process of changing, however. The economics and politics of gender equality have been issues in Icelandic politics for years, but during the 1980s the Women's List, a national political party, had some electoral success in parliamentary elections.

LAND TENURE. In medieval Iceland land tenure depended on being able to appeal to sufficient force to prevent others from taking the land one claimed. Chieftains built coalitions of commoners and entered into alliances with other chieftains. Commoners joined chieftains to insure their land claims. One of the contradictions of the period was an economic system based on concepts of landownership and stratification with no state system of governance to enforce it. From the thirteenth century on many landless people worked

HARVEST

*Icelanders raking hay into piles.
Since the growing season is too
short for other crops, grass is
cultivated as feed for cattle and
sheep. Mosfellsveit, Iceland.
(Ted Spiegel/Corbis)*

for wages or rented from the few landowners.
This system continued virtually until independence. In independent Iceland land tenure is less
important than sea tenure. In 1975 Iceland led the
way to the establishment of the international 200-
mile (333-kilometer) offshore limit, which resulted in its cod wars with Great Britain. This
limited the right to fish within these limits to Icelandic fishermen, thus reserving a rich fishing area
for Icelandic use. This has been and remains one
of the most important aspects of Icelandic foreign
policy.

Kinship, Marriage, and Family

KINSHIP. The modern kinship terminology
is made up of two systems. One is Ego-centered
with terms that indicate specific individuals. The
second is a set of collective terms that indicate
groups of kin. Each of these two systems is divided into two more or less classificatory or descriptive subsystems. Descriptive terms designate
individuals by generation, sex, and laterality.
Merging terms refer to individuals with others of
other positions of the same category. These systems have evolved from similarly complex medieval systems.

MARRIAGE. Documents of the literary-
historic tradition record instances of men having
multiple mates if not legal wives. Marriage has

never been considered as important in Iceland as
in some other societies. Since the early nineteenth
century when national statistics began to be
recorded, from 13 to 36 percent (in 1977) of
births have been illegitimate. Illegitimacy has
never been a stigma or hindrance. Of the Nordic
countries, Iceland has the youngest age at marriage (24.9 years for males, 22.7 years for females).
Divorce has always been easy. The rate of divorce
in 1977 was 9.12 per thousand married women.
Because of the high rate of cohabitation, this figure does not necessarily have the same social
meaning as it might in a society with a higher rate
of marriage.

DOMESTIC UNIT. In 1703 the average
household size was 5.6 persons and remained between 6 and 7 until 1901 when it was 6.2. In 1950
it was 3.8 and in 1960 3.9.

INHERITANCE. There is no kindred-based
land inheritance in Iceland. Personal decisions
outweigh structural obligations. The historical-
literary tradition records cases of contested inheritance, usually resolved by force in medieval times.

SOCIALIZATION. Modern Icelanders are
very aware of issues of child rearing, child welfare,
and education, and these issues sometimes become political. Public-health nurses make periodic house checks on newborns to ensure that
they are staying on their growth curves and to

Choral Singing may be one of the most popular art forms in Iceland.

help mothers with any problems they may encounter. Day care for preschool children is widely available in and near Reykjavik. In less metropolitan areas parents rely more on kin and friends for child care. Some rural and urban households have au pair girls to help with young children.

Sociopolitical Organization

Iceland has been a stratified society without a state and a colony of Denmark, and it is now an independent republic with an elected president as ritual head of state, a multiparty system, a parliament, and a prime minister who is the effective head of state.

SOCIAL ORGANIZATION. Iceland has a strongly egalitarian ideology and the distribution of income is more equal than in most other societies. Differences in economic status, however, have become greater in recent years under conservative economic policies. There are significant differences between male and female remuneration for similar work. There has never been any Icelandic royalty, though some people have been and remain in privileged positions relative to others. These differences are well documented and discussed, and they sometimes become political issues. Almost all workers belong to well-organized unions.

POLITICAL ORGANIZATION. Since its establishment as a republic in 1944, Iceland has never had a majority government. It is governed by a coalition of several parties that range from the Left to the Right in their political rhetoric and policies.

SOCIAL CONTROL. The small size of Iceland and its population makes for greater accessibility than in larger, more populous societies. People know each other and know of each other. This closeness operates as a kind of social control and may be characterized as stifling or as close. Icelanders tend to be tolerant and nonfanatical. When someone says "it is not fair," he or she gets an immediate hearing. The response is not "no one said life was fair." Appeal to egalitarian ideals, concepts of justice and fairness, are given weight rather than disregarded. Discussions and debates, like the political parties, tend to be many-sided rather than two-sided.

CONFLICT. The literary-historic tradition records many instances of conflict in medieval times. Today conflict tends to be verbal and legal rather than physical. Sometimes there are strikes. One definition of chaos is the interruption of normal middle-class patterns of life. There is no military. There is a small police force and coast guard.

There is no national guard. When there are strikes, the policemen's union is as likely as any other to be on strike, so they are not used to break strikes. Since most people belong to unions, nonunion workers are not available to break strikes.

Religion and Expressive Culture

RELIGIOUS BELIEFS AND PRACTICES. The Icelandic writer Sigrdur Nordal wrote, "We have been bad pagans for a century and bad Christians for ten." During early times, chieftains were also priests. As in many other primitive societies, their offices were both secular and sacred. After Christianity was introduced, clergy refused to abide by the rule of celibacy, bore arms, and entered feuds. The higher clergy functioned as another kind of chieftain. Most modern Icelanders are confirmed in the Icelandic State Church, a major rite of passage. The clergy have social as well as religious roles. The church is tax-supported, but individuals who do not want to support the church may so indicate on their tax returns and their taxes are used for other purposes. Nonstandard quasireligious movements such as spiritism and folk concepts such as elves and prophetic dreams have some support and go in and out of fashion from time to time.

ARTS. Choral singing may be one of the most popular art forms in Iceland. Rural as well as urban areas support choirs. There is an active theater community, symphony orchestra, new music movement, and visual arts community. There are several art museums, some of which are dedicated to individual artists. There is a small film-making industry. There is a state television station, two state radio stations, and one commercial television station. Icelandic rock-and-roll bands come and go in national and international popularity. One of the problems they must face is whether to perform in the Icelandic language, thus maintaining a strong sense of Icelandic identity but limiting their appeal to the island, or to perform in English (e.g., the Sugarcubes), thus appealing to an international audience but losing some of their national identity. Iceland is a nation of poets and writers. The most internationally known writer is the Nobel Prize winner Halldor Laxness, who has written only in Icelandic. Before he won the Nobel Prize, Icelanders gave him a cool reception because of his challenges to long-held myths of egalitarianism and romantic ideas of independence.

MEDICINE. Iceland has a modern and advanced healthcare system. All Icelanders participate in this system, and health care is available to all.

Bibliography

Durrenberger, E. Paul, and Gisli Palsson, eds. (1989). *The Anthropology of Iceland*. Iowa City: University of Iowa Press.

Gelsinger, Bruce E. (1981). *Icelandic Enterprise: Commerce and Economy in the Middle Ages*. Columbia: University of South Carolina Press.

Rich, George W. (1989). "Problems and Prospects in the Study of Icelandic Kinship." In *The Anthropology of Iceland*, edited by E. Paul Durrenberger and Gisli Palsson, 53–118. Iowa City: University of Iowa Press.

Tomasson, Richard F. (1980). *Iceland: The First New Society*. Minneapolis: University of Minnesota Press.

—E. PAUL DURRENBERGER

IRISH

Ethonym: Eireanneach

Orientation

IDENTIFICATION AND LOCATION. For the Irish and Ireland, identification and location are inextricably linked aspects of self-definition. Ireland, located between 51°30′ and 55°30′ N and 6°00′ and 10°30′ W, is an island 480 by 273 kilometers at its longest and widest (N–S and E–W, respectively). It is separated on the east from Great Britain by the narrow Irish Sea (17 to 192 kilometers wide). To the west is the Atlantic Ocean. The island consists mainly of low-lying land whose central lowlands support rich pastureland, agricultural regions, and a large central peat bog. The rim is mountainous, especially in the west, but elevations are rarely higher than 900 meters. Ireland's geographical location—combining proximity to England with peripherality vis-à-vis Europe—has played the major role in defining its historical experience. This relationship has also made the definition of just who and what is Irish problematic. Centuries of British rule culminated in the division of the island in 1922 into two political entities: the Republic (Free State from 1922 to 1949) of Ireland, comprising twenty-six counties and 70,550 square kilometers, and the Province of Northern Ireland, comprising six counties and remaining part of the United Kingdom. The population of the republic is 95 percent Catholic and that segment identifies itself unambiguously as Irish. Members of the Protestant minority may choose to emphasize their English ancestry, but they typically call themselves "Irish"—or "Anglo-Irish" as they are identified by their Irish Catholic neighbors. In Northern Ireland, however, the situation is more complex. The substantial Catholic minority—whatever their political affiliation—consider themselves ethnically Irish, while the subjective and objective identification of Protestants has been far more fluctuating and context-dependent. At various points, they may identify themselves as "Irish," "Ulster," "Ulster Protestant," or "British." The merging of religious, geographical, and ethnic labels is also applied from the outside. Irish Catholics may use a variety of such terms to identify their neighbors, and the choice of label nearly always has a political subtext.

DEMOGRAPHY. The population of the Republic of Ireland was 3,540,643 in 1986, representing an increase of 97,238 persons since the 1981 census. The population, which began a steep decline during the late 1840s famine, has been increasing since the 1961 census and has now been restored to the level of 1889–90. However, a recent decline in the birthrate and a leap in the emigration rate (at least 72,000 between 1981 and 1986), makes the demographic future uncertain. The high birthrate in the sixties and seventies has made Ireland one of the youngest countries in Europe, and migration to Dublin has made the population far more urban than it had been up until recently (57 percent urban, 43 percent rural), with close to a third of the population living in Dublin County.

LINGUISTIC AFFILIATION. Although Irish Gaelic is the official language of the republic, the vast majority of people on both sides of the border speak English. Irish is the daily language of only tens of thousands (disputed number) of inhabitants of scattered Gaeltacht zones mainly along the west coast. Irish Gaelic, a Celtic language, has three main dialects and is closely related to Scottish Gaelic. The Goidelic Branch of the Celtic languages also includes Manx (once spoken on the Isle of Man), while the Brythonic Branch is represented by Welsh and Breton. The language issue has played a central part in the ethnic identity issues previously mentioned. Although Irish Gaelic was by the late nineteenth century very much a minority language, proponents of Irish nationalism (Protestant and Catholic) favored the restoration of the "national language" as a critical element in the maintenance of a distinct national identity and culture. Government measures meant to ensure this restoration have gradually relaxed over the decades, however, and despite the persistence of Irish in a few enclaves and a lively

See also

English, Gaels, Highland
Scots, Lowland Scots, Welsh

After the bloody reaction to Catholic civil rights demonstrations in Northern Ireland, the British Army began to maintain a strong and active presence that continues to this day.

♦ **Celts**
An Indo-European people of Iron Age and pre-Roman Europe who ranged from the British Isles to Asia Minor. Modern-day descendants of the Celts include the Irish, Highland Scots, Welsh, Cornish, and Bretons.

Irish-language literary and cultural scene, English is clearly the de facto national language.

History and Cultural Relations

The earliest inhabitants of Ireland were Mesolithic hunter-gatherers whose sites are dated as early as 8980 B.P., but it is the extensive Neolithic settlement that has left a large number of impressive megalithic constructions. The exact origin point of "Celtic culture" in Ireland and its relation to preexisting cultures and/or populations is much disputed. By the first few centuries B.C., however, a clearly Celtic culture was established all over the island, with clear connections to continental Celts. Iron Age Celtic society established a lasting economic, political, social, and cultural framework for Irish society. Unhampered by the Romanization that transformed so much of continental Europe, Ireland's cattle-based chieftaincies remained the basic social unit through the early Christian period, giving Irish Christianity a Celtic construction that would give rise to Roman consternation at various historical junctures. Celtic Ireland was notably rural, and it was the Vikings who established the major port cities that would continue to play an important role in Irish history (e.g., Dublin, Cork, Waterford, Wexford). The English presence began with the twelfth-century Anglo-Norman expedition under the auspices of Henry II, in aid of one side in an internecine struggle in the south. The invaders settled, particularly in the southeast, bringing with them a manorial type of settlement and economy, as well as a new language and culture. The succeeding centuries brought much cultural borrowing between native Irish and Anglo-Norman cultures, particularly in areas distant from the capital. The Cromwellian and Williamite wars of the seventeenth century established Ireland as a fully colonial society, with political rule and most landownership in the hands of English-speaking Protestants, and with a native population of mainly Gaelic-speaking Catholics, the vast majority of whom were poor tenant farmers, seen and described by their overlords in increasingly "primitive" terms. The wars also brought the "plantation" of Northern Ireland, the importation of thousands of mainly Presbyterian Scots who took ownership of small farms and settled in areas from which Catholic Irish had been driven. There was also a very considerable influx of Protestant English into the south. For most Catholic tenants, the central issue through the eighteenth century was local land tenure, and a variety of locally based secret societies—such as the "White Boys"—were active in retaliatory guerrilla raids against landlords, agents, or collaborators. After the failure of the United Irishmen's rebellion in 1798, land tenure as well as cultural and religious identity came more and more to be linked with nationalism. The nineteenth century saw a series of attempts, armed and legislative, to win independence and/or redress land issues, culminating in the Easter Uprising of 1916 and the war of independence that followed. Ireland achieved independence as a Free State with the treaty of 1922, which left the six Protestant-majority counties of Ulster in the United Kingdom. The Free State became Eire, or the Republic of Ireland, in 1949. One faction of the Irish—represented thereafter by the Irish Republican Army (IRA)—refused to accept the legitimacy of the boundary. Within Northern Ireland most Catholics—and a few Protestants—are "nationalists" favoring a "United Ireland." The vast majority of Protestants—and very few Catholics—espouse "Unionism," seeking to remain a part of the United Kingdom. It is difficult to assess what proportion of either population supports the activities of violent paramilitary organizations, which continue to carry out assassinations and bombings. After the bloody reaction to Catholic civil rights demonstrations in Northern Ireland in 1969, the British Army began to maintain a strong and active presence that continues to this day.

In addition to the political developments already described, the eighteenth and nineteenth centuries brought tremendous economic and social upheaval to Ireland. The population increased at a tremendous rate and grew increasingly dependent on the potato for sustenance. The great potato famine of the late 1840s (numerous smaller ones occurred before and after) led to evictions and immigration that vastly increased the flow of Irish to America.

While significant numbers went to England—and, to a lesser extent, Canada and Australia—the large proportion of Irish in America has had a great and lasting impact on both the United States and Ireland. Even since 1973, when Eire joined the European Economic Community, cultural (as opposed to economic) attention has been focused on the United States, to which the current crop of emigrants have once again come.

Settlements

Settlement patterns have of course varied much over time and place. The dominant Celtic pattern seems to have been scattered fort/cattle pen/households (*rath*). Peasant communities following a mixed-cattle, agricultural regime, at least in the west of Ireland, lived in small hamlets (*clachan* or *clibin*), using a commonly held infield for grain and vegetables and an extensive outfield "mountain" for livestock. This pattern was generally eliminated (though there are a few survivals) through landlord intervention by the middle of the nineteenth century. The demise of such traditional patterns was also accelerated by the famine and emigration. The resulting pattern was of more or less dispersed households and farms, or more concentrated but separate rows of dwellings where geography and varying land type made that form appropriate. In either case, however, the "townland" (*baile fearainn*), which corresponds to the common holding of the traditional cluster settlement, may continue to operate as a socially significant "neighborhood" and its inhabitants may even continue to hold common rights to turf (for fuel) in bogs and grazing land on mountains. Elsewhere other agricultural and/or geographical factors made for other settlement types, including dispersed large farms, estate villages, or the street market towns, which mainly developed in the nineteenth century under landlord regimes.

Economy

SUBSISTENCE AND COMMERCIAL ACTIVITIES. Agriculture, until recently the overwhelming mainstay of the Irish economy, remains important, although a decreasing percentage of the population is engaged in such pursuits. Most arable land is devoted to pasture or hay production, and livestock and livestock products are the most important exports, sold in European and Near Eastern markets. The United States is also a major trading partner. Tourism, greatly promoted in recent decades, provides the single largest item in the country's net earnings. Since the 1960s, attractive conditions have brought many foreign-owned small factories to Ireland, and they along with Irish manufacturing and construction firms now employ around 27.5 percent of the labor force. While the city of Dublin has grown at a great rate, the lack of a large industrial or commercial base there has meant much unemployment. Membership in the European Common Market has benefited agricultural producers through subsidies and opened up new channels for emigration for professionals, but so far has not done much to change the economic peripherality of Ireland. The relative prosperity of the sixties and seventies seems to have been based on borrowed money, leaving Ireland with one of the highest per capita foreign debts in the world. Inflation and high unemployment fueled renewed emigration, mostly to the United States, in the late 1980s. In the west of Ireland, where most anthropological fieldwork has been carried out, small farms—where viable—continue to produce livestock and dairy products sold at marts or through local cooperatives. Much of the extreme west, including Gaeltacht zones, is characterized by underfarmed smallholdings, which support a subsistence crop of potatoes and vegetables, combined in varying degrees with sheep farming (whose economic viability depends on government subsidies). In a few areas small- or medium-scale fishing or rural factory employment adds to the income of such families or provides the total support of younger families. Government welfare and old-age pensions, however, contribute importantly to the maintenance of many households. Where the farm is viable, it absorbs the labor of the entire family. In smaller holding areas, however, younger family members are often engaged in subsidiary income pursuits. Where available, factory jobs are sought by young men and women. Areas of large farms, such as Meath and West Meath, and the city and suburbs of Dublin exhibit different sociocultural patterns, which are only recently being studied by anthropologists.

LAND TENURE. Although after the seventeenth century the mainly British landlords held proprietary rights, the Irish tenantry continued to pass on the right to these tenancies as if they were property. Land reforms in the late nineteenth and early twentieth century turned these tenants into peasant proprietors. Common rights were often retained in bogs (for peat fuel) and in extensive mountain pasturelands.

Kinship, Marriage, and Family

KINSHIP. *Clan* is an Irish word and traditionally referred to the agnatic descendants of a common ancestor (e.g., "the O'Donnells"). Such clans had a hierarchical territorial arrangement in traditional chiefdoms, wherein subgroups and individuals were linked to superiors through cattle clientship and/or tribute and service. The local kin group in this system was called a *fine*. In this way traditional commonage rundale (common land that is distributed among owners in such a way that an individual's holdings are scattered among those of others) was followed by divided inheritance in western Ireland, which gave way, again under landlord action, to enforced undivided inheritance. This continues to be the legal mode today, with the father naming a single son as heir to the farm. The social integrity and rela-

Agriculture, until recently the overwhelming mainstay of the Irish economy, remains important, although a decreasing percentage of the population is engaged in such pursuits.

tive autonomy of the household farm based on the single heir is a central concern of many influential studies of the culture. However, in some areas at least, the ethos of continuing obligation to and among all siblings makes "stem family" a misleading designation, even for the contemporary rural Irish family.

MARRIAGE. Sibling solidarity before and after marriage is a striking feature of daily life. In the west, in particular, individuals still marry close to home and tend to keep up frequent visiting patterns with siblings. In the extreme case men and women may even remain with their natal households after marriage. Unmarried siblings will very often live together and will frequently be joined by a widowed sibling late in life.

Sociopolitical Organization

SOCIAL ORGANIZATION. Although an increasing share of the population lives in Dublin, rural culture enjoys a disproportionate importance, and many urban dwellers retain ties to the countryside. While an egalitarian ethos prevails in most rural areas, there are large differences in the "objective" class situation of farmers, ranging from large numbers of very small farmers cultivating less than 6 hectares, mainly in the west, to graziers farming hundreds of hectares in the east. The class structure of the cities resembles that of other urban areas in western Europe.

POLITICAL ORGANIZATION. Eire is a parliamentary democracy with a nonexecutive president elected by direct vote. The parliament (Oireachtas) consists of a lower house (An Dail Eireann) elected through proportional representation by a single transferable vote, and an upper house (An Seanad Eireann). The government is headed by a prime minister (An Taoiseach) chosen by An Dail. The two principal political parties, Fine Gael and Fianna Fail, are both centrist in European terms and owe their origins to respective positions on the border question seventy years ago. There are a variety of other parties holding few seats, including the Labor Party and Sinn Fein (the political wing of the IRA). Local government is through the "county council," but recent changes in the structure of taxation have left that body with little real resources and hence little power, making Eire's political system an increasingly centralized one.

SOCIAL CONTROL. In rural areas, the local community and kin groups continue to play the most obvious role in daily social control. The Catholic church, especially in the person of the parish priest, typically continues to exercise con-

siderable authority, especially in the rural areas. In these same areas the "legitimacy" of the state to interfere with local practice may be more often questioned.

CONFLICT. Irish nationalists tend to sum up Ireland's history as "800 years of British oppression and Irish resistance." Academic histories currently debate whether the local uprisings and guerrilla activity of the eighteenth century, the 1798 rebellion, the Fenians of the nineteenth century, and the ongoing "troubles" can best be understood in terms of class, nationalism, or local interests. From any point of view, however, conflict continues to define the Irish experience, historically and currently.

Religion and Expressive Culture

RELIGIOUS BELIEFS AND PRACTICES. By any measure, Ireland is a profoundly Catholic country and culture. Weekly mass attendance continues at nearly 90 percent of the population, and the influence of the clergy on all social as well as narrowly religious questions is enormous. Ireland, alone with Malta in Europe, has no legal divorce, and abortion—never legal—has recently been made unconstitutional. The central tenets of the Catholic church are mainly accepted, but various local heterodox usages continue in some areas. Notably, holy well cults are still an important aspect of local practice. There are more than three thousand holy wells listed for Ireland, most of them associated with a Roman Catholic saint and with beliefs about curing, indulgences, honor, prayer, etc. Major pilgrimage points within Ireland (Knock, Croagh Patrick, Station Island, Lady's Island) attract tens of thousands annually, and the Irish are disproportionately represented at Lourdes.

ARTS. Language remains perhaps the most important form of expressive culture: from the oral narrative that still characterizes much local Irish life to one of the most vibrant literary traditions in Europe. Although less well-known, there is a lively visual art scene in the urban centers. Music, always important in the folk tradition, has made a great resurgence in recent decades with much creative interaction between folk and rock forms.

MEDICINE. Although most Irish avail themselves of whatever modern medical facilities are available, many will combine such treatments with propitiation of saints and/or pilgrimages to the above sites.

DEATH AND AFTERLIFE. For the vast majority of Irish, the rites of the Catholic church are

♦ **parliamentary
democracy**
*A form of democratic
government in which the
elected legislature has control
over the making and
administration of the law.*

followed scrupulously on the occasion of death. Wakes held in the home of the deceased for two or three days, however, continue to provide a central communal focus to the event in many areas. Appropriation of the powerful act and rites of death has characterized Irish political activity, especially in the twentieth century.

Bibliography

Arensberg, Conrad (1937). *The Irish Countryman*. New York: Macmillan.

Arensberg, Conrad, and Solon Kimball (1968). *Family and Community in Rural Ireland*. 2nd ed. Cambridge, Mass.: Harvard University Press.

Curtin, C., and T. Wilson (1989). *Ireland from Below: Social Change and Local Communities*. Galway: University College Galway Press.

Fox, Robin (1978). *The Tory Islanders: A People of the Celtic Fringe*. Cambridge: Cambridge University Press.

O'Kelly, Michael P. (1989). *Early Ireland*. Cambridge: Cambridge University Press.

Taylor, Lawrence J. (1989). "Bás InÉirinn: Cultural Constructions of Death in Ireland." *Anthropological Quarterly* 62:175–187.

—LAWRENCE J. TAYLOR

LOWLAND SCOTS

Ethonym: Scots, Scottish

Orientation

The Scottish Lowlands are made up of the southern portion of Scotland, the central region, the eastern coast, and most of the northeastern coast. The bulk of Scotland's population (about 80 percent) lives in the Lowlands, particularly in the urban and industrial areas around such major cities as Glasgow and Aberdeen, as well as in the capital city of Edinburgh. Taken as a whole, the Lowlands comprise some 48,648 square kilometers in land area and have a population in excess of 5 million. The climate is generally cool and wet, but there is variation across the region. There are few thunderstorms and little fog. Days are long in summer, short in winter.

Unlike that of the Highlanders, the language of Lowland Scots is not Gaelic but is rather a variant form of English introduced by Germanic settlers in the region as early as the sixth century A.D. The distinctiveness of what is now called "Scots" or Northern English, which was once called "Inglis," is great enough to merit its treatment as a language in its own right, rather than simply a dialect of the official or Standard English of southern Britain. Scots is a language with a long literary tradition, dating back to the 1300s. In the early 1700s English was made the official language, at least with regards to administration, for all of Britain, and Scots suffered a loss of prestige for a time. However, the linguistic tradition remained strong, borne in ballads, verse, and folk songs and preserved in the mid-seventeenth-century poetry of Robert Burns, perhaps the most famous of writers associated with the tongue.

History and Cultural Relations

The Romans arrived in the Scottish Lowlands in A.D. 80 but left few traces of their stay. During the period known as the Dark Ages, four groups emerged in Scotland: the Picts in the north; the Scots (of Irish origin) in the west; the Britons, who were related to the Welsh, in the southwest; and the Angles in the southeast. Linguistically, these groups were distinct from one another: the linguistic tradition of the Angles derived from Low German and Saxon English, the Scots and Britons spoke Gaelic, and the Picts possessed a language of their own. The formation of a unitary nation out of these disparate groups came about as a result of external pressures and the slow growth of Christianity in the region.

The first Scottish king, formally recognized, was Malcolm II (1005–1034), who inherited control of the southwestern portion of Scottish territory and won lands to the southeast through conflicts with England. But through the eleventh and twelfth centuries, rulership was frequently disputed among local leaders, and individual petty kings often sought English alliances to strengthen their causes. By the late thirteenth century, this state of affairs had resulted in increasing English control over the region. King Edward I of England arbitrated among claimants to the Scottish throne and installed John Balliol in that position for a time—though he was later to depose Balliol and assume personal control in 1296. The Treaty of Northhampton, in 1328, confirmed Scottish nationhood.

At about this time the house of Stuart arose, from which line came a succession of Scotland's leadership, nearly ending with Catholic Mary Stuart, who was beheaded in 1587. Her son became James I of England and James VI of Scotland. The last reigning Stuart was James II of England (James VII of Scotland), who was forced to abdicate in 1688, largely because the predominantly Protestant Scots rejected his devout Catholicism.

Once known for having higher wages and greater economic opportunities than the rest of Great Britain, the Lowland Scots area has suffered a decline since the mid-twentieth century.

See also

English, Gaels, Highland Scots, Irish, Welsh

The year 1707 brought about the formal Act of Union with England, linking the political entities of Scotland and England. While the political fortunes of the two nations have remained joined one to another since that time, the strong sense of a specifically Scottish national identity has never been erased, and to this day there are strong movements aimed at establishing Scottish independence.

Economy

The Lowlands consist of both rural and urban, agricultural and industrial, areas. Within the Lowlands, regional differentiation is marked in part by divergent economic practice. Although the county of Lothian, for example, is predominantly industrial, East Lothian is known as "corn country" and possesses some of the most prosperous farms of the region, while the Borders are associated with sheep husbandry. Glasgow is the industrial heart of the region, with its economy centered on the busy Clyde docks. It is thus difficult to describe some overall Lowland Scots culture, tradition, or economy. Once known for having higher wages and greater economic opportunities than the rest of Great Britain, the area has suffered something of a decline since the middle of this century, and unemployment has led to significant out-migration. Its traditional industries include shipbuilding and coal mining, both of which have grown less prosperous in recent years. Newer industries include electronics. Women working outside the home can be found today in all fields, but in the past they were associated largely with the textile industries and domestic work. In agricultural regions, a greater division of labor by gender was to be found, with women traditionally occupied in hand weeding and reaping with the sickle; culturally they were prescribed from working with horses. In the Scottish Lowlands, as elsewhere in industrialized regions, there is a marked difference in wage levels for men and women, with women often earning substantially less than their male counterparts.

Scotland as a whole has long honored the idea of education and equal access thereto. Public education, once controlled by the churches, came more and more under the control of the state during the nineteenth century. Higher education is highly valued, and the universities of St. Andrews, Edinburgh, and Glasgow are of world renown. It was not until the last decade of the nineteenth century that women were legally granted full-status access to university-level education.

HISTORIC EDINBURGH

The spires of a church look over some stone residences in Edinburgh. Around 80 percent of Scotland's population lives in the Lowlands. Edinburgh, Scotland. (Adam Woolfitt/Corbis)

Religion and Expressive Culture

Religious affiliation in Lowlands Scotland is pluralistic, and sissenting churches have included the Secession, Relief, Episcopal, and Roman Catholic churches. The Free Church of Scotland was created in the mid-1800s, and the Catholic church underwent a significant increase during roughly the same period, largely as a result of a major influx of Irish immigrants who fled to Scotland to escape the Irish potato famine. Also during this period, the Secession and Relief churches, which had formed in rebellion against the control of the Crown over the established Church of Scotland, were merged to form the United Presbyterian church. Church affiliation is to some degree linked to socioeconomic position in the Lowlands, with tradespeople predominating within the United Presbyterian church, the "landed gentry" associated most strongly with Episcopalianism, and rural laborers largely belonging to the Church of Scotland. Church influence in daily life was and remains strongest in rural areas as compared to urban ones.

The contribution of Scots to literature and the arts is immense. Lowlanders of world renown include R. L. Stevenson, Walter Scott, A. Conan Doyle, J. M. Barrie, David Hume, and Adam Smith. The Borders are famed as the heartland of minstrels and were the home of Walter Scott. Thomas Carlyle was born in the rural southwest. Burns wrote of the rich agricultural world of East Lothian.

Bibliography

Fraser, W. Hamish, and R. J. Morris, eds. (1988–1991). *People and Society in Scotland: A Social History of Modern Scotland in Three Volumes*. Edinburgh: John Donald Publishers.

—NANCY E. GRATTON

MONTENEGRINS

Ethonym: Crnogorci

Orientation

IDENTIFICATION. Montenegrins live predominantly in the region currently constituting the Socialist Republic of Montenegro, the smallest republic within modern-day Yugoslavia. Montenegrins speak the Štokavian dialect of Serbo-Croatian and call their republic "Crna Gora," meaning "Black Mountain." Culturally, they are closely related to the Serbs; some authors consider them to be of the same ethnic group. Montenegrins closely identify with the Serbs through common history and culture. Nonetheless, there are some important cultural, economic, and historical differences that distinguish the two groups. This entry focuses on aspects of Montenegrin life, history, and geography that differentiate them from Serbs. In general, however, there is little published research on contemporary Montenegrin culture. The reader should consult the entry under Serbs for additional information.

LOCATION. Montenegro is located between approximately 42 and 43.5° N and 18.5 and 20.5° E. It is bounded on the northeast and east by Serbia and the autonomous region of Kosovo, on the west and northwest by Bosnia and Herzegovina, and on the south by Albania and the Adriatic Sea. Terrain and climate are highly varied. Mountains rise from the seacoast, reaching inland heights of 2,400 meters in some parts of the republic. Rainfall varies from lows of only a few centimeters per year along the coast to highs of 200 centimeters in some mountainous areas. The growing season in the limited arable areas can last from April to October. Much of the republic is otherwise covered by barren limestone known as the *karst*. Even in areas with abundant rainfall, this geography limits the availability of surface water.

DEMOGRAPHY. The population of the Socialist Republic of Montenegro in 1981 was 584,000. People identifying themselves as ethnically Montenegrin constituted approximately two-thirds of the total population. Serbs make up about 11 percent of the republic's population, and there is a small but significant Muslim minority.

LINGUISTIC AFFILIATION. Montenegrins speak a dialect of Serbo-Croatian known as Štokavian (subdialect: Ijekavian), which is a South Slavic language from the Slavic Branch of Indo-European. Nearest related languages are Slovene, Macedonian (both spoken in other Yugoslav republics), and Bulgarian. Like other Orthodox Serbo-Croatian speakers, they traditionally employed the Cyrillic alphabet, although the Latin alphabet is now also widely seen.

History and Cultural Relations

Slavic settlement of the area dates to Slavic migrations of the sixth and seventh centuries. From 1389 and the Serbian defeat at Kosovo until 1516, Montenegro was nominally an independent principality. Montenegro was the last Balkan area to be subjugated by the Ottomans in the late fifteenth century and the first "liberated" when con-

♦ autonomous
region (AR)
An autonomous (usually, ethnically based) region of a Union republic.

See also
Serbs

trol passed to the Cetinje monastery and the hereditary prince-bishops around 1700, but it was never fully subjugated. Researchers note considerable variation from source to source in these dates, the degree of subjugation, and centers of political power. Montenegro was an independent kingdom for a brief time in the early 1900s before joining the Kingdom of the Serbs, Croats and Slovenes in 1918. Since the end of World War II it has been part of modern-day Yugoslavia.

Montenegrins have traditionally sided with the Serbs, with whom they share many cultural and historical links. This has remained true in the current conflict with Croatia begining in 1991; during this conflict Montenegrins supported Serbian guerrilla insurgencies in southern Croatia. At the national level Montenegro supported Serbian attempts to block Croatian ascendancy to the national presidency in the spring of 1991.

Settlements

Settlement patterns vary but most villages are small with populations of less than 1,000. Montenegro is the most sparsely populated republic in the country with only 42 persons per square kilometer in 1981 (as compared to 105 persons in Serbia). The two major village types are clustered and dispersed. Where land is arable, villages tend to be clustered on the borders of the cultivated basins. Elsewhere, the pattern is more one of dispersed family residences.

Nearly all houses traditionally were made of stone using lime mortar. One or two stories was the general rule. Windows are small and, in older houses, it is still possible to see the loopholes used in warding off Turkish attacks or blood feuding. Roofs were traditionally made of tile, straw, or stone, depending on local availability and economics. Since World War II, modern buildings have appeared, but home styles remain based on the old patterns. During the summer months when livestock are pastured on the high mountain grasses, the herders live in smaller summer cabins grouped together into *katuns*. These are typically also made of stone.

Economy

Historically, Montenegrins have been farmers, in the areas where agriculture is possible, and herders elsewhere. Major agricultural products include rye and barley, as well as other cereal crops. In coastal areas, olives, figs, and grapes are also grown. Most important, however, has been the herding of sheep, goats, and cattle based on seasonal movement of flocks.

SUBSISTENCE AND COMMERCIAL ACTIVITIES. Although post-World War II modernization has produced some industrialization, Montenegrin industry and agriculture remain under-developed and the population poor by Yugoslav standards. In the post-World War II period, Montenegro continued to rank last among

SOCIAL ORGANIZATION

Class structure is relatively undifferentiated in rural areas, but as elsewhere in Yugoslavia, the urban elite traditionally have wielded both internal and external political power.

Political Organization

Administrative divisions below the republic level have been reorganized several times since 1945. Below this level, however, the village and other local councils are important to local affairs. Village Council members are locally elected and are responsible for the exercise of federal and republic government policies at the local level; they also determine policy in local affairs. Traditionally,

bonds of kinship expressed in clan or tribal affiliations were important to defining political power.

Social Control

Honor, shame, and duty have traditionally been highly important concepts in defining proper behavior. Proper behavior is reinforced through violence, as evidenced by the high incidence of blood feuding, and gossip. Historically, capital punishment was common for a number of offensives, both major and minor by modern standards. In contemporary times, the federal court system has attempted to usurp many of the powers earlier vested in kin groups and less

formal clan and tribal courts, but informal settlement of disagreements (often through bloodshed) remains common.

Conflict

Montenegrin history is fraught with conflict, both internal and external. Montenegro fought in seven wars between 1850 and 1918. Revolt against Ottoman rule was continuous, and the area served as a refuge and staging area for revolts elsewhere in the region. Feuding between kin groups was endemic and continues in some areas even today.

the Yugoslav republics in the percentage of its work force employed in industry.

TRADE. In general, external trade was historically of only minimal importance. Because of the isolation generated by centuries of military conflict with the Ottomans and extensive raiding outside of the mountain strongholds, trade links did not develop as they had farther up the Adriatic coast.

DIVISION OF LABOR. Sex roles traditionally were well defined and women economically important but of low status.

LAND TENURE. Contemporary landholding laws and patterns are governed by Yugoslav law and mirror those in Serbia. However, according to late nineteenth-century reports, historical distinctions existed in grazing versus farming rights. Whereas arable holdings and their inheritance followed the traditional Serbian pattern, grazing rights were vested in the larger clan and tribal communities.

Kinship

KIN GROUPS AND DESCENT. One important point differentiating the Montenegrins from the Serbs is the existence of kin and social groups larger than the lineage. Both clan (*bratstvo*) and tribe (*pleme*) were important economic and social groups. The pleme was composed of several contiguous bratstvo. These larger groups have been important throughout Montenegrin political and economic history. Economically, they defined cooperative labor arrangements. Politically, they formed the basis of the alliances from which political and military power were generated. Fictive kin ties established through godfatherhood and blood brotherhood also figured prominently in kin relations.

Descent is patrilineal, and great emphasis is placed on the perpetuation of male lines.

KINSHIP TERMINOLOGY. Kinship terminology is parallel to that used in Serbia. On the first ascending generation, terminology is bifurcate-collateral for males and lineal for females. In general, terms for consanguineal kin are more specific than for affines.

Marriage and Family

MARRIAGE. Traditionally, marriages in Montenegro were almost always arranged by the parents. Family reputation, not love, was the primary factor in selecting a bride. Virginity before marriage was highly valued and in some areas the practice of displaying the bloodied wedding sheets as proof of the bride's chastity was common. Some sources note a pattern of "trial" marriage in which consumation of the union was delayed for a period of up to a year. Marriage was an important way to create bonds of friendship between families and to maintain or improve the family's status in the community. Unlike nearby Bosnia, the practice of *otmica*, or bride capture, was rare in Montenegro. When it did occur, the consent of both families had been quietly prearranged. There was likewise no pattern of brideprice. Although divorced individuals could remarry within the church, the actual incidence of divorce was low until after World War II and the establishment of secular reforms in marriage law. Among the most common causes of divorce were sterility or the failure to bear male offspring, both of which were always seen as the wife's fault. Women could not initiate divorce in the pre-Socialist period. Postmarital residence is typically patrilocal.

DOMESTIC UNIT. The basic household and family unit is the patrilocal extended family. Although the most basic term of reference is *kuća*, meaning simply "house," this area was characterized like much of the Balkans by *zadrugas*, large extended-family households.

INHERITANCE. Inherited property traditionally was divided equally among surviving sons, although a widow was entitled to usufruct. Traditionally, in cases where a man had no sons, property that passed instead to daughters was said to "come on the miraz." By contrast, post–World War II legal codes specify bilateral inheritance, although the laws are still frequently circumvented.

SOCIALIZATION. Corporal punishment is a common means of discipline. Traditional emphasis on respect for elders, concepts of honor and shame, and conformity to household goals has been eroded in the post–World War II period.

Sociopolitical Organization

The Socialist Federal Republic of Yugoslavia has separate heads of state and government. By 1991, however, the central government had disintegrated and the national Communist party, under its old framework, had been dissolved. In late 1991 Slovenia and Croatia, having declared themselves separate nations, were accepted as such by the European Community. In Montenegro, the old-line Communist government was forced from power by large-scale street demonstrations in January 1989. Montenegro aligned itself with Serbia in the creation of a new Yugoslav federation in May 1992.

Montenegrins have traditionally sided with the Serbs, with whom they share many cultural and historical links. This has remained true in the conflict with Croatia beginning in 1991.

Religion and Expressive Culture

RELIGIOUS BELIEFS. Traditionally, Montenegrin beliefs are a syncretic blend of Eastern Orthodox Christianity and pre-Christian practices. Although most people consider themselves Orthodox, there are significant Catholic and Muslim minorities. God (Bog), Saint Elijah, and the one or two patron saints associated with each clan are the most prominent supernatural figures. Other supernatural beings such as vampires, ghosts, and nature spirits often figure prominently in folk epics and stories.

RELIGIOUS PRACTITIONERS. In addition to Eastern Orthodox priests, there were historically large numbers of local "popes," lay priests frequently ignorant of written doctrine and tradition.

CEREMONIES. The religious calendar includes all the normal Christian holidays, with Easter being the most important church holiday. Life-cycle ceremonies, particularly those marking birth and death, are also important events. However, two other ceremonies also figure prominently in people's lives. The first is the ceremony establishing godfatherhood or *kumstvo*. The second is the *slava*, or the feast of the clan's (*bratstvo's*) patron saint. Today the slava has lost much of its former functions in promoting kin-group solidarity and reinforcing kin-group boundaries.

ARTS. As for the Serbs, the Montenegrin national instrument is the *gusle*—a single-horsehair wooden instrument stroked with a horsehair bow. The most important function of the instrument is to provide accompaniment for the singing of oral epic poetry. This tradition is wholly oral in the sense that, while the formula uses ten-syllable lines, each performance is a unique creation. Texts are not memorized. Common story themes include battles with the Turks, encounters with supernatural beings, the exploits of culture heroes, and the recounting of lineage ancestry.

Bibliography

Boehm, Christopher (1983). *Montenegrin Social Organization and Values*. New York: AMS Press.

Boehm, Christopher (1984). *Blood Revenge: The Anthropology of Feuding in Montenegro and Other Tribal Societies*. Lawrence: University Press of Kansas.

Denton, William (1877). *Montenegro: Its Land and Their History*. London: Daldy, Isbister & Co.

Durham, Mary E. (1928). *Some Tribal Origins, Laws, and Customs of the Balkans*. London: George Allen & Unwin.

Federal Statistical Office of Yugoslavia (1983). *Statisticki kalendar Jugoslavije* (Statistical pocket book of Yugoslavia). Belgrade.

Partridge, Monica (1964). *Serbo-Croatian: Practical Grammar and Reader*. New York: McGraw-Hill.

—RICHARD A. WAGNER

NORWEGIANS

Ethonym: Nordmenn

Orientation

IDENTIFICATION. The nation of Norway constitutes the western portion of the Scandinavian Peninsula. Its population is substantially of Scandinavian stock, with the exception of Saami and Finns in the north and recent European and other immigrants in the urban south.

LOCATION. Norway is a narrow, essentially mountainous strip, with an almost 3,200-kilometer coastline to the west and south on the Atlantic Ocean (Norwegian Sea), which is characterized by fjords and numerous islands. Norway shares a long border with Sweden to the east, and shorter boarders with Finland and the Russia to the north and east. Oslo is its capital. It is located at approximately 58° to 73° N and 3° to 31° E. The Gulf Stream assists in producing a continental climate in much of Norway. Despite its northerly location and a short growing season, agriculture and animal husbandry accompany fishing and timbering as primary traditional subsistence occupations. Average yearly rainfall (Oslo) is 68 centimeters.

DEMOGRAPHY. The population of Norway is approximately 4.1 million. The direction of population migration in Norway in recent years has been generally from the country and into the urban centers, the three largest cities currently accounting for approximately one-fourth of the population.

LINGUISTIC AFFILIATION. Norwegian is one of the languages of the North Germanic (i.e., Scandinavian) Branch of Germanic languages, which are in turn a branch of the Indo-European Language Family. It is written with the Latin alphabet and is closely related to both Swedish and Danish, the latter having had a strong historical influence on the Norwegian language beginning in the fourteenth century. Today there are two forms of standard written Norwegian. The Danish-influenced Bokmal is characteristic in urban and upper-class use. Nynorsk, based on Norway's rural dialects, is associated with independent

"Norwegianness" and social egalitarianism. In spoken usage, Norway's mountainous geography has spawned a multitude of local dialects (and local cultural variation in general), although recent urbanization has eroded dialect distinctiveness in some areas.

History and Cultural Relations

Norway was populated by people who are the forerunners of today's Norwegian ethnics as early as 10,000 B.C. Stone Age subsistence in southern Norway was characterized both by foraging and farming. The Bronze Age (1500–500 B.C.) and Iron Ages (500 B.C.–A.D. 400) are clearly demarcated in the archaeological record, the former characterized by rock art, the latter by expanded agriculture and population and by contact with the culture of the Roman Empire. The Germanic migrations of A.D. 500–800 affected primarily the coastal Norwegian population. The Viking Age (A.D. 800–1100), one of exploration, was accompanied by political unification of Norway under a line of kings and the arrival of Catholicism, although growing cultural unification of Norway was interrupted in the fourteenth century by the Black Death. Norway was politically unified with Denmark, as one of its provinces, from 1380 to 1814. Thereafter, it was politically unified with Sweden until 1905, when it gained independence. Norway experienced substantial emigration to North America in the late nineteenth and early twentieth centuries.

Norway is traditionally an ethnically homogeneous society, with the notable exceptions of the Saami and Finnish immigrants in the north and of recent urban immigrants in the south. Cultural and economic conflict characterizes Saami-Norwegian relations, with language use and resource use and allocation being commonly contested issues. Despite substantial cultural similarities with Sweden and Denmark, the colonial history that Norway has experienced with both has strained its relationships with them.

Settlements

Villages are nucleated settlements providing focal points (for marketing, schooling, and religion) for dispersed settlement in the area. Towns are increasing in size, complexity, and degree of interrelatedness to urban centers. The largest cities in Norway are Oslo (approximately 450,000), Bergen (approximately 200,000), and Trondheim (approximately 150,000), with universities in all three (a fourth university is located in Tromso).

Economy

SUBSISTENCE AND COMMERCIAL ACTIVITIES. Prior to World War II, the economy was based on timbering, fishing and whaling, metal production (i.e., aluminum, copper), agriculture, and the merchant marine. Since World War II energy production (gas, oil, electricity) has played an increasing role, and the service sector of the economy has grown. A mixed-subsistence base of wage labor and the primary occupations of fishing, farming, or animal husbandry was not uncommon, but it is becoming less prevalent with relative depopulation of rural areas. A typical diet consists of bread, butter, cheese, fish, and meat. Potatoes, cabbage, and carrots are the most common vegetables, and local berries (lingonberry, cloud berry) are supplemented by imported fruits as sources of vitamin C.

INDUSTRIAL ARTS. Many people, especially in the rural areas, produce crafts, such as knitted or woven goods and various wooden crafts (utensils, bowls, furniture). Regional costumes are a widespread manufacture.

TRADE. Open-air produce markets supplement established stores in the summer months.

DIVISION OF LABOR. The complementarity of female and male roles is a fundamental presumption of Norwegian social structure and is reinforced by a pattern of strong spousal solidarity. "Feminine" and "masculine" behaviors are not strongly distinguished, and decision-making authority is often shared in families. Informal social networks of males and females are, however, substantially segregated. The public/private division of labor is operative in rural areas, with the women performing the majority of domestic duties (i.e., baking, washing, weaving) while the men hold the primary responsibility for such tasks as chopping wood. Farm labor such as making silage, harvesting potatoes, or milking cows often is shared by the entire family.

LAND TENURE. Traditionally the small single-family farm was the prevailing type of landholding in rural areas. Gradually the size of these holdings has increased with rural depopulation.

Kinship, Marriage, and Family

KINSHIP. Kinship is cognatic, with the nuclear family (or less frequently the stem family) as the coresidential group. Residence patterns in rural areas tend to virilocality, whereas in larger towns and urban areas uxorilocality or neolocality are more frequent. Social ties with other cognatic kin living in close physical proximity are signifi-

Despite substantial cultural similarities with Sweden and Denmark, the colonial history that Norway has experienced with both has strained Norwegian relationships with them.

See also

Finns, Saami

cant, but friendship networks and ties of voluntary association also structure everyday interaction in important ways. In modern Norway, no kin-based corporate group exists beyond the nuclear family.

MARRIAGE.   After confirmation at about age 14, young Norwegians begin to engage in sexual relations in their mid- to late teens. At formal engagement, sexual relations are openly sanctioned and accompanied by partial or complete cohabitation. Pregnancy is the most common stimulus for marriage. Men are typically 25–30 years of age at marriage and women are typically 20–25 years of age. The divorce rate is relatively low, but it is rising. Personal friction and alcoholism are the most frequently cited reasons for divorce.

DOMESTIC UNIT.   The nuclear or stem family is the prevalent domestic unit. The stem family consists of a married pair and their unmarried children, plus the parent or parents of one of the spouses. These grandparents often live in a small separate apartment in the same house or in a small separate building near the main house.

INHERITANCE.   Traditional Norwegian inheritance patterns were based on both *odelsrett* (a principle of primogeniture and patriliny) and *asetesrett* (a principle of equal inheritance of all children). In practice in rural areas, eldest sons inherited farms, together with an obligation to pay monetary compensation to other siblings.

SOCIALIZATION.   Norwegian adults consider children as independent individuals who will not be very much influenced by adults, and thus they have a correspondingly democratic approach to child rearing. Harsh discipline, especially corporal punishment, is discouraged, with discussion used as a substitute. Early physical independence is not especially encouraged, but it is welcomed. Avoidance of direct confrontation characterizes relationships. Children construct role models on the behavior of adults rather than on the instructions adults give them for behavior.

Sociopolitical Organization

SOCIAL ORGANIZATION.   Norway's system of taxation and social welfare generally precludes extremes of poverty and wealth. Class distinctions between professionals, business people, and working-class people in urban areas are greater than social differentiation in rural areas (the rural merchant-king excepted). Rural elites were and are small in number.

POLITICAL ORGANIZATION.   Norway is a constitutional monarchy, divided into nineteen provinces (*fylke*). Of the nine major political parties (including a spectrum from Conservative to Center to Communist), the Labor party has dominated Norwegian politics since the 1930s. The current prime minister, Gro Harlem Brundtland (Labor party), leads a 157–member parliament. Norway's nineteen provinces are in turn divided into counties (*kommune*), each of which has a central administration. Debate of issues is highly valued in county councils. Villages do not have formal councils and local community consciousness may or may not be the norm, as individual independence is also strongly developed.

SOCIAL CONTROL.   Nonconfrontation and the maintenance of conformity are important Norwegian values. Breaches of law are handled by local sheriffs or by police and are adjudicated in the Norwegian judicial system. Personal relations are characterized by avoidance of expressing strong emotions, rather than open conflict.

CONFLICT.   Norway's early kings (especially Harold Fairhair, c. A.D. 900–940) prevailed in conflicts with local lords to establish centralized leadership; this pattern of internal armed conflict was congruent with simultaneous external Viking conquest. When Norway was ceded by Denmark to Sweden in 1814, the Norwegians attempted unsuccessfully to repel the Swedish army and establish an independent government. Norway's independence from Sweden in 1905 was achieved without military conflict. Norway was occupied by Germany in World War II.

Religion and Expressive Culture

RELIGIOUS BELIEFS AND PRACTICES. Lutheranism became the official state religion in Norway in the sixteenth century and remains such, although minority religions (Baptists, Catholics) are also evident. Although membership in the state church is high, many Norwegians are not regular churchgoers, with women generally putting more emphasis on church attendance. High festivals such as Christmas, Easter, and Norwegian Independence Day (Syttende Mai) are ritualized events with national costumes, festive foods, and church attendance integrated into the celebrations.

ARTS.   Various folk arts, such as rose painting and costume and clothing manufacture, are accompanied by modern forms of visual, literary, and theatrical arts.

MEDICINE.   State-supported socialized medicine fulfills health care needs, with hospital care as a norm for childbirth and serious illnesses. Almost all drugs are dispensed on a prescription basis in pharmacies (*apotek*).

◆ **primogeniture**
A rule of inheritance that gives the exclusive right of inheritance to the first-born son.

◆ **patriliny**
(patrilineal descent, agnatic descent) The practice of tracing kinship affiliation only through the male line.

DEATH AND AFTERLIFE. Funerals, like all life-and-death rituals (baptism, confirmation), are generally held in the church. The concept of a continuing spirit after death, which is in accordance with Lutheran theology, is however absent in a significant number of nonchurchgoing Norwegians, approximately 30 percent of the total population.

Bibliography

Barnes, John A. (1954). "Class and Committee in a Norwegian Island Parish." *Human Relations* 7:39–58.

Barnes, John A. (1957). "Land Rights and Kinship in Two Bremnes Hamlets." *Journal of the Royal Anthropological Institute* 87:31–56.

Barth, Fredrik, ed. (1963). *The Role of the Entrepreneur in Social Change in Northern Norway.* Oslo: Universitetsforlaget.

Eliot, Thomas D., et al. (1960). *Norway's Families.* Philadelphia: University of Pennsylvania Press.

Hollos, Marida (1974). *Growing Up in Flathill.* Oslo: Universitetsforlaget.

—KAREN A. LARSON

PERIPATETICS

Ethonym: Gypsies, and all corresponding terms in the various European languages (Bohémiens, Cigani, Cingaros, Gitanos, Gitans, Mustalainen, Tataren, Tsiganes, Zigeuner, Zingari, etc.)., Travelers or Travellers and all corresponding terms in the various European languages (Gens du Voyage, Rasende, Viajeros, Voyageurs, etc.)., Rom or phonetically similar terms (Beaš, Camminanti, Hantrika, Jenischen, Kale, Korrner, Manuš, Minceir, Pavé, Quinquis, Romanicel, Romanies, Rudari, Sinte or Sinti, Woonwagenbewoners, etc.)

Orientation

All complex societies (with a division of labor determined not solely on the basis of sex, with a hierarchical sociopolitical organization, with an economy capable of producing a surplus) leave a potential space for those people referred to, among other terms, as "groups that don't want in." Such a definition is to be understood in both a sociological and an epistemological sense: these groups "don't want in" (1) as far as the hierarchical organization of the society in which they live is concerned, and (2) as far as traditional anthropological categories are concerned. Regarding both these characteristics, one could say that they have been considered by Europeans as "good to think about" symbolically, "good to prohibit" politically, but "indigestible to study" anthropologically. Social anthropology has discovered them only in the last few decades, rejecting the results of the two main theoretical approaches with which they were previously studied: the sociopsychology of disadjustment and positivist, racist criminology. Beyond this rejection, however, no unanimous consensus exists as to how to categorize the "groups that don't want in"; certain scholars consider it erroneous to attempt to create a single defined category. Among the various terms proposed, "peripatetics" has had the greatest theoretical elaboration and today enjoys the greatest consensus. The three main characteristics of the peripatetic groups are: spatial mobility; subsistence based on the sale of goods and/or services outside the group; and endogamy. Since these three features may vary greatly from one group to another, some groups occupy marginal positions that are difficult to define in terms of such a theoretical elaboration. We could thus assert that the main characteristic of the "groups that don't want in" is their extraordinary structural flexibility. The "groups that don't want in" are those who can be categorized as "peripatetics" at certain historical-geographical junctures, but not at others.

IDENTIFICATION. Such groups are currently referred to in Europe as Gypsies and Travellers. The difference between the two categories would appear to reside in their "origin": the former are thought to come from India, the latter to be native Europeans. Since the "origin" is not always verifiable and since several present-day groups may be the result of a fusion between groups of autochthonous origin and groups of an extra-European origin, certain scholars have merged the two terms into "Traveller-Gypsies." In order to maintain the traditional distinction between Gypsies and Travellers, we can subdivide the former into two large sets based on self-denominations: (1) the "Rom" set includes all those groups whose autonym is Rom or one of its phonetic variants (Rom, Róma, Romá, Romje, etc.); (2) the "rom" set includes all those groups that, though having other autonyms, use or formerly used the term "rom," or its variants, with the meaning of "men" or "husband" (Kale, Manuš, Romanicel, Sinti). In some cases, among these last groups, "rom" can also mean "man of our group," thus becoming concurrent with the normally used autonym.

LOCATION. With the possible exception of Iceland and Malta, all European countries are

With the possible exception of Iceland and Malta, all European countries are host to a permanent presence of peripatetic groups.

host to a permanent presence of peripatetic groups. Although the three sets we have categorized—"Rom," "rom," and "Travellers"—are represented today in communities throughout the European continent, we can indicate, nevertheless, approximate areas of major concentration, historically speaking. An imaginary line (Rome-Vienna-Prague-Helsinki) divides Gypsy Europe into two parts: the western half is noted for its preponderance of "rom" groups, while in the eastern half there is a large majority of "Rom" groups. This line is only an indication of concentration tendencies—after the great migrations of the nineteenth and twentieth centuries some "rom" communities (especially Sinti) are found in the east and, more importantly, many "Rom" groups have moved to the west. The "Traveller" groups, though in general widely dispersed, also seem to be concentrated in specific regions, which are either marginal or enclaves of the "rom" zone. On the Celtic fringe (Ireland and Scotland), in Scandinavia (but not in Finland) and in the northern Alps (especially the Swiss part, inhabited mainly by Jenischen), these Traveller groups appear to be in the majority. From here, along a corridor running up through Alsace-Lorraine and the Rhine valley (where the Jenischen are outnumbered by "rom" groups, though their number is by no means negligible), we reach the Netherlands, where the local Travellers (Woonwagenbewoners) appear to outnumber the "rom" and "Rom" groups.

DEMOGRAPHY. Many estimates have been made as to the numbers of Gypsies and Travellers present in Europe. Here we cite only three: Puxon (1973) counts exactly 4,745,475; Vossen (1983) gives a minimum number of 1,988,000 and a maximum of 5,621,000; Liégeois (1986) calculates a minimum of 3,421,750 and a maximum of 4,935,000. More consistent estimates, however, can be obtained using the same authors' data for areas of larger concentration. Their presence seems concentrated in the Danubian-Carpathian region (the Czech and Slovak Federative Republic; Hungary; the former Yugoslavia; Romania; and Bulgaria) with percentages between 59.1 percent (Puxon) and 64.6 percent (Vossen) of the total European peripatetic population. The southwestern region (Spain and France) is also important with estimates between 15.2 percent (Liégeois) and 18.7 percent (Puxon), whereas percentage estimates for the nations of the former Soviet Union prove to be of little significance, given the lack of more precise data on concentration within this vast territory—between 6 percent (Liégeois) and 10 percent (Puxon). In the rest of Europe there

results a more dispersed presence amounting to a percentage somewhere between 12.2 percent (Puxon) and 14.3 percent (Liégeois) of the total Gypsy and Traveller population.

History and Cultural Relations

HISTORY. The presence of itinerant groups that lived by trade and handicraft in medieval Europe is fairly well documented. Certain *mangones* and *occiones*, horse dealers and metalworkers, were itinerant in Charlemagne's empire (eighth century). In twelfth-century Ireland, certain *tynkers* were to be found, and at the beginning of the fourteenth century nomads by the name of *sculuara* were the subject of one of the king of Sweden's decrees. In addition to the continual presence of these groups of presumably autochthonous origin, medieval Europe would seem to be scoured now and then by foreign groups: "Egyptian" acrobats visit Greece, Macedonia, and Spain, while an "Ethiopian" group given to magic artistry visits Italy, Spain, France, and England during the thirteenth century. However, undoubtedly at the start of the fifteenth century Western exotic nomads began to invade western Europe. Their presence in the Balkans had already been noted during the previous two centuries. Although Europeans used many names to describe these foreigners, two are by far the most common: "Egyptians" in the Atlantic regions, which was to become "Gitanos" in Spanish, "Gitans" in French, "Gypsies" in English, etc.; and "Cigani" (a term whose etymon is dubious—perhaps from the Greek word "Atsinganoi") used in central-eastern Europe with several variants: "Zigeuner" in German, "Zingari" in Italian, "Cingani" in modern Latin, etc. The two terms overlap in many regions. The relationships established between the newcomers and the local peripatetic groups do not appear to have been always univocal. Although it may be true that modern literature notes several cases of "counterfeit Egyptians," that is, people of the so-called "dangerous classes" joining bands of Gypsies or passing themselves off as Gypsies, it is equally true that foreign peripatetics often kept their identity distinct from that of the local ones. As far back as the sixteenth century, one anonymous author compared the two groups and demonstrated their diversity through ethnographic and linguistic data. Language research, in fact, dates back to the end of the eighteenth century and plays an important role in the study of the history of the exotic peripatetics' migrations, by making the connection between Romani (the language of the Gypsies) and the neo-Sanskrit languages of India. The race to discover the Gypsies' Indian origins (the region of India they came from) and the era of their departure was, thus, initiated. Different interpretations of certain phonological and lexicological features have resulted in moving the "country" of origin, from central India either to north-west India or to the region of present-day Afghanistan. The date of departure is still uncertain; the date currently proposed is A.D. 1000, though some scholars date this as far back as the seventh or eighth century A.D. Linguists maintain that the numerous terms in the Romani language of non-Indian origin (above all Persian, Armenian, and Greek) are proof of the journey undertaken from India to Europe. According to a recent hypothesis, however, during the Middle Ages, the Romani language could have been a sort of lingua franca, used along the trade routes connecting Europe to the East. This hypothesis implies that the present-day European Gypsies, albeit speakers of neo-Indian dialects, may not be the direct descendants of peoples living in India today. According to linguists, however, the Gypsies who came to Europe spoke an essentially unitary language, which then became more and more diversified as a result of the borrowings from the languages of the European people among whom they settled or among whom they practiced their nomadism. On the basis of these borrowings, the linguists identify six or seven major Romani dialectal groups, still in use today or spoken up to the last century.

CULTURAL RELATIONS. The patterns of Gypsy dispersion and settlement within modern Europe are practically unknown and consequently so are the modalities of the ethnogenesis of the Gypsy groups as they appear today. Nevertheless, two factors would appear to be at the basis of such modalities: the external relationships with non-Gypsies and the inter-Gypsy relationships. As far as the former are concerned, we can distinguish, very schematically, two political approaches adopted by European governments towards Gypsy populations: the "western" approach, aimed at the annihilation of the Gypsies, and the "Danubian" approach, aimed at the exploitation of Gypsy labor. The western approach consisted of thousands of banishments, mass imprisonment, deportation to American and African colonies, Gypsy hunting for rewards, with the resulting genocide, and, at the best, attempts at forced assimilation. The culmination of this tradition is the genocide of the Nazi period when more than half a million Gypsies were

ON THE ROAD

A Peripatetic family on a road near Tulcea. Peripatetics travel through Europe, offering their skills for employment. Danube Delta, Romania. (Barry Lewis/Corbis)

exterminated. This figure does not bear true witness, however, to the real proportions of the Holocaust, since the Gypsy presence in some areas occupied by the German forces and their allies was diminished by 80 percent. The "Danubian" approach, in contrast, saw the insertion of Gypsies in the servitude and slavery systems of southeastern Europe. Here the Gypsies were never submitted to the "western" type of mass extermination. Therefore, they have become an important part of the overall population in many eastern European countries—and not only in those countries where mixed marriages between Gypsies and non-Gypsies were formally forbidden by law—and have for the most part become sedentary. The Gypsy disequilibrium in demographic terms between the Danubian-Carpathian region and the rest of Europe is a result of these two different political approaches. This disequilibrium has had at least two consequences. In the west the Gypsy groups have subdivided themselves mainly on a regional basis, practicing a sort of commercial eclecticism consistent with their resistance to annihilation. The dozens of subdivisions derive from this situation: the Sinti, for example, call themselves "Prussian" Sinti, "German" Sinti, "Austrian" Sinti, "Marchigiani" Sinti (from the region in central Italy called the Marches), etc. In southeast Europe, on the other hand, the subdivisions, in addition to being regional, have also been of a professional nature. Compelled by public authorities or by economic expediency in the wake of growing demographic pressure to differentiate their professions, the Gypsy groups have often adopted ergonyms with the function of ethnonyms: Kalderaš and its variants (coppersmiths), Čurara (sieve makers), etc. This phenomenon has been seen by certain authors as a survival of the Indian caste system among the Gypsies, whereas we are, in all probability, dealing with a situation that has its origins in the Balkans. Another consequence of the demographic disequilibrium has been the Gypsies' periodic movements from the Danubian-Carpathian region to other parts of Europe, which tend to take place during periods of economic or political hardship suffered by the non-Gypsy population in the region. Thus large groups of Rom arrived in western Europe during the second half of the nineteenth century (after the abolition of slavery in Moldavia and Walachia, in 1865, but above all at the time of the Balkan states' struggle for independence against the Turks) and at the start of the twentieth century. Other groups, after a stay in Russia, took refuge in the West following the events of 1917; others from the south of Yugoslavia began to migrate to Western Europe from the beginning of the 1960s in order to escape from the local economic crisis; others continue to flee en masse from disaster-struck post-Ceausescu Romania.

These great migratory movements have always been accompanied by smaller, virtually imperceptible group movements from one region to another. In all probability, these smaller movements have contributed more than anything else to the present Gypsy disposition in Europe. One example will suffice: the Romanicel are today present only in Great Britain (apart from North America and Australia), yet the same ethnonym has been noted in Spain and France for the nineteenth century. This would lead us to believe that the Romanicel once frequented much vaster zones than they do today. Toward the end of the eighteenth century and the beginning of the nineteenth, for reasons still unknown, there was a sort of "explosion" of the Sinti present in the Germanic countries, who gradually penetrated into the neighboring states. In some cases, they remained in the minority in relation to the Gypsy groups already present, but sometimes they perhaps "Sinticized" the local Romanicel (this is probably the case for France). In both the greater and the smaller migratory movements, there also appears to be a sort of autoregulation, because of "internal" pressures of a politicoeconomic nature. The settlement in new territories is always, in fact, made simpler when the presence of other groups is scarce or when the newcomers start to occupy "economic niches" that have yet to be exploited. The Gypsy populations, though nowadays largely sedentary, without doubt have constituted and continue to constitute the main "producers" of peripatetic groups; however, the non-Gypsy populations have always been a potential reservoir. The Jenischen in the Germanic countries and certain Swedish Rasenede appear to have formed a distinct identity only as late as the seventeenth and eighteenth centuries, while Dutch Woonwagenbewoners seem to have an even shorter history, dating from the nineteenth and twentieth centuries.

Peripatetic groups therefore are useful as special observatories for the study of ethnogenesis in highly stratified societies. Furthermore, given their great capacity to adapt—which requires a structural flexibility that is hard to find in other populations and which enables them to escape any sort of systematic classification—they should be considered worthy of careful and urgent research.

Bibliography

Fraser, Angus (1990). "Counterfeit Egyptians." Paper read at the Annual Meeting of the Gypsy Lore Society, Staten Island, N.Y.

Gmelch, Sharon B. (1986). "Groups That Don't Want In: Gypsies and Other Artisan, Trader, and Entertainer Minorities." *Annual Review of Anthropology* 15:307–330.

Hancock, Ian (1987). *The Pariah Syndrome*. Ann Arbor, Mich.: Karoma.

Hancock, Ian (1988). "The Development of Romani Linguistics." In *Languages and Cultures*, edited by M. A. Jazayery and W. Winter, 182–223. New York: Mouton de Gruyter.

Liégeois, Jean-Pierre (1986). *Gypsies and Travellers*. Strasbourg: Council of Europe, Council for Cultural Co-Operation.

De Nubianis erronibus, quos Itali Cingaros appellant, eorumque lingua" and "De idiotismo quorundam Erronum a Nubianis non admodum absimilium" (1597). In *De literis et lingua Getarum siue Gothorum*, edited by C. Vulanius, 100–109. Lugduni Batavorun [Leiden]: Apud Raphelengium.

Okely, Judith (1983). *The Traveller-Gypsies*. Cambridge: Cambridge University Press.

Puxon, Grattan (1973). *Rom: Europe's Gypsies*. London: Minority Rights Group.

Rao, Aparna (1987). "The Concept of Peripatetics: An Introduction." In *The Other Nomads*, edited by A. Rao. Cologne: Böhlau.

Vossen, Rüdiger (1983). *Zigeuner*. Frankfurt: M. Ullstein.

—LEONARDO PIASERE

PORTUGUESE

Ethonym: none

Orientation

LOCATION. Continental Portugal occupies approximately one-sixth of the Iberian Peninsula in western Europe. It is bordered on the south and west by the Atlantic Ocean and on the east and north by Spain. Portuguese also inhabit the islands of the Azores and Madeira in the Atlantic. As a result of colonial expansion and of massive emigration in the nineteenth and twentieth centuries, Portuguese-speaking peoples live in Asia, Africa, South America, the United States, Canada, Australia, and northwestern Europe.

DEMOGRAPHY. In 1984 the population of continental and island Portugal was estimated at 10,128,000. The population increased during the twentieth century until the 1960s, when it declined by more than 200,000 because of the extensive emigration to northern Europe after 1961. In the 1970s, the population of continental Portugal increased by more than a quarter of a million, largely as a result of the *retornados*, the settlers who returned to Portugal from Africa after decolonization. By comparison with other nations of Europe, Portugal has a high birthrate, though this rate is regionally differentiated and has declined in recent years. In 1985 the birthrate was 12.5 and the death rate 9.6.

LINGUISTIC AFFILIATION. The Portuguese language has largely Latin roots, though some words are Arabic in origin. Portuguese was made the official language under the reign of King Dinis (1279–1325). Unlike Spain, continental Portugal demonstrates a high degree of linguistic homogeneity.

Economy

SUBSISTENCE AND COMMERCIAL ACTIVITIES. The subsistence and commercial activities of the Portuguese vary regionally. The Azores are largely agricultural, with some islands depending primarily on dairying and meat production and others on a combination of cattle raising, whaling, fishing, and small-scale agriculture (sugar beets, tea, tobacco, and vegetables). These activities have been supplemented by more than a century of emigration to the United States. Madeira also relies on agriculture (wine, bananas, sugarcane), fishing, and whaling, in addition to small-scale cottage industry and tourism. The embroidery industry, introduced by an Englishwoman in the middle of the nineteenth century, employs approximately 70,000 female workers. Large numbers of Madeirans have emigrated to South Africa and, to a lesser extent, to Canada. The people of the Algarve are engaged in agriculture, fishing, and tourism. Cash-crop agriculture (wheat, olives, cork) predominates in the Alentejo. In central continental Portugal, a variety of irrigated grains (wheat, corn, rice) are cultivated on medium-sized family farms. The peasants of northern continental Portugal cultivate maize (rye in the northeast), potatoes, wine grapes, and vegetables. Many also raise dairy cattle. Along the coastline are populations engaged in fishing. Fish canning is an important export-oriented industry. Like the Azores, the local economies of northern Portugal have been supplemented by centuries of emigration, and as a result men have developed artisan skills as masons, carpenters, etc. Around the cities of Braga, Porto, and Guimarães there is a population

The Portuguese language has largely Latin roots, though some words are Arabic in origin.

of worker-peasants who are employed in the old and important textile industry. Furniture making, food processing, winemaking, and pulp and paper production are among the other industrial activities in this region. Heavier industry (steelworking, shipbuilding, iron production) and the bulk of the industrial working class are concentrated in the Lisbon-Setubal region in the south. In recent years, the construction industry has become important in several parts of the country.

In 1984 there were 4,695,700 Portuguese counted in the labor force. Of these, 22 percent were engaged in agriculture, forestry, and fishing; 22 percent in manufacturing; 13 percent in distribution and hotels; 8 percent in construction; 27 percent in other sectors; and 8 percent unemployed. The estimated national income per person was $1,820. Labor force figures frequently underestimate the participation of women who, since Roman times, have been making important contributions to the rural economy of northern Portugal. Some anthropologists view these activities as the basis of significant economic and political power accorded to peasant women. Bourgeois and upper-class women, on the other hand, were at one time restricted to the domestic sphere. This situation has changed significantly in the last

twenty years as women have received advanced education, professional training, and full legal equality.

LAND TENURE. Portugal is characterized by significant regional variations in patterns of land tenure. In the southernmost district of continental Portugal, the Algarve, land-holding are small and cultivated by owners, tenants, or sharecroppers. The region between the Algarve and the Tagus River, the Alentejo, has traditionally been a region of low population density, latifundia that originated in the Roman estate system, and landless day laborers. Prior to 1974, approximately 500 absentee landlords owned the bulk of the land and were disinterested in capital investment and agricultural development. The agrarian reform movement of the post-1974 period altered the system of land tenure in the south, though some of the early "revolutionary" expropriations have been restored to their original owners. By contrast, the north of the country is characterized by much greater population density (higher in the northeast), land fragmentation, "minifundia" that originated with the system brought by the Germanic invaders of the fifth and sixth centuries and subsistence peasants. These peasants (*lavradores*) own, rent, and/or sharecrop several fields

HISTORY AND CULTURAL RELATIONS

Humans have inhabited Portugal since Paleolithic times. Over the course of prehistory and history, various peoples have settled in the region, though the modern Portuguese trace their descent to the Lusitanians, a branch of the Iberian populations that spread over the peninsula in the third millennium B.C. Lusitanians made contact with Celtic peoples who moved into the region after 900 B.C. Roman armies invaded the Iberian Peninsula in 212 B.C. The Romans established important towns at the present-day sites of Braga, Porto, Beja, and Lisbon. An invasion of Swabians in the fifth century A.D. and of Moors in the eighth century A.D. added new elements to the Portuguese population, though Moorish influence was much stronger in the south than in the north. Portugal emerged as an independent kingdom in 1140 with its capital in the northern city of Guimarães. As part of the reconquest, whereby the Moors were pushed out of the peninsula, Lisbon was made the capital in 1298 and the boundaries of Portugal as they exist today were definitively determined. Early statehood and a national identity with

deep historical roots are the basis of the relative homogeneity of Portuguese society. In the fifteenth century the Portuguese inaugurated their age of discovery and for three centuries built and expanded their empire. The loss of Brazil in 1822 and a series of economic and political crises led to a decline in the world position of the Portuguese during the nineteenth century. The monarchy was eliminated in 1910 with the establishment of the First Portuguese Republic, and this in turn was replaced by the authoritarian dictatorship of António Salazar in 1926. Salazar formed his New State in 1932 on corporatist political principles. The Salazarist regime survived until 1974, when it was overthrown by a group of military men frustrated by the hopelessness of the colonial wars in Africa, wars that had escalated after 1961. The entire African colonial system was dismantled after 1974. In the late 1980s the Portuguese turned their attention toward Europe to become part of the European Community. However, linguistic and other cultural ties with former colonies, including Brazil, are maintained.

◆ **latifundia**
Large estates of the Roman Empire that were often the local or regional centers of political and economic power. Large estates based on the latifundia model existed in many regions of Europe up to the present time, for example in Italy and Spain. Typically the land was owned by a single family and passed on through inheritance, with the land actually being worked by serfs.

scattered throughout a village and in neighboring villages. Most of the farms are of less than 3 hectares. Although they are not as numerous here as in southern Portugal, there is also a population of landless day laborers (*jornaleiros*) in northern Portugal, many of whom are women. Jornaleiros provide supplemental labor to the peasant household. In the much less densely populated region of northeastern Portugal, ethnographers have described a form of communal property ownership and communal farming that survived well into the twentieth century.

Kinship, Marriage, and Family

KINSHIP AND DOMESTIC GROUPS. Although all Portuguese reckon kinship bilaterally, the structure of domestic groups and the kinship links that are emphasized vary by both region and social class. Portuguese kinship terms have Latin roots, with the exception of the Greek roots of *tio* (uncle) and *tia* (aunt). In northern Portugal, nicknames (*apelidos*) are extremely important as terms of reference. Some anthropologists have suggested that they connote moral equivalence in otherwise socially stratified rural communities. In the northwest, nicknames serve to identify localized kin groups linked through females. In this region there is a preference for uxorilocality and uxorivicinality, both of which can be linked to male emigration. At some point in the domestic cycle, households in northern Portugal tend to be complex, many of them composed of a three-generation stem family. Some villages of the northeast follow a custom of natalocal residence for many years after marriage. In southern Portugal, however, a household usually is a nuclear family. The obligations between friends sometimes are felt to be more important than those between kin. Among the rural peasantry, particularly in the northwest, household headship is held jointly by a married couple, who are referred to as *o patrão* and *a patroa*. By contrast, among urban bourgeois groups and in the south the concept of a dominant male head of household is more prevalent. Spiritual kinship ties are established at baptism and marriage. Kin are frequently chosen to serve as godparents (*padrinhos*), and when this arrangement occurs the godparent-godchild relationship takes precedence over the kinship relationship.

MARRIAGE. The marriage rate has demonstrated a progressive rise during the twentieth century. Age at marriage has been characterized by both spatial and temporal variation—that is, marriage generally occurs later in the north than in the south, though differences are slowly disappearing. In southern Portugal there are significant numbers of consensual unions, and northern Portugal has had high rates of permanent spinsterhood. Although it has declined since 1930, the illegitimacy rate formerly was high in rural northern Portugal. It remains high in Porto and Lisbon. Marriage has generally been class-endogamous and there is a tendency, though by no means a rule, for villages to be endogamous. Although the Catholic church traditionally prohibited cousin marriage within the fourth degree (inclusive of third cousins), dispensations as well as unions between first cousins were by no means unusual among all classes of Portuguese society. This kind of marriage was traditionally associated with a desire to rejoin divided properties.

INHERITANCE. In accordance with the Civil Code of 1867, the Portuguese practice partible inheritance. Parents, however, have the right to dispose freely of a third share (*terço*) of their property, and women share the right to both receive and bestow property. (The Civil Code of 1978 did not significantly change the articles pertaining to these practices.) Among the peasants of northern Portugal, where inheritance is generally postmortem, parents use the promise of the terco as a form of old-age security by marrying a child, often a daughter, into the household. At their death, this child becomes the owner of the house (*casa*). The rest of the property is divided equally among all heirs. *Partilhas*, whether in the north or the south, can be an occasion for friction between siblings since land is variable in quality. Some peasants hold land under long-term lease agreements; traditionally these agreements also were passed on "for three lives" in one piece to one heir, their value being calculated against the total assets. The Civil Code of 1867 eliminated the system of entailed estates (*vínculos*) that made it possible for wealthier classes to pass on property to a single heir, usually by a rule of male primogeniture. Wealthier landowners have been able to keep property intact by having one heir buy out the interests of his siblings.

Sociopolitical Organization

SOCIAL ORGANIZATION. Salazarist Portugal was a hierarchical society with a small upper class composed of latifundists, industrialists, financiers, top military personnel, the Catholic episcopate, university professors, and other professionals; a small middle class composed of people in the service sector; and a mass of urban and rural poor. Since 1960, as urbanization has progressed, a lower-middle class of skilled workers and technicians has emerged.

Under the First Portuguese Republic, education was secularized, Catholic church properties were confiscated, folk celebrations were restricted, and religious orders were abolished.

♦ **partible inheritance**
An estate of inheritance that may be divided.

POLITICAL ORGANIZATION. Before 1974, the Portuguese state was based on corporative bodies that in theory channeled class interests but in practice were often circumvented by means of personal contacts. Electoral politics were absent. Between 1974—when the Salazar regime was bloodlessly overthrown—and 1976, the Portuguese established a constitutional democratic representative system. Recently, some of the more socialist clauses of the 1976 constitution have been revised. At the local level, villages are still run by a parish council (*junta da frequesia*), the members of which are elected by village households. Throughout the Salazar period, the juntas had little real power and few economic resources of their own, though the members had local prominence. They depended on the *câmara*, the administrative body in the county seat, and today the câmara is still the important unit of political organization and administration. Since 1974 political parties and agricultural cooperatives have assumed importance, though participation varies by region. The other important local social institutions are the religious brotherhoods (*confrarias*). Traditionally they served as lending institutions; today they are largely ceremonial and cover funeral expenses.

Religion and Expressive Culture

RELIGIOUS BELIEFS. The bulk of the Portuguese population is nominally Catholic. During its history, Portugal has experienced waves of political anticlericalism—in the latter half of the eighteenth century; during the 1830s, when religious orders were banned and church properties were confiscated; and under the First Portuguese Republic, when education was secularized, properties again confiscated, folk celebrations restricted, and religious orders abolished. Under Salazar, Portugal experienced a religious revival, and the position of the local priest in the villages throughout the country was greatly enhanced. Since 1974, however, this position has been challenged, and in recent years there has been a decline in the number of clergy. A form of "pious" anticlericalism exists among the people who view the priest as a spiritual leader on the one hand and a man like every other man on the other. Religiosity is generally weaker in Lisbon and in the south of continental Portugal and stronger in the center, in the north, and on the islands. Portuguese Catholicism has produced fewer mystics than that of Spain, and people develop personal relationships with particular saints who are never represented with the suffering and anguish that char-

acterizes some Spanish representations. Much of Portuguese religious life exists beyond the official structures of the Catholic church.

CEREMONIES. The rhythms of local village life are marked by various celebrations honoring the saints. *Romarias* (pilgrimages) to regional shrines are a central feature of religious practice, especially in northern Portugal. Portuguese villagers also celebrate an annual *festa* (generally but not always to honor the patron saint) that includes a procession and combines elements of both the sacred and the secular. In the Azores, the festas of the Holy Ghost (Espirito Santo) predominate. In conjunction with these festas people fulfill religious vows (*promessas*). Cults of death, magical practices, sorcery (*feitico*), witchcraft (*bruxeria*), which is largely associated with notions of illness and healing, and beliefs in envy (*inveja*) that invokes the evil eye are still part of the belief system of many Portuguese.

ARTS. Craftspeople can be found throughout Portugal. The rugs made in Arraiolas (in southern Portugal) are well known internationally. Women of the north and the island of Madeira produce embroidered goods, many of which are sold to tourists. This is also true of pottery, which varies in style according to geographic region. Artistic expression is also evident in the items that are produced for decorating the floats carried in religious processions.

MEDICINE. Modern medical practice now reaches all sectors of Portuguese society. Few women, for example, give birth at home, a practice that was common into the 1960s. Good health is often associated with what is natural, and changes in the diet (the consumption of unnatural and synthetic foodstuffs) are frequently cited as the cause of diseases such as stomach cancer. Folk medical practices are still prevalent in some parts of the country. Curers use a combination of prayer, religious paraphernalia, and traditional and modern medicines in their healing. Among some Azorean Portuguese at home and abroad there is a high incidence of Machado-Joseph disease. It is an inherited disorder of the central nervous system, colloquially known as the "stumbling disease" because the carriers demonstrate a staggering and lurching gait, spasticity, and uncoordinated body movements.

DEATH AND AFTERLIFE. Death is a fundamental part of Portuguese village life. Church bells toll to send the message that a neighbor (*vizinho*) has passed away. In some parts of Portugal the gates and doors of the dead person's house are opened to allow anyone to enter, and relatives begin to wail around a body prepared for viewing. Burial is in local cemeteries, and family graves are well tended by living kin. Each village has several burial societies (confrarias) to which individuals belong in order to help defray the costs of a funeral and help pay for commemorative masses that continue for several years after death. All Saints' Day is an occasion for special reverence for those who have departed. Mourning is signified by the wearing of black; a widow will generally wear black for the rest of her life, while other kin remain in mourning for varying lengths of time depending on their age and relationship to the deceased. Portugal is also characterized by various cults of death—for example, beliefs about souls in purgatory or incorrupt bodies. Such beliefs are by no means confined to rural areas; in Portuguese cities a network of spirit mediums who can contact the dead for the living has arisen.

Bibliography

Brettell, Caroline (1986). *Men Who Migrate, Women Who Wait: Population and History in a Portuguese Parish*. Princeton: Princeton University Press.

Cutileiro, José (1971). *A Portuguese Rural Society*. Oxford: Clarendon Press.

Keefe, Eugene K., et al. (1977). *Area Handbook for Portugal*. Washington, D.C.: Foreign Area Studies of American University.

O'Neill, Brian (1987). *Social Inequality in a Portuguese Hamlet*. London: Cambridge University Press.

Pina-Cabral, João de (1986). *Sons of Adam, Daughters of Eve: The Peasant Worldview of the Alto Minho*. Oxford: Clarendon Press.

Robinson, Richard (1979). *Contemporary Portugal*. London: George Allen & Unwin.

—CAROLINE B. BRETTELL

PROVENCAL

Ethonym: Provencal

Orientation

IDENTIFICATION. Provence is one of the twenty regions that constitute the Republic of France. These regions correspond to the pre-1789 division of the country into provinces. Provence refers to a region in the southeasternmost part of France and it includes the departments of the Alpes-de-Haute-Provence, the Hautes-Alpes (also known as the Basses-Alpes), the Alpes-Maritimes, the Bouches-du-Rhône, the Var, and the Vaucluse.

LOCATION. The region is delimited on the north by the departments of the Rhône-Alpes region and on the west by the departments of the region of Languedoc. The southernmost departments of Provence touch the Mediterranean Sea, and the principality of Monaco in the southeastern corner of Provence is generally considered part of the region. The Italian border represents the eastern boundary of the region. Provence is located approximately at 44° N and 6 to 8° E. Topographically, Provence can be divided into three zones—an alpine zone in the northeast, an intermediate zone of hills between the mountains, and a third zone of river valley plains in the west and the coast in the south. The hills and highlands are cut by gorges, rocky plateaus, and valleys of the Rhône, the Durance, and the Verdun rivers. Extending from the delta of the Rhône through Monaco to Italy is the famous narrow strip of coastline called the Côte d'Azur. The port cities of Marseille and Toulon and the well-known cities of the French Riviera, Cannes, Saint Tropez, and Nice, are all situated on this coast. The climate of the coast is Mediterranean in character consisting of long hot and dry summers, warm autumns, and relatively mild winters, though the mistral, a chilly wind from the inland mountains, prevails in the winter months. The interior of Provence has a climate that is more continental in character. Average annual precipitation ranges from 50 to 150 centimeters. The annual temperatures vary from highs averaging in the upper 20s to lower 30s Celsius. The average low temperatures for the region range from 15° C on the coast to 5° C in the interior.

LINGUISTIC AFFILIATION. Within Provence, French represents the official language; however, Provencal is often spoken for everyday purposes, especially among the rural elderly of the region. Provencal is a dialect of Languedoc or the Occitan language, a Romance language once spoken throughout southern France. "Languedoc" comes from the langue d'oc, a language using *oc* for "yes" (from the Latin *hoc ille*). The langue d'oïl was once spoken only in northern France. The Occitan dialects are more closely related to Spanish than to French. Provencal refers both to the dialect of Languedoc spoken in the region of Provence and to the literary language, the language of the troubadours of medieval twelfth- to fourteenth-century France and northern Spain. There is some degree of controversy over the extent to which Provencal is used in contemporary France. Recently, however, intellectuals and some politicians have launched campaigns to preserve local culture

♦ **literary language**
A language used for literature (e.g., poetry); a written form of a language used for newspapers, documents, etc.

and language. So Provencal has come to be taught in schools, and Provencal history, literature, poetry, and festivals are all undergoing revival.

DEMOGRAPHY. The population of Provence in 1990 exceeded 4 million, with about 75 percent concentrated along the coast. The rapid growth in population after World War II (from 2 million in 1950 to the current total) is attributed to the large numbers of immigrants who have settled in the Provence area. In the immediate post-World War II period, immigration from Italy and Spain rose to meet the demand for labor in reconstructing France. More recently, with the collapse of the French colonial empires in Indochina and North Africa, colonial subjects came to France in search of work. Many residents of Provence issue from the former French colonies in North Africa. In Marseille, for example, roughly one-sixth of the population is Muslim Arab, and a large number among them are recent immigrants to France. Refugees from Vietnam, Cambodia, and Palestine have come also to settle throughout France and in Provence.

History and Cultural Relations

At the end of the second century B.C., when what is now France was partly under Roman rule, Provence was the first Roman *provincia* (hence the name Provence) beyond the Alps. With the breakdown of the Roman Empire, about 536, Provence fell under Carolingian rule (in the second Frankish dynasty founded by Charlemagne), after suffering successive invasions by the Franks from the north. Following the collapse of the Carolingian Empire in the ninth century and until the beginning of the eleventh century, Provence formed part of a series of kingdoms set up between France and Germany. By the end of the tenth century, a local dynasty (which had led the defense against the invasion by Muslims) dominated the area and acquired for its leader the title of count of Provence. In 1113, this dynasty ended, the House of Barcelona gained the title, and Provence fell to Spanish rule from Catalonia for over a century. Under Catalonian-Spanish rule, Provencal cities grew, becoming important centers for trade with Spain. Troubadour poetry, Romanesque architecture, and the use of a language very similar to Latin were characteristic of this period. In the thirteenth century, the Albigensian crusade was launched by the Catholic church to suppress the Cathari sect of southern France, which was considered heretic. The crusade consolidated the influence of the papacy and northern France. The popes acquired certain ter-

ritories in northern Provence and took up residence in Avignon from 1309 to 1377. The domination of Provence by the north dates from around 1246, with the extension of the rule of the Angevin dynasty, started by Charles of Anjou, brother of Louis IX. During this period, the administrative autonomy of Provence prevailed, with the development of the estates that had the power to approve taxes and to help rule the province in times of disorder. In 1481, Provence was willed to the king of France, and from the sixteenth to the eighteenth century, control by the king grew and the power of the estates decreased. After the revolution of 1789, Provence lost all its political institutions, and in 1790 the first division of the province into departments occurred.

Contemporary France is inhabited by a culturally diverse population, though white native French represent the numerical majority. While Spanish and Italian immigrants have been more easily absorbed into the dominant culture, visible minority groups are less easily absorbed and tolerated. As the economic recession has reduced the demand for labor, resulting in job scarcity, ethnic tensions have grown. In the 1970s, racial intolerance became the political platform of the Right and ultra-Right parties of France. Interracial conflict is especially evident in areas with a large population of visible minority groups, such as Marseille, which represents one of the main ports of entry for the migrants from North Africa. In the rural areas, social interaction between French families and families of North African origin is highly attenuated and limited usually to the workplace.

Settlements

Roughly 65 percent of the population of Provence is concentrated in the urban areas surrounding Avignon in the Vaucluse, in Marseille, and on the Côte d'Azur. The remaining 35 percent of the population lives in villages scattered throughout the region. In the middle of the nineteenth century, the population of the hinterland of Provence began to decline as people migrated to the coastal areas in search of employment in a developing industrial and commercial economy. The inhabitants of rural Provence live together in nucleated villages that are surrounded by fields worked by local farmers and agricultural laborers. Older houses in Provence are constructed of stone and covered by red roof tiles, while more recent dwellings are made of brick and stucco and are also covered by red roof tiles.

♦ **Roman Empire**
The state centered in Rome, founded as a republic in 509 B.C., established as an empire in 27 B.C., the western half of which collapsed in the fifth century A.D. The Roman Empire was the dominant force in the Mediterranean region, North Africa, and much of Europe.

See also

French

SUBSISTENCE AND COMMERCIAL ACTIVITIES. The economy of Provence is based on a combination of agriculture, industry, and tourism. The agricultural economy is highly diversified, mixing the cultivation of cash and subsistence crops with animal rearing. Sheep, goats, and cattle are raised in the highlands and foothills of Provence. On the plateau of Valensole, which is cut by the Durance River, mixed grains are grown, including corn, wheat, sorghum, barley, and oats. Viticulture takes up the greatest proportion of the arable land, and vineyards cover almost all of the southern half of Provence, leaving a small area in the Rhône Valley and the river valley of the Durance for the cultivation of fruits and vegetables. Groves of fruit and olive trees as well as flowers are often found interspersed with vineyards. Half the agricultural output is exported outside the region to large urban centers within France and also abroad to Germany, the Netherlands, and Great Britain. The other half of the agricultural output is primarily sold in local markets and a small proportion is retained by the producers for home consumption. The number of people employed in agriculture has been declining since 1954.

Some small, older industries that were developed in the eighteenth and the nineteenth centuries, such as building-materials fabrication, food processing, and textile manufacture, are scattered throughout the region. However, more recently developed industries tend to be concentrated around Avignon, Marseille, Aix-en-Provence, and Toulon. These industries include the agro-alimentary, steel, armaments, electronics, energy, and chemical industries. Much of the immigrant population constitutes the labor force in the industrial sector of the Provence economy. The economic recession of the 1980s, economic restructuring, and the transformation of technology have resulted in a reduction of employment in industry. Tourism is also a significant sector of the economy of Provence. In contrast to both agriculture and industry, the tourist economy and the service sector of the economy have grown, absorbing much of the labor force rendered redundant in industry and agriculture.

TRADE. Periodic markets, supermarkets, and "hyper-markets" service the population of Provence. The small open-air markets in the villages of the hinterland and the tourist centers along the coast are outlets for the sale of local handicrafts, such as lace, perfume, sweets, pottery, and for local farm products.

DIVISION OF LABOR. In the division of labor in rural Provence, men are primarily responsible for executing the tasks of farm production, while women are responsible for the domestic tasks. This division represents the conceptual ideal and is seldom met in practice. Women often perform farm work in the fields on the family

PROVENCAL FEAST

Olive and garlic paté; for sale at a market in Saint Remy de Provence. Half of the agricultural output is sold in local markets. Department Bouches de Rhône, France. (Owen Franken/Corbis)

One of the main sources of Provencal social conflict is political allegiances, which often reflect class differences in the local population.

holding. Available children and the elderly are also enlisted to aid in the fields. Most rural households survive on the basis of mixing farm work with wage work, and husbands, wives, sons, and daughters may be involved in nonfarm wage work. While women are often involved in farm work, performing a range of light and heavy tasks, married men seldom perform domestic tasks such as cooking and cleaning.

LAND TENURE. Land is privately owned, rented, or sharecropped. A farmer may operate a holding that is partly sharecropped and partly owned. Sharecropping arrangements are often made with absentee owners who wish to maintain some agricultural land while not working it. The conditions of each sharecropping contract differ, but generally the owner receives one-third of the revenues generated on the sharecropped land. The sharecropper receives two-thirds of the revenues and provides the equipment and inputs, as well as labor. In rental arrangements, the tenant farmer pays a fixed rent to the owner of the land. The average size of the farms in this region is 11.5 hectares, which is half the national average. Sixty percent of the farming population operate holdings of less than 5 hectares. Because of the relatively small size of the holdings, most rural households combine some form of wage work with agricultural work.

Kinship, Marriage, and Family

KIN GROUPS AND DESCENT. The "conjugal unit" is commonly referred to as the *famille*. It consists of a husband and wife and their unmarried offspring. The term *ménage* refers to "household," which consists of a coresidential kin core and its dependents. It is usually used interchangeably with famille. Kinship or *parenté* is reckoned bilaterally, and it is applied to both affinal and consanguineal kin.

MARRIAGE. In rural Provence, women and men tend to marry in their early twenties. There is no strict postmarital residence rule, but the newly married couple tends to reside in a separate residence, close to the location of their principal source of income. In farm households this of course means close to the holdings operated by the farmer. In rural Provence, the preferred marriage partner is a person who owns land.

DOMESTIC UNIT. The ménage in rural Provence may consist of many arrangements. In some households, several generations may live together and grandparents, parents, and children may take meals together and participate in the running of the household and the farm. Other households may consist only of a couple and their unmarried children. Other domestic arrangements may involve kin living under the same roof, but in different quarters, forming separate households.

INHERITANCE. In the late eighteenth century, the Napoleonic Code abolished primogeniture, and all legitimate offspring, female and male, came to be legally entitled to an equal share of their parents' estate. The division of property in practice in rural Provence may take a variety of forms. For example, land may be distributed among sons and cash and movable property distributed among daughters. The different forms of property division respond to the pressure preventing, if possible, the further fragmentation of already small holdings.

Sociopolitical Organization

SOCIAL ORGANIZATION. The villages of Provence tend to be stratified on the basis of landownership. Families who own and operate large agricultural holdings tend to enjoy both wealth and prestige compared with the landless segment of the village population. However, wealth does not necessarily confer political rank and influence. Since the economies of rural villages are complex, with villagers earning incomes from diverse sources, some villagers may become relatively wealthy earning incomes as owners of local businesses, such as hotels, cafés, butcher shops, and hardware stores. The wealthiest members of the village do not necessarily monopolize local power, as efforts often are made to elect officials who reflect the diversity in wealth and occupation at the local level. Hence, landless agricultural laborers, housewives, and schoolteachers have been elected to serve on municipal councils, as well as large and small farmers.

POLITICAL ORGANIZATION. France is a constitutional republic, headed by an elected president, who forms the government. The president is responsible for the appointment of government ministers and the prime minister. France also has a parliamentary system, which is composed of two houses of elected representatives, the National Assembly and the Senate. The main units of local government are the departments, the communes, and the overseas territories. The department is composed of from 11 to 70 cantons. Cantons are in turn composed of communes, which are the smallest administrative units in France. Each commune has a municipal council headed by a mayor, which is composed of elected representatives who sit for six-year terms. The main political parties in France include the Gaullist party, the Rassemblement du Peuple Francais (RPR). The Socialist party of France (PSF) forms the current government of France headed by Francois Mitterrand. Other important parties are the Communist party (PCF) and the ultra-Right National Front party (PFN).

SOCIAL CONFLICT. One of the main sources of social conflict is political allegiances. These differences become most apparent around election time, when animosities between supporters of the various political parties at the local level can develop into brawls in public places as well as attacks on private property. Political allegiances often reflect class differences in the local population, as agricultural laborers as well as small farmers historically have tended to support the parties of the Left while large landowners have tended to support the parties of the Right. Conflicts between agricultural laborers and their employers revolve around wage rates, conditions of work, and terms of employment, and differences over these issues have often resulted in strikes and work stoppages.

Religion and Expressive Culture

RELIGIOUS BELIEFS. The dominant religion in rural Provence is Catholicism; however, because of the significant numbers of Muslim Arabic residents, Islam represents an important religious force. The majority of people in Provence observe the holy days and participate in the cycle of festivities of the Catholic church. Thus, Epiphany, All Souls' Day, Assumption, Candlemas, and Lent are celebrated. One of the most prominent festivals is Carnaval, which is held during Holy Week at Easter. Carnaval has enjoyed a revival in rural villages in Provence and Languedoc. While the specific rites and ceremonies may vary from one region to another and from one village to another, the reemergence of Carnaval is linked to a revival of Occitan customs, language, and culture. This revival has also occurred in the arts.

ARTS. The music and poetry of the troubadours is being revived in Provence as part of a movement to preserve regional identity against the dominant French identity. Written in the Occitan language, troubadour art forms flourished in medieval Provence. Occitan literature and the Occitan language itself also have become part of school curriculums at the local level.

MEDICINE. Villages are served by licensed medical practitioners (i.e., doctors and nurses), who make their rounds visiting patients in their homes as well as tending to them in their offices. One doctor or nurse may serve several villages in close proximity to one another. Most large villages contain a pharmacy that stocks standard pharmaceutical products as well as homeopathic medicines. Homeopathic remedies as well as naturopathy are used in conjunction with "scientific" medicine. Medical knowledge itself is not the strict domain of medical practitioners, as many villagers, especially the elderly, are familiar with the medicinal properties of a wide variety of herbal plants that grow wild in the countryside. These plants are collected, dried, and brewed into teas that are used as medical remedies for many ailments.

Bibliography

Atlas economie régional (1987). Marseille: Chambre Régionale de Commerce et d'Industrie, Provence Alpes Côte d'Azur Corse.

Busquet, Raoul, V.-L. Bourilly, and Maurice Agulhon (1986). *Histoire de la Provence*. Paris: Presses Universitaires de France.

Forster, R., and O. Ranum, eds. (1977). *Rural Society in France*. Baltimore: Johns Hopkins University Press.

Wylie, Lawrence (1956). *Village in the Vaucluse*. Cambridge, Mass.: Harvard University Press.

—WINNIE V. LEM

SAAMI

Ethonym: Saami, Sámi, Sapmi; formerly Fenni, "Finn," Lapp

Orientation

IDENTIFICATION. Saami speak various dialects of the Saami language, and/or the national languages, within northern Norway, Sweden, Finland, and Russia's Kola Peninsula, and nominally follow the religions of the dominant society. "Sapmi," or "Same-eatnam," refers to traditional Saami regions others have called "Lapland." The terms "Lapp" and "Lapland" were used mainly by non-Saami, and the derivations of both "Lapp" and "Saami" are contested. Contemporary areas designated "Finnmark" and "Lappmark" constitute but a small portion of Sapmi.

LOCATION. Saami inhabit much of the tundra, taiga, and coastal zones north of 62° N in Norway and Sweden, 66° N in Finland, and 67° N on the Kola peninsula. These arctic and subarctic regions enjoy a climate moderated by the gulf stream, with winters seldom dipping below

Because of the significant numbers of Muslim Arabic resdients in Marseille, Islam represents an important religious force in Provence.

−40° C (in the far north, without sun for up to two months), and summers occasionally reaching 25° C (sometimes with midnight sun for up to two months).

DEMOGRAPHY. There have been no adequate censuses of Saami. Any estimate of their population depends on the operational definition of Saamihood as much as on quality of sampling, but they number very roughly 1 percent of the populations in their overarching countries. Representative figures around 1982 suggest a total of 40,000 to 60,000 in Norway, 15,000 in Sweden, 4,000 in Finland, and less than 2,000 in Russia—of which about 70 percent speaks Saami and 10 percent breeds reindeer. All in all, the roughly 7,000 Saami dependent on reindeer management as a livelihood herd and husband around 450,000 head. While the majority of Saami resides in the traditional northern regions, the largest concentrations of Saami are today in their national capital cities, to which migration has been most intense in the period since World War II.

LINGUISTIC AFFILIATION. The Saami language is in the Western Division of the Finno-Ugric Branch of the Uralic Family. Its closest linguistic relatives include Finnish, Estonian, Livonian, Votic, Veps, Mordvin, Mari, and Permian. Northern, southern, and eastern dialects of Saami mirror traditional habits of resource utilization, cutting across contemporary national boundaries. Saami inflection (of nouns, verbs, pronouns, and adjectives) involves infixes, from alteration of intersyllabic consonant values as well as suffixes. Morphology is highly productive through noun-noun apposition, nuanced verbal and adverbial forms, prepositions, postpositions, and other deictic constructions. Stress is on the first and alternating syllables. Orthographies inspired by Scandinavian, Finnish, and Russian conventions were first devised and disseminated by missionaries in the sixteenth century. Mid-twentieth century efforts for Nordic Saami solidarity have resulted in refinement and consolidation of these orthographies by linguists and native speakers. This writing system follows the Roman alphabet with supplemental symbols and diacritics.

History and Cultural Relations

Hunting and gathering ancestors of present-day herding, farming, fishing, mixed-economy, and entrepreneurial Saami entered northern Fennoscandia from the east by several routes and separate migrations and over several millennia. During these waves, Saami traversed some areas already sparsely settled by other peoples and languages before establishing themselves in present-day Sapmi. Here, cultural and linguistic contact arose with the later northern movements of Scandinavian, Finnish, and Russian peoples in the current era. Earliest contacts in the historic period came through traders, tax collectors, and missionaries. Periods of intense proselytization and forced assimilation led some individual Saami as well as whole regional groups into the dominant national culture and language, facilitated by the phenotypic indistinguishability of the Saami. More pluralistic national policies in the late twentieth century have stemmed the trend of assimilation. Saami today have full rights as citizens and participate in the same educational, religious, and political institutions as other members of their dominant cultures, at the same time as they actively champion their ethnic status.

Settlements

Saami settlements range in size and permanence, since part of the population is seasonally nomadic. More permanent villages and towns range from a few families to a few thousand individuals. In the latter case, Saami inhabitants may be in the minority, being interspersed with members of the dominant culture, some of very recent entry. Both encampments and settlements are predicated on local resource utilization, and are often along waterways affording access by boat in summer and by sled and snowmobile on winter ice. Contemporary transportation relaxes these constraints on settlement, at the same time as social conventions such as schooling and consumer habits impose other demands and opportunities leading to centralization. In the literature, occasionally "village" refers to a reindeer-herding, an administrative, or a territorial unit, rather than to a settlement per se.

Various forms of permanent and portable housing exist, often juxtaposed in the same settlement or even on the same household plot. Earlier types of construction include tents, sod huts, and frame dwellings, and these persist as homes (or are diverted to other purposes such as storage of food and equipment, smoking of meat and fish, or work stations). Contemporary homes are built to national standards, with central heating and running water; social life centers on the kitchen. Particularly in the more mobile reindeer-breeding segment of the population, some families manage more than one permanent dwelling and numerous portable ones. The tents and huts are round, organized around a central, usually open, fire. Any

See also

Finns, Norwegians, Swedes

bare ground will be covered first with birch twigs and then by reindeer hides. Small items such as cooking utensils are stored in one or more chests opposite the entry.

Economy

SUBSISTENCE AND COMMERCIAL ACTIVITIES. The reindeer is best described as semidomesticated and half wild. Dogs assist in reindeer herding and are sometimes kept as pets. Less frequently, goats may provide milk for household consumption. Commercial farmers may raise sheep and cattle. Pets other than dogs are seldom encountered. Originally hunters, especially of wild reindeer, some Saami converted to domestic reindeer breeding in the most recent half-millennium. Today, several forms of reindeer management, all essentially oriented to a cash market, support as much as 35 percent of the population in some regions, while other regions have only some combination of farming, fishing, hunting, and commercial activity. Even though reindeer management is a minority occupation of this ethnic minority group, it has largely shaped the stereotype of Saamihood and has been recognized in law as the only justification for special Saami rights. Through both indigenous identification with the reindeer and extrinsic policies controlling but also privileging reindeer management, this occupation continues to be an emblem of the Saami despite some ambivalence and even resentment by the sedentary majority of Saami and other northern dwellers. Farming centers on sheep- and bovine-meat production and some dairy cattle; these animals require shelter and provisioning up to eight months a year. No grains other than barley thrive at these latitudes, but potatoes have been grown since their arrival in the early 1800s. Freshwater fishing focuses on salmon, char, trout, and whitefish, the smaller species available year-round and not just in the open water of summer. Ocean fishing brings in greater quantities of cod, halibut, haddock, coalfish, and sole. Some Saami hunt ptarmigan, small mammals, European elk, and reindeer predators. Wild berries, abundant in season, are collected by all.

INDUSTRIAL ARTS AND TRADE. Reindeer hide, antler, and bone provide raw materials for footwear, clothing, and utensils. Saami men etch distinctive decorations on the antler sheaths of their knives. Wood is also an important material, especially burls from birch for the carving of shallow cups and containers. Basketry and root-weaving artisans execute utilitarian and decorative wares, and other specialists spin pewter thread to be sewn onto leather and fabric. All these naturally harvested products and manufactures are used in the house-hold; they are also sold commercially and used in barter between sedentary and nomadic Saami and among Saami generally, with local and distant non-Saami, and with tourists. The post-World-War II road system has promoted the increase of communications, services, circulation of goods, tourism, and nonindigenous resource extraction. Larger towns have local shops and national chains as well as municipal offices, slaughterhouses, handicraft centers, and museums.

DIVISION OF LABOR. Today, the sexual division of labor is both more and less pronounced than in earlier times. Reindeer herding and husbandry now falls more into the hands of men, while women are tied down by the need to maintain and utilize the conveniences of modern housing, compulsory schooling for their children, and transportation. In the farming sector, women do most chores with seasonal assistance by men, who may spend other seasons in hunting, fishing, and/or wage labor. Overall, women do the majority of crafts with soft materials, men with hard materials; men slaughter; both genders cook and tend children; men control snowmobiles and women cars. It is common for at least one member of each family to contribute a wage income to the household economy. Higher education and nontraditional professions especially attract sedentary men and nomadic women.

LAND TENURE. The Saami reindeer-grazing regions of Fennoscandia are divided into administrative units, only sometimes commensurate with traditional utilization practices. The nation-states grant the Saami special resource privileges (including reindeer grazing, hunting, fishing, and use of timber) on these crown and public lands. However, state ownership of these lands is still contested by Saami organizations. Saami immemorial rights of usufruct have been confirmed in a number of important court cases. The issue of Saami land rights has continually been investigated by government commissions and brought before international courts of law. With but few exceptions, reindeer management is a right reserved for Saami in Norway and Sweden. Any Finnish citizen living in the Finnish reindeer herding region has the right to manage reindeer. On the Kola Peninsula, Saami herders mix with those of other native herding peoples.

Kinship

KIN GROUPS AND DESCENT. Traditionally, the basic kin group in the reindeer-management

In the past, if burdensome to the Saami family, the elderly boarded with sedentary people, wandered off, or were left behind to die.

Saami

SOCIOPOLITICAL ORGANIZATION

sector has been based on a flexible and seasonally fluctuating affiliation, usually consisting of consanguineal kin of the same generation living in a loosely defined territory. This kin group is called a *siida*. Variations of the siida organization persist today, though often subsumed by larger extrinsic units. Individuals resort to a kindred-type structure in locating friends, mates, assistance, and godparents. Descent is bilateral.

KINSHIP TERMINOLOGY. Kinship terminology is bifurcate in first ascending generation, with special terms for mother's older and younger sisters and for father's older and younger brothers. Cousins are classified as semisiblings, both differentiated by gender. Classificatory grandmother and grandfather terms generalize when addressing and referring to older persons. Affines have marked terms. Most individuals will be related to each other by more than one consanguineal, affinal, or fictive kinship link.

Sociopolitical Organization

SOCIAL ORGANIZATION. Saami society is open, fluid, acephalous, and relatively egalitarian. Members of the reindeer-breeding sector enjoy higher prestige within the society and more attention from without. In some regions dominated by non-Saami, the ranking has placed the reindeer breeders last. In their core areas, the nomadic and sedentary sectors integrate symbiotically. Saami reside in parliamentary democracies with and without constitutional monarchies, as well as in the former USSR. When expeditious, Saami can appear to defer to the national majority culture.

POLITICAL ORGANIZATION. In earlier times, the largest though noncorporate group, the siida, was based on resource utilization, and its consensual leader was, and still can be, active, but only in unusual circumstances. Although poorly represented in the governing structures of contemporary society, Saami have initiated a number of their own general- and special-interest organizations, the latter responsive to subsistence interests. Saami have also been active participants in the fourth-world movement since its inception in the early 1970s.

SOCIAL CONTROL. Until the eighteenth century, social control was informal and relatively nonproblematic. In the absence of any hierarchical regulating mechanisms, some disturbances such as reindeer theft could escalate. With the court and religious systems of the encroaching dominant societies, Saami found alternatives in formal administration and litigation while maintaining informal controls through persuasion, gossip, sorcery, and relocation (forced or voluntary).

MARRIAGE AND FAMILY

Marriage

Marriage is monogamous. Sometimes cross cousins or double cross cousins marry, which is advantageous for nucleation of herding groups. Constraints on marriage include compatibility of the partners' subsistence bases. The merging of two large reindeer livestock holdings or two very small holdings would each be marginally viable arrangements (given some combination of labor requirements, pasturage availability, and herd controllability), as would be the marriage of two persons having the responsibilities associated with ultimogeniture, or two persons committed to incommensurable livelihoods. Within these limits, individuals usually choose their own mates, marrying sometimes after a family has been started. Postmarital residence is neolocal, although flexible, as in the case of an ultimogeniture heir apparent, who remains at home. When a newly formed family continues in the subsistence livelihood of one or another of the spouses, they reside so as to take advantage of their familiarity with the area. Divorce seldom occurs, either formally or informally.

Domestic Unit

The domestic unit is the nuclear family, from which individuals disperse and regroup (also across household lines) owing to activities requiring constant mobility.

Inheritance

In reindeer-breeding families, each individual, regardless of age or gender, owns livestock. Saami inheritance is constrained by the various practices of the dominant society. Following Saami tradition, however, inheritance of parental dwellings, plots, livestock, resource-utilization locations, and other wealth—as well as the responsibility of caring for elderly parents—will commonly fall to the youngest child.

Socialization

Children learn at their own pace through opportunistic imitation. They are seldom explicitly instructed or disciplined. Versatility and individuality are rewarded.

CONFLICT. Saami history reveals little endemic conflict other than competition, often between reindeer-breeding units. The exception was a massacre in 1852 in which the two victims were non-Saami. In recent times, however, conflict is more prominent, centering on protests of encroachments on Saami areas through resource extraction (hydroelectric power, mining, logging), by communication networks (roads, snowmobile routes, boat and air lines, and power lines), through usurpation of land (by recreational, tourist, and military activities), and by pollution (most recently nuclear contamination from Chernobyl).

Religion and Expressive Culture

RELIGIOUS BELIEFS. The ecstatic shamanic tradition has been subsumed but not utterly eradicated by state churches, whose missionizing nominally converted most Saami by the end of the eighteenth century. Most Saami belong to the evangelical Lutheran faith of the dominant culture, while some retain a nineteenth-century syncretic institution named Laestadianism after its charismatic founder.

According to Saami traditions, various spirits reside in and around prominent geographical locales, such as natural outcroppings and encampment sites. The shamanic drum of old commemorated a host of cosmological forces associated with space, time, weather, animals, and social categories. Saami folklore contains abundant references to people of the underworld and a giant troll-like figure. Other spirits correspond to once-living beings, as do ghosts of infanticide casualties.

RELIGIOUS PRACTITIONERS. Male pastors from the dominant society service most Lutheran churches in Saami areas; Laestadian practitioners are usually recruited from the Saami and Finnish populations. Laestadian practitioners also perform in the folk-medicine arena, and are male. Self-styled shamans of both genders serve the medical and sorcery needs of their kin, friends, neighbors, and trading partners. Not all healers are shamans, however, and not all shamans are healers.

CEREMONIES. The most elaborate ceremony in former times, congruent with that of other circumpolar peoples, was associated with the bear hunt. The Saami observe the regular Christian life-cycle rituals. Laestadian meetings are held in some of the same places as church services and also in secular buildings and homes. Healing rituals, whether Laestadian or shamanic, usually take place in the home of a patient or during a meeting.

ARTS. Most utilitarian arts and crafts are done by all, while specialists such as knife makers, basket makers, and silver-smiths render decorative wares. Summer tourism and year-round exports have become important in the local economy. To protect themselves against imitation, Saami handicraft professionals mark their produce with a special seal. A number of Saami have attained international recognition in nontraditional graphic art forms and literature. The vocal arts are represented by the chantlike *yoik*, which has become a recognized musical form.

MEDICINE. Indigenous beliefs and practices (such as the stopping of blood) are grounded in the knowledge and skills of the patient, a family member, or a shaman. Remedies are readily available in nature for human, reindeer, and dog maladies. In addition and within limits, these sparsely settled outlying regions receive medical and veterinary services in line with those of the rest of the country.

DEATH AND AFTERLIFE. Saami have a higher-than-average incidence of cardiovascular disease; males in their early years are at risk for accidental death, and in earlier times, a certain toll was taken by childbirth. Barring such mortality, Saami are often active in their 80s. In the past, if burdensome to the family, the elderly boarded with sedentary people, wandered off, or were left behind to die. The funeral and burial follow national custom, usually Lutheran. Saami do not speculate much about afterlife. In pre-Christian and earlier Christian times, when frozen or rocky terrain precluded burial, interment or temporary interment utilized trees and cairns.

Bibliography

Anderson, Myrdene (1978). *Saami Ethnoecology: Resource Management in Norwegian Lapland.* Ann Arbor, Mich.: University Microfilms.

Beach, Hugh (1981). *Case of Tuorpon Saameby in Northern Sweden.* Uppsala Studies in Cultural Anthropology, 3. Uppsala: Almqvist & Wiksell.

Ingold, Tim (1976). *Skolt Lapps Today.* Cambridge: Cambridge University Press.

Paine, Robert (1965). *Coast Lapp Society.* Vol. 2, *Study of Economic Development and Social Values.* Oslo: Universitetsforlaget.

Pelto, Pertti J. (1962). *Individualism in Skolt Lapp Society.* Kansatieteellinen Arkisto, 16. Helsinki: Suomen Muinaismuistoyhdistys.

Vorren, Ornulv, and Ernest Manker (1962). *Lapp Life and Customs.* Oxford: Oxford University Press.

—MYRDENE ANDERSON AND HUGH BEACH

SERBS

Ethonym: Srbi

Orientation

IDENTIFICATION. Serbia is the larger of the two remaining republics that constitute the Federated Republic of Yugoslavia as of 1992. Ethnically homogeneous within Serbia proper, the republic also contains two autonomous provinces. The autonomous province of Vojvodina in the north is mainly Serbian but also contains large minorities of Romanians and Hungarians. The province of Kosmet (Kosovo-Metohija) is located in southern Serbia and has a majority Albanian Muslim population in which Serbs are a minority. Substantial Serbian populations live in the neighboring republic of Montenegro and in the independent states of Croatia and Bosnia and Herzegovina.

LOCATION. Serbia is bounded on the north by Hungary, on the east by Romania and Bulgaria, on the south by Albania and Macedonia, and on the west by the Yugoslav republic of Montenegro, Bosnia and Herzegovina, and Croatia. Its location is approximately 42–45° N and 19°30′–23° E. Geographically, Serbia is two-thirds highlands and one-third rolling plains. Šumadija, the agricultural heartland of Serbia, lies west of the Morava River valley, just south of Belgrade. The climate of the plains is markedly continental consisting of dry, warm summers, long, humid autumns, and cold, dry winters. The growing season begins in mid-March and runs through November. Average annual precipitation is 76 centimeters. Temperatures vary from an average high of 23° C in July to 1.6° C in January, the coldest month. Within these patterns, however, considerable variations exist, with recorded highs well over 38° C and lows down to below −10° C.

DEMOGRAPHY. The population of Yugoslavia in 1990 was estimated at 23,864,000. At this time some 8,591,000 individuals (36 percent) were identified as ethnically Serbian, making them the largest ethnic group in the country.

LINGUISTIC AFFILIATION. Serbs speak mainly the Ekavian Subdialect of the Štokavian Dialect of Serbo-Croatian, a South Slavic language from the Slavic Branch of Indo-European. Slovene, Macedonian (both spoken in other former Yugoslav republics), and Bulgarian are the closest related languages. The Serbs still prefer the use of the Serbian Cyrillic alphabet, which differentiates them from the Croats who use the Latin alphabet. In recent years this situation has changed somewhat with street signs, bus routes, etc. being written in both scripts, but Cyrillic remains the alphabet of choice for official documents and newspapers.

History and Cultural Relations

Early Serbian migration into the then largely unpopulated Balkan Peninsula dates to about A.D. 500–600. Moving south from the area adjacent to the Carpathian Mountains, these early settlers arrived with their flocks and herds. The first Serbian state dates to the middle of the ninth century. By the fourteenth and fifteenth centuries, however, internal warfare had facilitated Ottoman conquest of the region. For the Serbs, this conquest is still symbolically remembered today by the defeat at Kosovo Polje (Kosovo Plain) in 1389. Modern settlement of the region dates to the 1700s and the wane of Ottoman power in the area. Prior to this time, much of the population had fled Ottoman conquest and remained in the Dinaric Alps to the west. By 1830, after years of continuous rebellion including the First Revolt of 1804 and the Second Revolt in 1815, Turkey was forced to recognize Serbia as an autonomous principality. Serbia was later proclaimed an independent state in 1882, but it was not until 1918 that the first Kingdom of Serbs, Croats, and Slovenes was established. The modern socialist state of Yugoslavia emerged out of World War II and the concomitant civil struggle between Mihailovic's Chetniks and Tito's Partisans.

Modern former Yugoslavia was an ethnically diverse and complicated state. Recent economic hardships coupled with political tensions have resulted in the flaring up of historical ethnic tensions between Croats and Serbs and between Muslims and Serbs. With the Croatian moves toward independence in 1990–1991, full-scale civil war between Croatia and the Serbian-dominated federal army erupted in the summer of 1991, after Croatia and Slovenia declared their independence. Also threatening at the present time are the tensions in the Kosovo between Serbs and Albanians fueled by growing Serbian nationalism. Yugoslavia is formally nonaligned.

Settlements

Traditionally, neighborhoods or hamlets within villages were composed of closely related kin belonging to the same *vamilija* (lineage). Today, however, the population of Serbia is predominantly urban: over the past decades a tremendous shift of population to urban centers has occurred.

Only about one in every four Serbs now lives in the countryside. Peasant villages in the Šumadija tend to be dispersed in small clusters, with each house surrounded by its own orchards, fields, and outbuildings. Three other types of settlements are found also. Agglomerated villages, in which houses are crowded together along narrow, crooked streets, are found mainly in eastern and southern Serbia. The cross-road village, with its evenly spaced houses and well-planned appearance, can be seen near Belgrade and in the lower Morava Valley. Finally, the *ciflik*, walled and densely packed villages created by Turkish landlords during the period of Ottoman domination of the area, are found in southern Serbia near the Macedonian border.

Houses ideally are made of brick and stucco with tile roofs. Wood dwellings, which were common historically, are considered inferior. A pattern of paying as you go in building, rather than financing through mortgage, means that a new house sometimes takes years to build.

Economy

SUBSISTENCE AND COMMERCIAL ACTIVITIES. The pre-World War II economy was based primarily on subsistence agriculture with a concentration on wheat and maize. Oats and barley are grown as market crops. Raising of pigs, cattle, and sheep was also important. Postwar modernization and urbanization have resulted in decreased dependence on agriculture. Most rural households have a diversified economic base that includes at least some wage earning. Some Serbian males (between 4 and 5 percent) work outside the country, predominantly in western European industry. The former Yugoslavia as a whole was noted for its labor policy of worker self-management.

A typical diet historically consisted primarily of bread and a variety of stews in a lard base. Fruits and vegetables were normally available on a seasonal basis. Lamb was reserved for holidays and other festivities. Cheese is made and eaten, but milk is rarely drunk. (Kefir is more common.) An important change over the last few decades has been the switch to the use of sunflower oil in cooking.

INDUSTRIAL ARTS. Many people engage in part-time craftwork, particularly in the manufacture of wood and metal utensils, tools, and furniture.

TRADE. In addition to Western-style stores and shopping centers, open-air markets (*pijaca*) with an array of fresh meats and produce, as well as handicrafts, are common.

DIVISION OF LABOR. An emerging social pattern is the so-called "feminization" of agriculture as households with male factory workers maintain a diversified resource base. Previously, labor tended to be divided into inside (female) and outside (male) activities. For example, baking, cheese making, weaving, cleaning, and washing were almost exclusively female jobs while chopping wood and most agricultural tasks were men's work. In urban areas, a similar pattern of women working outside the household also has emerged.

LAND TENURE. Despite a Socialist government, the vast majority of land is held privately. Attempts in the late 1940s and early 1950s to socialize landholdings met with staunch peasant resistance and were eventually abandoned. Although a few large collectives remain, most peasants continue to work their own land. Current law limits private holdings to 10 hectares, but contiguous holdings by different family members often allow joint working of larger parcels. Recently, the government has made some attempts to develop plans for reorganizing private holdings, which have become increasingly fragmented, into more productive integrated holdings. This attempt has been poorly received.

Kinship

KIN GROUPS. The most important kinship group after the *zadruga*, or extended family household, is the vamilija (lineage). Tracing descent patrilineally from a common known ancestor, sharing a common last name, and having the same patron saint, a vamilija nonetheless lacks the corporate functions normally associated with true lineage structure. Lineages are exogamous, and the bonds created by marriages between them are socially important. In addition, the fictive kin relationships created by godfatherhood (*kumstvo*) and blood brotherhood (*pobratimstvo*) are important social ties.

DESCENT. Descent is strictly agnatic, and to die without male heirs is one of the worst personal tragedies that can befall a traditional Serbian peasant. Village society is built on the matrix of male kin relationships as expressed in lineage structures and the relationships between them. Knowledge of this matrix, and one's place in it, are important in knowing who you are and where you came from. It is common for rural men to be able to recall accurately several hundred living and deceased male relatives spanning eight, or even ten, generations.

KINSHIP TERMINOLOGY. Serbian kinship terminology is complicated and does not fit readily

Also threatening are the tensions in Kosovo between Serbs and Albanians fueled by growing Serbian nationalism.

See also
Bosnian Muslims, Croats, Montenegrins

into conventional categories. On the first ascending generation, however, terminology is bifurcate-collateral for males and lineal for females. In general, terms for consanguineal kin are more specific than for affines. For example, a cover term, *sna* or *snaja*, can be applied to all in-marrying females.

Marriage and Family

MARRIAGE. In rural Serbia where marriage and childbearing have remained important symbols of adult status, the age at marriage has remained low. Both men and women typically marry in their early twenties and immediately start a family. Postmarital residence is almost exclusively patrilocal. Matrilocal residence is a possibility only in cases where no sons are present. Such in-marrying males are commonly referred to as a *domazet*. Traditionally, marriages were often arranged. In urban areas, where living space is less available, marriage may be delayed until later. Legal abortion is a principal means of birth control. Divorce has become increasingly common in the postwar era.

DOMESTIC UNIT. The zadruga, or South Slavic extended-family household, is the most prevalent rural domestic unit even to this day. Even in cities, domestic units often contain extended-family members. Historically, zadrugas consisted of married brothers, their wives, and children.

Households of ten or more members were common. These extended-family households functioned as single units of production and provided a common defense. Normally, married brothers would remain together until after the death of their father, but as their own families matured, the household would be divided. Often this went so far as actually disassembling the dwelling and evenly dividing the building materials. Today these households are typically smaller and lineally, rather than laterally, extended. Nonetheless, most rural Serbs continue to live in extended-family households. There has not been the pattern of family nuclearization so often associated with modernization.

INHERITANCE. Historically, land inheritance was strictly through male lines of descent. Land was divided equally between a man's sons when the household was divided. Men without male heirs would frequently seek to find an in-marrying son-in-law (a practice counter to the norm of patrilocal residence). Post–World War II legal codes specify bilateral inheritance, although the laws are still frequently circumvented.

SOCIALIZATION. Corporal punishment is a common means of discipline. Emphasis has traditionally been placed on respect for adults and the aged and on conformity to household goals. It is not uncommon today, however, to hear people complaining that children no longer respect their parents and often ignore their wishes.

Sociopolitical Organization

Yugoslavia is a Socialist federated republic with separate heads of state and government. The Communist party as embodied in the National Front remained the principal political force in the country until the late 1980s. After Tito's death in 1980 and the establishment of a collective presidency to replace him, the head of the collective presidency had been rotated between members representing each republic and the two Serbian autonomous regions. By 1991, however, the central government was in danger of disintegrating and the national Communist party, under its old framework, had been dissolved. Late in 1991, Croatia and Slovenia withdrew from the republic and declared their independence. War between the Serb-dominated national army and Croatians has left Serbia in control of some territory within Croatia. The Serbian republic's government remains headed by ex-Communists, as of early summer 1992.

SOCIAL ORGANIZATION. The class structure of modern Serbia is occupational and simple.

Some pure agriculturalists remain in rural areas, but most households combine agriculture with some wage earning. Landless working people also exist. Successful peasant agriculturalists may still be esteemed, but the urban upper commercial class now wields real political power.

POLITICAL ORGANIZATION. Administrative divisions below the republic level have been reorganized several times since 1945. Village and other local councils are important to local affairs. Village council members are locally elected and responsible for the exercise of federal and republic government policies at the local level, as well as deciding policy on local affairs. Membership in the Communist party is not a prerequisite to being elected.

SOCIAL CONTROL. Public opinion and tradition, coupled with a well-developed federal court system, are important to conflict resolution and the maintenance of conformity.

CONFLICT. Serbian history is fraught with warfare, both internal and external. Centuries of war with the Turks is a common theme in traditional oral epic poetry and is an important symbol of solidarity against the outside world. Serbia, and the former Yugoslavia as a whole, were decimated in both the First and Second World Wars.

Religion and Expressive Culture

RELIGIOUS BELIEFS. Serbian Orthodoxy is the principal religion of Serbia. However, holiday (rather than weekly) church attendance is the norm. Easter is the most important general religious holiday.

RELIGIOUS PRACTITIONERS. In addition to the village priest and Western medical facilities, help may also be solicited from a *vračara*, typically an older woman.

SUPERNATURALS. The saints are highly revered in Serbian Orthodoxy, and in Serbia each clan or lineage has its own patron saint from whom help may be solicited.

CEREMONIES. The most important holiday in addition to the church calendar is the *slava*, or feast of the patron saint, held on the saint's day. Every family has a patron saint who is inherited through the male line. Formerly, these were lavish affairs often lasting three days.

ARTS. Serbian culture is noted both for its traditional oral epic poetry, recited with an accompanying *gusle* (a single-horsehair string instrument stroked with a bow), and its naive art painting movement.

MEDICINE. Modernization has meant increased access to Western medical facilities. Women now give birth in hospitals rather than at home. However, for some types of illnesses, help is still solicited from a vračear or vračeara. Illness may be attributed to many causes, and self-diagnosis has been important to the decision to seek help from a folk practitioner or Western-style physician.

DEATH AND AFTERLIFE. Peasant society readily accepts death as part of life, but in contrast to church theology its concept of the afterlife is more one of a continued life in heaven. Funerals are held the day after death. The dead continue to serve an important integrative function both in terms of lineage recall and lineage solidarity. Large graveyard feasts traditionally are held one week, forty days, six months, and one year after the death.

Bibliography

Federal Statistical Office (1983). *Statistički kalendar Jugoslavije* (Statistical pocket book of Yugoslavia). Belgrade.

Halpern, Joel M. (1967). *A Serbian Village*. Rev. ed., illustrated. New York: Harper & Row.

Halpern, Joel M., and Barbara Kerewsky-Halpern (1972). *A Serbian Village in Historical Perspective*. New York: Holt, Rinehart & Winston. Rev. ed. 1986. Prospect Heights, Ill.: Waveland Press.

Hammel, Eugene A. (1968). *Alternative Social Structures and Ritual Relations in the Balkans*. Englewood Cliffs, N.J.: Prentice-Hall.

Lodge, Olive (1941). *Peasant Life in Jugoslavia*. London: Seeley, Service & Co.

Simic, Andrei (1973). *The Peasant Urbanites*. New York: Seminar Press.

—RICHARD A. WAGNER

SICILIANS

Ethonym: Siciliani

Orientation

IDENTIFICATION. Sicily is the largest island in the Mediterranean Sea. The name derives from the Sicels, a people who settled Sicily in prehistoric times. Currently a semiautonomous region of the Republic of Italy, Sicily, for administrative functions, also includes adjacent minor islands.

LOCATION. Sicily is located at the center of the Mediterranean, between 36° and 38° N and 12° and 15° E. Triangular-shaped, the island has an area of 25,500 square kilometers. Only 144 kilometers from Tunisia in North Africa, Sicily

Sicilians

*Although often
classified as a
southern Italian
dialect, the native
language of most
Sicilians is often
unintelligible to
those who speak
Italian.*

has historically been a bridge between Africa and Europe, and between the eastern and western Mediterranean. The island is separated from the Italian mainland to the northeast by the Strait of Messina. Sicily is mainly mountainous and hilly. On the east coast, Mount Etna, an active volcano, is Sicily's highest peak. The largest lowland, the Plain of Catania, is located nearby. Other lowlands are also located along the coasts. Much of the topography in the interior consists of rugged, deforested hills. Sicily has a typical Mediterranean climate of moderate, wet winters and hot, dry summers; the lack of summer rain, together with insufficient irrigation, has profoundly affected agriculture.

DEMOGRAPHY. With an estimated population of slightly more than 5 million in 1987, Sicily contained somewhat less than one-tenth of the population of Italy. Emigration because of lack of work has depopulated the interior, whose towns and villages are composed mainly of the very young and the very old. The movement of people has proceeded from the interior to the coastal cities and from the island overseas. Waves of emigration from the island have been occurring for at least a century, initially to destinations such as the United States, and more recently to industrialized areas of northern Italy and Europe.

LINGUISTIC AFFILIATION. The native language of most Sicilians is a Romance language, derived mainly from Latin. The vocabulary includes many words borrowed from Arabic and from other cultures that influenced Sicily. Although often classified as a southern Italian dialect, the local language is usually mutually unintelligible with the national language. As a result of the past isolation of towns, noticeable differences in local vocabulary and pronunciation still persist and are important social markers to Sicilians. Owing to the influence of television, the school system, and other unifying phenomena, most Sicilians, particularly the younger people, are bilingual in their native language and in the national language of Italy.

History and Cultural Relations

Sicily's geographic position and formerly rich agricultural resources have made it a crossroads of cultures. For most of its long history, Sicily has been subject to foreign rule. The island was first populated perhaps before 20,000 B.C. Notable among the various groups of early colonizers and settlers were the Greeks, who arrived in the eighth century B.C. Sicily subsequently became the first province of Rome, which it served as a producer

of wheat. The Romans introduced latifundia, large estates owned by absentee landlords and farmed by a subject population. This method of organizing agriculture, in which those who actually work the land are separated from the owners through chains of middlemen or brokers, has been a feature of Sicily for much of its history and indeed persisted until fairly recently. Colonizers and settlers subsequent to the Romans include Byzantine Greeks in the sixth century A.D. and Muslims from North Africa, who ruled Sicily for approximately 200 years beginning in the ninth century. The conquest of the island by the Norman French in the eleventh century inaugurated a new pattern of rulers from northern and western Europe. Under the Normans and in the ensuing period, Sicily had a culture unique in Europe, based on a mixture of northwestern European, Arabic, and Byzantine elements. The island experienced a period of strong local rule under Emperor Frederick II in the thirteenth century. At the end of the thirteenth century, while Sicily was controlled by the Angevins of France, Sicilians rebelled in the Sicilian Vespers. However, this uprising resulted in a centuries-long period of rule by dynasties of Spain. Throughout the following centuries, while a representative of the foreign ruler nominally held authority, power was in fact exercised for the most part by the local nobility, the large landowners of the island. In the nineteenth century, Sicily was ruled from the Italian mainland by the Bourbon dynasty based in Naples, in a state called the Kingdom of the Two Sicilies. During the movement for national Italian unification, the Italian military hero Garibaldi joined Sicily to the mainland; in 1861, Sicily became part of the newly constituted kingdom of Italy whose ruling dynasty was the House of Savoy, based in Turin. In 1946 special autonomous status was granted by the government of Italy to the region of Sicily to appease a separatist movement that had been active at the end of World War II. Italy became a republic after World War II and is a member of the European Community.

Settlements

The capital of Sicily, Palermo, and other major cities such as Catania, Messina, Syracuse, and Agrigento are located along the coasts, which are the most densely populated areas of Sicily. In the interior, nucleated settlement patterns leave the countryside largely uninhabited. A typical Sicilian interior town is situated on a hilltop. The urban orientation is also reflected in the importance in every town of a large square or piazza, the center of the community's formal representation. Typically located in the piazza are the main church, the town hall, commercial institutions, and coffee bars. Often emerging from the piazza is the street on which Sicilians take their ritual stroll on Sundays, feast days, or in the evenings. This promenade (*passeggiata*) is an expression of the gregariousness of the people, their enjoyment in creating theater and in observing each other. Outside the main square, houses directly adjoin one another in dense settlements. Traditional peasant homes, usually one or two rooms, contained people and animals. Wages from migration are used to modernize and enlarge homes by adding floors. A typical home today might consist of several stories, with one or two rooms to a floor. While the piazza and other formal spaces are in normal hours reserved for the activities of women, who, especially in small towns, live in semiseclusion and venture into public spaces only for specific purposes. A recent settlement pattern made possible by emigrant remittances tends toward suburbanization on formerly cultivated land.

Economy

SUBSISTENCE AND COMMERCIAL ACTIVITIES. The interior economy is based on extensive dry agriculture, whereas more profitable irrigated agriculture and industries are located along the coast. Wheat has long been the major crop of interior Sicily. Herding of sheep and goats, important in the past, has declined. Other significant agricultural products are vines, olives, almonds, hazelnuts, walnuts, and garden crops. Sicily is Italy's largest producer of citrus fruits. Fishing, especially for tuna and sardines, is important to the regional economy. Industries based on petroleum are located in the southeast of the island. Other industries, such as those based on the transformation of agricultural and fishing products, are also located along the coasts. Services, retailing, and the public sector are major sources of employment. While Italy is one of the world's largest economic powers, Sicily and southern Italy in general experience underdevelopment and unemployment. Migrant workers are now the most important export of Sicily, and their savings are crucial to the economy. Staples of the Sicilian diet are bread and pasta, olive oil, tomato sauce, vegetables and fruit, cheeses such as *pecorino* and ricotta, nuts, and wine. Meat has recently become a significant addition to the diet.

INDUSTRIAL ARTS. Trades connected with construction prosper. While several towns are still noted for the production of colorful ceramics, other artisanal activity has almost entirely disappeared because of the availability of inexpensive imported consumer goods.

TRADE. Stores and open-air markets are supplemented by itinerant tradesmen who ply their wares with characteristic cries through local streets on foot or by truck.

DIVISION OF LABOR. Sicily has long had a rather rigid division of labor. Men have performed most agricultural work, with the exception of harvests, such as those of grapes and olives, in which the whole family participated. While women no longer spin, weave, or raise chickens, in the interior they still transform agricultural products for food, cook, maintain the home, and raise children. In the larger towns and cities, and as migrants, increasing numbers of women work outside the home.

LAND TENURE. In the past, most land was held by an absentee-landlord class of the nobility and their successors in large estates, called latifundia or *feudi*. The majority of the population had access to land either as sharecroppers on short-term contracts or as wage laborers hired for the day (*braccianti*). Following land redistributions, particularly in the post-World War II period, land is now more widely distributed among the population. However, most families own only several hectares of land, often plots of poor quality, lacking irrigation, and dispersed in the countryside. As a result of emigration, much of the land is once again owned by absentee landlords.

Kinship

KIN GROUPS AND DESCENT. The most important social unit is the nuclear family, the basis of self-identity and location in the community. The cultural concept of honor identifies loyalty to the family as the major social allegiance. Bilateral kin outside the nuclear family may share in a corporate reputation. Relations of spiritual kinship established during baptism, marriage, or confirmation extend alliances beyond the nuclear family.

KINSHIP TERMINOLOGY. Kin classification follows the Eskimo system.

Marriage and Family

MARRIAGE. Sicilians consider marriage socially necessary to attain full status as an adult. The most important achievement in the lives of parents is to establish their children in good marriages. Traditionally, people tended to marry within the town, although current patterns of mobility have been altering this situation. People still

Sicilians consider marriage socially necessary to attain full status as an adult. The most important achievement in parents' lives is to establish their children in good marriages.

marry within their social class. Although legal, divorce is infrequent.

DOMESTIC UNIT. The ideal domestic unit is the married couple and children living independently as a viable economic and social unit. It is also common for parents, in remodeling their home, to build separate floors for their married children. In a recent domestic pattern, parents working abroad send their children back to Sicily to live with grandparents so as to maintain the children's cultural identity.

INHERITANCE. Partible inheritance is traditional. Women have been more likely to receive a larger share of their inheritance at the time of marriage, as a dowry in the form of a trousseau of embroidered and lace white wear and household goods, or money, and possibly a house. Men usually received land and agricultural implements, and possibly a house, either at marriage or at the death of their parents. As part of their rapidly increasing integration into a market economy, many families now favor education for their children as a form of inheritance.

SOCIALIZATION. As children mature, they are taught to subject their wishes to the interests of the family. The Catholic church is an important agent of socialization, as is education. Most Sicilians now complete high school. Older generations have lost some of their authority to adolescent peer groups.

Sociopolitical Organization

SOCIAL ORGANIZATION. Sicily has long had a stratified social system. A small minority of the population controls material resources and the allocation of employment. The most salient factor in the lives of the majority of the population is lack of work. Most families pool earnings from agriculture, salaries, and wage labor, or emigrate in an attempt to better their condition. Recently, even some working-class families are turning to university education as a means of economic advancement.

POLITICAL ORGANIZATION. Sicily is an autonomous region of Italy with an elected parliament, which elects a cabinet and president. The island is divided into provinces and communes, which are the local administrative units. Communes hold elections for mayor and other administrative officials. The political parties control access to a large percentage of employment possibilities and to other necessities of life. Formal political authority lies almost exclusively in the hands of men.

SOCIAL CONTROL. Police forces and the judiciary, as well as public opinion with its mechanisms of gossip and ridicule, help maintain order. In addition, the dependence of the majority of the population on assistance from those in control of resources in order to survive creates vertical patron-client ties, which exert pressure against challenging the status quo.

CONFLICT. Western Sicily in particular is known for the existence of associations engaging in violent activities, often called "mafia." The origins of this phenomenon are often attributed to the important role played by intermediaries between the absentee large landowners and the dispossessed population, in the absence of other effective government. Organized crime has moved from its traditional rural base into urban, national, and international activities.

Religion and Expressive Culture

RELIGIOUS BELIEFS. Christianity was introduced to the island soon after the origin of the religion. Almost all Sicilians are Roman Catholic. Devotion to Mary in her maternal role is particularly strong, and she, as well as saints such as Joseph, Agatha, Anthony, Lucy, and Rosalia, are revered as intercessors. Many people engage in reciprocal exchange relations with these supernatural patrons, through vows that promise lighting of candles, participation in processions, or pilgrimages. Recently, Protestant denominations have been attracting converts.

RELIGIOUS PRACTITIONERS. Roman Catholic priests are the major religious practitioners.

CEREMONIES. Each town has a patron saint, whose feast day (*festa*) is considered the most important local holiday, the symbol of town identity. As migrants return from the north, markets or fairs are held and public entertainment is offered. On this date and for major church feast days, images of the sacred figures are taken out of the church and carried through the streets to the people in lengthy processions. On 19 March in many communities, women make elaborate altars of food in their homes to honor Saint Joseph.

ARTS. Traditional Sicilian arts included puppetry and peasant carts brightly painted with historic scenes. Itinerant story-tellers also kept themes of chivalry and honor alive. Sicily is known for its elaborate pastries and sweets, formerly made in some places by convent nuns. Women still embroider and make fine lace linens not only to dower their daughters, but also for sale. Noted Sicilian writers include Giovanni Verga, Luigi Pirandello, Giuseppe Tomasi di Lampedusa, and Leonardo Sciascia.

MEDICINE. Most Sicilians now have access to modern medical facilities. Folk healers may still be consulted by some people, often to supplement modern medicine.

DEATH AND AFTERLIFE. After death, the soul journeys to purgatory, and then to heaven or hell. In the funeral, the casket is carried through the town to the cemetery on a bed of rose petals. Periods of wearing black in mourning are rigidly prescribed by degree of relation to the deceased, and widows may wear mourning clothes for the rest of their lives as a symbol of family identity.

Bibliography

Chapman, Charlotte Gower (1971). *Milocca: A Sicilian Village*. Cambridge, Mass.: Schenkman.

Di Lampedusa, Giuseppe Tomasi (1960). *The Leopard*. New York: Pantheon.

Finley, M. I., Denis Mack Smith, and Christopher Duggan (1987). *A History of Sicily*. New York: Viking Press.

King, Russell (1973). *Sicily*. Harrisburg, Pa.: Stackpole.

Schneider, Jane, and Peter Schneider (1976). *Culture and Political Economy in Western Sicily*. New York: Academic Press.

—PAMELA QUAGGIOTTO

SLOVAKS

Ethnonym: Slováci, Slovák

Orientation

IDENTIFICATION. The Slovaks are Western Slavs who speak Slovak and live in Slovakia, the easternmost third of Czechoslovakia, in 1992 renamed the Czech and Slovak Federative Republic. Slovaks are most closely related to two other Slavic peoples located to their west: Moravians and Czechs.

LOCATION. Slovakia is located between 47° and 50° N and 17° and 23° E. Slovakia occupies an area of approximately 49,995 square kilometers and is bounded on the north by Poland, on the east by Ukraine, on the south by Hungary, on the southwest by Austria, and on the west by the Czech republic of the Czech and Slovak Federative Republic. The topography of Slovakia is extremely varied, ranging from the Carpathian Mountains in the north to the Danube Basin and fertile plains in the south and west. The climate is typical of continental Europe with hot summers and cold, snowy winters.

DEMOGRAPHY. The 1986 estimated population of Slovakia was 5,200,000 with Slovaks constituting 88 percent of that number. About 1,000,000 live outside Slovakia, with approximately 750,000 residing in the United States and others scattered throughout Europe, Canada, and South America. The population density in Slovakia averages 106 persons per square kilometer, and the population is growing at an estimated rate of 0.3 percent per year. Hungarians, Ukrainians (Rusins), Poles, Romany peoples, and Germans account for the remaining 12 percent of Slovakia's population.

LINGUISTIC AFFILIATION. Slovak is a Western Slavic language (along with Czech and Polish) of the Indo-European Language Family. It is most closely related to, but distinct from, Czech. Slovak is an inflected language, and stress is fixed on the first syllable of a word; words of more than three syllables also have a secondary accent. Generally, Slovak words have as many syllables as they have vowels. Some words appear composed entirely or mostly of consonants: *smrt'* (death); *slnko* (sun); *srdce* (heart); and *yrt* (bore, drill boring). There are three genders (masculine, feminine, neuter) and forty-three letters. The three main dialects represent western, central, and eastern subareas of Slovakia. The dialect spoken in central Slovakia was the one adopted by Slovak scholars as the norm.

Settlements

Slovaks live in small hamlets or colonies, villages, towns, and cities. The hamlet or colony (*osada*) typically contains less than ten households of closely related people, usually with a common surname, which may also be the name of the community. The village (*dedina*) can have upwards of 3,000 to 4,000 people, frequently including the inhabitants of the surrounding hamlets. A town (*mesto*) commonly has a population in excess of 5,000 and a city (*velkomesto*) many thousands more. The largest cities of Slovakia are Bratislava, the capital (417,100), and Košice (222,200). Traditional Slovak homes in hamlets and villages were constructed of plastered-over mud bricks in western Slovakia or wood in the heavily forested regions of central and eastern Slovakia. Roofs were thatched or shingled. Typical peasant homes built in the eighteenth and nineteenth centuries contain one room, or at most, two rooms: a kitchen that would also double as a bedroom, and

See also

Czechs

a separate room that would serve as a bedroom by night and a room to entertain guests by day. A large oven would be accessed from the kitchen, while the body of the oven would extend into the second room where it would provide a warm surface for children to sleep on. Sometimes additional rooms were added linearly to this basic design to accommodate families of married sons or daughters and/or provide for the sheltering of livestock. Many hamlets still exhibit this traditional Slovak house, though most now have tile roofs. Villages in present-day Slovakia usually contain a jumble of varied house types, from the basic two-room plan of a detached home to the newer four- or six-unit two-story apartment houses. Cinder blocks and fired bricks have replaced mud bricks and wood as building materials, and indoor plumbing has been the norm for three decades even in rural areas. Stepwise migration, with people leaving hamlets and villages for larger communities (cities), is ongoing throughout Slovakia. In some regions, nearly 10 percent of the hamlets have been abandoned over the past fifteen years.

Economy

SUBSISTENCE AND COMMERCIAL ACTIVITIES. During the many centuries of Magyar rule when nearly all the land of Slovakia was owned by Hungarian nobility, most Slovaks were peasants (actually landless serfs). They cultivated the land, growing and harvesting crops for the manor. Initially, the fertile plains in the west and south were heavily populated, but by the twelfth century A.D., Slovaks began moving into the central region, which was more suited to animal husbandry. Other Slovaks were court servants and their villages were named for their trades or occupations. They worked at making metal pots, being forest wardens, fishing, goldsmithing, etc. The

HISTORY AND CULTURAL RELATIONS

Slavs who became known as the Slovaks settled between the Danube River and the Carpathian Mountains of east-central Europe by the fifth or sixth centuries A.D. and have occupied that territory continuously. Evidence of growing cultural complexity, from tribe to prefeudal alliances to feudal state, is found in their permanent settlements in the Váh, Nitra, Torysa, Ipel', and Morava river valleys. The settlement of Nitra became the home of the Slovak princes and the location of the first Christian church in east-central Europe. During the reign of King Svatopluk (A.D. 870–894), the Great Moravian Empire of the Slovaks reached its greatest development and size, consisting of some one million inhabitants and 350,000 square kilometers, including Polish and Czech subjects. After Svatopluk's death and the defections of Czech and Polish peoples, the Magyars (Hungarians) began to invade Slovak lands. The Magyars controlled Slovakia from the time of the battle of Bratislava in A.D. 907 to the end of World War I. About midway into the millennium of Hungarian rule, the Turkish invasion of 1526–1683 reduced the Magyar kingdom to the size of modern-day Slovakia.

The first half of the nineteenth century marked the beginning of a Slovak national renaissance and desire for ethnic independence as a minority in the Austro-Hungarian Empire, but in 1868 the Hungarians initiated a formal program of assimilation or "Magyarization." Hungarian was declared the official language in Slovakia, the last three Slovak secondary schools were closed, and in 1869, the Matica Slovenská (the Slovak Institute of Sciences and Arts founded in 1863) was suppressed. As World War I got under way, Slovaks in the United States urged Czech-Americans to join in efforts to promote a joint nation and by 1919, the federated state of Czecho-Slovakia was established and recognized to be a union of two ethnic groups.

The Czechs, who were more numerous and powerful, soon insisted on Czechoslovak unitarism in an effort to eliminate the national individuality of Slovakia. Slovak relations with the Czechs worsened until Czecho-Slovakia disintegrated in 1938–1939. The Slovak Republic (1939–1945) was established as the result of growing international pressures and became dependent on Hitler's Germany. In 1944, anti-Nazi Slovak partisans mounted an armed rebellion, but they were quickly crushed by German forces who reportedly killed 30,000 Slovaks while Soviet troops waited in the nearby Carpathian Mountains. The nation of Czechoslovakia was reconstituted at the end of World War II; by 1949 Communists had gained total control of the country and Slovaks were once again placed in a subordinate position by the Prague government.

When the "Czech Spring" movement emerged in 1968 under the leadership of a Slovak, Alexander Dubcek, it was crushed by a Soviet-led invasion of Warsaw Pact troops who occupied the entire Czechoslovak Socialist Republic, including Slovakia. In November 1989, the Czech dissident playwright, Vaclav Havel, led the Civic Forum party in the "Velvet Revolution," a peaceful overthrow of the republic's Communist government. Public against Violence was the Slovak counterpart of Civic Forum. National elections were held in 1990, and the name of the country was changed to the Czech and Slovak Federative Republic. In 1991, a vocal Slovak nationalistic party called Movement for a Democratic Slovakia began to demand independence for Slovakia. Its showing in the June 1992 elections further widened the rift between the Czech and Slovak republics.

years of Magyar rule resulted in a mostly peasant Slovak population. Agriculture is still extremely important in late-twentieth-century Slovakia, with key crops such as rye, wheat, corn, clover, potatoes, and sugar beets being grown since the 1950s on large collective farms. Vineyards and wine making are important in the region surrounding Bratislava, while the spas of Piešt'any, Trenčianski, Teplice, and Bardejov still attract foreign visitors. Many rural families keep gardens, fruit trees, and livestock and thus do not experience the frequent shortages in urban stores. Barter is still active in Slovak villages, with families that keep chickens trading eggs for milk with neighbors who have cows. For several decades there also has been an active black market for all sorts of commodities, such as building materials, parts for motor scooters, and currency. In recent decades Slovakia received an economic boost during the tenure of Gustav Husak, a Slovak who took national office in 1968 and served as president of the Czechoslovak Socialist Republic from 1975 until 1989. However, the steelworks, chemicals industry, and aluminum works established in Slovakia during the Husak years are experiencing difficulties as the economy languishes in the post–cold war era.

INDUSTRIAL ARTS. Slovakia has a long tradition of ceramic manufacturing, lace making and embroidery, linen and wool garment making, wood carving, metalworking, and the sewing of traditional costumes.

TRADE. Prior to the twentieth century, Slovak trade was controlled by the Magyars. Routes leading into Slovakia from the west were popular entryways for enemies of the Hungarians, so these roads were frequently gated and guarded. On numerous occasions, the Slovak lands were devastated by invading armies. Therefore, growth of trade with neighboring groups was difficult. During the era of the Council of Mutual Economic Assistance, Slovakia was an active trade participant, but remained primarily agricultural. Light industry (underwear manufacturing) and the growing importance of the amount of electricity being generated by Slovakia's nuclear power facility in the village of Jaslovské-Bohunice have been emerging as significant economic factors in recent years, along with the development of some heavy industry. Now with the demise of COMECON, new trade problems have appeared and old ones have grown worse. Some Slovak collective farms are moving towards a farm-co-op type of arrangement, which will entail local control of production and the ability to enter directly into an assortment of economic relationships.

DIVISION OF LABOR. The traditional division of labor was by age and sex. In peasant agricultural life, adult males tended to the draft animals and performed the heavier tasks in the fields, such as plowing. Adult females would plant, weed, and help with the harvest. Children of both sexes could be placed in charge of the family's geese, cows, or other livestock to take to pasture. In addition, girls would be expected to help their mothers and boys would be sent to work alongside their fathers. In the home, the bulk of child-rearing responsibility fell to the females of the household. Women cooked, tended the household gardens, stripped the geese of feathers to make the featherbeds, cleaned the house and immediate yard areas, washed the clothes, wove, and performed all the other sorts of handiwork, such as lace making and embroidery.

Formal schooling for peasant children even in the first quarter of the twentieth century rarely went beyond the third grade. Learning a trade, such as tailoring, enabled boys to live in a village or town and not be locked into agricultural activities. Some men worked at trades in addition to cultivating crops and keeping livestock. Some girls might learn to be midwives or traditional curers from their mothers or grandmothers.

LAND TENURE. Prior to the onset of Magyar rule, property was probably held and used in common by related individuals, as is reported for many Slavic groups. Feudalism resulted in vast numbers of landless peasants, so that by the twentieth century, Slovaks were emigrating at a rate second only to the Irish. With the establishment of Czechoslovakia after World War II, land reform brought some degree of prosperity to those who held plots. In the 1950s, land was once again confiscated as large collective farms were established. There are now measures to repatriate land taken by the Communists, but few individuals expect to return to the agricultural pursuits of their fathers or grandfathers and will probably sell the land for cash.

Kinship

KIN GROUPS AND DESCENT. Modern Slovak kinship is bilateral, resulting in large numbers of relatives. In many regions, Slovaks can travel to village after village and continue to find individuals with whom they share some kin relationship. In the past, Slovaks were patrilineal, organized in male-headed units termed *rod* (sing.), and were virilocal. The term for a small village, dedina, is

A Slovak daughter ordinarily could not marry until her female relatives had completed a set of featherbeds for her, her prospective husband, and their first offspring.

derived from a kin term for elderly male relative or grandfather, *dedo*. Several families, closely related through males, formed residence colonies. This pattern survives today in the tiny hamlets that surround Slovak villages. The modern term for family in Slovak is *rodina*.

KINSHIP TERMINOLOGY. Although Slovaks now exhibit bilateral kinship and are moving toward an essentially Eskimo terminology, they retain a Hawaiian-type terminology for Ego's generation: terms for brother and sister are, respectively, *brat* and *sestra*, while male cousins are called *bratanec* and female cousins *sesternica*. In many parts of Slovakia and especially in rural areas, portions of what was once a descriptive kinship system is still in use. For example, there are different terms for father, mother, father's brother, mother's brother, father's brother's wife, mother's brother's wife, brother's son, sister's son, brother's daughter, and sister's daughter.

Marriage and Family

MARRIAGE. Slovaks practice monogamy, with divorce and remarriage becoming a frequent occurrence in the last quarter of the twentieth century. In the past, there was a high degree of village endogamy or, at least, local endogamy (marriage within a group of villages representing a particular regional enclave). Religious endogamy is still prevalent, but is growing less important. In the past, everyone married and staying single was not possible, save for those unable to secure a spouse because of disability. Dowry was important, with cash being the preferred item. A daughter ordinarily could not marry until her female relatives had completed a set of featherbeds for her, her prospective husband, and their first offspring. There was a strong emphasis on virilocal residence. On the day of the wedding, the groom and his entourage would arrive at the bride's home and, after her attendants had sent several imposters outside to "trick" him, they would finally send the bride out. She would then bid a ritual farewell to her parents and be carried off with her possessions in a wagon to the groom's home. At some point following the ceremony, her wedding headdress would be removed and the distinctive, folded cap of a married woman would be placed on her head, accompanied by the singing of another ritual song. Once she was in her husband's home, her mother-in-law would call her *nevesta* (bride) for several months, and she would be assigned many of the heavy household chores. Today postmarital residence is ambilocal and even neolocal when financial circumstances permit or

when employment cannot be secured near relatives.

DOMESTIC UNIT. Increasingly, the domestic unit is the nuclear family. However, the extended family, three generations deep, was once the norm and can still be found in villages and hamlets. Some homes have an additional room or two at the end of a house to provide a separate kitchen or bedroom for a son's wife and children.

INHERITANCE. Inheritance is partible. In the past, if a peasant family had some land, the brother or brothers might attempt to buy out the sister's share and thereby provide her with some dowry while keeping enough land to farm. Partible inheritance reduced landholdings in some areas to small ribbons of land that were ultimately too small to support a family. Today, grown children of deceased parents feud over shares in houses. The married offspring who occupies the parents' home is forced either to sell it and divide the proceeds or to come up with the cash to pay off the claims of siblings.

SOCIALIZATION. Babies remained under the care of their mothers, who would take them into the fields. Young children were placed in the care of their grandmothers, most commonly their father's mother. When they reached about the age of 7, children would be assigned chores usually specific to their gender; both boys and girls would be sent off with geese, cows, or sheep to tend. The Communist government established preschools throughout Slovakia by the 1970s, thus changing the old pattern of socialization. Liberal maternal leaves permitted new mothers to stay home with pay. These factors have combined to lessen the degree of cultural continuity across the generations. Today formal education is compulsory, but in the past it was common for Slovak peasant children to leave school in the early grades with many dropping out after the third grade to go to work.

Sociopolitical Organization

SOCIAL ORGANIZATION. In hamlets the basis of social organization is a loose grouping of related families and in villages, one or more groups of households. This local organization takes responsibility for villagewide events such as facilitating weddings and funerals. The leadership of the collective farms in the rural sector took over some of these activities and certainly was responsible for directing the work force in the villages. Informal, voluntary associations of amateur musicians exist on the village level and play for various events, including the end-of-the-school-year procession and the end-of-the-harvest celebration.

Males, related and unrelated, congregate nightly in the village bar to play cards, drink, and visit. Females, related and unrelated, visit in the evenings and do a considerable amount of the planning for communal events.

POLITICAL ORGANIZATION. Prior to 1990, the Slovak Socialist Republic of the Czechoslovak Socialist Republic was divided into eighteen administrative districts (*okres*), each with a large town or city serving as a district seat. The boundaries of the districts were drawn in 1949 and correspond somewhat to yet older political divisions, *župa*, that were in place from 1886. The Slovak Republic of the Czech and Slovak Federative Republic instituted a local government system of elected mayors and councils in 1990 several months after holding elections for national representatives, republic representatives, and national and republic leaders. Therefore, at least on the community level, the prospect is for more flexibility in local decision making.

SOCIAL CONTROL. Widely accepted expectations and obligations among the peasants who lived in virtual daily contact with one another resulted in broad compliance within the parameters of acceptable behavior. Antisocial behavior would ordinarily be dealt with directly by the offender's and victim's relatives in order to maintain harmony in the community. As communities grow larger and more diverse, disputes more frequently are settled in the courts.

CONFLICT. Today there is still conflict over inheritance and, with the changes since 1990, renewed conflict over land occurs as the government attempts to repatriate plots confiscated by the Communist government since the 1950s. Theft from the collective farms and from village construction may be overlooked if the offender is a local person, but intruders from other villages (operating at night) are confronted out-right by local men, who may beat the thief, relieve him of his loot, and then telephone the police the next morning when the post office opens. Villages do not have police in residence.

Religion and Expressive Culture

RELIGIOUS BELIEFS. Cyril and Methodius brought Christianity to the Slovaks in the ninth century, but there are numerous examples of an earlier, widespread, traditional religion characterized by a pantheon of supernatural beings. Among them is Morena, the goddess of death who, represented by a straw doll, is still ritually "drowned" in the first meltwater of the spring by a group of young girls in some mountain villages.

Some Christian Slovaks, even those educated beyond high school and holding professional positions in villages, still believe in the existence of witches, ghosts, and the evil eye. The vast majority of Slovaks are Roman Catholic, but there is a strong minority presence of Protestants (Evangelical Lutherans), especially in western Slovakia, where many villages have churches of both faiths and some have only a Lutheran one. Jewish Slovaks, once numerous in some villages, towns, and cities, lost their lives in the Holocaust; businesses and farm plots were confiscated and sold off to Christian Slovaks by banks and other agencies during the years of the independent Slovak Republic. Few synagogues remain and Jewish Slovak cemeteries in the villages are abandoned and in ruin.

RELIGIOUS PRACTITIONERS. Full-time religious practitioners, Roman Catholic priests and Evangelical (Lutheran) pastors, experienced diminished influence and authority between 1949 and 1989. Sermons or any departure from the prescribed liturgy were required to be tape-recorded for review by a government official. Secular authorities held full control over their activities and priests or pastors could be jailed if they held religious services during government-mandated harvest periods. In 1990, some Roman Catholic priests began taking an active role in local and national politics by promoting one candidate or one party over another to their parishioners. Slovaks also recognize part-time religious practitioners who are traditional curers and mostly female.

CEREMONIES. Historically, Slovaks observed an annual round of rituals common to European agricultural peoples that were ultimately linked with and incorporated into events in the Christian calendar. On the village level, these rituals involved virtually everyone and provided settings for village cohesion and solidarity.

ARTS. Wood carving, embroidery, lace making, burn etching in wood, egg painting, ceramics, and weaving were and still are the traditional arts. There are also very rich folk dance, folk music, and folk song traditions that distinguish one Slovak region from another, along with the sewing of distinctive regional costumes. The *fujara*, a shepherd's giant flute held vertically in front of the body when played, is a particularly Slovak instrument. Hviezdoslav (1849–1921), the pseudonym of Pavol Országh, is probably the best-known Slovak poet.

MEDICINE. Until fairly recent times, Slovak peasants relied on the knowledge of traditional

Until fairly recent times, Slovak peasants relied on the knowledge of traditional curers to diagnose their illnesses and provide them with appropriate remedies.

curers to diagnose their illnesses and provide them with appropriate remedies. Rural populations also shared popular cures among themselves and had extensive information about how to make teas and poultices to relieve certain symptoms and about which plants to use to stem bleeding. Curers were still diagnosing evil eye in the 1970s through a particular divination ritual. Modern Slovak medical care on the village level revolves around the clinic, a community building where patients come to be treated by the regional dentist, pediatrician, obstetrician/gynecologist, and general practitioner who stop by at regular intervals. Usually the resident health-care delivery system consists of a midwife aramedic and a nurse. Pharmacies in towns display colored charts bearing drawings of medicinal plants and urge people not to destroy them. Although modern medicine is mostly relied upon and doctors with formal educations are trusted, Slovaks in some areas still believe that certain illnesses and symptoms are the work of witches or the evil eye and will seek out traditional curers.

DEATH AND AFTERLIFE. Christian Slovaks believe in an afterlife, and burials are primarily inhumations in conventional cemeteries. Pre-Christian Slovaks apparently cremated the dead, placed the ashes in ceramic urns, interred them with grave goods of various types, and then covered these features with clay and stone mounds. Death is not borne lightly by the surviving relatives and friends. In the recent past, the deceased was washed and prepared for burial at home, with a wooden coffin being made as soon as possible and brought to the house. The family then kept vigil with the corpse through the night and visitors paid respects the next day, at which time a religious service would be held in the church and then the coffin would be carried off for burial. Normally, a funeral procession would form and walk through the village, accompanied by the village band. Widows would adopt black skirts, aprons, vests, and sweaters as permanent attire following the death of a spouse.

Bibliography

Kirschbaum, Joseph M., ed. (1978). *Slovak Culture through the Centuries*. Toronto: Slovak World Congress.

Mikus, Joseph A. (1977). *Slovakia and the Slovaks*. Washington, D.C.: Three Continents Press.

Oddo, Gilbert L. (1960). *Slovakia and Its People*. New York: Robert Speller & Sons.

Pleuvza, Viliam, and Jozef Vladár, general eds. (1984). *Slovenská Socialistická Republika: Encyklopedický prehl'ad. Priroda, dejiny, hospodárstvo, kultúra*. Bratislava: Slovensky Akademie Vied.

Seton-Watson, R. W. (1943). *A History of the Czechs and Slovaks*. Hutchinson & Co. Reprint. 1965. Hamden, Conn.: Archon.

—JANET POLLAK

SWEDES

Ethonym: none

Orientation

IDENTIFICATION. The origin of the name "Swedes" *(svenskar)* is *swaensker*, which means "from Svealand."

LOCATION. Sweden is located between 55° and 69° N and 24° E. Sweden lies in northwestern Europe in the Scandinavian Peninsula bounded by Norway in the west, Finland in the northeast, Denmark in the southwest, the Gulf of Bothnia in the east, the Baltic Sea in the southeast, and the North Sea in the southwest. Sweden's main regions are, from the north, the northern mountain and lake region named Norrland; the lowlands of central Sweden known as Svealand; the low Småland highlands and the plains of Skåne, both areas in Götaland. Sweden has a coastline that is sometimes rocky and consists of large archipelagoes, *skärgård*. About 15 percent of the country lies within the Arctic Circle, and the climatic differences in the country are substantial. Snow is found in the mountainous regions in the north for approximately eight months out of the year, but in the south only about one month. The waters of the west coast are almost always ice-free, but the northern Baltic is usually ice-covered from November to May. The growing period is about three months in the north and eight in the south.

DEMOGRAPHY. In 1990 the Swedish population was about 8,590,630, including a Saami population in Lappland and a Finnish-speaking group, Tornedalians, along the border of Finland, both consisting of approximately 15,000–17,000 persons.

LINGUISTIC AFFILIATION. The Swedish language belongs to the North Germanic (Scandinavian) Subgroup of the Germanic languages. It is related to Norwegian, Danish, Icelandic, and Faroese. It has been influenced by German, French, English, and Finnish. The Saami and the Tornedalians understand and speak Swedish, but they form special linguistic groups. Immigration to Sweden after World War II has created many new language groups.

History and Cultural Relations

It is most likely that the first migrations to Sweden occurred about 12,000 B.C. when tribes of reindeer hunters followed the herds from the Continent to Sweden. The Sviones (Swedes) are mentioned by Tacitus (A.D. 98); this indicates that trade links between the Roman Empire and Scandinavia existed. During the Iron Age (500 B.C.–A.D. 1050) the Lake Mälaren valley, in central Sweden, became an influential area, with the Svea tribe in the leading position. The Vikings (c. A.D. 800–1050) were traders who made voyages to many of the Christian countries of Europe. Many of them stayed in countries such as France, England, and Scotland. Many geographical names in these countries are of Scandinavian origin. The Vikings controlled several trade routes in contemporary eastern Russia, but from the tenth century they began to lose their foothold in this market. During the period of 800–1050 Sweden was frequently visited by Christian missionaries from France, Norway, Denmark, Russia, and Germany. Toward the end of the tenth century, Sweden had been transformed into a Christian kingdom and a united state. In the thirteenth-century Swedish "crusades," Sweden—with the double goal of Christianization and conquest—moved against Finland and the eastern Baltic coast. By the mid-thirteenth century, several Hansa merchants were established in Sweden, and an increase in trade with the Hansa cities followed. German involvement in Scandinavia led to the unification of Scandinavian countries in 1397 under the Kalmar Union; this lasted until 1448. In the following period Sweden was involved in wars with Finland and crushed a Danish attempt to recreate a union. During the seventeenth century Sweden constituted a major power consisting of present-day Sweden, Finland, Ingermanland, Estonia, Latvia, and smaller areas in northern Germany. The country was involved in war for over a hundred years, and Swedish soldiers were in Germany, Czechoslovakia, Russia, and the Baltic States. After 1721 all overseas Swedish provinces were lost with the exception of Finland and Pomerania. In the beginning of the nineteenth century, Sweden became involved in new wars with Denmark and Russia, and Finland was lost to Russia in 1809. This political border was drawn right through a former culturally homogeneous area—Tornedalen—and thus Sweden obtained a Finnish-speaking minority at the border with Finland.

From 1814 to 1905 Sweden was unified with Norway. During World War II, from which Sweden was spared, thousands of refugees came to Sweden, mainly from Denmark, Norway, and Finland but also from Estonia, Latvia, and Lithuania. Before this time Sweden was unusually homogeneous in language and ethnic stock, although it had had an immigration of Germans, Walloons, Dutch, and Scots from the Middle Ages on. But since World War II Sweden has had a net immigration of about 600,000 people, primarily from the European continent but also from Latin America, Asia, and the Middle Eastern countries.

Today there are representatives of 166 different nations living in Sweden. The number of ethnic groups is even higher. There is also a Swedish minority in North America. During the nineteenth century, over a million Swedes emigrated because of difficult living conditions.

Settlements

As a result of variations in ecological conditions and inheritance practices, there have been large variations between villages in different parts of the country. Traditionally, the largest villages were in Dalecarlia, in the valley of Norrland, and on the rich plains of Skåne. There are also variations in

SWEDISH PICNIC

A Swedish family picnics beside the Gota Canal. The canal traverses Sweden between Goteborg and Stockholm. Soderkoping, Sweden. (Macduff Everton/Corbis)

Characteristically, young children in Swedish peasant society participated in adult tasks, learning about working life through observation, imitation, and practice rather than education.

the form of the villages. In Dalecarlia the houses have often been built in irregular and open clusters (*klungbyar*, cluster villages). In other parts, the villages have had a more closed and regular structure, as for example in Svealand and Götaland where the villages were often built as a row of houses (*radbyar*, row villages). In Skane the villages have often been constructed around an open place (*rundby*, circle villages). There have been five main forms of traditional housing design in the Swedish villages. The northern Swedish farmyard consisted of several buildings around a grassy yard. In the central Swedish yards the main house and the farmhouse were separated by a building, often a stable with a gate. The third type (Gothic) had a long, rectangular form, with the farmhouse separated from the main house by a fence. The western Swedish type was an irregular and loose construction of houses. The southern Swedish farmyard consisted of four long row houses built together. These square houses in Skåne were built with brick, and clay was applied over a stick frame. In the rest of the country, wood has been the most common construction material. Houses built in contemporary Sweden are basically the same throughout the country. Because of urbanization many empty houses are now used as summer houses. The relatively few castles and manors are found only in southern and central Sweden.

Economy

SUBSISTENCE AND COMMERCIAL ACTIVITIES. Preindustrial Sweden was an agrarian country. Farming was the most common subsistence activity, always combined with stock raising and often with forestry, handicraft, trade, and transportation. Farming was combined with fishing along the coasts and around the many big lakes. Today agriculture has diminished. In 1990 it employed only 3.3 percent of the working population. The main agricultural products are dairy produce, meat, cereals, and potatoes.

INDUSTRIAL ARTS. Iron ore and lumber are the basic raw materials. Besides lumber, the modern forest industry produces paper, board, pulp, rayon, plastics, and turpentine. Sweden also is able to exploit hydroelectric power thanks to its many rivers with waterfalls. The country has two big car manufacturing companies (Volvo and Saab), a telecommunications industry (Ericsson), a manufacturer of roller and ball bearings (SKF), a producer of household appliances (Electrolux), and a company producing electric motors, steam turbines, and equipment for hydroelectric power plants (ASEA-Brown Bovery).

TRADE. About one-half of the industrial production is exported. Iron, steel, and forest products—such as paper and paper board—are important as well as different kinds of manufactured commodities, especially machinery and transportation equipment. Sweden's largest export markets are Germany, the United States, the United Kingdom, and Norway, in that order. Engineering products, cars and other motor vehicles, machinery, computers, chemical products, fuel, and crude oil dominate the imports to Sweden. The supplying countries are Germany, the United Kingdom, the United States, and Denmark.

DIVISION OF LABOR. In the old peasant society, cattle raising was female work, while horses were part of the male world. Threshing was regarded mainly as men's work, but in eastern Dalecarlia it belonged to the women's sphere. Women from this area even worked as professional threshers during seasonal work periods. Textile production has been a female job, except in Halland, where men, boys, and women traditionally produced knitwear for sale. The general tendency is that in areas where agriculture has been a sideline, women have carried out several tasks that traditionally belonged to the male sphere in typical agricultural areas. Child labor was usual in preindustrial Sweden as well as during the first period of industrialization (1850–1900). Children worked in the sawmills, factories, glassworks, and ironworks. In contemporary Sweden, ethnic niches have started to emerge. There are restaurants owned by Chinese, pizza shops, sweet stalls, and small grill-restaurants owned by immigrants from the Middle Eastern countries. Assyrians and Syrians are involved in traditional trades such as tailoring and shoemaking. Together with Kurds and Turks, they also trade in fruit and vegetables.

LAND TENURE. Before 1827, when a statute on enclosures (*laga skifte*) was passed, the fields of each farm were split up in several small lots in various places. The agricultural modernization of 1827 meant that the fields of each farm could be assembled together in a compact area. These enclosures of land took place during the entire nineteenth century and changed the countryside radically. At the end of 1940, a new wave of structural rationalization began with the goal of creating larger and more productive units. In 1988 only 8.7 percent of Sweden's land area was utilized for agriculture. The majority farms are privately owned. An estimated 69.6 percent of the country's area is covered by forest and woodland. Corporations and other private owners control at least three-quarters of the nation's forest land and timbering.

See also

Finns, Saami

Kinship

KINSHIP AND DESCENT. Swedish kinship is bilateral and cognatic. Generally the kinship system follows the same rules of other European peoples. Except for the family, kin groups have been of little importance as a focus of social organization during the most recent centuries.

KINSHIP TERMINOLOGY. Kin terms follow the Eskimo system with local and regional variations in terminology. In some regions in northern Sweden, cousins are numbered from first to fourth. They can be called, as for example in northern Värmland, *tvämänningar, tremänningar, fyrmänningar, femmänningar*. In central and southern Sweden the words *syssling, brylling, pyssling* are used instead of the number of the cousins.

Marriage and Family

MARRIAGE. In preindustrial Sweden, marriage was an economic agreement between two families and not, as today, a private affair. The marriage ritual included exchanges of gifts and economic transactions between the two families. The dowry that the bride should bring into the marriage was carefully stipulated. This dowry, as well as a gift she got from her husband, belonged to her. In cases of childlessness, the dowry went back to the wife's family. Because of economic and social differences in Sweden, there have been variations in the degree of parental control over marriage partners. Strategic marriages, even sibling exchange, have been much more common among the wealthy farmers in the south than among the poor forest dwellers in the north. During the last twenty years, cohabitation without marriage (to *sambo, sam* meaning "together with" and *bo* meaning "live") has increased. This form usually precedes a marriage, and it is not unusual to have children before marrying. In 1988 a law was passed making the partners in sambo relationships almost spouses. The divorce rate has risen during the last two decades: twice as many marriages end in divorce now as compared to 1960.

DOMESTIC UNIT. The dominant domestic units in the peasant society were the small, extended, and nuclear families. Today the most common type is the nuclear family.

INHERITANCE. Until 1845 peasant daughters inherited half as much as their brothers. In 1845 equal rights of inheritance were legally stipulated. In reality, however, there were variations in inheritance practice. Many farmers, for example, on the isle of Gotland, on the plains of Skåne, and in the valley of Mälaren, had male primogeniture. Male ultimogeniture also existed. Other families practiced partible inheritance, for example in Dalecarlia and certain parts of Norrland.

SOCIALIZATION. Characteristically, young children in Swedish peasant society participated in adult tasks. The children learned about working life through observation, imitation, and practice rather than by education. In three-generational domestic units, grandparents played an important role in raising children. In contemporary Swedish families it is common for both parents to work, and all children over 18 months are entitled to a place in a daily-care center up to the age of 6 years. There are also open preschools where preschoolers can meet a few times weekly in the company of a guardian. "Leisure time centers" are available for children ages 7–12 whose parents are working or studying. These centers are open before and after school and during vacations.

Sociopolitical Organization

SOCIAL ORGANIZATION. Strong patriarchalism was characteristic of the preindustrial family unit. In northern Sweden the master often kept his role until his death, but in the rest of the country it was normal for him to hand over the leadership to the younger generation during his later years. The older couple was then "retired" (*pa undantag, sytning*), and were supported for the rest of their lives. Even though the family was the basic production unit, there was also a great need for cooperation in larger units. In preindustrial Sweden there existed a large number of corporations, which were constructed through cooperation and/or joint ownership. The structure of these corporations was often nonhierarchical. If there was a leader, he was primus inter pares (first among equals).

POLITICAL ORGANIZATION. In preindustrial Sweden owning land was a condition for taking part in local policy. The communal villages were led by a council of the landed gentry. An alderman could be chosen, but it was more common that the job was shared by rotation. Contemporary Sweden has been famous for its "middle way"—a Socialist but non-Communist policy. Sweden is a constitutional monarchy. The hereditary monarch is head of state but has very limited formal prerogatives. Executive power rests with the cabinet (*regeringen*), which is responsible to the parliament (Riksdag). In 1971 the unicameral Riksdag was introduced. Its 349 members are elected for three years by universal suffrage. The country is divided into 24 counties and 279 mu-

Swedes

At birth all Swedes automatically become members of the Lutheran Protestant State Church.

nicipalities; local governments are responsible for important parts of public administration.

SOCIAL CONTROL. Since the 1930s, the relationship between Swedish employees and employers has been characterized by the "Swedish model." This model implies negotiations between the government, employers, and the trade unions, and as a result cooperation is typical in Swedish working life. Since the general strike in 1909, strikes have been rare.

CONFLICT. Sweden is not a member of any political or military alliance and pursues a policy of neutrality. The Swedes have lived in peace for over 170 years.

Religion and Expressive Culture

RELIGIOUS BELIEFS. At birth all Swedes automatically become members of the Lutheran Protestant State Church, but they have the right to leave the church. Ninety-two percent of the Swedish population belongs to it. The majority of people do not go to church regularly, but most children are baptized and confirmed, and most Swedes are married and buried by the church. During the nineteenth century there were many pietistic movements characterized by a puritan life-style. In the north of Sweden the Laestadian movement is still vital. Swedish peasant society believed that the landscape was crowded with various supernatural beings.

RELIGIOUS PRACTITIONERS. Shamans were part of the Saami religion and are considered prophets of the Laestadian movement. Today the ministers of the Lutheran Protestant State Church are both male and female.

CEREMONIES. There are not many religious ceremonies in contemporary Sweden. Certainly some celebrations have a religious origin—Advent, Lucia, Christmas, Easter, and Whitsuntide—but only a minority of the Swedes think of these celebrations as religious.

ARTS. Swedish folk art and handicrafts present many regional variations because of differences in the availability of raw materials. Straw products were usual in Skane, whereas birch-bark products were common in Norrland. The Saami made, and still make, richly ornamented knives and spoons from reindeer horn. In Dalecarlia human hair was used to produce rings, necklaces, and brooches, which were sold all over Sweden until 1925, when they went out of fashion. The traditional Swedish textiles are wool and flax. A weaving technique used mainly in south and western Sweden is *röllakan*. Dalecarlia is famous for its wall painting. Blacksmithing is another handicraft

with a long tradition. Folk art is noticeable in the modern design of glassware, ceramics, woodwork, textiles, furniture, silver, and stainless steel.

MEDICINE. Traditional folk medicine made use of magical objects as well as locally grown plants. As illness was often attributed to spirit possession, various kinds of healing rituals were also used. These were mainly readings, for example of charms, and various types of curing by local healers' or priests' touch. Medical knowledge was passed from one generation to the next. During the nineteenth century, several literate healers read official medical books. They picked up fragments of information from these books, which they combined with their traditional knowledge. Sometimes this led to conflicts between local healers and district medical officers and sometimes to a division of labor, with local healers often being respected for their ability to cure allergies and various skin diseases.

DEATH AND AFTERLIFE. Beliefs in a life after death certainly influenced the daily life in preindustrial Sweden. Currently, such beliefs are not integrated into everyday life but are privately held. The Tornedalians in the north still practice a funeral ritual, which in earlier days was common in several areas. Immediately after the death the family, neighbors, and close friends gather around the deceased, in his or her home, and "sing him/her out." Two weeks after this ritual, the formal funeral takes place in the church.

Bibliography

Bringeus, Nils-Arvid, ed. (1973). *Arbete och redskap: Materiell folkkultur på svensk landsbygd före industrialismen.* Lund: CWK Gleerup Bokförlag.

Daun, Åke (1989). *Svensk mentalitet: Ett jämförande perspektiv.* Stockholm: Raben & Sjögren.

Frykman, Jonas, and Orvar Löfgren (1987). *Culture Builders: A Historical Anthropology of Middle-Class Life.* New Brunswick and London: Rutgers University Press.

Hellspong, Mats, and Orvar Löfgren (1974). *Land och stad: Svenska samhällstyper och livsformer fran medeltid till nutid.* Lund: CWK Gleerup Bokförlag.

Himmelstrand, Ulf, and Göran Svensson, eds. (1988). *Sverige-vardag och struktur: Sociologer beskriver det svenska samhället.* Stockholm: Norstedts.

Stromberg, Peter G. (1986). *Symbols of a Community: The Cultural System of a Swedish Church.* Tucson: University of Arizona Press.

Svanberg, Ingvar, and Harald Runblom, eds. (1990). *Det mångkulturella Sverige: En handbok om etniska grupper och minoriteter.* Stockholm: Gidlunds Bokförlag.

—LENA GERHOLM

SWISS, GERMAN

Ethonym: Deutschen Schweiz, Schweiz, Swiss, Tütsch Schweiz

Orientation

IDENTIFICATION. The German Swiss are the linguistic majority in nineteen of Switzerland's twenty-six cantons and half-cantons. They call their country "Schweiz," which comes from the canton of Schwyz. They are generally either Roman Catholic or Protestant.

LOCATION. Switzerland is located between 46° and 48° N and 6° and 10.5° E. It is a small country of 41,295 square kilometers. The German Swiss occupy central, north, east, and a third of the south of Switzerland's land area. The west is French-speaking, while the southeast is either Italian- or Romansh-speaking. The geography of Switzerland is divided into three areas: the Alps, the Mitteland, and the Jura. The Alps are the mountainous spine of Europe forming the southern portion of Switzerland, while the Mitteland is a plateau between them and the Jura Mountains, which form the northern frontier along with the Rhine River. The German Swiss live principally in the Alps and the plateau.

DEMOGRAPHY. The population of Switzerland in 1982 was 6.5 million with 5.5 million of that figure being Swiss. German Swiss comprise 65 percent of the total population, and they represent 73.5 percent of the native Swiss. The population density is 153 persons per square kilometer, ranging from 9,868 persons per square kilometer in Geneva to 1.3 persons per square kilometer in Fieschental, in the canton of Valais. The population is growing at a rate of 40,000 persons per year or less than 1 percent per year. The three largest cities in Switzerland—Zurich (369,000), Basel (182,000), and Bern (149,000)—are in German Swiss cantons. Switzerland as a whole has become an industrialized urban nation with a large net internal migration from the mountain areas to the plateau (with 26 percent of the country's total population migrating in 1850, decreasing to 15 percent by 1950, but still comprising a significant amount). This is particularly true for German Switzerland. The urban population has shifted toward German Swiss cities, with Geneva and Lausanne both being larger than Zurich in 1850 and rating fourth and fifth in overall population size today.

Since 1976, German Switzerland has had a decreasing population. The reasons include reduced marriage rate, lower number of births, increase in childless marriages, unwed cohabitation, and postponement of births. The largest demographic problem in German Switzerland is considered to be the alien or foreign-worker problem (*Auslander Probleme*). Over 1 million non-Swiss work in the Swiss economy. This wave of immigrants is a post-World War II phenomenon. Most were, or are, unskilled workers who do the menial labor the Swiss refuse to do.

LINGUISTIC AFFILIATION. Swiss German (Schweizerdeutsch, Schwyzertütsch, or Schwyzerdütsch) represents a wide range of local and regional dialects that are derived from the Old Allemmanic, a West Germanic language. Most are classified as High Allemmanic, with exceptions such as Basel (Low Allemmanic) or Samnuan (Tirolean). The number of dialects has been estimated to be in the hundreds, but they are generally mutually intelligible, with rare exceptions—such as dialects spoken in the most remote valleys. High German, *Hoch-Sprache* or *Schriftdeutsch*, is taught in schools and used as the written language. Strangers are addressed in High German, and for the German Swiss it constitutes their true second language.

History and Cultural Relations

The German Swiss trace their ancestry to a Celtic tribe called the Helvetti, who were defeated by Rome in 58 B.C. This is suggested by the Latin name for the Swiss Confederation, "Confoederatio Helvetica." Romanized for centuries, the fall of the western Roman Empire in the fifth century A.D. brought Germanic tribes (Allemani and Burgundians) into Switzerland. These tribes were, in turn, conquered by the Franks, with the area of Switzerland becoming part of Charlemagne's eighth-century Holy Roman Empire. Under the vestiges of this polity during the Middle Ages, the Swiss lived under various duchies until 1291, the founding date of the first Swiss Confederation. Formed by the three German Swiss "forest cantons" of Uri, Schwyz, and Unterwalden, the nucleus of modern Switzerland was born as a defense league against the Hapsburg emperors. From this time until 1515, Swiss militarism enlarged the Swiss Confederation and fostered an export of mercenary soldiers primarily from the poor, mountain cantons. At the Battle of Marignano, Francis I of France forever punctured the bubble of Swiss invincibility with a crushing defeat wherein Swiss fought Swiss. During this period, Bern was ascendant, being the largest and most dominant of the thirteen cantons. During

As a rule, most German Swiss engaged in commerce are bilingual in English rather than any of the national languages.

See also

Swiss, Italian

The German Swiss temperament is characterized as (among other traits) orderly, practical, little given to abstractions, scrupulously honest, blunt, and implacable in the application of rules.

the Reformation, Geneva replaced Bern in international importance, being the home to Calvin and Voltaire. Napoleon occupied Switzerland in 1798, dissolving the old Swiss Confederation to form the Helvetian Republic with six more cantons. In 1815, the Congress of Vienna added Geneva, Valais, and Neuchâtel to a reconstituted neutral Switzerland. Only Jura (established in 1979) is of twentieth-century origin, being formed out of the German Swiss canton of Bern. Switzerland remains politically neutral today and is the home of the International Red Cross. German Swiss Bern is the capital of the modern Swiss Confederation.

Settlements

German Switzerland is a modern economic landscape of cities, towns, and villages. Urbanism is a feature of the plateau, while the mountains remain the domain of villages. Towns are found throughout the German Swiss area, being concentrated along the larger valley floors and plateau. The pre-World War II agricultural villages of the mountain areas are generally a thing of the past. Many villages of this type have shifted to tourism as their principal economic endeavor. Villages have post offices, *Gasthofs* (guest houses), churches, and houses with barns. Chalets and field buildings are found outside the alpine villages. Villages and towns are located on avalanche-free slopes. Tree lines and barriers are maintained to prevent avalanches. In the major valleys, villages and towns are along principal automobile routes or rail lines. Less and less construction of houses is of wood. Modern homes are brick or block, even in the most remote areas. The older homes in the mountain and foreland areas are wooden with shingled or tiled roofs. These houses have carved gables, other ornamentations and inscriptions. Regional styles differentiated the carved Bernese farmhouse from the rock-roofed, inscribed Valais home. With the advent of stone or masonry construction, these embellishments have all but disappeared on modern homes. The exceptions are chalets built by urban dwellers as vacation homes, which imitate the older rustic forms. Towns and cities are characterized by a center with older buildings. The newer homes, apartments, malls, and industrial buildings lie on the periphery. The train station or *Bahnhof* is still a central focus in the larger towns and cities.

Economy

SUBSISTENCE AND COMMERCIAL ACTIVITIES. The mountainous landscape of much of German Switzerland makes over a quarter of its land area unproductive for agriculture. Even before the addition of more modern agricultural aids, there was rarely little more than subsistence farming in the mountain areas. The agro-pastoralism of pre-twentieth century Switzerland gave rise to much that is considered "Swiss"—community, cooperative labor, frugality, provincialism—peasant values born out of a unique adaptation to a harsh environment. The shift away from agriculture is reflected in a comparison of 1860 and 1980 agricultural population percentages: 43.6 versus 6.2, for the German Swiss cantons. Nonetheless, Switzerland as a whole produces more than half its food. This output comes principally from the plateau, while the Rhone Valley is a major fruit and vineyard area. Stock farming is the most important part of agriculture, which results in two-fifths of the arable land being devoted to pasture, alpine or otherwise. As a result of this emphasis, milk and its by-products—especially cheeses—form the major agricultural export. Swiss wines are rarely exported and there are heavy subsidies for this and other agricultural products provided by the government.

Industrial products are four-fifths of the commercial output of Switzerland. The bulk of this is centered in German Switzerland at Zurich, Winterthur, Basel, and Oerlikon. The major products are chemicals and pharmaceuticals (Basel), with engineering, armaments, and optical products manufactured at the other centers.

Banking and insurance are major industries with principal centers in the German Swiss areas. Swiss industry is depauperate in raw materials and energy, with the exception of electricity. As a result, Swiss industry competes in foreign markets on the basis of quality rather than price. Because of its reliance on world markets, Swiss industry emphasizes English as the language of world commerce. As a rule, most German Swiss engaged in commerce are bilingual in English rather than any of the national languages.

DIVISION OF LABOR. German Switzerland emphasizes a traditional division of labor by sex. As in all Western countries, this division has been modified with women playing roles in all elements of Swiss society. Increasingly, women work outside the home, particularly in the urbanized cantons of the plateau. In the more conservative mountain cantons, the traditional roles were more varied as cooperative labor was necessitated by subsistence agricultural practices. Today, with men of these cantons involved in trade, the woman's roles have centered on the home or jobs in tourist-related fields, such as hostelry. Women work as nurses, teachers, and shopkeepers in rural areas and are part of industry, notably watch-making and electronics in the urban zones. Young German Swiss are encouraged to follow the pattern of a *Welschlandjahr*, a period of apprenticeship or domestic service outside German Switzerland. Both sexes participate in this practice.

LAND TENURE. Land is a limited commodity in German Switzerland as it is in the whole country. Dense population in the plateau and continued emigration from the mountain areas has increased property values throughout. Maintenance of property rights through inheritance predominates. In the rural areas, land has passed to developments or otherwise is not used for agriculture. "Alp rights," or access to pastures, are sold to urban dwellers to build chalets or homes for vacations. Decentralization of industry has produced industrial plants in smaller towns throughout the plateau and even the alpine foreland. Housing access, particularly in urban areas like Zurich, has led to unrest among younger German Swiss. While not necessarily a "landless" stratum, they represent a result of changes in land tenure and usage in modern German Switzerland. Property can be owned by non-Swiss, but it is controlled both by federal and cantonal regulations to limit foreign penetration.

Kinship

KIN GROUPS AND DESCENT. Descent is bilateral with a very slight emphasis upon the male side. Men never use the wife's maiden name, but women may include it in a hyphenated form after marriage. No attempt is made to distinguish patrilateral or matrilateral kin. A distinction is made between female and male first cousins. No distinction exists for more distant cousins, although distant relatives are considered to be of the *Stamm* or kin group. Fictive kin, such as godparents, have a specific role in religious ceremonies in Catholic areas. Affinal kin terms are noted in normal speech. Neither fictive nor affinal designations connote any special reinforcement of obligations within kin groups today.

Marriage and Family

MARRIAGE. Marriages are monogamous. Prohibitions on first-cousin marriage exist in Catholic cantons of German Switzerland. Neolocal residence is favored today, but newly married couples often reside with either the man's or woman's family. This practice reflects less on the role of kin ties than on the availability of housing

or land. Under Swiss law, married women have some of their premarital privileges proscribed or limited. A married woman needs her husband's permission to seek employment, to run for political office, or to open a bank account. Marriage ages have fallen to younger levels in rural and urban settings. Marriage in the mid-twenties for both sexes is common. In rural areas, there is a high level of endogamy to, for example, a specific valley. This practice is less prevalent today with out-migration to cities becoming more common. German Swiss tend to be endogamous to their language group as a whole. In 1960, a total of 51,800 German-French households were recorded. Divorce is more common in non-Catholic areas.

DOMESTIC UNIT. The nuclear family is the minimal family unit. In Catholic cantons, it can number between six and seven persons with fewer members in the urban, non-Catholic cantons. Family size has dropped since 1970 with the falling birthrate, and three or more children are increasingly rare. Men no longer exert the same control over their children as in pre-industrial days, although they are recognized as the family head.

INHERITANCE. Inheritance is both partible (equal divisions among children) and impartible. In rural areas, Swiss law requires agricultural operations to be inherited intact, if one of the male heirs who is capable of managing it makes the request. If an heir dies childless, the estate is divided among siblings and does not go to the surviving spouse. Landholdings within rural valleys do promote a certain level of endogamy as the joint inheritance of the partners provides for a certain security. Again, this is less important with the decreased importance of agriculture for subsistence.

SOCIALIZATION. Infants are reared by both parents and any relatives who are household members. Children live at home during schooling, until trade school or college age. The interest in children is strong at the commune level. Each canton is responsible for its educational program and, until recently, has seen considerable diversity in educational philosophy. For instance, the obligatory schooling is nine years, seven primary and two secondary. The Federal Maturity Certificate awarded after completion of upper-level secondary schooling at age 19 or 20 is recognized as qualification for entry into other sectors of higher education. Schooling acts as a primary agent in socialization and reflects the accepted standards of the community and nation as a whole. All Swiss males between the ages of 20 and 50—German or otherwise—are required to serve in the military. The importance of the military service in Swiss socialization is more appreciated today after its integrative role during two world wars, which produced great tensions between German Swiss and non-German Swiss. Many scholars credit the military with modeling the ethos of modern Switzerland. Still, socialization begins with family and continues through community (schooling, religion, service). Religion's socializing role is more important in Catholic areas of German Switzerland.

Sociopolitical Organization

Switzerland is a federal, constitutional democracy termed the Swiss Confederation (*Schweizerische Eidgenossenschaft*). Its head is a president chosen for one year from the Federal Council (Bundesrat) of seven members who serve four-year terms. These are elected by the 200-seat Federal Assembly (*Bundesversammlung*) composed of representatives of the twenty-six cantons and half-cantons.

SOCIAL ORGANIZATION. The German Swiss, by virtue of sheer numbers, have more influence than the non-German Swiss within the Swiss Confederation. All Swiss citizens, German or otherwise, consider themselves equal. No social classes exist within German Swiss society. Status is achieved rather than ascribed. If there is a tiering of German Swiss society, it is not recognized as such, although the farmer or peasant is unofficially recognized as the lower rung of the economic ladder. By extension, then, the industrialist, being more economically successful, holds a higher position. Few Swiss, German or otherwise, would publicly validate this hierarchy. The foreign worker or Auslander is the true lower class—isolated and often shunned.

Stereotypes exist, with the German Swiss temperament characterized as orderly, practical, little given to abstractions, capable of intense commitment to work, scrupulously honest, blunt and plain-spoken solid, unswerving, and implacable in the application of rules. Among the German Swiss, the most extreme form of this stereotype is applied to the residents of the alpine cantons. These hillfolk turn the negative aspects of the stereotype into virtues by emphasizing hard work, communal spirit, and religious conviction over what they perceive to be the lesser virtues of the

RELIGION AND EXPRESSIVE CULTURE

Religious Beliefs

German Switzerland is equally divided between Protestant (44.4 percent, 1980) and Catholic (47.6 percent, 1980). Religious divisions within the German Swiss reflect those of the confederation as a whole. These divisions have been a major source of internal tensions since the Reformation. The canton of Bern is over 75 percent Protestant, while the alpine zone is Catholic. Religion plays a structural role in countering the linguistic pluralism within German Switzerland itself and the confederation. Greater tensions exist between German Swiss Protestants and Catholics than between the German Swiss and French Swiss. Political affiliations crosscut these dimensions and tend to offset religious differences today. Alpine areas of German Switzerland have customs that relate to supernatural beliefs outside the traditional religions. In the mountains, natural forces are viewed as generally malevolent or, at best, neutral. These forces manifest themselves in

avalanches, landslides, mists, or storms. The *Föhn,* a warm, gusty wind blowing from the Alps and creating sudden temperature reversals, has been associated with madness. These beliefs are fading in the Alps today.

Ceremonies

Each canton and commune has ceremonies unique to it. To the non-Swiss visitor, German Switzerland must appear, at times, to be on some continual form of vacation. There are festivals to herald the coming spring, harvest festivals, major and minor religious days, founder's days, and the Swiss National Day, 1 August. The most famous carnival is the Baseler Fastnacht, a 48-hour festival with grotesque masks and garb and parades.

Arts

German Switzerland was particularly rich in folk arts. Today there is a renewed interest in this heritage. Many of the skills in native woodcrafts have disappeared, as the winterbound peasant farmer is essentially a thing of the past. Tourism and nostalgia have promoted activity in carving, weaving, embroidery, and traditional dressmaking (*Frauentracht*) among both urban and alpine German Swiss. Much of this craftwork is done at a cottage-industry level with commercial sale as the ultimate objective. The federal government encourages this activity, and authorized craft outlets (*Heimattwerke*) are found in the large cities. The arts and customs of dance and song have survived less affected by social and economic changes. Yodeling, which originated in ancient times, persists, and alp horns are played. The German Swiss hold a strong place in the literature, music, and art of modern Western culture. In particular, they have merged architecture and engineering into structural art, most notably with the bridges of Robert Maillart, Othman Ammann, and Christian Menn.

city dwellers. Social mobility is based mainly on education and acquired wealth.

POLITICAL ORGANIZATION. The smallest and most important administrative structure is the commune or *Gemeinde*. There are more than 3,000 of these independent bodies that raise taxes and maintain municipal councils. The German Swiss's first loyalty is to the Gemeinde. The next highest order is the canton, and then the Swiss Confederation. Under the 1874 constitution, no Swiss can be denied residence anywhere within the confederation unless he becomes an "undesirable" because of criminal activity. German Swiss have voting rights in the canton of residence. Bern is the federal capital of the Swiss government. The structure of Swiss federalism is predicated on initiative and referendum. To call a referendum, 30,000 signatures are required. For an initiative (proposed legislation), 100,000 signatures are needed. Any Swiss, age 20 or older, can initiate the process. Female suffrage came last to German Switzerland, with Appenzell being the last canton to grant it, although women were given the right to vote in federal elections in 1971.

SOCIAL CONTROL. A shared value system exerts the greatest social control in German Switzerland. This value system has been erected on foundations of the values of the past. Order and continuity are prized in social life. Still, control is not overt but discrete. Peer presence as much as overt pressure operates throughout German Swiss society. The German Swiss is rarely outside the community of his or her peers because of the small size of the country itself. Self-control is taught early by the family and reinforced throughout all stages of the German Swiss's life.

Bibliography

Friedl, John (1974). *Kippel: A Changing Village in the Alps.* New York: Holt, Rinehart & Winston.

Herold, J. Christopher (1948). *The Swiss without Halos.* Westport, Conn.: Greenwood Press.

Imhof, Eduart, ed. (1965–1978). *Atlas der Schweiz.* Wabern-Bern: Verlag der Eidgenössischen Landes Topographie.

Kennan, George F. (1989). "The Last Wise Man: Sketches from a Life." *Atlantic Monthly* 263(4): 51–52.

Luck, J. Murray, ed. (1978). *Modern Switzerland.* Palo Alto, Calif.: Society of Promotion of Science and Scholarship.

McRae, Kenneth D. (1983). *Conflict and Compromise in Multilingual Societies: Switzerland.* Waterloo, Ontario: Wilfrid Laurier University Press.

Suter, Marc R. (1976). *Switzerland, from Earliest Times to the Roman Conquest.* London: Thames & Hudson.

—ERVAN G. GARRISON

SWISS, ITALIAN

Ethonym: Graubunden, Grigioni Italiano, Italiani in Svizzera, Svizzera Meridionale, Svizzeri Italiani, Ticino

Orientation

IDENTIFICATION. The canton of Ticino was named by Napoleon in 1803 after the main river of the region. The name "Grigioni" is derived from the "grey league" founded in the fourteenth century.

LOCATION. Italian-speaking people in Switzerland reside in two cantons: Ticino and Grigioni (Graubunden in German) (Mesolcina, Calanca, Bregaglia, and Poschiavo valleys). Except for one village (Bivio, in Grigioni), they are all situated south of the Alps (Svizzera Meridionale). All the rivers lead to the Italian Lombardic plain of the Po River. The region is located at 46° N and between 8° and 11° E. To the north are the cantons of Valais, Uri, and Grigioni. Ceneri Mountain divides Ticino in two parts. To describe the climate, we have to distinguish among the plains, the hills/mountains, and the Alps: the differences in temperature, hours of sunshine, and altitude are considerable. The landscape is characterized by many steep and wooded valleys (such as the Centovalli). On the plains the lakes influence the climate so that even exotic plants grow in the open air. In general, the climate south of the Alps is characterized by dry, sunny winters, with little fog and sometimes heavy snowfall; rainy springs; sunny summers with frequent thundershowers; and autumns with dry periods, alternating with strong rainfalls. In recent years, air pollution has adversely affected the climate and its reputation.

DEMOGRAPHY. Before the nineteenth century, emigration from the valleys was seasonal or yearly and then mainly to cities in Switzerland and Italy, but there was also emigration to France, England, Germany, Austria, Hungary, Poland, and Russia. In the nineteenth century, permanent emigration took place to North and South America and to Australia. (In 1830, 12,000 passports were issued.)

Italian workers began coming to Switzerland to construct the San Gottardo railway at the end

Swiss, Italian

*The desire to control
the alpine transit
roads was the reason
for wars that greatly
affected the Swiss
Italian population.*

See also

Swiss, German

of the nineteenth and beginning of the twentieth century. During the twentieth century, the population of the Ticino (but not Grigioni Italiano and the Centovalli, Maggia, Verzasca, Leventina, Blenio areas) has doubled. There has been constant population growth in the cities so that today over 70 percent of the population lives there. In 1990 the population in the Svizzera Meridionale was about 6 percent of the Swiss population (i.e., 300,000 people). About 20 percent of the population in the Ticino is Italian by nationality.

If we define Swiss Italians on the basis of language, we must also count the 400,000 or so Italian migrants (beyond those who are naturalized citizens and their children) living in all parts of Switzerland. In most of the Swiss cantons, one will find Italian immigration centers, Italian consulates, private Italian schools, or other services to support Italian culture.

LINGUISTIC AFFILIATION. The identity of the Swiss Italians reflects the history of minorities within minorities. In Europe, Switzerland consists of German, French, Italian, and Romansch minority groups. Within Switzerland, French, Italian, and Romansch people are minority groups. The Grigioni Italiano live in a canton that has the smallest linguistic minority in Switzerland—the Romansch—besides the German-speaking majority.

Written Italian in Switzerland is the same as in Italy, with some dialectal differences. It has a Latin grammar, with Celtic, Gallic, and Lombardic elements. The dialects spoken by native Swiss Italians are an important element of their ethnic identity. To speak the Swiss Italian dialect affords a social distinction in most Swiss Italian regions, though the elite of Lugano emphasize standard Italian and the Locarnese prefer to use their own dialect. The Italian language is disappearing in two of the four valleys of the Grigioni Italiano (Bregaglia, Poschiavo), which are economically and politically dependent on the German-speaking capital of their canton. The valleys of Calanca and Mesolcina are geographically attached to Ticino, where their language is used in the press and in education.

History and Cultural Relations

The desire to control the alpine transit roads was the reason for wars that greatly affected the Swiss Italian population. The first alpine passages were the Passo di Spluga and the Bernina (Bregaglia) in the second century A.D. After the fall of the Roman Empire, Ticino was dominated in turn by the Lombardic lords, monasteries or the church,

and German rulers or lords; and from the fifteenth century to the French Revolution, it fell under the domination of the other Swiss cantons. Leventina and Blenio were independent and had a democratic political system for a short time in the twelfth century. With the creation of the different leagues of the Grigioni in the fourteenth and fifteenth centuries, the Bregaglia and the Mesolcina/Calanda were organized as independent regions.

Because of fear of foreign domination by France or Austria if the regions were integrated into the Napoleonic Republica Cisalpina, Ticino became a free republic and a canton of Switzerland in 1803. The end of tax-free trade with Italy in 1848 and the incorporation of Ticino into the bishopric of Basle and Lugano in 1888 bound Ticino to Switzerland.

The railway through the San Gottardo, which opened in 1882, brought little economic or industrial development. Only the German Swiss profited, as the taxes to use the trains were too high for the people of Ticino to pay. The attitude of the people of Ticino toward Italian unification and fascism displays another facet of Swiss Italian identity. During the Italian Fascist movement, sympathy for fascism grew and the desire for incorporation into Italy (*irredentismo*) grew in Ticino. But, as tradition changed into folklore, the Swiss Italian regional culture became a harmless "Ticinesità." Reasons for this shift may be related to post–World War II relations of Ticino with the German Swiss, Germany, and Italy and concern such issues as economic development, tourism, and migration.

Settlements

The first known settlers in Ticino were the Leponzi (Leventina), Brenni (Blenio), and Insubrii (Isole di Brissago). In the alpine valleys, the villages were situated on the steep slopes. The transhumance of the pastoralists in the alpine valleys involved residing in summer homes in the Alps (Monti, Rustici); during the winter months, people from Maggia and Verzasca descended to the lakesides of the Lago Maggiore. Today, houses are built closely together. In the Leventina and the Blenio, they are made of wood, while elsewhere they are constructed from stone. The roofs are of granite in the Sopraceneri and of bricks in the Sottoceneri. On the lakesides and in the Sottoceneri, the architecture of the houses is similar to the Lombardic style. Castles, market-places, and churches were built and maintained by the ruling families, the lords, and the church. They show the influence of Roman architecture. During the German Swiss occupation few public buildings were constructed, as the German Swiss lords did not want to invest in an occupied territory.

Economy

SUBSISTENCE AND COMMERCIAL ACTIVITIES. In 1900 about 60 percent of the population still lived by family-based agriculture. In the Sottoceneri, long-term land leasing to tenants was the primary economic arrangement and mode of production. Hunting at one time also played a role. Fishing was an economic activity on the lakesides, but as pollution has increased, fishing in the Lago Ceresio has been prohibited. Entire families are sometimes involved with a single trade such as bricklaying, plastering, carpentry, chestnut selling, chimney sweeping, or baking. Cottage industries also exist: for example, straw is woven in Valle Onsernone; cotton and silk, woven mainly in Sottoceneri and mainly by women, was another source of income until the 1930s. Mountain farming has now ended as it is not profitable. Today 80 percent of the farms are for second incomes, are smaller than 5 hectares, and produce less than 5 percent of the economic product. Some of the abandoned farms have been taken over by the *neorurali*, young urban German Swiss.

Industrialization in Ticino began in the second half of the nineteenth century. Capitalistic industrialization was, until the 1950s, local and traditional (half of the enterprises are still family-owned). Modernization of the economy in the 1950s and 1960s took place rapidly. Today, service (tourism, banking) is the most important sector. The banking sector grew explosively in the 1970s as foreign capital was transferred to Switzerland (Ticino is the Hong Kong of Switzerland). In general, industry in Ticino is oriented toward labor-intensive production, as the required pool of low-paid workers (Italian) is assured. Raw materials are imported from abroad, and half-finished industrial products arrive either from German Switzerland or from abroad. Export is to German Switzerland, Italy, or other countries. The banks have become internationalized (44 percent of the banks in the Ticino are foreign-owned). The industrial survival of the Ticino depends on reacting to the European marketplace.

INDUSTRIAL ARTS. Cattle, cheese (*formaggio di paglia*), wine, and other goods—game (in the nineteenth century), skins, fish, charcoal, larch, chestnut, crystal, marble, granite—are sold at Lombardic marketplaces. The main industries at the turn of the century were food, wood, clothing, railway production, hydroelectric power, granite, tobacco, and metallurgic products. The last three are threatened today by structural changes and low-cost production elsewhere. Microelectronic and precision instruments are manufactured today as well. Construction is one of the most stable activities.

TRADE. San Gottardo is the most important of the Swiss alpine passages. Today road transport (a street tunnel opened in 1980) of goods and tourist traffic during holidays is responsible for notorious traffic jams in Ticino. From Roman times the alpine passages have been used for warfare expeditions. Men were recruited as soldiers and as transporters of goods. Most of the time, taxes and tributes were paid to the respective regional lords and/or the church for protection from enemies.

DIVISION OF LABOR. Public prestige is afforded primarily to men (the vote was given to women in Switzerland only in 1971). The head of the traditional agricultural families were men but as they migrated, the main work in agriculture was done by women, elderly people, and children. Women performed all the farm work (household, cattle, hay making), while the same cannot be said of men. The traditional pattern of sharing work (general reciprocity, open networks) is taken over by families of the neorurali. Even though equality in employment is the law, the idea is still widespread that a man must earn more than a woman, and when spouses are taxed together, the official form is only addressed to the man. Average salaries in Ticino are 20 percent lower than in Switzerland in general, and some women earn half of what other women earn in German Swiss towns.

LAND TENURE. Land or forests in the communities can be owned privately, by several kin of the same family, or by the *patriziato* (the old community of the bourgeoisie). Land is attributed or loaned and work or profit is distributed by vote of the assisting persons. Land sharing (based on traditional Roman laws) is a barrier to land reform as agricultural plots become too small to be cultivated effectively.

With the development of tourism, the "sale of the Ticino" began. Since 1970 several laws have limited land sales—a limitation on selling to outsiders, a stipulation that agricultural land has to be used as such, and a limit on second residences.

Kinship

KIN GROUPS AND DESCENT. Children take their father's name if their parents are married.

The banking sector grew explosively in the 1970s as foreign capital was transferred to Switzerland.

The kinship system is cognatic, with a patrilineal preference. In general, the more people in a family rooted in the village context and the larger the family, the more important the kin group becomes. Traditionally, one's godfather and godmother were of social importance. Modernity, economic mobility, and urbanization have eroded the role of the localized kin group.

KINSHIP TERMINOLOGY. Cousin terms follow the Eskimo system.

Marriage and Family

MARRIAGE. Regional and village endogamy was the rule in the past. Young people met on church visits and at church festivals and feasts. Informal, secret meetings of the future spouses (*kiltgang*) existed in the alpine valleys. For the engagement, a man offered a gift (*dotta*) to the woman, which was taken as a promise of marriage. Today young people meet within peer groups, at discos and sporting events, at school, or at work. In urban centers young people often live together before marriage and get married when the woman is pregnant. Normally the wedding is of three parts: legal, religious, and celebratory. The bride and the groom are led to church by their witness. Rice as a sign of fertility is thrown on the spouses after the religious ceremony. The celebration takes place in a restaurant or in a community room and consists of a banquet, wedding cake, fireworks, and music. Depending on the importance of kin and on one's financial status, only the next of kin or also aunts and uncles and friends are invited to the party. Cousins are invited to the religious ceremony, for

RELIGION AND EXPRESSIVE CULTURE

Religious Beliefs

In the Swiss Italian region there was space for an autonomous, anarchistic, esoteric *monte verità*. Newspapers give a good view of popular beliefs, as they are full of advertisements by fortune-tellers, therapists, and problem solvers. Officially, most Swiss Italians are Catholic. Archaeological remains from graves provide evidence of Etruscan, Celtic, Gallic, and Roman customs and goddesses. The Swiss Italians were Christianized already in the fourth century and some villages still celebrate Ambrosian rites. In the alpine valleys (Leventina, Blenio) people were Christianized from the north. During the Reformation, Italian refugees were accepted in Mesolcina, Bregaglia, Poschiavo, and Locarno. As the Grigioni Italiano were under foreign domination, the Reformation could develop freely but it did not have a lasting influence. Catholic Ticino was influenced considerably by the Catholic Swiss cantons, which by law prohibited the Reformed church from remaining in dominated areas. Until the formal separation of church and state, the population was under the control of the churches and monasteries. Recently, many monasteries and community churches have been abandoned because of a shortage of priests. Italian priests are often found in the valleys.

Arts

The cultural (linguistic, intellectual, architectural, art-historical, and artistic) center of Swiss Italy lies in Italy (Milan). The sculptor Giacometti from Bregaglia (Stampa), who was known locally, had to exhibit first in Paris and Milan before he was recognized in Ticino. The same can be said of Brignoni, the artist and ethnographic collector. Swiss Italian literature emphasizes regional culture and identity. There are regional programs for theater, music, and arts education. There is no Swiss Italian university (four American universities around Lugano and business centers in nearby Lombardia were recently opened).

In the last thirty years nearly every valley has opened a local ethnographic museum. Many of the objects are also sold as souvenirs: wooden backpacks (*gerla*); copper pots; bast-covered chairs; *pergolas, peperonis*, and *maïs* of plastic; open wooden shoes (*zoccoli*); and special mugs (*boccalino*).

Medicine

Because of the climate, a growing segment of the economy focuses on the construction of private hospitals and old-age homes. At the beginning of the century hospitals for the treatment of tuberculosis were famous. Because of a lack of confidence in modern medicine, there is a movement among the middle class toward traditional methods of healing. Traditional knowledge about medical plants and healers is being studied. Modern medicine is still regularly used for major health problems.

Death and Afterlife

Beliefs about the afterlife are shaped by the Christian tradition. In villages today the deceased are no longer kept at home until the funeral, and wakes are less common. A community room is now used for this purpose. At funerals the church is more or less filled, depending on the public status of the dead. At times there is a "fanfare" played. After the service the procession goes to the churchyard, where the last prayers and rites take place. The churchyard is built at the edge of the village and protected by walls. The burial places show differences depending on traditional, economic, political, and social status.

a drink afterward, and for lunch. Postmarital residence depends on the working place of the husband and economic opportunities and is usually neolocal.

DOMESTIC UNIT. Extended nuclear families with grandparents or other kin in the same household are rather rare. Economic mobility encourages nuclear families or one-person households and second residences (*pendolarismo*).

INHERITANCE. Roman law as a historical base of inheritance rules demands a division of property. Sometimes this leads to a situation where houses cannot be renovated or sold because the heirs cannot be located or do not agree.

SOCIALIZATION. The growing role of public social institutions has reduced the socialization role of the family and has intensified generational conflicts. For young people, owning a car signifies freedom and also produces a high traffic-death rate among young men. In the valleys, family gatherings for Sunday lunches at the house of the grandmother (*mamma/nonna*) are common and highly valued.

Sociopolitical Organization

SOCIAL ORGANIZATION. Besides the local open-air restaurants (*grotto*), which serve as informal, public meeting places, in the villages there are a variety of associations, although they have lost their initial political or religious significance. On the level of regional ethnic identity, the ideals of conserving nature and preserving tradition are emphasized. The activities and ceremonies of the *confraternità* association are centered on a church patron. A Catholic movement with slightly fundamentalist or traditionalist tendencies, called "Communione e liberazione," supports them and the religious processions they organize. Traditional music bands (*fanfare*) with political significance (radical-liberal vs. Christian-Democrat bands of the villages in the nineteenth century) are today mostly apolitical. Shooting associations from the same epoch and sporting clubs, founded from the 1920s on, today organize carnivals, summer parties, and walking tours.

Quite a few cultural events and festivities (*festa dei fiori* as an imitation of the *fêtes des vendanges* of Vevey, the May dance, and polenta and risotto banquets) were introduced in Ticino. They are attempts to add a folkloric element to the culture and are also tourist attractions.

POLITICAL ORGANIZATION. The political organization of Switzerland is federalistic and democratic. It is structured on the levels of the confederation, the cantons, the districts (only juridical), and the community. There is a parliament (*gran consiglio del Ticino*, general assembly of the community) and an executive branch (*consiglieri dello stato*, *consiglieri della commune*), with members elected to four-year terms in a proportional election.

In the middle of the nineteenth century, Ticino was known as liberal and there was a broad support for the Lombardic liberation movement. The political pattern of the nineteenth century (liberals vs. conservatives) is still alive, despite the introduction of the Social Democratic party in the 1920s and its splinter groups. But neither the liberals (Partito Liberale Radicale) nor the Christian Democrats (PCD) can command an absolute majority today. In the last fifteen years four new parties joined in elections: Diritti Democratici Ticinesi; Partito Socialista dei Lavoratori; Partito Sozioliberale Federalisti Europei; and the Lega Lombarda. Those political groups show where the political future of Ticino lies. The elections are no longer major political battles, as the number of people who vote has shrunk (as everywhere else in Switzerland) to an average of a third or a half of the population.

SOCIAL CONTROL. In urban centers where anonymity is growing, publicity in the press has assumed a role in social control. Until recently, social control in the villages was exercised by the church, the political party, and the family. Today these institutions have weakened considerably.

CONFLICT. Coexistence with the German Swiss neorurali is an example of conflict in the village context today. They are also called *capelloni*, because of the long hair some of them once wore; today this term is used for any man wearing long hair and dressing alternatively. As the neorurali differ from the natives in ideology and values, their alternative life-style is subject to gossip, rumors, and even legal sanctions (prohibition of settlement). Thus, the presence of the neorurali triggers feelings of anger among the Italian Swiss about their own "miserable" past and the colonizing German Swiss of the past and the present.

Bibliography

Franscini, Stefano (1987). *La Svizzera italiana*. Edited by Virgilio Gilardoni. 4 vols. Bellinzona: Casagrande.

Frisch, Max (1981). *Der Mensch erscheint im Holozän*. Frankfurt: Suhrkamp.

Martini, Plinio (1970). *Il fondo del sacco*. Bellinzona: Casagrande.

Nessi, Alberto (1986). *Rabbia di vento*. Bellinzona: Casagrande.

Ratti, Remigio, et al. (1990). *Il Ticino—Regione aperta*. Locarno: Armando Dado Editore.

—BARBARA WALDIS

WELSH

Ethonym: Cymry (pronounced kamrī)

Orientation

IDENTIFICATION. The principality of Wales is one of the four "countries" constituting the United Kingdom of Great Britain and Northern Ireland. Though once ethnically homogeneous, Wales has had a steady influx of English-speaking settlers since the twelfth century. Prior to 1974 there were thirteen internal divisions or counties; in 1974 these were redrawn into eight counties.

Wales is a wide peninsula that extends into the Irish Sea on the west coast of the island of Great Britain. The northern shore begins at the Dee Estuary and Liverpool Bay, the western shore borders on Saint George's Channel and the Irish Sea, and the south shore consists of the Severn Estuary and the Bristol Channel. The peninsula consists of four major regions. The interior plateaus and uplands are characterized by a shorter growing season, relatively infertile acid soils, and high rainfall. The northwestern and west coastal lowlands or "Welsh Heartland" has a milder climate, longer growing season, and better soils. The "Anglicized Lowlands" along the south coast and the English border have relatively good soils and a more productive agricultural economy. Finally, "Industrialized Wales" is centered in the hills, valleys, and coastal cities of the south.

LOCATION. The Welsh climate is part of the North Atlantic maritime pattern with relatively heavy rainfall and high humidity throughout the year. Along the coast the amount of rainfall varies between 76 and 80.9 centimeters per year. The annual mean temperature is around 10.4° C with the January mean around 5° C and the July and August mean around 16° C. At times the higher uplands are subject to heavy winter snowstorms.

DEMOGRAPHY. As of 1988 the population of Wales was estimated at 2,805,000, of which 76 percent was urban and 24 percent rural. Given the official status of both the English and Welsh languages and the differing degrees of bilingualism, it is impossible to determine the exact numbers of individuals who ethnically identify as Welsh. The uplands, north, and west are relatively thinly populated. All the large cities (Cardiff, Swansea, and Newport) are in the relatively densely populated southern industrial belt.

LINGUISTIC AFFILIATION. Both Welsh and English are official languages. During the past two centuries the percentage of Welsh speakers has continued to decline. In 1901 about half the people spoke Welsh; today this is about 20 percent. Welsh is one of the Celtic languages. It is closest to Breton in France. Other related languages are Irish and Scottish Gaelic. In recent years there has been an increasing recognition and use of Welsh in Wales.

History and Cultural Relations

The Celtic conquest of Wales occurred only a few centuries before the Roman conquest of Britain in A.D. 70. The Romans withdrew in A.D. 383. This was followed by the arrival of Christian missionaries from Ireland and the Anglo-Saxon invasions vasions from the east. After the seventh century the Welsh were increasingly isolated from the rest of Europe by the expanding Saxon kingdoms. From this time until the arrival of the Normans, Welsh history can be characterized as a complex pattern of internal disputes between its small kingdoms, shifting alliances between different factions, and a constant series of petty wars between these groups and the Saxon kingdoms. During the ninth and tenth centuries, there was some success at unification, the establishment of a code of laws along with increasing Saxon legal and cultural influences. Between 1066 and the early twelfth century, Norman colonies, towns, and forts along the east and south further isolated the Welsh. In 1282 the Anglo-Norman conquest of Wales was completed, and between 1400 and 1410 the last Welsh revolt was suppressed. Finally in 1536 the Act of Union occurred whereby Wales was made a principality of England, English became the official language, and English law became dominant.

From about 1750 to 1900 much of Welsh life was greatly changed by the industrial revolution and the Methodist-Calvinist religious revivals. The development of coal and iron mining and smelting in the south resulted in massive movements of Welsh workers to the south. Large numbers of English workers also arrived. This division between the urban-industrial south and the rural-agrarian center and north still remains. The Wesleyan and nonconformist religious movements stimulated a shift away from the established church and provided a new core of Welsh ethnic consciousness.

Settlements

Traditionally, Wales was land of dispersed homesteads and small hamlets. The medieval Code of Hywell Dda specified that a hamlet could consist of no more than nine houses or hearths. This pattern was a reflection of the old economy based

♦ **United Kingdom**
Also known as Britain or Great Britain, the term refers to England, Scotland, Wales, and Northern Ireland.

See also

Gaels, Irish

upon subsistence farming and transhumance dairying with the winter base camp (*hendre*) at a lower elevation and the summer camp (*havod*) in the uplands. The earliest towns were those founded by the Normans in the south and the coastal strips. After the English conquest in 1292, county administrative and market towns were established, but these usually remained centers of English social life. During the industrialization of the south, larger towns and cities arose but the older rural pattern remained in the uplands and the north.

In the mining communities of the southern vales, slateroofed and stone-walled row houses often stretch for miles along the valley slopes. Most of these were built in the late nineteenth century.

Economy

SUBSISTENCE AND COMMERCIAL ACTIVITIES. Since the 1830s, the Welsh economy developed into a bifurcated pattern between the rural uplands and the southern industrial regions. In the uplands, the Welsh Heartland, and the north, the older self-sufficient agricultural, dairying, and sheepherding way of life was increasingly drawn into the larger regional and national economic networks. The most important agricultural products included wheat, barley, oats, dairy products, beef, mutton, and lamb. Potatoes, poultry, vegetables, and fruits were important for household use and local markets. In today's urban markets most of these are now supplied by English producers. Most dairy products are produced and marketed locally.

Beginning in the 1840s the Welsh economy increasingly shifted to coal mining, iron and steel production, and tin plating in the industrial south. Since 1950 these have drastically declined and are being replaced by light industry, plastics, and chemical- and electronic-equipment manufacturing. The recent development of the deep-water oil port, refinery, and petrochemical complex at Milford Haven has been the one major change. Slate mining remains important in the north.

INDUSTRIAL ARTS. Up to 1930 every locality had a wide range of local craftsmen such as blacksmiths, tanners, clog makers, coopers, etc. By the 1940s these were declining and by the 1950s they had virtually ceased to exist.

TRADE. Today one finds a mixture of traditional shops, open-air markets, supermarkets, shopping centers, large department stores, and weekly farmers' open-air markets.

DIVISION OF LABOR. In the rural areas women traditionally were in charge of food production, dairying activities, and care of the cattle

SLATE

A pile of slate above a Welsh town. Slate mining remains important in the north, whereas coal mining and steel production dominates the south. Wales. (Ferrell Grehan/Corbis)

and poultry, whereas men did the heavier work in the fields, pastures, and hedges. Cooperative exchanges of labor, farm machinery, and farm laborers were essential. With the commercialization of dairying and poultry raising, women's labor load has increased. Modern machines have almost ended the labor exchanges. Costly machines are cooperatively purchased.

LAND TENURE. Western and southern Wales was once a land of minor gentry; elsewhere there were small owner-occupied farms. Today the gentry is gone and the small farms predominate. A heavy turnover of ownership for small holdings is normal.

Kinship

KIN GROUPS AND DESCENT. The core kin group is the bilateral kindred. Within this group the household and relationships of the first degree (parents, siblings, and children) are the most important. Second-degree relationships (grandparents, uncles, aunts, first cousins, nieces, nephews, and grandchildren) are also important as are those of the third degree (siblings of grandparents and children of first cousins and of nieces and nephews). Both consanguineal and affinal links are important in tracing one's relationships to others in the locality and expressing "community solidarity,"

*The nineteenth and
twentieth centuries
have seen the rise of
a Welsh cultural
revival and ethnic
consciousness in the
face of a decline in
the use of the Welsh
language.*

reciprocal obligations, and needs. Ideally, people should remain loyal; otherwise, they risk social isolation. Interconnections between kindreds tend to bind everyone together into larger groups of "kin," which from the bases for local identity. Older individuals can often trace interrelationships between everyone in a locality back 130–150 years. The kindred also influences membership in religious groups, political affiliation, marriage alliances, and general social interaction. Marriage between kin closer than second cousins is rare. The oldest son in a family is commonly named after the paternal grandfather, the second son after the father, and the first and second daughters after the grandmothers.

KINSHIP TERMINOLOGY. Welsh kinship terminology follows a bifurcate-merging pattern as among the English. In some areas there are differing terms for consanguineal as opposed to affinal relatives. Personal or individual preferences often lead to stressing one side of the family as opposed to the other. Lifelong nicknames based upon negative or humorous traits are common.

Marriage and Family

MARRIAGE. Traditionally, a son's marriage was his important transition to independence and adulthood. This concluded his major economic obligations to his parents. At this time they provided him with a farm, the implements, and livestock. There was a tendency to marry within the local community if possible. Sons usually married in their late twenties or early thirties and daughters in their mid- or late twenties. The percentage of bachelors was relatively high. Courtship tended to be very lengthy. Today the number of children per family generally ranges between one and three.

DOMESTIC UNIT. The basic domestic unit is the nuclear family, which consists of either the husband and wife or the parents and their children. In the latter case this often includes unmarried adult sons acting as unpaid farm workers. A widow or widower who gave up farming traditionally preferred to live with a married daughter. A chosen son, in most cases a younger son, commonly inherited the parental farm.

INHERITANCE. From medieval times to the present each child has been entitled to his/her share of inheritance. Older siblings usually receive their shares in the form of purchased land, furnishings, and other goods at the time of their marriage; the chosen heir, often the youngest son, succeeds to the parental land. The sex of the children, movement to the city, and other cir-

cumstances can influence these inheritance patterns.

SOCIALIZATION. Traditionally discipline was maintained through a combination of corporal punishment, moral example, and religious teachings and exhortations, especially in the context of the nonconformist chapels. These were reinforced by an emphasis on the importance of schooling and knowledge in general.

Sociopolitical Organization

Wales is a principality that is governed from Whitehall in London. Since 1964, when the position of Secretary of State for Wales was established, an increasing degree of administrative autonomy for Wales has evolved. All British political parties are represented, although the Labor Party is strongest in the industrial south. The Welsh Nationalist Party (Plaid Cymru) and other separatist groups are small but vocal.

SOCIAL ORGANIZATION. Wales was and remains far less classconscious than England. After the Union of 1536, whereby authority was centralized in London, the aristocrats drifted away and Wales increasingly became a land of smallholders. The Acts of Enclosure were never applied in Wales. A large liberal-oriented working class and an egalitarian middle class have emerged in the industrial south.

POLITICAL ORGANIZATION. In 1974 the internal political organization of Wales was simplified and Monmouthshire, now Gwent, was transferred to Wales. Sparsely populated counties in the north and central uplands were amalgamated and Glamorgan was divided into three new counties. The eight counties were subdivided into thirty-seven districts, and Cardiff retained its status as a city and capital of Wales. Each county and administrative district has its own elected council.

SOCIAL CONTROL. On the local level gossip, religious values, and ethnic pride are the primary means of social control. Above this, the British court system prevails. Both English and Welsh are used in the courts.

CONFLICT. Welsh history was dominated by centuries of military and social conflict with the English and internal dissention. The nineteenth and twentieth centuries have seen the rise of a Welsh cultural revival and ethnic consciousness in the face of a decline in the use of the Welsh language. Much of this revival has centered around the musical and literary competitions of the Welsh *eisteddfod*, Welsh religiosity, literary societies, and the efforts to have Welsh recognized as one of the official languages in Wales.

Religion and Expressive Culture

RELIGIOUS BELIEFS. Various Protestant churches are dominant in Wales. In 1536 the Church of England became the official faith of the Welsh; by the early nineteenth century, the majority of the Welsh were nonconformists: Calvinist-Methodists, Congregationalists, Baptists, Presbyterians, Unitarians, etc. In 1914 the Church of England was declared no longer the official church of Wales, but the four ancient cathedrals retain their importance for all denominations.

RELIGIOUS PRACTITIONERS. Ministers are respected leaders and moral exhorters in their individual parishes.

CEREMONIES. The most important services are the weekly Sunday services and special evening prayer services. Others are Christmas eve and morning services, New Year's Eve, Palm Sunday, Easter, and Harvest Home. Saint David's Day (1 March) for the Patron Saint of Wales has increasingly become a secular holiday related to ethnic consciousness. Bible study, or Sunday schools with age-graded groups for young people and adults, have traditionally been important.

ARTS. The local and national literary, musical, and cultural eisteddfods are the core of the Welsh arts. The Welsh poetic tradition remains uniquely strong even today.

MEDICINE. Medical beliefs and practices are basically the same as those in modern England (i.e., socialized medicine with physicians, surgeons, modern clinics, and hospitals).

DEATH AND AFTERLIFE. Death and the ensuing funeral, with the gathering of the kindred, were traditionally the great reminder of family unity. Every local household was expected to have at least one representative at the funeral and the feast provided for by the family of the deceased afterwards. In the past, careful note was made as to who was and was not there. In some areas the list from the funeral guest book was published in the local newspaper. The basic Protestant belief in the soul going either to heaven or hell was common among the Welsh.

Bibliography

Jenkins, David, Emrys Jones, T. Jones Hughes, and Trefor M. Owen (1962). *Welsh Rural Communities.* Cardiff: University of Wales Press.

Jenkins, J. Geraint (1976). *Life and Tradition in Rural Wales.* London: J. M. Dent & Sons.

Jones, R. Brinley, ed. (1972). *Anatomy of Wales.* Peterston-Super-Ely, Wales: Gwerin.

Owen, Trefor M. (1974). *Welsh Folk Customs.* 3rd ed. Cardiff: National Museum of Wales, Walsh Folk Museum.

Rees, Alwyn D. (1950). *Life in a Welsh Countryside.* Cardiff: University of Wales Press.

—ROBERT J. THEODORATUS

Middle America and the Caribbean

ANTIGUANS AND BARBUDANS

Ethonym: none

Orientation

IDENTIFICATION. The country Antigua and Barbuda includes two of the Leeward Islands located in the eastern Caribbean Sea. Settled by English colonists in the seventeenth century, the islands have a history of slavery and British colonial rule. Antigua and Barbuda won independence in 1981. The national motto is "Each endeavouring, all achieving."

LOCATION. Antigua measures 281 square kilometers in area, and Barbuda 161 square kilometers. A third island, uninhabited Redonda (3.25 square kilometers), is a dependency of the state. Volcanic and comprised of limestone, Antigua is generally flat, except for the southwestern section, which is the site of the highest point, Boggy Peak (403 meters). The coastline has many fine white sandy beaches, some protected by dense bush, and many natural harbors. Antigua's vegetation is evergreen and deciduous forest and evergreen woodland. Most of the country's government buildings are located in the capital, Saint John's, together with a central market, schools, banks, shops and restaurants, a deep-water harbor, and, since the late 1980s, a modern tourist complex.

Relatively isolated Barbuda lies some 50 kilometers to the northeast. It is a coral island covered with open scrub. Cattle, deer, guinea fowl, and hogs roam freely through the bush. Barbuda's unsafe harbors have contributed to its isolation over the centuries; regular air service from Antigua began only in 1961. Almost all of Barbuda's 1,200 residents live in historic Codrington Village. The island has a few shops, some resort hotels where people find seasonal work, an elementary school, a health clinic, and several churches.

DEMOGRAPHY. Antigua and Barbuda's population, according to the 1991 census, was 60,840 persons (29,638 men and 31,202 women, a ratio of 105 females for every 100 males); of these, only 2 percent lived on Barbuda. The vast majority of Antiguans and Barbudans, 60,148 persons, live in private households. Most of the islanders are African Caribbean people, their ancestors having been brought as slaves in the seventeenth and eighteenth centuries. Other groups include a few remaining descendants of British colonists, the progeny of Portuguese indentured servants who came in the mid-nineteenth century under planter-inspired schemes to find field laborers, and the children of Syrian and Lebanese traders who arrived at the turn of the twentieth century. West Indians from other islands and a small group of expatriates from the United States, Canada, and England reside in Antigua as well.

LINGUISTIC AFFILIATION. Antiguans and Barbudans speak English, although there is a creole dialect most commonly heard in the countryside. Most citizens are literate.

History and Cultural Relations

Antigua and Barbuda's first indigenous people included Siboney and later Arawak Indians. These were hunting and fishing peoples whose settlements have been located at several sites on both islands. From their villages in Dominica and Saint Kitts, Carib Indians raided the Arawak and later the European colonists on Antigua and Barbuda. The first English colonists arrived in Antigua in 1632. They were led by Sir Thomas Warner, who had earlier headed an expedition to Saint Christopher (now Saint Kitts). These colonists and their indentured servants grew tobacco, cotton, and subsistence crops and defended themselves against the Carib and the French. Within a few years, they had devised a regular system of government, complete with elected assemblies, governors' councils, parish vestries, and a hierarchy of courts. By the early eighteenth century the colonists had adjusted their legal codes to the exigencies of managing an economy devoted to sugar and organized around plantation slavery (Lazarus-Black 1994). Gaspar estimates that 60,820 African slaves were imported to Antigua between 1671 and 1763 (1985, 75). Slaves accounted for 41.6 percent of the population in 1672; 80.5 percent in 1711; and 93.5 percent in 1774 (p. 83).

Unlike Antigua, Barbuda never developed sugar estates. Early attempts by English settlers to farm the island were unsuccessful, and the Carib proved a constant menace. In 1685 the Crown leased Barbuda to the Codrington family for a payment "unto her Majesty yearly and every year one Fat Sheep if demanded" (Hall 1971, 59). The Codringtons used the island as a supply depot, manufacturing center, and slave "seasoning" area. Until 1898, when the Antiguan legislature assumed responsibility for its government, the islanders, most of them descendants of Codrington's slaves, were without political representation or social services.

Slavery was abolished in 1834, but much of the political, social, and economic organization of

Antiguans and Barbudans take great pride in their music. Calypso and steel bands are very popular, and there are annual competitions during the July Carnival.

See also

English

Antiguans and Barbudans

*Historic windmills on the
island of Antigua. Antigua and
Barbuda. (Reinhard
Eisele/Corbis)*

these islands remained largely unchanged over the next century. Barbudans continued to reside in Codrington Village, working subsistence gardens, fishing, and hunting. In Antigua, there was little land available for purchase and few jobs beyond those offered on the estates. Workers remained in very impoverished conditions and most continued to plant and harvest sugarcane under the terms of the infamous Contract Act. Reform began with the legalization of trade unions in 1940, higher wages, and the extension of political representation in the 1950s and 1960s.

Settlements

The largest town, Saint Johns, is on the north-western coast of Antigua. It is the hub of island activity. Beyond Saint Johns, villages dot the rural Antiguan landscape. Many of these were founded immediately after Emancipation and adopted names such as "Liberta" and "Freetown." The freedmen built wattle-and-daub (wood frame and straw) houses for their families in preference to residing on the sugar estates. Churches became centers of religious and social life in these villages. Today the villages of Parham, Bolans, All Saints, and English Harbour are large enough to serve as centers for schools, police stations, courts, post offices, and other government services. Barbudans mostly reside in Codrington Village. Despite opposition from the government in Antigua, they continue to insist upon communal ownership of the land beyond the village.

Economy

SUBSISTENCE AND COMMERCIAL ACTIVITIES. Antigua's economy remained almost singularly devoted to sugarcane for more than two centuries. The last sugar factory closed in 1972, but there are periodic attempts to revive that industry. Agricultural production is moving toward greater diversification, which includes fruits, vegetables, and grains (World Bank 1985, 15–16).

Tourism began to develop haltingly in the early 1960s; by the 1980s it had become the single most important economic activity in Antigua. Its direct value now accounts for approximately 21 percent of the gross domestic product, and at least 12 percent of the labor force is directly employed in this sector (World Bank 1985, 24). Other economic sectors include the personal-service industries, distributive trades, construction, transport, agriculture, and fishing. The government employs some 30 percent of the total work force (p. 4). Unemployment remained at around 20 percent through the first half of the 1980s.

INDUSTRIAL ARTS. Industrial activity includes processing local agricultural produce; some manufacturing of clothing, furniture, and household goods; and production of rum and other beverages. In 1983 manufactured exports represented about 85 percent of total domestic exports (World Bank 1985, 20). A handful of firms produce more than half of the output and employ at least half of the industrial work force. Crude oil, machinery, automobiles, luxury consumer items, and clothing are imported.

TRADE. Antigua exports cotton, pineapples, live animals, rum, tobacco, and animal and vegetable products. Provision crops are consumed locally, with surpluses passed on to family and friends or sold for extra cash. The middle class depends heavily on imported foods and consumer items. People travel abroad specifically to shop for retail goods.

DIVISION OF LABOR. Holding multiple jobs and sharing jobs are common in Antigua and Barbuda. For example, a man may work as a carpenter, keep cows, and rent a house. The growth of tourism has enabled many more people, particularly women, to enter the labor force. For the most part, however, household chores, tending gardens and domestic animals, and child care remain women's work even if they hold full-time jobs.

LAND TENURE. The government owns nearly 60 percent of the available land in Antigua. The practice of offering short-term leases to individuals has not proved particularly conducive to land improvement. Barbudans individually own their homes in Codrington Village, but they hold in common lands beyond the village.

Kinship

KIN GROUPS AND DESCENT. Antiguans and Barbudans trace family relationships bilaterally through blood and law. Family is very important, both to one's social identity and for social, economic, and political support. A woman is said to have a child "for" a man, a way of noting that children create new social bonds and alliances. Marriage is the preferred form of union, but many persons marry later in life after their families have been established. Families are generally large, and they may include legitimate ("inside") as well as illegitimate ("outside") children who are socially acknowledged. Because of the small populations of these islands, people have extensive knowledge about kinship ties and histories.

KINSHIP TERMINOLOGY. Antiguans and Barbudans inherited the kinship terminology of the British colonists who settled these islands, but they do not make a linguistic distinction between "half" and "whole" siblings. "Aunty" and "uncle" may be used as terms of respect for elders. Another departure from English tradition is that men and women who have lived together for some time may refer to each other as "wife" or "husband" even though the couple is not legally married.

Marriage and Family

MARRIAGE AND FAMILY STRUCTURE. Scholars have gone to great lengths to try to explain the high rates of illegitimacy, the prevalence and popularity of three different conjugal forms (visiting unions, concubinage, and legal marriage), and the pervasiveness of female-headed households in the English-speaking Caribbean. Early efforts to explain these patterns centered on slavery; historians argued that bondage made marriage and a stable family life impossible. An alternative perspective suggested that slaves retained vestiges of African polygamy and matrilineal kinship practices. Others have attributed West Indian kinship and household organization to economic factors, particularly persistent poverty, male migration, and other social and demographic factors.

Historical investigations suggest there was never a single type of slave family form in the Caribbean (Higman 1984). As was true throughout the region, Antiguan slaves toiled in different socioeconomic contexts, and these influenced the content and forms of their conjugal and reproductive practices. Slaves on large estates, for example, might have experienced relative stability in their day-to-day lives and had access to a pool of potential conjugal partners on their own and nearby estates. Slaves who labored in towns, in contrast, were more likely to live in motherchild households than were field laborers (pp. 373, 371). The record shows a pattern in which most slaves had a number of partners early in life and later settled into long-term unions with single partners. Certain men of unusual talent, wit, or charisma, however, maintained multiple unions.

Religion and law exerted important influences on the marriage and kinship practices of Antiguans. By the end of the slave trade in 1807, for example, the missions claimed to have converted about 28 percent of the Black and Colored population in Antigua, Saint Kitts, Montserrat, Nevis, and the British Virgin Islands (based on Goveia 1965, 307). Early in the nineteenth century, free colonists, including free persons of color, married in the Anglican church in Saint Johns (Lazarus-Black 1994).

For much of Antigua's early history, there were three separate marriage laws, each corresponding directly to a person's role in the island's division of labor. Free Antiguans, for example, were married by Anglican ministers. These men generally married women of their own social standing in the community, but some also entered into nonlegal unions with women of color. In contrast, "respectable" free women married and refrained from extramarital affairs. Ministers were forbidden by law, however, from performing marriages for salves or indentured servants unless the latter had permission from their masters. After 1798, a special marriage law, only partially resembling that pertaining to free persons, governed the unions of slaves. A child of a slave marriage was not allowed to take the father's surname or inherit property. The law did provide for a public declaration of a couple's intention to live together, monetary awards from masters for marrying, and a brief ceremony in which the marriage was officially recorded in the estate records. After slavery ended in 1834, there was a single marriage code. Nevertheless, the establishment of families without formal legal confirmation remained commonplace across the social classes.

DOMESTIC UNIT. Married couples prefer to live in their own households, although needy relatives and friends are welcomed. If a couple is unmarried and the man is "visiting," the children usually reside with their mother. Kinship and the domestic unit are not coterminous; many children live away from their biological parents, and some children grow up in several different households. Parents make choices about where a child should reside, considering the economy of the household, people's work patterns, the need to care for the elderly, educational opportunities, and the simple fact that a relative may ask for a child to keep from being lonely.

INHERITANCE. Since 1987 it has been illegal to discriminate against a person because of birth status; a child born out of wedlock may readily be legally acknowledged by his or her father, and any child so recognized can inherit from the father's estate. The islanders usually divide inheritances equally among their children. A married man often remembers his illegitimate children in his will or with a gift made during his lifetime.

SOCIALIZATION. Children are desired by both men and women, although women have primary responsibility for children's early care. In the past, many children were cared for by female relatives or older siblings. Today day-care centers and preschools are an option. Nevertheless, the extended family remains crucially important in children's socialization.

Sociopolitical Organization

SOCIAL ORGANIZATION. The contemporary social structure consists of a small socioeco-

RELIGION AND EXPRESSIVE CULTURE

Religious Beliefs

There have been two major waves of missionary activity in Antigua. The first occurred at the end of the eighteenth century, spurred by the arrival of Methodist and Moravian ministers on the island. The second wave of proselytizing began around World War I and gained momentum during the years of the Great Depression. Today the Anglican church has the largest following. Other large congregations include the Moravian, Methodist, Catholic, Seventh Day Adventist, Pilgrim Holiness, and Pentecostal churches. Churches have historically played a very important role in the lives of Antiguans and Barbudans, and they remain very important today. Despite Barbuda's small size, more than half a dozen churches find congregations.

Some people also believe in a body of knowledge and set of rites called obeah. Deriving from Africa, obeah can be used for a variety of purposes including healing, causing sickness or other physical harm, determining who has been guilty of theft, "fixing" a court case, and ensuring that a loved one will remain faithful. It is illegal, but practitioners are mainly ignored by police.

Religious Practitioners

Ministers are accorded high prestige in the community. In addition to their roles as spiritual leaders, they provide psychological counseling and often mediate in conflicts among their parishioners.

Ceremonies

Antiguans and Barbudans celebrate with friends and relatives a child's birth, baptism, and marriage. Weddings and funerals are very important and elaborate events. Independence Day is celebrated on 1 November.

Arts

Cricket is the national sport. Antiguans and Barbudans also take great pride in their music. Calypso and steelbands are very popular, and there are annual competitions at Carnival at the end of July to determine the best songs, singers, and bands. During Carnival, troupes march in colorful costumes in the street and excited viewers "jump-up" enthusiastically to urge the revelers on. Visitors to Antigua can see an overview of the country's history at the Museum of Antigua and Barbuda in Saint Johns. Choral and theatrical groups perform occasionally.

nomic elite and two broad classes, middle and lower. The elite includes high-ranking political officials, local businessmen, major landholders, senior attorneys, and a few foreign entrepreneurs and expatriates who play important roles in the economy but who are noticeably absent from the official political process. The homes, cars, leisure activities, and family life of the elite are virtually indistinguishable from those of people in Antigua's middle class. The middle class includes young lawyers, landowners, teachers, clergymen, retailers, members of the civil service, and the few industrialists. The upper strata of the lower class consists of a petite bourgeoisie who own some productive resources and who may be self-employed. The large working class includes agricultural workers, fishermen, domestics, hotel workers, and common laborers. Barbudans are relatively homogeneous in terms of their homes and life-style; most are working class.

Political Organizations

Few Antiguans could meet the property qualifications for voting, much less running for office, until well into the twentieth century. Planters controlled local politics until labor unrest heralded a movement for political reform. Adult suffrage was granted in 1951. Shortly thereafter, election rules were changed to allow greater participation among the working people. Independence occurred through a series of stages that Henry (1985) refers to as "constitutional decolonization." In 1969 the islands became associated states, gaining control of their internal affairs. Since 1981, Antigua and Barbuda has become a parliamentary democracy with a bicameral legislature and an elected prime minister. The governor-general is the representative of the British Crown. The government has proclaimed a nonaligned foreign policy but maintains its strongest political and economic ties with Britain, Canada, and the United States. There are two major political parties, the Antigua Labour party and the United Progressive party. The former, led by V. C. Bird, Sr., has been politically dominant since 1946.

SOCIAL CONTROL. Antiguans and Barbudans pride themselves on being a law-abiding people; the crime rate remains low. A police force and a four-tiered court system presently serve the islands. The first tier consists of the magistrates' courts, which decide some family cases, disputes between persons over small property claims, personal grievances, traffic matters, and minor assaults. The High Court settles major civil and criminal cases. The Appellate Division of the Supreme Court of the Eastern Caribbean meets intermittently. Because Antigua and Barbuda is a member of the Commonwealth, cases decided by the Supreme Court may be appealed to the Privy Council in England.

Bibliography

Gaspar, David Barry (1985). *Bondmen and Rebels: A Study of Master-Slave Relations in Antigua*. Baltimore: Johns Hopkins University Press.

Goveia, Elsa V. (1965). *Slave Society in the British Leeward Islands at the End of the Eighteenth Century*. New Haven: Yale University Press.

Hall, Douglas (1971). *Five of the Leewards, 1834–1870*. Saint Lawrence, Barbados: Caribbean Universities Press.

Henry, Paget (1985). *Peripheral Capitalism and Underdevelopment in Antigua*. New Brunswick, N.J.: Transaction Books.

Higman, B. W. (1984). *Slave Populations of the British Caribbean 1807–1834*. Baltimore: Johns Hopkins University Press.

Lazarus-Black, Mindie (1994). *Legitimate Acts and Illegal Encounters: Law and Society in Antigua and Barbuda*. Washington, D.C.: Smithsonian Institution Press.

World Bank (1985). *Antigua and Barbuda Economic Report*. Washington, D.C.

—MINDIE LAZARUS-BLACK

ARUBANS

Ethonym: none: historical names for the island, of pre-Colombian or Spanish origin: Oirubae ("companion," that is, to Curaçao), Ora Oubao ("shell island"), Oro Ubo ("once there was gold")

Orientation

IDENTIFICATION. Aruba is a multicultural island society with both Caribbean and Latin American features in its culture and social structure. Its people have been strongly influenced by the globalization of world culture.

LOCATION. Aruba is the most southeastern island of the Caribbean archipelago. It is located 27 kilometers off the coast of the Venezuelan peninsula of Paraguana and 90 kilometers west of Curaçao. Together with Curaçao and Bonaire, it forms the Dutch Leeward Islands. Aruba's area is 193 square kilometers. The climate is tropical, with an average temperature of 28° C. The main rainy season is from October to January. Yearly rainfall usually does not exceed 50 centimeters.

*Insular nationalism,
strengthened by
cultural and racial
differences, has
caused Aruba to
strive for separation
from Curaçao.*

♦ **creole**
*A general, inconsistently
used term usually applied to
a spoken language or dialect
that is based on
grammatical and lexical
features combined from two
or more natural languages.
It is a first language,
distinct from a pidgin.*

See also

Dutch

DEMOGRAPHY. The population and housing census of 1991 showed that 66,687 people live on Aruba, not including an estimated 2,500 to 5,000 illegal aliens. Compared to the period 1972–1981, during which the population increased 4.2 percent, the growth rate climbed to 10.6 percent between 1981 and 1991, mostly owing to immigration after 1987. The proportion of foreign-born inhabitants has risen from 18.5 percent in 1981 to 23.9 percent in 1991.

LINGUISTIC ORIENTATION. The traditional language of Aruba is Papiamento (Talk), a creole language that is also spoken on Curaçao and Bonaire. The origins of Papiamento are much debated. Two points of view dominate the discussion. According to one, it originated as a lingua franca, based on Portuguese and West African languages, during the seventeenth-century slave trade. Others maintain that it developed during the interaction between the Spanish and the Dutch. Indian names of plants and places are included in its lexicon. Owing to 350 years of colonial domination, Dutch is the official language in education and public affairs. The oil industry, tourism, and subsequent migration brought English and Spanish to the island, which are the second- and thirdmost spoken languages. Most Arubans are multilingual.

History and Cultural Relations

Prior to European discovery, Aruba was inhabited by Indian populations. From 2000 to 1000 B.C. the island was populated by preceramic Indians. Around 1000 B.C. Arawak from the east of Venezuela migrated to Aruba, introducing pottery and agriculture.

Aruba was discovered by the Spanish around 1499. Because of the absence of precious metals, Aruba, Bonaire, and Curaçao were declared *islas inutiles* (useless islands). In 1515 their inhabitants were deported to Hispaniola to work in the mines. After an unsuccesful effort toward colonization by Juan de Ampíes (1526–1533) the islands were abandoned to their fate. Other Indians later migrated to Aruba, and Spanish priests from the Falcón region of Venezuela undertook to Christianize them.

The Dutch West India Company (WIC) took possession of Aruba in 1636, two years after the conquest of Curaçao. Colonization of the island was forbidden until 1754; the island was used to breed cattle for trade and to supply food for the residents of Curaçao. After the dissolution of the WIC (1792) and the English interregnum (1810–1816), colonization started on a more seri-

ous footing. A short-lived trade upheaval and, in 1824, the discovery of gold and the introduction of more liberal regulations of administration favored colonization. Although gold mining and (after 1879) phosphate mining temporarily supported economic growth, the elite were mainly active in commercial agriculture and (illegal) trade with the South American mainland. The Aruban peasantry remained dependant on small-scale agriculture, fishing, and labor migration to the mainland and the Cuban sugar estates. Slavery was marginal; colonists and Indians intermixed and formed the traditional Aruban population. Between 1816 and 1924 the population increased from 1,732 to 9,021.

The arrival of the oil industry in the 1920s resulted in rapid modernization and massive immigration of thousands of industrial laborers, merchants, and civil servants from the Caribbean, Europe, and the Americas. Aruba became a pluralistic society consisting of over forty nationalities. The Eagle Oil Refining Company (a Royal Dutch/Shell affiliate) ceased its activities in 1953. The Lago Oil and Transport Company changed hands several times and became part of the Standard Oil concern (later Exxon) in 1932. Lago began to automate in 1952 and closed its gates in 1985. Since then, tourism, which was first initiated in the 1950s, has strongly expanded, becoming the main source of income and employment. The need for labor resulted in a new wave of migration from the Caribbean, South America, and the Netherlands. In 1988 the Coastal Oil Company was established on the island.

As a relatively wealthy island, Aruba has strived for separation from the former colony of the Netherlands Antilles since 1933. Insular nationalism was and is strengthened by cultural and racial differences with Curaçao. In the 1970s this sense of nationalism resulted in a heightened cultural self-esteem and increased political participation on the part of the traditional Aruban population. In 1986 Aruba became an autonomous entity within the Dutch kingdom. The mass media and tourism are the agents of rapid change in Aruban cultural identity. Growing concern about this issue inclines some Arubans toward cultural conservatism.

Settlements

The capital, Oranjestad, is situated on the west part of the southern coast. San Nicolas, on the east side of the southern coast, is the second-largest town and the locus of the oil industry. Townships are spread over the rest of the island. The most important villages are Noord (located near the tourism area), Santa Cruz, and Savaneta. The hilly northeastern part and the rocky northern coast are uninhabited. Aruba has a population density of 354.7 (legal) inhabitants per square kilometer.

Economy

SUBSISTENCE AND TOURISM. Having scant natural resources of its own, Aruba has relied on oil refining and tourism as its main sources of income throughout the twentieth century. The government, the single largest employer on the island, has a payroll of approximately 5,000 persons. After the closure of the Lago refinery in 1985, the number of hotel rooms was more than doubled; a tripling is under way. The trade and construction sectors have expanded but are strongly dependent on tourism. The unemployment rate rose to nearly twenty percent after the closing of the refinery, but was less than 1 percent in the early 1990s. Of the total employed population of 29,220 persons in 1991, 10,604 worked in hotels, restaurants, and wholesale and retail companies. The construction and manufacturing sectors had 2,975 and 1,717 employees respectively.

The gross domestic product more than doubled between 1987 and 1992. Despite the economic recovery, serious concerns have arisen because of inflation and strains on the labor market, infrastructure, and the natural environment. Furthermore, the worsening competitive position in tourism, possible future claims on government guarantees of stalled hotel projects, and a recession in the United States add to the concern about future economic prospects.

Efforts to attract industry in the 1960s proved largely unsuccesful. After the closure of the Lago refinery in 1985, Coastal Oil Corporation renovated the remains of the old refinery and started operations in 1988. Oil transshipment is handled by Wickland Oil Company. Other industrial efforts are of minor importance. The construction sector, which largely depends on tourism and the need for housing and business offices, is booming.

TRADE. Apart from oil refining and transshipment, trade is mainly directed toward tourism and local consumption. A free zone is becoming increasingly important because of revenues related to port charges and services. Some nine offshore companies have been established on Aruba.

DIVISION OF LABOR. Labor participation of men and women between 20 and 54 is respectively 89.8 and 66.0 percent. All through the economy men possess the more important positions. An important division of labor is based on ethnicity. Nat-

uralized citizens and permanent residents of Lebanese, Madeirean, Chinese, and Jewish descent focus mainly on trade. Post-1985 migrants from the Philippines, Colombia, and Venezuela, whose residency may be temporary, hold the lower positions in tourism. Women from Santo Domingo, Colombia, and Jamaica work as live-in maids with upper- and middle-class families. Young Dutch migrants work mostly in business, especially in bars and restaurants. Civil servants are drawn mostly from traditional Arubans and migrants who arrived during the oil-boom years.

LAND TENURE. Since the decline of agriculture after the arrival of the oil industry in the 1920s, land tenure has been most important to the population for the construction of houses. Three types of land tenure occur: regular landed property, hereditary tenure or long lease, and the renting of government grounds. For economic purposes, especialy in the oil and tourism industries, government grounds are given in long, renewable leases of sixty years.

Kinship

KIN GROUPS AND DESCENT. Until the beginning of the twentieth century, the extended family and the conjugal nuclear-family household were the centers of kinship organization. Traditionally, as a result of patri- or matrilocal settlement, groups of brothers and/or sisters and their spouses lived near each other on family grounds. Marriage between close kin was common. Incest prohibition applied to the *primo carnal* (bilateral first cousin). Geographical and genealogical propinquity therefore were virtualy synonymous. A shortage of land and urbanization caused a decrease in patri- and matrilocal settlement and the weakening of the traditional type of kinship organization. Descent rules are bilateral.

KINSHIP TERMINOLOGY. Kinship terminology parallels that of Catholic canon law. The term *yui mayó* (oldest child) refers to the eldest offspring's special position as the first successor to the parents. Kinship terminology is also used to address oneself to nonrelatives, the terms *ruman* (brother), *primo* (cousin), and *swa* (brother-in-law) meaning "friend." Ritual kinship focuses around the godparents, the *padrino* and *madrina*, who each have clearly defined obligations regarding the godchild's baptism, first holy communion, and marriage.

Marriage and Family

MARRIAGE. Monogamy and legal marriage are the norm, but extramarital and premarital

*Aruban democracy
functions with a
certain degree of
patronage and
nationalistic
rhetoric. Political
parties carefully
select candidates
from different
regional and ethnic
backgrounds.*

relations are common. Concubinage doubled between 1981 and 1991. Teenage pregnancy is a growing concern. Intraethnic marriages are favored, but the census of 1991 showed that in 1990 and 1991, 45.2 percent of Aruban-born men married foreign spouses and 24.8 percent of Aruban women married non-Arubans. One cause of this is the great number of marriages of convenience ("fake marriages"). By marrying Arubans, foreigners can obtain the much-desired Dutch nationality.

DOMESTIC UNIT. The conjugal nuclear family is the most favored domestic unit. Nevertheless, one-person households, extended-family or composite households, and consensual nuclear-family households are socially accepted. The traditional household can be characterized as matricentric. The everyday authority lies with the mother, the ultimate authority with the father. In family affairs, the oldest child (yui mayó), who has special influence in situations of decision making and conflict.

INHERITANCE. Inheritance, like descent, is bilateral; normally, all children receive a share.

SOCIALIZATION. Socialization generally takes place within the family and social organizations as well as at school. Within the nuclear family, it is predominantly the mother who takes care of the children. A growing number of children attend day-care centers before going to school. The educational system is based on the Dutch model. At the age of 4, children attend kindergarten, and after age 6 primary school. They enroll in secondary or lower vocational school after age 12. Higher education is provided by a pedagogical institute, and the study of law or economics may be pursued at the University of Aruba. A hotel school is designed after the U.S. system. Many students leave for the Netherlands or the United States to attend institutions of higher education. Adult education is very popular and is provided by Enseñanza pa Empleo (Education for Employment), a development project cofinanced by the Aruban and the Dutch governments and a great number of for-profit institutes.

Social organizations are important loci of socialization and social participation for all age groups and classes. The most important organizations are sports and service clubs, scouting associations, community centers, and religious and professional organizations. Ethnic clubs were extremely important between approximately 1945 and 1970 but have lost their impact on later generations.

Sociopolitical Organization

SOCIAL ORGANIZATION. Aruba is divided along class, ethnic, and geographical lines, which in part overlap. Although the gap between rich and poor is significant, class lines are loosely defined. Anthropological research has devoted much attention to ethnic relations. Ethnic boundaries are not as rigid as in typical Caribbean plural societies such as those of Suriname or Trinidad but can be seen between (descendants of) traditional Arubans and Afro-Arubans. Trade groups, such as the Chinese and the Portuguese from Madeira, and the traditional elite hold their own position. Recent migration has created new boundaries between newcomers and older ethnic groups. Ethnic and geographical divisions can be seen in labor specialization, patterns of marriage and settlement, choice of language, and political affiliations.

POLITICAL ORGANIZATIONS. Aruba has been an autonomous part of the Dutch kingdom since 1986. The *gouvernor* is the local representative of the Dutch monarch and the head of the Aruban government. The kingdom's Council of Ministers consists of the complete Dutch cabinet and two ministers plenipotentiary, one representing Aruba and the other the Netherlands Antilles. It is in charge of joint foreign policy, defense, and justice and the safeguarding of fundamental rights and freedoms. Political autonomy in internal affairs is almost complete. Although it was decided in 1983 that Aruba would become independent and leave the Dutch kingdom in 1996, this is now being changed and Aruba will maintain its autonomous status within the kingdom. Execution of this resolution, however, is contingent on restructuring of the governmental apparatus, enhancing the quality of administration, and reducing public expenditures.

Aruba is a parliamentary democracy with a multiparty system. Elections are held every four years. Since achieving the Status Aparte, government has been dependent on coalitions between one of the two bigger parties and the smaller ones. The biggest parties are the Christian-democratic Arubaanse Volkspartij (People's party of Aruba) and the social-democratic Movimento Electoral di Pueblo (People's Electoral Movement). Democracy functions with a certain degree of patronage and nationalistic rhetoric. Political parties carefully select candidates from different regional and ethnic backgrounds.

National festive days are the Day of the National Anthem and the Flag on 18 March and

Queen's Day on 30 April. The first stresses Aruba's political autonomy, the second the partnership with the Dutch kingdom. Aruba's former political leader François Gilberto "Betico" Croes (1938–1986) is commemorated on his birthday, 25 January. Croes is the personification of Aruba's struggle for separation from the Netherlands Antilles. He was seriously injured in a car crash, a few hours before the proclamation of the Status Aparte, on New Year's Eve 1985. He died in November 1986.

SOCIAL CONTROL. The small scale of the society allows gossip to be an effective means of social control. Newspapers, of which Aruba has four in Papiamento, two in Dutch, and three in English, also function as such. Legal forms of social control are provided by the juridical system. Aruba has its own legislative powers but shares a Common Court of Justice with the Netherlands Antilles. The Supreme Court is situated in the Netherlands.

CONFLICT. Most public conflicts on the island arise from political and ethnic differences. Some labor conflict occurs but has virtually never led to serious threats to peace in the workplace or to economic stability. Massive migration and a shortage of adequate housing cause much social tension and resentment. The rise in criminality is often ascribed to the growing number of immigrants. Informants state that the kin group is the most important locus of social interaction but also the biggest source of social conflict.

Religion and Expressive Culture

RELIGIOUS BELIEFS. Catholicism is the prevalent religion on Aruba. In 1991, 85 percent of the population claimed to be Catholic. Church attendance is much lower. The first chapel on Aruba was built in 1750. Protestantism, the religion of the traditional elite, is embraced by less than 3 percent of the population. The Protestant Church of Aruba was founded by Lutherans and Reformed in 1822, who both had been without ministers or churches until then; Lutheran and Reformed communities ceased to exist as separate entities. Although, officially, it has no specific denomination, its present identity can be described as "Calvinistic." Twentieth-century migration led to the appearance of other groups such as Jehovah's Witnesses, Methodists, and evangelical sects (one having emigrated from Suriname during the oil-boom years, another originating in the United States), each comprising 2 percent or less of the population; as well as small communities of An-glicans, Adventists, Jews, Muslims, and Confucianists. Nearly 3 percent of the population claims to have no religion. The number of and participation in new religious sects and movements is increasing.

Traditional popular assumptions about the supernatural are called *brua*. Although the term probably originates from the Spanish word *bruja* (witch), brua is not to be equated with witchcraft. It includes magic, fortune-telling, healing, and assumptions about both good and evil. Magic is conducted by a *hacido di brua* (practitioner of brua) and can be applied for both beneficently and maliciously. As a counterpoint to Christian belief, the evil spirit is called *spirito malu*. Belief in brua is often not confirmed because of the low social esteem attached to it.

CEREMONIES. Traditional (semi-)religious ceremonies have a Catholic origin or orientation. On New Year's Eve, best wishes are delivered at homes by small bands singing a serenade called Dandé. Saint John's Day (24 June) is celebrated with bonfires and the ceremony of Dera Gai (the burying of the rooster). Traditionally, a rooster was buried, leaving its head under a calabash above the ground. At present the ceremony is carried out without the rooster. Blindfolded dancers from the audience try to hit the calabash with a stick while a small band plays and sings the traditional song of San Juan. Carnival was introduced on Aruba by Caribbean migrants but has become the preeminent festival of the entire population. Easter Monday is called Black Monday; at present people camp for up to a week at the beach in tents and shacks, but the custom originates from the yearly picnic held by Afro-Caribbean Methodists. Of special importance are the celebrations of an individual's fifteenth, fiftieth, and seventy-fifth birthdays.

ARTS. Of the fine arts, music, poetry, singing, theater, dance, painting, and other visual arts are the most important. Aruban artistic production can be divided into two spheres, one noncommercial and the other directed at tourism and local recreation. Numerous artists are active in both. Many noncommercial artists are inspired by Aruba's history, tradition, and natural landscape, reworking these in a modern form. A lack of funds and clear governmental policy results in tension between the commercialization of art for the benefit of tourism and the professionalization of local talent for noncommercial purposes. Aruba hosts an annual jazz and Latin music festival and biennial dance and theater festivals.

Easter Monday is called Black Monday in Aruba; at present people camp for up to a week at the beach in tents and shacks.

The name "bahamas" derives from baja mar *(Spanish for shallow water).*

MEDICINE. Most family doctors and specialists have been educated in the Netherlands, the United States, or South America. The Doctor Horacio Oduber Hospital has 350 beds. Traditional healing methods (Papiamento: *remedi di tera*) make use of herbs, amulets, and so on, and are practiced by a *curadó* or *curioso* (healer), who often also acts as hacido di brua. Some of the methods are legally forbidden. Modern natural healing methods seem to be growing in popularity.

DEATH AND AFTERLIFE. Opinions on death and the afterlife are in accord with Christian doctrine. The traditional wake is called Ocho Dia—"eight days," the duration of the customary mourning period. In a carefully closed room, prayer and singing around a small altar continue for those eight days. The wake is concluded by a ceremony in which close kin and friends participate: at the last evening of mourning, the altar is taken apart, and chairs are turned upside down. The windows are opened to make sure the spirit of the deceased is able to leave the house. The ceremony ends with a meal and storytelling. The wake, which has a medieval Spanish origin, is losing popularity in the course of modernization.

Bibliography

Alofs, Luc, and Leontine Merkies (1990). *Ken ta arubiano?: Sociale integratie en natievorming op Aruba* (Who is Aruban?: Social integration and nation building on Aruba). Antillen Working Papers, 15. Leiden: Koninklijk Instituut voor Taal, Land- en Volkenkunde, Caraïbische Afdeling.

Eelens, Frank C. H. (1993). *The Population of Aruba: A Demographic Profile.* Aruba: Central Bureau of Statistics.

Green, Vera (1974). *Migrants in Aruba.* Assen: Van Gorcum.

Kalm, Florence (1975). *The Dispersive and Reintegrating Nature of Population Segments of a Third World Society: Aruba, Netherlands Antilles.* Ann Arbor, Mich.: University Microfilms.

Koulen, Ingrid, and Gert Oostindie, with Peter Verton and Rosemarijn Hoefte (1987). *The Netherlands Antilles and Aruba: A Research Guide.* Royal Institute of Linguistics and Anthropology, Caribbean Series, no. 7. Dordrecht and Providence, R.I.: Foris Publications.

Phalen, John Harvey (1977). "Kinship, Color, and Ethnicity: Integrative Ideologies in Aruba, Netherlands Antilles." Ph.D. thesis, State University of New York at Stony Brook.

—LUC ALOFS

BAHAMIANS

Ethonym: none

Orientation

IDENTIFICATION. The name "Bahamas" derives from *baja mar* (Spanish: shallow water). The best-known islands in the Bahamas island chain, from northwest to southeast, are Grand Bahama, the Abacos, the Biminis, New Providence, Eleuthera, Andros, Cat, San Salvador, the Exumas, Long, Crooked, Acklins, Mayaguana, and Inagua. Turks and Caicos, at the southeast end of the island chain, are a British crown colony; the two islands were separated from the Bahamas in 1848.

LOCATION. The Bahama Islands, a chain of islands, reefs, and cays lying southeast off the Florida coast of North America, extend over 942 kilometers from 20°56′to 27°22′ N and between 72°40′ and 79°20′ W. Depending upon the count, there are twenty-nine islands and 661 cays. The total land area is approximately 14,000 square kilometers. (These measurements and figures do not include the Turks and Caicos.) The largest islands in the group are rimmed with sandy beaches and coconut groves. Low-lying hills, seldom exceeding a height of 30 meters, run the length of these islands. Pine forests grow on many of the ridges. The Bahamas have a subtropical climate, with an annual mean daily temperature of 25° C; the mean for the coldest month, February, is 22° C, and for the warmest, August, 28° C. Rainfall, concentrated in the late-summer months, averages about 125 centimeters per year.

DEMOGRAPHY. The population was estimated at 268,726 in July 1993. The official census of 1980 placed the population at 209,505. Of the thirty inhabited islands and cays, the most densely populated is New Providence, with 171,502 residents (almost 70 percent of the total population) in an area of only 208 square kilometers. Andros, the largest island, with an area of 5,980 square kilometers, had a population of 8,155. Approximately 85 percent of the population is of African origin. Of the Whites, some 25,000 are native Bahamians; the rest are largely British, American, and Canadian expatriates. Most White Bahamians live on New Providence, the Abacos, and Grand Bahama.

LINGUISTIC AFFILIATION. Standard English is the official language of the Bahamas. Creolized English, termed "Bahamian dialect," is the language of working-class Bahamians. Many White

Bahamians and middle-class Bahamians of African ancestry speak varieties of English that fall between Standard and creolized English. All Bahamians understand standard English, and many can converse in several dialects.

History and Cultural Relations

The Bahamas were discovered by Europeans in 1492, when Columbus made his first landing in the West Indies on San Salvador, or Watlings Island. The Spaniards transported the aboriginal population of Lucayan Indians to Hispaniola and Cuba to work in mines, and within twenty-five years of Columbus's arrival the islands were depopulated. During the latter half of the seventeenth century the islands were colonized by English settlers, who brought along their slaves. By 1773 the population, which totaled approximately 4,000, had an equal number of Europeans and people of African origin. Between 1783 and 1785 many Loyalists who had been expelled from the American colonies immigrated to the islands with their slaves. These slaves, or their parents, had originally been transported to the New World from West Africa during the eighteenth century to work on cotton plantations. This influx to the Bahamas increased the number of Whites to approximately 3,000 and the number of slaves of

African ancestry to approximately 6,000. Most of the slave plantations established by the Loyalists in the Bahamas were on the "Cotton Islands"—Cat Island, the Exumas, Long Island, Crooked Island, San Salvador, and Rum Cay. At first they were successful economic enterprises; after 1800, however, the production of cotton declined because the slash-and-burn technique used to prepare the fields for planting depleted the soil. Following the emancipation of slaves in the British Empire in 1838, some departing plantation owners gave their land to their former slaves, and many of these freed slaves adopted the names of their former owners in gratitude. At the time of Emancipation the English captured a number of Spanish ships transporting slaves taken in the Congo, the primary site of slave-trade activity after 1800, and brought their human cargo to special village settlements on New Providence and some of the other islands, including Long Island. The newly freed Congo slaves who went to the Exumas and Long Island intermarried with former slaves who were tilling the soil of the abandoned plantations. With the increased number of occupants on already depleted land, many were forced to migrate and Long Island and the Exumas experienced a decline in population after 1861. From the middle of the nineteenth century

ECONOMY

Subsistence and Commercial Activities

The Bahamian economy is based mostly on tourism and offshore banking. The commercial-agriculture and industrial sectors are comparatively small. From 1981 to 1990, tourist arrivals increased an average 8.5 percent per year, owing to an almost threefold increase in the number of cruise-ship visitors. In 1990, 3,628,372 tourists visited the islands; half of them arrived by sea and 1,561,600 stayed twenty-four hours or more. U.S. citizens comprise 85 percent of the tourist population. Expenditures by tourists totaled $369.1 million in 1981 and $1.26 billion in 1990. (The Bahamian dollar is kept equivalent to the U.S. dollar.) The government is promoting agricultural development to fill the gaps left by exploitive foreign companies that have pulled out of the Ba-

hamas. Subsistence farming has been carried on in the out islands since the first settlements. Two important crops are Indian maize, used for grits, and pigeon peas, which are added to imported rice to make the national dish, peas and rice. Some men in the out islands fish for their families and sell extra fish to neighbors.

Industrial Arts

Industry is scarcely developed. Two major exports are the spiny lobster and crude salt. Beer and rum are produced for local consumption and for export.

Trade

Nearly everything that Bahamians need is imported, from automobiles to food. Indeed,

over half of the government's revenue is derived from general import taxes. Total revenues exceed $600 million.

Division of Labor

The government is the number-one provider of employment. Hotels and resorts, as a group, are a major employer, and banks are primarily operated by Bahamians. In the out islands, men and women perform many of the same jobs. Most men are farmers and fishermen; their wives, housekeepers and farmers. To earn the cash needed to purchase groceries, clothes, and household furnishings, men and women must perform wage labor. Since there are few paying jobs in the out islands, most Bahamians go off to seek jobs in Nassau and Freeport, often leaving their children in the care of grandparents.

onward, Bahamians sought ways to bring prosperity to the islands. During the U.S. Civil War they engaged in blockade-running and gunrunning from New Providence to the southern states. Later attempts at large-scale export of agricultural products, such as pineapple and sisal, failed as more successful growers emerged elsewhere. Sponge gathering flourished early in the twentieth century but suffered a severe setback with the advent of a widespread sponge disease in the 1930s. Rum-running to the United States, a lucrative enterprise, ended with the repeal of Prohibition. World War II created a demand for migrant agricultural laborers to fill jobs abandoned by Americans newly recruited into industry and the military, and Bahamians seized the opportunity to "go on the contract" on the U.S. mainland. The most enduring prosperity for the Bahamas has come from tourism; New Providence has evolved from a wintering place for the very wealthy, as it was in the nineteenth century, to the center of a massive tourist industry that it is today.

Settlements

A rimless, many-spoked wheel superimposed upon the islands depicts the relationship of New Providence, where the capital, Nassau, is located, to the other islands (out islands, or the Family Islands, as the government prefers to call them); it also depicts the isolation of the individual islands. Nassau is a magnet for people from the out islands who seek both residence and employment. The second-largest city is Freeport, on the island of Grand Bahama (population: 41,035); like Nassau, it is a tourist center. The third-largest settlement is Marsh Harbor on Abaco Island. Most settlements are villages of scattered houses located near the shore (e.g., the settlement of Long Bay Cays consists of villages spread out over a distance of 11 kilometers). Nucleated villages are found on offshore cays such as Green Turtle Cay and Abaco. Mail boats, which also carry supplies and passengers, link the settlements to Nassau but not directly to one another.

Kinship

KIN GROUPS AND DESCENT. A person's kindred includes all known consanguineal relatives. In most areas of the Bahamas, a man will not marry a female member of his kindred. A person's descendants form an unrestricted descent group or a descending kindred. Land held in common by the descent group is called "generation property." Unilineal descent groups are absent.

KINSHIP TERMINOLOGY. Bahamian kinship terminology is of the Eskimo type, the same as that in use in England and the United States.

Marriage and Family

MARRIAGE. Unlike many of the peoples of the Caribbean, Bahamians have a mating system characterized by marriage and extraresidential unions but not consensual unions. A double standard of sexual morality regulates the behavior of men and women. A man is expected to have both premarital and extramarital affairs; a woman is not. Seldom do an unmarried man and woman live together. One-third of the children born in the 1960s were "outside," that is, illegitimate, and the percentage of illegitimate births has risen steadily.

DOMESTIC UNIT. The nuclear-family household is the ideal norm. With the migration of adults to Nassau and Freeport, households headed by one or both grandparents are common in the out islands. Single-parent and single-person households are also found.

INHERITANCE. Bahamians frequently follow the rule of primogeniture, a legacy of British colonialism. For most people, their home is the only item of value. On the death of the husband, the home becomes his wife's, to be used by her until her death, at which time it is inherited by the oldest son. Property may also be received by will.

SOCIALIZATION. The primary caretaker for most children is either the mother or grandmother. The caretaker not only provides for immediate needs but also acts as the chief disciplinarian. Women who fear the supernatural are more likely to use corporal punishment than those who view the supernatural as benevolent. The punishment itself does not seem to prevent the establishment of strong bonds of loyalty. Adult children frequently give gifts (often money) to their mothers, sometimes to help the older women raise their grandchildren. In the past, children in the out islands attended local schools for eight years, then went to Nassau for secondary education. Since independence, secondary schools, drawing from several settlements, have been introduced in many out islands where there had been only primary schools. These schools are staffed by teachers from other parts of the British Commonwealth as well as Bahamians.

Sociopolitical Organization

SOCIAL ORGANIZATION. Social organization is based primarily on kinship. The members of one's kindred provide both emotional and material support. The unrestricted descent group may even provide a building lot for a man. Growing up in the same settlement is likely to lead to life-long friendships, but school attendance fosters friendships among children from different settlements. The social-class system of the Bahamas prior to about 1960 can be characterized as a three-tiered pyramid, with Bahamians of African ancestry at the base, Bahamian Whites (known as "Conchs" or pejoratively as "Conchy Joes") in the middle, and the British official class, including wealthy expatriates, at the top. Many Bahamian Whites, particularly those residing in Nassau, have some African ancestry. Today the British are gone, many members of the business class are of African ancestry, and the Progressive Liberal party (PLP), the ruling party from 1968 to 1982, largely draws its membership from among Bahamians of African ancestry. The former opposition political party, the Free National Movement (FNM), draws its membership from both the White community and that of African ancestry.

POLITICAL ORGANIZATIONS. The Bahamas has a parliamentary government inherited from the British. From independence (10 July 1973) until August 19, 1992, the PLP controlled the forty-nine-seat House of Assembly. Sir Lynden Pindling, leader of the PLP, was the prime minister for this entire period. The FNM defeated the PLP on 19 August 1992 by obtaining thirty-two seats in the House of Assembly. Hubert Alexander Ingraham, leader of the FNM, became prime minister and Orville Alton Turnquest the deputy prime minister. In addition to the leadership, there are thirteen cabinet ministers. The Senate has sixteen members, with nine appointed by the governor-general on the advice of the prime minister, four on the advice of the leader of the opposition, and three on the advice of the prime minister after consultation with the leader of the opposition. The governor-general represents the British monarch, who is the titular head of government.

SOCIAL CONTROL. A well-developed legal structure was inherited from the British; English common law and much of English statute law were adopted almost word for word. The basic structure is entrenched in the constitution of the Bahamas. Three main functions are generally distributed under the authority of the law of the constitution: the executive function is entrusted to the prime minister and his cabinet, the legislative function is entrusted to parliament, and the judicial function is entrusted to the courts. The independent judiciary includes magistrates courts, the Supreme Court with a chief justice and five other justices, and a three-judge Court of Appeal; the constitution grants the right to appeal to the Judicial Committee of the Privy Council in England. In the out islands commissioners can act as magistrates. The administration of justice properly includes law enforcement (i.e., police functions) and lawful prosecutions (the sphere of the attorney general's office). Informal social control, particularly in the out islands, is based on fear of developing a bad reputation and fear of obeah, the practice of harmful magic.

CONFLICT. Except for the very early years (before 1718) when Nassau was a center for pirates, the Bahamas was a peaceful country for much of its history; there were no slave uprisings. The riots of 1942 were sparked by wage inequities. Verbal public confrontations, although common, seldom escalated into violence, and homicides were rare. In recent times, however, drug trafficking has brought crime and violence to the country.

Religion and Expressive Culture

RELIGIOUS BELIEFS. Three realms of the supernatural can be identified. Most Bahamians belong to a Christian church and frequently attend their own church as well as others. Most people believe God helps the faithful and punishes the wicked. The spirit of a person who dies "in Christ" goes to rest and can help the living; if an ungodly person dies, the spirit wanders about frightening and hurting people. Obeah is practiced to harm rivals, to protect one's property and person, and to raise the spirits of the dead.

RELIGIOUS PRACTITIONERS. Ministers and priests head the Christian churches. In the out islands local men, and sometimes women, serve part-time as preachers. Specialists in the practice of obeah are called obeah men; although never common, obeah practitioners are becoming even less numerous as young people turn away from old practices and embrace the modern world.

CEREMONIES. Junkanoo, once widespread in the Caribbean, is a cultural event similar to New Orleans's Mardi Gras. Its roots lie in pre-Emancipation days, when slaves were allowed a special Christmas holiday. The culmination of Junkanoo is a costumed parade with floats and bands, which takes place along Nassau's Bay Street on Boxing Day (26 December) and New Year's Day.

ARTS. Goombay is the calypso-style music of the Bahamas. In the out islands, local bands us-

Nearly everything that Bahamians need is imported, from automobiles to food. Indeed, over half of the government's revenue is derived from general import taxes.

♦ **English common law**
A legal system in which laws are based on the decisions rendered in prior judicial cases. Common law developed in England, beginning in the eleventh century.

ing guitars, goatskin-headed drums, and saws entertain at dances and weddings. The major decorative art is straw work. Women in the out islands plait "straw" from palm fronds into long strips, which are then sewn together to form hats, baskets, and purses. Raffia paper and seashells are typically sewn to the straw work in decorative patterns.

MEDICINE. Modern medicine is provided at the Princess Margaret Hospital in Nassau. In 1992 the out islands were served by 107 clinics; the seriously ill are flown to Princess Margaret Hospital. Many Bahamians, particularly those in the out islands, often rely on "bush" medicine; parts of selected plants are commonly boiled in liquid, and the resulting "bush tea" is then drunk. Love-vine (*Cuscuta americana*), for example, is said to produce a tea that gives a man "courage."

Bibliography

Collingwood, Dean W. (1989). *The Bahamas between Worlds*. Decatur, Ill.: White Sound Press.

Collingwood, Dean W., and Steve Dodge, eds. (1989). *Modern Bahamian Society*. Parkesburg, Iowa: Caribbean Books.

Craton, Michael (1986). *A History of the Bahamas*. 3rd ed. Waterloo, Ont.: San Salvador Press.

Craton, Michael, and Gail Saunders (1992). *Islanders in the Stream: A History of the Bahamian People*. Vol. 1, *From Aboriginal Times to the End of Slavery*. Athens: University of Georgia Press.

Dupuch, S. P., editorial director (1991). *Bahamas Handbook and Businessman's Annual, 1992*. Nassau: Etienne Dupuch, Jr. Publications.

Holm, John A., with Alison Watt Shilling (1982). *Dictionary of Bahamian English*. Cold Spring, N.Y.: Lexik House Publishers.

Hughes, Colin A. (1981). *Race and Politics in the Bahamas*. New York: St. Martin's Press.

LaFlamme, Alan G. (1985). *Green Turtle Cay: An Island in the Bahamas*. Prospect Heights, Ill.: Waveland Press.

Otterbein, Charlotte Swanson, and Keith F. Otterbein (1973). "Believers and Beaters: A Case Study of Supernatural Beliefs and Child Rearing in the Bahama Islands." *American Anthropologist* 75:1670–1681.

Otterbein, Keith F. (1966). *The Andros Islanders: A Study of Family Organization in the Bahamas*. Lawrence: University of Kansas Press.

Otterbein, Keith F. (1978). "Transportation and Settlement Pattern: A Longitudinal Study of South Andros." *Anthropology* 2(2): 35–45.

—KEITH F. OTTERBEIN AND
CHARLOTTE SWANSON OTTERBEIN

See also

English, Jamaicans,

Trinidadians and

Tobagonians

BARBADIANS

Ethonym: Bajans

Orientation

IDENTIFICATION. Barbadians are people born on the island of Barbados and people born elsewhere who have at least one Barbadian parent who maintains cultural ties to this island nation. Barbadian communities in Canada, the United Kingdom, the United States, and Guyana maintain active ties with their kin and friends in the West Indies.

LOCATION. Barbados, a coral limestone outcropping of the South American continental shelf, is located at 13° 10′ N, 59° 33′ W. Barbados thus lies in the western Atlantic Ocean, 150 kilometers east of the island of Saint Vincent and the geological fault line along which most of the Caribbean islands have emerged, and 275 kilometers north of Trinidad and the northern coast of South America. The island's shape resembles a leg of lamb 40 kilometers long. The north (shank) of the island exhibits a width of about 10 kilometers, the south a width of about 25 kilometers. In contrast with most West Indian islands of volcanic origin, which rise dramatically from the sea to elevations of more than 1,000 meters within a kilometer or so of the shore, Barbados has low, rolling hills that rise no higher than 300 meters, and, in the north and south portions of the island, extensive areas of relatively level ground. Nonetheless, like nearly all West Indian islands, Barbados exhibits significant microclimate variation. Rainfall averages more than 125 centimeters annually across the central portion of the island, but levels are higher on the windward (eastern) coast and the hilly interior, and lower on the leeward (western) coast. The northeast corner of the island, however, exhibits a semidesert biome. The southern portions of the island, characterized by little topographic variation, receive little rainfall, although more than the northeast corner. Barbados averages more than 3,000 hours of sunlight annually. Northeast trade winds blow year-round and significantly moderate a mean day-time temperature of around 27° C, which fluctuates little over the course of the year. Sugarcane and tourism have brought prosperity to Barbados, even in the face of occasional droughts, hurricanes, and world recessions.

DEMOGRAPHY. More than 260,000 people now live on this small island of some 443 square kilometers. Only Hong Kong, Singapore, and Bangladesh surpass Barbados's national population density of 586 persons per square kilometer. As early as 1680, the island was home to 70,000 people. Barbadians who couldn't find land on the island emigrated to other New World locations, including South Carolina, Antigua, and Jamaica. Whereas other island populations dwindled or grew slowly during the 1800s, Barbados sent more than 50,000 of its citizens elsewhere (especially to Guyana and Trinidad) and still experienced an extraordinary annual growth rate of about 1.2 percent between Emancipation in 1806 and the first years of the twentieth century.

Until 1960, high birth and death rates prevailed. The island's population consisted mostly of young people; Barbadians emigrated in large numbers to the United Kingdom and in smaller numbers to the United States and, later, to Canada. Barbados began demographic transition about 1960, reached replacement-level fertility in 1980, and fell to below-replacement levels quickly thereafter. Aided by continuing emigration of the young and a new stream of elderly immigrants, the population of Barbados aged rapidly in the succeeding decade. The population of elderly (aged 60 and over) grew 15 percent during the 1980s and comprised 15.3 percent of the total population by 1990. Barbadian projections suggest that, by the year 2050, the proportion of the population aged 65 and over will range between 25 and 33 percent of the total population.

LINGUISTIC AFFILIATION. Barbadians speak a dialect of English with tonal qualities that reflect the West African heritage of the vast majority of its people, and an English-West African pidgin called Bajan. The number of native Bajan speakers has declined precipitously since 1950.

History and Cultural Relations

Barbados was colonized by the English early in the seventeenth century. The English found the island uninhabited when they landed in 1625, although archeological findings document prior habitation by both Carib and Arawak Native Americans. By 1650, Barbados was transformed by the plantation system and slavery into the first major monocropping sugar producer of the emerging British Empire, and its fortunes were tied to sugar and to England for the next 310 years. In 1651, Barbados won from England most of the freedoms the United States gained only by revolution 100 years later, and established what was to become the oldest continuing parliamentary democracy in the world outside England. This significant degree of autonomy encouraged Barbadian planters to remain on the island rather than, as was typical elsewhere in the English and French West Indies, to return to Europe when their fortunes improved. Barbados continues to be distinguished in the West Indies by an unusually high proportion of population with a largely Eu-

Aided by continuing emigration of the young and a new stream of elderly immigrants, the Barbadian population began to age rapidly in the late twentieth century.

RUM REFINERY

Two men roll rum barrels at a Barbadian rum refinery. Sugar production declined in 1960 when tourism and industry began to grow. Barbados, West Indies. (Tony Arruza/Corbis)

The Barbadian economy stems from a diverse population, which is one of the world's most highly educated, with a literacy rate very close to 100 percent.

ropean ancestry. When West Indian sugar plantations disappeared elsewhere over the course of the 1800s, Barbadian plantations remained competitive. The improvement in living standards that had marked the nineteenth century was brought to an end by the creation of a merchant-planter oligopoly in the early twentieth century. The Great Depression precipitated massive labor disturbances. Subsequent investigations of living conditions, particularly the Moyne Commission Report, established grounds for fundamental political change. The franchise, which until the late nineteenth century had been restricted to propertied, White males, was made universal in 1943. By the 1950s, the descendants of former African slaves controlled the Barbadian Assembly and set in motion a series of actions that fundamentally transformed the island. Barbados opted for full independence in 1966, but it remains a member of the British Commonwealth.

Settlements

Bridgetown, founded early in the seventeenth century on the southern leeward (western) coast, is the island's capital and only city. Small towns exist at Holetown, 5 kilometers north of Bridgetown; Speightstown, 6 kilometers north of Holetown; and Oistens, 10 kilometers south of Bridgetown. Holetown, Speightstown, and Oistens, along with numerous other small communities along the leeward coast, now form one long megalopolis containing about 70 percent of the island's population. About 50 percent of the island's residents live in or south of Bridgetown. The southeastern region, formerly planted in cane, now has another 10 percent of the island's population and may be best described as a dispersed bedroom community for Bridgetown. The remaining 20 percent of the population lives amongst plantations and small farms in settlements that vary from dispersed homes to small, nucleated villages.

Economy

The Barbadian economy stems from a diverse population, which is one of the world's most highly educated, with a literacy rate very close to 100 percent. The currency is the Barbados dollar, which is linked to the U.S. dollar at a rate of BDS$2.00 to U.S.$1.00. Excellent public and private bus and taxi services take advantage of nearly 1,300 kilometers of roads and make it possible to move easily and quickly, and relatively cheaply, from any spot on the island to any other. Barbados supports one of the three campuses of the University of the West Indies (the others are

in Jamaica and Trinidad and Tobago). The local campus (Cave Hill) offers degrees in the physical, biological, and social sciences, in the humanities, and in law and medicine. Barbados Community College was modeled along lines originally established by the California community-college system; it offers a wide variety of courses in technical fields and the liberal arts. Advanced education is also available through a teacher-training college, a polytechnic college, the Extra Mural Centre of the University of the West Indies (which has branch campuses on all eastern Caribbean islands), and a hotel school. A large number of private and public primary and secondary schools offer educational programs modeled on those in the United Kingdom.

The year 1960 initiated a structural change in the Barbadian economy marked by decline in sugar production and the growth of industrial manufacturing and tourism. By 1980, the sugar industry contributed only about 6 percent of domestic output and accounted for less than 10 percent of employment and 10 percent of foreign-exchange earnings. At the same time, manufacturing and tourism contributed respectively about 11 percent and 12 percent of domestic output and about 18 percent and 41 percent of foreign-exchange earnings. These proportions remained about the same a decade later. Sugar plantations were turned into manufacturing sites, subdivided for new housing sites or small agricultural plots, or converted to the production of vegetables for a growing domestic market for food. Manufactured goods include garments, furniture, ceramics, pharmaceuticals, phonograph records and tapes, processed wood, paints, structural components for construction, industrial gases, refined petroleum, paper products, and solar-energy units. Data processing and assembly of electronics components also figure in the ecconomic array. Barbados served as a tourist destination as early as the 1600s; it advertises that George Washington was one of its more illustrious early visitors. The growth of tourism on Barbados, however, as throughout the world, depended on the rise of cheap, global transportation and rising proportions of discretionary income. Small numbers of tourists come from South America and other islands in the Caribbean. A significant stream of tourists come from northwestern Europe, primarily the U.K. Most tourists, however, come from the United States and Canada, which send many flights to the island daily, and, during the height of the tourist season, cruise ships call almost daily. Long known in the Caribbean as "Little England," many Barbadians now claim that the island's increasingly important ties to the United States have transformed it into "Little America."

Kinship

Barbadians trace descent and inheritance through both their father and their mother. They recognize no organized, corporate groups of kin. Barbadians use the Eskimo cousin terminology common to the United Kingdom, Canada, and the United States. Biological fathers and mothers are sharply distinguished from other adults who may serve various caregiving and economic-support functions for children.

Marriage and Family

A Barbadian household may consist of a single man or woman or of a mixed-gender group of as many as fifteen people. Barbadians idealize a household that consists of a married couple and their children, which characterizes about 45 percent of all households on the island. Around 35 percent of Barbadian households are organized around a mother and her children. These households occasionally encompass three generations of women; they may include brothers, uncles, sons, and the sexual partners of members of the core family unit.

Historically, in Barbados as elsewhere in the West Indies, sexual activity usually began at an early age. Women traded sex for economic support and children (called "visiting" or "keeper" relationships). Visiting unions gave way to common-law unions that, when a couple was older, a church ceremony might legitimate. Young people, however, were not the only ones who had visiting relationships. Historically, West Indian islands have been job-poor. Men left the islands in large numbers to look for work, which left significantly more women than men at nearly all ages. As a result, many women could not legally marry. Lower-class men might never marry. Moreover, no relationship implied men's sexual fidelity. Lower-class men commonly drifted from one temporary sexual partner to another. Married men in the middle and upper classes commonly engaged in a series of visiting relationships with "outside" women. Barbadian fathers, consequently, often were not husbands; even those who were frequently did not live with the mother and her children. When they did, they might contribute little to domestic life. Men often were not home. They spent time instead with girlfriends or other men, often in rum shops, which remain popular among older men. What they contributed, other than a house and money, all too often was violence directed at the mother and children.

Women, for their part, usually drilled into the children not only how much they sacrificed and how hard they had to work to raise them properly, but also that their labors were that much more arduous because they had no companion to help them. It was easy to explain family hardships. Men were irresponsible and abusive. Understandably, fathers could expect domestic help from their sons and daughters only incidentally, and the weak filial obligations that existed applied only to biological fathers. By contrast, childbearing was an investment activity for Barbadian women. In a woman's youth, children legitimated her claims on income from men, although establishing those claims required her subservience. As she moved toward middle age, daughters took over nearly all household chores, and sons provided financial support that could make her independent of spousal support and reduce or eliminate her subservience to an autocratic male. In her old age, financial and domestic support from children meant the difference between abject poverty and a moderate, or even comfortable, level of living. Indeed, these phases often transformed gender relations. Because men could expect support from their children only if they had maintained a relationship with their children's mother, the women dependent on men in their youth found men dependent on them by late middle age. Gender power relationships thus were contingent on historical conditions that made women dependent on men in their youth, and on their male children during and after middle age.

Since 1960, however, Barbadian kin relations have undergone a revolution that reflects global leveling processes that were set into motion by the Industrial Revolution in England 200 years ago. Growth in the world economy, spurred by the Industrial Revolution, was marked by increasing numbers of resource-access channels. Large numbers of resource-access channels imply high levels of competition. High levels of both international and regional competition offer selective advantages to technical skills and competencies and reduce power differentials both between nations and within societies. Gender and skin color have become less important determinants of social position.

Barbadian women experienced a conjunction of good job opportunities and increased educational levels that ushered in a revolution in the relations between generations and between genders. The West Indian marriage pattern of visiting,

*Barbados is
organized as an
independent
parliamentary
democracy within
the British
Commonwealth.*

common-law, and legal unions persists, but empowered women enjoy more domestic help, emotional support, and affectionate behavior than women who are not empowered, and they experience little or no family violence. Women freed from dependency on childbearing have fewer children. Women freed from dependency on men have markedly better relationships with their partners. The incidence of family violence on Barbados fell dramatically in just one generation.

Sociopolitical Organization

SOCIAL ORGANIZATION. Prior to 1960, Barbadian society was characterized by a small merchant-planter elite of largely European ancestry; a slightly larger class of accountants, lawyers, medical personnel, journalists, and teachers of diverse ancestry; and a huge lower class of field laborers and domestic servants with a largely African ancestry. The elite remains about the same size but has grown much more diverse in heritage. The lower class has all but disappeared. In its place, there now exists a huge middle class that encompasses skilled blue-collar workers employed in manufacturing firms and hotels, and a wide range of white-collar, professional, and managerial occupational groups employed directly or, in the case of public employees, indirectly in the manufacturing and tourist sectors of the economy.

POLITICAL ORGANIZATION. Barbados is organized as an independent parliamentary democracy within the British Commonwealth. For administrative purposes, the island is divided into the city of Bridgetown and eleven parishes: Saint Lucy, Saint Peter, Saint Andrew, Saint James, Saint Joseph, Saint Thomas, Saint John, Saint Philip, Saint George, Saint Michael, and Christ Church. The monarch of England is recognized as the head of state, and the highest court of appeals is the Supreme Court of the United Kingdom. The monarch appoints a governor-general, selected from among nominees put forth by the majority and minority political parties. Two principal political parties, the Barbados Labour party and the Democratic Labour party, compete for seats in the House of Assembly; members of the Senate are appointed by the governor-general. The leader of the majority party in the Assembly serves as prime minister. A cabinet appointed from among majority-party members of the Assembly assists the prime minister in carrying out executive functions of government. The judiciary consists of a national police force and three tiers of courts. Magistrates oversee Lower Courts, which adjudicate minor cases and hear preliminary evidence for major ones. Judges who sit in the Assizes hear cases involving allegations of major crimes. Barbados's chief justice heads a group of three judges who hear cases in the Court of Appeals. The last court of appeals is the Privy Council in England.

Religion and Expressive Culture

RELIGIOUS BELIEFS. More than 80 percent of the population claims adherence to one or another Christian denomination or sect. More than half of these belong to the Church of England and attend appropriate parish churches; Methodists, Roman Catholics, and Seventh Day Adventists constitute most of the remainder. A small East Indian community includes some Hindus, and a small number of people of diverse backgrounds practice Islam. A growing, albeit still small, number of people embrace Rastafarianism. A small Jewish community with Sephardic roots attends services in a synagogue originally built in A.D. 1640.

MEDICINE. Barbadians use two bodies of knowledge to prevent and treat illness. They rely heavily on a biomedical system organized on a Western model. The health-care system consists of physicians and other staff who practice in public, government-run hospitals, clinics, halfway houses, and long-term care facilities of various kinds, and physicians and other health-care workers who practice in a private system of hospitals, clinics, nursing homes, and private offices. Individual health-care providers frequently participate in both formal systems.

Barbadians also rely heavily on an indigenous ethnomedical system that makes use of "bush" teas and "home remedies." Around 70 percent of the population uses home remedies at rates that vary from daily to once or twice a year. Most of those who use this indigenous medicine regard it as an alternative to biomedical care; the remainder use indigenous medicine to supplement care available through the biomedical system.

When Barbadian economic development began in the 1950s, the island's health-care needs arose from high rates of acute infectious disease. Accordingly, the government of Barbados built an outstanding health-care delivery system directed at these problems. The medical school at the University of the West Indies is located at a 600–bed facility for acute care, Queen Elizabeth Hospital. Separate geriatric and psychiatric hospitals provide specialized care for the elderly and mentally ill. Smaller facilities are available for younger mentally and physically handicapped patients.

Public clinics, located in nearly every parish, and private clinics, concentrated in the heavily populated parishes of Saint Michael and Christ Church, serve primary healthcare needs. The accomplishments of this system included a reduction in infant-mortality rates from more than 150 per 1,000 in the early 1950s to around 15 per 1,000 in the early 1990s, and control over other infectious diseases, rivaling the developed regions of Europe, North America, and Asia.

Today, however, large numbers of Barbadians suffer from arthritis, hypertension, adult-onset diabetes and its complications, cancer, and heart disease. Often, these diseases remain untreated even after diagnosis. Disabilities grow more common and more serious with aging; the vast majority of disabilities can be traced to arthritis and to diabetes and its complications. Significant proportions of disabled Barbadians experience unmet needs for physical aids that bear on the most fundamental human needs—seeing, eating, and walking.

Barbadians tend to equate mental illness with being "crazy" and, therefore, deny they experience emotional disorders even in the presence of significant symptoms. Almost no one who displays symptoms of depression and anxiety seeks treatment. By creating intense emotional pain, family violence in particular leads to high-risk sexual behavior and the spread of sexually transmitted diseases like HIV/AIDS. Although the incidence of family violence has declined, much interpersonal violence still is within families. Still more violence comes from outside the family. The island suffers from an increasing use of crack cocaine and its accompanying patterns of violence.

Bibliography

Brathwaite, Farley, ed. (1986). *The Elderly in Barbados*. Bridgetown: Carib Research and Publications.

Dann, Graham (1984). *The Quality of Life in Barbados*. London: Macmillan.

Greenfield, Sidney (1966). *English Rustics in Black Skin*. New Haven: College and Universities Press.

Handler, Jerome S. (1974). *The Unappropriated People: Freedmen in the Slave Society of Barbados*. Baltimore: Johns Hopkins University Press.

Handwerker, W. Penn (1989). *Women's Power and Social Revolution*. Newbury Park, Calif.: Sage Publications.

Handwerker, W. Penn (1993). "Gender Power Differences between Parents and High-Risk Sexual Behavior by Their Children." *Journal of Women's Health* 2:301–306.

Karch, Cecilia A. (1979). *The Transformation and Consolidation of the Corporate Plantation Economy in Barbados: 1860–1977*. Ann Arbor: University Microfilms.

Massiah, Joycelin (1984). *Employed Women in Barbados*. Institute of Social and Economic Research (Eastern Caribbean) Occasional Paper no. 8. Cave Hill, Barbados: University of the West Indies.

Richardson, Bonham C. (1985). *Panama Money in Barbados, 1900–1920*. Knoxville: University of Tennessee Press.

Worrell, DeLisle, ed. (1982). *The Economy of Barbados, 1946–1980*. Bridgetown: Central Bank of Barbados.

—W. PENN HANDWERKER

COSTA RICANS

Ethonym: Tico (after a diminutive suffix Costa Ricans often add to Spanish adjectives and nouns)

Orientation

IDENTIFICATION. The country's name is attributed to Columbus's visit in 1502 and that of Gil González in 1522. "Rich Coast" (Costa Rica) was suggested by the abundant gold ornaments the Indians were wearing. By 1539, the territory had become officially known as Costa Rica. It borders with Nicaragua on the north and with Panama in the southeast, with the Atlantic Ocean on the north and east and the Pacific Ocean on the south and west. Tico culture is identified with that of the dominant Hispanic majority. There are social-class and regional variations as well as the influences of other distinctive cultural traditions of the country.

LOCATION. The country lies 10 degrees north of the equator. The land area is 51,100 square kilometers. There is great diversity of elevations. The volcanic mountain ranges Guanacaste, Tilarán, and Central rise, in that order, from the northwest to the center. From the center to the southeast lies the higher, Talamanca range whose highest peak is Chirripó, 3,820 meters above sea level. Fifty-two percent of Costa Ricans live in the central part (3.83 percent of the country's surface), now called Central Valley (formerly Central Plateau), at elevations between 800 and 1,500 meters. At lower elevations, there are plains in the Caribbean lowlands to the north (Alajuela and Limón provinces) and the Pacific lowlands to the west (Guanacaste Province), whereas valleys characterize the south Pacific region. The main rivers are the Tempisque, the Grande de Tárcoles,

The name "Costa Rica," attributed to Columbus, was suggested by the abundant goal ornaments worn by the Indians.

the Reventazón, the San Juan, the Diquís, and the Sixaola, but smaller rivers and creeks are plentiful. Plant and animal life is diverse and abundant. The main cities are the provincial capitals: San José (also the country's capital), Heredia, Alajuela, Cartago, Liberia, Puerto Puntarenas, and Puerto Limón.

DEMOGRAPHY. In 1991 the population was 3,087,700; it is projected to rise to 3,710,656 by the year 2000, and to 5,250,122 by the year 2025. In 1992 population density was 62.0 persons per square kilometer, and life expectancy at birth was 75 for men and 79 for women. The birthrate from 1985 to 1990 was 29.7 and general death rate was 3.9 per thousand; annual growth was 2.6 percent. The infant-mortality rate per 1,000 was 12 in 1992, and household average size 4.4. The literacy rate is 93 percent. In 1992 one out of every four Costa Rican households was classified as being below the poverty line. In genetic terms, Costa Rica has a trihybrid population. The three racial stocks from which this hybrid is derived are the Mongoloid Amerindian, the African Negroid, and the European and Near Eastern Caucasoid. The gene flow for this fusion has taken place over the course of the past 500 years. A study of genetic markers has shown that the Caucasoid component varies between 40 and 60 percent, the Negroid component varies between 10 and 20 percent, and the Amerindian component varies between 15 and 35 percent. In specific samples, the variations of these percentages are explained by regional and socioeconomic conditions.

LINGUISTIC AFFILIATION. Spanish is the official language. The national dialect is non-Castillian. It uses the pronoun *vos* rather than *tú* and particular verb endings for this second-person singular form of address. There are regional and urban-rural variations. English is the foreign language most widely known.

History and Cultural Relations

The Indian chiefdoms found by the Spaniards had achieved considerable skill in government, trade, agriculture, gold- and stonework, pottery, and weaving cotton textiles. After 18 September 1502, when Columbus landed in Limón, Spanish expeditions stayed close to the shoreline. Then, in 1562, Juan Vázquez de Coronado founded the first capital in Cartago. The Central Valley slowly became the nucleus of the nation. The Costa Rican political elite, to a great extent, has been proven to be descendants of Vázquez de Coronado and his companions. From 1569 to the end of the seventeenth century, the *encomienda* system

was in place, and it had at least two major effects on Costa Rican society. First, it divided the Spanish into two main classes: an elite of wealthy, dominant merchants and a larger class of poor *campesino criollos* (Central Valley peasantry of Spanish descent). Second, the Indian population, already diminished by the epidemics, battles, and various slavery policies of the early sixteenth century, grew even smaller under the encomienda system. Mestizos were not supposed to pay tribute, and intermarriage with Indians was not encouraged. For this reason, among others, there was not an important process of *mestizaje* (mestizoization) at the time Indians were living in the Central Valley.

Throughout the colonial period, Costa Rica was a poor, neglected, and isolated province of small farmers. The Spanish Crown decreed that no colony was allowed to trade with any country, except Spain. Foreigners were not permitted to enter. Restrictions on commerce were greatly responsible for this poverty. Costa Rica became independent from Spain in 1821. In 1829, the first newspaper appeared. By 1844, a university had been established, and, in the 1840s, a coffee-export and marketing structure built upon British shipping and credit was organized. From that time forward, the coffee economy has influenced all aspects of daily life from personal routines to government regimes, involving all aspects of international relations. The republican type of government and a sense of nationalism developed in the nineteenth century. In spite of national unity, class divisions were marked, from the oligarchy (the coffee-exporting elite) to the rural peasantry. A railroad to the Caribbean coast, built from 1876 to 1883, made commercial growing of bananas feasible. Bananas, like coffee, were dependent on foreign investment and markets. This crop increased economic dependence on the United States, as coffee had done with respect to England.

In the 1880s there began to predominate an ideology of government called *democracia liberal*. Its leaders were conservatives who stood for individual liberties, the separation of church and state, and the spread of formal secular education to all sectors. Many institutions and laws date from that time, such as the National Civil Registry, the National Museum, the National Theater, and the Civil Code. The full achievement of electoral democracy is attributed to the events of 1889. The election held that year had not been rigged by the government, and candidates had sought the popular vote. The president, however, tried to impose his candidate. Peasants angrily marched on the capital, demanding respect for their choice. The 1930s and 1940s brought the decline of the liberales and the new trends of *democracia social*, which meant activist government and the welfare state, especially after the armed revolt in 1948, when new institutions marked a break with the past. The banking system was nationalized, taxes were imposed on wealth, the army was abolished, the civil service was institutionalized, an impartial electoral system was crafted, the franchise was extended to women, and autonomous institutions (public corporations) were created to perform basic services. From the 1960s to the 1990s, the country has experienced different development schemes that have stressed diversified agriculture, industrialization, and state socioeconomic planning. The late 1980s and the 1990s have been characterized by policies of *economía neoliberal* and *democracia participativa*; these are attempts to reduce the role of government in the economy, limit state social programs, expand the free-market economy, join global markets, and obtain more citizen participation in decisions on public issues and solutions to national problems.

Settlements

Costa Rica's seven provinces are divided into *cantones* (townships), and the townships into districts. Each provincial capital is the largest city in the province. The townships' seats are smaller cities or towns in the central districts. The outlying districts had been more rural than urban; in the 1990s this pattern may be observed in the peripheral areas of the country, but it is uncommon in the Central Valley. Urbanization of the whole country has proceeded very rapidly. Even remote areas have electricity, piped water, bus service, telephones, and television. Some may even have computers in public facilities or in some homes. In rural areas as well as in urban ones, however, great differences in levels of income show in the homes and general life-style of the residents. In urbanized areas the neighborhoods are identified as barrios; in sparsely populated rural areas, the neighborhoods are called *caseríos*. The sense of community is associated more with these smaller units than with the larger towns or cities. San José dominates the rest of the country in politics, economic pursuits, and services. The city has grown haphazardly. Planning and zoning have not been very effective against crowded motor and pedestrian traffic, pollution, and constant razing and rebuilding. Most Ticos live in painted wooden or cement-block houses that have metal roofs and wood or tile floors. People prefer to own, rather than rent, their homes; a shortage of adequate housing is one of the problems addressed by government projects.

Economy

SUBSISTENCE AND COMMERCIAL ACTIVITIES. Ticos have mainly depended on agriculture, whether as a subsistence activity or as a large export business. Maize, beans, plantains, garden vegetables, cocoa, coffee, bananas, and flowers are examples of the crops. In addition, there is animal husbandry: beef and milk cattle, horses, pigs, goats, and birds (chickens, turkeys and, at present, even ostriches) are examples. Fishing has evolved into a major industry. In 1992 the gross national product showed the following percentage structure: primary sector (agriculture, forestry, mining, and fishing) 25.5; secondary sector (industrial) 19.3, and tertiary sector (services) 55.2. Agriculture generates over 28 percent of employment and accounts for close to 70 percent of exports. Tourism was the third source of income in 1989 and first in 1994.

INDUSTRIAL ARTS. Industry was mostly artisanal until the 1950s. One of its products, the painted wooden oxcart, became a symbol of the country. In 1957, 64.7 percent of industrial production and 68.5 percent of employment came from foods, shoemaking, clothing, and lumber products, with an average of three to ten employees per shop or factory. Larger industrial concerns were involved in printing and publishing, rubber products, and brewing plants. By 1963, Costa Rica had become fully integrated into the Central American Common Market. Industrial production became more mechanized in the 1960s and 1970s and grew rapidly. Chemical products, rubber, paper, and metal and electric items gained in importance. Foreign investment also influenced change; in the late 1950s it was 0.6 percent of total investment. By 1969 it was 21.1 percent of that total. By 1978 industry accounted for 24 percent of the gross national product, in contrast to 1 percent in 1950. By 1992, however, it accounted for only 19.3 percent. Costa Rica's Chamber of Industry was founded in July 1943. It had 700 affiliates in 1994, including business associations of the following industries: plastics, metals, vehicles, transportation, pharmaceuticals, shoes, textiles, foods, cosmetics, clothing, and graphic arts.

TRADE. In the 1960s Costa Rica greatly increased the exportation of "traditional" products such as coffee, bananas, sugar, and beef, plus some manufactured products. By 1970, however, industry demanded the importation of 76.9 percent of

Costa Rican laws are considered among the most advanced regarding equality of men and women. The gender movement toward making these laws apply in daily life is strong.

the value of raw materials and 98.6 of the value of capital goods. The rise of oil prices after 1973 increased the country's trade deficit. Economic growth was reduced in 1974 and afterward. Inflation and public debt increased greatly. The 1980s were marked by a severe economic crisis. The search for new markets became more imperative than in the seventies. By 1975 over half of manufactured goods came from abroad (10 percent from Central America and 43 percent from outside the Isthmus), whereas only 20 percent of industrial production was exported. In 1980 manufactured goods exported to Central America totaled U.S.$255 million but diminished to U.S.$160 million by 1982. Even in 1992, the 1980 value had not been recovered. Exports to markets outside the Isthmus, however, have increased. From 1984 to 1989, the main exported manufactured goods were clothing, jewelry and similar items, machinery and electrical appliances, canned fruits and vegetables, leather, tires, and seafood. In 1990, 25 percent of these "nontraditional" exports went to Central America, and 75 percent went to the rest of the world. The challenge faced in the nineties is to increase production and access to foreign markets, especially those of Mexico, the Caribbean, the United States, and Canada.

DIVISION OF LABOR.   In the generally prevailing pattern, women devote their time and training to their homes, husband, and children, and men to jobs outside the home. Specific variations of this pattern are numerous, however, for several reasons. Costa Rican laws are considered among the most advanced regarding equality of men and women. The gender movement toward making these laws apply in daily life is strong. Women increasingly combine wife-mother roles with student and work roles outside the home. They have entered practically all the trades, businesses, professions, and careers besides the traditional ones of jobs at home, teaching, social work, nursing, and office work. They have been appointed or elected to high political office; however, at this upper level men greatly outnumber women. Increasingly, men are helping with domestic chores, especially among young, well-educated couples.

LAND TENURE.   Private ownership is the norm. Arable land is unequally and inefficiently distributed, although programs for the redistribution of farmalands have been implemented since about the mid-twentieth century. The importance of small landholdings held by independent farmers is often mentioned as a main cause of the Tico

MARRIAGE AND FAMILY

Marriage

Legal marriages are civil or religious. Free unions comprise roughly one-quarter of the couples living together. The proportion of children born outside legal marriage is close to 40 percent. Ideals of mutual aid expected of family members (spouses, children, parents, grandparents, great-grandparents) are formally required by the Family Code of the country. Some forms of family behavior are attributed to machismo and to *marianismo* (moral and spiritual superiority of women), as well as to vestiges of the Spanish traditional sex roles. Modernity has brought changes in authority patterns. Divorce is no longer the scandal it once was; separation and desertion are common. For the most part, families take care of the aged, but a trend of placing them in homes for the elderly has arisen. The churches and the government have programs addressed to family life.

Inheritance

The law requires that a surviving spouse inherit half of the possessions of the couple and the other half be divided among the offspring; other relatives may inherit if there are no spouses or children. There is a strong tendency toward equal inheritance.

Socialization

Most Costa Ricans love and desire children. A child's first birthday is a great occasion. Besides parents, other relatives participate in the care of children. There may also be helpers for this task. The services of nursery schools and kindergartens are increasingly sought. In rural areas, 5– and 6–year-olds are given duties such as running errands or picking coffee. Eight- to 10–year-old girls may perform all the household chores. Young girls are expected to help around the house more than boys are. Punishments are less harsh in the late twentieth century than they were in mid-century. The Family Code obliges parents to be moderate. Upper-class parents emphasize responsibility, honor, loyalty, and self-esteem. The middle class stresses the values of occupational success, personal realization, individual independence, honesty, and generosity. Working-class parents expect obedience, respect, self-discipline, and honesty. Girls' fifteenth birthdays (*quinceañeras*) are well-defined rites of passage, celebrated with a religious ceremony and a party. School graduations of both sexes are likewise celebrated. Legal maturity is at age 18. Young men and women usually stay with their families until they get married. If they remain single, they are not asked to leave but may do so.

cultural distinctiveness; about half the farmers are in the small-holder category. The greatest amount of land surface, however, is taken up by large holdings in the hands of less than 10 percent of all owners. A pattern of large landholdings is known as *latifundismo*. The trend continues toward land concentration and toward tinier plots for the greatest number of owners (*minifundismo*). Wage laborers with miniplots or no land at all are many. Land invasions by "squatters" occur in rural and urban areas. For instance, in 1985 there were 936 cases of invasion.

Kinship

KIN GROUPS AND DESCENT. Nuclear-family households are predominant, but extended households are also widespread, and extended-family groups act as units in politics, business, and social affairs. Separate but related nuclear families attend christenings, weddings and, above all, funerals. The descent system is bilateral; people use both the paternal and maternal surnames.

KINSHIP TERMINOLOGY. Tico Spanish sibling-cousin terminology is of the Eskimo type: the same terms are used for cousins on the father's and the mother's side, and cousins are differentiated from siblings.

Sociopolitical Organization

SOCIAL ORGANIZATION. Ticos are oriented primarily to family, village, and neighborhood. Their community activities center around church, school, and sports. Informal groups for solving immediate problems are common, but Costa Ricans also cooperate through boards and committees, clubs, charity organizations, and community-development organizations. Registered associations for different purposes numbered more than 8,000 in 1991. Costa Ricans, however, are not characterized as joiners; individualism is said to be a trait of their national character, as is localism. Other values attributed to Tico culture are formal education, equality, democracy, freedom, peace, moderation, compromise, conformity, conservatism, caution, amiability, and courtesy.

POLITICAL ORGANIZATION. Presidents are elected by direct popular vote every four years, as are fifty-seven congressional representatives. Citizens of both sexes over eighteen are required to vote. The president appoints the ministers. Each of the provinces has a governor, also appointed by the president. The eighty townships elect their municipal councils. The constitution is highly respected. Reelection of presidents is not allowed. The Supreme Court of Justice is composed of seventeen magistrates chosen by the legislature for eight-year terms. The fourth power is the Supreme Electoral Tribunal. Government is characterized by a well-developed system of checks and balances.

SOCIAL CONTROL. Informally, the strongest social control is fear of what others will say. Gossip and *choteo* (mockery) keep people in line without violence. Choteo ranges from friendly to prejudicial statements. It may be done with humor or with unpleasant ridicule. The importance of making a good impression is another check on behavior. Religion is also widely regarded as such a check. Rates of crime, theft, burglary, narcotics offenses, and corruption have increased with cosmopolitanism. Police corps and the courts handle these problems.

CONFLICT. Ticos tend strongly to avoid overt conflict in interpersonal relations. Decision making implies constant bargaining in an effort to avoid conflict. When inevitable, domestic conflict (e.g., abandonment of children, alcoholism, child abuse, battering of women) is referred to special agencies that cope with the situation at family and community levels. Communities take collective action against immoral teachers or priests; they may set up road blocks to protest government inefficiency or lack of response to their needs. Everywhere in the country, some moderate political and religious rivalry may be observed. There is a free press in which problems and policies are discussed. Conflict is handled formally, through the judicial system. The *defensoría de los habitantes* (office for the defense of the inhabitants) controls or checks the exercise of public power. Its basic task is the defense of fundamental human rights. An administrative organization whose recommendations may be taken into account by the judiciary or other branches of government, it has access to all official files except state secrets.

Religion and Expressive Culture

RELIGIOUS BELIEFS. Costa Ricans take pride in religious tolerance, and support of ecumenism is widespread. The constitution guarantees freedom for all faiths. Catholicism is the dominant and official religion. Different Protestant denominations have relatively large memberships. There are all degrees of belief and practice among Catholics, but, nevertheless, it may be said that their religion permeates Tico culture. Some people become deeply faithful and committed to the church. Others simply express faith in God. The "will of God" is a guiding and explanatory concept. The cult of the saints, as intermediaries

Costa Ricans take pride in religious tolerance, and support of ecumenism is widespread. The constitution guarantees freedom for all faiths.

between supplicants and God, is a feature of the country's Catholicism. Villages and towns are named for saints, and major celebrations are conducted for each patron saint. Pilgrimages to some of the sanctuaries of the Virgin Mary and Christ on the cross are major events. Religious education is required in the public schools. Women are considered more devout than men. A minority believes in the efficacy of witchcraft in matters relating to love, illness, and misfortune. Clients and practitioners may be accused before the courts, however, because witchcraft is forbidden by law. In this matter, as in established religion, there are degrees of belief and practice.

RELIGIOUS PRACTITIONERS. Costa Rica is organized into four Catholic dioceses, each with a bishop; the bishop of San José is the archbishop. There are diocesan priests and religious orders. Priests are scarce—probably one for about every 6,000 Catholics. In 1979 the first lay deacons were authorized to preach sermons, baptize, and give Communion to the sick in the absence of a priest. There are twenty-six congregations of nuns. In the late twentieth century, training for priests, nuns, and the laity emphasized that religion is concerned not only with prayer, ritual, and salvation but also with social justice, community service, and awareness of—and solutions to—social problems.

DEATH AND AFTERLIFE. When a death occurs, friends and relatives are notified by telephone, by announcements in the newspapers, or by radio stations. Mourners attend a wake at the home of the deceased or at a funeral parlor. Funerals are usually held the day following the death. After the church service, mourners accompany the hearse or pallbearers to the cemetery. Someone may say a few words in praise of the deceased or lead a last prayer just before the coffin is placed in a niche or lowered into the grave. When the coffin is covered, the mourners leave. Religious and memorial ceremonies follow for nine days at home and at church, then every month, and again when a year has passed. Some families make public announcements of memorial masses for a few years after the first one. Black is the color of mourning. On 2 November, the Day of the Dead, flowers are placed on graves. Most people believe the life of the soul is eternal.

Bibliography

Biesanz, Richard, Karen Zubris Biesanz, and Mavis Hiltunen Biesanz (1982). *The Costa Ricans.* Englewood Cliffs, N.J.: Prentice-Hall.

Fondo de Población de las Naciones Unidas (1993). *Situación demográfica y políticas de población en Costa Rica.* Informe para la Conferencia Internacional sobre la Población y el Desarrollo. El Cairo, Egipto, setiembre 1994. San José: Ministerio de Planificación y Política Económca (MIDEPLAN).

Morera-Brenes B., and Ramiro Barrantes (1994). "Estimación de la mezcla racial en la población de Costa Rica mediante marcadores genéticos." *Memorias del Onceavo Congreso Latinoamericano de Genética,* Puerto Vallarta, Mexico.

Sibaja, Luis F., Jorge Rovira, Anabelle Ulate, and Carlos Araya (1993). *La industria: Su evolución histórica y su aporte a la sociedad costarricense.* Cámara de Industrias. San José: Litografía e Imprenta Lil.

—MARÍA EUGENIA BOZZOLI DE WILLE

CUBANS

Ethonym: none

Orientation

IDENTIFICATION AND LOCATION. Cuba is the largest of the Caribbean islands in the West Indies. Situated between 19°40′ and 23°30′ N and 74° to 85° W, the Antillean nation of Cuba comprises approximately 120,000 square kilometers of land, including over 1,500 islets and keys and the Isle of Pines southwest of the Gulf of Batabanó. Cuba measures 200 kilometers at its widest, southernmost point and under 35 kilometers at its narrowest point. Natural harbors and ports dot the northern coast's low marshlands, swamps, and bluffs, and mountain ranges define the southern coast.

Elevations of the Maestra, Escambray, and Guaniguanico mountain ranges—located in southeast Santiago de Cuba, south-central Villa Clara, and Pinar del Río provinces respectively—vary from 2,000 meters in the Sierra Maestra to 600 meters in Guaniguanico. Between these chains, which cover 35 percent of the island land mass, are hills and sea-level plains suitable for a wide variety of tropical agricultural cultivation, ranching, and forestry. The stable climate, with temperatures that seldom drop below 21° C and average rainfall of 137 centimeters a year, contributes to the production of tropical crops. Cuba has often been in the path of devastating tropical storms and hurricanes that negatively affect production.

LINGUISTIC AFFILIATION. Cuba's earliest inhabitants were the seminomadic Ciboney, and little information on their language remains. Their successors, the Arawak, dominated the island at the time of Spanish exploration and occupation. Terms taken from the Arawak language became incorporated into the major language of Cuba, which continues to be Spanish. By the end of the sixteenth century, most of the native population had ceased to exist, further homogenizing language, but African slaves from Bantu-language groups of West Africa have contributed many terms to Spanish as spoken in Cuba.

Other permanent immigrants from China, Germany, Great Britain, and the United States tended to adopt the Spanish language. After Cuba's separation from Spain in 1898, the English language was incorporated into school curricula and North American terms and commodity trademarks infiltrated Cuban speech. Beginning in 1961, as a consequence of closer ties with the Soviet Union, the government promoted learning Russian and Eastern European languages to facilitate business and diplomatic communication.

Before the 1959 Revolution, the urban literacy rate was high by Latin American standards, but the literacy rate in the countryside was particularly low. An intensive literacy campaign focused first on teaching the rural population the fundamentals of reading and writing Spanish, then on gradually improving levels of literacy. Cuba's accomplishment in this regard has gained universal recognition.

DEMOGRAPHY. In 1991 more than half of the Cuban population of 10.7 million was under the age of 30. This pattern is related in part to the emigration of over 1 million Cubans to other countries following the 1959 Revolution. The Cuban population is 51 percent mulatto, 37 percent White, 11 percent Black, and 1 percent Chinese. Forty percent of the population resides in the western provinces and the major urban areas of Havana, Matanzas, and Pinar del Río. Another 20 percent of the population resides in the provinces of Villa Clara and part of western Camagüey. Twenty percent resides in northwestern Santiago de Cuba and Camagüey, and the final 20 percent in the easternmost area of Santiago de Cuba. The eastern naval base of Guantánamo, leased to the United States in 1903, houses 6,000 U.S. military personnel and their families and is effectively separated from Cuba.

Since the late Spanish colonial period, the rural population has migrated to the major cities of Havana, Matanzas, and Santiago de Cuba. Following the 1959 Revolution, efforts have been made to emphasize services to the countryside and slow down the migration to cities. Although population growth has declined in Havana, the trend toward urbanization has continued: in the late twentieth century 62 percent of women and 58 percent of men reside in cities. In contrast to pre-1959 conditions, however, the rural population has enjoyed improved provision of health care, education, housing, and other basic needs.

History and Cultural Relations

The earliest known settlers in Cuba, the Ciboney (1000 B.C.) were joined by Arawaks from A.D. 1100 to 1450. From Christopher Columbus's first landing in 1492 to U.S. troop landings in 1898 during the final stages of the war for Cuban independence, the island was integrated into the Spanish colonial structure, producing as major export crops sugarcane, coffee, and tobacco. The island also served as an administrative center for Spanish political and economic control of the region and was therefore a significant arena of international rivalry over Spanish control of the Western Hemisphere. Population growth and economic and political activity centered on the Havana environs, marginalizing authority and economic growth in the eastern regions and restraining opportunities there even in the postcolonial period. In the second half of the nineteenth century, the Spanish government proved incapable of resolving conflicts over its policies, resulting in the Ten Years War (1868–1878) and the war for Cuban independence, which began in 1895.

Between 1899 and 1902 the United States occupied Cuba and appointed military governors as administrators; the republic was not formally established until a president was elected in 1902. The Cuban constitutional convention reluctantly incorporated the Platt Amendment (to a U.S. army appropriation bill of March 1901), which became the legal justification for U.S. control of the naval base at Guantánamo, ownership of Cuban land, and intervention in Cuba's internal affairs until the abrogation of the amendment in 1934. Between 1934 and 1959 the Cuban economy strengthened its economic and political ties with the United States. Persistent national conflicts generated the formation of various opposition movements. After the success of the July 26th movement in 1959, Cuba built a socialist system; even after the collapse of socialism in Eastern Europe and the Soviet Union, Cuba's government continued to be a rather stalwart adherent.

Revolutionary Cuban society has attempted to eliminate traditional vestiges of both racism and

Cuba is attempting to create a society in which neither class nor circumstances of occupation, income, race, or sex define social opportunities and rewards.

Cuba's Latin African mulatto culture manifests fewer racial tensions than more racially separated societies.

sexism. With a heritage combining descendants of Spaniards and other western Europeans, African slaves, and Chinese indentured laborers and immigrants, Cuba's Latin African mulatto culture manifests fewer racial tensions than more racially separated societies. The revolutionary government continues to make structural attempts to fully integrate and empower women and Afro-Cubans and to publicly address the foundations of bias.

Settlements

During the colonial period and prior to 1959, the major urban centers of Havana, Matanzas, Cárdenas, and Santiago de Cuba displayed patterns of growth associated with emphasis on the agro-export economy. Towns and villages organized around production of sugar, coffee, and tobacco exports expanded with markets. Migration of seasonal workers and subsistence farmers exerted strong pressures on urban centers as the concentration of landownership proceeded. Since 1959, the revolutionary government has attempted to reduce this migration in keeping with its agenda of providing more social services to rural areas and small cities and towns, radically reforming land-tenure patterns, and diversifying the economy.

As before the Revolution, rural dwellings of the poor, particularly in the mountainous regions, are constructed from palm thatch, cane, and mud with dirt floors. These *bohíos* traditionally dominated the countryside around sugarcane fields and areas where family subsistence plots persisted; they are only gradually being replaced with dweller-constructed, partially prefabricated cement multifamily housing. Cycles of increased construction have occurred from 1959 to 1963, in the mid-1970s, in 1980, and from 1988 to 1989 but have not kept pace with housing needs. In urban centers, housing combines single-family Spanish-style architecture, low-rise apartment units, single-story apartments joined in rows, and, in the oldest cities, some former single-family homes converted into multiple units. The Spanish patio arrangement is more predominant in the older dwellings. Construction of single-family housing has received less priority from the revolutionary government.

Economy

SUBSISTENCE AND COMMERCIAL ACTIVITIES. Since 1959, the Cuban government has endeavored to provide food security to its population and increase access to basic needs in housing, education, and medical care. Programs have been implemented to diversify and decentralize agri-

cultural production, exploit nickel reserves, develop light industries, expand the fishing and tourist industries, and increase export earnings to provide for other development needs.

Before the collapse of the socialist bloc, over 40 percent of Cuba's food supply was imported. The National Rationing Board attempted to assure distribution of minimum basic food needs based on demographics. The island suffered severe food shortages in 1993 and 1994, following climatic disasters and the loss of most of its oil imports and 30 percent of its agrochemical, machinery, and parts imports. Attempts to address the crisis included the transformation of state farms into worker-owned enterprises or cooperatives, the reintroduction of farmers' markets, and new trade arrangements for food imports from other countries. The government also legalized private markets and private vendors and suppliers of services in many industries.

INDUSTRIAL ARTS. Cuba is well known for its production of handcrafted wood and cane furniture as well as folk-music instruments.

TRADE. Until the 1990s, government-owned food stores set uniform prices for rationed foods. Prices remained fixed from the early 1960s to 1981, when they were increased slightly. Government nonrationed food markets were expanded in 1983 and 1994 to provide greater supplies and varieties of foods and to end black marketeering. Consumer goods remained under government ownership and control until 1994, when the government legalized the taxable, direct sale, without price controls, of crafts and surplus industrial goods by licensed private vendors. Price increases on services and some products followed the 1994 decriminalization of the dollar. Taxes were introduced in select areas.

DIVISION OF LABOR. The traditional division of labor by gender—*casa* (home) and *calle* (street)—ascribed to urban, upper-class Latin American societies began to change significantly during World War II, as more middle-class women entered professional fields. In the postrevolutionary period, transference between gender-traditional occupations has made limited strides. Although women have become more educated, have entered new job fields, and play a greater role in political organizations, they continue to be concentrated in the traditional fields of education and public health and remain underrepresented in politics. The labor force of 3 million presently includes 30 percent engaged exclusively in agriculture, 20 percent in industry, 20 percent in services, 11 percent in construction, 10 percent in commerce, and 5 percent in government.

LAND TENURE. Since eliminating foreign ownership and large private estates, which were legacies of the colonial system, agrarian reform has gone through several stages. By the mid-1980s, 80 percent of land had come under state ownership, 11 percent was organized into cooperatives, and 9 percent was held by private owners. Food crises forced alteration of this system in 1994. State farms were replaced by Basic Units of Cooperative Production, which are allowed to sell in farmers' markets any food they produce in excess of government requirements. To diversify the economy further and earn foreign exchange, the government entered into investment contracts with foreign enterprises in the fields of construction technology, consumer goods, mining, biotechnology, oil, sugar, and tourism.

Kinship, Marriage, and Family

KINSHIP. Prerevolutionary kinship ties and social ties of the Cuban upper class were based in part on patrilineal descent from the Spanish colonial aristocracy. The ability to trace family backgrounds sharing common names and patron saints became somewhat less significant in the decades following establishment of the republic and declined even more significantly after the 1959 Revolution and the exodus of large numbers of the upper class. Lower-class Cubans demonstrated much less regard for lineage than had the middle class but continued the Latin tradition of godparenting and maintaining close relationships with and responsibility for the extended family.

MARRIAGE. In the prerevolutionary period, within the framework of a Catholic-Latin society and rural/urban economic polarization, church-sanctioned marriage and baptisms assumed more importance in the cities than in the countryside. A relatively low marriage rate, cited as less than 5 per 1,000 in the late colonial period, reflected emphasis on common-law marriages in the countryside. Since the 1959 Revolution, rates of both marriage and divorce have tended to increase and become more similar for rural and urban areas. The marriage rate declined somewhat in the late 1970s, however, as the housing shortage limited the establishment of separate households. Postmarital residence tends to be patrilocal and has at times required doubling up of families. In 1979 extended families resided in 40 percent of Cuban households. Various types of birth control, including abortion, are available.

DOMESTIC UNIT. Efforts to strengthen family solidarity, stability, and female equality include the enactment of the 1975 Family Code, which identifies the nuclear family as the essential social unit responsible for improving the health and welfare of society. The code calls for equal sharing of responsibilities in household work, maintenance, and child rearing, as well as equal commitment to respect and loyalty in marriage. Legally mandated child-care centers and maternity leaves are among the projects and policies intended to reduce gender inequality and modify traditional gender-defined roles.

INHERITANCE. The Rent Reform and Agrarian Reform Laws of 1959 and subsequent legislation aimed at redistribution of wealth focused on limiting rent charges, foreign ownership of property, and private landownership, as well as nationalizing rural property, establishing cooperatives, and transferring land to sharecroppers and tenants. Legislation enacted with the objective of progressing toward abolition of private property has restricted the sale, mortgaging, and inheritance of land and has successfully increased state purchases of land. Other personal property assets may be inherited with some restrictions.

SOCIALIZATION. In addition to social conformity reinforced by traditional family relationships, Cubans find both overt and subtle pressures to conform to the values of revolutionary socialist ideology.

Sociopolitical Organization

Cuba is organized politically into fourteen provinces and 169 municipalities. Its socialist system is hierarchical and bureaucratic. The 525,000-member vanguard or cadre party, the Cuban Communist party (PCC) is led by Fidel Castro, the first party secretary, and his brother Raúl Castro, the second party secretary. The Political Bureau has responsibility for supervising economic, political, and military activities. In 1991 the 1,667 delegates to the Fourth Party Congress, acting on recommendations at local meetings attended by some 3.5 million people throughout the island, cut the staff of the 225-member Central Committee by one-half and reduced the number of departments by more than one-half. Alternates in the Political Bureau were abolished, and the Secretariat was terminated. The congress also called for increased review and recall of party officials and special sessions to deal with the economic crises at the provincial and municipal levels.

Secret-ballot elections to the municipal assemblies in 1992 and elections to the provincial and national assemblies in 1993 significantly reduced the number of incumbents who had been part of the decision-making bodies for decades. Membership in the Communist party was no longer a

The collapse of the Soviet bloc contributed to Cuban shortages of consumer goods, food, and medicine, as well as to blackouts and transportation and production problems.

requirement in selecting delegates. By 1993, half of the members of the National Assembly were directly elected municipal-assembly delegates; more and younger delegates represented the trades, medicine, and culture.

SOCIAL ORGANIZATION. In contrast to the prerevolutionary years, Cuba is attempting to create a society in which neither class nor circumstances of occupation, income, race, or sex define social opportunities and rewards. The most significant challenges for the Revolution since the collapse of the Eastern bloc are providing equal access to political and economic opportunities without creating a privileged group in society or loss of conscious socialist goals, and simultaneously moving the economy toward diversification and industrialization.

POLITICAL ORGANIZATION. Prior to 1959, participation in the national and local political processes was limited. Between 1959 and 1970, the revolutionary government largely centralized authority and provided limited representative or direct access to decision making. Reorganization of the political system in 1970 was designed to allow greater input into policy formation at all levels. Legislative reforms in 1976 and again in 1992 and 1993 were illustrative of a trend toward increasing participation in economic decision making at all levels. To ensure wider input and greater understanding of the potential effects of change prior to policy formation, it was required that meetings be held with mass organizations and constituencies.

Most citizens belong to at least one of the mass organizations (committees for the defense of the Revolution, the Confederation of Cuban Workers, the Federation of Cuban Women, the National Association of Small Farmers) or to specific professional or student associations. Several human-rights organizations, founded outside the established political process, are not recognized by the government. In 1994 the government announced the visit of the United Nations High Commissioner for Human Rights and the creation of an ad hoc committee within the National Assembly to review and report on political, social, economic, cultural, and individual rights.

CONFLICT. From 1898 to 1959, Cuba experienced several political and economic crises that resulted in armed revolts against government officials and in military and political intervention by the United States. Between 1953 and 1959, armed struggle in the cities and countryside culminated in a successful revolution. Subsequently, more than 200,000 mainly upper- and middle-class Cubans left the island. A small percentage of the exiles in the United States has established organizations that have actively sought the overthrow and/or destabilization of the Cuban government and have resisted U.S. rapprochement with Cuba.

U.S. opposition to Cuban expropriation of U.S. businesses, implementation of a socialist agenda, and relations with the Soviet Union strained U.S.-Cuban relations early in the revolutionary struggle. Immediate consequences included U.S. training and equipping of Cuban exiles in the Playa Girón (Bay of Pigs) invasion of 1961, attempts to isolate Cuba economically and diplomatically in the Western Hemisphere, and a U.S. trade embargo. The 1962 Cuban missile crisis and Cuban support of revolutions and anticolonial movements in Latin America and Africa contributed to further tensions between the United States and Cuba.

Dependence on Soviet support and trade with Eastern Europe complicated Cuban-Eastern bloc relations in the late 1980s as those nations disavowed socialism. Cuba has made substantive efforts to rebuild diplomatic and trade relations with Latin America and increase trade with other nonsocialist nations. Despite three separate votes in the United Nations condemning the U.S. embargo of Cuba as a violation of international law, the United States has determinedly continued the embargo.

Within Cuba, the most significant political conflicts center around perceptions of counterrevolutionary activity. Although criticism is encouraged within the socialist-revolutionary framework, individuals and organizations attempting to operate actively outside this framework or perceived as opponents of the socialist system are subject to legal proceedings that typically result in incarceration. Internal conflict in the 1980s was exemplified by the exodus of more than 125,000 Cubans to the United States from Mariel, the growth of various human-rights organizations, and the trials of high-echelon political and military leaders on drug-trafficking and other counterrevolutionary charges. The collapse of the Soviet bloc contributed to shortages of consumer goods, food, and medicine, as well as to blackouts and transportation and production problems resulting from fuel shortages. Emphasis on tourism to earn necessary foreign exchange and the decriminalization of the dollar were increasingly criticized for creating a dual standard of living and social problems such as prostitution. The economic decline resulted in heretofore rare public demonstrations against the government.

U.S. determination to see the Cuban government overthrown was reflected in the tightening of the embargo in 1992. An immigration policy that denied Cubans legal visas while allowing them entry through illegal means created an immigration crisis in the summer of 1994. Ultimately, the United States reversed its policy of preferential treatment for Cubans and sent those attempting to enter the United States illegally to camps at Guantanamo Naval Base and elsewhere. It also entered into new discussions with the Cuban government on immigration but rescinded many travel opportunities and tightened controls on dollar transfers.

Religion and Expressive Culture

RELIGIOUS BELIEFS AND PRACTICES. Catholicism has been the principal religion of Cuba, although Methodist, Baptist, and Presbyterian schools, churches, and missions and a number of other religious groups also thrived in the prerevolutionary period. Researchers contend that the Catholic church had less influence and significance in Cuban society than in many other Latin American countries, which in part accounts for reduced hostilities during the period of strong separation between religion and the revolutionary government (1959–1983). The emergence of liberation theology and Cuban government recognition of a role for religion in revolutionary society resulted in improved relations between the churches and the Cuban government in the latter part of the 1980s.

Afro-Cuban Santería, a syncretic religion that draws on both the Yoruba and Catholic cultural heritages, is deeply engrained in Cuban culture and has at least the tacit respect of practitioners of other religions.

ARTS. Under the revolutionary government, Cuba has expanded the number of libraries from 100 to 2,000 and of museums from 6 to 250. Workshops and institutes in music, dance, theater, art, ceramics, lithography, photography, and film are available to amateurs and professionals in the 200 *casas de cultura*. A new film industry and film school have produced internationally acclaimed works, and several publishing houses, of which the Casa de las Américas is the best known, have produced and reproduced an unprecedented number of publications. Political poster art, street theater, and experimental workplace theaters have been distinctive contributions of the revolutionary period. The rich Afro-Hispanic culture, including the traditional *guajiro* (folk) songs and dances, have been emphasized with new vigor since 1959.

MEDICINE. Between 1959 and 1964, almost one-half of Cuba's 6,300 physicians left the island, and the United States imposed a trade embargo that cut off essential medicines. As part of its campaign to increase the availability of medical care, Cuba has since trained more than 16,000 doctors. Medical care is completely free and available to all; Cuba has also sent many physicians and other health-care workers to more than twenty-six countries to provide care, training, and biomedical research. Using the medical-team approach and emphasizing preventative health care, the government expanded the former *mutualistas* (health-maintenance organizations) to include urban and rural polyclinics, more rural hospitals, and extensive neighborhood health-education and disease-prevention programs. Modern techniques and equipment available from the socialist bloc improved health-care delivery dramatically.

The rapid decline in the importation of medicine, equipment, and pharmaceutical-industry supplies from the former socialist bloc, and the limited availability of hard currency for purchases created a medical crisis in 1993–1994. Shortages of food and chemicals for water treatment led to outbreaks of diseases, including an optic and paralytic epidemic that was stemmed only with the help of the international community. Emphasis

HOLY MAN

A Santeria priest blows cigar smoke into the hands of a devotee. Santeria is an African religion influenced by Catholicism. Cuba. (Francoise de Mulder/Corbis)

The history of the Dominican Republic is marked by continued interference by international forces and a Dominican ambivalence toward its own leadership.

See also

Haitians

on herbal and traditionalist methods of treatment has increased with the loss of manufactured medications.

DEATH AND AFTERLIFE. Funeral rituals and beliefs regarding death and afterlife continue to reflect the combined Santería and Roman Catholic heritage.

Bibliography

Bremer, Philip, William LeoGrande, Donna Rich, and Daniel Siegel, eds. (1989). *The Cuba Reader: The Making of a Revolutionary Society.* New York: Grove Press.

Halebsky, Sandor, and John Kirk, eds. (1985). *Cuba: Twenty-Five Years of Revolution, 1959–1984.* New York: Praeger Special Studies.

Perez, Louis A. (1988). *Cuba: Between Reform and Revolution.* New York: Oxford University Press.

Thomas, Hugh (1971). *Cuba: The Pursuit of Freedom.* New York: Harper & Row.

—SUSAN J. FERNÁNDEZ

DOMINICANS

Ethonym: none

Orientation

IDENTIFICATION. "Dominicans" is the term used to describe the people of the Dominican Republic. The native population of Taino Indians was decimated during the Spanish Conquest, which began in 1492 and came to be characterized by forced labor and newly introduced diseases. Africans were imported as slaves to replace the Indians on the plantations and in the mines. Today Dominicans physically reflect the ancestry of Europe and Africa; over 70 percent of Dominicans are now officially considered mulatto. Even though the majority of the Dominican people are classified by the government as mulattoes, social status and skin color are correlated, with lighter-skinned Dominicans dominating business, government, and society. Mulattoes constitute most of the Dominican middle class; the working classes are mostly Black or dark mulatto. Other ethnic groups in the Dominican Republic are Lebanese, Chinese, Italians, French, Jews, Japanese, Haitians, and West Indians.

LOCATION. The island of Hispaniola, one of the Greater Antilles, lies between Cuba and Puerto Rico in the Caribbean Sea. The Dominican Republic occupies the eastern two-thirds (i.e., 48,464 square kilometers) of Hispaniola and is strikingly diverse geographically. The Dominican Republic contains mountain ranges interspersed with fertile valleys, lush rain forests, semiarid deserts, rich farmlands, and spectacular beaches. The western third of the island of Hispaniola is the nation of Haiti.

Many Dominicans have migrated to other countries in search of employment and increased opportunity. Between 5 and 8 percent of the population of the Dominican Republic live and work in the United States—most of them in New York City, but substantial numbers have also settled in New Jersey and Florida. Migration between the Dominican Republic and other islands of the Caribbean is less well documented.

DEMOGRAPHY. There were about 7,915,000 Dominicans in 1993. About half of them lived in the *campo* (countryside) and worked mainly as peasant farmers. Because of the relative poverty in the countryside, more and more Dominicans have migrated to cities such as Santo Domingo (the capital city), Santiago de los Caballeros, La Vega, San Francisco de Macorís, La Romana, and Puerto Plata on the north coast.

During the period of Rafael Trujillo's rule from 1930 to 1961, Dominican immigration to the United States was severely limited, given Trujillo's domestic agenda, which depended on a steady supply of an expendable labor source. Dominicans did migrate however, even with Trujillo's restrictive policies. Between 1950 and 1960, almost 10,000 Dominicans emigrated to the United States and became legal residents. Following the overthrow of Trujillo in 1961 and the lifting of his restrictive policies, migration to the United States increased substantially. Between 1961 and 1981, 255,578 legal immigrants entered the United States from the Dominican Republic. It is much more difficult to estimate the number of undocumented Dominicans in the United States. Reports suggest that Dominicans are third among immigrant groups from Latin America admitted into the United States. The economic crisis of the early 1980s has further increased the number of Dominicans seeking to emigrate to the United States. Research suggests that those Dominicans who succeed in doing so are most often young, predominantly urban in origin, often skilled and semiprofessional, and better educated than Dominican nonmigrants.

In 1993 the crude birthrate in the Dominican Republic was 25.2 per thousand, the crude death rate was 5.8 per thousand, the infant mortality rate was 49.3 per thousand, and total life expectancy at birth was 69 years.

LINGUISTIC AFFILIATION. Spanish is the language spoken by Dominicans. Although there are some regional dialects of Spanish in the Dominican Republic, Dominicans pride themselves on the "purity" of their Spanish. Dominican Spanish is considered by some to be perhaps the clearest, most classical Spanish spoken in Latin America. According to some authors, this may be the result of the virtual elimination of the native population and the fact that the Dominican Republic was the first Spanish-settled colony in the New World.

History, Politics, and Cultural Relations

The history of the Dominican Republic, both colonial and postcolonial, is marked by continued interference by international forces and a Dominican ambivalence toward its own leadership. Between the fifteenth and nineteenth centuries, the Dominican Republic was ruled both by Spain and France and occupied both by the United States and Haiti. Three political leaders influenced Dominican politics from the 1930s to the 1990s. The dictator Rafael Trujillo ran the country for thirty-one years, until 1961. In the years following Trujillo's murder, two aging caudillos, Juan Bosch and Joaquín Balaguer, vied for control of the Dominican government.

In 1492, when Columbus first landed in what is now the Dominican Republic, he named the island "Española," which means "Little Spain." The spelling of the name was later changed to Hispaniola. The city of Santo Domingo, on the southern coast of Hispaniola, was established as the Spanish capital in the New World. Santo Domingo became a walled city, modeled after those of medieval Spain, and a center of transplanted Spanish culture. The Spanish built churches, hospitals, and schools and established commerce, mining, and agriculture.

In the process of settling and exploiting Hispaniola, the native Taino Indians were eradicated by the harsh forced-labor practices of the Spanish and the diseases the Spanish brought with them, to which indigenous peoples had no immunity. Because the rapid decimation of the Taino left the Spanish in need of laborers in the mines and on the plantations, Africans were imported as a slave labor force. During this time, the Spanish established a strict two-class social system based on race, a political system based on authoritarianism and hierarchy, and an economic system based on state domination. After about fifty years, the Spanish abandoned Hispaniola for more economically promising areas such as Cuba, Mexico, and other new colonies in Latin America. The institutions of government, economy, and society that were established, however, have persisted in the Dominican Republic throughout its history.

After its virtual abandonment, once-prosperous Hispaniola fell into a state of disorganization and depression lasting almost two hundred years. In 1697 Spain handed over the western third of Hispaniola to the French, and in 1795 gave the French the eastern two-thirds as well. By that time, the western third of Hispaniola (then called Hayti) was prosperous, producing sugar and cotton in an economic system based on slavery. The formerly Spanish-controlled eastern two-thirds was economically impoverished, with most people surviving on subsistence farming. After the Haitian slave rebellion, which resulted in Haitian independence in 1804, the Black armies of Haiti attempted to take control of the former Spanish colony, but the French, Spanish, and British fought off the Haitians. The eastern part of Hispaniola reverted to Spanish rule in 1809. The Haitian armies once again invaded in 1821, and in 1822 gained control of the entire island, which they maintained until 1844.

In 1844 Juan Pablo Duarte, the leader of the Dominican independence movement, entered Santo Domingo and declared the eastern two-thirds of Hispaniola an independent nation, naming it the Dominican Republic. Duarte was unable to hold power, however, which soon passed to two generals, Buenaventura Báez and Pedro Santana. These men looked to the "greatness" of the sixteenth-century colonial period as a model and sought out the protection of a large foreign power. As a result of corrupt and inept leadership, the country was bankrupt by 1861, and power was handed over to the Spanish again until 1865. Báez continused as president until 1874; Ulises Espaillat then took control until 1879.

In 1882 a modernizing dictator, Ulises Heureaux, took control of the Dominican Republic. Under Heureaux's regime, roads and railways were constructed, telephone lines were installed, and irrigation systems were dug. During this period, economic modernization and political order were established, but only through extensive foreign loans and autocratic, corrupt, and brutal rule. In 1899 Heureaux was assassinated, and the Dominican government fell into disarray and factionalism. By 1907, the economic situation had deteriorated, and the government was unable to pay the foreign debt engendered during the reign of Heureaux. In response to the perceived economic crisis, the United States moved to place the

In the mid-Twentieth Century, the Dominican Republic became a ruthless police state in which torture and murder ensured obedience.

Dominican Republic into receivership. Ramón Cáceres, the man who assassinated Heureaux, became president until 1912, when he was in turn assassinated, by a member of one of the feuding political factions.

The ensuing domestic political warfare left the Dominican Republic once again in political and economic chaos. European and U.S. bankers expressed concern over the possible lack of repayment of loans. Using the Monroe Doctrine to counter what the United States considered potential European "intervention" in the Americas, the United States invaded the Dominican Republic in 1916, occupying the country until 1924.

During the period of U.S. occupation, political stability was restored. Roads, hospitals, and water and sewerage systems were constructed in the capital city and elsewhere in the country, and land-tenure changes that benefited a new class of large landowners were instituted. To act as a counterinsurgency force, a new military security force, the Guardia Nacional, was trained by U.S. marines. In 1930 Rafael Trujillo, who had risen to a position of leadership in the Guardia, used it to acquire and consolidate power.

From 1930 to 1961, Trujillo ran the Dominican Republic as his own personal possession, in what has been called the first truly totalitarian state in the hemisphere. He established a system of private capitalism in which he, his family members, and his friends held nearly 60 percent of the country's assets and controlled its labor force. Under the guise of economic recovery and national security, Trujillo and his associates demanded the abolishment of all personal and political freedoms. Although the economy flourished, the benefits went toward personal—not public—gain. The Dominican Republic became a ruthless police state in which torture and murder ensured obedience. Trujillo was assassinated on 30 May 1961, ending a long and difficult period in Dominican history. At the time of his death, few Dominicans could remember life without Trujillo in power, and with his death came a period of domestic and international turmoil.

During Trujillo's reign, political institutions had been eviscerated, leaving no functional political infrastructure. Factions that had been forced underground emerged, new political parties were created, and the remnants of the previous regime—in the form of Trujillo's son Ramfis and one of Trujillo's former puppet presidents, Joaquín Balaguer—vied for control. Because of pressure from the United States to democratize, Trujillo's

son and Balaguer agreed to hold elections. Balaguer quickly moved to distance himself from the Trujillo family in the realignment for power.

In November 1961 Ramfis Trujillo and his family fled the country after emptying the Dominican treasury of $90 million. Joaquín Balaguer became part of a seven-person Council of State, but two weeks and two military coups later, Balaguer was forced to leave the country. In December 1962 Juan Bosch of the Dominican Revolutionary party (PRD), promising social reform, won the presidency by a 2−1 margin, the first time that Dominicans had been able to choose their leadership in relatively free and fair elections. The traditional ruling elite and the military, however, with the support of the United States, organized against Bosch under the guise of anticommunism. Claiming that the government was infiltrated by communists, the military staged a coup that overthrew Bosch in September 1963; he had been president for only seven months.

In April 1965 the PRD and other pro-Bosch civilians and "constitutionalist" military took back the presidential palace. José Molina Ureña, next in line for the presidency according to the constitution, was sworn in as interim president. Remembering Cuba, the United States encouraged the military to counterattack. The military used jets and tanks in its attempt to crush the rebellion, but the pro-Bosch constitutionalists were able to repel them. The Dominican military was moving toward a defeat at the hands of the constitutionalist rebels when, on 28 April 1965, President Lyndon Johnson sent 23,000 U.S. troops to occupy the country.

The Dominican economic elite, having been reinstalled by the U.S. military, sought Balaguer's election in 1966. Although the PRD was allowed to contest the presidency, with Bosch as its candidate, the Dominican military and police used threats, intimidation, and terrorist attacks to keep him from campaigning. The final outcome of the vote was tabulated as 57 percent for Balaguer and 39 percent for Bosch.

Throughout the late 1960s and the first part of the 1970s, the Dominican Republic went through a period of economic growth and development arising mainly from public-works projects, foreign investments, increased tourism, and skyrocketing sugar prices. During this same period, however, the Dominican unemployment rate remained between 30 and 40 percent, and illiteracy, malnutrition, and infant mortality rates were dangerously high. Most of the benefits of the improving Dominican economy went to the already wealthy. The sudden increase in oil prices by the Organization of Petroleum Exporting Countries (OPEC) in the mid-1970s, a crash in the price of sugar on the world market, and increases in unemployment and inflation destabilized the Balaguer government. The PRD, under a new leader, Antonio Guzmán, once more prepared for presidential elections.

Since Guzmán was a moderate, he was seen as acceptable by the Dominican business community and by the United States. The Dominican economic elite and military, however, saw Guzmán and the PRD as a threat to their dominance. When the early returns from the 1978 election showed Guzmán leading, the military moved in, seized the ballot boxes, and annulled the election. Because of pressure from the Carter administration and threats of a massive general strike among Dominicans, Balaguer ordered the military to return the ballot boxes, and Guzmán won the election.

Guzmán promised better observance of human rights and more political freedom, more action in health care and rural development, and more control over the military; however, the high oil costs and the rapid decline in sugar prices caused the economic situation in the Dominican Republic to remain bleak. Even though Guzmán achieved much in terms of political and social reform, the faltering economy made people recall the days of relative prosperity under Balaguer.

The PRD chose Salvador Jorge Blanco as its 1982 presidential candidate, Juan Bosch returned with a new political party called the Dominican Liberation party (PLD), and Joaquín Balaguer also entered the race, under the auspices of his Reformist Party. Jorge Blanco won the election with 47 percent of the vote; however, one month before the new president's inauguration, Guzmán committed suicide over reports of corruption. Jacobo Majluta, the vice president, was named interim president until the inauguration.

When Jorge Blanco assumed the presidency, the country was faced with an enormous foreign debt and a balance-of-trade crisis. President Blanco sought a loan from the International Monetary Fund (IMF). The IMF, in turn, required drastic austerity measures: the Blanco government was forced to freeze wages, cut funding to the public sector, increase prices on staple goods, and restrict credit. When these policies resulted in social unrest, Blanco sent in the military, resulting in the deaths of more than one hundred people.

Joaquín Balaguer, nearly eighty years old and legally blind, ran against Juan Bosch and former interim president Jacobo Majluta in the 1986 election. In a highly contentious race, Balaguer won by a narrow margin and regained control of the country. He once more turned to massive public-works projects in an attempt to revitalize the Dominican economy but this time was unsuccessful. By 1988 he was no longer seen as an economic miracle worker, and in the 1990 election he was again strongly challenged by Bosch. In the campaign, Bosch was portrayed as divisive and unstable in contrast to the elder statesman Balaguer. With this strategy, Balaguer again won in 1990, although by a narrow margin.

In the 1994 presidential election, Balaguer and his Social Christian Reformist party (PRSC) were challenged by José Francisco Peña Gómez, the candidate of the PRD. Peña Gómez, a Black man who was born in the Dominican Republic of Haitian parents, was depicted as a covert Haitian agent who planned to destroy Dominican sovereignty and merge the Dominican Republic with Haiti. Pro-Balaguer television commercials showed Peña Gómez as drums beat wildly in the background, and a map of Hispaniola with a dark brown Haiti spreading over and covering a bright green Dominican Republic. Peña Gómez was likened to a witch doctor in pro-Balaguer campaign pamphlets, and videos linked him with the practice of Vodun. Election-day exit polls indicated an overwhelming victory for Peña Gómez; on the following day, however, the Central Electoral Junta (JCE), the independent electoral board, presented preliminary results that placed Balaguer in the lead. Allegations of fraud on the part of the JCE were widespread. More than eleven weeks later, on 2 August, the JCE finally pronounced Balaguer the winner by 22,281 votes, less than 1 percent of the total vote. The PRD claimed that at least 200,000 PRD voters had been turned away from polling places, on the grounds that their names were not on the voters list. The JCE established a "revision committee," which investigated 1,500 polling stations (about 16 percent of the total) and found that the names of more than 28,000 voters had been removed from electoral lists, making plausible the figure of 200,000 voters turned away nationally. The JCE ignored the findings of the committee and declared Balaguer the winner. In a concession, Balaguer agreed to limit his term in office to two years instead of four, and not to run for president again. Current President Leonel Fernandez Reyna defeated Peña Gómez in 1996.

*Throughout most of
its history, the
Dominican economy
has been based
largely on the
production and
export of sugarcane.*

Economy

SUBSISTENCE AND COMMERCIAL ACTIVITIES. Throughout most of its history, the Dominican economy has been based largely on the production and export of sugarcane. Sugarcane is still the biggest cash crop grown in the Dominican Republic, with coffee and cocoa being the other most important export crops. Agriculture continues to be the largest source of employment in the Dominican Republic, but mining has recently surpassed sugar as the biggest source of export earnings. Tourism is the most rapidly growing sector of the Dominican economy, with receipts in 1990 of U.S.$944 million. With the relative stability of Dominican democracy since the 1970s, tax incentives for building tourist facilities, the most hotel rooms of any country in the Caribbean, and beautiful uncluttered beaches, tourism is now the largest source of foreign exchange. Manufacturing, especially in the Free Trade Zones (FTZ), is also a rapidly growing sector of the Dominican economy.

INDUSTRIAL ARTS. The three main industrial activities in the Dominican Republic are mining, manufacturing, and utilities. In 1991 mining accounted for 33.5 percent of the total earnings from exports. Ferro-nickel is the major mineral mined in the country; bauxite, gold, and silver are also extracted. Manufacturing accounted for 16.1 percent of the Dominican gross domestic product in 1991. A rapidly growing part of the Dominican manufacturing sector are the FTZ being established by foreign multinational corporations. In these FTZ, the main activity is the assembly of products (mainly textiles, garments, and light electronic goods) intended for sale in nations such as the United States. Assembly industries locate in these zones because there they are permitted to pay low wages for labor-intensive activities and because the Dominican government grants exemptions from duties and taxes on exports from FTZ. Sixteen FTZ had been established in the Dominican Republic by 1991, comprising more than 300 companies, which employed around 120,000 workers.

TRADE. In 1991 the Dominican Republic had a trade deficit of U.S.$1,070.5 million, with the United States receiving 56 percent of Dominican exports. The other major trading partners of the Dominican Republic are Venezuela and Mexico. The main exports from the Dominican Republic in 1991 were raw sugar and ferro-nickel.

DIVISION OF LABOR. In 1991 an estimated 34.9 percent of Dominicans worked in the agricultural sector, 28.1 percent were employed in industry, and many others worked in the service sector, which caters mainly to tourism. Labor is divided along the lines of ethnicity, class, and gender. Light-skinned individuals control most of business, finance, government, and other high-status professions, whereas darker-skinned individuals are predominant in the military officer crops and constitute much of the new middle class. More than three-quarters of the workers in the free trade zones are women; employers can pay them low wages and keep them from forming strong labor unions.

LAND TENURE. Land-tenure patterns reflect both Dominican and international politics. Sugar and cattle are significant products for the Dominican economy, and land-tenure patterns associated with sugar production and cattle raising have changed over time. The 1916 U.S. invasion is often conceptualized an action under the Monroe Doctrine to protect regional security and counter European "interference" in the Americas, especially to stop German expansion in the region; however, the invasion was also a means to protect U.S. sugar producers in the Dominican Republic. World War I destroyed the European sugar-beet industry, allowing for the rapid expansion of Dominican sugar production. During the U.S. occupation, U.S. military authorities enacted legislation to facilitate the takeover of Dominican land by U.S. sugar growers. The 1920 Law Registration Act was designed to break up the communal lands and transfer them into private ownership. In 1925, one year following the withdrawal of U.S. troops, eleven of the twenty-one sugar mills in the Dominican Republic belonged to U.S. corporations, and 98 percent of the sugar exports went to the United States.

Cattle raising, an important source and symbol of wealth in the Dominican countryside, was feasible for many people because the animals were branded and then left to graze freely on open land. In the 1930s Trujillo expropriated large portions of land, reducing the amount available for free grazing. Those lands became further reduced in the 1950s when Trujillo established "La Zona," a law requiring the enclosure of large livestock that effectively prohibited free grazing. In the 1960s and 1970s the Balaguer government tried to increase cattle production for meat exports and, in so doing, created state-subsidized credits for cattle production. Some of these credits made it easier and more rewarding for people to buy parcels of land on which to graze their cattle.

KINSHIP

Kin Groups and Descent

Kinship in the upper classes of Dominican society is patrilineal, based on the Spanish model. The eldest man is the ultimate authority; brothers and unmarried sisters stay very close, and sons give their allegiance to their father and mother. Brothers and sons help to support their unmarried sisters and mother, whereas married sisters are expected to become part of their husband's families. The extended family is also the locus of social activity among the Dominican upper class. Kinship among the Dominican lower class, on the other hand, is more matrilineal. The eldest woman is the head of the family, with very close ties with her daughters and their children. Because of the practice of consensual unions among lower-class Dominicans, men are not as integral a part of the kin grouping.

Marriage and Family

MARRIAGE.   Three different types of marital union can be found among Dominicans: church marriage, civil marriage, and consensual or common-law union. Church and civil marriage are most prevalent among the upper classes of Dominican society, whereas consensual unions predominate among the poor. These patterns of marriage in Dominican society can be traced back to the Spanish-colonial and slave periods. Among the Spanish settlers that came to Hispaniola, there was a strong ethic of family solidarity, and the father was the dominant figure in the family structure. Among the slaves, however, families were frequently broken up, and marriages were often not allowed. There was also an established pattern of informal unions between Spanish-colonial settlers and African slave women. Reflections of these practices are present today in the range of skin tones and marriage practices among Dominicans.

There are also contemporary reasons for the strong class and racial basis of the different types of marital union. One reason is the high cost of church and civil-marriage ceremonies in the Dominican Republic. Another is that, as throughout the Caribbean, early pregnancies result from consensual relationships. Both sexes initially tend to form a series of consensual unions, each resulting in more children.

DOMESTIC UNIT.   The extended family, composed of three or more generations, is the predominant domestic unit among the Dominican elite. Within this extended-family structure, the oldest man holds authority, makes public decisions on all family matters, and is responsible for the welfare of the rest of the family. The eldest married woman commands her household, delivers the decisions in the private sphere, and is a source of love and moral support for the family. The family unit often includes grandparents, parents, and unmarried siblings, along with married brothers and their wives and children; married daughters become part of their husband's families.

The practice of consensual unions, more prevalent among the Dominican lower classes, creates a much more loosely structured domestic unit. Given that the father often does not live in the household, parental authority and responsibility fall to the mother. In this situation, the eldest woman becomes the center of both public and private authority and the main breadwinner, in contrast to the patriarchal public authority among the elite. The result of this pattern is that a lower-class household often becomes a kind of extended matrilineal family, with the matriarch at the head and her unmarried children, married daughters, and grandchildren constituting the household.

Sociopolitical Organization

SOCIAL ORGANIZATION.   Dominican society is organized strongly on the basis of class and race. Dominicans of the more powerful classes, who control the economic and political processes of the country, have historically been of European ancestry. The poorest of Dominicans are most often Black, descendants of the original African slave population or migrant workers from Haiti. Mulattoes make up the majority of the Dominican population and have created a burgeoning middle class. In the twentieth century the military and lower levels of government have provided avenues of advancement for darker-skinned men, and some have reached the level of general, and even president (i.e., Trujillo).

POLITICAL ORGANIZATION.   The Dominican Republic consists of twenty-six provinces, each run by an appointed governor, and the Distrito Nacional (DN), where the capital is located. The 1966 constitution established a bicameral National Congress (Congreso Nacional), which is split into the 30-member Senate (Senado) and the 120-member Chamber of Deputies (Camara de Diputados). Members of Congress are elected for four-year terms. There is an executive branch with a president who is elected by popular vote every four years, a vice president, and a cabinet. There is also a Supreme Court (Corte Suprema).

Although the Dominican political system has long been modeled after that of the United States, with a constitution and tripartite separation of power, the political reality is different. Dominican politics has been based on a system of presidential control since colonial times. Developed to its extreme under the totalitarian dictatorship of Trujillo, this system, even in its most liberal periods, has not strayed very far from its historical model.

In the 1990s the major political parties in the Dominican Republic were the Social Christian Reformist Party (PRSC), led by Joaquín Balaguer; the Dominican Liberation Party (PLD), led by Juan Bosch; the Dominican Revolutionary Party (PRD), led by José Francisco Peña Gómez; and the Independent Revolutionary Party (PRI), led by Jacobo Majluta.

Religion and Expressive Culture

RELIGIOUS BELIEFS. The Catholic church and Catholic beliefs are nominally central to Dominican culture. It is estimated that 98 percent of Dominicans are Catholic, even if not all of these people attend church regularly. Catholicism was introduced to the Dominican Republic by Columbus and the Spanish missionaries and has remained a force in Dominican society ever since. Toward the end of the twentieth century, the dominance of the Catholic church diminished because of a decrease in funding, a shortage of new priests, and a lack of social programs for the people. As a result, Protestant evangelical movements, with their emphasis on personal responsibility and family rejuvenation, economic entrepreneurship, and biblical fundamentalism, have been gaining support among some Dominicans. An unknown number of Dominicans practice synchronistic religions combining Catholicism and Vodun. Santería is also found among Dominicans.

MEDICINE. The Dominican Republic, like many other countries in Latin America and the Caribbean, has three parallel public health-care delivery systems. The largest is the government-funded Secretaria de Estado de Salud Publica y Asistencia Social (SESPAS), which serves the general population. Because of structural and economic constraints, SESPAS is concentrated in urban areas, has a focus on curative rather than preventive care, often has inoperative medical equipment, and is known for high absenteeism among physicians. These factors severely limit access to health care for the majority of Dominicans

in the rural areas. This system, which is inadequate for the needs of the majority of Dominicans, is a result of the Spanish-colonial tradition and the biomedical system put into place by the United States during its occupation from 1916 to 1924. The other health-care delivery systems in the Dominican Republic are the Instituto Dominicano de Sequros Sociales (IDSS), which is a social-security health system, and the Instituto de Seguridad Social de las Fuerzas Armadas (ISSFAPOL), which provides health care to members of the armed forces. Private health care is also available, primarily in the urban centers.

Bibliography

Ferguson, James (1992). *The Dominican Republic: Beyond the Lighthouse*. London: Latin America Bureau.

Georges, Eugenia (1990). *The Making of a Transnational Community: Migration, Development, and Cultural Change in the Dominican Republic*. New York: Columbia University Press.

Whiteford, Linda M. (1990). "A Question of Adequacy: Primary Health Care in the Dominican Republic." *Social Science and Medicine* 30(2): 221–226.

Whiteford, Linda M. (1992). "Contemporary Health Care and the Colonial and Neo-Colonial Experience: The Case of the Dominican Republic." *Social Science and Medicine* 35(10): 1215–1223.

Whiteford, Linda M. (1993). "Child and Maternal Health and International Economic Policies." *Social Science and Medicine* 37(11): 1391–1400.

Whiteford, Linda M., and Donna Romeo (1991). "The High Cost of Free Trade: Women, Work, and Health in Dominican Free Trade Zones." Manuscript.

Wiarda, Howard J., and Michael J. Kryzanek. (1992). *The Dominican Republic: A Caribbean Crucible*. 2nd ed. Boulder, Colo.: Westview Press.

World Health Organization (1993). *Demographic Data for Health Situation Assessment and Projections*. Geneva: World Health Organization, Division of Epidemiological Surveillance and Health Situation and Trend Assessment.

—LINDA M. WHITEFORD
AND KENNETH J. GOODMAN

GARIFUNA

Ethonym: Black Carib, Island Carib, Garinagu, Karaphuna

Orientation

IDENTIFICATION. The term "Garifuna," or on Dominica, "Karaphuna," is a modern adaptation of the name applied to some Amerindians of the Caribbean and South America at the time of Columbus. That term—"Garif," and its alternate, "Carib"—are derivatives of the same root. The label "Black" derives from the fact that during the sixteenth to eighteenth centuries considerable admixture occurred with Africans whom they captured, or who otherwise escaped being enslaved by Europeans.

LOCATION. Modern-day Garifuna live mostly in Central America, in a series of villages and towns along the Caribbean coastline of Belize, Guatemala, Honduras, and Nicaragua. Many have emigrated to the United States, where they live in large colonies in New York, Chicago, Los Angeles, and several other cities. Small groups survive in Trinidad, Dominica, and Saint Vincent. Although all of them recognize a distant kinship, the Central American and Caribbean groups are virtually distinct today.

LINGUISTIC AFFILIATION. In spite of their name, their language is basically of the Arawakan Family, although there is a heavy overlay of Cariban, which may once have been a pidgin trading language for them. Linguists term their language Island Carib to distinguish it from Carib as it is spoken among groups ancestral to them still living in the Amazon area of South America.

DEMOGRAPHY. Historical sources indicate that only about 2,000 Carib survived warfare with the British to become established in Central America in 1797. Because they reside in so many different countries, and because they are not counted as a distinct ethnic group except in Belize, it is difficult to state how many there may be today. Estimates vary from 200,000 to 500,000; high fertility rates and the absorption into their communities of many other Blacks in the Americas helped boost their population over the last 200 years.

History and Cultural Relations

Archaeologists have still not been able to sort out with precision the cultural history of the various Caribbean groups, except to note that all of them apparently derived from the tropical forests of South America, coming into the Caribbean in at least three waves, dating from about 5000 B.C. to about A.D. 1400. At the time of Columbus, the ancestors of the Garifuna occupied most of the habitable islands of the Lesser Antilles, but by the eighteenth century they were primarily found on Saint Vincent, Dominica, Saint Lucia, and Grenada. For Europeans, the term "Carib" became synonymous with "cannibal," and allega-

tions about such activities formed the justification for killing or enslaving them in the fifteenth and sixteenth centuries. Once agricultural plantations had been established by the various Europeans, Africans were brought in large numbers as laborers. On Saint Vincent, from the time of the first major British occupation in 1763, the Garifuna sided with the previously resident French colonists in a protracted conflict that ultimately ended in defeat for both of them. In 1797 those with the darkest skin color, (termed "Black Carib") mostly resident on Saint Vincent, were forcibly removed from that island and sent to Spanish Honduras. Many of the lighter-skinned individuals remained in the islands; most were absorbed into the local Creole populations. In Central America the Garifuna joined the Spaniards and at first fought against, but later temporarily joined, the Miskito Indians, who were firmly aligned with the British in opposition to the dominant Spanish colonization. They were quick to adopt whatever innovations they admired in other groups, so that today their culture is a new synthesis, unlike any of its immediate forbears.

Settlements

In aboriginal and early contact times, settlements were on the windward sides of the various islands, whereas gardens were inland on more fertile soil. The earliest houses were circular, and each was inhabited by a woman, her unmarried daughters, and her small sons. Teenage boys and men spent most of their time in centrally located communal houses, where they ate; slept; debated political decisions; made and repaired weapons, tools and utensils; and entertained guests. In Central America they have repeated this settlement pattern, except that they have favored locations close to European settlements and enterprises in which the men could find wage labor and the women could sell their agricultural produce. Today they live in some sixty settlements on the coastline between Gracias a Dios in Nicaragua and Dangriga, Belize. Some of these still harbor only Garifuna, but others are multiethnic towns and cities. In the United States the Garifuna do not necessarily cluster in the same city neighborhoods, although they remain in close contact with their fellows, especially Garifuna coming from the same country.

Economy

SUBSISTENCE AND COMMERCIAL ACTIVITIES. The Island Carib were fishers, hunters of small land animals, collectors of shellfish, and horticulturists; both sexes participated equally in

Garifuna women have long enjoyed considerable independence of word and action. They are, in general, as well or better educated than the men.

See also
Dominicans, Trinidadians and Tobagonians

539

food production. Only men engaged in offshore fishing and hunting, whereas the women were largely in charge of the fields after the initial clearing. Bitter manioc was the primary staple, of which the Garifuna made a flat, unleavened bread that, when properly stored, would keep for weeks and could be carried on the long sea voyages the men frequently made to other islands and to the South American mainland. Trading and raiding were important activities that often kept the men away for long periods of time. After the arrival of Europeans, the Carib began to trade with them and to sell their labor. They also turned increasingly to plantation agriculture of commercial crops, such as cotton, and, by the time they were deported from Saint Vincent, they seemed well on their way to dependence upon a cash economy. In Central America they were at first in great demand as mercenary soldiers for both the Royalists and the revolutionary Creole forces. They also worked in the mahogany camps in Belize, Honduras, and Nicaragua, both before and after independence in those areas.

After 1900, when the fruit industry had become the major employer along the coast, they worked as stevedores and in various semiskilled occupations in the major banana ports. During World War II many men worked in the U.S. merchant marine, which led them to seek continued employment in this sector later. This started what has become a migratory stream, with some individuals returning periodically to their home villages until final retirement there and others settling permanently in the United States. The second generation has produced many teachers, physicians, and engineers—professions they follow both in the United States and in their home countries. The largest part of the population, however, remains in the underemployed working-class sector. Women joined the men as migrants during the 1960s, most working as seamstresses, factory workers, or domestics in the large cities of the United States and Central America. The village economies have been bolstered by the remittances sent home to relatives, but little capital has been invested there. Many communities are largely made up of older folk and young children living on irregular and inadequate checks sent by the absent intervening generation.

INDUSTRIAL ARTS.   Aboriginal craft products included baskets, cotton cloth, sleeping mats, pottery, and a variety of wooden utensils, including graters for manioc, drums, and dugout canoes. All of these have survived in Central America except pottery, which was replaced by European earthenware and porcelain, probably during the eighteenth century in Saint Vincent. Most of the crafts have been forgotten today, and only a handful of persons in the more remote villages still manufacture the other items.

TRADE.   Although most scholars believe the Carib engaged in extensive trade in aboriginal times, it is not clear what products they exchanged. During the eighteenth century they were known among European residents in the Caribbean for their silk-grass woven bags, baskets, tobacco, fruits and vegetables, and various forest products. In Central America the women regularly appeared in town markets with superior agricultural produce, and the men sold fish, both fresh and dried. Their reputation as smugglers of arms, liquor, bullion, and consumer goods has survived to the present day.

DIVISION OF LABOR.   Women in aboriginal times were the primary farmers, dependent upon the men only for clearing the land. Women also caught land crabs and other shellfish, cared for pigs and chickens (known only after the arrival of Europeans), prepared the food, cared for the children, and wove cotton cloth and fiber mats on hanging looms. Men fished and hunted, made canoes, and engaged in trading and raiding excursions. They were also largely in charge of the ceremonial life, including public ritual and curing. After the middle of the twentieth century, women left behind while the men migrated took on more and more of the men's responsibilities. Today they are dominant in religious and curing rituals and ceremonies. Women have long enjoyed considerable independence of word and action. They are, in general, as well or better educated than the men and have begun to enter political life and some of the professions in their countries of origin.

LAND TENURE.   Because their agriculture was largely of a shifting nature, land tenure has not been a major issue for the Island Carib or the Garifuna. So long as there was sufficient land and a small population, tenure was determined by "first come." The very concept of landownership was problematic for them aboriginally, which no doubt worked against them in making treaties with the Europeans. Not until the twentieth century did land scarcity become an issue in Central America, and by then most of the Garifuna were adapted to an economy supported by male wage labor.

Kinship

KIN GROUPS AND DESCENT.   Both kinship terminology and early accounts suggest the former existence of a matrilineally oriented system, but it is not clear whether there were clans or sibs. Early European contacts seem to have altered the aboriginal system. Today they have informal nonunilineal kin associations, active primarily in religious activities and in mutual aid for domestic purposes.

KINSHIP TERMINOLOGY. Modern usage is Hawaiian when using the native language, but the Eskimo system of their neighbors is more prevalent.

Marriage and Family

MARRIAGE. The Island Carib may have preferred marriage between cross cousins, and men of higher rank were polygynous. Chiefs excepted, residence was uxorilocal. Today marriage is informal and brittle. Women commonly bear children before a permanent union is established, with or without a legal or religious ceremony. In both aboriginal and modern times, male travelers frequently had wives in more than one location.

DOMESTIC UNIT. What has been called the matrifocal household has been typical since at least the 1940s. This formerly was extended through at least three generations of women, but since the 1970s, probably owing to the massive emigration of both men and women, has often been reduced to a grandmother and her grandchildren under the age of puberty. Among more highly educated and affluent Garifuna, monogamy and the nuclear family are highly valued.

INHERITANCE. Modern Garifuna tend to dispose of their private movable property in the form of gifts to favored persons if and when they feel death is imminent. They favor children or grandchildren who have remained at home to care for them or who have sent back larger sums of money. To control the behavior of their descendants, older people commonly threaten to withhold an inheritance or to dispose of all their property before death.

SOCIALIZATION. Boys are raised permissively until early manhood, when they are suddenly shoved out of the maternal fold and expected to earn their own living as well as to support their mothers and sisters. Girls are required to "grow up" more quickly—to work at domestic tasks at an early age—and are more severly reprimanded when they transgress. In the absence of the men, women seem to have more difficulty disciplining their sons.

Religion and Expressive Culture

RELIGIOUS BELIEFS. Both Island Carib and modern Garifuna believe that human affairs are governed by a higher god, but also by the spirits of their deceased ancestors, whom they both love and fear. Since the nineteenth century, most

---

SOCIOPOLITICAL ORGANIZATION

Political Organization

Prior to contact with Europeans, there may have been incipient chiefdoms. Leaders were men who excelled in warfare or in supernatural affairs—the older ones usually having greater prestige. In European-colonized Saint Vincent and Central America, these leaders were endowed with greater derivative authority than they may have had aboriginally. Presently, the Garifuna engage in political action within their own countries but do not yet vote as an ethnic block. Few have achieved either elective or appointive office at any level, but recent revitalization efforts may change this.

Social Control

Persons who act in socially deviant ways may be subjected to public criticism, frequently in song or proverb. More serious infringements may be referred to the ancestors in religious rituals. The ancestors, when they assume human form by possessing a descendant, may loudly chastise the culprit and even call him or her to a face-to-face confrontation. Witchcraft, which is most often directed toward outsiders, is a force to be feared.

Conflict

The Island Carib were in an almost constant state of war against each other, against Arawakan groups in the Greater Antilles, and, later, against Africans and Europeans. After deportation to Central America, they hired themselves out as mercenaries and also engaged in isolated conflicts with Miskito Indians. Since the middle of the nineteenth century, however, they have largely eschewed violence in both their public and private lives.

have also been Roman Catholic. In addition to the ancestors, the shamans call upon "spirit helpers," who assist them in curing and locating lost objects. There may have been a belief in nature spirits in previous times, but today these have been replaced by a faith in Catholic saints and angels.

RELIGIOUS PRACTITIONERS. Called *buwiyes*, shamans are born to their calling, receiving training through dreams and apprenticeships. A very few have become Roman Catholic priests and nuns.

CEREMONIES. In addition to the usual Catholic rites, Garifuna have included some prayers and other rituals in their ceremonies in honor of their ancestors. They also sacrifice pigs and roosters, dance, sing, beat drums, and ritually drink alcohol in an effort to get the ancestors to pay attention to them and to assist them in their human trials and tribulations. Several other ritual occasions are celebrated during the year, but these are all taken from either the Catholic calendar or British secular observances. "John Canoe" is an important dance performance during Christmas and the New Year.

ARTS. Dancing and singing are the primary means of artistic expression, as they were aboriginally.

MEDICINE. A wide range of bush medicines is known and used by most Garifuna today, both at home and in their U.S. urban homes. They also respect and use modern Western medicine when they deem it appropriate, but when all else fails, they refer their illnesses to the ancestors, who can either save or doom them.

DEATH AND AFTERLIFE. All Garifuna anticipate a continuing interaction with their loved ones after death. They believe that if not properly propitiated, the dead ancestors can wreak great harm upon them, and they look forward to having such power in their own hands.

Bibliography

Gonzalez, Nancie L. (1988). *Sojourners of the Caribbean: Ethnogenesis and Ethnohistory of the Garifuna*. Urbana: University of Illinois Press.

Gullick, C. J. M. R. (1985). *Myths of a Minority*. Assen: Van Gorcum Press.

Kerns, Virginia (1983). *Women and the Ancestors: Black Carib Kinship and Ritual*. Urbana: University of Illinois Press.

Whitehead, Neil L. (1988). *Lords of the Tiger Spirit*. Leiden: Foris Publications Holland.

—NANCIE L. GONZALEZ

HAITIANS

Ethnym: Ayisyens, Haïtiens, Haytians

Orientation

IDENTIFICATION. The Republic of Haiti is the second-oldest independent nation in the Western Hemisphere, and it is the only one with a French-Creole background and an overwhelmingly African culture. large communities of Haitians exist outside Haiti, especially in the Dominican Republic, on other Caribbean islands, in Central America and northern South America, and in North America. The second-largest Haitian community, after Port-au-Prince, the Haitian capital, is in New York City, with about 500,000 members.

LOCATION. Occupying 27,750 square kilometers on the western third of the Caribbean island of Hispaniola, which it shares with the Dominican Republic, Haiti lies between 18° and 20° N and 72° and 74° W. It is 90 kilometers southeast of Cuba, 187 kilometers northeast of Jamaica, and about 1,000 kilometers from Florida. Its topography ranges from flat, semiarid valleys to densely forested mountains; about one-third of its area lies 200 to 500 meters above sea level, and the remaining two-thirds is covered by three mountain ranges. The highest point of elevation is La Selle Peak (2,680 meters). The mean temperature is somewhere between 24° C and 27° C; averages for the hottest and coolest months differ by perhaps 5° C, although temperature variations on any given day may be as great as 12° C. Temperature decreases three-quarters of a degree per 100 meters of elevation. Port-au-Prince, with an elevation of 40 meters, has a mean temperature of 26.3° C, but Pétionville, at 400 meters, records 24.7° C, and Kenscoff, at 1,450 meters, enjoys 18.5° C.

DEMOGRAPHY. Demographic information is at once scarce and unreliable. According to educated estimates, the total population of Haiti is about 6.5 million. Port-au-Prince has a population of about 740,000, and the second-largest city, Cap Haitien, has about 70,000 inhabitants. Regional cities that can boast populations of 10,000 to 50,000 are Les Cayes, Gonaïves, Port-de-Paix, Jacmel, Jérémie, Saint Marc, and Hinche. The single recent census for which information is generally available was conducted only in urban centers in 1971; a 10 percent sample survey was used to estimate the population in rural areas. The total population calculated from that census was 4,314,628, 79.6 percent of it rural.

LINGUISTIC AFFILIATION. The language spoken by all Haitians is usually referred to as Haitian Creole. For most of modern history, however, the official language of government, business, and education has been French. At best, only about 8 percent of the population, the educated elite, speaks French well—and then only as a second language. Another 2 to 7 percent uses French with a lesser degree of competence. Traditionally, the elite has used the requirement of fluency in French to exclude the general population from competing for positions in government and business. Haitian Creole, which has often been seen as a nonlanguage in which sophisticated thoughts cannot be expressed or, at best, as a poor imitation of French, is coming into its own, and the prestige of French is rapidly declining in Haiti. In the early 1990s both Creole and French were the country's official languages.

History

At the time of European contact, anywhere from 60,000 to 4 million Indians inhabited the island of Hispaniola. The indigenous population rapidly succumbed to the ravages of disease, slavery, and brutality, and the Europeans soon had to look to Africa for the labor they needed to work their plantations. In the colonial period (1492–1804) sugarcane plantations were established and slavery instituted in Saint Domingue, as the French called their territory on Hispaniola.

A series of minor uprisings culminated in the slave revolt of August 1791. By 1796, White supremacy was at an end, and within the framework of the French Republic, Black rule was established under the leadership of a former slave, the charismatic Toussain Louverture. In 1800 Napolian sent 28,000 troops under his brother-in-law, Gen. Charles Leclerc, to retake the colony and re-enslave the Blacks. By 1803, however, Haitians had defeated Napoleon's troops, and on 1 January 1804 Jean-Jacques Dessalines, Toussain's successor, proclaimed the independence of Haiti.

In the postindependence period (1820–1915) Haiti became a focal point of debates about the effect of emancipation and the capacity of Blacks for self-government. Many slave insurrections in the southern United States were consciously modeled after the Haitian example.

The U.S. military occupied Haiti from 1915 to 1934 for pressing economic and strategic reasons. The major, though certainly unintended, results of the occupation were the increasing Black consciousness of the elite, the suppression of peasant movements, the training of the army, and the con-

centration of sociopolitical power in Port-au-Prince.

The postoccupation period (1934–1957) was characterized by a succession of undistinguished administrations, with one notable exception: the government led by President Dumarsais Estimé (1946–1950), which many view as a highly progressive era in Haitian politics that probably spelled the end of mulatto political domination. Important developments during his presidency were the entrance of Blacks into the civil service, increased pride in the African heritage, greater interaction with other Caribbean nations, the beginning of peasant integration into the national polity, and, especially, the rise of the new Black middle class.

François "Papa Doc" Duvalier, president from 1957 to 1971, established his power base largely among this middle class. Duvalier carried out a brutal campaign of oppression against his opponents, and Haiti was increasingly isolated from the international community. When Duvalier's 19-year-old son, Jean-Claude ("Baby Doc"), became president in 1971, a new economic program guided by the U.S. government was put in place; U.S. private investment was wooed with such incentives as no customs taxes, a minimum wage kept very low, the suppression of labor unions, and

WOMAN'S WORK

A Haitian woman carries a steel bucket on her head in Port-au-Prince, Haiti. (Owen Franken/Corbis)

See also

Dominicans

the right of U.S. companies to repatriate their profits.

With little gain from fourteen years of rule by a second Duvalier, Haitians finally reached the end of their patience and overwhelming public protests led to the ouster of Jean-Claude on 7 February 1986. An interim government, the Conseil National de Gouvernement (CNG) headed by Lieut. Gen. Henri Namphy, took charge. Elections for president and for seats in the national assembly, set for 29 November 1987, were aborted by army-sponsored violence. In January 1988 the CNG held sham elections and announced that Leslie Manigat had won the presidency. About four months later, Manigat's attempt to play off one segment of the army against another led to his own ouster, and Namphy declared himself president. On 17 September 1988 Namphy was forced out of the National Palace and leadership was handed over to Lieut. Gen. Prosper Avril. Jean-Bertrand Aristide of the National Front for Change and Democracy (FNCD) was elected president on 16 December 1990 and assumed office on 7 February 1991 but was deposed on 30 September 1991. The military ousted him a little more than seven months later, but no state (except the Vatican) recognized the military government. After considerable vacillation, the administration of U.S. president Bill Clinton forced the military leaders to leave Haiti, and in October 1994 Aristide was reinstated under heavy U.S. military sponsorship. President Rene Garcia Preval was elected on December 17, 1995.

Settlements

With 75 to 85 percent of the population living in a rural setting, the majority of Haitians can be classified as peasants: they live in dispersed villages loosely connected by trade routes. Scattered within these villages are huts of wattle and daub surrounded by gardens, fields, and out-buildings. Regional centers once had considerable cultural and commercial importance, but since the first U.S. occupation, Port-au-Prince has become disproportionately dominant.

Economy

SUBSISTENCE AND COMMERCIAL ACTIVITIES. About 65 percent of the labor force are small landowners engaged in agriculture (one of the highest proportions of peasants in any country); only about 7 percent are in manufacturing. One percent of workers are involved in construction and 27 percent in other sectors. Agriculture is precarious because the countryside is 95 percent deforested, and 25 percent of the soil is undergo-

ing rapid erosion. Haiti's primary products are coffee, sugar, rice, and cocoa. Its light manufacturing enterprises produce shoes, soap, flour, cement, and domestic oils. Its export industries produce garments, toys, baseballs, and electronic goods for the U.S. market. Despite this small-scale industrialization, the annual per capita income is estimated at $380. The current instability of the government is having deleterious effects on the national economy.

INDUSTRIAL ARTS. Many people engage in part-time craft work, particularly in the manufacture of wood utensils, tools, and furniture. Formerly, many of these items were destined for the tourist trade.

TRADE. Most commercial exchange is carried out in open-air markets. The market women are justly famous both for carrying heavy loads of merchandise and for bargaining with great skill. Haiti's economy is closely tied to that of the United States; a sizable portion of its exports go to North America, and it is dependent on governmental and nongovernmental U.S. aid.

DIVISION OF LABOR. In rural areas, men generally handle agricultural production, and women take charge of the produce. The women depend on the men to provide a product to sell, and the men depend on the women for domestic labor.

LAND TENURE. A crucial problem facing the newly independent Haiti was access to land. Having failed in its attempt to reinstate the plantation system of colonial Saint Domingue, the government distributed much of the land among the former slaves. Currently, from 60 to 80 percent of the farmers own their own land, although few have clear title, and the plots are fragmented and small. Fairly large plantations do exist but not nearly to the same extent as in Latin American countries. The state owns land, but the government has rarely shown a sustained interest in agriculture.

Kinship, Marriage, and Family

MARRIAGE. The plantation system and the institution of slavery had a profound influence on domestic entities. Additionally, the laws of the early republic reinforced the tendency of the rural population to avoid legal and church marriages. The most recognizable kinship pattern in rural Haiti is the somewhat patrilineal extended family living in a cluster of households linked through legal, ritual, consanguineal, and affinal ties and headed by the oldest male member.

In addition to conventional church weddings, long-term monogamous unions, and neolocal nuclear-family households, there are socially accepted unions without formal sanction, couples who do not coreside, fathers who do not participate actively in rearing their children, and households without a nuclear family at their core.

In writing about Haiti, anthropologists often avoid the word "family"; instead they use "household," which embraces the wide range of relatives—direct and collateral, on the sides of both parents—that the Haitian "family" typically includes.

INHERITANCE. The complexity of the domestic unit and the varieties of household types do create inheritance problems. In general, all children from all the varieties of conjugal unions have equal rights of inheritance, but, in practice, residents, contacts, and personal feelings are important determinants of who inherits.

SOCIALIZATION. Because both adults and children may change residential affiliation with relative ease and frequency and enjoy a variety of temporary residential rights, children often come into contact with a relatively large number of adults who may discipline and train them. In general, a great deal of emphasis is placed on respect for adults, and adults are quick to use corporal punishment to ensure that they receive it. Fewer than half of the rural children attend school, and only about 20 percent of those complete the primary grades.

Sociopolitical Organization

In 1995 Haiti was in the process of reestablishing its political and social institutions under a democratic administration. Agreements with the U.S. government and international finance agencies had created a difficult set of parameters within which a move toward more social equality and justice was being attempted.

SOCIAL ORGANIZATION. One result of the land reform in the early 1800 was that the largely mulatto elite fled to the cities and, with no land of their own, made their living from taxing peasant markets and the nation's imports and exports. This elite also practiced the religion of the slave owners, Roman Catholicism. Driven by fear of a renewed French occupation, the bulk of the population retreated into the mountainous interior, inside a ring of magnificent forts. What emerged from these displacements was a nation with a very small European-oriented, Roman Catholic, mulatto elite residing in several coastal urban centers and a large, scattered Black population that farmed the interior and worshiped in the ancient African manner.

POLITICAL ORGANIZATION. The largely Black peasantry has always regarded the government as having little relevance to their lives. Haiti's regional political units, called *départements*, are further divided into several *arrondissements*, each with an administrative center. Arrondissements consist of several *communes*, which usually coincide with church parishes. Each commune is divided into *sections rurales*, each of which is headed by an appointed *chef de section*, who reports to the *commandant* of the commune, who in turn reports to the *préfet* of the arrondissement. The limited contact rural Haitians normally have with the government is, for the most part, with the chef de section.

SOCIAL CONTROL. Criminality is rare, and, for the most part, the rural population, in deference to village elders, polices itself. The urban areas have police and courts, mainly modeled after the French system.

CONFLICT. Governments in Haiti have been run primarily by members of the elite, and despite the early and heroic independence of Haiti from France and the elimination of slavery, the attitude of the elite classes of Haiti has traditionally been a neocolonial one. Nativism, negritude, and the increasing use of Creole have made all Haitians more aware of their Haitianness, but tensions exist between the affluent city dwellers and the poor peasants and shantytown residents. Aside from a very small but moderately influential group of Middle Eastern merchants, the population of Haiti is exceptionally homogeneous, both culturally and linguistically.

Religion and Expressive Culture

RELIGIOUS BELIEFS. Although the majority of the population is nominally Roman Catholic and although Protestant missionaries have won a number of converts in the poorer rural areas, the religion of Haiti is still Vodun, an ancient religion that focuses on contacting and appeasing ancestral spirits (*lwa*), which include both distant, stereotyped ancestors and more immediate relatives, such as dead parents and grandparents.

RELIGIOUS PRACTITIONERS. Vodun is a particularly egalitarian religion; both men and women serve as priests (*ougan-yo* and *manbo-yo*, respectively; sing. *ougan* and *manbo*).

CEREMONIES. As many of its rituals are performed in the context of sickness and death, Vodun is primarily a system of folk medicine that attributes illnesses to angry ancestors; it consists of appeasement ceremonies, including divination

The largely Black Haitian peasantry has always regarded the government as having little relevance to their lives.

rites, which are used to find the cause of illnesses; healing rites, in which a Vodun priest interacts directly with sick people to cure them; propitiatory rites, in which food and drink are offered to specific spirits to make them stop their aggression; and preventive rites, in which ancestors are offered sacrifices to help head off any possible future trouble.

ARTS. In the 1940s Haiti burst into the consciousness of the art world with an astonishing display of paintings, and its artists received worldwide attention for their so-called primitive or naive art. In 1944 the Centre d'Art was founded in Port-au-Prince.

Haiti is also renowned for its literature, despite its high rate of illiteracy (85 percent). Major themes include concepts of negritude, which foreshadowed the Black Power and post-World War II anticolonial movements, and Vodun. The most famous novel in Haitian Creole, Franketinne's *Dézafi*, is about the revolt of a colony of zombies.

MEDICINE. Although Western medicine has been available to the urban elite since the early 1960s, there were only 887 physicians in Haiti in 1988 (Wilke 1993, Table 804). In the rural areas, curing depends on a rich body of folk knowledge that includes herbal medicine and Vodun. The peasants nevertheless suffer from malnutrition and many diseases. Measles, diarrhea, and tetanus kill many children, and the daily per capita caloric intake for 1988 has been estimated at 2,011 (Wilke 1993, Table 824). Only about 38 percent of the population has access to potable water. Tuberculosis is the most devastating disease, followed closely by dysentery, influenza, malaria, measles, tetanus, and whooping cough. Eye problems are endemic in Haiti; the chief causes of blindness are cataracts, glaucoma, pterygium (a growth over the cornea), and scarring of the cornea.

Bibliography

Courlander, Harold (1960). *The Drum and the Hoe: Life and Lore of the Haitian People.* Berkeley and Los Angeles: University of California Press.

Ferguson, James (1987). *Papa Doc, Baby Doc: Haiti and the Duvaliers.* Oxford: Basil Blackwell.

Laguerre, Michel S. (1982a). *The Complete Haitiana: A Bibliographic Guide to the Scholarly Literature, 1900–1980.* 2 vols. Millwood, N.Y.: Kraus.

Laguerre, Michel S. (1982b). *Urban Life in the Caribbean: A Study of a Haitian Urban Community.* Cambridge, Mass.: Schenkman.

Laguerre, Michel S. (1993). *The Military and Society in Haiti.* Knoxville: University of Tennessee Press.

Lawless, Robert (1986). "Haitian Migrants and Haitian-Americans: From Invisibility into the Spotlight." *Journal of Ethnic Studies* 14(2): 29–70.

Lawless, Robert (1988). "Creole Speaks, Creole Understands." *The World and I* 3(1): 474–483; 3(2): 510–521.

Mintz, Sidney W. (1995). "Can Haiti Change?" *Foreign Affairs* 74:73–86.

Nicholls, David (1979). *From Dessalines to Duvalier: Race, Colour, and National Independence in Haiti.* Cambridge: Cambridge University Press.

Weinstein, Brian, and Aaron Segal (1984). *Haiti: Political Failures, Cultural Successes.* New York: Praeger.

Wilkie, James, ed. (1993). *Statistical Abstract of Latin America.* Vol. 30, Part 1. Los Angeles: UCLA.

—ROBERT LAWLESS

JAMAICANS

Ethnym: none

Orientation

IDENTIFICATION. The name of the island of Jamaica is derived from the Arawak word "Xaymaca," which may have meant "land of springs," "land of wood and water," or "land of cotton."

LOCATION. Jamaica is located in the Greater Antilles group of the West Indies, 144 kilometers south of Cuba and 160 kilometers west of Haiti. It has an area of 11,034 square kilometers and is the third-largest island in the Caribbean. The interior is very hilly and mountainous, with deep valleys and 120 unnavigable rivers, and the coastal plain is flat and narrow. The climate is generally hot and humid (tropical) but cooler and more temperate in the highlands.

DEMOGRAPHY. The population was 2,506,701 in July 1992, with an average annual growth rate of 0.09 percent and a density of 228 people per square kilometer. The ethnic composition of Jamaica is 76.3 percent Black, 15.1 percent Afro-European, 3.2 percent White, 3 percent East Indian and Afro-East Indian, 1.2 percent Chinese and Afro-Chinese, and 1.2 percent other. Approximately 22,000 Jamaicans emigrate every year, and roughly a million now live in the United States, Canada, and Great Britain.

LINGUISTIC AFFILIATION. Jamaica is officially English speaking, but it actually has what linguists call a postcreole linguistic continuum. An indigenous language, referred to as "patois" by Jamaicans and "Jamaican Creole" by linguists, evolved from contact between African slaves and

♦ **creole**
A general, inconsistently used term usually applied to a spoken language or dialect that is based on grammatical and lexical features combined from two or more natural languages. It is a first language, distinct from a pidgin.

English planters. Jamaican speech varies, by class, from Creole to Standard English, with many intermediate grades of variation.

History and Cultural Relations

About 60,000 Arawak Indians were living in Jamaica when Columbus landed in 1494, but they were exterminated by disease and enslavement during the Spanish occupation, which lasted from 1509 to 1655, when the island was seized by Great Britain. The British tried to populate the island with convicts and indentured servants from England, Scotland, and Ireland; they also persuaded buccaneers like Henry Morgan to establish their base at Port Royal, which became the center of trade for loot captured in raids on Spanish ships. Yeoman farming, with cocoa as the principal crop, soon gave way to cattle ranching and sugar, coffee, cotton, and pimento (allspice) estates and plantations. About 750,000 Africans were brought in to work the estates, but resistance to slavery was strong, and the society was in an almost constant state of revolt; a permanent population of runaway slaves (Maroons) established communities in the mountains. Production of sugar cane, the principal crop, peaked in the mid-eighteenth century, when Jamaica was regarded as England's richest and most valuable colony, but it began to fall in 1774. The declining economy and an increasingly influential antislavery movement in England led to the abolition of the slave trade by an act of parliament in 1807. A serious slave revolt, the "Baptist War" of 1831, and shocking reprisals against missionaries for their alleged involvement in it, encouraged passage of an emancipation act in 1833, but full freedom did not come until 1838, after a period of "apprenticeship." Many of the freed slaves left the estates, moving to the towns or becoming small farmers, and indentured servants from India (and later China) were brought in to replace them. After 1866, some abandoned sugar estates were turned over to the production of bananas, which rapidly replaced sugar as the leading export. The process of decolonization was set in motion by serious and widespread labor disturbances in 1938 that inspired nationalistic sentiments and led to the formation of the island's first trade union and political party. Large deposits of bauxite ore (the basis for aluminum) were discovered in the 1940s, and by 1960 Jamaica had become the world's leading producer of bauxite and aluminum. Many factories were built in the 1950s, and the value of manufacturing reached that of agriculture by 1960. The tourist industry also began to grow at a tremendous rate in the 1950s. Jamaica received its independence in 1962.

The island was a British colony for over 300 years, and many of its institutions (particularly legal, governmental, and educational) and ideals (for example, monogamy and the patriarchal nuclear family) are essentially English. Jamaican society was initially "pluralistic," embracing the African cultures of the slave majority and the English culture of their masters, but "creolization"—the gradual reshaping of English traditions by African traditions, and vice-versa—led to the emergence of a syncretic, indigenous culture. The African influence is particularly evident in language, cuisine, folklore, folk medicine, religion, and the arts, but rarely does it survive in true form.

Settlements

Urban centers are growing rapidly as a result of migration from rural areas. About 40 percent of the population is in the Kingston-Spanish Town conurbation in the southeast, where most of the factories are located. Another 15 percent live in forty-eight small towns, and the remaining 45 percent live in over one thousand rural settlements. Sugar estates are located in low-lying areas, generally along the coast. Bauxite mining and alumina processing are concentrated in the center of the island. The tourist industry is situated largely along the north coast, from Negril in the west to Port Antonio in the east. Small farms are dispersed throughout the rugged interior.

Economy

SUBSISTENCE AND COMMERCIAL ACTIVITIES. The gross domestic product was U.S. $1,400 per capita in 1991, up from $960 in 1987. The economy grew rapidly in the 1960s, declined steadily from 1973 to 1980, and recovered slowly in the 1980s. Sugar was the main industry until the slaves were emancipated, whereupon a peasantry and a dual economy came into being. Small farmers produce a variety of crops, such as yams and sweet potatoes, for local consumption. Bananas replaced sugar as the main export at the beginning of the twentieth century, but the peak production level attained in 1937 has never been surpassed. The primary cash crop today is marijuana (ganja), which is largely exported to the United States and had an estimated value of U.S. $3.5 billion in 1984. Marijuana cultivation is illegal (as is its use), but the economy is very dependent on it. The most valuable sector of the formal economy is bauxite mining and alumina processing. Light manufacturing

Jamaica is still highly stratified by wealth; it has a very small, prosperous upper class, a small middle class, and a huge, impoverished lower class.

See also
English

grew rapidly in the 1960s, and in 1984 there were 1,202 small factories (768 of them in the Kingston metropolitan area). The number of tourists fell sharply in the 1970s but rebounded in the 1980s; the island had over a million visitors in 1987. There was a marked decline in the number of tourists and in the rate of economic growth in 1991, as a result of the recession in the United States.

INDUSTRIAL ARTS.   Owing to its long history of plantation monoculture, the island has developed few industrial crafts, with the notable exception of basket making. Industrialization has been hampered by a shortage of skilled workers, due in part to emigration.

TRADE.   There are many small shops in the countryside and a few large grocery and department stores in urban areas. Agricultural products are distributed largely through a system created by slaves; about 20,000 higgler women buy produce from small farmers and sell it at some ninety marketplaces. The economy has always been export oriented and dependent on a few basic commodities. Guided by the philosophy of Mercantilism, the British developed the island for sugar production and as a market for their industrial exports. Jamaica was an important part of the infamous "triangular trade," which brought firearms and manufactured goods from Europe to Africa, slaves from Africa to the Caribbean, and sugar from the Caribbean to Europe. England was Jamaica's main trading partner until the development of the bauxite industry in the 1950s, when the focus of trade shifted to the United States.

DIVISION OF LABOR.   In 1989, 22.5 percent of the labor force was employed in agriculture, 41 percent in the service sector, and 19 percent in industry. The unemployment rate was high, at 17.5 percent, and highest among 20- to 24-year-olds. The proportion of women in the labor force is about 46 percent, one of the highest in the world; women work mainly in the service sector, as higglers, domestics, teachers, and office workers.

LAND TENURE.   Slave plantations were generally located in flat and fertile areas, such as valleys and the coastal plains. The hilly and less fertile interior was sparsely inhabited until Emancipation; seeking land as a symbol of freedom, former slaves settled there and became peasant farmers. These historical patterns still prevail to some extent. There are about 1,000 farms of over 40 hectares and 151,000 of under 2 hectares. Large farms occupy the best land and produce a single crop, principally for export. Small farms are generally located in hilly areas and produce a variety of crops, mostly for the domestic market. Ownership of land is greatly preferred to renting; some land is held in common by kindreds. All heirs to this "family land" have an equal right to live on and use a portion of it but cannot alienate it. Family land is an important symbol of security and family unity; it usually has little or no agricultural value, but kin are often buried on it.

Kinship

KIN GROUPS AND DESCENT.   There are no corporate kin groups, but kindreds are very important. Jamaicans maintain strong ties with consanguines that include regular exchanges of gifts such as produce. Descent is bilateral, although matrilateral ties are often stronger than patrilateral ones.

KINSHIP TERMINOLOGY.   Jamaicans have an Eskimo system, using basically the same kin terms as the English and the Americans, but they emphasize consanguines and often ignore affinal or conjugal relationships.

Sociopolitical Organization

SOCIAL ORGANIZATION.   Slave society was stratified into three castes: a small number of Whites, a smaller number of "free people of color" (generally mulattoes), and a huge Black slave population. White-minority rule led to the development of a "white bias": European phenotypic and cultural traits were more highly valued than their African or Creole counterparts. With Emancipation, the castes were transformed into classes, but the White bias persisted, resulting in a "color-class pyramid": a White upper class, a "Brown" middle class, and a Black lower-class majority. The addition of Chinese, East Indian, and Lebanese immigrants, who did not have a clear place in the color-class pyramid, made stratification more complex. Color and ethnicity still influence social interactions, but the White bias and the color-class pyramid have become less evident since the mid-twentieth century. Nevertheless, Jamaica is still highly stratified by wealth; it has a very small, prosperous upper class, a small middle class, and a huge, impoverished lower class. In the mid-1960s Jamaica had the highest rate of income inequality in the world.

POLITICAL ORGANIZATION.   Jamaica was ruled by a governor appointed by the Crown and an elected House of Assembly until the peasant uprising at Morant Bay in 1865. This event ignited fear among the White oligarchy that democracy would lead to Black rule; so the British abolished the assembly in 1866 and imposed a Crown Colony government, run by the governor and an imperial bureaucracy. Democracy was not restored until 1944, when an elected House of Representatives was created by a new constitu-

MARRIAGE AND FAMILY

Marriage

Legal marriage, monogamy, and the nuclear family are cultural ideals more often attained by the middle and upper classes than by the lower classes. Sexual relations generally begins during early adolescence among the lower-class majority. Extraresidential or "visiting" relationships are usually followed by several coresidential and neolocal "common-law" or consensual unions. Legal marriage occurs relatively late, after the birth of several children and the attainment of some degree of economic security. Marriage is monogamous; divorce is rare but extramarital relationships are common.

Domestic Unit

The composition of Jamaican households varies greatly. Matrifocal units are common, particularly in urban areas. Nuclear families are the norm among the middle and upper classes. Lower-class households often include children of previous relationships, children of poorer relatives, informally adopted children, and children of daughters who have migrated to urban areas or abroad.

Inheritance

Children generally receive equal shares of their parents' property, which, in the case of land, may be held in common.

Socialization

Men are affectionate toward children but are not usually involved in child care. Child rearing is the mother's responsibility, but it is often delegated to an older sister or, increasingly, to the maternal grandmother. Respect and obedience are very important to parents, who threaten or physically punish children when they are "rude." Girls and, to a lesser extent, boys are given many household chores. The emotional bond between a mother and her children, particularly her sons, is very strong and enduring.

tion, and full internal self-government was granted in 1957. Jamaica joined the short-lived Federation of the West Indies in 1959 but left it in 1961; the following year Jamaica became an independent nation in the British Commonwealth. The present system of government is a constitutional monarchy with two houses of Parliament. The ceremonial head of state is the governor-general, who is appointed by and represents the British monarch. The sixty members of the House of Representatives are elected for a term of five years—or less, if an early election is called. The leader of the majority party in the House becomes prime minister and selects a cabinet. The twenty-one members of the Senate are appointed by the governor-general on the advice of the prime minister and the leader of the opposition. The two major political parties are the People's National Party (PNP) and the Jamaican Labour Party (JLP). The National Workers Union (NWU) is affiliated with the PNP, and the Bustamante Industrial Trade Union (BITU) is affiliated with the JLP, giving each party a solid core of supporters. Jamaicans are fervently partisan and strongly identify with political leaders, but the political system is remarkably stable. Party support is not clearly related to racial, ethnic, class, or regional divisions; both the PNP and the JLP have gov-

erned at various times since the 1940s. Michael Manley, the leader of the PNP, succeeded Edward Seaga, the leader of the JLP, as prime minister after the 1989 elections. Percival J. Patterson became prime minister on 30 March 1992, and his PNP won a 52-to-8 majority in the lower house of Parliament in the March 1993 election. The PNP and the JLP agree that a president should replace the British Crown as constitutional head of state but disagree as to the precise role and scope of the presidency.

SOCIAL CONTROL. Ostracism, gossip, derision, and sorcery are the main sanctions in rural communities, where crime (with the exception of theft of crops) is relatively infrequent. In urban areas, however, crime has become a very serious problem. A rapidly escalating rate of violent attacks with firearms led to the passage, in 1974, of legislation providing severe penalties for gun offenders and creating a special Gun Court. The main function of the army (the Jamaica Defense Force) has been to augment the police (the Jamaica Constabulary Force), particularly in efforts to control unrest and suppress the drug trade.

CONFLICT. Jamaica has a history of organized violence, including many slave revolts, some peasant uprisings, and labor and urban unrest. Individual acts of violence were at one time relatively

Jamaica is a profoundly religious society, with a wide range of cults, sects, denominations, and movements.

uncommon; the recent increase in urban violence can largely be attributed to the gangs that protect ghetto neighborhoods and control the drug trade. During the 1970s, gangs also supported politicians and political parties. Over 700 people died in politically related violence during the election of 1980, but there were few fatalities in the 1989 election. The 1993 election was also marred by violence.

Religion and Expressive Culture

RELIGIOUS BELIEFS. Jamaica is a profoundly religious society, with a wide range of cults, sects, denominations, and movements. The religion of the slaves was based on African beliefs and practices, such as ceremonial spirit possession, spiritual healing, sorcery, and drumming and dance as forms of worship. An ancestor cult called Kumina and belief in obeah (sorcery) are living survivals of the African heritage. Missionization of slaves by Moravians, Baptists, Methodists, and Presbyterians began in 1754 and stimulated the development of syncretic, Afro-Christian cults, among them Zion Revival and Pocomania, or Pukkumina, which still exist. The Rastafarian movement, which reveres Haile Selassie as a messiah and regards marijuana as a sacrament, first appeared in 1933 but did not become widespread until the 1960s. American Pentecostalism has grown rapidly since World War II and is perhaps the most popular religion today. "Science," or "De Laurence," a form of magic based on a mail-order catalog from Chicago, developed during the same period. Jamaicans believe strongly in supernatural influence. Zion Revival incorporates such African notions as a supreme but distant creator who is generally uninvolved in human affairs and a polytheistic pantheon of angels who guide and protect people. Obeah is based on the belief that obeah men capture and use ghosts ("duppies") for malicious ends. Pentecostals seek the inspiration and power of the Holy Ghost, which protects them from Satan and demons. "Fallen angels" are said to be in league with De Laurence. Rastafarians worship Jah, a god who is within them.

RELIGIOUS PRACTITIONERS. Ministers of Christian churches are highly respected and influential. The leaders of Zion Revival cults are known as "daddies," "captains," or "mothers," and their authority is based on the "spiritual gifts" of possession, prophecy, healing, dream interpretation, and the like. Obeah men and "scientists" or "professors" are nearly always men, but many if not most traditional healers are women.

CEREMONIES. Zion Revival cults perform a circular, hyperventilative dance called "shouting" or "laboring" at feast ceremonies called "Tables,"

which resemble the "Altar" ceremonies of Pocomania cults. A meeting of Rastafarians is called a *grounation* or *nyabinghi.*

ARTS. Music and dance are very popular. Jonkonnu (or John Canoe) is a secular festival that began in the early 1700s, when masked and costumed dancers paraded in the streets during the Christmas season and gave performances at the houses of prominent citizens. Today, however, it is performed mainly on special occasions, such as the annual national Festival. Jamaica is the home of reggae music and its foremost exponent, the late Bob Marley. Jamaican contributions to literature, dance, drama, painting, and sculpture have won international recognition.

MEDICINE. Jamaican folk medicine is largely derived from African traditional medicine. Zion Revivalists operate healing centers called "balm yards" and often attribute illnesses to duppies and obeah. Balm practitioners are shamanic in that they use spiritual means to diagnose and treat illnesses, but they also use herbs ("bush"), candles, prayers, and tonics. Healing by the laying on of hands is very common in Pentecostal churches.

DEATH AND AFTERLIFE. Funerals are important events in Jamaica, and ghosts of the deceased are widely feared. The slaves believed in a good soul that went to Africa after death and a bad one that lingered as a duppy, particularly around cotton trees. A festive wake was held to pacify the deceased and render the ghost harmless, and this "set-up" or "Nine-Night" is still practiced in rural areas.

Bibliography

Hurwitz, Samuel J., and Edith F. Hurwitz (1971). *Jamaica: A Historical Portrait.* New York: Praeger.

Kaplan, Irving, et al. (1976). *Area Handbook for Jamaica.* Washington, D.C.: U.S. Government Printing Office.

Kuper, Adam (1976). *Changing Jamaica.* Boston: Routledge & Kegan Paul.

—WILLIAM WEDENOJA

KUNA

Ethonym: Cuna, Tule, Tulemala

Orientation

IDENTIFICATION. The Kuna are one of Panama's three major groups of indigenous peoples. Most of the Kuna live in the *comarca* (district) of San Blas, or Kuna Yala, along Panama's northern coast. Literally "Kuna Yala" means Kuna Land.

The comarca of San Blas is the legal name of the region, but the Congreso General Kuna has petitioned the Panamanian government to have the name of the region officially changed to Kuna Yala. "Cuna" and "Kuna" are Spanish designations; the ethnonyms "Tule" and "Tulemala" are in the Kuna language.

LOCATION. The comarca of San Blas lies along the northeastern coast of Panama. It is comprised of a long, narrow strip of mainland jungle extending 200 kilometers along the coast and 15 to 20 kilometers inland and an archipelago of 365 small islands. A single road links San Blas to the Pan-American Highway and to the rest of Panama. The road is only passable in a four-wheel drive vehicle and, as of 1985, had not been used for regular transport of people or agricultural produce. Because of road conditions, most travel in and out of the region is by plane or boat.

DEMOGRAPHY. According to the 1980 Panamanian national census, the total population of San Blas was 28,567. There are fifty-four communities ranging in size from 70 to over 2,000 inhabitants each. Forty-two of these communities are located on small islands, ten are situated on the mainland coast, and two are inland, on the riverbanks. All the inhabited islands are no farther than about 1.5 kilometers from the mainland coast and the mouth of a freshwater river. Proximity to the coast makes daily travel possible from the islands to the Kuna's agricultural field on the mainland. Freshwater mainland rivers provide an easily accessible source of water for drinking, bathing, and washing clothes.

In addition to the San Blas Kuna, or the Island Kuna, as they are called, there are Kuna who live outside the comarca. Approximately 10,000 Kuna live in Panama City and Colón, the two largest cities in Panama. Many of these individuals retain close ties with San Blas and consider the region their home. About ten other small villages, with a combined population of fewer than 2,000, are located in the Darién jungle.

LINGUISTIC AFFILIATION. Kuna, or Tule Kaya, is the primary language spoken in San Blas. Many Kuna also speak Spanish, Panama's official language. A considerable number of Kuna speak some English, especially those who have traveled internationally on trade boats in the Canal Zone. A few individuals know other languages such as French, Russian, or Chocó (spoken by the Chocó Indians who inhabit the Darién).

History and Cultural Relations

When the Spaniards arrived, the Kuna lived primarily near the Gulf of Urabá in what is today

Colombia. Contact with the Spanish, which began in the 1600s, was violent, and trade was limited. Fleeing from the Spaniards, the Kuna traveled up the jungle rivers and settled in the Darién region of what is now Panama. As early as the mid-1800s, entire Kuna villages started to relocate gradually to the sandy islands near the mouths of freshwater rivers. Moving to the islands gave the Kuna easier access to trade vessels plying coastal routes and freedom from disease-carrying insects.

When Panama became an independent nation in 1903, the new government attempted to impose by force a "national culture" on the Kuna. In 1925 the Kuna staged a rebellion (La Revolución Tule, or the Kuna Revolution), and with the backing of the U.S. government were able to negotiate a semiautonomous status for their region. In 1938 the region was officially recognized as a Kuna reserve, and their new constitution, known as *la carta orgánica de San Blas*, was approved in 1945. Legal recognition of San Blas as a territory collectively owned by the Kuna people had implications for the economic organization of the region. The carta orgánica prohibited non-Kuna from purchasing, renting, or otherwise using land within Kuna territory. This law has been used by the Kuna to try to ensure that all enterprise within the San Blas region is owned and operated by Kuna rather than by outsiders. A subsequent law (Ley 16), passed by the Panamanian government in 1953, further delineated the reserve's boundaries, as well as political and economic relations between the Kuna and the national government. Political and economic relationships between San Blas and the rest of Panama continue to be the subject of negotiation.

Settlements

Today most Kuna villages are located in four distinct areas. Most are situated in the comarca of San Blas. Three others are near the headwaters of the Río Bayano, and seven are located along the Río Chucunaque near a hydroelectric dam; all ten are in the Darién jungle. A few small communities can be found in Colombia. Kuna also live in Panama City and Colón and a few live abroad.

In San Blas, island communities are crowded; there is scant space between the houses, which are constructed of locally produced materials. The Kuna live in large matrilocal households composed of senior couples, their married daughters, grandchildren, great-grandchildren, and in-married, subordinate sons-in-law. Households usually span three or four generations. Generally, the compound includes a kitchen and one or more

The Kuna are one of Panama's three major groups of indigenous peoples.

sleeping houses. Most Kuna sleep in hammocks, which are strung from the supporting beams of the house. Clothes are draped over bamboo poles suspended from the rafters or are stored in wooden or cardboard boxes. Most houses have bamboo walls and thatched roofs, but some Kuna have built two-story cement houses with corrugated-metal roofs. These structures often house a store, in addition to providing living space.

Economy

SUBSISTENCE AND COMMERCIAL ACTIVITIES. The Kuna practice slash-and-burn agriculture and use intercropping techniques. Although plantains are now their primary subsistence crop, they also grow rice, maize, *yucca* (manioc), sugarcane, coconuts, fruits (such as mangoes, pineapples, lemons, limes, and oranges), and hot peppers. Fishing, hunting, and gathering supplement the Kunal diet. Some households keep a pig to slaughter for a special occasion.

The most common source of cash income is the export of coconuts to Colombia and *molas* (multilayered panels of cloth cut away to reveal intricate patterns and then carefully hand stitched) to the United States, Europe, and Japan. Coconuts have been exchanged with Colombian traders for goods or cash since the late 1800s. Mo-

las were commercialized in a major way starting in the 1960s. Kuna women sew mola panels into their blouses (also called molas), and sew panels and other items (e.g., small mola patches, animal pillows, pockets, purses, Christmas-tree ornaments) specifically for sale. Mola commercialization occurred concurrently with an increase in Kuna male migration in search of wage labor and a consequent decrease in subsistence-agriculture production. Lobsters and, to a lesser extent, crabs and octopuses began to be harvested for export starting in the 1960s; however, because diving for and preserving the catch require special equipment, and because only young men dive, the impact of this commercial activity has not been as widespread as that of the production of molas.

Kuna men seek wage labor opportunities especially in the Canal Zone, Panama City, Colón, and on Changuinola—a banana plantation. Outside San Blas, few job opportunities are available for Kuna women, but within the region, wage-labor opportunities are equally accessible to Kuna men and women. Such salaried government positions as those of teacher and health worker are filled by both sexes. A few positions, such as air-traffic controller, national guardsman, and agricultural-extension worker, are occupied only by men, but either men or women can be airport attendants, accountants, or store clerks within the community.

Tourism, primarily concentrated in the western third of San Blas, increased dramatically during the 1960s. Most tourists visit the region in luxury cruise ships. Some visit one of several Kuna- or foreign-owned small hotel resorts.

INDUSTRIAL ARTS. Sewing molas is the primary art form for Kuna women and for *omekits* (Kuna men who are socially defined as women). Some women have special gifts for creating and cutting mola designs and for fashioning *wini*, strings of tiny colored beads worn wrapped around the forearms and lower legs of Kuna women to form geometric designs. Wini, mola blouses, wraparound skirts, head scarves made from imported cloth, and a gold nose ring are considered "traditional dress" for women. Most women in San Blas dress "traditionally." A few elderly women still make hammocks and ceramic vessels, but these traditional crafts are rapidly disappearing as commercial goods become increasingly available. Kuna men make baskets, ladles, wooden stools, and fans that women use to keep the fires burning. Some men make their own clothing: a solid-colored shirt with pleats in the front and a pair of pants, also without designs.

Most Kuna men, however, wear Western clothing. Men who live in the area frequented by tourists carve small model boats and balsa-wood Kuna doll heads to sell to visitors. Dugout wooden canoes are handcrafted by men who have learned this special skill.

TRADE. Starting in the 1600s, the Kuna engaged in lucrative trade with the Scots, the French, and with the British colony of Jamaica. Kuna chiefs learned European languages and traveled throughout the Caribbean. The Kuna also traded with pirates as early as the 1600s. A Scottish colony was established in the area in 1698. Alliances and trade relations with Kuna communities were developed and maintained until the 1700s, when the Spanish expelled the Scots.

In the 1700s the French began to trade with the Kuna and to forge military alliances that protected both parties from the Spanish and British. Relations were sufficiently amicable to allow intermarriage. In the 1740s, however, the French began to cultivate cacao for export and, soon thereafter, to use Kuna labor. Relations between the two groups deteriorated; the Kuna rebelled, attacking the French settlers and driving them from the region. Taking over the production of cacao (about 100,000 trees on an estimated seventy-three properties), the Kuna began to trade with the British for guns, ammunition, tools, and cloth. By the 1850s, maritime trade with pirates and merchants was well developed, and trade continues to provide the Kuna with a steady source of goods.

Nowadays the Kuna are actively engaged in commerce with Colombians on boats; they trade coconuts for sugar, rice, cocoa, or cash. Trade boats, most of which are collectively owned by Kuna villages, travel to Colón (an international trade zone), returning to San Blas with a wide range of goods. Kuna storekeepers and itinerant traders acquire their merchandise either directly from Panama City or from the trade boats. Interregional trading of agricultural produce is minimal; plantains and roof thatch, abundant in the east, are mostly sold to communities in the west, where they are needed. Molas, coconuts, and lobsters are the region's primary exports. Although the Kuna still produce much of the goods they consume, they import a wide range of consumer goods including boat motors, cookware, clothing, shoes, certain staples (cocoa, rice, sugar), cement, guns, harpoons, lanterns, tape decks, and radios.

DIVISION OF LABOR. Concurrent with commercialization of coconuts and relocation of many mainland villages to the islands, Kuna men increasingly took over subsistence-agricultural production as women turned their attention to the coconut trade. This shift did not occur in all Kuna communities, nor did it happen all at once. Despite the variations, however, mean generally took increased responsibility for plantain, maize, rice, yucca, fruit, and sugarcane production. Both men and women still planted, weeded, and harvested coconuts, but the women from each household were usually the ones to exchange them for goods or cash.

Women continue to be responsible for child care; food gathering, preparation, and preservation; hauling water; and other tasks related to household maintenance. They also sew molas for themselves, their daughters, and elderly mothers. Men continue to engage in agricultural production and to hunt, fish, build houses, and craft many necessary household items. Women in the eastern region of San Blas and older women throughout the region are active in agricultural production. Women who spend most of their time sewing molas for sale are the least involved in agricultural and household-maintenance activities. Omekids usually work alongside women but may also participate in men's activities. Many omekids in the region are known as outstanding sewers of molas.

LAND TENURE. Private property did not exist among the Kuna until the mid- to late nineteenth century. Increased population pressure and the cash cropping of coconuts are factors that precipitated this change. Since 1938, all lands located within the comarca of San Blas have been owned collectively by the San Blas Kuna, although they do not own subsoil rights. The Kuna recognize individuals' rights to land. According to Kuna law, whoever first clears a plot may pass the land to his heirs. Because only men clear land, women generally inherit easily accessible, already producing fields. Women's brothers are expected to clear unclaimed land and often inherit fallow plots. Heirs retain their rights to land even if it has not been cultivated for many years.

Kinship

The Kuna kinship system is bilateral. Age and sex are reflected in kin terms. Cross and parallel cousins are not terminologically distinguished. Kinship terms are often used in place of personal names.

Marriage and Family

MARRIAGE. In the past, young people did not choose their own partners. A girl's father and

Private property did not exist among the Kuna, until the mid- to late nineteenth century brought increased population pressure and the cash cropping of coconuts.

Kuna

*A Kuna girl's
parents chose a
young man, based
on his ability to
work, and made
arrangements for the
marriage, usually
without the
knowledge of either
young person.*

mother chose a young man, based on his ability to work, and made arrangements for the marriage, usually without the knowledge of either young person. Today young people usually choose their own partners. Couples may "marry in the hammock"—a short ritual that is considered the "traditional" form of marriage. Alternatively, they may present themselves to the *congreso* (a politico-religious community gathering) and state their intention to marry. Unmarried men who move in with women are considered "married," and such couples are expected to notify the congreso. Some of the younger women who meet their future husbands in Panama City marry there according to civil law. Religious ceremonies either in San Blas or in Panama City are another possibility. Children take their biological father's surname unless he refuses to recognize his baby, in which case the child uses the mother's name. No apparent stigma is attached to the mother or to children bearing her name. Women retain their own names. No money, food, land, or other goods are exchanged between households before, during, or after the marriage. Island endogamy prevails, and interracial marriages are frowned upon.

Once married, a man is expected to reside in his mother-in-law's household and to work under the direction of his father-in-law. Any fish caught, game hunted, or produce harvested (even from fields to which he owns the rights) must be given to his mother-in-law to distribute.

DOMESTIC UNIT. The prototypical Kuna household is comprised of a senior couple, one or more married daughters with their husbands and children, and any unmarried children. Households may reorganize any number of times within the life span of any given generation. For example, a woman may return to her mother's household each time her husband goes to Panama City to work. Kin, unrelated children, visitors, teachers, or other government-paid employees working in the village—even an anthropologist—may join any given household for several days, months, or even years.

INHERITANCE. Inheritance of land is bilateral. Although Kuna sons and daughters inherit approximately equal amounts of land, men have greater possibilites for acquiring land than do women. Women inherit but do not lay claim to new plots of land. Only men clear uncultivated land. For example, virgin jungle may be claimed by clearing and cultivating a plot. Whoever clears the land retains usufruct rights, which are passed to his children. Spouses do not inherit land from one another. Husband and wife each retain rights to his or her own property and other resources. If one spouse dies, his or her property is distributed among his or her offspring.

Coconut groves, located on the mainland coast or on uninhabited islands, may be inherited by an individual or by groups (descended from a male or female ancestor) that collectively own and exploit coconut groves and, sometimes, agricultural lands.

SOCIALIZATION. Infants are raised primarily by their mothers and grandmothers with the help of other female relatives. At around the age of 5, boys start accompanying their fathers and other male relatives to the fields and on hunting and fishing trips. Girls stay with their female relatives. Adolescent girls help with the care of their younger siblings. Since about the 1960s, Kuna boys and girls have been required to attend primary school. Many youths go on to secondary school and high school; a few attend the university.

Sociopolitical Organization

SOCIAL ORGANIZATION. The Kuna are known for their egalitarian forms of social organization. Most agricultural labor in San Blas is organized at the community and household levels or through small collective entrepreneurial groups called *sociedades* (voluntary associations). All males and females of appropriate age are required to participate in community work projects and are fined if they do not. The senior male and female of each household are responsible for the organization of its labor. Sociedades, which are prevalent, consist of aggregates of friends, relatives, and neighbors. They are organized around specific activities such as selling gasoline, operating a retail store, or engaging in subsistence-agricultural production or coconut cultivation.

Kuna households and/or individuals may have different amounts of land or money. Factors affecting socioeconomic differentiation include the amount of land a household controls, ancestors' level of industriousness in planting coconuts, the extent to which current household members have planted coconuts, opportunities for paid employment, and income from mola sales. Age is another key variable in determining differences in wealth. Older men and women hold most of the land, whereas young migrant laborers obtain consumer goods and cash. Wealthier households in San Blas do not automatically accrue political power, nor do they usually appropriate the labor of poorer ones. Inheritance patterns tend to prevent the accumulation of wealth and ensure the redistribution of rights to land and to coconut trees among households across the generations.

POLITICAL ORGANIZATION. Each Kuna village has a local congreso (community meeting house). Every village in San Blas has four to six traditional or administrative *saklas*. Traditional saklas are considered political as well as religious leaders. Ranks and strata are absent, and very little social distance separates leaders and followers. Leaders are chosen for their wisdom and morality; leadership is not hereditary. After the 1925 Kuna uprising known as "La Revolución Tule," a Congreso General Kuna, comprised of local authorities representing each village, was established. The Congreso General Kuna created a unified political entity that can negotiate with the Panamanian government. Today it meets approximately every six months; emergency sessions are called if a crisis occurs. The region has three caciques (chiefs), each responsible for a particular subregion, and a regionwide *intendente* (administrator). Caciques are selected from Kuna leaders at the local level, whereas the intendente, until the 1990s always a non-Kuna, is named by Panama's president.

In 1968 new political boundaries were drawn throughout Panama. San Blas became politically and administratively separate from the province of Colón. Government ministries, previously administered through Colón, opened regional offices in San Blas. The comarca of San Blas was divided into four subareas called *corregimientos*. Each area elects one representative to the Asamblea Nacional de Representantes de Corregimientos. Local chapters of a wide range of political parties were organized within their communities. In most villages, women organized their own chapters and activities separately from the men's, even within the same political party. Women have become increasingly active in politics at the national level. In 1980 the Kuna elected a Kuna representative to the national legislature.

SOCIAL CONTROL. Within a household, the eldest man and woman exercise the most authority. He is responsible for organizing the labor of the men, she that of the women. At the village level, the local congresos are the loci for social control. In the past, public shamings were sufficient control mechanisms. Today congresos levy fines and require community labor in addition to public shaming. The region has several jails. Serious cases are referred to the Panamanian judicial system.

CONFLICT. Disputes that cannot be resolved within a household are taken to the local congreso. There is ongoing conflict both with the Panamanian national government and with outsiders (non-Kuna Panamanians or U.S. citizens) trying to establish businesses (usually hotels, tourist resorts, or stores) in the region or to con-

vert the Kuna to a particular religion. There are also occasional confrontations with *colonos* (settlers) from the interior who encroach upon Kuna land. The Kuna have developed the Project for the Study of the Management of Wildland Areas of Kuna Yala (PEMASKY) to help firmly establish the comarca's borders and to stop the deforestation of their rain forest. This project has received substantial support from international funding sources.

Religion and Expressive Culture

RELIGIOUS BELIEFS AND PRACTITIONERS. The Kuna creation myth includes references to both Pab Dummat (Big Father) and Nan Dummat (Big Mother). The Kuna religion is now called the "Father's Way." Communities alternate political meetings in the local congresos with singing gatherings where saklas and caciques chant religious and historical songs full of symbolism and myth, and the *arkar* (*vocero*, or chief's spokesman) interprets the meaning of the chants. Many Kuna attend Catholic and Protestant churches, in addition to the singing gatherings.

CEREMONIES. Kuna ceremonies include an *ikko inna* (needle ceremony), in which a baby girl's nose is pierced for a gold nose ring; an *inna tunsikkalet* (short ceremony), a puberty rite that usually lasts one or two days; and an *inna suit* (long ceremony), a ritual cutting of the hair that usually lasts three or more days. Once a young girl's hair is ritually cut short, she becomes available for marriage. Sometimes an inna suit is held for a very young girl even though she will not be ready for marriage for many years. There are no similar ceremonies for Kuna boys. Special chants exist for birth, death, and the healing of the sick.

ARTS. The Kuna are known internationally for their molas. Kuna verbal arts include three different types of chants: *pab ikar*, historical, religious and political material sung by Kuna leaders; songs sung by *kantules* (ritualists) during female puberty rites; chants used in curing ceremonies. Kuna women sing lullabies. Kuna dance groups are becoming increasingly popular among Kuna youth. Rattles and reed panpipes are used by the dancers.

MEDICINE. Kuna medicinal healers are called *inatulets* or *neles* (a nele is a seer). They use a combination of herbs and chants to heal their patients. Family, friends, and elderly women play an important role by sitting with patients while healers chant. Beginning in the 1970s, health centers staffed by a nurse or a Western-trained health paraprofessional were established on many islands. The region has one hospital. Many Kuna

Kuna ceremonies include an ikka inna *(needle ceremony) in which a baby girl's nose is pierced for a gold nose ring.*

♦ puberty rites
Ceremonies and related activities that mark the transition from childhood to adulthood or from secular status to being a cult member.

combine Western and Kuna approaches to healing when they are ill.

DEATH AND AFTERLIFE. Kuna women and children prepare the body for burial. Women are responsible for wailing and mourning; they review the deceased's life and character and refer to punishments or rewards that will be his or hers in the afterworld. To guide the deceased, a death chanter (*masartulet*) may be employed to sing a long narrative song describing the soul's journey through the underworld to heaven. Kuna cemeteries are located on the mainland. Small houses, many furnished with a table, dishes, and other everyday objects, are often constructed over the graves. These articles are for the deceased to use in the afterworld and to take as gifts to previously departed relatives. Kuna women (usually the elders) are responsible for visiting the dead, bringing them food, and keeping their houses clean.

Bibliography

Chapin, Mac (1990). "The Silent Jungle: Ecotourism among the Kuna Indians of Panama." *Cultural Survival Quarterly* 14(1): 42–45.

Herrera, Francisco (1972). "Aspectos del desarollo economico y social de los indios kunas de San Blas." *América Indígena* 32(1): 113–138.

Holloman, Regina (1976). "Cuna Household Types and the Domestic Cycle." In *Frontier Adaptation in Lower South America*, edited by Mary Helms and Franklin Loveland, 131–149. Philadelphia: Institute for the Study of Human Issues.

Howe, James (1986). *The Kuna Gathering: Contemporary Village Politics in Panama*. Austin: University of Texas Press.

Sherzer, Joel (1983). *Kuna Ways of Speaking*. Austin: University of Texas Press.

Stier, Frances Rhoda (1982). "Domestic Economy: Land, Labor, and Wealth in a San Blas Community." *American Ethnologist* 9(3): 519–537.

Stout, David (1947). *San Blas Cuna Acculturation: An Introduction*. New York: Viking Fund.

Tice, Karin E. (1994). *Kuna Crafts, Gender, and the Global Economy*. Austin: University of Texas Press.

—KARIN E. TICE

LADINOS

Ethonym: none

Orientation

IDENTIFICATION. "Ladino" is a term that was applied to the Old Castilian or Romance language to differentiate it from Latin, from which it was derived and of which it was considered to be a degenerate form. During the time that Muslims were in Spain, the term was applied to Muslims who spoke Castilian. In Mexico during the sixteenth century, Indians who had been educated by the friars and who knew the necessary Latin for the Catholic liturgy were sometimes called "Latinos" and, more generally, "Ladinos" or "Ladinizados." Later the term began to be applied to those Indians who learned Spanish. In a distorted sense, because of the cultural values attributed to the term "Ladino," the word came to be used to describe someone who was deceptive or malicious.

Despite the connotations of "Ladino" during the colonial period, the term took root; it persists only in Central American usage, with two distinct meanings. According to some authors who specialize in this area, the term "Ladino" is applied to any non-Indian. So, for example, the populations of Guatemala, and Honduras, and the Mexican state of Chiapas would be divided between Indians and Ladinos. North of the Isthmus of Tehuantepec, the term "mestizo" is now often used to refer to rural non-Indian people. According to other researchers, the classification is more complex: it is necessary to employ the more traditional colonial vocabulary and speak of Indians, criollos, mestizos, and Ladinos—including in the Ladino group those who have deliberately rejected any cultural link to Indian culture. "Criollo" is a term usually reserved for Whites born in the New World without any admixture of Indian. Mestizos are people with mixed Indian-Hispanic ancestry. Whatever their contact with Indian culture has been, Ladinos try to prove that they have no connection with it. Ladino identity is fragile because it is defined in negative terms—by what one is not; it is acquired by maintaining contact with the culture of more urban areas. In this article, we adopt the more restricted, but more complex, definition of "Ladino," as the culture of persons who have some degree of Indian culture in their background and who have turned away from it to seek a new, non-Indian, national, and urban cultural identity.

LOCATION. Ladinos are found intermixed with indigenous, mestizo, or criollo groups and with mestizos or criollos in the areas of Chiapas, Guatemala, and Honduras, mainly in the cities and larger villages of the region. They do not form communities identifying themselves as Ladino; rather they try to imitate or blend in with criollos or mestizos. Under the other definition of "Ladino," however, as "anyone with a non-Indian culture," many rural villages are characterized as "Ladino" by social scientists because they have no obvious indigenous cultural characteristics and, in particular, no indigenous language.

DEMOGRAPHY. According to the Guatemalan censuses of 1970 through 1990, 45 percent of the total population of the country is classified as "Ladino," amounting to approximately 4,500,000 people. In Chiapas, the category of "Ladino" is not registered in the census; in 1990, 240,429 non-Indian people resided in that state, constituting 19 percent of the population, but this is not a measure of the number of Ladinos in the cultural terms outlined here.

In the case of Honduras, the non-Indian population consists of around 4,200,000 people—that is, about 70 percent of the total population of the country; of these, only a few hundred thousand people on the urban periphery are Ladinos.

LINGUISTIC AFFILIATION. Ladinos are by definition speakers of Spanish, the language they use habitually. Spanish gives them a sense of identity, despite the fact that many learned it as a second language and can also speak an indigenous language. They try, however, to deny that they know their mother tongue—and try to forget it—and, of course, they will not teach it to their children. Yet their Spanish is filled with terms and words that have their origin in Indian languages spoken in the area.

History and Cultural Relations

Under the more restricted definition of the term, Ladinos emerged in the sixteenth century, when Spanish domination was consolidated. The first Ladinos were Indians who were faced with the dissolution of their communities because of loss of their lands, because of congregation into towns (a policy that the Spaniards carried out coercively and from which some Indians tried to escape), or because the community disappeared as a result of an epidemic. Later, some Indians abandoned their communities to look for a better way of life; they established themselves in cities and tried to assimilate to the culture and values of the conquerors. During the colonial period, Ladinos were members of the Indian community, experts in matters pertaining to criollo culture. They could continue being Indians in racial terms, but they were treated differently.

Ladinos who adopted the values of Spanish culture—and in this way ameliorated their social position—were not well regarded. Rather, they were feared and distrusted because they had rejected their own people, and they were never to-tally accepted by groups of purely European origin. In the colonial cities of Chiapas and Guatemala, distinct groups of criollos and Ladinos formed, although miscegenation, which is prevalent in the area, blurred the distinction and made it more difficult to define the borderline between one group and the other.

With no definite criteria for identifying their group, Ladinos began to relate to the nascent "national state" on an individual basis and adopted state institutions. Although they established relations with Spanish and criollo groups and, subsequently, with mestizos, and attempted to assimilate their cultural practices, Ladinos generally remained in a subordinate position. Relations were reestablished with Indian communities years after the initial rupture.

Settlements

There are no settlements that one might consider specifically Ladino, unless we adopt Adams's (1956, 1964, 1970) criterion and classify as "Ladino" every non-Indian city or town in Guatemala, Chiapas, and Honduras. There are family groups or individuals who live in the middle- or lower-class areas of cities and larger towns in the area, having adopted models of urbanization and settlement typical of these urban milieus. One frequently finds two- and three-generation families whose houses are located on the same land or on adjacent lands, but, in contrast to those who revindicate their Indian origin, Ladinos do not form migrant colonies originating from a single place.

Economy

SUBSISTENCE AND COMMERCIAL ACTIVITIES. Since precolonial times, the right to the usufruct of the land was linked to membership in a community. Ladinos originally gave up their agricultural rights in order to work at various occupations within urban areas, mainly in manufacture and commerce. In the nineteenth century Ladino laborers began to be employed in haciendas and, later, on coffee plantations, although only when there was a scarcity of indigenous labor. Nowadays it is unusual to find them performing agricultural labor; their presence is more noticeable in small-scale commerce and in the service sector. Some hold jobs as low- and middle-level public functionaries.

INDUSTRIAL ARTS. There is no handicraft production that might be considered typically Ladino; however, Ladinos are associated with agro-industrial and local industries; they partici-

Ladino families are isolated groups that can trace their descent back two or three generations but rarely maintain solid relationships with collateral kin.

pate as wage earners within mestizo establishments. In the highlands of Chiapas and isolated villages of Guatemala, Ladinos work in the production of *aguardiente* (a cane liquor), which they monopolize in a kind of clandestine emporium that illegally introduces the product to Indian communities.

TRADE. Most Ladinos are employed in commerce. They incorporate themselves within the system established by the urban majority, operating small stores or stalls in local markets or working as traveling salesmen in cities. Often they are also intermediaries between suppliers of agricultural products (especially rural Indian communities) and large-scale urban merchants. Some are small private entrepreneurs who transport cargo in their own trucks or vans, or drive passenger vehicles.

DIVISION OF LABOR. Ladinos have adopted models of division of labor that are predominant among mestizo groups: a father must provide for his family and a mother must dedicate herself to domestic work and the care of her children. Nevertheless, compelled by economic need, women are now increasingly having to find employment outside the home. They run family businesses or sell food or other items from ambulatory stalls.

Increasingly, sons and daughters of better-off Ladino families study at universities to become elementary-school teachers or occupy positions as public functionaries.

LAND TENURE. Neither members of indigenous communities nor well established in mestizo farming communities, Ladinos can own land only as private proprietors. Given their commercial orientation, however, their primary interest is not in working the land. If they do own property, it is more likely to be land in the city that they use for business ventures, as investments, to build and rent housing, or to leave to their children.

Marriage and Family

MARRIAGE. Mixed marriages, either between Ladinos and mestizos of other groups or between Ladinos and Indians, are the most common form of marriage. In urban marriages with mestizos, the Christian ceremony is performed in the church of which both bride and groom are members, and, in many cases, there is also a civil ceremony. In the case of marriage to an Indian woman, the indigenous tradition of asking for the woman's hand must be followed, and traditional ceremonies must be performed in each community, including a Christian religious ceremony.

KINSHIP

Kin Groups and Descent

Ladino families are isolated groups that can trace their descent back two or three generations but rarely maintain solid relationships with collateral kin. Their relationships tend to be extended through *compadrazgo*, which provides an opportunity for betterment, if not in economic terms, at least in terms of status.

Children of nuclear families, if both of their parents are living, carry the paternal name, and when they form their own families they frequently maintain their patrilocal residence. There are cases of single mothers, and among them a lack of continuity in family names is more frequent. Some children take the name of the putative father, others that of their mother.

Kinship Terminology

Ladino kinship terminology is the same as that used by other Spanish-speaking groups in the area. That is, one speaks of grandparents, parents, aunts and uncles, sons and daughters, brothers and sisters, cousins, brothers- and sisters-in-law, fathers- and mothers-in-law, and sons- and daughters-in-law in the same way in which these terms are used within Hispanic culture. The only unusual characteristic is the rather frequent incorporation of an *entenado*—a child given into someone's care by its parents, or semiadopted by another family for various reasons. The child may have been orphaned, been mistreated at home, or come from a family in dire economic straits. A child facing such circumstances may be sent to another family to be cared for in exchange for doing some work. The entenado is almost always a relative by marriage or a more remote family member—perhaps a godson or goddaughter.

With increasing frequency, lack of money to pay the cost of any type of ceremony leads to "stealing" the bride, which also obviates the need for gifts. As a rule, however, even though it might be several years later and the couple may already have had children, they will attempt to formalize the relationship and reestablish relations with the wife's family.

DOMESTIC UNIT. For people who have only recently become Ladinos, or first-generation Ladinos, neolocal domestic units and simple nuclear families are typical. With succeeding generations, however, extended families that include the husband's mother and some of the sons and their wives become more common. Sons take their spouses to their paternal home, but daughters do not. Sometimes the youngest daughter of the family remains in the home and does not marry so as to attend to the needs of her parents in their old age, but, more frequently, an entenada or an older granddaughter takes on this obligation.

INHERITANCE. There are no clear rules regarding inheritance; however, it is expected that the oldest son or several of the sons will continue working in their father's occupation and will inherit his business. Nevertheless, if a daughter or younger son takes care of the business, she or he will be the one to inherit it, albeit with an obligation to help one's brothers. Families who are in a position to do so try to leave houses, lands, and some kind of small business to each of their children, including married daughters.

SOCIALIZATION. Socialization of children—just as in the case of mestizos—takes place in schools, neighborhoods, and churches. Sometimes it occurs within the workplace, given that some of these children work from a very early age.

Sociopolitical Organization

SOCIAL ORGANIZATION. Ladinos are groups that consolidated and developed from the second half of the nineteenth century onward. Because of this short history, Ladino families have no extensive network of social relations. They have abandoned their communities of origin and the institutions that would have permitted them to build up a collective identity.

POLITICAL ORGANIZATION. Ladinos participate in the political system of the society as a whole. In Honduras, they do not take an active part in politics, but simply accept that the dominant system expects of them in terms of respect toward national institutions. They do not appear to be linked to any Indian organizations. In Guatemala and Chiapas, their political participation is mixed; some have opted for supporting the governing classes, actively setting themselves off from subversive indigenous organizations. In the Chiapas Indian mobilizations of 1994, however, Ladino groups supported the Indian movement in its demands, perhaps in opposition to the *coletos* (inhabitants of San Cristóbal de las Casas who consider themselves direct descendants of the old colonial aristocratic families).

SOCIAL CONTROL. Because the group does not identify itself as such, there are almost no mechanisms for social control beyond those established by the society at large.

Religion and Expressive Culture

RELIGIOUS BELIEFS. Ladinos are people whose syncretic processes have been deeply internalized. They come from Indian communities in which the customs of their grandparents persists; because the mainstream society holds these traditions in contempt, Ladinos reject them, yet, simultaneously, they are ashamed of the extent to which the costumbre still influences them. All of them are members of some Christian church—formerly it was only the Catholic church, but increasingly Ladinos have joined various Protestant churches or fundamentalist sects.

MEDICINE. Although Ladinos pride themselves on using only conventional allopathic medicine, in cases they consider to be serious, almost all will go to an herbalist, bone-setter, shaman, midwife, or curer in their community of origin or of some indigenous group in the city.

Bibliography

Adams, Richard N. (1956). *Encuesta sobre la cultura de los ladinos en Guatemala.* Guatemala City: Ministerio de Educación Pública, Seminario de Integración Social Guatemalteca.

Adams, Richard N. (1964). "La mestización cultural en centroamérica." *Revista de Indias* (Madrid) 95–96: 153–176.

Adams, Richard N. (1970). *Crucifixion by Power: Essays on Guatemalan National Social Structure, 1944–1966.* Austin: University of Texas Press.

Casaus Arzú, Marta (1992). *Guatemala: Linaje y racismo.* San José, Costa Rica: Facultad Latinoamericana de Ciencias Sociales.

Glittenberg, Joann Elizabeth Kropp (1976). "A Comparative Study of Fertility in Highland Guatemala: A Ladino and an Indian Town." Ph.D. dissertation, University of Colorado at Boulder.

Pitt-Rivers, Julian (1970). "Palabras y hechos: Los ladinos." In *Ensayos de antropología en la zona central de*

Chiapas, edited by Norman McQuown and Julian Pitt-Rivers, 21–42. Mexico City: Instituto Nacional Indigenista.

Spielberg, Joseph (1965). "San Miguel Milpas Altas: An Ethnographic Analysis of Interpersonal Relations in a Peasant-Ladino Community of Guatemala." Ph.D. dissertation, Michigan State University.

—MARÍA DE LA PALOMA ESCALANTE GONZALBO
(TRANSLATED BY RUTH GUBLER)

Martinique is part of a major world power (France) but set in a third world geographic region.

MARTINIQUAIS

Ethonym: Béké (the elite White minority descended from slave owners), Creoles (refers to both the non-White, mixed-heritage local population and to the local language), Metropolitans (refers to people of European descent who live in French-speaking former colonies)

Orientation

IDENTIFICATION. In many ways, Martinique is a unique island culture: it is part of a major industrial world power (France) but set in a third-world geographic region. With its neighbors, Martinique shares an important social history of slavery and a monocrop economy based on sugar. Like other Caribbean islands whose sugar production has dwindled since the late 1950s, Martinique also lacks the mineral and natural resources to support its own economic growth. Because of Martinique's political assimilation to France, however, the islanders' standard of living remains well above that of most Caribbean countries. Incorporation translates into French import subsidies, social transfer payments, and provisions for a large, highly paid local government sector.

LOCATION. Part of the eastern Caribbean chain of islands known as the Lesser Antilles, the French islands of Martinique and Guadeloupe constitute the French Antilles. Martinique is situated south of Dominica, and north of Saint Lucia, encompassing a total land mass of 1,100 square kilometers.

DEMOGRAPHY. The French, who first arrived in Martinique and Guadeloupe in 1635, found only a sparse population of native Carib Indians. At the hands of the colonists, these Indians were a short-lived labor source. Realizing the need for a cheap, abundant source of hardy laborers to work the sugar plantations, the settlers looked to Africa. Thus began more than two centuries of the Atlantic slave trade. By 1680, African slaves in Martinique outnumbered White planters two to one.

The forced migration of Africans to the New World, and specifically to Martinique, transformed the social order and composition of the local population. By the mid-1700s, all non-Spanish island populations were overwhelmingly Black but included a small number of mulatto Browns and an even smaller number of Whites. By 1770, 85 percent of Martinique's population were slaves, 12 percent masters, and 3 percent freed. The number of slaves imported to the island grew from 258,000 in 1810 to 365,000 in 1848, the year slavery was abolished in France.

Abolition created pressures to find a new source of plantation labor. Colonists turned to contract laborers, primarily from India, but also from China and Africa. Again, the composition of the population changed.

A demographic boom in Martinique occurred between 1930 and 1965 as a declining death rate and an increasing birthrate combined to double the population of the island. By the mid-1960s, the steady out-migration of Martiniquais to the Metropole (continental France) had reduced the impact of these changes on population growth. Once the birthrate began to decline in the late 1960s, net population growth began to lose momentum; a decade later, by the end of the 1970s, the growth of the island's population had slowed drastically.

Out-migration to France from Martinique peaked in the early 1970s and has continued to decline since 1980 as job prospects in the Metropole have become increasingly bleak. In fact, from 1982 to 1990, more people immigrated to the island than emigrated from it; some were return migrants, others were Metropolitan French coming to Martinique to live.

According to the 1990 census, there are approximately 360,000 residents of Martinique, an increase of almost 31,000 (or 10 percent) since 1982. As in Latin America and the neighboring Caribbean islands, rural-to-urban migration continues in Martinique. Today, more than half of all island households are situated in the general urban area of the capital city, Fort-de-France.

LINGUISTIC AFFILIATION. The official language is French, and most people take pride in their facility with the language. A French-based Creole, not intelligible to French speakers, is the historical mother tongue of Martiniquais, however. One is likely to hear more Creole than French in rural areas, at cockfights and storytelling events, and in informal and intimate settings of family and friends. In recent years, local linguists created a written French Creole grammar. Since then, a number of novelists and poets have published works in Creole.

History and Cultural Relations

Both the long-term continuity of a plantation economy and the Martiniquais assimilation to French culture have produced unique social as well as economic realities. Together, these forces of history forged new ideological and cultural foundations for a transplanted African people and generated a complicated sense of self-identity. Therefore, although the history of Martinique is the story of Caribbean colonization, of sugar plantations, and of slavery, it is also the story of how the French treated their Caribbean colonies: how they prized the riches they represented and how they assumed a proprietary interest in the people they claimed as their own.

The French colonization of the Caribbean began in the late sixteenth century as a way to break up Spanish dominance of the waterways from gold-rich Mexico to the Atlantic route home. The political strategy of Caribbean settlement took a decidedly economic turn in the early 1600s, however, when it became feasible to cultivate sugar on a large but labor-intensive scale. The need for laborers stimulated the Atlantic slave trade, which supplied African slaves to French, British, and Dutch Caribbean planters.

The other historic legacy that has shaped contemporary Martiniquais life was the assimilation-oriented nature of French colonization. Certainly, French colonists instituted a system of slavery no less brutal than other Europeans; unlike the British or Dutch, however, the French came to identify their own strength and international power with their colonies and the populations there.

In keeping with its colonial "mission," France declared Martinique, Guadeloupe, and the South American coastal area of French Guiana *départements outre-mers* (overseas departments, DOMs) of France in 1946. This status guaranteed the population of the French Caribbean the same rights and privileges that the citizens of France enjoy. The new status granted DOM residents representation in both the French National Assembly and Senate and made the three départements eligible for the extensive social-security-system allocations.

The legacies of the French assimilation ethic are easily visible today in Martinique and Guadeloupe. Following departmentalization, schools, hospitals and clinics, libraries, social-service and welfare agencies, and government bureaus were built to make the French feel at home and to pro-

FLOWERS FOR SALE

A Martiniquais woman balances a box of flowers on her head as she sells flowers along the street. Martinique. (Dave G. Houser/Corbis)

vide continuing evidence to the Martiniquais of the value of being French. A system of excellent roadways and an administrative infrastructure were designed to replicate Continental standards and are the envy of other Caribbean islanders.

Appearances suggest that the Martiniquais have indeed welcomed the assimilation to French life. They have incorporated the status markers of all things European: language, table manners, religion, fashion, cuisine, and education. Local advocates of independence from France have only gained credibility since about 1980, and they do not represent the prevailing view. Understandably, people of the French West Indies do not wish to be independent when their standard of living is kept artificially high through French subsidies and allocations.

Settlements

Because Martinique's three mountain ranges account for a considerable portion of the island's area, 90 percent of the population lives on one-quarter of the land. The island population is dispersed among thirty-four communes, most of which are coastal. The administrative capital is Fort-de-France.

Fort-de-France became the capital of Martinique when picturesque Saint Pierre was destroyed by

See also

French

The complex social structure of urban Martinique involves a combination of income, occupation, education, skin color, language, family organization, and religion.

the eruption of Montagne Pelée in 1902. Fort-de-France is situated at the edge of Caribbean waters and benefits from a calm, deepwater port that supports the island's import-driven economy. The urban center is comprised of several square kilometers of boutiques and offices, a large park, the cathedral, and government offices, banks, restaurants, and rented residences located on upper floors of the street-level storefronts.

Two classes of people were the first to populate the port town: the emerging group of *mulatre* merchants and a number of younger Békés whose families had invested their plantation fortunes in the import-export trade. By the 1950s, when agricultural workers began to stream into the city in search of wage labor, working-class neighborhoods sprouted up in the hills around the flat town center, eventually surrounding it on three sides. Today, the residents of Fort-de-France span all socioeconomic groups and ethnic identities.

The greater Fort-de-France area extends almost without interruption north to Schoelcher, a town of 20,000, and south to Lamentin, the industrial center of the island where 30,000 people live and where the international airport is located. Compared to the size and density of this urban sprawl, which continues to lead island growth, other settlements are quite small, most under 10,000 people. The population residing in the lush, mountainous northern area is thinning, but the island's southern end, with its agricultural possibilities, fine beaches, and tourist economy, attracts an increasing number of residents.

Economy

In slightly less than thirty years following departmentalization of Martinique in 1946, the entire basis of the economy had shifted. Where once agriculture had dominated the lives of islanders, tertiary production, including services and commerce, had come to employ nearly 70 percent of the active population.

Since World War II, there have been no new sectors of productive growth to accommodate the increased population of workers resulting from the demographic boom. Instead, growth has been centered on the public sector: in 1954 it accounted for 2 percent of employment, by 1974, 18 percent, and by 1986, 32 percent. Still, increases in the number of jobs in government and commerce have only served to offset the fall in agricultural and craft-related production.

Since the early 1970s, unemployment in Martinique has hovered around 30 percent. There is a thriving underground economy, however, that is

not accounted for in official statistics. In addition, French social-transfer payments have helped offset the economic hardships of irregular work or lack of work.

These transfer payments have meant that in spite of dramatic declines in self-sufficiency beginning in the 1950s, Martiniquais have enjoyed a constant rise in income, life expectancy, and overall living standards. For instance, whereas only half of all households had both water and electricity in the mid-1970s, by the early 1990s, 90 percent did. Most also have a refrigerator, a television, and a telephone, and more than half own a car. Between 1970 and 1985, the minimum wage guaranteed to full-time workers multiplied more than 7 times. As consumption has soared, dependency on credit purchases has also increased. Thus, economic dependency on France is deep and wide, and despite the fact that Martinique cannot sustain its own standard of living, Martiniquais live relatively affluent, consumer-oriented lives.

Kinship, Marriage, and Family

KIN GROUPS AND DESCENT. On Martinique, the system of kinship is bilateral, and informal adoption of children by relatives or close friends is fairly common. The only social group with rigid rules of kinship, marriage, and social affiliation is the Béké population; however, many East Indians also prefer to marry endogamously.

MARRIAGE. Traditionally, marriage was reserved for later in life, after the couple had successfully raised children, but today the situation is changing. The elite, for whom marriage prior to having children was the norm, have become the current model, leading a trend to marry early. In contrast to the commonly mixed marriages among other population segments in Martinique, Békés still carefully guard their aristocratic origins by continuing to practice endogamy. Their insistence on marrying only members of other Béké families has helped them maintain control of most arable land and economic power in Martinique.

DOMESTIC UNIT. In Martinique, household units may involve one-, two-, or three-generation family members, with or without a conjugal couple at the center of the group. The membership of a household is variable according to the group's resources and needs at the time. Neither nuclear families nor extended-family arrangements are the norm, but these represent possible units among a range of other, equally suitable groupings. Approximately one in three households is "female-headed," a pattern occurring mostly among lower-income and younger people.

SOCIALIZATION. Martiniquais children are considered a cultural treasure and represent an important source of status for parents, irrespective of socioeconomic level. Thus, children are indulged, and even parents with the most meager resources find it important to dress their children in smart, modern clothes.

Fewer than 40 percent of the population over 15 years of age holds any kind of school degree. As jobs become even scarcer, however, there is an increasing recognition that education is the key to social mobility and professional success. Enrollment in the island's only university remains modest because only programs in law and economics are offered. Those wishing to study other subjects generally attend college in France.

Sociopolitical Organization

SOCIAL ORGANIZATION. The complex social structure of urban Martinique involves a combination of the following factors: income, occupation, education, skin color, language, family organization, and religion. Distinctions of social class are primarily a matter of one's income/occupation and one's skin color. Refinements in the hierarchy are often determined by education, the success of one's children, the degree to which one can freely associate with lighter-skinned people, and the number of socially important parties one can host and attend.

Martiniquais informants describe the local color hierarchy in a precise system involving distinct linguistic terms, which identify a particular combination of skin color, cheekbone features, lip size, and hair consistency. In brief, the most common distinctions include the following: Mulatre, the offspring of a White and Black parent, generally with very light skin, smooth hair, and Caucasian facial features; Chabin/Chabine, the offspring of a mulatto and a Black parent, generally with light skin, broader features and light brown, kinky hair; Chappe cooli, pure East Indian parent and Black parent, generally with wavy hair, well-defined cheekbones, narrow nose, and small lips; Câpre/Câpresse, offspring of a Black parent and a mixed-race parent, such as Chappe cooli and Chabin, or Chabin and Brune, generally with kinkier hair and less well-defined cheekbones than the Chappe cooli; Brun/Brune, brown-skinned, of mixed-race parentage, generally with kinky hair and African facial features; Rouge/Marron, of Chabin ancestry and therefore with lighter skin but stronger African features;

Noir/Negre, pure Black parentage with very dark skin, kinky hair, and broad, African facial features.

Some color terms are used for political reasons. "Noir" may be used as the term "Black" is used by English speakers in the United States: for example, a Chabin man might refer to himself as "Noir." "Negre" is considered old-fashioned, and derivatives of it are used perjoratively in Creole, whereas "Metis," a deliberately nondescriptive term, is typically used by people who, for social or political reasons, prefer not to refer to their specific mix of parentage.

Skin color generally darkens as one follows the occupational ladder down to the least-skilled workers and the unemployed. Because of the early economic benefits accorded the mulatto offspring of unions between masters and slaves, the tradition of prestige associated with lighter-colored skin continues to exist today. Along with White Metropolitans from France, light-skinned blacks tend to dominate the professions and highest offices of government.

The small group of endogamous Békés, representing about 1 percent of the population, remains a dominant minority in terms of economic power and social status. In addition to their large-scale retail and import/export concerns, Béké families continue to hold the bulk of productive land and employ the vast majority of agricultural workers in production of bananas, rum, and tropical flowers.

POLITICAL ORGANIZATION. Political power in Martinique is in the hands of the Creole population, irrespective of the economic prominence of the Békés. Since the island's designation as a département outre-mers, its political pyramids have been effectively inverted so that the mixed-race, Creole majority of the population controls the local affairs of government and represents island interests in the French legislative bodies.

CONFLICT. The price of full French citizenship and economic dependency is high and takes a psychological toll on the Martiniquais. Underneath the overlay of aspirations to be European lies a recognition of a Creole reality made of truths that are neither wholly French nor African. These truths live in the native tongue of French Creole, are told by the old group of *conteurs* at traditional funeral rites, and are felt swelling up from a collective consciousness during the Chanté Noël songfest at Christmas.

This resilient Martiniquais culture offers the mixed-race majority both hope of self-understanding and despair of ever becoming completely French. The distinctly non-French or only

The Martiniquais culture offers the mixed-race majority both hope of self-understanding and dispare of ever becoming completely French.

Speakers of Mixtec live in the southern Mexican states of Oaxaca, Guerrero, and Puebla.

French-in-part traditions and attitudes of the Martiniquais recall hostilities and struggles for dignity born in a time of slavery.

Religion and Expressive Culture

RELIGIOUS BELIEFS. The vast majority of Martiniquais, both in Fort-de-France and throughout the island, consider themselves Catholic, although a rapidly declining proportion consider themselves "practicing" Catholics. Since the early 1970s, a small but increasing number of people have been shifting their religious affiliation to become Evangelists, Adventists, and Jehovah's Witnesses. In addition, there is a Muslim following among the minority population of Middle Easterners from Syria and Lebanon.

Martiniquais of all social classes also embrace many non-Christian beliefs, for example, in the power of sorcery. In contrast to sorcerers who are hired to inflict harm, shamans and folk healers generally are recruited to help people solve a variety of health and psychological problems.

CEREMONIES. Catholic holy days are observed in Martinique, as are numerous locally distinct ritual events and traditional ceremonies including funeral rites, Chanté Noël at Christmas, and Mardi Gras.

ARTS. Martiniquais society has a strong artistic tradition that has produced gifted, internationally recognized literary talents. Other creative and popular traditions include public storytelling, music and dance, costumes, and cuisine.

MEDICINE. Most urban dwellers prefer to treat serious illnesses and injuries at local clinics or hospitals, although herbal medicines and shaman healers are also recognized as effective sources of treatment for many health and personal problems.

Bibliography

Aldrich, Robert, and John Connell (1992). *France's Overseas Frontier: Départements et Territoires d'Outre-Mer.* Cambridge: Cambridge University Press.

Browne, Katherine E. (1993). *Factors Underlying Differential Participation in the Informal Economy.* Ann Arbor, Mich.: University Microfilms International.

Horowitz, Michael M. (1967). *Morne-Paysan: Peasant Village in Martinique.* New York: Holt, Rinehart & Winston.

Lirus, Julie (1979) *Identité antillaise.* Paris: Éditions Caribéennes.

Lowenthal, David (1972). *West Indian Societies.* London: Oxford University Press.

Massé, Raymond (1978). *Les adventistes du septiéme jour aux Antilles Françaises: Anthropologie d'une espérance*

milléneariste. Ste. Marie, Martinique: Université de Montréal.

Mintz, Sidney, and Sally Price (1985). *Caribbean Contours.* Baltimore: Johns Hopkins University Press.

Slater, Miriam (1977) *The Caribbean Family: Legitimacy in Martinique.* New York: St. Martin's Press.

—KATHERINE E. BROWNE

MIXTEC

Ethonym: Cloud People, Ñuu Savi

Orientation

IDENTIFICATION. Speakers of Mixtec live in the southern Mexican states of Oaxaca, Guerrero, and Puebla. Mixtec speakers usually refer to themselves as "Ñuu Savi" (people of the rain).

LOCATION. The Mixteca, the homeland of the Mixtec people, has traditionally been divided into three broad geographical zones: the Mixteca Alta, a mountainous, forested region; the Mixteca Baja, a high, dry area northwest of the Alta; and the Mixteca de la Costa, a low-lying tropical area bordering the Pacific Ocean. Within each of these zones, the sharply faulted topography has created a great deal of environmental diversity. A lack of economic opportunity has caused many Mixtec speakers to migrate from this area, and there are now substantial colonies of Mixtec speakers located in the Isthmus of Tehuantepec region, in Oaxaca City, in Mexico City, in Baja California, and in various places in the United States. Groups of Mixtec labor migrants have been reported to be working as far north as Alaska.

DEMOGRAPHY. Prior to the Spanish Conquest, the population of the Mixteca (which included non-Mixtec-speaking groups) was over 500,000. The plagues of the sixteenth century reduced the population by 90 percent. After reaching a nadir in the early seventeenth century, the population has steadily recovered, to the point where by 1980 there were 323,137 speakers of Mixtec in Mexico, making them the fourth-largest indigenous group in the country.

LINGUISTIC AFFILIATION. Mixtec is classified as an Otomaguean language, although sharp dialectal differences mean that the Mixtec spoken in one area is often not intelligible to speakers of Mixtec in other areas. The Summer Institute of Linguistics has identified twenty-nine "dialects" of Mixtec that fall below the 70-percent intelligibility level with one another.

See also

Zapotec

History and Cultural Relations

In the early sixteenth century the Mixteca was divided into numerous small kingdoms, or *cacicazgos*, ruled over by a hereditary elite. The Mixtec elite also ruled over non-Mixtec-speaking peoples, and some Mixtec kingdoms had, in turn, been conquered by the Central Mexican Triple Alliance. The Mixtec elite, related to one another by marriage and descent, patronized one of the finest artistic traditions in the New World. The area was conquered by the Spanish between 1522 and 1524. Owing to severe population decline in the wake of the sixteenth-century plagues, as well as to the region's lack of major mineral and agricultural resources, relatively few Spaniards settled in the area, however, and the pressures for change, although substantial, were not as great as in other areas in Mesoamerica. In the nineteenth and twentieth centuries outsiders began to move into the Mixteca in increasing numbers, and commercial agriculture was expanded. At the same time, the region became a center for several armed political movements, and Mixtec-speaking peoples actively participated in the struggle for independence, as well as in the Wars of the Reform and the Mexican Revolution of 1910–1920. Today, most Mixtec speakers are what anthropologists call peasants, but there is a growing Mixtec middle class, made up of teachers, government workers, technicians, politicians, health officials, and other professionals.

Settlements

Rural Mixtec speakers reside in village communities. Some of these communities form municipalities (the basic unit of political organization within Mexico), and some are hamlets within municipalities. In physical terms, most village communities have at their centers a main plaza surrounded by a church, a schoolhouse, and government buildings. Domestic dwellings are traditionally built of locally available materials. In higher, colder areas, most people tend to live in log cabins, but in the warmer, lower-lying areas, houses are usually made of cane and thatch. Adobe bricks are used throughout the region, and in some areas the waterproof husk of the banana is used as a roofing material. Today, many people construct their homes of cement cinder blocks and corrugated iron roofs.

Economy

SUBSISTENCE AND COMMERCIAL ACTIVITIES. Most rural Mixtec people are peasants who subsist chiefly on maize, beans, squash, chilies, local fruits, and other vegetables. In some areas, swidden, or slash-and-burn, agriculture is widely practiced; in other areas oxen-drawn plows are used. In favored areas, irrigation works have been developed. The *lama-bordo* technique of building hillside terraces to control erosion and bring fertile soil off the mountains onto agricultural plots appears to be unique to the Mixteca. In some areas, where virgin forests still exist, wild game (deer, squirrels, coati, iguanas, and birds) supplements the diet. Principal cash crops include coffee, wheat and other grains, tobacco, sugarcane, and fruits. In most areas, significant numbers of goats and sheep are raised, and the coastal area is known for the large number of cattle bred there.

INDUSTRIAL ARTS. In traditional Mixtec villages, there are adept weavers, candle makers, and house builders. In addition, many communities specialize in particular crafts such as pottery making, sugar and liquor production, baking, the manufacture of straw hats and mats, firework production, the manufacture of agricultural tools, leatherworking, and furniture making.

TRADE. Much of the trade within the Mixteca is carried out at weekly markets. Local trade involves the exchange of the crafts of different communities and the products of complementary ecozones. Long-distance trade between the Coastal Mixteca and other regions has traditionally focused on salt. Cotton, cacao, chilies, fish, and coconuts are also traded from the coast into highland areas, in exchange for pulque, squashes, herbs such as oregano, and temperate fruits. Pilgrimage centers also function as trading points in the Mixteca, as do sites of religious festivals. Some regions lack weekly markets, and traders simply go from house to house with their wares.

DIVISION OF LABOR. For rural peasants, the division of labor is by gender and age. Men are responsible for agricultural tasks and house building, whereas women cook and process food, maintain the house, and care for children. In some places, this division of labor is defined by taboos, such as the one arising from the belief that husbands become ill if their wives perform agricultural chores. Both sexes gather firewood; only men hunt. Children and older people are often assigned the task of caring for goats and sheep.

LAND TENURE. Patterns of land tenure vary greatly from place to place within the Mixteca, the result of Mexico's complicated agrarian history and local ecological factors. In some areas, land is held privately by individuals and can be freely bought and sold. Elsewhere, land is held privately but cannot be sold to outsiders. In still other places, no individual titles exist, although the same plots may stay within families for generations. In places where swidden agriculture is practiced and there is abundant land, fields are abandoned after a year or two, and the family that worked a plot may never again return to it. Most Mixtec communities maintain at least some communal lands, which are used by community members for pasturage, cutting timber, collecting wild plants, and gathering fuel.

Kinship

KIN GROUPS AND DESCENT. In the pre-Hispanic period, many local groups were organized as demes, a practice that continues in at least some communities in the area today. For purposes of inheritance, descent is reckoned bilaterally. *Compadrazgo*, or ritual kinship, is extremely important in all areas. There are several different kinds of compadrazgo relationships, but those deriving from baptism and marriage are considered the most significant. The compadrazgo tie extends beyond the immediate partners and the godchild to embrace a range of lineal and collateral relatives, who may then refer to one another by kinship terms.

KINSHIP TERMINOLOGY. Mixtec is characterized by Hawaiian cousin terminology. Three separate terms for siblings and cousins are used, depending on whether the persons are of the same or the opposite sex.

Marriage and Family

MARRIAGE. Parents traditionally selected mates for their children. Often people married before they were sexually mature. Today, marriage occurs much later, and the young people involved have much more influence over the decision about who and when to marry, although the older pattern can still be found in some areas. Bride-wealth payments are made, and in some places can amount to the equivalent of several years' wages. Bride-service, with residence by the groom in the father-in-law's house, is also required in some areas. Community endogamy is the predominant pattern, although members of the growing Mixtec middle class are as likely to marry someone outside their community as they are to marry an insider. Polygyny is practiced by wealthy individuals. Residence is usually virilocal. When divorce occurs, the woman returns to her parents' or brothers' households. If it occurs relatively soon after marriage, a portion of the bride-wealth must be repaid.

DOMESTIC UNIT. The ideal domestic unit for most Mixtec peasants is a husband and wife, their unmarried children, and their adult married sons, who bring their wives to live with them in their father's house. Often separate houses are erected, forming a residential compound, for each of the different nuclear families. There is, however, much variation in the composition of Mixtec households, depending on the phase of the developmental cycle, selective mortality, divorce, and other factors.

INHERITANCE. Traditionally, all sons inherited equally. Daughters inherited land only when a man died without any sons. In many places today, women are given the same rights to their parent's estate as their brothers.

SOCIALIZATION. All members of the household help raise children. Females with nursing infants may breast-feed one another's children, and older children often spend as much time caring for their younger siblings as do the parents. Once children reach the age of 4 or 5, they begin to leave the compound to play with other children. Boys are encouraged to roam freely with their peers, but girls are expected to stay near the household. Both sexes are given productive tasks to perform from a very early age. Marriage is often a difficult time for young girls, who are suddenly separated from their home and kin.

Sociopolitical Organization

SOCIAL ORGANIZATION. The basic social unit of Mixtec peasant communities today is the household. Households are linked to one another through reciprocal exchange of goods and labor, marriage, ritual kinship, and corporate interest. The municipal subunits of *ranchería* and *agencia*, as well as the barrio, often form intermediate organizations between household and community.

POLITICAL ORGANIZATION. In settlements where Mixtec speakers predominate, leadership and decision making rest in the hands of officers of the civil-religious hierarchy. It is often the case in these areas that ultimate authority rests with a group of *tañuu* and *ñañuu*, men and women who have passed through all the offices of the hierarchy and are now respected elders. Elsewhere, a single individual, or cacique, may control local government, often by being a broker between the state bureaucracy and the local village. In rural areas with mestizo populations, the power of Mixtec speakers in local government is usually limited.

SOCIAL CONTROL. Gossip, public ridicule, the threat of evil spells, and fear of being accused

---

◆ **deme**
A group based on the merging of locality, descent, and in-marriage.

◆ **cacique**
A local strongman or political boss. The word "cacique" was adopted into Spanish to designate a native chief. Today it is applied variously to Indians and non-Indians to designate a local political boss who leads and controls people through the more or less undemocratic exercise of political power.

◆ **mestizo**
A term used to refer to persons of mixed Indian and European ancestry. In most contexts, mestizo is in fact more a social than a racial classification.

of witchcraft are important mechanisms of social control in village life. The assignment of offices in the civil-religious hierarchy to those who violate community norms is another very effective form of punishment, since work in these offices requires a substantial expenditure of time and money. In the case of serious infractions, such as the theft of property, local authorities may decide that incarceration and the payment of fines is necessary. Habitual criminals may be subjected to banishment or some form of corporal punishment. In most areas, murderers are sent to the district capital for trial and punishment.

CONFLICT. Intervillage conflict is widespread throughout southern Mexico, but it is particularly intense in Oaxaca, where disputes between neighboring communities over land boundaries have continued for hundreds of years. These disputes have sometimes degenerated into open warfare, resulting in deaths and the destruction of property. Within communities, conflicts frequently take place between community members over land, with drunkenness and witchcraft accusations often playing precipitating roles. Some Mixtec communities have homicide rates that exceed those recorded in the most violent cities in the United States.

Religion and Expressive Culture

RELIGIOUS BELIEFS. There are several basic elements to contemporary Mixtec peasant religious beliefs. These include a cosmology divided between the Earth and the Sky; a monistic pantheon, wherein the distinction between a particular deity, such as the image of the rain god, and its manifestations in rain and water, is unimportant; a focus on the renewal and fertility of the world through acts of self-sacrifice; and a modeling of contemporary social interactions on those that occurred between humans and the gods in mythic times. At the center of many Mixtec rituals are the saints introduced by the Spanish during the colonial period, and almost every Mixtec town has a Catholic church at its center. Protestant missionaries have made inroads in some Mixtec communities since the 1930s, often dividing the community into factions based on religious affiliation.

RELIGIOUS PRACTITIONERS. Native religious practitioners are only rarely full-time specialists; they usually function as a combination of curer, diviner, and shaman, with individuals specializing in particular divinatory and curing techniques. Both men and women play these roles.

CEREMONIES. Ceremonial life in Mixtec communities is very rich and centers around the fiesta complex. Fiestas, held to celebrate the feast days of major saints, are often sponsored by a *mayordomo*. On these occasions, hundreds of people may be involved in the rituals, which include gift exchange, sacrifices, processions, a mass, and much eating and drinking. Fiestas are also held to commemorate the life crises of baptism, marriage, and death and may involve hundreds of participants in rituals, the exchange of gifts, and feasting. Other major events include Carnival, just before Lent, which often involves the performances of dance troupes, and rituals to bring rain and celebrate the return of the dead (the latter occurring at harvest time in late October and early November). Pilgrimage sites are scattered throughout the Mixteca, and Mixtecs often make pilgrimages to important places outside their region, such as Juquila, and to the Shrine of the Virgin of Guadalupe in Mexico City.

MEDICINE. Most people are familiar with a wide range of plant and animal products that have curative properties. Specialists are called to cure illnesses such as soul loss, evil eye, and those believed to be caused by witchcraft. Many sicknesses are attributed to moral failings by the sufferer or by the sufferer's immediate kin. The Mexican government has established free rural clinics throughout the Mixteca, staffed by trained nurses and doctors. These have been especially effective at reducing the mortality rate of young children and women of childbearing age who develop complications during pregnancy.

DEATH AND AFTERLIFE. Death is commemorated by elaborate mourning rituals, which involve gift exchange and feasting and seven or nine nights of prayer, depending on whether the deceased was a child or an adult. The world of the dead is the mirror image of the world of the living. Thus, one year for the living is one day for the dead; when it is night for the living, it is day in the land of the dead. In some places, the dead are said to reside on certain mountaintops. Many people subscribe to the ancient Mesoamerican belief that one's final resting place is determined by the manner in which one died. Thus, those who drown serve the rain deity; those who die in the forest serve the demon. Most of the dead are believed to return during the All Saints' observance to visit with the living.

Bibliography

Butterworth, Douglas (1975). *Tilantongo*. Mexico City: Instituto Nacional Indigenista.

Jansen, Maarten (1982). *Huisi Tacu*. Amsterdam: Centrus voor Studie en Documentatie van Latijns Amerika.

At the center of many Mixtec rituals are the saints introduced by the Spanish during the colonial period, and almost every Mixtec town has a Catholic church at its center.

Monaghan, John (1990). "Reciprocity, Redistribution, and the Transaction of Value in the Mesoamerican Fiesta." *American Ethnologist* 17:758–774.

Ravicz, Robert, and A. Kimball Romney (1969). "The Mixtec." In *Handbook of Middle American Indians*, edited by Robert Wauchope. Vol. 7, *Ethnology, Part One*, edited by Evon Z. Vogt, 367–399. Austin: University of Texas Press.

Smith, Mary Elizabeth (1973). *Picture Writing of Ancient Southern Mexico*. Norman: University of Oklahoma Press.

Spores, Ronald (1984). *The Mixtec in Ancient and Colonial Times*. Norman: University of Oklahoma Press.

—JOHN MONAGHAN

NAHUA OF THE HUASTECA

Ethnonyms: Aztec, Mexicano, Mexijcatl (pl., Mexijcaj), Nahuatl

Orientation

IDENTIFICATION. The Nahua are the most populous Native American group living in Mexico. The name "Nahua" is used by scholars to designate people who speak the Nahuatl language. The appellation derives from Nahuatl and appears to mean "intelligible," "clear," or "audible." Nahuatl speakers recognize the name "Nahua," but rarely employ it themselves. More commonly, they use the word "Mexicano" to refer to the Nahuatl language and as a general name for their ethnic group. "Mexicano" also derives from Nahuatl but has been Hispanicized and is pronounced and pluralized as in Spanish. Some writers use "Nahuatl" to refer both to the people and the language. Older-generation Nahua in the Huasteca sometimes refer to a member of their ethnic group as a "Mexijcatl," recalling the term of self-reference used by the ancient Aztecs. The name "Aztec" is properly used to refer only to the short-lived Mexica Empire that was forged by certain high-land groups of Nahua before the Spanish Conquest. Scholars commonly divide contemporary Nahua into subgroups based on the geographical area they inhabit. The Nahua described here live in the Huasteca region in east-central Mexico. William Madsen (1969) noted the relative lack of ethnographic studies of Huastecan Nahua culture at that time.

LOCATION. The Huasteca is a cultural-geographic region composed of portions of six states on the Gulf Coast of Mexico—Veracruz, San Luis Potosí, Tamaulipas, Hidalgo, Querétaro, and Puebla. The precise boundaries of the Huasteca are disputed by local inhabitants and experts alike. The region is bordered on the east by the Gulf of Mexico and on the west by the great Sierra Madre Oriental range. Many authorities agree that the Río Cazones defines the southern limit, and the Sierra de Tamaulipas forms the northernmost boundary. The Nahua generally occupy the hilly southern and western portions of this vast region; they are concentrated in northern Veracruz and northern Puebla, northeastern portions of Hidalgo, and southeastern San Luis Potosí. At lower elevations the climate is tropical and the territory well watered, with numerous rivers and arroyos flowing from the mountains and emptying into the Gulf. At higher elevations the climate becomes dryer and colder, supporting pine forests. There are distinct wet and dry seasons corresponding to summer and winter, respectively.

DEMOGRAPHY. It is impossible to determine the precise population of the Nahua of the Huasteca. Official counts are suspect because census takers usually do not have access to all members of the population. The Nahua live in communities scattered widely throughout hilly or mountainous terrain penetrated by few roads. Furthermore, when census takers determine linguistic affiliation, they count only people 5 years of age and older. Finally, there is the problem of deliminiting the boundaries of the Huasteca. Defining the Huasteca as consisting of ninety-two *municipios*, the 1990 census recorded 431,805 speakers of Nahuatl 5 years of age or older who live in the region.

LINGUISTIC AFFILIATION. Nahuatl belongs to the Uto-Aztecan Family and is related to several languages spoken in Mexico and North America. It was the language spoken by the Aztecs (Mexica-Tenochca), Toltecs, Tlaxcalans, and many other pre-Hispanic and contact-era peoples. Speakers are generally concentrated in the highland region of central Mexico. Linguists divide Nahuatl spoken in the Huasteca into eastern, western, and T dialects, although these are probably 95 percent mutually intelligible. The western dialect is spoken mainly in San Luis Potosí, Hidalgo, and a small area of Veracruz. Eastern Huastecan Nahuatl is spoken in extreme eastern Hidalgo, Veracruz, and the northern tip of Puebla. The T dialect (called Nahuat, as opposed to Nahuatl) is represented by an island of speakers

See also

Totonac

located in and around the town of Huejutla de Reyes in Hidalgo.

History and Cultural Relations

Neither the prehistory nor the history of the Huasteca is well known. A number of archaeological sites have been explored, and from these it appears that the earliest identifiable people to occupy the region were Huastec speakers. At the time of the Spanish invasion, the Huastec were struggling against Mexica expansion in their region.

Sometime probably during the late pre-Hispanic era, groups of Nahua, along with Otomí and Tepehua, migrated into the Huasteca. Ethnohistorical sources indicate that the first Nahua to settle on the Gulf Coast may have been refugees from the highlands escaping a great famine during the mid-1450s. Other sources mention that Motecuhtzoma II sent colonists to the coast to repopulate the area following a series of epidemics there. Documents record a number of military invasions launched by the Mexica and their allies. Archaeological evidence confirms a Mexica presence in the southern Huasteca; the best-known site is Castillo de Teayo. This ruin has not been excavated, nor even surveyed. It features a pyramid, ceramics, and at least fifty-two sculptures, all purportedly of Mexica origin. Dates for the site are uncertain, but the late fifteenth century seems reasonable. Based upon the few ethnographic studies conducted among the Nahua of the Huasteca, Nahua culture is linked to that of the highland peoples. Many rituals, deities, and beliefs, for example, are similar to those reported by sixteenth-century chroniclers of the Mexica. Nahua from more western regions of the Huasteca may originally have been part of the Aculhuacán Empire; they have remained largely independent of the Mexica.

During the colonial period, the Nahua of the Huasteca, along with most Native Americans in Mexico, experienced a cataclysmic decline in population owing to social disruption, forced labor, and disease. The scattered remnants of the population caused difficulties for Spanish administrators, who instituted a policy of establishing *reducciones* (areas where indigenous peoples were forced to settle) as early as 1592 in the southern Huasteca. These centralized locales were also known as *congregaciones* (congregations). Many contemporary Nahua communities are products of these colonial programs. Spanish missionary work began in the Huasteca prior to 1630, spearheaded by the Franciscans. Despite long exposure to missionaries, the southern Huasteca remains a conservative stronghold of pre-Hispanic religious beliefs and practices.

The Nahua areas of the Huasteca played an active part in the Mexican War of Independence in the early nineteenth century. Many people, probably including the Nahua, also participated in the war against France in the late 1860s and in the Mexican Revolution in the early part of the twentieth century. The Revolution brought land reform and the establishment of the *ejido* system, which effectively redistributed private land to many Native American communities, including some Nahua.

In 1901 the first government concessions were granted to oil companies to exploit reserves in the southern Huasteca. This development and other factors led to the building of roads into the interior and subsequent changes entailed by increased contact with urban Mexico. Prior to World War I, sugarcane was the major cash crop grown by people in the Huasteca. Following the war, people in the higher elevations, including many Nahua, began to grow coffee for the international market. Also during this time, cattle ranching became a lucrative business for people of the region. Most cattle ranches were owned by mestizos, but Nahua participated in production by acting as temporary laborers on ranches and, among the more affluent, by owning a few head of cattle that they raised in conjunction with their farming activities.

Population increases following World War II, along with economic and political instability, have caused a crisis for many Nahua farmers. Economic exploitation of small-scale village farmers and competition with cattle ranchers for arable land have led to a series of sometimes violent confrontations. Land invasions and military repression have given the Huasteca a reputation among urban Mexicans as being a lawless and dangerous region. Political crises, violence, and lack of economic opportunity have led increasing numbers of Nahua to leave the region and migrate to cities in search of employment. In 1992 the government of Mexico amended the land-reform laws established after the Revolution. It remains to be seen what effect this fundamental change in land tenure will have on Nahua of the Huasteca.

Settlements

In general, the Nahua live in villages that range in population from 200 to 800. Larger, more acculturated communities may be organized according

During the colonial period, the Nahua of the Huasteca experienced a cataclysmic decline in population owing to social disruption, forced labor, and disease.

to the Spanish model, with a church and plaza at the center. Smaller villages are often scattered groupings of houses belonging to kin. Dwellings of less acculturated people usually consist of a single room with a thatched roof. The floor plan is rectangular, although sometimes one of the short ends of the rectangle is curved. The walls are made from vertical poles tied to a framework with vines, and mud mixed with dried grass is sometimes applied to form a solid wall. Floors are of packed earth, kept clean by women who sprinkle them with water and sweep them daily. An architectural cycle is evident in which people use a newer house for sleeping and other activities while using the older habitation as a kitchen. Interiors are sparsely furnished with few manufactured items. Increasingly, houses have tar-paper or corrugated-iron roofs and may be constructed from cement block. Such houses frequently have cement floors as well. More acculturated villages may have electricity.

Economy

SUBSISTENCE AND COMMERCIAL ACTIVITIES. The Nahua of the Huasteca practice a mixed form of agriculture based upon the subsistence farming of maize. Members of some communities use a horse- or mule-drawn plow to turn the soil, whereas people in other communities, sometimes constrained by hilly terrain, use the slash-and-burn method with a dibble stick for seeding. Besides maize, the Nahua grow beans, chili peppers, squashes, onions, tomatoes, papayas, citrus fruits, tobacco, and condiments such as cilantro. Major cash crops include maize, sugarcane, and coffee. Animals raised include turkeys, chickens, pigs, bees, and, in well-to-do households, cattle. Virtually all Nahua families supplement their farming activities with secondary occupations.

INDUSTRIAL ARTS. The only widespread industrial production entails the manufacture of sugarloaf. A wooden, or, in the late twentieth century, a metal *trapiche* (cane press) is used to squeeze the cane stalks and extract the juice. This liquid is boiled until a thick syrup is rendered, then poured into molds and cooled, with the resulting loaf wrapped in cane leaves and sold in the market.

TRADE. Major trading takes place in weekly markets organized throughout the region. Many Nahua attend one or more markets, often at considerable distances from their home base.

DIVISION OF LABOR. The major division of labor is by sex. Women prepare food, make and repair clothing, attend to domestic chores, help with the harvest, and provide major care for children. They may also engage in one of a number of secondary occupations to help increase family income. These activities include baking bread, embroidering, gathering and selling firewood, pottery making, bonesetting, curing, midwifery, or operating a stall in a regional market. Men clear and plant fields, care for animals, build and maintain houses, weave fishing nets, hunt and fish, carry produce to the market for sale, and make sugarloaf. They may also engage in clearing forest and brush for regional cattle ranchers, picking coffee beans, temporarily working as a laborer in an urban area, playing music, curing, raising bees, or selling produce or animals at the regional market. Both men and women may choose to run a small one-room shop in their community as a means of earning extra money.

LAND TENURE. The land-tenure situation in the Huasteca is exceedingly complex. Many Nahua have rights to ejido land. Many others had invaded private ranch land and were in the process of applying for ejido status. Still others share-crop or farm as tenants, and many families combine several such approaches in order to gain access to farmland.

Kinship

KIN GROUPS AND DESCENT. The nuclear family is the most important kin group in Huastecan Nahua communities, but these units are often linked through male and sometimes female ties to form functioning extended families. Descent is determined bilaterally.

KINSHIP TERMINOLOGY. Huastecan Nahua kinship terminology has characteristics of both the Hawaiian and Eskimo systems. Parents are distinguished from parents' siblings, and grandparents are distinguished from their siblings, although not according the side of the family to which they belong. Cousins and those married to cousins are in some instances equated with Ego's siblings and their spouses.

Sociopolitical Organization

SOCIAL ORGANIZATION. Nahua social organization can be conceived of as a series of concentric rings surrounding the individual nuclear- or extended-family household. One step removed from the household is the nonresidential extended family. The next largest subdivision is a toponymic group composed of residents of a named subarea in a community. These subareas are based on residence, may entail shared ritual obligations, and usually include nonkin. In some cases, the toponym functions as a type of surname for residents. Smaller Nahua communities are often divided into upper and lower halves, which constitute an extension of the social circle beyond named subareas. Larger communities may be divided into two or more barrios, and these can be important extrakin groupings as well. The entire village or town constitutes the next encompassing circle. Daughter communities, usually established by families in search of land, extend the social circle outside of the local community. These may serve as a buffer between individual communities and the municipio and state levels of government.

POLITICAL ORGANIZATION. Larger towns are invariably led by mestizo elites, with Nahua occupying lesser positions in the hierarchy. A *cargo* system or civil-religious hierarchy often characterizes larger communities. In this system, individuals work their way up a series of unpaid political offices and sponsorships of saints' celebrations. In traditional villages, an informal council of male elders may be looked to for leadership, particularly in times of crisis. Ejidos are run by elected political officials as mandated by federal and state law.

SOCIAL CONTROL. Most social control is effectively handled within the community by means of gossip, accusations of sorcery, and the threat of ostracism. More serious offenses often result in the person having to leave the community for indefinite periods. In the severest cases, local authorities may bring an offender to officials of the municipio for trial and punishment.

CONFLICT. Disputes over access to scarce land resources are a common feature of many Nahua communities. Community members may band together in the face of external threats, but unsettled internal conflicts inevitably surface. Factions form along kinship lines and, if violence erupts, entire extended families may be forced to leave the community.

Religion and Expressive Culture

RELIGIOUS BELIEFS. Nahua religious beliefs are generally a syncretic mix of Native American traditions and Spanish Catholicism; however, even in areas where Catholicism appears to prevail, beliefs tracing to pre-Hispanic practices often remain strong. The sun has been syncretized with Jesus Christ and is seen as a remote creator deity. The moon-related Virgin of Guadalupe, a manifestation of the pre-Hispanic earth and fertility deity Tonantsin, is widely venerated. The pantheon incorporates a complex array of spirits

Among the Nahua of the Huasteca, factions form along kinship lines and, if violence erupts, entire extended families may be forced to leave the community.

MARRIAGE AND FAMILY

Marriage

Marriage customs vary according to degree of acculturation. In more remote communities, a couple may elope without the permission of the bride's parents, usually following a villagewide ritual or social occasion held for other reasons. Sometimes the bride's father feigns anger upon learning of the elopement, but he is eventually reconciled to the inevitable union. In some communities, marriage is a more formal affair in which an older kinsman of the husband-to-be acts as a go-between with the family of the potential wife. Gifts are exchanged, feasts may be held, and the two families enter into ritual kinship with each other. Weddings derived from Catholic or Protestant traditions are increasingly common in Nahua communities throughout the Huasteca. Postmarital residence is ideally patrilocal, but actual practice is in fact more flexible.

Domestic Unit

A majority of the domestic units in Huastecan Nahua communities are nuclear families. Related household heads often build their dwellings near one another, thus forming nonresidential patrilocal extended families. After marriage, young couples may live in the household of the groom's parents until they are able to build their own place of residence. This creates a temporary extended family living in the same household.

Inheritance

In theory, property is passed equally to male and female descendants; however, family lands usually pass to male heirs under the assumption that it is they who will farm them. Daughters acquire access to land through their husbands. In the absence of male heirs, daughters inherit land rights. In cases where arable land is scarce, the eldest son or daughter inherits the bulk of the estate, leaving younger siblings to face the problem of gaining access to additional fields. The house usually reverts to the youngest son with the expectation that he will care for his surviving aged parents.

Socialization

Nahua children are provided much attention, love, and support by both their fathers and mothers. Often an older sister cares for her younger siblings during the day, freeing parents to pursue their work unhindered. A child is normally surrounded by many relatives who are nearly the same age, and children have the run of the community and surrounding areas. Parents usually value education for their children and support local schools.

representing manifestations of a unified sacred universe: earth spirits associated with death and fertility, water spirits that distribute rain and provide fish, and celestial spirits that watch over people and also provide rain. A complex sacred geography is associated with mountains, springs, caves, lakes, arroyos, and the Gulf of Mexico. More acculturated communities may have a cult surrounding the saints. A significant religious development in the 1970s and 1980s was the conversion of increasing numbers of Nahua by U.S.-based Protestant-fundamentalist missionaries.

RELIGIOUS PRACTITIONERS. In more traditional Nahua communities, the primary religious specialist is the shaman, called *tlamatiquetl* ("person of knowledge"). These shamans may be either male or female, and they undergo an apprenticeship under an established master before practicing on their own. Other specialists include midwives, and, in more acculturated communities reflecting Catholic influence, catechists and prayer leaders. Few Nahua communities have a resident priest. During the 1980s, under the influence of North American missionaries, some Nahua have become lay Protestant pastors.

CEREMONIES. The Nahua have a rich ceremonial life that is partially synchronized with the Catholic liturgical calendar. Major occasions include a winter-solstice ritual devoted to Tonantsin, planting and harvest ceremonies, and important commemorations of underworld spirits at Carnival in the early spring and on the Day of the Dead in the fall. In more Hispanicized communities, celebrations of saints' days may be part of a civil-religious hierarchy. Noncalendrical observations include curing and disease-prevention rituals, ceremonies to control rain, pilgrimages to sacred places, ceremonial washing of newborn infants, the creation of ritual kinship ties, house blessings, divinations, and funerals.

ARTS. Nahua of the Huasteca generally do not recognize artistic expression as a separate sphere of activity. Women take pride in creating beautiful, colorful embroidery on their blouses and in constructing well-made clothing for their families. Men fashion headdresses from mirrors, folded paper, and ribbons and perform dances during important ritual occasions. Men also play musical instruments and are the ones most likely to engage in storytelling. Both male and female shamans engage in the practice of cutting intricate and aesthetically powerful images of spirits from paper; as part of their religious observations, they also construct complex altars designed to be beautiful places.

MEDICINE. Medical practices include the use of herbs to treat symptoms of disease, bonesetting through massage, and attendance by midwives at births. These pragmatic measures are supplemented by elaborate symbolic healing procedures orchestrated by shamans. The use of cut-paper figures to represent various spirits is characteristic of curing rituals held by the Nahua of the southern Huasteca. These rituals, which vary in complexity and length according to the seriousness of the symptoms, are usually preceded by a divination to determine the cause of the malady. In extreme or chronic cases, individuals may visit a regional clinic to seek help from a Western-trained medical specialist.

DEATH AND AFTERLIFE. Beliefs concerning the afterlife are in transition under influence from both the Hispanic dominant culture and late-twentieth-century Protestant proselytizing efforts. The fate of the soul is linked to the circumstances of death rather than being a reward or punishment for behavior. The *yolotl* soul, representing a person's life force, generally travels to an underworld place of the dead called *mictlan*, where it eventually dissipates. The *tonali* soul, linked to the personality, disappears at death. There is a widespread belief that the souls of those who die from water-related causes go to a kind of watery paradise. People who die prematurely are thought to become disease-causing wind spirits.

Bibliography

Beller, Ricardo N., and Patricia Cowan de Beller (1984–1985). *Curso del Náhuatl moderno: Náhuatl de la Huasteca.* 2 vols. Mexico City: Instituto Lingüístico de Verano.

Madsen, William (1969). "The Nahua." In *Handbook of Middle American Indians,* edited by Robert Wauchope. Vol. 8, *Ethnology, Part Two,* edited by Evon Z. Vogt, 602–637. Austin: University of Texas Press.

Medellín Zenil, Alfonso (1982). *Exploraciones en la región de Chicontepec o Huaxteca meridional.* Jalapa, Veracruz: Editora del Gobierno de Veracruz.

Ochoa, Lorenzo (1984). *Historia prehispánica de la Huaxteca.* Instituto de Investigaciones Antropológicas, Serie Antropológica, no. 26. Mexico City: Universidad Nacional Autónoma de México.

Reyes García, Luis (1960). *Pasión y muerte del Cristo Sol: Carnival y Cuaresma en Ichcatepec.* Cuadernos de la Facultad de Filosofía y Letras, no. 9. Jalapa, Veracruz: Universidad Veracruzana.

Reyes García, Luis, and Dieter Christensen, eds. (1976). *Das Ring aus Tlalocan: Mythen und Gabete,*

Lieder und Erzählungen der heutigen Nahua in Veracruz und Puebla, Mexiko; El Anillo de Tlalocan = Mitos, oraciones, cantos y cuentos de los Nawas actuales de los Estados de Veracruz y Puebla, México. Berlin: Gebr. Mann Verlag.

Sandstrom, Alan R. (1991). *Corn is Our Blood: Culture and Ethnic Identity in a Contemporary Aztec Indian Village.* Civilization of the American Indian Series, vol. 206. Norman: University of Oklahoma Press.

Schryer, Frans J. (1990). *Ethnicity and Class Conflict in Rural Mexico.* Princeton, N.J.: Princeton University Press.

Williams García, Roberto (1957). "Ichcacuatitla." *La Palabra y el Hombre* 3:51–63.

—ALAN R. SANDSTROM

PUERTO RICANS

Ethnonym: Puertorriqueños

Orientation

IDENTIFICATION. The people of Puerto Rico weave their distinctive ethnic identity from three historical traditions: Spanish colonial, Afro-Caribbean, and North American. Puerto Rican cuisine, religious beliefs, and other identifying components of their expressive culture draw heavily upon Spanish and Afro-Caribbean traditions. Puerto Ricans share rituals and practices with their neighbors throughout Latin America as well as with English- and French-speaking peoples of the Caribbean; yet Puerto Rican educational, political, and economic systems have had to incorporate many North American features owing to U.S. domination since 1898. Puerto Ricans identify strongly with their homeland, their history, and their place in the Caribbean. Although Puerto Ricans have a legal claim to U.S. citizenship, they rarely refer to themselves as "Americans," even while residing on the U.S. mainland. Puerto Rican attachment to their islands has endured despite large-scale emigration to the mainland since 1917, the year they were granted citizenship status (largely because the War Department wanted legal grounds to enlist Puerto Ricans into the World War I endeavor).

One segment of the population, derogatorily referred to as "Nuyoricans," are children born to Puerto Ricans living in New York City. The often impoverished condition and ambivalent cultural status of mainland Puerto Ricans adds yet another dimension to Puerto Rican identity, with some segments of the population incorporating urban street-survival methods and outlooks into their ways of life.

LOCATION. Lying on the eastern end of the Greater Antilles in the Caribbean, between Hispaniola and the U.S. Virgin Islands, Puerto Rico is so well situated in the sealanes that it was a prize territory of the Spanish from the earliest years of the Conquest. The main island is around 169 kilometers long and 56 kilometers wide, although the territory includes a number of smaller outer islands, the largest of which, Vieques, rivals Saint Croix (U.S. Virgin Islands) in size and serves, in part, as a base for the U.S. Navy. Puerto Rico has a land mass of 8,874.6 square kilometers, and its climate is subtropical.

Three overlapping mountain ranges—Cordillera Central, Sierra de Cayey, and Sierra de Luquillo—extend in an east-west direction along its interior. North of the chain of mountains, as with most Caribbean islands, the island is generally wetter and lusher; the southern slopes and plains tend to receive less rain and have a drier, savanna appearance. Its surrounding waters include the Mona Passage (just west of the main island)—a highly productive fishing ground and often treacherous channel for illegal immigrants crossing from the Dominican Republic—and the extremely deep Puerto Rican Trench, renowned in the tourist industry for its sportfishing.

DEMOGRAPHY. Puerto Rico is the homeland of between 6 and 7 million people, although only slightly more than half the population actually resides on the island. The 1990 census counted 3,522,037 Puerto Ricans living on the island, and estimates of those living in the continental United States range between 2.5 and 3 million. The Puerto Rican people thus constitute a diaspora—a dispersed people—residing in areas of New York City, such as the South Bronx, as well as in the Caribbean. Migration, a common demographic feature of the population at least since 1917, has been a means to escape domestic problems, seek education and fortune, and deal with economic woes. The Puerto Rican fertility rate—perceived to be high in relation to natural and economic resources—has been a matter of much social planning and dispute, leading to spotty and largely ineffective sterilization and other family-planning programs. Population density on the island is high, with 369.9 persons per square kilometer.

LINGUISTIC AFFILIATION. Puerto Ricans speak Spanish, although it is distinctly different from the Spanish spoken in other Latin American or Caribbean regions. The ability to speak English

Puerto Rico is the homeland of between six and seven million people, although only slightly more than half the Puerto Rican population actually resides on the island.

is widespread, owing to the high rates of migration between Puerto Rico and the U.S. mainland and to the practice of teaching English in many of the private and public schools. At the university level, much of the instruction is in English, and the exchange of faculty and students between U.S. mainland and Puerto Rican universities is quite common.

The teaching of English in the primary and secondary public schools has been a subject of much debate in Puerto Rico, since many regard the teaching of English instruction as an infringement upon Puerto Rican cultural autonomy. Others view the lack of English instruction in school as a barrier to statehood; still others view it as a mechanism for maintaining the island's status quo.

Settlements

Because Puerto Ricans constitute a diaspora, it is difficult to locate them in terms of defined territory. Their "settlement" patterns include New York City and other major metropolitan areas off the islands, and the dispersed households of Puerto Ricans may include members living in as many as three to five locations on the islands and the mainland.

The main island of Puerto Rico is most densely populated along its coastal fringe. The four major metropolitan centers are San Juan, Ponce (south-central coast), Mayagüez (west-central coast), and Arecibo (north coast). The San Juan metropolitan area, which includes several cities and districts, extends in all directions except north (the seaward side). Old San Juan retains its prominent position at the mouth of San Juan harbor. Bayamón and Cataño ajoin the western limit of the metropolis. The business and financial center of Hato Rey, along the Río Piedras, home of the main campus of the University of Puerto Rico, lie along the south end of the city, and the tourist districts stretch out aong the ocean to the east.

Most of the settlements depart from the usual grid pattern of Spanish settlement and instead extend outward from town squares that might have once been centrally located. The development of public housing and land-annexation schemes to accommodate the growing population have undermined the centrality of town squares. Government housing-development schemes have been implemented islandwide.

Economy

SUBSISTENCE AND COMMERCIAL ACTIVITIES. Puerto Rico emerged from a Spanish colonial past of haciendas and peasant farming to become dominated by large-scale farming of sugarcane, coffee, and tobacco following the U.S. annexation of the island, in 1898, during the Spanish-American War. During the first part of the twentieth century, the sugar industry in particular

HISTORIC DISTRICT

A street scene in the historic district of Ponce, one of Puerto Rico's four metropolitan areas. Ponce, Puerto Rico. (Macduff Everton/Corbis)

stimulated migrations of the small peasant farmers from the inland highlands to create a rural proletariat to work on the sugar plantations. Until after World War II, agriculture in general and sugar in particular dominated the economy, lending a seasonal dimension to the island's work that was common throughout much of the Caribbean. It became usual to work on the island during the later fall and winter months, when sugarcane and other crops needed their heaviest labor inputs, and then to migrate to the mainland during the summer months. This regime succeeded in converting much of the smallholding peasant population into wage laborers.

Puerto Rico retains the vestiges of a peasantry today, but few Puerto Ricans conform to the *jíbaro* stereotype of the strong, hardworking, independent farmer, which today serves as a Puerto Rican national symbol. For part of their subsistence, many of the island's inhabitants still rely on combinations of fishing, farming, and gardening with casual wage work. The Caribbean practice of "occupational multiplicity"—combining a number of odd jobs—is common enough in Puerto Rico that short-term, irregular jobs have been given their own term—*chiripas*. Puerto Ricans are eligible for some social assistance from the U.S. government. Although they receive fewer transfer payments per capita annually than the general population of the United States, transfer payments make up proportionately more of the incomes of Puerto Rican households that receive them.

INDUSTRIAL ARTS. Since the 1950s, agriculture as a cornerstone of the Puerto Rican economy has yielded ground to service industries, tourism, and manufacturing. A development program known as "Operation Bootstrap" was designed to industrialize the island following the decline of sugar production. Much of the growth in manufacturing has been the result of special provisions in the U.S. tax code that make it desirable for U.S. firms to operate assembly plants on the island. Most of the products of these plants are produced solely for export. They include optical equipment, pharmaceuticals, chemicals, shoes and clothing, and electronics.

Attracting industry to the island is also facilitated by a labor force perceived to be docile and generally antiunion. Owing to similarities between Cuban and Puerto Rican histories and the fear of a revolution like Cuba's, since the late 1950s there has been a subtle yet comprehensive suppression of socialist thought in Puerto Rico. The antiunion sentiments thus derive in part from the association of unionism with socialism.

Puerto Rico's tourist industry is centered around San Juan, which serves as a port for cruise ships. Old San Juan, with its Spanish-colonial cathedrals, fortifications, customs and merchant houses, and other impressive architecture, is a well-known shopping and historical district for tourists. San Juan is also known for its luxury resort hotels and casinos, which grew in favor after restrictions on travel between the United States and Havana. The promotion of other parts of the island, especially its beaches and two national parks—El Yunque (a tropical rainforest), and Bosque Seco (a dry forest on the southwest coast)—has intensified since the early 1980s.

TRADE. Puerto Rico's position in the sealanes established San Juan as an important port early in the island's European history. Today Puerto Rico competes with Miami as an international center of banking and commerce for many Latin American and Caribbean nations. Its political status as a U.S. territory, combined with the bilingual capabilities of most of its businesspeople, gives it an advantage over other Caribbean nations in acting as a liaison between Latin American and North American business interests. Its commerce is constrained, however, in that the same restrictions that apply to trade between the United States and other nations also apply to Puerto Rico. Puerto Rican politicians cannot negotiate trading and other international arrangements independently of the U.S. federal government.

DIVISION OF LABOR. Unskilled and semi-skilled labor has been one of Puerto Rico's principal exports since late in the nineteenth century. Migration between the mainland and the island, whether spontaneous or encouraged by the insular government, served the needs of low-wage industry and agriculture much more than it encouraged or facilitated upward mobility across generations or entrepreneurial behavior. The working histories of Puerto Ricans reveal cycles of work and rest, or employment and unemployment, owing to the hazardous or monotonous nature of many of the jobs Puerto Ricans obtain. Most civilian Puerto Ricans work either in the public sector or at low-wage jobs. Since 1917, the U.S. military has drawn upon Puerto Ricans as soldiers and civilian workers; the large number of Puerto Ricans involved in the Vietnam War is reflected in the fact that some neighborhoods bear Southeast Asian names.

Although much of the population remains a low-income proletariat, partially dependent on government transfer payments, the labor force includes a substantial professional and managerial

The working histories of Puerto Ricans reveal cycles of work and rest, or employment and unemployment, owing to the hazardous or monotonous nature of many of their jobs.

class because of the growth of the island's prominence in banking, insurance, and commerce. Many of these individuals have found work in Sunbelt cities such as Miami and Houston, where their bilingual skills are in demand because of growing Latino business transactions.

The island's labor force also includes those who occupy positions in the informal economy of petty commerce, small-scale manufacturing, food processing, fishing, and farming. Historically, within peasant farming and fishing families, there has been a division of labor by sex, although men and women tend to be capable of most of the same tasks required to pursue small-scale fishing and farming. Often these "informal sector" jobs are combined with government jobs, which tend to be allocated through political patronage.

LAND TENURE. The agrarian past and jíbaro identity make landownership a desirable goal for Puerto Ricans. In accordance with U.S. law, land in Puerto Rico is privately owned and available for sale or purchase on the open market. Yet there have been variations owing to Puerto Rico's special political status and circumstances. The state has owned and operated sugar plantations, for example, but more common have been government schemes designed to make land available to the poor for house construction. These schemes emerged as the sugar industry began to decline in importance, leaving many sugar workers unemployed or displaced from company housing. Called *parcelas*, the program consisted of providing plots of land to families with low incomes and then providing a number of contiguous plots with public services such as water, sewer, garbage collection, and electricity. The growth of squatters' settlements is not unknown to Puerto Rico; sometimes these precede parcelas development.

Kinship

Puerto Ricans trace their ancestry through both sexes, but have nothing corresponding to corporate lineal descent groups. Their kinship terminology conforms to the Eskimo system, with some local variations for the expression of deference, affection, respect, and fictive-kinship ties based on the common Latin tradition of *compadrazgo*. Compadrazgo, acknowledged as ritual coparenthood at the baptism of a child, is one of the principal institutions for establishing interhousehold relations.

Marriage and Family

MARRIAGE. Marriages in Puerto Rico are usually recognized by the Catholic church. Common-law or consensual unions, once typical in peasant regions, have become less common. Marriage takes place at a young age, usually in the teens, and most Puerto Ricans desire children shortly after marriage. Both marriage and the birth of children are important events in terms of forming bonds between families and households, with well-established visiting patterns among related households and compadrazgo relations formed between households at the baptisms of children.

DOMESTIC UNIT. The Puerto Rican diaspora has had a strong influence on the character of the domestic unit. Households may or may not be units bounded by dwellings, plots of land, or even the boundaries of the commonwealth. The 1990 census reports 3.31 persons per household in Puerto Rico, a figure that is probably an underestimate because of the dispersed nature of Puerto Rican households. Interdependent groups of individuals residing in a number of different locations characterize most Puerto Ricans' domestic units. Individuals come together and part over the course of seasons, years, and phases of the life cycle. In Puerto Rico, the typical unit consists of a woman and man and their unmarried children, yet it is not uncommon for unmarried or widowed parents to live with their children, and visiting patterns among households and dwellings are such that the lines between households often become blurred. On the mainland, there is a much higher incidence of households headed by women with small children than there is on the island.

INHERITANCE. In principle, all possessions of the deceased are to be divided into three equal parts: the *legitimá* (legitimate), which is divided equally among the children; the *mejora* (best), which is divided among the children according to the decisions of the deceased; and the *libre disposición* (freely disposable), which is given to the spouse. In real terms, possessions are divided among surviving kin and heirs based on access and residence. Specifically, heirs who have direct access to family land or fishing equipment because they farm or fish nearby plots or waters are likely to benefit from the inheritance more than heirs who have migrated to an urban area in Puerto Rico or emigrated to the U.S. mainland. The extent to which inheritance causes legal disputes among surviving family members varies with the size of the inheritance. A small inheritance generates few disputes, whereas great wealth is likely to be transferred from the dead to the living by careful legal documentation.

SOCIALIZATION. The socialization and enculturation of Puerto Rico's young occurs in the home and neighborhood, public and private schools, the Catholic church, and in the fluid social realms of the diaspora. In these varied social fields, Puerto Ricans are affectionate and loving toward their own and others' children. Much of the teaching is by example; corporal punishment is rare.

In the ghettos of the South Bronx, these ideals are difficult to uphold under the stress of poverty. Puerto Rican children on the mainland are as susceptible as any ghetto youth to the influences of the street: gangs, drugs, crime, the reification of sports as an escape, and pressures to leave school. Witnessing their children coming under these influences, many household heads choose to return to the island with their families or, failing that, send their children back to families still on the island once those children have reached adolescence. On the island, children from lower-class families who work in the informal sector, from fishing households, or from small farming households tend to learn the crafts of the household between the ages of 8 and 10.

Sociopolitical Organization

POLITICAL ORGANIZATION. Puerto Rico is a highly politicized society, with three main political parties that compete with one another in elections. For the first five decades of U.S. domination of the island, island politics were overseen by a series of U.S. government officials similar to colonial administrators. Just before, during, and after World War II, the Partido Popular Democrático (Popular Democratic Party, PPD) gained the strength necessary for Puerto Ricans to demand greater autonomy from Washington. Early in Puerto Rican party politics, the issue of the island's political status was at the forefront of its relationship with Washington. Prior to 1952, the political debate dealt with whether the island should become a state or become independent, but in 1952 the compromise status of commonwealth was granted, which allowed the islanders to continue receiving tax benefits and limited assistance from the United States yet elect their own governor. Luis Muñoz Marín oversaw the declaration of the new status; his legacy remains in Puerto Rican politics to this day. Today three political parties, differentiated from one another primarily over the issue of the island's status relative to the United States, compete for power in Puerto Rico. The most powerful party since 1952, the PPD, still prefers commonwealth status, and two others, the Partido Nuevo Progresista (New Progressive Party), and Partido Independentisa Puertorriqueño (Puerto Rican Independence Party), are prostatehood and proindependence, respectively. Elections often affect one's job prospects, as changing local and regional politics determine the distribution of jobs in the public sector.

SOCIAL CONTROL. Puerto Rico has its own civilian police force, along with a National Guard. The U.S. military maintains bases on the island as well. All this force is insufficient to control crime, which ranges from petty theft, larceny, and carjacking to murder and terrorism. The high crime rate has been linked to the island's poverty, high unemployment, high fertility levels (which have resulted in large proportions of juveniles), and the influence of New York City street culture on Puerto Rican youth. Many programs designed to alleviate poverty and unemployment are seen as social-control mechanisms, particularly the housing-development programs. The Catholic church has had a moderating influence on the island's crime rate.

CONFLICT. Conflict and conflict resolution occur on formal and informal levels. Formal conflicts involve crimes against people and property and are dealt with through police, judicial, and penal methods common throughout the United States. Informal conflicts arise within and between Puerto Rican households over moral and ethical behaviors, inheritance, courtship, and other issues important to Puerto Rican values. These types of conflicts often involve families, as opposed to individuals, in their resolution. Conflicts among groups quite often are resolved through combinations of negotiation, publicity, and civil disobedience.

Religion and Expressive Culture

RELIGIOUS BELIEFS. Puerto Ricans are predominantly Catholic, yet their beliefs, rituals, and practices often stray outside the orthodox boundaries of Catholicism. Puerto Ricans do not generally differentiate between official Catholicism and their rituals and beliefs and give little credit to African and Latin American influence on their religion. In addition to the rich homage paid to saints, as is common throughout Latin America, parts of the island still host beliefs in the evil eye, saints' miracles, faith healing, and witchcraft. Catholic icons are common in Puerto Rican households, often intermingled with photographs of family members and clusters of ceramic and porcelain figures. Protestant sects—particularly the Pentecostal church—have converted a small portion of the population.

CEREMONIES. Baptisms, marriages, weddings, vigils, processions, and funerals all come

Puerto Rico has a rich history of folk music, which incorporates Caribbean and Spanish influences and often involves storytelling, social critique, and joking.

within the scope of Catholic ceremonies. In addition to these, Puerto Ricans celebrate religious and political holidays with great enthusiasm—singing, playing music, drinking, and feasting in recognition of a sacred day, an historical event or figure, or a time of year. Often called "home fiestas," these observances tend to be private affairs that bring together close friends and family members. Public fiestas include those that honor patron saints and occasional folk-music festivals. Some towns, for commercial reasons, have invented festivals, for example, the seafood festival in Puerto Real, a fishing community on the west coast. Cockfights, which can assume as ritualist and ceremonial a flavor as other sporting events, bring large numbers of people together.

ARTS. Puerto Rican theater, dance, and other arts benefit from the culture's association with New York City yet combine with these influences more local cultural elements considered unique to the island. Puerto Rico has a rich history of folk music, which incorporates Caribbean and Spanish influences and often involves public storytelling, social critique, and joking. As in other Caribbean countries, there exist wood carving, doll making, and weaving traditions on the island, although many of these have come to be oriented toward the tourist trade.

The distinctive literary tradition of Puerto Ricans negotiates among Spanish, Latin American, and Nuyorican influences. Critics all too easily dismiss much of Puerto Rican literature and drama as overly political, obsessed with U.S. domination and the colonial past. For example, René Marqués uses rebellious and critical protagonists to illustrate the complex effects that imposed economic and political structures have on dislocated folk, but his work goes beyond a simple indictment of the status quo, tracing subtle and overt influences of social conditions on individual character. In personal essays, he acknowledges without apology his kinship with social critics throughout Western history.

In their poetry, Puerto Ricans have labored to free themselves from the formal qualities that characterized their verse during the years after U.S. occupation, when many poets withdrew into Spanish traditions in search of a defining cultural identity. Julia de Burgos internalized this struggle in her poems and marshaled it to confront the difficulties of romantic love and desire in a society dominated by Catholicism and machismo. Since the 1960s, growing attention has been given to the poetry originating from New York's Nuyorican Poets' Cafe: violent images in the work of

Miguel Piñero, pride in the Puerto Rican heritage overcoming despair in that of Pedro Pietri, or the strength that poverty and bitterness inspire in that of Jorge Lopez.

MEDICINE. Western medicinal practice is as firmly established in Puerto Rico as it is throughout much of the United States, yet the Latin American and Caribbean traditions continue to provide solutions where Western medicine is weak, especially in the realm of prevention. *Curanderos* (native curers) and *brujas* (witches) are still prevalent throughout the island; these individuals often mix herbal remedies with religious ritual and Western medicines in their cures.

DEATH AND AFTERLIFE. In Puerto Rico, death and the passage into afterlife are commonly marked by vigils, or wakes, and novenas, which are days of prayer for the dead. During the vigils, which occur between death and burial, the close friends and relatives of the dead gather around the body, which lies in state, and pray for the soul's passage into heaven. Throughout the night of the vigil, people who knew the deceased come and go while a small group of women and men who were particularly close to the dead say the rosary. Candles burn, and the prayers last until dawn of the day the person is to be buried. Following the funeral, the novenas begin. These nine consecutive days of prayer take place in the house of the deceased and constitute a means by which God's favor is solicited on behalf of the deceased's surviving kin and friends, as well as a means of reaffirming ties among households and community solidarity.

Bibliography

Bonilla, Frank, and Ricardo Campos (1981). "A Wealth of Poor: Puerto Ricans in the New Economic Order." *Daedalus* 110:133–176.

Buitrago Ortiz, Carlos (1973). *Esperanza: An Ethnographic Study of a Peasant Community in Puerto Rico.* Tucson: University of Arizona Press.

Griffith, David, Manuel Valdés Pizzini, and Jeffrey C. Johnson (1992). "Injury and Therapy: Proletarianization in Puerto Rico's Fisheries." *American Ethnologist* 19:53–74.

Koss-Chioino, Joan (1992). *Women as Healers, Women as Patients: Mental Health Care and Traditional Healing in Puerto Rico.* Boulder, Colo.: Westview Press.

Lewis, Oscar (1977). *La Vida; A Puerto Rican Family in the Culture of Poverty: San Juan and New York.* New York: Random House.

Mintz, Sidney W. (1974). *Worker in the Cane: A Puerto Rican Life History.* New York: W. W. Norton & Co.

Picó, Fernando (1986). *Historia general de Puerto Rico*. Río Piedras, P.R.: Ediciones Huracán.

Steward, Julian, Robert A. Manners, Eric R. Wolf, Elena Padilla Seda, Sidney W. Mintz, and Raymond L. Scheele (1956). *The People of Puerto Rico*. Urbana: University of Illinois Press.

—DAVID GRIFFITH

TOTONAC

Ethonym: Totonaca, Totonaco

Orientation

IDENTIFICATION. The word "Totonaco" is recognized as the name of this Amerindian ethnic group by its own members. According to oral tradition, "Totonaco" is derived from two words in their language: *tutu* (three) and *naku* (heart). The interpretation most frequently given, which is also noted by Kelly and Palerm (1952), is that the name refers to the three historical centers of the Totonac population. The exact locations of these three centers vary according to historical references and regional traditions. The area inhabited by the Totonac has been known as the Totonacapan since at least the sixteenth century.

LOCATION. The Totonacapan includes portions of the Mexican states of Puebla and Veracruz. In the former, the Totonac lived in the mountainous region known as the northern Sierra de Puebla. In Veracruz, the Totonac were found from the mountain highlands to the coastal plains, between the Río Cazones and the Río Tecolutla. Currently, this area continues to have the highest concentration of the Totonac population; however, a growing number have migrated to cities in search of higher wages. There are Totonac living in urban areas such as Mexico City, Poza Rica, Jalapa, Cholula, and Puebla de Zaragoza.

DEMOGRAPHY. According to the 1990 census, there were 207,876 speakers of the Totonac language who were 5 years of age or older. The state of Puebla had 86,788 speakers of Totonac, and the state of Veracruz had 111,305; 3,056 Totonac speakers resided in Mexico City. There are also Totonac migrants in the states of Tlaxcala and México.

LINGUISTIC AFFILIATION. The Mesoamerican language closest to that of the Totonac is Tepehua, the language of their nearby neighbors. Together they form a linguistic group known as Totonacan, which is related to the Huastec and Mayan linguistic groups, although the nature of this relationship is under discussion. Totonac has some dialectal variations, but these can be understood without difficulty by native speakers.

History and Cultural Relations

According to Totonac oral tradition, their ancestors helped build the ancient city of Teotihuacán, located 42 kilometers northeast of Mexico City; however, there is no archaeological evidence to support this claim. After the decline of the city, Totonac legend maintains, they migrated to the area that became known as Totonacapan. They established important centers of population at Cempoala and Tajin, in coastal Veracruz. Traditional deities are still worshiped at the temple complex at Tajin. Aztec warfare and domination weakened the Totonac rulers. Archaeologists have developed a different, more objective view of the early history of the people of this area, but this is the history the Totonac accept.

Eager to defeat the Aztec, the Totonac helped the Spanish invaders, as was noted by the chronicler Bernal Díaz del Castillo. Nevertheless, they fared no better than any other Indian group under Spanish colonial rule. In areas where the Spanish colonists resided, newly introduced diseases ravaged the Amerindian population, and forced labor occasioned a soaring mortality rate. The Franciscan clergy evangelized Totonacapan, building churches with Indian labor and converting the communities to a somewhat superficial Catholicism.

Fortunately for the Totonac, the region's hot, wet climate and uneven terrain made it unattractive to most of the Spanish colonizers, thus affording a certain amount of political and cultural autonomy for the indigenous people during the colonial period. Essentially self-governing, Totonac communities experienced limited external influence.

Following Mexican independence in 1821, the Totonac of Veracruz became enmeshed in conflict with mestizos over land and over interference with Totonac ritual life. In 1836 the bishop of Puebla, Francisco Pablo Vázquez, prohibited the Indians from celebrating their Holy Week rituals. The ensuing rebellion (1836–1838), led by Mariano Olarte, began at Papantla. Eventually, the establishment of *conduenazgos* (the legal term for the recognition of communal lands by the state) permitted the Indian communities of Veracruz to defend their lands for the remainder of the nineteenth century.

The Totonac of the northern Sierra de Puebla were able to maintain a greater autonomy. They

According to Totonac oral tradition, their ancestors helped buld the ancient city of Teotihuacán.

See also

Nanua of the Huasteca

proved to be valuable allies to the regional leaders, usually mestizos. The Totonac supported these strongmen as long as Totonac villages were left alone. They also contributed to the triumph of liberal forces at Puebla in the Batalla del Cinco de Mayo in 1863.

During the Mexican Revolution, Totonac villages were attacked and burned by different factions. People from remote areas entered Totonacapan, and growing numbers of mestizos entered Totonac villages. The situation of social unrest allowed mestizos to establish themselves and find economic opportunities in villages in which mestizos had been previously unwelcome, and conflict over landownership became acute.

A few Indian strongmen (*caudillos*) arose after the Revolution, but mestizos obtained political control with the help of regional leaders who were able to obtain power on a national level. The most notable case is that of Manuel Avila Camacho, who was president of Mexico in the 1930s and was from the northern Sierra de Puebla, where his wealthy family was prominent in mestizo society.

Economy

SUBSISTENCE AND COMMERCIAL ACTIVITIES. The principal crop, maize, is considered a basic part of every Totonac's diet. In the highlands, there is only one season for the cultivation of maize (March to September or October). In the lowlands, two crops per year are possible; however, land erosion and overuse of the soil have made double cropping more difficult. Agriculture is labor intensive. Other subsistence crops are beans, chilies, and, on a lesser scale, other vegetables that are grown on small family plots near the houses.

Sugarcane became an important commercial crop in Totonacapan during the colonial period, although production could not rival that of the great sugar plantations. Coffee began to be cultivated on a large scale around 1950. The ecological conditions in many communities are favorable for this plant, and production boomed in the following decades. Prices, however, are dependent on the international market for coffee beans, and cultivators suffer great losses when they go down.

SOCIOPOLITICAL ORGANIZATION

Social Organization

Community identity is not always related to ethnic identity because various locations have multiethnic populations. The most important obligation to the community is communal labor, but this tradition has been weakened in some areas owing to religious conflict between Catholics and Protestants.

Political Organization

All Totonac communities have elected political authorities, but the political process itself is subject to outside control. Indian participation varies greatly from one location to another. Those who are elected to office tend to speak Spanish and to have migratory experience and at least a grade-school education. Religious and civil hierarchies were once united in all the communities; they are now separate, but this development is more recent in some areas than in others.

Social Control

Municipal authorities are responsible for maintaining peace in the communities. Officials rely not only on their limited knowledge of the Mexican penal code but also base decisions on local customs that establish the parameters of socially acceptable conduct. The influence of elders was once important but has been greatly weakened. When offenders commit major crimes, they are now judged and sentenced by higher authorities outside the community.

Conflict

Unequal distribution of land remains a principal cause of conflict. Agrarian struggles continue, and political parties have become involved in them. Peasant movements are widespread. Elections are highly contested, and factionalism is prevalent. The federal government all too often resorts to force to end conflicts. Violence is commonplace; the charge on which Totonac are most frequently incarcerated is homicide.

In Veracruz, vanilla has traditionally been an important commercial crop. Because of a growing consumer rejection of artificial chemical substitutes for vanilla, the cultivation of this crop has expanded and may offer an alternative to dependence on coffee as the only cash crop.

The oil industry has created new jobs for many Totonac men living on the coastal plains of Veracruz, but it has damaged the marine environment and some agricultural lands.

INDUSTRIAL ARTS. Tools, household items, and clothing are made by family members. There is no external market for these goods.

TRADE. The Totonac rely on middlemen to take their agricultural produce to distant markets. Aware that these individuals were monopolizing the transport and distribution of produce to the detriment of the growers, the Mexican government created agencies to replace the middlemen, who had become local caciques, but corruption and mismanagement proved difficult to eradicate. The Instituto Mexicano del Cafe, a government agency for the purchase and marketing of coffee beans, was terminated in 1989. Attempts to create nonprofit marketing agencies that aid the small growers of cash crops continue, with varied results.

DIVISION OF LABOR. For many years, men were in charge of the maize fields and women took care of the household and the family vegetable plots. Coffee cultivation, which requires a great deal of labor, has altered these patterns; women, children—in fact, entire families—work together to harvest the delicate beans. Migration in search of wage labor has led to further changes: when the men are absent, women must work the fields themselves or find someone else to carry out the household agricultural labor.

LAND TENURE. Small private holdings are predominant in Totonac communities. There are few *ejidos* in the northern Sierra de Puebla. Communal lands, which do not fall within the category of government-granted ejidos, are also scarce. The distribution of land is unequal; mestizo cattlemen own large ranches, whereas many Indian families are landless rural laborers. Many owners of small plots of land have formed cooperatives, often with government aid, to obtain mutual benefits. Along the coast of Veracruz, Totonac fishers are also organized into cooperatives.

Kinship

KIN GROUPS AND DESCENT. Some Totonac communities in the northern Sierra de Puebla had patrilineal systems of descent that were based on residence in a specific location and on a common surname. Conflicts over land, a consequence of the Mexican Revolution, destroyed these systems, although they are still remembered by aged persons. Great importance is given to the relationship of *compadrazgo* (ritual coparenthood).

KINSHIP TERMINOLOGY. Few kinship terms in Totonac remain—only those for uncles, aunts, grandchildren, cousins, and members of the nuclear family. No distinction is made between maternal and paternal relatives.

Marriage and Family

Marriage was traditionally arranged by both families. Preferably, a high "price" was paid for the bride, in goods or the groom's labor. When this was not possible, couples eloped and negotiation of payment followed. A church-sanctioned marriage is an ideal today, but the cost of a wedding feast deters many couples.

DOMESTIC UNIT. The ideal domestic arrangement is a nuclear family living near the relatives of the husband. Extended families spanning at least three generations are also common. The practice of polygamy, which is considered a symbol of wealth, is diminishing because of the efforts of both Catholic priests and Protestant preachers.

INHERITANCE. Customarily, among the Totonac of the northern Sierra de Puebla, upon a man's death, his land is inherited by his eldest son. Among coastal Totonac, a father bequeaths land to all sons equally. Direct inheritance from father to daughter is highly exceptional.

SOCIALIZATION. From infancy, a child is educated by the extended family. All children must go to elementary school, but what is taught there is not always adequate to meet the needs of the communities. Bilingual education has rarely been fully implemented.

Religion and Expressive Culture

RELIGIOUS BELIEFS. Totonac popular Catholicism is a complex reelaboration of elements of both Iberian and Amerindian religion. The concepts of the deities and their relations to humans are not those of institutional Catholicism. According to the Totonac view, there are sacred beings that have power over aspects and places of the world. These include not only the images of saints in churches but beings with Amerindian attributes, such as the Dueño del Monte, a mountain god. Many Totonac have been converted to Protestantism, especially that of the Pentecostals, who are highly critical of popular

Prestige was traditionally accrued by those Totonac who sponsored religious festivals honoring the saints and their images. Participation by all families was obligatory.

Catholic beliefs. In some communities, this has created conflict.

RELIGIOUS PRACTITIONERS. Prestige was traditionally accrued by those who sponsored religious festivals honoring the saints and their images. Participation by all families was obligatory. Those persons who had held official positions in a *cargo* system (which governs sponsorship of festivals) received the important status of *principales*. The cargo systems were independent of the Catholic clergy.

Pentecostalism offered an opportunity for young people to obtain status outside the cargo system by becoming charismatic preachers. To counter the growth of Protestantism, the Catholic church also created pastoral programs for laypersons. Such programs often characterize traditional Indian religion with its Catholic borrowings as "superstitious."

CEREMONIES. Rising costs have affected the system of individual-family sponsorship of religious festivals. An alternative to individual-family sponsorship has been the establishment of collective groups to finance the ceremonies.

ARTS. The Totonac consider the Dance of the Voladores, in which the performers unwind from ropes attached to the top of a pole, to be an important symbol of their ethnic identity. Although other indigenous peoples of the region perform this dance, the Totonac regard themselves as the best performers. The dance is rich in symbolism; it represents birds descending from the sky. Professional troupes of Volador dancers travel to large cities within Mexico and abroad.

MEDICINE. There are various native health specialists. *Parteras* (midwives) are elderly women who attend pregnant women and supervise natural births, for which they enjoy high status. *Curanderos* heal through the use of medicinal plants and ritualized ceremonies. *Brujos* have knowledge of sorcery and can cast and break magic spells through contact with the supernatural. In the past, persons accused of sorcery often were murdered. Medical care is also given by doctors at government clinics that exist in most communities. The Totonac tend to consult either traditional or institutional medical practitioners, or both, depending on the circumstances.

DEATH AND AFTERLIFE. There are specific godparents (*compadres*) of death, who help pay the cost of burial. The Day of the Dead, on which spirits are said to return to the village, is an important feast. Protestants, like Catholics, arrange flowers on the tombs of the dead, although they do not celebrate with alcohol or incur excessive expenditures.

Bibliography

Garma Navarro, Carlos (1987). *Protestantismo en una comunidad totonaca de Puebla*. Mexico City: Instituto Nacional Indigenista.

Harvey, H., and Isabel Kelly (1969). "The Totonac." In *Handbook of Middle American Indians*, edited by Robert Wauchope. Vol. 8, *Ethnology, Part Two*, edited by Evon Z. Vogt, 638–681. Austin: University of Texas Press.

Kelly, Isabel, and Angel Palerm (1952). *The Tajin Totonac*. Washington, D.C.: Smithsonian Institution.

Masferrer, Elio (1986). "Las condiciones históricas de la ethnicidad entre los totonacos." *América Indígena* 46(4).

—CARLOS GARMA NAVARRO

TRINIDADIANS AND TOBAGONIANS

Ethonym: Trinidadians

Orientation

IDENTIFICATION. The name "Trinidad and Tobago" is a conjunction of the names of the two islands that comprise this independent state. "Trinidad" is often used alone to refer to the two islands as a political unit. Columbus, on his third voyage, in 1498, sighted three points of an island; in appropriating it for Spain, he called it "Trinidad," in honor of the Holy Trinity. This etymological history has subsequently been commemorated by various Christian authorities, including John Paul II during a 1986 papal visit. The name "Tobago" apparently derives from the Carib word for a smoking receptacle for tobacco, the plant that was reportedly the first item from Tobago to be exported to Europe.

LOCATION. The island of Trinidad is located in the Caribbean Sea at 10°30′ N and 6°30′ W, and 11 kilometers (at the nearest point) from the Venezualan coast. It has an area of 4,950 square kilometers. The island of Tobago lies 32 kilometers northeast of Trinidad and has an area of 290 square kilometers.

DEMOGRAPHY. The population of the two islands was 1,299,301 in 1992, with an average of 214 people per square kilometer. Life expectancy at birth is 70 years. The average annual growth rate from 1965 to 1980 was 1.3 percent, although the rate fluctuated with net annual migration, which reached a high of 17,370 in 1970 and a low of 2,200 in 1976. Brooklyn, London, and Toronto are the most common destinations for Trinidadians. Because many return after many years, and many move back and forth a number of times in a lifetime, the process is better described as one of transmigration rather than emigration.

LINGUISTIC AFFILIATION. Although Trinidad and Tobago is an English-speaking country, its speech forms are diverse. They vary with class and social context, from a local "dialect" that is substantially opaque to foreign English speakers to a Global Hegemonic English (G.H.E.) articulated by television newscasters and prescribed in schoolrooms. Moreover, almost all Trinidadians hear a substantial portion of the range of English used on U.S. television programs and in contemporary popular music by U.S. artists. In general, writing is in G.H.E., and there have been few efforts to establish a written form of the local dialect.

History and Cultural Relations

The pre-Columbian population of Trinidad has been estimated at nearly 30,000 to 40,000. Almost a century passed after Columbus's landing on Trinidad before the Castilian Crown attempted, in 1592, to establish a permanent European settlement. By then, intermittent contact had probably reduced the indigenous population by one-half. For the next two centuries, the island remained an insignificant and sparsely colonized outpost of Castile's empire in the Americas. In 1725 Trinidad's settler population included only 162 adult males. In the last three decades of the eighteenth century, during a period of alliance between Paris and Madrid, the Castilian government sought to fortify and increase profits from its colonies. Catholic planters from elsewhere in the Caribbean—largely from French colonies rocked by the Haitian Revolution, other slave uprisings, and the French Revolution—were encouraged to settle with their slaves in Trinidad. By 1797, the population of the island had reached nearly 18,000 persons, of whom 10,000 were slaves and just over 1,000 were Amerindians. It was during this period of French settlement, specifically in 1787, that the first sugar mill was built on Trinidad. Ten years later, however, approximately 130 mills were in operation. British forces took control of the island in 1797, and Trinidad, along with nearby Tobago, was formally ceded to Britain in 1802. Tobago had been largely ignored by Europeans until the early seventeenth century; thereafter, it was regarded as a strategic military site and shifted hands some twenty-two times between 1626 and 1802.

The British slave trade was abolished in 1807, and Emancipation was initiated in 1834, with a planned six-year period of "apprenticeship." At the time of Emancipation, the colonial state recorded a population of some 20,000 slaves; 3,200 Whites; 16,300 Coloreds; and only 750 Amerindians. Apprenticeship ended in 1836, some two years before the date scheduled by the British state, owing to resistance by the enslaved population. During the 1840s, the colonial state acted both to anglicize Trinidad (establishing the Church of England, for instance) and to ensure a continued supply of abundant, exploitable labor for plantation agriculture. Beginning in 1845, indentured laborers were brought to Trinidad from India, and, when such immigration ended in 1917, just under 144,000 indentured laborers had entered the colony. Beginning in 1868, these primarily Hindu and Islamic settlers—together termed East Indians—were missionized by Canadian Presbyterians.

In 1889 Tobago and Trinidad were for the first time joined as a unit of colonial administration. Commercial production of oil began in Trinidad in 1902, and by 1911 Trinidad's first refinery was in operation. Following labor protests in 1925, Trinidad's Legislative Council was reformed to include a small number of elected members, although suffrage was limited to approximately 6 percent of the population. Beginning in 1935, laborers struck the sugar plantations, and in 1937, the oil fields. The primary leaders of this working-class uprising were Adrien Rienzi and Tubal Uriah Butler. By the time of these strikes, petroleum had become the colony's most valuable export: in 1932 oil accounted for 50 percent of Trinidad's export earnings, and by 1943, 80 percent. Trinidad's petroleum was, moreover, a significant fraction of the British Empire's total production as Britain fought World War II: 44 percent in 1938, rising to 65 percent by 1946. The petroleum industry was not, however, significant in terms of direct employment—only 8,000 persons were so engaged in 1939, whereas some 40,000 were involved in farming and refining sugarcane in 1930, even though Trinidad's sugar industry was increasingly unprofitable. In 1941 Britain ceded land for two military bases to the United States. Over the next four years, Trinidad's economy was driven by the construction of the U.S. bases. Following a wartime ban on Carnival, victory in Europe was celebrated in Port-of-Spain by a V-E Carnival, at which bands of tuned petroleum drums—steelbands—were first seen in public performance.

In contrast to their espoused ideals, colonial elites among the Trinidadians and Tobagonians practiced a system of dual marriages or sexual unions.

In 1946 universal adult suffrage was introduced, and in 1956 the People's National Movement (PNM) led by Eric Williams, formed Trinidad's first home-rule government. In 1957, in the midst of negotiations to establish the Federation of the West Indies, Williams and Norman Manley of Jamaica each announced that they would not stand for election to the federal parliament, thereby foreshadowing their states' withdrawals from the federation. A year later, a structurally weak federation was established, comprised of all the British West Indian colonies except Guyana and Belize. In 1960, after leading nationalist demonstrations against the U.S. military bases, Williams negotiated leases for the bases. Within a decade, however, the United States concluded that the bases were of little importance and returned them to Trinidad. Following Jamaica's withdrawal from the federation at the end of 1961, Williams and the British made plans for Trinidad and Tobago to be established as an independent state. In January 1962 the British Parliament passed the acts granting independence to both Jamaica and Trinidad, and, in the same month, it passed the new Commonwealth Immigration Bill, which restricted entry from independent former colonies. Trinidad and Tobago became independent on 31 August 1962. In 1970, following a period of rising unemployment, Black Power demonstrators focused attention on continued racial discrimination in employment and on Trinidad's economic dependence. As a result of price increases instituted by the Organization of Petroleum Exporting Countries (OPEC), state revenues increased by 1,100 percent between 1973 and 1978. In the 1980s, however, the decline in the world oil price produced a severe recession. After thirty years of continuous rule by the PNM (1956–1986), Trinidad has had two changes of government during this recession: the 1986 elections were won by the National Alliance for Reconstruction (NAR); in 1992, the electorate returned the PNM to power. In 1995, the NAR and the United National Congress (UNC) formed a majority coalition.

Counting persons by "ethnic origin," the 1990 census reported that 43 percent of the population was African, 40 percent East Indian, 14 percent mixed, 1 percent White, 1 percent Chinese, and 1 percent other. In Trinidad, however, race and color identities are, to a great extent, shifters, which vary with observer and context. Thus, counts of ethnic groups give them a false concreteness: distinctions between "mixed" persons and others are particularly ambiguous and contested. Historically, African, East Indian, and European cultures interacted and were re-shaped in colonial society. Today these labels of ethnic origin are used for lifeways, worldviews, and values that are decidedly West Indian. Trinidadian culture has also been shaped by the society's historic porosity vis-à-vis the North Atlantic metropolises.

Settlements

Approximately 50 percent of the population lives in the east-west corridor that includes both Port-of-Spain and Arima. As much as 20 percent of the population lives in a second densely populated area around San Fernando, in the southeast. Oil refineries are located in the south of the island, oil rigs off the southern coast. Sugar fields are concentrated in low-lying areas on the western coast.

Economy

SUBSISTENCE AND COMMERCIAL ACTIVITIES. Since independence, per capita gross domestic product (GDP) has fluctuated with international oil prices. In 1973 per capita GDP was estimated at U.S.$1,180; the figure peaked in 1982 at $6,800 (using official exchange rates) but has declined since then, reportedly to $4,210 in 1987. Trinidad has a large middle class, but there are also extremes of wealth: the wealthiest quintile of the population has 50 percent of GDP, and the poorest, 4 percent. During the oil-boom years, the government sought to end the economy's dependence on the world oil market by establishing state-owned energy-based industries, including a steel mill and a fertilizer plant. The economy's performance in the 1980s indicates, however, that this diversification did not meet its goal. The costly steel mill is now owned and operated by Nucor, a U.S. company. Since the end of World War II, both commercial and subsistence agriculture have declined steadily, although there is evidence of increased food production during the continuing recession; most food, however, continues to be imported.

INDUSTRIAL ARTS. In 1980 Trinidad had a reported literacy rate of 96 percent, and three-quarters of the secondary-school-age population were enrolled in schools in 1986. As a consequence of state educational policies and employment in the petroleum industry, Trinidadians have become a highly skilled industrial labor force. Transemigration has, however, removed a disproportionate number of skilled laborers and professionals.

Trinidadians have also developed important organizational, manufacturing, and design skills through the production of the annual Carnival.

TRADE. Two local conglomerates import most consumer and commercial goods. Trinidad has some half-dozen large shopping malls, each with its own supermarket. Until the recession of the mid-1980s, the government restricted the importation of many items and levied large tariffs on others, for the purpose of promoting local production. Only in a very few cases did these policies lead to the development of alternatives to foreign imports. Moreover, large import companies were often able to obtain exemptions from trade restrictions. A "suitcase trade" in light goods—notably clothing—thrived, although such trade was largely outside the official economy. After the elections of 1986, the NAR government adopted a policy of increased trade liberalization, which has largely been continued under the PNM government since 1992. Throughout the postindependence era, the United States has been Trinidad's main trading partner.

DIVISION OF LABOR In 1982 some 21 percent of the population was employed in services (including public administration), 19 percent in commerce, 19 percent in construction, 16 percent in mining and manufacturing, and 8 percent in agriculture. Women constituted 33 percent of the labor force in 1982.

Kinship

Although Trinidadians follow the Euro-American pattern of reckoning genealogical relatedness, such relatedness is not, in social practice, a distinct principle of association or group formation: kinship and friendship merge in daily life. Descent is bilateral. Trinidadians use basically the same kin terms as the English and Americans.

Marriage and Family

MARRIAGE. Euro-American ideals of religiously sanctioned weddings and monogamy were avowed by colonial elites as signs of "respectability." For some, these ideals remain guides for conduct; for others, they are the basis for stigmatizing and stereotyping certain segments of society; and for still others, they are foreign values, largely irrelevant to local circumstances. In contrast to their espoused ideals, colonial elites practiced a system of dual marriages or sexual unions. Upperclass males characteristically married a status equal but had extralegal unions—some of long duration, some acts of rape—with women of lower status. The cultural distinction between "inside" and "outside" partners remains important.

DOMESTIC UNIT. There is great variation in the composition of Trinidadian households. Households of monogamous couples and their children are not culturally aberrant, but neither is one comprised of a middle-aged woman, her (transmigrant) son's former girlfriend, and the latter's child by a subsequent boyfriend. Such an example illustrates the open rather than distinctive character of "kinship." Attributional aspects of sexual difference are culturally emphasized: men and women are deemed fundamentally different. Concomitantly, husbands and wives generally have separate household roles and responsibilities.

INHERITANCE. Property generally passes from parents to children. Historically, the distinction between "inside" and "outside" children has been manifest in patterns of inheritance.

SOCIALIZATION. Women are regarded as more suited to the care of young children, although both men and women display great affection for children. It is not unusual for grandmothers and aunts, as well as mothers, to raise children. Formal education in schools, generally beginning by age 5, is highly valued.

Sociopolitical Organization

SOCIAL ORGANIZATION. Colonial society was organized hierarchically by the valorization of things European. The hierarchy of race and color was not, however, scalar: it did not rank all non-Europeans on a single social ladder. Rather, the discourse of race inscribed two very different principles of subordination to Europeans. Africans, deemed lacking an ancestral civilization, could, through both education and sexual "mixing" with Whites, become at least partially Europeanized; paradoxically, they could also be seen as becoming "West Indian" or "Creole" through this mixing. By contrast, East Indians were considered saturated with an (inferior) ancestral civilization of their own and therefore not amenable to "mixing," "Europeanizing," or becoming "West Indian"—even when they adopted and developed lifeways that reflected their presence in Trinidad. This ideological image prevailed, notwithstanding substantial social and sexual "mixing" of Indians with both Whites and Afro-Trinidadians. Historically, this complex system of racial distinctions and identities has shaped class relations. This system of racial typifications has served to naturalize the value placed on being "White" or "European," to divide subordinated classes by masking the social

In 1965 new legislation limited the right of Trinidadians and Tobagonians to strike, and since then the government has intervened to impose labor stability.

entanglements of East Indians in the West Indies, and to define Trinidad as a "mixed" and/or "plural" society, in contrast to the imagined purity and homogeneity of European nation-states. These racial typifications and their consequences have been contested throughout Trinidadian history, and, since independence, racial stratification has been substantially attenuated.

POLITICAL ORGANIZATION. Trinidad is a parliamentary democracy with a bicameral parliament comprised of an elected House of Representatives and an appointed Senate. Peaceful elections have taken place regularly since independence. The head of government is the prime minister; the presidency is a largely ceremonial position. For the first thirty years after independence, Trinidad had a single stable political party, the People's National Movement, and a frequently reorganized and renamed opposition alliance. During this time, political support broke roughly along racial lines, between Afro-Trinidians (in support of the PNM) and East Indian Trinidadians (in support of the opposition). Until his death in 1981, Eric Williams, an Oxford-trained historian, led the PNM. In 1986 opposition groups formed the National Alliance for Reconstruction. Under the leadership of A. N. R. Robinson, the NAR that year drew electoral support from nearly all classes

and ethnicities. Once in power, however, the alliance and its wide support quickly eroded. In 1992 the PNN returned to power, with Patrick Manning serving as the new prime minister.

SOCIAL CONTROL AND CONFLICT. In 1965 new legislation limited the right to strike, and since then the government has intervened, with substantial success, to impose labor stability. High unemployment in the late 1960s led to widespread unrest by the urban proletariat and lumpenproletariat in 1970. The resulting demonstrations, supported by a segment of the small military force, posed a serious threat to the government and were dispersed by police and military intervention. The unrelated rise in oil revenues that began in 1972 led to a decrease in unemployment, a dramatic increase in government patronage for the urban underclasses, and, consequently, a substantial increase in mass support for the state. This patronage, however, declined dramatically during the recession of the 1980s. In July 1990 an attempted coup by about a hundred members of the Jamaat-al-Muslimeen, a relatively small group of Afro-Trinidadian Muslims, led to four days of unrest and considerable loss of state control. Although the coup had little mass support, it was symptomatic of widespread disaffection from the state among workers and the urban unemployed.

Religion and Expressive Culture

RELIGIOUS BELIEFS. The 1980 census counted Catholics (32 percent), Hindus (25 percent), Anglicans (15 percent), Muslims (6 percent), Presbyterians (4 percent), Pentacostals (3 percent), as well as othe religious groups. What these figures fail to reveal, however, is the prevalent belief that these (and other) religions all worship the same God in largely valid ways. Most Trinidadians have attended, and to a greater or lesser extent participated in, services outside their own religion. For many in Trinidad, religious differences are understood as stylistically different routes to a shared divinity rather than as incompatible systems of values.

CEREMONIES. The world religious traditions present in Trinidad conduct their characteristic ceremonies in globally recognizable ways. With some exceptions, however, there is a modulation of religious piety. For example, although the pre-Lenten Carnival is intensely celebrated, Lent is not a time of dramatic self-denial, and neither is Ramadan.

ARTS. The most popularly practiced arts are associated with the annual Carnival. For each Carnival, topical calypsos are composed and performed, and costumes for new masquerade

ROAD MARCH

A Trinidadian man wears an elaborate gold costume in the great Road March, a musical celebration and competition for Carnival. Streets of Port of Spain, Trinidad, Trinidad and Tobago. (Pablo Corral V, 1996)

bands—some with as many as 2,500 persons—are designed and crafted. Steelbands, or *pan*, require meticulous tuning and rehearsal, activities which are aesthetically and socially complex. A number of other important musical forms and traditions—notably *tassa* drumming—are associated specifically with Indo-Trinidadians, although this ethnic identification is oversimplistic. Peter Minshall, who has designed masquerade bands and worked in other performance genres, has achieved wide renown within Trinidad, as well as among avant-garde elements of the international art world. Novelist and essayist V. S. Naipaul and political theorist C. L. R. James are internationally acclaimed writers. Saint Lucia-born Nobel laureate Derek Walcott has worked in Trinidad for much of his adult life, while maintaining an academic appointment in the United States.

MEDICINE. Medical care is provided primarily by physicians, dentists, and registered nurses. There is a mixed system of private and public financing of health care.

DEATH AND AFTERLIFE. Christians and Muslims are generally interred in cemeteries, as are some Hindus, although cremation is more common for Hindus. Ideas about the afterlife are highly diverse.

Bibliography

Brereton, Bridget (1981). *A History of Modern Trinidad*. London: Heinemann.

James, C. L. R. ([1963] 1983). *Beyond a Boundary*. New York: Pantheon.

Naipaul, V. S. (1962). *The Middle Passage*. New York: Vintage.

Segal, Daniel (1989). "Nationalism in a Colonial State." Ph.D. dissertation, University of Chicago.

Singh, Kelvin (1994). *Race and Class Struggles in a Colonial State: Trinidad, 1917–1945*. Calgary: University of Calgary Press.

Yelvington, Kevin, ed. (1992). *Trinidad Ethnicity*. London: Macmillan.

—DANIEL A. SEGAL

TZOTZIL OF CHAMULA

Ethonym: Batz'i Krisanoetike ("true people" in Chamula), Chamula, Chamo' (Chamula's civil-ceremonial center), San Juan Chamula

Orientation

IDENTIFICATION. San Juan Chamula is a Maya township located in the highlands of central Chiapas, the southern-most state of Mexico. Chamula's Tzotzil name is "Chamo'," or "[where] the water died." According to a myth, Chamula's civil-ceremonial center was built on the site of a lake that San Juan (the patron saint) had dried up in order to make it habitable. Chamula is the largest and most densely populated of more than thirty Maya-speaking communities in the Chiapas highlands.

LOCATION. Chamula occupies an area of 364 square kilometers and the average elevation of its lands is 2,300 meters. Most people live close to the lands they plant, in hamlets scattered along hills and basins across Chamula's eroded terrain. As a consequence of erosion, water holes, the main sources of water, tend to dry up before the rainy season. When this happens, the Chamula abandon their hamlets, temporarily or permanently, and find other places to live. The highest mountain in the region, the Tzontevitz, lies within Chamula and is sacred to the Chamula and neighboring indigenous groups.

DEMOGRAPHY. The Chamula number around 100,000, of which about one-half live in the township, and the rest have emigrated to establish new communities both within and outside the highlands. The emigration process began more than a century ago and continues today as land shortages and political and religious conflicts force people to leave.

LINGUISTIC AFFILIATION. The Chamula speak Tzotzil, a language belonging to the Tzeltalan Group (Tzotzil, Tzeltal, and Tojolab'al) of Mayan languages.

History and Cultural Relations

Recent archaeological studies place the arrival of Maya speakers into Chiapas around 100 B.C. Theories suggesting that the immigrants may have come from the Chuj region in Guatemala are not yet supported by archaeological findings. Dispersion over the area appears to have been relatively rapid. Highland Tzotzil and Tzeltal lived in proximity with Zoque groups to the west and other Maya groups to the north (Chontal and Ch'ol) and east (Tojolab'al and Chuj). Aggressive Chiapanec groups entered the region about A.D. 900, settling to the south and constantly pressuring Tzeltal and Tzotzil towns. During the late Postclassic period (A.D. 900 to 1250), central Mexico strongly influenced highland Chiapas's political ideology, organization, religion, and other aspects of its culture. The area functioned as regional intermediary of an extensive network of trade between Guatemala, Tabasco, and central Mexico.

The Tzotzil of Chamula maintain friendly relations with people from nearby indigenous communities, with whom they share many cultural traits.

See also

Ladinos, Yukateko

*The Tzotzil of
Chamula still define
themselves as
independent
agriculturists who
plant their small
milpas with the
sacred trilogy of
maize, beans, and
squashes.*

Upon the arrival of the Spanish, highland Chiapas was divided into small, warring petty states. Chamula was a large population center. The Chamula built a fort to confront the invaders, whom they attacked with bows and arrows, slingshots, stone-tipped spears, boiling water, and boiling resin. Aided by Zinacantec warriors, Bernal Díaz del Castillo besieged the town and finally succeeded in entering the fort and overwhelming its defenders. In order to control the indigenous population, the Spanish founded Ciudad Real (now San Cristóbal de las Casas) in 1528.

Since that time, the city has been a center of Ladino (non-Indian) political and commercial domination in the highlands. The defiant attitude of the Chamula toward the dominant society has remained constant for five centuries. Exploited and oppressed through exaggerated tribute and taxes and forced-labor arrangements, the Chamula managed to keep alive central elements of their culture and identity that have helped them resist invasive forces. When the abuses of Spanish-colonial, and later, Mexican societies became intolerable, the Chamula joined other indigenous groups to rebel openly against their oppressors. Major rebellions took place in 1712 and 1867, when the insurgents struggled for the right to their own religion and better living conditions. The rebellions were quelled, but the insurgents were able to secure a measure of religious freedom. The Zapatista rebellion of 1994 focused international attention on the plight of indigenous peoples in Chiapas. Although the Chamula did not participate directly in this uprising (in view of the alliance of the Chamula oligarchy with the ruling Mexican Institutional Revolutionary party), many Chamula sympathize with the movement and recognize that their situation will be deeply affected by the aftermath of this struggle.

The Chamula maintain friendly relations with people from nearby indigenous communities such as Zinacantan, Chenalhó, and Tenejapa, with whom they share many cultural traits. They visit these and other communities to trade and attend their celebrations. Most of their interaction with other indigenous people and with Ladinos takes place in San Cristóbal de las Casas, where they go to sell their produce or woven goods, buy necessities, and worship. Ladinos despise indigenous people and usually mistreat and humiliate them, making them feel unwelcome in the city. To combat this situation, the Chamula utilize quiet resistance, forbidding Ladinos to take up residence within their *municipio* and making their own presence in San Cristóbal felt in ever larger numbers, as more of them seek economic opportunities there.

Settlements

Chamula's contemporary settlement pattern represents a continuation of ancient Maya ones. Most of the people live close to their land, in about one hundred hamlets of varying size. The civil-ceremonial center, or *jteklum* as the Chamula call it, contains a small permanent population. Civil officials move into Chamula Center for one to three years to carry out their duties, whereas religious officials rent a house for a few weeks to celebrate the saint under their care. The Chamula flock into town for market days (Saturdays and Sundays) and for religious celebrations (several times a year). Before 1960, the Chamula built wattle-and-daub homes with thatched roofs. At present, only the poorest people live in such houses. Most Chamula eventually build homes with cement blocks and tile roofs. Dirt floors are the rule. The fact that emigrants found new colonies that reproduce fundamental cultural traits of the original community reveals the vitality of Chamula culture and society.

Economy

SUBSISTENCE AND COMMERCIAL ACTIVITIES. The Chamula still define themselves as independent agriculturists who plant their small milpas with the sacred trilogy of maize, beans, and squashes. Planting one's own land is still the most respected occupation for men, as it stresses independence and commitment to traditional values. This, however, has increasingly become an unreachable dream since the end of the nineteenth century, when large coffee farms in Chiapas started recruiting a cheap labor force from highland indigenous groups. The high elevation of lands in Chamula, the fact that they have been intensively planted for hundreds of years, and the fractionalization of land bestowed upon both male and female children have reduced the size of landholdings and their productivity. On average, the Chamula can produce only about 20 percent of their yearly food requirements on their own lands. Most Chamula depend upon wage labor on farms and plantations to support their families or to supplement their plots' production. Many rent lands at lower elevations to plant their foodstuffs—and move there during several months each year to care for their crops. The majority of households own sheep, an important economic asset, since they are the source of wool to weave the family's clothing. Most households also raise chickens, which are eaten occasionally during celebrations and as ritual food. Some households tend pigs to sell to Ladinos.

INDUSTRIAL ARTS. Some households produce utilitarian pottery, furniture, and candles, but weaving is a universal activity for Chamula women and is considered the quintessential female occupation. In the late 1970s many women learned to embroider and to produce more modern-looking garments for tourists.

TRADE. From Pre-Hispanic times, periodic local markets have been of central importance in the area. Everything is sold in these markets, from ritual objects, fresh produce, and cooked food to clothes, furniture, and other household needs. People attend the market with enthusiasm, for it is not only a place to buy and sell but also to exchange the latest gossip and visit with relatives and friends. Many Chamula peddle goods on the streets in some of southern Mexico's large cities.

DIVISION OF LABOR. A traditional, complementary division of labor between men and women existed in the past and still holds as the contemporary ideal; men are independent agriculturists, and women are weavers; they complement each other in household tasks. At present, men leave for wage labor, and women take charge of the household, domestic animals, and children, and plant their small plots.

LAND TENURE. Most lands within the township are individually owned, but forests and water holes are community property. Many Chamula have received *ejido* lands (i.e., lands granted by the government under agrarian reform laws) outside of the community.

Marriage and Family

MARRIAGE. Although the Chamula consider monogamy to be the moral way of life, many Chamula men have more than one wife. Polygyny has always been an option in this community. To contract marriage, a young man, assisted by his family and especially selected petitioners, goes to a woman's house to request her hand. Ideally, bride and groom have never spoken to one another, although they may have exchanged looks or words that signal their mutual interest. The young woman has a say in the decision, but parents may pressure her into accepting. Three weeks to a month go by from the beginning of the petition to the actual marriage (the "house-entering" ceremony), the process taking place according to Chamula tradition. Church weddings, in accordance with Catholic sacraments, are rare.

KINSHIP

Kin Groups and Descent

Patrilineages are constituted by two or more virilocal domestic units living in adjacent lands inherited from their ancestors. Strong in the past, patrilineages are rapidly losing ground because of a shrinking land base. Although there is still some preference for virilocality, the system now tends more toward bilocality. Young couples choose their residence near the groom's or bride's family, according to which family can offer them more land or space in the house; or, they establish residence close to either but manage their economy independently.

Kinship Terminology

Kin terms reflect the principles of age, gender, and generation, central organizing axes among the Chamula. People of a generation older than the speaker are addressed respectfully as "uncle" and "aunt." A Chamula couple establishes a fictive-kinship tie, or *compadrazgo*, with the godparents of their children. These ties are very important; they create or reinforce life-long friendships and foster respect and mutual aid among the people involved.

DOMESTIC UNIT. A household compound consists of several domestic units. The primary domestic unit consists of a couple, their unmarried children, their married sons, their sons' wives, and their son's children, all sharing a single maize supply and a house altar. This situation is changing because of the lack of land and other resources that supported the father's claim to his sons' and their families' labor; domestic units often manage their economy in an independent manner. The relationship of a woman to her in-laws may be strained; she tries to get her husband to build a new house for her and move out of his parents' house as soon as possible. Separation and divorce are common, especially during the first years of marriage. Major causes cited are the husband's drinking and domestic violence, his quest to acquire a second wife, the husband's or wife's laziness, or either spouse's conflict with in-laws.

INHERITANCE. Houses, land, and personal property are bequeathed in equal measure to male and female children.

*The Chamula
transformed imposed
Christian beliefs to
suit their central
Maya ideas.*

SOCIALIZATION. Children are viewed as sources of joy and important economic assets. Socialization takes place mainly within the domestic unit and extended family, with mothers, sisters, grandmothers, and aunts being the main socializing figures, given that men leave for months at a time for wage work. Fathers take their young male children with them to the fields in Chamula and to the farms or rented fields in the lowlands when the children are around 10 years old. Although more children are attending school now than were in the 1970s, children still participate actively, from a very tender age, in the household economy. They fetch water and wood, tend the sheep, help their parents at home and in the fields, grind maize, cook, spin, and weave. They start earning money from about age 15, when girls start selling their woven and embroidered goods, and boys begin wage work.

Sociopolitical Organization

SOCIAL ORGANIZATION. The extended family, compadrazgo, and the *cargo* system constitute the backbone of sociopolitical organization in Chamula. The cargo system in Chamula is a variant of civil-religious hierarchies in indigenous Mesoamerica, a system through which individuals alternate between civil and religious positions, thus climbing the ladder of prestige and power in their communities. The Chamula express their strong feeling of community by serving in this traditional hierarchy. Assisting the deities, they bring blessings upon their families and all the Chamula people.

POLITICAL ORGANIZATION. The regional town council, the traditional form of government, consists of several civil officials selected by a group of respected community elders. Its function is to uphold traditional Chamula values, arbitrate disputes over lands, and resolve intrafamilial problems. The regional town council also includes the religious hierarchy, a body of officials who sponsor public and private celebrations in honor of the saints. The regional town council represents a survival of the system of government that prevailed before the direct intervention of national and state controls in local affairs. Although Spanish and Mexican authorities had always encroached upon the affairs of Chamula, the government has intervened directly in its political life since the 1930s. Through the creation of the constitutional town council mandated by law, the government effectively manipulates the Chamula governing elite. A native elite has benefited from these ties, becoming rich and powerful while acting against

their own people. This new imposed system has diminished the influence of the traditional system of government in which community and religion were central guiding forces.

SOCIAL CONTROL. Shame is a powerful deterrent both for children who are learning Chamula ways and for adults who stray from the community's mores; hence, gossip acts as a central control mechanism. Minor offenses are punished by the regional council: the offender is shamed before a large audience at the town hall and is required to spend a few days in jail in Chamula. Rape and murder cases are adjudicated by the state authorities outside Chamula and punished by terms in state prisons.

CONFLICT. Since the early 1970s, political opposition against the ruling oligarchy in Chamula has taken the form of religious conversion to several evangelical sects. Converts oppose the authority of *ilols* (shamans), object to paying taxes for celebrations they consider pagan, and stop buying liquor. The ruling elite claims this behavior imperils the unity and cultural continuity of the Chamula people and, consequently, expels the converts. More than 15,000 people have been ousted in this way. The converts usually establish residence in colonies close to Chamula, on the outskirts of the Ladino town of San Cristóbal de las Casas. Conflict between traditional Chamula and expelled converts periodically erupts in violence and has become a major source of instability in Chamula.

Religion and Expressive Culture

RELIGIOUS BELIEFS. The Chamula transformed imposed Christian beliefs to suit their central Maya ideas. They merged Christ and Sun into the figure of Our Father, the Sun/Christ, and they merged the Virgin Mary, the Moon, and the Earth into a single female entity, Our Mother, the Earth-Moon/Virgin. Catholic saints, imbued with Maya characteristics, are viewed as helpers of Sun and Moon. Nature and topographic features of the landscape, such as mountains, caves, and water holes are infused with a sense of sacredness: they represent sources of life and places where human beings and deities come into contact. The Earth-lord, who lives inside mountains and "owns" all wild animals and water sources, must be propitiated before one partakes of his possessions. From birth, all human beings share a part of their soul with an animal. The Chamula interpret sudden death as the death of one's animal soul-companion.

RELIGIOUS PRACTITIONERS. Women or men ilols (i.e., "seers") conduct private healing rituals for individuals. Ilols obtain their gift for healing in dreams, directly from Our Father and Our Mother. They also preside over annual ceremonies at the water holes to ensure the water supply. Midwives conduct several ceremonies during a woman's pregnancy and labor to safeguard her soul and that of her baby.

CEREMONIES. Private curing rituals occur frequently and are held by the hearth in the patient's home or in the church in Chamula's civil-ceremonial center. Ilols entreat the deities, offering prayers, liquor, candles, and food to release their patients' souls from the hold of evil powers. Major and minor public ceremonies take place almost monthly to celebrate the day of a specific deity. Hundreds, sometimes thousands, of Chamula attend these long and complicated rituals, which include processions, dance, prayers inside and outside the church, and distribution of ceremonial foods at the religious official's home.

MEDICINE. The Chamula interpret illness as the result of the actions of an envious or ill-willed person who appeals to evil beings to seize his or her enemy's soul. The person targeted becomes "colder," loses his or her life force, becomes increasingly weak, and finally dies. "Heat," the essential component of life and health, must be restored through prayer (defined by the Chamula as "heated words"), liquor, nutritious foods such as chicken, ritual sweat baths, and coming under the life-giving influences of Our Father and Our Mother.

ARTS. Most Chamula women weave their own and their family's clothing on the backstrap loom; this ancient weaving technique has deep cultural and religious associations. The gift of weaving, like that of healing, is granted in dreams by Our Mother, the Earth-Moon/Virgin, to young women.

DEATH AND AFTERLIFE. Like illness, death is viewed as the result of the loss of one's soul through the schemes of malevolent individuals. The souls of dead people come back to visit their relatives and partake of their food offerings once a year, during the Festival of the Dead (K'in Santo), from 30 October to 1 November. Men and women intone special prayers beseeching the deities to release the souls of their dead relatives and inviting them to come to earth and enter their home.

Bibliography

Calnek, Edward (1988). "Highland Chiapas before the Spanish Conquest." In *Archaeology, Ethnohistory,* *and Ethno-archaeology in the Maya Highlands of Chiapas, Mexico.* Papers of the New World Archaeological Foundation, nos. 54–56. Provo: Brigham Young.

Eber, Christine, and Brenda Rosenbaum (1993). "'That We May Serve beneath Your Hands and Feet': Women Weavers in Highland Chiapas, Mexico." In *Crafts in the World Market,* edited by June Nash, 103–112. Albany: State University of New York Press.

Gossen, Gary H. (1974). *Chamulas in the World of the Sun.* Cambridge: Harvard University Press.

Gossen, Gray H. (1986). "The Chamula Festival of Games: Native Macroanalysis and Social Commentary in a Maya Carnival." In *Symbol and Meaning beyond the Closed Community: Essays in Mesoamerican Ideas,* edited by Gary H. Gossen, 227–254. Albany: State University of New York at Albany, Institute for Mesoamerican Studies.

Posas, Ricardo (1959). *Chamula: Un pueblo indio de los altos de Chiapas.* Mexico City: Instituto Nacional Indigenista.

Rosenbaum, Brenda (1993). *With Our Heads Bowed: The Dynamics of Gender in a Maya Community.* Albany: State University of New York at Albany, Institute for Mesoamerican Studies.

Wasserstrom, Robert (1983). *Class and Society in Central Chiapas.* Berkeley and Los Angeles: University of California Press.

—BRENDA ROSENBAUM

YUKATEKO

Ethonym: Máasehual, Maya, Mayero, mestizos

Orientation

IDENTIFICATION. The term "Maya" is of indeterminable antiquity and today is usually used by the Yukateko to refer only to their language, not to themselves. For self-identification, the terms used are "Mayero," which refers to a speaker of Maya; mestizo, which in Spanish means "mixed people"; or "Máasehual," an adapted Nahuatl word that denotes "poor people."

LOCATION. In pre-Columbian times and today, the Yukateko have inhabited much of the Yucatán Peninsula of Mexico, including the states of Yucatán, Quintana Roo, and Campeche. They live adjacently with other Maya groups such as the Kekchi and Mopan to the south near Belize, Guatemala, and the Mexican state of Tabasco.

DEMOGRAPHY. It is difficult to enumerate the Yukateko population because classification

♦ **mestizo**
A term used to refer to persons of mixed Indian and European ancestry. In most contexts, mestizo is in fact more a social than a racial classification.

See also
Tzotzil of Chamula

Most Maya feel helpless in the face of Hispanic domination.

criteria used by the Mexican government and those used by anthropologists differ, owing in part to the *mestizaje*, or Spanish/Maya "mixture" process, as well as the isolation of hundreds of communities. The best estimate is about 500,000, which suggests a recovery to near precontact levels.

LINGUISTIC AFFILIATION. Yukateko belongs to the Maya Language Family and is believed to have separated from other languages about 1000 B.C. Although there are regional Maya dialectal differences identifiable by native speakers, the language used among all Maya is rather homogeneous, the result of frequent population movements during colonial and contemporary times.

History and Cultural Relations

Archaeological evidence indicates that the earliest known settlements in the Yucatán Peninsula were fishing villages on the eastern coast, suggesting a Maya presence in the area for many thousands of years. The earliest Yukateko historical records in the form of hieroglyphic texts date to the fourth century A.D., with earlier texts found to the south. These Maya were probably Ch'ol speakers with a large-scale system of trading and warring city-states, ruled by priest/kings, at centers such as Tikal, Palenque, and Copán, which flourished and then declined during what has come to be known as the Classic period, from A.D. 250 to 900. The Yukateko were also present at Cobá, Ek'Balam, Edzná, Dzibilchaltún, and other centers, although the cataclysmic collapse of this system seems to have resulted in less depopulation in Yucatán than in other Maya centers. In fact, there is some evidence that when the sites in the Guatemala region were abandoned, through some combination of environmental abuse and internal discord, Yukateko people moved south to fill the void.

By A.D. 1000, the emerging central-Mexican Toltec apparently established dominance during what is called the Postclassic period at the previously Classic Maya site of Chichén Itzá, increasing their control of the Mesoamerican trade network. Following the demise of the Toltec, beginning about A.D. 1250, the Yukateko lived in regional chiefdoms until their first contact with the Spanish off the eastern coast in 1511. In 1526 Francisco de Montejo ("El Adelantado") began a military campaign that culminated in the official Spanish aquisition of the Yucatán in 1545, although many groups remained isolated. Thousands of years of indigenous cultural development were superseded by a European colonial system of *encomienda* (Spanish ownership of land inhabited by the Maya); forced religious conversion by Spanish friars, often through torture and Inquisition-style campaigns; and centuries of enslavement to the Spanish speakers.

Yucatán's attempt to secede from Mexico in 1846 and the use of Maya conscripts in the Yucatán militia led to a release of Yukateko resentment in what has come to be called the Caste War. Two years after the beginning of this organized Maya revolt in 1847, all Spanish-speaking Yukateko were driven to take refuge in the state capitals of Mérida and Campeche, but the arrival of the spring rains caused the Maya to return to the cornfields and thus to lose their military advantage. Skirmishes and retribution against the Maya continued until about 1910. During the Mexican Revolution, the Maya made their most recent attempt to "throw off slavery," by joining in local fighting against dominant landlords. Today, the development of tourism on the peninsula has put the Maya in increasing contact with North Americans and Europeans. The Maya generally regard these light-skinned people with respect for their socioeconomic prominence but consider their morality questionable or unclear.

Settlements

There is virtually no running water in the Yucatán Peninsula because of the karst (limestone-cap) topography with its maze of underground caverns; consequently, most settlements are found near naturally occurring sinkhole wells (Maya: *c'ono'ot*; Spanish: *cenotes*). Both the pre-Hispanic city-state and the colonial village or hamlet relied extensively on these cenotes for drinking water, although in the city-states, containment systems for rain water were built as well. Contemporary villages depend on wells dug in the twentieth century or on electronically run potable water systems installed by the Mexican government. The pre-Columbian village often clustered around a cenote, as did the administrative/ceremonial center of the nobility. Farmers and the general populace lived on the outskirts of such centers. Pre-Columbian centers, like contemporary hamlets, were constructed as quadrilaterals, with their four corners marking points aligned with the imagined four corners of the flat Maya earth. This quadripartite form provided a framework for integrating human living space within cosmological conceptions, through ritual activity that fostered human health and prosperity with supernatural assistance. Today, the thousands of communities, often isolated in the scrub brush of the north or the jungle of the south, can be contrasted with the few quasi-urban centers that also have considerable Maya habitation. In most of these, Maya is a lingua franca that many non-Maya must speak out of necessity.

Economy

SUBSISTENCE AND COMMERCIAL ACTIVITIES. For most of the thousands of years of occupation of the peninsula, the Yukateko have relied upon slash-and-burn (milpa, or *kòol*) horticulture. Evidence exists that pre-Hispanic Mayas supplemented kòol horticulture with other more intensive techniques such as raised fields. To make kòol, quadrilaterals of jungle are felled and burned in the dry spring. Planting occurs after the arrival of the first rains and continues for a total of three consecutive years. The fertilizing ash supplements the shallow soil. The field is then left fallow for fifteen to twenty years. This digging-stick-based system is perfectly adapted to the Yucatán environment, which does not favor mechanized agriculture. Maize, beans, and squashes have long been planted together. The maize tortilla (*wah*) is a dietary staple, and fruits and vegetables are often grown in house gardens. Since pre-Hispanic times, and to a lesser extent today, salt has been produced from coastal lagoons.

Today wage labor supplements subsistence or incomeproducing agriculture. In the northeast, residual estates producing henequen provide agricultural employment. Tourist resorts provide many low-paying construction jobs. These jobs have great allure for Yukateko men, however, because urban merchants pay below-market prices for their produce simply because they are Maya, a discriminatory practice that limits the potential for economic success through agriculture.

INDUSTRIAL ARTS. Certain communities have a reputation for producing high-quality hammocks (*k'áan*), hats, shoes, pottery, or *huipil* dresses, but such industry is highly localized.

TRADE. Pre-Columbian trade networks were both sea and land based, with the latter depending exclusively on foot transport, owing to the absence of draft animals. Markets as centers for exchange were more common in the past than they are today, with private or government-controlled capitalism requiring Mayas to transport their wares to urban centers. Village-level exchange, often based on Mexican currency, is usually preferred, given the difficulties of transport.

DIVISION OF LABOR. The Yukateko man is known by his profession of *kòolnàal*, or maize farmer, and is complemented by his wife, who is in charge of the domestic unit, usually venturing forth only to take her daily maize to the local grinder, collect firewood and water, go to market, go to church, or visit friends and family.

LAND TENURE. In pre-Columbian times, land use was controlled by political and kin groups. Today, the Maya have access to both private land, if resources allow, or federal *ejido* lands, which were made available through agricultural reform after the Mexican Revolution.

Kinship

KIN GROUPS AND DESCENT. Hieroglyphic inscriptions of the elite ruling class suggest that the centers of pre-Hispanic communities were inhabited by patrilineal and patrilocal extended families in which dynastic rulership would most often pass from father to son. Dynastic lineages are represented in great detail in hieroglyphic texts, tracing the right to rule back to cosmological creator deities and thereby linking kings with the supernatural realm and affording them divine authority. Spanish Conquest and subsequent subjugation removed this dynastic level from the social hierarchy, and a patrifocal system remains for the general populace.

KINSHIP TERMINOLOGY. Both Maya and Spanish terms are used in a patrifocal bilateral system.

Marriage and Family

MARRIAGE. Marriage is and has been expected of all adults, and in fact almost all Yukateko adults are married; those who are not are considered childlike in a number of contexts. Mexican law requires civil ceremonies for all, with those who can afford it also having a church service. In either, their parents' *compadres*, who are the couple's godparents, play a crucial role as they support and advise the couple, publicly and privately. First-cousin marriages are avoided. Postmarital residence is usually either neolocal or patrilocal, and divorce is uncommon.

DOMESTIC UNIT. Extended families are often still important, especially in maize production, but with wage labor at tourist centers increasing as an economic option, nuclear families, with spouses often separated for long periods of time, are becoming increasingly common.

INHERITANCE. As imposed by Spanish conquerors, Mayas acquire both of their parents' first surnames, with the father's being first. Property is divided only when both parents have died and the children have married.

SOCIALIZATION. Parents seem quite lenient, and although Maya life is typically very demanding,

For most of the thousands of years of occupation of the Yucatan Peninsula, the Yukateko have relied upon slash-and-burn (milpa, or kóol) agriculture.

great tenderness often exists between parents and children. A major paradox for parents is the conflict between maintaining pride in traditional culture and sensing the need for children to pursue economic opportunities outside the village. Toward this end, many parents will speak to their children in whatever little Spanish they know, although a high degree of Maya monolingualism is still evident. There is often great ambivalence for both parent and child if children leave, either to attend high school or to seek wage labor.

Sociopolitical Organization

SOCIAL ORGANIZATION. The more complex hierarchy of the pre-Columbian period changed to a system of local governance at the community or regional level, which has persisted from colonial times to today, as a result of the social and physical isolation of the Indians by the dominant Hispanics. Local prestige is attainable with age, by being skilled, or by having likable personal characteristics, such as being able to converse well. Formally organized social events center on the church, as during certain fiestas, where *gremios* (religious groups) carry the burden (*kúuc*) of celebrating their saint through the preparation of food and care of the saint's ritual paraphernalia. The *socios*, or those in charge of such groups, enhance their status by bearing this burden well. Organized cooperation is also characteristic of the ejido group, which is managed at the local level by the *comisario ejidal*, who coordinates access to federal ejido farmlands and assigns labor to be performed as service to the community.

POLITICAL ORGANIZATION. After the encomienda system of landlord rule ended with the Caste War and the Mexican Revolution, the new federal system became the political milieu for the Yukateko. The *municipio* is controlled by its largest community, which is called the *cabecera*, or head, and is governed by the municipal president. At the village level, a *comisario* (commissioner) represents local authority and is subservient to the president. He is elected for a multiyear term and is most effective if he is adept at negotiation and persuasion and refrains from trying to exert his power through coercion. Although mostly isolated in the bush and jungle of the peninsula, the Yukateko are integrated into the national political system, albeit at the bottom of the hierachy of power.

SOCIAL CONTROL. Yukateko communities are noted for hospitality and reserved behavior, with theft and other crimes being almost unknown, except in the larger cities. The only type of village disruption might be an occasional display of drunkenness, which is either handled informally or

by the police chief, who heads the community's *guardia* (unarmed police force). The guardia has a rotating membership, through which men fulfill their communal obligations and qualify for use of ejido land. Language also acts as a social-control mechanism: in the majority of bush communities, pressure is great for mestizos and Hispanics to speak Maya in public, strengthening Maya ethnic identity and countering external social domination.

CONFLICT. For some Maya and Hispanics, bitter memories linger of the killing that occurred during the Caste War. In general, however, violence across ethnic lines is very rare. Most Maya feel helpless in the face of Hispanic domination.

Religion and Expressive Culture

RELIGIOUS BELIEFS. The Pre-Columbian symbolic complex representing a worldview of the joined yet distinct realms of sky, earth, and underworld endures despite centuries of forced Christianization. Only recently have the Yukateko begun to call themselves "Catholics," because of the increased presence of various Protestant sects. The Catholic

rotestant division is a clear schism in the social fabric. Although from an external prespective Maya beliefs and ritual practices can be considered a syncretic mix of indigenous and European symbols, the Maya themselves make no such distinction, as they practice their religion daily.

Many pre-Hispanic deities are still significant today, although there is variation across the total population. The supreme creator deity of the past was probably a double-headed sky serpent representing the astronomical ecliptic. Today, Hahal Dios, or the "true god," is a syncretic combination of Jesus Christ and the sun. His assistants are the *càak* (rain deities) and the *báalam* (guardians), who, like all supernaturals, can punish as well as cure, "lest people forget that they exist." Punishments come to earth as illnesses in the form of "winds" and are expelled or prevented through elaborate ritual offerings.

RELIGIOUS PRACTITIONERS. In response to the brutal crusades of the first Spanish priests, Maya shamans went "underground" and continued the traditional roles of curer, counselor, and diviner. Today called *hmèen* or *ah k'ìin*, this individual occupies a dual social status: mediating between humans and supernatural forces yet being an ordinary farmer.

CEREMONIES. The central ritual has probably always been the rain ceremony, today called *c'a càak*, or "take càak," performed during the period of the summer when the maize fields are most in need of rain. The structure in time and space of this and all ritual activity is dependent on the four-corners concept, reflecting the centrality of the Maya worldview. Whether rain or a cure for an illness is being sought, the setting of the ritual—the maize field, community, house plot, or corral—is always a quadrilateral (i.e., a model of the cosmos). These hmèen-directed functions share this symbolic structure with public fiestas centered on the church.

ARTS. The monumental architecture, carved hieroglyphic texts, pottery, and other aspects of Maya material culture are mainly responsible for the worldwide attention focused on the Yucatán Peninsula. Today, the huipil, or women's garment, with its embroidered floral patterns, is the most visible form of Maya artistry.

MEDICINE. A hmèen has a sophisticated awareness of medicinal plants. These treatments, however, are always administered in the context of ritual, and the combination of ritual healing and organic remedy has apparently proven very effective over time. Governmental clinics notwithstanding, the Mayan hmèen continue to gain recognition for their curative capabilities and are sometimes even sought out by Hispanic Yucatecos.

DEATH AND AFTERLIFE. It is evident from funerary remains that the rulers of the past confirmed their divine qualities through pictographic renditions of their anticipated afterlife. Although the subterranean realm was a part of this spiritual domain, the flat-earth perspective and the constancy of astronomical motion within the earth and back into the sky added a celestial component to the assumed destination of souls. The contemporary hmèen still hold these beliefs, and general mortuary practices symbolically express the cosmological motion of the human soul after death.

Bibliography

Hammond, Norman (1982). *Ancient Maya Civilization.* New Brunswick, N.J.: Rutgers University Press.

Redfield, Robert (1941). *The Folk Culture of the Yucatan.* Chicago: University of Chicago Press.

Redfield, Robert, and Alfonso Villa Rojas (1962). *Chan Kom: A Maya Village.* Chicago: University of Chicago Press.

Sosa, John R. (1989). *Cosmological, Symbolic, and Cultural Complexity among the Contemporary Maya of Yucatán.* World Archaeoastronomy. New York: Cambridge University Press.

Villa Rojas, Alfonso (1945). *The Maya of East Central Quintana Roo.* Washington, D.C.: Carnegie Institution of Washington.

—JOHN R. SOSA

MAYA ARTISTRY

Yukatecos standing outside of their house. The women's garment, or huipil, with its embroidered floral patterns, is the most visible form of Maya artistry today. Yucatan Peninsula, Mexico.

ZAPOTEC

Ethonym: Ben 'Zaa, Binii Gula'sa', Tsapotecatl, Za, Zapoteco

Orientation

IDENTIFICATION. The Spanish name "Zapoteco" stems from the Nahuatl name for the Zapotec, "Tsapotecatl," which, in turn, was derived from the name of a fruit, the *zapote,* that was common in the region. Pre-Hispanic Zapotec referred to themselves as the "Ben 'Zaa" (cloud people). On occasion, modern Zapotec refer to themselves as "Za" (the people), but it is more typical of them to identify themselves as being from a particular community or region.

LOCATION. The Zapotec are the largest indigenous group in the Mexican state of Oaxaca. Oaxaca is located between 15° and 19° N and 94° and 99° W. The Zapotec inhabit four main areas of Oaxaca: the central valley, the Isthmus of Tehuantepec, the sierra region in the north, and the southern coastal mountain area called the Sierra de Miahuatlán. The central valley (average elevation 1,550 meters) has a temperate climate, the isthmus and other coastal areas are tropical and semiarid, whereas the sierra regions to the north and south, with variable elevations higher than the central valley, have a cooler climate than the temperate central valley. All regions experi-

See also

Mixtec

HISTORY AND CULTURAL RELATIONS

Today, the impressive ruins of Monte Albán, Mitla, and Yagul (among others) stand as testimony to the accomplishments of the pre-Hispanic Zapotec. Prior to the arrival of the Spanish, the Zapotec developed a powerful state system that flourished and then declined. Long before the rise of the state (ca. 8,000 to 1,500 B.C.), the Zapotec and the related Mixtec camped in small groups probably of twenty-five persons or less. Permanent villages appeared during the Formative period (ca. 1,500 to 100 B.C.) as did various new customs and practices, including loom weaving, adobe construction, stone masonry, pottery making, a 260–day calendar, human and animal sacrifice, and redistribution and reciprocal exchange systems. During the Classic period (ca. A.D. 300 to 900), Monte Albán was the metropolis of the Zapotec area, the center of a state organization that exerted its influence throughout southern Mexico. The Postclassic (ca. A.D. 900 to 1,520) was the time of competitive Zapotec city-states. During the fifteenth century, the Aztec occupied the central valley and founded a garrison that would later become the state capital, Oaxaca City. When the Spanish arrived in Oaxaca, this garrison served as their colonial headquarters. Compared with the Aztec invasion, the Spanish presence in Oaxaca was exploitative and religious rather than military; compared to many parts of Mexico, most Zapotec communities remained relatively autonomous. Presently, through the market system, the Zapotec have contact with other indigenous groups and mestizos.

ence dry and rainy seasons, the latter beginning in May and extending to October. Diverse microclimates exist in all of these regions.

DEMOGRAPHY. The indigenous populations of Oaxaca generally, and the Zapotec in particular, underwent a marked depopulation following the Spanish Conquest. For example, the population of the central valley, estimated at about 350,000 when the Spanish arrived, had declined to about 40,000 or 45,000 by the 1630s, and regained its pre-Conquest level only in the mid-1970s. In 1971 the state of Oaxaca had 307,245 Zapotec speakers; in 1960 the figure was 253,438.

LINGUISTIC AFFILIATION. Zapotec languages belong to the Otomanguean Language Family. There are probably at least nine separate, mutually unintelligible Zapotec languages: one in the central valley, one in the isthmus, four in the northern sierra, and three in the southern Sierra de Miahuatlán. Additionally, dialect differences often exist between communities.

Settlements

The Zapotec are primarily town-dwelling peasant farmers. In the central valley, for instance, communities are compact and most villages have fewer than 5,000 inhabitants. The mountain Zapotec also live in compact settlements, although in the southern sierra there are some scattered ranches. In the isthmus, in addition to rural villages, there are two urban centers that are primarily Zapotec in composition—Juchitán and Tehuantepec. A typical Zapotec community has a Catholic church, a central plaza, local governmental buildings, a primary school, perhaps a health clinic, and probably several small dry-goods stores. Depending on its history and size, the community may be divided into barrios or sections. Generally, narrow unpaved streets are lined with adobe house walls, fences of woven cane, or cacti planted in a row. Yards and patios are often only semiprivate, being visible from the street and neighboring compounds.

Economy

SUBSISTENCE AND COMMERCIAL ACTIVITIES. The majority of Zapotec in all regions are peasant farmers, practicing a mixture of subsistence and cash agriculture with some animal husbandry. This is also the case in the isthmus urban centers. The primary subsistence crops are maize, beans, and squashes; various other crops are grown, depending on the climate, the availability of irrigation sources, and soil conditions. The household is the basic production unit but it is linked to the outside through an elaborate, cyclical marketplace system that has operated for centuries. At times, maize may be sold as a cash crop. In the valley region, a limited number of farmers plant garbanzo beans or wheat as off-season crops, whereas maguey, which is used to make the liquor mescal, is widely planted as a cash crop. In the mountain regions, coffee is a cash crop; in the isthmus, cash crops are bananas, mangoes, and coconuts. Crops are sometimes irrigated, although many villages remain totally dependent on rainfall. In all regions, farmers use teams of oxen to plow their fields; however, when mountain slopes are too steep for oxen, planting may be accomplished with a digging stick. Tractor use is gradually increasing.

INDUSTRIAL ARTS. Many Zapotec communities are specialized by craft and industry. In the valley, for instance, village specializations include the production of pottery, wool serapes, grinding stones (metates), woven belts, baskets, and other goods. In the northern sierra, crafts are less prevalent but include leatherworking and cotton weaving. Dress varies both among and within the Zapotec regions, with women's clothing showing greater variety than men's apparel. The Zapotec can often identify a woman's village of origin by her style of dress.

TRADE. Oaxaca is known for its highly developed market system, and the Zapotec are renowned for their commercial activities. Since pre-Hispanic times, the Zapotec have maintained trade routes through much of Oaxaca. Products were carried by tumpline, a device that is still used by farmers to transport such loads as firewood. Certain localities, for example, the valley community of Mitla, specialized in trading activities. Presently, the Zapotec play a central role in the indigenous marketplace activities in both Oaxaca City and Tehuantepec.

DIVISION OF LABOR. In each Zapotec region, men and women engage in different activities, but the specific nature of the division of labor is somewhat variable. Generally, men farm, and women prepare food, perform domestic chores, and perhaps participate in commercial activities. The isthmus Zapotec women are well known for their commercial activities and are almost exclusively the traders in marketplaces. Selling is an activity closed to isthmus men, whereas in other regions both men and women produce and sell various goods. In the valley town of Teotitlán del Valle, only men weave and generally sell serapes. Some men are so successful as weavers (they now sell to an international market) that they hire farmers from neighboring villages to work their fields.

LAND TENURE. Prior to changes in the Mexican constitution in 1992, land tenure consisted of a mixture of private land, communal land, and *ejidos*. A farmer's private land usually consists of several small separate parcels, not one continuous holding. Local authorities grant permission to community members to farm or graze livestock on communal lands, which generally are of poor quality. Ejidos do not exist everywhere. They were established under the land reforms following the Mexican Revolution and are portions of communities (sometimes whole communities) that hold land in common under a special local authority structure. The large haciendas, common in other parts of Mexico, were relatively insignificant in Zapotec Oaxaca.

Kinship

KIN GROUPS AND DESCENT. The aboriginal Zapotec kinship system was bilateral and ambilineal, that is, descent was reckoned in both lines—and still is today. With variation from place to place, the system of ritual coparenthood, *compadrazgo*, is used by the Zapotec.

KINSHIP TERMINOLOGY. Zapotec kinship terms, ancient and modern, are closest to the Hawaiian type. Spanish terms are replacing some of the Zapotec designations.

Marriage and Family

MARRIAGE. Most Zapotec communities are endogamous, although this is by custom, not by rule, and there are exceptions in most locations. Monogamy is generally practiced. The Zapotec discuss at least two types of marriage: free union and church marriage. Divorce is not permitted by the Catholic church, but sometimes spouses simply separate and take other spouses. Young couples sometimes live together prior to a formal marriage. Often they are later married by the church, but sometimes they separate. A pregnancy often will prompt a marriage, either through the church or through common law. The most common residence pattern is patrilocal for young couples, but neolocality sometimes follows patrilocality, perhaps after the birth of the first child. Less commonly, residence may be matrilocal; for example, when a bride lacks brothers, her husband may come to live with her and assist his father-in-law in the fields.

DOMESTIC UNIT. Depending on his or her stage in the life cycle, a Zapotec may live in a nuclear or an extended family.

INHERITANCE. The rule is that all children should inherit equally, but in actuality, younger offspring who are still living with parents at the time of death may inherit more. Additionally, sons tend to inherit more land than do daughters. Land may be inherited at the parent's death, at an offspring's marriage, or when a parent becomes too old to work the fields.

SOCIALIZATION. There is considerable variation in socialization practices even among closely situated Zapotec communities. For instance, parents in two adjoining valley communities may have very different beliefs about the use of physical punishment on children and also have different expectations about their children's conduct. Generally, young children up to the age of 3 years

The Zapotec play a central role in the indigenous marketplace activities in both Oaxaca City and Tehuantepec.

The Zapotec worldview includes a cast of supernaturals: witches, male and female devils, images of Christ (as a child and as an adult), and animal guardians.

are treated affectionately, but often, corresponding with the arrival of the next sibling, parental affection is curtailed. Parents regularly frighten children by threatening that outsiders will take them away or eat them. Children are rarely instructed in how to accomplish a task or how to behave; rather, children are expected to observe, practice, and consequently learn. Older children are regularly the caretakers of younger children, which allows the adults to tend to their work.

Sociopolitical Organization

SOCIAL ORGANIZATION. From the Post-classic period onward, the local community has been the primary sociopolitical entity in Zapotec society. Post-Classic Zapotec society consisted of three groups: commoners, priests, and the nobility, with each community having a controlling lord. In modern Oaxaca, the community remains the essential unit of organization, bound together by an institutionalized form of exchange called the *guela uetza*, or *gozana*, which has several manifestations. It can involve the exchange of agricultural labor or the exchange of goods during celebrations such as weddings and saint's day fiestas. For example, when a son or daughter is going to marry, the father visits all the households that owe him some form of debt from past occasions (e.g., mescal or turkeys) and asks for repayment at the upcoming wedding.

POLITICAL ORGANIZATION. In most Zapotec communities, citizens are elected to fill positions in a *cargo* system. Zapotec Cargos are hierarchically arranged, age-graded religious and political posts in which adult men in the community serve terms of office without pay. The cargo system itself is consistently present in Zapotec communities, although variation exists as to details such as how officials are nominated and elected, the number of posts, and the duties of particular positions. Common posts include mayor, judge, and other officials such as treasurer and police captain. It is also noteworthy that the isthmus Zapotec women in particular wield considerable political power.

SOCIAL CONTROL. The Zapotec employ a variety of formal and informal social controls. Formally, disputes may be brought before the local or district authorities, who have the ability to fine and imprison wrongdoers. At the informal level, mechanisms such as the avoidance of conflict situations; the denial of hostility and anger; the internalization of ideals such as respect, cooperation, and responsibility; fear of witchcraft; gossip; envy; and the withdrawal of social support operate variably in different locations. One frequently noted Zapotec ideal involves respect for others. The renowned former Mexican president, Benito Juárez, a Zapotec, reflected the importance of respect in Zapotec thinking when he wrote, "respect for the rights of others is peace."

CONFLICT. Notwithstanding the Zapotec valuation of respect, they have been involved in conflict. For much of the Classic and Post-Classic periods, there is evidence that military conquest, coupled with the enslavement and at times sacrifice of captives, was a prevalent Zapotec institution. During the Mexican Revolution, some Zapotec communities, such as Ixtepeji in the northern sierra, became involved in the conflict, but others did not. Intervillage disputes over community boundaries, sometimes resulting in the loss of life, have periodically arisen in many areas for at least the last several hundred years. Interestingly, the level of intracommunity conflict is extremely variable; some Zapotec communities are very peaceful, whereas others are much more violent. Historical, social-structural, and psychocultural variables appear to be interrelated factors accounting for this pronounced variability.

Religion and Expressive Culture

RELIGIOUS BELIEFS. The pre-Hispanic Zapotec perceived their universe as consisting of the center surrounded by four quarters, each with a certain color and supernatural attributes. Time was viewed as cyclical, not lineal, and the Zapotec believed in gods associated with various natural elements, such as rain. The Zapotec rain god was worshiped in the northern sierra region until the mid-twentieth century. Presently, the Zapotec follow a form of Catholicism wherein saint worship plays a dominant part and pre-Hispanic beliefs have become fused with Catholicism. The Zapotec worldview includes a cast of supernaturals: witches, male and female devils, images of Christ (as a child and as an adult), and animal guardians (*tonos*). At birth, each person acquires his or her tono (e.g., a mountain lion). An unbaptized person risks becoming a *nahual*—an animal form assumed in the state of possession.

RELIGIOUS PRACTITIONERS. Aside from Catholic priests, specialized Zapotec ritual leaders, *hechiceros*, also conduct certain ceremonies, including offerings of flowers, food, poultry blood, mescal, money, cigarettes, and prayers at occasions such as weddings, funerals, and house initiations.

CEREMONIES. Traditionally, the Zapotec engaged in numerous rituals associated with their farming activities. Lightning, Cosijo, was seen as alive; the powerful deity was offered human blood, quail, dogs, human infants, and war captives in exchange for rain. Modern Zapotec mark major life-cycle events such as baptism, communion, marriage, and death with ceremonies in the church and in their homes. Important ceremonies occur on Todos Santos (All Saints' Day) and on the patron saints' days in each community.

ARTS. Pre-Hispanic Zapotec architectural achievements are especially evident from the temples, compounds, and courts of Monte Albán and Mitla. Some modern Zapotec towns are renowned for serape weavings, pottery, and other crafts.

MEDICINE. The Zapotec have an impressive repertoire of remedies and cures. Members of both sexes are curers, but only women are midwives, and only men mend bones. Illness may be attributed to improper religious conduct, soul loss, envy, anger, the evil eye, fright (*susto* or *espanto*), and witchcraft.

DEATH AND AFTERLIFE. The Zapotec distinguish between ordinary death and sudden violent death; in the latter, the deceased's soul does not make the transition to heaven. A distinction is also made in the death ritual for married and unmarried persons.

Bibliography

Chiñas, Beverly L. (1973). *The Isthmus Zapotec: Women's Roles in Cultural Context*. New York: Holt, Rinehart & Winston.

Flannery, Kent, and Joyce Marcus, eds. (1983). *The Cloud People*. New York: Academic Press.

Nader, Laura (1969). "The Zapotec of Oaxaca." In *Handbook of Middle American Indians*, edited by Robert Wauchope. Vol. 7, *Ethnology, Part One*, edited by Evon Z. Vogt, 329–357. Austin: University of Texas Press.

Whitecotton, Joseph W. (1977). *The Zapotecs*. Norman: University of Oklahoma Press.

—DOUGLAS P. FRY

Middle East

ARABS

Ethonym: none

Orientation

The Arab world is usually considered to be comprised of the following nineteen countries: Mauritania, Morocco, Algeria, Tunisia, Libya, Chad, Lebanon, Egypt, Sudan, Jordan, Syria, Iraq, Kuwait, Bahrain, Qatar, United Arab Emirates, Saudi Arabia, Oman, and Yemen. There are also significant Arab populations in Iran, Turkey, East Africa, South America, Europe, and Southeast Asia. The total population of Arabs in the world is roughly 160 million (Eickelman 1987), or about 3 percent of the world's population. This large ethnic group has a very heterogeneous population, but there are a number of characteristics that a majority of Arabs share.

Religion

Perhaps the most common Arab characteristic is adherence to the Islamic faith. Muslim Arabs comprize about 93 percent of the Arab population and belong to several different sects including Shia (Ithna Ashari and Ismaili), Alawi, Zaidi, and Sunni, which is the largest. The other 7 percent of Arabs are largely Christian or Druze.

The link between Arabs and Islam has deep historical roots. It was among Arabs early in the seventh century that Mohammed preached the tenets of Islam. Mohammed's successors quickly spread the word of Allah into Southwest Asia, across North Africa and into Spain, into Persia, Afghanistan, and Central Asia, and to the east coast of Africa. Wherever Muslims went, they left elements of Arab culture along with their religion. The cultures of the assimilated territories, which included Christian, Jewish, and Zoroastrian populations, were not only influenced by the Arab invaders and their religion, but, in turn, substantially influenced the nature of Arab culture.

The conquered populations were subjugated politically, but their administrative skills, crafts, arts, and worldviews gradually transformed their conquerors. This transformation of Arab identity and tradition has been a continuing process for over 1,300 years. Pre-Islamic poetry indicates that in the year 600 "Arab" referred to the Semitic-speaking tribes of the Arabian Peninsula. Quranic usage and other Arabian sources suggest that the word referred primarily to the pastoral Bedouin tribes of the region. Even though camel-herding pastoral nomads were only a minority during Mo-

hammed's lifetime, it seems clear that Arabs were an important social and political force. Their rich oral literature, especially their poetry, and their rejection of authoritarian political forms presented a powerful cultural ideal. Nevertheless, townspeople and others often used the term "Arab" in a pejorative sense. Southern Arabians, both farmers and urban residents, probably did not at first regard themselves as Arab. They probably only adopted this identity when there were political and economic advantages to doing so after the adoption of Islam.

The early Islamic period was a time when Arab identity meant that one belonged to an all-encompassing patrilineal descent system. Membership in an Arab descent group brought recognition, honor, and certain privileges, such as exemption from some taxes. The significance attributed to one's genealogical ties has not prevented Arab societies from assimilating non-Arabs into Arab society, a practice that has remained important throughout Arab history. In the first years after the Arab conquest, it was common to convert to Islam and become an Arab at the same time by forming a relationship with an Arab tribe. Later, converting to Islam and acquiring Arab identity became separate processes. Islamization continued, but it was no longer tied to Arabization.

Muslim Arab leaders created great empires that lasted hundreds of years. Following Mohammed, the Umayyid dynasty was established in Damascus in 661 and lasted until 750. Religious and ethnic minorities were given a large measure of self-rule under Umayyid domination. The succeeding 'Abbāsid dynasty ruled the Muslim world from Baghdad, its capital, for nearly 500 years, of which the first 200 (750–950) are called the Golden Age of Arab civilization.

Arab rulers brought intellectual Jews, Christians, Greeks, Persians, and Indians to Baghdad and other centers of learning during the 'Abbāsid dynasty. These foreign intellectuals contributed elements from their own cultures to the development of Arab culture. The works of Plato and Aristotle were translated from Greek into Arabic before they were translated into other European languages. Indian scientists brought the concept of "zero" to the Arabs, who combined it with Arabic numerals and transmitted the mathematical systems of algebra, geometry, and trigonometry to Europe. There are also many other important scientific discoveries that can be traced to the 'Abbāsid dynasty. 'Abbāsid scientists disproved Euclid's theory that the eye emanates rays, 'Abbāsid chemists introduced such concepts as "alkali" and

The most common Arab characteristic is adherence to the Islamic faith.

See also

Bedouin, Palestineans

After World War II, Arabs once again ruled their own lands, but by then the imported system of political nationalism had divided the Arabs into separate states.

"alcohol," and ʿAbbāsid medical scholars compiled the world's first medical encyclopedia. What was happening throughout the world at that time was being recorded and passed on to later civilizations by Arab historians.

The ʿAbbāsid Empire was declining by the thirteenth century. Largely because of European colonization of North and South America, European trade with the Arab world virtually stopped and did not resume until the opening of the Suez Canal in 1869. The outlying provinces of the empire were the first to break away. Then, the Arabs were pushed out of Spain. Invading Turks and Mongols from the north destroyed not only the cities and towns in their path, but also irrigation systems. The Arab economy never recovered from the destruction. By the sixteenth century, Seljuk and Ottoman Turkish invaders conquered the remaining Arab territories; they ruled until World War I, when the Turkish Empire in turn disintegrated.

Language

Another important and unifying characteristic of Arabs is a common language. Arabic, like Hebrew, is a Semitic language of the Afro-Asiatic Family. Evidence of its first use appears in accounts of wars in 853 B.C. Arabic became a high-status language in the early Islamic centuries. It also became widely used in trade and commerce. Over the centuries, it became the predominant religious language of the world's Muslims. Even though most Muslims cannot speak Arabic today, it is revered as the language that God chose to reveal the Quran, and, because of this, it has profoundly influenced the language and thought of all Muslims.

Arabic has developed into at least two distinct forms. Classical Arabic is the religious and literary language. It is spoken and written throughout the Arab world and serves as a bond among all literate Muslims. Colloquial Arabic, an informal spoken language, varies by dialect from region to region, and is not always mutually intelligible. Both forms of the language are in use today and provide an important force for Arab cohesion.

Urban Life

About half of Muslim Arabs live in cities and towns. They have a greater variety of occupations, weaker family ties, greater freedom for women to leave the home, fewer arranged marriages, and fewer social pressures to conform to religious practices than do nonurban Arabs. The social structure of the urban Muslim Arab is consider-

ably more complex than that of his desert or village counterpart.

Arabs who live in towns are also experiencing changes in their traditional patterns of living, but to a lesser degree than the city dwellers. Nomads, villagers, and urban traders meet in the *suq* (marketplace) to exchange goods and products. Representatives of government agencies (e.g., tax collectors, army conscriptors, police, and irrigation officers) make contacts with most of the population in the towns.

The townspeople are disdainful of the villagers. Town residents are more religiously conservative and more intimately involved in their kin network than urban dwellers are. The ideal values of the nomad are not so strong in the town. There is less concern with hospitality and defiance and more concern with symbols of economic prosperity—property, wealth, and education. Family honor remains important, however, and women continue to live a secluded life under the watchful eyes of husbands, brothers, and fathers.

Rural Life

Most Arabs are farmers who live between the two extremes of the desert on the one hand, with its conservative rigidity, and the cities and towns on the other hand, with their changing traditions and practices. The Arab village is usually composed of walled, mud-floored homes built of mud bricks. These homes hide the villagers' insecurities from strangers and provide an intimate environment in which strong family ties are nurtured.

Arab villagers grow only what they need to eat or trade—cereal grains, vegetables, livestock, and cotton. They are often in debt, and seldom have enough money to pay off their debts or to save for investments. Villagers live by tradition and lack the incentives, knowledge, or security to make changes. Change is seen as disruptive and threatening to the harmonious relationship that Arabs have established with their environment and their fellow villagers. Village values stem from the ideal values of the nomad. Unlike the Bedouin, villagers will relate to nonkin, but loyalty to the group is as strong as it is among the tribesmen. As among the Bedouin, village segments may also feud with each other. Similarly, standards of hospitality are high among villagers, as is awareness of family honor. The villager lives in an extended family in which family life is tightly controlled. Each family member has a defined role, and there is little individual deviation. Like the Bedouin, the villager finds security in the family during times of economic hardship and in old age.

◆ **Quran, Koran**
Divinely inspired holy book of Islam, written down by the Prophet Mohammed at the dictation of the Angel Gabriel in about A.D. 610-630.

Changes in individual roles, such as when a son goes off to work in a town, often weaken the family socioeconomic system.

Children are a family's greatest asset, providing the parents with a work force and social security. The patrilineal system is reflected by Islamic rules of inheritance, which give more to boys than to girls, particularly in terms of real estate. A girl's value is linked to her function of tying one family to another through marriage, and to her primary role as a mother. Births are celebrated, particularly those of boys. Births are often accompanied by non-Islamic rituals such as burying the placenta to protect the mother and baby from enemy spirits or dressing boys as girls to deceive evil spirits. A child's first possession is often an amulet to ward off malevolence, and the first word a baby hears is "Allah."

Boys are circumcised at age 7, a ritual event that formally brings the boy into the religious community. Animistic rituals may also accompany this ceremony. Circumcisions, or clitoridectomies of girls, if they are performed, are not accompanied by any public ceremonies.

Arab boys and girls are treated very differently. Boys are given great affection and are pampered by their mothers. Girls are also given affection, but are weaned much earlier than boys and are not pampered. A mother is viewed as a symbol of warmth and love throughout a child's life. A father is viewed as a stern disciplinarian who administers corporal punishment and instills a degree of fear within his children. Boys are especially taught—often harshly—to obey and respect older males.

Children are given adult responsibilities and sex-specific socialization early in life. Boys work in the fields, and girls help their mothers cook and care for siblings. Adolescents have no contact with the opposite sex outside the family, and girls are watched closely to protect their chastity. A girl's primary protector is her older brother, who continues to watch over his sister even after she is married.

Marriages are arranged by parents. Girls marry between the ages of 14 and 19, whereas boys are usually somewhat older. Marriages establish important ties within one's own kin group or with other lineages that have economic or status advantages. Marriage is endogamous within one's kin group. The preferred match is between brothers' children. Bride and groom often meet for the first time on the day of the wedding, when the

POLITICS

Although unified by language and some cultural attributes, Arabs have been politically divided since the first Islamic centuries. With the rise of the Ottoman Empire in the sixteenth century, most of the Arabic-speaking regions of the Middle East and North Africa were turned into Ottoman provinces. There were relatively few economic, political, or intellectual achievements that were inherently Arab during Ottoman rule. During the latter half of the nineteenth century, however, there were some attempts to emulate the perceived achievements of European civilization. It was at this time that the idea of Arabism, perhaps as a counterpart to European nationalist movements, began to emerge. It was not until after World War II, however, that Arabs once again ruled their own lands, and by then the imported system of political nationalism had divided the Arabs into separate states, which undermined the political unity (i.e., the Arabism), of the ethnic group as a whole.

Arab culture developed in the desert among the peoples of the Arabian Peninsula, who lived either as tribal nomads or town folk. Town folk were strongly influenced by Bedouin values and practices. Mohammed was a townsman, but his tribe, the Quraysh, included many Bedouin, and Mohammed and his followers adhered to many pre-Islamic tribal traditions. These traditions, arising within the harsh environment of the desert, included strict codes of proper economic and social behavior, which were legitimized by Islam and became part of Arab culture.

Traditionally, Bedouin moved often, living in tents and earning their living as stock breeders, transporters, or traders. They produced the livestock for much of the sedentary Arab world, raising camels, horses, and donkeys as beasts of burden and sheep and goats for food, clothing, and manure. As transporters, they moved products from the countryside to towns and between settlements not connected by roads. As traders, they provided a link between villages and towns, bringing to the villagers manufactured utensils and products that were not available locally. Their relationships with settled people were based on reciprocity and followed carefully defined rules of protocol.

A completely different facet of Arab culture developed along the Mediterranean shore, where Arabs had direct contact with the cultures of Europe. Compromise replaced rigidity, and religious fundamentalism gave way to accommodation and the acceptance of new ideas. There were thriving economies in the cities of Beirut, Cairo, Alexandria, Tunis, Algiers, and Casablanca, which offered the traditional Arab the possibility of entering new professions. Attending universities became an option for a changing population. European-styled nationalism replaced tribal allegiance and European imperialism.

bride-wealth (*mahr*) is determined and a marriage contract is signed.

The lives of Arab village men and women are very distinct. Men work in the fields, women in the home. For social contact, men go to coffee houses, but women visit neighbors and relatives or receive such visits in their own homes. Men and women often eat separately, and they always pray separately.

Arab villagers follow a mixture of Islamic folk beliefs and rituals. Religion provides explanation for many unknown and uncontrollable events in their lives. God's will dictates the direction of life and provides divine authority for action. Religion confirms changes in social status, for example, at circumcision and marriage. It provides hope for a better life after death. Religious festivals, such as 'Id al-Adhha, 'Id al-Fitr and, for Shia Arabs, Muharram, break the monotony of village life. Men worship at a mosque. Women, often not allowed in mosques, attend ceremonies conducted in a home by female religious leaders.

Cultural Change

Change is occurring at a rapid pace throughout the Arab world. The Bedouin have had to deal with the many changes arising from oil-based economies—oil fields, trucks, and other forms of transportation, for example. Road building has also decreased the degree of isolation of thousands of villages and increased the number of contacts between villagers and the outside world. Radios bring new ideas to Bedouin and villager alike. Land reform has brought new systems of landownership, agricultural credit, and new farming technology. Overcrowding and diminishing economic opportunities in the village have prompted many villagers to migrate to the towns and cities. Migration from poorer Arab countries to oil-rich states has also become an economic opportunity and an important source of revenue for millions of Arabs.

Bibliography

Atiyeh, George N., ed. (1977). *Arab and American Cultures*. Washington, D.C.: American Enterprise Institute for Public Policy Research.

Bacharach, Jere L. (1984). *A Middle East Studies Handbook*. Seattle: University of Washington Press.

Bates, Daniel C., and Amal Rassam (1983). *Peoples and Cultures of the Middle East*. Englewood Cliffs, N.J.: Prentice Hall.

Beck, Lois, and Nikki Keddie, eds. (1978). *Women in the Muslim World*. Cambridge: Harvard University Press.

Carmichael, Joel (1977). *Arabs Today*. Garden City, N.Y.: Anchor Press.

Eickelman, Dale F. (1987). "Arab Society: Tradition and the Present." In *The Middle East*, edited by Michael Adams. Handbooks to the Modern World. New York: Facts on File.

Eickelman, Dale F. (1989). *The Middle East: An Anthropological Approach*. Englewood Cliffs, N.J.: Prentice Hall.

Faris, Nabih Amin, ed. (1963). *The Arab Heritage*. New York: Russell & Russell.

Friedlander, Jonathan, ed. (1981). *The Middle East: The Image and the Reality*. Berkeley and Los Angeles: University of California Press.

Gulick, John, ed. (1965). "Dimensions of Cultural Change in the Middle East." *Human Organization* 24 (Special Issue).

Hopkins, Nicholas, and Saad Eddin Ibrahim, eds. (1985). *Arab Society: Social Science Perspectives*. New York: Columbia University Press.

Hourani, Albert (1991). *A History of the Arab Peoples*. Cambridge: Harvard University Press, Belknap Press. Reprint. 1992. New York: Warner Books.

Knapp, Wilfred (1977). *North-West Africa: A Political and Economic Survey*. 3rd ed. Oxford: Oxford University Press.

Lutifiyya, Abdulla M., and Charles W. Churchill, eds. (1970). *Readings in Arab Middle Eastern Societies and Cultures*. The Hague: Mouton.

Mansfield, Peter (1980). *The Middle East: A Political and Economic Survey*. 5th ed. Oxford: Oxford University Press.

Mostyn, Trevor, and Albert Hourani, eds. (1988). *The Cambridge Encyclopedia of the Middle East and North Africa*. Cambridge: Cambridge University Press.

Nydell, Margaret K. (1987). *Understanding Arabs: A Guide for Westerners*. Yarmouth, Me.: Intercultural Press.

Raban, Jonathan (1979). *Arabia: A Journey through the Labyrinth*. New York: Simon & Schuster.

Sweet, Louise E. (1971). *The Central Middle East*. New Haven: HRAF Press.

Weekes, Richard V. (1984). "Arabs." In *Muslim Peoples: A World Ethnographic Survey*, edited by Richard V. Weekes, 35–45. Westport, Conn.: Greenwood Press.

—RONALD JOHNSON

BAKHTIARI

Ethonym: none

The term "Bakhtiari" refers to a group of people and to the area they occupy. The Bakhtiari inhabit about 156,000 square kilometers in and near the central Zagros Mountains of Iran. The most recent estimates place their population at about 700,000 in the 1980s. The Bakhtiari are traditionally nomadic pastoralists who make their winter encampments in the low hills along the narrow fringe of the northeast Khūzestān plain and their summer pastures in the intermontane valleys. Some also find summer pastures at the western edge of the central plateau, which is also the permanent habitat for a sedentary village population. Other Bakhtiari live in permanent agricultural settlements throughout the larger area, except at the highest elevations.

Sheep and goats are the basis of the Bakhtiari economy, and Bakhtiari nomadism arises from the search for pastures. Sheep and goat products are used for subsistence and for economic exchange with the sedentary population.

The family is the basic unit of production and of flock- and landownership, as well as of political and social organization. Families cooperate in the sharing of pastures. At successive levels of segmentation, families regroup and redefine themselves under different political and kin headings. The smallest political/kin unit is the *rish safid*, and successively higher units include *kalantars* (headmen), *khans* (chiefs), and an *ilkhani* (paramount chief of the entire confederation).

The confederation, Il-i-Bakhtiari (*il*, tribe) is the unit that includes all those who live in the territory, speak a subdialect of the Luri dialect of Persian, and acknowledge the leadership of the khans and the ilkhani. Historically, the Bakhtiari have been divided into two major sections, the Haft Lang and the Chahar Lang, but in contemporary times the most important division has been Ilkhani and Hajji Ilkhani (two moieties from which the ilkhani were chosen).

Migration, competition for scarce resources, and the need for exchange with sedentary groups create potential for much conflict in Bakhtiari society. Add to that the pressures of external conflict with other tribes, including defending tribal territory, and the demands of the central government, and it becomes clear that there is a need for khans as mediators and intermediaries. Traditionally, the power of the khans and ilkhani comes from personal abilities as well as the inherent power of the position. It is based on the benefits they can provide, the respect they attain through birth, their coercive capabilities within the tribe, and the support given to them by the central government or by outside sources of power.

The Bakhtiari political system has been described as a hierarchy of khans, but it is similar to a segmentary lineage in that there are segmented levels that function in balanced opposition, with certain activities and responsibilities associated with each segment. The tribes and subtribes of the Bakhtiari use force against each other, their khans, and their ilkhani. Therefore, as in a segmentary lineage, intergroup and intragroup relations are based on a balance of power at each level. Tribes that fight each other at one time may unite to fight a third tribe at another.

The Bakhtiari confederation was once much more powerful than it is today. Reza Shah considered the Bakhtiari a direct threat to his sovereignty and, in the 1920s, took military, economic, and administrative actions to subjugate them. His policy of forced sedentarization, intended to break the tribal economy and prevent tribal identification, destroyed the political power of the ruling khans but was less successful in forcing the Bakhtiari to settle in one place.

The Bakhtiari now appear to be choosing sedentarism as a way of life much more than in the past. Formerly, only the richest and poorest lived a sedentary life-style; today many Bakhtiari not only settle in agricultural villages, they also work in the oil fields or urban centers. Although there is little reliable information on the Bakhtiari in post-Pahlavi Iran, it appears that changes are taking place. Along with increased sedentarism has come improved communications, and many government activities may be effectively transferring loyalty and identification from the tribe to the nation-state.

Bibliography

Case, Paul E. (1947). "I Became a Bakhtiari." *National Geographic Magazine* 91(3): 325–358.

Garthwaite, Gene R. (1983). *Khans and Shahs: A Documentary Analysis of the Bakhtiyari in Iran*. Cambridge: Cambridge University Press.

Garthwaite, Gene R. (1984). "Bakhtiari." In *Muslim Peoples: A World Ethnographic Survey*, edited by Richard V. Weekes, 81–84. Westport, Conn.: Greenwood Press.

Grimes, Barbara F., ed. (1988). *Ethnologue: Languages of the World*. Dallas: Summer Institute of Linguistics.

Johnson, Douglas L. (1969) *The Nature of Nomadism: A Comparative Study of Pastoral Migrations in Southwestern Asia and Northern Africa*. Chicago: University of Chicago, Department of Geography.

Migration, competition for scarce resources, and the need for exchange with sedentary groups create potential for much conflict in Bakhtiari society.

Bedouin societies traditionally eschew permanent settlement, preferring portable shelters that allow them the flexibility that their pastoral nomadic way of life requires.

BEDOUIN

Ethonym: A'raab, Bedu (sing. Bedawi)

Orientation

IDENTIFICATION. The term "Bedouin" is the anglicization of the Arabic "*bedu.*" The term is used to differentiate between those populations whose livelihood is based on the raising of livestock by mainly natural graze and browse and those populations who have an agricultural or urban base (*hadar*). Given that the opposition of bedu to hadar is a specifically Arab cultural tradition, it is arguable whether non-Arab-speaking pastoralists in the region should be termed "Bedouin." Most of these societies prefer expressions such as "A'rab ar-Rashaayida" (the Rashaayida Arabs), or "qabiilat Fed'aan" (the Fed'aan tribe), rather than the term "Bedouin." Among sedentary Arabs, another common term is "A'raab" which, since the beginning of Islam, has been synonymous with "nomad."

LOCATION. Bedouin societies are found in the arid steppe regions of Arabia and North Africa and along the margins of rain-fed cultivation. In some areas rainfall is very unpredictable and measures less than 5 centimeters per year. Bedouin living in such areas tend to move camp irregularly, as dictated by the availability of green pasture and seasonal occult precipitation (heavy morning dew). Often they have access to small date gardens for short periods of the year. In areas where winter rainfall is less unpredictable (in the Arabian Badia and the Nejd and in parts of Sudan, Egypt, southern Tunisia, and Libya), Bedouin groups move their animals to areas where pasture is regularly found. Often these societies plant grain along their migration routes, which they harvest on their return to their winter camping areas. In areas where winter rain falls predictably on mountain plateaus (Morocco), the Bedouin practice transhumance, planting their crops near their permanent homes in the valleys at the onset of the rains and then moving their livestock to the highland pastures.

LINGUISTIC AFFILIATION. Like other Arabs, Bedouin speak various dialects of Arabic, which belongs to the Semitic Language Group. Other living languages of this group are Modern Hebrew, Amharic and other spoken languages of Ethiopia (Harari, Tigre), Aramaic dialects (current in parts of Syria, Lebanon, and Iraq), and Maltese.

History and Cultural Relations

Agriculturists and pastoralists have inhabited the southern edge of the arid Syrian Steppe since 6,000 B.C. (Fagan 1986, 234). By about 850 B.C., a complex of oasis settlements and pastoral camps was established by a people known as "A'raab." These Semitic speakers were the latest in a succession of farming and stock-breeding societies. They were distinguished from their Assyrian neighbors to the north, however, by their Arabic language and by their use of domesticated camels for trade and warfare. These A'raab were the cultural forerunners of the modern-day Arabs. They carried out a caravan trade with their camels between southern Arabia and the large city-states of Syria. By the first century B.C., they had moved westward into Jordan and the Sinai Peninsula and southwestward along the coast of the Red Sea. The creation of a powerful Islamic state in western Arabia in the middle of the seventh century A.D. gave a dramatic impetus to Arab expansion. Thousands of Arab Muslims—many of them Bedouin—left the Arabian Peninsula to settle in the newly conquered lands around it. As a result, the bedu/hadar distinction was reproduced in those Arabized territories where such a regional division of labor was ecologically and geographically practicable.

Bedouin societies are always linked to other nonpastoral societies by economic, social, and political relations. In the local context, a "Bedouin" is a regional specialist in livestock breeding whose closest social and political ties are with his pastoral kinsmen. The sedentary Arab, by contrast, places less emphasis on relations with genealogically distant kin. During periods when premodern states were weak and large-scale irrigated agriculture declined, some settled cultivators increased their reliance on breeding of small stock and moved into Bedouin social circles. In modern times, strong centralized authority and the monetarization of the rural economy have prompted some Bedouin to seek wage labor in cities and become sedentary. Regardless of their occupation and residence patterns, however, they remain culturally Bedouin as long as they maintain close social ties with pastoralist kin and retain the local linguistic and cultural markers that identify them as Bedouin.

Settlements

Bedouin societies traditionally eschew permanent settlement, preferring portable shelters that allow

See also

Arabs

them the flexibility that their pastoral nomadic way of life requires. Kin-related domestic units or households generally migrate together during the spring and summer months and tend to converge with other households of near kin during the winter months. In the past, Bedouin residence units were composed exclusively of tents (*buyuut*; sing. *bayt*). Depending upon the season of the year and, more specifically, the quality of surrounding pastureland, as few as three buyuut, and sometimes as many as fifteen, formed a camping unit. Among some Bedouin groups that spend the winter months in the same place year after year, stone houses (*buyuut hajar*) are also common. In many cases, these winter encampments are only partially deserted during the spring and summer—the very young and the very old are left behind to benefit from government efforts to extend health care and schooling facilities to these settlements. In certain areas of North Africa where transhumance is practiced, the seasonality of movement is somewhat different, although the principle is the same. Structurally, the tent and stone dwellings are alike. Both are rectangular in shape and consist of two—or occasionally three—sections. One section is the women's domain, kitchen, and storeroom. The other section is almost exclusively the domain of men and visitors—where hospitality is extended to guests, clients, and kinsmen alike. Sometimes the Bedouin home includes a third section, where sick or very young animals are given care.

Economy

SUBSISTENCE AND COMMERCIAL ACTIVITIES. The primary economic activity of the Bedouin is animal husbandry by natural graze and browse of sheep, goats, and camels. This way of life, called pastoral nomadism, has been in existence for at least three millennia. At the core of pastoral nomadism is migration, the pattern of which is determined by a combination of seasonal and areal variability in the location of pasture and water. Because water and grass can be in short supply in a particular area at the same time that it is abundant elsewhere, survival of both herds and herders makes movement from deficit to surplus areas both logical and necessary. Pasture and water are seldom found randomly scattered about in a given region, but generally are distributed in a regular fashion in accordance with a particular seasonal pattern of climate. Since the 1960s, trucks and other motor vehicles have come to replace camels as beasts of burden; today a truck often serves to bring feed and water to the herds in the desert.

INDUSTRIAL ARTS. The pastoral adaptation to the ecological environment presupposes the presence of sedentary communities and access to their products. None of the essentials of metal or cured leather are produced by pastoralists. They are dependent on persons outside their own group for practically all specialized work. In some regions, roving Gypsy tinkers and traders provide specialized services and goods to Bedouin households.

TRADE. There are several traditional means utilized by Bedouin to guarantee themselves access to grain and other sedentary produce. A household may, if its tribal land is close enough to rain-fed cultivation, sow and harvest crops. More commonly, rent from oasis or agricultural land owned by the group is collected in kind. At one time, *khuwa* (tribute) was exacted from sedentary farmers in return for protection from raids by tribes in the region. This tribute/raid relationship was a simple business proposition whereby the pastoralists received a needed product (grain) and the farmer acquired a scarce commodity (security). In principle, it was not very different from the most widespread relationship today whereby animal products are exchanged for dates and grain.

DIVISION OF LABOR. As with most pastoral societies, the division of labor among Bedouin is determined by the type of animals that are herded. When both large and small domesticated animals are kept, the larger animals—camels and, in a few cases, cattle—are the responsibility of the men. Women are often barred from close contact with these animals. It is generally the responsibility of the women and older girls to herd, feed, and milk the smaller animals (i.e., goats and sheep). When only sheep and goats are kept, men tend to be the herders, and women help with the feeding and milking of the flock.

LAND TENURE. Each Bedouin group seeks to control a land area that contains sufficient resources to sustain communal life. Each has a definite zone with well-understood, though often variable, limits and has certain rights of usufruct denied to other Bedouin groups. Only in an emergency does a pastoral unit attempt to graze its herds outside of its traditional area, and this eventuality is often preceded by negotiations at a higher political level. Governments throughout the Middle East and North Africa no longer recognize Bedouin collective territory. These areas are now considered "state-owned" land.

In the small-scale, exclusive communities that constitute Bedouin society, face-to-face (as opposed to anonymous) relations are of paramount importance.

Kinship

KIN GROUPS AND DESCENT. Like all Arabs, the Bedouin are patrilineal. Names consist of a personal name, the father's name, and at least the agnatic grandfather's name. Women retain their father's family name unchanged even after marriage. The smallest residential unit (bayt) is named after its senior male resident. Unlike settled peoples, however, most Bedouin are also members of larger patrilineal descent groups (buyuut), which are linked by agnation to form even larger lineages (afkhaadh; sing. fakhadh; lit., "thigh"), tribes (qabaa'il; sing. qabila), and sometimes even tribal confederations (such as the 'Anayza and the Shammar of northwestern Arabia). Bedouin frequently name more than five generations of patrilineal ancestors and conceptualize relations among descent groups in terms of a segmentary genealogical model. This model of nested patrilineal groups, each unit included in a larger one and itself including smaller units that are internally divided, provides the main framework for discussing marital alliances and for resolving legal disputes and violent conflicts.

KINSHIP TERMINOLOGY. There are distinctive terms for kin on the mother's side and kin on the father's side in Ego's generation and the first ascending generation. All terms indicate the sex of the person designated.

Sociopolitical Organization

In a sense, the Bedouin form a number of "nations." That is, groups of families are united by common ancestry and by shared territorial allegiance. The exploitation and defense of their common territorial area is effected through a universally accepted system of leadership. For centuries, these "nations" of Bedouin tribes and their leaders operated in the ecologically and politically shifting landscapes of the Middle East and North Africa. Only in the course of the twentieth century has their traditional flexibility and mobility been checked. Factors foreign to their universe have damaged the territorial mainstay of their so-

MARRIAGE AND FAMILY

Marriage

Marriage is normally contracted within the minimal lineage (bayt). The ideal marriage is to the closest relative permitted by the Quran (surah 4:23). This is between a man and his father's brother's daughter. Not only is marriage to the *bint 'amm* (female parallel cousin) or the *ibn 'amm* (male parallel cousin) preferred, but, in addition, the father's brother's son has a customary right to his cousin. Although the female cousin may refuse to marry her father's brother's son, she may not marry anyone else without his consent first. Although parallel-cousin marriage is actively favored, in many of these marriages the term "first cousin" is only a classificatory one. In many cases, the bint 'amm or ibn 'amm is actually a second or third cousin. Nevertheless, these cousin marriages are seen as reinforcing the unity and authority of the minimal lineage. Although plural marriage is permitted, the incidence of polygyny is not particularly high. It is generally limited to those older men who are wealthy enough to maintain separate households for each wife. Divorce is frequent and can be initiated by either the husband or the wife. In either case, the wife will return to her father's home for protection and support until her marital crisis has been resolved.

Domestic Unit

The three-generation extended family is the ideal domestic unit. Although this group, averaging between nine and eleven persons, may sleep under more than one tent or shelter, its meals are generally taken together. The newly formed nuclear family of husband and wife tends to remain with the larger domestic unit until it has sufficient manpower and a large enough herd to survive on its own. On occasion, a combination of brothers or patrilineal cousins will join forces to form a single domestic unit.

Inheritance

Property is divided in accordance to Quranic precepts: among surviving children, a son receives half, a daughter a quarter, and other near kin the percentage specified (surah 4:12). Among some Bedouin groups the division of the animal holdings of the deceased is complicated by the fact that women may not look after the larger domesticated animals. Thus, if a woman receives an inheritance of a number of camels, these must be put in trust for her and are generally incorporated into a brother's or cousin's herd.

Socialization

Children and infants are raised by the extended family unit. Parents, older siblings, grandparents, aunts, uncles, and cousins all take part in the rearing of the young. By the age of 6 or 7, the child begins to take on simple household tasks and soon thereafter becomes a full working member of the family. Adolescence is hardly recognized; by the early teens, the individual is accepted as a full working member of Bedouin society.

cieties, necessitating the adoption of new bases of identification with their "nations" and its leaders.

SOCIAL ORGANIZATION. Bedouin society is organized on the basis of a series of real and fictive overlapping kin groups. The smallest unit is generally agreed to be the bayt (minimal lineage). Numerous buyuut, claiming descent from a common ancestor, form a fakhadh (maximal lineage). Theoretically, each male household head in a bayt or the larger fakhadh is the equal of all the other adult males. In practice, age, religious piety, and personal characteristics such as generosity and hospitality set some men above others in the organization of the group.

POLITICAL ORGANIZATION. The buyuut are the basic social and economic units of Bedouin society, but the leaders of these units generally form a council of elders, directed by the head of the tribe. In some larger tribes with more centralization, the fakhadh head is linked to a subtribe (*'ashiira*) leader, who comes immediately under the direction of the head (*shaykh*; pl. *shuyukh*) of the tribe (qabiila). Thus, traditional chains of command link the individual groups ultimately to the shaykh. He traditionally exercises authority over the allocation of pasture and the arbitration of disputes. His position is usually derived from his own astute reading of the majority opinion.

He generally has no power to enforce a decision and therefore has to rely on his moral authority and the concurrence of the community with his point of view.

SOCIAL CONTROL. In the small-scale, exclusive communities that constitute Bedouin society, face-to-face (as opposed to anonymous) relations are of paramount importance. The concepts of honor and shame are thus a constant preoccupation and, to a large extent, serve to control the social behavior of individuals. *Sharaf* (honor), which is inherited from the family, has to be constantly asserted or vindicated. A man's share of honor is largely determined by his own behavior and that of his near agnatic kin. Sharaf can be subject to increase or decrease, to development or deterioration, according to the conduct of the person and his kin. There is an exclusive term, *ird*, for the honor of the women of a kin group. This is used only in connection with female chastity. Ird differs from sharaf in that sharaf can be acquired or augmented through right behavior and achievement, whereas ird can only be lost by the "misconduct" of the woman; once lost, it cannot be regained. At the community level, the threat of *jalaa'* (expulsion) as punishment for a grave social offense tends to be regarded with great seriousness.

NOMADS

*Following a pastoral nomadic way of life, Bedouins typically live in tents. These rectangular structures have two or three sections to divide women's and men's areas. Iraq.
(Nik Wheeler/Corbis)*

Bedouin

CONFLICT. In the past, most tribal conflicts revolved about the rights to scarce pasture and water resources. Numerous tribal campaigns were once fought to acquire or defend pastures and watering holes. Since the middle of the twentieth century, however, the centralized political authority of the modern nation-states in the region has successfully pacified the Bedouin tribes.

Religion and Expressive Culture

RELIGIOUS BELIEFS. Although a few Bedouin societies in Jordan have remained Christian since the early Islamic period, the vast majority of Bedouin are Sunni Muslims. The Five Pillars of Islam are the declaration of faith, the five daily ritual prayers, almsgiving, fasting, and the pilgrimage to Mecca. Most Bedouin societies observe the fast of Ramadan, perform the obligatory prayers, and celebrate the two major Islamic holidays—'Iid al-Fitr and 'Iid al-Adhha. Some groups endeavor to make the hajj (the pilgrimage to Mecca) more than once in a lifetime, and individual piety is sometimes reflected in the number of pilgrimages an individual manages to undertake. The Bedouin societies throughout the region variously believe in the presence of spirits (jinn), some playful and others malevolent, that interfere in the life of humans. The "envious eye" is also very real to the Bedouin, and children are believed to be particularly vulnerable. For this reason, they often have protective amulets attached to their clothing or hung around their necks. Some Bedouin groups postulate the existence ogresses and of monstrous supernaturals (*ahl al-ard*, "people of the earth"), who are sometimes met by lone travelers in the desert.

RELIGIOUS PRACTITIONERS. There is no formal clergy in Islam and no center of "priests." Bedouin societies have no formal religious specialists. Bedouin groups traditionally arrange for religious specialists from adjacent settled regions to spend several months a year with them to teach the young to read the Quran. These specialists are often called "shuyukh" (sing. shaykh). Other rural or settled religious specialists that Bedouin seek out for curative and preventative measures are variously called *kaatibiin* (sing. *katib*), *shaatirin* (sing. *shatir*), and *mutawwi'iin* (sing. *mutawi*).

CEREMONIES AND RITUALS. In addition to the religious observances discussed under "Religious Beliefs," Bedouin ceremonies and rituals include elaborate celebrations of weddings, ritual namings of newborn infants, and the circumcision of children (boys universally, girls frequently). Those Bedouin who are influenced by Sufism (Islamic mysticism)—for example, the Bedouin of southern Sinai and Libya—also celebrate the Prophet's birthday and carry out pilgrimages to the tombs of saints. Hospitality is extensively ritualized. Whenever an animal is slaughtered for a guest, men ritually sacrifice it in accordance with Islamic law. Guests are ritually incorporated into their hosts' households; in case of armed conflict, guests must be protected as if they were family members. Other rituals contribute to the definition of household membership and household space. For instance, a newborn child is made a household member through rites of seclusion and purification, which new mothers observe for between seven and forty days after childbirth.

ARTS. Simple tattooing of the face (and in some cases the hand) is practiced. Drawing on sand is sometimes engaged in, particularly among children. Women weave sheep's wool—and occasionally goats' hair—into tent strips, rugs, blankets, saddlebags, and camel and horse trappings. Important artistic expression in design, color, and pattern is incorporated into these handicrafts. Most aesthetic expression, however, focuses on the recitation of poetry, some memorized and some composed for the occasion. Both men and women engage in contests of oral skills among their peer groups. Traditional musical instruments are mostly limited to the single-stringed instrument, various types of drums, and, in places, a type of recorder or wind instrument.

MEDICINE. Illness is attributed to a number of causes: imbalance of elements in the body and spirit possession, as well as germ invasion. Traditional preventative and curative measures include locally prepared herbal remedies, branding, the wearing of amulets, and the carrying of Quranic inscriptions. Western medical treatment is also sought out, particularly when traditional efforts fail.

DEATH AND AFTERLIFE. Islamic tradition dictates the practices associated with death. The body is buried as soon as possible and always within twenty-four hours. Among some Bedouin groups, an effort is made to bury the dead in one place (sometimes called the *bilaad*), although often it is impossible to reach it within the strict time limit imposed by Islamic practices. Funeral rites are very simple, and graves tend to be either unmarked or undifferentiated.

Bibliography

Abu-Lughod, Lila (1986). *Veiled Sentiments: Honor and Poetry in a Bedouin Society*. Berkeley and Los Angeles: University of California Press.

Asad, Talal (1970). *The Kababish Arabs: Power, Authority, and Consent in a Nomadic Tribe.* London: C. Hurst & Co.

"Badw" (1979). In *Encyclopedia of Islam.* Vol. 1, *A–B,* 872–882. New ed. Leiden: E. J. Brill.

Behnke, Roy (1980). *The Herders of Cyrenaica: Ecology, Economy, and Kinship among the Bedouin of Eastern Libya.* Urbana: University of Illinois Press.

Chatty, Dawn (1986). *From Camel to Truck: The Bedouin in the Modern World.* New York: Vantage Press.

Cole, Donald (1975). *Nomads of the Nomads: The Al Murrah of the Empty Quarter.* Chicago: Aldine Publishing Co.

Fagan, Brian (1986). *Peoples of the Earth: An Introduction to World Prehistory.* Boston: Little, Brown & Co.

Lancaster, William (1981). *The Rwala Bedouin Today.* Cambridge: Cambridge University Press.

Marx, Emanuel (1967). *Bedouin of the Negev.* Manchester: Manchester University Press.

Peters, Emrys (1968). "The Tied and the Free: An Account of a Type of Patron-Client Relationship among the Bedouin Pastoralists of Cyrenaica." In *Contributions to Mediterranean Sociology,* edited by J. G. Peristiany. The Hague: Mouton & Co.

—DAWN CHATTY AND WILLIAM YOUNG

CIRCASSIANS

Ethonym: Adyge

Orientation

IDENTIFICATION. The Circassians are a people indigenous to the northwestern Caucasus who are also found today as minority communities in four Middle Eastern countries: Turkey, Syria, Jordan, and Israel. They call themselves "Adyge," the term "Circassian" being the one used by outsiders ("Çerkez" in Turkish, "Sharkass" in Arabic) to refer, rather loosely, to a variety of groups from that region.

LOCATION. The Circassians migrated into the Ottoman Empire in the late nineteenth century after the Russian takeover of their homeland. They were first settled by the Ottoman state in the Balkans but were soon displaced again as the Ottoman Empire lost control of that region. They were then settled in Anatolia and in Bilād ash-Sham (the Syrian province). The general policy of the state was to settle immigrants to act as buffers against dissident local groups and also to extend agricultural settlements and push back the "desert line"; however, specific locations were determined by local exigencies such as the availability of agri-

cultural land. The major settlements were in the regions of the Black Sea coast, western Anatolia and Kayseri (Turkey), Aleppo (Syria), the Golan Heights (Israeli-occupied Syria), Amman (Jordan) and Tiberias (Israel). Circassians also live in the major urban centers of these areas.

DEMOGRAPHY. The number of Circassians is difficult to determine because census data are lacking. Estimates point to about 1 million in Turkey, 60,000 in Syria, 30,000 in Jordan, and 1,500 in Israel. There are also no statistics on the rate of intermarriage with non-Circassians, which tends to vary by location, class, and urban versus rural settlement.

LINGUISTIC AFFILIATION. The Circassian language, Adygebze, is one of the North-West Caucasian Group of languages and is divided into a number of different dialects. It is still spoken in all the Circassian communities, especially in the home and during community events, although the younger generation tends to feel more comfortable speaking in Arabic or Turkish, and many words have been adopted from these languages. There has been a convergence of the various dialects (notably Kabartey, Bzedugh, Shapsoug, and Abzekh) owing to intensive interaction and common residence. When Circassian is written, the adapted Cyrillic alphabet developed in the Soviet Union is used.

History and Cultural Relations

Circassian immigration into the Ottoman Empire began in 1850 and accelerated into a mass migration starting in 1864. There was an earlier Circassian presence in the Middle East, through the Mamluk "slave-dynasties" in Egypt, whose descendants, augmented by continued individual migration, came to form a Turco-Circassian elite ruling class in Egypt. This presence, although an entirely different phenomenon than the later mass migrations, points to important historical links between the Caucasus and various regional empires to which it provided slaves (both men and women) and warriors.

Circassian migration during the nineteenth century resulted from an Ottoman policy of encouraging immigration, both to overcome its shortage of manpower and to increase its Muslim population in turbulent regions. Religion was also a factor inducing the Muslim Circassians' emigration from under czarist Russian rule. In all, about 1.5 million Circassians settled in Ottoman lands. The relations that they established with their host communities were shaped by the nature of Ottoman rule and prevailing local economic condi-

♦ **Cyrillic alphabet**
A writing system developed in the ninth century for Slavic languages. Russian, Serbian, Bulgarian, and other Slavic languages today are written with somewhat different versions of the basic Cyrillic alphabet.

See also

Turks

tions. The commonality of religion was an integrative force. The provincial authorities were given instructions to allocate the migrants free land and building materials and to exempt them from most forms of taxation. Soon, however, the number of immigrants overwhelmed both the facilities provided and the capacity of the provinces to absorb them. Conditions quickly deteriorated. More and more immigrants tended to drift toward the cities.

In what was to become Jordan, for example, the areas of Circassian settlement were strongholds of large nomadic and seminomadic Bedouin tribes. Conflict arose over water and pastureland. Furthermore, Circassians refused to enter into the indigenous peasant/Bedouin relationship of paying protection money. Armed clashes ensued, mostly around harvest-time, and a kind of mutual respect grew out of these clashes. Soon treaties were negotiated between various tribes and the Circassians, and some judicious marriages of Circassian women to powerful Bedouin families were arranged.

The breakup of the Soviet Union and the accessiblity of the Caucasus after 140 years now allows third- and fourth-generation Circassians to revisit their "homeland" (the republics of Adygei, Cherkessk-Karachai, and Kabardino-Balkaria, all part of the Russian Federation). An estimated two hundred families, mainly from Turkey and Syria, have migrated back, and there is intense cultural activity between various organizations in the Caucasus and ethnic associations in the Middle East, as well as families seeking long-lost kin. The new links are marked by intense nostaligia and emotion, but also by a sense of rupture caused by divergent historical experiences.

Settlements

The different settlements were formed slowly through the waves of migration and were mainly agricultural. Today some are still primarily agricultural (as in Turkey). Others have become metropolitan centers (as in Jordan), and still others are abandoned (as in Syria, where, after the Israeli occupation of the Golan Heights in 1967, the inhabitants all became refugees). Some moved to urban areas in the early days of the immigration, others came as part of a wider rural-urban migration, particularly since the 1950s.

Circassian village neighborhoods initially reflected the different dialect groups and the time of settlement. As villages grew more heterogeneous, distinct Circassian and Arab neighborhoods tended to form, although the boundaries are becoming increasingly blurred as residential and economic mobility increase. Where urban centers formed, the Circassians eventually became a numerical minority, old neighborhoods broke up, and residence became defined by class rather than ethnicity.

Economy

SUBSISTENCE AND COMMERCIAL ACTIVITIES. Upon settlement, the Circassians were mainly engaged in agriculture, although they gradually became drawn into the network of internal trade controlled by merchants from nearby towns and cities. In Bilād ash-Sham, although Circassians were engaged in transporting goods such as barley cultivated by Bedouins, they remained essentially suppliers of agricultural goods and did not control trade. The construction of the Hejaz railway to Mecca provided wage-labor opportunities. A few Circassians were also employed in the Ottoman administration.

The changes wrought in the geopolitics of the region in the early twentieth century, with the dismemberment of the Ottoman Empire into present-day Turkey and several mandate governments (the French in Syria and the British in Jordan and Palestine), changed the economy and nature of Circassian settlements. New opportunities, notably in the armies and bureaucracies, became available to them and their settlements become more heterogeneous. Amman, for example, became the capital of the new Jordanian state. Later, with the transformation of the peasant economy, Circassians, as others, participated in the new avenues for wage labor in industry, agro-business and so on, although the military and bureaucracy remain the main occupations for the communities in Syria and Jordan.

INDUSTRIAL ARTS. Circassian traditional crafts included agricultural implements, especially their distinctive two-wheeled carts, silversmithing and other metalwork, and leatherwork. Very few are still involved in crafts production today, except in the form of "folkloric" items and attempts at the revival of traditional arts.

TRADE. The Circassians in the Middle East have largely not engaged in trade and attribute this to national character, saying that Circassians make good military personnel but bad traders. More likely it has to do with the nature of the opportunities that were available to them in their new environments. The Anatolian Circassians were engaged in some horse breeding and cattle trading, and some continue to work as truckers of meat and animals. Furthermore, in some places, such as Jordan, they are heavily engaged in real estate because their lands have gained in value as urban residential areas continue to expand into formerly agricultural land. The new opportunities opened up by the possibility of commercial links with the Caucasus have led some, especially in Turkey, to establish import-export companies as well as travel agencies.

DIVISION OF LABOR. Previously, the division of labor reflected the nature of agriculture in the areas of settlement. Women do not seem to have worked in the fields, although they cultivated orchards and gardens and raised animals. Where herding was an important activity, women also played a role in managing herds. Young men and women had well-defined duties serving elders at formal gatherings and ceremonies. Where a more urban economy is in place, such as in Syria and Jordan, the former peasant households have been transformed; men work mostly in the military and the bureaucracy. Within the sectors made available to them by the wider economy, women have also entered the urban workforce.

LAND TENURE. At the time of settlement, land was allotted to each household according to its size. In Jordan, this amount of land was 60 *donums* (6 hectares) for households of up to five people and 80 donums (8 hectares) for larger ones. Land was registered in the name of the head of the household. Later, each state undertook different types of land registration and distribution. In Jordan, land is generally privately owned, and until the 1980s, and especially in rural settlements, land was often held by the father until his death, whereupon it was divided among the children, according to Islamic inheritance rules. In those areas where land became valuable commercial property, younger family members pressured elders to divide the property among them. In a rather widespread phenomenon, many elderly women who own vast tracts of land inherited from their fathers are refusing to divide or sell them.

Kinship

KIN GROUPS AND DESCENT. In the past, the basic kin units among the Circassians were the patrilineal extended family and a wider patrilineal descent group. In the Caucasus, each descent group tended to live in a separate hamlet. Emigration and settlement broke up these groups, and the new villages included many different descent groups but were often comprised of families of the same dialect group, which, in turn, represented their original region in the Caucasus.

Nowadays, in places such as Jordan, descent groups are being organized in formal family associations.

KINSHIP TERMINOLOGY. Circassian kinship terminology is extremely descriptive and distinguishes matriline from patriline for both consanguineal and affinal kin. The terms used for "father-in-law" and "mother-in-law" mean "Master" and "Lady," the same terms used to refer to members of the nobility, illustrating the strict hierarchical relations involved between in-laws. The new bride is traditionally given a new personal name upon becoming part of her husband's household and gives new names to all the members of this household, by which she henceforth calls them. Nowadays Arabic or Turkish kinship terms are increasingly replacing Circassian ones, some of them "Circassianized" through a particular pronunciation.

Marriage and Family

MARRIAGE. Circassians are preferentially endogamous within the ethnic group but descent-group exogamous. Traditionally, marriage to kin, up to five generations bilaterally, was prohibited. This has led, in diaspora, to far-flung marriages across communities and settlements but is becoming difficult to maintain. More and more, the rule of exogamy is being ignored, although cousin marriage, which is a preferred form of marriage among Arabs, is still extremely rare among Circassians. A prevalent form of marriage is through elopement, erroneously seen as bride-capture by neighboring groups. Intermarriage with Arabs and Turks does occur, but interesting differences are found between communities. For example, in Jordan, Circassian women marry Arab men, but the reverse (Circassian men marrying Arab women) is rare, whereas in the Kayseri region of Turkey the opposite appears to hold.

DOMESTIC UNIT. The domestic unit used to be the patrilineal extended family, with each conjugal family living in a separate dwelling within a common courtyard. Circassians are largely monogamous; polygyny and divorce are rare, although remarriage after the death of a spouse is common. In general, family size—usually three to five children—is small as compared with that of the surrounding society.

INHERITANCE. Islamic Sharia precepts of inheritance are followed. In Syria and Jordan women inherit their share of property according to Sharia. In rural Turkey, despite the replacement of Sharia with civil codes that stipulate equal division of property among the progeny regardless of

Within sectors made available to them, Circassian women have entered the urban workforce.

*It is a source of
shame for a
Circassian man to
be seen playing with
or showing affection
to his children; the
same holds for
relations between
mothers and
children.*

sex, it appears that women often give up this inheritance in favor of their brothers, which is common practice in the Middle East.

SOCIALIZATION. Circassian families traditionally emphasize discipline and strict authoritarianism. Avoidance relationships are the rule between in-laws and between generations and different age groups. It is a source of shame for a man to be seen playing with or showing affection to his children (but not his grandchildren). Although tempered by necessities of everyday life, the same holds for relations between mothers and children. In the past, paternal uncles played an important role in instructing children in proper behavior. This behavior, both public and private, is codified in a set of rules known as Adyge-Khabze (*adyge* = mores) and is reinforced by the family as well as the kin group and the neighborhood as a whole. Nowadays ethnic associations sometimes make attempts to discuss the Adyge-Khabze with young people, and the term is almost always invoked at public gatherings. In Jordan, a Circassian school has been operating since the mid-1970s and has become an arena for socialization and reproduction of Circassian identity.

Sociopolitical Organization

SOCIAL ORGANIZATION. Displacement led to the amalgamation of the different groups with one another while, at the same time, separating families and descent groups. Emigration led to the breaking up of old authority relationships and the creation of new ones. Traditionally, Circassian society was ranked into nobles, warriors, free peasants, and bondsmen—each status maintaining strict endogamy. Emigration disrupted this stratification, and land distribution tended to equalize the communities until new, class-based stratification and rural-urban differences emerged; however, the older status ranking is sometimes still a consideration in deciding on acceptable marriage partners.

POLITICAL ORGANIZATION. The Circassian communities are encapsulated in different formal political systems that range from parliamentary democracies (Turkey and Israel), to one-party regimes (Syria), to constitutional monarchies (Jordan). Other than in Jordan, Circassians do not have a special quota of elected representatives in government. Informal politics of ethnicity and state policies toward minorities govern the political trends and types of participation in the communities. The ethnic associations are the primary arena for organizing the communities; elections may be hotly contested. For example, during the Abkhazian-Georgian war, aid for Abkhazia was collected by

such associations. Links with the Caucasus are generally established via these associations.

SOCIAL CONTROL. Avoidance relationships diffuse potential conflict, and control is reinforced by the strict discipline imposed through deference to the authority of elders. The latter, however, complain that the younger generation, being ignorant of customs and tradition, no longer respect them sufficiently.

CONFLICT. Disputes that do not involve civil law tend to be solved through negotiation and consensus by local-level leaders within the community, but intraethnic conflict sometimes involves complicated processes. In Jordan, Arab tribal law, in which not all Circassians are well versed, continues to play an important role in conflict resolution. To this end, a group of Circassian leaders in Jordan established a "Tribal Council" in 1981 to help Circassian individuals and to mediate on their behalf.

Religion and Expressive Culture

RELIGIOUS BELIEFS. The Circassians in the Middle East are all Muslims of the majority Sunni sect. Islam spread late into the northern Caucasus, after the sixteenth century, although a largely syncretic form of Islam, including Christian and local beliefs, continued to be practiced. Exposure to Islamic Orthodoxy occurred mostly during the immigration process, when the Ottomans sent imams to instruct the new immigrants in beliefs and practices.

RELIGIOUS PRACTITIONERS. There are Circassian imams and religious specialists, but, except where there are still ethnically homogeneous villages, there are no mosques where Circassians worship separately from fellow-Muslim Arabs and Turks. Some graveyards that were established before the settlements became heterogeneous continue to be favored by Circassians for burial, even if they do not reside nearby.

CEREMONIES. The main ceremonies that distinguish the Circassians from the wider society are those relating to weddings (especially when marriage is through elopement). Several days of dancing and feasting are divided into separate phases for the different age groups. Some other ceremonies (e.g., marking age grades) are now less frequently performed. Many occasions are now celebrated at ethnic organizations. In addition, the major Islamic rituals are observed.

ARTS. Folk dancing figures most prominently in Circassian expressive culture, partly because of weddings and other ceremonies in which it plays a major part. Ethnic organizations have focused on folklore troupes. In some cases, notably Turkey, Circassian dances have been incorporated into the national folklore "repertoire." In other countries as well, Circassian dancing is routinely presented at national festivals and occasions.

MEDICINE. Besides the use of herbs and poultices, traditional Circassian medicine emphasized forbearance of pain and the value of constant entertainment in distracting the ill or wounded from dwelling on their suffering. With the encroachment of Western medicine, these practices are being abandoned. There are no specialized Circassian healers.

DEATH AND AFTERLIFE. Contemporary Circassian beliefs about death and the afterlife are congruent with the Islamic faith, although vestiges of distinctive beliefs in immortality are reflected in the myths of the Narts (half-divine, giant ancestors of the Circassians) and in the tales of Susoruga, who brought fire to humankind. Distinctive funeral practices are still observed, including placement of a large, open pair of scissors on the chest of the deceased and the digging of a particular type of grave.

Bibliography

Abujaber, Raouf S. (1988). *Pioneers over Jordan.* London: I. B. Tauris & Co.

Karpat, Kemal (1977). "Ottoman Immigration Policies and Settlement in Palestine." In *Settler Regimes in Africa and the Arab World: The Illusion of Endurance*, edited by Ibrahim Abu-Lughod and Baha Abu-Laban, 57–72. Illinois: Medina University Press International.

Lewis, Norman N. (1987). *Nomads and Settlers in Syria and Jordan, 1800–1980.* Cambridge: Cambridge University Press.

Shami, Seteney (1992). "19th Century Settlements in Jordan." In *Studies in the History and Archaeology of Jordan.* Vol. 4, 417–421. Amman: Department of Antiquities; Maison de l'Orient Méditerranéen.

Shami, Seteney (1995). "Disjuncture in Ethnicity: Negotiating Circassian Identity in Jordan, Turkey, and the Caucasus." *New Perspectives on Turkey* 12 (Spring): 75–95.

—SETENEY SHAMI

JEWS OF ISRAEL

Ethonym: Yahudim (pl.), Yisraelim (pl.)

Orientation

IDENTIFICATION. The state of Israel came into formal existence on 14 May 1948. The United States recognized the new state on the same day, and the Soviet Union followed on 18 May. On 15 May 1948 the new state was invaded by the armies of Egypt, Iraq, Jordan, Syria, and Lebanon, along with smaller numbers of troops from other Arab countries. Hostilities continued until January 1949, when a cease-fire was negotiated. The boundaries determined by the cease-fire defined the state of Israel until the 1967 War (the "Six Day War"), when additional territories (East Jerusalem, the West Bank, the Golan Heights, and the Gaza Strip) came under Israeli control. On 11 May 1949 Israel was admitted to the United Nations as a member state.

LOCATION. Israel is located in southwestern Asia, at the eastern end of the Mediterranean Sea, at approximate latitude 31°30' N and longitude 35°00' E. It is bounded on the north by Lebanon, on the northeast by Syria, on the east and southeast by Jordan (the Dead Sea and the Gulf of 'Aqaba), on the southwest by Egypt (the Sinai Peninsula), and on the west by the Mediterranean Sea. Pre-1967 Israel had an area of approximately 20,700 square kilometers (about the size of the state of New Jersey). The territories captured after the 1967 War total about 7,500 square kilometers, including East Jerusalem which, along with the Golan Heights, Israel has formally annexed. Geographically, Israel is divided into four regions: the coastal plain, the central highlands, the Jordan Rift Valley, and the Negev Desert. The highest point in Israel is at Mount Meron (1,208 meters), in the Galilee (the central highlands) near the city of Safad. The lowest point is at the Dead Sea (in the Jordan Rift Valley) which, at 399 meters below sea level, is the lowest point in the world. Israel, located between a subtropical arid zone to its south and a subtropical wet zone to its north, has a Mediterranean climate with short, cool, and rainy winters and long, hot, and dry summers. About 70 percent of the rainfall occurs between November and March, but it is unevenly distributed, diminishing sharply to the south. During January and February, precipitation may take the form of snow at the higher elevations (including Jerusalem). About a third of the country (areas receiving more than 30 centimeters of rainfall a year—the coastal plain, the Jezreel Valley, and the Galilee) is cultivable.

DEMOGRAPHY. At the end of 1987, the total population of Israel was 4,389,600, of whom 82 percent (3,601,200) were Jews. (About 27 percent of the world's Jewish population lives in Israel.) The Jewish population in the late 1980s grew at the rate of about 1.4 percent (compared to

The state of Israel came into formal existence on 14 May 1948.

about 3 percent for the non-Jewish population). With a median age of about 27.6 (1986), the Jewish population is relatively young, but not so compared to Muslims (whose median age in the same year was 16.8). The Jewish population is skewed in age toward the very young and the very old; a relatively small percentage is in the 35–50 age group. This skewing is because of the effects of large-scale immigration in forming the Jewish population of Israel. Between 1948 and 1960, immigration accounted for almost 70 percent of the annual average population-growth rate. Many of these immigrants were older, and those who were younger were often single people who deferred marriage and child rearing until after their settlement.

LINGUISTIC AFFILIATION.   Hebrew is the major official language of Israel and the predominant language of Israel's Jews. Arabic is spoken by Israel's Arab minority, most of whom are bilingual in Hebrew as well. Arabic is also an official language and may be used in courts and the parliament (Knesset). The successful revival of Hebrew as a modern, spoken, and "living" language, a major thrust of the Zionist cultural program, was one of its major accomplishments. Nevertheless, because so many in the population are immigrants, many other languages are spoken by Jews, especially older people or recent immigrants. These include Arabic (or dialects of Judeo-Arabic), Yiddish, Ladino, Persian, English, Russian, French, Spanish, and other European, African (e.g., Amharic) and Asian (e.g., Malayalam, of Cochin, India) languages.

History and Cultural Relations

The Connection of the Jewish people to the land called "Palestine" by the Romans is one of the oldest religio-political claims in the world. Jews (and many Christians as well) will point to God's promise to Abraham in Genesis 15:17 and Deuteronomy 1:7 and 11:24 as proof of the sacred "birthright" of Jews to what they call the Land of Israel (Eretz Yisrael). Jewish presence in Palestine has been constant (if very small in number), even after the final Roman suppression of the Jewish revolt in 135 C.E. Throughout premodern times, pious Jews lived in Palestine, concentrated in the four "holy cities" of Jerusalem, Hebron, Safad, and Tiberias. They were supported by funds, called *halukkah*, collected by special emissaries sent from Palestine to Jewish diaspora communities.

The history of modern Israel, however, begins in the nineteenth century with the articulation in Europe of a program for Jewish national and cultural revival, called Zionism ("Zion" being one of the biblical names for Jerusalem). Zionism was a reaction to virulent and increasingly violent European anti-Semitism (which culminated in the terrible Holocaust of 1933–1945), but it was also a response to the nationalist movements of other, especially eastern and southern, European peoples throughout the nineteenth century. Zionism stressed the physical relocation of Jews to Palestine (in Hebrew, Aliya), and in 1882 the first wave of these "modern" immigrants—politically and ideologically, rather than religiously, motivated—arrived. This first wave effectively doubled the Jewish population of Palestine (from about 24,000 in 1881). Immigration continued to come in waves, mostly from eastern and central Europe, until the eve of World War II. Immigration was greatly curtailed by the war and, later, by restrictive British policies (Palestine had been a British Mandate since 1919), which sought to assuage Arab fears, which were based on the fact that, by early 1948, the Jews had succeeded in establishing a society in Palestine (called the Yishuv) that was in many ways autonomous and independent of both Arab society and British colonial constraints and that had many of the institutions of a state already in place. On the day Israel declared its independence, there were about 650,000 Jews in the country. Virtually the first act of the new government was to open its borders to unrestricted Jewish immigration. There was a massive influx between 1948 and 1960 from Middle Eastern and North African countries—almost the entire Jewish populations of Yemen, Aden, Libya, and Iraq, and large numbers from Egypt, Syria, Morocco, and Tunisia. Today these so-called "Oriental" (Afro-Asian) Jews and their children constitute the majority of the Jewish Israeli population, outnumbering Jews of European and North American origin. Nevertheless, it was not until 1975 that native-born Jewish Israelis (called "sabras") outnumbered immigrants of any kind.

Settlements

The Jewish population of Israel is overwhelmingly urban (about 90 percent), concentrated along the Mediterranean coast and in the three major cities—Tel Aviv, Jerusalem, and Haifa. About twenty-seven smaller cities called "development towns" were planned by the government, starting in the mid-1950s, as ways to settle large numbers of Oriental Jews, promote light industry, and disperse the population from the coastal strip. Today these areas, among the poorest Jewish areas in Israel, are sites of ethnic unrest. Of the small proportion of Jews who reside in rural areas, the majority live in collective (kibbutz) and cooperative (moshav) communities. The kibbutz, especially, is known worldwide as a distinctive Israeli institution whose members (*kibbutznikim*) historically have played a significant role in Israeli society. Nevertheless, today only about 3.5 percent of Israeli Jews live on the kibbutzim and 4.5 percent on the moshavim.

Economy

SUBSISTENCE AND COMMERCIAL ACTIVITIES.   Israel's economy in the past was influenced heavily by the centralized and socialist tendencies of the Labor governments that ruled the country between 1948 and 1977. Between 1977 and 1992, Likud-led governments favored privatization of enterprises and limitations on the large public sector. Labor was returned to power in 1992.

INDUSTRIAL ARTS.   The importance of Israel's industrial sector has continued to grow (proportional to agricultural production), and by the early 1980s industrial exports accounted for close to two-thirds of total exports. Tourism remains a major source of employment and foreign exchange.

TRADE.   Israel's merchant marine (numbering about 100 ships) is vital both to its economy and, given hostile relations with surrounding Arab countries, its sense of security. Israel's small size, lack of natural resources (particularly petroleum and water), and heavy commitments to defense expenditures have constituted obstacles to sustaining economic growth, and the country has become increasingly dependent on foreign inflows of capital, especially foreign aid from the United States.

DIVISION OF LABOR.   About 40 percent of the Jewish civilian labor force is female. The other great division of labor is between Jews and Arabs, with the latter concentrated in construction and agriculture. Occupational differences are also evident between Jews of Afro-Asian origins ("Orientals") and those of Euro-American descent (called "Ashkenzim"): about 65 percent of all Ashkenazim are concentrated in white-collar professions, whereas about 55 percent of Oriental Jews are concentrated in blue-collar occupations.

LAND TENURE.   Most of the land in Israel is owned by the state or state-sponsored institutions and is conceived as held "in trust" on behalf of the entire Jewish people.

Kinship

KIN GROUPS AND DESCENT.   Extended kin groups based on descent are not important among

WAILING WALL

People praying at the Western (Wailing) Wall, a Jewish holy site in Jerusalem, Israel. About 27 percent of the world's Jewish population is in Israel. (Richard T. Nowitz/Corbis)

Israel is overwhelmingly a nation of immigrants, who, despite their common identity as Jews, come from very diverse social and cultural backgrounds.

Jewish Israelis. Kinship is bilateral, and the nuclear family is its most important unit. Remnants of other patterns—for example, patronymic kin groups (*hamula*, pl. *hamulot*)—can be found in some moshav communities settled by North African Jews.

KINSHIP TERMINOLOGY. Kin terms conform to Western (cognatic) systems, translated appropriately into Hebrew.

Marriage and Family

MARRIAGE. The median age of marriage in 1986 for Jewish men was 26.4, for women 23.1. (Many men defer marriage until after their mandatory service in the Israel Defense Forces.) The age is considerably younger among ultra-Orthodox Jews, who are effectively exempted from army service, and for whom the biblical injunction to "be fruitful and multiply" is very important.

DOMESTIC UNIT. The nuclear family is the main domestic unit. The average family size is 4.7 among Jews of Oriental origin, versus 2.8 for Ashkenazim.

INHERITANCE. Inheritance, like all matters of personal-status law in Israel, falls for Jews under the jurisdiction of rabbinical courts that apply (sometimes controversially) rabbinic law (*halakha*).

SOCIALIZATION. Education in Israel is free and compulsory through tenth grade, tuition in high school (since reforms in 1984) has been set at about U.S.$10 monthly. Preschool is available to children between ages 3 and 6 and (given the high percentage of working women) is widely used. Education is sharply divided into three separate tracts: state-supported secular schools (about 72 percent of primary-school students), state-supported religious systems (about 22 percent), and a number of traditional, private religious schools (the yeshivas, or Talmudic academies) that cater to the ultra-Orthodox. These enroll about 6 percent of primary-school students. For the vast majority of Israel's Jews, service in the Israeli army is a crucial part of their transition to adulthood.

Sociopolitical Organization

SOCIAL ORGANIZATION. The key to Israeli Jewish social organization is the fact that Israel is overwhelmingly a nation of immigrants, who, despite their common identity as Jews, come from very diverse social and cultural backgrounds. The goals of Zionism included the "fusion of the Exiles" (as Diaspora Jews were called), and although

great strides toward this fusion have occurred—the revival of Hebrew has been mentioned—it has not, on the whole, been achieved. The immigrant groups of the 1950s and 1960s are the ethnic groups of today. The most important ethnic division is that between Jews of European and North American background, called "Ashkenazim" (after the old Hebrew name for Germany) and those of African and Asian origins, called "Sephardim" (after the old Hebrew name for Spain, and referring technically to Jews of the Mediterranean and Aegean) or "Orientals" (in modern Hebrew *edot hamizrach*; lit., "communities of the East"). The problem, as most Israelis see it, is not the existence of Jewish ethnic divisions per se, but the fact that they have become linked over the years to differences in class, occupation, and standard of living, with Oriental Jews concentrated in the lower strata of society.

POLITICAL ORGANIZATION. Israel is a parliamentary democracy. The whole nation acts as a single constituency to elect a 120-member parliament (the Knesset). Political parties put forth lists of candidates, and Israelis vote for the list, rather than individual candidates on it. A party's representation in the Knesset is based on the proportion of the vote it receives. Any party receiving at least 1 percent of the national vote is entitled to a seat in the Knesset. The majority party is asked by the president (the nominal head of state, chosen by the Knesset to serve a five-year term) to name a prime minister and form a government. This system entails coalition formation, and means there are many small political parties, representing all shades of political and ideological opinion, that play a disproportionate role in any government.

SOCIAL CONTROL. There is a single national police force and an independent, paramilitary, border police. National security is considered a top priority in Israel and, within the country, is the responsibility of an organization called the Shin Bet. The Israeli army has enforced social control in the Territories, particularly after the Palestinian uprising (*intifada*) of December 1987. This new role for the army has been very controversial within Israel.

CONFLICT. Israeli society is characterized by three deep cleavages, all of which have entailed conflict. In addition to the cleavage between Ashkenazim and Oriental Jews, and the deeper one between Jews and Arabs, there is a division in the society between secular Jews, the Orthodox, and the ultra-Orthodox. This last division cuts across Jewish ethnic lines.

Religion and Expressive Culture

RELIGIOUS BELIEFS. Judaism is the dominant religion, although the majority (about two-thirds to three-fourths) of Israeli Jews are nonobservant. There are ritual and liturgical (and, some claim, stylistic and emotional) differences between Ashkenazi and Sephardi traditions.

RELIGIOUS PRACTITIONERS. Rabbis are the predominant Jewish religious practitioners. Religious-court judges serve as state civil servants. There is a Ministry for Religious Affairs and a Chief Rabbinate, the latter divided into Ashkenazi and Sephardi offices.

CEREMONIES. All of the holidays of the Jewish religious calendar are celebrated in Israel. Some ethnic festivals (e.g., the North African Mimouna) are also celebrated, and some national holidays—for example, Israeli Independence Day (Yom Haatzma'ut) and Remembrance Day—are given a semisacred status.

ARTS. Both the "high arts" (classical music, dance, theater, and literature) and folk arts (dance, especially) are highly extolled.

MEDICINE. Good medical care is widely available, and medical insurance (kupat holim) covers virtually all Israelis.

DEATH AND AFTERLIFE. Traditional Jewish death rites are simple. At the grave site, a kaddish is said; on various occasions from then on it will be repeated by close relatives to memorialize the deceased. A seven-day full mourning period (shivah) follows. (Lesser mourning lasts thirty days, a full year for one's parents.) The anniversary of the death (yahrzeit) is celebrated by close relatives. The soul (nefesh) of the deceased is thought to return to God.

Bibliography

Avruch, Kevin (1981). *American Immigrants in Israel: Social Identities and Change.* Chicago: University of Chicago Press.

Deshen, Shlomo, and Moshe Shokeid (1974). *The Predicament of Homecoming: Cultural and Social Life of North African Immigrants in Israel.* Ithaca, N.Y.: Cornell University Press.

Elazar, Daniel (1986). *Israel: Building a New Society.* Bloomington: Indiana University Press.

Spiro, Milford E. (1970). *Kibbutz: Venture in Utopia.* Cambridge: Harvard University Press.

Weingrod, Alex, ed. (1985). *Studies in Israeli Ethnicity.* New York: Gordon & Breach.

—KEVIN AVRUCH

KURDS

Ethonym: none

Orientation

The Kurds have inhabited an area of rugged mountains and high plains at the headwaters of the Tigris and Euphrates rivers for over two thousand years. They are believed to be descended from the Medes who overthrew Nineveh in 612 B.C. Their traditional mode of subsistence is pastoralism and agriculture.

The territory Kurds conceive of as Kurdistan ("the land of the Kurds") is distributed across the present borders of Turkey, Iraq, Iran, and Syria. There are other pockets of Kurds living in these countries, but outside of Kurdistan. A large group of Kurds can also be found in contiguous parts of the former Soviet Union. The terrain of Kurdistan is formed by the Eastern Taurus and the Zagros mountains and includes the steppelike plateaus to the north and the foothills of the Mesopotamian plains to the southwest. The climate is prone to extreme temperature fluctuations, from −30° C in the winter, to 45° C during the summer. Some mountain villages are completely isolated by heavy snows for up to six months of the year.

Kurdish, an Indo-European language, is most closely related to Persian. It consists of four main dialects (northern, middle, and southern Kurmanji, and Gorani), which in turn include several local dialects.

Estimates of the number of Kurds living in Turkey, Iran, Iraq, Syria and the former USSR are unreliable owing to the census policies of the various countries. Estimates of the Kurdish population in the mid-1970s for all these countries combined ranged from 13.5 to 21 million.

Settlements

Traditionally, Kurds were either nomads who lived in tent camps and moved their herds between summer and winter pasturage, or settled agriculturists who lived in villages on the plains or in mountain valleys. Today most Kurds have settled. Those who have not live in heavy, black woolen tents, which remain standing at the winter pasturage, and use lighter tents when traveling to and from summer pastures higher in the mountains. Camps may consist of an entire clan or of a group of families who join to herd their flocks together.

Kurdish villages consist of low clay or stone houses with flat roofs. They are often built up the

The Kurds have inhabited an area of rugged mountains and high plains at the headwaters of the Tigris and Euphrates rivers for over two thousand years.

See also

Persian

HISTORY AND CULTURAL RELATIONS

The Kurds have a long and eventful history. The Greek historian Xenophon recounted his encounters with the "Karduchi" as early as 375 B.C. The Arabs who brought Islam to the area in the seventh century A.D. were the first to refer to "Kurds." Many important figures in the history of the Ottoman and Persian empires were Kurds, and the remote area inhabited by Kurds served as a buffer between empires. The Kurds have long fought for autonomy, either as self-governing provinces or as an independent nation-state.

This history has profoundly affected almost every aspect of Kurdish life and culture. Rapid social change has been occurring in the countries that divide Kurdistan, which affects the Kurds as well. The policies of the various governments have also had quite different kinds of impact on the Kurds. Whereas the Turkish government outlaws the use of the Kurdish language in public and the publication or possession of Kurdish writings or audio recordings, the Iraqi government allowed the use of Kurdish as the language of instruction for Kurdish schoolchildren during the 1970s and 1980s. Thus, the development of Kurdish literature prospered in Iraq but was severely hampered in Turkey. In addition to dialectal differences, written communication is further complicated by the use of the Latin, Arabic, and Cyrillic alphabets in the different countries. These examples illustrate the complexity of the situation and serve as a caution against overgeneralization.

sides of a slope such that the roof of one house serves as a terrace for the house above it. Some villages correspond to lineages, others contain members of several lineages or of both tribal and nontribal groups; many are not organized along any kind of kinship tie. Villages often own communal pasture land, and, in some villages, private property may be sold only to fellow villagers. Kurdistan also contains several urban centers where large landowners, professionals, government workers, and laborers reside.

Economy

The nomadic pastoralists raise sheep and goats and trade wool, meat, and dairy products for grain, tea, sugar, and other consumer products available through the local markets. Other domesticated animals include cattle, donkeys, mules, and horses.

In the agricultural villages, wheat, barley, and lentils are the staple crops. Tobacco is raised as a cash crop, and walnuts, fruits, and vegetables are cultivated according to local conditions. Most agriculturists also have livestock.

Domestic industry consists of spinning, weaving, plaiting ropes, and the production of unglazed clay storage vessels.

The distribution of labor is based on the distinction between male and female tasks and that between peasants and aristocratic landowners. Women are responsible for milking and the processing of butter and cultured milk. In addition to preparing food, housekeeping, and child care, they collect firewood and manure for use as fuel, fetch water, clean grain, spin, weave, make ciga-

rettes, harvest tobacco, carry the harvest to the threshing floor, and may help with plowing. Aristocratic women perform tasks within the home but have servants to do the work away from home, such as milking and fetching fuel.

Men plow, sow, and harvest, transport surplus grain to the town market, and make whatever purchases are needed at the market. Usually one shepeard is employed to herd the flocks for the entire village. Traditionally, the *agha* (lineage, clan, or village leader), was responsible for the upkeep of a guest house in which visitors to the village were lodged and entertained and where village men met to discuss recent events. In return for this service, the agha was paid a tribute of approximately 10 percent of the villagers' harvest. Village guest houses are no longer as important as they once were. As the village leaders have moved away to the larger towns, the village guest houses have begun to disappear, and the men socialize instead at local tea houses.

Kinship

Kurdish kin groups are based on patrilineal descent. Several generations of one man's descendants through the male line constitute a lineage. Several such lineages compose a clan. It is assumed that all members of a clan are related through a common male ancestor, but outside groups may attach themselves to a powerful tribe and, after several generations, be incorporated as full members into a clan and tribe. A tribe consists of several clans.

Kurdish kinship terminology does not distinguish between maternal and paternal grandparents. It does distinguish between father's and mother's brothers, and between their children. Father's sisters and mother's sisters, however, are categorized together, as are their children.

Marriage and Family

Kurdish marriages are arranged between the families of the bride and groom. Ideally, a man will marry his father's brother's daughter, to whom he has "first rights." The majority of Kurdish marriages in the 1960s were reported to be between the children of two brothers. This lineage endogamy "keeps the family together" but also weakens the ties between lineages, thus increasing the likelihood of conflict. If marriage to father's brother's child is not possible, the next best choice is one of the other cousins.

Marriage negotiations are first carried out between the women of the two families, and then finalized by the men when a marriage settlement is drawn up. It states the size of the bride-wealth and how it will be used. If the groom does not pay the agreed-upon bride-wealth or does not support and clothe her according to the standards of her own family, the bride has grounds for divorce. The only other way she may obtain divorce is by repayment in full of the bride-wealth, unless otherwise stipulated in the marriage settlement. The man may divorce his wife merely by renouncing her three times.

According to the Quran, a man may have up to four wives provided he can support them all and spends equal time with each; however, few men can afford even two wives. A childless marriage is the most common grounds for divorce or the taking of a second wife.

The wedding entails the fetching of the bride to the groom's home, where the new couple will live until they establish their own home. A Kurdish household thus consists of a man, his wife (or wives), children, and eventually daughters-in-law and grandchildren. In the case of polygyny, each wife may have her own section of the house, which she runs independently.

Inheritance from the father is divided equally between the sons. Daughters do not inherit.

Sociopolitical Organization

Tribal organization based on patrilineal descent is typical of Kurdish nomadic pastoralists. Pasturage is collectively held by the clan within the tribe's territory, and migrations are coordinated at the tribal level. Among the seminomads and in the sedentary villages, clans and lineages come into play only in response to conflict, often in the form of blood feuds; however, not all sedentary agriculturists are organized along kinship lines. A traditional distinction was made between tribal agriculturists, who owned the land they worked, and nontribal peasants, who were subservient to the landowning tribals. These peasants did not own the land—they were bound to it and "belonged" to the tribal leader who controlled it. They owed him their labor and/or a percentage of their crops. Thus, Kurdish society includes both tribal and feudal systems, with clan, lineage, or village leaders serving as feudal lords.

As most Kurds have settled and become agriculturists, and because of the impact of government policies such as land reforms, changes have occured in Kurdish social organization. Through his contacts with government authorities, the agha was able to register communal lands in his own name. Thus, whereas in some areas village membership includes the right to a plot of land, in others entire villages are owned by a single absentee landlord, for whom the villagers work as sharecroppers or wage laborers. The mechanization of agriculture has reduced the need for village labor, and villagers have sought wage employment in urban centers both within and outside Kurdistan. The following events have clearly also had a major impact on Kurdish social organization: the Iran-Iraq War, the forced resettlement of tens of thousands of Iraqi Kurds, Iraq's gas-bombing of Kurdish towns and villages, the Gulf War and the resultant flight of Kurds to Iran and Turkey, and the establishment of a U.N.-enforced safe haven; however, the long-term consequences of these events remain to be determined.

Because of its rugged terrain, Kurdistan acted as a buffer area between a series of competing empires. Kurdish political organization is therefore best understood as a response to the state. Kurdish tribal leaders were able to increase their power vis-à-vis one another by leading warriors in the service of the various empires. Their loyalty to the state was rewarded with titles and the backing of the central government in local disputes. Other tribal chiefs could submit to this paramount chieftain or establish relations with the competing states. Eventually, confederations of tribes arose that were ruled by a single *mir*. These emirates encompassed large territories and were granted considerable autonomy. In the 1500s many of the Kurdish emirates were incorporated into the Ottoman Empire. The mirs maintained local autonomy but were under the administration of regional governors who reported directly to the sultan. The emirates were abolished in the 1800s,

The Turkish government outlaws the use of the Kurdish language in public and the publication or possession of Kurdish writings or audio recordings.

and local rule reverted to several paramount chieftains.

In the 1900s government control penetrated further into the local level, and administrators dealt directly with the leaders of individual tribes and villages. Thus, Kurdish leaders are now found at the local level, and their influence is derived from personal attributes such as generosity, honor, and the ability to persuade and to deal with government officials. Tribal and lineage leadership is inherited, although there may be several contenders within the family, and other families may challenge and take over the position. Larger tribes generally choose their leader from a royal lineage, but different branches of the lineage may compete for the title. The *shaykh* (pl. *shuyukh*) also plays an important role (see "Religion and Expressive Culture").

The Kurds have been much affected by the different national policies and are now engaged in a long-term effort to gain some form of self-rule. Demands range from local autonomy to the formation of a Kurdish nation-state. Political parties and demands, guerrilla forces, and support from foreign governments are all part of modern Kurdish politics.

Religion and Expressive Culture

The Kurds converted to Islam in the seventh century A.D. Most Kurds are orthodox Sunni Muslims of the Shafi school; however, in southeastern and southern Kurdistan, some tribes are Shiite. Also found in southeastern Kurdistan is the Ahl-e Haqq sect, which, although based on Ismaili Shiism, is considered heretical by other Muslims. The Alawites (Alevis) of northwestern Kurdistan also practice an unorthodox form of Shiism. The majority of Alawites are Turks, but many are Kurds, some of whom speak the Zaza dialect. A syncretistic form of religion found only among the Kurds is the Yezidi sect. It is believed to be derived from Zorastrianism but influenced by Ismaili Shiism. Its practitioners have been referred to as devil worshipers and are subject to severe persecution. In addition to Muslims, groups of Jews and Christians (Armenians, Assyrians, and Syriacs) have lived among the Kurds.

Sharia (Islamic law) was enforced in religious courts throughout the Ottoman Empire. With its fall and the secularization of the Turkish state, the only clerics left are the mullahs. They continue to provide religious instruction and lead religious ceremonies at the village level. Their prestige and influence are no longer guaranteed, however, but is based upon their personal integrity and wisdom.

In addition to the clerics and the shuyukh, there are those who maintain that they are descendants of the Prophet Mohammed. Many of them are poor, living on a claim to financial support on the basis of their descent; some serve as itinerate peddlers of religious amulets and as soothsayers. They are accorded little respect unless they are also wealthy or powerful; in this case, their descent increases the prestige they have obtained through other channels.

The shuyukh obtain prestige and power as holy men and leaders of religious brotherhoods (Sufi or Dervish orders). After receiving instruction in the religious order, a man may be declared a shaykh by an already established shaykh. A shaykh's ability to perform miracles serves as proof that he is indeed a "favorite of God." This ability is believed to continue after death, giving rise to pilgrimages to the tombs of powerful shuyukh. Before the emergence of modern political parties, Dervish orders in Kurdistan—the Qadiri and the Nagshibandi brotherhoods—provided a basis for a level of organization wider than the tribe but independent of the state (van Bruinessen 1992, 210). For this reason, shuyukh performed an important function as mediators after the destruction of the emirates. They have thus been able to gain substantial power as leaders, especially in areas where tribal organization dominated and blood feuds prevailed.

In addition to the observances of the Islamic calendar, Kurds celebrate events of the pastoral seasons, which provide occasions for the strengthening of social bonds and negotiation of marriages. The Kurdish new-year celebration, Newroz, takes place on 21 March and commemorates the people's rebellion against a cruel and unjust king, and the return of light. Fires are lit on mountaintops and in villages, and a feast is held, followed by a ceremony mourning the dead. The Kurds consider Newroz their "national holiday," which they claim to have celebrated for over 2,500 years.

The Kurds are renowned for the rich colors and intricate designs of their wool rugs. These continue to fetch high prices on the international market but are sold by traders in urban centers far from Kurdistan.

The Kurds also have a rich oral tradition. Professional troubadours traveled from place to place recounting legends and singing ballads and epic tales. The art of storytelling was much appreciated until the radio and increased literacy began to compete. Kurds have therefore begun to write down their oral legends and songs in an effort to preserve them. Kurdish written literature consists

♦ **Sharia**
Quaranic law.

predominately of classical poetry dating from as far back as A.D. 1200. After the division of the Ottoman Empire, the new nation-states restricted or forbade the publication of Kurdish literature. Only in Iraq could it continue to develop freely. Kurdish exiles in Europe are now attempting to further the analysis and development of their literature.

The Kurds maintain that to be a Kurd is "to look Death in the eye" because expressing and passing on their culture has often entailed breaking laws and engaging in armed resistance. As agonizing as was the plight of Iraqi Kurds in the aftermath of the Gulf War, it was merely another chapter in the ongoing Kurdish struggle for self-rule in the face of the repression and violence employed by the various national governments to assimilate and/or control them. Men speak of having many children to ensure that some Kurds survive the violence to carry on the culture.

Kurdish funerals occur immediately after death. The corpse is washed by a member of the same sex, wrapped in white cotton, and covered with a prayer rug. It is carried to the mosque, where a blessing is given, according to the Shafi rite. It is then buried, facing Mecca, stones marking the head and feet. Following a death, friends and relatives visit the family of the deceased, to pay their respects. While in mourning, a person will not make visits outside the home unless there is a death in the family.

Bibliography

Barth, Fredrik (1953). *Principles of Social Organization in Southern Kurdistan*. Oslo: Universitetsforlaget.

Busby, Annette (1994). "Kurds: A Culture Straddling International Borders." In *Portraits of Culture: Ethnographic Originals*, edited by Melvin Ember, Carol Ember, and David Levinson. The Source One Custom Publishing Program. Englewood Cliffs, N.J.: Prentice-Hall.

Chaliand, Gerard (1980). *People Without a Country: The Kurds and Kurdistan*. London: Zed Press.

Entessar, Nader (1992). *Kurdish Ethnonationalism*. Boulder, Colo., and London: Lynne Rienner Publishers.

Hansen, Henny Harald (1961). *The Kurdish Woman's Life*. Copenhagen: Nationalmuseets Skrifter.

Leach, Edmund R. (1940). *Social and Economic Organization of the Rowanduz Kurds*. Monographs in Social Anthropology, no. 3. London: School of Economics and Political Science.

McDowall, David (1992). *The Kurds: A Nation Denied*. London: Minority Rights Publications.

Olson, Robert (1989). *The Emergence of Kurdish Nationalism, 1880–1925*. Austin: University of Texas Press.

van Bruinessen, Martin M. (1992). *Agha, Shaikh, and State: The Political Structures of Kurdistan*. London and Atlantic Heights, N.J.: Zed Press.

—ANNETTE BUSBY

PALESTINIANS

Ethonym: Filastinyoun

Orientation

IDENTIFICATION. Palestinians inhabit an area east of the Mediterranean Sea and south of Lebanon. The Jordan River, Lakes Huleh and Tiberias, and the Dead Sea separate Palestine from Jordan. Palestinian territory stretches as far south as the Gulf of Aqaba. Palestinians refer to their land as "Filastin," the name of an Aegean population (Philistines) who inhabited coastal Palestine before the Israelites. Christians refer to Palestine as "the Holy Land." Today Palestine is divided among Israel and the Palestine National Authority. Palestinian territory falls into two major geographic zones: the coastal area, and the northern extension of the Great Rift Valley.

LOCATION. Palestine is located between 30° and 33° N and 34° and 36° E. Its total land area is 27,128 square kilometers, divided between Israel and the two towns (Gaza and Jericho) administered by the Palestine National Authority. The total area under direct Palestinian control since 1993 is 135 square kilometers. Palestine lies at the southern tip of the fertile eastern Mediterranean region, and almost half of its total area is arid or semiarid. Only parts of the narrow coastal plain, the Jordan Valley, and the Galilee region in the north receive adequate rainfall. Palestine, on the whole, enjoys typical Mediterranean weather. The Great Rift Valley, or the Jordan Valley, has a semitropical climate. The main city in the Jordan valley, Jericho, is the lowest spot on earth—250 meters below sea level. The arid and semiarid areas to the south enjoy a desertlike dry and hot climate.

DEMOGRAPHY. Between 5.8 million and 6 million Palestinians live in Israel, on the West Bank, in the Gaza Strip, and dispersed all over the world. As of 1989, there were 900,000 living in the West Bank, 550,000 to 770,000 in the Gaza Strip, and 800,000 in Israel proper. East Jerusalem, annexed to Israel since 1967, is the home of 155,000 Palestinians. Those living under the Palestine National Authority since 1993

See also

Arabs

Palestinians

The Palestinians are a racial amalgam of the indigenous pre-Israelite population and later groups that settled in Palestine.

number 775,000 in Gaza and 20,000 in Jericho. There are also 1.7 million Palestinians living in Jordan, 350,000 in Lebanon, 225,000 in Syria, 70,000 in Iraq, 60,000 in Egypt, 25,000 in Libya, and 250,000 in Saudi Arabia. Until the Gulf War, there were 400,000 in Kuwait. There are other, smaller Palestinian communities in the Persian Gulf area, amounting to 113,543 people. It is estimated that 104,856 Palestinians live in the United States and another 140,000 around the globe. The highest ratio people to land is in Gaza, where there are 3,577 people per square kilometer. Many Palestinians live as refugees in camps: 248,000 in the Gaza Strip, 100,000 on the West Bank, 187,000 in Jordan, 143,300 in Lebanon, and 67,000 in Syria. Palestinians speak Arabic, but most are bilingual, their second language depending on their place of residence.

LINGUISTIC AFFILIATION. Arabic is a member of the Hamito-Semitic Family of languages. Modern Arabic is a South Semitic language. Palestinians speak a distinct dialect of Arabic but write classical Arabic, like the rest of the Arab world.

History and Cultural Relations

The Palestinians are a racial amalgam of the indigenous pre-Israelite population and later groups that settled in Palestine. Even though the Canaanite and Philistine city-states were defeated by the Israelites under King David in 1,000 B.C., their populations were not exterminated. The Muslim Arab conquest of A.D. 638 did not result in a large transfusion of Arabs, but the local inhabitants' culture became increasingly Arabized, and large numbers converted to Islam. The Peninsular Arab conquerors took great interest in Palestine because of the Prophet Mohammed's association with Jerusalem: his nocturnal journey there in A.D. 621 and his ascension to heaven from the spot where the Jewish Temple once stood bestowed a holy status on the city. When Muslims conquered Jerusalem, Caliph Omar came to receive the keys to the city from the Byzantine patriarch, Sophronius, and issued the Pledge of Omar: he vowed to protect the holy sites and freedom of worship of all religious communities. During the Umayyad dynasty (A.D. 661–750), Caliph Abd al-Malik ibn Marwan built a magnificent mosque (691–692) over the ruins of Solomon's Temple to commemorate Mohammed's ascension to heaven. Known as the Dome of the Rock, it is the oldest example of early Islamic architecture in the world. The Western Wall (the Wailing Wall), which is the only remaining portion of Solomon's Temple, was consecrated as a Muslim charitable trust in later years on the grounds that Mohammed tethered his steed, al-Buraq, at the wall. In view of its holy status, Jerusalem was never made into an Arab capital. Muslims also permitted the return of Jews to Jerusalem, from which they had been barred since the Roman period. Under the Abbasid Emperor, Harun al-Rashid (786–809), the number of hostels for European pilgrims increased. Jerusalem's religious status attracted foreign invaders, including the Christian Crusaders, who took over the city in 1099. Frankish invaders established the Latin Kingdom of Jerusalem, which lasted until 1187. Disputes between the Arabized eastern Christians, who coexisted peacefully with Muslims, and the European Crusaders cemented a lasting bond between Palestine's two religious communities. During the Latin Kingdom, the Dome of the Rock was converted into a Christian site known as Templum Domini. Jerusalem was liberated by Saladin (Salah al-Din) the Ayyubid sultan of Egypt and Syria in 1187. Muslim families were restored as the guardians of the holy sites, and Jews were permitted to return in large numbers. The Crusaders repossessed the city from 1229 to 1244. The Egyptian Mamluk dynasty liberated the city again, but in 1516 Jerusalem and Palestine fell to the Ottoman Turks. Under their rule, Palestine was divided into districts and attached to the province of Syria. In the nineteenth century European Jews began to settle in Ottoman-controlled Palestine. Jewish efforts to purchase the Wailing Wall and large areas of land with the help of foreign consuls were met with stiff resistance. With the financial support of European banking families, Jews fleeing Russian pogroms during the second half of the nineteenth century were able to establish collective farms. There was also significant Arab economic development. Following the Crimean War (1854–1856), Gaza emerged as a major grain-producing area. Cotton production expanded during the 1860s. Palestinians also became successful citrus growers, producing 33 million oranges in 1873. Jewish colonists who settled at Petach Tikva, near Jaffa, were exporting 15 percent of Palestine's total orange crop by 1913. Arab economic activity expanded around Nablus, an area specializing in olive oil and soap production. Jewish purchase of Arab land had a detrimental effect on Palestinian prosperity. Once bought, land became the perpetual property of Jews, and Arab laborers were thrown off. The land problem continued to be-devil Arab-Jewish relations after Britain took over Palestine. British interest in Palestine was the result of the strategic significance of the Suez Canal. During World War I, the British concluded several secret agreements regarding the future of Ottoman-held territories. One of these agreements, the Balfour Declaration, granted Jews the right to establish a national homeland in Palestine. In 1920, when the British acquired control over Palestine as a mandate under the League of Nations, they made the Balfour Declaration official policy, which was at variance with their responsibility under the mandate: to prepare the native population for eventual independence and majority rule. As a result, Palestinian demographics changed drastically. According to the 1922 census, the total population of Palestine was 752,000, of whom 660,000 were Arabs and 84,000 were Jews. The Arab population included 71,000 indigenous Christians who shared most of the sociocultural traits of the Muslim Palestinian population. By the end of World War II, the Palestinian population grew to two million. By 1946, there were 1,269,000 Arabs, as opposed to 608,000 Jews. Around 70,000 of the Jews were unauthorized immigrants who entered Palestine in the immediate postwar period. Throughout the mandate era (1920–1948), Arab despair over Jewish immigration fostered a policy of noncooperation with the mandate government. A proposed constitution offered in 1922 by the high commissioner, Sir Herbert Samuel, was rejected by both Muslim and Christian Palestinians. The only body that continued to represent the Palestinians was the Supreme Muslim Council, which supervised the Islamic charitable trusts and the court system. The appointed head of this institution, Amin Husseini, was the highest religious authority and emerged as the sole leader of the Palestinian community. He became the head of the Arab Higher Committee, representing both Christians and Muslims, following the 1936 Arab Revolt. The first major outbreak of Arab-Jewish violence was a result of attempts by Revisionist Zionists, led by Vladimir Jabotinsky, to expand Jewish rights over the Wailing Wall. This violence was investigated by British parliamentary commissions, which concluded that unrestricted Zionist immigration and land purchases led to the impoverishment and anger of the Palestinian peasantry. A general Arab strike and uprising in 1936 led the British to convene the Peel Commission, the first such commission to recommend the partitioning of Palestine into an Arab and a Jewish state. The Peel Commission allotted 20 percent of the most fertile land to the Jews, and 80 percent to the Arabs. The Commission also recommended the internationalization of Jerusalem and Bethlehem.

Both the Higher Arab Committee and Arab governments rejected this plan. By 1942, Zionist lobbying efforts shifted from Britain to the United States. A Zionist conference in 1942, which was held at the Biltmore Hotel in New York City, called openly for the establishment of a Jewish commonwealth in Palestine, and efforts were made to obtain the endorsement of major U.S. political parties and members of Congress. The Nazi Holocaust against European Jews succeeded in winning powerful world leaders, including U.S. president Truman, over to the cause of Israeli statehood. Once the British Government made the decision in 1947 to end its mandate over Palestine, the latter became the responsibility of the United Nations. A special eleven-member committee, known as UNSCOP, was organized to make recommendations to the General Assembly regarding the future of Palestine. These recommendations were made in the form of majority (8 votes) and minority (3 votes) reports. The majority report, which was adopted by the General Assembly on 29 November 1947, stipulated that Palestine be partitioned into a Jewish state and an Arab state, with Jerusalem and Bethlehem brought under a UN regime as a *corpus separatum*. Both the United States and the Soviet Union voted for General Assembly Resolution 181, the majority plan. Palestinians were outraged over the decision by an outside agency to give away half of their land without consulting them. Arab states in the United Nations did not oppose the Vatican-sponsored resolution on Jerusalem. During the following year, a U.S. State Department report by George F. Kennan predicted that the partition resolution could not be enforced without war. Clashes between Jewish armed forces and Palestinian and other Arab armies quickly followed. Jewish forces moved not only to consolidate their UN lands but to acquire additional areas in the Galilee and Negev areas. The UN partition plan granted one-third of the population—namely, the Jewish community—one-half of the total land area of Palestine. The Jewish community at the time owned 20 percent of all cultivable areas, amounting to 6 percent of the total land area of Palestine. At the end of this conflict, the Egyptian army remained in control of the Gaza Strip and the Jordanian Arab Legion maintained control over eastern Palestine and eastern Jerusalem. The Arab states signed separate armistice agreements with newly founded Israel. Soon thereafter, Transjordan changed its name to the Hashemite Kingdom of Jordan, naming the area east of the Jordan River the "East Bank" and the area west of the

Palestinians

WEST BANK

A Palestinian waits to cast his vote in the election of January 1996. In the West Bank and Gaza, Palestinians have been living under Israeli military rule since 1967. Israeli Occupied Territories. (David H. Wells/Corbis)

river the "West Bank." The 1947–1948 Arab-Jewish War produced one of the Middle East's major refugee problems. Palestinians who fled their homes or were driven out by Jewish forces numbered between 500,000 and 750,000 people. Some placed the percentage of Palestinians who became refugees at 80 percent of the total Arab population. Between 125,000 and 150,000 of the Palestinian peasantry retained their homes but lost their agricultural lands. The state of Israel continuously rejected UN resolutions calling for the return of the refugees or providing them with financial compensation. The only Arab country that granted citizenship rights to the Palestinians was Jordan. The League of Arab States created a seat for Palestine, which was occupied by the Gaza-based government of All Palestine until 1957. The Gaza government was a rump Palestinian authority that was directed by Amin Husseini's deputy, Ahmad Hilmi Abd al-Baqi; it existed under the watchful eye of the Egyptian military governor. By 1964, a new Palestinian authority—the Palestine Liberation Organization, headed by Ahmad Shuqairy—was created at the behest of President Gamal Abdel Nasser of Egypt. Conflicts with the Egyptians forced Shuqairy's resignation in 1968. Another PLO emerged during

that year and was soon headed by Yasser Arafat, the leader of Fatah, a militant underground organization. The new PLO rejected the need to rely on Arab governments and promoted the principle of the armed struggle. After a brief stay in Jordan, armed conflict with the Jordanian army drove the PLO to Lebanon, where it established itself inside Palestinian refugee camps. The launching of attacks against Israel from Lebanon's southern borders eventually resulted in a massive retaliation by the Israeli Defense Forces in 1982. The PLO was forced to evacuate its militias out of Lebanon under U.S. protection and relocate to Tunisia. The Israeli invasion of Beirut during the latter days of that war resulted in a Lebanese-led massacre of Palestinian refugees in the Sabra and Shatilla camps. The PLO's rehabilitation by the world community was a slow process, which began in 1974. During that year, the Arab summit meeting at Rabat, Morocco, recognized the PLO as the sole representative of the Palestinian people. Also in 1974, the United Nations confirmed this designation by granting the PLO observer status. The United Nations also recognized the inalienable rights of the Palestinian people, a gesture of enormous symbolic significance because it was the United Nations that divided the Palestinian homeland in the first place. The outbreak of the *intifada* (uprising) in 1987, in the West Bank and Gaza, provided the PLO with another opportunity to integrate itself with the international community. The PLO declared itself a state and sought recognition by the United States. This was granted upon the PLO's unilateral recognition of Israel and of Security Council Resolution 242. Following the Gulf War in 1991, the PLO agreed to participate in a U.S.-sponsored Middle East peace conference. In 1993 Israel and the PLO signed a "declaration of principles" that provided a framework for settling all issues pertaining to the Palestinian-Israeli conflict and granted the newly created Palestine National Authority autonomous rule over Gaza and Jericho. In January 1996, Palestinians in the Gaza Strip and the Palestinian-controlled parts of the West Bank elected a legislature and president. Little progress has been made in further peace talks.

Settlements

Until the establishment of Israel in 1948, the Palestinian coastline was dotted with Arab villages. The Galilee area in the north was also heavily settled. The Bedouin (nomadic) population was concentrated in the Negev Desert area. After the division of Palestine into Israel and the West

Bank, the coastal area became heavily Jewish. The Jordan Valley was less settled than the Mediterranean coast. After Israel's occupation of the West Bank and Gaza following the 1967 Arab-Israeli War, Israeli settlements were built on Palestinian lands, using up to 50 percent of these territories. Around 125,000 Israeli settlers began to live within the Arab area. Under international law, these settlements are considered illegal and may be dismantled as the price of a lasting peace settlement. There are also ancient cities in Palestine: Jerusalem (built by the Jebusites), Jericho (the oldest city in the world), Bethlehem, Beershiba, Gaza, and Nablus (ancient Samaria). Most of these urban centers have an old city surrounded by walls and modern suburbs in the nearby hills. Typical village dwellings are built of local building material, stone in the hills and mud and straw in the villages. Jerusalem's old city and ancient walls are built exclusively of Jerusalem limestone. Wood, which has always been in short supply, is rarely used.

Kinship

KIN GROUPS AND DESCENT. The basic unit in society is the family, with the village unit quite often being an extended family. Political upheaval over a long period of time strengthened the traditional family structure. Kin groups, as exemplified by the family or the clan (*hamula*), survived despite increased mobility and urbanization. Entire families and clans from the same village relocated together to the same refugee camps after 1948. Descent, as in all Muslim societies, is traced patrilineally.

KINSHIP TERMINOLOGY. Palestinians follow the Sudanese kinship terminology commonly found in patrilineal societies such as those in North Africa. Kinship terms referring to the mother's side of the family are distinguished from those referring to the father's side of the family.

Marriage and Family

MARRIAGE. Palestinians are, generally speaking, monogamous, although polygyny is sanctioned by Islam. Marriages are normally determined by families, but, increasingly, individual choice is accepted. Statistics for the 1931 census indicate that early marriages were rare. The average age of marriage within the Muslim community was 20 years for women and 25 for men. Until around the mid-twentieth century, the preferred match, in both the Christian and Muslim communities, was between first cousins.

DOMESTIC UNIT. Postmarital residence is patrilocal. A woman returns to her natal unit only in the event of divorce or widowhood. The authority of the male head of the family is exercised over matters of marital, educational, and occupational choice despite frequent geographic separation of members of the nuclear family. Grandparents and unmarried aunts and uncles frequently share the domestic unit. Women rarely establish independent places of residence.

INHERITANCE. Muslim law regulates division of the estate and does not ignore female members of the family. Land is divided equally among surviving males, but females inherit half of the male's share because they are not expected to support the family. Among the indigenous Christian population, inheritance customs are not regulated by church law and often mirror Muslim customs.

SOCIALIZATION. Children are socialized by various generations within the household, commonly along gender lines. The socialization of Palestinian children encourages a commitment to education and to family solidarity.

Sociopolitical Organization

Palestinians inhabiting the West Bank are under Israeli rule, but in Gaza and Jericho they live under the Palestine National Authority. In Jordan, where they constitute 60 to 70 percent of the population, they are full citizens. In other Arab countries, Palestinians are resident aliens, carrying temporary UN travel document. Palestinians in the West Bank and Jerusalem are still Jordanian nationals. In Gaza they are stateless, and within Israel they are citizens of the Jewish state.

SOCIAL ORGANIZATION. Before 1948, Palestinians were divided along class lines determined by private wealth. In the Christian community, class differentiation accorded more to educational level than to wealth. The Muslim and Christian communities were always allied in the national struggle. The Palestinian diaspora after 1948 had a great leveling impact. The massive loss of land weakened the landowning class. Education is highly valued as a movable form of wealth and the determinant of status. Today there is a large professional class that prospered as a result of employment in the Persian Gulf countries.

POLITICAL ORGANIZATION. In the West Bank and Gaza, Palestinians have been living under Israeli military rule since 1967. Those living in Arab Jerusalem, annexed to Israel in 1967, are allowed to participate in municipal elections but are barred from national elections. Because Jerusalem's Arabs are Jordanian citizens, they do not enjoy Israeli civil liberties. The Israelis permitted one round of municipal elections in the West Bank

After Israel occupied the West Bank and Gaza following the 1967 Arab-Israeli War, Israeli settlements were built on Palestinian lands, using up to 50 percent of them.

and Gaza in 1976, but since then most town councils have been headed by Israeli military officers. The Islamic religious institutions of Jerusalem and the West Bank, which are linked to Jordan, are still under the jurisdiction of the Supreme Muslim Council. Within Israel proper, Palestinians are full citizens, but they suffer from frequent land confiscations and exclusion from military service and from higher political office. The PLO, on the other hand, functions as a nonterritorial state, with a parliament in exile, an executive committee, and militia units.

SOCIAL CONTROL. Social control is exercised by the family, females being subjected to greater restrictions than males. In some refugee camps, social control was dictated by the PLO, which attempted to influence the patterns of female education and female morality.

CONFLICT. Palestinians suffer from harsh military rule in the West Bank and from constant police surveillance in Arab countries. Clashes with the Israeli military and with Israeli settlers are frequent. The mythology of the popular upris-

ing of 1987, the intifada, still exercises a powerful influence on the popular imagination.

Religion and Expressive Culture

RELIGIOUS BELIEFS. Muslims make up two-thirds of the population. The majority are Sunni, but there is also a small Druze community. Christians are almost one-third of the population. The largest denomination is Greek Orthodox, followed by the Greek Melkite Catholic, the Roman Catholic, the Episcopal, and the Lutheran. Muslim-Christian harmony was always the norm. The rise of militant Islamic groups like Hamas is a new phenomenon among people who have a powerful ecumenical tradition.

RELIGIOUS PRACTITIONERS. Palestinian Muslims view themselves as guardians of the Muslim holy sites, especially the Dome of the Rock, considered the third holiest in Islam. Christian Palestinians maintain a similar view of their role as guardians of the holiest places of Christendom, such as the Church of the Holy Sepulchre and the Church of the Nativity.

ECONOMY

Subsistence and Commercial Activities

Until the creation of Israel and the dispersal of the Palestinians, 60 percent of the population was engaged in agricultural activities and food processing. Village crafts included the rich and ancient tradition of embroidery. Mother-of-pearl and olive-wood artifacts were common in the cities. After 1948, Palestinians who became refugees subsisted on daily rations supplied by the United Nations Relief and Works Agency (UNRWA). Skilled and educated refugees became professional and white-collar workers in the Persian Gulf oil countries.

Industrial Arts

Along with food processing and tourist-related arts and crafts, Palestinians were engaged in oil refining, a British-run industry, in Haifa. After 1948, Palestinians lost access to this industry and turned to phosphate min-

ing in the Dead Sea area. There was also a thriving glass industry in Hebron.

Trade

Before 1948, Palestinians exported citrus fruits to Egypt and other parts of the Middle East. Fruits, vegetables, hand soap, and olive oil were the mainstay of trade with Arab markets after the West Bank was taken over by Jordan. Since 1967, this area has become a captive market for Israeli goods.

Division of Labor

Palestinian village women and Bedouin women always participated in agricultural work. In towns and cities, women have been increasingly integrated in gender-specific occupations such as teaching, nursing, and clerical positions. Palestinian women are also employed as teachers in the Persian Gulf area. Since 1967, many West Bank women have been proletarianized and work

as migratory laborers within Israel proper, employed in food processing and the garment industry. Women have also become heads of households as a result of the imprisonment or exiling of Palestinian men.

Land Tenure

Until the British period, there were three types of landholding: public lands (*miri*), privately owned land (*mulk*), and state and private lands cultivated by peasants as communal lands (*musha*). The cultivation of land by the peasants of an entire village was abolished by the British in the 1940s in order to facilitate the purchase and sale of land held by individuals. Jewish efforts to buy land were facilitated by the existence of absentee landlords in the Galilee region, such as the Lebanese Sursuq family. After 1967, public lands previously considered the property of the Ottoman, British, and Jordanian governments were transferred to Israeli settlers.

ARTS. Palestinian arts center around village group dances, such as *dabka*. Village music is performed on traditional instruments such as the flute (*nay*), drums (*tabla*), and the lute (oud). Since the rise of the PLO, Palestinian music and song have for the most part reflected patriotic themes. Art flourished after 1948, with several artists depicting the Palestinian refugee experience. The PLO has fostered political poster art and holds exhibits in many parts of the world.

MEDICINE. Modern medical facilities are badly lacking in the West Bank and Gaza. Most medical institutions are supported by Arab donations from outside and private donations from within the country.

DEATH AND AFTERLIFE. Funerals are conducted by the family and the entire neighborhood. Long periods of mourning are observed by the Muslim and Christian communities. Cemeteries are public lands. Both communities believe strongly in an afterlife. Muslims, who believe Jerusalem will be the site of the Day of Judgment, consider burial there to be greatly desirable.

Bibliography

Abu-Lughod, Ibrahim, ed. (1971). *The Transformation of Palestine*. Evanston, Ill.: Northwestern University Press.

Beatty, Ilene (1971). "The Land of Canaan." In *From Haven to Conquest*, edited by Walid Khalidi, 3–19. Beirut: Institute for Palestine Studies.

Boullata, Isa (1989). "Modern Palestinian Literature." In *Palestine and the Palestinians: A Handbook*, 72–76. Toronto: Near East Cultural and Educational Foundation of Canada.

Graham-Brown, Sarah (1980). *Palestinians and Their Society, 1880–1946*. London: Quartet Books.

Khalidi, Walid (1984). *Before Their Diaspora: A Photographic History of the Palestinians, 1876–1948*. Washington, D.C., Institute for Palestine Studies.

Nassar, Jamal, and Roger Heacock, eds. (1990). *Intifada: Palestine at the Crossroads*. New York: Praeger.

Near East Cultural and Educational Foundation of Canada (1989). *Palestine and the Palestinians: A Handbook*. Toronto: Near East Cultural and Educational Foundation of Canada.

Polk, William R., David M. Stamler, and Edmund Asfour (1957). *Backdrop to Tragedy: The Struggle for Palestine*. Boston: Beacon Press.

Said, Edward (1980). *The Question of Palestine*. New York: Vintage.

Smith, Charles D. (1988). *Palestine and the Arab-Israeli Conflict*. New York: St. Martin's Press.

Talhami, Ghada (1986). "From Palestinian Nationhood to Palestinian Nationalism." *Arab Studies Quarterly* 8:346–357.

Talhami, Ghada (1994). "The History of Jerusalem: A Muslim Perspective." In *The Spiritual Significance of Jerusalem for Jews, Christians, and Muslims*, edited by Hans Ucko, 21–31. Geneva: World Council of Churches.

—GHADA HASHEM TALHAMI

PERSIANS

Ethonym: Iranians

Orientation

Persians are an ethnic group defined primarily by language and location. The Persian language, also known as Farsi, which linguists classify in the Indo-Iranian Branch of the Indo-European Language Family, had about 23 million speakers in Iran in 1986 and 6 million in Afghanistan the same year (Grimes 1988). It is the official language of Iran, and also the language of Iran's government bureaucracy, educational institutions, mass media, and literature. A dialect of modern Persian is used as the language of elites in Afghanistan. Standard Persian, or Farsi, followed Middle Persian, or Pahlavi, which was the language of the Sāssānian period of Iranian history (A.D. 224 to 642). In the centuries that followed the Arab conquest of Iran, Pahlavi absorbed numerous Arabic elements. The addition of Arabic words into Persian is the primary difference between the language spoken today and that spoken thirteen centuries ago.

History and Cultural Relations

The Iranian plateau was inhabited by a hunting and gathering group by 10,000 B.C. Around 3000 B.C., waves of pastoralists from Eurasia drifted into the area searching for new pastures. Some of these pastoralists were warriors on horseback who supplanted the indigenous populations of the Iranian plateau. The first Iranians (Aryans) arrived about 1,000 B.C. They also penetrated the Iranian plateau in waves lasting several centuries, and, like their predecessors, they were pastoralists who also relied on agriculture to some extent.

The Iranians consisted of several tribal groups, including the Medes, Persians (Pars), Parthians, Bactrians, Soghdians, Sacians, and Scythians. For several centuries they absorbed the cultural influences of existing civilizations. In the seventh century B.C. they began to take over the known

See also

Kurds

world. Between 625 and 585 B.C., the Medes developed a powerful civilization, with its capital at Ecbatana, modern day Hamadān. They defeated the powerful Assyrians and sacked their capital, Nineveh, in 612 B.C. Those tribes that had settled near Lake Urmia moved south and occupied Persis (Parsa), the modern province of Fārs, from which they obtained their name. These loosely federated Persian tribes became a more cohesive political unit under the Achaemenian dynasty. In 553 B.C., Cyrus, the ruler of Persis, overthrew the Median dynasty and consolidated the Medes and Persians into the mighty Achaemenid Empire.

For 1,200 years Persia maintained a culture that grew increasingly complex and rigid. The social structure supported rulers, priests, warriors, artisans, scribes, pastoralists, agriculturists, and other producers. By the seventh century A.D., a small privileged class dominated a large mass of people who were blocked from attaining any upward social mobility; this was an important factor in setting the stage for a successful Arab conquest.

In the thirteen centuries since the Arab invasion, there has been a steady Persianization of the society. Persians have been able to maintain their independence from invaders and their dominance over non-Persian minorities. An intense nationalistic movement began in 1925, which included the official adoption of the name "Iran," the use of Farsi as a national language, and government encouragement to produce the best in Persian culture.

Economy

Persians are a sedentary people who have traditionally relied on agriculture as a means of subsistence. Much of the agriculture in Iran is based on dry farming. Farming methods and implements are primitive by Western standards, but well adapted to the steep and rocky terrain and shallow topsoil of much of the country. Important crops include wheat, barley, legumes, and a few cash crops such as tobacco, sugar beets, and sesame. Few villages have a substantial surplus.

The production of oil has added immensely to the economic base of Iran in the twentieth century. The role of oil in providing jobs for the labor market is clear, and Persians have certainly benefited from an expanded job market. The proportion of Persians involved in oil production and the effects of huge oil revenues on the daily lives of the Persian population are not clear at this point.

ANCIENT CITY

The ruins of Persepolis, once an ancient capital of Persia. Persepolis was used by Persian kings beginning with Darius I in the 6th century BCE. Takht-I Jamshid, Iran. (Charles & Josette Lenars/Corbis)

Kinship, Marriage, and Family

The basic social and economic unit in Persian society is the nuclear family. Some families combine into larger units comprised of a man, his wife or wives, and their married sons and their families. The Persian family is patriarchal, patrilineal, and patrilocal. Women defer to their husbands in public but may wield considerable decision-making power in private. The father is usually aloof and a disciplinarian, whereas the mother is permissive and affectionate, often acting as an intermediary between the children and their father. Men are the guardians and defenders of the family honor; they are responsible for protecting the chastity of their daughters and sisters. This obligation has sometimes led to the sequestering of women in the more traditional segments of society.

Marriages are arranged only after negotiation and approval by both sets of kin. Husband and wife usually have similar educational and socioeconomic backgrounds. Endogamy is the traditional practice, although it is avoided by the urban, educated people. There is a preference for marrying cousins.

Sociopolitical Organization

Persians are concentrated in and near several cities on the Iranian plateau—Kermān, Shirāz, Yazd, Eṣfahān, Kāshān, and Tehran—and in Herāt in Afghanistan. Each city is the economic and political center of dozens of towns, and each town integrates hundreds of villages into a regional economic network. Urban Persians can be grouped into distinct occupational and social classes based on their degree of control over economic and political resources. At the top of the hierarchy are real-estate investors and speculators and other industrial and commercial entrepreneurs. This class includes many deputies, senators, ministers, ambassadors, and governors. On the next rung of the hierarchy are high-ranking administrators, who derive their power from above. Merchants and shopkeepers, the Bazaaris, constitute the third level of the social system and are perhaps the most cohesive segment of Iranian society. The Bazaaris have been closely allied with the *ulama* (clergy), who comprise another step on the hierarchical ladder. They are the interpreters and practitioners of Islam and in the past have led successful protest movements against unpopular rulers. The fifth urban category might be considered the middle class. It includes a large proportion of the educated white-collar workers, civil-service employees, doctors, teachers, engineers, and other spe-

cialists, including the military. In the 1970s the middle class was growing rapidly in size and political importance. Below the middle class is the urban proletariat. They comprise more than a third of the urban population, including factory and construction workers, municipal employees, and menial laborers. On the bottom rung is the subproletariat—the unskilled and often unemployed. Primarily Persian, this group consists primarily of poor nomads and landless villagers who come to the city in search of wage labor.

Persian towns are far more homogenous than are the cities. Religious observances are practiced more regularly and fervently than in the city. Townspeople criticize urban dwellers because of their religious laxity and decadent Western behavior and values. At the same time, however, many townspeople, especially the more affluent, try to emulate the city life-style.

A large proportion of the Persian population still lives in thousands of villages and hamlets. Village populations vary between a few households and a thousand inhabitants. The size of a village depends on two critical factors, arable land and availability of water, both of which can be privately owned.

Like the Persian family, the social system is hierarchical, paternalistic, and authoritarian. Initiatives originate and decisions are almost always handed down from the top; subordinates seldom assume responsibility. This vertical system of social relations sometimes produces friendships between people of equal status that are very close and intimate but difficult to maintain over time.

Religion and Expressive Culture

The Islamization of Iran after the Arab conquest was possibly more far-reaching in its effects than were the linguistic changes. The Iranian religion prior to that time was Zoroastrianism, which was based on the belief that there was an eternal struggle between the forces of good and evil. Shiism became the national religion of Iran during the sixteenth century, at which time the ulama began to play an important role in the social and political life of the society. When Ayatollah Khomeini led the revolution that toppled the shah in 1979, he declared that the ulama were needed to purify Islam and apply its laws. As an Islamic republic, Iran is guided by the tenets of Islam as interpreted by the ulama. Most Persians today are Shia Muslims of the Ithna Ashari sect and adhere to Islamic laws and principles.

Persian art is found in a variety of forms ranging from intricately patterned tiles and Quranic

Persians believe that all unexplainable occurrences are the will of God, and that most things in life are controlled by fate rather than by humans.

inscriptions on the walls of mosques to handicrafts, miniature painting, and calligraphy. Poetry with well-defined meter and rhyme is a popular Persian art form. Persian poetry often deals with subjective interpretations of the past and sometimes satirizes social problems such as inequality, injustice, and repression.

A popular religious or philosophical theme that is expressed in Persian literature is *qesmet*, or fate. Persians believe that all unexplainable occurrences are the will of God, and that most things in life are controlled by fate rather than by humans. The unpredictable nature of life is sometimes used to justify the pursuit of pleasure.

Bibliography

Arasteh, A. Reza (1969). *Education and Social Awakening in Iran, 1850–1968*. Rev. ed. Leiden: E. J. Brill.

Beeman, William O. (1986). *Language, Status, and Power in Iran*. Bloomington: Indiana University Press.

Critchfield, Richard (1973). *The Golden Bowl Be Broken: Peasant Life in Four Cultures*. Bloomington: Indiana University Press.

English, Paul Ward (1966). *City and Village in Iran: Settlement and Economy in the Kirman Basin*. Madison: University of Wisconsin Press.

Fazel, Golamreza (1984). "Persians." *Muslim Peoples: A World Ethnographic Survey*, edited by Richard V. Weekes, 604–612. Westport, Conn.: Greenwood Press.

Grimes, Barbara F. (1988). *Ethnologue: Languages of the World*. Dallas: Summer Institute of Linguistic.

Keddie, Nikki R. (1971). "The Iranian Power Structure and Social Change, 1800–1969: An Overview." *International Journal of Middle East Studies* 2(1): 3–20.

Keddie, Nikki R., ed. (1982). *Religion and Politics in Iran: Shi'ism from Quietism to Revolution*. New Haven: Yale University Press.

Lambton, Ann K. S. (1969). *The Persian Land Reform, 1962–1966*. London: Oxford University Press.

Lambton, Ann K. S. (1984). "Dilemma of Government in Islamic Persia: The Siyasat-nma of Nizam al-Mulk." *Iran* 22:55–66.

Pierce, Joe E. (1971). *Understanding the Middle East*. Rutland, Vt.: Charles E. Tuttle.

Smith, Harvey H., et. al. (1971). *Area Handbook for Iran*. American University FAS, DA Pam 550–568. Washington, D.C.: Government Printing Office.

Szliowicz, Joseph S. (1973). *Education and Modernization in the Middle East*. Ithaca, N.Y.: Cornell University Press.

—RONALD JOHNSON

TURKS

Ethnym: Türken (German), Türkler (Turkish)

Orientation

IDENTIFICATION. Ethnically, the Turks are a cultural group united by a common language, but the term "Turk" has no clearly defined racial significance; it can be properly applied to those communities historically and linguistically connected to the nomadic people whom the Chinese identified as the "Tu-Kiu." Some scholars consider that the name "Hiungnu," which appears in Chinese sources of the second millennium B.C.E., refers to the Turks; however, it was probably a generic term that included both Turks and Mongols, and perhaps other peoples.

Today ethnic Turks constitute approximately 80 percent of the population of the Republic of Turkey. Turkish-speaking peoples can be found in Iran, Azerbaijan, Kazakhstan, Uzbekistan, Turkmenistan, Afghanistan, and China. Turks are linked by their common history and language, which are strong and persistent; additionally they are linked by their religion—Islam; with the exception of the Turkish tribe called the Yakut, who live in eastern Siberia and the Altai region, almost all Turks are Muslims.

LOCATION. Turkey is located in southwestern Asia and fits roughly between 36° and 42° N and 25° and 45° E. It is bounded on the west by the Aegean Sea and Greece; on the north by Bulgaria and the Black Sea; on the northeast by Georgia, Armenia, and Azerbaijan; on the east by Iran, and on the south by Iraq, Syria, and the Mediterranean Sea. The total area of the country is 780,580 square kilometers. The greater part of the country lies in Asia, specifically Asia Minor or Anatolia. About 8 percent of Turkey—called Turkish Thrace—is in Europe. Because of the mountainous terrain and the maritime influence, climates very greatly. The country has three main temperate climates: Mediterranean on the south and southwestern coasts, Black Sea in the north, and steppe throughout most of Anatolia.

DEMOGRAPHY. The population of Turkey in 1994 was estimated as 62,154,000. More than half the population lives in urban areas. Turkey has one of the highest rates of population increase in the world, as the result of a high birthrate, estimated in 1994 to be 25.98 births per thousand and an average death rate of 5.8 deaths per thousand. The current annual rate of growth is 2.02 percent. From 1923 to 1994, the population multiplied by approximately five. Large-scale migration to the cities since the middle of the century has led to overcrowding. In 1990, 65 percent of the population was urban. Istanbul is the cultural, industrial, and commercial center. Ankara is the capital. Other major cities are: Adana, Antalya, Bursa, Diyarbakir, Gaziantep, Izmir, Kayseri, Konya, and Samsun.

LINGUISTIC AFFILIATION. Turkish is the language of more than 90 percent of the population of Turkey. Until recently, some scholars contended that Turkish is part of the Ural-Altaic Language Group. Philologists today, however, consider Turkish an Eastern Turkic language. Turkish is an agglutinating language; words are made by adding strings of suffixes to a root that does not change. Perhaps the most striking characteristic of the Turkish language is vowel harmony. The vowels in a Turkish word are either all back vowels (a, ı, o, u) or all front vowels (e, i, ö, ü). Turkish is totally unrelated to Arabic or Persian, but it has borrowed many words from these two languages. In 1928 the Arabic script that had been used to write Ottoman Turkish was abandoned in favor of a twentynine letter Latin script. After the establishment of the modern Republic of Turkey in 1923, attempts were made to purify the Turkish language by creating new words to replace many Arab, Persian, and some French words. These attempts met with only limited success, and borrowed words are still very common.

History and Cultural Relations

The origins of the Turkish peoples are among the nomadic and pastoral peoples who lived east of the Eurasian steppes from the borders of China across Turkestan. Their earliest appearance in history was in what would be today Outer Mongolia, south of Lake Baikal and north of the Gobi Desert. The Turks were once part of a group of Altaic peoples, which includes the Mongols, the Manchu, the Bulgars, probably the Huns, and others. The first group known to be called Turks emerged in the sixth century C.E. The Tu-Kiu founded an empire stretching from Mongolia and the northern forntier of China to the Black Sea. In the seventh century the Arab conquest of Persia carried Islam to the Turkish fringes of Central Asia. In the ninth century and later, many Turks were recruited as slaves for the ʿAbbāsid armies and converted to Islam. Some rose to important administrative positions. The larger portion of Turks, however, still being essentially nomadic in Central Asia east of the Aral Sea, did not accept Islam until the tenth century. Bands of Turks joined in the gradual war of attrition that was being waged by Muslim warriors along the frontiers with the declining Byzantine Empire. A tribe of Turks called the Oghuz (Oğuz) wrested control of Persia from the Ghaznavids and founded the Seljuk Turkish Empire in 1037. The Seljuks took control of Baghdad from the Buyids in 1055. The Seljuk Turkish victory in 1071 over the forces of the Byzantines at Manzikert, northwest of Lake Van, led to the migration of Turkoman tribes into Anatolia. Within a very short time, the Seljuks had penetrated as far as Nicaea (present-day İznik), only 80 kilometers from Constantinople. Although driven away from this city in 1097, their hold on eastern and central Asia Minor was firmly established. By the early twelfth century, most of the Anatolian plateau was a Seljuk principality, which came to be called Rum. The capital of Seljuk Rum was Konya, and in this city there developed a hybrid Islamic culture that combined elements of Arab Sunni Islam with Persian Shia Islam and Turkish mystical humanism. The invasion of the Mongols in the thirteenth century ended the dominance of the Seljuks in Anatolia.

The Ottoman principality of Sogut was one among ten successor-states that survived from the Seljuk Empire and the Mongol protectorate. In the 1290s the ruler of this principality was Osman, from whose name comes that of the dynasty: Osmanli in Turkish. Sogut was located on the Byzantine frontier, closest to Constantinople. As Osman's emirate expanded, it created both the territorial basis and the administrative organization for an empire. Osman's grandson, Murad I, crossed the Hellespont to extend the young empire into the Christian Balkan states. He applied the principle of toleration to allow non-Muslims to become full citizens and rise to the highest offices of state, and thus, at this very early stage, established the character of the vast multilingual and multiethnic Ottoman Empire. In 1453 Sultan Mehmed II conquered Constantinople, and the city's name was changed to İstanbul. In its first two centuries, most of the ottoman Empire's energies had been directed toward Christian Europe; however, Selim I (r. 1512–1520), called "the Grim" by Westerners, turned his attention toward Asia. He transformed the Ottoman Empire from a Ghazi state on the western fringe of the Muslim world into the greatest empire since the early caliphate. Selim defeated the Safavids and moved fierce Kurdish tribes to eastern Anatolia to seal that border with the Persians. He defeated the Mamluks and took over their vast empire. The Ottomans became the rulers of Syria, Egypt and

Turks often marry their first cousins and other close kin, under the incest laws of Islam, to keep control of wealth within the extended family.

See also

Circassians

The Turkish educational system was modernized after the founding of the republic as part of an effort to Westernize the country.

the Hejaz—the heartland of Arab Islam. At its peak, the Ottoman Empire stretched from the Persian Gulf to Algeria. The empire reached its cultural zenith under the son of Selim I, Süleyman I, "the Magnificent" (r. 1520–1566). His reign also marked an Ottoman cultural renaissance. A considerable poet in his own right, Süleyman encouraged the arts at his court. Like all great civilizations, the Ottoman absorbed and transformed various external cultural influences. The first sultans took from the Byzantines. Selim and Süleyman brought artisans from Tabrīz, in western Persia, to beautify İstanbul. Under Süleyman, with the help of Sinan (the son of a Christian from Anatolia and one of the finest architects of all time), Istanbul became a city of true magnificence, at the point of confluence of Eastern and Western civilization. Immediately after Süleyman's death, the Ottoman Empire began to suffer a decline. In the eighteenth and nineteenth centuries it lost several wars to the expanding Russian Empire. It did enjoy another period of cultural renaissance during the reign of Sultan Ahmed III (r. 1703–1730), which is called the Tulip Period. Some reform of the government was accomplished at this time. Nevertheless, the empire lost territory around the Black Sea and in the Balkans during the last part of the eighteenth century and first half of the nineteenth. Russian ambitions were checked by Great Britain and France in the Crimean War (1854–1856), but the Russo-Turkish War liberated Bulgaria, Romania, and Serbia from the control of the sultan. The Ottoman Empire was drawn into World War I, on the side of the Central Powers. With its defeat and the abdication of its last sultan, Mehmed VI, the empire finally collapsed. The Allies sought to divide Turkey among themselves after their victory, but the country saved itself by waging a war of liberation directed by the empire's most successful general, Mustafa Kemal (who would later take the surname "Atatürk"). Turkey made a remarkable recovery under Atatürk's leadership. He abolished the sultanate and the caliphate, and Turkey became a republic on 29 October 1923. It was declared a secular state, and religious toleration was guaranteed by the new constitution. Many other reforms were set in motion to modernize Turkey along Western lines. Turkey remained neutral during World War II, until it joined the Allies in February 1945. It joined the North Atlantic Treaty Organization (NATO) in 1952. Turkey suffered political instability that led to military takeovers in 1960, 1970, and 1980. In 1982 a new constitution was promulgated that provided the reestablishment of democratic government.

Settlements

Although there are many large cities and towns in Turkey, Turkish Thrace and Anatolia are essentially rural. About 45 percent of the population lives in rural settlements. There are about 36,000 villages in Turkey. The houses in the villages vary from region to region. In Eastern Anatolia, the Aegean region, and in the Taurus Mountains, they are made of stone. In the Black Sea region, village houses are made of wood, and, on the Anatolian plateau, they are made of sun-dried bricks. A typical village house is two stories high and has a flat roof. The lower floor is used to shelter animals and for storage. Many villages in eastern Turkey lack running water, and some do not have electricity. The number of villagers who are migrating to urban areas continues to grow.

Economy

INDUSTRY AND TRADE Modern industry dates from the beginning of the republic. The government has played an important role in the development of industry from that time and in the late twentieth century owned 47 percent of the industries. Manufacturing accounts for about 20 percent of the nation's gross national product but employs only about 10 percent of the labor force. Turkish industries include textiles, food processing, mining, steel, construction, lumber, and paper. Antimony, borate, copper, and chrome are mined in sufficient quantities to be exported. Tourism is a growing industry and has become an important source of national income. Turkey has close economic ties with Western Europe and applied for full membership in the European Economic Community in 1987. At the same time, it has sought trading partners in the Middle East. Turkey controls the headwaters of the Tigris and Euphrates rivers and has had disputes with Syria and Iraq in this regard. In 1993 it was estimated that there were 1,800,000 Turks working outside of Turkey, mostly in Germany.

AGRICULTURE AND LAND TENURE. About 30 percent of Turkey's land area is considered arable. More than one-half of the land is devoted to cereals. Agriculture accounts for nearly one quarter of the gross national product and employs 48 percent of the population. The main cash crops include tobacco, cereals, cotton, olives, mohair, wool, silk, figs, grapes, nuts, citrus fruits, and sugar beets. Turkey is self-sufficient in food production, and it exports its surplus. Forests cover about 25 percent of the land and are protected by the state. Much of the wood that is harvested from these forests is used for fuel.

DIVISION OF LABOR. The mechanization of agriculture has relieved the burden of women's agricultural chores, but the harvest continues to be a time of hard physical labor for all of the members of families who make their living from agriculture. Women continue to do much of the hoeing of vegetables and the digging for potatoes. Girls and young women are involved in the weaving of rugs.

Kinship, Marriage, and Family

MARRIAGE AND DOMESTIC UNIT. Marriage continues to be a very important institution in Turkey. From the time parents have their first children, thought is given to their eventual marriage. Some of the marriages that take place are "love matches," but most of them are still being "arranged." In villages, girls are still usually married at a young age. In rural areas, large transfers of wealth are often involved in the marriage arrangement. Turks often marry their first cousins and other close kin, under the incest laws of Islam, to keep control of wealth within the extended family;

however, many marriages in Turkey today involve completely unrelated persons. Households in rural areas consist of a man, his wife, his adult sons and their wives, and his young children and grandchildren. In the city, households are usually smaller, being limited to the immediate family and paternal grandparents.

SOCIALIZATION. Parents assume primary responsibility for raising children, and they are assisted by members of the extended family. The educational system of Turkey was modernized after the founding of the republic as part of an effort to Westernize the country. Today education is compulsory for children ages 6 to 14, and in 1991 it was estimated that 78 percent of this age group do attend school. Instruction is co-educational, and, in state schools, free. The literacy rate among persons 15 years of age and older was estimated in 1990 to be 81 percent. Religious instruction in state schools, having been prohibited when the republic was established and then later made optional, is now compulsory. There are not sufficient numbers of elementary or secondary schoolteachers or school buildings. Many schools have a morning and an afternoon session, and often the number of students in a class is greater than forty.

SOCIOPOLITICAL ORGANIZATION

Social Organization

Strong class prejudice does not seem to be a part of the structure of modern Turkish society, which does, however, show very marked social divisions. This apparent paradox is explained by the fact that although there are very real differences between various social groups, the Turks do not usually think of themselves in terms of class. Political parties are not organized along class lines. The ideology of the republic has avoided class distinctions, and there is increasing social mobility. There is an educated elite in Turkey, which is basically located in the cities. It has been the ruling element in the country in both Ottoman and republican times.

Political Organization

Atatürk established the ideological basis for the modern Republic of Turkey. It has a re-

publican form of government and a democratic, multiparty system. His reforms included the disestablishment of the role of Islam in government and the adoption of the Swiss civil code. The voting franchise includes men and women aged 21 or older. Women were given the vote in national elections in 1934. The 1982 constitution provides for a democratic, parliamentary form of government. The president is elected for a seven-year term and is not eligible for reelection. The prime minister and his or her council of ministers hold executive power, although the president can veto legislation. Turkey is divided into eighty provinces (*iller*; sing. *il*), administered by governors (*valiler*; sing. *vali*).

Social Control

Turkey has long been familiar with military power. This is evident not only in the Seljuk, Ottoman, and republican governments, but

in the prestige patterns of Anatolian village societies. Early nomadic existence on the Central Asian steppe, where boundaries were not stable, created within those Turkish tribes a closer reliance on military force than was generally the case in more settled communities. A strong militaristic attitude continues to permeate Turkish society. The military is respected and, generally, trusted. Conscription, which is fifteen months for males at the age of 20, is viewed as a necessary duty.

Although Turkey is a secular state and has adopted the Swiss civil code, civic morality is still governed to a large degree by the laws and traditions of Islam.

The Muslim calendar is based on twelve lunar months and is therefore ten or twelve days shorter than the solar year.

Approximately 35 percent of high school graduates go on to higher education. In 1992 there were twenty-nine universities in Turkey.

Religion and Expressive Culture

RELIGIOUS BELIEFS AND PRACTICES. More than 99 percent of the population is Muslim, and most of them are Sunnites. Estimates of the number of Shiites fall between 5 percent and 35 percent of the population. There are approximately 50,000 Christians and 20,000 Jews in Turkey today. Villagers, although they are for the most part Muslims, continue to believe in superstitions like the evil eye, which is the ancient belief in the power of certain persons to harm or damage someone else with merely a glance. Beliefs in the power of jinn and *efrit*, as well as other supernatural phenomena, also persist in rural Turkey.

CEREMONIES. Most Turks celebrate the two most important Islamic holidays. Ramazan is the ninth month of the Islamic calendar; it is the holy month of fasting. Muslims celebrate the end of the fast with Çeker Bayrami (the Candy Holiday), during which visits of friends and relatives take place, and boxes of candy are taken as presents. Kadir Gecesi (the Night of Power) is the eve of the 26th of Ramazan. This is the night on which Mohammed was given the power of prophecy, and it is celebrated in the mosques by prayers and a nightlong service. Kurban Bayrami (the Festival of Sacrifice) comes during the month of Muharrem. If Muslims make a pilgrimage to Mecca, they must arrive there ten days before Kurban Bayrami. The pilgrimage ends when a sheep or a goat is sacrificed, and the meat is given to the poor. The sacrifice is performed whether the person goes to Mecca or stays at home. The Muslim calendar is based on twelve lunar months and is therefore ten or twelve days shorter than the solar year. This means that the months and the religious holidays fall a bit earlier each year. The Mevlevi dervishes, better known in the West as the Whirling Dervishes, are an order of Sufis that was established by the son of the great mystical thinker, Jalāl ad-Dīn ar-Rūmī, in the thirteenth century. Every year the Mevlevi dervishes have a ceremony in which they whirl for fifteen days before and on the anniversary day of Rūmī's death, which is 17 December.

CLOTHING. The Western style of clothing has been adopted by most Turks in large urban areas; however, in the rural regions men and women wear baggy pants. Village women enjoy wearing bright colors and flowered prints. The wearing of a turban or a fez by any man in Turkey was outlawed during Atatürk's administration. Many conservative Muslim women wear long coats and white head scarves. Wearing a veil is not against the law, but it is not a usual practice except in some areas of eastern Turkey. Nevertheless, women in villages anywhere will often make an effort to cover their faces in front of strange men, using a corner of their scarf or handkerchief.

ARTS. Seljuk and Ottoman Turkish culture is rich—and well represented in museums like the ethnographic museums in İstanbul and Ankara. They include fine examples of calligraphy, rug weaving, ceramics, metalwork, and miniature painting. The weaving of carpets is an industry that dates among the Turks from Seljuk times. Much of the symbolism in the design of Turkish rugs and kilims is pre-Islamic and shares its origins with the Turkish people in Central Asia. Nevertheless, these rugs have become an important part of the prayer ritual in Islam. Turkish culture, since the establishment of the republic, has been dominated by nationalism. Writers, authors, and musicians have left the tradition of Islam. Turkish folk music and dancing are popular. The ministry of culture was established in 1971, and the government extensively supports a national network of the arts, encompassing theater, opera, ballet, music, and fine arts, as well as popular art forms.

MEDICINE. Medical services provided by the government are free to the poor. Although health services are improving, rural areas suffer shortages of physicians and facilities. In 1992 there were 126,611 beds in 928 hospitals and health centers in Turkey.

DEATH AND AFTERLIFE. Death in Quranic terms is the beginning of a new life, which will be eternal. Muslims believe that it is a phenomenon like the phenomenon of life and is created by Allah (God). When an individual dies, according to Islamic teachings, the dead person begins a long wait that lasts until the day of resurrection. The grave becomes a garden in the garden of heaven or a well in the well of hell, depending on the life that the deceased has led. When Turkish Muslims die, they are buried the next day at the noontime *namaz*, or call to prayer. There are several rituals that are performed, including washing the body and covering it in a white cotton cloth. Then the body is taken to a nearby mosque and the funeral *namaz* is performed, after which it is taken to the cemetery and placed in a grave. The body must be attended to as quickly as possible, and people must abstain from exorbitant expenses.

Bibliography

Davidson, Roderic H. (1981). *Turkey: A Short History.* Walkington, Beverly, Eng.: Eothen Press.

Halman, Talat, et al. (1983). *Mevlana Celaleddin Rumi and the Whirling Dervishes.* Istanbul: Dost.

Kinross, Lord (1971). *Atatürk: The Rebirth of a Nation.* 5th ed. London: Wiedenfeld & Nicholson.

Kinross, Lord (1977). *Ottoman Centuries.* New York: Morrow.

Lewis, Bernard (1968). *The Emergence of Modern Turkey.* London: Oxford University Press.

Lewis, Geoffrey (1974). *Modern Turkey.* 4th ed. New York: Praeger.

Shaw, Stanford J., and Ezel Kural Shaw (1977). *History of the Ottoman Empire and Modern Turkey.* 2 vols. New York: Cambridge University Press.

Stirling, Paul (1965). *Turkish Village.* New York: John Wiley & Sons.

—ALAN A. BARTHOLOMEW

YEMENIS

Ethonym: none

Orientation

IDENTIFICATION. The Yemenis are a Muslim and Arabic-speaking people who are mainly Arabs, although a small percentage of the population has African and Asian ancestry. Yemeni values have traditionally relied on a hierarchical, tribally organized, and sex-segregated society. In 1962, following the overthrow of a conservative monarchy that had been supported by members of the Zaydi Islamic sect, the Republic was established, marking Yemen's entry into the modern world.

LOCATION. Yemen occupies the southern shore and the southwestern corner of the Arabian peninsula. Its western boundary is the Red Sea. The country has a mountainous interior with a temperate or subtropical climate. The central highlands divide Yemen into a coastal plain called the Tihama, which has a tropical climate with sparse rainfall, and a desert region that stretches into the Empty Quarter. A midlands area consists of valleys (wadis) and foothills that slope down to the lowlands. Southwest monsoons influence Yemen's climate. The southern highlands receive the most rainfall, particularly where mountains provide less of a barrier to precipitation.

DEMOGRAPHY. In the first national census that was conducted in 1975, the population of over 5 million included male laborers temporarily employed outside the country but excluded many Yemenis in the lowest servant groups. Population figures taken from various census reports between 1985 and 1989 range from more than 6 million to more than nine million. In the early 1990s the population of Yemen surpassed 10 million.

LINGUISTIC AFFILIATION. Yemenis speak the dialect of Arabic spoken in the region or urban center from which they originate. Regional variations in the pronunciation of certain Arabic phonemes (especially the phoneme /q/) differentiates the speech of northerners from southerners, for example. The speech pattern of Tihama residents is marked not only by dialectal variations but by characteristic accents, intonations, and inflections.

History and Cultural Relations

Yemen is an ancient country. In the millennia before Christianity, the two Yemens, known as South Arabia and Arabia Felix ("Happy Arabia"), were important points along the incense trade routes. South Arabian kingdoms dating from 1000 B.C. included the land from which the Queen of Sheba made her visit to King Solomon. Prior to the coming of Islam in the sixth century A.D., the South Arabian kingdoms declined, the conquests of Persian and Ethiopian rulers failed, and the famous dam at Ma'rib was destroyed. Remnants of the dam and pillars, reputedly from the queen's temple, are still to be found in the eastern desert of Yemen. Leadership under the Zaydi imams began in the ninth century. Between the eleventh and fourteenth centuries, various external and local dynasties struggled for power in different parts of Yemen. Among these were the Sulayhid (including the noted queen, Arwa), Ayyubid, and Tehirid dynasties. Yemen resisted foreign rule, but two occupations by the Ottoman Turks occurred—between the mid-sixteenth to early seventeenth centuries and from the 1870s to 1918. The imams then sought to reassert their political authority over the tribes of Yemen and against Saudi Arabia. The assassination of Iman Yahya in 1948 was eventually followed by a successful revolt of dissident army officers, intellectuals, and businessmen in 1962. Civil warfare lasted into the 1970s and reerupted in the 1990s. Troops loyal to the president won the war and the country remained united.

Settlements

Most Yemenis live in small, widely dispersed farming villages and towns. Three-quarters of the population lives in roughly 50,000 settlements with less than 500 inhabitants. The cities of Aden, Abyan, Al-Houta, Al-Hudaydah (a port), San'a,

Yemeni values have traditionally relied on a hierarchical, tribally organized, and sex-segregated society.

See also

Arabs

and Ta'izz have more than 100,000 residents each. Many foreign countries have assisted in the building of roads, hospitals, and schools, but improvements such as sanitary water facilities and power supply typically remain local development projects.

Economy

SUBSISTENCE AND COMMERCIAL ACTIVITIES. In the rapid transition from a subsistence to a cash economy, most families can no longer support themselves exclusively by farming. Yemen, once a chief exporter of Mocha coffee (from the port of the same name) now has a highly inflated economy that is dependent on imports. Yemenis who continue to plow their fields manually or with the aid of oxen do so not only because traditional methods are more efficient on narrow traces, but also because farmers are far too poor to own or even to rent the services of a tractor. Radical changes in the subsistence economy began in the 1970s with the export of male labor to Saudi Arabia. By the mid-1980s, remittances from abroad, including U.S. earnings, amounted to a billion dollars and resulted in a sharp rises in bride-price and the cost of land, food, modern consumer items, and professional services. Yemeni dependence on the oil-producing economies now means that staple grains (such as drought-resistant maize, sorghum, wheat, and barley), livestock (including goats, sheep, cattle, and chickens) and even cash crops (cotton and sesame, for example) cannot compete with high-yield commodities from the industrialized world. Oil was discovered in 1984 by the U.S. Hunt Oil Company. By fulfilling its potential to become a modest oil producer, Yemen would reduce its economic dependence on Saudi Arabia. Presently, the most important cash crop for local consumption is qāt (*Cathe edulis*), the mild leaf stimulant that Yemenis chew for its euphoric effects and which is an essential component of daily social and business gatherings. One measure of increasing affluence is the affordability of qāt, especially among town dwellers.

INDUSTRIAL ARTS. Yemenis are applying new skills to old trades or entering new occupations that were formerly reserved only for members of despised groups. Operating a sewing machine is an example of a new skill; women do the sewing at home, or, more often, men do the work in shops. Prior to their exodus from Yemen in the mid-twentieth century, Jews were the silversmiths. Now jewelry trades have been taken up by Yemeni Arabs. Returning migrant laborers apply the metal crafts they learned abroad in the making

YEMENI FAMILY

A Yemeni family sits together in their living room, or mafraj, the father holding a waterpipe and the son a rifle. Shaharah, Yemen. (Earl Kowall/Corbis)

of steel doors, which are much desired by Yemeni homeowners and shopkeepers. Certain regional crafts and services must compete with imports and modernity: weaving, pottery, and charcoal selling fall into this category. Selling goods in the market was formerly an occupation considered too lowly for individuals of tribal status, but now shopkeeping offers men one of the few opportunities to invest their foreign earnings. On the other hand, greater spending on meat consumption and the resultant increase in the demand for butchers has not meant an elevation in the social status of butchers despite their upgraded economic position.

DIVISION OF LABOR. Various tasks in the cultivation of crops are divided according to sex. Men, women, and children share responsibility for the care of livestock. Women gather firewood and water; in some regions, they now receive assistance from the men, who have acquired Japanese trucks. The family's livelihood may also depend on women selling homemade goods and produce in the marketplace.

LAND TENURE. Farmers either own their plots, which tend to be small, or they work as shareholders. No stigma is attached to non-landowners unless one is a member of a group that, in the past, was not permitted to buy land.

Kinship

KIN GROUPS AND DESCENT. In the northern highlands, tribal lineages are based on claims of descent from a named male (patronymic) ancestor. More characteristic of social organization in the southern and coastal regions are smaller alliances and/or greater association with others residing in the same vicinity.

KINSHIP TERMINOLOGY. Yemenis recognize the concept of "closeness" to describe desired relationships through marriage.

Marriage and Family

MARRIAGE. Islamic law and custom guide contemporary Yemeni marriages, although government regulations establishing ceilings on bride-price are often ignored. The legal marriage age of 16 for girls is also difficult to regulate because births are not routinely recorded. Arranged marriages prevail, but women do have veto power over a prospective groom. Fewer than 5 percent of Yemeni males exercise their option as Muslims to have up to four wives. The difficulty of supporting multiple wives equitably, as Islamic law requires, as well as the high cost of getting married, probably discourages polygyny. Divorce can be accomplished by men with far fewer restrictions than are imposed on women. Customarily, wives (through fathers or brothers) must remunerate their husbands if they wish to terminate the marriage. Legally, fathers' rights to the children after divorce supersede those of mothers.

DOMESTIC UNIT. Women preside over the work of the household, which may be comprised of blood relatives, neighbors, and members of client or servant groups in families of high social status. Women are valued members of the household unit as agricultural producers and are also crucial to the maintenance of the Yemeni ideal of domestic hospitality.

INHERITANCE. Landownership is concentrated within the dominant patrilineages, the result both of inheritance practices and marital strategies. Under Islamic rules, a woman's inheritance is only half that of her brother. In Yemen, women often do not renounce their claims of ownership. Thus the ideal marriage between patrilateral cousins would ensure that land remains within the patrilineage. Similarly, marriage to an outsider encourages the renunciation of claims to land that is too far away to farm.

SOCIALIZATION. In Yemeni society, the responsibilities of child care are willingly assumed by many others besides the mother, including older children and grandmothers. Once children are able to walk, they freely roam their village, observing the activities of any household. Physical punishment is reserved for more severe infractions, but mothers have ingenious ways of getting their children's attention.

Sociopolitical Organization

SOCIAL ORGANIZATION. Yemeni society is hierarchically organized on the basis of birth status and occupation. Until relative political stability was achieved in the late 1970s, birth and occupational statuses were legitimized as ascribed social categories. The elimination of practical barriers that restrict power and privilege—especially through marriage and education—to certain members of the society has only just begun. Under the system of ranked social categories, members of respectable groupings recognized their own noble descent and considered themselves the protectors of servants, former slaves, artisans, and certain farmers, all of whom were thought of as "deficient," either because they provided a service or craft—such as bloodletting, butchery, or barbering—that involved contact with polluting substances, or because their origins were discredited as ignoble. The tribal code of protection was also

Yemenis are applying new skills to old trades or entering new occupations that were formerly reserved only for members of despised groups.

extended to elites at the top of the social scale, especially to sayyids, the reputed descendants of the Prophet, who originally came to Yemen to serve as mediators between tribes and who are respected for their religious expertise. Another social category, that of legal scholars, also inherits high status in the ranking order. Scholars, along with *shuyukh* (sing. *shaykh*), who are tribal leaders, typically serve as village administrators. The majority of Yemenis use various equivalent or substitute terms to identify themselves within the social hierarchy, including *qabaʿil* in the northern highlands to connote tribal membership, *raʿiyah* in the south to mean "cultivators," and *ʿarab* along the coast to signify respectable ancestry. Former slaves continue to act as agents and domestics in the households of former masters, but the most menial jobs (e.g., removing human waste from the street) are reserved for Yemenis who are alleged descendants of Ethiopians of the pre-Islamic era. In addition, Yemen relies on a range of foreigners from the East and West for professional, technical, and custodial services.

POLITICAL ORGANIZATION. It is a continuing challenge of governmental strategies to achieve a stable balance between relatively autonomous tribes and the state. Alliance with dominant tribal confederation therefore may still be influential in the distribution of development projects by central authorities.

SOCIAL CONTROL. A strict and complex code of honor based on tribal values governs behavior among groups and proper decorum between the sexes, including veiling of women in urban or northern areas.

CONFLICT. The cultural concept of honor also regulates the handling of disputes, which depends on confirming significant kinship ties.

Religion and Expressive Culture

Islam is the major force that unifies Yemenis across social, sexual, and regional boundaries. Yet most adherents of the different schools of Islam reside in distinct sections of the country, and this fact has certain political implications. Zaydis, who belong to the Shia subsect of Islam, are located in the northern and eastern parts of Yemen, whereas Shafis, orthodox Sunnis, live in the southern and coastal regions. Location in the highlands apparently enables Zaydis more successfully to repel invasions than Shafis in the lower lying areas. A smaller Shia subsect, the Ismaili, and also the remnants of an ancient Jewish community, may still be found in certain parts of Yemen.

RELIGIOUS BELIEFS. As Muslims, Yemenis aspire to fulfill the five tenets of Islam: affirmation of the Islamic creed, prayer, fasting, charity, and pilgrimage.

In the Shafi areas of Yemen, the tombs of certain holy men are visited by believers for their special healing and other powers.

RELIGIOUS PRACTITIONERS. Being of sayyid status, even in contemporary Yemeni society, still validates (but does not necessarily guarantee) one's access to religious learning. Men gather at the mosque for prayers and sermons on the Sabbath, which in Yemen occurs on Friday. Strict segregation of the sexes usually does not permit women to worship in public.

CEREMONIES. Yemenis observe the major holidays, such as Ramadan, the holy month of fasting, as well as lesser festivals in the Arabian calendar.

ARTS. Despite the imposition of modernity, Yemenis remain proud of their architectural and oral-poetry traditions. Houses and mosques found in different regions of the country reflect unique stylistic and functional variations. Highlanders construct multistoried buildings from smooth, layered mud, mud brick, or cut stone. Dwellings in Sanʿa are particularly impressive with their decorative colored-glass windows. In the rural highlands, houses constructed atop terraced embankments were fortresses against enemy tribes. In cities along the coastal plain, the former elegance of houses and mosques can be seen in their elaborate doors and facades. Rural towns in the Tihama usually include a walled compound that contains mud and thatched-roof huts identical to those found in Africa, on the other side of the Red Sea. The interiors of Tihama houses may be highly ornamented. Buildings constructed of cinder blocks are routinely replacing the huts. Competitive poetry duels performed at weddings by men of tribal status are highly valued. In the past, celebrations for circumcision (required of all Muslim males) were particularly elaborate, but now government officials discourage postinfancy circumcisions, thereby undermining the importance of ceremonial specialists.

MEDICINE. Yemenis often continue to rely on traditional healers and midwives while simultaneously taking advantage of modern medical technologies. Illness is thought to be caused by such factors as fright—which many believe can be cured by branding (*misam*)—and possession by malevolent spirits (jinn), which requires the performance of the *zar* exorcism ceremony.

DEATH AND AFTERLIFE. On the occasion of a death, most households receive visits from those with whom they have social bonds. Such visits to the bereaved are part of the formal visiting networks that have been established, especially among women in towns and cities. Yemeni views regarding the Day of Judgment are far from simplistic, even though a fatalistic belief system is implicit in Quranic teachings of an allpowerful Allah. Yemenis also believe that whether one's soul spends eternity in heaven or hell is ultimately the responsibility of the individual Muslim.

Bibliography

Nyrop, Richard F. (1986). *The Yemens: Country Studies.* Washington, D.C.: U.S. Government Printing Office.

Swanson, Jon C. (1979). *Emigration and Economic Development: The Case of the Yemen Arab Republic.* Boulder, Colo.: Westview Press.

Weir, Shelagh (1985). *Qat in Yemen: Consumption and Social Change.* London: British Museum Publications.

—DELORES M. WALTERS

North America

AFRICAN AMERICANS

Ethnonyms: (contemporary): Black Americans, Afro-Americans; (archaic): Colored, Negro

Orientation

IDENTIFICATION. African Americans constitute the largest non-European racial group in the United States of America. Africans came to the area that became the United States in the sixteenth century with the Spaniards, but their first appearance as a group in the English colonies occurred in 1619, when twenty Africans were brought as indentured servants to Jamestown, Virginia. Subsequent importations of Africans from western Africa stretching from Morocco on the north to Angola on the south over a period of two hundred years greatly increased the African population in the United States. By the time of the Emancipation Proclamation in 1863, they numbered 4.5 million people. A composite people, comprised of numerous African ethnic groups including Yoruba, Wolof, Mandingo, Hausa, Asante, Fante, Edo, Fulani, Serer, Luba, Angola, Congo, Ibo, Ibibio, Ijaw, and Sherbro, African Americans have a common origin in Africa and a common struggle against racial oppression. Many African Americans show evidence of racial mixture with Native Americans, particularly Creek, Choctaw, Cherokee, and Pawnee, as well as with Europeans from various ethnic backgrounds.

LOCATION. African Americans were predominantly a rural and southern people until the Great Migration of the World War II era. Thousands of Africans moved to the major urban centers of the North to find better jobs and more equitable living conditions. Cities such as Chicago, New York, Philadelphia, and Detroit became magnets for entire southern communities of African Americans. The lure of economic prosperity, political enfranchisement, and social mobility attracted many young men. Often women and the elderly were left on the farms in the South, and husbands would send for their families, and children for their parents, once they were established in their new homes. Residential segregation became a pattern in the North as it had been in the South. Some of these segregated communities in the North gained prominence and became centers for culture and commerce. Harlem in New York, North Philadelphia in Philadelphia, Woodlawn in Detroit, South Side in Chicago, and Hough in Cleveland were written into the African Americans' imagination as places of high style, fashion, culture, and business. The evolution of the African American communities from southern and rural to northern and urban has been going on since 1945. According to the 1980 census, the largest populations are found in New York, Chicago, Detroit, Philadelphia, Los Angeles, Washington, D.C., Houston, Baltimore, New Orleans, and Memphis. In terms of percentage of population, the five leading cities among those with populations of over 300,000 are Washington, D.C., 70 percent; Atlanta, 67 percent; Detroit, 65 percent; New Orleans, 55 percent; and Memphis, 49 percent. (East St. Louis, Illinois, is 96 percent African American, but its population is less than 100,000.)

DEMOGRAPHY. The 1990 population of African Americans is estimated to be 35 million. In addition to those in the United States, there are approximately 1 million African Americans abroad, mainly in Africa, Europe, and South America. African Americans constitute about 12 percent of the American population. This is roughly equal to the percentages of Africans in the populations of Venezuela and Colombia. The largest population of African people outside the continent of Africa resides in Brazil; the second largest is in the United States of America. The following countries have the largest populations of Africans in the world: Nigeria, Brazil, Egypt, Ethiopia, Zaire, and the United States. The cities with the largest populations of African Americans are New York, 2.1 million; Chicago, 1.4 million; Detroit, over 800,000; Philadelphia, close to 700,000; and Los Angeles, more than 600,000. Seven states have African American populations of more than 20 percent. These are southern and predominantly rural: Mississippi, 35 percent; South Carolina, 30 percent; Louisiana, 29 percent; Georgia, 27 percent; Alabama, 26 percent; Maryland, 23 percent; and North Carolina, 22 percent.

LINGUISTIC AFFILIATION. African Americans are now native speakers of English. During the seventeenth century, most Africans in the Americas spoke West African languages as their first languages. In the United States, the African population developed a highly sophisticated pidgin, usually referred to by linguists in its creolized form as Ebonics. This language was the prototype for the speech of the vast majority of African Americans. It was composed of African syntactical elements and English lexical items. Use of this language made it possible for Africans from various ethnic and linguistic groups (such as Yoruba,

♦ **pidgin**
A second language very often made up of words and grammatical features from several languages and used as the medium of communication between speakers of different languages.

African Americans were stolen from the continent of Africa and transported, against their will, across the Atlantic.

Ibo, Hausa, Akan, Wolof, and Mande) to communicate with one another as well as with the Europeans with whom they came in contact.

The impact of the African American language on American society has been thorough and all-embracing. From the ubiquitous "O.K.," a Wolof expression from Senegal, to the transformations of words like "bad" and "awesome" into different and more adequate expressions of something entirely original, one sees the imprint of African American styles that are derived from the African heritage. There are more than three thousand words, place names, and concepts with African origins found in the language of the United States. Indeed, the most dynamic aspects of the English language as spoken in the United States have been added by the popular speakers of the African American idiom, whether contemporary rap musicians, past jazz musicians, or speakers of the street slang that has added so much color to American English. Proverbs, poems, songs, and hollers, which come with the historical saga of a people whose only epics are the spirituals, the great songs, provide a rich texture to the ever-evolving language of the African American people.

History and Cultural Relations

African Americans did not come freely to America. Theirs is not a history of a people seeking to escape political oppression, economic exploitation, religious intolerance, or social injustice. Rather, the ancestors of the present African Americans were stolen from the continent of Africa, placed on ships against their wills, and transported across the Atlantic. Most of the enslaved Africans went to Brazil and Cuba, but a great portion landed in the southern colonies or states of the United States. At the height of the European slave trade, almost every nation in Europe was involved in some aspect of the enterprise. As the trade grew more profitable and European captains became more ambitious, larger ships with specially built "slave galleries" were commissioned. These galleries between the decks were no more than eighteen inches in height. Each African was allotted no more than a sixteen-inch-wide and five-and-a-half-foot-long space for the many weeks or months of the Atlantic crossing. Here the Africans were forced to lie down shackled together in chains fastened to staples in the deck. Where the space was two feet high, Africans often sat with legs on legs, like riders on a crowded sled. They were transported seated in this position with a once-a-day break for exercise. Needless to say, many died or went insane.

The North made the shipping of Africans its business; the South made the working of Africans its business. From 757,208 in 1790 to 4,441,830 in 1860, the African American population grew both through increased birthrates and through importation of new Africans. By 1860, slavery had been virtually eliminated in the North and West, and by the end of the Civil War in 1865, it was abolished altogether. After the war, 14 percent of the population was composed of Africans, the ancestors of the overwhelming majority living in the United States today.

During the Reconstruction period after the Civil War, African American politicians introduced legislation that provided for public education, one of the great legacies of the African American involvement in the legislative process of the nineteenth century. Education has always been seen as a major instrument in changing society and bettering the lives of African American people. Lincoln University and Cheyney University in Pennsylvania, Hampton in Virginia, and Howard University are some of the oldest institutions of learning for the African American community. Others, such as Tuskegee, Fisk, Morehouse, Spelman, and Atlanta University, are now a part of the American educational story of success and excellence.

The Great Civil Rights Movement of the 1950s and 1960s ushered in a new generation of African Americans who were committed to advancing the cause of justice and equality. Rosa Parks refused to give her seat to a White man on a Montgomery city bus and created a stir that would not end until the most visible signs of racism were overthrown. Martin Luther King, Jr., emerged as the leading spokesperson and chief symbol of a people tired of racism and segregation and prepared to fight and die if necessary in order to obtain legal and human rights. Malcolm X took the battle a step further, insisting that the African American was psychologically lost as well and therefore had to find historical and cultural validity in the reclamation of the African connection. Thus, out of the crucible of the 1960s came a more vigorous movement toward full recognition of the African past and legacy. Relationships with other groups depended more and more on mutual respect rather than the African Americans acting like clients of these other groups. African Americans expressed their concern that the Jewish community had not supported affirmative action, although there was a long history of Jewish support for African American causes. Accepting the role of vanguard in the struggle to extend the protection of the American Constitution to oppressed people, African Americans made serious demands on municipal and federal officials during the civil rights movement. Voting rights were guaranteed and protected, educational segregation was made illegal, and petty discriminations against African Americans in hotels and public facilities were eradicated by the sustained protests and demonstrations of the era.

Economy

African Americans have been key components in the economic system of the United States since its inception. The initial relationship of the African American population to the economy was based upon enslaved labor. Africans were instrumental in establishing the industrial and agrarian power of the United States. Railroads, factories, residences, and places of business were often built by enslaved Africans. Now African Americans are engaged in every sector of the American economy, though the level of integration in some sectors is less than in others. A considerable portion of the African American population works in the industrial or service sectors. Others are found in the professions as opposed to small businesses. Thus, teachers, lawyers, doctors, and managers

account for the principal professional workers. These patterns are based upon previous conditions of discrimination in businesses throughout the South. Most African Americans could find employment in communities where their professional services were needed; therefore, the above-mentioned professions and others that cater to the African American population provide numerous opportunities for employment. During the past twenty years, the number of businesses opened by African Americans has begun to increase again. During the period of segregation, many businesses existing solely for the convenience of the African American population flourished. When the civil rights movement ended most of the petty discriminations and it became possible for African Americans to trade and shop at other stores and businesses, the businesses located in the African American community suffered. There is now a greater awareness of the need to see businesses as interconnected and interdependent with the greater American society. A larger and more equitable role is being played by women in the African American community. Indeed, many of the chief leaders in the economic development of the African American community are and have been women. Both men and women have always

RELIGION AND EXPRESSIVE CULTURE

Religious Beliefs

African Americans practice the three main monotheistic religions, as well as Eastern and African religions. The predominant faith is Christian, the second largest group of believers accept the ancestral religions of Africa—Vodun, Santeria, Myal—and a third group of followers practice Islam. Judaism and Buddhism are also practiced by some people within the community. Without understanding the complexity of religion in the African American community, one should not venture too deeply into the nature of the culture. While the religions of Christianity and Islam seem to attract attention, the African religions are present everywhere, even in the minds of the Christians and Muslims. Thus, traditional practitioners have introduced certain rites that have become a part of the practices of the Christians and Muslims, such as African greetings and liba-

tions to ancestors. The African American is spiritually oriented; having given to the American society the spirituals, the master songs, the African American people have learned how to weave religion into everything so that there is no separation between religion and life. Many of the practitioners of the African religions use the founding of Egypt as the starting date for the calendar; thus 6290 A.F.K. (After the Founding of Kemet) is equivalent to 1990. There is no single set of beliefs to which all African Americans subscribe.

Ceremonies

Martin Luther King, Jr.'s, birthday, January 15, and Malcolm X's birthday, May 19, are the two most important days in the African American calendar. Kwanzaa, a celebration of first fruits, initiated by the philosopher Maulana Karenga, is the most joyous occa-

sion in the African American year. Kwanzaa is observed from December 26 to January 1, and each day is named after an important virtue.

Death and Afterlife

There is no wide acceptance of cremation in the African American culture; the majority of African Americans choose burial. Funerals are often occasions of sadness followed by festivities and joyousness. "When the Saints Go Marching In" was made famous as the song to convery African Americans to the other world by African American musicians in New Orleans. Sung and played with gusto and great vigor, the song summed up the victorious attitude of a people long used to suffering on earth.

After the Civil War, African American politicians introduced legislation that provided for public education, one of the great legacies of the African American legislative involvement in the nineteenth century.

worked in the majority of African American homes.

Kinship, Marriage, and Family

MARRIAGE AND FAMILY. African American marriage and kinship patterns are varied, although most now conform to those of the majority of Americans. Monogamy is the overwhelming choice of most married people. Because of the rise of Islam, there is also a growing community of persons who practice polygyny. Lack of marriageable males is creating intense pressure to find new ways of maintaining traditions and parenting children. Within the African American population, one can find various arrangements that constitute family. Thus, people may speak of family, aunts, uncles, fathers, mothers, and children without necessarily meaning that there is a genetic kinship. African Americans often say "brother" or "sister" as a way to indicate the possibility of that being the actual fact. In the period of the enslavement, individuals from the same family were often sold to different plantation masters and given the names of those owners, creating the possibility that brothers or sisters would have different surnames. Most of the names borne by African Americans are derived from the enslavement period. These are not African names but English, German, French, and Irish names, for the most part. Few African Americans can trace their ancestry back before the enslavement. Those that can do so normally have found records in the homes of the plantation owners or in the local archives of the South. African Americans love children and believe that those who have many children are fortunate. It is not uncommon to find families with more than four children.

SOCIALIZATION. African American children are socialized in the home, but the church often plays an important role. Parents depend upon other family members to chastise, instruct, and discipline their children, particularly if the family members live in proximity and the children know them well. Socialization takes place through rites and celebrations that grow out of religious or cultural observances. There is a growing interest in African child socialization patterns with the emergence of the Afrocentric movement. Parents introduce the *mfundalai* rites of passage at an early age in order to provide the child with historical referents. Increasingly, this rite has replaced religious rites within the African American tradition for children. Although it is called mfundalai in the Northeast, it may be referred to as the Changing Season rite in other sec-

tions of the United States. This was done in the past in the churches and schools, where children had to recite certain details about heroines and heroes or about various aspects of African American history and culture in order to be considered mature in the culture. Many independent schools have been formed to gain control over the cultural and psychological education of African American children. A distrust of the public schools has emerged during the past twenty-five years because African Americans believe that it is difficult for their children to gain the self-confidence they need from teachers who do not understand or are insensitive to the culture. Youth clubs established along the lines of the African age-set groups are popular, as are drill teams and formal youth groups, often called "street gangs" if they engage in delinquent behavior. These groups are, more often than not, healthy expressions of male and sometimes female socialization clubs. Church groups and community center organizations seek to channel the energies of these groups into positive socialization experiences. They are joined by the numerous Afrocentric workshops and seminars that train young people in traditional behaviors and customs.

Sociopolitical Organization

SOCIAL ORGANIZATION. African Americans can be found in every stratum of the American population. However, it remains a fact that the vast majority of African Americans are outside of the social culture of the dominant society in the United States. In a little less than 130 years, African Americans who were emancipated with neither wealth nor good prospects for wealth have been able to advance in the American society against all odds. Considered determined and doggedly competitive in situations that threaten survival, African Americans have had to outrun economic disaster in every era. Discrimination against African Americans remains in private clubs, country clubs, social functions, and in some organizations. Nevertheless, African Americans have challenged hundreds of rules and regulations designed to limit choice. Among the major players in the battle for equal rights have been the National Association for the Advancement of Colored People (NAACP) and the Urban League. These two organizations have advanced the social integration of the African American population on the legal and social welfare fronts. The NAACP is the major civil rights organization as well as the oldest. Its history in the struggle for equality and justice is legendary. Thurgood Marshall, the first African American to sit on the Supreme Court, was one of the organization's most famous lawyers. He argued twenty-four cases before the Supreme Court as a lawyer and is credited with winning twenty-three. Although there is no official organization of the entire African American population, and no truly mass movement that speaks to the interests of the majority of the people, the NAACP comes closest to being a conscience for the nation and an organized response to oppression, discrimination, and racism. At the local level, many communities have organized Committees of Elders who are responsible for various activities within the communities. These committees are usually informal and are set up to assist the communities in determining the best strategies to follow in political and legal situations. Growing out of an Afrocentric emphasis on community and cohesiveness, the committees are usually composed of older men and women who have made special contributions to the community through achievement or philanthropy.

POLITICAL ORGANIZATION. African Americans participate freely in the two dominant political parties in the nation, Democratic and Republican. Most African Americans are Democrats, a legacy from the era of Franklin Delano Roosevelt and the New Deal Democrats who brought about a measure of social justice and respect for the common people. There are more than six thousand African Americans who are elected officials in the United States, including the governor of Virginia and the mayors of New York, Los Angeles, Philadelphia, and Detroit. A previous mayor of Chicago was also an African American. Concentrated in the central cities, the African American population has a strong impact on the political processes of the older cities. A former national Democratic party chairperson is of African American heritage, and some of the most prominent persons in the party are also African Americans. The Republican party has its share, though not as large, of African American politicians. There is no independent political party in the African American community, although it has remained one of the dreams of leading strategists.

SOCIAL CONTROL AND CONFLICT. Conflict is normally resolved in the African American community through the legal system, although there is a strong impetus to use consensus first. The idea of discussing an issue with other members of the community who might share similar values is a prevalent one within the African

American society. A first recourse when problems arise is another person. This is true whether it is a personal problem or a problem with family members. Rather than calling a lawyer first, the African American is most likely to call a friend and seek advice. To some extent, the traditional African notion of retaining and maintaining harmony is at the heart of the matter. Conflicts should be resolved by people, not by law, is one of the adages.

Bibliography

Asante, Molefi, and Mark Mattson (1990). *The Historical and Cultural Atlas of African Americans*. New York: Macmillan.

Baughman, E. Earl (1971). *Black Americans*. New York: Academic Press.

Frazier, Thomas R. (1988). *Afro American History: Primary Sources*. 2nd ed. Chicago: Dorsey Press.

Harding, Vincent (1981). *There Is a River*. New York: Vintage.

Henry, Charles (1990). *Culture and African American Politics*. Bloomington: Indiana University Press.

McPherson, James, et al. (1971). *Blacks in America: Bibliographic Essays*. Garden City, N.Y.: Anchor Books.

—MOLEFI KETE ASANTE

AMISH

Ethnonyms: Mennonites, Pennsylvania Dutch, Pennsylvania Germans

Orientation

IDENTIFICATION. Old Order Amish Mennonites in North America are a Germanic people with origins in the radical Swiss Anabaptist movement that developed between 1525 and 1536 during the Reformation. Among the Anabaptist groups who have persisted in their beliefs for over three centuries are the Amish, the Mennonites, and the Hutterites. These groups believe in adult baptism and pacifism, maintain a strict religious community and reject participation in the world to varying degrees. Their adherence to simple, or "plain," living is widely known.

LOCATION. The Amish migrated to America from Switzerland, Alsace-Lorraine, the Palatinate (in what is now western Germany), France, and Holland. During the first period of their migration, between 1727 and 1790, approximately five hundred Amish, along with other Germanic groups, settled in Pennsylvania. Between 1815 and 1865, a second influx of three

♦ **Reformation**
A revolution in the Catholic church in the sixteenth century that led to the development of Protestantism.

The Amish were established as a separate sect between 1693 and 1697 on the basis of religious principles that continue to guide their communities.

thousand Amish immigrated to Ohio, New York, Indiana, and Illinois.

DEMOGRAPHY. In 1990 there were approximately 130,000 Amish living in twenty states and one province of Canada (Ontario). Seventy percent of all Amish live in Pennsylvania, Ohio, and Indiana. At a 3 percent rate of population increase annually, the Amish are doubling their numbers every twenty-three years. This growth rate results from large families in which seven or eight children are typical.

LINGUISTIC AFFILIATION. The Amish speak a dialect of German among themselves, use biblical High German in religious services, and speak standard English with outsiders.

History and Cultural Relations

The Amish were established as a separate sect between 1693 and 1697 on the basis of religious principles that continue to guide their communities. These rules, laid down by Jacob Ammann, a leader of a dissenting faction of the Swiss Anabaptists, include shunning (the social avoidance of excommunicated members), ceremonial foot washing as part of the communion service, and simplicity in dress and grooming. Today the rules are interpreted locally by the members of each congregation. The Amish, like other Anabaptist groups in Europe, suffered severe persecution and imprisonment. If they remained in thier own countries, they were not allowed to own land and were denied citizenship. These restrictions prevented them from forming permanent settlements. As a result, those who stayed in their European homelands have largely been assimilated into the dominant religious groups there.

The bases for Amish existence as a distinct American subculture are their nonconformity in dress, homes, speech, attitudes toward education, and resistance to modernization and change. The Amish adhere to traditions that include living in rural areas, using horses for farming, marrying within the group, and dressing in a manner reminiscent of seventeenth-century Europeans. The Amish lead lives that are socially distinct as well. Since the Amish are secure in their tradition of separation from the outside world, their relations with their non-Amish neighbors appear to be free of the judgmental attitudes of other separatist sects. Rules for Amish living prohibit more than an elementary school education, the ownership (but not always the use) of automobiles and telephones, and the use of electricity and modern conveniences. The Amish are aware of their position with respect to the large cultural environment. Farmers especially consider that using technological farm implements would have a devastating impact on their ability to maintain a separate society.

Conformity to the consensual rules (*Ordnung*) for behavior serves to unify Amish communities. Their religious perspective emphasizes commitment to a self-sufficient community of believers who reject worldly values. As part of a religious ethic based on their interpretations of Biblical scripture, the Amish ideal is to provide totally for members of their congregations throughout the life cycle. The Amish therefore remain committed to the home as the locus of their church services and for the care of the sick, the orphaned, the indigent, the elderly, and the mentally retarded. Important values that are the result of socialization in the home rather than in school are the ability to cooperate with others and to work as a contributing member to the society.

Outside industries have moved to Amish districts in Indiana and Pennsylvania in order to take advantage of their reputation for hard and reliable work. The Amish, though, tend to maximize their interactions with members of their group through the spatial arrangements in their communities, for example, while reducing interactions with outsiders. Like other rural communities, the encroachment of industrialization has diminished the possibility of isolation desired by the Amish.

Settlements

The Amish are located in regions that are compatible with their ideal of continuing a farming life-style. Within a settlement, the church district encloses a certain area. The size of the district is determined by the number of persons who can be accommodated in a single farm dwelling for church services. About twenty-five to thirty-five married couples plus their children compose a district. The steady growth rate of the Amish population and the need for more farmland accessible to the younger generation for purchase have required movement to new settlements. Amish homes tend to be large, functional dwellings dedicated to simplicity. Interiors are neatly kept and, in compliance with church rules, there is minimal decoration or ornamentation other than quilts and decorative china. The emphasis is on functional space that will allow homes to become churches for the bimonthly Sunday worship.

Economy

SUBSISTENCE AND COMMERCIAL ACTIVITIES. Farming is the occupation desired by most Amish. All family members are integrated into an agricultural way of life. Beginning at an early age, the young assist in farm and household chores. The Amish keep their farms small enough to be handled by the family unit. Family-size farms have consistently been productive, serving to meet the needs of the community rather than to earn large profits. Farms average between fifty and ninety-six acres; the larger acreage occurs in midwestern areas rather than in eastern regions such as Lancaster, Pennsylvania. The lack of concern with high-income productivity is evident in Amish farmers' choosing to concentrate on raising livestock in small numbers and on growing a variety of crops. Farm size is limited not only by the amount of land that can be managed by one family but also by the prohibition on the use of electricity.

On New York farms, if tractors are used at all, they provide the power source for other types of farm machinery. Often these vehicles are outdated and have steel wheels instead of rubber tires. In some parts of Ohio, for example, the prohibition on technological dairy farming has meant the abandonment of farming, resulting in a change in the nature of the Amish community. Some nonfarming Amish work within their communities, serving traditional needs such as the repair of farm and household equipment and operating horse-and-buggy trades. Work outside of farming in some regions has become increasingly necessary because of the declining availability of affordable land. Ironically, however, nonagricultural employment has also created the financial security that allows many young families to remain within the Amish fellowship. Newer occupational opportunities include service industries and shops where Amish work for non-Amish ("English") employers, often saving their earnings to buy a farm. More women are now being trained as teachers for Amish schools.

The Amish depend on outsiders for medical and legal services. When making loans to Amish clients, bank managers rely on the system of mutual aid for church members to back up buyers who become financially overburdened.

DIVISION OF LABOR. Mainly, women are employed in the home. Besides attending to children, house, garden, and chickens, the Amish woman also sews clothes for her family, cooks and cans food, and engages in quilt and rug making and embroidery. Both sexes handle household finances; children have both parents as role models for learning behavior appropriate to Amish society. Members of the congregation, both male and female, work cooperatively to build and rebuild houses and barns.

LAND TENURE. The Amish are often forced to migrate to areas where cheaper farmland is available. They save to buy additional farms for their children, giving young married couples financial and other forms of assistance in establishing their own farms. It is not uncommon for members of the community to provide low-interest loans to young people starting out.

Kinship

KIN GROUPS AND DESCENT. The Amish tend to maintain social relations mainly but not exclusively with members of their group. Ingroup marriages and kinship solidarity reinforce the family-based social structure. Amish marriages occur in what is essentially a large kin group. The extent of intermarriage that has resulted in the intermingling of genealogies for more than two centuries is evident in various Amish localities by the relatively few surnames. In naming their children, Amish parents may recognize both maternal and paternal sides of the family. Children have their fathers' surnames and middle names that are often their mothers' maiden names.

Several hereditary diseases have been studied among Amish populations. Although they are not a single, genetically closed population, the Amish have separate inbreeding communities within the larger group. The inbred character is indicated by the history of their migration patterns, by the unique family names in each community, and by the distribution of blood types. Of at least twelve "new" recessive diseases ascertained, several are especially pronounced: dwarfism, a rare blood cell disease, hemophilia, muscular dystrophy, and diseases associated with metabolism. The low rate of some hereditary diseases that are common in the general population has also been noted.

Marriage and Family

MARRIAGE. Amish couples are expected to remain married to the mates they select as young adults. The Amish church depends on the biological reproduction of its members rather than on acquiring new members through proselytization. There is thus a strong commitment to marrying within the church, although females tend to move outside the district since males usually inherit the family farm. Despite the fact that mate choice is limited to other church members, the young people do not necessarily choose to marry close relatives. The high inbreeding of the Amish popula-

The Amish church depends on the biological reproduction of its members rather than on acquiring new members through proselytization.

tion results not from marriages between first cousins but from the inter-marriages that have occurred over generations within a genetically isolated group.

Baptism into the church is preliminary to marriage. Courtship tends to be a private matter prior to the wedding announcement by the minister. A wedding, on the other hand, is a public affair celebrated in anticipation of certain benefits that will accrue to the entire community. Members of the congregation see the marriage as an end to a sometimes spirited adolescence and expect to have the couple's home as a new place for the Sunday service; they also look forward to more children who will be raised in the Amish way. Guests give household gifts; parents may provide livestock, furniture, and equipment to help the young people get started.

Where a newlywed couple resides depends on the opportunity to continue farming in the traditional manner. This may mean working in a factory until enough savings have been accumulated to invest in a farm of their own. If the couple remains on the family farm, their parents may, at retirement, move to a separate house on the property and eventually leave the management of the farm to the younger couple. No provision is made for divorce, nor is separation a part of Amish ex-

pectations for conformity to church-based rules of behavior.

DOMESTIC UNIT. As previously mentioned, each family member contributes to the working of the family farm. Although married couples share in the responsibilities of child rearing and of running the household and farm, the prevailing authority rests with the husband.

INHERITANCE. Land tends to be kept within families and is usually passed on to sons rather than to daughters and to younger rather than to older sons.

SOCIALIZATION. Individuals are prepared for all stages of life, including aging, under Amish patterns of socialization. The primary goals of child rearing are the acquisition of practical skills, the instilling of responsibility to the Amish community, and an emphasis on respect for hard work. Young people may be hired out to relatives or other church members after they are trained on the family farm and in the household. Parents often allow adolescents to explore the outside world and test the boundaries of Amish identity. Family and community may therefore overlook the ownership of radios, cameras, even automobiles, by young people as well as their going to the movies and wearing non-Amish clothes. Such deviations are ignored in order that the young may freely decide on marriage and membership within the church community. About one-quarter leave the church, but most join more progressive Amish or Mennonite churches.

Sociopolitical Organization

SOCIAL ORGANIZATION. Amish communities are not entirely self-sufficient. Support for state and local government may be given through voting and paying taxes, but church rules prohibit them from participating in politics as officeholders. They also comply with church rules forbidding military service and government assistance in the form of insurance or subsidies.

Resistance to compulsory school attendance beyond the eighth grade is perhaps the most controversial issue that has brought the Amish into direct confrontation with state and local authorities recently. Amish in certain communities were subjected to fines and imprisonment because they rejected secondary school education for their children. Finally, the dilemma was resolved in the 1972 Supreme Court decision *Wisconsin* v. *Yoder et al.,* which found that laws that required Amish children to attend school beyond the elementary level were a violation of their religious convictions. Conflicts between Amish and mainstream

QUILT MAKER

An Amish woman prepares to sew a portion of a quilt. Finished quilts surround her. Berlin, Ohio, USA. (Clay Perry/Corbis-Bettmann)

American goals in education were not an issue when one-room schoolhouses were the norm in a primarily rural United States. Today, the change to consolidated schools and to a deemphasis on basic skills has prompted the Amish to establish their own schools. According to Hostetler there are more than seven hundred one- and two-room schools that uphold Amish traditions and lifestyles.

POLITICAL ORGANIZATION. Old Order Amish churches are not organized around a central authority. Rather, the church districts serve as the governing units for each congregation. Men who hold the offices of deacon (*Armen Diener*), preacher (*Diener zum Buch*), and bishop (*Volle Diener*) are chosen by lot from among the members of the congregation themselves. The three ministers have charge of various aspects of church activities. The bishop performs baptisms and marriages; the preacher assists in the communion service and delivers the bimonthly sermon when asked; the deacon is responsible for distributing funds to the needy. Bishops meet informally to discuss matters pertaining to their congregations, and visiting by congregants also helps maintain bonds between church districts.

SOCIAL CONTROL. When a member breaks a moral or church code, the minister presents the question of discipline to the congregation. It is the church community that has the final decision. Shunning (*Meidung*), an extreme censure placed on violators, requires that no church member engage in social dealings with the individual until the ban is lifted.

Religion and Expressive Culture

RELIGIOUS BELIEFS. The Amish conceive of their church-community (*Gemeinde*) as being composed of those who are truly repentant and duly baptized. Members are joined communally in an effort to become righteous Christians and reject worldly values. Amish moral imperatives also account for their desire to be close to the soil and to nature.

CEREMONIES. The communion service to celebrate the Lord's Supper is held twice a year in the fall and spring. Preparations for communion include prayer, meditation, and fasting. As part of the service, the ceremonial foot washing, introduced by Ammann in the seventeenth century, takes place as a sign of fellowship.

ARTS. Women combine quilt making and visiting as an acceptable means of artistic expression. Other forms of artistic endeavor, like photography, are forbidden. Whitewashed houses with decorative paint trim and brightly colored flowers are also evidence of artistry among the Amish.

MEDICINE. The Amish have access to a variety of practitioners, including folk healers as well as modern physicians and surgeons. They also consider the reputation of practitioners and, taking for granted the competency of providers, they select ones whom they feel they can trust.

DEATH AND AFTERLIFE. Death is a solemn occasion, but is accepted as a matter of course. The dead are usually buried on the third day after death. Respect for someone who has died is often shown in a large funeral attendance. Funeral establishments may be asked to prepare the body, but afterward, church members dress the body at home in special garments. Preparation of the grave, notification of the ministers, and selection of pallbearers are duties that are divided between more or less distant relatives, friends, and neighbors of the deceased. Amish bereaved are comforted by their belief in heaven and life after death. Although the Amish want to be ready for Judgment Day, they are not especially preoccupied with the nature of an afterlife.

Bibliography

Gallagher, Thomas E., Jr. (1982). *Clinging to the Past or Preparing for the Future? The Structure of Selective Modernization among Old Order Amish in Lancaster County, Pennsylvania.* Ann Arbor: University Microfilms International.

Hostetler, John A. (1980). *Amish Society.* 3rd ed. Baltimore: Johns Hopkins University Press.

Hostetler, John A. (1980). "Amish." In *Harvard Encyclopedia of American Ethnic Groups*, edited by Stephen Thernstrom, 122–125. Boston: Harvard University Press, Belknap Press.

Keim, Albert N., ed. (1975). *Compulsory Education and the Amish: The Right Not to Be Modern.* Boston: Beacon Press.

Kraybill, Donald B. (1989). *The Riddle of Amish Culture.* Baltimore: Johns Hopkins University Press.

McKusick, Victor A. (1978). *Medical Genetic Studies of the Amish.* Baltimore: Johns Hopkins University Press.

—JOHN A. HOSTETLER

ARAB AMERICANS

Ethnonyms: Arab Muslims, Chaldeans, Copts, Druze, Lebanese, Palestinians, Shia, Syrians, Yemenis

See also
MIDDLE EAST: Arabs

Arab Americans

Arab Americans share a common Arab cultural and linguistic heritage.

Orientation

IDENTIFICATION. Americans of Arab ancestry are a heterogeneous amalgam of national and religious subgroups. Their link is a common Arab cultural and linguistic heritage, which has profoundly influenced the Middle East for over fourteen centuries. Historically, "Arab" referred exclusively to the Arabic-speaking tribes of the Arabian Peninsula and parts of the Fertile Crescent. Today, the term is understood to be a cultural/linguistic and political designation. It embraces various national, religious, and regional groups that share overlapping histories and national political aspirations, although significant differences and regional loyalties remain strong. No single set of racial or physical traits defines all Arabs. Nor can they be identified with a single religion (Islam), as is often mistakenly done, for not all Arabs are Muslims (about 6 to 10 percent are non-Muslims, mostly Christians and some Jews). In fact, although Islam originated in the Arabian Peninsula, and the Qur'an (its holy book) was written in Arabic, the vast majority of Muslims are not Arabs, but Indonesians, Pakistanis, Asian Indians, and Persians.

Arab Americans hail from only a handful of the twenty-one countries that compose the modern Arab world: Lebanon, Syria, Palestine, Iraq, Egypt, Yemen, and Jordan. In terms of recency of arrival, Arab Americans fall into three diverse groups: recent arrivals, long-term immigrants, and native-born descendants of earlier generations of immigrants.

LOCATION. Arab Americans live primarily in cities or adjacent suburbs. Many recent arrivals tend to gravitate to Arab neighborhoods, where ethnic grocery stores, restaurants, bakeries, clubs, and religious centers are concentrated. These neighborhoods tend to be working class and lower middle class in character. The largest is found in the Detroit suburb of Dearborn, Michigan; others are located in New York and Chicago. These "Arab Towns" have largely replaced the "Little Syrias" of earlier immigrant generations. The more assimilated long-term immigrants and native-born Arab Americans tend to eschew the ethnic neighborhoods for the middle-class suburbs. The major concentrations of Arab Americans are found in Detroit, New York, Los Angeles, Boston, Chicago, and Houston. Smaller communities are also found throughout the Northeast and Middle West.

DEMOGRAPHY. Exact population figures are difficult to ascertain owing to imprecise immigration and census data. Scholars tend to agree on 2 million as the number of persons of Arab ancestry in the United States, with another 80,000 in Canada. In comparison, the population of the Arab world is over 150 million. The largest single concentration of Arabs in North America is in Detroit, which is reputed to have about 250,000 Arabs. Native-born Arab Americans and long-established immigrants make up the largest share of the population, which was fairly stable through the mid-1960s. Beginning in the late 1960s, the population in North America witnessed rapid growth owing largely to the influx of tens of thousands of new immigrants.

LINGUISTIC AFFILIATION. Most assimilated Arab Americans use English as their primary language or only domestic language. Many recent arrivals use Arabic as their primary language, employing English as needed in contacts outside the home and the ethnic community. Arabic speakers converse in the regional dialect of their home village or town. Some Iraqi Chaldeans speak Chaldean (a Semitic language) as their only domestic language; others know only Iraqi Arabic or combine the two languages. Second-generation Arab Americans usually reach adulthood retaining very little of their parents' native tongue.

History and Cultural Relations

The first Arabic-speaking immigrants in the United States were a handful of nineteenth-century adventurers and sojourners. It was not until the end of the century that significant numbers of Arab immigrants began making their way to the United States. Their numbers were minuscule by the standards of the day, averaging several thousand per year, with the highest recorded number reaching nine thousand in 1913–14. World War I brought immigration to a virtual standstill. In the years immediately following the war, Arab immigration returned to its prewar level only to be restricted again by the legislation of the 1920s.

Many of the early immigrants left homes in Greater Syria, an Arab province of the Ottoman Empire until the end of World War I. In the postwar period, the province was partitioned into separate political entities (Syria, Lebanon, Palestine, Transjordan) under British and French rule. Although the area remains predominantly Arab and Muslim culturally, Christian, Islamic, and Jewish ethnoreligious minorities constitute its cultural mosaic. Many of the early immigrants were drawn from these minorities, especially certain Christian denominations (Maronites, Melkites,

♦ **Ottoman Empire**
Empire created by Turkish peoples in what is now Asian Turkey from 1300 to 1922.

and Eastern Orthodox). Others included a small number of Muslims and Druze, as well as smaller numbers of Iraqi Chaldeans and Yemeni Muslims.

In general, the early immigrants were mostly illiterate or semiliterate, unskilled, single males, who emigrated without their families. Of the approximately 60,000 who entered the United States between 1899 and 1910, some 53 percent were illiterate, and 68 percent were single males. A notable exception was a small group of literati (writers, poets, artists, journalists) who settled in places like New York and Boston. Politically rather than economically motivated, this group spawned an important school of modern Arabic literature. They formed the Pen League (*al-Rabita al-Qalamiyya*) under the leadership of Kahlil Gibran (1883–1931), the celebrated author of *The Prophet*.

The early immigrants tended to settle in the cities and towns of the Northeast and Midwest, in states like New York, Massachusetts, Pennsylvania, Michigan, and Ohio. By 1940 about a fifth of the estimated 350,000 Arabs lived in just three cities—New York, Boston, and Detroit—mostly in ethnic neighborhoods ("Little Syrias"). Many worked their way across America as peddlers of dry goods and other sundry items, reaching virtually every state of the Union. Some homesteaded on the Great Plains, and others settled in southern rural areas.

A second wave of Arab immigration to the United States occurred after World War II. The influx included many more Muslims than the previous one. It also included refugees who had been displaced by the 1948 Palestine war, as well as professionals and university students who elected to remain permanently in the United States. These trends accelerated after the June 1967 Arab-Israeli War, a watershed for both the Middle East and Arab immigration to the United States. The 1970s and 1980s witnessed a massive influx of Arab immigrants from Lebanon, Iraq, the Israeli-occupied West Bank, Yemen, Egypt, and other Arab countries. Many had been displaced by war and political upheaval.

The early Arab immigrants followed a fairly smooth assimilation into mainstream society. Several generations later their descendants have achieved high social mobility. Some are household names: Danny Thomas, Ralph Nader, Christa McAuliffe, Paul Anka, Casey Kasem, Bobby Rahall, F. Murray Abraham. In comparison, the second-wave immigrants have had a mixed time of it. Many have prospered econom-ically, especially those in the professions and business. But others, particularly in the period following the June 1967 war, have had to contend with demeaning stereotypes, prejudice, and discrimination stemming from the oil crisis, Middle East terrorism, and U.S. involvement in the region. These problems are more pronounced in areas where large numbers of recent arrivals reside.

Economy

Arab Americans are highly integrated into the U.S. and Canadian economies. Both immigrant and assimilated Arabs are heavily involved in the retail business trade. In many urban areas, they own and manage grocery stores, supermarkets, candy stores, gasoline stations, and restaurants. Some native-born Arabs own small and medium-sized manufacturing and commercial enterprises; most, however, choose careers in the professions (medicine, law, accounting, engineering, teaching). Many unskilled immigrants, particularly recent arrivals, can be found working in factories or restaurants, but they usually remain in such jobs only until they accumulate sufficient means to enter the retail business world. Although Arabs as a group have not faced economic discrimination, individuals have encountered discrimination in hiring and on the job, mostly in the professions.

Sociopolitical Organization

SOCIAL ORGANIZATION. Traditionally, the primary loyalties and affiliations of Middle Eastern peoples have been to local areas, the village or urban quarter, which were usually homogeneous religious and ethnic units. Not surprisingly, Arabs in America tended to establish ethnically homogeneous church- and mosque-centered communities. In addition, they formed hometown and village clubs and associations. Because immigrants from the same village or town were often scattered in many parts of the United States and elsewhere, these associations often acquired a national or even international scope. Hometown and village affiliations remain strong among recent arrivals and the immigrant population generally, and less so among assimilated Arab Americans.

POLITICAL ORGANIZATION. There is no overarching political structure that groups all Arab Americans. The Christian denominations are separately organized in hierarchical groups that are essentially extensions of churches based in the Middle East. Lacking the hierarchical

Although Arabs as a group have not faced economic discrimination, individuals have encountered discrimination in hiring and on the job, mostly in the professions.

structure of the Christian churches, local congregations of Muslims are loosely federated with one another according to sect (Sunni, Shia) and to competing Islamic federations in the Middle East.

In the late 1960s Arab Americans began establishing national organizations that transcend religious and hometown/village affiliations. The Association of Arab-American University Graduates (AAUG), founded by a group of academics and professionals, was the first such organization. Eventually larger organizations appeared in the 1970s and 1980s (American-Arab Anti-Discrimination Committee; National Association of Arab-Americans; American Arab Institute). The impetus behind the emergence of these organizations was the perceived need to present an Arab-American voice on U.S. foreign policy, combat demeaning stereotypes and discrimination, and encourage Arab Americans to become actively involved in the electoral process. Although these groups are highly visible, they represent only a small fraction of the Arab American population.

SOCIAL CONTROL AND CONFLICT. Arab Americans generally resolve disputes through the legal system. The population is law-abiding, and contrary to popular images, Arab Americans have not been involved in terrorist activities. Rather, they have been the targets of sporadic intentional violence, including several bombings and arson fires that killed two people and injured nearly a dozen others in the 1980s.

RELIGIOUS BELIEFS AND PRACTICES. Islam is the youngest of the monotheistic religions. Established in the seventh century, Islam's central tenet is the oneness of God. Humankind is called on to obey God's law and prepare for the Day of Judgment. Muslims view the Prophet Muhammad as the last in a long succession of prophets going back to Abraham. Muslims accept Jesus as a prophet who possessed miracle-working powers. The Qur'an places emphasis on his virgin birth. Muslims do not, however, recognize the divinity of Christ or accept that he was crucified, claiming instead that God intervened at the last moment. Shia Muslims differ from Sunni (orthodox) Islam over the rightful succession of the Caliphate (leader) of the early Muslim community and over the role and powers of the *ulama* (religious scholars or clergy). The majority of Arab American Muslims are Sunni; Arab American Shia Muslims are mostly from Lebanon and to a lesser extent from North Yemen and Iraq.

Arab Christians are divided between Eastern rite churches (Syrian Antiochian Orthodox, Greek Orthodox, and Coptic) and Latin rite Uniate churches (Maronite, Melkite, and Chaldean). Originally, all Middle Eastern denominations belonged to churches that followed Eastern rites. The Uniate churches eventually split from the Eastern churches and affiliated with the Latin church in

KINSHIP, MARRIAGE AND FAMILY

Marriage and Family

Arab marriage and kinship practices vary somewhat by religion and recency of arrival, but usually stress lifelong marriages, a preference for religious and ethnic group endogamy, marriage of cousins, extended families, patrilineal descent, and bifurcate-collateral (descriptive) kinship terminology. Surnames are patrilineal. Data on inter-marriage with non-Arabs are virtually nonexistent. Generally, recency of immigration, degree of ethnic group cohesiveness, and religiousness mitigate against interreligious marriages, though marriages across Arab regional and national lines are allowed as long as religious group endogamy is maintained. Arab affiliation is usually traced patrilineally, though women are delegated the responsibility of transmitting ethnic and religious awareness to the children. In many mixed marriages, particularly of Arab men to non-Arab women, the wives often play important roles in promoting Arab cultural heritage within the family and the ethnic community.

Socialization

As with North Americans generally, early socialization takes place in the immediate family. Arab parents are extremely indulgent, though they may resort to physical punishment. Socialization as an Arab takes place in the home, through attendance at "Arabic school" on weekends, and in youth groups at the mosque or church. Weddings, funerals, and other community gatherings offer occasion for further socialization into the ethnic group.

Rome. Although they formally recognize the authority of the Roman pope and conform to Latin rites, the Uniate churches maintain their own patriarchs and internal autonomy. The Middle Eastern churches, Eastern as well as Uniate, allow priests to marry, though not bishops, and maintain their separate liturgies, often in an ancient language (Coptic, Aramaic, Syriac, and so on).

RELIGIOUS PRACTITIONERS. Islam lacks a hierarchical church structure. The ulama are essentially teachers or scholars, lacking real authority, though Shia Islam as practiced in non-Arab Iran invests the ulama with special occult powers and authority in social matters. The Middle Eastern churches are structured in rigid hierarchies, and priests often command substantial respect and authority in local affairs.

CEREMONIES. Strictly speaking, Islam recognizes only three religious holidays: Ramadan, Eid al-Fitr, and Eid al-Adha. Other holidays, like the Prophet's birthday, are celebrated by some communities and not others. Ramadan, the ninth month of the Islamic lunar calendar, is the time of fasting that precedes Eid al-Fitr. The fast requires complete abstinence from food, drink, tobacco, and sex from sunrise to sunset during the entire month. Eid al-Fitr ("End of the Fast") marks the end of Ramadan. Eid al-Adha ("Feast of the Sacrifice") commemorates Abraham's willingness to sacrifice his son Ishmael in obedience to God. The holiday at the end of the Hajj, or pilgrimage to Mecca, falls on a different day each year owing to the differences between the Islamic lunar calendar and the Western solar calendar. The Eastern rite churches differ from the Latin churches on the timing of Easter and Christmas celebrations. Easter is celebrated the Sunday after Passover, and Christmas is celebrated on the Epiphany, which falls on January 6.

Bibliography

Abraham, Sameer Y., and Nabeel Abraham, eds. (1983). *Arabs in the New World*. Detroit: Center for Urban Studies, Wayne State University.

Abu-Laban, Baha (1980). *An Olive Branch on the Family Tree: The Arabs in Canada*. Toronto: McClelland & Stewart.

Abu-Laban, Baha, and Michael W. Suleiman, eds. (1989). *Arab Americans: Continuity and Change*. Belmont, Mass.: Association of Arab-American University Graduates.

Hooglund, Eric J. (1987). *Crossing the Waters: Arabic-Speaking Immigrants to the United States before 1940*. Washington, D.C.: Smithsonian Institution Press.

Naff, Alixa (1985). *Becoming American: The Early Arab Immigrant Experience*. Carbondale: Southern Illinois University Press.

Orfalea, Gregory (1988). *Before the Flames*. Austin: University of Texas Press.

—NABEEL ABRAHAM

BLACKFOOT

Ethnonyms: Blood, Kainah, Northern Blackfoot, Peigan, Piegan, Pikuni, Siksika

Orientation

IDENTIFICATION. The Blackfoot of the United States and Canada consisted aboriginally of three geographical-linguistic groups: the Siksika (Northern Blackfoot), the Kainah (Blood), and the Pikuni or Piegan. The three groups as a whole are also referred to as the "Siksika" (Blackfoot), a term that probably derived from their practice of coloring their moccasins with ashes. The term *Kainah* means "many chiefs" and *Piegan* refers to "people who had torn robes." Although the three groups are sometimes called a confederacy, there was no overarching political structure and the relations among the groups do not warrant such a label. Actually, the three groups had an ambiguous sense of unity, and they gathered together primarily for ceremonial purposes.

LOCATION. Before the Blackfoot were placed on reservations and reserves in the latter half of the nineteenth century, they occupied a large territory that stretched from the North Saskatchewan River in Canada to the Missouri River in Montana, and from longitude 105° W to the base of the Rocky Mountains. The Plains Cree were located to the north, the Assiniboin to the east, and the Crow to the south of the Blackfoot. The Piegan were located toward the western part of this territory, in the mountainous country. The Blood were located to the northeast of the Piegan, and the Northern Blackfoot were northeast of the Blood. The Blackfoot now live mainly on or near three reserves: the Blackfoot Agency (Northern Blackfoot), the Blood Agency, and the Peigan Agency (Northern Peigan) in Alberta, Canada, and the Blackfeet Indian Reservation in Montana, inhabited by the Southern Piegan.

DEMOGRAPHY. In 1790 there were approximately 9,000 Blackfoot. In 1832 Catlin estimated that the Blackfoot numbered 16,500, and in 1833 Prince Maximilian estimated that there were 18,000 to 20,000. During the nineteenth

Blackfoot

The Blackfoot were nomadic hunter-gatherers who lived in tipis. The bison was the mainstay of their economy, if not the focus of their entire culture.

♦ **tipi (tepee, teepee)**
A conical-shaped portable dwelling of skin- or hide-covered poles, associated with the nomadic Plains Indians.

♦ **Sun Dance**
A ceremonial dance, connected with the summer solstice and often associated with Plains Indians, which lasted for four days and sometimes involved dancing until exhausted as well as inflicting wounds on oneself.

century, starvation and repeated epidemics of smallpox and measles so decimated the population that by 1909 the Blackfoot numbered only 4,635. Evidence indicates that the Piegan were always the largest of the three groups. In 1980 in Montana, the Blackfoot population was about 15,000 with 5,525 on the Blackfeet Reservation and the remainder living off the reservation. In Canada they numbered about 10,000.

LINGUISTIC AFFILIATION. Blackfoot is an Algonkian language and is on a coordinate level with Arapaho and Cheyenne. Dialects of Blackfoot are Siksika, Blood, and Piegan.

History and Cultural Relations

Horses, guns, and metal as well as smallpox were probably present among the Blackfoot early in the eighteenth century, although they did not see a White person until the latter part of that century. The introduction of horses and guns produced a period of cultural efflorescence. They were one of the most aggressive groups on the North American plains by the mid-nineteenth century. Allied with the Sarsi and the Gros Ventre, the Blackfoot counted the Cree, Crow, and Assiniboin as enemies. Warfare between the groups often centered on raiding for horses and revenge. The U.S. government defined Blackfoot territory and promised provisions and instructions in the Judith Treaty of 1855. The westward movement of White settlers in the following decade led to conflicts with the Blackfoot. By 1870 the Blackfoot had been conquered and their population weakened by smallpox. The bison had become virtually extinct by the winter of 1883–1884, and by 1885 the Southern Piegan had settled on the Blackfeet Reservation. The Canadian government signed a treaty with the Blackfoot in 1877. The three reserves were established some time later, and they are under jurisdiction of the Canadian Indian Department.

Settlements

The conical bison-hide tipi supported by poles was the traditional dwelling. During the summer, the Blackfoot lived in large tribal camps. It was during this season that they hunted bison and engaged in ceremonial activities such as the Sun Dance. During the winter they separated into bands of some ten to twenty households. Band membership was quite fluid. There might be several headmen in each band, one of whom was considered the chief. Headmanship was very informal, with the qualifications for office being wealth, success in war, and ceremonial experience.

Authority within the band was similar to the relationship between a landlord and a tenant. As long as the headman continued to provide benefits, people remained with him. But if his generosity slackened, people would simply pack up and leave. When bands congregated during the summer, they formed distinct camps, which were separated from other band camps by a stream or some other natural boundary when available. When the Piegan, Blood, and Northern Blackfoot joined together for ceremonial purposes, each one of the three groups camped in a circle.

Economy

SUBSISTENCE AND COMMERCIAL ACTIVITIES. The Blackfoot were the typical, perhaps even the classic example of the Plains Indians in many respects. They were nomadic hunter-gatherers who lived in tipis. The bison was the mainstay of their economy, if not the focus of their entire culture. They hunted other large mammals and gathered vegetable foods. Traditions indicate that the bison were hunted in drives, although hunting practices changed when horses and guns were introduced. Deer and smaller game were caught with snares. Fish, although abundant, were eaten only in times of dire necessity and after the disappearance of the bison. Today, the economy at Blackfeet Reservation, Montana, is based on ranching, farming, wage labor, welfare, and leased land income. There is potential for oil and natural gas production and for lumbering. Poverty is a major problem, with the more acculturated doing better economically than the less acculturated as a general rule. Describing the Blackfeet during the 1960s, Robbins refers to them as an "underclass" and their economic position as "neo-colonial." On the Canadian reserves the current economic situation is similar to that in the United States, with the Blackfoot now marginally integrated into the White economy.

INDUSTRIAL ARTS. In traditional times, the bison was the primary food source as well as the source of raw material for many material goods including clothing, tipi covers, cups, bowls, tools, and ornaments. After trade was established with Whites, metal tools and cloth rapidly replaced the traditional manufactures.

TRADE. Trade within the group or among the three Blackfoot groups was more common than trade with other groups. Horses, slaves, food, tipis, mules, and ornaments were common trade items. Trade with Whites involved the Blackfoot trading bison hides and furs for whiskey, guns, clothes, food, and metal tools.

DIVISION OF LABOR. There was a rigid division of labor on the basis of sex. Men hunted, made war, butchered animals, made weapons, made some of their own clothing, and painted designs on the tipis and shields. Women did most of the rest, including moving camp, bringing wood and water, preparing and storing food, cooking meals, making clothing, and producing most implements and containers.

LAND TENURE. Traditionally, there were no formal rules relevant to access or use of lands. Under the reservation system, about 15 percent of the reservation land is owned by the tribe, with the remainder allotted to individuals. In some cases, the inheritance by numerous heirs of what were once large parcels of land has resulted in ownership of small pieces of land of no economic value.

Kinship

KIN GROUPS AND DESCENT. The aboriginal kinship and social systems have been characterized as reflecting "anarchistic individualism." The kinship system was multilineal and multilocal, with a very slight tendency toward patrilineality. The basic social unit was the "orientation group," which consisted of the household of one's parents and one's own household.

KINSHIP TERMINOLOGY. Kin terms were of the Hawaiian type.

Marriage and Family

MARRIAGE AND DOMESTIC UNIT. Marriage brought increased status to both the husband and the wife. Although most marriages were monogamous, polygyny was practiced and was preferred, especially among wealthier men. Marital and kinship relationships in general were governed by rigid rules of etiquette and behavior including mother-in-law avoidance, age-grading, and the use of formal speech with older kin. Husbands were exceedingly sexually jealous, and a wife suspected of adultery might be beaten, mutilated, or even killed. Today, family relationships and structures remain amorphous, unstable, and fluid. At Blackfeet Reservation, the formation of large households made up of related families and the tendency for the families to live near each other is associated with the scarcity of economic resources. These groups of relatives from cooperative economic units. A similar situation obtains at the Northern Blackfoot Reserve, with independent households occurring only under conditions of financial security.

PARTED-HAIR SOCIETY

A ceremonial skewer of the Blackfoot, featured in the dances of the Kaispa, or Parted-hair Society. The skewer is made of wood, beads, feathers, and paint. Canada. (Werner Forman/Corbis)

INHERITANCE. Traditionally, men would leave their property to kin through a verbal will. Horses were the most valuable property and were most often left to the man's oldest brother. In the past, women inherited little, although today they more often receive an equitable share.

SOCIALIZATION. Children were and are viewed as individuals worthy of respect. They are expected to be quiet and deferential with adults but assertive with peers. Admonishing, teasing, ridiculing, and scaring are preferred to corporal punishment which is considered abusive. Girls are taught by women and boys by men, generally learning the appropriate sex-typed behavior and skills first by imitation, then by helping, and finally by instruction. The extended family plays a central role in child rearing and care; it is not uncommon for children to live with their grandmother or grandparents. Adoption or the "bringing up" of children raised by relatives is also fairly common.

Sociopolitical Organization

SOCIAL ORGANIZATION. Like other Plains Indian cultures, the Blackfoot aboriginally had age-graded men's societies. Prince Maximilian counted seven of these societies in 1833. The first one in the series was the Mosquito society, and the last, the Bull society. Membership was pur-

> *The Blackfoot feared the ghosts of the dead, and if a person died in a tipi, that tipi was never used again.*

chased. Each society had its own distinctive songs, dances, and regalia, and their responsibilities included keeping order in the camp. There was one women's society.

POLITICAL ORGANIZATION. For each of the three geographical-linguistic groups, the Blood, the Piegan, and the Northern Blackfoot, there was a head chief. His office was slightly more formalized than that of the band headman. The primary function of the chief was to call councils to discuss affairs of interest to the group as a whole. The Blackfeet Reservation is a business corporation and a political entity. The constitution and corporate charter were approved in 1935. All members of the tribe are shareholders in the corporation. The tribe and the corporation are directed by a nine-member tribal council.

SOCIAL CONTROL AND CONFLICT. Intragroup conflict was a matter for individuals, families, or bands. The only formal mechanism of social control was the police activities of the men's societies in the summer camp. Informal mechanisms included gossip, ridicule, and shaming. In addition, generosity was routinely encouraged and praised.

Religion and Expressive Culture

RELIGIOUS BELIEFS. Aboriginally, the religious life of the Blackfoot centered upon medicine bundles, and there were more than fifty of them among the three main Blackfoot groups. The most important bundles to the group as a whole were the beaver bundles, the medicine pipe bundles, and the Sun Dance bundle. Christianity is practiced now by most Southern Piegan with Roman Catholicism predominating. The Blackfoot apparently never adopted the Ghost Dance, nor is the Peyote Cult present. The Sun Dance and other native religious ceremonies are still practiced among most of the Blackfoot groups.

CEREMONIES. By the middle of the nineteenth century, the Sun Dance had become an important ceremony. It was performed once each year during the summer. The Sun Dance among the Blackfoot was similar to the ceremony that was performed in other Plains cultures, though there were some differences: a woman played the leading role among the Blackfoot, and the symbolism and paraphernalia used were derived from beaver bundle ceremonialism. The Blackfoot Sun Dance included the following: (1) moving the camp on four successive days; (2) on the fifth day, building the medicine lodge, transferring bundles to the medicine woman, and offering of gifts by children and adults in ill health; (3) on the sixth day, dancing toward the sun, blowing eagle-bone whistles, and self-torture; and (4) on the remaining four days, performing various ceremonies of the men's societies.

ARTS. Singing groups were an important form of social intercourse. Porcupine quillwork was considered a sacred craft and some men were highly skilled painters of buffalo-skin shields and tipi covers. Today, achievement in traditional arts and crafts is valued as a sign of Indian identity. Consequently, there are skilled Blackfoot dancers, artists, carvers, leather- and beadworkers, orators, and singers whose work is known both within and beyond Blackfoot society.

MEDICINE. Illness was attributed to an evil spirit entering the body. Treatment by the shaman was directed at removing the spirit through singing, drumming, and the like. Some practitioners specialized in treating certain illnesses, setting broken bones, and so on.

DEATH AND AFTERLIFE. The dead were placed on a platform in a tree or the tipi, or on the floor of the tipi. Some property was left with the body for use in the next life. The Blackfoot feared the ghosts of the dead, and if a person died in a tipi, that tipi was never used again.

Bibliography

Hanks, Lucien M., and Jane R. Hanks (1950). *Tribe under Trust: A Study of the Blackfoot Reserve of Alberta.* Toronto: University of Toronto Press.

Hungry Wolf, Adolf (1977). *The Blood People, a Division of the Blackfoot Confederacy: An Illustrated Interpretation of the Old Ways.* New York: Harper & Row.

Hungry Wolf, Beverly (1980). *The Ways of My Grandmothers.* New York: William Morrow.

McFee, Malcolm (1972). *Modern Blackfoot: Montanans on a Reservation.* New York: Holt, Rinehart & Winston.

Robbins, Lynn A. (1972). *Blackfoot Families and Households.* Ann Arbor, Mich.: University Microfilms. Ph.D. diss., University of Oregon, 1971.

Wissler, Clark (1910). *Material Culture of the Blackfoot Indians.* New York: American Museum of Natural History.

CAJUNS

Ethnonym: Acadians of Louisiana

Orientation

IDENTIFICATION. The Cajuns are a distinct cultural group of people who have lived mainly in south-central and southwestern Louisiana since the late eighteenth century. In the past, because of their Acadian heritage, residential localization, unique language, and Roman Catholicism, it was relatively easy to distinguish Cajuns from other groups in Louisiana. Today, their identity is less clear. It usually applies to those who are descended from Acadians who migrated in the late 1770s and early 1800s from Canada to what is now Louisiana, and/or live or associate with a Cajun life-style characterized by rural living, family-centered communities, the Cajun French language, and Roman Catholicism. Cajuns in Louisiana today are a distinct cultural group, separate from the Acadians of Nova Scotia. Like the Appalachians and Ozarkers, they are considered by outsiders to be a traditional folk culture with attention given to their arts and crafts, food, music, and dance. The name "Cajuns" is evidently an English mispronunciation of "Acadians." Cajun and Black Creole culture share a number of common elements, some of which are discussed in the entry on Black Creoles of Louisiana.

LOCATION. In 1971 the Louisiana legislature designated twenty-two parishes as Acadiana: Acadia, Ascension, Assumption, Avoyelles, Calcasieu, Cameron, Evangeline, Iberia, Iberville, Jefferson Davis, Lafayette, Lafourche, Pointe Coupee, St. Charles, St. James, St. John, St. Landry, St. Martin, St. Mary, Terrebonne, Vermilion, and West Baton Rouge. This region includes coastal marshes, swamps, prairies, and levee land. In recent decades, as the region has experienced economic development and population shifts, the boundaries of Acadiana have blurred. And the Cajuns are not the only residents of these parishes, which include non-Cajun Whites of various ethnic backgrounds, African-Americans, Black Creoles, and others.

DEMOGRAPHY. In the 1970s there were about 800,000 Cajuns in Louisiana. After Acadians began arriving in Louisiana, perhaps as early as 1756, the population increased rapidly, from about 6,000 in 1810 to 35,000 in 1815 to 270,000 in 1880.

LINGUISTIC AFFILIATION. Language use by Cajuns is a complex topic, with the relationship between the speakers and the social context often determining what language is spoken. Cajun French is the language commonly associated with the Cajun culture, though many Cajuns no longer speak it fluently and its use has declined markedly in the younger generation. Older Cajuns speak Cajun French in the home and with other Cajuns. Cajun French differs from standard French in the use of some archaic forms of pronunciation, the inclusion of various loan words from English,

American Indian, Spanish, and African languages, and a simplified grammar. Cajuns usually use English as the contact language and as the domestic language in an increasing number of homes. In some homes and communities, Creole French is spoken as well.

History and Cultural Relations

Cajun culture began with the arrival of French Acadians (the French-speaking people of the territory that is now mainly Nova Scotia in Canada) who migrated to and settled in what is now Louisiana mainly between 1765 and 1785. Some migrated directly from Acadia, whereas others came after stays in France and the West Indies. All came as part of the Acadian Diaspora, which resulted from their forced exile by the British from Acadia in 1755. Because of additional migrants who arrived in the early 1800s and a high birth rate, the Acadians increased in numbers rapidly and were soon the most numerous group in many locales where they settled. Once settled in Louisiana, in environments very different from Acadia and in contact with other cultures including Black Creoles, American Indians, Germans, Spaniards, and Italians, the Acadian culture began to change, eventually becoming what has come to be called Cajun culture. With the exception of those in the levee-land region who lost their land to Anglos, most Cajuns lived in relative isolation in rural communities where they farmed, fished, or raised cattle.

It was not until after World War I that mainstream society entered Acadiana and began to influence Cajun life. Mechanization of farming, fishing, and cattle raising, the building of roads linking southern Louisiana to the rest of the state, mass communication, and compulsory education changed local economic conditions and exposed Cajuns to mainstream Louisiana society. Contact also meant that the use of Cajun French decreased, and in 1921 it was banned from use in public schools.

The end of World War II and the return of Cajun veterans to their homes was the beginning of a new era in Cajun culture, one characterized by continuing involvement in mainstream life and by the birth of Cajun ethnicity, reflected in pride in one's heritage and efforts to preserve some traditional beliefs and practices. In 1968 Louisiana created the Council for the Development of French in Louisiana (CODOFIL) as a mechanism to encourage the teaching of French in public schools. Because of conflicts over which French to teach—standard French or Cajun

HISTORY AND CULTURAL RELATIONS

Cajun culture began with the arrival of French Acadians (the French-speaking people of the territory that is now mainly Nova Scotia) who migrated to and settled in what is now Louisiana.

French—the program has not been a total success, though many Cajun children do participate in French-language programs.

Acadians are one of a number of groups of French ancestry in Louisiana, which also include the French-Canadians, Creoles, and those who emigrated directly from France. Relations between the Cajuns and other groups in Louisiana including Anglos, Creoles, Black Creoles, and others were generally peaceful because the Cajuns were largely self-sufficient, lived in distinctly Cajun regions, were numerically dominant in those regions, and chose to avoid conflict. That they were Roman Catholic while others were mainly Protestant further contributed to group segregation. Within the regional class structure, Cajuns were considered better than Blacks but the lowest group of Whites. In general, they were seen as poor, uneducated, fun-loving backwoods folk. Cajuns generally viewed themselves as superior to the poor rural Whites referred to as Rednecks.

Settlements

Acadian settlements in the past varied in size, style, and structure among the four major environmental zones. Settlements included isolated houses, small farms, towns, ranches, and families living on houseboats. Population relocations, the arrival of non-Cajuns, and changes in economic activities have all produced changes in settlement patterns. In recent years, there has been a marked trend to settlement in towns and cities through migration from the rural areas. The Acadian cottage, a small, nearly square dwelling with a covered front porch and high-pitched roof, was a distinctively Cajun house type in the 1800s. It was raised a few feet above the ground and constructed from cypress wood and infilled with clay and moss. Some later styles of dwellings were elaborations on the basic style, though all have now been replaced by modern-style homes made from mass-produced materials.

Economy

SUBSISTENCE AND COMMERCIAL ACTIVITIES. In Canada, the Acadians lived by farming (wheat, oats, rye, vegetables), raising cattle, and fishing, and by selling surplus crops and cattle and buying manufactured products. Louisiana had a markedly different environment, with four environmental regions, none exactly the same as Acadia. These new environments led to the development of new subsistence and commercial pursuits in Louisiana as well as variation in activities from one region to another. In the levee-land region,

the early Cajun settlers grew maize and rice for consumption and cotton for sale. They also grew vegetables and raised cattle. Non-Cajuns began settling in the region around 1800, however, and took much of the land for large plantations. Most Cajuns moved elsewhere; those that stayed lived by subsistence farming in the backwaters until well into the twentieth century. In the swampland region, fishing and the hunting and gathering of crawfish, ducks, crabs, turtles, frogs, and moss were the major economic activities. By the late 1800s, most Cajuns in this region were involved in the commercial fishing industry, and many still are today, though they have modernized their equipment and methods and often live outside the swamps. The Cajuns who settled on the Louisiana prairies developed two economic adaptations. Those in the east grew maize and cotton, supplemented by sweet potatoes. Those in the west grew rice and raised cattle, with local variation in terms of which was the more important. In the marshland region, on the Chernier Plain, Cajuns raised cattle, trapped, and gardened; on the Deltaic Plain they farmed, fished, hunted, and trapped.

Regular contact with the outside economy, which influenced all regions by about 1920, has changed the traditional economy. Cattle ranching has declined, and sugar cane, rice, cotton, and maize are now the major crops. As towns have developed and compulsory education laws have been enforced, Cajuns have been employed in service-sector jobs, and many now work in the oil and gas industries that have entered the southern part of the region. With public interest in the Cajuns as a folk culture developing in the 1960s, tourism has also become a source of income.

INDUSTRIAL ARTS. Aspects of the traditional subsistence technology of the 1800s that draw attention today are mainly adaptations to life in the swamp and marshlands. The traditional technology has been modernized, although traditional knowledge and skills are still valued. Aspects of the traditional technology that are of interest today are the Cajun cottage, the various tools and techniques used in collecting crawfish, crabs, and moss, and the *pirogue* (a narrow canoe made from a dugout log or planks).

TRADE. The intinerant traders (*marchand-charette*) who once supplied most household supplies are a thing of the past. Most Cajun families are now integrated into the mainstream economy and purchase goods and services.

DIVISION OF LABOR. The traditional economy centered on cooperation among members of the extended family and kindred. Men generally had responsibility for subsistence activities, and women managed the household. As the Cajuns have been drawn into American society, traditional sex roles have weakened, with women now working outside the home and often taking the lead in "Americanizing" the family.

LAND TENURE. Despite their early settlement in Louisiana, Cajuns own relatively little land. This is the result of a number of factors, including dishonest land agents, Cajun ignorance or misunderstanding of real estate laws, and patrilineal inheritance of property coupled with patrilocal residence which meant that once sizable farms were divided into smaller and smaller units over the generations. Today, lumbering, fossil fuel, and agricultural corporations own much land in the Cajun region, and in some locales, many Cajuns lease the land they farm.

Kinship

The basic social and economic unit in traditional times was the patrilineally extended family, whose members often lived near one another. Nearby residence was encouraged by patrilocal postmarital residence which involved fathers giving newly married sons a piece of the family land. Wider ties were also maintained with the local community, which often involved homesteads located some miles from one another. Preferential community endogamy meant that others in the community often included the wife's kin. People were involved with this kinship network throughout their lives.

Marriage and Family

MARRIAGE AND DOMESTIC UNIT. Although community and in-group endogamy was preferred, some women did marry non-Cajun men who were rapidly and easily assimilated into the group. Marriage usually occurred at a young age. Divorce was rare and difficult to justify. Although the nuclear family unit lived in the same dwelling as part of the extended family, the extended family was the basic social and economic unit. Kin worked together, helped build each other's houses, went to the same church, had to approve the marriage of female kin, cared for each other's children, and socialized and celebrated together. Both the country butchery (*la boucherie de campagne*), where kin met every few days to butcher hogs for meat, and the weekly public dance (*fais do-do*) provided opportunities for regular socializing by family members. Men were the major decision makers in their homes, but if a man died, his wife, not his sons, assumed control. Children lived at home until they married.

This traditional pattern of marriage and family began to change after World War I and then changed even more rapidly after World War II. Today, nuclear families have replaced extended ones, with economic ties now far less important than social ones in kinship groups. Husbands no longer dominate families, as women work outside the home and establish lives for themselves independent of their families. The prohibition of the teaching of French in Louisiana schools has created a generation gap in some families with grandparents speaking Cajun French, parents speaking some Cajun French, and the grandchildren speaking only English. Marriage to outsiders has also become more frequent, and is often the reverse of the former pattern, with Cajun men now marrying non-Cajun women who acculturate their husbands into mainstream society.

SOCIALIZATION. Traditionally, children were raised by the extended family. Cajuns rejected formal education outside the home except for instruction provided by the church. Parents emphasized the teaching of economic and domestic skills and participation in the activities of the kinship network. In 1916 school attendance up to age fifteen became compulsory, although the law was not rigorously enforced until 1944. Public school education played a major role in weakening the traditional culture, as it resulted in many children never learning or even forgetting Cajun French and provided skills and knowledge useful in mainstream society, thus giving younger Cajuns the opportunity for upward socioeconomic mobility. Today, Cajun children attend both public and parochial schools and tens of thousands participate in French-language programs in elementary schools. The rapid growth of the University of Southwestern Louisiana, McNeese State University, and Nicholls State University is evidence that many Cajuns now attend college as well.

Religion and Expressive Culture

RELIGIOUS BELIEFS. The Cajuns were and are mainly Roman Catholic. Experts suggest that the traditional culture cannot be understood unless the central role of the Catholic church is considered. On the one hand, their Roman Catholic beliefs set the Cajuns apart from the surrounding population, which was mainly Baptist and Methodist. On the other hand, the church was a visible and active participant in family and social life in every community. The priest was often a major figure in the community, setting the moral

With their current status as a folk culture, considerable interest has developed in the expressive elements of traditional Cajun culture, especially in the music and food.

SOCIOPOLITICAL ORGANIZATION

Social Organization

Social cohesiveness in Cajun communities as well as a general sense of being Cajun was maintained through various informal mechanisms that brought Cajuns together both physically and symbolically. The Roman Catholic church was a major unifying force, as it provided the belief system that supported many Cajun practices as well as differentiated Cajuns from their mostly Protestant neighbors. As noted above, the extended family and the somewhat larger kinship network were the basic social groupings in Cajun society. These social units were maintained through daily participation of members and through regularly scheduled get-togethers such as the boucherie and the fais do-do and the cockfights that brought the men together. There was no formal class structure, though a Cajun elite, the "Genteel Acadians" emerged in the early 1800s. They were mainly a few families who had become wealthy as farmers, merchants, or professionals. They tended to marry non-Cajuns, lived among Anglos and Creoles, and looked down upon the poor, rural Cajuns. Within the Cajun group in general, there was a continuum of wealth, though most were poor. Today, as the Cajuns have shifted from being a distinct cultural group to an ethnic group, group cohesiveness has weakened, with a sense of "being Cajun" derived from membership in a group that shares a common tradition.

Political Organization

There was no overarching political structure governing Cajun life, nor was there any purely Cajun political organization at the local level. Rather, Cajuns generally participated in Louisiana and national politics as voters. Two governors and other state officials came from the Genteel Acadian ranks in the 1880s. In the 1900s, Edwin Edwards, "the Cajun Governor" was first elected in 1972.

Social Control and Conflict

Conflicts were preferably handled by the local group, through mediators, or through fighting between men when matters of honor were involved.

tone and serving as a confidant and adviser as necessary. All life events such as birth, marriage, and death required church rituals as did many daily events, with the blessing of fields, tools, boats, and so on an integral part of the work cycle. There were also numerous festivals and feast days of religious significance. Perhaps more important, the church teachings formed the belief system underlying Cajun social organization. Male dominance in the home, stable marriages, large families, and so on were all in accord with the requirements of the church. In addition, Roman Catholicism as practiced in Acadiana created an atmosphere that allowed the celebration of life, or "la joie de vivre," so characteristic of Cajun culture.

CEREMONIES. All the major Roman Catholic holidays were celebrated by the Cajuns. Mardi Gras was the most important festival, with local communities celebrating in ways often much different than that in New Orleans. Public dances (*bals*), festivals, and feasts were regularly held in Cajun communities. All usually involved community dinners, dancing, playing, drinking beer, and music making, and all were family affairs with the entire family participating. Although they occur now less often, public dances, especially the fais do-do, are still important social events for the extended family. Dances, parties, and other opportunities to have a good time are an integral element of the Cajun life-style. Numerous other festivals are held in Acadiana each year, many of which are harvest festivals focusing on local crops such as sugar cane, rice, crawfish, and shrimp.

ARTS. With their current status as a folk culture, considerable interest has developed in the expressive elements of traditional Cajun culture, especially the music and food. Both are unique cultural forms, with a French base combined with elements drawn from American Indian, Spanish, African, British, and German cultures. Both have also changed over the years as new features have been added. Today, Cajun music comes in a variety of styles, the two most prominent being the country-western style and zydeco, which reflects the influence of Black rhythm and blues. Cajun music involves a band, singing, and sometimes foot-stomping. The particular instruments vary with the style, though the fiddle and accordion have been basic instruments for some time. As with their music, Cajun food reflects the combining of elements from a number of cultural traditions on a rural French base. Traditional Cajun cuisine was also influenced, of course, by the foods grown or available locally. From this combination of influences, we find, for example, the heavy use of cayenne pepper for a piquant taste, an oil and flour roux, gumbo, dirty rice, jambalaya, *boudin* (stuffed hog intestine casings), and crawfish as distinctive elements of Cajun food.

Bibliography

Conrad, Glenn R., ed. (1983). *The Cajuns: Essays on Their History and Culture.* Lafayette: Center for Louisiana Studies, University of Southwestern Louisiana.

Del Sesto, Steven L., and Jon L. Gibson, eds. (1975). *The Culture of Acadiana: Tradition and Change in South Louisiana.* Lafayette: University of Southwestern Louisiana.

Dorman, James H. (1983). *The People Called Cajuns.* Lafayette: Center for Louisiana Studies, University of Southwestern Louisiana.

Rushton, William Faulkner (1979). *The Cajuns: From Acadia to Louisiana.* New York: Farrar, Straus & Giroux.

CHEROKEE

Ethnonyms: Chalaque, Cheraqui, Manteran, Oyata'ge Ronon, Rickahochan, Tallige', Tsa'lagi', Tsa'ragi

Orientation

IDENTIFICATION. The Cherokee are an American Indian group who now live in North Carolina and Oklahoma. The name "Cherokee" is apparently of foreign origin, perhaps from the Choctaw *chiluk,* meaning "cave," an allusion to the Cherokees' mountainous homeland. Historically the Cherokee sometimes referred to themselves as "Ani'-Yun'-wiya"' (real people) or "Ani'-kitu' hwagi" (people of Kituwha) in reference to one of their important ancient settlements.

LOCATION. Aboriginally the Cherokee occupied the region of the southern Appalachian Highlands from 34° to 37° N and 80° to 85° W, mainly in the present-day states of Tennessee and North Carolina in the southeastern United States. Most Cherokee now live in Oklahoma and North Carolina.

DEMOGRAPHY. In 1970 the Cherokee population was estimated at 66,150, with 27,197 in Oklahoma, 6,085 in North Carolina, and 32,878 in other states, mainly California, New Mexico, and Texas. In early postcontact times the Cherokee numbered approximately 20,000. In a 1989 Bureau of the Census publication, it was noted that in 1980 there were over 230,000 Cherokee enumerated, which would make them the largest Native American group in the United States.

LINGUISTIC AFFILIATION. The Cherokee language is classified in the Iroquoian family. In aboriginal and early postcontact times there were three dialects: the Eastern or Lower dialect is now extinct; the Middle or Kituwha dialect is spoken in North Carolina; and the Western or Upper dialect in Oklahoma.

History and Cultural Relations

Linguistic, archaeological, and mythological evidence suggest that the Cherokee migrated to the southern Appalachian Highlands from the north prior to European contact in 1540. Native groups bordering the Cherokee territory at that time included the Powhatan and Monacan to the northeast, the Tuscarora and Catawba to the east and southeast, the Creek to the south, the Chickasaw and Shawnee to the west, and the now-extinct Mosopelea to the north. Generally speaking, Cherokee relations with all these groups during the early historic period were contentious.

Continuous contact with Europeans dates from the mid-seventeenth century when English traders from Virginia began to move among native groups in the southern Appalachians. Following contact, the Cherokee intermarried extensively with Whites. Peaceful Cherokee-White relations ended when war broke out with South Carolina in 1759. During the American Revolution the Cherokee allied with the British and continued hostilities with Americans until 1794. White encroachments on their territory led a large number of Cherokee to migrate west between 1817 and 1819. In 1821, after many years of effort, Sequoyah, a mixed-blood Cherokee, developed a Cherokee syllabary, which had the important result of extending literacy throughout the population. In 1835 gold was discovered in the Cherokee territory and White encroachments increased.

In that same year the Treaty of New Echota arranged for the sale of Cherokee lands to the U.S. government and the removal of the Cherokee to Indian Territory (Oklahoma) and Kansas. As the treaty was opposed by most Cherokee, the removal had to be carried out by force involving seven thousand federal troops. Over four thousand Cherokee, intermarried Whites, and African-

In 1821, Sequoyah, a mixed-blood Cherokee, developed a Cherokee syllabary, which had the important result of extending literacy throughout the population.

Over four thousand people died as a result of the forced removal of the Cherokee form tribal lands in 1935.

American slaves died en route or as a result of the removal. A band of several hundred Cherokee escaped the roundup and in 1842 were granted permission to remain on land set aside for them in North Carolina. The descendants of these two groups make up the present-day Western (Oklahoma) and Eastern (North Carolina) Cherokee.

Settlements

In aboriginal and early-contact times settlements were clustered near streams and rivers. Because of the rugged topography, they were often separated by considerable distances but were linked by intricate trade networks. Up to sixty towns existed, with populations of 55 to 600, but averaging 250–300 persons. Larger towns were built around a council house and a field for stickball and served as economic, social, and religious centers for smaller surrounding towns. Warfare, disease, and trade attending European contact undermined the nucleated settlement pattern and resulted in more linear, dispersed settlements.

Since the removal, mixed-blood Cherokee in Oklahoma have tended to settle on rich bottomlands near railroad centers while full-bloods have tended to settle in small isolated villages in the Ozark foothills. At the Qualla Boundary Reservation in North Carolina, the Cherokee population is concentrated in four bottomland areas comprising five townships. Each township has a small center, but most families live on isolated farmsteads on the edges of the bottomlands and along creeks and streams. The community of Cherokee in the Yellow Hill township is the site of numerous tourist attractions, shops, and restaurants. The aboriginal Cherokee house was of wattle-and-daub construction, oval or oblong, with a single door, no windows, and a pitched roof of thatch, reeds, or poles. Today, much Cherokee wood-frame housing is substandard, although improvements have been made recently.

Economy

SUBSISTENCE AND COMMERCIAL ACTIVITIES.
The Cherokee were horticulturalists, raising cereal and vegetable crops on a swidden basis and supplementing their subsistence through hunting, fishing, and collecting. The primary cultigen was maize and the most important game animal the white-tailed deer. Contact with Europeans resulted in the addition of new grains, vegetables, and domesticated animals. During the seventeenth century the European fur trade became a central factor in the Cherokee economy.

But the trade declined in the mid-eighteenth century, and the Cherokee adopted more intensive forms of agriculture and animal husbandry.

Prior to contact each Cherokee town maintained a mutual aid society known as the gadu:gi (later known as the Free Labor Company), which coordinated agricultural activities. After contact the cooperative functions of the gadu:gi expanded to include relief to those in need of emergency assistance. In North Carolina the gadu:gi remained a permanent organization until very recent times, while in Oklahoma it became a temporary group constituted to perform specific tasks.

Today the majority of the Eastern Cherokee continue general subsistence farming, with tobacco, garden crops, and beef occasionally raised for cash. At Qualla Boundary, tourism provides income through retail shops, restaurants, motels, museums, and exhibitions; however, these are not sufficient to provide all families with adequate incomes. Other income is derived from logging, seasonal wage labor, and government assistance. Among the Western Cherokee there is little industry, tourist or otherwise, and they often rent their land to White ranchers rather than farm it themselves. Cash income is from ranching and other wage labor, government work projects, and government assistance.

INDUSTRIAL ARTS.
Aboriginal crafts included metalworking, potting, soapstone carving, and basket weaving. Copper, then brass, then silver were used by Cherokee metalsmiths. Today basket weaving persists among Cherokee women at Qualla Boundary, where the products are sold to tourists.

TRADE.
A considerable precontact trade was maintained with neighboring Indian groups. Trade with Europeans in the seventeenth century was indirect and inconsequential, but by the early eighteenth century it had become an integral part of the economy. Salt obtained by the Cherokee from saline streams and licks was an important trade item in both pre- and postcontact times.

DIVISION OF LABOR.
Prior to the mid-eighteenth century women did most of the farming, while men were responsible for hunting, fishing, and clearing fields for planting. Women also prepared food, made clothes, made pottery and baskets, and raised the children. Ritual and medicinal activities were carried out mainly by males. After contact, both men and women conducted trade with Europeans. The decline of hunting and the adoption of more intensive agriculture in the eighteenth century altered the traditional division of labor, and men replaced women in the

♦ **wattle-and-daub**
A method of house construction whereby a framework (wattle) of poles and twigs is covered (daubed) with mud and plaster.

fields and women's work was increasingly confined to the household. Today, at least among the Eastern Cherokee, most women continue to work in the home. Some, however, are employed in tourist services, crafts, factory work, and farm and domestic labor.

LAND TENURE. Aboriginally, individuals had the right to occupy, hunt, and cultivate the land with ownership vested in local clan sections. After contact the Cherokee were under constant pressure to sell their lands to Whites, and as a result in the early nineteenth century the Cherokee Nation adopted a system of property law, placing all Cherokee lands under tribal authority. In 1906, tribal land in Indian Territory was allotted to individuals by the U.S. government. In North Carolina after the removal the Cherokee were prohibited from owning land, and for a time all their lands were recorded under the name of their White benefactor, Will Thomas. Today, the federal government is the trustee of the Eastern Cherokee lands, with actual ownership vested in the Eastern Band itself.

Kinship

KIN GROUPS AND DESCENT. Cherokee society was divided into seven matrilineal, exogamous clans, or sibs. Within each town, clan sections formed corporate groups that held and allocated land, regulated marriage, and controlled conflict among local clan members. Age stratification within the clan section constituted the first level of local decision making. Clans rarely, if ever, acted as corporate groups on a tribewide basis. Since the time of contact, intermarriage with Whites and acculturation has gradually undermined the clan system. Among the Eastern Cherokee, clans are no longer meaningful social units except among the very elderly.

KINSHIP TERMINOLOGY. Traditional kinship terminology followed the Crow system.

Marriage and Family

MARRIAGE. In the traditional marriage system, members of the mother's and father's matrilineage were forbidden as marriage partners, while marriage to members of the father's father's and mother's father's matrilineage was permitted and even favored. Few modern Eastern Cherokee marriages conform to these rules. Marriages were usually monogamous, but polygyny was permitted and occasionally practiced. In the eighteenth century the marriage ceremony was an informal affair in which a man obtained the consent of the prospective bride and her mother before accompanying her to a previously prepared dwelling place. Matrilocal residence was the traditional norm. Divorce was common and could be affected easily by either party.

DOMESTIC UNIT. Until recently, small extended families were common. Among contemporary Cherokee the nuclear family tends to predominate. Owing to poverty and high rates of illegitimacy, however, three-generation households also are common.

INHERITANCE. Since the nineteenth century, property has usually passed to the person who took care of the owner in his or her last years. Since that person has often been the youngest son, ultimogeniture has prevailed by custom.

SOCIALIZATION. Generally speaking, children were and are raised permissively. Ostracism, ridicule, and the threat of external sanctioning agents—"boogers"—were and still are used to discipline and control children. Overt and direct expressions of hostility and aggression are discouraged. Parents, many of whom are themselves well educated, encourage their children to remain in high school and often to continue with postsecondary training.

Sociopolitical Organization

SOCIAL ORGANIZATION. In aboriginal and early-contact times age conferred status and the oldest, "beloved" men enjoyed the greatest prestige. Women occupied a position of equality with men, but as the traditional division of labor shifted during the eighteenth century their economic independence lessened and their influence and status diminished. Institutionalized slavery appeared in the form of African slaves before 1700 and became widespread in the nineteenth century. Intermarriage with Whites resulted in a class of mixed-blood Cherokee who, after the American Revolution, increasingly controlled power and wealth within the society. In the nineteenth century they formed a class of wealthy, educated, and acculturated planters set apart from full-blood Cherokee by language, religion, lifestyle, and values. This class division persists in contemporary Cherokee society.

POLITICAL ORGANIZATION. Prior to contact with Europeans each town was politically independent from the others and had two distinct governmental structures—a White, or peace, government and a Red, or war, government. During the course of the eighteenth century an overarching tribal government based on the traditional town model was created in response to European expansion. In 1827 a constitution was adopted creating a republican form of government modeled after that of the United States, which remained active until 1906 when it was abolished by the U.S. Congress. In 1948 the Cherokee Nation in Oklahoma was reestablished. The Eastern Cherokee incorporated as the Eastern Band of Cherokee Indians in 1889.

SOCIAL CONTROL. Eschewing face-to-face conflict, the Cherokee have employed gossip, ostracism, and social withdrawal as important forms of social control. Fear of divine retribution was a powerful form of social control in the past and remains so among some conservative Cherokee today. Conjuring or witchcraft declined in importance during the eighteenth century. In aboriginal and early-contact times serious crimes were adjudicated by the White government. Homicide often led to blood revenge by clan members. In 1898 the Cherokee judicial system was dissolved by the federal government and the group was placed under the jurisdiction of the U.S. federal courts.

CONFLICT. In the eighteenth century the Cherokee were divided mainly along lines of age over what the relationship to the European colonies should be. In addition, the introduction and gradual acceptance of the money economy and European values introduced an element of

aggression and competition between individuals and towns that previously was unknown in the society. Even more significant was the split over the removal to Indian Territory, first in 1817–1819 and then more seriously in 1838–1839. In general, mixed-bloods favored removal while full-bloods did not. This split broke out into civil war after arrival in Indian Territory and resurfaced during the American Civil War. Beginning in 1896 many full-bloods took part in the nativistic Nighthawk Keetoowah movement to resist the reallotment of tribal lands and mixed-blood support for reallotment. For several decades the Nighthawk movement exercised a powerful force among conservative full-blood Cherokee, but beginning about 1935 its influence waned, owing to internal divisions and the opposition of militant Christian Cherokee. Today the mixed-blood/full-blood division persists, and on occasion the hostility has erupted in violence.

Religion and Expressive Culture

RELIGIOUS BELIEFS. The aboriginal religion was zootheistic and guided by a deep faith in supernatural forces that linked human beings to all other living things. Evil was understood to be the result of a disharmony with nature. Beginning in the early nineteenth century Christian missionaries succeeded in driving native religious beliefs underground, and today the Baptist denomination predominates among Christian Cherokee in Oklahoma and North Carolina. The existence of a supreme being in the native religion is not clear; however, there were numerous animal, elemental, personal, and inanimate spirits. These spirits were believed to have created the world and to reside in seven successive tiers of heaven, on earth, and in the water, where they remain until the exercise of their powers is properly petitioned.

RELIGIOUS PRACTITIONERS. In aboriginal times priests received no special material considerations, although they did exercise considerable influence as a result of their divining and healing roles. In the nineteenth century Christian Cherokee pastors were an important factor in the conversion process.

CEREMONIES. The native ceremonial cycle consisted of a series of six festivals, the last three of which were held in quick succession in the autumn, simultaneously with important meetings of town councils. The Propitiation Festival, held ten days after the first new moon of autumn and the Great New Moon Feast, was the most important and was devoted to ritually eliminating ill will

**CHEROKEE
BASKETMAKER**

*The early craft of basket weaving persists today for many Cherokee women. Oconaluftee, North Carolina, USA.
(Richard A. Cook/Corbis)*

among villagers and promoting local unity. The six festivals have been collapsed into a single Green Corn Festival.

ARTS. Singing was an important part of aboriginal and postcontact ceremonial life. For religious and other purposes texts are sung in Cherokee, but tunes and the manner of harmonizing are derived from nonnative sources.

MEDICINE. In the aboriginal culture disease was understood to be the product of spiritual malevolence brought on by violating taboos. Curing techniques consisted of herbal medicines, ritual purifications, and the enlistment of spirit helpers to drive out the malevolent forces. Western clinical medicine is now the treatment approach, although native conjurors still persist.

DEATH AND AFTERLIFE. Native beliefs ascribed death, like disease, to evil spirits and witches. Death was feared and so, too, were the evil spirits connected with death. There was also a belief in an afterworld, or "nightworld," to which the ghosts or souls of the deceased desired to go. A successful journey to the nightworld, however, depended on one's actions in life on earth. Funeral ceremonies had great religious significance, and among Eastern Cherokee the funeral is the most important life cycle ritual.

Bibliography

Gearing, Frederick O. (1962). *Priests and Warriors: Social Structures for Cherokee Politics in the Eighteenth Century.* American Anthropological Association, Memoir 93. Menasha, Wis.

Gulick, John (1973). *Cherokees at the Crossroads.* Chapel Hill: University of North Carolina Institute for Research in the Social Sciences.

King, Duane H., ed. (1979). *The Cherokee Indian Nation: A Troubled History.* Knoxville: University of Tennessee Press.

—GERALD REID

CHEYENNE

Ethnonyms: Sha-hi'ye-la, Itasi'na, Chien, Schian, Chayenne, Shyenne

Orientation

IDENTIFICATION. The name "Cheyenne" derives from the Dakota word sha-hi'ye-la, meaning "red talkers" or "people of an alien speech." The Cheyenne refer to themselves as "Tsetsehese-staestse" (People), although today the Northern Cheyenne also are known as the "Notame-ohmese-heetse" (Northern-eaters) and the Southern Cheyenne are called "Heevaha-tane" (Rope-people).

LOCATION. Throughout the late-eighteenth and mid-nineteenth centuries, the Cheyenne occupied a region that extended from the Yellowstone River, Montana, to the upper Arkansas River in present-day Colorado and Kansas. In all, their territory extended over 500,000 square miles, covering nearly eight states. The high plains is characterized by shortgrass vegetation, occasionally interrupted by riparian forests and shrubs along the more perennial waterways. Evergreen stands predominate at higher elevations. The climate is one of hot summers and harsh, cold winters, with an average annual precipitation of ten to fourteen inches. Although the region was not conducive to horticulture, it did support a large bison population.

DEMOGRAPHY. At contact (c. 1780) population estimates indicate that there were about 3,500 Cheyenne. Despite four known major epidemics and a number of massacres inflicted by the U.S. military forces, the 1888 Cheyenne reservation population was 3,497. Of that number, 2,096 were Southern Cheyenne living in Indian Territory (now Oklahoma) and 1,401 were Northern Cheyenne residing on the Tongue River Reservation, Montana, and the Pine Ridge Reservation, South Dakota. In 1989, the Northern Cheyenne numbered 5,716. An exact Southern Cheyenne population figure is more difficult to obtain. Currently 9,525 Southern Cheyenne and Arapaho are enrolled at Concho Agency; at least 50 percent identify themselves as Southern Cheyenne.

LINGUISTIC AFFILIATION. The Cheyenne language is one of five main Algonkian languages spoken on the Great Plains. In the postcontact period, there were at least two major Cheyenne dialects, Tse-tsehese-staestse and So'taa'e, the latter spoken by a tribe incorporated into the Cheyenne. Today only Tse-tsehese-staetse is spoken, but So'taa'e words have been adopted into the language.

History and Cultural Relations

Cheyenne history and cultural relations are linked to their shifting adaptations from a woodland people to equestrian nomads on the Great Plains. Although the Cheyenne have never been associated with a specific archaeological focus, oral tradition and ethnohistorical evidence confirm that the protohistoric Cheyenne occupied the woodland-prairie country of the upper Mississippi Valley, where they inhabited semisedentary villages located along lakes and rivers. As early as 1680,

Cheyenne history and cultural relations are linked to their shifting adaptations from a woodland people to equestrian nomads on the Great Plains.

♦ **earthlodge**
A large, dome-shaped, partly underground dwelling constructed on a frame of posts and beams, thatched with bundled grass, branches, mats, and so on, and covered with earth.

the Cheyenne initiated contact with the French in an attempt to establish trade relations. Their desire for trade provoked attacks from the Sioux and Chippewa, who were competing for domination. Outnumbered and possessing no firearms, the Cheyenne were forced westward into the Minnesota Valley and eventually onto the northeastern plains. On the plains, the Cheyenne established at least twelve fortified earthlodge villages along the Sheyenne and Missouri rivers. Allied with the Mandan and Arikara, they continued to war with the Chippewa, Assiniboin, and expanding Sioux. During this period, the Cheyenne incorporated the So'taa'e, intermarried Arikara, and the Moiseyu, a Siouan group from Minnesota. Although forced out of the Great Lakes fur market, the Cheyenne continued to trade, serving as middlemen between more westwardly nomadic Plains groups and the Missouri River village people. Between 1742 and 1770, the Cheyenne acquired horses and became equestrian nomads. By 1820, the Cheyenne had stabilized their geographical and political position in the Black Hills region, allying themselves with the Arapaho and Oglala. From here, the tribe expanded in a southwesterly direction. Their separation into northern and southern divisions began as early as 1790 and was accelerated in the 1830s by the establishment of Bent's Fort on the Arkansas River and Fort William on the North Platte River.

Formal relations with the U.S. government was marked by the signing of the 1825 Friendship Treaty and White-Cheyenne relations were generally amicable until the 1840s. During this decade, the Cheyenne witnessed a flood of Whites migrating along the Oregon Trail and the destruction of their environment and bison herds; they also contracted infectious diseases at this time. The Cheyenne and their allies responded by conducting a series of minor raids. To end Indian-Indian and Indian-White hostilities, the U.S. government negotiated the Treaty of 1851, making the division between the Northern and Southern Cheyenne permanent. The reduction of their land base, the continuing invasion of Whites, and the construction of forts prompted the Cheyenne to fight. For the next twenty-five years, they waged war against the U.S. military and White settlers; the Southern Cheyenne surrendered in 1875 and Northern Cheyenne resistance ended in 1879. With the Southern Cheyenne settled on their reservation, the U.S. government attempted to reconsolidate the tribe by forcibly removing the Northern Cheyenne to Indian Territory. Culturally alienated, starving,

and infected with dysentery, measles, and malaria, 257 Northern Cheyenne broke out and avoided capture until crossing the North Platte River. There they divided into two bands, both of which were eventually captured, with the remnants allowed to relocate in 1881 from Indian Territory to Pine Ridge Agency. In 1884, the Tongue River Reservation was established by executive order in southeastern Montana and all the Northern Cheyenne were reunited. In 1892 the Southern Cheyenne-Arapaho Reservation was dissolved through allotment. The Northern Cheyenne Reservation was allotted in 1932, although the land was never opened to White homesteading, thus preserving the integrity of the reservation. Presently, both tribes continue to struggle to establish the legal and cultural rights they have lost over the centuries.

Settlements

For most of the year, the ten Cheyenne bands traveled independently throughout their territory. Camping locations were usually near the confluence of two waterways, near adequate game, wood, and grazing land for the horses. During the early summer, the bands congregated to conduct tribal ceremonies. Afterwards, the bands dispersed to their territories, settling in wooded areas along waterways for winter. After being placed on their reservations the Cheyenne continued to settle along waterways, although eventually communities were formed near government buildings or White towns. Aboriginal Cheyenne housing on the plains was a three-pole tipi replaced during the reservation period by cabins. Today, most Cheyenne live in governmental housing, mobile homes, or converted older reservation structures. Some of the homes are substandard, although improvements have been made since the 1960s.

Economy

SUBSISTENCE AND COMMERCIAL ACTIVITIES. Although casual gardening continued among some bands as late as 1850, the primary focus was the bison. Besides meat, the bison provided materials for shelter, clothing, and manufactured goods and was a trade item. Of over forty food plants gathered, the most important were the Indian turnip, chokecherries, and plums. European contact resulted in the adoption of trade foods into the Cheyenne diet. Coffee, sugar, bacon, and bleached flour became important commodities, especially during the dramatic decline of the bison. Cheyenne involvement in the nineteenth-century bison robe trade resulted in a further dependency on European goods. On reservations, rations, gardening, and marginal wage labor became the mainstay of the Cheyenne economy. Today the majority of the Southern and Northern Cheyenne income is derived through the federal government. Among the Northern Cheyenne, tribal enterprises such as logging, ranching, growing alfalfa, seasonal wage labor, and governmental assistance provide most of their income. The Southern Cheyenne are involved in wheat raising, oil exploitation, some ranching, and governmental work projects. Both tribes continue to be underemployed and dependent on governmental support. The most important domesticated animal was the horse, which was used for transportation, warfare, and hunting, and became a source of wealth in Cheyenne society.

INDUSTRIAL ARTS. Cheyenne skills included leatherworking, woodworking, quillworking, featherworking, and stone carving. After direct trade with Europeans, metal objects, glass beads, cloth, and other items to decorate replaced articles of native manufacture. Today the Cheyenne continue to make objects for personal use, powwows, ceremonial purposes, and sale to non-Indians.

TRADE. The extent of precontact trade is not fully known, but by the historical period the Cheyenne were involved in a complex trading network. As middlemen, the Cheyenne traded horses, dried bison meat, pemmican, dehydrated *pomme blanche*, and decorated robes, shirts, and leather pouches with the Missouri River tribes. In exchange, the Cheyenne obtained European items such as guns, powder, and foodstuffs as well as native maize and tobacco. By 1830, they had become involved in the bison robe trade with Europeans, which ended in the 1880s, leading to complete economic dependency on the U.S. government.

DIVISION OF LABOR. The division of labor was based on age and sex. Men's work included hunting, raiding, ceremonial activities, and manufacturing all items associated with these pursuits. Young boys and elder men in the household were often in charge of caring for the horse herd. Women's tasks were associated with domestic activities: gathering food and fuel, caring for children, butchering meat, making pemmican, erecting and dismantling the lodge, manufacturing all household objects, and preparing bison hides for use or trade. Young girls assisted their mothers with these tasks, and elder women relieved the mother of child-care duties. During the bison hide trade period, men's and women's labor focused on acquisition and production of hides.

During the reservation period, the division of labor was altered radically with women's work increasingly devalued and confined to the household. Since World War II, Cheyenne men and women have been employed in a variety of occupations ranging from trapping to law.

LAND TENURE. Aboriginally, any Cheyenne had the right to resources within their territory. Although portions of their territory were contested by other Plains Indians, the Cheyenne claimed and actively defended the region from the Yellowstone River to the Arkansas River. Within this territory, each band occupied and utilized a favored location, usually near major rivers.

Kinship

KIN GROUPS AND DESCENT. Descent was bilateral. Although clans probably existed when the Cheyenne resided in sedentary earthlodge villages during the 1700s, clans no longer existed after they became equestrian nomads.

KINSHIP TERMINOLOGY. Prior to the alteration of the kinship system during the reservation period, terminology followed the Hawaiian system, emphasizing horizontal classification along generational levels.

Marriage and Family

MARRIAGE. Marriage was a formal matter. Premarital sex was strictly prohibited and a girl's virginity was carefully guarded by her family. Because a young man postponed marriage until he had horses and a respectable war record, courtship often lasted for several years. The most respectable marriages were arranged between families, although elopement took place. Until the pattern was interrupted by epidemic disease and warfare, marriage was forbidden to a relative of any degree. Most marriages were monogamous, but polygyny was permitted, often of the sororal type, with the levirate also practiced. Today there is still concern about the degree of relatedness between a couple wanting to marry. Traditionally, postmarital residence was uxorilocal. With the incorporation of the Dog Soldiers into the tribal circle, residence shifted in that portion of Cheyenne society to patrilocality, resulting in two residence patterns after 1860. Divorce could be initiated by either the husband or wife for mistreatment, adultery, or other marital transgressions. A man could publicly disgrace his wife by "throwing her away" at a public gathering.

DOMESTIC UNIT. The primary unit of cooperation and subsistence was the *vestoz*, a residential extended family of related women and

Premarital sex was strictly prohibited by the Cheyenne and a girl's virginity was carefully guarded by her family.

their conjugal families. Although the nuclear family is the predominant pattern today, extended families still exist, often as an adaptation to the high unemployment rates, poverty, illegitimacy, and other socioeconomic factors associated with social disadvantage.

INHERITANCE. Some of a man's personal possessions were buried with him, but all the remaining property was given to nonrelatives. The widow and her children retained nothing. At funerals today, give-aways are still held before the body is buried and one full year after the death. Contemporary inheritance patterns are defined by legal stipulation and kinship.

SOCIALIZATION. Children were generally raised permissively. Social ideals were taught through advice, counsel, and demonstration. Although physical punishment was rarely used, gossip, teasing, and sometimes ostracism acted as negative sanctions if the child misbehaved. Many of these mechanisms are used today, but physical punishment is also now used to correct undesirable behavior.

Sociopolitical Organization

SOCIAL ORGANIZATION. Although kinship was the foundation of Cheyenne society, there coexisted four types of social organization: the

RELIGION AND EXPRESSIVE CULTURE

Religious Beliefs

The Cheyenne world was a dynamic, operative system with interrelated components. Within the Cheyenne universe (*Hestanov*), the world was divided into seven major levels. Spirit-beings (*maiyun*) reside in this universe and their sacredness is relative to their relationship to Ma'heo'o, the creator of all physical and spiritual life in Hestanov. These levels are intersected by the Maiheyuno, a personal spirit residing at each of the cardinal directions. Various animals, birds, and plants are manifestations of these spirit-beings. In Cheyenne religious expression, aspects of these spirit-beings or the spirit-beings themselves are entwined symbolically with plant and animal forms portrayed in Cheyenne ceremonies. Many Cheyenne today view the world's ecological crisis as an end to Hestanov. Christian missionary activity has been continuous among the Cheyenne for a century, especially the Mennonites and Catholics. Today there is a variety of religious beliefs and expressions including Christianity and the American Indian church, although Sacred Arrows (*Mahuts*) and the Medicine Hat (*Isiwun*) remain the most venerated sacred objects.

Religious Practitioners

Aside from the Keepers of Mahuts and Isiwun and the arrow priests, there were numerous Cheyenne shamans and doctors, each possessing a particular religious or healing power.

Ceremonies

There were four major religious ceremonies: the renewal of Mahuts, the *Hoxehe-voho-mo'ehestotse* (New Life Lodge or Sun Dance), the *Massaum* (Animal Dance), and Isiwun. Mahuts was given to the Cheyenne by their cultural hero, Mutsoyef (Sweet Medicine). The four Sacred Arrows included two "Man Arrows" for warfare and two "Bison Arrows" for hunting. The Arrows were renewed every few years, unless a murder took place or a pledger needed their blessing. Presently, the renewal of the Mahuts, the New Life Lodge, and ceremonies surrounding Isiwun are still performed.

Arts

Aboriginal arts featured a particular musical style, songs, and an artistic tradition, all important parts of Cheyenne social and ceremonial life. The Cheyenne artistic tradition reflected not only the sacred but the socioeconomic pursuits of men and women. Presently, there are a number of prominent Cheyenne artists, and Cheyenne songs are still performed at various functions.

Medicine

Disease arose from both natural and supernatural causes. Curing techniques involved the use of herbal and root remedies, ritual purification, the sweat lodge, smoking, prayer, and sometimes surgery. Both men and women were healers. Treatment of sickness was designed to restore the patient not only biologically but spiritually as well. Presently, most Cheyenne use Western clinical medicine to cure afflictions, but native healers are still used by many people.

Death and Afterlife

Cheyenne believed that death, like disease, could have a natural or spiritual causation. As a cultural phenomenon, death was a spiritual process. At birth, Ma'heo'o provided the child with the "gift of breath/power" (*omotome*) and "spiritual potential" (*mahta'sooma*). These two gifts are developed through life. As a person ages, the process is reversed. Mahta'sooma leaves the body, resulting in behavior and cognitive changes. Next omotome departs, bringing on death. The spirit of the deceased then travels up the long fork of the Milky Way to *Seana*, the camp of the dead. If the dead individual was an outcast, died in a violent accident or by suicide, or was an unredeemed sinner, he or she would travel the "suicide road," the short fork of the Milky Way. Others would return to earth as malevolent spirits. The concern for following the "good life," and so to have a "good death," is still prevalent among the Cheyenne.

vestoz (a camp), the *manhastoz* (a bunch), the *notxestoz* (military society), and the *manhao* (a sacred band). The manhastoz was structurally similar to the vestoz, but was larger and usually organized around a chief's household; it was organized for trade rather than strictly subsistence pursuits. The manhao, the largest traditional Cheyenne social unit, was composed of numerous vestoz and manhastoz led by council chiefs. Most important, these ten "sacred bands" were recognized as having a camping position in the Cheyenne tribal circle when they came together to conduct ceremonies. The 1849 cholera and 1850–1851 smallpox epidemics and White expansion resulted in three "sacred bands" becoming extinct and others being depopulated. In response, a notxestoz, the Dog Soldier Military Society, merged with the remnant Mas'kota band and was added to the Cheyenne tribal circle. Aside from kin-based groups, there were various sodalities for men and women. The most famous male sodality was the Contraries; other male sodalities included the Buffalo Men and Horse Men. Women's sodalities focused on skill and achievement in manufactured articles, the most important being the Quillwork Society. In modern times, the War Mothers Association was organized to honor Cheyenne veterans.

POLITICAL ORGANIZATION. Cheyenne political organization was unique among Plains equestrian peoples. They maintained a Council of Forty-four, leaders who made decisions for the entire tribe consisting forty headsmen (four from each of the ten bands) and four councilmen known as the old man chiefs. They were considered the wisest men and were often the tribal religious authorities. Each council member had equal authority and served for ten years. The Council of Forty-four met during the summer when the tribe congregated for ceremonies and decided on future tribal movements, relations with other tribes, the schedule of tribal ceremonies, and important internal tribal matters. To carry out their decisions, the Council of Forty-four relied upon the six Cheyenne military societies. Membership in any of the military societies was open to all young men, although most boys joined their father's society. In addition, each society selected several young women, known for their chastity and virtue, who served as assistants in society ceremonial functions.

SOCIAL CONTROL. The mechanisms of social control ranged from public ridicule, social withdrawal, songs, and ostracism to physical punishment carried out by the military societies.

Such mechanisms were replaced during the reservation period. After allotment and Oklahoma statehood in 1906, the Southern Cheyenne came under the legal jurisdiction of state law enforcement agencies. Since that time, the Southern Cheyenne, like the Northern Cheyenne, have instituted a tribal police force and tribal court system.

CONFLICT. Forced onto the plains through conflict, the Cheyenne, between 1790 and 1850, warred against the Crow, Shoshone, Pawnee, and numerous other tribes to establish hunting territories, to acquire new land, and to maintain an advantageous position in their trade relations with other tribes and Europeans. Other reasons for going to war were more individualistic, usually to acquire horses, take captives, or gain revenge. After 1850, the nature of warfare changed and the growing conflict with Whites became a fight for survival.

Bibliography

Grinnell, George Bird (1923). *The Cheyenne Indians: Their History and Ways of Life.* 2 vols. New Haven: Yale University Press.

Moore, John H. (1987). *The Cheyenne Nation: A Social and Demographic History.* Norman: University of Oklahoma Press.

Schlesier, Karl H. (1987). *The Wolves of Heaven: Cheyenne Shamanism, Ceremonies, and Prehistoric Origins.* Norman: University of Oklahoma Press.

Weist, Tom (1977). *A History of the Cheyenne People.* Billings: Montana Council for Indian Education.

—GREGORY R. CAMPBELL

CHOCTAW

Ethnonyms: Chacktaws, Chaquita, Chat-Kas, Tchatakes, Tchiactas

Orientation

IDENTIFICATION. The Choctaw are an American Indian group who lived aboriginally in Mississippi. "Chahta," the Choctaw's name for themselves, is probably a term of native origin derived from *Hacha Hatak*, "River People."

LOCATION. In the eighteenth century, the Choctaw population was centered in central and southern Mississippi. Most Choctaw now live in Oklahoma and Mississippi.

DEMOGRAPHY. Historically, the Choctaw were one of the largest tribes in the Southeast. In spite of major population losses through warfare

Choctaw

The Treaty of Fort Adams in 1801 had begun a pattern of progressive loss of Choctaw land, which resulted in removal thirty years later.

and disease in the early historical period, the population in 1831 was 19,554. In 1980, there were 6,000 Choctaw in Mississippi and 10,000 in Oklahoma. Over 100,000 people in Oklahoma claim some Choctaw ancestry, however. Small numbers of Choctaw have migrated to urban areas in Texas, California, and Illinois.

LINGUISTIC AFFILIATION. The Choctaw language belongs to the Muskogean family, which also includes Creek and Chickasaw.

History and Cultural Relations

Choctaw origin legends describe a migration of the Choctaw and Chickasaw from farther west, but there is no known archaeological evidence for this. Native groups bordering the Choctaw territory at the time of European contact included the Creek east of the Tombigbee River, the Chickasaw in northern Mississippi, and the Natchez to the west on the Mississippi River. Along the Gulf Coast were closely related Choctaw-speaking tribes: the Pascagoula, the Acolapissa, and the Bayogoula. Choctaw relations with other major tribes were characterized by customary warfare associated with the receiving of young males into adulthood.

The first written account of the Choctaw is in the chronicles of the Hernando de Soto expedition in 1540. Permanent European contact began with French settlements on the Gulf Coast in 1699. The Choctaw were rapidly plunged into a complicated colonial rivalry as European powers sought to utilize Indian allies to carry out their territorial designs and to profit from the trade in guns, deerskins, and slaves. The Choctaw allied with the French operating from New Orleans in efforts to get European goods as well as guns to protect themselves from the English and their allies. With the ending of colonial rivalry and the establishment of the American nation, warfare was curtailed.

The Choctaw joined with the United States in the War of 1812 against their traditional enemies, the Creeks, and the British. But the Treaty of Fort Adams in 1801 had begun a pattern of progressive loss of Choctaw land, which resulted in removal thirty years later. In each treaty, the Choctaw were forced to cede more land and more prerogatives to the United States. Choctaw leaders such as Pushmataha were aware of the threat imposed by the growing number of White settlers in the Southeast and consciously decided to adopt White ways as a means of survival. Missionaries established schools in response to a Choctaw request. With the spread of literacy, the Choctaw

adopted formal written rules passed in district councils in the place of customary law. But these changes did not affect the demand for Indian removal that resulted in the Treaty of Dancing Rabbit Creek in 1831 requiring the removal of the Choctaw to Oklahoma.

Under this treaty, Choctaws could elect to remain in Mississippi with individually owned lands, but when large numbers attempted to use this provision, the treaty agent deliberately failed to record their claims. In the coming years, the remaining Choctaw were robbed of their possessions, and most eventually were forced to go to Oklahoma. Some Choctaw remained as subsistence farmers on unoccupied marginal lands in east central Mississippi. The descendants of these two groups compose the current Oklahoma and Mississippi Choctaw populations.

Settlements

The basic Choctaw social unit was the town, usually located along tributaries of major rivers. Approximately ninety towns were divided into three major districts clustered in the upper reaches of the Pearl River, the western tributaries of the Tombigbee River, and the Chickasawhay River in southern Mississippi. Settlements ranged from fifty to five hundred people. Larger towns were fortified and had a physical center including a council house and field for stickball. These larger towns served as social, economic, and religious centers for surrounding settlements. With the end of colonial warfare, the population dispersed from the towns and from the centers of the districts. Following removal to Oklahoma, the more acculturated mixed-blood Choctaw settled in the rich bottomlands, while the more traditional Choctaw settled in isolated communities in hill country. The Mississippi Choctaw remained on marginal land protected by hills and swamps. The purchase of lands for the current Mississippi Choctaw Reservation centered on lands where Choctaw were located, resulting in a dispersed pattern of six major reservation communities. In Oklahoma, the Choctaw are concentrated in what was the old Choctaw Nation in southeastern Oklahoma. Here traditional Choctaw rural communities still exist on more marginal lands.

The aboriginal Choctaw house was of wattle-and-daub construction, oval or square, with a single door, no windows, and a steeply sloping roof of thatch. This was usually accompanied by one or more open roofed structures, referred to as summer houses, and by granaries. In this century, most rural Choctaw have lived in poorly constructed frame houses, but public housing programs have made great improvements.

Economy

SUBSISTENCE AND COMMERCIAL ACTIVITIES. In the latter half of the eighteenth century the Choctaw were among the most accomplished farmers in the Southeast, but this was only an intensification of the basic Southeastern pattern of maize, beans, and squash cultivation supplemented by hunting, fishing, and collecting. The arrival of Europeans brought additional vegetables, cattle, horses, and cotton. During the eighteenth century the trade in deer skins resulted in first an expansion of hunting and then an increase in agriculture and cattle as the deer population declined. In the nineteenth and early twentieth centuries, rural Choctaw remained subsistence farmers, often in debt to the cotton sharecropping system. Agriculture was supplemented by work in forestry and agricultural day labor. In the 1970s and 1980s, the Mississippi Choctaw successfully established tribal industries including construction and electronic component and greeting card assembly. Lacking a reservation land base, the Oklahoma Choctaw have been less successful in establishing economic enterprises and are largely dependent on employment in forestry, seasonal wage work, and governmental assistance.

INDUSTRIAL ARTS. Aboriginal crafts included pottery, carving of wood, stone, and shell, and basket and textile weaving. Today basket weaving continues among the Choctaw, but the number of skilled craftspeople is declining because of limited markets. Making traditional nineteenth-century Choctaw clothing to wear at special events remains important.

TRADE. The Choctaw participated in the complex of aboriginal trade linking the shell of the coastal areas with stone and related products of the interior. Competition over the trade for deerskins and guns was a major factor in eighteenth-century Choctaw affairs. By the nineteenth century, the replacement of Indians by African slaves and the decline in deer led to an expansion of peaceful trade in agricultural products and cattle.

DIVISION OF LABOR. Aboriginally, women and children cared for the crops, while the men cleared fields and helped with planting and harvesting. Women prepared food, made clothes, pottery, and baskets, and cared for the children. Men hunted, built houses, and performed ritual activities. Both women and men practiced medicine. Men became more involved in agriculture with the use of domesticated animals for cultivating crops, but subsistence farming involved both men and women in major shared activities. With the rise of an industrial economy, men and women were able to gain employment outside the home.

LAND TENURE. Aboriginally, individual ownership was limited to use rights for homesites and lands under cultivation or improvement. Although men cleared land and built houses, these were the property of the wife and her female descendants as long as the land and house were being utilized. Those Choctaw remaining after removal had to register land in the name of the male head of household, but most of these land titles were quickly lost, leaving the Mississippi Choctaw largely without land until the establishment of the Choctaw Agency in 1918. The reservation is held by the federal government as trustee for the Mississippi Choctaw. Individual homesites are allocated by the Tribal Council. In the Choctaw Nation in Oklahoma, the traditional land use patterns were lost with the abolishment of the Choctaw Nation and allocation of Choctaw lands to individuals by the U.S. government. Most of this land soon passed to White ownership leaving the Oklahoma Choctaw without a reservation land base.

Kinship

KIN GROUPS AND DESCENT. Choctaw society was divided into two matrilineal exogamous moieties and six matrilineal clans. The remaining kinship unit was the locality group similar to the "house names" of the Chickasaw. Members of different clans lived together in the same town. But since inheritance rules followed the female line, it is probable that residency was matrilocal. With the disruption of removal and increasing White contact, the clan system was undermined, and matrilineality was largely replaced by patrilineality.

KINSHIP TERMINOLOGY. Traditional terminology followed the Crow system.

Marriage and Family

MARRIAGE. In the traditional marriage system, exogamy applied to the matrilineally based moieties. Marriages were usually monogamous, but polygyny was permitted. Marriage required the consent of the bride and her mother, and involved a ceremony involving members of both kinship groups. Divorce was common and could be obtained easily by either party.

DOMESTIC UNIT. Until this century extended families were common. While the nuclear family predominates, three-generation families often occur because of poverty and illegitimacy.

Choctaw

TRADITIONAL DANCE

A Choctaw woman performs a traditional dance for tourists in Phoenix. Currently, the Choctaw live in Oklahoma and Mississippi. Phoenix, Arizona, USA. (Buddy Mays/Corbis)

♦ **moiety**
A form of social organization in which an entire cultural group is made up of two social groups. Each moiety is often composed of a number of interrelated clans, sibs, or phratries.

INHERITANCE. Traditionally, all property except individual personal property passed through the female line. After the abolishment of Choctaw governments in Mississippi in 1830 and Oklahoma in 1906, patrilineal patterns of inheritance came to dominate.

SOCIALIZATION. Children are raised permissively with little direct punishment or direct orders. Ridicule, ignoring, and threat of external forces are used to discipline children. Direct aggression and hostility are discouraged. Parents encourage their children to continue their education, but such encouragement rarely is expressed directly or forcefully.

Sociopolitical Organization

SOCIAL ORGANIZATION. Choctaw social organization was based on two geographic units: the three districts and ninety towns, and three social units: moieties, clans, and locality groups. The relationships among these units are not completely clear. Early descriptions of the Choctaw show a confusion of names of geographic division, moieties, clans, and locality groups. At all levels, leadership was by older proven warriors called "beloved" men.

POLITICAL ORGANIZATION. The two matrilineal exogamous moieties of the Choctaw resemble the White, or peace, moiety and the Red, or war, moiety of other Southeastern tribes. The moiety and clan divisions were basic to kinship, ceremony, and political affairs. The heads of respective clans were responsible for adjudicating disputes. If the principal men in two divisions could not agree on the outcome of a case, it was referred to the leading men of the next larger divisions. Major officials within a town were selected from the leaders of the local groups within the town. Each town had a chief who, with his spokesman, supervised civil affairs and ceremonies. A war chief and his assistants led the men in time of war. The leadership pattern at the town level was duplicated at the district level. Early in the eighteenth century there may have been a central district and head chief for the tribe as a whole, but if so this had been abandoned by mid-century as a result of civil strife. The primary means of achieving consensus on major courses of action was the council. District councils were called by the district chief, and national councils were called by the three district chiefs acting jointly. In 1834, the Choctaw adopted a constitution for the Choctaw Nation in Oklahoma that was in force until the Choctaw Nation was abolished as a territorial government by the U.S. Congress in 1906. Nevertheless, the Choctaw Nation of Oklahoma continues to exist as a nonterritorial organization conducting activities and enterprises for the Choctaw there. The remaining Mississippi Choctaw did not adopt a constitution until 1945, but since then they have operated a tribal government with jurisdiction over the reservation lands in Mississippi.

SOCIAL CONTROL. Avoiding direct conflict, gossip, and avoidance have been important forms of social control. Witchcraft declined in importance in the eighteenth century. Tribal judicial authority was ended in Mississippi with removal, and in Oklahoma with the abolishment of the Choctaw Nation in 1906. But local judicial control under tribal courts was reestablished on the Mississippi Choctaw reservations in 1978 through a ruling of the U.S. Supreme Court.

CONFLICT. In the eighteenth century the Choctaw were divided over the proper relationship with European powers. In the nineteenth and twentieth centuries the expansion of the money economy resulted in conflicts over participation in the White-dominated market economy. While this social class discord involved conflict between mixed-bloods and full-bloods in Mississippi prior to removal and later in Oklahoma, the same dissension exists among the predominantly full-blood Mississippi Choctaw. For the latter a major external conflict arose from the acute racism of surrounding White society, which did not noticeably improve until the 1970s.

Religion and Expressive Culture

RELIGIOUS BELIEFS. Choctaw traditional religion was largely unrecorded before early nineteenth-century Christian missionaries influenced traditional practices. The Choctaw maintain a deep faith in supernatural forces linking humans and other living creatures. The importance of maintaining harmony with nature, fellowmen, and the supernatural world is central to Choctaw beliefs. The status of a supreme being in traditional Choctaw religion prior to the spread of Christianity is not clear. Their belief in numerous animal and anthropomorphic spirits who influenced human affairs continued, however, after the coming of Christianity. Today the Baptist denomination predominates among Choctaw in Oklahoma and Mississippi.

RELIGIOUS PRACTITIONERS. In aboriginal times, the influence of Choctaw prophets and doctors was considerable, and the belief in witchcraft was strong. By the nineteenth century, the influence of Christian Choctaw pastors was important in most Choctaw communities in Oklahoma and Mississippi.

CEREMONIES. Choctaw ceremonies were similar to other Southeastern tribes, with the Green Corn ceremonies being most important. Observers noted that the Choctaw held fewer religious ceremonies and more social dances than their neighbors. Both dances and ceremonies were closely associated with the very popular stickball game similar to lacrosse.

ARTS. In addition to their industrial arts, the Choctaw were well known for singing and storytelling. In addition to traditional music, the Choctaw enjoy country music.

MEDICINE. The Choctaw believe serious persistent illnesses to be a product of spiritual evil often associated with witchcraft. Curing consisted of herbal medicines, ritual purifications, and the enlistment of spirit helpers to drive out evil forces. Western clinical medicine is generally used today, but native Choctaw doctors are still consulted.

DEATH AND AFTERLIFE. Death, like disease, could be the result of either natural or supernatural forces. Choctaw believed in an afterworld to which spirits of the dead go and in which individuals experience reward or punishment depending on their life on earth. Funeral ceremonies are the most important life cycle ritual.

Bibliography

Debo, Angie (1934). *The Rise and Fall of the Choctaw Republic*. Norman: University of Oklahoma Press.

DeRosier, Arthur H., Jr. (1970). *The Removal of the Choctaw Indians*. Knoxville: University of Tennessee Press.

Kidwell, Clara S., and Charles Roberts (1981). *The Choctaws: A Critical Bibliography*. Bloomington: Indiana University Press.

Peterson, John H. (1979). "Three Efforts at Development among the Choctaws of Mississippi." In *The Southeastern Indians since Removal*, edited by Walter L. Williams, 142–153. Athens: University of Georgia Press.

Swanton, John R. (1931). *Source Material for the Social and Ceremonial Life of the Choctaw Indians*. U.S. Bureau of American Ethnology Bulletin no. 103. Washington, D.C.

—JOHN H. PETERSON

CREE, WESTERN WOODS

Ethnonyms: Ne•hiyawak, Ne•hi⁶awak (we speak the same language), Maskegan {from omaske•ko•wak (swamp or muskeg)}, Rocky Cree or Asini•ska •wi⁶iniwak (people of the place where there is an abundance of rock), Bush Cree or Saka•wiyini-wak (bush people)

Orientation

IDENTIFICATION. The Cree are a Subarctic group whose name is derived from the name of specific bands in the region between Lake Superior and Hudson Bay, known to the French, from Ojibwa, as "Kiristino," later shortened to "Cree." The meaning is unknown. The regional designations are those by which they know themselves.

LOCATION. Aboriginally the Western Woods Cree occupied the subarctic or boreal forest from Hudson and James bays westward to the Peace River in what is now Canada. This is the Precambrian or Canadian Shield, except for westernmost northern Alberta, with a mixed-wood boreal forest. The subarctic has long cold winters, during which temperatures may fall to −60° F or lower, and short moderately warm summers. "Freeze-up," the period during which the lakes, rivers, and streams freeze over, is a time of limited travel, and "break-up," or spring thaw, is the harbinger of summer. The severity of the subarctic climate makes its mark on the cultures, which are closely

The importance of maintaining harmony with nature, fellowmen, and the supernatural world is central to Choctaw beliefs.

The Cree are a Subarctic group originally located between Lake Superior and the Hudson Bay in what is now Canada.

tied to the environment. In only a few favored areas is horticulture even marginally possible.

DEMOGRAPHY. Reliable population estimates are for recent times only, and these figures include only those having legal status under the provisions of the Indian Act. Cree were seriously affected by great smallpox epidemics in 1781 and later and other European-introduced diseases to which they had no immunity. After World War I, influenza epidemics struck at various times and places across the subarctic. In 1970, there were approximately forty thousand Western Woods Cree with legal status and an unknown number of people of mixed Cree and European ancestry who were not legally classified as Indian.

LINGUISTIC AFFILIATION. The Cree language or dialect group is the northern variant of Central Algonkian, extending from the Montagnais-Naskapi of the Labrador Peninsula to the Rocky Mountains. Swampy Cree is the /n/dialect, Rocky Cree the /ˡ/ dialect, and Bush and Plains Cree speak /y/ dialects. An /r/ dialect was spoken south of Lake Athabasca until the late eighteenth century.

History and Cultural Relations

Historical traditions, linguistic evidence, and a growing amount of archaeological data confirm oral traditions that the Cree occupied the boreal forest from Hudson Bay to approximately the Peace River, with some protohistoric, probably seasonal expansion north of Lake Athabasca to the south shore of Great Slave Lake. In addition, there may have been some expansion into Beaver areas near Peace River. The Cree were bounded on the north by Athapaskan-speaking peoples including the Chipewyan, on the northwest by the Slavey, and on the west by the Beaver. To the south were Algonkian speakers, including Blackfeet, Piegan, Blood, Ojibwa, and Gros Ventre. Later, Siouan-speaking Assiniboin occupied part of the adjacent prairies. Until the early nineteenth century, relationships with Athapaskan-speaking groups and those Inuit near Hudson Bay were hostile. Warfare on the Plains periphery continued until the late nineteenth century.

Earliest contacts with Europeans were with the French near Lake Superior, beginning after 1640, and with the English at Hudson's Bay Company forts on Hudson and James bays after 1670. French exploration reached the Rocky Mountains by 1751, but ended after the cession of New France to the British in 1763. Thereafter, fur trade competition involved the Scots partnerships that became the Northwest Company out of Montreal. European exploration increased in the western hinterland of Hudson Bay, and trading posts were established by the competing fur companies. The sanguinary contest was resolved in 1821 by the merger of the two companies under the royal charter of the Hudson's Bay Company. The stabilization of the fur trade economy coincided with the end of intertribal warfare and endured until the impact of Canada's national policies in the mid and late twentieth century was felt. The gradual diminishing of the big-game and fur-bearing animal populations in the late eighteenth century led many Cree, Ojibwa, and Iroquois to move west. Intermarriage between fur traders and Cree led to a new population element, and from the Algonkian-French combination emerged the first and culturally distinctive Metis of the Red River.

In 1870 the Hudson's Bay Company ceded Rupert's Land to the new Dominion of Canada and the era of treaty making began. Through treaties, Canada attempted to end aboriginal title to Indian lands in return for reserves and small annuities, but a number of remote and isolated Bush Cree bands were overlooked. They neither entered into treaty relations nor surrendered their lands or sovereignty; the discovery and exploitation of oil on their lands was the source of much tension later. In recent times, many Cree have received varying degrees of education and have taken positions of leadership with their own people and in the larger Canadian society in the economic, political, and artistic arenas.

Settlements

Cree settlement patterns varied seasonally. As nomadic hunters, local bands were widely distributed among camps in their small autumn-winter-spring hunting ranges. The camps were located near water, usually on the windward side of a lake where they were protected from the cold winds. In summer they gathered in large regional bands, widely spread out along the leeward side of a favorable lake, where winds blew the voracious flies and mosquitoes into the bush. The basic shelter was a conical lodge, made of moose or caribou hides. It usually held an extended family, including several hunters. Animal hides were later replaced by canvas coverings, often made into ridge pole tents. About the end of the nineteenth century log cabin settlements developed, reflecting a higher degree of sedentism. In very recent times, federal and provincial governments have provided relatively modern houses, band offices, schools, and health facilities.

Economy

SUBSISTENCE AND COMMERCIAL ACTIVITIES. The Cree were basically hunters of big game, especially moose. In some areas, moose were supplemented by woodland caribou or barren-ground caribou (reindeer), and in others by white-tailed or Virginia deer. Bear were hunted and were also ritually important. Waterfowl, geese, and ducks were seasonally available in favored localities and flyways. Fish were apparently taken by women in the vicinity of the camps, but fishing by men did not become important until the decline of big-game populations, especially among the inhabitants of the Shield. Except for beaver, small fur-bearing animals became valuable only after the beginning of the European fur trade. The early trade introduced an increasing variety of goods. Metal items were of great value and included awls, axes, kettles, knives, muskets, fish-hooks, and other items, such as alcohol, beads, and mirrors. Blankets and cloth were introduced and became common. Cree bands became oriented to specific trading post-mission complexes. Low-cost trade goods had ended with the establishment of the Hudson's Bay Company monopoly, but toward the end of the century independent or "free traders" entered the region. In the mid-twentieth century commercial fishing was added to trapping as a basis of the cash economy.

By the mid-twentieth century, government programs induced subarctic peoples to concentrate in nucleated villages, for "administrative convenience," where the social institutions of Canadian industrial society were located. This increasingly brought an end to or weakened traditional socioeconomic adjustments and social control mechanisms, as well as many cultural institutions; it also increased unemployment, alcohol abuse, and other social problems, leading to greater dependence upon social welfare programs.

The only aboriginally domesticated animal was the dog, used in hunting or as a pack animal. By the end of the nineteenth century, dog teams were increasingly used for hauling toboggans. In some areas on the southern margins of the forest, horses came into use as pack animals, saddle horses, and draft animals, until they were replaced by motorized toboggans and pickup trucks.

INDUSTRIAL ARTS. The women were expert in preparing hides and making clothing, storage bags, lodge coverings, and other items. They also made baskets of birchbark and were potters until ceramics were replaced by metal. Men made weapons, showshoes, and birchbark canoes.

TRADE. There was probably trade between friendly Algonkian-speaking bands in prehistoric times, although the archaeological record is incomplete. With the establishment of trading centers on the Great Lakes and Hudson and James bays, some Cree were employed seasonally as "home-guard" Indians, hunting, fishing, and carrying messages between forts. Others became middlemen, bringing furs to the traders and trade goods to the Indians of the interior. This phase lasted until the trading companies expanded throughout the forest. Trade was so important that many bands were oriented toward specific posts, and some new bands came into existence around such places.

DIVISION OF LABOR. Men were responsible for hunting, trapping, fishing with nets, and traveling to the trading posts. Women were responsible for processing the game, preparing food and hides, making clothing and other items such as baskets, and caring for girls and small boys. Shamans were usually men, and they were concerned with ritual, while female shamans were often skilled in the use of herbal medicine. As a result of concentration in villages and the decline of traditional activities, this division of labor is disappearing and new patterns may be emerging.

Kinship

KIN GROUPS AND DESCENT. The Cree were typical subarctic band societies. The basic unit was a small hunting group or local band made up of one or more extended families and numbering about twenty-five persons. Unity was based on father-son relationships, or cooperation among brothers. The life expectancy of such a band was limited, as sons became adults and developed highly valued personal autonomy. The leader was usually the eldest active male hunter. These winter bands dispersed to hunt the widely distributed nomadic game and to trap relatively sedentary fur-bearing animals. They were usually known by the name of the best-known lake. Regional bands were the largest and most permanent groups, named after some feature of the area, usually a lake at which the people assembled during the summer or some common animal. The regional band was a bilateral grouping, made up of individuals, families, and hunting groups related by primary ties of consanguinity and affinity. They probably numbered from one hundred to two hundred or more. Descent was bilateral, with paternal and maternal relatives equally recognized.

KINSHIP TERMINOLOGY. The kinship system was bilateral, with bifurcate merging terminology in

Traditional Cree hunting society was egalitarian, with status distinctions based on relative age or abilities, as in hunting success, and on one's sex.

the first ascending generation, and Iroquois cousin terminology in one's own generation. Males and females were both differentiated on the basis of relative age and sex.

Marriage and Family

MARRIAGE. Marriages were arranged by parents between opposite-sex cross cousins. Marriage with parallel cousins, first or classificatory, was prohibited, as they were considered siblings. Arranged marriages ensured that the son-in-law would be a good hunter and provider. The levirate and sororate were practiced. Sororal polygyny was permitted and was an indication of the bride's parental approval. Bilateral cross-cousin marriage tended to establish or maintain cooperative relations between hunting groups, and the marriage of sibling pairs (two brothers to two sisters, or a brother and sister to a sister and brother) was considered exceptionally good. Some marriages were arranged with more distant groups, and with the advent of the fur trade, marriage of a daughter to an important fur trader was highly desirable. Following marriage, there was temporary matrilocal residence involving brideservice, until a child was born. The groom hunted for his parents-in-law and performed other services. After the birth of a child, residence was patrilocal. Divorce in the past was highly informal, but marriages are now performed in Roman Catholic or Anglican churches or by civil authorities and are subject to religious restraints and civil law.

DOMESTIC UNIT. The typical residential unit was an extended family, adjacent to another related unit.

INHERITANCE. Property was minimal and on the death of an individual was abandoned. Later, as material goods accumulated, survivors inherited appropriate items, but Canadian law is now applicable in the new village and urban context.

SOCIALIZATION. Children were raised permissively, and control and discipline were instilled gradually. Mothers trained their daughters, and boys were gradually taught hunting and trapping skills by their fathers. A boy usually killed his first big game at about the age of fourteen, marking him a true hunter. Girls were secluded at first menses and regularly thereafter. These traditional practices are rapidly disappearing. In recent generations, many Cree children were sent to boarding schools, but now elementary and secondary schools are commonly found on the reserves, and some children go on to university or other postsecondary institutions.

Sociopolitical Organization

SOCIAL ORGANIZATION. Traditional Cree hunting society was egalitarian, with status distinctions based on relative age or abilities, as in hunting success, and on one's sex. In summer, regional bands were normally the largest social aggregation and gathered at lake shores. At the end of the summer, regional bands dispersed into constituent hunting groups to exploit the seasonally dispersed game. The pattern was only slightly altered when the Cree began to hunt and trap fur-bearing animals, although the orientation was to a trading post center which later included a Christian mission. Intermarriage with Whites created no problems until treaties were made, after which the patrilineal provisions of the Indian Act of 1869 separated status Indians from nonstatus or Metis.

POLITICAL ORGANIZATION. Leadership was based on age, with the eldest active male the head of the extended family, and informal councils of elders reaching consensus on behalf of the members of regional bands. During the treaty-making period, chiefs and councilors had to be elected. At first these were respected elders, but with the increase in importance of government authorities, younger and more articulate men skilled in English became the formal chiefs, principally acting as foreign ministers or ambassadors. The elders remained extremely important in decision making, however.

SOCIAL CONTROL AND CONFLICT. The socialization of children and informal pressures were usually enough to prevent serious problems. Face-to-face conflict was always avoided, and interpersonal tensions were resolved by families leaving one local band and realigning with another. Belief in conjuring and witchcraft was also important, but there is little information available about specific practices. In the contemporary period, order is maintained by special constables or the Royal Canadian Mounted Police.

Religion and Expressive Culture

RELIGIOUS BELIEFS. Throughout history, Cree have always been reticent about sharing their beliefs with scoffing outsiders. Beliefs in a Great Spirit (*misi-manito*) or Evil Spirit (*macimanito• w*) may be of postcontact origin. The cannibal giant (*wi-htiko• w*) was greatly feared. The religion was animistic, and all living beings and some inanimate objects had spirits, or *manitowak*. Humans, through dreams and visions, were able to secure the help of powerful animal spirits in such

♦ **levirate**
The practice of requiring a man to marry his brother's widow.

♦ **sororate**
The practice of a woman being required to marry her deceased sister's husband.

activities as hunting, warfare, and love. Since all beings, including humans, had spirits, there was no concept of the supernatural.

RELIGIOUS PRACTITIONERS. All individuals had some power, but some men or women had more. There was no priesthood.

CEREMONIES. No ceremonies are recorded for the earliest periods, but in recent history tea dances of thanksgiving were held in spring and autumn. Feasts and dancing were held following successful hunts. Christian rituals are now common.

ARTS. There was a rich oral tradition that included both sacred and secular tales. *Wi• sake• ca• hk* was the hero of the popular trickster or transformer tales. In the past, the face and body were tattooed and painted with elaborate designs. Women worked with quills and, later, beads.

MEDICINE. Sickness and injury were considered the result of personal malevolent forces, for which treatment by a shaman was necessary. Treatment included herbal medicines and setting broken limbs, but the spiritual help invoked in the ritual of the shaking tent or the sweatbath was equally important.

DEATH AND AFTERLIFE. Fatal illness was greeted with equanimity, but the dying person required that his survivors avenge his death, for death was believed to be the result of witchcraft. Burial was in a grave or on a scaffold. A gun was fired in the tent to drive away the spirit.

Bibliography

Helm, June, ed. (1981). *Handbook of North American Indians*. Vol. 6, *Subarctic*. Washington, D.C.: Smithsonian Institution.

Isham, James (1949). *Observations on Hudson's Bay, 1743–1749*, edited by E. Rich. Toronto: Champlain Society.

Mandelbaum, David G. (1940). *The Plains Cree*. American Museum of Natural History, Anthropological Papers 37, 155–316. New York.

Mason, Leonard (1967). *The Swampy Cree: A Study in Acculturation*. National Museum of Canada, Anthropological Paper no. 13. Ottawa.

Smith, James G. E. (1987). "Western Woods Cree: Anthropological Myth and Historical Reality." *American Ethnologist* 14:434–448.

Smith, James G. E. (1981). "Western Woods Cree." In *Handbook of North American Indians*. Vol. 6, *Subarctic*, edited by June Helm, 256–270. Washington, D.C.: Smithsonian Institution.

—JAMES G. E. SMITH

EAST ASIANS OF THE UNITED STATES

Ethnonyms: Chinese, Japanese, Koreans, Filipinos, Orientals

Orientation

IDENTIFICATION. The general category of East Asians in the United States includes Americans of Chinese, Filipino, Japanese, and Korean ancestry. Neither East Asians in general nor any of the four East Asian-American groups is a homogeneous cultural group in the United States. Within each are a number of identifiable subgroups, with perhaps the most significant being those who arrived before World War II and their descendants and those who have arrived since, the latter, except for Japanese-Americans, making up the overwhelming majority of East Asian-Americans. Other important divisions are based on the region of origin in the sending nation, language, religion, generation, and occupation.

LOCATION. Prior to the post-World War II population increase East Asian-Americans were concentrated in Hawaii and California, with small numbers in Washington and Oregon. Since World War II, the percentage of East Asians has increased dramatically, partly through immigration to the United States and partly through migration from Hawaii to the mainland. Japanese-Americans remain heavily concentrated in the West (80.3 percent in 1980), mainly in the Los Angeles, San Francisco, and San Jose areas, though sizable numbers now live in Chicago, Washington, D.C., and New York City. In 1980, 42.9 percent of Korean-Americans lived in the West, with the other 60 percent distributed almost evenly in the northeastern, north-central, and southern regions. In 1980, 52.7 percent of Chinese-Americans lived in the West with 26.8 percent in the East, with major communities in New York City and Boston. Filipino-Americans remain a largely West Coast group with 68.8 percent settled there in 1980. Large Filipino communities also exist in Detroit, Chicago, New York City, and Boston as well as in San Diego, Norfolk, New London, Connecticut, and other cities with large naval bases, reflecting a tradition of Filipino service in the U.S. Navy dating to 1901.

DEMOGRAPHY. Estimates for 1985 indicate that there were 1,079,400 Chinese, 1,051,600 Filipino, 766,300 Japanese, and 542,400 Korean-Americans in the United States. If immigration figures for 1986 through 1989 are considered, it is

In the second generation of recent immigrants, relatively few speak the native language regularly or remain fluent in it as adults.

After the bombing of Pearl Harbor 110,000 Japanese-Americans were classified as enemy aliens and placed in internment camps.

likely that Filipinos are now the largest East Asian group in the United States as the number of Filipino immigrants was more than double the number of Chinese ones during this period. The number of East Asians has increased dramatically since the 1950s. In 1940, there were 285,115 Japanese, 106,334 Chinese, 98,535 Filipino, and 8,568 Korean-Americans. Reflecting this heavy recent immigration, the East Asian population contains a majority of immigrants (in 1980, 63.3 percent of the Chinese, 64.7 of the Filipinos, 81.9 percent of the Koreans), and they are a young population (about 60 percent are under forty-four years of age in these three groups). Japanese-Americans were a larger population than the other groups before 1950 and have had a lower rate of immigration since then; thus they have a lower percentage of immigrants (28.4 percent) and are a somewhat older population group.

LINGUISTIC AFFILIATION. The first generation of East Asian immigrants generally spoke the language of their homeland. Thus, Japanese spoke Japanese; Koreans spoke Korean; Chinese spoke Cantonese, various Mandarin dialects, or Hakka; and Filipinos spoke Ilocano, Visayan, or Tagalog, with most recent immigrants speaking Tagalog, now the offical language of the Philippines. In the second generation of recent immigrants, relatively few speak the native language regularly or remain fluent in it as adults. Instead, they prefer to speak English. Native language maintenance is a major concern of the first generation of recent immigrants, though language school programs have met with only limited success.

History and Cultural Relations

The nature of East Asian immigration to and settlement in the United States is a function of a variety of factors including politics and economic conditions in the sending nation, the relationship between the sending nation and the United States, the need for cheap labor in the United States, and the racial prejudice encountered by East Asians in the United States. The Chinese were the first East Asian group to settle in America in significant numbers, with 322,000 arriving between 1850 and 1882. Most were men who worked as laborers in mines, in factories, and on farms to earn money that would enhance their economic status when they returned home. While initial settlement was in the western states, some later were sent east under a contract labor system designed to exploit the Chinese as a source of low-paid labor, and others settled in the south. In response to demands for control of Chinese immigration and settlement that began in California in the 1860s, Congress passed the Chinese Exclusion Act which in 1882 effectively ended their immigration until 1943. During this period, the Chinese population in the United States decreased from 107,448 to 61,639. It was also during this period, however, that Chinatowns developed in cities near where the men worked.

Unlike Chinese immigrants, the first influx of Filipino, Japanese, and Korean immigrants went to Hawaii where they were recruited to work on the sugar and pineapple plantations. Later, some moved on to California and the Northwest Coast while others immigrated directly from their homelands, again to work as laborers on farms and in factories and canneries. The Japanese came first, and by 1890 there were 12,000 in Hawaii and 3,000 in California. By 1920 300,000 had come to these two areas. The gentlemen's agreement between the United States and Japan in 1907 placed quotas on and slowed Japanese immigration. Between 1903 and 1905, 7,226 Koreans immigrated to Hawaii; however, Korean immigration virtually disappeared for forty years when the Japanese government (which then ruled Korea) ended emigration from the country in 1905. Filipinos were recruited and began immigrating to Hawaii in 1906 in place of the Koreans and Chinese. Between 1909 and 1931 113,000 Filipinos immigrated to Hawaii, with 55,000 settling there, 39,000 returning home, and 18,600 moving on to the mainland. Some Filipinos also immigrated directly to California and the Northwest Coast, where they were used as farmworkers in place of the declining numbers of Japanese and Chinese. The Immigration Act of 1924 through quotas virtually eliminated immigration from East Asia. Most immigrants between 1924 and the 1940s were wives of men already in the United States. Many of these were "picture-brides" selected through an exchange of photographs handled by a matchmaker. Nearly all East Asian men and women lived in distinctively Chinese, Japanese, or Filipino communities in which the native languages and many traditional beliefs and practices were maintained. The marriages also produced a second generation in the United States who were citizens and who spoke English and were much less interested in maintaining the traditional cultures.

During World War II, the four East Asian communities had different experiences. Filipinos were classified as nationals and therefore could not serve in the U.S. armed forces, though the rules were changed during the war to allow Filipinos to serve. The Chinese-American community benefited in some ways from the war, as job opportunities opened up. In 1943 the Exclusion Act was repealed, migration increased, and anti-Chinese sentiments lessened. Because Korea was ruled by Japan, Korean-Americans were classified as Japanese, although they were strong supporters of the war and vehemently anti-Japanese. Despite their being seen as Japanese, they were not classified as enemy aliens or removed to internment camps.

The bombing of Pearl Harbor served as a catalyst to turn years of anti-Japanese feeling on the West Coast into action designed to destroy the Japanese-American community on the mainland. Japanese-Americans (including those who were citizens) were classified as enemy aliens and rounded up; by the end of 1942 110,000 from California, Oregon, and Washington had been interned in camps in the California desert, Idaho, Arizona, Utah, and Arkansas. All except those who chose and were allowed to serve in the military and those who chose to resettle in the Midwest and East were kept in the camps until 1945. This mass violation of Japanese-Americans' civil rights nearly destroyed the Japanese community in the United States. After release from the camps most returned to California, with many reestablishing farms in the central part of the state. It was not until the late 1980s that the U.S. Congress voted to pay survivors of the camps $20,000 each as compensation for their losses.

As noted above, since the end of World War II, there has been a multifold increase in the number of East Asians immigrating to the United States. The repeal of restrictive immigration laws, closer ties between the United States and South Korea, the Philippines, Taiwan, and Japan, and the Hart-Cellar Immigration Act of 1965 which essentially ended the national-origin quota system all encouraged immigration to and settlement in the United States. East Asians who have come to America since World War II are a much different population than those who came earlier. They are younger, include a larger number of women and families, are often highly educated professionals and technicians, and expect to stay in the U.S.

The one constant in the settlement histories of the four groups was the economic exploitation and discrimination they experienced. In addition to major discriminatory actions—the Chinese Exclusion Act, the Immigration Act of 1924, and Japanese-American internment during World War II—East Asians were subject to numerous other discriminatory practices. For example, in California they were barred from certain businesses and professions, antimiscegenation laws prevented marriage to Whites, residential restrictions confined East Asians to their own communities, various laws limited their right to own land, Chinese miners (and Mexican miners) had their profits taxed, and so on. Today, although overtly racist policies and laws have essentially disappeared, racism continues. East Asian-American men, for example, make less than White counterparts with equal experience and education, and few have made it to the top level of American businesses. There is also growing resentment among other Americans about East Asian and especially Japanese investment in the U.S. economy and ownership of properties in the United States. The depiction of East Asian-American groups as "model minorities" troubles some East Asian-Americans, as it suggests that equality has been achieved while contrasting East Asian economic success with other minorities' alleged failures and thus creating conflict between the groups.

Settlements

East Asian-Americans are mainly an urban-suburban group, with the place of residence now largely determined by socioeconomic status. The two major nonurban groups are Japanese-Americans in the farming and nursery and related businesses in central California and Filipino-American farm workers in California. Today, Koreatown in Los Angeles is the center of Korean life for the 150,000 Korean-Americans in southern California and the home for many elderly Korean-Americans and recent immigrants. The large Chinatowns that developed early in the century in cities such as San Francisco, Portland, Boston, Los Angeles, and New York City have been transformed into major economic zones providing products and services both to the regional Chinese-American population and to the general economy. The tourist trade has also become a major source of income in Chinatowns. Their economic growth has been accompanied by or perhaps was stimulated by their decline as residential districts. As with Koreatown in Los Angeles, most residents are either elderly or are recent immigrants and many are poor. "Little Tokyo" in Los Angeles, which serves Japanese-American communities in southern California, has also undergone the same transformation. Filipino-Americans, except for the mostly male communities in

Korean-Americans have drawn considerable attention as owners of small businesses in minority neighborhoods.

*East Asian-
Americans are
mainly an urban-
suburban group,
with the place of
residence now
largely determined
by socioeconomic
status.*

♦ **middleman
minority**
*A term used to describe an
ethnic or racial group that
occupies a middle economic
position between the
supplier and the consumer
in a national, regional, or
local economy. Usually the
group is segregated from the
rest of society because of
racial or ethnic differences.*

Hawaii and California early in the century, have not formed distinct ethnic enclaves comparable to Chinatowns.

Economy

In general, the economic circumstances of Koreans, Japanese, Chinese, and Filipinos in Hawaii and on the mainland in the late nineteenth and early twentieth centuries were much the same. The majority were low-paid, unskilled, male workers on sugar plantations in Hawaii and in the railroad, agriculture, fishing, logging, and mining industries on the mainland. When demand for their work diminished and East Asian immigration decreased, those who remained in the United States and their children tended to settle in cities and became involved in service industries. Filipinos worked as domestics in hotels and as kitchen workers in restaurants and many men joined the Merchant Marine or the U.S. Navy where they worked as mess stewards or in other low-level service jobs. At the same time, many Filipinos were employed seasonally as farm workers and eventually became active in the unionization movement. The Chinese were also employed in service industries as well as founding their own businesses, with restaurants, laundries, and garment factories being most common. In Hawaii, many Chinese sugar workers went on to work in the rice industry, and a sizable percentage became business owners or professionals. The Japanese also found work as domestics, gardeners, and farmers, with some finding ways to circumvent laws that prohibited them from owning land. Many of those who owned farms returned to rebuild them after they were released from the World War II internment camps. Both the Japanese and Chinese businesses have been described as "middleman minority" adaptations characterized by self-ownership of family-staffed businesses that provide a unique product or service to the community.

The arrival of the post-World War II immigrants has changed the position of East Asian-Americans in the U.S. economy. Many of those who have arrived since 1965 have been highly educated professionals or skilled technicians, and the children of the earlier settlers have had greater access to advanced education and professional employment. These two developments have improved the economic position of East Asian-Americans. Both men and women are now employed at about the same rates as Americans in general. The percentages of East Asian-American women who work (55 percent of Koreans, 58

percent of Chinese, 59 percent of Japanese, and 68 percent of Filipinos in 1980) are especially noteworthy. As of 1980, the men were employed in significant numbers in managerial and professional positions (22.5 percent for Filipinos to 38 percent for Chinese), with the largest percentages of women being employed in administrative support and service jobs. Unique occupation patterns include 22 percent of Chinese-American men in service jobs, 30.4 percent of Filipino-American men in service and administrative support positions, and 14.4 percent of Korean-American men in sales. For women, 18.2 percent of Chinese-American and 24 percent of Korean-American women work in low-level laborer positions. Gross figures indicate that full-time Chinese-American and Japanese-American men have higher incomes and Filipino-American and Korean-American men have lower incomes than Whites. The Chinese and Japanese figures are somewhat misleading, however, in that they do not reflect the fact that men in these groups often have more education and work longer hours than do Whites. Korean-Americans have drawn considerable attention as owners of small businesses, often grocery stores or vegetable stands, in minority neighborhoods, suggesting a middleman minority role similar to the Chinese and Japanese earlier.

Kinship, Marriage, and Family

KINSHIP. In the early Korean, Chinese, and Filipino communities, which were composed almost entirely of men, ties to families and wider kin networks were maintained through return visits, correspondence, and the remittance of a percentage of the man's earnings. In the communities that formed in this country, the absence of East Asian women and antimiscegenation laws made marriage and the formation of families and kin groups difficult. Some community cohesion was created through fictive kin groups modeled on clan and extended family structures in the homeland. Chinese men formed fictive clans with recruitment and membership based on immigration from the same village or province or possession of the same surname. When Chinese families began to form later in the early twentieth century with the arrival of Chinese women, these clan associations became less important. Filipinos organized *compang*, fictive extended families composed of men who immigrated from the same village, with the oldest man usually heading the family. As more Filipino women immigrated to the United States, Filipino-American families became more common (though before World War

II Filipino-American men still outnumbered women by nearly three to one), and the *compadrazgo* (godparent) system was transferred to the United States with each individual then enmeshed in a network of actual and fictive kin.

The situation for Japanese-Americans was different, as beginning in 1910 stable families began to form and Japanese urban and rural communities also became relatively stable. Although the second-generation Japanese-Americans, the nisei, were being acculturated into American society, the first-generation-based family (issei) was still strong enough to maintain traditional beliefs regarding appropriate behavior between superiors and inferiors as well as filial duties.

MARRIAGE AND FAMILY. The most noteworthy trend in East Asian-American marriages is the shift from ethnic endogamous to ethnic exogamous marriage. In all groups since the 1950s there has been a large increase in the number of marriages to non-ethnic group members, and especially to Whites. Contemporary East Asian-American families are generally small nuclear families. Korean-American and Filipino-American households are somewhat larger because of the larger number of children in the former and the presence of non-nuclear family members in the latter. East Asian-American families are notably stable, with over 84 percent of children in all four groups living with both of their parents. Nonetheless, there are concerns in the Chinese-American community about juvenile delinquency and in the Korean-American about what is considered a high divorce rate. There is a major difference in household composition between those already settled in the United States and recent immigrants. Households among the latter frequently contain additional relatives beyond the nuclear family or friends, as these households are often part of the chain migration process through which relatives immigrate to the United States.

Within households in all four East Asian-American groups, decision making has become more egalitarian as patriarchal authority has diminished. Women, however, still bear the major responsibility for household tasks, even though a majority of both men and women are employed. Educational opportunities are afforded both boys and girls, and both sexes are encouraged to excel in school.

SOCIALIZATION. As with Americans in general, socialization takes place through the family, the local community, and the formal education system. Many East Asians in the past came to America with a high school education and many of the recent immigrants have college and/or professional education or technical training. The children of recent immigrants make full use of educational opportunities in the United States; in fact education for their children is a major reason many East Asians resettle. Programs designed to maintain the traditional culture, such as language classes, youth groups, and cultural programs are offered in all major East Asian communities by ethnic associations and churches. One major problem facing many recent immigrant families is a generational gap between parents who prefer to speak the native language and eat native foods, stress family obligations, and associate mainly with other ethnic group members and their children who see themselves as Americans, speak English, and make friends among non-Asian-Americans.

Sociopolitical Organization

SOCIAL ORGANIZATION. Each of the four East Asian-American groups is a diverse ethnic group composed of a number of distinct subgroups. Across all four groups, two internal divisions are most obvious. First is the distinction between those who settled before World War II and their descendants and those who arrived after the war. Second is the distinction in the post-World War II group between the parental and second generation, with the latter composed of those who were born in the United States or came when they were young. Beyond these two categories, each East Asian group displays additional diversity as well as various social institutions developed in the United States.

Chinese. Major divisions within the Chinese-American community include those based on place of origin (Hong Kong, Taiwan, Southeast Asia), Cantonese or non-Cantonese ethnicity, rural or urban residence, and support for Taiwan or recognition of the People's Republic of China. Localized in Chinatowns and excluded from full participation in American society for over one hundred years, Chinese-Americans developed a complex set of interlocking organizations that enabled them to maintain elements of their traditional culture while adapting to their new life. In the early years, when the population was mostly male, clan and regional associations with affiliation based on surname and region of origin served to affiliate men in the United States and maintain ties with the homeland. Other organizations including secret societies (tongs), guilds, and credit associations were also developed, all of which served economic, political, and social functions.

See also

APPENDIX: Chinese

With the arrival of more women and the formation of families in the twentieth century, the second generation of Chinese-Americans appeared. Although they were socially and economically isolated from mainstream society, they learned English in school and formed organizations based on mainstream models and interests. At the same time, they were less interested in the traditional culture, and membership in the clan and regional associations declined. In the post-World War II immigrant group, the clan and regional associations and tongs have declined in importance as the focus has shifted to forming organizations that will help Chinese-Americans secure full rights as American citizens.

Filipinos. For Filipino-Americans, the major internal distinction is based on the region from which one emigrated: the Ilocanos from northern Luzon, the Tagalogs from central Luzon, and the Visayans from the central Philippines. Although the three groups are no longer as separate as they once were, regional endogamy is still stressed by the post-World War II parental generation, and a preference for affiliation with people from the same region has contributed to the absence of a pan-Filipino organization in the United States. In the mostly male pre-World War II Filipino community, few social organizations developed. Instead, social cohesion was achieved through the maintenance of family and kin groups based on

traditional practices. Today, the Roman Catholic church is the social center of many Filipino communities, and kinship and friendship networks are also important agents of social cohesion.

Japanese. Within the Japanese-American community a major distinction is made on the basis of generation in the United States with the issei being the first generation, the nisei the second, the sansei the third, and the yonsei the fourth. These categories are applied to those who arrived before World War II. Those who arrived after the war are technically issei, but are not referred to as such. Japanese in the United States also include Japanese businessmen and wives or ex-wives of Americans who worked in Japan after World War II. Both these groups exist outside the Japanese-American community. In the prewar years in California, Japanese-Americans formed a network of interlocking businesses, such as rooming houses, laundries, groceries, and so on, which served the Japanese-American and other East Asian-American communities. At the same time, the issei maintained a cohesive community through educational and cultural organizations, a credit association, and regional associations. The nisei moved away from the more traditional groups and chose instead to form their own organizations often based on existing mainstream models and activities such as recreation leagues. Today, the Japanese-American community is socially com-

PRISONER

A Japanese-American woman visits the Tule Lake Internment Camp, where her parents were interned during World War II. Although there are close to a million Japanese-Americans today, this violation of rights nearly destroyed the Japanese community in the United States. California, USA. (Ted Streshinsky/Corbis)

plex with distinctions made on the basis of generation, age, political affiliation, life-style, and occupation. At the same time, Japanese values emphasizing group interests over individual interests, deference, loyalty, and reciprocity govern everyday behavior for many Japanese-Americans and are a major source of social cohesion.

Koreans. The Korean-American community today is composed mainly of people who immigrated to the United States after World War II and their children. One basic distinction in the community is made among those born in Korea (Ilse), those born in the United States (*Ese* or *samse*), and those who came to the United States when they were young. The Ilse tend to speak Korean rather than English, have strong ties to Korea, and emphasize the role and authority of the family and the husband/father. Those in the younger generation are more assimilated into American society. Unlike the other East Asian groups, organizations based on kinship or regional affiliations rarely formed among Korean-Americans. Rather, most organizations have formed on the basis of common interests and include clubs, churches, associations, and political groups. One of the more important are the alumni associations (high school and college) which enmesh Korean-Americans in lifelong social and economic networks. Living outside the Korean-American community are perhaps as many as 100,000 wives or ex-wives of American servicemen who served in Korea, their children, and thousands of Korean children adopted into White families.

POLITICAL ORGANIZATION. Because they were denied citizenship and the right to vote, East Asian-Americans before World War II were essentially powerless to directly influence local, state, or federal policies and actions that affected them. Within the mostly male, relatively isolated East Asian-American communities, social control and decision making were based on traditional beliefs and customs that usually accorded much authority to the older men in the community. At the same time, the regional and clan associations, guilds, secret societies, and other organizations served as special interest groups to advance the interests of their members. East Asian-American interests within American society were often handled by umbrella organizations, which included the Chinese Consolidated Benevolent Association and later the Chinese-American Citizens Alliance, the Japanese-American Citizen's League, and the Korean Association. A pan-Filipino political organization did not develop, though Fil-

ipinos were active in labor movements in Hawaii and California.

Politics in the homeland have been and continue to be a major concern and a source of conflict especially in the Chinese-American and Korean-American communities. Some Korean-Americans affiliate on the basis of ties to factions in Korea, and a major division in the Chinese-American community involves those who emphasize ties to Taiwan versus those who recognize and want ties strengthened with the People's Republic of China.

Japanese-Americans have been active in Hawaiian politics and hold many elective offices, a development that has sometimes led to conflict with other ethnic groups. On the mainland, especially since the 1960s and to some extent as a result of the civil rights movement, Chinese and Japanese-Americans especially have been more active in voicing their concerns, participating in the major political party politics, running for office, and seeking government employment.

Religion and Expressive Culture

RELIGIOUS BELIEFS. Religious beliefs and institutions have been a major force in all East Asian-American communities, both past and present, though the particular beliefs and institutions vary among the four groups. Most Koreans who settled in the United States had already been converted to Christianity (usually Protestantism) in Korea before arriving. In the contemporary Korean-American community the the Korean Christian churches are often the center of community activity and provide many programs of special appeal to women, the elderly, and children. They have also been the locus of language and cultural maintenance programs. In many churches the services are conducted in Korean.

Nearly all Filipinos in the United States are Roman Catholics, their ancestors having been converted some generations ago in the Philippines. Because of their dispersed residence pattern, Filipino-Americans do not form their own churches but instead affiliate with the local church.

The first generation of Japanese-Americans believed in Buddhism and/or Shintoism. Many were converted in the United States by missionaries to various Protestant denominations, and today the Japanese-American community has perhaps the widest range of religious affiliations of the four East Asian-American groups. Recent immigrants have brought with them some of the new Japanese religions, although all have roots in Buddhism and Shintoism.

Eskimos refer to themselves with terms that translate as "real people" or "authentic human beings."

The religious beliefs and practices of the early Chinese immigrants centered on ancestor worship, Buddhism, and Taoism. Ancestor worship was especially important as a source of community cohesion and as a mechanism to maintain ties with the homeland. Efforts by Protestant missionaries with these immigrants largely failed, and today only about 20 percent of Chinese-Americans are Christians. Recent immigrants have brought with them some of the revived Chinese folk religions and have formed Buddhist and Taoist associations.

EXPRESSIVE CULTURE. The post-World War II immigration has revitalized the expressive elements of East Asian culture in the United States. In all four groups, traditional dance, music, theater, and art are flourishing and are a major focus of ethnic solidarity and pride, as is the public celebration of traditional holidays. Some aspects of expressive culture have also become part of the mainstream culture, most notably Chinese and Japanese cuisines, martial arts, architecture, and artistic styles and designs.

Bibliography

Almirol, Edwin B. (1983). *Ethnic Identity and Social Negotiation: A Study of a Filipino Community in California*. New York: AMS Press.

Bonacich, Edna, and John Modell (1980). *The Economic Basis of Ethnic Solidarity: Small Business in the Japanese American Community*. Berkeley: University of California Press.

Daniels, Roger (1988). *Asian America: Chinese and Japanese in the United States since 1850*. Seattle: University of Washington Press.

Hurh, Won Moo, and Kwang Chung Kim (1984). *Korean Immigrants in America: A Structural Analysis of Ethnic Confinement and Adhesive Adaptation*. Rutherford, N.J.: Fairleigh Dickinson University Press.

Kendis, Kaoru O. (1988). *A Matter of Comfort: Ethnic Maintenance and Ethnic Style among Third-Generation Japanese-Americans*. New York: AMS Press.

Kim, Ilsoo. (1981). *New Urban Immigrants: The Korean Community in New York*. Princeton, N.J.: Princeton University Press.

Kitano, H. L. (1977). *Japanese Americans: The Evolution of a Subculture*. Englewood Cliffs, N.J.: Prentice-Hall.

Loewen, James W. (1971). *The Mississippi Chinese: Between Black and White*. Cambridge: Harvard University Press.

Pido, A. J. A. (1985). *The Pilipinos in America: Macro-Micro Dimensions of Immigration and Integration*. Staten Island, N.Y.: Center for Migration Studies.

Sung, Betty Lee (1967). *Mountain of Gold*. New York: Macmillan.

Takaki, Ronald (1989). *Strangers from a Different Shore: A History of Asian Americans*. Boston: Little, Brown & Co.

Thernstrom, Stephan (1980). *Harvard Encyclopedia of American Ethnic Groups*. Cambridge: Harvard University Press, Belknap Press.

Tsai, F. W. (1980). "Diversity and Conflict between Old and New Chinese Immigrants in the United States." In *Source-book on the New Immigration: Implication for the United States and the International Community*, edited by Roy S. Bryce-Laporte, 329–337. Washington, D.C.: Research Institute on Immigration and Ethnic Studies, Smithsonian Institution.

Wong, Bernard (1983). *Patronage, Brokerage, Entrepreneurship, and the Chinese Community of New York*. New York: AMS Press.

Xenos, Peter S., Robert W. Gardner, Herbert R. Barringer, and Michael J. Levin (1987). "Asian Americans: Growth and Change in the 1970s." In *Pacific Bridges: The New Immigration from Asia and the Pacific Islands*, edited by James T. Fawcett and Benjamin V. Cariño, 249–284. Staten Island, N.Y.: Center for Migration Studies.

Yanagisako, S. (1985). *Transforming the Past: Tradition and Kinship among Japanese Americans*. Stanford: Stanford University Press.

Yu, Eui-Young (1989). "Korean American Community in 1989: Issues and Prospects." *Korea Observer* 20:275–302.

ESKIMO

Ethnonyms: Esquimox, Esquimaux

The name "Eskimo" has been applied to the native peoples of the Arctic since the sixteenth century; ironically, it is not an Eskimo word. For close to a century both anthropological and popular sources, including the *Oxford English* and *Webster's New World* dictionaries, maintained that the name "Eskimo" derived from a proto-Algonkian root translating as "eaters of the raw flesh." In fact, the name originated in the Montagnais language and had no such meaning. Eskimos refer to themselves with terms that translate as "real people" or "authentic human beings." These self-names vary from one Eskimo language to another and include the names "Inuit," "Inummaariit," "Inuvialat," "Inupiat," "Yup'ik," "Suxpiat," and "Unangan." The strength of the belief by Eskimos themselves in the pejorative connotations of their name was a major factor in its replacement, in Canada and Greenland since the 1970s, by the designation "Inuit," an ethnonym used by eastern Arctic Eskimos and Canadian Arctic Eskimos. In Alaska and Siberia, however, the term has never taken root. Although the Eskimos of the western Arctic are indeed members of the larger family of Eskimo cultures, they refer to themselves in their own language as "Yup'ik," "Inupiat," or "Unangan." To call them "Inuit" is inaccurate, and there is no all-encompassing native name for the entire native population of the Arctic.

—ANN FIENUP-RIORDAN

EUROPEAN-AMERICANS

About 80 percent of Americans are descended from people of European ethnicity. The short summaries that follow present information on the population, distribution, migration history, and cultural persistence of thirty-seven European ethnic groups in the United States. Appended to some summaries are short lists of publications, most of which are recent studies of a particular ethnic community or a general historical or cultural survey of the ethnic group. Some of the information in these summaries is derived from *The Harvard Encyclopedia of American Ethnic Groups* and *We the People.* These are the basic reference resources for information about American ethnic groups and should be consulted for additional information and references.

ALBANIANS. In 1980, 21,687 Americans claimed Albanian ethnic ancestry and another 16,971 claimed Albanian and other ethnic ancestry. Because of underreporting in the past, this is likely an undercount, with Americans of Albanian ancestry probably numbering no less than 70,000. Pre-World War II Albania was inhabited by two major cultural groups—the Ghegs (Gegs) in the mountainous North and the Tosks (Toscs) in the South. Both groups spoke mutually intelligible dialects of Albanian, although there were clear economic, religious, and social differences between the two groups. In the United States, ingroup variation is reflected more in religious differences (Greek Orthodox, Muslim, Roman Catholic) than in the Gheg/Tosk dichotomy. Most Albanians settled in the United States in the early 1900s, with Boston the major community. Other communities formed in Detroit, Chicago, Worcester (Massachusetts), and Connecticut. After World War II, a community of Catholic Albanians formed in the Bronx, New York, and continues to exist as a distinct ethnic enclave. The traditional culture centered on the patriarchal family, a strong sense of family honor, clans, and blood feuds has mostly given way to an American middle-class life-style. But a strong sense of Albanian identity survives through ethnic associations, the church, traditional celebrations and foods, and kin ties. Albanian political identity is perhaps centered more on concern over the status of Albanians in the Kosovo region of Serbian Yugoslavia than on anticommunism.

Bibliography

Nagi, Dennis L. (1987). *The Albanian-American Odyssey: A Pilot Study of the Albanian Community of Boston, Massachusetts.* New York: AMS Press.

ARMENIANS. In 1980, 155,693 Americans claimed Armenian ancestry and another 56,928 claimed Armenian and other ethnic ancestry. In Europe and the Near and Middle East, Armenians have lived under the control of the Turks, Russians, and Iranians and have formed distinct ethnic minorities in countries such as Lebanon. Economic and cultural variations among Armenian groups in these locales was transferred by Armenian immigrants to the United States. Industrial cities in the East and Midwest, the California central valley, and Los Angeles are major Armenian population centers, with 42 percent of Armenian-Americans in 1980 living in California. Settlers in industrial cities first worked in the steel, automobile, and textile industries, but quickly moved up the economic ladder, using business and technical skills brought with them from Armenia to the New World. The first Armenians in central California were farm workers, and they, too, quickly moved up the economic ladder, as shop and landowners. In both locations, the rapid economic mobility was accompanied by rapid assimilation, reflected in the loss of the Armenian language and a high rate of intermarriage. The most recent arrivals are those who have emigrated from the Soviet Union (and indirectly from Turkey and the Middle East) since 1976 to the Los Angeles area. Since the 1960s, there has been a strong ethnic revival reflected in Armenian schools, language programs, contacts with Armenians in the Soviet Union, and concern over the continuing Armenian-Azerbaijani conflict there.

Bibliography

Henry, Sheila A. (1978). *Cultural Persistence and Socioeconomic Mobility: A Comparative Study of Assimila-*

See also

EUROPE: Albanians

tion among Armenians and Japanese in Los Angeles. San Francisco: R and E Research Associates.

Mirak, Robert (1983). *Torn between Two Lands: Armenians in America, 1890 to World War I.* Cambridge: Harvard University Press.

Phillips, Jenny K. (1987). *Symbol, Myth, and Rhetoric: The Politics of Culture in an Armenian-American Population.* New York: AMS Press.

Rollins, Joan H., ed. (1981). *Hidden Minorities: The Persistence of Ethnicity in American Life.* Washington, D.C.: University Press of America.

About 80 percent of Americans are descended from people of European ethnicity.

AUSTRIANS. In 1980, 339,789 Americans claimed Austrian ancestry and another 608,769 claimed Austrian and other ancestry. Unlike many other Euopean nations, Austria was not formed on a distinct ethnic population base, and thus Austrians are more accurately described as a nationality than as an ethnic group. Austrians who have settled in the United States, including a sizable minority of Jews, have assimilated rapidly into American society and tend to see their Austrian identity as a variant of German identity.

BELGIANS. In 1980 there were 122,814 Americans who claimed Belgian ancestry and another 237,463 who claimed Belgian and other ethnic ancestry. The nation of Belgium was and is inhabited by two distinct groups—the Flemish in the coastal northwest (in the region commonly called Flanders), who speak a language closely related to Dutch, and the Walloons in the east and southeast, who speak French. This distinction has been maintained in the United States and is reflected in the separate settlements established by immigrants from each group in the nineteenth and twentieth centuries. Most of the pre-1920 immigrants were Flemish and they tended to settle in areas already settled by the Dutch (especially in Michigan and Wisconsin), although they were often excluded from Dutch communities because of Dutch anti-Catholicism. Walloons tended to settle near French or French-Canadian communities, and the large Walloon community near Green Bay, Wisconsin, began in this way. Although some features of Walloon or Flemish culture survived into the mid-twentieth century such as cycling clubs, choral societies, and community newspapers, both groups are now largely assimilated into American society and are seen by others as of Belgian rather than of distinctively Flemish or Walloon ancestry.

CARPATHO-RUSYNS

(Carpatho-Russians, Carpatho-Ukrainians, Rusnaks, Ruthenians, Uhro-Rusyns). Carpatho-Rusyns in the United States today are mainly third- or fourth-generation descendants of Carpatho-Rusyns who immigrated to North America between 1880 and 1914. Carpatho-Rusyns spoke East Slavic dialects closely related to Ukrainian. In 1980 about 600,000 Americans were of Carpatho-Rusyn ancestry, although only 8,485 claimed such ancestry in the 1980 census. This is in part because many identify themselves as Ukrainians or Russians and because the U.S. census no longer considers the Carpatho-Rusyns as a distinct group. The homeland of the Carpatho-Rusyns is the Carpathian mountains in what are the modern nations of Poland and Czechoslovakia and the Ukrainian Soviet Socialist Republic. Initial settlement was in the mining and industrial regions of Pennsylvania, New York, New Jersey, Ohio, Illinois, and Connecticut. Ethnic identity was closely tied to their identity as Eastern Christians, expressed through membership in the Byzantine Rite Catholic church or Orthodox churches. Carpatho-Rusyn services contained a number of unique practices, most notably a liturgical chant using folk melodies still sung by groups today. Partly because of the absence of a distinct country of national origin, a sense of Carpatho-Rusyn ethnic identity has largely disappeared in the United States. In the Ukrainian Soviet Socialist Republic, people of Carpatho-Rusyn ancestry now see themselves as Ukrainians. In 1931, a subgroup called the Lemkians, composed of people from the Lemkian region of southeastern Poland formed a separate ethnic association. They have made a strong effort to maintain their ethnic identity through an active press, concern about their national identity, and the maintenance of some traditional practices.

Bibliography

Magocsi, Paul R. (1984). *Our People: Carpatho-Rusyns and Their Descendants in North America.* Toronto: Multicultural History Society of Ontario.

See also

EUROPE: Austrians, Flemish, Croats

BYELORUSSIANS (Belorussians, Kryvians, White Russians, White Ruthenians). There are about 200,000 people of Byelorussian ethnic ancestry in the United States today. This is very likely an underestimate, as those who arrived prior to World War I (and whose descendants are the majority of Byelorussians in the United States today) were identified as either Russians or Poles. Byelorussia is the region that today is located in the Soviet Union south and east of Lithuania and Latvia. As with many peoples from Eastern Europe, the Byelorussians arrived in two major waves: 1880 to World War I and after World War II. Both groups tended to settle in large industrial cities in the Northeast and Midwest. The descendants of the first wave are now much assimilated into American society. Those who arrived after World War II and their children have emphasized their Byelorussian identity through formation of their own church communities, parochial schools, associations, anti-Soviet sentiment, a language preservation program, and the celebration of ethnic holidays and life-cycle events following traditional customs.

Bibliography

Kipel, Vitaut (1982). *Byelorussian Americans and Their Communities of Cleveland*. Cleveland: Cleveland State University.

CROATS (Croatians). In 1980, 107,855 Americans claimed Croatian ancestry and another 145,115 claimed Croatian and other ethnic ancestry. This is probably a gross undercount, as many Croats are identified as Yugoslavians or Serbs. A figure of at least 500,000 is probably a more accurate estimate of the number of people of Croatian ancestry in the United States. Croatia is one of the six constituent republics of the modern nation of Yugoslavia. The U.S. census has usually classified Dalmatians, who live on the Adriatic coast of Yugoslavia, as Croats. In the late 1700s and early 1800s Dalmatian fishermen settled in Louisiana, where they were able to continue their maritime traditions. The major migration of Croats occurred between 1880 and World War I when they formed Croatian communities in industrial and mining towns and cities in Pennsylvania, Ohio, Illinois, and Indiana. Most Croats are Roman Catholic, although church membership did not play a major role in the establishment of Croatian communities as it did with other groups. Croats have assimilated more slowly into American society than many other groups, and it was not until the mid-1950s that inner-city Croatian neighborhoods began to break up through outmigration to the suburbs. Factors involved in the maintenance of Croat communities were strong extended family ties and a pattern of sons settling in the same community and working in the same factories as their fathers. Since World War II at least 60,000 Croats have settled in the United States and have led a renewal of Croat ethnic identity, through ties maintained with the homeland and a revitalized Croatian press.

Bibliography

Bennett, Linda (1978). *Personal Choice in Ethnic Identity Maintenance: Serbs, Croats and Slovenes in Washington*. Palo Alto, Calif.: R and E Research Associates.

Kraljec, Francis (1978). *Croation Migration to and from the United States*. Palo Alto, Calif.: Ragusan.

Prpic, G. J. (1978). *South Slavic Immigration in America*. Boston: Twayne.

CZECHS. In 1980, 788,724 Americans claimed Czech ancestry and another 1,103,732 claimed Czech and other ethnic ancestry. This figure may be somewhat inflated as it includes both ethnic Czechs and Czechoslovaks, some of whom may be ethnically Slovak rather than Czech. Czechs in the United States today are mainly descendants of people who emigrated from Bohemia and Moravia between 1850 and 1914, the two major regions of the Czech area of the nation of Czechoslovakia. Czechs settled both in farming communities (in Wisconsin, Minnesota, Nebraska, Iowa, South Dakota, and Texas) and in cities (New York, Cleveland, Chicago, and Omaha). Czech settlers differed from other European ethnic groups in a number of ways. First, they had an unusually low return-migration rate. Second, many left the Roman Catholic church and either converted to Protestantism or eschewed formal religious affilation altogether. Third, although they never were a unified group, they assimilated relatively slowly, in part because of values that stressed individual and family self-reliance and because of ties to the homeland. After the 1920s, Czech identity began to weaken as few new immigrants arrived, children attended public schools, and intermarriage became common.

After the communist takeover of Czechoslovakia in 1948, 35,000 Czechoslovakians fled to the United States and an additional 10,000 or so arrived after the failed 1968 revolution. These groups contained many professionals who often stayed apart from the established Czech commu-

See also
EUROPE: Czechs

Dutch Calvinists continue to be a major political-economic-social force in a four-hundred-square-mile region of southwestern Michigan.

nities in the United States. The Czech presence still reflects considerable internal diversity (rural/urban, early/later immigrants).

Bibliography

Bicha, Karel D. (1980). "Community of Cooperation? The Case of the Czech-Americans." In *Studies in Ethnicity: The East European Experience in America*, edited by C. A. Ward, P. Shashko, and D. E. Pienkos, 93–102. Boulder: East European Monographs.

Jerabek, Esther (1976). *Czechs and Slovaks in North America: A Bibliography*. New York: Czechoslovak Society of Arts and Sciences in America.

Skrabanek, R. L. (1985). *We're Czechs*. College Station: Texas A&M University Press.

DANES. In 1980, 428,619 Americans claimed Danish ancestry and another 1,089,654 claimed Danish and other ancestry. Most Danes immigrated to the United States in the last half of the nineteenth century. Mormon missionaries were active in Denmark after 1850, and a sizable contingent of Danes settled in farm communities in Utah and southern Idaho. The descendants of these Danish Mormons account today for about 9 percent of Danes in the United States. Most immigrants settled in the Midwest, primarily in Wisconsin, Iowa, and Minnesota. There is also a sizable Danish ancestry population in California, mostly the product of migration west following initial settlement elsewhere. Danes assimilated more quickly than other Scandinavian peoples, in part because of their relatively few numbers and wide dispersal, which encouraged marriage to non-Danes and a more rapid loss of the Danish language and adoption of English. Today, a sense of Danish ethnicity survives through the Dansk Samvirke (the Association of Danes Abroad), tours to Denmark, and Danish customs as part of the Christmas celebration.

Bibliography

Hale, Frederick, ed. (1984). *Danes in North America*. Seattle: University of Washington Press.

Mackintosh, Jette (1988). "'Little Denmark' on the Prairie: A Study of the Towns of Elk Horn and Kimballton in Iowa." *Journal of American Ethnic History* 7:46–68.

Nielsen, George R. (1981). *The Danish Americans*. Boston: Twayne.

DUTCH. In 1980, 1,404,794 Americans claimed Dutch ancestry and another 4,899,705 claimed Dutch and other ethnic ancestry. In the United States, Frisians, who form a distinct ethnic group in the Netherlands and West Germany, are classified as Dutch. After Henry Hudson "discovered" the Hudson River during his exploration of 1610–1611, the Dutch established the colony of New Netherland in the Hudson and Delaware river valleys and the city of New Amsterdam on lower Manhattan Island. Following the loss of the colony to the English in 1664, some Dutch settlers removed to adjacent areas in what are now New York State and New Jersey. Many people of Dutch ancestry still live in these areas, although their numbers have been swelled by later Dutch immigrants who worked in the factories in northern New Jersey. Most Dutch immigrants (80 percent) were Protestants, with the densest concentration being Dutch Calvinists who continue to be a major political-economic-social force in a four-hundred-square-mile region of southwestern Michigan. The major concentration of Dutch Roman Catholics is found across Lake Michigan in eastern Wisconsin. Other Dutch settlements were started and continue to flourish in Bozeman, Montana, and northwestern Washington State. The most recent Dutch immigrants are mostly native Indonesians who fled to the Netherlands from their country in the 1960s, with some subsequently immigrating to the United States. The large number of negative phrases with the word *Dutch* such as *Dutch treat* or *Dutch courage* can be attributed to the anti-Dutch sentiments of the early English colonists.

Bibliography

Bratt, James D. (1984). *Dutch Calvinism in Modern America: A History of a Conservative Subculture*. Grand Rapids, Mich.: William B. Eerdmans.

Swierenga, Robert P., ed. (1985). *The Dutch in America: Immigration, Settlement, and Cultural Change*. New Brunswick, N.J.: Rutgers University Press.

Van Hinte, Jacob (1985). *Netherlanders in America: A Study of Emigration and Settlement in the 19th and 20th Centuries in the United States of America*. Robert P. Swierenga, general editor. Adriaan de Wit, chief translator. Grand Rapids, Mich.: Baker Book House.

ENGLISH. In 1980, 23,748,772 Americans claimed English ancestry and another 25,849,263 claimed English along with other ethnic ancestry. These figures include those claiming Cornish ancestry but not those of Manx ancestry, who numbered 50,000 in 1970. Americans of English ancestry are sometimes referred to as White Anglo-Saxon Protestants (WASPs) and those in New England, as Yankees. The English were the primary colonizers of what became the United States and were the major shapers of the American economy, political system, society, and culture. Although American society is now a blending of beliefs and practices from dozens of cultures, the most fundamental features of American life, such as the use of the English language and the legal system, reflect English traditions. People of English ancestry are settled across the entire United States with major concentrations in Maine, the Appalachian and Ozark regions, and the Mormon region of Utah and southern Idaho. The few areas with relatively low percentages of English-Americans are New York City, areas of Southwest Texas with large Mexican-American populations, and those sections of Nevada and the Dakotas with large American Indian reservations.

Bibliography

Ewart, Shirley (1987). *Cornish Mining Families of Grass Valley, California*. New York: AMS Press.

ESTONIANS. Because emigrants from Estonia arriving before 1922 were usually listed as Russians, the number of Estonians who came to the United States and the number of current Estonian-Americans are unknown. Estimates place their number at about 200,000, with over half in the Mid-Atlantic and New England regions, 19 percent on the West Coast, and 15 percent in the Great Lakes area. The homeland is currently the Estonian Soviet Socialist Republic. The Estonian language is related to Finnish, and Estonian culture has been strongly influenced by Scandinavian traditions. Most Estonian-Americans are descendants of people who arrived between 1890 and World War I. An influx of about 15,000 Estonians after World War II has both increased the population and stimulated a rebirth of Estonian ethnic identity. The Estonians today are unified by strong nationalistic and anticommunist sentiments and active local, regional, national, and international ethnic associations. At the same time, a high intermarriage rate and a middle-class life-style are drawing many people in the younger generations into mainstream society.

Bibliography

Parming, Tönu, and Imre Lipping (1979). *Aspects of Cultural Life*. Estonian Heritage in America Series. New York: Estonian Learned Society in America.

Walko, Ann M. (1988). *Rejecting the Second-Generation Hypothesis: Maintaining Estonian Ethnicity in Lakewood, New Jersey*. New York: AMS Press.

FINNS. In 1980, 267,902 Americans claimed Finnish ancestry and another 347,970 claimed Finnish and other ethnic ancestry. Finnish immigration took place mainly from the 1860s on, with most settling and continuing to live in northern Michigan, Wisconsin, and Minnesota. In 1980, 38 percent of Finnish-Americans lived in this area. The original lure for many Finnish men was work in mining and the sawmills and on the railroads, although many eventually established small farms. Up to about 1920, Finnish identity remained strong and was maintained by the interlocking ties of churches, temperance groups, labor unions, and political parties. The membership and influence of these groups, however, waned after 1920, leading to rapid assimilation.

Bibliography

Finnish Americana: A Journal of Finnish American History and Culture. New York Mills, Minnesota.

Kivitso, Peter (1984). *Immigrant Socialists in the United States: The Case of Finns and the Left*. London, Ontario, and Toronto: Associated Universities Press.

FRENCH. In 1980, 3,504,542 Americans claimed French ancestry and another 10,168,192 claimed French and other ethnic ancestry. The general category of Americans of French ancestry includes people of French, French-Canadian, Acadian (Cajun), and Creole ancestry. It can also be stretched to include Bretons, Alsatians, and French Basques, although these groups are not French-speaking nor do they identify themselves as French; they are simply from areas that are today located in France. The two largest groups are the French-Canadians and those of direct French ancestry; the former outnumber the latter by a ratio of five to two. People who emigrated directly from France often came alone or in small groups and were rapidly assimilated into the general population through both intermarriage and wide dispersal, with a significant number settling in California. Those from the other French cultural traditions have tended to maintain their traditional culture for longer periods of time.

La Salle claimed what is now Louisiana for France in 1682, and Louisiana has since been known as the "French" region of the United States. The French influence in Louisiana is seen in the continued use of French in some areas, ad-

See also

EUROPE: Finns, French
RUSSIA AND EURASIA: Estonians
APPENDIX: French

Next to the English, the Germans are the largest ethnic population group in the United States.

herence to Roman Catholicism, French-style architecture and cuisine, and so on. This region was first settled by French-Canadians, who traveled down the Mississippi River and settled New Orleans, and then by Acadians, who fled from eastern Canada and numbered over 1,000 in Louisiana by 1800. Some of the Acadians eventually returned to Canada, but most remained in Louisiana and are today called Cajuns. They reside mostly in a region centered around Lafayette. These groups were added to by French arriving directly from France and French Creoles, Whites, and Blacks from French Caribbean colonies, most important, Saint Dominique (Haiti). In their travels south, the French Canadians also founded other French settlements including a number in Missouri.

The Northeast is the second major area of French settlement in the United States, with people of French-Canadian ancestry found in large numbers in the northern sections of Maine, New Hampshire, Vermont, and New York. The first French-Canadian settlers were mostly farmers, loggers, and traders. After 1860 they began moving farther south and found factory work in the leather goods, jewelry, cutlery, and brick industries that flourished in New England. They fought hard to maintain their French-Canadian heritage through inmarriage, residential isolation in distinctively French neighborhoods, use of the French language, and Roman Catholic parochial schools. But with the demise by the mid-twentieth century of the industries in which they worked, isolation from mainstream society became more difficult and assimilation increased.

Bibliography

Brault, Gerard J. (1986). *The French-Canadian Heritage in New England*. Hanover, N.H.: University Press of New England.

Breton, Raymond, and Pierre Savard, eds. (1982). *The Quebec and Acadian Diaspora in North America*. Toronto: Multi-cultural History Society of Ontario.

Carroll, R. (1987). *Cultural Misunderstanding: The French-American Experience*. Chicago: University of Chicago Press.

Dominguez, Virginia R. (1986). *White by Definition: Social Classification in Creole Louisiana*. New Brunswick, N.J.: Rutgers University Press.

GERMANS. In 1980, 17,943,485 Americans claimed German ancestry and another 31,280,661 claimed German and other ethnic ancestry. Next to the English, the Germans are the largest ethnic population group in the United States. German immigration began in the 1600s, was especially heavy during the early and mid-nineteenth century, peaking in the 1890s. Because relatively few Germans have arrived since then, most of them in the United States today are third-or fourth-generation Germans. Germans settled in rural areas, small cities, and urban centers. Today, areas with heavy German populations include Pennsylvania, southeastern Wisconsin, south-central Texas, and the Midwest. During the twentieth century, there has been a movement from rural areas to cities, with most recent arrivals also settling in cities.

Despite their large numbers and long settlement history, Germans are among the most assimilated of all European ethnic groups, and German neighborhoods, publications, associations, architecture, meeting halls, and so on have mostly disappeared. A number of factors account for this assimilation. First, German immigrants never formed a homogeneous linguistic, religious, or cultural group. Second, the early peaking of immigration in the 1890s means that few first- or second-generation Germans live in the United States. And, third, for some Germans, German ethnicity was a means to economic and political ends and, thus, became less important when German identity was not helpful such as during and after World Wars I and II.

A distinct group who have maintained their ethnic identity are the German-Russians (Russian-Germans, Germans from Russia). German-Russians are German-speaking peoples whose ancestors settled in the Volga and Black Sea regions of Russia in the 1700s. In the late 1800s, many of the Germans in Russia left in order to find political and religious freedom elsewhere. By the 1920s, at least 300,000 had settled in the United States. Those from the Volga region settled in Colorado, Kansas, and Nebraska where many were involved in sugar beet agriculture and processing. Many of those from north of the Black Sea became wheat farmers in the Dakotas. Today, there are over a million German-Russians in the United States. Their long tradition of independence, residential localizations, and desire to stay separate from other Germans has enabled them to maintain their distinct ethnic identity.

Bibliography

America and the Germans: An Assessment of a Three-Hundred-Year History. (1986). Philadelphia: University of Pennsylvania Press.

See also

EUROPE: Germans

APPENDIX: Germans

Arends, S. F. (1989). *The Central Dakota Germans: Their History, Language, and Culture*. Washington, D.C.: Georgetown University Press.

Miller, Randall M., ed. (1984). *Germans in America: Retrospect and Prospect*. Philadelphia: German Society of Pennsylvania.

Prewitt, Terry J. (1988). *German-American Settlement in an Oklahoma Town: Ecological, Ethnic and Cultural Change*. New York: AMS Press.

Rippley, LaVern J. (1976). *The German-Americans*. Boston: Twayne.

Sallet, Richard (1974). *Russian-German Settlements in the United States*. Translated by LaVern J. Rippley and Armand Bauer. Fargo: North Dakota Institute of Regional Studies.

GREEKS. In 1980, 615,882 Americans claimed Greek ancestry and another 343,974 claimed Greek and other ethnic ancestry. The nearly two-to-one ratio of full to partial Greek ancestry indicates that Greek-Americans continue to stress their Greek cultural identity. The first Greek immigrants arrived in Florida in 1768, although the current Greek-American population is composed mostly of the descendants of emigrants from Greece who arrived in the United States between 1880 and 1920. Greek-Americans were and remain a largely urban group and at 93 percent, have the highest urban-suburban settlement rate of any European-American group. Major concentrations of Greek-Americans live today in and around New York City, Boston, Washington, D.C., Chicago, and Tarpon Springs, Florida, with sizable populations in Los Angeles, San Francisco, Detroit, Pittsburgh, and Houston. In some locations the Greek population is associated with a particular economic specialization such as sponge fishing in Tarpon Springs and restaurant ownership in New England. Although Greektowns were never as prevalent as other ethnic enclaves, Greek identity was and is maintained through male socialization at coffeehouses, the Greek Orthodox religion and church, a strict division of labor with men working outside and women in the home, the continued use of the Greek language, marriage within the group, and economic cooperation among Greek-American businesspeople.

Bibliography

Georgakais, D. (1987). "The Greeks in America." *Journal of the Hellenic Diaspora* 14:131–143.

Kiriazis, James W. (1989). *Children of the Colossus: The Rhodian Greek Immigrants in the United States*. New York: AMS Press.

Patterson, George J., Jr. (1988). *The Unassimilated Greeks of Denver*. New York: AMS Press.

Psomiades, Harry J., and Alice Scourby (1982). *The Greek American Community in Transition*. New York: Pella Publishing.

Scourby, Alice (1984). *The Greek Americans*. Boston: Twayne.

HUNGARIANS. In 1980, 727,223 Americans claimed Hungarian and another 1,049,679 claimed Hungarian and other ethnic ancestry. Hungarians, also called Magyars, are ethnic Hungarians. The label "Hungarian" also sometimes includes people of Romanian, Slovak, Polish, Ukrainian, German, or Jewish ancestry who lived in what was the large territory that was Hungary prior to World War I. Ethnic Hungarians who came to the United States mostly between 1880 and World War I also displayed religious variation, with about 60 percent being Roman Catholic and the others Protestant, Greek Christian, and Eastern Orthodox. The immigrants, many of whom were single men, settled in regions offering the opportunity of heavy industrial work such as mining and steel production. Thus, the majority settled in four states—New Jersey, New York, Pennsylvania, and Ohio. Since 1950 there has been a gradual dispersal of Hungarians, especially to California and the South. The revolution against communist rule in Hungary in 1956 led the U.S. government to allow 35,000 Hungarians to immigrate since then. Better educated than Hungarians already settled in the United States, they tended to assimilate quickly into the American economy. Hungarians never established distinct neighborhoods comparable to those of other European immigrants. Rather, a strong sense of Hungarian identity resulted from the putting aside of religious and regional differences for economic solidarity and the formation of insurance associations, churches, and Magyar-language newspapers. Hungarian identity was further strengthened by Hungarian government programs designed to prevent assimilation in the United States and to encourage a return to Hungary. World War I was the effective end of this strong sense of Hungarian ethnicity in the United States, as Austro-Hungary was the enemy. After the war, ties to Hungary (now substantially reduced in size) weakened, and by the Second World War, English had essentially replaced or existed alongside Magyar in Hungarian associations, churches, newspapers, and schools. Although the post-1956 arrivals have remained concerned about Hungary and have been strongly

See also

EUROPE: Greeks, Hungarians

anticommunist, their presence has not produced a rebirth of Hungarian ethnicity.

Bibliography

Vardy, Steven B. (1985). *The Hungarian-Americans.* Boston: Twayne.

Weinberg, Daniel E. (1977). "Ethnic Identity in Industrial Cleveland: The Hungarians, 1900–1920." *Ohio History* 86:171–186.

People thought of as ethnic Irish in the United States today are the descendants of the Roman Catholic Irish who arrived mainly between 1830 and World War I.

IRISH. In 1980, 10,337,353 Americans claimed Irish ancestry and another 29,828,349 claimed Irish and other ethnic ancestry. Included in these figures are 17,000 people who claimed Scots-Irish identity (Northern Irish, Ulster Scots) who are mostly descended from Irish Protestants who settled in North America in the 1700s. This is probably a gross undercount as over half of the Irish in the United States are Protestants, and most of these are likely descended from the 1700s immigrants. Most people of Scots-Irish ancestry live in the rural South, Appalachia, and the Ozarks. Any unique Scots-Irish identity has now been lost, and they are generally lumped and lump themselves with other Americans of either Irish or English ancestry.

People thought of as ethnic Irish in the United States today are the descendants of the Roman Catholic Irish who arrived mainly between 1830 and World War I. Many of these immigrants were poor and fled to the United States to escape famine in Ireland. They formed distinctively Irish neighborhoods in eastern and midwestern cities, often centered around the parish church and large, stable families dominated by the wife/mother. It was in reference to these urban Catholic Irish that the negative stereotype of the drunken, violent Irishman developed. Involvement in the Roman Catholic church through social assistance programs, parochial schools, colleges and universities, and local and national religious leaders and involvement in local politics brought the Irish into the mainstream of American society. These involvements also benefited the Irish community and have given them much influence in American life.

The Irish are now dispersed across the United States in a pattern typical of the general American population. They were and remain a strongly urban-suburban group, however, with major concentrations in the Mid-Atlantic states, New England, Chicago, and Los Angeles. Despite their settlement across the nation, Irish cultural identity and influence on American society remains strong.

Bibliography

Akenson, Donald H. (1985). *Being Bad: Historians, Evidence, and the Irish in North America.* Port Credit, Ontario: P. D. Meany.

Cahill, Kevin M., ed. (1984). *The Irish American Revival.* Port Washington, N.Y.: Associated Faculty Press.

Clark, Dennis (1986). *Hibernia America: The Irish and Regional Cultures.* Westport, Conn.: Westview Press.

Greeley, Andrew M. (1982). *The Irish Americans.* New York: Harper and Row.

McCaffrey, Lawrence J., Ellen Skerrett, Michael F. Funchion, and Charles Fanning (1987). *The Irish in Chicago.* Urbana: University of Illinois Press.

Miller, Kerby A. (1985). *Emigrants and Exiles: Ireland and the Irish Exodus to North America.* New York: Oxford University Press.

ITALIANS. In 1980, 6,883,320 Americans claimed Italian ethnic ancestry and another 5,300,372 claimed Italian and other ethnic ancestry. Italian immigration to the United States can be divided into two periods. Prior to 1880, most immigrants were from northern Italy (Tuscany, Lombardy, Piedmont) and represented only a minority of those coming to the New World, with most settling in Brazil and Argentina. Most of the men were skilled craftsmen (masons and stone-cutters), and the families lived in small communities often composed of people from the same town in Italy. The second period, beginning in 1880 and continuing to World War I, was a time of major Italian immigration to and settlement in the United States. After 1880 most Italian immigrants were poor men or families from the southern provinces and Sicily. In competition for low-level factory jobs with Eastern European immigrants, the Italians tended to settle in cities where the Eastern Europeans were less numerous. Thus, Italian communities formed in Portland, Maine; Rochester, New York; Philadelphia, Pennsylvania; Newark, New Jersey; New Castle, Pennsylvania; Staten Island, New York; Chicago, Illinois; and New York City. Other Italian communities formed in midwestern cities, and a few farming communities formed in central California, Louisiana, Illinois, and Arkansas. But the Italian immigrants were mostly an urban group, with at least 85 percent settling in cities.

Italy became a unified nation only in 1870; thus Italian immigrants generally felt only a weak identity with Italy and lacked an overarching cultural tradition typical of other immigrant groups. This led to two unique developments in the

See also

EUROPE: Irish, Sicilians

APPENDIX: Irish, Italians

United States. First, strong ties were maintained with the town from which emigration took place, and a weaker sense of Italian identity prevailed. Second, within the first two generations of settlement, a syncretic Italian-American culture developed in the United States. Key features of the new cultural identity were an Americanized dialect of Italian that replaced the regional languages and dialects, a distinctly Italian tradition within the Irish-dominated American Roman Catholic church featuring a more "emotional-celebratory" set of practices, involvement in local politics, and the formation of associations, banks, and labor unions that served the Italian community. At the same time, the large patriarchal families were giving way to small families, with intermarriage to non-Italian Roman Catholics increasing in frequency.

Assimilation has progressed rapidly since World War II, and the Italians are now a middle-class, urban-suburban group. Although much of the population has shifted to suburbs, distinct Italian neighborhoods remain in many cities, including Philadelphia, New York, Chicago, St. Louis, Newark, and Providence. At the same time, the Italian-American cultural identity is maintained through extended family ties, the church, unique food preferences and practices, and a general sense of respect for the family and its oldest members.

Bibliography

Alba, Richard D. (1985). *Italian Americans*. Englewood Cliffs, N.J.: Prentice-Hall.

Belfiglio, C. V. (1983). *Italian Experience in Texas*. Austin: Eakin Press.

Cinel, Dino (1982). *From Italy to San Francisco: The Immigrant Experience*. Stanford: Stanford University Press.

di Leonardo, Micaela (1984). *The Varieties of Ethnic Experience: Kinship, Class, and Gender among California Italian-Americans*. Ithaca: Cornell University Press.

Martinelli, Phyllis C. (1987). *Ethnicity in the Sunbelt: Italian-American Migrants in Scottsdale, Arizona*. New York: AMS Press.

Mormino, Gary R. (1986). *Immigrants on the Hill: Italian-Americans in St. Louis, 1882–1982*. Urbana: University of Illinois Press.

Nelli, Humbert S. (1983). *From Immigrants to Ethnics: The Italian Americans*. New York: Oxford University Press.

Schoener, Allon (1987). *The Italian Americans*. New York: Macmillan.

Tomasi, Lydio F., ed. (1985). *Italian Americans: New Perspectives in Italian Immigration and Ethnicity*. New York: Center for Migration Studies.

Tricarico, Donald (1984). *The Italians of Greenwich Village*. New York: Center for Migration Studies.

LATVIANS. In 1980, 55,563 Americans claimed Latvian ancestry and another 36,578 claimed Latvian and other ethnic ancestry. Latvians are people who trace their ethnic identity to the territory that is now the Latvian Soviet Socialist Republic. Latvian is an Indo-European language closely related only to Lithuanian. Latvians came to the United States in two major migrations. The first group, composed mainly of peasants and artisans looking for better opportunities, emigrated from Russia between 1905 and World War I. They were mostly Lutherans or Baptists and initially took unskilled work in the Northeast and in communities in Wisconsin and Minnesota. Some returned to Latvia after the Russian Revolution, and the descendants of those who remained in the United States are now largely assimilated into American society. The second group contained about 40,000 emigrants who arrived after World War II, with many classified as displaced persons seeking refuge from war-ravaged Europe and Soviet rule. Because of their more recent arrival and strong Latvian nationalistic feelings, they have resisted assimilation and make up the majority of Latvian-Americans today. About 50 percent still speak Latvian and 85 percent are members of Latvian ethnic organizations. Latvian culture is a mix of native, Slavic, Scandinavian, and German elements that have been combined over the centuries into a unique Latvian cultural tradition. To outsiders, Latvian culture is most notable for its rich collection of folk songs (*dainas*), unique art and design motifs, and native peasant dress.

Bibliography

Karklis, Maruta, Liga Streips, and Laimonis Streips, comps. (1974). *The Latvians in America, 1640–1973: A Chronology and Fact Book*. Dobbs Ferry, N.Y.: Oceania Publications.

LITHUANIANS. In 1980, 339,438 Americans claimed Lithuanian ethnic ancestry and another 403,338 claimed Lithuanian and other ancestry. The majority of Americans of Lithuanian ancestry are descendants of immigrants who settled in the United States between 1880 and World War I. They came mainly from the eastern sections of the

Italian-American cultural identity is maintained through extended family ties, the church, unique food preferences and practices, and respect for the family.

See also

Latvians, Lithuanians

territory that is now the Lithuanian Soviet Socialist Republic. Most were Roman Catholics, and they often settled near Polish communities in industrial cities and towns in the Northeast and Midwest where the men worked in the mines and factories. Beginning about 1890, Lithuanians began to distance themselves from the Poles and distinct Lithuanian communities formed around their own parishes, kin and friendship networks, local and national associations, and the Lithuanian-language press. From about 1900 on, their economic role began changing, as Lithuanians were often involved in labor unions, strikes, and other efforts to improve working conditions. Since then, the Lithuanians have assimilated into American society, though distinct Lithuanian ethnic enclaves, such as the Marquette Park area of Chicago, still exist. New arrivals after World War I and World War II brought strong nationalistic and anticommunist sentiments with them. Even in this group, however, a distinct Lithuanian cultural identity is disappearing.

Bibliography

Baskauskas, Liucija (1983). *An Urban Enclave: Lithuanian Refugees in Los Angeles*. New York: AMS Press.

Gedmintas, Aleksandras (1988). *An Interesting Bit of Identity: The Dynamics of Ethnic Identity in a Lithuanian-American Community*. New York: AMS Press.

Jonitis, Peter P. (1983). *The Acculturation of the Lithuanians of Chester, Pennsylvania*. New York: AMS Press.

NORWEGIANS. In 1980, 1,260,997 Americans claimed Norwegian ancestry and another 2,192,842 claimed Norwegian and other ethnic ancestry. Starting in 1840, Norwegians began forming church-based farming communities in western Wisconsin, Minnesota, and North Dakota, regions that provided the settlers with affordable farmland. A migration of younger people from the Midwest farther west led to the formation of a Norwegian community in Washington. Today, over 20 percent of Norwegian-Americans live in Minnesota, mostly in and around Minneapolis. Beginning in 1853, the Norwegian Evangelical Lutheran Church (the Norwegian Synod) became the focal point for the continuation of Norwegian culture in the New World. In 1962, the church merged with the German and Dutch churches to form the American Lutheran church, though Norwegian identity continues in rural Norwegian communities in the Midwest.

Although most Americans of Norwegian ancestry are assimilated into American society, Norwegian ethnic identity is notably strong, because of a combination of factors including the rural church-based communities, Norwegian colleges, ethnic organizations, and Norwegian social and business networks in some Midwest cities.

Bibliography

Gjerde, Jon (1985). *From Peasants to Farmers: The Migration from Balestrand, Norway, to the Upper Middle West*. Cambridge: Cambridge University Press.

Lovoll, Odd S. (1984). *The Promise of America: A History of the Norwegian-American People*. Minneapolis: University of Minnesota Press in cooperation with the Norwegian-American Historical Association.

Strickon, Arnold, and R. A. Ibarra (1983). "The Changing Dynamics of Ethnicity: Norwegians and Tobacco in Wisconsin." *Ethnic and Racial Studies* 6:174–197.

PENNSYLVANIA DUTCH. This general label refers to the Amish, Mennonites, Moravians, Dunkers, Schwenkfelders, and others who settled mostly in Pennsylvania. These peoples, fleeing religious persecution, were either German or Swiss (all were German speakers), not Dutch. The reference to "Dutch" is a modern-day confusion resulting from the word *Deutsch* meaning "German." Thus, the Pennsylvania Dutch are actually Pennsylvania Germans and are sometimes correctly labeled as such. Most Pennsylvania Dutch are today found in Pennsylvania and North Carolina.

Bibliography

Reimensnyder, Barbara L. (1988). *Powwowing in Union County: A Study of Pennsylvania German Folk Medicine in Context*. New York: AMS Press.

Swank, Scott (1983). *Art of the Pennsylvania Germans*. New York: W. W. Norton.

POLES. In 1980, 3,805,740 Americans claimed Polish ancestry and another 4,422,297 claimed Polish and other ethnic ancestry. The Poles are one of the largest and, in some ways, the least assimilated of the European-American groups. Poles in the United States are mostly ethnic Poles whose ancestors spoke Polish, German, and Russian. Distinct ethnic minorities in Poland, including the Carpatho-Rusyns, Kashubians, Górali, Mazurians, Silesians, and Galicians are also represented in the United States, and they have tended to remain somewhat separate from the ethnic Polish majority. The majority of Poles have arrived

See also

EUROPE: Norwegians

NORTH AMERICA:

Amish

since 1850. The first large group of settlers was composed of German-speaking Poles who settled in cities already inhabited by Germans. Later arrivals, though from non-German sections of Poland, settled near those already in the United States. This migration pattern led to the formation of major Polish communities in cities with large German communities such as Buffalo, Milwaukee, Chicago, New York, and Cleveland. Other major Polish communities formed in Pittsburgh, Detroit, Philadelphia, and the Connecticut River valley in New England. Poles have remained an urban group, with 80 percent still living in urban areas. Small rural communities based on farming formed in south-central Texas, the northern Midwest, Missouri, and Nebraska.

Polish men generally found relatively low-level physical work such as mining, steel-working, meat-packing, automobile manufacturing, and factory labor. From 1865 through World War II the Poles remained a relatively homogeneous group, with their lives centered around the Roman Catholic parish and parochial schools, extended family ties, associations, multiple-family housing, Polish neighborhoods and stores, the Polish press, and Polish beliefs and customs at holidays and life-cycle celebrations. A religious schism developed around the turn of the century, leading to the formation of the independent Polish National Catholic Church of America, which now has about 300,000 members. Since the end of World War II, Poles have been assimilating more rapidly into American society, fueled primarily by upward social mobility from a working-class to a middle-class life-style. Today, the majority of Poles work in white-collar and skilled occupations. Still, Polish assimilation has been slower than among other groups, with intermarriage mostly with other Eastern European Catholics, a slower loss of the Polish language, the continued existence of Polish neighborhoods in large cities, and ties often maintained with relatives in Poland. A reaction to the negative stereotype of Poles and the Solidarity movement in Poland have also contributed to a strong sense of Polish identity in recent years.

Bibliography

Bodnar, John, Roger Simon, and Michael P. Weber (1982). *Lives of Their Own: Blacks, Italians, and Poles in Pittsburgh, 1900–1960*. Urbana: University of Illinois Press.

Obidinski, Eugene, and Helen Stankiewicz Zand (1987). *Polish Folkways in America: Community and Family*. Polish Studies Series 5. Lanham, Md.: University Press of America.

Mocha, Franck, ed. (1978). *Poles in America*. Stevens Point, Wis.: Worzalla Publishing.

Polish-American Studies: A Journal of Polish-American History and Culture. Binghamton, N.Y.: Polish American Historical Association.

PORTUGUESE

In 1980, 616,362 Americans claimed Portuguese ancestry and another 407,989 claimed Portuguese and other ethnic ancestry. Americans of Portuguese descent came either from Portugal or from the Portuguese Azores and Madeira islands. Portuguese immigration patterns are different from most other European-American groups in that a large percentage arrived in recent years (about 39 percent since 1959) and a large number (29 percent) settled in California. The Portuguese are essentially bicoastal with major concentrations in Hawaii (descendants of Azorean whalers and Madeiran sugar plantation workers), farming communities in central California, and fishing and industrial communities in southern New England and the northern Mid-Atlantic states. The early arrivals were mostly Azoreans and Madeirans who settled and formed communities populated by immigrants from the same islands. With life centered around the patriarchal family and family financial obligations, the traditional culture has survived to some extent even among the third and fourth generations. The more recent arrivals have resisted integration into these communities and have instead directed their efforts at maintaining political and economic ties with Portugal, activities of less interest to the descendants of the earlier settlers.

Bibliography

Cabral, Stephen L. (1988). *Tradition and Transformation: Portuguese Feasting in New Bedford*. New York: AMS Press.

Gilbert, Dorothy A. (1987). *Recent Portuguese Immigrants to Fall River, Massachusetts*. New York: AMS Press.

Pap, Leo (1981). *The Portuguese-Americans*. Boston: Twayne.

See also

APPENDIX: Poles

ROMANIANS. (Roumanians, Rumanians). In 1980, 141,675 Americans claimed Romanian ancestry and another 173,583 claimed Romanian and other ethnic ancestry. Most Romanians who arrived in the United States before 1895 were Jewish. Romanian immigrants since 1895 include Jews and non-Jews, with both groups included in the above figures. Romanians settled mainly in industrial cities such as Cleveland, East Chicago, Gary, and Detroit where men worked in the steel and auto industries. Although the Romanian church, clubs, and press were active for some years, the descendants of these immigrants are now largely assimilated into American society. More recent arrivals have lived apart from these communities and have focused their attention on anticommunist activities and Romanian-U.S. relations. The community has recently coalesced around the overthrow of the communist leadership of Romania in 1989–1990.

Bibliography

Bobango, Gerald J. (1978). "The Union and League of Romanian Societies: An 'Assimilating Force.'" *East European Quarterly* 12:85–92.

Roceris, Alexandra (1982). *Language Maintenance within an American Community: The Case of Roman-*
ian. Grass Lake and Jackson, Mich: Romanian-American Heritage Center.

RUSSIANS. In 1980, 1,379,585 Americans claimed Russian ancestry and another 1,401,847 claimed Russian and other ancestry. The category "Russian" generally includes people who emigrated from what was the Russian Empire and is now the Soviet Union. This includes a number of culturally distinct groups including ethnic Russians, Ukrainians, Georgians, Latvians, Lithuanians, Estonians, Belorussians (Byelorussians, White Russians), Galicians, Russian Jews, Doukhobors, Old Believers, Molokans, Carpatho-Rusyns, and Cossacks. Stretched to its limits, Russians can also include peoples from non-European regions of the Soviet Union such as the Azerbaijani, Kalmyk, and Turkestani who do not consider themselves Russian. In short, "Russians" is more correctly viewed as a territorial-political label than an ethnic one, except when applied specifically to ethnic Russians.

Russians immigrated to the United States in five stages. The first group was composed of traders who settled in Alaska to trade for furs with the local American Indian groups. When Russia sold Alaska to the United States in 1867, they either returned home or migrated to California.

See also
RUSSIA AND EURASIA:
Russians
APPENDIX: Russians

From the 1880s to World War I, Russians settled in industrial cities in the East and Midwest. After the Russian Revolution of 1917, a large influx of mostly middle-class, anticommunist Russians also settled in large cities. After World War II, Russian displaced persons and refugees made their way to the United States, often with stays in other countries first. Finally, a small number of Russians have immigrated to the United States since the 1950s. In the past, participation in the Eastern Orthodox church was a major factor in maintaining Russian ethnic identity. Red scares in the twentieth century (1919–1920, 1950s) led to sometimes hostile relations between Russian-Americans and mainstream society. But the cold war and the resultant interest in Russian life have somewhat lessened hostility toward Russian-Americans. Today, the Russians do not form a viable, cohesive ethnic entity in the United States, partly because of internal variations and partly because of the relatively few Russians who have arrived in the past forty years.

Bibliography

Gerber, Stanford N. (1983). *Russkoya Celo: The Ethnography of a Russian-American Community*. New York: AMS Press.

Townsend, Joan B. (1975). "Mercantilism and Societal Change: An Ethnohistoric Examination of Some Essential Variables." *Ethnohistory* 22:21–32.

SCOTS

SCOTS. In 1980, 1,172,904 Americans claimed Scottish ancestry and another 8,875,912 claimed Scottish and other ethnic ancestry. The distinction between Lowland and Highland Scots, though still important in Scotland, has not been of concern for some years in the United States. Because of their early settlement beginning in the late 1600s, high intermarriage rate, and dispersal across the entire United States, Scots are largely assimilated into American society and no longer display the degree of ethnic identity found in non-English-speaking ethnic groups of later arrival.

Bibliography

Chalker, Fussell M. (1976). "Highland Scots in the Georgia Lowlands." *Georgia Historical Quarterly* 60:35–42.

MacDonell, M. (1982). *The Emigrant Experience: Songs of Highland Emigrants in North America*. Toronto: University of Toronto Press.

SERBS. In 1980, 49,621 Americans reported Serbian ethnic ancestry and another 51,320 reported Serbian and other ancestry. These figures are probably a gross undercount, as many people of Serbian background often identified themselves as Yugoslavians. A more realistic estimate of Americans of Serbian ancestry is 200,000. Serbia is one of the regions of the modern nation of Yugoslavia. The other major regions are Slovenia, Montenegro, Bosnia, Macedonia, and Croatia. Most immigrants of Serbian background came from the Bosnia, Montenegro, Croatia, and Vojvodina regions, primarily between 1903 and 1909. While Serbs and Croats came from different villages in Europe, they tended to settle near one another in the United States, mainly in the iron and steel-producing cities of Detroit, Chicago, Milwaukee, and Cleveland and the western Pennsylvania and eastern Ohio regions, which provided men with employment opportunities. Since World War II, about 50,000 Serbs, many of them displaced persons, have settled in the United States. Better educated and more urban than the earlier generation of immigrants, they have tended to remain separate from the already established Serbian communities. Although many Serbs have assimilated into mainstream life, the opportunity for maintaining a strong Serbian identity is readily available for those who so choose. A strong, politically conservative Serbianism ethos still exists in the United States, ties are maintained with the homeland, Serbian social organizations at all levels are highly organized, and Serbian music, epic poetry, and traditions provide a unifying bond.

Bibliography

Brkich, Lazar (1980). "Serbian Fraternal, Social, and Cultural Organizations in America." In *Studies in Ethnicity: The East European Experience in America*, edited by C. A. Ward, P. Shashko, and D. E. Pienkos, 103–114. Boulder: East European Monographs.

Padgett, Deborah (1988). *Settlers and Sojourners: A Study of Serbian Adaptation in Milwaukee, Wisconsin*. New York: AMS Press.

SLOVAKS. In 1980, 361,384 Americans reported Slovak ethnic ancestry and another 415,422 reported Slovak and other ancestry. These figures are almost certainly undercounts, as Slovaks who reported Czechoslovakian ancestry were classified as Czechs. Slovaks are people from the Slovakia region, which is today part of the modern nation of Czechoslovakia. The major Slovak immigration to the United States began in the 1870s, with the Slovaks settling in the anthracite mining region of eastern Pennsylvania and the coal mining and steel areas of western Pennsylvania and eastern Ohio. By the 1920s, the Slovaks had settled in the towns and cities where they continue to live today, with the only major population shift being a movement by the post-World War II generation to the suburbs. The Slovaks display a high degree of geographical persistence, with only 3 percent living in California, the lowest percentage of any European ethnic group. The pre-World War II ethnic culture was centered on family-based communities, wage labor in what was often the only factory or mine in the town, the Roman Catholic church, local clubs, and home ownership. Cohesion was reinforced by a general disinterest in education and the settlement of people from the same Slovak villages near one another in the United States. Today, a strong sense of Slovak identity remains, focused on the church, Slovak cuisine, and holiday rituals, although intermarriage has increased, family visits have replaced the two-generation domestic unit, and Slovak is spoken by only a few.

Bibliography

Stolarik, Mark M. (1985). *Growing up on the South Side: Three Generations of Slovaks in Bethlehem, Pennsylvania, 1880–1976.* Lewisburg, Pa.: Bucknell University.

Stolarik, Mark M. (1988). *Immigration and Urbanization: The Slovak Experience.* New York: AMS Press.

SLOVENES (Slovenians). In 1980, 63,587 Americans claimed Slovenian ancestry and another 62,876 claimed Slovenian and other ethnic ancestry. Slovenes are people from Slovenia, the northwestern section of the modern nation of Yugoslavia. The major arrival of Slovenes took place before World War I with major population centers forming in the mining areas of Colorado, northern Minnesota, and western Pennsylvania and in the industrial cities of Cleveland and Chicago. Slovene cultural identity was maintained through the Roman Catholic church, fraternal insurance societies, singing societies, and the Slovene press. Assimilation has been slowed by the arrival of a second large wave of immigrants in the 1950s, who are much concerned about and involved in political developments in Yugoslavia.

Bibliography

Prisland, Marie (1968). *From Slovenia to America.* Chicago: Slovenian Women's Union of America.

Susel, Rudolph M. (1983). "The Perpetuation and Transformation of Ethnic Identity among Slovene Immigrants in America and the American-Born Generations: Continuity and Change." In *The Dynamics of East European Ethnicity outside of Eastern Europe*, edited by Irene P. Winner and Rudolph M. Susel, 109–132. Cambridge, Mass.: Schenkman.

Voynick, S. M. (1984). *Leadville: A Miner's Epic.* Missoula, Mont.: Mountain Press.

SORBS (Wends). The Sorbs are a distinct cultural group in Germany. The Sorbian territory is located in the Lusatia region in the southeastern corner of what was the German Democratic Republic (East Germany). Sorbian is a West Slavic language, with Lower and Upper dialects spoken in northern and southern Sorbia, respectively. The number of Sorbs in North America is unknown, as they have usually been counted as German. Most are descendants of Sorbs who emigrated in the last half of the nineteenth century and settled in Texas near already existing German communities in present-day Lee Country. Smaller communities also formed in Nebraska and Canada, although the Texas ones were the largest and most distinctly Sorbian. In recent years, some Sorbs have moved to cities in Texas, including Houston, San Antonio, and Austin. Initially close to the Germans through intermarriage, nearby residence, and language (most Sorbs also spoke German), self-identification as Americans began with World War I, in part as an effort to distance themselves from Germany. The traditional culture centered on distinct religious customs and holiday and life-cycle celebrations, although assimilation has increased rapidly in recent years.

SPANIARDS. Spaniards should be differentiated from Latinos who are people of Latin American ancestry. Because Spanish immigrants either were not counted at all or were at times lumped with Latinos, it is impossible to say how many Spaniards have immigrated to and settled in the United States—one estimate suggests about 250,000. Major population centers are in New York City, southern California, Louisiana, and Florida. The American Southwest has had an especially strong Spanish influence, dating to Coronado's expedition of 1540, though Mexican (which is also partly Spanish) and American Indian influences are also important in the region. For the most part, Spanish immigrants and their descendants have rapidly assimilated into American society and no strong sense of Spanish identity or culture has ever emerged. This is in part

See also
EUROPE: Catalans, Galicians

because they were few in number compared to other immigrant groups also arriving in the early twentieth century and in part because regional cultural identities (such as Galician, Catalonian) were more important in Spain than any sense of a national culture. In the United States these regional identities have been manifested in regional associations.

Bibliography

Brophy, Don, and Edythe Westenhauer, eds. (1978). *The Story of Catholics in America*. New York: Paulist Press.

Williams, James C. (1978). "Cultural Tension: The Origins of American Santa Barbara." *Southern California Quarterly* 60:349–377.

SWEDES. In 1980, 1,288,341 Americans claimed Swedish ancestry and another 3,057,051 claimed Swedish and other ethnic ancestry. Swedes began immigrating to the United States in sizable numbers after 1840, settling mostly in the Midwest, where they often formed communities based on kin ties, or in areas where work similar to that in Sweden (such as metalworking, iron mining) was available. Illinois, Minnesota, Wisconsin, Iowa, Nebraska, and Kansas were areas of heavy settlement, with smaller communities forming in New England and New York where specialized work was available. Chicago and Minneapolis were the major centers for urban Swedes, with ties maintained with the Norwegian and German communities. Although Swedes resisted intermarriage (except with Norwegians), they nonetheless rapidly assimilated into American society. They learned English quickly (most Swedes were literate), desired U.S. citizenship, valued public education, and were upwardly mobile, moving from the cities to the suburbs. The 1970s saw a revival of interest in Swedish identity, reflected in public celebrations of Swedish holidays, Scandinavian study programs at colleges, and the economic success of Swedish retail outlets.

Bibliography

Kastrup, Allan (1975). *The Swedish Heritage in America*. St. Paul, Minn.: The Swedish Council of America.

Moe, M. L., ed. (1983). *Saga from the Hills: A History of the Swedes of Jamestown, New York*. Jamestown, N.Y.: Fenton Historical Society.

Wheeler, Wayne (1983). *An Analysis of Social Change in a Swedish-Immigrant Community*. New York: AMS Press.

SWISS. In 1980, 235,355 Americans claimed Swiss ancestry and another 746,188 claimed Swiss and other ancestry. Switzerland is a pluralistic country populated by four linguistic-cultural groups: French speakers in the West, German speakers in the center and North, Romansch speakers in the East, and Italian speakers in the South. Nearly 90 percent of Swiss settlers in the United States prior to 1900 were German speakers (German-speaking Swiss are also the most numerous group in Switzerland), although some had lived in other European countries prior to their migration to the New World, which may have blurred their sense of Swiss identity. The concentrations of Swiss in the United States today represent four distinct cultural traditions. The largest concentration of Swiss is the Old Order Amish and Mennonites in Pennsylvania, Ohio, Indiana, and Kansas. A second large concentration is the Swiss Mormons in northern Utah whose ancestors converted to Mormonism in the 1880s. A third group is the Italian Swiss in northern and central California whose ancestors settled in the San Francisco area. Last is the best-known Swiss concentration centered in and around Madison, Wisconsin, known as "the Swiss capital of the United States" and a major tourist attraction. The first Swiss settlement was formed in 1845 by immigrants who at first made their living from dairy farming and cheese making, two occupations associated also with other Swiss settlements.

Bibliography

Kuhn, W. Ernst (1976). "Recent Swiss Immigration into Nebraska: An Empirical Study." *Swiss American Historical Society Newsletter* 12:12–20.

Lewis, Brian A. (1973). "Swiss-German in Wisconsin: The Impact of English." *American Speech* 48: 211–228.

UKRAINIANS. In 1980, 381,084 Americans claimed Ukrainian ethnic ancestry and another 348,972 claimed Ukrainian and other ancestry. The relatively low percentage of Ukrainians claiming mixed ethnic ancestry indicates that the Ukrainians continue to exist as a distinct cultural group in the United States. Among the Ukrainian immigrants who arrived between 1880 and World War I, 85 to 95 percent were classified as Carpatho-Rusyns (Ruthenians), and few saw themselves as ethnically Ukrainian. After the end of World War I and the establishment of the

Madison, Wisconsin is known as "the Swiss capital of the United States."

See also

EUROPE: Germans, German Swiss, Italian Swiss, Swedes

APPENDIX: Swedes

RUSSIA AND EURASIA: Ukrainians

Ukrainian Soviet Socialist Republic, descendants of this first wave of immigrants who were from Galicia have often preferred to define themselves as Ukrainian. The more than 100,000 Ukrainians who came to the United States after World War I were mainly from the center of the Ukraine, and their presence has strengthened Ukrainian identity. Fifty percent of Ukrainians lived in either New York State or Pennsylvania in 1980, with the New York City area being the major population and cultural center, especially with many immigrants since World War II settling there. The Ukrainians continue to exist as a distinct cultural group within American society, although many are, at the same time, active participants in the national economic system. Ukrainian schools, social clubs, associations, churches (Catholic, Protestant, and Orthodox), resorts, and publications all provide the opportunity for a full life within the Ukrainian community. A shared sense of identity is further maintained through continued use of the Ukrainian language, a high rate of endogamous marriage, and strong and active membership in fraternal organizations. External forces also play a role in maintaining group identity, especially involvement in political movements to establish a free Ukrainian nation and continued estrangement from the Polish- and Russian-American communities.

Bibliography

Stachin, Matthew (1976). "Ukrainian Religious, Social and Political Organization in the U.S. Prior to World War II." *Ukrainian Quarterly* 32:385–392.

WELSH. In 1980, 308,363 Americans claimed Welsh ancestry and another 1,356,235 claimed Welsh and other ethnic ancestry. Although the Welsh began arriving in North America in the late 1600s, the major migrations were in the mid- and late-1800s. Those who came first were largely farmers who sought to escape assimilation into English society by forming Welsh-speaking communities in North America. Those who came after 1880 were largely miners who settled in the coal-mining areas of northeast Pennsylvania, eventually moving from coal mining into work in the steel and related industries. Sizable populations of Welsh-Americans still live in this region, although most people of Welsh ancestry are assimilated into American society, as indicated by the high intermarriage rate and migration of many Welsh to the West Coast.

Bibliography

Ashton, Elwyn T. (1984). *The Welsh in the United States*. Shoreham, England: Elwyn T. Ashton.

Ellis, David M. (1973). "The Assimilation of the Welsh in Central New York State." *Welsh Historical Review* 6:424–447.

Thomas, R. D. (1983). *Hanes Cymry America: A History of the Welsh in America*. Translated by Phillips G. Davies. Washington, D.C.: University Press of America. (Originally published, 1872.)

EUROPEAN-CANADIANS

In 1986, about 78 percent of Canadians were descended from people of European ethnicity. The short summaries that follow present information on the population, distribution, migration history, and cultural persistence of thirty-three European ethnic groups in Canada. Appended to many of these summaries are short lists of publications, most of which are recent studies of a particular ethnic community or a general historical or cultural survey of the ethnic group. The population information in these summaries for 1981 is taken from the 1981 census of Canada, and that for 1986, from the estimates (based on a 20 percent sample) from the 1986 census of Canada as reported in the *Canada Year Book 1990*.

ALBANIANS. In 1981, 1,265 Canadians claimed Albanian ethnic ancestry. This is probably an undercount, as many Albanians do not identify themselves as such and others identify themselves as Yugoslavians. The distinction between Gheg and Tosk Albanians, which was significant in pre-World War II Albania, has disappeared in Canada. Most present-day Albanian-Canadians are descendants of Albanians who settled in Canada between 1900 and World War I. Given their small numbers and third- and fourth-generation status, they are now much assimilated into Canadian society. Ethnic identity is expressed mainly within the the context of small family groups.

ARMENIANS. In 1986, an estimated 22,525 Canadians claimed Armenian ancestry, 60 percent of whom lived in the Montreal area and 35 percent in the Toronto-Hamilton area. Armenia is today a unit of the Soviet Union, as the Armenian Soviet Socialist Republic, and in the past

See also

French Canadians

EUROPE: Albanians

RUSSIA AND EURASIA:
Armenians

APPENDIX: Welsh

Armenians have been under the control of various other peoples, including the Turks, Russians, and Iranians. Armenians began immigrating to Canada in the late 1880s, and by 1915 1,000 Armenians were living in the country. The major period of Armenian immigration came in the 1950s and 1960s when thousands arrived from the Middle East and Mediterranean countries. Many of these were professionals or business people who settled in urban areas. As in other nations where they have settled, Armenian ethnicity remains strong in Canada, centered around the memory of the genocide of 1915–1922 by the Turks and ongoing concern over the possible loss of their traditional homeland. Armenian institutions include the Armenian National Apostolic church, the Armenian National Committee, the Armenian-language press, and language-maintenance programs.

Bibliography

Kaprielian, Isabel (1987). "Migratory Caravans: Armenian Sojourners in Canada." *Journal of American Ethnic History* 6:20–38.

AUSTRIANS. In 1986, an estimated 24,900 Canadians claimed Austrian ancestry with over 40 percent living in Ontario. Unlike many other European nations, Austria was not formed on a distinct ethnic population base, and thus Austrians are more accurately described as a nationality rather than an ethnic group. Austrians who have settled in Canada, including a sizable minority of Jews, have assimilated rapidly into Canadian society and tend to affiliate with the much larger German community.

Bibliography

Keyserlingk, Robert H. (1983). "Policy or Practice: Canada and Austria 1938–1948." In *Roots and Realities among Eastern and Central Europeans*, edited by Martin L. Kovacs, 25–39. Edmonton, Alberta: Central and East European Studies Association of Canada.

BELGIANS. In 1986, an estimated 28,395 Canadians claimed Belgian ethnic ancestry. The nation of Belgium is inhabited by two distinct groups—the Flemish in the Northwest (in the region commonly called Flanders), who speak a language closely related to Dutch, and the Walloons in the South and Southeast, who speak French. This distinction was maintained in Canada, with the Walloons settling primarily in Quebec and the Flemish settling in Ontario and forming Belgian communities in the western provinces of Alberta, Manitoba, Saskatchewan and British Columbia. Because of their small numbers, wide dispersal, and cultural similarity to British and French Canadians, the Belgians are highly assimilated into Canadian society.

Bibliography

Magee, Joan (1987). *The Belgians in Ontario: A History.* Toronto and Reading: Dundurn Press.

BYELORUSSIANS (Belorussians, Kryvians, White Russians, White Ruthenians). Estimates place the number of people of Byelorussian ethnic ancestry in Canada today at from 30,000 to more than 100,000. No accurate count of Canadians of Byelorussian ancestry is possible, as those who arrived prior to World War I were often identified as either Russians or Poles and they were not enumerated separately in the census until 1971. Byelorussia is the region that today is located in the Soviet Union, south and east of Lithuania and Latvia. The Byelorussians arrived in three major waves. Those coming in the first decade of the twentieth century mainly settled in cities in northern Ontario where they worked as industrial laborers. Often identified by themselves and others as Poles, they were rapidly absorbed by the Canadian Polish community. The group that arrived after World War I settled in the prairies where they often established farming communities. The group arriving after World War II were more educated and skilled than the earlier groups and settled in cities. This latter group is also much involved in maintaining their Byelorussian identity through associations, festivals, Byelorussian publications, and a strong desire for an independent Byelorussian homeland.

Bibliography

Sadouski, John (1981). *A History of the Byelorussians in Canada.* Belleville, Ontario: Mika Publishing Co.

CROATS (Croatians). In 1986, an estimated 35,115 Canadians claimed Croat ethnic ancestry. Since it is estimated that at least 75,000 Croats have immigrated to Canada in the twentieth century, this figure is a gross undercount. Most Canadians of Croat ancestry are now identified by themselves or others as simply Canadians or Yugoslavians. (Croatia is one of six republics that

In 1986, about 78 percent of Canadians were descended from people of European ethnicity.

See also

EUROPE: Austrians, Croats, Flemish
RUSSIA AND EURASIA: Belarussians

form the modern nation of Yugoslavia.) Croats in Canada today are mostly people who immigrated there in the 1900s or are their descendants. The first wave of immigration preceded World War I and consisted mainly of men who took mining, railroad, and logging work in the western provinces. Those who came between the world wars settled in both rural and urban areas where they established distinctively Croat neighborhoods, displaying many of the communal and co-operative features of the *zadruga*, the extended family homestead common in rural Croatia. By the 1950s, the Croatian identity of these groups and their children had eroded, and many had adopted a middle-class life-style. After World War II, and especially after 1955, there was a third major immigration of Croats to Canada, which has led to a fragmentation of the Canadian Croat population into the assimilated earlier arrivals and the post-World War II group, which strives to maintain its Croat ethnic identity. The latter group is largely urban; its members have founded new Croatian Catholic churches, economic and political associations, social clubs, and music and art groups, and are served by a revitalized Croatian press, language maintenance programs, and family-based businesses and partnerships that rely on cooperative features of the zadrugas. There is also considerable interest and involvement in efforts to establish an independent Croatian homeland.

Bibliography

Rasporich, A. W. (1982). *For a Better Life: A History of the Croatians in Canada*. Toronto: McClelland & Stewart.

CZECHS.

In 1981, 67,695 Canadians claimed Czechoslovakian ethnic ancestry, but this figure requires a number of qualifications. First, Czechoslovakian is not an ethnic category, but a national one, referring to the citizens of the modern nation of Czechoslovakia (Czecho-Slovakia), whose two major ethnic groups are the Czechs and the Slovaks. Second, it is likely an underestimate of the number of ethnic Czechs and Slovaks in Canada, as prior to 1918 they were often identified as Austrians or Hungarians. And, third, the number of people of Slovak ancestry is probably two to three times greater than those of Czech ancestry. Substantial Czech immigration to Canada began in the 1880s, with the first settlers relocating from the United States to form farming communities in the prairies and to mine in the

Rockies. A large number came in the late 1800s and early 1900s, again from the United States, but also now directly from the Czech region of Austro-Hungary. They settled mainly in Alberta and Manitoba. The greatest influx occurred after World War I, with many of these immigrants working in factories in cities such as Toronto, Montreal, Windsor, Hamilton, and Vancouver, though distinctively Czech neighborhoods rarely formed. Following World War II and the establishment of communist rule in Czechoslovakia, more Czechs arrived in Canada. In the absence of ethnic communities, Czech identity was maintained through the church (Roman Catholic and Baptist), economic and political associations, social clubs, and the Czech and Czechoslovakian press. At the same time, Czechs have become well integrated into Canadian society.

Bibliography

Gellner, John, and John Smerek (1968). *The Czechs and Slovaks in Canada*. Toronto: University of Toronto Press.

Horna, Jarmila L. A. (1979). "The Entrance Status of Czech and Slovak Immigrant Women." In *Two Nations, Many Cultures: Ethnic Groups in Canada*, edited by Jean L. Elliott, 270–279. Scarborough, Ontario: Prentice-Hall of Canada.

DANES.

In 1986, an estimated 39,950 Canadians claimed Danish ethnic ancestry. Most Danes immigrated to Canada either between 1870 and World War I or in the 1950s. Those who came before World War I moved directly from Denmark or indirectly from Danish settlements in the United States. The former often settled in the Maritime Provinces and Ontario; many of the latter settled in the Prairie provinces. Those who came in the 1950s settled mainly in cities, especially in Alberta, British Columbia, and Ontario. Because many of these immigrants eventually returned to Denmark, the Danish population in Canada has been relatively unstable, doubling in the years between 1951 and 1961 and then decreasing by at least 50 percent between 1961 and 1986. Because of the previous residence of many in the United States, their wide dispersal across Canada, and the return of many to Denmark, Danes did not develop a distinct ethnic identity in Canada, and most are assimilated into Canadian society.

Bibliography

Paulsen, Frank M. (1974). *Danish Settlements on the Canadian Prairies: Folk Traditions, Immigrant Expe-*

riences, and Local History. National Museum of Man, Centre for Folk Culture Studies, Paper no. 11. Ottawa: National Museums of Canada.

DUTCH. In 1986, an estimated 351,765 Canadians claimed Dutch ethnic ancestry. Of these, 171,151 lived in Ontario, 62,945 in British Columbia, 55,920 in Alberta, and 27,875 in Manitoba. Dutch settlement in Canada can be divided into three periods. From 1890 to 1914 Dutch emigrated from the United States and the Netherlands mostly to the western provinces where they worked on or established farms. In the 1920s, the Dutch continued to settle in the West, but now sought industrial work in cities in the East as well, especially in southern Ontario. After World War II about 150,000 Dutch settled in cities with a heavy concentration in Ontario. Despite being the sixth largest ethnic group in Canada and the large number of recent arrivals, the Dutch are among the most assimilated of all ethnic groups in Canada. Dutch is rarely spoken anymore, the Dutch Catholic and Protestant churches, with the exception of the Dutch Calvinists, have become Canadian churchs, and associations attract only a minority of Dutch-Canadians. Integration into Canadian society has come through a strong work ethic, a willingness to intermarry, and little attachment to Dutch traditions that are sometimes seen as an impediment to full participation in Canadian life.

Bibliography

Ganzevoort, Herman, and Mark Boekelman, eds. (1983). *Dutch Immigration to North America.* Toronto: Multicultural History Society of Ontario.

Ishwaran, K. (1977). *Family, Kinship, and Community: A Study of Dutch Canadians, a Developmental Approach.* Toronto: McGraw-Hill Ryerson.

ENGLISH. The number of Canadians of English ethnic ancestry is unknown, as the English are classified as British, along with the Scots, Irish, and Welsh. Estimates from the 1986 census indicate that 6,332,725 Canadians claimed British ethnic ancestry. An additional 2,073,830 claimed mixed British ancestry and 3,401,870 claimed British and other ethnic ancestry. Prior to 1850, most English immigration to Canada involved soldiers stationed there to combat the French influence, Loyalists who fled north both before and following the American Revolution, and those encouraged to emigrate by the English government. English settlement in Canada accelerated after

DUTCH INFLUENCE

A Dutch-style windmill at Osoyoos in the Okanagan region, Canada. (Gunter Marx/Corbis)

1850, with immigrants arriving in three major groups. Between 1867 and 1920 many indigent English children were sent to live in the care of various societies in Canada. Between 1890 and 1914 many English also settled in the prairies, as did numerous other immigrants. After World War II, English immigration increased again. The English have settled heavily all across Canada, except in Quebec, with major concentrations in the Maritime Provinces, British Columbia, and Ontario. Modern Canadian society has been shaped in important ways by English institutions; these include the language, the legal system, the parliamentary form of government, the Anglican church, the Royal Canadian Mounted Police, social clubs, labor unions, and various cultural activities. Because English customs and beliefs are so common, if not dominant, English immigrants have easily and quickly assimilated into Canadian society.

Bibliography

Arnopoulos, Sheila, and D. Clift (1980). *The English Fact in Quebec.* Montreal: McGill-Queen's University Press.

Cowan, Helen (1967). *British Immigration to British North America.* Toronto: University of Toronto Press.

See also
EUROPE: Dutch, English

European-Canadians

German European-Canadians have never formed a cohesive ethnic group; rather, there have been a number of major divisions within the population.

See also

EUROPE: Finns, Germans
RUSSIA AND EURASIA: Estonians

Dunae, Patrick A. (1981). *Gentlemen Emigrants: From the British Public Schools to the Canadian Frontier.* Vancouver, British Columbia: Douglas & McIntyre.

Weaver, Jack W. (1986). *Immigrants from Great Britain and Ireland: A Guide to Archival and Manuscript Sources in North America.* Westport, Conn.: Greenwood Press.

ESTONIANS. In 1986, an estimated 13,200 Canadians claimed Estonian ethnic ancestry. Estonians are mostly recent arrivals in Canada, with 14,310 arriving between 1947 and 1960 and 11,370 of those between 1948 and 1952. Most were displaced persons who fled Estonia in 1944 and afterward for Sweden and Germany and then immigrated to Canada and other nations. The first permanent Estonian settlements were farm communities formed in Alberta in the first decade of the twentieth century. The subsequent arrival of other Canadians led to rapid assimilation into Canadian society. Today, Estonians are an urban group, with 85 percent living in cities such as Toronto, Montreal, Hamilton, and Vancouver. Many are professionals or entrepreneurs who own small or medium-sized businesses. While participating in Canadian society, the Estonians are attempting to maintain their ethnic identity through clubs, schools, summer camps, credit unions, the Estonian-language press, and associations who maintain contact with similar associations in other nations where Estonians have settled.

Bibliography

Aun, K. (1985). *The Political Refugees: A History of the Estonians in Canada.* Toronto: McClelland & Stewart.

FINNS. In 1986 an estimated 40,565 Canadians claimed Finnish ethnic ancestry. This is probably a large undercount, with Canadians of Finnish ancestry more likely numbering more than 100,000. Over 50 percent of self-identified Finnish-Canadians live in Ontario, and about 20 percent live in British Columbia. There have been three major eras of Finnish migration to Canada. The small number who came before World War I, either directly from Finland or after initial settlement in the United States, included some socialists who stressed community cooperation. A major influx occurred after World War I, but these Finns were mainly antisocialist and often formed rural communities centered around the Finnish Lutheran church. Between 1950 and 1960, a third group arrived. More urban and skilled than the earlier settlers, they more often settled in cities. The Finns have been active participants in the Canadian economy and political system. At the same time, a strong Finnish identity has been maintained, especially in smaller towns that were initially settled by Finns emigrating from the same areas in Finland. In the early years, temperance societies, the churches, sports and social clubs, a Finnish-language press, and participation in national organizations were sources of Finnish identity. More recently, as the use of Finnish has declined and the Finns have become economically assimilated, Finnish identity revolves more around such core values as personal freedom, pride, determination, and strongly held political and religious views that both Finns and others see as uniquely Finnish in the Canadian context.

Bibliography

Karni, Michael G., ed. (1981). *Finnish Diaspora. Vol. 1, Canada, South America, Africa, Australia and Sweden.* Toronto: Multicultural History Society of Ontario.

Nilsen, Kirsti (1985). *The Baker's Daughter: Memoirs of a Finnish Immigrant Family in Timmins.* Toronto: Multicultural History Society of Ontario.

Roninila, Mike (1987). "Language Retention in the Finnish Identification of Winnipeg's Finnish Population." *Siirtolaisuus-Migration* 2:6–11.

GERMANS. In 1986, an estimated 896,720 Canadians claimed German ethnic ancestry. Germans are the third largest ethnic population group in Canada, behind the British and French. German-Canadians are heavily concentrated in the western provinces, with 182,870 in Alberta, 148,280 in British Columbia, 128,850 in Saskatchewan, and 96,160 in Manitoba. There are also 285,155 in Ontario. The majority of German-speaking people who came to Canada emigrated not from territory that is now part of the two German nations but from territory now in other nations such as Austria (and the Austro-Hungarian Enmpire), Switzerland, the Netherlands, Russia, and the United States. German immigration to Canada goes back to the seventeenth century when German soldiers who fought with the French and then the British settled in Canada. In the eighteenth century, German settlement in Canada continued, but then by families from Europe and others resettling from the United States. In the first half of the 1800s most settlement was in Ontario. From about 1880 to World War I immigration was mainly to the western provinces, and it was during this period that many German communities were founded in the West.

Germans have never formed a cohesive ethnic group in Canada. Rather, there have been a number of major divisions within the German population group, including those based on religion (Roman Catholic or Protestant), nation or region of origin, rural or urban settlement in Canada, and social class. In addition, intermarriage with non-Germans has been common, Germans are highly integrated into the Canadian economy, and German identity became less desirable during and after World War I when Germans were often treated as the enemy. Only in the last twenty years as part of the revival of ethnic pluralism in Canada has a strong sense of German ethnic identity reemerged. German ethnicity has perhaps been stronger in rural communities where land is often seen as family property, the traditional division of labor by sex prevails, and children are raised less permissively. Despite their almost full participation in Canadian society, Germans are generally not seen by experts as fully assimilated, perhaps because of their large numbers and also because of their large concentrations and visibility in the western provinces.

As much as 25 percent of the German-Canadian population is of German-Russian (Russian-German, Germans from Russia) ancestry. They are German-speaking peoples whose ancestors settled in the Volga and Black Sea regions of Russia in the 1700s. In the late 1800s, many of them left Russia in order to find political and religious freedom elsewhere, some of them in western Canada. Others arrived later, after World I and again after World War II. Because of their rural background in Russia and settlement of farm communities in western Canada, they are perhaps somewhat less assimilated than other German-Canadians.

Bibliography

Bassler, Gerhard (1986). *The German Canadians, 1750–1937: Immigration, Settlement and Culture*. Translated by Heinz Lehmann. St John's, Newfoundland: Jesperson Press.

Eberhardt, Elvire (1985). "The Growth of the German Population in Medicine Hat, Alberta, from 1885 to the Present." *Deutsch Kanadisches Jahrbuch/German-Canadian Yearbook* 6:62–65.

Helling, Rudolf A. (1984). *A Socio-Economic History of German-Canadians: They, Too, Founded Canada*. Edited by Bernd Hamm. Wiesbaden: Franz Steiner Verlag.

Kloberdanz, Timothy J. (1988). "Symbols of German-Russian Ethnic Identity on the Northern Plains." *Great Plains Quarterly* 8:3–15.

Lee-Whiting, Brenda (1985). *Harvest of Stones: The German Settlement in Renfrew County*. Toronto: University of Toronto Press.

GREEKS. In 1986 an estimated 143,780 Canadians claimed Greek ethnic ancestry. Of these, 80,320 lived in Ontario, 47,450 in Quebec, and 7,295 in British Columbia. Most Greeks came to Canada after 1900, with perhaps no more than 1,000 arriving before then. From 1900 to 1945 Greek immigration to Canada was relatively steady, with Greeks generally settling in cities. After 1945, in reaction to the political and economic instability in Greece, the immigration increased, leading to the formation of distinct neighborhoods with a strong sense of Greek identity in cities such as Montreal, Toronto, and Vancouver. With the Greek population today composed of many of these post-World War II immigrants and their children, Greeks remain relatively unassimilated into Anglo-Canadian society. Greek is still spoken by many of them, they have a relatively low level of identification with Canadian society, they tend to socialize mostly with other Greeks, and they are not highly integrated into the work force. Factors leading to the persistence of Greek culture include Greek schools, the Greek Orthodox church, the family and its strong resistance to exogamy, the Greek-language press, and the survival of Greek neighborhoods. In addition, traditional Greek values focusing on hard work, economic cooperation, and family authority have been maintained while more mainstream Canadian values have been rejected. Although the Greeks in Canada form a relatively homogeneous cultural group, it should be noted that the Macedonians are culturally distinct and see themselves as a separate ethnic group. In 1986 there were an estimated 11,355 Canadians of Macedonian ancestry, with nearly all residing in Ontario.

Bibliography

Chimbos, Peter D. (1980). *The Canadian Odyssey: The Greek Experience in Canada*. Toronto: McClelland & Stewart.

Chimbos, Peter D. (1987). "Occupational Distribution and Social Mobility of Greek-Canadian Immigrants." *Journal of the Hellenic Diaspora* 14:131–143.

Constantinides, Stephanos (1983). *Les Grecs du Québec*. Montreal: Les Éditions Le Métèque.

Ioannov, Tina (1983). *La Communauté Grecque du Québec*. Quebec: Quebecoise Recherche sur la Culture.

See also
EUROPE: Greeks

The many Irish European-Canadians are now assimilated into Canadian society and no longer see themselves as members of a distinct ethnic group.

Vasiliadis, Peter (1988). *Whose Are You? Identity and Ethnicity among the Toronto Macedonians.* New York: AMS Press.

HUNGARIANS. In 1986, an estimated 97,850 Canadians claimed Hungarian ethnic ancestry. Of these, 51,255 lived in Ontario, 12,780 in Alberta, and 13,000 in British Columbia. Hungarian immigration to Canada has taken place in three stages. From 1885 to World War I, Hungarian peasants, many of whom moved north from the United States, established rural farming communities in the plains. Settlement was so concentrated in Saskatchewan that before 1914 it was labeled Little Hungary. Between World Wars I and II, Hungarian immigrants settled in cities across Canada, leading to a more dispersed and more urban Hungarian population. Following World War II, Hungarian immigration increased again and included Jews, Nazi sympathizers, anticommunists, and those who fled after the 1956 revolution. These new arrivals have produced a far more heterogeneous Hungarian population and have stimulated a revitalization of Hungarian ethnicity manifested in schools, clubs, theater and dance groups, and a Hungarian-language press. At the same time, the internal diversity has hindered a broad sense of shared Hungarian identity.

Bibliography

Blumstock, Robert (1985). "Est Vita Hungariam: Hungarians in Canada." *Hungarian Studies Review* 12(1):33–41.

Dreisziger, N. F. (1985). "The Hungarian Experience in Toronto." *Hungarian Studies Review* 12:1–88.

Dreisziger, N. F., with M. L. Kovacs, Paul Bödy, and Bennett Kovrig (1982). *Struggle and Hope: The Hungarian-Canadian Experience.* Toronto: McClelland & Stewart.

Miska, John, comp. (1987). *Canadian Studies on Hungarians, 1886–1986: An Annotated Bibliography of Primary and Secondary Sources.* Regina: Canadian Plains Research Centre, University of Regina.

IRISH. There are at least 2 million people of Irish ethnic ancestry in Canada today. The exact number of Irish-Canadians is unknown, as the many descendants of Irish immigrants who arrived in the early 1880s are now assimilated into Canadian society and no longer see themselves as members of a distinct ethnic group. The Irish have been a sizable population and major contributor to Canadian society since Canada was under French control in the seventeenth century. But

ICELANDERS

Contemporary Icelanders are descendants of Norwegians who migrated to Iceland and established an independent republic there in A.D. 874. After failed attempts in 1873 and 1874 to establish settlements in Quebec and Ontario, a group of Icelanders settled in the interlake region of what is today Manitoba in 1875 where they founded the republic of "New Iceland." Later arrivals settled in and around Winnipeg where they were joined by people moving south from New Iceland. When the boundaries of Manitoba were extended northward, New Iceland became part of the province.

The major unifying feature among Icelanders in Canada has been their rich oral and written literary tradition, with many sagas recounting the settling of Iceland in the ninth century. Icelanders are partially assimilated into Canadian society in that most speak English as their primary language, are highly educated, intermarry readily, and often hold professional positions. At the same time, a long history of factionalism involving kin group and regional distinctions, Lutherans versus Unitarians, and political differences has kept much of the group focus inward and helped maintain Icelander identity.

Bibliography

Lindal, Walter J. (1967). *The Icelanders in Canada.* Ottawa and Winnipeg: National Publishers and Viking Printers.

Matthiasson, John S. (1979). "The Icelandic Canadians: The Paradox of an Assimilated Ethnic Group." In *Two Nations, Many Cultures: Ethnic Groups in Canada*, edited by Jean L. Elliott, 195–205. Scarborough, Ontario: Prentice-Hall of Canada.

the major period of Irish immigration was the first half of the nineteenth century. Those who came before 1840 tended to settle in the Maritime Provinces where they often worked as laborers. Those who came after 1847, the "Famine Irish," more often settled in towns and cities across Canada, but especially in Ontario and the Maritime Provinces and less so in the West.

The Irish who came to Canada included both Protestants and Roman Catholics who represented different cultural traditions and experi-

See also

EUROPE: Hungarians, Irish

enced different assimilation processes. The Protestants associated with the British tradition and quickly and easily assimilated into British Canadian society. There probably never was and certainly is not now a distinct Protestant Irish ethnic group in Canada. Many of the Catholics arrived later than the Protestants, were less educated and less well-off economically, and were at odds with both the Protestants and the Catholic French-Canadians, making assimilation more difficult. Nevertheless, assimilation did occur for several reasons: they spoke English, the Catholic church was a major force in Canadian society, and, from the 1860s on, many Irish Catholics moved south to the United States. Thus, Irish urban neighborhoods rarely formed in Canada. Today, both the Protestants and the Catholics are integrated socially, economically, and politically into Canadian society.

Bibliography

Akenson, Donald H. (1984). *The Irish in Ontario: A Study in Rural History*. Kingston and Montreal: McGill-Queen's University Press.

Elliott, Bruce S. (1988). *Irish Migrants in the Canadas: A New Approach*. Montreal: McGill-Queen's University Press.

Nicolson, Murray W. (1985). "The Irish Experience in Ontario: Rural or Urban?" *Urban History Review/Revue d'Histoire Urbaine* 14:37–45.

O'Driscoll, Robert, and Lorna Reynolds, eds. (1988). *The Untold Story: The Irish in Canada*. 2 vols. Toronto: Celtic Arts of Canada.

ITALIANS. In 1986, an estimated 709,590 Canadians claimed Italian ethnic ancestry. Italians are the fourth largest ethnic group in Canada. They are a largely urban group with the largest concentrations in 1981 in Toronto (297,205) and Montreal (156,535) and sizable communities in Hamilton, Vancouver, St. Catherines, Windsor, Ottawa, Calgary, and Edmonton. Although Italian contact with Canada goes back to the late fifteenth century, most immigration occurred between either 1900 and 1914 or 1950 and 1970, with the majority of Italian-Canadians having entered or descended from people who entered in the latter period. Over 90 percent of Italian-Canadians are Roman Catholics. About three-quarters of all immigrants came from southern Italy, mainly from Abruzzi-Molise and Calabria, and the majority were peasants.

Italians have participated in and contributed to Canadian society, but they have also resisted as-

similation and in important ways remain a distinct cultural group. Ethnic associations, clubs, the Roman Catholic church, the Italian press, and language programs have all played a role since the early 1900s in maintaining Italian ethnicity. Perhaps more important were the Italian neighborhoods ("Little Italies") that formed in cities with large Italian populations. These communities were often based on extended family and nuclear family ties as well as ties to regions and villages in Italy that provided a social context in which basic core values such as loyalty, reciprocity, respect for the elderly, and family honor could be expressed. Although there has been considerable population relocation to the suburbs and second- and third-generation Italian-Canadians have moved rapidly up the socioeconomic ladder, kin and family ties and obligations remain strong as does a shared sense of Italian identity.

Bibliography

Campenella, M., ed. (1977). *Proceedings of Symposium '77: On the Economic, Social and Cultural Conditions of the Italian Canadian in the Hamilton-Wentworth Region*. Hamilton: Italian Canadian Federation of Hamilton.

Harney, Robert F. (1978). *Italians in North America*. Toronto: Multicultural History Society of Ontario.

Multicultural Society of Ontario (1985). "Italians in Ontario." *Polyphony* 7(2):1–147.

Razzolini, Maria (1983). "All Our Fathers: The North Italian Colony in Industrial Cape Breton." *Ethnic Heritage Series* 8:1–55.

Sturino, Franc, comp. (1988). *Italian-Canadian Studies: A Select Bibliography*. Toronto: Multicultural History Society of Ontario.

Zucchi, John E. (1988). *Italians in Toronto: Development of a National Identity*. Montreal: McGill-Queen's University Press.

LATVIANS. In 1986, an estimated 12,615 Canadians were Latvians—people who trace their ethnic identity to the territory that is now the Latvian Soviet Socialist Republic. Latvian is an Indo-European language closely related only to Lithuanian. Most Latvians in Canada are immigrants who arrived after World War II, many of them classified as displaced persons seeking refuge from war-ravaged Europe and Soviet rule. Most settled in Ontario and especially in Toronto where many who were professionals integrated easily into the Canadian work force. Because of their recent arrival and strong Latvian nationalistic feelings, they have resisted cultural assimilation and have formed associations, clubs, language schools, and

See also

RUSSIA AND EURASIA:

Latvians

churches (mostly Lutheran). Latvian culture is a mix of native, Slavic, Scandinavian, and German elements that have been combined over the centuries into a unique Latvian cultural tradition. To outsiders, Latvian culture is most notable for its rich collection of folk songs (*dainas*), unique art and design motifs, and native peasant dress.

LITHUANIANS. In 1986 an estimated 14,625 Canadians claimed Lithuanian ethnic ancestry. Lithuanians are people from the territory that is now the Lithuanian Soviet Socialist Republic in the Soviet Union. Lithuanian-Canadians can be divided roughly into those or the descendants of those who arrived before World War II and those who came after. Many of those who arrived before World War II (mainly early in the century and in the 1920s and 1930s) settled initially in rural areas, but many eventually relocated to cities (usually Toronto and Montreal) where the men often worked in factories. Those who came after World War II numbered about 20,000 and were primarily displaced persons and refugees. They tended to settle in cities, with most Lithuanians now in Ontario but some also in Quebec, Alberta, and British Columbia. Lithuanian ethnic identity remains strong in Canada, with perhaps a majority still speaking Lithuanian, a strong sense of national community, and numerous well-organized clubs, associations, and societies that promote Lithuanian identity, culture, and language.

Bibliography

Danys, Milda (1986). *Lithuanian Immigration to Canada after the Second World War*. Toronto: Multicultural History Society of Ontario.

NORWEGIANS. In 1986, an estimated 61,575 Canadians claimed Norwegian ethnic ancestry. During the nineteenth century hundreds of thousands of Norwegians immigrated to Canada, although very few stayed as most continued on to the United States. The Norwegians who settled in Canada did so mostly before 1930. From 1886 to 1929, Norwegians arriving from both Norway and the United States settled mostly in rural communities in the western provinces where they farmed, logged, mined, and worked for railroads. The rate of Norwegian immigration increased again after World War II but decreased and has remained low since about 1960. Up to about fifty years ago, Norwegians maintained a strong sense of ethnic identity centered around the rural communities, membership in the Lutheran church, associations and

clubs, and ties to the Norwegian community in the United States. Over time, however, the effects of relocations to cities, intermarriage, public education, and the use of English in place of Norwegian have led to assimilation into Canadian society. In recent years there has been a marked revival of Norwegian ethnic identity, tied less to the past and the traditional culture than to an association with the modern nation of Norway.

Bibliography

Loken, Gulbrand (1980). *From Fjord to Frontier: A History of the Norwegians in Canada*. Toronto: McClelland & Stewart.

POLES. In 1986, an estimated 222,260 Canadians claimed Polish ethnic ancestry. Of these, 117,570 lived in Ontario, 28,500 in Alberta, 19,305 in British Columbia, 18,835 in Quebec, and 13,325 in Saskatchewan. Nearly 90 percent of Poles live in urban centers, with Toronto, Winnipeg, Montreal, Edmonton, Hamilton, and Vancouver having the largest numbers. Today, there are no uniquely Polish urban ghettos nor any Polish rural communities. In the early years of immigration, Poles were often distinguished as Kashubians, Galicians, German Poles, and so on. These distinctions have now largely disappeared. The first wave of Polish immigration took place from 1858 to 1913, with most arriving after 1895 and settling on farms in the prairie provinces. Those who arrived in the interwar years also settled on the prairies. The end of World War II brought a third wave of Polish immigrants, including many men who had served in the Polish military, displaced persons, and refugees. From 1957 on, Poles have continued to settle in Canada, many immigrating in search of better economic conditions and political freedom. Most of the post-World War II immigrants have settled in cities, about half in Ontario. The Roman Catholic church (about 70 percent of Canadian Poles are Roman Catholic; others are mainly United church or Polish Catholic) and various Polish associations and clubs have played a major role in maintaining Polish ethnic identity. There is considerable variation within the group regarding the strength of Polish identity, with the strongest identity expressed by those who have arrived since World War II and share an interest in and concern about the Polish homeland.

Bibliography

Boski, Pawel (1987). "On Turning Canadian or Remaining Polish: Stability and the Change of Ethnic

See also
RUSSIA AND EURASIA:
Lithuanians
EUROPE: Norwegians

Identity among Polish Immigrants to Canada." *Przeglad Polonijny* 13:25–54, 128.

Heydenkorn, Benedykt (1985). *A Community in Transition: The Polish Group in Canada*. Toronto: Canadian Polish Research Institute.

Kusharska, Jadwiga (1986). "Kaszubi W Kanadzie: Mechanizmy Identyfikacji Ethniczncj" (Kashubs in Canada: The mechanism of ethnic identification). *Etnografia Polska* 30:163–179.

Radecki, Henry, and Benedykt Heydenkorn (1976). *A Member of a Distinguished Family: The Polish Group in Canada*. Toronto: McClelland & Stewart.

Renkiewicz, Frank, ed. (1984). *Polish Presence in Canada and America*. Toronto: Multicultural History Society of Ontario.

PORTUGUESE

PORTUGUESE. In 1986, an estimated 199,595 Canadians claimed Portuguese ethnic ancestry, with about 139,220 living in Ontario, 29,700 in Quebec, and 15,535 in British Columbia. About 38 percent live in Toronto. The Portuguese have been coming to maritime Canada since the late 1400s, first as explorers and later as fishermen. Few actually settled there, however, and in 1951 there were only about 1,000 Portuguese in Canada. After 1950, Canada became a preferred place for Portuguese settlement, and large numbers of immigrants arrived from mainland Portugal and the Azores. Much of the migration was in the form of chains of extended family members who formed communities and neighborhoods populated mostly by people from the same communities or regions in Portugal. Portuguese communities are mainly working class (the first generation often found only unskilled work), although there has been a steady movement into small-business ownership, and jobs in the service, technical, and professional sectors. With nearly all Portuguese being either first- or second-generation Canadians, ethnic identity remains strong and is a major concern of the first generation. This identity is reflected mainly in Portuguesismo, "being Portuguese." Among central elements of this identity are a strong sense of family, distinct sex roles, respect for the elderly, and food and music preferences. At the same time, however, a strong pan-Canadian Portuguese cohesiveness has not developed, perhaps because Portuguese regional distinctions are still important and because of the social class cleavages appearing in the Portuguese community.

Bibliography

Anderson, Grace M., and Davis Higgs (1976). *A Future to Inherit: The Portuguese Communities of Canada*. Toronto: McClelland & Stewart.

Joy, Annamma (1988). *Ethnicity in Canada: Social Accommodation and Cultural Persistence among the Sikhs and the Portuguese*. New York: AMS Press.

ROMANIANS

ROMANIANS (Roumanians, Rumanians). In 1986, 18,745 Canadians claimed Romanian ethnic ancestry. This is probably an undercount, as some who arrived around the turn of the twentieth century came from Austria, Hungary, and Russia and were not listed as Romanian. The largest number of Romanians live in Ontario (7,385), with concentrations also in Saskatchewan (2,695), Alberta (2,790), and British Columbia (1,840). The major periods of Romanian immigration to Canada were the late 1880s to World War I, the 1920s, and post–World War II. Early immigrants settled in rural communities mainly in the western provinces, whereas the post–World War II group more often settled in cities in Ontario. The Romanian Orthodox church, the Romanian press, and local units of national organizations have long provided a focus for Romanian identity, but such identity has weakened in recent years, especially in urban areas, where many post–World War II immigrants settled.

Bibliography

Patterson, G. James (1977). *The Romanians of Saskatchewan: Four Generations of Adaptation*. National Museum of Man, Canadian Centre for Folk Culture Studies, Paper no. 23. Ottawa: National Museums of Canada.

RUSSIANS

RUSSIANS. In 1986, an estimated 32,080 Canadians claimed Russian ethnic ancestry. Russians in Canada live mainly in the western provinces, with 14,170 in British Columbia (many of whom are Doukhobors), 4,185 in Alberta, 4,130 in Saskatchewan, and 1,755 in Manitoba. There are also 5,780 in Ontario. Russians in Canada represent a number of distinct groups: (1) White Russians who fled after the Russian Revolution in 1917, (2) Old Believers, (3) Doukhobors, (4) Russians from Poland, (5) Russian peasants, (6) displaced persons and refugees after World War II, and (7) Russian Jews. Russian immigration to Canada began in the late eighteenth century with fur trappers and traders in Alaska, then a Russian territory, and on the Pacific coast; they, however, moved elsewhere after the sale of Alaska to the United States. After the Russian Revolution a large number immigrated to Canada, as did many displaced persons and refugees after World War II. Most of these latter two groups settled in cities. Russians have never

The Portuguese have been coming to maritime Canada since the late 1400s, first as explorers and later as fishermen.

See also

EUROPE: Portuguese
RUSSIA AND EURASIA: Russians

formed a cohesive ethnic entity in Canada, partly because of internal variations and partly because of the relatively few Russians who have arrived in the past forty years. In those areas where a sense of Russian identity does exist, it tends to center on participation in the Russian Orthodox church or in anticommunist organizations.

Bibliography

Jeletzky, T. F., ed. (1983). *Russian Canadians, Their Past and Present*. Ottawa: Borealis Press.

Jones, David C. (1987). "So Pretty, So Middle Europe, So Foreign—Ruthenians and Canadianization." *History of Education Review* 16:13–30.

Tarasoff, Koozma J. (1988). *Spells, Splits, and Survival in a Russian Canadian Community: A Study of Russian Organizations in the Greater Vancouver Area*. New York: AMS Press.

SCOTS. The number of Canadians of Scottish ethnic ancestry is unknown, as the Scots are classified as British, along with the English, Irish, and Welsh. Estimates from the 1986 census indicate that 6,332,725 Canadians claimed British ethnic ancestry. An additional 2,073,830 claimed mixed British ancestry and 3,401,870 claimed British and other ethnic ancestry. In 1961, 1,894,000 Canadians claimed Scottish ancestry. The earliest sizable groups of Scottish settlers were the men from the Orkney Islands who worked for the Hudson's Bay Company in western Canada and soldiers who served in the British army. From 1770 to 1815 a substantial number of Roman Catholic, Gaelic-speaking Highland Scots settled in eastern Canada where their distinctive communities continued to exist for a number of generations, though most have now disappeared into mainstream society. Since about 1815, Scottish migration to Canada has been dominated by the Protestant, English-speaking Lowland Scots who have settled all across Canada except for Newfoundland and Quebec. Since that time Scots have constituted about 10 percent of the Canadian population. Scots have been successful at both playing a major role in the development of Canadian society and maintaining a distinct sense of ethnic identity. Scots have participated in all areas of Canadian life but have been most visible in the religious, educational, business, and political sectors where they have brought such values as respect for education, intellectual inquiry, hard work, and thrift into the Canadian national culture. Today, Scottish identity is manifested through proud self-identification as a Scot as well as Scottish literary traditions, music, dance, sports such as curling, and educational and other institutions.

Bibliography

Emmerson, Frank (1987). *Peoples of the Maritimes: The Scots*. Four East Publications.

Hill, Douglas (1972). *The Scots in Canada*. London: Gentry Books.

McRae, Ellen (1986). "The Glens of Glengarry: 'Aye, 'Tis Not Scotland, but, Achh Now It'll Do!'" *Canadian Geographical Journal* 106:66–71.

Reid, W. Stanford, ed. (1976). *The Scottish Tradition in Canada*. Toronto: McClelland & Stewart.

SERBS. In 1986, an estimated 9,510 Canadians claimed Serbian ethnic ancestry. They are people from the territory that is now Serbia, one of the six republics of the modern nation of Yugoslavia. Serbs in Canada, since they first arrived, have been sometimes misidentified, first as Hungarians, Austrians, or Turks, and later as Yugoslavians (a political, not a cultural category). Thus, the figure above underestimates the number of people of Serbian ancestry in Canada. Serbs began immigrating to Canada (both from Serbia and other regions of Yugoslavia and later from the United States) in 1850, and those who arrived before the early 1900s settled mainly in the western provinces. Those who arrived afterward—before World War I, between the wars, and since World War II—have more often settled in cities in Ontario. Serbian identity remains strong in Canada and is supported by associations, clubs, societies, Serbian-language radio, numerous publications, and the Serbian Orthodox church. The majority of Serbs in Canada still speak Serbian.

Bibliography

Skoric, Sofija, and George Vid Tomashevich, eds. (1987–1988). *Serbs in Ontario: A Socio-Cultural Description*. Toronto: Serbian Heritage Academy.

SLOVAKS. In 1981, 67,695 Canadians claimed Czechoslovakian ethnic ancestry. This figure requires a number of qualifications. First, Czechoslovakian is not an ethnic category, but a national one, referring to the citizens of the modern nation of Czechoslovakia (Czecho-Slovakia), whose two major ethnic groups are the Czechs and the Slovaks. Second, it is likely an underestimate of the number of ethnic Czechs and Slovaks in Canada, as prior to 1918 they were often identified as Austrians or Hungarians. And, third, the

See also

EUROPE: Scots, Serbs, Slovaks

number of people of Slovak ancestry is probably two to three times greater than those of Czech ancestry, with 43,070 Canadians being identified as of Czech ancestry in 1981. Slovaks came to and settled in Canada during four periods. Those who came first, from 1885 to World War I, settled in the West, where they farmed, mined, and worked for railroads. The second group came after World War I, and they too farmed and mined, settling in the West and also in Ontario and Quebec. The third and fourth waves of immigration took place after World War II and after the revolt against communist rule in 1968 and brought displaced persons and refugees to Canada. Although more than a third of the Slovaks in Canada have married non-Slovaks and Slovaks value Canadian citizenship, the Slovaks remain a distinct ethnic group. Their ethnic identity has been maintained in a variety of ways, including participation in ethnic organizations and church parishes and a shared concern about their homeland.

Bibliography

Kirschbaum, Joseph M. (1967). *Slovaks in Canada.* Toronto: Canadian Ethnic Press Association.

Stolarik, M. Mark (1988). "From Field to Factory: The Historiography of Slovak Immigration to the U.S. and Canada (1976–1987)." *Ethnic Forum* 8:23–39.

Sutherland, Anthony X. (1984). *The Canadian Slovak League: A History, 1932–1982.* Toronto: Canadian Slovak League.

SLOVENES. (Slovenians). In 1986, an estimated 5,890 Canadians claimed Slovenian ethnic ancestry. Slovenes are people from the territory that is now Slovenia, one of the six republics of the modern nation of Yugoslavia. Slovenes in Canada, since they first arrived, have been sometimes misidentified, first as Hungarians, Italians, or Turks, and later as Yugoslavians (a political, not a cultural category). Thus, the figure above underestimates the number of people of Slovenian ancestry in Canada. Slovenian immigration to Canada can be divided into two periods: before and after World War II. Those who came before the war, especially in the late 1800s and early 1900s, settled mainly in rural communities, often in the western provinces. Many of those who came after World War II were political refugees who settled mainly in cities, especially Toronto. They have stimulated a revival of Slovenian ethnic identity, centered around their Roman Catholic parishes and anticommunist sentiments.

SPANIARDS. In 1986, an estimated 57,125 Canadians claimed Spanish ethnic ancestry. This figure includes both Spaniards and Latinos. Spaniards are people who migrated directly from Spain (perhaps with a short stop elsewhere) or whose ancestors did so. They should be differentiated from Latinos who are people of Latin American ancestry. But because Spanish immigrants either have not been counted at all or were at times lumped with Latinos, it is impossible to say how many Spaniards have settled in Canada. The major population centers are Ontario and Quebec, with 78 percent of the Spanish population in those two provinces. For the most part, Spanish immigrants and their descendants have rapidly assimilated into Canadian society, and no strong sense of Spanish identity or culture has ever emerged. Assimilation has been especially rapid in French Canada. This is in part because Spaniards were few in number compared to other immigrant groups also arriving in the twentieth century and also because regional cultural identities (Galician, Catalonian, and so on) were more important in Spain than a sense of a national culture.

Bibliography

Anderson, Grace M. (1979). "Spanish and Portuguese-Speaking Immigrants in Canada." In *Two Nations, Many Cultures: Ethnic Groups in Canada*, edited by Jean L. Elliott, 206–219. Scarborough, Ontario: Prentice-Hall of Canada.

SWEDES. In 1981, 78,360 Canadians claimed Swedish ethnic ancestry. The major period of Swedish settlement in Canada was from 1868 to 1914. Most of these people came after having first settled in Minnesota and North Dakota. In Canada, they settled mainly in the western provinces, with Winnipeg becoming the hub of Swedish activities and British Columbia today having the largest Swedish population. The majority of these early settlers were farmers, although many of their descendants have moved to cities where they work in industry and business. Other, smaller influxes of Swedes followed World Wars I and II, with these people settling mainly in Ontario. The rural Swedish communities were joined together through various organizations including the Swedish Lutheran church, labor unions, temperance groups, societies, and clubs. Today, Swedes are much assimilated into Canadian society, a result of their movement to cities, active participation in the public education sys-

See also

EUROPE: Swedes

*Welsh immigration
to Canada began
with Welsh soldiers
who served with the
British in the
American
Revolution.*

tem, and the relatively few new arrivals in the last few decades.

SWISS. In 1986, an estimated 19,130 Canadians claimed Swiss ethnic ancestry. Ontario is home to the largest number, followed by British Columbia, Alberta, and Quebec. The Swiss came to Canada from both Switzerland and the United States, and a substantial number arrived before the twentieth century. The majority were from the German-speaking region of Switzerland, and they tended to affiliate with Germans in Canada; those from the French-speaking region affiliated with French-Canadians. Today, a strong sense of Swiss identity has disappeared, and the Swiss are generally assimilated into Canadian society.

WELSH. In 1981, 46,620 Canadians claimed Welsh ethnic ancestry. This is almost certainly a large undercount (only twenty years earlier nearly three times as many claimed Welsh ethnicity) and is mostly the result of many Welsh being classified as British or as English (they had departed from Liverpool). Welsh immigration to Canada began with Welsh soldiers who served with the British in the American Revolution. The influx peaked after 1862 when gold miners settled in British Columbia, in 1902 when the Patagonian Welsh relocated from Argentina, after World War I, after World War II, and in the mid-1950s. The Welsh in Canada have never formed a national organization, although local societies and associations have existed since the early days of settlement in Canada. Perhaps the most visible signs of Welsh identity today are the Gymanfa Ganu (hymn-singing festival) and *eisteddfod* (arts festival) regularly held by various Welsh societies. In general, the Welsh lump themselves and are lumped by others under the general category of British, and, as such, are much assimilated into Canadian society.

Bibliography

Bennett, Carol (1985). *In Search of the Red Dragon: The Welsh in Canada.* Renfrew, Ontario: Juniper Books.

Thomas, Peter (1986). *Strangers from a Secret Land: The Voyages of the Brig "Albion" and the Founding of the First Welsh Settlements in Canada.* Toronto: University of Toronto Press.

FRENCH CANADIANS

Ethnonyms: Francophones (outside of Quebec), Québecois

Orientation

IDENTIFICATION. French Canadian is a generic term applied to all descendants of French settlers in Canada. They form two groups: Québecois in the province of Quebec, and Francophones outside of Quebec. The former identify themselves as a distinct society and culture. The latter form a diaspora having a minority status, namely, Acadians in the Maritime Provinces and French Canadian communities in Ontario and the western provinces.

LOCATION. Quebec Province is bounded by Hudson Bay and Ontario on the west, New Brunswick on the east, Labrador and the Arctic Ocean on the north, and New York on the south. Its area is 1,540,680 square kilometers. Geographically, the St. Lawrence lowlands separate the Canadian Plateau from the Appalachians. An Arctic climate, vegetation, and fauna are found in the north; subarctic climate in the center; and continental humid with mixed forest and a growing season of 60 to 160 days in the south.

DEMOGRAPHY. The total population is about 6.4 million persons in Quebec and 500,000 outside Quebec. Francophones form 90 percent and Anglophones 10 percent of the population of Quebec. The Francophone population is now mainly urban, living in Montreal and Quebec City metropolitan areas. The remainder of the population of Quebec is sparsely distributed in regional cities of less than 10,000 persons and in rural areas. Francophones outside Quebec live in small localities and rural areas, but some have migrated recently to cities.

LINGUISTIC AFFILIATION. French has been the official language of Quebec Province since 1974. In the 1970s the status of the French language became an important political issue: Quebec governments adopted linguistic laws. In other provinces, French Canadian communities must struggle to have their own institutions in order to preserve their language and culture and avoid assimilation. In New Brunswick and Ontario they now have access to French-language governmental services, education, and radio and television. The language spoken in Quebec differs from that in France in its vocabulary and pronunciation. The Quebec government decided in 1979 to translate English technical terms and promote Frenchification of all enterprises in Quebec so that French would be predominant. A special effort was also made to introduce immigrants to the language in order to protect the French character of the province.

History and Cultural Relations

In 1534, a French navigator took possession of the eastern part of Quebec in the name of France. Because of France's involvement in wars, it was not until 1608 that Samuel de Champlain, following the St. Lawrence River, founded Quebec City, the first settlement of the colony named New France. From 1608 to 1760, only ten thousand persons migrated from France to the colony, and present-day French Canadians are almost all descended from these first settlers. New France differed from New England in significant ways. France was a feudal society, which transplanted the seigneurial system, French law, and the Roman Catholic church to New France. The territory was divided between seigneuries headed by a seignor collecting seigneurial dues for granting land to *censitaires*, or peasant settlers. The New France economy rested on subsistence agriculture and the fur trade, all furs being exported to France. The territory was then much larger than now, covering the Maritime Provinces, the Great Lakes region, the central part of the United States along the Mississippi River, and Louisiana.

In 1760, New France became an English colony. Since French Canadians formed a distinct society and culture, they resisted assimilation, and in 1774 the English compromised, with the Act of Quebec recognizing French Canadian distinctiveness and affording them the right to live by their laws, religion, and language. From 1774 to 1854, the seigneurial system and the Catholic church dominated the social and economic life of French Canadians. The church allied itself with the seignors and English rulers. This situation was resented by the professional and merchant class, leading to the 1837–1838 revolt, which was put down by the English army. The leaders were killed or jailed and the peasant population demoralized and subordinated to the Catholic church. From 1840 to 1867 the colony had two governments: Upper Canada with Anglophone settlers, and Lower Canada, the French Canadian territory. Each had its own somewhat autonomous parliament to manage its internal affairs. In 1867, a federation of five provinces was founded. Lower Canada then became the province of Quebec. From 1867 to 1949, five other provinces joined Canada. In the federation, Quebec Province maintained its cultural distinctiveness.

A strong nationalist movement seeking more political autonomy for Quebec has developed since 1945. The Duplessis government (1945–1959) obtained its own provincial taxation system. In 1960, a Liberal party government decided to modernize the economic, educational, and health systems, marking the end of the social and political power of the Catholic church and the beginning of a secular society in which the state plays the dominant role. Nationalist aspirations reached their high point in the 1970s. The *Parti Québecois* was elected in 1976 on a nationalist platform. It lost a referendum to negotiate the independence of Quebec in 1980 but remained in power until 1984. The Liberal party government was elected in 1984 and governed until 1994 when the Parti Quebecois once again won a majority of seats in the National Assembly.

Isolated for one hundred years from France, *franco-québecois* cultural, economic, and political relations have existed since the 1960s and have been extended to all Francophone countries in Europe and elsewhere through the regular participation by the Quebec government in the Francophone Summit for the past twenty years. Québecois have been influenced almost equally by France and the United States, and their intellectual and organizational life is a synthesis of the two. Relations with English Canada have been more limited because of cultural and linguistic differences but also because of strained relations.

Settlements

Two settlement patterns have shaped the Quebec landscape. Since the St. Lawrence River and its tributaries were once the only means of transportation, all farms fronted the river in a pattern called *rangs*. Social life took place in these rangs and small villages. Settlements spread from the river to interior lands. From 1608 to 1850, the French Canadians lived in the rangs of seigneuries on each shore of the St. Lawrence River between Quebec and Montreal. In the 1840s, Scottish and Irish settlers colonized the eastern townships outside the seigneuries according to the English pattern. In the 1860s, peripheral regions of Quebec were colonized from the seigneuries. During this same period, thousands of French Canadians migrated to work in New England factories where they formed the Franco-American diaspora.

Kinship, Marriage, and Family

KINSHIP. French Canadians reckon descent bilaterally. Kinship terminology distinguishes the paternal from the maternal line by adding the term *paternel* and *maternel* to terms like uncle, aunt, or cousin. First, second, and third cousins are recognized. Genealogical knowledge is an im-

The Act of Quebec in 1774 recognized French Canadian distinctiveness and afforded them the right to live by their laws, religion, and language.

portant social asset in which women excel. In rural areas, women can easily state every kinship tie they have with hundreds of persons for five or six generations. Residence was traditionally patrilocal for the son inheriting the paternal farm but neolocal for other sons and daughters. Now it is neolocal for all.

MARRIAGE. Traditionally, men and women had to either marry or remain celibate, taking care of their elderly parents or entering religious communities. Marriage was religious and divorce prohibited by the church. Sexuality was severely repressed and only allowed as a means to produce children. Married couples felt obligated to have a great number of children to ensure the survival of the French Canadian nation. A radical change has taken place since 1960, with fewer men and women entering religious communities and civil marriage, birth control, and divorce now the norm. The typical family now has only two children, and 50 percent of new marriages end in divorce. Sexuality has been liberalized, and a woman's economic status in marriage has been recognized by civil law in marriage contracts and in divorce settlements.

DOMESTIC UNIT. *Famille-souche*, consisting of a married couple, their numerous children, grandparents, and unmarried brothers or sisters on the paternal farm, was the traditional pattern. For sons and daughters leaving the famille-souche, the nuclear family was the rule. The nuclear family with five persons or less is now prevalent, with a growing proportion of single-parent families as a consequence of the large number of divorces. Agricultural families have followed the urban pattern.

INHERITANCE. Patrilineal land transmission was the rule, with only one son (usually one of the younger ones) inheriting the paternal farm, the other sons having been given land earlier by their father. Women were not allowed to inherit land, though they now can. For inheritance of other goods, English practices have been followed since the nineteenth century.

ECONOMY

Subsistence and Commercial Activities

Quebec has been industrialized since the 1920s. Before 1939, more than 20 percent of the population worked in agriculture, industry being mostly textile- and local-market-oriented. World War II accelerated industrialization. Today, Quebec is an industrially advanced society. Since 1960, Quebec governments have encouraged a diversified industrial base of Québecois-owned enterprises through a social-democratic policy (social assistance, free health services, Health and Security Commission) and an interventionist economic policy (statist financial institutions; direct subventions to industries; nationalization of electricity, automobile insurance, and asbestos companies; construction of dams). Agriculture has been modernized and only 2 percent of the population is now engaged in farm work. The main products are milk, pork, beef, fruits and vegetables, grains, and greenhouse crops. Forests have attracted pulp and paper companies.

Industrial Arts

French Canadians make traditional and modern crafts. The traditional crafts focus on re-creations of folk objects. The modern is creative and functional. Craftwork is taught in technical schools and organized in associations holding annual expositions.

Trade

Cities and suburbs have shopping centers and American-style stores. There are also open-air markets during the summer for fruits and vegetables, but most people buy their food in supermarket chains. A recent trend, however, is to buy fruits, vegetables, and meat directly from the farm.

Division of Labor

Traditionally, women working on the farm performed a great variety of tasks. Many handled all the farm responsibilities while their husbands lumbered in the forests for months. They also received more education than men and managed the family money. Outside of agriculture, they could work only as teachers, nurses, or industrial workers. This rigid division of labor was challenged by a strong feminist movement during the 1970s. Since 1975, steps have been taken to give women equal access to university education, professions, and traditionally male jobs. The Quebec government has followed affirmative action guidelines for women since 1981, and the feminist movement has been institutionalized through the formation of a Consultative Council on the status of women in 1977, and a Feminine Condition Ministry in 1979. Important changes have resulted in the division of labor between the sexes in the workplace and in the family, with the younger generation now taking sexual equality for granted.

Land Tenure

Quebec is a capitalist society. Private ownership is the rule for agricultural, industrial, and commercial property. Family farms are predominant with a single farm owner or a partnership between spouses or among relatives.

SOCIALIZATION. Traditionally, children in rural areas received only a minimal formal education for three to six years. They worked on the farm from the age of twelve to the time of their marriage. Emphasis was placed on capacity to work hard and on respect for adults and church authority. Only a minority had an opportunity to attend the colleges and universities controlled by the clergy. Since 1960, religious educational institutions have been nationalized, and universal access to formal education has been promoted. Familial education is more liberal and permissive since families are now smaller. With the changing roles of men and women, a greater emphasis has been put on the socialization of boys and girls free of sexual stereotypes in families and at school.

Sociopolitical Organization

SOCIAL ORGANIZATION. The class structure of modern Quebec is complex and consists of several strata: (1) an Anglophone bourgeoisie; (2) a French Canadian middle bourgeoisie having interests in financial institutions, middle-sized industries, and controlling statist economic institutions, which supports the federalist political position with minimal nationalist claims; and (3) a petty bourgeoisie including public-sector managers and employees, professionals, and small entrepreneurs in industry and commerce, which supports the nationalist party. The working class is numerically important and is divided into two groups: workers organized in strong assertive unions that have won acceptable salaries and working conditions, and poorly paid nonunionized workers. In agriculture, family farms are the majority. Farmers are organized and control the sale of agricultural products through quotas. Quebec has more unemployed persons than other provinces; almost 15 percent of the population collects unemployment insurance or social security payments.

POLITICAL ORGANIZATION. Quebec is a province with its own parliament within a federation. According to the Canadian Constitution, the provincial parliament has jurisdiction over educational, health, agricultural, economic, and social policy in the province. Quebec governments have sought additional autonomy from the federal government since the 1940s. The political system is bipartisan with two major political parties and a third and fourth of marginal influence. The dominant political party has been the Liberal party (1960–1976; 1984–1994). A conservative party in power in the 1950s disappeared in the 1970s, replaced by the *Parti Québécois*, which governed from 1976 to 1984 and regained control of the government in 1994.

PRO-SEPARATISTS

"Oui" signs for the Pro-Separatist Canadian Party (Parti Quebecois) hang at the party headquarters in Montreal, Quebec, Canada. (Library of Congress/Corbis)

The Quebec government makes decisions concerning education, health, and economic matters. Municipalities have power over local matters. All decisions regarding zoning, the environment, transportation, and economic development are centralized at the government level. Municipalities receive a part of their budget from the central government and are grouped into regional units to coordinate decision making. Deputies are important intermediaries between the people and the government. Ministries have delegated some of their power to semi-autonomous commissions like the Health and Security Commission, the Right of Persons Commission, the Agricultural Markets and Agricultural Credit Commission, the French Language Commission, and the Zoning Commission.

SOCIAL CONTROL. Quebec operates under two legal systems: French civil law and English criminal law. The provincial court system has three levels: the Ordinary Court, the Provincial Court, and the Superior Court. Since 1981, a provincial Charter of Person's Right predominates over all laws. Quebec citizens can obtain a Supreme Federal Court judgment when they have passed through the three levels of provincial courts. A national police corps has jurisdiction over all of Quebec.

CONFLICT. Armed conflict has been rare in Quebec history with the exception of the 1837 revolt. In 1970, when a terrorist group kidnapped two politicians, war powers were enacted by the federal government, leading to the arrest of hundreds of persons and the military occupation of Quebec. The main conflicts in Quebec are not ethnic, but protracted conflicts involving unions are a consequence of the unions' aggressiveness in defending their interests. Racism and any kind of discrimination are overtly condemned and they occur only rarely. Québecois are on the whole tolerant and pacific people who will fight for respect but who generally live in peace with other groups.

Religion and Expressive Culture

RELIGIOUS BELIEFS. The Catholic religion occupied a central place in French Canadian life from the beginnings of New France until 1960. The authority of the Catholic church was not only religious but also social through the religious community's monopolization of educational and health institutions; economic through the wealth of the clergy; political through the partisan position and alliance of the clergy with English rulers and seignors in the nineteenth century and with the conservative federal and provincial governments in the 1940s and 1950s; and ideological because of the church's strong opposition to liberal and democratic ideas, helping those with conservative and elitist ideas to remain in control. With the Quiet Revolution in the 1960s, the Catholic church lost its social and political influence. Québecois abandoned religious practices and beliefs en masse and rapidly accepted a pluralistic value system. But schools remained confessional, and the governments have lost the battle for the complete secularization of the school system.

ARTS. Québecois culture has been flourishing during the last thirty years in literature, poetry, popular songs, theater, cinema, painting, sculpture, and music. The Quebec government encourages arts with subsidies and aid for travel abroad. Cultural relations with France have helped artists to become known in Europe and to build an international reputation. Quebec culture is now celebrated internationally for its diversity and creativity. Canadian Francophones outside Quebec followed the same path. Acadians have developed their own literature, theater, and popular song, as is the case with Franco-Ontarians and Franco-Manitobans.

MEDICINE. The Quebec health system was nationalized in 1960, and in 1969 the Health Insurance Commission was created by law to provide free health services for the people. Physicians are paid for their services by the commission. With the aging of the population, a debate has now begun because the costs are constantly increasing. Alternative medical practices are developing, but most are still illegal.

DEATH AND AFTERLIFE. Traditionally, the deceased was displayed at home or later in funeral homes for two days for viewing by kin and friends. A religious funeral ceremony was performed on the third day and a banquet organized after the ceremony. Catholic funerals have been the norm for many years. Recently, cremation was introduced as an alternative with the religious ceremony retained. Beliefs regarding life after death followed the teachings of the Catholic church, which insisted in the 1960s that those who did not conform were condemned to eternal fire. This view was rejected as a manipulative attempt by the church to maintain its waning power.

Bibliography

Anthropologie et sociétés. Quebec: Presses de l'Université Laval.

Hamilton, Roberta (1988). *Feudal Society and Colonization: The Historiography of New France*. Gananoque, Ontario: Langdale Press.

Moniere, Denis (1981). *Ideologies in Quebec: The Historical Development*. Translated by Richard Howard. Toronto: University of Toronto Press.

Recherches sociographiques. Quebec: Presses de l'Université Laval.

Revue d'histoire de l'Amérique française. Montreal: Institut de l'Amérique français.

Ryan, William F. (1966). *The Clergy and the Economic Growth of Quebec, 1896–1914*. Quebec: Presses de l'Université Laval.

Sociologie et sociétés. Montreal: Presses de l'Université de Montréal.

Wade, Mason (1968). *The French Canadians, 1760–1967*. 2 vols. Toronto: Macmillan.

—LISE PILON

HOPI

Ethnonyms: Moqui, Tusayan

Orientation

IDENTIFICATION. The Hopi are an American Indian group in Arizona. The term "Hopi" means "one who behaves" or "one who follows the proper way."

LOCATION. The Hopi lived aboriginally in the same location they now inhabit, the northeastern quadrant of Arizona. Their reservation is completely surrounded by the Navajo reservation.

DEMOGRAPHY. The Hopi tribal enrollment was 6,624 in 1988. At first contact in 1540, there may have been a similar number. The population estimate in 1887 was about 2,200. Until recently, intermarriage with outsiders was rare, with only an occasional Navajo or person from another tribe marrying in.

LINGUISTIC AFFILIATION. The Hopi language belongs to the Shoshonean branch of Uto-Aztecan. There are minor dialectical differences among the three Mesas (First, Second, and Third) on which Hopi villages are situated.

History and Cultural Relations

Hopi culture as known from the time of first contact came out of long tradition of Pueblo and pre-Pueblo culture, known archaeologically as Anasazi. Francisco Vasquez de Coronado's expedition in 1540 brought them their first contact with the Spanish. After a few other brief contacts, three missions were established, the first in 1629. These were destroyed in the Pueblo Revolt of 1680; after that date, there was little effort toward resuming contact and the Hopi were left alone. Contact with Americans began in the early nineteenth century and became intensive after 1850. An agency under the Department of the Army was established at Keams Canyon, near First Mesa, in 1873, and a reservation was set up in 1882. The first school was opened in 1887, and schooling became a central issue in the early factions of "Hostiles" and "Friendlies," or those opposed to or favorable toward accommodation with the Americans. Oraibi, the largest Hopi village, split in 1906 with much acrimony over this and other issues. A tribal constitution was adopted in 1936, providing for a tribal council with elected representatives from each village.

Settlements

The Hopi lived in compact villages, ranging in population from less than a hundred to perhaps two thousand persons. In 1850 there were seven villages; now there are eleven. Today as formerly, houses cluster about a central plaza where public ceremonies take place. Interspersed among the houses are kivas, or ceremonial chambers, which function as centers for esoteric ceremonies and as clubhouses for men. Traditional houses were built of stone and plastered with mud. Today, many people live in housing constructed of modern materials.

Economy

SUBSISTENCE AND COMMERCIAL ACTIVITIES. Aboriginal Hopis were horticulturalists, hunters, and gatherers. The major crop was maize. Hopis traded widely with neighboring peoples and were well known for the textiles that men wove of the cotton they grew. European articles were accepted and traded; and after coming under American rule, Hopi participated enthusiastically in wage labor and established numerous small businesses. Today, wage labor, commercial cattle ranching (begun in the 1920s), pensions, and welfare are major economic resources for those who live on the reservation. Commercial craft production has been a supplementary source of income for both men and women since the 1860s, and tourism is a major source of income for a small percentage of the population. Dogs were used for hunting aboriginally. Sheep and cattle supplemented hunting until the early twentieth century.

INDUSTRIAL ARTS. Cotton garments were woven for home consumption and external trade. Basketry was important for home use and for ceremonial exchange. Painted pottery, a traditional craft that had fallen into decline, was revived as a commercial craft in the late nineteenth century. Modern clothing, tools, and household goods began to be used in the late nineteenth century. Today, the traditional crafts are made for ceremonial use, sale, and to some degree household decoration.

DIVISION OF LABOR. Men did most of the subsistence labor, in addition to weaving textiles and working wood and leather. Women performed mainly processing tasks and made pottery and baskets. After contact, both sexes took advantage of wage labor opportunities on and off the reservation. Today, women and men hold a variety of jobs in teaching, administration, clerical tasks, and commerce as well as skilled and unskilled labor. Both sexes did and do perform ritual activities.

LAND TENURE. Land close to the village was owned by clans and was divided up among matrilocal clan households. Men cultivated land they received through their wives, and the harvested crops belonged to their wives. In addition, plots of land accompanied certain ceremonial positions. Since the horse and wagon and later the pickup truck were introduced, men have cleared fields in unclaimed territory farther from the village. These become their private property, which is often passed on to their sons.

Kinship

KIN GROUPS AND DESCENT. Hopi society is divided into exogamous matrilineal ranked

See also

Pueblo Indians

clans, the number varying over time. Clans are associated into exogamous phratries. Clans own farmland close to the villages and claim eagle-nesting grounds away from the village where eagles are captured for ceremonial use. High-ranking clans control ceremonial and traditional political offices and are in charge of ceremonies. Clan affairs are directed by a male and female pair, the clan elder and the clan mother. The elder is responsible for directing any male activities and ceremonies controlled by the clan and for representing the clan to the village, particularly in land boundary disputes. The clan mother directs female activities and ceremonies, makes the final decision in clan land distribution, and is responsible through prayer and ritual for the well-being of clan members. Although most clans are represented in most of the villages, each clan is a corporate group only within its village. Today, the importance of clans has diminished as land ownership and political office are achieved through other means, although clans are still active in ceremonial matters and exogamy is still the norm.

KINSHIP TERMINOLOGY. Hopi kin terms follow the Crow system.

Sociopolitical Organization

SOCIAL ORGANIZATION. The Hopi community could be seen as a federation of ranked clans. Upward mobility by a clan occurred when a lower-ranking clan took over the position of a higher-ranking one within the phratry. Women were equal to men, each gender having its own area of control: women controlled most aspects of the economy through their control over land and produce, and men controlled most aspects of village decision making. The ideology of gender gave women a higher value than men. Sexual equality still exists, although gender roles have changed considerably.

POLITICAL ORGANIZATION. Prior to the late nineteenth century, each village was autonomous and was governed by a chief and a council of elders from the leading clans. The major areas of political discussion were clan land disputes, over which the chief had final adjudication, and warfare. Every man belonged to a kiva, which he used as a social club; and through kiva discussions the village leaders could read village opinions. Women played an active, although indirect, role in decision making, as men represented the wishes of sisters and wives as well as their own. The traditional system was undercut by the reservation system and suffered a death blow with the establishment of an elected tribal council.

SOCIAL CONTROL. Before contact, control was probably informal: gossip, teasing, fear of being labeled a witch, and mocking by ceremonial

MARRIAGE AND FAMILY

Marriage

Marriage was monogamous and was believed to last into the afterlife. In theory, people chose their own spouses, but high-ranking families to some extent controlled the marriage choices of their children. The marriage ceremony involved a short period of groom-service by the bride and an elaborate exchange of goods from both sides. The leading families of high-ranking clans tended to intermarry. Today, social class rather than clanship is a factor in selecting mates as it is in mainstream society, and some persons marry Whites or Indians of other tribes whom they meet at college or at work. Matrilocal residence was the rule. By the mid-1920s, a number of people lived in neolocal households, which predominate today. Marriages dissolved with some frequency. Sexual fidelity was expected, but infidelity was known and often a subject of gossip and conjecture. It was not punished, though separation frequently resulted.

Domestic Unit

During the early nineteenth century, the small extended family was probably most common. By the late nineteenth century and into the twentieth, the matrilocal stem family was the accepted form, with usually the youngest daughter remaining as older daughters and their husbands built houses contiguous or near to the maternal home.

Inheritance

Clan land and ceremonial and political positions pass within the clan. Livestock usually goes from parents to children of both sexes, most commonly sons. Daughters inherit houses.

Socialization

Early socialization was permissive. After about age four, children were expected to begin to do small tasks and were shamed or threatened if they did not obey. Boys were treated more harshly than girls, the preferred sex. From the 1880s to about the 1920s, there was much conflict over sending children to school, and even children eager to go were sometimes taken out to work on the family farm or to prevent them from being acculturated. In recent years, education has been recognized as valuable.

clowns at village ceremonies. Today, local crimes and misdemeanors are handled through the tribal court system. Serious crimes like murder are adjudicated in federal court.

CONFLICT. Before American domination, war sometimes erupted between villages over land boundaries or vengeance. Navajos raided Hopi villages from the 1700s until they were pacified in the late nineteenth century. Warfare involved all village males under the leadership of the hereditary war chief. Since American pacification, much conflict within and between villages is expressed in terms of acceptance or rejection of accommodation to White ways, although its causes may lie elsewhere. In recent years, conflict with Navajos has intensified as the two tribes dispute their share of jointly held land, but this time the conflict is being resolved through the U.S. federal court system rather than by warfare. The Hopi have a reputation for nonviolence, but domestic and other forms of interpersonal violence seem to have increased in recent years.

Religion and Expressive Culture

RELIGIOUS BELIEFS. The Hopi universe consists of earth, metaphorically spoken of as "our mother," the upper world, and the under world from which the Hopi came and to which their spirits go after death. Although the concept of original creation is unclear, there are various accounts of the Emergence into this present world from three preceding ones, the place of emergence, or the *sipapu*, being located in the Grand Canyon. Each of the preceding worlds came to an end because of some evil done by witches, and the present world will someday come to an end also. In order to forestall this and to keep the world in harmony, ceremonies are performed by ceremonial societies and by kiva members. The universe is balanced between a feminine principle, the earth, and a masculine one, manifested in the fructifying but dangerous powers of sun, rain, and lightning. Evil is caused by the deliberate actions of witches, called "two-hearts" because they have bargained away their hearts for personal gain and must steal another's heart to prolong their own lives. When a ceremonial leader is believed to "steal" the heart of a relative to ensure that the ceremony will be successful, there is an element of magical human sacrifice in this belief.

There are three major classes of supernatural. The most individualized are the gods and goddesses, each having his or her special area of concern. Figures or impersonations of these deities are used in ceremonial activity. The next category is the kachinas. A few of the kachinas are individuals, but most of them are classes of beings each with its different character and appearance. In kachina dances the dancers wear the costume appropriate to the kachina type they portray. Some types are more popular than others; new ones are invented and old ones drop out of use. Finally, there are the generalized spirits of natural objects and life-forms, who will be offended if one of their earthly representatives is treated improperly. Thus, when a game animal is killed, its spirit, and the generalized spirits of that animal type, must be placated.

RELIGIOUS PRACTITIONERS. The leaders of the clans that control ceremonies are the chief priests or priestesses of these ceremonies and clan members take leading roles in them. Every Hopi is initiated into one of the two kachina societies, which are responsible for putting on the kachina dances. In former times, every man joined one of the four fraternities that put on the Emergence ceremony, and most women joined one of the three sororities. There are also special-purpose societies, controlled by clans but open to membership to anyone in the village, which conduct ceremonies. Villages vary in the number of societies still in existence, but all put on kachina dances, which are organized through kiva membership.

CEREMONIES. The Hopi follow a ceremonial calendar determined by solar and stellar positions. The ceremonial year begins with Wuwtsim, the Emergence ceremony, in November. Soyal, occurring at the time of winter solstice, is conducted by the village chief, and its officers are the men holding the leading ceremonial positions in the village. It is at this time that ceremonial arrangements for the coming year are planned. Powamuya, in February, is a planting festival in which beans are sprouted in the kivas in anticipation of the agricultural season. This is a great kachina festival, with many types being represented. Kachina dances begin after Soyal and continue until July, when Niman or Home Dance is held. This celebrates the return of the kachinas to their unearthly homes in the mountain peaks and the under world. Snake-Antelope and Flute Dances alternate biennially in August, the first emphasizing war and the destructive element and the second emphasizing the continuity of life after death. In September, Mamrawt, or the principal women's ceremony, is held. This contains many elements found in Wuwtsim. The other women's societies hold their ceremonies in October. Along with these ceremonies, there are some that are held only from time to time and others that have been defunct for many years. In addition,

Clans own farmland close to the villages and claim eagle-nesting grounds away from the villages, where eagles are captured for ceremonial use.

The League of the Iroquois was originally a confederacy of five North American Indian tribes: the Mohawk, Oneida, Onondaga, Cayuga, and Seneca.

there are many small rituals. Accounts of the late nineteenth century indicate that hardly a day passed without some ritual activity taking place somewhere in each village. While ceremonies have specific purposes, all are in some way thought to bring rain, which is valued both for itself and as a symbol of abundance and prosperity. The kachinas, especially, are rain-givers. Kachina dances are joyous public events, consisting of carefully choreographed dance sets interspersed with comical performances of clowns. The clowns, like ignorant children, mock everything and understand nothing. Social deviants are shamed by the clowns' mockery.

ARTS. Traditional objects are produced as art objects as well as for use. Kachina dolls, nonsacred representations of kachinas given to girls and women as symbols of fertility and for toys, became tourist items in the late nineteenth century and have undergone several stylistic revisions since then. Modern techniques of silverwork were introduced by American artists associated with the Museum of Northern Arizona in Flagstaff in the 1920s. Using Hopi designs, this is a flourishing craft. There are several contemporary Hopi painters in oil and other media, as well as poets and art photographers. Aesthetic standards for dance, song, and costume are high and clearly articulated.

MEDICINE. Sickness can be brought on by witchcraft, by contact with dangerous forces like lightning, or, more commonly, by sad or negative thoughts, such as anger or jealousy, which disturb the harmony of the body. Curing is done by shamans who diagnose and heal the ailment or by members of ceremonial societies that control the cures for certain diseases. Today, most Hopis make use of government hospitals along with native home remedies and shamanistic treatment.

DEATH AND AFTERLIFE. A peaceful death in old age is a natural death. Other deaths may be attributed to witchcraft or the other factors causing disease. Burial by a son or other close relative is completed as soon as possible outside of the village. During its journey to the under world, the spirit of the dead may try to induce others to come with it, and various rites protect against this. Once safely in the under world, the dead are friendly to the living and will return to earth along with the kachinas to bring rain.

Bibliography

Laird, W. David (1977). *Hopi Bibliography*. Tucson: University of Arizona Press.

Nagata, Shuichi (1960). *Modern Transformations of Moenkopi Pueblo*. Urbana: University of Illinois Press.

Schlegel, Alice (1977). "Male and Female in Hopi Thought and Action." In *Sexual Stratification*, edited by Alice Schlegel, 245–269. New York: Columbia University Press.

Titiev, Mischa (1944). *Old Oraibi: A Study of the Hopi Indians of Third Mesa*. Papers of the Peabody Museum, Harvard University, 22(1) Cambridge.

—ALICE SCHLEGEL

IROQUOIS

Ethnonyms: Five Nations, League of the Iroquois, Six Nations

Orientation

IDENTIFICATION. The League of the Iroquois was originally a confederacy of five North American Indian tribes: the Mohawk, Oneida, Onondaga, Cayuga, and Seneca. A sixth tribe, the Tuscarora, joined the League in 1722 after migrating north from the region of the Roanoke River in response to hostilities with White colonists. In the 1980s members of the six Iroquoian tribes lived in Quebec and Ontario, Canada, and New York, Pennsylvania, Wisconsin, and Oklahoma in the United States.

LOCATION. On the eve of European contact the Iroquois territory extended from Lake Champlain and Lake George west to the Genesee River and Lake Ontario and from the St. Lawrence River south to the Susquehanna River. Within these boundaries each of the original five tribes occupied a north-south oblong strip of territory; from east to west, they were the Mohawk, Oneida, Onondaga, Cayuga, and Seneca. The region was primarily lake and hill country dissected by numerous rivers. Deciduous forests of birch, beech, maple, and elm dominated the region, giving way to fir and spruce forests in the north and in the higher elevations of the Adirondack Mountains. In aboriginal times fish and animal species were diverse and abundant.

DEMOGRAPHY. In 1600 the population of the Five Nations is estimated to have been about fifty-five hundred and that of the Tuscarora about five thousand. By 1904 the six Iroquois tribes numbered at least sixteen thousand, not including several thousand persons of mixed blood. In the 1980s the total population of the six tribes was estimated to be over twenty thousand.

LINGUISTIC AFFILIATION. The languages of the six tribes are classified in the Northern Iroquoian branch of the Iroquoian language family. The languages of all six tribes are still spoken.

History and Cultural Relations

The Iroquoian confederacy was organized sometime between 1400 and 1600 for the purpose of maintaining peaceful relations between the five constituent tribes. Subsequent to European contact relations within the confederacy were sometimes strained as each of the five tribes sought to expand and maintain its own interests in the developing fur trade. For the most part, however, the fur trade served to strengthen the confederacy because tribal interests often complemented one another and all gained from acting in concert. The League was skillful at playing French and English interests off against one another to its advantage and thereby was able to play a major role in the economic and political events of northeastern North America during the seventeenth and eighteenth centuries. The Iroquois aggressively maintained and expanded their role in the fur trade and as a result periodically found themselves at war with their neighbors, such as the Huron, Petun, and the Neutral to the west and the Susquehannock to the south. Much of the fighting was done by the Seneca, the most powerful of the Iroquoian tribes.

From 1667 to the 1680s the Iroquois maintained friendly relations with the French, and during this time Jesuit missions were established among each of the five tribes. Iroquois aggression and expansion, however, eventually brought them into conflict with the French and, at the same time, into closer alliance with the English. In 1687, 1693, and 1696 French military expeditions raided and burned Iroquois villages and fields. During Queen Anne's War (1702–1713) the Iroquois allied with the English and at the war's end were acknowledged to be British subjects, though they continued to aggressively maintain and extend their middleman role between English traders at Fort Orange (Albany) and native groups farther west. The victory of the English over the French in North America in 1763 weakened the power of the Confederacy by undermining the strategic economic and political position of the tribes and by promoting the rapid expansion of White settlement.

When the American Revolution broke out in 1775 neither the League as a whole nor even the tribes individually were able to agree on a common course of action. Most of the Iroquois allied

IROQUOIS CHIEF
*Sa Ga Yeath Qua Pieth Tow,
chief of the Maquas (Iroquois).
USA.
(Michael T. Sedam/Corbis)*

with the British and as a result during and after the Revolution were forced from their homelands. In the period following the American Revolution the members of the Iroquois tribes settled on reservations in western New York state, southern Quebec, and southern Ontario, where many of their descendants remain today.

Settlements

Villages were built on elevated terraces in close proximity to streams or lakes and were secured by log palisades. Village populations ranged between three hundred and six hundred persons. Typically, an enclosed village included numerous longhouses and several acres of fields for growing crops; surrounding the village were several hundred more acres of cropland. Longhouses were constructed of log posts and poles and covered with a sheathing of elm bark; they averaged twenty-five feet in width and eighty feet in length, though some exceeded two hundred feet in length. Villages were semipermanent and in use year round. When soil fertility in the fields declined and firewood in the vicinity became scarce, the village was moved to a new site. This was a gradual process, with the new village being built as the old one was gradually abandoned. The settlements of the five tribes lay along an east-west axis and were connected by a system of trails.

Long before European contact the Iroquois were involved in an intricate trade network with other native groups; clay pipes were an important trade item.

Economy

SUBSISTENCE AND COMMERCIAL ACTIVITIES. Traditionally, the Iroquois were farmers and hunters who practiced a slash-and-burn form of horticulture. In addition, they fished and gathered berries, plants, and roots. Before the arrival of Europeans the primary weapons were bows and arrows, stone axes, knives, and blowguns; however, by the late seventeenth century European trade goods had almost completely replaced the traditional weapons and tools. The principal crops were maize, beans, and squash which, in addition, were prominent in ceremonial activities. In good years surplus crops were dried and stored for future use. After the harvest of crops in the late summer, the seasonal round included fall hunting that lasted until the winter solstice, early spring fishing and hunting of passenger pigeons, and then spring and summer clearing and planting of fields. Farming has now been largely abandoned by the Iroquois, although the annual cycle of festivals and ceremonies associated with planting, harvesting, and other traditional economic activities persist. In the 1980s most Iroquois who are employed work off the reservations because economic opportunities are so limited on them. Some men, for example, work in high steel construction, which has been an important source of employment for the Iroquois since the late nineteenth century.

INDUSTRIAL ARTS. The Iroquois knew how to bend and shape wood when green or after steaming. House frames, pack frames, snowshoes, toboggans, basket rims, lacrosse sticks, and other wood products were made using these techniques. Rope was made from the inner bark of hickory, basswood, and slippery elm, and burden straps and prisoner ties were made from the braided fibers of nettle, milkweed, and hemp. Pipes of fired clay were among the many types of items manufactured by the Iroquois. They are known for making ash and maple splint baskets, although this craft may be of European origin.

TRADE. Long before European contact the Iroquois, as mentioned above, were involved in an intricate trade network with other native groups. Clay pipes were an important trade item that reached other native groups all along the east coast of North America. The aggressive behavior the Iroquois exhibited toward their neighbors during the fur trade period has been interpreted by some as the result of their aim to protect and expand their middleman role. Others have suggested that the behavior was related to the scarcity of furs in their own territory and the resulting difficulty in obtaining European trade goods. According to this theory, the Iroquois warred primarily to obtain the trade goods of their neighbors who were in closer contact with Europeans. After the center of fur trading activities had moved farther west, the Iroquois continued to play an important role as voyageurs and trappers.

DIVISION OF LABOR. Traditionally, men hunted and fished, built houses, cleared fields for planting, and were responsible for trade and warfare. In addition, men had the more visible roles in tribal and confederacy politics. Farming was the responsibility of women, whose work also included gathering wild foods, rearing children, preparing food, and making clothing and baskets and other utensils.

LAND TENURE. Matrilineages were the property-holding unit in traditional Iroquoian society.

Kinship

KIN GROUPS AND DESCENT. Matrilineages were organized into fifteen matrisibs. Among the Cayuga, Onondaga, Seneca, and Tuscarora, the matrisibs were further organized into moieties. Among the Mohawk and the Oneida, no moiety division was recognized. Descent was matrilineal. In modern times, the stress placed on patrilineal inheritance by Canadian authorities has undermined the traditional system.

KINSHIP TERMINOLOGY. Traditional kinship terminology followed the Iroquoian pattern. In one's own and the first ascending and descending generations parallel relatives were classed with one's lineal relatives and cross relatives were referred to separately.

Marriage and Family

MARRIAGE. At one time marriages were a matter of individual choice, but in the historic period the matrilineage, particularly the mother, played an increasingly important role in the arrangement of marriages. Postmarital residence was matrilocal. Polygyny was practiced, but by the late eighteenth century had entirely disappeared. Divorce was possible, and when it occurred the mother retained full control over her children.

DOMESTIC UNIT. The basic economic unit consisted of matrilineally extended family groups of women, their spouses, and their children. Each extended family group occupied a longhouse within which individual nuclear families occupied designated sections and shared common hearths. Each long-house was under the control and direc-

♦ **moiety**
A form of social organization in which an entire cultural group is made up of two social groups. Each moiety is often composed of a number of interrelated clans, sibs, or phratries.

tion of the elder women in the extended family group.

INHERITANCE. Traditionally, property was inherited matrilineally. In the 1980s matrilineal inheritance continued to be practiced among Iroquois on reservations in the United States, but not so for those in Canada, where the government has enforced a patrilineal system of inheritance.

SOCIALIZATION. The life cycle pattern of the Iroquois is not well understood. There was a clear dividing line between the activities of men and women and the ideals of male and female behavior, and roles were communicated to children by elders through oral traditions. Except for those who achieved political office, no formalized rites of passage marked the transition to adulthood for boys or girls.

Sociopolitical Organization

SOCIAL ORGANIZATION. The members of matrisibs cooperated in economic activities and were obligated to avenge the death or injury of any other member. Moieties had reciprocal and complementary ceremonial functions and competed against one another in games. Matrisibs cut across tribal boundaries so that members were found in each tribe and village and often within each longhouse.

POLITICAL ORGANIZATION. The Iroquois confederacy operated under a council of fifty sachems representing the five original tribes. When the Tuscarora joined the League in 1722, no new sachem positions were created for it. The council was a legislative, executive, and judicial body that deliberated only on the external affairs of the confederacy, such as peace and war, and on matters common to the five constituent tribes. The council had no voice in the internal affairs of the separate tribes. Tribal representation on the council was unequally distributed among the five tribes, although abuse of power was limited by the requirement of unanimity in all council decisions. Below the level of the League council were separate tribal councils concerned with the internal affairs of each tribe and each tribe's relations with external groups. The tribal council was composed of the sachems who represented the tribe on the League council. Sachem positions were hereditary within each tribe and belonged to particular matrisibs. The women of the matrisib nominated each new sachem, who was always a male, and had the power to recall or "dehorn" a chief who failed to represent the interests of his people. Theoretically, each sachem was equal to the others in power, but in practice those with better oratorical skills wielded greater influence. After the confederacy had been functioning for a period of time a new, nonhereditary office of pine tree chief was created to provide local leadership and to act as adviser to the council sachems, although later they actually sat on the League council and equaled the sachems in power. Pine tree chiefs held their position for life and were chosen by the women of a matrisib on the basis of skill in warfare. Iroquois involvement in the fur trade and war with the French increased the importance and solidarity of the League council and thereby strengthened the confederacy. Its strength continued to grow until the time of the American Revolution when Iroquois alliances were divided between the British and the American colonists.

SOCIAL CONTROL. Part-time religious specialists known as keepers of the faith served in part to censure antisocial behavior. Unconfessed witches detected through council proceedings were punished with death, while those who confessed might be allowed to reform.

CONFLICT. Witchcraft was the most serious type of antisocial behavior. The Iroquois believed that witches, in concert with the Evil Spirit, could cause disease, accident, death, or other misfortune. Because witches were thought to be able to transform themselves into other objects, they were difficult to catch and punish.

Religion and Expressive Culture

RELIGIOUS BELIEFS. The supernatural world of the Iroquois included numerous deities, the most important of which was Great Spirit, who was responsible for the creation of human beings, the plants and animals, and the forces of good in nature. The Iroquois believed that Great Spirit indirectly guided the lives of ordinary people. Other important deities were Thunderer and the Three Sisters, the spirits of Maize, Beans, and Squash. Opposing the Great Spirit and the other forces of good were Evil Spirit and other lesser spiritis responsible for disease and other misfortune. In the Iroquois view ordinary humans could not communicate directly with Great Spirit, but could do so indirectly by burning tobacco, which carried their prayers to the lesser spirits of good. The Iroquois regarded dreams as important supernatural signs, and serious attention was given to interpreting dreams. It was believed that dreams expressed the desire of the soul, and as a result the fulfillment of a dream was of paramount importance to the individual.

Around 1800 a Seneca sachem named Handsome Lake received a series of visions which he

The Iroquois believed that witches, in concert with the Evil Spirit, could cause disease, accident death, or other misfortune.

believed showed the way for the Iroquois to regain their lost cultural integrity and promised supernatural aid to all those who followed him. The Handsome Lake religion emphasized many traditional elements of Iroquoian culture, but also incorporated Quaker beliefs and aspects of White culture. In the 1960s, at least half of the Iroquoian people accepted the Handsome Lake religion.

RELIGIOUS PRACTITIONERS. Full-time religious specialists were absent; however, there were part-time male and female specialists known as keepers of the faith whose primary responsibilities were to arrange and conduct the main religious ceremonies. Keepers of the faith were appointed by matrisib elders and were accorded considerable prestige.

CEREMONIES. Religious ceremonies were tribal affairs concerned primarily with farming, curing illness, and thanksgiving. In the sequence of occurrence, the six major ceremonies were the Maple, Planting, Strawberry, Green Maize, Harvest, and Mid-Winter or New Year's festivals. The first five in this sequence involved public confessions followed by group ceremonies which included speeches by the keepers of the faith, tobacco offerings, and prayer. The New Year's festival was usually held in early February and was marked by dream interpretations and the sacrifice of a white dog offered to purge the people of evil.

ARTS. One of the most interesting Iroquoian art forms is the False Face Mask. Used in the curing ceremonies of the False Face Societies, the masks are made of maple, white pine, basswood, and poplar. False Face Masks are first carved in a living tree, then cut free and painted and decorated. The masks represent spirits who reveal themselves to the mask maker in a prayer and tobacco-burning ritual performed before the mask is carved.

MEDICINE. Illness and disease were attributed to supernatural causes. Curing ceremonies consisted of group shamanistic practices directed toward propitiating the responsible supernatural agents. One of the curing groups was the False Face Society. These societies were found in each village and, except for a female keeper of the false faces who protected the ritual paraphernalia, consisted only of male members who had dreamed of participation in False Face ceremonies.

DEATH AND AFTERLIFE. When a sachem died and his successor was nominated and confirmed, the other tribes of the League were informed and the League council met to perform a condolence ceremony in which the deceased

sachem was mourned and the new sachem was installed. The sachem's condolence ceremony was still held on Iroquois reservations in the 1970s. Condolence ceremonies were also practiced for common people. In early historic times the dead were buried in a sitting position facing east. After the burial, a captured bird was released in the belief that it carried away the spirit of the deceased. In earlier times the dead were left exposed on a wooden scaffolding, and after a time their bones were deposited in a special house of the deceased. The Iroquois believed, as some continue to believe today, that after death the soul embarked on a journey and series of ordeals that ended in the land of the dead in the sky world. Mourning for the dead lasted a year, at the end of which time the soul's journey was believed to be complete and a feast was held to signify the soul's arrival in the land of the dead.

Bibliography

Fenton, William N. (1971). "The Iroquois in History." In *North American Indians in Historical Perspective*, edited by Eleanor B. Leacock and Nancy O. Lurie, 129–168. New York: Random House.

Fenton, William N. (1978). "Northern Iroquoian Culture Patterns." In *Handbook of North American Indians*. Vol. 15, *Northeast*, edited by Bruce G. Trigger, 296–321. Washington, D.C.: Smithsonian Institution.

Morgan, Lewis H. (1901). *League of the Ho-de-no-sau-nee or Iroquois*. Edited by Herbert M. Lloyd. 2 vols. New York: Dodd, Mead. Originally published, 1851.

Oswalt, Wendell H. (1966). "The Iroquois." In *This Land Was Theirs: A Study of North American Indians*, edited by Wendell H. Oswalt, 397–461. New York: John Wiley.

Tooker, Elisabeth (1978). *The League of the Iroquois: Its History, Politics, and Ritual*. In *Handbook of North American Indians*. Vol. 15, *Northeast*, edited by Bruce G. Trigger, 418–441. Washington, D.C.: Smithsonian Institution.

—GERALD F. REID

JEWS

Ethnonyms: Ashkenazim, Hebrews, Sephardim

Orientation

IDENTIFICATION. The Jews of North America are a relatively assimilated ethnic group in the United States and Canada. The name "Jew" is an

Anglicized version of the Hebrew word *yehudi*, meaning "Hebrew, the language of the kingdom of Judah," and originally referred to the members of the tribe of Judah, one of twelve tribes of Israel in the Middle East about four thousand years ago. Jewish self-identity rests on a number of factors including a unique set of religious beliefs and practices, ancestry from Jewish peoples, a shared understanding of the Holocaust, and a belief in Israel as the Jewish homeland.

LOCATION. Jews in North America live primarily in cities or adjacent suburbs. Although urban Jewish ghettos no longer exist, a pattern of residential isolation persists, with many city neighborhoods or suburban communities defined as "Jewish" because of the large number of Jews who reside there and the Jewish institutions such as synagogues, community centers, and kosher food stores located there. Sixty percent of Jews live on the East Coast of the United States and about 20 percent on the West Coast, with relatively few, save those in major cities, in the South and Midwest. In Canada, the same pattern holds, with two-thirds of the Jewish population living in or near Toronto or Montreal.

DEMOGRAPHY. In 1986 the Jewish population in North America was about 6.3 million, with 5.9 million in the United States and 305,000 in Canada. Thus, North American Jews constitute about 43 percent of the 14.5 million Jews in the world. By way of comparison, in Europe there are 4.1 million Jews, in Asia 3.3 million, in South America 600,000, in Africa 159,000, and in Oceania 72,000. The United States has the largest Jewish population in the world and Canada the seventh largest. In North America, the majority of Jews live in twelve large cities, with 1.9 million in the metropolitan New York City region (over 30 percent of U.S. Jews), 500,000 in Los Angeles, 300,000 in Philadelphia, 250,000 each in Miami and Chicago, over 100,000 each in Boston, Washington, D.C., Montreal, and Toronto, and over 50,000 each in Baltimore and San Francisco. In Canada, the other Jewish population centers are Winnipeg, 15,000, and Vancouver, 14,000. The Jewish population has been relatively stable for the past decade, despite a relatively low birth rate, offset somewhat by recent emigrations of Jews from the Soviet Union and Israel to the United States and Canada.

LINGUISTIC AFFILIATION. The overwhelming majority of North American Jews use English as their primary or only domestic language, or French in the French-speaking provinces of Canada, with about 20 percent of Canadian Jews bilingual in the two languages. Recent immigrants from Europe and the Middle East often speak the language of their homeland, those from the Soviet Union speaking Russian, those from Syria speaking Arabic, and those from Israel speaking Hebrew. Hasidic Jews use Yiddish, written with Hebrew characters, and some Jews of central and eastern European ancestry speak Yiddish at home. Yiddish, the traditional language of Jews of Eastern Europe, shares common medieval roots with High German and contains Slavic loan-words, although it is usually written with Hebrew characters and from right to left as is Hebrew. A number of Yiddish words have become part of the U.S. English lexicon, including *blintze*, *chutzpah*, *goy*, *kibitz*, *landsman*, *mensh*, *nebbish*, *shlemiel*, *shlock*, *shnook*, and *shmooz*.

Hebrew is the religious language for Orthodox and some Conservative Jews, with prayerbooks written in and prayers chanted in Hebrew. Hebrew is a branch of the Canaanite group of Semitic languages. Reform Jews use English in their religious services.

History and Cultural Relations

The immigration history of Jews to the U.S. and Canada differs as does the nature of cultural relations between Jews and other groups in those nations.

United States. The first Jews in North America—23 Sephardic Jews from South America—arrived in New Amsterdam (now New York City) in 1654. Since then Jews have continued to immigrate to North America, with the bulk arriving in three periods: 1830–1880, 1881–1924, and 1935–1941. Prior to 1830 most Jews in North America were Sephardic (see "Social Organization" below) and numbered about six thousand in 1830. From 1830 to 1880 the Jewish population increased to 250,000, most of whom were Ashkenazi Jews who emigrated from Germany, as part of a larger movement of Germans to North America. Not only did these immigrants, largely young, rural or small-town peoples escaping religious persecution, swell the Jewish population, but they also spread across the continent establishing communities in dozens of cities. The second period of migration from 1880–1924 closed with a Jewish population of over 4 million in the United States, mostly urban and mostly on the East Coast. This time the immigrants were mostly Ashkenazi Jews from eastern and central European countries such as Poland, Romania, Hungary, and especially western Russia. These

The first Jews in North America—23 Sephardic Jews from South America— arrived in New Amsterdam (now New York City) in 1654.

See also
MIDDLE EAST: Jews of Israel
RUSSIA: Ashkenazim

Jews

*Judaism is the
oldest monotheistic
religion to survive to
modern times. To
Jews, God is the
Supreme Being,
Creator of the
Universe, and
ultimate Judge of
Human Affairs.*

immigrants were the forebears of about 80 percent of Jews in North America today. Restrictive immigration laws in the United States and the depression slowed immigration, but beginning in the mid-1930s until the late 1940s, some 200,000 Jews fleeing Nazi-controlled Europe and extermination in concentration camps arrived in the United States. The 1900–1950 period was also a time of upward (socially and economically) and outward (from the cities to the suburbs) mobility for the eastern European Jews. Since the establishment of the state of Israel in 1948, Jews have arrived in the United States mainly from the Middle East, the Soviet Union, and most recently from Israel. One key feature of Jewish immigration is that most of the immigrants stayed, with only one in fourteen returning to their homelands as compared to about one in three returns for most other ethnic groups.

Despite overt discrimination in education and employment in the past and organized anti-Semitism in some sectors of American society, laws have generally guaranteed Jews religious freedom and relations with other ethnic and religious groups have been generally peaceful if not friendly. Political ties to the African-American community are no longer as strong as they once were. Current tensions with the African-Americans reflect, in part, Jewish concerns over African-American support for the Palestinians in the Middle East and African-American concerns over Jewish ties to South Africa and lack of Jewish support for affirmative action programs. Jews generally distinguish themselves from all non-Jews who are classified and referred to as *goyim,* commonly understood to mean "non-Jew." Some scholars suggest that Jews in the United States today are more apt to stress the secular aspects of Jewishness, such as the use of Yiddish words, as opposed to the religious aspects such as following Jewish law regarding dietary restrictions.

Canada. In contrast to the immigration history in the United States, the majority of Jewish immigrants to Canada arrived after 1945, with about 40 percent of the current Canadian Jewish population composed of recent arrivals as compared to about 20 percent for the United States. In 1900 there were 15,000 Jews in Canada, but by 1915 the population had grown to 100,000 through mass emigrations from eastern Europe. Few Jews immigrated to Canada in the years before World War II, and about 200,000 have arrived since then. These include Jews fleeing war-torn Europe, Hungarian Jews escaping from Hungary in 1956, French-speaking Jews coming

from North Africa, and, most recently, about 22,000 arriving from Israel and 8,000 from the Soviet Union.

Largely because Canada is a bicultural nation with distinct French- and English-speaking populations and because of greater acceptance of cultural diversity, Jews in Canada, like other ethnic groups, are relatively less assimilated than their counterparts in the United States. While this has led to a more visible emphasis on religious elements of Jewishness and the survival of European customs, it has also placed Jews outside the two mainstream Canadian religious traditions of Catholicism and Protestantism. This position as a third religion and other factors have sometimes subjected Jews to laws interfering with traditional religious practices. Laws introduced after World War II removed most of these restrictions. Today, Canadian Jews are slowly becoming more like U.S. Jews, with the use of European customs and languages disappearing.

Economy

Jews are now largely integrated into the U.S. and Canadian economic systems. Although they work in most trades and professions, they are overrepresented (as a percentage of the population) in several, including ownership of small and middle-sized businesses, the communication and entertainment industries, public service, and professions such as medicine, dentistry, law, accounting, teaching, and scientific research. Past and present discrimination has been cited by some as the cause of the relatively few Jews found in the upper echelons of the banking industry and large corporations in general. Civil rights legislation of the 1960s and 1970s has outlawed old laws and private covenants that restricted Jewish ownership of land or membership in private associations. The traditional Jewish division of labor with men working outside the home and women working in the home has given way to many women having professional employment.

Sociopolitical Organization

SOCIAL ORGANIZATION. Today, Jews are highly integrated into the North American class system, with Jews found in the upper, middle, and working classes. Upward social mobility is an important value, and has been achieved for about three generations largely through education. Although Jews are often thought to be concentrated in the upper-middle and lower-upper classes, there is still a sizable number in the working class and some elderly Jews live below the poverty line.

Vestiges of discrimination remain and Jews are still excluded from some social organizations open to non-Jews. In communities with large Jewish populations, exclusively or largely Jewish social organizations such as community centers, the Young Men's and Young Women's Hebrew Associations (YMHA, YWHA), B'nai B'rith, and Hadassah are important. And in some communities the synagogue (*shul*) plays an important social and recreational role. Many Jews are also involved in or contribute to national or international organizations that support Jewish causes such as the Anti-Defamation League of the B'nai B'rith, the United Jewish Appeal, and the United Jewish Welfare Fund.

Internally, Jews have no formal social or political organization, although they can be and are often divided into subgroups on the basis of three overlapping criteria: degree of religiousness, place of one's own or one's ancestor's birth, and Ashkenazic or Sephardic ancestry. Degree of religiousness is reflected in the labels Orthodox, Conservative, or Reform Judaism. Orthodox Jews generally follow and resist changes in traditional religious beliefs and practices, which they base on the *halakhah*, the Jewish literature that covers ethical, religious, civil, and criminal matters. Conservative Judaism comprises a combination of thought reflecting different philosophical, ethical, and spiritual schools. In general, Conservatives stress change from within, Zionism, and an ingathering of all Jews. Because of the diversity of opinion, Conservative religious practices run a wide gamut, although most are less traditional than those of Orthodoxy. Reform Judaism, as the name suggests, reflects a modification of Orthodoxy in light of contemporary life and thought. Thus, Reform Jews do not believe that Jewish law is divinely revealed and eschew many practices central to Orthodoxy such as eating only kosher foods, wearing a skull-cap (*yarmulke*) when praying, and using Hebrew in prayer. The differences among Orthodox, Conservative, and Reform Jews go well beyond religion and are manifested in many day-to-day activities and events and the degree to which members of each are assimilated into North American society. Other categories of Jews based on degree of religiousness include Hasidic (ultra-Orthodox) Jews, Reconstructionists, and "Civil" Jews.

As mentioned above, Jews arrived in North America in waves, largely from European nations and these places of ancestry are used to delineate one Jew or group of Jews from another. Thus, for example, one speaks of German Jews, Russian Jews, Polish Jews, Syrian Jews, and so on, or in a more general sense, eastern, central, or southern European Jews. These distinctions are no longer especially important, although German Jews are still looked upon as wealthier and of higher status than other Jews.

The final major distinction is between Jews of Ashkenazic (Ashkenazim) or Sephardic (Sephardim, Sfardim) ancestry. Ashkenazim Jews are those descended from the Ashkenazic Jews of eastern and central Europe and currently make up about 90 percent of North American Jews. Sephardim are descended from the Sephardic Jews who lived in southern Europe from about the seventh to the fifteenth century when they were expelled from Spain by Queen Isabella and King Ferdinand. Most of the exiles settled in the Middle East and North Africa. Beyond a difference in place of ancestry, Ashkenazic and Sephardic Jews differed and in some ways continue to differ in language (Yiddish or European languages versus Judeo-Spanish or Middle Eastern languages), the pronunciation and spelling of Hebrew, liturgy, and surnames. But members of both groups freely acknowledge that members of the other group are Jews, although some Ashkenazim were less accepting of Sephardim in the past. Although North American Judaism is dominated by Ashkenazim because of their large numbers, there are important Sephardic communities in New York, Los Angeles, Seattle, Atlanta, Chicago, Montreal, Rochester, and Indianapolis. These communities derive from a migration occurring from 1900 to 1925 when Sephardic Jews left areas that are now Turkey, Greece, Yugoslavia, Rhodes, and other territories of the Ottoman Empire.

Finally, mention should be made of other Jewish groups such as Karaites (Qaraites), Israeli, and Russian Jews who have recently immigrated to North America from their respective countries, and Black Jews who have formed their own sects (though by Jewish-defined criteria most of these sects are not considered Jews). These groups, who sometimes follow an ultra-Orthodox life-style or a life-style different from that of assimilated Jews, also sometimes choose to live in relatively isolated urban communities and form their own synagogues. The recent emigrants from Israel are looked upon by some with puzzlement, as they seem to be rejecting the *aliyyah*, or ascent to the land of Israel, a marker of Jewish identity if not a goal for many Jews.

POLITICAL ORGANIZATION. Although North American Judaism has no overarching

The majority of Jewish immigrants to Canada arrived after 1945, including Jews fleeing war-torn Europe.

political structure similar to that of Roman Catholicism or the Church of the Latter-Day Saints (Mormons), the Orthodox, Conservative, and Reform synagogues are aligned with central organizations—the Union of Orthodox Congregations of America, the United Synagogue of America (Conservative), and the Union of American Hebrew Congregations (Reform). Although in the past the synagogue played an important organizational and leadership role, it no longer does so for most Jews. Similarly, the rabbi, the spiritual and moral leader of the synagogue congregation, now rarely plays a leadership role in the community, based solely on his status as the rabbi.

Jews have been seen (often by anti-Semitic commentators) as aligned with liberal or radical political philosophies including socialism, communism, unionization, and the New Deal and tended to vote heavily in favor of candidates of the Democratic party in the United States; in the past decade or two, a marked trend toward conservatism and identification with the Republican party has been noted among a minority of Jews. Jews, despite being only about 2 percent of the population, are an important voting bloc because large numbers vote and because they make up a sizable percentage of the population in some large states such as New York and Florida and the Canadian provinces of Ontario and Quebec. Jews run for and have been elected to numerous local and state offices.

SOCIAL CONTROL AND CONFLICT. Integrated as they are into U.S. and Canadian society, Jews generally resolve legal conflicts with Jews or non-Jews through the legal system. Legal remedies available through Jewish agencies are rarely used. Among the Orthodox there is recourse to some religiously sanctioned social control such as Orthodox divorce. Although overt discrimination against Jews is waning in North America, there is a long tradition of anti-Semitism, reflected in limited access to certain professions and residential isolation. Within the Jewish communities in both nations, there are long traditions of supporting Jewish causes and institutions through charitable donations to and work for synagogues, schools, community centers, social welfare agencies, and the state of Israel.

Religion and Expressive Culture

RELIGIOUS BELIEFS. Judaism is the oldest monotheistic religion to survive to modern times. To Jews, God is the Supreme Being, the Creator of the Universe, and ultimate Judge of Human Affairs. Some importance is also given to particular prophets and angels. The Hebrew calendar is a lunar calendar (based on the movement of the moon around the earth) and has 354 days, 12 months of 29 or 30 days each with extra days added so that the lunar calendar conforms to the solar (Gregorian) calendar, and seven days in a week. The Hebrew calendar is based on the date 3761 B.C.E., the year traditional Jewish scholars believed the world began. Thus, the years 5748–5749 are the equivalent of 1989 in the Gregorian calendar. Jewish weekly synagogue attendance is relatively low at about 20 percent compared to other religions. Because of the wide divergence of religious belief and practice (Orthodox/Conservative/Reform, Ashkenazic/Sephardic, and so on), no single all-encompassing system of Jewish belief and practice can be described.

RELIGIOUS PRACTITIONERS. There is no hierarchy of religious leaders. The rabbi (master, teacher) is the spiritual leader of the synagogue congregation. Today, the role and status of the rabbi is roughly the same as that of a Protestant minister or Catholic priest and involves pastoral, social, educational, and interfaith responsibilities. Reform Jews and Reconstructionalists permit women to be ordained as rabbis. Cantors are also important, leading the congregation in the chanting of prayers (prayers are chanted, not recited) and in training boys for the Bar Mitzvah.

CEREMONIES. Rosh Hashanah (New Year) and Yom Kippur (the Day of Atonement), the High Holy Days, usually fall in September. Pesach (Passover), Shavout (Festival of Weeks), and Succot (Feast of the Ingathering) were originally harvest festivals involving pilgrimages to the Temple. Passover today marks the escape of the Hebrews from ancient Egypt about 3,500 years ago and is widely celebrated. Minor holy days or festivals include Hanukkah (dedication Feast of Lights), Purim (Festival of Lots), and Tisha B'Av (Ninth Day of Av). Although of less importance today, Rosh Hodesh (Beginning of a New Moon) is still noted and marked by special prayers. Shabbat (the Sabbath) is the only Holy Day mentioned in the Ten Commandments and is celebrated from sundown Friday to sundown Saturday each week of the year. The Sabbath is a day of rest and reflection. In addition to these Holy Days and festivals, all major life-cycle events—birth, age of religious majority, marriage, and death—are marked by prayer and ritual observances.

DEATH AND AFTERLIFE. Jewish law requires that the deceased be buried within twenty-

♦ **Gregorian calendar**
A slight revision of the Julian calendar that was adopted in Great Britain and the American colonies in 1752. Most Roman Catholic countries adopted it immediately, with Protestant countries adopting it later, and Eastern Orthodox countries in the twentieth century.

four hours of death. Some Reform Jews allow cremation. For close relatives there is a seven-day mourning period (shivah) involving prayer and restrictions on the activities of the mourner. Regular prayer in memory of the deceased follows at set intervals following the mourning period. Jewish beliefs concerning the soul and afterlife are vague and vary from one group to another.

Bibliography

Cohen, Steven (1983). *American Modernity and Jewish Identity*. New York: Tavistock.

Goren, Arthur A. (1980). "Jews." In *Harvard Encyclopedia of American Ethnic Groups*, edited by Stephan Thernstrom, 571–598. Cambridge: Harvard University Press, Belknap Press.

Gross, David C. (1981). *The Jewish People's Almanac*. Garden City, N.Y.: Doubleday.

Rosenberg, Stuart E. (1970–1971). *The Jewish Community in Canada*. Toronto: McClelland & Stewart.

Rosenberg, Stuart E. (1985). *The New Jewish Identity in America*. New York: Hippocrene Books.

Tillem, Ivan L., comp. and ed. (1987). *The 1987–88 Jewish Almanac*. New York: Pacific Press.

Weinfeld, M., W. Shaffir, and I. Cotler, eds. (1981). *The Canadian Jewish Mosaic*. Toronto: John Wiley.

—DAVID LEVINSON

LATINOS

Ethnonyms: Central Americans, Chicanos (alternative for Mexican Americans), Cuban Americans, Dominicans, El Salvadorians, Guatemalans, Hispanics, Marielitos, Mexican Americans, Nicaraguans, Puerto Ricans

Orientation

IDENTIFICATION. Latinos in the United States are a diverse group and, collectively, the second largest ethnic minority population in the country. Latino groups include, principally, Mexican Americans, who are the largest and (in historic terms) the oldest group; Puerto Ricans, Cuban Americans, Dominicans (from the Dominican Republic) and in recent years Central Americans, mainly from El Salvador, Nicaragua, and Guatemala. Most Latino Americans came to the United States as a result of one of the many wars of the last 150 years. Puerto Ricans and many Mexican Americans are descendants of residents whose homelands were annexed by the United States; many more Mexican, Cuban, and Central American refugees fled from civil wars and revolutionary upheavals. Others, however, came with or without government visas to seek economic opportunities. The U.S. Bureau of the

KINSHIP, MARRIAGE AND FAMILY

Marriage and Family

Jewish marriage and kinship practices conform to those of mainstream North American culture: monogamous marriage, nuclear families, bilateral descent, and Eskimo-type kinship terms. Surnames are patrilineal, although there is a trend toward women keeping their own surnames at marriage or hyphenating their husbands' surnames and their own. The importance of family continuity is emphasized by the custom of naming children after deceased relatives. Although marriage with non-Jews (goyim) was proscribed and sanctioned by ostracism in the past, the intermarriage rate today is increasing as among North Americans in general. Though Jewish families have fewer children, they are often described as child-oriented, with family resources freely expended on education for both boys and girls. Jewish identity is traced matrilineally. That is, if one's mother is a Jew, then that person is Jewish according to Jewish law and entitled to all the rights and privileges that status brings, including the right to emigrate to and settle in Israel as citizens.

Socialization

As with most Americans and Canadians, early socialization takes place in the home. Jewish parents are indulgent and permissive and rarely use physical punishment. Socialization as a Jew takes place in the home through storytelling and participation in Jewish rituals, and through attendance at Hebrew school in the afternoon or evening and participation in Jewish youth groups at the synagogue or community center. Orthodox Jews often run their own grammar and high schools, whereas most non-Orthodox Jews attend public or private secular schools. Acquisition of knowledge and the open discussion of ideas are important values and activities for Jews, and many attend college and professional schools.

The Bar Mitzvah ceremony for a boy at age thirteen is an important rite of passage as it marks him as an adult member of the community for religious purposes, and the Bat Mitzvah ceremony for a Reform or Conservative girl at age twelve or thirteen serves the same purpose. In the past the Bar Mitzvah ceremony was much more elaborate and spiritual in focus; today both ceremonies have become important social as well as religious events for many Jews.

Census has used the term "Hispanic" to designate all such persons, and use of the label has become widespread. An Hispanic is anyone in the United States who has a Spanish surname and comes from a Spanish-speaking background. Most people, however, prefer other labels that reflect where they came from, where they live, when they came, and how they have adapted to the dominant culture of the United States. In short, there are many Hispanics, and even within the broader subgroupings, there are very wide spectrums of historical experience and tradition. An understanding of the way these spectrums have come into being requires an appreciation of the importance of time, place, and history. Thus, "Latino" (a generic term created by the people themselves) identity is a varied and complex process that has created a fascinating mosaic.

LOCATION. Place has been crucial to the formation of the many Latino identities. For one thing, geography determines proximity to cultural roots in Latin America. Just as important, the U.S. government's acquisition and integration of Latinos was episodic, and the political and social conflicts that resulted from that process varied by region and by time period. Mexican Americans live principally in the southwestern states of California, Texas, Arizona, Colorado, and New Mexico, all of which were, before 1848, part of northern Mexico. Puerto Ricans outside of the island territory have settled mostly in New York City and large midwestern cities. Dominicans are located principally in New York, Cuban Americans, in Florida, and Central Americans, in California and Houston. Beyond these concentrations, members of each group also live in most major American cities.

DEMOGRAPHY. Estimates of the 1989 population based on 1985 figures indicate that there were 21 million Latinos constituting just under 10 percent of the U.S. population. The estimated 1989 populations of the largest Latino groups were 13 million Mexican Americans, 3 million Puerto Ricans, 1 million Cuban Americans, and 4 million other Latin American immigrants and their descendants. In recent decades, the influx of immigrants has sharply increased the total Latino population, so that 12 percent of Mexicans, for example, are first-generation immigrants. The immigration and settlement experiences of Latinos have varied from one group to another and also over time within groups. At the beginning of this century, Mexican immigrants were largely a rural, migrant worker population who joined a settled population that predated the 1846–1848

Mexican-American War by 250 years. Since the 1950s, however, Mexican Americans have become about 90 percent urban, concentrated in California and Texas. Among Puerto Ricans and Cubans, in contrast, initial migration was primarily to the urban areas, with the major Puerto Rican immigration beginning between the two world wars and Cubans mostly arriving after the 1959 Cuban Revolution. Central Americans, primarily settling in California and Houston, have arrived after the social upheavals of the 1970s and 1980s in their countries.

LINGUISTIC AFFILIATION. Spanish is the national language of each of the nations from which Latinos emigrated and in which their cultures developed. The Spanish spoken by American Latinos, however, has been transformed by the cultural changes, mixtures and attitudes, and other local and historical accidents and syncretisms that marked conditions in the New World. Mexican, Puerto Rican, Cuban, and other national language habits and customs differ; features of American Indian and African languages, for just one example, have variously influenced each of them. Many regional and urban/rural linguistic contrasts exist within each of the groups. With exposure and integration into American society, however, many Latinos' Spanish-speaking abilities and styles have been "Anglicized" (been affected by the English language), and many even forswore the use of Spanish to speak English, especially Latinos raised primarily in the United States.

Language usage is an important component of Latino ethnic identity. Certain Latino populations, especially recent immigrants and those of high social status, derive much pride from their ability to speak fluent Spanish. Where Spanish usage is expected, some enjoy the opportunity to demonstrate their bilingual flair. For both social and political (as well as aesthetic and practical) reasons, proficiency in Spanish has become a key component in an emerging ethnic "management" style, particularly in the border areas or where Latinos are heavily concentrated such as in Los Angeles (Mexicans and Central Americans), New York (Puerto Ricans and Dominicans), and Miami (Cubans). Speaking Spanish has also resulted at times in negative personal and group experiences, for it has been used by outsiders to stigmatize many people because they are different.

History and Cultural Relations

Mexicans can trace their roots to settlements in what is now the southwestern United States as

See also

MIDDLE AMERICA
AND THE CARIBBEAN:

Cubans, Dominicans, Puerto
Ricans

APPENDIX: Mexicans

early as 1598; this area was once the northern reaches of Mexico proper and was colonized before the settlement of New England by people from Europe. The region was prospering when Anglo-Americans began arriving in the early nineteenth century, setting in motion events that led to the Mexican-American War of 1846–1848. In the aftermath of the war, relations between Anglo-Americans and Mexicans were often characterized by culture conflict and intercultural hostility. With increased immigration in the wake of the 1910 Mexican Revolution, the Mexican population burgeoned in all previously established settlements, a process that has continued to this day.

Puerto Ricans and Cubans became associated with the United States as a result of the 1898 Spanish-American War. Puerto Rico became a territory of the United States and now has limited sovereignty within its commonwealth status. A migrant stream, increasing considerably after World War II, connected Puerto Ricans with the city of New York and brought the eastern seaboard its first large Latino population. Like Mexicans, Puerto Ricans have had a problematic relationship with Anglo-Americans, in their case further aggravated by the issue of national independence versus commonwealth status, which has strained both intergroup and intragroup relations. Cubans immigrated to the United States in large numbers after the socialist revolution of 1959. The first waves were primarily from the upper-middle and upper classes and most immigrants were people of European racial backgrounds; the second wave began in 1980 and involved mostly poorer, darker-hued "Marielitos," including many expelled from Cuban prisons. American foreign policy and actions have been affected by events in Cuba, especially the rise of anticommunism.

Large-scale immigration from the Dominican Republic occurred in the early 1960s. Central Americans, mostly from Guatemala, Nicaragua, and El Salvador, made their entrance in the late 1970s and early 1980s. Coupled with the changes brought by Cuban events, the radical upheavals in Central America have tended to generate even more anticommunist fears. Political and economic refugees from these nations have accounted for a substantial proportion of recent immigration to the United States.

American military conquests in the nineteenth century made Mexican residents of the southwest and Puerto Ricans on their island subjugated peoples. For subsequent migrants from Mexico and Puerto Rico, this intensified the scorn and discrimination that has been the traditional lot of poor immigrant populations in the United States. Cuban immigrants were initially comparatively well-off economically, especially because of federal government subsidies for refugee resettlement, which ameliorated economic problems for them. In all instances, however, the dynamic processes of immigration and adaptation have affected all groups in the direction of assimilation and acculturation. Latinos' relations with other racial minorities have been less antagonistic than with Anglo-Americans, although not tension-free, largely because Latinos and other minorities internalize Anglo-American stereotypes of each other. Civil rights measures and changing public attitudes over the last twenty-five years have substantially reduced these interethnic problems, but tensions remain, especially with regard to language and immigration issues.

Settlements

Initially, Mexicans established missions and small rancherias (hamlets) in what is now the Southwest; in California, a mission-pueblo-presidio structure ordered religious, civil, and military life for both American Indians as well as the Spanish/Mexican newcomers. In the twentieth century, immigration enlarged some of these locales, but more often new settlements were established near work sites such as ranches, mines, railroad tracks, cash crop fields, and light industries. The railroad network helped create a migrant stream to the Midwest to Chicago and other industrial cities. The word *barrio* (neighborhood) came to be associated with these settlements in both rural and urban regions. Since the end of World War II, the Latino population has become increasingly urban, a trend that continues today, though pockets of traditional culture still exist, especially in areas such as New Mexico and south Texas. Puerto Ricans have established their own barrios in the eastern and midwestern cities. World War II was a watershed period as it created a demand for more workers and soldiers, and Puerto Rican communities expanded as a result. A unique arrangement facilitating travel between the mainland and island has tended to strengthen Puerto Rican culture and community. Arriving much later than the other Latino groups, Cubans and Central Americans have settled mainly in cities. Cubans, in fact, have achieved major economic and political influence in Miami, Florida. The U.S. government attempted to widely disperse the recent Marielitos wave, but in time even these immigrants gravitated to established Cuban enclaves.

Cubans immigrated to the United States in large numbers after the socialist revolution of 1959.

Economy

SUBSISTENCE AND COMMERCIAL ACTIVITIES. Small pockets of Mexican Americans who trace their heritage to the early centuries have maintained their self-sufficient ranches and farmlands, but the majority earn wages as mine, farm, railroad, construction, and light industry laborers. Puerto Ricans have filled the garment district and light industry jobs of the cities. Cubans arrived with some money but, more important, with skills and training and have had much success in various business enterprises and professions. In recent decades there has been a slight increase in employment in white-collar service and professional occupations, but Latinos generally lag behind the Anglo population in employment in these sectors. A large agricultural migrant-worker population exists in states such as California, Texas, and Florida. Mexican Americans were a major force in the unionization effort by farm workers in California.

Latino foods vary and reflect the syncretic Spanish/Indian/African mixture noted above, but beans, rice, and various stews prepared with pork, beef, and seafood are found in all groups. Chilies are also widely used in Latino cuisines. Corn products are of particular importance in Mexican and Mexican American culture (although bread and wheat flour tortillas have replaced corn tortillas on many Mexican American tables). Cubans and Puerto Ricans, as islanders, generally favor various seafood dishes characterized by Latino methods of preparation and spices.

INDUSTRIAL ARTS. The original settlements in New Mexico produced excellent wood carving, weaving, jewelry, and other artistic traditions. Today, this Latino bent is found among auto paint-and-body, upholstery, and seamstress craftspeople.

TRADE. Barrios have shopping centers and stores that cater to the tastes of the local population, and some of these districts have become ethnic centers for social, cultural, and political activities. Latinos also use many of the malls that dot urban and suburban regions. Small family-operated stores are common among Latino entrepreneurs, and some have grown into multimillion-dollar enterprises. The Cuban American community has become a major economic force in the Miami area.

DIVISION OF LABOR. A shift from low-skilled to skilled blue-collar jobs has emerged as an important trend, as has the increase of two-wage-earner households with many women now having the dual roles of breadwinner and breadmaker. Although the middle class has grown, with many professionals and educated people, especially among Cuban Americans, there are still relatively few Latinos of middle- or upper-class status. Because of traditional beliefs and the Spanish colonial influence, there has been particular strain involving changing gender relations and traditionally defined status in Latino communities. Many women have moved out of traditional female roles, and some men have found it very difficult to adjust to this change. Similarly, status distinctions based on the traditional "patron-peon" arrangements are slowly disappearing in an open, class-structured society.

LAND TENURE. Since the late nineteenth century, most of the extensive land holdings owned by Mexican Americans have been lost to Anglo-Americans. The few pockets that remain are in rural areas such as New Mexico. As recently as 1966, attempts to raise public attention to the corrupt way in which these lands were acquired have failed. Nevertheless, Chicano (an ethnic name for Mexicans in the United States) activists still offer reminders of the abrogation of the Treaty of Guadalupe Hidalgo of 1848, which ended the Mexican-American War with assurances that land rights would be respected. Puerto Ricans have largely retained ownership of both large and small farms in Puerto Rico, but are predominantly renters in their urban U.S. communities. Cuban Americans, in contrast, are rapidly purchasing large blocs of real estate in Miami.

Kinship

KIN GROUPS AND DESCENT. Family life is important to Latinos, especially extended kin networks, even though Anglo-American influences have altered traditional patterns. Family interests are valued over individual well-being. A syncretic mixture of indigenous and Catholic religious beliefs and practices undergirds this sense of familism. Although somewhat revamped in the United States, the *compadrazgo* (co-parenthood) institution of Latin America is widely practiced in baptisms, where godmothers and godfathers become *comadres* and *compadres* of the baptized child's parents. Descent is bilateral with a strong emphasis on patriarchy in how the family sets standards for status, respect, and authority. Generally, a sex and age hierarchy prevails, and often elder kin, especially grandparents, are vested with complete authority in family affairs; they sometimes take over primary care of grandchildren when parents falter. There are some intragroup Latino differences in family structure that stem from time, place, and history. For example, female-headed households are more common among Puerto Ricans; Mexican Americans have larger families on average, and Cuban Americans tend to have the smallest families. Mexican Americans in rural enclaves in south Texas and New Mexico generally embrace traditional family practices and beliefs, such as are found in Mexico proper.

Marriage and Family

MARRIAGE. Each person is allowed to seek his or her own mate, but traditionally the elder family members keep close watch to make sure that the choice is an appropriate one. The average age of marriage has increased lately, but typically it is lower than the overall average in the United States. Separate Latino groups have their own marriage customs, but even with American innovations, the wedding and celebrations are large, well-attended, often catered affairs hosted by the bride's family. Postmarital residence is almost always neolocal, although financial necessity allows for temporary living arrangements with either the bride's or the groom's parents. American-born Latinos who are upwardly socially mobile tend to intermarry more with Anglos, and exogamous marriage is slightly more common among Latinas of a higher status.

DOMESTIC UNIT. Modernization and Americanization, of course, have changed Latino households. Nevertheless, the sense of obligation and responsibility that one owes to family elders and parents remains. This takes many forms, but emphasizes affording them respect and caring for them until death. Machismo, or manliness, is among the traits associated with the patriarchy complex, and male-female relations are often conditioned by the public assertion of male control, especially the positive qualities of providing care and protection for one's home and family. These practices are tempered somewhat by Marian Catholic ideology which places females, especially mothers and wives, in an exalted position.

INHERITANCE. Land and property is usually transferred to the eldest son, although senior females also have rights. Most traditional practices in the area, however, have given way to American practices.

SOCIALIZATION. Social class differences account for considerable variation among the Latino groups in their approaches to child rearing. But beliefs in personal honor, respect for the aged, and proper courtship behavior are still stressed by many people in all groups. The bulk of the population follows working-class practices, and new immigrants attempt to continue native ways. Social and economic pressures on family life, however, have weakened parental control in many communities, with juvenile and adolescent street peers taking on many tasks of socialization.

Sociopolitical Organization

SOCIAL ORGANIZATION. There are a small number of well-to-do Latinos, with Cuban Americans disproportionately represented among them. The number of Latino entrepreneurs and professionals in the middle class is also relatively small, but increasing. The majority of the population is divided almost equally between American-born, working-class families and immigrant families headed by low-skilled and unskilled workers.

"Mestizaje," the mixing and amalgamation of Spanish, Indian, and African racial groups, was widespread in various places in Latin America. Terms like *mestizo, mulatto, cholo, moreno,* and *castizo* were originally created to categorize the subtle differences in the "hybrid" population mixes. Thus, there is a wide spectrum of racial appearance reflected within the Latino communities. Historically, such diversity has created considerable strain and conflict. As racial appearance and racial attitudes became increasingly important in interpersonal relations, people were made to feel different on the basis of their racial appearance. A kind of "pigmentocracy" was established throughout much of Latin America to shape people's attitudes—about others and, even more important, about themselves. Feelings of inferiority and superiority were implanted in people's heads and these feelings helped determine the extent to which they would have a common heritage and shared experiences.

POLITICAL ORGANIZATION. Latinos vary widely in their access to and inclination toward participation in the political process in the United States. Undocumented and documented aliens—who are unable to vote—are limited to publicizing their concerns. Many avoid even these activities out of fear of deportation. Recent immigrants often follow political developments in their homelands more closely than those of the United States. Latinos are sharply underrepresented in federal, state, and local governments despite the efforts of organizations such as NALEO (National Association of Latino Elected and Appointed Officials), which have attempted, with

Family life is important to Latinos, especially extended kin networks, even though Anglo-American influences have altered traditional patterns.

*Latinos vary widely
in their access to
and inclination
toward participation
in the political
process in the United
States.*

some success, to unite all Latinos and especially to find common ground for political lobbying. Latinos are also profoundly divided in political orientations. Cuban Americans are largely drawn to conservative causes, especially on foreign affairs issues. A majority of Mexican Americans and Puerto Ricans align themselves with the Democratic party, but the issues that concern them in part reflect their regional differences. Two political positions that Latinos largely support are improved, less punitive immigration legislation and increased support for bilingual education programs.

SOCIAL CONTROL AND CONFLICT. Traditional familial constraints and respect for authority and, of course, the local, state, and federal legal systems operate to maintain social order. But there is still a residue of instability and uncertainty remaining from the past and especially from the negative side effects of immigration. Racial diversity has contributed to continuing social conflict, and frictions with major social control institutions, such as schools and police, have also persisted.

Local, regional, and sometimes national efforts to resist and change discriminatory practices are common occurrences. The Latino social movements of the 1960s, however, have resulted in continued improvements in such areas as bilingual education, increased hiring in public jobs, and a rise of public interest in Latino issues. The wars

of the past continue to affect Latino-Anglo relations in the United States: Mexican Americans deplore violations of the Treaty of Guadalupe Hidalgo; many Puerto Ricans aspire to statehood or independence; Cubans, because of its recency, talk of recapturing the "revolution"; and Central Americans lament the contemporary wars from which many are refugees.

Religion and Expressive Culture

RELIGIOUS BELIEFS. As with the Spanish language, Roman Catholicism dominates throughout Latin America, but varies in form and practice from country to country and region to region, owing largely to syncretic mixing with other religious traditions. Latinos in the United States also display this variation, with patron saints, special days of observance, and rituals of baptism, marriage, and death varying among different Catholic Latino groups. For example, the Virgin of Guadalupe, a brown-appearing icon associated with the Indian-Mestizo segment of the population in Mexico, is of little interest among Cuban Americans and Puerto Ricans, and *santeria* (worship of African gods clothed in Catholic dogma) beliefs and practices in those groups are far less common among Mexican Americans. Although most Latinos adhere to the Catholic church, evangelical Protestantism has gained many followers in recent decades.

CELEBRATION!
Two Latino women dance during a festival at the Seattle Center. Seattle, Washington, USA.
(Mike Zens/Corbis)

ARTS. Folk art traditions in murals, woodwork, music, oral lore, and pottery, as well as modern stylized forms reinterpreting these traditions, characterize a rich artistic cultural element. Afro-Cuban and Puerto Rican percussion instruments and rhythms have effected a new American salsa style of music. Recently an increase in Latino American plays, theater, and cinema has brought a new awareness to the population; particularly important are the sociopolitical content of these works, such as demonstrated by the early Teatro Campesino (Peasant Theater) "actos" (politically charged skits) during the United Farm Worker movement in California.

MEDICINE. Traditional folk practices continue to vie with Western medicine in many Latino communities, although most Latinos seek medical help for serious injuries or acute illness. Still, one can readily find *curanderos* (folk healers) who offer old indigenous and syncretized herbal and physical remedies for virtually any ailment.

DEATH AND AFTERLIFE. Latinos generally subscribe to Christian beliefs of an afterlife in which one is rewarded or punished for having led a good or evil life. The significance of death and afterlife is symbolized most clearly in Mexican American celebrations of *El Dia de Los Muertos* (literally "Day of the Dead," but known as All Saints' Day in English), which feature masks, dolls, and cakes adorned with figures of skulls and skeletons. Funeral rites vary as other syncretized religious ceremonies do among Latinos, but typically include large gatherings of real and fictive kin.

Bibliography

Borjas, G., and M. Tienda, eds. (1985). *Hispanics in the U.S. Economy*. New York: Academic Press.

Boswell, Thomas D., and James R. Curtis (1984). *The Cuban-American Experience*. Totowa, N.J.: Rowan & Allanheld.

Hendricks, Glenn L. (1974). *The Dominican Diaspora: From the Dominican Republic to New York—Villagers in Transition*. New York: Teachers College Press.

Moore, Joan W., and Harry Pachon (1985). *Hispanics in the United States*. Englewood Cliffs, N.J.: Prentice-Hall.

Padilla, Felix (1987). *Puerto Rican Chicago*. South Bend, Ind.: University of Notre Dame Press.

Rodriquez, Clara (1989). *Puerto Ricans: Born in the U.S.A.* Boston: Unwin Hyman.

Vigil, James Diego (1984). *From Indians to Chicanos: The Dynamics of Mexican American Culture*. Prospect Heights, Ill.: Waveland Press.

—JAMES DIEGO VIGIL

MORMONS

Ethnonyms: Latter-day Saints, LDS, Saints

Orientation

IDENTIFICATION. The Mormons are a religious-based cultural group founded in western New York State in 1830. They were one of a number of such groups founded in this part of the country during the first half of the nineteenth century. Others included the Shakers, Campbellites, the Oneida Community, and the Community of the Publick Universal Friend. All groups were based in part on a communal lifestyle or value system and a reemphasis of New England Puritan beliefs. Unlike the other groups, however, Mormonism has flourished and is now a worldwide religion. The name "Mormon" is commonly applied to members of the Church of Jesus Christ of Latter-day Saints and splinter groups such as the Reorganized Church of Jesus Christ of Latter-day Saints (founded in 1860) and the Church of Jesus Christ (Bickertonites). The Mormons apply the term *Gentile* to all those who are not members of the church and often refer to themselves as LDS or Saints.

LOCATION. The majority of the Mormon population is located in the intermountain region of the western United States, especially in the state of Utah, in a distinct cultural region labeled by cultural geographers as the Mormon Region. The region consists of a core, domain, and sphere. The core is the zone of the most dense, continuous Mormon population and runs about sixty-five miles north to south in the Wasatch Oasis, centered on Salt Lake City. The domain runs from the upper Snake River country of Idaho south to the lower Virgin River area and southeast Nevada and includes most of west-central Utah and sizable sections of southeast and northeast Utah. The sphere encompasses those areas where Mormons live in clustered communities within the general population. In addition to Utah, it includes parts of Oregon, Idaho, Montana, Nevada, Colorado, New Mexico, and Arizona. Finally, many Mormons live among the general population, especially in urban areas, with sizable numbers in Los Angeles, San Francisco, and Portland. There are also significant numbers of members in South America, Asia, Afric, Europe, and Oceania.

DEMOGRAPHY. As of the 1980s the church claimed more than 5 million members around the world. Because of a high birth rate, longer than average life expectancy in the United States, and

The Mormons apply the term Gentile to all those who are not members of the church and often refer to themselves as Saints.

recruitment of new members through worldwide missionary work, the Mormon church has a very high growth rate. In 1989, there were about 4 million members of the Church of Jesus Christ of Latter-day Saints in the United States and over 200,000 in splinter groups.

LINGUISTIC AFFILIATION. Mormons in the United States speak English and the basic church documents are written in English. In other nations, members usually speak the native language of the country or of their cultural group.

History and Cultural Relations

The church was officially organized in 1830 by Joseph Smith, Jr., and five followers. Smith, known as "The Prophet," claimed to receive his authority and guidance through divine revelation, and he taught that he was the instrument through which God had restored the church instituted by Jesus Christ. He called others to join him in building the "City of Zion" in preparation for the second coming of Christ. The early years of the church were marked by a series of migrations as hostilities between Mormons and their non-Mormon neighbors caused the Mormons to abandon settlements and move westward. The first temple was built in Kirtland, Ohio, in 1836. In 1841 the group moved to Independence, Missouri, then to northern Missouri, and then across the Mississippi River to what became the Mormon settlement of Nauvoo. In 1844 Joseph Smith was killed by a Gentile mob in Illinois. His death was followed by a brief period of division and dissension within the church over the election of his successor.

Eventually the majority coalesced behind Brigham Young who headed the church until his death in 1877. Under his leadership the Mormons undertook their last forced migration, arriving in the Salt Lake Valley of Utah in 1847. Young named the region "Deseret" and in 1849 sought recognition from the federal government as a state. Congress refused, and designated a much smaller region as Utah Territory. Troubles with the government, other settlers, and Indians continued, and in 1857, the U.S. Army was sent to the area to confront Young and the Mormons he had gathered together in Salt Lake City. The confrontation was peaceful, though the federal presence was continued through the establishment of Fort Douglas overlooking Salt Lake City in the 1860s.

From this base the Mormons then spread and settled throughout the intermountain region, primarily through the formation of farming communities and towns. The church hierarchy played a key role in planning and organizing the settle-

♦ **polygyny**
The marriage of one man to more than one woman at a time.

ment and development of this region. An important factor in the growth and development of the church and the Mormon settlement of the West was the large influx of migrants assisted by the church's Perpetual Emigrating Fund. Converts were actively sought and encouraged to migrate to Utah. It is estimated that between 1850 and 1900 the church helped some 90,000–100,000 people immigrate to the United States, primarily from England, Denmark, and Switzerland. Today, there are a number of counties within the Mormon region with markedly high Danish and Swiss-ancestry populations.

The Mormons remained fairly isolated in Utah and adjacent areas until the late 1860s when mining, railroads, and manufacturing attracted non-Mormons to the area in ever-increasing numbers, leading once again to conflicts over social, political, economic, and religious matters. Major issues included the church's role in political affairs, the church's financial holdings and policies, and polygynous marriage by Mormons. This time the U.S. government became actively involved, passing and enforcing legislation aimed at restricting the church's financial practices and Mormon polygyny. By the end of the nineteenth century, the church had made major concessions in its policies as an accommodation to the non-Mormon society within which it had to operate. The conflicts that marked Mormon-Gentile relations over the first seventy years of the church's existence then gave way to the peaceful relations that have existed since. By 1900 the Mormon region as it now exists was basically settled, with the possibility of future expansion limited by the surrounding Gentile settlements.

Settlements

Mormon communities established in the 1800s in Utah and Mormon buildings displayed stylistic features that have been identified as uniquely Mormon. These included a N-S-E-W grid plan with large rectangular blocks, wide streets, roadside irrigation ditches, open fields around towns, cattle and sheep pastured together, unpainted farm buildings, red and light-brown or white houses, brick houses, hay derricks, central-hall house plans, tree-lined streets, and Mormon-style chapels. Buildings constructed since about 1900 generally lack these features and more often reflect outside architectural and stylistic influences.

Economy

COMMERCIAL AND SUBSISTENCE ACTIVITIES. The Mormons are participants in the U.S.

economy. Historically, however, the Mormons attempted to develop their own economic system and to achieve economic independence from non-Mormons. The Mormon economic ideal, based on the biblical notion of stewardship, was communal ownership. According to this ideal, church members would consecrate all their property and surplus earnings to the church. The church in turn would distribute to each member household that which it needed to survive. Although this ideal was never fully implemented, the values placed on communalism and cooperation and the central economic function of the church were influential in Mormon economic activities and experiments. At present, Mormons in good standing give tithes (10 percent of their income) to the church and 2 percent to the ward, but private property is the norm. In the initial phases of settling the Utah territory, the development of irrigation and agriculture were of primary importance. Mormon leaders were also concerned with developing essential small-scale industries. As the U.S. economy has grown and industrialized, so has the economy of Utah. At present, the majority of Mormons work in industry, commerce, and the professions with agriculture remaining an important though secondary source of income.

The church is often reported to be enormously wealthy, although the actual value of church property and investments is unknown. Still, it is no secret that the church owns considerable real estate in the western and southern United States and a variety of businesses such as banks, insurance companies, hotels, newspapers, and radio stations. The church also has large expenses involved in constructing and maintaining church property and in supporting missionary activities around the world.

DIVISION OF LABOR. Mormons have tended to follow societal norms with men working outside the home and women responsible for most domestic tasks. Since the beginning, Mormons have stressed sexual equality, and though women cannot be priests, they are actively involved in other church organizations. There is also an emphasis on age, as reflected in the power held by older men in the church hierarchy.

LAND TENURE. Property rights are seen as a temporary trust held by humans as stewards for the Lord. Individual property ownership is the norm, with a strong value placed on communal effort under church authority.

Kinship, Marriage and Family

MARRIAGE AND FAMILY. Mormons place high values on marriage and family and kinship ties, with large, close-knit, nuclear families the ideal. These values are supported by customs such as annual family reunions, weekly home nights for family activities, and group rather than individually oriented recreational activities. The practice of polygyny was a matter of church doctrine and commonly practiced in the nineteenth century. Harassment from non-Mormons and the U.S. government over the issue led church officials to renounce the teaching in 1890. The practice of polygyny persists among some fundamentalists, but they are subject to excommunication from the official church, and the overwhelming majority of Mormons are opposed to polygyny.

SOCIALIZATION. Mormons stress education and have perhaps the highest percentage of college graduates among their members of any religious group in the United States. Early socialization takes place within the family, extended kin network, and church framework. Regular involvement in group activities with other Mormons is perhaps the most important activity. Many Mormons attend college at Brigham Young University, the largest church-affiliated university in the United States. High school and college programs are supplemented by seminary and institute programs, both designed to stress Mormon beliefs and values and to keep the adolescents involved in Mormon group activities.

Sociopolitical Organization

SOCIAL ORGANIZATION. The Mormons emphasize close relationships among church members and social distance between themselves and nonmembers. The church sponsors a number of social groups and social occasions for its members. Particularly important groups are the church auxiliary organizations such as the Women's Relief Society, the Young Men's Mutual Improvement Association, and the Young Women's Mutual Improvement Association. These organizations combine social, recreational, educational, and religious functions. Although a formal class structure is absent within the church framework, wealth differences between Mormons or between families are noted, and those among the very wealthy enjoy access to the leaders of the church. Although Mormons, in a general sense, are part of the American class system, their self-identity as Mormons is far more important and takes precedence in social situations. The place of American Indians and African-Americans in the church for some time has been equivocal. Both groups are represented in the membership, but not in the church hierarchy. Similarly, the leaders have always been men.

The Mormon economic ideal, based on the biblical notion of stewardship, was communal ownership; church members would consecrate all their property and surplus earnings to the church.

Mormons

TEMPLE HEADQUARTERS

Salt Lake Temple in Temple Square, the world headquarters of the Church of Jesus Christ of Latter-Day Saints, otherwise known as Mormons. Salt Lake City, Utah, USA. (Scott T. Smith/Corbis)

POLITICAL ORGANIZATION. The organization of the Church of Jesus Christ of Latter-day Saints is both lateral and hierarchical and exceedingly complex. Laterally, the church is organized territorially into wards and stakes (called respectively branches and missions in areas where membership is too small to warrant full-scale organization). Wards are local-level units, roughly equivalent to a parish, with an average of about six hundred members each and presided over by a ward bishop and his two counsellors. Wards are organized into stakes, with an average of about five thousand members each, which are governed by stake presidents, his two counsellors, and a stake council. Above the stakes are the general authorities of the church, who include the First Presidence (the first president and his two counsellors), the Quorum of the Twelve (the Apostles), the First Council (the Council of the Seventies), the presiding bishopric, and the patriarch of the church. The first president is the apex of religious and administrative authority within the church. He is considered the successor to Joseph Smith, Jr., bears Smith's title—"prophet, seer, and revelator"—and holds office for life. When the office of the first president falls vacant, the senior member of the Quorum of the Twelve succeeds to the office which he holds until he dies. Since the founding of the church, authority has rested with White males, a source of discord today, particularly among some women and African-American members.

Mormons have always been involved in local, state, and national politics and are a major force in Utah politics. They have usually managed to achieve a workable balance between loyalties to the state and to the church, both on the group and individual levels.

SOCIAL CONTROL AND CONFLICT. As noted above, it was not until about 1900 that Mormon conflicts with Gentiles and the federal government were resolved. Mormon relations with Indians (the Ute in Utah) were generally friendlier than between Indians and other settlers. This arose mostly from the Mormons' belief that American Indians are of Hebraic origin and that one goal of Mormonism is to reconvert Indians to Christianity. The Mormons and the Ute were also allies in conflicts with non-Mormon settlers. The Mormons emphasize work and personal development and discourage activities such as alcohol and tobacco consumption that might interfere with that goal. Drinking coffee and tea are also discouraged. As marriage and the family are key social institutions, divorce and birth control are also discouraged, although neither is uncommon. In general, internal social control is achieved through lifelong involvement in Mormonism.

Religion

RELIGIOUS BELIEFS. The Mormon religion is based on Judeo-Christian Scriptures (the Old and New Testaments), the Book of Mormon, said to be a scriptural account of events in the New World between 600 B.C. and A.D. 421, and teaching believed to have come to their prophets through divine revelation as reported in the Doctrine and Covenants and the Pearl of Great Price. The Mormons believe in a three-person Godhead, the immortality of the human spirit, and salvation of the soul through baptism, proper behavior, and repentance of sin. They believe they have the "gifts" or powers outlined in the New Testament including those of healing, speaking in tongues, and prophecy. They also believe that Jesus Christ will return to rule the earth. Like many modern religions, there are conflicts within the church regarding religious interpretation and the degree of literalness with which the Scriptures should be regarded.

RELIGIOUS PRACTITIONERS. There is no professional priesthood within the Mormon church. Rather, any "worthy" practicing Mormon male may become a priest when he reaches the age of twelve or so. There are two levels of the priesthood: the Aaronic, or lower, priesthood and the Melchizidek, or higher, priesthood. Ideally, boys enter the Aaronic priesthood at the age of twelve and move through the three offices within this priesthood (deacon, teacher, priest) by the age of twenty. "Worthy" adult males enter the Melchizidek priesthood, which also has three offices (elder, seventy, and high priest). Members of the higher priesthood have greater authority and wider ritual prerogatives than do members of the lesser priesthood.

CEREMONIES. Mormons believe that "worship is the voluntary homage of the soul." Religious services are relatively sedate and involve prayer, singing, and blessings. Baptism and the marriage ceremony are particularly important ceremonies, and individual prayer is a central element of many Mormons' lives. Private religious ceremonies may be more elaborate and emotional than public ones.

Bibliography

Arrington, Leonard J. (1966). *Great Basin Kingdom: An Economic History of the Latter-day Saints, 1830–1900.* Lincoln: University of Nebraska Press.

Francaviglia, Richard V. (1978). *The Mormon Landscape.* New York: AMS Press.

Green, Doyle L., and Randall L. Green (1974). *Meet the Mormons: A Pictorial Introduction to the Church of Jesus Christ of Latter-day Saints and Its People.* Salt Lake City: Deseret Book Co.

Meinig, D. W. (1965). "The Mormon Culture Region: Strategies and Patterns in the Geography of the American West, 1847–1964." *Annals of the Association of American Geographers* 55:191–220.

O'Dea, Thomas F. (1957). *The Mormons.* Chicago: University of Chicago Press.

Shipps, Jan (1985). *Mormonism: The Story of a New Religious Tradition.* Urbana: University of Illinois Press.

Talmage, James E. (1976). *A Study of the Articles of Faith; Being a Consideration of the Principal Doctrines of the Church of Jesus Christ of Latter-day Saints.* 51st ed. Salt Lake City: Church of Jesus Christ of Latter-day Saints.

Turner, Wallace (1966). *Mormon Establishment.* Boston: Houghton Mifflin Co.

NAVAJO

Ethnonyms: Apaches de Nabaju, Dine, Dineh, Dinneh, Navaho, Nabajo, Nabaju

Orientation

IDENTIFICATION. The Navajo are a large American Indian group currently located in Arizona and New Mexico. In sixteenth-century Spanish documents the Navajo are referred to simply as "Apaches," along with all the other Athapaskan-speaking peoples of the New Mexico province. The more specific designation "Apaches de Nabaju" appears for the first time in 1626 and sporadically thereafter until the end of the seventeenth century. From about 1700 on, the people are always called "Navajo" (or "Nabajo") in Spanish documents, and the name has been retained throughout the Anglo-American period. The source of the name is uncertain, but is believed to derive from a Tewa Pueblo Indian word for "cultivated fields," in recognition of the fact that the Navajo were more dependent on agriculture than were other Athapaskan peoples. The spelling "Navaho" is common in English-language literature, but "Navajo" is officially preferred by the Navajo Tribe itself. In their own language, however, the Navajo refer to themselves as "Dine," meaning simply "the people."

LOCATION. In the Southwest, the traditional home of the Navajo has been on the Colorado Plateau—the arid and deeply dissected upland of northwestern New Mexico and northeastern Arizona. Elevations range from thirty-five hundred to more than ten thousand feet, with hot summers, cold winters, and relatively scant rainfall. Most of the area is covered by a scattered growth of piñon and juniper trees and sagebrush, but there are also extensive pine forests at the highest elevations and open grasslands at the lowest. The earliest known home of the Navajos was in the area between the Jemez and Lukachukai mountains, in what today is northwestern New Mexico, but subsequently the people expanded westward and northward into portions of present-day Arizona and Utah. The present Navajo Reservation occupies about twenty-five thousand square miles in the Four Corners area where Arizona, New Mexico, Utah, and Colorado come together.

DEMOGRAPHY. The Navajo population in 1864 was probably somewhere between 16,000 and 20,000. By 1945 it had increased to about 55,000, and in 1988 it was estimated at about 200,000. The Navajo are the largest Indian tribe in North America today. There are large off-reservation Navajo populations in many cities of the Southwest, but the great majority of Navajo still live on the Navajo Reservation.

LINGUISTIC AFFILIATION. The Navajo language belongs to the Apachean branch of the Athapaskan family and is particularly close to the languages of the Tonto and Cibecue Apache tribes.

♦ **piñon**
(pinyon) Pine trees (Pinus edulis and Pinus monophylla) of western North America whose large seeds were once an important food source.

Settlements

Unlike other agricultural peoples of the Southwest, the Navajo have never been town dwellers. In the late prehistoric and early historic periods they lived in small encampments clustered within a fairly restricted area in northwestern New Mexico. Later, increasing warfare with the Spanish forced them to adopt a more mobile existence, and bands of Navajo might range over hundreds of miles between the Rio Grande and the Colorado River. Since their pacification in the 1860s, the Navajo have lived in extended-family encampments, usually numbering from two to four individual households, that are scattered over the length and breadth of the vast Navajo Reservation. Many extended families maintain two residential encampments a few miles apart. The summer camps are located close to maize fields and therefore are concentrated to some extent in the more arable parts of the reservation; the winter camps are more scattered and are located primarily for easy access to wood and water.

Economy

SUBSISTENCE AND COMMERCIAL ACTIVITIES. The society and economy of the Navajo have been continually evolving in response to new opportunities and challenges since their first arrival in the Southwest, so that it is difficult to speak of any traditional economy. During most of the reservation period, from 1868 to about 1960, the people depended on a combination of farming, animal husbandry, and the sale of various products to traders. The cultivation of maize was considered by the Navajo to be the most basic and essential of all their economic pursuits, although it made only a relatively small contribution to the Navajo diet. The raising of sheep and goats provided substantial quantities of meat and milk, as well as hides, wool, and lambs that were exchanged for manufactured goods at any of the numerous trading posts scattered throughout the Navajo country. Additional income was derived from the sale or exchange of various craft products, especially rugs, and of piñon nuts. Beginning

HISTORY AND CULTURAL RELATIONS

Ancestors of the Navajo and Apache peoples are thought to have migrated to the Southwest within the last one thousand years, probably from somewhere in the prairie regions of western Canada. They were originally hunters and foragers, but some of the groups, most particularly the Navajo, quickly adopted agriculture, weaving, and other arts from the sedentary Pueblo peoples of the Southwest. There then developed a kind of symbiotic relationship in which the Navajo supplied hides, piñon nuts, and other goods to the Pueblo villages in exchange for agricultural products, woven goods, and pottery. The coming of Spanish rule in 1598 created a new political and economic order, in which the Pueblos were directly under Spanish rule, whereas the Navajo and Apache were never subjugated but remained intermittently at war with the colonial overlords for the next two and a half centuries. From the newcomers the Navajo soon acquired sheep and goats, which provided them with a new basis of livelihood, and also horses, which greatly increased their ability to raid the settled communities both of the Pueblo Indians and of the Spanish settlers. By the end of the seventeenth century, the Navajo as well as the Apache had become widely feared raiders throughout the Southwest. The American annexation of New Mexico in 1848 did not immediately alter the pattern of Navajo raiding on the settlements of the Rio Grande Valley, and it was not until a decisive military campaign in 1864, led by Col. Kit Carson, that the Navajo were finally brought under military control, and the Navajo wars came to an end. About half the tribe was held in military captivity at Fort Sumner, in eastern New Mexico, until 1868, when a treaty was signed that allowed the people to return to their original homeland along the Arizona-New Mexico border. Since that time the tribe has steadily increased both in numbers and in territory, and the original Navajo Reservation has been enlarged to more than four times its original size.

Modern Navajo culture exhibits a unique blend of Athapaskan, Puebloan, Mexican, and Anglo-American influences. The Navajo preference for a scattered and semimobile mode of existence, in marked contrast to the Pueblo neighbors, is part of the original Athapaskan legacy, as is the ceremonial complex centering on the treatment of disease. On the other hand, much of the Navajos' actual mythology and ritual is clearly borrowed from the Pueblos, along with the arts of farming and weaving. From the Mexicans came the dependence on a livestock economy and the making of silver jewelry, which has become one of the most renowned of Navajo crafts. From the early Anglo-American frontier settlers the Navajo borrowed what has become their traditional mode of dress, as well as an increasing dependence on a market economy in which lambs, wool, and woven blankets are exchanged for manufactured goods.

in the early 1900s, a few Navajo were employed by the Bureau of Indian Affairs and in off-reservation towns and ranches, but wage work did not become a significant feature of the Navajo economy until after World War II. By the 1980s, wage work was contributing about 75 percent of all Navajo income, although the more traditional farming and livestock economies were still being maintained throughout the reservation as well. Tourism, mineral production, and lumbering are the main sources of cash income on the Navajo Reservation.

INDUSTRIAL ARTS. The oldest of surviving Navajo crafts is probably that of pottery making. Only a few women still make pottery, but they continue to produce vessels of a very ancient and distinctive type, unlike the decorated wares of their Pueblo neighbors. The art of weaving was learned early from the Pueblos, but the weaving of wool into heavy and durable rugs in elaborate multicolored patterns is a development of the reservation period and was very much stimulated by the Indian traders. For a time in the late nineteenth century the sale of rugs became the main source of cash income for the Navajo. While the economic importance of weaving has very much declined in the twentieth century, most older Navajo women and many younger ones still do some weaving. Apart from woven goods, the most celebrated of Navajo craft products were items of silver and turquoise jewelry, combining Mexican and aboriginal Southwestern traditions. Although many Navajo still possess substantial quantities of jewelry, the silversmith's art itself has nearly died out. Other craft products that are still made in small quantities are baskets and brightly colored cotton sashes, both of which play a part in Navajo ceremonies.

TRADE. In the prehistoric and early historic periods there was a substantial institutionalized trade between the Navajo and many of the Pueblo villages, and this persists on a small scale today. Since the later nineteenth century, however, most Navajo trade has been funneled through the trading post, which in most respects resembles the old country general store. Here clothing, housewares, bedding, hardware, and most of the other material needs of the Navajo are supplied in exchange for livestock products or, more recently, are sold for cash. Traditionally, most Navajo families lived on credit for much of the year, paying off their accounts with wool in the spring and with lambs in the fall.

DIVISION OF LABOR. In the traditional Navajo economy there was a rigid though not to-tal division between male and female tasks. Farming and the care of horses were male activities; weaving and most household tasks were female activities. More recently, however, both sexes have collaborated in lambing, shearing, and herding activities, and both men and women are now heavily involved in wage work. Although males played the dominant roles in Navajo ritual activities, there has always been an important place for females as well.

LAND TENURE. Families traditionally have exclusive use rights to agricultural land as long as they actually farm it; if it lies uncultivated for more than two years another family may take possession. All range land, however, is treated as common and collective property of the whole community and is unfenced.

Kinship

KIN GROUPS AND DESCENT. Every Navajo belongs to one of sixty-four matrilineal clans, but is also said to be "born for" the clan of his or her father. Strict exogamy is practiced on both sides. Apart from the clans, there are no formally designated units of kinship in Navajo society; people are known by the household or extended family in which they reside rather than by membership in a named kin group. Property, like clan membership, is inherited mainly in the female line.

KINSHIP TERMINOLOGY. Kin terms conform to the basic Iroquoian system.

Marriage and Family

MARRIAGE. Navajo marriages are the result of economic arrangements between kin groups. The great majority of marriages were always monogamous, but polygyny was permitted until recently, and it is estimated that about 10 percent of Navajo men had two or more wives. By far the most common form of polygyny was sororal. Residence for newly married couples was ideally uxorilocal, but there were many departures from this practice when economic circumstances made another arrangement preferable. It was also fairly common for couples to move from the wife's to the husband's residence group, or vice versa, at some time after their marriage. Neolocal residence was very unusual in the past, but is becoming increasingly common today, as couples settle close to where there are wage work opportunities. Both marriage and divorce involve very little formality, and the rate of divorce is fairly high. But the great majority of divorces take place between spouses who have been married less than two years.

From the early Anglo-American frontier settlers the Navajo borrowed what has become their traditional mode of dress, as well as an increasing dependence on a market economy.

Navajo

*The most respected
of Navajo ritual
practitioners are
called "singers,"
men (or occasionally
women) who can
perform the major
Navajo ceremonies.*

♦ **hogan**
*A conical, hexagonal, or
octagonal dwelling of the
Navajo with a framework
of logs and sticks covered
with sod, mud, and adobe.*

DOMESTIC UNIT. The basic domestic unit in Navajo society is the biological or nuclear family. Its members traditionally live together in a single hogan (an earth-covered log dwelling) and take their meals together. The basic economic unit is the extended family, a group of biological families who live close together and share productive resources such as a maize field and a flock of sheep and goats in common. An extended family unit most commonly comprises the household of an older couple, plus the households of one or more of their married daughters, all situated "within shouting distance" of one another.

INHERITANCE. Basic productive resources are the collective property of the extended family and are not alienable by individuals; they are passed on from generation to generation within the group. Jewelry, saddles, horses, and many kinds of ceremonial knowledge are treated as personal property, however. Individuals have considerable freedom in disposal of these, although it is always expected that a woman will leave most of her personal property to her daughters and that a man will leave much of his property to his sister's children.

SOCIALIZATION. Children were and are raised permissively, and there is a marked respect for the personal integrity even of very young children. The main sanctioning punishments are shaming and ridicule. Children receive a good deal of formal training in various technical and craft activities from their parents, and boys may be schooled in ceremonial lore and ritual practice by their fathers or by their mothers' brothers. The recitation of myths by grandparents and other elders also contributes to the education of Navajo children.

Sociopolitical Organization

SOCIAL ORGANIZATION. There was no ranking in traditional Navajo society; social obligations were determined entirely by kinship and residence. Both men and women had fairly specific, lifelong obligations toward the family into which they were born as well as toward the family into which they were married. The father in each household was the recognized household head, and the father in the oldest household was the headman of each residence group, with considerable authority over the allocation of labor and resources among all the members of the group. The status of women was notably high.

POLITICAL ORGANIZATION. There was no system of formal authority among the Navajo except that embodied in kinship relationships. In the prereservation period, however, the population was divided into a number of localized bands, and each of these had its recognized leader, although he had no coercive powers. In the reservation period, the organization into bands disappeared, but respected singers (medicine men) may act informally as local community leaders and as arbitrators of disputes. Political organization of the tribe as a whole was instituted only in 1923 and is modeled on the institutions of European and American parliamentary democracy rather than on aboriginal tradition. There is a tribal chairman and a vice chairman, elected by reservationwide popular ballot for four-year terms, a Tribal Council made up of elected delegates from each of about one hundred local "chapters," and an Executive Committee elected by the members of the council. In most parts of the reservation there are also locally elected chapter officers who attend to the political needs of the local community.

SOCIAL CONTROL. The principal mechanism for the maintenance of order has always been the concept of collective responsibility, which makes all members of a family, or even of a clan, responsible for the good behavior of any individual member. Maintaining the good name of the family or clan within the community is an important consideration for all Navajo. In addition, the accusation of witchcraft was likely to be directed against persons who were considered to be "bad characters"; this in effect defined them as public enemies.

CONFLICT. Conflict between individuals or families might arise for a variety of reasons. Disputes over the possession of farmland and disputes arising from poor marital relations were especially common in earlier times. All infractions except incest and witchcraft were treated as private wrongs, to be settled by negotiation between the kin groups involved. Locally respected medicine men might be called upon to arbitrate or advise in these disputes. There is, in addition, a system of Navajo Tribal Courts and a code of offenses adopted by the Navajo Tribal Council, but most Navajo still prefer to settle disputes without recourse to these institutions.

Religion and Expressive Culture

RELIGIOUS BELIEFS. Navajo gods and other supernatural powers are many and varied. Most important among them are a group of anthropomorphic deities, and especially Changing Woman or Spider Woman, the consort of the Sun God, and her twin sons, the Monster Slayers. Other supernatural powers include animal, bird, and reptile spirits, and natural phenomena or wind, weather, light and darkness, celestial bodies, and monsters. There is a special class of deities, the *Yei*, who can be summoned by masked dancers to be present when major ceremonies are in progress. Most of the Navajo deities can be either beneficial or harmful to the Earth Surface People, depending on their caprice or on how they are approached. Navajo mythology is enormously rich and poetically expressive. According to basic cosmological belief, all of existence is divided between the Holy People (supernaturals) and the Earth Surface People. The Holy People passed through a succession of underworlds, each of which was destroyed by a flood, until they arrived in the present world. Here they created First Man and First Woman, the ancestors of all the Earth Surface People. The Holy People gave to the Earth Surface People all the practical and ritual knowledge necessary for their survival in this world and then moved away to dwell in other realms above the earth. However, they remain keenly interested in the day-to-day doings of the Earth Surface People, and constant attention to ceremonies and taboos is required in order to keep in harmony with them. The condition of *hozoji*, or being in harmony with the supernatural powers, is the single most important ideal sought by the Navajo people.

RELIGIOUS PRACTITIONERS. The most respected of Navajo ritual practitioners are called "singers." These are men (or, very occasionally, women) who can perform in their entirety one or more of the major Navajo ceremonies. They are not shamans but priests who have acquired their knowledge and skills through long apprenticeship to an established singer. They are the most highly respected individuals in traditional Navajo society and frequently act as informal community leaders. Men with a lesser degree of ritual knowledge who can perform only short or incomplete ceremonies are referred to by another term, which might be translated as "curers." There is in addition a special class of diagnosticians, or diviners, who use various shamanistic techniques to discover the source of a person's illness or misfortune and who then prescribe the appropriate ceremonial treatment.

CEREMONIES. In aboriginal times there were important Navajo ceremonies connected with war, hunting, agriculture, and the treatment of illness. In the reservation period, nearly all of the major public ceremonies have come to focus on curing in the broadest sense—that is, on the restoration of harmony with the supernaturals. There are, or have been, at least sixty major ceremonies, most of which involve an intricate combination of songs, prayers, magical rituals, the making of prayer-sticks and other paraphernalia, and the making of an elaborate dry-painting using colored sands. Masked dancers also play a part in some ceremonies. Ceremonies may last for two, three, five, or nine nights, depending partly on the seriousness of the condition being treated.

ARTS. The artistic creativity of the Navajo finds expression in a wide variety of media, including poetry, song, dance, and costume. The most celebrated of Navajo artistic productions are the brightly colored rugs woven by women, and the intricate dry-painting designs executed by the singers as a part of each major ceremony. Dry-paintings were traditionally destroyed at the conclusion of each ceremony, but permanent reproductions of many of the designs are now being made on boards for sale commercially. In the present century, a number of Navajo have also achieved recognition as painters and have set up commercial studios in various western cities.

MEDICINE. In traditional Navajo belief, all illness or misfortune arises from transgressions against the supernaturals or from witchcraft. Consequently, medical practice is essentially synonymous with ceremonial practice. There are particular kinds of ceremonies designed to treat illnesses caused by the patient's transgressions, by accidents, and by different kinds of witchcraft. Apart from ceremonial practices, there was formerly a fairly extensive materia medica of herbs, potions, ointments, and fumigants, and there were specialists who collected and applied these.

DEATH AND AFTERLIFE. Traditionally, Navajo were morbidly afraid of death and the dead and spoke about them as little as possible. The dead were buried promptly and without public ceremony, although a great many ritual taboos were observed by the close kin of the deceased and by those who handled the corpse. Ideas about the afterlife were not codified in a systematic way, but varied from individual to individual. There was no concept of rewards and punishments for deeds done in this life; it seems that the afterworld was not thought of as a happy or desirable place for anyone.

Bibliography

Kluckhohn, Clyde, and Dorothea Leighton (1946). *The Navaho*. Cambridge: Harvard University Press.

Leighton, Dorothea, and Clyde Kluckhohn (1948). *Children of the People*. Cambridge: Harvard University Press.

Locke, Raymond F. (1976). *The Book of the Navajo*. Los Angeles: Mankind Publishing Co.

Ortiz, Alfonso, ed. (1983). *Handbook of North American Indians*. Vol. 10, *Southwest*, 489–683. Washington, D.C.: Smithsonian Institution.

Underhill, Ruth (1956). *The Navajos*. Norman: University of Oklahoma Press.

—WILLIAM Y. ADAMS

*The name "eskimo"
is of foreign
derivation, although
there is considerable
disagreement about
where and when it
originated.*

NORTH ALASKAN ESKIMOS

Ethnonyms: Iñupiat, Malemiut, Nunamiut, Tariurmiut

Orientation

IDENTIFICATION. The North Alaskan Eskimos are located along the coast of northern Alaska. The name "Eskimo" is of foreign derivation, although there is considerable disagreement about where and when it originated. The North Alaskan Eskimos refer to themselves collectively as "Iñupiat," or "authentic people." "Nunamiut" was and is used as a general designation for people who spend the winter inland, and "Tariurmiut" is the corresponding term for coast dwellers. "Malemiut" is derived from a Yup'ik Eskimo word from Norton Sound that was formerly used to denote the speakers of an Iñuit dialect from Kotzebue Sound. The term was frequently used erroneously in late-nineteenth-century and early- twentieth-century literature to refer to a tribal entity of some kind. Its use is now restricted in the technical literature to the name for a regional dialect.

LOCATION. Aboriginally, the North Alaskan Eskimos occupied the coast of northern Alaska from the western tip of Kotzebue Sound to the mouth of the Colville River, and the entire hinterland drained by rivers reaching the sea between those two points. In the late nineteenth century they expanded eastward along the Arctic coast to beyond what is now the Canadian border, and southward to the eastern shore of Norton Sound.

DEMOGRAPHY. The population at the beginning of the 1800s was probably about eight thousand to nine thousand people. There was a decline of some 75 percent in the last quarter of that century, but the population began to recover early in the twentieth century. By about 1975 it had reached its traditional level, and it has continued to grow since.

LINGUISTIC AFFILIATION. The language of the North Alaskan Eskimos belongs to the Eskimo branch of the Eskaleut language family. More specifically, it is an Iñuit Eskimo language, which is spoken from Bering Strait across northern North America to Greenland. Within North Alaska, the Malemiut dialect is spoken in eleven villages of the Kotzebue Sound drainage and three on the shore of Norton Sound, and the North Slope dialect is spoken in the eight villages north of Kotzebue Sound.

History and Cultural Relations

When they were first encountered by Europeans in the second decade of the nineteenth century, the people were organized in nineteen autonomous societies, or tribes. They welcomed the few explorers and shipborne traders who ventured into their area as long as they were interested in trade. Otherwise, they tended to be hostile, although bloodshed was rare. Relations with Europeans improved with more familiarity. A greater threat to native life was posed by American whalers after 1848; over the next two decades they decimated the bowhead whale and walrus populations, which previously had been major sources of food and other raw materials. In the 1870s the natives themselves decimated the caribou population with newly introduced firearms. Widespread famine followed. European epidemic diseases also arrived about this time, with catastrophic effect. The demographic decline and ensuing chaos resulted in the destruction of the traditional social boundaries and in extensive interregional movement of families trying to find productive hunting and fishing grounds.

In the late nineteenth century, missionaries and miners made their way to the region. Between about 1900 and 1910, schools were established at several locations. The new mission-school villages subsequently became focal points for the natives, resulting eventually in the formation of twenty-two permanent villages distributed across their expanded late-nineteenth-century territory. Domesticated reindeer were introduced to fill the void left by the nearly extinct caribou, and reindeer herding and fur trapping became the basis of a new economic order lasting until the 1930s. The fur trade collapsed during the Great Depression, and reindeer herding declined as the caribou population began to recover. Welfare payments and seasonal wage employment for men, usually far from home, subsequently became the major sources of cash income, while hunting and fishing continued to provide the raw materials for food and some clothing. Increasing economic and political stability, combined with improved medical care, has resulted in a steady population increase since 1910.

The period 1960–1990 has seen major economic and social changes. The Alaska Native Claims Settlement Act (ANCSA) led to the formation of two native regional corporations, NANA Corporation, in the region focused on Kotzebue Sound, and the Arctic Slope Regional Corporation (ASRC) to the north. Oil and mineral development provided a substantial tax base leading to the formation of modern political units: the North Slope Borough (in the general territory of the ASRC) and the Northwest Arctic Borough (in the general territory of NANA). As they approach the end of the twentieth century the people are involved in the general political and economic life of Alaska, but continue to rely to a considerable extent on hunting and fishing for food. Increasing numbers of nonnatives have moved into North Alaska since the 1960s, but Eskimos still constitute a substantial majority of the permanent resident population.

Settlements

During the early contact period each society had a distinctive settlement pattern, but the several forms can be grouped into two broad categories, a whaling pattern and a nonwhaling pattern. In the former, relatively large villages were located at Point Hope, Icy Cape, Ukpiarvik, and Point Barrow, places where spring ice conditions favored hunting the bowhead whale. Smaller satellite villages were distributed along the coast and on the lower reaches of rivers elsewhere within the societal territory. In both types of settlement, the semisubterranean sod house was the sole type of dwelling. After the conclusion of whaling, in June, the inhabitants of these villages dispersed to spring seal-hunting camps scattered along the coast. After the sea ice left in late June or early July, they dispersed even more widely to hunt caribou and fish along the rivers or to trade at one of the annual trade fairs. These travels usually concluded in late August or early September, at which time people returned to their winter villages.

The nonwhaling settlement pattern was characterized by the autumn dispersal of the population in small villages, primarily along rivers, but in a few cases along the coast or around lakes. These villages were usually located in areas likely to be visited by caribou, but at specific sites that were particularly well suited for fishing; in a few instances, they were at good fall seal-hunting locations. Houses in these settlements were constructed of wooden frames covered by one of a variety of materials: sod, moss, or a tarpaulin made of skins. As the winter progressed, people stayed in their fall settlements if food supplies lasted, but they usually had to move around eventually in search of game. In the spring, there was a fair amount of variation. In some societies, people moved to the coast to hunt seals; in others, they moved to lakes and sloughs to hunt muskrats and migratory waterfowl and/or to fish. After the river ice broke up, the members of several societies moved to the coast to trade, hunt sea mammals, and fish, but the members of several others remained inland to fish and to hunt caribou. In all areas summer was a time of movement during which people lived in tents. The two patterns persisted into the twentieth century, but the native population gradually became more sedentary, especially after the end of the reindeer herding and trapping era.

Economy

SUBSISTENCE AND COMMERCIAL ACTIVITIES. The entire economy was based on hunting and fishing and, to a much more moderate extent, on the gathering of plant products. Whales, seals, caribou, several species of fish, and a variety of fur-bearing animals, small game, and birds provided them with all the raw materials they needed for food and clothing and, to a significant extent, for tools, weapons, and utensils as well. Wood was used in house construction and in the manufacture of some weapons and tools; leaves, berries, and some roots were collected for food. Hunting, fishing, and gathering continue to be important sources of food today, but are significantly supplemented by foodstuffs imported from regions farther south. Gardening is carried on to a very limited extent in a few villages where soil and summer weather conditions permit. Cash income is derived from welfare payments and by employment in a variety of private commercial enterprises—particularly in the oil, mining, and service industries—and government agencies. Traditionally, the only domesticated animals were large dogs. In winter they were used to pull sleds; in summer, to track boats along the seacoast and rivers and as pack animals. For about half a century, beginning in the 1890s, imported reindeer were raised on a relatively large scale, but that industry has declined to only a few small herds today. Cats and dogs are now kept as pets; teams of sled dogs are kept only for racing.

INDUSTRIAL ARTS. The North Alaskan Eskimos were noted for the quality of their work in

Increasing numbers of non-natives have moved into North Alaska since the 1960s, but Eskimos still constitute a substantial majority of the permanent resident population.

North Alaskan Eskimos

KEEPING WARM

North Alaskan Eskimo woman in her warm fur coat. Kotzebue, Alaska, USA. (Dave Bertruff/Corbis)

ivory and flint. Skin sewing was developed to a high level. Beautiful birchbark baskets were made in the southern interior. Except for work in flint, these traditional manufactures are perpetuated today, skin sewing primarily for personal or family use, ivory and bone carving and basket making as a source of cash income.

TRADE. Aboriginally there was a well-developed intersocietal trade network in North Alaska. It was based upon trading partnerships and implemented through two major summer fairs and a system of winter feasts during both of which partners from different societies came together. The whole system was connected by similar links with Athapaskan Indian societies in the Alaskan interior, with other Eskimos in the Bering Strait area and southwestern Alaska, and with Eskimos and Chuckchees in easternmost Asia.

DIVISION OF LABOR. Aboriginally there was a sharp division of labor based on gender. Men hunted big game, built houses, and manufactured weapons, tools, and utensils. Women looked after most game from the time it was killed: retrieving it, storing it, and performing whatever processing chores were required prior to ultimate consumption. Women also did the sewing and child rearing. Fishing, trapping, and hunting birds and small game were either men's work or women's work, with regional and seasonal variations in the precise allocation of duties. The traditional division of labor based on gender persisted with only a few modifications until the 1960s. Since then, although the pursuit of large game is still carried out primarily by men, the great increase in the opportunities for local employment in teaching, government, and service industries has changed the primary basis of the division of labor to one's level of education and technical training rather than gender.

LAND TENURE. Aboriginally, land ownership was vested at the societal level; it was owned in common by all the members of the society. Within the territory of a society, its members were free to live, hunt, and fish where they wished, subject only to the provision that people who first occupied a place had the primary right to use it until they abandoned it. There was no other private ownership of land, nor were there individual or family hunting or fishing territories. Today land ownership in North Alaska follows the pattern that exists generally in the United States; the region is a patchwork of properties owned by individuals and corporations—much of it by native corporations established under ANCSA, local governments, the state of Alaska, and various agencies of the U.S. government.

Kinship

KIN GROUPS AND DESCENT. Traditionally, the North Alaskan Eskimos were organized in terms of bilocal extended families. Typically they involved about a dozen people, but many were larger, and some involved as many as sixty to eighty. Unilineal descent groups were absent. Bilocal extended families are still important today, although in recent decades the conjugal family has become the dominant kinship unit.

KINSHIP TERMINOLOGY. In the nineteenth century kinship terminology conformed to the Yuman type. Today, as a result of acculturation, the Eskimo type is beginning to predominate.

Marriage and Family

MARRIAGE. Traditionally, incest prohibitions applied absolutely to siblings, strongly to first cousins, and rather weakly beyond that. Parents attempted to control, and certainly to influence, their children's choice of a spouse, but there was no institutionalized betrothal system. Monogamy predominated, with polygyny practiced by a few wealthy men, most of whom had two wives, but a few of whom had as many as five.

Polyandry was permitted, but was extremely rare. Postmarital residence was bilocal. Divorce was common, especially during the early years of adult life. It could be effected by either party.

DOMESTIC UNIT. A household could consist of a single conjugal family, but usually comprised two or more conjugal families connected by sibling or cousin ties reckoned through either the female or male lines, or both. Adjacent houses were usually occupied by people who were closely related and often were connected to one another by tunnels or passageways, the whole being a single economic and political unit managed by the family head and his wife. Three-generation households were common. This general pattern prevailed until the late 1960s, after which the population increase and the imposition of the U.S. system of land ownership and of clearly bounded property lines in the villages made it difficult to perpetuate.

INHERITANCE. Individually owned movable property was buried with the deceased. Houses, boats, and other items owned by the family as a whole continued to be used by the surviving members of that family.

SOCIALIZATION. Traditionally, the ratio of adults to children was high, and children received a great deal of individual attention and supervision. Discipline was permissive. Children were encouraged to learn by a combination of admonition, example, and especially practice. The traditional approach is still preferred in native households. As the ratio of children to adults increased in the twentieth century, however, it became less effective because there were too many children to look after with the same level of care. Jobs now take one or more parents out of the house for several hours each day, and much socialization takes place outside the family context, primarily in schools.

Sociopolitical Organization

SOCIAL AND POLITICAL ORGANIZATION. Aboriginally, there were no governments, tribal councils, chiefs, or other forms of centralized authority. The traditional societies were organized in terms of large extended families that were politically and economically self-sufficient to a high degree. The several families were linked to one another by various kinship, namesake, and partnership ties to form the society as a whole. Most settlements were occupied by the members of only a single extended family. Larger settlements, including each of the whaling villages, were occupied by the members of several families who lived in close proximity to one another, but who maintained a high level of autonomy nevertheless. Each extended family served as a redistribution network in which the family head and his wife served as foci. Men who demonstrated superior hunting, managerial, and leadership skills, and who were married to women of commensurate ability, attracted more and more relatives to join their family groups. The heads of large families were often wealthy, and they typically had at least two wives. At the opposite extreme, couples who were lazy or incompetent either had to shift for themselves or become affiliated with a large family in some kind of marginal and subservient capacity.

SOCIAL CONTROL. Affiliation with a particular family head was voluntary; both individuals and conjugal families could strike out on their own whenever they wished. This served as a check on disruptive behavior by the family head. Life in isolation was precarious, however, and the only realistic option to belonging to one extended family was to belong to a different one. These facts, which were well understood, served as important constraints on disruptive behavior by ordinary family members. Additional constraints took the form of admonition by family elders, ridicule, and gossip. In cases where these were ineffective, family members might shun an individual or, in extreme cases, even kill the person. There were fewer controls on disruptive behavior between families, since there were no individuals or organizations with authority to mediate interfamily disputes. Over the decades a kind of balance of power seems to have developed among the families in a given society, with smaller units forming alliances to offset the dominance of larger ones. Interfamily relations in traditional times were often tense, especially in the whaling villages, but only rarely erupted into violence.

CONFLICT. Within societies, interfamily feuds did occasionally result in murder. When that occurred, the male relative closest to the deceased had the obligation to kill the assassin. If he was successful, the obligation for vengeance passed back to a man on the other side. At the intersocietal level, warfare was relatively common. It seems to have been undertaken solely for the purpose of avenging a wrong of some kind, and the objective was the death of as many people as possible on the enemy side—men, women, and children. War was not conducted for the purpose of acquiring territory, booty, or slaves. Nighttime raids were the preferred form of attack, although organized warfare, with battle lines, tactical maneuvers, and

The traditional North Alaskan Eskimo religion was animistic. Everything was believed to be imbued with a spirit.

clearly developed fire and shock tactics, also occurred.

Religion and Expressive Culture

RELIGIOUS BELIEFS. The traditional religion was animistic. Everything was believed to be imbued with a spirit. There was, in addition, an array of spirits that were not associated with any specific material from. Some of these spirits looked kindly on humans, but most of them had to be placated in order for human activities to proceed without difficulty. Harmony with the spirit world was maintained through the wearing of amulets, the observance of a vast number of taboos, and participation in a number of ceremonies relating primarily to the hunt, food, birth, death, the life cycle, and the seasonal round. In the 1890s a few natives from Southwest Alaska who had been converted by Swedish missionaries began evangelical work in the Kotzebue Sound area. About the same time, Episcopal and Presbyterian missionaries from the continental United States began work in Point Hope and Barrow, followed by members of the California Annual Meeting of Friends in the Kotzebue Sound area. After some difficulties, the Friends were successful in converting a large number of people, and these converts laid the foundation for widespread conversions to Christianity throughout North Alaska. Today, practically every Christian denomination and faith is represented in the region.

RELIGIOUS PRACTITIONERS. In traditional times, shamans interceded between the human and spirit worlds. They divined the concerns of the spirits and advised their fellow humans of the modes of behavior required to placate them. They also healed the sick, foretold the future results of a particular course of action, made spirit flights to the sun and the moon, and attempted to intercede with the spirits when ordinary means proved ineffective. Around 1900, the shamans were replaced by American missionaries. Most of them, in turn, have been replaced by natives ordained as ministers or priests in the Christian faiths to which they adhere.

CEREMONIES. The traditional ceremonial cycle consisted of a series of rituals and festivals related primarily to ensuring success in the hunt. Such events were most numerous and most elaborate in the societies in which whaling was of major importance, but they occurred to some degree throughout the region. Intersocietal trading festivals were also important. The traditional cycle has been replaced by the contemporary American sequence of political and Christian holidays.

ARTS. Traditional arts consisted primarily of the following: (1) making essentially utilitarian objects (such as tools, weapons, and clothes) in a particularly elegant fashion; (2) storytelling; and (3) song and dance. Since the advent of store-bought products and television, all the traditional art forms have declined considerably.

MEDICINE. There were two forms of traditional medicine. One, which involved divination and intercession with the spirits, was conducted by shamans. The second involved the massage and/or manipulation of various body parts, particularly the internal organs. The former has given way to Western clinical medicine. The latter, after several decades of being practiced in secret, has recently experienced a revival.

DEATH AND AFTERLIFE. Life and death were believed to be a perpetual cycle through which a given individual passed. When a person died, his or her personal possessions were placed on the grave for use in the afterlife, although it was understood that, in due course, the soul of everyone who died would be reanimated in the form of a newborn infant. The traditional beliefs about death and the afterworld have been replaced by an array of Christian beliefs. Whereas funerals were not well defined or important rituals in traditional times—the observance of special taboos was much more important—they have in recent decades become elaborate events in which hundreds of people from several villages often participate, particularly when the death of an elder is involved.

Bibliography

Burch, Ernest S., Jr. (1975). *Eskimo Kinsmen: Changing Family Relationships in Northwest Alaska.* St. Paul, Minn.: West Publishing Co.

Burch, Ernest S., Jr. (1980). "Traditional Eskimo Societies in Northwest Alaska." In *Alaska Native Culture and History*, edited by Yoshinobu Kotani and William Workman, 253–304. Suita, Osaka, Japan: National Museum of Ethnology.

Gubser, Nicholas J. (1965). *The Nunamiut Eskimos: Hunters of Caribou.* New Haven, Conn.: Yale University Press.

Rainey, Froelich G. (1947). "The Whale Hunters of Tigara." *Anthropological Papers of the American Museum of Natural History* 41 (2):230–283.

Spencer, Robert F. (1959). *The North Alaskan Eskimo: A Study in Ecology and Society.* U.S. Bureau of American Ethnology Bulletin no. 171. Washington, D.C.

—ERNEST S. BURCH, JR.

OJIBWA

Ethnonyms: Anishinabe, Bungee, Bungi, Chippewa, Mississauga, Northern Ojibwa, Plains Ojibwa, Saulteaux, Southwestern Chippewa, Southeastern Ojibwa

Orientation

IDENTIFICATION. The Ojibwa are a large American Indian group located in the northern Midwest in the United States and south-central Canada. "Ojibwa" means "puckered up," a reference to the Ojibwa style of moccasin. The Ojibwa name for themselves is "Anishinabe," meaning "human being."

LOCATION. Aboriginally, the Ojibwa occupied an extensive area north of Lakes Superior and Huron. A geographical expansion beginning in the seventeenth century resulted in a four-part division of the Ojibwa. The four main groups are the Northern Ojibwa, or Saulteaux; the Plains Ojibwa, or Bungee; the Southeastern Ojibwa; and the Southwestern Chippewa. At the end of the eighteenth century the Northern Ojibwa were located on the Canadian Shield north of Lake Superior and south and west of Hudson and James bays; the Plains Ojibwa, in southern Saskatchewan and Manitoba; the Southeastern Ojibwa, on the lower peninsula of Michigan and adjacent areas of Ontario; and the Southwestern Chippewa, in northern Minnesota, extreme northern Wisconsin, and Ontario between Lake Superior and the Manitoba border. The Canadian Shield country is a flat land of meager soil and many lakes and swamps. The country of the Plains Ojibwa is an environment of rolling hills and forests dominated by oak, ash, and whitewood. The homeland of the Southeastern Ojibwa and the Southwestern Chippewa, also a country of rolling hills, includes marshy valleys, upland prairie, rivers and lakes, and forests of maple, birch, poplar, oak, and other deciduous species. Throughout the region, winters are long and cold and summers short and hot.

DEMOGRAPHY. The Ojibwa are one of the largest American Indian groups north of Mexico. In the mid-seventeenth century they numbered at least 35,000, perhaps many more. Today the Ojibwa who are located in Ontario, Manitoba, and Saskatchewan in Canada and Michigan, Wisconsin, Minnesota, North Dakota, Montana, and Oklahoma in the United States, number about 160,000; the majority of them live in the Canadian provinces.

LINGUISTIC AFFILIATION. The Ojibwa languages are classified in the Algonkian language family.

History and Cultural Relations

Contact with Europeans was initiated in the early 1600s, and by the end of the century the Ojibwa were deeply involved in the fur trade and heavily dependent on European trade goods. As a result, the Ojibwa underwent a major geographical expansion that by the end of the eighteenth century had resulted in the four-part division of the tribe. Their migration in some cases led to significant modifications in their aboriginal hunting, fishing, and gathering subsistence pattern. These modifications were most evident among the Northern Ojibwa, who borrowed extensively from the Cree and adopted a subarctic culture pattern, and the Plains Ojibwa, who took up many elements of the Plains Indian way of life. During the first half of the nineteenth century the Southeastern Ojibwa were forced by White demands for farmland to cede their territory for reservation status. Similarly, in the mid-nineteenth century the Southwestern Chippewa and in the late nineteenth and early twentieth centuries the Plains Ojibwa and the Northern Ojibwa were resettled on reservations and reserves in the United States and Canada. Since the 1950s a major theme of Ojibwa cultural change has been migration off the reservations to urban centers where the people have become integrated into the Canadian and American work forces. The 1960s, however, saw a resurgence of native consciousness among the Ojibwa on many of the reservations in the United States and Canada, as the people saw their traditional culture eroding under the impact of government education programs, urban migration, and other acculturative forces.

Aboriginally and in the early historic period the Ojibwa were closely tied to the Huron to their south. After the Huron were defeated by the Iroquois in 1649–1650 in their contest for control of the western fur trade, the Ojibwa came under strong pressure from the Iroquois. By the end of the seventeenth century, however, some Ojibwa were pushing southeastward, sometimes by force, at the expense of the Iroquois. Those who moved into the lower peninsula of Michigan became closely allied with the Ottawa and Potawatomi. During the eighteenth century Ojibwa, who had obtained European firearms from French traders, expanded to the southwest where they had a strategic military advantage over their neighbors

The Ojibwa are one of the largest American Indian groups north of Mexico.

Ojibwa men and women shared responsibility for numerous economic activities, such as fishing and trapping, and sometimes cooperated in the same tasks, such as canoe construction.

and displaced the Dakota, Cheyenne, Hidatsa, and other groups from their traditional homelands. Intermittent and sometimes costly warfare between the Southwestern Ojibwa and the Dakota persisted for more than a century until ended by U.S. government-enforced treaties in the 1850s. The Northern Ojibwa who moved onto the Canadian Shield became closely associated with the Cree peoples to their north and west. With the acquisition of the horse, the westernmost of the Ojibwa had by 1830 evolved a pattern of seasonal migration to the open plains and adopted many elements of the Plains Indian way of life, including the preoccupation with bison hunting, the Sun Dance, and decorative tailored skin clothing.

Settlements

The prehistoric and early historic Ojibwa maintained semipermanent villages for summer use and temporary camps during the remainder of the year, as they moved to exploit fish, game, and wild plant resources. This pattern of seasonal settlement and movement persisted to some extent among all the Ojibwa groups, but especially so among the nineteenth-century Southeastern Ojibwa and Southwestern Chippewa, who in their seasonal round returned each summer to permanent village bases to plant gardens. The typical dwelling of the early Southeastern Ojibwa was the traditional conical hide-covered lodge, but as they adopted farming and a more settled way of life, log cabins and wood frame houses came into widespread use. Among the Southwestern Chippewa the most common dwelling was a dome-shaped wigwam covered with birchbark and cattail matting. The Northern Ojibwa spent much of their year moving in dispersed groups in search of subsistence, but during the summer they congregated at fishing sites in close proximity to trading posts, where they procured their supplies for the coming year. Their basic dwelling was a conical or ridge pole lodge covered with birch and birchbark. A high degree of mobility also characterized the Plains Ojibwa, who adopted bison-skin tipis and a pattern of seasonal movement involving concentration on the open plains in the summer to harvest the bison herds.

Economy

SUBSISTENCE AND COMMERCIAL ACTIVITIES. In the summer when they gathered in their villages, the aboriginal and early historic Ojibwa fished, collected wild nuts and berries, and planted small gardens of maize, beans, squash, and pumpkins. In some areas wild rice was harvested in the fall. In the winter the bands dispersed and moved to hunting grounds where they subsisted on deer, moose, bear, and a variety of small game. In the spring maple sap was gathered and boiled to produce maple syrup. By the late 1600s, the Ojibwa were heavily involved in the exchange of mink, muskrat, beaver, and other animal pelts for European trade goods. Among the Southeastern Ojibwa and the Southwestern Chippewa this subsistence pattern persisted, but with a greater emphasis on wild rice harvesting among the latter and more intensive farming among the former. Among the Plains Ojibwa bison and bison hunting became the basis of life. The Northern Ojibwa fished, gathered wild foods, and hunted game and waterfowl, but were beyond the environmental range of wild rice and the sugar maple, and so the exploitation of those resources was not part of their subsistence pattern.

INDUSTRIAL ARTS. Birchbark was a multipurpose resource for most of the Ojibwa, providing the raw material for canoes, lodge coverings, and storage and cooking containers. Various types of wood were used for snowshoes, canoe frames, lacrosse racquets, bows and arrows, bowls, ladles, flutes, drums, and fishing lures. Among the Plains Ojibwa bison were the principal source of raw materials for clothing, shelter, and tools.

TRADE. Aboriginally, furs and maple sugar were traded to the Huron for maize and tobacco. After becoming involved in the European fur trade Ojibwa traders made annual treks to Quebec and later to Montreal to trade furs for blankets, firearms, liquor, tools, kettles, and clothing. As trading posts were established by the French at Detroit and other closer points the distance of the trading expeditions was gradually reduced. Fur trapping and trading remained an important source of income among the Northern Ojibwa until the mid-twentieth century.

DIVISION OF LABOR. Men and women shared responsibility for numerous economic activities, such as fishing and trapping, and sometimes cooperated in the same tasks, such as canoe construction. Men's labor focused on hunting, trapping, and trading, and women's labor was most concerned with processing hides, making clothes, preparing food, caring for children, and collecting plant foods and firewood.

LAND TENURE. With the development of the European fur trade, bands tended to exploit a particular hunting and trapping territory. Gradually, these vaguely defined areas evolved into territories in which hunting and trapping groups had exclusive rights over fur resources.

Kinship

KIN GROUPS AND DESCENT. Except for the Northern Ojibwa, Ojibwa society was divided into numerous exogamous totemic clans. Among the nineteenth-century Southwestern Chippewa in Minnesota there were twenty-three such clans, groups of which were linked and divided into five phratries. Clan membership was reckoned patrilineally.

KINSHIP TERMINOLOGY. Ojibwa kinship terminology followed the Iroquois pattern. Parallel cousins were merged terminologically with siblings and cross cousins were classed separately. Parallel aunts and uncles were merged terminologically by sex with mother and father and cross aunts and uncles were classed separately.

Sociopolitical Organization

SOCIAL ORGANIZATION. In aboriginal and early historic times the Ojibwa were divided into small autonomous bands of interrelated families. Band organization was loose and flexible, and social relations, apart from divisions along the lines of age and sex, were egalitarian. With involvement in the European fur trade, band organization was modified. Among eighteenth-century Southeastern Ojibwa and Southwestern Chippewa, bands numbered several hundred people; among the Northern Ojibwa, bands were smaller, with about fifty to seventy-five mem-

bers. Plains Ojibwa bands were loose, shifting units.

POLITICAL ORGANIZATION. Each Ojibwa band was headed by a chief whose position was earned on the basis of hunting ability, personal appeal, and religious knowledge, but was also dependent on kinship connections. Shamans were respected and feared individuals who sometimes also functioned as band leaders. Among the eighteenth-century Southeastern Ojibwa, bands were headed by chiefs, but as farming and a more permanent settlement pattern were adopted local political organization evolved to include an elected chief, assistant chiefs, and a local council. This form of political organization was in part a government-imposed system. Among the Northern Ojibwa band leadership was supplied by a senior male whose kin group formed the basis of the band's membership. In addition, he was usually also a skilled trader. Among the Plains Ojibwa each band had several chiefs, one of whom was recognized as the head chief. The head chief usually inherited his position, held it for life, and was assisted by councillors elected by the adult male members of the band. Secondary chiefs among the Plains Ojibwa achieved their position by virtue of their deeds in war, skills in hunting, generosity, and leadership ability.

SOCIAL CONTROL. Censure by means of ridicule and ostracism was the primary mechanism of social control. In addition, among some Ojibwa groups mutilation and execution were punishments for certain offenses. Among the

MARRIAGE AND FAMILY

Marriage

Marriages were arranged by parents or guardians and involved little formal ceremony. Cross-cousin marriage was practiced, but not preferred. Polygyny was possible, but most marriages were monogamous. Divorce was permitted and a simple matter to effect for either husband or wife. Remarriage was permitted after divorce and after the death of a spouse following a mourning period of one year.

Domestic Unit

Traditionally, the basic social unit was the

extended family. Over time, however, it has given way to the nuclear family.

Inheritance

No single principle of inheritance appears to have prevailed among the Ojibwa. Instead, it seems to have been bilateral and a matter of residence and affection.

Socialization

Children were raised in a permissive fashion and rarely reprimanded or punished physically. The most important phase of a boy's life occurred at puberty when he sought a

guardian spirit through a vision quest. The quest involved several days (ideally four) of isolation, fasting, prayer, and dreaming undertaken to contact a guardian spirit to provide aid and protection. Through frequent offerings of food and tobacco the boy could maintain rapport with his guardian spirit and retain its aid and protection throughout his life. At the time of first menstruation the girl was isolated, but not required to undergo a vision quest. If, however, she did receive a vision during her isolation, it was regarded as a special blessing. Among the Plains Ojibwa girls visited by a spirit in this way were believed to possess curing powers.

Plains Ojibwa a wife found to have committed adultery could be mutilated or killed by her husband, and among the Southeastern Ojibwa mutilation was the prescribed punishment for violating mourning taboos. Chiefs among Plains Ojibwa sometimes mediated serious disputes, and when the people gathered on the open plains, camp police, or *okitsita*, composed of war heroes, maintained peace and order.

CONFLICT. Overt face-to-face hostility was rare in Ojibwa society. However, alcohol consumption seems to have increased the frequency and intensity of interpersonal conflict and physical violence. The Ojibwa believed sorcery to be the cause of individual misfortune and often employed sorcery in retaliation against their enemies. Suspicion of sorcery was a cause of conflict and could result in long-lasting feuds between families. Conflict also stemmed from encroachments on hunting and trapping territories.

Religion and Expressive Culture

RELIGIOUS BELIEFS. For the Ojibwa the supernatural world held a multitude of spiritual beings and forces. Some of these beings and forces—Sun, Moon, Four Winds, Thunder, and Lightning—were benign, but others—ghosts, witches, and Windigo, a supernatural cannibalistic giant—were malevolent and feared. Presiding over all other spirits was Kiccimanito, or Great Spirit, although this belief may have been a product of European influence. Ojibwa religion was very much an individual affair and centered on the belief in power received from spirits during dreams and visions. For this reason, dreams and visions were accorded great significance and much effort was given to their interpretation. The power obtained through them could be used to manipulate the natural and supernatural environments and employed for either good or evil purposes. Missionization by the Anglican and Roman Catholic churches began during the nineteenth century, but conversion and Christian influence were limited prior to the twentieth century. In the mid-twentieth century the religious orientation of many Ojibwa was a mixture of Christian and traditional native elements.

RELIGIOUS PRACTITIONERS. In their vision quests, some young men received more spiritual power than others, and it was they who in later life became shamans. Several different types of shamans existed, the type being determined by the sort of spiritual power received.

CEREMONIES. The most important religious ceremony for the Southeastern Ojibwa and the Southwestern Chippewa was the Midewiwin, or Medicine Dance, of the Medicine Lodge Society. The Midewiwin ceremony was held semiannually (in the late spring and early fall among the nineteenth-century Wisconsin Chippewa) and lasted for several days. The Northern Ojibwa did not practice the Midewiwin ceremony, although the Plains Ojibwa did. Among the latter, however, it was exceeded in importance by the Sun Dance, performed annually in mid-June in order to bring rain, good health, and good fortune.

ARTS. Ojibwa music was individualistic. Musical instruments included tambourines, water drums, rattles, and flutes. Songs were derived from dreams and had magical purposes, such as ensuring success in hunting and other economic activities, invoking guardian spirits, and curing sickness. Among the Southwestern Chippewa porcupine quill work employing a floral motif was an important technique in the decoration of buckskin clothing and leather bags. After European contact glass beads replaced quills in decorative applications, although the floral motif was maintained.

MEDICINE. Disease and illness were thought to be caused by sorcery or as retribution for improper conduct toward the supernatural or some social transgression. Curing was performed by members of the Midewiwin, or Medicine Lodge Society, into which both men and women were inducted after instruction by Mide priests, payment of fees, and formal initiation. Shamans, with their powers derived from dreams and visions, were curers of sickness, but so, too, were others knowledgeable in the use of medicinal plants.

DEATH AND AFTERLIFE. Upon death the corpse was washed, groomed, dressed in fine clothing, and wrapped in birchbark before burial in a shallow grave. Following death, the soul of the deceased was believed to journey westward for four days to an afterlife in the sky. Among the Southwestern Chippewa the deceased was also painted prior to burial and lay in state in a wigwam. The funeral ceremony was attended by friends and relatives and was conducted by a Mide priest, who talked to the deceased and offered tobacco to the spirits. After the ceremony was concluded the body was removed through a hole in the west side of the wigwam to the grave site, where it was buried along with personal possessions. The door of the wigwam was not used when removing the deceased for fear that the departed soul would return through the door. In later times a long, low, gabled plank house was constructed over the grave. The Plains Ojibwa also employed the gabled grave house and left offerings of food and water at the grave house for four days after burial for the soul's subsistence on its journey to the afterlife.

Bibliography

Barnouw, Victor (1977). *Wisconsin Chippewa Myths and Tales and Their Relation to Chippewa Life.* Madison: University of Wisconsin Press.

Buffalohead, Patricia (1986). "Farmers, Warriors, Traders: A Fresh Look at Ojibway Women." In *The American Indian,* edited by Roger L. Nichols, 28–38. 3rd ed. New York: Alfred A. Knopf.

Densmore, Frances (1979). *Chippewa Customs.* St. Paul: Minnesota Historical Society. Originally published, 1929.

Howard, James H. (1965). *The Plains Ojibwa or Bungi: Hunters and Warriors of the Northern Prairie, with Special Reference to the Turtle Mountain Band.* University of South Dakota, South Dakota Museum, Anthropological Papers, no. 1. Vermillion, S.D.

Ritzenthaler, Robert E. (1978). "Southwestern Chippewa." In *Handbook of North American Indians.* Vol. 15, *Northeast,* edited by Bruce G. Trigger, 743–759. Washington, D.C.: Smithsonian Institution.

Rogers, Edward S. (1978). "Southeastern Ojibwa." In *Handbook of North American Indians.* Vol. 15, *Northeast,* edited by Bruce G. Trigger, 760–771. Washington, D.C.: Smithsonian Institution.

Rogers, Edward S., and J. Garth Taylor (1981). "Northern Ojibwa." In *Handbook of North American Indians.* Vol. 6, *Subarctic,* edited by June Helm, 231–243. Washington, D.C.: Smithsonian Institution.

—GERALD F. REID

PUEBLO INDIANS

"Pueblo Indians" is the generic label for American Indian groups of the Southwest who are descended from the Anasazi peoples who inhabited the American Southwest continuously from the eighth century A.D. Prior to Spanish arrival in and settlement of the Southwest beginning with Francisco Vásquez Coronado's expedition of 1540–1542 there were ninety or more Pueblo groups in northern Arizona and New Mexico. Today, twenty-one groups still exist, with all but two (the Hopi in Arizona and the Tigua in Texas) in northern New Mexico. Among distinguishing features of the Pueblo culture are long-term occupation of the region, permanent villages, distinctive stone or adobe pueblo dwellings built around central plazas, semisubterranean ceremonial chambers (*kivas*), a traditional subsistence economy

CLIFF DWELLINGS

These cliff dwellings are made of bricks and were built into the cliff face by Pueblo Indians who inhabited the area in the 1400s. Bandelier National Monument, New Mexico, USA.
(Macduff Everton)

See also

Hopi, Zuni

Pueblo Indians

Extensive archaeological research indicates that ancestors of some contemporary Pueblo groups had moved north from Mexico by at least 1000 B.C.

based on the irrigated cultivation of maize, squash, and beans, and extensive use of highly stylized coiled pottery. Of the extant Pueblo groups, seven speak Keresan, six speak Tewa, five speak Tiwa, and one each speak Hopi, Towa, and Zuni languages. For the purpose of discussion, the Pueblo groups are categorized on the basis of location: Eastern (near the Rio Grande in New Mexico) or Western (in mesa and canyon country in western New Mexico and eastern Arizona). Cultural variations among groups, however, do not conform neatly to these linguistic and geographical divisions.

Extensive archaeological research indicates that ancestors of some contemporary Pueblo groups had moved north from Mexico by at least 1000 B.C. Descendants of these groups then progressed through a series of cultural traditions culminating in the distinctive Anasazi culture, whose most notable feature was the cliff dwellings found in canyons in northern Arizona and New Mexico and southern Utah and Colorado. The contemporary cultures of the surviving Pueblo groups are an amalgam of the traditional culture as modified by Mexican, Spanish, Roman Catholic, Protestant, and European-American influences. Despite centuries of external influence, however, each group has maintained its identity as a distinct people. There are important differences among groups and sometimes within groups as regards adherence to traditional beliefs and practices, degree of integration into European-American society, and economic well-being. Today, Pueblo groups and manifestations of their culture, such as pottery, jewelry, dances, and so on, are an important tourist attraction and a major element in the New Mexico State economy. Pan-Pueblo interests are represented by the All Pueblo Council, though each group retains and emphasizes its cultural and political autonomy.

Acoma. There were 2,681 Indian inhabitants of the 245,672-acre Acoma Indian Reservation in 1980. The reservation is located about sixty-five miles west of Albuquerque, New Mexico. Acoma Pueblo, located atop a 350-foot mesa, has been occupied for as long as a thousand years, making it, along with Oraibi, a Hopi village in Arizona, the two oldest, continuously occupied settlements in North America. Acoma is a western Keresan language and is still spoken, along with English. The current economy rests on cattle raising, tourism, the sale of pottery and other craft items, and mining on reservation land. The Acoma have retained much of their traditional culture.

Cochiti. There were 613 Indian inhabitants of the 28,776-acre Cochiti Indian Reservation in 1980. The reservation is about thirty miles southwest of Santa Fe, New Mexico. Cochiti is an eastern Keresan language and is spoken today, along with Spanish and English. Much of the traditional culture is still followed, including the traditional form of government, religious and other ceremonies open only to the Cochiti, and the wearing of traditional-style clothing. At the same time, attempts have been made at economic development to take advantage of mineral wealth on reservation land.

Laguna. There were 3,564 Indian inhabitants of the 412,211-acre Laguna Indian Reservation in 1980 (the reservation is actually in three parcels). It is located about forty-five miles west of Albuquerque, New Mexico. The major segment of the Acoma Reservation borders the Laguna Reservation on the west. Their name for themselves is "Kawiak," and Laguna is a western Keresan language. Laguna was settled by migrants from a number of other pueblos in 1697. Unlike other groups who live primarily in or near one village, the Laguna live in more than a half-dozen villages on the reservation. The group derives much income from royalties on uranium ore-mining leases and has invested strongly in economic development. Although more assimilated into Anglo society than most other Pueblo groups, the traditional language, religion, crafts, and ties to other groups are maintained.

San Felipe. There were 1,789 Indian inhabitants of the 48,853-acre San Felipe Indian Reservation in 1980. It is located twenty-five miles north of Albuquerque, New Mexico. Their name for themselves is "Katishtya." The San Felipe speak an eastern Keresan language. The contemporary culture represents a mix of the traditional culture, modern Anglo culture, and Roman Catholicism.

Santa Ana. There were 407 Indian inhabitants of the 45,527-acre Santa Ana Indian Reservation in 1980. It is located twenty-three miles north of Albuquerque, New Mexico. The Santa Ana name for themselves is "Tanava," and they speak an eastern Keresan language. They now live mainly in the village of Ranchos de Santa Ana on the reservation, returning to the traditional village for religious ceremonies.

Santo Domingo. There were 2,139 Indian inhabitants of the 69,260-acre Santo Domingo Indian Reservation in 1980. It is located about twenty-five miles southwest of Santa Fe, New Mexico. The Santo Domingo name for themselves is "Kiua," and they speak an eastern Keresan langauge. Despite regular contact with outsiders and participation in the regional and national pottery and silver jewelry market, Santo Domingo remains one of the most conservative of the Pueblo groups. Their adherence to tradtional ways is manifested in the strength of the traditional religion, the regular use of the native language, the retention of traditional clothing, and the maintenance of traditional kin ties.

Zia. There were 524 Indian inhabitants of the 112,511-acre Zia Indian Reservation in 1980. It is located about twenty miles southwest of Santa Fe, New Mexico. Their name for themselves is "Tseya," and they speak an eastern Keresan language. The Zia are known for their distinctive pottery and for the accommodation they have forged between their traditional culture and Roman Catholicism.

Nambe. There were 188 Indian inhabitants of the 19,073-acre Nambe Indian Reservation in 1980. It is located fifteen miles northeast of Santa Fe, New Mexico. The Nambe speak Tewa, a Tanoan language. The Nambe were much influenced by neighboring Spanish communities, and much of the traditional culture has disappeared.

Pojoaque. There were 94 Indian residents of the 11,599-acre Pojoaque Indian Reservation in 1980. It is located fifteen miles north of Santa Fe, New Mexico. They speak Tewa, a Tanoan language. Almost extinct in the late 1800s, the Pojoaque have slowly increased in numbers, although they are largely assimilated into Anglo society.

San Ildefonso. There were 488 Indian inhabitants of the 26,192-acre San Ildefonso Indian Reservation in 1980. It is located eighteen miles northwest of Santa Fe, New Mexico. The San Ildefonso name for themselves is "Poxwogeh," and they have lived in their current location for seven hundred years. They speak Tewa, a Tanoan language. San Ildefonso was the center of the rebirth of American Indian arts and crafts in the 1920s, primarily through the world-famous black-on-black pottery of Maria Martinez. The modern pueblo combines traditional beliefs and practices with integration into the local economy and modern, adobe-style community buildings.

San Juan. There were 851 Indian inhabitants of the 12,232-acre San Juan Indian Reservation in 1980. It is located twenty-four miles northwest of Santa Fe, New Mexico. The San Juan name for themselves is "Okeh," and they speak Tewa, a Tanoan language. They are closely related to the neighboring Santa Clara. The San Juan have in-termarried more with the Spanish than any other Pueblo group, though the traditional culture and language remain strong.

Santa Clara. There were 1,839 Indian inhabitants of the 45,744-acre Santa Clara Indian Reservation in 1980. It is located thirty miles northwest of Santa Fe, New Mexico. The Santa Clara name for themselves is "Xapogeh," and they speak Tewa, a Tanoan language. Although the language is still spoken and the traditional religion is practiced, the Santa Clara have been much involved in the external economy, primarily through tourism and the sale of Santa Clara pottery.

Tesuque. There were 236 Indian inhabitants of the 16,810-acre Tesuque Indian Reservation in 1980. It is located ten miles north of Santa Fe, New Mexico. Their name for themselves is "Tetsugeh," and they speak Tewa, a Tanoan language. The Tesuque have lived in their current location for over seven hundred years. Roman Catholicism is followed, though it exists alongside the traditional religion. The Tesuque operate a large bingo hall and campground for tourists.

Isleta. There were 2,289 Indian inhabitants of the 210,937-acre Isleta Indian Reservation in 1980. It is located fifteen miles south of Albuquerque, New Mexico. Their name for themselves is "Tuei," and they speak southern Tiwa, a Tanoan language. The Pueblo was built around 1709 and counts as its current residents descendants of a number of Pueblo groups including the Hopi, Laguna, Acoma, and Isleta. Despite the closeness to Albuquerque, the Isleta have managed to maintain much of their traditional culture.

Picuris. There were 125 Indian inhabitants of the 14,947-acre Picuris Indian Reservation in 1980. It is located forty miles northeast of Santa Fe, New Mexico. Picuris Pueblo was founded nearly seven hundred years ago. The Picuris were influenced by the Spanish, Plains Indians, and Apache and have been attempting to maintain the traditional culture. They speak northern Tiwa, a Tanoan language, and are closely related to the nearby Taos.

Sandia. There were 227 Indian inhabitants of the 22,884-acre Sandia Indian Reservation in 1980. It is located fifteen miles north of Albuquerque, New Mexico. The Sandia name for themselves is "Nafiat," and they speak southern Tiwa, a Tanoan language. Although much of the traditional culture survives, it is under increasing pressure since the Sandia are much involved in tourism.

Jemez. There were 1,504 Indian inhabitants of the 88,860-acre Jemez Indian Reservation in

The contemporary cultures of the surviving Pueblo groups are an amalgam of the traditional culture as modified by Mexican, Spanish, Roman Catholic, Protestant, and European-American influences.

*In general, South
and Southeast
Asians of the United
States are
concentrated in the
warmer areas of the
country, particularly
California.*

1980. It is located forty-five miles northwest of Albuquerque, New Mexico. The Jemez name for themselves is "Walatowa," and they speak Towa, a Tanoan language. Jemez is also the home of the descendants of the people of Pecos Pueblo, southeast of Santa Fe, which was abandoned in the late 1880s. The Jemez were active participants in the Pueblo Revolt of 1680 amd subsequent revolts. The Jemez maintain ties to the Navajo, which can be traced back to their alliance in the 1696 revolt against the Spanish.

Tigua. There were 365 Indian inhabitants on or near the three small (73 acres in all) state reservations near El Paso, Texas, in 1980. The Tigua migrated from Isleta in 1862 and are therefore not considered a distinct group by some experts. The Tigua have been much influenced by the nearby Mexican society and have retained less of the traditional culture than the other Pueblo groups to the north.

Bibliography

Ortiz, Alfonso, ed. (1979). *Handbook of Indians of North America*. Vol. 9, *Southwest*. Washington, D.C.: Smithsonian Institution.

SOUTH AND SOUTHEAST ASIANS OF THE UNITED STATES

Ethnonyms: South Asians: Asian Indians, Bangladeshis, Bhutanese, East Indians, Nepalese, Pakistanis, Sri Lankans; specific cultural groups— Gujaratis, Sikhs, Tamils. Southeast Asians: Burmese, Cambodians, Indonesians, Laotians, Malaysians, Thais, Vietnamese; specific cultural groups—Chinese of Southeast Asia, Hmong, Indos, Khmer, Malays

Orientation

IDENTIFICATION. The terms *South Asian* and *Southeast Asian* refer to broad ethnic and cultural categories, each comprised of a number of ethnic and national groups. Almost all South Asians in the United States came from or are descendants of those who came from Bangladesh, India, Pakistan, or Sri Lanka. There are a few people from Nepal and Bhutan. A number are secondary migrants from the South Asian diaspora who lived in Africa, South America, and islands in the Indian and Pacific oceans before coming to the United States. Most individuals define themselves as being Indian, Pakistani, Tamil, Bengali, and so on, rather than as being South Asian. Southeast Asians in the United States are mainly immigrants from Cambodia, Laos, and Vietnam, with substantial numbers also coming from Thailand and to a lesser extent from Myanmar (Burma). Those coming from Myanmar, Thailand, and Vietnam are usually either ethnic Burmese, Thai, Vietnamese, or Chinese. Those coming from Laos and Cambodia (Kampuchea) are mainly ethnic Lao or Khmer, respectively, although some are Chinese or of other ethnic groups.

The nations of South and Southeast Asia contain a rich variety of cultural, religious, and occupational groups. Broad labels such as "South Asian" and "Southeast Asian" and even national labels such as "Indonesian" often obscure the variety and complexity of ethnicity in this part of the world as well as the cultural background of immigrants to the United States.

LOCATION. In general, South and Southeast Asian-Americans are concentrated in the warmer areas of the country, particularly California, with local concentrations in large metropolitan areas in other regions. Except for special cases, such as that of Vietnamese refugees after the fall of that country to the Viet Minh, initial settlement by immigrants has usually been in urban centers. Over time, however, secondary migration within the United States generally increases.

DEMOGRAPHY. In early 1990, the U.S. Bureau of the Census reported that heavy immigration of Asians from 1980 to 1988 had increased their total population by 70 percent to about 6.5 million. A significant portion of this increase has been South and Southeast Asians and a great number of these have settled in California. In general these new immigrants, particularly the South Asians, have far higher educational and professional qualifications than those of earlier groups. Major factors in immigration to the United States may be the lack of job opportunities for skilled professional workers in the sending nations as well as political violence there. Large numbers of the immigrants were admitted under family reunification priorities in order to join relatives already in the United States.

In 1980 the number of South Asian-Americans was probably underestimated when the U.S. Bureau of the Census counted about 375,000 Indians, 25,000 Pakistanis, and a few thousand each of Bangladeshis and Sri Lankans. Some experts believe that the Indian population at that time alone may have been in excess of 700,000. Most of the approximately 450,000 Southeast Asian-Americans enumerated in the 1980 census were post-1960 immigrants. The proportion of Vietnamese in this group up to the mid-1980s was steadily increasing.

LINGUISTIC AFFILIATION. Because of British colonial dominance, in most South Asian nations English was used as the language of the educated classes or as a national language. Other major languages used were and are Gujarati, Hindi, Punjabi, Urdu, Bengali, Malayalam, Sinhala, Tamil, and Telugu. Hundreds of other languages are spoken on the subcontinent. Most U.S.-born South Asian-Americans can understand the mother tongue of their parents, but few

are fully fluent in it. The situation with many Southeast Asian-Americans is much the reverse, as few immigrants knew English, and a significant number presently do not have effective command of it. Many of those coming from former Indochina, a French colonial area, have some command of French, but this is of little use in the United States. Among the major languages are Vietnamese, Khmer, Lao, and Cantonese, which is a commercial lingua franca in the area. In the southern part of the area, Malay and Bahasa Indonesia are the major languages. Other languages spoken are Burmese, Thai, and the languages of numerous smaller ethnic groups, with among the latter groups, only Hmong or Yao spoken by significant numbers in the United States.

HISTORY AND CULTURAL RELATIONS

Most of the nineteenth- and early-twentieth-century immigrants were South Asians who saw themselves as temporary laborers who would return home after working hard in the United States to make as much money as possible. Most, however, remained. The number of South and Southeast Asian immigrants began increasing in the early 1900s. Asian Indians formed the majority, usually taking low-paying farming and laboring jobs in the western states. Strict immigration laws after the First World War closed off immigration from these areas, and until the 1960s most immigrants were wives or family members of men already in the United States. After the immigration law amendments of 1965, which essentially eliminated the restrictive annual quotas of the earlier laws, immigration increased greatly, especially of Asian Indians and Indochinese.

The more recent migrants from South Asia have included many well-educated middle-class professionals (often doctors, engineers, and nurses). The ethnic, national, and class backgrounds of South Asian immigrants have widened greatly in this recent period. Their resettlement in the United States has mostly been smooth, although there have been instances of prejudice and intolerance. Social and cultural links with the parent countries are usually strong. Relations between the various ethnic and national groups are not strongly developed, however, except where religious and other needs require them. The sharing of common or closely related languages also tends to strengthen relations among groups, particularly when the groups are small.

In contrast to the South Asians, most Southeast Asians have come to the United States since 1965, particularly since the end of the war in Vietnam in 1975. The earlier immigrants in this period were usually well-educated skilled workers. A large proportion of the immigrants since 1975, however, have been poorly educated and unskilled farm workers and laborers escaping from their parent areas. After their initial spread across the United States, most have relocated to major cities and other core areas, particularly on the West Coast, in order to be near relatives and to have better access to jobs and public welfare assistance. Adjustment to life in the United States has been difficult for most of these later immigrants since they had neither desired nor planned to emigrate. In general, there is a greater likelihood of quicker and easier adjustment among voluntary Southeast Asian-Americans than among those forced to flee their homeland. Nevertheless, many have since become U.S. citizens.

Today, South and Southeast Asian-American groups form a heterogeneous population of different cultural groups displaying a wide variety of life-styles and adaptations to life in the United States.

Bibliography

Allen, James Paul, and Eugene James Turner (1988). *We the People: An Atlas of America's Ethnic Diversity.* New York: Macmillan.

Baizerman, M., and G. Hendricks (1989). *A Study of Southeast Asian Refugee Youth in the Twin Cities of Minneapolis and St. Paul, Minnesota.* Minneapolis: University of Minnesota, Southeast Asian Refugee Project.

Fawcett, James T., and Benjamin V. Cariño, eds. (1987). *Pacific Bridges: The New Immigration from Asia and the Pacific Islands.* Staten Island, N.Y.: Center for Migration Studies.

Haseltine, P., comp. (1989). *East and Southeast Asian Material Culture in North America: Collections, Historical Sites and Festivals.* Westport, Conn.: Greenwood Press.

Thernstrom, Stephan, ed. (1980). *Harvard Encyclopedia of American Ethnic Groups.* Cambridge, Mass.: Harvard University Press, Belknap Press.

Long Beach,
California has been
the main Khmer
center since 1975.

ASIAN INDIANS. In 1980, about 375,000 Americans claimed Asian Indian ethnic ancestry. This, however, is likely a gross undercount, with the actual population closer to 700,000. There were only about 700 Asian Indians in the United States before 1900 and fewer than 17,000 before 1965. Between 1917 and 1946 almost all Asian Indian immigration was barred. Most immigrants have arrived since 1965, though there have been Asian Indian-American communities in California since the early part of the twentieth century. Asian Indians have come mostly from the Indo-Gangetic plain of northern India, from Gujarat in western India, and from Dravidian southern India. Asian Indian-Americans are concentrated in metropolitan areas with a wide dispersal in the warmer areas. The bulk of the immigrants before 1920, generally Punjabi Sikhs, worked on farms in the Central Valley of California, which enabled some to eventually own their own farms and orchards. The more recent immigrants have tended to settle in urban areas across the country, particularly around New York City, Chicago, San Francisco, and Los Angeles, but also with a large number scattered across the country. Many new immigrants entered the Central Valley of California in the 1970s, with the younger people often moving to the cities in search of commercial or professional jobs. Many of the Sikhs became prosperous farmers and sponsored immigrants, and the Sikhs in California as a whole form a large and separate social community.

The majority of the post-1965 immigrants are Hindus. Caste distinctions are less important than in India, but social bonds are strongest within each of the many language and religious groups. Hindus tend to categorize Asian Indians in terms of region of origin within India, whereas non-Hindus categorize fellow immigrants in terms of religion. Many male post-1965 immigrants have returned to India to marry and bring their wives back to the United States. A large number of the recent immigrants have completed college and graduate education and have found positions as engineers, doctors, professors, and so on. Many have become small businessmen, travel and insurance agents, restaurant owners, and operators of motels and hotels, particularly in the warmer parts of the United States and in rural areas.

Bibliography

Dasgupta, Sathi (1988). *On the Trail of an Uncertain Dream: Indian Immigrant Experience in America.* New York: AMS Press.

Fenton, John Y. (1988). *Translating Religious Traditions: Asian Indians in America.* New York: Praeger Publishers.

Jain, Usha R. (1988). *The Gujaratis of San Francisco.* New York: AMS Press.

Jensen, Joan M. (1988). *Passage from India: Asian Immigrants in North America.* New Haven, Conn.: Yale University Press.

Saran, Parmatma (1985). *The Asian Indian Experience in the United States.* Cambridge, Mass.: Schenkman Publishing Co.

Saran, Parmatma, and Edwin Eames, eds. (1980). *The New Ethnics: Asian Indians in the United States.* New York: Praeger Publishers.

Xenos, P., H. Barringer, and M. J. Levin (1989). *Asian Indians in the United States.* 1980 Census Profiles, no. 111. Honolulu: East-West Center, East-West Population Institute.

BANGLADESHIS. There are probably about 8,000 Americans of Bangladeshi origin, with 6,859 immigrants having arrived between 1960 and 1984. The People's Republic of Bangladesh was known as East Pakistan before becoming independent from Pakistan after a civil war in 1971. Eighty-three percent of the population of Bangladesh are Sunni Muslim, with the remaining non-Muslim 17 percent consisting of Hindus, Buddhists, or Christians. The same general distribution holds for the immigrants to the United States. Most immigrants speak Bengali, although English is the official language of Bangladesh. Many of the earlier immigrants were refugees from the civil war of 1971. The more recent immigrants arrive seeking escape from the continuing sociopolitical and economic stresses in the homeland, one of the world's poorest nations. There are Bangladeshi settlers in nearly every state, with the largest concentrations in California, Illinois, Texas, and the New York Metropolitan area. A large proportion of the immigrants are professionals and white-collar urban dwellers. As a result, most of them have had an easier time in finding employment than immigrants and refugees from other Asian countries. The bulk of the immigrants have been under forty years of age. There have been fewer opportunities for women to gain an education or to work in the homeland; thus the women are not well prepared for the competitive way of life in America. Most men and women marry other Bangladeshis in this country or are married when they arrive. As a result of chain migration, there are many extended families among the settled immigrants. Groups living in the same area have tended to form civic

◆ **Dravidian**
The language family of the darkest-skinned people in South Asia, mainly found in southern India and Sri Lanka.

See also

EAST AND SOUTHEAST ASIA: Burmese, Lao, Hmong, Khmer, Malay, Vietnamese

SOUTH ASIA: Bengali, Gujarati, Sikh, Tamil

associations that form a focus for various activities and mutual support for adapting to life in the United States.

Bibliography

Hossain, M. (1982). "South Asians in California: A Sociological Study of Immigrants from India, Pakistan, and Bangladesh." *South Asia Bulletin* 2:74–83.

BHUTANESE, MALDIVIANS, AND NEPALESE. These groups are discussed together, as so few in each have immigrated to the United States. From 1960 through 1984, 90 immigrants arrived from the Kingdom of Bhutan, 12 from the Republic of Maldives, and 977 from the Kingdom of Nepal. Buddhism is the state religion in Bhutan, Sunni Islam in the Maldives, and Hinduism in Nepal. The basic languages are different as well, with Dzongkha being official in Bhutan, a dialect of Sinhalese in the Maldives, and Nepali in Nepal. All three countries maintain close contacts with India, and many immigrants arrived speaking some English. Little is known about the adaptation of these peoples to life in the United States.

CAMBODIANS. In 1980, 16,052 Americans claimed Cambodian (Kampuchean) ethnic ancestry and another 2,050 claimed Cambodian and other ethnic ancestry. Most people of Cambodian ancestry belong to the Khmer ethnic group, although some Chinese and members of other ethnic groups may have reported themselves as Cambodian. This reporting is a serious undercount, since by September 1986, 138,900 refugees and immigrants had come to the U.S. and certainly a significant number arrived before 1980. Most Cambodian-Americans immigrated after 1970 to escape war, starvation, the Pol Pot-Khmer Rouge reign of terror, and the Vietnamese invasion in 1979. In the United States, Long Beach, California, has been the main Khmer center since 1975. It has a commercial district, with Cambodian markets, tailors, and jewelry stores, but homes, churches, a Buddhist temple, and various organizations are scattered throughout the city. Ethnic Chinese from Cambodia have more often settled in various Chinatowns. There are large Cambodian-ancestry populations in other parts of the Los Angeles area, in San Diego and in or near Seattle, Houston, and Providence. Additional concentrations are found in Texas, Washington State, and Arlington, Virginia. In the early 1980s the U.S. government established a program to settle Cambodian refugees in twelve cities outside California, including Rochester, New York, Richmond, Virginia, Phoenix, Arizona, and a large number of metropolitan centers that did not have a significant number of Cambodians already living there.

The Khmer are overwhelmingly Theravada Buddhists and were peasant farmers in Cambodia. Adjustment to American life has been difficult, and there is a marked tendency to maintain close ties to the extended family and the ethnic communities in order to cope. When problems become overwhelming, they tend to relocate, usually to other low-rent areas or to California to be with friends and relatives.

Bibliography

Ebihara, May M. (1985). "Khmer." In *Refugees in the United States: A Reference Handbook,* edited by D. W. Haines, 127–147. Westport, Conn.: Greenwood Press.

Gordon, Linda W. (1987). "Southeast Asian Refugee Migration to the United States." In *Pacific Bridges: The New Immigration from Asia and the Pacific Islands,* edited by James T. Fawcett and Benjamin V. Cariño, 153–174. Staten Island, N.Y.: Center for Migration Studies.

BURMESE. There are about 20,000 Americans of Burmese ethnic ancestry, of whom 13,197 arrived between 1970 and 1984. Immigrants from Myanmar (the official name of Burma since 1989) began to arrive in the United States in the early 1960s, with significant numbers coming in the 1970s. Most of the immigrants have been fairly young professional, technical, and white-collar workers. Since Myanmar has been a politically isolated nation, the number of immigrants has been small. There do not seem to be any sizable Burmese ethnic communities in the United States, with the largest numbers of Burmese-Americans living in California, New York, Illinois, Maryland, Pennsylvania, and Texas. Because of their small numbers and occupational skills, assimilation into mainstream society has been relatively easy.

BRUNEIANS. Only 164 immigrants arrived in the United States from Brunei between 1975 and 1984, with none identified as having arrived before then. Earlier immigrants may have been attributed to other countries since Brunei became a sovereign and independent state only in 1984. Malay is the official language of the country, with English and Chinese also spoken. Two-thirds of

South and Southeast Asians of the United States

Many Hmong have settled in Missoula, Montana, which is similar to their Laotian homeland.

the inhabitants are Muslim, with the remainder being divided among Buddhist, Christian, and other religions. Since so few Bruneians have arrived in this country, there are no data available on their adaptation to life in the United States.

INDONESIANS. There are probably a little over 30,000 Americans of Indonesian descent in the United States today, a small portion of them being former Dutch colonials who left Indonesia when the country gained its independence from the Netherlands. Almost all the remainder are native Indonesians who spoke Malay, Bahasa Indonesian (a variety of Malay), Javanese, or one of a number of Austronesian languages in their homeland. Most of the population are Sunni Muslims, although there are small groups of other denominations. The immigrants, except for students, tend to arrive in family groups and are usually professional, technical, or white-collar workers.

There are also about 60,000 "Indos," people of mixed European and Indonesian ethnic ancestry in the United States. Most Indos came prior to 1962 after having fled Indonesia during the domestic crises in 1947 and 1951. For many, the trip to the United States was a secondary migration, as most had initally fled to the Netherlands.

Bibliography

Kwik, Greta (1989). *The Indos in Southern California.* New York: AMS Press.

LAOTIANS. In the 1980 census, 53,320 Americans claimed Laotian ancestry and another 2,278 claimed Laotian and other ethnic ancestry. This is a serious underreporting, however, since immigration records show that 110,840 Laotians came into the United States during the 1960 to 1984 period, principally as refugees from the wars in Southeast Asia. As of September 1986 about 162,000 refugees, about one-third of whom were of the Hmong ethnic group, had arrived in the United States. Most Laotian-Americans now live on the West Coast and are mainly composed of two distinct ethnic groups, the Lao of the Laotian lowlands and the Highland Hmong, with minor numbers of other ethnic groups also represented.

The distribution of Laotians in the United States in the early 1980s was mainly determined by various voluntary resettlement agencies and the location of sponsoring groups and families. Many found work in low-paying jobs, such as in meat packing and clothing manufacturing. There was much secondary migration after first settlement in the United States, with members of extended families rejoining one another and with the formation of new communities. Linguistic and cultural barriers are the main reasons that Laotian-Americans have generally achieved only slow occupational advancement, have resorted to public welfare, and have remained socially isolated. In addition, many have sought a return to a farming way of life and have moved to smaller towns and rural areas where they garden or work as farm laborers. The major resettlement area has been California, because of the location of relatives and economic opportunities. Many of the Hmong have settled in California's Central Valley, with particular concentrations in the cities of Fresno and Merced. The Hmong in Merced have formed neighborhood, extended family, and church organizations, as well as an official mutual assistance agency. Many Hmong have settled in the Missoula, Montana, area, which is similar to their Laotian homeland. Other centers of settlement have been in or near Portland, Oregon, and Minneapolis-St. Paul.

Bibliography

Dunnigan, Timothy, and D. P. Olney (1985). "Hmong." In *Refugees in the United States: A Reference Handbook,* edited by D. W. Haines, 111–126. Westport, Conn.: Greenwood Press.

Gordon, Linda W. (1987). "Southeast Asian Refugee Migration to the United States." In *Pacific Bridges: The New Immigration from Asia and the Pacific Islands,* edited by James T. Fawcett and Benjamin V. Cariño, 153–174. Staten Island, N.Y.: Center for Migration Studies.

Hendricks, G. L., B. T. Downing, and A. S. Deinard, eds. (1986). *The Hmong in Transition.* Staten Island, N.Y.: Center for Migration Studies.

Schein, Louisa (1987). "Control of Contrast: Lao Hmong Refugees in American Contexts." In *People in Upheaval,* edited by Scott M. Morgan and Elizabeth Colson, 88–107. New York: Center for Migration Studies.

Van Esterik, John L. (1985). "Lao." In *Refugees in the United States: A Reference Handbook,* edited by D. W. Haines, 149–165. Westport, Conn.: Greenwood Press.

Yang, D., and D. North (1988). *Profiles of the Highland Yao Communities in the United States: Final Report.* Washington, D.C.: CZA.

MALAYSIANS. There are probably fewer than 10,000 Americans of Malaysian ethnic ancestry in the United States today. Between 1960 and 1984 about 8,400 came. Malays make up about 60

♦ **Austronesian languages**
A large group of languages (formerly called "Malayo-Polynesian") including about 450 in Oceania. They are found mostly on the coasts in Melanesia and New Guinea, but otherwise throughout Polynesia and Micronesia.

percent of the host country's population, Chinese about a third, and East Indians the remainder. They are predominantly Muslim, with many Hindus, Buddhists, Confucians, and Taoists. Most of the immigrants have been professionals, white-collar workers, and students who have settled in urban areas. Little is known about the life of Malaysians in the United States, however.

PAKISTANIS. In the 1980 census, 22,615 Americans claimed Pakistani ethnic ancestry and another 3,348 claimed Pakistani and other ethnic ancestry. Most Pakistanis in the United States have entered since 1965. The immigration rate remains high, as evidenced by the more than 56,000 arriving between 1960 and 1984. The distribution of these immigrants in the United States generally follows that of Asian Indians in recent years. Areas with large Pakistani populations include New York City, Los Angeles, Chicago, Houston, and Fairfax, Virginia. The new settlers have generally had high educational and occupational levels and a preference for living in large metropolitan areas. They have usually assimilated easily into the American economic system. Some have not, however, and are working in various unskilled jobs. About three-fourths of Pakistani-Americans are Sunni Muslims, with small percentages following other religions. Most are Punjabi- or Urdu-speaking and have some background in English as well. More than two hundred Pakistani civic and cultural organizations have been established, largely in urban areas, and several Pakistani periodicals are published.

Bibliography

Ghayur, M. Arif (1981). "Muslims in the United States: Settlers and Visitors." *Annals of the American Academy of Political and Social Science* 454:157–177.

Malik, Iftikhar H. (1988). *Pakistanis in Michigan: A Study of Third Culture and Acculturation*. New York: AMS Press.

SRI LANKANS. There are probably about 6,000 Americans who claim Sri Lankan ethnic descent. They are almost all from Tamil- or Sinhalese-speaking ethnic groups. Most have some knowledge of English as well and are Hindu or Buddhist depending on their ethnic affiliation. Many are well educated and have secured professional and white-collar employment. Very little has been published about their life in the United States and their adaptation to American culture. They are identified by many Americans as Asian Indians.

THAIS. In the 1980 census, 52,214 Americans claimed Thai ethnic ancestry and another 11,700 claimed Thai and other ethnic ancestry. The total of 64,000 is probably an undercount since 70,459 immigrants came into the United States between 1960 and 1984. Few Thais immigrated to the United States before the 1960s. The majority of the people of Thailand are ethnic Thai, with Chinese accounting for about 12 percent of the population and tribal peoples making up 11 percent. Most Thais came to the United States not as refugees but as students, temporary visitors, or spouses of U.S. military personnel (mainly the air force). Generally, the Thais in the United States are ethnic Thai, but others are Thai Dam (usually not from Thailand but from the upland valleys of northern Vietnam and Laos). Some ethnic Chinese from Thailand may also have listed themselves as Thai. The Los Angeles area has by far the largest concentration of Thais. Other concentrations can be found in Chicago, New York City, and around military bases, such as Fort Bragg, North Carolina, and Fort Huachuca, Arizona. In Los Angeles, Thai businesses and houses have been clustered in the Hollywood area. Thais own banks, gas stations, beauty parlors, and other small businesses, especially Thai restaurants. Most Thai immigrants have been between the ages of twenty and forty upon arrival. In addition to the family members of the servicemen, there have been many students, professional and white-collar workers and most have found employment in America. The major settlement of the Thai Dam has been in the vicinity of Des Moines, Iowa, where most have found work in low-paying jobs with little hope of advancement. Most Thais are Hinayana Buddhists, although some are Muslims.

Bibliography

Desbarats, J. (1979). "Thai Migration to Los Angeles." *Geographical Review* 69: 302–318.

VIETNAMESE. The U.S. Bureau of the Census reported that in 1980 about 260,000 Vietnamese were living in the United States. At that time many were located in southern California (Los Angeles, Orange, and San Diego counties) with concentrations also around Brockport, Texas, Arlington, Virginia, Amarillo, Texas, and Fort Smith, Arkansas. It is reported, however, that in the period 1960–1984 over 387,000 immigrants had arrived from Vietnam, thus making them by far the largest population group in the

See also

EAST AND SOUTHEAST ASIA

United States of Southeast Asian origin. A fairly large proportion (as high as 15 percent in California) were Vietnamese Chinese—members of the Chinese minority community in Vietnam. Most of these have settled in various Chinatowns around the country.

The Vietnamese are one of the newest ethnic communities in the United States, most of them having immigrated because of the Vietnam War and its aftermath. As of September 1986, over 500,000 Vietnamese had entered the United States as refugees. They usually have found sponsoring families and communities (many churches were active in sponsoring immigrants) and were originally widely scattered around the country, usually in nuclear family households. This was less than satisfactory, as most had lived their lives as members of extended families. Soon after settlement, they began to reunite their original extended families, with a very large percentage of them resettling in California, with another focus in Texas.

Few refugees were prepared for life in the United States, and they faced serious language and cultural barriers. Many have had difficulties because most of the jobs available to them were low-paying ones like janitor, laborer, busboy, or dishwasher. Some have found work in factories (electronics assembly) or in restaurants and other small businesses. Many of the recent arrivals are supported at least in part by government programs. The unemployment rate of earlier arrivals, who were usually better educated, is quite low, however. Fishermen have concentrated on the Gulf Coast from Texas through northwestern Florida and have done well through a combination of working hard and taking on the less attractive jobs. In the Monterey area of California, fishermen have also done well by not competing for the same species with local fishermen. Vietnamese Catholics made up a large percentage of the early refugees, and many have settled in the New Orleans area. The largest Vietnamese communities in the eastern states are around Washington, D.C., with many working for the government or for international agencies.

Bibliography

Gold, Steven J. (1987). "Dealing with Frustration: A Study of the Interactions between Resettlement Staff and Refugees." In *People in Upheaval*, edited by Scott M. Morgan and Elizabeth Colson, 108–128. New York: Center for Migration Studies.

Gordon, Linda W. (1987). "Southeast Asian Refugee Migration in the United States." In *Pacific Bridges:*

The New Immigration from Asia and the Pacific Islands, edited by James T. Fawcett and Benjamin V. Cariño, 153–174. Staten Island, N.Y.: Center for Migration Studies.

Kelly, Gail P. (1977). *From Vietnam to America: A Chronicle of the Vietnamese Immigration to the United States*. Boulder, Colo.: Westview Press.

Montero, Darrel (1979). *Vietnamese Americans: Patterns of Resettlement and Socioeconomic Organization in the United States*. Boulder, Colo.: Westview Press.

Orbach, M. K., and J. Beckwith (1982). "Indochinese Adaptation and Local Government Policy: An Example from Monterey." *Anthropological Quarterly* 35:135–145.

TETON

Ethnonyms: Dakota, Lakota, Sioux, Teton Sioux, Titunwan, Western Sioux

Orientation

IDENTIFICATION. The Teton are an American Indian group now living predominantly on reservations in South Dakota and in Saskatchewan. The name "Teton" is a corruption of *Titunwan*, which conventionally is glossed "dwellers of the prairie" but which actually connotes the setting up of campsites. The root *ti* gives rise to the name of the popular dwelling *tipi*. Teton designates seven subdivisions of Lakota-speakers who migrated from aboriginal homes in the Great Lakes region to the Northern Plains. They are called "Oglala," "Sicangu" (or "Brule"), "Hunkpapa," "Itazipco" (or "Sans Arcs"), "Sihasapa" (or "Blackfeet Sioux"), "Oohenunpa" (or "Two Kettle"), and "Mnikowoju." The Teton in turn are one of seven larger divisions collectively known as the "Oceti Sakowin," or "Seven Fireplaces," all of which lived originally in the Great Lakes region. The others are known as "Mdewakanton," "Sisseton," "Wahpeton," and "Wahpekute," collectively known as "Santee" and who speak Dakota; and the "Yankton" and "Yanktonais," who are called "Wiciyela" and speak Nakota, a dialect today associated with the Assiniboins. The only proper tribal designation for this group is "Titunwan," the Anglicized form "Teton," or the linguistic designation, "Lakota." All other terms are misnomers or redundant.

LOCATION. Although the Teton's parent stock migrated from the Southeast, arriving in the region of Milles Lacs, Minnesota, in the sixteenth century, the term *Teton* and its variant forms, particularly the erroneous designation *Dakota* (proper for the eastern division only), were not identified until 1640, after which time migrating bands occupied a large swath of the northern plains in what is now North and South Dakota, parts of Montana, Wyoming, Colorado, and Nebraska. Today, most Teton live on reservations in South Dakota, while others, mainly descendants of fugitives of the Custer battle, fled to small reserves in Canada. A large segment of the population lives in urban areas such as Chicago, Denver, Los Angeles, Rapid City (South Dakota), and San Francisco.

DEMOGRAPHY. Early population estimates are meager and largely unreliable. In 1825, however, the Brules were estimated at three thousand; the Oglala at fifteen hundred; and the combined other five at three thousand. These estimates are probably much too low. The current population is similarly difficult to estimate because of intermarriage between Teton and other Indians and non-Indians. But based on estimates derived from population figures for the predominantly Teton reservations in South Dakota and Canada, a current population of sixty-five thousand seems reasonable.

LINGUISTIC AFFILIATION. The Teton speak a dialect of a newly proposed subfamily of the Siouan language family called Shakowinian, whose other two members include Dakota and Nakota. Today Nakota (or Nakoda) is spoken almost exclusively by the Assiniboins, and most Yankton and Yanktonais speak Dakota. Traces of the Nakota dialect, however, are still found among contemporary Lakota- and Dakota-speakers.

History and Cultural Relations

By the beginning of the sixteenth century the Teton and other members of the Oceti Sakowin had established themselves on the headwaters of the Mississippi River, where they lived in semisedentary villages raising maize, squash, and beans and supplementing their diets by hunting and fishing. They were first encountered by Jean Nicolet, who named them "Sioux," a French corruption of an Algonkian word, *Nadowesiih*, meaning "snakes" or "enemies," which, despite its prevalent use in historical and anthropological literature, is a derogatory term.

After wars with Cree and Ojibwa enemies, who by 1750 were better armed through European contact, some of the Oceti Sakowin began migrating onto the prairies and plains. Within a generation they became acclimated to a nomadic, bison-hunting way of life. By this date they also had obtained horses from the Arikara and other riverine tribes and soon became adapted to an equestrian way of life.

Although the term *Lakota* translates as "allied" or "affiliated," early observers reported that when the Tetons were not fighting other tribes, they were fighting each other. By 1778, according to their own hide-painted calendars known as winter counts, they had chased out almost all aboriginal inhabitants of the Black Hills region except the Cheyenne and Arapaho and had taken over the land as their own.

The Teton are also known for various skirmishes and battles with the U.S. government during the Indian wars of the 1860s and 1870s. Most notable of these was the Battle of the Little Big Horn, or "Custer's Last Stand," when on June 25, 1876, Custer and most of the Seventh Cavalry were annihilated by a combined force of Tetons, Cheyennes, and Arapahos. Most infamous was the Wounded Knee Massacre of December 19, 1890, where 260 men, women, and children mainly of Big Foot's band were massacred by remnants of Custer's Seventh and Ninth Cavalries during the Ghost Dance movement of 1889–1890. The names of great Teton leaders include Red Cloud, Crazy Horse, Sitting Bull, Rain in the Face, Gall, American Horse, and Young Man Afraid of Horse.

Settlements

In aboriginal times, the Teton lived in tipi camps that fluctuated according to the seasons. During winter, camps were smaller and clustered in wooded ravines where small herds of bison and other game were hunted. In summer, the bands joined for their annual religious ceremony, the Sun Dance, and for the communal bison hunt. In 1868, the Treaty of Fort Laramie between the Great Sioux Nation and the U.S. government established the boundaries of the Great Sioux Reservation located primarily in South Dakota. The roving bands settled down to form the nuclei of the present towns on the reservations. After 1887, Indian land was divided into individual ownership and the Great Sioux Reservation was severely diminished. Today, the Teton live predominantly on six reservations: Pine Ridge (the second largest reservation in the United States), Rosebud, Cheyenne River, Lower Brule, Crow Creek, and Standing Rock (the latter lying partly in North Dakota). Other Tetons live on small reserves in Saskatchewan, mainly remnants of Sitting Bull's band, who fled to Canada after the Custer battle. Over time, tipis gave way to four-

At the infamous Wounded Knee Massacre in 1890, 260 Teton men, women, and children were massacred by remnants of Custer's cavalry.

walled tents, and then to log cabins and frame houses. Although tipis and tents are still used at ceremonial events, most Tetons live in frame and brick houses on the reservations.

Economy

SUBSISTENCE AND COMMERCIAL ACTIVITIES. The Teton are primarily associated with bison hunting. In aboriginal times, men, women, and children stampeded herds over cliffs where they would be killed in the fall and then butchered. Later, after the advent of the horse, bison hunting was an equestrian pursuit, both dangerous and thrilling. Most bison were originally hunted with bows and arrows and lances, and later with rifles. The entire bison was utilized for food, clothing, and shelter. Additionally, various species of roots and berries, such as *pomme blanche* or prairie turnips, and chokecherries, buffalo berries, and sand cherries were dried and used through the hard winters. Small game, deer, and elk were also stalked by individual hunters, and their meat and hides were utilized.

After the establishment of the reservations and land allotments, many Teton turned to farming and ranching, both successful enterprises until the Great Depression hit, when many lost their source of income and were never able to recoup. Since World War I, many Teton landowners have made their living by leasing their rich pastures to non-Indian ranchers. Others have invested in individual enterprises such as service stations, grocery stores, and small appliance stores, although many of the larger businesses such as supermarkets are owned by non-Indians. Arts and crafts provide a living for a few who continue to make quillwork and beadwork. About one-third of the work force is employed by the federal government in various agencies of the Bureau of Indian Affairs and the Indian Health Service. An undisclosed number are welfare recipients. Pursuant to treaty stipulations, all enrolled members of the various Teton reservations are eligible to receive annuities, mainly in the form of food, each month.

INDUSTRIAL ARTS. Aboriginal crafts include pictographic hide painting and ornamentation with porcupine quillwork. After the introduction of trade goods, Teton women were particularly known for their elaborate and voluminous beadwork. One of the most outstanding art forms associated with Teton today are their handmade star quilts, originally learned while at school and modeled after those made by the Amish of Pennsylvania. The star quilt is used for all sorts of traditional occasions from cradle to grave, and many of them are in great demand by trading posts and stores catering to the South Dakota tourist trade. The Red Cloud Indian Art Show, sponsored by the Holy Rosary Mission at Pine Ridge, is one of the largest in the country and has produced a number of outstanding Teton artists.

TRADE. During the latter part of the eighteenth century, the Teton engaged in trade fairs with other Plains tribes. Trade with Europeans began at the turn of the nineteenth century, and for the first quarter of that century trade was monopolized by French traders from St. Louis. Many Teton bear French surnames today as a result of marriages between French traders and Teton women. Later, the Teton traded with the American Fur Company and the Rocky Mountain Fur Company, and by 1850 trade goods such as beads, blankets, hair pipes, and metal axes, blades, and cooking utensils dominated Teton culture.

DIVISION OF LABOR. The harsh vicissitudes of the plains required cooperation between males and females. Although men actually hunted bison, women and children accompanied them on the hunt to help kill animals wounded in the chase. Butchering was the primary job of women, but men assisted them when necessary. Women were responsible for collecting fruits, berries, and tubers, but some fruits were collected by men. Making the tipi and clothing was in the domain of females, but men made and decorated ceremonial and war objects. After marriage, however, the tipi and its belongings were considered the property of the woman, and hunting and war implements were owned by men. Today, both men and women share equal positions in the business place as well as in tribal politics, the judicial system, the Indian Health Service, and the reservation school system. A fairly larger percentage of women attend colleges and universities located on and off the reservations.

LAND TENURE. Being nomadic, the Teton did not have a concept of land tenure until after the Indian Allotment Act of 1887, when reservation lands were issued in fee patent.

Kinship

KIN GROUPS AND DESCENT. Although kinship terminology suggests that the Teton earlier were organized into matrilineal clans, once they had migrated onto the plains their descent system gave way to a bilateral form of organization. Somewhat reminiscent of an earlier clan system is the Teton unit called *tiyospaye*, a named

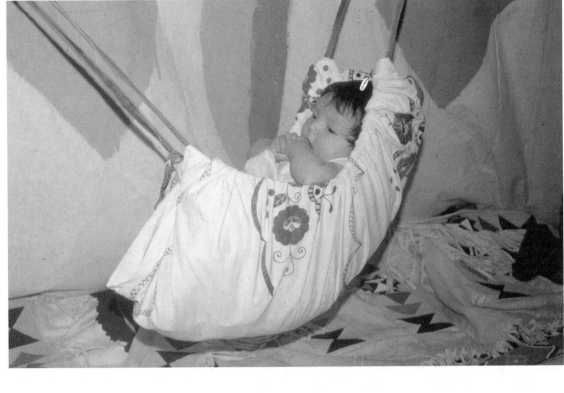

NEXT GENERATION

A Teton baby sleeps in a hammock in Canada. (Charles & Josette Lenars/Corbis)

unit into which people are born and within which men and women cannot intermarry. Although age stratification exists among a number of surrounding plains tribes, the Teton do not exhibit such characteristics.

KINSHIP TERMINOLOGY. Traditional kinship terminology follows the Iroquoian system.

Marriage and Family

MARRIAGE. Although there is evidence for an earlier form of preferred cross-cousin marriage, once the Teton reached the plains males and females who did not share a common grandfather were eligible to marry. The ceremony itself was essentially an exchange of gifts between the parents of the couple. Frequently, the marriage was solidified when the groom gave horses to his prospective in-laws, and the female made a tipi and moccasins for her intended husband. Occasionally, the husband provided bride-service for his in-laws for a year. Upon marriage, the parents of the couple adopted a special relationship of co-parenthood. Polygyny was socially acceptable but rare.

DOMESTIC UNIT. Tiyospayes were divided into groups of extended families called *wicotis*, a pattern maintained today.

INHERITANCE. Inheritance was irrelevant to nomadic living. After the establishment of the reservation, however, inheritance followed local American law.

SOCIALIZATION. Values were instilled in girls by their mothers and grandmothers, and in boys, by their fathers and grandfathers. Ridicule was the strongest form of control, and corporal punishment was eschewed.

Sociopolitical Organization

SOCIAL ORGANIZATION. The Teton were divided into seven tiyospayes prior to the reservation period: the *Payabya*, "head circle"; *Tapisleca* "spleen"; *Kiyaksa*, "breakers of the rule"; *Wajaje*, "Osage"; *Itesica* "bad faces"; *Oyuhpe*, "untidy"; and *Wagluhe*, "loafers." Each tiyospaye was in turn divided into a constantly changing number of wicotis, themselves composed of extended monogamous or polygynous families. The minimal social unit is called *tiwahe*, "family."

POLITICAL ORGANIZATION. Prior to contact, Teton wicoti were under the ad hoc leadership of a chief proficient in hunting and warfare. In the summer, however, when the bands came together for the communal hunt, the entire camp was under the supervision of a group of chiefs called *wakicunze*, who determined when the camps should move and hunts and ceremonials begin. After the reservation period, some of these wakicunze represented their tribes in treaties with the United States. But it is generally accepted that the position of head chief never existed in aboriginal times. After the Indian Reorganization Act of 1934, the Teton reservations formed tribal councils whose officers were elected by ballot every two years. This is the present form of government.

SOCIAL CONTROL. During the summer encampments, various sodalities called *akicita* (soldier or marshal) were in charge of policing the camp and ensuring that the bison hunt would not be jeopardized by overzealous individuals. Under the authority of the wakicunze, the akicita could severely punish or even kill offenders. A number of these sodalities, known by such names as Strong Hearts, Foxes, Crow-Owners, and Badgers, also waged personal vendettas against tribes in retaliation for those lost in battle. Members were elected, and great prestige accrued to them.

CONFLICT. After the establishment of the reservation, conflict arose between several of the Teton chiefs. Sitting Bull and Crazy Horse, both heroes of the Custer battle, were assassinated by their own people as a result of jealousy and a rising fear among Whites that they might regain power. Red Cloud was perhaps the most controversial in that he advocated friendly relations with the United States after earning the reputation of being the only Indian to win a war against the U.S. government. A number of tiyospayes engaged in rivalry with each other, and much factionalism on the Teton reservations still persists along earlier lines of social and political organization.

Religion and Expressive Culture

RELIGIOUS BELIEFS. The Teton have a subterranean origin story in which humans were led to the surface of the earth by Inktomi, the trickster-culture hero, who then abandoned them. The earth and sky were formed after the supernaturals were sent there by Takuskanskan, the prime mover, partly as punishments and rewards for social transgressions. All animate and inanimate objects are capable of having a soul, and supernatural beings and objects are propitiated to maintain or restore harmony between good and evil. The earth is called the lodge of the wind, in which reside the Four Directions, the spirits of the zenith and nadir, and the center of the universe, each of which maintains animal and bird guardian spirits whose help may be invoked through smoking the sacred pipe. Although nearly every Christian denomination is represented on the reservations, most Tetons are only nominal Christians and still respect the beliefs of their ancestors.

RELIGIOUS PRACTITIONERS. Teton differentiate between *wapiye*, or people who mediate between the common people and supernaturals through prayer and self-abnegation, and *pejuta wicasa/winyan*, medicine men and women who cure by means of prayer and herbs. Many of the men and women became active in the Ghost Dance movement of 1889–1890, and still later as lay catechists at mainly Jesuit missions. To a much lesser extent, some Teton also conduct meetings of the Native American church.

CEREMONIES. There are seven major ceremonies believed to have been brought to the Teton by the White Buffalo Calf Woman in aboriginal times: Sweat Lodge, Vision Quest, Sun Dance, Ghost-Keeping Ceremony, Making of Relatives, Girl's Puberty Ceremony, and Sacred Ball Game. Other contemporary ceremonies include the pipe ceremony and *Yuwipi*, a modern curing ceremony.

ARTS. Music and dance play an important part in Teton performance arts. Songs continue to be composed in the native idiom, and the Teton produce some of the best singers on the northern plains. Individual reenactments of visions, such as the Horse Dance, are still occasionally performed.

MEDICINE. Although the Indian Health Service maintains hospitals and clinics on Teton reservations, Native wapiye and medicine men and women continue to provide treatment to patients through the implementation of at least eighty kinds of herbal medicines. The sweat lodge is still used for spiritual and salutary purposes.

DEATH AND AFTERLIFE. The Teton believe that each individual has four aspects of soul. The last may be inhered in another individual at birth, and thus this constitutes a reincarnation system. Some deceased are forever required to be ghosts. Twins are considered special and are believed to preexist and select the families into which they wish to be born. The Milky Way is considered the path of the campfires of the deceased en route to the Spirit Village. In aboriginal times, the dead were buried mainly on scaffolds, but since the reservation, Christian cemeteries have been used. Funeral rites tend to be a mixture of traditional and Christian belief and ritual, and traditionalists continue to ritually keep the spirit of the deceased for one year, after which it is released at a memorial feast.

Bibliography

Hyde, George E. (1937). *Red Cloud's Folk: A History of the Oglala Sioux Indians.* Norman: University of Oklahoma Press.

Hyde, George E. (1961). *Spotted Tail's Folk: A History of the Brule Sioux*. Norman: University of Oklahoma Press.

Powers, Marla N. (1986). *Oglala Women: Myth, Ritual and Reality*. Chicago: University of Chicago Press.

Powers, William K. (1977). *Oglala Religion*. Lincoln: University of Nebraska Press.

Powers, William K. (1982). *Yuwipi: Vision and Experience in Oglala Ritual*. Lincoln: University of Nebraska Press.

Vestal, Stanley (1957). *Sitting Bull: Champion of the Sioux*. 2nd ed. Norman: University of Oklahoma Press.

—WILLIAM K. POWERS

TLINGIT

Ethnonyms: Thlinget, Thlinkets, Tlinkit, Lleeengit

Orientation

IDENTIFICATION. The Tlingit are an American Indian group located in southern Alaska. "Tlingit" means "in the people."

LOCATION. The Tlingit continue to occupy many of their aboriginal village sites along the southeastern coast of Alaska from Ketchikan to Yakutat—54°40′ N to about 60° N—and from the coast to Lake Atlin, or as the Tlingit say, the "second mountain range." This area includes many offshore islands, numerous streams emptying into inlets, and rugged mountains that jut up from the edge of the sea and whose snow-capped serrated peaks cover most of the area.

DEMOGRAPHY. Conservative population estimates place the precontact population at ten thousand. The present Tlingit population numbers about twenty-five thousand.

LINGUISTIC AFFILIATION. The Tlingit language is classified in the Na-Dene phylum. Among the coastal Tlingit, northern, central and southern dialects are still spoken by the elders.

History and Cultural Relations

Archaeological data suggest that a Tlingit or proto-Tlingit population inhabited the coast of southeastern Alaska by seven thousand B.C. Oral history traces several migration routes of Tlingit clans down various rivers that flowed from the interior to the sea, and linguistic data reveal a close affinity with interior groups. While the neighboring Haida and Tsimshian tribes were pushing some southern Tlingit northward, the northern Tlingit were expanding in Eyak and Eskimo territory. British, French, and Russian interests vied for control of Alaska with the United States acquiring final control over the rich Alaskan resources in 1867. Gunboat diplomacy instituted by the United States undermined local Tlingit autonomy and opened up the territory to outside settlers and gold prospectors. Alaskan natives fought back by organizing the Alaskan Native Brotherhood in 1912 to fight for their civil rights and subsistence resources. In 1929 the Tlingit began a struggle to regain control of their natural resources, resulting in the Alaska Native Claims Settlement Act of 1971 transferring some 100 million acres back to Alaskan natives.

Settlements

Early Tlingit settlers selected village sites near heavily resourced areas along protected sections of coastline ideal for beaching canoes, digging clams, acquiring drinking water, and catching migrating salmon. An expanding Tlingit population, increasing competition for local resources, and intensifying patterns of warfare contributed to the progressive development of four types of villages: the local household village, the localized clan village, the local moiety village, and the consolidated clan village. In early times, people lived in one large community longhouse, which served as shelter, storage place, and fort. Population increases and mounting tension contributed to the breakup of the large household into several smaller related lineage households sharing a common fort. Later, in a third settlement stage, two intermarrying clans from the two moieties moved together to reduce distances, share resources, and increase village security. Depopulation and depletion of subsistence resources following European contact contributed to the rise of a fourth settlement pattern, the consolidated clan village, composed of two or more clans from both moieties.

Economy

SUBSISTENCE AND COMMERCIAL ACTIVITIES. The Tlingit hunted deer, bear, seals, and goats; fished for salmon, halibut, and herring; and gathered roots, berries, and shellfish. Runs of salmon choked the local streams each year as five species of salmon migrated to their spawning grounds. Fishnets and gaffing hooks were used to haul in large quantities of salmon for smoking and drying for winter consumption. The rapid depletion of the population by foreign diseases and increased reliance upon proceeds from fur trapping reduced subsistence resources while increasing dependence upon foreign trade goods. Today, the Tlingit value education, resulting in many

Archaeological data suggest that a Tlingit or proto-Tlingit population inhabited the coast of southeastern Alaska by 7000 B.C.

members working in business, industry, government, and the professions.

INDUSTRIAL ARTS. Carving, basket making, Chilkat blanket weaving, beading, and metalworking were sources of income. Gold and silver coins shaped into bracelets, pendants, and rings were embellished with clan symbols. The active arts and crafts trade that began with the arrival of the early steamship tourists has grown in volume over the years, and several Tlingit villages now have dancing groups that perform for local ceremonies and for tourists.

TRADE. An aboriginal trade network flourished between the interior Athapaskans and the Tlingit, between coastal and island Tlingit, and with the neighboring Eyak, Haida, Tsimshian, and Kwakiutl. Native trade goods such as coppers, shells, slaves, canoes, carvings, oulachan oil, and furs were later replaced by European trade goods, including guns, ammunition, knives, axes, blankets, and food.

DIVISION OF LABOR. Prior to the decline of the traditional culture around 1880, Tlingit men hunted, fished, and carved, and women cleaned fish, gathered food, tanned hides, and wove baskets and blankets. Today, men drive diesel-powered boats equipped with hydraulic hoists and large nets, and women work in modern canneries and make button blankets or beaded moccasins from commercial materials.

LAND TENURE. The localized clan was the basic holder of rights to fishing streams, tidelands, and hunting grounds in traditional Tlingit villages. Today, clans own ceremonial and symbolic ritual items. The 1971 Alaska Native Claims Settlement Act organized the Alaska Tlingit into one large regional corporation, called Sealaska. Sealaska received title to 330,000 acres of land and 660,000 acres of mineral rights; it had total assets of $216 million as of March 1988. Sealaska governs nine village corporations each of which received title to 20,040 acres of aboriginal land and hundreds of thousands of dollars in cash payments, depending upon the number of tribal members.

Kinship

KIN GROUPS AND DESCENT. Tlingit society is divided into two large exogamous moieties—Raven-Crow and Eagle-Wolf (Crow for Inland Tlingit and Wolf for Southern Tlingit). Each moiety contains some twenty autonomous matriclans. Aboriginally, each exogamous localized matriclan had its own village and formed marriage alliances with other communities. Matriclans that intermarried with considerable frequency within a given region formed a *Kwaan*, or district, of which there were fourteen. Following depopulation and the depletion of resources, scat-

MARRIAGE AND FAMILY

Marriage

The preferential marriage pattern was patrilateral cross-cousin marriage—to father's sister's daughter; the second choice was a member of the paternal grandfather's or great-grandfather's clan; and a third choice was a member of any clan in the opposite moiety. Marriage within one's clan and moiety were strictly forbidden under penalty of death or ostracism. Arranged marriages have rapidly decreased during this century, although patrilateral marriages are still encouraged. Monogamy was the general rule among the lower classes, and polygamy was practiced by a few high-status men and women. Divorce was rare, as it was seen as an offense against the clans of both spouses. Marriage prohibitions within the clan and moiety are still subscribed to in principle, though broken frequently in practice.

Domestic Unit

Until the turn of the century, the lineage community longhouse served as the residential unit. Recent government housing projects have largely eliminated the need for community households. Presently, lineage and clan households have more symbolic than economic significance, serving as the repository for the ceremonial objects and as a symbol of clan identity.

Inheritance

Formerly, property was passed on within the matriclan with much of the wealth going from uncle to nephew. Presently, material possessions are inherited in typical American fashion, although ceremonial goods are still expected to be passed on in conformity with traditional rules.

Socialization

Many elders played an active role in the education of Tlingit youth. Aunts extolled the virtues of respectable clan leaders, and maternal uncles rigorously and rigidly guided their nephews through adolescence, teaching them basic hunting, fishing, carving, and fighting skills. Grandmothers or maternal aunts spend considerable time with pubescent girls, preparing them for childbearing and teaching them clan history and domestic skills such as food preparation, basket weaving, and basic hygiene. Elders still maintain a strong influence even among the large number of members who have attended college.

tered clans within Kwaans moved together to form consolidated clan villages like Angoon, Hoonah, and Yakutat. Local matriclans were corporate groups holding title to property, real estate, and ceremonial objects. A matriclan consisted of one or more community longhouses in which descent was traced matrilineally. Lineage, clan, and moiety affiliations are still important for marriage and ceremonial purposes.

KINSHIP TERMINOLOGY. Crow-type kinship terminology, once a characteristic of Tlingit society, is little used by younger members today.

Sociopolitical Organization

SOCIAL ORGANIZATION. The Tlingit were stratified into three social classes: (1) high-class *anyaddi*, (2) commoners, or *kanackideh*, and (3) low-class *nitckakaku*. Individuals and groups were also ranked within the clan and between clans, depending upon their wealth, titles, and achievements. High-class people managed and controlled strategic resources and used them to promote individual and group status. Class and rank remain important in Tlingit villages.

POLITICAL ORGANIZATION. Each aboriginal settlement was owned by a localized clan whose claims were documented through stories and symbols, with other clans residing in their village viewed as guests. Leadership and councils at the household, clan, and local moiety levels were traditional political units and remain influential. Today, three ethnic associations address Tlingit concerns. The Alaska Native Brotherhood serves as cultural broker and advocate; the Tlingit-Haida Organization with some 14,500 members of Tlingit descent promotes housing and social welfare; and Sealaska, the largest corporation in Alaska, provides growing economic and political clout.

SOCIAL CONTROL. Shame and rank were powerful motivators for enforcing traditional social norms. Individuals were said to define their status by the way they conducted themselves, with all ill-mannered persons bringing shame upon their lineage and clan. Thus, elders held a tight rein on youths. Fear of accusation of witchcraft or ridicule also influenced behavior. Several Tlingit villages now have their own mayor, city council, police force, and school boards along with other administrative services.

CONFLICT. Aboriginally, conflicts arose over assaults, insults, or damages suffered by individuals and groups to themselves or their property. Such conflicts were usually resolved through payment of wealth or, in some cases, killing the offender. Conflicts with Whites over the past century centered around aboriginal resources, civil rights, and civil liberties. The persistence of these conflicts contributes to alcohol abuse and other drug abuse.

Religion and Expressive Culture

RELIGIOUS BELIEFS. Early records suggest that the Tlingit believed in a creator, Kah-shu-goon-yah, whose name was sacred and never mentioned above a whisper. This primordial grandfather, or "divisible-rich-man," controlled the sun, moon, stars, and daylight in addition to creating all living things. Little more is known of him. The sacred past centers upon Raven (cultural hero, benefactor, trickster, and rascal) who was credited with organizing the world in its present form and in initiating many Tlingit customs. Raven was never represented, symbolized, or made equal with the supreme being who transcended Tlingit legends. The Tlingit inhabited a world filled with spirits, or *jek*. These spirits could manifest their power through individuals, animals, or things. Since every material object or physical force could be inhabited by a spirit, Tlingit were taught to respect everything in the universe. The penalty for disrespect was the loss of ability to obtain food. Properly purified persons could acquire spirit power for curing illnesses, for protection in warfare, for success in obtaining wealth, and for ceremonial prerogatives. Each Tlingit had a mortal and an immortal spirit.

RELIGIOUS PRACTITIONERS. Two options open to youths were to seek good power and help the community or to seek evil power and threaten the community. Every Tlingit had a personal guardian spirit, or *tu-kina-jek*. Spirit doctors, or *ichet*, received more powerful spirits and therefore could treat the sick with herbs, discern the presence of evil, predict the future, and protect the community from evil forces. Witches, or *nukw-sati*, sought evil power and used it to harm others.

CEREMONIES. Dancing societies never gained a major foothold in Tlingit society as they did in neighboring Northwest Coast tribes. The Tlingit sought their power primarily through their clan spirit doctor whom they trusted to help and not to harm them. Politicoreligious ceremonies called potlatches, or *koolex*, marked significant events in the life of the clan and its members. Sacred songs, dances, symbols, and stories accompanied all changes in social stature, political leadership, and ceremonial objects within the clan.

ARTS. Carving of house posts, heraldic screens, chiefs' hats, chiefs' staffs, and weaving of Chilkat blankets were highly acclaimed. Wood-

Western Apaches for the most part avoided direct conflict with American settlers and the military after the 1850s.

carvers, metalworkers, and blanket weavers continue to use their traditional clan symbols (*kotea*) to indicate ownership and identity.

MEDICINE. Every family possessed a basic knowledge of herbs and principles of hygiene and for the most part were medically self-sufficient. Occasionally, a spirit doctor, who possessed superior knowledge of herbal medicines and special spirit power, was called in for difficult cases after household remedies failed. Contemporary Tlingit do not hesitate to consult modern medical facilities when the need arises.

DEATH AND AFTERLIFE. Spirits of the dead traveled to the appropriate level of heaven commensurate with their moral conduct in this life. Morally respectable people went to the highest heaven, *Kiwa-a*, a realm of happiness; moral delinquents went to a second level, or Dog Heaven, *Ketl-kiwa*, a place of torment. Individuals remained in the afterworld for a period of time and then returned to this world as a reincarnation of some deceased maternal relative.

Bibliography

Krause, Aurel (1970). *The Tlingit Indians.* Translated by Erna Gunther. Seattle: University of Washington Press. Originally published, 1885.

Laguna, Frederica de. (1972). *Under Mount Saint Elias: The History and Culture of the Yakutat Tlingit.* Washington, D.C.: Smithsonian Institution Press.

Oberg, Kalervo (1973). *The Social Economy of the Tlingit Indians.* Seattle: University of Washington Press. Originally published, 1937.

Tollefson, Kenneth (1976). "*The Cultural Foundations of Political Revitalization among the Tlingit.*" Ph.D. diss., University of Washington.

—KENNETH TOLLEFSON

WESTERN APACHE

Ethnonyms: Dził ghạ'i, Dilzhẹ'é, Dził t'aadń, Ndeé

Orientation

IDENTIFICATION. The name "Apache" first appears in the historical record in 1598. There is no undisputed etymology, although Zuni is often cited as its source. The Western Apache include the subtribes White Mountain, San Carlos, Cibecue, Northern Tonto, and Southern Tonto. They were defined as a single cultural unit because dialect variation among them was minor, they were horticultural to a degree, and they were linked through matrilineal clans, although they themselves recognized no such superordinate

level of organization. All used the word *Ndeé,* or "man, person, Indian," to refer to their specific subtribe, but they did not necessarily include the other "Western Apache" in such a designation.

LOCATION. Since the late seventeenth century the Western Apache have occupied the mountains of the Mogollon Rim, and the high desert transition zone of the Colorado Plateau, including the headwaters of the Verde, Salt, and Little Colorado rivers, and part of the Gila River. The area is between 32° and 35° N and 109° and 112° W. Today, most Western Apache live on the Fort Apache (White Mountain), San Carlos, Camp Verde, and Payson reservations.

DEMOGRAPHY. According to the 1980 census the Indian populations of the three major reservations were Fort Apache, 7,010; San Carlos, 6,013; and Camp Verde, 136. Estimates of the nineteenth-century population total less than 5,000.

LINGUISTIC AFFILIATION. Western Apache is one of the Apachean (Southern Athapaskan) languages, classified in the Athapaskan stock of the NaDené phylum.

History and Cultural Relations

Linguistic and cultural evidence indicates that the Western Apache migrated from Canada between A.D. 1400 and 1500 and arrived in Arizona no earlier than the 1600s where they came into contact with the native Pueblo populations. Pueblo influence was particularly strong after the Pueblo Revolt of 1680 when numerous Pueblos took up residence among Apacheans. Severe pressure from Utes in the early 1700s and again in the mid-1800s along with the U.S. campaign led by Kit Carson resulted in groups of Navajo moving south and coming into contact with or even taking up residence among Apaches. It is likely that it was during these times that the Navajo introduced horticulture and matrilineal clans. Relations with both Western Pueblos and the Navajo alternated between trade and raid up through the nineteenth century. Relations with Spain also alternated between war and peace, though relations with Mexico were generally hostile. Although some new technical items were added to the Apache inventory along with their Spanish names, Spanish and Mexican cultures had little significant impact.

The Western Apache were much less affected than other Apacheans by the changes brought about by the 1848 Treaty of Guadalupe Hidalgo and the subsequent Gadsden Purchase of 1853, probably because their lands in north-central Arizona were not astride major routes of travel, nor, except in the Tonto area, were there major mining activities. They accepted without resistance the presence of forts within their territory, and the White Mountain and Cibecue groups in particular made peace and cooperated with the new conquerors. This quiescent state was marred by two major incidents—the Camp Grant Massacre in 1871, in which at least seventy-five San Carlos women and children were killed by residents of Tucson and their Papago allies, and the Cibecue Fight in 1881, which resulted in the death of a prominent shaman along with a number of soldiers and Apache scouts.

Settlements

With the adoption of horticulture Western Apaches became permanently associated with farming sites. This association was seasonal with local groups composed of several matrilineal-matrilocal extended families (*gotah*) moving from place to place in a yearly round of hunting and gathering—returning in the spring and fall to the farm area and in the winter moving to lower elevations. Local groups varied in size from thirty-five to two hundred individuals and had exclusive rights to certain farm sites and hunting localities. Adjacent local groups, loosely linked through marriage, areal proximity, and dialect, formed what have been called bands controlling farming and hunting resources primarily in a single watershed area. There were twenty of these bands in 1850, each composed of about four local groups. Their ethnographic names, such as Cibecue Creek Band or Carrizo Creek Band, reflect their watershed specificity.

Contemporary Apache communities are an amalgam of these older, territorially defined units, which during the reservation period concentrated near agency headquarters, trading posts, schools, and roads. On the White Mountain Apache Reservation there are two major communities at Cibecue and Whiteriver, and on the San Carlos Reservation there are two at San Carlos and Bylas. Traditional housing was the wickiup (*gogha*); contemporary housing consists of a mixture of older frame homes, modern cinder block or frame tract houses, and mobile homes. Some housing is substandard relative to general U.S. standards, though vast improvements have been made in the last twenty years. The White Mountain Apaches have had a particularly aggressive development program and own a shopping center, motel, theater, sawmill, and ski resort.

Economy

SUBSISTENCE AND COMMERCIAL ACTIVITIES. In traditional times, about 40 percent of the diet came from gathered wild plant foods, 35 percent from meat (especially deer), and 25 percent from horticulture. Wild food products included sahuaro fruit, mescal (agave), acorns, mesquite beans, juniper berries, and piñon nuts. Horticulture was practiced in fields often less than an acre in size, with small dams and channels used for irrigation. After the establishment of the reservations a few Apaches took advantage of government allotment programs to develop cattle herds, but those who did often came into conflict with Whites who grazed cattle through a permit system on the reservations. By the 1950s most of the non-Indians who were running livestock on Indian land had been forced off, and the tribes themselves started cooperative herding operations with stock owned by individuals but managed by tribal employees.

Subsistence farming has continued up to the present day only on the Fort Apache Reservation. The White Mountain Apache Tribe has started an irrigated farming operation, and both reservations have a variety of tourist facilities to profit from camping, boating, fishing, and hunting by non-Indians along with lumbering. The Fort Apache Reservation has been more successful in these enterprises than San Carlos because it has more resources and a better climate. San Carlos has developed a jojoba nut industry, and some Apaches mine and sell the semiprecious stone peridot, which is found relatively close to the surface in one area of the reservation. All these activities provide jobs and income for at least part of the population. Other income derives from off-reservation employment, government jobs, small businesses, and public assistance.

INDUSTRIAL ARTS. Traditional activities such as tanning skins, basket making, and the manufacture of cradle boards and pitch-lined water jars are still done on a limited basis. Beadwork, painting, and doll making have been added to the repertoire.

TRADE. In the past, Apaches traded with some of the surrounding tribes for a variety of items. Individual handicrafts are still occasionally traded to local stores or sold to dealers, but for the most part the economic system on the reservations is part of the larger American cash economy.

DIVISION OF LABOR. Although hunting, raiding, and warfare were usually men's tasks, and gathering, basket making, child rearing, and cooking, women's, the division of labor was flexible. Both sexes worked fields and continue to do so. Both work at public gatherings. Both could function in leadership roles and as shamans, although men did so more often. Today both sexes run for and are elected to tribal office. There is,

♦ **mescal**
A strong alcoholic beverage distilled from a species of maguey (Agave) cactus. When the cactus is mature, the base of the leaves is cut into chunks and baked in a pit oven with heated rocks. Water is added to the sealed oven to produce steam that helps to cook the chunks. When done, the chunks are cooled and taken to the distillery to be beaten into a mash. The mash is squeezed to extract a juice, which is then fermented.

♦ **piñon**
(pinyon) Pine trees (Pinus edulis and Pinus monophylla) of western North America whose large seeds were once an important food source.

777

however, marked physical separation of men and women in a variety of contexts, and to preserve their reputations a man and a woman must not be alone with each other.

LAND TENURE. Aboriginally, the bands controlled resources within their territories, and farmlands were owned by the individuals who were members of the various local groups. Individuals could will their land to any of their offspring or to their surviving spouse and could also lend land to any of their relatives. Only if they wished to lend land to a nonrelative was approval of local leaders needed. Today land is held in trust by the U.S. government, and individual-use rights are controlled by rules based on a mix of tradition and tribal law.

Kinship

KIN GROUPS AND DESCENT. There are over fifty named exogamous matrilineal clans, which form three unnamed phratries. Clans were named after farm sites, and the phratries no doubt formed as a result of population spread and settlement of new farm sites. Clans functioned to regulate marriage, sponsor and support the ritual activities of their members, enact revenge, and aid in day-to-day cooperative work groups. Since clans tended to be localized within the same band, they operated at a restricted geographic level, but because the phratries were represented in all the subtribes, they provided weak cross-cutting ties among all the Western Apaches. Clans continue today to play some role in Western Apache politics, feuds, and ritual; the clan, however, is being supplemented by friendships for mutual economic support in ritual activities, and clan endogamous marriages occur.

KINSHIP TERMINOLOGY. Cousin terminology is of the Iroquois type, with bifurcate collateral parental generation terms, emphasis being placed on parental-generation matrilateral kin with parental-generation patrilateral kin being merged into one category regardless of gender.

Marriage and Family

MARRIAGE. Distant patrilateral cross cousins in the father's clan or phratry were considered ideal and some marriage partners reflect such exchange in several successive generations. Sororal polygyny, levirate, and sororate marriages all occurred. Chastity was highly valued and girls were extremely shy when interacting with boys. During the first few days of a marriage the couple did not necessarily sleep together and sometimes were chaperoned by a female relative of the wife.

Residence was matrilocal with the son-in-law responsible for hunting, protection, and labor on his in-law's farm. Rather strict mother-in-law avoidance is still practiced by many Apaches. Divorce was easy and could be effected by either party.

DOMESTIC UNIT. Gotah were composed of several generations with a core of matrilineally related women. Some contemporary residence units still reflect this structure, but with jobs frequently requiring sons-in-law to be elsewhere, many families have other arrangements. But, even in families living in tract-style houses it is not unusual for a number of matrilineally related relatives to be close neighbors and for unmarried daughters with small children to compose part of a household. This pattern reflects both high rates of illegitimacy and poverty and traditional views of kinship and residence patterns.

INHERITANCE. Personal property was often destroyed or buried with an individual, but possessions could be given to any close relative or friend prior to death. Today some items are buried with the body, but the bulk of the estate is divided among a person's children.

SOCIALIZATION. Apaches value above all else the autonomy of the individual. This applies to children as well as adults, and thus children are often indulged.

Sociopolitical Organization

SOCIAL ORGANIZATION. The only groups were those based on kinship, territoriality, and co-residence. Individuals who were leaders of these various units were titled *nant'an*. Occasionally the prestige of some of these leaders exceeded the boundaries of their respective units, and they might be recognized outside their own local group. Depending on the unit involved, leadership was either inherited matrilineally or achieved. Leaders had no power and little formal authority because of the high value placed on individual autonomy, and they were primarily spokespersons and wealthy individuals with the largest farms in their area. Being wealthy gave them economic clout, and their charisma and their ability to talk and make good decisions meant that they were listened to and highly respected. Relatives often supplied labor for their farms in exchange for being provided for. The only other prominent role in the society was that of shaman.

POLITICAL ORGANIZATION. Today San Carlos, Fort Apache, and Camp Verde have tribal councils and governments based on constitutions

◆ **phratry**
A social group consisting of two or more clans joined by some common bond and standing in opposition to other phratries in the society.

authorized under the Indian Reorganization Act of 1934. Elections are vigorously contested.

SOCIAL CONTROL. The general Athapaskan value of individual autonomy is evidenced here as well. Traditional social control focused heavily on the threat of witchcraft accusation, which if supported by community consensus resulted in execution. Witchcraft accusation still plays a role in social control, and some murders may be explained as witch executions. Positive role models for behavior are provided by stories repeated by elders in reference to events that have taken place at specific locations in the area. Apaches refer to this as being "stalked by stories." Gossip and indirect criticism also are traditional means of enforcing conformity to accepted standards of behavior. Only when under the influence of alcohol do individuals directly confront each other. Both federal and tribal laws and ordinances are enforced by tribal police and government agents.

CONFLICT. Western Apaches for the most part avoided direct conflict with American settlers and the military after the 1850s. Minor problems were caused by nativistic movements in the late nineteenth and early twentieth centuries. Traditional feuds between territorial or kinship groups sometimes were carried on through shamans trying to counteract the magic believed to be emanating from the adversary groups. In some cases feuds resulted in violence. Contemporary elections often take on an atmosphere that involves conflict, and accusations of ballot stuffing may be leveled. Some contemporary vandalism is rumored to be reflective of old feuds. There has recently been some conflict between the leadership of the White Mountain Apache Tribe and business leaders and citizens in neighboring communities over issues relating to reservation boundaries, income from tourists, and leased land within the reservation. There has also been some conflict over land and water use with the federal government.

Religion and Expressive Culture

RELIGIOUS BELIEFS. Apaches believe that a number of supernatural powers associated with natural phenomena exist. These powers are neutral with respect to good and evil, but they can be used for various individual purposes. Control of these powers can be either sought after and developed or thrust upon one. Belief is supported by a mythology that explains the creation of the world and includes several deities. Most important are Life Giver, sometimes identified with the sun; Changing Woman, a source of eternal youth and life; and her twins, Slayer of Monsters and Child

INAUGURATION

Western Apache man dressed in traditional clothing for the Apache Tribal Chairman Inauguration Ceremony on White Mountain, Arizona, USA. OCEANIA (Tom Bean/Corbis)

of Water. These are sometimes syncretically identified with God, Mary, and Jesus. Also important are anthropomorphic mountain spirits called *gaan* who in form and symbolism were no doubt borrowed from the Pueblos. Other important figures in myth are Coyote and Old Man Big Owl.

For many Apaches traditional religion has been supplemented or replaced by a variety of Christian sects. Lutherans and Catholics were the first groups to proselytize, and they have been joined by Mormons, Baptists, Assemblies of God, and the pentecostal Miracle church. Wycliffe Bible Translators has provided an Apache translation of the Bible and has an ongoing literacy program to promote it. Various nativistic movements have characterized Apache life, the most recent of which is the Holy Ground cult centering on regular gatherings at specified "holy grounds" and led by individuals who learned specific prayers and songs recorded in an original style of picture writing developed by a leader, Silas John.

RELIGIOUS PRACTITIONERS. Agents of powers are called *diyin* (shaman). Those who have their knowledge secretly and use it for their own ends are witches, *'iłkashn.*

CEREMONIES. In the past there were a large number of curing ceremonies each related to a specific power. These were performed as individual treatment seemed warranted. The only major ceremony still performed is the girl's puberty ceremony, both a rite of passage and a community ritual. It harnesses the power of Changing Woman to ensure individual health and long life and community health. In the last twenty years this ceremony has been elaborated, with expensive gift exchanges continuing between relatives of the girl and relatives of her godparents for several years after the initial ceremony.

MEDICINE. Traditional curing consisted of shamans' singing ceremonies to restore the balance upset by accidental contact with or disrespect shown toward a power to reverse witchcraft attacks. Herbal medicines were also used. In the recent past both Western medicine and traditional ceremonies were used in various combinations. Today contemporary Western medicine is the primary form of medical treatment, although Changing Woman's power is sought after at puberty rites, and some individual Apaches know songs and prayers to powers, which they use primarily within their immediate families.

DEATH AND AFTERLIFE. Everyone is given an allotted life span, which, unless violence or witchcraft intervenes, will end because of old age. Concepts of an afterlife are vague. Special actions are taken to make sure the dead do not return and try to lure the living to come with them.

Bibliography

Basso, Keith H. (1970). *The Cibecue Apache.* New York: Holt, Rinehart and Winston.

Basso, Keith H. (1983). "Western Apache." In *Handbook of North American Indians.* Vol. 10, *Southwest,* edited by Alfonso Ortiz, 462–488. Washington, D.C.: Smithsonian Institution.

Goodwin, Grenville (1942). *Social Organization of the Western Apache.* Chicago: University of Chicago Press.

Kaut, Charles R. (1957). *The Western Apache Clan System: Its Origins and Development.* University of New Mexico Publications in Anthropology, no. 9. Albuquerque: University of New Mexico Press.

—PHILIP J. GREENFELD

ZUNI

Ethnonyms: Ashiwi, Cibola, Cuñi, Narsh-tiz-a (Apache), Nashtezhe (Navajo), Quini, Saray (Tiwa), Seven Cities of Cibola, Siyo (Hopi), Sumi, Sunyitai or Su'nyitsa (Keres)

Orientation

IDENTIFICATION. The Zuni Indians live today on the Zuni Reservation in west-central New Mexico. The name "Zuni" appears to have derived ultimately from Keresan, wherein Acoma and Santa Ana *su'ny* denotes "a Zuni Indian." It first appears in Spanish as Suñi and Zuni in the entrada reports of Augustín Rodriguez and Francisco Sánchez Chamuscado (1581–82). Alternative spellings occur thereafter. The Zuni refer to themselves as "Ashiwi" and their pueblo as "Itiwana" (Middle Place), "Halona:wa," name of Halona Pueblo, or most commonly now, Zuni.

LOCATION. The Zuni have occupied the Zuni River valley of western New Mexico and eastern Arizona since at least A.D. 700. The present reservation comprises approximately 655 square miles divided into three areas: the main reservation, Zuni Salt Lake (one square mile added in 1978), and Zuni Heaven (*Kolhu/wala:wa*) (fourteen square miles added in 1984).

DEMOGRAPHY. Historically, the Zuni population at European contact in 1540 has been estimated at over 6,000. Population was greatly reduced by diseases such as smallpox, influenza, and measles. Since 1903, when medical doctors arrived, the population has steadily increased. Reservation population in February 1988 was 8,299 Zuni (3,984 men, 4,315 women) and 460 non-Indians. Of the Zuni, 2,469 were less than sixteen years old. Many Zuni live off the reservation, but precise figures are lacking.

LINGUISTIC AFFILIATION. The Zuni language is an isolate that may possibly be related to Penutian of central California. If so, glottochronology suggests a separation minimally of seven thousand years.

History and Cultural Relations

Archaeological evidence indicates a resident population within the Zuni River drainage for well over a millennium. In 1540 the Spanish entrada led by Francisco Vásquez de Coronado came in search of gold to Zuni (the fabled Kingdom of Cibola) described by Fray Marcos de Niza after his 1539 sojourn with Esteban, a Black slave. Coronado and his party defeated the Zuni at Hawikkuh but found that women, children, and most provisions had been removed to the sacred stronghold mesa, Dowa Yalanne. The men escaped and soon followed. The entrada wintered in the Rio Grande, but passed through Zuni again on the way back to Mexico, having found no gold. Several Mexican Indians remained and were reported alive by later Spanish explorers, Chamuscado (1581), Antonio Espejo (1583), and Juan de Oñate (1598). Colonization of the Southwest by the Spaniards under Oñate in 1598 involved the Rio Grande valley. The Zuni were largely unaf-

♦ **puberty rites**
Ceremonies and related activities that mark the transition from childhood to adulthood or from secular status to being a cult member.

See also

Pueblo Indians

fected until 1629, when they accepted the Franciscans. A mission was built at Hawikkuh in 1629 and another at Halona:wa by 1632. Hostility towards the friars led to the Zuni's killing them at Hawikkuh in 1632. Apparently the missions were then left unattended until after 1660. In 1672, Apaches killed the priest at the rebuilt Hawikkuh mission with suggestions of Zuni complicity. The Pueblo Revolt of 1680 drove the remaining Spanish settlers and priests from the Southwest, and missions and their accouterments were destroyed. The reconquest by Diego de Vargas in 1692, however, revealed the Zuni were the only Indians to have preserved Christian ritual objects. De Vargas found the Zuni living atop Dowa Yalanne. They resettled only Halona:wa in 1700, rebuilding the mission. Early in the 1700s, the Zuni killed three Spaniards and briefly fled to Dowa Yalanne. There were also problems with the Hopi, and mutual raiding of villages occurred (the Hopi Wars).

Throughout the eighteenth and most of the nineteenth centuries, Apache and Navajo raiding parties were a problem. Zuni reprisals in a number of instances involved joining with Spanish militia, later Mexican troops (1821 to 1846), and finally the U.S. Army (1846 to 1865). From the outbreak of the Mexican War, the Zuni were allied to the United States and assisted numerous expeditions/militia with food, shelter, and warriors. Stephen Watts Kearny (1846), John Marshall Washington and James H. Simpson (1849), Lorenzo Sitgreaves (1851), Amiel W. Whipple (1858), and Edward F. Beale (1857–1858, with twenty-five camels!) were among those assisted.

With Americanization came tremendous encroachments on what were recognized as Zuni lands during the Spanish and Mexican periods— about 15 million acres were involved. The Zuni reservation boundary was officially established in 1877 and reflected less than 3 percent of the original area utilized. Reservation lands were officially extended beginning as early as 1883 through the assistance of the Bureau of American Ethnology ethnologist Frank Hamilton Cushing. He accompanied Matilda Coxe and James Stevenson, fellow anthropologists, in 1879 and stayed at Zuni for several years, becoming an adopted tribal member and a bow priest. These early anthropologists began a century-plus collaboration with the tribe. Recently, anthropologists have taken an active role in assisting the Zuni in land claims cases and other endeavors.

Economy

SUBSISTENCE AND COMMERCIAL ACTIVITIES. The Zuni were horticulturists, with maize of several colors, beans, and squash as the primary cultigens grown in dry, floodwater, or irrigated fields. Crops were supplemented by the gathering of numerous wild plants and the hunting of animals (mule deer, rabbits, antelope, mountain sheep, and others, including bison on the plains). Communal hunts, which involved considerable ritual activity, were not uncommon. Following Spanish contact, wheat, melons, peaches, and other plants were introduced, as were sheep, goats, cattle, horses, and burros. Aboriginally, turkeys and dogs were domesticated, and eagles were caged or tethered for ritual use of their feathers. Sheep quickly became the dominant animal (for both wool and meat).

Today, all available range land (95 percent of the reservation) has been assigned in ninety-five grazing units/sheep ranches and four cattle pastures operated by two cattlemen's associations. The reservation was fenced in 1934. Range improvements are ongoing, and sheep and cattle provide a growing source of income. Although trading in turquoise, shell, piñon nuts, salt from Zuni Salt Lake, plants/herbs, and other materials has not ceased, with the coming of the railroads (to Gallup in 1882) and Americanization, there was a shift from bartering to a cash economy. Employment on the reservation is limited to positions associated with federally funded tribal programs, trading posts, and other commercial enterprises. During the 1970s a candle factory and a subsidiary plant of a major electronics company were established, but were short-lived. Cottage industry involving jewelry and other craft production began to be an important source of income during the 1920s and reached a zenith in the 1970s; today, most households are involved on either a part- or full-time basis. Events of the 1970s, particularly the "jewelry boom," nearly brought an end to subsistence farming pursuits. Sources of off-reservation employment include fire fighting with the U.S. Forest Service and a variety of jobs in Gallup.

INDUSTRIAL ARTS. Crafts included pottery, blanket and belt weaving, basketry, fetish carving, turquoise (and shell) bead making, and metalworking after Spanish contact. Although silversmithing began in the late nineteenth century, it did not reach major importance until the 1920s with the assistance of reservation and Gallup traders. A progression from clusterwork to mosaic inlay and, more recently, needlepoint and channel work has brought international prominence to Zuni. Fetishes, glass beadwork, kachinas, paintings, prints, and ceramics are available to the trader and tourist market. Sash and belt weaving is being revitalized, but basketry is near extinction.

TRADE. Since prehistoric times, Zuni have maintained an important position in trade with other Pueblos, Navajo, Apache, Mexican Indians, and other groups. Hawikkuh, ethnohistorically, was the nexus of trade; present-day Zuni (Halona:wa) continues the tradition. While major trade in wheat and other crops no longer exists, trade in jewelry and other crafts, as well as salt and piñon nuts, continues.

DIVISION OF LABOR. There has been a major shift from traditional patterns (men worked in fields, harvested crops belonged to the women) to a nonagricultural cash economy wherein both women and men are frequently involved in wage earning. Expectations are that a husband will give his wife his earnings. Livestock ownership traditionally resided with males, with related males sharing flock/herd duties and dividing proceeds after sales. Today, women may be involved via inheritance from their fathers. Within households many married couples work together in jewelry production, dividing the work by personal preference. Preparing food for ceremonial occasions and bread baking continues to be women's work, and wood gathering and chopping generally resides with males.

LAND TENURE. Since Americanization, land has been passed down through either male or female lines, rather than being controlled by matrilineal clans. Today, land associated with houses and farming tends to be viewed as personal property with surveyed boundaries. Cattle and sheep grazing areas are divided among tribal members with registered use rights.

Kinship

KIN GROUPS AND DESCENT. As of 1977 there were fourteen matrilineal, exogamous, and totemically named clans. A child is born into the clan of his or her mother and is viewed as a child of the father's clan. Clans with large memberships may have subclans within them. Although there has been some intermarriage with non-Zunis, the clan structure remains strong and viable. Its most conspicuous workings may be seen during ceremonies.

KINSHIP TERMINOLOGY. A basic Crow system operates with some modification in kin terms. The Zuni system incorporates blood kin and conjugal relatives, as well as clan and ceremo-

SETTLEMENTS

The original area used by the Zuni contains sites indicating Paleo-Indian occupation dating approximately 10000 to 6000 B.C. The Archaic period follows with more numerous sites reflecting a foraging way of life. The introduction of maize from Mexico in 1500 B.C. eventually resulted in a shift from foraging to horticulture. The traditional ancestral Zuni area embraces both Mogollon and Basketmaker-Pueblo (Anasazi) developments, beginning about A.D. 200. At this time, villages of several pit-structures, the introduction of ceramics, and greater dependence on maize are noteworthy. Population and site frequency increased through time. Within the Zuni River drainage proper, painted ceramics developed about A.D. 700, and by 1000, above-ground masonry pueblos appeared. From about 1000 to 1150, the area was incorporated into the Chacoan system centering in Chaco Canyon to the north, with numerous outliers reflecting well-planned masonry structures featuring Great Kivas (one can see, at Zuni, the Village of the Great Kivas and other sites). With the collapse of the Chacoan system, the ancestral Zuni be-

gan to build larger, aggregated pueblos, often with over a thousand rooms. Irrigation to ensure crop production probably began at this time. At Spanish contact the Zuni resided in six pueblos along a twenty-five-mile section of the Zuni River. One of the sites, Halona:wa, is present-day Zuni.

Following reconquest, the present Zuni was the focus for Zuni life and culture, but a number of seasonally occupied sites were constructed and used in the central area early in the seventeenth century. These villages were associated with farming and peach orchards; they were also outposts for grazing livestock and places where religious ceremonies could be held without Spanish interference. During the latter part of the nineteenth century, after Navajo and Apache raiding ceased, farming villages were established at Nutria, Pescado, and Ojo Caliente where excellent springs for irrigation exist. These villages, though largely in ruin, continue to be occupied, as does Tekapo, founded early in the twentieth century at the terminal point of an irrigation canal associated with Blackrock Dam on the Zuni River.

nial kin, and appears highly complex with inconsistencies to non-Zunis.

Marriage and Family

MARRIAGE. One does not marry within one's clan, and though one should not marry within the father's clan, this does occasionally occur. Marriage traditionally could take place with or without courtship, but it always entailed gifts, discussions with the girl's mother or father, and the girl's own choice. Since the 1970s, courting has followed basic American mainstream patterns; marriages are formalized by a church ceremony, by a justice of the peace with a tribal marriage license, or by living together. Divorce is easy, although with a cash economy and nontraditional material possessions, separation can be more complicated. A male returns to his mother's house with his personal possessions and little else. Children belong to their mother's matrilineal clan, and therefore illegitimacy does not exist. Alimony payments are unknown.

DOMESTIC UNIT. Traditional extended matrilocal households continue; however, nuclear housing has become common with federal HUD assistance. Subdivisions fan out around the village, and much development has occurred at Black Rock, two miles east of Zuni.

INHERITANCE. Matrilineality continues to play a significant role in inheritance of homes and personal property, though males have considerably more say about sheep and cattle disposition. Modernization of the pueblo, especially since the 1970s, has tended to alter traditional division patterns. Bitter disputes within extended families, in part a result of nuclear family housing, are not uncommon.

SOCIALIZATION. The "Zuni Way" begins with infants being tightly bound to a hard-backed cradle board. Childhood is characterized by general permissiveness. Mother's brother may be asked to assist in reprimands, and threats of visits by Boogie Man kachinas are not uncommon for repeated naughty behavior. Aggressive and hostile acts are discouraged. Education—from Head Start through high school—is emphasized as a key factor to improved opportunities in life. The University of New Mexico has a vocational branch at Zuni.

Sociopolitical Organization

SOCIAL ORGANIZATION. The interconnectedness of the Zuni social, political, and religious systems and their complexities have been described as almost impossible for non-Zunis to comprehend. In essence, no part of the system can be isolated. At the base is the maternal household; it is the social, economic, and religious unit composed of elder members of the maternal lineage, their daughters with their children, unmarried sons, and male in-laws. Within this setting, the status of women is high, particularly for matrons. Males joining households as husbands may achieve relatively high status almost immediately because of knowledge and skills that bring financial support to the family, but their ties and obligations to their maternal households continue.

POLITICAL ORGANIZATION. Aboriginally, members of the bow priesthood controlled both internal and external political matters. The functioning of the bow priests as a council, an arm of the all-powerful religious priests, may date to precontact times. The Spanish instituted the positions of governor (with a cane of office), lieutenant governor, and assistants perhaps as early as the late 1500s and certainly by 1692 (the reconquest). The head bow priest normally would be governor. Installation by the head priests involved presenting the individual with the Spanish cane and, later, another one from Abraham Lincoln (the Lincoln cane). Selection and appointment by the religious hierarchy continued until 1934, when a nominating committee was selected to present two nominees to the priests. At a public meeting, the individual receiving the most "male stand-up" votes was installed as governor; the other, as lieutenant governor. They then had some say about the remaining members of the council. Women, although not officially excluded, did not vote until 1965, when secret balloting was also initiated.

Significant changes occurred in 1970, when the Zuni constitution was ratified. Terms of office for the governor and council were set at four years, and salaries for the first time were guaranteed from federally derived funds via the Bureau of Indian Affairs. On July 1, 1970, the Tribal Council, following application, gained control of all functions of both the Tribal Council and the reservation with an Indian agent (the secretary of the interior's representative) acting as adviser to tribal programs. This was part of an overall comprehensive development plan whereby Zuni would receive increased funds to bring numerous improvements and job opportunities to the reservation. Funding was based on Federal Law 25 U.S.C. 48, passed in 1834; Zuni was the first to apply. The funding led to forty-three modernization programs, and today the pueblo, with its paved streets, sidewalks, and streetlights, appears little

Both Zuni men and women are frequently involved in wage earning. Expectations are that a husband will give his wife his earnings.

different outwardly from other Southwestern communities its size.

SOCIAL CONTROL. Aboriginally, the bow priests were central figures in social control. Many infractions were directly tied to accusations of witchcraft; punishments included public whipping and even death. The last public trials of witches were held in 1925, but belief in witchcraft continues. Now it is resolved privately between the person who catches the witch in the act and the witch. Any infractions against the gods are punished directly by them. Gossip and ridicule play an active role in social control; sacred clowns may publicly expose improper behavior in the plaza on various occasions. Zuni also has a tribal police force and jail, as well as access to the state police, the sheriff's office, and federal agents (the FBI in Gallup) as needed.

CONFLICT. Internal problems appear to have been minimal given the functioning theocratic aboriginal system. During the twentieth century, factionalism, involving pro- and anti-Catholic groups, religious hierarchy versus political groups, and various combinations, has been a problem. Political differences in 1940 resulted in the Sun Priest (highest priest) refusing to serve; he moved to Gallup and the office lapsed with his death in 1952. In 1984, the religious hierarchy, acting on behalf of the people, requested the return of the canes of office from the Tribal Council, citing gross neglect of duty. The priests appointed an interim council, but it was not recognized by the Bureau of Indian Affairs until an election was conducted. Most recently, in 1990, the religious hierarchy objected to the Tribal Council's plan with the National Park Service for the first cultural park on a reservation after it was approved by Congress. A pueblo-wide vote was taken, and negative results ended the plan.

Religion and Expressive Culture

RELIGIOUS BELIEFS. The "Zuni Way" is an all-encompassing approach to the universe. Everything within it is sacred, and through religion, harmony and balance are maintained. Ancestors, nature, and zootheism are major aspects. Offered are numerous prayers and prayersticks and the sprinkling of sacred white maize meal with bits of turquoise, shell, and coral in order to give thanks and to maintain balance and harmony. Disharmony is caused by infractions of proper behavior, and evil per se is equated with witchcraft. Spanish missionaries attempted to destroy the native religion, and some converted to Catholicism and other Christian faiths. But though many have

compartmentalized Christianity with Zuni religion, the latter remains strong and viable. Stability is provided through four interlocking subsystems: clans, kivas (kachina society), curing societies, and priesthoods. Each operates independently, but synchronically, to fulfill both psychological and physical Zuni needs. Within the Zuni supernatural order, "The Ones Who Hold Our Roads" are supreme; these are Sun Father and his wife, Moon Mother. Earth Mother is also of great importance. Another deity, Old Lady Salt, is Sun Father's sister, and White Shell Woman is his mother (or maternal grandmother). Other deities include Turquoise Man, War Gods, Beast Gods, and a number of kachinas who require impersonators of the highest character.

RELIGIOUS PRACTITIONERS. In reality, all Zuni are religious practitioners and religion begins in the home. One's clan may determine positions within the religious system. All males are initiated into the kachina society and become members of one of six kiva groups. The father or mother selects his kiva when he is born, but he may change membership. Initiation occurs in two stages: between ages five and nine, and between ten and fourteen; after this, the male can dance and wear a kachina mask. The kachina society is headed by kachina chief and the kachina spokesman, each of whom has a kachina bow priest assistant. There is also a dance chief for each of the six kivas. Twelve curing societies (Cults of the Beast Gods) are open to both male and female members—individuals may join by choice, by being guilty of trespass, or by being cured of illness. Each has four officers. Membership normally is for life. Sixteen rain priesthoods (six daylight and ten night priests) exist; most have from two to five ranked assistants and may also have one or two female assistants. Some priests come from specific clans either because sacred bundles associated with them are housed by these clans or because clan affiliation is mandatory (for example, the sun priest and the house chief). The final two priesthoods are bow priesthoods (cult of the war gods), and the priest must have taken a scalp.

CEREMONIES. All of the above groups perform calendrical ceremonies and rituals; some are public, others are secret. Each kiva group normally dances four times a year (summer, prior to the harvest, prior to the winter solstice, and winter proper). The internationally famous Shalako ceremony and feast in late November or early December requires year-long preparation and has reportedly brought five thousand or more visitors

♦ **kachina**
Supernatural persons, often the mythical ancestors of human beings, who visit the earth periodically; a doll, mask, or other object representing such a person, used for ritual purposes by the Hopi and other Pueblo groups.

annually in recent years. But as of June 1990, Shalako has been closed to the public and non-Indians. In addition to numerous annual pilgrimages, quadrennial rituals and ceremonies include the boys' initiation into the kachina cult and pilgrimages to Zuni heaven, the home of most kachinas and some ancestors.

ARTS. Numerous items are made for religious purposes: highly elaborate masks and costumes, kachina dolls presented to girls and women who represent them, bows and arrows to boys, jewelry worn by dancers, moccasins (painted or dyed red), women's leggings, fetishes, prayersticks, images of the war gods (*Ahayuda*), wood slat altars, and various insignia of societal membership. Dancing, religious text recitation, and singing (both newly created kachina songs as well as older ones, some of which are in Keresan or archaic Zuni) are also important.

MEDICINE. Sickness is caused by taboo infractions or witchcraft. A tremendous variety of medicinal plants, which are either collected or traded for with other tribes, is used in curing. These are administered in a variety of ways—internally, often as teas, rubbed on the skin, or smoked. The curing societies are associated with specific maladies and effect specific cures. A modern hospital (U.S. Public Health Service) is located at Black Rock for general health, dental, and eye care. Serious problems involve ambulance transport to the Gallup Indian Hospital or air service to Albuquerque's Bernalillo County Indian Hospital.

DEATH AND AFTERLIFE. Witchcraft is commonly viewed as causing death; but kachina dances, which continue for an extended series of days, and dreams wherein the dead appear to lure the living can bring about death as well. Infractions of religious rules can cause either the individual or someone close to that person to die. Thunderstorms in January and observed landslides foretell the death of rain priests within a year. Likewise, a Shalako impersonator who falls, especially during the final races, is expected to die within a year. The time of an individual's death is predetermined by a person's "invisible road." If one commits suicide or dies from grief or other premature cause, the individual may not enter the afterworld until "the road" is fully traversed. Following death, the deceased lies in state at home for an evening. During this time, the body is washed by specific female clan relatives and dressed in traditional clothing. Blankets and clothing brought by the assembled group are buried with the individual during the morning. It is preferred that burial occur within twenty-four hours of death. Rather than the overly crowded Campo Santo in front of the mission, the new Panteah cemetery south of the village is the final resting place. The spirit ("wind") of the deceased remains within the home for four days following death. It passes out the open door and resides at one of several locations. Bow priesthood members become lightning makers; rain priests join their kind "in the waters of the world"; medicine society members go to Shipapulima, Place of Emergence. The majority of others go to kachina village/Zuni heaven to participate in activities there or return as clouds or "invisibly" to Zuni while dancing is going on. Following death, the name of the deceased ceases to be used, except for rain priests, whose names are invoked by extant members to bring rain.

Bibliography

Crampton, C. Gregory (1977). *The Zunis of Cibola*. Salt Lake City: University of Utah Press.

Ferguson, T. J., and E. R. Hart (1985). *A Zuni Atlas*. Norman: University of Oklahoma Press.

Leighton, Dorothea C., and John Adair (1966). *People of the Middle Place: A Study of the Zuni Indians*. New Haven, Conn.: Human Relations Area Files Press.

Ortiz, Alfonso, ed. (1979). *Handbook of North American Indians*, Vol. 9, *Southwest*. Washington, D.C.: Smithsonian Institution.

Wright, Barton M. (1985). *Kachinas of the Zuni*. Flagstaff, Ariz.: Northland Press.

—THEODORE R. FRISBIE

ASMAT

Ethnonyms: Asmat-ow, Samot

Orientation

IDENTIFICATION. The Asmat are hunting, fishing, and gathering people who inhabit an area which they refer to as *Asmat capinmi*, the Asmat world. The term "Asmat" (or "As-amat") means "we the tree people." In anthropological usage, the term Asmat labels the people (collectively), the language, and the geographic area. A single individual is referred to as an "Asmatter."

LOCATION. The Asmat live within the Indonesian province of Irian Jaya (previously known as West Irian), which in turn occupies the western half of the island of New Guinea. Scattered over an area of some 25,000 square kilometers, these people inhabit a tropical lowland, alluvial swamp, and rainforest zone. The geographic coordinates are approximately 6° S and 138° E. Irian Jaya is located at the periphery of the monsoon region, with the most prevalent winds in Asmat blowing from November through April. The hottest month is December, the coolest June. Rainfall regularly exceeds 450 centimeters annually.

DEMOGRAPHY. It is estimated that there are approximately 50,000 Asmat people. Village size currently ranges from about 300 to 2,000. While extremely variable, the estimated average rate of growth has been about 1 percent during the past thirty years. There is very little migration into or out of the area. Demographic factors of importance in the pre- and early-contact eras included the practice of infanticide, *papis* (ritual wife exchange), intra- and intervillage adoption of children and widows of war, and deaths associated with warfare. During the contact era, diseases such as cholera, influenza, and yaws have impacted growth.

LINGUISTIC AFFILIATION. The determination of which scattered groups constitute the Asmat is, in part, an artifact of outside intervention and classification processes dating to the pre-1963 era of Dutch occupation. Five dialects are spoken in the Asmat language, which is a member of the Asmat-Kamoro Family of Non-Austronesian languages. Bahasa Indonesia, the national lingua franca of the country, also is spoken by many.

History and Cultural Relations

As an indigenous Papuan people, the Asmat are descended from groups of lowland, swamp-dwelling people whose still-earlier ancestors likely settled portions of New Guinea as far back as 30,000 years ago. Owing to accurate accounts kept by explores and traders, virtually all of the earliest contacts made with the Asmat by Europeans are known. The first was made by the Dutch trader, Jan Carstensz, on 10 March 1623. Next to arrive, almost 150 years later on 3 September 1770, was Captain James Cook. Occasional contacts were made during the next 150 years, but it was not until 1938 that a Dutch government post called Agats was opened. Permanent contact has been maintained since the early 1950s. Agats has grown into Asmat's central administrative, trading, and mission town.

Settlements

Villages (in the strictest sense of the term) have arisen during the contact era. There has been a trend toward the spatial consolidation of traditionally more disparate *yew* (the maximal social/kin unit, each centered around a men's house and based on principles of patriambilineal descent). Settlements usually are located either along outer perimeters of sweeping river bends, or along small tributaries near points where they join large rivers. These locations afford both strategic and resource advantages. Mission and government posts are based near some villages.

YOUNG CARVER

*An Asmat boy carves a figure from a block of wood with a stone chisel, under the supervision of an aged man. Irian Jaya, Indonesia
(Peter Arnold, Inc. / BIOS)*

♦ **monsoon**
Regular and persistent winds that blow in the Indian Ocean, coming from the southwest between June and August and from the northeast between October and December. The southwest monsoon is the main rain-bearing one.

The Asmat are descended from groups of lowland, swamp-dwelling people whose still-earlier ancestors likely settled portions of New Guinea as far back as 30,000 years ago.

Economy

SUBSISTENCE AND COMMERCIAL ACTIVITIES. The Asmat traditionally were subsistence-based, relying upon a combination of hunting, fishing, and gathering activities, which continue today. Horticultural activity first was introduced in the late 1950s. Processed stipe of the sago palm remains the dietary staple. First under Dutch and then Indonesian auspices, a partial wage-based economy has been introduced. Exportable hardwoods and crocodile hides are among the most valued items, reaching Singaporean and Japanese markets.

INDUSTRIAL ARTS. Traditionally the craft emphasis was upon wood carving. The *wowipits*, "master carver," was renowned for his technical skill and creativity. *Perindustrian*, the Indonesian term for "cottage industry," has been introduced to aid production and marketing activities. Asmat carvings are sought by collectors worldwide.

TRADE. During the precontact era most trade was intraregional, with the primary items being of ritual value (e.g., triton shells). One exception was stone for use in axes. This was obtained through an extended network reaching to the foothills of the central highlands. Current trade patterns now include manufactured items as well and also involve merchants (primarily Indonesians of Javanese and Chinese heritage), missionaries, and the occasional tourist.

DIVISION OF LABOR. This largely is based on gender. Women are responsible for net fishing, gathering (assisted by children), the transport of firewood, and most domestic tasks. Men are responsible for line and weir fishing, hunting, most horticultural activities, the felling of trees, and construction projects. Both sexes assist with sago processing.

LAND TENURE. Local, autonomous sociopolitical aggregates of equal status are associated with more or less defined tracts of land. Rivers and river junctions constitute key points of demarcation. Boundaries are not rigid, changing as intervillage alliances and resources fluctuate. Sago palm groves, as well as individual hardwood trees, constitute inheritable and rigidly controlled resources. In recent decades major disputes have arisen with the government owing to differing conceptions of land tenure.

Kinship

KIN GROUPS AND DESCENT. The yew is the nexus of Asmat kin and social/ritual organization. It is complemented by a complex yet flexible patriambilineal descent system (i.e., one wherein male lines predominate but female lines also are traced and actively recognized). Strong residential/spatial and dual organizational features are found. The tracing of actual and putative genealogical relationships beyond the great-grandfather is perceived to be superfluous and rather dysfunctional. Being a member of a domiciled core constitutes sufficient proof of being a relative.

KINSHIP TERMINOLOGY. Each yew is divided into named halves or moieties, termed *aypim*. These moieties are reflected in the positioning of fireplaces within the men's houses. The kinship system is classificatory, with certain terms crosscutting generational lines. What the authors have termed "residential override" is operative, in that (despite an essentially bilateral recognition and naming of kin) once a young man enters the men's house he progressively has less to do with his mother and her consanguineal relatives. The terms *cemen* (literally, "penis") and *cen* (literally, "vagina") are used to clarify certain male and female kin relations, respectively.

Marriage and Family

MARRIAGE. In principle, marriage is yew-endogamous and aypim-exogamous. Strict incest prohibitions only cover the nuclear family. Bride-price, provided by the groom in installments, traditionally consisted of such items as stone axes, bird of paradise feathers, and triton shells. Tobacco and small Western goods now are being included. Polygamy continues to be practiced by a few of the most prestigious males, although governmental and mission pressure against it has been intense. Similar pressure has been exerted against the practice of papis. While not a common occurrence, divorce does take place. Occasionally it is precipitated (in polygamous households) by inter-wife tensions, but more often it is caused (in monogamous as well as polygamous households) by problems between husband and wife. Some wives cite physical abuse as the primary cause. Some husbands cite inadequate cooking skills. A woman's return to her original yew and aypim signifies divorce; there is no formal ritual.

DOMESTIC UNIT. At marriage a woman becomes more closely affiliated with her husband's aypim, and takes up residence there. Individual houses are built, occupied, and maintained by extended families in the vicinity of the men's house. The informal adoption of children, even those whose parents remain viable members of the same village, is relatively common. This is perceived to be a means of maintaining "yew balance."

INHERITANCE. Certain important ritual items, such as *bipane* "shell nosepieces," are heritable. Principles of primogeniture do not pertain. Of primary importance are songs and song cycles, which can be inherited by a *soarmacipits,* a "male song leader," a *soarmacuwut,* a "female song leader," or other yew leaders. Leadership positions per se are not heritable, but they tend to run in families.

SOCIALIZATION. The primary responsibility for child rearing rests with female members of the extended family. Apart from socialization occurring through government- or mission-run school programs, most takes place through informal extended family and yew contexts.

Sociopolitical Organization

SOCIAL ORGANIZATION. Traditionally, social organization (often involving ritual) revolved around activities of the yew and its associated men's house. The yew was the largest stable unit of social organization. Since the 1950s this focus has diminished somewhat. Some men's houses have been replaced by community houses, open to all.

POLITICAL ORGANIZATION. For this traditionally egalitarian society, political organization was based upon the interplay of yew-prescribed activity (including warfare and ritual) and the dictates of the *tesmaypits,* ascribed charismatic leaders. Ascribed leadership, based on a combination of skill, generosity, and charisma (*tes*), is still important today; but the government's appointment of an Asmatter who does not possess tes to a local post can create a great deal of friction. The ability of tesmaypits to develop flexible intersettlement alliances and confederations, once so important to the waging of war and peace, has been curtailed.

SOCIAL CONTROL. Traditionally, social control largely was exerted by the various tesmaypits and was tied to allegiances that they had developed over time. While attenuated, this practice continues. Strong processes of peer sanction are operative, including gossip and the open berating of husbands by their wives. Wife beating occurs and is implicitly condoned.

CONFLICT. Ritualized warfare, head-hunting, and cannibalism were distinctive features of Asmat life through the early 1950s. Strikes, ambushes, and skirmishes still occur occasionally, and—as with ritual warfare in the past—they are aimed at revenge. The latent function is seen to be the rectification of cosmic and also population balance.

Religion and Expressive Culture

RELIGIOUS BELIEFS. Traditionally an animistic society, the Asmat have developed an intricate pattern of rituals that pervades village life. Various Catholic, Protestant, Islamic, and government programs (introduced since 1953) have attenuated but not erased beliefs in a complex spiritual system based on the conception of a dualistic, balanced cosmos. Spirit entities are thought to inhabit trees, earth, and water. The spirits of deceased ancestors mingle among the living, at times aiding or hindering activities and bringing sickness. Cyclical rituals—such as those involving the carving of elaborate ancestor (*bis*) poles—and rituals that accompanied head-hunting raids, the death of great warriors, and ceremonies of peace and reconciliation can be related to the appeasement of the ancestral spirits.

PRACTITIONERS. Sorcerers and shamans (*namer-o*) mediate between humans and the spirit world. These statuses represent visionary callings requiring long apprenticeships. Practitioners perform magic, exorcisms, and healing. Tesmaypits organize and supervise rituals, employing head singers and providing food for ceremonies. In recent years, cargo-cult leaders also have emerged.

CEREMONIES. Villages celebrate major rituals on a two- to four-year cycle. Ritual warfare (and the activities that preceded and followed each battle) traditionally was understood as integral to the cosmology of dualism, reciprocity, and checks and balances. Feasting, dancing, the carving of artworks, and lengthy song cycles continue to reflect this perspective. Mythological, legendary, and historical heroes are extolled in epic song-poems lasting several days. Initiation, papis, adult adoption, and men's house construction are also accompanied by ceremonies.

ARTS. Asmat art, music, and oral literature are closely bound to ceremonial and socioeconomic cycles. The master carvers (wowipits) have been recognized as among the best of the preliterate world. Exuberance of form, shape, and color characterize ancestor (bis) poles, war shields, and canoe prows. Drums and head-hunting horns are considered to be sacred objects, although only singing is viewed as "music." Music serves as a vehicle of possession, social bonding, political oratory, therapy, cultural transmission, and recreation.

MEDICINE. Most curers also are religious practitioners. They employ herbal remedies (including tobacco), sorcery, and magic. The introduction of Western medicine has been systematically promoted by missionaries but only erratically promoted by the Indonesian government. Earlier Dutch programs were deemed superior.

DEATH AND AFTERLIFE. Virtually all sickness and death is attributed to spiritual intervention or cosmic imbalance. Such imbalance leads to vulnerability. Upon death, family and close friends grieve openly and intensively for several hours, flinging themselves down and rolling in the mud of the riverbank. Mud is believed to mask the scent of the living from the capricious spirit of the dead. The body traditionally was bound in pandanus leaves, placed on a platform, and left to decay. Relatives retrieved certain bones; the skull of one's mother often was worn on a string around the neck or used as a pillow. The spirits of the dead enter *safan*, "the other side." Most Asmat now rely upon burial, with some deaths accompanied by Christian funerals.

Bibliography

Amelsvoort, V. F. P. M. (1964). *Culture, Stone Age, and Modern Medicine*. Assen, The Netherlands: Van Gorcum.

Van Arsdale, Kathleen O. (1981). *Music and Culture of the Bismam Asmat of New Guinea: a Preliminary Investigation*. Hastings, Nebr.: Crosier Press, Asmat Museum.

Van Arsdale, Peter W., and Carol L. Radetsky (1983–1984). "Life and Death in New Guinea." *Omega* 14:155–169.

Voorhoeve, C. L. (1965). *The Flamingo Bay Dialect of the Asmat Language*. The Hague: Martinus Nijhoff.

—PETER VAN ARSDALE AND
KATHLEEN VAN ARSDALE

BAU

Ethnonyms: Kubuna, Mbau, Tui Kaba

Orientation

IDENTIFICATION. The name "Bau" was originally that of a house site (*yavu*) at Kubuna on the Wainibuka River in the interior of Viti Levu, the main island of Fiji, but today "Bau" usually refers to the small offshore islet, home of the paramount chiefs, and "Kubuna" to those who claim kinship with the chiefly families, or those who "go with" Bau in the wider politics of all Fiji.

LOCATION. The Kubuna moved down the Wainibuka and then the Wailevu (Rewa) river valleys to occupy the northeastern coast of the Rewa Delta and the Kaba Peninsula before making a home for their chiefs on the small islet of Bau, at 17°58′ S, 178°37′ E. This islet is no more than 8 hectares in extent and 15 meters above sea level at the highest point.

DEMOGRAPHY. When Bau was at the height of its power, the population on the islet is said to have been 4,000. The paucity of available data permits no more than a guess as to the number of its supporters. Mid-nineteenth-century estimates varied between 100,000 and 300,000 for all of Fiji, of whom perhaps half supported Bau, but traditions tell of disastrous epidemics—associated with the earlier arrival of Europeans—ravaging the population by as much as 40 percent. The 1986 census revealed Fijians in the provinces that "go with" Bau totaling 175,000.

LINGUISTIC AFFILIATION. The language is one of 300 "communalects" (dialects largely confined to one community) that exist among the contemporary population of 300,000 Fijians. In the early nineteenth century, a lingua franca based on the communalects of Bau and Rewa was used by Fijians from different parts of the islands when they wished to communicate, and European missionaries chose Bau for translation of the Bible. Europeanized Bauan, sometimes also called Old High Bauan, has now become the basis for Standard Fijian, which is in the Oceanic Branch of Austronesian languages.

History and Cultural Relations

Although Fiji has been inhabited for at least 3,500 years, much intervening history has been lost to memory. All of the great chiefdoms of eastern Viti Levu trace their founding ancestors to the Nakauvadra Mountains near the north coast, but existing genealogical information cannot be held to relate to earlier than the sixteenth century. The Bau had two great chiefly lines, that of the Rokotui Bau, the sacred chiefs, and the Vunivalu, war chiefs and executive chiefs. After moving to the islet, the Bau began extending their influence. The Vunivalu Naulivou exploited musket-bearing European beachcombers to such effect that at the time of his death in 1829, Bau seemed well on the way to establishing a Fiji-wide hegemony. Rebellion in 1832 halted this inexorable rise, and as the century advanced, relationships between Bau and other chiefdoms, and between Fijians and Europeans, became increasingly complex. Missionaries arrived at Bau in 1839. Their progress was limited during the early stages of the war between Bau and Rewa, which dominated Fiji's politics during the middle years of the century, but in 1854, the Vunivalu Cakobau converted to Christianity, and the climactic battle of Kaba, in 1855, took on the character of a struggle between pagan and Christian power in Fiji. Thereafter, European influence increased. Fiji was ceded to Great Britain in 1874, with Cakobau signing the deed as King of Fiji. The British colo-

♦ pandanus
Definition here

nial administration adopted a fairly benign paternalism towards all Fijians. Alienation of land was stopped, but evolution of Fijian society and adaptation to change were severely limited. The old chiefdoms such as Bau became relatively insignificant, although some of the chiefs were involved in administration. With independence in 1970, and even more so after the military coups of 1987, however, the chiefly confederations have once again come to the fore.

Settlements

Although the focus of the chiefdom was Bau Island, there were many tributary towns and villages, each with their own territory up and down the Tailevu coast, along the north coast of the delta, and on nearby islands in the Koro Sea. During the period of greatest turbulence, villages were elaborately defended. Those in the swamplands of the delta, in particular, were surrounded with impenetrable barriers of fences and ditches strengthened with concealed and upraised spikes. Special structures included the temple to the ancestral god of the paramount chiefs, the house sites of the most important families, which were built on rock-stepped platforms, and the stone-bordered canoe docks, representing political supremacy. In order to provide more land, terraces were leveled and foreshore reclaimed, and a bridge was built to connect the islet with the mainland more than a kilometer away. During the time of friendship with Rewa, a 2-kilometer canal was dug linking adjacent channels of the great river to provide easier access between the two centers of power.

Economy

SUBSISTENCE AND COMMERCIAL ACTIVITIES. Bauan Fijians were subsistence horticulturists, raising root crops such as taro and cassava on a swidden basis on the drier Tailevu coastal lands, but planting swamp taro in carefully mounded and ditched plots in the Rewa Delta. Fishing and collecting the resources of mangroves and the nearby reefs provided important additional food. Trading with Europeans began when the latter discovered stands of sandalwood on the northern island of Vanua Levu in the first decade of the nineteenth century, and it greatly intensified when the technology associated with the drying of sea slugs (trepang) was brought to Fiji from China in the 1820s. The chiefs of Bau deployed their supporters in order to acquire the cash they needed to buy guns, ammunition, and, in the case of the Vunivalu Cakobau of Bau, a schooner for his personal use. Today, 60 percent of the total population lives in villages, largely still with a subsistence economy and the continued obligations of communal life, but rural-urban drift is creating problems. More Fijians work for wages and seek employment in towns, resulting in a lack of housing, employment, and education opportunities and a weakening of the resources of the villages. Since the coups of 1987, the Fijian-dominated government has sought to redress imbalances that it perceives between Fijians and Indians, originally brought to the country by the colonial administration in 1878 to work in the plantation sugar industry that eventually became the basis of the colonial economy.

INDUSTRIAL ARTS. Traditional crafts of Fiji included the making of pots, woven mats, and fine bark cloth by the women, and, by the men, the carving of whalebone ivory (sometimes inlaid with pearl shell) and a wide variety of wooden artifacts, including spears and clubs, bowls for the ceremonial drinking of kava, and the great seagoing double-hulled canoes that permitted speedy passage between the islands of Fiji and to Samoa and Tonga to the east.

TRADE. Bauan power rested on the ability to maintain a wide network of tributary relationships that involved the supplying to it of all the resources of the land and sea, including the crafts mentioned above. Europeans were integrated into the system whenever possible, particularly in the first half of the nineteenth century.

DIVISION OF LABOR. In traditional times, family units spread widely over the land, cultivating and collecting. The division of labor was according to both age and sex. Men produced a far greater proportion of the family's food, for agriculture was and remains the domain of men. Young girls might collect taro leaves, but otherwise they would not go to the gardens. Fishing by line or net and the collection of molluscs and other products of the reef are women's work, as is the fetching of water, most cooking, and the care of house and children. Young children of 8 or 9 might help their parents, but lack of responsibility usually lasts until 14 or so. The heavier tasks fall on the younger men and women. The domestic seniority system serves to organize household production; this arrangement was especially true of the traditional extended family.

LAND TENURE. Land was held by the "family," which was defined more or less inclusively in different parts of Fiji. During the period of its rise to power, Bau struggled with Rewa for control of the delta and sought to impose a tributary

The Bau chiefly clan was supported and defended by two groups of hereditary fishers, who had the role of defending the chiefs from attack by land or sea.

♦ trepang
A sea slug found in shallow tropical waters.

relationship on those they conquered. The colonial government defined principles of land tenure retrospectively, creating homogeneity in place of a system built on dynamism and change. They based their system at least in part on Bauan norms.

Kinship

KIN GROUPS AND DESCENT. Fijian society is organized into a hierarchy of kinship groups of increasing orders of inclusiveness. At Bau, the chiefly *yavusa* was divided into four patriclans: the two chiefly *mataqali*, a warrior clan, and a herald clan divided into two subclans associated with each of the chiefly lines. With the rise to political importance of the chiefly confederations since the 1987 coups, clan relationships at the individual level are becoming more important once again.

KINSHIP TERMINOLOGY. The system is of the Iroquois type, with some special features. There is the usual sharp distinction between cross and parallel relatives, but bifurcate merging occurs in all but the second descending generation, in which kinship reckoning is simply generational. Among the chiefly families of Bau, the *vasu* relationship, between ego and mother's brother, was used to cement ties with other chiefdoms. The vasu was able to make particular demands on the material wealth of his maternal uncle's kin group, frequently doing so in the interests of his own chiefdom.

Sociopolitical Organization

SOCIAL ORGANIZATION. The social organization of the chiefdom was extraordinarily complex, with all aspects of its existence ringed with ceremony. Each individual identified with a hierarchy of increasingly inclusive groups: extended family, subclan, clan (yavusa), federation of clans (*vanua*), and political confederation (*matanitu*). The focus of the chiefdom was the chiefly clan, which was supported and defended by two groups of hereditary fishers, who also had the role of defending the chiefs from attack by land or sea.

POLITICAL ORGANIZATION. As head of the political confederation, the chiefly clan of Bau sought to maintain a network of tributary relationships through its subclans. This arrangement implied a degree of political instability, and, indeed, the history of the first half of the nineteenth century was one of a ceaseless struggle for power. Warrior subclans were spread as a shield along the north coast of the Rewa Delta and at the base of the Kaba Peninsula, separating Bau and Rewa. More distant ties were based on acknowledged an-

MARRIAGE AND FAMILY

Marriage

Traditionally, the preferred marriage alliance was between cross cousins; marriage between tribes was possible only after formal request. Nonsororal polygyny was practiced, and a man's status was defined by the number of his wives. The great chiefs married many times, usually in the interests of extending political power. This meant that all of the chiefly families of Fiji were closely related, often many times over in succeeding generations. In such situations, the status of the first wife was distinctly superior. The title of the principal wife of the Rokotui Bau was "Radi ni Bau," and his second wife was titled "Radi Kaba." The principal wife of the Vunivalu was called "Radi Levuka." Marriage ceremonial was more or less elaborate depending on the rank of the participants. Patrilocal residence was the norm, and divorce could be effected easily by either party.

Domestic Unit

The traditional extended family consisted of several married pairs and their children, inhabiting separate dwellings but sharing and cooperating in one cook house. Typically, men of the family would be closely related to the paternal line, but a daughter and her husband might also belong. The senior male would use the ancestral house site (yavu).

Inheritance

Dwelling houses are allocated by the family head and remain under his control, as do garden plots and other family property such as canoes. At his death, his surviving senior sibling determines the disposition of the house if the deceased has no mature sons. In the case of the great chiefs, the council of the whole tribe (yavusa) would determine succession and with it all rights to property.

Socialization

The rigor and principles of family ranking are a microcosm of larger kin groups and communities. Children are subordinate to their parents, but they are also ranked relative to each other by birth order. Aboriginally, they were ranked first by order of marriage of their mothers and then between full siblings by birth order. The first child (ulumatua) has a special status. Obedience and respect are demanded of the child by the father; after infancy the child is constantly taking orders. Punishment by the father is the main disciplinary mechanism, and the mother is more indulgent than the father, particularly towards boys and young men of the family.

cestral kin relationships. As such, they required to be constantly reinforced within the contemporary play of political forces. The colonial administrative system and that of the immediate postindependence period divided the old chiefdom of Bau between several new administrative units, but in postcoup Fiji the chiefly confederations are again assuming political significance.

SOCIAL CONTROL. Reflecting a preference for avoiding direct confrontation, gossip, ostracism, and social withdrawal have always been important forms of social control. Fear of divine retribution was and remains a powerful sanction at both the individual and the community level. The colonial government made Fijians subject to its judicial system, but since the 1987 coups there has been an attempt to reincorporate traditional principles into the legal system.

CONFLICT. There were ceremonial ways of asking forgiveness where there was a wish for reconciliation, ending with the drinking of kava. The vasu could also defuse potential conflict, being able effectively to represent the female side in a patrilineal society.

Religion and Expressive Culture

RELIGIOUS BELIEFS. In traditional times, religious belief centered on the deified founders of clans, frequently worshipped in animal form. In addition, each group had its own set of animal and plant totems, deemed to be inhabited by ancestral spirits. The missionaries succeeded in driving ancient beliefs underground, but they surfaced several times at the end of the nineteenth century, usually in the form of atavistic cults as vehicles for anticolonial opposition. Today, Methodism claims the support of most Fijians, although there is an important Roman Catholic minority.

RELIGIOUS PRACTITIONERS. Traditionally, priests formed hereditary clans, exercising important divinatory and healing roles and acting as the voice of the ancestral gods.

CEREMONIES. These were mainly associated with life cycles and with intergroup relationships. In ancient times, there was a ceremony of first fruits, when the various tributaries of Bau brought offerings of food to the Rokotui Bau and later to the Vunivalu, these usually being in the form of delicacies for which particular groups were well known. This ceremony was conducted according to the traditional calendar.

ARTS. Singing and chanting, dancing, and joke telling were the traditional arts. The sexes never danced together and had quite different dances. Both danced standing and sitting. The women used delicate hand movements, while the men often danced with fan and spear or club, or with sticks.

MEDICINE. Disease was understood as deriving from malevolence of the spirits, particularly after the violation of taboos. Women collected and compounded herbal cures, while men applied them—a reflection of the belief that men possessed heavenly power (mana) whereas the strength of women came from the earth. Massage was also an important healing technique, but women massaged only women, and men only men.

DEATH AND AFTERLIFE. The ceremony associated with death was extremely elaborate, particularly when the status of the deceased was high, reflecting its importance in traditional belief. Tributary groups would come to pay homage to the corpse and to the bereaved family, cementing ties in the process. After the burial of a high chief, a taboo was laid on the waters around Bau, and the women, having kept vigil over the corpse for four to ten days, would cut their hair; only after 100 nights of mourning would the taboos be lifted. Wives were strangled to go with their husbands into the spirit world, for on the way lurked Ravuyalo, who killed the spirits of those who failed to accompany their spouses. The unmarried were buried with a club for their own defense.

Bibliography

Nayacakalou, R. R. (1975). *Leadership in Fiji*. Melbourne: Oxford University Press.

Ravuvu, Asesela D. (1988). *Development or Dependence: The Pattern of Change in a Fijian Village*. Suva, Fiji: University of the South Pacific.

Thomson, Basil (1908). *The Fijians: A Study of the Decay of Custom*. London: Heinemann. Reprint. 1968. London: Dawsons.

Williams, Thomas (1858). *Fiji and the Fijians*. Vol. 1, *The Islands and Their Inhabitants*. London: Alexander Heylin. Reprint. 1982. Suva: Fiji Museum.

—DAVID ROUTLEDGE

CHIMBU

Ethnonyms: Kuman, Simbu

Orientation

IDENTIFICATION. The Chimbu live in the Chimbu, Koro, and Wahgi valleys in the mountainous central highlands of Papua New Guinea. An ethnic and linguistic group, not traditionally a political entity, the Chimbu are speakers of Kuman and related dialects. Most people living in the Chimbu homeland identify themselves first

♦ **mana**
A term with cognates in numerous Melanesian and Polynesian languages for a type of spiritual power, energy, or energizing capability believed to be physically resident in objects, persons, or places.

Chimbu

The Chumbu live in the mountainous central highlands of Papua New Guinea.

♦ **Papuan languages**
Also called Non-Austronesian languages, these number over 700 and are found mostly in New Guinea, the Bismarck Archipelago, and Bougainville.

and foremost as members of particular clans and tribes—identification as "Chimbus" is restricted primarily to occasions of interaction with nonethnically Chimbus. The term Chimbu was given to the people by the first Australian explorers (in the early 1930s) who heard the word *simbu* (an expression of pleased surprise in the Kuman language) exclaimed by the people at first meetings with the explorers.

LOCATION. The Chimbu homeland is in the northern part of Simbu Province, in the central Cordillera Mountains of New Guinea, around the coordinates 6° S and 145° E. They live in rugged mountain valleys between 1,400 and 2,400 meters above sea level, where the climate is temperate, with precipitation averaging between 250 and 320 centimeters per year. To the east live the Chuave and Siane, and to the north live the Bundi of the upper Jimi Valley. In many ways culturally very similar to the Chimbu are the Kuma (Middle Wahgi) people living to the west. South of the Chimbu in the lower Wahgi and Marigl valleys are Gumine peoples, and farther south are lower altitude areas, lightly settled by Pawaia and Mikaru (Daribi) speakers.

DEMOGRAPHY. Approximately 180,000 people live in the 6,500 square kilometers of Simbu Province. Of those, more than one-third live in the traditional homeland areas of the Kuman-speaking Chimbu. In most of the northern areas of the province, population densities exceed 150 persons per square kilometer, and in some census divisions population densities exceed 300 persons per square kilometer.

LINGUISTIC AFFILIATION. Kuman and related languages (SinaSina, Chuave, Gumine) are part of the Central Family of the East New Guinea Highlands Stock of Papuan languages.

History and Cultural Relations

Little archaeological evidence exists for the Chimbu area proper, but data from other highland areas suggest occupation as long as 30,000 years ago, possibly with agriculture developing 8,000 years before the present. It is believed that the introduction of the sweet potato (*Ipomoea batatas*) about 300 years ago allowed for the cultivation of this staple food at higher altitudes with a subsequent increase in the population of the area. Oral traditions place the origin of the Chimbu at Womkama in the Chimbu Valley, where a supernatural man chased away the husband of the original couple living in the area and fathered the ancestors of the current Chimbu tribal groups. First Western contact occurred in

1934 when an expedition, led by gold miner Michael Leahy and Australian patrol officer James Taylor, passed through the area, and soon afterward an Australian government patrol post and Roman Catholic and Lutheran missions were established. The initial years of colonial administration were marked by efforts to curtail tribal fighting and establish administrative control in the area. Limited government resources and staff made this goal difficult, and by the beginning of World War II only a tenuous peace had been imposed in parts of Simbu. Following the war, Australian efforts to extend and solidify administrative control continued, local men were recruited as laborers for coastal plantations, and coffee was introduced as a cash crop. Establishment of elected local government councils after 1959 was followed by representation of the area in a territorial (later national) legislative body and by the creation of a provincial legislature. Local tribal politics remain important and tribal affiliation greatly influences the participation in these new political bodies.

Settlements

In contrast to highland areas to the east, Kuman Chimbu do not arrange their houses into villages but rather have a dispersed settlement pattern. Traditionally, men lived in large men's houses set on ridges for purposes of defense, apart from women, girls, and young boys. Each married woman and her unmarried daughters, young sons, and the family's pigs lived in a house that was situated some distance from the men's house and in or near the family's gardens. By situating their houses near the gardens, women were able to remain close to their work and better manage their pigs, a family's greatest economic asset. Although this housing pattern still exists to some extent, reduction in the segregation of the sexes, reduction in tribal fighting, and economic development have resulted in more men living with their families in houses that are located near coffee gardens and roads. Most Chimbu houses are oval or rectangular, with dirt floors, low thatched roofs, and walls woven from flattened reeds.

Economy

SUBSISTENCE AND COMMERCIAL ACTIVITIES. The primary subsistence crop in Simbu is the sweet potato. Grown in fenced and tilled gardens, sometimes on slopes as steep as 45°, sweet potatoes provide food for both people and pigs. Sweet potatoes are the main food at every meal, comprising about 75 percent of the diet. Over

130 sweet potato cultivars, or varieties, are grown in different microenvironments and for different purposes. Sweet potato gardens are usually made in grass or forest fallow areas by digging ditches in a gridwork pattern to form a checkerboardlike pattern of mounds 3 to 4 square meters in size on which vine cuttings are planted. Gardens are planted throughout the year, with impending requirements for food, such as the need for more sweet potatoes for upcoming food exchanges and increased pig herds, influencing planting as much as climate seasonality. In addition to sweet potatoes, other crops grown for consumption include sugarcane, greens, beans, bananas, taro, and nut and fruit varieties of pandanus. Pigs are by far the most important domesticated animal to the Chimbu and are the supreme valuable, sacrificed to the ancestors in pre-Christian times and blessed before slaughter today. Pigs, killed and cooked, are the main item used in the many ceremonial exchanges that are crucial to creating and cementing the many social relationships between individuals. By giving partners pork, vegetables, money, and purchased items (such as beer) the contributors create a debt that the receivers must repay in the future in order not to lose valued prestige. These exchanges occur at various times, for various reasons—for example, to celebrate marriage, to compensate for injury or death, or to thank a wife's natal kin group for the children born into the husband's clan. By far the largest of these exchange ceremonies is the pig ceremony (*bugla ingu*), at which hundreds or even thousands of pigs are slaughtered, cooked, and distributed to friends and affines at the final climax of events. Money has become an increasingly important item exchanged in these ceremonies. For most rural people, money is primarily earned through the growing of coffee in small, individually controlled gardens. In addition to coffee, money is acquired through the selling of vegetables in local markets and, for a small minority, through wage employment.

INDUSTRIAL ARTS AND TRADE. Crafts of clothing and tool making are now largely abandoned, their products replaced with items manufactured beyond the local communities and purchased in stores. All subsistence work, before contact, relied upon the skillful use of local woods, fibers, canes, stone and bone materials, and a few trade items. In general, men made the wooden tools and weapons and constructed fences and houses; they also made artifacts of cane, bamboo, and bark.

DIVISION OF LABOR. As in precolonial times, the division of labor remains based primarily upon gender. Men fell trees, till the soil, dig ditches, and build fences and houses; women do the bulk of the garden planting, weeding, and harvesting, care for the children, cook, and care for pigs. Men are also responsible for political activities and, in time of tribal warfare, defense of the territory. The production of coffee is primarily the responsibility of men, and the few Chimbu with wage employment are almost exclusively men. Predominantly, women sell items (mostly fresh vegetables) in the local markets.

LAND TENURE. Each family's land is divided among a number of different plots, often on different types of soil at different altitudes. Land tenure in Chimbu is marked by relative fluidity. Most commonly land is jointly inherited from a father to his sons. But it is not unusual for associations with more distant agnates and with kin or affines in other clans to result in rights to use their land. Rights to land in fallow remain in the hands of the previous user so long as those rights are defended. Despite the high population densities in most parts of Chimbu, absolute landlessness is unknown because of the ability of individuals to acquire land through any of a number of different contacts. But the advent of cash cropping has led to a lack of land suitable for growing coffee and other tree crops. Therefore, although land for food is available to all, access to the means to earn money through commodity production has become limited. This lack of land suitable for cash crops has led a large number of Chimbus, over 30 percent in some higher altitude areas, to migrate away from their home territories to towns and lower, less crowded rural lands.

Kinship

KIN GROUPS AND DESCENT. Chimbu view their kin groups as consisting of patrilineal segments, "brother" groups, which have descended from a common patrilineal "father" ancestor. The clan, with an average population of 600–800, is the usual unit of exogamy. Clan names are often taken from the ancestral founder's name combined with a suffix meaning "rope." Clans are further divided into subclans, kin groups with between 50 and 250 persons. The subclan group is often the main organizing unit at ceremonial events, such as marriages and funerals, and subclan members undertake some joint agricultural activities. Smaller groups are sometimes identified within the subclan. These "one blood" or men's house groups consist of close agnates or lineage mates.

KINSHIP TERMINOLOGY. Kinship terms are classificatory by generation and bifurcate merging, distinguishing sex and relative age among siblings and father's siblings.

Marriage and Family

MARRIAGE. Marriage in Chimbu, as in many parts of the world, represents a social and economic link between the groom's kin group and the bride's kin group. The ceremony reflects this with a large number of valuables, primarily pigs and money, negotiated and arranged by senior members of clan segments and given as bride-price. Men are usually in their early twenties when they are first married, women are usually aged 15 to 18. Residence after marriage is usually patrivirilocal. Polygyny is still common, although the influence of Christian missions has reduced its occurrence. Having more than one wife is economically advantageous for men because women are the primary laborers in the gardens. Until the birth of children, marriages are very unstable, but divorce occurs sometimes years after children are born.

DOMESTIC UNIT. Until recently, men always lived separately from their wives in communal men's houses, joining their wives and children most often in the late afternoon at mealtime. Coresidence of a married couple in a single house is becoming more common. If a man has more than one wife, each wife lives in a separate house and has her own gardens. An individual man and his wife or wives are the primary productive unit. Often closely related men will cooperate in the fencing and tilling of adjacent garden plots. Households commonly join others during short visits.

INHERITANCE. Brothers jointly inherit their father's land in crops as well as rights to fallow and forest land. Usually most of the land is distributed to sons after they are married, when the father gets older and becomes less active. Other valuables are distributed to other kin after a man dies. Land of childless men is redistributed by senior men of the clan segment.

SOCIALIZATION. Infants and children of both sexes are cared for primarily by their mothers and other sisters. At about the age of 6 or 7, boys move in with their fathers if they live in a separate men's house. Starting at about age 7, about half of Chimbu children begin to attend school. Up to adolescence Chimbu girls spend large amounts of time with their mothers, helping in daily work. Boys form play sets with others of similar age from the same area, and these sets of related boys form relationships that last through adulthood. The initiation ritual for males, held during the

preparation for the pig ceremony, involved the seclusion and instruction of boys and young men at the ceremonial ground in the meaning of the *koa* flutes and other ritual questions and proper behavior. Since the festivals were held at intervals of seven to ten years, and all youths who had not previously participated were taken, it was a men's group rite rather than a puberty ceremony. The initiates were subject to bloodletting and painful ordeals. These ceremonies have ceased, except for revealing the flutes to young people at the time of the feast. At first menstruation, girls were secluded and for a few days (or weeks) instructed in proper behavior, and then their passage was celebrated with a family feast including members of the local subclan and kinsmen. Some girls are still secluded and celebrated in a family rite.

Sociopolitical Organization

SOCIAL ORGANIZATION. Chimbu society is organized around membership in agnatic kin groups with small groups at the lower level combining with other groups to form larger inclusive memberships, much like a segmentary lineage system. Individual loyalties and associations are generally strongest at the smallest, least inclusive level associated with common residence areas and shared resources. The clan, the largest exogamous group, commonly acts as a unit in large ceremonial activities and does have a common territory. The largest indigenous sociopolitical organization is the tribe. The tribe, numbering up to 5,000 people, acts as a defensive unit in times of tribal fights with people from other tribes. The marriages contracted between members of different clans and tribes are fundamental in establishing political and economic relationships beyond the local level.

POLITICAL ORGANIZATION. In traditional times the tribe was the largest political unit, but parliamentary democracy, begun in the late 1950s and early 1960s, created constituencies much larger than the traditional kin-based political units, but the influence of small local groups centered on leaders, called "big-men," has not diminished. These men are influential in organizing ceremonial exchanges of food and money, as well as rallying support for the candidacies of those standing for election. Typically more than one man from each tribal group stands in elections, fracturing support among many local candidates and allowing the successful candidate to win with often less than 10 percent of the total votes. In many ways modern parliamentary politics has not increased the scale of Chimbu political groups—

♦ **men's house**
A structure, common in New Guinea and Melanesia, usually housing the young adult males and adult men of a community. A men's house typically serves as both a residence and ceremonial center.

even national-level politicians can gain office with a following not much larger than those supporting some traditional leaders in the past.

SOCIAL CONTROL AND CONFLICT. Although the possibility of violence, between family members as well as between large tribal groups, serves to control people's actions, mediation by third parties, often politically important men, is more often used to prevent or resolve disputes. Accusations of witchcraft are also levied against those who are perceived to be threatening agnatic group strength, usually against women, who marry into the group and are seen sometimes to have divided loyalties. Warfare occurs between different tribes and occasionally between clans within a tribe. Traditionally, the relations between tribes were characterized by a permanent state of enmity, which served as an important contributing factor to the unity of a tribe. In the decades following colonial contact warfare at first diminished, only to reappear in the 1970s. Although the incidence of warfare is related to competition over scarce land, often the incident that precipitates fighting is a dispute over women, pigs, or unpaid debts.

Religion and Expressive Culture

RELIGIOUS BELIEFS. The indigenous Chimbu religion had no organized priesthood or worship. The sun was seen as a major spirit of fertility. Supernatural belief and ceremonies concentrated on appealing to ancestral spirits who, if placated through the sacrifice of pigs, were believed to protect group members and contribute to the general welfare of the living. Although many traditional supernatural beliefs still exist, various Christian sects claim the majority of Chimbus as members.

CEREMONIES. Of the most important traditional ceremonies, initiation of boys into the men's cult is no longer practiced (having been actively discouraged by missionaries); the large pig-killing ceremonies (bugla ingu) are still held but with less emphasis on the sacrificing of pigs to ancestral spirits.

ARTS. The visual arts are concentrated on body decoration with shells, feathers, wigs, and face paint being worn at times of ceremonial importance. Songs, poetry, drama, and stories are important as forms of entertainment and education. Musical instruments include two types of bamboo flutes, wooden and skin-covered drums, and bamboo Jew's harps.

MEDICINE. Illness and sudden death are attributed to witchcraft, sorcery, and transgression of supernatural sanctions. There was a very limited traditional herbal medical technology, but for most illnesses the people now make use of the government medical aid posts and hospitals.

DEATH AND AFTERLIFE. Although Christian beliefs have modified traditional beliefs, it is still thought by many that after death one's spirit lingers near the place of burial. Deaths caused by sorcery or war that are not revenged result in a dangerous, discontented spirit that can cause great harm to the living. Chimbu stories are replete with accounts of deceiving ghosts.

CHIMBU CHIEF

In the highlands of Papua New Guinea, a Chimbu chief wears traditional costume and carries a staff. Chimbu, Papua New Guinea.
(Jack Fields/Corbis)

Bibliography

Bergmann, W. (1971). *The Kamanuku.* 4 vols. Mutdapilly, Australia: The Author.

Brookfield, Harold, and Paula Brown (1963). *Struggle for Land: Agriculture and Group Territories among the Chimbu of the New Guinea Highlands.* Melbourne: Oxford University Press.

Brown, Paula (1972). *The Chimbu: A Study of Change in the New Guinea Highlands.* Cambridge, Mass.: Schenkman.

Nilles, J. (1943–1944; 1944–1945). "Natives of the Bismarck Mountains, New Guinea." *Oceania* 14: 104–123; 15:1–18.

Nilles, J. (1950–1951). "The Kuman of the Chimbu Region, Central Highlands, New Guinea." *Oceania* 21:25–65.

Nilles, J. (1953–1954). "The Kuman People: A Study of Cultural Change in a Primitive Society in the Central Highlands of New Guinea." *Oceania* 24: 1–27; 119–131.

Ross, J. (1965). "The Puberty Ceremony of the Chimbu Girl in the Eastern Highlands of New Guinea." *Anthropos* 60:423–432.

—KARL RAMBO AND PAULA BROWN

DANI

Ethnonyms: Akhuni, Konda, Ndani, Pesegem

Orientation

IDENTIFICATION. Dani is a general term used by outsiders for peoples speaking closely related Papuan (Non-Austronesian) languages in the central highlands of Irian Jaya, Indonesia (formerly Netherlands New Guinea, West New Guinea, Irian Barat).

LOCATION. The various Dani groups live in and around the Balim River, approximately 4° S, 138° to 139° E. The greatest concentration of Dani is in the Grand Valley of the Balim. To the north and west of the Grand Valley, in the upper Balim and adjacent drainage areas, live the Western Dani. This is generally a rugged, mountainous country, with a temperate climate. Because of the high altitude and the sheltering ranges, the Dani area is temperate and unaffected by monsoon cycles. In the Grand Valley, the mean range of temperature is from 26° C to 15° C. Rainfall in the Grand Valley is about 208 centimeters per year, but wet and dry periods occur irregularly. For all practical purposes, the Grand Valley Dani do not recognize any yearly seasonal cycles, nor do they shape their behavior around them.

DEMOGRAPHY. The broad floor of the Grand Valley, at 1,500 meters, has about 50,000 people, or about half of the entire estimated Dani population. It is densely populated, one of several such broad valleys found across the central ranges of the island. The other Dani are scattered across the rough mountain terrain from about 900 meters to about 1,800 meters above sea level. The major concentration of non-Dani in the area is in Wamena, the Indonesian administrative center, a town of some 5,000 people at the southern end of the Grand Valley.

LINGUISTIC AFFILIATION. The half-dozen languages and dialects of the Great Dani Family are related to other Non-Austronesian language families of the Irian Jaya Highlands Stock, which belongs to the Trans-New Guinea Phylum.

History and Cultural Relations

The western half of the island of New Guinea, where the Dani live, was part of the Netherlands East Indies until 1949. With the independence of the rest of Indonesia, the Dutch held on to Netherlands New Guinea until it was transferred to Indonesia in 1963 via a United Nations Temporary Executive Authority. It is now the Indonesian province of Irian Jaya. Even as the Javanese component of the population is being increased through the resettlement program (*Transmigrasi*), a small Free Papua movement continues to demand independence from Indonesia. But neither the new settlements nor the insurgents have had any direct effect on the Dani. No archaeology has been done in the Dani area. Some Dani groups were contacted briefly by expeditions prior to World War II, but the first permanent outside settlements were established by Western Christian missionaries in the 1950s. By 1960, the Dutch government was carrying out its program of pacification and development in the Grand Valley. This has been continued and intensified by the Indonesian government since 1962.

Settlements

Dani compounds are scattered across the floor of the Grand Valley. The basic compound is one round men's house, a smaller round women's house, a rectangular common cook house, and a rectangular pig sty. The largest compounds may have up to half a dozen more women's houses. The structures are linked together by fences and open onto a common courtyard. Behind the houses, and enclosed by an outer fence, are casual household gardens. The houses are built of wood and thatched with grass. Compounds vary greatly in size. They may contain just a single nuclear family or many families and assorted others. A compound may stand by itself or it may be physically attached to several other compounds. The compound itself is a social unit, at least in terms of intensity of social interaction. These largest compound clusters may house well over 100 people, but they do not form social units. The population of the compound is fairly unstable, as people often move about from one place to another, usually in the same general area, for a variety of reasons. Although a few Dani now live at the government centers in houses with sawn-lumber walls and corrugated-zinc roofs, most settle-

The basic Dani compound is one round men's house, a smaller round women's house, a rectangular common cook house, and a rectangular pig sty.

ments in the Grand Valley have changed little in forty years.

Economy

SUBSISTENCE AND COMMERCIAL ACTIVITIES. About 90 percent of the Dani diet is sweet potatoes. They are grown in the complex, ditched field systems surrounding the compounds. The men prepare the fields with fire-hardened digging sticks, and women do most of the planting, weeding, and harvesting. The ditch systems capture streams and run the water through the garden beds. In wet periods, the ditches drain off excess water. These gardens usually go through a fallow cycle, and when they are again cleared, the rich ditch mud is plastered on the garden beds. Dani living near the edges of the Grand Valley may also practice slash and burn horticulture on the flanking slopes. Because of the absence of marked growing seasons, the sweet potatoes are harvested daily throughout the year. In addition to sweet potatoes, Grand Valley Dani grow small amounts of taro, yams, sugar cane, bananas, cucumbers, a thick succulent grass, ginger, and tobacco. Pandanus, both the kind with brown nuts and the kind with red fruit, is harvested in the high forests, and now the trees are increasingly planted around the valley floor compounds. Although the Western Dani had adopted many Western fruits and vegetables, especially maize, before actual contact, the Grand Valley Dani are more conservative and even by the 1980s only minor amounts of a few Western foods were grown there. Domestic pigs are an important part of the Dani diet, as well as being major items in the exchanges at every ceremony. The pigs live on household garbage, and forage in forests and fallow gardens. Pigs are tempting targets for theft and so are a major cause of serious social conflict. The Grand Valley itself is so densely populated that little significant wildlife is available for hunting. A few men who live on the edge of the Valley keep dogs and hunt for tree kangaroos and the like in the flanking high forests. In the Grand Valley, there were no fish until the Dutch began to introduce them in the 1960s. The only water creatures which the Dani ate were crayfish from the larger streams.

INDUSTRIAL ARTS. Until the 1960s, when metal tools were introduced by outsiders, the Grand Valley Dani tools were of stone, bone, pig tusk, wood, and bamboo. Ground ax and adz stones were traded in from quarries in the Western Dani region, and the Jale, or Eastern Dani,

got their stones from even further east. Other tools were made locally. They made no pottery or bark cloth. Gourds were used for water containers and also for penis covers. String rolled from the inner bark of local bushes was used extensively to make carrying nets, women's skirts, and ornaments. Rattan torso armor for protection against arrows was made by Western Dani but the Grand Valley Dani neither made it nor traded for it. Spears and bows and arrows were the weapons of war. The arrows were unfletched, with notched, barbed, and dirtied (but not poisoned) tips. By the 1980s, cloth, metal axes, knives, and shovels, as well as the detritus of modern life—cast-off tin cans and plastic bottles—had partially replaced traditional Dani crafts.

TRADE. Even before contact, various seashell types had been traded up from the coasts of the island into the entire Dani area. Ax stones and flat slate ceremonial stones, bird of paradise feathers, cassowary-feather whisks, and spear woods were traded into the Grand Valley in exchange for pigs and salt produced from local brine pools.

DIVISION OF LABOR. Gender and age are the major bases for division of labor. There are no full-time specialists; but there is some spare-time specialization. A few people are known as expert arrow makers or curers. Generally, men do the heavy work like tilling gardens or building houses, while women do the tedious work like planting, weeding, harvesting, and carrying thatch grass. Men weave the tight shell bands used in ceremonies, women make carrying nets, and both make string. Because of the very relaxed atmosphere between men and women, there is little activity totally hidden from either sex.

LAND TENURE. Quite informal usage rights are the rule. Although there is little or no population pressure in the Grand Valley, the extensively ditched sweet potato gardens on the broad valley floor do represent quite a considerable labor investment, but even so, rights are casually and informally transferred. Large garden areas are usually farmed by men of a single sib or a single neighborhood. Fields are controlled by men, not women.

Marriage and Family

MARRIAGE. Weddings take place only at the time of the great pig feast, which is held in an alliance area every four to six years. Moiety exogamy is invariably observed. Marriages tend to take place between neighbors, if not within a

♦ **tapa**
A fabric (or bark cloth) made by soaking and beating the inner bark of trees, especially the paper mulberry (Broussonetia papyrifera), Ficus spp., or Hibiscus spp. Tapa was traditionally used in much of Oceania for protective cloaks or clothing.

♦ **clan, sib**
A unilineal descent group in which people claim descent from a common ancestor but cannot demonstrate this descent.

KINSHIP

Kin Groups and Descent

The Grand Valley Dani have exogamous patrilineal moieties and exogamous patrilineal sibs. Some sib names can be found also in groups outside the Grand Valley and there are hints, perhaps remnants, of a moiety system in Western Dani. In the Grand Valley, people are born into the sib of their father, but at birth all Grand Valley Dani are considered to be of the *wida* moiety. Before marriage, those whose fathers are of the *waiya* moiety "become waiya," the boys through an initiation ceremony, the girls without ceremony. The chief function of the moieties is to regulate marriage. Sibs are associated with one or the other moiety, never both. There are sib-specific bird totems and food taboos. Local segments of sibs keep their sacred objects in common, store them in the men's house of the most important man, and hold renewal ceremonies for these objects. Grand Valley Dani are not much concerned with tracing genealogy. Common sib membership is assumed to mean common ancestry, but people rarely know their ancestors more than a couple of generations back.

Kinship Terminology

The Dani have Omaha-type kinship terminology.

neighborhood at least within a confederation. Some marriages are arranged by the families, while others are love matches arranged by the individuals. Marriage begins a series of relatively equal exchanges between the two families, which continues for a generation, through the initiation and marriage of the resulting children. These exchanges consist of pigs, cowrie shell bands, and sacred slate stones. Immediate postmarital residence is patrilocal, although within a few years the couple is likely to be living neolocally within the neighborhood or confederation where both sets of parents live. Divorce is fairly easy, but long-term separation is more common. At early stages of tension, the wife, or the junior wife, moves out to another relative's compound for a time. Nearly half the men are involved in polygynous marriages. The Grand Valley Dani have remarkably little interest in sexuality. A postpartum sexual abstinence period of around five years is generally observed by both parents of a child. The minority of men who are involved in polygynous marriages may have sexual access to another wife, but for most men and all women there are no alternative outlets nor any apparent increased level of stress for those subject to the abstinence. Ritual homosexuality is absent. This extraordinarily long postpartum sexual abstinence has not been reported among the Western Dani.

DOMESTIC UNIT. It is easy to identify both nuclear families and extended families, but these units are usually less important than the compound group as a whole.

INHERITANCE. There is little real property to inherit. As boys grow up they join with their fathers in maintaining the sacred objects held by the local patrilineal sib segment. In a more general sense, sons—and to some extent daughters—of the wealthier and more powerful men benefit from their father's position.

SOCIALIZATION. Child rearing is very permissive. Toilet training is casual. Children are rarely, if ever, physically disciplined and even verbal admonishment is rare. There is almost no overt instruction. Children learn by participating but not by asking questions. Since the late 1960s, government-sponsored schools, usually run by missionaries, have been teaching more and more Dani children to read and write in Indonesian.

Sociopolitical Organization

SOCIAL ORGANIZATION. In the Grand Valley the largest territorial sociopolitical unit is the alliance, with several thousand people. Warfare and the great pig feast are organized at the alliance level. Each alliance is composed of several confederations, which are also territorial units containing from several hundred up to a thousand people. Confederations are usually named for the two sibs with the strongest representation. Many ceremonies, and the individual battles that constitute warfare, are organized on a confederation level, initiated by the confederation-level leaders. Within the confederation territory there are usually recognizable neighborhoods, but these are not true, functioning social units. Contiguous clusters of compounds, also making up physical units, are not social units. Each individual compound, although lacking formal organization, is the venue of the most intense social interaction. Moieties and sibs are nonterritorial, unilinear descent groups which crosscut the territorial units. The two moieties, being exogamous, are represented in every compound. A couple of dozen sibs may be represented in a confederation, even though it is dominated by members of only a few sibs. In Dani areas outside the Grand Valley, the confederation is the largest unit and alliances are absent.

POLITICAL ORGANIZATION. Dani leadership is relatively informal, vested in nonhereditary "big-men" (that term is used in Dani). The leaders of the confederation and the alliance are well known, but they are not marked by special attire or other artifacts. They are men of influence, not power, and they emerge as leaders through consensus. Leaders take responsibility for major ceremonies and for initiating particular battles. The leader of the alliance announces the great pig feast and directs the final alliance-wide memorial ritual. Leaders are believed to have unusually strong supernatural powers.

SOCIAL CONTROL. Grand Valley Dani have no formal judicial institutions, but leaders, using their influence, can resolve disputes up to the confederation level, assessing compensation for pig theft and the like. But beyond the confederation, even within a single alliance, disputes often go unresolved because rarely does anyone's influence extend across confederation boundaries. Norms were not expressed in explicit formal statements. Now the Indonesian police and army have taken over dispute settlement.

CONFLICT. Until the early 1960s, interalliance warfare was endemic in the Grand Valley. Each alliance was at war with one or more of its neighbors. Wars broke out when the accumulation of unresolved disputes became too great. A war could last for a decade. Then, as the original grievances began to be forgotten, fighting would slack off. At that point an alliance that had built up unresolved interconfederation grievances could split apart, resulting in re-formation of alliances and ties, whether of war or of peace, between alliances. The confederation itself remained relatively stable, but alliance groupings shifted. It was the ritual phase of war that lasted for years. Once begun, it was fueled by the belief that ghosts of the killed demanded revenge. Since both sides were Dani, with virtually the same culture, and the same ghost beliefs, the killing went on, back and forth. In the ritual phase of war, formal battles alternated with surprise raids and ambushes at the rate of about one incident every couple of weeks. Battles might bring 1,000 armed men together for a few hours on a battleground. A raid might be carried out by a handful of men slipping across no-man's-land hoping to kill an unsuspecting enemy. But a war would begin with a brief, secular outburst that had no connection with unplaced ghosts. Some confederations in an alliance would turn against their supposed allies and make a surprise attack on villages, killing men, women, and children indiscriminately. The alliance would be broken apart, and both sides would withdraw from a kilometer-wide area, which would become a fallow no-man's-land on which the periodic battles of the ritual phase of war would be fought. By the mid-1960s, the Dutch and then the Indonesians were able to abolish formal battles of the ritual phase of war, but sporadic raids and skirmishes continue in isolated parts of the Grand Valley.

Religion and Expressive Culture

RELIGIOUS BELIEFS. The Grand Valley Dani explain most of their ritual as placating the restless ghosts of their own recent dead. These ghosts are potentially dangerous and cause misfortune, illness, and death. Thus, attempts are made to keep them far off in the forest. Dani also believe in local land and water spirits. In the 1950s, the Western Dani region experienced nativistic cargo cult-like movements that swept ahead of the Christian missionary advance. But these movements had no effect on the more conservative Grand Valley Dani. Now, in the 1990s, many Dani—Grand Valley as well as others—are practicing Christians. Islam, the majority religion of the larger nation, was not able to cope with Dani pigs and has had little success there.

RELIGIOUS PRACTITIONERS. Various people, mainly men, are known for their magical curing powers. Ritual as well as secular power is combined in the leaders at various levels. Leaders of alliances seem often to have exceptionally strong and even unique powers.

CEREMONIES. During the time of war, ceremonies were frequent. Battles themselves could be seen as ceremonies directed at placating the ghosts. There were also ceremonies celebrating the death of an enemy or funerals for people killed by the enemy. At the cremation ceremony for someone killed in battle, one or two fingers of several girls would be chopped off as sacrifices to the ghost of the dead person. Men might occasionally chop off their own fingers or cut off the tips of their ears, but these actions were signs of personal sacrifice and mourning. Funeral ceremonies as well as wedding ceremonies continued at intervals after the main event. Both were con-

Until the early 1960s, interalliance warfare was endemic among the Dani of Grand Valley.

♦ **cargo cult**
A millenarian or nativistic movement, found mostly in Melanesia and New Guinea during the first half of the twentieth century in the context of colonialism and World War II. The cults usually focused on the prophesied arrival of trade goods ("cargo") heralding a new era of material plenty and native control.

cluded in the great pig feast held every four to six years, in which the entire alliance participated.

ARTS. The Grand Valley Dani have practically no art beyond decorations on arrow points and personal ornaments of furs, feathers, and shells. Formal oratory was not important, but casual storytelling was a well-developed skill.

MEDICINE. The Grand Valley Dani have no internal medicine, but they do rub rough leaves on the forehead to relieve headaches. For serious battle wounds, they draw blood from chest and arms. Until the recent introduction of malaria and venereal diseases they were quite healthy.

DEATH AND AFTERLIFE. The Grand Valley Dani conceive of a soullike substance, *edai-egen* or "seeds of singing," which is seen throbbing below the sternum. It is considered to be fully developed by about two years of age. Serious sickness or wounds can cause it to retreat towards the backbone, whence it is recalled by heat and by curing ceremonies. At death, this feature becomes a *mogat*, or ghost, and it must be induced to go off into the forest where it cannot harm the living. Death itself is considered to be caused by magic or witchcraft but, although witches are known, there is no particular fear of them in the Grand Valley. Similar patterns of witchcraft belief occur among the Western Dani, but there witches are lynched.

Bibliography

Broekhuijse, J. Th. (1967). *De Wiligiman-Dani*. Tilburgh: H. Gianotten.

Gardner, Robert (1963). *Dead Birds*. Film. Produced by the Film Study Center, Harvard University. New York: Phoenix Films.

Heider, Karl G. (1990). *Grand Valley Dani: Peaceful Warriors*. 2nd ed. New York: Holt, Rinehart & Winston.

Larson, Gordon Frederick (1987). "The Structure and Demography of the Cycle of Warfare among the Ilaga Dani of Irian Jaya." Ph.D. dissertation, Department of Anthropology, University of Michigan Ann Arbor.

Matthiessen, Peter (1962). *Under the Mountain Wall: a Chronicle of Two Seasons in the Stone Age*. New York: Viking.

O'Brien, Denise, and Anton Ploeg (1964). "Acculturation Movements among the Western Dani." *American Anthropologist*, 66 no. 4, pt. 2:281–292.

Stap, P. A. M. van der (1966). *Outline of Dani Morphology*. Verhandelingen van het Koninklijk Instituut voor Taal-, Land- en Volkenkunde, vol. 48. The Hague: Martinus Nijhoff.

—KARL G. HEIDER

♦ **Polynesia**
A general term (from Greek for "many islands") for the islands located within the huge triangle formed by the Hawaiian Islands, New Zealand, and Easter Island.

EASTER ISLAND

Ethnonyms: Isla de Pascua, Pito-O-Te Henua, Rapa Nui

Orientation

IDENTIFICATION. Easter Island, the easternmost island in Polynesia, was so named by Jacob Roggeveen who came upon it on Easter Sunday in 1722. Easter Islanders evidently never had a name of their own for the island. "Rapa Nui" (also Rapa-nui, Rapanui) came into use in the 1800s and eventually became the preferred name for Easter Island throughout Polynesia. The origin of Rapa Nui is unclear but the name was evidently given by people from another island, perhaps Rapa. In 1862 and 1863 Easter Island experienced a severe depopulation that led to the destruction of much of its traditional culture. Subsequent contact with Chile, which took possession of Easter Island in 1888, has produced a culture containing many elements borrowed from South America. Easter Island is currently a dependency of Chile.

LOCATION. Easter Island is located at 27°8′ S and 190°25′ W, about 4,200 kilometers off the coast of Chile and 1,760 kilometers east of Pitcairn Island, the nearest inhabited island. It is a triangular-shape volcanic high island with a total area of 180 square kilometers. The most prominent physical features are the three volcanic peaks, each located at one corner of the island. The land is either barren rock or covered by grass or shrubs, although parts were heavily forested in the past. Only flocks of sea birds and the Polynesian rat were indigenous to the island, with chickens, dogs, pigs, sheep, and cattle introduced by people from other islands or Europeans. The climate is tropical. Water was obtained from springs and by collecting rainwater.

DEMOGRAPHY. Population estimates by European explorers in the eighteenth and early nineteenth centuries ranged from 600 to 3,000, although none can be considered reliable. There are indications that the precontact population could have been as much as 10,000 people. From 1862 to 1871 severe depopulation resulted from the kidnapping of about 1,000 men by Peruvian slavers, a smallpox epidemic, and relocation to Mangareva and Tahiti. In 1872 reliable missionary reports indicated only 175 people on Easter Island. The population continued to decline until the late 1880s and then slowly increased to 456 in 1934. In 1981, there were about 1,900 Easter Islanders on Easter Island and others living in Chile, Tahiti, and the United States. Easter Islanders make up about two-thirds of the island population, with the others being mainly Chilean military personnel or government employees.

LINGUISTIC AFFILIATION. Easter Islanders speak Rapa Nui (Pascuense), a Polynesian language that has been described as closely related to the languages spoken on Tahiti, Mangareva, and by the Maori in New Zealand. Since contact, words from French, English, and Spanish have been added to the lexicon. Because of the Chilean presence, many Easter Islanders also speak Spanish. There is debate over whether symbols found carved in wood boards called *rongorongo* are a precontact written language, pictographs, symbolic ornamentation, or copies of Spanish documents left by early explorers.

History and Cultural Relations

The settlement of Easter Island has been a topic of considerable conjecture and debate. Thor Heyerdahl's *Kon-Tiki* expedition showed that the island could have been settled from South America, although linguistic and archaeological evidence suggests settlement from other Polynesian islands perhaps as early as A.D. 400. Wherever the first Easter Islanders migrated from, it is likely that, given the remote location of the island, they were relatively isolated from other Polynesians. First contact with Europeans was with the Dutch explorer Jacob Roggeveen in 1722. There is some evidence that because of deforestation and wars between subtribes, the population was already declining and the culture disintegrating at this time. The island was subsequently visited, usually infrequently and briefly, by a succession of Spanish, English, French, American, and Russian explorers, traders, and whalers. The first major and the most significant contact occurred in 1862 when Peruvian slavers raided the island and kidnapped about 1,000 men to the guano islands off the Peruvian coast. There the Easter Islanders were forced to mine guano for one year during which time 900 died. Facing an international scandal, the Peruvian government sent the remaining 100 men home, although only 15 survived the trip. Infected with smallpox, they spread the disease to those on the island, further reducing the population to perhaps 25 percent of what it had been in 1862. The depopulation, disease, fear of outsiders, and death of many leaders led to cultural disintegration and a loss of much of the traditional culture within a decade. Catholic missionaries arrived in 1863, beginning a small though

continuous European presence to this day. Within ten years, all surviving Easter Islanders were converted to Roman Catholicism, with many of the economic and social practices taught by the priests replacing traditional culture practices. In 1888 Chile annexed the island and subsequently leased 160 square kilometers to the Williamson and Balfour Company, which established sheep ranching for wool. The remaining 20 square kilometers were set aside for use by the Easter Islanders. In 1954 governance of the island and the sheep-ranching business was turned over to the Chilean navy, and in 1965, in response to islander complaints, the island was put under civilian control. Easter Island is currently a dependency of Chile and Easter Islanders are Chilean citizens.

Settlements

Since 1862 the Easter Islanders have lived in or around the village of Hangoroa in the southwest corner of the island. European-style stone and wood houses have completely replaced the traditional forms. Before 1862, villages were located along the coast, leaving the interior mostly uninhabited. Dwellings included thatched huts, semi-subterranean houses, and caves. Wealthier Easter Islanders evidently lived in larger houses, often with stone foundations. In addition to dwellings, villages often contained cooking shelters, underground ovens, stone chicken coops, turtle watchtowers, and stone-walled gardens.

Economy

SUBSISTENCE AND COMMERCIAL ACTIVITIES. Prior to 1862, Easter Islanders subsisted mainly on cultivated crops, with sweet potatoes being the most important. Taro, yams, sugarcane, bananas, gourds, turmeric, and arrowroot were also grown while berries and seabird eggs were gathered. Fish provided some protein, although fishing was never a major subsistence activity. Easter Islanders continue to farm small plots today, although maize is now the major crop and Chilean cuisine has replaced the native diet. Since the introduction of sheep ranching, sheep and cattle on the island have been the primary sources of meat. Most material goods are now obtained from the store on the island and from the Chilean government. In addition to farming and fishing, Easter Islanders now work for the government, in a few small businesses, and in the tourist industry.

INDUSTRIAL ARTS. Easter Islanders were highly skilled stone-cutters and stone-carvers, masons, woodcutters, and canoe makers. Today, some carve wood images for the tourist trade. The

Easter Island is located about 4,200 kiometers off the coast of Chile. It is a dependency of Chile.

stone-carving tradition had already been abandoned at the time of contact, though the large stone statues survived and drew the attention of visitors to the island. Easter Islanders also made various utensils, implements, and tools from stone and wood, baskets, nets, mats, cordage, tapa (a cloth made from bark), and body ornaments.

TRADE. Because of their isolation, Easter Islanders evidently did not trade with other groups in Polynesia. There has been conjecture that some culture elements developed through contact with South America, most notably the facial images on the stone monuments. These ideas remain unproven.

DIVISION OF LABOR. Men were responsible for planting the gardens, fishing, and building the stone structures. Women harvested crops and handled most domestic chores. There was also a well-defined occupational hierarchy, with expert reciters of genealogies and folklore, stone-carvers, wood-carvers, and fishermen paid for their services with produce. Stone-carvers were a privileged group with the role and status passed from father to son.

LAND TENURE. In traditional times, land was owned by lineages with dwelling and farm plots alloted to families. Since 1888 Chile has maintained ownership of all of Easter Island and has restricted the Easter Islanders to land in and around Hangoroa. Newlyweds are given a few acres of land for their use by the Chilean government.

Kinship

KIN GROUPS AND DESCENT. The population of Easter Island was divided into ten subtribes or clans (*mata*), each of which evidently occupied a distinct territory in precontact times. By historic times, subtribe members were more widely dispersed as a result of exogamous marriage, adoption, and capture during war. The ten clans formed two larger divisions, with one controlling the western half and the other the eastern half of the island.

KINSHIP TERMINOLOGY. Traditional kin term usage followed the Hawaiian system, which has been modified over time to reflect changes in family organization.

Marriage and Family

MARRIAGE. In traditional times, most marriages were monogamous, though some wealthy men had more than one wife. Marriages were generally arranged, with infant betrothal not uncommon. Today, marriage is by free choice, although the fathers of both the groom and bride are involved in approving and making arrangements for the marriage. Marriages are marked by three ceremonies—a civil ceremony, church ceremony, and a large feast hosted by the groom's father—reflecting the survival of a traditional practice. Upon marriage, the couple generally live with one family or the other until materials can be obtained to build their own home. In the past, many marriages ended in divorce, which could be initiated by either party for virtually any reason. The Roman Catholic church has made divorce more difficult and less frequent.

DOMESTIC UNIT. In the past, the basic family and residential unit was the laterally extended family composed of brothers, their wives, and their children. Today, the nuclear family is the norm, although other relatives such as grandparents and brothers might also be present. In the past and today, the father was the authority figure, although today the wife's father has more power than the husband's father and a son-in-law will often seek his father-in-law's approval for educational and career decisions. Under Chilean influence, the role of godparent (*compadre*) has developed, and godparents often play a role in child rearing.

INHERITANCE. In the past and today, both men and women could inherit and both men and women could leave property.

SOCIALIZATION. Puberty in traditional times was marked for boys and girls by secluding them on an island for some months and then holding large separate feasts at the end of the seclusion period. These rites disappeared long ago, and puberty is no longer marked by ritual. The Chilean government provides a school for elementary education and some Easter Islanders attend high school in Chile.

Social and Political Organization

SOCIAL ORGANIZATION. In addition to social distinctions based on kinship, Easter Island traditionally had four distinct social classes: noblemen (*ariki*); priests (*ivi-atua*); warriors (*matatoa*); and servants and farmers (*kio*). The ruler was the main high chief (*ariki-mau*) who traced his status to descent from Hotu-matua, the founder of the island. In reality, ariki were invested with considerable mana and were subject to numerous taboos, although they had little actual power. Little is known about the activities of priests, as the role had disappeared by the time missionaries arrived. Kio were war captives who worked for others or paid tribute in the form of percentage of their crops.

POLITICAL ORGANIZATION. As noted above, the nominal rulers came from the ariki class, with succession to the position of high chief going to the oldest son at the time of his marriage. However, since this marriage was often delayed many years beyond that of most Easter Islanders, chiefs often held their position for some years. At the time of sustained contact, warriors were the actual political leaders, reflecting a long history of fighting among the subtribes and the almost continuous fighting that followed the kidnapping of men in 1862. Today, the Easter Islanders are governed by Chile, with a Chilean governor, civil service, and police force providing services. Easter Islander representation is through the mayor of Hangoroa.

SOCIAL CONTROL. Most early observers described theft as a common occurrence, with items stolen both from Europeans and from other Easter Islanders. Revenge was the major form of social control (actually it often led to warfare rather than peace) in early historic times. Taboos on the king, nobles, various foods, places, crops, death, and so on were a major aspect of everyday life and were rigorously enforced. Taboo violators were subject to beatings and even death. Although traditional taboos have now disappeared, they were still a strong infuence in the 1860s. Today, the laws of Chile are enforced by the Chilean police and government officials on the island.

CONFLICT. Wars were evidently common between the subtribes and especially between the eastern and western factions. Wars were often for revenge and involved ambushes, burning and looting villages, and the taking of captives, some of whom were tortured. War with Europeans was short-lived, and after the kidnapping in 1862 many Easter Islanders fled to inland caves upon the arrival of European ships.

Religion and Expressive Culture

RELIGIOUS BELIEFS. The traditional pantheon included at least ninety different named gods and spirits divided into the two categories of high gods and lesser gods. High gods included the creator, the rain god, and the superior god (Makemake). Lesser gods included gods with more restricted powers, nature spirits, demons, and ancestor spirits. Religious ritual included offerings of food and tapa, communication through priests, and chanting. Traditional beliefs have now been completely replaced by Roman Catholicism.

RELIGIOUS PRACTITIONERS. Priests, who could be men or women, were evidently drawn from the noble class. Little is known of the role

GOODBYE SONG

A native of Easter Island plays a good-bye song on the guitar. Easter Island. (James L. Amos/Corbis)

and status of priests other than the fact that they acted as healers and communicated with the supernatural world through possession trance. Priests could also place curses that were considered especially harmful. There were also sorcerers whose skills were used to influence or cause harm to others.

CEREMONIES. Ceremonies were held to bring rain, sanctify new houses, and to ensure a rich harvest as well as to mark all major life-cycle events. The annual feast of the bird cult (*tangata-manu*) and the feast of the Bird-Man were the most important ceremonies.

ARTS. The best-known of the traditional arts centered on stoneworking and stone carving. The most dramatic expressions of this tradition are the 600 large (from 20 to 60 feet high) carved stone statues mounted on stone platforms called *ahu*. The statues are most likely portraits of ancestors and chiefs. Statue carving had ceased by the time of European contact, with some 150 statues sitting unfinished in the quarry and many toppled over. Petroglyphs have been found on the island, and some interior stone walls of houses are decorated with paintings. Traditionally, various body ornaments were carved and both men and women wore body tattoos. The carving of wooden images, which was a common activity in early times, has evolved into a tourist-based

♦ **mana**
A term with cognates in numerous Melanesian and Polynesian languages for a type of spiritual power, energy, or energizing capability believed to be physically resident in objects, persons, or places.

economic activity with human images much in demand.

MEDICINE. Healing was done by the priests who used steaming, massage, binding, a limited pharmacopoeia, and contact with spirits. Today, Easter Islanders use Western medical care provided by Chile.

DEATH AND AFTERLIFE. In the past, the body of the deceased was placed on the ahu platform and left to decompose. The bones were then buried in the ahu vault. Much behavior that would normally occur in the vicinity of the ahu was taboo during the time the body was displayed. The funeral ceremony involved a large feast with singing and dancing. Today, Roman Catholic practices have replaced the traditional ones, although the latter survived into the twentieth century, far longer than many other cultural traits. The body is now displayed in the home, followed by the church rite and burial in a coffin in the church cemetery. Interment is marked by hysterical grief. In the evening there is a feast with food taboos for the family of the deceased.

Bibliography

Barthel, Thomas (1978). *The Eighth Land: The Polynesian Discovery and Settlement of Easter Island.* Honolulu: University of Hawaii Press.

Cooke, Melinda W. (1984). "Easter Island." In *Oceania: A Regional Study*, edited by Frederica M. Burge and Melinda W. Cooke, 371–375. Washington, D.C.: U.S. Government Printing Office.

Ferndon, Edwin N., Jr. (1957). "Notes on the Present-Day Easter Islanders." *Southwestern Journal of Anthropology* 13:223–238.

Metraux, Alfred (1940). *Ethnology of Easter Island.* Bernice P. Bishop Museum Bulletin no. 160. Honolulu.

HAWAIIANS

Ethnonym: Hawaiian Islanders

Orientation

IDENTIFICATION. Hawaiians are the indigenous people of the Hawaiian Islands. Now a disadvantaged minority in their own homeland, they are the descendants of Eastern Polynesians who originated in the Marquesas Islands. The name "Hawai'i" is that of the largest island in the chain. It came to refer to the aboriginal people of the archipelago because the first Western visitors anchored at that island and interacted predominantly with Hawai'i Island chiefs.

LOCATION. The populated Hawaiian Islands are located between 15° and 20° N and 160° and 155° W. The climate is temperate tropical, and weathered volcanic features dominate the terrain. Rainfall and soil fertility may vary significantly between the windward and leeward sides of the islands.

DEMOGRAPHY. The aboriginal population is estimated at 250,000–300,000. Because of recurrent epidemics of introduced diseases, the native population had been reduced by at least 75 percent by 1854. In the late 1880s Hawaiians were outnumbered by immigrant sugar workers. According to the state's enumeration, Hawaiians today number about 175,000, or 19 percent of the state's population. Because of historically high rates of Hawaiian exogamy "pure" Hawaiians number only about 9,000.

LINGUISTIC AFFILIATION. Hawaiian is closely related to Marquesan, Tahitian, and Maori. The use of Hawaiian was suppressed in island schools during the territorial period, and the language fell into disuse during the mid-twentieth century. Few Hawaiians can speak the language today. The colloquial language of most Hawaiians is Hawai'i Islands Creole, informally known as "Pidgin." Since the 1970s the University of Hawaii has been the center of attempts to revive the Hawaiian language through education. A few hundred children are enrolled in language-immersion preschools where only Hawaiian is spoken.

History and Cultural Relations

The date of first colonization is constantly being revised, but Polynesians are believed to have reached Hawai'i by about A.D. 300. There may have been multiple settlement voyages, but two-way travel between Hawai'i and other island groups was never extensive. By the time of Captain James Cook's arrival late in 1778, the Hawaiian chieftainship had evolved a high order of political complexity and stratification, with the Maui and Hawai'i Island dynasties vying to control the eastern portion of the archipelago. In their first encounters with the Hawaiians Cook's men introduced venereal disease. At Kealakekua, on the leeward side of Hawai'i Island, Cook was greeted as the returning god Lono, but he was later killed in a skirmish over a stolen longboat. Europeans nevertheless began to use the islands as a provisions stop, for Hawai'i was uniquely well situated to supply the fur trade and, later, North Pacific whalers. The Hawaiian chiefs became avidly involved in foreign trade, seeking to accu-

While descendants of the Asian sugar workers have lived the American dream in Hawai'i, native Hawaiians suffered increasing poverty and alienation during the territorial period.

See also

Tahiti

mulate weapons, ammunition, and luxury goods. In 1795 Kamehameha, a junior chief of Hawai'i Island, defeated the Maui chiefs in a decisive battle on O'ahu Island, thereby unifying the windward isles. This date is taken to mark the beginning of the Hawaiian kingdom and Hawai'i's transition from chiefdom to state. An astute and strong-willed ruler, Kamehameha consolidated his rule and established a bureaucratic government. His successors were weaker and were continually pressured by foreign residents and bullied by colonial governments. High-ranking chiefly women and their supporters convinced Kamehameha II to abolish the indigenous religion shortly after his father's death in 1819. Congregationalist missionaries arrived a few months later and came to exert tremendous influence on the kingdom's laws and policies. In the 1840s resident foreigners persuaded Kamehameha III to replace the traditional system of land tenure with Western-style private landed property. The resulting land division, the "Great Máhele," was a disaster for the Hawaiian people. The king, the government, and major chiefs received most of the land, with only 29,000 acres going to 80,000 commoners. At the same time foreigners were given the right to buy and own property. Within a few decades most Hawaiians were landless as foreign residents accumulated large tracts for plantations and ranches. The 1875 Reciprocity Treaty with the United States ensured the profitability of sugar. Planters imported waves of laborers from Asia and Europe, and Hawaiians became a numerical minority. A clique of white businessmen overthrew the last monarch, Queen Lili'uokalani, in 1893. Although President Grover Cleveland urged that the monarchy be restored, Congress took no action and annexation followed in 1898. While descendants of the Asian sugar workers have lived the American dream in Hawai'i, native Hawaiians suffered increasing poverty and alienation during the territorial period. Hawaiian radicalism and cultural awareness have been on the upsurge since the mid-1970s. Citing the precedent of American Indian tribal nations, activists now demand similar status for Hawaiians, and the movement for Hawaiian sovereignty has gained increasing credibility among the state's political leaders.

Settlements

In precontact times Hawaiians lived in dispersed settlements along the coasts and in windward valleys. Inland and mountain areas were sparsely populated. Hawaiian houses were thatched from ground to roof ridge with native grass or sugarcane leaves. Commoner houses were low and sparsely furnished with coarse floor mats. The dwellings of the chiefs were more spacious, with floors and walls covered thickly with fine mats and bark cloth. Because of taboos mandating the separation of men and women in certain contexts, a household compound consisted of several dwellings for sleeping and eating. The most important developments affecting Hawaiians since the mid-nineteenth century have been land alienation and urbanization. Small Hawaiian subsistence communities practicing fishing and farming persist in isolated rural areas of Maui, Moloka'i, and Hawai'i. On O'ahu, the leeward Waianae coast is a center of Hawaiian settlement. Significant numbers of Hawaiians also live on leased house lots in government-sponsored Hawaiian Home Lands communities within the city of Honolulu. Dwellings in the style of plantation housing predominate in working-class communities and neighborhoods throughout Hawai'i, and Hawaiian settlements are no exception to this pattern. In most Hawaiian villages and neighborhoods the houses are of single-walled wood construction, sometimes raised off the ground on pilings, with corrugated iron roofs. Rural Hawaiians may have small houses for cooking and bathing behind the main dwelling, a pattern that appears to be a holdover from Polynesian culture.

Economy

SUBSISTENCE AND COMMERCIAL ACTIVITIES. The first Polynesian settlers in Hawai'i subsisted largely on marine resources. In the ensuing centuries the Hawaiians developed extensive and highly productive agricultural systems. The staple food was taro, a starchy root that the Hawaiians pounded and mashed into a paste called *poi*. In wetland valleys taro was grown in irrigated pond fields resembling rice paddies. Intricate networks of ditches brought water into the taro patches, some of which doubled as fish ponds. In the late precontact period, concurrent with increasing political complexity, large walled fish ponds were constructed in offshore areas. These were reserved for chiefly use. The lee sides of the islands supported extensive field systems where Hawaiians grew dry-land taro, sweet potatoes, breadfruit, and bananas. The Polynesians brought pigs, dogs, and chickens to Hawai'i. Goats and cattle were introduced by Westerners before 1800. In the early 1800s, to avoid the chiefs' growing demands on the rural populace, some Hawaiians turned to seafaring, peddling, and various jobs in the ports. The shift from rural subsistence to wage labor intensified in the latter half of the century. Hawaiians—men and women—made up the bulk of the sugar plantation labor force until after 1875. According to 1980 state figures, about 23 percent of Hawaiians today are employed in agriculture. Some are independent small farmers who produce the traditional staple, taro, for sale to markets. But most Hawaiians are engaged in service jobs. Hawaiians are underrepresented in management and professional occupations and overrepresented as bus drivers, police officers, and fire fighters.

INDUSTRIAL ARTS. Indigenous Hawaiian crafts included mat and bark-cloth making, feather work, and woodworking.

TRADE. Although the traditional Hawaiian local group was largely self-sufficient, there was specialization and internal trade in canoes, adzes, fish lines, salt, and fine mats. In the postcontact period Hawaiians have tended to leave store keeping and commerce to other ethnic groups.

DIVISION OF LABOR. Most agricultural labor was performed by men in ancient Hawai'i, as was woodworking and adz manufacture. Women made bark cloth for clothing and mats for domestic furnishings, chiefly tribute, and exchange.

Men did the deep-sea fishing while women gathered inshore marine foods. In most Hawaiian families today both spouses have salaried jobs outside the home.

LAND TENURE. In the native Hawaiian conception land was not owned but "cared for." Use and access rights were allocated through the social hierarchy from the highest chiefs to their local land supervisors and thence to commoners. The most important administrative unit was a land section called the *ahupua'a*, which ideally ran from the mountain to the sea and contained a full range of productive zones. Typically a household had rights in a variety of microenvironments. The introduction of private land titles resulted in widespread dispossession in part because Hawaiians did not understand the implications of alienable property. The lands of the Kamehameha chiefly family descended to Princess Bernice Pauahi Bishop, whose estate supports the Kamehameha Schools in Honolulu for the education of Hawaiian children. The Hawaiian Home Lands, established by Congress in 1920, are leased to persons who can prove 50 percent Hawaiian ancestry. Originally conceived as a "back to the land" farming program, the Hawaiian Home Lands are now used primarily for house lots.

SOCIOPOLITICAL ORGANIZATION

At the time of Western contact in 1778 the Hawaiian islands were politically divided into several competing chiefdoms. Hawai'i was an independent kingdom from 1795 to 1893 and a United States territory from 1898 until statehood in 1959.

Social Organizations

Precontact Hawai'i was a highly stratified society where the chiefs were socially and ritually set apart from the common people. Rank was bilaterally determined and chiefly women wielded considerable authority. The commoner category was internally egalitarian.

Political Organization

Each island was divided into districts consisting of several ahupua'a land sections.

Districts and ahupua'a were redistributed by successful chiefs to their followers after a conquest. The chief then appointed a local land agent to supervise production and maintenance of the irrigation system. The commoners materially supported the chiefs with tribute at ritually prescribed times. Rebellions and power struggles were common. In legendary histories cruel and stingy chiefs are deserted by their people and overthrown by their kinder younger brothers.

Social Control

The chiefs had absolute authority over commoners. They could confiscate their property or put them to death for violating ritual prohibitions. In practice, however, chiefs were constrained by their reliance on the underlying populace of producers. In Hawaiian communities today there is no sense of inborn rank and an egalitarian ethic prevails. Pretensions are leveled by the use of gossip and temporary ostracism.

Conflict

Warfare was endemic in the Hawaiian chieftainship in the century or two preceding Cook's arrival. After Kamehameha's conquest the Hawaiian warrior ethic declined to the extent that the monarchy could be overthrown in 1893 by a company of marines. Interpersonal conflicts among Hawaiians today typify the tensions present in any small-scale community, and they are for the most part resolved through the intervention of family and friends. Hawaiians are very reluctant to call in outside authorities to resolve local-level conflicts.

Kinship

KIN GROUPS AND DESCENT. There were no corporate kin groups among Hawaiians at the time of contact. The chiefs could trace their genealogies back many generations through bilateral links, opportunistically linking themselves to particular ancestral lines as the political situation demanded. Commoners recognized shallow bilateral kindreds augmented by stipulated and fictive kin.

KINSHIP TERMINOLOGY. In the Hawaiian language no distinction is made between parents and parents' collateral kin. Same-sex siblings are ranked by relative age, but brother and sister are terminologically unranked.

Marriage and Family

MARRIAGE. In pre-Christian Hawai'i both sexes enjoyed near-complete freedom to initiate and terminate sexual attachments. Marriage was unmarked by ceremony and was hardly distinguished from cohabitation and liaisons, except in chiefly unions. The birth of children was the more important ceremonial occasion. Marrying someone of higher rank was the ideal for both men and women. Polygyny was the norm among the ruling chiefs, permissible but infrequent among the common people. Postmarital residence was determined by pragmatic considerations.

DOMESTIC UNIT. Both commoners and chiefs lived in large extended-family household groups with fluid composition. The indigenous religion mandated that men and women had to have separate dwelling houses and could not eat together.

INHERITANCE. Men were more likely to inherit land rights than women, while women were privileged in the inheritance of the family's spiritual property and knowledge. Since the legal changes of the nineteenth century land inheritance among Hawaiians has been mostly bilateral.

SOCIALIZATION. In Hawaiian families today grandparents have an especially close relationship with their grandchildren, and they frequently take over parenting duties. As in other Polynesian societies, children may be adopted freely without emotional turmoil or secretiveness. Emphasis is placed on respect for age and mutual caring between family members.

Religion and Expressive Culture

The religion described in ethnohistorical sources was largely the province of male chiefs. Sacrificial rites performed by priests at monumental temples served to legitimate chiefly authority.

RELIGIOUS BELIEFS. Chiefs were genealogically linked to gods and were believed to have sacred power (mana). Under what was called the *kapu* system women were denied many choice foods and could not eat with men. Pre-Christian beliefs persisted at the local level long after the chiefly sacrificial religion was overthrown. The indigenous religion recognized four major gods and at least one major goddess identified with the earth and procreation. Kū, the god of war, fishing, and other male pursuits, was Kamehameha's patron deity. Another god, Lono, represented the contrasting ethos of peace and reproduction. Women worshipped their own patron goddesses. Commoners made offerings to ancestral guardian spirits at their domestic shrines. Deities were also associated with particular crafts and activities. Although Congregationalists were the first to missionize in Hawai'i, the sect has few adherents among Hawaiians today. Roman Catholicism has attracted many Hawaiians, as have small Protestant churches emphasizing personal forms of worship.

RELIGIOUS PRACTITIONERS. Before the *kapu* abolition younger brothers normatively served their seniors as priests. Major deities had their own priesthoods. The volcano goddess Pele is said to have had priestesses. Among the commoners there were experts in healing and sorcery, known as "Kāhuna," and such specialists are still utilized by Hawaiians today.

CEREMONIES. The Hawaiian ritual calendar was based on lunar phases. Kū ruled the land for eight months of the year. Lono reigned for four winter months during the Makahiki festival when warfare was suspended and fertility was celebrated.

ARTS. Chiefly men were sometimes tattooed, but this was not a general custom and most of the details have been lost. The carved wooden idols of the gods are artistically impressive, but few survived the dramatic end of the native religion. The hula, the indigenous dance form, had numerous styles ranging from sacred paeans to erotic celebrations of fertility. Various percussion instruments used included drums, sticks, bamboo pipes, pebbles (like castanets), gourds, rattles, and split bamboo pieces.

MEDICINE. Hawaiians today utilize Western medicine but may also consult healers and spiritual specialists, some linked to Hawaiian cultural precedent and others syncretic, drawing on other ethnic traditions. Hawaiians are particularly prone to spirit possession, and many believe that evil thoughts have material consequences on

Hawaiian Chiefs were genealogically linked to gods and were believed to have sacred powere (mana).

other people. Illness is linked to social grievances or imbalances.

DEATH AND AFTERLIFE. Ancient Hawaiians secreted remains of the dead in burial caves. The deceased's personal power or *mana* was believed to reside in the bones. Chiefs were particularly concerned that their enemies not find their remains and show disrespect to them after death. Those who broke the taboos, on the other hand, were killed and offered to the gods, and their remains were allowed to decompose on the temple.

Bibliography

Kirch, Patrick V. (1985). *Feathered Gods and Fishhooks: An Introduction to Hawaiian Archaeology and Prehistory.* Honolulu: University of Hawaii Press.

Kuykendall, Ralph S. (1938). *The Hawaiian Kingdom.* Vol. 1, 1778–1854. Honolulu: University of Hawaii Press.

Linnekin, Jocelyn (1985). *Children of the Land: Exchange and Status in a Hawaiian Community.* New Brunswick, N.J.: Rutgers University Press.

Valeri, Valerio (1985). *Kingship and Sacrifice: Ritual and Society in Ancient Hawaii.* Chicago: University of Chicago Press.

—JOCELYN LINNEKIN

KAPAUKU

Ethnonyms: Ekagi, Ekari, Me, Tapiro

Orientation

IDENTIFICATION. The Kapauku live in the central highlands of western New Guinea, now Irian Jaya. Although they are generally treated as a single cultural group, there are variations in dialect and in social and cultural practice across Kapauku territory. The name "Kapauku" was given them by neighboring groups to the south, and the Moni Papuans, their neighbors to the north, call them "Ekari," but they call themselves "Me," which means "the people."

LOCATION. The Kapauku occupy an ecologically diverse region of the west-central highlands, between 135°25′ and 137° E and 3°25′ and 4°10′ S. Most of the region is above 1,500 meters, with three large lakes (Paniai, Tage, and Tigi), and five vegetation zones, including much tropical rain forest. Rainfall is plentiful and the average daily temperature ranges from 20° C to 60° C.

DEMOGRAPHY. In the 1960s, the Kapauku population was estimated at about 45,000; today they number about 100,000.

LINGUISTIC AFFILIATION. The Kapauku language (Ekagi) is classified within the Ekagi-Wodani-Moni Family of Papuan languages.

History and Cultural Relations

There is little information available regarding the history of the Kapauku prior to European contact, but they have long been horticulturalists (both intensive and extensive) and traders in the region. An important intertribal trade network linking the south coast of New Guinea to the interior ran directly through Kapauku territory, bringing the people of the region into contact with peoples and goods from far beyond their own territorial borders. European contact with the Kapauku did not occur until 1938, when a Dutch government post was established at Paniai Lake. It was quickly abandoned with the Japanese invasion of New Guinea. In 1946 the post was reestablished, and a few Catholic and Protestant missionaries returned to the area.

Settlements

The Kapauku village settlement is a loose cluster of about fifteen dwellings, typically housing about 120 people. Houses are not oriented to one another in any formal plan, as individuals are free to build wherever they please, as long as proper title or lease is held to the piece of land upon which the house is to be built. Dwellings consist, minimally, of a large house (*owa*), an elevated structure with a space beneath in which to shelter domesticated pigs. This building is divided into halves separated by a plank partition. The front half is the *emaage*, or men's dormitory. The back section is subdivided into *kugu*, or individual "apartments," one for each woman and her children. If the *owa* is insufficient to provide space for wives and children, outbuildings (called *tone*) are added.

Economy

Leopold Pospisil, the leading authority on the Kapauku, labels their economy as "primitive capitalism" characterized by the pursuit of wealth in the form of cowrie shell money, status distinctions based on such wealth, and an ethic of individualism.

SUBSISTENCE AND COMMERCIAL ACTIVITIES. Kapauku subsistence is based on the sweet potato, to which about 90 percent of cultivated land is devoted, and pig husbandry. Sweet potatoes are grown both for human consumption and to feed the pigs that, through sales, are a basic source of income and wealth. Commonly grown, but constituting a far smaller portion of the diet,

---

◆ **Papuan languages**
Also called Non-Austronesian languages, these number over 700 and are found mostly in New Guinea, the Bismarck Archipelago, and Bougainville.

are a spinach-like green (*idaja*), bananas, and taro. In the densely populated Kamu Valley, hunting is of small importance due to a paucity of large game animals, but it is indulged in by men as sport. Edible fish are absent from the lakes, but crayfish, dragonfly larvae, certain types of beetles, and frogs augment the diet, as do rats and bats. Farming is done both on the mountain slopes and in the valleys. Upland gardens are given over to the extensive cultivation of sweet potatoes, with long fallow periods between plantings. In the valleys a more intensive method is followed, using both mixed cropping and crop rotation. Households will generally cultivate at least one of each type of garden.

INDUSTRIAL ARTS. Kapauku manufacture is limited and, for the most part, not specialized. Net bags, for utilitarian and for decorative purposes, are made from woven tree bark, as are the armbands and necklaces worn by both men and women. Also made from this bark are women's aprons. Kapauku also manufacture stone axes and knives, flint chips, and grinding stones. From bamboo they make knives for the carving of pork and for surgical use. Other carving tools are fashioned from rat teeth and bird claws, and agricultural tools include weeding, planting, and harvesting sticks. Weaponry consists of bows and arrows, the latter of which may be tipped with long blades of bamboo.

TRADE. Trade is carried out intra- and interregionally and intertribally, with trade links extending to the Mimika people of the coast. The two most important trade commodities are pigs and salt. Trade is generally conducted in shell currency, pigs, or extensions of credit, and the bulk of trading occurs during pig feasts and at the pig markets. Barter is a relatively unimportant means by which goods may be transferred. All distributions of food incur a debt on the part of each recipient to repay in kind to the giver. Pospisil notes that the Kapauku are lively participants in the selling of pigs and pork. Shell money (and sometimes an obligation to provide pork) is required in payment to a shaman for the performance of magic.

DIVISION OF LABOR. There is a sexual division of labor. Tasks held to be the exclusive province of men include the planning of agricultural production, digging ditches, making garden beds, felling trees, building fences, planting and harvesting bananas, tobacco, chili peppers, and *apuu* (a particular variety of yam), while the burning of gardens, planting sugarcane, manioc, squash, and maize, as well as the harvesting of

sugarcane, manioc, and ginger, are preferentially but not necessarily done by males. Exclusively female tasks include the planting of sweet potatoes and *jatu* (an edible grass, *Setaria palmifolia*) and weeding. Other tasks, such as planting and weeding taro and harvesting sweet potatoes, are usually done by women. All other tasks relating to agriculture are carried out by members of both sexes. The gathering of crayfish, water beetles, tadpoles, dragonfly larvae, and frogs is largely the task of women; the hunting of large game is an infrequent enterprise and is done only by men. Small game is hunted by young men and boys. Pigs and chickens, while usually owned by males, are tended by women or adolescent children, but only males are allowed to kill and butcher them. The weaving of utilitarian net bags is a woman's job, while the production of the more ornate and colorful decorative bags is the province of males.

LAND TENURE. A particular piece of land is the property of the house owner, always male, with use rights accorded to members of his household. Sons inherit land from their fathers. Ownership implies rights of alienation of the land as well as usufruct rights.

Kinship

KIN GROUPS AND DESCENT. Kapauku reckon descent along both maternal and paternal lines, but villages are patrilineal and exogamous, with postmarital residence generally patrilocal. The most important Kapauku kinship group is the sib, a named, ideally exogamous, totemic, patrilineal group whose members share a belief in a common apical ancestor. Two or more sibs group into loosely united phratries that have common totemic taboos but are not exogamous. Many of the sibs are further split into moieties. Kinship ties with other lineages (through affines) give rise to larger, political amalgamations known as "confederations."

KINSHIP TERMINOLOGY. Kapauku kinship terminology is of the Iroquois type, but it diverges in the way in which parallel and cross cousins are differentiated: the sex of the nearest and the most distant link connecting the individual to his or her cousin determines cross- or parallel-cousin status. Kapauku kinship terms differentiate among paternal and maternal relatives, affinal and consanguineal relatives, and generationally.

Marriage and Family

MARRIAGE. Marriage is ideally arranged between the families of the prospective groom and brothers and mother of the prospective bride. The

The Kapauku live in the central highlands of western New Guinea.

◆ **usufruct**
The right to use land or property without actually owning it.

Kapauku

Kapauku leadership is based on personal influence, developed through the accumulation of wealth in shells and pigs, particularly through sponsoring pig feasts.

♦ clan, sib
A unilineal descent group in which people claim descent from a common ancestor but cannot demonstrate this descent.

preferences of the woman are considered secondary to the possibility of collecting a high bride-price but, in practice, her mother may set a forbiddingly high bride-price to discourage an unacceptable suitor. Elopements, while considered improper, occur with some frequency. In such cases the families of the eloping couple will likely accept the union by negotiating a bride-price after the fact. Courtship is often conducted in the context of the pig feast, when young men and women arrive at the host village from neighboring villages to dance and to be seen by members of the opposite sex. Premarital sex, while not approved of because of its possible negative effect on a woman's bride-price, is generally not punished. Premarital pregnancy, however, is severely disapproved. Divorce involves the return of bride-price, and the children generally remain with their mother until they reach the age of about 7, at which time they join their father's village. Polygyny, as an indicator of the husband's ability to pay multiple bride-prices, is the ideal. A widow is expected to remarry within a suitable period following the death of her husband, unless she is quite old or very sick, but the levirate is not assumed.

DOMESTIC UNIT. The household consists, minimally, of a nuclear family, but it more commonly also includes consanguineal or affinal kinsmen and their wives and children as well. In the case of wealthy and prestigious men, there may also be apprentices or political supporters and their wives and children. The household is the basic Kapauku unit of residence and, to a large extent, of production and consumption. Within the household, the house owner is titular head, responsible for organizing production activities and maintaining cooperation among the male household members. However, each married male has sole authority over the affairs of his wife or wives and his offspring, an authority which even the head of household cannot usurp.

INHERITANCE. Personal items, such as bows and arrows, penis sheaths, etc., are interred or otherwise left with the corpse of the deceased. Land and accrued wealth is inherited by males through the paternal line, ideally by the deceased's first-born son. If there is no son, a man's eldest brother inherits. Women do not inherit land.

SOCIALIZATION. Children learn adult roles through observation and by specific training. Boys leave their mothers' apartments at the age of about 7 to live in the men's dormitory, at which time they are explicitly exposed to the expected adult male behaviors. There is no male initiation ceremony. Girls, upon achieving their menarche,

undergo a brief period (two days, two nights) of semiseclusion in a menstrual hut during the time of their first two menstruations. During this time they are instructed in the responsibilities and skills of adulthood by close female relatives. After these periods of seclusion, girls put aside the skirtlike apparel of childhood and begin to wear the bark-thong wrap of adulthood.

Sociopolitical Organization

SOCIAL ORGANIZATION. The Kapauku patrilineage is a nonlocalized grouping whose membership claims descent from a common apical ancestor. Its dispersed character makes it inutile for political purposes; rather, its functions pertain to the regulation of marriage, the establishment of interpersonal obligations of support (both personal and economic), and religion. The sib establishes shared totemic taboos that involve its members in relations of mutual ritual obligation, particularly in the matter of redressing taboo violations. Most day-to-day rights and obligations are incurred within the localized patrilineal group; it is to members of this group that an individual will turn for assistance in amassing the bride-wealth necessary for marriage, as well as for allies in conflicts arising with outsiders. Within the village, households are relatively autonomous, as each household head is able to call on fellow members for support in economic and ritual endeavors.

POLITICAL ORGANIZATION. Kapauku leadership is based on personal influence, developed through the accumulation of wealth in shells and pigs, particularly through sponsoring pig feasts. A headman (*tonowi*) uses his prestige and wealth to induce the compliance of others, particularly through the extension or refusal of credit. Again, the principle of organization is based upon the tracing of at least putative kinship ties, and the larger the group of individuals united in a political unit, the more these ties are based on tradition rather than demonstrable links. The most inclusive politically organized group is the confederacy, which consists of two or more localized lineages that may or may not belong to the same sib. Such groups unite for defense as well as for offense against nonmember groups. The leader of the strongest lineage is also the leader of the confederacy, and as such this leader is responsible for adjudicating disputes to avoid the possibility of intraconfederacy feuding. He is equally responsible for representing the confederacy in dealings and dispute settlement with outsiders, deciding upon the necessity of war, and negotiating terms of peace with hostile groups. Leadership is ostensibly the province of men only, but in practice considerable influence may be wielded by women.

SOCIAL CONTROL. Social control is effected in Kapauku local groups by inducement rather than by force. The primary form of inducement is the extension or withdrawal of credit. Since a headman's supporters are tied to him through his economic largess, the threat of a withdrawal of credit, or of a premature demand for repayment, provides strong inducement for others to accede to the headman's wishes. Sanctions such as public scolding or shooting an arrow into a miscreant's thigh are common, but in such cases the party being punished has the opportunity to fight back. Kin-based obligations to seek vengeance for the death of a lineage member are often invoked. Less frequently, to punish sorcerers, ostracism or death may be inflicted.

CONFLICT. Kapauku do not care for war, but members of a lineage are obligated to avenge the death of their kin. Warfare almost never occurs below the level of the confederacy, and it is most frequently occasioned by divorce. Wars are fought exclusively with bows and arrows. At the more localized level, disputes over economic interests or factional splits between two powerful headmen may lead to outbreaks of hostility to the point of violence. Such occasions may require the intervention of confederacy headmen.

Religion and Expressive Culture

RELIGIOUS BELIEFS. The Kapauku believe that the universe was created by Ugatame, who has predetermined all that occurs or has occurred within it. Ugatame is not, strictly speaking, anthropomorphized, although a creation myth—in which disease and mortality were first brought to the Kapauku—attributes to Ugatame the combined characters of a young woman and a tall young man. Ugatame dwells beyond the sky and is manifested in, but is not identical to, the sun and the moon. It is believed that, along with the physical universe, Ugatame created a number of spirits. These spirits, essentially incorporeal, frequently appear to Kapauku in the form of shadows among the trees, which can be heard to make scratching or whistling sounds. Less commonly, they will appear in dreams or visions, at times assuming human form. They can be enlisted by the dreamer or visionary as guardians and helpers, for good or for ill. The souls of the dead can similarly be persuaded to help their surviving kin.

RELIGIOUS PRACTITIONERS. Magical-religious practitioners are of two classes: shamans (who practice magic for good purposes) and sorcerers (who practice "black magic"). Both men and women can become shamans or sorcerers through the acquisition of spirit helpers in dreams or visions and through the successful (as gauged by perceived results) use of magic. The shaman practices curative and preventive magic, while the sorcerer is concerned with causing harm to others (through illness, death, or economic failure). Ghouls are older women whose souls have been replaced during sleep by rapacious spirits hungry for the taste of human flesh. The ghoul, by all appearances a normal woman during the day, travels abroad in the night to dig up the corpses of her possessing spirit's victims and make a feast of their flesh. Women believed to be possessed in this way are not killed, for their death would simply release the possessing spirit to find a new hostess. Rather, ghouls are held to be the helpers of sorcerers, whose black magic is held responsible for the women's condition. It is the sorcerer's magic that must be countered, or the sorcerer must be killed, to stop the depredations of a ghoul.

CEREMONIES. One of the most important Kapauku ceremonies is the *juwo*, or pig feast. This begins with a series of rituals associated with the construction of a dance house and feasting houses, after which follows a period of nightly dances, attended by people from villages throughout the area. After about three months a final feast is held wherein the sponsors slaughter many pigs and pork is distributed or sold. During this final feast day, trade in items of manufacture is also conducted.

ARTS. Visual arts are not heavily represented in Kapauku culture, apart from the decorative net bags made by the men and the armbands and necklaces worn as bodily adornment. Dances, as part of the pig feast, are frequent. There are two principal dances, the *waita tai* and the *tuupe*. The *ugaa*, which is a song that begins with barking cheers, is followed by an individual's extemporaneous solo composition, the lyrics of which may contain gossip, local complaints, or a proposal of marriage.

MEDICINE. Illness is attributed to sorcerers or the spirits. Cures are accomplished by a shaman, who seeks a diagnosis and treatment from a spirit helper. Treatment includes the recitation of spells or prayers, the manipulation of magical plants, purification through the washing of body parts in water, and, at times, the extraction of bits of foreign matter from the body of the victim. Should an individual believe that he or she may be the

Magical-religious practitionars of two classes: shamans (who practice magic for good purposes) and sorcerers (who practice "black magic").

target of sorcery, a preventive cure may be sought before the actual onset of illness.

DEATH AND AFTERLIFE.   Death, regardless of the outward cause, is thought always to be caused by sorcerers or spirits. The soul goes to spend its days in the forest, but it returns to the village at night to assist its surviving kin or to seek vengeance in the case of wrongful death. There is no concept of an afterworld, in the sense of some "other" place in which the dead dwell. A principal concern of Kapauku funerary practices is the enlistment of the soul of the departed as guardian of its surviving kin. The more beloved or prestigious the deceased, the greater the care taken, through burial practices, to tempt them to such a role. The head is left exposed, sheltered under a cover of branches, but provided with a window. Cremation for fallen and unclaimed enemies and complete interment for those of little social status constitute the lower range of funerary attention.

Bibliography

Pospisil, Leopold (1958). *Kapauku Papuans and Their Law*. Yale University Publications in Anthropology, no. 54. New Haven, Conn.

Pospisil, Leopold (1960). "The Kapauku Papuans and Their Kinship System." *Oceania*, 30:188–205.

Pospisil, Leopold (1963). *Kapauku Papuan Economy*. Yale University Publications in Anthropology, no. 67. New Haven, Conn. Reprint. 1972. New Haven, Conn.: Human Relations Area Files.

Pospisil, Leopold (1978). *The Kapauku Papuans of West New Guinea*. 2nd ed. New York: Holt, Rinehart & Winston.

—NANCY GRATTON

KIRIBATI

Ethnonyms: Gilbertese (Gilbert Islands), I-Kiribati, Tungaru

Orientation

IDENTIFICATION.   Almost all of the citizens of Kiribati have at least some I-Kiribati ancestors and have inherited land rights in the Gilbert Islands. The indigenous inhabitants of Banaba (Ocean Island) speak a Gilbertese dialect and practice a variant of Gilbertese culture but consider themselves a separate people politically. Most of the Banabans have lived on Rabi Island in Fiji since 1945. Another Gilbertese dialect is spoken on Nui in Tuvalu. The Gilbert Islands were named in honor of Thomas Gilbert, a British captain whose ship sighted some of the islands after transporting convicts to Australia in 1788. In default of a generally acceptable indigenous name, it was decided at the time of independence to adopt "Kiribati" (pronounced "kiribass"), the local respelling of "Gilberts," for the new nation. The poetic "Tungaru" usually connotes the ancestors and their savage or superhuman feats.

LOCATION.   The Gilberts comprise sixteen inhabited coral reef islands and atolls between 3° N and 3° S and between 173° and 177° E. The territory of the Republic of Kiribati also includes the raised coral island of Banaba, about 400 kilometers west of the Gilberts, and the Phoenix and Line Islands lying as much as 2,800 kilometers to the east. The average annual rainfall diminishes from north to south. The islands south of the equator and Banaba suffer from periodic droughts.

DEMOGRAPHY.   According to the 1985 census, Kiribati had a total population of 63,883. The average population density for the Gilbert Islands, which have a combined area of 279 square kilometers, was 219 persons per square kilometer. The growth rate averaged 2.0 percent per annum in the 6½ years between censuses. A third of the population was enumerated in the urbanized area of South Tarawa.

LINGUISTIC AFFILIATION.   I-Kiribati and Banabans speak a single language, usually known as Gilbertese. Linguists agree that Gilbertese belongs to the Oceanic Branch of the Austronesian languages, and its closest relatives are the other Nuclear Micronesian languages: Trukese, Ponapean, Kosraean (Kusaian), and Marshallese. The more distant connections of Nuclear Micronesian within Oceanic Austronesian are still being debated, but they seem to point toward the southern Solomon Islands and Vanuatu, with the languages of San Cristobal and Malaita as perhaps the strongest candidates. The pioneer American missionary, Hiram Bingham, Jr., devised a written form of Gilbertese based on the Latin alphabet that is still in general use, having undergone only minor modifications.

History and Cultural Relations

On linguistic and archaeological grounds, it is likely that voyagers from southern Melanesia arrived in the Gilberts long before A.D. 600, the earliest radiocarbon date obtained up to now. Kiribati language and culture show signs of borrowing from western Polynesia at some time after the islands were settled. The political and social structure of all the islands except for Butaritari-Makin and Banaba was forcibly unified, possibly in the seventeenth century, when armies led by Kaitu, Beru, and Uakeia of Nikunau introduced the meetinghouse organization. Regular contacts with Europeans and Americans began when merchant ships sailing new routes across the Pacific, New England whalers, and exploring expeditions discovered or rediscovered all the islands between 1765 and 1826. Resident traders bought coconut oil from 1846 to the 1870s and then switched to copra, which remains Kiribati's sole agricultural export. A British protectorate was proclaimed over the Gilberts and their Polynesian neighbors, the Ellice Islands, in 1892. The Japanese occupation of the Gilberts early in World War II ended with an American victory in the "particularly bloody battle at Tarawa" (as Richard Overy has aptly termed it) fought in November 1943. The phosphate mine on Banaba provided most of the colony's revenue and employment for its people from 1900 until the deposits were exhausted in the year of independence; I-Kiribati still mine phosphate on the neighboring independent island of Nauru. Since 1967, the Marine Training School has made it possible for many young men to get jobs as seamen on West German ships and to add greatly to their families' incomes through remittances. Four years after the Ellice Islands had separated from the colony to become the state of Tuvalu, the Gilberts also became independent as the Republic of Kiribati on 12 July 1979.

Settlements

Precolonial villages were social and political units centered on a meetinghouse (*te mwaneaba*). The settlement pattern was one of dispersed hamlets on descent-group lands, which usually ran across islets from west to east. Around 1900 the Resident Commissioner and government agents ordered villages consolidated along a road running parallel to the western (leeward) shore of each inhabited islet, even if that meant forcing people to move off their hereditary lands. They also compelled the islanders to build houses according to a uniform pattern. A house consists essentially of a roof covered with coconut- or pandanus-leaf thatch and supported by four or six wooden posts. Unlike most precolonial houses, the new-style ones have raised floors of split coconut-leaf midribs and can comfortably accommodate only one nuclear family. Following a colonial regulation, each family still builds separate houses for sleeping and eating. In the 1980s some relatively affluent people, such as the families of merchant seamen, and members of clubs organized for that purpose were erecting cement-block houses with galvanized-iron roofs and facilities for catching rainwater. Large meetinghouses are still constructed in more or less the traditional style, not only as sites for village councils and festivities but also by church congregations and neighborhoods.

Economy

SUBSISTENCE AND COMMERCIAL ACTIVITIES. The only crop that I-Kiribati cultivate regularly is the atoll taro *Cyrtosperma chamissonis*, which is grown in gardens dug down to the level of the freshwater lens or in natural swamps. The slower-growing varieties are often fertilized for years with mixtures of humus and leaf compost sprinkled into "pots" of plaited coconut fronds or braided pandanus leaves, until the leaves are as much as 3.5 meters high. The huge corms that develop as a result of this treatment are suitable for feasts and formal presentations. Smaller varieties, allowed to clone and not usually fertilized, are an everyday food on the northern islands. The only other important native vegetable foods are tree crops—coconuts, pandanus, and, mainly in the north, breadfruit. The coconut palm is also the source of toddy, the juice of the unopened flower spathe which is collected in a coconut shell as a fresh drink, boiled into molasses, or allowed to ferment. The numerous fishing methods include trolling behind a canoe furnished with a sail or an outboard motor, unrolling a line with baited hook into deep water from a smaller paddling canoe, catching flying fish with a coconut-leaf torch or kerosene lantern and a scoop net, searching the holes and pools of the nighttime reef with a scoop net and machete, netting on the reef at high tide, angling from the edge of the reef, and trapping fish behind a stone weir. Domestic animals, all of which are eaten, include dogs, chickens, and introduced pigs.

INDUSTRIAL ARTS. There are part-time builders of canoes, houses, and meetinghouses in every village. These men, like the few remaining navigators, enjoy respect and deference, but they receive no pay except their food while at work and perhaps a waist cloth when the job is finished.

TRADE. Most adults hold shares in their village cooperative store, which is affiliated with a national federation. There are many even smaller general stores belonging to individuals, partnerships, and clubs. Women sell or give away all of their husbands' catches of tuna, flying fish, and shark that exceed household requirements.

DIVISION OF LABOR. Men cultivate and harvest *Cyrtosperma* in the south, where the corms

The Kiribati have inherited land rights in the Gilbert Islands, sixteen inhabited coral reef islands and atolls.

♦ toddy
Palm wine, the fermented sap of the palmyra (Borassus flabellifer) and other palms, such as date, coconut, or sago.

♦ weir
A wall of sticks or rocks placed in a body of water, river, or stream to prevent fish from passing.

A good deal of personal independence is conceded even to young Kiribati children, who theoretically have the right to own property and to decide with whom they will live.

are a luxury food. In the north women do most of the routine fertilizing, and the custom that only a woman may dig up a corm is used as an argument for marriage. The I-Kiribati also believe that only men should climb trees. Men do the bulk of the fishing; women collect shellfish and catch land crabs, but occasionally they engage in other kinds of fishing as well. Work with leaves is restricted to women, who make mats, baskets, and thatch and produce cordage from fiber obtained from coconut husks. Men build houses and canoes and make smaller wooden objects. Women normally fetch water, cook meals, and wash clothes. The division of labor is not rigid, but persons who habitually perform tasks associated with the opposite sex are regarded as having changed their gender identity, like North American Indian *berdaches*.

LAND TENURE. Both men and women inherit land rights from both parents, rights that are inseparable from one's status as a blood relative and a member of the community. The colonial administration abrogated the old rules, under which sons received larger shares than daughters and an eldest son (and sometimes an eldest daughter) more than younger children, in favor of an equal division. Parents customarily divide their lands in a way that assures each of their children of rights in as many of the parental descent groups as possible. If someone dies without leaving natural or adopted children, his land will be divided among his siblings or, lacking these, will revert to the estate of his father and mother. Most of the lands (though not the *Cyrtosperma* gardens) on Butaritari and Makin are the joint property of descent groups, necessitating a system of annual or weekly turns for collecting coconuts. A widespread Micronesian distinction between provisional titleholders or caretakers (who actually work the land and utilize its products) and residual titleholders (whose claims must be acknowledged by gifts and assistance) is the basis for several social relationships, such as those between brother and married sister and between guardian and ward.

Kinship

KIN GROUPS AND DESCENT. Descent, like inheritance, is ambilineal. Everyone is affiliated with the descent groups (ramages) of several ancestors, although he or she is most active in a group associated with his or her own or the parents' place of residence. Before the introduction of lands registers, inactive memberships tended to lapse after a few generations, especially if the link to the group was a female ancestor. Members of a

descent group who together with their spouses and children occupied a communal dwelling or hamlet on its estate constituted a residential group (*te kaainga*, a term used for a descent group conceived of as a landholding corporation and also for the land itself). Each descent group has traditionally been associated with a place in the meetinghouse (*teinaki*, literally "a vertical row of thatch," or *te boti*).

KINSHIP TERMINOLOGY. Cousin terminology is Hawaiian-type: everyone with whom one shares an ancestor an equal number of generations removed can be referred to by the terms for "sibling of the same sex" or "sibling of the opposite sex." Other cognatic and affinal relatives are also classified by generation. Native kinship terms are not used in address.

Marriage and Family

MARRIAGE. First marriages, in particular, ideally are arranged by the parents or at least require their consent, but elopements are becoming more common. In theory, persons who share an ancestor within three generations, or who trace descent from a more distant common ancestor but themselves belong to different generations, are forbidden to marry. In practice, reaction to a proposed marriage that would join together distant relatives depends on whether the immediate families of the young people have been treating one another as kinsfolk. Some families still follow the old custom of rejoicing publicly when a bride has demonstrated her virginity. Most young married people reside with the husbands' parents until they are considered ready for independent life. Until recently, they were also expected to reside permanently on land the husband had inherited either through his father or through his mother. A man who agreed to live with his wife's kin was thought to yield much of his authority over his household. A permanently separated couple is regarded as divorced by the community if not by the church. Once children have been born, kin on both sides will put pressure on the spouses to reconcile or will try to persuade an unmarried sibling to act as stepparent. Sororal polygyny is dying out.

DOMESTIC UNITS. The people who cook and eat meals together are considered a family. The teenage boys and young unmarried men of the neighborhood often sleep in an unoccupied house but eat with their families. A nuclear family or a currently unmarried woman and her children are ordinarily the minimal family units. As their own children grow up and leave home, couples often begin rearing a second family of grandchildren or wards. Other helpful or dependent kinsfolk may be present as well. Families outside South Tarawa average 5.8 persons.

INHERITANCE. Parents leave their house to one of their children, often when they retire to stay with each of their children in turn. Portable artifacts are probably distributed informally, but large canoes tend to be treated like land. Items of esoteric knowledge, which are considered a kind of personal property, may be bestowed on a favorite child, on another young relative, or even on an outsider.

SOCIALIZATION. A good deal of personal independence is conceded even to young children, who at least in theory have the right to own property and to decide with whom they will live. Small children are treated indulgently by everyone, even when they act aggressively. Older children are expected to help with household tasks, to show respect for senior kinsfolk, and to refrain from calling attention to themselves when adults are present. Physical punishment is acceptable once a child has reached the age of reason. Threats, ridicule, and scary stories about punitive agents from outside the family are commoner sanctions, however.

Sociopolitical Organization

Kiribati is a democracy with a popularly elected president and House of Assembly.

SOCIAL ORGANIZATION. Chiefs were present in the central and northern Gilberts, but on several islands no single chief managed to hold undisputed power for very long. The most stratified societies in the late precolonial and early colonial periods were Butaritari-Makin and Abemama, which had conquered the neighboring islands of Aranuka and Kuria. The Butaritari-Makin hierarchy, which resembled those of other Micronesian societies to the north, was headed by a high chief who was a focus for redistributive activities. Below the high chief and his siblings and children were aristocrats, commoners, and descendants of strangers from other islands. Since the 1970s life-styles have reflected differences in family incomes, even in the villages.

POLITICAL ORGANIZATION. The government of the republic provides a system of courts and health, educational, and agricultural services on the national and island levels. Elected island councils are responsible for repairing roads, maintaining schools, granting permission to build new houses, and filling some off-island jobs. Lands courts approve the inheritance and transfer of real property and resolve disputes over boundaries and the rights of coowners. Especially since independence, many of the powers of the island councils have been assumed by unofficial bodies of village elders that developed out of the traditional councils of heads of descent groups. The elders legislate on matters ranging from trips by the local soccer team to the prohibition of alcohol. They punish violators with fines, beatings, and occasionally exile. Wider consensus is reached by inviting delegates from other villages to a joint meeting or, as on Nonouti in the late 1960s, by organizing a single council for the whole island.

SOCIAL CONTROL. The Kiribati ethos holds that an adult should be prepared to fight if challenged and be ready to avenge an injury or insult against himself or a member of his family. On the other hand, the wisdom and control over the passions that comes with age gives some older people the status of acknowledged peacemakers. Any assembly is thought to assert social norms over the selfish or shortsighted impulses of individuals. The fear of gossip and of secret or open mockery by neighbors are commonplace checks on deviant behavior.

CONFLICT. In the past, villages and intervillage factions fought to avenge offenses, to seize land, and to gain a chieftainship for their candidate. Wars became more destructive in the nineteenth century, when steel weapons and firearms were widely available and the activities of labor recruiters, traders, and missionaries weakened the social order and created new causes for conflict. In the presidential election preceding independence, the voters of Kiribati decided against having an army.

Religion and Expressive Culture

RELIGIOUS BELIEFS. The forerunners of the present-day Kiribati Protestant Church (K.P.C.), the American Board of Commissioners for Foreign Missions and the London Missionary Society, arrived in the northern and southern islands, respectively, in 1857 and 1870. The French Roman Catholic fathers of the Order of the Sacred Heart began work on Nonouti in 1888. Catholics (53 percent of the indigenous population) are in the majority from Tarawa northward. The K.P.C. (41 percent) holds a near-monopoly on Arorae and Tamana and retains majorities on a few of the other southern islands. About 2½ percent of the I-Kiribati adhere to the Baha'i faith. Mormons, Seventh-Day Adventists, and members of other Christian sects make up the remainder of the population. A good deal of social, recreational, and even economic activity centers on the churches.

RELIGIOUS PRACTITIONERS. The expatriate (mostly French) Catholic clergy has been

The Kiribati ethos holds than an adult should be prepared to fight if challenged and to avenge an injury or insult against himself or a family member.

largely replaced by I-Kiribati priests and nuns. Local catechists conduct services on most islands between occasional visits by a priest. K.P.C. ministers are all I-Kiribati (except for a few from Tuvalu) but do not serve on their home islands. The priests of the old pagan religion interpreted omens and made offerings to deities that descended from time to time onto pillars of coral limestone and other shrines or took animal forms. Spirit mediums are probably still active, although they are possessed by recently introduced supernaturals and are regarded with great ambivalence. I-Kiribati deities (some with western Polynesian names) were believed to have been ancestors of descent groups that obeyed their taboos and relied on them for protection. Their associations with animals and natural phenomena gave them significance for the community as a whole.

CEREMONIES. Early in the colonial period, indigenous dancing was permitted only on Christmas, New Year's, and the Queen's birthday. These holidays, with Independence Day replacing the Queen's birthday and Easter and Youth Day added, are still occasions for public feasting and dancing. Catholics celebrate the major feasts of the church in the same ways and sometimes by mass visits to their coreligionists in other villages.

ARTS. The patterns of plaited sleeping mats, created by alternating light- and dark-colored strips of dried pandanus leaf, show off women's esthetic sense as well as their technical skills. Durable ornaments are made of spondylus, mother-of-pearl, and marine snail shells; in former times, dolphin, whale, and human teeth were also used. Kiribati sitting and standing dances, accompanied by singing and by clapping hands or beating on a box, are famous. Songs are still composed by traditional methods, although usually on a Western tonal scale.

MEDICINE. Illness is generally attributed to material causes, although attacks by ghosts, retribution for offending a parent or other superior, sorcery, soul loss, and divine punishment are advanced as explanations in particular cases. Indigenous curing methods include the use of proprietary herbal medicines and systems of massage and cautery.

DEATH AND AFTERLIFE. Nineteenth-century travelers reported that the body was kept in the house for three to nine days and even longer if the deceased had been prominent. Some months after burial the skull was removed and thereafter oiled and offered food and tobacco. Mission influence has been opposed to drawn-out funerals and

**CEREMONIAL
DANCE**

*Kiribati men and women performing a dance at a ceremony, wearing traditional headbands and sashes. Kiribati.
(Charles & Josette
Lenars/Corbis)*

of course to the custom of keeping a relative's skull on a shelf or carrying it around. The wake is still attended by a large number of kinsfolk, who contribute *Cyrtosperma* corms and money and eulogize the departed. Burial is in a village cemetery or in a grave next to the house. Despite strong Christian beliefs in an afterlife of rewards or punishments, people remember the old story that the god Nakaa welcomes souls at the north end of the Gilberts.

Bibliography

Geddes, William H. (1977). "Social Individualisation on Tabiteuea Atoll." *Journal of the Polynesian Society* 86:371–392.

Macdonald, Barrie (1982). *Cinderellas of the Empire: Towards a History of Kiribati and Tuvalu.* Canberra: Australian National University Press.

Silverman, Martin G. (1971). *Disconcerting Issue: Meaning and Struggle in a Resettled Pacific Community.* Chicago: University of Chicago Press.

Watters, Ray, and Nancy J. Pollock, project directors (1983). *Atoll Economy: Social Change in Kiribati and Tuvalu.* 6 vols. Canberra: Australian National University Press.

—BERND LAMBERT

MALAITA

Ethnonyms: 'Are'are, Fataleka, Kwaio, Kwara'ae, Langalanga, Lau, Sa'a, To'aba'ita

Orientation

IDENTIFICATION. Malaita is one of six large islands in the double chain that forms the Solomon Islands, formerly the British Solomon Islands Protectorate. As the most populous island in the Solomons, Malaita has long been a source of plantation labor, and in earlier decades its people were famed and feared for their violent resistance to European invasion. The island remains noteworthy for its strong cultural conservatism.

LOCATION. Running northwest to southeast and being about 160 kilometers long and up to 40 kilometers wide, Malaita lies at 9° S and 161° E. The island is mountainous (rising to 1,540 meters) and comprised of rain forest, with lagoons along parts of both coastlines. The island of Maramasike is separated from Malaita proper by a narrow channel.

DEMOGRAPHY. Malaita had a population in 1986 of about 80,000, with some 20,000 more Malaitans living elsewhere in the Solomons.

LINGUISTIC AFFILIATION. Malaita languages fall into the Malaita-San Cristobal Group

of the Southeast Solomonic (Oceanic Austronesian) languages. Southeast Solomonic may turn out to fall within a subgroup of Eastern Oceanic languages, along with North-central New Hebridean, Fijian, Polynesian, and Nuclear Micronesian languages; but so far the evidence is inconclusive, clouded by the shared retention in all these languages of many Proto-Oceanic features. Malaita is divided into a series of languages or dialects (mainly running in stripes across the island) although their precise relationship is not yet established. The most recent subgrouping establishes a subgroup of Northern Malaita languages, consisting of a northern dialect cluster (To'aba'ita, Baelelea, Baegu, Lau, Fataleka), Kwara'ae (with 18,000 speakers, the largest language group), Langalanga, and Kwaio. (There is some evidence that the latter two, along with two smaller language groups, form a separate Central Malaita Group.) 'Are'are and Sa'a (spoken on Maramasike) seem to form a subgroup with the Makira (San Cristobal) languages, although on cultural and other grounds a closer affinity of 'Are'are with the Malaita peoples to the northwest (Kwaio, etc.) seems likely.

History and Cultural Relations

Malaita was largely avoided in the early whaling and trading period (pre-1860) because of its inhospitable coastline and inhabitants. About 1870, Malaitans began to be kidnapped (and were later indentured) in the labor trade to Queensland, Fiji, Samoa, and New Caledonia plantations, a process notable for violent confrontations and heavy loss of life. Mission enclaves were established at the turn of the century. Pacification of Malaita began in 1909 but was not completed until 1927, after the assassination of a district officer by Kwaio warriors. Malaita was mostly spared the direct ravages of World War II, but laborers working with American troops were central in a postwar anticolonial resistance movement, Maasina ("Marching") Rule, focused on recognition of customary law and the codification of custom, indigenous representation in the process of administration, improved pay, dignity, and working conditions, and communal reorganization along military lines. The Solomon Islands gained independence in 1978, and today Malaitans play many important roles in national life.

Economy

SUBSISTENCE AND COMMERCIAL ACTIVITIES. In bush areas of Malaita, taro was the primary subsistence crop, grown in a continuous

SETTLEMENTS

Very sharp contrasts in ecological adaptation distinguish the "bush" peoples of the Malaita interior from those of the lagoons of the northeast coast (Lau speakers, who also have a colony on Maramasike) and the lagoons of the central west coast (Langalanga speakers). The former, living on islets and on coral platforms dredged from the lagoon floor, specialize in fishing (in the lagoon and the open sea) and in bartering fish and other marine products for root vegetables and forest products offered by peoples of the adjacent mountains. The Langalanga speakers may earlier have had a similar adaptation, but in recent centuries their fishing has been complemented and overshadowed by the specialized production and export or barter of shell valuables. What follows deals primarily with the numerically preponderant "bush" peoples, but it also briefly examines the "saltwater" variants on common cultural themes (the contrast between *tolo* or "bush" and *asi* or "sea" is widely drawn in Malaita languages). In bush areas, settlements were scattered homesteads or tiny hamlets, clustered close enough for collective defense and frequently moved because of pollution violations or gardening cycles. Each settlement mapped out a cosmological pattern in which the men's house above and the menstrual hut below became symbolic mirror images, with domestic houses in between. During the colonial period, missions, labor recruiters, and the government encouraged movements to the coast; and these movements were accelerated by the postwar Maasina Rule anticolonial movement. Nowadays, the Malaita population is mainly concentrated along the coast in substantial villages, except in remaining pagan areas (notably the east Kwaio interior) where old patterns still prevail; large Malaita populations have also resettled around Honiara, with pockets elsewhere in the Solomons.

cycle in forest swiddens. Yams were a secondary subsistence crop, but because they were grown in an annual cycle, they were accorded ritual importance. Plantains and a range of other cultigens and forest products augmented these starchy staples. (The taro plants were devastated by viral and fungal blights after World War II, and sweet potatoes—culturally disvalued but convenient—have become the dominant staple.) Animal protein came from fish, grubs, birds, cuscus, opossums, and other game, as well as domestic pigs. The latter (and their theft and defense) were a focus of cultural attention; the pigs were used mainly in sacrifices, mortuary feasts, bridewealth, and compensation payments. Strung shell beads and dolphin teeth served as mediums of exchange, used in bride-wealth, homicide payments, compensation, and mortuary feasts. Red-shell discs produced in Langalanga (especially the ten-stringed *tafuli'ae* of northern Malaita) were widely used, but Kwaio produce their own white-shell beads, which in standard lengths and combinations (denominations) serve as an all-purpose medium of exchange. For 120 years, Malaitans have been locked into a system of circulating male plantation labor (originally to Queensland, Fiji, Samoa, and New Caledonia, and, in this century, to internal plantations). In the last 20 years, this adaptation has increasingly given way (except for the diehard pagans) to peasant production of copra, cocoa, and livestock, to petty entrepreneurship, and to wage labor in urban settings. Today, Malaitans occupy every rung of a developing class system, ranging from prosperous businesspeople and parliamentarians to a marginalized and violently predatory urban underclass.

INDUSTRIAL ARTS. Traditionally, chipped chert adzes were the primary felling and cutting tools. Other elements of early Malaita technology included pouches and bags woven from bush fibers, river fish and bird nets, intricate fishhooks, and large composite seagoing canoes with caulked planks and high prow and stern. In contrast to the relative elaborateness of their weaponry and some aspects of their maritime technology, Malaita bush peoples specialized in a kind of throwaway tool technology: crudely chipped chert adze blades were used in place of older ground basalt blades; giant bamboo was used for water, cooking, and construction; today, digging sticks are not even fire-hardened (at least among the Kwaio). With highly uneven access to education and Westernization on Malaita during the last forty years, Malaitans now span a technological range from engineers, doctors, and pilots to subsistence cultivators using magic and digging sticks.

TRADE. Precolonial trade systems included the far-flung Langalanga networks, through which shell valuables were traded for pigs, produce, and other items, and the well-organized

♦ **cuscus**
A type of marsupial found in New Guinea and highly prized for its meat and fur.

markets (especially on the northeastern coast) where Lau bartered fish and marine products for taro, yams, *Canarium* almonds, and forest products with interior populations (Baegu, Baelelea, Fataleka, To'aba'ita). Chert for adze blades and other scarce materials seem also to have been traded.

DIVISION OF LABOR. Men and women had complementary roles in the division of labor, with women doing the bulk of everyday garden work, foraging, domestic labor, and child care and men felling trees, fencing land, fishing, and fighting.

LAND TENURE. Primary rights to land are obtained through tracing patrifiliation, but secondary rights are also granted to those with maternal links to ancestors.

Kinship

KIN GROUPS AND DESCENT. Throughout the Malaita interior, descent-based local groups having primary interests in estates in land and primary connections to ancestors are the most important sociopolitical units. Everywhere, the ideal pattern is for virilocal residence and patrifiliation, with children growing up in their father's place and developing a primary attachment there to lands and ancestors. Ideally, then, members of the group should all be connected to the founding ancestors through patrifilial chains (and those who are, are distinguished as "agnates"). However, throughout Malaita, connections with maternal relatives (and, through them, to lands and ancestors) are regarded as very important and complementary to connections to and through paternal relatives. "Nonagnates" are recognized as having secondary rights of residence and land use. Such ties are extended through father's mother, mother's mother, and more distant kin; and ancestors related through such links were commonly propitiated. Life circumstances—uxorilocal residence, parental divorce, or widowhood—can lead children to grow up with maternal kin. When they do, they are accorded de facto rights of residence and land rights as though they were agnates: what matters is commitment to lands, ancestors, and kin and intimate knowledge of a place and its rituals and taboos. Given the ideological emphasis on agnation (at least in some contexts) and countervailing ideologies of symmetric bilaterality, and given the varying statistical composition of groups, it is no wonder that ethnographers have differed in characterizing Malaita social structure. Among the Lau speakers of the lagoons, densely concentrated in large villages, descent groups are quite squarely agnatic. In some parts of Malaita, segmentary ritual and political relationships above the level of local descent-based groups were accorded importance. In the north, eight clusters of descent groups were recognized, with the politically dominant and ritually senior "stem" groups of each cluster connected to one another by putative agnatic links (but with some other groups within each cluster connected to the "stem" group by nonagnatic links). In Kwaio, such higher-level linkages operate only through ritual links between shrines and their priests.

KINSHIP TERMINOLOGY. Kinship terminology ranges from a symmetric Iroquois-type pattern in Kwara'ae (systematically distinguishing cross from parallel kin in the middle three generations according to relative sex of the last connecting links) to a basically Hawaiian-type pattern in Kwaio (broken only by a self-reciprocal mother's brother/sister's child category). Intermediate are systems (such as To'aba'ita) with a partial Omaha-like skewing in which the mother's brother/sister's child category is incorporated into the grandparent/grandchild category (which occurs in all the Malaita terminologies).

Marriage and Family

MARRIAGE. Marriage is generally serially monogamous, although polygyny is possible in some places. Bride-wealth is universal. Prohibitions on marriage generally are bilaterally based, with marriage between close cousins normatively prohibited. As noted previously, postmarital residence was initially virilocal, although in some areas later flexibility in residential attachment was possible. Divorce was possible but difficult because of bride-wealth.

DOMESTIC UNIT. Domestic family groups (prototypically nuclear families but often augmented by widows, bachelors, spinsters, and foster children) are the primary units of production and consumption.

INHERITANCE. Inheritance assigns rights to those who create property and transmits these rights to and through children. Normatively, although sons and daughters inherit rights, sons transmit primary rights to their children and daughters transmit secondary rights. A steward, ideally a senior agnate, acts as a spokesperson for collectively held land and other property.

SOCIALIZATION. Children are highly valued and caringly nurtured, with women having the primary responsibilities for early child care and training. Sexual polarization early separates boys' and girls' life experiences (though there are no

Malaita was largely avoided in the early whaling and trading period (pre-1860) because of its inhospitable coastline and inhabitants.

Blood feuding was endemic on Malaita, with larger-scale warfare infrequent but dramatic and culturally celebrated in epic chants of ancestral deeds.

formal initiations), with boys being much more free to hunt and play and girls beginning early a regimen of hard labor and child care. Boys spend progressively more time with men, stay in men's houses, and participate in ritual.

Sociopolitical Organization

SOCIAL ORGANIZATION. In bush areas, a fierce egalitarianism based on achievement rather than rank traditionally prevailed. However, in some coastal areas (e.g., Lau and Maramasike) ideas of hereditary rank had some currency.

POLITICAL ORGANIZATION. A pervasive ideology on Malaita distinguishes three leadership roles: that of "priest," who acts as the religious officiant of the descent group (see below); that of "warrior-leader" (*ngwane ramo*), a bounty hunter and fighting leader; and that of a secular leader (in the Northern Malaita dialect, *ngwane inoto/inito'o*). Characterizations of the latter range from a hereditary chief (*araha* in Maramasike) to a smallish big-man in the most politically fragmented bush areas, such as Kwaio and northwestern 'Are'are. Other areas combined an ideology that the senior agnate of a descent group acted as its secular leader with a recognition of de facto leadership achieved through entrepreneurial success. In Lau and southeastern 'Are'are, hereditary leaders commanded prestige and had considerable authority in peacemaking and other intergroup relations. The colonial government appointed headmen as agents of administrative control. Partly in counter to this, in the Maasina Rule movement Malaitans put up a hierarchy of chiefs to lead them in an anticolonial struggle. The leaders were imprisoned in 1947, then released and incorporated into the process of gradual, indigenous-led participation in government, culminating in national independence in 1978. Today, Malaita (including Polynesian outliers) forms the Province of Solomon Islands, with a premier and a Provincial Assembly. Interest in "custom" remains strong, even in relatively Westernized areas, and "paramount chiefs" are being given legitimate status, even in bush areas where variant big-man systems prevailed.

SOCIAL CONTROL AND CONFLICT. Blood feuding was endemic on Malaita, with larger-scale warfare infrequent but dramatic and culturally celebrated in epic chants of ancestral deeds. Using bows and arrows, clubs, and spears, warriors challenged one another in direct combat or sometimes launched attacks in force against an enemy group in a fortified refuge, led by a shield-bearing fight leader. More often, killings were stealthy executions to gain vengeance, often on behalf of another group, to collect a bounty of valuables and pigs. Cannibalism was apparently practiced at least sporadically everywhere on Malaita; it seems not to have been primarily motivated by a quest for spiritual power, or even for protein, but rather represented a relegation to animal status of enemies or of social offenders (such as adulterers) whose conduct took them out of the bounds of human society. In northern Malaita, sorcery accusations were a common cause of killings; in central Malaita, sorcery was a less-central theme, and seductions were the most common cause of killings (a puritanical sexual code enjoined the execution of adulterers and often led to the killing by their own kin of young women whose sexuality had been invaded, even by a proposition). Curses and other insults also triggered brawls and killings. Principles of collective accountability in blood feuding often led to the killing of a substitute victim, a close or sometimes distant relative, if the seducer or sorcerer could not be killed himself. A cultural distinction was made (at least among the Kwaio and 'Are'are) between powers of productivity (and associated magic and ritual) and powers of destruction (warfare, theft, vandalism): a kind of uneasy tension existed between groups whose primary commitments were to stability and prosperity (and whose safety lay in their capacity to put up blood money against transgressors) and groups whose ancestors incited and supported killing, theft, and destruction (and whose living was consequently too unstable to allow sustained productivity).

Religion and Expressive Culture

RELIGIOUS BELIEFS. The precolonial religious system on Malaita centered on the propitiation of ancestral spirits (*akalo*, *agalo*, *adalo*) through the consecration and sacrifice of pigs. Each descent group had one or more focal shrines where religious officiants sacrificed; hierarchies of shrines and priesthoods marked higher levels of segmentary connection between groups and bonds to common ancient ancestors. In communities with maritime orientations (Lau, Langalanga, Maramasike), sharks were seen as spirits and were accordingly propitiated. Some Malaita peoples, particularly those in the north and south with maritime orientations, had extensively elaborated cosmologies positing multiple levels of creation and elaborated bodies of myth. Cosmologies and myth were less developed in bush areas, especially in central Malaita. Divination, dreams, and omens provided daily communication with the spirits. When displeased with their descendants, the ancestral shades visited sickness and death on the living; when pleased, they supported and protected them from malevolent "wild" spirits and empowered their efforts (in production and violent deeds) by "*mana*-izing" them. {In Malaita languages, cognates of *mana* were used mainly verbally: "be effective, be potent, be true, be realized" and (speaking of or to ancestors) "support, empower." They were also used as verbal nouns, such as "*mana*-ness," "*mana*-ization," or "truth."} The sacred (*abu*) men's houses and shrines where men symbolically gave birth to spirits through mortuary rites were a mirror image of the dangerous (*abu*) menstrual huts and childbirth areas where women gave birth to infants, a cosmological scheme that was mapped in the spatial layout of settlements. The traditional religious system functions still in pockets of pagan settlement, particularly the mountainous Kwaio and 'Are'are interiors. Elsewhere on Malaita, Christianity (principally the South Sea Evangelical, Catholic, Anglican, and Adventist churches) holds sway. Fundamentalist Christians, in particular, see themselves as being in continuous struggle with the ancestors that are viewed as manifestations of Satan.

RELIGIOUS PRACTITIONERS. Traditionally kin groups had "priests" (in North Malaita, *fataabu*) who took primary responsibility for conducting sacrifices and other rites and maintaining relations with the spirits. Divinitory powers were believed to be quite commonly distributed, but certain persons were thought to have extraordinary powers and were widely sought.

CEREMONIES. The death of an important or sacred person plunged a descent group into an intense and dangerous communication with the dead. This liminal separation from other living people was gradually ended by rites of desacralization and an eventual mortuary feast (north Malaita *maoma*, Kwaio *omea*), which was also an occasion for largess and competition involving large-scale exchanges of prestations (particularly shell valuables and pigs) in the fulfillment of kinship obligation.

ARTS. The most notable artistic achievement on Malaita consisted of panpipe music, with orchestras of eight or more musicians playing matched sets of scaled pipes. The contrapuntal structures of this music are beautiful and complex, using as many as seven or eight melodic voices. In some genres, the panpipers accompanied formations of dancers, and they themselves performed intricate movements while piping. An-

other noteworthy musical genre is epic chanting, in which deeds of ancestors are recounted with harmonized accompaniments. Other musical forms include stamping tubes, Jew's harps, and other flute varieties. The most striking graphic arts took the form of bodily ornaments—women's heirloom jewelry (chest pendants, nose sticks, earrings, necklaces), intricately plated ornamental combs worn by men, arm shells, chest pendants, belts, and bandoliers. Weapons, batons, betel mortars, bowls, and other items were carved and/or decorated with nautilus inlay.

MEDICINE. Magic was highly elaborated, and it followed the sharp cultural separation between productive and destructive powers. Gardening, feast giving, fishing, fighting, and stealing all called for elaborate magic.

DEATH AND AFTERLIFE. Throughout Malaita, the souls of the dead were believed to travel to the land of the dead (associated with a small island off the northwestern tip of Malaita), while their shades hovered about the community, propitiated by the consecration of pigs and placated by purificatory sacrifice. The shades of the dead monitored the strict pollution taboos that compartmentalized menstruation and childbirth and sharply separated men's and women's realms, and they also supervised the strict observance of ritual procedures.

Bibliography

Hogbin, H. Ian (1936). *Experiments in Civilization*. London: Routledge & Kegan Paul.

Ivens, Walter J. (1927). *Melanesians of the South-East Solomons*. London: Kegan Paul.

Ivens, Walter J. (1930). *The Island Builders of the Pacific*. London: Seeley & Service.

Keesing, Roger M. (1982). *Kwaio Religion*. New York: Columbia University Press.

Keesing, Roger M. (1983). *'Elota's Story: The Life and Times of a Solomon Islands Big Man*. New York: Holt, Rinehart & Winston.

Ross, Harold (1972). *Baegu: Social and Ecological Organization on Malaita*. Urbana, Ill.: University of Illinois Press.

—ROGER M. KEESING

MANUS

Ethnonym: Manusian

Orientation

IDENTIFICATION. The terms "Manus" and "Manusian" denote people native to Manus

Manus

Province, Papua New Guinea. Manus also denotes the Titan-speaking people of the coast and offshore islands of the southeastern part of the province, who had the most intense early contact with White colonists. People can refer to each other by their language, village, or local area names, often the same. Also, they can use terms that denote other significant differences. Examples include electoral district names, terms denoting "islanders" (historically fishing and trading people) or "mainlanders" (historically agriculturalists) and terms denoting residents or those who have migrated elsewhere.

LOCATION. Manus Province consists of a mainland (the main island of Manus and the barely separated island of Los Negros) and offshore islands, mostly to the southeast and north. It also includes several islands to the far west, inhabited by a set of ethnically distinct people not discussed here. Manus is in the Admiralty Islands at about 2° S and 147° E. The mainland is about 96 kilometers long and 24 kilometers wide, about 272 kilometers north-northeast of the Madang coast on the main island of New Guinea. It and some larger, volcanic islands are relatively fertile, but many smaller islands are infertile sand cays. The seasons are those of the southeast trade winds (April to October) and the northwestern monsoon (October to April). The monsoon has higher tide levels, greater cloudiness, and frequent storms, but the whole year is hot and wet.

DEMOGRAPHY. In 1980, there were about 26,000 Manus people, of whom about 6,000 lived elsewhere in Papua New Guinea. This is more than twice the population reported in the first reliable estimates, early in the twentieth century.

LINGUISTIC AFFILIATION. Manus languages are a distinct family of Austronesian languages, with four subfamilies: Eastern Mainland Manus (the largest), Western Mainland Manus, Northern Islands, and Southeastern Islands. There is little agreement on the origin of the languages. Estimates of their number range from eighteen to forty, and they share some grammatical and vocabulary elements. Many people from small, linguistically unique villages may understand three or four different languages; almost all speak Melanesian Pidgin; most speak some English.

History and Cultural Relations

Earliest European contact with the Manus mainland was in the sixteenth century, but first substantial contact was in the nineteenth century, with pearlers, whalers, and bêche-de-mer fishermen. Germany annexed Manus with the rest of German New Guinea in 1884 and was replaced by Australia in 1915. Colonial administration was based on appointed village headmen. Resistance to colonization was fierce in some areas: control was not complete until about 1920. A few copra plantations were established by 1910 and mission activity began shortly after. However, relatively little land was alienated for plantations. By World War II, most Manus were Christian—primarily Catholic, Seventh-Day Adventist, or Lutheran—but Christianity supplemented rather than displaced indigenous beliefs. After World War II, there was agitation for social, economic, and political improvement. Partly as a result, education provision increased, village officials were elected rather than appointed, and there was encouragement of village cooperatives. Public services expanded through the early 1980s, when government financial difficulties led to slight contraction. Shortly after the independence of Papua New Guinea in 1975, the province acquired an elected assembly.

Settlements

Villages rarely have more than 400 residents. They frequently are made of hamlets, sets of houses built around a central clearing, often with an associated patriclan's men's house. Hamlets and village sections are connected by paths. These hamlet clearings and the areas around houses are cleaned carefully. Households often maintain a dwelling house with a separate house for cooking. Houses may be built on the ground or on posts (up to about 6 feet) and may be of one or two stories. The household usually is a nuclear family, though a married child may build a house adjacent to the parents' dwelling. Manus has two urban areas. Lorengau, the provincial capital and market center, is a harbor town with about 4,000 people. Lombrum, a Defense Force naval base, has about 1,500 people. Both were built during Australian control with commercial housing materials.

Economy

SUBSISTENCE AND COMMERCIAL ACTIVITIES. The household is the basic economic unit. The subsistence base for rural villagers is arboriculture and swidden agriculture (traditional for mainland villagers) or fishing (traditional for islanders). Agriculturalists harvest sago palms and various tree fruits and nuts, and they grow taro, sweet potatoes, leafy greens, and bananas. Fishing people catch many varieties of reef fish and some pelagic species, as well as the occasional shark or sea turtle. Almost all villages maintain coconut palms: coconut is an important food and source of cooking oil; many households use it to produce copra for occasional sale and in some areas it is an important commercial crop. Cocoa is also an important commercial crop in a few areas. Many households grow small quantities of leafy greens, squash, sugarcane, and bananas, and areca (betel) nuts, and betel peppers. Pork is important for feasts, and so in most villages a few pigs are reared. Indigenous food sources are supplemented by imported items, especially rice, tinned fish and meat, biscuits, tea, coffee, sugar, beer, cigarettes, and twist tobacco. These are available in small village shops and in greater variety more cheaply in Lorengau and Lombrum.

INDUSTRIAL ARTS. Before colonization, people produced a range of manufactured items. By the mid-1900s, imported substitutes displaced most indigenous manufacture, though most houses and canoes are still made of local materials. Handicraft production is reviving in some areas, for sale to tourists.

TRADE. Manus originally had a complex system of trade that reflected village ecological differences, primarily between mainland agricultural villages and island fishing villages. This fish-for-starch trade weakened after World War II as mainland villagers, and in some instances islanders, moved to the coast and took up both agriculture and fishing. However, there remain many markets between pairs of island and mainland villages, but by about 1970 these generally had become cash-only rather than barter markets. In addition, many villages had access to special natural resources: clay for pots, obsidian for knives and spear points, beds of shell for shell money, etc. By about 1970, imported manufactures replaced these items and trade for them largely disappeared. Some villages carry fish and agricultural produce to Lorengau and Lombrum for sale in the marketplaces, and they buy and sell there from each other as well.

DIVISION OF LABOR. The sexual division of labor is pronounced, though weaker than it had been. Men make housing (including village buildings like aid posts, schools, and churches), canoes, and sails, tend coconut and sago palms, and do some preparation of gardening land. Women do much other agricultural work, including pounding and washing sago, splitting and scraping coconuts, and preparing oil. Women also clean the house and its nearby area and village paths. In fishing villages, both men and women fish in nearby waters, but usually only men fish outside the surrounding reef. In some villages, different fishing techniques are clearly restricted to men or women. Although men claim formal control, in many villages women exert strong informal influence on much ceremonial activity. Villagewide cooperation for communal projects is difficult, as the villagewide structures that could be activated to induce cooperation are relatively recent and weak. An important division of labor for many villagers is between migrants and residents. Migrants remit money, important for the economic well-being of residents. In return, residents perform ritual and social activities necessary for the social and spiritual well-being of migrants (e.g., life-crisis and healing rituals).

LAND TENURE. Land rights are inherited and there is almost no land sale. Parcels of land belong to agnatic groups, with sections of such parcels controlled by the group members who garden or build on them. In fishing communities, agnatic groups commonly hold marine rights, but the complexity of the system of tenure varies. Usually, areas of the surrounding reef and sea are claimed by agnatic groups, but specific parcels are not controlled by individuals in the way land is. In some villages there is ownership of fishing techniques of different sorts and of the right to catch certain species of fish. In the past these rights may have been of economic significance, but presently they are of little significance among subsistence fishing people. In principle, land in urban areas can be bought and sold by individuals as private property. However, some village groups claim to be ancestral owners of urban land and they have tried to assert that ownership.

Kinship

KIN GROUPS AND DESCENT. The politically dominant kin groups are village-based, patrilineal descent groups that can loosely be called patriclans, internally differentiated into lineages. These groups are concerned primarily with land and sea tenure, but they also participate in exchange. People inherit group membership from their fathers; in some areas women adopt their husband's on marriage. There are also province-wide matriclans that do not have complex internal differentiation, though their importance varies around Manus. These matriclans are concerned mainly with health: treating pollution caused by contact with forbidden items, purification at stages of the life cycle. In addition there are local cognatic stocks (with patrilateral biases), one descending from each married couple in the past and present. These relationships are activated pri-

Manus villages rarely have more than 400 inhabitants. They frequently are made of hamlets, sets of houses built around a central clearing and connected by paths.

marily during ceremonial exchanges, and as exchanges are frequent and important economically, these stocks are important. Villagers inherit all the stock memberships of both parents.

KINSHIP TERMINOLOGY. Terminology varies, but it commonly stresses the relationship between the descendants of brothers and of sisters. Generational skewing of the Crow type occurs.

Marriage and Family

MARRIAGE. Village endogamy and patriclan exogamy seem to have been enduring marriage preferences (matriclans are not significant here). In addition, other patterns have appeared at different times and places, shaped by political and economic interests. Notable among these is cross-cousin marriage and intervillage marriage (especially among elite families). Since conversion to Christianity, patterns have been shaped by church rules as well. Marriage entails payment of bride-price, which in the past made it susceptible to the manipulation of entrepreneurial big-men and in the present makes it an important conduit through which money passes from migrants to residents. Patrivirilocal residence is commonly preferred. Acceptability of divorce and illegitimacy vary widely, shaped in part by religious affiliation.

DOMESTIC UNIT. The domestic unit is the married couple and their unmarried children. Husband and older sons are no longer expected to sleep routinely in the patriclan's men's house, but they may do so occasionally.

INHERITANCE. The right to make decisions about real property is inherited patrilineally. Personal property can pass from parents to children or from sibling to sibling.

SOCIALIZATION. The main institutions that socialize children are parents, schools, and churches (the last two at times being the same). As well, certain classes of relatives often have special responsibility for the child's welfare. Parents and other relatives, schools, and churches frequently are seen to have distinct spheres of competence: traditional and village skills, urban and Western skills, and Christian morality, respectively. Physical punishment of children is expected only in restricted circumstances. While some socialization may have occurred during initiation procedures in the past, these rites no longer exist.

Sociopolitical Organization

SOCIAL ORGANIZATION. Villages are organized around the structure of patriclans, which shape rights in real property, and the structure of cognatic stocks, which shape participation in exchange. (Matriclans are relatively unimportant here.) Patriclans and stocks are localized and do not facilitate intervillage relationships. Patriclans are small (at times no more than five or six resident adults), and lineages are even smaller. Thus, they commonly recruit nonmembers for productive and ceremonial activities, typically from cognatic stocks descended from out-marrying patriclan (or lineage) women of earlier generations. This is often described as a distinction between the line (descendants) of the man (the brother) and the line of the woman (the out-marrying sister). A distinction between a line of the man and a line of the woman first appears at marriage, between the line of the groom and of the bride. For the children of the marriage, the distinction is between the line of the father and of the mother. In subsequent generations, it is the line of the man and of the woman. Villagers also distinguish residents and migrants, though this is reflected in practices rather than structures. Many ceremonial exchanges are organized to accommodate the schedules and wishes of important migrants, and the rules and practices of contribution and distribution help assure that migrants' contributions remain in the hands of residents.

POLITICAL ORGANIZATION. Village political organization revolves around patriclans and village factions. Hereditary patriclan leaders are supposed to lead patriclan activities and influence patriclan political decisions, though within a general framework of consensus. Often, different village patriclans were responsible for villagewide activities, such as making war, making peace, and village governance. Patriclans and their leaders are more powerful in those villages where clan land is of prime economic significance, not overshadowed by introduced economic resources that are beyond the control of villages (especially wage labor). Village factions often reflect patriclan differences, but also reflect different orientations to contemporary conditions and issues. Most common are different orientations to modernization, tradition, and Christianity. Villages have formal governments, including an elected village leader and assistant, elected magistrates and constable, and usually an elected representative to the local subprovincial governing body. Electoral districts for provincial and national parliaments include more than one village, and elections for these bodies often unite villagers in support for the candidate from their village. Provincial party allegiance is weak and people often say that representatives are swayed by gifts and favors.

SOCIAL CONTROL.   Ideally, relations within the patriclan are amicable. This is less true of relations between patriclans and villages, which may be tense and even violent. Behavior is controlled in three ways. One is the sanction of agnatic ancestors, who monitor the acts of their living descendants and in cases of unresolved grievance may inflict illness, which can be fatal. Someone suspecting an ancestral illness will call a meeting of relatives, where all are to confess their hidden grievances and resolve them. As ancestors monitor migrants as well as residents, this helps tie migrants to their natal village. Second is the power of specific classes of ego's kin (especially classificatory father's sister, father's sister's daughter, and father's sister's son). These have the power to bless or curse, and can use their power to ensure ego's proper behavior. Third is the village court system. Cases of slander and petty theft, as well as more serious matters, are routinely heard by village magistrates. Higher-level courts are seldom used.

CONFLICT.   Prior to colonial control, raiding and open warfare between villages were common. Conflict was common when mainland or island groups moved to coastal land, and so it helped maintain the ecological division of villages and the related trade system. Intravillage, interclan fighting occurred, but such conflicts seem to have been unusual and informal, though sorcery attacks among villagers did occur. Such fighting could lead to village fission. Modern intervillage conflict is not common, occurring mainly when residents of one village use the land or seas of other villages. There is conflict between villages and government over the imposition of taxes and, more recently, over provincial government policies. Such conflicts reflect a recurring regional division between southern and northern Manus.

Religion and Expressive Culture

RELIGIOUS BELIEFS.   Indigenous religion revolves around the dead rather than gods. Ancestors monitor the acts of their agnatic descendants and punish wrongdoing by taking the substance of an individual's soul. A recently dead ancestor could be adopted as household patron and protector. There are also malevolent spirits, which can be controlled by sorcerers. Most Manus are Christian, and denominational beliefs have been modified in different ways by their mixture with indigenous cosmology.

RELIGIOUS PRACTITIONERS.   Divining in various ways is common, and many villages have two or three practitioners, who are not distinguished by special title or ritual. Some people are thought to control malevolent spirits, but few admit to this activity. Many people have entered the service of the church as catechists and lay officials, and some have been ordained.

CEREMONIES.   Dancing and feasting are performed only as part of other activities, especially men's-house raising, marriage and brideprice exchange, visits by important government and church officials, major provincial occasions, and important sporting events. Exchanges are frequent and are always accompanied by a degree of ceremonial activity, especially speech making and feasting. Church services are well attended.

ARTS.   Everyday objects, houses, and canoes could be carved and painted in the past, though this is less common in the present. Woven mats and baskets, lime gourds, and lime sticks frequently are decorated. Indigenous valuables (shell money and dogs' teeth) were and are treated as decorative as well as valuable. They are mounted on beadwork belts made with bright designs. People also make decorative beadwork-and-shell bracelets and necklaces.

MEDICINE.   Before colonization there was extensive use of plant matter as medicine, and some is still used. Much illness is thought to be caused by ancestors and much medical practice involves locating and resolving the source of such illness. Illness caused by contact with matriclan totems, potentially fatal, is usually not worrisome as it is treated easily by the invocation of matriclan ancestors by matriclan women. With colonization, church and government health services spread; now they are often the treatment of first resort, though failure of nurses or physicians to diagnose and treat a complaint quickly can be taken to mean that an ancestral illness exists.

DEATH AND AFTERLIFE.   Almost all deaths, even of the very old, are laid to ancestral illness or sorcery. The human spirit reluctantly leaves the body after death, usually before burial. Spirits exist in a parallel, invisible world, where they continue to act as normal people. As already described, they monitor the behavior of their agnatic descents, punishing where necessary. In addition, they may take revenge on some of the living to redress old complaints or their own death. The most recent dead are the most active, and after three or four generations the spirit no longer affects the living. This set of beliefs overlays Christian beliefs in Heaven and Hell, angels being the spirits of the dead.

Bibliography

Carrier, James, and Achsah Carrier (1989). *Wage, Trade, and Exchange in Melanesia: A Manus Society in the Modern State.* Berkeley: University of California Press.

Fortune, Reo (1935). *Manus Religion.* Philadelphia, Pa.: American Philosophical Society.

Mead, Margaret (1934). "Kinship in the Admiralty Islands." *American Museum of Natural History Anthropological Papers* 34:189–358.

Mead, Margaret (1930). *Growing Up in New Guinea.* New York: William Morrow. Reprint. 1963. Harmondsworth, England: Penguin.

Schwartz, Theodore (1963). "Systems of Areal Integration: Some Considerations Based on the Admiralty Islands of Northern Melanesia." *Anthropological Forum* 1:56–97.

Schwartz, Theodore (1962). "The Paliau Movement in the Admiralty Islands." *American Museum of Natural History Anthropological Papers* 49:211–421.

—JAMES G. CARRIER

Maori youth enjoyed premarital sexual freedom and were expected to have a series of discreet love affairs before marrying.

MAORI

Ethnonym: Te Maori

Orientation

IDENTIFICATION. The Maori are the indigenous inhabitants of New Zealand. Culturally, they are Polynesians, most closely related to eastern Polynesians. After contact with Europeans, the people now known as the Maori began using the term *tangata maori*, meaning "usual or ordinary people," to refer to themselves.

LOCATION. The Maori were originally settled primarily in the northern parts of North Island, New Zealand. South Island was much more sparsely settled.

DEMOGRAPHY. When Captain Cook visited New Zealand in 1769 the indigenous population was probably between 200,000 and 250,000. The population declined after contact with Europeans, but it began to recover at the beginning of this century and now approaches 300,000.

LINGUISTIC AFFILIATION. Maori is classified as part of the Polynesian Group of the Eastern Oceanic Branch of the Austronesian languages. Approximately one-third of the Maori still speak their ancestral language, with the vast majority fluent in English as well.

History and Cultural Relations

New Zealand was evidently settled in three waves by travelers from Polynesian islands in A.D. 950,

1150, and 1350. The early arrivals, the Moriori, subsisted mainly by fishing and hunting the moa and other birds that are now extinct. The final (pre-European) immigration was that of the "seven canoes of the great fleet." The people of the great fleet assimilated the original inhabitants by marriage and conquest. The immigrants of 1350 arrived with their own domesticated plants and animals (several of which did not survive the transition from a tropical to a temperate climate), and they subsequently developed into the Maori of the present historical period. Whalers and sealers were common visitors to New Zealand in the 1790s and their relations with the Maori were generally unfriendly and often violent. The first missionaries arrived in 1814 and by the 1830s large numbers of Europeans and Australians were settling in New Zealand. With the Treaty of Waitangi, signed in February 1840 by many (but not all) of the indigenous chiefs, the Maori relinquished sovereignty over New Zealand land and in turn received British recognition and protection, as well as guaranteed rights to their native lands. A period of rapid acculturation ensued, lasting until 1860. The years 1860–1865 saw many battles between the Maori and the government of New Zealand, mainly over questions of land rights and sovereignty. By 1900 their population slide had reversed and the Maori began to play a more active role in New Zealand society. They received permanent Maori seats in the national legislature, and most discriminatory laws were repealed. At present the Maori are a legally recognized minority group (about 10 percent of the population), and they receive special legal and economic considerations on these grounds. Since the 1960s there has been a move to revitalize the Maori language and the Maori are attempting to preserve their cultural heritage while living side-by-side with the "Pakeha" (New Zealanders of European descent). This summary focuses on traditional Maori culture.

Settlements

Today the Maori are overwhelmingly an urban population, located primarily in towns and cities of the northern sections of North Island. In the past there were two types of Maori settlements: fortified (*pa*) and unfortified (*kainga*). Pa, in which people took refuge in wartime, were usually located on a hill and were protected by ditches, palisades, fighting platforms, and earthworks. Houses in the pa were closely crowded, often on artificial terraces. Kainga were unfortified hamlets consisting of five or six scattered houses (*whare*), a cooking shelter (*kauta*) with an earth oven (*hangi*), and one or two roofed storage pits (*rua*). Most farmsteads were enclosed in a courtyard with a pole fence. Most buildings were made of pole and thatch, but some better-made ones were constructed of posts and worked timber.

Kinship

KIN GROUPS AND DESCENT. The largest kin groups in Maori society were the so-called tribes (*iwi*). The iwi were independent political units that occupied discrete territories. An iwi was a large, bilateral descent group encompassing as its members all descendants, traced through both male and female links, of the tribe's founder (by whose name most tribes were known). The Maori were organized into some fifty iwi, of varying size and prestige. The iwi, in turn, were made up of a number of sections known as *hapu*. The hapu also owned a discrete territory and consisted of all individuals bilaterally descended from a founding ancestor. The hapu were much more important than the iwi with regard to land use and communal projects among their members. Most of the members of a hapu lived, along with in-marrying spouses and slaves, in one or two communities. Since they were defined bilaterally, an individual was often a member of and could affiliate with more then one hapu. A household became officially affiliated with a particular hapu by demonstrating a genealogical link conferring membership and by participating fully in the group's daily life. Descent was reckoned bilaterally, with a patrilateral emphasis, especially in chiefly families.

KINSHIP TERMINOLOGY. Maori kin terminology was of the Hawaiian type.

Marriage and Family

MARRIAGE. Maori youth enjoyed premarital sexual freedom and were expected to have a series of discreet love affairs before marrying. The choice of a marriage partner was made by the senior members of the whanau (household). Marriage served to establish new relations with other kin groups and brought new members into the hapu. Aristocrats often betrothed their children as infants. Marriages were nearly always between members of the same tribe and often between members of the same hapu. First and second cousins were ineligible as marriage partners. Most marriages were monogamous, though chiefs often took several wives. Gifts were exchanged by both partners at the weddings of commoners while aristocratic women brought a dowry often in the form of land and slaves. Divorce was common and easy, based simply on an agreement of husband and wife to separate. Residence was flexible, but often patrilocal. Children were greatly desired and commonly adopted from relatives. Abortion, infanticide, and postpartum sexual abstinence were the primary methods of population control.

DOMESTIC UNIT. The basic social unit was the household (whanau), often comprised of an extended family, including a male head (*kaumatua*), his spouse (s), their unmarried children, and their married sons, along with the latter's spouses and children. Many households also had resident slaves.

INHERITANCE. A dying person would make a final testament disposing of his or her property. Most of the estate was divided fairly equally among the surviving children, except that certain types of hunting, fishing, and craft equipment went only to the offspring of the same sex.

SOCIALIZATION. Children were generally educated by their relatives, especially grandparents, through songs and stories. Games often imitated adult activities and were competitive. Aggressiveness and competitiveness were encouraged.

Sociopolitical Organization

SOCIAL ORGANIZATION. The interrelationships among households, hapu, and iwi has been described above. While iwi were fixed in composition and number, new hapu were created through fission. When a hapu grew too large to function effectively some of its members would break off and establish a new hapu under the leadership of one of the chief's sons or younger brothers. The tribes whose ancestors arrived in New Zealand in the same canoe were considered to constitute a *waka*, literally "canoe." A waka was effectively a confederation whose members felt some obligation to help one another. This special relationship did not, however, rule out warfare between two tribes of the same waka. The Maori were ranked into three social classes, determined by the source of one's line. Members of the two highest classes were both free people, while those descended from the oldest males of each generation formed the aristocracy (*rangatira*). Those from more junior lines, or whose ancestors had lost status, were considered commoners (*tutua* or *ware*). The question of precisely where a particular line stood in these two classes was often a source of controversy. Difference in rank was directly correlated with degree of sacredness (*tapu*) and mana of each individual and group. Finally, there were the slaves (*taurekareka*), mainly war captives, who stood outside the descent system.

POLITICAL ORGANIZATION. Each hapu had a chief (from the rangatira). The rangatira of the most senior hapu was the paramount chief (*ariki*) of that tribe. The tribe was therefore the highest politically integrated unit in Maori society. Both chieftainships were passed on patrilineally to the first son in each generation. In some tribes a senior daughter was also given special recognition. Chiefs were of high rank and generally quite wealthy. They exercised great influence but lacked coercive power. The chiefs organized and directed economic projects, led *marae* ceremonials, administered their group's property, and conducted relations with other groups. The chiefs were often fully trained priests with ritual responsibilities and powers, most importantly the right to impose tapu. The rangatira and ariki were, in their persons, very tapu and had much mana. The household heads or kaumatua as a group constituted the community council (*runanga*) which advised and could influence the chief.

SOCIAL CONTROL. Penalties for crimes ran from gossip, reprimand, and sorcery to seizure of property, beating, and execution.

CONFLICT. Conflict between different hapu and different tribes was common and often led to warfare. The defeated were most often enslaved, killed, or eaten. Women and children were the most likely persons to be spared.

Religion and Expressive Culture

RELIGIOUS BELIEFS. The Maori held an essentially spiritual view of the universe. Anything associated with the supernatural was invested with tapu, a mysterious quality which made those things or persons imbued with it either sacred or unclean according to context. Objects and persons could also possess mana, psychic power. Both qualities, which were inherited or acquired through contact, could be augmented or diminished during one's lifetime. All free men were tapu to a degree directly proportional to their rank. Furthermore, an object or resource could be made tapu and therefore off-limits. The

ECONOMY

Subsistence and Commercial Activities

Maori subsistence depended on fishing, gathering, and the cultivation of sweet potatoes, or *kumara* (*Ipomoea batatas*), some taro, yams, and gourds. Fishing was done with lines, nets, and traps, while fowling was done with spears and snares. Items gathered include shellfish, berries, roots, shoots, and piths. Rats were also trapped and eaten. In infertile areas or in harsh seasons uncultivated fern roots provided an important starchy supplement. Kumara was planted in October and harvested in February and March; winter was the most important hunting season. Getting food was a time-consuming and arduous business.

Industrial Arts

The Maori made tools from stone and wood. Important mechanical aids were wedges, skids, lifting tackles, fire ploughs, and cord drills. Most material items were highly decorated. Major manufactures included flax mats, canoes, fishing equipment, weapons, elaborate digging sticks, cloaks, and ornaments, among others.

Trade

Goods and services were conveyed or compensated through gift giving between individuals. Items and services did not have set values, and the Maori lacked any form of true money. Items most often exchanged were food, ornaments, flax coats, stone, obsidian, and greenstone. Generosity was valued as it enhanced a person's mana, or psychic power. There was a coastal-interior exchange of sea and agricultural products for forest products and greenstone from the west coast of South Island was exchanged for finished goods from the north.

Division of Labor

Men were responsible for felling trees, clearing ground for cultivation, planting, trapping birds and rats, digging fern roots, deep-sea fishing, canoe making, carving, stonework-ing, tattooing, and performing esoteric rites. Women were responsible for gathering, weeding, collecting firewood, carrying water, cooking, plaiting, and weaving. Especially skilled individuals could become specialists (*tohunga*) as carvers, builders, and raft makers. The Maori preferred to work cooperatively, with particularly odious jobs left to the slaves.

Land Tenure

Nearly all land was owned by the various descent groups or tribes. Each group controlled a parcel of tribal territory and granted rights of usufruct and occupation to its members. Only the group could alienate the descent group's land, and then only with the permission of the entire tribe. Border disputes were a common source of fighting. The nuclear family (*whanau*) of a descent group held rights to specific resources and parcels of land, which could be conveyed to the members' children. Rights of use could be extended to nonmembers only with the permission of the entire descent group.

punishment for violating a tapu restriction was automatic, usually coming as sickness or death. The Maori had a pantheon of supernatural beings (*atua*). The supreme god was known as Io. The two primeval parents, Papa and Rangi, had eight divine offspring: Haumia, the god of uncultivated food; Rongo, the god of peace and agriculture; Ruaumoko, the god of earthquakes; Tawhirimatea, the god of weather; Tane, the father of humans and god of forests; Tangaroa, the god of the sea; Tu-matauenga, the war god; and Whiro, the god of darkness and evil. There were also exclusive tribal gods, mainly associated with war. In addition, there were various family gods and familiar spirits.

RELIGIOUS PRACTITIONERS. The senior deities had a priesthood (*tohunga ahurewa*), members of which received special professional training. They were responsible for all esoteric ritual, were knowledgeable about genealogies and tribal history, and were believed to be able to control the weather. Shamans rather than priests served the family gods whom they communicated with through spirit possession and sorcery.

CEREMONIES. Most public rites were performed in the open, at the marae. The gods were offered the first fruits of all undertakings, and slaves were occasionally sacrificed to propitiate them. Incantations (*karakia*) were chanted in flawless repetition to influence the gods.

ARTS. Most of the material objects of the Maori were highly decorated. Their statues and carvings, especially with filigree motifs, are admired worldwide and are the frequent subject of art museum exhibitions.

MEDICINE. Sickness was believed to be caused by sorcery or the violation of a tapu. The proximate cause of illness was the presence of foreign spirits in the sick body. The medical tohunga accordingly exorcised the spirits and purified the patient. The therapeutic value of some plants was also recognized.

DEATH AND AFTERLIFE. The dying and dead were taken to a shelter on the marae. The body was laid out on mats to receive mourners, who came in hapu or tribal groups. After a week or two of mourning the body was wrapped in mats and buried in a cave, in a tree, or in the ground. Often after a year or two the ariki would have the body exhumed, and the bones scraped clean and painted with red ochre, to be taken from settlement to settlement for a second mourning. Afterward, the bones were given a second burial in a sacred place. The spirits of the dead were believed to make a voyage to their final abode, a vague and mysterious underworld.

Bibliography

Best, Elsdon (1924). *The Maori.* 2 vols. Memoirs of the Polynesian Society, no. 5. Wellington.

Buck, Peter (1949). *The Coming of the Maori.* Wellington: Maori Purposes Fund Board and Whitcombe & Tombs.

Firth, Raymond (1929). *Economics of the New Zealand Maori.* Wellington: Government Printer.

Hanson, F. Allan, and Louise Hanson (1983). *Counterpoint in Maori Culture.* London: Routledge & Kegan Paul.

Metge, Joan (1967). *The Maoris of New Zealand, Rautahi.* London: Routledge & Kegan Paul. Rev. ed. 1976.

—CHRISTOPHER LATHAM

MURNGIN

Ethnonyms: Miwuyt, Wulamba (Cultural Bloc), Yolngu, Yuulngu

Orientation

IDENTIFICATION. Yolngu has generally replaced the term Murngin to refer to the indigenous people of the northeastern part of Arnhem Land in Australia. "Murngin" was the term that the anthropologist Lloyd Warner adopted in the 1930s to identify the region and its culturally similar peoples. Linguists working in the area in the 1960s and 1970s introduced the term "Yolngu language," since *yolngu* is the word for "Aboriginal human being" in all the dialects. Aboriginal people in the Yolngu-speaking area refer to themselves as yolngu (as well as identifying all Aboriginal Australians as yolngu). Within the Yolngu area are some twenty such language-named, land-owning groups. In addition to the names of language groups, Yolngu people describe and name themselves in a number of other ways, including the location and features of the land they own or where they live (for example, "beach people" or "river people").

LOCATION. The Yolngu area is roughly triangular and is located between 11° and 15° S and 134° and 137° E. The northern and eastern "sides" are coastal and the third "side" runs inland southeast from Cape Stewart on the north to south of Rose River on the east. Northeastern Arnhem Land is monsoonal, with northwest winds bringing rain from about December until April or May.

DEMOGRAPHY. The Aboriginal population within the Yolngu area is estimated at 3,500; the population is largely in developing towns and settlements that were formerly Protestant missions.

*It is likely that the
Yolngu (Murngin)
have lived in
northeastern
Arnhem Land for
50,000 years.*

♦ **moiety**
*A form of social
organization in which an
entire cultural group is
made up of two social
groups. Each moiety is often
composed of a number of
interrelated clans, sibs, or
phratries.*

LINGUISTIC AFFILIATION. Yolngu languages are classified as Pama-Nyungan along with others covering seven-eighths of Australia, but they are isolated geographically from other Pama-Nyungan languages. Yolngu speakers classify their languages according to their pronominal systems into some nine groups, and each group is labeled by their shared demonstrative "this/here." Two of the largest groups, in terms of number of named languages, also classify their speakers by moiety: *dhuwal* languages are all Dhuwa moiety, and *dhuwala* languages are all Yirratja moiety. Since the 1970s and the development of adult education and bilingual education programs, a substantial amount of written material is being produced in the Yolngu languages.

History and Cultural Relations

In Western Arnhem Land, an area to the west of the Yolngu, archaeologists have excavated several living sites more than 30,000 years old and one that may be more than 50,000 years old. It is likely that the Yolngu have been in northeastern Arnhem Land for a comparable period of time. Yolngu had only sporadic contacts with non-Aboriginal people until European occupation of the Northern Territory was under way in the last quarter of the nineteenth century, except for regular visits by Macassans, traders from the Celebes, who gathered bêche-de-mer annually from the late seventeenth century until 1907. Yolngu assisted the Macassans in gathering and processing the bêche-de-mer, and they obtained from them iron tools, cloth, tobacco, and the techniques of dugout-canoe construction. In the nineteenth century, explorers and prospectors began to make their way overland; around the coast government customs boats patrolled. The Arnhem Land Aboriginal Reserve, created in 1931, includes the Yolngu area. Hostilities involving Japanese bêche-de-mer collectors and a police expedition in 1932 led to the establishment of a mission station on the Gove Peninsula to serve as a buffer between the Yolngu and the increasingly frequent incursions of non-Aborigines into the area. Other missions had been established earlier, two on the north coast and one on the south coast. Each of these missions became centers of gradually increasing Yolngu population. During World War II some Yolngu were killed in Japanese air attacks, some served in an Australian unit in Dutch New Guinea, and many become acquainted with Europeans. After the war, increasing numbers of missionaries and government personnel were based in the Yolngu settlements, and efforts to implement the federal policy of assimilation were intensified. Although gradually accepting Christianity, Yolngu generally resisted complete assimilation into the dominant British-derived society. Federal governments espousing multiculturalism and favorably disposed to some degree of Aboriginal self-determination enacted land-rights legislation in 1976 (which made the Arnhem Land Reserve an inalienable freehold, also called "Aboriginal Land") and began to support a widespread decentralization movement as Yolngu started to move back to their traditional lands. Settlements established there, although increasing in number and intended to be permanent, remain attached to the larger towns (formerly missions) and are serviced by them. Yolngu people are committed to the development of economic independence, although it must be based to some extent on mining on their land, to which in principle they object. They are also committed to the development of a bicultural society at a rate of change under their control.

Settlements

Population of the four major Yolngu towns (called "townships") ranges from approximately 1,000 to 2,000, including the permanent or semipermanent residents of the outstations or homeland centers serviced from the towns. The towns reflect their origins as missions, with a central area containing administration buildings and usually a church, as well as substantial well-constructed houses. Nearby, sometimes in the center and radiating away from the center, are the houses of the Yolngu people. This housing was at first of traditional shelter design, seasonally appropriate; subsequently, it was made of bush timber and corrugated iron; later, framed corrugated iron on cement slab was used. Increasingly houses have been built closer to standard Australian outback design, and still more recently they are of cement-block construction. At homeland centers, construction remains predominantly of bush timber or corrugated iron, with earth or sand floors, although some "kit houses" are now being erected. The largest center in the Yolngu area is the mining town at Nhulunbuy, with an estimated population of 3,500; fewer than 50 are Yolngu. In the other centers, non-Aboriginal residents are about 8 percent of the population and are mostly employees of the Yolngu towns and organizations.

Economy

SUBSISTENCE AND COMMERCIAL ACTIVITIES. The Yolngu economy was based exclusively on hunting and gathering until the establishment of the missions and the gradual introduction of market goods. Hunting and gathering remain important for Yolngu both in terms of subsistence (especially at the homeland centers) and of identity, even though motor vehicles, aluminum boats with outboard engines, guns, and other introduced objects have replaced indigenous tools. Small amounts of cash were introduced in the 1940s and 1950s; in 1969 federal training grants began to provide limited wages, and social service benefits were generally being paid. Standard wages were in place by the mid-1970s, but social services remain the major source of cash income for Yolngu and unemployment (in European-Australian terms) remains at over 50 percent. Most employment is provided by government agencies in administrative and service jobs. Yolngu on the Gove Peninsula have established business enterprises mainly related to contract work for the mining company.

INDUSTRIAL ARTS. For a few men and women in each Yolngu town or outstation the production of arts and crafts—bark paintings, carvings (chiefly but not exclusively made by men), woven net bags and baskets (exclusively produced by women)—is a significant source of income, but it is not nearly sufficient to preclude the need for social-security support.

TRADE. Yolngu traditionally had trading partners who exchanged scarce commodities such as highly prized stone, ochres, and other objects of ritual value; trading relationships were important both socially and economically, and the network of trade, although attenuated, remains.

DIVISION OF LABOR. In the past, women regularly gathered and processed vegetable foods as well as provided substantial amounts of protein (shellfish at coastal sites, small animals such as goannas and snakes at inland sites), while men provided less regularly taken but highly prized large animals (turtles, dugongs, and fish at coastal sites, and kangaroos, wallabies, emus, opossums, bandicoots, and echidnas at inland sites). This division of labor still exists, although women as well as men now line fish and men continue to use the spear and spear thrower for fishing. The division of labor in wage and salary jobs tends to follow the Euro-Australian pattern.

LAND TENURE. Land is owned by language-named clans; the parcels comprising a clan's estate may not all be contiguous, and ideally they include both coastal and inland areas. Individuals inherit ownership rights in the clan estate from their father and responsibilities for and use rights in their mother's estate. They may also have subsidiary rights in an area where they were conceived (where their father found their spirit before it entered their mother) and also where they were born. In addition, individuals have interests in and responsibilities for their mother's mother's estate, including the potential right of inheritance should there be no males in their mother's mother's clan. Federal legislation in 1976 formally recognized Yolngu title along with the Aboriginal title of all Aboriginal reserve lands.

Kinship

KIN GROUPS AND DESCENT. The main corporate kin groups are patrilineal clans that own land and the ritual objects and ceremonies that validate their title. In the case of large clans, this function may be assumed by subclan or lineage groups. Kinship provides the primary medium of social identity in the Yolngu social domain; each person is reckoned as kin to every other person, and kin links may thus be traced through several different relatives. Matrilineally defined relationships establish rights and duties complementary to those of patrilineal descent but not corporate landowning groups.

KINSHIP TERMINOLOGY. Yolngu use some twenty-four kin terms (as well as some optional extras) to distinguish lineal and collateral, marriageable and nonmarriageable relatives; the analysis of their system of kin classification continues to provide fertile ground for anthropological debate.

Marriage and Family

MARRIAGE. Polygynous marriages, formerly regarded as most desirable, are increasingly rare. Moiety and clan exogamy are observed, and within these parameters, families arrange marriages: ideally a young man is assigned a mother-in-law who is his mother's mother's brother's daughter (most likely and most desirably a classificatory relative in this category). Marriages in the past and to a large extent today maintain or extend alliances between lineages. A young man performs bride-service. Divorce was not formerly institutionalized, but permanent separation of spouses was not uncommon.

DOMESTIC UNIT. A man and his wife or wives, who are often sisters, and their children eat and sleep together, whether living in houses in towns, or in houses or shelters at homeland centers. Brothers with their wives and children frequently live in close proximity. Women in such a

Yolngu infants are almost always in physical contact with caretakers; children are not physically punished or threatened, and they are never overtly denied whatever they wish.

*Yolngu religious
beliefs center on the
myths that tell the
travels and activities
of spirit beings "in
the beginning."*

hearth group or household forage together, and brothers often hunt together.

INHERITANCE. Joint rights in land inhere in the patrilineal group into which each person is born; in the same way, ownership of a language is inherited. A lineage is a potential inheritor of land belonging to the patrilineal group of a real or classificatory mother's mother, should there be no males remaining in that group. Movable property is disposed of through exchange. Formerly a deceased person's personal property was destroyed, but now if such property is valuable it is ritually purified and distributed to relatives on the basis of their attachment to the deceased.

SOCIALIZATION. Infants are almost always in physical contact with caretakers, children are not physically punished or threatened by adults, and infants and very young children are never overtly denied whatever they wish. Yolngu are proponents of bicultural education ("two-way education") and some are gaining university degrees and designing their own school curricula as well as administering and teaching in their schools.

Sociopolitical Organization

From the point of view of the Australian government, the Yolngu are citizens of Australia, although the entitlements of citizenship have been acquired piecemeal. As citizens they are subject to the administration of both Australian commonwealth and Northern Territory law. Special status exists in terms of the legislative provisions defining "Aboriginal land" and in limited recognition of some aspects of customary law. Yolngu towns receive financial support for their infrastructure maintenance and development from federal funding authorities and/or from the Northern Territory, depending on the legislation under which they are incorporated.

SOCIAL ORGANIZATION. Yolngu society is based on principles of descent and the categories and groups within it are related through the idiom of kinship. In addition, the factors of age (both absolute and relative), birth order, and gender all influence the organization of social groups. Thus, through the operation of pervasive dualism, the universe is divided into two mutually exclusive but complementary name moieties, Dhuwa and Yirritja, and each individual is by birth a member of the moiety of his or her father. Each language-named clan is either of the Dhuwa or the Yirritja moiety; clans of the same moiety are linked through a shared myth while clans of the opposite moiety, through lineages within them, are linked by marriage alliances. Clans or particular lineages

of alternate generation defined by matrifiliation are closely linked—or merged—through shared interests in land and ritual performance. Yolngu place a high value on personal autonomy and individual achievement.

POLITICAL ORGANIZATION. Leadership roles in Yolngu society are defined by seniority, which is determined by birth order. The oldest man in a sibling set exercises (or should exercise) primary authority over his brothers and sisters and their families. The oldest man in a clan should be its head, with his next-younger brother "second" to him. The expectation that the oldest man in a clan will be its head mitigates the strict ranking lineages, and in practice if the first son of the first son is still regarded as too young to assume the headship, a younger brother of a deceased head will usually assume the headship. Here exist the grounds of competition for the headship. The rule of seniority operates with respect to both men and women; except that in public men usually exercise authority, birth order is more salient than gender in Yolngu political process. Leaders should be skilled orators, and have the obligation to "look after" all the people who acknowledge their position as leader. To be implemented, a decision must represent a consensus; until a consensus is reached, no decision has been made. These principles of authority and decision making still govern Yolngu political life, even though elected councils are responsible for administering the towns. Yolngu are increasingly active in Northern Territory politics, both through the activities of the Northern Land Council and interaction with elected officials of the territory government. A Yolngu man is currently serving as an elected member of the Northern Territory Assembly.

SOCIAL CONTROL. One of the chief responsibilities of a Yolngu leader is to manage the procedures of dispute settlement. When a member of his clan requests his help to gain satisfaction for some grievance, he may intervene personally to attempt to bring about a resolution; he may convene family meetings or clan moots to ensure the involvement of all those whose concurrence in the matter in dispute and the appropriate outcome is necessary for settlement. People may call attention to a grievance by a public and very loud announcement; if they also threaten physical assault, certain kin should immediately respond: a sister and/or brother-in-law to provide physical restraint, and a lineage leader or clan head to urge calmness and to undertake to arrange satisfaction for the grievance.

CONFLICT. In the past, blood revenge (payback) prevailed; it was incumbent on certain kinsmen of a deceased person to avenge his or her death. Since deaths were rarely attributed to a "natural" cause, at almost any time people were planning a revenge expedition or were fearful of being subjected to one. It has frequently been said that the only sources of conflict among Yolngu (or Aborigines in general) were women and corpses. Yolngu deny this; rather, they say that serious disputes concern interests in land. The *makarrata*, which has been described as a "peace-making" ceremony, or as a "trial by ordeal," is ritualized revenge. A successful outcome is signaled by blood flowing from a wound inflicted in the thigh of a principal offender and is accepted as balancing accounts, at least during the time required for the performance of the ceremony. A custom referred to as *mirrirri* relates to special kinds of avoidance behavior expected between brothers and sisters regarding a reference to a woman's sexuality—a reference which, if made in the hearing of her brother, causes him to attack that sister or any other woman he calls sister. Nowadays, while a man might not attack his sister or "sisters" with a spear, people are still very circumspect about any reference to a woman's sexuality in the presence of her brother.

Religion and Expressive Culture

RELIGIOUS BELIEFS. Religious beliefs center on the myths that tell the travels and activities of spirit beings "in the beginning." The earth was much as it is now, but the acts of the spirit beings at that distant time in the past set the patterns of proper behavior for the Yolngu who would follow, and left signs of their presence in the land. "Wangarr" refers both to spirit being and distant time past; it is comparable to what has been called "the Dreaming" or "the Dreamtime" in other accounts of Aboriginal religion. The spirit beings named plants and animals in the language of the people on whom they bestowed the land and performed ceremonies that present-day owners of the land should perform. They transformed parts of the landscape during their journey. At what would be a clan's most important sacred site, they left a part of themselves; in some cases they stayed and "are always there." For the Yolngu, Wangarr continue to exist and to manifest themselves in both the seen and the unseen world. For individuals, the most important ones are those of their father's and their mother's clans. Healers (*marrnggitj*) have spirit familiars, often referred to as their "spirit children," who assist them in their curing

practices. Since the arrival of the missions, all Yolngu have some knowledge of Christianity and to a varying extent have become active church members.

RELIGIOUS PRACTITIONERS. Since all Yolngu are expected to participate in religious ritual—and most do—all are practitioners. All men sing the ritual songs and at some time do the appropriate dances; all women perform the women's dances that are required for the enactment of some phases of ceremony. Traditional ritual specialists are men who commit to memory a large corpus of sacred names (sometimes called "power names")—names of clan lands, sites, spirit beings, and their appurtenances—and who intone them in the manner of invocations at certain junctures in ritual performance. Some Yolngu men have been ordained as ministers in the Uniting Church (the successor of the original mission Methodist church); for most Yolngu it is important that their Christianity has been Aboriginalized. Some of the ritual of Yolngu ceremony and its sacred objects have been incorporated in the iconography of the Yolngu Christian churches.

CEREMONIES. The major ceremonies of the Yolngu focus on death; their mortuary rituals are an elaborate and important part of their culture,

A bark painting by David Malangi. Men paint the designs that represent or symbolize their heritage. Arnhem Land, Northern Territory, Australia. (Penny Tweedy/Corbis)

although they have undergone certain changes since the advent of the missions. The initial phases of induction into ritual adult manhood were often conducted at this time too, when ritual paraphernalia had been renewed and all the appropriate relatives were gathered. Marriage arrangements, trade, and other negotiations were also conducted during the time of ceremonies, which tended to be at the end of the dry season. Rituals at which the clans' most sacred ritual objects are freshly decorated, displayed, and their meanings explained are the most restricted of all: these ceremonies are directed by the oldest men; only mature men who have demonstrated their worthiness are admitted; and the meanings are imparted incrementally. These objects are of the greatest importance to Yolngu, their significance indicated by their having been called "title deeds" to land.

ARTS. Performance of ritual is judged by canons of aesthetics which make it a form of art as well as religious practice; individual dancers, singers, and drone pipe players are noted and praised for their performance style. Men learn to paint the figures and designs that represent or symbolize their clan's and their mother's clan's heritage, both ritually on bodies on religious occasions and at present on sheets of prepared bark as commercial fine art. Women have also produced commercial fine art since the 1970s. In the houses of Yolngu living in towns, bark paintings and carvings are displayed for the aesthetic pleasure they give as well as for their religious meaning.

MEDICINE. Yolngu may now avail themselves of Western medicine and also call on the services of a marrnggitj for diagnosis and/or treatment, especially if the cause of illness is suspected to be sorcery or inadvertent entry into a spiritually dangerous place. Yolngu have in addition a large pharmacopoeia based mainly on indigenous plants, the knowledge and use of which most people have some familiarity with.

DEATH AND AFTERLIFE. At the time of death, the soul, or its malign aspect, remains about the place of death and is a threat to close family members. One objective of the purificatory rites performed to "free" both survivors and material objects associated with the deceased, including houses, is protection from the malignity of the soul. During the extended course of the mortuary ritual, the soul is guided to some particular area or site on its own clan land, usually a place where, along with other souls of its clan, it awaits reincarnation.

Bibliography

Berndt, R. M. (1952). *Djanggawul; an Aboriginal Cult of North-Eastern Arnhem Land.* London: Routledge & Kegan Paul.

Berndt, R. M., and C. H. Berndt (1954). *Arnhem Land: Its History and Its People.* Melbourne: F. W. Cheshire.

Morphy, H. (1984). *Journey to the Crocodile's Nest: An Accompanying Monograph to the Film "Madarrpa Funeral at Gurka'wuy."* Canberra: Australian Institute of Aboriginal Studies.

Warner, W. L. (1937). *A Black Civilization: A Social Study of an Australian Tribe.* New York: Harper & Bros. Rev. ed. 1958. New York: Harper & Brothers.

Wells, A. E. (1963). *Milingimbi.* Sydney: Angus & Robertson. Reprint. 1976. *Life in the Crocodile Islands.* Adelaide: Rigby Seal Books.

Williams, N. M. (1986). *The Yolngu and Their Land: A System of Land Tenure and the Fight for Its Recognition.* Stanford, Calif.: Stanford University Press.

Williams, N. M. (1987). *Two Laws: Managing Disputes in a Contermporary Aboriginal Community.* Canberra: Australian Institute of Aboriginal Studies.

—NANCY M. WILLIAMS

SAMOA

Ethnonym: Tagata Sāmoa

Orientation

IDENTIFICATION. There is no generally agreed upon explanation of the meaning of the name "Samoa." According to one Samoan version, the name is compounded of "Sā," meaning "tribe, people of," and "Moa," which means "chicken," referring to the "family" of the Tui Manu'a, the highest-ranking titleholder of eastern (American) Samoa. Another proposal suggests that linguistic evidence points to the meaning of Samoa as "people of the ocean or deep sea."

LOCATION. The Samoan Archipelago (about 3,000 square kilometers in land area) lies in western Polynesia in the central Pacific, from 13° to 15°S to 173°W. The Manu'a group (Ta'ū, Ofu, and Olosega), Tutuila, and 'Aunu'u comprise the Territory of American Samoa; 'Upolu, Manono, Apolima, and Savai'i make up the Independent State of Western Samoa. The islands are of volcanic origin. Beyond the coastal plains, the mountain ranges rise steeply to a maximum of 1,859 meters on Savai'i. The climate is tropical with abundant rainfall. Humidity averages 80 percent. The average monthly temperature ranges from 22° to 30° C.

DEMOGRAPHY. In 1980, the Samoan population was about 188,000 (American Samoa: 32,000; Western Samoa: 156,000). In the middle of the nineteenth century, the aboriginal population of Western Samoa was estimated at 35,000; the aboriginal population of Tutuila was estimated at 3,900 in 1865. The Samoan Islands are the home of the largest concentration of full-blooded Polynesians in the world. Today, many Samoans live and work abroad, mainly in New Zealand, Australia, Hawaii, and California.

LINGUISTIC AFFILIATION. The Samoan language belongs to the Polynesian Group of Austronesian languages. There are no dialects; except for minor local variants the same language is spoken on all the Samoan Islands.

History and Cultural Relations

Settlement of the Fiji-Tonga-Samoa area by people belonging to the prehistoric Melanesian Lapita culture took place between about 1500 and 1000 B.C. Genealogical, mythological, and linguistic evidence suggests that relations with both Tonga and Fiji were maintained throughout the prehistoric period, with intermarriage occurring among the upper classes especially of the Samoan and Tongan population. The first European to sight the Samoan Islands in 1722 was the Dutch explorer Jacob Roggeveen, though he did not land there. In about 1800 some isolated European sailors and escaped convicts settled on Samoa, bringing with them the first notion of Christianity. In 1830, the missionary John Williams of the London Missionary Society (LMS) landed in Savai'i during a power struggle among factions, bringing with him native Polynesian missionaries from Tahiti and the Cook Islands. The first permanent European missionaries arrived in 1835 (LMS and Methodists), followed by Roman Catholic priests in 1845. During the nineteenth century, Germany, Great Britain, and the United States strove for influence among the diverse Samoan factions. In 1900, Western Samoa became a German colony (until 1914) and Eastern Samoa was claimed by the United States. From 1914 to 1962, New Zealand administered Western Samoa, which became an independent state in 1962, with kings Malietoa Tanumafili II and Tupua Tamasese Mea'ole serving as joint heads of state. Before World War II, administrative policies by the New Zealand administration led to the "Mau," a resistance movement (1926–1936) that mustered the support of about 90 percent of the Samoan population at its height. American Samoa remains a United States territory. After constitutional changes, Peter Tali Coleman became the first elected native Samoan governor in 1977.

Settlements

The Samoans have been mainly a coast-dwelling people living in self-governing, autonomous towns (*nu'u*) linked by political and ceremonial alliances. Households center on the sacred central place (*malae*) of each nu'u where the ranking high chief's assembly house is also situated. Town populations range between 300 and 1,200 persons and average 450 to 600 persons. In the middle of the last century, town populations averaged 200 to 500 persons. However, a census taken of twenty-two towns in the district of Aana, Western Upolu, Manono, and Apolima in 1867 shows that town populations ranged between 40 and 310 persons only, the mean being 164 persons. In the nineteenth century, there were a few inland settlements, too. In recent years, there has been a tendency to give up settlements along the coast and to shift towns to newly built roads farther inland.

Economy

SUBSISTENCE AND COMMERCIAL ACTIVITIES. The Samoans are horticulturalists, raising tubers (taro and yams) on a swidden basis. They also grow bananas, breadfruit, and coconuts and supplement their diet through fishing. They raise chickens and pigs, too, but pork is reserved as a special food for ceremonial occasions. Hunting for runaway pigs is still practiced with the help of dogs, but it's probably done more for sport than for food. Pigeon snaring also formerly served as an entertainment and as a sporting event. Terracing and irrigation are not practiced. There are small house gardens for raising staple foods in the back of the households, but the main taro gardens often lie 3–4 kilometers farther inland. The primary cultigens are taro and breadfruit. Contact with Europeans resulted in the addition of new sorts of bananas and vegetables, which are grown today mainly by the small Chinese population for consumption and sale. Many Samoan families earn a small income by selling coconuts to the Western Samoan Trust Estate Corporation, which does the processing. There are many small family businesses, shops, and guest houses, the majority of them in Apia, the capital of Western Samoa. In many local communities there is a small shop where locals can buy a limited range of products, many of them imported.

INDUSTRIAL ARTS. Aboriginal crafts included the making of bark cloth, house building,

The climate in the Samoan Archipelago is tropical with abundant rainfall. Humidity averages 80 percent.

See also

Tonga

Samoan children are expected to obey their parents and elders at once, without hesitation and without asking questions.

♦ **kava**
A fermented beverage traditionally consumed ritually or ceremonially (though sometimes merely for its euphoric and soporific effects) in Melanesia, New Guinea, and Polynesia. The drink is made from the dried and ground root of the kava plant (Piper methysticum) mixed in water.

boat building, and tattooing. House builders, boat builders, and tattooers were organized in guilds. They met the demands of prestige consumption, since small boats and houses were and are built by the male members of each household. Mat weaving is practiced by women.

TRADE. There was only a limited amount of interregional trade in precontact times. Samoan fine mats (*'ie tōga*) were exchanged for parrots and red parrot feathers from Tonga and sometimes from Fiji. Intraregional trade, too, was limited. Some regions and places were noted for their products, such as nets, which are said to have been made mostly by towns in the interior. Some places were noted for their boats, adzes, and kava bowls. After contact with the Europeans, trade of coconut products (oil and copra) was encouraged by the missionaries, but it became a regular and important activity only after the German firm of Godeffroy and Son from Hamburg founded a branch in Apia, Western Samoa, in 1857. Traders were stationed in Samoa and on other Pacific islands, but there was also direct trading with the Samoans. In 1865, the firm established its first coconut plantations. Today, Western Samoa is dependent on the world market, its three most important export items being copra, cocoa, and bananas. Western Samoan governments seek to promote tourism, and beer brewing may develop into a profitable enterprise, at least for the regional market.

DIVISION OF LABOR. Men do the more strenuous agricultural work, such as clearing and planting with a pointed hardwood digging stick, while women may weed and help in harvest activities. Men are responsible for fishing beyond the reef and for cooking; they engage in toolmaking, house and boat building, and ornament making. Women look after the household, raise the children, and plait mats and fans; formerly they also made bark cloth. They collect edible wild plants to supplement the diet and they forage in the lagoon and reef for small sea animals.

LAND TENURE. Aboriginally, the widest social unit for landownership was the community (nu'u). Its domain included all the territory from the central mountain ridge to the reef. The heads (*matai*) of the different descent groups ('āiga) of the community were entitled to claim blocks of land for themselves and their dependents. Overall authority over lands, however, was vested in the council of matai (*fono*), whose members could revoke ownership of the respective 'āiga. Individuals had the right to occupy and cultivate the land of the descent group to which they belonged. When

Western Samoa became independent, 80.5 percent of its territory was still considered customary land, administered outside the statute law in accordance with traditional principles of tenure; 3.7 percent of the land was freehold; 11.3 percent was government land; and the Western Samoan Trust Estate Corporation owned 4.5 percent. American Samoa, too, has provisions that restrict ownership of land to Samoans.

Kinship

KIN GROUPS AND DESCENT. In Samoa there are overlapping cognatic descent groups ('āiga) with an emphasis on agnation. Each descent group has a localized section in a community where its lands and chiefly (matai) titles traditionally belong; other members live in other communities on the lands of other 'āiga. Localized sections hold and allocate land to their members, regulate marriage, and control conflict among members. Between the descent groups there exist multifarious relationships that are genealogically explained, forming ramified descent structures, both at the community and at the supracommunity level. Not all of these structures are descent groups in the strict anthropological sense of the term, however, since in some of them only matai are members. These structures are 'āiga in a metaphorical sense only. They play an important part in supracommunity territorial integration.

KINSHIP TERMINOLOGY. Kin terms follow a Hawaiian-type system.

Marriage and Family

MARRIAGE. Members of the father's and mother's descent groups are forbidden as marriage partners, and community endogamy is also discouraged. Bride and groom should be of similar rank. Today, a church wedding is an important and costly affair, but many marriages are still customary ones, man and wife living together with their parents' consent after the appropriate exchange of goods. Premarital virginity is highly valued and a girl's moral code prohibits sexual relations with a man unless she is recognized as his wife. Customary marriages among younger people frequently end in divorce, however, and the partners may have undergone several such marriages before eventually contracting a church wedding. Residence tends to be virilocal, but during the early stages of married life a couple frequently resides with the wife's family. In pre-Christian times, polygyny was practiced, although probably only by matai of high rank.

DOMESTIC UNIT. The localized section of a descent group, forming an extended family and living in a group of houses clustered around a common hearth, is the customary domestic unit. In modern times, the nuclear family has become more frequent.

INHERITANCE. Members of the descent group retain rights to use and control of customary land occupied and cultivated by their 'āiga, regardless of where they live. The same applies to matai titles that are not subject to any automatic inheritance rule. A family council will decide to confer a vacant title upon a member—usually male—whom they consider to be the best choice. Especially with regard to high titles, however, agnatic succession is preferred.

SOCIALIZATION. Starting at about 1½ years of age, children become subject to an education Europeans would label as "authoritarian." They are expected to obey their parents and elders at once, without hesitation and without asking questions. Overt and direct expressions of hostility and aggression are discouraged, but *musu*, the state of sullen unwillingness to comply with orders, is a culturally tolerated outlet. Much of the actual education work takes place in the peer groups where older brothers and especially sisters are made responsible for the behavior of their younger siblings. Formal education in schools is considered essential for the well-being of the entire family today and parents usually encourage some of their children to remain in high school.

Sociopolitical Organization

SOCIAL ORGANIZATION. Rank goes with age and the position a matai title holds within the complicated title structure. An older sister ranks higher than her brother. The descendants of a sister still enjoy a special respected status within the descent group. Christianity has emphasized the status of the wife, however, and the sister's position is not as pronounced today as it once was. Within most descent groups, there are two sets of matai: aristocrats

RELIGION AND EXPRESSIVE CULTURE

Religious Beliefs

Today, Samoans are devout Christians, following diverse Protestant denominations, as well as the Roman Catholic church. Pre-Christian beliefs in ancestor-spirits (*aitu*) are still widespread, but they are not openly confessed vis-à-vis Europeans. Aitu formerly were family gods, and they have retained their character as locally associated and kinship-bound deified ancestors. There was a belief in a supreme being, Tangaloa, but Samoa probably never developed a national cult like that of the Society Islands or Hawaii. Tangaloa was a *deus otiosus* who withdrew after having caused the emergence of the islands and set in motion the process which led to the evolution of natural phenomena and, ultimately, humans. Aitu were the active numinous beings who interfered directly in everyday life.

Religious Practitioners

In aboriginal times, each matai was a religious practitioner responsible for the worship of the family aitu. Some matai played paramount roles as oracles of particular aitu of supralocal importance. Today, matai continue to lead family prayers (to the Christian God), but there are also native pastors, trained in local theological seminaries, and priests who conduct formal church services.

Ceremonies

Many native ceremonies focus on life-cycle rites. Attendance is an expression of the rank of the persons involved. The kava ceremony, in which a beverage prepared from the *'ava* root (*Piper methysticum*) was consumed in ceremonial style, was performed to honor important guests and to mark important social events, such as the deliberations of the fono.

Arts

Oratory, dancing, singing, and tattooing continue to be means of aesthetic expression. Today, hymns for church services are an important outlet for expressive needs. The traditional art of bark-cloth (*siapo*) making and printing is not very widespread today.

Medicine

In aboriginal times, disease was supposed to be caused by the wrath of some particular aitu. Treatment was sought with the aid of the special matai, Taulaitu (whose name means "anchor of the Aitu"). They were asked to intercede with the aitu they represented. Various herbs and plants were administered and massage was also applied.

Death and Afterlife

Samoans believe in the dichotomous character of human nature. The separation of the "soul" (*agāga*) and body (*tino*) is tantamount to death. That the agāga continued to live after death as an aitu was the focal topic of the pre-Christian religion. There are various accounts of an afterworld, but no uniform picture of its nature can be gleaned from the historical and ethnographic sources.

(ali'i), who embody the group's dignity; and orators (*tulāfale*), who take a more official role when they speak on behalf of the ali'i at certain formal public events. Each matai supervises and looks after the family under his immediate control and is responsible for it vis-à-vis the community.

POLITICAL ORGANIZATION. Communities (nu'u) are politically independent but are organized into districts and subdistricts for ceremonial purposes. Aboriginally, war, too, was a supracommunity concern. Ceremonies on a supracommunity level often focus on the life-crisis rites of certain very high-ranking titleholders, the *tama-a-'āiga*, which are not to be confused with matai and should rather be called kings. Formal political control within the community is exercised by the council of matai (fono) with the *'aumaga* (the untitled men's organization) serving as executive body. Women's committees exist today in all communities, playing an important role in community affairs as an unofficial arm of local government. They replace or complement the *aualuma*, the group made up of the sisters and daughters of the community, which played an important ceremonial role in former times.

SOCIAL CONTROL. Informal social control is exercised through gossip and was formerly aided by the open Samoan houses, which prevented privacy. Formal control is exercised through the fono, which retains the right to expel individuals and, in rare cases, entire 'āiga from the community and its lands.

CONFLICT. In aboriginal times and throughout the nineteenth century, conflicts over titles and lands often resulted in wars. Such cases are adjudicated today by special law courts. Competitiveness—such as evidenced in, for instance, the zeal of untitled men to distinguish themselves as good servants to their matai, in oratory, in donations to the church, etc.—adds areas of conflict to social life.

Bibliography

Cain, Horst (1979). *Aitu. Eine Untersuchung zur Autochthonen Religion der Samoaner.* Wiesbaden: Franz Steiner Verlag.

Finney, Joseph C. (1973). "The Meaning of the Name Sāmoa." *Journal of the Polynesian Society* 82: 301–303.

Gilson, R. P. (1970). *Samoa 1830 to 1900. The Politics of a Multi-Cultural Community.* Melbourne: Oxford University Press.

Holmes, Lowell D. (1974). *Samoan Village.* Case Studies in Cultural Anthropology. New York: Holt, Rinehart & Winston.

—THOMAS BARGATZKY

See also

Hawaiians

TAHITI

Ethnonym: Society Islands

Orientation

IDENTIFICATION. The name "Tahiti"—or, as Bougainville first wrote it in 1768, "Taiti," and Cook in 1769, "Otaheite"—was the name the natives gave their island and which Europeans came to apply to the indigenes. If the Tahitians had a name specifically identifying themselves, it is not known. What is known is that all of those living in the Society Archipelago, including Tahiti, referred to themselves as "Maohi."

LOCATION. The island of Tahiti upon which the Tahitians lived is the largest of the Society Islands and is located in the windward segment of that group at 149°30' W and 17°30' S. It is a high island of volcanic origin with peaks rising above 1,500 meters. The mountainous interior is covered with forest and ferns while the lower slopes, especially on the leeward side, are brush and reed covered. In the inhabited valleys and coastal plains open stands of indigenous trees and tall grasses were scattered between the cultivated fields of the Tahitians. Wild fowl were said to have been relatively scarce and limited to a few species, pigeons and ducks being specifically mentioned. Wild four-legged creatures were limited to a few small lizards and the Polynesian rat, the latter probably brought by Polynesians.

LINGUISTIC AFFILIATION. The Tahitic language of the Tahitians belongs to the Eastern Polynesian Subgroup of the Malayo-Polynesian Subdivision of the Austronesian languages.

DEMOGRAPHY. Estimates of Tahiti's population in the later years of the eighteenth century varied from as few as 16,050 to approximately 30,000 persons, and thus these estimates are of little factual value. A nineteenth-century decline in population due to wars and diseases is known to have occurred. However, by 1907, after which it was no longer possible to segregate indigenous totals from those of foreigners and immigrant Polynesians from other islands, the number of Tahitians was said to number 11,691.

History and Cultural Relations

Present archaeological evidence supports the view that the Society Islands, of which Tahiti is a part, were the first to be populated in eastern Polynesia from an eastern Polynesia dispersal center in the Marquesas, perhaps as early as A.D. 850. Whether later prehistoric migrants ever reached the Society

Islands is an open question. Limited archaeological data and tradition suggest the occurrence of prehistoric Society Island emigrations to New Zealand and Hawaii. However, by contact times Tahitian voyaging, primarily for political and trade purposes, was limited to the islands of the archipelago and the atolls of the western Tuamotus. In contrast to prehistoric culture change on Tahiti, which had occurred in small increments, the discovery of the island by Wallis in 1767 marked the beginning of strong European acculturative forces impacting on the traditional lifeways of Tahitians. Except for material goods, the most notable changes occurred with the arrival of Protestant missionaries in 1797. Within several years after their arrival a number of Tahitians, including the paramount chief, Pomare II, had been taught to read and write, and the Christian faith and mores had begun to be accepted. However, objections by more conservative members of the society resulted in a series of internecine wars and it was not until 1815 that Pomare II crushed his opponents and, with the aid of the missionaries, successfully guided a religious and political modification of the older traditional order. With the development of American and European whaling and sealing activities Tahiti became a prime distribution center for goods. By 1840 South American currencies had come to be accepted as a substitute for the old trading techniques. At the same time, foreign immigrants and investments on the island produced a variety of problems for which the Tahitians were ill prepared. Foreign government overtures to Queen Pomare to establish a protectorate resulted in the French moving quickly to annex the island in 1842 and thus dissolving Tahitian native rule.

Settlements

Prior to European intervention, Tahitians followed a pattern of dispersed settlements, dwellings being scattered along the coastal plain and up the broader valleys. By the nineteenth century missionary activities and the use by European vessels of safe harbors on the island resulted in the formation of villages near these locations. The Tahitian house resembled a flattened oval inground plan, the long sides being parallel and the two ends rounded. The thatched roof extended down on all sides from a central ridgepole extending lengthwise along the house. Most dwellings were enclosed by a wall of vertically lashed bamboo poles, a space being left open in the middle of one long side to serve as a doorway. Such structures averaged about 6 meters in length with a

width of 3.6 meters and a ridge height of 2.7 meters. However, important chiefs might have buildings measuring as much as 91 meters in length and proportionately wide, with a ridgepole resting some 9 meters above the tamped earthen floor.

Economy

SUBSISTENCE AND COMMERCIAL ACTIVITIES. Tahitians were horticulturalists raising a variety of tree and tuberous crops as well as plantains, all of which, except sweet potatoes, originated in southeast Asia or Melanesia. Domesticated animals included pigs, dogs, and chickens. Fish, caught by a variety of techniques, were a dominant source of protein. Contact with Europeans resulted in the addition of several American and Old World plants and domesticated animals. During the early nineteenth century a successful pork trade with New South Wales was carried on and this was followed later by exports of coconut oil, sugarcane, and arrowroot. Provisioning of European ships became a major nineteenth-century source of income.

INDUSTRIAL ARTS. Decorated bark cloth was a major aboriginal industrial art created by women and used as clothing, as formal gifts, and for export trade. Bark-cloth production continued into the twentieth century, but such cloth is no longer manufactured.

TRADE. Regular aboriginal trading was carried on with the leeward islands of the Society Archipelago and the western atolls of the Tuamotus. The principal item for exchange was bark cloth, to which was added provisions in the case of the Tuamotu atolls. With the arrival of Europeans, iron became the dominant item traded to those atolls. In exchange, Tahitians obtained dog hair, pearls, and pearl shells from the Tuamotus and coconut oil and canoes from the leeward islands.

DIVISION OF LABOR. Traditionally, general construction work and manufacturing of tools, weapons, canoes, and fishing gear was men's work, as was fishing, major ritualism, and warfare. Women created bark cloth, wove mats, and fashioned clothing from both materials. Farming was shared by both sexes.

LAND TENURE. At the time of contact landownership with the right of inheritance was recognized for those of the chiefly and commoner classes, with only the lower class, known as *teuteu*, being excluded. Such lands were subject to taxation in kind by the ruling chiefs who could banish an owner if such taxes were not forthcoming. Missionary activity in the nineteenth century

Tahitian marriage was not permitted between those of different social classes; children resulting from a sexual relationship between partners of differing classes were killed upon birth.

seems to have resulted in at least some of the teuteu class obtaining land rights.

Kinship

KIN GROUPS AND DESCENT. Descent was bilateral with social weight tending to favor patrilateral ties. Consanguineal and, perhaps, affinal kin were grouped in what have been referred to as kin congregations who worshiped their own tutelar deity at their group religious structure, referred to as a *marae*. Primogeniture was important in ranking within the kin congregation. While women were excluded from the marae of the large kin congregations, that was not always true for marae of smaller kin congregations.

KINSHIP TERMINOLOGY. The term *matahiapo* was applied to firstborn as well as all representatives of a family stock descended in the line of the firstborn. *Teina* was used to distinguish younger brothers, sisters, and cousins who were not matahiapo; otherwise, the Hawaiian type of kinship terminology was used.

Marriage and Family

MARRIAGE. Tahitians disapproved of marriage between close consanguineal kin, but how close was never made clear. However, marriage was not permitted between those of differing social classes. Therefore, children resulting from a sexual relationship between partners of differing classes were killed upon birth. In the eighteenth century young couples were required to obtain the permission of their parents before marriage, and among the chiefly class early betrothal was said to be the norm and concubinage was common. Marriage ceremonies, when present, consisted of prayers at a marae. There appeared to be no fixed residency requirement and divorce was by common consent.

DOMESTIC UNIT. The nuclear family was the dominant unit.

INHERITANCE. The firstborn son became the head of the family at birth and succeeded to his father's name, lands, and title, if any. The father then served as the child's regent until he became of age. In the event of the firstborn dying, the next son succeeded him. There is some indication that in the absence of male offspring, an oldest daughter might be the inheritor.

SOCIALIZATION. Children were raised permissively by their parents, although those of the chiefly class were given a degree of education through teachers of that class. Men and women ate separately, and there was a variety of restrictions regarding who might prepare another's meal.

Sociopolitical Organization

SOCIAL ORGANIZATION. During the eighteenth century, there were basically three social classes: the *ari'i*, or chiefs; the commoners, variously known as *manahuni* or *ra'atira*; and the laboring and servant class known as teuteu. Only the last group could not own land. By the beginning of the nineteenth century, perhaps because of European influence, a fourth class called *titi*, consisting of slaves derived from warfare, had been added.

POLITICAL ORGANIZATION. In the early years of European contact Tahitian tribes were grouped into two major territorial units. One constituted the larger northwestern portion of the island and was known as Tahiti Nui, while the other consisted of the southeastern Taiarapu Peninsula and was known as Tahiti Iti. Each maintained a paramount chief of socioreligious power. Below this highest position were chiefs who ruled over what may be likened to districts. These were divided into smaller units and managed by inferior ranked chiefs. A paramount chief's power was not unlimited, since important matters affecting most or all of his region were decided by a council of high-ranking chiefs. Para-

♦ **marae**
A stone plaza, platform, or walls regarded throughout Polynesia as a sacred enclosure. Traditionally a marae was a center of ceremonial rituals and the focal point of community life.

mountcy was not totally preordained, as wars and kinship alliances served to maintain such a status. It was with European aid and combinations of these factors that the Pomare paramountcy was maintained well into the nineteenth century.

SOCIAL CONTROL. Fear of divine retribution was a major control, while human sacrifice and a variety of corporal punishments for secular antisocial behavior were also used as sanctions. Justice in the latter cases was determined by a district chief, and the right to appeal to one's paramount chief was available.

CONFLICT. Confusion regarding tribal territories and overindulgence of chiefly demands for products and services were sources of irritation. At the time of European contact, warfare for chiefly aggrandizement, rather than territorial acquisition, was dominant. By the close of the eighteenth century the European tradition of warfare for territorial gain had been added to the traditional theme of warfare. Minor interpersonal conflicts were resolved by each antagonist being allowed to exhibit publicly his strong resentment of whatever indiscretion had caused the conflict, after which both parties soon reconciled. However, more important conflicts were settled by a district chief, the antagonists having the right to appeal his decision to the paramount chief if not satisfied.

Religion and Expressive Culture

RELIGIOUS BELIEFS. Just as with Tahitian society, native religion recognized a ranked series of gods starting with one supreme deity and passing down through lesser gods and subordinates to individual family spirits of departed relatives. Religion was centered on regional, tribal, and kin tutelar deities, although a few of the gods transcended such limitations and were, in effect, supratribal deities. Gods required a wide variety of appeasements in order to ensure the continued welfare of the individual as well as the tribe. Early nineteenth century missionary activity successfully substituted Christian beliefs for the earlier traditional ones.

RELIGIOUS PRACTITIONERS. Aboriginally, priests were of the chiefly class and were of two kinds. There were those who conducted formal rituals during which the gods were prayed to and appeased by gifts in order to gain their favor. Others were inspirational priests through whom particular gods spoke and offered oracular advice. All priests received some sort of payment for their activities and many were believed to have powers of sorcery. With the nineteenth-century acceptance of Christianity, various Tahitians, not all neces-

sarily of the chiefly class, were trained by the missionaries to become lay preachers.

CEREMONIES. Religious ceremonies were carried out in marae, most of which were tabooed to women. Some ceremonies were seasonal affairs, while others pertained to war and peace, thanksgiving, atonement, and critical life-cycle events of chiefs. The degree of ceremonialism was dependent upon the deity and the importance of the marae, those for commoners in districts and smaller land divisions being the least elaborate.

ARTS. Drums—and, in the early nineteenth century, shell trumpets—were the only musical instruments used during ceremonies. The raised platforms of certain marae were decorated with carved boards, while the god, Oro, was personified by a wickerwork cylinder enclosing sacred feathers. The culture-hero god, Maui, was represented by a large humanoid wicker figure covered with patterns of feathers. Plaited masks were worn during certain ceremonies on the Taiarapu Peninsula.

MEDICINE. Obvious ailments such as sores and open wounds were treated with herbal medicines and poultices, and splints were applied to broken bones. Less obvious illnesses were thought to occur as a result of sorcery, contact with a sacred individual or object, or the anger of one's god. Curing was attempted through priestly prayers and offerings. Among the chiefly class, these cures were performed at the patient's marae and might include human sacrifices.

DEATH AND AFTERLIFE. Untimely death was thought to be because of the anger of one's god, while death through aging was regarded as a natural process. Rank determined the extent of expressions of mourning and the length of time the corpse was exposed on a platform before burial. In the case of high-ranking members of the chiefly class, this time factor was greatly extended by evisceration and oiling of the body. Simple burial, secretive for those of high rank, was customary. There is some indication that cremation was employed for certain individuals on the Taiarapu Peninsula. Among the upper classes human relics were preserved. For some, the afterlife was seen as a state of nothingness, but for others it was believed to be a happy life, for rank in the spirit world remained the same as in life.

Bibliography

Ferdon, Edwin N. (1981). *Early Tahiti as the Explorers Saw It*. Tucson: University of Arizona Press.

Untimely death was thought to be because of the anger of one's god, while death through aging was regarded as a natural process.

See also
Samoa

Newbury, Colin (1980). *Tahiti Nui: Change and Survival in French Polynesia, 1767–1945*. Honolulu: University Press of Hawaii.

Oliver, Douglas L. (1974). *Ancient Tahitian Society*. 3 vols. Honolulu: University Press of Hawaii.

—EDWIN N. FERDON

TONGA

Ethnonyms: None

Orientation

IDENTIFICATION. The Kingdom of Tonga, located in the South Pacific Ocean, was under the protection of Great Britain from 1900 to 1970. Tongans have had a constitutional monarchy since 1875 and in 1970 Tonga became an independent country, joining the British Commonwealth of Nations. The islands of Tonga (known to eighteenth-century Europeans as the "Friendly Islands" because of the friendly reception given to explorers) have a total area of approximately 646 square kilometers. The word *tonga* means "south" in many Polynesian languages.

LOCATION. In 1887, the territorial boundaries of the kingdom were established to encompass an ocean area from 15° to 23° S by 173° to 177° W. The islands fall within a rectangle some 959 kilometers from north to south and 425 kilometers from east to west. The three principal island groups, from north to south, are: the Tongatapu group (*tapu* means "sacred"); the Ha'apai group; and the Yava'u group. Tongatapu Island, the largest island in the kingdom, is the seat of Tongan government. The Tongan Islands are the low coral type, with some volcanic formations. The highest point in the Kingdom of Tonga is 1,030 meters on the uninhabited volcanic island of Kao. Tongatapu Island has a maximum elevation of 82 meters along the southern coast and the island of Yava'u reaches to the height of 305 meters. Average temperature in the Kingdom of Tonga in the winter months of June–July is 16–21° C and in the summer months of December-January it is about 27° C. The island chain of Tonga is classified as semitropical even though in the northern islands there is a true tropical climate and rainfall on Yava'u can be as much as 221 centimeters per year. Rainfall on Tongatapu averages 160 centimeters per year, with November to March being the local hurricane season. Because of the destructive powers of hurricanes striking mainly in the northern Tongan Islands, the southern island of Tongatapu became the place where Tongan culture was established with relative permanency.

DEMOGRAPHY. It has been estimated that in the year 1800 there were approximately 15,000 to 20,000 Tongans residing throughout the islands. In 1989 the resident population of the Kingdom of Tonga was estimated to be 108,000, with Tongans comprising 98 percent of the population and the remainder being other islanders or foreign nationals. The capital and principal city of the kingdom is Nuku'alofa, with an estimated population of 30,000, located on Tongatapu Island. Tongatapu Island itself has an estimated island population of 64,000. There are 48,000 Tongans who are ages of 0–14 (45 percent); 54,000 ages 15–59 (50 percent); and 6,000 (5 percent) over the age of 60. There are also approximately 40,000 to 50,000 Tongan nationals residing in Australia, New Zealand, and the United States of America.

LINGUISTIC AFFILIATION. The Tongan language is derived from a proto-Fijian-Polynesian language originally spoken by Fiji islanders about 1500 B.C. Linguistic and archaeological evidence points to the migration of people into Tonga from locations north and west of the islands.

History and Cultural Relations

Through the use of carbon-14 dating techniques, a date of 1140 B.C. is the given date for the beginning of human occupation of Tongatapu. The first Europeans to visit the Tongan Islands were Dutch navigators in 1616 (Willem Schouten and Jacob LeMaire) and additional contacts occurred as other Europeans explored the Pacific throughout the seventeenth and eighteenth centuries. Contacts between Europeans and Tongans lasted for periods of a few days to several weeks. Publications by Europeans about Pacific Islanders placed Tonga firmly on the map of the world. These published accounts, coupled with the great evangelical revival that swept Europe in the nineteenth century, caused organizations to send individuals to convert the peoples of the Pacific. Tonga, along with the South Pacific islands of Tahiti, was one of the first island groups to receive European missionaries specifically for the purpose of converting the native inhabitants to Christianity. After European missionaries landed in Tahiti in 1797, additional missionaries continued on to Tongatapu. Other missionaries also arrived in Tonga in 1822 and in 1826 two Tahitians who had converted to Christianity in their native islands arrived on Tongatapu while en route to Fiji and began their Christian work among the

Tongan natives. There is no indication that Tongans had extensive trading voyages with other Polynesian island groups. Modern Tonga, an ethnically homogeneous Polynesian kingdom, is attempting to find its way into the twenty-first century. Tongans in the islands are extremely dependent upon relatives living overseas who send money back to family members. In recent years, funds sent back to Tonga from relatives living abroad amounted to ten times the amount of income the kingdom generated from the export of agricultural products such as copra, vanilla, and bananas. Attempts at solving the inherent economic problems of the kingdom have included oil exploration since the 1960s, foreign aid, and increased tourism ventures. Tourism is the primary source of hard currency earnings. Through these efforts, the government hopes to vary the economy and provide additional jobs for Tonga's growing population.

Settlements

Prior to European missionaries, Tongans lived in dispersed settlement patterns that were kin-based and kin-related territorial units. A typical Tongan residential site included a home (*fale*), with a thatched roof and sides made from woven coconut-palm fronds, as well as a separate area for cooking purposes that would have an earthen oven (*'umu*). Today, in addition to some traditional thatched homes, numerous nontraditional or European-American homes (made of wood, concrete, and metal) are located throughout the islands.

Economy

SUBSISTENCE AND COMMERCIAL ACTIVITIES. Prior to the establishment of a market economy, Tongans were subsistence farmers and fishers who had adapted to the environment of their relatively small groups of islands. Because of the relatively low population density of the islands in traditional times, Tongans were essentially self-sufficient horticulturalists and fishers who traded for foodstuffs and material goods among themselves. In the late 1980s, earnings from the tourism industry, accompanied by funds received from Tongans living abroad, accounted for the majority of all personal income in the Kingdom of Tonga. In traditional Tonga, tropical products such as yams, breadfruit, taro, and coconuts were all cultivated on small farms. Tongans fished the surrounding waters by spear fishing, by

net fishing, and by hand. In recent years the pressures of population growth and tourism have forced Tongans to import much of their foodstuffs, including canned meats and fish.

INDUSTRIAL ARTS. Contemporary Tongans are small-scale handicraft manufacturers for the tourist industry and there are still independent artisans, manufacturers of basketry and wood carvings, on the islands. In traditional times, Tongans carved small statues and bowls and manufactured other items, such as baskets, mats, and sails, from tropical materials.

TRADE. Evidence indicates that, in traditional times, Tongans had large double-hulled canoes called *kalia* that could carry provisions for up to 200 people, and in them Tongans made extensive trading voyages between Fiji and Samoa.

DIVISION OF LABOR. Young males in traditional Tonga followed their father's occupation, with the eldest son receiving the title to the trade. Hereditary occupations included canoe building, fishing, and cooking; some trades could be hereditary or not, such as tattooing and barbering. Both men and women could be priests, and women also gathered reef fishes and fished with nets in the lagoon. Women manufactured valuable items (*koloa*), such as basketry, mats, and tapa, and women prepared kava. Kava, the nonnarcotic drink made from the roots of the *Piper methysticum* plant, continues to be an important social and ceremonial drink and elaborate rituals involving kava drinking exist for various ceremonial occasions such as marriages and funerals. Tapa, a clothlike material made from the bark of the paper mulberry tree (*Broussonetia papyrifera*), is still widely manufactured today for sale to tourists. Mats in traditional Tonga, woven for floors and walls, could also be worn as waist garments (*ta'ovala*) or used as sails for canoes. With a cash economy and increased sales of female-produced items for the tourist market, certain women now make more money than men, and tensions between the sexes have increased in contemporary Tonga.

LAND TENURE. Current Tongan law guarantees that every male over the age of 16 should receive an allotment of land: an *'api* of 3.3 hectares for agricultural purposes and 0.16 of a hectare as a site for a home. Because of population growth and limited natural resources, however, thousands of Tongan males are landless today. Prior to the Tongan constitution, established in 1875 by King George Tupou I (1797–1893), land rights in Tonga were vested with an extended kinship group, the *ha'a*, a corporate landholding and property-sharing descent group. The leadership of the ha'a distributed resources to members. In 1875, however, all land was acquired by the Crown for redistribution to a newly created class of hereditary nobles (*nopele*) for eventual redistribution to the people.

Kinship

KIN GROUPS AND DESCENT. Divided into various ha'a, traditional Tongan society had a patrilineal descent system, yet matrilineal lines were also taken into consideration for decisions involving chiefs. Tongan society was—and continues to be—an extremely rank-conscious society, with rank being based on age or birth order, gender, and kinship affiliation. There was a great deal of mobility in traditional Tongan society, and the rank of an individual on any given occasion was relative to the other individuals present at that occasion.

KINSHIP TERMINOLOGY. Kinship terminology was extended to collateral relatives, though to a lesser degree than in the Hawaiian system.

Marriage and the Family

MARRIAGE. Monogamy was and is the norm in Tonga, but in traditional times multiple marriages were not uncommon and marriage dis-

solutions and subsequent remarriages often occurred.

DOMESTIC UNIT. Traditionally, a wife became part of her husband's lineage upon marriage and set up residence in the territory of her husband's ha'a or in the area of a smaller kindred group (*kainga*). Large families were the rule in Tonga, and children were frequently adopted by individuals. The extended family was—and continues to be—an important organizing group in Tonga.

INHERITANCE. Currently there are strict rules of male primogeniture in Tonga, but in traditional times adopted and fictive kin could inherit various titles and possessions. Much of traditional Tongan consensus and flexibility was eliminated with the introduction of Tongan law codes and the constitution of 1875.

SOCIALIZATION. That which occurs in Tonga in day-to-day existence is *fakatonga*, or the Tongan way of life or doing things; Tongans have continuously adapted to changing environmental situations to the best of their abilities. The most important agents of socialization in traditional Tonga were members within the immediate family and then individuals of the ha'a: parents, siblings, and near relations were key. In contemporary Tonga, in addition to family relations, criteria

COCONUT HALVES

A young Tonga coconut harvester sits among split coconuts in Nukualofa. In traditional Tonga, tropical products such as coconuts and yams were cultivated on small farms. Nukualofa, Tongatapu, Tonga. (Dave Bartruff/Corbis)

such as religious affiliation, educational background, and whether one is of the nopele class or "commoner" class contribute to day-to-day socialization activities. Perhaps the most important expression of Tongan reality is the concept of 'ofa, literally "to love" or have a fondness towards an individual; the phrase 'ofa atu (literally, "love to you") can be heard on many important ceremonial occasions.

Sociopolitical Organization

SOCIAL ORGANIZATION. Tongan society was and is hierarchical in nature. There is an administrative class consisting of the agreed-upon titleholders or rulers, currently personified by the nobles (nopele) and the reigning monarch. Experts in traditions or spokespersons (matapule) are next, followed by the bulk of the populace, the commoners. Before the Europeans arrived in Tonga, the embodiment of all that was sacred and secular (and leader of all Tongans) was the individual designated as the "Tu'i Tonga." In approximately the fifteenth century, as Tongan society expanded in size, a division was made between the sacred and secular aspects of managing the islands. An individual who was the brother of the Tu'i Tonga was designated the "Tu'i Ha'a Takalaua," the administrator of the secular aspects of Tongan society. Approximately 200 years later, the Tu'i Ha'a Takalaua delegated some of his secular authority to his son and created the lineage known as the "Tu'i Kanokupolu." In traditional times, the fourth major Tongan individual was the sister of the Tu'i Tonga, designated the "Tu'i Tonga Fefine," given the title of "Tamaha." All Tongans, including the reigning monarch of the modern Kingdom of Tonga, theoretically trace their kinship affiliations, and hence their rank relative to one another, from these four chiefly titleholders. In traditional Tonga, succession to a title and chieftainship depended upon a variety of factors, especially the decision of the corporate landholding and property-sharing descent group. Any individual who had a position of authority in traditional Tongan society and had a title as evidence of rank did not have the title because of any inherent rights but only because he or she had the consensus of the governed group. The titleholder operated within a system of checks and balances that ensured that the governed were willing to be influenced and led by these individuals.

POLITICAL ORGANIZATION. Tongan culture began to change in the seventeenth century, when the first European explorers landed in the islands. The culmination of these changes took place in 1875 when the Tongan constitution was introduced. By the nineteenth century, a traditional and flexible system of titles and inheritance, which had been in operation for hundreds of years, passed out of existence. In 1875, a rigid father-to-son inheritance system was instituted and the inherent consensus and flexibility concerning the rights of leadership or chieftainship passed out of existence.

SOCIAL CONTROL. Informal social control could take the form of gossip when there was inadequate social reciprocity on various occasions. Tonga operates under a constitutional monarchy and in addition to the current reigning monarch there is an executive branch (consisting of the prime minister and a cabinet appointed by the king) as well as the legislative and judicial branches. The twenty-nine-member Legislative Assembly or parliament consists of the governors of Ha'apai and Yava'u, nine cabinet ministers, nine nobles, and nine commoners. Tonga also maintains the Tonga Defense School of 400 individuals, charged with maintaining public order, patrolling coastal waters, and engaging in various Kingdom of Tonga projects.

CONFLICT. Although Tongan oral histories report some traditional conflicts relating to political situations, Tongans were essentially peaceful islanders prior to the coming of European missionaries. In early nineteenth-century Tonga, the Christian missionaries made numerous efforts to convert the chiefs to the new religion, since if the chiefs converted, their people would follow. As word of missionary successes in the islands spread, other missionaries arrived and religious wars of intense fury began in 1826. Although it may not have been a deliberate nineteenth-century missionary plan, a divide-and-conquer policy saw non-Christian Tongans fighting against Christian Tongans, and there were additional conflicts in 1837, 1840, and 1852. With the aid of missionaries, three Tongan law codes were introduced to Tongans in 1839, 1850, and 1862. The culmination of all missionary involvement was the Tongan constitution of 1875. Tonga continues to have problems: its economy remains unsound and the lack of serious planning for its improvement may lead to political unrest in the future.

Religion and Expressive Culture

RELIGIOUS BELIEFS. Traditional Tongans believed in a multideity world including Tangaloa, who pulled up certain islands from the sea.

Tongan society was—and continues to be—an extremely rank-conscious society, with rank being based on age or birth order, gender, and kinship affiliation.

There were traditional gods of various trades (such as fishers or artisans) and gods of various ha'a. In observance of the strictures of fundamentalist Christianity, it is written into the Tongan constitution that the Sabbath is a legal day of rest in the Kingdom of Tonga, and no commercial activities or entertainment are officially allowed. It should be pointed out, however, that these legal regulations do not coincide with actual activities.

ARTS. In traditional Tonga, tattooing was an important form of ornamentation, but with European contact this traditional art has all but vanished. One of the highest forms of traditional arts that has survived into the twentieth century is tapa artistry. Tapa continues to play an important role in gift giving, being redistributed among Tongans on important occasions. Other forms of the expressive arts in Tonga surviving into the twentieth century include dances and kava preparation.

MEDICINE. Tongans practiced traditional medicinal techniques, utilizing local products and the assistance of Tongan specialists who interceded with the deities for good health. Today there are modern hospital facilities on Tongatapu.

DEATH AND AFTERLIFE. In traditional times, after a Tongan titleholder died the body would be interred in a royal tomb (*langi*) on Tongatapu Island, and the soul was believed to go to Pulotu, the home of Tongan deities and the location where Tongans were thought to reside with their principal gods in the afterlife. Prior to the introduction of Christianity, commoners were believed not to have souls, but this way of thinking appears to have changed. Tongan kinship ties are truly demonstrated at times of death, and each individual who is related to the deceased has a specific task to perform during the funeral activities. Black is the color of mourning in Tonga.

Bibliography

Connelly-Kirch, Debra (1982). "Economic and Social Correlates of Handicraft Sellers in Tonga." *Annals of Tourism Research*. 9:383–402.

Ferdon, Edwin N. (1987). *Early Tonga: As the Explorers Saw It, 1616–1810*. Tucson: University of Arizona Press.

Gifford, Edward W. (1929). *Tongan Society*. Bernice P. Bishop Museum Bulletin no. 61. Honolulu.

Tanham, George K. (1988). *The Kingdom of Tonga*. [RAND: N-2799-OSD, prepared for the Office of the United States Secretary of Defense.] Santa Monica, Calif. Rand Corporation.

Urbanowicz, C. F. (1977). "Motives and Methods: Missionaries in Tonga in the Early Nineteenth Century." *Journal of the Polynesian Society*. 86: 245–263.

Urbanowicz, C. F. (1979). "Changes in Rank and Status in the Polynesian Kingdom of Tonga." In *Political Anthropology: The State of the Art*, edited by S. L. Seaton and H. J. M. Claessen, 224–242. The Hague: Mouton.

Urbanowicz, C. F. (1989). "Tourism in Tonga Revisited: Continued Troubled Times?" In *Hosts and Guests: The Anthropology of Tourism*, 2nd ed., edited by Valene Smith, 105–117. Philadelphia: University of Pennsylvania Press.

—CHARLES F. URBANOWICZ

TROBRIAND ISLANDS

Ethnonyms: Kaileuna, Kilivila, Kiriwina, Kitava, Vakuta

Orientation

IDENTIFICATION. The Trobriand Islands were named for Denis de Trobriand, the first lieutenant in one of D'Entrecasteaux's frigates when this group of populated atolls and hundreds of islets was sighted in 1793. Traditionally, Kiriwina—the largest and most heavily populated island—and three other neighboring islands—Kaileuna, Kitava, and Vakuta—were each divided into discrete, named political districts. Although these divisions still exist, the islands now form a more unified political unit as parts of Milne Bay Province, Papua New Guinea.

LOCATION. The Trobriands (approximately 8°30′ S, 151° E) are situated about 384 km by sea from Port Moresby, the capital of Papua New Guinea, in the northern tip of the Massim. Kiriwina is 40 kilometers long but only 3.2 to 12.8 kilometers wide, and the other islands are much smaller. Except for Kitava, where cliffs rise sheer for 90 meters, the islands are relatively flat, crosscut by swampy areas, tidal creeks, and rich garden lands that abut rough coral outcroppings. Reefs may extend up to 10 kilometers offshore; anchorage is often dependent upon high tides and careful navigation. Temperatures and humidity are uniformly high. Rain showers, heavy but usually of short duration, average from 25 to 38 centimeters each month. Yet unexpected droughts can occur, causing severe food shortages.

DEMOGRAPHY. At the beginning of this century, the population in the Trobriands was about 8,000, but by 1990 it had increased to approximately 20,000. Although many young people leave the islands to find wage labor or to attend

♦ Massim
A region consisting of islands and island groups off the southeastern tip of New Guinea characterized by distinctive art styles and interisland exchange links, especially the kula system.

850

technical schools or the University of Papua New Guinea, a large percentage of them eventually return to resume village life.

LINGUISTIC AFFILIATION. The Kilivila language belongs to the Milne Bay Family of Austronesian languages. Although Kilivila is spoken on a few other Massim islands, the major speakers are Trobrianders. Mutually understandable local dialects are used in which different phonological rules are employed without affecting the syntax. Since the time of first contact, many English words have been incorporated into the Kilivila lexicon. Tok Pisin is rarely heard, although, along with Motu, it is often learned by Trobrianders who have resided elsewhere in Papua New Guinea. English is taught in the local grammar schools as well as the high school on Kiriwina, but less than half of the young population attend school.

History and Cultural Relations

The origin stories for each matrilineage describe how different groups arrived in the Trobriands from under the ground or by canoe and claimed garden and hamlet lands as their own. These claims were often contested by others who arrived later, so that subdivisions of matrilineages occurred. American whalers were in the northern Massim during the 1840s, and twenty years later Queensland's blackbirding ships made frequent kidnapping excursions to other islands in the vicinity. In the 1890s, Germans periodically sailed from New Britain to purchase tons of Trobriand yams, while wood carvings, decorated shells, and canoe prows were already becoming part of museum collections. The turn of the century marked the establishment of the Methodist Overseas Mission (now the United Church Mission) on Kiriwina, followed in 1905 by the arrival of Dr. Rayner Bellamy, the first Australian resident government officer. Bellamy spent ten years in charge of the government station on Kiriwina and assisted C. G. Seligman with ethnographic information during Seligman's Massim research. Following his mentor, Bronislaw Malinowski stopped on Kiriwina and then stayed for two years between 1915 and 1918. The Sacred Heart Catholic Mission arrived in the 1930s but during World War II all resident Europeans were evacuated. Australian and U.S. troops set up a hospital and two airstrips on Kiriwina. Although no battles were fought the area served as a staging ground for planes en route to Rabaul and the Coral Sea. In 1950, when Harry Powell arrived to undertake ethnographic research, surprisingly few fundamental cultural changes had occurred. Even in 1990, *kula*, the interisland exchange of arm shells and necklaces, was as intense as ever, while yam harvests and women's mortuary distributions remain as politically dynamic.

Settlements

Trobrianders live in named hamlets associated with specific garden, bush, and beach lands. Usually, from four to six hamlets are grouped together to form a discrete village with populations ranging from 200 to 500. Yam houses stand prominently around a central clearing, dwarfing the individual dwellings built behind this plaza. Chiefs may decorate their houses and their yam houses with ancestral designs and hang cowrie shells indicating differences in ranking. If a chief is polygynous, each wife will have her own separate house. In all other cases, husbands and wives live together with their young children while adolescent boys, and sometimes girls, have their own small sleeping houses close by their parents' living quarters. These are the houses widows and widowers retire to when they are too old to remarry. Hamlets look much as they did in Bronislaw Malinowski's photographs. Roofs are still thatched (although some metal roofs are in evidence) and the walls are made from plaited coconut-palm fronds. The interior of the house is private, with a fireplace and sleeping areas, while most social life takes place on the verandas. Burial plots are at the edge of the hamlet. From there footpaths provide quick communication between villages. On Kiriwina, only one vehicular road (with several spurs) bisects the island.

Economy

SUBSISTENCE AND COMMERCIAL ACTIVITIES. Trobrianders are yam growers par excellence. Through slash-and-burn technology, large yam harvests are produced once a year. Taro, sweet potatoes, bananas, sugarcane, leafy greens, beans, tapioca, squashes, coconuts, and areca palms are also grown. The pig population is small; pork is usually eaten only at special feasts. Few chickens are raised and fish provides the major protein source. There is almost no game, except for birds that are sometimes hunted; children catch and eat frogs, grubs, insect eggs, as well as mollusks they collect along the reefs. Since colonization, government attempts at developing cash crops have failed (except for a period of copra production) and only within the past few years has a local market run by women been installed on Kiriwina. Fishing provides many coastal men

♦ **Tok Pisin**
A lingua franca (sometimes called Neo-Melanesian Pidgin) that is now one of the official languages of Papua New Guinea.

♦ **blackbirding**
A form of labor recruiting, often involving coercion or deception. From the 1840s to the end of the nineteenth century thousands of male Pacific islanders were taken to Australia or South America as laborers to be returned home (though many were not) after a period of years in service.

*The strength of
Trobriander
matrilineal identity
is embodied in the
belief that
conception occurs
when an ancestral
spirit child enters a
woman's body.*

with cash incomes and a fishing cooperative has been successful on Vakuta Island. In the 1970s, weekend tourist charters resulted in increasing carving sales, but over the past decade tourism has declined dramatically. Ebony wood, once prized for fine carvings, is depleted and must be imported from other islands. A few Kiriwinans own successful trade stores; a guest lodge and two other trade stores are owned and run by expatriates. Today, remittances from children working elsewhere in the country provide villagers with their main source of cash. Women's bundles of dried banana leaves act as a limited currency when villagers buy trade-store foods, tobacco, kerosene, or cloth and sell such things to other villagers for payment in bundles. In this way, those without cash can purchase Western merchandise.

INDUSTRIAL ARTS. Most garden and other tools are metal. Canoes still are built in the traditional way, with their elaborately carved prows. Pandanus sleeping and floor mats, baskets, and armbands are woven; so are traditional women's skirts, which, although only worn on special occasions, are considered as wealth and are vital for mortuary exchanges. Bundles of dried banana leaves are also produced by women and as wealth are necessary for mortuary distributions. A few men still make arm shells for kula exchanges as well as decorations, such as *Spondylus* earrings and necklaces.

TRADE. Stone axe blades are men's wealth; in the last century the stones were traded in from Muyua Island and polished in the Trobriands. Large cooking pots, also used in local exchanges, come from the Amphlett Islands. Canoes from Normanby and Goodenough islands arrive periodically with sacks of betel nuts that are sold at the Kiriwina wharf. Kula voyaging also enables partners to bring back exotic goods from other islands.

DIVISION OF LABOR. Women and men work together in clearing new garden land. Men tend to planting yams and staking up the vines, as well as building garden fences and harvesting. Women produce other garden foods, although occasionally a woman decides to make her own yam garden. Men fish and butcher pigs. Women attend to the daily cooking, while men prepare pork and cook taro pudding for feasts. Men and women weave mats but only women make skirts and the banana-leaf bundles that are women's wealth.

LAND TENURE. Provisionally, hamlet, garden, bush, and beach lands are owned by a founding matrilineage and are under the control of the

lineage's chief or hamlet leader. Rights to residence and the use of land are given by these men to others, such as their sons, who are not members of the matrilineage. Land disputes are frequent and, because the court cases are public, they are fraught with tensions that sometimes lead to fighting. Knowledge of the history of the land from the time of the first ancestors legitimates a person's claim, but competing stories make the arbitrating chiefs' decisions difficult.

Kinship

KIN GROUPS AND DESCENT. The strength of matrilineal identity is embodied in the belief that conception occurs when an ancestral spirit child enters a woman's body. All members of the matrilineage are believed to have the "same blood" and also to have rights to the "same land." Land, ancestral names, body and house decorations, magic spells, dances, and taboos are all owned by members of individual matrilineages. Although men may lend the use of land and names to their children, they must be reclaimed by men's sisters at a later time. From birth, Trobrianders belong to one of four exogamous matriclans that are not corporate groups. Clan membership determines marriage categories, bringing together in alternating generations members of different matrilineages within the same clan who view themselves as close kin. These are the people who support each other in important exchange events.

KINSHIP TERMINOLOGY. Kin terms are a modified Crow type with a number of atypical features. For example, the same term is used for ego's mother and mother's brother's wife and the terms for parallel siblings-in-law are merged with parallel siblings.

Sociopolitical Organization

SOCIAL ORGANIZATION. Trobrianders are divided between those born into chiefly and commoner matrilineages. Chiefly matrilineages, ranked among themselves, own rights to special prerogatives surrounding food prohibitions and taboos that mark spatial and physical separation as well as rights to wear particular feather and shell decorations and to decorate houses with ancestral designs and cowrie shells. For all villagers including chiefs, the locus of social organization is the hamlet with networks of social relations through affinal and patrilateral ties to those living in other hamlets within the same village. Women and men also consider themselves kin to those whose ancestors came from the same place of origin. Traditionally, only members of chiefly lineages and their sons participated in kula, but now many more villagers (although by no means all) engage in kula. Chiefs remain the most important kula players.

POLITICAL ORGANIZATION. Each ranking matrilineage is controlled by a chief but the highest-ranking chief is a member of the *tabalu* matrilineage and resides in Omarakana village. The most important chiefly prerogative is the entitlement to many wives. At least four of each wife's relatives make huge yam gardens for her and this is the way a chief achieves great power. But if a chief is weak, he will have difficulty finding women to marry. The villagers of all the islands elect councillors who are members of the Kiriwina Local Government Council. Chiefs sit at the Council of Chiefs, and the Omarakana chief presides over both councils. Chiefs' kula partners are the most important players in other kula communities, and chiefs have the potential to gain the highest-ranking shells.

SOCIAL CONTROL. Disputes most often arise over land tenure, usually before the time of planting new yam gardens. Other causes of conflict concern cases of adultery, thefts, physical violence and, more rarely, sorcery accusations. The Council of Chiefs arbitrates most problems but some cases are referred to formal courts.

CONFLICT. Because of the many intermarriages that occur within a village, conflicts are quickly resolved by public debate. Warfare between village districts was a common occurrence prior to colonization. Such fighting, undertaken by chiefs, most often took place during the harvest season when political power or its absence was exposed. Today, fights sometimes erupt for the same reasons, but the presence of government officials usually holds these incidents in check. The most dangerous conflict is the traditional yam competition where the members of one matrilineage line up their largest and longest yams to be measured against the yams brought together by the members of a rival matrilineage. Lengthy speeches made by intervening kin or affines will usually stop the competition from proceeding. Once a winner is declared, the losers become the most dangerous enemies of the winning matrilineage for generations.

MARRIAGE AND FAMILY

Marriage

Most marriages occur between young people living in different hamlets within the same or neighboring villages. By marrying a father's sister's daughter—usually three generations removed—a man marries someone from another matrilineage within his father's clan. Endogamous clan marriages sometimes occur but they are regarded as incestuous and are not discussed openly. Only when a young man may inherit the leadership of the matrilineage will he live avunculocally in his mother's brother's hamlet. Other married couples usually reside virilocally in the young man's father's hamlet. The major commitment that follows each marriage is the annual yam harvest produced by the woman's father and eventually by her brother in the woman's name. These yams obligate her husband to obtain many bundles of banana leaves for her when she participates in a mortuary distribution. Divorce has few obstacles and although the couple's kin may seek to prevent the dissolution of the marriage there is little they can do if either spouse is adamant about their separation. If a divorced man wants one of his children to remain with him, he must give his wife's kin valuables. Remarriage is usual for both spouses. There are a few permanent bachelors but women do not go through life unmarried.

Domestic Unit

Nuclear families live together in one household. Older people usually take one of their grandchildren to live with them.

Inheritance

A villager's personal property, including magic spells, are given to those who have helped him or her by making yam gardens and assisting with other food. This is the way sons inherit from their fathers. Matrilineal property, such as land and decorations, is given to a man's sister's son, while a woman may inherit banana trees, coconut or areca palms, magic spells, and banana-leaf wealth from her mother. Among kula men, shells and partners are inherited either by a son or a sister's son. When a man dies, his house and yam house are destroyed and his wife usually returns to her natal hamlet.

Socialization

Young children are cared for by both parents. Because marriages often take place among people living in the same village, gradparents also provide child care. A man's sister performs beauty magic for his children and acts as a confidant when they reach puberty and seek out sexual liaisons. Children who attend the Kiriwina high school board during the week, while others who go to high schools on the mainland only return for holidays.

*Because of the many
intermarriages that
occur within a
Trobriander village,
conflicts are quickly
resolved by public
debate.*

Religion and Expressive Culture

RELIGIOUS BELIEFS. Trobrianders believe in spirits who reside in the bush who cause illness and death, but their greatest fear is sorcery. Only some people are believed to have the knowledge of spells that will "poison" a person and such experts can be petitioned to exercise their power for others. Counterspells are also known; chemical poisons obtained from elsewhere are thought to be prevalent. In addition, magic spells are chanted for many other desires, such as control over the weather, love, beauty, carving expertise, yam gardening, and sailing. Mission teachers have not disrupted the strong beliefs in and practice of magic. Recently, villagers from two hamlets have introduced a new fundamentalist religion whose tenets negate the practice of magic.

RELIGIOUS PRACTITIONERS. Most villagers own some magic spells, but only certain women and men are known to have the most sought after and powerful spells for gardening, weather, and sorcery. The most powerful spells are owned by the Omarakana chief. Some villages have resident mission catechists who conduct Sunday church services.

CEREMONIES. A series of rituals are performed for a pregnant woman, and for several months after birth the mother and infant remain secluded. Their emergence is marked by a feast. The largest festivities occur during the annual harvest season after the yams are brought from the garden and loaded into yam houses. Led by a chief or hamlet leader, a village may also host cricket matches, dancing, or competitive yam exchanges, all of which culminate in a huge feast for participants. Kula activities are surrounded by many rituals and feasts.

ARTS. Dances first brought by the original ancestors are still owned by the members of individual matrilineages. Drums are the only traditional musical instruments for these dances. Jew's harps or flutes made from bush materials are played for personal enjoyment. String bands are now common. Traditional songs are still sung when someone dies. Traditionally, only certain special people had the magical knowledge necessary to make them expert carvers of canoe prows, war shields, dancing paddles, large bowls, and betel chewing implements. Today, many other villagers carve tourist items.

MEDICINE. Some women and men are renowned curers, depending upon plants and herbs from the bush that they use with magic spells. A small hospital is located near the government station on Kiriwina, and medical aid posts (usually poorly stocked) are within walking distance of most villages. Adequate medical care is still a grave problem.

DEATH AND AFTERLIFE. When a person dies, the spirit goes to live on the distant island of Tuma where the ancestors continue their existence. At the end of the harvest period, the ancestors of a matrilineage return to the Trobriands to examine the well-being of their kin. The mourning and exchanges following a death are the most lengthy and costly of all ritual events. When a person dies, an all-night vigil takes place in which men sing traditional songs and the spouse and children of the deceased cry over the body. A series of food and women's wealth distributions takes place after the burial, and then the close relatives of the spouse and father of the dead person shave their hair and/or blacken their bodies while the spouse remains secluded. On Kiriwina, about six months later, women of the deceased's matrilineage host a huge distribution of skirts and banana-leaf bundles to repay the hundreds of people who have been in mourning. (On Vakuta Island, only skirts are exchanged.) The woman who distributes more wealth than anyone else is a big-woman. Today, trade-store cloth is sometimes used in place of bundles, and such cloth is central when a women's distribution is held in the capital by Trobrianders living there. Annual distributions of yams, pork, taro pudding, sugarcane, or betel nuts take place each year after an important person dies. When a harvest is especially large, a villagewide distribution is held that honors all the recently deceased from one clan.

Bibliography

Leach, Jerry W., and Edmund Leach, eds. (1983). *The Kula: New Perspectives on Massim Exchange.* Cambridge: Cambridge University Press.

Malinowski, Bronislaw (1922). *Argonauts of the Western Pacific.* London: Routledge & Kegan Paul.

Munn, Nancy (1986). *The Fame of Gawa: A Symbolic Study of Value Transformation in a Massim (Papua New Guinea) Society.* Cambridge: Cambridge University Press.

Scoditti, Giancarlo M. G. (1990). *Kitawa: A Linguistic and Aesthetic Analysis of Visual Art in Melanesia.* Berlin: Mouton de Gruyter.

Seligman, C. G. (1910). *The Melanesians of British New Guinea.* Cambridge: Cambridge University Press.

Weiner, Annette B. (1976). *Women of Value, Men of Renown: New Perspectives in Trobriand Exchange.* Austin: University of Texas Press.

Weiner, Annette B. (1988). *The Trobrianders of Papua New Guinea.* New York: Holt, Rinehart & Winston.

—ANNETTE B. WEINER

Russia and Eurasia

ARMENIANS

Ethnonyms: Self-designation: Hay. Other names include Armyanin (Russian) and Somekhi (Georgian). The land of Armenia is called Hayasdan.

Orientation

IDENTIFICATION. Historically, the Armenian nation has been situated in the Anatolian highlands of Asia Minor. Greater Armenia, as identified by the ancient Romans, once lay to the east of the Euphrates River, while Lesser Armenia lay to the west. At different times Armenian kingdoms have occupied territory within the present-day boundaries of modern Turkey, Iran, and Azerbaijan, as well as the Soviet Socialist Republic of Armenia. As recently as the early nineteenth century, Eastern Armenia was controlled by Persia and Western Armenia by the Ottoman Empire. In 1828 Eastern Armenia came under Russian rule. The transition to Soviet rule was marked by a brief and difficult period of independence (1918–1921). In 1915 many Armenians fled persecution and genocide in eastern Turkey (Western Armenia) and came as refugees to Eastern Armenia. This genocide and the subsequent seventy years of Soviet rule have played a major role in shaping contemporary Armenian culture and consciousness, in addition to determining the geography and demography of present-day Armenia.

LOCATION. The Armenian Republic (formerly the Armenian Soviet Socialist Republic) is in the southwestern region of the former Soviet Union, bordered on the east and west by Azerbaijan and Turkey, respectively, and on the north and south by Georgia and Iran, respectively. Its territory comprises 29,740 square kilometers, and its border is 1,422 kilometers long. Armenia encompasses multiple climatic zones, varying seasonally in temperature from −13° C to 25° C. Much of the land is dry and arid, which has made large-scale cultivation difficult.

The Armenian Republic consists of thirty-seven administrative regions and twenty-seven towns and has its own constitution and governmental institutions. The official language of the republic is Armenian. The three main industrial centers are the capital city, Erevan; the pre-Soviet capital city, Gumri (formerly Leninakan, and before that, Alexandropol); and Kirovakan. The republic consists of six economic regions: Ararat, Shirak, Lori, Agstev, Sevan, and Sjunik. Since the 1920s the Soviet republics of Armenia and Azer-baijan have opposed each other in a violent border dispute over the fertile region of mountainous Karabagh (the Nagorno-Karabagh Oblast), which by Soviet law is an autonomous region within the jurisdiction of Azerbaijan, but which is populated by a majority of Armenians (80 percent in the 1970s) and is, according to Armenian accounts, traditionally Armenian.

DEMOGRAPHY. In 1990 the population of the Armenian Republic was 3,515,000, with the second-highest population density in the Soviet Union. The ethnic composition of Armenia is highly homogeneous, with Armenians constituting 93.5 percent of the population. Russians make up 2.7 percent, and Kurds account for 1.5 percent. The remaining 2.3 percent is composed of other nationalities. Nearly 66 percent of the Armenian people live in urban areas, and 60 percent (1.5 million) live in Erevan, the republic's capital.

LINGUISTIC AFFILIATION. The Armenian language represents an independent subgroup of the Indo-European Language Family. The Armenian alphabet was devised in the early fifth century by Mesrop Mashtots, for the purpose of translating biblical texts and Christian liturgical materials. In the twentieth century, written Armenian has undergone two spelling reforms in Soviet Armenia, to improve the phonetic relationship between the written and spoken languages and to standardize the grammar. There are many spoken dialects in Armenia today.

History and Cultural Relations

The first known textual reference to the Armenians is by the Greek historian Xenophon, dated approximately 400 B.C. From this time on Armenians were a noted cultural presence in the Mediterranean world. Centered in eastern Anatolia, now within the boundaries of modern Turkey, historic Armenia was a buffer zone between successive empires: first between the Roman and Persian empires, and then between the Byzantine and Muslim empires. By the sixteenth century, Greater Armenia had been absorbed into the Iranian and Ottoman empires. This is the source of the division of Armenia into two cultural and linguistic halves: eastern and western. Today two dialects have been standardized: one for the Eastern and one for the Western Armenian peoples. Eastern and Western Armenia have distinctive cultural and literary traditions reflecting their linguistic differences. Today, Western Armenian is characteristically spoken in the Armenian diaspora by Armenians deriving from

Genocide and the subsequent seventy years of Soviet rule have played a major role in shaping contemporary Armenian culture and consciousness.

♦ **Asia Minor**
Also known as Anatolia, the peninsula of land that forms the Asian portion of Turkey.

See also

MIDDLE EAST: Persians, Turks

According to legend, Armenia was the first nation to convert to Christianity, between the years 301 and 330.

Turkey, Lebanon, Syria, and other countries of the Middle East—primarily those displaced by the genocide of Armenians in Turkey in 1915. Contemporary speakers of Eastern Armenian are characteristically indigenous to the region of historic Armenia (the current Armenian Republic) or belong to the Armenian communities of Iran. Yet the split between Eastern and Western Armenians predates the Soviet period; indeed, it goes back to the sociopolitical context of the Middle Ages.

According to legend, Armenia was the first nation to convert to Christianity, between the years 301 and 330, when a Parthian missionary, Saint Gregory the Illuminator, met the Armenian King Trdat. Prior to the national conversion, the first Christian Armenian church was founded by the saints Bartholomew and Thaddaeus in the first century. Despite the pressures of Zoroastrian Iranian, Islamic Seljuk (1063–1072) and Mamluk, Mongol (1242–1244 and 1400), Russian, and Soviet occupiers over the centuries, the Armenians have retained their Apostolic church to the present day. Although the church was at first subordinate to Constantinople, it broke away at the Council of Chalcedon in 451 to follow a Monophysite doctrine. Armenians nevertheless continued to make a significant cultural contribution to the Byzantine Empire, notably through their distinctive tradition of church architecture. In fact, it is rumored that when the Hagia Sophia Basilica was damaged by an earthquake, the Patriarch Basil sent for the Armenian architect Trdat to come to Constantinople and direct the repairs. Squinches, small archlike structures that make the structural transition from four walls to a circular dome (and upon which the dome rests), are often attributed to the Armenian architectural tradition, or even specifically to the architect Trdat.

Another major challenge to the authority of the Armenian church began in the late nineteenth century when, as part of a policy of Russification, the czarist government attempted to convert Armenians to the Russian Orthodox church with tactics such as the imprisonment of the Armenian clergy and the confiscation of church property. Yet the church has survived and is today enjoying a renaissance in its leadership of the Armenian people. Today several distinctive Armenian churches have formed in the diaspora, including a Protestant church (which originated under the influence of Presbyterian missionaries in Turkey in the nineteenth century); an Apostolic church with a *catholikosate* at Antelias, Lebanon; and an Armenian Catholic church. The majority of Arme-

nians both in the diaspora and in the Armenian Republic, however, belong to the Armenian Apostolic church, with its *catholikos* (primate) at Echmiadzin in the Armenian Republic.

Today, in the context of *perestroika*, and *glasnost*, the conflict with Azerbaijan over the Nagorno-Karabagh region, an Armenian nationalist movement is growing in the republic. Born out of conditions of oppression and persecution in the late nineteenth century, Armenian nationalist parties last dominated Armenian politics in the republic during the period of independence. Often having a Socialist agenda, these parties stated as their goal the liberation and improvement of the Armenian people. These groups retained some power among Armenians in the diaspora throughout the Soviet period.

Settlements

Traditional Armenian villages generally consisted of two or three hundred households or, in the mountainous regions, twenty to thirty farms. Although separate, the households were interdependent. When village families could not produce enough to meet their own subsistence needs they engaged in barter. Individual houses were often arranged around a central courtyard or were grouped together around a communal space in which fruit trees were usually grown. The flat roofs of contiguous houses provided a space where neighbors and relatives might gather socially (although in some regions subterranean houses might have domed or cone-shaped roofs with a central opening called *yerdik'*). Most often, the individual houses each consisted of a stable and two rooms: one for the reception of guests and one for general living. Part or all of the structure was often subterranean, a building feature derived from defense tactics. External walls were built of either mud bricks or the indigenous *tuf* (tufa, a kind of volcanic rock). Kitchens and bathrooms (outhouses) were usually located in external structures. There was usually a special oven, called a *t'onir*, in the center of the earthen floor of the reception room. The t'onir is a round hole dug in the ground, which can be used for baking Armenian flat bread (*lavash*) and for heating the home in winter. In some households, the fire in the t'onir was never extinguished and was said to symbolize the family. The t'onir is still common to Armenian village households today.

Living arrangements, accommodations, and architectural styles differed from village to village and were altogether different in the towns of Alexandropol (later Leninakan, now Gumri) and

♦ **Byzantine Empire**
The eastern half of the Roman Empire that survived the fall of the western half and lasted until 1453, when it fell to the Turks. The capital at Constantinople was established in A.D. 330.

Erevan, where people participated much less in their neighbors' daily lives. In the towns, family units were smaller and men were primarily artisans, merchants, and traders by profession. Residents of the villages might come to the towns to visit the bazaar, where most business was conducted. Traditionally, in addition to the Armenian populations of Alexandropol and Erevan, there have been large Armenian populations in the cities of Tbilisi (the capital of Georgia) and Baku (the capital of Azerbaijan). Generally these Armenians were also artisans, merchants, and businessmen.

Kinship

KIN GROUPS AND DESCENT. Traditional Armenian cultural practices have changed dramatically since the 1915 genocide and subsequent dispersal of Armenians from eastern Anatolia. Many traditional elements still characterize contemporary Armenian life, however, particularly in rural villages of the former Soviet Union. The most general category of Armenian descent was the *azk*, a nonresidential community of Armenians with kinship and political loyalties. The largest unit of Armenian kinship was the clan (*gerdastan*). While this term may refer to the immediate relatives of a single parent or grandparent, it is also used to describe patriarchal, patrilineal clans that included ancestors in the male line, sometimes extending as far back as six or eight generations. These clans resembled other European and Caucasian clan organizations dating back to the Middle Ages. Among the many responsibilities of the head of the clan were the maintenance of clan honor, consent for all marriages, the burial of deceased clan members, and the avenging of blood feuds. Clans often served the purpose of self-defense against other clans and other peoples.

Although the clans were not characteristically residential, they sometimes occupied a particular territory within a village. In such cases, a network of blood ties constituted a cooperative economic unit, and consensus was required among male members for the disposal of any property. Both residentially and nonresidentially based clans were exogamous, with strict taboos against marriage between second cousins and between god kin and against levirate.

Marriage and Family

MARRIAGE. Armenian families were traditionally patrilocal, requiring that the bride move to the home of the groom's parents at the time of marriage. In traditional Armenian society marriages were arranged by the families of the bride and groom or by a matchmaker hired by the groom's family. In-law (*khnami*) relations were very important to social life in the village, and therefore the wedding was a social event involving the entire community. The average age of a bride

ECONOMY

Subsistence and Commercial Activities

Less than one-third of the land of historic Armenia was arable, and cereals were the staple crop. Although the crops were the responsibility of the men, the women often helped during the harvest if extra hands were needed.

Clothing

For nearly 200 years European styles of dress have been popular in Armenian towns and cities. Until the Soviet period, however, traditional dress could be found in many villages. For both men and women traditional garb consisted of baggy trousers covered by long shifts and overcoats. Men in particular might wear sheepskin hats and elaborate metalwork belts made in the style of their particular region. It was popular for women to wear their hair in long braids until marriage and to wear gold and silver jewelry (especially coins), which represented the family's wealth and investments. Most clothing was made of wool, although cottons and silks were used when they were available. Many features of traditional Armenian dress are common to other peoples of the Caucasus.

Food

The Armenian diet was somewhat monotonous, consisting largely of grains and cereals. Bulgur, pilaf, porridge, and flat bread were staple items. Dairy products were also commonly eaten, such as yogurt, milk, butter, and cheese. A popular Armenian drink to this day is *tan*, a mixture of water and soured yogurt. Fruits such as apricots and figs were dried for consumption in the winter and were often eaten with nuts. Other fruits, such as berries, were canned, and vegetables were pickled. Grapes were very commonly grown in Eastern Armenia, where there is a long history of wine production. Meat was eaten rarely, usually only when an animal could not be sustained through the long winter. Livestock were kept primarily for dairy products, and in winter they shared living quarters with the family.

Prior to an Armenian burial, the body is kept at home, and the coffin lid is placed upright by the front door of the house.

(*hars*) was between 14 and 16 years, while the average age of the groom (*p'esa*) was between 15 and 20. The bride and groom were generally, but not always, acquainted prior to the engagement. The engagement began as a series of negotiations between families and did not involve the participation of either the bride or groom. When the boy's father ascertained the approval of the girl's father for the marriage, the "word was tied" (*khosgab*, i.e., preengagement, occurred), and the female relatives on both sides began visiting one another. With the first visit of the girl's entire family to the home of the boy, the actual engagement and in-law relationship was established. The engagement usually lasted from several months to two years, during which the boy and girl were prohibited from talking with one another during family visits. If the girl had older, unmarried sisters, it was considered important for her to wait for them to marry first. A party to celebrate the formal betrothal was hosted by the girl's parents, and at this party the boy's mother placed gold coins or some other ornament (like a ring) on the girl (*nshan*), thus instigating the period of her initiation as bride in the boy's household.

The wedding celebration itself (*harsanik'*) was commonly held in autumn (approximately one year after the engagement). It would begin on a Friday and last between one and seven days, with the consummation occurring on a Sunday evening. On the wedding day the groom and his party would go to the home of the bride, where she would be dressed by his godmother or, if dressed by her own female relatives, she would be veiled by the godmother. An outer veil was removed after the wedding ceremony; an inner veil was not removed until after consummation of the marriage. After she was dressed, the bride was escorted to the church by the groom and his relatives. The marriage took place there, and the godparents (*k'avor* and *k'avorkin*) of the groom usually presided over the ceremony as well as over the subsequent festivities. These festivities were conducted at the home of the groom, where all the guests gathered. Upon entering the house, the bride and groom would break dishes, jars, or sometimes eggs to symbolize good luck in the new home. Also during their entrance to the house, the bride and groom wore lavash (traditional Armenian flat bread) draped over their shoulders to ward off evil spirits. The wedding festivities usually included (and still do in some regions of Armenia) the pre-Christian practice of jumping over a fire three times to ensure fertility.

The bride and groom would "fly" (*t'rrch'il*) over the fire together, while the guests circled around them, holding hands and dancing. The bride was expected to remain quiet throughout the party, both in respect for her in-laws and husband and in sorrow at leaving her own family. The period directly preceding the wedding ceremony was one of joviality for the groom and of lamentation for the bride, who was about to permanently leave her home. On the day following the wedding ceremony the groom's parents would send a red apple to the parents of the bride, to recognize the bride's virginity. The bride was prohibited from seeing her family for the first week after marriage but on the seventh day her parents would visit her at the home of her in-laws, bringing symbolic gifts or sometimes the trousseau. This practice is known as "head washing" (*gloukha laval*). The bride herself was not permitted to visit her parents until after the birth of her first child or, with the permission of her mother-in-law, after forty days. Many of these practices pertaining to marriage are still common today in the Armenian Republic, although generally engagements are shorter, lasting one to two months. Similarly, whereas autumn was traditionally the season for weddings—because fruits and vegetables were still available, because the summer's wine was ready to be drunk, and because animals that could not be supported during the long winter could be slaughtered—today weddings take place year-round.

DIVISION OF LABOR. Labor in the household economic unit was strictly divided according to the principles of gender and generation: the patriarch managed communal work and the incomes of all family members, while domestic work and the household itself were supervised by the wife of the head of the family. The rigidity of the domestic labor hierarchy and the pertinence of gender and generation to the associated social roles are best illustrated by the subordinate position of the new bride. Upon entering the household of her in-laws, the bride was expected to serve all of its members. Because cooking was the privileged work of the mother-in-law, the bride's responsibilities included menial tasks such as cleaning the shoes of all household members. Her face was usually veiled in public for at least one year (and sometimes it was tightly bound, a practice known as *mounj*), and during a ritual period of silence she was allowed to speak to no one except children and her husband (should they find themselves completely alone). After the birth of her first child, she was sometimes permitted to speak to the women of her household. Some women maintained a period of ritual silence for ten years or for life. The other responsibilities of the bride included kissing the hands of elders, never falling asleep if her father-in-law was still awake, and helping him to dress and undress. Humiliating tasks were considered an initiation of the new bride into the household. In general, women's responsibilities included the preparation of food, clothing, and domestic items such as candles, soap, and pottery; the weaving of rugs; and the tending of dairy animals and poultry. While women were working, the eldest children of the household would care for the younger children. This required little work in the case of infants, who were swaddled. Men were responsible for the heavy agricultural work, the building of houses and furniture, and the working of leather. The vast majority of labor was organized by family units, although occasionally an entire village might undertake a project. Hospitality, regarded by Armenians as a great virtue, was considered to be the obligation of everyone, male and female.

DOMESTIC UNIT. Within a village, families resided either in extended family (clan, or gerdastan), or nuclear (*untanik`*) units. Extended family residences were usually multigenerational and consisted of somewhere between fifteen and fifty relatives who were bound together by principles of patrilineal descent. Residential nuclear families usually consisted of an elder married son who had left the extended family home with his wife and older children.

INHERITANCE. The extended family home was typically inherited by the youngest son, who remained there with his wife and children and cared for his parents after his elder brothers had moved away. Property was nevertheless generally distributed evenly among brothers. The senior male of the domestic family was usually succeeded by his eldest son, and the wife of the family head was typically succeeded by the eldest son's wife.

Sociopolitical Organization

Village organization was often distinct from clan organization. The traditional Armenian village (*kiwgh*) was governed by a local patriarchal headman, usually a senior representative of the wealthiest family in the village. However, the village headman (*tanouter*) was elected by residents, who usually cast votes by placing a nut or a bean in the hat of their candidate. The headman's responsibilities included mediating domestic and village-level quarrels, distributing tax loads, and punishing violations of custom.

Religion and Expressive Culture

RELIGIOUS BELIEFS AND PRACTICES. Most rituals in Armenian tradition follow the calendar of the Armenian Christian church, so that, for example, Easter and various saints' days are often celebrated. The new year is celebrated on 1 January in Soviet tradition, and it is customary for people to go visiting from house to house on that day to wish each other luck and success for the new year. At midnight of New Year's Eve, it is common to go to the cemetery to visit and drink a toast to deceased family members. Christmas is celebrated by Armenians on 6 January, which is also the date of Christmas in the Orthodox church. Like other peoples of the Near East, Armenians believe in the evil eye and have various ritual means of diverting it, such as wearing blue clothing or a clove of garlic.

ARTS. Education and the arts have traditionally been held in high esteem in Armenian society. In the late nineteenth and early twentieth centuries, many young men were sent abroad for education and made significant contributions to international education, letters, and business. In the former Soviet Union, Armenians were particularly recognized for their contributions to science and the arts. A Western Armenian literary tradition has flourished in the diaspora, and Armenians have achieved a worldwide reputation for literature and painting. Armenians have been active in the government and politics of many countries of the world. Armenian folk arts notably include metalwork, woodwork, rug weaving, and verbal arts.

MEDICINE. In the nineteenth century Armenians practiced various healing rituals, but today medical care is primarily of the Soviet type. Exceptions are the treatment of colds or small wounds: the remedy for a sore throat is to take lemon with honey, and yogurt is used as a salve for the treatment of skin wounds.

DEATH AND AFTERLIFE. Armenian funerals generally take place three days after death. Prior to the burial, relatives and close friends gather at the home of the deceased; the men might stand and talk while the women take coffee and pastries together. The body is kept at home until the burial, and the coffin lid is placed upright by the front door of the house as a sign to neighbors that there has been a death in the family. The grave is visited by close friends and relatives on the seventh and fortieth days after death and on the anniversary, as well as at New Year. Until the visit on the fortieth day, male members of the family are prohibited from shaving. Food, alcoholic beverages, and flowers are common offerings for the dead.

Bibliography

Hoogasian-Villa, Susie, and Mary Kilbourne Matossian (1982). *Armenian Village Life before 1914.* Detroit: Wayne State University Press.

Matossian, Mary Kilbourne (1962). *The Impact of Soviet Policies in Armenia.* Leiden: E. J. Brill.

Suny, Ronald G. (1983). *Armenia in the Twentieth Century.* Chico, Calif.: Scholars Press.

UNIDO (1990). *Industry Brief: Armenia—"Towards Economic Independence and Industrial Restructuring."* United Nations Industrial Development Organization.

—STEPHANIE PLATZ

ASHKENAZIM

Ethnonym: Yevrei

Orientation

IDENTIFICATION. "Ashkenaz" refers to the first settlements of Jews in northwestern Europe, on the banks of the Rhine, and to the culture, conservative of sources and customs, as developed through study of Torah (which can refer to the first five books of the Old Testament, the entire Old Testment, or all of Jewish law) and Talmud (a collection of laws and traditions). Since at least the fourteenth century, "Ashkenazim" has referred to German Jews and their descendants anywhere in the world. Ashkenazim share with Jews worldwide an origin myth based on the cycle of stories about the Ten Lost Tribes, according to which Jews came to Germany after the destruction of the first temple in Jerusalem (586 B.C.). Ashkenazi culture then spread from Germany and northern France to Poland and Lithuania and then to Russia, among other countries. Ashkenazi society was based on the monogamic Jewish family and governed itself on community and synod levels.

This article focuses on Ashkenazim residing in areas of the Russian, Belarussian, and Ukrainian republics (formerly centers of the Jewish Pale of Residence of the Russian Empire), which were Soviet territory from before World War II until 1990 (between 75 and 90 percent of Soviet Jews).

The actions of others and their images of Jews have strongly influenced Jewish culture. Limitations on Jews' ability to express ethnicity have almost eradicated knowledge about their religion and history and have accelerated their assimilation into the dominant society. Paradoxically, these limitations have also intensified the feeling of difference that Jews experience. Jewish identity is constructed as much in "opposition" to what is felt to be a hostile environment as in terms of common lineage and history. Vital to Ashkenazi culture are characterizations of Jews as seen through the eyes of others—for example, "Zionist" (especially since 1967), "conspiratorial" (Slavophile), "Western and materialist" (Revolutionary), "capitalist" (Stalin era), "rootless cosmopolitans," and exploitative and profiteering middlemen; also contributing to Ashkenazi culture has been the image of the Jew in literature: the sickly, cowardly, pushy, avaricious, curly-haired individual with a long hooked nose, grotesque and provincial, taking the best jobs in Russia, having secret allegiances elsewhere. The "Jewish accent," influenced by Yiddish expressions, phonetics, intonation, and syntax, is common in the Ukraine, less so in Russian cities and among the highly educated. Many jokes are made about the Jewish manner of speech, so it can be a matter of irritation, self-consciousness, or both.

Clothing styles that had hardly changed for centuries disappeared after 1917. Nevertheless, "differences" may exist between Jewish and Soviet styles, perhaps as slight nuances in tailor- or homemade clothes, and because some Jews save money and purchase goods from abroad. Despite being the most extremely assimilated Jews in the former USSR, the Ashkenazim maintain a distinct identity, involving a combination of desires to preserve their Jewishness and at the same time to be as invisible in it as possible.

LOCATION AND DEMOGRAPHY. Census figures underestimate the Jewish population because younger Jews or those with greater social aspirations often want to hide their Jewish identity. At age 16, children of mixed-nationality marriages may choose to have either parent's nationality on their passports, and it is considered less advantageous to be known as a Jew. "How is he on the fifth point?," referring to the fifth point, nationality, on Soviet official documents, means "Is he a non-Jew?" or, in other words, "Can we hire him?" Thus, although the 1979 census showed a population of 701,000 Jews in Russia (38.7 percent of Soviet Jews, 0.5 percent of the Russian population), 634,000 in the Ukraine (35 percent

See also

EUROPE: Ashkenazic Jews
MIDDLE EAST: Jews in
Israel

of Soviet Jews, 1.3 percent of the Ukrainian population), and 135,000 in Byelorussia (7.5 percent of Soviet Jews, 1.4 percent of the Byelorussian population), a more accurate total is between 1.5 and 2 million.

Because of emigration, mixed marriage, and the relatively high percentage of older Jews (26.5 percent of Jews are over 60, but only 12 percent of ethnic Russians are), Ashkenazim are one of the very few groups with a declining population. Since as early as 1926, Jews have had the lowest birth rate of any major ethnic group in the USSR.

Nearly all Ashkenazim are now urban, a phenomenon that began at the end of the nineteenth century because of pogroms and poverty caused by village overpopulation. Small Jewish villages essentially ceased to exist after World War II. Emigration further diminished the population.

Anti-Semitism is felt to be strongest—and more constitutive of Jewish identity—in the Ukraine, Belarus, and Russian cities and towns than in the Baltic states, Caucasus, and Central Asia, but Moscow is widely considered to be the most attractive place in the former USSR (there were 8,473 Jews in Moscow in 1897; at present there are about 250,000); most Jews born there remain there or emigrate, and over one-half of Jews moving from other regions move to Moscow. Leningrad's Jewish population is about 160,000. On the opposite extreme is the Ukraine, where only about one-half of Jews born there stay.

EMIGRATION. About 2 million Jews emigrated to the Americas and Palestine between 1881 and 1914. After the Six Day War in 1967 the attempt to emigrate accelerated; 30.9 percent of Jews in the Ukraine requested visas, 12.6 percent of Jews in the Russian Republic requested visas, and in Byelorussia 18.7 percent of Jews submitted requests (a total of 125,788 requests were granted for the three republics). From 1979 to 1985 about 12 percent of Soviet Jews emigrated, of which 60 percent settled in Israel. Interest in emigration continues to increase, motivated by desires to relate to Jewish tradition, rejoin family or friends, improve one's financial position, or (most common) to live free of discrimination. The state of Israel is valued as a symbol of historical and cultural unity and continuity.

The Six Day War was a turning point in many Jews' self-images and the beginning of a renewal of interest in Jewish culture, although much emigration is not to Israel: from 1973 to 1976, only 25 percent of those emigrating from Moscow, Leningrad, and Kiev and 6 percent of those emigrating from Odessa on Israeli visas went to Israel, though this tendency changes in different emigration waves.

LINGUISTIC AFFILIATION. In czarist Russia, Jews spoke Yiddish in everyday life and knew Hebrew, the language of Jewish religion. Now children speak Russian as a first language, and in the Ukraine and Belarus they study Yiddish and Hebrew also and often speak them fluently. Before and after the 1917 Revolution the Jewish community debated whether Yiddish or Hebrew had primacy in Jewish life. In 1918 Yiddish was officially recognized as the "proletarian" Jewish language, and the instruction of Hebrew was forbidden in secondary schools. In 1909, 96.9 percent of all Jews of the Russian Empire considered either Hebrew or Yiddish their native tongue. By 1979 this had dropped to 14.2 percent (almost all older people), with Yiddish considered a second language by 5.4 percent. In Russia, the Ukraine, and Belarus the decline is much more dramatic. After the Revolution, Hebrew was taught only to a limited extent in universities. Currently, it has begun to be taught again by some 100 teachers across the former republics, with about 500 students (one-half the USSR total) in Moscow and about 200 in Leningrad. Among educated city Jewry, Hebrew is preferred over Yiddish, perhaps because it carries associations with ancient history and biblical tradition rather than with a more recent, "degrading" past.

Yiddish formed during the tenth to twelfth centuries in Germany, is based on German dialects, and contains much Hebrew (taken from the Bible and the Talmud), Russian, Polish, and Ukrainian. In a 1932 attempt to "dehebraize" the culture, Yiddish orthography was changed by transcribing Hebrew loanwords phonetically and eliminating the five final letters of the alphabet. Until after World War II Yiddish was spoken openly on the street. Everyday use of Yiddish has largely disappeared, with knowledge of Yiddish being greater with each higher age group; some older people spoke it as a first language and use it at home; later generations were hardly exposed to it.

History and Cultural Relations

Ashkenazi travelers and traders were in Russia before the twelfth century, but significant movement east from Germany and Bohemia occurred slowly over the thirteenth to sixteenth centuries, first to Poland-Lithuania (where at the end of the fifteenth century the Jewish population was only 10,000 and 15,000) and then to the Ukraine, Belarussia, and Russia, where the first legislation mentioning Jews was in the sixteenth century.

During World War II many of the most traditional Ashkenazim were killed (estimates vary between 1.2 and 2.5 million).

Ashkenazim

Yiddish, formed during the tenth to twelfth centuries, is based on German dialects, and contains much Hebrew, Russian, Polish, and Ukrainian.

Small Jewish communities, *shtetls* rarely had large-scale industry, surviving on trade with peasants. The central communal organization of the shtetl surveyed weights and measures, interacted with professional groups (such as midwives and town musicians) and with scribes, teachers, and other professionals to regulate fees, wages, and so forth, and also governed artisan guilds, which often combined social, administrative, religious, and economic institutions. Rabbis regulated aspects of everyday life governed by Jewish law: butchers and food preparation; ritual baths; tiny scrolls for door posts; observation of the Sabbath, of weddings, and other ceremonies; and the administration of justice. Myriad charities and philanthropic groups were supported by donations even from poor Jews. Shtetls had no public places of amusement; life centered on the *beis hamidrash* ("house of study") and the synagogue, where morning, afternoon, and evening prayers were attended by male community members.

In the eighteenth century Jews were first banished from Russia and from Ukrainian and Belarussian territories; then, on the basis of mercantilist theories, there was some readmission. Settlements increased after 1772, augmented by partitions of Poland, which added thousands of Jews to the empire. Catherine II established a Jewish "Pale of Residence." Jews were allowed to do business only in certain regions. The "Black Hundreds" anti-Semitic movement encouraged pogroms and massacres in the Ukraine.

In the nineteenth and early twentieth centuries, pauperization of villagers caused men to travel for work, move to cities, and emigrate. Of those who moved to the cities, a small number advanced in banking, industry, and the professions, but poverty and crowding in the ghettos increased. Jewish communities had always had internal class conflicts, but they grew in severity as economic conditions worsened. Jews were active in the two large anticzarist and other revolutionary movements. Theodore Herzl's writings and the formation of the World Zionist Organization fueled a nationalist movement among all groups of Jews. The Marxist-Socialist Bund, General Alliance of Jewish Workers, was an important component of Russian Social Democracy and the Revolutionary movement. In 1903 and 1905 pogroms, about 1,000 Jews were killed and thousands wounded, despite a new self-defense movement. The 1917 revolutions abolished anti-Semitism along with all national and religious discrimination. Economic changes undermined the role of the shtetl, increasing migration to cities. Even in the traditional Pale, youth and intellectuals were attracted to Bolshevik internationalist, socialist ideals; there were Jews at the top of the Communist party (e.g., Sverdlov, Zinoviev, Yoffe, Litvinov, Radek, Trotsky) and in the party ranks: in 1927 Jewish party members numbered 44,155 in the three republics; Jews comprised the largest group of party members after ethnic Russians and Ukrainians. In 1926, 4.4 percent of the Red Army officers were Jewish. The Revolution and communism were and are now again perceived by many as non-Russian phenomena, occurring under the influence of "foreigners," especially Jews. From 1917 to 1921 over 50,000 Jews were killed in Ukrainian pogroms. Many shopkeepers and independent craftsmen adapted well to the opportunities for private economic initiative allowed in the "New Economic Policy" (1920s) but were later held up as symbols of bourgeois exploitation. The percentage of Jews in agriculture dropped from its 2.33 percent level in 1897, but when NEP failed to help economic distress and thousands of families were surviving on help from Western Jewry, Jewish agricultural settlements were established in the Ukraine, Byelorussia, and the Crimea. By 1930, 11 percent of Jews made their living on these settlements, but these tens of thousands of families had moved back by 1939. For example, in 1928 Birobijan, a 36,000-square-kilometer territory in southeast Siberia, was established as an "Autonomous Jewish Region" giving Jews the territory required by the definition of a nationality and as an "alternative" to Zionism, but by 1933, 11,450 of the 19,635 Jews who had moved to Birobijan had returned; the population has declined since.

During World War II many of the most traditional Ashkenazim were killed (estimates vary between 1.2 and 2.5 million), including 33,771 killed within thirty-six hours and up to 90,000 in the following months at Babi Yar, a ravine outside Kiev in 1941. Yevtushenko's poem "Babi Yar," a rare affirmation by a non-Jew, was important for the Soviet Jewish self-image. Two hundred thousand Jews died in the Red Army. What remained of Jewish collective farms in the Ukraine was almost totally destroyed by Nazis and Ukrainian collaborators.

After World War II, under the auspices of Stalin's campaign against "cosmopolitanism," remaining synagogues, schools (in 1949, the last Yiddish school, in Birobijan, was closed), and publications were closed; literature and religious objects were confiscated and destroyed; rabbis, writers, and Jews of all professions were harrassed, attacked in the press, imprisoned, de-

♦ **Siberia**
Territory from the Ural Mountains to the Pacific Ocean and from the Arctic Ocean to the borders of Kazakhstan, Mongolia, and China.

ported to Siberia, and killed. Twenty-four Jewish writers were executed on 12 August 1952. In 1953 a group of doctors was tried for terrorism, followed by an anti-Semitic campaign. After Stalin's death this campaign was cut back and some of the accused and executed were "rehabilitated." The charge of "economic crimes," however, has often (particularly during the 1960s Krushchev regime) been brought against Jews.

Assimilation of Ashkenazim into Russian culture has at various points in history been imposed from the outside and desired by some within the community: Czar Nicholas I undertook to Russify the Jews by a combination of methods: Christianization, deportation, assigning prolonged army service, granting some the right to study in Russian schools, and establishing state schools for Jews. Alexander II liberalized the right of Jewish merchants of the first guild, graduates of Russian schools, and skilled artisans to exit the Pale and facilitated the promotion of Jews in professions formerly closed to them. After Alexander II's assassination, this Russianization was replaced by renewed distinctions made between Jews and others. In the mid-nineteenth century the "Haskalah" Jewish enlightenment movement supported assimilation, opposing as "separatist" aspects of Judaism such as the education system and traditional dress.

Because the culture underwent specific changes during successive political and cultural eras in the twentieth century, contemporary Ashkenazim can be seen in terms of "generations"; most born at the end of the nineteenth century and the beginning of the twentieth were raised with traditional Jewish educations, speaking Yiddish and observing religious and dietary laws. Forty-six percent of employed Jews were artisans, home workers, and factory workers; 39.4 percent were merchants, shopkeepers, and commercial agents; 2.33 percent were farmers; and 4.38 percent professionals and civil servants. Unemployment was high. Jews represented 72.8 percent of all tradesmen, 31.4 percent of artisans (primarily tailors, cobblers, and other clothing workers, stereotypical Jewish professions, but also many metalworkers, gold- and silversmiths, and barbers), and 20.9 percent of those engaged in transportation. This profile is radically different from that of other nationalities: 38.6 percent of Jews were in trade and only 3.7 percent of Russians.

In the generation between 1917 and World War II, the employed Ashkenazi population was entirely redistributed from commerce and craftsmanship to industry and "nonphysical labor." In 1918 the Yevsektsii (Jewish sections of the Communist party) were designed (under Stalin, commissar for Nationality Affairs) to help find a proletarian answer to the "Jewish question." Yevsektsii, in cooperation with Jewish local officials, were responsible both for an initial upsurge in theater, newspapers, and schools and for closing synagogues and other traditional institutions and staging trials to dramatize failings of the religion. Russian language and culture became the principal modes of life, Jewish sociopolitical and cultural activity disappeared or went underground, Jewish cultural activity in Russian declined, and the officially supported use of Yiddish was limited. The generation of the 1920s and those following were raised as Russian Communists; there was danger and little interest in consciously passing down to the next generation information about Judaism. Jews born in the 1940s and 1950s who were interested in rediscovering Jewish culture resorted to books, but the extreme difficulty of obtaining such materials made this rare. Since the mid-1960s there has been some renewed interest in Judaism, and since the mid-1980s materials, classes, and study groups have become more available.

Responding to what was called "the excessive number of Jews in establishments of secondary education," quotas were established for matriculation in 1885, but the 1917 Revolution initially suppressed them (the number of Jewish students tripled between 1917 and 1926, reaching 26 percent of university students and 46 percent of medical students in the Ukraine). This resulted in more Jews getting Russian educations, accompanied by a break with tradition. Education has in a sense absorbed the value of the rest of tradition as well as of a homeland, making the experience of encountering institutional quotas in the Soviet and post-Soviet eras particularly painful for them.

Absence of ritual slaughterers, food shortages, and lack of interest have eliminated the practice of keeping kosher at most homes, although a few individuals have recently learned kosher slaughter; others have become vegetarian so as to avoid nonkosher meat. Kosher observances have basically been transformed into a generalized desire for cleanliness in food preparation. Jewish-style fish, chicken, and other dishes have remained and influenced local cuisine. Many families mark holidays only with a meal of traditional foods, including ethnic Russian or Ukrainian dishes.

Sociocultural Organization

Jews traditionally help each other in matters such as obtaining goods and maintaining contacts.

Religion was traditionally the center of the Jewish community, and men were at the center of ritual life.

Most Jews still count many or a majority of Jews among their friends, a tendency strongest in people over 40, Ukrainian- and Belarus-area Jews, lower social classes, and certain groups of higher social classes. Preference for Jewish associates is strengthened by an awareness of shared weakness, of being a persecuted people, strangers wherever they are; the everpresent possibility of "things getting worse for the Jews" is a frequent topic of conversation.

Religion was traditionally the center of the community, and men were at the center of this ritual life. Girls' educations were usually rudimentary, and they learned religious and practical aspects of keeping a home and raising children by helping their mothers. Marriages were often arranged between parents by a marriage broker. If necessary, a woman might be a contributing or even principal wage earner; now as in the past, a strong element of matricentrism runs through this formally male- and father-centered culture. Currently a couple and their children often share the small apartment of whichever set of grandparents has room for them, though if it is feasible, they may live separately. Jews traditionally had many children, but now one or two is the norm, a slightly lower average than that of surrounding nationalities. Russians help grown children and grandchildren monetarily and otherwise for an indefinite time; this tendency is even stronger in the Jewish family. The family preserves some of its value as the highly autonomous and self-contained unit it was traditionally; social activity is often with other relatives. Women cook and clean but husbands may help, which is uncommon in Russian families. The home may contain inherited objects and books that are valued, even if they are not specifically Jewish in content, as connected to the past, understood as a time when Jews had a more substantive identity; "Jewish objects" from abroad are cherished as a form of "remembering who we are." A Hebrew-Russian dictionary published in the 1960s has long been considered necessary in many homes where no one speaks a word of Hebrew. As in the humblest Jewish home before the Revolution, there are many books, seen as investments both in one's family's education and as difficult-to-obtain treasures whose value increases.

ECONOMY. Education is fundamental to Jewish religion; the unavailability of religious education, books, and objects has resulted in a transformation of that center of identity. Primary responsibility for children's education traditionally rested with parents, who were also responsible for

their own continuing studies. Judaism's basis in Torah, the sense that Jews are the people of the book, has been transformed into a sense that books "gave birth to the people." Prevalent among Jews is an emphasis on education, on the relation of people to books, and on a tradition of analytical thought (a common joke is that a Jew answers a question with another question). This tradition has survived among Jews, who, it is assumed by both Jews and non-Jews, will pursue higher education if possible. Both Jews and Russians would find the idea of a Jewish janitor incongruous; indeed, very small percentages of Jews work in service and housekeeping; in agriculture, less than 1 percent. Jews get more education than other groups, with 47 percent of employed Jews in the Russian Soviet Federated Socialist Republic (RSFSR), 28 percent in the Ukraine, and 25 percent in Belarus having higher education; the number of Jews entering higher and secondary technical education is falling as a result of demographic decline, an aging population, and quotas in university admissions.

Currently, Jewish men and women are approximately equally educated and employed. Men are slightly more likely to receive higher education, and their income levels are higher, even in similar occupations. Women tend to enter less prestigious occupations. Choices of professions have evolved in interaction with a changing political situation, which often determines which schools Jews enter; in addition, the humanities and social sciences have been quite ideologized and reserved to a large extent for Communist party members and Russian ethnics. Jews make up 0.9 percent of the population but 6.1 percent of its scientific workers and 13.8 percent of holders of the degree of "candidat." Jews are often acting factory heads with a Russian or Ukrainian holding the title above them. Jews favor careers in the exact sciences, biology, education, culture, health care, industry, transport, and construction. Technical-cultural-scientific occupations were, in Soviet terminology, upper socioeconomic levels; Jews have tried to use professional success to make a place for themselves.

Kinship, Marriage, and Family

MARRIAGE. At this time it is estimated that, at least among Moscow Ashkenazim, as many as 50 percent (and possibly more) of marriages involving one Jewish partner are to a member of another nationality; men tend to "marry out" more than women, and Jewish women marry slightly later than those of other nationalities. Divorce is common. Intermarriage is more common among the educated and professionals. Endogamy is preferred, not only by Jews with a positive attitude to religion; the reason for this is not connected with religion but rather formulated (as is the preference for Jewish friends and business associates) in terms of the relative safety of marrying one's own kind, often in reference to possible future "hard times" when, under pressure, a non-Jew might "call you a Zhid" (the archaic term for Jew, now highly derogatory). Marriage to ethnic Russians is preferred over that to other non-Jews because of the notion that Russians are less nationalistic than, for example, Ukrainians or Belarussians. Jews between 25 and 30 years of age with higher educations and higher-status jobs and RSFSR residents have less objection to intermarriage. As early as the 1930s it was said that non-Jewish girls preferred Jewish husbands, who supposedly "drank less, took good care of and did not beat their wives."

KINSHIP TERMINOLOGY. Russian has different kin terms for husband's and wife's sides of the family, but these distinctions are disappearing from Russian speech and even more rapidly from Jewish usage. A woman may take her husband's surname at marriage, as is traditional, but many keep their father's names (a common choice in the Soviet era). A strong survival of tradition is that a child inherits the given name of a deceased relative of the family's choice. Even antireligious Jews do not tend to name a child after a living relative. If the relative's name was a Jewish one not acceptable to Russians, a more acceptable or Russian name with the same first initial is given. After the Revolution, distinctively Jewish names became less desirable; many began to choose Russian names, using Jewish nicknames at home. Everyday usage of patronymics preserves names for a generation: "Davidovich" or "Abramovich" clearly indicate Jewish nationality.

Religion and Expressive Culture

A consistent effort since the Revolution to dissociate religion from culture has in many ways been successful, as the vast majority of Jews feel themselves Jewish but in no way religious. It should be borne in mind that in the former USSR, expression of Jewishness and especially religiosity was felt to be an act requiring courage, and was thus less likely in conservative parts of society. Some people attended gatherings at the synagogue and other places without telling their families. Since World War II, the vast majority of Ashkenazim have not observed Jewish holidays, the result of assimilation, commitment to communism, fear of anti-Semitism, or lack of information about the significance of holidays and their proper observance. Others bitterly resent the past unavailability of religious materials and opportunities for religious education and practice. Reading material related to Jewish culture, religion, and the cycle of observances is rare and immensely valued; the traditional respect for books is augmented by the fact that only through books do Soviet Jews see a possibility of rediscovering and revitalizing their Jewish identity. Since the 1960s, Jews have attended readings, skits, musical programs, and synagogues without understanding the Yiddish or Hebrew in which the performance is presented; there has also been a movement to establish study groups and seminars for Jews to educate each other in and discuss Jewish culture, music, literature, and languages, although laws have proscribed many such activities, including the teaching of religion to children. Since the late 1970s there have been a few Jewish kindergartens formed in apartments.

RELIGIOUS PRACTITIONERS AND PRACTICES. Since the Revolution, rabbis have required permission to celebrate holidays. For the ninety-one (Orthodox) synagogues the authorities claim, they claim fifty rabbis; in fact only about sixty synagogues function and thirty-five rabbis serve them; the fact that Judaism allows for worship with a quorum of ten adults (*minyan*) keeps worship possible in some places. Congregations have functioned separately, with no regular meetings of rabbis sanctioned. Of the sixty synagogues, fifteen are in Russia (one in Leningrad and one large and one small in Moscow) for a population of over 701,000 Jews, eight are in the Ukraine for a population of over 634,000 Jews, and three are in Belarus for over 135,000 Jews. Laws allow religious ceremonies to be held in apartments or open places such as forests only with special permission, but a number of services and celebrations are held in such places. A one-room yeshiva at the Moscow synagogue was inaugurated in 1957, then closed until 1974. To date not a single rabbi has graduated. A few students from the USSR study in Budapest. The Hasidic sect, which originated in the eighteenth century and stresses enthusiastic piety, claims as many as a few thousand adherents in the former USSR. These Hasidim conduct their own services alongside others in the synagogue; some men wear side curls, beards, prayer shawls, and head coverings.

Although education and high-ranking occupations have a negative correlation to religiosity, and the roles of the rabbi and synagogue with respect

At least among Moscow Ashkenazim, as many as 50 percent of marriages involving one Jewish partner are to a member of another nationality.

to legal, cultural, and religious life have been altered, synagogues remain rare visible symbols, gathering places even for antireligious Jews on holidays, seen as celebrations of Jewish history and identity. Another form of recent collective expression has been to gather at a site where large numbers of Jews were killed in World War II. A great number of Ashkenazim use what are usually considered religious forms to express not belief but rather nonreligious identification with Jewish culture. On some holidays streets around synagogues fill with Jews who stand together, sing, and talk—for many, a public gesture of defiance. It is estimated that in 1981 20,000 Jews gathered at the Moscow synagogue on Simhas Torah, 5,000 at Passover, and many on the Jewish New Year.

CEREMONIES.   Sabbath services throughout the 1980s were sparsely attended, mostly by older people. Religious marriages are not recognized by the state, and rabbis have rarely performed them. Recently, some religious weddings have been celebrated at home, with the traditional canopy, breaking of a glass, Jewish music, and a wedding bread. Some Jews take advantage of foreign rabbis traveling through for the celebration of marriages and bar mitzvahs.

In the 1920s and 1930s even antireligious Communists observed the custom of burying Jews only in Jewish cemeteries, but now Jewish cemeteries and Yiddish inscriptions on gravestones are rare; some cemeteries have Jewish sections. Many elders dying now were Communists, perhaps atheists. The kaddish is sometimes said.

A new awareness that the thirteenth birthday has significance is spreading, and some bar mitzvahs are marked by family celebration and per-

haps a speech made by the 13–year-old when it is not known what else to do. The bat mitzvah for girls is an American innovation adopted by Russian Jews. When it is known that the ceremony involves study, reading in Hebrew, and explication of a passage of the Torah, and this is a possibility, it is done. The ceremony is easy to perform at home, as it does not require a rabbi.

Passover has been, for some Jews, a once-a-year "heroic act" since the 1970s: to go to the synagogue and buy matzo, unleavened bread that commemorates the Jews' exodus from Egypt, and to light candles, which started becoming the practice again in the mid-1980s. The making of matzo has long been suppressed. Baked secretly in the 1930s and 1940s, it was unavailable in the late 1950s and early 1960s; since 1964 limited production has been permitted at certain synagogues (in some places people bring their own flour).

Circumcision, affirming the biblical covenant with the God of Israel, should be performed, according to Jewish law, on the eighth day following birth. Although some circumcisions were secretly performed even during the Stalin era, they have been rare since World War II, owing to a lack of trained individuals, (*mohalim*), legal proscription of religion-related surgical procedures ("which may damage citizens' health"), and fear that if a boy were discovered to be circumcised in school or during a medical exam, there would be problems. There has been some interest lately in circumcision: a very few men at the time of their bar mitzvah or in their twenties have chosen to be circumcised as a gesture affirming their commitment to Judaism.

When possible, outdoor shelters have been built for the autumn festival of Sukkes, the last

PRAYERS

Ashkenazi men pray and read from the Torah. There are only fifteen synagogues in Russia for over 701,000 Jews. Grand Choral Synagogue, St. Petersburg, Russia. (Steve Raymer/Corbis)

day of which, Simhas Torah, "Rejoicing in the Law," marks the completion of a year's cycle of weekly Torah readings and the beginning of a new one. The celebration involves dancing, singing, and processions dancing with and honoring the Torah. Since the 1960s it is the holiday most celebrated (even by atheists), an expression of national solidarity, and a favorite festival of youth with huge emotional gatherings in the streets around synagogues. In the late 1970s the tradition of *purimspiels*—plays related to the story of Esther and Mordechai, who avoided a massacre of Jews under a Persian king—was revived in Moscow and Leningrad.

ARTS.   Since the mid-1800s there have been dramatic changes in Jewish artistic culture (e.g., there have been important visual artists, though visual representation was interpreted as tantamount to idolatry according to the Old Testament). Bakst and Chagall (before his 1923 emigration, when he joined other Russian Jewish painters such as Soutine in the École de Paris) were among artists prominent in stage design; Marc Antokolsky was an important sculptor; Isaak Levitan was considered a great Russian landscape painter. Eisenstein was a world-famous film director.

The first influence of Jewish culture on Russian (then East Slavic) literature was in the eleventh century with both an account of the Old Testament story of the tower of Babel in the *Primary Chronicle* and a translation of Josephus's *The Jewish War*. Odessa was home to a flourishing writing culture from the 1860s until well past the Revolution, when Moscow also became a center of Jewish creativity. In 1934, at the first conference of Soviet writers, Jews accounted for 20 percent of participants. Yiddish writers wrote poetry, novels, and literary and historical criticism; these and popular classics were published and translated. Prominent in Russian literature were Babel', Mandelshtam, Bagritsky, P. Antokolsky, Ilf, and Ehrenburg; popular Yiddish writers and playwrights were Itzik Fefer, Peretz Markish, "Der Nitzer," Max Erik, Shmuel Persov, David Bergelson, Zelik Axelrod, and others. Most of these were executed or died in prison or in exile during the Stalin era. Unofficial samizdat publications dealing with Jewish issues were passed from hand to hand at great personal risk by individuals. At the end of the Soviet era the only Yiddish magazine was the monthly literary and artistic review *Sovietish Heimland* (Soviet Homeland), first published in 1961. It is accessible only to those who read Yiddish (although each issue contains a Yiddish lesson) and is considered one of the best such journals in the world but is also government-controlled and not representative of Jewish interests. The *Birobidjaner Shtern* is a Yiddish translation of the Russian-language *Birobijan* newspaper. Some Yiddish books are published. In the 1980s a Yiddish primer and a Russian-Yiddish dictionary (with all words pertaining to Zionism and religion omitted) were published.

In the nineteenth century, the Rubenstein brothers influenced musical performance and education, and Leopold Auer founded a school that produced violin virtuosi Yascha Heifetz, Mischa Elman, Nathan Milstein, and Efrem Zimbalist. Serge Koussevitsky was an important conductor and music publisher. Pre–World War II Jewish playwrights were Yitzhak Peretz, Moiher Sforim Mendele, Sholem Asch, Haim Bialik, and Avraham Goldfaden and Sholem Aleikhem, whose "Tevye the Milkman" has been watched by all nationalities for decades in Russian theaters with Russian actors; a new musical based on it was popular in Moscow in 1989–1990. Pre-Revolutionary Yiddish plays are popular and often performed for audiences who do not understand Yiddish; even some performers of Yiddish songs do not speak the language. In 1982 the Soviet company Melodiya began recording Jewish music. A Hebrew and Yiddish chorus was organized in 1980; Jewish music festivals have become more common since the mid-1970s. The "Habimah" Hebrew theater began in Moscow after the Revolution and left in 1926 to become the national theater of Israel. Yiddish theaters remained in Kiev, Minsk, Odessa, and Moscow. Since 1970 theatrical and music-theatrical groups have been forming; all are amateur except the Musical-Dramatic People's Theater (Jewish Chamber Theater) and the Moscow Jewish Dramatic Ensemble (Birobijan); they perform music and dances and show rituals such as traditional weddings.

Bibliography

Altshuler, Mordecai (1987). *Soviet Jewry since the Second World War: Population and Social Structure.* Studies in Population and Urban Demography. New York: Greenwood Press.

Baron, Salo W. (1987). *The Russian Jew under Tsars and Soviets.* New York: Schocken Books.

Encyclopedia Judaica, s.v. "Ashkenaz" and "Russia."

Ettinger, Shmuel (1984). "The Position of Jews in Soviet Culture: A Historical Survey." In *Jews in Soviet Culture*, edited by Jack Miller. London: Institute of Jewish Affairs.

Fain, Benjamin (1984). *Jewishness in the Soviet Union: Report of an Empirical Survey.* Jerusalem: Center for Public Affairs.

Gitelman, Zvi (1972). *Jewish Nationality and Soviet Politics.* Princeton, N.J.: Princeton University Press.

Gitelman, Zvi (1988). *A Century of Ambivalence.* New York: Schocken Books.

Hindus, Milton (1971). *A World at Twilight: A Portrait of Jewish Communities of Eastern Europe before the Holocaust.* New York: Macmillan.

Levin, Nora (1988). *The Jews in the Soviet Union since 1917.* Vols. 1–2. New York: New York University Press.

Pinkus, Benjamin (1988). *The Jews of the Soviet Union.* Cambridge: Cambridge University Press.

Rozenblum, Serge-Allain (1982). *Être Juif en U.R.S.S.* Paris: Collection de la RPP.

Sawyer, Thomas E. (1979). *The Jewish Minority in the Soviet Union.* Boulder, Colo.: Westview Press.

Weisel, Elie (1968). *The Jews of Silence: A Personal Report on Soviet Jewry.* London: Valentine, Mitchell. English translation. New York: Holt, Rinehart & Winston.

—DALE PESMEN

AZERBAIJANI TURKS

Ethnonyms: Azerbaijanis (used since 1937 in Soviet Azerbaijan), Azeris.

Orientation

IDENTIFICATION. Historic Azerbaijan is today divided into the independent Republic of Azerbaijan (Azerbaijan Soviet Socialist Republic until 30 August 1991) in the north and the East and West Azerbaijan provinces of Iran in the south. The Araxes (Aras) River forms most of the boundary between the two sides.

LOCATION. Azerbaijan occupies the western shore of the Caspian Sea, extending west to approximately 45° longitude (which runs through the middle of the Caucasian isthmus and west of Lake Urmia in Iran) and from the foot of the Caucasus Mountains in the north to just south of Lake Urmia (37° latitude) in the south. The Kura River crosses the republic from northwest to southeast. Elevation varies greatly, from the coastal lowlands and basins of the Kura and Araxes rivers in the east and southeast (at and below sea level) to the Greater Caucasus mountains (to 4,243 meters) in the north at the Daghestan border, and to the Lesser Caucasus (to 3,581 meters) in the west. In the lowlands, the climate is mild (average temperature is 14–14.5° C with 20–40 centimeters of precipitation annually), but in the mountains winters are severe (average temperature is 2–10° C; with extremes to −13°, and 100–160 centimeters of precipitation). The Azerbaijan Republic, with its capital at Baku, includes the (mostly Armenian) Nagorno-Karabagh region and the noncontiguous Nakhjivan Autonomous Republic (separated from the rest of the republic by a strip of Armenia). Iranian Azerbaijan is entirely mountainous: elevations are over 2,000 meters, with some ranging as high as 5,000 meters near Ardebil in the east. Climate is correspondingly severe. It is separated from the Caspian coast by the Gilan region. In the south, the main city, Tabriz, is located near Lake Urmia.

DEMOGRAPHY. The population of the Azerbaijan Republic was about 7 million in 1989; Baku had a population of 2.5 million. The birthrate is high (43.7 per thousand between 1959 and 1969, as contrasted with 19 per thousand for Russians), with the median age of the population in 1979 at 15. The Azerbaijan SSR had become more ethnically homogeneous in the last three decades, both because of the emigration of non-Azerbaijanis and because of the relatively higher birthrate of the Azerbaijanis. The other major groups in the republic are Russians and Armenians. These three groups account for approximately 90 percent of the population. Other groups are Georgians, Jews, and northern Caucasians. Comparable demographic data are not available for Iranian Azerbaijan. Tabriz has a population of over half a million, and East Azerbaijan Province, about 4 million. Estimates of the total number of Azerbaijanis in Iran, however, vary from 6 million to more than twice that figure. In West Azerbaijan Province, there is a large Kurdish population and also Assyrian and other Christian minorities. Some nomadic groups still exist, although their former migration patterns were disrupted by the restrictions on moving southward across the Araxes River. Most prominent among these groups are the Shahseven.

LINGUISTIC AFFILIATION. Azerbaijani is a dialect of Turkish, although on the northern side of the border the Soviet state officially called it a separate language starting in 1937; on the Iranian side it is called simply "Türki," as are Turkish dialects in Central Asia. Azerbaijani is closely related to Turkmen and Anatolian Turkish; it is intelligible to most speakers of Turkish dialects and is a lingua franca in much of Daghestan. The Azerbaijan Republic has used the Cyrillic orthography since the late 1930s, after about a decade of Latin orthography, which replaced the earlier

♦ **SSR**
Soviet Socialist Republic. In the former Soviet Union there were fifteen SSRs.

See also

MIDDLE EAST: Persians, Turks

Arabo-Persian script. The republic's government plans to reinstate Latin orthography in 1993. Azerbaijani is a language with an important literature. Azerbaijanis have a low level of linguistic Russification, with over 98 percent claiming Azerbaijani as their first language. On the Iranian side of the border, the Arabo-Persian script is still in use. Prior to the creation of this script, Turkish had been written in other alphabets, the earliest of which was the so-called runic script of the eighth century Orkhon-Yenisei inscriptions.

History and Cultural Relations

Present-day Azerbaijanis north of the Araxes River regard themselves as descendants of the ancient Caucasian Albanians (Albania is the former name of the area), whose kingdom occupied eastern Caucasia from antiquity to the Muslim conquests; they also claim descent from Turkish nomads who first migrated to the steppe north of the Caspian in pre- or early Christian times and thereafter penetrated and mingled with the existing population of Azerbaijan. Decisive Turkicization occurred in the eleventh century. In Iran, however, as a result of the Persianization campaigns of the Pahlavi dynasty (1925–1979), official history insists that the Turks of the Azerbaijan provinces are "Turkicized Aryans." Because of the restrictions on higher education and publishing in Iranian Azerbaijan, there has been little exploration of this contention in Iran; Soviet Azerbaijani scholars have denounced it. Over the centuries, Azerbaijan has been overrun by its neighbors (Byzantium and Iran) and more distant invaders (Khazars, Arabs, Seljuks, Mongols, Timurids, and Russians). For much of its history, Azerbaijan has been ruled as part of Iran by successive groups including the Sasanids (third to seventh century); the Arab caliphate (at various times); the Turkish Seljuks (eleventh century); the Chingizid Ilkhanids (thirteenth-fourteenth centuries); the Central Asian Timurids (fourteenth and fifteenth centuries); and Safavids from southern Azerbaijan (sixteenth-eighteenth centuries).

Among historically important cities are Barda, Ganje, Ardebil, Tabriz, and Maragha. Local dynasties have occasionally exerted considerable independence, notably the Shirvanshahs of the north, who ruled during the sixth to sixteenth centuries despite the loss of suzerainty to imperial rulers in Iran or Central Asia. The region they ruled was known simply as "Shirvan" or "Sharvan." After a period of fragmentation into semi-independent khanates in the eighteenth century, northern Azerbaijan was conquered by the Russians early in the nineteenth century. The border was fixed in 1828 at roughly its present position. Northern Azerbaijan constituted two provinces of the Russian Empire (the Baku and Elisavetpol provinces) and part of the Erevan Province. It experienced rapid (if one-sided) industrial development as Baku's oil wealth was exploited from the last quarter of the nineteenth century well into the twentieth; because of the "oil rush," northern Azerbaijan received thousands of Russians, Caucasian mountaineers, Armenians, and southern Azerbaijani Turks as workers, many of whom were organized into the Socialist movement. Northern Azerbaijan became an independent republic in 1918, in the wake of the Russian Revolution and World War I, but it was reconquered by the Red Army in 1920. Southern Azerbaijan was one of the richest provinces of Iran and, under the Qajars, was ruled by the heir to the Iranian throne. It became a center of protests against the shah's foreign concessions in the 1890s and of the Constitutional Movement (1905–1911) that led to the short-lived constitutional period. This history of protest, however, so weakened the old regime that the path was paved for the coup by Reza Khan (later Shah) Pahlavi in the 1920s. Cross-border relations remained strong. During World War II, Soviet troops occupied part of southern Azerbaijan, but they withdrew in 1946. Thereafter an autonomous local government was destroyed by the Shah's troops.

The culture of Azerbaijan has historically been a rich and complex admixture of pre-Islamic Turkish, Iranian, and Islamic elements. The mix is reflected in the *dastan*, or "ornate oral history," which preserves history, customs, values, and the language itself. Later forms (dating from about the fourteenth century) of these ancient works are known today: *The Book of Dede Korkut* and *Köroglu*. "High culture" is also strongly in evidence in the form of poetry, scholarship, visual arts, and architecture. The eleventh to thirteenth centuries were the golden age, during which the poets Khagani Shirvani (1120–1199) and Nizami Ganjevi (1141–1209) and the scholar Muhammad Nasr al-Din Tusi (1207–1274) lived and worked. Later luminaries included the poet Fuzuli (1498–1556). They were internationally known and many traveled far beyond the borders of Azerbaijan. Maragha, in the south, boasted a fourteenth-century observatory and library. Mausoleums, bridges, and other structures survive from the eleventh century and later. Some remaining structures are even older. Russian influence had some impact on the upper classes in the

♦ **steppe**
Open grassland, relatively treeless plain.

871

The culture of Azerbaijan has historically been a rich and complex admixture of pre-Islamic Turkish, Iranian, and Islamic elements.

north during the nineteenth century and far more under Soviet power. Certain members of the Azerbaijani intelligentsia in the nineteenth and early twentieth centuries were educated in France, Germany, or the Ottoman Empire; those desiring religious training went to Iran or Ottoman Iraq. Under Soviet rule, the Azerbaijan SSR became increasingly insulated, and cultural policies were determined by the Soviet Communist party. In addition to the alphabet changes, many works of oral and written literature were banned and denounced as "feudal-clerical" or "bourgeois." Writers, composers, and poets perished in the purges. In the south, Persianization was emphasized and Azerbaijani Turkish culture regarded as primitive, "folk" culture. Major historical personages were called "Persian" regardless of their place of birth, parentage, or self-identification. Literacy in Turkish was not counted in the 1962 Iranian census.

Settlements

The northern Azerbaijani population has been about half urban since the middle of this century. The traditional division of towns into *mahalle* (quarters) based on the ethnicity or region of origin of the inhabitants, which the names of the mahalle may reflect, survives to some degree to the present. Rural villages are numerous on both sides of the border and tend to be ethnically homogeneous. In the north, the descendants of nineteenth-century Russian settlers still remain in a few areas. The transfer of large Armenian populations from Iran after the Russian conquest has led to large Armenian concentrations in some western and central regions of Caucasia, including many parts of the present-day Armenian Republic and the Karabagh region of the Azerbaijan Republic.

Economy

SUBSISTENCE AND COMMERCIAL ACTIVITIES. Agriculture is a key component of the economy on both sides of the border; the region encompasses several climatic zones and produces tea, grapes, wheat, tobacco, and pomegranates, as well as mulberry trees and cocoons (for silk) and forest products. Sheep, cattle, and goats are kept. Among natural resources are copper, salt, iron ore, and, in the north, the most famous—oil. Black caviar is produced by the sturgeon off the Azerbaijan coast, but severe pollution in the Caspian Sea has virtually destroyed this industry and fishing. Industrial development, consisting of oil and petrochemical industries, is confined to the north.

Pesticide use, especially on grapes and cotton, has been excessive and has caused serious health and environmental damage.

INDUSTRIAL ARTS. Azerbaijan has long been famous for its silks and carpets. Tabriz is known for carpets and has famous schools of miniatures and calligraphy; Shemakhi in the north was a major producer of silk cloth; various towns produced rugs. Machine production has largely, but not entirely, replaced handicrafts.

TRADE. Trade in silk, carpets, wax, and oil has been important to the towns of Azerbaijan throughout its history. Baku is located on the south side of the Apsheron Peninsula and has the best natural harbor on the Caspian. It has been a commercial port for more than a millennium. Ruins of caravansaries reflect trade with South Asia as well as the Middle East. The towns of the south lay on major overland trade routes. Since the early nineteenth century the economy of each part of Azerbaijan has been integrated into the state of which it is a part.

DIVISION OF LABOR. The traditional division of men's and women's work generally prevails, with the latter including unusually onerous tasks in nomadic and rural areas. In the twentieth century, especially with losses of male population in northern Azerbaijan after the abortive battle for independence, collectivization, purges, and World War II, women increasingly filled the work force. Intellectual or white-collar employment for females is acceptable in northern Azerbaijan, but physical labor is disdained by women and will be accepted only by the very poor.

LAND TENURE. There was no private land in the Azerbaijan SSR, but in rural areas the population was able to use land to build houses and keep private gardens. There is sufficient flexibility in the system for a thriving black market in fruit and flowers. The republican government is committed to privatization of land, but the process is proceeding slowly. In the south, the abortive land reforms of the last Pahlavi shah did not alter the landowning pattern in Azerbaijan; land tends to be concentrated in the hands of the wealthy.

Kinship

A patrilinear pattern is characteristic. Language reflects details of relations, with different terms for the mother's brother and sister, the father's brother and sister, spouses and avuncular relatives, and so forth. Marriage bonds are very important, with clear definition of relations between children and paternal and maternal relatives. These obligations are recognized even among urban populations. Extended families are preferred, even in cities.

Sociopolitical Organization

The Azerbaijan Republic, unlike its Soviet predecessor, is characterized by various political and social organizations and parties. Its leaders have confirmed their willingness to grant cultural autonomy to ethnic minorities. Iran does not recognize ethnic or national differences nor grant autonomy to nationalities.

SOCIAL ORGANIZATION. Although much of the society has been peasant and nomadic, the cities in Azerbaijan have produced a small but vigorous urban culture and merchant class. The upper class traditionally was composed of landowners or merchants, but in the north industrialization in the nineteenth century also created an industrial bourgeoisie. In the north, there was a secular cultural-intellectual movement in the nineteenth and twentieth centuries.

POLITICAL ORGANIZATION. The Azerbaijan Republic realized aspects of its sovereignty only slowly because of the continued control of the government by former Communists during its first months of independence. The 1978 constitution remained in force. During the spring of 1992, the former Communists lost power and were supplanted by the Azerbaijan Popular Front, the major opposition force since its founding in 1989. Its leader, Abulfez Elchibey, was elected president (7 June 1992) in the first democratic elections since 1919. In June 1993, Heydar Aliyev of the New Azerbaijan Party was elected president.

SOCIAL CONTROL. Traditional norms are enforced by the family and by community opinion. Religious values can be enforced by the religious establishment in the south. In the north, the pressure by the Communist party apparatus and Ministry of Internal Affairs is gradually being replaced by new laws.

CONFLICT. The main conflict is between Azerbaijani Turks and non-Azerbaijanis. The czarist period was marked by continual but only sporadically violent resistance to Russian control, laws restricting non-Christians, and Christianization and Russification campaigns. Resistance to Russification continued under Soviet rule. The use of force by the Soviet state to mobilize the population at harvest time led to occasional violence against the authorities. Sporadic but intense periods of conflict with Armenians characterized the first quarter of the twentieth century and the late 1980s

MARRIAGE AND FAMILY

Marriage

People commonly marry in their early twenties, and within each family are expected to marry in order from eldest to youngest. If marriages are not specifically arranged (arranged marriages are increasingly unlikely in urban areas), Azerbaijani Turks are expected to marry someone whose family is known by or related to their own family. The first child is expected to be born in the first year of marriage, although there is no convention concerning the timing of subsequent children. Higher education may cause marriages to be deferred and may also result in marriage outside the usual circles. Nonetheless, marriage outside the national community is rare. In those instances when official "mixed" marriages are recorded by Soviet statistics, the match is usually with another Turk (a Tatar, Uzbek, etc.) or non-Turkish Muslim (Legzhi, etc.) rather than a non-Turk and non-Muslim. Intermarriage between Turks and Persians in Iran is more likely for those outside Azerbaijan. Abortion, though legal in the north, is virtually unheard of; divorce is rare, and social pressures against it are enormous. Polygamy was illegal in the Soviet Union but existed sporadically in a few rural areas under various guises (such as civil divorce, followed by a civil and religious second marriage).

Domestic Unit

An extended patrilocal family is preferred and is often necessary because of housing shortages in towns in the north. Women constitute a subculture within the household and share in housekeeping and childrearing duties, even if employed outside the household. They may play an important role in decision making, especially concerning children.

Inheritance

Inheritance was traditionally determined by Islamic provisions that require all offspring to inherit, although males were favored. Now the laws of each state govern inheritance.

Socialization

The family is the main instrument of socialization, and public opinion exerts a powerful force. Both the Russians (under czarist and Soviet power) and Persians have tried to use schools as a means to socialize Azerbaijani Turks into the majority culture. The Russians had limited success; the Persians have had more, especially among those Azerbaijanis who leave Azerbaijan.

and early 1990s. The latter confrontation concerns a territorial dispute over Nagorno-Karabagh (the first word means "mountainous" in Russian, the second is "black garden" in Turkish), which both nations regard as their historic patrimony.

Religion and Expressive Culture

RELIGIOUS BELIEFS AND PRACTICES. Today Azerbaijan is more than three-quarters Shiite, less than one-quarter Sunni. Azerbaijan has been Islamic since the eighth century and Shiite since the sixteenth century, when Shah Ismail, founder of the Safavid dynasty, adopted Shiism as state religion. Secularization is far more in evidence in northern Azerbaijan, probably as a result of the Russian conquest. The veiling and segregation of women, common throughout Iran, is not practiced in former Soviet Azerbaijan, nor among nomads on either side of the border, although modesty in dress is the norm. Rural women often wear large black shawls but leave their faces uncovered.

In accordance with pre-Islamic belief systems common in Central Asia, including animism and shamanism, Azerbaijani Turks display reverence for nature and the elements. According to Harry H. Walsh (in Weekes, 1984, 65–66), "in rural areas of Azerbaijan, pre-Islamic practices may still be encountered among the Azeris. Holy places (*pir*) are still revered. The holiday Su Jeddim, in which Azeris seek communion with their ancestors through bathing in sanctified streams, has been observed in recent times. Certain trees, especially the oak and the iron tree, are venerated and may not be felled. Pieces of bark from the iron tree are worn about the neck of persons and horses as amulets, and are tied to cribs in order to ward off illness and the evil eye. A cult of fire, which is regarded by the Azeris as the holiest and purest element in nature, has had many adherents, and there has been a cult of rocks, particularly of a certain kind of black rock to which curative powers are attributed."

RELIGIOUS PRACTITIONERS. Islam has no "clergy" in the Christian sense, as Islam is not a sacramental religion. Mullahs are prayer leaders; *ulema* (pl. of *alim*, "scholar") act as judges (*qadis*), interpreters of the law. These practitioners were driven out of northern Azerbaijan or subordinated to the Ecclesiastical Boards created in the 1840s. The Bolsheviks destroyed these boards in the 1920s. They were reestablished in the 1940s and still exist in the republic. Under the Soviet regime, these boards controlled the education, practices, and publications of official mullahs in Soviet Azerbaijan. Consequently, the populace

PLOWING THE FIELDS

An Azerbaijani boy plowing a field with buffalos along the Banab-Miandoab road, where agriculture is a key component of the economy. Azerbaijan area, Iran.
(Roger Wood/Corbis)

looked upon the mullahs with suspicion and sometimes turned to "holy men." There are about 300 holy places in Azerbaijan, and pilgrimages to them are common in the countryside (i.e., there are notable differences in religious practices between rural and urban areas). With the fall of communism, interest in religion has revived but plays no significant role in political life. In Iran, on the other hand, the ulema were and continue to be a powerful and independent force.

CEREMONIES. Novruz Bayram, a holiday celebrating the beginning of spring, survives from the pre-Islamic period. Another significant ceremony is Ashura, devoted to the martyr Imam Hussein. Muharrem (Shiite commemoration) and other Islamic rituals are common in the south; they were legal but discouraged in Soviet Azerbaijan.

ARTS. Traditional music is extremely popular throughout Azerbaijan. The north also has a twentieth-century tradition of operas based on traditional music; most famous among these are the operas and comic operettas of Uzeir Hajibeyli (1885–1948). His national march, written for the first republic in 1918, has been adopted by the present republic. Prominent singers enjoy enormous celebrity. Hajibeyli and many singers, composers, and traditional reciters of dastans and poetry come from Karabagh, which is regarded as a cradle of music in Azerbaijani culture. Folk plays, often with religious content, are performed in Iranian Azerbaijan. Plays with secular, often social-satirical themes were first produced in the north by Mirza Fath Ali Akhundzade (1812–1878). These and similar later works are still performed.

MEDICINE. In the north, remnants of the inadequate Soviet system prevail. The south has the same system as elsewhere in Iran, which is also inadequate. Herbal folk medicines are still used, mainly by the rural population.

DEATH AND AFTERLIFE. Islamic ceremonies in mourning and burial appear to be practiced universally (and were practiced even by Communist party members in the north). A commemoration is held at the fortieth day after death.

Bibliography

Altstadt, Audrey L. (1985). "Baku, 1813–1914: Transformation of a Muslim Town." In *The City in Late Imperial Russia*, edited by Michael F. Hamm. Bloomington: Indiana University Press.

Altstadt, Audrey L. (1992). "Azerbaijani Turks." In *Modern Encyclopedia of Religions of Russia and the Soviet Union*. Vol. 2. Sea Breeze, Fla.: Academic International Press.

Altstadt, Audrey L. (1992). *The Azerbaijani Turks: Power and Identity under Russian Rule.* Stanford, Calif.: Hoover Institution Press.

Bennigsen, Alexandre, and Chantal Lemercier-Quelquejay (1964). *Islam in the Soviet Union.* Translated by Geoffrey Wheeler. London: Pall Mall Publishers.

Bennigsen, Alexandre, and S. Enders Wimbush (1986). *Muslims of the Soviet Empire: A Guide.* Bloomington: Indiana University Press.

Golden, Peter (1983). "The Turkic Peoples and Caucasia." In *Transcaucasia: Nationalism and Social Change*, edited by Ronald Grigor Suny. Ann Arbor: Michigan Slavic Publications.

Walsh, Harry H. (1984) "Azeris." In *The Muslim Peoples: A World Ethnographic Survey.* 2nd ed., edited by Richard V. Weekes. Westport, Conn.: Greenwood Press.

—AUDREY L. ALTSTADT

BELARUSSIANS

Ethnonyms: Belorussians, Byelorussians, White Russians

Orientation

IDENTIFICATION. Belarussians are a majority in the nation of Belarus. Large groups of Belarussians also live in Russia, the Baltic states, Kazakhstan, and the Ukraine. The overall population of Belarussians in the territory of the former USSR was 10,036,000 in 1991. In Poland, the United States, Canada, Argentina, and Australia there are from 300,000 to 2 million people of Belarussian ancestry, according to different estimates. Linguistically the Belarussians belong to the East Slavic Subgroup of the Indo-European Language Family.

LOCATION. The ethnic territory of the Belarussians occupies the westernmost part of the eastern European plain in the basin of the western Dvina River, the middle Dnieper, and the upper Neman. The peculiarities of the landscape were formed under the influence of the anthropogenic ice. Alternation of hills and plains with glacial low grounds, often covered with lakes or swamps, is typical. The peculiarities of Belarus's mild continental climate are determined by the heavy influence of air masses from the Atlantic. The average annual temperature ranges from 7.4° C in the southwest to 4.4° C in the northeast; the

♦ **continental climate**
In the Köppen system, a climate characterized by large seasonal temperature variations, with hot summers, cold winters, and year-round precipitation.

Belarussians

The war with Russia (1654–1667) led to a catastrophic loss of Belarussian population.

◆ Slavs (Slavic peoples)
A generic term for peoples who speak Slavic languages: in Europe, it encompasses Serbs, Croats, Slovenes, Bulgarians, Macedonians, Czechs, Slovaks, Sorbs, Poles, Russians, Ukrainians, and Belorussians.

amount of rain and snow ranges from 52 to 71 centimeters per year. The period of vegetation is 180 to 208 days. A characteristic feature of the hydrography is the abundance of lakes (over 10,000); the largest is Narotch (79.6 square kilometers). The predominant type of soil is turf-ash (up to 60 percent), and approximately 5 percent is turf-humus with a large percentage of humus. Marshlands make up nearly 20 percent of the territory and swamps 12 percent; over 30 percent of the territory is forest. Among trees, pines are the most common (56.5 percent); broad-leaved ones (oak, hornbeam, maple) constitute almost 5 percent. The fauna are typical of the forest zone of Europe. A peculiar representative of the fauna is the relict animal *bison bonasus*, whose picture is often used to symbolize Belarus.

DEMOGRAPHY. Sharp fluctuations of the population level, caused by social and political events, characterize the demographic history of Belarus. In the middle of the seventeenth century Belarus lost more than 50 percent of its inhabitants, in the beginning of the eighteenth century up to 30 percent, and in the beginning of the nineteenth century 12 to 15 percent. In the period during World War I and the civil war the population was diminished by 18 percent; the Stalin genocide and World War II took the lives of 40 percent of the population. Currently, demographic dynamics are determined by the combination of a low birth rate and a low death rate, with natural growth at 4.9 percent. The average life span is 71.7 years. Urban residents constituted 66 percent of the population in 1991. Besides Belarussians, Russians (1,342,000—13.2 percent), Poles (418,000—4.1 percent), Ukrainians (291,000—2.9 percent) and Jews (112,000—1.1 percent) live in Belarus.

LINGUISTIC AFFILIATION. Seventy-one percent of Belarussians living in the territory of the former USSR, 64 percent of Poles, and 5.5 percent of Ukrainians residing in the Republic of Belarus consider Belarussian their mother tongue. Many phonetic, grammatical, and lexical peculiarities bring Belarussian close to Russian and, even more, to Ukrainian. Peculiar phonetic features include the affricates *dz* and *ts* appearing in place of the soft *d'* and *t'*; nonsyllabic *y* in place of the etymological *l* and *v*; hard *r*; proteic sounds *v* before labial vowels; *a, i* before consonant clusters; hardening of labial vowels before *j* and in word-final position; and lengthening of consonants before *j* and between vowels. In morphology, features include the alternations between *c, k,* and *x* and *z, g,* and *s* in words of feminine gender; drop-

ping of the final *t* in the third-person singular present verb forms; gender distinctions in the declension of numerals; and dropping of the final *y* in adjectives, participles, and ordinal numerals in the nominative masculine forms. Syntactic peculiarities of Belarussian include preference for descriptive constructions over participial ones. The lexicon is composed of words of Common Slavic and Indo-European origin, Belarussian neologisms, and borrowings from Polish, Latin, German, Lithuanian, and Tatar languages.

Two main dialects of the Belarussian language can be distinguished: the Northeastern (the Polotsk and Vietbsk-Mogilev group of dialects) and the Southwestern (the Grodno-Baranovichi and Slutsk-Mozir dialects). There is also a transitional group of middle Belarussian dialects between them. Especially distinctive is the West Polesk dialect region, the dialects of which come close in many phonetic and grammatic features to the northwestern Ukrainian dialects. The modern literary language has been formed on the basis of the transitional middle Belarussian dialects, the writing system mostly on the basis of the Cyrillic alphabet. In the period between the sixteenth and beginning of the twentieth centuries the Polish version of the Latin alphabet was also used.

History and Cultural Relations

The early stage of the ethnogenesis of Belarussians is linked to the Slavic colonization of eastern Europe in the seventh to ninth centuries A.D., which was accompanied by the assimilation of the ancient Baltic population. Tenth- to twelfth-century sources register several ethnic formations on the territory of Belarus, the identities of which are still in dispute: Slavic Kriviches in the northeast, Dregoviches in the center and south, Radimiches in the southeast, and Baltic speakers in the southwest. In the eleventh to thirteenth centuries they were replaced by territorial entities—"lands" (*zemli*) and kingdoms. The local group of Kriviches, Polochans who were centered in Polotsk (the city was first mentioned in 862), established the earliest of these kingdoms. During the period of its prime (eleventh to twelfth centuries) the Polotsk Kingdom became one of the three largest political and cultural centers of East Slavs. The conversion of the population of Belarus to Christianity, which began at the turn of the tenth to eleventh centuries, contributed to the development of the culture. In the thirteenth to fourteenth centuries the Belarussian and Lithuanian lands were united into the Great Kingdom of Lithuania, Russia, and Zemotia. Its creation allowed both nations to retain their political independence in the struggle against the Tatar-Mongol invasion and the German expansion. Historic Lithuania—a region in the northwest of Byelorus with a mixed Slavic and Baltic population—became the center of the new state. Belarussians made up the majority of the population of the kingdom, and their language, peculiarities of which are noted in written documents beginning in the thirteenth century, became official.

In connection with east Belarussian lands, White Rus was first mentioned in the beginning of the fourteenth century. In the sixteenth to seventeenth centuries the names "Byelorus," "Belarus," and the self-name, "Belarussians," had finally became associated with the territories of the Vitebsk, Mogilev, and Smolensk regions. There are several interpretations of the etymology of the name. It is linked to the predominance of the color white in the traditional costume, the fair anthropological type, independence from Tatars in the thirteenth to fifteenth centuries, the relatively early adoption of Christianity relative to the other region—Black Russia, to the west of the ethnic territory of Belarussians. The term "Polessje" was used for the southern part of Byelorus from the thirteenth century on. In the fourteenth to seventeenth centuries the Belarussians created a complex system of ethnonymic names, which combined local territorial forms (Belarussians, Chernorussians, Litvins, Paleshuks) with confessional (Litvins-Catholics and Ruthens-Orthodox) and common-state (Litvins) forms that were independent of the place of residence or confession. The name "Litvins," as applied to Belarussians, became accepted by Poles, Russians, and Belarussians in the fifteenth to seventeenth centuries. Lithuanians called the Belarussians "Gudasi" and the Latvians called them "Krives."

Belarussian Renaissance culture attained its zenith at the end of the fifteenth and the beginning of the sixteenth centuries. The marked transformation of traditional state structures contributed to this process: trade was developing rapidly because of the disintegration of communal agriculture beginning in the middle of the sixteenth century; the peasantry became involved in the trade network, and the number of cities and the urban population increased. The development of printing in Belarussian (1517), the spread of Protestantism and humanistic ideology, the creation of an extensive network of educational establishments—all promoted the process of national consolidation, the codification of literary language, and the formation of ethnic self-consciousness.

The continuing expansion of the Moscow kingdom, however, forced the Great Kingdom of Lithuania to enter into a federal union with Poland. The creation of a new state—"Retch Pospolitaja"—together with the development of the Counter-Reformation, led to a noticeable strengthening of the position of the Catholic church and Polish culture, especially among the landed aristocracy. In 1596 in Brest the church Unia was proclaimed, as a result of which the Orthodox church, although retaining its rituals, became part of the Catholic church. In the first half of the seventeenth century Belarussian gradually lost its dominant position in the social sphere. The war with Russia (1654–1667) led to a catastrophic loss of population, mainly in the urban areas, and to the final ethnocultural separation of the feudal elite from the peasantry. This conversion of Belarussians into a "small" nation with an incomplete social structure greatly complicated the process of national consolidation in the nineteenth to twentieth centuries.

The slow rate of national formation was also determined by a number of other factors. The occupation of Belarus by Russia toward the end of the eighteenth century slowed down social and economic development—up to the beginning of the 1960s. In the nineteenth century almost 80 percent of the population were peasants. The Russian administration enacted a policy of assimilation with regard to the Belarussians, who were considered a separate ethnic group, but part of the Russian nation, "spoiled" by Polish influence. In 1839 the Uniate church was abolished. The Belarussian political movement was repressed. The anti-Russian insurrection of 1863–1864 had a national character; on its eve the Belarussian primer and a clandestine newspaper (1862) were published. Between 1860 and 1870 a Belarussian political organization of Socialist trend was formed in St. Petersburg. In its journal *Gomon* the main postulates of national ideology were presented in full for the first time. National ideology started to form in the 1910s. The appearance of literary works in Belarussian can be traced to this period.

Toward the end of the nineteenth century the structure of Belarussian ethnic self-consciousness underwent considerable change. The terms "Belarussian" and "Belarussians" replaced most local names. The name "Lithuania" at this time stabilized in its use relative to the Lithuanian ethnic territory. Belarussians did not have a national identity and were affected by religious tensions between Catholic Poles and Orthodox Russians.

Belarussians

By the middle of the 1980s practically all of the structures that provided the ethnocultural identity of Belarussians were either destroyed or heavily deformed.

♦ **Russification**

Assimilation to Russian language, culture, political control; process of encouraging or enforcing the spread of Russian influence, sometimes including the forced relocation of ethnic populations, the settlement of Russians in republics other than Russia, the use of Russian, and Russian control of politics and economics.

In the northwest the self-name "Tuteishia" (locals) was relatively widespread. National consciousness per se was common only among the relatively narrow stratum of intellectuals. In 1903 national parties appeared. In 1906 legal newspapers and publishing houses and national artistic culture took shape rapidly. The sign of the maturity of this Belarussian movement was the declaration of a national state—the Belarussian Peoples Republic (February to November 1918) and the Byelorussian Soviet Socialist Republic (January 1919 to August 1919). These events, however, could not prevent the disruption of the territorial integrity of the Belarussians. In 1919 the lands of East Byelorussia were alienated by the Communist leadership in favor of Russia, and in 1921 West Byelorussia was given to Poland.

Despite this, the 1920s became the period of the highest national activity in the history of Belarussian people. The relatively liberal character of the political regime of that time allowed the creation of a national infrastructure in the Byelorussian Soviet Socialist Republic (BSSR): a system of public education, including university education; mass media; artistic culture; and research institutions. The Belarussian language was granted its dominant role constitutionally. At this time the Belarussian national movement within the territory of Poland was particularly extensive. As a result of the establishment of a totalitarian regime in the USSR by the end of the 1920s, the ethnic crisis of Belarussians became global. By the 1930s the national intellectual elite was near complete destruction, the use of Belarussian was restricted, and Belarussian history was rewritten. As a consequence of the Soviet-German division of Poland, West Byelorussia was returned to the BSSR. This event was accompanied by mass repressions against the activists of the national movement and mass deportations.

A considerable acceleration in Russification in the postwar period entailed the replacement of the Belarussian language in the official sphere and in education. By the beginning of the 1960s Russian-based culture occupied a dominant position in urban life. Its high social status determined a rapid deethnicization of migrants from the rural areas during the period of great urbanization of the 1960s through the 1980s. The dominating Communist ideology, which was oriented toward an integration of nations, was the vehicle of this unimpeded development.

By the middle of the 1980s practically all the structures that provided the ethnocultural identity of Belarussians were either destroyed or heavily

deformed. There was not a single Belarussian school left in the cities. The Belarussian language was retained only by a small number of intellectuals and in the rural areas. On a mass level, national self-consciousness lost its ethnic identity and acquired instead an administrative-regional character. The national artistic culture, which was retained by the regime for purposes of propaganda, lost its link with the consumer and turned into a self-contained system. At the same time, in the 1970s the first signs of a national rebirth of the Belarussian became apparent. At first, this took the form of cultural resistance to the regime by the intellectual elite. In the beginning of the 1980s the first informal national-cultural educational organizations appeared, and in 1988 political organizations (the Belarussian National Front) appeared, as did an uncensored mass press. The development of the national democratic movement resulted in the restoration of the Belarussian language as the official one, the declaration of independence in 1990, and a noticeable growth of national self-consciousness on a mass scale. In September 1991 the new name—Republic of Belarus—was adopted, and the white-red flag and the coat of arms "Pogona" were introduced as national symbols.

Settlements

Classical descriptions of the traditional culture of the Belarussians date back to the second half of the nineteenth and beginning of the twentieth centuries. At this time peasants constituted almost 90 percent of the total population of Belarus, and their life-style remained relatively unchanged under the influence of the urbanized culture. Typical rural settlements were small household villages (5 to 100 households) and villages whose distinctive features were a church, school, or local administration. They were of several types: nonsystematic (the oldest), linear, and street. Also widespread were settlements of the hamlet type, called *okolitsi* (neighborhoods) where the land-starved nobility (*shl'akhta*) lived; *folvarki* (a complex consisting of a mansion and several peasant households) and peasant hamlets as such existed.

The traditional peasant household included a house (*khata*) and numerous household constructions: for the cattle (*khlev*) and for the storage of grain (*klet'*), food (*puna*), vegetables (*istopka*), and agricultural tools (*povet'*). Apart from the house there was a place for threshing grain (*gumno*) and a bathhouse (*bana*). Two types of household plan became common: a wreathlike plan (in the north and northeast), in which all the buildings were located along the perimeter of the household, creating a closed space, and a straplike plan (in the west), in which all the buildings were constructed in one or two rows under one roof. A free-plan type also existed, with the buildings 10–15 meters from the house. The traditional Belarussian dwelling was a two- or three-room log cabin built of pine or spruce logs. Usually the house was raised off the ground with stones or wooden blocks. Up to the middle of the nineteenth century small houses with two rooms with an earthen or clay floor, arched beam ceiling, and a stove with no chimney were prevalent. Later on there appeared chimneys, hardwood floors, and flat, board roofs with one or two longitudinal beams. The roofs were two- or four-pitched, most frequently of a rafter construction; they were covered with rye or reed thatches, more rarely by shingles or boards.

The traditional architectural decor was noted for its conservatism. It was exemplified by carved window panels and artistic pediments of thin planking (*shalevka*). A characteristic feature of the interior of a peasant home was its compositional integrity throughout the whole ethnic territory of the Belarussians. The stove, made of brick, was in the right or left corner by the entrance, and its orifice was turned toward the side wall with windows. A wooden floor for sleeping was built by the stove along the blank wall with no windows. In the "red" corner—the one diagonally across from the stove—there was a table and above it an icon; next to it there were wide benches. Hanging shelves for kitchenware were attached to the walls. Clothes and linen were kept in wooden trunks. In winter the *krosni* (a loom) was put in the house and, if necessary, a hanging wooden cradle. The house was lit with a splinter that was fixed on a wooden or metal stand, a suspended metal frame that had its own chimney.

Economy

Belarussians are a typical agricultural people. The most important traditional agricultural crops were rye, oats, barley, buckwheat, flax, and from the second half of the eighteenth century, potatoes. The three-field system was the dominating one in agriculture. In the northeast in the second half of the nineteenth century, orchards and horticulture played an important role (for example, cabbages, beets, carrots, maize, legumes, and tobacco). The main agricultural tools were a two-tooth wooden plow of the *sokha* type and a harrow. Plows had started to appear by the end of the

nineteenth century; at first they were wooden, with metal only at the points. In the northeast horses were used as draft animals, and in the southwest oxen were so used. The crop was harvested with the help of a sickle. The scythe was used for hay and to harvest oats, buckwheat, and peas. The stacks of the cut-down crops were tied into sheaves and dried either in the fields or in special buildings. Threshing was done by hand or with the help of wooden staves. Flour was ground in watermills or windmills or sometimes in the household itself with the help of millstones or in wooden mortars.

Animal husbandry traditionally was subordinate to agriculture. Its main purpose was to provide draft animals and, to a lesser degree, to provide dairy or meat products, wool, or leather. Belarussians bred horses, oxen, cows, goats, sheep, and pigs. Most of the year the cattle were fed forage crops; in winter they were kept in special premises. During the period when they were penned in, cattle were most often fed straw; horses and sheep were fed hay; and pigs were given chaff fortified with potatoes and flour.

In the north (Poozerje) and south (Polessye) fishing played an important role in the traditional economy. Nets of various kinds (for example, sweep nets) were in widespread use, as were stationary and mobile traps, harpoons, and hook tackles.

Hunting was much less important. Its objects were boars, moose, deer, and hare. Bear spears, rifles, traps, and snares were used in hunting. Gathering forest and swamp berries, mushrooms, and nettles was an additional economic occupation in summer and autumn. Beekeeping traditionally played an important part in the economy. Boats were the main means of water transportation.

INDUSTRIAL ARTS. Home trades and crafts were an important addition to the main occupations of the Belarussians. The timber industry was oriented toward the production of tools and implements, means of transportation (sleighs and sledges), and household utensils (barrels, churns, cooking appliances, and trunks). Weaving was highly developed—linen, hemp, and wool fabrics for clothes, linen, tablecloths, towels, and bed covers were produced. Such weaving equipment as the distaff (*kolovrot*) and the vertical loom (*krosni*) were widespread. Braiding and plaiting were also widespread. Containers for storing grain and clothes were made out of straw and willow, footgear (*lapti*) and bags were made out of bark, household utensils and caskets were made out of tree roots, headgear and toys of straw, and furniture of willow. Usually, there was one blacksmith for several villages. He made the metal parts for agricultural tools, joiner's and fitter's tools, parts of the interior (locks and screens), and furniture. Pottery was highly evolved. Ceramic kitchenware—pots, bowls, and mugs—was made and then burnt on potter's wheels. Leather making was also developed to a high degree.

CLOTHING. Local variations, in the traditional costume of Belarussians were congruent with the composition and style of dress throughout the ethnic territory. The main part of the woman's costume was a tunic shirt (*kashul'a*) made of bleached linen fabric. The sleeves, collar, and cuffs of this shirt had an embroidered or fabric ornament, usually of red thread. The skirt (*spadnitsa*) was of two kinds: the summer skirt (*letnik*) was made of linen, with a fabric ornament of hemp or red wool; the winter skirt (*andrak*) was made of wool, checkered or striped, with a red, blue, or dark-green background. In the southeast the archaic form of costume consisting of two separate sheets (*poneva*) was retained. A long white linen apron was a necessary part of the costume; it had an ornament and lace. Often a short woolen vest (*garset*) was added to the costume. *Namitki*— long linen sheets wrapped in a peculiar way around the head and neck—were a characteristic feature of the woman's costume. The man's costume included a linen shirt and pants made of cloth or wool (*spodni*), often also a vest (*kamizelka*) and headgear—a straw hat (*bril'*) or a felt cap (*magerka*). Men's and women's seasonal clothes consisted of a long, Ukrainian-style outer garment *svita* made at home out of a white, gray, or (rarely) brown felt wool fabric and decorated with an embroidery of woolen threads. In the cold time of the year men and women wore sheepskins. An ornamented belt woven with woolen threads was a necessary part of the costume. Woven linden or willow lapti were a universal peasant footgear; at the same time leather shoes became popular, too. In winter felt boots were worn. Within the ethnic territory of the Belarussians up to thirty local types of traditional costume were known, differing in the color pattern, technique of weaving, and the character of decorative ornaments.

FOOD. Cereals constituted the basis of the traditional diet of the Belarussians: bread, blinis, and rye, rye sourdough, oatmeal, buckwheat, and pea-flour pancakes. Cereals formed the basis of kissel or blancmange (*zur*), porridge (*culaga, saladukha*), and various soups (*kalatukha, kulesh*). Potato dishes became a characteristic feature of traditional Belarussian cuisine (there were over 500 different ways of preparing them). Potatoes were fried, baked, or boiled and cooked in a casserole; *draniki* (pancakes made of minced potatoes) as well as *kletsks* and dumplings were consumed. Meat, pork mostly, was eaten relatively rarely, primarily on winter holidays. Meat was used to make sausages and aspic, cooked in casseroles in a sauce, and eaten with buckwheat pancakes (*machanka*). Dairy products were mostly fresh and sour milk, sour cream, farmer's cheese, and butter. Farmer cheeses became common. Among the traditional beverages there were bread, birch, and linden juice kvass; herbal infusions; and dried-fruit compote (*uzvars*). Of alcoholic beverages vodka (*garelka*) was the most popular one; beer and mead *medovukha* were less so. The traditional Belarussian food was seasonal: in winter and in the autumn the food was most nutritious and plentiful; in summer vegetarian food prevailed. Belarussian peasants would usually eat three or four times a day. Breakfast (*snedanje*) was very early and nutritious: it included first courses (e.g., soups), a main course, and always porridge. Dinner included several very high-calorie dishes. The afternoon snack (*padvacherja*) and supper (*vacherja*) were lighter meals, but they also included several courses.

DIVISION OF LABOR. There was a clear division of labor in the economy of the Belarussians. Men would plow the land; sow and mow; take in the hay and sheaves from the fields; thresh; store timber; construct and repair buildings; make carts, sledges, and boats; and weave lapti (boat shoes) and baskets. The women would reap; harvest hay, hemp, flax, and potatoes; take care of cattle; prepare the food; and provide the family with clothing. Beginning at ages 5 to 6 children would take care of the younger ones. From the ages of 7 to 8 boys worked as shepherds, and by age 12 they helped with the haying. From the age of 15 they mowed and threshed, and after about 16 they had to do every kind of job. This rule was also applicable to young women relative to women's jobs.

TRADE. As a rule the traditional Belarussian economy was not closely connected with the large markets; it was a semisubsistence economy. *Mestechki* were local market centers where goods were sold once or twice a week; fairs (*kirmash*) were held several times a year. Trade operations were an activity mainly of members of the Jewish ethnic group.

Kinship, Marriage, and Family

The Belarussians had several types of families in the nineteenth and twentieth centuries. The small family (six or seven people) was prevalent; at the same time there were large patriarchical families that consisted of several generations of relatives and also fraternal families. Marriage was usually virilocal—although the husband moving in with the family of his wife (*primachestvo*) was a fairly frequent alternative. The unity of two unrelated groups or the adoption of a nonrelative (*zdolnik*) into the family for the purposes of making the economy more effective were peculiar forms of family relations. Relations both in the large patriarchical family and the small families were based on the authoritarian power of the eldest man (*batsko*) and his wife.

Religion and Expressive Culture

RELIGIOUS BELIEFS. Traditional knowledge of Belarussians was represented by the folk calendar that was oriented toward the phases of the moon, relative to which the starting point of various stages in agricultural work was defined. Weather watching at certain calendar days made long-term meteorologic forecasts possible, whereas observations of animal behavior and natural phenomena were used for short-term forecasts. Traditional meteorology relied on length, space, weight, and volume measures.

CEREMONIES. The family was the main institution through which Belarussians socialized in the nineteenth and twentieth centuries. The entire population of the village would participate in the celebration of holidays. The most important events of the year-long cycle were Christmas festivities (*kaladi*), calling the spring (*gukanje*), the first driving of the cattle to the pasture on Yuri day, Easter (*balikden*), Trinity (*semukha*), summer solstice (the feast of Ivan Kupala, or Saint John the Baptist), and the beginning and the end of harvest (*zazhinki, dazhinki*).

ARTS. Traditional Belarussian art was very diverse. In the seventeenth through eighteenth centuries, within the framework of the early Baroque style, the Belarussian Uniate school of icon painting and sculpture was formed: it combined features of professional art and folk art. Applied decorative art was the main development in the nineteenth and twentieth centuries; it was represented by weaving, embroidery, pottery, artistic forging, and wood carving. Straw weaving is a type of decorative art peculiar to the Belarussians. This technique was used for making ornaments, toys, boxes, and even architectural details of church interiors—the "czar's gates of the iconostasis." Traditional music was represented by two forms—songs and instrumental music. Archaic forms of vocal art are monophonic. Polyphony started to spread mostly at the end of the nineteenth century in the south. The most popular instruments were the violin, cymbals, different kinds of bagpipes, flute (*zalejika*), "lyre" (a string instrument with the body of a violin but with a keyboard), and the *basetla* (double bass). Puppet theater (*batlejika*) was a characteristic form of theater. Performances of a carnival character were also known. The repertoire included plays with biblical themes, for example *King Herod*.

MEDICINE. Folk medicine was based on a developed system of beliefs and treatments in the fields of hygiene, epidemiology, pharmacology. The most common drugs were made from herbs, dried root and bark infusions, animal fat, bile, and preparations of mineral origin. They were quite successfully used to prevent the spreading of infections and diseases (notably cholera) and to treat colds, wounds, and bruises. Baths were considered a kind of physiotherapeutical treatment.

DEATH AND AFTERLIFE. The funeral ritual of Belarussians included many magical elements. The dead person was buried on the third day after death. Salt, a pipe, and copper coins were usually put into the coffin. After the funeral and also on the sixth, ninth, and fortieth days and after half a year after the memorial, ritual dinners (*trapeza*) were held. *Kutsa* (a sweet barley porridge) was a necessary dish at these events. According to the traditional beliefs of the Belarussians, the next world is separated into two parts: heaven in the south, where summer is eternal, and hell in the north. God assigned people to either parts, depending on the good and bad deeds they had accomplished during their lives. Four times a year Belarussians held commemorative feasts for all the dead ancestors (*dzadi*), who returned home on these days. Every participant at the ritual left some food for them (three pieces or three tablespoons of each course). There was a belief that the late relatives patronize the family and ensure its success.

Bibliography

Krushinsky, S. (1953). *Byelorussian Communism and Nationalism: Personal Recollections.* New York: Research Program on the USSR, East European Fund.

Shamiakin, I. P., et al., eds. (1989). *Etnahrafiia Belarusi: Entsyklapediia* (Encyclopedia of Belarussian ethnology). Minsk: Belaruskaiia Savetskaia Entsyklapediia.

Vakar, Nicholas P. (1949). "The Name White Russia." *American Slavic and East European Review* 8: 201–213.

—PAVEL TERESHKOVICH
(TRANSLATED BY OLGA BELODED)

Traditional knowledge of Belarussians was represented by the folk calendar that was oriented toward the phases of the moon.

♦ **czar**
Ruler of Russia before 1917.

CHECHEN-INGUSH

Ethnonyms: Chechen: Nokhchiy (sing., Nokhchuo);
Ingush: Ghalghay

Orientation

IDENTIFICATION. The Chechens and Ingush are the most numerous northern Caucasian group and territorially one of the largest. In view of their numbers, the strategic location of their territory, and the strong leading role of the Chechens in the resistance to the Russian conquest of the Caucasus, they figure with particular prominence in Russian artistic literature depicting the northern Caucasus. Although Chechen and Ingush are distinct languages and are not mutually intelligible, in areas of population overlap communication is achieved through passive bilingualism. Learning to communicate smoothly in an unfamiliar dialect area may require several days' time. There are Chechen communities in Jordan, Syria, and Turkey, formed when many Chechens and Ingush emigrated to Muslim countries after the Caucasus Wars in the mid-nineteenth century. These émigré communities retain the language (basically Chechen dialects, although some of the émigrés are of Ingush descent) and much of the culture. The language is especially well retained in Jordan, where children still learn it as their first language.

The Chechens and Ingush are relatively tall, with fair skin and hair color ranging from black to blond, with reddish shades being common. Stereotypically, in their own view, the Chechens and Ingush are thin and long-limbed, with thick hair and little male baldness. The two groups see themselves as physically identical to each other and physically distinct from their neighbors.

This article is based on available published sources—which are neither extensive, recent, nor of even quality—and on some elicitation and extremely limited field observation. The past tense is used for patterns reported of traditional life (some of which may still be observed) and the present tense for those reported or observed now (most of them traditional). The word "apparently" marks inferences.

LOCATION. The traditional territory lies on and to the east of the principal road crossing the central Caucasus (leading to the Darial Pass and the Georgian Military Highway) and extends from just north of the Terek River in the southern part of the north Caucasian plains to the snow line; a few villages, speaking the distinctive Kisti dialect, are found to the south of the Caucasian crest, in eastern Georgia. At its greatest extent this territory reaches from about 42° to 44° N and about 45° to 46° E. The land ranges from plains and rolling foothills in the north to alpine terrain in the south. The northern lowlands enjoy rich soil, ample precipitation, and a long growing season; the mountain valleys also offer fertile soil and adequate-to-ample precipitation, with increasingly alpine conditions at higher elevations. The climate is continental, with hot and often humid summers and cold (though not harsh) winters. Much of the land is heavily forested. Lowland settlements are in natural plains; in mountain valleys there has been some clearing (presumably extensive in some areas).

DEMOGRAPHY. The population in 1989 was 1,194,317 (956,879 Chechens and 237,438 Ingush); in 1979 it was 941,980 (755,782 Chechens and 186,198 Ingush); in 1926 it was 392,619 (318,522 Chechens and 74,097 Ingush). The birthrate is—and apparently always was—high.

LINGUISTIC AFFILIATION. Chechen and Ingush, together with closely related Batsbi (or Ts'ova-Tush; spoken in Georgia), form the Nakh, or North-Central Caucasian, Branch of Northeast Caucasian (Nakh-Daghestanian), a stock not demonstrably related to any other (although connections to Hurrian-Urartian and to Northwest Caucasian have been sought). Typologically, Chechen and Ingush are verb-final, agglutinating, ergative, and case-marking languages, with six to eight nominal genders and with fixed initial stress, numerous vowels (phonemic length, diphthongs, sometimes nasalization), numerous consonants (three manners of articulation, including ejectives; eight points, including *c, ch,* uvulars, pharyngeals, glottals), but a simple root and syllable canon with geminate consonants and few clusters. Ingush has little or no internal dialect differentiation. Chechen comprises a number of dialects; a central lowlands dialect now serves as the official literary language and is the basis for the orthography. Chechen and Ingush were not traditionally written; prior to the Revolution, writing was in Arabic. Chechen and Ingush are now separate written languages. Latin orthographies were created in 1923 and replaced by Cyrillic in 1938. Both Latin and Cyrillic orthographies grossly underdifferentiate the vowel phonemes but render consonants well and economically. At present there is fairly extensive publication of textbooks, newspapers, and literature (as well as radio and television broadcasts and theater per-

*The Chechens and
the Ingush are
relatively tall, with
fair skin and hair
color ranging from
black to blond, with
reddish shades being
common.*

formances) in Chechen and Ingush, but almost no technical or scientific publication. Much of the population (especially among the Ingush) is fluent in Russian, and some (especially those who received primary or secondary education in Central Asia during the period of exile, 1945–1956) are bilingual and Russian-dominant.

Settlements

A typical lowland village consists of single-story wood or brick houses on rectangular fenced lots in a compact and generally rectangular arrangement. Modern brick now replaces adobe—which traditionally was tempered with straw and manure, sun-dried, and, once in place, covered with stucco—although the adobe (said to be of Ukrainian origin, brought to the Caucasus by the Cossacks) is probably superior to all other materials in preserving an even, comfortable temperature. A fence or wall encloses the house, outbuildings, work space, and the household's garden and fruit trees. In high mountain villages the layout is less regular. Mountain houses were traditionally multistory structures of hewn and fitted stone interspersed with similar stone defense towers up to five stories in height; they were owned and maintained by clans. Both houses and defense towers were inhabited. The stone buildings are no longer inhabited, and many were destroyed during the period of deportation. Village populations range from a few hundred in the mountains to a few thousand or (in a few cases) a few tens of thousands in the

HISTORY AND CULTURAL RELATIONS

According to both archaeological and linguistic evidence, Northeast Caucasian speakers have inhabited the northeastern Caucasus since about 6000 B.C. The Nakh languages exhibit a few words of early Indo-European provenance, testifying to relations with the Bronze Age steppe populations. There is surprisingly little lexical evidence of interaction with the Iron Age Iranian-speaking steppe tribes. The Nakh languages have numerous loanwords from adjacent Ossetic (Iranian) and Kumyk (Turkic). Native vocabulary suggests ancient connections with the high mountain languages of southern Daghestan, later (but still early) interaction with the Lak of the northeastern lowlands, and relatively recent interaction with the adjacent Avar. Present Chechen-Ingush territory largely coincides with the entry route along which steppe peoples and cultures penetrated the mountains and from which mountain culture periodically spread to the steppe. Inferable prehistory, with its fluctuation between mountain and steppe influences, is consistent with this picture. After the weakening of the Golden Horde in the sixteenth century, a substantial descent to the lowlands began, including the abandonment of some high mountain villages, a process that must have been periodically repeated throughout prehistory and continues to the present day. History can be traced to the seventeenth century and the first recorded interaction with Cossacks, and it begins in earnest with the Russian invasion of the Caucasus, of which there are extensive Russian records—literary, historical, military, and ethnographic. With the introduction of literacy after the Revolution, an intelligentsia, a written literature, and a remarkably strong scholarly tradition of descriptive philology were quick to form, but these developments were gutted in the purges of the 1930s. Ingushetia and Chechnia were separate autonomous regions (autonomous oblasts) until 1934, when they were joined and eventually made an autonomous republic (ASSR). During World War II the front extended to Chechen-Ingush territory. From 1944 to 1956 the Chechens and Ingush were exiled to Central Asia (with considerable loss of life), ostensibly for having collaborated with the Nazis but in all likelihood to clear Muslims and possible sympathizers with Turkey from major routes of military movement in the event of an invasion of Turkey. During this period their republic did not exist and the languages were removed from the status of literary languages. Upon "rehabilitation" most survivors returned to the Caucasus; many settled in cities instead of their ancestral villages, and most high mountain villages were not resettled. In 1991 the Chechens declared their independence and their secession from the then-USSR; the Ingush supported their right to self-rule, and demanded for themselves the status of a republic in Russia with the return of territory (on the right bank of the upper Terek, including suburban Vladikavkaz) that had been removed to North Ossetia during the exile.

The Chechens and Ingush had close and generally peaceable relations with their neighbors to the west (Ossetes and, in the lowlands, Kabardians), south (Georgians), and east (Avars, speakers of Andi-Didoic languages; in the lowlands, Kumyks). Available sources depict warfare as occasioned only by attacks by steppe tribes; in high mountain areas, land shortages and population pressure led to tension between clans and between Chechen-Ingush and other ethnicities. In recent decades there has been some local tension between Ingush and Ossetes, the result of dual claims to territory that was Ingush until the deportation and has been Ossetic since. Major literary influence has come from Ossetic (epic verse), Kumyk or other Turkic languages (lyric songs), and, presumably via Georgian, Persian (lyric songs). The culture is solidly North Caucasian overall. Most Chechen-Ingush speakers today live in the Chechen and Ingush Republic; outside of it are Vladikavkaz (Soviet Orjonikidze) in North Ossetia, the Kisti villages in eastern Georgia, and outlying villages in northwestern Daghestan.

lowlands. There are two true cities, both with sizable Russian populations and both originally Russian military forts: Groznyi in the Chechen lowlands and Vladikavkaz in the Ingush and Ossetic highlands. In villages, but not in cities, settlement is kin-based, with members of the same clan occupying the same street or neighborhood.

Economy

SUBSISTENCE AND COMMERCIAL ACTIVITIES. Raising livestock, especially sheepherding, was the traditional economic mainstay in the highlands; grain agriculture was the mainstay in the lowlands. High mountain villages were not self-sufficient in grain because of the short alpine growing season and the scarcity of arable land, so they traded livestock and eggs for grain in lowland bazaars. Where this trading did not suffice, some horse thievery and other robbery (especially from Georgian nobility, to judge from folklore) rounded out the economy. There was, and is, a renowned bazaar in Nazran´ in the Ingush lowlands and a lesser but still sizable one in Vladikavkaz. The lowlands were more than self-sufficient in grain, which was exported to the highlands. The staple grain since approximately the seventeenth century has been maize. There apparently was no traditional production of manufactured items for trade. In the modern economy, some 40 percent of the population remains rural and primarily agricultural. Nearby oil fields have made Groznyi a center of industry and urban employment.

The traditional diet relied on grains and dairy products. Traditional ethnic foods include unleavened corn bread (*siskal*); meat in dough casings boiled in stock (*khingal*; the dish and a term resembling this one are also found among other peoples of the Caucasus); pancakelike, unleavened-wheat pan bread stuffed with cheese, squash, or other dairy or vegetable products and brushed with melted butter (*ch'ä:pigish*); cheese, curds, sour cream, yogurt, butter; fruits (including apples, pears, plums; medlars were harvested from wild trees); nuts; and meat, typically mutton. The proportion of fat, especially dairy fat, was high by modern urban standards.

DIVISION OF LABOR. Men were responsible for livestock, fieldwork, construction, and defense; they sometimes took salaried work in lowland villages. Women were responsible for poultry and gardens, as well as for cooking, weaving, sewing, preserving, and caring for young children. In the modern urban household the woman generally remains in full and exclusive control of the kitchen, whereas the man makes purchases and does all heavy work and most household repair.

LAND TENURE. Lots, gardens, and orchards were privately owned by households. Fields were communally owned by clans or villages (except that cleared land belonged to the household or head of household that had cleared it). Pastureland, at least for cattle, was communally owned by villages. Livestock was privately owned by households. Virgin land was not owned and was open to use by anyone (subject to strict cultural controls, for example on what species of tree could be cut). Roads and paths apparently were not owned. Food, once harvested and prepared, or livestock, once slaughtered, were to some extent subject to distribution by the owner to guests, neighbors, kin, people held in deference, and to fellow clan or subclan members with whom the owner had mutual obligations of support and hospitality. In high mountain villages where land was scarce, there was a strict limit on the number of livestock a household could own. When a herd exceeded this limit, the entire herd was confiscated and redistributed. (The Kisti and Batsbi settlements in Georgia are said to have received some of their population from highland people emigrating to avoid confiscation.) Land was not in short supply in the northern lowlands, but periodic incursions of steppe tribes are thought to have made expansion dangerous.

Kinship

KIN GROUPS AND DESCENT. Descent, in the form of clan membership, was reckoned through the male line. Clans (*taip*) were grouped into tribes that generally corresponded to dialects; tribes were not considered kin groups, though they were traced to mythic ancestors. Clan fission could occur if a feud or other serious disagreement led a family to adopt a different name or if a family needed to hide its identity from the authorities (as happened in czarist times), but in general clans strove to become as large as possible. Modern family names are said to derive generally from the clan name among the Ingush but from the first name of a paternal ancestor (the paternal grandfather, when family names were fixed, and by now a more distant ancestor) among the Chechens.

KINSHIP TERMINOLOGY. The kinship system is minimally classificatory: basic terms (mother, father, brother, sister, son, daughter, wife, husband) are combined to yield transparent phrases such as "mother's father," "father's father's sister," etc. The only simplex classificatory terms appear to be *nuskal* ("daughter-in-law"—the element *nus-* is pan-Caucasian and an evident Indo-Europeanism), *shicha* ("first cousin," male or female), and *meakhcha* ("second cousin," male or female); the latter two have the Turkic suffix **chi*.

Marriage and Family

Marriage was obligatorily clan-exogamous and usually tribally endogamous. The socially sanctioned form of marriage was by arrangement, but elopement was probably more common. Elopement outwardly resembled capture but was usually arranged in advance with the knowledge and cooperation of the girl's mother; to judge from folklore sources, the girl took the more active role in choosing her partner and making arrangements for the elopement. In arranged marriages the groom, his family, and the bride's family agreed on the union; the consent of the bride was not traditionally required. There was a bride-price, usually payable in livestock. Marriage by kidnapping to avoid the high bride-price, although it could trigger a feud, is reported in some nineteenth-century sources. Among urban families the bride-price now often takes the form of a negotiated gift, usually paid to the young couple in currency, apparently often with a fund-matching contribution from the bride's parents. Divorce is increasingly common, especially in cities. Divorce settlements are made by clan elders; the bride-price can be returned to the husband's family if the wife is deemed to have been at fault, or it may be retained by the wife if the husband was at fault. A divorced or widowed woman with children can generally hope to remarry only if she leaves the children with the husband's family; if she keeps the children, her chances of remarriage are slim because she would be bringing children of another clan into her new husband's household.

A man avoids contact with his wife's parents and observes the etiquette of deference with her brothers and sisters. A woman at first avoids her husband's parents, but after some time—typically by the time the first child is born—she can converse with them. She never mentions the names of her husband's parents or siblings, whether in or out of their presence.

There was no formal adoption. Orphaned children were raised by a father's brother or by the nearest relative in the clan. A childless family might raise a son of the husband's brother as its own. In such cases children were raised in their own clan (and never, for instance, in their mother's clan).

The usual household consists of a nuclear family when space and resources permit.

Sociopolitical Organization

SOCIAL ORGANIZATION. Traditional Chechen-Ingush society is highly egalitarian. The only hierarchical relationships are those of age, kinship, and earned social honor. Hierarchical relationships are signaled and maintained by two partly intersecting forms of behavior that can be called "deference" and "formality." Deference is a form of interaction; it includes rising (by men) or standing (by women) in the presence of the deferree, maintaining silence to some extent, and markedly formal behavior; details of deference differ depending on the situation and kin relation between the individuals. A man gives deference to older males in his own clan (including his own father and older brothers) and to all males of his mother's clan (since to all of them he is a nephew and hence counts as younger). A woman similarly gives deference to elders, to members of her mother's clan, and to in-laws. All members of society, even children, offer deference to people who have earned particular respect. Formality is not necessarily a form of interaction; it is triggered by the mere presence of a relevant person. One is formal in the presence of elders (especially deferrees). Formality involves dignified behavior, erect posture, measured speech, and refraining from any form of intimacy (expression of one's personal feelings, displays of affection, etc.). Proper observance of formality and deference are particularly important to the institution of hospitality. Hospitality remains central even in modern urban life. To fail or refuse to give hospitality is unthinkable; to decline to take it (or, more generally, to fail to maximize others' opportunities to offer it) is ill-mannered and offensive. Observance of all aspects of the etiquette of deference and formality is an essential part of ethnic identity. Proper behavior and the code of etiquette are not explicitly taught to children, who are expected to observe for themselves and learn.

POLITICAL ORGANIZATION. Villages were traditionally autonomous (although villages, or perhaps clans, apparently held mutual defense obligations in times of warfare). Clans were also autonomous in their respective spheres. Each clan had a headman, typically a respected elder. Clans had religious and legal responsibilities, which to some extent they still retain, as well as shared economic interests. Clans or subclans had support obligations in vendettas. Clans still have their own traditional cemeteries. In villages, elders held collective adjudicatory responsibilities.

Traditional Chechen-Ingush society is highly egalitarian. The only hierarchical relationships are those of age, kinship, and earned social honor.

SOCIAL CONTROL AND CONFLICT. Social control in this egalitarian society was effected by a system in which bringing honor to one's household, clan, and ancestors was highly valued, and bringing dishonor was avoided even at high cost. A man could bring honor to his line by scrupulous lifelong observance of formality and deference, generous hospitality, and economic productivity. He could bring dishonor by failure to observe formality or deference, failure to extend hospitality, and apparently also by failure to receive hospitality (or create opportunities to receive it). Women were credited with maintaining harmony within household and community and with making hospitality possible; thus they indirectly brought honor to their households and ultimately to their husband's clan. A woman could dishonor clan and household by immodest public behavior or by nonchastity (especially nonvirginity at marriage); rape brought dishonor to the woman's household and clan (the man risked retaliation but not dishonor). The system was enforced by feuding: offenses against deference, the rape of a marriageable woman or public questioning of her chastity, the kidnapping of a bride, murder, and perhaps grave offenses against hospitality could all trigger feuds.

Women were, for all practical purposes, owned by the immediate head of household (father or brother, husband) and ultimately by his clan. Their chastity, especially their virginity before marriage, was jealously guarded. Rape made a woman unmarriageable (and since elopement was minimally distinguishable from rape, a change of mind on the man's part in the first days could render the woman permanently unmarriageable). A nonvirgin bride was rejected and left disgraced and unmarriageable (but traditional custom seems to have given young men little experience that would enable them to judge virginity with great accuracy). Nevertheless, especially prior to the conversion to Islam, a certain amount of sexual freedom for married women is suggested in some folklore and historical sources.

Religion and Expressive Culture

RELIGIOUS BELIEFS. From about the ninth to sixteenth centuries, there is thought to have been missionary activity by the Georgian church (Eastern Orthodox), chiefly among the Ingush. Only traces remain of this tradition—ultimately Greek names for days of the week and an occasional abandoned medieval church in the high mountains. The indigenous traditional religion was basically animistic, with a number of nature and patron deities (the head of the pantheon was simply Deela, "God"), an ancestor cult (the prob-

HUMAN COST

Chechen Muslim men pray and grieve at the funeral of a friend killed in the conflict with Russia. The Chechnya conflict lasted from 1994–1996. Grozny, Chechnya. (David Turnley/Corbis)

able source of patron deities), a hearth cult, and belief in an afterlife where the well-being of one's deceased ancestors was determined by one's behavior on earth. Funerals were held the day after death, a few days later (a feast with contests enabling the deceased to rise from his bed in the afterworld), two years later, and three years later. A widow resumed regular dress and could remarry (usually a brother of the first husband) after the third-year funeral. She was buried with her first husband in his family tomb and belonged to him in the afterworld. There were no funerals for women since they did not pass down the clan name. The lowland Chechens converted to Islam (transmitted by the Kumyks) in the eighteenth century and the Ingush in the early nineteenth century. The conversion is described as originally political in motivation, a move to identify and ally oneself with the Caucasian resistance to the Russians. By now, Islam (specifically, Sunni Islam of the Hanafi school) is devoutly professed as religion by most of the population and is widely considered an essential element of ethnicity. Bennigsen and Wimbush describe a system of conservative Islam that takes the form of clandestine brotherhoods (*tariqa*). Islam spread to the Chechen-Ingush via these brotherhoods along clan and subclan lines; the Soviet repression of Islam, including wholesale destruction of mosques during and after the period of deportation, only strengthened the brotherhood organization. Tariqa are described as fulfilling in modern society a number of the functions traditionally performed by clans and subclans (e.g., determination of preferred patterns of marriage, legal and religious responsibilities, etc.). I have not been able to replicate this information, nor the claim of "an absolute confusion between religious, clan, and national loyalties" (Bennigsen and Wimbush 1986, 188).

ARTS. Perhaps the most conspicuous art form is architecture, represented by the finely built tall defense towers in the high mountains. None have been built in historical times, and their construction is sometimes attributed to semimythical previous inhabitants. Wood carving, weaving, felt making, leatherwork, and other crafts were traditionally practiced. Music includes instrumental dance music (now mostly played on the accordion, plus drum) similar to that of Daghestan and (to a lesser extent) Georgia. Dance of the Caucasian type is highly developed. There are lyric songs (*yish*) primarily for solo voice, occasional polyphonic choral songs suggesting Georgian influence, and long epic song-poems (*illay*);

solo music is sung to the accompaniment of a three-stringed strummed instrument (*pondar*). Traditional music and dance continue to flourish. Novels and lyric poetry, some of distinct merit, have been published in recent decades. There are theaters of note, both Ingush and Chechen, in Groznyi; they perform both Chechen-Ingush and translated dramas, all in Chechen or Ingush.

Bibliography

Akiner, Shirin (1986). *Islamic Peoples of the Soviet Union: An Historical and Statistical Handbook.* 2nd ed., 175–180, 197–201. London: KPI.

Bazorkin, Idris (1976). *Iz t'my vekov* (Out of the darkness of the ages) [A novel; thinly disguised Ingush ethnography]. Grozny: Checheno-Ingushskoe Knizhnoe Izdatel'stvo.

Beerle-Moor, Werner (1988). "Studien zum Cardakischen: Phonologie und verbale Formenbildung." Ph.D. dissertation, University of Zurich.

Bennigsen, Alexandre, and S. Enders Wimbush (1986). *Muslims of the Soviet Empire: A Guide*, 181–190. Bloomington: Indiana University Press.

Dalgat, Bashir (1893). "Pervobytnaia religiia chechentsev" (The aboriginal religion of the Chechens). *Terskii Sbornik* (Vladikavkaz: Terskii Oblastnoi Statisticheskii Komitet) 3(2.2): 41–132.

Genko, A. N. (1930). "Iz kul'turnogo proshlogo ingushei" (From the cultural past of the Ingush). *Zapiski Kollegii Vostokovedov pri Aziatskom Muzee* (Leningrad: Akademiia Nauk) 5:681–762.

Jabagi, M. (1935). *Textes populaires Ingush (Traduits, commentés et précédés d'une introduction grammaticale par G. Dumézil).* Paris: Adrien-Maisonneuve.

Maksimov, E. (1893). "Chechentsy" (The Chechens). *Terskii Sbornik* (Vladikavkaz: Terskii Oblastnoi Statisticheskii Komitet) 3:(2.1).

Margoshvili, L. Iu. (1969). "Kisty pankisi (Istorikoetnograficheskoe issledovanie)" (The Kist'is of P'ank'isi: A historical-ethnographical study). Summary of candidate's Ph.D. dissertation, Georgian Academy of Sciences, Tbilisi.

Moses, Larry W. (1984). "Chechen-Ingush." In *The Muslim Peoples: A World Ethnographic Survey.* 2nd ed., edited by Richard V. Weekes. Westport, Conn.: Greenwood Press.

Vertepov, G. (1892). "Ingushi: Istoriko-ekonomicheskii ocherk" (The Ingush: A historical-economic sketch). *Terskii Sbornik* (Vladikavkaz: Terskii Oblastnoi Statisticheskii Komitet) 2:71–138.

Wixman, Ronald (1980). *Language Aspects of Ethnic Patterns and Processes in the North Caucasus.* University of Chicago Department of Geography Research Paper no. 191.

Wixman, Ronald (1984). *The Peoples of the USSR: An Ethnographic Handbook.* Armonk, N.Y.: M. E. Sharpe.

—JOHANNA NICHOLS

ESTONIANS

Ethnonym: Eesti

Orientation

IDENTIFICATION. The Estonians are a nominally Lutheran and Orthodox people inhabiting their own nation on the Baltic Sea and having their own language and culture despite having been dominated by foreign powers over most of their history.

LOCATION. The nation of Estonia, with an area of 45,125 square kilometers, is located between 57°30′ and 59°49′ N and 21°46′ and 28°13′ E. It is bounded on the north and west by the Baltic Sea, on the east by Russia, and on the south by Latvia. The climate is maritime and cool, the topography is flat, and there are many rivers and lakes. The precipitation (61–71 centimeters annually), together with a very low evaporation rate and flat topography, often results in saturated soil. The soil is also very rocky, especially in the north. Forty percent of Estonia is forested, and 80 percent of the trees are coniferous.

DEMOGRAPHY. The population of the nation of Estonia was estimated at 1,581,000 in 1991. Ethnic Estonians constitute 61.2 percent of this total, Russians 30.3 percent, Ukrainians 3.1 percent, Belarussians 1.8 percent, and Finns 1.1 percent; there are small numbers of Jews, Tatars, and Germans as well. The birthrate was 14 per 1,000 persons, and infant mortality was 25 per 1,000 live births in 1989. More than 72,000 Estonians left Estonia in August and September of 1944, fleeing the Soviet forces who were following the retreating Germans. Most of these people went to Germany and Sweden, although the majority of those in Germany have since emigrated to the United States and Canada.

LINGUISTIC AFFILIATION. Estonian belongs to the Baltic-Finnic Division of the Finno-Ugric Branch of the Uralic Language Family; it is mutually intelligible with Finnish and is thus related to Livonian, Mordvin, Zyrien, Karelian, Votic, Ingrian, and Veps and distantly to Hungarian. Estonian is famous for its three degrees of consonant and vowel length. The vocabulary currently contains many German loanwords. Structurally, inflection is primarily by use of suffixes. Estonian has two main dialects, the southern or Tartu, and the northern or Tallinn; the latter is spoken by the majority of Estonians and is the standard Estonian literary dialect. Some subdialects show the influence of other languages; for example, the western subdialect of the northern dialect exhibits Swedish influence. All of the Estonians plus .3 percent of the other people living in Estonia (i.e., 61.5 percent in all) speak Estonian as their native language. Since independence from the Soviet Union in 1991, it has been necessary to demonstrate proficiency in Estonian to acquire Estonian citizenship.

History and Cultural Relations

Archaeological evidence suggests that present-day Estonia was peopled by 6000 B.C. and probably earlier. The Neolithic transition had little effect on the region, save for small changes in stoneworking and the introduction of pottery; agriculture was not adopted here as elsewhere. Moreover, neither the Bronze Age nor the early Iron Age had much effect on the people of the region because it is poor in metal resources and because trade with southern peoples was insubstantial. Instead, the people made tools of stone, bone, and wood, and most continued a hunting, fishing, and gathering life-style. During the later Roman Iron Age the ancestors of modern Estonians began extensive overland trade with peoples to the south and sea trade with the Goths. It was during this period as well that hunting, fishing, and gathering were replaced by agriculture, animal husbandry, and trade, and people left the valleys to settle on more arable lands. During the Middle Iron Age Estonia and most other regions of Europe experienced economic distress as a repercussion of the fall of the Roman Empire.

During the Later Iron Age (A.D. 800–1200) Estonia prospered, owing in large part to its strategic location between western and northeastern Europe. In addition to animal husbandry and agriculture, the peoples of the area became skilled in handicrafts and ironworking. Society at this time was stratified. The small farmers were freemen but had less influence than the nobility, who were called "betters." There were also slaves, people who had been taken from other countries. Political affairs were run by the "elders," one or more of whom controlled each state. During foreign wars, several or all of the states would form a confederacy. These confederacies were responsible for a successful repulsion of the Russians and, during the period of A.D. 1000–1200, for successful raids on Sweden and Denmark.

◆ **Bronze Age**
The third stage in the development of Western civilization, characterized by the production and use of bronze tools and objects. The Bronze Age, which began in Europe in Greece about 3000 B.C. and ended about 1000 B.C., followed the Neolithic period and preceded the Iron Age.

◆ **Iron Age**
The fourth stage in the development of Western civilization, characterized by the production and use of iron tools and objects. Beginning in southeastern Europe in about 1200 B.C., the Iron Age followed the Bronze Age.

The Estonians, who were politically and militarily uncentralized, lost their independence in 1227, when they were conquered by Christian forces. Along with the Latvians, the Estonians had opposed conversion to Christianity since that would have meant relinquishing political control to the church. In 1202 Bishop Albert of Riga formed the crusading Order of the Military Brothers of Christ, to conquer Estonia. In their long war with the Estonians, this order, also known as the Knights of the Sword, were allied with the Danes after 1219.

Northern Estonia came under the rule of the Danes. Southern Estonia was controlled by the Knights of the Sword and, later, by the Order of Teutonic Knights. The Danes sold northern Estonia to the Order of Teutonic Knights in 1346, largely because of Estonian rebelliousness. The Teutonic Knights put down the insurrections, taxed their Estonian subjects heavily, and created large landed estates, which they rented to tenants. The tenants gained increasing legal control over the lives of the peasants and gradually transformed them into serfs and, later, slaves.

Ivan IV began a war against the Teutonic Knights in 1558, and the Muscovites rapidly took Estonia. The Teutonic Knights, the city of Tallinn and the northern Estonian nobles took an oath of loyalty to the king of Sweden in 1561. Sweden fought the Muscovites and removed them from Estonia by 1582. The reign of Gustavus Adolphus, beginning in 1625, saw numerous reforms including the abolition of landowners' jurisdiction over criminal legal cases, the creation of courts in which peasants could take action against their landlords, and the founding of schools.

Peter the Great of Russia went to war and took Estonia in 1710. He obliterated the reforms of the Swedes and returned to the German nobles their control over the lives of the peasants. In 1740 the Russian judiciary ruled that serfdom was legal. Estonians later rioted. Czar Alexander I supported protections for the serfs, however, and in 1816 Estonian serfs were freed. The former serfs courted the czar's protection from the Lutheran landlords by becoming members of the Orthodox church. Land reform ensued in 1856: peasants were given the right to buy and own freehold estates. Czar Alexander II made a law in 1866 removing the authority of landowners over peasant communities and in 1868 decreed the payment of rent by service abolished. The liberal influences of the Russian czars also led to the availability of schooling for all, with the result that by 1870 the Estonian literacy rate was 95 percent.

An Estonian nationalist movement began in the 1860s, and by the 1870s it had split into two factions. The more moderate faction, composed mostly of university-educated people, favored a slow pace for reform, whereas the majority of people adhered to a more extreme program that sought immediate equality with the German upper class. Czar Alexander III responded by attempting to Russify Estonia, making Russian rather than German the official language of the courts, the schools, and the police. In the 1890s, Tartu University students initiated the next significant wave of nationalism, which led to slow but peaceful reforms. In 1905, however, the Russian Revolution took place, and some Estonians took this as an opportunity to attack German landowners. Russia responded by establishing martial law from 1905 to 1908. The February Revolution of 1917 brought into power a liberal Russian government, which in April 1917 granted Estonian unification and autonomy. In June the Estonians elected a national council, but this was quickly and forcefully dissolved by the Bolsheviks. On 24 February 1918 the Estonian Council of Elders declared Estonian sovereign independence, but the next day a German occupation force dissolved the new provisional government. The German Revolution put an end to German designs on Estonia, and on 9 November 1918 Germany recognized Estonian rule over Estonia.

What followed is known as the Estonian War of Independence, which began 28 November 1918 with a Bolshevik attack. The Estonians were aided in their defense by British weapons and naval forces and by Finnish troops. After many difficult battles the Estonians prevailed, and the Soviets concluded a peace treaty on 2 February 1920. Following the war, Estonia gradually rebuilt its industry and economy.

Unfortunately for Estonia, the country and its people were annexed by the USSR in 1940 under the secret provisions of the Molotov-Ribbentrop Pact. On 6 August 1940 Estonia became a Soviet republic. The Soviets nationalized businesses and industries without compensation and deported 60,000 people. Most of the men were sent to perform hard labor (e.g., cutting timber) in Siberia, where many died; a few were conscripted by the Red Army. Germany captured Estonia in 1941 and drafted into its military those young men who had not managed to escape to Finland. In 1944 the Soviets reconquered Estonia. The Soviets

Following independence, Estonia embarked upon an ambitious program to enter western European markets, particularly those of Finland and Germany.

then proceeded to collectivize Estonian agriculture. When the process looked to be going too slowly to suit the Soviets, they punished Estonia by deporting Estonians to Siberian labor camps; from 1944 through 1949, an estimated 40,000 to 50,000 Estonians were forcibly removed from their homeland. In 1955 those who survived were allowed to return to Estonia. The Soviets carried out a policy of cultural and social Russification after World War II, despite encountering guerrilla resistance well into the 1950s.

As the Soviet Union began to crumble, Estonia pressed for its independence. Resentment of Soviet control took the form not only of anger over political domination but also of outrage over the pollution and despoliation caused by Soviet-style industrialization. After Lithuania declared independence in 1990, the Estonian congress renamed the country and adopted its pre-Soviet coat of arms. After the attempted coup against Gorbachev, Estonia formally declared independence on 20 August 1991, which the USSR recognized on 6 September of that year. Eleven days later, Estonia joined the United Nations. The postindependence period has thus far been characterized by political and economic instability.

Settlements

The settlement pattern is typically European, with people living in villages, towns, and four major cities (Tallinn, Tartu, Narva, and Köhlta Jarve). Since the late 1920s houses in rural areas have been constructed of bricks, rather than the traditional wood, so as to conserve timber resources.

Economy

SUBSISTENCE AND COMMERCIAL ACTIVITIES. Primarily agrarian until Soviet domination in 1940, the Estonians were a nation of farmers who produced grains, flax, potatoes, and animal products. There are also the historically important timber, shipping, and fishing industries. Industrialization took many years to establish itself following independence in 1920 because Estonia had little money, had been kept undeveloped by the landed nobility, and had little fuel for factories. It was fortunate for Estonia that it has large oil-shale deposits, which have been used to supply industrial needs. Soviet control turned Estonia into a primarily industrial nation; 60 percent of the gross national product and more than 65 percent of employment is provided by

SOCIOPOLITICAL ORGANIZATION

Social Organization

During the period of independence between the world wars, Estonia had three social classes. There was a small upper class, composed primarily of businessmen and government and military officials. The middle class was much larger than the other two, counting among its members teachers, clerks, doctors, lawyers, and independent farmers. There was also a working class. Movement between classes was relatively easy to accomplish at that time.

Political Organization

The Republic of Estonia's legislature is a unicameral assembly, the Riigikogu, whose 102 members are directly elected by the people to four-year terms. For any political party to put its elected members into the Riigikogu,

however, it must receive 5 percent of the vote. The government is the Council of Ministers, headed by a prime minister. The head of state is the president, who is elected by a majority of the popular vote; should no one candidate receive a majority, the president is elected by the Riigikogu. All Estonians over the age of 18 may vote in national elections. Those who are not Estonian citizens may vote only in municipal elections.

Social Control

After independence in 1920, the Estonian legal system was still under the control of ethnic Russians; consequently, great emphasis was placed on the training of ethnically Estonian law teachers. Two of the advances made by the Estonian legal authorities were to make all administrative decisions subject to the law and to make legal decisions conform to precedent, neither of which had been the case theretofore.

Conflict

Many of Estonia's internal conflicts arise from Estonians' hatred of Russians. Many Russians remain in Estonia, and they are essentially unable to become Estonian citizens. Both Russians in Estonia and within the Russian nation have protested this situation as a violation of human rights, and the withdrawal of Russian troops has slowed. The Estonians, in response, have brought up the issue of past Russian human-rights violations. Much political conflict has come about over the associations that people in government once had with the Soviet government and over questions as to whether those in power are sufficiently anti-Russian in their actions.

manufacturing. Much of the industrial output of Soviet Estonia went to the USSR; most of the Estonian oil shale, for example, went to provide gas for Leningrad.

INDUSTRIAL ARTS. Prior to Soviet domination, Estonia had a modern and well-developed industrial base, even though the country was at the time primarily agricultural. Estonia produced the following in quantities sufficient to export: butter, bacon, eggs, potatoes, flax, timber and lumber, pulp, paper, shale oil, textiles, glass, and artificial (casein) horn. Much of the required electrical power came from the burning peat, of which Estonia has large stores. The Soviets established many new industries in Estonia, which produce concrete, scientific instruments, industrial chemicals, electrical equipment, refined oil, agricultural tools, and mining machinery.

TRADE. Under the Soviets, nearly all of Estonia's trade was with the Soviet Empire. Following independence, Estonia embarked upon an ambitious program to enter western European markets, particularly those of Finland and Germany. Several Swedish companies have purchased such goods as automobile parts and cigarettes from Estonian companies. In January 1993 Estonia made an advantageous trade agreement with the European Community. Estonia, like all recently freed former Soviet republics, has been hindered by its earlier interconnectedness with the internal economy of the Soviet Empire. In one respect, however, the long-established trade routes with Russia and the largely open borders between the two countries have helped Estonia; they have led to a great deal of smuggling of Russian goods, which in Russia are sold at far below world prices. The nationalism that Estonia has experienced since independence has been growing, and as a result foreign investment in Estonia has rarely been welcome, despite a high unemployment rate.

DIVISION OF LABOR. Women in urban areas traditionally remained at home to care for children and perform domestic tasks, whereas men worked outside the home. In rural areas women did this same work but also tended gardens and cattle and sometimes worked in the fields when needed. The traditional roles of women and children were altered by the Soviets. Women were "liberated" from the capitalist system so that they could be put to work in the oil-shale mines and at other physically onerous tasks. The Soviets also imposed a labor duty on boys of 14 to 17 years of age; this duty required them to attend industrial schools for six months and then to work wherever they were needed within the Soviet Union.

LAND TENURE. The husband traditionally owned all of the family's property. During the period of freedom between the world wars, the new government embarked on a program of land reform. Approximately 750 of the great estates that had survived so long under the Russian government were expropriated by the Estonian government and divided into 55,000 parcels. Also, the 23,000 Estonians who had rented land were given freehold title to those lands. Real property was nationalized under the Soviets. Farms were collectivized in 1949, and the 140,000 Estonian farms were reorganized into 2,300 kolkhozy and 127 sovkhozy. By 1991 many of these had been combined so that there were a total of only 300 collective and state farms. The new Estonian government has already begun to dismantle these farms and to privatize farm ownership. By mid-1993 it aims to break all but 50 of the collective and soviet farms into 15,000–16,000 private farms. Moreover, all kinds of real property nationalized by the Soviets is being privatized by the Estonian Department of State Property. Those who lost their property to Soviet nationalization in 1940 may either take possession of the property they lost or accept compensation for it. Land not returned to previous owners is being put up for sale and may be purchased by Estonians. Estonians are being given vouchers for the years they have worked, at a rate of 300 kroon per year of employment; they may use these vouchers either to purchase their residences or to invest.

Kinship, Marriage, and Family

Traditionally, nuclear families have lived separately in cities. In rural areas, on the contrary, it was not uncommon for as many as three generations to live together. It was often the case, however, that older couples built themselves a new house near their old home, which was left to a married son or daughter who was to begin having children. Since World War I and perhaps earlier, there has been a trend throughout Estonia toward separation of nuclear families. During the period of independence between the world wars, the fertility rate fell, and the government tried to stimulate births by means of financial bonuses.

Prior to independence in 1918, Estonian schooling was not well developed because of the harsh economic conditions imposed on the people by the ruling class of landlords. After independence, and after a sufficient number of school buildings were erected, education became compulsory for those between 8 and 16 years of age. English, German, French, and Russian were

◆ **kolkhoz**
A collective farm in which the land is owned by the government and its use given to the kolkhoz members who work it communally, the products being shared somehow by the government and member households. Each household has a small private plot for its own use.

◆ **sovkhozy**
State farms owned by the government and from which the government takes all that is produced, the workers being paid wages and given a small plot for their own use.

Many of Estonia's internal conflicts arise from Estonians' hatred of Russians. Many Russians remain in Estonia and are essentially unable to become Estonian citizens.

taught as foreign languages. In addition, there were colleges and lyceums as well as an entire network of vocational schools. The Soviet occupation in 1940 abolished this system entirely and substituted the Soviet system. Although many students attended Estonian-language schools, they were required to study Russian as well; others attended Russian-language schools. No Estonian history was taught until 1957, and after that only small amounts. Political indoctrination was of prime importance in the curriculum.

The contemporary Estonian formal educational system is free of charge. Attendance is compulsory for eleven years. Primary education spans eight years, the secondary level four years, and the university level five years.

Religion and Expressive Culture

RELIGIOUS BELIEFS. A Danish monk by the name of Fulco introduced Christianity to the Estonians in the twelfth century, although it was not until later that the Estonians converted. Moreover, it was not until the eighteenth century that beliefs concerning the supernatural became more or less fully Christian. In 1934, before Soviet domination, nearly 80 percent of Estonians were Lutherans, and almost 20 percent were listed as Orthodox. There were also very small numbers of Baptists, Methodists, Jews, and Catholics.

RELIGIOUS PRACTITIONERS. During the period of independence between the world wars, the Estonian Lutheran Church was governed by the Church Assembly, composed of the members of the various synods, the members of which in turn were the pastors and lay officials of the parishes. Each parish was controlled by provosts, prominent pastors elected from among the synod membership. The Church Assembly elected its bishop, the head of the church, and legislated church rules. Some of the more prominent clerical and lay people together formed the Consistory, which made decisions on the basis of religious rules.

After independence in 1920, the Orthodox Church of Estonia broke from the Russian church and became the independent Estonian Apostolic Orthodox Church. The head of the church was the metropolitan, who approved the executive decisions of the synod and who was consecrated by the patriarch of Constantinople. The Church Assembly, made up of church members, elected the metropolitan, the bishops, the membership of the synod, and the priests.

Recently another denomination, the Free Estonian Church, has become an important link between Estonians in exile.

CEREMONIES. The most important rituals, in terms of the amount of effort expended in celebrating them, are baptisms, confirmations, and weddings. In rural areas wedding celebrations could last a week.

ARTS. Traditional Estonian folklore has as its subjects animals, witchcraft, and humorous material. Estonian folksongs are of two kinds. The older, traditional, style is known as *runo* and is characterized by short and simple musical phrases that are repeated again and again as the epic lyrics are sung. The newer style, influenced by German choral music, is more lyrical and has longer musical phrases and a wider range of rhythms. The modern Estonian musical had its start in the choirs and brass bands that were first established in the early nineteenth century. Estonians have a penchant for large musical festivals, and in some of these celebrations there are as many as 21,000 performers and 100,000 spectators. The larger festivals may have a choir with as many as 15,000 voices or a band of 2,000 musicians. During the period of independence, Estonia established several symphony orchestras and theaters and two music schools. The arts in general were supported by grants from the federal government during this era.

Much of Estonian literature has been influenced by foreign trends, and foreign literature continues to be popular. Early literature (1200–1700) was often the work of resident foreigners who had little proficiency in the Estonian language. Only in the late eighteenth and early nineteenth centuries did fiction by Estonians begin to appear, including that of the poet Kristian Jaak Peterson. During the national renaissance of the late nineteenth century, physical conditions had improved to the point that authors were free to write, although Russian political domination also included heavy literary censorship. During this time poetry, particularly epic poetry, became the most popular form of literature; the most popular poet of the era was Lydia Koidula. The realist period of 1890–1905 saw the introduction of modern foreign literature into Estonia, the publication by Estonians such as Eduard Vilde of historical-political novels, and the performance of political plays by August Kitzberg and others. Neoromantic and symbolic poetry became popular in the period 1905–1920, and names such as Gustav Suits, Marie Under, and Friedebert Tuglas became famous. After World War I, the neorealist novel became preeminent. Some of the more important authors of the period are Anton Tammsaare, Albert Kivikas, and August Jakobson. Soviet domination from 1940 on all but destroyed Estonian literature; only approved Soviet Communist themes were tolerated. Many Estonian authors escaped to the West, where they continued to write, but of those who remained many were imprisoned or had their works banned.

The Estonian pictorial arts followed a similar pattern of mixing foreign influences with indigenous invention. In the late nineteenth and early twentieth centuries, painters and sculptors were trained in St. Petersburg, and later in Paris and Germany. Some of the most important names are Eduard Jakobson (who established Estonian graphic arts) and the "Young Estonians" Mägi, Triik, Koort, Jansen, and others. The 1930s saw the rise of three important wood engravers: Wiiralt, Mugasto, and Laigo. Soviet political control later resulted in uncreative work, although some good works have been created in exile.

Bibliography

Konstantin Päts Fund (1974). *Estonia: Story of a Nation.* New York: Konstantin Päts Fund.

Parming, Tönu, and Elmar Järvesoo, eds. (1978). *A Case Study of a Soviet Republic: The Estonian SSR.* Boulder, Colo.: Westview Press.

Raud, Villibald (1953). *Estonia: A Reference Book.* New York: Nordic Press.

Raun, Toivo U. (1991). *Estonia and the Estonians.* 2nd ed. Stanford, Calif.: Hoover Institution Press.

Selirand, J., and E. Toñisson (1984). *Through Past Millennia: Archaeological Discoveries in Estonia.* Tallinn: Perioodka.

Uustalu, Evald, ed. (1961). *Aspects of Estonian Culture.* London: Boreas Publishing Co.

—DANIEL STROUTHES

GEORGIANS

Ethnonyms: Kartveli (Georgian person), Sakartvelo (Georgia). Names for the country in other languages include Gruziya (Russian), Gurjistan (Persian), Iberia (Latin), Vrastan (Armenian).

Orientation

IDENTIFICATION. Georgians are one of the most numerous peoples of the Caucasus region, which divides Russia from Turkey and Iran. Georgians speak a group of languages that are not known to be related to any others. They have lived in Caucasia for at least three millennia and are counted among the area's native peoples. Most Georgians are Orthodox Christians, but some are Sunni Muslims. Georgians are the majority people of the Georgian Republic, which declared its independence in 1991.

LOCATION. Georgians live at the east end of the Black Sea in a wedge of land between the Caucasus Mountains and the Armenian plateau. To the south and east are Turkey, Armenia, and Azerbaijan. Northeast across the mountain crests live Circassian, Karachay, Balkar, Ossetic, Chechen-Ingush, and Daghestanian peoples in autonomous regions and republics of the Russian Republic. Georgia itself is divided into about twenty traditional provinces marked by distinctive landscapes, dialects, histories, cooking, folklore, and architecture. Kakheti and Kartli are the principal eastern provinces; Imereti, Mingrelia, and Guria the largest western provinces. The Georgian Republic also includes the Ajarian Autonomous Republic in the southwest next to Turkey, the Abkhazian Autonomous Republic in the northwest, and the South Ossetian Autonomous Region in the middle Caucasus. Ajarians are Muslim Georgians. Ossetes and Abkhazians are non-Georgians, many of whom wish to secede from Georgia.

Georgia covers 70,000 square kilometers, mostly hills and mountains. Across the north, the main chain of the Caucasus makes a wall of snowcapped peaks, the highest reaching above 5,000 meters. The Surami range then divides the southern lowlands in two: a wet, western crescent where rivers flow down toward the Black Sea, and long, drier eastern valleys that lead into Azerbaijan. The countryside is thus extremely varied and includes mountain slopes with rocky river gorges, alpine meadows, and old pine forests; a southern highland area of upland steppe, extinct volcanoes, and scrub-covered hills; a central, temperate band with fields, orchards, vineyards, and deciduous forest—the heartland of the country; and, in the far west, a subtropical coastal strip of tea and citrus plantations and forests thick with undergrowth. Georgia's capital, Tbilisi, stands in the east on the Mt'k'vari River (also known as the Kura or Cyrus).

DEMOGRAPHY. As of 1989 the Republic of Georgia had a population of 5,456,000, of whom 538,000 live in Abkhazia, 382,000 in Ajaria, and 99,000 in South Ossetia. Georgians make up about 69 percent of the total, Armenians 9 percent, Russians 7 percent, Azerbaijanis 5 percent, Ossetians 3 percent, Greeks and Abkhazians each 2 percent, and Ukrainians and Kurds each 1 percent. Russians and Armenians are concentrated in

◆ **Caucasus**
A system of mountain ranges running from northeast to southwest between the Black and Caspian seas; the general geographical-cultural area between the Black and Caspian seas and the south Russian steppe and the Iranian plateau.

◆ **steppe**
Open grassland, relatively treeless plain.

cities; Abkhazians and Greeks live mostly in Abkhazia. Ossetes are the majority of South Ossetia (Shida Kartli), but a greater number live in other parts of Georgia. Only 4 percent of the Georgians in the Soviet Union, some 200,000 people, live outside Georgia, mostly in major cities. An estimated 150,000 Georgians, or people who recognize Georgian ancestry, are in Iran, and another 150,000, including 50,000 Laz, in Turkey. In the thirteenth century Georgians numbered some 5 million people, but waves of invasion and war reduced that figure to around 500,000 in 1800; Russian rule then allowed a recovery.

The birth rate in the Georgian republic is 16.7 per 1,000 people, the death rate 8.6. Infant mortality is 19.6 per 1,000 live births; life expectancy is 76 years for women, 68 for men. In 1917 about 25 percent of Georgia's population lived in cities; by 1989 this had risen to 56 percent. Tbilisi alone has a population of 1.2 million. In fact, some rural Georgians commute to city jobs, and urban dwellers spend much time with relatives in the country. Nearly all Georgians are literate in Georgian, and 15 percent have completed higher education, one of the highest percentages in the former Soviet Union. According to the 1989 census, 98 percent of Georgians considered Georgian their native language, and 33 percent claimed mastery of Russian. Most Georgians know some Russian, but for children, grandparents, and those in rural areas this may amount to very little. Nine percent of Georgian men and 6 percent of Georgian women marry people of other nationalities.

LINGUISTIC AFFILIATION. The Georgian language, together with the less widely spoken Mingrelian, Laz, and Svan languages, makes up the Kartvelian (or South Caucasian) Family. Mingrelian and Laz are closely related, and neither is intelligible to those who speak only Georgian; Svan is quite different and apparently diverged from the others at an earlier date. Mingrelians live in Georgia's western lowlands, and Svans in two valleys up in the highest parts of the Caucasus; both peoples now also speak Georgian. Despite their linguistic differences Mingrelians and Svans regard themselves as Georgians, and Mingrelia and Svanetia are counted among Georgia's provinces. Almost all of the Laz live just over the Turkish border in Artvin and Rize provinces; they sometimes consider themselves distinct from Georgians. Scholars have tried to relate the Kartvelian languages to the neighboring Northwest and Northeast Caucasian families, to Indo-European, and even to Basque, but this question remains open.

Georgian is written in an alphabet of its own; there are three related scripts, only one of which is in current use. The order of the letters and their numerical values are based on those of the Greek alphabet, but the shapes of the Georgian letters themselves indicate no regular correspondences to other alphabets. The first surviving literature in Georgian dates from the fifth century, soon after the country was Christianized; before this time, Georgians wrote in Greek, Persian, and other languages. There may have been a pre-Christian Georgian literature that was lost or destroyed. The Georgian language is conventionally divided at the eleventh century into Old and Modern periods; Georgians today can read even the oldest texts with fair comprehension. The speech of Kartli Province is the basis of a standard literary language, developed in the nineteenth century; the north Georgian mountain dialects (Pshavian, Khevsurian, Rachan) have more archaic grammatical features, and western ones (Gurian, Ajarian) share some grammatical features with Mingrelian. Mingrelians, Svans, and the few Laz in Georgia use Georgian as their written language. Modern Georgian has twenty-eight consonants and five vowels, each represented by a single letter. Up to eight consonants may cluster together at the beginning of a word; however, Georgian favors open syllables and polysyllabic words. Stress is weak; Georgian verse utilizes lines with a fixed number of syllables and makes much use of alliteration and rhyme. Georgian has seven noun cases, ten basic tense-aspects, and four classes of verbs. The verbal system is complex: verbs are agglutinative and mark both subjects and objects. The grammar is sensitive to animacy and plurality, but there is no grammatical gender. Georgian has borrowed words freely from Arabic, Persian, Greek, and the modern European languages.

The Russian language was formerly a mandatory school subject in Georgia, and the urban intelligentsia speaks it fluently. Many, even in villages, also know some German, English, or Turkish; linguistic facility is a cardinal virtue, along with bravery and intelligence. Nonetheless, Georgian remains the dominant language in all aspects of people's lives and a national rallying point. Government, business, and university classes are conducted in Georgian; most newspapers, books, and television programming are also in Georgian. In 1978 the Communist party proposed giving Russian and minority languages equal status with Georgian under the Georgian constitution but backed down in the face of demonstrations.

History and Cultural Relations

Humans have been living in Georgia for an extremely long time, as attested by the recent discovery near Tbilisi of a Homo erectus jawbone that may be over a million years old. Stable agricultural and stock-raising cultures left archaeological remains beginning around 5000 B.C. In the third millennium B.C. these cultures were in contact with Akkadian Mesopotamia and then with the Hittites in Asia Minor; trade networks developed and the people learned to work in bronze. Around 2000 B.C. Indo-European groups began passing through Caucasia, mingling to some extent with the native population. Between the twelfth and seventh centuries B.C., according to Assyrian and Urartian records, there were a number of proto-Georgian tribal unions: Colcha and Diaokhi, also Mushki and Tabal, and possibly the biblical Meshech and Tubal. By 500 B.C. the first Georgian kingdoms took shape—Colchis (or Egrisi) in the west and Iberia in the east. These were at first tributaries of the Achaemenid Persian Empire, then independent states; the first ruler described in Georgian chronicles, King Parnavaz, lived in these times. In the first century B.C. Romans invaded and established weak control over both kingdoms. Over the next four centuries Romans and the Iranian Parthians fought over Caucasia while Georgian princes sided with one or the other and tried to preserve as much independence as possible. Beginning in the seventh century B.C. Greeks established trading colonies along the Black Sea, where they played a leading role in commerce into this century. In the first century B.C. Strabo described four social classes in Georgia: rulers, priest-judges, soldiers and farmers, and common people.

In A.D. 337, according to tradition, Saint Nino of Cappadocia converted King Mirian, and Christianity became the state religion of Iberia. Over the next 300 years, however, Christian Byzantium fought the Mazdaist Sassanids for control of Georgia's various principalities. In the fifth century, King Vakhtang Gorgasali repelled Ossetian and Khazar raids and brought an era of strength and security; according to legend, he also founded Tbilisi. Arabs conquered Georgia in the seventh century, decimating the people and splintering the land into tiny kingdoms. By 1008 the Bagration dynasty managed to unite all of Georgia except Tbilisi, only to have the country de-stroyed again by Seljuk Turks. King David the Rebuilder drove the Seljuks from Georgia and portions of Armenia, Azerbaijan, and the Black Sea littoral, recapturing Tbilisi after 400 years of Muslim domination. He invited Kipchaks and Armenians to settle depopulated areas in Georgia and proclaimed religious toleration. In the twelfth and thirteenth centuries Georgia enjoyed a golden age under Queen Tamar and her son Giorgi Lasha. Tamar Mepe (King Tamar), as she is known, conquered all Transcaucasia from the Black Sea to the Caspian, including present-day northeastern Turkey. She made the northern mountaineers her tributaries, built many churches, and brought the Georgian feudal system to its zenith of complexity and centralization. In the thirteenth and fourteenth centuries, however, Georgia was invaded and conquered by waves of Mongols. With the fall of Constantinople in 1453, Georgia's Christian kings lost their main ally; soon after, the country split into three kingdoms and numerous principalities. In the following years the Ottoman Turks, Safavid Persians, and occasionally the Russian czars fought over Georgian lands. Especially in western Georgia, slave trading and constant warfare drastically reduced and impoverished all classes of society.

In the early eighteenth century, King Vakhtang VI codified the laws of Georgia and brought a cultural revival. Despite repeated betrayals, Georgia's kings were convinced that their only hope for survival against the Turks and Persians lay with Russia. In 1783 King Irakli II signed the Treaty of Georgievsk, placing the Kakheti-Kartli kingdom

Humans have been living in Georgia for an extremely long time, as attested by the recent discovery of a Homo erectus jawbone that may be over a million years old.

WEDDING TRADITIONS

A traditional Georgian wedding dance. The day of the wedding, the groom and his best man will drink a glass of wine in the bride's house with the bride and her bridesmaid, before the civil ceremony. Georgia.
(Chris Hellier/Corbis)

under Russian protection; in 1801 Czar Paul I annexed it to his crown. By mid-century all of Georgia was under Russian rule. The nobility became Russianized, but there were also repeated anti-Russian plots and popular revolts. In the 1860s, Georgian serfs were emancipated but remained burdened with debts to their former lords. Many nobles were themselves heavily in debt to a rising urban class of merchants and capitalists. In the late 1800s, the writer Ilia Ch'avch'avadze headed movements to improve the lot of serfs, bring universal education, and unite all classes into a Georgian nationality. In the 1890s, the "third group" (*mesame dasi*) of Georgian poets and intellectuals took up Marxist ideas; the young Stalin was linked with this third group, but later parted ways with it. In 1917 local revolutionary groups arose and took power as the czarist government collapsed. Georgia was briefly part of a Transcaucasian federation and then became an independent democratic state for three years under Social Democratic (Menshevik) leadership. The new government established close relations with Germany; the British, victorious in World War I, then replaced German troops and advisers. France and England eventually recognized Georgia, but offered no concrete support. In 1920 Lenin and Georgia's president, Noe Zhordania, signed a nonaggression pact; early in 1921, apparently at Stalin's instigation, the Red Army invaded and conquered Georgia.

An insurrection in 1924 was crushed, leaving an estimated 10,000 dead and 20,000 deported to Siberia. Under Stalin—an ambiguous, highly charged figure, a Georgian who became Russianized—many more people were imprisoned, exiled, or killed. A period of enforced political conformity ensued. It was not until Eduard Shevardnadze became secretary of the Georgian Communist party in 1972 that moderate reforms were instituted. In 1988 Georgian nationalist groups began demonstrations in the center of Tbilisi. Soviet troops killed nineteen protestors on 9 April 1989, and the groundswell of revolutionary feeling accelerated. In autumn 1990, as Mikhail Gorbachev's policies swept the Soviet Union, Zviad Gamsakhurdia's Mrgvali magida ("Round Table") coalition defeated the Communists in Georgian parliamentary elections. In spring 1991 a referendum on Georgian independence gained 99 percent approval, and on 9 April 1991, invoking the act of independence of 26 May 1918, the parliament redeclared Georgia a sovereign state. President Gamsakhurdia began dismantling Soviet institutions, replacing local councils with prefects.

At the same time he acknowledged that Georgia remained de facto part of the Soviet Union. In parliament, the former Supreme Soviet, Gamsakhurdia's Round Table coalition held 155 seats, the former Communist party 60, and liberals and independents 26. Radicals and intellectuals formed an alternative National Congress that advocated an immediate, complete break with the Soviet Union. Gamsakhurdia's opponents pointed to press controls and political arrests as evidence that he was becoming a dictator; he, in turn, accused them of being agents of the KGB and emphasized his popular support (he was elected with 86 percent of the votes cast). In early 1992 a coalition of opposition groups, joined by many former members of Gamsakhurdia's administration, mounted an uprising in Tbilisi, which after several weeks succeeded in overthrowing the government and forcing Gamsakhurdia into exile. Shortly after consolidating their power, the new government asked Eduard Shevardnadze to be the new head of government. He was elected chairman of Parliament in 1992 and elected president in 1995.

Georgia's northern mountaineers traditionally raided the Muslim tribes across the crests, and also each other. Nominally Muslim and Christian villagers in the mountains had many shared traditions and habitually attended each other's festivals. Across the south and around Tbilisi, Azerbaijani, Armenian, and Turkish communities blend into Georgian ones, making Georgians sometimes feel overrun. Ajarians, Laz, and other Muslim Georgians, however, feel ties to Turkey. In 1944 Muslims in the province of Meskheti, including some Georgians, were deported to Central Asia; they still seek permission to return. Jews have lived in Georgia for twenty-six centuries without persecution, but they are now emigrating to Israel. The merchants and craftsmen in Georgia have always been largely of other nationalities, especially Armenian. Greek and Turkish influences are strong in western Georgia, whereas eastern regions have borrowed more of Persian culture; Russian and German ties are also important today. In earlier centuries, rulers often changed religions and orientations depending on which foreign power was in ascendance. In the nineteenth century Georgia was a common place of exile for Russian officers; Pushkin, Lermontov, and Tolstoy all spent time in Georgia and wrote works about the Caucasus that became popular in Russia. Educated Georgians, in turn, immersed themselves in Russian and Western literature and ideas.

◆ **KGB**
The Committee for State Security, which was formed by the Soviet government in 1954 to manage both internal security and foreign intelligence-gathering activities; successor to the Cheka and other prior organizations.

In the late 1980s, as Georgia began seeking independence from the Soviet Union, Abkhazians and Ossetes renewed campaigns to secede from Georgia. The Abkhazians are a minority in their republic and complain that Georgians have not supported their culture and economy. Ossetes wish to form a single entity with their compatriots in the North Ossetian Autonomous Region of Russia. In 1990 the South Ossetian Autonomous Region declared its independence, and in 1991 fighting broke out between small groups of Ossetes and Georgians. Gamsakhurdia abolished South Ossetia's sovereignty (restoring the province's ancient Georgian name of Shida Kartli) and sent in Georgian troops; Soviet authorities responded with troops of their own. Both sides agreed to a cease-fire in 1992.

Settlements

Georgia's central valleys and coastal regions are thickly settled with towns and villages of from 50 to 50,000 inhabitants. Town suburbs often sprawl out and divide into clusters of houses, like villages themselves. In the mountains and hills, villages rarely exceed 1,000 people and are often at a considerable distance from one another. Even the smallest villages typically consist of several named areas, each originally settled by a different family. In eastern Georgia, houses cluster compactly, with both private plots and collective-farm fields surrounding them; in the west, each sits in its own large garden. A small village usually includes a stone water fountain, a shop, a kindergarten, and a threshing ground, also used for summer meetings and dances. Larger villages may have a recreation hall, a bath-house or café, clinics, grammar schools, and one or two factories or workshops.

A standard house in eastern Georgia is square, two stories high, and built of cement or brick with a tile roof. In the west the older style, still preserved, favors wide, one-story, all-wood houses with elaborate carvings. Houses often have eight or ten rooms; the kitchen is on the ground floor with its own entrance, the best room is on the second floor. All houses have verandas, outside staircases, and balconies, where people work and eat in the summer months. Each house, or sometimes several dwellings belonging to a father and his sons, stands in a courtyard with a fence and a gate. The gates are now usually metal, painted blue or green (once regarded as protection against the evil eye); a visitor pauses at the gates and calls to the people inside. The garden invariably includes a grape arbor and rose bushes as well as fruit trees and vegetables. Men build their houses carefully over a period of years, as they have the time and can buy the materials.

In Tbilisi most people live in apartments, either fivestory prewar buildings or modern highrises. The center of the city is Rustaveli Prospect, a wide avenue of public buildings, theaters, and stores, where crowds stroll in summer. Nearby is the old town with its jumbled balconies and courtyards, the old sulfur baths, and the most important churches. A traditionally Armenian quarter lies across the river, along with the central market and most of the city's industry. Abandoned cliff and cave dwellings, refuges during the wars of earlier centuries, remain across southern Georgia. In mountain villages many houses still have old stone defense towers, some dating from the twelfth century or perhaps earlier. Into the twentieth century, poorer western Georgians lived in ancient-style round houses with central hearths.

Economy

SUBSISTENCE AND COMMERCIAL ACTIVITIES. Most Georgian families have gardens or private plots in which they grow beans, maize, fruits, vegetables, and spices for their own consumption. Men make wine and sometimes keep bees; women make condiments, pickles, and preserves and may raise chickens and pigs. In mountainous regions, people are mostly engaged in raising sheep and cattle. Only potatoes, barley, rye, and oats can be grown in the highest villages, so vodka and beer take the place of wine. The staple food of eastern Georgia is fresh, flattish white bread, now usually bought from stores; in the west the staple is cornmeal, either in cakes or as porridge. A meal also commonly includes various bean dishes (*lobio*), cheese or yogurt, and fruits and vegetables in season. Among the most popular Georgian dishes are shish kebab (*mts'vadi*) with sour plum sauce (*t'q'emali*), chicken with spicy walnut sauce (*satsivi, bazhe*), lamb-stuffed dumplings, and cheese bread (*khach'ap'uri*).

In previous centuries Georgian cities had highly disciplined guilds of merchants and craftsmen, including armorers, tailors, blacksmiths, butchers, bakers, and wine merchants. Tbilisi was known for its sharp-tongued street hawkers, roaming musicians, and cellar restaurants. Today professional craftsmen are few, but private cooperative stores and restaurants are once again allowed. State stores offer staples, including bread; open markets and specialty stores have a wide variety of produce, nuts, and preserved meats, but at much higher prices. Clothing, toys, and house-

Traditionally, all Georgian wage workers put their earnings into a common fund kept by the senior woman of the household.

hold items appear in stores randomly or not at all, and may cost weeks, months, or years of the average person's wages. Georgians, while participating in the cash economy, thus rely heavily on the assistance of relatives, friends, and co-workers to obtain inside access to goods and services.

In this century the Soviet policies of collectivization and industrialization have commercialized Georgia's economy and increased the standard of living. Large state farms in the lowlands now grow warm-weather, labor-intensive crops for export: tobacco, tea, and citrus in the west; wine, fruit, and vegetables in the east. In other areas collective farms produce more varied crops, mostly for local consumption. Georgia has one of the world's largest manganese mines (at Ch'iatura) and significant reserves of coal, timber, and various minerals. Other industries across the country include food processing, clothing production, steel works, and oil refineries. Tourism is also a major industry; Georgia has many natural mineral water spas in addition to its coast and mountains. Russian workers in Georgia are concentrated in tourist services and in industry.

TRADE. Georgia produced over 90 percent of the tea and citrus consumed in the Soviet Union and much highly prized wine. Owing to its increasingly specialized agriculture, the country is now dependent on imports of grain. Batumi in Ajaria is a major port, especially for oil that comes by pipeline from Baku. Overland routes to Russia are limited: the only railway runs along the Abkhazian coast, and the main road—the Georgian Military Highway—is through the difficult Darial Pass into North Ossetia. (Plans to blast a tunnel through the Caucasus to allow a more direct rail link between Russia and Tbilisi were abandoned after a popular outcry over the environmental and cultural consequences.) In Russia, Georgians have earned a reputation as entrepreneurs and speculators.

DIVISION OF LABOR. Georgian family members cooperate economically, even though some may have official jobs and residences in the city and others in the country. Traditionally, all wage workers put their earnings into a common fund kept by the senior woman of the household. When major purchases were to be made, the whole family conferred, with the oldest man having final say. In Tbilisi nowadays, family members simply give each other money as needed. In rural areas men do most of the fieldwork, cut hay, and take animals to high pasture in summer. Women do the cooking, washing, and cleaning and have the primary responsibility for taking care of chil-

dren. Only men slaughter animals and serve as priests (in the Georgian Orthodox church or in pre-Christian ceremonies still observed in many remote parts of the country). Women are expected to teach their children to read and to ensure that they do well in school. Both men and women usually have nonagricultural jobs, sometimes in a neighboring larger village or town. One typical pattern is for grandparents to remain in the village, registered in the collective farm, while some of their grown children work or get training in town.

LAND TENURE. Collectivization in the 1930s eliminated differences in family landholdings and competition for scarce arable land. Most fields and pastures now belong to collective farms, with individuals drawing wages and portions of the harvest in proportion to hours worked. About 30 percent of the agricultural land belongs to the state, which pays workers a fixed wage. Under Soviet law, people have the right only to use their houses and individual plots, with inheritance based on coresidence. In practice, however, Georgians ensure that sons or other appropriate heirs are official residents, thus keeping property within the family. In pre-Soviet times, fields belonged to families, pastures to villages, and forests to nobles, churches, or to all for free use.

Marriage and Family

MARRIAGE. Marriages are initiated by the groom's side, but require the eventual consent of both young people and both families. A boy in love may simply ask a girl to marry him, then tell his parents. More often, a young man's female relatives arrange for him to meet potential brides on various pretexts, then open formal negotiations. If the bride and her family consent, the groom or one of his relatives brings a gold watch or ring as a sign of betrothal. The two families feel bound to help each other because they will share the same grandchildren. A bride should be a virgin, a good worker, and have done well in school; the groom's family should offer a reasonable standard of living and not be difficult to get along with. Ideally, the two families should be of the same class and region. Divorce was unusual in Georgia, but is now increasing. A divorced woman's family is supportive, but it is hard for her to remarry.

On the wedding day, the groom and his best man drink a glass of wine in the bride's house, then drive off with the bride and her bridesmaid for the civil ceremony. This is often accompanied, even today, by a service in church with an exchange of rings. At the threshold of the groom's

♦ **collectivization**
A process by which peasant farms were converted into large-scale, mechanized economic units. The process began in the late 1920s and during the early 1930s resulted in a great loss of life and economic displacement (through famine and deportation). The system of state farms (sovkhozy) and collective farms (kolkhozy) began to break up in the 1990s.

house, the groom's mother gives him a plate to break under his foot (in another variant of this practice, the bride and groom compete to be the first to crush the plate; this is believed to be indicative of who will have the upper hand during their married life). Then both bride and groom are offered wine and something sweet. The couple preside as "king" (*mepe*) and "queen" (*dedopali*) at a lavish banquet of toasts, with singing and dancing for up to three days. In some areas the bride and groom are expected to sit with lowered eyes and eat little. In villages, the morning after the wedding the bride is asked to sweep the courtyard and fetch water from the spring, where other women come to greet her. A new wife is treated kindly and given only light work to do; in return she does

not show too much how much she misses her family. The husband's relatives call her "little daughter-in-law" (*p'at'ardzali*) until she has had her first child; only then is the marriage considered consummated. A Georgian man still sometimes abducts his bride, nearly always with her tacit consent. Urban Georgians will run off together to another town, then return in a week to tell their parents. In rural areas, the groom and a few friends bring the bride first to one of the groom's paternal relatives' houses and then to his own. The groom's family quickly swallow their surprise and rally behind him; the bride's family are very angry, particularly her brothers. Intermediaries then try to calm the bride's family and win their consent to the usual marriage banquet. Once

KINSHIP

Kin Groups and Descent

Georgian families are typically of three generations: an older couple and married sons with children, plus unmarried sons and daughters. Increasingly, however, married sons may work in separate places and so form semi-independent households. Families are grouped together into patrilineages (*sadzmo*), or "branches" (*sht'o*) of four to seven generations. In villages, families of a single branch occupy a section of adjacent houses. A branch also refers to all relatives up through the seventh degree, with whom marriage is prohibited by the church. In addition, people with the same surname (*mogvare*) assume they are related and do not marry. Families from western Georgia tend to have surnames ending in -*dze*, those from eastern Georgia in -*shvili*; Mingrelian, Svan, and some aristocratic family names have other endings. Many surnames are further identified with specific regions and villages.

Membership in all kin groups is patrilineal, marriage is exogamous, and residence patrilocal. Thus a villager grows up among his father's kin and sees his mother's relatives as guests. Nonetheless, Georgians consider their mothers' and grandmothers' relatives close "blood" kin, the same as their fathers', and visit them frequently if they live in the same town. Adults call on both their

fathers' and mothers' relatives for help and in both groups enjoy the reassurance of being among kin. A man's honor is closely bound up with his mother, and his conduct reflects back on her most of all. A woman usually does not take her husband's name when she marries. She remains under her father's and brothers' protection throughout her life, but she is buried with her husband.

Georgians also recognize several categories of "spiritual" kin. In pre-Soviet times a nobleman sometimes gave his child to be suckled and raised by a peasant's wife. The child and the mother's own children would then be "milk brothers/sisters" (*dzudzumt'e*), binding the families for generations. As a variation, a grown man could publicly touch his lips to the breast of a woman, and so become adopted into a family. Even today two people who feel strong affection for each other cut their fingers, let their blood intermingle, and swear siblinghood. In a form of ritual kinship contracted between a man and woman, the couple could have affectionate, even intimate relations; on the other hand, since they were considered kin, they could not marry (this custom, known as *ts'ats'loba* in the mountain province of Pshavi, and as *sts'orproba* in the neighboring district of Khevsureti, was practiced up to the early years of the twentieth century). All Georgian children today have godparents; those of the first child are the mother's and father's life-

long best friends, who stood with them at their wedding. Parents' and godparents' descendants should not marry for fourteen generations.

Kinship Terminology

A Georgian names relatives by their relation to his or her ancestral line; maternal and paternal lines are not distinguished. Blood uncles are called by a special term (*bidza* or *dzia*) and their wives by another (*bitsola*). All other relatives are referred to by compound terms of the form "mother's sister," "grandfather's brother's wife," "brother's child's child," and so on. Terms distinguish gender when counting up generations, but not down. "Uncle" and "mother's sister" (*deida*) are general terms of respect for older people; an older woman of the same village is "uncle's wife." A wife has a set of terms to call her husband's mother, father, brother, and sister; and the husband likewise has a separate set for his wife's immediate kin (e.g., husband's mother, *dedamtili*; wife's mother, *sidedri*). All the members of each family then reciprocate with a single term. Husbands of sisters, wives of brothers, a married couple, and the parents of a married couple each have a reciprocal term. There is also a complete set of terms for families joined through godparenthood.

*Georgians have a
strong, sacred
tradition of family
hospitality. A family
marks weddings,
funerals, birthdays,
holidays, or the
arrival of any guest
with a ritual
banquet.*

a man and woman are known to have spent the night together, it is assumed that they have had sex and so must marry. Thus the bride's family always eventually relents, and the birth of a child heals remaining hard feelings.

DOMESTIC UNIT. Two to four generations usually eat together and share the same house or courtyard. Large families are considered fortunate. Traditionally, the oldest man heads the household, supervises other men's work, and has the final say in all matters; he therefore tends to reserve his opinions. The oldest woman manages the house's money and food, apportions work among other women, and has the largest hand in arranging her children's jobs and marriages. When a young couple marries and has children, however, their own small family is understood to become their primary focus. Georgians usually marry in their twenties and have two or three children; they hope for at least one son. New mothers take a year's maternity leave; after that the grandmother often stays with the children while the parents work. Husbands and wives avoid displaying affection openly; brothers and sisters are typically very close. The men and women of a family have a sense of gender solidarity, but do not keep separate from each other.

Georgians have a strong, sacred tradition of family hospitality. A household marks weddings, funerals, birthdays, holidays, or the arrival of any guest with a ritual banquet (*supra*). The supra may be a banquet for hundreds or just two friends sitting and talking, but it shows a family's honor and prosperity. The table is spread with rich and beautifully arranged food. The host, or an older man with authority and eloquence, raises a glass of wine and begins to lead the table in certain standard toasts, as well as some of his own invention. Guests elaborate each toast in turn, growing gradually drunker and more sentimental. Standard toasts are to the house, to parents, to children, to siblings, to the reason for gathering, to each of the people present, to women, to the departed, and finally, to "the holiest of all" (*q'ovelta ts'minda*, an epithet originally referring to the Virgin Mary). Strangers learn about each other's lives; enemies must find something kind to say about each other. Older women may participate fully, but younger women keep quiet and concentrate on serving food.

INHERITANCE. A family's house and land are common property; even after a man dies his married sons and their wives prefer to live together. In villages, a family that grows too large builds houses nearby for the older sons and leaves

the old house to the youngest son and the grandparents; other property is divided equally. Women may inherit land, especially if they live in the village and head households; otherwise the property reverts up the patriline. Old people often distribute their property before they die to forestall arguments. In the highlands, a woman used to have a personal fund of land, stock, jewelry, or linens, which passed to her daughters.

SOCIALIZATION. Georgians believe people learn slowly, with age, experience, and good teachers. Babies and small children receive much love and attention from all their relatives. They are encouraged to do things for themselves, not to wander away or cry too much, to know how the other gender behaves, and to be polite to elders. When a child misbehaves he or she is not punished severely, but is considered to be still learning. Until recently, schoolchildren were taught a Soviet version of history and morals with which their parents usually did not agree, but were afraid to question too openly. Without being told explicity, a child learned to read between the lines of official publications and not to speak of family business to strangers.

Older children usually act as their parents would wish, without needing to be told. By around age 15, children take a considerable share of the household work, and by age 20 they and their parents start thinking about future careers and spouses. Young men had been required to spend two years in the Soviet army, but many managed to bribe their way out or simply never reported. For children of the intelligentsia, the years at university, especially the general exams, are the great rite of passage. All young people are considered prone to strong emotions of love, jealousy, and anger, which temper when they marry. For both men and women, becoming a parent, and then a grandparent are felt to be life's happiest, most important achievements.

Sociopolitical Organization

SOCIAL ORGANIZATION. Georgian society is patriarchal: the head of a Georgian table is by custom always a man, and the men of a family are protective of the women. On the other hand, mothers are especially revered, and the language contains far more idiomatic expressions that refer to mothers than to fathers: the world is "mother Earth" (*deda mits'a*), Georgian is the "mother tongue" (*deda ena*), and so on. The Georgians revere the twelfth-century Queen Tamar as the symbol of their nation at its apex, and all mothers for the power to give life. Georgians expect men and women to have distinct natural inclinations, but regard each other as equals. Most doctors, teachers, and philologists are women, whereas men dominate in government, science, and heavy industry; many other professions are mixed. Georgians respect all older people's wisdom and control; in return they expect parents and grandparents to watch over children and be patient with their mistakes. People pay attention to each other's ages and sit and toast at suppers in roughly decreasing order of age. In general, Georgians do not enjoy eating meals or going places without the company of relatives or close friends.

Georgia has a large, loosely defined class of leading families whose members are academics, doctors, writers, artists, and political leaders. Old Tbilisi families have the highest status, but every village has an intelligentsia, usually including the former nobility. Communist party members, some from leading families and some not, formed a special class, at once elite and outcast, now disintegrating. Working and farming families receive respect insofar as they are large, prosperous, established, and honorable. Georgians feel working in business or any kind of service job is degrading, even if sometimes necessary. The Russians, Armenians, Azerbaijanis, and Jews who fill these jobs are therefore considered tainted by them or marked as separate people with separate roles. People recognize and reward individual merit, but access to education and employment also usually involves family guidance and patronage, thus replicating existing social divisions. The Communists, while they were in power, followed this traditional system, their ideology to the contrary notwithstanding.

The control exercised by Soviet offices, factories, schools, and clubs was to some extent circumvented by private ties that were the bases of society. People were accustomed to using their connections and paying bribes to gain government permission to build houses, change residence, or travel outside their republic. In general, Georgians consider it natural and moral to favor relatives and friends, provided that the beneficiaries are worthy. Under feudalism, the king, the church patriarch, and a few dozen princely families commanded lesser nobles as warriors and attendants; nobles, in turn, ruled farming families, who owed them labor, crops, and respect. City dwellers were organized into guilds, and foreign prisoners of war became slaves. In some areas peasant families were essentially free, watched over by village elders; elsewhere princes exploited their serfs, even selling them into slavery. Nobles

were usually raised in local peasant families, and all classes carried arms, fought in battle, and had a sense of honor.

POLITICAL ORGANIZATION. Under Soviet rule, Communist party leaders, government officials, and heads of institutions and industries effectively formed a single ruling body. Party members, supervisors, collective-farm chairmen, and schoolteachers represented this authority in everyday life, earning respect according to their individual qualities. Major decisions were made in Moscow, and formal opposition was not tolerated. Factions of the local *nomenklatura* schemed aggressively against each other for government wealth and favor, however. In earlier centuries, nobles, members of the royal family, and rulers of neighboring states formed shifting alliances. The central monarchy and the Christian church became closely tied to the idea of a unified, independent Georgia. Strong kings developed a feudal system similar to that of Europe, with hereditary land rights conditional on services rendered to a lord. However, princes and local leaders also made wars and alliances as extensions of their private affairs, building power by tradition, kinship ties, and personal ability.

SOCIAL CONTROL AND CONFLICT. Disputes are mediated by older men in the families involved or by third parties who have the respect of both sides; occasionally they simply simmer unresolved. Soviet police and courts were politically controlled and sometimes instruments of terror. People avoided litigation and resorted to bribery and influence when arrested. This system is now breaking down but has not been replaced. Georgia's traditional law codes, administered by nobles, bound offending families to pay fixed restitutions for death, injury, and loss of property; there was no distinction between purposeful and accidental wrongs. Parties took oaths on icons or brought witnesses to swear support. Families also took justice into their own hands, retaliating back and forth over generations. Georgians who feared revenge or official punishment sometimes fled to the forest and became bandits.

Georgia was thus historically a land of blood feuds and frequent raiding and warfare. A dagger belted around the waist and cartridge belts across the chest were standard elements of dress. This was balanced by a chivalric code of honor and strong traditions of kinship and hospitality. With the weakening of Soviet control, people are again dividing along political, national, and family lines, and leaders are building private armies. Georgian banquet tables may erupt into drunken fights, but

Georgia was historically a land of blood feuds and frequent raiding and warfare.

*The eleventh to
thirteenth centuries
were Georgia's
artistic golden age.*

can also heal rifts through adroit toasting; the supra is ideally "the academy," a place to learn and discuss. A fight most often starts between young men; older men, friends, or women then step in and try to calm them. A man's relatives and close friends may, however, also feel obligated to take his side. Formerly a woman could stop a fight by throwing her kerchief between the combatants.

Religion and Expressive Culture

RELIGIOUS BELIEFS AND PRACTICES. Most Georgians belong to the Georgian Orthodox church; Ajarians and the Georgians of Turkey are Sunni Muslims of the Hanafi rite. A small group of Georgians in Azerbaijan, the Ingilos, are Shiites, as are the Fereidanian Georgians of Iran. About 25,000 Georgian Jews live in Georgia. Georgians, especially those of the mountains, also maintain cults of local deities and traditions of honoring the spirits of ancestors. These older traditions, Christian beliefs, and even Mazdaist and Muslim ideas, have fused in different proportions in different regions. In addition, Georgian academies of the golden age embraced Neoplatonism and established a strong tradition of humanism that continues today. The autocephalous Georgian Orthodox church was incorporated into that of Russia in czarist times, then mostly suppressed under Soviet rule; celebrations in the countryside have thus been left to families. Georgians are now renovating churches and reestablishing services. The church patriarch (presently Ilia II) has reemerged as an important national figure.

Georgian churches are dominated by an iconostasis, traditionally made of elaborately carved stone, pierced by three ceremonial doors and set with icons of Mary, Christ, John the Baptist, and other saints and angels. Georgians associate knowledge, faith, light, and the Holy Spirit; baptism and subsequent mysteries (sacraments) are understood as growing enlightenment. Major Georgian Orthodox holidays are Easter, Christmas, New Year's, the Day of Souls, and days to honor Mary, Saint Nino, Saint George, and Georgia's old capital and religious center, Mtskheta. Holidays are celebrated with processions, special services, sacrifices, offerings of wine and bread, and periods of fasting and feasting.

Georgia's traditional pantheon consisted of an all-encompassing god (*ghmerti*) and a host of lesser deities called angels, saints, or icons (*khat'i*). Most likely these represent the cults of earlier pagan deities modified and renamed under the influence of Christianity. These included the many in-

carnations of Saint George, dragon slayer and chief protector of humankind; the Svan hunting goddess Dali; Tamar, queen and conqueror, associated with the sun; Saint Barbara, patron of fertility and healing; K'op'ala, victor over the race of demons; Saint Mary; the Archangel Michael; and even Christ as ruler of the underworld. Each saint (or version of a saint) has its own sanctuary, holiday, and (in pre-Soviet times) lands and families of attendants. The sanctuary belongs to the local community, but pilgrims from other regions (including representatives of some non-Georgian peoples) also bring sheep to sacrifice and join in feasting. Many churches have been built on mountains or near sacred trees and groves. According to myth, the shrines are linked to heaven by invisible chains, along which the saint travels in the form of a bird, winged cross, or light. In the mountains, standards topped with crosses were kept in the sanctuaries and were carried on raids and used to draw out drowned souls. In some mountain localities one can still see stone shrines adorned with antlers, drinking horns, and other offerings (metal objects, bullets) left by petitioners.

ARTS. Through the eighteenth century, the Georgian high arts developed in connection with those of Persia, Byzantium, and Armenia. Old churches, still revered and reproduced today, are cruciform or octagonal with alternating square and rounded masses piling up to a central tower with a conical roof. Doors, friezes, and altar screens are carved with geometrical designs, human figures, and birds and beasts; inside walls have frescoes in red and blue. Medieval Georgia is also famous for cloisonné enamel icons and repoussé metal frames, crosses, cups, and arms in silver and gold; the country retains many fine metalsmiths and jewelers. Men's traditional dress was a tightly belted woolen tunic and trousers tucked into soft leather boots; women wore silk or cotton gowns with flared hems and sleeves. Only the mountaineer Khevsur now wear their embroidered costumes in ordinary life, but tailoring and leather-working traditions remain strong. Pottery, wood carving, and knitting are also all old and popular arts in Georgia.

The eleventh to thirteenth centuries were Georgia's artistic golden age. The masterpiece of this period, Shota Rustaveli's romantic verse-epic *Vepkhist'q'aosani* (The Knight in the Leopard Skin) remains the Georgians' most beloved work of literature, both for its language and for the ideal picture of society it presents. Other classical works, many still read today, are lives of saints, historical chronicles, works of philosophy, love lyrics, and narrative poems of romance, history, and reflection. There are also many translations and retellings of literature from other countries. The silver age of the fifteenth to eighteenth centuries brought a renaissance of poetry, the introduction of printing, the first monumental dictionary of the Georgian language, and works of history and criticism that established modern scholarship. Georgian folklore includes myths, historical tales, stories featuring literary characters, fairy tales, fables, battle epics, love poems, songs of mourning, work songs, humorous poems, lullabies, and hymns. Festive suppers are favorite times for songs, and winter evenings for stories.

Georgians have a distinct tradition of polyphonic a cappella folk singing, sung by men divided into two or three main voices and up to four additional voices. Other song styles need just one voice and are sung to instrumental accompaniment. Tbilisi has given rise to a genre of urban folk songs, many written by nineteenth-century poets. Traditional Georgian instruments include three-stringed mandolins and lutes, pipes, clarinets, drums, and, in various areas, bagpipes, panpipes, and harps. Medieval Georgians enjoyed chamber music and had a system of musical notation. In Georgian dances men imitate the art of war—leaping, spinning, and battling with swords; women move proudly and gracefully, with elaborate movements of their hands. Men and women never touch each other while dancing. Often the company makes a ring, clapping or revolving while individuals show off in the center. In sports Georgians excel at wrestling, fencing, equestrian events, and chess (especially women's chess, which has been dominated by Georgians for the past two decades); soccer is also extremely popular.

Beginning in the early nineteenth century, Georgian arts came under Western influence. Many Georgians have excelled in painting, sculpture, lyric and narrative poetry, fiction, symphonic music, opera, ballet, theater, and cinema. Professional artists draw heavily on folk themes, and their work is known to people from all walks of life. Georgian painters and sculptors favor portraits and scenes of gatherings; many use strong, sharp lines and give their subjects an impression of weight. Among painters of the post-war period, Lado Gudiashvili has pride of place; the naive painter Niko Pirosmanishvili has become famous for his murals in cellar restaurants depicting scenes from urban and village life. Over the course of the nineteenth century, Georgian poets

and novelists turned from romantic to realistic styles; common subjects remain the fate of the country, historical episodes, everyday life, and intense portraits of character and emotion. Important poets of earlier generations include Nikoloz Baratashvili, Ak'ak'i Ts'ereteli, Galak't'ion T'abidze, and those of the symbolist "blue horn" circle. Perhaps the greatest poet of the modern period is the early-twentieth-century writer Vazha-Pshavela, whose poems were inspired by the epic oral literature of his native mountains.

MEDICINE. Georgians go both to state clinics and to doctors who use traditional remedies. Certain families are famous for their knowledge of curing; recipes and rituals are also found in old books. Georgians traditionally had shamans who fell into trances and prescribed cures in the voice of a local deity. Similarly, some women could speak in the voices of the dead. Some Georgians fear old women's curses and unhappy local and ancestral spirits, blaming them for illness or bad fortune. Many believe in the healing powers of mineral-water drinks and baths. Old women see their families' futures written in dreams in standard sets of signs; some are also known as fortune-tellers. Many women like to get together in winter, drink coffee, and tell fortunes from the grounds. Mountain priests used to divine the future from shoulder bones of sacrificed animals. Many Georgians consider certain days of the week lucky or unlucky for doing certain household tasks or for individuals in their lives.

DEATH AND AFTERLIFE. Georgians want very much to die in the company of their families and be buried in their native land. As a person is dying, relatives place a bowl of water beside the bed and open a window, so the soul can be clean and fly away. On the third, fourth, and fifth days after death, hundreds, or even thousands, come to pay their respects; a priest is also called, if one is available. A candle burns behind the head of the corpse and grains of wheat are strewn alongside; the women of the family sob and lament, the men stand quietly. For the burial, the pallbearers carry the coffin three times around the room, then knock on the door and let themselves out. The family follows with wine and special dishes. That evening neighbors organize a large funeral banquet; the toasts must total an odd number. Forty days after death, the family celebrates the soul's departure for the other world; on the first anniversary, they mark the end of mourning. Thereafter, on anniversaries, on holidays, and especially on the Day of Souls, people return to the cemetery

The years of massive collectivization, for the pastoral Kazakhs, were accompanied by enforced settlement, epidemics, and many Stalinist repressions that killed millions of people.

and have a small supper, including toasts and offerings to those who have passed away. A person in mourning consumes no milk or meat and wears black. Some women mourn husbands or brothers their entire lives, but young widows and widowers often remarry. In folklore Georgians associated death with journeys to the west, into caves, and through water. They envisioned the afterlife as a dim, shadowy replica of the present one: the dead sit at a vast banquet at which they do not eat, drink, or speak. Souls maintain family loyalties and still crave food, drink, and, according to some, clothing and entertainment. Their well-being depends on their character in this world, and their relatives' continuing care. Georgians also have Christian ideas of a heaven and hell.

Bibliography

Allen, W. E. D. (1932). *A History of the Georgian People.* London: Kegan Paul. Reprint. 1971.

Charachidzé, Georges (1968). *Le système religieux de la Géorgie paienne.* Paris: Maspéro.

Davitaia, F. F. (1972). *Sovietskaia Gruziia* (Soviet Georgia). Moscow: Progress.

Dragadze, Tamara (1988). *Rural Families in Soviet Georgia.* London: Routledge.

Grigolia, Alexander (1939). *Custom and Justice in the Caucasus: The Georgian Highlanders.* Philadelphia: University of Pennsylvania Press.

Lang, David Marshall (1966). *The Georgians.* New York: Praeger.

Papashvily, George, and Helen Papashvily (1946). *Yes and No Stories: A Book of Georgian Folk Tales.* New York: Harper.

Suny, Ronald G. (1988). *The Making of the Georgian Nation.* Bloomington: Indiana University Press.

Tuite, Kevin (in press). *Violet on the Mountain: An Anthology of Georgian Folk Poetry.* Madison, N.J.: Fairleigh Dickinson University Press.

Volkova, N. G., and G. N. Dzhavakhishvili (1982). *Bytovaia kultura gruzii XIX-XX vekov: Traditsii i inovatsii* (Georgian domestic culture in the 19th-20th centuries: Tradition and innovation). Moscow: Nauka.

—ELISA WATSON

KAZAKHS

Ethnonym: Kazaks

Orientation

IDENTIFICATION. Kazakhs are a Central Asian people who live mainly in Kazakhstan, for-

merly the Kazakh SSR. The so-called Kirghiz SSR was established as part of the Russian Soviet Federated Socialist Republic in 1920 and renamed the Kazakh SSR in 1926. In 1991 it declared its sovereignty and independence and began to be called the Republic of Kazakhstan. Toward the end of 1991 it voluntarily joined the other states that formed the Commonwealth of Independent States. The Republic of Kazakhstan is a multicultural state, with members of numerous different ethnic groups living there. A significant portion of the population is Slavic, mainly Russians and Ukrainians, who constitute nearly half the population in some northern areas. Also living in Kazakhstan are Uzbeks, Kyrgyz, Tajiks, Turkmens, Uighur, Tatars, Dungans, Germans, Koreans, Greeks, Kurds, Turks, Mordvins, and many peoples from the Caucasus, especially the northern Caucasus.

The self-name of the Kazakh people—"Kazakh" or "Kazak"—has existed, according to written sources, since the seventeenth century and was generally known to neighboring peoples by the seventeenth and eighteenth centuries. The Russians, who called them "Kazakhs" or "the Kazatskaye" (or also "Kazattskaya"), subsequently began to call them "Kyrgyz" (although the actual Kyrgyz are the Karakyrgyz or Will Stone Kyrgyz), "Kazak-Kyrgyz," "Kyrgyz-Kaisak," and "Kyrgyz-Kazakh." This occurred because the Russians sought to differentiate the Kazakhs from the Russian Cossacks who had settled in neighboring regions of Siberia at the beginning of the eighteenth century, or in Kazakh territory itself. Only in 1926, when the Kazakhs gained national autonomy, was the name of the Kirghiz ASSR changed to Kazakh and did the Kazakhs regain the use of their traditional name.

LOCATION. The territory of the Kazakhs, known as Kazakhstan, is quite large. It stretches from the Balkhash Lowlands in the east to the Ural River in the west (about 3,000 kilometers) and from the Syr Darya and Chu river systems and the Tobol River in the south to the Imum and the Irtysh rivers in the north (about 2,000 kilometers). Basically the region consists of steppe, desert, and semidesert lands, which in the east and southeast are bounded by the Altai and Tianshan massifs. In the extreme northwest are the southern marshes of the Common Syrt; in the south the wide, flat Pre-Caspian Lowlands and, further on, the desert peninsula of Mangyshlak. The Ural River flows almost all the way across the Common Syrt and the Pre-Caspian Lowlands, emptying into the Caspian Sea. To the west, Eu-

◆ **SSR**
Soviet Socialist Republic. In the former Soviet Union there were fifteen SSRs.

904

rope begins at the Ural Mountains, and Asia is to the east.

The Mangyshlak Peninsula, along with the low mountain ridges of the Aktar and Karatar, is distinguished by deep hollows, the deepest of which—Karagie—is 132 meters below sea level. To the east from Mangyshlak there extends the desert plateau of Ust Urt. Both of these places are now used by the Kazakhs for winter pasturage. To the northeast lie the Pre-Caspian Lowlands bordering the spurs of the Urals and the low mountain massif of Mugogzhari. Further east lie the Turgay plateau and, south of it, the Tuvan Lowlands filled by the desert of Kyzylkum. To the north of the Aral Sea are the sandy massifs of the great and small Balger. The desert of the Pre-Aral Kanakum is north of the Aral Sea. The Aral Sea has recently become well known, as it is gradually growing shallow and creating an ecological crisis. Since ancient times, the Kazakhs have used this region for winter pasturage for their cattle.

Further to the east, the Kazakhs occupy the southern region of the western Siberian plain, to the south of which spreads the fine summer pasturage that the Kazakhs affectionately call the Sary-Arka. Yet further to the south is the desert of Betpak-Dala. The Chu River, its waters flowing from the west, separates the southern part of Betpak-Dala from the sands of Muyunkum. From the southeast to the northwest the land is framed by the mountain ridges of the Karatay. To the east of the Betpak-Dala Desert lies Lake Balkhash and, to the south of the lake, the well-known province of Gernirechye, or, as the Kazakhs call it, Jetys.

The wide variation in the landscape and variable distances from the oceans have led to a climate that is basically continental but with marked regional variation. In the north the winters are cold and long, with temperatures dipping to as low as −45° C. In the central regions winters are moderate, and in the south they are gentle and short, almost without snow. Summers are dry and range from warm in the north to hot in the south.

Precipitation is rare almost everywhere other than the mountains, and especially so in the desert regions, where it is less than 10 centimeters per year. Only in the foothills and mountains is rainfall plentiful, ranging from 40 to 160 centimeters per year. Winds blow across the entire region; in the steppe lands these winds turn into severe snowstorms (*buran*) in the winter, and in the fall (and less often in the summer) into dust storms. The variations in topography and climate have also produced marked variation in the distribution of water sources. Although there are about 85,000 lakes, many are in the mountains in the north, with hardly any in the desert and semidesert regions. The water level in lakes and rivers rises and falls markedly with the seasons, and during droughts some dry up completely in the summer months. The water in the great majority of lakes is saline. Fresh water is found only in the steppe lands and the mountains and in the flatland along the major rivers and lakes. The two seas—the Caspian and Aral—and the largest lakes, including Balkhash, are isolated basins. Only major rivers such as the Ishim, Irtysh, and Tobal cross the Kazakh region and extend into other regions.

The flora is diverse. Many varieties of grain (feather grass, wormwood, and *tipchak*—an oatlike grass that grows in steppes and deserts) flourish in the steppe in the north; the main summer pasturage is found here. Wormwood and grasses predominate in semidesert regions. Most of Kazakh territory is desert covered by drought-resistant bushes, small brush, and different grasses called salt grass (*solyanka*). In the sandy deserts are sand wormwood, sage, acacias, and haloxyon (*saksaul*). In the flatland are *tugainye* woods, and around the lakes reeds are found in abundance. The foothills are covered with poppies and tulips. Higher up in the mountains are bushes and mixed woods of aspen and birch and, even higher, coniferous forests. In the forest belt, fed by the glacial streams, are alpine and subalpine meadows with a rich variety of flora. The soil in Kazakhstan is mostly fertile. In the north it is *chernozem*, to the south *chermits* soils are most common, and in the desert regions there is a mix of red-brown, grey-brown, and sandy soils. Agriculture in the desert regions requires irrigation.

As with the flora, there is also a rich variety of fauna including 155 varieties of mammals, 480 of birds, 49 of reptiles, 11 of amphibians, 150 of fish, and many invertebrates.

DEMOGRAPHY. According to the 1989 census, there were 8,136,000 Kazakhs in the lands of the Soviet Union, with 6,535,000 in Kazakhstan. Kazakhs also live in Uzbekistan, Turkmenistan, Kyrgyzstan, and Tajikistan in Central Asia and in Russia. Over 1 million live in other countries, mainly China, Mongolia, and Turkey, and in Europe.

LINGUISTIC AFFILIATION. The Kazakh language belongs to the Northwest or Kipchak Group of Turkish languages of the Ural-Altaic Family. Together with Karakalpak and Nogay it forms the Kipchak-Nogay Subgroup of the Kipchak

The Kazakh language has become the state language of Kazakhstan, although Russian continues to be the language of international relations.

languages. Kazakh has three dialects—Western, North-Eastern, and Southern.

History and Cultural Relations

Much archaeological and documentary evidence establishes the continuous history of Kazakhstan from the Late Paleolithic era. In the late Bronze Age (end of the second to the beginning of the first millenia B.C.) the inhabitants of the steppe region began practicing nomadic animal husbandry, mining, and the production of bronze wares. More than 100 settlements dating to the Bronze Age, with foundaries for the fusion of metals and the manufacture of weapons, tools, and ornaments, have been discovered. In the following period (roughly from the first millenium B.C. to the Christian Era) the nomadic tribes of Kazakhstan began to consolidate into larger units—the Saks (Scythians) tribal union in southern (Semirechie), eastern, and central Kazakhstan, and the Savromat Confederacy to the west and partly to the north. Ideologically, the cults of the sun and fire dominated worship of the goddess-guardian of the domestic hearth and of fertility and totemism, and magical practices were retained. The well-known Scythian-Saksian style flourished, renowned to this day for its artistry and expressivity. Subsequently, new, more powerful tribal unities developed, these showing early signs of centralized state power: Usuni, and Kangyugi (in southern Kazakhstan the Semirechie), which maintained contacts with Bactria and the empires of Kushan, Panthia, and China.

In the second 500 years of the first millennium A.D. a process of feudalization took place. Powerful feudal states such as the Old Turkish, Tyurgesh, Karluk, Oguz, Kumak, and Kipchak ruled the region, with each tending to replace the next. In 1219–1220 Mongol Tatars conquered the region; their rule restricted cultural and economic development. The emergence of the Kazakhs as a distinct ethnic group occurred in the fourteenth and fifteenth centuries with the rise of the Kazakh Khanate. There were three powerful entities called zhuz (Russian: *orda*): the Old Zhuz in southern Kazakhstan and the Semirechie, the Middle Zhuz in central and northern Kazakhstan, and the Young Zhuz in western Kazakhstan. At the start of the nineteenth century the Bukeev Zhuz broke away from the Young Zhuz and occupied the Pre-Caspian steppe between the Volga and Ural rivers. Each of the zhuzes consisted of a number of tribes, which were further subdivided into smaller tribes and clans within the tribes. The clans were unified internally by common ancestry.

During the fifteenth to seventeenth centuries the "traditional" culture of the Kazakhs was established, including house type, furnishings, utensils, clothing, food, rituals, art, and oral tradition. All customs and beliefs were strongly influenced by the nomadic and seminomadic animal husbandry that was the basis of Kazakh life.

In the first quarter of the eighteenth century the survival of the Kazakhs was threatened by invasions of the Jungans from the east in 1713, 1718, and 1722–1723, a period known as "the years of the great disaster." The Jungans seized a significant amount of Kazakh land, and some Kazakh tribes and clans fled west and established protective ties with the Russians. In 1731 the Kazakhs of the Young Zhuz (Khan Abulkhair) and some from the Middle Zhuz accepted Russian citizenship. The unification of Kazakhstan with Russia was completed by the 1860s, and, as a result, the Kazakh steppe was ringed by Russian military lines and fortifications, which served to strengthen the Russian Empire. The basic military force was drawn from Cossack settlements, to which were given over 67 million hectares of the best Kazakh land. During the unification process the power of the Kazakh khans was weakened (the Young Zhuz in 1824 and the Nukeev Zhuz in 1845), and a new administrative system based on the rule of the czar was introduced. The new system delineated the following territories: West-Siberian, later Steppe (with the Akmolinsk and Semipalatinsk regions); Orenburg, with its Ural and Tungai provinces; Turkestan territory, with its Syr-Dal'in and Semirechie provinces. In turn the provinces (*oblasts*) were subdivided into regions (*uezds*) and the regions into districts (*volosts*). Kazakh lands were declared to be state property and granted for usufruct without a time limit.

During this period, the Kazakh economy also changed markedly. Trade increased, agriculture developed, and the first industrial enterprises, mainly devoted to the processing of agricultural raw materials, were developed. The territory was also settled by large numbers of peasants from European Russia, and Kazakhstan became a multicultural region. The presence of the Russians affected the Kazakhs in a variety of ways. On the one hand, they lost large tracts of the best pasturage because this land was allotted to the settlers. On the other hand, the settlers were involved in the development of Kazakh agriculture and the emergence of a Kazakh ethnic consciousness. A Kazakh bourgeoisie was born, and a working class began to emerge—both entirely new social groupings for the Kazakhs.

♦ **usufruct**
The right to use land or property without actually owning it.

During World War I large numbers of Kazakhs were mobilized for rear-echelon work. In 1916 an anticolonial movement flared up, only to be harshly suppressed; 300,000 Kazakhs were forced to migrate beyond the boundaries of Russia, some to China and Mongolia. During the 1917 Revolution and the civil war and in subsequent periods, the Kazakhs shared the same fate as other peoples of the USSR. On the one hand, a backward, agrarian region was transformed into an agricultural, industrialized republic. As a result, a high culture emerged, characterized by literature, art, science, and technology. These years, however, were also marked by cruel famines, especially during the years of massive collectivization, which for the pastoral Kazakhs was accompanied by enforced settlement, epidemics, and many Stalinist repressions that killed millions of people. For example, during the famines of the 1930s the populations of entire villages perished—hundreds of thousands of Kazakh families. Those who survived left their property and herds behind and set off for Siberia, Central Asia, and other regions. Approximately 1 million Kazakhs dispersed in China, Mongolia, Afghanistan, and other countries. Nearly 200,000 of these returned in 1934; the rest remained abroad. During the 1930s, mass purges and campaigns against "enemies of the people" were carried out among the Kazakhs, as among the other peoples of the USSR. As a result of all these tragic events, 1.75 million Kazakhs perished—nearly 40 percent of the total population.

Despite these horrific human losses, the national economy of Kazakhstan nevertheless developed steadily. In the prewar years, 200 large-scale industrial enterprises were established, land-tenure regulations for the former Kazakh nomads and seminomads were implemented, and livestock raising and agriculture were improved.

World War II interrupted the peaceful development of the Kazakh Republic. More than 1.2 million citizens of Kazakhstan were drafted into military service and participated in the defense of the USSR. According to data from 1946, 96,638 Kazakh veterans received decorations and medals of distinction.

During the war the Kazakh homeland also played a vital role in the country's economy, providing coal, oil, and various metals and furnishing the army with food products. Also during the war, Kazakhstan accommodated more than 1 million Russians, Ukrainians, Belarussians, and other peoples of the Soviet Union evacuated from frontline areas.

In the postwar period, the Kazakhs endured several unfortunate events. In the mid-1950s, there was a mass "opening up" of the virgin steppe lands. With the help of 640,000 immigrant workers who arrived to aid the Kazakhs, more than 1.8 million hectares of land were plowed and sown—that is, approximately 60 percent of the total area of the country's newly opened land. In 1956 Kazakhstan provided the state with more than 1 billion *puds* (36 billion lbs/16.38 billion kg) of bread. This was more than in the eleven preceding years combined. The virgin land epic was ill-conceived, however. Over a huge area the most fertile layer of soil (humus) was destroyed by erosion. In addition, the lands previously used for pasture, the best ones, were reduced, which seriously undermined the basis of the Kazakhs' traditional occupation, livestock raising. The ecological situation in Kazakhstan deteriorated, as the plowing up of the steppes resulted in a reduction of the number of livestock and the stocks of wild animals and birds and the drying up of the rivers and lakes.

In the rural areas, less than one-half of all children are provided with preschool institutions; most medical facilities are ill-equipped, lacking medicine and medical supplies; and hospital beds are poorly distributed. The homes of rural Kazakhs, as a rule, lack running water and sewer systems; more than 700 settlements use imported water. Many cities, including large ones, are experiencing a severe shortage of water. In remote districts, where mainly Kazakhs dwell, a low standard of living remains: there is a high infant and maternal mortality rate and a high rate of disease in general.

Not every aspect of the development of industry was well received. Although Kazakhstan is an industrially developed country, the structure of the national economy is one-sided: the principle emphasis has been on the attainment and initial processing of raw materials. All of these factors led to serious socioeconomic complications and to a shortage of industrial goods and food products.

To this one must add the irreparable changes in the ecosystem as a result of 40 years of systematic nuclear testing in the Semipalatinsk region. The air, earth, rivers, and lakes of the once-blossoming region were contaminated with radioactivity in a large area around the testing ground; the people, especially the children, as well as the animals and plants are suffering from the effects of these acts.

An ecological tragedy is coming about with the unprecedented drying up of the Aral Sea. Because

The drying up of the Aral Sea is causing an ecological tragedy for the inhabitants of the area.

Kazakhs accustom children to work from an early age. They teach a boy to ride a horse at age three and to tend it and other livestock at five or six.

of the shortage of water, the dispersal of poisonous chemical fertilizers, and the general contamination of the land and water, everyone living within a few kilometers of the Aral Sea is perishing. The tragedy affects not only Kazakhs but other peoples as well—the Turkmens, the Uzbeks, and the Karakalpaks who live in the basin of the Aral Sea.

The events outlined above have led to an exacerbation of socioeconomic and political problems and to dissatisfaction manifesting itself in various ways. On 17 December 1986 student disturbances broke out in the capital of Kazakhstan, Alma-Ata. As a result of provocation, clashes between youths and the militia flared up, causing numerous casualties. Nearly 1,700 people were injured and more than 8,000 arrested and detained, many of whom were convicted. At the present time these events have been reappraised as struggles for democratic freedom. December 17 has been proclaimed Kazakhstan's Day of Democracy.

In June 1989 long unresolved social problems in the city of Novyi Uzen' (Mangyshlak Peninsula) led to interethnic conflicts—members of seventy ethnic groups, many from the Caucasus, live in the city alongside Kazakhs. As a result of the riots, lives were lost and strikes were held repeatedly at the mines of the Karagandin coal basin.

The modern political life of the Kazakhs is very active. Legislators are passing a series of laws that are fundamentally changing the lives of the people of Kazakhstan. The president of the Republic of Kazakhstan, Nursultan Nazarbaev, was popularly elected and enjoys the support of most of the population, especially the Kazakhs. In September 1991, the Communist party of Kazakhstan was renamed the Socialist party. Other parties have arisen, including the Social Democratic party, the Alash Party of National Independence, and the Republican party, along with many social movements. Testing at the atomic proving ground of Semipalatinsk Oblast has been discontinued. The Aral Sea Basin has been declared a zone of ecological disaster, and measures are being taken to rectify the aftereffects of this catastrophe. Among the laws adopted by the Parliament of the Republic of Kazakhstan, notable are the laws connected with the development of the culture and language of the Kazakh people as well as those of other ethnic groups living in the territory of Kazakhstan. The Kazakh language has become the state language, although Russian continues to be the language of international relations. Legis-

lation about teaching and record keeping in the languages of other nationalities in areas where they live in dense concentration has also been passed.

Fundamental economic changes have come about. Joint-stock companies, cooperative works, and the privatization of businesses have been authorized. The number of farm-based economies is growing. Land is given to farmers for unlimited use, including the right to inherit it. On collective and state farms, leases are receiving widespread distribution; anyone may rent a portion of land to cultivate crops, in return for a portion of the harvest but is entitled to sell the remainder at market price. Since 1992, in Kazakhstan as in many other republics of the former USSR, free prices for food and industrial products have been introduced, with the exception of products of primary necessity. In short, a market economy is being developed.

Economy

In the pre-Revolutionary period the Kazakhs were prominent on the Eurasian Steppe, leading nomadic and seminomadic life-styles. Their chief occupation was livestock raising; the animals were kept in pastures year-round. These pastures were divided according to season—summer, spring/fall, and winter, based on when grass was sufficient, in turn depending on climatic conditions. The summer pastures were located in the north, in the steppe zone, with abundant, lush grass. It was impossible to remain there during the winter, however, as the huge amount of snow would not permit the livestock to graze. Therefore the nomadic livestock breeders were required to move with their herds far to the south to the desert and semidesert zones in the winter, where vegetation flourished after the autumn rains and where there was little snow. Sometimes the migration reached upwards of 1,000–1,500 kilometers. En route, the nomads would stay for a short while at the spring/fall pastures when they were migrating to the north in the spring and to the south during the fall. Such a migratory system was quite widespread among the Kazakh nomads and seminomads; it has been designated "meridianal" in the literature.

In the mountainous regions the nomadic and seminomadic Kazakhs passed the winter in the valleys of the mountain rivers and ravines, where there was little snow, whereas in the summer they and their herds went high into the mountains to the alpine and subalpine meadows. This type of migration is called "vertical."

The particular nomadic life-style determined the specific makeup of the herd. The domesticated animals had to withstand travel during the lengthy migration and, crucially, had to be able to procure food for themselves from under the snow during the winter. The horse was most suited to these conditions and was thus highly prized among the Kazakhs. The horse was also the main transport and riding animal, able to cover a long distance in a relatively short time. The horse also supplied kumys, which has been revered since the days of the Scythian nomads. Horse meat was also considered most tasty and nutritious; horse hair was used in the preparation of strong, thick ropes.

In early childhood the Kazakh nomad was given a colt, which she or he called by name, looked after, and by the age of 5 to 7 was already riding. Adult Kazakhs, both men and women, were spectacular riders; so great was their skill that several researchers noted that the rider seemed to become one with the horse. The importance of the horse in the life of the Kazakh nomads is further attested by the fact that instead of "to the left" the Kazakhs say "mounting side" (*minar yak*); instead of "to the right" they say "whip[-holding] side" (*kamshi yagt*). From as early as the Scythian-Sak period, nomadic livestock breeders have revered the horse as a totemic animal.

Sheep have no lesser significance to the Kazakh nomads and seminomads. As with the horse, the Kazakhs had their own particular breed of sheep, which was well suited to the conditions of year-round pasturing without warm refuge during the winter. "Fatty-tail" sheep were particularly prized—that is, sheep that instead of a tail had a large fatty growth that reached a weight of 10–16 kilograms. Kazakhs get all that is necessary for life from sheep. From its wool they make felt, with which they cover the traditional nomadic dwelling, the yurt, and make felt carpets decorated with multicolored ornamentation. They cover the earthen floor in the yurt with these carpets. In the winter the Kazakhs put stockings of thin felt in their boots for warmth. Felt is also used as a saddlecloth.

From sheepskins, which the Kazakhs, as a rule, process themselves, they sew warm coats, hats, and sometimes men's trousers. The pelts of domestic animals, including sheep, are sent to market. A minority of Kazakhs also raise goats, from which they also get milk, meat, wool, and pelts.

Camels serve as the basic beast of burden among the Kazakh nomads and seminomads. During the migrations they load all domestic goods on them, including the dismantled parts of the yurts. Kazakhs keep fewer camels than they do other domestic animals, however. Even rich families possess no more than fifty to sixty camels; other households, the poorer ones, have no more than three or four—that is, only as many as are required to transfer all domestic items during the migrations. In several regions of Kazakhstan—on the Mangyshlak Peninsula, for example—the Kazakhs drink *shubat* (the sour milk of camels), which is their preferred beverage. Camel's wool is valued for its great warmth. Like the horse and the sheep, the camel is highly esteemed by the Kazakhs. Muslims view it as a holy animal.

The Kazakhs also raise cattle. Among the nomads, it is true that there are only a few, and often none, because they are not suited for long and rapid migrations and are not capable of procuring food for themselves from underneath the snow. Relatively more cattle are found among the seminomads, who, in contrast with the nomads, undertake shorter migrations and prepare hay for the livestock to eat during winter. Cattle are not only a source of milk, meat, and leather; they are also the principle beast of burden in agricultural endeavors.

In general, the Kazakhs grew a variety of grains: wheat, millet, a little rye, barley, and others. At present Kazakh farmers, for the most part, raise the best kinds of wheat: the so-called hard (durum) wheats. The cultivation of rice, peas, corn, and industrial crops, especially cotton and tobacco, is widespread. In the south of Kazakhstan, the cultivation of fruits and vegetables is developing.

In a number of regions of Kazakhstan where the conditions are suitable for irrigation agriculture—along large rivers and lakes, for example, or in foothill regions where streams abound—the Kazakhs have always practiced agriculture.

FOOD. Kazakhs make butter and various types of curds and cheese from sheep's milk. The most widespread is a dry cheese from sour milk, *kurt*. It is one of the chief means of nourishment for the average Kazakh in the winter months, when there is no milk. The Kazakhs always boil sheep or cow's milk; only mare's milk is used fresh and, in this case, always soured. The most beloved and widespread Kazakh dish is boiled lamb, in Kazakh *bes barmak* ("five fingers," since the Kazakhs, like many other Eastern peoples, eat with their hands). They give the specially prepared lamb's head to the most esteemed guest.

DIVISION OF LABOR. The community is divided into smaller units, auls, which consist of closely related families headed by the senior member, an *aksakala* ("white beard"). Usually this is the father, although the adult married sons head the other households. After the father's death, his oldest son becomes head of the aul.

The households of the aul cooperate in many labor-intensive activities, such as tending the livestock. The most difficult jobs necessitate the strength of many workers; for example, the shearing of sheep in spring and fall requires the combined efforts of the households and auls of the entire nomadic community. At present, Kazakhs are trying to preserve the traditional forms of the family, especially in rural areas; under urban conditions, this is obviously more difficult.

LAND TENURE. The summer pastures are usually under the governance and use of individual clans, which consist of several nomadic kin groups or communities. The winter pastures, as a rule, are in the common use of the small nomadic community. Water sources for livestock are a chief concern of the nomadic breeders. Best of all are natural sources: rivers, streams, lakes, and so forth. Frequently, however, livestock can slake their thirst only from wells; therefore these are the property of the individual households that dug them, or of the aul. The right to use the pastures nearest to the well follows from this. There are also wells that belong to the entire clan. As a rule, such wells were dug long ago. The land-use pat-

tern of the seminomadic Kazakhs is similar, but in contrast with the nomads, they also have hay-growing areas for the preparation of winter fodder. As a rule, these hay-growing areas are under the control of individual households and are spread out near the winter pastures. Also located here are the arable lands: seminomadic Kazakhs engage in varying degrees in agriculture along with raising livestock. The poorer a household is, the more it relies on agriculture. The poorest families, who have no livestock, have abandoned seminomadism and live year-round in one location, engaging in agriculture or some other business. Thus, they constitute the settled population among the Kazakhs.

INDUSTRIAL ARTS. In addition to raising livestock and practicing agriculture, the Kazakhs engage in a variety of manufactures. Only women process wool and prepare various items from it, but both men and women process leather and pelts. Woodworking and metalwork are in the domain of the men. Traditionally, only Kazakh men were occupied with tending the livestock (including the milking of the horses), whereas women performed all domestic tasks, including the erecting and dismantling of the yurts during the migrations. Notable for their quality are the preparation of various felts and the working of leather and pelts for clothing, various types of skin vessels, saddles, and so forth. Woodworking is wide-

A YURT

A Kazakh woman outside her felt yurt, a transportable dwelling consisting of a wooden frame covered in felt. Yurts are mainly used by shepherd families who follow their herds to summer pastures. The Kazakhs live in both Russia and China. Sinkiang Uighur, China. (Ric Ergenbright/Corbis)

spread, including the preparation of the wooden parts of the yurt, saddles, trunks, and wooden vessels, which like the skin vessels are indispensible in nomadic conditions. Many wooden products are adorned with carvings. One of the most ancient trades of the Kazakhs is metalwork: the fabrication of weapons and instruments of labor as well as household items. The art of silver adornment is highly refined.

The years of Soviet dominance were marked by the fostering of a nihilistic attitude toward national culture; as a result, many traditional Kazakh trades disappeared almost completely. Only in the present has a rebirth of traditional Kazakh trades occurred, in conjunction with a general rebirth of national culture.

CLOTHING. The traditional Kazakh national costume was closely tied to their nomadic life-style. Thus, the oldest materials used in clothing preparation were cloths woven from camel or sheep wool, thin felts, skins, and fur. In ancient times, however, they had already begun sewing clothing from manufactured fabrics—cottons, silks, and wools from Central Asia, China, and, from the eighteenth century on, from Russia. In our own time, fabrics of industrial manufacture have supplanted all others. The men's outfit traditionally consisted of an undershirt and pants, which in the summer also served as work clothes. Over the shirt, men wore long *beru kavkas* or *beshmets* (quilted coats, narrow but widening toward the bottom, knee-length with long sleeves). The *shapan*—a robe with long sleeves tapering from the shoulder to the fingers, with a stand-up collar, worn open and therefore always with a belt—was ubiquitous. Poor Kazakhs fashioned their shapans from homewoven camel wool; the rich, however, made them from velvet, heavy cloth, or silk of bright colors. Depending on the weather, Kazakhs would wear one shapan over another. In the wintertime, they wore coats sewn from sheepskin—either double-sided or not—or from skins of lamb, ferret, marten, and fox. The outer trousers were made of skins adorned with ornaments, especially among the rich. When setting off on a long journey, the Kazakh horseman inserted the flaps of all the robes he was wearing into these trousers. Their high-heeled boots, sewn of strong skins, were well suited to riding.

The traditional winter headgear of the Kazakhs was a pointed fur cap (*tymak*) with earflaps of lamb's wool or even sable fur, with a felt base covered by heavy cloth. Factory-made caps with earflaps have almost completely supplanted them. In the summer Kazakhs wore hats made from thin white felt with bent-back flaps (*kalpak*); recently such hats have also been replaced by factory-made ones, including ones of felt. It has again become fashionable, however, especially among youths, to wear the traditional felt caps which, incidentally, provide better protection against the cold. These caps have turned into a distinctive "ethno-designative" feature. *Bashlyks* with a crown with a small peak and flaps to cover the ears and neck were sewn from felt and later from cloth. It was usual that the head was always covered, even at night during sleep, if only with a *tyubeteika* (Central Asian embroidered skullcap).

Traditionally, all Kazakh men shaved their heads as well as their mustaches and beards around the lips. At present, only elderly men shave their heads, and most men let their mustaches and beards grow.

The belt was an indispensable part of the traditional costume; Kazakhs tied it over the shapan or trousers, especially when they were preparing to ride. Belts were of silk fabric or skins—the latter were decorated with metallic plates, of silver and sometimes even precious stones, among the rich.

The Kazakh women, like the men, wore a shirt and trousers as undergarments. Sometimes, however, the shirt was long and tunic-shaped and served as a dress. Fashioned out of cotton fabric, the shirt-dress was white (but dark for older women and of bright and variegated colors—usually red—for younger women). Beginning in the middle of the nineteenth century, Kazakhs began to sew these brought in at the waist, to which they attached a wider lower part at the gathers. As an adornment to this lower part of the dress, younger women sewed on two or three frills of the same material. Sometimes they embroidered them and covered them with braids and silk ribbons.

Over the dress women wore sleeveless tunics extending down to the knees, with an open collar and a clasp at the belt. They also wore beshmets. These were sleeveless ones, fashioned of thick cotton, wool, silk, or velvet fabrics. Red, green, or raspberry beshmets of velvet were particularly prized. The women, like the men, wore robes when out and about and sheepskin overcoats in the winter.

Women's footwear consisted of leather boots sewn for one foot—that is, without distinguishing the left side from the right. They also sewed soft boots of green and red leather and adorned them with embroidery. Women's trousers were of almost the same cut as the men's.

A great diversity existed in women's headgear. Variations pointed to age differences, family position, or membership in a given clan. Thus, girls wore elegant caps with a cloth crown, which they decorated without fail, and a fur cap-band (*boryuk*). The decoration was finished with eagle-owl feathers, which had a protective function. The young women wore the most expensive female headdress, *saukele*. This consisted of a tall (up to 70 centimeters) cone of felt, covered in expensive fabric and richly ornamented with various pendants, fur, and precious stones. Along the sides of the saukele descended corals, pendants of beads, and other decorations. From the back of the saukele women attached long, richly embroidered and adorned ribbons or kerchiefs of expensive fabric. Among the rich, the worth of the saukele could reach up to 2,000 silver rubles. Therefore, the saukele passed from one generation to the next in Kazakh families.

In the year after marriage, the young woman donned the headdress of the married woman, which represented a type of cowl of white fabric covering the head, shoulders, breast, and back. Kazakhs call such a headdress *kimeshek*. Young and middle-aged women decorated theirs with embroidery on the outward-facing side; those of the elderly were not embroidered. Among the various Kazakh clan groups, this headgear was differentiated according to cut, form, and dimensions of the part covering the back. Women wore the kimeshek when at home, and, when going out, they put on a white turban of great width over it.

In the second half of the nineteenth century, multicolored silk shawls with tassels imported from Russia came into fashion. Today, particularly in rural areas, women wear headgear according to their age; if young girls or women appear in public without headgear, they meet with great disapproval from the older generation. Girls do not necessarily wear a headdress at home, especially the daughter of the master of the house. If a young woman wears a headdress, it indicates that she is marriageable.

Women and girls also differed from one another in hairstyle. The former braided their hair into two or three plaits, whereas the girls had many thin braids, sometimes as many as thirty. Young women and girls adorned their braids with shells, metallic plates, pearls, and coins. Rich Kazakh women sported many silver adornments—rings, bracelets, earrings, breast pendants, and so on. Some of these adornments had a sacred significance. Thus, the arms of a woman were considered unclean if she wore no bracelets. As with men, an indispensible attribute of the female costume was a richly ornamented belt of beautiful fabric or even skin.

Many researchers note the influence of the Tatar outfit on both the Kazakh men's and women's attire and, from the mid-nineteenth century, of Russian-style clothing, especially in the cities. In the present, as was noted above, individual parts of the traditional Kazakh attire that serve as ethno-designative features have been preserved. The national costume has been retained to a great degree in rural areas and among the elderly population, especially by the women, as well as among those who most uphold the occupations of the traditional branches of the economy—shepherds, for example. In general, however, Kazakhs today wear clothes of urban cut and of factory manufacture.

Kinship

KIN GROUPS AND DESCENT. Rather close kin relations were preserved between persons counting back to the seventh generation. Men who were united by this kinship group were not allowed to select a wife from it. In other words, an exogamic clan up to the seventh generation existed among the Kazakhs. Several such clans constituted an even larger clan, which also had one common ancestor. In turn, these clans were united into even larger groupings, groups of which formed tribal unities, entering into three zhuz. The Kazakhs considered all these clans and tribes to have a common origin or forefather. Specialists maintain that although the ancestors of the exogamic clans were actual personages, those of the larger clans and tribes were legendary or fictitious. The oldest zhuz of the Kazakhs consisted of eleven large tribes, namely Dulat, Alban, Suan, Sary-Uysun, Srgeli, Ysty, Oshakty, Chaprashty, Canyshkly (Katagan), Kangly, and Zhalair. All these tribes in ancient times entered into a union of tribes, headed by an *usun*. In turn, each of these enumerated tribes consisted of several large clans. Thus, the Dulat tribe consisted of four clans: Botpay, Chmyr, Saikym, Zhamys. These also consisted of several clans. For example, the Botpay clan had four subclans: Xudaykul, Chagay, Bidas, and Kuralas; the Saikym clan had ten; the Chmyr clan, three; and the Zhamys clan, seven. Each of these subclans was divided into yet smaller groupings down to the exogamic clan and family-kin groups. Every Kazakh knew his own genealogy, at least to seven generations. Thus, the Kazkahs could always determine their kinship ties to one another. Large tribes of Kazakhs entered into the Middle Zhuz: Kipchaks, Argyns, Naimans, Kere, and Uaki. Three large tribes constituted the Younger Zhuz: Bayul, Alimul, and

Zetyru. Historical tales and legends associated with the origin of a given clan or tribe also exist. Every Kazakh clan and tribe had its own *tamgy*, a clan symbol, as well as a war cry, the *uran*.

The memory of membership in a given tribe or clan still persists among the Kazakhs, even down to the smallest grouping. The Kazakhs of the oldest generation know this particularly well. In connection with the growth of national self-awareness, the interest in one's past has awakened among the youths as well.

Kinship ties among the Kazakhs were traced along both the male and female lines. The children of the daughters or sisters of a woman were called *zhien* by her other relatives, whereas the latter were called *nagashi* by the former. In accordance with centuries-old traditions, the Kazakhs attempted not to offend their zhiens and not to refuse them anything, insofar as was possible. According to customary laws, the zhien could take any valuables from the relatives of the mother up to three times.

SETTLEMENTS

As of 1989, 16,528,000 people live in Kazakhstan, of which 57 percent are urban dwellers and 43 percent rural residents. The capital of the republic, Alma-Ata, was founded in 1854 and is situated at a height of 700-900 meters by the northern slopes of the Zailiiski Altai range; its population is 1,132,000. There are 82 cities and 132 urban-type settlements in Kazakhstan. The 17 provinces (oblasts) include 218 rural and 33 urban districts. In the cities Kasakhs live in large apartment buildings, paying monthly rent, as well as in houses of the rural type, which, in general, they own. In the rural settlements and *auls* of rural areas, Kasakhs live in houses of their own construction. A portion of rural dwellers use houses built for them on collective or state farms. At the present time, measures are being undertaken toward the privatization of all housing. A distinguishing feature of the Kazakhs living in rural areas is the retention of the traditional transportable dwelling—the yurt—in several regions of Kazakhstan (the Mangyshlak Peninsula, the areas around the Syr Darya, etc.), even up to the present. The yurt is a round, collapsible dwelling consisting of a wooden frame covered in felt. The basis of the frame is several sliding wooden lattices (*kerge*), which fold up when collapsed. The bigger these lattices are, the bigger are the yurts themselves. Long curved poles (*uuk*) are attached to these lattices from above, the sharp upper ends of which are put into a wooden hoop (*shangyrak*). Thus the roof of the yurt has a dome-shaped appearance. In one place between

the lattices Kazakhs fasten a wooden bi-valved door frame. A flap of felt on the hoop of the yurt's dome is tied back to form an opening for smoke from the hearth, which is traditionally positioned in the center of the yurt, slightly closer to the door. Today yurts are used mainly during the summer. They serve as dwellings chiefly for families of shepherds who set off with their herds for the summer pastures. Other rural inhabitants set up yurts near their homes in the summer.

The entire internal space of the yurt is strictly arranged according to tradition. Opposite the door by the wall is the *zhuk*, where trunks filled with household items are stacked; during the day the bedding is also piled up there. The place in front of the zhuk is considered the most honored (*tor*). The most esteemed guest occupies this spot and, in the event no guest is present, the master of the yurt does so. The floor of this area is covered with fleece carpets or even fur bedding over the usual felt. The woman's half of the yurt is located to the left of the tor, where she stores household tools and food supplies as well as the large skin bag (*saba*) for *kumys* (a beverage prepared from sour mare's milk). The bedding of the master and his wife is located nearer to the tor. The area to the right of the tor is considered the male half, where the horse harness, saddle, and the master's tools are found. Closer to the door is the place reserved for the younger members of the family, including sometimes even a married son. The door of the Kazakh yurt always faces south. Kazakhs still try to

preserve the traditional layout of the yurt's interior as much as possible.

Among the settled and semisettled Kazakhs (among the latter during their winter camp), permanent dwellings are found, differing according to the climatic conditions of the vast Kazakh homeland and depending on the influence of neighboring settled peoples. Thus, among the northern Kazakhs, a permanent dwelling in a yurtlike form was originally widespread, as is common among peoples of western Siberia. In the south and west of Kazakhstan, the ancient form of dwelling was the adobe cottage. In the middle of the nineteenth century, however, quadrangular buildings with flat roofs covered with earth and turf appeared. As a rule, these were built without a foundation and had an earthen floor, which was covered with felt and carpets. They utilized turf, adobe bricks, wood, and stone as building materials.

Today the rural dwelling of the Kazakhs is a rather large accommodation with several rooms. Usually there is a room for the elderly, in which they maintain the traditions particularly strongly. There is also a guest room with modern furnishings. The kitchen is set off separately. Even now, however, the whole life of a family is spent in a single room, especially during the winter. Many rural homes have their own steam heating.

Despite the predominance of a nomadic or seminomadic life-style among the Kazakhs, they did construct a large number of "cult" monuments—funerary buildings (see "Death and Afterlife").

KINSHIP TERMINOLOGY. Kazakh kinship terminology shared many features with that of other Turkic peoples of Central Asia, such as differentiation of age within generations, recognition of many degrees of lineal and collateral agnates, and recognition of maternal as well as paternal lines. Consonant with their penchant for calculating kinship, Kazakhs had numerous terms designating consanguinity and affinity.

Marriage and Family

MARRIAGE. A variety of forms of marriage existed among the Kazakhs. The most widespread was marriage via matchmaking and purchase of the bride for a *kalyn* (bride-price). For an individual to enter into marriage, the observance of certain restrictions tied to the exogamic norms—social, national, and sometimes that of the clan/tribal denomination—were required. The exogamous barrier generally was in effect up to the seventh generation. The Kazakhs still uphold this restriction. Traditionally, those who violated the exogamic barrier were severely punished, to the point of expulsion from the clan and even death. In social relations, the parents tried as much as possible to become related to families of standing equal to themselves. Historically, in Kazakh marriages ethnicity and religious factors held great significance. Marriages of mixed ethnicity were encountered, however, especially between Kazakh men and Turkic-speaking women who followed Islam. Less frequently did the Kazakhs take wives from among followers of other faiths. According to Sharia (Islamic law), Muslims could marry nonbelievers only if the latter publicly renounced their faith and adopted Islam. Marriage of Kazakh women to nonbelievers was strictly forbidden. Even in the present, such restrictions generally continue to operate among the Kazakhs.

One form of arranged marriage was the so-called cradle-betrothal, in which the fathers of the future bride and groom negotiated their marriage immediately following the birth of the children.

One of the most ancient forms of marriage among the Kazakhs was abduction, in which, under certain circumstances, the young man abducted his future wife either with her agreement or without it.

As a rule, patrilocal marriage predominated among the Kazakhs. There were instances, however, in which the groom went to live among the relatives of the bride, usually when the daughter was the only child in the family.

Levirate (*emengerlik*) and sororate (*baldyz alu*) exist among the Kazakhs. In accord with the custom of levirate, after the death of her husband, the widow, together with the children and all the property of the deceased, is inherited by his brother (i.e., she becomes his wife). If the wife or a betrothed bride died, the widower husband/groom, according to the custom of sororate, had the right to marry the younger sister of the deceased. Although this custom was not as strongly observed as levirate, individual instances persist in the present day.

There are also remnants of ancient variants of "cousin marriages" among the Kazakhs. The so-called cross-cousin marriage is one in which a man married the daughter of his mother's brother or his father's sister. The "orthocousin" marriage was one in which a man married the daughter of his father's brother or of his mother's sister. The latter, of course, would have been a violation of the exogamic norms and therefore was not encountered among the Kazakhs; marriage between children of sisters, however, was frequently encountered, as the exogamy was observed only along the male line.

A necessary condition of Kazakh nuptials was the custom of recompense payment, the kalyn, from the groom's family to the father of the bride. In general, the bride-price consisted of livestock. In response to the bride-price, the bride brought a rich dowry to the home of her intended, which by tradition obligatorily included a yurt.

In accord with custom, Kazakhs could have several wives; Islamic doctrine permitted up to four wives. Kazakhs turned to polygamy, however, only when the first wife was barren; if there were no male heir; by virtue of the tradition of levirate; or because of the inability of the first wife to lead the domestic household, owing to illness, for example. A rich man could have several wives in order to increase the number of his descendants, have sufficient labor resources available, and other reasons. According to custom, the husband had to care completely for all his wives and children.

The senior wife in the house (*baybishe*) occupied a special position with respect to the second and third wives (*tokal*). This often led to strained relations among them and their children. Therefore the Kazakhs tried to separate them into individual households or even auls, insofar as possible.

The wedding ceremonies began with the matchmaking, at which the size of the bride-price and the order of its payments were agreed upon. From this moment on the preparation of the dowry was set into motion in the bride's home. As a rule, the parents carried out the selection of the bride, since frequently the bride and groom did not know each other. Only after payment of part of the bride-price could the groom "secretly" visit the bride.

After the payment of the kalyn, the wedding day (*toy*) was designated. Usually the groom first came to the bride's aul, where the wedding ceremony took place with the aid of a mullah. This was followed by festivities at which various ceremonial songs were sung and everyone was treated to kumys.

The bride departed from her own aul and set off for the groom's home accompanied by the groom and numerous relatives. When the bride approached the groom's home, she covered her face. Entering the house, she greeted the fire at the hearth. Those who gathered for the celebration, generally the groom's relatives, sang songs called *bet ashar* (uncovering the face). They also sang songs in which the obligations of the young wife were enumerated. Then one of the groom's young relatives raised the veil slightly from the bride's face with a small stick. At this time, those who gathered counted the gifts for the bride-inspection (*smotriny*).

In the wedding celebrations of the Kazakhs, many ceremonies bear a religio-magical character, for example the showering of the newlyweds with sweets and the "uniting" ceremonies—the drinking of water by the bride and groom from one cup, for instance.

The ceremonies associated with the wedding are generally preserved today, but sometimes, especially in the cities, so-called youth weddings are organized. At these the acquaintances and relatives simply gather with the bride and groom around a common table, and lavish refreshments are presented. In recent years, however, there has been a tendency toward returning to traditional wedding ceremonies.

Still rather widespread, especially in rural areas, is marriage through abduction. This is today only an imitation of abduction, however, since the girl, as a rule, willingly goes to the groom's home "surreptitiously." In such instances, the wedding is arranged immediately. The groom's parents ask forgiveness from the bride's parents, who give it. After the wedding the bride's dowry is brought.

Among the Kazakhs a young wife must behave very modestly; she does not have the right, especially at first, to call her husband's relatives by name, especially the older ones, or show them her face; she must make way for them, let them pass by, and do other acts of obeisance. These taboos, for the most part, are kept even today, just as the survival of clan exogamy up to the seventh generation continues.

DOMESTIC UNIT. Among nomadic Kazakhs the small, individual family predominated, consisting, as a rule, of a married couple, their unmarried children, and elderly parents. In accordance with custom, the oldest son was able to marry first, followed by the other sons in descending order of age. The father allotted livestock (*enshi*) to the married son and in this way created a new household (*otay*). According to the ancient customs of the *minorat*, the youngest son was not allotted a household, even after marriage. He remained the heir to the ancestral hearth. Among the seminomadic and settled Kazakhs, there were extended families in which several closely related families lived in one household. Usually this was the family of the head of the household, as well as his married sons, and, after his death, the families of his married brothers. As a rule, however, after the death of the household master, the married brothers parted company. The daughters went to live with the families of their husbands after marriage.

Elements of patriarchal relations were preserved in certain ways, however. Married sons, even when they had their own individual households, did not break ties with the paternal household completely. Many labor-intensive tasks, such as pasturing of livestock, shearing of sheep, preparation of felt, and so on, were accomplished through the efforts of several households with close relations along paternal lines. This was especially important in defending livestock and pastures from the encroachment of others. Such a unification of families, the basis of kinship ties, is called in the literature a "family-kin" group. In Kazakh, these groupings are called *bir ata baralary* (children of one father). If a family-kin group was called Koshenbaralary, for example, then their ancestor was called Koshen, and the families of this group had heads who were grandsons and great-grandsons of Koshen. Among the Kazakhs, such family-kin groups formed communities. The heads of families were considered close relatives up to the fourth or fifth generation.

SOCIALIZATION. The Kazakhs attach great significance to the birth and raising of children. A Kazakh family is not considered happy without children, especially sons—the continuers of the clan. There are many customs and ceremonies associated with birth and raising of children. These customs arose from centuries of experiences and from the Kazakh worldview. Thus, they protected a pregnant woman from the evil eye with the aid of amulets and did not allow her to leave the house alone at night; weapons, wolves' teeth, eagles' bills, and owl talons were forbidden wherever she lived. All this was necessary to protect her from impure forces. The pregnant woman herself had to observe a multitude of taboos. In order not to tangle the child's umbilical cord, for example, she could not step over the staff for raising the dome of the yurt (*bakan*), the device for catching horses (*kuruk*), rope (*arkan*), and many other items. She was also forbidden to eat camel meat because it was thought that, were she to do so, she would carry her child for twelve months, like a she-camel. Kazakhs protect pregnant women from heavy labor, especially in the later months.

Kazakhs carefully guard the woman and child during the actual birth and the first forty days thereafter, which are regarded as especially dangerous for the baby. Various rituals are followed—placing the child in the cradle on the seventh day, for example. The fortieth day after birth is seen as especially festive because the danger is deemed to have passed. Only women gather at this celebration.

Kazakhs accustom children to work from an early age. They teach a boy to ride a horse at age 3 and to tend it and other livestock at age 5 or 6. The shaving ceremony, strongly upheld in modern times, is conducted when a boy has reached age 3 to 10. Girls are taught to sew, embroider, and carry out other household activities. In the past, Kazakhs believed that at age 13 to 15 they were ready for independent life and could have their own family; at present girls marry at age 16 to 18.

Religion and Expressive Culture

RELIGIOUS BELIEFS AND PRACTICES. The Kazakhs are Sunni Muslims. Islam began to appear in southern Kazakhstan in the eighth to ninth centuries, after the Arab conquest of Central Asia. After the foundation of the Kazakh khanate in the fifteenth century, Islam became the predominant religion among the Kazakh people. Its influence was especially strengthened after the Russian colonization of the Kazakhs in the eighteenth to nineteenth centuries because the czarist government attempted to solidify its position in Kazakhstan through Islam. During this period many mosques were constructed and *madrasahs* (Islamic secondary schools) opened. Pre-Islamic beliefs—the cults of the sky, of the ancestors, and of fire, for example—continued to a great extent to be preserved among the common people, however. The Kazakhs believed in the supernatural forces of good and evil spirits, of wood goblins and giants. To protect themselves from them, as well as from the evil eye, the Kazakhs wore protection beads and talismans. Shamanic beliefs were widely preserved among the Kazakhs, as well as belief in the strength of the bearers of this cult—the shamans, which the Kazakhs call *bakhsy*. In contradistinction to the Siberian shamans, who used drums during their rituals, the Kazakh shamans, who could also be men or women, played (with a bow) on a stringed instrument similar to a large violin.

At present both Islamic and pre-Islamic beliefs continue to be found among the Kazakhs, especially among the elderly. Following the severe Soviet persecutions, in which the mullahs were annihilated, there are few today who have received special religious training. For this reason, literate elderly people who know the prayers fulfill the role of mullahs in rural areas. Quite frequently these are school teachers on pension or other people with higher education.

DEATH AND AFTERLIFE. The Kazakhs observe funerary rites that are a mixture of Muslim customs with pre-Islamic beliefs. Mainly the relatives and neighbors of the deceased take part in the funeral ceremonies; they place the deceased, washed and wrapped in a white shroud, into a separate yurt specially put up for this event and do not leave him or her unattended for a single minute until the burial. Those who gather for the funeral pray under the guidance of a mullah. The women bemoan the deceased. The mourners bring the deceased to the cemetery on special stretchers; after further prayers, they lower the body into the grave and bury it. Among the Kazakhs, as among many other Eastern peoples, women are not allowed at the cemetery. After interment, ablutions are enacted at home and the clothing of the deceased is distributed to funeral participants; refreshments are prepared for all. Near the yurt of the deceased they set up a spear with a mourning flag, which is red if the deceased was a young person, black if middle-aged, and white if elderly. They do not remove this spear throughout the entire period of mourning—that is, the whole year. Funeral banquets for the deceased are held on the third, seventh, and fortieth days. Kazakhs observe the first anniversary funerary feast especially solemnly, with as many people as possible coming together. For this day, they slaughter the favorite horse of the deceased, whose mane and tail they had shaved on the day of its master's death. They also slaughter a good deal of other livestock for the feast.

This anniversary funeral banquet is celebrated quite ceremonially; many people gather—representatives come from various tribes and clans, sometimes several hundred people. For this reason, they set up many additional yurts and organize equestrian races, the victors receiving rich prizes. At present the Kazakhs are attempting to preserve all customs and ceremonies associated with the funerary rites.

The Kazakhs set up domed monuments on the graves, frequently mausoleums of stone, adobe bricks, and clay. The simpler grave constructs are clay or brick fences in a rectangular shape, or sometimes simply a pile of stones with a pole to which they attach bundles of horse hair. They also make sacrifices at the graves, laying bones of animals on them.

ARTS. Oral folk art is widely developed among the Kazakhs: songs, epic tales, folktales, heroic epics, and so forth. The Kazakhs greatly value their performers: the storytellers (*zhyrsy*) and improvisational poets (*akyn*). Several of these achieved great popularity, including Bukharzhyrau Kalmakanov (1693–1787) and the improvisational poet Makhambet Utemisov (1803–1846), who along with his friend Isatay Taymanov led the Kazakh uprising in the Bukeevsky Horde in 1836–1837.

The work of the eminent Kazakh educator and scholar Chokan Valikhanov (1835–1865), who painstakingly gathered and attentively studied the national poetic works of the Kazakhs, had great significance for the development of Kazakh literature. Kazakh written literature took shape under the influence of Russian literature in the second half of the nineteenth century. The renowned pedagogue Ibray Altynsarin (1841–1889) made a great contribution to the development of Kazakh literature as well. He created the first Kazakh chrestomathy for Russian/Kazakh schools and published his own works, those assembled by him from the national oral literature, and translations from Russian. Abay Kunabaev (1845–1904) was also a prominent figure of the Kazakh literary movement. From the beginning of the twentieth century a plethora of Kazakh poets and writers has produced works in Kazakhstan. Among them are the giants of Kazakh literature Mokhtar Auezov (1897–1961), Saken Seyfullin (1894–1939), Beymbet Maylin (1894–1939), and others. The modern Kazakh writers are successfully continuing the traditions of Kazakh national art and of the founders of Kazakh literature.

The folk music traditions are an inseparable part of the spiritual culture of the Kazakh people: the songs, the vocal accompaniment of the professional improvisational poets, the instrumental works, and so on. Popular musical instruments include the *dombra*, a "plucked" string instrument, and the *kobyz*—an instrument played with a bow. The favorite wind instrument is the *sybyzgy*, in the shape of an elongated flute; as for percussion instruments, the *dauylpaz*, a small drum, is favored. Since the second half of the nineteenth century, new musical instruments have appeared: the accordion and the violin. In the twentieth century professional musical arts have arisen and developed greatly among the Kazakhs. In 1934 the first musical performance took place, and in 1935 the Kazakh State Philharmonic opened. In 1937 the Abay State Academic Theater of opera and ballet opened.

Formerly there were no professional theatrical arts among the Kazakhs. Only in the beginning of the twentieth century and during the years of Soviet dominance did amateur forms of Kazakh theater begin to grow. The first Kazakh theater opened in 1926 in Orenburg (at that time the capital of the Kazakh Republic). At present, Kazakh drama and theatrical arts, as well as the national cinema, have achieved a great deal of success in a short period of time.

Until recently the decorative arts of the Kazakhs have focused mainly on the details of Kazakh dwellings, clothing, and other everyday objects. One can find original Kazakh ornamentation on teased and unteased carpets, strips, the yurt, and felt coverings. Kazakh women decorate their clothes and embroider.

Woodworking, leatherwork, and metalwork have occupied places of distinction within the Kazakh national arts, but a professional decorative arts industry developed only in the twentieth century. Moreover, the first professional artists in Kazakhstan were Russians. The openings of the Kazakh State Artists Gallery in 1935 and the Artistic-Theatrical Gallery in 1938 played a large role in the development of art in Kazakhstan. The communications media have greatly expanded, including print, radio, and, in recent times, television.

Academics have developed intensively in the course of the twentieth century; this includes the study of a variety of disciplines from mathematics and mechanics to various social sciences. In Kazakhstan today there are hundreds of scientific institutions where tens of thousands of scholars work. There is also a Kazakh Academy of Science.

Oral folk art, like songs, epic tales, folktales and heroic epics, are widely developed among the Kazakhs.

Bibliography

Grodekov, N. I. (1889). *Kirgizy i Karakirgizy Syr-Dar'inskoi Oblasti* (The Kazakhs and Kirgiz of the Syr Darya Region). Tashkent: Typolithography of S. I. Lakhtin.

Hudson, Alfred E. (1938). *Kazak Social Structure*, 1–109. Yale University Publications in Anthropology, no. 20. New Haven: Yale University Press.

Konovalov, Aleksei V. (1986). *Kazakhi i Iuzhnogo Altaia problemy formirovaniia etnichesko i gruppy* (Problems in the ethnic and group formation of the Kazakhs and Southern Altai). Alma-Alta: Izdvo Nauka Kazakhskoi SSR.

Murdock, George P. (1934). "The Kazakhs of Central Asia." In *Our Primitive Contemporaries*, 135–153. New York: Macmillan.

Vostrov, Veniamin V., and I. V. Zakharova (1989). *Kazakhskoe Narodnoe Zhilishche* (Dwellings of the Kazakh people). Alma-Alta: Nauka Kazakhskoi SSR.

—VADIM P. KURYLĔV
(TRANSLATED BY PAUL FRIEDRICH AND
GREGORY S. ANDERSON)

KYRGYZ

Ethnonyms: Kik-Kun, Kirghiz, Kirgiz

Orientation

IDENTIFICATION. The Kyrgyz are a Turkic-Mongol people who live primarily in the mountainous regions of Central Asia, where their traditional livelihood was that of pastoral nomadism. The ethnonym "Kyrgyz" is derived from the Turkic *kyrk + yz*, "the forty clans," reflecting their patrilineal clan kinship system. In early twentieth-century texts, the term "Kyrgyz" was also used in reference to the Kazakhs, a group with quite similar ethnic characteristics.

LOCATION. The majority of the modern Kyrgyz (about 2 million) live in Kyrgyzstan (the former Soviet republic of Kirghizia), located in the southeastern part of the Tianshan range and the northwestern area of the Pamir-Altai Mountains. These two mountain ranges separate the north and south of Kyrgyzstan not only geographically but also in terms of their economic, religious, and political orientations. Well-adapted to living in the higher elevations, some Kyrgyz fled to Afghanistan, Pakistan, and eastern China during various land disputes among the Russians, Chinese, and Afghans over the regulation of pasturage. More so than their Soviet counterparts, the Kyrgyz diaspora still practices nomadic pas-

toralism. Kyrgyzstan is a landlocked country in the center of Asia—with China bordering on the east, Kazakhstan on the north, Uzbekistan on the west, and Tajikistan on the south and southwest. Occupying 198,500 square kilometers, Kyrgyzstan is situated at elevations between 1,000 meters and 7,400 meters with only about 7 percent of its land being desert, steppe, and arable river valleys. Located between 39° and 43° N, Kyrgyzstan has a harsh continental climate with temperatures as low as −23° C and as high as 41° C. More than 600 glaciers cover 6,578 square kilometers of the country. Lakes and rivers abound in this part of Central Asia, including one of the largest lakes in the world, Lake Issyk Kul. This unique saltwater lake—at an elevation of 1,500 meters—covers about 6,000 square kilometers, has a maximum depth of nearly 700 meters, and is geothermally heated. Sometimes referred to as the "little Switzerland of Central Asia," Kyrgyzstan, with its exceptionally high mountain ranges and intense seismic activity, is a major site for the study of the geology of Central Asia.

DEMOGRAPHY. Kyrgyzstan's population of 4.5 million is 52.4 percent Kyrgyz. Other major ethnic groups living there include Russians, Uzbeks, Ukrainians, Germans, Tatars, Dungans, Kazakhs, Uighur, and Tajiks. Since Kyrgyzstan's independence in 1991, there has been a large exodus of Russians, Germans, Ukrainians, and Jews who are migrating to other parts of the Commonwealth of Independent States, Germany, and Israel. In 1989 Kirghizia had the third-highest rate of reported abortions (86 percent of women reporting at least one abortion) of the Soviet republics, with Russia and the Ukraine first and second. Prior to 1990 Kirghizia had one of the lowest rates of emigration in the Soviet Union. Approximately 83% of the population of Kyrgyzstan live in the rural regions around Lake Issyk Kul, the Fergana Valley, Naryn River valley, and the low-lying areas of the Tianshan and the Pamir-Altai Mountains. The other 17 percent live in Biskek, the capital city, or Osh, which is on the former Silk Road and is one of the oldest cities of Central Asia.

LINGUISTIC AFFILIATION. The Kyrgyz language belongs to the Northwestern (Kipchak) Division of the Turkic Branch of the Altaic Language Family. It is closely related to Kazakh, Nogay, Tatar, Kipchak-Uzbek, and Karakalpak and should not be confused with Yenisei Kyrgyz. Kyrgyz was not a written language until the late nineteenth century. Before that, "Turki," a written form of Uzbek, was the script in use. At the turn of the century, Kyrgyz was first written using the Arabic alphabet, and in 1924, the Arabic alphabet was modified for writing Kyrgyz. In 1928 Arabic was dropped and the Latin alphabet substituted. In 1940, under Soviet influence, the Kyrgyz adopted the Cyrillic alphabet.

The official language recognized by the 1993 constitution of Kyrgyzstan is Kyrgyz. Although all urban dwellers know Russian because it was the language of instruction in the Soviet educational system, the rural population has maintained Kyrgyz as the primary language. Recently, the five Central Asian nations of Azerbaijan, Turkmenistan, Uzbekistan, Kazakhstan, and Kyrgyzstan have all agreed to adopt the Latin alphabet by 1995 in order to smooth trade and increase affiliation among themselves.

History and Cultural Relations

Archaeological remains indicate that Kyrgyzstan was first inhabited by humans about 300,000 years ago, during the Lower Paleolithic period. Stone implements and stone quarries of the Middle Paleolithic period have been located in several primitive sites. Settlements from the Neolithic period have been found in caves near the city of Naryn and also on the northern shore of Lake Issyk Kul. Archaeologists infer from the burial sites and settlements that during the Bronze Age both agricultural and pastoral groups inhabitated the valley regions in what is now Kyrgyzstan. By the fifth century B.C., iron tools and weapons were in use, indicating that the economy had shifted more toward nomadic herding. The Scythians' domestication of the horse (1000 B.C. to A.D. 900) made Kyrgyzstan an important transcontinental trade route. Later in the Middle Ages, Kyrgyzstan was one of the several routes for the Silk Road through the Tianshan and the Pamir-Altai Mountains. Religious artifacts of the Zoroastrians, Buddhists, early Christians, and Muslims, who transversed these well-traveled mountain valleys, are found at Burana Tower outside of Tokmak. This strategic garrison of early tribes was one of the few sites not destroyed by the Mongol conqueror Chinggis (Genghis) Khan (eleventh century) on his many warring expeditions to the western parts of Central Asia and eastern Europe.

The nomadic history of the Kyrgyz is more difficult to trace. The modern history of the Kyrgyz is currently undergoing revision, as Soviet-period accounts were formulated to support Marxist ideals. The Kyrgyz were not originally from the area that is now Kyrgyzstan. Most frequently, their cultural origin is traced to the region around the Yenisei River in southern Siberia. Similar cultural elements, including the practice of animism, certain burial customs, and animal husbandry suggest common roots with other nomadic peoples of Siberia. The existence of a Kyrgyz people is believed to date to at least 200 B.C. In the eighth century A.D. they were mentioned in the Orkhan inscriptions. In 840 the Kyrgyz tribes defeated the Uighur tribes and inhabited their lands in what is now northwestern Mongolia. The Kyrgyz were themselves dispossessed of these lands by the Khitai in the tenth century.

Most historians specify the sixteenth century as the time when the Kyrgyz tribe migrated in large numbers into the area now known as Kyrgyzstan. The tribal history of Central Asia is marked by continuous upheavals between warring tribes. Throughout the last millennium, the Kyrgyz tribes utilized vast areas of land from the eastern shores of the Aral Sea to the western border of China for herding their sheep and horses. In southern Kyrgyzstan, caravans of traders moved along the Silk Road, bringing silk and spices to the West. Bennigsen and Wimbush (1986) have argued that because of the relative geographic isolation of Kyrgyzstan, the Kyrgyz have been less influenced by the pan-Turkic and pan-Islamic ideologies that are especially deep-rooted in Uzbekistan. It is nevertheless important to realize that the Tianshan range divides the southern Kyrgyz from the northern Kyrgyz, who have maintained a seminomadic economic existence much longer than those in the south and have been less influenced by Islam. Southern Kyrgyzstan historically has had a sedentary, agricultural economic base, with the Fergana Valley as its center, a region the Kyrgyz share with the Uzbeks and Tajiks. The southern city of Osh is where Islam took hold in the Middle Ages.

In the early nineteenth century the Kyrgyz were defeated by the Uzbeks in 1845, 1857, 1858, and 1873. These intertribal conflicts were among the factors that led the Kyrgyz to ally themselves with the Russians in the mid-nineteenth century. As the Russians colonized the Kyrgyz and surrounding ethnic groups, they also confiscated the better agricultural lands. Competition for lands for farming and herding, along with compulsory service in the Russian army, resulted in a revolt by the Kyrgyz in 1916. They were disastrously defeated by the Russians, who burned villages and killed many Kyrgyz. Thereafter, about one-third of the Kyrgyz fled to eastern Turkistan (the western region of China). The Kyrgyz continued their

The traditional nomadic lifestyle made the Kyrgyz self-sufficient. They were isolated by mountains, which made trade less viable.

resistance to the Russians even after the 1917 Revolution, but eventually, in 1924, the new Soviet regime established Kirghizia (the Russified name of Kyrgyzstan) as an oblast within the Russian Soviet Federated Socialist Republic (RSFSR), and in 1926 it was declared a Soviet autonomous republic.

During Stalin's collectivization of 1927–1928, Kyrgyz pastoralists were forcibly settled on collective and state farms; many responded by slaughtering their livestock and moving to Xinjiang, China. Between 1926 and 1959 the Soviets moved many Russians and Ukrainians into the republic, and for a time the Kyrgyz were in the minority. Kirghizia joined the USSR as a Union republic in 1936. The capital, Bishkek, was called Pishpek until 1925 and Frunze from 1925–1991. Kyrgyzstan declared itself independent on 31 August 1991, joined with ten other former Soviet republics in the Commonwealth of Independent States on 21 December 1991, and achieved complete independence with the dissolution of the USSR on 25 December 1991.

Settlements

Until recent decades, the Kyrgyz were nomadic, as they needed to move their livestock from one grazing area to another. The Soviet government has both encouraged and forced settlement, first into *kyshtaks*, villages intended to be transitional, and then into permanent Soviet-style settlements in cities and towns and on collective and state farms. Many kyshtaks remain, however, and not all Kyrgyz have been settled. Most Kyrgyz living on kolkhozy and sovkhozy were only partially settled.

Economy

SUBSISTENCE AND COMMERCIAL ACTIVITIES. The Kyrgyz have long been transhumant nomadic pastoralists who raise primarily sheep, but also horses, goats, cattle, Bactrian camels, and yaks; in some areas swine are important. Horses provide not only transportation, but also meat and milk, the latter of which is fermented to make *koumiss.*

In the warm months the higher meadows are grazed, and in the colder months the people and their animals move to lower elevations. Transhumant pastoralism has survived under the Soviets because it is the most efficient way to raise livestock, given the ecological conditions. During the 1960s Khrushchev acknowledged the importance of nomadic pastoralism and launched an economic plan that included the production of fac-

tory-made yurts, the traditional dome-shaped tents of Central Asian nomads.

Under the Soviets, the previously self-sufficient Kyrgyz families became enmeshed in the Soviet imperial economy. Their production efforts were collectivized and controlled by the central Communist party in Moscow, and the products they made went to other republics and to foreign markets. The Kyrgyz also became dependent on foreign manufactured goods, especially medical supplies, which they do not manufacture themselves and which, over the last several years, they have been unable to afford.

INDUSTRIAL ARTS. The Soviets introduced a great complex of industries, including food processing, oil drilling, coal and gas mining, lumbering and woodworking, textiles, leatherworking, sugar refining, agricultural and electrical machinery production, and various others. Two industries have been especially well developed in Kyrgyzstan: hydroelectric power and the extraction and processing of nonferrous metals, notably mercury, antimony, zinc, tungsten, and uranium. Kyrgyz agricultural products include wheat, cotton, maize, grapes, sugar beets, poppies, hemp, potatoes, fruits, nuts, tobacco, wool, silk, and sheep.

TRADE. The traditional nomadic life-style made the Kyrgyz self-sufficient. They were isolated by mountains, which made trade less viable. Under Soviet rule the Kyrgyz became enmeshed within the great Soviet interdependent trade network as producers and consumers.

DIVISION OF LABOR. The traditional division of labor in the Kyrgyz nomadic pastoralist household was unique among Central Asian groups. It was often noted in historical records that Kyrgyz women were less conservative in behavior and dress than were other Muslim women of Central Asia. The transhumant life-style required that both men and women operate independently of one another; thus, both sexes rode horses and knew how to hunt and prepare food. Women were principally in charge of putting up and striking the large yurt, caring for all domestic animals used as food sources, and shearing sheep for wool to construct felted rugs (*shurdak*). Both men and women herded nondomestic animals as well. Although tribal organization of the clan system included a de facto male army to protect pasturelands, there are legends of Kyrgyz women warriors. Three prominent historical women were very popular among the Kyrgyz: Konikey, the powerful wife of the legendary figure Manas; Kurmanjon Datka, the Kyrgyz leader who signed

♦ **oblast**
Province, an administrative division of a Union republic. In the former Soviet Union there were 121 oblasts, some of which contained autonomous areas.

♦ **Union republic**
Soviet socialist republic of the former Soviet Union.

the original treaty between the Kyrgyz and the Russians in the late nineteenth century; and Jongil Misar, the female warrior who conquered khans in the sixteenth century. These Kyrgyz women, despite Islamic ideals, are all perceived as self-sufficient, powerful, and wise advisers to their people.

After the 1917 Revolution, the collectivization of farms and pastures changed the division-of-labor strategy. Women were relegated to the more traditional roles of dairy work and textile manufacture. With an increase in literacy, both men and women had the opportunity to train in specialized fields. Although Soviet socialist policy was to treat women and men as equals in all arenas, economic demands more than ideological guidelines set out by Marx and Engels have historically influenced Soviet women's involvement in the work force. Not until *perestroika* were questions raised about the economic and social welfare of women rather than the economic welfare of the state.

LAND TENURE. Each family traditionally had its own pasturage, which it defended from use by others. This continued under the Soviets, although it was then each brigade that guarded its own interests. The Soviets exerted rather rigid control over production, including land use, and so reduced the expression of tensions between groups over land use. Since independence, Kyr-gyzstan has embarked on a privatization program in which people are given coupons with which they may purchase state property; preference has been given to the employees of each business concern.

Kinship

KIN GROUPS AND DESCENT. Kyrgyz society is organized on agnatic descent principles. The basic, and in some respects, most important social group is the *oey*, or patrilineally extended family. The oey includes a man, a wife or wives, all sons and unmarried daughters, and the wives and offspring of the married sons. All of these people typically live together in a single yurt. Several oeys, all sixth- or seventh-generation descendants of the same apical male ancestor, belong to a *kechek oruq* (patrilineage) which is also conceptualized as a large exogamous patrilineally extended family known as *bir atanyng baldary*, or "children of the same father." Members of this group often live together in one camp and assist each other in trade, herding, migration, and religious activities. Above this level, Kyrgyz are organized by *chung oruq* (clan) and *orow* (tribe). Kyrgyz place great emphasis on being able to trace their patrilineal ancestors seven ascending generations, in order to prove membership in an oruq. In earlier times, those who could not prove oruq membership in this fashion were made slaves (*qul*).

KYRGYZ SHEPHERDS

Transhumant pastoralism survived under the Soviets because it is the most efficient way to raise livestock, given the ecological conditions of the region. Kyrgyzstan. (William James McDonald/Corbis)

There is a distinction between the religious practices of Islam and the everyday cultural practices of Islam.

Marriage and Family

MARRIAGE. The traditional Kyrgyz marriage was arranged by parents and extended family members. Young adults often courted, however, and their wishes frequently influenced or determined the choice of mate. In the past, marriage was often highly endogamous for clans and lineages in areas in which the hated Uzbeks, Uighur, and Tajiks were predominant. Only marriages to other Kyrgyz or Kazakhs were acceptable, and children of marriages between Kyrgyz and people of other ethnic groups were often assigned low-status positions in the clan.

Traditional marriage practices in the rural regions maintain pre-Soviet sentiments and have been little affected by Soviet domination, although couples undertake both civil and traditional marriage rituals. Patrilocality remains the norm, and the groom's family in some instances pays a modified form of bride-price. Under the Soviet system, bride-price payments were illegal; the Kyrgyz simply substituted "gifts."

DOMESTIC UNIT. The basic residential unit is the oey, or patrilineal extended family, which traditonally shared a yurt.

INHERITANCE. Under Islamic law men own property, and a man's sons inherit his property. Under Hanafi law, however, which pertains to the Kyrgyz, women may also own property and may inherit their husband's property, although only one-half of the amount inherited by his sons.

SOCIALIZATION. Prior to the 1917 Revolution, the Kyrgyz were primarily illiterate. The institutionalization of Soviet education throughout the rural and urban areas of Kirghizia in the 1920s and 1930s rapidly brought literacy to the country.

Sociopolitical Organization

SOCIAL ORGANIZATION. Kinship and descent principles play the preeminent role in social organization. Kinship may be real or fictive; fictive kin include milk kin, people who were nursed by the same woman and are forbidden to marry each other. Differences in wealth were traditionally relatively small. The wealthy are expected to assist poorer kin materially.

POLITICAL ORGANIZATION. Politics within the Kyrgyz ethnic group follows tribal lines. Each tribe, which is made up of clans, belongs to one of two large federations. The larger of the two federations, Otuz Uul (thirty sons) has two *kanats* (wings). The right wing (Ong Kanat) of the Otuz Uul is located in northern, western, and southern Kyrgyzstan. One of its member tribes is the Tagay, who are the political and intellectual leaders of the Kyrgyz people. The Tagay have thirteen clans. Other tribes within the right wing are the Adigine and the Mungush. The left wing of the Otuz Uul has eight clans. The other federation is the Ich Kilik, which is composed of ten major and several minor tribes. The tribes of the Ich Kilik live in the southern Ferghana Valley in southern Kyrgyzstan and in Tajikistan. Some of the left wing and Ich Kilik tribes are of Mongol origin.

The qualities traditionally necessary for leadership, which was a male role, are: possession of good character, observance of Islamic laws, courage in battle, success as a herdsman, wealth, membership in a large lineage, and a good oratorical ability.

In Soviet times, members of each kolkhoz belonged to the same clan, and local Communist party organizations were composed of people belonging to the same clan or tribe. Soviet political and economic structures simply incorporated indigenous social structure unchanged.

Since independence in 1991, Kyrgyzstan has become a constitutional republic, with an elected president who acts as head of state. In April 1993 the first Kyrgyz constitution was ratified by the parliament.

SOCIAL CONTROL. Within the oey, the head of the household exercises authority. Beyond the oey, but also governing its members' behavior, is the authority of Islamic law and Islamic courts, which is similar to that found in other Muslim areas.

Religion and Expressive Culture

RELIGIOUS BELIEFS. The Kyrgyz are Sunni Muslims of the Hanafi school of law, but the degree to which the north and south adhere to religious practices must be considered when understanding the role of Islam in Kyrgyzstan. The distinction is often made between the religious practices of Islam and the everyday cultural practices of Islam. Islamic mosques and *madrassah* were built by the sixteenth century in the southern regions of Kyrgyzstan. One of the most important holy places for Muslims in Kyrgyzstan is the Throne of Suleyman in the southern city of Osh. It is sometimes referred to by Soviet Muslims as the "second Mecca." By contrast, Islam infiltrated northern Kyrgyzstan in a slower, less encompassing manner. Many ancient indigenous beliefs and practices, including shamanism and totemism, coexisted syncretically with Islam. Shamans, most of whom are women, still play a prominent role at funerals, memorials, and other ceremonies and rituals. This split between the northern and southern Kyrgyz in their religious adherence to Muslim practices can still be seen today. Likewise, the Sufi order of Islam has been one of the most active Muslim groups in Kyrgyzstan for over a century.

The Sufi orders represent a somewhat different form of Islam than the orthodox Islam, and their adepts are generally more extreme in their views and in their intolerance of non-Muslims. The four Sufi *tariqas* (paths to God, or Sufi brotherhoods) that brought Islam to the Kyrgyz and remain in Kyrgyzstan are: the Naqshbandiya, which is Bukharan and very popular and powerful; the Qadiriya, an ancient tariqa; the Yasawiya, a south Kazakhstan tariqa; and the Kubrawiya, a Khorezm tariqa. In addition, there are two newer indigenous orders that sprang from the Yasawiya. The earlier of the two is the Order of Lachi, which formed in the late nineteenth century. It opposed the older orders and was oppressed by them in return. As a result of this enmity, the Lachi initially supported the Bolsheviks but later came to oppose them. The Lachi went underground, and the Soviets could not find them again until the 1950s. Several villages in the Osh Oblast are composed entirely of Lachi members. Another indigenous Sufi order is the Order of the Hairy Ishans, which formed in the 1920s and was intensely anti-Soviet. As a result of its opposition, the Soviets attacked them in 1935–1936 and again in 1952–1953, killing some of their leaders. The Hairy Ishan order, unlike other Sufi orders, allows women to participate in the zikr (prayers) and to form their own female-only subgroups. On the whole, however, under the Soviets the practice of Sufism became highly secretive, even to the point that the silent zikr has replaced the zikr said aloud.

Under the Soviets, religious activity and belief were strongly discouraged, although not eradicated. The Soviets printed anti-Islamic books for Kyrgyz consumption (sixty-nine titles between 1948 and 1975) and gave antireligious lectures (45,000 in Kirghizia in 1975 alone). Antireligious propaganda was seen or heard in the opera, the ballet, the theater, and over the radio. The Soviets also formed motor clubs, whose task it was to bring antireligious propaganda to isolated regions. Reforms in the 1980s made open religious observance possible for the first time in many decades. A significant number of Kyrgyz observe Muslim practices in their everyday lives but not in a religious sense. Kyrgyz women do not wear veils, nor do they avoid men to whom they are not related.

RELIGIOUS PRACTITIONERS. The Kyrgyz Muslims have the standard Islamic clerics. In addition, the Sufi orders have their own *murshids*, or leaders.

CEREMONIES. The Kyrgyz practice standard Islamic ceremonies and rituals. Births, circumcisions, weddings, funerals, and Islamic holidays occasion celebrations. The wealthy and the politically powerful also hold large, well-attended festivals for weddings and to commemorate the death of a family member.

ARTS. Kyrgyz cultural arts are rich and varied. From acrobatic horseback riding by both men and women to the fine craftsmanship of leather saddles and silver jewelry, the Kyrgyz have remembered their nomadic roots in keeping such traditional arts prominent in their everyday lives. One of the more significant cultural arts of the Kyrgyz is the recitation of their epic poem *Manas*, one of the longest epic poems in the oral tradition of the world's peoples. It is at least one million lines long and is said to take six months to perform. *Manas* is part of the Turkic *dastan*, a genre of literature that served as an educational medium by which the Kyrgyz transmitted from generation to generation their history, values, customs, and ethnic identity. The bard, called a *manaschi*, chanted *Manas* without musical accompaniment. This storytelling role was performed by an individual with shamanlike capabilities and in whom the community would confide. The Russian historian Basilov describes a nineteenth-century manaschi as one who used episodes of *Manas* as a curative ritual. Listening to the epic was reputed to have the power to cure a woman of infertility.

The Kyrgyz also have a long and popular tradition of informal recitation of folklore. The singing of folk songs is often accompanied by the three-stringed instrument *akomuz*. Among some of the most famous Soviet writers of the last thirty years, Kyrgyz writer Chingis Aitmatov has distinguished himself as the author of books and screenplays. His works include *Dzamilya*, *A Day Lasts Longer than One Hundred Years*, and *The White Steamship*.

Soviet influence in Kirghizia has included the formation of a Kyrgyz orchestra; the publication of books, magazines, and newspapers in Kyrgyz and Russian; the establishment of libraries; radio and television broadcasts; and the creation of a feature-film industry to disseminate cultural material.

MEDICINE. Traditional Kyrgyz medicine, Chinese acupuncture, and Soviet rest sanitoriums

Kyrgyz arts are rich and varied, ranging from acrobatic horseback riding by both men and women to the fine craftsmanship of leather saddles and silver jewelry.

♦ tariqa
Sufi religious brotherhood (clandestine in the Soviet period).

offer the major methods of healing available to people in Kyrgyzstan. Since 1991 Western aid has focused on providing pharmaceutical medicines and medical training to the country. Medical help is inadequate in the rural mountainous regions, especially since the breakup of the Soviet infrastructure in 1991 and the earthquake in August 1992.

Bibliography

Abramzon, C. M. (1990). *Kirghizia i ix ethnogenetich-eskie i istoriko-kulturnie svyazi* (Kyrgyzia and its ethnogenetic and historico-cultural relations). Frunze: Kyrgyzstan.

Aitmatov, Chingis (1989). "The Grain and the Millstones." In *Time to Speak*, 67–70. New York: International Publishers.

Akiner, Shirin (1986). *Islamic Peoples of the Soviet Union: An Historical and Statistical Handbook.* London: KPI.

Altay, Azamat (1964). "Kirghizia during the Great Purge." *Central Asian Review* 12(2).

Attwood, Lynne (1990). *The New Soviet Man and Woman: Sex-Role Socialization in the USSR.* Bloomington: Indiana University Press.

Bennigsen, Alexandre, and S. Enders Wimbush (1986). *Muslims of the Soviet Empire: A Guide.* Bloomington: Indiana University Press.

Buckley, Mary (1989). *Women and Ideology in the Soviet Union.* Ann Arbor: University of Michigan Press.

Crisp, Simon (1990). "Kirgiz." In *The Nationalities Question in the Soviet Union.* London: Longman.

Fierman, William, ed. (1991). *Soviet Central Asia: The Failed Transformation.* Boulder, Colo.: Westview Press.

Mote, Victor (1978). "Kirgiz." In *Muslim Peoples: A World Ethnographic Survey*, edited by Richard V. Weekes, 215–220. Westport, Conn.: Greenwood Press.

Omurkulov, Kadyr (1987). *Kirghizia.* Moscow: Novosti Press Agency Publishing House.

Poliakov, Sergei P. (1992). *Everyday Islam: Religion and Tradition in Rural Central Asia.* Armonk, N.Y.: M. E. Sharpe.

Shahrani, M. Nazif (1979). *The Kirghiz and Wakhi of Afghanistan.* Seattle: University of Washington Press.

Shahrani, M. Nazif (1984). "Kirghiz." In *Muslim Peoples: A World Ethnographic Survey.* 2nd ed., edited by Richard V. Weekes, 405–411. Westport, Conn.: Greenwood Press.

—KATHLEEN RAE KUEHNAST AND
DANIEL STROUTHES

LATVIANS

Ethnonyms: Latvieši, Latvji, Letten, Letts

Orientation

IDENTIFICATION. Latvians are one of two Baltic ethnolinguistic groups (the other is Lithuanians). Their name for their country is "Latvija" or "Latvijas Republika." Latvians call themselves "Latvieši" or "Latvji."

LOCATION. Latvia spans an area of 64,600 square kilometers and is located between 55°40′23″ and 58°5′12″ N and 20°58′7″ and 28°14′30″ E. The country is more than twice as long between the eastern border and western seashore (450 kilometers) as it is from the northern to the southern border (210 kilometers). On the west and northwest, the country is bounded by the Baltic Sea. On the north, east of the Gulf of Riga, is Estonia. Russia is to the east of Latvia, Belarus to the southeast, and Lithuania to the south. Latvia is located in the central part of the Baltic Sheet, a geological formation underlying Scandinavia and the Russian plain. The terrain is characterized by gently rolling hills. The mean elevation is 89 meters above sea level; 75 percent of the countryside is lower than 120 meters above sea level. The highest hill is Gaiziņš, 312 meters.

Latvia has 777 rivers longer than 10 kilometers. Its greatest river, Daugava (Düna), is 1,020 kilometers long, but only 357 kilometers of it flows through the country. Most rivers freeze for two to three-and-a-half months during an average winter. Most of the major rivers flow northward, and floods during the spring thaw are common. There are 2,500 lakes larger than 5 hectares, covering about 1.6 percent of the country's surface. Of these, 16 are greater than 10 square kilometers and represent approximately half of the area covered by lakes. Latvia is located in the turf-podzol soil area.

CLIMATE. The climate is influenced by the Atlantic's Gulf Stream, the Baltic Sea, and the country's latitude. In December, the sun rises 9° to 10° above the horizon, and days are six to seven hours long. In June, the sun rises to 55° and days are seventeen to eighteen hours long. There are four seasons—fall (September to mid-December), winter (mid-December to mid-March), spring (mid-March to the end of May), and summer (June to the end of August). The annual growing season is 200 days, but only July and August are completely frost-free. The climate is warmer, moister, and the growing season 10 days longer in the west than in the east. Eastern Latvia has twice as many days with snow as the western part, 130 and 65 days respectively. The highest temperature recorded is 36° C; the lowest is −42.2° C. January temperatures average between −6.6° C in the east and −2.8° C in the west. July temperatures average between 16.7° C in the west and 17.6° C in the east. Annual precipitation averages between 60 and 80 centimeters, with 20 percent occurring as snow. Precipitation is minimal in February and maximal in August. Because of the predominantly cloudy weather, the country receives only 37 percent of possible sunshine.

DEMOGRAPHY. Worldwide there are 1,620,000 Latvians. Of these, 1,388,000 live in Latvia, and some 232,000 reside outside of the country. The largest concentrations of Latvians abroad are in the United States (86,000), the former Soviet Union (71,000), the ten West European countries (30,000), Australia (25,000), and Canada (20,000). Latvians comprise only 52 percent of their country's 2,680,000 population. The largest ethnic minority is the Great Russians (34 percent of the total population). Other minorities (Belarussians, Ukrainians, Poles, Lithuanians, etc.) together constitute 14 percent of the total. Latvians predominate in rural areas (71.5 percent of rural inhabitants) but account for only 44 percent of the urban population. Latvians make up only 36.5 percent (332,000) of Riga's population; the Great Russians constitute the largest ethnic group in the city (431,000 or 47.3 percent). Only in Ogre (pop. 29,926), the ninth-largest city, do Latvians have a slight majority. In the fourth-largest city, Jelgava (pop. 74,704), Latvians fall just short of a majority (49.7 percent).

The ethnic composition is the result of World War II and postwar population policies. In 1935, 77 percent of the population was Latvian. During World War II, a significant number of Latvia's residents were killed or deported, or left voluntarily. By the war's end, the percentage of Latvians rose to 80 percent. After World War II, the Soviet government recruited immigrants for Latvia. As a result, the proportion of ethnic Latvians decreased to the current level.

LINGUISTIC AFFILIATION. Latvian, Lithuanian, and the now-extinct Old Prussian make up the Baltic Branch of the Indo-European Language Family, a part of the Nostratic Macro-Family. Latvian uses the Latin alphabet. Spelling of foreign words is modified to reflect Latvian phonemic values. The literary language is based on the dialect spoken in the middle of the country. With the advent of mass media and compulsory universal education, local dialects are disappearing. Most Latvians are bilingual; 68.3 percent of Latvians in Latvia report knowing Russian, and most Latvians residing outside the country are bilingual.

History and Cultural Relations

It is generally held that the ancestors of modern Latvians entered Latvia during the second millennium B.C. They were farmers and raised livestock. Extensive written documents about events and individuals in Latvia begin in the twelfth century. At that time, most of the peoples of Latvia were pagans, and the country was inhabited by four Baltic tribes (Kurši or Courlanders; Latgaļi, from whom the Latvian ethnonym has been derived; Sēļi; and Zemgaļi) and a Finno-Ugric tribe, the Livs, who, since they were the first indigenous people contacted by Westerners, provided the early name, Livonia, that was used for the Latvian and Estonian area.

Riga was founded by Germans in A.D. 1201 as a base for commerce, missionizing, and military conquest. Latvia's thirteenth-century history is one of interactions and wars between the indigenous tribes and the Lithuanians, Poles, Russians, Germans, Catholic ecclesiastical authorities, Germanic crusading orders, and merchants. By 1300 Germans had gained political and economic control over the country by conquest, and the people were converted to Christianity. For the next several centuries Latvia's neighbors (i.e., Lithuanians, Poles, Russians, and, later, Swedes) attempted to annex the country, and the locals resisted these efforts.

In the late sixteenth century, Livonia was partitioned. Only the duchy of Kurland and Zemgale (1562−1795) retained independence under Polish-Lithuanian suzerainty. In 1721 the country was conquered by czarist Russia, although the duchy of Kurland and Zemgale maintained a separate status for a while. Starting in the thirteenth century, rural Latvians were gradually reduced in legal status, until by 1458 most had become serfs. Latvians living in cities retained free status but were not numerous. Legal vestiges of the serf status were abolished in 1861.

On 18 November 1918, as World War I ended, Latvians declared independence. A war of independence was fought against both Germany and Russia. The war against Germany ended with a peace treaty on 15 July 1920, and the war against the Federal Socialist Republic of the Russian Soviets was concluded by a peace treaty on 11 August 1920. By then Latvia had lost 25 percent of its pre−World War I population, 25 percent of its

Latvians perceive a real danger of becoming a minority in their own country and feel they have been abused and have suffered greatly for the past fifty years.

Between 1940 and 1991, the Soviet Union made a determined effort to sever West European ties and to reorient Latvian culture toward the Russian.

farm buildings were completely or partially destroyed, 29 percent of its arable land lay fallow, and its industry had virtually disappeared. A period of rebuilding followed; by 1940 per-capita income approximated that of Finland, Hungary, and Italy, and Latvia was emerging as a democratic republic with a constitution based on those of France, Germany, and Switzerland.

After an armed coup d'état on 15 May 1934, however, Latvian Prime Minister Karlis Ulmanis instituted a dictatorship. The German-Soviet nonaggression treaty of 23 August 1939 assigned Latvia to the Soviet sphere of influence. Projecting an uncertain future, the Latvian government transferred its gold reserves to Western banks and issued extraordinary powers to the Latvian minister in London. On 17 June 1940 Latvia was occupied and on 5 August 1940 incorporated into the Soviet Union as the Latvian SSR. The country's economic, political, and social structures were transformed to the Soviet pattern. This culminated on the night of 13–14 June 1941, when 15,600 individuals were deported to labor camps.

On 22 June 1941 Germany attacked the Soviet Union and occupied Latvia until 8 May 1945. The return of Soviet rule to Latvia meant the reimposition of a harsh totalitarian political and economic system with tens of thousands of new political prisoners being sent to the gulag. With the advent of Gorbachev's *glasnost* and *perestroika*, the Soviet Union began to disintegrate, and on 21 August 1991, the Supreme Council of Latvia declared the Republic of Latvia independent again. On 17 September 1991, Latvia was admitted as a member of the United Nations.

Latvia is on the border of Western European and Russian cultural areas. Between 1200 and 1945, the predominant influences on Latvian culture were Western European. The majority of Latvians were members of religions stemming from the West—Lutheranism and Roman Catholicism. The predominant influences in the fine arts, education, and science were Western. Between 1940 and 1991, the Soviet Union made a determined effort to sever West European ties and to reorient Latvian culture toward the Russian. Literary and scientific works, for example, had to be translated from Russian versions rather than from the original language. With the dissolution of the Soviet Union, the Western orientation is resurgent.

Settlements

Before World War II, some street villages with associated strip fields could still be found in the east. In the rest of the country, scattered single farms were the norm. The farmstead consisted of separate structures surrounding an open farm yard with the house fronting the road. Beginning on 17 June 1940 private farms were nationalized and confiscated, and state and collective farms were formed. After World War II, new rural settlements with apartment houses and large farm buildings were built. The country has been urbanized; 71 percent of the population lives in cities. Riga (pop. 915,106) is the country's capital and the seat of the Lutheran and Roman Catholic bishops. The next two largest cities—Daugavpils (pop. 126,680) and Liepāja (pop. 114,462)—are barely one-seventh that size. Latvia has three cities with 50,000 to 75,000 inhabitants (Jelgava, Jūrmala, and Ventspils) and twenty-six cities with 5,000 to 43,000 inhabitants. The vast majority of city dwellers live in apartments. Because of the proximity of services, the center of the city is considered to be the most desirable residential area.

Economy

SUBSISTENCE AND COMMERCIAL ACTIVITIES. Of the total population, 54.7 percent are employed. Of this percentage, three-quarters work in goods production and one-quarter in service. Between 1945 and 1991, Latvia's economy was an integral part of the Soviet Union's. This resulted in relative stagnation of the agricultural sector and overexploitation of forest resources. Industry is dependent on energy, labor, and raw materials imported from elsewhere, and the products manufactured are exported. The industrial sector employs 30.7 percent of all those employed. Heavy industry produces 54 percent of the country's gross national product; light industry, 19 percent; and agricultural and food processing, 25.4 percent. Among industrial products are diesel engines and generators, electrical railroad and street cars, radios, telephone equipment, other electrical and electronic items, pharmaceuticals, and textiles. Of all those employed, 15.1 percent work in agriculture. Farming has been mechanized and requires energy from outside sources. Most land is farmed by large state and collective farms. The private farming sector is just resuming. The agricultural emphasis is on animal husbandry to produce eggs, meat, and milk, and on field crops (e.g., barley, flax, oats, peas, potatoes, rye, sugar beets, and wheat). Economic restructuring according to market principles began in mid-1990, but only 1 percent of the labor force is thus far employed in the nonstate sector. Latvia has very little mineral wealth and no coal, natural gas, or oil. Its economy in the future probably will be based on farming, forestry, light industry, and service.

TRADE. There is strife between the people who constituted the power structure under the autocratic Soviet regime with its command economy and those attempting to establish a market economy with private ownership. In order to retain their status and influence, the former struggle to establish a neocolonial situation; the latter attempt to open the economy to private entrepreneurs. Still present is the old Socialist trade network, with government-owned stores and distribution network, and farmers' markets. Simultaneously, newly established private manufacturing and retail establishments vie for resources.

DIVISION OF LABOR. Legally there is equality between the genders. In fact, men occupy the more prestigious and better-remunerated jobs. Women employed outside the home are still responsible for the "second shift" of family shopping and household chores; they receive little or no help from the men and do without the convenience of modern appliances. There is also an ethnic division of labor. Latvians predominate in agriculture, forestry, printing, and communication; non-Latvians are concentrated in industry (Russians make up more than 41 percent of industrial workers), sea and railroad transportation, and white-collar jobs.

LAND TENURE. All real estate was acquired by the Soviet government and was owned by "the people" (i.e., the government). Since 13 June 1991, there has been an effort to return real property to its former owners or their heirs. Private owners' rights over property and duties toward society are in the process of being established.

Kinship, Marriage, and Family

KINSHIP. The kinship system and terminology are of the Eskimo type. The most common kin unit is the nuclear family, although there are also stem extended families. Kinship beyond the nuclear and small extended family is recognized, but it is not an important principle for organizing society, except that truncated kindreds may assemble for weddings and funerals.

MARRIAGE. In Latvia, the majority (67.8 percent of men and 56 percent of women) of

RELIGION AND EXPRESSIVE CULTURE

Religious Beliefs and Practices

Religion in Latvia has been politicized, making it difficult to know what the current belief system is. The population was converted by "fire and sword" to Roman Catholicism by A.D. 1300. In the sixteenth century most Latvians converted to Lutheranism. Those living in the part of Latvia incorporated into the Polish-Lithuanian Commonwealth, however, remained Catholic. In the nineteenth century, some seeking economic advantage joined the Russian Orthodox church. Between 1940 and 1991, the Communist Soviet government actively opposed religious activities and encouraged atheism. As a result the "mainstream" churches' (i.e., Lutheran, Roman Catholic, and Russian Orthodox) leadership and membership have declined, and their moral and ideational influence has eroded. The culture has become secularized. Many individuals are not so much atheistic as agnostic. One recent development is active proselytizing by charismatic and Pentecostal churches, sects, and cults.

Arts

Production of authentic folk arts and crafts has almost fallen into desuetude. Current production is a commercialized fine art on folk-art themes. This decline applies to the performing arts as well. An important part of Latvian performing arts are song festivals organized in Latvia and other countries with significant Latvian populations. These events feature folk music performed by choirs of hundreds and dances by folk-dance troupes. Because of Russian political domination of the country for the past three centuries, Latvian artists and popular culture have been influenced by the artistic fashions and trends of Russia. But, except for the Soviet period, Latvian fine arts and popular culture have been more oriented toward Western Europe. During the Soviet period, the government promoted propagandistic art and suppressed art styles and artists deemed unde-sirable. Now Latvians are once again exploring other styles and approaches.

Medicine

The medical-care delivery system consists of clinics, hospitals, sanatoria, and dispensaries and pharmacies staffed by physicians, nurses, dentists, pharmacists, and support staff. Because of the general economic breakdown and lack of resources, however, the medical system is in a state of virtual collapse. Although there seems to be an adequate number of physicians, there is a shortage of trained support staff and a critical lack of medicines, vaccines, equipment, and supplies. Medical workers, too, are trying to make the change from a system that discouraged initiative and forbade private enterprise to one featuring these characteristics. The need for medical services is acute, life expectancy is decreasing, and birth defects are increasing.

those 16 years of age and older are married. The ideal is a monogamous marriage for life, but many people engage in serial monogamy. In recent years, there have been 10,000 to 11,000 divorces annually. The preferred residence is neolocal, but, owing to a housing shortage, many couples live with their parents. Most families (72.5 percent) consist of members of the same ethnic group.

DOMESTIC UNIT. For Latvians in Latvia, the average family size is 3.09. In Latvia, the predominant family type (74.4 percent of all families) is a married couple either with children (55 percent of all families) or without children. One-fifth of these families have another relative, usually a parent of one of the spouses, living with them. Single-parent families are becoming common (the number has increased 20 percent in the past ten years) because of the rising rates of divorce and births to single mothers.

INHERITANCE. Inheritance is governed by law. Testamentary disposition and an ambilineal inheritance from parents to children, grandchildren, and other lineal descendants is recognized.

SOCIALIZATION. The family stresses tenderness and a moral code of loyalty to its members, relatives, and friends. The mother is seen as nurturant and affectionate; the father is the disciplinarian. The father is conceptualized as the head of the family, whereas the mother is its heart. Peer groups (for youth) and circles of friends (for adults) stress loyalty, helpfulness, and strong emotional support among their members. The Soviet schools advocated a Communist-oriented "official message"—loyalty and obedience to the state, hard and selfless work—whereas the students stressed loyalty to schoolmates and rivalry against teachers and adults. The official and ubiquitous Soviet government propaganda affected the local population's worldview.

Sociopolitical Organization

SOCIAL ORGANIZATION. Between 1940 and 1991, the Soviet state severely curtailed the activities and membership of any organization or social unit not directly controlled by it. When Latvia regained independence, many organizations such as the Communist party, Communist youth organizations, and the secret police (KGB) were abolished or collapsed because of a lack of support by their members. New groups are encountering organizational difficulties—small memberships, lack of public awareness regarding their goals and activities, and a lack of leaders with organizational and administrative experi-

ence. For the individual, personal relationships are important elements in manipulating the political and economic systems. These connections are marshaled to gain access and to influence people in a position to grant favors.

POLITICAL ORGANIZATION. The political system is in transition from a repressive totalitarian government to a democracy. There is a battle between the old Soviet *nomenklatura* who used to run the country and nationalistically and democratically inclined people who were barred from positions of authority by the Communist regime. There is no agreement regarding the rights and duties of the various administrative and political bodies and offices or on how their personnel are to be selected. Making the task of building institutions more difficult are the public's distrust of politicians and centralized authorities and skepticism regarding their ability to solve society's problems. There is also the ethnic factor. Latvians perceive a real danger of becoming a minority in their own country and feel they have been abused and have suffered greatly for the past fifty years. The Russians resent the recent changes because these reduce the privileges they had enjoyed as an occupying and dominating nationality in a colonial situation. Most likely what will eventually emerge will be a system consisting of a parliament (probably unicameral), a president, and a government headed by a prime minister.

SOCIAL CONTROL. Social control has its formal and informal aspects. Among the family, peer group, and circle of friends, emotional withdrawal and social isolation are common sanctions. Physical violence may occur when psychological pressures do not result in desired behavior. Police and other legal armed forces exist in the country, but their duties are not clear and their competencies overlap. No reliable statistics are available regarding criminal activities.

CONFLICT. Many wars have touched Latvian territory and caused much destruction and death. Except for the 1918–1920 war for independence, Latvians have not conducted wars since 1300. They have, however, participated in the wars and armies of others. During World War II, both the Soviet and German governments drafted Latvians for their respective militaries. Civilian ethnic relations in Latvia were not characterized by mass physical violence, lynchings, pogroms, or riots. Latvians who did participate in such activities (e.g., crimes against humanity during and after World War II) did so individually or as members of armed units formed by and at the direction of foreign governments.

Bibliography

Bilmanis, Alfred (1951). *A History of Latvia*. Princeton, N.J.: Princeton University Press.

Carson, George B., ed. (1956). *Latvia: An Area Study*. Vols. 1 and 2. New Haven: Human Relations Area Files.

Gimbutas, Marija (1963). *The Balts*. New York: Frederick A. Praeger.

Ligers, Ziedonis (1954). *Etnographie Lettone*. Basel: Société Suisse des Traditions Populaires, vol. 35.

Plakans, Andrejs (1984). *Kinship in the Past: An Anthropology of European Family Life*. New York: B. Blackwell.

Simanis, Vito Vitauts, ed. (1984). *Latvia*. St. Charles, Ill.: Book Latvia.

—ANDRIS SKREIJA

LITHUANIANS

Ethnonyms: Lietuva, Litawen, Litva, Litwa

Orientation

IDENTIFICATION. Lithuania is a Baltic nation bounded on the west by the Baltic Sea, on the north by Latvia, on the east and south by Belarus, and on the southwest by Poland and Russia. The ethnonym "Lietuva" is the Lithuanian term for "Lithuania" and "Litva" is the Russian term.

LOCATION. Lithuania lies at 54° to 56°30′ N by 21° to 26°30′ E and covers an area of 64,445 square kilometers. It is a low plain with glacial moraines and is covered by meadows, forests (25 percent of the land), peat bogs, and swamps (7 percent of the land). Lithuania has 3,000 lakes, and its rivers drain into the Baltic Sea. The country's major natural resources include dolomite, gypsum, peat, limestone, gravel, sand, clay, and amber. Its climate is quite moderate, owing to its proximity to the Baltic Sea—the average January temperature is −4.8° C, and the average July temperature is 17.2° C. Annual precipitation normally varies between 58 and 79 centimeters, peaking in August.

DEMOGRAPHY. The Lithuanian population has undergone significant fluctuations owing to two world wars and to Nazi and Soviet occupations. By 1939, when the Soviets took control, the Nazis had deported or caused the emigration of 200,000 to 300,000 of the approximately 3,000,000 people in Lithuania. Fear of the Soviets caused many Lithuanians to emigrate to the West during World War II. The Soviets implemented large deportations in 1940–1941 and 1946–1950; dispersals, killings, and concentra-

tion camps were used to gain obedience. This policy resulted in a decline of 500,000 in the population of Lithuania. By 1970, the Lithuanian population had rebounded to 3,100,000, though only 80.1 percent of these were ethnic Lithuanians—the balance were Russians, Poles, Byelorussians, Gypsies, and others who had entered from the Soviet Union. In 1992 the population was estimated at 3,700,000, of whom 79.6 percent were ethnic Lithuanians. The average annual rate of natural increase is 0.4 percent, and the birth rate is 15 per 1,000 people. Approximately 70 percent of the population is urban, a percentage that is increasing annually; many people are moving to the planned cities of Alytus, Kapsukas, Plunge, Utena, and others. The capital, Vilnius, has a population of 587,000.

LINGUISTIC AFFILIATION. The Lithuanian language belongs to the Baltic (or Letto-Lithuanian) Branch of the Indo-European Language Family. The close relationship of this language to Latvian mirrors an overall similarity of the Lithuanian and Latvian cultures. In common with all Baltic languages, Lithuanian preserves several Proto-Indo-European language characteristics, including the distinction of dual number for nouns and verbs.

The Lithuanian language is written using the Roman alphabet and additional diacritical marks. After the 1863 rebellion, the Russians retaliated by forbidding the printing of anything in the Roman alphabet (1864–1904), and the use of the Cyrillic script was encouraged instead. The Lithuanians responded by printing most of their literature during that period with the Roman alphabet in the Prussian-dominated region of Lithuania and by smuggling books and publications across the border.

Lithuania has had a literary language since the sixteenth century. The first of these was used only for religious writings until the end of the eighteenth century; it differed from later standards in grammar, vocabulary, and pronunciation. By the early nineteenth century, three literary dialects had emerged, each used in a different part of the country.

Language and Literacy

Formal education is important to Lithuanians, who had a 98.5 percent literacy rate in 1959 (up from 77 percent in 1939). There are three official languages of instruction in Lithuanian schools: 84 percent of the students study in Lithuanian, 12 percent in Russian, and 4 percent in Polish—recently the percentage in Russian has decreased

There are three official languages of instruction in Lithuanian schools: 84 percent of the students study in Lithuanian, 12 percent in Russian, and 4 percent in Polish.

Lithuanians

For much of their history, Lithuanians have been dominated or have tried to avoid domination by other people.

greatly. Education in the country's one university in Vilnius is almost entirely in Lithuanian. In 1971 there were 581,000 students attending school in Lithuania, and 15,826 of those attended the university.

Lithuania leads most other former Soviet republics in the publication of books, pamphlets, and periodicals. In 1970, 2,186 books and pamphlets were published, approximately 60 percent of which were in Lithuanian. In that year as well, ninety-one newspapers were published, seventy-four of which were in the Lithuanian language. Lithuania has numerous radio and television stations, and its people, because of contacts with the West, are better supplied with receivers than people in many other parts of the former USSR.

History and Cultural Relations

For much of their history, Lithuanians have been dominated or have tried to avoid domination by other peoples. By the early thirteenth century, the Lithuanians were united under the feudal control of five families. Though at first protected by the heavy forests, the Lithuanians were eventually threatened by the Teutonic Order. In response, they united under Mindaugas, who was crowned in 1253. Gediminas, who ruled from 1315, expanded Lithuanian control into Byelorussian regions and made Vilnius the capital by 1323. He divided the empire among his seven sons, although in relatively little time only two were still in power—Algirdas, who controlled the Lithuanian empire and defended it against the Tatars and the Russians, and Kestutis, who controlled ethnic Lithuania and defended it against the Teutonic Order. Algirdas died in 1377 and left the empire to his son Jogaila. In 1381 Kestutis took the empire from Jogaila, but Jogaila retook it and imprisoned Kestutis until the latter died. In 1385 Jogaila married Jadwiga, Poland's queen, and became king of Poland; he united Poland, Kievan Russia, and all parts of Lithuania by 1392. Jogaila was baptized in 1386. His forces roundly defeated the Teutonic Order in 1410. The Lithuanian-Polish union survived for more than three centuries, during which the Belarussian and Lithuanian nobility was almost assimilated into the Polish culture, whereas the peasants retained their native languages and customs.

Russia's power was growing: in 1772 and 1793 it annexed two major portions of the grand principality of Lithuania, and in 1795 it annexed ethnic Lithuania, with the exception of the province of Suwalki (Suvalkai), which was joined to the kingdom of Prussia. Suwalki later became part of the Duchy of Warsaw, which the Russians annexed in 1815. Poles and Lithuanians rebelled together in 1830–1831 and in 1863, but both times the Russians put down the rebellions; in 1863 the suppression was particularly brutal. Lithuanians pushed to regain some rights, including freedom of religion and of speech. In 1905 they were granted the right of free speech and of instruction in the Lithuanian language in schools.

Germans controlled much of Lithuania during World War I. Following the war, the Lithuanians, Poles, and Russians vied for control of various parts of ethnic Lithuania. Józef Pilsudski, the leader of Poland, disputed with the Lithuanians about the borders of the Lithuanian state, wanting some Polish control over Vilnius, which at that time had a mostly Polish population. In 1919 Pilsudski took Vilnius from the Russians, and Kaunas became the substitute capital of Lithuania. The Lithuanians entered into a treaty with the Soviet state in 1920, in which the former received Vilnius and other areas. The Lithuanians controlled Vilnius for a few months until the Polish army retook it. In 1921 Lithuania became a member of the League of Nations; in 1923, the Council of the League of Nations decided that Vilnius was to remain part of Poland. The Lithuanians adopted a constitution in 1922, and held elections to the Seimas (parliament). The mix of parties represented in the Seimas led to political instability, however. A moderate to right-wing coalition held power until 1926, when Kazys Grinius was elected president, representing, in part, a coalition of Polish, Jewish, and German minorities. Antanas Smetona, who had been Lithuania's first president, reacted to the leftist government by taking dictatorial control of the country in a military coup in December 1926 and banning opposition parties. Smetona was fiscally conservative, kept a balanced budget, and encouraged agricultural development at the expense of industrial development.

In 1938 Lithuania normalized diplomatic relations with Poland. During the 1930s, Nazis attempted to take control of the Klaipeda region of Lithuania, and in 1938 they won a majority of seats in the Klaipeda Landtag. In March 1939 Nazi Germany demanded and received Klaipeda, and this cost Smetona's government so much support that he was compelled to form a new and politically more moderate cabinet.

Although Lithuania had chosen a course of neutrality in World War II, a secret protocol to the German-Soviet treaty of nonaggression of 23 August 1939 placed Lithuania within the Soviet sphere of influence. In October 1939 Lithuania signed a mutual assistance treaty with the USSR, which gave the latter the right to place military bases on Lithuanian soil. On 15 June 1940 Lithuania was occupied by Soviet military forces and compelled to form a government that would rule in accordance with Soviet wishes. Large numbers of Lithuanians fled to the West, but tens of thousands were caught and sent to Siberia. In August of that year Lithuania became a Soviet republic. In June 1941, 30,455 Lithuanians of political importance were sent to Siberia and about 5,000 political prisoners lost their lives. But by the end of the month, Lithuania was in Nazi hands. In October 1944 it was retaken by the USSR. Some 80,000 Lithuanians attempted to escape to the West, but tens of thousands were captured in the eastern zone of Germany and returned. In order to Russify the Lithuanians, secure their submission, and force the acceptance of collective agriculture, Stalin deported about 145,000 people in 1945–1946, and in 1949 about 60,000 more were sent various places in Siberia.

Lithuanian partisans fought guerrilla wars against the Soviets until at least 1955. Although guerrilla warfare ended at that time, Lithuanian opposition to Soviet rule did not. Lithuanians often refused to speak or understand Russian. In 1956 people in the Kaunas region supported the uprising in Hungary by rioting. Educators were purged in 1959 for nationalism. In 1968 samizdat publications appeared and later became more numerous. At the same time, Catholic priests began to send letters to Soviet and church leaders protesting the restrictions on the numbers of priests who could be trained. In 1970 the first priests were arrested. As priests were tried, parishioners began to send letters and petitions to the Soviet government protesting the removal of their priests. Eliciting no response, over 17,000 Lithuanian Catholics sent a petition of protest to Secretary General Kurt Waldheim of the United Nations in January 1972, along with instructions to send it on to CPSU General Secretary Brezhnev; the signatures on the petition included full addresses and some were even accompanied by telephone numbers. In 1972 there were three self-immolations in protest, after which large riots took place. Two of the three attempted hijackings of Soviet planes in 1969–1970 were made by Lithuanians, one successfully.

The Lithuanian independence movement gathered momentum in 1988. On 12 February 1990 the Lithuanians elected Vytautas Landsbergis, previously the head of the large Sajudis popular move-

ment, to parliament, and on 11 March 1990, to the presidency. It was also on 11 March that the Lithuanian parliament unanimously declared independence from Soviet rule. On 2 September 1991 the United States gave full diplomatic recognition to Lithuania and the other two Baltic countries, Estonia and Latvia. The USSR recognized Lithuanian independence on 6 September 1991, and Lithuania became a member of the United Nations on 17 September of that year. Guntis Ulmanis was elected president on 18 June, 1993.

Economy

Traditionally an agrarian land, Lithuania became extensively industrialized as a result of Soviet programs in the 1960s. By 1989 it had a labor force of 1,853,000. Forty percent of workers are employed in industry and 20 percent in agriculture and forestry.

During the nineteenth century, industrialization was hampered by a shortage of natural resources and absence of good port facilities. Much of the land was held in large estates given to the raising of grain, flax, and horses. Much of what industry had developed was destroyed during World War I. During the period of independence between the world wars, the government emphasized the production of high-quality meats, dairy products, and eggs, and it pursued a vigorous program of land reform that resulted in greater productivity. This emphasis on animal husbandry in agriculture remains today.

The imposition of Soviet rule, which led to guerrilla warfare against the Soviets and forced collectivization of the farms, caused a marked decline in agricultural productivity that lasted until 1955. Prior to Lithuanian independence in 1991, there were approximately 310 state and 740 collective farms. Farm production today is geared toward raising pigs and dairy cattle; half of the crops raised are for fodder. Lithuanian farms also produce significant quantities of flax, sugar beets, potatoes, and vegetables. In recent decades, farms have been expanded through land reclamation and swamp drainage. Most of the country's farming is done in the northern and southern regions.

Following the establishment of Soviet control, and especially during the 1960s and after, industrial production grew rapidly. Lithuania produces electricity from several plants, including a hydroelectric and a nuclear plant. It makes ships, machine tools, chemicals, building materials, petroleum products, cement, welding equipment, plastics

Traditionally an agrarian land, Lithuania became extensively industrialized as a result of Soviet programs in the 1960s.

and synthetic fibers, chemical fertilizers, cotton cloth, knitted garments, and electronic devices. Lithuanian factories also process meat, fish, sugar, and butter. In addition, there is significant light industry, including metalworking and woodworking, and Lithuania boasts several large resorts. Most of Lithuania's shipbuilding and fish processing is done in the west, metalworking and light industry are primarily concentrated in the east, and most of the hydroelectric generation and food processing is done in the south. There is a Chernobyl-type nuclear reactor in Ignalina in the north, which presents a great danger to the entire region.

Eighty percent of Lithuania's trade is with countries belonging to the Commonwealth of Independent States. Other important trading partners are Germany, Great Britain, Denmark, Belgium, Poland, Cuba, the Czech Republic, Slovakia, and Italy. Goods transported by ship usually go through the port of Klaipeda, and Vilnius has the major airport, but most of the country's goods move by rail.

Kinship

Lithuanian kinship is bilateral and follows the Eskimo kinship system. In earlier times a quite extensive system of kin terms distinguishing cate-

gories based on marriage and sex (e.g., *dédiené,* father's brother's wife) existed. These terms varied regionally. Today kin terms have been reduced, reflecting the predominance of the nuclear family.

Marriage and Family

In preindustrial Lithuania, marriage was arranged by matchmakers. Especially for the landholding classes, it was largely an economic union with the bride providing a bargained dowry. During Lithuanian independence, arranged marriages slowly disappeared and were replaced by love matches. The extended family was especially important in rural areas in these periods. In Soviet times, family size was reduced to one or two children per family, and the nuclear family became the norm. These changes took place due to urbanization, collectivization of farms, alcoholism, and the high divorce rate. Eight percent of adult women worked outside the home, in addition to bearing the brunt of the household work. Furthermore, there were extreme housing shortages, and ideological considerations made women unwilling to send children to large, state-run nurseries. In the last twenty years, many couples have married at a younger age, either to register for the very scarce housing or because of premarital pregnancy owing to the lack of birth control. Separate housing was available only to married couples—after an average wait of fifteen years. Abortion was the main means of population control; the typical woman had eight in her lifetime. Divorce rates increased to six out of every ten marriages. Since the turbulent political and economic changes following the reestablishment of independence, marriage and familial trends seem to parallel those of the proximate western European nations—cohabitation and a further decline in the birthrate.

Sociopolitical Organization

Lithuania is a democracy governed by a parliament, known as the Seimas; its president, the head of state, selects the prime minister (subject to the approval of parliament).

Religion and Expressive Culture

RELIGIOUS BELIEFS AND PRACTICES. Lithuania was pagan, worshiping forces of nature, until 1387, and was the last country in Europe to accept Christianity. Today ethnic Lithuanians in Lithuania are 94 percent Catholic. Most of the other 6 percent are Lutheran descendants of Germans and Austrians who immigrated after the Great Plague (1710); Lutheran worship also re-

FOLK DANCE

A Lithuanian folk dancer prepares for a performance. Lithuanian folk and fine arts have been strongly influenced by Western art traditions. Vilnius, Lithuania. (Dean Conger/Corbis)

flects residence in areas under German control. Catholic clergy regulated the educational system when Lithuania was under Russian control in the nineteenth century, and the Catholic political parties held considerable power during the period of Lithuanian independence between the two world wars. Clergy frequently supported anti-Soviet warfare. In more recent times, popular opinion opposed Soviet harassment of Catholic clergy. Radio Vatican is received in Lithuania and was opposed by the Soviet regime. Catholicism is an inseparable and vital part of Lithuanian culture.

ARTS. Lithuanian arts, both folk and fine, have been strongly influenced by Western art traditions. Traditional folk arts include ceramic work, woodcuts, embroidery, and amber work. Characteristic Lithuanian decorations include geometric and floral motifs, and the use of natural colors is preferred. Lithuanians are famous for their melodious folksongs (*dainos*), a genre shared with the Latvians. The Lithuanians hold dancing and singing festivals throughout the country each summer, and every five years there are national singing competitions that draw up to 40,000 contestants. Each generation hands down to the next a large number of traditional folktales, proverbs, and aphorisms.

Lithuanian fine arts traditions have been and continue to be influenced by the Vilnius school of drawing, established at the university in 1866. Lithuania's most famous artist is Mykolas Čiurlionis (1875–1911), a forerunner of the abstractionist and surrealist schools. There were many abstract artists in Lithuania during its domination by the Soviets, but they rarely had the opportunity to show their work publicly. Lithuanian architecture has its own character, which may be seen not only in newer buildings but also in the older Gothic and neoclassical structures. Lithuania has eleven professional theaters—including drama, ballet, and opera theaters—as well as thirty-three museums. The Lithuanian Film Studio has produced feature films since 1952.

Lithuanian literary figures include several renowned novelists, short-story writers, and poets. Its literature is considered to have begun with the works of Kristijonas Donelaitis (1714–1780); his *The Seasons* is a story of peasant life. Many consider Adam Mickiewicz (1798–1855) Lithuania's greatest poet, despite the fact that he wrote in Polish. In the first half of the nineteenth century a movement to invent a new Lithuanian literary language and to write about the early history of Lithuania arose, a movement that was influenced by Western countries after the French Revolution. Many writers during the second half of the nineteenth century pushed the development of a nationalist, anti-Russian trend; some of these were members of the Catholic clergy, including the important writers Antanas Baranauskas (1835–1902) and Maironis (1862–1932). Following liberation in 1918, many Lithuanian authors were concerned with promoting a national culture. Most Lithuanian literature has not been critically acclaimed because of Soviet influence and domination that began in the 1940s. Notable exceptions to this generalization are the following: the 1962 poetry collection *Žmogus* (Man) by Eduardus Mieželaitis, the 1957 novel *Parduotos vasaros* (Bartered Summers) by Juozas Baltušis, and the 1960 poem "Kraujas ir pelenai" (Blood and Ashes) by Justinas Marcinkevičius.

Bibliography

Butkus, T. (1964). *Take a Look at Soviet Lithuania*. Vilnius: Mintis.

Gerutis, Albertas, et al. (1969). *Lithuania: 700 Years*. New York: Manyland Books.

Jurgela, Constantine R. (1948). *History of the Lithuanian Nation*. New York: Lithuanian Cultural Institute.

Stukas, Jack J. (1966). *Awakening Lithuania*. Madison, N.J.: Florham Park Press.

Vardys, Stanley, ed. (1965). *Lithuania under the Soviets*. New York: Praeger.

—DANIEL STROUTHES AND KRISTINA KELERTAS

RUSSIANS

Ethnonyms: Russkiy, Velikorusskiy; formerly Rus', Ross

Orientation

IDENTIFICATION. Russians are the largest subdivision of the Eastern Slavs, the other members of which are Ukrainians and Belarussians. The Russian language emerged from the common East Slavic tongue, Ancient Russian or Old Church Slavonic, by the fourteenth century A.D. in the Rostov-Suzdal' area of central Russia.

LOCATION. In 1979 eight administrative provinces (oblasts) of central Russia were over 97 percent Russian; in addition, over 90 percent of the population in a north-south ellipse encompassed by St. Petersburg, Arkhangel'sk, Gorki, Volgograd, Rostov-na-Donu, Belgorod, and Smolensk was Russian. Three areas in the Urals

Since the fifteenth century, the Russian state has been distinguished by centralized, generally autocratic rule, strongly dependent upon a service class.

and western Siberia—Kurgan, Novosibirsk, and Kemerovo oblasts—likewise were over 90 percent Russian.

These Russian areas are flat or rolling, with a mix of forests and steppes, mostly glaciated in European Russia and loessial in western Siberia. They have cold, snowy winters and summers ranging from cool to very hot. Soils are podzolic in the north and chernozemic in the south. The Russian lands are transected by important rivers, the Oka, Volga, Don, Donets, and Severnaya Dvina in Europe and the Ob system in western Siberia. Peripheral waters include Lakes Ladoga and Onega, the White Sea, and the Gulf of Finland in the European North and the Sea of Azov in the south.

Natural conditions in the Russian environment have been profoundly altered by agriculture, which has left only residual forests south of Moscow; by extensive water development, especially on the Volga and Don; and especially by urbanization. In 1989 only fourteen of thirty primarily Russian oblasts were under 70 percent urban. Tambov, 56 percent urban, was the most rural Russian area in Europe. Conversely, St. Petersburg, Moscow, Ivanovo, and Yaroslavl in Europe and Kemerovo in Siberia were over 80 percent urban. The largest primarily Russian cities were Moscow (9.0 million), St. Petersburg (5.0 million), Nizhny Novgorod (1.4 million), and Novosibirsk (1.4 million).

Despite the degree of urbanization, Russians remain deeply attached to their natural environment. A dacha in the countryside, even if it is a humble cabin, is much sought after and often obtained. Russian poetry, which remains a highly esteemed expressive form (and a mainstay of education), often celebrates the beauty of the land. Contrast Pushkin's "Winter Evening" and Yesenin's "The Golden Grove Has Ceased to Speak." Although these poems were written years ago, the environment to which they refer—birches, oaks, pines, feather grass, nightingales and cranes, and the Russian rivers—has deep and pervasive meaning to this day.

DEMOGRAPHY. Expanding with the rise of Muscovy, the Russian people numbered more than 8 million by 1678. Concentrated in central and northern Russia and thinly settled in the Urals and Siberia, they formed about 40 percent of the population of the Russian Empire of the eighteenth and nineteenth centuries. By 1917 their numbers had grown to about 76 million, with somewhat less than half of these in their an-

cient core area but only 10 percent outside the boundaries of today's Russia. Prior to World War II the Russian population was characterized by high fertility and mortality—a crude birth rate of 33 per 1,000, a death rate of 23.6 per 1,000, and life expectancy of about 44 years. World War II and its aftermaths had disastrous effects: the 1959 census reported that, for the ages 35 and over, there were only 54 men for 100 women, the absolute deficiency of men in these ages coming to 12.2 million. By 1979–1980 the Russian population had reached 137.4 million, with 25 percent of the gain between 1939 and 1979 coming from Russification, but the natural increase rate, with dropping fertility, averaged only about 6 per 1,000 over the same period. Recent Russian life expectancies at birth are among the lowest for any urbanized population: the 1988 figures were 69.9 years for both sexes, 64.8 years for men, and 74.4 years for women. Infant mortality for the Russian Republic in that year was 18.9 per 1,000 births (three-quarters of the USSR average). By 1979 one-third of the Russian population of 137 million lived in the old core area, another half elsewhere in the Russian Republic, and only 17 percent in the other parts of the USSR, where, however, they often constituted a large minority or a near majority (Estonia). Today the population is 150 million. The Russian population has grown at a historic rate of 0.9 percent annually.

Cardiovascular stress associated with smoking, alcoholism, the workplace, and family life is the major cause of death today. For women, the combination of heavy domestic work loads and full-time employment contributes to the death rate. This, as well as poor housing, spouse abuse (associated with alcoholism), and unplanned pregnancies partly account for a lifetime average of five abortions per woman—more than twice the number of live births. Fewer than 60 percent of Russian women practice a contraceptive method other than withdrawal or the rhythm method; the total number of women suffering from the consequences of abortions and related medical practices is hard to assess but certainly high.

Migration, particularly to and from Siberia, has had a marked effect on the population, with only 10 to 20 percent of the migrants remaining in their adopted homes after five years. Such movements of population are of course associated with social and political stress.

LINGUISTIC AFFILIATION. Speakers of Russian form the largest East Slavic speech community, the other members being Ukrainian and Belarussian. After the Common Slavic, Common East Slavic, and Old Russian stages, the Russian language emerged in about the fourteenth century in central Russia (centered on Rostov-Suzdal'). The Russian language has historically been divided among northern, central, and southern dialects and by marked differences between the popular, administrative, and ecclesiastical styles, which are still evident in vocabulary and syntax. Russian has also been influenced by other languages, notably Finno-Ugric in its early stages, Germanic, Turkic, Greek, Polish, and, above all, French and, most recently, English.

History and Cultural Relations

Since the fifteenth century, the Russian state has been distinguished by centralized, generally autocratic rule, strongly dependent upon a service class (*oprichnina*, *dvoryanstvo*, Communist party). This was particularly developed by Peter I. Even in 1987 a party monograph stated that "it is important that not only directors, but rank and file workmen, collective farmers, and intellectuals understand their place and role in *perestroyka*" (Laptev, ed., 1987, 22). Although alternative foci of power (the Orthodox church, the National Assembly Zemskiy Sobor, the high aristocracy, the local Zemstva) have emerged from time to time, they have been repeatedly co-opted and controlled. Only the widely dispersed, deeply devoted, and secretive Old Believers have resisted control despite persecution since the seventeenth century.

The rise and expansion of the Russian state, in a context of hostile states and peoples, has been at enormous cost in wars and rebellions, famines and epidemics. The Tatar raids, the Time of Troubles (a period of dynastic conflict, 1598–1613), the Swedish War, the Napoleonic Wars, the Crimean War, the Russo-Japanese War, and World Wars I and II brought great misery. For 150 years, the drafting of serfs for 25 years of military service was deeply mourned in every village. Peter I instituted a modest vehicle for military and civilian upward mobility, through the system of progressively earned ranks. A modern-day parallel was the *nomenklatura*, a system of specified ranks in the former USSR.

Autocratic, often capricious, political power has combined with other elements of Russian social culture to limit the extent and stability of social stratification. In earlier times, estates were constantly being dispersed because of falls from favor and the equal inheritance rights of all sons (as opposed to primogeniture). Although there were many merchant families, some of them extremely wealthy, trade was in general not highly valued and was prohibited for those of noble descent. Modest alternative avenues of social ascent (as defined in the Tables of Rank) were open even to Jews, who were otherwise a persecuted minority confined to the western Pale.

Serfdom, which began during the medieval period, reached its nadir in the eighteenth century when Aleksandr Radishchev's *A Journey from St. Petersburg to Moscow* disclosed appalling abuses. Conditions on the great estates, particularly for household serfs, were those of true slavery, although they were better for the land-working serfs, particularly those under the quitrent (*obrok*) system (the other system being to work on shares). Because, as in other frontier lands, there was no serfdom in Siberia, it provided an escape and some relief—hence the continuing stream of fugitive serfs, who settled these regions and often became Cossacks.

From the 1930s in the former USSR, the collective farmer represented a dispossessed class lacking the internal passport needed for urban residence. Only collective-farm chairmen—party appointees after 1956—were in a position to control farm resources and incomes. Virtually the only area of collective-farm freedom was the de facto possession of small private plots that produced an extraordinary share of Russian foodstuffs, including meat, dairy products, and vegetables. This is increasingly the case today. Within this rural domain, incidentally, elements of customary law have persisted with remarkable vitality. Despite the partial privatization of land and various programs and projects, many Russian peasants are primarily interested in more effective production (e.g., by working together) than they are in private ownership of land as a matter of principle.

Russian industrialization has varied between periods of intensive development and those of prolonged stagnation. In the Kievan period, the cities, as archaeology shows, were centers of local and even international trade and of production through many sophisticated crafts. By the sixteenth century Muscovy's trade with England and other parts of Europe had stimulated technological development. But it was not until Peter I that a strategically oriented program of industrialization was initiated and pushed forward with considerable success. Its central and continuing weaknesses were the dependence on facilities granted to court favorites and on serf (i.e., slave) labor. Despite these weaknesses, there was, in the eighteenth century, phenomenal growth in many areas, the opening of mines and factories, and, among central and northern peasants, the growth of large cottage industries with an enormous inventory of goods such as wooden spoons for export to Asia via Kazan. By the nineteenth century steam power was used, especially in the growing textile industry; during the latter part of the nineteenth and first part of the twentieth centuries, Russia experienced the most rapid industrial growth in modern world history. In general, though, government efforts failed to help rising small entrepreneurs, and the subsidization of inefficient favorites went on. By the eve of World War I, Russia had become an industrial world power, comparable to France, Germany, and the other Western powers that had aided it with their capital.

Although permanent urbanization encompassed barely 10 percent of the Russian population in 1913, a great part of the central and northern Russian population was engaged in migratory industrial labor as well as crafts. This permitted very rapid economic growth in the 1920s. With the rise of German and Japanese militarism, Soviet industrialization took a strategic direction, stressing widely dispersed heavy industrial production, which has continued to dominate to this day. Vast numbers of workers were essential for the huge tasks, and forced labor was a basic recruitment mechanism from 1933 to 1957. In addition, between 1940 and 1957, the State Labor Reserves drafted millions of young people, whose barracks life greatly depressed family formation, induced cultural discontinuity, and encouraged alcoholism and violence.

Generally, the new cities built standardized housing—apartment blocks with central play areas for children. But housing rarely approached real needs, nor did it provide the desired privacy. In 1984 in Kemerovo, about 40 percent of the population lived in apartment blocks, another 40 percent resided in traditional wooden houses without running water or plumbing but with electricity, and the remainder were in dormitories.

The class of intellectuals, despite attrition through oppression, censorship, and internal conflicts, has been of great significance in modern times. With its origins mainly in the educational reforms of the eighteenth century, and drastically enlarged through the intellectual explosion and political tensions of the nineteenth century, the intelligentsia, defined partly by intellectual and

partly by political criteria, became a decisive factor in the revolutions of the twentieth century and remains peculiarly powerful in the chaotic scene of the 1990s.

Economy

In 1985 the Russian Republic had about 83.8 million persons of working age (men reckoned from 16 to 59 years of age; women from 16 to 54). The number employed as workers and service personnel was about 63 million, whereas collective farmers numbered 4.5 million. Fifty-two percent of this civilian employment was female. Eighty-one percent of the working-age population was working. Nonworkers, unemployed, and people working exclusively in the private sector composed the remainder—or somewhat more, since a fair proportion of older men were still employed. The total labor force, including that concerned with private agricultural plots, was divided as follows: industry and construction, 42 percent; agriculture and forestry, 14 percent; transport and communications, 10 percent; trade and food services, 8 percent; health, physical education, social security, and science, 18 percent; governmental administration, 3 percent; housing and miscellaneous, 5 percent.

Economic returns included pay and entitlements, which depended on the place of employment, party status, and other determinants. In 1985 pay averaged 210 rubles per month, running highest in water transport (287 rubles) and lowest in "cultural work" (123 rubles). Service in remote areas, such as the Arctic, led to large bonuses; all Siberians get "northern percentages" (but prices are higher in Siberia). Entitlements covered housing, health care, day care, vacation sites, and even the right to purchase luxuries such as Volga cars, but these benefits were all but absent for the "unorganized" population, which included children not attending nurseries and schools, the unemployed, and the retired, particularly in rural areas.

The state and cooperative retail trade, including food services, provide only a partial picture of consumption; the unofficial shadow economy is not measured in the official statistics, although it involves a large part of the economy; nor are the large price differences for various social groups included. Official figures for 1985 indicate that 51 percent of the total volume of sales was for foodstuffs, including 5 percent on meat and fowl and 3 percent on bologna. Dairy products took about 3 percent; fats, 2.4 percent; eggs, almost 2 percent. Bread, heavily subsidized, accounted for 2.6 percent; vegetables and fruits, for 3.5 percent. Potatoes continue to be a mainstay of the diet, and most families seem to have a supply of them. Of nonfood items, clothes, footwear, and cloth were the largest component at 21.4 percent. Consumer durables (i.e., cars, furniture, carpets, bicycles, and motorcycles) came to 8.4 percent, whereas soap, detergents, and perfume took 1.6 percent. Printed matter—Russians are avid readers—was 1.4 percent. All else came to 15.7 percent.

These statistics reflect the austere way of life of the majority of the Russian population. Only occasionally can an average Russian enjoy traditional foods such as *pirozhki* (meat- or cabbage-filled turnovers) or go to the circus, enjoy tapes or concerts, or travel freely by car or motorcycle to escape overcrowded housing. This context gives rise to high rates of alcoholism and family violence.

Kinship, Marriage, and Family

In the eighteenth and nineteenth centuries the bilateral kindred was the basic Russian social unit among both peasants and aristocrats (such as the Aksakov family on the Ural frontier). This kindred was delimited in Russian kinship terminology by the exogamic units set by churchly canon: four "links" for consanguinal kin, two for affinal; only the archaic term *dyadina* (father's brother's wife, mother's brother's wife) extended further. The terminology is isolating, except that no distinction is made among consanguinal kin between male and female lines of descent; cousin terms derive from sibling terms; gender suffixes distinguish the sexes among the consanguinal kin of ascending generations and among affinal kin (except daughter's husband and son's wife); and the terms for daughter's husband and sister's husband are merged. Within the kindred, patterns of behavior other than exogamy were largely determined by the specific coresidence patterns of each household. The nuclear family, often supplemented by a grandmother or aunt, was particularly important in the south, but in the central regions patrilocally or fraternally extended families were common, and in the north the large extended family, often numbering more than twenty persons in the household, was typical. Within these households, whatever their size, parental, especially paternal, authority prevailed. To this day on the collective farms, and to a lesser extent in the cities, various joint household budgets persist. Christenings, reverence of icons, and parental blessings of various kinds strengthen human relations. A basic, endearing term for all types of kin is *rodnoy* or *rodnaya* (kinsman, kinswoman), from *rod* (clan). Until recently, at least, godparenthood (*kum*, *kuma*), often by a relative, constituted a lifelong tie of central importance.

Although premarital sex and single parenthood were always common among Russian peasants and workers, marriage continues to be a major socioreligious act. Traditionally it was mainly

RELIGION

The Christianization of Russia in A.D. 988 was a formal royal act that signified the continuing closeness of church and state. Even during Mongol domination, the church was exempt from taxation and enjoyed vast possessions. Through ritual, saintly example, and legal innovations, the church promoted such values as the cardinal importance of love, the respect due to parents, the obligation to give alms, and the abhorrence of suicide. Much of the customary law, including aspects of women's rights, came from the church. The veneration of icons (e.g., in the "red corner" in peasant homes) was adopted in various figurative ways by the Communist party for its own sacred imagery. Prayers and blessings by family elders on important occasions, religious processions, and fasting as a major expression of religious devotion became deeply embedded in peasant and worker culture. Christening and burial in consecrated ground have retained much of their significance, even though priests as ritualists were never very close to peasant or worker life. Such non-Christian practices as soothsaying on New Year's have persisted. Today over half of all Russians, particularly in Europe, appear to be active religious believers, their Orthodox dogma and ritual having changed very little. Weddings and other rituals still have a traditional character; Easter ritual trappings such as painted eggs and *kulich* cake are retained in a quasi-secular setting. The revitalization of Orthodoxy has gone hand in hand with the rapid growth of various Eastern religions, mysticisms, parapsychology, and belief in "paranormal phenomena" (some of the latter being regarded as "scientific").

an economic contract between the heads of two households, reinforced by the payment of the wedding costs by the groom's household and the provision of a substantial dowry by the mother of the bride. Both patrilocal and matrilocal marriage were practiced, although the former was preferred and more frequent. In matrilocal marriages, parents without sons adopted a son-in-law under a contract that stipulated that he support them for the remainder of their lives and give them a decent burial. Although marriages today are individual commitments, they are often associated with obligations to older female relatives. In Kemerovo, for example, families can gain prized housing rights by means of a coresident grandmother, real or adopted, who is thus protected and in turn helps with child care and household tasks. (This "structural *babushka*" may be a grandparent's sister or other older female relative.)

Sociopolitical Organization

In contrast to the abundance of pre-Revolutionary data, recent materials on Russian social structure are fragmentary. Clearly much has changed since 1985. It may be surmised, however, that traditional kin groups, informal networks, and elements of customary law have persisted to a considerable extent in areas least disturbed by migration (e.g., Ryazan and Tambov provinces). The pervasive social controls of the Communist party, designed to suppress alternative sources and processes of power, seem to have had major limitations and were often mitigated by kindred and friends acting in a "handshake all around" (*krugovaya poruka*)—that is, exchanging and sharing food and other commodities in informal networks.

Bibliography

Berezovskiy, V. N., and N. I. Krotov (1990). *Neformal'-naya rossiya: O neformal'nykh politizirovannykh dvizheniyakh i gruppakh v RSFSR* ("Nonformal" Russia: On "nonformal" politicized movements and groups in the RSFSR). Moscow: Molodaya Gvardiya.

Bruk, S. I., and V. M. Kabuzan (1982). "Dinamika chislennosti i rasseleniya Russkikh posie Velikoy oktyabr'skoysotsialisticheskoy revolutsiyi" (Dynamics of the number and distribution of the Russians after the Great October Socialist Revolution). *Sovetskaia* Etnografiia 5:3–21.

Bruk, S. I., and V. M. Kabuzan (1982). "Dinamika chislennosti i rasseleniya Russkogo etnosa (1678–1917)" (Dynamics of the numbers and distribution of the Rusian ethnic population, 1678–1917). *Sovetskaia Etnografiia* 4:9–25.

Budina, O. R., and M. N. Shmeleva (1982). "Traditsiya v kul'turno-bytovom razitiyi sovremennogo Russkogo goroda" (Tradition in the development of daily culture in the contemporary Russian city). *Sovetskaia Etnografiia* 6:27–39.

Filin, F. P. (1981). *Istoriya leksiki Russkogo literaturnogo yazyka: Kontsa xvii-nachala xix veka* (History of the lexicon of the Russian literary tongue: End of the seventeenth to the early nineteenth centuries). Moscow: Nauka.

Frolov, A. V. (1987). "Osobennosti smertnosti detey v vozrosti do i goda na domu v sel'skoy mestnosti" (Peculiarities of infant deaths at home in a rural locality). *Sovetskoye Zdravookhraneniye* 6:18–21.

Katkova, I. P., and I. S. Shurandina (1987). "O rabote uchastkovogo vracha-pediatra s semey po preduprezhdeniya sluchayev smerti detey" (On the work of a primary care pediatrician with families at risk of child death). *Sovetskoye Zdravookhraneniye* 6:21–24.

Kiparsky, V. (1971). "On the Stratification of the Russian Vocabulary." *Oxford Slavonic Papers*, n.s. 4:1–11.

Laptev, I. D., ed. (1987). *Sovetskoye obshchestvo segodnya* (Soviet society today). Moscow: Izd. Politilit.

Miliukov, Paul (1962). *Russia and Its Crisis*. New York: Collier.

Oblensky, Dimitri (1962). *The Penguin Book of Russian Verse*. Harmondsworth: Penguin Books.

Radishchev, Aleksandr N. (1958). *A Journey from St. Petersburg to Moscow (1790)*. Cambridge: Harvard University Press.

Reznokov, S. G., and A. P. Denisov (1987). "Medikosotsial'nyye osobennosti formirovaniye semye i zdorovya vnebrachnogo rebenka v zapadnoy Sibiri" (Medical-social peculiarities of family formation and the health of children of unmarried mothers in western Siberia). *Zdravookhraneniyi Rossiyskoy Federatsiyi* 6:24–26.

Shimkin, D. B. (1963). "Current Characteristics and Problems of the Soviet Rural Population." In *Soviet Agricultural and Peasant Affairs*, edited by R. Laird, 79–130. Lawrence: University of Kansas Press.

Shimkin, D. B., and P. Sanjuan (1953). "Culture and World View: A Method of Analysis Applied to Rural Russia." *American Anthropologist* 55:329–348.

Sokolov, Y. M. (1950). *Russian Folklore*. New York: Macmillan.

Volin, Lazar (1943). "The Russian Peasant and Serfdom." *Agricultural History* 17:41–61.

Zenkovsky, Serge A. (1957). "The Ideological World of the Denisov Brothers." *Harvard Slavic Studies* 3:49–65.

—DIMITRI SHIMKIN

TAJIKS

Ethnonyms: Tadjiks, Tadzhiks

Orientation

IDENTIFICATION. Tajiks are a Central Asian people who live in Afghanistan, in republics of the former Soviet Union, and in China. Within the former Soviet Union, they are concentrated in the Republic of Tajikistan, although important populations also live in Uzbekistan. Tojikistoni shuravi (Soviet Tadzhikistan), a sovereign republic, was formed in 1929. The distinguishing features of Tajiks are their language, sedentary lifestyle, and Islamic-Iranian culture. The widespread use of "Tajik" as an ethnopolitical term emerged with Soviet usage; prior to that, regional rather than linguistic affiliation held the key to self-identity. In Soviet usage, the term "Tajik" also includes speakers of non-Persian Iranian languages who inhabit mountain valleys in the Pamir mountain area such as Sarikolis, Wakhis, and Shugnis.

LOCATION. Tajik-inhabited areas fall roughly between 65° and 75° W and 35° to 42° N. Tajikistan is the southeasternmost of the republics of the former Soviet Union and is bordered by Uzbekistan and Kyrgyzstan to the west and north, the Xinjiang Uigur Autonomous Region of the People's Republic of China to the east, and Afghanistan to the south. The total area of Tajikistan is 143,100 square kilometers. The entire Tajik-inhabited region is very mountainous with narrow valleys; agriculture is nourished by mineral silt and irrigation waters from fast-flowing rivers fed by melting snows. The rivers form tributaries of the Panj, which flows into the Amu Darya (Oxus River). Northern Tajikistan includes parts of the Ferghana Valley, where the waters eventually meet to flow into the Syr Darya (Jaxartes River).

Geographically, the Tajik Republic is trifurcated by mountains that are impassable by road in winter. The northern portion is dominated by the town of Khojent, formerly Leninabad; the capital, Dushanbe, known from 1930 to 1931 as Stalinabad, is in the south. To the east, but still part of the Tajik Republic, is the Gorno-Badakhshan Autonomous Region, a sparsely populated area inhabited mainly by small, valley ethnic groups including Kyrgyz. The major urban center of this area has become Khorog.

The climate falls within the temporal continental high-altitude range with about 320 days of sunlight. Precipitation occurs as rain and snow, mainly between November and April. Summers are hot and dry with mean daytime temperature in July ranging from 23 to 30° C.

DEMOGRAPHY. The world Tajik population is more difficult to analyze than that within the republics of the former Soviet Union, although this too has been subject to manipulation, especially outside Tajikistan. The 1989 census placed the number of Tajiks within the Soviet Union at 4,217,000, 3,168,000 of these residing within their own republic and 932,000 in Uzbekistan; in other words, about 99 percent of the Tajiks reside in these two republics. Together with the estimated 4 million Dari speakers in Afghanistan, who may also be identified broadly as Tajik, and smaller numbers in the People's Republic of China, the world Tajik population may be estimated at about 9 million. Since the 1959 Soviet census, Tajiks have increased in number by 201.9 percent, making them the fastest-growing major ethnic group of the former Soviet Union. They constitute 62.25 percent of the population of Tajikistan and 4.7 percent of that of Uzbekistan (Uzbeks constitute 23.52 percent of that of Tajikistan). The number of Russians in Tajikistan is declining (7 percent in 1989).

LINGUISTIC AFFILIATION. The standard Tajik dialect is mutually intelligible with the Persian of Iran and the Dari of Afghanistan and is increasingly being called either Farsi-Tojiki or Farsi (Persian), all of which form the major living branch of the Iranian Language Family. In addition to standard Tajik, nineteen dialects exist, which differ from each other morphologically and phonetically. Rural mountain valley people cannot be readily understood by urban Tajiks, who generally use the standard dialect. Tajik intellectuals are monolingual (Russian), bilingual (Tajik and Russian), or trilingual (Tajik, Russian, and Uzbek). The Tajiks, on the whole, are one of the least Russified Muslim communities of the former Soviet Union; in 1979, only 22,666 claimed Russian as their "first native language."

History and Cultural Relations

Tajik historical development is intertwined with that of the other sedentary people of Central Asia, especially the Uzbeks. Before the coming of the Turks to the area and their eventual sedentarization, Iranian groups dominated the urban oases. Islam eventually became universally accepted and Turkic conquerors adjusted their religious and literary culture to that of the local inhabitants whom they ruled. Local (Tajik) administrators continued to dominate in public life

The distinguishing features of Tajiks are their language, sedentary lifestyle, and Islamic-Iranian culture.

under Turkic tribally affiliated rulers. This hybrid Turko-Iranian culture dominated the important oases towns, especially Bukhara and Samarkand. Bilingualism—Tajik and (Turkic) Chagatay or Uzbek—was widespread both on the literate and nonliterate level through the early twentieth century. Most Tajik areas fell under the Bukharan and Khokand khanates until the latter was destroyed by czarist forces in 1876 and incorporated into the Turkestan governor-generalship. Resistance to czarist, then Bolshevik rule gained strength in Tajik areas where Basmachi bands of Uzbeks and Tajiks were finally stamped out only in 1932. With the division of Soviet Central Asia along ethnolinguistic lines in 1924, a Tajik Autonomous SSR was set aside within the Uzbek SSR and this, by 1929, became a full-fledged Tajik SSR. Most of the educated and elite Tajiks lived in Bukhara and Samarkand and made the transition to Dushanbe and other Tajik territory with reluctance. Both the status and the size of the Tajik population in these two cities are sources of conflict; many Tajiks feel that these cities, together with Khiva, as traditional Tajik centers of culture, should be part of Tajikistan.

Disentangling a distinct Tajik culture from the Uzbek culture around it—and from non-Soviet Persian culture—became the focus of cultural activity during the Stalinist period. Separate Tajik institutions, organized on the All-Union model, labored to use valley dialects, history, and especially archaeology to create a Tajik history delinked from Islam and distinct from other Central Asian culture. Thawing of Soviet-Iranian relations led to ever-closer Iranian-Tajik cultural relations; the Soviet invasion of Afghanistan (1979) saw increasing Tajik tutelage of Afghans in Kabul as well as in Dushanbe. Important in this international cultural linking have been Russians and Russianized Tajiks. The Uzbek-Tajik bilingual pattern has been replaced by a Tajik-Russian one. In the mid-1990s, a civil war broke out in Tajikistan. After four years of conflict, a peace agreement was signed in 1997.

Settlements

Most of Tajikistan is rural; 85 percent of the population lives in valleys and mountain areas up to 1,600 meters in elevation. Most of these settlements are organized in the kolkhoz/sovkhoz pattern superimposed on former villages (*deh kishlaq*, which are sometimes equivalent to loosely extended families practicing endogamy). There are pockets of industrialization in rural areas where non-Tajiks as well as Tajiks work. In the north and south population density runs from 50 to 150 per square kilometer, whereas in the mountains it is as low as 5 to 10. New urban settlements have expanded from former villages. Urban administrative centers, especially Dushanbe, have grown along Western patterns, with roads for motorized vehicles, apartment blocks, parks, and industries. Old villages retain extended family homes, often placed within orchards and vineyards. Walled compounds ensure household privacy.

Economy

SUBSISTENCE AND COMMERCIAL ACTIVITIES. The Tajik economy was seriously disrupted by four years of civil conflict. Cotton, a commercial product developed during the czarist period, has dominated Tajik agriculture—Tajikistan ranks second among former republics of the Soviet Union in cotton production. Other agricultural products, geared to the western, urban Soviet centers, include grapes and orchard fruits and nuts, vegetables, grain, and flowers. Greenhouse production, especially in the Surkhan Darya region, is flown to colder parts of the former USSR. Stock breeding, chiefly by Kyrgyz and Uzbeks, also contributes to the economy in mountainous regions. A black-market economy in produce, more recently expanded to manufactured goods smuggled from Afghanistan, also thrives.

INDUSTRIAL ARTS. Hydroelectric power and mining/processing form the main heavy industries in Tajikistan. Large dams (Qairoqqum, Nurek, Sarband, Boighazi, Markazi, and Sharshara) supply power to Soviet Central Asia and Afghanistan. Industrial manufacture is in cotton-related machinery. Together with light industry in textiles, furniture, and food processing, the industrial sector employs most non-Tajiks, especially Russians.

TRADE. Under the Soviet system, trade within the union was conducted on a nonmonetary basis. Thus, Tajik cotton, hydroelectric power, and other products were traded by Moscow on the world market for hard currency or as barter items. In turn, Tajikistan received needed commodities and services. On a lower level, trade in fresh agricultural produce on private plots has flourished in urban areas where the government has constructed new bazaars to facilitate private trade.

DIVISION OF LABOR. Labor patterns have undergone transformation under the Soviet system in two important ways: the importation of labor (Slavs, Koreans) and the mobilization of women into the formal labor force. This imposed

RAKING COTTON

*A Tajik man raking cotton in
Vaksh Valley. Cotton developed
as a commercial product during
the czarist period and dominates Tajik agriculture.
Tadzhikistan.
(Dean Conger/Corbis)*

system of labor has resulted in nominal universal
employment. Most women, however, do agricultural work. The fast-growing Tajik rural population shows signs of having outpaced agricultural
employment capacity. Entry into light or heavy
industry appears barred by lack of training and
aptitude. Women, regularly visible in high positions, continue to be the only ones who perform
domestic labor.

LAND TENURE. Under collectivization, little
land remained private, although private homes
were frequently retained. As collectivization is
dismantled, the problems of commercial crop
production, the small amount of arable land for
the large rural population, and the desire for private housing all create problems in a new economic order.

Kinship

KINSHIP GROUPS AND DESCENT. Extended families sharing adjacent houses or a single compound were the norm in traditional Tajik
society. This pattern has been interrupted by the
construction of apartment complexes in which
units are distributed based on place of employment. Descent is determined through the father,
although women retain their own family names.

KINSHIP TERMINOLOGY. Relationships are
distinguished by gender and also (reflecting borrowings from Uzbek) by age among siblings.

Marriage and Family

MARRIAGE. Marriage patterns differ between urban and rural areas and over the past sixty
years. In urban settings and among young people,
Soviet influence on marriage may be seen in the
exercise of choice in marriage partners and the importance of civil ceremonies. The couple may live
with the groom's parents until a suitable apartment
is located. In rural areas, the older pattern of
arranged marriages with religious/traditional marriage celebrations continues to be honored. The
couple will live with the man's family until a house
is constructed. Divorce is rare in both settings.

DOMESTIC UNIT. The size of the rural domestic unit is large: the average rural household
numbers seven to eight children as well as a
grandparent or other relations. In urban areas the
domestic unit is far smaller, averaging three to
four children and possibly a paternal or maternal
parent. According to Bennigsen and Wimbush
(1986, 89) "traditional customs such as the *kalym*
[bride-price], the early marriage of girls, the levirate and sororate, preferences of marriage between

*In the late Soviet era
the pattern of
political
organization had
begun to move
toward gradual
entrenchment of
Tajiks into positions
of real power within
the Communist
party.*

cousins, sexual segregation, *aksakalism* [local rule by 'white beards'] and even polygamy are observed by Tajiks more generally than by any other Muslim nationality of Central Asia."

INHERITANCE. The residence, if privately owned, and its contents are often inherited by the oldest son (or the one with whom the parent lived). Inherited property is infrequently sold.

SOCIALIZATION. Tajiks rarely send children to institutions for care, even if both parents work away from the home. Accommodation is made within the extended family for the care of young children. Children are raised to value family life, religious or ethical standards, their ethnic identity, and within this, their regional ties. Young Tajiks intermarry with Uzbeks and other cultural Muslims at a far higher rate than with Russians, despite the extensive Russification of urban elites.

Sociopolitical Organization

SOCIAL ORGANIZATION. Tajik society retains few objects of cohesion except as determined by general Central Asian customs and recent history. Cleavage among urban and rural groups rests also on place of origin and descent. Bukharan immigrants socialize with each other, as do people of various valleys. Soviet institutions and the workplace have brought them together, as has a common language, but without the economic and political institutions, the social fabric is fragile and susceptible to influence from emergent Islamic, nationalistic, and other forces. The core of social organization remains the extended family and region.

POLITICAL ORGANIZATION. In the late Soviet era the pattern of political organization had begun to move toward gradual entrenchment of Tajiks into positions of real power within the Communist party.

SOCIAL CONTROL. Modes of social behavior ingrained within the family function within society at large. These include loyalty to family members and fellow villagers. Other forms of social control exercised by the state have served to create tight groupings to preserve the welfare and safety of the group. Increasingly difficult socioeconomic conditions arising from population growth and ecological damage have begun to strain public order.

CONFLICT. Tension between the Communist controlled government and anti-Communist and Islamic opposition groups led to a four-year civil war, 1992–1997. Tens of thousands of people died

in the fighting and the Tajik economy has been gravely weakened. In 1997, the government and opposition leaders signed a peace agreement to end the civil war.

Religion and Expressive Culture

RELIGIOUS BELIEFS. Most religiously minded Tajiks belong to the Sunni sect, and within this to the Hanafi juridical school. Small, isolated groups, especially among the Pamir peoples of Iranian but not Tajik language, are devotees of Isma'ili Shiism, and yet a smaller portion follow the Ithna Ash'ari sect. As such, with the exception of Bukharan Jews, Slavs, other Christian-associated groups, and the urban-dwelling Koreans, the people of Tajikistan generally follow Islamic belief patterns. Belief in the supernatural, outside of formal Islam, falls into several categories: curative customs, fortune-telling, and ascription of bad fortune to the power of fate or of evil beings called jinn.

RELIGIOUS PRACTITIONERS. Strong evidence exists of the growth of Islamic practice among rural Tajiks, particularly the educated leadership on collective farms. In the absence of formal religious schools within Tajikistan (such as are found in Uzbekistan), individual Tajiks demonstrate a surprising familiarity with formal Islamic theological and juridical doctrine, owing in part to unregistered mullahs, Sufi brotherhoods, and a special category of half-Sufi-half-shaman; about a dozen shrines to saints are major religious centers (Bennigsen and Wimbush 1986, 91). Fasting during Ramadan, and especially the fast-breaking feast of Eid-e Fitr are popular and more public than in earlier years. Family ownership of a copy of the Quran is valued despite the lack of facilities for instruction in its contents. Informal teachers not recognized by the state or the Spiritual Directorate of Central Asia and Kazakhstan in Tashkent function throughout society on a semisecret level.

CEREMONIES. Rites of passage include circumcision of male children, marriage, and funerals. Holidays include the Islamic Eid-e Qorban and Eid-e Fitr, as well as Nowruz, the traditional Iranian new year celebrated at the vernal equinox.

ARTS. Literature, especially poetry rooted in the brilliant classical culture that Tajiks share with other Iranian peoples, is foremost among traditional Tajik arts. Architectural decoration (*gach kari*), carpet weaving, metal decoration, embroidery, and calligraphy have continued to be valued, although all these arts have acquired some level of

Soviet content to conform with political dictates. In the fields of music, dance, and theater, innovations are widespread as Western arts have been introduced and local arts have been adapted.

MEDICINE. Tajik medicine, like other medicine in Central Asia, falls into two branches: the Western-oriented branch represented by the Gastrointestinal and Chemistry Institutes of the Tajik Academy of Sciences established in 1955, and the traditions of folk medicine passed within particular families by word of mouth but based also on written works of medieval scientists such as Ibn Sina. The two branches have drawn closer together as the herbal cures offered by folk medicine have become the object of study of the scientific institutions and the medical properties of cumin and the like have been recognized.

DEATH AND AFTERLIFE. Formal ideas of death follow either the nonreligious pattern or the Islamic one. It is customary for funeral proceedings for Tajik Communists to be conducted according to Muslim custom and for the burial to take place in a Muslim cemetery. Among the traditional populace, the afterlife is firmly held to be a time for reward and punishment for conduct in the present life.

Bibliography

Atkin, Muriel (1989). *The Subtlest Battle: Islam in Soviet Tajikistan*. Philadelphia: Foreign Policy Research Institute.

At the Foot of the Blue Mountains: Stories by Tajik Authors (1984). Moscow: Raduga Publishers.

Bennigsen, Alexandre, and S. Enders Wimbush (1986). *Muslims of the Soviet Empire: A Guide*, 89, 91. Bloomington: Indiana University Press.

Naby, Eden (1975). "Transitional Central Asian Literature: Tajik and Uzbek Prose Fiction from 1909 to 1932." Ph.D. dissertation, Columbia University.

Rakowska-Harmstone, Theresa (1970). *Russia and Nationalism in Central Asia: The Case of Tadzhikistan*. Baltimore and London: Johns Hopkins University Press.

—EDEN NABY

TURKMENS

Ethnonyms: Turcomans (from the Persian usage), Türkmens

Orientation

IDENTIFICATION. The Turkmens are one of the major ethnic groups of Central Asia, where they had their own Soviet Socialist Republic (SSR), also referred to as Turkmenia or Turkmenistan. The majority of Turkmens of the former USSR live within the present-day republic of Turkmenistan, although some communities are found in neighboring Uzbekistan and Tajikistan. In addition, large numbers of Turkmens reside outside the former Soviet Union, in northeastern Iran, northwestern Afghanistan, northern Iraq, and eastern Turkey.

LOCATION. Turkmenistan is the southernmost republic of the former Soviet Union. It is bounded on the west by the Caspian Sea, on the south by Iran and Afghanistan, on the northwest by Kazakhstan, and on the north and east by Uzbekistan. The Amu Darya forms much of the border with Uzbekistan. The dominant geographic feature of the republic is the largely uninhabited Kara Kum (lit., "Black Sand") Desert, which occupies almost 90 percent of Turkmenistan. Human habitation is concentrated on the fringes of the Kara Kum, especially along the southern border of the republic, in the foothills of the Kopet Dagh, and in the oases of the Murgab and Tejen rivers, as well as along the Amu Darya in the east, the Caspian shore in the west, and the western border of Khorezm in the north.

Turkmenistan tends to have hot, dry summers; mild winters; short, humid springs; and dry autumns. Temperatures range from an average high of 2° C in January to 30° C in July, with highs near 50° C recorded in the Kara Kum Desert. Precipitation averages only 20 to 30 centimeters annually. Both temperature and precipitation vary considerably within the republic.

DEMOGRAPHY. The Turkmen population of the Soviet Union as of the 1989 census was 2,718,297, an increase of 34 percent over the 1979 population of 2,027,913, and 78 percent over the 1970 population of 1,525,284. The Turkmens are therefore one of the fastest-growing ethnic groups of Central Asia, largely owing to very high birthrates; they presently average over five children per family. The increase among the Turkmens contrasts with a declining Slavic population in Turkmenistan. In 1979 Slavs accounted for 13.9 percent of the republic's overall population, in 1989 only 10.5 percent. With well over 50 percent of the population residing outside of urban areas, the Turkmens are among the most rural inhabitants of the former Soviet Union.

LINGUISTIC AFFILIATION. The Turkmens speak a language belonging to the Oghuz or Southwest Branch of the Turkic Language Group. Thus, they are closer linguistically to the

See also

Kazaks, Uzbeks

Azerbaijanis and the Turks of Turkey than to the neighboring Turkic peoples of Central Asia, such as the Uzbeks and Kazakhs. Distinct tribal dialects exist among the Turkmens. Elements of an emerging Turkmen literary language can be found as early as the eighteenth century in the common Turkic (or Chagatay) literature of Central Asia. The modern literary Turkmen language is a relatively new creation, however, developed in the 1920s under Soviet supervision and based on the Yomut and Teke dialects. Initially the Soviets opted for modifying the traditional Arabic script of the Turkmens, but in the late 1920s a shift was made to the Latin alphabet and, after 1939, to the modified Cyrillic alphabet. There have been calls to return to the Arabic script, which Turkmens living outside the former Soviet Union have continued to use.

History and Cultural Relations

The Oghuz Turkic ancestors of the Turkmens first appeared in the area of Turkmenistan in the eighth to tenth centuries A.D. The name "Turkmen" first appears in eleventh-century sources. Initially it seems to have referred to certain groups from among the Oghuz that had converted to Islam. During the thirteenth-century Mongol invasion into the heart of Central Asia, the Turkmens fled to more remote regions close to the Caspian shore. Thus, unlike many other peoples of Central Asia, they were little influenced by Mongol rule and, therefore, Mongol political tradition. In the sixteenth century the Turkmens once again began to migrate throughout the region of modern Turkmenistan, gradually occupying the agricultural oases. By the middle of the nineteenth century, the majority of Turkmens had become sedentary or seminomadic agriculturalists, although a significant portion remained exclusively nomadic stockbreeders.

From the sixteenth to nineteenth centuries the Turkmens repeatedly clashed with neighboring sedentary states, especially the rulers of Iran and the khanate of Khiva. Divided into more than twenty tribes and lacking any semblance of political unity, the Turkmens managed, however, to remain relatively independent throughout this period. By the early nineteenth century the dominant tribes were the Teke in the south, the Yomut in the southwest and in the north around Khorezm, and the Ersari in the east, near the Amu Darya. These three tribes constituted over one-half the total Turkmen population at that time.

In the early 1880s the Russian Empire succeeded in subjugating the Turkmens, but only af-

ter overcoming fiercer resistance from most Turkmens than from other conquered groups of Central Asia. At first the traditional society of the Turkmens was relatively unaffected by czarist rule, but the building of the Transcaspian Railroad and the expansion of oil production on the Caspian shore both led to a large influx of Russian colonists. The czarist administrators encouraged the cultivation of cotton as a cash crop on a large scale.

The Bolshevik Revolution in Russia was accompanied by a period of rebellion in Central Asia known as the Basmachi Revolt. Many Turkmens participated in this rebellion, and, after the victory of the Soviets, many of these Turkmens fled to Iran and Afghanistan. In 1924 the Soviet government established modern Turkmenistan. In the early years of Soviet rule, the government tried to break the power of the tribes by confiscating tribally held lands in the 1920s and introducing forced collectivization in the 1930s. Although pan-Turkmen identity was certainly strengthened under Soviet rule, the Turkmens of the former Soviet Union retain their sense of tribal consciousness to a great extent. The seventy years of Soviet rule have seen the elimination of nomadism as a way of life and the beginnings of a small but influential educated urban elite. This period also witnessed the firm establishment of the supremacy of the Communist party. In October 1991, Turkmenistan declared its independence from the Soviet Union and joined other republics in a loose association called the Commonwealth of Independent States.

Settlements

Turkmens traditionally lived a seminomadic life, with the summer encampment considered to be the "homeland." The encampments were contractual in nature, although they almost always were composed primarily of close relatives. The basic settlement was the *oba* (Russian: *aul*), which consisted of a group of households associated with a definite territory that they held in common. The traditional dwelling of the Turkmens was the round, collapsible tent (*oy*), consisting of a wooden frame with felt and sometimes reed coverings that could be erected or dismantled in about an hour. The Turkmens retained this dwelling even after becoming completely sedenterized. To this day these yurts, now serving as summer quarters or guest rooms, can be seen alongside modern brick homes.

Collectivization has replaced the oba with the kolkhoz, yet the basic family and tribal structure is intact. Movement to urban areas naturally weakens these traditional settlement patterns. The cities, however, are still primarily non-Turkmen; for example, Ashkhabad, the capital and largest city of the republic, is only 41 percent Turkmen.

Economy

SUBSISTENCE AND COMMERCIAL ACTIVITIES. Traditional Turkmen society was characterized by a distinctive division along economic lines between pastoralists (*charwa*) and agriculturalists (*chomur*). This division was found within almost every tribe and settlement and even within families. Individuals constantly alternated between these two life-styles, although the pastoralism was somewhat preferred. The traditional stock animal was the dromedary camel, well-suited to the climatic conditions of Turkmenistan. Only in the nineteenth century, with increased sedenterization, did sheep become the main animal in the Turkmen herds.

In the twentieth century Soviet planners have dictated the cultivation of cotton to the virtual exclusion of most other crops in Turkmenistan. The serious ecological repercussions of this cotton "monoculture," in terms of soil exhaustion and excessive water usage, have only recently been acknowledged. For example, the Kara Kum Canal, a Stalinist-era project to convey water for irrigation from the Amu Darya to the Turkmen Desert, has been shown to lose up to 50 percent of its water in transit (through seepage and evaporation) and to have significantly contributed to the dessication of the Aral Sea, formerly the world's second-largest inland sea, which is now rapidly disappearing. Very little industry has been developed in Turkmenistan and what does exist mainly employs ethnic Slavs.

A brisk trade is carried on in the bazaars of the republic, where many products not easily found in state stores, including fruits and vegetables from private plots and meat from privately held livestock, are readily available, although at much higher prices.

INDUSTRIAL ARTS. Many samples of Turkmen craft work can be found, especially in the bazaars. These include metal and wood household utensils, tools, and furniture. In modern times the traditional Turkmen practice of hand-weaving beautiful carpets has been transformed into a state industry with factories mass-producing carpets.

TRADE. Since Turkmenistan is heavily oriented toward agriculture, the republic relies on other regions of the former Soviet Union for imports of most finished goods. In return, the republic exports virtually all of its raw materials, especially cotton and natural gas, to other former Soviet republics.

DIVISION OF LABOR. Turkmen men and boys were traditionally responsible for tending the herds and performing heavy agricultural work, whereas women managed domestic affairs. Women and girls contributed to the household economy through weaving carpets. In modern times, men generally drive the machinery on the kolkhozy and manage the transport and sale of goods in the bazaar. Women and children represent the backbone of cotton harvesting, which is still mainly done by hand.

LAND TENURE. Historically, pastures and natural water sources were held in common by the oba, whereas plowed fields and dug wells were considered private property. After sedentarizing, some Turkmen tribes developed a system of land tenure known as *sanashik*, in which there existed an equal division of land and water between tribes and tribal subdivisions. This system included an annual redistribution between all eligible landholders (i.e., married males) in the tribe. During the Soviet period, land was declared the property of the state and collectivized.

Kinship

KINSHIP GROUPS AND DESCENT. The Turkmens are organized into a segmentary system of territorial descent groups. The largest descent groups are usually referred to as tribes. Each tribe is further subdivided into increasingly smaller and more closely related descent groups. Descent is traced patrilineally to a common ancestor, Oghuz Khan. The Turkmens preserve knowledge of their descent group and its relation to other groups in oral genealogies. Individual Turkmens know their recent genealogy—at least five to seven generations—very well, although they often conceal knowledge of the fifth and sixth generations to avoid becoming embroiled in more distant blood fueds. When two strangers first meet, they inquire about each others' descent group to establish their relationship to each other. When households that are not closely related camp together in the same oba, a tenuous kinship tie is often discovered. Marriage does not serve an important function in linking Turkmen descent groups. Although agnatic ties are very close and require political, social, and economic cooperation, uterine and affinal ties seldom go beyond limited economic assistance.

Among the Turkmens five sacred lineages exist, which trace their descent not to Oghuz Khan

When two strangers meet, they inquire about each others' descent group to establish their relationship to each other.

*Historically,
Turkmen society has
been highly
egalitarian, with
little notion of class
distinction. There
are very few
examples in
Turkmen history of
exceptionally rich
individuals.*

but to the first four caliphs in Islamic history. These groups, known as Owlad tribes, are strictly endogamous, rarely intermarrying with other Turkmens, although they live interspersed among all Turkmen tribes. The Owlad are especially revered by the Turkmens and carry out important religious and social functions in the communities where they live.

KINSHIP TERMINOLOGY. Turkmen kinship terminology is highly specific and serves to indicate the important distinctions in Turkmen society. For example, separate terms differentiate agnatic and nonagnatic relationships, as well as the important societal distinction of senior and junior positions between and within generations. Affinal and uterine relations are often addressed with broad classificatory terms.

Marriage and Family

MARRIAGE. The Turkmens are generally endogamous, choosing spouses from within their own tribe. This contrasts with the strict exogamy of other Central Asian peoples such as the Kazakhs and Kyrgyz. Marriage ceremonies are conducted according to Islamic rites, although this practice was often discouraged by Soviet authorities. Women traditionally marry very young (in their early teens), but their spouses can be much older. This is because of the practice, which continues to this day, of asking relatively high bride-prices for daughters. This forces men to wait until they can earn enough to afford to marry. The high bride-price historically also served as a means of leveling income by redistributing wealth. Traditionally, newlyweds would not actually live together until two or three years after the wedding, when the bride would come to live with her husband and his family. Polygamy, though allowed under Islamic law, has always been rare among the Turkmens. Modern Soviet life weakened—but did not eliminate—many of the traditional marriage practices of the Turkmens. To this day Turkmens almost never marry non-Turkmens, especially Russians or other Slavs.

DOMESTIC UNIT. The Turkmens maintain a traditional extended family with the fathers accorded formal authority within the home, although wives and elder sons may exert considerable informal influence. As sons marry and establish their own households, they continue to live in close proximity to their father and practice economic cooperation. Soviet housing shortages and internal passport laws to some extent strengthened rather than weakened the traditional Turkmen extended family.

INHERITANCE. The Turkmens follow traditional custom rather than strict Islamic law regarding inheritance. Each son receives his portion of inheritance after he marries and forms a separate household with his own children, usually sometime between ages 30 and 40. The youngest son remains with his father until the latter's death and then receives all remaining property. Naturally, the Soviet legal system provided other possibilities in determining inheritance.

SOCIALIZATION. In accordance with the value system of Turkmen society, men are expected to show great respect and deference to their elders, especially their father, grandfather, and even elder brothers. Women are expected to show even greater subordination, traditionally covering their mouths with their headcloth in the presence of male guests or even their own in-laws. Turkmen women, however, have never worn veils as was common in neighboring Islamic societies. Historically, women would sit in less honorable places within the yurt. Even in modern times, Turkmen women often remain in separate parts of the home when the husband is entertaining guests.

Sociopolitical Organization

SOCIAL ORGANIZATION. Historically, Turkmen society has been highly egalitarian, with little notion of class distinctions. Unlike other Turkic groups of Central Asia, Turkmens had no traditional aristocracy. There are very few examples in Turkmen history of exceptionally rich individuals, and the Turkmen custom of aiding relatives in times of economic need ensured that few people remained impoverished for long. There did exist a differentiation between people of pure Turkmen origin (*igh*) and those of slave (*qul*) or mixed (*yarim*) origins. Practically speaking, however, this distinction meant very little except for purposes of social ceremony. As elsewhere in Soviet Central Asia, a kind of "Soviet aristocracy" developed, consisting of families of famous writers, artists, and other members of the urban intelligentsia, as well as leading members of the Communist party.

POLITICAL ORGANIZATION. Turkmen society has never been marked by strong political leaders or tribal chiefs. Men gained influence through such personal qualities as military valor, but their authority was limited to their ability to persuade others to join them and was seldom of long duration or conferred to their descendants. The Communist party remains the dominant political organization. At the same time, however, tribal loyalties continued to play important roles in granting positions within the party and government. For example, the Teke tribe long dominated the upper echelons of the Turkmen party apparatus, as well as appointments at the state university.

SOCIAL CONTROL. Turkmen society is strongly influenced by the desire to maintain tradition (*adat*). Historically, tribal elders made decisions in councils that were designed to achieve consensus within the entire community. This practice is often employed in Turkmenistan even today.

CONFLICT. The Turkmens were renowned throughout their history for their warlike tendencies and their devastating raids (*alamans*) against sedentary neighbors, especially Iran. Within Turkmen society, there is an important responsibility for close agnates to come to the defense of each other in any conflict. The Owlad tribes have an equally important responsibility to serve as neutral mediators between potential Turkmen combatants.

Religion and Expressive Culture

RELIGIOUS BELIEFS. The Turkmens are Sunni Muslims of the Hanafi branch. Despite the claims of some observers that their nomadic heritage created a certain laxness or heterodoxy in their religious practice, Turkmens are devout. The incorrect perception stems in part from the fact that in the past few mosques were found among the Turkmens, a phenomenon not uncommon among traditionally nomadic societies, where religious practice is centered more in the movable home than in a stationary mosque. The Turkmens saw themselves as resolute defenders of Sunni orthodoxy against the Shiism prevalent among their southern neighbors in Iran.

During the Soviet period the authorities repeatedly tried to eradicate religious belief, without success. Among the most persistent traditions has been that of *ziyarat*, or pilgrimage to the tombs of Muslim saints, a practice that was always strong among the Turkmens and that increased in popularity because of the difficulty for Soviet Muslims of performing the pilgrimage to Mecca. Later Soviet policies allowed for more openness in religious practice and permitted the opening of several new mosques.

RELIGIOUS PRACTITIONERS. Turkmens respect the mullahs, who teach and lead the faithful in their religious life. In the past, these mullahs received their training in the urban centers of Khiva and Bukhara. For much of the Soviet period mullahs and their activities were strictly controlled by the authorities, a policy that increased the influ-

ence of the more secretive leaders (*ishans*) of mystical Sufi orders. These latter, who are often closely tied to the sacred Owlad tribes, have traditionally played a significant role in the spiritual life of the Turkmens and have functioned as unofficial preservers of the Turkmens' Islamic heritage during the more oppressive periods of Soviet rule.

CEREMONIES. The Turkmens keep all the major ceremonies of the Islamic calendar, with the feast of Kurban Bairam perhaps the most important for them. This has been true despite strong official disapproval in years past.

ARTS. The Turkmens have a rich oral epic tradition held in common with other Oghuz Turks, including the epic of *Dede Korkut* (*Gorkut Ata* in Turkmen). They also have produced numerous poets renowned for their eloquence, the most famous being Maqtum Quli (eighteenth century). Their weavings, which include everything from large floor rugs to saddle bags, purses, and other domestic utilitarian items, are considered to be among the finest examples of decorative art in the world. Many scholars see the preservation of tribal markings and religious symbols in the designs found in Turkmen weavings.

MEDICINE. Only late in the Soviet era did authorities admit the poor state of medical care in Turkmenistan. For example, the infant mortality rate in the republic, which is estimated to be between 60 and 100 per thousand, is the highest of the former Soviet republics and among the highest in the world. Perhaps for this reason amulets to protect children from evil spirits and other folk medical practices have remained common, despite the advent of modern medical treatment.

DEATH AND AFTERLIFE. Funerals among the Turkmens are performed according to Islamic rites, even by avowedly atheistic party members. Special feasts and remembrances are held forty days and one year after a death. Turkmens usually bury their dead in cemeteries built up around the tomb of an Islamic saint or an Owlad tribesmen, who serves as a guide and helper in the afterlife for those buried near him.

Bibliography

Barthold, V. V. (1962/1929). "A History of the Turkman People." In *Four Studies of the History of Central Asia*, by V. V. Barthold. Translated by V. and T. Minorsky. Vol. 3. Leiden: E. J. Brill.

Irons, William (1975). *The Yomut Turkmen: A Study of Social Organization among a Central Asian Turkic Speaking Population*. University of Michigan Museum of

Anthropology, Anthropological Paper no. 58. Ann Arbor.

Saray, Mehmet (1989). *The Turkmens in the Age of Imperialism: A Study of the Turkmen People and Their Incorporation into the Russian Empire.* Ankara: Turkish Historical Society Printing House.

—WILLIAM A. WOOD

UKRAINIANS

Ethnonym: Ruthens

Orientation

IDENTIFICATION. Ukrainians are the second-largest Slavic group in the world and they form the sixth-largest nation in Europe. They comprise the majority of the population of the Republic of Ukraine, which declared its independence on 24 August 1991. According to the census of 1989, Ukrainians constitute 37.4 million or 72.7 percent of the total population of Ukraine, estimated at 51.7 million people. In addition, there were 6.8 million Ukrainians living in the former republics of the Soviet Union and at least 2 million living in the countries of Europe, the United States, Canada, and Australia.

Ukraine is a polyethnic republic. Over a quarter of its population is not Ukrainian (22 percent are Russians, 0.9 percent Jews, 0.8 percent Belarussians). These groups have played an important role in the economic, political, and cultural development of the Ukrainian nation. Ethnic influences are especially pronounced in multicultural regions (Transcarpathia, Odessa region, Donbass, and the Crimea). Development has occurred in conjunction with the ethnic consolidation of the Ukrainian people, the growth of their national self-awareness, an increase in the social mobility of the population, and the formation of common features of its culture and life-style. The Ukrainian language is used more and more in everyday speech.

A number of state laws have stimulated these changes, in particular the Law on Language, which not only establishes Ukrainian as the national language but creates conditions for the preservation of the languages of all the ethnic minorities (opening of national schools, chairs in universities, radio, optional language instruction), freedom of religion, opening of national communal centers, and so on.

LOCATION. Ukraine is in the southwest of the eastern European plain. It is famous for its beauty and picturesque scenery; its lands, mostly plains, are bounded by the Carpathian and the Crimean mountains on the west and south. The Black and Azov seas wash its southern borders. Its soil is extremely fertile, especially the chernozems. Ukraine is rich in natural resources: there are large reserves of coal (in the Donetsk region) and abundant deposits of iron ore and manganese. Within the Ukrainian "Cristalline Shield" are titanium, nickel, chromium, mercury, aluminum, uranium, chemical resources, and building materials ranging from granite and marble to limestone and fire clay. There are relatively large deposits of oil and natural gas in the Precarpathian and other regions. The Dnieper, Dniester, and the Danube rivers flow through Ukraine into the Black Sea. Neighboring seas that do not freeze have permitted the construction of trading routes; these routes were known to the Vikings, Greeks, Romans, and other peoples of Europe and Asia. During the last decades, however, human activities have harmed Ukrainian lands, causing the impoverishment of the environment, disruption of the ecological balance and, above all, the meltdown of the nuclear reactor at the Chernobyl power station.

DEMOGRAPHY. Presently Ukrainians are dispersed evenly over the territory of the republic, which, with the exception of the Autonomous Republic of Crimea and some industrial regions of the southeast, is noted for the high density of its population (85.6 people per square kilometer). In most regions Ukrainians constitute more than 70 percent of the urban population. The percentage of Ukrainians is even higher in rural areas: in almost all regions, it is over 90 percent.

The growth of cities was accompanied by a decrease in the rural population, especially since the second half of the 1920s. While the urban population of the Ukraine multiplied nearly sevenfold between 1920 and 1991, the rural population dropped from 21.3 million to 16.9 million people (i.e., from 80.7 to 32.7 percent of the population).

These changes were caused by migration and the reorganization of rural villages into urban ones or the merger of rural villages with cities. During the 1970s alone, the urban population of the Ukraine rose by 4.8 million people (2 million as result of natural growth in cities and 2.8 million as a result of reorganizing rural villages into urban ones and migration to cities).

The decrease in natural growth and the demographic losses of the 1930s had a negative impact on the size of the rural population of the Ukraine. At the end of the nineteenth century the birthrate in the Ukraine was one of the highest in Eu-

Ukrainians are the second-largest Slavic group in the world and they form the sixth-largest nation in Europe.

rope—7.5 children per woman; in 1989 it was only 1.9 child, which was the lowest of all the republics of the Soviet Union. The drop in the birthrate, which began in the 1920s, is still taking place. Since 1979, moreover, depopulation has also occurred in the rural areas, and thus now affects the entire republic.

LINGUISTIC AFFILIATION. The Ukrainian language belongs to the East Slavic Branch of the Slavic Stock of the Indo-European Language Family. In the early period of the formation of the Ukrainian nation, the traditions of the literary language of Kievan Rus' were dominant. Alongside the language that grew from local dialects, there was a literary language common to the East Slavs and close to the modern language of South Slavs. Later, when a large portion of Ukrainian and Belarussian lands were part of the Lithuanian principality, a common Ukrainian-Belarussian language began to emerge based on Old Russian. It was used on many written monuments in both nations and played an important part in different spheres of their public life.

In 1989, 40 million people (78 percent of the population) in the Ukraine spoke Ukrainian fluently, 1.5 million more than in 1979. Thirty-two million Ukrainians consider their national language their mother tongue. Tens of thousands of Russians and Poles and a large number of Czechs, Slovaks, Moldavians, and Romanians who live in Ukraine also speak Ukrainian as their primary language. More than 4 million people consider Ukrainian their second language and speak it fluently. In mixed ethnic regions, multilingualism is common. Its extent is determined by the location of the ethnic groups and the duration of ethnocultural contacts. Such factors have also been taken into consideration during the formulation of the Law on Language and its implementation.

In the sixteenth through seventeenth centuries there were two literary languages in the Ukraine: Slavic Russian, resulting from the interaction of Old Church Slavonic and the Old Russian literary language (used mostly in church literature) and the so-called common one based on the Old Russian literary language, which has absorbed much from the Ukrainian language.

The Ukrainian language acquired specific Ukrainian features and retained an internal dialectical division (middle Dnieper, Polessk, Podolsk, Transcarpathian, etc.). These dialects are conventionally classified into three groups: northern, southwestern, and southeastern. The Middle-Pridnieper (Poltava-Kiev) dialects of the turn of the eighteenth and nineteenth centuries formed the basis of the modern Ukrainian literary language, which gradually absorbed elements of other regional Ukrainian dialects.

History and Cultural Relations

The ancient history of Ukraine is rich, as the many archaeological remains testify. Kurgans, ancient villages, ramparts, and ruins of castles and monastery walls abound. Here, in the territory of Ukrainian Transcarpathia in the village of Beregovo in the Korolev region, the oldest human settlements in Europe—over 6,000 years old—were found. In the Stone Age, one of the oldest agricultural centers was organized on the lands of Pridnieper.

During the disintegration of primitive society feudal relations began to occur, tribal unions appeared (Polyans, Severyans, Drevlyans, White Croatians, Dulebs, Ulichs, Tivertses, etc.), and later, principalities (*knyazhestvas*) formed. Those of Kiev and Novgorod united as one state—Kievan Rus'—which became one of the most powerful in medieval Europe. In the fifteenth to sixteenth centuries Ukrainian territory expanded owing to the settling of the southwestern outskirts by peasant refugees and the founding of the Zaporozh Cossacks—the settlement of Slobozhanshina—in northeastern parts of the Ukraine and neighboring territories. The formation of Ukrainian Cossacks (Zaporozh Sech) stimulated the development of the lower Dnieper and the protection of the southeastern borders. The Sech

A Ukrainian policy encouraging autonomy for all ethnic groups, regardless of their nationality, religion, or language, has been officially declared and is being implemented.

UKRAINIAN STAPLE

A young Ukrainian woman carries barrels of milk on her back. The cuisine of Ukraine includes wheat breads, dumplings, vegetable dishes, and dairy products. Rahovo, Carpatho-Ukraine. (Scheufler Collection/Corbis)

was a military-administrative organization with broad democratic principles, self-government, and distinctive cultural features. It is likely that the Cossacks played a major role in the shaping of Ukrainian national identity.

The Ukrainian ethnic group consists of three components. The first is the main settlement of Ukrainians that generally coincides with the territory in which the Ukrainian ethnic group formed, the present administrative borders of the republic, and the regions of dense Ukrainian settlement beyond these borders. The second component encompasses Ukrainians who live outside the main ethnic settlement and who are territorially separated from it—both elsewhere in the former Soviet Union and abroad—as a result of increasing migration since the end of the nineteenth century. Recently, the word "diaspora" has been used in reference to these people. The subcultural groups—ethnic groups within the Ukrainian nation that have distinct cultural features (Gutsuls, Lemks, Boyks, Polyshuks, etc.)—comprise the third component.

The ratio of the size of the main settlement of the Ukrainians to the diaspora communities changes continually. From 1917 to 1989 the percentage of Ukrainians within the modern borders of the republic fell from 85.6 to 81 percent. Of the total number of Ukrainians, the percentage living in other countries of Europe rose from 6.6 to 11.1 percent. At the same time, the percentage of Ukrainians living in North America rose from 0.6 to 3.1 percent. The overall decrease in the number of Ukrainians in the world during this period—from 57,398,000 to 46,136,000 people—was caused by a number of factors, including the absence of a separate state and Ukrainian political disunity within different countries, great losses from wars that took place in the Ukraine, famine, and other demographic factors. Beyond the borders of the republic the total number of Ukrainians has decreased significantly as a result of the policy of national and territorial demarcation of Soviet republics in the beginning of the 1920s. At that point, large concentrations of Ukrainians, numbering in the millions, were left outside the borders of the Ukraine in the neighboring regions of Kuban, the northern Caucasus, Priazov, the central Chernozem region, and elsewhere.

The above-mentioned ethnic groups of Ukrainians differ in the level of their social and economic development and in other aspects. Under these circumstances, ethnic self-consciousness becomes very important—as long as it persists, the group continues to exist. A change in Ukrainian self-consciousness occurred in two spheres: the ethnogenetic one (i.e., starting from the onset of the Ukrainian nation they transformed their name from "Rusks" to "Ruthens" to "Ukrainians") and the spatial or territorial one, which developed as a consequence of their ethnic history.

The main formative centers of the Ukrainian nation were Middle Prednieper, the right bank of Kievshina, Periaslavshina, and Chernigov-Sivrshina. It was here that the name "the Ukraine" (meaning the "land" or "country") was established in the twelfth century, a term that afterward spread to incorporate the whole area of Ukrainian settlement and that became the cultural ethnonym. Almost until the seventeenth century (and in the western Ukrainian regions until the last decades), the older East Slavic names for the land and the people—"Rus'," "Ruska land," "Rusks," "Ruthens," and others—were still used.

The many interpretations of the origins of the Ukrainians can be coalesced into two general theories. The first, emerging from Russian historiography and promulgated in the former Soviet Union, postulates that Ukrainians—as well as the other Eastern Slavs-Russians and Belarussians—come from a single proto-Russian nation ("common cradle") that was part of the feudal state of Kievan Rus (ninth through twelfth centuries). Feudal relations, according to this theory, led to the breakup of this state and resulted in new economic, political, and cultural centers as early as the second half of the twelfth through the thirteenth centuries; specific conditions led to the formation of the three East Slavic groups—Russians, Ukrainians, and Belarussians. During the development of the Old Russian nation, the most important cultural characteristics evolved, common to all East Slavs; their common name ("Rusks") was preserved as well as a consciousness of their common origins and close ethnic ties. The Old Russian nation was a complex of local languages and cultural traditions, which later played a differentiating role in the formation of East Slavs. Unfavorable events abroad and destructive invasions temporarily slowed the economic and political development of ancient Russian lands and even exacerbated their feudal disunity. Within these ancient Russian lands, it was in the southwest that the early history of Ukraine began, in the territories of the Kiev, Peryaslav, Chernigov-Siversk, and Galician principalities. Adherents of the common cradle theory date the onset of the Ukrainian nation to the end of the fourteenth or the beginning of the fifteenth century. At this time the ancient Russian state had already broken into separate feudal principalities; northwestern Russia (Rostov-Vladimir, Suzdal, and [later] Moscow) played a decisive role in the formation of another East Slavic nation—that of the Russians, which became more powerful.

An ethnogenic theory of Ukrainian ethnicity based on autochthonous origins has been put forward in the twentieth century and has been gaining support. The theory was proposed by M. Grushevsky, a historian of the twentieth century. He considers Ukrainians direct descendants of the most ancient population of the territory that is now Ukraine, from which Russians and Belarussians subsequently separated and formed distinct nations. The existence of a single Old Russian nation is denied, as is the disintegration of one common Slavic unity into three ethnically separate East Slavic countries. On the basis of this, Grushevsky dates the history of the Ukrainian nation back to the fourth, not the twelfth, century and links Ukrainians with the East Slavic tribes, Ants. The anthropological, psychophysical, linguistic, and other features of Ukrainian culture are explained by this differentiation.

According to the ethnogenic theory, the earliest name for Ukrainians was "Ruthens," which in the tenth through twelfth centuries was used only for Ukrainians, and later by other East Slavs. The northeastern group, however, adopted the general name "Russians" in the original meaning of "governed by Rus'."

Subgroups of Ukrainians have formed over the centuries, and they retain certain distinctive cultural features. The best known among them are the Ukrainian highlanders (Gutsuls, Lemks, and Boyks); in western Ukraine, the Polishuks, Pinchuks, and Litvins; and in the Ukrainian marshland, the Polesye. Lemks live in the northwestern regions of Transcarpathia and some regions of neighboring Poland. They got their name from using the particle *lem* (only) in their speech. A theory of the origin of the names "Lemks" and the neighboring "Boyks" has recently been proposed that suggests that the names were taken from "Lemko" (hypothetically, the founder of a kindred or a tribal leader). Some researchers make a connection between the origins of the Lemks and the tribes of White Croatians, the majority of whom, in the sixth through seventh centuries, moved from the Carpathian region to the Balkans. There are questions about the origin of the name "Gutsuls"; the people of this subgroup are noted for the distinctive features of their life-style and are famous for their crafts—metalwork, pottery, and rug making. Some link it with the Romance term *guts* (bandit), which originated in connection with a mass upheaval of "national avengers" (*oprishky*) in the seventeenth through eighteenth centuries. Others trace the word back to *kochul* (shepherd), or tie it to the Old Russian tribe of Ulichs.

The "Litvins"—in the past an ethnonym of a group of Ukrainians widespread in the marshlands of the Ukraine—are associated with political and state relations of the twelfth through sixteenth centuries, when this part of the Ukraine belonged to the Lithuanian principality; the name "Polishuks," first noted in seventeenth-century documents and maps, denotes the Ukrainian and Belarussian population within the marshland Polesye.

Certain names of groups of people, unities, and collectives reflect complex ethnogenetic processes. These are *tuteyshie* (local) names of separate groups in Polesye and Volin that do not have a defined ethnic identity. "Cherkasy," a name popular in official Russian documents of the sixteenth through seventeenth centuries, was used for a large segment of the Ukrainian population of the middle Pridnieper, the Zaporozh Cossacks in particular. Some researchers associate it with the city of Cherkasy, around which there were many Cossack settlements, others with the northern Caucasian Adygs, Black Klobuks, and other Turkish-speaking peoples. At least as late as the second half of the seventeenth century the Sevruks—descendants of the ancient tribes of the Silver land, who inhabited the valleys of the Desna, Seim, and Sula rivers—maintained their own name and distinctive culture. It is believed that they played a role in the formation of the Eastern Slavs and that they are genetically related to the "severa" of the manuscripts.

As noted above, the old name for Ukrainians, "Ruthens," is still popular in western Ukraine. According to the latest Ukrainian laws in those regions, such as Transcarpathia, this name may be used in defining ethnic origins. Some names of Ukrainians are etymologically related to religious factors: "Latinniks" (Ukrainians who adhere to the Roman Catholic religion, classified with the Ukrainian-speaking Poles), "Kalakuts" (groups of Kholmshina and Podlashie who adopted Roman Catholicism and Polish self-awareness but retained Ukrainian as their language), "Volokhs" (the Orthodox population of Bukovina, both the Roman- and Ukrainian-speaking).

*In a December 1991
referendum, more
than 90 percent of
the Ukrainian
population
supported the idea of
national
independence.*

In the past, there were smaller ethnographic groups among Ukrainians. In the last decades the number of such groups has decreased and their members have tended to assimilate into neighboring groups. The majority of them, such as the Opolyans, Nistrovyans, Sotaks, Pidgoryans, and others in the regions of the western Ukraine, were actually local groups with some unique cultural features rather than distinct ethnic groups. Nowadays regional peculiarities of culture more or less exist alongside a gradual spreading of common customs and beliefs brought about by the ethnic consolidation of the Ukrainians.

In the past, interethnic relations in the Ukraine were influenced by a variety of factors, especially the political disunity of the territory; Ukrainians lived in several countries (Poland, Austria-Hungary, Russia) and were thus dependent on the rulers of these nations (Russians, Poles, Austrians, Romanians, etc.). Often relations between nations were determined by the social statuses of groups in the population; thus, interactions between the enslaved Ukrainians and the ruling ethnic groups (Germans, Bulgarians, Greeks, Serbs, etc.) were difficult. At the same time, comembership in a social-status category led to much interethnic contact (between Ukrainians and Moldavians, for example). Mixed marriages were common among such groups, which were linked by common economic and political interests.

There are some tensions between the Orthodox and Greek Catholic churches in the western regions, and between the Moscow Patriarchy and the Orthodox church in Ukraine, although, officially, by the decision of the council of the Russian Orthodox Church of 25–27 October 1990, the Ukrainian Orthodox Church was granted independence.

Currently, a policy encouraging autonomy for all ethnic groups, regardless of their nationality, religion, or language, has been officially declared and is being implemented. All the parties and social groups support these ideas. The Law on National Minorities adopted in 1992 grants all citizens of Ukraine equal civil, political, social, and economic rights and freedoms, including national and cultural autonomy, education in the native language, the creation of national cultural societies, and so on. In a referendum held on 1 December 1991, more than 90 percent of the population supported the idea of national independence. On December 1991, the Soviet Union was dissolved and Ukraine joined the Commonwealth of Independent States.

Settlements

The founding of most of the settlements in the Ukraine and their subsequent growth were influenced by agricultural and industrial requirements—including the relative potential of the land to be cultivated, the availability of transportation routes and water resources, the landscape, and the nature of the soil. Villages are located along rivers, lakes, or ravines or dried-up riverbeds.

The following types of village plans may be distinguished, depending on the type of construction and the arrangement of streets, squares, and houses: clusters, unplanned-dispersed, and by row and by street. The oldest settlements in the Ukraine were near rivers. A village that grew out of a single household might develop without any plan at all. Villages like this were the most common in the Ukraine. Later, buildings were constructed in a row along rivers or roads, eventually to be expanded with planned streets. Beginning with the end of the eighteenth century, state controls often stipulated that villages in the steppes be built with streets and blocks and that the streets be straight and the blocks rectangular.

The names of settlements in the Ukraine come from a variety of sources. The oldest names are of Iranian, Fracian, Illirian, Baltic, and Old Germanic origin. Most of the Old Russian and medieval names are connected with properties of the environment or the activities of an individual. The names that were introduced during the Soviet period were not indigenous. Usually they were part of Soviet propaganda and symbolism. As a result, such names as Zhovtneve, Pershotravneve, Proletarskoe, Pionerskoe, Lenino, and Lenino Pervoe appeared on the map; now they are being replaced.

Traditional Ukrainian life-styles and family structures were closely connected with the village territorial community, the *gromada*, which developed in ancient times. In the Middle Ages it was called *kop* and was the local unit of government. The spread of a commodity-money economy and serfdom contributed to the disintegration of this form of community organization, although at different rates in different regions of the Ukraine. With the gradual shift from collective to private forms of ownership and the replacement of feudalism with capitalism, the gromada's economic basis was completely undermined. By the beginning of the twentieth century most households in the Ukraine were privately owned. There were, however, residues of traditional communal patterns, which figured prominently in the organization and democratization of the peasantry and in its struggle for its rights. These included a system of legal traditions and norms, a tradition of communal use of land and mutual assistance in labor-intensive work (*toloka, supryaga*), recreation for youth connected to their labor (*vechornitsy, dosvitky*), and a system of ethics.

The most common types of dwelling consist of three parts and have four pitched roofs, either of straw or reed; these are typical in regions with well-developed agriculture. The interiors of Ukrainian household conform to a remarkably uniform plan: the stove (*pech*) faces the long wall, the table is diagonally opposite it in the corner where the icons are placed, and the flooring where the family sleeps is behind the stove. This uniformity is also found in the tradition of double-sided whitewashing of walls and bright decorative painting.

Economy

SUBSISTENCE AND COMMERCIAL ACTIVITIES. Ukraine is one of the largest agricultural nations in the world. A favorable natural environment allowed the evolution of complex farming systems, which have existed there since the fourth through sixth centuries B.C. There were various methods of utilizing the soil, of growing crops, and of collecting and processing agricultural produce. Today the major crops are cereal grains, sugar beets, and potatoes. Ukraine also has a large industrial sector centered on steel, chemicals, machinery, vehicles, and cement.

Ukrainian agricultural tools and practices were original, in particular the heavy Ukrainian plow, different ways of growing and preserving crops, and the means of transportation (*mazha* of the Chumaks, *chovni* [the boats of Zaporozhie], Carpathian rafts).

Apart from agriculture and cattle breeding, great attention was traditionally given to subsidiary forms of production (fishing, hunting, and apiculture), as well as to household craftsmanship. Also prominent were the wood-working industry (making barrels, sleighs, and carts); building construction; fiber (flax, hemp); wool processing; pottery; glassmaking; stone- and metal-forging; stone-, metal-, and leatherwork; and the salt industry. Traditional industries are today being restored.

During the second half of the nineteenth century, because of the industrial development of the Ukraine (especially in large cities and industrial centers of the south), powerful combinations and syndicates were coalescing, social stratification of the society sharpened, and mobility increased. Different types of property that appeared in the past years have radically changed the industrial and social relations and life-styles of Ukrainians.

CLOTHING. The traditional national Ukrainian costume has prominent features that vary from region to region. Embroidery displays wide local stylistic variation but everywhere exemplifies picturesque design and clear composition. The national outfit, consisting of a shirt, waist garments, and seasonally varying ornamentation for the shoulders, reflects highly sophisticated techniques of producing handwoven fabrics and extensive experience in creating and decorating clothes.

FOOD. The cuisine of Ukraine is well known beyond its own borders. The fare includes huge wheat breads, curd or fruit dumplings (*varenikis*), plain dumplings, (*galushki*), vegetable dishes (especially the famous Ukrainian borscht made with more than twenty ingredients), potato and bean dishes, dairy products (including various cheeses, especially Carpathian ones), and all kinds of fruit and berry liqueurs. Traditional features encompassing the structure of meals, mealtime, ceremonial and everyday food, traditional dishes, and customs connected with cooking and eating have been firmly retained in modern Ukrainian cuisine.

TRADE. Ukrainians have always been traders. Domestic trading gradually came to be concentrated in cities. The most important trading routes known since ancient times are the Salt, Chumak, and Iron, which stimulated foreign trade. The river way "from the Vikings to the Greeks" played an extremely important role in this activity; it was formed in the ninth century and connected the Baltic and Black seas. In the early feudal period, shops and organizations of craftsmen and traders appeared in Ukrainian cities. At the end of the seventeenth century, guilds of craftsmen and traders were begun; these had a clearly hierarchic social structure (masters, apprentices, etc.), regulations, and unique symbols. In the regions of the western Ukraine that had belonged to Poland since the nineteenth century, there has been a process of strong social differentiation among the population, including both the Polish and Ukrainian populations.

Religion and Expressive Culture

Rational knowledge acquired throughout centuries played an important part in the life of

The most important Ukrainian folk morals have always been respect for and love of free labor, ideals of kindness, beauty, and knowledge of one's genealogy and civil duties.

Ukrainians. Some of this knowledge, especially in the fields of medicine, veterinary medicine, pharmacology, agriculture, meterology, and astronomy, has been recognized by modern science. In folk medicine, this includes the use of plants and medications of animal and mineral extraction as a preventive treatment, physiotherapy (compress, massage, bath), folk methods for back problems, and so on. The same is true about the system of common law—ancient legal traditions that determined relations between people and their behavior. Among the Carpathian highlanders, for example, methods of electing the head of the highland *gromada* (deputy), conditions of collective cattle breeding and distributing the produce,

KINSHIP, MARRIAGE, AND FAMILY

Domestic Unit

The large extended family is the oldest family form in the Ukraine. It was composed of several generations and was characterized by a collective household and common property. Relations in the family were regulated by norms of common law, and the head of the family saw to it that they were observed. The relatively early formation of commodity-money relations (sixteenth to seventeenth centuries) and, subsequently, serfdom, caused Ukrainian families to disintegrate at a faster rate than in Belarus and Russia, although in some regions (Carpathia, Left Bank) traces of extended families were present in the nineteenth century. Most dispersed into separate households (*dims*). From the eighteenth century to the present, the small, nuclear family of parents and children has been the primary type.

Certain features of extended families were retained in the nuclear family: the bridegroom paid the wedding expenses, marriages were sanctioned by the traditional legal settlement, men controlled the family, the head of the family maintained his special role, and so on. The modern Ukrainian family has fewer children than did the traditional family. The number of ethnically mixed marriages has increased, especially in the cities.

Marriage

Many traditional customs are in evidence in family life and in the celebration of family holidays. These include the lavish wedding ceremony, its traditional foods, and the custom of uniting the bride with the bridegroom. There are no wedding ceremonies without the *trial* music (violin, tambourine, and dulcimer). The Ukrainian wedding ceremony retained features peculiar to it alone, both in the ceremony itself and in the overall character of the wedding, which reflected unique aspects of the Ukrainian family. Patriarchal traces were less pronounced in Ukrainian than, for example, in Russian weddings. The Ukrainian wedding did not have wedding lamentations of the bride; she neither covered her head with a scarf nor tearfully beseeched her father not to give her away into a strange family. In some regions, as noted by the sixteenth-century French author Beauplan, the woman took the initiative during the engagement. Before the nineteenth century there was a custom that, as a sign of rejection, the young woman gave the proposing party a pumpkin. This is the origin of the expression "to get a pumpkin" (i.e., to get rejected). In modern Ukrainian weddings, there are many regional differences regarding beliefs, magical gestures, traditional food, the degree to which archaic traits are retained, and the role of the parents in the wedding ceremony. In modern marriages the prewedding cycle and the wedding ceremony itself are shorter, although some traditional elements (e.g., the repertoire of songs) are retained. Especially in the cities, some forgotten traditions (folk symbols, elements of humor, the wedding bread) are reappearing. Customs connected with the birth of a child were more common in the Ukraine than in Russia or Belarussia, especially the rite of purification and customs symbolizing the acceptance of a child into the family.

Inheritance

In certain regions of the Ukraine (Left Bank, the south, Slobozhanshina), the father's property was traditionally distributed evenly among all the members of the family, including the daughters. In the Right Bank regions, where the traditions of the Lithuanian state were maintained, women's inheritance was restricted but even there a woman had the right to personal property and *materizna*—that part of the land that was inherited through the female line of the family. The latter is considered unique to family relations in the Ukraine.

Traditions, public morals, and norms of common law determined inheritance practices. For example, unmarried people inherited less. In the marriage contract the amount of the bride's dowry, which consisted of a trunk and cattle, was specified, as were the bridegroom's ransom and the parents' and relatives' donations. In most parts of the Ukraine a son-in-law who was accepted into a family with no sons was equal with other members of the family in his rights to property. With the advent of capitalism the role of parents in the management of family relations decreased.

Kinship Terminology

The extensive kinship terminology reflects the ramification of the kinship system: in addition to the usual East Slavic lineal terms for great-grandparent (e.g., *pradid* [grandfather]), there are terms for in-laws (e.g., machukha [mother-in-law]) and other affines, depending on the linking spouse (e.g., *svekor* [husband's father], *tesha* [wife's father]), including the husband's brother's wife (*yatrov*).

as well as paying the shepherds, were mainly indigenous.

RELIGIOUS BELIEFS.   In the past, Ukrainians held cosmogonic concepts about the origins of the earth and the universe and personified natural phenomena. Nature was perceived as a living world inhabited by magic powers, and humans were a fundamental part of it. There were also ancient totemistic and animistic concepts about the life of plants, animals, and the environment. Fire and its purifying power were very important in the beliefs and superstitions of the Carpathian highlanders in particular. Pagan cults were dominant before Christianity was adopted in Kiev Rus'. Along with the deification of natural phenomena and stars, ancient Slavs created a multitude of gods, the most powerful among which were the gods of the sky (Svarog), the sun (Dazhbog), the wind (Stribog), and fertility and cattle breeding (Veles).

Beliefs related to evil forces, demonic creatures of forests and water, and the power of people endowed with magical capabilities date to antiquity. Christianity has coexisted with different pre-Christian ideas (beliefs in magic, evil eye, etc.). Although these beliefs have mostly lost their original meaning, they retain a certain aesthetic appeal or serve as entertainment.

The most important folk morals have always been respect for and love of free labor, ideals of kindness, beauty, and knowledge of one's genealogy and civil duties; negative features such as drunkenness, laziness, insincerity, robbery, and stinginess were condemned. According to folk conceptions of the world, a human was an inalienable part of nature. Even age was associated with the seasons of the year (childhood with spring, youth with summer, etc.). From early childhood, a Ukrainian was taught to value singing, folk poetry, and his or her land.

At least by the second century B.C., Christianity was widespread in Ukrainian lands, although it was officially adopted only in 988 under Prince Vladimir to replace paganism as the official religion. The Kiev metropolis was under the canonical jurisdiction of the patriarch of Constantinople, and since the 1680s, under the patriarch of Moscow. After the Brest Unia (1596) and the unification of the Orthodox church with the Vatican under the condition of preserving the Eastern ritual, the Ukrainian population of the western regions comprised the Uniats or the Greek Catholics. The Russian czars and later the Soviet regime banned the Greek Catholic religion and repressed others many times. In 1946 the Lwiw church council decided to abolish the Brest Unia and return to Orthodoxy. After independence and the declarations of freedom of conscience and religion, the Ukrainian Greek Catholic church and the Ukrainian Autocephalous Orthodox church (which was legalized within the period 1920 to 1930) were restored.

Alongside these religions the so-called Rodnaya Ukrainskaya Natsional'naya Vera has become widespread in Ukraine; it was born within the Ukrainian communities of the United States and Canada about thirty years ago and it worships nature and a single god of nature, Dazhbog.

CEREMONIES.   Ukrainians have created an original folk calendar—cycles of social agricultural festivities and traditions, symbolizing the beginning and end of industrial labor. The most popular holidays are Christmas, Shrovetide, and Easter. New Year and Christmas carols—*shedrivkas* and *kolyadkas*—were original. In the eastern Ukraine carols were sung with a star, in the western Ukraine with a *vertep*—a box in the form of a multistoried house with the help of which different puppet shows of a religious or secular character were shown. Ukrainians celebrated spring holidays more frequently than other East Slavs. There are picturesque festivals at the end of the harvest and, in the Carpathian Mountains, at the return from the alpine pastures.

The so-called Soviet holidays and traditions created after the October Revolution have not become very popular because of their artificiality. These were usually celebrated formally and almost never recognized, although some of them, based on traditional customs (the holiday of the first haystack), are still celebrated.

ARTS.   Ukrainian folk art is distinct and extensive. In choreography there are round dances and dances that mimicked everyday activities, the famous *gopak* among them. The best known musical instruments are the stringed *kobza* and *bandura*, and they accompany the singing of the *dumas* (folk epics glorifying heroic deeds of the people). Professional music in the Ukraine was formed mostly on the basis of folk music. High professionalism is seen in church music both in one-and two-part singing. The development of professional theater was influenced greatly by the concepts of the folk puppet theater (*vertep*). Various forms of folk art continue to evolve on the basis of centuries-old folk experience. In Dniepropetrovsk Province, for example, painting under glaze on ceramic tiles is as common as before, pre-Carpathian folk artists are successfully adapting the traditions of decorative carving and etching in

The proportion of indigenous Central Asians in Uzbekistan has been growing, wereas that of the Russians has been declining.

wood, and those from Lwiw are making difficult kinds of glass. Ukrainian decorative art (fabric prints, bright rugs, wooden objects, ceramics, paintings, and murals) is popular in many countries, and the best works of Ukrainian artists have received international awards.

In the last few decades, many forms of western European culture have become popular among Ukrainians, and many folk traditions that fell into disuse during the Soviet era are being revitalized.

DEATH AND AFTERLIFE. The complexity of funeral customs relates to the cult of ancestors and the necessity of ensuring a successful transition of the dead "soul" into the world of ancestors. Death brought about a change in the behavior of people and the use of cultural markers (a white sheet was hung out, young women let their hair down, men did not wear any headgear). In the funerals of unmarried young men and women, wedding customs are observed. Since death is not considered the end of existence but a transition into a new state, it is not preceived as a tragedy, which explains why funerals are accompanied by various games. After the funeral, as well as on the ninth and fortieth day after death, commemorative feasts are held.

Bibliography

Allen, W. E. D. (1941). *The Ukraine: A History*. Cambridge: Cambridge University Press.

Beauplan, Guillaume Le Vasseur (1990). *La description d'Ukranie de Guillaume Le Vasseur de Beauplan*. Edited and annotated by Dennis F. Essar and Andrew B. Pernal. Ottawa: Presses de l'Université d'Ottawa.

Friedberg, Maurice (1991). *How Things Were Done in Odessa: Cultural and Intellectual Pursuits in a Soviet City*. Boulder, Colo.: Westview Press.

Krawchenko, Bohdan, ed. (1983). *Ukraine after Shelest*. Edmonton: Canadian Institute of Ukrainian Studies, University of Alberta; Downsview, Ontario: University of Toronto Press.

Lewytzkyj, Borys (1984). *Politics and Society in Soviet Ukraine, 1953–1980*. Edmonton: Canadian Institute of Ukrainian Studies, University of Alberta; Downsview, Ontario: University of Toronto Press.

Marples, David R. (1991). *Ukraine under Perestroika: Ecology, Economics, and the Workers' Revolt*. Houndmills, Basingstoke, Hampshire: Macmillan.

Mirchuk, I., ed. (1949). *Ukraine and Its People: A Handbook with Maps, Statistical Tables and Diagrams*. Munich: Ukrainian Free University Press.

Putro, Aleksei I. (1988). *Levoberezhnaia Ukraina v sostave Rossiiskogo gosudarstva vo vtoroi Polovine XVIII Veka: Nekotoryi voprosy sotsiaslno-ekonomicheskogo i obshchestvenno-politicheskogo Razvitiia* (Left-bourgeois Ukraine in the composition of the Russian state in the second half of the 18th century: Some questions on socioeconomic and labor-political development). Kiev: Vyshcha Shkola.

Santsevych, A. V. (1984). *Ukrainska radianska istoriohrafiia, 1945–1982* (Ukrainian historiography, 1945–1982). Kiev: Vyshcha Shkola.

—VSEVOLOD IVANOVICH NAULKO
(TRANSLATED BY OLGA BELODED)

UZBEKS

Ethnonyms: none

Orientation

IDENTIFICATION. Uzbekistan ranks third in population of the former republics of the USSR and is the largest of the four republics (Uzbekistan, Tajikistan, Turkmenistan, and Kyrgyzstan) formerly referred to as Soviet Central Asia. The republic is comprised of twelve regions (oblasts) and one autonomous republic, the Karakalpak Republic. The vast majority of Uzbekistan's population belongs to Turkic-speaking Muslim groups, with a relatively small population of Slavs and other nationalities.

LOCATION. Uzbekistan is a landlocked area nestled between the republics of Turkmenistan to the west, Kazakhstan to the north, Kyrgyzstan to the east, and Tajikistan to the east and south; it shares one relatively short international border with Afghanistan to the south. With a territory of roughly 447,400 square kilometers, it is located between 37° and 45° N and 56° and 73° E. Few rivers feed the republic—only the Syr Darya, Amu Darya, and Zeravshan—and rainfall is slight. Uzbekistan's population, therefore, tends to be clustered along these rivers, concentrated in the oases of Tashkent, Samarkand, and Bukhara, and in the Fergana Valley. The vast majority of Uzbekistan's territory is steppe or desert. Toward the south and east Uzbekistan becomes more mountainous in the vicinity of the Tianshan and Pamir ranges. Overall, Uzbekistan has a hot, dry climate, with temperatures ranging in some places up to about 51° C in the summer.

DEMOGRAPHY. The population of Uzbekistan in 1989 was 19,810,000, of which 14,142,000, or roughly 71 percent, are Uzbek and almost 90 percent are of various Muslim nationalities. Uzbekistan's population is characterized by a very high rate of natural growth—at least three to four times that of the Russians—and very low migration. For that reason, the population of Uzbekistan has been growing ever more rapidly and has been becoming more ethnically homogeneous over the past several decades. Whereas Uzbekistan's population grew by 28 percent over the twenty-year period from 1939 to 1959, for example (from 6.3 to 8.1 million people), it grew by almost 90 percent over the next twenty-year period, to more than 15 million people, and then by another 29 percent between 1979 and 1989. Central Asian demographers project that by the year 2005, 30 million people will be living in Uzbekistan—roughly the population of the entire Soviet Central Asian region today—and that by 2010, Uzbekistan's population will reach 33 million people.

The proportion of indigenous Central Asians has been growing, whereas that of the Russians has been declining. Although from the 1920s until 1959 Russians had comprised a consistently growing share of Uzbekistan's population (rising from less than 2 percent of Uzbekistan's population in 1917 to 13.5 percent in 1959), by 1989 that proportion had fallen to 8.3 percent, or to 1,653,000 people.

Demographic pressures have become one of the most serious and controversial problems in Uzbekistan, as they are increasingly straining the system's ability to provide basic goods and social services. Some Soviet officials and scholars in Central Asia advocated expansion of family planning, but this was initiated on only a rudimentary level and was strongly resisted by the local populations. There is a great need for economic and social reform. The steady decline of Russians in the republic's population and the growth of an increasingly homogeneous Uzbek and Central Asian population fueled Uzbekistan's demands for greater autonomy and, finally, sovereignty from Moscow.

LINGUISTIC AFFILIATION. Modern literary Uzbek is a Turkic language that is quite close to other Turkic languages of Central Asia, especially Uighur. In a sense, it is the successor to the Chagatay language, which was used for literary purposes (along with Persian) in the region prior to the Bolshevik Revolution. Modern literary Uzbek, however, is an artificial conglomerate of a variety of Turkic dialects. The origin of most of the Uzbek vocabulary is Turkic, but there are also many Arabic and Persian elements—and "international" words, usually borrowed from Russian. During most of the period from 1930 to 1989, the Communist party (which held a monopoly on the mass media and educational institutions) attempted to increase the Russian stratum of vocabulary and decrease the others, as well as to promote greater use of the Russian language. The Soviet period has also witnessed extensive change in Uzbek writing systems. During the 1920s a new modified version of the Arabic alphabet was introduced to write Uzbek. Then, at the end of the decade, Arabic letters were replaced with Latin ones; in 1940 Uzbek writing shifted to a slightly modified form of the Russian alphabet. Many of the trends of the period 1930 to 1989 are now being changed or reversed. Many international words are being replaced by Turkic, Arabic, and Persian equivalents; lessons in the Arabic writing system are now being introduced in the schools; and in October 1989 Uzbek was officially declared the state language of Uzbekistan.

History and Cultural Relations

The Central Asian region, which includes what is today Uzbekistan, has a rich history. Lying at the heart of the Silk Road, the region was both a major commercial and spiritual center: trade flourished; agriculture was well advanced; in this area arose great centers of education, art, architecture, poetry, religion, and scientific thought.

Throughout its long history, however, the region has also been the object of repeated invasions and conquests. These include the conquests of Alexander the Great in the fourth century A.D.; the Arab invasions of the seventh to eighth centuries, which introduced Islam and the Arabic script, classical learning, and a new worldview to the region; the occupation of the Turks from the seventh to ninth centuries, from which the region took the name "Turkestan"; and the Mongol invasions of the thirteenth century under Chinggis (Genghis) Khan. The conquest by Timur, or Timur the Lame (Tamerlane), in the late fourteenth century began the last and perhaps finest period of a flowering of culture and learning in the region, which included the emergence of perhaps the greatest of Central Asia's poets, Alisher Navoi, the astronomer Ulugh Bek, and the construction of architectural masterpieces the remains of which are still visited today in such Uzbek cities as Samarkand and Bukhara.

Beginning in the sixteenth century, however—as oceans became a more important means for transporting goods and as European merchants began to turn their attention more toward the New World—Turkestan entered a long period of decline. The political order that had been established under such leaders as Timur at the height

Most Uzbeks, especially those in rural areas, live under one roof with several generations, and families still tend to be very large.

of the region's glory was supplanted by warring principalities. The Bukharan Emirate and the Khivan and Kokand khanates emerged as the major political units. They held sway until the Russian conquest that occurred from the mid-1860s through the mid-1880s.

The czarist conquest not only secured Russian rule of the territory, but also brought an influx of Russians. The total number of Russians living in Central Asia at the turn of the century, however, was small, comprising only about 2 percent of the population, and the lives of the Russians and Asians rarely overlapped. Loyalties of the indigenous nationalities rarely extended beyond the family, tribe, or clan. This changed dramatically with the Bolshevik Revolution when, despite a long period of resistance by Central Asians (highlighted by the armed opposition to the Soviet regime of the "Basmachi," which continued well into the 1930s), the new Bolshevik government consolidated its power and created the Uzbek Soviet Socialist Republic in 1925. Uzbekistan saw an increasing flow of Russians into the republic and the beginning of strong government efforts to eradicate religion, educate the population, make Russian the common language, and supplant local traditions with Soviet mores. Uzbekistan became independent in 1991 after nearly 70 years as a republic of the Soviet Union. Islam A. Karimov, a former Communist leader, was elected president on 29 December, 1991.

Settlements

Traditionally, there were two kinds of groups in what is now Uzbekistan: the sedentary farmers and the nomadic herdsmen. The farmers and city dwellers were largely merchants and craftsmen, whereas the herdsmen lived largely by their flocks of sheep and herds of horses, cattle, camels, and goats. The basic social unit was the village, the nomadic village being called an *aul*, and the sedentary agricultural village being called a *kishlak*. Both were based on kinship ties: the auls were relatively small, moving from winter to spring camps on their way to summer pastures, whereas kishlaks were somewhat larger. The kishlak traditionally had a closely knit settlement pattern: houses were built within a small radius of each other. The houses were made of clay, and most had a courtyard in which family and social activities largely took place. The streets of the kishlak ran between the clay walls enclosing the courtyards.

The onset of Soviet power saw the construction of collective and state farms in the country-side, settlement of nomadic tribes, and mass efforts to urbanize the population. In the "European" sectors of cities—and in some entire cities and towns—the buildings resemble those found in the European parts of the former USSR. Many of the villages, smaller cities, towns, and sections of large cities, however, have retained the features of the kishlak. Uzbekistan has become over 40 percent urban, with Tashkent, Uzbekistan's capital, now the third-largest city of the former USSR, having a population of over two million. According to demographers, however, roughly 80 percent of all Uzbeks still live in rural areas.

Economy

SUBSISTENCE AND COMMERCIAL ACTIVITIES. The economy of Uzbekistan is very much specialized on a single crop, cotton, and on the infrastructure to serve the cotton industry—such as irrigation networks, branches of the machine-building and chemical industries that support cotton growing and harvesting, and cotton-ginning and textile mills. Uzbekistan is also rich in other raw materials, including natural gas, some coal, and important nonferrous metals, including what was, at least until recently, the largest gold mine in the world. In the early 1980s some estimates indicated that Uzbekistan and Turkmenistan alone accounted for as much as one-half of the former USSR's total gold output.

But Uzbekistan has not reaped the benefits of these rich resources. Instead, control of all resources has been in Moscow's hands, and most processing has been conducted outside of the republic. Thus, Uzbekistan today is one of the poorest republics of the former USSR, with an estimated 40 percent of its population living in poverty. The republic, moreover, has become riddled with the often devastating environmental and health consequences of cotton production. For example, the misuse of water resources, largely for irrigation, has led to the drying up of the Aral Sea, once the world's sixth-largest inland sea; in the past twenty years, it has shrunk by roughly 40 percent. The drying up of the Aral and resulting salinization has ruined fertile soil in the surrounding areas and has had severe health repercussions for the local populations. Likewise, the population's extensive exposure to pesticides, fertilizers, and defoliants used in the cotton fields and the contamination of drinking water with these chemicals has led to a severe increase in death and disease. As but one indication, over the past fifteen years infant-mortality rates in Uzbekistan have risen by over 50 percent to among the highest in the world: in some areas over 100 out of every 1,000 babies born die before reaching the age of 1.

INDUSTRIAL ARTS. Uzbek artisans still ply the handicrafts passed down from generation to generation. These include ceramics, copper embossing, carpet weaving, silkcraft (including silk tapestry), embroidery of headgear, wood carving, and the like.

TRADE. By custom Uzbeks are merchants and traders. Although a network of Soviet stores and cooperatives has opened, the traditional open-air markets, with an array of foodstuffs, textiles, and other goods, still tend to remain the center of much commerce. Since the beginnings of *perestroika* in the USSR, Uzbeks have increasingly attempted to enter world markets, attract Western partners for joint ventures within Uzbekistan, and sell more goods abroad.

DIVISION OF LABOR. Traditionally in Uzbekistan, there has been a broad division of labor between Uzbeks and Russians, just as there has been between men and women. Uzbeks have tended to be concentrated in the agricultural, service, and light-industrial sectors, whereas Russians have tended to dominate heavy industry and key government and party posts. Uzbek women have tended to predominate in household work and in the lower-skilled and manual jobs, often segregated from men.

But this began to change in the late Soviet era as Uzbeks demanded more economic autonomy from Moscow and developed broader skills, while unemployment, particularly among Central Asians, soared. According to one estimate from Central Asia, between 1.5 and 2 million people are currently unemployed; according to another, roughly one in ten able-bodied people in Uzbekistan are now without jobs, with almost one-quarter of a million young people entering the labor market every year. High unemployment is considered to be one of the key reasons for the many outbreaks of ethnic violence over the past several years, including the bloody violence that erupted in 1989 and 1990 between Uzbeks and Meshketian Turks and between Uzbeks and Kyrgyz.

LAND TENURE. Under the Soviet system, there was no private ownership of land anywhere in the USSR. Instead, most agricultural land was held as part of collective and state farms. Farmers were allowed to cultivate small private plots, and these accounted for a disproportionate share of total agricultural production—by some estimates, as high as almost 30 percent of Uzbekistan's total

agricultural output. The development of perestroika and efforts toward economic reform over the past few years have brought with them increasing debates over questions of ownership of land and resources. These efforts, coupled with independence, may greatly change the system of land tenure in Uzbekistan in the future.

Kinship

KIN GROUPS AND DESCENT. Uzbek society was traditionally organized patrilineally, with members of individual families carefully graded according to order of birth and precedence. Descent lines for Uzbeks were traditionally traced along patrilineal lines to the founding ancestor of the clan. Although each clan possessed its own territory, single leader, and center of authority, clan genealogy was often amended. Thus, with the combination of two clans in an economic or military alliance, the leader of one might recognize the leader of the other as a brother. Although to a lesser extent than among the Kazakhs or Kyrgyz, many Uzbeks today are still conscious of clan identities, and, to some extent, these still maintain political importance.

KINSHIP TERMINOLOGY. The Uzbek language has a very complex kinship terminology. It differentiates, for example, between older and younger brothers, older and younger sisters, patrilineal and matrilineal uncles, and patrilineal and matrilineal aunts.

Marriage and Family

MARRIAGE. Marriage of children was traditionally contracted between the bride's and groom's family through a third party. At the time of marriage, the bride-price (*kalym*) was transferred and the bride left to join the groom's family. Marriages were marked with feasting, competitions, the actual wedding ceremony, and other rituals. Although for many years the Communist party actively discouraged the kalym, religious weddings, and extravagant banquets, all of these practices survive in some form. It is common for young couples to recite religious wedding vows as well as to comply with the obligatory civil registration.

DOMESTIC UNIT. Most Uzbeks, especially those in rural areas, live under one roof with several generations. Likewise, in rural areas, families still tend to be very large. Over 40 percent of all Uzbek families have seven or more children. Upon marriage, women leave their parents' home to live with their husband's family. This means that the households of families with several married sons

The onset of Soviet power saw the construction of collective and state farms in the Uzbek countryside, settlement of nomadic tribes, and mass efforts to urbanize the population.

can be quite large. Although housing constraints have affected this practice, even sons who move out of their parents' homes tend to live nearby. The traditional Uzbek family was polygynous, at least in theory. In fact, however, few families could afford the bride-wealth for more than one wife per son.

INHERITANCE. The physical property of a family was traditionally divided among the sons in roughly equal proportions. Each son normally received part of his share when he married and part upon the death of the father.

SOCIALIZATION. Despite the Soviet government's promotion of nurseries and kindergartens, most small Uzbek children are raised by their mothers and grandmothers. This is one of the major reasons for the conservation of cultural and religious traditions in Uzbekistan.

Sociopolitical Organization

SOCIAL ORGANIZATION. The same Soviet social organizations that were created throughout the USSR—for example, Octobrists and Pioneers (for children), women's organizations, and labor unions—have all existed in Uzbekistan. The neighborhood (*mahalla*) committees, however, were much stronger in Uzbekistan than any analogous institution in Russia. Another very important social institution is the *chaykhana* (teahouse), where Uzbek men still gather.

POLITICAL ORGANIZATION. Uzbekistan has a president, a prime minister, a Cabinet of Ministers, and a one-house legislature whose members are elected to five-year terms. A republic, presidential rule is authoritarian with little power outside the executive branch.

SOCIAL CONTROL. Public opinion, especially the views of local elders, has been a powerful means for social control. In Soviet times, such formal organizations as the Ministry of Internal Affairs (MVD), Committee on State Security (KGB), the Communist party, and the social organizations played central "control" functions. Although the Communist party treated the traditional forms of control with distrust throughout most of Soviet history, in recent years it turned to these for help in fighting such maladies as crime, alcoholism, and drugs.

CONFLICT. Numerous states have conquered the territory that comprises modern-day Uzbekistan. The most important conquests by foreign invaders were those of the Mongols in the thirteenth century and the Russians in the twentieth. Until the twentieth century there were frequent wars among smaller states established in the region. The nineteenth-century internecine wars among these entities facilitated Russian conquest

ISLAMIC SCHOOL

Several ornate Islamic schools border the public Rigestan Square. Because of the Communist Party's antireligious policy, many Uzbeks were reluctant to participate in Islamic rituals until 1988. Samarkand, Uzbekistan. (Michel Gotin)

of the territory. Under Soviet rule there have been no open wars among the republics or regions of Central Asia. Beginning in the spring of 1989, however, there have been a number of violent mass disturbances involving Uzbeks clashing with members of other ethnic groups.

Religion and Expressive Culture

RELIGIOUS BELIEFS. Uzbeks are Sunni Muslims. Because of the region's complex history, however, some beliefs and practices date back to the pre-Islamic past, in particular to Zoroastrianism. A belief in demons and other spirits was widespread in traditional Uzbek society.

RELIGIOUS PRACTITIONERS. The Muslim Religious Board of Central Asia (located in Tashkent) supervises the "official" religious life and institutions in Uzbekistan and trains the "official" clergy. However, because the official institutions have been popularly viewed as coopted by the Communist party and because of limitations on training clergy, a large number of unofficial mullahs perform services. Since 1988, as relations between the party and official religious institutions have improved, many new mosques have opened and antireligious propaganda has drastically decreased. Historically, many Uzbeks belonged to Sufi *tarigat* (mystic orders). It is very difficult to judge how many adherents these organizations have today.

CEREMONIES. Uzbeks, even those who do not consider themselves "believers," participate in a number of Muslim religious ceremonies. The most important are a few life-cycle rituals, in particular, weddings, male circumcisions, and funerals. In addition, many Uzbeks observe other Islamic practices, such as fasting during Ramadan. Only a handful have had the opportunity to perform the hajj to Mecca. The cult of tombs (*mazar*) of holy men is widespread in Central Asia. Commonly observed pre-Islamic rituals (e.g., those performed during the New Year, Navroz) are popularly considered Islamic. Because of the Communist party's antireligious policy, however, many Uzbeks were reluctant to participate openly in Islamic rituals until 1988.

ARTS. Uzbekistan has a rich variety of art forms, reflecting the cultural influences of the many groups that have crossed Central Asia. During much of Soviet history, especially during the Stalin years, many of these were labeled "feudal." Moreover, the Soviet government encouraged artificial "mixing" of Uzbek and other cultures, usually as a cover for Russification. Nevertheless, in the late twentieth century the Uzbeks

are paying renewed attention to study and development of traditional literature (especially poetry), music, and applied arts such as ceramics, calligraphy, metal crafting, and embroidery.

MEDICINE. Although some modern medicine was introduced into Uzbekistan during the Soviet period, the standard of health care—especially for the predominantly rural Uzbek population—is far below that in most European parts of the former USSR. Many of the serious health problems (e.g., a soaring cancer rate, a high infant-mortality rate, and hepatitis) are direct or indirect results of the reckless pursuit of cotton cultivation (including depletion of water supplies and use of large doses of toxic chemicals). Uzbeks have a rich tradition of folk medicine, but until late in the Communist era the party did not encourage its use.

Bibliography

Akiner, Shirin (1986) "The Uzbeks." In *Islamic Peoples of the Soviet Union: An Historical and Statistical Handbook.* 2nd ed. London: KPI.

Allworth, Edward (1964). *Uzbek Literary Politics.* The Hague: Mouton.

Bennigsen, Alexandre, and S. Enders Wimbush (1986). "The Uzbeks." In *Muslims of the Soviet Empire: A Guide.* Bloomington: Indiana University Press.

Montgomery, David C. (1984). "Uzbeks." In *Muslim Peoples: A World Ethnographic Survey*, edited by Richard V. Weekes, 833–839. Westport, Conn.: Greenwood Press.

—NANCY LUBIN AND WILLIAM FIERMAN

VOLGA TATARS

Ethnonyms: Bulghar, Kazanlï, Mishär, Mösälman, Tatar

Orientation

IDENTIFICATION. The Volga Tatars are the westernmost of all Turkic ethnic groups living in the former Soviet Union. Among them, there are two major groups, the Kazan Tatars and the Mishars, who share a common literary language and culture despite ethnogenetic and linguistic particularities. The Volga Tatars live mainly in Tatarstan and Bashkirstan in Russia, but they can also be found in large numbers in other areas of Russia as well as in the republics of Uzbekistan, Kazakhstan, and Kyrgyzstan in particular. As late as the second half of the nineteenth century,

Volga Tatars

HISTORY AND CULTURAL RELATIONS

Regardless of dialect, Volga Tatar retains a Persian and Arabic influence in its vocabulary, in addition to the strong influence of Russian.

♦ khanate
A territory in eastern Russia, Central Asia, or Siberia that was under the control of a khan—many were formed following the Mongol conquest in the thirteenth century. The three major khanates were the Crimea, Astrakhan, and Kazan.

Volga Tatars preferred to identify themselves and to be identified by others as "Mösälman" (Muslims), in addition to using ethnonyms such as "Kazanlï," "Bulghar," and "Mishär." The Russians and other peoples identified them simply as "Tatars," a practice which often led to confusion, since Russians used the ethnonym to designate any Muslim of Turkic ethnic background living in European Russia and the Caucasus. The ethnonym "Tatar" was less than universally embraced because the popular as well as official identification of the Volga Tatars with the Mongol Tatars of the thirteenth century was at the root of the stigma attached to it. The ethnonym "Tatar" was controversial then, a quality it retained into the 1990s, when *glasnost* and *perestroika* made possible the renewal of the ethnonymic debates. The name of their homeland has changed since the tenth century from "Bulghar" to "Kazan," "Idel-Ural," and "Tatarstan" or "Tataria." In the Soviet system, their titular republic was called Tatarstan Avtonomiyale Sovet Sotsialistik Respublikase. Tatarstan is presently part of the Russian Federation formed in 1992.

LOCATION. Most Volga Tatars live in the middle Volga's forest and forest-steppe zone (Tatarstan) and in the southern Ural Mountains (Bashkirstan), an area encompassing 211,600 square kilometers. The ecology, economy, culture, and history of the region have been shaped to a great extent by the rivers that cross it: Volga, Kama, Viatka, Sura, Sviaga, Belaia, and Samara.

DEMOGRAPHY. According to the 1989 census data, there were some 6,645,588 Volga Tatars in the Soviet Union, a 7.4 percent increase compared to their numerical strength in 1979. Of these, less than 50 percent live in their historic homeland, the middle Volga-Ural region. The average population density per square kilometer is approximately 50.5 in the middle Volga region and 26.8 in the southern Ural area. Volga Tatars are one of the most urbanized ethnic groups of the former Soviet Union: 62.1 of those Volga Tatars who live in Tatarstan proper live in cities, compared to 50.3 of those Volga Tatars who live in other parts of Russia. Those who live in the republics of Central Asia enjoy levels of urbanization below 30 percent.

LINGUISTIC AFFILIATION. Volga Tatars speak a language belonging to the West Turkic, Kïpchak, or Kïpchak-Bulghar Group. Volga Tatars have a single literary language, based on the Kazan dialect, but there are three main dialectal divisions based on lexical, phonetic, and morphological differences: Central (around Kazan),

Western or Mishar (spoken by Tatars outside Tatarstan), and Eastern or Siberian. Regardless of dialect, Volga Tatar retains a Persian and Arabic influence in its vocabulary, in addition to the strong influence of Russian. The Arabic script, which the ancestors of the Volga Tatars adopted when they chose Islam as their religion in 922, was for more than a millennium the vehicle for the development of a rich literature, and indeed, the backbone of Tatar culture and civilization. In 1927, in the aftermath of the decision of the 1926 Turcological Congress held in Baku, it was replaced with a Latin script, which was, in turn, replaced with a Cyrillic script in 1939. Today Volga Tatars still use the Cyrillic script, but recent debates in the press have challenged the wisdom of the two previous alphabet changes.

History and Cultural Relations

The Volga Tatars are the descendants of the Kïpchak Turkic peoples who inhabited the western wing of the Mongol Empire, the *ulus* of Dzhuchi. Despite the fact that the issue of their ethnogenesis is still being hotly debated among scholars, Soviet and Western alike, there is agreement that by the sixteenth century, Volga Tatars were living in the area of the middle Volga River, which included the northern lands of the former Muslim state of the Turkic people called "Bulghar." Displaced from the Azov steppes by frequent Arab campaigns, the Bulghars had penetrated the middle Volga and lower Kama river regions in the first half of the eighth century. When their territory was conquered and devastated by the Mongol army of Batu Khan in 1236, most of the survivors moved north, to the land beyond the Kama River. The Mongol conquerors, who organized their possessions north of the Black and Azov seas into a state that came to be known as the Golden Horde, never aimed at transforming the conquered lands in accordance with a Mongol weltanschauung. As a result, the area became a veritable melting pot and the ancestors of the Volga Tatars, the Bulghars and the Kïpchak Turkic tribes inhabiting the lands of the Horde, participated in the ethnic and cultural syntheses that emerged.

The people of the khanate of Kazan that emerged in 1445 after the disintegration of the Golden Horde, were the product of these syntheses, and they wrote an important chapter in the history of the Volga Tatars. Despite the brevity of its life as a free political entity, (1445–1552) the khanate of Kazan exhibited socioeconomic dynamism and cultural vitality. It was during this period that the process of the ethnogenesis of the people we identify today as the Volga Tatars entered its final stages, and their language took shape as a distinct branch of the Turkic languages.

Ivan's conquest of Kazan in 1552 brought about the demise of the khanate as an independent political entity. The assimilationist policies imposed by the Russian state on the population of the khanate between the sixteenth and nineteenth centuries ranged from forced conversion to economic coercion and cultural assimilation through education. The Tatars responded by fueling the social unrest of their homeland with their discontent, joining peasant rebellions such as those of S. Razin (1667–1771) and E. Pugachev (1773–1775).

By the end of the nineteenth century, the Volga Tatars were articulating new responses to the Russification policies of their government: they embarked upon a multifaceted movement of cultural reform and renewal called *jadidism* (from *usul-u-jadid*, "the new method of teaching"). The main goal of the movement was to achieve a harmonious balance between secularism and religion and between isolation and integration in their search for solutions and correctives to the socioeconomic, political, and cultural problems that preoccupied their communities. This movement received an added impetus during the years of political pluralism that followed the Russo-Japanese War of 1904–1905. It was further aided by the emergence of a dynamic Tatar-language press and book-publishing businesses. Journals such as *Shura* and newspapers such as *Vagt* were known among the Muslims of the Russian Empire and beyond. Religious reformers such as Sh. Merjani, M. J. Bigi, R. Fahreddin, A. Bubi, and others sought to bring about a renewal from within by returning to the pristine purity of the dogma, whereas poets such as A. Tukay—the national poet of the Volga Tatars—and intellectuals and politicians such as Y. Akchura and S. Maksudi addressed issues concerning Volga Tatar identity and political life. In the brief intermezzo between 1905 and 1917 the Volga Tatars actively participated in the political life of the empire, providing the bulk of the Muslim deputies for the four Russian dumas, becoming the main force behind the emergence of a Muslim political caucus (Ittifak-al-Muslimin), and joining parties that belonged to the entire breadth of the Russian political spectrum.

The revolutions of 1917 brought about hopes of establishing a Volga Tatar state. Their attempt to set up an independent Idel-Ural (Volga-Ural) state as a federation of the Turkic peoples living in that region failed, however. Instead, on 27 May 1920, the territory at the confluence of the Volga and the Kama—where only approximately 40 percent (1,169,342) of the Volga-Ural Tatars lived—was organized as the Tatar Autonomous Soviet Socialist Republic, one of the constituent units of the Russian Federation. The bulk of the remaining Volga Tatars were placed under the jurisdiction of the Bashkir Republic, organized on 23 March 1919, and others under those of the adjoining territories of western Siberia, beyond the Urals and Central Asia.

The demise of the plans for a Volga-Ural federation, as well as the renewal of Russification policies under the guise of proletarian internationalism, contributed to the emergence of national communism in the 1920s. The theoretician of national communism was M. Sulvan Galiev (purged in 1928); one of its most remarkable cultural manifestations was the defense of Tatar national culture (language, Arabic script, religion, traditions).

The purges of the 1930s eliminated national communism as a political issue among the Volga Tatars, but in the post–World War II years its cultural manifestations endured in scholarship, as well as literature and the arts.

Today, the Volga Tatars participate actively in the economic life of their region, which is rich in gas and oil resources and a leader in the heavy machinery and chemical industries. Since 1985 they have been actively using the openness of the glasnost era in an attempt to both reclaim their past and participate in the decision-making process that will affect their future. Some of the most spectacular developments since the mid '80s are an upsurge of interest in Islam, coinciding in 1989 with the celebration of 1,100 years since the adoption of Islam by their ancestors; rehabilitation of major cultural and political figures such as M. J. Bigi, A. Ishaki, and M. Sulvan Galiev; defense of the national language, which unfolded in the campaign to make Tatar the official language of Tatarstan; and sovereignty for Tatarstan.

Settlements

The rural Tatar population of the Volga-Ural region resides mostly in the 1,659 villages of Tatarstan and Bashkirstan (807 and 852 respectively). Today there are no villages with an exclusively Tatar population. Even as only one of the components of the physiognomy of multiethnic villages (usually of the strip-and-cluster type), Tatar houses are easily identifiable, however, because of their architecture and decoration. The main construction material, for rich and poor alike, is wood. Stone gained popularity with the well-to-do peasants only in the nineteenth century. The houses of the Volga Tatars are built according to two main floor plans: simple one-room dwellings with an attached planked porch (average size: 6 by 8 meters, including the porch); two-room, hexagonal-shaped dwellings, actually constructed by linking with a corridor two traditional one-room houses. The room used by the family every day faces the street and is called *kara yak* (the black side), whereas the room reserved for guests is called *ak yak* (the white side). Houses were surrounded by high fences and gates.

Well-to-do peasants built two- and even three-story houses, observing the same floor plan. The houses of the rich were distinguished not only by their size, building material (sometimes stone), and the lavish decorations, but also by the fact that they were laid across the property, rather than being parallel to the street. Toward the end of the nineteenth century, the distance between the houses (of rich and poor peasants alike) and the streets began diminishing, and today there are many houses whose walls stand on the property line facing the street.

Economy

SUBSISTENCE AND COMMERCIAL ACTIVITIES. Agriculture, crafts, cattle breeding, hunting, fishing, and trade represented the backbone of the economic life of the Volga Tatars for centuries. Beginning with the second half of the nineteenth century, and most dramatically after 1917, the traditional economic patterns changed: collectivized agriculture and industrialization were responsible for changes in rural areas and cities alike. As Tatars acquired industrial skills, entered the professions in larger numbers, and took white-collar jobs, the ratio of the urban population grew.

The Volga region has rich soil, suitable for agriculture, and rich oil and gas resources. Modern agricultural technology penetrated the area only in the twentieth century. Until then, the basic implements were the heavy metal plow with a single blade (*saban*), effective for the chernozem, and the light wooden plow used for podzol. For centuries, the traditional crops of the area were barley, wheat, and millet, and these continue to be the main crops today. Domestic animals include chickens, geese, sheep, and large cattle.

Industrial development accelerated in the Volga-Ural region, particularly after World War II; in addition to the oil and gas industries, and related to them, strong petrochemical and auto industries emerged. The Volga Tatars were known throughout their history for their active involvement in trade. Besides trading regionally, they acted as intermediaries between the Muslim states on the eastern and southern frontiers of the Russian state and the Russian merchants. Tatar

SOCIOPOLITICAL ORGANIZATION

Tatarstan and Bashkirstan—the lands where most of the Volga Tatars live—were autonomous republics (they received this status in 1919 and 1920) of the Russian Republic, which in turn, was one of the fifteen republics that comprised the Soviet Union. Today, following the demise of the USSR, the Russian Federation is comprised of eighteen of the twenty former autonomous republics. Tatarstan has chosen to remain independent.

Political Organization

In the Soviet era the major political-administrative units of the Volga-Ural area within the autonomous republics were districts (*raions*), cities, urban settlements, and villages. The local branches of the Soviet government and institutions were in charge of all aspects of life, from law enforcement to education and health services. What characterized them all was the still-strong level of centralization, despite promises of increased local autonomy.

Social Control

There were two levels of social control: official (through a set of Soviet institutions that promoted the socialist value system) and unofficial (through the family unit, which emphasized the traditional values of Tatar society).

Conflict

Family conflicts are usually arbitrated by the elders. Marriage conflicts that could not be solved within the family had to be submitted to the arbitration of Soviet organs, however.

merchants sold leatherwork, furs, fish, honey, and, until the sixteenth century, slaves. In the nineteenth century they became involved in the book trade, in addition to participating in the grain, soap, and candle trades.

INDUSTRIAL ARTS. The ancestors of the Volga Tatars (the Bulghars) were experts in processing the hides and pelts that were abundant in a hunting/agricultural economy. A certain type of leather even came to be known as "Bulghari." Leather craftsmen, along with potters, blacksmiths, coppersmiths, carpenters, stonemasons, jewelers, tanners, and tailors, remained a fixture of Tatar rural and urban communities into the twentieth century. Most of these crafts survive today.

TRADE. All types of commercial enterprises were represented among the Volga Tatars. There were merchants of the first guild and large firms such as those of Saidashev, midsize and small enterprises, itinerant traders in rural areas, and peddlers of used clothing and food in large cities.

DIVISION OF LABOR. The traditional division of labor assigned home tasks to women. They cooked and were in charge of producing the cloth to cover the personal and household needs of the entire family. They also tended vegetable gardens and were involved in preserving and preparing meats and dough products for winter consumption. Tending babies and raising the female children of the family until marriage was exclusively the domain of women. Men usually plowed, harrowed, engaged in trade and industry, and took charge of the education of male children. The division of labor is no longer rigidly observed, but most traditional approaches still endure.

LAND TENURE. Land was collectively owned in the former Soviet Union. Agricultural land was either organized in kolkhozy or sovkhozy. Peasants working in these units were either members of a collective enterprise or state employees. Today, private ownership of land, industrial and commercial enterprises, and natural resources is one of the major issues in Tatarstan.

Kinship

KIN GROUPS AND DESCENT. Volga Tatars traditionally lived in extended-family, multihousehold units. In these hexagonal-type dwellings, parents and their sons, or at least one of their sons, shared work responsibilities, as well as wealth. Today, even in villages, the nuclear family is becoming more prevalent.

KINSHIP TERMINOLOGY. The kinship terms of the Volga Tatars resemble those of other Turkic peoples in at least two ways: the emphases on age and on the male/paternal line of the family. Thus, there are separate terms for older and younger sisters—*apa* and *senel* respectively—and special terms to distinguish patrilineal and matrilineal kin.

Marriage and Family

MARRIAGE. Tatar culture and society have been shaped by the imperatives of Islamic laws and traditions. Hence, Sharia, which sanctions polygamy, has governed the sphere of marriage and family life. Despite the fact that a man was permitted to marry up to four wives, until the end of the nineteenth century most men had no more than two wives. At the onset of the twentieth century, monogamous marriages were gaining ground, but religious endogamy was strictly observed until 1917. Today, monogamous marriage is the norm and arranged marriages are rare, but ethnically mixed marriages are no longer an exception, although their number has been decreasing. Housing shortages in the cities are responsible for the fact that more and more often young couples reside with one or the other of their two families for an extended number of years.

DOMESTIC UNIT. All those who share the same ancestry, usually including the members of three generations, are considered a family, regardless of their place of residence. A family unit is usually comprised of those individuals belonging to either a nuclear or extended (including grandparents) family who reside together, share responsibilities, and pool their resources.

INHERITANCE. Male children traditionally received a larger share of their parents' property, and the responsibility of caring for the parents usually fell to one of them. Girls received a dowry, which, according to Islamic law, they continued to control fully, even after entering the families of their husbands. Although the laws of the former Soviet state applied to all citizens and provided for equal division of property, the force of tradition endured in many Tatar communities.

SOCIALIZATION. Children are raised by mothers and female siblings. During the Soviet period, government-owned nurseries and kindergartens were available. In the family, emphasis is placed on respect for and deference to the opinion of the elders, whereas in the nurseries and kindergartens emphasis was on the importance of the collective and deference to its needs.

Religion and Expressive Culture

RELIGIOUS BELIEFS. Islam, which the ancestors of the Volga Tatars adopted in 922, has

Islam, which the ancestors of the Volga Tatars adopted in 922, has been the religion that shaped their lives and culture for more than a millennium.

♦ **Sharia**
Quaranic law.

Volga Tatar music differs drastically from the music of other Turkic peoples because of its monophonic structure that traditionally lacked instrumental accompaniment.

been the religion that shaped their lives and culture for more than a millennium. Volga Tatars belong to the Sunni branch of Islam, and within it, to the Hanefite legal school. In the Soviet era they were under the jurisdiction of the Religious Board for the Muslims of European USSR and Siberia. The seat of the Board (Muftiat) was in Bashkiria, in the city of Ufa. The head of the Muftiat, Talgat Tadzhuddinov, was appointed to this post in 1980 and was actively involved in using the opportunities offered by the era of openness to secure more freedom of worship for the Volga Tatars. The celebrations of 1,100 years of Islam in the middle Volga that took place in the summer of 1989 mark the high point of this new era. Other developments include opening new mosques, returning to the use of the believers old mosques that had been given secular uses, teaching the Arabic script and the fundamentals of religion, and printing new editions of the Quran and prayer books, as well as rehabilitating some of the leading religious figures of years past, such as M. J. Bigi. At the parish level, the most prominent figures are the mullahs and imams who are responsible for the performance of rituals and the religious education of their parishioners. Women cannot occupy these positions, but as in years past, wives of mullahs and imams or older women conversant in the ritual and dogma lead prayers for women and instruct them in the dogma and ritual. They are called *abïstays*.

Strict adherence to monotheism is required of every Muslim, and this fundamental obligation is expressed in the Shahadah (the profession of the creed): there is no God but God, and Mohammed is His Prophet. While adhering to this creed, Volga Tatars also honor saints and holy places, tombs associated with people whose lives were marked by special deeds and religious devotion. Some beliefs in supernatural forces still endure as remnants of the pre-Islamic history of the Volga Tatars, but overall, their influence on everyday life is minimal. One of these pre-Islamic traces is belief in the evil eye and the power of various amulets worn to annihilate its effect.

CEREMONIES. The religious calendar of the Volga Tatars includes several major events: the month of Uraza (fasting [one of the most important ceremonial obligations of all Muslims]); the feast that follows it, Uraza Bäyram (the feast of sacrifice); and Gait Kurban; as well as the celebration of the birth of the Prophet, marked by prayers called Mäwliud. In addition, Volga Tatars celebrate two other festivals, both echoes of their pre-Islamic culture: Navruz (New Year), the cele-

bration of the arrival of spring on March 21, and Sabantui, the Festival of the Plow. This festival is held before the beginning of the spring agricultural cycle and consists of a week-long ritual that culminates with a day of athletic competitions, song, and dance.

ARTS. Religious prohibitions were responsible for the absence of representative art among the Volga Tatars. Until the end of the nineteenth century, calligraphy and applied arts were the only forms that Volga Tatars embraced and developed. Of the calligraphers who specialized in the production of a religious art form—*shämail* (ornamented verses from the Quran)—the most famous in the nineteenth century was Ali Makhmudov.

Representational art had its beginnings at the beginning of the twentieth century when Volga Tatars were engaged in the jadidist reform movement. The main thrust of this movement was to forge a symbiosis between tradition and modernity without altering the essence of the religious creed. The Volga Tatars emerged from this search with a restored sense of their identity and dedicated their efforts toward renewal of their educational system, art, and literature. Hence, their first representational artists emerged at the beginning of the twentieth century. They were M. Galeev and G. Gumerov. With every decade, new names were added: S. S. Akhun, N. K. Valiullin, B. M. Al'menov, F. Sh. Tagirov, I. V. Rafikov, G. A. Rakhmankulova, L. A. Fattakhov, I. M. Khalilullov, Kh. A. Iakupov, and B. I. Urmanche—painter and sculptor, the doyen of Tatar art, who was active into the ninth decade of his life.

Volga Tatar music differs drastically from the music of other Turkic peoples because of its monophonic structure that traditionally lacked instrumental accompaniment. Its modal basis is the pentatonic scale. Several genres of folk songs exist: *ozïn koi* (lyric-epic), *qïsqa koi* (dance songs), *avïl koe* (village song), *shekher koe* (city song), and *bäit* (narrative epic). Twentieth-century singers, however, have opted for musical accompaniment. The instrument of choice is the accordion (*garmun'* or *baian*); some Volga Tatars also play the mandolin.

Before the appearance of professional music at the beginning of the twentieth century, folk music dominated the musical life of the Volga Tatars. Tatar folk songs were first written down by Tatars such as G. Kh. Enikeev and G. G. Saifullin and Russians such as S. G. Rybakov in the nineteenth century. They have been collected and published since the 1930s, although some of the best collections, such as that of M. N. Nigmetzianov, were published in the 1970s.

The first Tatar opera (*saniya*) was staged in 1925, but the operatic art has blossomed only since the 1930s. Ballet and symphonic music also developed, particularly after World War II. Among the most prominent Tatar composers are M. Z. Iarullin, A. G. Valiullin, F. A. Akhmetov, and D. I. Iakupov.

Tatar literature developed along two lines, oral folk literature and a written literature. Islam influenced both, but the Arabic script was the vehicle for the development of written literature, whether religious or secular, until the end of the 1920s.

Some of the earliest monuments of Tatar written literature are Kol Gali's narrative love poem *Yusuf and Zuläikha* (thirteenth century) and Mukhammediar's didactic poems (sixteenth century). The literature of the seventeenth and eighteenth centuries was dominated by the religious (Sufi) poetry of Mävliya Kulï, Utïz Imäni, and Shamsetdin Zäki. In the nineteenth century, writers such as A. Kargalï and G. Kandalïy introduced themes of everyday life but also continued the tradition of religious odes.

The Tatar learned men of the nineteenth century were responsible for triggering the movement of reform and renewal that came to be known as jadidism. They were critics of scholasticism and some advanced anticlerical ideas, but all had an appreciation for enlightenment. Of these, A. Kursavi (1776–1818), Sh. Märjani (1813–1889), and Kayyum Nasiri (1825–1902) can be called the founders of modern Tatar culture. In the first decades of the twentieth century the Tatar national poet G. Tukay (1886–1913), romantic poets such as S. Ramiev (1880–1926) and Z. Ramiev (1859–1921), and revolutionary poets and writers such as G. Kulakhmetov (1881–1918), G. Ibragimov (1887–1937), and others flourished.

The literature of Socialist Realism, which dominated the Soviet literary scene from the 1930s to the 1980s, did produce, despite the confining imperatives of ideology, some enduring names in Tatar letters: G. Bashirov, Sh. Mannur, F. Khusni, and I. Gazi.

Musa Jalil, whose World War II experiences were recorded in his *Moabit Notebook*, may be the best-known writer of the war period but there are many others such as S. Khakim, Isanbet, Sh. Mudarris, and N. Fattakh.

The most notable developments of the post–World War II literature were the emergence of the "thaw" literature of the 1960s, represented by poets and writers such as I. Iuzeev, R. Kharisov,

I. Aminov, T. Minnullin, and Zölfat, and the cultural explosion of the perestroika period, characterized by an effort to revitalize and retrieve the cultural values of the past and by a determination to save from extinction the main vehicle for the transmission of Tatar culture—the Tatar language.

Bibliography

Bennigsen, Alexandre, and S. Enders Wimbush (1986). *Muslims of the Soviet Empire: A Guide.* Bloomington: Indiana University Press.

Gulova, F. (1983). *Tatarskaia natsional'naia obuv'* (Tatar national footwear). Kazan.

Karimullin, A. (1988). *Tatary: Etnos i etnonim* (Tatars: People and ethnonyms). Kazan.

Mukhametshin, Iu. G. (1977). *Tatary Kriasheny* (Kriashen Tatars). Moscow: Nauka.

Rorlich, A. A. (1986). *The Volga Tatars: A Profile in National Resilience.* Stanford, Calif.: Hoover Institution Press.

Suslova, S. V. (1980). *Tatarskie iuvelirnye ukrashenia* (Tatar ornamental jewelry). Kazan.

Urmancheev, F. (1984). *Geroicheskii epos Tatarskogo naroda* (Heroic epics of the Tatar people). Kazan.

Valeev, F. Kh. (1984). *Narodnoe dekorativnoe iskhusstvo Tatarstana* (Decorative art of the people of Tatarstan). Kazan.

—AZADE-AYSE RORLICH

YAKUT

Ethnonyms: Sakha, Urangkhai Sakha, Yakutians

Orientation

IDENTIFICATION. The Yakut, who prefer to call themselves "Sakha," live in Yakutia, the Sovereign Sakha Republic of the Russian Federation formed in 1992. The Yakut are the farthest-north Turkic people, with a consciousness of having once lived farther south kept alive by legends and confirmed by historical and archaeological research. The Yakut, spread through Yakutia yet concentrated in its center, have become a minority in their own republic. The majority is of Slavic background. Other minorities include the dwindling Yukagir of northern Yakutia, the Even, the Evenk, and the Dolgan, a mixed Yakut-Evenk group.

LOCATION. Yakutia is a 3,100,000-square-kilometer territory (over four times the size of Texas) in eastern Siberia (the Soviet Far East). Located at approximately 56 to 71° N and 107 to 152° E, it is bounded by Chukotka to the northeast, Buriatia in the south, and the Evenk region

♦ perestroika
("reconstruction")
Part of Mikhail Gorbachev's policy set in motion in 1987.

Yakut

Yakutia is notorious for extremes of cold, long winters, and hot, dry summers.

◆ **taiga**
Area of heavy forest, both coniferous and deciduous, often with poor soil and bogs and marshs in low-lying drainage areas; an ecological zone across nothern Eurasia, south of the tundra belt.

to the west. Its northern coast stretches far above the Arctic Circle, along the East Siberian Sea, and its southern rim includes the Stanovoi Mountains and the Aldan plateau. Its most majestic river, the Lena, flows north along cavernous cliffs, into a long valley, and past the capital, Yakutsk. Other key river systems where major towns have developed include the Aldan, Viliui, and Kolyma. About 700,000 named rivers and streams cross Yakutia, which has some agricultural land but is primarily nonagricultural taiga with vast resources of gold, other minerals, gas, and oil. Tundra rims the north, except for forests along the rivers. Notorious for extremes of cold, long winters, and hot, dry summers, Yakutia has two locations that residents claim to be the "coldest on earth": Verkhoiansk and Oimiakon, where temperatures have dipped to -79° C. More typical are winters of 0° to −40° C and summers of 10° to 30° C.

DEMOGRAPHY. The 1989 Soviet census recorded a population of 147,386,000 for the Russian Republic, and 1,081,000 for the Yakut Autonomous Republic. The Yakut numbered 382,000, an increase from 328,000 in 1979. In the 1920s they constituted about 82 percent of their republic's population; by 1989 they were only 35 percent. The Yakut have become increasingly urban in the past twenty years, although at a slower rate than the majority (Slavic) population. Whole villages in central and northern Yakutia remain solidly Yakut, whereas the major cities of Yakutia are heavily Russian. The population of Yakutia was 65 percent urban in 1989. As many as 10 percent of marriages were between Yakut and other nationalities in the 1970s and 1980s, although this percentage was declining by 1990.

LINGUISTIC AFFILIATION. The Yakut speak Yakut, a Northeast Turkic language of the Altaic Language Family. It is one of the most divergent of the Turkic languages, closely related to Dolgan (a mixture of Evenk and Yakut sometimes described as a Yakut dialect). The Yakut, over 90 percent of whom speak Yakut as their mother tongue, call their language "Sakha-tyla." Their current written language, developed in the 1930s, is a modified Cyrillic script. Before this, they had several written forms, including a Latin script developed in the 1920s and a Cyrillic script introduced by missionaries in the nineteenth century. Yakut lore includes legends of a written language lost after they traveled north to the Lena Valley.

History and Cultural Relations

Yakut oral histories begin well before first contact with Russians in the seventeenth century. For ex-

ample, *olonkho* (epics) date at least to the tenth century, a period of interethnic mixing, tensions, and upheaval that may have been a formative period in defining Yakut tribal affiliations. Ethnographic and archaeological data suggest that the ancestors of the Yakut, identified in some theories with the Kuriakon people, lived in an area near Lake Baikal and may have been part of the Uighur state bordering China. By the fourteenth century, Yakut ancestors migrated north, perhaps in small refugee groups, with herds of horses and cattle. After arrival in the Lena Valley, they fought and intermarried with the native Evenk and Yukagir nomads. Thus, both peaceful and belligerent relations with northern Siberians, Chinese, Mongols, and Turkic peoples preceded Russian hegemony.

When the first parties of Cossacks arrived at the Lena River in the 1620s, Yakut received them with hospitality and wariness. Several skirmishes and revolts followed, led at first by the legendary Yakut hero Tygyn. By 1642 the Lena Valley was under tribute to the czar; peace was won only after a long siege of a formidable Yakut fortress. By 1700 the fort settlement of Yakutsk (founded in 1632) was a bustling Russian administrative, commercial, and religious center and a launching point for further exploration into Kamchatka and Chukotka. Some Yakut moved northeast into territories they previously had not dominated, further assimilating Evenk and Yukagir. Most Yakut, however, remained in the central meadowlands, sometimes assimilating Russians. Yakut leaders cooperated with Russian commanders and governors, becoming active in trade, fur-tax collection, transport, and the postal system. Fighting among Yakut communities decreased, although horse rustling and occasional anti-Russian violence continued. For example, a Yakut Robin Hood named Manchari led a band that stole from the rich (usually Russians) to give to the poor (usually Yakut) in the nineteenth century. Russian Orthodox priests spread through Yakutia, but their followers were mainly in the major towns.

By 1900 a literate Yakut intelligentsia, influenced both by Russian merchants and political exiles, formed a party called the Yakut Union. Yakut revolutionaries such as Oiunskii and Ammosov led the Revolution and civil war in Yakutia, along with Bolsheviks such as the Georgian Ordzhonikidze. The consolidation of the 1917 Revolution was protracted until 1920, in part because of extensive opposition to Red forces by Whites under Kolchak. The Yakut Republic was not secure until 1923. After relative calm during Lenin's New Economic Policy, a harsh collectivization and antinationalist campaign ensued. Intellectuals such as Oiunskii, founder of the Institute of Languages, Literature, and History, and Kulakovskii, an ethnographer, were persecuted in the 1920s and 1930s. The turmoil of Stalinist policies and World War II left many Yakut without their traditional homesteads and unaccustomed to salaried industrial or urban work. Education both improved their chances of adaptation and stimulated interest in the Yakut past.

Settlements

As horse and cattle breeders, the Yakut had a transhumant pattern of summer and winter settlements. Winter settlements comprised as few as twenty people, involving several closely related families who shared pastureland and lived in nearby yurts (*balagan*) with surrounding storehouses and corrals. The yurts were oblong huts with slanted earthen walls, low ceilings, sod roofs, and dirt floors. Most had an adjoining room for cattle. They had substantial hearths, and furcovered benches lining the walls demarcated sleeping arrangements according to social protocol. Yurts faced east, toward benevolent deities. In summer families and their animals moved to larger encampments. The most ancient summer homes, *urasy*, were elegant birch-bark conical tents. Some could hold 100 people. Their ceilings soared at the center point, above a circular hearth. Around the sides were wide benches placed in compartments that served as ranked seating and sleeping areas. Every pole or eave was carved with symbolic designs, the motifs of which included animals, fertility, and lineage identities. By 1900 urasy were rare; summer homes were yurts or combination yurt–log cabins. By 1950 yurts were also obsolete, found only in a few museums. Yet collectives still send workers to summer sites to graze cattle away from large villages. Housing is Russian style, often rough-hewn log huts with broad, raised stoves. Many families, even in large towns, rely on outhouses and outdoor water pumps. Some collectives, however, are gradually letting workers build more substantial individual family homes with modern amenities. Another style is the "village of the urban type," with low, concrete apartment buildings and indoor plumbing. The largest city is Yakutsk (with a population of 187,000 people in 1989). The towns of Viliusk, Olekminsk, Neriungri, and Mirny grew rapidly in the 1980s.

Economy

SUBSISTENCE AND COMMERCIAL ACTIVITIES. Traditional pastoralism in central Yakutia required homestead self-reliance, with intense dependence on calves and foals in a harsh climate. Stables, corrals, and haying developed in conjunction with hardy breeds of cattle and short, fat, furry horses. Richer families owned hundreds of horses and cattle; poorer ones raised a few cattle or herded for others. A huge variety of dairy products, including fermented mare's milk (Russian: *kumys*), was the staple food; meat was reserved for special occasions. The diet was augmented by hunting (bears, elk, squirrels, hare, ferrets, fowl), fishing (salmon, carp, *muksun*, *mundu*), and, under Russian influence, agriculture (cereals). Wealthy Yakut hunted on horseback, using dogs. The poorest Yakut, those without cattle, relied on fishing with horsehair nets and, in the north, herded reindeer like their Evenk and Yukagir neighbors. Yakut also engaged in the fur trade; by the twentieth century hunters for luxury furs had depleted the ermines, sables, and foxes, and they were relying on squirrels. Yakut merchants and transporters spread throughout the entire northeast, easing communications and trade for natives and Russians. They sold luxuries like silver and gold jewelry and carved bone, ivory, and wood crafts in addition to staples such as butter, meat, and hay. Barter, Russian money, and furs formed the media of exchange. Guns were imported, as was iron for local blacksmiths.

INDUSTRIAL ARTS. Before iron was imported, ironworkers used ore from local marshes. Similarly, ceramics made from local clay preceded Russian pottery. Most homemade crafts were for household use: decorated birch-bark containers, leather bags, dairy-processing equipment, horsehair blankets, fur clothing, benches, hitching posts, and elaborately carved wooden containers (including *chorons* for kumys).

DIVISION OF LABOR. Although occupations within a household were divided by gender and status, the atmosphere was usually one of productive group activity. All participated in hay making, cattle herding, and milking, but, in general, horses were a male preserve and cattle a female responsibility. Women tended children and fires, prepared food, carried water, and made clothing and pottery. Men handled more strenuous firewood preparation, house building, sled making, hunting, fishing, and mowing. Ivory carving and wood- and metalworking were male tasks. These divisions have held through the twentieth century in households of rural collectives, although possibilities have also expanded. Women now hunt, fish, and engage in crafts once associated with men. They have become doctors, nurses, teachers, engineers,

Traditional pastoralism in central Yakutia required homestead self-reliance, with intense dependence on calves and foals in a harsh climate.

♦ yurt
A usually portable multifamily dwelling with a circular ground plan and sides of felt or skins attached to a folding wooden lattice framework.

bookkeepers, and politicians. Some women work in the growing industrial sector. Men are engineers, tractor drivers, geologists, teachers, doctors, managers, and workers in the lucrative energy, metallurgy, gold, diamond, and building industries. In the 1980s a Yakut man was director of the Yakutia gold ministry and a Yakut woman was head of the republic legislature. The intelligentsia of Yakutia is dominated by Yakut men and women in prestigious cultural, scientific, and political jobs.

Kinship

Key kin relations are based on a patrilineage (*aqa-usa*) that traces membership back nine generations. Within this, children born to a specific mother are distinguished as a group (*ye-usa*), and may form the basis for different households (*korgon*). Historically, more distant kin were recognized on two levels, the *aimak* (or territorial *nasleg*), with one to thirty lineages, and the *dzhon* (or territorial *ulus*), composed of several aimak. These larger units were united by alliances, including for common defense, and by economic relations; these links were renewed at councils and festivals. Kin terms reflect gender and age distinctions and distinguish senior from junior paternal lines. Any relation, affinal or consanguinal, is called *uru*, which is the word for "wedding."

Marriage and Family

MARRIAGE. Traditionally, for wealthy Yakut, marriage could be polygamous. More common, however, was monogamy, with occasional remarriage after the death of a spouse. Arranged marriages were sometimes politically motivated. Patrilineage exogamy was reckoned strictly; those one could marry were called *sygan*. Until the 1920s many marriage arrangements were complicated and protracted, involving financial, emotional, and symbolic resources of the bride's and groom's extended families. This included the matchmaking ritual; several formal payments of animals, furs, and meat to the bride's family; informal gifts; and extensive dowries. Some families permitted poor grooms to work in their households as a replacement for the bride-price. Occasionally bride-capture occurred (it may have been more common in pre-Russian times). Wedding ceremonies and their attendant feasts, prayers, and dancing, were held first at the household of the bride's parents, then at that of the groom's. The couple usually lived with the groom's parents or settled in a nearby yurt. Since the 1970s interest in limited aspects of ritual and gift exchange has revived, although few couples are paired through matchmakers. In the 1980s one young man was chagrined to find that a woman he had fallen in love with on a train was a distant cousin, a forbidden marriage partner according to kin rules still observed.

INHERITANCE. By customary law, land, cattle, and horses, although used by households, were controlled by the patriline. Animal or land sale and inheritance were approved by elders. But by the twentieth century smaller families were keeping resources, in part because of the decline of large horse droves. Men owned most of the wealth and passed it to their sons, especially elder sons, although the youngest son often inherited the family yurt. Mothers could pass on dowries to daughters, but the dowry could be forfeited by bad behavior. In theory, dowries included land, as well as goods, jewelry, and animals, although in practice elders rarely gave land to another lineage. Soviet law limited inheritance to goods, and non-state housing could be bequeathed at individual discretion. Most apartments and summer houses were kept in families.

Sociopolitical Organization

SOCIAL AND POLITICAL ORGANIZATION. Kinship and politics were mixed in the hierarchical council system that guided aqa-usa, aimak, and dzhon. Yakut explanations of dzhon in the nineteenth century included concepts like "people," "community," or "tribe," territorially defined. Councils were composed of ranked circles of elders, usually men, whose leaders, *toyons*, were called nobles by Russians. A lineage head was *bis-usa-toyon*; respected warriors and hunters were *batyr*. Lineage councils decided major economic issues, interfamily disputes, and questions of blood revenge for violence committed against the group. Aimak and dzhon councils were infrequent, dealing with issues of security, revenge, alliance, and, before Russian control, war. Through war, slaves were captured for service in the wealthiest toyon households. Kin-based councils were rare by the nineteenth century and had little influence on twentieth-century politics. Yet in the Soviet period Yakut remained aware of regional and kin ties and helped kin obtain jobs and political positions. In this period the Yakut elite, some of whom were Communist party members, revived certain traditions, participating in wedding ceremonies and annual festivals once associated with council meetings. To avoid doing so would have been impolitic. Yakut have demanded greater economic and political autonomy from Moscow, and some Yakut politicians, including the elected president, are reformers implementing the new republic constitution. A major ecological movement and democratically elected councils are trying to redress local grievances.

SOCIAL CONFLICT AND CONTROL. In the Soviet period the Communist party controlled the courts and congresses of the Yakut, most of whom felt removed from policy making until the Gorbachev period. Demonstrations erupted on Yakutsk streets several times in the 1980s, mostly by young Yakut protesting police inaction over violent incidents involving Russians and Yakut. Tensions exist between newcomers and natives, developers and ecological activists, and "internationalists" and "nationalists." In addition, minorities, such as the Evenk, Even, and Yukagir, have demanded greater cultural and political rights. In response, a precedent-setting national district within Yakutia, the Even-Bytantaisk Raion, was established in 1989.

Religion and Expressive Culture

RELIGIOUS BELIEFS. Yakut religion derives from Turkic, Mongolic, Tungusic, and Russian ideas. Labels like "animist," "shamanist," or "Russian Orthodox" do not suffice. Ideas of sin are syncretized with concepts of contamination and taboo. Saints and bears are seen as shamanic spirit helpers. Christ is identified with the Yakut Bright Creator Elder God, Aiyy-toyon. A pantheon of gods, believed to live in nine hierarchical eastern heavens, was only one aspect of a complex traditional cosmology that still has meaning for some Yakut. Another crucial dimension was the spirit-soul (*ichchi*) of living beings, rocks, trees, natural forces, and objects crafted by humans. Most honored was the hearth spirit (*yot ichchite*), still fed morsels of food and drink by pious Yakut. Giant trees (*al lukh mas*), deep in the forest, were especially sacred: their ichchi are still given small offerings of coins, scarves, and ribbons. Belief in ichchi is related to ancient ideas of harmony and equilibrium with nature, and to shamanism. Yakut shamanism is a Turkic, Mongolic, and Tungusic blend of belief in the supernatural, with emphasis on the ability of "white," or benign, shamans to intercede, through prayers and séances, with eastern spirits for the sake of humans. "Black" shamans, communing with evil spirits, could both benefit and harm humans.

RELIGIOUS PRACTITIONERS. As with other Siberian peoples, Yakut shamans (*oiun* if male, *udagan* if female) combine medical and spiritual practice. Despite centuries of Russian Orthodox and Soviet discrediting of shamans as greedy

STRONG WOMEN

*A Yakut woman in traditional dress. Although some rural areas still follow a traditional division of labor, women now hunt and fish, and have become doctors, engineers, and politicians. Verkhoyansk, Yakutia, Siberia, Russia.
(Dean Conger/Corbis)*

charlatans, some Yakut maintain belief in shamans and supernatural powers. Others, struggling to recover spirituality after rejecting Marxist-Leninist materialism, accept aspects of shamanic philosophy. Still others, influenced by Soviet education and science, reject all religion as superstition. In the nineteenth century a few Yakut leaders financed the building of Russian Orthodox churches, and many Yakut declared themselves Christian, but this did not mean that they saw Christianity and shamanism as mutually exclusive. The Yakut also believed in the spiritual power of blacksmiths. By the 1980s shamans in Yakutia were rare and more likely to be Evenk than Yakut. Yet rituals once associated with spirit belief were being revived by urban as well as rural Yakut.

CEREMONIES. The most important ceremony, associated with a founding Yakut ancestor named Ellei, is the annual summer *yhyak* festival, a celebration of seasonal change, of kumys (fermented mare's milk), and of kin solidarity. Once a religious celebration led by a shaman, the ceremony has been adapted since World War I into a secular commemoration of Yakut traditions. Practiced in villages and towns, it features opening prayers (*algys*) and libations of kumys to the earth. Although some Yakut debate its "authenticity," the festival still includes feasting, horse rac-

Yakut

*Despite centuries of
Russian Orthodox
and Soviet
discrediting of
shamans as greedy
charlatans, some
Yakut maintain
belief in shamans
and supernatural
powers.*

♦ **permafrost**
*Land that is permanently
frozen, with only the top
few milimeters thawing in
the warmer months.*

ing, wrestling, and all-night line dancing to improvised chants. It lasts three joyous days in Suntar, where it is especially famed. Wedding rituals, pared down from previous eras, center around memorial hitching posts (*serge*), carved for the occasion, with couples honored by prayers, special food, and dancing. New rituals marking wedding anniversaries and graduations at all educational levels include the placement of serge, on which the names of those honored are carved. But traditional rituals of birth, supplicating the goddess of fertility, Aiyyhyt, have become less popular, with some Yakut women even mocking the restrictions that were once associated with beliefs about female impurity. Russian Orthodox holidays are rarely celebrated.

ARTS. Yakut art takes many forms, sometimes rooted in ritual life, but, in the Soviet period, often secular and commercial. Silver and gold jewelry, once considered talismanic, is enjoyed for its aesthetic value. Famed for ivory- and woodcarving, Yakut artists have branched into graphic art, painting, and sculpture. Filmmakers, theater groups, and opera and dance companies enrich cultural life in Yakutia and beyond. Continuity of folk art is strongest in exuberant improvisational poetry that accompanies line dancing (*ohuokhai*) and in a revival of mouth-harp (*khomus*) playing. But few young people memorize the olonkho that once took days to tell. Instead, olonkho heroes are memorialized in other art forms.

MEDICINE. With the decline of shamanism, most Yakut rely on Western medicine administered in hospitals and clinics. Yet rumors persist of faith healing, described as spiritual or hypnotic. A few Yakut with shamanic family backgrounds attend medical school, supporting the belief among Yakut that healing talent can be inherited. Traditional healers (who had long periods of apprenticeship) were specialized, with herbal experts, bonesetters, shaman's assistants, and various grades of shamanic power. Sources vary as to whether male or female shamans were more powerful. Drumming and the music of the khomus enhanced a shaman's trance during séances to ascertain the cause of illness. Each person was believed to have three souls, which were necessary to maintain health.

DEATH AND AFTERLIFE. At the demise of all three souls, especially *tyn* or "breath," a person was declared dead. On the deathbed, the family sometimes dressed the dying in funeral attire. Before burial, the deceased's spirit visited every place he or she had traveled in life. On the third day, bearers took the body to the graveyard, where a grave was prepared deep enough to touch permafrost and shallow enough to be seen by escort spirits. A horse, steer, or reindeer was sacrificed, to help the deceased travel to the land of the dead and to provide food for family and grave preparers. One of the deceased's souls, *kut*, was believed to travel skyward to a lush greenery-filled heaven. People feared that souls could stay on earth, becoming *yor* capable of haunting kin. Fears of yor, especially yor of shamans, lingered in the 1980s. Burials were mixtures of pre-Soviet and Soviet ritual, with traditional symbolism observed more in villages than in cities.

Bibliography

Gogolev, Anatoli Ignatevich (1983–1986). *Istoricheskaia etnografiia Iakutov* (Historical ethnography of the Yakuts). 2 vols. Yakutsk: Yakutsk University Press.

Gurvich, Ilya Samoilovich (1977). *Kul'tura severnykh Iakutov-olenevodov* (Culture of the northern Reindeer-Yakuts). Moscow: Nauka.

Jochelson, Waldemar (1933). *The Yakut.* American Museum of Natural History Anthropological Papers 33. New York.

Kulakovsky, Aleksei Eliseevich (1979). *Nauchnye trudy* (Scientific works). Compiled by N. V. Emelianov and P. A. Sleptsov. Yakutsk: Institute of Languages, Literature, and History, Academy of Sciences.

Okladnikov, Aleksei Pavlovich (1970). *Yakutia before Its Incorporation into the Russian State.* Translated by Stephen P. Dunn and Ethel Dunn. Edited by Henry Michael. Anthropology of the North series, 8. Montreal and London: McGill-Queen's University Press.

Seroshevskii, V. L. (Sieroshevski, W.) (1896). *Iakuty* (Yakuts). St. Petersburg: Imperial. Russkoe Geograficheskoe Obshchestvo. Adapted as "The Yakuts," edited by W. G. Summer. 1901. *Journal of the Royal Anthropological Institute* (London) 31:65–110.

Tokarev, S. A., and I. S. Gurvich (1964). "The Yakuts." In *Peoples of Siberia*, edited by M. G. Levin and L. P. Potapov, 243–304. Translated by Stephen P. Dunn and Ethel Dunn. Chicago: University of Chicago Press. Originally published in Russian in 1956.

—MARJORIE MANDELSTAM BALZER

South America

ARAUCANIANS

Ethnonyms: Huilliche, Lafquenche, Mapuche, Pehuenche, Picunche, Promaucae

Orientation

IDENTIFICATION. The name "Araucanian" is of Spanish origin. Historically, Mapuche or "people from the land" was the term used to designate the Araucanians occupying the south-central area of the Chilean territory but now is the term used by all Araucanians. The terms "Huilliche" (people of the south), "Pehuenche" (piñon-eating people of the mountains), "Lafquenche" (people of the coast), and "Picunche" (people of the north") were used by the Araucanians to differentiate their regional areas. The term "Promaucae" (rebellious people) was given to the Araucanians by the Incas.

LOCATION. Aboriginally, the Araucanians occupied the region between the Río Choapa (32° S) and Chiloé Island (42°50′ S). The majority of Araucanians live in the Chilean provinces of Arauco, Bío-Bío, Malleco, Cautín, Valdivia, Osorno, and Llanquihue between 37° and 40° S. (In 1975 the twenty-five Chilean provinces were reorganized into thirteen regions. Arauco, Malleco, and Cautín are now in the ninth region; Bío-Bío is in the eighth region; Valdivia, Osorno, and Llanquihue are in the tenth region.) Within this area summers are warm and the winters characterized by heavy rainfalls. The annual average rainfall is over 200 centimeters and the average temperature is 10° C. In Argentina, the Araucanians are found in the provinces of Buenos Aires, Río Negro, Mendoza, Chubut, La Pampa, Santa Cruz, and Neuquén (between 41° and 36° S and 73° and 78° W. Neuquén has the largest concentration of Araucanians.

DEMOGRAPHY. The aboriginal population of the Araucanians has been estimated to have been between 500,000 and 1,500,000 at the time of the Conquest. Today it is estimated that there are about 400,000 Araucanians in Chile and 40,000 in Argentina.

LINGUISTIC AFFILIATION. The Araucanian language, Mapudungun, belongs to the Mapuche Stock and is comprised of several dialects. In Chile these are: Mapuche proper, Picunche, Pehuenche, Huilliche, and Chilote. Mapuche proper was spoken from the Bío-Bío to the Tolten rivers at the time of the Conquest; at present it is spoken in the provinces of Bío-Bío, Maule (in the seventh region), Arauco, Cautín and Ñuble (in

the eighth region). Picunche was spoken from Coquimbo to the Río Bío-Bío. Pehuenche is spoken from Valdivia to Neuquén. Huilliche is spoken in Chile in the province of Valdivia and in Argentina in the Lake Nahuel Huapí region. In Argentina, Moluche or Nguluche and Ranquelchue are also spoken. Moluche is spoken from Limay to Lake Nahuel Huapí. Ranquelchue was spoken on the plains of La Pampa and can now be heard in Chalileo, General Acha, and on the Río Colorado.

History and Cultural Relations

Archaeological evidence suggests the existence of an Araucanian culture by 500 B.C. in the territory of present-day Chile. The aboriginal Araucanians were hunters and gatherers and practiced horticulture and incipient agriculture. At the beginning of the sixteenth century, the Araucanians were divided into three geographically contiguous ethnic groups: the Picunche in the north, the Mapuche in the central-south, and the Huilliche in the southern section. At this time the Incas invaded the Araucanian territory, dominating the Picunche. The Picunche were influenced more by the Central Andes cultures in their material culture and technology than were the Mapuche and the Huilliche, but the organization of their economic, social and religious life was like that of the other Araucanian groups. The Inca invasion was stopped at the Río Maule by the Mapuche and the Huilliche.

In the mid-sixteenth century the Spanish arrived and established a military outpost in central Chile. Only the Picunche were conquered by the Spanish. They were forced to work in the gold mines and to perform agricultural tasks. The Picunche eventually mixed with the Spanish rural population, and by the seventeenth century the Picunche had completely disappeared as an ethnic group. The Mapuche and the Huilliche managed to keep their independence from the Spanish and the Chileans for almost four centuries by waging guerrilla warfare. The horse was adopted by the Araucanians soon after the middle of the sixteenth century and it was used effectively in warfare and hunting.

In the eighteenth century the Mapuche and the Huilliche started to migrate to Argentina in search of horses to continue their battle against the Spanish. In their search for horses, they began their geographical and cultural expansion in the Argentinian territory, which lasted 150 years. Three Indian groups were Araucanized: the Pehuenche, the Puelche, and the Pampa. By the end

Archaeological evidence suggests the existence of an Araucanian culture by 500 B.C. in the territory of present-day Chile.

♦ **incipient agriculture**
The growing of crops by the slash-and-burn method while supplementing the diet with the products of hunting, fishing, or gathering because the garden produce alone is insufficient.

975

Araucanians

In Chile, the present reservation system was established in 1884, and the Araucanians were relocated to reservations; in Argentina they were arrested and confined to isolated areas.

of the eighteenth century, all these groups spoke the Mapuche language and had acquired Araucanian beliefs and traditions. The Mapuche and the Huilliche controlled all the area between the vicinity of Buenos Aires, Córdoba, San Luis, and the Río Negro from the cordillera to the sea. Three permanent chiefstainships were established in the Argentinian territory. In Chile, the Mapuche and the Huilliche continued their war with the Spanish for over two centuries. Two major treaties were signed between the Araucanians and the Spanish in which the Spanish Crown recognized the independence of the Araucanian territory. The conflict between the Araucanians and Whites was rekindled, however, after Chile became independent from Spain in 1818.

The Chilean government promoted European colonization of the Araucanian territory by establishing the reservation policy of 1866, which favored White colonists. The Mapuche and especially the Huilliche lost a great deal of land to German settlers. With the loss of land, the Huilliche began to lose their traditional way of life. Two major rebellions were staged by the Mapuche, both of which were defeated by the Chileans. Following the last major rebellion (1880 to 1882), the Mapuche lost their political autonomy and military power. In Argentina, the military campaigns under generals Julio Roca and Conrado Villegas in 1879–1883 completely defeated the Indian confederates and drove most of the Indian survivors beyond the Río Negro and into Neuquén.

In Chile, the present reservation system was established in 1884, and the Araucanians were relocated to reservations; in Argentina they were arrested and confined to remote areas. At the present time, they form two relatively differentiated modern ethnic groups: the Argentinian Araucanians and the Chilean Mapuche.

Settlements

Prior to the arrival of the Spanish, the Araucanians lived in small clusters of semipermanent to permanent settlements arranged in a dispersed pattern. Three to eight patrilocal families or households inhabited each settlement, each living in its own dwelling. The settlements were located mostly in valleys or plains along rivers and streams. The Araucanians never lived in towns. Their dwellings consisted of huts (*rukas*) situated in prominent places so approaching visitors could be seen and the animals could be observed. The typical ruka had a timber or cane framework; an oval, polygonal, or rectangular ground plan; and a

thatch roof extending nearly to ground level. Dimensions ranged from 3 to 6.5 meters in length and from 3 to 4 meters in breadth. There were one or two smoke holes at one or both ends of the roof. Although this type of ruka can still be found, modifications involving the use of shingles, cement, brick, or wood instead of thatch are becoming common. The number of rukas determines wealth: poor Mapuche live in one ruka, whereas wealthy ones have separate rukas for sleeping, eating, and storage.

Economy

SUBSISTENCE AND COMMERCIAL ACTIVITIES. Between A.D. 500–1000 and 1500 Araucanian subsistence was based on a combination of food gathering, hunting, fishing, horticulture, and incipient agriculture. Their diet was and continues to be predominantly vegetarian. Horticulture is believed to have developed among the aboriginal Araucanians between 500 and 1500. In the valleys, horticulture and incipient agriculture were combined with hunting and gathering, whereas in the highlands only hunting and gathering were practiced. In the coastal areas, fishing and gathering shellfish were supplemented with hunting. The plants cultivated by the Araucanians of the valleys were maize, kidney beans, squashes, quinoa, oca, peanuts, chili peppers, and white potatoes. The latter are believed to have been domesticated by the Araucanians. Irrigation agriculture was practiced by the Picunche in the northern part of the Araucanian territory. The Araucanians were herders as well as farmers, raising llamas for meat and wool. By the end of the eighteenth century, llamas were replaced by horses, mules, sheep, pigs, and other domesticated animals introduced by the Spanish.

Contemporary Araucanian agriculturists cultivate European crops using steel plows and farming techniques learned from the Chileans, such as the three-field system of land rotation and crop rotation. Woven blankets, pottery, and wood- and stone-work are sold to tourists in the markets of cities near the reservations. Women sell part of the produce from their gardens in the local markets.

INDUSTRIAL ARTS. Ceramics were probably introduced in the northern cultures of the Araucanian territory in the last 500 years prior to the arrival of the Spanish. By the time of their arrival, the Araucanians were skilled in fashioning baskets, blankets colored with native dyes, cordage and netted objects, pottery, and wood and stone objects. With the introduction of sheep by the

Spanish, weaving became more important. Silver-smithing was introduced in the late eighteenth century and became highly developed. Today, the Araucanians make textiles, baskets, and stone- and wood-work both for domestic use and for cash sale in the local markets.

TRADE. Exchange between the Araucanians consisted of reciprocated favors. Chilean Araucanians traded with the Argentinian Araucanians for salt and animals in exchange for weavings and alcohol. Trade between the Araucanians and the Spanish and, later, the Chileans, was fairly common in the eighteenth and nineteenth centuries; however, there were no established markets. Generally, Araucanians traded animals and weavings for alcohol and European goods.

DIVISION OF LABOR. When swidden agriculture was practiced, men cut down and burned the forest, whereas women did the planting, weeding, and harvesting of the gardens. During times of war farming was performed primarily by women. Since the relocation to reservations, farming has become the main occupation of men. Women, in addition to their domestic work, engage in the smallscale cultivation of vegetable gardens. Children start to help their parents in farm activities when they are young. At an early age, they begin by taking care of the animals. As they grow older, boys help their fathers with farm activities, whereas girls help their mothers with domestic tasks. *Minga*, a communal form of reciprocated labor in which kin members and neighbors participate, was and continues to be resorted to for the construction of houses and agricultural tasks.

LAND TENURE. Among aboriginal Araucanians land lacked importance because their economy did not emphasize extensive agriculture. In the second half of the eighteenth century, land was owned communally by a group of families. Each family owned the land they cultivated and grazed. Property was administered by chiefs, who apportioned plots to families. Reservation settlement in 1884 changed this situation, weakening common holding and strengthening individual holding and inheritance. Three thousand small reservations were mapped by surveyors from 1884 to 1920. The Chilean authorities gave the head of a kinship group a land deed (*título de merced*) granting use to him and to the (named) group members. The reservation policy of 1884 gave chiefs an opportunity to receive more land if there was division. Under this policy, upon petition of one-eighth of the households, the reservation would be disbanded and the land given in sever-alty title to household heads, with additional land given to chiefs as inducement.

In the early part of the twentieth century, this policy, combined with the increase in population and diminishing agricultural productivity, produced the greatest pressure to divide land. In the 1920s, however, the division of land came almost to a standstill. The Mapuche resisted disbandment. The government continued its efforts to attempt to appeal to individual Mapuche and bypass the authority of the chiefs. In 1927 the law pertaining to the disbanding of reservations was changed to require only the appeal of a single household. After this measure failed, the government decreed that even this single vote was not necessary and that it could disband reservations at its own discretion. In 1931 the law was again changed; it stipulated that the votes of one-third of the households of a reservation were needed. In March 1979 Decree-Law 2568 went into effect, providing for the division of Mapuche communal land into individual plots if only one occupant demands it, whether Mapuche or non-Mapuche. The majority of the Mapuche now live on reservations (the number of reservations has decreased to under 2,000). They can bequeath their land, lend it, or rent it, but they cannot sell it or dispose of it in any permanent way. The sale of land is possible only after the reservation is divided.

Kinship

KIN GROUPS AND DESCENT. The system of descent is patrilineal, tracing back to a mythical ancestor who is believed to be a creator of the lineage. Until the nineteenth century the *kuga* kinship and naming system existed: each lineage, or kuga, had its own name, which was given to its male children shortly after birth. Members of each group had a particular loyalty to one another and sided with one another during arguments.

KINSHIP TERMINOLOGY. Traditional kin terms follow the Omaha system insofar as a man will call his mother's brother's daughter "mother," and she will call him "son."

Sociopolitical Organization

SOCIAL ORGANIZATION. Prior to pacification, the Araucanians derived personal prestige and personal rank from martial prowess, wealth, generosity, and eloquence of speech. The modern Araucanians are divided into three loosely separated classes: the wealthy, the commoners, and the poor farm workers.

MARRIAGE AND FAMILY

Marriage

The ideal marriage was and continues to be the "mother's brother's daughter" marriage. Sororal polygyny, sororate, and levirate marriage customs were common. The basic marriage process involved negotiations over a bride-price, a dramatized capture of the bride-to-be, the payment by the prospective groom, and then the marriage ceremony. Divorce was common, most often occasioned by sterility, infidelity, desertion, or ill-treatment. In all cases, the bride-price was returned to the husband. At present, these traditional practices have been almost completely replaced by monogamy.

Domestic Unit

Until the nineteenth century the domestic unit was a patrilocal extended family composed of a central male, his wives, and their children and grandchildren. Currently, a domestic unit generally consists of a couple and their children and may include one of the couple's parents.

Inheritance

Position and inheritance were patrilineal, passing from father to son. Before settlement on the reservations, inheritances consisted mainly of herds and movable goods. Now the importance of land ownership has made property the most consequential inheritance, and both men and women inherit land.

Socialization

In aboriginal times boys had to sleep outside, bathe daily, and abstain from certain foods in order to toughen themselves. They were trained in the use of arms, swimming, horsemanship, and oratory and accompanied their fathers to drink with the rest of the men. Today oratory and farming skills are taught to young boys. Girls are taught to take care of the home and their younger siblings. *Datura stramonium* and *Latua pubiflora* are used by the Mapuche and Huilliche as personality tests for their children; a mild tea is brewed from these plants and the parents observe the child's reactions and draw conclusions regarding the character traits she or he will develop.

POLITICAL ORGANIZATION. Kinship heads, called *lonko*, controlled agricultural labor and other cooperative (minga) ventures. A lonko's power extended only over his own household, and his prestige partly depended upon his generous hospitality. There was no overall chief in peacetime. When necessary, military commanders were elected by these lonko. After settlement in reservations, the political power of the chiefs was temporarily strengthened. The chief's role in land allocation gave him control over marital and postmarital residence. The consequent division of land and the inability of the original chiefs to transfer their reservation land title to their heirs decreased their newly acquired political power. Modern chiefs share their authority with councils of elders and heads of lineages. The chief's authority is restricted to inter- and intrareservational matters.

SOCIAL CONTROL. During prereservation times, crimes of adultery, murder, and sorcery within the community were punishable by death. With the exception of sorcery, however, compensation was commonly made through payments. At present, troublemakers and people suspected of sorcery are usually evicted from the reservation as punishment. Since pacification, the Araucanians have been under the Chilean judicial system.

CONFLICT. Prior to settlement on the reservations, feuds and raids between Araucanians were common. Each household defended its farm lands against trespass and avenged death or sorcery by means of blood feud.

Religion and Expressive Culture

RELIGIOUS BELIEFS. The maintenance of a sustained and responsible link between the living and the dead is the central concept of Araucanian religious morality. The living are responsible for the propitiation of their ancestors, and rituals are performed to maintain a positive relationship with them. Dreams, the vehicle of contact with the supernatural, are an important aspect of the Mapuche spirtual life. Araucanians interpret their dreams daily to understand their present situation and learn about their future.

In aboriginal times, the Araucanians are believed to have had an animistic religion. At present, the Araucanian religion is polytheistic, with the highest god located at the highest level of

♦ **blood feud
(vendetta)**
A conflict between two groups (usually families or other kin groups) in a society. The feud usually involves violence or the threat of violence as a means of avenging some wrongdoing against a member of one of the groups. Feuds often are motivated by a desire to protect or restore a member's honor.

heaven. The family set of the highest god is formed by two couples, one young and one old. The most important of these gods is the male of the old couple. Located in descending order within this hierarchical heaven, there are the gods of fertility, of the morning star, of the stars, of the past warriors, of the rituals, of music, and of the cardinal points and climatic and metereological forces. On the lowest levels there reside the spirits of the Araucanian ancestors and the spirits of the volcanoes. The *perrimontu* are beings with ambivalent association with the forces of good. They aid shamans in their profession and cause sicknesses. The evil forces are called *wekufe* and are of three major types: natural phenomena, ghosts, and those of zoomorphic form. In spite of the prolonged contact with missionaries and Whites, Araucanian religion has been little affected and Christianization has been minimal.

RELIGIOUS PRACTITIONERS. A *kalku* is both a sorcerer and a witch. Kalkus, who are usually women, are trained in their arts by other kalkus. Their powers are obtained through dreams and visions. The forces of evil are activated when envious people ask kalkus to use the evil spirits to attack persons who are the objects of their envy. Shamans (*machi*), aided by their auxiliary spirits, ward off these evil forces. Although men used to practice shamanism during prereservation times, at present the majority of shamans are women. Selection as a shaman and the acquisition of shamanistic power is believed to occur in dreams and visions. Candidates are those who have suffered a prolonged and dangerous illness, display a greater ability to dream than others, and experience visions. The novice receives her training from a senior shaman. The training lasts anywhere from two to four years, during which time the trainee demonstrates obedience and works hard to learn herbal lore, ventriloquism, diagnosis of illness, and divination. After the training has been completed, the neophyte must demonstrate her expertise to other shamans and to the community in a ceremony called *machiwüllun*. The shamanic paraphernalia consist of a drum (*kultrun*) and carved pole (*rewe*). Shamans are assisted by the *thungunmachife*, or shaman interpreter, who translates the language of the shaman while she is in a trance.

CEREMONIES. The most important ritual among the Araucanians is the *ngillatun*. In the prereservation era, the emphasis of the ngillatun was militaristic, but with pacification it became mainly agricultural, except in times of crisis. The ngillatun celebrated near harvest time consists principally of agricultural rites conducted for the purpose either of thanking the gods for the harvest received or asking for a plentiful one. The ngillatun usually involves the participation of more than one community, and some involve as many as four communities, preferably neighbors. The frequency of this ceremony varies, but if several communities should cooperate as members of a ngillatun, they will take turns in hosting each other. In times of stress this ritual is conducted as soon as a catastrophic event has occurred and may or may not involve the participation of other communities.

ARTS. The traditional art most practiced among contemporary Araucanians is oratory; it is characteristic primarily of chiefs, but ordinary people also engage in it. Mapuche oral narrative can be classified into five categories: *epeus* (mythological tales, animal tales, and legends), *peumas* (dream reports), *nut'amkans* (narratives that recount the heroic deeds of past Araucanian warriors), *weupins* (formal speeches made by men at social and religious events), and *qulkatuns* (improvised sung narratives usually expressive of strong emotions). The main musical instruments are the kettle drum, flute, and trumpet. Men and women dance—but rarely together—imitating animals with masks and movement. Men and women engage in spontaneous singing at social gatherings.

MEDICINE. In earlier times all sicknesses were believed to be caused by supernatural agents. Among contemporary Araucanians, however, there are two kinds of sickness: one caused by supernatural agents, the wekufe and the perrimontu, and the other by natural agents or environmental factors. Shamans treat all sicknesses with herbs and rituals.

DEATH AND AFTERLIFE. After death, the soul is believed to undergo a series of transformations on its journey to the *wenu mapu* (the place of final rest). The soul has the potential of becoming an agent of evil if captured by the evil spirits on this journey. Special ceremonies are conducted by the relatives of the dead to ensure the safety of the soul. At its final destination the soul becomes an ancestral spirit. Through dreams and visions the ancestor visits the living and helps them. Funeral rites involve the gathering of friends and relatives of the deceased, ceremonial wailing, tearing of the hair, shamanistic autopsy, temporary preservation of the cadaver, and the heavy drinking of alcohol.

Bibliography

Cooper, John (1946). "The Araucanians." In *Handbook of South American Indians*, edited by Julian Steward.

The maintenance of a sustained and responsible link between the living and the dead is the central concept of Araucanian religious morality.

Vol. 2, *The Andean Civilizations*, 687–766. Bureau of American Ethnology Bulletin 143. Washington, D.C.: Smithsonian Institution.

Degarrod, Lydia Nakashima (1990). "Coping with Stress: Family Dream Interpretation in the Mapuche Family." *Psychiatric Journal of the University of Ottawa* 15(2): 111–116.

Faron, Louis (1968). *The Mapuche Indians of Chile*. New York: Holt, Rinehart & Winston.

Stuchlick, Milan (1976). *Life on a Half Share*. London: C. Hurst & Co.

—LYDIA NAKASHIMA DEGARROD

AYMARA

Ethnonyms: none

Orientation

IDENTIFICATION. The name "Aymara" is of unknown origin. Historically, the Aymara referred to themselves as "Jaqi," meaning "human beings," or as "Colla." This term "was extended loosely by early Spanish chroniclers to include all the Aymara-speaking tribes of the 'Collao' or Collasuyo division of the Inca empire" (La Barre 1948).

LOCATION. The Aymara are presently concentrated on the altiplano, the Andean high plateau, a geographical zone of approximately 170,000 square kilometers at a medium elevation of 4,000 meters above sea level. Although located in the center of the South American continent, the altiplano has far from a tropical climate, owing to the extreme elevation—surrounding mountains range up to 7,000 meters. The temperature varies more between night and day than between seasons. Normally the summer season (November to March) has daily rainfalls, the winter (May through September) a complete drought. The population is mainly spread around Lake Titicaca in Peru and Bolivia, extending into southern Bolivia, southern Peru, and northern Chile. There is evidence that in the pre-Inca period Aymara speakers were geographically spread over a substantially larger area.

DEMOGRAPHY. In 1950 the Aymara population was estimated to be between 600,000 and 900,000, with the majority living in Bolivia. More recent estimates claim that the Aymara number between two and three million, of which around half a million live in Peru (approximately 2.3 percent of the Peruvian population). The Bolivian Aymara are about 30 percent of the population.

♦ **Inca**
A preindustrial civilization that flourished in what is now Peru, Bolivia, Ecuador, and Chile from about 1438 until its final destruction in 1572.

For these reasons, the Aymara tend to be linked more closely to the history of Bolivia than to that of Peru.

LINGUISTIC AFFILIATION. The Aymara language, one of the three most widely spoken (with Quechua and Guaraní) Indian language in South America, belongs to the Andean-Equatorial Language Family, more specifically to the Jaqi Language Group. There are three Jaqi languages: Jaqaru and Kawki, spoken only in Peru, and Aymara, spoken primarily in Bolivia and Peru.

History and Cultural Relations

The Aymara are considered descendants of some of the earliest inhabitants of the continent and possible founders of the so-called Tiahuanaco (Tiwanaku) high culture, estimated to have existed from between 500 and 200 B.C. to around A.D. 1000. For unknown reasons this culture suddenly collapsed in the thirteenth century (i.e., before the Inca Empire reached its peak toward the end of the fifteenth century). By then most people of the Andes, from Equador into Chile, were linked in a tightly controlled economic and political system in which the Quechua language of the Incas dominated. But the Aymara, as an exception from Inca practice, were allowed to retain their own language. This contributed to the still-persisting cultural and social separation of the Aymara.

After the Spanish Conquest in 1533 the Aymara shared the fate of most South American peoples—centuries of suppression. In what later became Bolivia, the Spaniards started the extraction of metals, mainly silver, at the price of ruthless exploitation of the Indian population, which was forced to work in the mines. The eighteenth century was a period of great unrest among various Indian groups in what was then called Upper Peru (part of Bolivia today). Lacking coordination, these uprisings had little effect upon the lives of the Aymara in the area. Nor did the fifteen-year long war of independence, which in 1825 resulted in the proclamation of the Republic of Bolivia.

The status of the Bolivian Aymara remained virtually unchanged until the revolution in 1952, which led to economic and social reforms such as universal suffrage and land reform. A continuing stormy political scene has, however, resulted in an underdeveloped economy, poor communication, and social problems; these conditions primarily affect the Indian population, whose situation is not likely to change rapidly. Culturally related peoples are the Quechua, the Uru, and the

Chipaya. Their languages are unrelated (in spite of the common belief to the contrary). but there has been extensive mutual linguistic and cultural borrowing.

Settlements

As the Aymara switched to pastoralism and agriculture, they settled in small clusters throughout the altiplano area. Several millennia later, during the colonial period, two types of highland communities came into existence in Bolivia: the hacienda-dominated community (inhabited by *colonos*) and the marginal, freeholding community (inhabited by *comunarios*), which contributed to the development of diverging settlement patterns. Homesteads in the comunario community are often widely dispersed, whereas in the colono community living quarters are mostly built in close-knit clusters. The buildings of each unit (for an extended family or some related families) are surrounded with a wall. Aymara frequently own dwellings in more than one location because of their traditional engagement (landholdings, trade, or barter) in different places. In the 1950s, when the Aymara began substantial migration to urban centers, they kept their settlement pattern, including having a wall around the dwelling of a nuclear or extended family.

Economy

SUBSISTENCE AND COMMERCIAL ACTIVITIES. Early Aymara began practicing animal husbandry and subsistence agriculture possibly around 2500 B.C. Climate, elevation, and poor soil limit the range of plants and food crops that can be cultivated. The Aymara adapted to their harsh environment by engaging in the domestication of animals and crops, some of which are still unique to the Andes (the Andean cameloid, llama, and the native grain, quinoa) and others of which (e.g., potatoes and maize) have spread throughout the world. A method for food preservation was developed early: dehydration (freeze-drying) of the staple food, potatoes, and other Andean tubers. This allowed long-term storage, necessary in a region of seasonal production, as well as the accumulation of a surplus to free labor for nonsubsistence activities. The dramatic differences in elevation create substantial climatic variations in geographically close areas. As insurance against the failure of a single crop and to get access to a greater variety of products, the Aymara have developed a method of agricultural diversification: they keep land in different ecozones. This diversification technique is used also in commercial activities (e.g., trade and wage labor). Trade is by tradition dominated by women, who bring agricultural produce to central markets, where today most products are sold, not traded. Early patterns of seasonal migration (mainly by men) for wage labor have contributed to the engagement in the cash economy by most present-day Aymara. However, there are rural villagers still living mainly through subsistence agriculture.

INDUSTRIAL ARTS. Pottery making and weaving are performed by both men and women.

KINSHIP

Kinship Groups and Descent

According to a common Andean bilateral kinship system, Aymara trace descent through both male and female ancestors within a certain number of generations, usually to the great-grandparents (*t'unu*). It is unclear when this cognatic system developed, but ethnographers (e.g., Lambert 1977) at present agree that earlier reports of a patrilineal system are the results of misinterpretations and that the pre-Hispanic kinship system rather was parallel, or dual, in its nature (Collins 1981). Kin groups were traditionally organized into an ayllu, described as a "subtribe," "one or several extended families," "extended lineages," "a unit within which certain bonds of kinship are recognized" or, according to Zuidema (1977), as "any social or political group with a boundary separating it from the outside." The ayllus and the current corresponding *comunidades* display strong tendencies of endogamy. A high rate of endogamy between urban migrants and members from their community of origin is reported.

Kinship Terminology

According to Lounsbury (1964), the kinship system was a rarity of the Omaha type. This is based on Ludovico Bertonio's early-seventeenth-century *Vocabulary*. Today there is assimilation to a Spanish bilateral system, but with vestiges of the older system.

*Aymara males and
females are
considered equal in
status, decision
making, and rights,
as well as in
inheritance, labor
division, and
cooperation.*

Works of highly skilled architects and sculptors from the Tiahuanaco culture can still be seen at that site.

TRADE. Despite lagging development of infrastructure and poor communications, Aymara men and women traditionally keep long-distance trading partners, which enables them to acquire produce from other ecological zones. In institutionalized reciprocal relationships, such as *ayni* (exchange of labor, goods, and services) and *compadrazgo* (godparenthood, coparenthood, ritual kinship), labor may be exchanged for food products or meals. Urban traders exchange, for example, salt, *sultana* coffee, rice, or vegetables grown at low elevation for several kinds of potatoes and dried beans with their rural partners.

DIVISION OF LABOR. Labor is divided equally between married spouses (i.e., husbands and wives work the fields together, although they may have different tasks). But no task is so sex specific that the other cannot take it on. Among urban "Westernized" Aymara, however, the traditional labor cooperation seems to be vanishing.

LAND TENURE. In early days a form of collective landownership was practiced by the members of an *ayllu*, a basic social, political, and geographical unit. Grazing land was used in common, whereas the agricultural land was rotated and distributed yearly among ayllu members according to the needs of each extended family. Only land on which the families had their houses was privately owned. As land became permanently divided and privately owned by separate families, the tradition of working in common-labor groups has been weakened.

Marriage and Family

MARRIAGE. Most marriages derive from the choice of the young couple but are regarded as an economic union with binding reciprocal obligations among three households: those of the parents of the groom, the parents of the bride, and the newlyweds. A marriage is entered through a series of stages and wedding ceremonies, earlier mistakenly apprehended as "trial marriages." Marriages are monogamous and divorce is fairly easy.

DOMESTIC UNIT. The basic unit is the nuclear family with extended family networks for cooperation. Nuclear families with separate households often live on the same premises as their extended kin. Virilocal or neolocal residence is typically practiced.

INHERITANCE. Inheritance is traditionally bilateral (i.e., males and females inherit property

separately from their father and mother). The equal inheritance rules, legalized in Bolivia in 1953, have sometimes led to extreme splitting up of land, resulting in the bending of the rules in practice.

SOCIALIZATION. Children are regarded as complete human beings and are brought up with guidance rather than with rebuke or force. They are treated with respect, and, although seldom excluded from any situation, they are taught to be quiet when grown-ups talk.

Sociopolitical Organization

SOCIAL ORGANIZATION. The idea of equality, embraced by all Aymara, is a component of most relationships in rural society. The social system is flexible, and on the lowest levels of the social structure, the family and the ayllu, individuals are interchangeable (i.e., men and women can change roles). Males and females are considered equal in status, decision making, and rights, as well as in inheritance, labor division, and cooperation.

POLITICAL ORGANIZATION. In pre-Conquest time, when the Aymara dominated the Andean highlands, a number of Aymara-speaking "nations," divided into "kingdoms" or "chiefdoms," developed. An Andean type of endogamous moiety organization with stratification of ethnic groups (Aymara and Uru) has been reported (Murra 1968). The independence of these nations was lost as the Quechua-speaking Incas extended their influence, but on the local level little of Aymara life changed. Decision making in the traditional ayllu was of the consensus type. Leadership authority was executed by the *jilaqata*, chosen yearly among adult men according to a rotating system. In the new community organization, connected to the national governments, the headman is theoretically chosen by the subprefect in the provincial capital, but in practice he is often elected by his community members. He is merely the "foremost among equals," and actual decisions are made by the *reunión* (assembly), where consensus is still a goal. An Aymara, Víctor Hugo Cárdenas, served as vice president of Bolivia from 1993 to 1997.

SOCIAL CONTROL. The flexible and ideally egalitarian Aymara system has resulted in relatively few rules and taboos and consequently a low degree of social control. In case of personal conflict, the common forms of social control are used—gossip and ostracism (e.g., in the form of exclusion from dancing, drinking, and eating with the well-demarcated fiesta group).

CONFLICT. Individual and family disputes, often over land or inheritance, were settled by the jilaqata, who also arbitrated in inter-ayllu conflicts. In today's organization, conflicts are solved at assembly meetings, or if intractable, referred to central authorities. Physical arguments or regular fights usually occur only under the influence of alcohol. On the ayllu or village level the Aymara have a strong sense of collective identity and "community orientation" at times resulting in prejudice, mistrust, and suspicion toward "outsiders." Competition, mistrust, and conflict between other bonded units, such as family groups and village or community sections, is also not uncommon.

Religion and Expressive Culture

RELIGIOUS BELIEFS. The majority of the Aymara today are nominally Roman Catholic. In practice their religion is a syncretistic blend of Catholicism and indigenous religion, based on a parallelism, in which supernatural phenomena were classified similarly to natural ones. Such phenomena, as well as religious leaders, were ranked in vaguely hierarchical and relatively unstructured and flexible orders. Some indigenous rites are still practiced, mostly in addition to established Catholic ceremonies. Spirits, in the indigenous Aymara cognition, inhabit not heaven but surrounding high mountains, rivers, lakes, and so on, or rather, those sacred places are personified spirits.

RELIGIOUS PRACTITIONERS. Intermediaries between the natural and supernatural spheres are several kinds of magicians such as *yatiri* (diviner) and *laiqa* and *paqu* (practitioners of black or white magic). The aim of their activities is to bring about a balance between human and natural phenomena. Magic is used (e.g., in courtship, at childbirth, to cure illness, at planting and harvest rituals, and in weather-controlling rites).

CEREMONIES. Reciprocity, the basic and most salient feature of all Aymara social relations, is culturally institutionalized in several systems (e.g., those of ayni, compadrazgo, and fiesta). Ayni, compadrazgo, and the two types of fiestas (religious and life-cycle) are all surrounded by specific rules and ceremonies. Although there has been much debate over the origin, development, and meaning of these systems, it is evident that in the form they exist today, they serve to extend and maintain an individual's personal network and fulfill his or her occasional need to express group cohesion and feelings of cultural identity.

ARTS. Performing arts in the form of band music and dancing are important parts of every ceremony and fiesta. Most common are brass instruments, completed with drums, Andean flutes (*kena* and *sampoña*), and a minimandolin (*charango*) made of armadillo hide.

MEDICINE. Illness is considered to be caused by both natural and supernatural phenomena and may be cured accordingly—with the help of medicine and/or a curer. Most medicines derive from plants; roots, leaves, or flowers are administered as infusions or herbal teas. Animal parts and minerals are also used. Indigenous methods are applied along with Western medicines prescribed by clinical doctors or obtained at the drugstore.

DEATH AND AFTERLIFE. Formalized passage rites are staged for a deceased, in which food and drink are important elements. This series of rituals (extending over a period of three to ten years) includes mourning wake, funeral, *cabo de año* (end of the mourning year), and yearly celebrations at Todos Santos (1–2 November). The souls of the departed are then believed to return to earth, where they must be treated properly (i.e., fed) so they will refrain from vengeance. For the interment, the common practice is to send a number of items along with the deceased, mostly clothing and food, for use during the difficult journey into the highlands, where the spirits dwell.

Bibliography

Albó, Xavier (1976). *Esposos, suegros y padrinos entre los aymares.* 2nd ed. La Paz: Centro de Investigación y Promoción del Campesinado.

Bolton, Ralph, and Enrique Mayer, eds. (1977). *Andean Kinship and Marriage.* American Anthropological Association, Special Publication 7. Washington, D.C.

Buechler, Hans C., and Judith-Marie Buechler (1971). *The Bolivian Aymara.* New York: Holt, Rinehart & Winston.

Carter, William E., and Mauricio Mamani (1982). *"Irpa Chico": Individuo y comunidad en la cultura aymara.* La Paz: Libreria-Editorial "Juventud."

Collins, Jane L. (1981). "Kinship and Seasonal Migration among the Aymara of Southern Peru: Human Adaptation to Energy Scarcity." Ph.D. dissertation, University of Florida.

Hardman, M. J., ed. (1981). *The Aymara Language in Its Social and Cultural Context.* Gainesville: University of Florida Press.

La Barre, Weston (1948). "The Aymara Indians of the Lake Titicaca Plateau, Bolivia." *American Anthropological Association Memoirs* 68:250. Washington, D.C.

Lambert, Bernd (1977). "Bilaterality in the Andes." In *Andean Kinship and Marriage,* edited by Ralph

♦ **ayni**
A Quechua word designating the practice of loaning goods or performing services with the expectation of receiving back in kind.

♦ **compadrazgo**
Ritual coparenthood. It involves two married couples. One couple becomes godparents of something— typically but not necessarily a child—belonging to the other couple. Compadrazgo establishes a special bond between the two couples through a ritual of godparenting and engenders a special form of trust and respect between the two couples, each of which refers to the other as "compadres." Compadrazgo goes well beyond the godparenting of children to include godparenting of religious images, objects, and life-cycle events such as graduation, death, and marriage.

♦ **Todos Santos**
A festival beginning on the evening of 31 October and lasting for several days. It coincides with the Catholic All Saints' Day but has other origins in the Aztec Days of the Dead at the end of the secular Mesoamerican year. It is celebrated by all classes in all parts of Mexico and is one of the most universal Mesoamerican festivals. People believe that the souls of departed family members visit the earth for a day. The souls are welcomed by an altar filled with food offerings. It is an important time for strengthening family bonds.

Bolton and Enrique Mayer, 1–27. American Anthropological Association, Special Publication 7. Washington, D.C.

Lounsbury, Floyd (1964). "A Formal Account of the Crow- and Omaha-Type Kinship Terminologies." In *Explorations in Cultural Anthropology*, edited by Ward Goodenough, 351–393. New York: McGraw-Hill.

Murra, John (1968). "An Aymara Kingdom in 1567." *Ethnohistory* 15:115–151.

Tschopic, Harry, Jr. (1946). "The Aymara." In *Handbook of South American Indians*, edited by Julian H. Steward. Vol. 2, *The Andean Civilizations*, 501–573. Bureau of American Ethnology Bulletin 143. Washington, D.C.: Smithsonian Institution.

Zuidema, R. Tom (1977). "The Inca Kinship System: A New Theoretical Outlook." In *Andean Kinship and Marriage*, edited by Ralph Bolton and Enrique Mayer, 240–281. American Anthropological Association, Special Publication 7. Washington, D.C.

—MICK JOHNSSON

CANELOS QUICHUA

Ethnonyms: Alama (pejorative), Canelo, Canelos, Pastaza Quichua, Pastaza Runa, Quijos (incorrect and misleading), Runapura, Yumbo (incorrect, misleading, and pejorative)

Orientation

IDENTIFICATION. The name "Canelos Quichua" is of foreign origin. It designates the mission site of Canelos that ranged historically from near Puyo to its present Río Bobonaza location. "Runa" means "human being" in Quichua, and "Runapura" means "people among ourselves," "us." "Ala" is a form of address among people acknowledged as "us," but use of "Alama" as a reference to Canelos Quichua people is pejorative.

LOCATION. The Canelos Quichua occupy the territory south and east of Puyo, capital of Pastaza Province, and the Río Bobonaza region north of the Curaray and Villano river regions in Ecuador. The territory south of the Bobonaza, from the Río Yatapi east, is Achuar Jivaroan territory, and the territory north of the Curaray from its conjunction with the Río Villano is Waorani territory. The climate is equatorial rain forest that ranges from 300 to 1,000 meters in elevation.

DEMOGRAPHY. Ten thousand is a reasonable estimate of the contemporary, expanding Canelos Quichua population. Historically, severe population decline was experienced on many occasions because of infectious diseases.

LINGUISTIC AFFILIATION. Quechua was the language of the imperial Inca. All Quechua dialects, including those known as Quichua (Kichwa, Kichua) are frequently, although erroneously, associated exclusively with the high Andean regions of Ecuador, Peru, and Bolivia. Quichua was a language of conquest in Andean Ecuador in the fifteenth century, but its entry into what has become Canelos Quichua territory and its eventual domination over Jivaroan and Zaparoan languages in parts of Ecuador's Amazonian regions remain an intriguing problem. It may have been introduced from the southeast (Amazonian) region. Related dialects are found on the upper and lower Río Napo. Today it is estimated that at least 20 percent of the Canelos Quichua speak Achuar Jivaroan as a second language, and speaking Spanish as a second or as a third language is common. In a few areas some Zaparoan-Quichua bilingualism also exists.

History and Cultural Relations

Myth, legend, archaeology, and history indicate that the Canelos Quichua migrated into their current area from the east and/or southeast. The ceramics found at Charapa Cocha, on the Río Pastaza, are identified by the Canelos Quichua as made by their ancestors and appear to be a transition from other red-banded Tupí ware to historical and contemporary Canelos Quichua pottery. While the Quichua language was penetrating the upper Napo region from the Andes through conquest, Canelos Quichua was spreading northwestward, replacing Jivaroan and Zaparoan languages. Sporadic contact with Europeans at sites along major rivers was characterized by patterns of indigenous concentration followed by indigenous dispersion. The vast areas away from the major rivers remained virtually out of the Eurosphere of sporadic influence, although exploration by friars began as early as 1581. Since the early nineteenth century the Canelos Quichua have experienced waves of foreign intrusion and exploitation, the most recent being the Amazon rubber boom (1870–1910), exploration for petroleum (1920–1940), World War II, and the rediscovery of petroleum in the early 1970s.

Settlements

Historically, the Canelos Quichua lived in dispersed residential patterns and aggregated in refuge areas during times of upheaval. Such refuge zones probably attracted the first Catholic friars, who established missions there and visited them sporadically. The emergence of a formative culture occurred 200 to 300 years ago and radiated out of such riverine sites as Puyo, on the Puyo-Pindo rivers, and Canelos, Pacayacu, Sarayacu, Teresa Mama, and Montalvo, on the Río Bobonaza, spreading north from the Bobonaza to the Curaray and Villano rivers. Today the largest population concentration, with perhaps 3,000 people divided into twenty-two hamlets, is on the Comuna San Jacinto del Pindo, south of Puyo. The settlements of Canelos, Pacayaca, Sarayacu, and Curaray have the next largest populations. Kindred segments from these settlements periodically trek to distant garden, fishing, and hunting sites, where they reside for part of the year. All settlements, whether dispersed or nucleated, are divided into sections of about 25 people to (usually) no more than 150. All modern hamlets have a central plaza with a school; some have a Catholic or Protestant chapel. All of the sites mentioned above (except the Comuna San Jacinto), and many others, have an airstrip built by either Catholic or Protestant missionaries.

Economy

SUBSISTENCE AND COMMERCIAL ACTIVITIES. The Canelos Quichua practice upper Amazonian swidden horticulture, focused especially on manioc and other root crops. Women are in charge of all root-crop production, and men are the cultivators of maize and tobacco. Both sexes fish; men hunt game and birds; men, women, and children collect fruits, wild seeds, snails, shrimps, crabs, tortoises, and turtles. Men plant palms, which provide material for house construction and net and net-bag weaving and natural herbariums for palm weevils and their larvae. Men also plant *huayusa* trees, the combination of palm and huayusa trees serving as markers for territories established by powerful shamans. Contact with Europeans resulted in acquisition of plantains and bananas, which became male crops. Chickens and foreign ducks were acquired and used in the internal economy. Sporadic demand for the *naranjilla* (*Solanum quitoense*) fruit led to its specialized cultivation by men (but with the help of women) in swidden gardens cleared specifically for it. Near Puyo indigenous people have moved heavily into cattle raising and timber cutting. Many also cut rough planks and boards with chain saws and sell them by the roadside. Other income derives from sporadic seasonal labor on plantations or for petroleum-exploration companies and from traditional and ethnic arts. Protestant missionaries put special emphasis on cattle raising in areas far beyond the reach of the expanding road system, but so far have had little success with the Canelos Quichua.

TRADE. Extensive trade networks have long characterized this area of greater Amazonia. There is archaeological documentation of trade networks linking the Andes, upper Amazonia, and coastal Ecuador some 4,500 years ago and coterminous pottery traditions 3,500 years ago with expanded trade networks. The archaeology of Ecuador reveals that agricultural development and ceramic manufacture occurred 1,000 years earlier than in Peru or Mexico. The Canelos Quichua long traded with indigenous neighbors, especially with Zaparoan and Jivaroan (Shuar, Achuar, Huambisa) peoples, with whom they also exchanged raids, as part of a far-flung, regional head-taking system. Trade with the Europeans began in the sixteenth century, and the Canelos came to corner the market for broom fibers and cinnamon bark, which they traded west to Puyo. Prior to large-scale disruption during the Amazon rubber boom, and later because of the Ecuadoran-Peruvian war of 1941, some Canelos Quichua traveled eastward and southward to the region of the Río Marañón to obtain salt and then returned to their territory to trade it up and down

The Canelos Quichua long traded with indigenous neighbors, with whom they also exchanged raids, as part of a far-flung, regional head-taking system.

PANNING FOR GOLD

A Canelos Quichua man panning for gold. Men hunt, tend crops, and explore labor possibilities outside of the village. Ecuador.
(Nik Wheeler/Corbis)

the rivers. Such expenditions to obtain salt would take from one to several years.

DIVISION OF LABOR. Division of labor by gender is pervasive. Women do most of the gardening, except for the cultivation of tobacco, bananas, and maize. Men hunt, clear the swidden of large trees and vines, tend their three principal crops, and explore labor and other financial possibilities in the economic sectors. Women prepare and cook food, mend clothes, and care for children. They also brew manioc mash, store it, and serve *chicha* (home brew) on a continuous basis. Pottery manufacture is part of this manioc complex, a strictly female domain. Women plant, harvest, and store special black beans to plant with the maize, but such beans are not eaten; they are utilized solely for nitrogen fixation. Hunting for forest game is strictly a male pursuit, as is acquisition of large fish with spears, hooks, or dynamite. Women and men join together in fish-poisoning and -netting expeditions when the rivers are low. Long-distance trade is undertaken by men and by husbands and wives traveling in pairs. Cosmologically speaking, men are predators, women are domesticators. Shamanism, for males, is the paradigmatic complement to female pottery manufacture, and women "help" their shaman fathers and husbands in very specific ways by preparing their tobacco and "clarifying" their visions.

LAND TENURE. Aboriginally, large territories were established by powerful shamans who were able to keep both their sons and daughters-in-law, and their own daughters and sons-in-law. From a great oval house in a strategic position, a powerful kindred would grow within three generations to lay claim to considerable territory. As more and more intermarriage occurred, with Achuar to the south and Napo Quichua to the north, such territories became subdivided, with a mission hamlet or condensed region as a permanent, geographical focus. By the 1940s the region that was to become the 17,000-hectare territory of the Comuna San Jacinto del Pindo began to sprout a few hamlets on its periphery; they grew to twenty-two in the late 1980s. In the early 1990s the struggle for land is incessant, as people confront contradictory laws and shifting agencies responsible for various kinds of nationally recognized social organizations including parishes, communes, colony-support systems, and cooperatives. The rhetoric of a given organizational mode is often contradicted by indigenous activity in a specific territory. Basically, though, in the indigenous system the residential kin unit (*ayllu*) derives

from a shamanic ancestor who laid claim to a territory (*llacta*).

Kinship

KIN GROUPS AND DESCENT. The ayllu is the bilateral kinship system as reckoned with a patrilateral bias for a maximum of three to four generations by male and female individuals and small intermarried groups. This system may be modified cognitively through the use of adjectives such as *quiquin* (one's own) or *caru* (distant) or a suffix such as *pura* (among us, ourselves). Ayllu means "kindred," "extended clan," and "maximal (dispersed) clan." The kinship system is intimately and inextricably tied to male shamanic nodes that merge and separate through time at levels of kindred, territorial clan, and maximal clan. Each powerful shaman is closely connected by consanguinity and/or affinity to a master potter. Affinal relationships of the grandparental generations, both demonstrated and stipulated, are very important in reckoning contemporary kinship structure and transmission patterns. A parallel system of kin-class transmission and cultural transmission takes place: men through men by the vehicle of shamanism, women through women by the vehicle of pottery manufacture.

KINSHIP TERMINOLOGY. The primary term for mother's brother is extended to father's sister's husband; mother's brother and father's sister's husband are always in the same kin class. Affinity is important in reckoning consanguinity ties. Affinal and consanguineal kin terms indicate an ideology of parental or grandparental cousin marriage and a kin equation suggesting sibling exchange. These structural features, combined with the bifurcate-merging nature of avuncular terminology, raise the unsolved issue of prior terminological separation of parallel and cross cousins.

Marriage and Family

MARRIAGE. Marriage is about a three-year process; monogamy is the norm. From the male perspective it is *warmiyuj* (to possess a woman); from the female perspective it is *cariyuj* (to possess a man). Marriage may result from romantic love and elopement, but preferably it occurs through highly structured exchanges of sons and daughters arranged by parents and even grandparents. In Canelos and Pacayacu, and formerly in Puyo, a visiting friar or priest would marry couples in traditional ceremonies controlled by the clergy. Many couples throughout the area marry in traditional ceremonies without clergy. Some couples register their marriage at a civil registry, and some couples

♦ **ayllu**
A social unit of the Inca period that may have begun as a unilineal, probably patrilineal, kinship unit but later evolved, owing to conquest and population displacements, into a primarily territorial unit of several unrelated kinship groups.

marry in the church in Puyo. Divorce prior to "legal" marriage involves undoing all of the structured consanguineal and affinal ties constructed during the new incorporation of the couple into the minimal kindred and territorial clan and involves great acrimony on the part of many relatives and neighbors. Formal divorce by use of lawyers is rare and expensive and engenders great and lasting hostility between rival kin groups. There is a strong kinship idiom in marriage ideology. Men and women try to marry so as to perpetuate their own male and female inherited and acquired soul and body substances coming to them, in a parallel manner, from the times of the grandparents.

DOMESTIC UNIT. The Canelos Quichua traditional house is distinct from the house forms and symbolisms of Shuar and Achuar Jivaroans and of Zaparoans. Until the early 1980s traditional large oval houses with three-generation patrilocal extended families, many of which included Achuar sons-in-law (the Achuar are uxorilocal except for the families of the "great men" or shamans), were characteristic. As of the mid-1980s colonist-style rectangular houses are rapidly replacing the large traditional opensided dwellings that were oriented on cardinal axes with virtually every portion a representation of cosmic order, but the latter still exist.

INHERITANCE. The spouse of the deceased inherits all of his or her property, including land. Transmission of property, except land, from a parent to siblings is idiosyncratic. Land is distributed by the rule that the youngest son of a deceased parent inherits land not already distributed, and the oldest daughter of a deceased parent inherits land not already distributed.

SOCIALIZATION. Socialization practices are geared to the basic male/female division of labor, to the stress on acquisition of knowledge through many sources, and to learning to live successfully within their special environment. Permissiveness in breast feeding, elimination, and exposure to adult experiences is tempered by immediate, unequivocal reprimands, usually verbal, and sometimes reinforced physically, for transgressions such as an older sibling hitting a younger one. Children are loved and valued, and affection is lavished on babies and toddlers by men as well as women. The ability to sustain hard work intelligently in a very harsh environment is taught in myriad ways.

Sociopolitical Organization

SOCIAL ORGANIZATION. Traditionally, it is reported, men dominated women; today strong male-female egalitarianism is characteristic. The *yachaj*, "one who knows" or shaman, was and is the apex of any three-generational kinship-territorial system. Traditionally, such shamans were themselves the connecting links between the indigenous, dispersed, egalitarian social order and the hierarchical order that placed indigenous people on the bottom, which was characteristic of church and state. Today it is sons-in-law or sons of powerful shamans who have become the cultural brokers, but the modern structure of relationships is a transformation of the traditional. Every minimal territory is organized as a habitat distribution based on kinship and marriage patterns leading to cooperation in swidden-garden allocation (including ample room for forest fallow). The same people of the dispersed habitat and its traditional upper Amazonian organization are incorporated into hamlets that are based in part on the maintenance of hierarchical relationships with dominating governmental, educational, political, and religious personnel.

The structure of social relations is at the same time egalitarian and hierarchical. It is part of a regional organization that may be understood by reference to a five-generational model of cultural-ethnic-linguistic identity extending through the dispersed rain-forest settlements to urban Puyo, and includes marriage interchanges among Canelos Quichua, Napo Quichua, Achuar, and Zaparoan peoples through time and across space. In its nucleated dimensions the hamlet replicates features of the national political economy, including a structure of internal ethnicity reflecting divisions of Black, Indian, White, and many variants.

POLITICAL ORGANIZATION. *Comunas* operate with an elected *cabildo* (governing board) or *directiva*, consisting of five officers. The Catholic clergy sporadically dominated many political organizations through the colonial *varayuj* system, wherein staffs of authority are passed out to four or five indigenous political officers who then serve as liaison to the church and, through the church, to the Ecuadoran nation-state. In some areas, U.S. Protestant evangelists have taken over the role of domination, trying to work with indigenous "leaders" contacted through bilingual school systems that they (the evangelists) introduced. In 1976–1978 polarized indigenous organizations began to form: on one side were anti-Protestant, anti-government secular movements; on the other side were proevangelical and progovernment ones. By the late 1980s a set of confederations had emerged that extended downward from the

*Outright killing of
powerful Canelos
Quichua shamans
by small groups,
and threats of
killing, may have
curtailed shamanic
activity or kept it
partially in check.*

national indigenous organization in Quito to the Confederation of Amazonian Organizations housed near Puyo on the edge of Comuna San Jacinto territory, to the Organization of Indigenous Peoples of Pastaza Province (OPIP).

In the early 1980s OPIP was charged by the governor of Pastaza Province with responsibility to speak politically for all the peoples of that province. Since then OPIP has allied closely with Socialist and pro-Socialist parties and with the Catholic church in violent antagonism to other religious organizations and against the national bureaucracy and dominant political party of the president of the republic. Tensions manifest in the national political economy were replicated within OPIP, and many rival organizations of various political and religious persuasions now exist.

SOCIAL CONTROL. Gossip, face-to-face public encounters, and social withdrawal (as with the periodic treks to distant swiddens) are ordinary mechanisms of traditional social control. A more powerful mechanism is shamanism and the accusation of shamanic activity. Outright killing of powerful shamans by small groups, and the threat of such killing, may have curtailed shamanic activity or kept it partially in check. Religious figures are often asked to resolve "manageable disputes." By the 1980s not only were police asked to exercise social control between members of rival political-economic organizations, but even the military has been called in on some occasions. Lawsuits filed by indigenous people involve accusations of murder and cattle theft, boundary disputes with encroaching colonists, and witchcraft.

CONFLICT. Shamanism, accusation of shamanic activity, killing, and the accusation of killing, or hiring a killer constitute traditional sources of fission. No two families or kindreds can be on both sides of a shamanic or killing vendetta. Added to the traditional domains of conflict are new causes of struggle: control of land, control over sectors of the political economy and indigenous activity, religious control, and struggles engendered by rival indigenous organizations in alliance with extraneous forces.

In 1990 some Canelos Quichua participated in a nationwide indigenous uprising (*levantamiento indígena*). In April–May of 1992 representatives of Canelos Quichua culture led a march from Puyo to Quito and staged a camp-out in a major park of the capital to demand legalization of their territory, as well as that of the Achuar and Shiwiar. The march and camp-out had clear mil-

lenarian dimensions and resulted in large-scale land transfers from the nation-state to indigenous organizations of Pastaza Province.

Religion and Expressive Culture

RELIGIOUS BELIEFS. Transformation (*tucuna*) is crucial in understanding relationships among animate essences of inanimate substances and spiritual essences in interaction with soul substances. *Unai* (mythic time-space) provides a rich cosmographic source of contemporary and ancient knowledge; *callarirucuguna* (beginning times-places) embraces the period of transformation from unai to times of destruction and times of the ancestors. The future is thought of both as a continuation of the past and present and as a pending transformation of the initial chaos of unai. One origin myth of the Canelos Quichua is that of an incestuous brother-sister relationship between the moon (male) and the Potoo bird (female); part of this myth involves the origin of pottery clay.

The origin of the kinship system is told in mythic segments that deal with the transformation of the Anaconda from the human penis. Soul (*aya*) and spirit (*supai*) are fundamental concepts that apply to both eschatological knowledge and quotidian life. Humans and spirits interact when one or the other moves to a new plane of existence. Spirits have souls, just as humans do. Three spirit masters serve as focal symbols by which patterned transformations in the spirit would occur. Amasanga is forest-spirit master; his/her transformation is the dangerous master spirit of other people who live in other territories. Sungui is the spirit master of the hydrosphere and first shaman. Nungwi, a strictly feminine spirit, is master of garden soil and pottery clay. Canelos Quichua must balance experiential knowledge (*ricsina*) with cultural knowledge (*yachana*) and visionary experience (*muscuna*) with learning (*yuyana*). Central to the transformative paradigm involving these critical concepts is the yachaj, the "one who knows," the "possessor of knowledge." This concept often means "shaman" when applied to males, but may also be used to refer to master potters.

RELIGIOUS PRACTITIONERS. Shamans (male) and master potters (female) constitute the twin nodes of ongoing interpretation through which the system of parallel transmission of cultural knowledge takes place.

CEREMONIES. The ayllu festival is held once or twice a year in all hamlets where a Catholic chapel or shrine exists. In it is enacted the cosmogony of the Canelos Quichua, their embeddedness in Catholic and national hegemony, and the invocation of the ultimate source of power, the hydrosphere, as embodied by the Anaconda (*amarun*), which may break all bonds of hegemony but contains within itself the genesis of destruction and reemergence of chaos.

ARTS. All Canelos Quichua women are potters who manufacture a very fine ware that seems, according to archaeological evidence, to derive from ancient red-banded ware associated with westward-moving Tupí migrations. The potters make black ware for cooking and serving cooked foods, and polychrome ware for storing and serving manioc brew (*asua*). The sporadic art markets for fine and crude ceramics provide income to many families, and there is considerable innovation, within traditional boundaries, regarding the size and shapes of vessels made for sale. Men make blowgun quivers, darts, net bags, fish nets, traps, canoes and paddles, carving boards, feather headdresses, and wooden bowls and pestles for pounding manioc mash. Many men and women traditionally wove small bands for blowgun quivers. Blowguns are usually acquired from the Achuar, as is curare dart poison which, in turn, the Achuar acquire from the Cocama.

In 1975 Canelos Quichua men in the Puyo area began experimenting with carved animals and birds for the ethnic-arts market, and carving balsa birds has become a major occupation of many families, allowing them a degree of financial independence.

MEDICINE. Shamans use *Banisteriopsis caapi*, called ayahuasca (soul vine), in curing and diagnosing illness. Individuals occasionally use *Brugmansia suaveolens* (*wanduj*) in lone quests within the spirit world. Many other medicines from the rain forest are known and utilized.

DEATH AND AFTERLIFE. Death is associated with the malign action of evil individuals in interaction with evil spirits. The soul leaves the dying person through the mouth as death approaches and remains in the vicinity of the corpse for the one to three days and nights of a wake. To interact with the soul, those not in the immediate ayllu of the deceased play games, some with maize or black beans, but the major one being with a carved die called "canoe." The body is interred along a west-east cardinal line and begins an underground and underwater trip with its soul, over the course of which many transformations of the soul's inanimate existence take place. Souls visit the living, may be captured by a spirit, and may exist in various domains.

Bibliography

Reeve, Mary-Elizabeth (1985). *Identity as Process: The Meaning of Runapura for Quichua Speakers of the Curaray River, Eastern Ecuador*. Ann Arbor, Mich.: University Microfilms.

Whitten, Dorothea S., and Norman E. Whitten, Jr. (1988). *From Myth to Creation: Art from Amazonian Ecuador*. Urbana: University of Illinois Press.

Whitten, Norman E., Jr. (1985). *Sicuanga Runa: The Other Side of Development in Amazonian Ecuador*. Urbana: University of Illinois Press.

Whitten, Norman E., Jr., with the assistance of Marcelo Naranjo, Marcelo Santi Simbaña, and Dorothea S. Whitten (1976). *Sacha Runa: Ethnicity and Adaptation of Ecuadorian Jungle Quichua*. Urbana: University of Illinois Press.

—NORMAN E. WHITTEN, JR.

CHIRIGUANO

Ethnonyms: Ava, Izoceño, Simba, Tapui, Tembeta

Orientation

IDENTIFICATION. The name "Chiriguano" is of foreign origin, most commonly believed to be of Quechuan derivation. A more probable explanation, however, is that this term refers to the mixed ethnic origin of the Chiriguano. Historically, the Chiriguano referred to themselves as "Ava" (men).

LOCATION. Before the Conquest the Chiriguano occupied a vast territory that ranged from the upper Río Pilcomayo to the upper Río Grande in Bolivia. Presently, the Chiriguano are settled in dozens of communities in the foothills of the Bolivian Andes, in the Izozo region of Bolivia, and in several communities near the city of Santa Cruz. Other groups have settled, since the beginning of the twentieth century and particularly during the Chaco War (1932–1935), in border towns of Paraguay and in the provinces of Salta and Jujuy in northwest Argentina.

DEMOGRAPHY. In the eighteenth century the total Chiriguano population was between 100,000 and 200,000. Today in Bolivia it is estimated at 22,000, in Argentina at about 21,000, and in Paraguay at approximately 3,000.

LINGUISTIC AFFILIATION. The Chiriguano language belongs to the Tupí-Guaraní Family. All four Chiriguano ethnic groups (Ava, Izoceño, Simba, and Chane) speak the same language with

♦ **blowgun**
A weapon constructed of a long length of wood with a bore down the center, through which curare-tipped and nonpoisonous wooden darts or other objects are projected by a puff of the shooter's breath.

♦ **curare**
A poisonous liquid extracted from the various vines of the Strychnos species and applied to arrows and blowgun darts.

*Chiriguano
relations with the
Spanish and the
Creoles were marked
by warfare and
uprisings, some of
these characterized
by their messianic
tradition.*

♦ **wattle-and-daub**
*A method of house
construction whereby a
framework (wattle) of poles
and twigs is covered
(daubed) with mud and
plaster.*

slight differences in pronunciation and vocabulary.

History and Cultural Relations

Present-day Chiriguano are the descendants of Guaraní people who migrated from Brazil, and of the Chane, an Arawak group. The Guaraní initiated a series of massive migrations that are known to have begun at the end of the fifteenth century. These migrations were driven by the desire to acquire metal objects and by messianic motives—the search for a mythical "land without evil"—and augmented because of internal conflict. Upon entering Bolivian territory, the Guaraní encountered the peaceful Chane. They reduced them to slavery, took their wives, and thus initiated a process of intermarriage. The result of the fusion of the Guaraní with the Chane is what we know as the Chiriguano. The Chiriguano were fierce warriors who conquered other ethnic groups and were not subjugated by the Inca Empire. Their relations with the Spanish and the Creoles were marked by warfare and uprisings, some of these characterized by their messianic tradition. The encounter with Whites, however, led to a drastic decimation of the population through warfare, slavery, and disease. Chiriguano were employed by White settlers on their large estates.

In 1892 the last great uprising took place, conducted by a Chiriguano known as Apiaguaiqui Tumpa, who was believed to possess supernatural power. He decided to fight against the settlers and reinstall the traditional Chiriguano life-style, but the local government sent in troops from Santa Cruz de la Sierra, Apiaguaiqui was killed, and the uprising was suppressed. The Chiriguano have been subjected to concerted efforts at conversion. Since colonial times the Jesuits and then the Franciscans have established missions throughout Chiriguano territory. At first the Chiriguano burned the missions, but eventually the Franciscans were successful in establishing a vast network of mission stations that lumped groups together and instituted schools and agricultural production. In the nineteenth century (as a result of the political and economic situation of Bolivia), the missions underwent a period of economic and organizational crisis and finally collapsed. Present-day Chiriguano are divided into two major groups: the Ava Guaraní, who inhabit the foothills of the Andes, and the Izoceño, who inhabit the Izozo region and are considered to have a greater Chane influence in their culture. The two minor groups include the traditional Simba, who inhabit a village in the Andean foothills, and the Chane of

Argentina, who are completely Guaranítized. Chiriguano communities have few mestizo inhabitants; although permitted, intermarriage with Whites and mestizos is infrequent.

Settlements

In aboriginal and early contact times Chiriguano settlements were villages along rivers. Each settlement was formed by one or several *malocas* (communal long houses), which could be inhabited by up to 300 people. Population density was high; villages ranged from 50 to up to 1,000 inhabitants. Towns had a large central plaza used for religious festivities and assemblies. The influence of Chane culture and contact with the missionaries and Whites changed the housing structure to small-household, extended-family units, which persist today. The traditional Chiriguano house was of wattle-and-daub construction, with a pitched roof of thatch reeds or poles. A storehouse for maize and other crops was built on piles near the dwelling. Currently, the same type of construction exists side by side with houses made of adobe brick and zinc roofs. Each village features a small primary school, a dispensary, and a grocery cooperative or several small grocery stores. In most Chiriguano villages there is neither running water nor electricity.

Economy

SUBSISTENCE AND COMMERCIAL ACTIVITIES. The Chiriguano were traditionally horticulturists and hunter-gatherers. They incorporated new methods of cultivation from the Chane. The Ava Chiriguano are settled in a rich agricultural area, although water is scarce. The Izoceño inhabit an arid region of the Gran Chaco, where strong winds, erosion, and a lack of water hinder agricultural production. The former inhabitants of the region, the Chane, developed a system of irrigation, digging canals up to 5 kilometers long from the river to the fields, thus providing a source of water to improve productivity. Nowadays the Chiriguano practice swidden agriculture and complement their diet with fishing during the rainy season and hunting. Fruit collecting, which was an important source of food, has diminished in certain communities as a result of cultural and ecological changes. The most important crops are maize, beans, and squash, which constitute the basis of the Chiriguano diet. Other plants, such as sweet potatoes and manioc, complement the diet. Vegetables such as tomatoes, cabbage, lettuce, and onions have been introduced through contact with the missionaries, White settlers, and development agencies. The Chiriguano also raise chickens, turkeys, sheep, and goats.

Since the beginning of the nineteenth century the Chiriguano have migrated in search of work, which they could not find in their homeland. Hundreds of Chiriguano families migrated to northern Argentina to work on the farms and sugarcane plantations. This migration, which constitutes an important aspect of their society, has produced numerous changes in the culture. Because of the economic crisis in Argentina, the Chiriguano do not migrate there anymore, but to the cotton and sugarcane harvest near Santa Cruz de la Sierra and to northern Bolivia for work in the timber mills. These temporary migrations, which in some cases last up to six months, have produced a deterioration in local agricultural production. Nongovernmental development agencies have been implementing development projects to revitalize agriculture and allow people to obtain a source of income in their communities without having to migrate or depend upon *patrones* (employers).

INDUSTRIAL ARTS. Aboriginal crafts included basket weaving, pottery, and loom weaving. Today, weaving of fishing nets and bags persists and loom weaving of hammocks, ponchos, and handbags constitutes an important source of income for many women. Chiriguano weaving, especially that in the Izozo region, is well known for its quality and designs.

TRADE. Precolonial trade was maintained between the Chiriguano and other ethnic groups. During the fifteenth and sixteenth centuries the Chane served as intermediaries to the Guaraní, trading metal objects made in the highlands. Until the 1940s trade continued to take place between different groups. The Izoceño would trade their weavings to the Ava in exchange for corn. Cheese and salt were important tradegoods.

DIVISION OF LABOR. Women attend to household chores; in the fields they do the harvesting and planting of beans, squash, and watermelon. Men are responsible for hunting, fishing (women also participate in fishing but to a smaller degree), and clearing, burning, and planting of the fields. Women prepare food, raise the children, and weave. In some Ava communities women participate more actively in agricultural tasks. When a Chiriguano family migrates, the men and the male children work the fields. Women usually stay at home engaging in household activities.

LAND TENURE. After contact Chiriguano territory was reduced, and since then there has been constant conflict over the right to obtain land titles, which the Chiriguano have struggled for a long time to obtain. They have gone to the capital of Bolivia in epic walks, hoping to impel officials to initiate the paperwork. Land titles were obtained for some communities—the agrarian reform of 1952 helped to some degree, but it has been manipulated and incorrectly implemented. This, together with the difficult ecological conditions and reduced access to roads and transportation, has caused the Chiriguano to lose some of their good lands. Most Izoceño communities have obtained communal land titles, whereas the Ava and Simba communities are still struggling with government bureaucracies. In northern Argentina most communities are under the jurisdiction of the missions and are involved in obtaining land titles.

Kinship

KIN GROUPS AND DESCENT. Chiriguano society was based on the principle of an exogamous patrilineage living in a *maloca* (the smallest settlement unit). Each lineage held and allocated lands, maintained a system of alliances, regulated marriage, established reciprocity, and controlled conflict among lineage members. After colonial times uxorilocality replaced virilocality; patrilineality was maintained and villages continued to be constituted by extended-family groups.

KINSHIP TERMINOLOGY. Kinship terminology is of the Hawaiian type.

Marriage and Family

MARRIAGE. In the traditional marriage system members of the mother's and father's lineage were forbidden as marriage partners. Marriages were monogamous with the exception of two leaders who had the right to several wives. Up to the beginning of the twentieth century, in order for a man to be accepted by a woman, he had to leave a log of firewood in front of her house. If she accepted him she would take the log into the house; if not, she would not touch the firewood. A welcome suitor had to talk with the woman's parents and provide them with game and crops. Uxorilocal residence was preferred; the young couple would build their house near that of the bride's parents. Nowadays, there is no specified residence pattern, marriage is by mutual accord of the couple, and divorce is common.

DOMESTIC UNIT. Extended families in three-generation households are still common.

INHERITANCE. In the 1980s property was passed to all of the sons and daughters. A will was

Agricultural production has been inhibited by the Chiriguano tendency to migrate, temporarily, in search of work.

written with specific instructions as to the inheritance of property and possessions. Preference was given to the last-born child.

SOCIALIZATION. Children are raised permissively. Both parents participate actively in the raising of the children, as do the members of the extended-family group. Grandparents play an important role in the upbringing of children. Overt and direct expressions of hostility and aggression are discouraged. Children are rarely beaten. Modern children attain a better level of education than that of their parents and are learning to speak Spanish as a second language with a higher degree of fluency.

Religion and Expressive Culture

RELIGIOUS BELIEFS. Native beliefs in zootheistic deities were guided by a deep faith in supernatural forces. In spite of the persistent influence of Christian missionaries, the Chiriguano still hold on to the basic tenets of their beliefs; nevertheless, they do acknowledge a principal creator God. This belief in a Supreme Being is a result of early missionization; however, the traditional Chiriguano pantheon includes numerous spirit beings of various kinds. Spirits are believed to have created the world and to be the guardians of plants, animals, rivers, stars, and so on. Evangelical sects have a profound influence and have been able to replace some traditional beliefs, although the Chiriguano have maintained their large corpus of myths and tales.

RELIGIOUS PRACTITIONERS. Chiriguano shamans were known to be powerful; they acted as intermediaries between humans and the deities and had the power to cure, attract the rain, or stop pestilence. They exercised influence on the chiefs and on the general decision-making process of a

SOCIOPOLITICAL ORGANIZATION

Social Organization

Chiriguano society was organized on the basis of the maloca, followed by the *tenda* (village) and the *guara* (a group of villages). Each local group was a homogenous entity, with no internal division, but there was specialization by sex, age, and kinship position. Some groups were wealthier and more powerful than others. The maloca was under the authority of a head of household or family group. Chiriguano society conferred status on a group of men known as the *queremba*, who were specialized warriors. They enjoyed greater privileges and prestige, as did shamans and leaders. As a rule, they did not participate in political affairs. Although some women are known to have been leaders, women in general were preoccupied with household and economic activities. Institutionalized slavery began with the domination of the Chane.

Political Organization

Chiriguano society continues to maintain a strong political organization based on the traditional system. Single Chiriguano towns were under the leadership of a *mburuvicha* or *tubicha* (chief), whereas a group of several villages was governed by a *mburuvicha guasu* or *tubicha mburuvicha* (paramount chief). The specific characteristic of this system is that the chiefs do not hold the power of coercion; they cannot give orders, make decisions, or compel people to obey. Instead, all the men of the village or group of villages must take decisions together in an assembly. The principal role of the chief was as peace mediator, gift giver, and orator. The present political system of the Chiriguano is known as the *capitania* (*capitán* in Spanish means "captain"). The capitania is a well-structured organization, composed of chiefs, advisers, and mayors. Chiriguano chiefs must acquiesce to the demands of the people, and they are well known in Chiriguano history for their struggle to obtain land titles and other benefits for the communities. The position of the mburuvicha guasu is patrilineally inherited. The local chiefs are democratically elected by the community. If a chief does not fulfill his obligations, he may be discharged from his position.

Social Control

Gossip, ostracism, social withdrawal, and eschewing face-to-face conflict have always been important forms of social control. Witchcraft continues to be practiced in Chiriguano society, and fear of witchcraft remains a powerful form of social control. The political organization of the Chiriguano acts as a judicial system: it judges and applies sanctions in cases of breach of the law (e.g., robbery, gossip, invasion of lands). Federal courts intervene in cases such as homicides.

Conflict

The major source of conflict in Chiriguano society has been their relations with White settlers. Some Chiriguano joined the missions and others worked for the White settlers, but another group waged a permanent war. Conflicts over land as well as labor exploitation persist. The introduction of evangelical sects in the Chiriguano communities since the beginning of the nineteenth century is a source of division between evangelists and Catholics. The Catholics are traditionalists and want to maintain the traditional beliefs and religious festivities and support the shamans. Conflicts regarding traditional and political matters are frequent.

village. They had immense prestige and privileges. Today they continue to exert influence, although in villages where the majority is evangelical, their role is diminishing. Chiriguano evangelical pastors are an important factor in the evangelization of the Chiriguano. They are beginning to exert a political role.

CEREMONIES. The *arete*, or feast, was a ceremony related to the maize harvest, among other things. This feast was transformed into the Carnival but maintained many of its traditional elements. Men wear wooden masks and costumes depicting the ancestors and animals spirits returning to meet with their relatives. Easter has been transformed by the Chiriguano, through the incorporation of dancing and singing.

ARTS. Music and singing in the Guaraní language occurred during all the Chiriguano festivals; these genres persist, but with the influence of colonial music. Native instruments such as flutes and drums have been retained, but the violin and the guitar have been incorporated.

MEDICINE. Disease is understood as the result of natural forces (wind, heat, cold), supernatural forces (spirits of the forest or of the river), or witchcraft. Curing techniques consist of herbal medicines, sucking, massage, diagnosis by blowing tobacco, and long therapeutic séances to drive out the evil. Witchcraft is believed to be a basic cause of illness, death, or any other misfortune. The shaman is the only one who can counteract the evil power of the witch. Western medicine has been introduced, and both systems persist side by side.

DEATH AND AFTERLIFE. Death is believed to be the result of disease, spirits of nature, or witches. There is a belief in an afterworld, to which souls go. Until the beginning of the twentieth century, the deceased were buried in funerary urns under the house. After death, the soul was believed to go to a heavenlike place after a hazardous journey. Presentday Chiriguano have incorporated Christian beliefs regarding the afterlife.

Bibliography

Métraux, Alfred (1948). "Tribes of the Eastern Slopes of the Bolivian Andes." *Handbook of South American Indians*, edited by Julian H. Steward. Vol. 3, *The Tropical Forest Tribes*. Bureau of American Ethnology Bulletin 143. Washington, D.C.: Smithsonian Institution.

Riester, Jürgen, Brigitte Simon Bárbara, and Schuchard Bárbara (1979). *Los chiriguanos*. Asunción: Suplemento Antropológico, vol. 14, nos. 1–2.

Susnik, Branislava (1968). *Chiriguanos: Dimensiones etnosociales*. Paraguay: Museo Etnográfico Andrés Barbero.

—SILVIA MARIA HIRSCH

EUROPEANS IN SOUTH AMERICA

Ethnonyms: none

Peoples of European ancestry are unevenly distributed across South America. A majority of the population in some countries, a minority in others, they wield considerable economic and political power throughout South America. Among the countries with the largest number of Europeans, they comprise 97 percent of the population in Argentina; 90 percent in Uruguay; 50 percent in Brazil; 25 percent in Chile; 20 percent in Paraguay, Venezuela, and Colombia; 15 pecent in Ecuador; 14 percent in Bolivia; and 12 percent in Peru. It should be noted, however, that the definition of the term "European" and who is categorized as such are often not clear in the South American context, especially in countries that have large Indian and mestizo populations, such as Peru or Bolivia. European identity is less confused in countries with large populations of African ancestry, such as Brazil, or in countries with small Indian and mestizo populations, for example, Argentina or Uruguay. In general, a South American is considered European—in contrast to Indian, mestizo, or Afro–South American—if he or she can trace European ancestry through both descent lines or, depending on the social, economic, and political context, if he or she lives a "European" life-style, associates socially with other Europeans, and is defined as such by others.

The first European contact with South Americans occurred in 1498, with the arrival of Columbus's third expedition to the New World. Subsequent explorations, including those led by Cabral in 1500 to Brazil, Magellan in 1519 through what came to be called the Straits of Magellan, Pizarro in 1531 to Peru, Jiménez de Quesada in 1536 to northwestern South America, Valdivia in 1541 along the southwestern coast, Mendoza in 1535 to Argentina, and Garay in 1580 to Argentina and Uruguay, paved the way for the Spanish and Portuguese colonization of South America. The Spanish gained control of

See also

EUROPE: English, Irish, Germans, Portuguese, Welsh

Europeans in South America

A majority of the population in some countries and a minority in others, Europeans in South America wield considerable economic and political power.

the western one-third of the continent, the Portuguese of the northeast coastal region and what is now eastern Brazil. The interior and the southern portions of what came to be Chile and Argentina were largely ignored during the colonial era. Although Spanish and Portuguese colonial domination officially ended in the early to mid-nineteenth century, numerous European influences are still major factors in modern-day South American culture. These include language (Spanish is the national language in most nations and Portuguese is the national language in Brazil); Roman Catholicism; the political boundaries of South America's modern nations and provinces; the basic social structure; and the economic system, which still emphasizes the export of raw materials and the import of consumer goods.

Under Spanish and Portuguese doctrines, immigration and settlement by other Europeans was forbidden. Thus, settlement by other Europeans began only after South American nations gained national independence beginning in the early 1800s. The first and major period of other than exclusively Iberian immigration was between 1870 and 1930, during which some 11 to 12 million immigrants arrived in South America. Most came from Italy and Portugal and settled mainly in Argentina, Uruguay, and Brazil. Although many eventually returned to Europe, most Europeans in these nations today are descendants of these immigrants. In addition to the large number of Ital-

ians and Portuguese, there were also Germans who settled in Argentina, Chile, and Brazil; German Mennonites who settled in Paraguay; British who settled in Chile, Peru, Argentina, and Brazil; and Welsh and Irish who settled in Argentina. Gypsies also began arriving in this period, although little is known about their settlement history or current situation. In general, these European settlers tended to form their own localized communities and often specialized in specific economic activities—for example, the Welsh in ranching, the British in commerce, the Mennonites in farming. Over time, those who remained in their new land became involved in politics and the professions, and individuals identified as Europeans are today key figures in many South American nations. Most early immigrants settled in cities, a pattern that is now changing as their descendants move to rural areas, villages, or towns. Immigration to South America was on a much smaller scale than immigration to North America, mainly because the tropical climate was less appealing, free land was limited in many nations, and political instability created concerns about safety. In addition, return migration was encouraged by government policies that awarded immigrants nearly all rights of citizenship without requiring citizenship and by the opportunity to accumulate wealth for transfer to the immigrants' country of origin.

In the 1930s and 1940s immigration expanded to include larger numbers of central and eastern

EXPATRIOTS

Two German colonial farm workers stand on a farm in Missiones Province. Europeans comprise 97 percent of the population in Argentina. Missiones Province, Argentina. (Hubert Stadler/Corbis)

Europeans, a pattern that continued in the years following World War II. Many of these immigrants settled in Venezuela, Colombia, Argentina, and Brazil. In the early 1990s, in the most recent phase of European immigration, some South American governments (e.g., that of Venezuela) and businesses were actively recruiting workers from eastern Europe to fill a perceived need for engineers and technicians. It is as yet unknown whether they, like guest workers elsewhere in the world, will remain and build their own ethnic communities.

Bibliography

Collier, Simon, Thomas E. Skidmore, and Harold Blakemore, eds. (1992). *The Cambridge Encyclopedia of Latin America and the Caribbean.* 2nd ed. Cambridge: Cambridge University Press.

Levinson, David (1994). *Ethnic Relations.* Santa Barbara, Calif.: ABC-Clio.

—DAVID LEVINSON

GUAJIRO

Ethnonym: Wayuu

Orientation

IDENTIFICATION. The Guajiro are an Indian group living in Colombia and Venezuela. The name "Guajiro" is probably of Spanish origin.

LOCATION. The traditional Guajiro territory, with a land area of approximately 16,000 square kilometers, consists of a peninsula called "La Guajira" located in the Caribbean Sea between 11° and 12°30′ N and between 71° and 72°30′ W. The peninsula is divided by the Colombia-Venezuela border; although only one-fifth of its surface area is Venezuelan, roughly half of the Guajiro population lives on the Venezuelan side. This is a region of brush savanna and xerophytic vegetation, dotted with desert zones, that also includes several mountain ranges reaching upwards of 850 meters (Makuira, Kusina, Jala'ala, and Kamaichi). Rainfall is abundant from October to November (the period called *juyapu*) and sometimes also in April or May (the period of *iiwa*). The major dry season (called *jouktai-jamü*, "hunger-wind") lasts from May to September and sometimes even longer, preempting the rainy season and imperiling the lives of animals and people. In the north of the peninsula annual mean precipitation is approximately 20 centimeters; it can reach 60 centimeters in the south. The amounts are irregular, however, and the regional variations great.

LINGUISTIC AFFILIATION. Guajiro is part of the Arawak Language Family. The speech of Wüinpumuin (the northeastern region) is distinct from that of Wopumuin (the southeastern region), although the two are mutually intelligible.

DEMOGRAPHY. A full census has not been taken. It is generally accepted, however, that the Guajiro number more than 100,000 (without taking into account mestizos or those who do not speak the language and are outside the lineage system). In 1938, as in 1981, there were approximately 47,000 Guajiro in Colombia. There are an estimated 60,000 in Venezuela, about two-thirds of whom live on the margins of the territory, in the city of Maracaibo, or in other areas.

History and Cultural Relations

In the southern part of the peninsula, there existed a population from around 1500 B.C. to just before the Conquest that, like the Guajiro, had a custom of double funerals; however, there is nothing to indicate that they were the ancestors of the Guajiro, who, from the linguistic evidence, originated in Amazonia. The Spaniards reached the coasts of Guajiroland in 1499 and began their penetration into the peninsula in 1526. According to chroniclers, there were several indigenous groups coexisting in the area (e.g., Anate, Atanare, Canoa, Caquetio, Cocina, Guanabucare, Makuira), but it is possible that they attributed several names to a given society, each one referring to various economic and social aspects of that society. The only other group that exists in the vicinity of the Guajiro today is the lacustrine Paraujano, who speak a closely related language and who are on the road to extinction.

Settlements

In the traditional territory, the settlements are widely dispersed. The residential unit (*miichipala*, "place of houses") is an aggregate of dwellings, often separated by many tens of meters, that provides shelter for nuclear families sharing the same water source. There are generally between a few dozen and several hundred persons in a miichipala. The latter are all named, and sometimes divided into subunits, which are themselves named. The miichipala are, on average, several kilometers distant from one another, and large stretches of the interior of the Guajira Peninsula remain uninhabited. Traditional dwellings are comprised of a small house where hammocks are hung at night; a kitchen, which consists of a

Groups of Apüshi (matrilineal relatives) are the dominant functional units of Guajiro society.

surrounding wall of cactus or branches, sometimes covered by a roof; and a porch roof, made of a flat overhang on posts, under which daily activities and the entertainment of visitors take place. Located farther out are the sheep and goat pens and the garden, which is protected by a fence.

Economy

SUBSISTENCE AND COMMERCIAL ACTIVITIES. Formerly, Guajiro society was probably egalitarian, based on an economy of horticulture, gathering, hunting, and fishing, depending on the region. Today, it is a strongly hierarchical pastoral culture. The first livestock arrived from Europe around the beginning of the sixteenth century. Hungry, curious, and adventurous, some of the Guajiro obtained livestock by raid and theft until they had semiwild herds of cattle and horses. Pastoralism progressively became widespread, probably facilitated by missionaries, who made many attempts at pacification; by Dutch, French, or English pirates hostile to the Spanish and in quest of food; and finally by the Black slaves who, by choice or by force, settled among the Guajiro. At the end of the nineteenth century, pastoralism was nearly general except, it seems, in the region of the Sierra Kusina, where it has developed since. The keeping of cattle, sheep, and goats is still the principal source of livelihood for the majority of the Guajiro on the peninsula. Horticulture, hunting, and fishing have become marginal as opportunities for smuggling and occasional wage labor have developed, even assuring essential income for mestizo families or families that have emigrated to urban zones. Livestock are destined for consumption or the market, but they are also a prestige item that is good to accumulate. Formerly, horses and mules were, along with cattle, the most valued animals. The former have practically disappeared. The wealthiest Guajiro now buy trucks or pickups.

INDUSTRIAL ARTS. Women weave hammocks of cotton with very rich motifs and coloring and belts decorated with similar motifs. They also crochet small bags that they sell at local markets or in Maracaibo. Men principally make sandals and produce colorful wool rugs using the saddleblanket technique.

TRADE. For centuries the Guarjiro have sold Whites brazilwood (*Hematoxilon brasiletto*) to make dyes, divi-divi fruits (*Caesalpinia coriara*), and skins. In the northwest of the peninsula, they fished for lobster and pearls and produced salt, an activity that still continues. There are weekly markets in many localities along the margins of the peninsula.

DIVISION OF LABOR. Women tend to domestic chores, make the essential items of material culture, and work beside the men in pastoral activities and horticulture. Some occasionally hold political office. In the late 1980s eight of every ten shamans were women.

LAND TENURE. Land is not owned, but its usufructs are associated with pasturage rights for visiting groups.

Kinship

KIN GROUPS AND DESCENT. The Guajiro are organized into some thirty nonlocalized clans (matrisibs) called *eiruku*, a term that also means "flesh" or "meat." Each one is associated with a proper name (or "flesh name," *sünülia eiruki*) and a totemic animal, a "clan animal" (*uchii shiiruku*). These clans are actually agamic and noncorporate, however. Filiation is matrilineal. Persons recognized as relatives, designated by the general term *wayuu kasa tanain* ("the people who are something for me"), constitute two groups: *apüshi* and *oupayu*. The former are uterine relatives in the strict sense—an Egocentric group or matrilineage, depending on the author—who gather together in the same cemetery the bones of their dead and act as a corporate group. The term "oupayu" refers to the close uterine relatives (apüshi) of Ego's father. The complementarity of these two groups becomes apparent: at the time of bride-price negotiations (in general, the price is determined by the father of the bride if it is his first daughter or, for the other girls, by their uterine relatives), in situations of conflict (in general, compensation is claimed by the victim's father if the wound is superficial, and by the victim's maternal uncle if the injury is serious or mortal), and, finally, in funeral arrangements (it is often the father or other uterine relatives of the deceased who are responsible for organizing the first obsequies, since the second funeral is always the responsibility of the apüshi).

KINSHIP TERMINOLOGY. Guajiro kinship terminology is of the Crow type.

Marriage and Family

MARRIAGE. Marriage entails a bride-price (*apan'na*). The amount varies greatly according to the hierarchical position of the bride's lineage as well as her specific qualities (e.g., skillfulness in weaving and commerce, beauty). Matrimonial exchanges are generally limited to certain very limited circuits. Virginity is valued. It was long believed that the Guajiro adhered to a rule of matrilocal residence (a new couple living in the same miichipala as the bride's mother). No single rule, however, is strictly applied. A couple can change residence several times during a lifetime, the previous configuration corresponding to the most stable situation. For the majority of young couples, residence is initially uxori-matrilocal; then it can change several times, possibly to patrilocal (patri-uxorilocal or patri-virilocal) or neolocal. The coresidence of sisters and brothers is the next most common form. The choice of residence is the result of two processes: the mode of marriage and the logic of household formation. Polygyny is highly valued and characteristic of rich men.

DOMESTIC UNIT. An individual is affiliated with three distinct groups—two of kinship and one of residence. This explains the great mobility of Guajiro society. A common household consists of a cohabiting group of siblings.

INHERITANCE. Property is owned both by lineages and individuals. Men and women both possess their own animals. The animals of a dead man not sacrificed during his funeral are generally distributed to his brothers and uterine nephews, who often share their portions with their sisters. A woman's children inherit her livestock at her death. Maternal uncles usually offer animals to their nephews. A father can also give animals to his children, a tendency that has developed during the twentieth century. In fact, the transmission of property is a complex process, varying according to the status of the lineage involved.

SOCIALIZATION. Children are raised in a rather permissive fashion, but they participate in economic activities at a very young age—little girls in household tasks, boys in tending the livestock. Pubescent girls were formerly subjected to a period of seclusion, which today is sometimes more symbolic than real.

Sociopolitical Organization

SOCIAL ORGANIZATION. The dominant functional units of Guajiro society are the groups of apüshi, the matrilineal relatives in the strict sense.

POLITICAL ORGANIZATION. One or several groups of apüshi, in general not localized, can recognize a dominant male figure, an *alaüla*, a term that designates a maternal uncle, an "elder," and, by extension, a "chief." In fact, the alaüla of a matrilineage functions in all three capacities. He is the keeper of "Guajiro custom" (*sükuaitpa wayuu*). The group to which he gives coherence is an economic unit. All of its members contribute to the payment of compensation for a misdeed caused

on the outside by one of its members, to members' burial costs, and to the bride-price obligations of male members. In theory, the office of alaüla is inherited by one of the sons of the former's eldest sister, or failing that, by the most competent of his uterine relatives. In fact, situations of conflict among the constituent lineages can arise. The alaüla from the minimal lineage that considers itself the most wealthy can lay claim to the office, and fission can result.

SOCIAL CONTROL. An alaüla is responsible for maintaining daily order in the domestic unit in which he resides.

CONFLICT. Serious offenses (homicide, body wounds) committed against members of different lineages are no longer, as formerly, subject to retaliation. Theoretically, there is always a way to arrive at a peaceful settlement. Each person who has suffered a wrong (*aainjala*) is a victim (*asirü*). The dispute (*putchi*) is submitted to a go-between (*pütchipu*, *püchejachi*, or often an alaüla), chosen by lineages in conflict and considered neutral. The dispute is settled by the payment of compensation (*maüna*) consisting of livestock, jewels, and money. The sum is accumulated by the lineage of the wrongdoer (*womuyu*) and remitted to the victim's familial group. The amount paid depends on the recognized worth of the victim, that is to say on the status of the victim's lineage. On the other hand, Guajiro history shows that if the groups in conflict are unequal, the stronger can refuse all mediation in order to appropriate the weaker's assets and capture and enslave certain of its members.

Religion and Expressive Culture

RELIGIOUS BELIEFS. The Guajiro are little inclined to religious practices. They do not appeal to their divinities directly, and their rites are few. Although their conception of the world is extremely dualistic, the Manichaeism of the Christian religion has made little impact on them.

The Guajiro invoke Maleiwa, their culture hero born from the remains of his mother, who was devoured by Jaguar. After having rejected Jaguar in the wilderness of Nature, which he personifies, Maleiwa created humans and differentiated the world, in which originally everything was anthropomorphic and related. Maleiwa, who is sometimes confused with the God of the Whites, is of little importance today. Guajiro mythic concepts are based on an opposition between two fundamental supernatural beings: Juya (rain), the hypermasculine hunter, and Pulowi, the subterranean woman, mistress of animals, who is associated with drought and death and who manifests

If Guajiro groups in conflict are unequal, the stronger can refuse all mediation in order to appropriate the weaker's assets and enslave certain of its members.

herself in numerous places such as holes or little rises, which are called *pulowi* and are avoided by the Guajiro for fear of disappearing or falling gravely ill. The elements of the symbolic world are divided into two equivalent and complementary classes of which Juya and Pulowi, who are husband and wife, are the representations and relevations. Several other supernatural beings are also recognized: *wanulüü, akalpui, keeralia, juyain,* and others. The Guajiro also accord great importance to the ghosts of the dead, the *yoluja,* who haunt their dreams, dictate much of their behavior, and are the cause of many illnesses.

RELIGIOUS PRACTITIONERS. Shamans as well as diviners still continue to corroborate traditional representations and beliefs, for example by curing sickness or epizootic disease or foretelling the appropriate site of new houses.

CEREMONIES. Formerly, collective horticultural work was accompanied by a ceremony, which has today disappeared, called *kaa'ülayawaa* (goat dance), often accompanied, among the wealthy, by courses of horse meat (*awachira ama*). It was an occasion for competitions, games of skill and team games, and for rendezvous between young people. Today the *yonna* dance, which is danced by a couple to the beat of a drum, is the most common collective demonstration. It is organized to celebrate an economic success; the visit of an important person, Guajiro or foreign (*ali-juna*); the end of a period of seclusion; and similar events. The dance is also frequently prescribed by a shaman at the end of a cure. But funerals, both first and second, remain the most important Guajiro ceremonies.

ARTS. Songs (*jayeechi*), sung as solos, often accompany gatherings; they can last for hours and so can become for men a true test of endurance. Their content can be biographical, historical, or anecdotal (love stories, lullabies, etc.). The Guajiro also play, also in solo, several types of flute and the Jew's harp.

MEDICINE. The Guajiro distinguish two types of sickness. Beyond a certain threshold of pain and when the domestic treatments by plants, firebrands (*asijai*), and the like are found to be ineffective, the sickness is considered to be of the *wanülüü* type: its cause is supernatural. Nosology is of the etiological type. It distinguishes three great types of causes: encounters with or aggression by supernatural beings (*oustaa*), aggression by ghosts of the dead (*yolujasiraa*), and contamination (*kapülainwea*) by animals or by those who have handled remains of the dead or the bodies of murder victims. Traditionally, only shamans could assure a cure. Today many Guajiro follow winding therapeutic itineraries that take them from shamans to doctors at "health centers" and, in passing, to the healers or "sorcerers" of the neighboring rural areas.

ENTERTAINERS

*Guajiro musicians at a festival in Uribia. The Guajiro are indigenous to the La Guajia Peninsula, between Colombia and Venezuela. Uribia, Colombia.
(Jeremy Horner/Corbis)*

DEATH AND AFTERLIFE. According to the Guajiro, humans are part of a fatal cycle. When they die, their souls cross the "way of the dead Indians," the Milky Way, and they go to Jepira, the peninsula of the dead, passing from the state of person (*wayuu*) to that of yoluja. To Jepira, the yoluja constitute a society comparable or opposed to that of the living, and then, "a long time after," "they are lost." Everything happens as though Juya and Pulowi were assimilating them. Long-dead Guajiro are then found on earth in the form of rain, which assures the rejuvenation of vegetation and life, or in the form of wanülüü, who bring sickness and death. The double funeral corresponds to the double fate of the dead. At the time of the second burial, to which the Guajiro accord extreme importance, the remains of the members of the same matrilineage are reunited, signifying anonymity and oblivion but also the force and the permanence of the group.

Bibliography

Goulet, Jean-Guy (1978). *Guajiro Social Organization and Religion*. Ann Arbor: University Microfilms. Translated as *El universo social y religioso guajiro*. 1982. Caracas and Maracaibo: Universidad Católica Andrés Bello.

Gutiérrez de Pineda, Virginia (1950). "Organización social en La Guajira." *Revista del Instituto Etnológico Nacional* (Bogatá). Translated as Social Organization in La Guajira. 1960. New Haven: HRAF.

Perrin, Michel (1976). *Le Chemin des indiens morts: Mythes et symboles guajiro*. Paris: Payot. Translated as *The Way of the Dead Indians*. 1987. Austin: University of Texas Press.

Perrin, Michel (1982). *Antropólogos y médicos frente al arte guajiro de curar*. Caracas and Maracaibo: Universidad Católica Andrés Bello; Corpozulia.

Picon, François-Reneé (1983). *Pasteurs de nouveau monde: Adpotion de l'élevage chez les indiens guajiros*. Paris: Maison des Sciences de l'Homme.

—MICHEL PERRIN

JIVARO

Ethnonyms: Aents, Chívari, Chiwaro, Gíbari, Givari, Gívaro, Híbaro, Jibaro, Jívara, Jívira, Macusari, Mainu, Shuar, Shuara, Síwaro, Xívari, Xivaro, Zíbaro

The 30,000 to 32,000 Jivaro live in the foothills of the Andes Mountains of Ecuador, particularly on the Zamora, Upano, and Paute rivers in Morona-Santiago Province (2° to 5° S, 77° to 79° W). There are four major subgroups: the Antipa, the Aguaruna, the Huambiza, and the Achuale. They speak a language belonging to the Jivaroan Family, but some speak Quechua in addition. When the Spanish first contacted them, the Jivaro were repelling the hostile advances of the Inca, who sought the gold in Jivaro territory. Later, the Jivaro fought off the Spanish, who also came to their territory looking for gold. A gold rush to the area in the 1930s caused the Jivaro to fight the new arrivals; the Roman Catholic Salesians, who had a mission among the Jivaro, were able to stop the war by persuading the Ecuadoran government to provide the Jivaro a reservation. Since then, relations between the Jivaro and Whites have been essentially peaceful, although the Jivaro cannot be considered completely pacified. The Jivaro are nowadays swidden horticulturists who produce sweet manioc, maize, and other crops. They have acquired a strong taste for trade goods, and many of them have entered the work force as laborers to earn the money necessary to buy such items.

Traditionally, the Jivaro raised sweet manioc, maize, sweet potatoes, peanuts, tuber beans, *macabo* (*Xanthosoma* sp.), pumpkins, plantains, tobacco, cotton, and, later, the introduced species of banana, sugarcane, taro, and yam. Planting and other horticultural rituals are very important. The Jivaro fish and forage for wild fruits, cacao, nuts, and other foods. They used to hunt deer and tapir, but in the middle of the twentieth century they gave up eating these animals out of fear of the spirits in them. Hunting is done with bows and arrows, spears, and atlatls. Larger game is hunted by groups of people accompanied by dogs; blowguns are used for small game. There is much magic associated with hunting, including the use of pepper in the eyes of hunters and dogs to improve vision. The Jivaro traditionally domesticated llamas and guinea pigs and later the introduced dog, chicken, and pig.

An entire Jivaro community of from 80 to 300 people (30 to 40 people in the twentieth century) lives in one house (*jivaría*), which, for defensive purposes, is built on a steep hill at the upper end of a stream. The house itself is approximately 13 meters by 26 meters, elliptical in shape, and has a thatched roof. Men and women sleep at opposite ends.

Each community is politically independent and has its own headman. It is located 4 or more kilometers from its nearest neighboring community. The community is made up of people patrilineally and affinally related. In times of war, two

The Jivaro have acquired a strong taste for trade goods, and many of them have entered the trade force as laborers to earn the money necessary to buy such items.

The Mataco have always lived in northern and central Gran Chaco, in central South America.

or more villages may unit to fight a common enemy, as was the case when the Spanish attempted to conquer them.

There are rituals for both boys and girls upon reaching puberty. Men may marry their cross cousins and their sisters' daughters. Polygyny is common, and this would appear to be adaptive since so many men die in warfare. Levirate is obligatory. Men either pay a bride-price or perform bride-service. Deceased adults are buried in hollowed-out logs in special buildings and are given food and drink for two years, after which they are believed to transform into animals or birds. Children are interred in urns.

Bibliography

Gippelhauser, Richard (1990). *Die Achuara-Jivaro: Wirtschaftliche und soziale Organisationsformen am peruanischen Amazonas*. Vienna: Österreichische Akademie der Wissenschaften.

Harner, Michael J. (1973). *The Jívaro: People of the Sacred Waterfalls*. New York: Doubleday.

Karsten, Rafael (1935). "The Head-Hunters of Western Amazonas: The Life and Culture of the Jibaro Indians of Eastern Ecuador and Peru." *Societas Scientiarum Fennica, Commentationes Humanarum, Litterarum* (Helsinki) 8(1).

MATACO

Ethnonyms: Churumatas, Coronados, Mataco-Güisnay, Mataco-Noctenes (Oktenai, Nocten), Mataco-Véjoz (Bejoses, Wejwos, Hueshuos), Mataguayo, Wenhayek wikyi', Wichi, Wikyé

Orientation

IDENTIFICATION. The fact that the Mataco have been identified with a series of denominations indicates the fragmentary knowledge that we have of all their different dialects and subsections. The name "Mataco" seems to be derived from Spanish *montaraces* (bush people), a pejorative word for those living in the little-known dry forests of the Gran Chaco.

LOCATION. Ever since their habitat was first established, the Mataco have lived in northern and central Gran Chaco, roughly in the area between the Pilcomayo and Bermejo rivers, from the foothills of the Andes in Bolivia to the town of Las Lomitas in Argentina. This part of the Gran Chaco is known as the hottest region of South America, and, apart from a few chilly days during the period from June to August, day tem-

peratures range between 30° and 40° C, with the average summer temperature ascending to more than 30° C. Precipitation is normally sparse, around 60 centimeters per year, which results in a semidesert climate with xerophytic vegetation.

LINGUISTIC AFFILIATION. The Mataco language belongs to the Mataco-Mak'á Branch of the Macro-Guaicuruan Language Family. Lately, the latter has been associated with the Ge-Pano-Carib Language Group. Mataco has for centuries been divided into three dialects: Noctenes, Güisnay, and Véjoz, but this partition may prove insufficient.

DEMOGRAPHY. According to official figures, there are 12,000 Mataco in Argentina and some 2,000 in Bolivia. These numbers are most certainly too low, however. In 1988 an Argentine newspaper *El Nuevo Diario* assessed the number of Mataco in Argentina alone to be about 60,000.

History and Cultural Relations

Comparative studies by Erland Nordenskiöld in the early years of this century suggest that the Macro-Guaicuruans are descendants of the first immigrants to South America. They were well established in the Gran Chaco before the Guaraní immigration in the sixteenth century and the arrival of the Spanish in the seventeenth. The first recorded contact between the Mataco and the Spaniards took place in 1628, but White penetration was slow, and the area cannot be considered to have been fully "colonized" until after the Chaco War (1932–1936).

Archaeological, ethnographic, and linguistic evidence show that the Mataco had extensive, early contacts with the Andean peoples, chiefly with the Quechua. In historical times, the Mataco traded with and worked for the Chiriguano. During the late nineteenth century and the first half of the twentieth, they migrated to the cane mills of northern Argentina. Nevertheless, they have exchanged fairly little by way of language and culture with other peoples. In most parts of their territory, the Mataco have resisted integration or interacted very reluctantly with the Whites and the mestizos. This attitude has made them the object of numerous negative evaluations by development planners, missionaries, and the local population.

Settlements

The Mataco live in villages of varying size, comprised of from 1 to 100 extended families. Because of lack of water and the abundance of fish, most settlements are situated along the rivers. Those who are not riverine Mataco also prefer the vicinity of waters. The spatial layout of the village reflects the social relations, usually family ties, of the inhabitants. The traditional beehivelike grass hut disappeared as a permanent dwelling around the time of the Chaco War and is seen only occasionally at temporary fishing camps. Today the Mataco live in square wattle-and-daub houses or, if residing in urban areas, in adobe or brick houses.

Kinship

KIN GROUPS AND DESCENT. Mataco society was traditionally divided into a series of *wikyi'*, or groups (i.e., named, geographically localized and exogamous social units). Each group was regarded as a single entity, but each split into bands that varied in size according to the season. After the Chaco War, these groups developed into wikyi' categories and are now spread out over large areas. Nevertheless, it is easy to find a correlation between a concentration of wikyi' members and its traditional locality. Apart from wikyi' membership, there is little emphasis on descent. There is no descent ideology, and when a person dies, he or she is immediately cut out of the kinship system. Even his or her name is quickly ignored and sometimes tabooed.

KINSHIP TERMINOLOGY. The system of kinship terminology is based on cognatic principles and could be classified as a variant of the Hawaiian type. Almost all kinship terms are generational and can be used in several genealogical positions. No difference is made between full siblings and first cousins. However, six core terms are specific (Ego, wife, mother, father, daughter, sister). These represent key concepts in Ego's family of orientation and that of procreation.

ECONOMY

Subsistence and Commercial Activities

The Mataco are gatherers, fishers, and hunters, but supplement these activities with a simple agriculture. Women gather tree fruits, tubers, herbs, and roots, whereas men forage for honey. The Mataco know over twenty species of honey-producing bees. Men fish with several techniques but most often with nets. The most common and economically important catches are of *sábalos*, *dorados*, and *zurubís*. Hunting decreased in importance after the Chaco War, and communal hunts have disappeared. Today the customary practice is to hunt with dogs. The most frequently taken game are armadillos, rheas, and iguanas. Slash-and-burn cultivation has been replaced by a more permanent cultivation. The main crops are maize, pumpkins, squashes, watermelons, and cassava. In the 1970s the northernmost Mataco developed a fishing industry, based on seine fishing. The Mataco adopted the idea from a missionary and based the work organization on traditional collective barring-net fishing. Since then commercialized fishing has become the single largest source of income for these Mataco. In other areas, lumbering and unskilled day labor provide the Mataco with the necessary cash.

Industrial Arts

Aboriginal crafts include pottery, making of *caraguatá* string bags, basketry, and the production of items from calabash and tools and ornaments from wood, bark, skin, bone, and teeth. The string bags have received special attention because of their beauty and variety of design; they are now also produced for sale. In the 1950s the Mataco started producing wickerlike furniture, and in the 1960s they started a home industry of baskets and balsa wood. In both cases, commercialization has been very successful, and these products constitute the second-largest source of income for the Mataco in the northern half of their habitat.

Trade

The group maintained a considerable pre-contact trade with the Quechua and the Chiriguano; there was probably an Amazon-Pampean trade route that passed through the Gran Chaco. Today the Mataco buy kerosene, maté, macaroni, rice, sugar, and clothes from the mestizos and sell fish, handicrafts, honey, some agricultural products, and labor.

Division of Labor

Women are responsible for the gathering of most foods and light firewood, fetching water, cooking, and making handicrafts out of clay, *caraguatá* fibers, palm leaves, wool, and cotton. Men gather honey and heavy firewood; they fish, hunt, and manufacture handicrafts of wood, bark, skin, leather, bone, and metal. Men also undertake most of the activities that relate to the national society: employment, work migrations, contacts with authorities, and trade. Both sexes help out in agriculture, and women sometimes sell their own handicraft products.

Land Tenure

Individuals have the right to occupy, hunt, and cultivate any unoccupied land. This right of possession lasts as long as the land is cultivated or inhabited. There is no individual ownership as regards land. With the help of missions or national agencies, Mataco village communities have acquired legal rights to portions of their former territory.

*Some Mataco
philosophers believe
in metempsychosis,
the successive
transformation of
humans into ghosts,
bats, and spiders
before they vanish
totally.*

Marriage and Family

MARRIAGE. The formation of a matrimony extends over considerable time, and the couple may follow any of the following procedures. According to the Mataco codex, discussions should precede initiatives toward sexual liaisons, and these should be followed by a phase of trials. Only thereafter do the parents celebrate the wedding or consider the couple to be married. Another, and nowadays more common, alternative is to escape for some time after the first, passionate encounter. The period away from home is equivalent to the trial, and if the liaison proves to be durable, the couple is regarded as "married" upon returning to the original community. Marriage should be followed by bride-service until the first child is born. After the initial, uxorilocal residence, the couple may move to any place they wish. Divorce is fairly frequent, especially among those contracting marriage at an early age.

DOMESTIC UNIT. The basic socioeconomic unit is the extended family, which lives in a single or several adjacent huts. It may be constituted by one or two pots, but is characterized by generalized reciprocity and close cooperation in all socioeconomic activities.

INHERITANCE. There is no inheritance among the Mataco. When a person dies, his or her property is destroyed.

SOCIALIZATION. Children are supposed to learn through imitation and instruction, not by correction or punishment. An increasing percentage of them now attend primary school. Until the 1980s, however, no Mataco had ever gone beyond secondary school.

Sociopolitical Organization

SOCIAL ORGANIZATION. All Mataco, men and women, young and old, are supposed to be equal; all share the right of free speech and partake in all activities. Nevertheless, eloquence (only acquired with age) is crucial; therefore elders, and often old men, enjoy a special status.

POLITICAL ORGANIZATION. Formerly, each wikyi' was an autonomous political entity, guided by the community council and represented by the *niyat*, the spokesman. The council, which was constituted of all the adults of the group, handled all kinds of political, judicial, and legal issues. Today, the village council fulfills these roles.

SOCIAL CONTROL. Within the family or the community, open face-to-face conflict, as well as gossip, slander, ostracism, and social withdrawal are, and have been, important forms of social control. Taboos and fear of supernatural powers cannot be disregarded, however. Between wikyi' and extended families severe crimes, like homicide, were settled through negotiations or blood revenge.

CONFLICT. There are no means of external intervention in internal familial controversies. Disputes between families often evolve into open clashes, necessitating the intervention of the village council. In these fights or scuffles, women, more often than men, are the protagonists. In bygone days, clashes between wikyi' could result in armed aggression, but such tension was often prevented by recurrent games of hockey.

Religion and Expressive Culture

RELIGIOUS BELIEFS. The Mataco believe in an interrelationship between humans and animals, the sky and the earth, and the natural and the supernatural. A distant and vague Creator is complemented by a rich pantheon of zoomorphic and anthropomorphic figures who intervene very little in a person's life if he or she adheres to the Mataco codex or keeps to the human zones. Breaking of taboos, or any other type of border crossing, brings a person in direct contact, or even conflict, with the supernatural. A characteristic feature of Mataco religion is the existence of "lords" over different phenomena central to the Mataco, like honey, caraguatá, or peccaries. The Mataco worldview is expressed, outlined, and explained in their rich mythology and in their oral tradition. There are numerous supernatural individuals and categories in the Mataco cosmos. Some of the most important are Lawo', the rainbow or giant serpent, who controls tempests, storms, and cyclones and is easily irritated; Ahââtaj, the head of all evil; Ijwala, the sun and the evil master; and Thokwjwaj, the feared but cherished trickster who represents "Mataconess." Most Mataco adhere to a type of parallelism, a combination of traditional beliefs and Christian faith spread through Anglican and Pentecostal missions.

RELIGIOUS PRACTITIONERS. The only religious specialists are the shamans, who have advisory as well as curative functions. Through shamanic trips, they have knowledge of the supernatural and the unknown and pass this information on to the people. Whenever a person fears supernatural intervention, he or she goes to a shaman for advice or curative rituals. Shamans have no direct political authority, but may, through their extensive knowledge, influence decisions. Missionary teachings have diminished the number of shamans and their caseloads.

CEREMONIES.　Traditional rituals included a rite of passage for girls, a wedding ceremony, and a funeral. Besides these, there were several types of shamanistic rites. Most of these have disappeared as a result of the influence of Christianity.

ARTS.　Mataco artistry reaches its supreme height in the string-bag designs, based on natural or symbolic patterns and closely related to their mythology. Several natural dyes are used and some fifteen basic patterns, with hundreds of variants. Aesthetic expression is also found in carvings, pottery, and, in bygone days, facial paintings.

MEDICINE.　The Mataco are familiar with a large number of herbs that are used for most somatic ailments. Aside from these, there are natural and supernatural forces that are accessible only to the shaman.

DEATH AND AFTERLIFE.　When a Mataco dies, he or she is buried with a jug of water, an important item for a trip in the barren Chaco. The deceased is supposed to initiate a long journey and must do so to avoid disturbing or molesting the living. The deceased will continue his or her afterlife in the underworld, much as he or she lived on earth. Some Mataco philosophers believe in metempsychosis, however (i.e., in successive transformation of humans into ghosts, bats, and spiders before they vanish totally).

Bibliography

Alvarsson, Jan-Åke (1988). *The Mataco of the Gran Chaco: An Ethnographic Account of Change and Continuity in Mataco Socio-Economic Organization.* Uppsala Studies in Cultural Anthropology, no. 11. Uppsala and Stockholm: Almqvist & Wiksell International.

Fock, Niels (1982). "History of Mataco Folk Literature and Research." In *Folk Literature of the Mataco Indians*, edited by Johannes Wilbert and Karin Simoneau, 1–33. Los Angeles: University of California, Latin American Center.

Métraux, Alfred (1946). "Ethnography of the Chaco." In *Handbook of South American Indians*, edited by Julian Steward. Vol. 1, *The Marginal Tribes*, 197–370. Bureau of American Ethnology Bulletin 143. Washington, D.C.: Smithsonian Institution.

Ortíz Lema, Edgar (1986). *Los mataco noctenes de Bolivia.* La Paz and Cochabamba: Editorial Los Amigos del Libro.

—JAN-ÅKE ALVARSSON

MATSIGENKA

Ethnonyms: Anti, Ashaninka ("our kind"), Kogapakori (isolated, uncontacted Matsigenka referred to as "wild ones"), Machiguenga, Nomatsigenka (an enclave residing within Campa territory)

Orientation

IDENTIFICATION.　"Matsigenka" means "people." It refers to a closely related group of people with minor local differences in dialect and material culture. They are sometimes considered a subgroup of the neighboring Campa, although both groups regard each other as distinct.

LOCATION.　The Matsigenka inhabit the tropical rain forest of the upper Amazon of southeastern Peru, primarily the eastern foothills of the Andes Mountains, along the Río Urubamba and its tributaries, and in the headwaters of the Río Madre de Dios. These Amazon headwaters originate near the ancient Inca capital of Cuzco and flow past abandoned Inca roads and terraces to the high forest (*selva alta*) of the Matsigenka. Here there is profuse rainfall (250 to 500 centimeters per year), spread evenly through a wet season from October through March and a less wet, but still rainy season from April through September. Temperatures range from 14° C on the coolest nights to 32° C during the hottest days, with an annual average around 24° C. The high-forest habitat is mountainous tropical rain forest with steep inclines, rushing mountain rivers, and hazardous trails, making interregional travel difficult.

DEMOGRAPHY.　The Matsigenka population is estimated at between 7,000 and 12,000. The population is steadily growing in size after suffering staggering losses from European diseases and social atrocities during the rubber boom of the early 1900s. Historically, they were pressed from the Andes by farmers who established farms in the upper reaches of their territory to grow coca and other tropical crops and from the north and east by neighboring groups competing for hunting and fishing territories. Today they are again being pressed by highlanders moving into their lands, driven by overpopulation and poverty in the highlands.

LINGUISTIC AFFILIATION.　Matsigenka is an Arawakan language of the Pre-Andean Subgroup, which also includes Campa, Piro, and Amuesha. Current opinion favors the view that these societies are descendants of the ancient inhabitants of this region, who migrated to it at

Most Matsigenka households continue to be scattered in traditional hamlets in order to avoid competition over resources.

least several thousand years ago. Despite evidence of historical contact with Andean culture, there is very little language borrowing from Quechua.

History and Cultural Relations

The Matsigenka have inhabited their present territory since long before the Spanish Conquest. It may be called a "refuge zone," in the sense of being a niche in a somewhat less favorable environment than surrounding ones, where they have sought to live peaceably and to be left alone. The Matsigenka were surrounded to the north, east, and south by Arawakan and Panoan groups, among whom warfare was endemic. Evidence of Panoan pottery in the Arawakan zone indicates the groups traded with one another. At least as early as the mid-nineteenth century, the Matsigenka were described as less fierce than their neighbors and more likely to avoid violence.

Contact between the forest people of the high forest and the highland groups of the Andes predates the Inca empire. Matsigenka and their neighbors provided the highlanders with cacao, bird feathers, palm wood, cotton, herbal medicines, and tropical fruits. In return they received stone and metal tools and bits of silver used in jewelry. Otherwise, the influence of highland culture was very slight. The uninhabited cloud forest has been an effective barrier separating the highlands and the high forest. Furthermore, low population density and an absense of regional political organization made it impossible for the Inca to exercise effective control over the Matsigenka. Consequently, the Matsigenka historically were able to maintain their distance from both the Inca Empire and the Spanish Conquest. Catholic missionaries also had little influence in the region, often being martyred in raids by Matsigenka and Campa.

In the early 1900s, however, the rubber boom and slave trade had a significant disruptive impact, abetted by Matsigenka strongmen who traded their own people into slavery in exchange for shotguns and steel tools. Although the rubber boom collapsed after a few years, the practice of raiding continued on a smaller scale until the 1950s because colonists persisted in their demand for laborers and household servants. By the 1960s, Peruvian police, development agencies, and missionary programs finally curtailed the slave trade. Despite their growing dependence on Western medicine, clothing, steel tools, and aluminum pots, present-day Matsigenka retain most of their traditional culture.

Settlements

The Machiguenga traditionally live in small semipermanent settlement clusters of 7 to 25 individuals, composed of one to four families, situated on hilltops and ridges for fear of slave raids. In the past, charismatic leaders or shamans attracted several hundred people along a tributary stream. Since the 1960s, Matsigenka schoolteachers, trained in Pucallpa by the Summer Institute of Linguistics (a Protestant group), have successfully drawn people out of their isolation into school communities with airstrips. But most Matsigenka households continue to be scattered in traditional hamlets to avoid competition over resources. Individual families periodically leave on foraging trips for several days or weeks at a time. Matsigenka school communities range in size from 100 to 250 individuals and consist of nuclear and extended family households averaging approximately 6 individuals per household. Houses are constructed entirely from local materials; they are built with heavy hardwood posts tied with bark, palm-wood walls, and a thatched palm-leaf roof. Houses were traditionally low, oval-shaped structures; today many have raised palm-wood floors and are larger and rectangular in shape. Houses are located at the edge of a river or a stream and are usually surrounded by a clearing with a small kitchen garden at the perimeter.

Economy

SUBSISTENCE AND COMMERCIAL ACTIVITIES. The Matsigenka are slash-and-burn horticulturists; the main cultivated crops are manioc, maize, plantains, and pineapples. Garden activities produce about 90 percent of all calories, supplemented by hunting, fishing, and collecting, which provide the most highly prized foods. Most hunting is done with bows and arrows and traps. Individuals with shotguns are more successful and share their catch with local households to offset resentment. The most common game include monkeys, birds, peccaries, and tapir. Fishing is done with hooks and lines, nets, and *barbasco* poison; the latter is the most successful but requires communal effort in damming up waterways. Commercial activities have been almost nonexistent in traditional communities. Communities with schools typically try to develop commercial crops such as coffee, cacao, peanuts, and beans for sale, but as of the early 1980s these provided only a small proportion of household income. Money has only recently been introduced into the local economy.

INDUSTRIAL ARTS. The Matsigenka manufacture nearly everything they use except machetes and axes, and now aluminum pots and factory-made cloth. Men make houses, bows and arrows, and fiber twine for netting used in fishnets and carrying bags. Women primarily spin cotton and weave cloth, but also make mats for sleeping and sitting and plaited sifters and strainers used in food preparation.

TRADE. Historically, trade with the Inca was important. Today Western goods such as machetes, axes, aluminum pots, and cloth are obtained through barter, by working for farmers in the major river valleys, or through the schoolteacher, who serves as a link with the commercial world.

DIVISION OF LABOR. Women provide most child care, prepare nearly all the food, manufacture cotton cloth, and grow certain "women's crops," such as yams and *cocoyam* (*Xanthogoma nigra*). Men do all the hunting, most fishing, and the bulk of agricultural work, accounting for the vast majority of calories in the diet. Men and women occasionally work together in the garden or on foraging trips, complementing one another's tasks. Starting at age 5, children begin to acquire adult skills by accompanying the parent of their sex to work. The only other division of labor is on an individual basis, as people with particular skills such as hunting or bow manufacture share their products with others in exchange for material goods or prestige.

LAND TENURE. Although land is not owned as such, territories are informally demarcated. Men announce in advance their intentions to clear gardens in specific locations; later, abandoned gardens revert to the public domain. Hamlets may remain in the same vicinity for several generations, although individuals frequently travel and visit to learn of prospects for resources or mates.

Kinship

KIN GROUPS AND DESCENT. The Matsigenka do not have named kin groups. At most, they have bilateral kindreds, in the form of hamlets of intermarrying families, but these hamlets frequently split for periods of time when nuclear-family households go off on their own. Newly married couples initially prefer matrilocal residence, so that a woman can be near her mother when her first child is born. Afterwards, residence is highly fluid and opportunistic. There are no descent rules determining access to group membership (no kin groups), territories, or ceremonial rights. Most material possessions are destroyed by burning upon an individual's death, so inheritance rarely arises as an issue. Kin relations are traced bilaterally through both parents.

KINSHIP TERMINOLOGY. The Matsigenka kinship system is a straightforward Dravidian system with the cross/parallel ("lineal vs. affinal") distinction maintained in Ego's generation and those immediately preceding and following it. Opposite-sex cross cousins are defined as potential spouses.

Marriage and Family

MARRIAGE. Some marriages are arranged at an early age, although in communities with schools it is more common for girls to marry after puberty. Everyone on Ego's generation is either a sibling or a cross cousin, with prescriptive cross-cousin marriage. The system favors a pattern of two families intermarrying over time and living together in the same hamlet or vicinity. Demographics often falling short of this ideal, unmarried individuals of both sexes must visit other settlements seeking mates. Marriage is initiated when each partner addresses the prospective spouse's relatives as "in-laws" and the male assumes bride-service responsibilities.

DOMESTIC UNIT. The typical domestic unit is a nuclear family household in a 5-by-10 meter house, situated in a clearing either alone or near other households in a hamlet. In the small number of cases of polygyny, each wife has a separate hearth at her own end of the house, which is considered her living space. Co-wives are cordial but separate: they tend to manage their own food supplies, rear their own children, and control the distribution of the products of their own labor. Single relatives, including widowed elders, may live in the household as additional members, but not with their own hearth. Households of more than one married couple are temporary arrangements occasioned by death, divorce, or migration into a new area.

INHERITANCE. Generally, property is not inherited. Durable valuables, such as an axe or a mirror, may be passed on from mother to daughter or father to son.

SOCIALIZATION. Infants are fed on demand and coddled and enjoyed. Discipline after 1 year of age is by verbal reprimand and the rarely enforced threat of corporal punishment. Weaning is between 3 and 4 years of age and is loudly protested by the child, but parents do not relent. After age 5, children gradually acquire adult, gender-appropriate behaviors. Scolding is common, but the process is gentle and gradual.

♦ **Dravidian**
The language family of the darkest-skinned people in South Asia, mainly found in southern India and Sri Lanka.

♦ **cross cousin**
Children of one's parent's siblings of the opposite sex— one's father's sisters' and mother's brothers' children.

Gossip and ostracizing are used to try to prevent serious wrongdoing such as homicide or incest.

Sociopolitical Organization

SOCIAL ORGANIZATION. The nuclear-family household is the basic social unit. Each household is virtually self-sufficient, even when aggregated in hamlets of several related households. Wild foods, particularly game and fish, are shared generously within the hamlet, and cross-cousin marriages may tie the hamlet group together over the years, even when households take up separate residence for periods of time. Hamlet dwellers exchange visits, but larger groups are amorphous and unstructured.

POLITICAL ORGANIZATION. The basic rule of political organization is household autonomy. There are no headmen or councils to set policy, and the Matsigenka are notorious for leaving an area when their autonomy is compromised. Traditionally, charismatic leaders and shamans did become centers of loose regional aggregates of households, brought together through beer feasts with meat sharing, singing, and dancing. Today, communities that have schools strive with limited success to overcome individualism. The government supplies a school curriculum that emphasizes Peruvian nationalism and political participation in the nation-state, and these communities register as Native Communities under Peruvian law. The Matsigenka have formed a multicommunity union and an elected council head to deal with oil exploration and other extractive industries moving into their territory.

SOCIAL CONTROL. No overarching legal system exists to punish wrongdoing. Gossip and shaming are used to try to prevent serious breaches such as homicide or incest. Individuals who commit such crimes are punished by being ostracized or expelled from the community. Early socialization and shaming are quite effective in teaching people to control aggressive impulses.

CONFLICT. Late in the twentieth century, conflict with outside groups is at a minimum. Conflicts within the household and hamlet occur occasionally, usually after drinking at a beer feast. Arguments take the form of verbal fights with limited physical contact. Fights usually result in one or more members leaving the community, either temporarily or for good.

Religion and Expressive Culture

RELIGIOUS BELIEFS. A Creator made the world by mounding up mud into land. He contended with a Trickster figure who created the bad things of this world, like biting flies. Many animals are the degenerated descendants of humans who violated norms in the past, for instance by theft or incest. Not all, but many features of the world are imbued with spirit. Animals have spirit rulers that must be appeased if one of their kind has been killed. Various demons, often with enlarged penises, haunt the forests and are especially dangerous to women, whom they can impregnate with a demon child. The alkaloid hallucinogen ayahuasca (*kamarampi*; lit., "death medicine") is ingested to allow the spirit to fly to the land of the Unseen Ones, spirit helpers who can inhabit one's body and perform cures, divine the future, and give instruction. The soul also lives on after death and can reach a better layer of the cosmos if not eaten by dangerous spirits during its postmortem journey. The heroically good (and bad) figures who created the world are no longer active. Good and bad spirits continue to be present, especially away from inhabited areas. Some shamans practice sorcery to bring harm to others, but these are generally thought to reside far away in other communities.

CEREMONIES. Ceremonial life is minimal. Curing and spiritual encounters are conducted by individuals in the privacy of their homes. Beer feasts are occasions for drunkenness, music and dance, and ribald humor blending into ridicule and humiliation, but they do not invoke spiritual forces. Calendrical festivals and ancestor worship are absent.

ARTS. The Matsigenka are good singers; they sing in groups of up to four, with hypnotic repetitions and counterpoint. Drums, flutes, and panpipes are widely used. When drinking manioc beer, men drum in rapid 4/4 time and dance by darting and whirling around the clearing. Women dance by walking behind the men, holding hands, and singing. Men and women occasionally decorate their faces with *achiote* (annatto). In the most traditional areas, women still wear small silver nosepieces. Cotton cloth is usually decorated with small geometric designs in the weave. Sculpture, painting, and other plastic arts are lacking, as is pottery.

MEDICINE. A large number of herbal remedies are known, many of the most common from plants raised for that purpose in kitchen gardens. Shamans identify spiritual causes of illness and treat them by sucking magic darts or blowing smoke and by invoking the powers of friendly spirits.

DEATH AND AFTERLIFE. Death can occur through natural or supernatural causes. If the soul dies through attack by an evil spirit, the body will wither and die. In any case, the soul will linger in sorrow near the house of the deceased. The house must be burned down and the remainder of the family must move away so the soul will have no reason to linger and will begin its journey to the higher level of the cosmos, where people live just as they do here on earth but without suffering or death.

Bibliography

Baer, Gerhard (1984). *Die Religion der Matsigenka Ost-Peru*. Basel: Wepf & Co.

Johnson, Allen, and Orna R. Johnson (1987). *Cross-Cultural Studies in Time Allocation*. Vol. 1, *Time Allocation among the Machiguenga of Shimaa*. New Haven: Human Relations Area Files.

Johnson, Orna R. (1978). "Interpersonal Relations among the Machiguenga of the Peruvian Amazon." Ph.D. dissertation, Columbia University.

Johnson, Orna R., and Allen Johnson (1975). "Male/Female Relations and the Organization of Work in a Machiguenga Community." *American Ethnologist* 2:634–648.

Renard-Casevitz, France-Marie (1991). *Le banquet masqué: Une mythologie de l'étranger chez les indiens matsiguenga*. Paris: Lierre & Coudrier.

—ORNA R. JOHNSON AND ALLEN W. JOHNSON

OTAVALO

Ethnonyms: Indígenas de Otavalo, Otavaleños, Runa (Quichua for "people") de Otavalo

Orientation

IDENTIFICATION. The name "Runa" dates from the post-Inca Conquest, whereas the names "Otavaleño" and "Indígena" date from the post-Spanish Conquest. The main tribes in the area when the Incas arrived in the late-fifteenth century were the Caranqui and Cayambi.

LOCATION. Aboriginally, these groups occupied the Andean cordilleras and the valleys of what are now Imbabura and Pichincha provinces from the contemporary border of Colombia to Carapugno (modern Calderón) at the northern edge of Quito. Most Otavalo still live in the Otavalo Valley in Imbabura Province, but there are large numbers in Quito and smaller colonies in every Ecuadoran population center; in Bogotá, Popayán, and Pasto, Colombia; and in Venezuela, Brazil, and Spain. The Otavalo wear a distinct costume combining pre-Hispanic, Spanish colonial, and modern elements. This dress has changed over the centuries, but serves to identify wearers as members of the Otavalo ethnic group. It is possible for Indians to hide their ethnic identity by adopting White-style dress, but this is rare.

DEMOGRAPHY. In 1990 the indigenous population of the Otavalo Valley was estimated at 45,000 to 50,000, including 3,000 in the town of Otavalo, with another 5,000 to 8,000 Otavalo living in expatriate communities in Ecuador and abroad.

LINGUISTIC AFFILIATION. The pre-Inca aboriginal language has been lost except for a few place-names, patronyms, and loom terms. It was affiliated with the Barbacoa Group of the Chibchan Language Family, as is the language spoken by the contemporary Cayapa in the western lowlands. Quichua was introduced into Ecuador in the fifteenth century by the Incas and was spread by Spanish missionaries as a lingua franca. According to the 1974 Torero classification, the Otavalo speak the Quichua B dialect of the Quechua II Language Group. (Linguists disagree whether Quichua B is a dialect or a separate language.) The Otavalo call Quichua *runa shimi* (the people's tongue). Most Otavalo are bilingual in Quichua and Spanish (*castellano*) and a few also speak Portuguese, English, French, or German.

History and Cultural Relations

The Caranqui and Cayambi lived in small, socially stratified city-states. They united to resist the Inca invasions of Ecuador in the second half of the fifteenth century but were finally defeated around A.D. 1495. Sarance (modern Otavalo) and Caranqui became Inca administrative centers. Before the Incas had a deep hold on the region, the Spanish, under Sebastián de Benalcázar, conquered Ecuador in 1534. By 1535 land in the Otavalo region was being given to Spanish settlers. Because Ecuador lacked the mineral resources of Peru and Bolivia, the Spanish put the indigenous population to work in Crown-owned and private textile factories under highly abusive conditions. By the mid-1550s a conquistador had been given a large *encomienda* (population grant), which included Otavalo. He set up an *obraje* (weaving factory) in Otavalo that employed up to 500 males at its height, but it reverted to the Spanish Crown in 1581. Other obrajes were also established in the region. The encomienda system evolved into large, privately owned landholdings (haciendas), and in the eighteenth century Indians were conscripted to work in hacienda textile factories through the *mita*, a system of forced labor. Ultimately, many Indians became permanently attached to the haciendas under a system

The Otavalo wear a distinct costume combining pre-Hispanic, Spanish colonial, and modern elements.

♦ **encomienda**
A large tract of land granted to Spanish settlers in America by the Spanish government. In return, the landholders were expected to convert the indigenous peoples to Roman Catholicism, make them work the land, and maintain order in the region.

of debt servitude (*wasipungu*), which included weaving for the hacienda in obrajes as well as agricultural work. Textile production in Ecuador was the mainstay of the colonial economy, with exports to what are now Bolivia, Peru, and Colombia. In 1964 debt servitude was outlawed, and some land reform was realized under the Law of Agrarian Reform and Colonization. The contemporary prosperity of the Otavalo through their involvement in the manufacture and marketing of textiles has resulted in more respectful and equitable treatment of them by Whites.

Settlements

Aboriginal settlements probably consisted of small towns where chiefs and priests resided, surrounded by small farms. Today there are about seventy-five small, dispersed communities, usually organized along a Spanish model around a central plaza with a church and school. Tile-roofed adobe or concrete-block houses are set among gardens or farmland. The town of Otavalo is a major tourist center with White- and Indian-owned hotels, restaurants, tour agencies, and craft shops.

Economy

SUBSISTENCE AND COMMERCIAL ACTIVITIES. The production of textiles has been im-

portant for centuries in the Otavalo region. Until the twentieth century, when a full-time weaving and merchant class arose, most textile activity was integrated into the agricultural cycle, and the Otavalo were subsistence farmers raising potatoes, corn, *haba* beans, quinoa, cherries (all indigenous crops), garden vegatables, and guinea pigs. Since the Spanish Conquest the Otavalo have also raised wheat, pigs, chickens, cattle, sheep, and occasionally horses.

INDUSTRIAL ARTS. Even before the arrival of the Incas, the Indians of the Otavalo Valley were known as weavers and merchants, using such indigenous technology and materials as the hand-held spindle, backstrap loom, and cotton and possibly camelid fibers to weave clothing and blankets. The obrajes, although oppressive, introduced production weaving and the technology upon which the modern economy is based: hand carders, walking spinning wheels, treadle looms, and sheep's wool. Because of a wool shortage, cotton and such synthetic fibers as acrylic are also used. Modern textile production is primarily a cottage industry with family members helping with production. About 25,000 males and females over age 16 work part- or full-time in the textile industry. Children also help after school. Involvement ranges from families who make two hand-spun wool backstrap loom-woven ponchos a month to families who produce hundreds of acrylic shawls a day on electric looms with the help of hired workers. The Otavalo produce clothing for themselves, for other Ecuadoran Indians and Whites, and high-fashion clothing for the export and tourist markets, as well as blankets, bedspreads, tapestry wall hangings, handbags, and electric machine-knit socks, to give a partial list. There are some wage workers in textiles but there is no industrial proletariat. Those not working in the textile cottage industry are subsistence farmers, day laborers in farming or construction, or both farmers and producers of other crafts. Families and villages have specialties. Mats are made from *totora* reeds in communities around San Pablo Lake; others fashion pottery, leather goods, and baskets.

TRADE. From pre-Inca times through the early Spanish colonial era, a separate merchant group (*mindalaes*) traded cotton textiles, beads, and other luxury goods throughout the sierra. Later, nonhacienda Indians continued to travel and market textiles. Today there are part- and full-time merchants who travel throughout Ecuador and to other Latin American countries, North America, and Europe selling textiles made

FRIENDLY FACE
An Otavalo Indian wearing a low brimmed hat and a dark gray shawl. Ecuador. (Victor Englebert)

by the Otavalo and by Whites and Indians from other parts of Ecuador, including wool or cotton sweaters hand-knit by White women in Ibarra, Mira, San Gabriel, and Cuenca. Substantial merchandising also occurs at the Saturday and Wednesday Otavalo markets.

DIVISION OF LABOR. Women traditionally spun with the hand-held spindle and men did the weaving. Today men predominate as weavers, but women also weave on both the pre-Hispanic stick loom and the European treadle loom. Both sexes spin, dye yarn, sew, finish textiles, garden, herd, farm, and sell items in the market and in stores. Women generally cook and care for infants, but men help. There is a high degree of gender equality, which was probably even greater before the Spanish Conquest. From a very early age children of both sexes help with textile and agricultural tasks, carry water, wash clothes, gather firewood, and care for their younger siblings.

LAND TENURE. Information is lacking on Caranqui and Cayambi and land tenure. Under the Inca empire land was communally owned and redistributed annually, with parcels farmed for the Sun (region), the Inca, and individual family consumption. Landownership has always been important to the Otavalo, and in the twentieth century, even before the agrarian reform, they bought back hacienda land whenever possible. In the 1990s small, individually owned landholdings are the norm.

Kinship

KIN GROUPS AND DESCENT. It is not known if the Caranqui or Cayambi had clans or moieties, but if so they have disappeared. Colonial documents mention the *ayllu*, a Quechua term for a corporate landholding group based on presumed common ancestry, but today "ayllu" simply means "family." There is no rule of village exogamy. Most Otavalo marry within the ethnic group, but there are some marriages with Whites. Descent is bilateral. Children have a patronym and matronym, and men and women keep both names after marriage. The practice of extending the family network through *compadrazgo* (coparenthood, fictive kinship) has religious, social, and economic importance. Godparents to a child at baptism, first communion, or confirmation became *compadres* to the child's parents. Compadres recognize an obligation to help one another in various ways, including economically, so families frequently choose compadres from a higher socioeconomic bracket. Godparents are supposed to supervise the religious education of their godchil-

dren but usually help the godchild with secular matters (gifts, money for education, jobs) and may be asked to raise the child if he or she is orphaned.

KINSHIP TERMINOLOGY. Evidence from the 1940s suggests that Otavalo Quichua kinship terminology was similar to that of the Inca: a bifurcate-merging system with classificatory three-generation cycles in both maternal and paternal lines. Today Spanish and some Quichua terms are used according to a European system, except that an affinal or consanguineal aunt is called *pani* (Quichua for sister) as well as *tía* (Spanish for aunt). The Quichua *mama* and *taita* (mother and father) are used for parents and as honorifics for elderly people in general, whereas the Spanish *tía* and *tío* (aunt and uncle) are used for these kin and as honorifics for younger adults. Children often call their godparents by the Quichua terms *achimama* or *achitaita* (godmother or godfather).

Marriage and Family

MARRIAGE. A person is not considered an adult until he or she marries, and marriage is the norm. It appears that aboriginally there were trial marriages; children resulting from such unions were considered legitimate. There is still no stigma attached to children born out of wedlock nor is virginity in either partner particularly valued. Until the mid-twentieth century most marriages were arranged by the couple's parents. Today young people meet and court at the Otavalo market, while running errands in town, at fiestas, or while attending high school. They generally marry between the ages of 18 and 24. The traditional giving of food by the groom's family is still practiced, together with the procession of the young man's parents to the home of his prospective bride to discuss the marriage. The food does not necessarily represent bride-wealth, since the bride's family does not lose her labor and the young couple may reside with them. Nor is a dowry given.

Exchanges of food between the families after marriage as agreed upon are a recognition of the reciprocity and the complementarity of opposites, which are core values in indigenous society. Appropriate marriage partners include anyone of the opposite sex except a first cousin or closer consanguineal relative. The mayor of the community places a rosary around the necks of the couple in a short ceremony and the union is recognized. Later, civil registration of the marriage is followed by a church wedding and fiesta if the man's family has the money to pay for the celebration. Divorce is rare.

An Otavalo is not considered an adult until he or she marries.

To the Otavalo, illnesses are considered hot or cold and are believed to be caused by fright, evil wind, evil spirits, or the entry of a foreign object.

DOMESTIC UNIT. Neolocal residence is the ideal, but until a young couple can build or buy their own house, they live with either set of parents depending on the families' resources; extended families are common. Unmarried or handicapped adults usually live with their parents or another relative, and orphaned children live with relatives.

INHERITANCE. Land and property are divided equally among all children, resulting in successive divisions of landholdings and a proliferation of tiny plots. The youngest child usually is given the parents' house while they are alive, with the understanding that he or she will care for them in old age.

SOCIALIZATION. Children are given much attention and affection and are raised relatively permissively. They are included in all activities, but they are also expected to help with household, farm, and textile chores; to obey adults promptly; and to respect them. Physical discipline, such as spanking, is infrequent. Ridicule, stern looks, or harsh words are usually sufficient to ensure proper behavior. Most children attend primary school. Increasing numbers are going on to high school and some to the university.

Sociopolitical Organization

SOCIAL ORGANIZATION. There is scant information on aboriginal social organization, but it appears that age was respected. Genders were equal, but priests and hereditary leaders (*kurakas*) had high rank. Today wealthy weaving and merchant families are beginning to form an indigenous upper class.

POLITICAL ORGANIZATION. The village (*parcialidad*) is an unofficial subdivision of the parish (*parróquia*), with no single authority. Instead, kinship and reciprocity bind the community. Each village has two mayors (*alcaldes*), appointed by the local political chief, and an elected council (*cabildo*). The political mayor calls collective work parties for such jobs as road repair but has no formal mechanism for enforcement. Indians have the right to vote and participate in politics at the local, provincial, and national level. Some Otavalo are active in nationwide indigenous federations.

SOCIAL CONTROL. The most common and effective mechanism for social control is the disapproval of one's family and community. Outside authorities such as the civil guard or town police are rarely, if ever, called in. Relatives and compadres informally mediate many marital and familial conflicts. Intractable conflicts, especially those over landownership or money, often end up in the local courts.

CONFLICT. The Caranqui and Cayambi forcibly resisted both the Inca and Spanish conquests. In the colonial era, there was an uprising in the Otavalo area against the Spanish in 1777. Through the 1970s and 1980s there have been conflicts with local haciendas over land, including the 1978 occupation of the Hacienda La Bolsa by Indians until they were dislodged by the army.

Religion and Expressive Culture

RELIGIOUS BELIEFS. The Spanish converted the Indians to Roman Catholicism, and indigenous celebrations were adapted to Catholic feast days. Today most Otavalo are Catholics with a substrate of pre-Hispanic beliefs. Since about the 1960s evangelical Christian sects and the Latter Day Saints have made converts through their missions in Otavalo.

Catholic saints, the Virgin Mary, and the Holy Trinity are worshiped, but the last drops of liquid in a glass are always poured on the ground as an offering to Pachamama (Earth Mother). Offerings are also made by women wanting children to a *lechero* tree on a hill overlooking Otavalo to the east. There is some belief in nature spirits, especially in the spirits of streams and waterfalls. The rainbow is feared as an evil omen that can cause flesh to petrify or lead to insanity or death. The two dormant volcanoes that dominate the Otavalo Valley are called Taita Imbabura and Mama Cotacachi; they figure in folktales and legends but are not worshiped as such. A smaller peak, Mojanda, is considered their *wawa* (baby).

RELIGIOUS PRACTITIONERS. Because of colonial conversions to Christianity and Spanish suppression of indigenous religion, there are no practitioners of *aboriginal* religion per se, although there are traditional healers.

CEREMONIES. The aboriginal ceremonial cycle was organized around solar events and the agricultural cycle. Today Christian feasts (Christmas, Holy Week, Easter, etc.) are observed, but the most important fiesta is that of San Juan on 24 June, which coincides with the winter solstice. For this fiesta men wear elaborate costumes and the celebration includes all-night music and dancing and ritual drinking for nearly a week. Until about the middle of the twentieth century a ritual battle between the men of different communities was held in front of the chapel of San Juan at the edge of Otavalo, and the blood of the wounded or dead was considered an offering to the Earth Mother. The fiesta of San Luis Obispo, called Coraza, was observed in Otavalo on 19 August until the 1940s, but by the early 1990s it was limited to the community of San Rafael. Various saints' days and local fiestas are celebrated in different communities throughout the year. Music, dancing by men and women, quantities of food, and the ritual consumption of alcohol are considered essential at all fiestas. The sponsorship of a fiesta by a couple has traditionally been a source of great prestige, although success in the textile business is now another route to high status.

ARTS. Besides textiles, traditional music is an important art form. Young Indians form folklore groups (*conjuntos*). Men play indigenous wind and percussion instruments as well as European stringed instruments, whereas both men and women sing traditional Quichua and some Spanish songs. Otavalo conjuntos play locally, compete in national music festivals, and sometimes record their music and perform abroad.

MEDICINE. Aboriginal and medieval Spanish beliefs have been syncretized in Otavalo culture. Illnesses are considered hot or cold and are believed to be caused by fright (*susto* or *espanto*), evil wind (*huyrashka* or *malviento*), evil spirits, or the entry of a foreign object. The town of Iluman is especially noted for its traditional healers. Male or female healers (*curanderos* or *brujos*) treat illnesses with herbal remedies or rituals to suck out the foreign body, absorb the evil wind, or drive out the evil spirits. Healers often travel to the Amazon or coastal lowlands to study with jungle healers. Local midwives (*patiras*) attend childbirth, and women stay in bed and observe a special diet for a month after giving birth, attended by a relative or a paid helper. Indians sometimes resort to Western-trained doctors in Otavalo, Quito, and Ibarra in addition to local healers.

DEATH AND AFTERLIFE. Syncretism is also evident in Otavalo concepts of death and the afterlife. The Otavalo believe in the Catholic heaven and hell, but many bury the dead with objects to help them in the afterlife. Baptized children are believed to go straight to heaven and become angels. On 2 November (the Day of the Dead) and on Holy Thursday, families carry offerings of wreaths, food, and drink to the cemetery. Food is shared with relatives and friends, given to beggars who say prayers for the dead, and left on graves because of the belief that the souls of the dead return for twenty-four hours and must be propitiated.

Bibliography

Meisch, Lynn (1987). *Otavalo: Weaving Costume and the Market.* Quito: Ediciones Libri Mundi.

Murra, John V. (1946). "The Historic Tribes of Ecuador." In *Handbook of South American Indians*, edited by Julian Steward. Vol. 2, *The Andean Civilizations*, 785–821. Washington, D.C.: Smithsonian Institution.

Parsons, Elsie Clews (1945). *Paguche, Canton of Otavalo, Province of Imbabura, Ecuador: A Study of Andean Indians.* Chicago: University of Chicago Press.

Salamon, Frank (1973). "Weavers of Otavalo." In *Peoples and Cultures of Native South America*, edited by Daniel R. Gross, 460–492. Garden City, N.Y.: Doubleday; Natural History Press.

—LYNN A. MEISCH

PÁEZ

Ethnonym: Paez

Orientation

IDENTIFICATION. The Páez live in southwestern highland Colombia and speak the Páez language. They call themselves "Nasa" to distinguish themselves from neighboring ethnic groups, including the Guambiano, the Guanacas, and the townspeople of mixed Spanish and indigenous or African descent.

LOCATION. The Páez heartland of Tierradentro in Colombia is comprised of some 1,300 square kilometers, located on the eastern slopes of Cordillera Central, at 2°30' N and 76° W. Páez settlements can also be found on the western slopes of the cordillera, and some Páez colonists have recently settled in the Caquetá lowlands to the southeast. Over 80 percent of Tierradentro lies above 2,000 meters in elevation, with one-third of the territory in the *páramo*, the high northern Andean swampy plateau that begins at 3,000 meters. This cold, mountainous country is crosscut by deep valleys, most notably those of the Páez, Moras, and Ullucos rivers, confining settlements to the mountain slopes overlooking these waterways. In Tierradentro, the rainy season extends from May to November, with the heaviest rains in May to June and October to November; on the western slopes of the Cordillera seasons are reversed.

DEMOGRAPHY. The 1972 census calculates a Páez population of only 35,724 persons, with 40

The Páez live in southewestern highland Columbia and speak the Páez language.

Páez

*Most Páez
settlements are
linked by unpaved
highways
constructed in the
1970s and 1980s;
individual
households are
connected to towns
by bridlepaths and
footpaths.*

percent living in Tierradentro. Nevertheless, most experts estimate that there are between 60,000 and 80,000 Páez. An excessively high rate of infant mortality on the western slopes of the Cordillera has resulted in a negative rate of population growth in some communities.

LINGUISTIC AFFILIATION. There is no agreement among scholars on the affiliation of the Páez language. Although it has been traditionally associated with the Chibchan Family, some linguists hesitate to classify Páez as a Chibchan language; it has been suggested that it is a linguistic isolate, together with neighboring Guambiano. According to some estimates, 75 percent of the Páez are bilingual in Páez and in Spanish, and 25 percent are monolingual Páez speakers. But in many communities more than half the population is composed of monolingual Spanish speakers. Páez is an unwritten language, and native linguists are beginning to develop an alphabet for purposes of bilingual education.

History and Cultural Relations

At the time of the 1537 Spanish invasion, the Páez were organized in a series of warring chiefdoms coexisting in Tierradentro with other ethnic communities, including the Guambiano, the Pijao, and the Yalcón, and linked with them through relations of warfare, trade, and marriage. During the first century of the Conquest, the aboriginal population of approximately 10,000 was halved through war and disease. The Spanish forced the Indians into centralized villages so that they would be more easily exploitable as a source of labor and tribute. Communities began to migrate to the western slopes of the cordillera, founding new towns. In the early eighteenth century native leaders validated their political authority and the territories under their dominion through the creation of reservations, or *resguardos*, legitimized through titles granted by the Spanish Crown. During the nineteenth century the communal landholdings of the resguardo were challenged by non-Indian landowners, by gatherers of quinine bark, by the ravages of civil war, and by national legislation that sought to privatize landownership throughout the country. At the turn of the century the Páez joined a political movement led by sharecropper Manuel Quintín Lame, who fought to reclaim lost lands and to free Indian sharecroppers from paying rent for the plots they tilled. Non-Páez sharecroppers evicted from their lands in neighboring regions colonized Tierradentro in the 1930s, arousing heightened militancy among the land-poor Páez. During the 1950s, Tierradentro was beset by violence and civil war, and some communities were forced to disperse.

Settlements

The Páez live in twenty-one settlements with populations ranging from 100 to 4,500 inhabitants. Although most communities are marked by towns, the majority of the population follows a dispersed mode of settlement, building adobe or wattle-and-daub houses with tile or thatch roofs, located near their fields on the mountain slopes. Some towns are composed of only ten to twenty sporadically inhabited houses, a school, a church, and a few tiny stores, whereas others are regional urban centers with large non-Indian populations and a governmental infrastructure. All of these towns are built in the traditional Spanish style, with a central plaza and, if there is more than one street, in a grid pattern. Most settlements are linked by unpaved highways constructed in the 1970s and 1980s; individual households are connected to towns by bridle- and footpaths.

Economy

SUBSISTENCE AND COMMERCIAL ACTIVITIES. The Páez are peasant farmers; they raise potatoes, coffee, or hemp (depending on the altitude at which they live) for sale and grow plantains, manioc, maize, or Andean tubers for domestic consumption. There is also some coca grown in the lower reaches of Tierradentro, consumed by the ever-shrinking number of older people who still chew it. Crops are generally cultivated with hand tools available on the regional market; commercial technology is used for processing hemp and coffee for sale to intermediaries. Crops raised for domestic consumption are generally grown on small plots, using slash-and-burn techniques; coffee, coca, and hemp are more permanent crops. In the nineteenth century quinine bark and laurel wax were gathered in many communities; most of the quinine forests were severely depleted at this time. Domestic animals include pigs, cattle, turkeys, and chickens.

TRADE AND LABOR. In most settlements a number of small stores stock commercial goods, but the population sells most of its produce and purchases goods at regional markets. Individual households are also connected by barter relationships with other communities, as well as with the neighboring Guambiano. Some of these relationships provide households with products grown in other ecological zones, as in the exchange of coca for potatoes. In other instances, exchange relationships link households on the two slopes of the cordillera, thus ensuring a steady supply of maize even in times of shortage between harvests. The Páez economy is also characterized by multiple modes of labor exchange that connect households in a web of reciprocal obligations; festive labor exchanges also characterize communal work projects. In some communities a considerable proportion of the population has migrated either temporarily or on a more long-term basis to nearby cities, as well as to coffee plantations to work as wage laborers.

LAND TENURE. Seventy percent of the land in the Páez region is resguardo territory, meaning that it is communal land granted in usufruct to community members and administered by an elected council, or *cabildo*. The vast majority of the Páez are resguardo members, although between 15 and 20 percent are landless; land-claim activities have done much to integrate the land-poor into the community economy, especially on the western slopes of the cordillera.

Kinship

KIN GROUPS AND DESCENT. The most basic social and economic unit of Páez society is the nuclear family. Families are related to one another through networks of exchange of labor and agricultural products, community political processes, and ritual. Members of each community have a limited number of surnames. Although some scholars have suggested that in the pre-Columbian era descent was patrilineal, among the contemporary Páez descent is bilateral, and this also appears to have been the case in colonial times. Exchange partners are recruited out of each individual's personal kindred.

KINSHIP TERMINOLOGY. Although Páez kinship terminology displays many of the characteristics of the Dravidian systems found in the Colombian northwestern Amazon, there is no indication that it was ever accompanied by bilateral cross-cousin marriage.

Sociopolitical Organization

SOCIAL AND POLITICAL ORGANIZATION. Páez sociopolitical organization is similar to that of other native highland populations in Colombia because it conforms to the dictates of national Indian legislation. The Páez live in resguardos, the boundaries and historical legitimacy of which are founded on eighteenth-century titles granted to native communities by the Spanish Crown. The

MARRIAGE AND FAMILY

Marriage

The Páez marry, for the most part, within their own communities or with individuals from neighboring resguardos; marriages seldom take place between Páez from distant communities. There are almost no instances of marriage with the neighboring Guambiano or with local non-Indians, and it is said that Juan Tama, the Páez culture hero and an eighteenth-century chief, ordered his people to marry only within their ethnic community. Marriages are performed by Roman Catholic priests based in the urban centers of each municipality. Residence is virineolocal: after a short period of residence with the husband's parents, a couple will build its own house, generally in the husband's community.

Domestic Unit

The domestic unit is usually composed of a nuclear family that shares a house and works the land communally. The average domestic unit has 5.5 members, although with an infant mortality rate of 36 percent in some communities, many more children are born to a family than survive to adulthood.

Inheritance

Inheritance of resguardo land is regulated by Colombian law. Use-rights are legitimized and passed from one individual to another through the mediation of the cabildo. The cabildo is also authorized to mediate disputes over the inheritance of movable property.

Socialization

Infants and children are raised by the members of the nuclear family. Children accompany parents in all activities. Into the 1930s women were confined at childbirth and first menstruation to a small hut and isolated there for a specified period of time, whereas young men were initiated at sacred lakes. Primary schools have been built in most communities, frequently under the supervision of the church, and most children are now receiving at least two to three years of formal education.

cabildo, elected annually, serves as an intermediary between the Colombian government and the native community, administering usufruct rights to communal lands. Eighteenth-century cabildos enjoyed considerably more authority than do their modern counterparts. Cabildo authorities receive no remuneration for their services, and all men are expected to serve at least once in their lifetime. Cabildo members carry staffs of office to identify themselves as community authorities, a Spanish symbol ubiquitous throughout the Andes. Parallel to the cabildo is the *capitán*, or captain, whose office is hereditary; the capitán organizes communal work projects to maintain bridle paths, churches, cemeteries, and other community holdings.

The Páez resguardo differs from its counterpart in other native communities in its ideological underpinnings. It is based on an oral history that centers around culture heroes and heroines and the chiefs (caciques), who are said to be of supernatural origin and to have saved the Páez from indigenous and European invaders, founded the resguardos in which the Páez live, and then disappeared into highland lakes. The mythic narratives that recount the exploits of the caciques are elaborations upon the Spanish resguardo titles, the contents of which provide a framework for recasting Conquest-era mythology.

SOCIAL CONTROL. The cabildo mediates disputes over land. Other areas of social control have been usurped by the non-Páez political authorities appointed by the Colombian government, although until the late twentieth century cabildos still used stocks and whipping to punish minor offenses. Colombian police, mayors, judges, and the army clash frequently with cabildos in struggles over the means of social control.

CONFLICT. Memories of valiant Páez warriors have led members of the dominant Colombian society to enlist Páez participation in the conflicts of the broader society. The Páez fought in the civil wars that raged throughout the nineteenth and into the twentieth centuries. Tierradentro has also been a stage for political organizing by the Indians themselves, who recently formed pan-Indian ethnic rights organizations to reclaim land and political autonomy. Because of the success of their agenda, the Páez have become targets in the political violence that characterizes contemporary Colombia.

Religion and Expressive Culture

The majority of the Páez were converted to Roman Catholicism by the eighteenth century, and a church stands in each Páez town. A significant number of people have been converted to evangelical Protestantism.

RELIGIOUS BELIEFS. Although the Páez have been Catholic for at least three centuries, the landscape of Tierradentro is populated with a variety of supernatural beings. Seventeenth-century Spanish chroniclers noted the importance among the Páez of highland lakes, sometimes the abode of Kpish, the Thunder. Colonial sources also mention hilltop oracles into which the sun rose and set. Pre-Columbian ceramics display images of snakes and serpents. Many of these ancient symbols are articulated today in the political arena. The mythic caciques are the children of the star, a wedding of the pre-Columbian symbol of divine heavenly bodies with the legal titles that legitimize post-Conquest communal landholdings. Those caciques not fished from the waters in which they float are transformed into serpents that eat villagers. The caciques defend their people with slings given to them by Kpish. They disappear into highland lakes from whence they have returned to defend the Páez against interlopers, just as Kpish sometimes does. In addition to these politically inspired beings, there are numerous water and mountain spirits that inhabit the landscape, inflicting harm on unwary passersby. Pre-Columbian burial sites are considered to be the abode of the *pijao*, dangerous spirits of the ancestors.

RELIGIOUS PRACTITIONERS AND MEDICINE. Just as myths of caciques and Kpish are political expressions of the belief system, shamans operationalize this wedding of myth and politics in everyday life. Called to their profession by the caciques, shamans perform divination and cure diseases caused by supernatural beings, assist the cabildo in ceremonially cleansing its staffs of office each year, and act as intermediaries between the supernatural and the human worlds. They are, moreover, active participants in the ethnic-rights movements through which land claims and cultural revitalization are coordinated.

CEREMONIES. Each Páez community celebrates a number of Catholic saints' days, as well as Christmas, Easter, and Corpus Christi; festival sponsors go to great expense to organize communal festivities. Each January cabildos used to withdraw to highland lakes to commune with their caciques and bless their staffs of office; in the late twentieth century this custom is being reintroduced by the ethnic-rights movement. Important ceremonies take place on such occasions as the completion of the construction of a house, when mythic history is reenacted by households.

DEATH AND AFTERLIFE. The Páez bury their dead in shaft-tombs, after having given them a Catholic wake. Shamans are charged with ceremonially cleansing the house of the impurities that come with death.

Bibliography

Findji, María Teresa, and José María Rojas (1985). *Territorio, economía y sociedad páez*. Cali: Universidad del Valle.

Hernández de Alba, Gregorio (1946). "The Highland Tribes of Southern Colombia." In *Handbook of South American Indians*, edited by Julian Steward. Vol. 2, *The Andean Civilizations*, 915–960. Bureau of American Ethnology Bulletin 143. Washington, D.C.: Smithsonian Institution.

Ortiz, Sutti (1973). *Uncertainties in Peasant Farming: A Colombian Case*. London: Athlone Press.

Rappaport, Joanne (1990). *The Politics of Memory: Native Historical Interpretation in the Colombian Andes*. Cambridge: Cambridge University Press.

Sevilla Casas, Elías (1986). *La pobreza de los excluidos: Economía y sobrevivencia en un resguardo indígena del Cauca-Colombia*. Quito: Ediciones ABYA-YALA.

—JOANNE RAPPAPORT

SARAMAKA

Ethnonyms: Saramacca, Saramaka Bush Negroes, Saramaka Maroons

Orientation

IDENTIFICATION. The Saramaka are one of six Maroon (or "Bush Negro") groups in Suriname. ("Maroon" derives from the Spanish *cimarrón*, itself derived from an Arawakan root; by the early 1500s it was used throughout the Americas to designate slaves who successfully escaped from slavery.)

LOCATION. The Republic of Suriname, formerly Dutch Guiana and independent since 1975, is located between 1° and 6° N and 54° and 58° W. The Saramaka live in the northern extension of the Amazonian forest along the upper Suriname River and its tributaries, the Gaánlío and the Pikílío, and—since the 1960s—along the lower Suriname River in villages constructed by the national government after the flooding of approximately half of tribal territory for a hydroelectric project.

DEMOGRAPHY. The 22,000 Saramaka are one minority within the multiethnic nation of Suriname, which includes approximately 37 percent Hindustanis or East Indians (descendants of contract laborers brought in after the abolition of slavery); 30 percent Creoles (descendants of Africans brought as slaves); 16 percent Javanese (descendants of contract workers brought during the early twentieth century from Indonesia); 3 percent Chinese, Levantines, and Europeans; 2 percent Amerindians; and 12 percent Maroons. Together with the other Maroons in Suriname and neighboring French Guiana—the Djuka (22,000), the Matawai, the Paramaka, the Aluku, and the Kwinti (who together number some 6,000)—the Saramaka constitute by far the world's largest surviving population of Afro-American Maroons.

LINGUISTIC AFFILIATION. The Saramaka, the Matawai, and the Kwinti (in central Suriname) speak variants of a creole language called Saramaccan, and the Djuka, the Paramaka, and the Aluku (in eastern Suriname) speak variants of another creole language, called Ndjuka. Both are closely related to Sranan-tongo (sometimes called Taki-taki), the creole of coastal Suriname. About 50 percent of the Saramaccan lexicon derives from various West and Central African languages, 20 percent from English (the language of the original colonists in Suriname), 20 percent from Portuguese (the language of the slave masters on many Suriname plantations), and the remaining 10 percent from Amerindian languages and Dutch. The grammar resembles that of the other (lexically different) Atlantic creoles and presumably derives from African models.

History and Cultural Relations

The ancestors of the Saramaka were among those Africans sold into slavery in the late seventeenth and early eighteenth centuries to work Suriname's sugar, timber, and coffee plantations. Coming from a variety of African peoples speaking many different languages, they escaped into the dense rain forest—individually, in small groups, and sometimes in great collective rebellions—where for nearly 100 years they fought a war of liberation. In 1762, a full century before the general emancipation of slaves in Suriname, they won their freedom and signed a treaty with the Dutch crown. Like the other Suriname Maroons, they lived almost as states-within-a-state until the mid-twentieth century, when the pace of outside encroachments increased. During the late 1980s a civil war between Maroons and the military government of Suriname caused considerable hardship to the Saramaka and other Maroons; by mid-1989

FAST WATER

Two Saramaka men paddle a canoe through rapids on a river in Suriname.
(Adam Woolfitt/Corbis)

access to the outside world had become severely restricted for many Saramaka in their homeland.

Settlements

Traditional villages, which average 100 to 200 residents, consist of a core of matrilineal kin plus some wives and children of lineage men. Always located near a river, they are an irregular arrangement of small houses, open-sided structures, domesticated trees, an occasional chicken house, various shrines, and scattered patches of bushes. (The so-called transmigration villages, built to house the 6,000 Saramaka displaced by the hydroelectric project, range up to 2,000 people and are laid out in a grid pattern.) Horticultural camps, which include permanent houses and shrines, are located several hours by canoe from each village, and are exploited by small matrilineal groups of women. Many women have a house in their own village, another in their horticultural camp, and a third in their husband's village. Co-wives live in separate houses. Men divide their time among three or four houses, built at various times for themselves and for their wives. Saramaka houses are barely wide enough to tie a hammock and not much longer from front to back; with walls of planks and woven palm fronds and roofs of thatch or, increasingly, of corrugated iron, they are windowless but often have elaborately carved facades.

Economy

SUBSISTENCE AND COMMERCIAL ACTIVITIES. The economy is based on full exploitation of the forest environment and on periodic work trips by men to the coast to bring back Western goods. For subsistence, the Saramaka depend on shifting (swidden) horticulture, hunting, and fishing, supplemented by wild forest products and a few key imports such as salt. Gardens are planted most heavily in dry (hillside) rice, but include many other crops, among them cassava, taro, okra, maize, plantains, bananas, sugarcane, and peanuts. Villages have domesticated trees such as coconut, orange, breadfruit, papaya, and calabash. Garden produce, game, and fish are shared among kin. There are no markets.

INDUSTRIAL ARTS. The Saramaka produce the great bulk of their material culture. All men build houses and canoes and carve a wide range of wooden objects for domestic use, such as stools, paddles, winnowing trays, cooking utensils, and combs. All women sew and embroider clothing and carve calabash bowls. Some men also produce baskets, and some women make pottery.

TRADE. Men devote a large portion of their adult years to earning money in coastal Suriname or French Guiana to provide the Western goods considered essential to life in their home villages, such as shotguns and powder, tools, pots, cloth, hammocks, soap, kerosene, and rum. Since the 1960s small stores have sprung up in many villages, and outboard motors, transistor radios, and tape recorders have also become common.

DIVISION OF LABOR. Once the men have cleared and burned the fields, horticulture is mainly women's work. Hunting, with shotguns, is the responsibility of men, who do most of the fishing as well. Wage labor outside the tribal territory is a male prerogative.

LAND TENURE. Land is owned by matrilineal clans, based on claims staked out in the early eighteenth century as the original Maroons fled southward to freedom. Hunting and gathering rights belong to clan members collectively. Within the clan, temporary rights to land use for farming are negotiated by village headmen. The establishment of transmigration villages has led to land shortages in certain regions.

Kinship

KIN GROUPS AND DESCENT. Saramaka society is firmly based on matrilineal principles. A clan (*lö*)—often several thousand individuals—consists of the matrilineal descendants of an original band of escaped slaves. It is subdivided into lineages (*bêè*)—usually 50 to 150 people—descended from a more recent ancestress. Several lineages from a single clan constitute the core of every village.

KINSHIP TERMINOLOGY. In keeping with matrilineal ideology, a strongly generational pattern is broken by bifurcate merging of males. Joking relationships prevail between consanguineal and affinal kin of alternate generations.

Marriage and Family

MARRIAGE. The application of complex marriage prohibitions (including bêè exogamy) and preferences is negotiated through divination. Demographic imbalance owing to labor migration permits widespread polygyny. Although cowives hold equal status, relations between them are expected to be adversarial. Marriages tend to be brittle; men average seven wives and women four husbands during their lifetime. The Saramaka treat marriage as an ongoing courtship, with frequent exchanges of gifts such as men's woodcarving and women's decorative sewing. Although many women live primarily in their husband's village, men never spend more than a few days at a time in the matrilineal (home) village of a wife.

DOMESTIC UNIT. Each house belongs to an individual man or woman, but most social interaction occurs outdoors. The men in each cluster of several houses, whether bêè members or temporary visitors, eat meals together. The women of these same clusters, whether bêè members or resident wives of bêè men, spend a great deal of time in each others' company, often farming together as well.

INHERITANCE. Matrilineal principles, mediated by divination, determine the inheritance of material and spiritual possessions as well as political offices. Before death, however, men often pass on specialized ritual knowledge (and occasionally a shotgun) to a son.

SOCIALIZATION. Each child, after spending its first several years with its mother, is raised by an individual man or woman (not a couple) designated by the bêè, girls normally by women, boys by men. Although children spend most of their time with matrilineal kin, father-child relations are warm and strong. Gender identity is established early, with children taking on responsibility for sex-typed adult tasks as soon as they are physically able. Girls often marry by age 15, whereas boys are more often in their twenties when they take their first wife. Protestant missionary schools have existed in some villages since the eighteenth century; such elementary schools came to most villages only in the 1960s. Schools ceased to function completely during the Suriname civil war of the late 1980s.

Sociopolitical Organization

The Saramaka, like the other Maroon groups, maintain considerable political autonomy within the Republic of Suriname.

SOCIAL ORGANIZATION. Saramaka society is strongly egalitarian, with kinship vertebrating social organization. No social or occupational classes are distinguished. Elders are accorded special respect and ancestors are consulted, through divination, on a daily basis.

POLITICAL ORGANIZATION. The Saramaka have a government-approved paramount chief (*gaamá*), a series of headmen (*kabitêni*), and assistant headmen (*basiá*). Traditionally, the role of these officials in political and social control was exercised in a context replete with oracles, spirit possession, and other forms of divination, but the national government is intervening more frequently in Saramaka affairs (and paying political officials nominal salaries), and the sacred base of these officials' power is gradually being eroded. These political offices are the property of clans (*lö*). Political activity is strongly dominated by men.

SOCIAL CONTROL. Council meetings (*kuútu*) and divination sessions provide complementary arenas for the resolution of social problems.

Each Saramaka child, after spending its first several years with its mother, is raised by an individual man or woman (not a couple).

*A large proportion of
Saramaka have
some kind of
specialized ritual
expertise for which
they are paid in
cloth or rum.*

Palavers may involve the men of a lineage, a village, or all Saramaka and treat problems ranging from marriage or fosterage conflicts to land disputes, political succession, or major crimes. These same problems, in addition to illness and other kinds of misfortune, are routinely examined through various kinds of divination as well. In all cases, consensus is found through negotiation, often with a strong role being played by gods and ancestors. Guilty parties are usually required to pay for their misdeeds with material offerings to the lineage of the offended person. In the eighteenth century people found guilty of witchcraft were sometimes burned at the stake. Today, men caught in flagrante delicto with the wife of another man are either beaten by the woman's kinsmen or made to pay them a fine.

CONFLICT.   Aside from adultery disputes, which sometimes mobilize a full canoe-load of men seeking revenge in a public fistfight, intra-Saramaka conflict rarely surpasses the level of personal relations. The civil war that began in 1986, pitting Maroons against Suriname's army, brought major changes to the villages of the interior. Members of the "Jungle Commando" rebel army, almost all Djuka and Saramaka, learned to use automatic weapons and became accustomed to a state of war and plunder. Their reintegration into Saramaka (and Djuka) society remains problematic.

Religion and Expressive Culture

The Western category "religion" encompasses every aspect of Saramaka life. Such decisions as where to clear a garden or build a house, whether to undertake a trip, or how to deal with theft or adultery are made in consultation with village deities, ancestors, forest spirits, and snake gods. The means of communication with these powers vary from spirit possession and the consultation of oracle-bundles to the interpretation of dreams. Gods and spirits, which are a constant presence in daily life, are also honored through frequent prayers, libations, feasts, and dances. The rituals surrounding birth, death, and other life crises are extensive, as are those relating to more mundane activities, from hunting a tapir to planting a rice field. Today about 20 percent of Saramaka are nominal Christians—mainly Moravian, but some Roman Catholic and, increasingly, evangelicals of one or another kind.

RELIGIOUS BELIEFS.   The Saramaka world is populated by a wide range of supernatural beings, from localized forest spirits and gods that reside in the bodies of snakes, vultures, jaguars, and other animals to ancestors, river gods, and warrior spirits. Within these categories, each supernatural being is named, individualized, and given specific relationships to living people. Intimately involved in the ongoing events of daily life, these beings communicate to humans mainly through divination and spirit possession. *Kúnus* are the avenging spirits of people or gods who were wronged during their lifetime and who pledge themselves to eternally tormenting the matrilineal descendants and close matrilineal kinsmen of their offender. Much of Saramaka ritual life is devoted to their appeasement. The Saramaka believe that all evil originates in human action: not only does each misfortune, illness, or death stem from a specific past misdeed, but every offense, whether against people or gods, has eventual consequences. The ignoble acts of the dead intrude daily on the lives of the living; any illness or misfortune calls for divination, which quickly reveals the specific past act that caused it. Rites are then performed in which the ancestors speak, the gods dance, and the world is once again made right.

RELIGIOUS PRACTITIONERS.   Major village- and clan-owned shrines that serve large numbers of clients, the various categories of possession gods, and various kinds of minor divination are the preserve of individual specialists who supervise rites and pass on their knowledge before death. A large proportion of Saramaka have some kind of specialized ritual expertise, which they occasionally exercise, and for which they are paid in cloth or rum.

CEREMONIES.   Saramaka ceremonial life is not calendrically determined but rather regulated by the occurrence of misfortune, interpreted through divination. The most important ceremonies include those surrounding funerals and the appeasement of ancestors, public curing rites, rituals in honor of kúnus (in particular snake gods and forest spirits), and the installation of political officials.

ARTS.   Saramaka life is permeated with aesthetic concerns, and activities from planting a garden to verbal repartee are judged in aesthetic terms. All men are woodcarvers and some are adept at the related art of engraving the exterior surfaces of calabash containers. Women are responsible for the decorative sewing on clothes and the carving of calabash bowls. Body arts include hairstyling and complex cicatrizations. The arts of performance—singing, dance, drumming, tale telling—are widespread and highly appreciated.

MEDICINE. Every case of illness is believed to have a specific cause that can be determined only through divination. The causes revealed vary from a lineage kúna to sorcery, from a broken taboo to an ancestor's displeasure. Once the cause is known, rites are carried out to appease the offended god or ancestor (or otherwise right the social imbalance). Since the 1960s, Western mission clinics and hospitals have been used by most Saramaka as a supplement to their own healing practices.

DEATH AND AFTERLIFE. The dead play an active role in the lives of the living. Ancestor shrines—several to a village—are the site of frequent prayers and libations, as the dead are consulted about ongoing village problems. A death occasions a series of complex rituals that lasts about a year, culminating in the final passage of the deceased to the status of ancestor. The initial rites, which are carried out over a period of one week to three months depending on the importance of the deceased, end with the burial of the corpse in an elaborately constructed coffin filled with personal belongings. These rites include divination with the coffin (to consult the spirit of the deceased) by carrying it on the heads of two men, feasts for the ancestors, all-night drum/song/dance performances, and the telling of folktales. Some months later, a "second funeral" is conducted to mark the end of the mourning period and to chase the ghost of the deceased from the village forever. These rites involve the largest public gatherings in Saramaka and also include all-night drum/song/dance performances. At their conclusion, the deceased has passed out of the realm of the living into that of the ancestors.

Bibliography

Herskovits, Melville J., and Frances S. Herskovits (1934). *Rebel Destiny: Among the Bush Negroes of Dutch Guiana.* New York and London: McGraw-Hill.

Price, Richard (1975). *Saramaka Social Structure: Analysis of a Maroon Society in Surinam.* Río Piedras, P.R.: Institute of Caribbean Studies.

Price, Richard (1983). *First-Time: The Historical Vision of an Afro-American People.* Baltimore and London: Johns Hopkins University Press.

Price, Sally (1984). *Co-Wives and Calabashes.* Ann Arbor: University of Michigan Press.

Price, Sally, and Richard Price (1980). *Afro-American Arts of the Suriname Rain Forest.* Berkeley and Los Angeles: University of California Press.

—RICHARD PRICE AND SALLY PRICE

SHIPIBO

Ethnonyms: Chama, Chipeo, Conibo, Cunibo, Pisquibo, Setebo, Shipiwo, Sipibo, Ssipipo, Xipibo

Orientation

IDENTIFICATION. The Shipibo are a South American Indian group in Peru. The name "Shipibo" is derived from the Shipibo word *shipi*, their name for a marmoset (*Cebuella pygmaea*). Hence, they have been referred to as the "little monkey people."

LOCATION. The Shipibo occupy the central Río Ucayali region of eastern Peru and its major western tributaries from Bolognesi to Contamana, with Pucallpa in its geographical center. Among the most significant of these rivers are the Sheshea, Pachitea, Tamayo, Aguaytía, Pisqui, and Cushabatay.

DEMOGRAPHY. Population reports for the Shipibo vary, with estimates as high as 20,000 to 30,000. A census in 1974 reported the existence of 9,000 Shipibo and another 6,000 Conibo.

LINGUISTIC AFFILIATION. The Shipibo language belongs to the Panoan Family. Dialectic differences exist between those who live along the Río Ucayali and others who occupy its tributaries, such as the Pisqui.

History and Cultural Relations

Archaeological evidence suggests that the origins of Shipibo culture lie in the Cumancaya tradition of the ninth century A.D., meaning that Shipibo culture, or something similar to it, has existed in the region for over 1,000 years. There are indications (the presence of head binding, panpipes, raised beds, and fire fans) that some Shipibo may have experienced contact with the Inca. Contact with Westerners began in the seventeenth century, when Franciscan missionaries entered the region. During this time, the Shipibo and Tupí-speaking Cocama/Cocamilla tribes were resettled in neighboring missionary-created villages. Because of their contact with Spanish colonists and their strategic location on the Río Ucayali, the Shipibo had access to guns and, in the nineteenth century, raided other Panoan and Arawakan tribes who lived nearby along "back-woods" interfluves. Shipibo were employed as wage laborers during the rubber boom of the nineteenth century and as *peones* (laborers) in agriculture and timber extraction for mestizo *patrones* (bosses) during this century. Other contacts with Whites have come from physicians and nurses, Protestant missionaries,

The Shipibo are known worldwide for the complicated geometrical motifs with which they decorate objects.

and representatives of the Peruvian government. Today, the Shipibo range from the well-accultur-ated, such as those living near the frontier city of Pucallpa, to moderately acculturated groups who reside in remote areas downriver.

Settlements

In the past the Shipibo lived in dispersed extended-family homesteads along rivers. Today they reside in villages with houses distributed along one side of a street, opposite *cocinas* (kitchens) and roughly parallel to the water. Villages are usually located on a beach alongside a river or a large ox-bow (i.e., crescent-shaped) lake. Some small households have their own cocina, whereas larger extended or polygynous family households may share a cocina, with each married woman maintaining her own earthen hearth. Today there are about 120 Shipibo settlements ranging in size from 100 to 500 inhabitants. Houses and cocinas are constructed entirely of materials extracted from the surrounding forest. Houses have raised floors of split palm wood and palm-thatched roofs; some are enclosed by bamboo walls. Cocinas are constructed of the same materials, but without elevated floors or walls.

Economy

SUBSISTENCE AND COMMERCIAL ACTIVI-TIES. The Shipibo practice slash-and-burn agriculture and subsist primarily on plantains and bananas, together with some sweet manioc, potatoes, and maize. These crops are supplemented with fish, game, and other wild foods collected from the forest. Now that some Shipibo are producing rice to sell in regional markets, they are hunting and fishing less. Moreover, greater participation in a cash economy seems to be affecting traditional exchange relationships between kinsmen. For example, whereas in the past it was a man's responsibility "to serve" his parents-in-law by supplying food and labor, men are now refusing to lend their fathers-in-law money.

INDUSTRIAL ARTS. The Shipibo are known worldwide for the complicated geometrical motifs with which they decorate objects. Women make ceramics, cotton textiles, baskets, and bead work, both for personal use and for sale to tourists. Men still manufacture wooden articles such as canoes and paddles, tobacco pipes, cooking utensils, animal figures, and clubs, although clubs are made only for sale to tourists.

TRADE. Historically, Shipibo traded with each other for items that were not locally available. For example, Shipibo on the Pisqui traded salt, vines for making houses and baskets, palm fiber for bow strings, whetstones, baskets, and fish; in exchange they received white earthen pigments used to decorate ceramics and wild cane used for arrow shafts, brought by Ucayali Shipibo. This activity has been discontinued; trade is now restricted to exchanges of food among matrilineal kin living in close proximity within the village.

DIVISION OF LABOR. Both men and women traditionally performed all aspects of agricultural work with the exception that men did the arduous task of felling trees. Both men and women fish and collect wild foods, although the latter is more often done by women. Hunting with shotgun or bow and arrow is strictly men's work. Women also cook, care for children, perform most of the housework, and manufacture ceramics, textiles, and bead work. Men build houses, make canoes, manufacture weapons, and carve wooden artifacts but more typically work as wage laborers and may be away from their families for weeks at a time.

LAND TENURE. Others' claims to land are ascertained before one establishes a garden on fallow garden land. As long as a garden is still producing crops, a man must ask permission of its owner before he can clear it. Permission to use old fallow garden land is not necessary, however. Men often mark valuable trees on their trips through the forest, and another must ask permission from its "owner" to cut and sell a tree that has been marked. In principle, all have equal access to hunting and fishing grounds, but certain men are recognized as being more knowledgeable than others about the animals in particular regions of the forest. Also, the owner of fish poison can regulate the number of participants on fish-poisoning expeditions by limiting the number of invitations he extends to others. In the 1970s Shipibo communities petitioned the Peruvian government for titles to land, but few titles have actually been acquired.

Kinship

KIN GROUPS AND DESCENT. The Shipibo term for "people" is *jonibo*, and they divide their social world among *noa jonibo* (we people) and *nahua jonibo* (less than people). *Rarëbo* includes kin, whereas *huëtsabo* are "others (like us)"—Shipibo who live a long distance away. Although some have claimed the possible earlier existence of Shipibo clans, there currently exists no evidence to support the existence of any descent or corporate groups based on relation to a common ancestor, fictive or real.

KINSHIP TERMINOLOGY. Shipibo kinship terminology has been classified as being Hawaiian in one's own generation and Sudanese in the first ascending and descending generations. No distinction of others in one's own generation is made other than whether the sex of the other is the same or different (i.e., Hawaiian cousin terms). Separate reference terms are used for mother, father, and their siblings. Great-great grandparents/grandchildren are referred to by the same terms as great-grandparents/grandchildren.

Marriage and Family

MARRIAGE. Rules stipulate that one should not marry descendants of grandparents, who are distinguished as *kikín rárëbo* (true family) rather than *ochó rárëbo* (distant family). In the past Shipibo marriages were arranged by both sets of parents. The future bride was expected to deliver beverages to her future husband's family each day, and he to contribute fish and game to her family and sleep with her each night. This trial period usually lasted six to twelve months, after which time the two were married. Although young men and women seem to enjoy more freedom to select their own mates, marriage has never had an elaborate ceremony; a man, or his mother, merely moves his mosquito net to the house of his wife's mother and he assumes residence there. Marriages dissolve just as unceremoniously when men simply leave their wives and return to their own families.

Men traditionally tended to marry between the ages of 19 and 25, whereas women usually married when 14 to 16 years of age, after completing the female initiation ritual. Girls are no longer initiated, and there is a trend for men to marry at a younger age (15 to 20 years); thus they are marrying women closer to their own age. Polygynous marriages are not as common as they once were, possibly because of the influences of missionaries and resident government officials. There is also some evidence of levirate and sororate in the past. Marriage is most common among people living in villages located along the same river.

DOMESTIC UNIT. In the past, large extended families lived together in the same house. In the early 1980s, smaller extended families were becoming more common, and some men were establishing nuclear-family households, albeit in the vicinity of their wife's family.

INHERITANCE. Men and women each "own" those things that they tend to use most. In the past, when a man or woman died, he or she was buried under his or her house and then the house was set afire. All articles that belonged to the deceased were disposed of, usually by burning them or immersing them in the river. This was done so that relatives would not suffer the heartbreak of thinking of the deceased one so often. Now that adults accumulate money and objects purchased with it, items are left to one's spouse and children, which, according to some informants, has caused disputes. These days, the scarcity of building materials prevents many from burning the deceased's house, and some corpses are even buried in cemeteries.

SOCIALIZATION. Children are socialized at home and in their bilingual school. Infants are always in the company of their mother or matrilineal kin, whereas fathers have less direct physical contact with their children. By Western standards, parents tend to raise their children in a permissive fashion. Social codes of behavior, particularly between certain classes of kin, are well recognized among the Shipibo—a child learns these early in his or her life. Corporal punishment is rarely administered; when it is, it is usually by those who have spent more time with mestizos and Whites. Most Shipibo place a high value on formal education, and at about age 5 children begin school.

Sociopolitical Organization

SOCIAL ORGANIZATION. Traditionally, Shipibo society was egalitarian, with the male heads of the largest families exercising the most influence. The men with the highest status were the ones with the most wives or those who were respected for their oratorical skills, knowledge of herbal medicines, or hunting and fishing abilities. Although men are more active in political matters, women often exercise their will in private by influencing the opinions of their fathers and husbands. The Peruvian government has imposed a political structure on the Shipibo, but these elected positions carry little authority. These tend to be filled by younger men who speak Spanish, and this has begun to undermine the status and influence traditionally wielded by elders.

POLITICAL ORGANIZATION. Communities are linked primarily by kinship and marriage, although the establishment of bilingual schools in many communities has linked them to administrative centers. Some attempts have been made to organize communities at a tribal level by creating artisan guilds and a Shipibo federation. Distance and lack of communication between villages, however, have made these organizations largely ineffective.

SOCIAL CONTROL. Rules for proper conduct between classes of kin are recognized. One

During a trial period, a future bride was expected to deliver beverages to her future husband's family each day.

Shipibo

RELIGION AND EXPRESSIVE CULTURE

In the past, when a Shipibo died, he or she was buried under his or her house and then the house was set afire.

♦ **ayahuasca**
A hallucinogenic beverage prepared from the stem of the vine Banisteriopsis caapi.

such relationship that demands extreme respect is that between a man and his in-laws. Tempers sometimes flare but kin usually intervene before disputes escalate to violence. Acts of infidelity and wife abuse occur; however, such behavior is met with social disapproval and the offender comes to know the power of public censorship. In the past grievances between men were often aired in public drinking ceremonies and settled with duels. Although these rarely resulted in fatal injury, the use of knives and clubs has all but disappeared under the influence of missionaries and government officials. Sometimes those who become ill after social misconduct are thought to have become the targets of male or female witches acting on behalf of the offended person.

CONFLICT. Wars and raids on neighboring Cashibo and Shipibo for wives and slaves were common, and placenames often refer to great battles that were fought there. First contacts with soldiers and Catholic missionaries created tensions that resulted in numerous attacks on missions in the seventeenth century, sometimes after the Shipibo formed alliances with other groups like the Cocama. After several massacres, missionaries ceased activities in the area until the mid-eighteenth century when, once again, Shipibo insurrection resulted in the destruction of a mission. It was not until almost the beginning of the nineteenth century that Catholic missionaries were able to establish a permanent presence; Protestant missionaries entered the region around 1930.

Religion and Expressive Culture

RELIGIOUS BELIEFS. It is difficult to separate traditional from Christian-influenced beliefs among the Shipibo; there is a blend of animism with Christianity. Moreover, accounts of religious concepts are often vague and vary among villages. Generally, it is believed that spirits and "gods" reside in the sky, and there is a stairway that joins the sky and earth along which spirits pass. Under the influence of ayahuasca, a *vegetalista* (herbalist) may climb this stairway and enter the spirit world. The Shipibo refer to supernatural beings as *yoshinbo*. These are spirits that reside in animals and plants and against which one must constantly be on guard. Those who have undergone religious instruction at nearby missions have adopted Christianity and its supernaturals.

RELIGIOUS PRACTITIONERS. Vegetalistas traditionally possessed the most esoteric knowledge about the spirit world and the use of medicinal plants. To become a vegetalista, a man served an apprenticeship and observed strict dietary prohibitions. Some men who have worked for Protestant missionaries have established churches in their communities and function as self-ordained pastors.

CEREMONIES. In the past, the *ani shrëati* (big drinking) was the most important ceremony, a time when young women were initiated into society and men settled disputes. This ceremony often lasted for three or four days and involved much drinking, fighting, dancing, and singing. It has all but disappeared and has been replaced by national fiestas.

ARTS. The Shipibo are known for their intricate rectilinear designs on pottery, clothes, paddles, and the human body. Old men and women still tell vivid stories about the discovery of fire and crops and of legendary "great" floods. Traditional line and circle dances are gradually being replaced by more modern forms. Many old men and women are known for their songs, and the power of a vegetalista is, in part, determined by the "force" of his chants. Flutes and drums are still played during fiestas, but these, too, are gradually being replaced by modern recorded music.

MEDICINE. According to the Shipibo, there are two categories of disease—those of the "flesh" and others caused by yoshinbo. Although Western medicines are recognized as being effective for treating the former, one seeks the curing powers of a vegetalista to treat the latter. To effect his cure, a vegetalista must travel to the spirit world, where he can divine the cause of his patient's illness. The vegetalista's techniques include chanting, blowing tobacco smoke, and massaging. It is believed that one becomes sick when a foreign object has entered the body; by applying the above treatments, the object can be moved to an appendage where the vegetalista can "suck it out" and throw it away.

DEATH AND AFTERLIFE. After one dies, his or her soul passes into a spirit world, but this spirit may frequent a family's house for some time afterward. If a spirit is thought to be malignant, one may seek the assistance of a vegetalista to drive it away.

Bibliography

Behrens, Clifford A. (1989). *Shipibo Time Allocation.* Cross-Cultural Studies in Time Allocation, vol. 4. New Haven: Human Relations Area Files.

Bergman, Roland (1980). *Amazon Economics: The Simplicity of Shipibo Indian Wealth.* Syracuse, N.Y.: Dellplain Latin American Studies.

Roe, Peter G. (1982). *The Cosmic Zygote: Cosmology in the Amazon Basin.* New Brunswick, N.J.: Rutgers University Press.

—CLIFFORD A. BEHRENS

WARAO

Ethnonyms: Ciawani, Guaraúnos, Tiuitiuas, Waraweete

Orientation

IDENTIFICATION. The Warao Indians, fishermen and incipient agriculturists, inhabit the labyrinthine arms of the Orinoco Delta of northeastern Venezuela and adjacent areas. "Warao" is an autodenomination meaning "lowland people" or "marshland people" from *waha,* "lowland," and *arao,* "inhabitant people." All non-Warao, whatever their origin, are *hotarao,* "dryland people," from *hota,* "high" or "dryland," and arao. "Guaraúno" is a Hispanicized version of the ethnonym, and "Tiuitiua" is the name given the Warao by the Otomac Indians, referring to a type of sandpiper, *waharomu* (*Tringa flavipes*), with which the Warao identified mythologically. Sir Walter Raleigh, the sixteenth-century English explorer, refers to the Tiuitiuas as divided into "Ciawani" and "Waraweete" ("real Warao").

LOCATION. Politically, the Orinoco Delta forms part of the Venezuelan Federal Territory of Delta Amacuro (Territoria Federal Delta Amacuro), which spreads over 40,200 square kilometers and is located between 7°38′ and 10°3′ N and 59°48′ and 62°30′ W. The area is at the northern tip of the vast lands between the Orinoco and Amazon rivers, called in colonial times the "Island of Guayana." More than half of the Warao population lives in a coastal strip of mangrove and *moriche*-palm (*Mauritia flexuosa*) swamps, about 80 kilometers deep, along some 200 kilometers of seashore between the Río Marosa (Mariusa) of the central delta and the Río Amacuro (Amakoro) south of the Río Grande del Orinoco. The warm and humid climate of the delta produces a mean annual temperature of 26° C, but early mornings can be chilly. The area is under the influence of twice-daily tides, which during the dry season between January and April bring brackish water upriver. After the sudden onset of the rainy season around May, the annual flooding of the Orinoco reaches a peak in August and September and fills the adjacent Gulf of Paria up to the island of Trinidad with fresh water to such an extent that it made Columbus suspect he had happened on a great continent when he touched the Spanish Main for the first time on his third voyage in August of 1498.

DEMOGRAPHY. Today the total Warao population is estimated at 22,000, of which, according to the Venezuelan indigenous census of 1982, 19,573 live in Venezuela, and 17,654 in the Territorio Federal Delta Amacuro, where they constitute about one-third of the total population. The Warao form the second-largest indigenous group in the country after the Guajiro (Wayuu). Although indigenous peoples make up less than 1 percent of the country's estimated 17,000,000 population, they inhabit over one-third of its surface, mainly in strategic border areas. After holding at an estimated 8,000 during colonial times and into the twentieth century, the Warao population has about tripled, possibly because of improved health service regarding infectious and gastrointestinal illnesses; but new endemic diseases such as tuberculosis are bringing this growth to an end.

LINGUISTIC AFFILIATION. All Warao speak mutually intelligible variants of the same language. Warao has traditionally been considered an isolate, without affiliation with one of the great South American language families such as Tupí, Carib, or Arawak. Nevertheless, some scholars suggest a possible connection of Warao, together with Yanomaman and Barían, to the Chibcha Language Family, whose speakers live mainly in the Colombian Andes. More likely, all these unaffiliated languages belong to a common substratum and are only tenuously related. Originally an unwritten language, Warao today is spelled in a variety of ways, all in the Roman alphabet.

Settlements

Traditional villages range in population from an extended household of 25 to clusters of household groups with 250 persons. Acculturated Indians may live in isolated homesteads around sawmills and palmetto factories. Until the early decades of the twentieth century, most settlements were located in the moriche-palm groves, where the Warao lived in small, 3-by-3-meter huts thatched with moriche leaves and with floors of stems from the same palm, but after the introduction of ocumo, many groups moved to the open river shores, where most villages are now located. These consist of clusters of 8-by-12-meter houses with a number of smaller kitchens and, in traditional settlements, menstruation huts, dancing

The Warao Indians inhabit the labyrinthine arms of the Orinoco Delta of northeastern Venezuala.

HISTORY AND CULTURAL RELATIONS

According to Warao oral tradition, relations with the neighboring Lokono, an Arawak-speaking population, were peaceful, but not so with the Carib-speaking Cariña ("red faces"), or Musimotuma, who are still feared today. From the beginning of colonial times the Río Orinoco (Wirinoko in Warao) was the main entrance for explorers, missionaries, and scientists to the lands of El Dorado, which supposedly lay farther upriver. Located at the limits of the Spanish colonial empire, the Warao worked for and traded with the Spanish and the neighboring Dutch alike, but from a secure home base in the swampy interior of the deltaic islands, where they lived by exploiting the starchy pith of the moriche palm, a relative of the *Metroxilon* or sago palm of Oceania. Until the decline of the rubber boom earlier in this century, the Warao suffered greatly, serving as forced laborers. After the

agreement in 1922 between the Capuchin order and the Venezuelan government, Spanish missionaries arrived in the Orinoco Delta and in 1925 established the mission of Divina Pastora de Araguaimujo, the first organized effort to permanently penetrate the Warao heartland. In the meantime, migratory Warao from the Río Sakobano with family ties among the Lonoko south of the Río Grande had imported from there a new cultigen suitable for growing in the swampy delta environment, the tarolike "Chinese" *ocumo* or *ure* (*Colocasia* sp.). This freed the Warao from their dependence on palm starch and the swamps and allowed them to establish themselves in the open river arms of the delta. It also made them available as a cheap labor pool for newly established sawmills and palmetto factories as well as commercial rice-growing operations.

floors, and two-story ritual structures. Warao homes there are composed of two independent sections: the floor, built like footbridges on stilts above the highest tide with a covering of *manaca*-palm trunks and *anare ahorohoro* (*Euterpe* sp.) and the saddle roof thatched with *temiche*-palm leaves (*Manicaria saccifera*).

Economy

SUBSISTENCE AND COMMERCIAL ACTIVITIES. Traditional Warao subsistence is based on fishing and, to a lesser extent, on hunting, supplemented by gathering fruits, larvae, and crustaceans in a marked yearly cycle. Since the substitution of ocumo for palm starch as a staple, gathering activities have diminished and been supplanted by wage labor in lumbering and fishing. Incipient agriculture other than ocumo includes some sugarcane, bananas, and, where suitable soil is available, bitter manioc and maize. There is also some commercial rice growing.

TRADE. The allocation of the domestic product is affected by delayed reciprocity and prestations inside local groups, whereas trade with outsiders is based on direct exchange, either through barter or the occasional use of money. Items sold by the Warao include hammocks made of moriche-palm fiber and other handicraft objects, as well as hunting dogs and pets such as parrots and macaws. Acquisitions consist mainly of metal tools such as axes and machetes, fish hooks, and iron pots, as well as some clothing.

DIVISION OF LABOR. There are no full-time specialists, although some persons are more proficient in a craft than others. Among the men, the expert builder of canoes, *moyotu*, is an important personage with considerable knowledge of rituals and oral tradition. Among the female population, the weaving of hammocks is practiced from childhood; this activity is a demonstration of how an old and sometimes blind woman can continue to perform useful labor. Along with the expert weaver of basketry, male or female according to area, such a man or woman is known as *uwasi*, with important implications for that person's afterlife. There is a whole range of religious practitioners with special knowledge. Other than the "guardian of the rains" (*naharima*) and the owners of specific ritual songs and musical instruments, there are three shamanic specialists who, according to their age, carry a lighter work load. Work is assigned on the basis of age and sex, girls aiding their mothers from an early age in the important gathering activities that contribute heavily to food production and female prestige. With the introduction of wage labor, female status has declined, as has the role of religious practitioners.

Kinship

KIN GROUPS. Kin groups as such play a role only as expressed in the domestic unit built around a group of real or classificatory sisters. The principal woman, *hanoko orotu* or "owner of the house," enjoys considerable prestige, and the important daily decisions are made by the core group of sisters and classificatory sisters. The work group is commanded by the old father-in-law, *arahi*, through the husband of his oldest daughter, *dawa awahabara*, who serves as foreman over the inmarrying husbands, *harayabas*, of the former's daughters and granddaughters. Descent is bilateral and fictive kinship is frequent.

KINSHIP TERMINOLOGY. Warao kinship terminology is different from that of all neighboring indigenous groups, which use Dravidian or two-line systems. Warao cousin terminology is of the Hawaiian type, according to Murdock's classification, resulting in the same kin terms for brothers/sisters and cousins. Male and female Ego, however, use different kinship terms, and address and reference terms are not distinguished. The ascending generation has a bifurcate-collateral terminology, whereas in the descending generation only a man's sister's children are distinguished from sons and daughters. There is a complete set of affinal kinship terms that structure social behavior inside the residence group.

Marriage and Family

MARRIAGE. Marriage is endogamous in relation to the local group, based on descent from one or several common ancestors (*ahokonamu*), but exogamous to the domestic unit. Residence is uxori-matrilocal with the young son-in-law moving into his mother-in-law's house, which is as close to the household of origin as possible. A prestigious head of a domestic unit may take a second wife by marrying his principal wife's "assistant" (*atekoro*), usually her brother's daughter, but polygynous marriages also come about by default, as when a man marries his wife's widowed sister. After a number of early trial unions, couples with several children are extremely stable and divorce is infrequent. A widowed man moves to another domestic unit, but must leave his children behind; they are brought up by a foster parent (*aidatu*), generally a maternal grandfather.

SOCIALIZATION. Children are taught by example rather than through formal instruction. Religious practitioners such as shamans and those who aspire to be expert boat builders serve apprenticeships. Both parents show affection to infants, but older siblings frequently take charge of routine child care. Role behavior, however, is learned from the same-sex parent. An important point in a child's life is when "consciousness strikes" at about the age of 4 and the individual is counted as a "human being." Life passages are marked by natural events such as menarche, when, at a special ceremony, a girl passes from *anibaka* to nubile young woman, *iboma*, and at the birth of the first or second child from iboma to adult woman, *tida*.

Sociopolitical Organization

SOCIAL ORGANIZATION. Although consanguineal kinship constitutes the framework for Warao social organization, specific rights and duties are determined by affinal kinship. The most important traditional relationship is the long-term social contract between father-in-law (arahi) and sons-in-law (*dawatuma*), with the former becoming over time the head of a large domestic unit that may grow to over 100 persons and constitute a separate settlement. Such an arahi then becomes the *aidamo* (village head) as well.

POLITICAL ORGANIZATION. Holding political office was traditionally equivalent to the role of a major shaman, but since colonial times headmen and other officeholders have been appointed by outside authorities. A *kabitana* (captain) was usually the head of the strongest domestic unit of the village and the *bisikari* (derived from the Spanish *fiscal*) or *borisia* (derived from the Spanish *policía*) head of a minor one. The native governor (*kobenahoro*) presided over an area such as a delta river arm. Although there is no concept of exclusive land tenure, the leader of an inmoving Warao group must subordinate himself to the local kobenahoro. Political offices are assigned on the basis of prestige, according to the number of dependent workers (*nebu*) and public acclaim during ritual dances like the moriche ritual (*nahanamu*) or the fertility ritual of the "little rattles" (*habi sanuka*). Thus, a hierarchical ranking is established in an otherwise classless society. In recent years the Venezuelan administration has nominated paid police *comisarios*, but they have little influence on day-to-day activities.

SOCIAL CONTROL AND CONFLICT. There is little coercive control available to headmen and other political officeholders. Gossip and complaining in an even-toned monologue serve to attract attention to grievances. Ridicule of antisocial behavior is very effectively aimed. Shamans, however, especially *hoarotu* shamans, exercise considerable influence through the threats of witchcraft and punishment by the supernaturals. The Warao do not wage war; traditionally, they have retreated deeper into the moriche-palm swamps when threatened by neighbors or invaders. They are known to be very pacific, but there are occasional outbursts of violent reactions to abuses by

The Warao do not wage war; traditionally, they have retreated deeper into the moriche-palm swamps when threatened by neighbors or invaders.

outsiders. The concept of *knauobe*, literally "the retribution of the head," is very important to the Warao and implies an ideal equilibrium with nature and between persons, but also vengeance. Intragroup conflicts are mediated through public hearings (*monikata*), with the aim that "all should be satisfied." Intergroup conflicts are handled by the Warao through the use of witchcraft (*hoa*). "We kill each other with hoa," the Warao say. Among interrelated groups a quite peaceful contest with shields (*isähi*) is used to vent anger.

Religion and Expressive Culture

RELIGIOUS BELIEFS. Although Catholicism and, in some areas of the western delta, evangelical Christianity, have made some inroads into Warao religious attitudes in recent decades, the vast majority of the indigenous population continues to adhere to traditional beliefs and values. The Warao possess a well-developed ancestor cult. Important spiritual beings are the life forces of great deceased *wisiratu* shamans (*hebu araobo*), who occupy the cardinal points of the edge of the world (*aitona*). Their subordinates are materialized in sacred ancestor stones (*kanohotuma*, "our old ones"), which are cared for locally in ritual huts by their "guardians" (*kanobo arima*), a task carried out by experienced wisiratu shamans. Trees and other plants and natural phenomena are animated, and *hebu* spirits roam the forests and rivers. Mythical *nabarao*, "people of the river depths" in a mirror image of human life, mate with Warao women to engender monsters (at times justifying infanticide). Metamorphoses (*anamonina*) are frequent, transforming "forest people" (plants and animals) and men into jaguars. The Warao worldview is an immanent one, and the concept of kanonatu, "our creator," seems of recent origin.

Principal spiritual beings, *hebu aidamo* or *hebu araobo*, together with their principal wives and a coterie of subordinates, occupy the edge of the Warao world, especially whatever higher elevations there are in Trinidad and south of the Orinoco, such as Naparima in the former area and Karosima in the latter. Each religious practitioner looks to a particular hebu spirit and its location as a destination for his life force (*mehokohi*) after death. Hebu spirits may be beneficial or malevolent and are mediated by wisiratu shamans. Especially feared are the *hebu masisikiri*, known among Carib speakers as *kanaima*, and the *kanobo himabaka*.

RELIGIOUS PRACTITIONERS. Virtually all Warao adults exercise a religious function or are tied into one as craft experts, but the three basic religious offices are those of *bahanarotu*, who controls *bahana* or *hatabu* (arrows); the hoarotu, who kills by means of hoa sickness for the voracious Hoebo spirits on the western world edge but also can counteract hostile hoarotu; and the wisiratu shaman, who mediates between the Warao and their ancestor spirits (hebu) and cares for the sacred rock, their material expression (*kanobo*). Women may become shamans after menopause.

CEREMONIES. Of vital economic and religious importance is the moriche ritual (nahanamu), which stretches over some six months from the collection of palm starch to its distribution. The habi sanuka dance, which takes different forms throughout the Guiana region, is a fertility ritual that formerly included sexual activities with an *amuse*, the wife of a close associate.

MEDICINE. Women are familiar with a number of curative herbs, but all sickness is considered to have a supernatural origin. Shamans both inflict and cure illnesses. Western medicine is available to a limited degree.

DEATH AND AFTERLIFE. When a Warao dies the life force leaves his or her body and returns symbolically to the maternal womb, and the person thus becomes a hebu spirit. Sometimes tarrying around its former dwelling place, the life force ultimately moves to the abode of the Supreme Kanobo corresponding to the magicoreligious specialty or craft that he or she exercised in life. Hence the Warao look to the end of their lives with a certain tranquility. Men are buried in their dugouts.

Bibliography

Barral, Basilio de (1964). *Los indios guaraunos y su cancionero: Historia, religión y alma lírica.* Madrid: Concejo Superior de Investigaciones Científicas, Departamento de Misionología Española.

Heinen, H. Dieter (1988). *OKO Warao: Marshland People of the Orinoco Delta.* Münster: Lit Verlag.

Heinen, H. Dieter (1988). "Los Warao." In *Etnología contemporánea.* Vol. 3, edited by Jacques Lizot. Los Aborígenes de Venezuela, edited by Walter Coppens and Bernarda Escalante. Monograph no. 35. Caracas: Fundación LaSalle de Ciencias Naturales, Instituto Caribe de Antropología y Sociología.

Murdock, George P. (1949). *Social Structure.* New York: Macmillan.

Osborn, Henry (1966a). "Warao I: Phonology and Morphophonemics." *International Journal of American Linguistics* 32:108–123.

Osborn, Henry (1966b). "Warao II: Nouns, Relationals, and Demonstratives." *International Journal of American Linguistics* 32:253–261.

Osborn, Henry (1967). "Warao III: Verbs and Suffixes." *International Journal of American Linguistics* 33:46–64.

Wilbert, Johannes (1970). *Folk Literature of the Warao Indians: Narrative Material and Motif Content.* Los Angeles: University of California, Latin American Center.

Wilbert, Johannes (1972). *Survivors of Eldorado: Four Indian Cultures of South America.* New York: Praeger.

Wilbert, Johannes, and Miguel Layrisse, eds. (1980). *Demographic and Biological Studies of the Warao Indians.* Los Angeles: University of California, Latin American Center.

—H. DIETER HEINEN

YANOMAMÖ

Ethnonyms: Guaica, Guajaribo, Shidishana, Shiriana, Shori, Waica, Waika, Yanoama, Yanomama, Yanomami, Xiriana

The names "Sanema" and "Sanima" are autodenominations of people to the north and east who are culturally and genetically very closely related and who speak a partially intelligible dialect of Yanomami.

Orientation

IDENTIFICATION. The Yanomamö are a South American tribal people who straddle the border between extreme southeastern Venezuela and upper northwestern Brazil. Their name may be derived from the Yanomamö word *yano*, which designates a provisional house made during treks. Alternative names such as "Shamatari" or "Waica" (Waika) are relative terms used by some Yanomamö to refer to other Yanomamö living to the south or north, respectively.

LOCATION. In Venezuela the extension of the Yanomamö is delimited to the north by the headwaters of the Erebato and Caura rivers, east along the Serra Parima, and west along the Padamo and Mavaca rivers in a direct line to the Brazilian border. In Brazil they are concentrated near the headwaters of the Demini, Catrimani, Araçá, Padauiri, Uraricoera, Parima, and Mucajaí rivers. In Brazil and Venezuela the total area inhabited is approximately 192,000 square kilometers. Dense tropical forest covers most of the area, but there are sparse savannas at higher elevations. The topography is flat to gently rolling with elevations ranging from 250 to 1,200 meters.

DEMOGRAPHY. Although ethnographers have done extensive and excellent demographic research on Venezuelan Yanomamö, a complete census for Venezuelan and Brazilian Yanomamö is lacking. Current estimates indicate about 12,500 and 8,500 Yanomamö in Venezuela and Brazil, respectively, for a total of 21,000. There are approximately 363 villages ranging in size from 30 to 90 residents each with some Venezuelan villages in

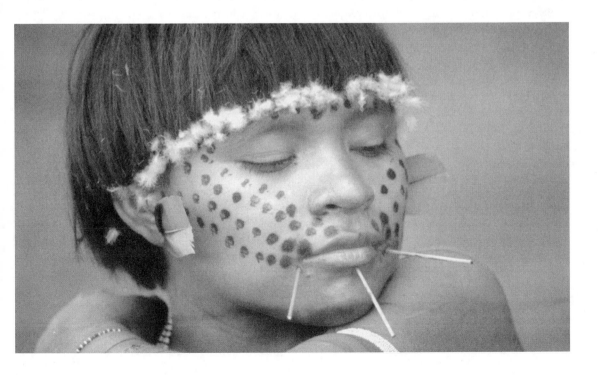

RIGHT OF PASSAGE

A Yanomamö boy wears pins in his lips and has painted dots on his face. Brazil (Claudia Andujar)

the Mavaca drainage reaching 200 and more. Population density ranges from about 6.7 square kilometers per person to 33.5 square kilometers per person.

LINGUISTIC AFFILIATION. Linguists have been unable to conclusively affiliate the Yanomamö language with any major South American language family. A linguist divides Yanomaman into four major dialectal groups: Sanema (3,262 speakers), Yanam (856 speakers), Yanomam (5,331 speakers), and Yanomami (11,752 speakers). The last two dialects, accounting for 81 percent of the total, are mutually intelligible, whereas the others may not be.

History and Cultural Relations

Archaeologists have done little research in the Yanomamö area. Ethnographers believe that the homeland of the Yanomamö lies in the Parima highlands of the Venezuelan-Brazilian border, and that they have recently expanded from there as a result of the decimation of Carib speakers who occupied the upper Orinoco and its major tributaries. Initial contact with Westerners may have begun as early as the mid-1750s, but it was not until the mid-1950s that missionaries and anthropologists made sustained contact. Some Yanomamö have had sustained contact with the Yekuana Indians for at least a hundred years, which has led to warfare, intermarriage, and establishment of partially integrated cosettlements. The contact situation differs sharply between the Brazilian and Venezuelan Yanomamö. In Venezuela, Yanomamö interaction with foreigners is largely limited to Yekuana Indians, missionaries, anthropologists, and government workers. In Brazil, significant portions of Yanomamö lands have been invaded by miners, which has led to the introduction of a variety of diseases that have taken a huge toll in Yanomamö lives and, in some places, open warfare occurs between the Yanomamö and Brazilians.

Settlements

The Yanomamö live in large single houses that, in close juxtaposition, look like a giant circular lean-to with a large central plaza. Families live in quarters that are not separated by internal walls. This communal dwelling is constructed of poles lashed together to form a framework that is thatched with palm leaves. In higher elevations the house may be reduced in diameter to form a pitched roof to adapt to cooler temperatures. The Yanomamö traditionally located villages near small, nonnavigable streams; since about 1970, however, many Yanomamö have chosen to occupy large river sites to maintain easy contact with missionaries.

Economy

SUBSISTENCE AND COMMERCIAL ACTIVITIES. The Yanomamö may be characterized as foraging horticulturists. Crops, most notably plantains and bananas, compose up to 75 percent of the diet calorically and are cultivated through pioneering shifting cultivation. Wild resources gained through gathering, hunting, and fishing supply important protein needs. Typically, the Yanomamö devote two to three times more effort (measured in hours per day) to these subsistence tasks than to horticulture. Many Yanomamö trek for a month or more during the year, living in provisional camps some distance from their village and depending heavily on wild resources. The Yanomamö associated with missions engage in light commercial trade or wage labor, but such Yanomamö probably amount to no more than 15 percent of the entire population.

INDUSTRIAL ARTS. The few technological items the Yanomamö make are mostly used for subsistence tasks. They include burden and food-serving baskets, bows and arrows, and a variety of single-use items such as tree-climbing thongs, leaf containers, and vine hammocks. Western manufactures have nearly replaced many traditional artifacts such as crude clay pots and fire drills. Where the Yanomamö have close contact with the Yekuana, they are adept at making tools necessary for manioc preparation and dugout-canoe construction.

TRADE. Internal trade among the Yanomamö is extremely well developed. Some trade is the result of differential distribution of primary resources (e.g., hallucinogenic plants) or a temporary surplus of prime domesticates (e.g., cotton or good hunting dogs), but in other instances trade is the exchange of material tokens to symbolize alliances between individuals. Since about 1970, most Yanomamö have become totally dependent on outside sources of axes, machetes, aluminum cooking pots, and fishhooks and line. Most of these items have come from missionaries as gifts and wages. Through mission-organized cooperatives, the Yanomamö recently have begun to market baskets and arrows and some agricultural products. Trade has a much longer history where the Yanomamö are in close contact with Yekuana.

DIVISION OF LABOR. Weapon making, tree felling for gardening, and hunting are the only exclusively male activities. Women spin cotton thread and plait baskets. Nearly all other activities may be done by either sex, although in many, one sex tends to be predominant. Women do most of the weeding, harvesting, food processing, and collecting of fuel and water. Both sexes frequently cooperate in gathering and fishing. When working cooperatively, however, one sex may concentrate on a particular phase. For example, in house construction men collect heavy poles and lash them together to form the structure, and women collect endless bundles of palm thatch that the men intermesh and tie for the roof.

LAND TENURE. Individuals are free to clear and cultivate any forest land near their village. Once land has been cleared of trees and a garden has been planted, it is owned by the cultivator. Theft of garden produce (tobacco, in particular) is a serious offense. Village mobility is such that semiproductive garden plots may be at a considerable distance from one's current village. Owners of such plots may find it difficult to assert ownership to valuable crops such as peach palms.

Kinship

KIN GROUPS AND DESCENT. The Yanomamö practice patrilocal residence and trace descent patrilineally. Patrilineal descent does not lead to the development of named kinship groups. Members of the same patrilineage refer to themselves as *mashi*, which simply means "people who are related patrilineally." Kin groups tend to be localized in villages, and their genealogical depth is rather shallow. Kinship is critical in the arrangement of marriage, and very strong bonds develop between kin groups who exchange women.

KINSHIP TERMINOLOGY. Yanomamö kinship terminology is bifurcate merging with Iroquoian cousin terms. Relations between brothers-in-law (cross cousins) are close and intimate, whereas relations between same-age parallel cousins are cool and reserved. A son-in-law should avoid his mother-in-law and be deferential and respectful to his father-in-law.

Marriage and Family

MARRIAGE. Yanomamö marriage rules are prescriptive in that marital partners must be cross cousins. Ideally, mates are double cross cousins, a result of the practice of sister exchange. Women typically marry soon after their first menses with men in their early twenties. Although marriage is patrilocal, a husband must live with his parents-in-law for several years and perform bride-service. This rule may be relaxed for high-status males. Polygyny is permitted and 10 to 20 percent of all males at any time are polygynists. Ideally, polyg-

yny is sororal, and levirate and sororate are practiced. Men and women average 2.8 marital partners during their lifetime, with about 75 percent of those marriages ending as a result of divorce and the balance as a result of death of one of the partners.

DOMESTIC UNIT. Monogamous or polygynous nuclear families are the rule among the Yanomamö. Deviations from this pattern occur when aged parents live closely associated with married children or when newlyweds dwell with one or the other's parents.

INHERITANCE. Neither status nor property is inherited among the Yanomamö. At death, kin incinerate the personal property of the deceased.

SOCIALIZATION. Mothers dominate in the care of infants, who spend most of their time suspended in a simple sling that runs diagonally from the caretaker's right shoulder to just above the left hip. During this time the mother carries her infant to forest and garden as she works. While the child is being weaned it is more frequently cared for by older sisters and female relatives. Weaning from the breast and the sling may occur abruptly, especially if the mother is pregnant, and is occasioned by howls of protest by the child. Although fathers will affectionately play with infants, they spend very little time (less than five minutes per day) in care-giving activities. In contrast to boys, girls begin making important economic contributions by the age of 6 as they accompany mothers in gardening and gathering excursions and assist in food preparation. Boys spend most of their time playing rough-and-tumble games, shooting toy bows, and roaming in the nearby forest in same-sex groups. Parents encourage sons and daughters to be assertive and to respond to insults with physical or verbal aggression. Physical punishment (slapping, punching, or striking with objects) is not uncommon. The girl's puberty ceremony (*yobomou*) begins immediately during her first menses. During this time a girl is secluded for a few weeks in a small shelter near her parent's hearth and is restricted to a special diet; her head is shaved upon departure.

Sociopolitical Organization

SOCIAL ORGANIZATION. Each Yanomamö village is an autonomous political entity, free to make war or peace with other villages. Coalitions between villages are important; nevertheless, such coalitions tend to be fragile and ephemeral. Although the Yanomamö are an egalitarian people, age, sex, and personal accomplishments are important in status differentiation. High status is

♦ **cross cousin**
Children of one's parent's siblings of the opposite sex— one's father's sisters' and mother's brothers' children.

The Yanomamö lack any formal mechanisms to prevent aggrieved parties from exacting the amount of vengeance or countervengeance they deem sufficient once a conflict has started.

acquired through valor in combat, accomplished oratory, and expertise in shamanism. High status cannot be inherited; it must be earned. Mature men virtually monopolize positions of political authority and religious practice. Local descent groups play important roles in regulating marriages and settling disputes within the village.

POLITICAL ORGANIZATION. The village headman is the dominant political leader and comes from the largest local patrilineage. When a village is large or when two local descent groups are approximately equal in size, a village may have several headmen. To be a successful leader, the headman must rely on demonstrated skills in settling disputes, representing the interests of his lineage and dealing with allies and enemies. Styles of leadership vary: some headmen lead through practiced verbal skills, whereas others resort to bullying tactics. Concerted action requires the consensus of adult males. An individual is free, however, to desert from collective action if it suits him.

SOCIAL CONTROL. Conflicts typically arise from accusations of adultery, failure to deliver a betrothed woman, personal affronts, stinginess, or thefts of coveted garden crops such as tobacco and peach-palm fruits. For men, if such a conflict moves beyond a boisterous shouting match, a variety of graded, formal duel may occur. If a fight becomes serious, respected men may intervene to cool tempers and prevent others from participating. Frequently, a duel ends in a draw, with each contestant preserving his dignity. For women, dueling is rare. Instead, a direct attack is made by the aggrieved using hands and feet or makeshift weapons.

CONFLICT. Warfare or feuding is endemic among the Yanomamö. Although the initial cause of a conflict may frequently be traced to a sexual or marital issue, feuds as such are self-perpetuating because the Yanomamö lack any formal mechanisms to prevent aggrieved parties from exacting the amount of vengeance or countervengeance they deem sufficient once a conflict has started. The primary vengeance unit is the lineage, but coresident nonkin have some obligation to assist since coresidence with a feuding faction is seen as implicit support of the faction by the faction's enemies. Most combat is in the form of surreptitious raids. The goal is to quickly dispatch as many of the enemy as possible (who are frequently found on the outskirts of the village engaging in mundane activities), abduct nubile women if possible, and return quickly home. Although the primary goal is to kill mature men be-

lieved to be responsible for a previous depredation or their patrilineal kin, unrelated covillagers may be killed if there is no safe opportunity to kill primary targets. Endemic warfare has a profound effect on politics and settlement size and location. Each village needs at least one allied village it can call upon for assistance if it is overmatched by a more powerful enemy, and village size and distance between villages tend to increase with the intensity of conflict. Peace between villages may develop if conflict has remained dormant for a long period, and there is a mutual need for an alliance in the face of a common enemy. It begins with a series of ceremonially festive visits. If old antagonisms do not flare, visits may lead to joint raids and intermarriage between villages that strongly solidify an alliance. Proximity of missions and government agencies has had little impact on warfare.

Religion and Expressive Culture

RELIGIOUS BELIEFS. The Yanomamö believe that the cosmos consists of four parallel planes or layers. The uppermost layer is empty but was once occupied by ancient beings who descended to lower layers. The second layer, or sky, is the home of spirits of dead men and women, and it resembles the earth except that the hunting is better, the food tastier, and the spirits of people are young and beautiful. The third layer is the earth, and below the earth is the fourth layer, or underworld. In the underworld live the Amahiteri, ancient spirits that bring harm to living humans. The Yanomamö have multiple souls that exist in a complex relation to one another. All shamans can use demons over which they have personal control to cure or cause illnesses. Catholic and evangelical Protestant missionaries have been in steady contact with the Yanomamö since the late 1950s but have had very little success in making converts.

RELIGIOUS PRACTITIONERS. The shaman is called upon to divine the causes of illness or misfortune, cure the ill, and sicken the enemy by sending demons that he controls. Shamans are also expert at using wild and domesticated plants that are useful for casting spells. Only men can become shamans, and they must complete an arduous training period requiring food deprivation and abstinence from sex.

CEREMONIES. Perhaps the most important and certainly the most dramatic ceremony is the *reahu*, or mortuary ceremony. It culminates when the bone ash of the deceased is mixed in a plantain puree and consumed by mourners in a demonstration of respect for the dead and in consolation to the close relatives of the deceased. This ceremony has considerable political implications if the deceased was a valiant warrior (*waiteri*) slain by enemies and when attended by members of allied villages.

ARTS. Yanomamö graphic art is limited and simple. Sparse geometric designs, usually black or red, adorn common objects such as baskets, arrow points, and bodies. The verbal and vocal arts such as oratory, chanting, and myth telling are much esteemed and developed among the Yanomamö. Although these acts may have political and social significance (e.g., when village leaders, employing esoteric metaphors and archaic words, ritually exchange chants), performers are admired and gain status based on their talents.

MEDICINE. The Yanomamö believe most serious illness to be the handiwork of independently acting hekura or enemy shamans who have caused their *hekura* to sicken a body. A shaman must diagnose the cause and sometimes figuratively pull the demon out, often with the help of his own demons. To prepare, a shaman frequently decorates himself and his surroundings handsomely and invariably inhales a hallucinogenic snuff to aid contact with hekura. Illness may also be caused by the breach of a ritual regulation or taboo. The Yanomamö employ a variety of herbal remedies as cures.

DEATH AND AFTERLIFE. The Yanomamö attribute a large fraction of deaths to the actions of malevolent shamans who send demons to consume the souls of people. Upon death, there are instantaneous lamentations, singing, and chanting. Usually the corpse is very quickly burned by the men, while women and children absent themselves from the village lest they become polluted by the smoke. The men then collect and pulverize the bones and pour the ash into a set of gourds that are stored in the village. After about a year the Yanomamö stage an elaborate mortuary ceremony (reahu). Close relatives, covillagers, and sometimes allies consume the ash, which is mixed into a large trough of plantain soup. This endocannibalism demonstrates affection for the dead and solidarity with the deceased's relatives. It also helps insure that the soul of the dead will find its way to *hedu*, a Yanomamö paradise above the earth.

Bibliography

Albert, B. (1988). "Temps du sang, temps des cendres: Représentation de la maladie, système ritual et espace politique chez les yanomami de sud-est (Amazonie brésilienne)." Ph.D. Dissertation, Université de Paris X—Nanterre.

Chagnon, Napoleon (1983). *Yanomamö: The Fierce People*. 3rd ed. New York: Holt, Rinehart & Winston.

Chagnon, Napoleon (1990). "Reproductive and Somatic Conflict of Interest in the Genesis of Violence and Warfare among Tribesmen." In *The Anthropology of War*, edited by Jonathan J. Haas, 77–104. New York: Cambridge University Press.

Early, J., and R. Fox (1990). *The Population Dynamics of the Mucajai Yanomama*. San Diego: Academic Press.

Hames, Raymond (1983). "The Settlement Pattern of a Yanomamö Population Bloc: A Behavioral Ecological Interpretation." In *Adaptive Responses of Native Amazonians*, edited by Raymond Hames and William Vickers, 393–427. New York: Academic Press.

Lizot, J. (1984). "Histoire, organisation et évolution du peuplement yanomamî." *L'Homme* 24:5–40.

Ramos, Alcida R. (1987). "Reflecting on the Yanomami: Ethnographic Images and the Pursuit of the Exotic." *Cultural Anthropology* 2:284–304.

Wilbert, Johannes, and Karin Simoneau (1990). *Folk Literature of the Yanomami Indians*. Los Angeles: University of California, Latin American Center.

—RAYMOND HAMES

South
Asia

BALUCHI

Ethnonyms: Baloch, Baluch

Orientation

IDENTIFICATION. The Baluchi are predominantly Sunni Muslim, seminomadic pastoralists, whose homelands straddle the Iran-Pakistan border as well as including a small portion of southern Afghanistan.

LOCATION. Baluchistan is the name of the westernmost province of Pakistan, as well as of the transnational territory of the traditional Baluchi homeland. This larger region was carved up by the imperial powers concerned more with ease of administration than with recognition of the territorial limits of the inhabitants. The traditional Baluchi territory extends from the southeastern portion of the Iranian Plateau across the Kirman Desert to the western borders of Sind and the Punjab, and from the Gumal River in the northeast to the Arabian Sea in the south. This is a largely inhospitable land, much of it barren desert or harsh mountainous terrain. Baluchi territory lies outside the monsoon belt, and annual rainfall is very low, not exceeding 16 centimeters. Throughout the region, winters are harsh and cold, and summers are very hot. In the mountains, the rains come in October and March, while in the lowlands they come in July and August.

DEMOGRAPHY. Population figures for the Baluchi are somewhat suspect, in part because of the unreliability of census-taking procedures across the three major political units that now control Baluchi territory, and partly because the criteria for ascribing Baluchi identity are not tightly defined. On the strength of linguistic criteria, there are an estimated 5 million or so Baluchi speakers living in eastern Iran, southern Afghanistan, and in Pakistan. However, Baluchi have in some areas become linguistically assimilated to neighboring peoples while retaining a specifically Baluchi cultural identity; this means that if sociocultural rather than purely linguistic criteria were used, the population count could easily exceed 9 million. Many Baluchi have migrated to Pakistan's Sind and Punjab provinces, and to the emirates of the Persian Gulf.

LINGUISTIC AFFILIATION. The Baluchi language is a member of the Indo-Iranic Language Family, having some affinity with Kurdish. There are three distinct divisions: Eastern, Western, and Southern Baluchi. Until the nineteenth century the language had no written form, because Per-

sian was the language of official use. Illiteracy is extremely high among the Baluchi.

History and Cultural Relations

Legend has it that the Baluchi people are directly descended from Amir Hamza, one of Mohammed's uncles, and migrated into the transnational region of Baluchistan from somewhere in the vicinity of Aleppo, in Syria. The migrations that brought them to their current territory began as long ago as the fifth century and were more or less complete by the end of the seventh. Prior to the twelfth century, theirs was a society of independent, more or less autonomous seminomadic groups, organized along principles of clan affiliation rather than territorial association. As the population of the region increased, access to land assumed greater and greater importance, giving rise to a system of tribes, each with a territorial base. The first successful attempt to unite several Baluchi tribal units was accomplished by Mir Jalal Han, who set up the First Baluchi Confederacy in the twelfth century, but this unity did not long survive his rule. Warfare between various Baluchi tribes and tribal confederacies was frequent during the fifteenth century, largely owing to economic causes. By the sixteenth century the Baluchis were roughly divided up into three separate political entities: the Makran State, the Dodai Confederacy, and the khanate of Baluchistan (the Kalat Confederacy). In the eighteenth century, Mir Abdullah Khan of the Kalat Confederacy succeeded in reuniting all of Baluchistan, providing a centralized government based on *Rawaj*, the customary law of the Baluchi people. The arrival of the British in the region had profound effects on the future trajectory of Baluchi development. Uninterested in the region economically, the British were solely concerned with establishing a buffer zone that could forestall the encroachment of the Russians upon the rich prize of India. To further this end, the British relied on the manipulation of Baluchi tribal leaders, cash handouts, and the establishment of garrisons, but they paid no attention to the economic development of the region itself.

Settlements

The Baluchi have two types of settlements, consistent with their seminomadic way of life. Village settlements are clusters of mud houses, loosely oriented around the house of the local chief. These permanent settlements are found in the mountains and valleys, and they are occupied chiefly in the summer. In winter the people migrate to the

Although the Baluchi are largely an illiterate people and their language was until quite recently unwritten, they have a long tradition of poetic composition.

♦ **monsoon**
Regular and persistent winds that blow in the Indian Ocean, coming from the southwest between June and August and from the northeast between October and December. The southwest monsoon is the main rain-bearing one.

plains and the coastal areas, seeking pasturage for the livestock that are central to the traditional Baluchi economy. During this time, the Baluchi live in tents, moving freely across the landscape as conditions favor the care of their herds, and settlements are smaller, consisting of closely related kin.

Economy

SUBSISTENCE AND COMMERCIAL ACTIVITIES. The traditional Baluchi economy is based on a combination of subsistence farming and seminomadic pastoralism (cattle, sheep, and goats). Because of the harshness of the environment, agriculture is somewhat limited, but it nonetheless constitutes a significant part of the economy. The principal crop is wheat. Wild fruits and vegetables also form a part of the household economy, and chickens may be raised as well. When the local economy cannot provide adequate opportunities, young men may migrate out in search of paid labor.

INDUSTRIAL ARTS. The Baluchi are a self-sufficient lot, as a whole, and they rely on their own skills to construct their houses and many of the tools necessary in their day-to-day life. Rugs are woven for household use and as items of trade also.

DIVISION OF LABOR. The entire household participates in the work of tending the family's herd, but in other aspects of the economy there is a division of labor by sex: women work in groups to thresh and winnow the grain harvest, while plowing and planting are men's work. The gathering of wild foods, water, and firewood is done by groups of women.

LAND TENURE. By tradition, land is not privately owned but rather is vested in the subsection of the tribe to which one belongs. It therefore is inalienable by the individual. However, during the British period, tribal leaders often managed to have title to some property conveyed in their own names.

Kinship

Baluchi kinship is patrilineal, tracing descent through one of several lineages, ultimately back to the putative apical ancestor, Amir Hamza. Clan membership is based on familial ties, while tribal membership has a more specifically territorial referent. For both males and females, one remains a member of one's patrilineal group for life—even after marriage, for example, a woman's "real" home is that of her father, and her position in her husband's house brings to her only very limited rights.

Marriage and Family

Baluchi marriages are arranged between the bride's father and the prospective groom upon the payment of a bride-price consisting of livestock and cash. On marriage, a woman passes from the

RELIGION AND EXPRESSIVE CULTURE

Religious Beliefs

The Baluchi today are Sunni Muslims but, according to many of the traditional ballads of the Baluchi, they have in the past claimed to be followers of Caliph Ali and thus were once Shia Muslims. Prior to the coming of Islam, the Baluchi were probably followers of Zoroaster, and traces of earlier, non-Islamic beliefs are still retained in current religious observance. In any case, and unlike the situation found in much of the Muslim world, religious belief and practice are considered to be a private affair—there is no Baluchi concept of a "religious state." Secular authority is quite distinct from the spiritual authority vested in religious leaders. It appears that their religious orientation (Sunni versus Shia) has something of a political component to it: when Iran was aligned with the Sunni sect of Islam, the Baluchi professed for Shia; whereas, when Iran embraced Shia, the Baluchi promptly realigned themselves as Sunni.

Religious Practitioners

Religious instruction and observance are led by the local mullah.

Arts

Although the Baluchi are largely an illiterate people and their language was until quite recently unwritten, they have a long tradition of poetic composition, and poets and professional minstrels have been held in high esteem. Their oral literature consists of epic poetry, ballads of war and romance, religious compositions, and folktales. Much composition is given over to genealogical recitals as well. This poetic creativity traditionally had a practical as well as aesthetic aspect—professional minstrels long held the responsibility of carrying information from one to another of the scattered Baluchi settlements, and during the time of the First Baluchi Confederacy these traveling singers provided an important means by which the individual leaders of each tribe within the confederacy could be linked to the central leadership. The earliest securely dated Baluchi poem still known today dates to the late twelfth century, although the tradition of such compositions is no doubt of much greater antiquity.

control of her father to that of her husband. Marriage is monogamous and is expected to be for life. Adultery was traditionally punishable by the death of both parties involved. Marriage to a non-Baluchi is rigidly proscribed. Postmarital residence is patrilocal.

INHERITANCE. All heritable property passes from father to sons.

SOCIALIZATION. Baluchmayar, or "the Baluchi Way," is the guiding principle of proper conduct for the Baluchi people. It is a sort of honor code, entailing the extension of hospitality, mercy, refuge, and honesty to one's fellows, and it is reaffirmed in the oral traditions of Baluchi song and poetry. Children learn proper behavior through observing their elders and through being subject to taunt and gossip should they behave badly.

Sociopolitical Organization

Baluchi society is organized both into kin-based clans and territorially defined tribes. One could claim a rough correspondence between the clan and the social hierarchy as distinct from the tribe and the more specifically political sphere, but this correspondence is not absolute. The Baluchi people are an amalgam of many large units, or chieftaincies, each one of which is itself composed of a nested set of smaller organizational units. From largest to smallest, these constituent units can best be understood as clans, clan sections, and subsections—with smaller segments of this last division being the level that most closely corresponds to actual settlement units. At each level of this hierarchy, leadership is in the hands of a male elder. At the least comprehensive level, such leadership is as likely to be achieved as inherited, but over time authority at the more inclusive levels has devolved to the elders of what have become hereditary "chiefly clans" (*Sardarkel*). By the fifteenth century, the Sardarkel formed the organizational foci of a loosely understood feudal system, which had developed into a set of semiautonomous sovereign principalities by the eighteenth century. During the imperial period, the Sardarkel served as mediators between British and local interests, losing a great deal of their original autonomy in the process. However, as a result of their participation in securing the interests of the ruling power, much land and wealth accrued to these groups, establishing a new and more purely economic basis for their leadership role, as well as allowing them to develop something of a monopoly over access to the larger political systems within which the Baluchi people now found themselves. As a "stateless" people, the Baluchi political presence is today somewhat attenuated. In the 1970s and 1980s, a number of groups sprang up in the name of Baluchi nationalism, but their activities have been largely of a guerrilla nature and, as yet, they have been unable to secure international support for their cause.

SOCIAL CONTROL. Although Muslim, the Baluchi do not invoke *Sharia* (Islamic law) to deal with social transgressions. Rather, secular authority is vested in the traditional tribal leaders (*Sardars*) and conducted according to Rawaj, which is based on the principles of Baluchmayar. The ultimate traditional sanction was provided by the mechanism of the blood feud, invoked by the clan to avenge the wrongful death of one of its members. Capital punishment was also traditionally applied in cases of adultery or the theft of clan property. Refusal to comply with the socially prescribed norms of hospitality is punishable by fines imposed by the local elders. Pardon for many social infractions can be obtained by the intercession of female representatives of the offender's family. In the case of all offenses except that of adultery, the offender may seek refuge in the household of a nonrelated clan, which obligates the household providing sanctuary to fight to the death to defend the refugee. Petitions for such sanctuary must be granted, according to the code of Baluchmayar. Formal public taunting, in verse as well as in direct speech, provides a further mechanism by which compliance with the Baluchi code of behavior is enforced.

CONFLICT. The warrior tradition of the Baluchi extends back throughout their history, reaching its fullest flowering in the eleventh to fourteenth centuries, at a time coincident with their need to establish a settlement base from which to conduct their seminomadic way of life. During the imperial period the British imposed a policy of pacification upon the region and enforced it by maintaining a substantial garrison presence. The Baluchi reputation for producing fierce warriors is today recalled primarily in the activities of the "free fighters" of the Baluchi nationalist movement.

Bibliography

Baloch, Inayatullah (1987). *The Problem of Greater Baluchistan: A Study of Baluch Nationalism*. Stuttgart: Steiner Verlag Wiesbaden.

Pastner, Stephen L. (1978). "Baluch Fishermen in Pakistan." *Asian Affairs* 9:161–167.

Pehrson, Robert N. (1966). *The Social Organization of the Marri Baluch*. Viking Fund Publications in

Anthropology, edited by Fredrik Barth, no. 43. New York: Wenner-Gren Foundation for Anthropological Research.

Salzman, Philip C. (1971). "Movement and Resource Extraction among Pastoral Nomads: The Case of the Shah Nawazi Baluch." *Anthropology Quarterly* 44:185–197.

Wirsing, Robert (1981). *The Baluchis and Pathans.* London: Minority Rights Group.

—NANCY E. GRATTON

BENGALI

Ethnonyms: Bangali, Bangladeshi (formerly Bengalee, Baboo)

Orientation

IDENTIFICATION. The Bengali people speak the Bengali (Bangla) language and live in the Bengal region of the Indian subcontinent located in northeastern South Asia, and most follow either the Hindu or the Muslim faith. The Bengal region is divided politically between the nation of Bangladesh and the Indian state of West Bengal. Bengalis themselves refer to their region as *Bangla desh*, meaning simply "the Bengali homeland," a term adopted by the people of eastern Bengal when they won sovereign independence for the nation of Bangladesh in 1971. The native ethnic term for themselves is Bangli—of which "Bengali" is an anglicization. However, Bengalis who are citizens of Bangladesh will also most readily call themselves Bangladeshi.

LOCATION. Lying at the north of the Bay of Bengal and roughly between 22° and 26° N and 86° and 93° E, the Bengal region consists largely of a vast alluvial, deltaic plain, built up by the Ganges River and watered also by the Brahmaputra River system originating in the eastern Himalaya Mountains. As in much of South Asia, monsoon winds bring a rainy season that can last from April to mid-November. Bengal's total area is approximately 233,000 square kilometers, of which about 38 percent (just under 89,000 square kilometers) is in India, the remaining 62 percent (144,000 square kilometers) constituting the nation of Bangladesh.

DEMOGRAPHY. According to the last available (1981) censuses, India's West Bengal contained some 47 million people (35 percent) and Bangladesh 86 million people (65 percent) claiming to be primary speakers of the Bengali language, with the total of around 133 million constituting the "core" ethnic Bengali population. To this total must be added at least another 7 million Bengali speakers living in adjacent or nearby states of India—Assam, 3 million; Bihar, 2 million; Tripura, 1.4 million; Orissa, 378,000; Meghalaya, 120,000; and Nagaland, 27,000—forming a kind of "Bengali diaspora" that, although concentrated in northeastern South Asia, is actually worldwide, with large numbers of Bengalis living as immigrants in the United States, United Kingdom, and Canada. In sum, Bengalis comprised a population of about 140 million in 1981, one which can be expected to have grown by at least 25 percent by the time data from 1991 censuses becomes available. Bengali speakers make up 85 percent of the population of West Bengal, which otherwise is home to an additional 9 million non-Bengali people. Most of these are from other parts of India, living in the metropolis of Calcutta, the state capital, but there are significant numbers of non-Bengali people locally classed as "tribals" in rural West Bengal as well. Bangladesh is far more homogeneous; all but 1 percent of its people identify themselves as Bengali. Most of the remaining 900,000 consist of non-Bengali ethnic groups also locally designated as "tribal," and the majority of these are speakers of Tibeto-Burman and other minority languages, often living in border areas of the country. Some speakers of dialects of Hindi-Urdu remain in Bangladesh as well. Overall population densities in West Bengal were recorded at 615 people per square kilometer in 1981, ranging from 466 in some rural areas to 56,462 in urban localities (especially Calcutta). In Bangladesh overall densities reached 624 persons per square kilometer by 1981, rising to 2,179 in the urban areas (especially Dhaka, the nation's capital), but also registering a quite high 693 persons per square kilometer in part of the countryside.

LINGUISTIC AFFILIATION. Like most of the languages of northern South Asia, Bengali belongs to the Indo-Iranian (sometimes also called Indo-Aryan) Branch of the Indo-European Family. Descended from ancient Sanskrit, Bengali contains forty-seven sounds: eleven vowels, twenty-five consonants, four semivowels, and seven "breath sounds" (including sibilants and aspirates). Its script, also Sanskrit-derived, contains fifty-seven letter symbols. The Bengali language is associated with a long literary tradition, pride in which is a major factor in Bengali ethnic and national identity. A Bengali, Rabindranath Tagore, was the first Asian to receive the Nobel Prize for literature (in 1913). The literary language with which educated speakers are familiar is, however,

♦ **Tibeto-Burman**
A subfamily of languages found mainly in Tibet, Myanmar (Burma), Nepal, and northeastern India. The larger family is called Sino-Tibetan and also includes the Chinese languages.

quite distinct from the urban and rural speech of the less well educated. The eastern dialects of Bengali, notably those spoken in the Sylhet and Chittagong districts of Bangladesh, differ quite noticeably from those heard in West Bengal.

History and Cultural Relations

Bengal is mentioned as a distinct region of South Asia in some of the earliest Hindu texts, and throughout the first millennium A.D. it was governed by a succession of Buddhist and Hindu rulers. Islamic armies arrived in the region in the late twelfth and early thirteenth centuries, and gradual Muslim conquest—culminating in Mughal rule after 1576—set the stage for widespread conversion of the local population to Islam, especially in eastern Bengal. Not long thereafter, European contact with, and competition for power on, the Indian subcontinent began, and the British period of India's history is usually dated from England's takeover of the administration of Bengal in 1757. Lasting until 1947, British rule had a profound impact on Bengali culture and society, especially with the introduction of English as the medium of higher education after 1835. Hindus responded more rapidly than did Muslims to opportunities provided by English education, and the nineteenth and early twentieth centuries saw the rise of a highly Westernized elite, mostly, but not exclusively, Hindu in composition, whose intellectual attainments were coupled with efforts at sociocultural and political reform. Bengali elites provided major leadership to the Indian nationalist movement as a whole, which began to develop in force after the mid-1800s. Bengali Hindus tended to support a nationalist party called the Indian National Congress in its vision of a free, secular India to follow British rule. But most Bengali Muslims believed, as did many Muslims throughout India at that time, that they had benefited less than Hindus under British rule and feared that they would suffer discrimination in a free India dominated by the country's Hindu majority. The Muslims of Bengal were thus more attracted to another nationalist organization, the Muslim League, which in 1940 advocated a separate postindependence state for Muslims, to be known as Pakistan. The British acceded to India's independence in 1947, at which time the subcontinent was partitioned into two separate nation-states: India, with a Hindu majority, and Pakistan, with a Muslim majority. The predominantly Hindu western districts of Bengal then comprised the Indian state of West Bengal, whereas the mainly Muslim districts of eastern Bengal

formed the eastern province of Pakistan (called East Pakistan). Pakistan's national unity was based on common religious identity of its citizens as Muslims, but it was undermined by the nation's linguistic diversity and growing conflict between the country's ethnic groups. Over time the Bengali Muslims of East Pakistan came into increasing confrontation with the non-Bengali Muslim groups of West Pakistan, where a preponderance of the economic wealth and political power of the country was concentrated. In 1971 the schism between East and West Pakistan erupted into a civil war—a national liberation struggle from the Bengali point of view—resulting in the breakup of Pakistan and the emergence of Bangladesh as a new nation. This history helps to explain why the Bengali population is divided into its two major political entities: the Hindu-majority Indian state of West Bengal, with its capital at Calcutta; and the Muslim-majority independent nation-state of Bangladesh, with its capital at Dhaka.

Settlements

Throughout the Bengal region the officially recognized unit of rural settlement is known as a *mauza* or "revenue village," which has surveyed boundaries determined during the British imperial period for purposes of taxation and general administration. There are more than 40,000 such villages in West Bengal, and some 68,000 in Bangladesh, but it is important to recognize that these officially designated villages do not necessarily always correspond to actual rural communities as locally and socially defined. Peasant communities range from 100 to 1,000 people, and a typical village in the low-lying Bengal delta consists of one or more hamlets (*para*) of peasant homesteads (*bari*) built on land deliberately raised so as to avoid monsoon flooding. Along canals and other waterways the pattern of settlement is more linear, and in areas of the country where monsoon inundations are especially great the pattern tends to be more dispersed. Peasant homesteads are usually composed of extended families, broken down into households most often consisting of a man and his dependents, who form an independent landholding and/or cultivating and consuming unit. Interspersed throughout one finds a network of periodic rural markets, and in the multivillage area served by each local market—what some anthropologists have called the "standard marketing area"—the market functions not only as the focus of commercial activity but also as the social and political center that unites the village communities served by the market into a certain degree of

Lasting until 1947, British rule had a profound impact on Bengali culture and society, especially with the introduction of English as the medium of higher education.

Bengali dwellings are most commonly constructed from the dense mud of the Bengal Delta, and sometimes are raised to two or three stories in height.

wider regional identity. Dwellings are most commonly constructed from the dense mud of the Bengal Delta and local, indigenous construction engineering is sometimes sophisticated enough to allow the raising of homes of two and three stories in height. Animal shelters and fruit-bearing trees are common fixtures in a homestead area, and the excavation of mud for construction often results in a human-made pond that serves the residents as a source of fish as well as water for bathing and laundering. Thatch grass typically provides roofing, but wealthier families can afford roofs of corrugated iron; the poorest families often have homes primarily made of bamboo only.

Economy

SUBSISTENCE AND COMMERCIAL ACTIVITIES. Statistical data for 1981 indicate that some 83 percent of the people in the Bengal region as a whole resided in the rural areas (89 percent in Bangladesh, 74 percent in West Bengal), and it is unlikely that the rural-urban distribution of the population or the occupational breakdown of the labor force has changed markedly over the past decade. Two-thirds (67 percent) of the labor was engaged in agriculture, more so in Bangladesh (74 percent) than in West Bengal (55 percent). The region is largely homogeneous in the kinds of crop its people grow, wet rice agriculture being the hallmark of the Bengali economy. There are three cropping seasons: (1) a spring season marked by the onset of monsoon rains in April, during which varieties of rice classed as *aus* are typically grown along with jute, the region's major commercial crop, until mid-July; (2) the *aman* season, which accounts for the bulk of annual rice production, lasting to November; and (3)

the dry winter season, lingering through March, in which types of rice called *boro*, which can grow under irrigated conditions, are sown, along with pulses and oilseeds. Wheat and potatoes represent relatively recent food crop innovations in Bengal. The raising of farm animals for food and labor is not usually an occupational specialization, although whether or not a farm family will possess any of the animals commonly found throughout Bengal—cows, oxen, bullocks, water buffalo, and goats—will depend on its wealth. Some small-scale fishing may be engaged in by farm families with homestead ponds, but extensive fishing is an occupational specialty of particular Hindu castes or castelike groups among Muslims.

INDUSTRIAL ARTS. Preindustrial manufacture and the provision of nonagricultural goods throughout Bengal has always been carried out by specialized, mostly Hindu, artisan caste groups—weavers, potters, blacksmiths, carpenters, and so forth. Because Bengali villages usually are small, it is rare for a full complement of artisan castes to be present in them, but these artisans are usually sufficiently dispersed throughout standard marketing areas to make their wares generally available. It should also be emphasized that industrial manufacturing is widespread in Bengal, concentrated primarily in its major cities.

TRADE. As noted above, periodic local markets dot the Bengal countryside, and these in turn are linked to permanent, daily markets in larger provincial towns and ultimately to major urban commercial centers. Many peasants engage in petty marketing to supplement their primary occupation, but large-scale accumulation and transportation of major crops, especially rice and jute, and artisan products are typically carried out by wholesalers who move from market to market. As elsewhere in South Asia, some Hindu caste groups specialize in certain kinds of trade and commercial transactions (e.g., those related to gold and other jewelry or specific consumption items other than rice). Because Bengal possesses a labyrinthine network of rivers, providing boat transportation to and between riverside centers is a major activity for many. Commerce is overwhelmingly male-dominated, since adult women are usually required to limit their activities to their homesteads and immediate surroundings and thus are not permitted to engage in significant trading activity.

DIVISION OF LABOR. The division of labor by both gender and occupational specialization is highly marked throughout South Asia, including Bengal, particularly so in the rural areas. Regard-

FISHERMEN

Bengali fishermen on a river near the Deiura Road. Their fishing nets are suspended over the river on bamboo poles. Bangladesh.
(Roger Wood/Corbis)

less of a rural family's occupational specialty, men engage in activities that take place outside the home, while women are limited to those that can be performed within its confines. Thus, for example, in rice-farming families men perform all the work in the fields—plowing, planting, weeding, and harvesting—and once the crop is brought into the homestead women take up the tasks of threshing, drying, and husking the crop. A similar kind of intra- (versus extra-) homestead division of labor by gender occurs in families with non-agricultural occupational specializations. Not surprisingly, domestic and child-rearing tasks fall within the women's domain as well. The degree to which women are permitted to work outside the home is, however, related to the economic and social status of the family. A poor or landless farmer's wife may spend part of her day processing agricultural goods in a wealthier household, for example, to supplement her family's meager income, and among the lower-ranked service castes the taboo on women working outside the home is considerably less strict. In the urban middle class and upper classes, it is by no means uncommon for women to have a profession, especially in the teaching and medical fields (nearly all gynecologists are women), and to work outside the home. The other major feature of the Bengali division of labor is occupational specialization by caste, already mentioned and discussed more fully below. In traditional Bengali Hindu society, nearly every occupation is carried on by a ranked hierarchy of specialized caste groups—not only the artisan and trading occupations already discussed but also personal and domestic service functions (e.g., barbering, laundering, latrine cleaning) as well as nonmenial tasks such as those related to public administration and, of course, the priesthood. There is some caste-based specialization among Muslims as well. In the modern sectors of Bengal's economy, the division of labor is not formally organized by caste. But the caste hierarchy tends to be visible in the distribution of the work force nonetheless; the professions and management jobs are likely to be taken up by persons of higher caste background, whereas laborers and lower-level service workers are most often members of the traditionally lower-ranked castes.

LAND TENURE. Land has always been individually owned and small family farms, typically little more than a single hectare in size, are found throughout Bengal. Farm holdings are often highly fragmented, consisting on average of between seven and nine separate plots per holding. Recent land tenure surveys from Bangladesh indicate that around 80 percent of the cultivated area is owned by only 35 percent of the land-owning households; 30 percent of rural households are landless and 10 percent more own farms of less than half a hectare. No significant land reform has been attempted in Bangladesh in the past forty years. Two decades ago, only 20 percent of the landholdings in West Bengal accounted for some 60 percent of the total cultivated area, and a large number of cultivating families were landless laborers, tenants, and sharecroppers as well; since then West Bengal has made a significant effort at land reform with some beneficial results.

Kinship

KIN GROUPS AND DESCENT. The commonest kin group in rural Bengal is the homestead-based patrilineal extended family, whose members jointly own homestead land and may—but usually do not—also own agricultural land in common. The homestead is typically composed of a senior male head, his married sons with their families, unmarried children and grandchildren, and other dependents.

KINSHIP TERMINOLOGY. In conventional classifications, the Bengali kinship terminology is of the bifurcate collateral type in terms of first ascending generation terminology, and it is of the Sudanese type from the point of view of cousin terminology. Thus, each of Ego's parental siblings is denoted by a separate term, and so therefore is each parental sibling's child (i.e., "cousin" in English terms). In this respect, Bengali terminology does not differ from that found across north India and the Middle East. Although both Bengali Hindu and Bengali Muslim terminologies share the same pattern, Muslims employ seven kinship terms that are found in Urdu and in several cases are actually derived from Arabic and Persian, all of which languages are distinctively identified with Islamic rather than Hindu civilization. (Recent discussions of Bengali kinship, however, suggest that the conventional anthropological classification system has limited utility for understanding the basic cultural categories of kinship in Bengali culture.)

Marriage and Family

MARRIAGE. Bengali marriages are arranged, but Hindu and Muslim marital practices differ in certain key respects. Among Hindus, considerations of caste rank are important; that is, marriage usually occurs between persons of the same caste. Hypergamous unions—between members of closely ranked castes, with women marrying upward—

*West Bengal is a
federal state within
the Republic of
India, with its own
elected governor and
legislature.*

are not forbidden. But hypogamous marriages—
in which a woman marries a man of a lower
caste—are strongly discouraged and rarely occur.
Because of the egalitarian ideology of Islam,
caste-related restrictions are not formally required
for Muslims. But since Bengali Muslim society as
a matter of fact reflects some castelike features,
social rank is also a strong consideration in the selection of mates, and there are some low-ranked
Muslim occupational groups that are perforce
highly endogamous. Among Hindus also lineage
exogamy is the basic rule and matrilateral cousin
marriage is also forbidden. By contrast, as Islam
raises no barrier to cousin marriage, its occurrence
among Bengali Muslims is common, although
empirical studies show that it is neither pervasive
nor necessarily preferred. Similarly polygyny, rare
and strongly discouraged among Bengali Hindus,
is of course permitted to Bengali Muslims, although its actual rate of occurrence is not high.
Divorce among high-caste Hindus is strongly
discouraged and, at least until recently, has always brought great stigma. Islam discourages but
nonetheless permits divorce, and thus its rate
among Bengali Muslims is much higher than
among Bengali Hindus. Finally, among high-
caste Hindus, widow remarriage—despite a century of legislation outlawing the ancient custom
of proscribing it—is still greatly frowned upon.
Islam places no barrier on remarriage for either
sex after spousal death or divorce, although the
incidence of remarriage of elderly Muslim widows is not high. For both Hindus and Muslims
patrilocal/virilocal postmarital residence patterns
are much preferred and almost universally practiced, at least in the rural areas. Neolocal nuclear-
family households are much more common
among urban professional families in both West
Bengal and Bangladesh.

DOMESTIC UNIT. Throughout rural Bengal
the patrilineally extended family homestead is
subdivided into its natural segments, called
paribar, consisting of men, their wives, their children, and other dependents, who form the basic
subsistence-producing and consuming kinship
units. The economic and social "jointness" of the
paribar is underlined by the sharing of a common
kitchen or hearth, as well as the ownership or control of land and/or other productive assets, if any.

INHERITANCE. Among Bengali Hindus, inheritance is governed by the *dayabhaga* system of
customary law in which a man has sole rights in
all ancestral property until his death and can in
principle pass it on to his survivors in any manner
that he wishes. Unless he makes a will to the con-

trary, upon his death a man's sons are to inherit
equally all property as a matter of survivorship,
not a matter of right; his wife and daughters have
no claim by right to any of his property, but they
do have the right to maintenance so long as they
are dependent on their sons or brothers. Among
Muslims inheritance is of course governed by Islamic law, which permits a man's female dependents to inherit a portion of his property; since
sons are expected to be the sole providers for their
families, the law permits them to receive more of
a father's property than do daughters. In actual
Bengali Muslim (at least rural, peasant) practice,
however, daughters commonly forgo or are deprived of their inheritance of immovable property
in favor of their brothers, assuming that if they
need to return to their natal homes after widowhood or divorce their brothers will take care of
them. Although joint retention and use of the father's property by his sons is the cultural ideal for
both Hindus and Muslims, in practice the subdivision of a man's property begins not long after
his death, and the formation or further proliferation of the domestic units discussed above begins.

SOCIALIZATION. Children learn proper behavior from parents and older siblings, gradually
becoming differentiated according to gender as
they mature. The pattern of older children caring
for their younger siblings is widespread. While
small children of both sexes are warmly indulged,
as girls approach physical maturity their movements outside the household are gradually curtailed in anticipation of the relative restrictions
that both high-caste Hindu and Muslim adult
women will experience for most of their childbearing years. Schools abound throughout Bengal, but whether and how long a child will attend
depend much upon gender as well as the social
standing and financial condition of the family.
Schools for religious education—Hindu *pathsalas*
for boys and Islamic *madrassas* open to both
sexes—are found everywhere and commonly attended, at least during childhood years.

Sociopolitical Organization

West Bengal is a federal state within the Republic
of India, with its own elected governor and legislature; it also sends representatives to a bicameral
national parliament. Bangladesh is an independent sovereign republic with an elected president
and a unicameral, elected national assembly (the
Jatiya Sangsad).

SOCIAL ORGANIZATION. Bengali Hindu
society is organized along the lines of the Hindu
caste system, in which every individual is a mem-

ber by birth of a corporate, ranked, endogamous occupational group, called a caste (*jati*). One's place in society is determined by the rank of one's caste, and the latter is determined by the relative prestige—measured by the degree of ritual purity or impurity—associated with the caste's traditional occupation. The castes traditionally associated with religious leadership are considered to be the most pure ritually and so have the highest rank. At the bottom of the hierarchy are found those castes whose occupations, because they involve direct or indirect contact with such defiling substances as blood and human excreta or may be associated with death in some way, are considered to be the most ritually impure. The customs governing much of the individual's existence are those of his or her caste community; the wealth of one's family is also correlated with one's caste ranking; the probability that a person will receive a high degree of education is also related to caste status, and of course most people marry a member of their caste as well. Individual upward social mobility is highly restricted in this kind of social system, but it is possible for a whole caste to elevate its actual rank in its local hierarchy if its members become wealthy and attempt to emulate norms and customs of the higher castes. Certain castes found elsewhere in India, notably those associated in the past with royalty (i.e., the Kshatriya varna) and the performance of traditional ruling functions, have not been historically present in Bengal. Anywhere from six to a dozen caste groups might be found in a typical Bengali Hindu village, but villages in Bengal tend to be less highly stratified, in the sense that they tend to have a smaller number of castes than Hindu communities in other parts of India. In the most populous southern areas of the Bengal Delta, Hindu village communities are often dominated numerically and politically by one of several low-ranked cultivating castes: the Namasudras, the Mahisyas, and/or the Pods. In part because Islam is an egalitarian religion and in principle forbids hereditary distinctions of social rank, one does not find among Bengali Muslims whole communities organized along the lines of caste, and the social system is more open and fluid from the point of view of social mobility. The vestiges are still found of a traditional South Asian Muslim system of social rank that distinguished between "noble" (*ashraf*) and low-ranked (*ajlaf* or *atraf*) status groups, and some of the latter still exist and tend to be occupationally endogamous. Today, however, Muslim village communities, at least in Bangladesh, are most often populated by ordinary cultivators, among whom well-marked castelike distinctions are not found and who emphasize distinctions in wealth as the basis for social rank.

POLITICAL ORGANIZATION. West Bengal is divided into sixteen districts, and below the district level (as everywhere in India) there is a three-tiered council system known as *panchayati raj*, whose purpose is to administer village and multi-village affairs and to carry out development projects consistent with statewide plans and goals. Each village elects a village assembly (*gram sabha*), whose executive body is the village council (*gram panchayat*). Usually these village councils are controlled by the numerically and/or economically dominant caste group in the villages electing them. Several village councils in turn elect an area council (*anchal panchayat*), which has jurisdiction over the village councils. The heads of the various area councils, along with nominated members of the state legislative assembly, form the district council (*zilla parishad*), which, linked to the state government, has control over the entire local government system. Parallel to the local councils at each level is a three-tiered judicial system as well. In Bangladesh, which undertook administrative reforms in 1982, the 68,000 officially designated "villages" or mauzas are amalgamated into around 4,300 unions with governing councils known as *union parishads* constituting the lowest levels of the national government and administration, to which the villagers elect members. Unions are further grouped into nearly 500 *upazillas* or "subdistricts," governed by *upazilla parishads*, whose memberships are composed by the chairmen of the union parishads (except that the chairman of an upazilla parishad is directly elected). Upazillas in turn are united into some sixty-four districts, and these again into four divisions. The key to this administrative scheme is supposed to be the upazilla parishad, which has many local decision-making powers, especially those relevant to community development. Social scientists who have studied the local government system in Bangladesh have found that it is usually dominated by the more wealthy sections of the peasantry and locally powerful village elites.

SOCIAL CONTROL. In both West Bengal and Bangladesh, formal social control mechanisms are provided by the units of local government described above, in conjunction with police and civil court administration. However, informal mechanisms have traditionally been important as well. Among Hindus, intervillage caste *panchayats* (councils), headed by the elders, regulate marriages and otherwise govern the affairs and mediate disputes of the members of the same caste in several adjacent villages. Among Muslims, similar traditional councils, called *samaj*, of village elders perform similar functions, and sometimes these groups may encompass several contiguous villages. These traditional sociopolitical groupings may overlap with the official units of local government described above, in that the leaders of these indigenous groups are sometimes elected to membership in the governmental bodies too.

CONFLICT. Anthropologists have conducted many studies of conflict in South Asian villages, including those of Bengal. They have found that conflict often occurs not only between the various castes but also between factions, each composed of members of various caste groups. Competition for scarce land is a major source of conflict, as well as rivalry between landowners for power and influence in local, regional, and even state and national affairs. Wealthy landowning families will often exercise control over their tenants and the landless people who work on their land, relying on the support of the latter in conflict situations. The outcomes of elections for both local and upper-level councils are influenced by factional conflict, as are the polls in each constituency for state and national legislative bodies.

Religion and Expressive Culture

Hinduism and Islam are the two major religions of Bengal, and religious identification was the basis for the political division experienced by the Bengalis with the departure of British rule in 1947. In West Bengal, Hindus constituted 77 percent of the population in 1981, and Muslims 22 percent. Some 85 percent of Bangladeshis are Muslim, about 14 percent Hindu. Less than 1 percent of Bengalis are Christians; one can also find a few isolated Bengali Buddhist villages in southern Bangladesh.

RELIGIOUS BELIEFS. Bengali Hinduism by and large conforms to the orthodox Vedantic variety of that faith, although in response to the cultural impact of the British in the last century there emerged certain modernistic variants (e.g., the Brahmo Samaj, to which some Westernized high-caste elites were drawn). The Shaivite cult, focusing on worship of the god Shiva and his female counterparts, is widespread among the upper castes, while Vaishnavism, involving devotion to the Lord Krishna, is popular among the lower castes. Bengali Muslims belong overwhelmingly to the Sunni division of Islam and generally conform to the Hanafi school of Islamic law. Popular religion in Bengal often displays syncretism, a mixing of both Hindu and Muslim folk beliefs, deities, and practices. Bengal is famous for its wandering religious mendicant folk musicians (e.g., the Bauls, who disdain caste and conventional Hindu/Muslim religious distinctions in their worship and way of life). In addition to formal worship at Hindu temples and Muslim mosques, popular worship involving religious folk music is widespread, especially at Vaishnavite gatherings (*kirtan*) and among Muslim followers of several Sufi orders (*tarika*) present in Bengal. Bengali Muslims are also known for their practice of "pirism," the cultic following of Muslim saints or holy men (called *pirs*).

RELIGIOUS PRACTITIONERS. The Hindu clergy is drawn from the highest (Brahman) castes and is thus a matter of birthright, although not all Brahmans actually practice as priests (*pandit, purahit*). Practitioners within the Hindu system also include persons who withdraw from conventional society to become religious mendicants in search of personal salvation (*sadhus*). By contrast, in Bengali Islam, recruitment to the clergy is voluntary; any man who has the desire and opportunity to study the Quran (for which he must learn to read the classical Arabic language) can eventually become the worship leader (mullah or imam) of a local mosque if so chosen by the congregation. Further study of the Quran and of Muslim law (the *sharia*) may qualify a man to be a religious leader with a wider following, greater stature, and sometimes significant political influence.

CEREMONIES. The Bengali Hindu religious calendar is replete with worship ceremonies (*puja*) devoted to the deities of both the Great and Little Traditions. Especially important is the annual festival (or *gajan*) of the Lord Shiva, as are those of his counterpart goddesses, Kali and Durga. The goddesses Lakshmi (of wealth and good fortune) and Saraswati (of learning and culture) also have annual ceremonies. Important folk deities propitiated by Hindus and Muslims alike include the "goddesses of the calamities"—Sitala, goddess of smallpox; Olabibi, goddess of cholera; and Manasa, goddess of snakes—all of whom have their annual festivals. Bengali Muslims celebrate the major festivals of Islam: the Id al-Fitr, which marks the end of the Muslim month of fasting (Ramadan); the Id al-Adha, or "feast of the sacrifice," coterminous with the annual pilgrimage (*haj*) to Mecca and commemorating the story of the prophet Ibrahim's willingness to sacrifice his son at God's command. Even though Bengali Muslims are Sunnis, they also observe the

◆ **Shiva**
The Destroyer, who with Brahman and Vishnu forms the Hindu Trinity of gods.

◆ **Vaishnavism**
Following Vishnu as the preeminent Hindu deity.

festival of Muharram, usually associated more prominently with the Shia division of Islam, in which the death of Hussain, grandson of the Prophet Mohammed and martyr of the faith, is mourned. Bengalis also celebrate the well-known Hindu rite of spring called Holi; for members of all religious faiths, the annual new year ceremony on the first day of the Hindu (and Bengali) month of Baisakh, coming between April and May and marking the onset of spring, is a joyous occasion.

ARTS. Urban Bengali elite culture has produced one of South Asia's finest literary traditions, including not only the novel, short story, and poetry but drama and film as well. Some of India's best classical musicians and greatest exponents of the dance have been Bengalis. Bengalis have also made major contributions to Indian and world cinema. Rural Bengal has an old and well-developed folk literature, including narrative poetry (*puthi*), drawn from history, myth, and legend, as well as a very popular itinerant theater (called *jatra*). There is also a strong tradition of religious folk music, particularly associated with the more devotional and mystical practices of popular Hinduism (e.g., worship of the goddess Kali and the Lord Krishna) and of popular Islam (e.g., the devotional gatherings of the various Sufi orders). Terra-cotta temple and mosque architecture throughout Bengal is much admired, and there is a folk tradition of painting, seen in Hindu religious scrolls and in the flowery, and often obscure, religious symbols (*alipana*) commonly daubed in white rice paste on the walls and floors of homesteads by Hindu village women. Finally, despite industrialization and the spread of commercially manufactured products throughout the region, the Bengali rural economy still depends on the services of traditional craftspeople—weavers, potters, carpenters, blacksmiths, metalworkers, and the like—whose wares often represent a high quality of both technique and aesthetic design.

MEDICINE. Although modern scientific medicine has long been known and accepted in Bengal, the homeopathic, allopathic, and the Hindu Ayurvedic and Muslim Unani medical traditions continue to exist as alternatives. There also remains a host of folk beliefs and curing practices among both the urban immigrant poor and the peasantry as a whole. Folk healers (*ojha* or *fakir*) are commonly called upon to treat everything from temporary illnesses and chronic diseases to bone fractures and snakebite, as well as to counteract ethnopsychiatric afflictions resulting from sorcery and ghost possession. Folk curing practices stress the use of magical verses (mantras), often combined with indigenous medicinal concoctions. Traditional healers also provide amulets for protection against devilry and sorcery, the wearing of which is ubiquitous not only among the peasantry and the urban poor but also among the Bengali middle classes as well.

DEATH AND AFTERLIFE. Bengali Hindus, of course, accept the doctrine of samsara, or the transmigration of souls from one earthly life to another. Funerary cremations, practiced by nearly all Hindu castes, are thought to release the individual's spiritual essence or soul from its transitory physical body. Bearing the influence (karma) of all the actions of its just terminated earthly embodiment, the soul then is reincarnated into a new worldly form and way of life shaped by those past actions. Normally a man's eldest son carries out the funerary rites, lighting the funeral pyre after first placing a burning stick in the mouth of the deceased. Muslim beliefs require that at death the person be ritually bathed, shrouded, and buried in a coffin with the head facing the holy city of Mecca, after which there follows a funerary prayer ceremony ideally led by either a relative or a recognized leader of the local Muslim community. The dead are thought to enter an indefinite transitional state—during which the wicked begin to experience punishment and the virtuous to receive their reward—between time of death and an eventual Day of Destruction, upon which the world will come to an end. There will then be a Day of Judgment, whereupon all beings will be restored to life, and humans will be brought before God (Allah) to have their lifetime deeds—which have been recorded by Allah's angels in a Great Book—reviewed and counted. Should one's good deeds outbalance the evil one has done, Resurrection Day will lead to everlasting life in Heaven; if vice versa, the outcome is a purifying, remedial period in Hell, whereupon, purged of its past iniquities, the soul may qualify for entry into Paradise.

Bibliography

Aziz, K. M. Ashraful (1979). *Kinship in Bangladesh.* Monograph Series, no. 1. Dhaka: International Centre for Diarrhoeal Disease Research.

Bertocci, Peter J. (1980). "Models of Solidarity, Structures of Power: The Politics of Community in Rural Bangladesh." In *Ideology and Interest: The Dialectics of Politics,* Political Anthropology Yearbook no. 1, edited by Myron J. Aronoff, 97–125. New Brunswick, N.J.: Transaction Books.

Chaudhuri, Nirad (1951). *The Autobiography of an Unknown Indian.* London: Macmillan.

Davis, Marvin (1983). *Rank and Rivalry: The Politics of Inequality in Rural West Bengal.* Cambridge: Cambridge University Press.

Inden, Ronald B., and Ralph W. Nicholas (1977). *Kinship in Bengali Culture.* Chicago: University of Chicago Press.

Islam, A. K. M. Aminul (1974). *A Bangladesh Village: Political Conflict and Cohesion.* Cambridge, Mass.: Schenkman. Reprint. 1990. Prospect Heights, Ill.: Waveland Press.

Östör, Ákos (1980). *The Play of the Gods: Locality, Ideology, Structure, and Time in the Festivals of a Bengali Town.* Chicago: University of Chicago Press.

Raychaudhuri, Tarak C., and Bikash Raychaudhuri (1981). *The Brahmins of Bengal.* Calcutta: Anthropological Survey of India.

Roy, Manisha (1972). *Bengali Women.* Chicago: University of Chicago Press. Reprint. 1975.

—PETER J. BERTOCCI

BHIL

Ethnonyms: none

Orientation

IDENTIFICATION. The Bhils are the third-largest (after the Gonds and Santals) and most widely distributed tribal group in India. Although their racial origin remains undetermined, they have been variously classified as Gondids, as Proto-Australoid Veddids, and as a subsection of the "Munda race." The name "Bhil" is believed to have been derived from *villu* or *billu*, which in most Dravidian languages is the word for "bow," in reference to the weapon that, until recent times, they seemed almost always to be carrying. Many Urdu speakers, however, equate the term "Bhil" with the English "aboriginal," leading to speculation that the term is a generic one associated with a number of tribes in contiguous areas bearing cultural similarities. Recent work on the Bhils appears to indicate that what has always been treated as one tribal group in fact is heterogeneous in nature. This is reflected in the 1961 census by the numerous tribes that are to be found under the name of "Bhil." It seems best to consider the term "Bhils" as covering a number of subtribes that include the Barelas, Bhagalia, Bhilalas, Dhankas, Dholi, Dublas, Dungri, Gamits or Gamtas, Garasias, Mankars, Mavchis, Mewasi, Nirle (Nilde), Patelia, Pathias, Pavadas, Pawra, Rathias, Rawal, Tadvis, Talavias, Vasavas, and

Vasave. The Dhankas, Tadvis, Pavadas, and the Gamits or Gamtas may refer to themselves as separate tribes, or at least as distinct from the main stock, with the Dhankas even having an origin myth that upholds their derivation from the Rajputs. The Bhilalas are generally acknowledged as a mixture of Bhils and Rajputs. Yet the members of each tribe regard themselves as belonging to an ethnic unit separate from their neighbors and have developed a shared tribal consciousness. The areas inhabited by the Bhils remain some of the more remote and inaccessible parts of India today. Their unique scattered settlement pattern has hindered government efforts to provide services as has their general distrust of government officials. Recent studies of the progress made by the Hindu Bhagat movement appear to indicate that there may be a process of transformation from tribal group to caste under way among the Bhils.

LOCATION. The area occupied by the Bhil is the forested lands of the Vindhya and Satpura hills in the western portion of central India between 20° and 25° N and 73° and 77° E. Straddling the borders of Andhra Pradesh, Gujarat, Madhya Pradesh, Maharashtra, and Rajasthan states, most of this territory, traditionally referred to as "Rewakantha" (a Gujarati term for the drainage of the Rewa, another name for the Narmada River), is the homeland of peoples collectively referred to as the Bhil.

DEMOGRAPHY. A total number of 5,172,129 people are to be found under the heading of "Bhils including other subtribes" in the 1971 census. The largest concentration, 1,618,716 strong, is found in Madhya Pradesh. In Gujarat there are 1,452,987 Bhils, while there are 1,431,020 in Rajasthan. In Maharashtra 678,750 registered as members of the tribal group. The Bhils as a whole recorded an astounding 64.5 percent increase in population (from 2,330,278 to 3,833,331) during the decade 1951–1961, but this remarkable rate may be in large part attributable to the reclassification of the tribal group in the census. Between 1961 and 1971, the Bhil population registered a much more moderate 45.9 percent growth rate.

LINGUISTIC AFFILIATION. The numerous and varied Bhili dialects spoken by the Bhil belong to the Indo-Aryan Family of languages and exhibit divergent levels of Rajasthani and Gujarati influence. A radius of 32 to 48 kilometers appears to be the limit of each dialect's boundaries.

History and Cultural Relations

Although empirical evidence is lacking, the Bhil are credited with the earliest occupation of their

♦ **Munda, Mundari, Austroasiatic, Mon-Khmer**
A language family, formerly called "Kolarian"; its main distribution is throughout Southeast Asia. In India the family is represented by only a number of tribal languages spoken in the east-central parts of the country, notably Santali, Munda, and Oraon.

area, with successive immigrations of Rajputs and conflicts with periodic waves of Muslim invaders believed to have driven them farther into the refuge of the forested central Indian highlands. The Rajputs, in feuds, periods of truce, and even alliances against the Muslims, were a constant source of interaction. By the end of the tenth century, most of Rewakantha was under the rule of either Bhil or Koli (a neighboring tribal group) chieftains. Between the eleventh and fourteenth centuries, the Bhil were supplanted by chiefs of Rajput or mixed descent. In recognition of the Bhil's prior occupation of the land, many Rajput ascensions of the throne in recent times necessitated validation by the performance of a *tika* or consecration ceremony, by representatives of the Bhil chiefs of the area. Around 1480, Rewakantha came under Muslim administration, leading to conversion to Islam among many Bhils. However, these Tadvi Bhils, as they came to be known, maintain many of the traditions as well as the religious beliefs of the past. A political system of rulership is ascribed to the Bhils from the earliest times. From the sixteenth century, which coincides with the Rajput supplantation, the Bhil political leadership fragmented into several chieftainships, leading to speculation that the Hindu encroachment, driving the Bhil into the hinterland, was a dynamic force that led to sociopolitical change. During the eighteenth century, deprived of their lands and finding their subsistence base greatly reduced, the Bhils resorted to looting and pillaging in large, armed bands. This led to conflict with the Maratha invaders and local rulers who retaliated by attempting to eradicate them. The Bhils were killed by the hundreds, and the survivors took refuge even deeper in the hills; this move resulted in greater disintegration of their leadership but increasing self-reliance and individualism. These developments are reflected in today's egalitarian structure of social relations, quite different from the system of rulership that is believed to have existed prior to the successive waves of immigration into Rewakantha. It took the intervention of the British imperial administration to restore peace and order in the Rewakantha territory, enticing the Bhils back through the extension of an amnesty and persuading them to settle down as cultivators. An agreement hammered out by a Mr. Willoughby, a British political agent and Kumar Vasava of Sagbara, a powerful Bhil chief, ensured a semiautonomous status for the Bhil under Rajput territorial administration and provided them with land for cultivation, loans with which to purchase

seed and bullocks, as well as rights to resources of the forest. Similar pacts were worked out in Khandesh. At present, the Bhils are a settled agricultural people whose short history of brigandage undeservedly besmirches their image on occasion. Those who have lost their lands now work as laborers. Extensive deforestation that has now reduced the forest to portions of the eastern highlands has considerably diminished Bhil dependence on forest resources.

Settlements

A Bhil village, whose boundaries are clearly marked by bundles of grass tied to trees along paths and roads, is composed of anywhere from three to forty families inhabiting houses set far apart from each other. A man's grown son may, on occasion, build his hut next to his father's, but generally a distance of 70 to 230 meters separates individual houses. Clusters of homes, usually made up of related families, are not, however, infrequent. The Bhil erect their houses on the tops of the hills with their fields surrounding them, thereby allowing them to maintain constant security over their crops. Where fields extend farther from the households, the Bhil build improvised field houses. The scattered pattern of household distribution results in Bhil villages occupying an area of about 3 to 4 square kilometers. Each village has land reserved for communal use, such as for cattle pasture, for roads, for a village cemetery, and for the community threshing floor. Most Bhils live in rectangular two-storied structures of timber frame with bamboo walls daubed with a plaster made of water, clay, and cattle dung, material valued for its cooling and insect-repelling properties. The windowless abode is provided with an entrance on the front wall that is usually the only opening into the building, although a rear entry for the exclusive use of the resident family may at times be built in. The roof is generally thatched with grass or teak leaves and bamboo, material that often requires annual replacement. Built 0.5 to 1.0 meter above the ground on a plinth of earth and stone or timber, the structure is essentially a cattle shed and domicile, with regional variations on the division and utilization of space.

Economy

SUBSISTENCE AND COMMERCIAL ACTIVITIES. As hunters and gatherers, the Bhils traditionally relied primarily on the bow and arrow, although spears, slings, and axes were also used. Game hunted by the Bhils included rabbits, foxes,

During the eighteenth century, deprived of their lands, the Bhils resorted to looting and pillaging in large, armed bands.

*Among the Bhils of
Khandesh and
Rajpipla, care of
their cattle is
entrusted to the
Gori, members of an
Untouchable caste.*

deer, bear, lizards, pigs, birds, rodents, and wild cats. The same weapons were also used for fishing, along with weir baskets, stone and bamboo traps, nets, and poisons. Edible plants, tubers, and fruits gathered from the forest supplemented their diet or their income, as also did honey, wild fruits, and firewood. The *mahua* tree (*Bassia latifolia*) is an important source of berries and flowers. When they converted to agriculture, the Bhils used slash-and-burn techniques until the method was declared illegal to prevent extensive destruction of the forests. Today fields are farmed continuously, although the lands that were allocated to the Bhils, as enticement to settle down in the nineteenth century, were generally poorer fields that lacked water. Crops planted include maize, millet, cucumbers, cotton, eggplants, chilies, wheat, chickpeas, wild rice, lentils, barley, beans, tobacco, and peanuts. Many Bhils today are landless and make a living working as laborers, primarily in clearing forests and in road repair. The primary draft animal is the bullock, of which each family owns at least a pair, as well as cows with which they may be bred. Buffalo are rare, but goats are kept for their milk and meat, as are pigs and chicken. Most Bhils are nonvegetarian, consuming all forms of game and raising pigs, poultry, and goats for their meat. Although all families own herds of cattle, they are never eaten but are kept for their milk, from which curds and ghee may be made. Maize, rice, wheat, and assorted kinds of millet are staples in the Bhil diet, supplemented with the various vegetables they grow as well as a variety of edible forest products.

INDUSTRIAL ARTS. The Bhil have no tradition of weaving cloth, making pottery, or metalworking and are dependent on trade for the procurement of the products of these crafts.

TRADE. The Kotwals, a caste of basket weavers, are an important trading partner from whom the Bhils obtain mats, baskets, winnowers, and grain containers woven from the bark of bamboo. Clothing is bought ready-made. Earthenware vessels need to be traded for from neighboring potter castes. Vohra and Vania traders that set up shop in weekly markets are the Bhils' primary sources for iron implements, spices, salt, and ornaments. For all these products, the Bhil trade excess agricultural produce, such as grain and vegetables, as well as products of the forest, such as wild honey and mahua flowers. The uncertain nature of the Bhil economy has on many occasions made them dependent on moneylenders for funds to make it through periods of scarcity, as well as to pay for ceremonies associated with important rit-

ual occasions. For these loans, collateral may be in the form of future crop harvests or indentured labor.

DIVISION OF LABOR. The father, as head of the household, controls the pooled income of all members of the family and distributes the daily work among them. The mother assigns and supervises the work among her daughters and daughters-in-law. These duties include the preparation of the family meal and its delivery to the men in the fields. Drawing water from its source, milking the cows, cleaning the cattle shed, and gathering firewood and wild fruits are some of women's daily work. In agriculture, the women assist in transplanting, weeding, and harvesting. The children are generally assigned the task of taking the cattle out to pasture. The agricultural work of plowing and sowing is done by the men and hunting is primarily a male activity.

LAND TENURE. The peaceful solution to the conflict between the Bhils and their neighbors in the late nineteenth century provided the tribals with land for cultivation. Shifting agriculture that the Bhils practiced was ended by government measures that brought pressure to settle permanently and farm the lands allocated to them. Landholdings range from 1.2 to 6 hectares with fruit and nontimber trees considered as part of the property if the owner's father had harvest rights to them. Timber trees are the property of the state. Property taxes are paid to the government annually and the Bhils rarely fall behind in these payments, for fear of offending the goddess of earth and bringing misfortune upon their crops.

Marriage and Family

MARRIAGE. Extensive regional variations of the marriage restrictions exist, although clan exogamy is strictly enforced everywhere. In some areas, such as Sabar Kantha and the Panch Mahals, cross-cousin marriage with the daughter of one's father's sister is permitted or even preferred. Polygyny among the Bhils is quite frequent. In the Ratanmal area, where lowland Bhils express displeasure at the thought of marrying off their daughters to the highland Bhils, a high incidence of this intermarriage occurs nevertheless, almost all as a result of elopement. This practice invariably results in dissatisfaction and bitterness, especially where negotiations for the bride-wealth are involved. Bhils marry young, at around 14–16 years for boys and 11–13 years for girls. A boy's first wife is expected to be a virgin. Residence is not established until after the girl's first menstruation, and the couple remain in most respects highly dependent on their parents for guidance and assistance for several more years. Clan exogamic injunctions are strictly enforced. Additionally, tribal endogamy is preferred, therefore intermarriage is often spatially restricted to a 35- to 40-kilometer radius. Although polygyny is accepted, the high bride-price to be paid, especially for a virgin first wife, is an important reason for the prevalence of monogamy among the Bhils. Sororal unions often occur among polygynous marriages, but although leviratic alliances are allowed they are quite rare. Most marriages fall in one of five categories: contract marriages, elopements, mutual attraction, marriage by service, and abduction.

A married woman sets up residence in her husband's village, in a new house built near his father's homestead. A son is generally given some farmland and a few head of cattle with which he may subsist and provide for his own family. The new couple function as a distinct economic unit and are expected soon to be independent of his parents, but mutual assistance occurs frequently, especially in such farming activities as plowing, sowing, and harvesting. It is not uncommon for related men to cultivate land jointly with the express purpose of sharing the harvest equally.

Among polygynous families, each wife is entitled to her own abode, but all are considered members of one household. The senior wife maintains a position of authority and determines the equitable distribution of the labor requirements of the homestead. The annulment of a marriage is formally recognized by all parties with the return of the bride-wealth. The dissolution of a marriage is often initiated by the woman, who, dissatisfied with her husband, abandons him, frequently eloping with another man.

DOMESTIC UNIT.   The basic coresidential unit is the nuclear family, comprising a couple and their unmarried children. Within polygynous families, several contiguous homes may constitute the homestead. As sons marry, the nuclear family loses its commensal nature but solidarity continues as a joint family evolves with corporate characteristics, wherein the patriarch maintains ultimate control and authority over the landholdings.

INHERITANCE.   Upon the death of the patriarch, his property and debts are divided among his sons, the size of the allotment increasing in direct proportion to a son's seniority. A daughter receives an inheritance only if she has no male siblings, although her father's brother's sons may receive an allotment as well. Property owned by her is inalienable and reverts back to the lineage upon

KINSHIP

Kin Groups and Descent

Within each 32- to 40-kilometer radius, the limits of a tribal and dialectal boundary, the Bhil are divided into *ataks* (clans), patrilineal exogamous descent groups. Clans are led by chiefs who have paramount power in matters concerning the clan or caste. These clans may be segmented, with each portion distributed among similar divisions of other clans over a wide area. A process of fission appears to be quite actively involved, resulting in dispersion of the polysegmentary clans. Clanship appears to have practically no regional or corporate function. The structural importance of clanship is limited, apparently, to serving as guidelines for determining the extent of exogamy as well as for purposes of identification in reckoning descent. Within the clans are generally vici-

nage-based *nal*, or lineages, that are corporate in character. Disputes between members of the lineage are resolved by male elders of the lineage who also control activities within the group. In theory, the lineage reserves residual rights to its members' property. Examples of both cognitive and unilineal descent systems occur among the Bhils. Males always belong to their father's joint or extended family, lineage, clan, and village. Upon marriage into a lineage, women are assumed into their husband's kinship group.

Kinship Terminology

Among the Bhils of the Ratanmal hill area of Vadodara District in Gujarat, kinship terminology is classificatory. A man's relatives fall into at least one of four categories: (1) his patrilineage, (2) other cognatic kinsmen, de-

scended from women of his lineage, which include his father's sister as well as his own sister, (3) his *haga*, or wife's relatives now related to him by marriage, and (4) his *haga-sambandhi*, a term for those not directly related to him who are cognatically or affinally related to his immediate relatives. In the Panch Mahals and Sabar Kantha districts of Gujarat, descriptive kinship terms also occur for such categories as grandfather (the older father or aged father) and grandmother (the older mother or aged mother), for whom there are no classificatory names. The Bhils in the former state of Rajpipla (now Nandod taluk of Bharuch District, Gujarat) and in West Khandesh, Dhule District, Maharashtra, reflective of preferential cross-cousin marriage, have one term, *mama*, by which they refer to their father's sister's husband or mother's brother.

The Bhils' history of interaction with the British imperial government is characterized by alternating periods of submission and of sporadic, isolated rebellion.

her death if she in turn has no heirs. In instances where there are no direct heirs, the property is inherited by the deceased person's closest collaterals.

SOCIALIZATION. Although formal submissiveness is rarely stressed, discipline is maintained by frequent beatings or threats, and the child is expected to contribute to the household economy very early, often accompanying the parents in their daily rounds by the age of 6. Babies are weaned from the mother's breast and fed solid food after 10 to 11 months. Among the Bhils, the shaving of the head occurs when the child reaches the age of 5 years.

Sociopolitical Organization

The Bhils' history of interaction with the British imperial government is characterized by alternating periods of submission and of sporadic, isolated rebellion. The overall objectives of their uprisings were to protest the erosion of agrarian and forest rights as well as to demand the attainment of higher social status and political self-determination. Tribal peoples were among the last to become politicized and thus their participation in national politics was much delayed. Until the early 1940s, awareness of tribal concerns among Indian leaders, with the exception of Mahatma Gandhi and Rajendra Prasad, was rare, and tribal issues were never addressed in resolutions passed in Congress.

SOCIAL ORGANIZATION. Among the Bhils, a social distinction is conceptualized by the different subtribes, including a division between Ujwala (or pure) Bhils in Kotra Bhomat and Kalia (impure) Bhils. A cleavage is also evident between the plains and hill Bhils, with the former considering themselves superior. Bhil villages consist of two or more extended families (*tad* in Ratanmal), each with a depth of six to seven generations and inclusive of cognates such as sisters' children, a pattern that tends to promote cooperation and unity among the extended family. In Ratanmal, a village's population may be made up entirely of members of one lineage, but in many villages several lineages may be represented and one lineage, claiming descent from the village founder and thus ownership of the village, becomes the dominant lineage. The members of the subordinate lineages in this case enjoy restricted privileges, and their rights to the lands they till, in theory at least, are subject to revocation by the dominant lineage. Dominant (*bhaibeta*) lineages reserve for their use the most fertile lands, the choicest pastures, most fruit trees, and other valuable trees

even when they stand on the subordinate (*karhan*) lineage's plots of land. In general, the karhan are considered as mere tenants and are excluded from participation in the management of the affairs of the village. Bhils recognize the concept of caste purity and impurity in transactions with artisan castes; and among Hinduized Bhils, their dependence on ritual specialists such as sweepers and handlers of cattle carcasses has increased. Among the Bhils of Khandesh and Rajpipla, care of their cattle is entrusted to the Gori, members of an Untouchable caste.

POLITICAL ORGANIZATION. Each village is under the leadership of a headman (*vasawo* in Gujarat; *gammaiti* among the Palia Bhils; *gaddo* among the Kalia Bhils; *tadavi* in Ratanmal; *mukhi* in Kotra Bhomat), a hereditary position whose functions include being the head both of the dominant lineage and of the local *pancha* or village assembly. The headman represents not only the lineage but also the village in functions beyond the community, and he is also the local conduit for transactions between the villagers and the government. He is assisted by one or two functionaries whom he generally appoints from among his kin. In some large Bhil villages in Gujarat, the *pardhan* (another hereditary office, but confirmed by the government) is subordinate only to the vasawo. During a headman's absence, he assumes many of the functions of the vasawo's office relating to government. The amount of power vested in the office of the headman varies greatly on a regional basis, but his dependence on the village *panchayat* (council) is constant in Bhil society.

SOCIAL CONTROL. The village council is composed of all the senior men of the village, and when they meet on important matters that concern the village, its members are of equal status, be they members of the dominant lineage or of the subordinate lineages. Indeed, since almost all important matters are discussed within the council before a decision is reached regarding their resolution, the subordinate lineages, which often are numerically and economically stronger, are able to assert themselves politically as equals of the dominant lineage. The headman settles disputes, imposes sanctions on dissidents, gives advice, arranges the settlement of debts, and mediates conflicts within the family. The presence of the headman is essential in validating any transaction, with negotiations being sealed and held binding by the eating of opium. Where serious punishment such as ostracism, banishment, or trials by ordeal are indicated, council acquiescence and support is essential before the headman delivers the verdict. Serious crimes that would have merited these punishments in the past, however, are at present brought before a local magistrate.

CONFLICT. Apart from their history of resistance to successive waves of invasion and domination by Rajputs, Muslims, Hindus, and the British, the Bhils had a brief period of brigandage and a series of rebellions during which their martial skills were put to the test. Their most efficient weapons of war were those that they employed for exploiting the forest environment—their bows and arrows. They sometimes also carried muskets, swords, and daggers.

Religion

RELIGIOUS BELIEFS. The Bhils have traditionally been classified as animists; this classification is reflected in the 1901 census, wherein 97.25 percent were labeled as animists and the remainder were associated with the Hindu faith. The process of Hinduization has, however, been a long-term process, and the lower level of Hindu belief integrates much animistic belief for which the Bhils would have found much affinity. There are localized deities, such as Wagh deo, the tiger god. Nandervo, the god of agriculture, is paid homage to after the rains have brought a new growth of grass. Shrines to lesser gods are built on slightly elevated and secluded land that is believed to preserve their sanctity by keeping them away from the pollution of the lower regions. Images of deities are also kept near their agricultural fields, to be propitiated with offerings to ensure the safety and quality of the crops. Today Christianity, Islam, and Hinduism are the major faiths that the Bhils adhere to, with the latter two having had the most impact on the belief systems. Among the Ratanmal Bhils, Hinduism is widespread, with four main elements predominating. (1) The few Hindu gods that they have adopted are powerful but benevolent rather than malevolent. (2) They believe in the existence of an afterlife where one's senior relatives maintain authority and control over events in this life, even in death. (3) There are many spirits of the earth, some that unite in bands with maleficent intentions and require personal devotion and regular propitiation. (4) There are malicious individuals among them that wield supernatural powers in the form of witchcraft and sorcery that must be neutralized. Bhagwan is the predominant name for the supreme deity among the Bhils, although in Ratanmal he is also referred to as Mahaveda. Kalika, the "earth mother," is another deity who evokes reverence and fear. Holi, an important postharvest festival, is celebrated for her. A person who did not die of natural causes—a murder or a suicide, for example—is believed to become a malevolent spirit who will consume people. Twins and babies with unusual features or deformities are believed to be manifestations of an evil spirit that must be destroyed immediately lest they be a source of danger to their kin (the practice is now illegal). Two Muslim sections of the Bhils are the Tadvi of Madhya Pradesh and the Nirle or Nilde in Maharashtra. They maintain, apart from the main body of Islamic faith, a belief in a *pir* or guardian spirit of the village for whom a shrine (*mazar*) is built, and this is the focal point for the annual *urs* or *jatra* festivals that celebrate the death anniversary of the spirit.

RELIGIOUS PRACTITIONERS. A priest (*badava*) among the Ratanmal Bhils plays the role of medium, diviner, and healer as well as worshiper. Only males may become priests as women are considered to be ritually impure and also believed to have insufficient strength of character. A person is born a priest but requires a long period of training under a master who imparts the wisdom and technical intricacies of the priesthood. The culmination of the rigorous period of discipline is a trial by ordeal. He may then undergo possession or induce possession in others. In essence, he officiates in functions that involve the gods. Below him are the more numerous priests who do not possess the spiritual strength to undergo the ordeal and as such are competent only in rituals that involve malignant ghosts. Lowest in rank are those who only possess powers that allow them to divine the causes of illness, heal certain diseases, or offer sacrifices and worship. Priests are generally no match for witches and are immune to witches' powers only if they are under the possession of a deity. To deal with these dangerous and formidable persons, villagers call on the aid of a witch doctor (*kajalio badava*) who has developed the power of divining the witches and sorcerers, neutralizing their powers, and, on occasion, destroying them. Sorcerers are believed to be persons who have trained for priesthood but, lacking the moral fortitude to resist, have succumbed to temptations to use their skills for personal gain (either monetary or in terms of power over others). Witches are believed to be persons (usually women) with low moral integrity who, lacking spiritual strength, have become agents of evil

♦ **Holi**
A Hindu spring festival marked by much merriment, especially the throwing of colored water or powders at passersby.

spirits in exchange for the occult powers of flight and transformation.

CEREMONIES. Apart from the main festivals of Holi and urs mentioned above, as well as rituals associated with childrearing, other festivals celebrated by the Ratanmal Bhils include the Akhatrij, when offerings are made to Mahadeva, the god of destruction; Indraj, the sky god; and Hadarjo Kuvar, the guardian spirit of fertility of the earth and women. These are joyous occasions marked by feasts, singing, and dancing. An *anabolkham* or ghost ritual, in contrast, is marked by tension, performed as a gesture of appeasement or propitiation to a spirit and is prompted by a series of unfortunate events. *Gundaru kadvanu* (exorcism of the cattle shed) is one major ghost ritual that takes place in a clearing in the jungle, during which offerings are made to all punitive and malignant spirits. In such rituals, active participation is limited to the headman, a ritual specialist, and a priest, while others attending maintain distance and silence. Women of all ages are barred from being present or anywhere near the site. In the Panch Mahals, the Bhils observe Gol Gadhedo six days after Holi. In a central place in the village, a pole is raised at the top of which some jaggery (crude sugar, or *gur*) is tied. Men attempt to climb the pole and reach the gur even as the women, drunk and armed with sticks, try to deny them access to the pole. He who succeeds in reaching the gur is considered clever and throws the prize down to the crowd. The Muslim Tadvi Bhils continue to observe local and regional festivals such as Adhujee, Holi, Dassara, and Divali (the lamp festival) but have minimized their religious significance.

ARTS. There is very little representational art among the Bhils. Rough wooden posts of carved human figures are sometimes used as memorials to the deceased. Some Bhils sport tattoos, many in the form of crescent moons, stars, and flowers. Music is perhaps the area of greatest artistic elaboration, with songs playing a central role in the celebration of festivals and in such ceremonies as weddings.

MEDICINE. In Gujarat most diseases have an associated god who must be appeased to relieve illness. For epidemics, Bhils may resort to building a toy cart that they consecrate and take to another village, whose people in turn take it to the outskirts of another, and so on, until the cart has reached a remote portion of the forest. By doing so they hope to drive out the plague. Since Bhils believe that illness is caused by the displeasure of

the spirits, they are indifferent to practitioners of modern medicine.

DEATH AND AFTERLIFE. The traditional method of disposing of the body was by burial, but Hindu influence has made cremation much more prevalent with a secondary burial of the charred remains. People raise memorial markers made of either stone or wood, with heroic figures often carved into the material. Ceremonies are performed three and twelve days after cremation, and food is set out for the deceased up to a year after death. All the dead of a house are offered food during important occasions. The Ratanmal Bhils believe in an afterlife where the spirits, endowed with human attributes that correspond to those of their past life, hover about the area that they lived in and maintain interest in their surviving kin. Thus, "good" persons who died of natural causes are believed to become benevolent spirits. Those who were mean or spiteful, practiced witchcraft, or died violently are believed to become malevolent spirits that cause misfortune among the living.

Bibliography

Ahuja, Ram (1966). "Marriage among the Bhils." *Man in India* 46:233–240.

Bhandari, Bhagwat (1989). *Tribal Marriages and Sex Relations: Customary Laws of Marriage in Bhil and Garasias Tribes.* Udaipur: Himanshu.

Carstairs, G. Morris (1954). "The Bhils of Kotra Bhomat." *Eastern Anthropologist* 7:169–181.

Koppers, Wilhelm (1948). *Die Bhil in Zentralindien.* Wiener Beiträge zur Kulturgeschichte und Linguistik, vol. 7. Vienna: Institut für Völkerkunde. Translated by Theodore Ziolkowski. *The Bhil in Central India.* 1958. New Haven, Conn.: Human Relations Area Files.

Moore, Grace Wood (1965). *Bhil Cultural Summary.* New Haven, Conn.: Human Relations Area Files.

Naik, T. B. (1956). *The Bhils: A Study.* Delhi: Bharatiya Adimjati Sevak Sangh.

Nath, Y. V. S. (1960). *Bhils of Ratanmal: An Analysis of the Social Structure of a Western Indian Community.* Baroda: Maharajah Sayajirao University.

Navlakha, Surendra Kumar (1959). "The Authority Structure among the Bhumij and Bhil: A Study of Historical Causations." *Eastern Anthropologist* 13: 27–40.

Rao, Adityendra (1988). *Tribal Social Stratification.* Udaipur: Himanshu.

—ANGELITO PALMA

BRAHMAN AND CHHETRI OF NEPAL

Ethnonym: Bahun

Orientation

IDENTIFICATION. Brahman and Chhetri are high Hindu Nepalese castes. They have played a more dominant role than have any other group in the formation of the modern Nepalese state. Their moral values and social and political strength continue to play a commanding part in contemporary Nepalese life. Brahmans are known in Nepali as "Bahuns." Chhetri is the Nepali equivalent of Kshatriya, the second of the four *varnas* into which classical Indian society was divided.

LOCATION. Brahmans and Chhetris are found throughout Nepal. Those living in the Terai (the low, level strip in the southern part of the country) are much like their counterparts across the border in northern India. This article describes those who inhabit the middle hills of Nepal. Here the climate of their villages depends primarily on elevation, which varies from 300 meters or so in the valley bottoms to as high as 2,500 to 3,000 meters on the hillsides and tops of ridges.

DEMOGRAPHY. Because the Nepalese census does not record the caste status of citizens, it is impossible to know how many Brahmans and Chhetris inhabit the country; but probably the two castes together constitute the largest group in Nepal. Their percentage of the population declines from the western hills, where they comprise well over half the population, to the east, where they are usually one among many minorities.

LINGUISTIC AFFILIATION. Brahmans and Chhetris speak the national language, Nepali, as their mother tongue. This is an Indo-European language closely related to Hindi and other North Indian languages. Like Sanskrit, the language from which it is descended, Nepali is written in the Devanagari script, which is a syllabary rather than an alphabet. The rate of literacy among Brahman men, whose traditional priestly role required them to read sacred Hindu texts, is well above the national average.

History and Cultural Relations

Brahmans are thought to have begun emigrating to the far western Nepalese hills in the twelfth century after they were dislodged by Muslim invasions in India. In the Nepal hills they encountered the Khas, people of the same general background as the Brahmans, who nevertheless ranked low in the caste order because of their deviance from orthodox caste rules. Both the Khas and the progeny of unions of Brahman men and Khas women, called Khatri, were granted the status of Chhetri. The existence of Matwali Chhetris (those who drink liquor), who do not wear the sacred thread, is evidence that not all Khas were accorded Chhetri status.

Settlements

Brahmans and Chhetris live in villages, hamlets, and isolated homesteads. The walls of their small houses are constructed from stone or mud brick, painted red ocher around the base, whitewashed above, and topped with a thatched roof. The floors and interior walls are made from a mixture of cow dung and mud, which dries to a clean, hard surface. The houses of those living in towns, such as Kathmandu, the capital, are larger and are made of brick and cement.

Economy

SUBSISTENCE AND COMMERCIAL ACTIVITIES. Rural Brahmans and Chhetris keep a few cattle and raise crops in their terraced fields. Brahmans also act as family priests, and Chhetris serve in both the Nepalese army and the Gorkha (Gurka) brigades of the British and Indian armies. In urban areas both castes are prominent in government service, financial services, and politics.

INDUSTRIAL ARTS. Any needs that Brahmans and Chhetris experience for craft and industrial products are met by lower-ranked artisan castes, such as blacksmiths, tailors, and leather workers.

TRADE. In rural areas Brahmans and Chhetris typically rely on others, such as Newar shopkeepers, for their commercial requirements.

DIVISION OF LABOR. Only Brahman males may act as priests, but much of the daily household *puja* (worship) is done by women. The day-to-day agropastoral activities of Brahman and Chhetri families are shared between men and women. Both sexes work in the fields, but overall women spend more hours per day in agricultural and domestic labor than men. They perform most of the child care, preparation and cooking of food, and weeding and tending of crops. Men do the plowing and maintain the terrace walls. Both are active at harvest time.

LAND TENURE. Brahmans and Chhetris are often landowners. Fields are often terraced and mostly have been fractionated into small plots

Brahmans and Chhetri have played a more dominant role than have any other group in the formation of the modern Nepalese state.

♦ **Sanskrit**
The sacerdotal Indo-Aryan language of South Asia in ancient times, as contrasted with the Prakrits or common speech. Sanskrit is still used by Brahmans in their prayers, but otherwise is hardly spoken.

Brahman and Chhetri of Nepal

KINSHIP

CHHETRI WARRIOR

A Nepali woman of the Chhetri, or warrior, caste, wears a large, jeweled stud in her nose. Brahmans and Chhetris are Hindu. Annapurna Sanctuary, Nepal. (Craig Lovell/Corbis)

through inheritance over generations. Large-scale absentee landlordism is not common in the hills of Nepal.

Kinship

KIN GROUPS AND DESCENT. Brahmans and Chhetris are members of two kinds of clans, the *thar* (indicated as a surname) and the *gotra*; the former is exogamous if a relation can be traced, but the latter is strictly exogamous. Descent and inheritance follow the male line exclusively.

KINSHIP TERMINOLOGY. All first cousins are addressed by sibling terms. Siblings are designated as either older or younger brothers or sisters: there is no generic term for brother or sister. Unrelated persons, including strangers, are also often addressed by kinship terms.

Marriage and Family

MARRIAGE. Most marriages are monogamous, but polygynous unions were traditionally frequent and are still occasionally found. Second and subsequent wives are often members of other ethnic groups, such as the Gurungs, Magars, Tamangs, Sherpas, and Newars, but not low-caste artisan groups. With the exception of Thakuris, the self-proclaimed aristocrats among the Chhetris who practice matrilateral cross-cousin marriage,

cousin marriage is not practiced. Brahman girls traditionally married by the age of 11, and Chhetri girls a few years later; but educated urban dwellers now marry in their late teens or early twenties. Grooms are normally a few years older than their brides. Village exogamy is usually observed, and parents arrange their children's marriages with the help of an intermediary. An astrologer also is consulted to ensure that the couple make a good match. The boy's family priest, in consultation with the bride's family, sets an auspicious date and time, based on the lunar calendar (several months of the year are inauspicious for marriage). The entire wedding ceremony lasts a full day, from the time the members of the groom's party arrive at the bride's home till they leave the next day with the bride. The most important part of the ritual is *kanyadan*, the gift of the bride to the groom by her parents. A married woman always wears vermilion powder in the parting of her hair, so long as her husband is alive.

DOMESTIC UNIT. The newly married couple ideally, and usually, live with the groom's family, along with his parents, brothers and their wives (if any), and unmarried sisters. A new bride enters this household in a lowly position, and her mother-in-law usually gives her the most onerous chores. Her status rises after she has given birth to a child, particularly if it is a son. Eventually she herself succeeds to the powerful position of mother-in-law.

INHERITANCE. Except for what a daughter may receive as dowry, all property, particularly all landed property, is inherited by sons. If a joint family is dissolved before the senior parents die, a woman is entitled to a share of her husband's property.

SOCIALIZATION. Mother and child are considered polluting until the eleventh day after birth, when a purifying ceremony is conducted and the baby is given a name. The first feeding of rice, called *pasni*, is given after 5 months for a girl and 7 months for a boy. A boy's head is shaved at about 7 years of age (a small tuft of hair is left on the back as a sign that he is a Hindu), and he is formally initiated into full caste membership when he receives the sacred thread, either at the time of the haircut or a few years later. At her first menstruation a girl is removed to another house, where she is shielded from the sight of any men in her family and from the sun. Both parents participate in raising their children, but women perform most of the child care, especially in the preteen years. Fathers act as disciplinarians as their children grow older.

Sociopolitical Organization

SOCIAL ORGANIZATION. A caste system prevails, with the Brahmans and Chhetris occupying a very high position in it.

POLITICAL ORGANIZATION. Village political life tends to follow its own dynamic, regardless of changes in the national political scene. Village affairs tend to be managed by formal or informal councils of village elders in which Brahmans and Chhetris, by virtue of their status as landholders and their relatively higher education, often play prominent roles. Nationally the king, whose ancestor unified the country in roughly its present form at the end of the eighteenth century, has always been a Thakuri, an aristocratic section of Chhetris. The Rana family, which provided all prime ministers from 1846 till 1950 and is still powerful in the government and army, is also Chhetri. The movement to overthrow the Ranas and subsequent political movements aimed at democratic or socialist reform have frequently been led by Brahmans and Chhetris.

SOCIAL CONTROL. Until 1963 Nepal's Mulki Ain (national code) explicitly stated which activities were proper for each caste group and prescribed penalties for infractions of the law. Since the code's revision in 1963, the Mulki Ain treats all citizens equally under the law.

CONFLICT. Those conflicts that cannot be settled through informal means at the village level are referred to the legal and judicial system of Nepal.

Religion and Expressive Culture

RELIGIOUS BELIEFS. All Brahmans and Chhetris are Hindus and subscribe to most of the basic Hindu beliefs. At a minimum these include three notions. One is dharma—the idea that each person has a specific duty, moral code, and set of behaviors which are entailed by virtue of membership in a group (such as a caste group). Another idea is that of karma—sometimes likened to "cause and effect," because it explains whatever present state of affairs exists in terms of the events in previous lives that produced it. The third is *moksha* (salvation)—release from the round of rebirths that reincarnation involves.

RELIGIOUS PRACTITIONERS. Brahmans may act as family priests (for Brahman and Chhetri households, but not for other castes and ethnic groups), as well as officiate at shrines and temples and at rituals associated with major festivals. They also handle all the rituals performed during marriage. They are generally present on religious oc-

casions and read excerpts from the Vedas or other Sanskrit texts. They also recite from the Puranas and from the two great Hindu epics, the *Ramayana* and the *Mahabharata*.

CEREMONIES. All Brahmans and Chhetris are Hindus and observe festivals, perform rituals, and worship deities associated with Hinduism. One of the more important annual festivals is Dasein (or Durga Puja), in which the goddess Durga (Kali) is worshiped over a fortnight in the month of October. Many ritual offerings and animal sacrifices are made at this time, and there is much feasting and visiting among immediate family and extended kin. On the tenth day of the fortnight each individual male and female pays respect to senior relatives, who then reciprocate by placing a colored *tika* on the forehead of the junior person. Also observed is Phagu (called Holi in India), the spring rite of Hindu culture related to fecundity and the god Krishna. It comes in the month of Phagun (February-March) and is a riotous time when men, women, and children sing, dance, and throw colored powder and water at each other. Other annual festivals include Tihar (Dipavali, the festival of lights), Janai Purnima (changing of the sacred thread), and Tij-panchami (a purificatory rite for women). Rituals in addition to those mentioned above (under Socialization and Marriage) include worship of the household god (*kuldevta*), worship of brothers by sisters (*bhai tika*, celebrated during Tihar), and daily (morning and sometimes evening) worship of various of the Hindu deities, including Ganesh, Shiva, Vishnu, Ram, Krishna, Saraswati, Durga, Parvati, Narayan, Bhairab, and many others. Some Chhetris of west Nepal worship Mashta through shamans (*dhamis* or *jhankris*) and know little or nothing about traditional Hindu deities and festivals.

ARTS. Brahmans and Chhetris are not known for their artistic interests or abilities. Music, dance, and visual and plastic arts are traditionally the domain of other, generally lower castes, and except among educated urban people Brahmans and Chhetris do not indulge themselves in these activities. Their simple, mostly undecorated houses reflect this lack of artistic bent.

MEDICINE. Brahmans and Chhetris will accept medical help from any available source, whether it is an Ayurvedic doctor (a specialist in herbal medicine), a passing Buddhist lama with a reputation for effective medicines, a shaman who prescribes treatment after going into a trance, or a practitioner trained in modern scientific medicine.

DEATH AND AFTERLIFE. Someone whose death appears to be imminent is taken to a river-

The Brahman and Chhetri of Nepal are not known for their artistic interests or abilities. Music, dance, and visual arts are traditionally the domain of other, generally lower, castes.

♦ **dharma**
The duties proper to one's station in Hindu life.

♦ **karma**
The effect of former deeds, whether done in this life or in a previous existence. These are thought to determine a Hindu's future and his or her social condition.

♦ **Vedas**
The four oldest documents of Hinduism, written in early Sanskrit in north India. They are the Rig Veda (perhaps 1200–900 B.C.), the Yajur Veda, the Sama Veda, and the Atharva Veda. Collectively these books are known as "Samhitas."

All Gonds are in some way or other engaged in agriculture or work in the forest. They would not dream of accepting any other occupation.

bank to die, as all rivers are considered sacred. Even if death occurs elsewhere, within hours the corpse is cremated beside the river, into which the ashes are finally cast. Mourning restrictions (including elimination of salt and other items from the diet) for the death of a close relative are observed for thirteen days. Men shave their heads and are considered polluting during this time. At the end of the mourning period a big feast takes place. Food and other items for the deceased in the next life are given as gifts to the officiating priest. For one year a monthly *shraddha* ceremony is performed. Thereafter an annual shraddha ceremony commemorates the person who has died. Without funeral rites—which must be performed by a son—the deceased cannot proceed to either Heaven or Hell and instead will plague survivors as an evil spirit.

Bibliography

Bennett, Lynn (1983). *Dangerous Wives and Sacred Sisters: Social and Symbolic Roles of High-Caste Women in Nepal.* New York: Columbia University Press.

Bista, Dor Bahadur (1987). *People of Nepal.* 5th ed. Kathmandu: Ratna Pustak Bhandar.

Fürer-Haimendorf, Christoph von (1966). "Unity and Diversity in the Chhetri Caste of Nepal." In *Caste and Kin in Nepal, India, and Ceylon,* 11–67. London: Asia Publishing House.

Hitchcock, John T. (1978). "An Additional Perspective on the Nepali Caste System." In *Himalayan Anthropology: The Indo-Tibetan Interface,* edited by James F. Fisher, 111–120. The Hague: Mouton Publishers.

Prindle, Peter H. (1983). *Tinglatar: Socio-Economic Relationships of a Brahmin Village in East Nepal.* Kathmandu: Ratna Pustak Bhandar.

Sharma, Prayag Raj (1971). "The Matwali Chhetris of Western Nepal." *Himalayan Review* 4:43–60.

—JAMES F. FISHER

GOND

Ethnonym: Koi

Orientation

IDENTIFICATION. The Gonds are an important and numerous tribe, residing at the present time mainly in Gondavana, "the Land of the Gonds," the easternmost districts of Madhya Pradesh, formerly the Central Provinces of India. They were first called "Gonds" (hill men) by the Mogul rulers. They call themselves Koi or Koitūr; the meaning of the latter name is unclear.

LOCATION. While the Gond live mainly in Madhya Pradesh, important clusters live also in the adjoining districts to the north, west, and south of Gondavana. Many of these subsections have assumed different tribal names so that their identity with the Gond tribe is not always clear.

DEMOGRAPHY. The latest available Census figures are from 1971, when there were 4,728,796 Gonds—one of the largest tribal groups on earth. In fact, the number of Gonds is really much higher, since many Gond communities have been fully accepted into the Hindu caste system, have adopted another name, and have completely abandoned their original tribal ways of life. While some Gond subsections thus have been lost to the tribe, some communities of different origin may have been incorporated into the Gond tribe. The Bisonhorn Marias of Bastar may be such a tribe.

LINGUISTIC AFFILIATION. If the Gonds ever had a language of their own, they have lost it completely. Half of the Gonds speak a Dravidian language called Gondi at present, which is more akin to Teluga than to Karmada. In the southern parts of Gondavana the Gonds speak a language called Parsi or Parji (Persian), also of the Dravidian family. In the northern regions the Gonds often speak the local language, a dialect of Hindi or Marathi.

History and Cultural Relations

The racial history of the Gonds is unknown. From their physical appearance it is obvious that they differ from the Aryan and Dravidian speakers settled in the country. According to B. S. Guha, they are Proto-Australoids by race like the Oraons and Maler of Chota Nagpur Plateau. It is unknown when and by which route they arrived in this part of India. At one time they must have been settled in the hills between Tamil Nadu and Karnataka, because their dialect, Gondi, is closely related to the languages of those regions. R. V. Russell and Hira Lal maintain that only between the ninth and thirteenth centuries A.D. did the Gonds come and settle in present-day Gondavana. They became progressive and wealthy farmers and were gradually transformed into Ragbansi Rajputs. When the ruling Rajput dynasties in these regions declined, Gonds established themselves as rulers at four centers. The zenith of their might was from the sixteenth to eighteenth centuries. Then the Marathas under a Bhonsle ruler of Nagpur overran their country and completely dispossessed them of their power except in the hill fastnesses, which held out against all invaders.

Settlements

The Gonds invariably live in villages. But in each village the Gonds live in a hamlet of their own. The hamlet is not a closed cluster of huts, for the Gonds' homesteads are spread over a large area within the hamlet. Each homestead houses a family, often a joint family consisting of the families of the married sons living with their parents. In the plains where the Gonds are more Sanskritized, or influenced by high Hindu culture, some have adopted Hindu ways and begun to live in closed villages, yet apart from the other castes and tribes.

Economy

All Gonds are in some way or other engaged in agriculture or work in the forest. They would not dream of accepting any other occupation. Originally they must have been nomadic hunters and food gatherers and then switched to shifting cultivation, retaining, however, their close connection with the forest. Shifting cultivation is not merely one type of agriculture but a complex cultural form, a way of life. It requires no draft animals and allows the cultivators more leisure time for work in the forest, hunting, fishing, and the collection of jungle produce. However, most Gonds have been forced to abandon shifting cultivation by the government because it is harmful to the forest, and some Gond sections had already voluntarily changed over to plow cultivation and even to terrace cultivation. They prospered economically and acquired a high social standing.

Kinship

KIN GROUPS AND DESCENT. The Gonds have a pronounced patrilineal and patriarchal clan system. They call it *gotra* or *kur*. A Gond clan comprises a group of persons who believe that they are descendants in the male line from a common ancestor. While a male can never change his clan, a woman on marriage is taken into the clan of her husband. The Gonds practice clan exogamy, considering intermarriage within a clan to be incest. They believe the gods would punish such a sin with a skin disease, worms in a wound, or leprosy. Offenders against the law of exogamy are excluded from the tribal community and can only be readmitted after separation. Many of the

SOCIOPOLITICAL ORGANIZATION

Social Organization

Since the Gonds are spread over a wide area, there are many local subsections that have no social contact with each other. The more Sanskritized these sections are, the higher is the social rank they claim. But the highest rank is given to the descendants of the Gond rajas and their retainers, the Raj-Gonds and Katholias. Among these two sections we find the greatest number of Gonds with substantial landholdings. Other Gond sections outside of Gondavana are the Kisans, in the south of Bihar and in the neighboring districts of Orissa. The Gonds reached even the hills along the southern bank of the Ganges. There they are known as Majwars or Majhis (headmen). Akin to the Gonds are a number of other tribes, such as the Bhattras, Koyas, Konda Kapus, Konda Deras, and Halbas. The Khonds of Orissa, another important tribe, also may originally have been Gonds.

Political Organization

The entire Gond tribe was never a political unit. Tribal solidarity does not extend beyond the confines of a subsection. The basic political unit is the Gond village community. It is a democratic organization in which the headman and other officials are chosen by the villagers. Each village has its council, with officials like the headman, the priest, the village watchman, and four or five elders. More important affairs are discussed and decided upon by all the men of the community. A village has also its servant castes, such as the Ahir (cowherds), Agaria (blacksmiths), Dhulia (drummers), and Pardhan (bards and singers). At the towns of Garha-Mandla, Kharla, Deogarh, and Chanda, the leading headmen managed to rise to the rank of rulers (*rajas*) and to establish dynasties that lasted for centuries. But the very fact that these rajas surrounded themselves with Hindu officials and eagerly adopted Hindu or Mogul methods of administration proves that royalty was alien to tribal democracy. In the present political situation the Gonds are, despite their numbers, politically powerless, which is partly because of this tribal disunity but also because of their comparative lack of education and drive, and their great poverty. Those few Gonds who are members of the legislative assemblies or even the national parliament (Lok Sabha) are either alienated from their tribal culture or easily manipulated by other politicians.

Conflict and Social Control

In settling disputes the court of first instance is the village council (*panch*), which is presided over by the headman. Usually it strives to restore harmony between the litigants rather than to implement customary law. A settlement commonly involves a fine, or excommunication in varying degrees. Those who offend against the rule of clan exogamy incur supernatural sanctions.

Gond clans bear animal or plant names, which suggests a totemic origin of the clans, and some Gond clans still observe totemic taboos. But generally, except for the observance of exogamy, the clan system has no important function. In the Mandla District at least, eighteen clans have been combined into a phratry. The combination of the clans varies locally, but the number—eighteen—is always retained. The phratry too observes exogamy, but with the payment of a fine the marriage prohibition can be waived.

Marriage and Family

MARRIAGE. A normal marriage among the Gonds is the monogamous union of a man and a woman based on mutual choice, sanctioned by the ceremonial exchange of vows, with the approval of the tribal council, witnessed by the relatives of the partners and the village community, and concluded with a festive wedding dinner. Although the Gonds have liberal views on premarital sex, they are strict in the observance of married fidelity. They believe that adultery is punished by the ancestral spirits that can cause crop failure or an epidemic among humans and cattle. A Gond wedding is solemnized with many significant ceremonies. The essential wedding rite consists of the groom walking with his bride seven times around a wedding post erected in the center of the wedding booth. Marriage is obligatory. Originally Gond boys and girls married on reaching physical maturity. Nowadays the Gonds increasingly follow the example of the rural Hindu population and parents arrange the marriage when children are still young. The father of the groom has to pay a bride-price, the amount of which depends on the position and wealth of the two families. Cross-cousin marriages are much preferred, so much so that a youth has to pay a fine if he refuses to marry an available cross cousin. A Gond can have more than one wife, polygyny being restricted only by the capability of the man to support a number of wives. The Gonds practice the sororate and the levirate. Widow marriage is forbidden only among the Sanskritized Gonds. Gonds who are too poor to pay the bride-price and the wedding expenses contract a service marriage. Families with no sons prefer such a marriage arrangement. Other more irregular forms of marriage among the Gonds are the elopement of an unmarried girl with a boy or the capture of a girl and her forced marriage to her captor. Marriage by capture was in the past a popular form of marriage among the Gonds. The marriage must later be legalized by the relatives and village councils of the partners. The Gonds permit divorce and easily resort to it for various reasons. For instance, a man may obtain a divorce if his wife is barren, quarrelsome, or negligent in doing her assigned work. Likewise, a woman may elope with another man if her husband is a bad provider, a drunkard, or a wife beater, or if he is habitually unfaithful. A divorce requires the legal sanction of the tribal council of the village.

DOMESTIC UNIT. Gond marriages are as a rule happy and lasting if the husband is able to provide a frugal livelihood for wife and children and if the wife is competent in her household tasks and field work. Gond men and women are affectionate toward children and enjoy having large families.

INHERITANCE. Property, primarily land, descends patrilineally to the sons equally (unless one son should move elsewhere, in which case he forfeits his rights). Daughters inherit next to nothing from their fathers. A widow usually remains in the house, which is inherited by her youngest son (ultimogeniture). If not too old, the widow may be remarried to a close relative of her deceased husband.

SOCIALIZATION. The ambition of every Gond woman is to bear a son. Barrenness in a woman is considered a curse. Pregnancy and birth are surrounded with protective rites against magic spells and evil influences. Children are generally welcome and treated with affection. Although sons are preferred, daughters are welcome too. Children grow up without much restriction, but the community teaches them correct behavior. Children are early invited to take over some tasks, first playfully, then in earnest. Boys spontaneously seem to prefer male company, while girls seem to gravitate naturally toward other females. The change to adulthood is gradual; there is no initiation ceremony. The first menstruation of a girl is not specially celebrated, but she does learn in advance what prohibitions she has to observe. Only three Gond sections in the south have youth dormitories, and only the Murias use the dormitory for the education of youth in married and civic life. The other Gond sections have no dormitory system.

Religion and Expressive Culture

RELIGIOUS BELIEFS. The religion of the Gonds does not differ much from that of the numerous other tribes in central India. Like them, the Gonds believe in a high god whom they call either by his Hindu name, "Bhagwan," or by his tribal name, "Bara Deo," the "Great God." But he is an otiose deity and is rarely worshiped, though his name is often invoked. He is a personal god—eternal, just, merciful, maker of the fertile earth and of man—though the universe is conceived as coexisting with him. In the Gond belief system, besides this high god there also exist a great number of male and female deities and spirits that personify various natural features. Every hill, river, lake, tree, and rock is inhabited by a spirit. The earth, water, and air are ruled by deities that must be venerated and appeased with sacrifices and offerings. These deities and spirits may be benevolent, but often they are capricious, malevolent, and prone to harming human beings, especially individuals who have made themselves vulnerable by breaking a rule of the tribal code. The deities and spirits, especially the ancestor spirits, watch over the strict observance of the tribal rules and punish offenders.

RELIGIOUS PRACTITIONERS. Gonds distinguish between priests and magicians. The village priest is appointed by the village council; however, his appointment is often hereditary. His responsibility is to perform all the sacrifices held at certain feasts for the village community for which he receives a special remuneration. Sacrifices and religious ceremonies on family occasions are usually performed by the head of the family. The diviners and magicians, on the other hand, are unofficial charismatic intermediaries between the supernatural world and human beings. The Gonds, like the other tribals of central India, believe that most diseases and misfortunes are caused by the machinations of evil spirits and offended deities. It is the task of the soothsayers and diviners to find out which supernatural agencies have caused the present sickness or misfortune and how they can be appeased. If soothsayers and diviners cannot help, magicians and shamans must be employed. Magicians believe that by magic formulas and devices they can force a particular deity or spirit to carry out their commands. Shamans are persons who easily fall into trances and are then believed to be possessed by deities or spirits that prophesy through their mouths. These frequent ecstasies do not seem to have any detrimental mental or physical effects on the shamans, who may be male or female. Magic may be "white" or "black": it is white if it counteracts black magic or effects a cure when a sickness has been caused by black magic. Gonds also believe in the evil eye and in witchcraft. A witch is usually a woman who by her evil power brings sickness and death to people in the neighborhood. When dis-covered, she is publicly disgraced and expelled from the village or even killed.

CEREMONIES. The Gonds celebrate many feasts connected mainly with the agricultural seasons and with life-cycle events (birth, marriage, sickness, and death). On all festive occasions sacrifices and offerings are performed either by the official village priest, by the soothsayers and magicians, or by the head of the family that is celebrating an event. All these sacrifices are accompanied by appropriate ceremonies of symbolic significance. The offerings and sacrifices can be either animal or vegetable; it depends on the type of deity being addressed. Female deities generally demand that blood be spilled; the victims are usually chickens or goats, sometimes male buffalo, and, occasionally in the past, human beings. Vegetable offerings include fruits (especially coconuts), flowers, colored powder, and strings.

ARTS. Like most tribals, the Gonds are accomplished artisans and can manufacture almost all the implements they require for their work on the farm and in the forest, all furniture in house and kitchen, and all of their ornaments and decorations. They are artistically gifted: they paint their house walls with artistic designs, and they carve memorial pillars in wood and stone for their dead. They have invented various original dances and are passionate dancers. They are good musicians on the drum, the flute, and other instruments. They are good singers, though the melodies of their songs sometimes sound monotonous and may not be of their own invention. They are inventive in composing new songs, folktales, legends, and myths and in retelling them dramatically. They have composed a great epic celebrating the origins and exploits of a culture hero named Lingo.

MEDICINE. The Gonds are fully aware that certain diseases have a natural cause, and they know many jungle medicines to cure such diseases. But when these remedies remain ineffective, they resort to magical devices.

DEATH AND AFTERLIFE. After death an adult Gond man or woman is cremated; children are buried without much ceremony. Ceremonies are performed at the funeral to prevent the soul of the deceased from finding its way back to its house and village. The Gonds believe in an afterlife. They believe each human being has two souls, the life spirit and the shadow. The shadow must be prevented from returning to its home, or it will harm the surviving relatives. The life spirit goes to Bhagwan to be judged and rewarded by reincarnation into a higher form or punished in a pool of biting worms; after a while the soul is reborn and begins a new life. Others believe that the soul joins the other ancestors of the clan, especially after a stone memorial has been erected. Still others believe that the soul is absorbed in Bhagwan or Bara Deo. The belief in the survival of the ancestral spirits is, however, quite strong. These ancestor spirits watch over the moral behavior of the living Gond and punish offenders of tribal law. Thus they act as strict guardians of the Gond community.

Bibliography

Elwin, Verrier (1943). *Maria Murder and Suicide*. London: Oxford University Press. 2nd ed. 1950.

Elwin, Verrier (1944). *The Muria and Their Ghotul*. London: Oxford University Press.

Fuchs, Stephen (1960). *The Gond and Bhumia of Eastern Mandla*. Bombay: Asia Publishing House. 2nd ed. 1968. Bombay: New Literature Publishing Co.

Fürer-Haimendorf, Christoph von (1948). *The Aboriginal Tribes of Hyderabad*. Vol. 3, *The Raj Gonds of Adilabad*. London: Macmillan.

Fürer-Haimendorf, Christoph von, and Elizabeth von Fürer-Haimendorf (1979). *The Gonds of Andhra Pradesh: Tradition and Change in an Indian Tribe*. New Delhi: Vikas Publishing House.

Grigson, William (1938). *The Hill Marias of Bastar*. London: Oxford University Press.

Russell, R. V., and Hira Lal (1916). "Gond." In *The Tribes and Castes of the Central Provinces of India*. Vol. 3, 38–143. London: Oxford University Press. Reprint. 1969. Oosterhout: Anthropological Publications.

Singh, Indrajit (1944). *The Gondwana and the Gond*. Lucknow: University Publishers.

—STEPHEN FUCHS

GUJARATI

Ethnonyms: none

Orientation

IDENTIFICATION. Gujaratis are the inhabitants of Gujarat, one of the federal states of the Indian Republic.

LOCATION. Gujarat covers 195,984 square kilometers and is situated on the west coast of India between 20°6′ N to 24°42′ N and 68°10′ E to 74°28′ E. Geopolitically and culturally Gujarat can be divided into five regions: (1) north Gujarat, the mainland between Mount Abu and the Mahi River; (2) south Gujarat, the mainland between the Mahi and Damanaganga rivers; (3) the Saurashtrian Peninsula; (4) Kachchh; and (5) a hilly eastern belt consisting of the outliers of the Aravalli system, the Vindhyas, the Satpuras, and the Sahyadris. The state lies in the monsoon area with a monsoon climate. The rainfall period is confined to four months from the middle of June to the middle of October. The amount of annual rainfall varies considerably in different parts of the state. The southernmost area receives annual rainfall as high as 200 centimeters. The rainfall in central Gujarat is between 70 and 90 centimeters; and Kachchh and the western part of Saurashtra receive less than 40 centimeters. The maximum temperature in the year occurs in May, when it is as high as 40° C in north Gujarat, Saurashtra, and Kachchh. January is the coldest month of the year, when the temperature does not exceed 30° C.

DEMOGRAPHY. At the time of the 1981 census, the population of Gujarat was 34 million. The population density averages 174 persons per square kilometer; it is highest in central Gujarat and lowest in Kachchh. The population is growing at the rate of 2.7 percent per year. Gujarati-speaking people constitute 91 percent of the population of Gujarat, which also includes 1.5 percent Kachchh-speaking people. There are three main religious groups in Gujarat: Hindus (89.5 percent), Muslims (8.5 percent) and Jains (1 percent). A majority of the Muslims speak Gujarati, though there is a small Muslim section that speaks Urdu. Around 14 percent of the Gujarati population are tribals who predominantly live in the eastern hilly belt. Sixty-nine percent of the population live in rural areas and 31 percent live in urban areas. Ahmadabad, Surat, Vadodara, and Rajkot are large cities.

LINGUISTIC AFFILIATION. Gujarati is considered by linguists to be a member of the outer circle of Indo-Aryan languages: it is partly Prakritic and partly Sanskritic in origin. A number of Arabic, Persian, Urdu, and European—particularly Portuguese and English—words have become part of the language. There are several dialects. Important among them, based on region, are Kathiawadi, Kachchh, Pattani, Charotari, and Surati. There are also caste- or community-based dialects, such as Nagari, Anavla or Bhathala, Patidari, Kharwa, Musalmani, Parsi, etc. Different tribal groups have their own dialects that bear a close affinity to Gujarati. The distinctive Gujarati script has thirty-four consonants and eleven vowels.

History and Cultural Relations

The territory was known as "Gurjara Bhoomi," "Gurjara Desh," "Gurjaratta," or "Gurjar Man-

♦ **Indo-Aryan**
The easternmost subfamily of the Indo-European language family. Its ancient languages were first introduced into South Asia by the Aryans, and today Indo-Aryan languages are spoken throughout most of Pakistan, Nepal, Bangladesh, Sri Lanka, and northern India. Seventy-four percent of the Indian population speak an Indo-Aryan language; Hindi, with over 200 million speakers, is one of the world's leading languages.

See also

Bhil

dal"—meaning abode of the Gurjar people—between the fifth and ninth centuries A.D. The name of the area known as "Gujarat" was recognized from the tenth century during the Solanki period, when Mulraja laid the foundation of his kingdom with its capital at Anhilwad Patan. During British rule the area was divided into a number of native states and estates and British administrative districts, which were a part of the Bombay presidency. After independence in 1947, the native states merged into the Indian Union. A group of states formed Saurashtra State; the mainland Gujarat became a part of Bombay State and Kachchh was centrally administered. But as a result of further reorganization of the states in 1956, Saurashtra and Kachchh were dissolved as separate states and became a part of Bombay State. Then, because of demands for a separate linguistic state, Gujarat, Saurashtra, and Kachchh formed the separate state of Gujarat in 1960.

Settlements

Among 18,114 villages, 8 percent are small with a population of less than 200 persons; and 49 (0.2 percent) are large with more than 10,000 people in each. The settlement pattern of each village is either clustered or dispersed. Clustered villages are divided into subclusters consisting of a group of families belonging to the same caste or community. The dominant caste resides in the center, and traditionally Untouchable castes live on the periphery of the village. In the dispersed pattern mainly found among tribals, each family—nuclear or joint—lives on its own farm. A temple or public platform under a large tree is a central place where males from upper and middle castes meet and spend their spare time. Today, most of the middle-sized and big villages have primary schools, one or two shops, grazing land, and a cremation ground. There are 255 towns or urban agglomerations. All but eleven of these towns have a population under 100,000. Many of them are expanded villages where caste or community clusters form neighborhood localities. Two styles of housing are common in urban and rural Gujarat. The first is the sturdy modern kind made of brick and concrete, with more than two rooms and a separate kitchen. The second is a tenement of mud, stone, and wood. The roofs are of locally made tiles or thatch. (Numerical data from 1981 census.)

Economy

SUBSISTENCE AND COMMERCIAL ACTIVITIES. Despite rapid industrial development, agriculture occupies a prominent place in the economy of the state. It contributes an average of 35 to 40 percent of the state's domestic products. Sixty-two percent of the workers engaged in agriculture are either cultivators or laborers. Although agriculture is not fully mechanized, use of tractors has increased considerably in recent years. The major food crops are *bajri, jowar*, rice, and wheat. Cotton, groundnut, tobacco, and sugarcane are major commercial crops: they occupy about 40 percent of the total cultivated area of the state. Cattle, buffalo, sheep, goats, chickens, horses, camels, monkeys, donkeys, and pigs are the main domestic animals. Bullocks are used for agriculture, cows and buffalo for milk. A cooperative dairy industry has developed.

INDUSTRIAL ARTS. Artisans in rural areas are engaged in pottery, silver- and brass-ornament making, embroidery, handloom construction and furniture making. Despite government support, these crafts are rapidly disappearing. Gujarat is one of the most highly industrialized states in India. The major industries are textiles, plastics, chemicals, and engineering. In terms of income generated from manufacturing, Gujarat ranks second in the country.

TRADE. Trade is a primary occupation of Gujaratis. The Hindu and Jain Banias are the trading castes. In this century the Patidars have emerged as entrepreneurs. In addition, the Parsis and Muslim Bohras are also traders. Gujarat has been well connected by trade routes within the continent and also with other countries. Historically, the Gujaratis possessed a remarkable spirit of enterprise that led them in search of wealth to Java and Cambodia during the sixth and seventh centuries A.D. and to Siam, China, Sri Lanka, and Japan at about the end of the seventh century A.D. Some Gujaratis emigrated to Africa in the last century, and from there they have moved to Europe and the United States.

DIVISION OF LABOR. Except among the tribals, work is clearly divided between men and women. Gujaratis continue to believe that "a woman's place is in the home": a woman's main tasks are cooking, washing, other household work, and child rearing. However, among the poor, women also participate in economic activities, engaging in cultivation and agricultural labor.

LAND TENURE. With the introduction of various land reforms in the 1950s, land was given to the tillers. Intermediary tenures were legally abolished. Nevertheless, concealed tenancy continues. Land distribution is uneven. According to the 1976–1977 agriculture census, the average

The Gujarati possessed a remarkable spirit of enterprise that led them to several other countries in search of wealth as early as the sixth century.

size of holdings for the state was 3.71 hectares. Nearly 46 percent of the cultivators have less than 2 hectares of land, which holdings constitute only 13 percent of the total area holdings; but only 6 percent of cultivators hold 10 hectares or more of land, which altogether constitutes nearly 25 percent of the total holdings. The Patidars and the Brahmans are rich peasants. The Kolis, the Scheduled Castes (or "SC," viewed as "Untouchables"), the tribals, and the Muslims are poor peasants and agricultural laborers.

Kinship, Marriage, and Family

KIN GROUPS AND DESCENT. Descent is agnatic and patrilineal.

MARRIAGE. Among the Hindu Gujaratis, marriage is a sacrament. It is arranged by parents. Certain castes (*jatis*) follow the principle of endogamy in which a man must marry not only within his jati but also within his subjati, which is divided into *ekdas* and *gols* (i.e., circles). However, among certain castes exogamy restricts the circle within which marriage can be arranged. It forbids the members of a particular group in a caste, usually believed to be descended from a common ancestor or associated with a particular locality, to marry anyone who is a member of the same group. Another custom among the Rajputs, Patidars, and Brahmans is hypergamy, which forbids a woman of a particular group to marry a man of a group lower than her own in social standing and compels her to marry into a group of equal or superior rank.

DOMESTIC UNIT. The family is generally considered to be the parents, married as well as unmarried sons, and widowed sisters. The joint family is a norm particularly among the trading and landed castes and also among the Muslims in rural areas. In the traditional joint family, three generations live together. All the family members eat from one kitchen and cultivate land jointly. Even if the kitchens become separate, cooperative farming continues in many cases. A joint family may have more than thirty members, although such cases are exceptional. A typical joint family has from eight to twelve members in rural areas and six to eight members in urban areas. Joint families are becoming less common. The head of the family—the father or grandfather—exercises authority over all family members. Women and even married sons have no independence and can do little without first obtaining consent or approval from the head. This situation is now changing.

INHERITANCE. Among the Hindus, consanguinity is the guiding principle for determining the right of inheritance. The following are heirs in order of precedence: sons, sons' sons, sons' grandsons, the widow of the deceased, daughters, daughters' sons, mother, father, brothers, brothers' sons. Although inheritance is based on patrilineal principles, two women—the widow and the daughter—are very high on the scale of priority.

SOCIALIZATION. Infants and children are raised by the mother and grandparents, though the role of the father in bringing up the children has recently increased. A girl is not closely looked after and she is involved in household chores from a very young age, whereas a boy is protected and indulged.

Sociopolitical Organization

SOCIAL ORGANIZATION. Gujaratis are divided into a number of social groups. The Hindus who constitute the largest group are divided into a number of jatis, which have a hierarchical order based on the principles of purity and pollution. The Brahmans are in the highest position, while the Scheduled Castes occupy the lowest position in the hierarchy. The SCs constitute 7 percent of the population, and they are scattered throughout the state. The Brahmans constitute nearly 4 percent. The other upper castes are the Vanias (traditionally traders) and Rajputs (traditionally warriors). They and some other upper castes together represent 8 percent of the total population. The Patidars, who belong to the middle strata of the caste hierarchy and were earlier known as the Kanbis, constitute around 12 percent of the population. Comprising about 24 percent of the population, the Kolis form the largest caste cluster among the Gujaratis and are distributed throughout the state. Broadly they can be divided into Kolis of the coastal and mainland belts. The latter prefer to be identified as Kshatriyas. The other low castes, such as the Bhois, Machhis, Kharvas, etc., together constitute about 7 percent of the Gujaratis. The Scheduled Tribes, generally known as the Adivasis, constitute 14 percent of the population and are mainly in the eastern belt. There are several tribal groups, some of the major ones being the Bhils, Dhodiyas, Gamits, and Chaudharis. The jatis have traditional *panchayats*, which are councils consisting of elders that regulate social customs and resolve conflicts. The importance of such panchayats in conflict resolution has declined over the last four decades.

POLITICAL ORGANIZATION. Gujarat is one among twenty-one federal states of the Indian republic. It is governed by representatives elected by universal adult franchise who constitute a *vidhan* *sabha* (legislative assembly). A majority party forms the government. The head of the state is the governor, appointed by the president of India. The state government has very wide powers for maintaining law and order, levying taxes, and carrying out development work. It also shares resources with the union government. Gandhinagar is the capital city of the state. The state is divided into 19 districts, which are further subdivided into 184 *talukas*. Local self-government by elected representatives functions at village, taluka, and district level and also in towns and cities. The local government performs functions related to public amenities, education, and development. It raises resources by levying taxes and income from property and also receives aid grants from the state government. Industrial investment is strongly encouraged.

SOCIAL CONTROL. Gujarat today has the usual institutions of a state police force and a hierarchy of law courts, ranging from the submagistrate's court to the state supreme court. In all courts the central writ is the Indian Penal Code. But in addition to these institutions, which were first developed under the British administration of the old Bombay Presidency, there is also an indigenous system of caste and village councils. The caste council is found in any village or small town where the numbers of any one caste or caste bloc are sufficient to warrant it. This council consists of the male heads of the most prominent families in the caste, and its function is to maintain equanimity with other castes by seeing that traditional patterns of behavior (the caste's dharma) are followed. Fines and minor physical punishment may be handed down to those who offend against these patterns. Public humiliation, such as a beating with sandals, is a usual punishment. There is also a village council (*gram panchayat*) which is headed by the village headman (*patel*) and contains leading representatives of each of the caste groups. Its function is partly to conduct formal community affairs, such as seasonal festivals, and partly to resolve intercaste disputes and offenses.

CONFLICT. Because there has been little labor unrest in recent times, Gujarat has become a relatively prosperous state. Public life has however been marred by several riots led by upper-caste students, in protest against the government policy of reserving places in the colleges for Scheduled Castes and Scheduled Tribes.

Religion and Expressive Culture

Gujarati Hindus are divided into a large number of religious sects. There are two broad categories: those who worship one or a combination of some of the great Vedic deities or of the Puranic accretions to the orthodox pantheon; and those who deny the regular deities and prohibit idol worship. The former are the Shaivites, Shaktas or Devi Bhaktas, Vaishnavites, and the followers of minor deities. The latter belong to the Arya Samaj, Kabir Panthi, and other such fairly modern sects. These sects are not mutually exclusive.

RELIGIOUS BELIEFS. A Gujarati Hindu attaches the greatest importance to bathing. He or she observes fasts once a week and every eleventh day in a fortnight. A Gujarati Hindu believes in Heaven, Hell, and the transmigration of the soul. One hopes to better one's position in this and the life to come by one's devotion to God, by *dan* (charity), and by *daya* (mercy toward fellow human beings and cows, etc.). Gujarati Jains, though few in number, occupy an important place in Gujarati society and the economy. Jainism rejects the authority of the Vedas and the spiritual supremacy of the Brahmans. The highest goal of Jainism is nirvana or *moksha*, the setting free of the individual from the *sanskara*, the cycle of birth and death. The Jains are divided into two sects, Digambaris and Svetambaris. The cow is worshiped and considered sacred by Hindus. Besides worshiping various idols, an average Hindu worships animals, trees, fire, etc. and believes in *bhuts* (possessing spirits). Belief in omens is also common. Hindus believe that the result of every undertaking is foreshadowed by certain signs and hints.

RELIGIOUS PRACTITIONERS. The life-cycle ceremonies are performed by Brahmans. Wandering holy men, however, are revered irrespective of their caste, religion, or origin. Gujaratis also patronize men who have a reputation for being able to rid the individual of bhuts.

CEREMONIES. Ceremonies are performed at birth, marriage, and death when relatives are invited for feasts. Among the important festivals are: Diwali, the festival of lamps; Hindu new year's day, which is the next day after Diwali; Utran or Sankrant, a festival of the harvest; and Navratra, a festival of the "nine nights" involving a folk dance called *Garba*.

ARTS. *Ras* and Garba are important folk dances performed by both males and females. *Melas*, fairs either at pilgrimage places or on the bank of a river during certain festivals, attract a large crowd where people dance, sing, and watch bullfights or cockfights. *Bhavai* is a popular folk drama, generally performed in open spaces in villages and towns. Wood and stone sculptures decorating temples, palaces, and private buildings are

> *A Gujarati Hindu attaches the greatest importance to bathing.*

well known. Paintings called *sathia* and *rangoli*, done by using powdered chalk, are made by women at the threshold of their houses for festivals and other ceremonies. The calico printing of Gujarat is famous. Tattooing is common among certain castes in Saurashtra and north Gujarat.

MEDICINE. Traditionally, disease was believed to be caused by an imbalance of elements in the body, as well as by several supernatural causes such as the displeasure of a god or goddess or spirit possession. Although home remedies and concoctions of local herbs are still used, modern medicine has been increasingly accepted and used.

DEATH AND AFTERLIFE. Normally a corpse is not kept more than twelve hours. It is taken in a procession mainly of males to the cremation ground. There the body is laid upon the pyre with its head to the north. The chief mourner lights the pyre. The period of mourning varies from a fortnight to a year according to the age of the deceased and the closeness of the relationship. A caste dinner is given on the twelfth and thirteenth days afterward as a part of the death rites. Certain religious rituals are performed and Brahmans are given gifts according to what the mourners can afford.

♦ **pyre**
The pile of logs on which a Hindu is cremated.

Bibliography

Desai, R. B. Govindbhai (1932). *Hindu Families in Gujarat.* Baroda: Baroda State Press.

Gujarat, Government of. Bureau of Economics and Statistics (1982). *Statistical Atlas of Gujarat.* Vols. 1–2. Gandhinagar: Government of Gujarat.

Majumdar, M. R. (1965). *Cultural History of Gujarat.* Bombay: Popular Prakashan.

Shah, Arvind M. (1973). *The Household Dimension of the Family in India: A Field Study in a Gujarat Village and a Review of Other Studies.* Berkeley: University of California Press; New Delhi: Orient Longman.

Shah, Ghanshyam (1989). "Caste Sentiments and Dominance in Gujarat." In *Dominance and State Power in Modern India*, edited by Francine Frankel and M. S. A. Rao. Delhi: Oxford University Press.
—GHANSHYAM SHAH

JAT

Ethnonyms: Jāṭ, Jaṭ

Orientation

IDENTIFICATION AND LOCATION. Primarily endogamous communities calling themselves and known as Jat live predominantly in large parts of northern and northwestern India and in southern and eastern Pakistan, as sedentary farmers and/or mobile pastoralists. In certain areas they tend to call themselves Baluch, Pathan, or Rajput, rather than Jat. Most of these communities are integrated as a caste into the locally prevalent caste system. In the past three decades increasing population pressure on land has led to large-scale emigration of the peasant Jat, especially from India, to North America, the United Kingdom, Malaysia, and more recently the Middle East. Some maintain that the sedentary farming Jat and the nomadic pastoral Jat are of entirely different origins; others believe that the two groups are of the same stock but that they developed different life-styles over the centuries. Neither the farmers nor the pastoralists are, however, to be confused with other distinct communities of peripatetic peddlers, artisans, and entertainers designated in Afghanistan by the blanket terms "Jat" or Jaṭ; the latter terms are considered pejorative, and they are rejected as ethnonyms by these peripatetic communities. In Pakistan also, among the Baluchi- and Pashto-speaking populations, the terms were, and to a certain extent still are, used to indicate contempt and lower social status.

DEMOGRAPHY. No reliable figures are available for recent years. In 1931 the population of all sedentary and farming Jat was estimated at 8,377,819; in the early 1960s 8,000,000 was the estimate for Pakistan alone. Today the entire Jat population consists of several million more than that.

LINGUISTIC AFFILIATION. All Jat speak languages and dialects that are closely connected with other locally spoken languages of the Indo-Iranian Group. Three alphabets are used, depending primarily on religion but partly on locality: the Arabic-derived Urdu one is used by Muslims, while Sikhs and Hindus use the Gurmukhi (Punjabi) and the Devanagari (Hindi) scripts, respectively.

History and Cultural Relations

Little is known about the early history of the Jat, although several theories were advanced by various scholars over the last 100 years. While some authors argue that they are descendants of the first Indo-Aryans, others suggest that they are of Indo-Scythian stock and entered India toward the beginning of the Christian era. These authors also point to some cultural similarities between the Jat and certain other major communities of the area, such as the Gujar, the Ahir, and the Raj-

See also
Baluchi, Punjabi, Sikh

put, about whose origins similar theories have been suggested. In fact, among both Muslims and Sikhs the Jat and the Rajput castes enjoy almost equal status—partly because of the basic egalitarian ideology enjoined by both religions, but mainly because of the similar political and economic power held by both communities. Also Hindu Jat consider the Gujar and Ahir as allied castes; except for the rule of caste endogamy, there are no caste restrictions between these three communities. In other scholarly debates about the origins of the Jat, attempts have been made to identify them with the *Jarttikā*, referred to in the Hindu epic the *Mahābhārata*. Some still maintain that the people Arab historians referred to as the *Zuṭṭ*, and who were taken as prisoners in the eighth century from Sindh in present-day southern Pakistan to southern Iraq, were actually buffalo-herding Jat, or were at least known as such in their place of origin. In the seventeenth century a (Hindu) kingdom was established in the area of Bharatpur and Dholpur (Rajasthan) in northern India; it was the outcome of many centuries of rebellion against the Mogul Empire, and it lasted till 1826, when it was defeated by the forces of the British East India Company. Farther north, in the Punjab, in the early years of the eighteenth century, Jat (mainly Sikh) organized peasant uprisings against the predominantly Muslim landed gentry; subsequently, with the invasion of the area—first by the Persian King Nadir Shah and then by the Afghan Ahmad Shah Abdali—they controlled a major part of the area through close-knit bands of armed marauders operating under the leadership of the landowning chiefs of well-defined territories. Because of their martial traditions, the Jat, together with certain communities, were classified by British administrators of imperial India as a "martial race," and this term had certain long-lasting effects. One was their large-scale recruitment into the British-Indian army, and to this day a very large number of Jat are soldiers in the Indian army. Many Sikh Jat in the Indian part of Punjab are involved in the current movement for the creation of an autonomous Khalistan.

Settlements

The Jat as a whole are predominantly rural. Depending on whether they are sedentary or nomadic, the Jat of various regions live in permanent villages or temporary camps. Over the last 200 years there has been increasing sedentarization of nomadic Jat; this trend began in the last decades of the eighteenth century when many pastoralists settled in the central Punjab under the auspices of Sikh rule there, and it continued over a very large area with the expansion of irrigation in British imperial times. With the consequent expansion of cultivation all these pastoralists are facing increasing difficulties in finding grazing lands for their herds. The buffalo breeders face the maximum difficulties in this respect, since their animals need to be grazed in areas with plentiful water, and these are precisely the areas in which agriculture has expanded most. They still live in the moist region of the Indus Delta, but many have had to settle permanently. Formerly the camel breeders migrated over larger areas, but increasingly they are restricted to the delta region of the Indus River, the desert areas of the Thar and the Thal, and the semideserts stretching west of the Indus to Makran and Baluchistan. The camel drivers were, at least a few decades ago, fairly widespread in most parts of Sindh and the western Punjab, and Kachchh. While in some less densely populated areas each Jat clan has a compact geographic area of its own, elsewhere several clans may inhabit the same village. Most Jat peasants live in flat-roofed houses made of baked or unbaked bricks in large compact villages, with few open spaces within the inhabited area; all villages have cattle sheds, village commons, and wells or ponds. Depending on the region and the precise community, Jat nomadic pastoralists use a variety of huts, mostly made of reed mats and wood, that are fairly easy to dismantle. The reed mats are woven by the women.

Economy

SUBSISTENCE AND COMMERCIAL ACTIVITIES. The mainstay of sedentary Jat economy is and has always been agriculture, and there are several proverbs and sayings in local languages that emphasize both the skill and industry of the Jat peasant, as well as the traditional attachment of this community to the soil. Cereals such as wheat, maize, and types of millet, as well as pulses and the cash crop sugarcane, are grown by Jat cultivators; in certain areas they increasingly grow fruits and vegetables also. In most areas of India where the Jat farmers live cultivation is now fairly mechanized, but in some areas the plow is drawn by oxen and harvesting is done by hand. Most crops are grown both for subsistence and for commerce. In addition to land the peasant Jat own water buffalo and cows for milk; male buffalo are often used for carrying loads. Milk is for household consumption and is not generally sold. The cattle are grazed on the village commons. The pastoral Jat

Because of their martial traditions, the Jat, together with certain other communities, were classified by British administrators of imperial India as a "martial race."

consist of three distinct groups of water buffalo breeders, camel breeders, and camel drivers (often known as Mir-Jat, rather than simply Jat). The buffalo breeders sell their herd animals for slaughter or as draft animals, especially for the Persian wheel; they also sell excess butterfat but never sell milk. The camel breeders do sell milk, but their main income is from the sale of young male camels, which are much in demand for purposes of transport. The camel drivers hire themselves out with their trained animals, either working for a fee or for a share of the profit. In many areas where former pastureland has come under the plow, due to irrigation facilities, they are obliged to ask local farmers for the rights to graze their herds on their lands; in return they often have to give their labor during the harvest. The women of the pastoral Jat of the north also sell mats and ropes made from the leaves of dwarf palms. The army has been a major source of income for the peasant Jat since the late nineteenth century, and in recent decades many Sikh Jat are in the motorized transport business. Remittances from Jat immigrants in North America and elsewhere also contribute much to the income of a very large proportion of the population.

INDUSTRIAL ARTS AND DIVISION OF LABOR.
Among the agricultural Jat, traditionally only the men work in the fields, while the women are entirely responsible for the household. In recent times more prosperous families hire non-Jat, primarily landless labor from other regions, as farmhands, partly as full-time workers but especially as part-time workers in peak seasons. Among the buffalo-breeding nomads, the men graze and milk their animals, and they sell these animals and their butterfat. Their women prepare milk products and do all the housework—cooking, cleaning, fetching water and fuel, rearing the children, sewing and embroidering all textiles for household use, and weaving the reed mats for their huts. Among the camel breeders all work connected with the animals is carried out by the men—grazing the herds, milking, shearing, spinning and weaving the camel's wool into coarse blankets and bags, and selling animals. Household work is done by the women, and encompasses the same tasks as among the buffalo breeders. No food products are made from camel's milk, and in the months when the milk is plentiful enough to provide sole subsistence, little or no cooking is done.

LAND TENURE. The landowners of a village stand collectively for the entire land of the village, but within the village each individual head of household has discrete rights within the various lineage segments. Generally, all landowners in a village are descended from a common ancestor who founded the village; his ownership of all the village lands is never forgotten, and by this token all individuated rights are successive restrictions of more general rights, applicable at all levels of genealogical segmentation. Common land is that which has not been brought under cultivation.

Kinship, Marriage, and Family

KIN GROUPS AND DESCENT. All Jat are divided into several large, usually dispersed clans, whose localized segments are often geographically compact, but among peasants they are sometimes equally dispersed, due to the population pressure on land. Most clans are de facto maximal lineages, which are further segmented; among Jat peasants this segmentation takes place at four broad levels. The minimal lineage is composed of a group of households, which had formed a single household two or three generations previously; they may still share a common courtyard and have joint rights to a well.

MARRIAGE. While among Muslim Jat the practice of exchange marriage takes place at various levels of lineage organization, among Hindu and Sikh Jat no such exchange marriages are allowed, and the rule of exogamy is such that a man may not marry a woman who has any of her four grandparental clans in common with his. Polygyny is allowed though not common, and the custom of adelphic polyandry, or the sexual access by an unmarried man to his brother's wife—which was often practiced by at least non-Muslim peasant Jat, in order to prevent further fragmentation of land—has declined in recent decades. Among all Jat, widow remarriage is permitted; either levirate is required or a widow is not allowed to remarry outside the maximal lineage, especially when she has children by her late husband. The practice of female infanticide, also known among the peasants, has dropped sharply. A woman's relationship with her husband's kin is organized according to a basic pattern of avoidance with seniors and of joking with those younger than the husband. Brothers share a common duty toward their sisters and their children.

DOMESTIC UNIT. Most Jat peasant households consist of lineal joint families, with the parents and one married son; many units are nuclear and some are collateral-joint, with two married brothers and their offspring living together. Among nomadic Jat the nuclear family and the lineal joint family are the most common domestic units.

INHERITANCE. Among those with land, all sons inherit equal shares in terms of both quantity and quality. Formerly, a man's wives shared equally on behalf of their sons, irrespective of the number of sons each had. Although in theory inheritance of land follows a strictly agnatic principle and daughters and sisters do not inherit, daughters' sons have been observed de facto to be among the inheritors in many cases.

Sociopolitical Organization

SOCIAL AND POLITICAL ORGANIZATION. All Jat are divided into patriclans; among the sedentary communities, each of these has a hereditary headman. By and large, the villages in which Jat farmers live, together with non-Jat, are under the jurisdiction of a clan council, and this council, of which every clan headman is a member, is the decision-making unit at the community level. Traditionally in these villages Jat farmers were integrated as patrons into the patron-client system prevalent in the area. Their clients were members of various service castes; however, this system has largely broken down today. Wealthy Jat landowners have entered local, regional, and even national politics since the beginning of this century, and in many areas they are still active as influential representatives of farmers and rural folk in general. Among the pastoral Jat of the Indus Delta, the clans are organized on the hierarchical principle of age, with the oldest man of the oldest lineage being at the head of the pyramid, followed by the eldest men of the younger lineages. Institutionalized authority over this entire group rests not with a Jat but with a Karmati-Baluch.

CONFLICT. A frequent source of conflict within the minimal lineage is land; such conflicts often take place between agnatic collaterals, since their lands usually border each other. Factional conflict is fairly common at a broader level.

Religion and Expressive Culture

RELIGIOUS BELIEFS AND CEREMONIES. A Jat can be Hindu, Muslim, or Sikh, and in 1931 over 50 percent of the entire Sikh population was constituted by Jat. Many ceremonies, especially those accompanying the rites of passage, are common to all Jat, irrespective of religious denomination. Among Hindu Jat there are in addition numerous local or more widely prevalent religious beliefs and observances. These include knowledge of certain but by no means all major mythological figures (gods and goddesses) of the Sanskritic tradition and the celebration of several festivals, both seasonal and annual, both of the all-Indian Hindu Great Tradition and of the localized Little Tradition. The Muslim Jat populations have a strong tradition of venerating a large number of local saints (*piīr*). Although most are officially Sunni, they have a large number of Shia traditions, and one group of Jat are Ismaelis. Till recently Sikh Jat, though very conscious of their distinct religious identity, were not very meticulous in their observance of the precepts of Sikhism. Most of them still observe Hindu marriage rites and till recently followed Hindu funeral customs; the majority also employed Brahmans as family priests. In most villages inhabited by Sikh Jat is the shrine of a Sikh martyr of old that acts as an ancestral focus for the minimal lineage. Various supernatural beings play a role in Jat life and are common to most Jat irrespective of creed; belief in many of them is widespread in the region as a whole.

ARTS. The women of the nomadic Jat are very skilled in needlework and embroider various textiles using threads of many colors in the delta region but mainly black and red in the north; tiny pieces of mirror are also used to decorate these textiles.

DEATH AND AFTERLIFE. Jat hold conflicting views on life after death. Some believe in the traditional Hindu concept of rebirth, others believe in going to Hell or Heaven, but many believe that there is no existence after death and that there is no form of life besides the present one on Earth.

Bibliography

Hershman, Paul (1981). *Punjabi Kinship and Marriage.* Delhi: Hindustan.

Kessinger, Tom G. (1974). *Vilayatpur, 1848–1968: Social and Economic Change in a North Indian Village.* Berkeley: University of California Press.

Lewis, Oscar (1958). *Village Life in Northern India.* New York: Random House.

Pettigrew, Joyce (1975). *Robber Noblemen: A Study of the Political System of the Sikh Jats.* London: Routledge & Kegan Paul.

Pradhan, M. C. (1966). *The Political System of the Jats of Northern India.* Delhi: Oxford University Press.

Rao, Aparna (1986). "Peripatetic Minorities in Afghanistan—Image and Identity." In *Die ethnischen Gruppen Afghanistans*, edited by E. Orywal. Wiesbaden: L. Reichert.

Westphal-Hellbusch, Sigrid, and Heinz Westphal (1968). *Zur Geschichte und Kultur der Jat.* Berlin: Duncker & Humblot.

—APARNA RAO

◆ **collaterals**
A person's relatives not related to him or her as ascendants or descendants; one's uncle, aunt, cousin, brother, sister, nephew, niece.

JATAV

Ethnonyms: Jadav, Jatava, Jatua; also known as Chamar, Harijan, Scheduled Caste, Untouchable

Orientation

IDENTIFICATION. The Jatavs are an endogamous caste of the Chamar, or leather worker, category of castes in India. Because of the polluting occupation of leather worker they rank among the Untouchable castes close to the bottom of India's caste hierarchy. Some say the name "Jatav" is derived from the word *jat* (camel driver), while others say it is derived from "Jat," the name of a non-Untouchable farming caste. Many Jatavs themselves say it is derived from the term "Yadav," the lineage of Lord Krishna. They are also known as a Scheduled Caste because, as Untouchables, they are included on a schedule of castes eligible for government aid. Mahatma Gandhi gave to Untouchables the name "Harijans" or "children of god," but Jatavs reject the term and its connotations of Untouchable childlikeness and uppercaste paternalism.

LOCATION. Jatavs live mostly in the states of Uttar Pradesh, Rajasthan, Haryana, and Punjab, as well as in the Union Territory of Delhi in northwest India. This is a semiarid area with rainfall mostly in the monsoon season of June to August and lesser rains in January–February. Temperatures range from 5.9° C in January–February to 41.5° C in May-June.

DEMOGRAPHY. Jatavs are not listed separately in the census of India but along with other Chamars. In the four states mentioned above Chamars numbered 27,868,146, about 9.9 percent of those states' population (1981).

LINGUISTIC AFFILIATION. Jatavs speak related languages of the Indo-Aryan Family of languages including Hindi, Rajasthani, and Braj Bhasha, all using the Devanagari script, as well as Punjabi using the Gurmukhi script. Chamars in other parts of India speak other languages of the Indo-Aryan Family and languages of the unrelated Dravidian Family, such as Tamil and Telugu.

History and Cultural Relations

Origins of the Jatavs, as well as most other Chamar and Untouchable castes, are mythical. Some say the Jatavs are the product of marriage of upper-caste Jats with Chamar women. Jatavs themselves deny such origins. In preindependent India they claimed upper-caste Kshatriya or warrior origin. In post-independent India many have claimed to be descendants of India's ancient Buddhists. This claim is in part a rejection of Untouchable status and in part an assertion of a political identity of equality rejecting the caste system.

Settlements

In villages, where 90 percent of India's Untouchables live, Jatavs live in hamlets separate from non-Untouchable castes, while in cities they live in segregated neighborhoods. In larger settlements in cities these may be broken down into subsections with separate leadership. Houses are densely grouped in a nucleated pattern. Housing style is of two types: *kacca* and *pakka*. Kacca homes are generally one room made of mud, sometimes mixed with a special clay for strength, or of unbaked mud bricks. Roofs are flat, although some have sloping thatched roofs to protect against rain. Kacca homes are painted with a mixture of slightly antiseptic cow dung and mud. Pakka homes, mostly found in cities, are of baked brick and cement, the better ones with walls, floors, and flat roofs also coated with cement. Pakka homes frequently have more than one room, a small interior courtyard where cooking is done, and a second story.

Economy

SUBSISTENCE AND COMMERCIAL ACTIVITIES. Jatavs, and all other Chamars in India, are traditionally leather workers, tanners, and shoemakers. Nevertheless, in villages they are primarily agricultural laborers hereditarily attached to landowners (*jajmans*) for whom they work, often upon demand. Payment was traditionally in shares of grain, food, and items of clothing. In recent years increased payment in cash has weakened the obligations of landowners toward them and progressively reduced them to wage laborers. Population increase, the use of mechanical devices such as tractors, and land reform measures have caused further unemployment and destitution. Many migrate to cities where Jatavs are skilled shoemakers. A number of the educated younger generation have found jobs in government service where a certain percentage of jobs are reserved for Scheduled Castes. Differences based on class and education have begun to appear among, but not yet to divide, them. Those who can afford it may keep a cow or water buffalo for milk.

INDUSTRIAL ARTS. In addition to being skilled leather workers and shoemakers, Jatavs are also skilled masons and building contractors.

TRADE. Shoes are manufactured, often on a putting-out system in which individual workers are given raw materials to make shoes in their homes, sold to wholesalers in a market. A few Jatavs in cities own large factories. Shoes are supplied to the domestic and a growing foreign market. However, since they do not control the wholesale and distributive networks, Jatavs do not reap the major profits of their craft.

DIVISION OF LABOR. Division of labor by sex is strict. Males alone make shoes, plow and do heavy work in the fields, and freely move outside of the hamlet or neighborhood to shop in a market or attend caste councils and other public functions. Married women wear a veil (*ghunghat*) before their husband's elder male kinsmen and in his village or neighborhood; the women draw water, cook, and care for the home. They may also work at harvest time in the fields and separate scraps of leather.

LAND TENURE. On the whole, Jatavs, like most Chamars, were until recently unable to own land in villages. In some villages a house tax is paid to the landowner. In cities, however, many have been able to purchase land for homes and factories.

Kinship

KIN GROUPS AND DESCENT. Kin groups are formed patrilineally. The smallest coresidential unit is the nuclear or extended family (*parivar*, *ghar*). Extended families are most often composed of parent(s), married sons and their wives, and grandchildren. Otherwise they are composed of married brothers, their wives, and their children. Minimal patrilineages (*kutumb*) of nonresidential brothers and cousins are expected to support one another in conflicts. The maximal lineage (*khandan*) consists of all male descendants of a known or fictive ancestor. The "brotherhood" (*biradari*) consists of all members of the caste (*jati*). All members of the same neighborhood or village are real or fictive kin in an exogamous *bhaiband*. Descent is formally patrilineal, although the mother's role in procreation is acknowledged.

KINSHIP TERMINOLOGY. Hawaiian-type cousin terms are used, while the first ascending generation uses bifurcatecollateral terms reflecting the lower status of girl-giving affinals (*nice rishtedar*) and the higher status of girl-receiving affinals (*unce rishtedar*). Affinals (*rishtedar*) are distinguished from agnates (*natedar*). Kin terms are fictively extended to all in a bhaiband.

Marriage and Family

MARRIAGE. Most marriages are monogamous, but a very few polygamous marriages still occur. Parents arrange most marriages, although a few educated today may be allowed some say in the match. Totemically named categories (*gotras*) exist but their exogamic function is not strictly observed. Marriage is exogamous for the khandan but endogamous for the caste. As a practical rule, marriages are not allowed with anyone having a remembered relationship through both paternal and maternal patrilineages. Members of the village or city neighborhood are fictive kin for whom marriage is also exogamous. Also forbidden is giving girls to lower-ranked families, villages, or neighborhoods from which girls have previously been taken. A dowry must be offered to the boy's family on behalf of the girl. Divorce is possible at the instigation of either party, but it is infrequent and must be approved by the caste council. Widows, widowers, and divorced persons may remarry, but women may not remarry in a formal wedding ceremony (*shadi*). The ideal is patrilocal residence in the extended family of the husband; the reality is often a majority of nuclear families.

DOMESTIC UNIT. Those who live in the same house share living space, cooking, and expenses. When an extended family disintegrates—usually because of conflicts between brothers or their wives—separate living, cooking, and expense arrangements are made in the house if it is large enough; otherwise, new living quarters are sought. Sons are expected to care for aged parents who are unable to work.

INHERITANCE. Property is divided equally among sons; daughters because of the dowry customarily receive nothing. Inheriting brothers are expected to provide dowry for unmarried sisters. Eldest sons may succeed to any offices, such as headman, held by their fathers.

SOCIALIZATION. Parents raise children affectionately, and elder siblings, usually sisters, are caretakers for younger siblings. Boys, however, are preferred and tend to receive better care and attention than girls. At around the age of 6 same-sexed parents become stricter disciplinarians. Children are not separated from most adult activities and easily move into adult occupations in early teens. Emphasis is on socialization for dependence upon the family, and boys are socialized especially to be dependent upon the mother, who may in turn become dependent upon them in old age.

Sociopolitical Organization

SOCIAL ORGANIZATION. In India's villages the caste system is an organic division of labor, each caste having a traditionally assigned and distinct occupation and duty. Because Jatavs, as

Division of labor by sex is strict.

♦ **endogamy**
Marriage within a specific group or social category of which the person is a member, such as one's caste or community.

Chamars, do the polluting and polluted tasks of removing dead cattle from the village and of working with leather, they are ranked as Untouchables at the bottom of the system. Traditionally, their major occupation in the village was agricultural and other menial labor for landowners. In cities, where the traditional interdependencies of the caste system are virtually nonexistent, Jatavs are more like a distinct and despised ethnic group.

POLITICAL ORGANIZATION. In preindependent India Jatavs gained considerable political expertise by forming associations and by developing a literate cadre of leaders. They tried to change their position in the caste system through "Sanskritization," the emulation of upper-caste behavior. Jatavs claimed Kshatriya or warrior-class origin and rank, and they organized caste associations to reform caste behavior and lobby for their claims. After independence India legally abolished the practice of untouchability, established the universal franchise, and developed the policy of "protective discrimination." That policy reserves electoral constituencies for Scheduled Caste candidates according to their percentages of population in the nation and the states; it does likewise for jobs in the national and state civil services; and it offers educational benefits to them. Jatavs have taken advantage of that policy and turned to active participation in India's parliamentary system of government. At times they have elected members of their caste to various state and national legislatures. In villages they have been less successful at influencing local political institutions and capturing funds meant for developmental projects. A major influence upon Jatavs was the Untouchable leader Dr. B. R. Ambedkar (d. 1956) who encouraged Untouchables to fight for their rights, and, as first minister for law in India, provided a powerful role model. Through their political efforts his statue and picture may be found in public parks and bus stations, symbolically asserting their quest for equal citizenship in the nation.

SOCIAL CONTROL. Everyday control and leadership of local communities was traditionally

RELIGION AND EXPRESSIVE CULTURE

Religious Beliefs

In general, Jatavs and other Chamars are Hindus. They reject, however, the Hindu teaching that makes them Untouchables, as well as the Brahman priests who wrote the sacred texts so defining them. Most major Hindu festivals, particularly Holi, are observed, as are major life-cycle ceremonies. In postindependent India Jatavs may enter major Hindu temples and visit pilgrimage spots. Some Chamars are devotees of the Chamar saint Ravi Das. A number of Jatavs have followed Dr. Ambedkar and converted to Buddhism as a rejection of the caste system and as an assertion of the equality of all individuals. Buddhism for them is a political ideology in religious form. Ambedkar himself has been apotheosized as a bodhisattva; his birthday is the major public Jatav festival. Belief is in the major deities of Hinduism, especially in their localized forms. The Buddha and Dr. Ambedkar have become part of the pantheon. Ghosts of those who died before their time (*bhut*) and other spirits are believed to be able to possess or harm living people; fear of the evil eye is also widespread.

Religious Practitioners

Brahman priests traditionally have not served Jatavs and other Untouchables. Instead local headmen have officiated at rituals. Shamans (*bhagat*), who are sometimes Jatavs, have been known to be consulted in cases of spirit possession and other illness.

Ceremonies

Life-cycle ceremonies at birth, first hair cutting, marriage, and death are the major public ceremonies. Marriage is the most important ritual as it involves public feasts, the honor of the girl's family, cooperation of neighbors and specific kin, and gift giving over years to the families of married daughters. Death rituals also require participation of agnates and male neighbors to cremate the corpse immediately and of women to keen ritually. Very small children are buried.

Memorial feasts or meals for the dead are given over a period of a year.

Arts

The verbal arts, particularly the composition of various forms of poetry, are cultivated, as is the skill in singing various forms of song.

Medicine

Folk remedies are used and practitioners of Ayurvedic, Unani, and homeopathic medicines are consulted. Modern medicines and physicians are used when affordable.

Death and Afterlife

Belief in transmigration of souls is widespread, and some believe in an afterlife in Heaven (Svarg) or Hell (Narak). A son to perform the funeral obsequies is essential. The dead soul lingers after death but passes on after a number of days.

in the hands of hereditary headmen (*chaudhari*). Serious cases of conflict, breaches of caste rules, and other caste-related problems were decided by councils of adult men (*panchayat*) in each locality. In the past, higher-level councils existed for more serious cases or for appeals. The council system and the powers of hereditary headmen have gradually eroded, especially in cities where the courts and the more educated and politically involved leaders and businessmen have become more prominent and influential.

CONFLICT. Conflicts arise within and between families and individuals over money, children, inheritance claims, drinking, insults, and the like. In recent years conflicts, both in cities and villages, have taken a political turn as Jatavs, and other Untouchables, have tried to assert their rights. Non-Untouchable castes have reacted negatively. Serious riots between Jatavs and upper castes have occurred in cities, such as Agra, and dangerous conflicts have also occurred in villages. Jatavs feel that the pace of change is much too slow, while upper castes have rejected it as too fast, unjustified, and contrary to orthodox Hindu teaching.

Bibliography

Briggs, George W. (1920). *The Chamars.* Calcutta: Association Press.

Cohn, Bernard (1954). "The Camars of Senapur: A Study of the Changing Status of a Depressed Caste." Ph.D. dissertation, Cornell University.

Lynch, Owen M. (1969). *The Politics of Untouchability: Social Mobility and Social Change in a City of India.* New York: Columbia University Press.

Lynch, Owen M. (1981). "Rioting as Rational Action: An Interpretation of the April 1978 Riots in Agra." *Economic and Political Weekly* 16:1951–1956.
—OWEN M. LYNCH

KHASI

Ethnonyms: Cassia, Cossyah, Kasia, Kassia, Kassya, Kasya, Khasía, Khasiah, Khassia, Khassu, Khosia, Ki Khási

Orientation

IDENTIFICATION AND LOCATION. The Khasi (who call themselves Ki Khási) live in two districts of Meghalaya State, India (21°10′ to 26°05′ N, 90°47′ to 92°52′ E), an area of some 16,000 square kilometers. This region is home to several Mon-Khmer-speaking groups. The Khasi themselves live in the upland center of this large area. The Khasi designation for the Khasi Hills section is Ka Ri Khásí and that of the Jaintia Hills section is Ka Ri Synten. Other matrilineal and Mon-Khmer-speaking groups found in this region include the Lyngngams (Lynngam) who occupy the western part of the area, the Bhois who inhabit the north-central region, the Wars who occupy the district's southern expanse, and the Jaintia (also called Pnar or Synteng) in the southeast of the region.

DEMOGRAPHY. According to P. R. T. Gurdon, who first studied the Khasi in 1901, the total population then numbered 176,614. Their number had risen to 463,869 by 1971.

LINGUISTIC AFFILIATION. The Khasi speak a Mon-Khmer language (belonging to the Austroasiatic Family). Khasi is believed to form a link between related languages in central India and the Mon-Khmer languages of Southeast Asia. While dialectal variation may be noted within different villages, the major Khasi dialects are Khasi, Jaintia, Lyngngam, and War.

History and Cultural Relations

In the mid-sixteenth century there were twenty-five separate Khasi chiefdoms along with the separate kingdom of Jaintia. Before the arrival of the British, the Jaintia were vassals to a series of dominant kingdoms from the thirteenth to the eighteenth centuries (e.g., the Kachari, Koch, and Ahom). At the beginning of the sixteenth century Jaintia rule was extended to Sylhet and this marked the beginning of Brahman influence on the Jaintia. The annexation of Sylhet in 1835 (instigated by the seizing of British subjects for human sacrifice) preceded the subjugation of the Khasi states by some twenty or more years. By 1860, the British had annexed all of the Jaintia Hills region and imposed taxes on it as a part of British India. The Khasi states had limited cultural relations before the arrival of the British, characterized in large part by internal warfare between villages and states and raiding and trading in the Sylhet and Brahmaputra valleys. The incorporation of the markets at Sylhet into the British colonial economy in 1765 marked the beginning of Khasi subjugation. Khasi raids in the 1790s led to the rise of British fortifications in the foothills and an eventual embargo on Khasi-produced goods in Sylhet markets. In 1837 the construction of a road through Nongkhaw State linking Calcutta to the Brahmaputra Valley led to the eventual cessation of Khasi-British hostilities, and by 1862 treaties between the British and all of the

Khasi villages are built a little below the tops of hills in small depressions to protect against storms and high winds, with houses built near each other.

Khasi states (allowing Khasi autonomy and freedom from British taxation) were signed. A significant amount of cultural change (e.g., an increase in wealth, decline of traditional culture, rise in educational standards, and frequent intermarriage) occurred after the British made Shillong the capital of Assam. In 1947 there was constituted an autonomous tribal area responsible to Assam's governor as an agent of the president of India. However, the native state system with its various functionaries remains intact, and Khasis now have their own state, Meghalaya, in which they predominate.

Settlements

Khasi villages are built a little below the tops of hills in small depressions to protect against storms and high winds, with houses built in close proximity to one another. In addition to individual houses, family tombs and memorial stones (*mawbynna*) are located within confines or nearby. Internal division of the village based on wealth does not obtain; rich and poor live side by side. Sacred groves are located near the village between the brow of the hill and the leeward side, where the village's tutelary deity is worshiped. Pigs wander freely through a village, and some villages (e.g., those of the high plateau) also feature potato gardens protected by dry dikes and hedges. Narrow streets connect houses and stone steps lead up to individual houses. The upper portion of a Khasi village may be as much as 100 meters higher in elevation than the lower portion. A village site is rarely changed. The typical Khasi house is a shell-shaped building with three rooms: the *shynghup* (porch for storage); the *nengpei* (center room for cooking and sitting); and the *rumpei* (inner room for sleeping). The homes of wealthy Khasi are more modern, having iron roofs, chimneys, glass windows, and doors. Some have European-style homes and furniture. A marketplace is located outside a Khasi village (close to memorial stones, by a river or under a group of trees, depending on the region). Within Khasi villages one may find a number of public buildings, Christian churches, and schools.

Economy

SUBSISTENCE AND COMMERCIAL ACTIVITIES. Cultivation is the major Khasi subsistence activity and the family farm (managed by a single family with or without the assistance of outside labor) is the basic operating unit in crop production. The Khasi are multioccupational and their economy is market-based. Marketing societies exist to facilitate trade and to provide aid in times of personal need. Crops are produced for consumption and trade. There are four types of land utilized for cultivation: forest; wet paddy land (*hali* or *pynthor*); homestead land (*ka 'dew kyper*); and high grass land (*ka ri lum* or *ka ri phlang*). Forest land is cleared by cutting trees, burning them, and planting seeds with hoes in the ground thus fertilized (*jhum* agriculture). Paddy land in valleys is divided into compartments by banks and flooded by irrigation channels. Proper soil consistency is obtained by using cattle and hoes. Crops produced by the Khasi include vegetables, pulses, sugarcane, maize, rice, potatoes, millet, pineapples, Job's tears, bay leaves, yams, tapioca, cotton, oranges, and betel nuts. Other crops known in the region include turmeric, ginger, pumpkins, gourds, eggplants, chilies, and sesame. The Khasi also engage in other subsistence activities such as fishing (by poisoning or with rod and line), bird snaring (quail, partridge, lapwings, coots, and wild geese), hunting (deer, wild dogs, wolves, bears, leopards, and tigers), and the raising of goats (for sacrifice), cattle (cows and oxen for manure, field cultivation, and dairy products), pigs, dogs, and hens (for sacrifice), chickens and ducks (largely for eggs), and bees (for larvae, wax, and honey).

INDUSTRIAL ARTS. Industrial specialization by village obtains to some extent among the Khasi, but generally they practice a great diversity of industrial arts. Cottage industries and industrial arts include cane and bamboo work, blacksmithing, tailoring, handloom weaving and spinning, cocoon rearing, lac production, stonecutting, brick making, jewelry making, pottery making, iron smelting, and beekeeping. Manufactured goods include: woven cloth, coarse cotton, *randia* cloth, quilts (made of beaten and woven tree bark), hoes, plowshares, billhooks, axes, silver work, miscellaneous implements of husbandry, netted bags (of pineapple fiber), pottery (made without the use of the potter's wheel), mats, baskets, rope and string, gunpowder, brass cooking utensils, bows, arrows, swords, spears, and shields.

TRADE. Trade takes place between villages, with the plains areas, and between highland and lowland areas. Barter (though to a lesser extent now) and currency are the media of exchange. There are local markets (village-based) in addition to a large central market in Shillong, and a large portion of Khasi produce is exported. Within a typical Khasi market one may find the following for sale: bees, rice beer, rice, millet, beans, sugarcane, fish, potatoes, oranges, lemons, mangoes, breadfruit, pepper, bananas, cinnamon,

♦ **paddy**
The rice plant (Oryza sativa), grown either in irrigated fields (wet rice) or in rain-fed fields (dry rice). Rice is the staple food of Sri Lanka, Bangladesh, Kashmir, and Dravidian India. Elsewhere wheat is more important.

goats, sheep, cattle (live and slaughtered), and housing and cultivation products (roofing grass, cut beams, bamboo poles, latticework, dried cow manure, spades, baskets, bamboo drinking cups, gourd bottles, wooden mortars, water pipes made of coconut, clay pipe bowls, iron pots, and earthen dishes). Large markets, like Shillong, contain goods from foreign markets (e.g., from Europe).

DIVISION OF LABOR. Men clear land, perform jhum agriculture, handle cattle, and engage in metalworking and woodworking. Women weave cloth, act as vendors in the market, and are responsible in large part for the socialization of children. Women are credited with being the growers of provisions sold at market. Men also participate in market activities by selling articles which they manufacture and produce (e.g., ironwork), raise (e.g., goats, sheep), or catch (e.g., birds). They also bring provisions to women at market and exercise some degree of control over the market by acting as accountants. For example, a husband may be responsible to his own family (by working the fields for his wife) while at the same time keeping his sister's mercantile accounts. A woman's uncle, brother, or son may function in a similar capacity on her behalf, though this is more likely to be the case if the woman's business is on a large scale.

LAND TENURE. There are four kinds of public land: *ka ri raj* (Crown lands); *ka ri lyngdoh* (priestly lands); *ki shong* (village lands for the production of thatching grass, firewood, etc.); and *ki 'lawkyntang* (sacred groves). There are two types of private land: *ri-kur* (land owned by a clan) and *ri-kynti* (land owned by families or acquired; it is inherited by a woman from her mother or is acquired by a man or a woman). Ancestral land must always be owned by a woman. Men may cultivate the land, but the produce must be carried to the house of the mother who divides it among the members of her family. Usually, if a man obtains land, upon his death it is inherited by his mother (i.e., if he is unmarried). There is, however, a provision made for a man to will land acquired after marriage to his children.

Kinship

KIN GROUPS AND DESCENT. The Khasi are a well-known instance of matriliny. The maximal matrilineage among them is the clan (called *kur* or *jaid*). The Khasi speak of a family of great-grandchildren of one great-grandmother (thus, four generations) as *shi kpoh* (one womb). Clans trace descent from ancestresses or *kiaw* (grandmothers) who are called *ki lawbei-tynrai* (grandmothers of the root, i.e., of the clan tree). In some instances the actual name of the ancestress survives. She is revered greatly and her descendants are called *shi kur* (one clan). Below this division are the subclan or *kpoh* (as already mentioned,

SHELTER

Khasi villages are built near the tops of hills to protect against storms; houses are built close to one another, and rich and poor live side by side. Khasi Hills, Meghalaya State, India.
(Nazima Kowall/Corbis)

The Khasi wedding ceremony includes the taking of the bride to the house of the groom's mother, where a ring is placed on the bride's finger by her mother-in-law.

descendants of one great-grandmother) and the *iing* (house or family), usually made up of a grandmother, her daughters, and her daughters' children. Together these are said to be *shi iing* (one house).

KINSHIP TERMINOLOGY. Kinship terminology employed for first cousins follows the Iroquois pattern.

Marriage and Family

MARRIAGE. The Khasi are, for the most part, monogamous. Their social organization does not favor other forms of marriage; therefore, deviation from this norm is quite rare. Marriage is a purely civil contract. The ceremony consists of a betrothal, the pouring of a libation to the clan's first maternal ancestor, the taking of food from the same plate, and the taking of the bride to the house of the groom's mother where a ring is placed on the bride's finger by her mother-in-law. Males are between the ages of 18 and 35 when they marry, while women's ages range from 13 to 18. Although parentally arranged marriages do occur, this does not appear to be the preferred form. Young men and women are permitted considerable freedom in the choice of mates and in premarital sexual relations. Potential marriage partners are likely to have been acquainted before betrothal. Once a man has selected his desired spouse, he reports his choice to his parents. They then secure the services of a male relative (or other male unrelated to the family) to make the arrangements with the female's family (provided that the man's parents agree with his choice). The parents of the woman ascertain her wishes and if she agrees to the arrangement her parents check to make certain that the man to be wed is not a member of their clan (since Khasi clans are exogamous, marital partners may not be from the same clan). If this is satisfactory, then omens are taken. If the omens are favorable, then a wedding date is set, but if the omens are negative, the wedding plans are abandoned. Divorce is frequent (with causes ranging from incompatibility to lack of offspring) and easily obtainable. This ceremony consists of the husband handing the wife 5 cowries or paisa which the wife then hands back to her husband along with 5 of her own. The husband then throws these away or gives them to a village elder who throws them away. According to Gurdon, postmarital residence is matrilocal, with the husband and wife leaving the wife's mother's residence after the birth of one or two children. C. Nakane makes a further distinction between two types of marriages, the first being marriage to

an heiress, the second marriage to a nonheiress. The type of marriage is, for Nakane, the determining factor in marital residence. This practice is the result of rules and regulations governing inheritance and property ownership. These rules are themselves related to the structure of the Khasi iing. In short, postmarital residence when an heiress is involved must be uxorilocal, while postmarital residence when a nonheiress is involved is neolocal. Khasi men prefer to marry a nonheiress because it will allow them to form independent family units somewhat immune to pressures from the wife's kin. A Khasi man returns to his iing upon the death of his spouse (if she is an heiress). If she is not an heiress, he may remain with his children if they are not too young and if he plans to marry his wife's younger sister. Marriage to a deceased wife's elder sister is prohibited. This is the only form of the sororate found among the Khasi. The levirate does not obtain in Khasi society. It has been suggested that the increasing monetization of the Khasi economy and availability of jobs for men beyond village confines may have altered postmarital residence patterns.

DOMESTIC UNIT. Around the turn of the century, the basic Khasi domestic unit was a single household made up of a grandmother, her daughters, and her daughters' children (the grandmother being the head of the household during her lifetime). In mid-century, Nakane distinguished between four types of Khasi households: (1) a household comprised of wife, husband, their children, and wife's unmarried sisters and brothers; (2) a household composed of nearly all the iing members (but not including their spouses) or a larger household (including wives and husbands) that contains all descendants of three or more generations from one woman (in which case the iing corresponds to the kpoh); (3) an intermediate type of household, between types 1 and 2, that is popular among newly married couples before the birth of children, in which a husband is supposed to live in the wife's house but often returns to his sister's house for meals and to sleep, and in which the husband is responsible for working his wife's fields and may also work those of his mother and sister; and (4) one nuclear family unit (usually when the man marries a nonheiress). According to Nakane, most Khasi households are of types 1, 3, and 4. All three types are usually found in one village. Type 2 was prominent at one time among the Jaintias.

INHERITANCE. With regard to real property, inheritance goes to the youngest daughter of the deceased mother and upon the youngest daughter's death in turn to her youngest daughter. Other daughters are entitled to a smaller share of the inheritance of their mother, but the largest share goes to the youngest daughter. When the mother has no daughters, the inheritance goes to her sister's youngest daughter. If the sister has no daughters, then the mother's sisters and their female kin receive the inheritance. Men are prohibited from inheriting real property. All property acquired by a man before marriage belongs to his mother. Property acquired by him after marriage belongs to his wife and children. Of these children, the youngest daughter will receive the largest share of the inheritance upon the death of the man's wife. If the man has no daughters, then his sons receive his property upon the death of their mother. Christian conversion has had and may continue to have a deleterious effect on the Khasi system of inheritance. Khasi heiresses who converted to Christianity lost their right to inherit at one time in Khasi social history. With the gradual acceptance of Christianity, these rights were restored. However, there is a tendency for heiresses who convert to Christianity to discontinue their sacerdotal functions within the family. It has been suggested that this may threaten the institution of ultimogeniture. It has also been suggested that the availability of nonland-based employment for males may undermine the economic basis of matrilineal inheritance.

SOCIALIZATION. Naming occurs one day after birth. Family activities center on the performance of religious rites, management of family property, and the maintenance and protection of kin relations. Men, women, and children participate fully in these and other labor-related activities. Women, however, are the chief agents of socialization.

Sociopolitical Organization

SOCIAL ORGANIZATION. Khasi villages tend to be endogamous units, each one containing a number of matrilineal clans (kur). Members of these clans trace their descent from a common female ancestor. Solidarity is manifest largely on this level of social organization. There are three class-defined lineages—nobles, commoners, and slaves. Elderly men and men of importance wear turbans as a sign of status, and men who have sponsored a great feast may wear silver armlets above the elbows. Wealth can be demonstrated in a number of ways, including the size of the mawbynna (monument) one has constructed at the burial site of a deceased person and the ownership of decorative gongs (wiang). In some sense, the lyngdohship (priesthood) may also be treated as a sign of status. The matrilineal clan is perhaps the most important primary institution. The position of women is more prominent than that of men. As member of a clan, a man will be lost to his mother's clan when he marries, his status shifting from that of *u kur* (brother) in his clan to that of *u shong ka* (begetter) in his wife's clan. He is not allowed to participate in the religious observances of his wife's clan and when he dies he is not buried in his wife's family tomb. Women also assume leadership in secondary institutions (e.g., religion) as evidenced by their management of the family cults and the performance of its attendant rituals.

POLITICAL ORGANIZATION. The Khasi state system arose originally from the voluntary association of villages or groups thereof. The head of state is the *siem* (chief). He has limited monarchical powers. He may perform certain acts without the approval of his *durbar* (an executive council over which he presides). He also possesses judicial powers. Those who sit on the durbar are called *mantris*. These individuals are charged with the actual management of the state. Some states have officials called *sirdars* (village headmen) who collect labor, receive *pynsuk* (gratification) for the siem, and settle local cases. In Nongstoin there is an official called a *lyngskor* who acts as supervisor of a number of sirdars. In most states the siem is the religious and secular head of state. He conducts certain public religious ceremonies, consults oracles and acts as judge (the durbar being the jury) in legal cases, and in times past was the literal head of the army in battle. The siem was chosen by popular election in Langrim, Bhoval, and Nobosohpoh states. The British attempted to impose this system on all Khasi states but the results of their efforts were questionable. Little was accomplished save the confirmation of an electoral body that itself elected the siem. Succession to siemship is always through the female side. A new siem is elected from a siem family (of which there is one in every state) by an electoral body that may be composed of representatives from certain priestly and nonpriestly clans, village headmen, and *basams* (market supervisors).

SOCIAL CONTROL. Interpersonal tensions, domestic disagreements, and interclan disputes account for the major part of conflict within Khasi society. Other sources include the swearing of false oaths, incest, revenge, conversions to other religions, failure to maintain the family religious cults, adultery, rape, arson, and sorcery. Social control is maintained by clan, village, state,

*Today over half of
all Khasis have
adopted
Christianity.*

and national authorities. The traditional means used to maintain order included exile, monetary fines, curses, disinheritance, enforced servitude, imprisonment, capital punishment, confinement (e.g., in the stocks), imposition of fetters, and confinement to a bamboo platform under which chilies were burnt.

CONFLICT. Conflict between states and regions (e.g., between the Khasi and the peoples of the plains) was prevalent before the arrival of the British. The taking of heads (associated with the worship of the war god U Syngkai Bamon) was also practiced by the Khasi. In their conflict with British imperial forces, the Khasi relied heavily on ambush and guerrilla tactics. Little is known of traditional Khasi contacts with other groups.

Religion and Expressive Culture

RELIGIOUS BELIEFS. Christian missionary work among the Khasi began in the late nineteenth century with the efforts of the Welsh Calvinistic Methodist mission. The effects of their endeavors and those of other Christian bodies have been considerable. Today over half of all Khasis have adopted Christianity. The missionary impact may be noted on almost all levels of culture. However, the core of traditional Khasi religious beliefs remains intact. The Khasi believe in a creator god (U Blei Nong-thaw) who is considered feminine in gender (Ka lei Synshar). She is invoked when sacrifices are offered and during times of trouble. The propitiation of good and evil spirits is also part of this system, as is the worship of ancestors. The following major spirits are worshiped: Ulei Muluk (god of the state); Ulei Umtang (god of drinking water and cooking water); Ulei Longspah (god of wealth); and O Ryngkew or U Basa Shnong (tutelary deity of the village).

RELIGIOUS PRACTITIONERS. The propitiation of the spirits is carried out by the *lyngdoh* (priest) or by old men knowledgeable in the art of necromancy. Other practitioners include the *soh-blei* and *soh-blah* (male functionaries with limited sacerdotal functions), the *ka soh-blei*, also called *ka-soh-sla* or *ka-lyngdoh* (female priests who must be present at the offering of all sacrifices), and the *nongkhan* (diviners). The lyngdoh—who is always appointed from a special priestly clan, who holds his office for life, and who may be one of several within a state—is the chief functionary of the communal cults. He also has certain duties in conjunction with marital laws and household exorcism. In some states, the lyngdoh subsumes the responsibilities of siem (chief) and rules with the

assistance of a council of elders. The duty of performing family ceremonies is the sole responsibility of the head of the family or clan who usually fulfills them through the agency of the *kni* (maternal uncle). Female priests must assist at all sacrifices and, in fact, are the only functionaries in possession of full sacerdotal authority. The lyngdoh exercises his duties as appointed agent of the ka soh-blei (female priest). It is believed that this system is an archaic survival from a period in Khasi history when the female priest acted as her own agent in the offering of sacrifice. In some states (e.g., Nongkrem), there is a high priestess who functions sacerdotally and as head of state. She delegates temporal responsibilities to a son or nephew who then exercises them as a siem. The adoption of Christianity by a large segment of Khasi society has resulted in important changes. The sacerdotal function of the youngest daughter (responsible, in traditional Khasi culture, for conducting burial services on behalf of her parents and for acting as chief practitioner of the family cult) has been threatened by Christian teaching and practice (i.e., the youngest daughter, if a Christian, is less likely to fulfill her priestly responsibilities to her family).

CEREMONIES. Dancing and music are important parts of Khasi ritual, and the Nongkrem Dance (part of the *pom-blang* or goat-killing ceremony) is the major festival on the Khasi calendar. It is dedicated to Ka lei Synshar, for the ruling of the Khasi. Its purpose is to ensure substantial crop yield and good fortune for the state. It is held in late spring (usually in May). A number of state and communal rituals are also performed, in addition to many ceremonies associated with the human life cycle (birth, marriage, death, etc.).

ARTS. Examples of decorative art include metal gongs (with animal engravings), implements of warfare (arrows, spears, bows, and shields), and memorial slabs (with engravings). To a limited extent woodwork, jewelry, and other industrial manufactures may be so classified. Music is an important part of Khasi religious ceremonies (both communal and clan-related), hunting expeditions, and athletic events (e.g., archery contests). Musical forms include extemporaneous verse that is said to resemble, in form and content, magicoreligious incantations. Drums, guitars, wooden pipes and flutes, metal cymbals, and various harps are among the instruments used in Khasi musical performance. As was mentioned previously, dancing also accompanies most ceremonies in public and private life. With regard to literature, a considerable body of oral and written material exists. This includes proverbs, myths, legends, folktales, songs, and agricultural sayings.

MEDICINE. In traditional Khasi medical practice magicoreligious means are used to prevent and treat sickness. The only indigenous drugs used are chiretta (a febrifuge of the Gentianaceae order—*Swertia chirata*) and wormwood. Native medical specialists are not present. Generally illness is believed to be caused by one or more spirits as a result of a human act of omission. Health, within this system, can be restored only by the propitiation of the spirits or, if the spirits are not able to be appeased, by calling on other spirits for assistance. Divination is done by breaking an egg and "reading" the resulting signs.

DEATH AND AFTERLIFE. In Khasi eschatology, those who die and have proper funeral ceremonies performed on their behalf go to the house (or garden) of God, which is filled with betel-palm groves. Here they enjoy a state of endless bliss. Those who do not receive proper burial are believed to roam the Earth in the form of animals, birds, and insects. This idea of soul transmigration is believed to have been borrowed from Hindu theology. Unlike Christian eschatology, that of the Khasi is not characterized by a belief in any form of eternal punishment after death.

Bibliography

Assam, Department of Economics and Statistics (1955). *Report on Rural Economic Survey in United Khasi and Jaintia Hills.* Shillong: Government Press.

Becker, Cristofero (1924). "Familienbesitz und Mutterrecht in Assam." In *Zeitschrift für Buddhismus und verwandte Gebiete* 6:127–138, 300–310. Reprint. 1925. Munich and Neubiberg: O. Schloss.

Godwin-Austen, H. H. (1872). "On the Stone Monuments of the Khasi Hill Tribes, and on Some Peculiar Rites and Customs of the People." *Journal of the Anthropological Institute of Great Britain and Ireland* 1:122–143.

Gurdon, P. R. T. (1904). "Note on the Khasis, Syntengs, and Allied Tribes, Inhabiting the Khasi and Jaintia Hills District in Assam." *Journal of the Asiatic Society of Bengal* 73, pt. 3:57–74.

Gurdon, P. R. T. (1907). *The Khasis.* London: D. Nutt. 2nd ed. 1914. Reprint. 1975. Delhi: Cosmo Publications.

Hunter, William W. (1879). "Statistical Account of the Khasi and Jaintia Hills." In *Statistical Account of Assam.* Vol. 2, 201–255. London: Trübner.

McCormack, Anna P. (1964). "Khasis." In *Ethnic Groups of Mainland Southeast Asia,* edited by Frank M. Lebar et al., 105–112. New Haven, Conn.: HRAF Press.

Nakane, Chie (1967). *Garo and Khasi: A Comparative Study in Matrilineal Systems.* Paris: Mouton.

Roy, David (1938). "The Place of the Khasi in the World." *Man in India* 18:122–134.

Stegmiller, F. (1921). "Aus dem Religiösen Leben der Khasi." *Anthropos* 16–17:407–441.

Stegmiller, F. (1924). "Opfer und Opferbräuche der Khasi." *Anthropologischen Gesellschaft in Wien, Mitteilungen* 54:211–231.

Stegmiller, F. (1925). "Pfeilschiessen und Jagdgebräuche der Khasi." *Anthropos* 20:607–623.

Stegmiller, F. (1928). "Das Marktleben der Khasi." In *Festschrift.* Publication d'hommage offerte au P. W. Schmidt. 76 sprachwissenschaftliche, ethnologische, religionswissen-schaftliche, prähistorische und andere Studien. . . . Edited by Wilhelm Koppers, 703–710. Vienna: Mechitaristen-congregations-buchdruckerei.

—HUGH R. PAGE, JR.

LINGAYAT

Ethnonym: Virasaiva

Orientation

IDENTIFICATION. The Lingayats speak Kannada, one of the four major Dravidian languages spoken in the south of India. They are called Lingayats because they worship *istalinga,* the symbol of Shiva, and they always wear it around their necks or across their chests. They are also called Virasaivas because of their deep love and commitment to their God, "the Omni-present and Ever Compassionate."

LOCATION. Lingayats live in all nineteen districts of Karnataka State in south India, which stretches from 11°05′ N to 19°00′ N and from 74°00′ E to 78°06′ E and along the Arabian Sea. The north and central regions are their heartland, although Lingayats are found also in the four neighboring states of Maharashtra and Goa to the north, Andhra Pradesh to the east, and Tamil Nadu to the south. The climate is basically a tropical monsoon type and the temperatures change periodically, varying between 15° and 40° C.

DEMOGRAPHY. The census of 1981 places the Karnataka population at 37,135,714 with a population density of 194 persons per square kilometer. Assuming that the Lingayat population has grown at the rate of the general population of Karnataka, the Lingayat numbered about 5,600,000 then.

LINGUISTIC AFFILIATION. The Kannada language is classified in the Dravidian Family, and the Lingayats fully identify with it. It is related to the Tamil, Telugu, Tulu, and Malayalam languages but it has its own script, which consists of thirty-four consonants and fourteen vowels. Its first poetics, *Kavirajamarga*, and first grammar, *Bhasa Bhusan*, were written in the early ninth and eleventh centuries, respectively, and its literary history spans well over 1,000 years.

History and Cultural Relations

The contribution of Lingayats to the cultural heritage of Karnataka is significant. Kannada literary historians have identified some 1,148 Kannada writers between the eighth and the end of the nineteenth century; of these, there are 453 Lingayats, 377 Brahmans, and 175 Jains, while the rest represent other groups. Basava, the founding father of Lingayat religion, was also in some ways the first to lead a successful crusade in the early part of the twelfth century A.D. against domination by the Sanskrit language in order to make Kannada, the language of the common man, the medium of literary expression. He set an example by recording his *Vacanas* (sayings) in Kannada and the tradition set by him continues to flourish in

modern Lingayat writings. The ideology of the Lingayat culture also begins with Basava, who rejected the feudal orientation of Hindu Brahmanism and substituted for it a new social order similar to Gandhian populism and based upon the principles of individuality, equality, and fraternity. The cooperative, communitarian movement initiated by Basava continues to flourish in the modern political life of Karnataka. The Lingayat monasteries, spread across contemporary Karnataka's small and large towns, run schools and colleges with free room and board for needy students. These monasteries serve not only as centers of religious culture but also as centers of education; they can claim a record of fifty years of contribution to the educational progress of the state, unrivaled by other educational institutions. The Shiva worshiped by the Lingayats does not belong to the Hindu pantheon. He is formless, qualityless, and an embodiment of love and compassion. Lingayats worship him as a symbolic manifestation of the universe and call him their personal God, istalinga. For them Sanskrit (like church Latin) is the vehicle of feudal values, inherited inequalities, and priestly prerogatives; so they identify with Kannada and contribute to its literary richness and variety. Their cultural heritage there-

ECONOMY

Subsistence and Commercial Activities

The economy of a Lingayat village, which is predominantly agricultural, reflects the Lingayat culture. Their social structure is populistic, with birth and occupation intertwined. Lingayats are engaged in an entire range of occupational activities—agriculture, commerce and trade, teaching and scholarship, blacksmithing, carpentry, weaving, oil pressing, hairdressing, etc. Traditionally, Lingayat farmers produced partly for local consumption and partly for a market economy, and plowed their land with metal-shod wooden plows powered by pairs of bullocks. Much of economic life was regulated by the *aya* system, in which exchange of goods and services took place. The local artisan groups and labor depended upon the farmers for their survival. With independence in 1947 and the launching of five-year plans and community development projects, the traditional mode of cultivation is being gradually modernized by the use of chemicals, fertilizers, lift pumps, irrigation, etc.

Rural life, once characterized by exchange relationships, is giving way to competitive interests revolving around the economic realities of supply and demand. For example, the artisan community in the village has nearly closed its doors to local customers, as it now seeks new opportunities in the nearby city market in its traditional specialities. And the village washerman's family also is involved in the city electric laundering establishment, the cobbler in its shoe stores, the blacksmith in tool-making jobs, and the goldsmith in the jewelry store. So traditional work is becoming modern work, and traditional skills are becoming modernized in the process. The village farmers, who once produced primarily for domestic and local purposes, now prefer cash crops such as sugarcane, cotton, chilies, fruits, and vegetables for export. But such concerns do not seem to have eroded traditional values as indicated by the increasing number of cooperative societies in Lingayat villages. Urban Lingayats are found equally in all occupations and dominate small trade, commerce, and the textile industry in Karnataka.

fore follows neither the *marga* (way of seeking) nor the *desi* (way of instruction) traditions; it rejects the institutions, cultural prescriptions, notions, and values characteristic of both these Hindu traditions. It represents, in fact, partly a selective blending and partly a selective conflict between the two. It comes very close to a populistic tradition, with its own institutions and values rooted in the 27,000 villages and some 300 towns of Karnataka.

Settlements

Lingayat villages are usually nucleated with houses built close to each other. The population of a village may vary anywhere from 250 to 3,500 persons. Villages are dispersed and connected by paths and main roads that link them to the national highways. Farmers' houses are made of either mud, stone, or cement. A well-to-do Lingayat farmer's house, made out of mud and stone, consists of three sections. The first section is a porch with a raised platform, usually open but sometimes closed, which is used for visitors and resting. A threshold and a door frame with carved figures of Basava lead to the second section, which consists of units used for housing the cattle and for domestic purposes, including a kitchen, a store-room, and a *puja* (worship) room. The third section of the house, the backyard, is used for storing hay, fuel, etc.

Kinship

KIN GROUPS AND DESCENT. The kinship universe of the Lingayats can be described in terms of two categories: effective and noneffective. Relationships among effective kin are close, intimate, obligatory, and reciprocal, whereas those among noneffective kin are less intimate and functionally insignificant. Effective kin are those closely related by descent and marriage, and mate selection among such kin is preferential. Noneffective kin are remotely related and rarely remembered, and meaningful interaction between them is absent. Ideally, Lingayat kinship emphasizes the patrimonial principle, but in reality matrilineal orientations prevail both in sentiments and obligations. Kin groups among rural Lingayats maintain and reinforce their kinship relations through uncle-niece, cross-cousin, and exchange marriages. Affinal relationships are recognized only if they are involved in preferential marriages.

KINSHIP TERMINOLOGY. Lingayat kinship may be described as multilateral with partly descriptive and partly generic kin terms. Father's brothers and sisters, for example, are described as "big" or "little" "fathers" and "mothers" depending on relative age; terms for paternal and maternal grandfathers and grandmothers are treated in the same way.

Marriage and Family

MARRIAGE. A common practice among Lingayat parents is to arrange their children's marriages. About five decades ago, a bride and bridegroom could see each other's face only at the marriage pedestal, but increasing education and widespread urbanization have crept into the villages and slowly affected the ways of traditional matchmaking. These days "love" marriages are heard of even in the countryside. In educated Lingayat families, younger generations enjoy some freedom in the choice of partners, a practice unheard of half a century ago. The use of horoscopes is conspicuously absent among the Lingayats. Divorce and separation are uncommon and marital breakdowns are frowned upon. Precautions against possible disintegration are taken by arranging interkin marriages, which help to strengthen the marital bonds. In the event of a breakdown, however, Lingayat attitudes toward divorce, especially in comparison with some other religious groups, are liberal and tolerant. They are equally liberal in encouraging widow remarriages, which are condemned by the Hindu-Brahmanic society. Residence is patrilocal among rural Lingayats. Upon marriage, the bride goes to live with the groom's household. Among urbanites they are expected to live independently. For an educated Lingayat couple, neolocal residence is the norm.

DOMESTIC UNIT. The extended family is regarded as the ideal arrangement among rural Lingayats, although the nuclear family is actually more common and there are occasional instances of conjugal family arrangements. Nuclear or conjugal, the family does not live in isolation, as it is always embedded in the larger kin group. Since the collective solidarity of the kin group is the prime value in the community, family autonomy and privacy are never its concerns. All related families are held together by a sense of mutuality and complementarity. Such interdependence is seen on occasions of births, weddings, fairs, and festivals. The urban Lingayat family is primarily nuclear but it too maintains its ties with its rural kin by providing shelter, hospitality, and employment opportunities, when needed.

INHERITANCE. Traditionally, legal rights favored the patrilineage. Upon marriage, a girl took her husband's surname and all the legal claims that went with it. Her loss of a share in her

Lingayat

SOCIOPOLITICAL ORGANIZATION

The Lingayat monasteries, spread across contemporary Karnataka's small and large towns, run schools and colleges with free room and board for needy students.

parental family property, however, was met through adequate gifts of jewelry and gold during her marriage and on successive visits to the natal family. Her parents and siblings fulfilled their moral obligations to her, especially in times of crisis. Such customs and conventions generally created an environment in which brother-sister relations continued even after the parents' deaths. The Succession Act of 1956 that gave guaranteed equal rights to surviving children of deceased parents altered the bonds that once united the conjugal and natal families and brother-sister relationships. It is not uncommon these days for brothers and sisters to behave like rivals over the sharing of parental property and to take their claims to court.

SOCIALIZATION. The socialization of a Lingayat child begins immediately after birth when the priest, the *jangama*, visits the home, names the child, and initiates him or her into the Lingayat faith by tying a *linga* around the child's neck. His role in communicating the values of his faith continues throughout the life of the named child, especially during some major life stages. Among other agents of socialization, mother, grandmother, father, siblings, and other extended relatives are significant, in that order. Among the nonfamilial agents, priest, peer group, elders, and teachers are effective. Socialization within the family is primarily informal and learning occurs there mostly by observation and imitation. Obedience and respect for elders, trust in their god and religion, hard work, and generosity are some of the values that Lingayat parents like to see in their children.

Sociopolitical Organization

SOCIAL ORGANIZATION. The Lingayat system of social stratification is built largely around wealth, power, and prestige in both secular and religious spheres. Occupational and social mobility are open to everyone. Lingayats are therefore involved in all sectors of the economy. Their work ethic flows directly from their ethic of *kayaka* (rites and observances performed with the body, hence the spiritual value of labor); their role in community building comes from their practice of *dashoha* (community sharing of one's own labor), and their identification with society at large from their notion of *aikya* (being with the linga is being with society). Lingayat economic behavior therefore stems from the values enshrined in their ideology.

POLITICAL ORGANIZATION. Lingayats are actively involved politically through participation in the democratic establishment in Karnataka. Its political history records the successful mobilization of Lingayats in achieving power at the village level, in unifying a single united Karnataka that was divided among several adjoining states prior to 1956, and in promoting village links with the center. In carrying this out, they have long been aware that social mobilization could not be achieved without a political orientation. The hundreds of biographies of successful Lingayats (published by the Gadag Tontadarya monastery) provide ample evidence of this awareness. The secular and religious leaders steer their community, mediated by its middle- and lower-middle-class core, well beyond communal polities into the universal polity, and from premodern polities to a modern, liberal one.

Religion and Expressive Culture

RELIGIOUS BELIEFS. The Lingayat religion is the largest established religion in Karnataka. Other established religions include Brahmanism, Jainism, and Islam. Lingayats do not label themselves Hindus and claim an independent status for their faith. The Lingayat theological doctrine of *saktivisistadvaita* (a qualified monistic philosophy characterized by Sakti, the spiritual power of Shiva); its socialization agents, the guru and the jangama (monk); and its notion of istalinga are distinctively Lingayat in character. Its system involving *astavarnas* (eight supportive systems), *panca acaras* (five principles of conduct), and *sat stalas* (six stages related to social and religious progress) has helped to transform Lingayatism into a distinct framework. Their ethical and behavioral norms have given them a capacity to coexist with other sociocultural groups and at the same time preserve their religious and cultural homogeneity and identity. The beliefs and behavioral patterns of Lingayats are expounded in the compositions of Basava, whom they regard as their founding father as well as a dominant influence in the works of his colleagues. These compositions, collectively known as the *Vacanas*, have the status of sacred literature, are taught to Lingayats from childhood, and are internalized by them. Lingayats believe in a one-and-only God and worship him in the form of istalinga, which resembles the shape of a globe. Lingayats are antimagic and antisupernatural in their religious orientation. They do not worship stone images and the deities of the desi tradition. They believe that devotion to Basava and the other Lingayat saints will bring them their blessings and guard their lives.

RELIGIOUS PRACTITIONERS. They have their own priests who officiate at the various life-cycle rites, of which the prominent ones are those dealing with birth, marriage, and death. Priesthood among Lingayats is not ascriptive and is open to all irrespective of sex. Lingayats do not consider the world as *maya*, an illusion, and reject the Hindu notions of karma, rebirth, purity, and pollution.

CEREMONIES. The Lingayat ritual calendar gives prominence to the birthdays of their saints, the first in importance being the birthday of Basava. In addition, they celebrate Hindu festivals such as Dipavali, Yugadi, and Sankramana. Their centers of pilgrimage are at Kalyan, Ulive, and Srisaila, the places where Basava, his nephew Cennabasava, Allama Prabhu, and Akka Mahadevi are laid to eternal rest.

ARTS. Although Lingayats in past centuries were noted for their religious poetry and philosophical writings, today the chief arts are the singing and playing of hymns. There is no marked ability shown in the visual arts.

MEDICINE. Lingayat priests (called *ayya* or *swami*) are also astrologers and medicine men, often dispensing herbal remedies to sick villagers. This is a useful craft for them to possess, rather than a learned profession.

DEATH AND AFTERLIFE. For Lingayats there is no life after death. They believe that there is one and only one life and that a Lingayat can, by his or her deeds, make this life a hell or heaven. At death, he or she is believed to have returned to God and to be united with him. They call this state *aikya* (unity with linga). Since the dead person is believed to have attained the status of Shiva, the body is washed, clothed, decked with flowers, worshiped, and carried in a procession to the burial yard accompanied by singing in praise of Shiva.

Bibliography

Beals, Alan R. (1967). "Pervasive Factionalism in Namhalli." In *Divisiveness and Social Conflict: An Anthropological Approach*, edited by Alan R. Beals and Bernard J. Siegel, 117–138. Stanford: Stanford University Press.

Chekki, D. A. (1974). *Modernization and Kin Network.* Leiden: E. J. Brill.

Desai, P. B. (1968). *Basveshwar and His Times.* Dharwar: Karnatak University.

Ishwaran, K. (1968). *Shivapur: A South Indian Village.* London: Routledge & Kegan Paul.

Ishwaran, K. (1977). *A Populistic Community and Modernization in India.* Monographs and Theoretical Studies in Sociology and Anthropology in Honour of Nels Anderson, no. 13. Leiden: E. J. Brill.

Ishwaran, K. (1983). *Religion and Society among the Lingayats of South India.* Leiden: E. J. Brill.

Ishwaran, K. (1989). *Basava and the Lingayat Religion.* Leiden: E. J. Brill.

Nandimath, S. C. (1942). *A Handbook of Vīraśaivism.* Dharwar: The Literary Committee, Lingayat Education Association.

Nanjundayya, H. V., and L. K. Ananthakrishna Iyer (1931). "Lingāyat (Vīrasaiva)." In *The Mysore Tribes and Castes*, edited by H. V. Nanjundayya and L. K. Ananthakrishna Iyer. Vol. 4, 81–124. Mysore: Mysore University.

Parvathamma, C. (1972). *Sociological Essays on Veerasaivism.* Bombay: Popular Prakashan.

Ramanujan, A. K. (1973). *Speaking of Siva.* Harmondsworth: Penguin.

—K. ISHWARAN

MARATHA

Ethnonyms: Kanbi, Kunbi, Mahratta

Orientation

IDENTIFICATION. Marathas are a Marathi-speaking people found on the Deccan Plateau throughout the present state of Maharashtra and nearby areas. The word "Kunbi" derives from the Sanskrit "Kutumbin" or "householder" (i.e., a settled person with home and land). Marathas/Kunbis are the dominant caste in Maharashtra State. They are landowners and cultivators, and they make up about 50 percent of the population. The distinction between Marathas and Kunbis is confused, and the former consider themselves superior to the latter. The Marathas were traditionally chieftains and warriors who claimed Kshatriya descent. The Kunbis are primarily cultivators. The distinction between them seems mostly one of wealth, and we may assume a common origin for both.

LOCATION. Maratha territory comprises roughly one-tenth the area of modern India and is of interest as the southernmost area where an Indo-Aryan language is spoken in India. It is bounded on the west by the Arabian Sea, on the north by the states of Gujarat and Madhya Pradesh, on the east by tribal pats of Madhya Pradesh, and on the south by Andhra Pradesh and Karnataka states, as well as Goa. Maharashtra therefore is a culture contact region between the Indo-Aryan north and the Dravidian south, and so it reveals a mixture of culture traits characteristic of

The Marathas were traditionally chieftains and warriors who claimed Kshatriya descent.

any region that is a buffer between two great traditions. Besides occupying the heartland of Maharashtra, Marathas have also penetrated southward through Goa into Karnataka. The area is watered by many rivers, including the Tapti, the Godavari, the Bhima, the Krishna, and their tributaries, which divide the land into subregions that have been important historically and culturally. There is also the fertile coastal plain of Konkan and thickly forested regions on the north and east.

DEMOGRAPHY.   According to the 1981 census, the population of Maharashtra was 62,784,171.

LINGUISTIC AFFILIATION.   All Marathas speak Marathi or a dialect of it. Historically Maharashtri, a form of Prakrit, became the language of the ruling house in the Godavari Valley; and from it modern Marathi is derived. People in the various subregions speak the following dialects: Khandesh has Ahirani, Konkan has Konkani, the Nagpur Plateau has Varhadi, the southern Krishna Valley has Kolhapuri, and an unnamed dialect that is found along the banks of the Godavari became the court language and rose to be the literary form of Marathi.

History and Cultural Relations

The early history of the Marathas is a tale of the rise and fall in the importance of the dynasties ruling the various regions. Over time the center of political influence shifted south from the Godavari Basin to the Krishna Valley. From the 1300s on, the Maratha rajas held territories under Muslim kings and paid tribute to them. Feuds among the local Muslim kingdoms and later their confrontation with the Mogul dynasty, which was eager to extend its power to the Deccan, allowed Maratha chieftains to become independent. One such successful revolt was that of Shivaji, a Maratha prince who fought against his Muslim Bijapur overlords in the name of establishing a Hindu kingdom. The local Muslim rulers, weakened by their fights with the Moguls, succumbed to the guerrilla attacks of Shivaji's light infantry and cavalry. Shivaji's military success also depended to a great extent on the chain of fortifications he built to guard every mountain pass in his territory and the system he devised for garrisoning and provisioning them. With the death of Shivaji (1680) the Maratha ranks were split between the claimants to his throne; his son Shahu set up his capital at Satara and appointed a chief minister with the title "Peshwa." The title and office became hereditary, and within a short time the Peshwas became the leading Maratha dynasty themselves. In the 1700s the Peshwas rose to be a powerful military force supported by the Maratha

**INFLUENTIAL
CULTURE**

Nineteenth-century portrait of Marathas. In cities and small towns, some Marathas have high positions in government service, giving the group political power. Bombay, India. (Hulton-Deutsch Collection/Corbis)

Confederacy, a group of loyal chieftains including the houses of Bhonsla, Sindhia, Holkar, and Gaekwar. With their support the Peshwas extended their territories all the way north to the Punjab. Their power came to an end with their defeat at the battle of Panipat in 1761. Infighting among the confederacy members at the death of the Peshwa led to the entry of the East India Company into the succession disputes among the Marathas. The British fought the three Maratha wars, supporting one faction against the other, and in each case the British gained territory and power over individual chiefs. At the end of the Third Maratha War in 1818 the British routed the Peshwas so completely that they abolished their position and directly incorporated vast areas of Maratha territory into the British Empire as a part of Bombay Presidency. In 1960 by an act of Parliament the modern state of Bombay was divided into the linguistic states of Maharashtra, with Bombay as its capital, and Gujarat. The legacy of the Maratha State lingers on in the memory of the people, who revere Shivaji as a modern hero. A more negative aspect of Maratha consciousness has led to intolerance of other communities who have settled in Bombay, the premier commercial, industrial, and cultural center of India. Political parties like the Shiv Sena, a labor union–based organization, have sought to politicize Maratha consciousness by demanding the ouster of "foreigners" like Tamils and Malayalis from Bombay.

Settlements

A Maratha village in the coastal lowlands is not a well-defined unit. A village (*kalati*) consists of a long street running north-south with houses on either side, each with its own yard. This street is also the main artery joining a village to the neighboring ones north and south. Hence the perimeter of the village is not well defined. Each house stands in its own walled or fenced enclosure; but the rice fields that stretch all around are bounded by narrow earth *bunds* zigzagging in all directions, which make communication between houses in the growing season difficult. In contrast, villages in the plateau ranges are tightly clustered, and the village boundaries are sharply defined. An outstanding structure in such a village might be a temple or the big house (*wada*) of a rich landlord. The typical house is a rectangular block of four walls, with the bigger houses being made up of more than one such rectangle. Frequently an open square in the center of the house serves as a sun court. Some of the rooms leading off this court-

yard have no inner walls, so that there may be one or two rooms which can be closed and private and the rest of the house is a space with or without divisions for different purposes, like a kitchen, an eating area, etc. The houses had very small and very high windows and faced inwards onto the court. A village of such wadas is surrounded by fields with temporary shelters in them called *vadi*. Individual fields are large, and worked with draft animals. The use of the land has been dramatically affected in recent times by the building of dams for hydroelectric and irrigation purposes. Much of the previously arid inland areas can now grow sugarcane. Since Maharashtra is one of the most urbanized areas of India (35 percent urban in 1981), the Marathas have gravitated to the urban centers for jobs as well as farm-related services.

Economy

In general, the majority of Marathas are cultivators. They are mainly grant holders, landowners, soldiers, and cultivators. A few are ruling chiefs. For the most part the *patils* (village headmen) in the central Deccan belong to this caste. Some are traders, and many are in the army or other branches of government service. In the plateau region the fields are plowed with the help of bullocks. Almost every farmer except the poorest has cattle and takes great pride in them. The greatest agricultural festival is Bendur or Pola, when the cattle are decorated and taken in procession. The cattle are kept on the farm in a shed (*gotha*), and it is not unusual for them to share the house space with people, so that a corner of the sun court may be given over to them. This is to avoid both theft and predation by wild animals, which once were common on the plateau. Staple foods are wheat cakes, rice, lentils, clarified butter, vegetables, and condiments. Less affluent people usually eat *jowar* (sorghum), *bhajari* (spiked millet), and lentils, while the poorest will subsist on millets seasoned with spices. All Marathas eat flesh and fish, though not beef or pork. Marathas seldom drink liquor, though no caste rule forbids liquor or narcotics. *Beedi* smoking is common among the men.

Kinship, Marriage, and Family

Marathas practice *kul* or *devak* exogamy. Devaks are totemic groups that worship a common devak symbol. Kul is literally defined as a "family," and it is actually a lineage made up of extended families. Devak is an alternative name for this. Although they claim to have *gotras*, gotra exogamy is not essential. These are clan categories adopted from

*In the cities and
small towns some
Marathas have risen
to very high
positions in
government service,
which has given
them political power.*

north India; but most of the Marathas do not know to which gotra they belong. Similarly, north Indian village exogamy is not practiced by Marathas. Cross-cousin marriage is allowed; so is marriage with a deceased wife's sister. Two brothers may marry two sisters. Polygyny is allowed and practiced, but polyandry is unknown. Boys are generally married between the ages of 12 and 25, and girls traditionally before they attain puberty. As in much of southern India, bride-wealth is paid to the bride's family, and gift exchange after the marriage between the two families is more reciprocal than in the north. Gifts are also required to fetch a wife back after visiting her natal home. The third, fifth, and seventh months of pregnancy are celebrated. A girl goes for her first confinement to her parents' home. Widow remarriage and divorce are strictly prohibited.

The laws of inheritance that prevailed in Maharashtra were governed by *Mitakshara*, a medieval commentary on *Yajnyavalkya Smriti*. The property was held and transmitted by males to males. When no male heir existed, adoption of one was the usual rule: a daughter's son could be adopted. Property was owned jointly by all male family members in certain proportions. Widows and unmarried daughters had rights of maintenance.

Sociopolitical Organization

Marathas claim to be Kshatriyas descended from the four ancient royal *vanshas*, or branches. In support, they point out that many of their kula, or family names, are common clan names amongst the Rajputs, who are indubitably Kshatriyas. In the past royal Maratha houses have intermarried with the Rajputs. They also observe certain Kshatriya social practices like wearing the sacred thread and observing purdah. These claims are made only by the Marathas proper (i.e., the chiefs, landowners, and fighting clans). The Maratha cultivators, known as Kunbis, and other service castes, such as Malis (gardeners), Telis (oil pressers), and Sutars (carpenters) do not consider themselves Kshatriyas. Nevertheless, the fact that the Kunbis and Marathas belong to one social group is emphasized by common occurrence of Maratha-Kunbi marriages.

SOCIAL ORGANIZATION. Maratha social organization is based on totemic exogamous groups called kuls, each of which has a devak, an emblem, usually some common tree that is worshiped at the time of marriage. The devak may also be an animal, a bird, or an object such as an ax. The Maratha proper, who claim descent from the original four royal houses, belong to 96 named kulas,

although much disagreement exists about which kula belongs to which vansha. Further, quite a few kulas have the same name as the Kunbi kulas with whom the aristocratic Marathas deny all identity. Some of the Marathas also claim to have gotras, which is a north Indian Brahman social category; but strict gotra exogamy does not exist, and this fact might suggest that the gotras, like the vanshas, might have been adopted at some time in the past to bolster Maratha social status.

POLITICAL ORGANIZATION AND SOCIAL CONTROL. In the cities and small towns some Marathas have risen to very high positions in government service, which has given them political power. Positions of importance in the cooperative sugar mills, in the managing committees of schools, in the municipalities, and in the *panchayat samitis* are held by Marathas in most cases. As the Marathas are the majority agricultural community with smallholdings in this region, they still belong to the lower-income groups as a whole; but there has arisen among them a stratus of educated elite who are in higher administrative services and in industry and who hold political power. This power to a great extent has its basis in the votes of the small rural landholder.

Religion

Marathas worship the god Shiva and his consort Parvati in her many guises as Devi or the mother goddess. At the same time, unlike other Shiva devotees in India, they may also worship Vishnu as Vitthal, by observing fast days sacred to both. Shiva worship is particularized by the worship of some of his specific incarnations, especially Khandoba, Bhairav, Maruti, etc., as family gods. The Devi or mother goddess is worshiped in many of her varying forms, such as Gawdi, Bhavani, Lakshmi, or Janni Devi. Marathas also worship as personal gods other Brahmanic, local, and boundary deities. They visit places of Hindu pilgrimage, such as Pandharpur. Maharashtra also has a whole line of saints who are worshiped, such as Namdev, Tukaram, and Eknath, who have written magnificent *bhakti* (devotional) poetry. Marathas also pay respect to holy men who may have been of humble origin but whose personal spirituality attracts reverence. An outstanding example of such a person was Sai Baba of Shiridi. In addition to the deities just mentioned, the Marathas believe in spirit possession and the existence of ghosts (*bhutas*).

RELIGIOUS PRACTITIONERS. The village temple priest may be a Brahman or a man belonging to another caste, depending on the type of temple and the deity. Temples of Vishnu, Rama, Ganapati, and Maruti generally have Deshasth Brahman priests, whereas temples of Shankar (Mahadev) generally have a Lingayat or Gurav as a priest. Khandoba generally has a Maratha or Dhangar priest. Mari-ai or Lakshmi has a Mahar priest. Devi and Maruti also may sometimes have non-Brahman priests. At the village level, the priest at the main village temple is a recognized hereditary servant of the village. In the more important shrines, like the Vithoba temple at Pandharpur, there are different classes of priests serving a shrine, and these are all hereditary priests. The priesthood and the temple it serves are completely autonomous and not connected to any others.

CEREMONIES. The life-cycle ceremonies regularly celebrated by the Marathas are birth, "mother's fifth and sixth" day after delivery, first hair cutting, an elaborate twenty-four-step marriage ceremony, of which the installation of the devak is the most important rite, and death ceremonies that follow the same rites as a Brahman funeral.

Bibliography

Carter, Anthony (1974). *Elite Politics in Rural India: Political Stratification and Alliances in Western Maharashtra.* Cambridge: Cambridge University Press.

Enthoven, Reginald E. (1922). "Marathas." In *The Tribes and Castes of Bombay*, edited by R. E. Enthoven. Vol. 3, 3–42. Bombay: Government Central Press. Reprint. 1975. Delhi: Cosmo Publications.

Karve, Irawati (1968). *Maharashtra State Gazetteer, Government of Maharashtra: Maharashtra—Land and Its People.* Bombay: Directorate of Government Printing.

Russell, R. V., and Hira Lal (1916). "Maratha." In *The Tribes and Castes of the Central Provinces of India*, edited by R. V. Russell and Hira Lal. Vol. 4, 198–214. Nagpur: Government Printing Press. Reprint. 1969. Oosterhout: Anthropological Publications.

—W. D. MERCHANT

NAYAR

Ethnonym: Nair

Orientation

IDENTIFICATION. The Nayars are one of a number of caste groups living in Kerala State, India. Most of the description given in this article refers to Nayar society as it existed around 1900. Traditionally they were warriors, landowners (who supervised but rarely worked the land), and rulers. Toward the end of the eighteenth century they began to abandon their role as warriors and gradually lost their political power. They took to Western education early on and came to form a significant proportion of the professional and white-collar class by the middle of the twentieth century.

LOCATION. Traditionally Nayars belong to the southwest coast of India, in what is now the state of Kerala. It is a long, narrow area bounded on the west by the Arabian Sea and on the east by the high ranges of the Western Ghats. The area may be divided into (1) a narrow alluvial coastland extending only a few miles from the sea and mostly confined to the area south of Ponnani (the lower two-thirds of the coastline); (2) low lateritic plateaus and foothills between 75 and 200 meters above sea level, covered with grass and scrub; and (3) the highlands. The central region forms the main area of traditional village settlement as well as the main area for rice cultivation. It consists of a continually undulating countryside, with long, narrow, winding paddy fields surrounded by hills and slopes that were earlier covered by thick vegetation. The climate is monsoonal with heavy rains from both the southwest (oncoming) and northeast (retreating) monsoons. The average temperature is 27° C.

DEMOGRAPHY. The state of Kerala has the highest rural population density in India with 1,244 persons per square kilometer in Alleppey District, 1,182 in Trivandrum District, 1,052 in Ernakulam District, and over 800 in Trichur and Kozhikode districts (1981). Despite an exceptionally successful family planning program, these densities are expected to be even higher in the 1991 census because of the demographic pyramid. Sex ratios in Kerala approximate those in the "developed world," with 1,032 females to every 1,000 males (1981 census). Extrapolating from the census of 1911, which gave great detail about caste, it can be estimated that the Nayars make up approximately 15 percent of the present population of Kerala, or a number close to 3.8 million (as of 1981) or 4.3 million (based on approximate figures for 1990).

LINGUISTIC AFFILIATION. Nayars speak Malayalam, a language belonging to the Southern Branch of the Dravidian Family.

History and Cultural Relations

The early history of Kerala is very complicated and there are many problems remaining to be

The Nayars took to Western education early on and came to form a significant portion of the professional and white-collar class by the middle of the twentieth century.

♦ **toddy**
Palm wine, the fermented sap of the palmyra (Borassus flabellifer) and other palms, such as date, coconut, or sago.

resolved by historians. The region was united between approximately A.D. 216 and 825, when the Malayalam era is said to have begun. By the beginning of the ninth century A.D. the area was divided into a number of small kingdoms, each ruled by a Nayar or Kshatriya (higher matrilineal subcastes related to Nayars) royal family. Those families were relatively autonomous, owing little allegiance to any overlord. Between the thirteenth century and 1498 (when the Portuguese arrived in Kerala) two Nayar chiefdoms, Kolattiri in the north and Travancore in the south, expanded into small kingdoms. In the central part of the coast the Zamorin of Calicut was in the process of establishing ascendancy over many of the petty rulers and was slowly expanding his territory through an alliance with the local Muslims and Arab traders. Although the Portuguese and later the Dutch and the British built up the ruler of Cochin (another central Kerala coastal kingdom), the Zamorin's kingdom remained powerful until the invasions of the Mysoreans in the eighteenth century. After defeating the Mysoreans in 1792, the British amalgamated the seven northern kingdoms (including the reduced domain of the Zamorin) to form the Malabar District of the Madras Presidency. The kingdoms of Cochin and Travancore remained independent, though each had a British resident and many British businesses. When India became independent in 1947, Malabar District became part of Madras Province and Travancore-Cochin became a separate state; in 1956 the state of Kerala was formed, uniting the district of Malabar with the state of Travancore-Cochin.

Settlements

In Kerala prior to the British period, communication was extremely difficult. There were no roads, wheeled vehicles, or even pack animals. Travel and the transportation of goods depended on human porters and boats plying the numerous rivers and backwaters as well as the seacoast. Only local rulers and petty chieftains could ride on elephants or horses, and even then their use was primarily confined to processions. Since Indian independence and especially since the formation of Kerala State, roads have been built linking all parts of the state and all villages by bus. A railroad now links the southern city of Trivandrum to Mangalore in the South Kanara District of Karnataka (apart from links to Madras and the rest of India); there is one international airport (at Trivandrum) and two regional airports (at Cochin and Calicut). By the mid-1980s all of the villages were electrified.

The settlement pattern in Kerala has always been dispersed, with the house of each landowner standing on its own patch of higher ground. The actual physical features of the countryside do not encourage the formation of compact settlements, though today there is a tendency for some parts of settlements to hug the roads. It is impossible to tell where one village ends and another begins. The ideal Malayali house was set in its own compound with its food-producing trees, so that the dwelling space did not subtract from cultivation space. Formerly (prior to the twentieth century) the large Nayar house, set in its own compound with its walls for protection, was a veritable fortress. Nambudiri Brahman houses as well as middle-class Tiyyar houses followed the same pattern. Every home had a name and the individuals belonging to a given house were known by that name. The members of low and Untouchable castes attached to a Nayar house were known also by the name of that house. Today settlements are still dispersed, though because of population growth many of the spaces in between have been filled in.

Economy

SUBSISTENCE AND COMMERCIAL ACTIVITIES. Traditionally the Kerala economy was extremely complex. The main subsistence food was rice. It was supplemented by a wide variety of root vegetables and some leafy ones, eggs, fish, poultry, goat meat, and for most of the population (apart from Nayars and Nambudiri Brahmans) beef or water-buffalo meat. All of the Brahmans (about one percent of the population) and some of the higher-ranking Nayars (especially those that intermarried with Brahmans) were vegetarian. Today, the diet includes bread and many other wheat products as well as Western vegetables such as carrots and potatoes. It is hard to separate commercial activities from trade, but it is important to note that every village supports a large number of tea shops, toddy shops, general stores, and rice mills, as well as numerous other enterprises. Kerala has probably more small-size printing and publishing establishments than anywhere in the world.

INDUSTRIAL ARTS. Industrial arts unique to Kerala include a wide variety of products made from coconut fiber, the very advanced manufacture of traditional Ayurvedic medicines for worldwide distribution, the crafting of exceptionally fine gold jewelry in intricate traditional designs, bell metalwork, until recently very delicate ivory work, and the construction of traditional seagoing boats and ships. The newer products made in the region are discussed in the next section.

TRADE.   Apart from the fact that the society was extremely hierarchical with several layers of nonworking overlords, the region was not self-sufficient in rice production (the main subsistence grain) even in the fifteenth century. (Vasco da Gama reported seeing ships carrying rice in the port of Calicut in 1498.) However, the port of Calicut and many lesser ports were grand emporiums for export by sea in this period. Traders came from China, from the Middle East, and even from Rome. Because of the great demand in Europe for black pepper (at that time grown only in Kerala), one of the places Columbus was trying to reach when he sailed west was the port of Calicut. Apart from black pepper, many other items were traded there: other spices, copra, gems of many kinds, peacock feathers, rice (used medicinally in ancient Rome), teak and mahogany, elephants and ivory, and cloth of various kinds, including both cotton and silk. Today Kerala exports pepper, cashew nuts, frozen freshwater fish and seafood, woven textiles, and (to other parts of India as well as many third-world countries) paper and paper products, condoms and other rubber products, coir rope and other coir products, radios and watches, fruits, and fertilizers. However, Kerala's major export today consists of people, primarily educated people, both to the Middle East and to the developed world. There are large numbers of Nayars working as doctors, lawyers, nurses, scholars, and other professionals in the United States, Canada, and Great Britain.

DIVISION OF LABOR.   Since the Nayars are part of an extremely hierarchical society with complex caste and class distinctions, it is hard to describe the division of labor simply. Traditionally, Nayars formed the militia of the countryside, as well as functioning as landlords. In some villages they were the highest level of landowners, in other villages they held the land on lesser tenures. In the extreme north of Kerala and in some parts of Cochin-Travancore, poor Nayar households actually worked the land. But in the rest of Kerala, while Nayars (both males and females) might supervise production, they did not work in the fields. This arrangement has changed to some extent in very recent times. Where Nayars worked in agriculture, the division of labor between the sexes was the same as that followed by other Malayali groups within a given region (though there were and are regional differences between the north and the south).

LAND TENURE.   Traditional Kerala land tenure resembled the feudal system in Europe, with several levels of subfeudation and infeuda-tion. Land was owned either by an individual, an unpartitioned family, or a temple. The owners derived their income from rents or customary payments by their tenants and lesser tenants or subtenants. Often the Nayars were the tenants, the Tiyyars or Ezhuvas the subtenants, and the agrestic slave castes the manual laborers. However, there were some Nayar owners and some Nayar subtenants. A series of land-tenure laws was passed starting in the late 1920s in Travancore, culminating in major land-reform laws in the early 1970s and a series of supreme court decisions that provided not only for permanence of tenure but also for the gift of actual ownership rights to the lowest rung of tenants in the former hierarchy. As a result, one finds today a large class of small landowners, an even larger class of landless laborers, and a small number of larger landowners (some of whom were former tenants and held land from a number of higher-ranking landowners) who have found ways to circumvent the legal land ceilings.

Marriage and Family

MARRIAGE.   Marriage customs among the Nayars have evoked much discussion and controversy in India among both jurists and social scientists. There was considerable subregional variation as well as variation by subcaste and family prestige. Details presented here refer to south Malabar and the former Cochin State. There were two kinds of marriage: *talikettu kalyanam* (*tali* [necklet]-tying ceremony); and *sambandham* (the customary nuptials of a man and woman). The tali-tying ceremony had to be held before puberty and often the ceremony was held for several girls at the same time to save on expenses. Depending on the group the tali could be tied by a member of a linked lineage (often two Nayar lineages that frequently intermarried were linked to one another and called *enangar* lineages), by a member of a higher subcaste of Nayars, by one of the matrilineal Ambilavasi (temple servant) castes, or by a member of a royal lineage. By the mid-1950s, it became common for some girls to have the tali tied by their mothers. It is still controversial as to whether this ceremony was ever a formal marriage or if originally it was simply an age-grade ceremony, since it often included a large number of girls ranging in age from 6 months to 12 or 14 years. Women did observe formal mourning practices for the men who tied their talis, and in some instances—for example, if the girl was close to puberty—it was possible that the marriage might be consummated during this

KINSHIP

Kin Groups and Descent

The Nayars were traditionally matrilineal. The traditional Nayar *taravad* consisted of all the matrilineally related kin, male and female, descended from a common female ancestor, living in one large taravad house and compound. The property was held impartible, and the several members each were entitled to maintenance within the taravad house but could not claim a separate share. This has all changed since the 1930s, when partition became legally possible. A traditional taravad was composed of a woman, her children, her daughters' and her granddaughters' children, her brothers, descendants through her sisters, and her relations through her dead female ancestors. Within each taravad a significant subgroup consisted of the set of individuals headed by a living female ancestor called a *tavari*. When partitions became possible, they originally occurred on tavari lines.

Kinship Terminology

Kinship terminology follows the Dravidian pattern, with the exception that kin terms traditionally were not used for paternal kin. Today, usage is completely of the Dravidian pattern with a clear distinction between matrilateral and patrilateral kin. Mothers' sisters are called elder or younger mothers, and cross cousins are distinguished from parallel cousins, who are equated with one's own brothers and sisters.

ceremonial period. How often this occurred is unknown. By contrast, sambandan involved a man having a "visiting husband" relationship with a woman. While such relationships were considered to be marriages by the woman's family, especially when they occurred with males of higher subcastes or castes, the males tended to view the relationships as concubinage. Traditionally Nayar women were allowed to have more than one "visiting husband" either simultaneously or serially.

DOMESTIC UNIT. The size and composition of the domestic unit have varied over time. Before partition was permitted it could consist of as many as 50 to 100 people. However, once partition was allowed, the size of units decreased rapidly, so that by the late 1950s and 1960s the normal unit consisted of one or more married women with their children, their mother (if living), and possibly some adult male members of the matrilineage. Traditional Nayar family organization provided one of the relatively unique exceptions to the near universality of the nuclear family. The "visiting husband" had very little importance in his wife's family and had no responsibility for any children he might sire. His main responsibilities were for his sister's children. The practice of polyandry also placed a limitation on relationships between men and their own biological children. Today households are even smaller, consisting often of only the nuclear unit, though a matrilineal relative of the woman might often reside with a married couple.

INHERITANCE. Traditional inheritance was in the matriline only. Any property a man possessed went to his sisters and their children. As men took to modern, Western professions and started accumulating personal wealth as opposed to family property, they began passing it on to their own biological children. As a result, there are today slightly different laws regulating inherited and acquired wealth. However, even today it is customary for a man to put his self-acquired property in his wife's name so that it can then be inherited matrilineally. Furthermore, a man feels greater responsibility for his sister's children than for his brother's children. Even men living away from Kerala in Delhi or New York are more likely to sponsor a sister's son or daughter than a brother's.

SOCIALIZATION. Traditional socialization patterns involved a strong emphasis on the use of shaming as a technique of control. Traditionally, in all but the poorest taravads, children (female as well as male) were expected to learn to read and write Sanskrit written in the Malayalam alphabet, and as soon as English education came to the region, boys started learning English. Girls only started learning English later. Socialization training strongly emphasized what people knew (i.e., keeping up appearances) rather than superego (i.e., internalized conscience and values).

Sociopolitical Organization

SOCIAL ORGANIZATION. Society in traditional Kerala was highly hierarchical, with a fairly close (though not one-to-one) correlation between caste and class. Most of the landless, land-attached laborers were from the Untouchable castes and tribal groups. The semi-Untouchable Tiyyars or Ezhuvas tended to be tenants, and the Nayars (as noted above) generally held land on various levels of infeudation and subfeudation. Socially, each middle- or upper-class Nayar taravad was a core for social as well as political organization. Today this has all changed, as taravads have split into smaller and smaller units, as population increase has blurred village boundaries even more, and as there are now areas where the normal Indian rural/urban distinction does not apply. Social ties today tend to be closest among members of the same caste and socioeconomic position, though among the educated elite caste distinctions are less prevalent. The Nayars were divided into a number of subcastes all hierarchically placed, though the subdivisions varied from one place to another. In central Kerala, the highest-ranking ones were often referred to as Samantans. Some Samantans were powerful rulers. (The Zamorin of Calicut was a Samantan from the Eradi subcaste.) The Samantan women marry either other Samantans or Nambudiri Brahmans. The Nayars themselves included: Stani Nayars (local chieftains), high-caste Nayars who traditionally served in the military or in some other important capacity for Nambudiri Brahmans, Kshatriyas, or Samantans; the middle-ranking Nayars who did not intermarry or interdine with those higher than themselves, and who performed various tasks for the temple; and the small group of low-caste Nayars who served other Nayars as washermen, barbers, and oilmongers. The majority of Nayars belongs to the high-caste groups.

POLITICAL ORGANIZATION. The traditional political organization was feudal in nature with many small states. Rulers had only limited control. After the British occupation of Malabar and the posting of British resident officers in Cochin and Travancore, the state came to have greater influence. Since Independence, large units of approximately 10,000 to 12,000 people have been governed by an elected *panchayat* (village council). There is a large bureaucratic structure and an elected legislative assembly in the state. Politics and political parties, especially those of the left, have penetrated into every nook and cranny of the state.

SOCIAL CONTROL. Social control is effected through the family, through a general concern about what people will think or what people will say and a strong emphasis on bourgeois values.

CONFLICT. Traditionally, conflicts were handled by the caste elders. In the Middle Ages, many of the Nayar men were warriors, fighting against neighboring principalities. Today, local conflicts are handled by the village panchayats, and large-scale ones by the police and the courts.

Religion and Expressive Culture

RELIGIOUS BELIEFS. The Nayars themselves are Hindus. However, in Kerala there are also many Christians (of various denominations) and Muslims.

RELIGIOUS PRACTITIONERS. Nayars frequently attend Hindu temples. The main *pujaris* (temple priests) are Tamil Brahmans or Brahmans from South Kanara, though in a few temples there are also Nambudiri or Kerala Brahmans. Kerala has been innovative in providing training and certification for well-trained lower-caste pujaris.

CEREMONIES. The most important ceremonies celebrated in Kerala among Hindus are Vishu, Onam, and Thiruvathira. Traditionally, these were the three ceremonial occasions when a "visiting husband" was expected to bring new clothes to his wife. Vishu occurs at the same time as the Tamil New Year in mid-April. It is a time for wearing new clothes and also is considered the beginning of the summer. The first things a person sees that morning upon arising are said to influence his or her life throughout the year. Onam (in August-September) is the harvest festival associated with the first paddy harvest. It is also the Malayali New Year. For Nayars it is extremely important not only as a time for getting new clothes but also because of the many rituals associated with it. Thiruvathira is in December, and it is said to be especially important for Nayar females, who have to take a bath in the family tank in the early morning before sunrise, sing a number of special songs, and perform a dance said to be especially beneficial as exercise for women.

ARTS. Nayar culture is closely associated with the Kathakali dance dramas that developed in the 16th century. They involve elaborate headdresses and makeup. It takes many years to master the intricate dance techniques (traditionally performed by males only, though today some females are involved in them). Other arts associated with Nayars include the famous Kalari *pattu* (Kalari or armed gymnasium play) and female Kaikuttikali (a kind of dance). All art forms traditionally were related to caste. Nayars were often patrons of art forms that they themselves did not practice.

MEDICINE. The traditional medicine in Kerala is Ayurveda. It has been highly developed there, especially by the Variars, an Ambilavasi (temple servant) caste group that is also matrilineal and

The traditional Nayar taravad consisted of all the kin, male and female, descended from a common female ancestor, living in one large house and compound.

As early as 1817 the agriculturist militia of Orissa revolted against the British in one of the first regional anticolonial movements.

shares many traits with Nayars. Today they run Ayurvedic medicine factories, nursing homes, and dispensaries. In addition, Kerala has a well-developed scientific medical system. Kerala doctors (including many Nayar doctors) and nurses may be found all over the world. There is no clash between Ayurvedic and modern or allopathic medicine, as they tend to be used to treat different diseases.

DEATH AND AFTERLIFE. As among all Hindus there is a strong belief in reincarnation. The dead are usually cremated.

Bibliography

Fuller, Christopher J. (1976). *The Nayars Today.* New York: Cambridge University Press.

Gough, E. Kathleen (1959). "The Nayars and the Definition of Marriage." *Journal of American Folklore* 71:23–34.

Gough, E. Kathleen, and David M. Schneider (1961). *Matrilineal Kinship.* Berkeley: University of California Press.

Logan, William (1887). *Manual of Malabar.* 2 vols. Madras: Government Press. Reprint. 1961. *Malabar.* 3 vols.

Mencher, Joan P. (1965). "The Nayars of South Malabar." In *Comparative Family Systems,* edited by M. F. Nimkoff, 163–191. Boston: Houghton Mifflin.

Mencher, Joan P. (1966). "Kerala and Madras: A Comparative Study of Ecology and Social Structure." *Ethnology* 5:135–171.

Mencher, Joan P. (1978). "Agrarian Relations in Two Rice Regions of Kerala." *Economic and Political Weekly* 13:349–366.

—JOAN P. MENCHER

ORIYA

Ethnonyms: Odia, Odiya; adjective: Odissi, Orissi (Orissan in English)

Orientation

IDENTIFICATION. In Orissa State in India, the Oriya constitute the regional ethnic group, speaking the Oriya language and professing the Hindu religion, to be distinguished from an Oriya-speaking agricultural caste called Odia found in central coastal Orissa. Some Oriya live in the adjoining states. The Oriya language and ethnic group are presumably derived from the great Udra or Odra people known since Buddhist and pre-Buddhist *Mahabharata* epic times.

LOCATION. The state of Orissa is located between 17°49' and 22°34' N and 81°29' and 87°29' E, covering 155,707 square kilometers along the northeastern seaboard of India. The large majority of the Oriya live in the coastal districts and along the Mahanadi and Brahmani rivers. Orissa falls in the tropical zone with monsoon rains from June–July to September–October. Western Orissa is afflicted with recurring drought.

DEMOGRAPHY. The last national census in 1981 records the population of Orissa as 26,370,271 persons, with a population density of 169 persons per square kilometer as compared to 216 for India as a whole. Of the total population of Orissa, 84.11 percent speak Oriya. Although rural, Orissa's urban centers with 5,000 or more persons rose from containing 8.4 percent of the population in 1971 (81 towns) to 11.79 percent in 1981 (108 towns). Most of the ninety-three Scheduled Castes, which constitute 15.1 percent of Orissa's population, speak Oriya. Of the 23.1 percent of Orissa's population categorized as Scheduled Tribes, many speak Oriya as their mother tongue. With 34.23 percent literacy in 1981 compared to 26.18 percent in 1971, Orissa trails behind many Indian states, especially in female literacy.

LINGUISTIC AFFILIATION. Oriya belongs to the Indo-Aryan Branch of the Indo-European Family of languages. Its closest affinities are with Bengali (Bangla), Assamese (Asamiya), Maithili, Bhojpuri, and Magahi (Magadhi). The Oriya spoken in Cuttack and Puri districts is taken as standard Oriya. The Oriya language has a distinctive script, traceable to sixth-century inscriptions. It has thirteen vowels and thirty-six consonants (linguistically, spoken Oriya has six vowels, two semivowels, and twenty-nine consonants).

History and Cultural Relations

Orissa has been inhabited since prehistoric times, and Paleolithic, Mesolithic, Neolithic, and Chalcolithic cultural remains abound. By the fourth century B.C. there was a centralized state in Orissa, though the hill areas often nurtured independent princedoms mostly evolving out of tribal polities. In 261 B.C., Orissa, then known as Kalinga, was conquered by the Emperor Ashoka after a bloody Kalinga war, leading to the conversion of the king into a nonviolent Buddhist who spread Buddhism in Asia. In the early second century B.C. Emperor Kharavela, a Jain by religion and a great conqueror, had the famous queen's cave-palace, Ranigumpha, cut into the mountain near Bhubaneswar, with exquisite sculptures depicting dancers and musicians. Both eastern and western Orissa had famous Buddhist monasteries, universities, and creative savants. Starting in the first century A.D., according to Pliny and others, there was extensive maritime trade and cultural relations between Orissa (Kalinga, Kling) and Southeast Asian countries from Myanmar (Burma) to Indonesia. Orissa was ruled under several Hindu dynasties until 1568, when it was annexed by the Muslim kingdom of Bengal. In 1590, Orissa came under the Mogul empire, until the Marathas seized it in 1742. In 1803 it came under British rule. As early as 1817 the agriculturist militia (Paik) of Orissa revolted against the British in one of the first regional anticolonial movements. In 1936 Orissa was declared a province of British India, and the princely states with an Oriya population were merged into Orissa in 1948–1949. The cultures and languages of south India, western India, and northern India— and also those of the tribal peoples—have enriched the cultural mosaic and the vocabulary of the Oriya.

Settlements

In 1981, 88.21 percent of the people of Orissa lived in villages. In 1971, 51,417 villages of Orissa ranged in population from less than 500 persons (71.9 percent), 500–900 persons (18.8 percent), 1,000–1,999 persons (7.5 percent), to more than 2,000 persons (1.78 percent). The Oriya villages fall into two major types: linear and clustered. The linear settlement pattern is found mostly in Puri and Ganjam districts, with houses almost in a continuous chain on both sides of the intervening village path and with kitchen gardens at the back of the houses. Cultivated fields surround the settlement. In the cluster pattern each house has a compound with fruit trees and a kitchen garden. The Scheduled Castes live in linear or cluster hamlets slightly away from the main settlement, with their own water tanks or, today, their own wells. In the flooded coastal areas one finds some dispersed houses, each surrounded by fields for cultivation. In traditional Orissa, two styles of houses (*ghara*) were common. The agriculturists and higher castes had houses of a rectangular ground plan with rooms along all the sides (*khanja-ghara*), leaving an open space (*agana*) in the center. Mud walls with a gabled roof of thatch made of paddy stalks or jungle grass (more durable) were common. The more affluent had double-ceiling houses (*atu ghara*) with the inner ceiling of mud plaster supported by wooden or bamboo planks. This construction made it fireproof and insulated against the summer heat and winter chill. The entrance room was usually a cowshed, as cattle were the wealth of the people.

Men met villagers and guests on the wide front veranda. Poorer people had houses with mud walls and straw-thatched gable roofs, without enclosed courtyards or double ceilings. The smoke from the kitchen escaped under the gabled roof. The Oriya had, in common with eastern India, a wooden husking lever (*dhenki*) in the courtyard for dehusking paddy rice or making rice flour. Nowadays houses with large windows and doors, roofs of concrete (tiled or with corrugated iron or asbestos sheets), walls of brick and mortar, and cement floors are becoming common even in remote villages. In the traditional house, the northeastern corner of the kitchen formed the sacred site of the ancestral spirits (*ishana*) for family worship.

Economy

SUBSISTENCE AND COMMERCIAL ACTIVITIES. Subsistence cultivation of paddy is ubiquitous as rice is the staple food. Double-cropping, sometimes even triple-cropping in irrigated fields, and single-cropping in drought-affected or rainfed areas are all common. Large-scale farming with heavy agricultural machinery is still uncommon. Plowing with two bullocks or two buffalo is usual, with a wooden plow. Only recently have iron plows been coming into use. Cash crops like sugarcane, jute, betel leaves on raised mounds, coconuts and areca nuts (betel nuts) are grown in coastal Orissa, and pulses and oil seeds in droughtprone areas. Recently coffee, cocoa, cardamom, pineapples, and bananas have also been raised on a commercial scale. Fish are caught in traps and nets from village tanks, streams, rivers, coastal swamps, and also in the flooded paddy fields. Fishing boats with outboard motors and trawlers are nowadays used at sea. The domestic animals include cows, goats, cats, chickens, ducks, and water buffalo among the lowest castes, as well as pigs and dogs among the urban middle class.

INDUSTRIAL ARTS. Most large villages had castes of artisans who served the agricultural economy in former times. Carpenters, wheelwrights, and blacksmiths were absolutely necessary. Some villages had potters with pottery wheels and weavers with cottage looms (cotton was formerly grown and yarn spun). Today, industrial products are displacing the village products except for the wooden plow and cart wheels. Some cottage industries, especially the handloomed textiles (including the weaving of *ikat*, cotton textiles that are tied and dyed), are producing for export. Brass and bell-metal utensils and statues and silver and gold filigree ornaments have a wide clientele.

Traditional Oriya society is hierarchically organized primarily on the basis of caste (and subcaste) and occupations and secondarily on the basis of social class.

TRADE. In villages, peddling and weekly markets were the usual commercial channels. Since World War II ration shops have sold scarce essential commodities.

DIVISION OF LABOR. Men plow, sow, and carry goods with a pole balanced on the shoulder, whereas women carry things on their head, weed, and transplant the fields. Harvesting is done by both sexes. While men fish and hunt, women perform household chores and tend babies. Traditionally, among higher-caste and higher-class families, women did not work outside home. Nowadays men and some women are engaged in salaried service, but only lower-caste and lower-class women undertake wage labor.

LAND TENURE. Before Independence land under agriculture had increased substantially. However, because of the high rate of population growth and subdivision of landholdings, the number of marginal farmers and the landless increased sharply thereafter. Following Independence some land above the statutory ceiling or from the common property resources was distributed among the landless, weaker sections of society. Large-scale industrial and irrigation-cum-power projects displaced people and added to the ranks of the landless. All of this has resulted in various categories of tenancy and contractual lease of land for subsistence cultivation.

Kinship

KIN GROUPS AND DESCENT. Traditionally and currently, three patterns of family organization have obtained: (1) the multihousehold compounds where the separate families of the sons of the common father are housed as an extended family; (2) joint families with all the brothers living together, with a common kitchen, with or without the parents living (more common in villages than towns); (3) several families belonging to a patrilineage among whom kin obligations continue, residing in neighboring villages. Descent is patrilineal.

KINSHIP TERMINOLOGY. The social emphasis on seniority in age and differentiation by sex and generation are observed. Kinship terminology follows the Hawaiian system. Fictive or ritual kin terms are used widely and are expressed in respect and affection and also in meeting appropriate kin obligations.

Marriage and Family

MARRIAGE. Although polygyny was practiced earlier, most marriages today are monogamous. Most marriages even now are also arranged by parents, though some are based on the mutual choice of the marriage partners. Only in western Orissa and southern Orissa is cousin marriage practiced. Marriage partners must not belong to the same *gotra* (mythical patrilineal descent group). Bride-price among the lower and middle castes has been replaced by a more costly dowry for the bridegroom among all classes and castes. After marriage, residence is patrilocal, with the bride assuming the gotra of the husband. Nowadays residence tends to be neolocal near the place of work. The Hindu marriage was ideally for this life and beyond, but since 1956 divorce has been permitted under legal procedures.

DOMESTIC UNIT. Living in a family is considered normal and proper. Most families today in both villages and towns are nuclear, though some are joint families. Members working and living outside usually visit the residual family and shrines occasionally. Often land is cultivated jointly by sharing the farm expenses. Recently there has been a tendency to reduce the size of the rural household through family planning.

INHERITANCE. Traditionally only sons inherited land and other immovable properties. The eldest son was given an additional share (*jyesthansha*). Since 1956 the widow and daughters have been legal cosharers in all property.

SOCIALIZATION. Parents, grandparents, and siblings care for infants and children and provide informal—and, recently, formal—education before school. Education of girls is still not common beyond primary school. Physical punishment to discipline a child is common, though infants are usually spared and cuddled. Respect for seniors in all situations and the value of education are emphasized, especially among the higher classes.

Sociopolitical Organization

Orissa is a state in the Republic of India, which has an elected president. The governor is the head of Orissa State, and the chief minister is the elected head of the government of Orissa.

SOCIAL ORGANIZATION. Traditional Oriya society is hierarchically organized primarily on the basis of caste (and subcaste) and occupations and secondarily on the basis of social class. The highest castes, Brahman, are priests and teachers of the Great Tradition. Below them in descending order of status are: the Kshatriya, warriors and rulers; the Vaisya, or traders; and the Sudra, or skilled and unskilled workers and service holders. The occupations involving manual and menial work are low in status, and polluting occupations like skinning dead animals or making shoes are associated with the lowest castes, the Untouchables. Ascriptive status in the caste system is sometimes checked now by acquired status in the class system. In rural Orissa patron-client relationships are common and social mobility is difficult.

POLITICAL ORGANIZATION. Orissa is divided into thirteen districts (*zilla*), and each district is divided into subdivisions (*tahsils*) for administrative purposes, into police stations (*thana*) for law-and-order purposes, and into community development blocs (*blok*) for development purposes. There are village-cluster committees (*panchayat*) with elected members and a head (*sarpanch*) for the lowest level of self-administration and development. The community development bloc has a *panchayat samiti* or council of panchayats headed by the chairman, with all the sarpanch as members. Each caste or populous subcaste in a group of adjacent villages also had a *jati panchayat* for enforcing values and institutional discipline. The traditional *gram panchayat*, consisting of the leaders of several important castes in a village, was for maintaining harmony and the ritual cycle.

SOCIAL CONTROL. Warfare between adjacent princedoms and villages came to a stop under British rule. The police stations (thana) maintain law and order in the rural areas.

Religion and Expressive Culture

Hinduism of various sects is a central and unifying force in Oriya society. The overwhelmingly important Vaishnava sect have their supreme deity, Jagannatha, who lords it over the religious firmament of Orissa. Lord Jagannatha's main temple is at Puri on the sea, where the famous annual festival with huge wooden chariots dragged for the regional divine triad—*Jagannatha, Balabhadra*, and *Subhadra* (goddess sister)—draws about half a million devotees. The famous Lingaraja temple of Lord Shiva at Bhubaneswar, the famous Viraja goddess temple at Jaipur, both in coastal Orissa, and Mahimagadi, the cult temple of the century-old Mahima sect of worshipers of Shunya Parama Brahma (the absolute soul void) at Joranda in central Orissa, are highly sacred for the Oriya people.

RELIGIOUS BELIEFS. The people of Orissa profess Hinduism overwhelmingly (96.4 percent), with Christianity (1.73 percent), Islam (1.49 percent), Sikhism (0.04 percent) and Buddhism (0.04 percent) trailing far behind. Obviously many tribal groups have declared Hinduism as their religion. Apart from supreme beings, gods, and goddesses of classical Hindu religion, the Oriya propitiate a number of disease spirits, village deities, and revered ancestral spirits.

RELIGIOUS PRACTITIONERS. In the villages each Brahman priest has a number of client families of Kshatriya, Vaisya, and some Sudra castes. There are also magicians (*gunia*) practicing witchcraft and sorcery. *Kalisi* or shamans are consulted to discover the causes of crises and the remedies.

CEREMONIES. A large number of rituals and festivals mostly following the lunar calendar are observed. The most important rituals are: the New Year festival (Bishuba Sankranti) in mid-April; the fertility of earth festival (Raja Parab); festival of plowing cattle (Gahma Punein); the ritual of eating the new rice (Nabanna); the festival worshiping the goddess of victory, known otherwise as Dassara (Durga Puja); the festival of the unmarried girls (Kumar Purnima); the solar-calendar harvest festival (Makar Sankranti); the fast for Lord Shiva (Shiva Ratri); the festival of colors and the agricultural New Year (Dola Purnima or Dola Jatra); and, finally, the festival worshiping Lord Krishna at the end of February. In November–December (lunar month of Margashira) every Thursday the Gurubara Osha ritual

FESTIVITIES

Oriya dancer dressed in an elaborate costume. Numerous rituals and festivities are observed following the lunar calendar. Orissa, India. (Jack Fields/Corbis)

for the rice goddess Lakshmi is held in every Oriya home.

ARTS. The ancient name of Orissa, Utkala, literally means "the highest excellence in the arts." The Oriya are famous for folk paintings, painting on canvas (*patta-chitra*), statuary and sculptures, the Orissan style of temple architecture, and tourist and pilgrim mementos made of horn, papier-mâché, and appliqué work. Classical Odissi dance, the virile Chhow dance, colorful folk dances with indigenous musical instruments (percussion, string, and wind) and also Western instruments, dance dramas, shadow plays (Ravana-Chhaya) with puppets, folk opera (*jatra*), mimetic dances, and musical recitation of God's names are all very popular. Orissi music, largely following classical (*raga*) tunes, and folk music, are rich and varied.

MEDICINE. Illness is attributed to "hot" or "cold" food, evil spirits, disease spirits, and witches; and mental diseases to sorcery or spirit possession. Leprosy and gangrenous wounds are thought to be punishment for the commission of "great" sins, and, for general physical and mental conditions, planets and stars in the zodiac are held to be responsible. Cures are sought through herbal folk medicines, propitiation of supernatural beings and spirits, exorcism, counteraction by a gunia (sorcery and witchcraft specialist), and the services of homeopathic, allopathic, or Ayurvedic specialists.

DEATH AND AFTERLIFE. Death is considered a transitional state in a cycle of rebirths till the soul (*atma*) merges in the absolute soul (*paramatma*). The god of justice, Yama, assigns the soul either to Heaven (*swarga*) or to Hell (*narka*). The funeral rites and consequent pollution attached to the family and lineage of the deceased last for ten days among higher castes. The dead normally are cremated.

Bibliography

Das, Binod Sankar (1984). *Life and Culture in Orissa*. Calcutta: Minerva Associates.

Das, K. B., and L. K. Mahapatra (1979). *Folklore of Orissa*. New Delhi: National Book Trust India. 2nd ed. 1990.

Das, M. N., ed. (1977). *Sidelights on History and Culture of Orissa*. Cuttack: Vidyapuri.

Eschmann, A., H. Kulke, and G. C. Tripathi (1978). *The Cult of Jagannath and the Regional Tradition of Orissa*. New Delhi: Manohar Publications.

Fisher, E., S. Mahapatra, and D. Pathy (1980). *Orissa Kunst und Kultur in Nordost Indien*. Zurich: Museum Rietberg.

Ganguly, Mano Mohan (1912). *Brissa and Her Remains—Ancient and Mediaeval (District Puri)*. Calcutta: Thacker, Spink & Co.; London: W. Thacker & Co.

Mahapatra, L. K. (1987). "Mayurbhanj, Keonjhar, and Bonai Ex-Princely States of Orissa." In *Tribal Polities and Pre-Colonial State Systems in Eastern and Northeastern India*, edited by Surajit Sinha. Calcutta: K. P. Bagchi.

Marglin, Frédérique Apffel (1985). *Wives of the God-King: The Rituals of the Devadasis of Puri*. New Delhi: Oxford University Press.

Orissa, Government of. Revenue Department (1990). "History" and "People." In *Orissa State Gazetteer*. Vol. 1. Cuttack: Orissa Government Press.

—L. K. MAHAPATRA

PAHARI

Ethnonyms: none

Orientation

IDENTIFICATION. "Pahari" can refer to any mountain-dwelling people, but in north India it generally designates the Indo-European-speaking peoples of the Himalayas who, however, generally prefer regional ethnic designations. In India these include, among many others (from west to east): Churachi, Gaddi, Kinnaura, Sirmuri (all in Himachal Pradesh); Jaunsari, Garhwali, Kumauni (all in Uttar Pradesh); etc. Crosscutting these are terms distinguishing religions (e.g., Hindu, Muslim), caste categories (e.g., for low castes: Dom, Kilta, Shilpkar; for high castes: Khas, Khasiya), and specific castes (e.g., for low castes: Bajgi, Lohar, Mochi, etc.; for high castes: Brahman, Baman, Rajput, Chhetri, Thakur). There are also terms associated with specific noncaste ethnic groups and livelihoods, such as Gujjar (transhumant cattle herders, some groups of which are Hindu, others Muslim). In Nepal distinctions among Paharis are more often reported to refer to caste than to region: that is, the high-caste category, Khas, and the low-caste category, Dom or Damai, with their specific caste names. These caste names distinguish them from Tibeto-Burman-speaking neighbors whom they identify by ethnic terms (e.g., Magars, Gurungs). The term, "Pahari" comes from the Hindi word *pahar*, meaning "mountain," and so literally it means "of the mountains."

LOCATION. The Pahari occupy the outer, lower ranges of the Himalayas—generally between about 600 and 2,100 meters above sea level—adjacent to the Indo-Gangetic Plain, in a

1,600-kilometer crescent not more than 80 kilometers wide, stretching from Kashmir in the northwest to central Nepal in the southeast. These geologically young mountains are the result of the Indian tectonic plate pushing under the Asian one. This upthrust results in frequent landslides and rapid erosion, creating precipitous topography with sharp peaks and *V*-shaped ravines rather than alluvial valleys or lakes. The massive scarp, which even the lower Himalayas present to the flat Indo-Gangetic Plain, forces the northward-moving summer monsoon clouds abruptly upward, generating heavy precipitation each year and ensuring a rich postmonsoon harvest. Winters tend to be cold with moderate to slight snowfalls at the upper limits of Pahari habitation (at 1,800 to 2,400 meters) and comparable rainfall at lower elevations.

DEMOGRAPHY. Reliable population figures on Pahari speakers are not available, but my estimate is in the neighborhood of 17 million: 6 million in Himachal Pradesh and Kashmir, 6 million in Uttar Pradesh, and 5 million in Nepal. Their population density is not great, perhaps 58 persons per square kilometer, but the annual growth must be around 2.5 percent.

LINGUISTIC AFFILIATION. The people of the outer Himalayas are culturally and linguistically distinct from their plains-dwelling Hindi-, Punjabi-, and Urdu-speaking Hindu, Sikh, and Muslim neighbors to the south and from the higher-elevation-dwelling Tibetan-speaking Buddhist Bhotias to the north. G. A. Grierson, in his classic *Linguistic Survey of India*, labeled their Indo-European language "Pahari" and identified its main sections: Western Pahari, found west of the Jumna River (i.e, now Himachal Pradesh) and into Kashmir; Central Pahari, between the Jumna and the Maha Kali rivers (i.e., in Garhwal and Kumaon, now comprising the Himalayan districts of Uttar Pradesh State; and Eastern Pahari (generally called Nepali), extending from Nepal's western border (the Maha Kali) into central Nepal. Less sharply drawn than the northern and southern linguistic boundaries are those to the east, where Pahari gives way to Tibeto-Burman, and to the west, where it meets Dardic languages, mainly Kashmiri. Also, along the southern border of the eastern half of the Pahari domain, in the *terai* (the narrow band where the Himalayas meet the plains), live the tribal Tharu with their distinctive language.

Settlements

Throughout most of the Pahari region the population is clustered in small villages, usually of well under 350 people. These are situated adjacent to open hillsides, near pasturage, forested land, and a reliable water source—either a stream or a spring. The hillsides are terraced for agriculture, the terraces irrigated where possible from upstream

The Pahari people probably derive from mountain movements out of the plains into the mountains, as refugees from political oppression, natural disasters, and other events.

HISTORY AND CULTURAL RELATIONS

The Pahari people probably derive from population movements out of the plains into the mountains. It is widely believed that they have come during the past 3,000 years as refugees from population pressure, plagues, famines, droughts, political oppression, military and civil conflict, and the like. Muslim invasions, from about A.D. 1000 to 1600, may have accelerated such movements, which need not have been characteristically massive but likely included many small-scale, even familial, migrations. Residents of Sirkanda, the Garhwali village in which I have worked for many years, say that their ancestors began coming some 300 years ago in extended family groups from still-known mountain villages in the Pahari heartland to the northeast in search of new land and pastures. Whatever the sources, it is clear that over time the Pahari population has been geographically mobile and numerically variable. The very name of "Garhwal" suggests this, for it means "land of fortresses"—referring to the ruins that are to be found throughout the region (including two in Sirkanda) and that are as much a puzzle as the people who built them. The Eastern and Central Pahari languages form a dialectal continuum, but there is a relatively sharp break in mutual intelligibility between Central and Western Pahari. Other cultural differences between the Eastern/Central and Western speech communities, together with some demographic evidence, also suggest that long ago there was a frontier, located somewhere between the Jumna and Ganges watersheds. As recently as the first decade of the nineteenth century, the small princely principalities that comprised the Pahari region east of present-day Simla in Himachal Pradesh were conquered by the Nepalese. A decade later the British drove them back, decreed the Maha Kali River to be the western border of Nepal, and laid the foundation for the present administrative subdivisions of the Indian Himalayas.

sources through systems of canals and flumes that also serve to power water mills. Houses are rectangular, of two or occasionally more stories, made of 46-centimeter-thick stone and adobe mortar walls and reinforced by wooden beams (in some regions the upper stories are made largely or entirely of wood), with gabled (but in some areas flat) roofs of slate, heavy wooden shakes, or thatch. They are no more than two rooms deep, but vary greatly—up to six rooms—in length. In many regions, as in Sirkanda, they characteristically have a large open central living room (*tibari*) or veranda near the middle, on the front (downhill) side, supported by ornamentally carved columns. Doors, door frames, and windows—and often rafters and beams as well—are also likely to be ornately carved and sometimes painted. Next to the living room is a kitchen; other rooms serve as bedrooms and storage rooms. Occupants, comprising an extended family, live on the second floor in anywhere from two to six rooms reached by one or more external stone stairways; livestock live on the ground floor. Within a village houses tend to be arranged along the contour of the land in parallel rows of several houses each.

Many landowning families own additional houses (*chaan*) situated near fields or pastures at a distance from the village sufficient to make tending them difficult from there. Chaans are usually of a single story shared by livestock and people, separated by a wooden curb or sometimes a partition. They may be occupied seasonally or year-round depending upon circumstances: often a family will have a higher-elevation chaan for use in summer and a lower-elevation chaan for use in winter. The hills are alive with movement when the seasons change and people, goods, and animals are moved from one location (chaan, village house) to another. Chaans provide a way to separate family members without dividing the family. Clusters of chaans may evolve into villages as population increases—the names of many villages reveal their former chaan status.

Economy

SUBSISTENCE AND COMMERCIAL ACTIVITIES. Pahari economy is based on subsistence agriculture, engaged in by landowning high castes (Brahmans and Kshatriyas). Extended joint families cultivate terraced fields that produce two crops per year. The winter crop, primarily wheat and barley, is planted in October–November and harvested in March–April; the rainy-season crop, primarily millets but also including substantial amounts of amaranth, maize,

dry and wet rice (where irrigation permits), and a variety of lentils and vegetables, is planted in April–May and harvested in September–October. Fields are kept productive by intensive fertilizing with animal manure and systematic fallowing. Milk and milk products, along with potatoes, ginger, and some vegetables, are produced for sale as well as for consumption where markets are accessible. Apricots are a cash crop in some areas, and near Kotgarh, north of Simla, apples have also become so. Opium is another, notably in Himachal Pradesh.

Buffalo and cattle are kept both for the milk they produce and for the manure. In Sirkanda, agricultural households averaged three to four buffalo and sixteen to eighteen cattle. In villages more remote from markets, fewer of these livestock are kept. Buffalo produce more and richer milk than cows, but they are harder to maintain because they eat more, must be kept well watered and cool, and unlike cattle must be stall-fed and watered because they are regarded as too clumsy to fend for themselves. Most highly prized of all livestock are the small but sturdy Pahari bullocks used as draft animals: there are usually one to three pairs per household (depending upon the size of landholdings). Goats and in some areas sheep are kept largely for sale but also for domestic sacrifice (and subsequent consumption). About half of Sirkanda households keep an average of fifteen of these animals per household. Horses or mules, one or rarely two, are kept by about a third of the landed families in Sirkanda, for transport of products to and from markets.

INDUSTRIAL ARTS. What might be called "industrial arts" are engaged in only for domestic use, not sale or export. Low castes of artisans are to be found in most regions if not in most villages: smiths (blacksmiths, silversmiths, goldsmiths), carpenters, lathe turners, masons, weavers, tailors, rope makers, shoemakers. Traditionally they did their work not by the piece and not for cash but in the well-known South Asian *jajmani* relationship, as clients to a landed patron who compensated them for their service and loyalty with agricultural produce. Where no specialist caste is available to supply a required product or service, another low caste will generally be pressed into service or the high-caste community members will take the job. As transportation has enhanced contact with markets, piecework and cash purchases have impinged on this system, to the advantage of the consumers and the disadvantage of the providers (who are rendered superfluous by the availability of commercial products).

TRADE. See preceding subheadings under "Economy."

DIVISION OF LABOR. The fundamental divisions of Pahari labor are by sex and caste. The high castes are landowning farmers who do all of the work required to grow and process crops and to husband domestic animals. The low castes are their hereditary landless servants. The latter are defined as artisans, as is suggested by their derogatory-descriptive appellation, *shilpkar* (literally, "handworker"). They include, in addition to the artisan specialties described above, service specialties such as musician, entertainer, and barber. Service castes are required as well to perform any domestic service their patrons may demand of them. Among themselves, they exchange their special products and services. The one high-caste specialty is that of the Brahman priest. Most people of this caste are farmers like their Kshatriya village mates, but some men—often only one in an extended family or in a village—specialize in priestly activities. These men tend to rituals—annual or periodic rites, life-cycle rites, horoscopes, temple worship, etc.—for their fellow high castes in the same jajmani relationship to those they service as is found among the artisan castes—except that here the Brahman server may be more accurately regarded as the patron and the person served as the client.

The sexual division of labor varies somewhat by caste. High-caste men and women share the agricultural labor, but men alone do the tasks entailing the use of draft animals (plowing, harrowing) and sow the seed, while women prepare the manure to be used as fertilizer, winnow and handmill the grain, and handle all phases in the preparation of food for eating. Men build and maintain houses and other structures and the terraces, transport goods into and out of the village, and handle the trading and all dealings with outsiders. Women care for the children, do the housekeeping, and handle most of the day-to-day maintenance and provisioning of persons and animals that farming households require. Among the service castes, the division of labor is the same except that men do most or all of the activities that their occupational specialty requires (essentially substituting such activities for the exclusively male agricultural activities of the high castes). Low-caste women perform a few special tasks to support their menfolk's caste specialties, but for the most part they have the same tasks and responsibilities as high-caste women: they process and prepare the food, care for the children, keep house, and do much of the care of animals.

It is important to note that the position of women in Pahari society is distinctly superior to the position of women in plains society. Both women and men are aware and proud of this feature of their society. Pahari women play an essential and recognized role in almost all aspects of the economy. They are not secluded, they are not limited in their movements within and around the village, and they participate fully in ritual and religious activities, except those reserved for priests and those which take place outside the village in which they live. They also participate fully in recreational activities including traditional dancing. Their marriage brings a bride-price to their family rather than costing a dowry. They can divorce and remarry as easily as men. Widows are not constrained by widowhood and routinely remarry. Pahari women are noticeably more outspoken and self-confident in the presence of others, including strangers, as compared to women of the plains. As the culture of the politically, economically, educationally, and numerically dominant plains society increasingly impinges upon Pahari people, their worldview is inevitably affected. Sanskritic standards of the plains distort or replace Pahari customs, to the point that not only plainspeople but expatriate Paharis as well become critical, even ashamed, of Pahari traditions. Thus traditional Pahari religious and ritual activities, which are matters of pride for many, have become matters of shame and denial for those seeking the approval of plainspeople. Among such customs are animal (especially buffalo) sacrifice, bride-price, marriage, female-initiated divorce, widow and divorcée remarriage, polygyny, polyandry (where it occurs), female singing and dancing in public—in fact, almost all expressions of female freedom of action, options, participation, and assertiveness in social life. Division of labor by age and familial status (e.g., daughter vs. daughter-in-law) also exists but harbors few surprises for those familiar with Indian society, and in any case it cannot be examined within the limitations of this space.

LAND TENURE. This topic is too complex to discuss in detail here. Suffice it to repeat that traditionally only the high-caste (Brahman and Kshatriya) categories were allowed to own land. Independent India has abolished this rule, and efforts have been made to provide land to the landless, but the overwhelming preponderance of low-caste people still own very little and very poor land, if any at all. The problem of bonded labor and "debt slavery" among low castes remains endemic in many Pahari areas.

Pahari women are noticeably more outspoken and self-confident in the presence of others, including strangers, as compared to the women of the plains.

In the vicinity of my research, there is very little in the way of sharecropping, renting, absentee landlordism, and the like. These are true extended joint-family subsistence farms, worked by the members of the owner families with the assistance of artisan castes and an occasional hired servant. But in other Pahari regions one can discover instances of virtually every conceivable alternative system of ownership and subsidiary rights to the land, as well as every manifestation of subinfeudation and exploitation.

Kinship

KIN GROUPS AND DESCENT. As with most South Asian societies, Pahari society is composed of named, ranked castes, membership in which is determined by birth (i.e., by ancestry). Castes are with few exceptions endogamous, and therefore they comprise very extended kin groups. Each caste is made up of exogamous patrilineal, patrilocal sibs (or clans). Each sib is made up of numerous extended joint families, usually including two generations but ranging from one to as many as three or even four. Brothers are expected to keep the family and its patrimony intact, but even if they succeed in doing so, upon their deaths their children, who are cousins, generally divide it up.

KINSHIP TERMINOLOGY. Kinship terminology reflects this social structure: there are detailed terminological distinctions on the basis of affinity and consanguinity, of seniority (generation, birth order, and age of self or husband), etc. But cousins are not terminologically distinguished from siblings, nor first from second cousins, etc. (i.e., all are regarded as siblings). Therefore, it is a system employing standard Hawaiian-type cousin terms. In short, Pahari kinship organization and terminology are typical of those found throughout north India.

Marriage and Family

MARRIAGE AND DOMESTIC UNIT. Marriage must be within the caste and outside the patrilineal sib (clan). It is ceremonialized in a way well within the range of variation found through north India except that, unlike that of most high castes elsewhere, it does not entail a dowry. Rather, it entails a bride-price, which in fact is the traditional necessary component of a valid marriage. Polygyny is permitted (most often occasioned by the levirate), with an incidence of about 15 percent in the region of my work; about 20 percent of polygynous unions are sororal. Unmarried men never marry previously married women (although unceremonialized elopement occasion-

ally occurs). Any subsequent marriage is ceremonialized only if the woman has not been previously married. Divorce, initiated by husband or wife, is easy and frequent, requiring only the return of the bride-price (by the wife's family or new husband). Children, however, belong to and stay with their father and his family, a major deterrent to divorce for women with children.

A major distinctive feature of the Western Pahari area is that fraternal polyandry—strictly prohibited in the Central and Eastern Pahari areas—is permitted and in fact is the preferred form of marriage in some regions such as Jaunsar Bawar and scattered localities in Himachal Pradesh.

Throughout the Pahari area, postmarital residence is prescriptively patrilocal (virilocal). Exceptions occur for economic reasons, but some stigma is attached to them.

SOCIALIZATION. Children are nursed to the age of 3 or 4 and are given the breast occasionally up to age 5 or 6. Socialization is permissive and relaxed, especially in the early years. Boys are socialized together with girls, in a largely female environment, up to the age of 7 or 8, at which time they begin to interact mainly with males. Never are the sexes as segregated as in the plains, however. Girls assume household responsibilities earlier and these are more taxing than for boys—in short, boys are indulged more than girls. Not until puberty are caste distinctions and restrictions rigorously enforced. The marriage ceremony may take place at an early age (8 to 10) but nowadays usually not until later, and in any case the couple does not begin to live together until puberty has been attained: girls by about age 13 or later, boys by age 16 or later. Schooling is a recent phenomenon, restricted primarily to high-caste boys from prosperous families and usually not pursued beyond the first three to five years. Learning for both sexes and all castes is by participation, in effect by apprenticeship.

Sociopolitical Organization

SOCIAL ORGANIZATION. Most features of social organization have been covered above under the headings "Division of Labor," "Kinship," and "Marriage and Family." The remaining point requiring explanation is the Pahari system of caste categories. The pan-Indian system of castes and caste categories comprises innumerable localized castes (*jati*), hierarchically ranked according to their inborn purity. Castes, in turn, are grouped into five ranked categories called *varnas*: Brahman, Kshatriya, Vaisya, Sudra, and Achut. The first three are called "twice-born," indicating a higher order of ritual purity than the other two, while the Sudra, in turn, are purer than the Achut, who are regarded as woefully polluted (*achut* literally means "untouchable") and in fact are scripturally described as outside of the varna system, although structurally they comprise a fifth varna. Brahmans are traditionally the priestly castes; Kshatriyas are the royal, administrative, and warrior castes; Vaisyas are the yeoman farmer castes (who in historic times have come to be identified primarily as mercantile castes); Sudras are the "clean" artisan and service castes; and Achut are the castes that perform the most polluting tasks (e.g., scavengers, latrine cleaners, leatherworkers). In Pahari society, by contrast, generally only three varnas are represented—Brahman, Kshatriya, and Achut. Proportions in each category vary locally and regionally, but 75 to 90 percent of the Pahari population is Kshatriya. The Pahari social organization can be understood, in a rough way, by saying that there are no Vaisya castes, and all of those castes that in most of India are Sudra are in Pahari society classified as Achut, creating in effect a tripartite varna system. But indigenous terminology, at least in the Central Pahari region, suggests that the varna system is or in origin was in fact binary, comprising simply "twice-born" and "untouchable" categories. Pahari Brahmans and Kshatriyas are often collectively termed "Khas" or "Khasiya"; Pahari low castes are collectively termed "Dom." The social reality of this seems confirmed by the fact that marriage between Pahari Brahmans and Kshatriyas is tolerated (although reluctantly and without ceremony), something that plains society does not countenance, and marriage among low castes is similarly allowed.

POLITICAL ORGANIZATION, SOCIAL CONTROL, CONFLICT. At the village level, each caste is organized to handle internal conflicts and transgressions. However, heads of high-caste households (or some of them) traditionally constitute a council that decides matters of policy and social control for the village at large and intervenes as well in low-caste disputes or transgressions. Since independence, various kinds of councils have been established by the national governments of the nations in which Paharis live. In India, these are elected bodies, with an elected headman and with seats reserved for women and members of Achut castes. Their actual powers, however, tend to be limited to official matters, while social control remains with the traditional high-caste councils. As is true throughout India, low-caste individuals and collectivities are subject to stern measures, including violent physical sanctions of the most dire sort, to enforce the constraints placed on them by the high castes.

Religion and Expressive Culture

RELIGIOUS BELIEFS. Because the overwhelming preponderance of Paharis are Hindus, only that religion is described here. There are also Muslim Paharis, but they have been little described in the literature. Presumably their Islamic religion is that of the rest of South Asia, with a distinctly Pahari cast to it, notably as a result of beliefs and practices, pervasive in Pahari culture, that are neither identifiably Islamic nor Hindu in origin.

Pahari Hinduism shares most of its content with pan-Indian Hinduism, including some degree of belief in dharma (intrinsic individual and collective duty or "right behavior"), karma (just desserts contingent on fulfillment of dharma), samsara (reincarnation in accord with karma), maya (the illusory nature of existence), nirvana or *samadhi* (ultimate escape, if karma permits, from the wheel of reincarnation into oneness with the universe). Similarly there is an awareness of the scriptures, the great deities of Hinduism, the holy places, the holy days, the periodic and life-cycle rituals, the values, the prescriptions and proscriptions enjoined upon the faithful, etc. But there are also distinctive Pahari traditions regarded by their practitioners as the consequence of social and environmental circumstances of their alpine existence. In contrast to villages of the plains, there is little systematic difference among Pahari castes in religious belief and practice. In the eyes of outsiders, expatriates, and sophisticates, these traditions are often seen as rustic and therefore embarrassingly unorthodox and in need of reform. The dominant aspect of this rusticity is a lack of rigor in following the behavioral injunctions of Sanskritic Hinduism: dietary restrictions are virtually ignored, except for the taboo on beef; many of the great deities of Hinduism and the rituals associated with them are overlooked; niceties in the expression and maintenance of ritual purity are treated casually; most Sanskritic restrictions on high-caste women are not observed; and life-cycle rites and periodic rituals are understood and observed in a distinctly Pahari manner.

Supernaturals are of many types and innumerable manifestations—as suggested by the frequently quoted description of Hinduism as a "religion of 330 million gods." Deities (or gods) are the most powerful of supernaturals and must be placated to avoid their destructive wrath. Placa-

Pahari

The famous (now outlawed) rope-sliding ceremony is an attempt to appease the wrath of the most powerful deity of the Pahari region.

tion takes the form of honoring them with worship, especially by making offerings to them (prominently through animal sacrifice). In Sirkanda a number of household deities (associated with, affecting, and therefore worshiped by household members) are worshiped by each family at shrines in the dwelling. In addition, there are village deities, worshiped by most villagers on ritual occasions at a shrine in or near the village. Among the latter deities are the five Pandava brothers, known to every Hindu as heroic warriors of the *Mahabharata* epic, but to my knowledge worshiped as major deities only, and universally, by Paharis. Polyandrous Western Pahari societies cite the polyandrous Panduvas as the precedent for their own marriage rules. There are in addition a variety of other categories of supernaturals: ancestral spirits, ghosts or demons, sprites or fairies, etc. As with deities, each of these has dangerous powers that must be avoided, warded off, or properly attended to. Various diviners, exorcists, curers, and other specialists capable of dealing with the malevolence of such supernaturals are to be found in every locality.

RELIGIOUS PRACTITIONERS. Pahari religious practitioners, as throughout Hindu society, are of two major types. The first type includes those of the priestly (Brahman) caste, exclusively entitled by birth to their profession, whose responsibilities are to convey, oversee, perpetuate, and perform the scripturally prescribed aspects of Hinduism necessary to the long-term maintenance of relations between the faithful and the supernatural. The second type includes the individually gifted and supernaturally inspired practitioners of folk traditions, who, while not incompatible with Hinduism and in fact universally associated with it, are not enjoined by it: namely, the shamans (called *baki* in the Central Pahari region, and *bhagat* in the north Indian plains), diviners, exorcists, curers, and a variety of other practitioners—most often of low caste but potentially of any caste and either sex—who serve the immediate, pragmatic needs of people by dealing via the supernatural with the fateful, unpredictable aspects of their lives.

CEREMONIES. Ceremonies are numerous and often complex. They honor and placate deities and ancestors, celebrate or ward off the effects of astrological concordances, memorialize and celebrate life-cycle events, protect and perpetuate the well-being of individuals and groups, etc. Among several peculiar to the Pahari region (all well within the range of Hindu ceremonies) is

the famous rope-sliding ceremony. Too complex to describe adequately here—and now outlawed—it is worth mentioning because it incorporates the features of all Hindu ceremonies in a unique and spectacular Pahari idiom. Basically, it is an attempt to appease the wrath of the most powerful deity of the region, who has wrought dire and persistent misfortune on a village, by offering him a magnificent and expensive entertainment accompanied by many subsidiary sacrifices and supplications carried out by scores of priests, shamans, and other specialists before hundreds of worshipful participants and spectators. The climactic event occurs when a ritually prepared low-caste man who has been secured to a saddle astride a gigantic oil-soaked rope that is stretched between a tree at the top of a cliff and another at a distance below to form a steep incline, is released to careen down the rope, smoke streaming behind, to an uncertain fate at the end of his ride. If the spectacle is successful, the rider survives, the god is pleased, the community is relieved of its misfortune, the many who contributed to the event are benefited in proportion to their material or financial contribution, and everyone who witnessed it is blessed.

ARTS. Pahari artisan castes are the artists of this society, best known for wood carving of doors, windows, columns, rafters, etc. and ornamental stone carving. Carpenters and masons are noted for their architectural achievements through ingenious and beautiful use of wood and stone. The artistry of gold- and silversmiths, expressed primarily in women's jewelry, is also notable. Tailors and shoemakers are responsible for the colorful traditional Pahari clothing. The distinctive Pahari music has recently been selectively adapted to a popular idiom without entirely losing its traditional qualities, and it has achieved popular attention and commercial success in India. This music derives from folksongs known to all elements of Pahari society, rendered and preserved by the musician castes.

MEDICINE. Traditional practitioners employ a wide variety of herbal and ritual treatments for illnesses, injuries, and discomforts. In every village there are specialists known for their success in healing: herbalists, masseuses, curers of pustular diseases, bone setters, laceration healers, midwives, shamans, exorcists, etc. Elements of conventional Ayurvedic medical belief and practice are discernible but do not generally form a tightly organized system in rural villages. Government programs have brought medical personnel—

employing variously Ayurvedic, Unani, and scientific medical treatments—to many villages and health clinics to many regions. Hospitals are available in major centers. Still, however, most treatment is by traditional, indigenous practitioners. When medicines are sought from outside they are almost always patent remedies rather than prescribed medicines. Mortality, especially infant mortality, remains extremely high in the Pahari areas.

DEATH AND AFTERLIFE. Among Hindu Paharis, death and afterlife are understood and dealt with in characteristically Hindu fashion. (Muslims bury their dead and attend to death in ways prescribed by Islam, but here I am able only to discuss Hindu customs in the matter.) Among Hindus, small children are buried, as are those who die of particular virulent diseases and the rare holy individual who has achieved samadhi. Others are cremated, preferably by the side of a stream, with the remains being committed to the water. The ceremonies attending death, cremation, and the postcremation period are complex but not notably different from those prescribed in Hinduism. Women do not attend the funeral cremation, but they, like all relatives, participate in mourning according to the closeness of their kinship to the deceased. It is believed that the station of one's next life in the cycle of reincarnation—one's karma—is a consequence of fulfillment of one's dharma—the donation to charities, the performance of austerities, etc.

Bibliography

Berreman, Gerald D. (1972). *Hindus of the Himalayas: Ethnography and Change*. 2nd ed. Berkeley: University of California Press.

Grierson, G. A. (1916). *Linguistic Survey of India*. Vol. 9, pt. 4, 1. Calcutta: Superintendent of Government Printing.

Majumdar, D. N. (1972). *Himalayan Polyandry: Structure, Functioning, and Culture Change, a Field-Study of Jaunsar Bawar*. New York: Asia Publishing House.

Newell, William H. (1967). *Census of India, 1961*. Vol. 20, *Himachal Pradesh*, pt. 5-B, *The Gaddi and Affiliated Castes in the Western Himalayas*, Report on Scheduled Castes and Scheduled Tribes. Delhi: Manager of Publications.

Parry, Jonathan P. (1979). *Caste and Kinship in Kangra*. London: Routledge and Kegan Paul.

Raha, Manis Kumar, ed. (1987). *The Himalayan Heritage*. Delhi: Gian Publishing House.

Raha, Manis Kumar, and Satya Narayan Mahato (1985). *The Kinnaurese of the Himalayas*. Memoirs of the Anthropological Survey of India, no. 63. Calcutta.

—GERALD D. BERREMAN

PATHAN

Ethnonyms: Afghan, Pashtun, Pukhtun, Rohilla

Orientation

IDENTIFICATION. The Pathan inhabit southern and eastern Afghanistan and western Pakistan. Their language is Pushto (Pashto) and, except for a small minority, they are Sunni Muslims. Pathan dynasties constituted and, until recently, have controlled the tribal kingdom of Afghanistan, and during some periods Pathan or Afghan monarchs established their rule on the Indian plains.

LOCATION. The Pathan inhabit an area roughly bounded by Kabul in the northeast and Herat in the northwest. It extends as far east as the Indus River and in the south an approximate boundary can be drawn from Sibi through Quetta to Qandahar. Pathan tribes like the Mohmand, Wazirs, Sulemankhel, and Achakzais actually straddle the international border. The topography of the area is primarily mountainous, consisting of a part of the Alpine-Himalayan mountain range in central Afghanistan and the Sulaiman range in Pakistan. To the east Pathan territory extends onto the Indus Plain and in the south onto the Iranian Plateau. The climate of Afghanistan is semiarid with cold winters and dry summers. The eastern Pathan areas are affected by the humidity and rain of the Indian monsoons. In addition Pathan live in and contribute to social life in certain areas of India such as Rampur (Rohilla) and cities like Bombay.

DEMOGRAPHY. The 1984 population of Pushto speakers was approximately 20 million. This includes 11 million native to Pakistan and 9 million originating in Afghanistan. Because of the civil war that has persisted in Afghanistan since 1979, roughly 2 million Pathans have left for Pakistan as refugees. The Pathan constituted from 50 to 60 percent of the population of prewar Afghanistan. As the largest and most influential ethnic group, the Pathan have dominated the society and politics of that country for the past 200 years. Other important ethnic minorities in Afghanistan include the Hazaras, Tajiks, and

The Pathan inhabit southern and eastern Afghanistan and western Pakistan.

Pathan

Uzbeks. Since the separation of Bangladesh from Pakistan, the Pathan constitute Pakistan's second-largest ethnic group. According to Pakistan's 1981 census 13 percent of the nation's households are Pushto-speaking. Punjabis make up the majority of Pakistan's population; other important linguistic groups are Sindhis, Baluchis, and Urdu speakers.

LINGUISTIC AFFILIATION. Pushto is in the Iranian Branch of the Indo-European Language Family. The two principal dialects, which differ in pronunciation, are Southwestern or Qandahari Pushto and Northeastern or Peshawari Pukhto. Most Pathans in Afghanistan speak Dari, a dialect of Farsi or Persian, as a second language, and it has had a strong influence on Pushto. Both languages are written in the Arabic script, modified to accommodate consonants that do not occur in Arabic.

History and Cultural Relations

The origin of the Pathan is debated. Linguistic evidence indicates Indo-European ancestry, while some tribal genealogies claim Semitic links. The regions of Afghanistan, eastern Iran, and western India have been some of the most heavily invaded in history and so the Pathan of today are probably a heterogeneous group. Among the invaders who have entered and established empires in the area have been Iranians, Greeks, Hindus, Turks, Mongols, Uzbeks, Sikhs, British, and Russians. The first historical reference to the Pathan (A.D. 982) refers to Afghans living in the Sulaiman Mountains. The first significant impact they had outside of that area was as troops in the armies of Mahmud of Ghazni, a Muslim Turk, who led a number of invasions against the Hindu kings in north India around the year 1000. Nearly 300 years later Afghan kings themselves took power in Delhi. The Pathan Khaljis and later Lodhis ruled there until displaced by Babur, the first of the Mogul emperors, in the early sixteenth century. It is ironic that Pathan kings ruled India before they ruled the mountainous areas to the west that are their homelands. That feat was not accomplished until 1747 when, from a base in Qandahar, Ahmed Shah Abdali fused together an empire that encompassed parts of Iran and India as well as Afghanistan. Members of his tribe ruled a more truncated Afghanistan until 1973. British involvement in Pathan areas was a consequence of efforts to protect the western borders of their Indian empire and check the southern advance of the Russians. In 1879, following the Second Anglo-Afghan War, the Afghan government conceded control of all the passes into India to

the British and in 1893 the Durand Line was established, delineating the spheres of responsibility of the two governments. It is now the international border dividing the Pathan between two nation-states.

Settlements

While some Pathan are nomadic and others urban, the majority dwell in villages of 2 to 400 families. Frequently the villages cluster around a larger town and are always located with concern for the availability of water and for defense. Settlement patterns reflect lineage politics with dominant lineages holding the choice or strategic lands. Genealogical closeness determines a group's location relative to them. Nomadic groups are primarily cattle herders who move with the seasons to follow pasture. They follow set routes and have traditional camping sites. Like the villages, camps are structured around the tents of the senior lineages. Houses are generally constructed of mud or sun-dried mud bricks covered with mud plaster. The only valuable parts of the house are the doors and the wood beams that support a flat roof of mats covered with mud and twigs. In small villages households consist of high-walled compounds frequently resembling fortresses, complete with towers on the corners. A clear and strict demarcation is observed between the areas (*hujra*) where the public may enter and be entertained and the family's living space. Women are secluded from the former (according to the Islamic custom of purdah) and animals and grain stores are kept in the latter. In the traditional style nomadic tents are woven from black goat's hair and supported by posts or arched poles and guy ropes.

Economy

SUBSISTENCE AND COMMERCIAL ACTIVITIES. Agriculture, primarily grain farming, and animal husbandry are the most important activities in the Pathan economy. The practice of agriculture is largely limited by the rough terrain and arid climate to river valleys; elsewhere, it depends on the scant rainfall. The most important crop is wheat, followed by barley and maize. Cultivation is done primarily by hand or with animals, though, where possible, mechanization is taking place. Traditional irrigation techniques such as *kareezes*, a series of wells connected by an underground tunnel, are in many cases being replaced by tube wells. Other important agricultural products are fresh and dried orchard fruits, nuts, veg-

♦ **purdah**
Seclusion of women; mainly a Muslim custom in South Asia and the Middle East.

etables, opium, and hashish. In addition to raising stock, nomads as well as some farmers engage in trade and moneylending. The presence of the border dividing Pathan territory into two countries also makes smuggling a lucrative pursuit. Domesticated animals include both fat-tailed and short-tailed sheep, goats, cattle, water buffalo, chickens, camels, donkeys, and horses.

INDUSTRIAL ARTS. Many industrial activities such as carpentry, bricklaying, and shoemaking are done by part-time Pashtun specialists who also farm. However, in many areas non-Pathan occupational groups carry out these activities, as well as others such as weaving, blacksmithing, and goldsmithing. An exception is the manufacture of guns; in certain areas, notably Darra Adam Khel south of Peshawar, Pathans produce guns in small factories.

TRADE. Villages in Pathan areas have until recently been largely self-sufficient. Traditionally trade and even farming were activities looked down upon by Pathans who saw raiding, smuggling, and politics as honorable pursuits. In areas where such attitudes persist, trade is carried out by non-Pathan (frequently Hindu) shopkeepers and peddlers or through barter with nomads. Despite these traditions, in large towns and urban areas Pathans have earned reputations as successful traders and businessmen.

DIVISION OF LABOR. The strict observance of purdah results in a marked division of labor between the sexes. Although rural women may participate in the harvesting of crops, they remain primarily inside the compound where they are expected to do the traditional home tasks of rearing children, maintaining the house, cooking, etc. Indeed, purdah is frequently observed to such an extent that women are not allowed to go out in public to do the shopping; thus, the shopping is all done by men. Purdah is less strictly observed by nomadic groups.

LAND TENURE. In the arid, low-yield regions the small landholdings are self-cultivated by the *malik* (petty chief or household elder) and his sons. In areas of greater productivity, where khans (village or tribal chiefs) own larger tracts, tenants do the work. Tenants receive about 20 percent of the product if they only supply labor and higher percentages if they supply implements or draft animals. Until early this century in the Swat and Mardan valleys the equality of the Pathan clans was underlined by the custom of *wesh* by which they periodically redistributed land between themselves. This involved physically shifting households and belongings to other parts of the valleys. Excess population from Pathan areas has traditionally left the area to serve as mercenaries in the armies of India, to work as tenants on the lands of others or,

MARKETPLACE

Pathan vegetable vendors spread their merchandise between two railroad tracks. Agriculture and animal husbandry are the most important activities in the Pathan economy. Peshawar, Pakistan. (Mike Zens/Corbis)

Purdah is frequently observed to such an extent by the Pathan that women are not allowed to go out in public to do the shopping; thus, the shopping is all done by men.

more currently, to act as laborers or entrepreneurs in the cities of Pakistan or the Persian Gulf states.

Kinship

KIN GROUPS AND DESCENT. Segmentary tribal structure and unilineal descent define Pathan kin groups. Genealogical and geographic divisions generally coincide. The most pertinent division within the tribal structure is the clan subsection, that is, the children of one man, generally encompassing four or five generations. It is within this sphere that one marries, makes alliances, and is in conflict. The smallest unit is the *kor*, or household, and it implies cohabitation with a living grandfather. This is the major economic and social unit; its members may cohabit in a village, a single compound, or a nomadic group. Descent is patrilineal.

KINSHIP TERMINOLOGY. Aspects of the Eskimo system, in which avuncular and cousin terms are uniform, are present, though certain collaterals are distinguished. For example, while all other female cousins carry the same term as do all other male ones, the father's brother's daughter (potential or preferred bride) and father's brother's son (rival for inheritance and thus potential enemy) are given distinct terms.

Marriage and Family

MARRIAGE. Although polygamy with up to four wives is permitted under Muslim law, monogamy is prevalent. Marriages are overwhelmingly endogamous within the clan and to a large degree within the subsection. Parallel-cousin marriage with father's brother's daughter is preferred among some tribes. Marriages are arranged by the couple's parents and their plans are generally fulfilled. The union is commonly contracted on the basis of bride-price. Frequently the bride's parents spend the money received in bride-price as dowry to meet the future domestic needs of the couple. A common practice is exchange marriage between close agnatic kin in which a sister or daughter is given and one simultaneously taken. Residence after marriage is virilocal, the bride coming to live in a single compound with the son, who receives separate quarters within it. The death of the patriarch of a family is frequently the time when such joint or compound families divide themselves into separate compounds. Despite the ease of obtaining a divorce under Muslim law, it is very rare among Pathans. The bride-price and the man's honor are lost if the woman remarries.

DOMESTIC UNIT. The household (kor) is the primary unit of consumption and cooperation and is conceived of as those who share a hearth or as a man and/or his sons. Three main types of domestic unit are found: (1) the nuclear family; (2) the compound family, in which a patriarch and/or his sons and their wives live together and share expenses; and (3) the joint family, in which the nuclear families in a compound, frequently brothers, keep independent budgets.

INHERITANCE. Land is divided as inheritance only among the males and on the basis of equality. The eldest brother is generally given an extra share to be used for the upkeep of the family guest house (hujra). It is over the inheritance of land that rivalry develops between brothers and, in the next generation, cousins. Despite Islamic injunctions, neither wives nor daughters inherit property.

SOCIALIZATION. With the separation of the sexes inherent in Islam, children are raised primarily by their mother and elder sisters. In the segregated atmosphere that prevails there is a great deal of competition for attention and affection, though men tend to be indulgent toward children. Boys are circumcised by their seventh year.

Sociopolitical Organization

The Pathan are divided into a number of different politicoadministrative structures. In Afghanistan the state, itself evolved from the tribal system, has historically exerted only loose control except in the major cities. In Pakistan several different systems prevail that are largely the legacy of British imperial administration. Although most Pathans live in districts where Pakistan's civil and criminal laws prevail, some tribes, such as the Mohmand and Wazirs, are within Federally Administered Tribal Areas (FATA), while others, such as those in Malakand in the North-West Frontier Province or those in Zhob Agency in Baluchistan, are within Provincially Administered Tribal Areas (PATA). In FATA and PATA tribal and customary law holds sway.

SOCIAL ORGANIZATION. Despite administrative divisions Pathan maintain a conception of their cultural and ethnic unity. This idea stems from the segmentary tribal structure and the associated notion of descent from a common ancestor. A. S. Ahmed has identified two principles of social organization among the Pathan, *nang* (honor) and *qalang* (taxes or rent). In areas where nang prevails traditional values are practiced, there is little social stratification, and there is no central political authority. In qalang areas landownership, not lineage membership, gives status and social stratification is prevalent, along with political centralization in the hands of an aristocracy. In both contexts mullahs, Sayyids (descendants of the Prophet Mohammed), and occupation groups play their special roles in Pathan society but stand outside Pathan genealogy.

POLITICAL ORGANIZATION. To varying degrees Pathans are assimilated into the administrative structure of the area in which they live. In the last twenty-five years Afghanistan has officially moved from being a constitutional monarchy to a republic and finally to a democratic republic. Despite these changes (and until the current civil war) the relationship between the government and the rural population changed little. Since the government's presence has usually been for the purpose of extracting taxes or conscripts, the villagers' attitude toward it has generally been defensive and noncooperative. To some extent the same was true on the other side of the border where there was ongoing resistance to British rule, though British administration was accepted in some areas and British subsidies in others. Although most Pathans supported the movement for the creation of Pakistan, others wanted to reunite Pathans on both sides of the border in a country to be called "Pakhtunistan." Since then the Pakhtunistan movement has smoldered in various forms in both countries. An important political role is played by indigenous decision-making councils called *jirgas*. They are made up of maliks and decide various intra- or intertribal matters on the basis of tribal custom and, to a lesser extent, Islamic law. In Afghanistan the institution extends to the national level where the Loya Jirga, made up of tribal, ethnic, and religious leaders, meets to decide important issues.

SOCIAL CONTROL. Traditionally social control was maintained by a code of behavior and honor called Pakhtunwali. It combines the principles of revenge, hospitality to guests, defense of those who have sought protection in one's care, the chastity of married women, and restraint toward those considered weak or helpless (Hindus, women, and boys). Pakhtunwali in some cases contradicts and generally takes precedence over Islamic law. It is harsh—the penalty for illicit sexual behavior, for example, is death—and it is enforced by strong social pressure. Violations of law outside of the activities the code encompasses are dealt with by the jirga or the government administration.

CONFLICT. As noted, the rivalry with father's brother's son for property, power, and wives is a constant source of conflict, as is Pakhtunwali

itself, since even petty quarrels can escalate to a point where honor is involved. Efforts to encapsulate the Pathan into political systems seen as alien are also a source of conflict. It is frequently at such times of external threat that religious leaders assume political importance since resistance takes the form of a holy struggle or jihad. Conflict resolution is done through the jirga or through the intervention of religious figures.

Religion and Expressive Culture

RELIGIOUS BELIEFS. Islam is an essential and unifying theme in Pathan life, and it also unites the Pathan with an international community of believers. The overwhelming majority of Pathan is Sunni Muslim of the Hanafi legal school. Some groups, notably in the Kurram and Orakzai agencies of Pakistan, practice Shia Islam. A number of supernatural figures reside among the Pathan. *Jinn* are spirits born of fire that can enter and possess people. Other negative beings include the ghosts of disturbed or cursed souls, witches, and fairies. The souls of pious figures can also return to Earth to play a more positive role.

RELIGIOUS PRACTITIONERS. While Islam has no ordained priesthood, religious leaders are recognized. At the village level this role is played by the mullah, a man who has attained some religious training. Besides tending the mosque and making the call to prayer five times a day, he officiates at the rites of passage that mark the stages of life, birth, circumcision, marriage, and death. Another important figure is the Sayyed who stands outside the tribal structure, since his genealogy extends to the Prophet himself and not to the ancestors of the Pathans. Not bound by the Pashtun code of honor, Sayyeds are saintly figures who can arbitrate between conflicting groups.

CEREMONIES. Besides ceremonies at the various rites of passage, the religious calendar includes: three days of celebration at the end of Ramazan, the month of fasting; a day observed by the ritual slaying of sheep in memory of Ibrahim slaying a sheep in place of his son on Allah's order; and the birthday of the Prophet Mohammed.

ARTS. Poetry is the art most esteemed by Pathans. Their greatest poet, Khushhal (d. 1689), wrote both love poems and patriotic poems. Embroidered waistcoats and elaborately decorated rifle butts were traditionally the major visual arts.

MEDICINE. While some medical facilities are being introduced, people customarily go to the mullah or traditional herbalist for cures. A jinn possessing the patient is commonly held to be the cause of disease. Indigenous treatment is in a

The term "Punjabi" signifies both an inhabitant of the Punjab and a speaker of the predominant language of the region.

tradition said to be of Greek origin or in a religious tradition worked out centuries ago. A common cure consists of the wearing of talismans around the neck composed of magic formulas or verses of the Quran sewn up in cloth or leather.

DEATH AND AFTERLIFE. In Islam the body is to be buried ritually pure so that the soul is prepared to enter Heaven on Judgment Day. After death the body is washed and wrapped in a white sheet. A mullah performs the death rites, leading the congregated mourners in a special prayer. The body is buried with the face pointing toward Mecca. Mourning obligations continue after the burial. The deceased's relatives gather at the grave on the first few Fridays and on the fortieth day after the death, and they observe the first year's anniversary of the death with a final memorial ceremony.

Bibliography

Ahmed, Akbar S. (1976). *Millennium and Charisma among Pathans: A Critical Essay in Social Anthropology.* London: Routledge & Kegan Paul.

Ahmed, Akbar S. (1980). *Pukhtun Economy and Society: Traditional Structure and Economic Development in a Tribal Society.* London: Routledge & Kegan Paul.

Barth, Fredrik (1972). *Political Leadership among Swat Pathans.* London School of Economics Monographs on Social Anthropology, no. 19. London: Athlone Press.

Caroe, Olaf (1958). *The Pathans 550 B.C.–A.D. 1957.* London: Macmillan; New York: St. Martin's Press.

Dupree, Louis (1980). *Afghanistan.* Princeton, N.J.: Princeton University Press.

—AKBAR S. AHMED WITH PAUL TITUS

PUNJABI

Ethnonym: Panjabi

Orientation

IDENTIFICATION. The term "Punjabi" signifies both an inhabitant of the Punjab and a speaker of the predominant language of that region, Punjabi. The name is from the Persian *panj*, "five," and *ab*, "river." The Punjab is defined by the Indus River and the five rivers to the south that flow out of the Himalayas to join it: the Jhelum, Chenab, Ravi, Beas, and Sutlej. These define five *doabs*, which differ culturally and linguistically. A doab is the land between two converging rivers. Culturally, Punjab actually extends southward still more, to the bed of the largely extinct Ghaggar,

which also traces from the Himalayas to the Indus and joins it about where the Sutlej does. The Punjab culture region includes the states of Punjab in Pakistan and in India as well as portions of present-day North-West Frontier Province in Pakistan and Jammu, Rajasthan, and Himachal Pradesh in India.

LOCATION. The region lies between 28° and 34° N and 70° and 74° E. It is mainly a nearly level plain, dropping in elevation from 300 meters in the northeast at the edge of the Siwalik range to about 100 meters at the point where the Indus becomes a single stream. Above the plain, the culture region includes the mountains of the Salt range in Pakistan and parts of the lower Himalayas in India. Its area is about 270,000 square kilometers. Of this, 205,344 square kilometers are in Pakistan Punjab and 50,362 square kilometers in Indian Punjab.

The climate is warm to temperate. The hottest season is May–June, when maximum daytime temperatures are about 40° C. The coolest months are January and February, when light nighttime frosts are common. Rainfall is monsoonal, with more than two-thirds falling in the summer rainy season. It is heaviest near the Himalayas. Along the Himalayan edge of the plains annual amounts of about 1 meter are normal. At Lahore, 100 kilometers out into the plain, rainfall is about 50 centimeters, and at Multan, about 500 kilometers from the mountains and in the center of the southeastern portion of the region, it is about 18 centimeters. There are two major agricultural seasons marked by two dry, hot harvest periods in April-May (*rabi*) and September–October (*kharif*). The winter monsoon, although light, is vital for the wheat crop that provides the traditional staple of the region.

DEMOGRAPHY. The combined population of Indian and Pakistan Punjab in 1981 was about 64.1 million, compared to about 36.6 million in 1961. Population densities in rural areas range from over 1,900 persons per square kilometer in the highly urbanized Lahore District in Pakistan to about 10 persons per square kilometer in the desert of the Thal Doab between the Indus and the lower portion of the Chenab (Mianwala District). Indian Punjab had about 333 persons per square kilometer.

LINGUISTIC AFFILIATION. Punjabi is Indo-European with close relations to surrounding languages, particularly to Pahari to the east. It is divided into six major dialects, localized in the major doabs. The Majhi and Malwa dialects are considered the most "pure." Majhi occupies the

See also
Sikh

upper half of the Bari Doab, the plain region between the Ravi and the Sutlej rivers, which includes the cities of Lahore and Amritsar. The Malwa tract is just south of this between the Sutlej and Ghaggar, centering on Bhatinda. The other dialects are Doabi, spoken around Jalandhar between the Beas and the Sutlej; Powadhi, spoken in the eastern portion of the doab between the Sutlej and Ghaggar, centering on Sirhind; Dogri in Jammu District of Jammu and Kashmir and Kangra District of Himachal Pradesh; and finally Bhattiani, extending southeast from the Malwa tract across the eastern tip of Haryana State and into Ganganagar District of Rajasthan. North and west of Majhi, Punjabi gives way to Lahnda, also called Western Punjabi, which is spoken all across the western half of the Pakistani Punjab. While linguistically distinguishable, Lahnda speakers generally consider themselves Punjabi. Lahnda and Bhattiani have been attenuated further by large migrations to the canal colonies of Shahpur, Lyallpur, Montgomery, and Multan and to Ganganagar District in Rajasthan. These schemes comprised almost 2.5 million hectares of new agricultural land by 1930, and by far the largest numbers of settlers were Jat farmers from around Lahore, Amritsar, Ludhiana, and Jalandhar.

History and Cultural Relations

The Punjab is an ancient center of civilization. Historically it has been the main route of invasion and migration into India, going back beyond the Harappans. Harappa itself is on the Ravi in Punjab near present-day Montgomery, while Mohenjo Daro is on the Indus in Sindh just outside the natural gateway to Punjab that is formed as the Suliman range curves southward to squeeze the five rivers together. Remains of numerous Harappan communities extend from there to Gujarat in the west and to the upper Jamuna in the east. Invaders since the Harappans have included the ancient Aryans who are responsible for the *Rig Veda*, Scythians, Greeks (Alexander the Great came as far as the Ravi), Arabs, Persians, Afghans, Pathans, Baluchis, Mongols, and Europeans. Each group has left its marks.

The chief historic cities of Punjab are Lahore, Amritsar, Ludhiana, Jalandhar, and Patiala. They are part of a line of commercial and military centers that lie along ancient routes from the Khyber Pass through the Ganges Plain. Along this route, rainfall is reliable, soils are deep, groundwater is accessible, and the climate is moderate. Cities in this belt south and east of Punjab include Delhi,

Varanasi, Lucknow, Meerut, Allahabad, and Patna. These linkages keep Punjab in constant communication with surrounding regions. Punjabi culture has never been isolated.

Modern Punjabi culture has been shaped profoundly by the partitioning of India and Pakistan that accompanied independence in 1947. This event resulted in massive migrations that separated Muslims from Hindus and Sikhs, drove the Sikh cultivators who had been the backbone of the canal colonies to India, made Sikhs for the first time an actual majority in rural areas of central Indian Punjab, and initiated divergent government policies that have had far-reaching effects on all areas of life.

Settlements

Compared to surrounding regions, Punjab's population is evenly spread and dense, particularly in the central areas. In Indian Punjab the rural population is consistently 60–70 percent of the total. It is similar in the adjoining districts of Pakistani Punjab except for Lahore District, which is 84 percent urban. Urban settlements now are sprawling towns, growing rapidly in both Punjabs but faster in Pakistan. Formerly they were walled and compact, with many-storied houses and narrow lanes for defense and shade. The towns are educational and administrative centers, and they have active agriculture trading sectors as well as numerous and diverse types of manufacturing. The estimated 1981 populations of the principal towns were as follows: Lahore, 2,922,000; Lyallpur (Faisalabad), 1,092,000; Multan, 730,000; Sialkot, 296,000; Amritsar, 595,000; Ludhiana, 607,000; Jalandhar, 408,000; and Patiala, 206,000.

Villages in the Punjab plains are nucleated. In the older villages—apart from the canal colonies, where villages were laid out in blocks at crossroads—houses are built together in a compact area and the outer walls are joined together to make a common rampart, with limited points of entry. Houses abut one another along narrow lanes, sharing many common walls. One can reach much of the village by going over rooftops, but the only access to the rooftops is from the inside of houses. Close outside this wall are work areas and areas for storage, or perhaps a village mill. Beyond this the agricultural fields lie open; only valuable orchards would be fenced. At some distance in the fields there are always one or two cremation grounds and some ritual sites. In larger villages, there are commonly separate sides or neighborhoods for upper- and lower-caste groups,

The main entry to a Punjabi village is commonly through a masonry gateway, which arches over the main road and limits the size of vehicles that can enter.

and there may be concentrations of households of specific caste or lineage groups in a particular lane or area.

Stereotypically, and commonly, the main entry to a village is through a masonry gateway, called the *durwaza*, which arches over the main road and limits the size of vehicles that can enter. It may be up to 20 meters long. Inside, along the roadway on both sides, it has wide raised plinths, where people can sit. The durwaza is always an important meeting place and the preferred stopping place for visiting artisans and traders.

The average population of a village in the central area is about 990 persons, but the distribution is highly skewed. About two-thirds of the villages are of less than average size.

Since independence many houses have been built outside the former rampart, and farmers have begun building houses directly in their fields, particularly at well sites. Many small new hamlets have also been established. The changes in settlement patterns reflect increased geographical mobility and regional integration. In India's Punjab all villages have been electrified and connected by paved roads. Almost all now have some kind of private motorized transport vans, motor rickshaws, or minibuses. Pakistani Punjab has a similar density of infrastructure in the central canal colonies, but it also has many areas that lack both electricity and paved roads.

Economy

SUBSISTENCE AND COMMERCIAL ACTIVITIES. The Punjab has long been one of the world's most important agricultural regions. Pakistan's Punjab, which comprises 25.7 percent of its total land area, is its most important agricultural area by far. Its principal crops are cotton and wheat. Indian Punjab, although only about 1.7 percent of the total area of India, produces about 21 percent of India's wheat and 8.5 percent of its rice. The agriculture has several distinctive features, beginning with heavy reliance on irrigation and exceptionally high cropping densities and levels of investment.

Punjab agriculturalists cannot be divided into subsistence and commercial sectors. Even farmers who sell most of what they grow still obtain most of what they consume from their own fields. The agricultural system involves intensive multicropping and most of the major commercial crops are also traditional food crops. The diet is simple, based on winter and summer "typical" combinations of a bread made of grain from the last season with a pulse from the last season or a veg-

etable from the present season. Thus, for example, the typical meal in the cold months is a maize *roti* (a flat bread cooked on an iron skillet, without oil) with *sarson ka sag* (mustard greens with spices, onions, garlic, and clarified butter cooked into a thick soup). In the other months, the most common meal is wheat roti and a side dish such as curried lentils, chick-peas, potatoes, squash, or okra.

The main exceptions to the general rule that marketed crops are simply food crops produced in excess of the family needs are rice in Indian Punjab and cotton in Pakistani Punjab. Cotton is a historic cash crop grown for export; taking advantage of the dry climate and rich soils, it requires about the same amount of water as wheat and can be readily grown with canal irrigation. It has been largely abandoned in Indian Punjab because it carries about a 50 percent risk of loss. Rice was introduced as a response to widespread flooding in the Amritsar area in the mid-1960s, caused by new canals traversing the area. It has since spread to other areas as electrification has become available for private bore wells, but it has not been adopted into the diet.

From about 1965 to 1978, both parts of Punjab underwent a "green revolution." This is a blend of advanced university-based seed production, relatively small-scale machine and storage technologies, and a system of rural support institutions suited to family-owned peasant management. Since their consolidation in Punjab, these technologies and institutions have been steadily spreading outward. Punjabi migrants are prominent leaders of agricultural innovation in many surrounding regions. Punjab agriculture is also characterized by a large cattle population. Major animals are oxen (*Bos indica*), camels, and buffalo.

Cattle population densities are higher in Punjab than surrounding regions, and the cattle are generally larger and more productive, except that Haryana, to the south, is known for producing even larger oxen as plow animals. With mechanization accompanying the green revolution technologies, the densities have increased and the proportions have changed. The number of camels, oxen, and Indica cows has been reduced, and that of milk animals, mainly buffalo, has greatly increased. Their size and quality have also been increased by artificial insemination programs. Many farmers have also obtained new Indica-Jersey or Indica-Holstein cows.

INDUSTRIAL ARTS AND TRADE. Associated with this agricultural base is an extensive economic infrastructure, including agroprocessing and agroservice industries, along with light and medium manufacturing. Ludhiana is widely known for very large scale bicycle manufacturing as well as the production of agricultural tools of many types. The infrastructure includes a vigorous truck transport industry, major agricultural universities in both Punjabs, and, in Indian Punjab, an extensive system of cooperatives engaged in obtaining input materials and distributing them to farmers as well as large-scale buying and transport of commodities on behalf of the national food-grain pools. Other cooperatives are engaged in sugar manufacturing, dairying, transport, and various small-scale industries such as the production of cotton and woolen textiles and clothing. Heavier production, both publicly and privately owned, includes farm tractors, railroad cars, cement, tools, and bicycles.

In Pakistani Punjab the agricultural infrastructure is weaker but heavy manufacturing is stronger. Major products include textiles, machinery, electrical appliances, surgical equipment, floor coverings, bicycles and rickshaws, and foodstuffs.

DIVISION OF LABOR. Urban areas in Punjab have the full range of occupations that exist in any comparable economic system: doctors, lawyers, teachers, government workers, engineers, mechanics, construction workers, shopkeepers, bankers, truck drivers, street sweepers, and so on. There is a high degree of industrial and craft specialization. Women as well as men participate in the labor force and in the professions. The proportion of women is lower in Pakistani Punjab.

In rural areas, the main occupational groups are: agriculturalists (landowner/farmer), about 50 percent; agricultural laborers, about 30 percent; and specialized artisans, about 20 percent—carpenters, masons, blacksmiths, mechanics, millers, operators of cotton gins. Large villages also have one or two shopkeepers, teachers, tailors, a mail carrier or postmaster, religious professionals, and perhaps a medical practitioner of some kind. Agriculturalists now commonly hire themselves out with their equipment for custom work such as plowing or harvesting with a combine.

The household division of labor is based on sex and seniority. In better-off households, men usually deal with the main property from which the family obtains its income: land, a shop, or the husband/father's individual vocation. The wife or mother of the senior man heads the women's side of the household. She takes direct charge of the internal household budget, oversees stores, takes care of young animals, directs the activities of other women and girls in the house, manages household servants, and oversees the daily preparation and distribution of food and the care of children. Sons are under the care of their mothers until about school age, when they begin to accompany their fathers at their work. In laboring

CRAFT SPECIALIST

A Punjabi man making a basket from tree branches. Urban occupations tend to be medical and educational, while rural occupations center around agriculture and specialized artisans. Near Chandigarh, Punjab, India.
(Nazima Kowall/Corbis)

households, both men and women work, although usually at different tasks. Men receive higher pay and do work that is physically more difficult. It is becoming common for women to take salaried work, but it would be considered very odd for a woman to set up an independent household.

Kinship

KIN GROUPS AND DESCENT. The most important descent/kinship groups in Punjab, in order of comprehensiveness, are caste (*jati*), clan (*got*), village (*pind*), division (*patti*), and family (*parivar*). In Punjab a caste is described as a group of families in an area, with common ancestry, who marry among themselves and have a common traditional occupation based upon a common type of inherited productive property.

Castes generally have origin stories that explain how they came into the area and/or into their present occupational position. Lower castes are described either as original landholders who were defeated and subordinated by later invaders (who became the present landholders), or alternatively as latecomers who were given their present occupation by the landholders in exchange for being allowed to settle. Higher castes are described as successful invaders or as a group given the land of an area by some past ruler for notable services.

In villages, castes commonly fall into higher and lower groups. Traditionally, members of the lower caste would have been considered unclean by the upper, and they might have been denied house sites and access to public wells on the upper-caste side of the village, and they also might have had to use different ritual specialists for marriages and other life-cycle rituals. Exactly which castes are put in each group varies by area, but the upper castes usually are Brahmans, landowners, and skilled artisans, while the lower groups do work such as handling dead animals and sweeping up offal. Landowning castes include Jats, Rajputs, Sainis, Kambohs, Brahmans, Gujars, and Ahirs. The term "Rajput" literally means "son of a king," but most of the other names are purely ethnic in connotation. There is no caste group literally named "landowner" or farmer. Artisan castes include carpenters, masons, blacksmiths, barbers, operators of cotton gins, and perhaps weavers. The lower group contains leatherworkers and sweepers. People often do not actually perform the work their caste name suggests. Leatherworkers, for example, are a numerous group who usually do agricultural labor. People of lower castes often use different caste names according to reli-

gion; for example, a Mazhbi is a leatherworker who is a Sikh.

In Punjab, caste discrimination is not generally supported by religion. It is specifically rejected in all forms of Islam and Sikhism. Many local Hindu sects and movements, such as Radhoswami, reject it as well. Each jati is divided into an indefinite number of clans (got). A got is a group descended from a common ancestor, not specifically known, whose members are more closely related to each other than to other members of the caste. Gots are exogamous; one must not marry a person from the gots of any of one's four grandparents. People commonly use the name of their got as part of their personal name.

Villages are also exogamous, and people of one's village are addressed with kinship terms as though they were people of one's own family, irrespective of caste or got. A patti—literally, a division—is the largest group of families with actual common ancestry within a caste or got in a single village. A family (parivar) is the basic and most important unit of Punjab society. The complementary roles of men and women in the household division of labor are based upon complementary rights and duties in terms of the kinship system, particularly complementary rights over property (see below).

KINSHIP TERMINOLOGY. The Punjabi kinship terminology distinguishes just four superior generations and four inferior generations, but there is no limit to the relationships that may be considered collateral.

In Ego's own generation, all males are addressed as *bhai* (brother) and all females are *bhain* (sister). These terms include all of those who would be called "cousin" in English, and many more. In the first ascending generation, the terminology distinguishes mother, mother's brother, and mother's sister, and each of their respective spouses, all of which are further distinguished from father, father's elder brother, father's younger brother, and father's sister and their respective spouses. From an English speaker's point of view, Punjabi thus demarcates ten distinct relations where English has only "uncle" and "aunt." But the offspring of these relations are all either "brother" or "sister," according to sex.

The terms above +1 continue to separate the matrilateral and patrilateral sides: all the terms of the mother's side are built up on the stem -*nan*-. On the father's side the stem is -*dad*-. Prefixes and suffixes distinguish generation and sex only. Thus the father of the father is *dada*, mother of father is *dadi*. Dada also applies to any male relative through the dada or dadi, and dadi to any female through the dada or dadi. Thus dada is "grandfather," "great-uncle," and indeed all of their siblings, spouses, or siblings of spouses or spouses of siblings of whatever remoteness. *Nana* and *nani* are those similarly related on the mother's side. Father of dada is *pardada*, his wife/sister is *parnani*, and these terms too are similarly extended. Their counterparts on the mother's side are *parnana* and parnani. The father or mother of parnana or parnani has no term (i.e., is not a relative). The term-pair superior to parnana-parnani on the father's side in turn is *nakarnana-nakarnani*. Above this no further relations are recognized on the father's side.

The system of terms for relatives below the generation of Ego is more complex. Each position is distinguished by generation, sex, and whether the person was brought into the family by birth or marriage. Further, lines of descent through males only are separated from those through females, beginning with distinguishing Ego's own sons and daughters from those of Ego's sister's on the one hand and Ego's brother's on the other. The line of direct descendants that remains with a man in his village is also separated out from all others. The terminology for men is the same as for women. In address, only terms for one's own and superior generations are used. Genealogical inferiors are addressed by name.

Marriage and Family

MARRIAGE. Marriage is considered universal and necessary among all religious communities. Residence is patrilocal. The bride comes to live with her husband in his natal village and house. Marriages are arranged by parents, with wide consultation. Although there is no formal rule, families who have more than one son who in turn have sons will generally divide, and just one son and his family will remain with the parents. If a family has so many sons that its property cannot be divided and still be useful, it is customary in Punjab, particularly among Jats, for some of the sons to remain single and stay in the house with one of the brothers who marries. Dividing the house in marriage has no necessary connection to the division of ancestral property.

Although laws in both Punjabs provide for legally registered marriages, these are seldom used. Marriages generally occur according to customary forms, whether Hindu, Sikh, or Muslim. The ceremonies vary by caste and region, but generally they symbolically represent the ideal that a marriage is a free gift of the girl from the girl's family to the groom, with nothing taken back in exchange. Expenses of the wedding are borne by the girl's parents, and substantial gifts by way of dowry are given by the parents to the girl to take with her to her new house. They should be enough to provide for her upkeep (or the equivalent of it) for two or three years. By that time, having children will have established her permanently as part of her new household.

There is provision in the customary rituals for de facto divorce. Immediately after the marriage ceremony the girl returns to her parental home, and she should be fetched by her husband to return. She may refuse. Otherwise, she may in any case come home and refuse to return. The husband's family should then return her property. Once children are born, however, divorce is effectively impossible, since there is no way parental rights or responsibilities can be abrogated or reassigned. The parents' relations to each other are set by their common offspring. On the other hand, if children are not born, the marriage will probably dissolve. Since the only old-age security most people have is that which is provided by descendants who inherit their property and maintain it for them, the groom's family will be forced to send the bride away (although adoption is also common and easy). If sent away, her parents will have an obligation to receive her back, although this will be considered awkward for her brothers and their wives. In any case, from a traditional point of view it will be less a matter of divorce than a matter of the marriage not being completed.

Polygamy is accepted, but rare. There are no organized or legal sanctions against intercaste marriages.

DOMESTIC UNIT. The domestic unit is the parivar, as discussed above. A parivar is a group of related people who have a common interest in some ancestral property, which they jointly operate. Ideally and most commonly a parivar will consist of a senior man, his wife, perhaps his aged parents and unmarried brothers or sisters, his children, and some or all of their wives and children. There is no domestic cycle, or a changing sequence of forms for the family as a whole. Rather, the family structure is considered constant, and the members move through it according to their individual life cycles.

INHERITANCE. As with marriage, Punjabis may choose to be governed in matters of inheritance by custom or by religious laws as formalized in governmental acts: Christian, Hindu, or Muslim. Most follow custom, which varies by caste and/or region. This commonly makes all males

Although laws in both Punjabs provide for legally registered marriages, these are seldom used. Punjabi marriages generally occur according to customary forms.

equal sharers of their father's property from birth. If a man has one son, from the birth of that son they each have a half share in whatever was his ancestral property. If a second son is born, they all have a third, and so on. If there are four sons and one dies, all the survivors and the father divide his share equally. If a father sells his son's share or his own while the son is too young to formally agree, the son may, on reaching maturity, preempt the sale and reclaim the land by paying only the original purchase price.

Women have no birthrights in property, but they have a right to maintenance. In addition, a son's most sacred obligation is considered to be to his mother. For Hindus this idea is embodied in the notion of a sacred cow, worshiped simply because she is "like" mother. But the basic value is held by Muslims and Sikhs as well. For a son to refuse to care for his mother is almost unthinkable.

Within this general pattern, the customary laws of different communities differ in the way possible applications or interpretations are ordered. For example, in Hindu law generally, a son may demand a legal partition and take his share of the ancestral property at any time. In Jat customary law, the division will not take place unless the father agrees to it.

SOCIALIZATION. Both Punjabs have modern school systems, although Indian Punjab's is more extensive. In 1981 rural Indian Punjab had a literacy rate of 38 percent; Pakistani Punjab had a rate of 17 percent. In addition to public education, each state has extensive religiously sponsored educational institutions. But in both, the main locus of socialization is still the family itself, and the discipline imposed by the knowledge that all family members are also part of a common economic enterprise, on which they are mutually dependent. Girls are trained in their economic tasks by accompanying their mothers; boys, after about age 5, accompany their fathers.

The different religious communities have various concepts of initiation to adulthood, but there is no general Punjabi concept as such.

Sociopolitical Organization

SOCIAL ORGANIZATION. Both Punjabs have a multitiered administrative system with a centuries-long history. The basic units in this system are village, block or circle, *tehsil* (subdistrict), district, and state. For the last 150 years, the district has been the most important unit of administration and the lowest unit controlled by the elite national administrative service officers. In the imperial period, these district commissioners combined all the administrative functions: police, revenue, and judicial. Since independence the functions have been separated in both countries. Both governments also recognize an important legal distinction between villages, which are under direct state administration and in which land revenue is collected, and towns, which are under chartered municipal committees and which collect a wide range of property and business taxes, but not land revenue. (Information on caste is provided above in the section on kinship.)

POLITICAL ORGANIZATION. Early writers on Punjab often reported that villages and caste groups in villages were governed by *panchayats*, village councils. Beginning in 1952, Indian Punjab built on this tradition by establishing an elected panchayat for every village. Representatives from the panchayats in turn met in *panchayat samitis* at block and district levels. This system grew to play an important role in the agricultural planning that produced Punjab's green revolution. But the panchayats had no power to change their own mandates or control their own elections. When Punjab came under central administrative control during the prime ministership of Indira Gandhi, the panchayats, along with other elected bodies, were legally disbanded. Although they had no legal power to continue on their own, many still did so informally.

Pakistani Punjab has not supported village-level government. Instead, in the 1960s the government established "Basic Democracies," a system of councils from the "circle" level up to the province that began with the election in each village of one "basic democrat" per 1,000–1,500 voters. The councils were remote from villages and dominated by large landlords and administrators. The result is that Pakistani Punjab continues to have a much less egalitarian distribution of power as well as resources, retaining a much clearer two-class system. Since independence both Punjabs have had provision for legislatures, although Pakistani Punjab, with the rest of Pakistan, has been under military rule for much of the time and the provincial assembly has been suspended. The chief executive is a governor, appointed by the president of Pakistan, assisted by an administrative secretariat. Indian Punjab established its legislature on the basis of direct elections, and electoral districts with large numbers of lower-caste voters are designated as "reserved" seats for members of those groups, to ensure minority representation. Except when under central rule, the chief executive of the state is the chief minister, elected by a majority of the legislative assembly. Both Punjabs have organized political parties, which go back historically to the late nineteenth century.

Both Punjabs also have active factional systems, beginning at the village level and extending upward to motivate much of the statewide party activity. In villages, these groups are considered "secret" and are not publicly acknowledged. They reflect alliances among households, commonly focusing on efforts to gain or protect land or other major resources. At higher levels, local factions engage with regional political figures or other influential persons in a complex and fluid system of exchanges that shows little regard for ideology.

Finally, organized religious establishments have an important role in social and political mobilization. They provide a public forum to discuss government policies that government itself cannot control. Each year, many tens of thousands of people customarily travel to attend religious fairs at major shrines, and those who speak on such occasions normally apply precepts of the religion to events of the day, including events involving government. In Indian Punjab, the most important forum of this type is the Sikh Gurdwara system. In Pakistani Punjab, mosques have similar functions.

SOCIAL CONTROL AND CONFLICT. There is no one system of social control. Rather, each system of institutions has its own set of sanctions and its own discipline: commerce, household management, politics, the civil administration, kinship, law and customary law, and the religious organizations.

Generally, village life is highly competitive even while it is cooperative. Villagers know each other well. Thus conflicts seldom arise by miscalculation. Slights are assumed to be deliberate, and they usually are. Such conflicts tend to persist. Village factions serve to structure and manage them; there is seldom a means for resolving them.

According to a Punjabi saying, the sources of all conflicts are land, women, and water. More exactly, it is the need to control the means to perpetuate one's family and property. Thus the sources of conflict are indistinguishable from the bases of social control.

Religion and Expressive Culture

RELIGIOUS BELIEFS. As of the 1981 census, the population of Indian Punjab reported itself as being 37 percent Hindu, 61 percent Sikh, 1 percent Muslim, and a little more than 1 percent Christian, with smaller portions of Buddhists, Jains, and others. Pakistani Punjab is about 97 percent Muslim and 2 percent Christian, with small numbers of others.

RELIGIOUS PRACTITIONERS. Each religion has its own taxonomy of practitioners, and in addition there are many kinds of folk or customary practitioners. For example, a *jyotshi* would be a Brahman who professed some kind of ability to foretell the future, by astrology or other means. A *nai* is a barber. Since the last Sikh Guru enjoined his followers to leave their hair and beards uncut, nais in principle have little work in Sikh villages. But they commonly serve as ritual managers of weddings, while their wives work as midwives. There are Muslim and Hindu *sants* who obtain reputations for holiness and may attract supporters for activities such as maintaining or rebuilding a local shrine or for curing diseases. And there are storytellers, poets, singers, and preachers who go from village to village or from one religious event to another throughout the region.

CEREMONIES. Rural Punjabis of all religions share many ceremonies considered customary, associated with the individual life cycle, village life, and the round of the seasons. Most of the specific ceremonies associated with marriages come under this heading, as do ceremonies of birth, naming, and death. An important sequence of annual rituals celebrates the successive roles a woman plays in her life. The ceremony of *tij* is celebrated as the rains begin by young girls and their brothers in the house of their parents; in the fall harvest season *karue* is celebrated by newly married and older married women in the house of the young woman's parents or in-laws; and in March (in Punjab a time of pleasant weather and steady growth of the all-important wheat crop) *behairi* is celebrated by mothers and their young children in the house of the husband. On the night of Diwali, in October/November, all buildings and structures of a village are outlined in little oil lamps (*diwas*) and people ask God for prosperity; and in midwinter there is a ceremony called "Tails" (meaning cattle), when men go in the evening to collect sweets from houses where boys have been born in the village, build a fire of dung (the traditional cooking fuel) at the village gate, pray to God for the health of the boys and more in the future, and distribute the sweets to the village children who come to collect them. Farmers commonly offer first fruits at village shrines, and almost any start of a venture or stroke of good fortune is an occasion for distributing sweets.

ARTS. Punjab has generated distinctive forms of virtually all the arts, from dance to architecture, bawdy folk epics to sublime theological poetry.

According to a Punjabi saying, the sources of all conflicts are land, women, and water.

Religion is viewed as a source of strength and inspiration to meet the obligations of this world more than as a gateway to another.

The best-known folk dance is lively and complex *bhangra*, named for *bhang* (marijuana). In architecture, the most distinctive major form is that of the Sikh Gurdwaras, which blend Mogul and Rajput elements. In literature, the most famous and prominent forms are romantic epic poems. The main ones are *Heer Ranjha*, *Sassi Punun*, and *Mirza Shahiban*, all by Muslim authors. Older than these are thirteenth-century theological *sufi* poems of Shaik Farid. In the Sikh tradition, closely allied in sentiment and style to the sufi, the most notable groups of poems are by Guru Nanak (1469–1539) and Guru Arjun Dev (1563–1606). There are also numerous modern poets and writers on both secular and religious topics and an active film industry that relies heavily on melodrama, folksong, and dance.

MEDICINE. Punjabis support all the forms of medical practice available in India, and when they can afford it, generally prefer the Western.

DEATH AND AFTERLIFE. The main formalized beliefs concerning death and the afterlife are those of the three major religious traditions, but the Punjabi versions of these traditions are generally austere, individualistic, and pragmatic. Religion is viewed as a source of strength and inspiration to meet the obligations of this world more than as a gateway to another. Funeral practices vary according to religion.

Bibliography

Brass, Paul (1974). *Religion and Politics in North India*. Cambridge: Cambridge University Press.

Darling, Malcolm Lyall (1925). *The Punjab Peasant in Prosperity and Debt*. 4th ed. 1947. Bombay: Oxford University Press. Reprint. 1978. Columbia, Mo.: South Asia Books; New Delhi: Manohar Book Service.

Eglar, Zekiye (1960). *A Punjabi Village in Pakistan*. New York: Columbia University Press.

Kessinger, Tom G. (1974). *Vilayatpur, 1848–1968: Social and Economic Change in a North Indian Village*. Berkeley and Los Angeles: University of California Press.

Leaf, Murray J. (1984). *Song of Hope: The Green Revolution in a Panjab Village*. New Brunswick, N.J.: Rutgers University Press.

Michel, Aloys A. (1967). *The Indus Rivers: A Study of the Effects of Partition*. New Haven and London: Yale University Press.

Sims, Holly (1988). *Political Regimes, Public Policy, and Economic Development: Agricultural Performance and Rural Change in the Two Punjabs*. New Delhi: Sage Publications.

—MURRAY J. LEAF

SANTAL

Ethnonyms: Santhal, Saonta, Saonthal, Saunta

Orientation

IDENTIFICATION. The Santal are the largest of the tribal populations in South Asia. Santals are found in the three adjoining Indian states of Bihar, West Bengal, and Orissa. Migrants work in the tea plantations of Assam, with smaller groups elsewhere in India. There are also Santal communities in northeastern Bangladesh and in the Nepal Terai. Traditionally mixed farmers with a recent past of hunting and gathering, Santals have found their way to employment in agriculture and industry all over eastern South Asia. "Santal" is the only term currently used by outsiders for the tribe. It is also recognized as an ethnic term by the Santals themselves. *Hoṛ hopon ko* (human children) and *Hoṛ ko* (men) are used by them in a more traditional or ritual context.

LOCATION. The Santal heartland is the area known as the Chota Nagpur Plateau, a hilly area of crystalline Cambrian rocks, strewn with laterite and covered by deciduous forest. The area lies in northeastern India approximately between 22° and 24°30′ N and stretches from 84° to 87° E. Elevation ranges from 200 to 500 meters with mountains over 1,000 meters. Rainfall, concentrated in the July monsoon, totals about 100 to 130 centimeters. Mean temperatures range from 15° to 21° C in January to 26° to 29° C in July.

DEMOGRAPHY. The Indian census counted 3,640,946 Santals in 1971 (but did not count tea workers in Assam), and today the total number of Santals must be somewhat more than four million. It is difficult to say much about their population history, except that they are the largest tribal group in South Asia. The regions of the core Santal area seem to have been settled by different clans. Further migration led to a subdivision of land among subclans, still unevenly distributed over the area. In practice, however, each region today contains a number of clans, possibly the result of an ongoing process of migration.

LINGUISTIC AFFILIATION. The Santal language, Santali, belongs to the North Mundari Group of languages, itself part of the Austroasiatic Language Family. Writing was introduced by Norwegian missionaries in the late nineteenth century, and so Santali literature uses Roman characters. More recently, Santali has been written in Devanāgari.

History and Cultural Relations

The original home of the Santals is believed to have been the Champa Kingdom of northern Cambodia, which explains their affinities with the Mon-Khmer groups. Physical anthropologists usually classify them under the Austro-Mongoloid type. They probably entered India well before the Aryan invasions and came by way of Assam and Bengal, as their traditions indicate. They assume the existence of a Santal kingdom, a tradition which is supported by the collections of medieval Santal weapons at the Oslo Ethnographic Museum and by the remains of what may be identified as Santal hill forts from the medieval period. Little else is known of this kingdom to which Santal mythic traditions allude. Moreover, the mythic tradition recalls a war between the Santals and a part-Hindu prince, Mandho Singh, who was born of a Santal mother. Mandho Singh succeeded in recruiting followers among the Santals who followed him to the south of Nagpur, settled there, and became more Hinduized. Early contacts with the British led to the Santal rebellion of 1854–1856, in which some ten thousand Santals were killed. They became an important source of plantation labor, while missionary efforts introduced writing and had some influence on their culture. Only small numbers were actually converted to Christianity. Today, the Santals are among the main sources of support for the Jharkhand "tribalist" movement, in which they collaborate to some extent with other Mundari-speaking groups.

Settlements

Santals typically live in their own villages, laid out on a street pattern, and numbering from 400 to 1,000 inhabitants each. While separate villages are preferred, various groups sometimes live more or less separately in the tribal or low-caste quarters of mixed villages or towns. Santals never live in Untouchable quarters. In the large industrial towns of the Indian coal and iron belt, there are separate Santal quarters.

Santal houses are mud structures, but they are sturdily built and often decorated with floral designs. Roofs are tiled and slope toward all four sides. Houses have verandas and at least two rooms; the "inner room" (*chitar*) contains the ancestors and the granary protected by them. The main post (*khunti*), located at the center of the house, to which sacrifices are made on building the house, is of considerable ritual importance.

Economy

SUBSISTENCE AND COMMERCIAL ACTIVITIES. It is probable that Santals originally were hunters and gatherers, as their near relatives and neighbors, the Birhors, still are. Their knowledge of plants and animals is reflected in their pharmacopoeia (see below). In hunting technology, their past is evidenced by the use of some eighty varieties of traps. Later, their main economic base shifted to slash-and-burn agriculture and husbandry. Today, wet rice is grown in terraced fields; on the plains, irrigation by canals and ditches is used. Several varieties of rice are grown along with some sixteen varieties of millet. Leguminous vegetables, fruit, mustard, groundnut (in Orissa), cotton, and tobacco are important crops. The Santals keep cattle, goats, and poultry and are nonvegetarian. Fishing is important whenever they have access to rivers and ponds. The economy of the Santals is biased toward consumption, but they sell or barter (in Bihar) goats, poultry, fish, rice and rice beer, millet, groundnut, mustard seed, vegetables, and fruits when a surplus is available.

Migrant labor plays an important role; many Santals have migrated to work in plantations, mines, and industries. In Bengal, some are gardeners or domestic servants. A small educated elite includes politicians, lawyers, doctors, and engineers, while considerable numbers of Santal women work as nurses. Seasonal or temporary migration is particularly important for women, who are working in construction or mining.

INDUSTRIAL ARTS. Santals are expert at wood carving, but this craft, like ironwork, is declining both in quality and importance. Such products were mainly made for their own ceremonial use. Basketwork, weaving of mats, and manufacture of dishes and cups from *sal* leaves (*Shorea robusta*) are crafts still of commercial importance, as are rope making and the manufacture of string beds (*charpay*). Santal woodwork formerly included the building of impressive carts and advanced wooden utensils. They still make a large number of musical instruments. While industrial arts have declined, beautiful artifacts are still found, cherished as private heirlooms. Santal women also brew rice beer and alcohol, made from mohua flowers (*Madhuca indica*).

TRADE. Santals sell their products for cash or barter at tribal markets; rice money was still in use in Bihar in the 1970s. Some trade is also done with Hindu villages and towns, mainly the marketing of agricultural and craft products. Women

The Santals have a long tradition of suspicion in regard to the diku, "foreigners," above all toward the dominant Hindu population of the area.

♦ **terraced fields**
A technique of forming narrow but more or less level fields along steep hillsides. Where the fields are for irrigated rice they have to be absolutely level to hold the water, but for other grain crops and potatoes they simply hold the soil to prevent erosion and allow access by the farmers and their equipment.

dominate this trade, while the main male preserve is the sale of goats and cattle.

DIVISION OF LABOR. Hunting was always a male activity, gathering activities being dominated by women. In agriculture, men plow and sow, while women transplant and weed; division of labor by gender extends through most agricultural work. Boys and young men herd the cattle; women do the milking, collect the dung, and collect fuel in general. Poultry is tended by women, who also catch freshwater crabs, shrimps, etc. in the ponds; fishing by boat or with large land nets is done by the men. Women, as noted, dominate most trade. Ironwork, woodworking, and rope making are male activities; basketwork, weaving, and leafwork are done by women. Ritual specialists are traditionally male; women are formally excluded from such activities.

LAND TENURE. Traditionally land was held by usufruct, for slash-and-burn agriculture. With the introduction of wet rice cultivation, local descent groups descended from the clans of the original settlers divided village lands between themselves. The village priest got an additional allotment. The British introduced individual holdings (*ryotwari*). Members of subclans, not represented among the village founders, were originally landless and are still accorded inferior status.

Kinship

KIN GROUPS AND DESCENT. The Santals are divided into 12 clans and 164 subclans. They are patrilineal and strictly endogamous; their principal function is ceremonial and referential. The clans (*paris*) are ranked according to old functional divisions: the Kisku were kings, the Murmu priests, etc. There is an allusion to mythical wars between clans, ending in a ban on intermarriage. The ranking of clans is reflected in a slight tendency to hypergamy. Subclan hierarchy is expressed in terms of senior/junior distinctions as well as pure/impure; subclan identities focus on modes of sacrifice. On the village level, the local descent group is of major organizational importance. Here genealogical knowledge extends backward for only three to four generations. In some areas, there is a tendency for certain clans to intermarry unilaterally over several generations, forming a marriage alliance, but this practice never assumes the form of prescriptive marriage. Of greater importance, however, is the principle of alternate generations, which explains a whole range of joking and avoidance relationships. Politically, kinship is overshadowed by the functions of local chiefs and priests.

KINSHIP TERMINOLOGY. The two main principles of the terminology are the distinctions between consanguine relatives and between affines. In address, there is a merging of all cousins into the sibling category. Despite the lack of a clear prescriptive alliance system, there is a tendency to marry the classificatory mother's brother daughter. The most distinctive Munda feature of the system is the alternation of generation (which recalls very clearly the Australian tribes). There is a slight tendency to have clan hypergamy—possibly a result of Hindu influence.

Sociopolitical Organization

SOCIAL ORGANIZATION. Although, as noted, there is a traditional hierarchy of clans, the Santals are basically egalitarian, thus contrasting strongly with their Hindu neighbors. Economically, however, there are considerable differences in wealth and status. The clans and subclans, on the one hand, and the villages and regions, on the other, are the most important internal divisions. The senior male member of the local descent group enjoys a certain authority and prestige derived from ritual functions, as do the religious specialists (priests and *lojhas*) and the chiefs. Proficient hunters and orators likewise acquire prestige. Political leaders in the modern arena, like the charismatic leaders of the past, become sources of authority. District chiefs (*parganas* and *désmanjhis*) may enjoy a considerable status when successful in the settlement of disputes. Differences of wealth are expressed in the ability to employ servants. The well-to-do Santal families employ laborers on a contract basis and sometimes grant them land.

POLITICAL ORGANIZATION. In general, authority tends toward a charismatic rather than a traditional pattern. At the village level, the most important political institution is the village assembly, which has no head. This institution directly confronts the "council of the five elders," who represent the "five brothers" of the Santal tradition and are the village chief, the messenger of the village, the one responsible for young people's morals, the village priest, and his assistant.

At the intervillage level, the pargana (chief of twelve villages), who is sometimes enthroned as a petty king, presides over the tribal court. He also leads intervillage ceremonial hunting, with the "hunting priest" at his side. The hunt is the occasion for a court. Likewise, the pargana is assisted by the "country chief" and the messenger who both carry out his orders.

For Indian Santals, villages and districts are subjects of *panchayati raj* (local government),

♦ **usufruct**
The right to use land or property without actually owning it.

sometimes overlapping and sometimes in competition with the traditional institutions.

SOCIAL CONTROL. The sources of conflict among Santals can be summarized as: sexual offenses, land disputes, conflicts over money, cases of evil eye, jealousy, and witchcraft. Many cases are settled by compensation, usually through tribal assemblies, which still function parallel to, and sometimes in competition with, the Indian courts. The most general of these traditional assemblies is the Santal Lo bir Sendera, "the judgment of the burnt forest," which is convened at the time of the traditional intervillage hunts. Village assemblies likewise play an important role in the settlement of disputes. Witchcraft accusations are common. The witch is identified by ritual specialists, either a *janguru* or an ojha. Traditionally this naming led to the death of the witch.

While some sexual offenses, including rape, are usually settled by compensation through the mediation of the village assembly, the major offenses of incest and breach of tribal endogamy are primarily the responsibility of the local kin group, which excommunicates and—at least traditionally—kills the offenders. Excommunicates, like witches, are ostracized by their relatives. Land disputes may be cited as the main example of conflicts that are settled by Indian courts.

CONFLICT. The Santals have a long tradition of suspicion in regard to the *diku*, "foreigners," above all toward the dominant Hindu population of the area. This is clear not only from history (e.g., the Santal rebellion) but even more from the content of their myths and folklore, where the foreigner is the source of death, sickness, and other calamities. In practice, there has certainly been a history of exploitation by Hindu merchants, moneylenders, and labor brokers. Today this conflict continues mainly within the framework of the Indian political system, where Santals tend to support either the Jharkhand "tribalist" movement, working for a semiindependent state, or the Maoist Communist party, working for land reform and control of the means of producing, especially mines and plantations.

Religion and Expressive Culture

RELIGIOUS BELIEFS. The Santal pantheon includes about 150 spirit deities, generally called boṅgas. These deities include a large number of separate classes, impossible to enumerate here. Some relate to the subclan, but even here we must distinguish between the boṅga of the place of origin of the clan and its ancestral boṅga. Each village has a sacred grove, where we find represented the boṅgas common to the Santal tradition. They are generally benevolent. The forest boṅgas, however, are malevolent, and include the souls of people who died an unnatural death.

Hindu influence is particularly notable in the appearance of Hindu goddesses as tutelary deities of Santal ojhas. On the one hand, these goddesses patronize Santal witches and introduce disease; on the other hand, their patronage is necessary to combat the same evils. Hindu symbols, such as the trident, have become potent ritual paraphernalia of the Santal ojha.

RELIGIOUS PRACTITIONERS. The village priest (*naeke*) is identified, with his wife, as representative of the original Santal couple. Their functions are mainly related to festivals and recurrent annual ceremonies. He consecrates the animals offered to the sacred grove deities. He often compares himself with the Brahman of the encompassing society.

The Santal ojha, a healer and diviner, has several functions. He drives away the malevolent deities, divines the causes of disease, administers remedies according to considerable medical knowledge, and expels pain from the body. He learns his basic magical formulas (mantras) from his master, but he also adds to them from his own experience. An important element in his repertoire is the sacrifice of his own blood (conceived as menstrual blood) to the boṅgas, for which he receives a fee. In the rationalization of his practice he employs several Hindu concepts, yet remains fundamentally within the Santal cultural framework. This position between two cultures enables him to interpret his own culture and society.

CEREMONIES. Life-cycle rituals, such as initiation, marriage, and burial are celebrated individually. But after burial, the final ceremony of gathering the bones and immersing them in water becomes a collective rite. Other collective rites are related to the agricultural cycle: sowing, transplanting, consecration of the crops, and harvest festivals, as well as the annual festival of the cattle. Another cycle concerns the old hunting and gathering traditions, notably the seasonal hunts. The most important, however, of the festivals related to the old hunting and gathering society is the flower festival, which is also the festival of the ancestors and related to the fertility of women. Rainmaking rituals, held in the spring, involve the ritual participation of the village priest, who has the power to produce rain.

ARTS. Santal oral literature is rich and includes folktales, myths, riddles, and village stories, and much of it has been recorded or written.

*Witchcraft
accusations among
the Santal are
common. If
identification is
confirmed by ritual
specialists, the witch
is put to death.*

Publication began in 1870 with the work of the Norwegian missionaries, who also left large archives of texts written by the Santals themselves. There is also a certain amount of literature in Santali: newspapers, Christian books, and schoolbooks.

Traditional songs are many and various, including ritual texts, dances in homage to the boṅgas, obscene songs sometimes related to hunting or the punishment of offenders, etc. They are classified according to tunes that in turn relate to content. Christian songs have been composed to the same pattern. Each type of song is accompanied by a particular type of traditional dance. The sexes dance separately except when love songs are performed.

More recently, a tradition of folk theater, often with political overtones, has developed. The main plays have been written by cultural reformers like Ragunath Murmu, and together they present a message of modernization and tribal uplift for the Santal tribe as a whole. Among the visual arts, we may mention the designs decorating houses, the traditional wood carving, and the traditional jewelery, sometimes made of iron and silver.

MEDICINE. Traditional medicine is highly developed among the Santals and implies a surprising range of botanical and zoological knowledge; more than 300 species each of plants and of animals are identified and used in the pharmacopoeia. There is even, in the organization of botanical knowledge, a hierarchization based on the morphology of plants. The making of remedies implies again a considerable practical knowledge of chemistry.

This medical knowledge is described in a Santal text from the turn of the century, which establishes a complete pathology defining and ranking symptoms and disease according to consistent criteria. Recent fieldwork data corroborates the value of this work, though there is a tendency nowadays to replace such remedies by ritual invocations.

For the Santals, modern medicine sometimes provides an alternative for healing without in any way replacing or superseding traditional medicine.

DEATH AND AFTERLIFE. Santal souls become boṅgas three generations after death, provided that the correct rituals have been performed. At cremation, some bones are collected by the main mourner (usually the eldest son) and kept for awhile under the rafters of the house. They are washed and fed ritually by female mourners with milk, rice beer, and sacred water. Thus, the mourning ritual displays the central Santal symbolism of flower and bone. The feeding of bones that are crowned by flowers expresses the complementarity of the principle of descent (bone) and the principle of affinity (flower = uterus). The chief mourner is possessed by and impersonates the dead and is questioned by the village priest. This dialogue aims at providing the deceased with the wherewithal of the other world. A year later, the bones are immersed in water, a ritual involving sacrifice of a goat. The dead now becomes an ancestor known by name; one month later the recitation of a ritual text releases him from identity to become a nameless ancestor. He now joins other ancestors in the ancestral room of the house and partakes in the offering of rice beer to the ancestors. Now his shadow, which was roaming between the worlds, goes to Hanapuri, the abode of the dead. Here Jom Raja, king of the dead, rules; the passage from there to the state of becoming a bonga is never made explicit.

The land of the dead is conceptualized as a place where certain individuals acquire the source of magic powers, while others are simply rewarded according to the way they have acted during their life. While the yogi returns to the world and achieves immortality, simple men endure the justice of Jom Raja. The idea of afterlife shows both Hindu and Christian influence.

Bibliography

Archer, William G. (1974). *The Hill of Flutes: Life, Love, and Poetry in Tribal India; A Portrait of the Santals.* London: Allen & Unwin.

Archer, William G. (1984). *Tribal Law and Justice: A Report on the Santal.* New Delhi: Concept.

Bodding, P. O. (1927). *Santal Folk-Tales.* Vols. 1–3. Oslo: Aschehoug.

Bodding, P. O. (1932–1936). *A Santal Dictionary.* Vols. 1–4. Oslo: Det Norske Videnskaps Akademi.

Bouez, Serge (1985). *L'alliance chez les Ho et les Santal de l'Inde.* Paris: Société d'Ethnographie.

Carrin-Bouez, Marine (1986). *La Fleur et l'Os: Symbolisme et rituel chez les Santal.* Paris: École des Hautes Études en Sciences Sociales.

—MARINE CARRIN-BOUEZ

SIKH

Ethnonym: Sardarji (address)

The approximately 18,000,000 Sikhs who reside in the Punjab and in scattered communities across the world share a reverence for "the ten gurus" (from Guru Nanak to Guru Gobind Singh) and the teachings of their scripture, the *Adi Granth* or *Guru Granth Sahib.* Worship is central for all

Traditional medicine is highly developed among the Santals and implies a surprising range of botanical and zoological knowledge.

devotees of Sikhism, India's youngest monotheistic religion, either in the form of daily observances at home or in corporate worship at the *gurdwara*, a building designated for congregational ceremonies and social events such as communal kitchens (*langar*) providing free food. Many Sikhs also observe a code of conduct and discipline that includes males wearing recognizable marks of orthodoxy (unshorn hair, a comb, a dagger, a steel bangle, and a pair of breeches), a ban on tobacco, and the use of common titles for male and female converts (Singh, "lion," and Kaur, "princess," respectively). This orthodox group, which has gradually grown to dominate the public life of the community, consists of *amritdhari* Sikhs (those who have undergone baptism). Other Sikhs in the community do not participate fully in the code of conduct but are accepted as Sikhs because of their devotion, participation in worship, and respect for the gurus.

The Punjab was and remains the homeland for Sikhs. There Sikhism evolved, incorporating various tribes and castes including a preponderance of Jats, rural agriculturalists, who along with others have shown great courage in times of persecution and political turmoil. The first guru and founder of the faith was Guru Nanak (A.D. 1469–1539). By early in the seventeenth century the following had grown to such an extent in the Punjab area that it was seen as a threat to the Mogul rulers. Within a

century the last of the ten gurus had died (by 1708), and open rebellion had broken out. By the middle of the eighteenth century bands of Sikh guerrillas were hastening the collapse of the Mogul administration in their area, while keeping Afghan invaders at bay (1747–1769). These military struggles continued, but by the end of that century Ranjit Singh had emerged as leader of the Sikhs and maharaja of the Punjab, a position he retained until his death in 1839. This continuing military activity had greatly encouraged a tradition of constant military readiness in the community, and it largely explains the role of Sikh men in the modern armies of India, Pakistan, and Great Britain.

The numerous shrines and holy spots associated with major events in Sikh history, most notably the Golden Temple at Amritsar, are primarily found in districts now in Pakistan or the Indian Punjab. In the late nineteenth century, Sikhs began migrating to Southeast Asia, Africa, Europe, and North America, and nowadays large and often very affluent and highly educated Sikh communities can be found in those areas. A new group of Western Sikh converts, the *gora* or "white" Sikhs led by Harbajan Singh, are associated with many gurdwaras (houses of worship) in North America and also have their own organizations. Although the centrality of the Punjabi language and culture within the daily lives of Sikhs sometimes divides those with roots in the Punjab

The frustrations of their minority status, coupled with economic problems, helped foster growing Sikh militancy in the 1970s, culminating in the demands for a separate Sikh nation.

ORTHODOX GROUP

Sikh children practice writing Punjabi on slates near Jhulunder. Sikhs have separated themselves from Hindus in areas such as politics, ritual, social practice, and theology. Punjab, India. (Earl Kowall/Corbis)

See also

Jat, Punjabi

from these new converts, common worship, beliefs, and a shared code of discipline tend to overcome the divisions aroused by ethnicity.

Sikh identity and institutions have been strengthened and at times modified by experiences over the last century. Organizing themselves into Singh Sabhas in the late 1800s, Sikhs have emphasized their separateness from Hindus in areas such as theology, ritual, social practice, and politics. These efforts culminated in the dramatic, nonviolent campaign (1920–1925) to wrest Sikh gurdwaras from the hands of British-supported managers, often Hindu, and to place responsibility for all shrines in the hands of the community. Since 1925, the Sikh Gurdwara Protection Committee (a central management committee) has supervised the shrines and also played an important role in Sikh politics. The frustrations of their minority status, coupled with economic problems, helped foster growing Sikh militancy in the 1970s, culminating in the demands for a separate Sikh nation, "Khalistan." The resulting government attack on armed militants in the Golden Temple (1984) led to a period of continuing political chaos in the Punjab, sparked dramatic episodes such as the assassination of Prime Minister Indira Gandhi and the resulting massacres of many Sikhs, and fostered debate among Sikhs about ideology and strategy. Despite this turbulence, Sikhs still maintain a positive outlook and continue to provide leadership in public institutions and professions wherever they reside.

Bibliography

Barrier, N. Gerald (1970). *The Sikhs and Their Literature*. New Delhi: Manohar.

Barrier, N. Gerald, and Van Dusenbery, eds. (1990). *The Sikh Diaspora*. New Delhi: Chanakya.

McLeod, W. H. (1990). *The Sikhs*. New York: Columbia University Press.

McLeod, W. H. (1990). *Who Is a Sikh*. Oxford: Oxford University Press.

O'Connell, Joseph, et al., eds. (1988). *Sikh History and Religion in the Twentieth Century*. South Asia Series. Toronto: University of Toronto Press.

—N. GERALD BARRIER

SINHALESE

Ethnonyms: Singhlese, Sinhala

Orientation

IDENTIFICATION. The Sinhalese speak the Sinhala language, live in the southwestern portion of Sri Lanka (formerly Ceylon), and are predominantly of the Theravada Buddhist faith. The name derives from the term for "dwelling of lions," an allusion to the mythical founder, an Indian princess who mated with a lion.

LOCATION. Sri Lanka is located between 5°55′ and 9°51′ N and 79°41′ and 81°5.3′ E. Sinhalese traditionally make their homes in the wet zone of the central, south, and west provinces of Sri Lanka, where they are divided into two regional subgroups, the Kandyan Sinhalese of the central highlands, and the Low Country Sinhalese of the maritime provinces. With the rise of government-sponsored internal colonization projects after 1945, considerable internal migration has occurred to the central and northeastern dry zone.

DEMOGRAPHY. In 1989 the population of Sri Lanka was estimated as 17,541,000. The population density averages approximately 252 persons per square kilometer and the population is growing at the rate of 1.8 percent per year. Sinhalese constitute 75 percent of the population of Sri Lanka. Sri Lanka's principal ethnic minority, the Sri Lanka Tamils, comprise an additional 11 percent, while the Sri Lanka Moors, a Tamil-speaking Muslim group, constitute 6.5 percent. Other minorities include the so-called Indian Tamils, descendants of tea plantation workers imported by the British, who comprise 8 percent, and small communities of Malays and Europeans.

LINGUISTIC AFFILIATION. Sinhala is an Indo-European language of the Indo-Aryan Group and was brought to Sri Lanka by North Indian settlers in approximately 500 B.C. Subsequently Sinhala evolved in isolation from its North Indian origins but in close proximity with the Dravidian tongues of southern India, which gave it a distinct character as early as the third century B.C.

Settlements

Only about one of five Sinhalese lives in a city; Sri Lanka is still predominantly rural country, and—unlike most Third World countries—its rural-urban balance has not changed significantly in this century. Educational and medical facilities are available in most rural areas and a very low rate of industrialization gives rural villagers little reason to migrate to the cities. In the traditional "one village, one tank" pattern, the village (*gama*) is situated downstream from an artificial reservoir. Ringed around the paddy fields are the traditional two- to four-room houses, each situated in its own garden and separated from others. Traditional houses are made of mud and plaster and thatched with woven palm fronds. Wealthier villagers construct stucco houses roofed with ceramic tiles.

Economy

SUBSISTENCE AND COMMERCIAL ACTIVITIES. Subsistence agriculture, supplemented by marginal employment in service-related occupations and government employment, characterizes the economic life of most rural Sinhalese villagers. Rice holdings are small and marginally economic at best. Plowing is often done with water buffalo; tractors are numerous but more often used for light transport. Seed is sown and the young shoots are transplanted by hand; harvesting and threshing are also done manually. "Green revolution" hybrids are widely used but are underfertilized. Additional subsistence food crops include fruit (jackfruit, breadfruit, and coconut), vegetables, and manioc, which has become a significant staple-of-last-recourse for the poor. Domestic animals include cattle, buffalo, goats, sheep, chickens, and pigs. There is significant nonplantation, as well as village-based cash crop activity, especially in the highlands, that produces chilies and other spices, poultry and eggs, goats, honey, herbs employed in Ayurvedic medicine, onions, tomatoes, pulses, cereals, vegetables, *ganja* (marijuana), and potatoes. A major supplement to the village economy is direct government income for schoolteachers and village officials. Low Country Sinhalese achieved early prominence in coconut, rubber, and low-elevation tea plantation agriculture as well as trade and light mining. Marginal employment is available for many in tea, rubber, and coconut processing.

INDUSTRIAL ARTS. The classical Sinhalese achieved remarkable feats in irrigation engineering, but the technology was lost in the collapse of the dry zone civilizations and Sinhalese today show little interest in engineering, mathematics, or science, preferring liberal arts subjects. "Hands-on" technical work is stigmatized by linkages to low-caste occupations, serving to inhibit children's hobbies, vocational education, and

HISTORY AND CULTURAL RELATIONS

Sinhalese dynastic chronicles trace their origins to the exile of Prince Vijaya and his 500 followers from his father's kingdom in north India. According to the chronicles, which portray Sri Lanka as a land destined to preserve Buddhism, Vijaya (the grandson of a Hindu princess and a lion) arrived in Sri Lanka at the moment of the Buddha's death. In the third century B.C., the Sinhalese king converted to Buddhism. By the first century B.C. a Sinhalese Buddhist civilization, based on irrigated rice agriculture, arose in the dry zone, with capitals at Anuradhapura and Pollunaruva. By the thirteenth century A.D., however, a major civilizational collapse occurred for reasons that are still debated (malaria, internal conflict, and South Indian invasions are possible causes), and the population shifted to the southwest. At the time of first European contact in 1505 there were two Sinhalese kingdoms, one in the central highlands at Kandy and one along the southwestern coast near Colombo. The Portuguese deposed the southwestern kingdom (but not Kandy) and won converts to Roman Catholicism among fishing castes

along the coastal littoral, but they were driven out of Ceylon by the Dutch in 1656–1658. A legacy of Portuguese times is the popularity of Portuguese names such as de Silva, Fernando, and de Fonseca among Low Country Sinhalese. The Dutch instituted the Roman-Dutch legal system in the maritime provinces (but not Kandy, which remained independent) and cash crop plantation agriculture, including coffee, cotton, and tobacco, but few Sinhalese converted to Protestant Christianity. The British took over the island's administration in 1798, brought down the Kandyan Kingdom in 1815, and favored the growth of a European-owned coffee and tea plantation sector in the central highlands. By the early twentieth century a new elite of English-speaking, largely Low Country Sinhalese rose to prominence in trading, petty industry, and coconut and rubber plantation agriculture. In 1932, universal adult suffrage and internal self-rule were granted. Without having to fight for its independence, Ceylon was granted freedom in 1948 becoming a constitutional democracy on the Westminster model. The country was

governed for eight years by an ostensibly panethnic national party of unity, but in 1956 a Sinhalese populist politician won a landslide victory on a platform to make Sinhala the sole official language of government affairs. Tensions rose as Tamils resisted this move, and communal riots occurred in 1958. Sinhalese youths also grew disaffected as the economy stagnated and unemployment mounted in the 1960s. A 1971 insurgency by an ultraleftist Sinhalese youth group called the Janatha Vimukthi Peramuna (the "People's Liberation Army," or JVP) nearly toppled the government. There were significant Tamil-Sinhalese riots again in 1977, 1981, and 1983; by 1984 a violent Tamil separatist movement had all but driven Sinhalese security forces out of the Tamil north and east; a 1987 accord with India brought 60,000 Indian peacekeeping troops to the Tamil provinces but set off a violent antigovernment campaign by the JVP, which now articulates right-wing Sinhala-chauvinist ideology in addition to its ultraleftist doctrine. More than 17,000 Sri Lankans have died in communal and political violence since 1977.

*"Hands-on"
technical work
among the Sinhalese
is stigmatized by
linkages to low-caste
occupations,
hampering
vocational
education and
technological
literacy.*

See also

Tamil of Sri Lanka

technological literacy, while Western imports have all but wiped out traditional arts and crafts. Efforts to industrialize Sri Lanka have met with little success, and the country shows one of the lowest rates of industrial growth of any South Asian country since its independence. Severe and growing unemployment and landlessness, particularly among rural youth, has contributed to the JVP youth militancy.

TRADE. Apart from the prevalence of subsistence agriculture, the Sri Lankan rural economy is almost completely cash-based, with barter and reciprocity restricted to kin-group transactions. Village boutiques involve villagers in debt that frequently results in an impecunious farmer becoming little more than a tenant on his own land; village shopowners are thus able to amass large landholdings. Shops in town sell additional consumer items, and weekly village markets provide marginal economic niches for itinerant traders and village cash-crop agriculturalists. Transport is provided by bullock carts, tractors pulling flatbed trailers, old automobiles, and light trucks. Internal trade, foreign investment, tourism, and economic growth are all casualties of the Tamil rebellion and the JVP insurgency.

DIVISION OF LABOR. Traditional Sinhalese society is male dominated and patriarchal, with a strong division of labor by sex and a tendency to stigmatize female roles (women are considered to be ritually impure at times owing to the "pollution" of puberty, childbirth, and menstruation). Men are responsible for the provision of food, clothing, shelter, and other necessities, while women prepare food and care for children. Traditionally, a family lost status if it permitted its women to engage in extradomestic economic roles, such as menial agricultural labor or cash-crop marketing. Men and women led separate lives aside from the convergence brought about by their mutual obligations. The entry of women into higher education and the professions is beginning to alter this pattern.

LAND TENURE. Traditionally the descendants of the village founder owned inheritable (but not marketable) shares (*panku*) of the village paddy lands. The actual holdings were sensitively adjusted to suit water availability and to reduce inequities in water distribution; when holdings were reduced below the economic level, a group of villagers hived off into the wilderness, constructed a new tank, and founded a new village. British reforms that defined all wilderness as Crown land and eliminated multiple claims to existing plots of land seriously eroded this system

and, as land came on the market, a new class of rice land investors (called *mudalalis*) acquired substantial holdings but left the farming to clients holding the lands by a form of traditional sharecropping tenancy (*ande* tenure). Population increase has led to severe and still growing landlessness.

Kinship

KIN GROUPS AND DESCENT. The largest kin group is the "microcaste" (*pavula*), an endogamous and corporate bilateral kin group that represents the convergence of several families' bilateral kindreds. Pavula members share paddy lands, often dwell together in a hamlet, and cooperate in agriculture, trade, and politics. A pavula's members share a unique status within the caste; the group's internal equality is symbolized through life-cycle rites and communal feasts. Descent is fully bilateral in practice, but noncorporate agnatic descent lines linking families with aristocrats of the Buddhist kingdoms may be maintained for status purposes.

KINSHIP TERMINOLOGY. The Sinhalese, including Moors, use Dravidian terms, which are associated with symmetrical cross-cousin marriage.

Marriage and Family

MARRIAGE. Most marriages are arranged between the two families, with a strong preference for cross-cousin marriage. Marriage implies caste equality, but with a double standard: to preserve the status of a microcaste (pavula), women must marry men of equal or higher status within the caste; men, however, may have sexual relations with women of inferior status without threatening their family's status. Among the Kandyans, who are governed by Kandyan law, polyandry is rare, though villagers say it can be convenient for all concerned. Polygyny is also rare and may amount to no more than the husband's appropriation of sexual services from a low-ranking female servant. The bride normally comes to live with her husband, and this pattern (called *deega*) establishes a relationship of mutual aid and equality between the husband and his wife's kin. In the less common *binna* residence, in contrast, the groom—who is usually landless—goes to live with his wife's parents (matrilocal residence) and must work for his father-in-law. Dowry is rarely paid unless a woman marries a man of higher status within the caste (hypergamy). The marriage may not involve a ceremony if it occurs between equals and within a pavula. Among the Kandyans, property is held individually and is not fragmented by the dissolution of marriage, which is easy and common. Among the Low Country Sinhalese, who are governed by Roman-Dutch law, matrilocal residence is very rare and hypergamy, coupled with dowry, is more common. After marriage the couple's property is merged and in consequence the allied families resist the marriage's dissolution.

DOMESTIC UNIT.   The smallest kin group is the commensal unit or nuclear family: a wife, unmarried children, and husband. Among traditional Kandyan Sinhalese, there may be more than one commensal unit in a house, but each has its own cooking area. Westernized families adopt the European pattern even for complex households.

INHERITANCE.   In sharp contrast to Indian practices property is divided equally among all children, including women, although wealthy families control a daughter's property and use it as an instrument of marital alliance; among wealthy families, dowry may be paid in lieu of inheritance.

SOCIALIZATION.   There is a strong preference for male children, who may receive better care; the infant mortality rate for girls is higher. Girls are expected to work harder than boys and may be given significant household chores as young as age 5 or 6, and they may be taken out of school at an early age even though education is compulsory for all children aged 5 to 14. Children are cared for by their mother, with whom they sleep except in highly Westernized households. Children are expected to show respect to their elders. Curiosity, initiative, and hobbies are not encouraged. Schools repeat this pattern by emphasizing rote instruction and avoiding vocational subjects. Especially among the landed and high castes, the family is strongly authoritarian: deference to one's parents and acceptance of their decisions is required, on penalty of excommunication.

Sociopolitical Organization

Sri Lanka is a parliamentary democracy with a president as the head of the state. There is a strong two-party system in which politics are dominated by the centrist United National party (UNP, in power since 1977) and the center-to-left Sri Lanka Freedom party (SLFP). Both are dominated by Sinhalese politicians and appeal to Sinhalese sentiment.

SOCIAL ORGANIZATION.   The Sinhalese caste system is milder than its Indian counterpart; it lacks Brahmans and the stratifying ideology of Hinduism. Most Sinhalese villages lack caste organizations (*panchayats*) which, in India, punish

transgressions of caste; enforcement of caste endogamy, for instance, is left up to families. Because property is inherited bilaterally, however, families have very strong incentives to enforce endogamy (this is one reason for their authoritarian nature). The Sinhalese ideology of caste is derived from precolonial feudalism, in which castes of almost all statuses were granted lands, contingent on their performing services for the king and local aristocrats. The highest caste, the agricultural Goyigama, comprise about half the population and count among their ancestors the aristocrats of the precolonial kingdoms. Among the Kandyans, additional castes include service castes, such as the Hena (washers), Berava (drummers), Navandanna (metalworkers), and the "lowest castes," such as the Rodiya, who were formerly itinerant beggars. Among the Low Country Sinhalese, three highly entrepreneurial maritime castes (Karava, Salagama, and Durava) have risen to economic and political prominence in this area, which has long been under European influence. Most Sinhalese continue to see caste as a positive principle of social affiliation but deny that castes should be ranked or given special privileges. A major consequence of the colonial period was the development of an achievement-oriented national elite based on education and especially knowledge of English. Persons of low caste have won membership in this elite. However, local elites continue to be dominated by high castes or locally powerful castes.

POLITICAL ORGANIZATION.   The Sri Lankan state, an artifact of colonial rule, is excessively centralized and politicized; the country's provinces are governed by agents appointed by the president, and virtually all services—roads, railways, education, health services, tax collection, government-owned corporations, land registry and allocation—are administered by centrally controlled ministries. Efforts to devolve power and resources to the provinces, including the Tamil Northern Province and Eastern Province, have been opposed by Sinhalese chauvinists who see devolution as an erosion of Sinhala sovereignty. Members of parliament select the candidates for government positions, including even the lowliest menial jobs, on the basis of political loyalty. Politicization has severely eroded the autonomy of the civil service and judiciary. The JVP insurgency and its popular support can be seen in part as a broad-based rejection of an unresponsive and corrupt political system, but the JVP offers few solutions.

SOCIAL CONTROL.   Within the village gossip and ridicule are strong forces for social conformity.

In sharp contrast to Indian practices property is divided equally among all children including women.

Most Sinhalese continue to see caste as a positive principle of social affiliation but deny that castes should be ranked or given special privileges.

The family regulates behavior through the threat of excommunication (deprivation of lands and family support in seeking employment). With growing landlessness and unemployment, however, many families are increasingly unable to deliver on their material promises and the threat of excommunication has become an empty threat. The JVP insurgency is in part a rejection of parental authority.

CONFLICT. Traditionally, violence occurred within families, often as the result of long-standing grudges and obsession with one's "enemies," real or imagined. In the absence of sustained economic growth, aspirations for social mobility cannot be fulfilled, and as competition and anomie grow more intense, ethnic and political violence occurs as various groups compete for state resources. A late-nineteenth-century riot occurred between Buddhists and Christians; later clashes pitted Sinhalese against Muslims (1915). After the "Sinhala only" language act of 1956, communal riots involving Tamils and Sinhalese occurred in 1958, 1977, 1981, 1983, 1987, and 1990. There was an aborted military coup in 1963, and violence often occurred during and after elections. Political violence has now become institutionalized in the form of youth insurgencies and government "death squads."

Religion and Expressive Culture

Sri Lanka is remarkable in that almost all major world religions are practiced there (Buddhism, Hinduism, Islam, and Christianity), but Buddhism has received special state protection under Sri Lankan constitutions since 1973. Nearly wiped out by Christian conversions and neglect in the late nineteenth century, Buddhism was revived by reformers who borrowed techniques of proselytization and political activity from Christian missionaries—and in so doing altered Buddhism by expanding the role of the laity and emphasizing a rigid Victorian morality.

RELIGIOUS BELIEFS. More than 70 percent of Sinhalese are Theravada Buddhists, but there are substantial (and largely non-Goyigama) Roman Catholic communities in the maritime provinces. Often thought by foreign observers to contradict Buddhist teachings, the worship of Hindu gods in their temples (*devale*) meets religious needs *bhikkus* (Buddhist monks) cannot address, and the pantheon's structure symbolically expresses the pattern of traditional political authority. At the lower end of the pantheon are demons and spirits that cause illness and must be exorcised.

RELIGIOUS PRACTITIONERS. In Theravada Buddhism, a true Buddhist—a monk, or bhikku—is one who has renounced all worldly attachments and follows in the Buddha's footsteps, depending on alms for subsistence. But few Sinhalese become bhikkus, who number approximately 20,000. Buddhist monastic organizations are known collectively as the *sangha*, which is fragmented into three sects (*nikayas*); most bhikkus live in the sect's temple/residence complexes (*viharas*). The largest and wealthiest sect, the Siyam Nikaya, is rooted in the precolonial Kandyan political order and is still limited, in practice, to Goyigama aspirants. The smaller Amapura Nikaya emerged from the nineteenth-century social mobility of the Karava, Salagama, and Durava castes of the maritime provinces. The smallest sect, the Ramanya Nikaya, is a reform community. Traditionally, the sangha was interdependent with Sinhalese kingly authority, which both depended on and supported the monastic orders, which in turn grew wealthy from huge land grants. The veneration of the famed Tooth Relic (a purported tooth of the Buddha) at Kandy was vital to the legitimacy of the Kandyan king. Bhikkus continue their tradition of political action today and are influential in right-wing chauvinist organizations. At village temples of the gods (*bandaras* and *devas*), non-bhikku priests called *kapuralas* meet the needs of villagers in this life.

CEREMONIES. Holidays include the Buddhist New Year (April), Wesak (May), the anniversaries of the birth, death, and enlightenment of the Buddha, the annual procession (*perahera*) of the Tooth Relic at Kandy (August), and the Kataragama firewalking pilgrimage (August).

ARTS. Classical Sinhalese civilization excelled in Buddhist architecture, temple and cave frescos, and large-scale sculpture. In colonial times artisans, now few in number, produced fine ivory carvings, metalwork, and jewelry. A mid-twentieth century school of Sinhalese painting called "The Forty-three Group" sparked an impressive renaissance of Sinhalese art, expressed in a traditional idiom in the temple paintings of George Keyt. A twentieth-century tradition of Sinhalese fiction and poetry has attracted international scholarly attention. A government-assisted Sinhala film industry produces many popular films, and a few serious ones have won international awards.

MEDICINE. The Indian-derived traditional sciences of Ayurveda (herbal medicine) and astrology, taught and elaborated at Buddhist schools (*piravena*) and practiced by village specialists, provide a comprehensive traditional explanation of health and illness.

DEATH AND AFTERLIFE. The possibility of enlightenment and freedom from rebirth is restricted to those withdrawn from the world; a layperson hopes for a more advantageous rebirth based on a positive balance of bad against good acts (karma) and performs meritorious acts (such as supporting the sangha) toward this end. In popular belief a person who dies without fulfilling cherished dreams may become a spirit and vex the living. The dead are cremated, unless Christians.

Bibliography

Gombrich, Richard F. (1971). *Precept and Practice: Traditional Buddhism in the Highlands of Ceylon.* Oxford: Clarendon Press.

Gunawardana, R. A. L. H. (1979). "The People of the Lion: The Sinhala Identity and Ideology in History and Historiography." *Sri Lanka Journal of the Humanities* 5:1–36.

Roberts, Michael (1982). *Caste Conflict and Elite Formation: The Rise of a Karava Elite in Sri Lanka, 1500–1931.* Cambridge: Cambridge University Press.

Yalman, Nur (1967). *Under the Bo Tree: Studies in Caste, Kinship, and Marriage in the Interior of Ceylon.* Berkeley: University of California Press.

—BRYAN PFAFFENBERGER

TAMIL

Ethnonyms: Tamiḷar, Tamilian

Orientation

IDENTIFICATION. Indian Tamils are those who speak Tamil. Their homeland in India from ancient times was known as "Tamiḷ Nāḍu" (land) or "Tamiḷ akam" (home), now largely coterminous with the state of Tamil Nadu plus the small territory of Pondicherry. Tamils are also found in Sri Lanka, Malaysia, Fiji, Britain, and North America.

LOCATION. Tamil Nadu is the southwesternmost state of India, extending from Madras city to the southern cape, between about 8° and 13° N and 76° and 80° E. The state is 130,058 square kilometers in area and was formed along with other linguistic states after the independence of India. It is mostly a sunny plain draining eastward with the Kaveri River basin in its center. The Western Ghats are mountains separating Tamil Nadu from Kerala; these rise to 2,400 meters in two places, near the mountain towns of Ootacamund and Kodaikanal. The rest of the state is tropical and moderately hot, with virtually no winter. Most of the rain comes with the northeast monsoon beginning in October, while the southwest monsoon begins in June. Rainfall is roughly 75 centimeters per year, but with the high evaporation and runoff, much of the state is semiarid, with large stretches of thorn-tree wasteland. There is no apparent source of more water for the state's agriculture, industry, and cities—nor is there enough water to support further population growth—and shortages are already occurring.

DEMOGRAPHY. There are about 60 million Indian Tamils. The 1991 census counted 55.6 million persons in Tamil Nadu and 8 million in Pondicherry, and it had an undercount of about 4 percent. There are perhaps 5 million Tamils around Bangalore and elsewhere in India, and a lesser number of Telugus and other ethnic groups in Tamil Nadu. The state has 1,024 males per 1,000 females, a marginal surplus compared with all of India. The density is 461 persons per square kilometer, compared with 267 for India as a whole. Literacy of persons above age 7 is 64 percent. Annual population growth has come down to 1.3 percent. Tamils are about 38 percent urban, the highest such percentage of any major ethnic group in India.

LINGUISTIC AFFILIATION. Tamil belongs to the Dravidian Language Stock, which includes at least 21 languages mostly in south and central India and is altogether different from the Indo-Aryan languages of north India. The four largest Dravidian languages are spoken in the four linguistic states comprising south India. The language and script of modern Tamil are directly descended from the Tamil of more than 2,000 years ago, and because of high consciousness about the purity of the language there has been some tendency to resist incorporation of Sanskrit or Hindi words. The modern regional spoken dialects of Tamil, including the Tamil of Sri Lanka, do not differ widely, but standard literary Tamil as taught in schools does differ grammatically. Malayalam, the language of Kerala, was considered in the ancient literature as Tamil, but in medieval centuries it gained status as a separate language.

HISTORY AND CULTURAL RELATIONS. Tamils consider their language to be the "most pure" of the major Dravidian languages. Its roots are from western India, Pakistan, and further westward. Dravidian must have been spoken in the Indus Civilization around 2500 B.C., diffusing through Maharashtra to the south, especially after 1000 B.C. with adoption of the horse and iron and with the black-and-red pottery dating from a few centuries B.C. There is no hint of the earlier lan-

See also

Tamil of Sri Lanka

Tamil

In the twentieth century the tendency has been to reject features ascribed to north India and to reemphasize Tamil identity in language, deities, foods, and state politics.

guages that might have been spoken in south India by cattle-keeping cultures or the hunters. The ancient literature defines Tamil Nadu as reaching from Tirupati (a sacred hill northwest of Madras) to Cape Comorin. Writing, urbanization, classical kingship, and other aspects of complex Indian civilization came to Tamil Nadu about the fifth to second centuries B.C. by sea, appearing on the southern coast in a progression parallel to diffusion of those features from Gujarat to Sri Lanka. There are also legends of early cities, including an ancient city of Madurai on the coast. The earliest Tamil inscriptions are in Buddhist and Jain caves of about the second century B.C. The present Madurai, capital of the enduring Pāṇḍiya kingdom, had an academy that produced the Tamil Sangam literature, a corpus of unique poetical books from the first to third centuries A.D. that mention sea trade with Europeans. Other Tamil kingdoms were the Cōḷas in the Kaveri Basin, the Cēras of Kerala, and from the seventh to ninth centuries the Pallavas at Kanchipuram near Madras. The Cōḷas developed a magnificent civilization in the tenth to thirteenth centuries, and for a time they ruled Sri Lanka, the Maldives, and large parts of Indonesia. Tamils were never absorbed by a north Indian kingdom, but from the sixteenth century the land was ruled by Telugu-speaking dynasties from the Vijayanagar Empire. The British built a trading center, Fort Saint George, in Madras in 1639 and ruled all Tamil Nadu from 1801 to 1947. The French, having lost to the British in south India, held Pondicherry and Karikal, now administered as a separate Union Territory within India. The process of Sanskritization, partial assimilation into the overarching Indian pattern of civilization, progressed in late medieval centuries. But in the twentieth century the tendency has been to reject features ascribed to north India and to reemphasize Tamil identity in language, deities, foods, and state politics.

Settlements

The predominant settlement pattern is one of nucleated unwalled villages, often having 2,000 persons or even more than 5,000, while traditionally retaining a village character. The layout usually has well-defined streets, with sections for separate castes, each marked by one or more little temples for their respective deities. House types range from one-room huts of mud and coconut-leaf thatch of the laboring and low castes to larger houses with courtyards and two-story brick and tile houses of the higher castes or landowning

families. Tamil villages look relatively neat, with most houses whitewashed. Early each morning the women of a house apply cow-dung wash on the street before the front door and create a pattern design on the ground with chalklike powder. A large village usually has several open wells, one large temple, a common threshing floor with big trees, a piece of land or two for cremation or burials, and in many cases a catchment reservoir for irrigating its rice land. Now nearly all villages have electricity, but only a minority of houses use it.

Economy

SUBSISTENCE AND COMMERCIAL ACTIVITIES. Land is classified into wet land growing mostly irrigated rice and dry land growing rainfed or well-watered crops. Large irrigation systems were built from at least the second century B.C., especially on the Kaveri River, and there was an elaborate political economy supporting agricultural productivity especially developed by the medieval Cōḷas. The kings also built catchment reservoirs for growing rice and gave them to the villages to maintain, as recorded in temple inscriptions; there are 40,000 such reservoirs in Tamil Nadu. The main field crops are rice, pearl millet and several other millets, sorghum, several types of pulses and oilseeds, coconuts, bananas, Indian vegetables, and condiments. Mango and tamarind trees abound. The oxen plow and harrow, pull ox carts, draw buckets of irrigation water, and turn oilseed presses, while cows yield milk that is given to children and made into curds and buttermilk. A village may have chickens, buffalo, goats, sheep, and donkeys that carry the washers' clothes. Fishing castes occupy the long coast. Money was issued by ancient kings so there is a long tradition of moneylending, capitalism, and overseas trade; rural economic transactions became monetized in the nineteenth century. Since the 1960s farmers have installed many thousands of electric irrigation pumps and have taken up commercial crops such as sugarcane, cotton, and peanuts. But now agricultural growth is beginning to lag compared with industries and urbanization.

INDUSTRIAL ARTS. Artisan castes still make fine products of clay, leather, reeds, cotton, wood, iron, brass, silver, and gold. Ox carts are sturdy and still numerous. Tamils are known for their fine weaving, which even the ancient Romans imported, and today they have the most successful handweavers' cooperatives in India, though power looms are taking over. Great brass water vessels are given at weddings, though plastics are becoming popular. Bricks, roofing tiles, cement artifacts, and wooden furniture are now in demand everywhere.

TRADE. The streets of large villages and towns are lined with shops, and there are still many weekly markets. Complex networks of wholesalers, agents, and financiers deal with all types of products. Now auctions are common for moving produce, and the trucking industry is intensively developed. Muslim traders are prominent in trade.

DIVISION OF LABOR. Men plow, harrow, and handle the rice harvest, but women do transplanting and weeding for which their daily wage is less than that of men, and they may also milk cows. Tools of trade such as an ox cart, potter's wheel, fishing net, or nowadays a taxi are not handled by women. Women do kitchen work, cleaning, washing, and child care, but men may also do all these tasks, and professional cooks and washers are men. Women now may be teachers, nurses, and office employees.

LAND TENURE. Landownership is well established with a system of official recording. Agricultural land is increasingly held by dominant farmer castes, while every village has its cadre of landless low-caste laborers available for fieldwork. There are few estates of great landowners, though temples and mosques still own some land for income. Sharecropping and tenancy are moderate, simply part of the socioeconomic dynamics. Because of population pressure and speculation, in many areas the market value of land now exceeds its productive economic value.

Kinship

KIN GROUPS AND DESCENT. The Dravidian kinship system with its preference for cross-cousin marriage has been the subject of wide anthropological theorizing. The household is linked by a network of kin alliances established through marriage within the caste. Fictitious exogamous clans (*gotras*) are found in only a few Brahmanized castes. Lineage depth beyond three generations is not important in most families. Most Indian Tamils are patrilineal and patrilocal, though the Dravidian system equally accommodates matrilineal descent as among some Sri Lanka Tamils, including Muslims, and some castes in Kerala. But patriliny is less strong than in north India, and matrilateral links remain important. A woman is expected to go to her natal home for childbirth, especially for the first child, and may remain there for a few months for nurturance and to gain confidence and training in infant care.

KINSHIP TERMINOLOGY. For a male, all females are classified as sister (or parallel cousin, unmarriageable) or as female cross cousin (marriageable). The preferred marriage for a male is generally to his mother's brother's daughter, while in some groups his father's sister's daughter and his own elder's sister's daughter are also quite acceptable, as are more distant cognates classifiable as female cross cousins. Kin terms are few compared with north Indian languages; for example, *māman* is wife's father/father-in-law, mother's brother (who may be the same person), and father of any female cross cousin or anyone so classified. For a man, *makan* is own son, brother's son, and son's male parallel cousin. Terms distinguish between elder and younger siblings, or those so classified, and between some elder and younger siblings of the parents, or those so classified. Some classical scholars tried to force explanations in terms of the north Indian system and Indo-Aryan languages, in which the bride's family is wife giver and hypergamy is built-in, but this misses the essence of the Dravidian system. About half of Tamil marriages now are between such kin, but the categories are so strongly maintained in the language that the kinship pattern is imposed on all interpersonal relations. This has been structurally analyzed by anthropologists. Louis Dumont sees it as essentially a matter of affinities established by marriage, in which women are exchanged among families that define the kin network; this has political and economic implications. Others see it as essentially a system of marriage rules that is an ideal or a mental representation. Still others have tried to explain it in terms of heritable body substances and biological ideas. The system has also been analyzed in terms of Freudian psychology: a man will want a marriage union enabling him to continue the warmth and protection of his mother, namely, through his mother's brother together with his daughter. For Tamils, as Thomas Trautman and others show, the whole conceptual structure is as much in the language as in the actual behavior. A recent approach proposed by Margaret Trawick is that the pattern itself is something like an art form that is perpetuated as any form of expressive culture; moreover, it creates longings that can never be fulfilled, and so it becomes a web of unrelieved tensions and an architecture of conflicting desires that are fundamental in the interpersonal relationships of Tamils.

Marriage and Family

MARRIAGE. Marriages are arranged by elders, ideally by a sister and brother for their respective

Tamils are known for their fine weaving, which even the ancient Romans imported.

*For a Tamil male,
all females are
classified as sister
(or parallel cousin,
unmarriageable) or
as female cross
cousin
(marriageable).*

♦ **sacred thread**
*A continuous cotton thread
worn across the right
shoulder by males of the
Brahman varna, once they
have undergone initiation
(upanayana). It should be
worn at all times, and it is
highly symbolic. A sacred
thread may also be worn by
Kshatriyas and Vaishyas,
but in these latter two cases
it should be made of wool
and linen, respectively.*

son and daughter. A girl is technically able to marry soon after the ceremony of her first menstruation, but now her marriage may be postponed a few years, and boys often do not marry until their twenties. The marriage is performed by a Brahman priest or by a caste priest in the home of the bride. Her family bears expenses and provides a modest dowry, though in some castes there is more bride-wealth given than dowry. Recently among educated classes the expectation of dowry has vastly increased, in line with the costs of education and the presumed benefits of the marriage for the girl and her family. Ideally a married couple sets up its own house, usually in the boy's village, but if necessary they may move in with the boy's or alternatively the girl's family until this is possible. Marriage is a religious ceremony and only a few register it with the state. Divorce is quite difficult for higher castes with strict social expectations, but separation and new alliances or marriages are common among castes whose prestige is not so damaged thereby. Widow remarriage is forbidden or rare among castes having Brahmanic values, but not among lower castes.

DOMESTIC UNIT. The average household size is five to six people, with preference for an extended nuclear family. It is not unusual for an old person or couple to live alone, especially if they have few assets. Occasionally there are joint families when there is land or a business to keep intact. Most influential families also have a live-in servant or servant family. When Tamil men migrate to a city for work, they try to take their wives and children along, so there is not a severe deficit of females in Tamil cities, but this means that urbanized families find their rural roots weakening.

INHERITANCE. Under Tamil Hindu tradition, sons divide the land because they may live by cultivating it, and daughters get the mother's gold and jewels either as dowry or as inheritance, but there are many exceptions and people can arrange their own wills.

SOCIALIZATION. Tamils are a child-friendly society, and they socialize children so that they grow up with a firm sense of well-being. There is less tension than in many societies, and hospitality is often genuine. Men and women play with small children easily, pass them around, and may take in relatives' children temporarily or even adopt them. Several male gods have important child forms whose pictures are in houses everywhere, and Tamil literature creates abundant images of children. Toilet training is early and seemingly natural, with little use of diapers. The first rice is fed at about 6 months, and weaning is sudden after a

year or so. Giving of food is important in relationships, and a mother may feed rice with her hand to a child up to the age of 6 or more. Adults frequently treat children with benevolent deceit and verbal ambiguity, and within the dynamic family context the child learns a wide range of verbal and emotional expression and body language. Children of school age are occasionally punished by tweaking of the ear or beatings given by the father. Girls are expected to help in household work as soon as they are able, and boys not in school may do agricultural activities or herd animals from about age 10. Most villages have their own elementary schools, and many now have middle schools also, so most children now become literate. There are no initiation rites except for high-caste boys at the time they put on the Brahmanic sacred thread. Girls have an important life-stage ceremony at the time of their first menstruation; a feast is given to relatives and friends, who bring presents. At this time the girl puts on a sari and is technically marriageable. This ceremony is found associated with the Dravidian kinship and marriage system.

Sociopolitical Organization

SOCIAL ORGANIZATION. Within a village, society is ordered principally by caste. Particular castes or blocks of castes occupy sectors of a village, with the ritually lowest castes sometimes in satellite hamlets. Large villages or towns may have a Brahman street with a temple at the end, formerly off-limits to low castes, and in the past Brahmans would generally avoid eating food not prepared at home. Ritual pollution and purity differentiate a wide range of human interaction, though not as strongly as in the nineteenth century and hardly at all now in public life in towns. Village coffee shops until the 1980s had benches for middle castes, low seats for the low laboring castes, and places on the floor for the lowest sweeper caste; there were separate cups for these three groups. Now rank by caste ascription is slightly declining even in villages, while the more numerous agricultural castes are increasing their landholdings and using elections to enhance their political power. Brahmans have for decades used their education to enter urban life, while many landless laboring caste people also have migrated to cities for urban labor and service jobs. The urban educated class and government officers utilize English to preserve their power and privileges, so now even in small towns many Tamils are demanding that schools offer English-medium education for their children.

POLITICAL ORGANIZATION. Traditionally many castes, or the larger ones, had caste *pan-*

chayats (councils) that enforced caste behavioral norms, and sometimes there were informal village panchayats. In recent decades the state government has set up elected village panchayats, which were supposed to take over village government and development. But these have been neglected because state politicians tended to view them as threatening. Statewide political parties competing for people's votes have infiltrated most rural institutions, and in the main members of state-level parties espousing Dravidian identity are elected. Dominant and landholding families manage to enhance their economic and political power through these new mechanisms, while the relative position of the laboring and low castes remains about the same as before.

SOCIAL CONTROL. Sources of tension in a village are family and caste norms of behavior, caste differences, and disputes over land. Caste or village elders can pronounce embarrassing punishment for violators of behavioral norms, particularly in sexual matters. Caste conflicts sometimes erupt over scarce resources, such as the rights of certain castes to use wells in time of water scarcity. Families basing prestige on land may engage in long litigation. An individual who feels wronged may wield a sickle against another, which may be occasion to call the police. The lowest administrative level is the *taluk*, usually centered in a particular town, with offices for police, land registration, and electricity supply, a local court, and usually high schools for boys and girls. The second level of administration is the district, of which there are twenty in Tamil Nadu; as throughout India, the district is headed by a collector, who has wide powers. The third level is the state, with Madras as its capital.

CONFLICT. Tamils have no destructive conflict with adjacent linguistic or ethnic groups, nor do Hindus have much conflict with the 6 percent Christian and 5 percent Muslim Tamil minorities. They tend to sympathize with the Sri Lanka Tamils in their struggle for political autonomy or independence. Tamils are suspicious of the overwhelming numbers and political power of north Indians and resent any attempts to "impose" Hindi on them, so Tamil Nadu does not require teaching of Hindi in schools. English is in fact favored over Hindi. The modern political system with its elections has provided a new arena for verbal conflict.

Religion and Expressive Culture

RELIGIOUS BELIEFS. Village Hinduism is vibrant, as are the imposing, large, and ancient temples in the center of all the old towns. Village beliefs are focused on a large number of deities, with most castes or social groups claiming a special deity. Female deities are more numerous and are worshiped for their power to intervene in healing, fertility, and other life situations. Male deities are protectors and dominate the landscape, especially Murugan, whose image stands on many stone hillocks and especially on Palani Hill, where people make special pilgrimages to him as protector of Tamil Nadu. By the process of Sanskritization over many centuries, most local deities acquired linkage with Sanskritic or Brahmanic deities. Among Brahman castes the distinctions between the sects of Shiva and Vishnu are maintained, but not always in village religion. It is very common that a person needing assistance of the power of the deity to solve some problem in life will make a vow to bend the will of the deity; for example, one may promise that if one's son passes his examination, if a disease is cured, or if an infertile woman gives birth, one will undertake some pilgrimage or make some gift to the deity. Tamil Catholics make similar vows. There is a strong stream of devotionalism (*bhakti*) in Hindu literature and in the practice of modern Hindus, Christians, and Muslims.

CEREMONIES. Among the most important religious events in villages are the birthdays of the special deities, which are celebrated with processions in which the deity is taken from the temple and carried around the village and with night entertainment performances. Festival days of the deities of major temples, as of Madurai or Palani, are regional Tamil festivals in which hundreds of thousands of pilgrims throng those places. Pongal is a distinctive Tamil festival, in which kin groups boil rice in front of their special temple and eat it communally. This occurs in January, along with Māṭṭu Pongal, in which oxen are honored, their horns painted red and green, and garlanded. North Indian festivals such as Holi and Dassara are far less important, though Tamils celebrate Dīpāvali (Diwali), the festival of lights. The Tamil New Year is widely celebrated, in mid-April.

ARTS. South Indian music, dance, and architecture were enhanced in Tamil Nadu in late medieval centuries by royal patronage, while north India was under the Moguls. There is no question that Bharatanāṭyam dance, preserved in the temples, along with south Indian classical instrumental and vocal music, are among the highest classical art forms anywhere; they are far too complex to discuss here. Tamil temples, immediately distinguishable by the soaring towers (*gōpuram*) above the gateways, are imposing living institutions. Large temples have tanks, thousand-pillared halls of stone, passages for circumambulating the deity, and an infinite number of sculpted images and figures, all done according to ancient architectural rule books. In villages today, troupes are commissioned to perform all-night musical narrations of epics such as the Tamil version of the *Rāmāyaṇa*, itinerant drama troupes are popular, and there may be magician entertainers, transvestite dancers, and fortune-tellers.

MEDICINE. The medical systems are: Ayurveda, based on Sanskrit texts; Siddha, a south Indian system using strong chemicals and herbs; Unani, the Muslim system; and Mantiravāti, the use of magical phrases (mantras) and herbal medicine that are found in villages everywhere, whose practitioners also prepare amulets many people use to ward off disease. Allopathic (scientific) medicine is available in towns in government hospitals and private clinics. Disease etiology may be analyzed as multiple, with proximate and ultimate causes. There are multiple possible cures including herbs, medicines, mantras, diet, psychological change, and divine intervention. Tamils believe that bodily qualities should be in balance, and they classify foods as "hot" or "cold." Vegetarianism is widely practiced by upper and middle castes on grounds of both religion and health.

DEATH AND AFTERLIFE. The doctrine of rebirth is not actively held by the majority of Tamils, though those who tend to orthodoxy are likely to assert that the doctrine is taught. But according to an old belief or longing, a child who dies has a soul that will be reborn in the same household, and therefore on death burial may be under or near the home. Many Tamil castes bury their dead, but those influenced by Brahmanic tradition cremate them. At a burial in a middle-rank caste, the corpse is wrapped in a cloth and lowered into the grave, whereupon the male relatives carrying pots of water circumambulate the grave counterclockwise (an inauspicious direction), then break their clay pots in the grave, while the women stand by watching. Death pollution lasts for a number of days that varies by caste; after that the house is cleansed and there is special food. For an important man, a brick structure may mark the grave, and there is an annual ceremony of offering food on the death anniversary.

Bibliography

Clothey, Fred (1978). *The Many Faces of Murukan: The History and Meaning of a South Indian God*. The Hague: Mouton.

PILGRIMAGE

Tamil pilgrims sit at an entrance to the Sri Minaskshi Hindu Temple. The temple attracts people from all over the country. Madurai, Tamil Nadu, India.
(Jeremy Horner/Corbis)

Daniel, E. Valentine (1987). *Fluid Signs: Being a Person the Tamil Way*. Berkeley: University of California Press.

Dumont, Louis (1983). *Affinity as Value: Marriage Alliance in South India, with Comparative Essays on Australia*. Chicago: University of Chicago Press.

Dumont, Louis (1986). *A South Indian Subcaste*. Delhi: Oxford University Press.

Trautmann, Thomas R. (1981). *Dravidian Kinship*. Cambridge: Cambridge University Press.

Trawick, Margaret (1990). *Notes on Love in a Tamil Family*. Berkeley: University of California Press.

Wadley, Susan, ed. (1980). *The Powers of Tamil Women*. South Asian Series, no. 6. Syracuse, N.Y.: Syracuse University.

—CLARENCE MALONEY

TAMIL OF SRI LANKA

Ethnonyms: Tamiḻarkaḷ (Tamil people), Tamilian

Orientation

IDENTIFICATION. Linguistically and culturally related to the Tamil- and Malayalam-speaking peoples of southern India, Sri Lankan Tamils have long resided in their traditional homelands (the northern and eastern cultural regions of Sri Lanka), and interacted with the neighboring Sinhalese. The products of their unique geographical and historical circumstances are a distinct culture and society. Predominantly Hindus, Sri Lankan Tamils call their traditional homelands Tamil Eelam, a term that originally meant "Tamil Sri Lanka" but has now become virtually synonymous with the Tamils' quest for a separate state in the predominantly Tamil-speaking Northeastern Province. Sri Lankan Tamils distinguish themselves from the so-called "Indian Tamils," who are Tamil-speaking descendants of south Indian Tamil laborers brought to Sri Lanka to work nineteenth-century British tea plantations, as well as from the indigenous, Tamil-speaking Muslim population of Sri Lanka, the Sri Lankan Moors, who dwell in the eastern coastal region and in the central highlands.

LOCATION. Sri Lanka is located between 5°55′ and 9°51′ N and 79°41′ and 81°53′ E. Sri Lankan Tamils traditionally made their homes within the present Northern and Eastern provinces of Sri Lanka, within the dry zone. The center of Sri Lankan Tamil population and culture is the densely populated Jaffna Peninsula of the extreme north; other Tamil population concentrations are found on the island of Mannar

and along the eastern coastal littoral, stretching from north of Trincomalee to Batticaloa. In recent times, many Sri Lankan Tamils have migrated to the North Central Province and to Colombo; almost half the Sri Lankan Tamil population dwells outside the group's traditional homelands. Significant overseas communities of Sri Lankan Tamils in London, Australia, and Malaysia maintain close ties with families back home; foreign remittances are a significant element in the Sri Lankan Tamil economy.

DEMOGRAPHY. In 1989 the population of Sri Lanka was estimated at 17,541,000, with an average population density of 252 persons per square kilometer and a growth rate of 1.8 percent per year. Sri Lankan Tamils constitute approximately 11 percent of the island's population. Many—perhaps as much as 60 percent of the population—are refugees from nearly a decade of fighting.

LINGUISTIC AFFILIATION. The Tamil spoken by Sri Lankan Tamils is a distinct regional dialect of mainland Tamil, but the two are mutually intelligible; Sri Lankan Tamils consider their dialect to be purer than that of the mainland. They fear that their language's survival is threatened by a Sri Lankan government that, in 1956, made Sinhala the sole official language of government affairs and, in 1973, elevated Sinhala to the status of the national language. Although subsequent measures were taken to allow for the legitimate administrative and educational use of Tamil within the predominantly Tamil areas and Tamil was also made a national language by the 1978 constitution, Tamils nevertheless believe that Tamil speakers are subject to rampant discrimination and cannot effectively participate in Sri Lanka's national affairs.

History and Cultural Relations

The unique culture of Sri Lankan Tamils took on distinctiveness early from its close proximity to the Sinhalese and from waves of immigration from diverse regions of southern India. Many features of Sri Lankan Tamil culture, including village settlement patterns, inheritance and kinship customs, and domestic and village "folk religion," stand in sharp contrast to mainland Tamil customs. One possible reason is that the immigrants who created the first Tamil settlements in Sri Lanka appear to have come not just from the Tamil region of south India but from the Kerala coast as well. It is not known when Tamils first settled in Sri Lanka; fishing folk doubtless visited the coasts, seasonally or permanently, from an

Tamil of Sri Lanka

HISTORY AND CULTURAL RELATIONS

The unique culture of Sri Lankan Tamils took on distinctiveness early from its proximity to the Sinhalese and from waves of immigration from diverse regions of southern India.

See also
Tamil

early date, either for their own fishing needs or to engage in the pearl trade between Sri Lanka and Rome. During the period of the classical Sinhala dry zone civilizations (about the first twelve centuries A.D.), there is evidence that Tamil-speaking Buddhist merchants settled widely in the northern and eastern seacoast regions, where they built towns and shrines. By the thirteenth century, in the wake of the collapse of the Sinhalese dry zone civilizations, a Tamil Hindu kingdom arose in the Jaffna Peninsula, with a Hindu king and a palace. The Portuguese subdued the Hindu king in 1619, and as their geographic control was only over the coastal region, they left their legacy in coastal Catholic communities that persist today. In 1658, the Dutch followed the Portuguese. The Dutch codified the traditional legal system of Jaffna, but in such a way that they interpreted indigenous caste customs in line with Roman-Dutch definitions of slavery. Taking advantage of the situation, agriculturalists of the dominant Vellala caste turned to cash-crop agriculture using Pallar slaves brought from southern India, and Jaffna soon became one of the most lucrative sources of revenue in the entire Dutch colonial empire. In 1796, the British expelled the Dutch from the island. During the first four decades of British rule, few changes were made with the exception of granting freedom of religious affiliation and worship, a move that was deeply appreciated by the Tamil population. Slavery was abolished in 1844, but the change in legal status brought few meaningful changes to the status of Pallar and other low-caste laborers. More threatening to the structure of Tamil society was a sedulous conversion campaign by Christian missionaries, who built within the Tamil areas (especially Jaffna) what is generally considered to be the finest system of English-language schools to be found in all of Asia during the nineteenth century. In response to a tide of Christian conversions, Arumuka Navalar (1822–1879), a Hindu religious leader, reformulated Hinduism in line with austere religious texts so that it omitted many practices Christian missionaries had criticized as "barbarous," such as animal sacrifice. Navalar's movement was resented by many Hindus who felt that sacrifice and other practices were necessary, but his reformed Hinduism stemmed the tide of Christian conversions and gave educated Hindus access to a textual tradition of Saivism (called Saiva Siddhanta) that gave them pride in their religious traditions. Benefiting from the missionaries' English-language schools without converting to Christianity, many Sri Lankan Tamils (except those of low caste) turned away from agriculture—which became far less lucrative as the nineteenth century advanced—and toward government employment in the rapidly expanding British colonial empire. In this adaptation to foreign rule, an accommodative, utilitarian culture arose that stressed rigorous study in professional fields, such as medicine, law, and engineering, together with staunch adherence to Hindu tradition. Family support of educational achievement led to extraordinary success in the British meritocracy but to disaster later: after Sri Lanka's independence in 1948, many Sinhalese came to feel that Tamils were disproportionately present in Sri Lanka's esteemed civil service, professions, judiciary, and business affairs. In 1956, S. W. R. D. Bandaranaike won a massive electoral victory by appealing to these sentiments and promising to implement Sinhala as the sole official language of government affairs. Tensions over the language act led to the appalling 1958 riots, in which Sinhalese mobs attacked Tamils living in Sinhalese areas. The subsequent imposition of university and employment quotas radicalized Tamil youths; the first Tamil youth organizations included many unemployed graduates. In 1974, the Tamil political parties unified and called for the peaceful creation, through negotiation, of a separate Tamil state in the Northern and Eastern provinces, but largely because the Colombo government made few concessions and political moderates seemed content to wait the situation out, Tamil youths rejected their elders' politics and began a wave of violent assassinations, mainly aimed at Tamils who were suspected of collaborating with Sinhalese organizations. In 1981, Sinhalese security forces went on a brutal rampage in Jaffna, burning down Jaffna's library and terrorizing the population, which came to the conclusion that only the youth groups could protect them. The 1983 Colombo riots, which appeared to have the unofficial guidance and support of some sections of the government, effectively eliminated the Tamil business presence in Colombo and throughout the Sinhalese sections of the island, which further radicalized the Tamil people. After almost two decades of violence, the Colombo government has yet to make genuine concessions to the Tamil community and apparently believes the Tamil militants can be defeated by force. In the meantime, many Tamils have become refugees, hundreds of temples and schools have been destroyed, the Tamil middle class and intelligentsia have fled abroad, and tens of thousands of inno-

SETTLEMENTS

Sri Lankan Tamil regions are predominantly rural; even the towns seem like overgrown villages. The rural-urban balance has not changed significantly in this century, thanks to Sri Lanka's vigorous rural social service program and to an almost complete lack of industrial development. Traditional villages are nonnucleated and are internally differentiated by hamlets, in which members of a single caste reside. The only obvious center of the village is the temple of the village goddess. Lanes wander chaotically through the village, and homes are hidden behind stout, living fences (trees), which provide copious green manure for gardens. Land is traditionally divided into three categories: house land, garden land, and paddy land. Traditional houses are made of mud and thatch; wealthier villagers construct stucco houses roofed with ceramic tiles. Houses are situated within a private, fenced, almost secretive compound, which is usually planted with mangoes, coconut palms, and palmyras.

cents have died, often in massacres of unspeakable brutality.

Economy

SUBSISTENCE AND COMMERCIAL ACTIVITIES. Subsistence agriculture, supplemented by marginal employment, characterizes the economic life of most rural Sri Lankan Tamils. A significant source of income for many families today is foreign remittances. Save in the eastern coastal region, where irrigation produces high rice yields, rice agriculture in Tamil areas is extensive but rainfall-dependent and only marginally economic at best. Under import restrictions following Sri Lanka's independence, Jaffna became a major source of garden crops, including tomatoes, chilies, onions, tobacco, gourds, pumpkins, okra, *brinjal* (eggplants), betel, potatoes, manioc, and a variety of grams and pulses. Traditional agricultural practices make intensive use of green and animal manures, although the use of chemical fertilizers and pesticides is increasingly common. In coastal regions with limestone bedrock (and particularly in Jaffna), groundwater is intensively used to supplement rainfall; irrigation is rare, save in the eastern coastal region. Domestic animals include cattle and chickens. Significant foods of last recourse include manioc and the ubiquitous palmyra, which supplies starch from seedlings, molasses, jam, and a mildly alcoholic beverage called toddy. Rapid growth in the service section (especially retailing, transport, communications, banking, public administration, education, health services, repair, and construction) has created significant new employment opportunities.

INDUSTRIAL ARTS. Some members of the artisan castes (goldsmiths, blacksmiths, carpenters, potters, and temple builders) still create traditional goods, such as jewelry, ox carts, hoes, and cooking pots, although such goods face stiff competition from industrially manufactured plastic and aluminum goods, so that traditional goods are increasingly used only for ceremonial purposes. Very few industrial enterprises are located in Tamil regions, with the exception of the state-owned cement factory at Kankesanthurai along the northern coast, the chemical factory at Paranthan, and a paper factory at Valaichenei in the east. Private-sector ventures include manufacturing or assembly of garments, toys, candies, bottled juices, and soap. But indigenous goods are regarded as shoddy and receive stiff competition from imports and rampant smuggling.

TRADE. The rural economy is thoroughly cash-based. Village boutique owners and wealthy villagers often engage other more impecunious villagers in what eventually becomes debt servitude. Shops in town sell needed consumer items, and weekly village markets provide marginal economic niches for itinerant traders and village cash-crop agriculturalists. Transport is provided by bullock carts, tractors pulling flatbed trailers, old automobiles, light trucks, and the ubiquitous Ceylon Transit Board (CTB), the nation's bus service.

DIVISION OF LABOR. Traditional Sri Lankan Tamil society is male-dominated and patriarchal, with a strong division of labor by sex, arranged marriages, and a tendency to demean female roles. Female seclusion is a concomitant of family status, thus discouraging women from travel or work without a constant chaperone. However, significant new employment and educational opportunities for women cause many families to moderate the traditional division of labor as they seek additional income. In general, women are responsible

At age 5, an authoritarian relationship begins in which parents assume the right to determine the child's interests, prospective career, friends, attitudes, and spouse.

for domestic affairs while men work outside the home in agriculture, transport, industry, services, and government.

LAND TENURE.   Land is held outright but holdings tend to be both minute and geographically fragmented. Bilateral inheritance, coupled with population increase, compounds subdivision. Landlessness is increasingly common and delays or prevents marriage because traditional dowry customs require the married pair to be given lands and a house.

Kinship

KIN GROUPS AND DESCENT.   The largest kin group is the "microcaste" (called "our caste people" in Tamil), a section of a larger caste category within which people recognize common descent and a shared status. The microcaste is often distributed among several hamlets or wards in adjoining (or in some cases separated) villages; within the hamlet microcaste members cooperate in agriculture, ritual, trade, and politics. In sharp contrast to south Indian Tamil culture, descent is fully bilateral, save in the eastern coastal regions, where matrilineal descent is common.

KINSHIP TERMINOLOGY.   Dravidian terms, which strongly encourage symmetrical cross-cousin marriage, are used.

Marriage and Family

MARRIAGE.   Marriages among the "respectable" castes are arranged by parents and are accompanied by a large dowry—which, again in sharp contrast to the mainland Tamil pattern, includes lands and a house as well as movables and cash. Boys are expected to delay marriage so that they can help their parents accumulate enough wealth to marry off their sisters. A girl is technically eligible to marry after puberty but marriages are increasingly delayed, often into a woman's mid- to late twenties, owing to the difficulties involved in assembling the dowry and finding a suitable groom. The ideal groom is an educated, English-speaking, and government-employed man from a good, respectable family of the same microcaste; again ideally, he is terminologically a cross-cousin of the bride, but this is by no means necessary. The traditional Hindu wedding is a lavish affair that proclaims the family's status. For most couples the marriage is strictly an unromantic relationship, though it may grow into love later; a "good wife" submits to her husband's authority and serves him humbly and obediently. If a boy's parents discover that he has fallen in love, they take offense at this erosion of their authority

and try to break up the relationship; if a girl's parents discover that she has fallen in love, they express their disdain for her and take advantage of the situation by trying to strike a marriage deal that involves little or no dowry. More rarely, broad-minded parents may try to arrange what appears to be a traditional marriage even if the pair are in love. Residence after marriage is neolocal, the determining factor being the availability of lands and a house. "Love marriages" are increasingly common. Poorer and low-caste families can afford neither the dowry nor the ceremony, so their marriages are far more casual. Although wife abuse is thought to be common, it is publicly discouraged and, in strong contrast to India, women have a moderate degree of economic recourse in that they retain property rights under traditional Tamil law (which is upheld in the courts). Divorce is exceptionally uncommon and quite difficult legally, but among the poor and lower castes desertion and new, casual relationships are common.

DOMESTIC UNIT.   The average household is five or six persons; a married couple may be joined by elderly parents after these parents relinquish their lands and homes to other children in a form of premortem inheritance.

INHERITANCE.   In contrast to the mainland Tamil pattern, property is divided equally among all children—if any property is left after paying dowry at the going rates.

SOCIALIZATION.   Small children are treasured by most adults, who play with them, tease them, and create homes that are structured around their needs. A first rice-feeding ceremony takes place at approximately 6 months. Toilet training is relaxed and untraumatic. But there is a pronounced change at approximately age 5, when the parents begin the task of bending the child to their will. At this age there begins an authoritarian relationship in which the parents assume the right to determine the child's school interests, prospective career, friends, attitudes, and spouse. Tradition-minded families may force girls to leave school at puberty, following which there was formerly a ceremony (now done privately or not at all) that declared the girl to be technically eligible for marriage; she dons a sari and is no longer free to go about unchaperoned. Both the family and school declare to children, in effect, "Do what we tell you to do and we will take care of you in life." However, families and schools are increasingly unable to deliver on this promise. In the 1970s, Tamil youths found themselves receiving authoritarian pressure from their families to conform but faced bleak prospects; this double bind apparently contributed to a tripling of suicide rates, giving the Tamil areas of Sri Lanka one of the highest recorded suicide rates in the world. The rise of youthful Tamil militant groups is not only a political phenomenon but also a generational revolt; Tamil youths are rejecting not only Sinhalese rule but also the moderate politics and social conservatism of their parents.

Sociopolitical Organization

Sri Lanka is nominally a parliamentary democracy with a president as the head of state. The two-party parliamentary system is, however, dominated by Sinhalese, and the Sri Lankan Tamils are not sufficiently numerous to affect the outcome of elections. As a result moderate Tamil politicians who endorsed a parliamentary solution to Tamil grievances were ineffective and were swept away during the rise of Tamil youthful militancy.

SOCIAL ORGANIZATION. Sri Lanka's Tamil regions take on their distinctiveness owing to the presence of a dominant agricultural caste—the Vellala in the Jaffna Peninsula and the Mukkuvar in the eastern coastal region—on which the entire caste system is focused. In contrast to the Tamil mainland, Brahmans are few, and although they are considered higher than the dominant caste in ritual terms, they are generally poor and serve the dominant caste as temple priests or temple managers. Traditional intercaste services focused on the dominant caste and were both sacred and secular; the sacred services, such as the services provided by barbers and washers at life-cycle rites and by agricultural laborers at sacrificial rituals, served to define and regulate the low status of serving groups, while the secular ones created patron-client linkages that could endure for generations. Once bound to these sacred and secular relations, the artisan castes freed themselves by taking advantage of British liberalizations, the expanding service economy, and their urban residence. The rural service and labor castes remained in traditional relationships with the dominant castes until the mid-twentieth century, when the rise of a service economy created new marginal economic niches for these groups at the same time that mechanization rendered their labor unnecessary. Coastal fishing groups were never incorporated into the compass of agricultural caste solidarity, and in consequence they have long maintained their independence and resisted the stigma of low status. Prior to the twentieth century, caste statuses were upheld by a huge variety of sumptuary regulations, such as a rule prohibiting low-caste women from covering the upper half of their bodies. Caste discrimination in such matters, including temple entry and the use of public facilities and conveyances, is now illegal but persists in rural areas. In the face of the brutal occupation of Tamil areas by Sinhalese security forces in the early 1980s, caste rivalry diminished in intensity as the Tamil community pulled together. Prominent in many Tamil militant organizations are leaders from low or marginal castes; Tamil youthful militancy is thus a rejection of traditional caste ideology as well as a generational and ethnic revolt.

POLITICAL ORGANIZATION. The Sri Lankan state is partly an artifact of colonial rule: excessively centralized, it was devised to suppress regional rebellions as the British were consolidating their power. The failure of this overly centralized political system to devolve power to the provinces is one of the reasons for the rise of militant Tamil separatism. Unable to win concessions from the Colombo government, Tamil parliamentarians lost credibility and were pushed out of the Tamil community by militant youth groups, which were composed mainly of unemployed graduates as well as unmarried and rootless youth. Fractious and focused on a single, charismatic leader, these groups competed with each other—sometimes violently—until the 1987 incursion by Indian troops under the provisions of an accord between Colombo and Delhi; the Marxist-oriented groups, unlike other factions, accommodated to the Indian security forces, whose presence and actions in the Sri Lankan Tamil community were resented as much as those of the Colombo forces. After the departure of the Indian troops, those Marxist groups lost credibility. At this writing the Liberation Tigers of Tamil Eelam (LTTE), a nationalist group, has effectively eliminated—through attrition, fear, assassination, and massacre—all other potential sources of political leadership within the Tamil community. They have won support among peasant folk who believe that no one else can protect them from the Sri Lankan security forces, but expatriate Tamils frequently voice concern that LTTE rule will amount to a brutal dictatorship.

SOCIAL CONTROL. Within traditional Sri Lankan Tamil villages gossip and ridicule were potent forces for social conformity. The family backed its authoritarian control through threats of excommunication (deprivation of lands, dowry, and family support). With growing landlessness and unemployment, however, many families are unable to deliver on their material promises and

Many Sri Lankan Tamils have become refugees; their temples and schools have been destroyed; the middle class and intelligentsia have fled abroad; and thousands have been massacred.

the threat of excommunication has become increasingly empty. Suicide and youthful militancy are both manifestations of a general rejection by youth of traditional forms of authoritarianism.

CONFLICT. Traditionally, conflicts occurred within families and between castes. Interfamily conflict often arose from status competition, particularly when a wealthy ward attempted to cease relations with its "poorer relations" in pursuit of new, more lucrative ties with a similarly-endowed group. Long-standing grudges and obsession with "enemies," real or imagined, sometimes have led to violence. Dominant castes routinely used violence to punish subordinate groups that were taking on high-caste life-style attributes (such as using umbrellas), often by burning down huts or poisoning wells. Since the late 1970s, the ineffectiveness of moderate Tamil politicians has led many Tamil youths to conclude that the only solution to their problems lies in violence. The result has been the rise, not only in Tamil areas but throughout Sri Lanka, of a culture of violence, in which unspeakable acts of slaughter and massacre are commonplace. It has even spilled over into India where, in 1991, Sri Lankan Tamils assassinated the former prime minister, Rajiv Gandhi. Official estimates are that approximately 20,000 have died in Sri Lanka's civil war but unofficial estimates place the toll at two to three times that figure.

Religion and Expressive Culture

RELIGIOUS BELIEFS. Sri Lankan Tamils are predominantly Hindus, but there are significant enclaves of Roman Catholics and Protestants (mainly Methodists), who consider themselves to be full members of the Sri Lankan Tamil community. Discussed here is the Hinduism of Tamil Sri Lanka, a Hinduism that is at once utilitarian, philosophical, and deeply devotional. Shiva is the supreme deity but is not worshiped directly; Shiva bestows his grace by running your life so you aspire to nothing other than reunification with him. The perspective taken toward the other deities is frankly utilitarian: they are approached for help with mundane problems, such as illnesses, university exams, job applications, conflicts, legal problems, or infertility. Commonly worshiped deities include Shiva's sons Murukan and Pillaiyar, the several village goddesses (such as Mariyamman and Kannakiyamman), and a host of semidemonic deities who are thought to demand sacrifices. Of all deities, most beloved is Murukan, who bestows boons even on those who may be unworthy, to the extent that they devote themselves to him.

RELIGIOUS PRACTITIONERS. In temples that conform to the scriptural dictates of the medieval temple-building manuals (called *Agamas*), the priests are Brahmans. A small caste of non-Brahman temple priests called Saiva Kurukkals performs the rites at non-Agama temples, particularly shrines of the goddess Amman. The officiants at village and family temples, called *pucaris*, are ordinary villagers with whom the temple's god has established a spiritual relationship, often through a form of spirit possession. Here and there one finds temple priests who open a shrine to the public and try to solve medical, legal, and social problems for all comers, without regard to caste. The very few holy men are revered but may attract more foreign than indigenous disciples. Astrologers are numerous and are routinely consulted at birth, marriage, and times of trouble; Hindus believe that one's fate is "written on one's head" (*talai viti*) and cannot be fully escaped, although some intelligent finessing and divine assistance can help one avoid some problems or calamities.

CEREMONIES. Households celebrate a rich repertoire of calendrical and life-cycle rituals that bring the family together in joyous, festive holidays. Village temples offer annual "car" festivals, in which the deity is carried around the temple atop a huge chariot; these ceremonies occur on a much larger scale in regional pilgrimage, which used to attract visitors from all over the country.

ARTS. With its utilitarian ethos, Sri Lankan Tamil culture does not encourage young people to pursue careers in the arts. Even so, young people today may receive instruction in traditional Tamil music or dance as a means of impressing on them the antiquity and greatness of Tamil culture; music and dance were formerly associated with low-caste status.

MEDICINE. There is a pronounced division of labor between scientific medicine and Ayurvedic medicine, which is thought to be more effective for mental illness, snakebite, paralysis, and listlessness.

DEATH AND AFTERLIFE. Westerners who believe Hindus are focused on a better life after reincarnation are inevitably surprised by the almost complete disinterest that Tamil Hindus show in the afterlife. It is thought, though, that someone who dies without having fulfilled a great longing will remain to vex the living. Cremation is the norm and is followed, for most castes, by a period of death pollution lasting thirty-one days; subsequently there is an annual death observance with food offerings. For the few highly educated

Hindus familiar with the Saiva Siddhanta tradition, an oft-expressed goal of afterlife is reunification with Shiva.

Bibliography

Banks, Michael Y. (1961). "Caste in Jaffna." In *Aspects of Caste in South India, Ceylon, and North-West Pakistan*, edited by E. R. Leach, 61–77. Cambridge: Cambridge University Press.

Helleman-Rajanayagam, Dagmar (1988–1989). "The Tamil Militants—Before the Accords and After." *Pacific Affairs* 61:603–619.

Holmes, W. Robert (1980). *Jaffna (Sri Lanka): 1980*. Jaffna: Jaffna College.

McGilvray, Dennis (1982). *Caste Ideology and Interaction*. Cambridge: Cambridge University Press.

O'Ballance, Edgar (1989). *The Cyanide War: Tamil Insurrection in Sri Lanka, 1973–1988*. London: Brassey's.

Pfaffenberger, Bryan (1982). *Caste in Tamil Culture: The Religious Foundations of Sudra Domination in Tamil Sri Lanka*. Syracuse: Maxwell School of Foreign and Comparative Studies, Syracuse University.

Schwarz, Walter (1988). *The Tamils of Sri Lanka*. 4th ed. London: Minority Rights Group.

Skonsberg, Else (1982). *A Special Caste? Tamil Women of Sri Lanka*. London: Zed Press.

—BRYAN PFAFFENBERGER

TELUGU

Ethnonym: Andhra

Orientation

IDENTIFICATION. Speakers of the Telugu language inhabit Andhra Pradesh State in south India as well as border areas of the neighboring states of Orissa, Madhya Pradesh, Maharashtra, Karnataka, and Tamil Nadu. There are also substantial numbers of Telugu speakers in the interior of Tamil Nadu, especially in the central and northern regions. In addition there are small Telugu communities in the United States, the United Kingdom, and countries formerly part of the British Empire—Fiji, Guyana, Malaysia, Myanmar (Burma), Mauritius, Singapore, and South Africa.

LOCATION. Andhra Pradesh is located in tropical latitudes (between 12° and 19° N and 76° and 86° E) similar to mainland Southeast Asia or southern Mexico. Important features of the land include a palmyra-dotted coastal plain extending 960 kilometers along the Bay of Bengal, lush deltas of the Godavari and Krishna rivers, a strip of forested hill country paralleling the coast, and a rolling upland plain strewn with eroded rocky outcrops. The major rainfall is supplied by the southwest monsoon, its winds prevailing between June and September.

DEMOGRAPHY. In 1981 the population of Andhra Pradesh was 53,550,000, with an average density of 195 persons per square kilometer and a decennial growth rate of 23.1 percent. The population is mainly Hindu (87 percent) but with important Muslim and Christian minorities (8 and 4 percent, respectively).

LINGUISTIC AFFILIATION. The Telugu language is a member of the Dravidian Language Family concentrated in the south of the Indian peninsula. Other related major languages are Tamil, Kannada, and Malayalam. Telugu possesses its own distinctive, curvilinear alphabet and a voluminous and venerable literary tradition. It is also the primary language of South Indian classical music.

History and Cultural Relations

Two millennia ago the Telugu country was a stronghold of Buddhism, a legacy of the empire of Asoka (ca. 250 B.C.). The Andhra Kingdom, with its capital in Paithan (now in Maharashtra), followed. Among the various dynasties that next held sway were the Pallavas, the Eastern Chalukyas, the Kalingas, the Kakatiyas, and the Cholas. The Muslim period saw the establishment of the Bahmani Kingdom and its successor, the sultanate of Golkonda. Hindu Vijayanagar in the southern part of the Telugu country was conquered by Muslims in 1565. European traders—Dutch, French, and English—attracted by textiles and spices began arriving on the scene in the sixteenth century. The British ultimately prevailed in the eighteenth century, acquiring control from the rulers of Golkonda over extensive tracts in the northeast coastal belt of the Telugu country. Later these territories were linked with those they acquired in the south and ruled from the city of Madras. The northwestern part of the Telugu-speaking lands remained in what became the state of the Nizam of Hyderabad, whose foreign affairs and defense came to be controlled by the British.

Political trends since Indian independence in 1947 include three decades of dominance by the Congress party. This was followed by the ascent of the regional Telugu Desam party, spearheaded by a former Telugu movie idol, N. T. Rama Rao.

Settlements

Telugu villages range in size from several hundred in population to many thousand, with larger ones resembling small towns. Frequently several

Andhra Pradesh is located in tropical latitudes similar to mainland Southeast Asia or southern Mexico.

Telugu society with its Hindu caste system has a highly developed tradition of family transmission of manufacturing and food-processing skills.

"hamlets" are affiliated together as a single village. In some cases, the constituent settlements have been designated a village by the government for purposes of taxation, economic development, and political representation. Typically the main settlement of the village has the widest variety of castes (or *jatis*, endogamous groups often associated with particular occupations), with a temple, small shops, tea and drink stalls, a weekly market, a post office, and a village school. Quarters of former Untouchable castes are traditionally segregated from the other houses of a settlement.

Telugu house types vary considerably even within the same village. Differences in construction materials usually indicate differing economic statuses. Dwellings range from mud-walled, single-family houses with palm-thatched roofs to houses made of brick and mortar—or stone in some regions—with flat, cement roofs. All houses have at least one inner room where the family valuables are stored, ceremonial brass vessels (dowry) are displayed, and deities are worshiped at a small shrine. A roofed veranda with cooking nook lies outside this inner room. For the highest castes, for whom it is important that cooking take place beyond the polluting gaze of outsiders, the cooking area is adjacent to the back of the dwelling in a walled compound.

Economy

SUBSISTENCE AND COMMERCIAL ACTIVITIES. The food grain held in highest esteem is rice, cultivated intensively in the Krishna and Godavari deltas as well as extensively throughout other parts of the coastal zone and in scattered parts of the interior. Away from streams irrigation is by reservoirs known as tanks. These are formed with earthen dams that hold rainwater in the wet season. Other food grains, grown on nonirrigated lands, are also important. Mung beans, lima beans, and black-eyed peas are widely cultivated, as are sesame seeds and peanuts for oil. Popular garden vegetables, grown for home use and for sale, include tomatoes, eggplants, onions, garlic, chilies, bitter gourds, pumpkins, okra, yams, ginger, and corn. Widely grown fruits include mangoes, tamarinds, guavas, bananas, coconuts, custard apples, sapodillas, limes, toddy-palm (palmyra, *Borassus flabellifer*), cashews, and pineapples. Turmeric root is also cultivated, as is mustard, fenugreek, coriander, and fennel. In addition to rice, important commercial crops are sugarcane, tobacco, and cotton. Chilies are cultivated throughout the state for sale. Fishing is important along the coast as well as in inland tanks.

Cultivation is mainly unmechanized, except for gasoline-powered pumps used by wealthier farmers to aid irrigation. Bullocks or water buffalo are used to pull wooden plows reinforced with iron tips. Crops are harvested by hand.

In addition to cattle and water buffalo—which are used not for meat but for dairy products—numerous other domestic animals are raised. These include chickens, ducks, turkeys, goats, sheep, and pigs. Dogs are kept by some villagers for hunting.

INDUSTRIAL ARTS. Telugu society with its Hindu caste system has a highly developed tradition of family transmission of manufacturing and food-processing skills. Among these are blacksmithing, carpentry, goldsmithing, cotton and silk weaving, basket making, pottery, and oil pressing. Many villagers weave their own baskets, make their own rope from palm fiber, and thatch their own roofs.

TRADE. Village markets selling fresh vegetables, meat, spices, cloth, and bangles are typically held one day each week. Generally one particularly large weekly market on a main bus route serves as a magnet for an entire rural region. Women of farmer castes often bring produce from their families' farms, and their husbands engage in petty trading, offering chickens for sale. Potters and sellers of bangles and clothing also offer their wares. Professional merchant castes maintain small provision stores, which are open daily in the villages.

DIVISION OF LABOR. To a great extent, women's time is taken up with child rearing and food preparation. However, among the middle and lower castes women engage in strenuous physical agricultural labor such as transplanting rice shoots and harvesting. In towns, women work on construction sites, carrying heavy baskets with cement or bricks or breaking rocks. But among the higher castes there are restrictions on women going out of their homes or even appearing in public unescorted.

In Telugu society labor is most strikingly divided by caste. Castes are economically interdependent endogamous groups often associated with particular occupations or crafts—barbering, washing, and oil pressing, for instance.

LAND TENURE. Land is held by households and passes patrilineally along the male line, in equal shares between brothers. Land is not owned by all families but rather held mainly by members of farmer castes, as well as by members of higher castes who employ lower castes to cultivate it. Food is traditionally distributed throughout the rural population via exchange of grain or cash for services. Landless lower-caste members of society who cannot support themselves in the village economy frequently migrate to urban areas to work for wages. They then usually maintain ties with their home village.

Kinship

KIN GROUPS AND DESCENT.   An individual is a member of the following groups: (1) a family residing in a household generally headed by the eldest male; (2) an endogamous subclan or branch of a patrilineage; (3) an exogamous clan (sharing a patrilineally transmitted family name); and (4) an endogamous caste with a particular hierarchical status, customs of diet, prohibitions on food exchange with other castes, and often a traditional occupation. Descent is patrilineal.

KINSHIP TERMINOLOGY.   Dravidian kinship terms are used; the terminology emphasizes relative age. For example, terms differ according to the ages of the speaker and the person spoken of; there are separate terms for "older brother" and "younger brother." The terminology also divides relatives into marriageable and unmarriageable categories. On the one hand, one calls one's parallel cousins "brothers" and "sisters." They are not considered to be potential spouses. On the other hand, one's cross cousins are designated by terms implying that they are potential affines.

Marriage and Family

MARRIAGE.   Marriages are monogamous, polygyny having been prohibited since Indian independence. Marriages are generally arranged by parents and relatives, though potential mates may get to meet each other or may already be acquainted if they are related or live in the same village. As mentioned, marriage with cross cousins is common, and a man's maternal uncle is viewed as a preferred donor of a wife. Wives are considered responsible for the well-being of their husbands and are felt to be at fault if their husbands die before they do. The theme of the inauspiciousness of widowhood recurs in many ritual contexts. Marriages are generally patrilocal. The fission of individual households is a gradual process, beginning with a man's sons marrying and bringing their wives to live with him and his wife. Eventually separate hearths are established, followed later by a division of lands. A sharing of tasks

SOCIOPOLITICAL ORGANIZATION

Andhra Pradesh, one of the largest states in the Republic of India, is led by a chief minister and a governor and has an elected legislature. Its capital is Hyderabad.

Social Organization

The primary organizing principle of Telugu society is hierarchy, based on age, sex, and social group. Each endogamous caste group reckons its relationship to other castes as either one of superiority, equality, or inferiority. While these relative rankings produce a hierarchy, this is in some cases a matter of dispute. To some extent the relative positions are perceived to be achieved on the basis of mutual willingness to engage in various sorts of symbolic exchanges, especially of food. Caste members do not accept food prepared by a caste they consider to be inferior to their own. In addition, castes maintain distinctive diets—the highest refuses to eat meat, the next level refuses to eat domestic pork or beef, and the lowest eats pork and beef. There are clusters of castes of similar status—such as farmers—that accept each other's food, as well as pairs of similar-status castes—such as the two major former Untouchable castes—that reject each other's food. There is also a group of castes—the Panchabrahma, artisans in gold, brass, iron, and wood—that claim to be higher than the highest Brahmans. But while they refuse food from all other castes, no other castes accept food from them.

Political Organization

The state of Andhra Pradesh is divided into twenty-one districts (*zilla*). Districts were traditionally subdivided into *taluks* until 1985 when a smaller subdivision, the *mandal*, was instituted by the Telugu Desam party. The mandal, whose leader is directly elected, serves as a functionary of revenue administration and of government development projects. Towns with taluk headquarters are the seat of courts, police, and government health-care programs. The political culture of democracy among the Telugus is highly developed, with frequent elections for state and national representatives.

Social Control and Conflict

In times of conflict the authority of elder males is respected. A male household head rules on a dispute within his household. Next, an informally constituted group of elder males of the same caste arbitrates difficult disputes within or between families in the caste. Cases involving members of different castes are often referred to higher castes for settlement, in a pattern of ascending courts of appeal. When conflicts begin there is often much commotion and shouting of accusations or grievances. This attracts the participation of bystanders and triggers the process of arbitration.

around agricultural field huts near their lands is the last tie to be maintained. Different castes have varying attitudes toward divorce. The highest in status prohibit it entirely. Next down in the hierarchy are castes that permit divorce if no children have been born. These are followed by castes permitting divorce relatively unrestrictedly. Agreements are reached regarding the return of marriage gifts and property. Formal written documents of release are drawn up and exchanged by the parties, leaving them free to remarry.

DOMESTIC UNIT. The basic unit is a nuclear family. A household, defined as those who share food prepared at a common hearth, is led by a household head. During the course of its development, a household can include additional members—spouses and offspring of sons, or widows and widowers.

INHERITANCE. Property, such as land, is divided equally among brothers, though the less economically established youngest son also often inherits the family home.

SOCIALIZATION. Infants and small children are raised by the women of the household. Older siblings and other cousins also often tend children younger than themselves. Children are encouraged to accompany their parents everywhere and begin learning sex-specific tasks and caste occupations from an early age.

Religion

The vast majority of Telugus are Hindus. There are also some Telugu castes that have converted to Christianity and Islam. Each village has its main temple—often dedicated to a great Hindu god, usually Rama or Siva—as well as small shrines to numerous village deities, most of which are female. Preeminent among the regional shrines in the Telugu country is the temple of Sri Venkatesvara in the town of Tirupati, a major pilgrimage center.

RELIGIOUS BELIEFS. Hinduism lacks a centralized ecclesiastical hierarchy or unified authority officially defining doctrine. The specifics of religious customs vary widely from one locality to another and even between different castes in the same village. Among the major types of ritual are family ceremonies, caste ceremonies, and village ceremonies. In addition the range of deities worshiped varies between localities. Many deities are associated with particular places or specialized powers or seasons. But a unifying theme is a system of worship called *puja* in which offerings are presented to a deity in return for protection and help. The offerings imply a subordination by the worshipers and include the receiving back of part of the items offered—after their spiritual essence has been partaken of by the deity. Overarching the host of specific deities is a transcendent divinity, *bhagavan* or *devudu*, responsible for cosmic order. People conceive of this deity in personified forms such as Vishnu and his associated circle of gods—including his ten incarnations, among whom are Rama and Krishna, and their various female consorts, such as Lakshmi, Sita, and Rukmini. Shiva and gods associated with him include his sons Ganapati and Subrahmaniam and his wife Parvati. Settlements, villages or towns, have a tradition of female "village deities" (*grama devatas*) who protect their localities as long as they are properly propitiated but cause illnesses if they are not. Ghosts of deceased humans, especially those of people who died untimely deaths, can hover about and interfere with people, as can other malevolent forces such as inauspicious stars and evil spirits. These thwart people's plans or render their children ill.

RELIGIOUS PRACTITIONERS. A person acting as the officiant in a temple, conducting or assisting the worship, is known as a *pujari*, or priest. Brahmans serve as priests in temples to deities associated with the scriptural deities known throughout India, such as Rama, Shiva, or Krishna. But members of many other castes, some of quite low social rank, act as priests for a wide range of lesser deities.

CEREMONIES. There is little uniformity in the celebration of festivals across the Telugu country. Each region presents a kaleidoscopic variation of interpretations and emphases on common themes. In the northeast, Makara Sankranti is the principal harvest festival. It features castes worshiping the tools of their trades and a period of fairs featuring elaborate nightlong operatic drama performances. In the northwest, Dasara and Chauti are the festivals during which castes worship their implements. Farther south, near the Krishna River, Ugadi is a time when artisans worship their tools. All regions have festivals that honor Rama, Krishna, Shiva, and Ganapati.

Village goddess festivals, celebrated on dates unique to individual settlements, are also among the most elaborate celebrations of the year. These rituals—entailing the offering of chickens, goats, or sheep—mobilize extensive intercaste cooperation to ensure the health of the whole community. Also important in the worship of village goddesses is the practice of making vows to achieve specific personal benefits, such as the curing of ailments or finding of lost objects. Periodically when emergencies arise—in the form of epidemics, a spate of fires, or sudden deaths—these goddesses are believed to require propitiation.

Life-cycle rituals vary greatly between castes and regions. All serve to define social statuses, marking the transitions between immaturity and adult (married) status, as well as between life and death. They also serve to define circles of interdependent relatives and castes. Weddings stand out as the most elaborate and significant life-cycle rites. They are highly complex, involve huge expenditures, last several days, and entail the invitation and feeding of large numbers of guests. Funerary rites are also highly significant, defining the lineal relatives who share ritual pollution caused by the death of a member. In addition, they mark social statuses by treating the body of a man differently from that of a woman (cremating it face up or face down, respectively) and by disposing of the body of an immature child differently from that of a married adult (by burial or cremation, respectively).

Bibliography

Dube, S. C. (1967). *Indian Village*. New York: Harper & Row.

Hiebert, Paul G. (1971). *Konduru: Structure and Integration in a South Indian Village*. Minneapolis: University of Minnesota Press.

Tapper, Bruce Elliot (1987). *Rivalry and Tribute: Society and Ritual in a Telugu Village in South India*. Delhi: Hindustan Publishing Corp.

—BRUCE ELLIOT TAPPER

American Immigrant Cultures

CHINESE

Most of the Chinese in the United States were traditionally Cantonese from the Guangdong Province of southern China. After the implementation of the U.S. Immigration Act of 1965, however, there were significant changes in the Chinese immigration population. Cantonese continue to dominate the Chinese immigrant population in the United States today, but there are also Fujianese (Fukienese), Taiwanese, Shanghainese, and Chinese from the northern regions of China.

Stories of the immigrants, their failures and successes, were circulated in their home communities in China. Since the new immigration laws of 1965 emphasized family reunification, the home communities of these early immigrants were favored sources of new immigrants, who often had kinship connections and were linked to the established ethnic community in the United States.

The History of Chinese Immigration

Some sources claim that the Chinese were present in America as early as the fourth century C.E., long before Christopher Columbus. Other sources claim that the Chinese arrived in the tenth century C.E. However, according to reliable historical records, the first large influx of Chinese immigrants to America dates from the 1850s. The number of immigrants steadily increased over the years, peaking in 1890 with a population of 107,488. Discriminatory legislation such as the Chinese Exclusion Act of 1882, the anti-Chinese Scott Act of 1888, and the Geary Act of 1892 were designed to prohibit the entry or reentry of Chinese immigrants who were laborers, thus ending the influx of Chinese immigration. By 1920 there were only 61,639 Chinese in the United States. Racism and fear of economic competition from the Chinese were the principal factors contributing to discriminatory legislation. It was not until after World War II that Chinese immigration recommenced, although significant influxes did not become apparent until the passage of 1965 immigration laws. By 1990 the Chinese population had grown to 1,645,472.

Initially, in the 1850s, the Chinese settled on the West Coast, where they found jobs as railroad workers, miners, farmers, and domestics. They have been a presence in the state of California ever since. Upon completion of the Central Pacific Railway in 1869 and the closing of many mining companies, Chinese and white laborers alike had to look for other forms of employment in California. Economic competition with whites led to various anti-Chinese campaigns in California and the passage of discriminatory legislation. One example of anti-Chinese legislation was the Sidewalk Ordinance of 1870, which outlawed the Chinese pole method of peddling vegetables and carrying laundry. Traditionally, the Chinese carried heavy loads balanced on a pole that rested on their shoulders. The pole functioned as a fulcrum. The Sidewalk Ordinance was directed specifically against the Chinese since non-Chinese people used wagons or carts to peddle their goods.

There were ordinances against the use of firecrackers and Chinese ceremonial gongs, which were important symbols of luck and necessary implements for Chinese festivities. In 1871 the Cubic Air Ordinance was enacted, requiring each adult to have at least five hundred cubic feet of living space. The law was specifically directed against the Chinese who were living in cramped quarters in extended family living situations. The Queue Ordinance, passed in 1873 in San Francisco, was another example of legislation specifically targeting Chinese. Under Manchu law, Chinese men were required to comb their hair into long braids called queues. Cutting off their queues was a serious violation of Chinese Law. After the passage of the anti-Queue law, gangs began to attack Chinese people with long hair, cutting off their braids and wearing them as trophies on their belts and caps.

There were numerous laws prohibiting the Chinese from working in federal, state, county, or city governments. The Chinese were barred from the fishing industry. There were laws prohibiting the education of Chinese children in the public schools, as well as laws prohibiting the use of Chinese people as witnesses against white defendants in court. Chinese were barred from purchasing property outside of San Francisco's Chinatown. In addition to these laws, in 1882 Congress passed the Chinese Exclusion Act, which prohibited Chinese laborers from entering the country.

The Chinese responded to these sentiments and legislative acts by entering into businesses, such as Chinese restaurants and laundries, that were not directly competitive with white enterprises. They organized self-help, community, and protective societies. Many moved to the major metropolitan areas of the United States, such as San Francisco, Los Angeles, and New York City, where they could attract a large clientele for their ethnic businesses. As a result of this movement, Chinese enclaves known as Chinatowns developed. From the 1880s to 1965, the Chinese depended entirely on ethnic businesses for their survival. In Chinatown they developed an ethnic economy that catered to both Chinese and non-Chinese customers. Their protective societies and associations were based on kinship, friendship, place of origin, trade, and dialect. Through these associations the Chinese mediated their own disputes, promoted their own economic interests, and socialized among themselves. Although the establishment of Chinatowns proved to be an adaptive strategy, their creation was necessary as a result of racism. Discrimination, nonacceptance, and exclusion of the Chinese by the larger society compelled them to engage in limited economic activities within the confines of Chinatown. By 1940, there were twenty-eight Chinatowns in the United States. As discrimination against the Chinese diminished and they became more accepted by the larger society, Chinese were able to move out of the Chinatowns and to pursue other economic activities. By 1955 there were only sixteen Chinatowns remaining in the United States. With the influx of new immigrants after 1965, some Chinatowns expanded. The already existing Chinatowns of San Francisco, Los Angeles, and New York all got a boost to their populations as new arrivals tended to move into preexisting Chinatowns.

In San Francisco, 20 percent of the Chinese live in Chinatown; the rest of the Chinese population is dispersed throughout the city. Similar phenomenon occurred in the Chinatowns of New York, Chicago, and Los Angeles. Additionally, a new Chinatown in Monterey Park, near Los Angeles, has been created by the new Chinese immigrants.

Among the new Chinese immigrants, many are highly educated and trained in various professional careers. Professionals tend to live outside of Chinatowns in the metropolitan areas of cities such as New York, San Francisco, Los Angeles, Houston, San Diego, Dallas, Boston, and Chicago. According to the 1990 U.S. Census, in terms of spatial distribution, among the 1,645,472 Chinese in America, 704,850 live in California, and 284,144 live in New York. Hawaii, Illinois, New Jersey, and Texas also have more than fifty thousand Chinese each.

Language

Before 1965 the Chinese in the United States were a rather homogenous group in terms of place of origin and linguistic background. Most of the Chinese immigrants came from the rural area of the Guangdong Province in southern China, particularly the Sze Yap and the Sam Yap districts. The various dialects from Sze Yap and San Yap were used. However, the lingua franca used in the Chinese community in the United States was the Taishan dialect. Since 1965, with the arrival of the new immigrants from different parts of China, the most commonly used dialect in the Chinese immigrant community is the standard Cantonese used in the areas of Hong Kong, Macao, and Guanzhou. However, there are also Mandrian, Shanghainese, or Fukienese speakers in the community. Many of the new immigrants are bilingual or even multilingual; they speak English and one or more Chinese dialects. Since the writing system is uniform throughout China, it is understandable to all Chinese immigrants regardless of where they came from. In general, first-generation Chinese immigrants can speak and write in Chinese. As times goes on, the second generation tends to lose the ability to read and write Chinese. Although some can still speak a Chinese dialect, many have become monolingual English speakers. With the recent emphasis on multiculturalism and the emergence of China as a world power, some second-generation Chinese Americans are learning the official language of China, namely, the Mandarin (or Pu Tung Hua dialect.)

Since 1965 most of the immigrants have come from either the Cantonese- or Mandarin-speaking area of China, causing these two dialects to become the dominant ones. The Chinese television stations in New York and San Francisco have programs in both Cantonese and Mandarin. There are many Chinese newspapers circulated among the immigrant Chinese. The two most important ones are *Sing Tao Daily* and the *World Journal*. The former caters principally to the Chinese from Hong Kong and China, while the latter one caters to the Chinese from Taiwan. There are different political persuasions among the immigrants. Some identify with the Kuomingtang of Taiwan, some are sympathetic with the People's Republic of China, and some are for establishing roots in the United States. These different political persuasions are reflected also in the ethnic press of the Chinese. There are more than five dailies in New York's Chinatown and four dailies in San Francisco's Chinatown. Additionally, Chinese newspapers from mainland China, Taiwan, and Hong Kong are available in the major Chinatowns in the United States. Chinese immigrants are sensitive to domestic and international events and are eager to learn about the different perspectives.

All the Chinese language newspapers have impressive news coverage. *Sing Tao Daily* has an English supplement with news specifically targeted to young Hong Kong Chinese who have difficulty reading Chinese characters. Apart from local and American news, the contents of *Sing Tao Daily* are transmitted from Hong Kong via satellite. The *World Journal* is a pro-Taiwan newspaper that receives daily communications via satellite as well. The new immigrants in general are quite well educated and have an international mind-set. The Chinese newspapers inform immigrants about their homelands and provide reliable coverage about the social and political events around the world and in the United States.

The Old Immigrants and the New

The coastal regions of southeastern China principally the provinces of Fujian and Guangdong, have been the main suppliers of Chinese immigrants. Traditionally, the South Seas had been a favorite destination for the Fujianese. Most of the Chinese of Guangdong Province, however, immigrated to the United States. Today the new Chinese immigrants come from different parts of China. Immigrants from Taiwan and mainland China face separate quotas imposed by the United States. The People's Republic of China has a quota of twenty thousand immigrants per year, while Taiwan has a separate quota of twenty thousand. Hong Kong, as a colony of Great Britain, had a colonial quota of six hundred slots per year. This quota for the Hong Kong natives was increased by the United States in August 1985 to five thousand per year. However, residents of Hong Kong who were born in China are included in the quota for mainland China.

Legal immigrants are admitted into the United States on three types of visas. One is the family reunion quota, the second is the special talents quota, and the third is the quota for political refugees. Illegal entrants from China do exist, but the number is relatively small as many of them have relatives in the United States. As it turns out, the illegal Chinese immigrants tend to be those from the economically deprived rural area of Fujian Province. In 1985, 95 percent of all visa applications cited family reunification as their classification preference. Since 1965, there has been a drastic increase of Chinese immigrants in the United States. There are several reasons that account for the increase. First, the Immigration Act of 1965 started to treat the Chinese more equitably. An equal quota was extended to nations from different parts of the world. Second, educational, political, and economic factors played important roles.

There are vast motivational differences between immigrants from Taiwan and Hong Kong and those from mainland China. Immigrants from mainland China seek economic opportunity and political freedom, whereas many immigrants from Hong Kong and Taiwan leave a strong economic situation to find political stability and educational opportunities in the United States. University education is highly competitive in the homeland of the Chinese. There are only two major universities in Hong Kong, and they can admit only eight hundred students per year, from a population of five million. For years Taiwan has sent many students to the United States to receive higher education, as Taiwan also has a limited number of universities; many do not even give doctoral degrees. These educational and political considerations of the new Chinese immigrants differ significantly from the overriding economic concerns of the nineteenth-century Chinese immigrants.

The kinds of structural principles used to organize the immigrant Chinese community in the United States were those common to rural China: kinship, place of origin, regionalism, and dialect similarities. During the pre-1965 era, many immigrants were sojourners who had no intention of staying in America permanently. They reasoned that after they had made enough money in America they would return to China to become entrepreneurs or they would lead blissful lives of retirement.

Initially, the Chinese worked mostly as laborers. After 1884, Chinese financial survival was entirely dependent on ethnic niche businesses such as Chinese restaurants, laundries, grocery stores, and gift shops. In general, the early immigrants were less educated than post-1965 immigrants and mostly came from rural areas of southern China. They were predominantly men who had left their families in China, as various pre-1945 immigration laws prevented the entry of Chinese women into the United States. After 1945 however, the War Bride Act and the G.I. Fiancees Act enabled Chinese women to enter the United States. Still, only Chinese G.I.'s benefitted from these new legal provisions. As a result, in the pre-1965 era, the sex ratio between males and females was highly uneven, with males dramatically outnumbering females. The Chinese community was labeled a "bachelor" community. The lack of family life and children was a principal reason that juvenile delinquency was not a problem.

Since 1965 the Chinese community in the United States has changed dramatically. Of major importance was the enactment of the Immigration Act of 1965, which abolished "national origins" quotas and established a system of preference whereby immediate relatives, skilled and unskilled workers, refugees, scientists, and technical personnel were listed under different categories of preference. For the first time Chinese immigrants were treated equally with other nationalities by United States immigration law, thus ending some eighty-five years of bias against the Chinese. How has the 1965 law affected Chinese immigrants? First, any Chinese citizen who has family connections in America can be sponsored for migration by their relatives in the United States. Family reunions are a major way in which these immigrants can immigrate to the United States. New immigrants can also bring their spouses and children under the age of twenty one. This practice helped to even out the sex ratio between males and females.

Another effect of the new immigration law has been the influx of skilled immigrants. This law specifically favored the entrance of skilled persons trained in science, technology, the arts, and other professions. New immigrants are relatively well-educated, and many are from urban areas of China: Taiwan, Hong Kong, or Macao. The new immigrants are also interested in making America their permanent home; they are not sojourners. The new immigrants' attitudes toward the United States is reflected in the phrase *Lo Di Sheng Gen* (after reaching the land, grow roots). Whenever they can, these new immigrants apply for United States citizenship. In fact, 48 percent of the Chinese in the San Francisco Bay Area are United States citizens. These immigrants wish to establish roots and commit themselves entirely to their new country, and they come relatively prepared to do so. The majority of the Chinese from Hong Kong belong to the middle class, and some arrive with a significant amount of savings or capital.

Given their resources, many of the new immigrants avoid traditional paths to employment through ethnic businesses such as restaurants, groceries, or gift shops. Some own or are employed in garment factories. Some are employed in Caucasian establishments. Others have branched out to areas of manufacturing, transportation, construction, wholesaling, finance, insurance, and agricultural services. Thus, there is more diversity in the economic pursuits of these new immigrants. The traditional images of Chinese coolies and penniless immigrants do not apply to the majority of the new Chinese immigrants. However, economically disadvantaged immigrants do exist, especially among those from mainland China.

Chinatowns in the United States

Today, there are about a dozen Chinatowns in the major metropolitan areas in the United States. While immigrants in the past tended to confine themselves in Chinatowns, the new immigrants who speak English and are professionals neither live nor work in the traditional Chinatowns. However, the Chinese immigrants who do not speak English still tend to move to Chinatowns or Chinese neighborhoods in the major metropolitan areas. These immigrants also depend on the traditional ethnic niche of the Chinese composed of Chinese restaurant, garment factories, gift shops, grocery stores, and laundromats. The ethnic economy of the Chinese and Chinatowns in the United States are an adaptation of the Chinese in the United States and, at the same time, the vestiges of racism and discrimination.

According to the 1990 U.S. Census, the San Francisco Bay Area's Chinese population was 315,345, while the Chinese population in the New York Metropolitan Area was 261,722. The Chinatowns in these two cities are the symbols of Chinese culture in the United States, housing many of the traditional Chinese organizations that coordinate many cultural activities relevant to the immigrant culture. Most of the traditional Chinese associations in various Chinatowns have their headquarters in New York or San Francisco.

Chinatown U.S.A. is a neighborhood, a work place, a social center, and a place that helps immigrants to adjust to a new land. It is an entry port for newcomers to the New World and, as such, is continually replenished with the traditional culture of the homeland. The newly arrived immigrants to the community get their first experiences with the United States and learn how to obtain employment, a social security card, open a bank account, sign up to learn English, understand their rights and obligations as members of U.S. society. America's Chinatown is an acculturation agent for the new immigrants. The community has bilingual social service agencies, translation services, Chinese stores, familiar food supplies, Chinese mass media, and information networks. All these social agencies and institutions fill the needs of the new immigrants. Newcomers can visit traditional herbal medicine stores, temples, and churches, which provides tremendous security to new Chinese immigrants, especially those who do not speak English.

Chinese Associations

Chinatown's traditional social structure was organized according to principles that are familiar to the immigrants. Everyone in the community has an opportunity to join one or more of these associations. There are also modern associations such as alumni associations, labor unions, social agencies, political parties.

Traditional Associations. In all the major Chinatowns in the United States, there are the traditional associations organized according to the traditional principles of kinship, clanship, place of origin, dialect, trade, and regionalism. These associations formed themselves into an associational structure. At the top of this structure is the Consolidated Chinese Benevolent Association (CCBA), known in San Francisco as the Chinese Six Companies. At one time, the CCBA, an overall community organization established in 1869, functioned as a consulate for the Chinese. The Chinese Six Companies in San Francisco were composed of Chinese from the six major district associations: the Ning Yung, Kong Chow, Young Wo, Shiu Hing, Hop Wo, and Yan Wo. The Six Companies served as spokesmen for the Chinese in San Francisco. Before the establishment of the Chinese Chamber of Commerce in 1910, the Six Companies also regulated the business activities of the Chinese, mediating business disputes and arbitrating conflicts between various family and district associations. The Six Companies arranged the shipment of bones of deceased immigrants back to China for reburial. They also issued clearance for immigrants to return to China, making sure that all returnees first paid their debts in America. The Chinese Six Companies still run a hospital and Chinese schools. They also are responsible for organizing the celebration of the Chinese New Year and various fundraising activities for the community. Although many of their functions are no longer needed, the Chinese Six Companies remain the highest authority, at least symbolically, of the San Fran-

cisco Chinese community. This is also the case of the CCBA in other Chinatowns in the United States.

The CCBA adopted an anti-Communist stance and are strong supporters of Nationalist China. This is perhaps because the CCBAs are controlled by the older Chinese who either suffered under Communism or embraced an anti-Communist ideology. Historically, the CCBA assisted the Kuomintang in their overthrow of the Manchu government in China. The CCBA in various Chinatowns have been under attack from radical students and community workers for being too slow to adapt and meet the needs of the new immigrants. Most of the traditional associations were established before 1965 to serve the needs of the adult, male Chinese, and they are not prepared to tackle contemporary social problems such as housing, Medicare, and juvenile delinquency.

The various family or clan associations in Chinatowns recruit members on the basis of common surname. The largest family associations are the Lee, Chan, and Wong. Within the family name associations are the *Fongs,* which group people according to both common surname and common village or place of origin. The family name or surname group in China was a clan group whose members were assumed to have descended from a common ancestor, and members addressed each other as "clan brothers." In China, the Fongs were a localized clan group and membership was based on patrilineal clansmen and descent from a common ancestor associated with a village. Many family name associations in San Francisco also maintain temporary lodging quarters for their members. These common lodging rooms are called common Fong. Thus the word "Fong" has two meanings: (1) common kinship origin in China and (2) the living quarters in the family name associations. What is significant here is that kinship has been used as a principal of social organization to address the needs and problems of the Chinese community. Within the family name associations, there were once informal credit-rotating clubs (*hui*). In the past, some members of a family name association could voluntarily participate in a hui. Members of the hui would agree on the amount of the deposit. Thus, for instance, ten members of the hui might agree to deposit $1,000 each and form a total pool of $10,000. The member entering the bid of the highest interest rate would get the money for his use. In return, he promised the $1,000 in return to each member plus interest. After repayment to all of the members, say, in ten months, the hui will be dissolved. This kind of informal credit arrangement is no longer practiced by the family name associations for it is rather risky and is not enforceable by law. Credit unions and banks are now the institutions for loans for the new immigrants. One association, the Lee Family Association, has its own credit union for members.

Multifamily name associations exist among the Chinese in the United States. One of the most important multifamily name associations is the Four Brothers Association, which was organized by the Liu, Kwan, Chang, and Chao families because their forebears swore brotherhood by the Peace Garden Oath two thousand years ago for the purpose of saving the Han

Dynasty. Another multifamily name association is the G. Ho. Oak Tin Association, which is composed of the Chan, Hu, Yuan, and Wang families, all of whom claim descent from the Shun Emperor. Chee Tuck Same Tuck Association is composed of the Wu, Tsai, and Chow families who were once neighbors in China. Similarly, the historical friendships among neighbors in China led to other associations; Loui, Fong, and Kwon families united to form Soo Yuen Association, and the Gon, Lai, and Ho families became the San Yick Association. Perhaps the most interesting of all is the Chew Lun Association, which united the Tam, Tan, Hsu, and Hsieh families based on a similarity (a common radical) in the Chinese characters used to spell their names.

In all the family name associations, both single family and multifamily, kinship ideology has been deliberately embraced, and kinship terms are used to address one another. The family name associations still exist today, attracting mostly older immigrants, to provide recreational facilities such as reading rooms and mahjong tables, to perform limited relief services, and to organize scholarship funds and ancestor worships.

Another level of organization is that of regional associations, which are composed of members from a certain county or region in China. The functions of the regional associations are similar to those of the family associations. They are basically mutual aid societies rendering welfare and employment assistance; the larger associations generally offer temporary lodging facilities, and some provide aid for burial service. The Vietnam Chinese Association has an informal insurance company that collects fees from members to form a fund to help families afford funeral services.

Business and trade associations form another cluster of associations in the social structure of Chinatown. The Chinese Art Goods Association, Chinese Chamber of Commerce, Chinese Apparel Contractors Association, Chinese Laundry Association, and Golden Gate Neighborhood Grocers' Association are some examples. These associations often negotiate with the larger society on matters of concern to Chinese businesses. As information centers, they channel information and regulations on taxes, sanitation, wages, licenses, and legislation. For example, the Chinese Chamber of Commerce voiced community-wide concern about the removal of Highway 480 in San Francisco, asking for the city government's assistance with the traffic flow through Chinatown and for parking facilities for customers of Chinatown businesses.

Another group of associations are called Tongs. The Tongs had much notoriety in the Tong Wars days. The Tongs have their roots in China as secret societies that fought against the Manchu government. In the past, the Tongs in Chinatown were involved in many illegal activities such as prostitution, gambling, and opium smoking. The Tongs have dissociated from their criminal past and today many call themselves fraternal organizations or merchant associations. On Leong Association, Suey Sing Merchant Association, Hip Sing Association, Yee Ying Merchant Association, and Ying On Association are some examples of Tongs.

Many of these traditional associations were important in the past, but they are gradually being replaced by modern associations such as alumni associations, political parties, social agencies, and the like. Organizations such as the Chinese American Citizens Alliance, Chinese for Affirmative Action, Chinese Newcomers Service Center, Chinatown Youth Center, Chinatown Neighborhood Improvement Resource Center, and On Lok Health Services for the elderly now play an important role in the life of the new immigrants.

The traditional Chinese associations exist mostly for social and recreational purposes. Some of these associations offer scholarships to students and maintain a place for ancestral tablets; some even have cemeteries. In fact, these associations tend to be particularly significant for the Chinese who have leadership capabilities or aspirations but have no opportunity to join any civic or social organizations in the larger society due to a lack of English fluency. Many well-to-do Chinese are particularly interested in joining the associations and aspiring to leadership positions that will bring recognition or prestige. In general, the new immigrants from Hong Kong and Taiwan who speak English and live outside the confines of Chinatown have little or no interest in becoming members of these Chinese associations.

New Associations. The second, larger block of formal organizations are called the new associations, for they differ from the traditional associations in many respects. First, the new associations have been organized recently and are not included within the umbrella of CCBA. Second, the new organizations recruit members from different social, economic, and educational backgrounds. Due to the influx of immigrants since 1965, the new associations have multiplied in size and number. New regional associations, alumni, political, commercial, and religious associations have been established, such as the Taiwan Association, the Hong Kong Student Association, the Lingnam University Alumni Association, and the Taiwan University Alumni Association. These associations have many highly educated members with cosmopolitan outlooks. Thus they differ markedly from the old sojourners who filled the rank and file of the traditional associations. The principal functions of most of these associations are generally social and recreational. Although all of them proclaim to protect the interests of Chinese Americans, these associations are generally apolitical. A small number of these associations, however, are actively concerned with Chinese civil rights. The notable ones are the Organization of the Chinese Americans, the Association for Progress, the Association for Equal Employment, and Chinese for Affirmative Action.

Social Agencies and Labor Unions. Social agencies and labor unions are oriented to the larger society and have their roots in the U.S. society. In fact, many of these organizations have direct connections with the government, churches, labor unions and nonprofit and charitable organizations of the larger society. They serve as bridges between Chinatown and U.S. society. The emergence and proliferation of their social services were related to the new resources available to the Chinese since 1965, including manpower and new funding available through the Economic Opportunity Act; consciousness of ethnicity; and the multiplication of social problems as a result of the influx of the new immigrants since 1965.

Cultural Continuity and Culture Change

The Chinese in the United States are not homogeneous. In terms of cultural identity, some adhere to the Old World culture, some are in favor of assimilation, and others are for the development of a hybrid identity (i.e., the Chinese-American identity). Politically, some are pro-Kuomintang, some are for the People's Republic of China, and some are committed to establishing roots in the United States. Increasingly, the trend is toward greater participation in the social, political, and economic life in America. In recent years, there has been an emphasis on diversity and multiculturalism in America, which encourages the celebration of one's ethnic roots and traditions. Among the Chinese, some want to be accepted wholeheartedly by the larger society and still retain their cultural heritage as Chinese. This tendency of emphasizing ethnic pride and at the same time wanting to be accepted by the larger society has met some practical difficulties. First, there is the problem of lack of education about the Chinese culture. Many second-generation Chinese Americans are so much concerned with economic mobility in the United States that they have not paid attention to learning the Chinese language and culture. In recent years, some of the American-born Chinese are taking ethnic studies courses. However, their knowledge of Chinese language and culture tend to be limited. Second, the residents of Chinatown who are new immigrants are more comfortable in speaking Chinese and are more at ease in following the Chinese patterns of interaction than the American ones. These new immigrants are so busy trying to make ends meet that they are not interested in the multiculturalism movement. The old immigrants are die-hard followers of old Chinese traditions. some of these old immigrants suffered severe discrimination in the past, and they see nothing worthwhile in assimilating to American life.

However, two important political changes in the larger society have affected the lives of the new immigrants. One is the enactment of the Immigration Act of 1965. The second is the civil rights movement in the United States and the subsequent passage of the Equal Opportunity Act and the Affirmative Action Program. The new Immigration Act of 1965 abolished the inequitable national quota system. Chinese and non-Chinese were to be treated equally under the new law. Chinese immigrants were no longer barred from bringing along their families. Since the new immigrants arrived with their spouses, they were also responsible for a new generation of native-born Chinese Americans. By 1996, there were more native-born Chinese Americans than any time before. The estimates of many experts about this population are around half a million. These native-born Chinese Americans will be the facilitators for future integration of the Chinese in America. As indicated by many social scientists, the local-born members of an ethnic community have always played an important role in the assimilation of minority populations.

Today, as a whole, there is more willingness among the Chinese immigrants to participate in American society than previously. Several reasons explain this kind of willingness to be part of America. First, they now immigrate to the United States with the intention of staying permanently. Second, many of them come from urban backgrounds. They are thus Westernized and more in tune with Western lifestyles. Many, in fact, want to assimilate into American culture and are looking forward to participating in American democracy. Third, many are well educated and knowledgeable about the American political process. They are eager to use American methods such as voting, petitioning, and demonstrating to pursue the "good life" in America. Thus there is a predisposition among the new immigrants to participate fully in American society, politically and socially. This kind of attitude will indeed help them enter into the larger society.

Politically, there have been relatively more new immigrants participating in U.S. politics than old immigrants. This is partly because new immigrants are better educated and more familiar with the political process in modern states. The new immigrants realize that they are rooted in Chinese culture but not in Chinese politics. They want to establish themselves in America, to protect their new life, and to obtain equal treatment in U.S. society. These new immigrants are eager to exercise their political rights. New organizations have been formed to sponsor political rights, to sponsor political candidates for elected offices, and to lobby for the interests of Chinese Americans. These organizations are not merely indications of the Chinese interest in establishing themselves politically; their participation in the democratic process is an important index of integration.

The normalization of the relations between China and the United States affected the assimilation of the Chinese in the post-1965 era. First, the People's Republic of China advocated explicitly that overseas Chinese should acquire the nationality of the host country. Second, as a result of normalization of relations, Chinese Americans became keenly aware of their peculiar situation. They live in America and are committed to its lifestyle. Culturally, however, their roots are Chinese. Socially and economically, they embrace the American system. They became convinced that America was their true home when confronted with the question of "belonging." Thus, contrary to popular perception, Chinese Americans, especially the new immigrants, have not become more "sinicized" or developed more allegiance to the People's Republic of China as a result of normalization of relations. Instead, as a whole they have become more Americanized, increasing participation in U.S. society. This kind of change has had a great deal to do with the awakening of their ethnic identity in the midst of the triangular relations among the People's Republic of China, Taiwan, and the United States.

The economic conditions of the Chinese Americans have improved. However, there are three major aspects that need to be clarified. First, there is a relatively large group of professional Chinese people. This group of people are high wage earners. Second, there is a group of people among the immigrants from China who have to toil in the labor intensive ethnic enterprises such as restaurants and garment factories. The income for these immigrants is relatively meager. Third, there are elderly immigrants who depend on the U.S. welfare system, although the size of this group is relatively small. These divisions still allow the average income of the Chinese immigrants to look better than many other ethnic groups. It is misleading, however, to use the term "model minority" to describe the Chinese immigrant group as a whole, for it obscures the social and economic differences among the Chinese.

Many second-, third-, or fourth-generation Chinese Americans have attended college or professional schools, and after graduation they usually prefer to work for American establishments according to their professional capacity. In fact, the professional Chinese tend not to be related to Chinatown economies and thus not to be connected to Chinatowns in general, living instead in middle-class neighborhoods.

Working and living among middle-class Americans allows the Chinese to have more contacts with U.S. society through education, institutions, careers, neighborhood connections, professional associations, churches, and other secondary institutions. They even have the same middle-class aspirations: better jobs, better housing, better cars, better education for their children, better house-hold appliances, and better economic mobility. Even the family system resembles that of the majority of middle-class Americans: a neolocal residence and the nuclear family. Siblings are no longer required to address each other by traditional kinship terminology. Relationships within the nuclear family focus on the husband and wife bond rather than the father and son bond that exists in the traditional Chinese family. The lifestyle of these professionals who are not connected to Chinatown is principally a product of their careers, which are intimately connected with the American economy and society. There is also a significant increase of interracial marriages between the Chinese and members of the larger society; the increase of out-marriage among Chinese males went from 7.4 percent (1940–1949) to 13.5 percent (1950–1959) to a high of 17.7 percent (1960–1969). Correspondingly, the out-marriages among the Chinese females for the same periods rose from 5.6 percent to 10.2 percent and finally to 18 percent. Increased interracial marriage among the Chinese is also an indication of their increased assimilation. Furthermore, Chinese professionals with a higher education are more likely to marry interracially, another example showing that Chinese professionals are more assimilatable than other Chinese in the Chinese ethnic enclave.

Forces for maintaining the culture in the ethnic enclave emanate from a variety of sources, one of which is the Chinese press. Others include the Chinese school, the traditional associations, and their leaders. The influx of the new immigrant also serves to reinforce Chinese culture in America. Last, but not least, is the celebration of traditional festivals in various Chinese communities. Some of these festivals are celebrated in public, and others are celebrated privately, either at home or in association halls. Cultural festivities in various Chinatowns tend to unite the inhabitants and are symbols of Chinese culture in America. The major festivals are the Chinese New Year, Chingming (Festival of the Tombs), Chungyang (Festival of the Kites), the Dragon Boat Festival, and the Mid-Autumn Festival. By far, the most popular of them all is the Chinese New Year, which attracts many tourists to the Chinatowns of New York and San Francisco.

Barriers to Further Assimilation

Increased participation in U.S. society by the Chinese since World War II should not imply that discrimination against the Chinese has ceased. While there has been great improvement, the Chinese still experience legal, social, and economic discrimination. Even the Chinese who are U.S. citizens find obtaining federal employment extremely difficult; the fact that their mother country is a communist country is a barrier for many government jobs. It is still assumed in some quarters that the Chinese are clannish and cannot be made good citizens of the United States, in spite of the fact that they have fought and died for the United States in World War I, World War II, the Korean War, and the Vietnam War. Some Chinese families have been in America for five or six generations, yet they are often considered foreigners because of their Chinese ethnicity. Socially, there are educational institutions that still turn away qualified students of Chinese descent. In the job market, Chinese often encounter subtle discrimination. Once employed, Chinese workers often find it difficult to be promoted to higher rank, especially to managerial positions. This phenomenon has been referred to as "topping out," meaning that they have reached the point where further promotion is extremely unlikely. This explains why some Chinese leave their jobs after working many years for a company. Realizing that it is a "dead-end" job, they leave and open their own firms. This strategy of becoming self-employed echoes the old strategy of the Chinese during the exclusion era; in adversary climates, their forebears withdrew from competition with the white labor market by opening their own ethnic restaurants or laundries. Economically, the lifeline for many Chinese immigrants is still tied to the ethnic niche. The 1990s also saw an increase in the number of "hate" crimes committed against the Chinese. Poverty still exists in various Chinatowns, but the model minority image created by the media often obscures the social reality of the Chinatowns' pressing problems: a decaying housing situation, crowding, aging, juvenile delinquency, deficient health care, underemployment, and restrictive economic opportunities.

As a whole, in examining the social and economic conditions of the Chinese, improvement can be seen. The gradual elimination of social, legal, and economic injustices throughout the years by legislative means has helped foster Chinese participation in American society. The continued elimination of these external barriers will likely entice further participation and contribution by Chinese Americans.

Bibliography

De Guignes, J. (1761). *Researches Sur Les Navigations des Chinois du Cote de L'Amerique.* Paris: Academie des Inscriptions.

Fang, Zhongpu. (1980). "Did Chinese Buddhists Reach America 1,000 Years Before Columbus?" *China Reconstruct* 29(8):65.

Hsu, F. L. K. (1981). *American and Chinese: Passage of Difference.* Honolulu: University Press of Hawaii.

Lee, R. H. (1947). "The Chinese Communities in the Rocky Mountain Region." Ph.D. diss., University of Chicago.

Lee, R. H. (1960). *The Chinese in the United States of America.* Hong Kong: Hong Kong University Press.

Sandmeyer, E. E. (1973). *The Anti-Chinese Movement in California.* Urbana: The University of Illinois Press.

Steiner, S. (1979). *Fusang: The Chinese Who Built America.* New York: Harper & Row.

Wong, B. P. (1979). *A Chinese-American Community: Ethnicity and Survival Strategies.* Singapore: Chopmen Enterprises.

Wong, B. P. (1982). *Chinatown: Economic Adaptation and Ethnic Identity of the Chinese.* New York: Holt, Rinehart and Winston.

Wong, B. P. (1988). *Patronage, Brokerage, Entrepreneurship, and the Chinese Community of New York.* New York: AMS Press.

Wong, B. P. (1994). "Hong Kong Immigrants in San Francisco." In *Reluctant Exiles?,* edited by R. Skeldon. Armonk, NY: M. E. Sharpe.

Wong, B. P. (1996). *Ethnicity and Entrepreneurship: Immigrant Chinese in the San Francisco Bay Area.* Boston: Allyn & Bacon.

Wu, C.-T. (1958). "Chinese People and Chinatown in New York City." Ph.D. diss. University of Michigan, Ann Arbor.

—BERNARD P. WONG

DUTCH

Compared to other European countries, the Netherlands did not see many of its inhabitants go to the United States as immigrants. The nation had a reputation for social and economic stability, as well as a long history of tolerance; relatively few of its citizens responded to the lures of life in the New World. By 1996, fewer than 300,000 Dutch immigrants to the United States had been recorded, compared to more than a million each from the smaller nations of Sweden and Denmark and far greater numbers from Germany, England, and Ireland.

Early Immigration

From the American Revolution until 1845, the number of Dutch immigrants to America averaged fewer than one hundred a year. These early immigrants, arriving in small groups of individuals or in families, sometimes found homes in the well-established Dutch colonial community of upstate New York, which had begun in the days when New York City was still called New Amsterdam. More often, however, Dutch immigrants settled in small towns or isolated agricultural enclaves; North Carolina, Ohio, Wisconsin, Texas, and Oregon were among their destinations. Such immigrants typically merged into the existing population and, except for their surnames, retained little of their Netherlandic culture.

Between 1847 and 1857, in contrast, more than a thousand people a year arrived, establishing towns and farming communities, and setting up cultural institutions that continued to welcome new immigrants, in even greater numbers, for more than a century. These midcentury arrivals were mostly Calvinists, members of a group (the Seceders) that had broken away from the state church of the Dutch government. To understand their situation, it is necessary to outline a bit of their history in the Netherlands. The Dutch government, reacting to rationalist influences and a new monarchy in the years after Waterloo, had changed the way the church was run.

William I had appointed key people to the Synod, a centralized ruling body, thus diminishing the autonomy of local congregations. The Synod had changed the songbooks used during worship by adding hymns, which struck many people as being less holy than their traditional Psalms taken from the Genevan Psalter. It had also tinkered with the doctrines of historic Calvinism, especially the Canons of Dort and the Belgic Confessions, whose strong hostility toward Catholics and Baptists had become something of an embarrassment to the Crown. For a time in the 1830s, in fact, the government had imposed a regimen of fines, harassment, and imprisonment on those Seceders who protested too loudly. By 1840, however, under a new set of religious laws and a new king, the harsh treatment had largely disappeared.

Although it is not accurate to say that the Seceders were the only American immigrants to flee a spirit of tolerance in their native land, it has often looked that way. The image of the Netherlands as a prosperous, open-minded, humane, and stodgily progressive nation has persisted to the present. This brief spate of official intolerance was very much out of character in a land where since the age of Erasmus (a Catholic humanist), Spinoza (a secular Portuguese Jew), and Rembrandt (an Anabaptist), people of widely divergent ideas had lived together peacefully. Much of the Seceders' resentment was aimed at the treatment the government guaranteed to Catholics, Baptists, and Jews, who enjoyed social and legal rights often lacking in other European nations.

The outlines of these ideological disputes should not obscure the issues of bread and butter. To Albertus Van Raalte and Hendrik Scholte, pastors who became the most influential leaders of Dutch settlers in America, the need for freedom of religion (as they saw it) was of utmost importance. But many of their followers were poor, and in their view the trip across the Atlantic offered a new economic beginning as well. Especially in the aftermath of the potato blight, which had hit the Netherlands with demoralizing thoroughness in the summer of 1845, poverty was a compelling reason for considering emigration. Many rural Hollanders had seen their entire potato crop destroyed and, with the blight still raging in the summer of 1846, there was little hope for a quick recovery. Complicating the farmers' plight were a profound change in European economies; a high rate of taxation; and an outmoded, fragmented national infrastructure.

The port cities of Amsterdam and Rotterdam dominated the nation's economy. The outlying provinces did not keep pace with market requirements and found themselves increasingly isolated from the centers of activity. For many farmers life was becoming difficult, sometimes desperate. Even those who could avoid poverty were worried about the future. Prospects for their children were bleak.

Van Raalte and Scholte, each working separately with other prominent leaders of the Seceders, formed cooperative associations, sought financial support, and began looking into possible places to live in America. Van Raalte was the first to leave the Netherlands. Late in the summer of 1846, he led several hundred settlers to the United States, intending to purchase land in Wisconsin, where a few Hollanders had already achieved a foothold. Travel delays, an early winter, and a chance meeting with Dutch Catholics on their way to Wisconsin helped persuade him to remain in Michigan. He soon explored the land around what is now the city of Holland, Michigan, and there he established a *kolonie*, which, over the ensuing decades, attracted thousands of Dutch immigrants. In 1847, Scholte followed Van Raalte; however, Scholte was unwilling to bring his band of people into Michigan, despite several invitations. The land in western Michigan was swampy and heavily wooded, making it difficult for agriculture. Scholte preferred the rolling plains of northwestern Iowa, and chose to settle there, in what became the city of Pella. Western Michigan and northwestern Iowa thus became the centers of a new sort of Dutch colony, based on agriculture, with churches and schools controlled by Calvinist Seceders.

Fewer than one in five of the immigrants came from cities, the rest having lived in rural provinces. In the century of great European emigration, when entire regions of countries such as Ireland were depopulated, the proportion of Hollanders to join the tide never amounted to as much as 1 percent of the population, although the land was small and crowded.

Those settlers who immigrated to America were not desperately poor. More than 65 percent of them were from the middle classes, although as many as one-fifth had sought public assistance from the Dutch government. In some ways, however, they followed traditional patterns. Like most immigrants, they normally arrived in groups rather than as individuals. They moved as part of an extended chain forged by family and church. They followed the folkways they had known back home and, despite the strangeness of the new land, found much that was familiar to them. Many letters tell of meeting old neighbors or long-lost relatives from the Netherlands:

> "I took a trip to the colony," says Marcus Nienhuis in 1854, in a letter back home, "and met a friend of yours. I saw the woman standing in her doorway and asked some directions. As soon as she opened her mouth, I could tell that she was from Drenthe and I asked if she was the wife of Harm Smidt. In surprise she answered. 'Yes'" [Brinks, 1986, p. 36].

People continued to speak in their regional dialects, and formed villages that were virtual transplants from the rural provinces of the Netherlands. Within a few years of the first arrivals, the towns around Holland had sprouted Dutch names: Overisel, Drenthe, Vriesland, Staphorst, Harlem, and Groningen, among others. Sometimes as many as two hundred people would arrive at once, putting a strain on the welcome that was extended to them. However, they kept coming.

Settlement Patterns

Van Raalte had chosen the land around Holland partly because of its isolation—in that way he thought he would keep "foreign" influences on his flock at a minimum. The very difficulty of the place appealed to him. Although the Treaty of Chicago (1833) had displaced most Native Americans from this part of Michigan, there were a few Indians still living in the region. Aside from occasional clearings and oak openings, the land was heavily wooded and swampy. Existing farms were scarce, but since farming was the only way of life most of the settlers knew, and since it was the desire even of those who could not afford land in the Netherlands, they worked clearing acreage and planting crops. By 1900, these settlers and their offspring had acquired more than two thousand square miles of land in Michigan, an immense tract by Dutch standards. In their homeland, thirteen thousand square miles had been parceled out among eleven million inhabitants.

Being primarily agricultural people, or at least aspiring to that condition, the settlers utterly failed to comprehend the ways of the Indians they met, a loosely mixed group of Ottawas and Catholic Potawatamies. Now and then a Hollander would find a deer hanging in a tree and take it home. More often the newcomers would gather up items the Indians had apparently abandoned in the woods, such as axes or troughs for making maple syrup, not knowing that the owners intended to return and use them the next year. Van Raalte, among his other duties as church father, oversaw the return of several thousand maple troughs, with negotiated settlements being reached for those items that had been lost or destroyed.

It was from individual Indian landowners that many of the original tracts of land were purchased, and the settlers worked at maintaining good relations with them, despite misunderstandings. But the late 1840s was a time when the Indian presence in Michigan was diminishing. Most of the Potawatamies had been resettled outside of the state, and the Ottawas were being pushed toward enclaves farther north. An outbreak of fevers, some of them malarial, in the summers of 1847 and 1848 speeded the process of Indian displacement. Some settlers saw God's will behind the high rate of Indian mortality during these bouts of sickness; more likely, however, the cause was a combination of low resistance and a folk remedy for fever that included sudden immersion in cold water.

New settlers kept arriving in a steady stream. Holland, the heart of the kolonie, with about fifteen hundred people in 1850, was spreading its influence through the surrounding villages and had sent many young workers and families to urban satellite communities. The Dutch in Michigan, despite their hardships, were living out an American success story.

Religious Conflicts

Scholte, in Iowa, seemed to favor a less isolationist approach to the experience of America than his counterpart in Michigan, but Scholte, too, wanted his followers to remain true to the vision that had brought them to America. He recognized that if people moved in sufficient numbers and stayed together, they would be able to control the institutions of religion, education, and local government, allowing them to retain the religious and social stability they desired. His followers in Iowa, settling on land that did not require clearing and draining, created productive farms almost immediately, and established trading relations with towns and cities as far away as St. Louis, Missouri. Both these leaders, and many others in smaller towns, insisted on the religious nature of their community. Title deeds routinely required that the owners be Christians, with the added proviso (in practice if not in writing) that they could not be Catholic.

Despite, or perhaps because of, such doctrinal strictness, religious conflicts soon arose in the new communities. The Dutch had long been known for a proclivity to theological squabbling. "Is there a mongrel sect in Christendom," asked one seventeenth-century onlooker, "which does not croak and spawn and flourish in their Sooterkin bogs?" "They are so generally bred up to the Bible," said another, "that almost every cobbler is a Dutch doctor of divinity . . . yet fall those inward illuminations so different that sometimes seven religions are found in one family" (Schama, 1987, p. 266). Religion did lend a special cast to the earliest settlements. Although fewer than 2 percent of the Dutch population belonged to this fringe religious group, Seceders accounted for almost 50 percent of the immigrants before 1850. Even among these conservative folk, however, more than 90 percent listed economic reasons, not religion, as foremost among the causes for their move.

Assimilation and Cultural Persistence

Concerning secular issues, there was virtually no disagreement. A certain amount of assimilation was inevitable and was welcomed. A commitment to a new country cannot be founded simply on disaffection with the old. The farmers worked to adopt current American agricultural practices, which sometimes differed from the Dutch ways, and their letters home show genuine pride in their accomplishments. The villages hired English-speaking teachers for both adults and children to ensure the removal of language barriers.

They established relationships with "Yankee" merchants in nearby cities. They showed a uniquely northern American sentiment on the issue of slavery, going so far in 1855 as to request "humbly and kindly" that a group of southern churches founded by Dutch-American slaveholders be kept out of their religious fellowship. And when the Civil War began, just thirteen years after the founding of Holland, Michigan, hundreds of their young men fought for the Union. These people were dedicated to the idea of becoming Americans—not merely Hollanders on foreign soil—and of making contributions to the life of their new nation. R. T. Kuiper expressed his feelings in a letter to the Netherlands:

"Life is more roomy here," [he wrote], "freer, easier, more common; there is more open-heartedness. . . . There are far fewer formalities and rules of conduct. Everyone associates on a more equal level. True, everyone is called 'mister,' but no one 'sir,' with the exception of the preacher, who is still addressed as 'Dominie.' But no one removes his hat for him" [Brinks, 1986, p. 231].

In one respect, then, they assimilated quite successfully.

However, another attempt at assimilation met with shattering opposition. The earliest Dutch churches affiliated themselves with the Reformed Church of America (RCA), a denomination whose history went back to the days of Peter Stuyvesant. In the eyes of many settlers, the RCA had become too Americanized (i.e., impure in doctrine); this group, almost half the existing community, formed the Christian Reformed Church (CRC) in 1857. Debates about minor details of religious doctrine and practice raged within the community, leaving outsiders mystified. It seems apparent to most historians that these family quarrels were less about religion than about ethnic identity. One group (the RCA) wished to effect a rather significant level of assimilation, while the other (the CRC) emphasized the need to retain moral purity by remaining separate. The real question was how to be American yet Dutch, or vice versa.

By 1900, more than 100,000 new immigrants had been added to the midwestern Dutch communities. The scarcity of available farmland in the original settlements caused two clear changes: First, many new farm villages sprang up in northern areas of Michigan and Wisconsin, on the lowlands to the east of Chicago, in southern Minnesota and South Dakota, and in settlements around Lynden, Washington, and Bellflower, California; second, many families found themselves settling in cities instead of on farms. During this era the communities gained an increasing economic and cultural self-sufficiency, creating or consolidating many of their institutions—hospitals, nursing homes, churches, and schools. Because of divided loyalties between the RCA and the CRC, these institutions tended to develop in pairs. Even the smallest villages supported two churches; the community also developed parallel systems of higher education. The RCA founded Hope College (1866) in Holland. Michigan: the CRC countered with Calvin College (1876) in Grand Rapids, Michigan. Both colleges added seminaries for the training of elergymen.

The divergent strategies of these two conservative cultures appear, in a superficial way, in the makeup of the student bodies at their respective schools. Today, Hope College in Holland enrolls about 40 percent of its students from the Dutch community, while Calvin in Grand Rapids attracts twice the percentage of undergraduates with Dutch surnames. Both communities remain somewhat precariously related to their Dutch heritage and to each other. The expending of so much energy on parochial issues continues to reinforce their insularity.

When historians describe the Dutch communities of Michigan, they are either scrupulously dispassionate or modestly glowing in their assessments. Neat and amply reasoned documents, well-ordered and comprehensible patterns of development, have an innate appeal to historians. Novelists of Dutch descent, writing about the same community, arrive at radically different conclusions, many of them unflattering. In dozens of short stories and novels, Peter De Vries has spent a sizable portion of his narrative time lampooning the midwestern Dutch. Especially in *The Blood of the Lamb,* he shows a society with infinite talent for fragmentation along doctrinal lines. The protagonist's father, in fact, sees this tendency as a sign of health: "Rotten wood you can't split," he boasts.

Novelists such as Feike Feikema and David Cornel De Jong emphasize the painful crushing of independent spirits by a narrow, often boorish culture, doomridden and bleakly ministerial. The filmmaker Paul Schrader, screenwriter and director of such films as *The Last Temptation of Christ, American Gigolo, Raging Bull,* and *Cat People,* often has fun with the community in sly visual asides.

Historians and artists perceive the community in vastly different ways. The nature and purpose of a wellorganized society is to promote group survival, not to nurture individual talent. This quality is what historians—students and employees of cultural institutions—seek and admire. Artists, on the other hand, approach society from the bottom up, often finding their identity in the delicious freedom to revolt and rebel.

Artists, despite the fact that they constitute only the tiniest segment of a community, suggest the possibility of a third immigrant strategy for coping with American society: to maintain a certain distance from the ethnic community without exactly losing touch. Population figures show that Dutch descendants in the United States in 1996 numbered about four million, mostly clustered in the areas of the historical settlement, where they prospered in a wide variety of economic pursuits. Ethnic membership in the RCA and the CRC combined amounted to approximately 500,000.

Continued Contributions

Traditional immigration from the Netherlands slowed to a trickle in the years after World War II, but in the early 1980s there was one notable exception. A group of dairy farmers from the northern provinces of the Netherlands began moving to West Texas, where they established family farms that were well funded and technologically sophisticated.

These farm families, more than four hundred of them by 1996, with religious and cultural connections to midwestern Hollanders, helped move Texas from thirty-fifth place to sixth place in the volume of its milk production, adding yet another small piece to America's cultural mosaic.

Bibliography

Bratt, J. D. (1984). *Dutch Calvinism in Modern America: A History of a Conservative Subculture.* Grand Rapids, MI: W. B. Eerdmans.

Brinks, H. J. (1986). *Write Back Soon: Letters from Dutch Immigrants in America.* Grand Rapids, MI: CRC Publications.

De Jong, G. F. (1975). *The Dutch in America, 1609-1974.* Boston: Twayne.

Hinte, J. v. ([1928] 1985). *Netherlanders in America: A Study of Emigration and Settlement in the Nineteenth and Twentieth Centuries in the United States of America,* translated by A. De Wit. Grand Rapids, MI: Baker Book House.

Lucas, H. S. (1955). *Netherlanders in America.* Ann Arbor, MI: University of Michigan Press.

Mulder, A. (1947). *Americans from Holland.* Philadelphia: Lippincott.

Schama, S. (1987). *The Embarrassment of Riches: An Interpretation of Dutch Culture in the Golden Age.* New York: Knopf.

—LARRY TEN HARMSEL

ENGLISH

England, the homeland of the English, is unlike Scotland, Wales, or Northern Ireland because it does not constitutionally exist; it has no separate rights, administration, or official statistics. The Church of England is its main distinctive institution. The English in England maintain their separate identity in sports (soccer, cricket, and rugby) and heritage, which are manifest in the monarchy, aristocracy and associated pageantry, Parliament, pride in their country, and love for their local community (with the local pub being an integrating institution). Also, English poetry, prose literature, and art are distinctive.

Although there are a lot of similarities, English culture differs from that of the United States in that the English place greater emphasis on maintaining traditions, self-restraint, control of aggression, discipline, insularity from Continental Europe and other cultures, and pride in their ability to deal rationally with diverse situations.

In the United States, an English person is one who has emigrated from or traces ancestral roots to England, even if the ancestry is not exclusively English. Unlike American ethnicity, which is based on the concept of soil (because of the inherent definition of the United States as an immigrant nation), English ethnicity is based on the concept of blood. In other words one had to trace one's blood or ancestry to those who claimed to be and were accepted as being racially English.

Immigrants from England have a unique place among the ethnic communities in America because their initial and ongoing cultural influence has been pervasive. Because English culture has survived as the base of U.S. culture, a unity has been maintained in spite of the cultural diversity resulting from immigration. Specifically, English culture forms the basis for U.S. society and culture in terms of language, literature, social customs, law, and political thought.

In addition to the English cultural concepts that contributed to the early success of the United States, people of English descent such as George Washington, John Adams, and Benjamin Franklin contributed directly by signing the Declaration of Independence and providing leadership for the drafting of the U.S. Constitution and Bill of Rights.

English culture continues to exert its influence, if somewhat less obviously, on American society. For example, WASP (white Anglo-Saxon Protestant) continues to connote traditional wealth and power, and assimilation to U.S. culture is still referred to as "Anglo-conformity." Some, like the "Boston Brahmins," take special pride in their English ancestry and the contribution their English ancestors have made to the growth and development of the United States, but the English-based foundation is being challenged by the ideology of multiculturalism.

Immigration and Settlement History

England constitutes the largest land area and has the highest population density of any of the four units of the United Kingdom. It is also the most intensely industrialized region. Located off the western coast of Continental Europe, it is bounded on the north by Scotland and on the west by Wales. Geographically, England constitutes 50,332 square miles, or 53 percent of the land area of the United Kingdom.

Other than the Native Americans, the English were the first to settle what is now the United States. They established the first permanent colony at Jamestown in 1607; other early settlements were at Plymouth and Massachusetts Bay in 1620-1622. Many immigrated to obtain cheap land and avail themselves of better economic opportunities, although others were looking for religious freedom. Most colonies came under royal control, established the Church of England, and had the English system of law, governmental administration, education, commerce, financial management, agriculture, arts, and entertainment.

Three settlements emerged as social models: Pennsylvania, where all white Europeans would be welcomed on equal terms; Massachusetts, where the "religiously pure" would be accepted; and the Virginia structure, where a plantation economy based on cheap workers, especially slaves, developed. The Pennsylvania model eventually became the basis for the U.S. Constitution and American society.

The settlements in southern New England, with their emphasis on Puritan ethics and conformity, possessed a zeal for democracy, a passion for education, and an intention for their values to be the values of the entire nation. Divergence was more characteristic of the indentured workers and relatives of indentured workers who lived in the settlements of the Tidewater region of Virginia and Maryland. However, tobacco dominated the economy of these middle Atlantic settlements, making the settlers dependent on the English market and perpetuating their ties to the homeland. The settlements of Pennsylvania emphasized "acceptance," creating a greater heterogeneity among their population. The distinctive traits of these three original settlement regions followed their residents who moved west. New Englanders migrated across New York and through northern Ohio to form settlements in Michigan, Wisconsin, northern Indiana, and northern Illinois. The Tidewater people moved across Pennsylvania to southern Illinois and down into the hill country of Kentucky and Tennessee. Pennsylvanians followed a similar pattern, moving into southern Indiana and Illinois.

Initially, single men were sent to America by the Virginia Company to find gold (which did not materialize) and create a profitable trade. By the late 1620s, agriculture and tobacco-raising stabilized and became profitable, while England began to suffer economically, all of which resulted in several thousand individuals immigrating annually, a stream that included women and children. In the Chesapeake to Charleston region, indentured servants trained as farmers, tradesmen, laborers, and craftsmen were the primary immigrants. Indentured servants who brought their families to or joined their families in America were likely to remain. But the indenture system was gradually replaced by slavery, which provided cheaper labor.

In 1690, 90 percent of the seaboard colonies were English by birth, and in the 1790 U.S. Census, 60 percent of the population of that region had English names.

Between the American Revolution and 1825, England's involvement in India, Latin America, and the War of 1812 ("America's Second War of Independence") contributed to a reduction in English immigration. Also, it was a period when London restricted the number of English craftsmen and settlers each ship could transport to America. Except for the period during the U.S. Civil War, however, English immigration increased steadily after 1825 and peaked in the 1880s. Family units became more prominent in the immigration stream after 1835. English immigration increased to 60,000 a year by the 1860s and rose to 75,000 annually in 1872, after which it began to decline. This wave that began in the 1820s was largely due to unrest in England caused by tenant farmers and urban laborers fleeing depressed areas affected by industrial changes. Although some people had dreams of a utopian society, most were attracted by new land, textile factories, railroads, and the expanding mining industry. By the end of the nineteenth century, the middle Atlantic states had the largest number of English Americans, followed by the north-central states and New England. However, a growing number were moving to the West, the Pacific Coast, and the South.

Despite the fact that England was the largest investor in American land development, railroads, mining, cattle ranching, and heavy industry throughout the nineteenth century, the English comprised only 15 percent of the great nineteenth-century European immigration to America. In fact, of those who left England between 1820 and 1920, only 10 percent went to America. During the first four decades of the twentieth century, English immigration declined to 6 percent of the total influx because there were better economic opportunities and favorable immigration policies in Australia and Canada. The percentage of skilled workers and professionals entering the United States, however, increased dramatically. It was a time when English culture, literature, and family connections were desired—the marriage of wealthy Americans to English aristocrats was well publicized, and colleges and universities emphasized America's English heritage in history and literature courses.

During the Great Depression of the 1930s, more English returned than entered the United States, although it was a time when more English women entered than men. The decline reversed in the decade after World War II, when more than 100,000 people, many of them war brides, entered the United States. This was less than 12 percent of the European influx. In the 1960s, the term "brain drain" was coined to refer to the outflow of English engineers, technicians, medical professionals, and other specialists being lured to America by large corporations. Thus, since 1970, partly due to the implementation of the Immigration Act of 1965, English immigrants have been about 12 percent of the total flow arriving from Europe. These individuals, usually unmarried and professionally trained, have, like their predecessors, continued to merge almost imperceptibly into American society. This is true not only because of their cultural compatibility but also because the immigration stream is dominated by professionals, managers, and technically skilled people who have found good jobs in metropolitan areas.

Demography

A total of 25,836,397 Americans claim English as their first ancestry, and 10,819,382 claim it as their second ancestry; in 1980, a total of 23,748,772 claimed it as their single ancestry. The type of immigrant has changed over the years. Initially settlers were primarily single males, with a large number being indentured laborers. In the nineteenth century, families and technically skilled individuals became more prominent. It was a time when there was a push factor of poor economic conditions and social unrest in England and the pull of opportunities in the United States. As of the mid-1990s, the highest percentage of English settlers is found in the counties of the Appalachian Mountains, especially in Tennessee, Kentucky, and southwestern Virginia. The English are the third-largest ethnic group in the United States (after the Germans and the Irish). The southeastern region of the United States has the largest number of people claiming English descent, while California, Texas, Florida, New York, and Ohio host the largest number of English Americans among individual states.

Language

When English immigrants arrive in the United States, they enter a country where the national language is the same as their own: English. The English language is of the Indo-European family. Its parent tongue is the West Germanic group of Proto-Indo-European. The nearest related languages are German, Netherlandic, and Frisian. There is considerable dialectal variation, the most distinctive in England being in Lancashire, Cornwall, and parts of East London.

English spoken by recent immigrants from England is identifiable by the accent. The accent, however, is largely lost after several decades in the United States. The greater distinction between English spoken in England and that spoken in the United States has to do with several hundred vocabulary words. Some of the differences include petrol for gas, crisps for potato chips, and ring off for hanging up the telephone.

Cultural Characteristics

The English are indistinguishable from the mainstream of American white society. Besides, American culture is based on English values and institutions; thus American institutions and behavioral patterns are similar to those of the comparable class in England. As a result, adjustment to life in the United States for English immigrants is minimal. They do not form residential enclaves, nor are their houses or lifestyle noticeably different from other Americans of a comparable class. The English in America do not have visible symbols that distinguish them from mainstream American society.

During the nineteenth and early twentieth centuries, English immigrants tended to be technically trained or agriculturalists. Most worked in industry. Small groups of English skilled workers in industrial and mining communities in the East and Midwest did attempt to form labor unions, but the unions were generally short-lived. During the post-World War II period, especially after the Immigration Act of 1965 was implemented, English immigrants were not numerous—in fact, the quota from England was seldom filled—but they were generally highly skilled and technically trained. Their contribution to the quality of life and the high technological position of the United States was and is very high.

English family life focuses on the nuclear family of husband, wife, and children, with an occasional relative living with them. This structure was set during the Colonial era. Even separatist groups, such as the Puritans, were comprised of nuclear families. In New England, laws such as Sunday "blue laws" were designed to sanctify the Sabbath by prohibiting drinking, dancing, and work-related activities on the Sabbath while at the same time encouraging prayer, charity, and missionary activities. Outside of New England, entertainment in the forms of dancing, sports, and singing were not only more prevalent but often were sponsored by the church. During the large waves of nineteenth-century immigration, English immigrants joined communities of other English in small towns and re-created the traditional pub as well as choral societies, sports clubs, self-help societies, and fraternal organizations.

Generally, women dominate the domestic and social life of the family as well as relations with friends and extended family. It is their role to maintain connections with relatives in England. Men control the business and public aspects of family life. This sexual division of duties in the English-American family has been decreasing since World War II, especially in the 1970s and 1980s, when the women's liberation movement gained a following in the United States. English-American women, like the rest of the American female population, joined in the cause of obtaining equal rights for females, which had the side effect of decreasing the sexual division of duties within the English-American family.

For most English immigrants, the church is central to their identity. Virtually all Christian religious denominations present in England are also present in the United States, and the liturgy and Scriptures are similar in both countries. Therefore, most English immigrants can practice the same form of religious expression in America that they practiced in England.

Another institution emphasized by the English immigrant is education. Many groups, including the Quakers and Puritans from England, advocate free public education for all. Professionals favor private schools and colleges; they also value sending their sons for a junior year abroad at a British university. Thus there are many endowments to subsidize education in England, the most famous being the Rhodes scholarship program.

Higher education has been a concern of English immigrants since the Colonial era. Thus a large percentage of early colleges in America were founded by British immigrants or their descendants, especially in New England and the Southeast. In many of these colleges, they emphasized traditional English sports such as sculling (team rowing) and rugby. However, three English aristocratic pastimes that enjoy the greatest popularity in America and have "become American" are tennis, horse racing, and sailing. Also, scattered throughout the United States are rugby, cricket, and English football (soccer) teams, where the uniquely English sports heritage is kept alive.

English immigrants and their descendants have included many leading philanthropists who have supported museums, colleges, medical societies, cultural organizations, and academic exchange programs.

Assimilation

The English in the United States have become a "hidden community" in that they have not developed or maintained an identity that is distinctive from the mainstream of American society. In fact, since the beginning of the civil rights movement, the English have become more "hidden" because identifying with or being WASP (a derogatory term also used to imply being English) resulted in connotations of being a racist or an exploiter. Because they have blended so easily into the American mainstream, there is very little written about the English as an ethnic community.

Bibliography

Berthoff, R. T. ([1953] 1968). *British Immigrants in Industrial America, 1790–1950.* New York: Russell & Russell.

Blumenthal, S. (1980). *Coming to America: Immigrants from the British Isles.* New York: Delacorte Press.

Boston, R. (1971). *British Chartist in America, 1830–1900.* Manchester, Eng.: University of Manchester Press.

Campbell, M. (1955). "English Emigration on the Eve of the American Revolution." *American Historical Review* 61:1–20.

Cohen, R. (1994). *Frontiers of Identity: The British and Others.* London: Longman.

Erickson, C. ([1972] 1990). *Invisible Immigrants: The Adaptation of English and Scottish Immigrants in 19th-Century America.* Ithaca, NY: Cornell University Press.

Johnson, S. C. ([1914] 1966). *A History of Emigration from the United Kingdom to North America, 1763–1912.* New York: E. P. Dutton.

Kirk, R. (1994). *America's British Culture.* New Brunswick, NJ: Transaction.

Noble, A. G., ed. (1992). *To Build a New Land: Ethnic Landscapes in North America.* Baltimore, MD: Johns Hopkins University Press.

Robertiello, R. C. (1988). *The WASP Mystique.* New York: Donald I. Fine.

Shepperson, W. S. (1957). *British Emigration to North America.* Minneapolis: University of Minnesota Press.

Shepperson, W. S. (1965). *Emigration and Disenchantment: Portraits of Englishmen Repatriated from the United States.* Norman: University of Oklahoma Press.

Snowman, D. (1977). *Britain and America: An Interpretation of Their Culture, 1945–1975.* New York: New York University Press.

Taylor, A. M. (1965). *Expectations Westward: The Mormons and the Emigration of Their British Converts in the 19th Century.* Ithaca, NY: Cornell University Press.

Yearly, C. K. (1957). *Britons in American Labor: A History of the Influence of United Kingdom Immigrants on American Labor, 1820–1914.* Baltimore, MD: John Hopkins University Press.

—ARTHUR W. HELWEG

FRENCH

French-born immigrants in America are sometimes called "Franco Americans." This term, however, characterizes essentially French Canadians. The term "French American" stresses that these immigrants came directly from France and cannot be mixed with other French-speaking groups in the United States (i.e., Louisiana Cajuns, Creoles, and French Canadians). The history, language, and culture of the French Canadians and Louisiana Cajuns often differ from those of the French Americans. Other French-born immigrants came as members of groups seldom associated with France (e.g., Amish and Mennonites) and share their history with these groups. The history of French-speaking immigrants from other countries (e.g., Switzerland and Vietnam) is also comparable to that of other immigrants from these areas. It is sometimes difficult to differentiate the contributions of the members of each of these groups.

Discovery and Settlement

"America," the name of the entire continent containing the United States, appeared in print for the first time in 1507, in Saint-Dié-des-Vosges (France), when the authors of the *Introduction to Cosmography* named the lands mapped earlier by Amerigo Vespucci. French merchants soon came to the realization that this discovery offered a potential source of income. In 1523, the French king Francois I sent Verrazano on a discovery mission. The first French explorers who ventured into the newly discovered lands followed the rivers (the Saint Lawrence River in particular). Members of the Jesuit order, the only religious group allowed in the French colonies at that time, came along with traders and explorers. The Jesuits' goal was to convert the Indians to Roman Catholicism; the goal of other Frenchmen in North America was to develop trade with the Indians. These two approaches were contradictory; the Jesuits often disrupted trading activities because they saw them as detrimental to the spiritual well-being of the Indians. The Jesuits enjoyed their monopoly until 1698. Their efforts brought limited results and often led to violence and warfare between Indian tribes or between the French and the Indians.

The regions of North America where French explorers, soldiers, and missionaries were active became known as New France. It included eastern Canada, the Great Lakes, and the valleys of the Ohio and Mississippi rivers. The seventeenth century marked a key period in the development of New France. The French king Louis XIV oversaw a transformation of the administrative structures of these regions that led to an increase in French efforts at discovery and trade. In addition to a reinforcement of the French presence in what is today the Canadian province of Quebec, the French colonies of Illinois and Louisiana emerged during this period.

The *coureurs des bois* (literally, "messenger of the woods"; here it means traders, in contrast to explorers and Jesuits) were the first Frenchmen to reach many of the Indian tribes during the westward development of New France They were often associated with explorers and Jesuits. The coureurs des bois accused the Jesuits of hampering their trade efforts; the Jesuits accused the coureurs des bois of corrupting the Indians with their alcohol and their bawdy lifestyle; the explorers saw the other two groups as necessary but unreliable allies. The best-known French figures of this period were explorers. In 1673, Jacques Marquette and Louis Jolliet were the first to enter the Mississippi River and travel southward until reaching the Arkansan tribes; Daniel Greysolon, sieur du Luth, explored Lake Superior in 1678; Cavelier de la Salle descended the Mississippi to the Gulf of Mexico in 1682; and Étienne Venyard, sieur de Bourgmont, explored Kansas in 1724. These early explorations did not bring immigrants but led to the creation of a few military and trading outposts. In addition to Quebec and its surrounding regions, the only noticeable areas of French settlement in the late seventeenth and early eighteenth centuries were the Illinois and Louisiana areas.

The evolution of the Illinois region during the second half of the seventeenth century was atypical. After several decades marked by hunting, fishing, and trading, the area (including the valleys of the Ohio and northern Mississippi rivers) became an agricultural region, thus entering the second stage in the development of the frontier. The creation of these French settlements complicated the military protection of French interests. The Fox Indians had been opposed to the French and renewed their attacks on the Illinois settlements. From 1712 to 1737, the French army waged an unsuccessful war against the Fox.

In Louisiana, the late seventeenth and the early eighteenth centuries were marked by military actions against the Indians (the Natchez Wars) and by efforts to attract settlers to ensure the survival and the growth of the colony. The French authorities deported poor men and women, robbers, and other French prisoners to Louisiana. They also provided the poorest women with a "dowry" so they could find a husband once they arrived in America. In addition, the French brought black slaves from Haiti to add to their work force. In 1727, the Ursuline Sisters established a convent in New Orleans (founded in 1718), introduced strict education among Creole and French young ladies, and contributed to an in-depth transformation of French society of Louisiana. The emergence of a moneyed class of traders and planters accelerated the establishment of slavery following enactment of the Black Codes in 1724.

The Seven Years' War began in 1754 in America with the defeat of George Washington at Fort Duquesne, near present-day Pittsburgh. After encouraging actions in 1756 and 1757 against the British, the French forces were progressively put on the defensive. Quebec fell on September 18, 1759, and the rest of New France crumbled progressively. In 1763, the Treaty of Paris took away all the French possessions in America and gave Louisiana to Spain.

Other Early French Settlers

During the early sixteenth century, Protestantism attracted a significant number of French followers. The opposition of the Catholic Church and edicts of the French king encouraged the French Huguenots to look for other places of settlement. Between 1555 and 1559, groups of explorers sailed without success to Brazil, Florida, and Canada. Jean Ribaut's first expedition to Florida failed; a second, more successful one was launched in 1564.

French Huguenot immigration to America began in earnest during the seventeenth century. The first French Huguenots left from Holland (the Dutch had founded New Amsterdam between 1610 and 1620) and, progressively, from French ports (La Rochelle in particular). By the late seventeenth century, several thousand French Huguenots had sailed for America. They settled in British colonies around New York City (New Rochelle in particular), in New England (Oxford, Salem), in Virginia, and in the Carolinas. The impact of these French-born Huguenots was hardly noticeable in America because they were readily assimilated by the society in which they had found refuge. The Colonists usually welcomed these French newcomers. The "Americanization" of the majority of French Huguenots was thorough because of their religious beliefs and because of their social standing (many French Huguenots were nobles or skilled craftsmen). Today, however, there is still an identifiable trace of the French Huguenot heritage in South Carolina (in and around Charleston).

Revolutionary Years

The revolutionary years include the 1770s, 1780s, and 1790s, when revolutionary wars spread in America and France. The French involvement was significant during the American War of Independence. Military support from the French army and navy as well as financial support from the French Crown sustained the American efforts until the British surrendered at Yorktown (in 1781). The results of these actions were felt differently by the French who were in America. The Marquis de Lafayette's popularity throughout the newly founded United States was a direct result of his own involvement in the War of Independence. For the French settlers in Illinois and the northern Mississippi River valley, these decades meant the end of their independence and prosperity. Their lands in Illinois and Missouri were progressively taken away from them by American settlers, and by the end of the eighteenth century, there were no significant French settlements left in the northern Mississippi River valley.

During the late 1780s and 1790s, the French Revolution forced French nobles out of France, and many found refuge in America. They settled primarily in urban areas (New York, Boston, Philadelphia, Charleston, New Orleans), with a few venturing westward. Several outlandish schemes were concocted by these nobles. One such example was Asylum, a settlement built in northeastern Pennsylvania with the hope of bringing Queen Marie Antoinette to America and re-creating a version of the French court of Versailles. By the early 1800s, as soon as the revolutionary violence diminished in France, most of these émigrés had abandoned their American homes and projects and had returned to France.

Nineteenth and Early Twentieth Centuries

The number of French settlers in the United States at the beginning of the nineteenth century was small and increased slowly during the nineteenth and early twentieth centuries (54,000 in 1850; 116,402 in 1870; 104,197 in 1900; 153,000 in 1920). This minimal increase was due to several reasons. First, since the Treaty of Paris, the French had no lands left in North America. Second, France had never had a strong pattern of immigration. Third, the French colonies easily absorbed those who wanted to try their luck outside France.

Several factors contributed to the arrival of noticeable small French groups to the United States. The de-

velopment of maritime transportation during the nineteenth century helped French immigrants cross the Atlantic to eastern harbors (New York City, Boston, Philadelphia) and southern ports (New Orleans, Mobile). The defeat at Waterloo led to the arrival of former Napoleonic soldiers who tried to create self-sufficient settlements in Alabama (Démopolis and Aigleville) and in Texas (Champ d'Asile). Those experiments, however, failed rapidly. The second group was composed of French whose goal was the creation of settlements in new lands where a new lifestyle would lead to happiness and well-being. Whether disciples of Étienne Cabet (the Icarians) who settled in Illinois, Iowa, and Missouri, or followers of Charles Fourier (the Phalanxists) who settled in Texas, these small groups encountered limited success. Some remained where they had settled and were absorbed into the neighboring American society; others returned to France after their failure. The third group included the French "forty-niners" who arrived in California during the Gold Rush. These immigrants were attracted by the promise of riches. Their impact, however, was felt only indirectly. After the rush, those who stayed behind planted vineyards and helped establish California's wine country.

A fourth group came later in the nineteenth century and attempted to organize workers in factories, mines, and workshops. These were socialists and anarchists who settled primarily in and around New York City and spread into the neighboring regions in the 1870s and 1880s. Their small numbers and pressures from their bosses as well as workers from other ethnic groups limited their success. The utopians came from urban locales where they were artisans and industrial workers; they attempted to create rural utopias in America and failed. The socialists and anarchists were also industrial workers or miners, and their efforts in America resembled those of their European counterparts. Their success was limited among a varied work force in a climate of uncertainty and tension.

Only a few areas of France provided significant numbers of immigrants. Four provinces sent identifiable contingents to the United States during the nineteenth century. Central France provided a stream of immigrants during the last decades of the nineteenth century; several areas in Brittany also sent regular groups to America. The largest groups came from northeastern France (Alsace, Lorraine, Franche-Comté). Alsace had been confiscated by the Germans after the French defeat of 1870–1871. Migrants from Alsace settled in rural zones between the East Coast and the frontier or in urban areas (Denver, Chicago, Detroit, etc.), where they often associated with German-speaking people, whose language they shared. The Basque migration that began in the 1880s was smaller, more focused, and confined primarily to Nevada and California, where the newcomers played an important role in raising and herding sheep and cattle.

French-born immigrants made a noticeable contribution to the history of Roman Catholicism in the United States. Between 1800 and 1900, many newly created dioceses were headed by French-born bishops. This trend is noticeable, as the creation of these dioceses paralleled the westward expansion of the United States. These early French-born bishops were often succeeded by bishops reflecting more closely the ethnic makeup of the Roman Catholic congregations within the diocese. During the nineteenth and early twentieth centuries, other French-born immigrants came alone, sometimes for specific reasons (Civil War volunteers, scientists, artists), and were often assimilated into the surrounding American society, whether they encountered fame or not.

From the 1920s to the 1990s

The impact of World War I caused a total break in the French migration patterns. There was a great need for workers, scientists, farmers, and teachers in France, and emigration slowed. In addition, the American Immigration Act of 1924 limited the number of French immigrants to 3,000 per year. The 1920s and 1930s were somber decades for French Americans. Their overall influence was waning, the cohesion of their communities was diminishing, and French-language publications began to disappear. With the growth of American public education, the active use of the French language became confined to familial or fraternal surroundings and diminished progressively. The end result was the assimilation of the French Americans.

World War II brought a new wave of French immigration to America. Artists, writers, actors, intellectuals, and politicians from diverse political allegiances (from Gaullists to socialists and collaborationists) fleeing Nazism settled in eastern cities. Many continued their original activities and brought an aura of distinction to the French-American group. After the war, French-born brides of American soldiers constituted a noticeable group of new immigrants.

The general migration patterns of French Americans changed during the postwar decades. Many French who immigrated to America after 1950 were active in teaching and abstract research (in secondary schools and universities), business and commerce (restaurant owners, chefs, designers), and industrial or applied research (computer specialists, software designers). In 1980, among the 120,200 French Americans, there were 160 women for every 100 men, settled primarily in the states of California (23,764) and New York (20,852); there were, however, French Americans in every state of the United States. The French Americans were part of the 2.6 million French-speaking Americans making up the fifth-largest linguistic group in the country.

Conclusion

The overall impact of French Americans was limited in past centuries. Today their impact on the social, scientific, artistic, and intellectual life of the United States is hardly noticeable. There is no French-language press of national scope in the United States, and French Americans have few relational or organizational networks (the Alliance Française seems to be an exception). They wield little power within the American political, religious, and economic systems. In 1980, 67 percent of

French Americans had become American citizens; the "melting pot" had really led to their absorption into American society.

Bibliography

Allain, M., and Conrad, G., eds. (1973). *France and North America: Over 300 Years of Dialogue.* Lafayette, LA: University of Southwestern Lousiana Press.

Allain, M., and Conrad, G., eds. (1974). *France and North America: The Revolutionary Experience.* Lafayette, LA: University of Southwestern Louisiana Press.

Allain, M., and Conrad, G., eds. (1978). *France and North America: Utopia and Utopians.* Lafayette, LA: University of Southwestern Louisiana Press.

Creagh, R. (1988). *Nos cousins d'Amérique: Histoire des Francais aux Etats-Unis.* Paris: Payot.

Golden, Richard M. (1988). *The Huguenot Connection.* Doordrecht, The Neth.: Martinus Nijhoff.

Louder, D., and Waddell, E., eds. (1993). *French America: Mobility, Identity, and Minority Experience Across the Continent.* Baton Rouge, LA: Louisiana State University Press.

McDermott, J. F., ed. (1969). *Frenchmen and French Ways in the Mississippi Valley.* Urbana: University of Illinois Press.

Mathy, J.-P. (1993). *Extrême-Occident: French Intellectuals and America.* Chicago: University of Chicago Press.

Nasatir, A. P. (1945). *French Activities in California: An Archival Calendar Guide.* Stanford, CA: Stanford University Press.

Parkman, F. (1851–1892). *France and England in North America: Being a Comprehensive History.* Boston: Little, Brown.

Zoltvany, Y. F. (1969). *The French Tradition in America.* New York: Harper & Row.

—ANDRÉ J. M. PRÉVOS

GERMANS

Traditions remain firmly rooted among many transplanted German Americans. More than a century and a half after settlement, Lutheran parishioners from Frankenmuth, Michigan, maintain routine contact with their parent congregation in the old country. As they have through the decades, church members still start each written letter with the same Old-German greeting, "I send you greetings in the name of the Father and Son and Holy Ghost." However, outside of a few enclaves such as Frankenmuth and in the "German triangle"—the areas between Cincinnati, Milwaukee, and St. Louis—and in Pennsylvania, German languages and customs have disappeared. For most contemporary Germans, social isolation and the ethnic tie to a small clan have been largely extinguished. Ethnic diversity among fellow Germans, religious and political differences, and two world wars fought against Germany encouraged German Americans to assimilate rapidly. The same forces also caused others to withdraw into isolated rural and urban ethnic enclaves. Diversity and fragmentation within German-American societies challenge those who intend to construct a common history of German settlement in America. Generalizations must be made carefully, stereotypes questioned, and historical observations often must be made with caution and qualification.

Today, ethnic traditions among Germans, when they do exist, are selective. The best German characteristics are often celebrated as part of tradition and economics—to attract visitors to Old World celebrations. German immigrants, better than most, successfully struggled and sacrificed to provide their children with a sense of belonging. Once later generations mastered the English language, secured employment, and transcended local parochialism, they looked back at their heritage. Most German Americans did not prolong ethnic sentimentality, and they should be viewed as descendants of those who struggled to become real Americans.

The contradictory image between cultural preservation and assimilation among German-speaking peoples is best explained by the sheer number of German immigrants and their places of origin. In 1990, fifty-three million Americans claimed some degree of German descent. Between 1820 and 1900, nearly five million immigrants from Germany settled in the United States. Between World War I and 1963, German arrivals outnumbered those from any other single country. In the last quarter of the twentieth century only Britain could claim more ethnic offspring (14% of all Americans) than those identifying themselves as descendants of Germans (12%). Nearly seven million Germans, settled in America, or 15 percent of the total immigration. Their numerical strength made it inevitable that sizable numbers would readily Americanize.

Besides numbers, religious, cultural, and geographic heterogeneity also encouraged assimilation. Nineteenth- and twentieth-century wars continuously shifted the boundaries of Germany and made it difficult to identify all Germans geographically. For the purpose of this entry, German immigrants are defined as those arriving from the territory of imperial Germany as formed in 1871, and the state that succeeded it after the Treaty of Versailles in 1919. Unless they arrived in masses as religious congregations or villages from one province and settled together in America, cultural differences among Germans coupled with widespread geographical settlement patterns in America dispersed common culture identity and facilitated acculturalization.

Germans are also exceptional among immigrant groups because of their religious differences. The most obvious religious identity divided northern Germans, dominantly Protestant Lutheran, from southern Germans and Rhinelanders, mostly Catholic. Even within these broad geographical zones, smaller sects were central to German identity. Moravians, Mennonites, Pietists, and Jews often were motivated by religious intolerance or missionary zeal to emigrate. Religion reinforced group identity in the New World and buttressed German churches, schools, and languages, especially in the mid-Atlantic and midwestern settlements.

German immigrants were politically and economically diverse. They were not all conservatives from an authoritarian empire, but freethinkers, political reformers, and some revolutionaries. And unlike poverty-driven Irish or Poles, many Germans arrived in America with some major or substantial savings and agricultural or mechanical skills. Also, many German immigrants had acquired some education.

Eighteenth-Century Immigration

Initially German settlers arrived in Virginia, recruited by the London Company; however, it was not until seventy years later, in 1681, that William Penn brought thirteen German and Dutch Mennonite families to settle Germantown, Pennsylvania. Although this was the earliest specifically German settlement, large-scale immigration did not begin until the early eighteenth century, in 1709, when heavy taxation and harsh winters led several thousand Palatinate Germans to immigrate, via England, to the Hudson River region of New York and to Pennsylvania. Word-of-mouth promotion, letters, and "newland" agents persuaded thousands of southwestern Germans to travel to America. Perhaps as many as half to two-thirds arrived in America as "redemptionists"—individuals bound to New World masters as servants, usually for four years, for payment of their passage across the Atlantic.

German immigration continued, reaching a peak in midcentury, until the Seven Years' War (1756–1763), imperial prohibition in 1768, and the American Revolution (1775–1783) brought it to a fifty-year standstill. The immigrants entered mostly through Philadelphia, and, like the experiences encountered in later centuries, these eighteenth-century pioneers immigrated to America for a variety of reasons.

The early Germantown settlers were Dutch and Swiss German-speakers, and mostly Lutheran and Reformed Church members. And while religious motives played a role in emigration—some Mennonites, Baptists, Dunkers, Schwenkfelders, and Moravian Brethren arrived before 1740—economic factors overwhelmingly motivated most German newcomers. Old Country inheritance customs that continuously divided small land parcels forced many farmers into marginal existence by the 1730s. Skilled and semiskilled artisans, day laborers, and former landholders were attracted to the opportunities in America promoted by ship captains, advertisements by proprietors in America, and "letters from Pennsylvania."

Those seeking a better life crowded the port city of Rotterdam, Holland. Often with little savings left after their four-week trip down the Rhine from southwestern Germany, these refugees remained willing to hazard the last of their resources on the transatlantic voyage; 7 to 10 percent of them died in crossing or shortly after their arrival. It is estimated that as many as 50 percent of the young children whose families attempted to settle along the tidewater coast between Baltimore and South Carolina also died.

Most German-speakers, though, fanned out in and around Philadelphia. The early arrivals took the best farmland or settled into the skilled or market trades in Germantown. In time others moved westward into Lancaster County and down the Shenandoah Valley into Virginia and South Carolina. New York, Maryland, and New Jersey also attracted significant numbers. Benjamin Franklin, just before the Revolutionary War, estimated that German-speaking settlers made up one-third of Pennsylvania's population. Still, while they were one of the largest sources of immigration, only about 100,000 Germans arrived in the colonies. In the 1790 U.S. Census, about 8.6 percent of the population in the United States was of German decent.

Franklin expressed the anxiety evident among many Pennsylvanians, where an alarming number of Germans threatened traditional English-speakers: "Why should *Pennsylvania* founded by the *English,* become a colony of *Aliens,* who will shortly be so numerous as to Germanize us instead of our Anglifying them?" (Dinnerstein and Reimers, 1988, p. 2). To assimilate the newcomers the state set up a number of English-language-only schools.

German-speakers assimilated into the cultural mainstream at a moderate pace in the eighteenth century. Rural areas originally settled by church groups or village migrations maintained their ethnic identity. The German language was used in the home and at religious services. A German press that supported thirty-eight German newspapers prior to 1800 flourished in urban areas. Many German-language schools and societies also were established to resist secularization and loss of the language. Marriage partners remained largely German-speakers at the end of the century, although patterns of religious commonality in marriage were beginning to break down.

As rural German settlements grew and settlers moved away from the cities, integration diminished German culture. The English language was necessary for trade and commerce, law, and politics. Germantown residents began to Anglicize their names, and church and business records were soon kept in English. German immigration, almost nonexistent for half a century at about the time of the American Revolution, encouraged assimilation as ties with Germany were loosened or severed.

Nineteenth-Century Immigration

Large-scale emigration from the German provinces began again after the Napoleonic wars in 1815. Until 1834, southwestern Germany continued to provide the bulk of the emigrants. They still departed from Dutch port cities; however, by the 1830s, Antwerp, Rotterdam, and Amsterdam acquired poor reputations because residents frequently exploited emigrants by charging high fees for provisions and lodging during the long wait for passage. On January 1, 1834, provincial toll barriers between German states were lowered nationwide. The Zollverein, or tariff union, facilitated movement to the German harbors of Bremen and Hamburg. Now others, both paupers and the more prosperous, joined the southwesterners on the journey to America.

By midcentury, passengers arrived in German port cities from the Rhineland, Westphalia, Oldenberg, and Saxony. The eastern regions of Prussia and Mecklenburg, heretofore recipients of German émigrés, likewise began to export people to America. Steamship and cheap, subsidized railway travel further diverted emigrants from the Rhine River corridor to Bremen and Hanover. American insistence on clean and safer ships, coupled with the efforts German emigration societies made for shorter waiting periods—only three or four days before departure—quickly dispelled many hazards once associated with the legendary journey.

Geographical diversification also reflected a change in the socioeconomic status of the travelers. Impoverished, surplus populations of the Southwest continued to emigrate, but now an increasingly more prosperous emigrant emerged from the North. Here farms and small shops could be passed on in total to heirs. Those who did not benefit through inheritance, as well as craftsmen, small merchants, and manufacturers who could not compete within a changing industrial economy, saw their future in the New World. Emigration for these people was a way to preserve and sustain Old World family and economic habits. Between 1830 and 1850, a higher proportion of comfortable, skilled, and educated emigrants left Germany than in any other period.

War and military service also influenced emigration. Decades-long conscription terms in the provincial armies coupled with frequent wars fought for German unification after midcentury spurred thousands of young men to travel abroad. "Forty-eighters," men who fled as fugitives from the aborted democratic revolutions in 1848 and 1849, likewise numbered several thousand. Bavarian Jews—some 10,000—fled from the Southwest to escape social and religious discrimination. Pietists continued to leave; they settled in communal societies such as Harmony and Economy, Pennsylvania; Amana, Iowa; Ora Labora, Michigan; and Zoar, Ohio. Chancellor Otto von Bismarck's *Kulturkampf* against Catholics encouraged many clergy and religious individuals to leave.

Albert Wolff, a "forty-eighter" who was the commissioner of emigration from Minnesota, reported from Bremen in 1870 that the city remained "alive with emigrants." Shipping firms, he noted, were able to dispatch emigrants quickly to America. Two passenger liners left for New York each week, and while many travelers seemed to know their destinations, an equal number were perfectly set "to go wherever they pleased." Wolff reported that these were often the better classes, well educated, and well dressed. The coming war between Prussia and France in 1870 "frightened thousands of well-to-do and peaceable people" (Johnson 1981, p. 160).

While there was a diversity of motives compelling emigration, annual numbers fluctuated sharply throughout the century. From 1820 to 1860, the numbers moved steadily upward—nearly a million German-speakers arrived in the peak decade prior to the U.S. Civil War. Immigration dropped off slightly in the 1860s and 1870s but resumed to more than a million in the 1880s. A sharp downturn occurred in the last decade of the century, but movement increased until World War I. Thereafter in the twentieth century it continued at reduced levels.

The most effective nineteenth-century factor in spurring German immigration is now believed to have been chain migration. One immigrant cluster, family, or church would write, encouraging letters to friends and relatives in Germany. These "letters from America" would bring others to an established midwestern settlement, and gradually more would follow in this chain to create a community of like-minded immigrants.

German settlement patterns in the New World depended not only on chain letters, but also on time of arrival, transportation routes to the interior, economic opportunities, and nineteenth-century advertising and state-recruitment efforts. Some German settlers continued to stop in the mid-Atlantic states and the Northeast. Only a few were attracted to the South, except for Texas and New Orleans. Most were drawn to the Midwest: Ohio, Michigan, Illinois, Wisconsin, Minnesota, and Missouri became the new centers of German settlement.

The earliest arrivals, those before the Civil War, followed migration chains to the open and free farmlands and frontier cities of the Midwest. Flowing from western Pennsylvania down the Ohio, Germans settled in Cincinnati and Louisville. They continued down the Mississippi to Missouri and northward into Illinois. The Erie Canal and the Great Lakes pointed them to Michigan, Wisconsin, and Minnesota. Later, railroad companies such as the Northern Pacific advertised the upper Midwest through thousands of brochures distributed by land agents hired by Michigan, Wisconsin, or Minnesota. Soon a chain of urban German communities stretched from Buffalo to Detroit to Milwaukee and into Minnesota. In between, they created hundreds of mostly rural, small agricultural communities often bound together by common religion, family, or place of origin.

The chain migration westward often was tied to immigrant churches. Though the churches seldom directed recruitment efforts, new arrivals frequently were of the same religion, geographic region in Germany, and social-political disposition. These strong religious affiliations explain the persistence to this day of certain settlement patterns. But deeply divided religious differences among German-speakers served to isolate antebellum German immigrants from one another as well as from Americans. Even among concentrations of Germans, Catholics, Pietists, or Lutherans—with their various synods—had little to do with one another. A good many of these small settlements represented religious theocracies, where the minister often remained a benevolent overlord. Also, because many of these midwestern settlements were peopled by immigrants with some means, skills, or entrepreneurial experience, they were easily able to establish and maintain self-supporting agricultural villages. These villages clung to their form of the German language and established parochial schools to protect their culture. Well into the twentieth century rural settlements such as Frankenmuth, Michigan; Saint Nanzcanz, Wisconsin; and Stearns County and New Ulm, Minnesota, remained largely isolated German enclaves.

After the Civil War, German-speakers settled more often in urban areas. Fewer farming opportunities (except for the Volga Germans of Colorado, the Dakotas, and Michigan's reclaimed Saginaw Valley), more skilled immigrants, and individualistic immigration trends channeled settlers toward pockets of German-speakers in the cities. Midwestern urban centers often became characteristically German. In Milwaukee and St. Louis, more than 30 percent of the residents were German-born by the Civil War. Cincinnati, Louisville, and to a lesser extent Chicago, Detroit, Cleveland, and Toledo also maintained important German communities.

Obviously, the reception given German-speakers varied according to religious affiliation, origin, and place of settlement in the new land. Those who arrived as family units and settled as groups often talked of building a new Germany in the United States. Although these efforts at state-building failed, many unassimilated pockets of Germans remained in the rural Midwest. In the cities, by the late nineteenth century, German dominance created sections known as *Kleindeutschlands* (little Germanys). These ethnic pockets boasted Lutheran or Catholic German-speaking churches, German newspapers, beer gardens, and a number of German mystical, fraternal, and mutual-benefit societies. Educational clubs, political societies, and patriotic organizations, modeled on similar groups in Germany, also dotted the Kleindeutschland neighborhoods.

Americans often defined rural Germans by their church, while urban Germans were more commonly identified by the clubs, social, or political organizations they joined. Regardless of the identity, these concentrations of Germans—both rural and urban—increased nativist fears that the Germans were unwilling to assimilate into traditional American culture. Nativists warned that the German colonies were put together without any mixing with Americans and were controlled by their ministers or politicians. Traditionalists also worried that monolithic German voting blocs would upset traditional party alignments.

Many nativists in the middle Atlantic and lower New England states, fearing alien influences, especially by German Catholics, joined the Know-Nothing party at midcentury. The Know-Nothings, who received their name from their familiar denial, "I know nothing," when asked about attacks on German Catholics, were opposed to any immigrant holding public office and to continued immigration, and they supported a naturalization period of up to twenty-one years. By 1856, following the formation of the Republican party in 1854, the Know-Nothings were absorbed by the new political organization.

Although German-speakers had a reputation for political apathy, when they did get involved, they generally supported Democratic candidates. Prior to the Civil War some Germans abandoned the Democrats for antislavery fusion parties and later the young Republican party. However, in the 1860 Presidential election, only in states such as Missouri, Illinois, and Minnesota, where the Republicans were not identified with the nativists, did the Germans support Abraham Lincoln in significant numbers. Elsewhere, and through the rest of the nineteenth century, the Republicans' support for prohibition, their affiliation with anticlerical German liberals, and the party's defense of the freedmen kept conservative Lutherans and German Catholics in the Democratic party. Only in 1896 did sizable numbers of Germans shift to the Republican party, out of concern for William Jennings Bryan's moralism and free silver advocacy.

Nativism carried over into surges of moralistic legislation against customs and institutions associated with German-speaking immigrants. Anti-liquor legislation and temperance movements flourished in Wisconsin, Ohio, and Nebraska in the 1870s. The spread of German-language parochial schools encouraged state legislators to require English-only public schools; however, so loud was the public outcry that most of those laws were quickly repealed. Not until World War I was the German language largely removed from public and parochial schools.

By the turn of the twentieth century, second-generation Germans, especially in the cities, were rapidly melding into the American mainstream. The pace of assimilation, though, varied by region. In the eastern port cities skilled workers found more employment opportunities, but competition from unskilled, immigrant labor often forced common German laborers to move to midwestern cities. Here, where the pace of assimilation was slower, the sons of German immigrants now found white-collar employment in increasing numbers. In businesses such as breweries, food-related industries, export-import businesses, and chemical and machinery manufacturers, Germans found entrepreneurial success. German women and their daughters did not enter the work force as often as other immigrants, but when they did, they began as laborers, servants, peddlers, shopkeepers, or tailors. Most German women avoided factory jobs; by century's end a good many found employment as nurses, clerical workers, sale.sladies, and teachers—opportunities that required education and the ability to speak English. For both men and women, economic opportunities spurred patterns of assimilation that continued into the twentieth century.

Even as German Americans experienced upward mobility, the family unit remained strong. The father, always a dominant figure, maintained that role despite a working wife and public-school-trained offspring. Nonetheless, children left school early—at twelve to fourteen years old—to take jobs to support the family. Germans, more often than many other immigrant groups, relied on child labor. Kinship and ethnicity enabled German city dwellers to survive hard times and eventually to build and buy homes. By the turn of the twentieth century, Germans owned their own homes at rates higher than similar-status immigrants or native-born urban residents. The nuclear family persisted despite children beginning to marry outside the ethnic

clan. Lutheranism or Catholicism nurtured the family circle and provided some continuing identity among German Americans in the larger cities.

Distinctive patterns of German culture persisted in insular and isolated rural communities into the twentieth century. Centered around the local Lutheran or Catholic church, the German language, education, and family orientation marked the tightly contained German rural social unit. Since Germans owned nearly 11 percent of all American farms in 1900, there were sufficient numbers to perpetuate for four and five generations these agricultural communities. By 1950, German descendants were still the single largest immigrant group engaged in agriculture. Even at the end of the twentieth century there are several remnants in the Midwest of these rural, self-contained, German religious and social enclaves.

The Twentieth Century

As World War I approached, there was a popular revival among both urban and rural German Americans of interest, preservation, and pride in things German. The paradox within the German community was evident: Gradual but persistent assimilation encouraged many people now to glorify and defend the fatherland. The German press—dependent on a readership that was rapidly diminishing—almost unanimously supported the German Empire and demanded strict American neutrality. The German-language press, which peaked at almost 800 newspapers in 1894, had shrunk to 554 in 1910. World War I was about to accelerate that decline, but in the meantime the press became even more stridently pro-German as it attempted to keep America out of the war and defeat the Anglophile Woodrow Wilson in 1916.

The German-American Alliance, a loose federation of more than three million members in forty states, led the heightened ethnic consciousness. Originally founded as a league to fight prohibition, it was financed by German brewers and led by businessmen, clergymen, journalists, and educators. The alliance and other organizations lobbied for an arms embargo, sponsored rallies, collected for German war relief, and organized speakers and writers to oppose American involvement. To many Americans, the activities of the alliance and the ethnic press implied German disloyalty.

When the United States joined the Allied powers against Germany in 1917, American patriots received a mandate to eradicate any semblance, especially among Germans, of any dual allegiance. Rumors about sabotage and disloyalty began to circulate throughout the states with significant German populations. Local defense committees, the National Americanization Committee, and the American Protective League created a climate of harassment and distrust. Communities by the hundreds dropped the German language from their schools; renamed streets, foods, and towns; banned German music; and burned German books. A German in Collinsville, Illinois, was even lynched in April 1918.

In response to the anti-German hysteria many Germans withdrew into their ethnic communities and at the same time tried to reassure themselves and their neighbors of their loyalty. Religious pastors were divided. Some remained openly against the war while others often encouraged young men to show their patriotism by enlisting. German voters switched to the Republican party to vote against President Wilson, and German cultural and social organizations quickly disappeared. German-language newspapers shrunk by half by 1919. The war finally forced assimilation on many urban and rural German churches that dropped the use of the native language and closed parochial schools.

Following the war, and until 1932, some 500,000 German-speakers entered the United States. The war, industrial expansion, and rapid cultural dissipation eliminated German communities in many cities. German identity was rapidly set aside when status as an American was challenged. Some resentment, economic mobility, and industrial leaders who preached acculturation encouraged many Germans to move out of cities to residential areas in and around large industrial communities. The automobile and improved roads abetted assimilation in urban as well as rural areas.

During the Great Depression years of the 1930s, some postwar German immigrants and "unchastened" second-generation residents were attracted to the racial views and anti-Semitism of the Nazi party. Father Charles Coughlin, Detroit's "radio priest," attracted thousands of German listeners in the Midwest with his neo-isolationist views and attacks on international bankers and Jews. The German-American Bund also attracted support among postwar immigrants. Fritz Kuhn, a decorated German war veteran, who immigrated to Detroit in 1927, organized the bund in 1936. Kuhn reportedly worked for the Ford Motor Company, where Henry Ford's anti-Semitism and strong antiunionism encouraged hate groups, especially during the union-organizing years among the auto-workers in the 1930s. Membership in the bund reached twenty-five thousand and was concentrated in Detroit and the Northeast, especially New York, where many unmarried and unemployed postwar immigrants settled. Kuhn moved to New York in 1936 but was convicted and imprisoned in 1939 for embezzling bund funds. Only a small percentage of German Americans ever joined the bund. Unlike during World War I, German ethnicity was not rekindled by Nazi success or failure. Little repression was evident as the remnants of German American were quickly disappearing.

The discovery of a "new ethnicity" in the 1960s enabled some third- and fourth-generation Germans to revive their Old World heritage. "Little Bavarias" sprouted as tourist attractions, German Day was still celebrated in Chicago, harvest processions, Oktoberfests, and singing festivals were common wherever Germans gathered. Folk customs and crafts experienced a revival, and whole towns redesigned themselves as German village replicas. Churches continued to preserve traditional customs and imagery.

The collapse of East Germany and the reunification of the homeland in 1990 likewise sparked a renewed interest in Germany's past. The establishment of a reunited and economically strong Germany as a leader among nations has finally enabled many German Americans to set aside the ethnic cloud of two world wars. Confronting and apologizing for the Holocaust likewise lessened the burden of German history. A resultant surge in genealogical research also occurred that revived interest and pride in things German.

Still, there is only a passing revival of interest in German-American culture. At the end of the twentieth century German Americans still essentially choose their ethnicity. Although little of the paradox between assimilation and cultural preservation remains, some Germans painstakingly—especially in rural areas—struggle to maintain their identity. In celebrating their ethnicity the lost culture is remembered, but what also should not be forgotten is that Germans, unlike any other immigrant group, in sheer numbers successfully transcended ethnicity and helped to define Americanism. Millions of German-speakers thoroughly assimilated and became Americans, but in doing so they contributed to that constantly changing identity of what it is to be an American.

Bibliography

Bennett, D. H. (1988). *The Party of Fear. From Nativist Movements to the New Right in American History.* Chapel Hill: University of North Carolina Press.

Conzen, K. N. (1976). *Immigrant Milwaukee, 1836–1860. Accommodation and Community in a Frontier City.* Cambridge, MA: Harvard University Press.

Dinnerstein, L., and Reimers, D. (1988). *Ethnic Americans: A History of Immigration and Assimilation,* revised edition. New York: HarperCollins.

Faust, A. B. ([1909] 1969). *The German Element in the United States,* 2 vols. New York: Arno Press.

Gatzke, H. W. (1980). *Germany and the United States. A "Special Relationship"?* Cambridge, MA: Harvard University Press.

Hawgood, J. A. ([1940] 1970). *The Tragedy of German-America.* New York: Arno Press.

Johnson, H. B. (1981). "The Germans." In *They Chose Minnesota,* edited by J. D. Holmquist. St. Paul: Minnesota Historical Society Press.

Keil, H., and Jentz, J. B., eds. (1983). *German Workers in Industrial Chicago, 1850–1910: A Comparative Perspective.* De Kalb: Northern Illinois University Press.

Levine, B. (1992). *The Spirit of 1848: German Immigrants, Labor Conflict, and the Coming of the Civil War.* Champaign: University of Illinois Press.

Luebke, F. C. (1990). *Germans in the New World. Essays in the History of Immigration.* Champaign: University of Illinois Press.

O'Connor, Richard. (1968). *The German Americans.* Boston: Little, Brown.

Trefousse, H. L., ed. (1980). *Germany and America. Essays on Problems of International Relations and Immigration.* Brooklyn, NY: Brooklyn College Press.

Trommler, F., and McVeigh, J., eds. (1985). *America and the Germans. An Assessment of a Three-Hundred-Year History,* 2 vols. Philadelphia: University of Pennsylvania Press.

—JEREMY W. KILAR

IRISH

The Irish experience in America, now almost three centuries long, is sometimes regarded as the stereotypical "immigrant experience." Like other immigrants, they were pulled toward the New World by its chance for individual opportunity and religious freedom, and like others, they have demonstrated intergenerational upward mobility and gradual acceptance into the mainstream. Nonetheless, the experience of the Irish stands apart, shaped by circumstances unique to their homeland and influenced by the environment in America whenever they arrived.

Ireland: The Background

Ireland had a troubled history, long marked by foreign conquest and colonization. When immigration to America began, a majority of the people in Ireland were still descendants of the Celts from northwestern Europe who settled on the island between 350 and 250 B.C.E. And, since the time St. Patrick visited Ireland in the fifth century C.E., most Irish were Roman Catholics. Outsiders had gradually settled in, however, once English kings and armies started asserting control over Ireland in the twelfth century. By the seventeenth century, English kings and Parliaments were newly eager and able to make Ireland serve their own Protestant and colonial purposes. The British government transplanted whole colonies of Scottish and English families to "plantations" on land confiscated from Irish Catholics. Although these resettled Protestants were concentrated in Northern Ireland, especially in Ulster, and in seaport towns such as Dublin, their power and influence reached all but the most isolated corners of the island. In the early 1700s, Parliament passed the Penal Laws, which limited the religious and civil rights of Catholics and favored the minority among the Protestants—those Anglicans who belonged to the British-imposed Church of Ireland. Even Scotch-Irish and Quakers faced discrimination, but the Irish Catholics suffered the most. A few converted to win British favoritism, but the vast majority insisted on their Catholic faith and persisted in their native Irish language. Still they had little chance but to become tenants on their own former farms, living on tiny allotments that had to be further subdivided when the children reached adulthood. By 1750, only 5 percent of all Irish land remained in Catholic hands, even though about 80 percent of the population was Catholic. This was the Ireland early emigrants left, a land so unequal that the majority could not afford to go even if they wanted to.

Irish Immigration Before 1845

The Irish were among the first immigrants to North America. By the Revolutionary War, there were more Irish in the thirteen colonies than any other white foreign-born group but the English. From the 1600s until the mid-1840s, the immigrants who recorded their place of birth as Ireland overrepresented the Protestants. According to best estimates, only about 20 to 25 percent of the Irish immigrants in this era were Catholic. By contrast, about three-fifths were Scotch-Irish Presbyterians or, less frequently, Quakers. As "dissenters" from the established Church of Ireland, they had suffered periodic religious restrictions, and their ministers began to encourage or even organize emigration among the young in their congregations. The Scotch-Irish—often the artisans, craftsmen, and "middling" farmers in Ulster—also had economic cause to emigrate once industrialization began to alter Northern Ireland's woolen and linen trades and farm conditions. The less advanced American colonies seemed a chance for them to maintain their trades and status. America had an appeal also among the sons of Anglican-Irish landholders, professionals, and businessmen. A fifth of the early Irish immigrants were Church of Ireland members, often young and anxious to take advantage of opportunities available in the colonies to men of their class and religion.

As they left for America, emigrants took their animosities along. Irish Anglicans joined the English colonists in their continuing dislike for Irish Presbyterians and Catholics. Pitted against one another for land and jobs at home, Presbyterian and Catholic Irish hated the English and each other. Conditions in the New World enabled the Irish Anglicans, Presbyterians, and Quakers to settle in more readily than the Irish Catholics. Early in the Colonial era, "the Irish" came to mean the Irish Catholics, a negative image that persisted.

Most of the Irish Catholic immigrants, men and women, could only pay for their passage by agreeing to be indentured servants in America. These poor Irish began to seem so conspicuous that some colonies enacted laws to restrict the importation of "papists" before the end of the seventeenth century. Only a few Irish Catholics arrived in the colonies with wealth. One, Thomas Dongan, served as governor of New York in the 1680s, and New York City as well as Philadelphia had prosperous Irish families. The Carrolls and their descendants, landed aristocrats who first settled in Maryland in the late 1600s, became the most important Irish family in colonial America. Charles Carroll III was the only Catholic to sign the Declaration of Independence, Daniel Carroll was a delegate to the Constitutional Convention, and John Carroll became the first Catholic bishop in the United States.

When the American Revolution began, most Irish Dissenters and Catholics were eager supporters of the cause and fought alongside each other against their common enemy, the English. Their revolutionary participation helped the Irish identify more firmly with the new nation, and an exodus developed once the War of 1812 settled any lingering fears that Britain might retake the former colonies. Between 1815 and 1845, about one million Irish immigrated to the United States; the small island was contributing nearly one-third of all arrivals each year.

It was Protestants, most of them from Northern Ireland, who continued to make up more than their share of the early nineteenth-century emigration. The English generally began to decide that America was a good place for the Irish Catholics, however, and the government lifted restrictions on emigration in 1827. Lower ship fares also began to enable more Irish to afford passage. By the 1840s, about nine out of ten Irish emigrants were Catholics, and they were coming now from poor as well as rich counties.

By their actions, the Irish Catholics contributed to their visibility as an identifiable group in the United States. They spoke English, but often imperfectly and with a "brogue" that invited caricature. They usually arrived young and single; a self-protective preference to marry and associate with each other led to charges of "clannish" behavior. The Irish also displeased British sympathizers by starting clubs to support homeland causes of Catholic emancipation. American temperance advocates despised the Irish neighborhood saloons, and established interests objected to Irish involvement in American politics. If Irish individuals or groups insisted on standing up to "their betters," became too vocal in political contests, or got involved in brawls, it convinced their detractors that Irish Catholics were an aggressive, hot-tempered, and "uncivilized" lot.

Above all, their religion set Irish Catholics apart and fueled prejudice against them from the outset. Wherever they settled, Irish families organized Irish churches and insisted on priests of their own nationality, a habit that resulted in the separate ethnic parishes that soon came to characterize the American Catholic Church. Meanwhile, Irish priests and bishops gained permanent dominance within the Church hierarchy. Irish Catholic nuns arrived to care for children in orphanages and to teach; the children of immigrants began to learn precepts of the faith their parents and grand-parents had followed in Ireland out of habit and defensive hatred for the English.

When evangelical revivals reinvigorated American Protestantism in the 1820s and 1830s, religious enthusiasts turned their holy wrath on the "papist" Catholics who had been their adversaries since the days of the Protestant Reformation. Catholic foes maintained that foreign despots were using immigrants in America to undermine democracy. These "nativists" began to justify their attacks on Catholics in the name of loyalty to the nation. A mob struck out the "enemy" Roman pope by burning a convent in Charlestown, Massachusetts, in 1834, and another mob vandalized a Catholic Church in Philadelphia in 1844. Anti-Catholics enthusiastically exploited fabricated tales about sexual misconduct between priests and nuns. A few Irish Catholics converted to eliminate the religious problem while, on their part, Irish Protestants deliberately became less "Irish" and more Protestant to distance themselves from any taint.

Like the children's nursery rhyme, the Irish had their "rich man, poor man, beggar man, and thief," but most of the generation who came into Jacksonian America busied themselves carving out opportunities somewhere amid the American "middling" classes. Irish lawyers, architects, teachers, and accountants contributed to the ranks of the professional classes. Irish businessmen catered to their countrymen in saloons, boarding-houses, and groceries. Immigrant craftsmen found jobs as carpenters or blacksmiths, and Irish laborers found work on the docks and on street, railroad, and canal-building crews. A small but significant share

of the Irish merged with Yankee Protestant migrants heading to farmland in the Old Northwest (the area of Ohio, Indiana, Illinois, Michigan, and Wisconsin) or to towns on the urban frontier.

Despite prejudice and enemies they could not appease, Irish Catholics had established a foothold in America by the mid-1840s. They were beginning to experience upward occupational mobility, and they were establishing themselves in neighborhoods proudly centered around their churches. They might have consolidated their gains and conciliated their critics more smoothly in the following years but for the potato famine that struck Ireland in 1845.

The Famine Irish Immigrants, 1845–1870

When the potato crop turned out to be rotten in 1845, it was just the beginning of the Great Famine that lasted until the early 1850s. Nearly every year, if the recurring fungus did not destroy the crop, discouraged peasants had planted so few potatoes that the yield was not enough to feed them. Most Irish peasants had been living entirely on a diet of boiled potatoes, eating an average of ten or twelve pounds a day. The famine was so severe and relief efforts were so inadequate that, out of a population of fewer than nine million, more than one million Irish died of malnutrition, scurvy, or fever. Irish Catholic peasants had often vowed to live and die in their homeland, but now their attitude toward emigration reversed and they tumbled out. The most destitute made it only as far as Britain, but Canada or the United States became the destination for 1.8 million. These were the "famine Irish," a generation especially desperate to leave Ireland and particularly disadvantaged in America because they arrived in such a huge wave.

They came, unsettling Protestant-dominated America, just at a time when urbanization, industrialization, and mass political participation were taking hold. All classes of Irish continued to arrive, but for the first time, immigration mirrored the mass of people who lived in Ireland. The famine Irish were generally poor, unskilled, anti-British, and defensively religious. Now, too, most of the immigrants came as families rather as single individuals, as had been the previous habit. Their financial and psychological resources exhausted by the ocean trip on "coffin ships," they stayed in the cities where their boats landed. Sudden Irish ghettos swelled Boston, New York, Philadelphia, and New Orleans. Landlords profited by cramming the new immigrants into dismal corners, attics, and basements. Such situations bred cholera, tuberculosis, mental illness, alcoholism, and vice. Even Catholic bishops and priests misunderstood how few alternatives poverty-stricken immigrants had; the chorus swelled, decrying Irish indifference to morality and a lack of self-help.

The only work these famine immigrants could get was at the bottom of the economic ladder. By their numbers they helped advance industrialization, holding the low-paying, unskilled, and dangerous jobs in the cities or joining railroad, canal, and road-building crews. Husbands wandered off in search of work or just away from agonizing responsibilities. Deserted mothers joined unmarried Irish women and widows to swell the ranks of domestic servants and sweatshop workers. "No Irish Need Apply" notices appeared in East Coast advertisements and in store windows, but other employers took advantage of the thousands of desperate Irish. They fired any troublesome employees or those who threatened to strike for better wages, and they hired Irish replacements who would take whatever wage was offered. Displaced workers turned their anger on the Irish. Pitched street fights regularly resulted in permanent injuries and deaths. A stereotyped notion of Irish Catholic immigrants took permanent form now, based on the poor who were so visible.

The lot of the immigrants was not so gloomy away from the crowded milltowns and city slums, however. From the 1820s, Irish immigrants had filtered westward, and they encouraged friends and relatives to join them. Bishops in Dubuque, Iowa, and St. Paul, Minnesota, urged the famine immigrants to go inland. New York's Irish Emigration Society made efforts to propel newcomers from ocean steamer to inland-bound ship. Some studies calculate that 25 out of every 100 immigrants left East Coast cities for points farther west. By 1850, 15 percent of the Irish-born immigrants in the United States lived in the Midwest, most in towns along the Great Lakes and inland rivers.

The plentiful mass of job-seeking Irish workers helped change the American landscape; they cleared Michigan forests as lumberjacks, dug coal in Pennsylvania, went down into copper or iron ore mines, headed for the California gold fields, and laid railroad tracks along the way. States such as Kansas were dotted with rural churches named after St. Bridget or St. Patrick, centers for the Irish farm communities that plowed the Midwest.

The economic and social opportunities of the booming frontier helped the Irish find a wider range of jobs and greater acceptance once they were away from the East Coast. Also, there were differences between those who could manage to go west and those who stayed behind. Young single Irish males and females and family heads with skills or education were better able to move than the older or unskilled famine Irish. At midcentury in Detroit, half of the Irish males were laborers, but half were skilled tradesmen, businessmen, or professionals. This contrasted sharply with the situation of Irish in places such as New York and Boston, where to be Irish was almost synonymous with being among the poor laboring class. Critics who blamed Irish poverty on a "weak character" failed to appreciate that in this "land of opportunity" it was important to be in the right place at the right time and that advantages of background, youth, and good health often fostered success.

Irish stereotypes based on the highly visible urban poor and on the long-standing Protestant animosities toward Catholics were reinforced by the role the Irish played in politics. The sudden famine influx of Irish Catholics occurred at a time when mass political participation was taking hold. In most states, residence rather than citizenship was enough to qualify men to vote. From almost the minute they stepped off the boat, the urban Irish were courted, usually by Democratic political machines such as New York's Tammany Hall, which offered low-level political positions, jobs, relief, and drinks in return for loyalty at the polls. But the Irish became Democrats not only because of such organized efforts; the party appealed to them because of its emphasis on the rights of the "common man."

The Irish mingled interests of the Democrats with particular interests of their own and, in so doing, became especially obnoxious to old-stock Protestant Americans who were championing reforms such as temperance, abolition, women's rights, and public education. Many Irish and Catholic leaders were urging voluntary temperance, but Irish, like German immigrants, opposed temperance laws that would outlaw saloons and breweries, eliminating not only neighborhood centers but also jobs. The Irish were uninterested in the abolitionists' antislavery crusades and sometimes were even hostile, worrying that freed slaves would present more job competition. Moreover, the Irish also opposed Sabbath laws, and their priests declared that women's rights advocates were threats to the home.

It was the religious education of their children that proved to be the most divisive and lasting issue separating Catholics and Protestants. In the 1850s, the "school wars" erupted between them. Public, tax-supported schools were just organizing in many communities at midcentury; Catholics protested, however, because the Protestants' King James Bible and Protestant teachers usually dominated the curriculum. Unable to achieve any acceptable accommodation with local public school boards, Catholics demanded a share of tax money to provide their own separate parochial schools. In some communities, the controversy split Protestant Democrats from Catholic Democrats and fractured the party. When one state legislature after another rejected the Catholics' request, Irish, German, French, and Belgian Catholic parishes proceeded to build parochial schools alongside their churches at their own expense.

Meanwhile, the controversy had added fuel to the wave of nativism and bigotry sweeping the country. The new party commonly termed the "Know-Nothings" maintained that the Catholics' position on education was convincing evidence that "papists" posed a dangerous threat to the very foundations of democracy in America. The party's supporters wanted to limit or eliminate the influence of Catholic immigrants as voters and candidates for office, maintaining they would take direction from the foreign pope. Know-Nothing adherents merged their cause with the hodgepodge of diverse political interests that created the Republican party by the late 1850s. Their presence amid the otherwise reform-minded temperance and abolitionist Republicans gave the Irish Catholics even more reason to find permanent shelter as staunch Democrats.

As Democrats, Irish Catholics joined in issues broader than their own. Dating from the late 1850s, Irish in the North and Irish in the South adopted their particular section's position on slavery and war. Once the Civil War erupted, there were Irish-born officers and Irish regiments on each side. Since most Irish lived in the North, however, the great majority of Irish soldiers fought on that side. While they believed in saving the Union, the Emancipation Proclamation made it a war to free the slaves and, at about the same time, the draft started in the North. It seemed, with some accuracy in places such as New York City, that Irishmen were drawn for the draft more often than was their share. Further, few Irish could afford the option of paying substitutes. They sent letters home warning countrymen not to be fooled by recruiters from America who might promise them jobs but would, in fact, be signing them up for the army. Scapegoated, blacks became victims of draft riots in cities across the North. The most serious occurred in New York City, where, during four days of mob violence in 1863, blacks were beaten, hanged, and their orphan asylum was burned. For years after, critics and history books emphasized the part the Irish played in the draft riots, failing to acknowledge the heavy death toll among Irish soldiers and the decisive role Irish regiments played on Civil War battlefields.

For a generation, the massive famine emigration helped focus public attention on the poor and the "troublemakers" who seemed to confirm previous notions that the Irish were a dangerous element. Irish gamblers and prizefighters dominated headlines and scandalized the genteel Yankees. Protestant middle and upper classes were outraged by Irish-American labor activists and imported "radical" causes. Young Ireland collected money in America to support revolutionaries across Europe in 1848; the Fenians launched efforts from American soil in 1866 and 1870, aiming to seize Canada and then offer it to the British in trade for Ireland; a secret Irish society, the Molly Maguires, horrified the establishment by employing bombs, murder, and intimidation on behalf of Pennsylvania coal miners in the 1860s and 1870s.

Although they drew less notice, Irish immigrants established dozens of mutual aid societies for insurance, burial, and poor funds to take care of their own. As early as the 1840s, Irish women in New York City became the first to establish institutionalized care for orphans. The famine Irish grew old, still disproportionately concentrated in unskilled jobs, but thousands of Irish families had pooled their hard-earned salaries to fashion respectable lives centered around the neighborhoods, churches, schools, and institutions their children inherited.

The Postfamine Irish, 1870-1921

The famine had initiated a habit of mass emigration, and by the late nineteenth century, there were nearly as many Irish-born in the United States as there were in Ireland. By 1920, more than one million people in the United States had been born in Ireland; more than three million were the American-born children of Irish immigrants.

Ever after the famine, most Irish in America were Catholics, with origins in the twenty-six counties of southern Ireland. Entire families continued to arrive together, but about four out of five Irish immigrants in the last decades of the nineteenth century were young and single. In many years, young single females outnumbered males among the immigrants. Since Irish Americans put off marriage, sometimes into their thir-

ties, single women now became a significant part of the work force. Coming from the poorer counties of Ireland, they had little to offer but a willingness to work and so moved into domestic service, printing, meat packing, garmentmaking, and textile factories. Irish women were active in the labor movement; organizers such as Mary Harris Jones—"Mother Jones"—defied "polite society's" notions about acceptable female behavior. Young Irish men, fluent in English and with friends and relatives already here, found it easier to advance by the end of the nineteenth century; employers chose them over the newest wave of Polish and southeastern European immigrants.

Irish families often gave their daughters more education than their sons; accordingly, second-generation Irish women were able to take advantage of opportunities becoming available to females. They were religious sisters, store clerks, secretaries, and nurses. Catholic women, most of them Irish, made up a fifth to a quarter of the teachers in public schools in nearly all American cities by about 1910. Catholic religious orders of men initiated colleges that filled with Irish sons. Notre Dame athletic teams captured widespread headlines for the "Fighting Irish," but of greater permanent significance, Catholic college graduates were moving into the ranks of middle-class professionals.

Their successful intrusion into new jobs, their continued insistence on having Catholic parochial schools, and the swelling of Catholic ranks with new immigrants such as the Poles led to waves of nativism in the 1890s and again in the 1920s. In the 1890s, the American Protective Association (APA) attacked Catholicism as "alien" and wanted to restrict the flow of immigration. In the 1920s, tensions in society helped revive a new version of the Ku Klux Klan, which targeted Catholic, Jewish, and black Americans as dangers to democracy. Both the APA and the Klan capitalized on long-standing prejudices, but thanks to their efforts to prove respectability and patriotism, Catholics won broad-based support. Protestants rallied to the defense of Catholics in several states where nativists tried to outlaw parochial schools by constitutional amendments. The 1920s marked the end of the last organized nativist movements.

Irish Immigration After 1921

The number of foreign-born Irish in the United States began to diminish after World War I. The old immigrants died, the creation of the Irish Free State in 1921 gave the young more reason to stay at home, and the Great Depression of the 1930s choked off job opportunities in the United States. Emigration did not soar again until the 1950s, a period when the American economy was strong and the Irish economy was stagnant.

It was the children, grandchildren, and greatgranchildren of immigrants who gave shape to the Irish-American experience for most of the twentieth century. As from the time of the famine, the Irish Catholics still represented "the Irish" in the popular imagination. Auto industrialist Henry Ford, the son of Irish Protestant immigrants, became an American folk hero. Yet the press generally hailed him as an "American" success story.

Most Irish Americans began blending the heritage of their ancestors with their experiences in the United States, sometimes railing against Irish Catholicism as a disability and sometimes embracing it as a strength. The plays of Eugene O'Neill and the novels of James T. Farrell and Edwin O'Connor were just part of a literary outpouring that told of lives familiar to many Irish Americans; yet such portrayals captivated Americans who had grown up in families not Irish. Reflecting other interests, novels by the third-generation and Princeton-educated F. Scott Fitzgerald revealed the American upper-class Protestant society he knew.

In one arena after another from the 1920s onward, Irish Americans moved between the immigrant world of their parents or grandparents and their own more plural, class-based society. Screen stars such as Spencer Tracy and Bing Crosby took on both stereotypical Irish roles and roles without any "ethnic" character. Labor leaders Philip Murray and George Meany, whose ancestors were Irish immigrant laborers, presided over powerful unions and spoke for working-class interests that crossed lines of ethnicity and religion.

Certain Irish Catholics were embarrassed by the famous 1930s "radio priest" Father Charles Coughlin, who blamed the Depression and its lingering effects on an "international Jewish conspiracy." And in the early 1950s, when Wisconsin's Republican senator Joseph R. McCarthy launched the national "Red Scare" and a witch-hunt for Communists, many critics attributed his cause and tactics to his Irish Catholicism. Each man did gain important support from among Irish Catholics, but their wider appeal reflected bigotry, fear, and an enthusiasm for easy answers shared by many Americans in times of political tension.

Whereas earlier immigrant politicians gained power in urban politics based on a bloc of Irish votes, the second and third generation moved into positions of national influence because they managed to have broader appeal, albeit often among Catholic and working-class voters. In 1928, Governor Alfred E. Smith of New York became the first Irish Catholic nominated for president. Throughout his presidency, Franklin D. Roosevelt rewarded Irish Democratic loyalty by appointing an unprecedented number of Irish Catholics to judgeships and important New Deal posts. In many states Irish Americans were winning election to the Senate and House of Representatives. Nonetheless, old-style Irish bosses such as Boston's James Michael Curley reinforced prevailing stereotypes of manipulative Irish politicians, an image still perpetuated by Chicago's mayor, Richard J. Daley, in the 1960s.

In 1960, John F. Kennedy became the first Catholic president. Kennedy's great-grandfather was a famine emigrant, but his maternal grandfather was mayor of Boston in the classic tradition of urban Irish politicians, and his wealthy father was ambassador to Great Britain from 1937 to 1940. Harvard-educated and already a U.S. senator, Kennedy was hardly typical. To win, moreover, he made it clear that he was more a loyal "American" than a Catholic. Nonetheless, Irish Catholics felt they had cleared the last hurdle to full acceptance.

Indeed, after Kennedy died and other Irish Catholics sought the office, including Robert Kennedy and Eugene McCarthy in 1968, opponents no longer made Catholicism an issue.

Their identity had begun to wane when Irish Catholics celebrated having "arrived" with Kennedy. Immigrant legislation in the 1960s reversed previous favoritism to northwestern Europeans, and admission became more difficult for the Irish. Fewer than 40,000 Irish entered the United States between 1971 and 1989. Meanwhile, decades of intermarriage meant many second-, third-, and fourth-generation families were only partially Irish and Catholic. Uncritical religious attachments were weakened, variously, by changes in the old Latin Mass after Vatican II, by papal pronouncements against birth control, and by the continuing subordination of religious sisters and laywomen. Upward mobility brought an end to old Irish neighborhoods; families settled in class-based suburbs, and their children attended public schools. Social and economic changes added up, even, to an "Irish Catholic vote" that was no longer predictably Democratic.

Paradoxically, the third, fourth, and fifth generations show interest in rediscovering their heritage, part of American society's growing appreciation for diverse cultures that emerged in the 1960s. They search genealogical records for Irish ancestors and travel to Ireland. They register for Irish history courses and listen to Irish musical groups. A few study the Irish language, and a few donate to the Irish Republican Army's ongoing battle against the "Brits" in Northern Ireland. They sometimes create new romanticized stereotypes.

If the old Irish Catholics are a "vanishing breed," as some among them fear, gone, too, are the "No Irish Need Apply" signs, the nativists' anti-Catholic campaigns, and the informal agreements to keep Irish Catholics out of upper-class neighborhoods, elite clubs, and prestigious corporate boardrooms. Current generations enjoy wider opportunity and greater freedom than their Irish immigrant ancestors ever anticipated when they set sail for America. There can be only a measured lament for a past that was, in fact, often frightening, hard, and unfair.

Bibliography

Adams, W. F. (1960). *Ireland and the Irish Emigration to the New World from 1815 to the Famine.* New York: Russell & Russell.

Clarke, D. (1973). *The Irish in Philadelphia: Ten Generations of Urban Experience.* Philadelphia: Temple University Press.

Conzen, K. N. (1976). *Immigrant Milwaukee, 1836–1860: Accommodation and Community in a Frontier City.* Cambridge, MA: Harvard University Press.

Diner, H. R. (1983). *Erin's Daughters in America: Irish Immigrant Women in the Nineteenth Century.* Baltimore, MD: Johns Hopkins University Press.

Dolan, J. P. (1975). *The Immigrant Church: New York's Irish and German Catholics, 1815–1865.* Notre Dame, IN: University of Notre Dame Press.

Greeley, A. M. (1981). *The Irish Americans: The Rise to Money and Power.* New York: Harper & Row.

Handlin, O. (1979). *Boston's Immigrants: A Study in Acculturation,* revised edition. Cambridge, MA: Harvard University Press.

Kennedy, R. E. (1973). *The Irish: Emigration, Marriage, and Fertility,* Berkeley: University of California Press.

McCaffrey, L. J. (1976). *The Irish Diaspora in America.* Bloomington: Indiana University Press.

McCaffrey, L. J. (1987). *The Irish in Chicago.* Champaign: University of Illinois Press.

Miller, K. A. (1985). *Emigrants and Exiles: Ireland and the Irish Exodus to North America.* New York: Oxford University Press.

Schrier, A. (1958). *Ireland and the American Emigration, 1850–1900.* Minneapolis: University of Minnesota Press.

Shannon, W. V. (1963). *The American Irish.* London: Macmillan.

Vinyard, J. M. (1974). *The Irish on the Urban Frontier: Detroit, 1850–1880.* New York: Arno Press.

—JOELLEN MCNERGNEY VINYARD

ITALIANS

Between 1880 and 1920, the period of large-scale emigration from Italy to the United States, some four million Italians entered America. Before the 1880s, Italians had been arriving in America in small numbers as far back as the seventeenth century. Indeed, in 1610, only a few short years after the first English settlement at Jamestown, several Italian craftsmen immigrated to Virginia. They were followed in 1622 by a group of Venetian glassmakers, who took up their trade in the colony. With unsettled conditions in sixteenth- and seventeenth-century Italy, many Italians left for political and religious reasons. A group of Italian Protestants known as Waldensians fled persecution in northern Italy and sought refuge in America. Many Italian intellectuals and revolutionaries immigrated to the United States for the same reason. One of the most prominent was the political philosopher Filippo Mazzei, a friend of Thomas Jefferson. Mazzei wrote a series of articles in which he espoused the idea of the equality of all men and of a true democratic government. Denouncing the British government as tyrannical, Mazzei's arguments had a significant influence on America's revolutionary leaders. Another famous Italian-American revolutionary leader was William Paca, a signer of the Declaration of Independence. In 1782, Paca became the governor of Maryland, the first governor of Italian heritage in the nation.

In the years preceding the Civil War, Italian immigrants arrived chiefly from the northern and economically more advanced areas of Genoa, Tuscany, Venetia, Lombardy, and Piedmont. Many were farmers from rich Piedmont and Liguria and were attracted to California, where they developed rich citrus and wine enterprises. Several hundred Italians were attracted by the 1849 Gold Rush in California, while others settled in Louisiana, where they worked as seamen at the port of New Orleans. In Milwaukee, many Italian artisans worked for Casper Hennecke, a nationally known statuary maker.

The turning point in the history of Italian immigration to the United States was 1880. Of the nearly four million Italians who entered America between 1880 and 1920, the vast majority emigrated from the poor agricultural regions of the South, the provinces of Abruzzi, Campania, Apulia, Basilicata (Lucania), Calabria, and the island of Sicily. A combination of "push-pull" factors caused this massive emigration from southern Italy. The "push" factors were conditions in Italy that undermined opportunities for economic improvement and social mobility. The "pull" factors were those conditions in the receiving society that attracted emigrants by offering them opportunities for employment and social and economic mobility.

The "push" factors causing the great post-1880 emigration included extremely low wages; infertility of the soil and primitive agricultural methods; overpopulation and poor health conditions; slow industrial growth; a system of heavy, indirect taxation; an unresponsive and distant national government; corruption in local government; and the exploitation of landless peasants by wealthy land-owners. The problems associated with southern agriculture were the most severe. Almost all property was owned by a landed elite, who left management of their estates to hired foremen. Most Italian peasants did not work their own land but labored for the benefit of others. Creating further pressure on the land was the Italian population, which doubled between 1861 and 1901, reaching twelve million, and increasing to eighteen million by 1916.

In the late 1880s, the Italian economy experienced three major setbacks that triggered emigration. Italians were faced with a ruined economy when the United States cut its imports of Italian citrus fruits due to improved production in California and Florida. At the same time, plant lice invaded Italian vineyards, leaving thousands of acres destroyed. In addition, France set up high tariffs, which cut off a major market for the grape growers of Apulia, Calabria, and Sicily.

Emigration offered an important means of upward mobility for Italians. Industry in the United States was burgeoning, and the promise of jobs beckoned many Italians. While America was the major destination for most Italians who left their homeland, it was not the only one. Italians went to South America, especially Brazil and Argentina, where they had been arriving in fairly large numbers since the early nineteenth century.

A large number of Italians who left southern Italy after 1880 were men between sixteen and forty-five whose goals were to work in America for a short time, save as much money as possible, and return to their native country to buy their own land. Italian patterns show that emigration and return migration were much more frequent when land was for sale than when it was not. Between 1899 and 1924, a total of 3.8 million Italians landed in the United States, but some 2.1 million departed in the same period. These people were labeled "birds of passage" by Americans who looked disapprovingly at this practice. Immigration gradually became more stable after the turn of the twentieth century as women and children joined men and families began to form.

Settlement Patterns

The majority of Italians settled on the East Coast, in New York, Rhode Island, Connecticut, Massachusetts, and New Jersey. Other Italian communities grew in Detroit, Pittsburgh, San Francisco, Milwaukee, and Chicago. During the decades of large-scale immigration, 97 percent of Italian immigrants landed in New York City, making it the city with the largest number of Italian immigrants.

According to census figures, there were nearly fifteen million Italian Americans in the United States in 1990. More than 50 percent (7,517,801) of all persons of Italian ancestry lived in the Northeast. Fewer than 20 percent lived in any of the other three regions—the Midwest (2,443,004), South (2,482,645), and West (2,271,489). Continuing the trend that began earlier in the century, 92 percent (11,450,322) lived in urban areas, about 36 percent (4,102,207) lived in central cities, while 64 percent (7,348,115) lived in the urban fringes of cities.

In 1990, Italian Americans comprised the fourth-largest immigrant group in America. (This count does not include African Americans or Hispanics.) In New Jersey, New York, Rhode Island, and Connecticut, Italians remain the largest ethnic group.

The data on family structure from the 1980 U.S. Census provides support for the hypothesis that family relationships are very strong among the Italian population. In New York as well as in New Jersey and Pennsylvania, the proportion of families in 1980 who were married couples (both husband and wife present) were higher among the Italians than among the total population. The proportion of persons under eighteen years living with both parents was higher for Italians than for the total state population. Also, the proportion of older persons living in families was higher among Italians than the total population sixty years or over of the states in this study.

A 1974 study found that Italian-American Catholics had the second lowest divorce rate (2%) of the ethnic groups reviewed. However, the Italians' rate of divorce in 1979 was not significantly different from that among the total U.S. population. In 1980, married Italian women age thirty-five to forty-five in New York, New Jersey, and Pennsylvania had approximately 2.5 children, which was slightly below the U.S. average of 2.8 children.

Family

In Italy the social structure of the rural village was founded on the family (*la famiglia*), whose interests and needs determined individuals' attitudes toward church, state, and school. Each member was expected to uphold family honor and to fulfill his or her particular duties and responsibilities. In America as in Italy, the family was a tightly knit unit, encompassing a wide range of relationships and retaining close ties even after the marriage of the children.

The obligation to support the aged is very important in Italian-American families. In the early days of immigration the father was recognized as head of the household. However, while Italian women were quick to acknowledge their husbands as the family head, they almost invariably had a strong hand in the important decisions of the family. They were particularly influential in the social and religious lives of their children.

Families discouraged marriage with non-Italians, while divorce, at least among the first generation, was almost unknown.

Religion

While the family has traditionally been the most important institution of Italian society, the church also has exerted profound influence on Italian life. When Italians arrived in America they found a church organization and culture that was totally outside their experience. Dominated by the Irish, American Catholicism appeared cold, stern, and disciplined, unlike the casual attitude of worship practiced by Italians.

In his article "Prelates and Peasants" (1969), Rudolph Vecoli describes Italians as nominally Roman Catholics but explains that theirs was a folk religion, a fusion of Christian and pre-Christian elements such as animism, polytheism, and sorcery with the sacraments of the church. Southern Italians transplanted their religious practices to America. Religious lucky charms, especially in the shape of horns (*corne*), were worn by Italian women in America to ward off evil spirits. The "evil eye" (*il mal occhio*) was greatly feared, for many Italians believed that certain people had powers to give the "evil eye" to others, resulting in ill health or other misfortune.

Southern Italians, especially, attributed special powers to individual saints. These local saints were believed to be significant personages whose favors were valuable to the peasants. One of the most significant aspects of religion for Italians was the feast day (*festa*) of the Madonna or a patron saint. This was the high point in the life of the village and the most authentic expression of Italian culture transplanted to the New World. With processions, bands, and fireworks, these celebrations exalted the miraculous powers of the patron saint and invoked his or her protection on the village. In every Italian community the feast day continues to be an important expression of Italian-American Catholicism.

Economics

Although the majority of Italians did not travel to America motivated by a desire to pursue agriculture, there were a significant number who desired to work the land. Some emigrations from Italy were undertaken for the express purpose of agricultural colonization. In Independence, Louisiana, nearly three hundred Italian immigrants from Palermo bought the land at low prices from native farmers because it was considered too wet to be productive. The Italians constructed ditches and drainage canals, converting the swampy land into fruitful soil. In another, much smaller, colony in Genoa, Wisconsin, several Italian families settled in 1863 and started dairy farming. Eventually more families joined the colony.

Italian colonies were especially successful in market and truck gardening. As early as 1844, Italians were engaged in market gardening near Providence, Rhode Island, and later in upstate New York and on Long Island. In California Italians grew oranges, lemons, and other fruits, while grape growing and wine manufacturing were undertaken on a large scale.

Even before the end of the nineteenth century the fruit trade in New York City was controlled by Italian entrepreneurs. The same was true for Milwaukee, Wisconsin, where Italians gained prominence in supplying fruits and vegetables to the city. In every city of significant Italian population their role as suppliers of fruits and vegetables became part of the business establishment.

Most Italians who were skilled workers practiced their trades and crafts in the ethnic neighborhoods and cities in which they lived. Italians worked as masons and stonecutters, mechanics, shoemakers, barbers, tailors, and musicians. Most immigrants at the turn of the twentieth century, however, were not skilled workers and were forced to take jobs as common laborers or as unskilled factory workers. Many single men, in particular, were itinerant workers, following jobs from one state to another. Many newcomers worked as common laborers on railroads, in shipyards, as ditch diggers and hod carriers. They worked in the coal mines of Pennsylvania, Illinois, and West Virginia; in the iron ore mines of Michigan, Wisconsin, and Minnesota; in the precious-metal mines of the Far West; in the phosphate mines of the South; and in the stone quarries of New England. In New York City, Italians help build the subways and entered the garment trades.

Many southern Italian immigrants knew little about American life and had no way of contacting potential employers for work. The Italian *padrone* (labor boss) played an important role in securing work for Italian immigrants. Some padrones recruited men in Italy, paid for their passage, and arranged work for them in the United States. In return, the padrone was paid a fee. The padrone also wrote letters and acted as banker and translator for Italian immigrants. Although he often played an important role helping immigrants bridge the Old World with the New, the padrone was viewed as one who exploits his own people for monetary gain.

Italian immigrants received less pay than the native worker, and since Italians usually had larger families, their standard of living was necessarily lower. Since fathers alone could rarely maintain the family, Italians had to depend on other sources of income. Wives and children contributed to the economic well-being of the family. Italian women took in boarders and worked at home in the finishing trades. They also entered the work force. In New York City the majority of workers in the garment trade were Italian women. In Endicott, New York, they were employed in the shoe factories; in Paterson, New Jersey, they worked in the silk mills; in Ybor City (Tampa, Florida), they worked in the cigar factories. Italian women also operated their own grocery stores, dry goods stores, restaurants, and saloons. Italian children often worked as soon as the law permitted. This pattern was part of the tradition brought from Italy, where everyone worked for the well-being of the family.

Ethnic Community Development

Immigrants seldom left their homelands without knowing exactly where they wanted to go and how to get there. Relatives and friends constantly sent information back regarding locations to live and potential places of employment. Italian immigration has always been a "chain" phenomenon. The first to leave from a particular village attracted others to the New World. From the very beginning the Italians settled in what have been termed "Little Italys." In these ethnic enclaves immigrants spoke and heard a familiar language, built their own churches, and operated grocery stores that specialized in imported food items.

Neighborhoods often were settled by Italian immigrants according to their native province, town, or village of origin. In New York City, for example, Calabrians lived on Mott Street, Sicilians lived on Prince and Elizabeth streets, Neapolitans lived on Mulberry Street, and the Genovesi on Baxter Street. These immigrants were called Italians, but they identified themselves as belonging to a particular province or village in Italy. They were Siciliani, Barese, or Ferrazzani. They possessed a fierce pride and loyalty to their provincial customs and dialects. Most were not able to understand immigrants from other regions of Italy. Even though the standard language of Italy is expressed in the Tuscan dialect, most immigrants arriving in America after 1880 had little education and arrived knowing only the dialect of their region. Consequently they were reduced to speaking a mixture of standard Italian with regional dialect combined with newly learned English words.

Ethnic Press

In 1849, the first newspaper printed entirely in Italian in America was founded: *L'Eco d'Italia* in New York City. Italian newspapers would not flourish until after the 1880s, when an expanding Italian population was substantial enough to sustain an immigrant press. Between 1880 and 1921, twenty Italian language newspapers appeared in Chicago. The country's leading Italian newspaper was *Il Progresso Italo-Americano* (first published in 1880) of New York, which became the most important in the community and, still in print, the most long-lived among foreign-language newspapers in the country. The immigrant press promoted Italian national pride and helped strengthen ties with Italy. It also assisted with the assimilation of immigrants to American society and served as an intermediary between the immigrants and their new homeland.

Home Ownership

When Italians settled in ethnic neighborhoods in large cities such as New York or Chicago, they were often restricted to tenement living. Later, second- and third-generation inner-city Italian Americans moved to suburban areas and purchased their own homes. Italians who migrated to smaller cities and towns, however, were more likely to achieve home ownership in their own lifetime. Studies of social mobility in communities throughout the United States reveal that home ownership represented a major marker of success among immigrants. Italians have had one of the highest percentages of home ownership of all immigrant groups in America. In addition to providing a sense of status, it has given them greater control over their environment, offered a form of enforced savings with a resultant equity, and offered the potential of providing a source of income. For Italian Americans home ownership has been the cornerstone of their conception of stability, respectability, and independence.

Mutual Aid Societies

Italians transplanted many Old World traditions to America. One tradition that took on even greater importance in America was the mutual aid society. John Briggs discovered that mutual aid societies existed in southern Italy soon after Italian unification. In *An Italian Passage* (1978), he noted that southern Italians maintained voluntary associations and recognized the possibilities for promoting individual goals through their associative endeavors. Among these were health, life, and unemployment insurance; education; support of the economic and trade interests of members; advancement of local communal interests; and maintenance of social centers. Italians met the realities of unemployment, widowhood, burial, and even social activities through their membership in mutual aid societies. The largest and most influential Italian organization in the country, the Order of the Sons of Italy in America, originated in New York City in 1905. By the 1920s, its membership had soared to 300,000.

More recently, Italian-American organizations have moved into underwriting programs, supporting the creation and dissemination of publications, films, and exhibits about the history and contemporary status of Italian Americans. Other organizations, such as UNICO (Unity, Neighborliness, Integrity, Charity, Opportunity) and the National Italian-American Foundation, support education by offering scholarships and research awards for Italian-American students.

Discrimination

Perhaps more than other European ethnic groups, Italians faced considerable prejudice in America. They were hired for low wages and, along with other southern Europeans of dark skin, labeled as "swarthy." Italians became a significant factor in the growth of American nativism. In the 1880s and 1890s, Italians played a role in American life that lent itself to nativist interpretation. They were to symbolize the social and economic ills with which the nativists generally identified the immigrants. Italian immigrants in the post-1880 period had the distinction of having all three nativist impulses directed against them: anti-radicalism, anti-Catholicism, and racial nativism.

The wave of Italian immigration came during an era of intense social and economic upheavals that "native" Americans did not understand. The development of

slums and a variety of social problems coincided with an increasingly urbanized America. Increasingly, industrialization led to millions of skilled and unskilled workers crowding into the cities. At the turn of the twentieth century more than 50 percent of Italian immigrants lived in cities. Thus reformers fixed on the immigrants in general, and the Italians in particular, as the major source of social disorders in the city. Nativism reemerged when the movement to redeem the cities became an organized crusade. To nativist reformers the Italian immigrants were the source of the squalor and corruption of the cities. To workmen they were a threat to their livelihood, while militant Protestants saw them as tools of Rome. Thomas Nixon Carver, a conservative economist, blamed them for causing the widening gulf between capital and labor. The major strikes of the period evoked references to dangerous foreign radicals who menaced orderly freedom. This was reinforced by the Haymarket riot in 1886, which convinced Americans that immigration, radicalism, and lawlessness were parts of the same whole.

During the 1880s, the American press often associated southern Italians with criminality and a lowering of the standard of living. Antiforeign sentiment filtered through a specific ethnic stereotype when Italians were involved. They suggested the Mafia and deeds of impassioned violence.

As the 1880s closed, an initial distrust born of contact with different cultures swelled into hatred and violence. Italians were viewed as a class hostile to the nation's institutions or to its best interests. The rapid increase in their numbers raised fear among nativists. In addition, Italians were perceived by many as a dangerous people. The press accounts and descriptions added that Italians were lazy, cruel, ferocious, and bloodthirsty. But cruel and ferocious behavior was more often experienced by the immigrants themselves, who were often victims of rabid discrimination.

Italians were victims of violence, as evidenced in 1891 when the leading citizens of New Orleans led a lynching party into a prison and systematically slaughtered eleven Italians who had just been found not guilty of murder. During the years of the "Red scare" in America, two Italian anarchists, Nicola Sacco and Bartolomeo Vanzetti, were arrested for a murder committed in connection with a payroll robbery in Massachusetts. They were found guilty and sentenced to death. The actual evidence against them was not conclusive, and the suspicion grew that they had been convicted not because they had committed the crime but because of their political beliefs. The judge's conduct of the trial, in which he made little secret of his feelings about anarchists, only deepened suspicion of the verdict. When Sacco and Vanzetti were sent to the electric chair in 1927, in the midst of worldwide protest, millions were convinced that guilty or innocent, they had not been given a fair trial.

The negative images that have plagued Italian Americans are most pointedly expressed in the word "Mafia." Since 1890, Italians have been connected in the public's imagination with criminality and violence. The very small percentage of Italian Americans who have been involved with organized crime have colored public perceptions of law-abiding Italian Americans, who comprise the vast majority of the group.

Italians in Public Life

Italian Americans have made notable contributions to American public life in music, theater, sports, entertainment, science, and politics. Several have had an especially significant impact on American culture, such as Frank Capra, acknowledged master of American filmmakers and producers. In music the dean of Italian-American composers is Giancarlo Menotti, founder of the Festival of Two Worlds at Spoleto, Italy, and its American counterpart in Charleston, South Carolina.

Italian-American writers have poignantly depicted the Italian-American experience. Among them, the 1938 novel *Christ in Concrete* by Pietro di Donato is a classic. This critically acclaimed work portrays hardworking Italian immigrants on the Lower East Side of New York before the Great Depression. Mario Puzo, best known for *The Godfather,* achieved great success as a novelist from writings molded by his experience growing up during the Depression in New York's "Hell's Kitchen," which resulted in his second novel, *The Fortunate Pilgrim.*

In science, Italian Americans have played a significant role from the nineteenth century, when Antonio Meucci perfected a workable telephone (prior to the work of Alexander Graham Bell), to the twentieth century, with the construction of the first atomic bomb. Enrico Fermi was the first person to achieve a nuclear chain reaction and was one of the top scientists engaged in the construction of the atomic bomb at Los Alamos.

Italians faced great challenges breaking into politics. Fiorello LaGuardia, the mayor of New York City from 1934 to 1945, was the first to win a highly visible public office. Representative Geraldine Ferraro was the first woman to run for vice president of the United States, while Associate Justice Antonin Scalia was the first Italian American appointed to the U.S. Supreme Court.

For Italian Americans the immigrant era has long since passed. It has been more than a century since southern Italians began to arrive in the United States in large numbers. The period of large-scale immigration lasted until the early 1920s, when federal legislation severely restricted entry into America.

Italian Americans have been responsible for extensive accomplishments and have achieved significant economic success. Italians are attending college in ever-increasing numbers. Typically, the children of Italian storekeepers and small-businessmen went to college and became professionals. By the 1970s, Italian Americans comprised approximately one-third of students enrolled in the City University of New York and half of the student body at Fordham University. As a result of their strong qualifications and better educational background, the children and grandchildren of Italian immigrants moved into the white collar fields.

Italians remain loyal to the Catholic Church, although they do not exert leadership within it in America proportionate to their numbers. Intermarriage, once discouraged by first-generation immigrants, is now commonplace. Today's Italian Americans are not only more likely than members of earlier generations to marry outside the ethnic group, they also are more likely to divorce. The Italian-American family tends to resemble the smaller, more egalitarian, child-centered family typical of the American middle class with fertility rates among Italian-American women lower than those for other American women.

Of all the contributions of Italians to American life, perhaps the most influential has been Italian cuisine. Pizza, introduced by Neapolitans, is as popular as the all-American hamburger. Spaghetti and meatballs have been replaced by the healthier pasta dishes, using fresh tomatoes and fresh herbs. Cooking with olive oil and drinking a glass of wine a day (which Italians have been doing for centuries) are now heralded as good for one's health.

Bibliography

Briggs, J. (1978). *An Italian Passage: Immigrants to Three American Cities, 1890–1930.* New Haven, CT: Yale University Press.

Campisi, P. (1948). "Ethnic Family Patterns: The Italian Family in the United States." *American Journal of Sociology* 53:443–449.

Gallo, P. (1981). *Old Bread, New Wine: A Portrait of the Italian Americans.* Chicago: Nelson-Hall.

Iorizzo, L., and Mondello, S. (1980). *The Italian Americans,* revised edition. New York: Twayne.

Kessner, T. (1977). *The Golden Door: Italians and Jewish Immigrant Mobility in New York City, 1880–1915.* New York: Oxford University Press.

Lopreato, J. (1970). *Italian Americans.* New York: Random House.

Mormino, G., and Pozzetta, G. (1987). *The Immigrant World of Ybor City.* Urbana: University of Illinois Press.

Nelli, H. S. (1975). *Italians in Chicago, 1880–1930.* New York: Oxford University Press.

Pisani, L. (1957). *The Italian in America.* New York: Exposition Press.

Vecoli, R. (1969). "Prelates and Peasants: Italian Immigrants and the Catholic Church." *Journal of Social History* 2:217–286.

Yans-McLaughlin, V. (1982). *Family and Community: Italian Immigrants in Buffalo, 1880–1930.* Urbana: University of Illinois Press.

—DIANE C. VECCHIO

MEXICANS

Mexicans immigrating into the U.S. Southwest are moving into territory that was once part of Mexico. Many Mexican Americans (Americans of Mexican descent, also called Chicanos) can trace their roots to settlements in the U.S. Southwest as early as 1595. For these Mexican Americans, the history of immigration included the movement of U.S. citizens into Mexican territory, resulting in the eventual loss of that territory after the Mexican War (1846–1848). Immigration of

Mexicans into what was now U.S. territory began shortly after 1848 but did not emerge as a major movement until the twentieth century. In the latter half of the nineteenth century, the United States relied on immigrants from Europe, China, and Japan to satisfy the growing demand for immigrant labor in its rapidly expanding industrial and agricultural economy. However, resentment toward these immigrant groups grew, leading to dramatic restrictions on their immigration in the early part of the twentieth century, after which Mexican immigrants became an even more important source of labor in the economy of the United States.

The Roots of Mexican Immigration

An understanding of contemporary Mexican immigration requires a brief history of its origins. Porfirio Diaz, president of Mexico from 1876 to 1911, laid the groundwork for both the Mexican Revolution and Mexican immigration to the United States. One of Diaz's goals was to modernize Mexico. To accomplish this he invited foreign investment from Europe and the United States and separated the Mexican *campesino* (peasant) from the land, thus creating a mobile labor force for capitalist development. By the time his presidency came to an end with the revolution, five million rural Mexicans had lost their rights to land. In villages and towns across the Mexican countryside, upwards of 98 percent of the farmers had no land to farm. During this time, the railroads were built, with U.S. financing, connecting the interior of Mexico with U.S. and European markets. The railroads also provided the rural labor force with a cheap means of transportation to Mexico's growing urban-industrial centers and to the northern border.

The growing demand for labor in the American Southwest was attractive to Mexicans. In the early part of the twentieth century, New Mexico, Arizona, Colorado, and Oklahoma needed workers for their booming coal and copper mines. In California, the deserts of the Central and Imperial valleys were being transformed into rich, labor-hungry, agricultural lands. A growing population and economy meant large-scale construction in expanding cities throughout the Southwest, but especially Los Angeles, San Diego, San Francisco, and Denver.

In its search for a labor force to meet these new labor demands in the Southwest, the United States turned to international sources. Chinese immigrants were brought to work in the agricultural fields and mines and on the railroads. Their immigration was virtually stopped with the Chinese Exclusion Act of 1882, a response to the "Yellow Peril" campaigns against the Chinese. The Japanese followed, but they, too, were characterized as a competitive threat due to their success in farming, fishing, and other economic endeavors. The "Gentlemen's Agreement" with Japan in 1907 closed the door on their immigration.

In the early 1900s, Mexicans became a preferred alternative labor force in the Southwest for a number of reasons. Mexican culture was not so different from American culture, relative to Asian cultures. U.S. employers already had experience with Mexicans through their investments in Mexico. And Mexicans had a long history in the area; their presence was not new or exotic. In addition, Anglo Americans commonly characterized Mexicans as indolent, passive, noncompetitive, inferior "half-breeds" who lacked ambition and who were satisfied with their lot in life, or at least believed there was little they could do to alter their future (they were, in other words, fatalists). They were portrayed as people who would not become economic competitors with their employers. And finally, Mexicans were viewed as the quintessential temporary immigrants who would return like "homing pigeons" to Mexico rather than stay permanently in the United States. With such characteristics, Americans viewed Mexicans as providing ample labor at little cost.

So pervasive were these perceived characterizations of Mexicans that in 1911 the Dillingham Commission, which was established to study the immigration issue, argued that Mexican immigration should be promoted as the best solution to the Southwest's labor needs. It even went so far as to exempt Mexicans from the head tax for immigrants that was established under the immigration laws of 1903 and 1907. With the higher wages offered in the United States compared to Mexico, and with active recruitment campaigns by American employers, Mexicans with few opportunities in Mexico became attracted to jobs in the United States.

By the 1920, a pattern of immigration had been established, and the stage was set for the first large immigration of Mexicans to the United States. The postrevolutionary years in Mexico were chaotic and violent, especially in the countryside. Across the border, the United States needed labor. The American economy was growing, but perhaps more important for Mexicans, the United States shut the door to low-skilled labor from Europe. The immigration laws of 1921 and 1924 severely restricted the immigration of southern and eastern Europeans. Once again, Mexicans became a suitable alternative for America's labor-hungry agricultural fields and factories. American businesses often sent recruiters to Mexico in search of laborers for work in the Midwest, including Chicago, where the communities they established continue today.

Immigration from Mexico and the rest of the world came to a virtual stop during the Great Depression of the 1930s. In fact, many Mexicans returned to Mexico—some willingly, others unwillingly. Anti-immigrant, especially anti-Mexican, sentiments flourished during the early 1930s. President Herbert Hoover even blamed the Depression on the presence of Mexican immigrants, providing another example of scapegoating of immigrants during difficult economic times. As a consequence, the U.S. Immigration and Naturalization Service (INS) routinely rounded up Mexicans and repatriated them to Mexico, forcing them to take their American-born children, who were U.S. citizens, with them. Close to 500,000 Mexicans were repatriated during the Depression.

Although Mexicans were eschewed during the 1930s, the 1940s witnessed a renewed recruitment of Mexican labor. World War II ushered many American men and some women out of the labor force and into military service. Many other women entered the workplace, but a labor shortage still existed. The United States turned to Mexico for unskilled and semiskilled laborers who would work in the United States on a contract basis for a few months. Beginning in 1942, this program became popularly known as the "Bracero Program," *bracero* meaning "arms" in Spanish. Although the Bracero Program was to last only during the war years, its advantages as a ready source of cheap labor, especially in agriculture, proved irresistible. The program continued until 1964.

During the course of the twenty-two-year Bracero Program, hundreds of thousands of Mexicans were recruited to work in the United States. Mexican workers came from many states, but principally from the highly populated central states of Jalisco, Michoacán, Zacatecas, Querétaro, Guanajuato, and Puebla. While in the United States, bracero workers learned about opportunities in the American labor market and they established contacts with American employers. When the Bracero Program ended in 1964, the demand for the labor these workers provided did not vanish. Employers still needed the workers in their fields and on their ranches, only the workers could no longer immigrate to work legally as braceros. Not surprisingly, the number of illegal immigrant workers rose dramatically after the termination of the Bracero Program. The system of employer-employee contacts, immigration routes, and social networks continued to operate, only clandestinely. The same Mexican states that supplied workers for the Bracero Program are the principal source of most Mexican immigration today.

Since the 1960s, use of Mexican labor has diversified, especially in the Southwest. Once working primarily in agriculture, undocumented Mexicans are now found in many urban and suburban jobs, performing work that pays low wages and offers few benefits and that therefore is not generally attractive to U.S. citizens.

A Demographic Profile

The Mexican-American population has grown rapidly. Between 1980 and 1990, Mexican Americans increased by approximately 7.75 million persons, a 54.4 percent increase over the decade. The dramatic growth in the Mexican-American population is, to a significant degree, due to immigration. Between 1980 and 1988, a total of 625,690 Mexicans legally immigrated to the United States, more than from any other Latin American country. In 1981 alone, 101,268 Mexicans legally immigrated, almost double the numbers of the year before and after. Since 1984, the number of legal Mexican immigrants entering the United States has continued to rise steadily, with a new peak reached in 1988, when 95,039 Mexicans legally immigrated. Mexicans accounted for 14.8 percent of the 643,025 immigrants admitted in 1988.

The years of 1989 and 1990 were unusual due to the large numbers of Mexicans admitted as legal immigrants under the legalization program authorized by the 1986 immigration law—the Immigration Reform and Control Act (IRCA). Fully 405,172 Mexicans were admitted as legal immigrants in 1989, and another 679,068 in 1990.

Legal Mexican immigrants live in similar geographic areas as Mexican Americans generally. California alone absorbs at least half the total flow of legal Mexican immigrants, averaging about 67,000 legal immigrants per year since 1981. Looking at one year provides a good example of where Mexican immigrants intend to reside. More than half (56.4%, or 53,622) of the 96,039 legal Mexican immigrants in 1988 chose California as their state of intended residence. Mexican immigrants that year also intended to reside in Texas (23.9%), Illinois (6.2%), Arizona (3.6%), New Mexico (1.8%), and Colorado (1.2%). Therefore, most (80.7%) legal Mexican immigrants in 1988 intended to reside in one of the southwestern states of California, Texas, Arizona, New Mexico, and Colorado. Thus the Southwest is both the region with the largest Mexican-American population and the area that attracts most legal Mexican immigrants. Almost 90 percent of Mexican immigrants choose to reside in a metropolitan area. The municipality of Los Angeles-Long Beach attracted one out of three (33.6%) legal Mexican immigrants in 1988. Other key urban destinations for Mexicans included Chicago, San Diego, El Paso, and Houston.

The traditional picture of the Mexican immigrant was of a young, single, male agricultural worker who immigrated for a few months and then returned home. This characterization was an accurate reflection of many Mexican immigrants during the early part of the twentieth century, and well into the 1940s, 1950s, and 1960s, when thousands of men immigrated as temporary contract laborers under the Bracero Program. Although men may have predominated in those earlier immigration flows, Mexican women also immigrated, both legally and illegally, to the United States, where they helped establish Mexican communities throughout the Southwest and Midwest. In 1988, women made up 43.9 percent of the legal immigrants from Mexico.

In the past, the immigration literature characterized women as appendages to their immigrating husbands; women immigrated to reunite with their husbands who were already in the United States. Today, single women from Mexico immigrate to the United States for economic as well as social reasons. They immigrate to find "a better life," seeking employment in the rapidly growing service sector, especially in domestic work. They often have family remaining in Mexico who rely on the money they send back. Some Mexican women are single parents who leave their children with parents or siblings when immigrating to the United States. In some cases these women may have intended to work in the United States for a short time, but their stay became extended. Thus, they often bring their children from Mexico to join them in the United States. If current trends persist, women will continue to make up a significant proportion of the Mexicans who immigrate to the United States well into the twenty-first century.

Undocumented Immigration

Many people immigrate to the United States without documentation from the INS. Popularly called "illegal aliens," these undocumented immigrants often are in the United States for relatively brief periods. Some, however, do settle and add to the existing population. Because undocumented immigrants are a clandestine population, making accurate estimates of their numbers is difficult. Some reasonable assessments are, however, available. For example, data from the 1980 U.S. Census were used to estimate the number of undocumented immigrants in the country during the early 1980s at between 2.5 million and 3.5 million. This number was dramatically reduced by the approximately 3 million undocumented immigrants legalized under the 1986 immigration law, about 75 percent of whom were Mexicans. On average, between 200,000 and 300,000 undocumented immigrants settle in the United States each year, a range that has been consistent for many years.

Undocumented immigrants come from many countries, such as China, Ireland, and Colombia. Mexicans, however, make up a large proportion of the undocumented population. For example, Mexicans made up about 70 percent of the undocumented population in 1988. Undocumented Mexicans tend to be relatively young—most are eighteen to thirty-four years of age. Historically, most undocumented immigrants were males, but the proportion of females has increased to more than 40 percent. Undocumented Mexicans on average have six to seven years of education.

California attracts the largest proportion of undocumented immigrants of all nationalities. For example, California had approximately half (1.74 million) of the nation's undocumented immigrants in 1987. Although undocumented immigrants accounted for only 1.4 percent of U.S. residents in 1980, they made up 6.3 percent of California's total population. Not surprisingly, about half of the approximately 100,000 undocumented Mexican immigrants entering the United States each year choose California as their state of residence. Although many undocumented immigrants are attracted to California, they also reside in many other states, including Washington, Texas, Illinois, New York, and Florida.

Families and Immigration

Families play an important role in the immigration process. Family networks extend well beyond the immediate household, often linking family members across national borders. Although the availability of jobs in the United States may fuel Mexican immigration, it is the transnational links of Mexican families that make immigration possible. Because of the extensiveness of these transnational social networks, established immigrant families often serve as landing pads for later immigrating family members, especially females. New immigrants turn to family for a place to live while they get settled, information about jobs in the local area, and insights into the cultural norms of the community. Therefore, Mexican immigrant households often consist of extended family members. Undocumented immigrants who have formed a family in the United States face additional pressures that contribute to their household composition. Having other adults in the household helps undocumented immigrants survive despite low wages, high rents, child-care needs, and sudden absences from the family due to apprehension by the INS.

Families form the key links in what is known as "chain migration." Countless examples exist of this process. Typically, a pioneer from a Mexican community immigrates to work in the United States. He or she then helps relatives and friends immigrate, who then help others. The reproduction of community in this way means that many friends and family from the same community or region in Mexico soon come to live near each other in the United States. As this process unfolds over time, Mexican immigrants develop a multiplicity of ties to other families, friends, and societal institutions in the United States. These ties create a sense of community among Mexican immigrants that both emerges from and fosters family settlement rather than return migration to Mexico.

Mexican women are particularly apt to desire to settle in the United States, often in contrast to their male counterparts. Why this is so has to do with many factors. First, Mexican women often immigrate once and then stay in the United States, whether they originally arrived to join husbands or were on their own. Mexican men, on the other hand, have often made many trips to the United States. Mexican immigrant women typically get year-round jobs in domestic work, hotels, restaurants, or manufacturing. In addition, undocumented women often fear recrossing the border clandestinely. Crossing the border at night, over hillsides and through ravines, is a dangerous undertaking, one that many undocumented women would rather avoid, even if it means not returning to Mexico as often as they would like. Moreover, the experience of working for wages, which they may not have done in Mexico, may lead to changes in women's relations with their fathers and husbands. Their independent earnings and contributions to their family's welfare increase their sense of independence and often lead to a greater role in the family's decision making. All these factors lessen traditional family patriarchy—male dominance—and contribute to Mexican women's reluctance to return "back home" permanently. Finally, if Mexican immigrant women form a family in the United States, either by having children or bringing their children from Mexico, they are more likely to desire to stay in the United States. Add to this the increasing sense of community felt by Mexican women as they develop friends among their neighbors, some of whom may be relatives or friends from Mexico, and the reasons for gender differences in desires for return migration and settlement become apparent.

Legalization and Citizenship

Many Mexicans immigrate to the United States legally. For undocumented immigrants, however, acquiring legal resident status is an important step toward working and living in the United States in relative security. Many undocumented immigrants manage to acquire legal resident status—that is, to become legal immigrants. They do this in a number of ways. For example, a relative who is a citizen of or legal resident in the United States can sponsor an undocumented immigrant's application for legal resident status. An employer can sponsor an undocumented worker if the work he or she performs qualifies and proves not to affect U.S. citizen job seekers negatively. An undocumented immigrant might also qualify for a government-sponsored legalization program such as that created by the 1986 immigration law. Finally, an undocumented immigrant might marry a U.S. citizen who then sponsors his or her application for legal residence. Given these various opportunities for legalizing one's immigration status, an undocumented immigrant may not be stuck in that status indefinitely.

Members of the same family can acquire legal resident status at different times, which often leads to families of mixed immigration status. The following scenario is typical of such families. The pioneer immigrant in the family, the one with the most time in the United States, acquires legal resident status through an employer or relative who has become a U.S. citizen. He or she then brings his or her spouse to the United States along with any children. Finally, he or she has a child born in the United States, making the child a U.S. citizen. The family now consists of one parent who is a legal immigrant, one parent who is an illegal immigrant, children who are undocumented immigrants, and a child who is a U.S. citizen. In all likelihood, the undocumented immigrants in the family will also one day find a way to become legal residents.

With legal resident status comes the opportunity to naturalize and obtain U.S. citizenship. Mexicans historically have had low naturalization rates, for several reasons. Mexican immigrants often believe that gaining U.S. citizenship would place obstacles to their dream of returning to Mexico someday, possibly to retire. For others, it is the emotional issue of nationalism, of losing one's national identity.

Over the years, however, larger numbers of Mexicans have sought U.S. citizenship. Between 1979 and 1988, there was an increasing trend in the number of Mexicans who became naturalized citizens, reaching a peak in 1986 and then decreasing somewhat before stabilizing and then increasing again in 1995 and 1996. These results reflect a positive movement toward becoming a U.S. citizen, perhaps a result of the efforts of groups such as the Southwest Voter Registration Program. The negative portrayal of immigrants that has characterized much of the public debate since the late 1970s may also have raised interest among Mexican immigrants to acquire the benefits of U.S. citizenship.

Cultural Continuity and Acculturation

Mexican immigration during the last half of the twentieth century has changed the profile of the Mexican-American, or Chicano, population. Eighteen percent of the Mexican-American population in the United States was foreign-born in 1970. In 1990, in contrast, 33 percent of the Mexican-origin population was foreign-born. Because of immigration, the proportion of immigrants among Chicanos in the nation almost doubled during the 1970s and 1980s. In California, Mexican immigrants accounted for 41.7 percent of the Mexican-American population in 1990. Mexican immigrants bring with them the Spanish language, values, and behavior that reinvigorate Mexican-American culture in communities in the Southwest and throughout the United States.

Without immigration, Chicanos would retain some of the immigrant generation's cultural beliefs and behaviors. By the third generation, however, the overwhelming majority of Mexican Americans born in the United States are dominant in English rather than Spanish. Immigration from Mexico and other Latin American countries keeps Spanish alive. Mexican immigrants also bring with them values of family solidarity, religion, and hard work that sometimes stand in sharp contrast to American values of individualism and secularism. Behavior patterns among Mexican immigrants are also relatively healthy. For example, only 5 percent of the babies born to Mexican immigrant mothers were of low birthweight despite having risk factors such as low levels of education, low income, and lack of medical insurance. Positive birth outcomes have been attributed to low consumption of alcohol and other drugs and low use of cigarettes by recent immigrant women. Moreover, they are particularly unlikely to use drugs during pregnancy. Mexican immigrants continue behaving in these ways in the United States, but eventually fall victim to acculturation. Moreover, there is growing evidence that this is also true for attitudes about education. Mexican immigrant children bring with them positive attitudes toward and respect for education, only to have them erode into the cynicism found in the urban youth culture in the United States. In short, it appears that acculturation may be bad for immigrants' health and educational attainment.

Mexican immigrants have also added creatively to the cultural life of the communities they settled in. As they mixed with other members of American society, the result has often been the production of ways of life that have become "American" rather than "Mexican." In the nineteenth century, the Mexican *vaquero* became the American cowboy, who retained much of the basic material culture and language of the vaquero (the saddle, the lasso, the rodeo). Mexicans in southern Texas borrowed the accordion and polka rhythms of their German immigrant neighbors and created *Norteño* music. This music continues as a popular musical form throughout the U.S. Southwest and Mexico, but for many Americans it was unknown until the murder of the popular Texas singer Selena. Spanish-language television and radio are extremely popular throughout the Southwest. Still, much of the musical and artistic production of Mexican immigrants and their descendants remains outside the American mainstream. Mexican Americans are not well represented in national television and movies, nor is there much variation in the presentation of thematic issues surrounding their lives. The dramatic range rarely extends beyond a gang and drug lifestyle.

Bibliography

Allen, J. P., and Turner, E. J. (1988). "Where to Find the New Immigrants." *American Demographics* 9:23–60.

Borjas, G. J., and Tienda, M. (1993). "The Employment and Wages of Legalized Immigrants." *International Migration Review* 27:712–747.

Cardoso, L. A. (1980). *Mexican Emigration to the United States, 1897–1931.* Tucson: University of Arizona Press.

Chavez, L. R. (1992). *Shadowed Lives: Undocumented Immigrants in American Society.* Fort Worth: Harcourt Brace Jovanovich.

Cornelius, W. A.; Martin, P. L.; and Hollifield, J. F. (1994). *Controlling Immigration: A Global Perspective.* Stanford, CA: Stanford University Press.

Craig, R. B. (1971). *The Bracero Program: Interest Groups and Foreign Policy.* Austin: University of Texas Press.

Donato, K. M. (1993). "Current Trends and Patterns of Female Migration: Evidence from Mexico." *International Migration Review* 27:748–771.

Hoffman, A. (1974). *Unwanted Americans: Mexican Americans in the Great Depression, Repatriation Pressures, 1929–1939.* Tucson: University of Arizona Press.

Hondagneu-Sotelo, P. (1994). *Gendered Transitions: Mexican Experience of Immigration.* Berkeley: University of California Press.

Massey, D. S.; Alarcon, R.; Durand, J.; and Gonzalez, H. (1987). *Return to Aztlan.* Berkeley: University of California Press.

Mendoza, I.; Ventura, S.; Valdez, R.; Castillo, R.; Saldivar, L.; Baisden, K.; and Martorell, R. (1991). "Selected Measures of Health Status for Mexican-American, Mainland Puerto Rican, and Cuban-American Children." *Journal of the American Medical Association* 265:227–232.

Portes, A., and Bach, R. L. (1985). *Latin Journey: Cuban and Mexican Immigrants in the United States.* Berkeley: University of California Press.

Suárez-Orozco, C., and Suárez-Orozco, M. (1995). *Transformations: Immigration, Family Life, and Achievement Motivation Among Latino Adolescents.* Stanford, CA: Stanford University Press.

—LEO R. CHAVEZ

POLES

Upon their arrival in North America, the people identified as Poles spoke Polish and belonged to the Catholic Church. They traced their heritage to historic Poland, a country that did not exist as a political and independent unit from 1795 to 1918.

Immigration History

Although there are unsubstantiated claims of Poles in North America earlier, the first known Poles arrived in Jamestown, Virginia, in 1608. Subsequent Polish immigration history can be divided into five periods. The first period extends to approximately 1800, when relatively few Poles arrived as individuals seeking fortune, freedom, or adventure. The second period, 1800 to 1860, saw an increase in numbers, with some arriving in groups of several hundred political exiles or peasants seeking land. Many settled where land was cheap (e.g., Panna Maria, Texas, founded in 1854 by a contingent of Silesian Polish peasants).

During the third period, 1860 to 1914, Polish immigration to the United States became a major wave of some two million people, with primarily economic and religious motivations for leaving Europe. This immigration reached a peak in 1912-1913, when 174,365 ethnic Poles immigrated, with men outnumbering women two to one.

The annual numbers of immigrants were relatively small during the fourth period, 1914 to 1988, because of the two world wars and the fact that under the U.S. Immigration Act of 1924 Poland's quota was 5,982 immigrants per year. However, there were 151,978 individuals admitted between 1945 and 1953 under various refugee legislative acts and presidential directives, and approximately 40,000 Polish ex-servicemen and underground insurgents were admitted between the end of World War II and 1968.

Combining various sources and best estimates, it appears that a total of 1,780,151 Poles immigrated to the United States between 1885 and 1972. Another 297,590 arrived and later returned to Poland, and 669,392 were nonimmigrant, temporary visitors to the United States.

The fifth period of Polish immigration consists of that since 1988. The number of legal immigrants has increased and is augmented by people staying in the United States after their visas have expired (the *wakacjusze*). The change in numbers of legal immigrants has been dramatic, from a total of 52,000 in the five years between 1982 and 1987, to 15,101 in 1989; 20,537 in 1990; 19,199 in 1991; and 25,504 in 1992.

These numbers of Polish arrivals and returnees are estimates at best; it is impossible to be accurate. The problem is that even when records are available they list an individual's country of origin and not ethnic affiliation. Before World War I, Poles would be included among immigrants originating in Austria, Germany or Prussia, and Russia. After World War I, minority groups living in Poland were included in Polish numbers.

The Polish immigration shows the characteristics of any large-scale immigration. Before the steamship and later the airplane became common means of transportation, few who crossed the Atlantic returned to Europe. However, beginning with the last part of the nineteenth century, a differentiation exists between the life histories of the political and the economic immigrants.

The refugees and émigrés arrived intent on carrying on the struggle for their political goals from abroad and returning when conditions in their homeland improved. In fact, they seldom returned. Economic immigrants frequently followed a chain migration, joining friends, relatives, or fellow villagers who had preceded them and established residence in the new country. In 1908, virtually all Poles arriving in the United States claimed they were joining relatives or friends. Frequently the immigrants planned to stay in the United States only long enough to save sufficient money for a specified end, such as to buy some livestock or a piece of land or to build a new house on the family farm in Poland. Between 1906 and 1914, about 30 percent of Polish immigrants returned home to Europe. At times, upon returning home new needs arose and the individual left for America again, becoming a "pendulum immigrant." Eventually a portion of the sojourners became settlers. Officials did not track such individuals and recorded only the total number of arrivals and departures. This practice adds another element of uncertainty to the immigration statistics.

Since a portion of the Polish immigration was due to political causes, there was the expectation that when Poland regained independence a large number would return. This massive return did not happen. In 1920–1921, a total of 42,207 returned; in 1921–1922, a total of 31,004 returned.

There is wide disagreement regarding how many individuals residing in the United States should even be considered Poles. The 1990 U.S. Census reported 723,000 individuals who spoke Polish at home. Estimates, by even apparently trustworthy sources, vary widely. In 1969, the federal government estimated that there were 4,021,000 Poles, but the 1990 U.S. Census categorized 9,366,000 as being Polish.

The difficulty with numbers stems from the fact that official census data are not based on unchanging definitions; the criteria for including or excluding an individual in any given group vary over time. Similarly, categories are added as they become politically important, and discontinued as they become politically less relevant.

Settlement Patterns

Polish settlements in the United States reflect the economic conditions existing at the time of arrival. Since most of the Poles arriving after the Civil War were peasants and immigrated to the United States *za chlebem* (for bread), they were attracted to areas of the country where jobs for unskilled laborers were plentiful.

In 1911, 10 percent of foreign-born Poles were engaged in agriculture. Some took up farming, settling in places where they were "abandoned" by employers. An example of this is the Polish settlement in the Connecticut River Valley, where some Polish railroad construction workers were laid off in 1887 due to a depression.

Others settled where land was cheap—northern Michigan, Minnesota, Wisconsin, and Nebraska. For example, Sherman County in Nebraska has a high percentage of residents of Polish ancestry, enabling Loup City, the county seat, to dub itself the Polish capital of America based on the percentage rather than the numbers. As generations and economic conditions changed, agricultural employment decreased. While 11 percent of second-generation Poles were engaged in agriculture, only 1 percent of their children were.

Many Poles worked in the meatpacking industry. Since Chicago; Kansas City, Kansas; and South Omaha, Nebraska, were important meatpacking centers, they developed sizable Polish settlements. However, the majority of Poles in the United States obtained work in industry and mining and settled in the industrial "rust belt" north of the Mason-Dixon Line and the Ohio River valley, south of the Great Lakes, and east of the Missouri River. The major settlements were and continue to be Chicago, New York, Pittsburgh, Buffalo, Milwaukee, Detroit, Cleveland, and Philadelphia. According to the 1990 U.S. Census, 37 percent of Poles lived in the Northeast and the same percentage in the Midwest, while 15 percent lived in the South and 11 percent in the West.

During the period of greatest immigration—between the Civil War and World War I—Polish society in the United States was essentially a working-class Roman Catholic society. The individuals who immigrated were not typical peasants or a cross section of Polish urban populations. They were predominantly young, unmarried males. They were not members of organized communities immigrating as a group. The values and needs of the community they created in various locations in the United States were essentially the same across settings, and it was not until after World War II that members of the group began to differentiate according to education and occupation. This was due, in part, to the fact that the new arrivals were middle-class and primarily politically rather than economically motivated immigrants and, in part, because some members of the group already established in the United States were second- or third-generation, continuing their education and beginning to move into professional and white-collar jobs and, thus, into the middle class. The results of this move into the middle class were employment and residence in places where few were of Polish background, leading to aspirations and behavior patterns similar to those of the wider society. In short, increasing numbers were becoming acculturated and socially assimilated to American society.

This assimilation into the structure of the larger society and acculturation to its culture is evidenced by various indicators. Starting in 1929, the Polish ethnic press has continued to decline. In 1977, there were one hundred Polish periodicals; in 1987, ninety-five; but in 1995, only forty.

By 1969, educational, occupational, and social differentiation could be seen in the Polish-American society. Some 16 percent had attended college and 45 percent of the males had white-collar jobs. About 25 percent were skilled workers, and 30 percent were semi-skilled or unskilled laborers. Their incomes approximated the national average of the time. By 1980, a total of 23.9 percent had four or more years of college. This is significantly above the average for the United States, where in 1980, 16.2 percent of the total population and 17.1 percent of whites had achieved this level of education. In employment, 23.5 percent of Poles in the United States were in the managerial or professional categories and 31.8 percent in technical or administrative positions, while only 18 percent were operators, fabricators, or laborers.

Polish-American Identity and Culture

It is becoming increasingly difficult to decide who Poles—or more accurately Polish Americans—are. Is it decided by ethnic descent in a "blood" type of relationship, meaning individuals who either consider themselves Poles or whose ancestors considered themselves Poles? In that case, Polish Americans are a varied lot, and many of them have little in common except shared descent. In such an "ancestrally derived" group there would be individuals who themselves immigrated, but come from a variety of backgrounds and classes, and who in Poland would have little to do with one another. There are also individuals whose ancestors have lived in the United States for two, three, four, or more generations or who come from ethnically mixed marriages where the only Polish ancestor may be a grandparent or even a great-grandparent. Where should the line be drawn?

The operative answer would be that each individual decides. When someone feels that he or she is Polish, then they are. If they do not, then they are not—regardless of antecedents.

Another way of viewing the issue is to look at the group's culture and the individuals who participate in it. Which groups participate? To what degree? With what frequency? Does the main interest lie in the rapidly disappearing group of first-generation immigrants (predominantly old men)? In 1990, a total of 39.4 percent of first-generation Polish immigrants were sixty-five or older. In this group, Polish culture probably predominates. Are individuals who did not move to the suburbs but who reside in ethnic neighborhoods in large cities the main interest? These people live in Polish-American neighborhoods, interact primarily with other Polish Americans, and continue to observe the customs, festivals, and interaction patterns they always have followed. This is a rapidly dwindling population. Is there concern about the population that has moved to the suburbs, where both husband and wife work and there are two or three children? In other words, should the focus be on people who are living as most Americans live?

In 1914, everyone knew who the Poles in the United States were. The vast majority had immigrated from Poland and resided in large industrial cities. Their neighborhoods formed communities around their own churches. The men supported families through their blue-collar jobs. Wives did not work outside the home after their first child. They lived in houses where, besides the owner and his family, there were often one or more boarders or roomers. The families were large, with about five children. On the whole, education was not particularly valued, and people preferred to send children to work rather than school. Their attitudes, customs, and worldview were shared with rural inhabitants in the areas of eastern Europe from whence they came.

In the Polish residential areas of Buffalo, Chicago, or Milwaukee just prior to World War I, there was an essentially Polish community. Polish was the language spoken in the streets, churches, other public gatherings, businesses, and homes. Polish food was produced, sold, and served at public gatherings and in homes. Religious holiday traditions such as Wigilia (Christmas Eve supper), with the essential *opłatek* wafer, Święconka (Easter food blessing), or *kolendy* (group Christmas caroling), or customs associated with farming, such as Dożynki (harvest festival) and Wianki (wreath tossing), were observed with pageantry and ritual very similar, if not identical, to such occasions in Poland. In short, the culture of Polish communities in the United States was a modified version of that of the Polish village or Polish city.

These traditions and customs are still observed, though perhaps not as frequently and ubiquitously as earlier. The difference is that they no longer are automatic actions but rather are matters of choice and of expression of ethnicity and a common bond in the community and among the individuals participating.

However, even in the early 1900s, these communities were neither miniature transplanted Warsaws or Krakows, nor were they replications of Polish villages or the localized cultures of the areas inhabited by Poles at that time. The Polish-American culture was unique, created by the integration of rural Polish cultures with the surrounding American culture. Therefore, one must not think of Polish-American culture as an attenuated or corrupted form of the "real" or "genuine" Polish culture, nor is it a modified version of the "real" American culture of its time. It was and is a unique creation.

One indicator of the magnitude of differences between the cultures found in Poland and in the United States is that whenever sizable numbers of individuals returned to Poland, the majority reimmigrated to the United States. For instance, of the 24,000 or 30,000 (authorities differ) Polish men recruited in the United States to fight in Poland at the end of World War I, some 19,000 returned to the United States. During World War II there were only 772 Polish volunteers for a similar unit. Second, there is some evidence that when Poles did return to Poland, they returned more as American missionaries intent on reproducing American economic and political systems rather than as native sons reintegrating into their society and continuing where they had left off before immigrating to the United States.

Today, there is a question whether a uniquely Polish culture exists in the United States. Some scholars feel that Polish-American culture is a U.S. ethnic subculture—a version of the general American culture. Others see it as distinct unit. It is clear that there are few if any areas in the United States where one could live one's entire life among fellow Poles without having to learn more than a smattering of English or to be exposed to the internal culture of the larger society. Among Polish subgroups, Górali, Kashubians, and Mazurians have retained the strongest and most distinctive identity, while immigrants from Galicia and Silesia have retained a less strong identity.

Can a recognizable Polish-American culture be identified? If the answer is yes, what are its characteristics? How widespread is it? How numerous are the people who have it? There are no clear answers to these questions. It is not eating *czarnina* or *szczawiowa zupa*, or speaking Polish the way an individual in Warsaw would, and wishing *smacznego* when serving food or entering a room where people are eating, or men kissing married women's hands. Rather, it consists of three elements.

One of the elements of Polish-American culture is participating in the community's life by attending church services, being a member of and actively participating in various organizations, and being involved in the social life of the group. Are the individual's friends Polish Americans? Has or is it likely that the individual will marry a fellow Polish American? Do the individuals or their children attend (or are they attending if of proper age) one of the 310 parochial schools associated with Polish-American parishes or the *szkoły dokształcające* (supplementary schools for children attending regular schools where Polish is not a major subject) sponsored either by *rady oświatowe* (educational councils) or some fraternal organizations? Similarly, does the individual attend or participate in *obchód* (celebrations consisting of parades, addresses, performances by choral societies and dance groups in national costumes)? Usually these are held to commemorate some important event in Polish history, such as the adoption of the Polish Constitution of 1791 (May 3) or the restoration of Poland's independence in 1918 (November 11); or to mark Pulaski Day (October 11); or to honor a visiting personage.

Is the individual one of the two million persons who are members of the five hundred Polish-American parishes in the Catholic Church or the Polish National Catholic Church and attend their services? Similarly, is the individual one of the 755,000 persons belonging to Polish-American fraternal organizations? These organizations sponsor Polish-language schools, celebrations, and other social activities aiding preservation of the ethnic culture and cultural creativity, and are the financial base of the Polish American Congress. The most important of these are the Polish National Alliance, the Polish Roman Catholic Union, and the Polish Women's Alliance. In 1993, there were some thirty-six Polish fraternal and non-fraternal organizations, with 650,000 members organized in 3,250 groups across the United States.

The second element of Polish-American culture is the attitudes one has toward Poland, the United States, and the Polish-American community. What group serves as the basis for one's identity? Is the identity that of a Pole who happens to be living abroad? Does one see herself or himself as an American whose ancestors happened to be Polish, in part or completely? In the United States there are a great many individuals who will mention that their ancestors were of various nationalities, but this has little or no bearing on their life except as an amusing element of their background. Or does the individual see herself or himself as a member of a distinct group stemming from Poland but living in the United States, fully integrated into the local society, similar to other groups, but with their own shared, specific, and unique ancestry and culture?

Internal culture is the third element. There is a belief in a Polish national character that is transmitted over generations. By all available data, individuals seeing themselves as Poles are more family-oriented than is the norm for the general population in the United States. They see themselves as highly individualistic and uncooperative. Human nature is considered to be prone to sin and evil, requiring strong external controls, and shame is seen as an effective way of socializing people. There is a feeling that people in Poland belong to two different classes, peasants and gentry, with an unbridgeable gap between them. But there is also an insistence on the equality of individuals within a class.

There are some other unusual elements in Polish cultural in the United States. One of them is that since initially the vast majority saw themselves as sojourners rather than settlers, their orientation was toward the society in Poland and later Polish-American community, rather than American society. This made the Poles one of the less readily assimilating ethnic groups in the United States. They derived their sense of identity and status from fellow members of the Polish-American community rather than from members of the larger society. They were not all that concerned with their image in American eyes. For instance, it was not until the late 1960s and early 1970s that the Polish-American community took active steps to improve its image in the larger society and organized a press campaign against "Polish jokes."

Another such element was their attitude to Poland and its fate. One important factor was the fact that Poland was divided among three countries, and the struggle for regaining independence was cultural as well as political. Consequently the Poles arriving in the United States were already more self-consciously Polish than those immigrant groups where most of them discovered their ethnicity in America only after coming in direct contact with people of other backgrounds. Also, since Poland was not free, the Polish-American community was seen as a fourth province, with the duty to speak for the country, which could not. Paradoxically, this meant that Poles in the United States had less of an identity problem and an easier time in their relationship with Poland when the country was not free than they do now that the country is free and "can speak for itself."

When Poland was not free, then clearly one of the purposes for the existence of the Polish-American community was to support Poland's struggle for freedom. This needed support was used to unify and mobilize Polish Americans. But now that Poland is free, what common goal is there? A goal that is considered moral, worthy, and supported by almost all. Should the Polish-American community become but another ethnic group in the United States, with the certainty of ultimate absorption into the larger society? What should be the attitude and interaction of the average Polish-American individual toward other ethnic groups in America? And how should the individual interact with the people and society in Poland?

This factor also complicates the relationship of the Polish-American community and its leaders with the leaders of independent Poland. How do they establish a common set of goals and ensure that they do not act at cross purposes? Who should lead? Who must follow? The relationship at times has been rather strained. In 1924, the largest Polish-American fraternal association refused full membership to citizens of Poland.

The question of who should lead also has a bearing on the internal social structure of the Polish-American community. When political refugees and educated Poles arrived in the United States, they expected to take over leadership among Polish Americans. They also expected help in adjusting to the new conditions. Most of them were disappointed on both counts. The individuals who already were leaders in the United States did not surrender their positions, feeling that they knew the local situation and had established contacts with leaders of the larger society. Also, material help was relatively sparse. The Poles already established in the United States felt that they had had to struggle, and there was no reason to spare the newcomers the same experience.

The Future

Will there be a Polish-American community in the United States in the year 2000, 2100, or 2200? The answer is that it depends. Does the question mean, Will there be individuals in the United States who identify themselves as Poles? Certainly there will be in 2000; after that the question becomes much more difficult to answer, and the answer hinges on several factors. Will the descendants of the people in the United States who today are considered and consider themselves Poles continue this identity? If the past is any guide, the answer is that few will so identify themselves. Despite the unfavorable image that the American has of "Polaks" and the popularity of Polish jokes, there is not much prejudice against Poles as such, certainly nothing comparable to the prejudice exhibited toward some other ethnic groups. This means that as the cultural and social distances between the Polish community and "mainstream America" lessens, the Poles will ultimately assimilate. All indicators show that the process to date has not been smooth and uniform, but it is there. With each generation there is more intermarriage with other ethnic groups and a lessening of the cultural differences.

A second factor is whether Poles will continue to immigrate to the United States in sizable numbers. The larger the future immigration, the more certainty of the persistence of the Polish-American community. The assimilation of future generations of the majority of individuals stemming from the present community is almost inevitable. Thus its persistence will be contingent on "fresh blood." If in the future sizable numbers of Poles continue to arrive, they will provide a critical mass of members for organizations to function and thus provide a way for those who were born in the United States to express their ethnic affiliation.

Another element in the equation is the activities of the government in Poland. If the government fosters personal, artistic, and cultural contacts between Polish Americans and Poland, then Polish-American community may persist for a long time. Again, the important element will be the maintenance of an organizational and activities framework so that individuals can participate if they so wish.

A final element in the equation is the United States and the attitudes and actions of its government and people. If Americans become xenophobic and there is strong condemnation or legal prohibition of the use of non-English languages and of ethnic organizations, then Polish culture in the United States will rapidly disappear.

Bibliography

Bukowczyk, J. J. (1987). *And My Children Did Not Know Me: A History of the Polish-Americans.* Bloomington: Indiana University Press.

Duscak, T. (1994). "The Polish Presence in North America." *Choice* 32(3):399–419.

Gladsky, T. S. (1992). *Princes, Peasants, and Other Polish Selves: Ethnicity in American Literature.* Amherst: University of Massachusetts Press.

Gory, D. E. (1995). "Polish Immigration to America: Before and After the Fall of the Berlin Wall." *The Polish Review* 40(1):73–79.

Obidinski, E. E., and Zand, H. S., eds. (1987). *Polish Folkways in America: Community and Family.* Polish Studies Series, Vol. I. Lanham, MD: University Press of America.

Poitrowski, T. (1995). *Vengeance of the Swallows: Memoir of a Polish Family's Ordeal Under Soviet Aggression, Ukrainian Ethnic Cleansing and Nazi Enslavement, and their Emigration to America.* Jefferson, NC: McFarland.

Pula, J. S. (1995). *Polish Americans: An Ethnic Community.* New York: Twayne.

Renkiewicz, F. (1973). *The Poles in America, 1608–1972: A Chronology & Fact Book.* Dobbs Ferry, NY: Oceana.

Renkiewicz, F., ed. (1982). *The Polish Presence in Canada and America.* Toronto: Multicultural History Society of Ontario.

Sanders, I. T., and Morowska, E. (1975). *Polish-American Community Life: A Survey of Research.* New York: Polish Institute of Arts and Sciences in America.

Thomas, W. I., and Znaniecki, F. (1984). *The Polish Peasant in Europe and America,* edited and abridged by E. Zaretsky. Urbana: University of Illinois Press.

Wytrwal, J. (1977). *Behold! The Polish Americans.* Detroit, MI: Endurance Press.

Znaniecka-Lopata, H. (1994). *Polish Americans,* 2nd, revised edition. New Brunswick, NJ: Transaction.

Zubrzycki, J. (1988). *Soldiers and Peasants: The Sociology of Polish Immigration.* London: Orbis.

—ANDRIS SKREIJA

RUSSIANS

The name "Russian" is and was adopted by people irrespective of their ethnic background who were citizens of the Russian Empire or of the Soviet Union (USSR). The Cossacks are mainly ethnic Russians, though many of them are of mixed ancestry. Carpatho-Rusyns from pre-World War I Austria-Hungary identified themselves with Russians. Like the United States, Russia was and continues to be a melting pot. People of many nationalities, ethnic backgrounds, and religious affiliations speak Russian at home, are immersed in Russian culture, and call themselves Russians or Russian-speakers.

Orientation

IDENTIFICATION. Russians belong to the Eastern Slavs, a group that also includes Belarusans and Ukrainians. The name "Russian" originates from the name Rus, or Kievan (after the city of Kiev) Rus, the ancient group of principalities that spread across present-day European Russia, Belarus, and Ukraine.

LOCATION. Of the persons who claimed Russian ancestry in the 1990 U.S. Census, 44 percent resided in the Northeast, 16 percent in the Midwest, 18 percent in the South, and 22 percent in the West. Areas where Russians are clustered are indicated by the locations of churches listed in telephone books as Eastern Orthodox or Russian.

DEMOGRAPHY. U.S. Census figures (which had 2.95 million Americans claiming Russian ancestry in 1990) are insufficient to provide data on the number of *ethnic* Russians in the United States. The estimated total population for ethnic Russians in the United States ranges from 750,000 to 2,000,000. A poll conducted in 1996 among 1,110 Russian Americans shows that 26 percent of them are younger than twenty years, 40 percent are twenty-one to sixty-five years old, and 34 percent are more than sixty-six years old; 39 percent were born in the United States, 53 percent in Russia or the USSR, and 8 percent in other countries; 28 percent have a college education. There are 10 percent more females than males. Between 1991 and 1996, there was only 1 birth per 1.6 deaths, which shows a demographic decline within the ethnic group.

LINGUISTIC AFFILIATION. Russian is the official language in an area that stretches from the Baltic Sea to the Pacific Ocean and from the Arctic Sea to the Black Sea. In the Russian Federation, 150,000,000 people speak Russian. More than 25,000,000 ethnic Russians live in other republics of the former Soviet Union. A total of 284,000,000 people worldwide speak Russian. However, in the United States only 242,000 people have command of Russian. This indicates the degree to which assimilation has progressed, which usually takes its toll in the third generation and is enhanced by mixed marriages.

During the period of Russian rule, education in primary schools in Alaska was in Russian and in one of the native languages. As a result of these cultural contacts, the modern Aleut language contains 700 Russian words, the Aleutiik 600, the Tanaina 500, the Yup'ik 200, and the Eskimo 150. Many places in Alaska have Russian names.

In the United States, Russian is still studied in a number of Sunday schools affiliated with the Russian Orthodox Church Outside Russia.

History and Cultural Relations

RUSSIAN AMERICA. The first Russian trappers, traders, and missionaries reached America from Siberia. They immigrated east, like the Americans, who were moving west. In 1741, two Russian ships under the command of Vitus Bering and Alexei Chirikov reached the coast of the North American continent. The first permanent Russian settlement in America was founded without official government approval on Kodiak Island in 1784 by Gregory Shelikhov, a fur trader. His enterprise developed into the Russian-American Company, which received a charter from the imperial government in 1799. Russian America appeared on maps next to British America (Canada) and the United States. Eight missionaries from Valaam Monastery arrived in Alaska in 1794. They built churches and started schools, studied the indigenous languages, converted the Aleuts and Indians to Orthodox Christianity, and interceded on their behalf before the Russian administration in cases of unjust treatment. Russians of all ranks married local women without prejudice. In addition to primary schools, there was a theological seminary and a junior college. Medical service was provided, farming was introduced, and ship-building started in 1807. Some ships traveling from Europe to Alaska made the long journey around South America and even Africa.

By order of the governor of Russian America, Alexander Baranov, Fort Ross was founded in 1812 in northern California to trade with the Spaniards and to provide agricultural products for Alaska. However, the fort was sold in 1848 to John Sutter and is now a state historical park. From 1815 to 1817, there was an unsuccessful attempt to colonize Hawaii by building Fort Elizabeth (Yelisaveta), now also a state park, on the island of Kauai.

The Russian possessions in Alaska were sold to the United States in 1867 for $7,200,000. The Russian government considered Alaska unprofitable because of a decline in the fur animal population and the potential risk of a territorial conflict with Britain. Most of the Russians returned to Russia, but some of them resettled in California and Canada. A total of 12,000 Orthodox Christian Alaskans, including many descendants of mixed marriages with Russian surnames, came under American jurisdiction.

EARLY IMMIGRATION. Fedor Karzhavin crossed the Atlantic in 1776 and outfitted three ships with supplies for the Revolutionary Army at his own expense in French Caribbean possessions. In 1792, Prince Demetrius Galitzin arrived in America, where he became a Roman Catholic missionary and helped to settle frontier lands in Pennsylvania.

During the nineteenth century small groups of Russian immigrants started congregating in New York and San Francisco. Most of them were educated and had command of at least one European language. This made it easier for them to adopt to the new country. A few arrived with some knowledge of English. They also experimented with communal farming. During the American Civil War, Russia sided with the North and sent squadrons of warships to New York and to San Francisco. John Basil Turchin (Turchaninov), a former Russian colonel, arrived in 1861 and fought in the Union army, retiring as a brigadier general. Turchin is also known as the founder of the city of Radom, Illinois, where the first settlers were Polish. Peter A. Dementieff (Demens), also a former Russian officer, started as a laborer, then became a businessman and railroad builder, and founded St. Petersburg, Florida, in 1888.

MASS IMMIGRATION. During the second half of the nineteenth century, immigrants from Russia started arriving in America. Of these, 60 percent were Jews escaping the Pale (a region, established in 1786 after the partition of Poland, in which the Jews were compelled to live); the rest were Poles, ethnic Russians, Ukrainians, Belarusans, Lithuanians, and German Mennonites. As soon as all these immigrants landed on American shores, they joined their respective ethnic and religious groups, which assisted them in integrating into the American way of life. There were 100,000 Russian-speaking people in the United States in 1914.

From 1898 to 1899, a total of 50,000 pacifist Dukhobors, who were in conflict with the Orthodox Church and the Russian government, left Russia with the help of Leo Tolstoy and started farming in Canada. A small number of them moved to the United States. Russian Molokans, another pacifist sect, arrived between 1905 and 1907; 17,000 of them settled in Los Angeles and 3,000 in San Francisco and in Oregon. A group of Molokans moved to Mexico, where they founded the Guadelupe Colony. There are also 8,000 Old Believers, dissenters from the official church in Russia since the seventeenth century. Some immigrated to the United States before World War I. Others arrived after escaping from the Communists in Russia and China. One group arrived from Turkey, where they had lived for more than two hundred years while preserving the Russian language and their religion. The Old Believers settled in Pennsylvania, New Jersey, Oregon, and Alaska (where in 1967 they founded the village of Nikolaevsk on the Kenai Peninsula).

In the 1920s, 20,000 Russian anti-Communist refugees arrived in America, forming the second wave of immigrants. These people were military men, engineers, scientists, actors, intellectuals, and representatives of the Russian nobility. After the end of World War II, 30,000 ethnic Russians formed the third wave of immigrants to the United States. Many of these Russians were already expatriates living outside Russia, and many were born in foreign countries. According to the 1945 Yalta agreement, "displaced persons" (prisoners of war, laborers, and refugees) from the Soviet Union who wound up in the territories occupied by the Allies had to be returned to the USSR regardless of their desires. This resulted in forced repatriations, with violations of human rights and suicides. Displaced persons of other nationalities had the option to return to their native lands or to resettle to other countries. Eleanore Roosevelt interceded at the United Nations on behalf of displaced persons from the USSR. As a result, they were granted safety and freedom in the United States.

Russians from Manchuria and the rest of China became refugees in 1949–1950 due to the Communist takeover and immigrated in great numbers to the United States and Canada. Since the establishment of the Communist regime in Russia, and during the period of the Cold War, there was no legal way for Soviet citizens to emigrate. The enactment of the Jackson-Vanik amendment to the 1974 Trade Act was aimed at Soviet restrictions on the emigration of Jews. As a result, the Soviet government yielded and started issuing exist visas. This did not apply to ethnic Russians unless they could prove that they were subject to discrimination. A new wave of immigrants started arriving in the 1970s and formed communities in major cities of America, with many intellectuals, scientists, writers and poets, businesspeople, and artists.

War Veterans. A large number of Russians served in the U.S. Army during World War I, World War II, the Korean War, and the Vietnam War. Memorials to American veterans contain names of fallen Russian immigrants and of their descendants. Russian veterans of foreign wars (World War I and the Russian Civil War) also had organizations that faded away with time.

Religion and Expressive Culture

RELIGION. When Alaska was sold to the United States in 1867, Russian Orthodox priests remained to continue their duties and to start spreading their activities over the entire country. The services in Alaska were originally in Church Slavonic and native languages. Gradually English was introduced. This created a cross-ethnic spiritual and cultural liaison. All Orthodox churches in America are of traditional architecture and are adorned with icons and frescoes on the inside walls.

In the United States the Orthodox Church is represented by dioceses that belong to three jurisdictions—the Orthodox Church in America, which has three theological seminaries; the conservative Russian Orthodox Church Outside Russia, with one seminary; and the Russian Orthodox Church, under the jurisdiction of the patriarch of Moscow. The churches are the principal centers of religious, social, and cultural life of Russian Americans. Because of religious differences, groups of Old Believers, Molokans, Dukhobors, and Baptists live separate from the Russian-American communities.

TRADITIONS. Ethnic and religious customs are preserved in families and communities. The annual cycle includes the twelve most important religious holidays, especially Easter, as well as birthdays, name days, and wedding anniversaries. The holidays, preceded by periods of fasting, feature lavish dishes prepared according to recipes brought from the old country. The preparation of food is seen as an art to be passed on with love from one generation to another. Some women and girls wear national dress during festivals. The Old Believers and Molokans wear Russian peasant costumes, and the men have beards.

SCIENCE AND ENGINEERING. Russian professors teach in many American universities. Russian studies and research are conducted in two hundred American universities and colleges. Outstanding contributions to American technology and culture were made by Vladimir V. Zvorykin (the "Father of Television"), Igor I. Sikorsky (designer of airplanes and helicopters), Vladimir N. Ipatieff (author of seventy American patents for petroleum refining, which helped America and the Allies win World War II), Wassili Leontief (Nobel Price laureate in economics), George Kistiakovski (creator of the explosive device for the atomic bomb), Stepan P. Timoshenko (researcher in strength of materials), and many others. Nina Fedoroff, a geneticist, was elected in 1990 to the National Academy of Sciences.

ARTS. Art in America has been greatly enriched by the works of Russian immigrants. Nine museums in the United States are dedicated to the Russian historical and military heritage and to the arts, including five museums founded by immigrants. Eight state parks and one national park commemorate Russian-American heritage and history. Several museums and galleries, especially the National Gallery of Art and the Hillwood Museum of Russian Art in Washington, D.C., exhibit paintings and precious objects from Russian museums and churches that were sold abroad by the Soviets.

Marriage and Kinship

Traditional marriages do not differ much from American customs, except for the religious rites, which are followed by sumptuous receptions. The stability of Russian-American families is reflected in the comparatively low ratio of divorces. According to a poll conducted among parishes in 1996, there was only one divorce in ten marriages. Intermarriage with individuals from other ethnic backgrounds is on the rise.

Kinship was important among immigrants before World War I. It served as a form of support for the new arrivals. Wars and Communist repressions in the USSR decimated many families. Survivors who managed to escape abroad tried to restore families and searched for missing members in the former USSR. New kinships developed among young generations through interethnic marriages.

Economy

Russians, including those Belarusans and Ukrainians who arrived before World War I, usually identified themselves as Russians. They were young peasants who wanted to stay and to work in factories or mines and on farms. After they established themselves in the new country, they were joined by family members and relatives. However, some of them were circular immigrants. They lived in the United States only for limited periods of time sufficient to earn enough funds to improve their economic standards in the old country. In the 1930s, most of these returnees were deprived of their property and sent by the Soviets to forced labor camps. Those who stayed in the United States became American citizens. They adapted fully to the American way of life while preserving some of their ethnic traditions. Their descendants are engaged in various fields, as engineers, educators, government employees, and workers. Some blue-collar workers live in the same neighborhoods where their parents settled. There are almost no farmers among Russian Americans. Those who escaped Communist persecution in the 1920s took jobs as factory workers, with some later returning to prominence in industry, science, and society. Immigrants of the 1950s were engineers, teachers, and white-collar workers, with a minority of blue-collar workers. Almost all preferred to live in one-family houses. The average income of a Russian-American household today corresponds to that of the American middle class. Less than 1 percent of ethnic Russians are on welfare.

Sociopolitical Organization

SOCIAL ORGANIZATIONS. Russian organizations started appearing in the United States in 1872. The Russian Orthodox Society of Mutual Aid was founded in 1895, the Russian Brotherhood Society in 1900, the Society to Help Russian Children in 1926, and the Tolstoy Foundation in 1939. Others include the Orthodox Theological Fund in New York, the Ivan Koulaeff Foundation in San Francisco, and the Association of Russian-American Scholars. There are also organizations of alumni from Russian schools that existed outside the Soviet Union until World War II. A number of social and cultural clubs operate in areas with major concentrations of Russians. Since 1972 the Congress of Russian Americans has represented the interests of American citizens of Russian descent. There are three organizations of Russian Scouts.

POLITICAL ORGANIZATIONS. A broad spectrum of Russian political organizations ranged from social-democratic to conservative and monarchist; many strove to expose the dangers of communism in memorandums, lectures, books, and periodicals. The Democratic party is popular among the descendants of blue-collar workers who arrived before World War I. Those who arrived after World War II and their children prefer the Republican party. November 7, the day when the Bolsheviks abolished democracy and seized power in Russia in 1917, is designated by the Congress of Russian Americans and other Russian organizations as the "Memorial Day for Victims of Communism."

DISCRIMINATION. Before World War I, immigrants from Russia were met with prejudice and characterized as being backward and having a low IQ. After the Bolshevik Revolution, Russians in the United States were treated with suspicion as potential Bolshevik sympathizers. Many who were active in labor unions or had socialist leanings were rounded up and deported without proper hearings.

Public Law 86–90, known since 1956 as the Captive Nations Law, listed nations under Communist rule as victims of "Russian communism." The Russian nation, the first victim of communism, was not included in the text of the law. News media routinely equated the names "Russian" and "Soviet" or even "Communist." The image of ethnic Russians, especially that of women, in the press and even in commercial advertisements was presented as an ugly caricature with racist overtones.

RUSSIAN PRESS IN THE UNITED STATES. The first bilingual newspaper, the *Alaskan Herald,* was published in San Francisco by a priest, Agapius Goncharenko, on March 1, 1868, to introduce Russians to the U.S. Constitution. About two hundred Russian newspapers, bulletins, and journals existed in the United States for various periods. They served as liaison among various groups of immigrants and represented a broad spectrum of trends, ranging from liberal and socialist to moderate and conservative-monarchist. Many publications have also been dedicated to the military history of the twentieth century and to religious life. A daily newspaper published in Russian since 1910 is *Novoye Russkoye Slovo* (The New Russian Word) in New York; another is *Russkaya Zhizn* (Russian Life), founded in San Francisco in 1920. Hundreds of books in Russian were published in the United States during the twentieth century, thus enriching the multiethnic culture of the country.

Bibliography

Chevigny, H. (1965). *Russian America: The Great Alaskan Venture, 1741–1867.* New York: Viking Press.

Eubank, N. (1973). *The Russians in America.* Minneapolis, MN: Lerner.

Gibson, J. R. (1978). "Old Russia in the New World: Adversaries and Adversities in Russian America." In *European Settlement and Development in North America,* edited by J. R. Gibson. Toronto: University of Toronto Press.

Jeletzky, T. F., ed. (1983). *Russian Canadians: Their Past and Present.* Ottawa: Borealis Press.

Klimenko, G. (1977). "Russians in New Jersey." In *The New Jersey Ethnic Experience,* edited by B. Cunningham. Union City, NJ: Wm. H. Wise.

Magocsi, P. R. (1987). *The Russian Americans.* New York: Chelsea House.

Mohoff, G. W. (1993). *The Russian Colony of Guadelupe Molokans in Mexico.* Montebello, CA: George Mohoff.

Reardon, J. (1972). "Nikolaevsk. A Bit of Old Russia Takes Root in Alaska." *National Geographic* 142(3):400–425.

Smith, B. S., and Barnett, B. J., eds. (1990). *Russian America: The Forgotten Frontier.* Tacoma: Washington State Historical Society.

Starr, S. F., ed. (1987). *Russia's American Colony.* Durham, NC: Duke University Press.

Tarasar, C., gen. ed. (1975). *Orthodox America, 1794–1976.* Syosset, NY: Orthodox Church of America.

Tolstoy, N. (1977). *The Secret Betrayal, 1944–1947.* New York: Scribner.

Westerman, V. (1977). *The Russians in America: A Chronology & Fact Book.* Dobbs Ferry, NY: Oceana.

Williams, R. C. (1980). *Russian Art and American Money, 1900–1940.* Cambridge, MA: Harvard University Press.

—EUGENE A. ALEXANDROV

SCOTCH-IRISH

The Scotch-Irish ethnic group is defined by the two geographical regions of the British Isles in which they once lived: Scotland and Ireland. The group has been also referred to as Scots-Irish, Ulster Scots, Ulstermen, and Northern Irishmen. Since they were originally Lowland Scots, they were somewhat less Scotch than Highland Scotsmen. And having come from Scotland, they were far less Irish than Irishmen. Yet they were nearly as Celtic as other northern and western peoples of the British Isles. Are they Scotch or Scot? The adjective "Scotch" identifies whiskey, or plaid cloth, or candy such as butterscotch. But "Scot" meaning Scotsman could lead to the possible term "Scots-Irish." However, throughout the literature and here as well, "Scotch-Irish" is the proper and widely accepted term. While in Northern Ireland's Ulster Province, they thought of themselves as the "Irish of the North." Upon arrival in America they probably identified themselves as "Irish," as the term "Scotch-Irish" was so rare. It was not until much later that they would become known as the Scotch-Irish people and even then not without controversy. In eighteenth-century America outsiders called the Scotch-Irish people "Ulster Irish," "Northern Irish," "Presbyterian Irish," or simply "Irish" because the ships they came in had embarked from Irish port cities. Twentieth-century American descendants of the Scotch-Irish have been called "mountaineers," "hillbillies," and "rednecks." Derogatory terms such as "poor whites" and "white trash" have been applied to some Scotch-Irish descendants based on their economic status and, unfortunately, what others think of them.

The history of the term "Scotch-Irish" is clouded in mystery. The first recorded use of the term was on April 14, 1573, when Queen Elizabeth I used "Scotch-Irish" to refer to the intermarrying of Scottish Highlanders with Irish native folk in County Antrim in Ireland. The queen's use of the term did not refer to the genuine Scotch-Irish people, who, beginning in 1610, immigrated as Lowland Scots to Northern Ireland's Ulster Province. The first record of the term in America was in 1695, when Sir Thomas Lawrence, secretary of Maryland, reported of "Scotch-Irish" people there wearing linen and wool clothing and living in Dorchester and Somerset counties, Maryland. This use of the term preceded the major immigrations of the folk to America by twenty-two years! While they were immigrating to America from 1717 to 1775, they were rarely called "Scotch-Irish" but rather were most often referred to as "Irish." Between 1776 and 1850, the term "Scotch-Irish" virtually disappears from the record and is not revived until the mid-nineteenth century, and then only as a term of prejudice. Following the Irish potato famine in Ireland in the 1840s, thousands of Irish immigrants poured into Eastern Seaboard cities. The distinction was then made between the older, more established, quite Americanized Scotch-Irish and the newly arrived, impoverished, foreign Irish. Unlike the Irish of the 1840s, the Scotch-Irish did not linger in eastern ports. Between 1717 and 1775, they quickly migrated westward and southward in an ever-widening dispersal, all the while becoming more and more American as they developed the way of life of the frontier-people in the wilderness interior of colonial America.

Immigration and Settlement History

The Scotch-Irish originally were groups of Celtic folk of a Scottish nature who came from the Lowlands and the hill areas of southern Scotland, the border country between Scotland and England, and the western Scottish coast and Hebrides Islands. Beginning in 1610, they moved a mere twenty miles across the North Channel in the Irish Sea to Northern Ireland (Ulster), where they were situated on "plantations," colonies of settlements established by King James 1 (for whom the King James Bible and Jamestown, Virginia, are named). In spite of several generations of successful development in agriculture and the woolen and linen industries, the group came under attack by English trade policies and by rent-racking schemes of local landlords so that many Scotch-Irish immigrated to America during much of the eighteenth century.

From 1717 to 1775, the Scotch-Irish and their descendants began major immigrations to the Americas. Contrary to popular belief, the Scotch-Irish immigration did *not* uniformly land on the Atlantic shores in eastern North America and sweep directly westward but formed two widely separated streams that entered through the ports of Philadelphia and Charleston, South Carolina. Through the ensuing generations, the population streams grew toward each other, creating an arc of Scotch-Irish settlement in colonial America. The larger, more important stream entered through Philadelphia and established a cultural hearth, a gathering place and staging area in the Susquehanna River valley just west of Philadelphia between 1710 and 1730. The subsequent migration went as far as the Allegheny Plateau escarpment, where it took a major course southward, following the Great Valley in the Ridge and Valley Province to southwestern Virgina by 1735. From interior Virginia the routes took several divergent courses. One continued straight down the valley trend toward northeastern Tennessee and later threaded northwestward through the Cumberland Gap to lead settlers deep into Kentucky. A larger route went southeasterly, passed through the Roanoke and New River gaps, and spilled immigrants out onto the Piedmont region of North Carolina. An important hearth of Scotch-Irish settlement formed here between the Yadkin and Catawba River valleys in the 1740s and 1750s.

A secondary stream from the southeastern Pennsylvania hearth pushed directly westward to form another Scotch-Irish hearth, in the Pittsburgh vicinity, between 1768 and 1790. From this Pittsburgh hearth, continuing migrations would lead into the Ohio River Valley in the late eighteenth and well into the nineteenth centuries.

In South Carolina, another migration stream of Scotch-Irish began from the port of Charleston as early as 1732 and pushed seventy-five miles northward, to the Kingstree settlement. As more people arrived, the migration streams pushed inland to the upcountry in the South Carolina Piedmont to form another Scotch-Irish hearth. From this interior South Carolina hearth, smaller streams pushed southwestward to Georgia and northeastward to North Carolina to eventually link up with the North Carolina Piedmont hearth in the Catawba and Yadkin River valleys.

Throughout the region, other migration routes formed, and the settling process continued. From the North Carolina Piedmont hearth, settlers led by Daniel Boone, James Robertson, and John Sevier in 1771–1772 crossed the Blue Ridge Mountains of southern Appalachia and followed the Watauga River directly westward to settle northeastern Tennessee. From these Watauga settlements of early Tennessee, additional westward migration was carried directly overland and via the Tennessee River in 1779–1780 to establish settlement in the Nashville Basin. Meanwhile, many settlers coming down the Great Valley turned northwestward through the Cumberland Gap to dominate the Blue Grass Basin in central Kentucky. Migrations continued down the valley trends toward the areas that were to become Knoxville, Chattanooga, and Birming-

ham as threats of Indian attacks lessened and lands were opened for permanent settlement. Out of the South Carolina hearth, settlers migrated northward through the Blue Ridge Mountains through the Saluda Gap to forge their way into the Asheville Basin and eventually westward to Tennessee. The southern Appalachian region was the homeland of Cherokee and other Native American groups, so much of the land was closed to European settlement until after the 1790s. Much of the South's interior to the west and south was Chocktaw, Chickasaw, and other Native American-held territory that prevented major European incursions until after 1830. Once in America, the Scotch-Irish quickly made a home for themselves and did not make circular or return migrations to the British Isles.

Demography

It is unclear how many Scotch-Irish immigrated to America. An estimated 114,000 immigrants arrived in the colonies between 1718 and 1778, but the estimates for the period 1707–1783 range between 102,000 and 125,000. Even in America, Scotch-Irish populations had to be estimated because the census for 1790 did not identify persons of Scotch-Irish ancestry. In 1902, Charles A. Hanna used the 1790 census to proportion the population from 1775 to estimate a total of 335,000 Scotch-Irish *and* Scots for the following states: Pennsylvania, 100,000; Delaware, 10,000; Maryland, 30,000; Virginia, 75,000; North Carolina, 65,000; South Carolina, 45,000; and Georgia, 10,000.

Attempts to determine the populations of early groups from the British Isles continued in disagreement. In 1909, the U.S. Census Bureau estimated the Scotch-Irish population to be 14.3 percent of the 1790 total population of 3,172,444, or 453,659 persons with an apparent Scotch-Irish identity. In 1931, a committee of historians estimated the Scotch-Irish to be 6.7 percent of the 1790 population, thus accounting for about 212,554 persons as Scotch-Irish. Modern historians have attempted to separate the immigrants by Scotch, Irish, and Welsh surnames, while other scholars continue to make percentage estimates. Still, it is unclear. Which Scots came from Ulster? Which Scots were directly from Scotland, and were they Highland or Lowland Scots? Which Irish were exclusively from Ulster? Which immigrants were truly Irish, from southern Ireland, and which were English? There is no clear way of knowing. However, the general pattern after 1790 and until about 1860 shows that about half the population in the American South was composed of Scotch, Irish, and Welsh, and about one-fourth of the population had come from western and northern England.

To simplify, approximately 200,000 Scotch-Irish immigrants arrived in what was to become the United States during the major years of immigration between 1717 and 1775. By 1790, the Scotch-Irish population had grown to about 250,000, making it the second-largest group next to the English in the United States at that time. The best opportunity to take the pulse of this elusive group is in the 1990 U.S. Census, in which the U.S. population expresses its ancestry in the clearest terms yet. The response is a current population of 5,617,773 Americans who claim Scotch-Irish ancestry. This represents approximately 2.3 percent of the total population of 248,709,873 for 1990 in the United States. Urban populations of Scotch-Irish account for 4,026,024 people, while rural populations total 1,591,749. One might expect the rural populations to be larger, but they are not. For example, only 92,456 people with Scotch-Irish ancestry live in places with a population of less than 1,000; and for places with a population of 1,000 to 2,999, the total is 178,739. Those living in rural areas who are still farmers account for 101,876 people.

The 1990 U.S. Census identifies a smaller subgroup of native, American-born Scotch-Irish to be 4,303,899 people, which divides into 2,021,654 males and 2,282,245 females in the native population. The population is composed of three major age groups. There are 926,316 children and young people, whose ages range from less than one year to twenty-one years. Those in the primary working age group, between twenty-two and sixty-four, account for 2,421,916. People sixty-five or over total 955,667 persons.

A valid Scotch-Irish representation in the population endures in those areas of first effective settlement. Strong concentrations of contemporary Scotch-Irish can be found in the old areas of initial settlement in Pennsylvania (270,299 Scotch-Irish descendants), North Carolina (343,345), and South Carolina (159,534), with concentrations in some of the adjacent states such as Ohio (217,478), New York (165,952), Virginia (195,722), Tennessee (197,942), Missouri (129,228), Georgia (192,187), Alabama (127,826), and on to Texas (495,886), to which nineteenth-century migrations took numerous Scotch-Irish. Concentrations of Scotch-Irish in parts of Ohio and especially Michigan (157,483) and Illinois (173,035) are largely attributed to movements of Scotch-Irish descendants from southern states to industrial factories in the North during and after World War II. The Washington State (154,566) concentration is tied to two phenomena: (1) the movement of southern Appalachian Scotch-Irish descendants who established rural farming communities in Washington State between 1884 and 1937, and (2) a later movement by those attracted to the logging industry and to aircraft manufacturing in the Pacific Northwest. The huge California contingent of 546,496 Scotch-Irish descendants is explained by several migrations of peoples from the East, the South, and from the Plains states. The California Gold Rush of 1849 brought many Scotch-Irish settlers to the West. In the 1930s, thousands of Scotch-Irish descendants from poor southern states and from the dust bowl states during the Great Depression migrated to California looking for work, much like the fictitious Joad family in John Steinbeck's *The Grapes of Wrath*. After World War II many Scotch-Irish descendants made new homes in California as many returning servicemen chose to live on the West Coast. From the 1950s to the 1970s, southern and eastern Scotch-Irish descendants migrated to California to seek the perceived good life. Additional migrations have been made by retirees who reflect a pattern of settlement, especially in Florida (320,217) and California.

Language

The Scotch-Irish on arrival in America spoke a form of Gaelic and/or English with a distinctive brogue or accent. Scholars have since discovered in the southern Appalachians that the folk speech there is English, too, The word *hit* (as in "*Hit don't matter*") is the third person singular neuter pronoun for *it*, a proper form of Old English. Words such as yonder and nigh for over there and near, respectively, are still widely used. His'n, our'n, your'n, and her'n are possessives much like mine and thine and were quite proper English in another century. Colorful speech with analogies and sayings pervade Scotch-Irish speech: "Hit's blue cold out thar!" "He's quick as double-geared lightnin'." "She's as slow as molasses but near 'bout as sweet."

There are no major or official language maintenance programs for preserving the accents of southern mountain speech. Isolation was and still is the best preserver of dialect. Articles such as "Folk Speech Is English, Too" and booklets on southern mountain English described as "The Queen's English" along with various publications on how to talk like a "redneck" can be found, but most are used for entertainment. Preservation practices of a more serious nature have been instituted since the mid-1930s, but mainly to collect folk songs and folk stories.

Cultural Characteristics

When the Scotch-Irish immigrated to America, the majority of them were small subsistence farmers, as the Industrial Revolution had not yet taken place. For two centuries thereafter the Scotch-Irish were still largely identified as small, independent farmers and until the 1950s, some were still eking out a living on subsistence farms. Current trends in the total work force of 2,067,143 people above age sixteen show a diversity in occupations: 28 percent in health, education, or other professional services, 15 percent in retail trade, 14.7 percent in manufacturing, and 9.3 percent in construction or transportation. A mere 2.5 percent of the work force continues in agriculture/forestry/fisheries. When divided by sex, the figures are 36.2 percent of all work force females and 34.3 percent of the males are in managerial occupations, 44.3 percent of the females and 24.5 percent of the males are in technical/sales/administrative support occupations, and 14 percent of the males and 4.9 percent of the females are in operator/fabricator/laborer occupations.

Historically, the Scotch-Irish in America were known for their fierce independence by living in isolated log cabins on the backwoods frontier. Folk house types largely followed the pattern of the English pen tradition, for which a pen represents an individual room unit, much like a one-room cabin. In the typology, houses evolved from single-pen houses; to double-pen houses with two rooms and called dogtrot, saddlebag, or Cumberland houses; to I-houses that were two stories tall, two rooms wide, and one room deep; to four-pen houses that had four rooms over four rooms. Construction techniques and materials were either horizontal, rounded, or squared hewn logs with corner notches, or later framed sawn lumber, but rarely brick or stone. Log construction, the primary building method, was introduced early to America by Swedish, Finnish, and German immigrants and was quickly adopted by Scotch-Irish settlers and their descendants. The many types of corner notching included saddle notch, saddle V notch, V notch, half dovetail notch, full dovetail notch, square notch, half notch, diamond notch, and half-log or semilunate crown notch.

Scotch-Irish independence continues to be reflected in their choice of contemporary housing. According to the 1990 U.S. Census, of the 1,994,366 total housing units occupied by native Scotch-Irish descendants, there were 1,345,919 single-unit, freestanding dwellings, representing 67.5 percent. Another 135,319 shelters were mobile homes. There were 1,433,903 owner-occupied housing units and 510,463 renter-occupied units. In the owner-occupied units, 4,925 places lacked complete plumbing facilities. In the renter category there were 2,274 units that lacked complete plumbing facilities.

The religion of the Scotch-Irish originally was Presbyterian in Ulster and remained Presbyterian for generations in America. Over time, numerous Scotch-Irish adopted other denominations, chiefly Baptist, Methodist, and Church of Christ, and founded numerous fundamentalist splinter groups. Their worldview in the past was extremely limited, perhaps restricted to just a hollow, a ridge, or a county, and would have continued in this narrow direction were it not for wars fought in foreign lands, improved transportation, and television and other forms of electronic communication that now reach nearly everyone. In the past, family and kinship ties were very strong for the Scotch-Irish. In rural isolation, clans formed enclaves of kin and kindred folk and stuck by each other, enduring all types of hardships together. Many of the older generations still hold to these values, and marriages remain strong. The 1990 U.S. Census indicates that there were 2,113,946 married Scotch-Irish descendants over age fifteen whose spouse currently lived with them. However, the national trend embracing easy divorce also affects families of Scotch-Irish ancestry. The 1990 U.S. Census shows that 130,903 males and 206,105 females over age fifteen are divorced.

For centuries the Scotch-Irish were not a group known for fine arts of any kind. But their folk art has been distinctive. Of particular note are the rich traditions in storytelling and folklore. Their folk songs have evolved into the broader realms of country and bluegrass music. Other artistic contributions are in folk dancing, especially clogging, and crafts such as quilt-making and woodworking.

Illness, death, and hardship are main points on the compass of conversation. The Scotch-Irish as well as the Scots have had a tendency to "enjoy poor health," meaning that when asked about their health, they like nothing better than to tell all the details of what is ailing them.

The Scotch-Irish have mostly avoided the national political arena, often choosing instead to deal with political matters using frontier justice. However, some of America's leaders came from Scotch-Irish stock. James Buchanan, fifteenth president of the United States, was from Scotch-Irish ancestry in Pennsylvania. Jimmy Carter, America's thirty-ninth president, came from Scotch-Irish folk who had migrated early from Virginia to Georgia, where the Carters became peanut farmers. As political parties developed, most Scotch-Irish identified with grassroots politics, following the lines of the Democratic party.

Extent of Assimilation

The Scotch-Irish are probably the most rapidly and most thoroughly assimilated ethnic group in America. Their identity was clouded and uncertain for more than 140 years until the 1850s, and by then the Scotch-Irish were already probably the most Americanized of ethnic groups. Their identity was never quite clear in the British Isles either, and it was virtually lost in America until the arrival of Irish potato famine survivors in the 1840s. By then, most people of Scotch-Irish ancestry were already American. Today cultural persistence remains in regional dialect, religion, and independence, but to a lesser degree in the material culture. While they are economically and socially stratified, the Scotch-Irish are in an ethnic mist, so clouded by their Americanism and so poorly identified except for the 1990 U.S. Census that they rarely experience direct ethnic discrimination. Their relations with other groups have been wry, but when it comes to dealing with them on a one-to-one basis—in the South, at least—the underlying question still comes down to "Who's yer daddy?"

Bibliography

Cunningham, R. (1987). *Apples on the Flood: The Southern Mountain Experience.* Knoxville: University of Tennessee Press.

Dial, W. P. (1970). "Folk Speech Is English, Too." *Mountain Life and Work* 46(March):15–17.

Green, E. R. (1992). *Essays in Scotch-Irish History.* Belfast: Ulster Historical Foundation.

Green, S. S. ([1895] 1970). *The Scotch-Irish in America.* San Francisco: R & E Research Associates.

Hanna, C. A. ([1902] 1985). *The Scotch-Irish, or The Scot in North Britain, North Ireland, and North America,* 2 vols. Baltimore, MD: Genealogical Publishing Company.

Jackson, C. (1993). *A Social History of the Scotch-Irish.* Lanham, MD: Madison Books.

Johnson, J. E. (1966). *The Scots and Scotch-Irish in America.* Minneapolis: Lerner.

Jordan, T. G., and Kaups, M. (1989). *The American Backwoods Frontier.* Baltimore, MD: Johns Hopkins University Press.

Kennedy, B. (1995). *The Scots-Irish in East Tennessee.* Londonderry, Ireland: Causeway Press.

Kingsmore, R. K. (1995). *Ulster Scots Speech: A Sociolinguistic Study.* Tuscaloosa: University of Alabama Press.

Lehmann, W. C. (1978). *Scottish and Scotch-Irish Contributions to Early American Life and Culture.* Port Washington, NY: National University Publications.

Leyburn, J. G. (1962). *The Scotch-Irish: A Social History.* Chapel Hill: University of North Carolina Press.

Rehder, J. B. (1992). "The Scotch-Irish and English in Appalachia." In *To Build in a New Land: Ethnic Landscapes in North America,* edited by A. G Noble. Baltimore, MD: Johns Hopkins University Press.

Reid, W. ([1911] 1970). *The Scot in America, and the Ulster Scot.* San Francisco: R & E Research Associates.

Wells, R. A., comp. (1991). *Ulster Migration to America: Letters from Three Irish Families.* New York: P. Lang.

—JOHN B. REHDER

SCOTS

The ethnic group known as Scots in the United States refers directly to those people who over several generations, from the mid-seventeenth century through the late eighteenth century, immigrated directly from Scotland to the Americas. Commonly used names for Scottish immigrants have been either Highland Scots or Highlanders or for those from southern Scotland, Lowland Scots. Although Lowland Scots were certainly part of the immigrations, more attention has been given to Highland Scots, the clans from northern Scotland known symbolically for their tartans, bagpipes, Highland games, and rich, thick Gaelic language and brogue accents. When Scottish people first arrived in America, they were called "Scots," "Scotsmen," even "Scotch." In nineteenth- and twentieth-century America they have been referred to as "blue bloods," as in "blue-blooded Scots," at the perceived upper end of the social scale, but at the lower end of the scale some have been called "rednecks." The Scots are not to be confused with the Scotch-Irish. Scots were from Scotland pure and simple. The people known as Scotch-Irish were an ethnic group that originated as seventeenth-century Presbyterian Scots from Lowland Scotland and immigrated to "plantations" established by King James I in Northern Ireland's Ulster Province after 1610. Additional Scottish immigrants came to Ulster from the area that borders present-day southern Scotland and northern England, while others were from the western coastal Highlands of Scotland and the Hebrides Islands. Collectively these Scottish immigrants to Ulster remained in Ireland for more than one hundred years before immigrating to America from 1717 to 1775. Once in America the Scotch-Irish were difficult to define because the early census did not identify them as Scotch-Irish. Still, the Scotch-Irish have received more attention from historians than the less numerous but potentially more easily identified Scots. There were times when Scottish immigrants were counted along with Scotch-Irish. In 1902, for example, Charles A. Hanna examined the 1790 U.S. Census and adjusted the figures for the year 1775 to estimate a total of 335,000 Scotch-Irish *and* Scots for the following states: Pennsylvania, 100,000; Delaware, 10,000; Maryland, 30,000; Virginia, 75,000; North Carolina, 65,000;

South Carolina, 45,000; and Georgia, 10,000. While this combines the two similar ethnic groups, the information can be used to view the immigrant population on a state-by-state basis. Modern historians Forrest and Helen McDonald examined surnames in the 1790 U.S. Census and calculated that 32.9 percent of the South Carolina population were Scots in 1790.

Immigration History

The Scots who immigrated to what was to become the United States began their travel somewhat slowly. Before 1650, only a few hundred Scots were in America. By the 1770s, there were thousands of Scottish immigrants arriving, and according to some estimates as many as 10,000 arrived each year for several consecutive years. Because of the lack of solid documentary evidence, scholars have been forced to estimate the number of immigrants, especially for those from the British Isles. The simplest, best conservative estimate for numbers of Scottish immigrants to America is approximately 150,000 by 1785. This compares favorably with the conservative estimate of about 200,000 Scotch-Irish immigrants for the same period.

For centuries Scots had been emigrating from Scotland to such locations as Poland, the Netherlands, England, and, of course, Northern Ireland's Ulster Province, but until the late 1600s and 1700s, few had found their way to colonial America. Many of the seventeenth-century Scottish immigrants had no choice, as they were criminals and prisoners. Numerous Scottish prisoners were sent to Virginia, New England, and the West Indies. Other Scots were seeking religious freedom in the 1680s, such as the attempt to settle a Scottish Presbyterian settlement in South Carolina and the movement of Scottish Quakers into New Jersey. Economic trade factors were important motivations for emigration, as English trade restrictions affected Scottish trade. Furthermore, the Scots were becoming aware of the market potential of American raw materials and agricultural products in a European market.

The major Scottish immigrations to America occurred in the 1700s. Among the first groups were Jacobite prisoners who were banished from Scotland to occupy American "plantations" of settlements in 1715 and again in 1745. Waves of Lowland Scots arrived next, as individuals and their families voluntarily sought freedom and economic prosperity in the New World. Beginning in the 1730s, however, Highland Scots, traveling in groups, perhaps clans, immigrated to colonial America.

Scots initially settled in pods or small enclaves in the midst of the English-settled Atlantic coastal regions. Many Lowland Scots were merchants, craftsmen, traders, and others associated with urban occupations and focused their settlements in English colonial coastal cities from New England, down the coast to Georgia; they especially settled in Virginia. Highlander Scots established new frontier settlements on the interior edges of English-held areas in the Carolinas, New York, and Georgia. Although the Highlander Scots may have thought that they were going great distances inland, their migrations were not nearly as deeply penetrating as the movements of the Scotch-Irish into the frontier wilderness. But unlike the ever-moving Scotch-Irish, the Highland Scots stayed put in the places where they initially settled. This sedentary way of life in enclaves on the edge of the wilderness helped to preserve their Scottish traditional culture. A good example is North Carolina, where, in the vicinity of the present-day cities of Fayetteville (Cumberland County), Aberdeen (Moore County), and Laurinburg (Scotland County), the initial Highlanders began to arrive in 1739. This region experienced continual arrivals of additional Scots from Scotland for many years into the nineteenth century. The Scottish presence is still vigorously felt in the area.

Scottish immigration in the second half of the eighteenth century came in many different forms. In 1746, nearly 1,000 men, women, and children were banished from Scotland to be sold as indentured servants in America. During the French and Indian War, between 1754 and 1763, Highland regiments entered the fight, but after the war many Scottish soldiers chose to settle the Mohawk River Valley in upstate New York. In 1782 and 1783, failed crops in the Scottish Highlands drove many Highlanders to seek their fortune in America. In Canada the Maritime Provinces of New Brunswick, Prince Edward Island, and particularly Nova Scotia (New Scotland) were richly populated by Scots beginning in the 1760s and especially up to 1785. Once the Scots had initially settled a region, permanent settlement generally followed, so that patterns of return migration to Scotland were uncommon. This was true among Scotch-Irish immigrants as well. However, contemporary interests in "all things Scottish" have drawn many Scottish Americans and non-Scots to choose Scotland as a travel destination. Genealogical searches also have become major activities for Scottish Americans.

Demographics

In the first U.S. Census, which was the one taken in 1790, the total population of the United States was 3,172,444 persons. The ethnic composition was as follows: English, 2,605,699; Scotch, 221,562; Germany, 176,407; Dutch, 78,959; Irish, 61,534; French, 17,619; Hebrew, 1,243; all others, 9,421. Controversy surrounds the census because the Scotch-Irish population, which was surely present in the new country, was not specifically identified. So it is not known how many of the "Scotch" and how many of the "Irish" were actually "Scotch-Irish," and more important here, how many Scots were in the "Scotch" category.

In the 1990 U.S. Census, 5,393,581 people claimed Scottish ancestry. In previous years census figures have shown far more Scots than for 1990. For example, it was estimated in 1979 that fourteen million of the U.S. population were of Scottish ancestry, but when the official 1980 U.S. Census was completed, ten million people were identified as having Scottish ancestry. The 1990 U.S. Census figure is much smaller but is possibly more accurate because it clearly separates Scots from Scotch-Irish, and both of these from those of Irish ancestry.

Of the total 5,393,581 people with Scottish ancestry, urban populations account for 4,013,188, while rural populations total 1,380,393. One might expect the rural populations to be larger, but they are not. For example, only 67,617 people with Scottish ancestry live in places with fewer than 1,000 population; and for places with 1,000 to 2,999 population, the total is 154,025. Those living in rural areas who are designated farmers account for 82,329 people.

The 1990 U.S. Census indicates a subgroup of native, American-born Scottish people to be 3,162,610, which divides into 1,688,870 males and 1,473,740 females in the native population. The current Scottish native, American-born population can be divided into three major age groups. There are 730,816 children and young people, whose ages range from less than one year to twenty-one years. Those in the primary working age group, between twenty-two and sixty-four, account for 1,913,449. People sixty-five or over total 518,345 persons.

Some of the Atlantic coastal states show concentrations of Scots owing to the ports of entry during the initial phases of early Scottish settlement. New York with 266,312 people of Scottish ancestry stands out especially for this reason. However, Massachusetts (199,489), Pennsylvania (223,544), Virginia (166,959), North Carolina (177,699), and Georgia (141,833) reflect relatively large numbers of Scottish descendants. North Carolina had the largest Scottish population in America from 1732 to 1776, and the state maintains a population of 177,699 people claiming Scottish descent. The interior states of Ohio (224,351), Michigan (252,104), and Illinois (176,096) reflect both early eighteenth- and nineteenth-century westward migration patterns. More important, they reflect twentieth-century patterns of people seeking employment in northern industrial cities from 1930 to 1960. The large contingent of Scots in Texas (306,854) reflects the nineteenth-century migrations of people from the Atlantic Seaboard states as well as some from interior states such as Tennessee and Kentucky. California has the largest population of Scottish descendants, with 646,674 people, accounting for about 12 percent of the total of 5,393,581 persons claiming Scottish ancestry. Here again, sporadic migrations over time account for the ethnicity in the state. The Gold Rush to California in 1849 would have attracted Scottish folk probably as much as the Great Depression of the 1930s drove many out of the South and Midwest to seek employment in California. Post-World War II migrations would have brought peoples of Scottish descent to California, Washington State, and Florida for employment, amenities, or retirement.

Language

Upon arrival in America many Scottish immigrants spoke Gaelic. In the initial phases of settlement in eighteenth-century North Carolina, existing groups complained about the newly arrived Scots' unintelligible Gaelic speech. In 1756, Hugh McAden reported that several Scots scarcely knew one word of English. Even as English speech took over, there were survivals of Gaelic in America for more than a century. There are few if any formal language maintenance programs for the preservation of the Scottish dialect or brogue accent. However, some Presbyterian churches have made the effort to secure clergymen directly from Scotland to feature the "Scottish" brogue in church sermons. In the South, characteristic Scottish speech can be heard in words such as whar, that, dar, fahr in place of where, there, dare, and fire, respectively. In the vernacular of the inner coastal plain of North Carolina one might hear "Far engines run on rubber tars, and we fix 'em with bailing war and plars" (Fire engines run on rubber tires, and we fix them with boiling wire and pliers).

Cultural Characteristics

When the Scots immigrated to America, many of those who settled in places such as North Carolina were men of wealth who had brought a level of prosperity with them from Scotland. Many had the agricultural skills and Scottish thrift that helped them later develop large, prosperous farms. For two and a half centuries thereafter in North Carolina, Scots were still largely identified as independent farmers with large holdings that had passed from generation to generation but clearly kept within the family. For example in Scotland County, North Carolina, the largest farms in cotton, tobacco, and cattle are still held by "blue-blooded Scots" with names such as McNair, McArthur, and McLloyd.

Employment trends in the total work force of 1,673,890 people above age sixteen show a diversity in occupations: 27 percent are in health/education/other professional services, 14.4 percent in retail trade, 15.8 percent in manufacturing, and 9.8 percent work in construction or transportation. Only 2.5 percent of the work force continues in agriculture/forestry/fisheries. When divided by sex, the figures are 38.1 percent of the females in the work force and 37.1 percent of males are in managerial occupations, 42.9 percent of the female work force and 24.3 percent of the males are in technical/sales/administrative support occupations, and 12.5 percent of the males and 4.4 percent of the females in the work force are in operators/fabricators/laborers occupations.

In eighteenth-century America, the initial Scots lived in relatively crudely constructed pine log houses. Very soon thereafter, houses of sawn planks came into vogue as sawmills were built. More important, the English from quite early on emphasized building with sawn lumber, so it was natural for the Scottish immigrants to adopt the construction techniques already established. House types in the Scottish communities began following the pattern of the English Pen tradition, in which a pen represents an individual room unit, much like a one-room cabin. In the typology, houses evolved from single-pen houses to double-pen houses (two rooms) to I-houses that were two stories tall, two rooms wide, and one room deep to four-pen houses that had four rooms over four rooms. Construction techniques and materials were originally horizontal round logs with corner saddle notches, or later framed sawn lumber, but rarely brick or stone.

Scottish independence continues to be shown in their choice of contemporary housing. According to the 1990 U.S. Census, of the 1,456,998 total housing units occupied by American-born Scottish descendants there were 994,055 single-unit, freestanding dwellings, representing 68.2 percent. There were 86,055 mobile homes. Owner-occupied housing units accounted for 1,050,181 places. There were 415,817 renter-occupied units. In the owner-occupied units, 3,445 places lacked complete plumbing facilities. In the renter category there were 1,838 units that lacked complete plumbing facilities.

The religion of the Scottish immigrant groups was predominantly Presbyterian in Scotland, and it remained Presbyterian for generations in America. Over time some Scots adopted other denominations, chiefly Baptist, Methodist, or fundamentalist splinter groups. Historically the Scottish world-view was limited to a community or a county and would have continued to be so were it not for America's participation in foreign wars, improved transportation, and forms of electronic communication via telephone, radio, and television. The Scots in America use illness, death, and hardship as main points of conversation. Scotch-Irish *and* Scots have a tendency to "enjoy poor health," meaning that when asked about their health, they like to tell all the details of what is ailing them.

Family and kinship ties have always been strong for Scots. Much like the clans in Scotland, groups in America formed enclaves of kinfolk who lived in close proximity to each other. Primary families and extended families were often very very close, working together, protecting each other, enduring hardships, and visiting together. Most get-togethers were devoted to visiting kinfolk on Sunday afternoons. Many of the older Scottish generations still hold to these values, and marriages remain strong. The 1990 U.S. Census indicates that there were 1,649,136 married people of Scottish ancestry over age fifteen who were still living with their spouse. However, the national trend for divorce also affects families of Scottish ancestry. The 1990 U.S. Census indicates that 104,893 males and 117,586 females over age fifteen are divorced.

Scottish Highland games and Scottish festivals are among the fastest-growing interest activities among Scottish descendants and non-Scots in North America. There are 194 annual scheduled events in Scottish games and festivals in North America with 168 in the United States and 26 in Canada. In Scotland about 40 events are held annually. Highland games, also called Caledonian games, are athletic events that originated in the Scottish Highlands as part of the traditional gathering of the clans. Competitions are held in foot-races; jumping events; hill racing; wrestling; hammer throwing; shot-putting with a heavy stone; and caber tossing, which involves throwing a tree trunk that weights one hundred pounds and is sixteen to nineteen feet long end over end. Kilts are worn, bagpipes are played, and Scottish terriers are shown amid much pageantry and ceremony.

In addition to the growing interest in Highland games are the organized Scottish clans and families that celebrate their Scottish heritage. There are 81 formal Scottish clan organizations in the United States and Canada. Scottish-American clans and families seek kin and kindred interests in all things Scottish. This important step in the preservation of the culture and the search for cultural heritage and ethnicity leads to genealogical research, tourism to Scotland, and the collection and promotion of "all things Scottish," such as bagpipes, pipe and drum corps, kilts, tartan plaid fabrics, tams, Scotch whiskey, haggis (a delicacy made from various ingredients boiled in the stomach of sheep), Scottish folk songs, Scottish folk stories, Gaelic language, Scottish accents, and Scottish terriers.

The social organization of Scots in America has closely matched but does not mirror exactly the social structure in Scotland. Families and kinships were and remain strong in both Scotland and North America. However, clans remain much stronger in Scotland than in America because of the greater freedom and mobility of American groups. Clannish, yes, but in varying degree are the Scots. Politically, the Scots in America are known to be largely conservative, partly owing to their tradition of thriftiness.

Extent of Assimilation

The extent of assimilation of the Scots has not been as rapid or as thorough as that of the Scotch-Irish in America. Scottish identity was relatively good and, for some, it has remained so for more than three centuries. Scottish identity has always been quite clear in the British Isles, and while it has been diluted in greater measure in America, still there were enclaves of Scots who made certain that while they were becoming Americanized, they would hold to their ethnic Scottish identity, even if only in memory. The Scottish cultural persistence is still strong in religion, independence, and especially in the resurgence of interest in material culture, Scottish Highland games, and Scottish festivals.

Bibliography

Aspinwall, B. (1984). *Portable Utopia: Glasgow and the United States, 1820–1920*. Aberdeen: Aberdeen University Press.

Black, G. F. ([1921] 1972). *Scotland's Mark on America*. San Francisco: R & E Research Associates.

Brownlee, R. (1986). *An American Odyssey: The Autobiography of a 19th Century Scotsman, Robert Brownlee, at the Request of His Children: Napa County, California, October 1892*. Fayetteville: University of Arkansas Press.

Dobson, D. (1984). *Directory of Scottish Settlers in North America, 1625–1825*, 4 vols. Baltimore, MD: Genealogical Publishing Company.

Dobson, D. (1994). *Scottish Emigration to Colonial America, 1607–1785*. Athens: University of Georgia Press.

Erickson, C. (1972). *Invisible Immigrants: The Adaptation of English and Scottish Immigrants in Nineteenth-Century America*. Coral Gables, FL: University of Miami Press.

Graham, I. C. C. (1956). *Colonists from Scotland: Emigration to North America, 1707–1783*. Ithaca, NY: Cornell University Press.

Johnson, J. E. (1966). *The Scots and Scotch-Irish in America*, Minneapolis: Lerner.

Jordan, T. G., and Kaups, M. (1989). *The American Backwoods Frontier*. Baltimore, MD: Johns Hopkins University Press.

Karras, A. L. (1992). *Sojourners in the Sun: Scottish Migrants in Jamaica and the Chesapeake, 1740–1800*. Ithaca, NY: Cornell University Press.

Landsman, N. C. (1985). *Scotland and Its First American Colony, 1683–1765*. Princeton, NJ: Princeton University Press.

Lefler, H. T., and Newsome, A. R. (1963). *North Carolina: The History of a Southern State*, revised edition. Chapel Hill: University of North Carolina Press.

Lehmann, W. C. (1978). *Scottish and Scotch-Irish Contributions to Early American Life and Culture*. Port Washington, NY: National University Publications.

Maclean, J. P. ([1900] 1978). *An Historical Account of Settlements of Scotch Highlanders in America Prior to the Peace of 1783*. Baltimore, MD: Genealogical Publishing Company.

Meyer, D. G. (1961). *The Highland Scots of North Carolina*. Chapel Hill: University of North Carolina Press.

Redmond, G. (1971). *The Caledonian Games in Nineteenth-Century America*. Rutherford, NJ: Fairleigh Dickinson University Press.

Reid, W. ([1911] 1970). *The Scot in America, and the Ulster Scot*. San Francisco: R & E Research Associates.

Scarlett, J. D. (1976). *The Tartans Spotter's Guide*. New York: Van Nostrand Reinhold.

—JOHN B. REHDER

SWEDES

The Swedes have a long presence in North America. In 1638, Sweden, then a great European power, established a colony on the Delaware River. New Sweden remained under the Swedish flag for only seventeen years, during which its Swedish and Finnish population—Finland then being a part of the Swedish realm—came to fewer than four hundred individuals. They continued to increase, however, under Dutch and, from 1664, under English rule, so that they and their offspring were estimated at about one thousand by 1700. Many Americans are descended in part from them, even if unknowingly. Perhaps the most significant thing about Sweden's seventeenth-century American colony has been the pride it has inspired among later Swedish and Finnish Americans by identifying them with the early colonial history of their new homeland.

The Great Emigration

THE FIRST PHASE. Individual Swedes continued to arrive in America during the eighteenth and earlier nineteenth centuries. By 1840, there began to be grave concern over growing impoverishment in Sweden. Much new land had been brought under cultivation since the beginning of the century, and yields had greatly increased with the introduction of improved farming methods. Still, population grew faster, more than doubling between 1800 and 1900, most rapidly among the poorer, landless classes of the countryside. The proportion of the population engaged in farming and related rural occupations meanwhile remained practically constant, at about three-quarters of the total, as late as the 1870s. Available farmland became ever scarcer. Although industrialization increased from mid-century, it was long unable to keep pace with population growth.

Just when the great emigration from Sweden to America may be considered to have properly begun remains open to varying interpretation. In 1838, the five Friman brothers (John, William, Herman, Adolph, and Otto) went out to the Wisconsin frontier. Their letters to their father (Carl) were printed in the widely read liberal Stockholm newspaper *Aftonbladet,* together with reports of the emigration then getting under way from neighboring Norway. In 1841, Gustaf Unonius from Uppsala, together with his bride and three others, established their short-lived "New Upsala" at Pine Lake, Wisconsin. His enthusiastic letters, which likewise came out in *Aftonbladet,* aroused widespread interest, especially in educated circles, encouraging various idealists and restless souls to follow him out to Pine Lake.

Among those who were impressed by Unonius's letters was the miller Peter Cassel, who in 1845 led a group of peasant farmers and their families from Kisa parish, östergötland Province, in south-central Sweden—twenty-one persons in all—out to Iowa Territory. They established their "New Sweden" in Jefferson County, the first lasting Swedish settlement in the American Midwest. Cassel's letters, widely publicized in the Swedish press, were particularly influential among the Swedish peasantry, coming from a respected man of their own background and experience, while arousing serious concerns among the ruling classes. Beginning in 1846, a growing stream of peasants from Cassel's home region made their way out to Iowa and neighboring northwestern Illinois.

These early immigrants were soon overshadowed by the arrival in 1846 of more than twelve hundred religious dissenters, followers of the self-proclaimed prophet Eric Jansson, mainly from north-central Sweden. At Bishop Hill, in Henry County, Illinois, Jansson's sect established its Utopian community, which survived until 1860, achieving considerable prosperity in the mid-1850s.

Meanwhile, numerous onetime Janssonists left to settle in other northwestern Illinois localities, in turn drawing to them new arrivals from Sweden, many of whom soon moved on in search of available land. Bishop Hill, together with the Swedish Lutheran settlement at Andover, also in Henry County, Illinois, dating from 1847, and Peter Cassel's New Sweden in Iowa would thus be the original "mother colonies" established by emigrants directly from the old country, from which new groups constantly ventured farther west and north to the advancing frontier—mainly in Iowa, Minnesota, Kansas, Nebraska, and the Dakotas. During the 1850s, Swedes, mainly living in the Midwest, also took part in the California Gold Rush, establishing a lasting presence on the Pacific Coast.

Such stage migration resulted in a spreading network of "daughter" colonies, which before the century was over would extend to the Pacific Coast and up into the Canadian prairies. Chicago and the Twin Cities, in Minnesota, meanwhile began to emerge as the main Swedish-American urban centers.

THE PEAK YEARS OF EMIGRATION. Emigration from Sweden reached a first, modest peak in 1854, when it came to more than four thousand persons. Thereafter it fell off during the hard times in America, beginning in 1857 and lasting through the U.S. Civil War (1861–1865)—during which many Swedish immigrants served in the Union forces. Between 1867 and 1869, Sweden was afflicted with serious crop failures. Thanks largely to already established contacts with America, improved and cheaper transport on steamships and railroads, and the American Homestead Act of 1862, emigration rapidly increased to previously unimaginable proportions, totaling more than thirty-two thousand persons in 1869. An increasingly important factor now was the energetic promotion of emigration by American state governments and land companies, and especially steamship lines and railroads with networks of local agents conveniently dispersed throughout Sweden.

Swedish emigration declined over the next few years, with the return of better times in Sweden and the financial panic of 1873 in the United States. By the late 1870s, however, Sweden, with its overwhelmingly rural population, faced a longterm economic crisis. Steam transport opened up vast new areas overseas, particularly in the American Midwest, to settlement and grain production for export. It thus became increasingly difficult for Swedish peasant farmers to compete, even at home. Increasing numbers sold their small acreages and departed for America.

Up to this time, most Swedish emigrants had been farmers with land to sell to pay for their families' emigration. By the 1880s, the social composition of the emigration began to change as increasing numbers of poorer persons without means of their own were leaving individually for America. This became ever more possible as the costs of transportation fell and as growing numbers of relatives and friends already there were able to advance money or prepaid tickets to poor persons eager to join them. Emigration from Sweden reached its all-time high in 1888, when more than 45,500 departed.

The increasing numbers of immigrants who could not afford to go directly into farming upon their arrival were largely employed in railroad construction, logging, harvesting, and other types of menial labor. Young unmarried women were in high demand as domestic servants in American homes. After earning enough money to get themselves started, Swedes generally sought in this period to acquire land and become farmers, often following periods of urban residence and employment. Swedish settlement spread to new locations: Texas, the Rocky Mountain states, the West Coast, Alaska, and, in growing numbers, New England and New York State.

This mass exodus aroused both indignation and sorrow in Sweden. It seemed to prove that something was grievously wrong, either with Swedish society or with the Swedes themselves. From the 1860s through the 1880s, there was widespread pessimism that Sweden was virtually helpless in the face of America's overwhelming material attractions. Although some persons urged the outright prohibition of emigration, the government steadfastly rejected this as a violation of fundamental civil rights.

THE END OF THE GREAT EMIGRATION. Emigration remained sizable until America was overtaken by a new, grave economic crisis beginning in 1893. Meanwhile, Sweden entered into a dynamic phase of its own industrial development, stimulating a new optimism that the country both could and should provide adequately for the needs of all its people. By the late 1890s, it appeared that America could no longer offer the same advantages as before and that the great Swedish exodus was at last drawing to a close. However, such hopes proved premature, for emigration rose again, to more than 35,400 in 1903, leading to a full-scale government inquest into its causes and the organization of the National Society Against Emigration, both beginning in 1907.

By now, as good farmland became harder to acquire, growing numbers of Swedes entered nonagricultural occupations in America, frequently in newer areas of settlement—for instance, as factory workers or miners in the Northeast and Great Lakes states, or as lumberjacks in the Pacific Northwest. By 1910, more than half of America's Swedish-born population had become urban dwellers. By now there were sizable concentrations of Swedes in Duluth, Seattle, San Francisco, and Brooklyn, as well as such smaller cities as Rockford and Moline, Illinois; Jamestown, New York; and Worcester, Massachusetts.

World War I brought Swedish emigration practically to a standstill. Emigration increased when peace returned, reaching a final peak of nearly 24,000 in 1923. Thereafter the American immigration quota laws of 1924 and 1927 reduced it, first to 9,561 per year, then to 3,314 per year (not including family members). By the late 1920s, however, even these modest quotas were no longer being filled. The main reasons for the decline were Sweden's own rapid industrialization, urbanization, and comprehensive system of social welfare during the 1920s, which convinced working-class Swedes that their future lay at home. Nonetheless, a limited emigration of Swedes has continued to the present, since World War II consisting mainly of persons in highly qualified occupations.

Even from the beginning of the emigration, there were always some who in time returned permanently to their homeland. Return migration is estimated to have amounted to about 18 percent during the height of the emigration, between 1875 and 1925. During the Great Depression of the 1930s, it became greater still, far surpassing immigration.

Ethnic Life and Institutions

THE SWEDISH-AMERICAN ELEMENT. It has been said that the great emigration created both a "Sweden in America" and an "America in Sweden." It brought approximately 1.25 million Swedes to the United States, some four-fifths of whom stayed. By 1910, it was commonly estimated that one Swede out of five was in the United States. Chicago was then reckoned to be the world's second-largest "Swedish" city, after Stockholm. Only Ireland and Norway had experienced greater emigration in proportion to their total population.

America's "Swedish element," officially described as the first and second generations, peaked in the 1930 U.S. Census at more than 1.5 million. Since then census figures have reflected its aging and numerical decline. However, the number of Americans with at least some Swedish ancestry are estimated in the 1990s at 8 million to 12 million. During the first two generations the great majority married within their own group. Although this has become less common in later generations, they have tended to intermarry primarily with Anglo Americans, other Scandinavian Americans, and German-American Protestants.

ASSIMILATION VERSUS CULTURAL RETENTION. As northern European Protestants with closely kindred origins and traditions, Swedish and other Scandinavian immigrants were generally welcomed by the older Anglo-American population, particularly from the 1880s, when growing numbers of southern and eastern Europeans began arriving in the United States. The Swedes were widely praised as the "best Americanizers." Swedish immigrants nonetheless brought with them their own cultural traditions and values, which—adapted to American conditions—found expression not only in their personal lives but also in a multitude of Swedish-American religious organizations, schools and colleges, newspapers, publishing houses, business enterprises, societies, and clubs of every kind.

RELIGION. As Lutheranism was the state religion of Sweden, most church-affiliated Swedish immigrants and their descendants have been Lutherans. In 1860, thirty-six pioneer Swedish and Norwegian congregations formed the Augustana Lutheran Synod. As congregations increased rapidly with rising immigration, the synod divided in 1870 into separate Swedish and Norwegian bodies. From the first years of the immigration, many other Swedish immigrants became Methodists or Baptists, organizing their own Swedish conferences within these denominations. In Sweden, Mormon missionaries made converts who immigrated to Utah. In 1884, a split within Swedish-American Lutheranism led to the establishment of the Swedish Evangelical Mission Covenant, part of which in turn became the Evangelical Free Church. There have also been Swedish-American branches of the Episcopalian and Pentecostal churches, and the Salvation Army. Many Swedish Americans meanwhile joined Anglo-American or in some cases other Scandinavian-American churches or did not formally affiliate with any denomination, even if they occasionally attended services.

EDUCATION. In 1860, the year of its founding, the Augustana Lutheran Synod established its Augustana College and Seminary in Chicago. With the withdrawal of the Norwegian congregations in 1870, it divided into the present Augustana colleges in Rock Island, Illinois (Swedish), and in Sioux Falls, South Dakota (Norwegian). Thereafter numerous other Swedish-American colleges and academies were founded, many of which have not survived. These now include the Lutheran-affiliated Gustavus Adolphus College in St. Peter, Minnesota, and Bethany College in Lindsborg, Kansas, as well as the Mission Covenant's North Park College in

Chicago and the Baptist Bethel College in St. Paul. While some early pioneering settlements organized their own schools to begin with, the Swedes—unlike certain larger immigrant groups, such as the Irish and the Germans (both Lutheran and Catholic)—did not favor ethnic parochial schools. The Swedes did, however, commonly organize congregational summer, or "Swede," schools to prepare children for confirmation and teach them to read and write Swedish. Some of these existed at least into the 1920s.

JOURNALISM AND LITERATURE. Following *Skandinaven,* briefly published in Swedish, Danish, and Norwegian by a Swede in New York in 1851–1852, the first purely Swedish newspaper in America, *Hemlandet* (The Homeland), was established in 1855 in Galesburg, Illinois, moving soon thereafter to Chicago, which quickly became the center of Swedish-American journalism. It is estimated that some twelve hundred Swedish-language periodicals have been published at various times in the United States, the largest number for any ethnic group except the Germans. The presently surviving Swedish-American newspapers include *Nordstjernan* in New York, *California Veckoblad* in Los Angeles, *Vestkusten* in San Francisco, and *Svenska Amerikanaren-Tribunen* in Chicago, the latter still entirely in Swedish. Numerous devotional works, magazines, yearbooks, practical manuals, and translations from English were published, chiefly in Chicago and Rock Island, as well as poetry and prose fiction by both Swedish and a remarkably large number of Swedish-American authors.

ORGANIZATIONS. Clubs and societies of every description flourished, for mutual benefits, choral singing, theatricals, sports, literary activities, charity, and for immigrants from particular provinces, all of them involving a lively social life and dedicated, at least in part, to the preservation in the new homeland of Swedish language and culture. In time many joined into broader regional or national federations, such as the Svithiod Order (1880), the Order of Vikings (1890), the American Union of Swedish Singers (1892), and the Vasa Order of America (1896), the last still the largest Swedish-American organization, with some thirty thousand members and with lodges in Canada and Sweden.

ETHNIC PRESERVATION. Since the end of the great emigration in the 1920s, many of these ethnic institutions—oriented as they were to the cultural needs of Swedish-born and Swedish-speaking immigrants—have gradually died out. Today Swedish is spoken by few Americans of Swedish origin, as compared with more recent immigrant groups. In 1966, Joshua Fishman rated Swedish thirteenth among non-English "mother tongues" in terms of prospects for maintenance in the United States, behind Norwegian (twelfth) but ahead of Danish (twenty-first).

But loss of the old language has by no means ended the lively interest of Swedish descendants in the land, culture, and traditions of their ancestors. This is amply proven by the constant establishment, from at least the 1920s, of new American-Swedish organizations that foster—now in English—ethnic pride and identification with the old homeland. The Swedish Council of America, founded with three participating societies in 1972, includes well over 160 Swedish-interest groups and continues to grow. Swedish- and Scandinavian-American museums in Philadelphia, Chicago, and Seattle, as well as in certain smaller communities; the American-Swedish Institute in Minneapolis; the Swenson Swedish Immigration Research Center in Rock Island; and the Swedish-American Historical Society in Chicago are of central importance in maintaining the ethnic heritage. Well-preserved Swedish traditions in America include the celebration of St. Lucia Day on December 13, old Christmas customs, Midsummer festivals, and not least the smorgasbord, with its many familiar dishes.

SOCIAL AND OCCUPATIONAL STATUS. As a long-established element in the American population, Swedish descendants would be described today as predominantly middle-class and comparatively well educated. A relatively high proportion are still rural, engaged in agricultural and related occupations, especially in the upper Midwest; in this regard they are surpassed only by Norwegian and German Americans. Many of those of Swedish descent are in skilled trades (often in construction and precision industries), in business, and in the professions. Historically they have tended to be churchgoers and to identify primarily with the Republican party. The newer immigrants, since World War II, consist mainly of highly trained professionals, technicians, and businesspeople, located in the larger metropolitan areas, especially on the East and West coasts. Frequently they return to Sweden. Culturally they have tended to have relatively little contact with the older working-class immigrants and their descendants.

Conclusions

The great emigration averted the threat of overpopulation and mass impoverishment in Sweden, allowing both those who left and those who stayed home to attain a more abundant and fulfilling life. Already by the 1880s appeals were heard in the homeland to "bring America to Sweden"—that is, to adopt America's political democracy, social equality, economic and technological skills, optimism, initiative, and work ethic—to counterbalance the fatal lure from across the sea. With time, American values, practices, and innovations have become so strongly rooted there that it is now claimed that the United States is the second-most Americanized country in the world—after Sweden! Materially and culturally, conditions have become ever more similar on both sides of the Atlantic. There nonetheless remains among Americans of Swedish origin a warm sympathy for the old homeland. They value those traits of character and culture they consider to be typically Swedish, and in their families, communities, and organizations, they cherish those customs that have proved adaptable to the American setting and that keep alive their sense of Swedish ethnic identity and pride.

Bibliography

Barton, H. A. (1990). *Letters from the Promised Land: Swedes in America, 1840–1914,* revised edition. Minneapolis: University of Minnesota Press.

Barton, H. A. (1994). *A Folk Divided: Homeland Swedes and Swedish Americans, 1840–1940.* Carbondale: Southern Illinois University Press.

Beijbom, U. (1971). *Swedes in Chicago: A Demographic and Social Study of the 1846–1880 Immigration.* Chicago: Chicago Historical Society.

Elmen, P. (1976). *Wheat Flour Messiah: Eric Jansson of Bishop Hill.* Carbondale: Southern Illinois University Press.

Hasselmo, N. (1976). *Swedish America: An Introduction.* New York: Swedish Information Service.

Janson, F. E. (1931). *The Background of Swedish Immigration.* Chicago: University of Chicago Press.

Johnson, A. (1911). *The Swedish Settlements on the Delaware, 1638–1664.* Philadelphia: University of Pennsylvania Press.

Kastrup, A. (1975). *The Swedish Heritage in America.* Minneapolis: Swedish Council of America.

Lindmark, S. (1971). *Swedish America, 1914–1932: Studies in Ethnicity with an Emphasis on Illinois and Minnesota.* Chicago: Swedish Pioneer Historical Society.

Ljungmark, L. (1996). *Swedish Exodus,* 2nd edition. Carbondale: Southern Illinois University Press.

Nelson, H. (1943). *The Swedes and the Swedish Settlements in North America.* Lund, Sweden: Gleerups Förlag.

Ostergren, R. C. (1988). *A Community Transplanted: The Transatlantic Experience of a Swedish Immigrant Settlement in the Upper Middle West, 1835–1915.* Madison: University of Wisconsin Press.

Runblom, H., and Norman, H., eds. (1976). *From Sweden to America: A History of the Migration.* Minneapolis: University of Minnesota Press.

Stephenson, G. M. (1932). *The Religious Aspects of Swedish Immigration.* Minneapolis: University of Minnesota Press.

Swedish-American Historical Quarterly (before 1982 the *Swedish Pioneer Historical Quarterly*), published since 1950 by the Swedish-American Historical Society, Chicago.

—H. ARNOLD BARTON

Cultures by Country

Afghanistan
Baluchi
Kyrgyz
Pathan
peripatetics
Tajiks
Turkmens

Albania
Albanians

Algeria
Arabs
Jews
Tuareg

Alsace
Ashkenazic Jews

Angola
Kongo
Lunda
San-speaking peoples

Antigua
Antiguans and Barbudans

Aomoro Islands
Swahili

Arctic
Eskimo
Saami

Argentina
Araucanians
Chiriguano
Japanese
Mataco

Armenia
Armenians
Greeks
Kurds

Aruba
Arubans

Australia
Ashkenazic Jews
Latvians
Murngin
Ukrainians
Vietnamese

Austria
Ashkenazic Jews
Austrians
Germans
peripatetics

Azerbaijan
Armenians
Azerbaijani Turks
Kurds

Bahama Islands
Bahamians

Bahrain
Arabs

Bangladesh
Bengali
Santal

Barbados
Barbadians

Barbuda
Antiguans and Barbudans

Belarus
Ashkenazic Jews
Ashkenazim
Belarussians
Germans
Poles

Belgium
Flemish
peripatetics

Belize
Garifuna

Benin
Ewe and Fon
Sonhay
Yoruba

Bhutan
Tibetans

Bolivia
Aymara
Chiriguano
Japanese
Mataco

Bosnia-Hercegovina
Bosnian Muslims
Croats
Serbs

Botswana
San-speaking peoples
Tswana

Brazil
Japanese
Koreans
Otavalo
Yanomamö

Bukovina
Ashkenazic Jews

Bulgaria
Bulgarians
peripatetics

Burkina Faso
Mossi

Burundi
tropical-forest foragers

Cambodia
Chinese in Southeast Asia
Khmer
Vietnamese

Cameroon
Kanuri
tropical-forest foragers

Canada
Albanians
Amish
Armenians
Ashkenazic Jews
Austrians
Basques
Blackfoot
Cree, Western Woods
Croats
Czechs
Danes
Dutch
English
Eskimo
Estonians
European-Canadians
Finns
French Canadians
Germans
Greeks
Haitians
Han
Icelanders
Irish
Iroquois
Jews
Koreans
Latvians
Lithuanians
Norwegians
Ojibwa
Poles
Portuguese
Russians
Serbs
Sikhs
Slovaks
Swedes
Swiss, Italian

Canada (*continued*)
Ukrainians
Vietnamese
Welsh
Central African Republic
tropical-forest foragers
Zande
Chad
Arabs
Kanuri
Chile
Araucanians
Aymara
Easter Island
China
Central Thai
Hakka
Han
Kachin
Kazakhs
Koreans
Kyrgyz
Miao
Mongols
Shan
Tajiks
Tibetans
Uzbeks
Zhuang
Colombia
Guajiro
Otavalo
Páez
Congo
Kongo
tropical-forest foragers
Costa Rica
Costa Ricans
Croatia
Croats
Serbs
Cuba
Cubans
Czech and Slovak Federative Republic
Czechs
peripatetics
Slovaks

Denmark
Danes
peripatetics
Dominica
Garifuna
Dominican Republic
Dominicans

East African coastline
Swahili
Ecuador
Canelos Quichua
Jivaro
Otavalo
Egypt
Albanians
Arabs
Bedouin
Palestinians
peripatetics
England
English
Equatorial Guinea
tropical-forest foragers
Estonia
Estonians
Ethiopia
Amhara
Fulani

Fiji
Bau
Finland
Finns
peripatetics
Saami
France
Ashkenazic Jews
Basques
Bretons
Catalans
Flemish
French
Provençal
Tahiti
Vietnamese

Gabon
tropical-forest foragers
Gambia
Fulani
Georgia, Republic of
Armenians
Georgians
Greeks
Jews
Kurds
Germany
Ashkenazic Jews
Estonians
Germans
peripatetics

Ghana
Akan
Ewe and Fon
Mossi
Songhay
Greece
Albanians
Greeks
peripatetics
Greenland
Eskimo
Guatemala
Garifuna

Haiti
Haitians
Honduras
Garifuna
Ladinos
Hong Kong
Hakka
Hungary
Ashkenazic Jews
Hungarians
peripatetics

Iceland
Icelanders
India
Bengali
Bhil
Gond
Gujarati
Jat
Jatav
Kachin
Khasi
Lingayat
Maratha
Nayar
Oriya
Pahari
Punjabi
Santal
Sikh
Tamil
Telugu
Tibetans
Indonesia
Asmat
Balinese
Batak

Chinese in Southeast Asia
Dani
Iban
Javanese
Kapauku
Makassar
Minangkabau
Iran
Arabs
Azerbaijani Turks
Bakhtiari
Baluchi
Georgians
Kurds
peripatetics
Persians
Iraq
Arabs
Kurds
Palestinians
peripatetics
Turkmens
Ireland
Gaels
Irish
peripatetics
Israel
Ashkenazic Jews
Circassians
Jews of Israel
Palestinians
peripatetics
Italy
Albanians
peripatetics
Sicilians
Swiss Italian
Ivory Coast
Akan
Mossi
Songhay

Jamaica
Jamaicans
Japan
Ainu
Burakumin
Japanese
Koreans
Jordan
Arabs
Chechen-Ingush
Circassians
Palestinians
peripatetics

Kazakhstan
Germans
Greeks
Kazakhs
Koreans
Kurds
Poles
Volga Tatars
Kenya
Fulani
Kikuyu
Luyia
Maasai
Nandi and other
       Kalenjin peoples
Korea
Koreans
Kuwait
Arabs
Palestinians
Kyrgyzstan
Germans
Koreans
Kurds
Kyrgyz
Volga Tatars

Laos
Chinese in Southeast Asia
Hmong
Lao
Vietnamese
Latvia
Latvians
Poles
Lebanon
Arabs
Palestinians
peripatetics
Leeward Islands
Antiguans and Barbudans
Arubans
Libya
Arabs
Bedouin
Palestinians
Tuareg
Lithuania
Ashkenazic Jews
Lithuanians
Poles

Madagascar
Swahili
Mafia Island
Swahili

Malaysia
Chinese in Southeast Asia
Dusun
Iban
Malay
Mali
Songhay
Tuareg
Martinique
Martiniquais
Mauritania
Fulani
Mexico
Guarijío
Ladinos
Mixtec
Nahua of Huasteca
Totonac
Tzotzil of Chamula
Yukateko
Zapotec
Moldova
Germans
Mongolia
Mongols
Montenegro
Montenegrins
Serbs
Morocco
Arabs
Bedouin
Berbers
Mozambique
Lozi
Shona
Swazi
Myanmar (Burma)
Burmese
Hmong
Kachin
Karen
Shan

Namibia
Khoi
San-speaking peoples
Tswana
Nepal
Brahman and Chhetri of Nepal
Santal
Tibetans
Netherlands
Dutch
peripatetics
New Caledonia
Vietnamese

New Zealand
Maori
Nicaragua
Garifuna
Niger
Hausa
Kanuri
Sonhay
Tuareg
Nigeria
Hausa
Igbo
Kanuri
Songhay
Tiv
Yoruba
Northern Ireland
Irish
Norway
Norwegians
peripatetics
Saami

Pakistan
Baluchi
Jat
Kyrgyz
Pathan
Punjabi
Panama
Kuna
Papua New Guinea
Chimbu
Manus
Trobriand Islands
Paraguay
Chiriguano
Japanese
Koreans
Pembar Island
Swahili
Peru
Aymara
Japanese
Matsigenka
Shipibo
Philippines
Chinese in Southeast Asia
Filipino
Ifugao
Tagalog
Poland
Poles
Portugal
Portuguese
Puerto Rico
Puerto Ricans

Qatar
Arabs

Romania
Ashkenazic Jews
peripatetics
Russia
Ainu
Albanians
Ashkenazic Jews
Ashkenazim
Chechen-Ingush
Germans
Greeks
Kurds
Mongols
Poles
Russians
Saami
Volga Tatars
Yakut
Rwanda
tropical-forest foragers

Saint Vincent
Garifuna
Saudi Arabia
Arabs
Palestinians
Scotland
Highland Scots
Lowland Scots
Senegal
Fulani
Wolof
Serbia, Republic of
Albanians
Croats
Sicily
Albanians
Sicilians
Sierra Leone
Mende
Temne
Singapore
Chinese in Southeast Asia
Han
Slovakia
peripatetics
Slovaks
Slovenia
Croats
Solomon Islands
Malaita
Somalia
Somalis

South Africa
Ashkenazic Jews
Khoi
Swazi
Tswana
Zulu
Spain
Castilians
Catalans
Galicians
Otavalo
peripatetics
Sri Lanka
Sinhalese
Tamil
Sudan
Arabs
Fulani
peripatetics
Zande
Suriname
Saramaka
Swaziland
Swazi
Sweden
Estonians
peripatetics
Saami
Swedes
Switzerland
German Swiss
Italian Swiss
peripatetics
Syria
Arabs
Chechen-Ingush
Circassians
Kurds
Palestinians
peripatetics

Taiwan
Hakka
Han
Tajikistan
Germans
Koreans
Kurds
Tajiks
Turkmens
Tanzania
Maasai
Nyamwezi and Sukuma
Thailand
Central Thai
Chinese in Southeast Asia
Hmong

Please see index for specific page numbers

Karen
Lao
Shan
Vietnamese
Togo
  Ewe and Fon
  Songhay
  Yoruba
Tonga
  Tonga
Trinidad and Tobago
  Garifuna
  Trinidadians and Tobagonians
Tunisia
  Arabs
  Bedouin
Turkey
  Albanians
  Arabs
  Chechen-Ingush
  Circassians
  Georgians
  Kurds
  peripatetics
  Turkmens
  Turks
Turkmenistan
  Greeks
  Koreans
  Kurds
  Turkmens

Uganda
  Ganda
  Luyia
  Nandi and other Kalenjin peoples
  tropical-forest foragers
Ukraine
  Ashkenazic Jews
  Ashkenazim
  Germans
  Greeks
  Poles
  Ukrainians
United Kingdom
  English
  Highland Scots
  Irish
  Lowland Scots
  peripatetics
  Welsh
United States of America
  African Americans
  Albanians
  Amish
  Arab Americans
  Armenians
  Ashkenazic Jews

Austrians
Basques
Blackfoot
Burmese
Cajuns
Cherokee
Cheyenne
Choctaw
Circassians
Croats
Czechs
Danes
Dutch
East Asians
English
Eskimo
Estonians
European Americans
Finns
French
Garifuna
Germans
Greeks
Haitians
Han
Hawaiians
Hmong
Hopi
Hungarians
Irish
Iroquois
Jews
Koreans
Latinos
Latvians
Lithuanians
Malaysians
Mormons
Navajo
North Alaskan Eskimos
Norwegians
Ojibwa
Palestinians
peripatetics
Poles
Portuguese
Pueblo Indians
Russians
Samoans
Serbs
Slovaks
South and Southeast Asians
Swedes
Swiss Italian
Tlingit
Ukrainians
Vietnamese
Welsh

Western Apache
Zuni
Uzbekistan
  Germans
  Greeks
  Koreans
  Kurds
  Tajiks
  Turkmens
  Uzbeks
  Volga Tatars

Venezuela
  Guajiro
  Otavalo
  Warao
  Yanomamö
Vietnam
  Chinese in Southeast Asia
  Hmong
  Vietnamese

Wales
  Welsh
Western Samoa
  Samoans

Yemen
  Arabs
  peripatetics
  Yemenis
Yugoslavia
  Albanians
  Bosnian Muslims
  Circassians
  Croats
  Montenegrins
  peripatetics
  Serbs

Zaire
  Kongo
  Lunda
  tropical-forest foragers
  Zande
Zambia
  Bemba
  Lozi
  Lunda
  Tonga
Zanzibar
  Swahili
Zimbabwe
  Lozi
  Shona
  Tonga
  Tswana

Index